CALIFORNIA *CONTROVERSIES*

Major Issues in the History of the State

Second Edition

Leonard Pitt

California State University, Northridge

Harlan Davidson, Inc.

Arlington Heights, Illinois

To Michael, Adam, and Marni

Library of Congress Cataloging-in-Publication Data

California controversies: major issues in the history of the state / [edited by] Leonard Pitt.
p. cm.
Originally published: San Rafael, Calif. : ETRI Pub. Co., 1987.
Includes bibliographical references.
ISBN 0-88295-879-8
1. California—Politics and government—1951- 2. California—Politics and government.
I. Pitt, Leonard.
F866.2.C3427 1990
979.4—dc20

90-3954
CIP

Cover design: Roger Eggers
Cover photo: Art Brewer

Manufactured in the United States of America

94 93 92 91 90 3 4 5 6 7 MG

Acknowledgments

Permission to reprint the following is gratefully acknowledged: Map of "Mission Santa Barbara," from p. 179 of the Sunset Book, *The California Missions*, copyright (c) 1979, 1964, Lane Publishing Co., Menlo Park, California; Maynard Geiger, O.F.M., *Mission Santa Barbara*, 1782-1965 (Santa Barbara: Franciscan Fathers of California, 1965), pp. 28-33, 61-68, 70-74, reprinted by permission of publisher; Three paragraphs from the letter from Indian Bar in "The Shirley Letters," from *The Shirley Letters from the California Mines*, 1854-55, by Louise Amelia Knapp Smith Clappe, published by Peregrine Smith Books, reprinted by permission of Gibbs M. Smith, Inc.; A paragraph from a letter by Thomas Oliver Larkin, July 18, 1846, in George Hammond, ed., *The Larkin Papers* (Berkeley: University of California Press), V, 140-141, reprinted by permission of the publisher; Sherburne F. Cook, *The Conflict Between the California Indian and White Civilization* (Berkeley: University of California Press, 1943), excerpts from vol. I, pp. 11-157, reprinted by permission of the publisher; Quote from Pedro Font's *Diary*, 1775-1776, in Herbert E. Bolton, ed., *Anza's California Expeditions* (Berkeley: University of California Press), IV, p. 179, reprinted by permission of the publisher; Adaptation of pp. 273-322, *Frémont: The West's Greatest Adventurer*, by Alan Nevins, reprinted by permission of Harper & Row, Publishers, Inc.; Bernard DeVoto, *The Year of Decision: 1846* (Boston: Houghton Mifflin & Co., 1942), copyright 1961 by Houghton Mifflin Company, condensed and adapted from pp. 111-472, reprinted by permission of the publisher; Paul W. Gates, "California's Embattled Settlers," *California Historical Society Quarterly*, XLI (June 1962), condensed from pp. 99-125, reprinted by permission of The California Historical Society; R.L. Duffus, "The Two States of California," *New York Times Magazine*, December 18, 1955. Copyright (c) 1955 by The New York Times Magazine Co. Reprinted by permission; Paul S. Taylor, "The Fight for Water," *American Federationist*, December 1970, reprinted by permission of the publisher, the AFL-CIO; one paragraph from *The Destruction of California*, by Raymond F. Dasmann, p. 145. Copyright (c) 1965 by Raymond F. Dasmann. Reprinted with permission of the publisher, MacMillan Publishing Co.; Rowell-Shortridge exchange, "Non-Partisan Ballot Acts," *Transactions of the Commonwealth Club of California*, X (1915), pp. 463-486, reprinted by permission of the Commonwealth Club of California; Dean E. McHenry, "Pattern of California Politics, *Western Political Quarterly*, I (March, 1948), excerpts from pp. 46-47, 49-53, reprinted by permission of the publisher; Morrow Mayo, *Los Angeles* (New York: Alfred Knopf, Inc., 1933), excerpts from pp. 221-246, reprinted by permission of Maxim Lieber, Wickham Apartments, 11-D Racebrook Drive, East Hartford, Conn. 06108; Don J. Kinsey, *The Water Trail* (Los Angeles: Department of Water and Power, 1928), condensed from pp. 7-39; The Mono Lake Committee, "Endangered Oasis: Position Paper" (Lee Vining, California: The Mono Lake Committee, 1983), condensed and adapted, with permission of the publisher; Morton Grodzins, *Americans Betrayed: Politics and the Japanese Evacuation*, excerpts from pp. 121-128. Copyright (c) 1949 by The University of Chicago. Reprinted by permission of the publisher; Jacobus ten Broek, Edward N. Barnhart, and Floyd W. Matson, *Prejudice, War and the Constitution: Japanese Evacuation and Resettlement* (Berkeley: University of California Press, 1954), condensed and adapted from pp. 85-334, reprinted by permission of the publisher; "Two Sections of the State Diametrically Opposed," *Los Angeles Times*, Nov. 7, 1962, part I, p. 2; "In Unity There is Strength," Nov. 7, 1962, part II, p. 4; "Should California Be Chopped in Half?" *U.S. News and World Report*, February 8, 1965, copyright 1965 by U.S. News and World Report, Inc.; Lynn Ludlow and Will Hearst, "The Paper Farmers," *San Francisco Examiner*, January 11-18, 1976. Excerpts reprinted by permission of the publisher; E. Phillip LeVeen, "Reclamation Policy at a Crossroads," *Public Affairs Report* vol. 19, no. 5, October 1978 (Berkeley: Institute of Governmental Studies, University of California, 1978). Excerpted by permission, (c) 1978 by the Regents of the University of California; Excerpts from *The Berkeley Student Revolt* by Seymour Lipset and Sheldon S. Wolin, pp. 201-215, 245-251, 257-263, 264-267. Copyright (c) 1965 by Seymour Martin Lipset and Sheldon S. Wolin; reprinted by permission of Doubleday & Co., Inc.; Excerpts from *California Monthly*, February 1965, reprinted by permission of The California Alumni Association; Tristan E. G. Krogius, "Role of the Corporate Grower," *Produce Marketing Almanac*, 1985, reprinted by permission; Jeannine Guttman and David Judson, "S. California Ready for New War on Water," *The Stockton Record*,

February 16, 1986, reprinted by permission of the publisher; Dick Miester article on illegal farm workers, Los Angeles *Herald-Examiner*, April 1, 1984, by permission of the author; Article on water development, peripheral canal, *Stockton Record*, December 18, 1985; Sen. John Doolittle, opinion piece Sacramento *Recorder*, January 3, 1985, reprinted by permission of the author; Harry Dennis, *Water & Power: The Peripheral Canal* (San Francisco: Friends of the Earth, 1981), condensed from pp. 9-15, 16-44, 133-135, reprinted by permission of the author; *California Farmer*, editorial on 160-acre limit, April 17, 1976, and article by Messrs. Razee, Porteous, Pryor and Leach, January 7, 1978, reprinted with permission of *California Farmer* (c) 1976 (8), California Farmer Publishing Co.; "Aria: A Memoir of a Bilingual Childhood," by Richard Rodriguez. Copyright (c) 1980 by Richard Rodriguez. First published in *The American Scholar* (Winter 1980-81). Excerpts reprinted by permission of the author; Marcos de Leon, "Wanted: A New Educational Philosophy for the Mexican American," *Thrust for Educational Leadership* (formerly, *California Journal of Secondary Education),* XXXIV (January, 1959), excerpts from pp. 398-402, reprinted by permission of the publisher; M. M. Swanson and P. W. Quig, op-ed page exchange on bilingualism, *San Jose Mercury News*, January 3, 1979, reprinted by permission of the publisher; Dolores Litsinger, *The Challenge of Teaching Mexican-American Students* (New York: D. C. Heath & Co., 1973), condensed and adapted from pp. 141-146. Reprinted by permission of the publisher; Bill Press, opinion piece on bilingual ballots, *Los Angeles Times*, October 24, 1984, reprinted by permission of the author; John R. Haynes and Edward F. Adams, "Direct Legislation," *Transactions of the Commonwealth Club of California*, VI (September, 1911), condensed from pp. 286-290, 292-296, reprinted by permission of the Commonwealth Club of California; Daryl Arnold's letter in *Bakersfield Californian*, May 29, 1983 and his letter in *Los Angeles Times*, February 3, 1986, reprinted by permission of Western Growers Association; Peggy Wayburn, "Time Has All But Run Out for the Virgin Redwoods," *Sierra Club Bulletin*, October, 1975, March 25, 1986; Simpson Timber Co., et al., *Proposed Expansion of the Redwood National Park: The Industry's View* (Arcata, Calif.: Simpson Timber Co., April, 1975), by permission of the author; Maps no. 6 and no. 7, from Susan Schrepfer, *The Fight to Save the Redwoods* (Madison: University of Wisconsin Press, 1983), reprinted by permission; C. C. Bruno, "I Refuse to Bow to the UFW," *The Humanist*, November-December, 1979; "Chavez and Bruno Continue to Differ," ibid., March-April, 1980; Cesar Chavez, address to Commonwealth Club of California, November 9, 1985, reprinted from *Food and Justice*, publication of United Farm Workers, AFL-CIO, January, 1985, and author's ms., courtesy the author; Cesar Chavez letter to the *Los Angeles Times*, June 29, 1985, permission of the author; Sunne Wright McPeak, opinion piece, *Oakland Tribune*, January 25, 1985; Joseph P. Harris, *California Politics* (4th edn.; San Francisco: Chandler Publishing Co., 1967), excerpts from pp. 94-110, reprinted by permission of Arthur Harris; David Kirp, "Is Comparable Worth Worthwhile?" *The Sacramento Bee*, June 25, 1984. Copyright, *The Sacramento Bee 1984*; Article by Joanne Jacobs, *San Jose Mercury News*, October 12, 1984, reprinted by permission of the publisher; Four paragraphs quoting Phyllis Schlafly and Betty Friedan, in *Common Cause Magazine*, March/April 1983, reprinted by permission of Common Cause; California Chamber of Commerce, *Alert*, vol. 9, no. 10 (March 11, 1983), excerpts reprinted by permission of the publisher; Georgia-Pacific Co., "Yes, America's Majestic Redwoods Have Already Been Saved," newspaper ad, *Wall Street Journal*, January 24, 1968, Sierra Club Collection, Bancroft Library, U.C. Berkeley, abridged version reprinted by permission of Georgia-Pacific Co.; Sierra Club, "Legislation by Chainsaw," newspaper ad, *Wall Street Journal*, January 26, 1968, abridged, Sierra Club Collection, Bancroft Library, U.C. Berkeley, abridged version reprinted by permission of the Sierra Club; Claude Fletcher, opinion piece on comparable worth, *San Jose Mercury News*, July 15, 1981, reprinted by permission of the author; Rick Rodriguez, series on farm labor, *Sacramento Bee*, March 31-April 4, 1985. Copyright *The Sacramento Bee*, 1985. Excerpt reprinted by permission of the publisher; "Fighting to Finish State Water Project," *San Diego Evening Tribune*, December 18, 1984, reprinted by permission of the publisher; AFSCME District Council 57, "San Jose Comparable Worth: Position Paper Presented to California Commission on the Status of Women, San Francisco, May 1981." Excerpts reprinted by permission of Nancy Clifford, District Council 57, American Federation of State, County, and Municipal Employees (AFL-CIO).

Preface

This is a revised and expanded version of a book that first appeared nearly two decades ago. As a collection of readings on issues covering a large span of California history, with each controversy arranged on an essentially pro-and-con basis, it has proved rewarding to many who study and teach the history of this state.

Any work of this sort must be premised on the belief that there are more questions than answers in the study of history, and that genuine mastery of the subject lies in identifying and weighing the issues rather than strictly in amassing factual knowledge. The object of this book, then, is to stimulate a careful consideration of the major controversial issues in California history, issues which still cause dispute among scholars and laymen. Although a good many of the issues presented are strictly historical (in the sense that they deal with institutions and forces having little practical impact on the present), other issues dwell on the topics which still plague the state today and may do so for some time to come.

Thus, a book of this sort may at once sharpen the capacity for historical interpretation and contribute to an understanding, and thus to a solution, of continuing problems. It does not pretend to exhaust the list of issues but to merely present some of the pivotal ones.

This book is perhaps best considered as supplement to, rather than a replacement for, the customary tools employed in teaching and studying California history, government, and society. It usually will not replace the basic textbooks which are more comprehensive, yet it does contain much historical information which will enable a student to delve more deeply into the topics only lightly touched on in his text.

In the long run, this work may be most useful to the instructor who seeks to introduce a certain amount of discussion into the classroom routine while maintaining the lecture-and-textbook system. Whenever possible, the selections in this work are paired and opposite. In fact, some selections are deliberately inflammatory and will, if nothing else, provoke discussion or even argument. An attempt has been made to choose selections for their informational value, conciseness, color, and power to evoke discussion.

Many of the topics from the first edition, like those on the missions, Frémont, and the internment of the Japanese, remain unchanged. Some of the previous chapters, as on agricultural labor, have been completely revised. New topics have been added on the redwoods, the peripheral canal, comparable worth, and bilingualism.

Chapter introductions help clarify the issues and suggest connections among the selections which follow. Headnotes help explain the context of the various separate items, indicate what has been deleted from the original version, or supply a few salient details about the author. Maps are introduced where the geographic view is most important and least available elsewhere. Certain chapters are divided into more than two parts—for there are sometimes more than two sides to every question. In general, footnotes in the readings have been deleted unless they are especially pertinent.

Chapters touch upon many facets of society—political, economic, social, and cultural. All chapters are arranged chronologically to conform as much as possible to the customary one-semester or two-quarter course covering the Spanish and Mexican eras and California's history as a state. Much attention is focused on the outstanding problems of the twentieth century.

I wish to express appreciation to the people who have helped me in the research or writing of this book:

Professor Lawrence J. Jelinek, Loyola-Marymount University; Paul Koistinen, California State University, Northridge; Roy Merrins, and the late Walton Bean, University of California, Berkeley, read parts or all of the manuscript and made valuable comments.

I should like to give a special thanks to the late Frederick G. Knell. We first met twenty years ago when he worked for Scott, Foresman and Company, publishers of the first edition. Fred was knowledgeable about many things, witty, friendly and likeable, and deeply attached to a lively wife and family. We kept in touch over the years even after we both severed our connection with Scott, Foresman. He believed in the book and in each conversation kept after me to work on a second edition. Unfortunately, he did not live to see the final product. I am grateful to have known him and I will miss him.

For helping to find and make items available, or in preparing the manuscript I also must thank:

Robert Anderson, William Sommerfield, Nancy Johnson and Jane Martha Barcus;
Debbie Ballard and Nancy Clifford, American Federation of State, County, and Municipal Employees, AFL-CIO; William Camp and Barbie Clark, California Agricultural Labor Relations Board;
Richard Chavez, United Farm Workers Union, AFL-CIO; Franz Enciso, Bancroft Library, U.C. Berkeley;
Ed Freudenberg, Los Angeles Department of Water and Power; Gay Hayden;
Dora Knell and Frederick Knell, ETRI Publishing Co.;
Tristan E.G. Krogius, Tenneco Corp.;
Alice Krueper, Defenders of the San Gorgonio Wilderness;
Joann Lundgren, Metropolitan Water District;
Joseph Leitsinger, Simpson Timber Co.;
Eugene Mornell, County of Los Angeles Commission on Human Relations;
Steven Osgood, Mono Lake Committee;
Debbie Rizzo and Patricia Van Pelt, California Commission on the Status of Women;
Christie Robinson;
Maynard Robinson;
Susan Schrepfer, Rutgers University;
Elton R. Swartz, U.S. Bureau of Reclamation;
Tanis Thorne;
Betty Trotter;
Victor Van Bourg;
Sandra Walton, National Farm Workers Ministry;
Msgr. Francis J. Weber, Catholic Archdiocese of Los Angeles;
and
Dorothy Wells, U.C.L.A. Library.

Finally, I owe a debt of thanks to my students at California State University, Northridge, who used the book in manuscript form and offered critical advice, and, not least, to my wife Dale Pitt, who lovingly edited all the copy in both editions.

Table of Contents

Maps

State of California

Know that on the right hand of the Indies there is an island called California, very near to the Terrestrial Paradise...
—García Ordóñes de Montalvo, 1510.[1]

California is different from Iowa and this difference means that it is possible to dress differently without being regarded as a crank or a freak.
—Carey McWilliams, historian.

CHAPTER **1**

CALIFORNIA'S UNIQUENESS
Nature vs. Culture

A topic long fascinating to students of history is man's interaction with nature. But the exact nature of the linkage between historical events and geography is a recurrent puzzle; granting that man's material and intellectual culture is powerfully shaped by the natural environment, precisely how does one meaningfully describe the connection? If the physical environment is relatively static while the social environment is relatively fluid, what casual connection can there be between them?

To take an example close at hand, the Feather River has been of great significance in California history. But while that stream has changed little over the centuries, the groups of men who have come within its sphere have differed vastly—Indians fishing or hunting along its banks, Forty-niners panning for gold, farmers taking water in irrigation ditches, construction crews building the world's greatest earthfill dam to divert water for use as far south as San Diego. If the river is a constant factor or a great influence, should it not have had more or less uniform social effects over long periods of time? Yet there have been enormous societal changes from one generation to the next in Feather River country. To say that the river was of no consequence to man because no two generations responded to it similarly would be nonsense; to say that it was the controlling influence in its sphere is plainly false. Geography, then, is not the sole determinant, but neither is its impact on history negligible (or California would not be spending billions of dollars in the Feather River Project).

It was this sort of problem in causality that haunted California historian Hubert Howe Bancroft when he wrote despairingly, "We may fully recognize the mighty power of environment without being able to analyze it."

Yet analyze it we do. In America, where the battle to subdue the frontier has had a special meaning in the interpretation of history, there have always been writers looking into the meshing of history and geography. Under the influence of Charles Darwin in the nineteenth century, writers in many fields began to attribute all manner of consequences to human struggles with the elements, even the shaping of political systems and social ideals (as revealed, for example, in the widespread popularity of the catch phrase "survival of the fittest.") When this environmentalist thinking spread among historians, its chief evangelist was Frederick Jackson Turner. In 1893 he propounded the thesis that the American wilderness, a vast treasure-house of free land, was the

[1]García Ordoñez de Montalvo, *Las Sergas de Esplandián*, Toledo, Spain, 1510.

prime source of political democracy. "The existence of an area of free land," he asserted in his essay on *The Significance of the Frontier in American History*, "its continuous recession and the advance of American settlement westward, explain American development." Turner's particular brand of geographic determinism profoundly influenced the entire generation of historians until the 1940's.

The study of geography in the United States, although never dominated by one thinker as history was dominated by Turner, took on a similar deterministic coloration. One example of this is the work of Ellen Churchill Semple, whose *American History and Its Geographic Conditions* (1903) remained a standard text for decades.

Today, with the exception of a few speculative writers like Arnold Toynbee, most scholars reject grandiose hypotheses of geographic determinism. Most of them make less sweeping claims for the natural setting as a cultural force. Yet they do not thereby minimize its importance. By saying less, in a sense they say more: by making no claims for a fixed general relationship, they leave open the possibility of many subtle and complex connections between people and their surroundings. Thus the geographic determinism so prevalent half a century ago has given way to what one writer has called "geographic possibilism."

In the case of California, many questions arise about the relationship of environment to society. What kinds of uses could the Indian make of natural resources, and did lack of these resources keep the level of his material culture low? Did the Spaniards and Mexicans cope successfully with California's isolation and remoteness, or did those factors cripple them? Has the climate stimulated people or made them more "lazy"; has it made them more inclined to work or to play? On balance, modern technology has contributed more than nature to the shaping of "California civilization," or is it the other way around—a bountiful nature giving of itself generously and people just lapping up the rewards? Why does California seem to be a special and unique part of America; is this uniqueness a matter of appearances or of reality; if it is reality, what are the reasons?

Although the following essays on this problem touch a variety of questions, they have most to say about California's uniqueness. Usually the issue is *why* California is special rather than *whether* it is special, for nearly everybody agrees that it is unique.

The essay by Josiah Royce illustrates a style of thinking which tends to be impressionistic, poetic, and romantic. It is also deterministic in that it assumes that nature's influence over its people is overwhelming and rigid. James Parsons' essay, by contrast, is more scientific and empirical than Royce's, and his outlook may be termed "possibilistic" in that he gives more importance to cultural factors than to natural factors in evolution. A close reading of both articles will make students of California history aware that when they approach geography they are not dealing with remote "background" but with material pertinent to the very core of their discipline. *(Editor's note)*

1.
Josiah Royce's Geographical Determinism

Born in Gold Rush California, in 1855, Josiah Royce went on to become professor of Philosophy and Literature at Harvard and, for a time, the nation's most influential philosopher. His early life in a tumultuous mining town made him keenly aware of the problems of individualism and social responsibility. As a Hegelian with strong personal overtones of Yankee Puritanism, he would later write extensively about those subjects in a philosophical work, The World and the Individual *(1900-*

1901), and in his only work of history, California, from the Conquest in 1846 to the Second Vigilance Committee in San Francisco *(1886). Ironically, when Royce died in 1916 he lost almost completely his stature as a philosopher while his book on California assured him a lasting position as a historian.*

The present selection is from an address prepared for the National Geographic Society in 1898,[2] *when Royce was at the peak of his influence at Harvard. In it he asks whether nature dictated distinctive social, political, and "psychological" traits in California; his answer is yes. Royce would closely link such "typically Californian" traits as "individuality," "industriousness," "hospitality," "union of man and the visible universe," and the "vagrancy of children," with the state's isolation, mountainous terrain, and semiarid climate.*

Much of what appears here in the name of psychology or social commentary will be dismissed by scholars as antiquarian, but it is interesting to note that many laymen would accept on face value Royce's impressionistic style and deterministic beliefs. In this vein one commonly hears quips and theories connecting California's "zany" policies with its smog, its abundant sunshine with its "wild" styles of dress, its suitability for outdoor living with "friendliness toward strangers." The student is well-advised, then, to ask whether his own "common sense" notions about the relationship between people and nature will withstand close scrutiny.

I have been asked to describe some of the principal physical aspects of California, and to indicate the way in which they have been related to the life and civilization of the region. The task is at once, in its main outlines, comparatively simple, and in its most interesting details hopelessly complex. The topography of the Pacific slope, now well known to most travellers, is in certain of its principal features extremely easy to characterize. The broad landscapes, revealing very frequently at a glance the structure of wide regions, give one an impression that the meaning of the whole can easily be comprehended. Closer study shows how difficult it is to understand the relation of precisely such features to the life that has grown up in this region. The principal interest of the task lies in the fact that it is our American character and civilization which have been already moulded in new ways by these novel aspects of the far western regions. But we stand at the beginning of a process which must continue for long ages. Any one interested in the unity of our national life, and in the guiding of our destinies by broad ideals, desires to conceive in some fashion how the physical features of the Pacific Coast may be expected to mould our national type. Yet thus far we have, as it were, only the most general indications of what the result must be.

In endeavoring to distinguish between what has already resulted from physical conditions and what has been due to personal character, to deliberate choice, or to the general national temperament, or to what we may have to call pure accident, one is dealing with a task for which the data are not yet sufficient. We can but make a beginning.

. . .[A] student of my own habits and prejudices feels at once disposed to pass directly to the inner life of the Californian and to ask himself what influence the nature and climate of such a region seem to have upon the life of the individual mind and body, and, indirectly, upon the social order. Here of course one treads upon ground at once fascinating and enormously difficult. Generalization is limited by the fact of great varieties of personal character and type with which we are dealing. But after all, I think that in California literature, in the customary expressions of Californians in speaking to one another, and, to a very limited degree, in the inner consciousness of any one who has grown up in California, we have evidence of certain ways in which the condition of such a region must influence the life and, I suppose in the end, the character of the whole community. I feel disposed, then, to try to suggest very briefly how it feels to grow up in such a climate, to live in such a region, thus separated by wide stretches of country from other portions

[2]Josiah Royce, "The Pacific Coast: A Psychological Study of the Relations of Climate and Civilization," in Josiah Royce, *Race Questions: Provincialism and Other American Problems* (New York: The Macmillan Co., 1908), pp. 169-225.

of our own land and from the world at large, thus led by the kindliness of nature into a somewhat intimate, even if uncomprehended, relation to the physical conditions, and thus limited to certain horizons in one's experience. I speak of course as a native Californian, but I also do not venture to limit even for a moment my characterization by reference to my own private experience. Californians are rather extraordinarily conscious of the relation between their home and their lives. Newcomers who have grown up elsewhere are constantly comparing their natural surroundings with those that they knew before. The natives, for reasons that I shall suggest in a moment, are put into a relation with nature which, whether they are students of nature or not, and whether they are observant or not, is in feeling a peculiarly intimate relation. . . .

The most familiar account of the California climate in literature is Bret Harte's characterization of the seasonal changes in his poem, "Concepción Argüello." The scene is here at the Presidio at San Francisco, close by the Golden Gate, where the heroine waited for her lover during the long years that the poem describes.

"Day by day on wall and bastion beat the hollow empty breeze—
Day by day the sunlight glittered on the vacant, smiling seas;
Week by week the near hills whitened in their dusty leather cloaks—
Week by week the far hills darkened from the fringing plain of oaks;
Till the rains came, and far-breaking, on the fierce southwester tost,
Dashed the whole long coast with color, and then vanished and were lost.
So each year the seasons shifted, wet and warm and drear and dry;
Half a year of clouds and flowers—half a year of dust and sky."

The nature which is thus depicted has of course many other aspects besides this its fundamental rhythm; but prominent in all the literary descriptions is the stress laid upon the coming of the rains, —an event which occupies, very naturally, the same place in the California poet's mind that the spring occupies elsewhere.

IV

. . . [M]any instances. . . might be given of the emotional reactions of sensitive minds in the presence of California nature. But now the outer aspect of nature unquestionably moulds both the emotions and the customs of mankind, insensibly affects men's temperaments in ways which, as we know, somehow or other tend to become hereditary, however we may view the vexed question concerning the heredity of acquired characters. Moreover, the influence of nature upon custom which every civilization depicts, is precisely the kind of influence that from moment to moment expresses itself psychologically in the more typical emotions of sensitive souls. Thus, one may observe that if we are considering the relation between civilization and climate, and are endeavoring to speculate in however vague a manner upon the future of a society in a given environment, we may well turn to the poets, not for a solution of our problem, but for getting significant hints. . . .

Now what all this poetry in general psychologically means, quite apart from special moods, is that the Californian, of necessity, gains a kind of sensitiveness to nature which is different in type from the sensitiveness that a severer climate would inevitably involve, and different too in type from that belonging to climates mild but moist and more variable. In the first place, as you see, such a climate permits one to be a great deal out of doors in the midst of nature. It permits wide views, where the outlines are vast and in general clear. As, when you are on a steamer it is a matter of some skill to understand what are the actual conditions of wind and sea, while, when you are on a sailing vessel you constantly feel both the wind and the sea with a close intimacy that needs no technical knowledge to make it at least appreciated, so in the case of such a climate as the one of California, your relations with nature are essentially intimate, whether you are a student of nature or not. Your dependence upon nature you feel in one sense more, and in another sense less,—more, because you are more constantly in touch with the natural changes of the moment; less, because you know that nature is less to be feared than under severer conditions. And this intimacy with nature means a certain change in your relations to your fellow men. You get a sense of power from these wide views, a habit of personal independence from the contemplation of a world that the eye seems to own. Especially in country life the individual Californian consequently tends toward a certain kind of independence which I find a strong and subtle contrast to the sort of independence that, for instance, the New England farmer cultivates. The New England farmer must fortify himself in his stronghold against the seasons. He must be ready to adapt himself to a year that permits him to prosper only upon decidedly hard terms. But the California country proprietor can have during the drought, more leisure, unless, indeed, his ambition for wealth too much engrosses him. His horses are plenty and cheap. His fruit crops thrive easily. He is able to supply his table with fewer purchases, with less commercial dependence. His position is, therefore, less that of the knight in his castle and more that of the free dweller in the summer cottage, who is indeed not at leisure, but can easily determine how he shall be busy. It is of little importance to him who his next neighbor is. At pleasure he can ride or drive a good way to find his friends; can choose, like the southern planter of former days, his own range of hospitality; can devote himself, if a man of cultivation, to reading during a good many hours at his own choice, or, if a man of sport, can find during a great part of the year easy opportunities for hunting or for camping both for himself and for the young people of his family. In the dry season he knows beforehand what engagements can be made, without regard to the state of the weather, since the state of the weather is predetermined.

The free life and interchange of hospitality, so often described in the accounts of early California, has left its traces in the country life of California at the present day. Very readily, if you have moderate means, you can create your own quiet estate at a convenient distance from the nearest town. You may cover your house with a bower of roses, surround yourself with an orchard, quickly grow eucalyptus as a shade tree, and with nearly equal facility multiply other shade trees. You become, on easy terms, a proprietor, with estate and home of your own. Now all this holds, in a sense, of any mild climate. But in California the more regular routine of wet and dry seasons modifies and renders more stable the general psychological consequences. All this is encouraging to a kind of harmonious individuality that already tends in the best instances toward a somewhat Hellenic type.

A colleague of my own, a New Englander of the strictest persuasion, who visited California for a short time when he was himself past middle life, returned enthusiastic with the report that the California countrymen seemed to him to resemble the ancient, yes, even the Homeric, Greeks of the Odyssey. The Californians had their independence of judgement; their carelessness of what a barbarian might think, so long as he came from beyond the border; their apparent freedom in choosing what manner of men they should be; their ready and confident speech. All these things my friend at once noticed as characteristic. Thus different in type are these country proprietors from the equally individual, the secretively independent, the silently conscientious New England villagers. They are also quite different from the typical southern proprietors. From the latter they differ in having less tendency to respect traditions, and in laying much less stress upon formal courtesies. . . .

The geographical isolation is added to the absence of tradition. To my own mind, in childhood, every human being was, with a few exceptions, whatever he happened to be. Hereditary distinctions I appreciated only in case of four types of humanity. There were the Chinamen, there were the Irishmen, there were the Mexicans, and there were the rest of us. Within each of these types, every man, to my youthful mind, was precisely what God and himself had made him, and it was distinctly a new point of view to attach a man to the antecedents that either his family or his other social relationships had determined for him. Now, I say, this type of individuality, known more or less in our western communities, but developed in peculiarly high degree in California, seems to me due not merely to the newness of the community, and not merely to that other factor of geographical isolation that I just mentioned, but to the relation with nature of which we have already spoken. It is free and on the whole an emotionally exciting, and also as we have said, an engrossing and intimate relation.

In New England, if you are moody, you may wish to take a long walk out-of-doors, but that is not possible at all or even at most seasons. Nature may not be permitted to comfort you. In California, unless you are afraid of the rain, nature welcomes you at almost any time. The union of the man and the visible universe is free, is entirely unchecked by any hostility on the part of nature, and is such as easily fills one's mind with wealth of warm experience. Our poet just quoted has laid stress upon the directly or symbolically painful aspects of the scene. But these are sorrows of a sort that mean precisely that relation with nature which I am trying to characterize, not the relation of hostility but of closeness. And this is the sort of closeness determined not merely by mild weather, but by long drought and by the relative steadiness of all the climatic conditions.

Now, I must feel that such tendencies are of vast importance, not merely today but for all time. They are tendencies whose moral significance in the life of California is of course both good and evil, since man's relations with nature are, in general, a neutral material upon which ethical relations may be based. If you are industrious, this intimacy with nature means constant cooperation, a cooperation never interrupted by frozen ground and deep snow. If you tend to idleness, nature's kindliness may make you all the more indolent, and indolence is a possible enough vice with the dwellers in all mild climates. If you are morally careless, nature encourages your freedom, and tends in so far to develop a kind of morale frequently characteristic of the dwellers in gentle climates. Yet the nature of California is not enervating. The nights are cool, even in hot weather; owing to the drought the mildness of the air is not necessarily harmful. Moreover, the nature that is so uniform also suggests in a very dignified way a regularity of existence, a definite reward for a definitely planned deed. Climate and weather are at their best always capricious, and, as we have seen, the variations of the California seasons have involved the farmers in much anxiety, and in many cases have given the farming business, as carried on in certain California communities, the same sort of gambling tendency that originally vitiated the social value of the mining industry. But, on the other hand, as the conditions grew more stable, as agriculture developed, vast irrigation enterpises introduced once more a conservative tendency. Here again for the definite deed nature secures a definite return. In regions subject to irrigation, man controls the weather as he cannot elsewhere. He is independent of the current season. And this tendency to organization—a tendency similar to the one that was obviously so potent in the vast ancient civilization of Egypt,—is present under California conditions, and will make itself felt.

Individuality, then, but of a peculiar type, and a tendency despite all this individualism toward agricultural conservatism and a definite social organization—these are already the results of this climate.

V

I have spoken already several times of the geographical isolation of this region. This has been a factor that was felt of course in the social life from the very outset, and more in the early days than at present. To be sure, it was never without its compensating features. It shows its influences in a way that varies with pretty definite periods of California history. In the earliest days, before the newcomers in California supposed that agriculture was possible on any large scale, nearly everything was imported. Butter, for instance, was sent around the Horn to San Francisco. And throughout the early years most of the population felt, so to speak, morally rooted in the Eastern communities from which they had sprung. This tendency retarded for a long time the development of California society, and made the pioneers careless as to the stability of their social structure; encouraged corrupt municipal administration in San Francisco; gave excuse for the lynching habit in the hastily organized mining communities. But a reaction quickly came. After the general good order which as a fact characterized the year 1849 had gradually given place, with the increase of population, to the disorders of 1851 and to the municipal errors of the years between 1850 and 1856 in the city of San Francisco, there came a period of reform and of growing conservatism which marked all the time of the later mining period and of the transition to the agricultural period. During these years many who had come to California without any permanent purpose decided to become members of the community, and decided in consequence to create a community of which it was worth while to be a member. The consequence was the increase of the influence of the factor of geographical isolation in its social influence upon the life of California. The community became self-conscious, independent, indisposed to take advice from without, very confident of the future of the state and of the boundless prosperity soon to be expected; and within the years between 1860 and 1870 a definite local tradition of California life was developed upon the basis of the memories and characters that had been formed in the early days. The consequence was a provincial California, whose ideals at last assumed that form of indifference to the barbarians beyond the border which my friend noticed as surviving even to the time of the visit of which I have spoken. . . .

VI

. . . From the very outset, climate and geographical position, and the sort of life in which men were engaged, have encouraged types of individuality whose subtle distinction from those elsewhere to be found we have already attempted in a very inadequate fashion to suggest. Accordingly, from the first period down to the present time, the California community has been a notable theatre for the display of political and financial, and, on occasion, of intellectual individuality of decidedly extraordinary types. The history of both earlier and later California politics has been a very distinctly personal history. The political life of the years before the war had as their most icturesque incident the long struggle for the United States Senatorship carried on between David Broderick and William Gwin. This contest involved personalities far more than principles. Gwin and Broderick were both of them extremely picturesque figures,—the one a typical Irish-American, the other a Southerner. The story of their bitter warfare is a familiar California romance. The tragic death of Broderick, in duel with the once notorious David S. Terry, is a tale that long had a decidely national prominence. Terry himself is an example of a type of individuality not elsewhere unknown in border life, but developed under peculiarly Californian conditions. Terry was, very frankly, a man of blood. Regarding him as a man of blood, one finds him in many ways, and within his own limits, an interesting, even a conscientious and attractive personality. He was at one time upon the Supreme Bench of the state of California. He warred with the Vigilance Committee of 1856 in a manner that certainly wins one's respect for his skill in bringing that organization into a very difficult position. He carried on this warfare both as judge of the Supreme Court and as wielder of a bowie knife. When he slew Broderick, he did so in a fashion that, so far as the duelling code permitted, was perfectly fair. He lived for years with a disposition to take the unpopular side of every question, to fight bitterly for causes for which no other man cared, and it was precisely for such a cause that he finally died. His attempted assault upon Judge Stephen J. Field, and the controversy that led there to, and that resulted in Terry's death, was, a few years since, in everybody's memory.

It would be wholly wrong to conceive California individuality as at all fairly represented by a border type such as Terry's. Yet when one looks about in California society and politics, one finds even at the present day picturesque personalities preserving their picturesqueness amidst various grades of nobility and baseness, in a fashion more characteristic, I think, than is customary in most of our newer communities. The nobler sort of picturesque personality may be the public benefactor, like James Lick or Adolph Sutro. He may be the social reformer of vast ideals, like Henry George. Or again the baser individual may be the ignorant demagogue of the grade of Dennis Kearney. Your California hero may be the chief of the Vigilance Committee of 1856, or some other typical and admired pioneer, growing old in the glory of remembered early deeds. He may be the railway magnate, building a transcontinental line under all sorts of discouragements, winning a great fortune, and dying just as he founds a university. But in all these phases he remains the strong individual type of man that in a great democracy is always necessary. It is just this type that, as some of us fear, the conditions of our larger democracy in more eastern regions tend far too much to eliminate. In California, such individuality is by no means yet eliminated. . . .

And now we have seen the various ways in which this sort of individuality is a product of the natural features of the state as well as of those early conditions which themselves were determined by geographical factors. On the other hand, in addition to this prevalence of individuality and this concomitant severity of the judgment of prominent individuals, there are social conditions characteristic of San Francisco which can also be referred to geographical and climatic factors. Early in the development of San Francisco a difficulty in the education of the young appeared which, as I fancy, has not yet been removed. This difficulty had to do with the easy development of vagrancy in city children. Vagrancy is a universal evil of cities, but the California vagrant can easily pass the night out-doors during the greater part of the year. A friend of mine who was connected with the management of San Francisco public schools for a number of years, laid stress upon this climatic factor and its dangers in official communications published at the time of his office. The now too well-known name of ''hoodlum'' originated in San Francisco, and is said to have been the name adopted by a particular group of young men. The social complications of the time of the sand-lot, when Dennis Kearney led laborers into a dangerous pass, were again favored by climatic conditions. Public meetings out-of-doors and in the sand-lot could be held with a certain freedom and persistency in California that would be impossible without interruption elsewhere. While such factors have nothing to do with discontent, they greatly increase the opportunities for agitation. The new constitution of California, adopted in 1879, was carried at the polls by a combination of the working men of San Francisco with the dissatisfied farmers of the interior. This dissatisfaction of the farmers was no doubt due in the main to the inadequacy of their comprehension of the material conditions under which they were working. The position of California —its geographical isolation again—has been one complicating factor for the California farmer, since luxuriant nature easily furnished him, in case he should use wise methods, with a rich supply, while his geographical isolation made access to market somewhat difficult. This difficulty about the market long affected California political life in the form of dissatisfaction felt against the railway, which was of course held responsible and which in fact for years was more or less responsible for an increase of these difficulties of reaching the market. Well, this entire series of complications, which in 1879 combined San Francisco working men with the farmers of the interior, and changed the constitution of the state, is an example of the complex way in which the geographical situation and the factors of climate have acted to affect social movements.

On the other hand, the individuality aforesaid, when brought into the presence of such social agitations, has frequently proved in California life a conservative factor of great importance. The mob may be swept away for a time by an agitating idea. But the individual Californian himself is suspicious of mobs. The agitations in question proved transient. Even the constitution, designed to give the discontented whatever they most supposed they wanted, proved to be susceptible of a very conservative construction by the courts, and public opinion in California has never been very long under the sway of any one illusion. The individuality that we have described quickly revolts against its false prophets. In party politics, California proves to be an extremely doubtful state. Party ties are not close. The vote changes from election to election. The independent voter is well in place. Finally, through all these tendencies, there runs a certain idealism, often more or less unconscious. This idealism is partly due to the memory of the romance due to the unique marvels of the early days. It is also sustained by precisely that intimacy with nature which renders the younger Californians so sensitive. I think that perhaps Edward Rowland Sill, whose poems are nowadays so widely appreciated, has given the most representative expression to the resulting spirit of California, to that tension between individualism and loyalty, between shrewd conservatism and bold radicalism, which marks this community.

2.
James J. Parsons Takes a More Flexible View

Every nation, every province on earth can claim special geographic qualities, for no two places are alike. And yet a few places like California manage somehow to generate an unusual aura of separateness, a distinctiveness which is universally recognized. The extent to which California is justified in considering itself a "land apart" is the main subject of this second essay.[3]

Professor James J. Parsons, of the Department of Geography at the University of California, Berkeley, bases his writing on a good deal of recent research. In a way he obeys Royce's admonition that others make new studies of the subject of geographic uniqueness.

Parsons gives as much credence to California's claim to distinction as does Royce and agrees that the state is unified by climate and geographical remoteness. But Parsons' basic premise and his mode of reasoning are quite different from Royce's. For one thing, the geographer is more aware of subregionalisms within California—more conscious of "aberrant cultural groups and distinctive landscape types." For another, he gives greater weight to the influence of cultural factors.

His basic assertion is that the most important cultural distinctions spring not from native soil, as it were, but from "the peculiar nature of the settlement of the state." The brewing in the "melting pot" and the "fusion of ideas, cultures and skills" which come from every part of the nation are largely responsible for the sense of newness and experimentalism and for other traits that typify California. This statement of causality is more rigorous, though "colder" and less romantic, than Royce's. Parsons' suggestion—that a blending of natural and cultural influences has molded California—is more in keeping with latter-day scholarly thinking.

There is general agreement that California, like Texas or New England, is a land apart. In the popular mind it is somehow different, a state with distinctive qualities both of the physical environment and of the human spirit which give it a personality of its own. It has mountains, deserts, valleys, beaches, and rocky coasts in magnificent profusion. Its boisterous and romantic past, its cornucopia harvests, its moving pictures, its ferry boats and cable cars, the brash geometric newness of its stuccoed cities and suburbs, even the very name "California," mellifluous and of mysterious origin, all symbolize a way of life or a state of mind if not a geographical area to most of the world's people.

The regional consciousness of Californians, remarkably strong for so restless and rootless a population, has had its origins in the common problems and interests imposed by geography. An off-side geographical position and a unique and gentle climate have strongly influenced the settlement history of the state and the character of its economy and culture. And the steady stream

[3]James J. Parsons, "The Uniqueness of California," *American Quarterly*, VII, No.1 (Spring 1955), 45-55. Footnotes deleted.

of promotional literature from the professional romanticists seems, if anything, to have made the outside world more convinced and aware of the uniqueness of California than are Californians themselves.

Among the factors of the physical environment it is probably climate, especially water availability, which ties more things together than anything else. It so happens that California's arbitrarily conceived boundaries outline the only area of winter rain and summer drought in North America with rather remarkable accuracy. Northward from the Siskiyous and Mount Shasta summer rains of cyclonic origin occur with increasing frequency; on the deserts of the Great Basin and the Colorado River drainage summer thundershowers are relatively common. But the cold upwelling ocean water off the California coast during the summer months so cools the layer of air above it that the fog-laden, on-shore moving air masses have an unusual stability. Precipitation of any kind is a rare occurrence anywhere in the state between June and October except in the higher mountains and on the extreme southeastern desert. During the rainy season it may range from as little as eight inches in San Diego County to a drenching 100 inches or more along the northern Redwood Coast, but throughout the length and breadth of the state drought turns the hillside grasses a golden yellow by the end of June. Only the deeper-rooted oaks, pines and chaparral-type brush retain their greenness. This is the classical Mediterranean or West Coast subtropical climate of the geographers, though California summers are drier and, except along the coastal fringe, hotter, than those of Italy, Greece or Spain. They are more comparable to those of North Africa or Israel.

Although the moderating influence of the Pacific Ocean makes extreme winter cold unknown in the lowlands, local temperature contrasts are nevertheless considerable. February weather may range from the warm and sunny days of Imperial Valley or coastal Southern California to raging blizzards in the Sierra Nevada and the persistent tule fogs of the Central Valley; summertime brings a shimmering dry heat to the interior lowlands while only a few miles away the coasts are bathed in cool sea breezes or sea fog.

This distinctive climatic pattern has had obvious and far-reaching importance for agriculture, industry, and the entire mode of life within the state. It has lured legions of new settlers. Without it there could scarcely be a California.

Much of California's highly specialized agriculture is directly dependent on either the mild winters and long growing season or the rainless, low-humidity summers. Citrus, avocados, dried fruits, cotton and winter truck crops are all conspicuous examples. Among the major agricultural crops only winter grains and the prunes and dry wine grapes of the north coast valleys are unirrigated. The recent widespread adoption of the overhead sprinkler for previously unwatered upland fields is permitting a further expansion of irrigation that will probably be arrested only by the exhaustion of available water supplies. The stakes in such farming are high and a large share of the production has always been from corporate farms, administered by professional farm managers who, with their labor force, typically live in the valley cities, commuting to these "factories in the field" as the crop calendar dictates. One of the distinguishing features of California agriculture, which for the most part lies outside of the rural farm tradition of the rest of the country, has been its dependence on a pool of mobile, foreign-born farm labor, but this is now rapidly disappearing with increased mechanization.

Although agriculture in the arid West is everywhere dependent on irrigation, most of its techniques and legal institutions were developed in California—Western water law, the control of alkali, deep-well drilling and pumping techniques, big dam building, joint stock irrigation districts, and legislation restricting the dumping of mining debris in streams. Further, it has been only in California among the Western states that such extensive irrigable soils have been associated with the supplies of water, a temperate winter climate and other resources of forest, mine and sea that could attract and support a large urban, non-agricultural population.

Climate also has had a direct bearing on the industrial development, not only in the well-known localization of the motion picture and aircraft industries but also in such burgeoning lines as garment and furniture making which produce goods "styled for Western outdoor living" for the national market. The recently discovered prestige value of the "Made in California" label has become one of the major assets of many of the state's new consumer goods manufacturers. The magic of the name derives, of course, from the way in which the people east of the Rockies have come to think of California as a sort of "never-never" land of sunshine and flowers and unlimited opportunity, the sort of place where the entertainers, artists and authors, for instance, who can serve a national market from any place in the country, so often choose to live. And it has been a cumulative process. The upsurge of population on the Pacific Coast has created new mass markets which have opened opportunities for additional industries best able to benefit from the economies of large-scale production.

The state's unparalleled population growth, to an extraordinary degree an urban phenomenon, can beyond dispute be very largely explained in terms of the lure of the climate, of mild winters coupled with relatively cool summers, low rainfall and abundant sunshine. As America has grown more wealthy it has grown more footloose and leisure-conscious so that the amenities of those regions which have pleasant outdoor climates the year around have become increasingly significant considerations in the redistribution of population. The Florida tropics and Arizona provide the closest parallels to California's climatic "pull," although both have hotter summers than the California coast, but these areas have lacked the diversity of resources with which this state has been able to absorb and support its new millions. For the last fifty years, at least, the well-advertised attractions of the climate have been a more important attraction to newcomers than opportunities in mining, agriculture and industry. This has been more especially true of Southern California which today, despite its later start, has the larger share of the state's population.

Although the railroad, and more recently the airplane, solved the physical problem of transportation for the West, the economic problems have remained. The fight against discriminatory freight rates has been continuous. The farmer, needing to market his oranges, his wine, his perishable truck crops in competition with producers located closer to the massed Eastern population, has until recently been more vocal than the industrialist in defending Western interests. The high cost of transportation has been a powerful influence pushing California towards industrial self-sufficiency. The freight charges on Eastern-made goods moving West are, in effect, a sort of protective tariff for the California manufacturer who would cater to the local, Western market. Today, when the three Pacific Coast states represent a market area with a population as large as all of Canada, the economies of mass production are becoming available to many more local producers. Like Canada, California has become a sort of branch-plant empire for consumer goods producers, but the absence of coal and iron ore and the threatened eventual shortages of cheap water, hydroelectric power sites, natural gas, and even petroleum will all tend to keep it from ever assuming the industrial dominance of the Eastern Manufacturing Belt states. Only the widespread application of low-cost nuclear or solar energy to peacetime ends could change the prospect. . . .

Competition between crops often involved more than elementary economics. Oranges, for example, had attained considerable importance in Southern California very soon after the completion of the Southern Pacific Railroad from New Orleans in 1881 and the arrival of the Santa Fe in 1886, but ownership of a lush green citrus grove set against a backdrop of snow-covered mountains carried a prestige value which left the profit motive often subordinate. The orange tree, as a symbol of California's sub-tropical climate and fertility, must have brought nearly as much money into the state in the form of retired Eastern and mid-Western industrialists and farmers as it has from sales on the citrus exchanges. . . .

II

The geographical remoteness of California from the rest of the nation and the world, as much as the climate, helps account for whatever quality of regional identity, of uniqueness, that here exists. The impoverished culture of aboriginal California was in considerable part caused by barriers imposed by distance, desert and mountain. (Climate likewise was involved, for the food crops of the American Indians were virtually all adapted to warm-season growth. On the summer-dry West Coast, agriculture was impossible prior to the introduction of irrigation techniques and Old World winter grains.) During the Spanish period and, indeed, until the completion of the Central Pacific Railroad in 1869, California was one of the truly isolated portions of the inhabited earth. China and Australia were closer, in time, in cost, and in comfort of travel than were Chicago or New York. Getting to California was then an undertaking of major proportion which must have exerted a significant selective influence on its early settlement. It was the more footloose and restless of the adventurers who came, whether from East of the Rockies, from Europe, from Chile, or from China. The problem of communication with the rest of the nation was from the beginning a common concern of all Californians, whether it was the clipper service 'round Cape Horn, the Pony Express, the transcontinental telegraph or the railroad. The construction of the Central Pacific Railroad may well have been hurried in an effort to counter secessionist rumors emanating from California.

III

As more and more elements of our culture become universalized and the influences of government on men's lives increase, political areas, states and provinces as well as nations tend increasingly to be the forms into which regional identities are cast. This is notably so in California where the state's boundaries are more in accord with geographic reality than almost any other of the 48 states. With reason it has been called "an island on the land."

The 42nd parallel, the state's most northern limit, was first recognized in 1819 as the boundary between Spanish and American rule. In effect, this was a delineation of the limits of the Louisiana Purchase of 1803 and cut across what was then, as it remains today, a region of mountains and lava beds for the most part uninhabited. On the south the present line between California and Mexico, recognized by Spain as an ecclesiastical boundary as early as 1804 was confirmed as an international line in 1848. At the time it ran through essentially unoccupied mountains and deserts; today, a century later, it stands as a supreme example of the decisive role of politics in geography, a line drawn arbitrarily by men on the surface of the earth that has become one of the world's sharpest, most clearly defined cultural boundaries.

The eastern boundary of the state was set by the California State Constitutional Convention of 1849 largely because at the time there seemed nothing but worthless desert to the East. It was considered important then to control the west bank of the navigable Colorado River and the timber resources on the eastern slopes of the Sierra. The concern for water which marks our day had not yet developed, the Nevada mines had not been discovered nor had the well-watered Carson and Truckee valleys been settled. Despite countless local controversies, threats of secession and annexation movements, California's frontiers seem today, after a century of trial, still to make reasonably good sense — something that cannot be said with similar force for many of the other American states.

IV

Although in one sense California can properly be thought of as approximating a physical, economic and cultural unit, it probably contains as many aberrant cultural groups and distinctive landscape types as any like area on earth. There is not one California, but many. One need not look far for diversities and contrasts. The different ways in which man has used and modified his environment are demonstrated alike by the San Gabriel Valley citrus belt, Kern County's forest of oil wells sprouting from the midst of great cattle, cotton and potato ranches, the rolling red up-lands of the Mother Lode fruit districts, the vineyards of Napa or of Fresno, the asparagus beds of the dusty Delta peat lands, Salinas' lettuce fields bordered by eucalyptus windbreaks, the green, forest-fringed meadows of Humboldt County, Coachella Valley's rich checkerboard of winter crops. Or consider San Francisco and Los Angeles themselves.

The Transverse Ranges (popularly if less properly, "the Tehachapi") which cut across the state just north of Santa Barbara have long symbolized the division of California into two sections, the North and the South, separated by well-recognized physiographic, historical, social and cultural barriers. Even during the Mexican period divisionist sentiment was sufficiently strong to give rise to serious political schisms. The same tension between North and South continued into the period of American rule. In considering California's admission to the Union, Congress thought seriously of a division of the state into two parts and the issue was also debated at the State's Constitutional Convention in 1849. Ten years later the legislature authorized the secession of the six southern most counties and their establishment into a proposed "Territory of Colorado" as its residents had requested in a referendum, but the Civil War intervened before the proposal could be placed before the Congress of the United States. In the state's first decades the preponderance of wealth and population was in San Francisco, the Central Valley and the Mother Lode. The South was thinly settled, Spanish speaking and isolated, without mines or large cities. Until 1876, when a branch of the Southern Pacific Railroad finally reached it, the Los Angeles area was linked with San Francisco only by coastwise shipping operating out of a poorly protected roadstead at San Pedro. As transplanted Easterners, oil and citrus, motion pictures, aircraft and long-distance aqueducts made the South strong, the divisionist sentiment gradually subsided. By then highway, pipeline and aircraft had united the state sufficiently to hold it together even in the face of a strong sectional rivalry. But Southern California is still "South of Tehachapi," another land with a distinctive climate, ocean, landforms, and even people. While culturally Northern California is Western, the South is Eastern, settled later by older people who came with the real estate booms and who maintained their cultural ties with the "folks back home." What the "Native Sons of the Golden West" encampments are to Northern California, the Annual Iowa Picnic at Long Beach is to the South.

In the mountain counties the pace has been slower. Most typically the earliest farm settlers seem to have been attracted by the abundance of wood and water there and by nostalgic reminders of more familiar landscapes from which they had come. Although the green hills may have reminded them of home during the spring months, the Eastern farmers who moved onto the land in the years immediately after the Gold Rush were prepared to cope with neither the severe summer dryness nor the capricious nature of the winter rains. Once the worst of the flood-control and drainage problems had been solved (and with them the threat of malaria which had sent many early settlers into the hills) the gradual down-slope migration of agriculture began which left in its wake so many abandoned farms throughout the Coast Range and the Sierra foothills. . . .

V

When contrasted with the humid East, the extraordinary character of the California environment can scarcely be denied; nor can the extraordinary character of its culture. Inevitably the temptation has been strong to link the two in the direct cause and effect of environmental determinism, arguing that the California land and climate breeds special forms of religious, political and social organizations, or architecture, dress and other cultural institutions. I should rather suggest, as Carey McWilliams so effectively does in his *California: The Great Exception*, that it has been the peculiar nature of the settlement of the state, the continued flow of restless immigrants across its borders from the Gold Rush to the post-war boom, that has been responsible for whatever distinctive cultural qualities it possesses.

The Gold Rush, which had sent California off to its flying start within a year after the annexation from Mexico, attracted peoples from every state and from every corner of the earth, obliterating almost overnight the leisure-loving, pastoral civilization of Spanish-California. Unlike other such booms, either before or since, California continued to grow long after the lure of gold had ceased to be effective. Wave after wave of immigrants have continued to arrive, with but brief interruptions, for more than a century. In every census outsiders have been in the majority; in 1950 two out of every three persons in the state had been born elsewhere. Significantly, a substantial portion of the new arrivals have always come with time on their hands and money in their pockets, thus contributing to what at times suggests a sort of self-perpetuating economy.

It is precisely such a melting pot where old ways and traditions are most easily discarded and where innovation and experimentation have their freest rein. "The fact is," writes McWilliams, "that Californians have become so used to the idea of experimentation. . .that they have had to experiment so often. . .they are psychologically prepared to try anything. . .California is different from Iowa and this difference means that it is possible to dress differently without being regarded as a crank or a freak". . .or, one may add, to build, to cook, to write, to paint, or to think differently. This willingness to experiment, associated with the disruption of family ties, social customs and traditions, is reflected to varying extents in its regional architecture, religious cults, pension plans, sportswear design, tract developments, the junior college movement, motels, drive-in restaurants, even in its branch banking organizations. In some cases, as with architecture and gardening and the flourishing desert and beach cults of Southern California, it has been given special emphasis by the novelty of the environment.

At one time California had a world-wide renown for the new mining techniques developed in the gold fields—hydraulicking, dredging, a dozen new types of cradles and rockers for placer mining, the California stamp mill, the Pelton water wheel and many specialized types of ore processing equipment. More recently these have been overshadowed by accomplishments in the field of agriculture—new techniques for water control (irrigation), for frost control, for pest control, the selection and improvement of new varieties of sub-tropical fruits, marketing cooperatives, forcing of early fruit and vegetables, mechanization of virtually every "stoop" and "reach" operation in field and orchard crop production. Inevitably, too, Californians have had a common concern for such geographically-conditioned problems as water supply, land reclamation, earthquake-proof construction, forest fire and flood, migratory farm labor, communication with the East, absentee ownership, freight rates, port development and foreign trade and the general adaptation to living in the only Mediterranean-type climatic area in the Western Hemisphere outside of Chile. But this background, it should be emphasized, involved primarily sectional self-interest rather than any evolving "psychic unity" of the group.

A sense of separateness and apartness from the rest of the nation, a regional awareness, gives California much of its distinctive character. We are scarcely dealing here, however, with the sort of deeply-rooted ties and affections for the land that have characterized those longer settled areas which have been most conspicuously identified with the concept of the "regional culture." For one thing, that sort of regionalism has its true roots in the rural countryside and California has had an essentially urban society since 1850. There is here neither the homogeneity of culture nor of physical environment for which the regionalist so fondly seek. Heterogeneity instead is the more conspicuous quality. Physiographic diversity and cultural contrast are among California's most obvious identifying features; the famed susceptibility of its inhabitants to unorthodox religions, architectural and political movements suggests as much. Yet there remains a conspicuous regional quality to the land and its people which stems from the political fact of the state, the isolation which the barriers of desert and distance have imposed, its distinctive combination of landforms, climate and natural vegetation and, especially, the recency and rapidity of its settlement and the diversity and origins of its settlers.

All manner of people from all sections of the country and the world have been thrown recently together here in a spectacular physical environment that is different and challenging, inviting new techniques and new adjustments at every turn. The resultant fusion of ideas, cultures and skills seems to have produced not only a buoyant optimism and self-confidence but also a sort of hybrid vigor, unfettered by conventions, which may account for many of the contradictions and paradoxes within the state. . . .

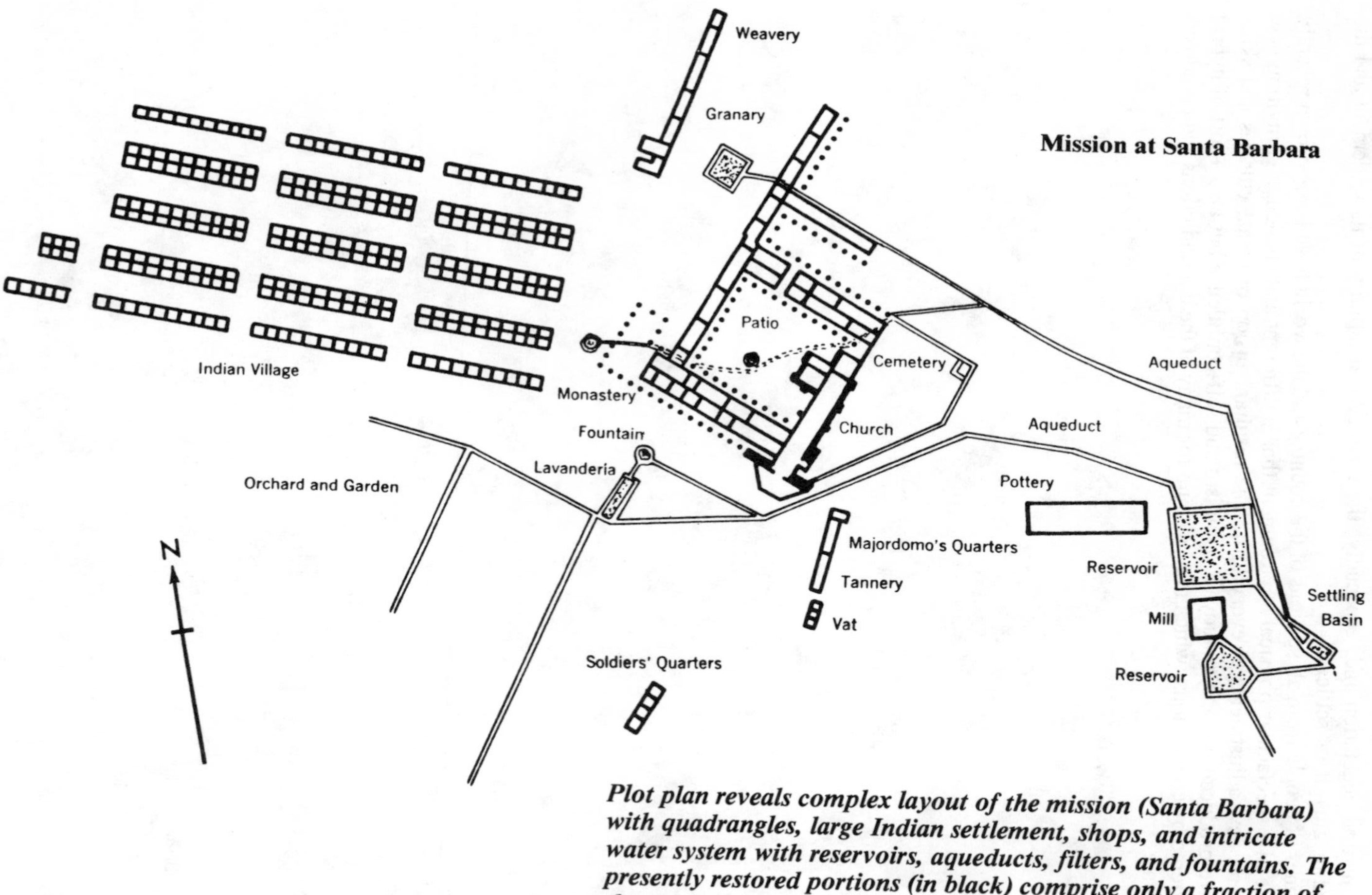

Plot plan reveals complex layout of the mission (Santa Barbara) with quadrangles, large Indian settlement, shops, and intricate water system with reservoirs, aqueducts, filters, and fountains. The presently restored portions (in black) comprise only a fraction of the original plant.

The method which the [Franciscan] fathers observe in the conversion is not to oblige anyone to become a Christian, admitting only those who voluntarily offer themselves, and this they do in the following manner: Since these Indians are accustomed to live in the fields and the hills like beasts, the fathers require that if they wish to be Christians they shall no longer go to the forest, but must live in the mission; and if they leave the rancheria, as they call the little village of huts and houses of the Indians, they will go to seek them and will punish them. With this they begin to catechize the heathen who voluntarily come, teaching them to make the sign of the cross and other things necessary, and if they persevere in the catechism for two or three months and in the same frame of mind, when they are instructed they proceed to baptize them.

—Fray Pedro Font's Diary, 1775–1776.[1]

The monks, by their answers to our different question, left us ignorant of no part of the government of this religious community [Mission San Carlos]. . . the day consists in general of seven hours labour, and two hours prayer; but there are four or five hours prayer on Sundays and festivals, which are entirely consecrated to rest and divine worship.

Corporal punishment is inflicted on the Indians of both sexes who neglect the exercises of piety, and many sins, which are left in Europe to the divine justice, are here punished by irons and the stocks. And lastly . . . the moment an Indian is baptized, the effect is the same as if he had pronounced a vow for life. If he escape, to reside with his relations in the independent villages, he is summoned three times to return, and if he refuse, the missionaries apply to the governor, who sends soldiers to seize him in the midst of his family, and conduct him to the mission, where he is condemned to receive a certain number of lashes, with the whip. . . .

—J. F. G. de la Pérouse, September 1786.[2]

CHAPTER 2

FRANCISCAN MISSIONARIES
Saviors or Exploiters?

So much praise has been given the Franciscan missionaries of California that it may be hard to imagine anybody speaking ill of them. With the publication of Helen Hunt Jackson's *Ramóna* in 1884, which called attention to the demise of the mission-bred Indians, the Franciscans in California began to assume the sacrosanct position attained by the Puritans in New England—that of the founders of an entire civilization. The mission era, 1769 to 1834, did indeed have many ingredients of which heroes and legends are made, including the narrow success of the "sacred expedition" of 1769, the starving time that followed, and the heroic efforts of Fr. Junipero Serra and his band to establish a chain of outposts on the farthest reaches of the Spanish Empire.

Although many accounts of mission history have been fanciful, it must be conceded that the missions held the center of the stage in early California. Never had Spanish missionaries faced a more difficult challenge in the New World, for the California frontier was remote and isolated, exposed to potential enemies, and relatively crowded with Indians. Nor was there apparently any gold or silver in California so that the missionaries thought agriculture would have to be developed to feed the large mission population. The natives numbered as many as 300,000 (an astonishing one

[1] Fray Pedro Font, "Diary of an Expedition to Monterey by Way of the Colorado River 1775-1776," in Herbert E. Bolton (trans. and ed.), *Anza's California Expeditions* (5 vols.; Berkeley: University of California Press, 1930), IV (Font's Complete Diary), 179.

[2] J. F. G. Pérouse, *A Voyage Round the World, Performed in the Years 1785, 1786, 1787, and 1788* (2 vols.; London: G. G. and J. Robinson, 1799), I, 448.

sixth of the total Indian population of the area that would become the United States) and generally lived in tiny isolated villages which were remarkably stable and peaceful. At the peak of mission influence, about 1810, the Franciscans held sway over 20,000 neophytes in twenty-one separate establishments scattered along the coast from San Diego to San Francisco, and also over hundreds of thousands of head of livestock on millions of acres of land. The secular village settlements, the ranchos, and the military installations were subsidiary to the missions. The Franciscans needed considerable administrative skill, physical stamina, and political know-how—not to speak of religious dedication—to endure a life of isolation and physical danger while also engaging in commerce, manufacture, and agriculture. There were seldom more than 30 or so friars to manage this entire system. Thus an imperial task that usually required expensive military conquest and occupation was successfully achieved through religious conversion and economic dependency.

Nevertheless, tension between church and state erupted early in the form of a mild but perpetual verbal duel between the military governors and mission heads. Governor Pedro Fages was already sparring with his opposite number, Fr. Serra, in 1770. Other governors followed suit, and the Mexican officials who sought and got the secularization of the missions by 1834 carried the struggle further. Moreover, from the time of the visit of the Frenchman La Pérouse in 1786, outsiders also offered criticism, some of it motivated by natural-rights idealism, some of it by ethnic myopia or religious bigotry. Nor were the nineteenth century historians, like Hubert Howe Bancroft, as appreciative of the Franciscan effort as the friars themselves would have liked. Finally, in the twentieth century, a host of scholars portraying what they feel to be the Indian side of the story have made new critical appraisals.

The major charges against the Franciscans have fallen into four general categories. The first charge is that the Franciscans did not carry out their original mission, which was to prepare the Indians for civilization within twenty years or so and then abandon their establishments and look for new frontiers and new converts. Second, critics say that the wealth amassed by the missionaries and their worldly preoccupations with the agriculture and the hide-and-tallow trade comported badly with their sacred vows of poverty. Third is the charge that the Franciscans accomplished far less than they claimed in the way of instruction in language and vocational skills and even in religious conversion. The fourth accusation is that their system of labor exploitation required armed repression of "wild" Indians and physical punishments for neophyte transgressors and these restraints vitiated the entire civilizing purpose of the missions. The latter charge is the most crucial, for it brings into question the Franciscans' reputation as benign masters of a group of willing subjects. Whether and to what extent the fourth charge is an accurate one comes into focus in the following pair of selections, each by a highly qualified observer.

Sherburne Cook's investigation of the matter is made with the penetrating analytical tools of a social scientist. He feels that the friars did not succeed in adapting the Indians to a more demanding society. He concludes that the Indians must have regarded the system of work as a stringent one. He believes, moreover, that their religious conversion may have been superficial.

Fr. Maynard Geiger's examination of similar data results in quite the opposite view. The records of a large and important mission, Santa Barbara, prove to his satisfaction an outcome of successful persuasion and adaptation.

For many years Fr. Geiger was responsible for assembling the official documentary evidence for the Church officials to use in determining whether Junipero Serra should be declared a saint. At latest count over 7500 pages of Serra's writings, as well as the works of numerous scholars and others, have been turned over to a panel of clerical judges for evaluation. In 1985 the Pope officially declared Serra "venerable," meaning that he led a life "of heroic virtue," and that his candidacy, first for beatification and finally for sainthood, is still proceeding. The Serra canonization question, which first arose formally half a century ago, ranks as perhaps the oldest unresolved California controversy. How Serra and his fellow Franciscans dealt with the Indians two centuries ago is, therefore, still a matter of ecclesiastical as well as academic concern.

The question having to do with mission labor and punishment bring other issues to mind. Did Spain have other practical alternatives for dealing with the Indians of California? How did the Indian policies of New Spain compare with those of the Yankees a generation later? More broadly: can there be absolute values in the comparison of entire cultures, as the Franciscans naturally assumed, or must one take a relativistic stance, as Cook seems to do? Finally, we may ask if there can ever be a completely dispassionate point of view on an issue involving religion or the clash of cultures; what role do the interpreter's own religious or cultural preferences play in interpreting historical events, and what role should they play? *(Editor's note)*

3. Sherburne Cook Takes a Hard Look at Mission Life

The California Indian has been the subject of more intensive study than probably any other comparable group of primitive people in any part of the world, mostly by investigators at the University of California, Berkeley. One of them, Berkeley physiologist Sherburne Cook, set himself the task of writing at length on The Conflict Between the California Indian and White Civilization. *He wished to see the Indians as physiological beings responding to a drastically changing natural environment. He uses such factors as reaction to physical restraint, incidence of disease, birth rate, death rate, and sex ratios as a measurement of Indian well-being. Cook's work is a masterful attempt to use modern analytical techniques to investigate a historical subject on which the records leave much to be desired.*

The work excerpted here is titled The Indian Versus the Spanish Mission:[3] *the very title portends a negative report. Cook's conclusions are, by and large, damaging to the Franciscans' reputation. His conclusions about the Indian responses to Anglo-American culture in California are not one whit more complimentary.*

Using such techniques as demographic analysis, Cook sees the death rate as notably high and the birth rate as significantly low. To Cook, these statistical levels indicate the Indians' inability to adapt to the demands of an alien society. Indian efforts at open resistance seem to him quite frequent. He surmises that the most comfortable adaptation may have been achieved in the spiritual sphere, where customary values and Christian concepts could exist together without, as in the daily occupations, one set of ideas and habits having to displace the other.

. . . The extent of fugitivism and rebellion is the key to the response of the individual, whereas population trends indicate the response of a group.

. . . In a recent paper the data bearing on this question [population trends] have been examined and critically analyzed. The chief conclusions were set forth as follows:

> Primarily as a result of consistent wholesale addition by conversion, the total population rose rapidly until approximately 1800. Thereafter the increase continued, but more slowly, up to an equilibrium point near 1820, subsequent to which a definite decline set in. These observed changes, which were based upon a large gentile immigration, mask the true situation with respect to the converted population. The latter was subject to very great real diminution in the beginning. This is clear from the falling birth rate and the huge excess of deaths over births

[3] Sherbourne F. Cook, *The Conflict Between the California Indian and the White Civilization* (Berkeley and Los Angeles: University of California Press, 1943), I, 11-157.

which was present throughout the mission era. Actually the critical and determining factor was the death rate, for it has been shown that the decline in gross or crude birth rate may be accounted for largely by the constantly increasing sex ratio (males to females). Since the latter was invariable at unity for children under ten, the change must have been due to a differential death rate between males and females during adolescence and maturity, which would result in a relative decline in the number of child bearing women. The death rate as a whole was always remarkably high, even, for some as yet unexplained reason, at the very start of the missions. It tended definitely, however, to fall during the last thirty years and, at the existing rates of change, would probably have come into equilibrium with the birth rate ultimately. These aspects of the total death rate were due primarily to the state of the child death rate, since the adult death rate did not alter so materially in sixty-odd years.

The chief conclusion of a more general nature is that the Indian population, which presumably had been in a more or less steady equilibrium prior to missionization, underwent a profound upset as a result of that process, a process from which it was showing signs of recovery only at the time of secularization. The indications are, indeed, that several further generations would have been necessary to recast the race, as it were, and bring about that restoration of biotic equilibrium which eventually would have occurred.

. . . The group response of the natives to the mission environment was therefore a very marked decline in numbers, referable primarily to the high mortality rate and secondarily to a reduced birth rate and altered sex ratio. . . .

Another response to the mission environment was an attempt to escape from it. The following items constitute the testimony of certain Indians who escaped but were caught. On their return each was asked to state why he absconded. The arabic numerals below indicate the individual reasons given:

1. He had been flogged for leaving without permission.
2. The same reason.
3. The same reason. Also, he ran away because he was hungry.
4. He had been put in jail for getting drunk.
5. He had run away previously and had been flogged three times.
6. He was hungry. He absconded previously and, when he returned voluntarily, he was given twenty-five lashes.
7. He was frightened at seeing how his friends were always being flogged.
8. Because. . .of the great hunger he felt.
9. When he wept over the death of his wife and children, he was ordered whipped five times by Father Antonio Danti.
10. He became sick.
11. His wife and one son died.
12. Because of hunger; also, he was put in the stocks while sick.
13. He wanted to go back to his country.
14. His wife, one son, and two brothers died.
15. His wife and a son had run away to their country, and at the mission he was beaten a great deal.
16. Because of a blow with a club.
17. They beat him when he wept for a dead brother.
18. He went to see his mother.
19. His mother, two brothers, and three nephews died, all of hunger, and he ran away so that he would not also die.
20. Lorenzo went away.

21. His father died.
22. Being bad, they whipped him.
23. His wife sinned with a rancher, and the priest beat him for not taking better care of her.
24. They made him work all day without giving him or his family anything to eat. Then, when he went out one day to find food, Father Danti flogged him.
25. His wife and two sons died, and he had no one to look after.
26. His little niece died of hunger.
27. He was very hungry.
28. After going one day to the presidio to find food, when he returned, Father Danti refused him his ration, saying to go to the hills and eat hay.
29. When his son was sick, they would give the boy no food, and he died of hunger.
30. Twice, when he went out to hunt food or to fish, Father Danti had him whipped.

Much of the above-cited Indian testimony will obviously be heavily discounted. Several of the accusations are absurd, and many of the reasons advanced are trivial and irrational. Yet they ring true to the primitive psychology of the Indian, as most persons who have had dealings with this and similar races will admit, and they merit at least a fair examination.

If we examine the opinions expressed by competent white observers, we find that they exhibit a uniform trend. They all ascribe Indian aversion to mission life to love of liberty, distaste for their surroundings, longing for their native home, or revolt against all forms of restraint or compulsion. In other words, the white man, thinking of the Indians as a group, conceives their responses in terms of pure abstractions. These abstractions are those in which his own thoughts are likely to be cast. In the early nineteenth century the rights of man and human liberty were dominant among politico-social ideas. Hence the emphasis laid on them by the white commentators.

The Indian neophyte, on the other hand, possessed no such philosophical background not such a ready-made system of concepts to which he might refer his condition and his actions. The new convert had no comprehension of liberty as opposed to servitude or slavery because he had known only one type of social status and had no basis for comparison with anything else. Furthermore, aside from small family or tribal affairs he had never encountered a situation which demanded expression in terms of abstract social concepts. Consequently, when called upon to give an account of his reasons for a specific line of conduct, he was totally unable to go beyond the concrete events of daily life. We must, therefore, regard Indian testimony as rationalization of underlying discontent in terms of sharp personal experience with definite environmental factors. Viewed in this light, Indian testimony makes sense. Moreover, it is no longer incompatible with the testimony of the white man. Both groups approach the same solution of the problem, but they approach it by different pathways and in different modes of expression. Where the Frenchman or the American assigns love of liberty as the cause for flight or resistance, the Indian says he ran away because he was put in jail. Where the white man talks about slavery, the Indian says he objected to being made to work by some individual, for instance, some particular father in the mission.

From the statements given here and many more which might be adduced certain factors emerge as possessing definite weight in the mission environment. The most important, and yet by far the most difficult to assess, is that called loss of liberty, by which is meant the restriction of the Indian's freedom of action, particularly with respect to the freedom they had previously enjoyed. Under the missions they were under no greater physical restraint or social compulsion than many civilized groups today; yet with their background the loss of personal license was a severe blow. Perhaps the best analogy is not that of slavery, which implies rigorous physical exactions, but captivity. . . .

To summarize some of the foregoing discussion it may be stated that, apart from demographic changes, the missionized Indians responded to their environment primarily by numerous individual attempts to escape from it, or to resist it, in the physical sense. One group of factors which was at least partially responsible for the observed response was associated with the spatial restrictions imposed by the missions. In particular one may distinguish within this group: (1) emotional or material resistance to any type of compulsory conversion; (2) the emotional tendency to return to the familiar ancestral habitat which we have termed "homesickness," (3) a revolt against over-aggregation in the missions which ran counter to a centripetal drive on the part of the Indians or urge to reestablish the pristine, lower population density; and, (4) a probable resistance to any confinement, especially to the custom of mass incarceration of both sexes at night. Further resolution of the components in this group of factors might be achieved if an exhaustive study were attempted. . . .

In spite of individual differences arising from personal experiences or political bias all observers, not only those cited above but others as well, are agreed with respect to certain essential points. There can be no doubt that the standard working week consisted of from 5 to 6 days at 6 to 8 hours per day, let us say, 30 to 40 hours per week. Nowhere do we find any claims that more than 40 hours were required, except under extreme provocation. The actual tasks were those characteristic of rather primitive agriculture and strictly home industry. Much of this work would beclassed today as light labor. It is very significant that even the bitterest opponents of the missions never accused the clergy of giving the Indians work which might cause either excessive fatigue through extremely long hours or physical injury through intense exertion and occupational hazard. The worst they could do was the charge that pregnant women were too severely treated. There is no doubt that by modern standards the work was very reasonable both as to hours and nature . One need only to compare the mission labor condition as set forth in the excerpts quoted with modern civilized labor conditions such as are encountered by the average farmer or worker in heavy industry. We may conclude immediately therefore that, as far as the adult neophyte was concerned, he was not obliged to perform labor which could in any way be injurious physically in either the individual or racial sense. . . .

The mental and moral aspects of labor, however, belong in an entirely different category. The compulsion placed on the Indian, the restriction upon his daily activity through obligatory physical effort is important. But it is not the whole story. His reaction to labor itself, in the abstract, must be considered, since mental or bodily exertion of the type demanded by white civilization was completely new to him. It constituted an environmental factor, of the nonmaterial type, with which he had never come in contact and which therefore required an emotional and intellectual readjustment or adaptation very difficult for him to make. Labor, with its associated complex system of rewards and penalties, has perhaps constituted a more serious obstacle to the racial reorientation of the Indian than brutal but quite comprehensible physical conflict. We may focus attention on the aspect of compulsion in labor among the mission Indians, keeping continually in the background the idea that labor in any form was alien to their disposition, their social heritage, and their biological environment.

Despite innumerable lamentations, apologies, and justifications, there can be no serious denial that the mission system, in its economics, was built upon forced labor. Any cooperative system of support, any organization which is economically self-sustaining, as were the missions, must of necessity be founded upon the productive toil of its members. This very necessity is the primary compulsion, but if the corporate members are of sufficient intelligence, the compulsion becomes rationalized and there is an appearance of willingness and volition. On the other hand, if the mass is stupid and ignorant, then the hierarchy of authority at the top must exercise force, moral or physical, to obtain the essential effort on the part of the mass. Compulsion then becomes personal, and we begin to speak of "forced labor." Thus in its essence the mission system predicated forced labor by the neophytes, but with little success. The next step was moral suasion, and it must be admitted that, in general, such measures were adequate. When, however, they failed, physical means became necessary, for the economic discipline of the community had to be maintained at all costs. It was very natural that many neophytes, not in the least comprehending the ideals of the Church and its servants or the complexities of administrative theory, should regard necessary "forced labor" as directed personally at themselves and should rebel against it. On the other hand, it is noteworthy that of all the complaints and grievances of the neophytes, relatively few were directed against the work itself. . . .

Turning now to a more fundamental aspect of the labor problem, we observe that the California tribes shared with other Indians the characteristic, or the vice, of whole-hearted aversion to physical labor. Whether the labor was compulsory or voluntary, the Indian—at least at the time of his first contact with the white man—preferred not to perform it. Hence he has been universally termed lazy and indolent. Now there is very little to be gained by applying opprobrious epithets to a race or a group without analyzing, at least in a cursory fashion, the reasons for such inherent traits as call forth the epithets.

In their wild state the Indians underwent extensive physical exertion. Even in California, where life was easier than in the eastern forests or on the central plains, much hard work was devoted to the obtaining of food, whether through fishing and hunting or by gathering acorns, nuts, and other plant materials. The processes involved in preparing the food were likewise laborious and tedious. Furthermore, the building of shelters and the manufacture of clothing, utensils, and weapons demanded much time and effort. No Indian group ever survived a year in a state of complete indolence and inactivity. Indeed, among numerous tribes extraordinary exertions and hardships were necessary for simple survival. It is therefore inaccurate to assume that the Indian disliked to work because muscular exercise was involved. He disliked it because of the conditions under which it was performed. The whole basis of the aboriginal labor system was the idea of intermittent effort rather than steady, consistent exertion. This, in turn, was associated with the facts that, first, the food supply was highly seasonal and, second, no preparative measures were required. The fish ran at a certain time, the acorns were ripe in a definite month. Hence the native worked hard to accumulate these materials when they were available. He strove mightily and without stint for a brief period. Then he rested and loafed until his environment demanded another expenditure of energy. Even the women, upon whom devolved the domestic tasks, operated on much the same basis. Hence there was developed a tremendously powerful tradition of labor only when necessity demanded. There was no concept of continuous effort over a long period of time, directed toward a consistent production of commodities or an end to be achieved in the relatively distant future. In a sense the Indian style and method of labor was admirably adapted to his environment and to the needs of his way of life.

Now, place him in a so-called civilized environment, surrounded by a race with an utterly different tradition, that of the value of labor performed throughout the year. In order to conform to the new type of culture he is forced—in the widest sense—to alter his inherited method of work. Whether in a mission, on a reservation, or as an independent agent he is obliged to work every day, a certain number of hours, at tasks the immediate value of which are obscure to him. Since he sees no direct necessity for ploughing the wheat field or weeding the vegetable garden, he feels no internal compulsion to perform these tasks. He is thus regarded as lazy and improvident, and pressure is brought to bear from without. Since he cannot appreciate the value of the work, it becomes irksome to him, and he resents the pressure which forces him to do it. In other words, he tends to carry over into the new environment the habits of thought and the methods of labor which served him adequately under aboriginal conditions. As a result, not only the external compulsion but the labor itself acts as a stimulus which generate negative or adverse responses.

At this point a vicious cycle, similar to those already discussed, begins to form. In response to disinclination toward the new type of labor and to either impersonal economic compulsion or personal moral and physical pressure, the mission Indian takes one of two courses. He exercises passive resistance by stalling or "soldiering" on the job or by malingering and inventing all sorts of excuses for not working. Alternatively, he avails himself of the flight mechanism and runs away. No matter which course he adopts, he is regarded by the white race, clerical and secular alike, as indolent, improvident, and exasperatingly oblivious to his true economic welfare. To correct this failure in racial, social, and environmental adjustment, the missionaries, soldiers, and civilians respond by doing exactly the worst possible thing under the circumstances; increasing the extent and severity of the pressure, which in turn forces a little more labor from the Indian but also intensifies his own trend toward refusal to work or toward escape. . . .

Apart from the strictly mission enterprise, as well as including it, the California Indian race proved itself a total failure as far as the labor system was concerned. From the point of view of population changes the race was doomed to severe depletion, if not extinction, in free competition with the whites simply because it could not sufficiently rapidly and successfully adapt itself to the labor system basic to white economy. This in turn is referable to the inherent attitude of the Indian toward consistent, long-continued physical exertion, an attitude built up through generations of adjustment to the wild environment, not to any genetically ingrained moral turpitude or reprehensible intellectual backwardness.

In short, the . . . offenses committed by the neophytes were of the same species as are perpetrated by every racial, political, or religious group which is at odds with the governing order at the time. Furthermore, it was as difficult for the Indian as for the members of any other repressed group to perceive the immorality or essential sinfulness of his behaviour. His reaction to chastisement for such acts was a normal, healthy resentment, directed chiefly against the individuals who were personally instrumental in applying the chastisement, whom he endowed, by extension, with responsibility for all his woes, of whatever nature. . . .

The type of disciplinary measures was frequently degrading and offensive to the Indian. Corporal punishment, or flogging, was of course standard practice in the eighteenth century among all white civilizations, particularly when used upon so-called inferior races. Nevertheless it has been singularly ineffective for, unless the physical effects are so terrific as to break down utterly the spirit of a man, the result is usually to inspire him with an undying, implacable hatred, which in turn communicates itself to all his friends. Imprisonment, or other curtailment of liberty, if properly carried out, does not result in bodily harm, and is much more dreaded by a race to whom freedom means the breath of life. It was therefore unfortunate that the lash was so quickly resorted to by the Spanish administration and applied with such severity. The relative frequency with which corporal punishment was employed may perhaps be gauged by the data in table 5 (although the absolute frequency would have to be determined from more extensive information). The items in the table which were taken from the prison records of the years 1809-1817 (Estudillo Docs.) must be omitted from any such calculation, since they state no more than that the offenders were in jail. These persons, therefore, constitute a selected group. Moreover, many of these culprits may have been flogged in addition to incarceration. Apart from this group there were 209 persons. Of these 71 were flogged, 46 imprisoned, 75 both flogged and imprisoned, and 17 executed. That is, 70 per cent suffered corporal punishment, 57 per cent imprisonment, and 36 per cent both.

Granting that discipline was often necessary and inevitable and that it took the form, as a rule, of confinement and whipping, we must inquire as to the extent and severity of the punishment inflicted. Quite obviously disciplinary measures of a conservative type, inflicted fairly and justly without personal spite for offenses generally conceded to be flagrant, would not be likely to affect the mass of the neophytes as adversely as irrational chastisement, administered for no good cause, in excessive amount, or by cruel methods. Now it so happened that this particular point was seized upon by the enemies of the mission system (both at the time and subsequently) as an argument against the missionaries. Consequently, the verbal testimony, from documentary sources, is conflicting in the extreme. In fact, some of the generalities set forth by the missionaries on the one hand and by some of the military men and civilians on the other are mutually exclusive. Moreover, individual cases have been cited which, perhaps, may have occurred but which alone by no means prove any rule. . . .

Retention of Customs and Religion

Apart from law and language there exists in any society, primitive or otherwise, a vast body of traits which may for convenience be grouped under the terms customs and religion. Herein will be included the entire complex of beliefs, myths, and superstitions, on the one hand, and, on the other, the activities associated with them, such as costumes, rites, dances, ceremonies of all kinds, together with the necessary social structure for their administration. Needless to add, the entire group life is based upon and bound up in this interlocking set of traits. Furthermore, as the experience of centuries has demonstrated, it is extremely difficult to eradicate such traits from the collective mind of any human racial unit, and if the process is successful, it will probably be accompanied by the spiritual and intellectual disintegration of that unit. A people may achieve adaptation to a new physical environment, they may overcome obstacles of war, economics, and pestilence, but they are very likely to retain a considerable amount of the original nonmaterial culture.

The mission Indians appear to have been no exception to the general rule, despite the fact that great and peculiar difficulties were placed in their path....

The operation of the mission system...involved an immediate, powerful restriction on the social and intellectual expression of the Indians comparable with those previously discussed which affected liberty, space, diet, and sex relations. One might expect that the responses to this restriction would follow the same lines of resistance or escape as characterized the other types of restriction. Although this was doubtless true to some extent, the situation was modified by certain factors which did not operate in the other cases.

The first of these was the possibility of a new avenue of escape. Physical, spatial confinement could be enforced by purely corporal methods. Spiritual confinement, so to speak, provided the Indian was genuinely obdurate, could not be enforced at all. It was impossible to prevent the converted gentile from thinking of his folkways, from respecting the fellow neophyte who was a former shamen, from clandestinely carrying on his ancient ceremonies. Nor could the missionary prevent the Christian mother from passing on to her child the unforgotten lore and tradition of the tribe. The most elusive, the most tenacious thing in the social order of the world is tradition, which can be kept alive in the face of the bitterest persecution and which constitutes a region into which the most oppressed can always escape with impunity.

The second factor was the form of the Christian religion. It is no accident that Catholicism has been uniformly successful among primitive peoples. Its effective, simple dogma can be readily taught to minds of limited comprehension, and its system of observances can be dramatized so as to appeal to the primitive emotion. Moreover, the proselyting orders in the New World, through their vast experience, were wonderfully adept at presenting their religion in its most attractive form. Christianity, therefore, itself provided a line of escape from the restriction placed on the older gentile spiritual culture. It was the hope of the clergy that the Indians would all avail themselves of this resource, and it is to their credit that so many did. In theory, there was not a complete restriction but a redirection, a recanalization of social and emotional energy. Unfortunately, the process, actually, was too swift, too sudden, to be complete. The Indian mentality was too fixed and rigid to give ground, to make the shift and adapt itself within one or even two generations. Consequently, in many instances, the effect was one of absolute restriction rather than an easy redirection.

To what extent the course of conversion was complete—using "conversion" to imply conversion in the whole way of life rather than in the limited theological sense—can be judged only by those records of the missions which give evidence of tendencies to retain or revert to aboriginal custom. These records include only statements of opinion and overt acts of sufficient consequence to require official attention.

Concerning the general question of the retention of primitive belief and custom by the neophytes, we have two very authoritative sources. The first is (Geronimo) Boscana, that thorough student of Indian religion. He says, "Superstitions of a ridiculous and most extravagant nature were found associated with those Indians, and even now in almost every town or hamlet the child is first taught to believe in their authenticity." The second source is the "Contestación" of 1811. One of the questions asked was whether the neophytes adhered to their former customs. Six missions replied, the statements being unanimous that great tenacity in this respect was to be observed. Several other questions concerned specific cultural traits; the answers to these were, likewise, without exception in the same tenor. In fact, I know of no competent contemporary authority who vouchsafed the unqualified assertion that the neophytes had to a significant degree given up the primitive customs and superstitions. . . .

Assimilation of Christianity

Although, as has been stated, the Indian did not "surrender his ways" in order to substitute for them the introduced ritualism and religion, there is no *a priori* reason to assume that he may not have added some of the latter to his own system. The two are not mutually exclusive, as are Indian law and European law. Christianity of a sort can be superposed on a substratum of cultism and ceremonialism and indeed, in the long run, it can be incorporated with the primitive system.

. . . Did the mission group really assimilate Christianity to the extent that it in any way altered their belief or their spiritual equipment? This is an exceedingly difficult question to answer, and in fact probably cannot be answered at all. Obviously, there are no objective criteria; mere observance of form is no valid index to the spiritual motive behind the actions. Written opinion is untrustworthy, since it was difficult for a contemporary to go below the surface and since at that period every observer was influenced by racial, national, and religious prejudices. For manifest reasons the missionaries were prone to be optimistic concerning the success of their spiritual endeavors, although they did deplore the extent to which apostasy showed itself. Most of the Protestant Americans were contemptuous of both the missionaries and neophytes and suffered from a tendency toward extreme superficiality in their observations. It is probably best to attempt no categorical answer but to suggest that the neophytes must have absorbed a great deal of the form and spirit of Christianity. Moreover, it is highly probable that the ceremonial of the Catholic Church went far toward satisfying the innate love of the Indian for ritual. . . .

If the concept of assimilation of religion by fusion is valid, it follows that racial conflict in this particular cultural sphere was resolved by adaptation in the reverse sense. That is, the primitive group adapted the introduced culture to fit its own mold, rather than changed its own culture to conform to the other. The pattern of religion, therefore, constitutes a noteworthy exception to the usual rule in the relations between the mission Indian and the white man. In summary, it becomes evident that with respect to cultural factors the interracial contact or conflict led to quite different results, depending upon the degree to which a given cultural factor involved material relationships. In the field of personal relationships, laws and codes of behavior, the two systems were mutually exclusive and irreconcilable. For purely pragmatic reasons, the Indians were forced to make a rapid and very difficult adaptation which cost them dear in lives and suffering. With respect to religion (in its most general sense), ceremonialism, and shamanism, the opposite was true. Despite the most intensive moral suasion and pressure, the Indians retained the basic pattern of their culture intrinsically unaltered. Indeed, they went so far as to adopt and modify Christianity and to incorporate it in such a way as to conform to their own manner of thought. In this one respect, therefore, the Indians achieved an adaptational success, which stands unique in their history.

4.
Rev. Maynard Geiger, O.F.M., Replies

Professor Cook's work on Indian-missionary relations has been neither directly challenged nor widely accepted. This is symptomatic. The numerous defenders of the missions have traditionally either ignored any negative findings or, like Fr. Zephryn Engelhardt, who for years was the official apologist-historian of the Franciscans, have used bombast against all opponents, even the most innocuous. Neither variety of apologist has been very persuasive among the serious students of California history.

A different approach is represented by Fr. Maynard Geiger, who has the capacity to tell the affirmative side of mission life in a manner that hints at familiarity with negative sources and that tries to deal coolly with their charges.

Fr. Geiger served for years at the mission archives in Santa Barbara. His labors there produced a modern translation of Fr. Francisco Palóu's classic Life of Serra, *and an original work,* The Life and Times of Fray Junípero Serra *(1959), generally considered the best work on the founder of the system.*

A selection from his authoritative history, Mission Santa Barbara, 1782-1965,[4] *is included here because it touches upon the disputed points in this problem—the degree and effect of repression in the Franciscan system. Although it deals with Santa Barbara only, parts of it can be extended by inference to the entire mission system. Fr. Geiger interprets the records as showing that the Indians entered their new life voluntarily, had the option of leaving almost at will, found the work easy, and suffered little punishment. In fact, he is convinced that they enjoyed their association with the Spanish padres and profited from it considerably.*

Revealing Facts from Registers and Reports

Santa Barbara's register preserves the names and statistics of 4,771 Indians who entered the Church between December 31, 1786, and September 14, 1858. This volume testifies eloquently that there was no rush on the part of Indians or missionaries for quick or mass conversions. This fact is corroborated by Governor Fages who in 1787 stated that the missionaries accepted for baptism only those who spontaneously insisted on receiving it. Thus also is underscored the declaration made by Father Estevan Tapis in 1805 that the Indians after viewing mission life as catechumens and realizing what such living would entail could "with full liberty return to their villages and remain in their pagan state."

If one compares the population of the native *rancherías* of 1769 with the number of Indians of those same villages who entered the mission system, it becomes clear that over half of the Chumash did not become Christians at all. The greater number of baptisms administered to Indians were those born in the Christian pueblo alongside the mission, namely, 1,497 out of a total of 4,771, or nearly a third of all the baptisms in the Hispanic period.

It took twenty-two years to bring into the mission system those Indians who lived in the immediate vicinity of Santa Barbara.

. . . [I]t may be stated that all the Indians from the coastal villages between the Rincón and Point Concepción entering Mission Santa Barbara were baptized by 1812; those of the interior valleys and mountain ranges by 1822, and those from the islands by 1828. This was the work of forty-two years. San Buenaventura and Santa Inés completed their work by 1818. After 1828 Santa Barbara's baptisms represented children of already Christianized parents. In 1835 there was a short spurt of baptisms from far-away places, probably including the Tulare region.

At Santa Barbara the strenuous years of evangelization were between 1786 and 1804. The

[4]Maynard Geiger, O.F.M., *Mission Santa Barbara, 1782-1965* (Santa Barbara: Franciscan Fathers of California, 1965), 28-74.

1,000th baptism was conferred on November 3, 1796; the 2,000th on January 12, 1803; the 3,000th on June 8, 1804. In the next fifty-five years only 1,771 baptisms were administered. The reason for this was the gradual extinction of the native villages and the preponderance of deaths over births from about 1812. The banner year for baptisms at Santa Barbara was 1803 when 832 Indians received the sacrament.

Not all baptisms recorded in the register were actually administered in church or even at the mission itself. Nor did all the baptized Indians become members of the Christian community at the mission village. The first seventy-two baptisms occurred at the presidio. A significant number of Indians, 638 of the total 4,771, were baptized in their native villages by padres, soldiers, civilians or native catechists. Those baptized in this manner were infants and adults in a dying condition or very old people who could not be transported. Most died at the place where they had been baptized. Each, however, was carefully noted in the register.

Spanish soldiers and civilians as well as the better trained Indians were well aware of their duty of baptizing anyone in danger of death when no missionary was available. Thus, José Raimundo Carrillo baptized a son of Chief Yanunali at Siujtu on September 3, 1788; José María Domínguez, soldier and interpreter, baptized at Miquigui on September 16, 1794. Members of the Ortega family, including the wife of the retired captain, María Antonia, frequently baptized in the neighborhood of their ranch in Refugio Pass, at Casil, Miquigui, Sisuchí and in the Santa Inez Valley where they had a grain field.

The greater number of such emergency baptisms however, were performed by competent Indian catechists and interpreters. Thus, Venancio Malasuit administered twenty-six baptisms at various times; Gaspar María, forty-nine. On November 30, 1814, Francisco Jalauehu, a well-versed neophyte, went over to Santa Cruz Island and baptized thirty-nine Indians who because of their age and infirmities could not be transported to the mainland.

The first sponsors at Indian baptisms were soldiers and their wives. The first Indian sponsor to serve was Rosalía María on July 8, 1787. One godparent was required for each baptism, a male for a man, a female for a woman. When groups were baptized on a single day, one sponsor stood for the whole group, the sexes being baptized separately. The Christian names bestowed at baptism were as varied as those contained in the Roman Martyrology.

The marriage register contains the record of 1,427 Christian weddings of Indians between February 3, 1787, and July 5, 1857. The first nuptial ceremony took place in the presidio chapel when Joséph Manuel and Catalina María were united in marriage by Padre Paterna. The data in this register is less detailed than in that of baptisms for the reason that most of the information would have been repetitious. Moreover, after 1815, the individual's entry number in the baptismal register was given in the marriage book so that the biographical data on the spouses could be easily found.

Register No. I of Burials contains the data on the deaths and burials of 3,997 Indians between August 8, 1787, and December 31, 1841. Register No. II merges with that of the *gente de razón* of the presidio. This latter contains the data on deaths and burials of all whites from December 29, 1782, to November 13, 1873, and includes the Indians who died between 1842 and 1873.

Father Antonio Jimeno in using the same register for the *gente de razón* and Indians declared that "because the register for burials of neophytes of this mission is full, we will begin to place in this [presidio] register for whites also the entries of Indians who will be buried in the future." Hence this volume contains the deaths and burials of 657 Indians beginning with January 9, 1842. The total number of Indians buried in Santa Barbara and its vicinity between 1786 and 1872 was 4,645.

In the case of Indian burials the missionaries gave both the Christian and pagan names of the deceased where the pagan names were remembered; the names of parents, husband or wife; whether the person was married or single, adult or child. At times the Indian's occupation is noted, such as interpreter, chief, *alcalde*. Then follow the place of death, place and date of burial and place of the individual's origin. Finally, it was noted which sacraments the deceased had received just before death if these were unusual and then the signature of the officiating priest.

Not all Christianized Indians were buried at the mission. Some, in remote *rancherias*, had been baptized in danger of death, most of these expiring where they were. Then they were buried in their native locales, generally by Christians. Usually, a cross was put above the grave to distinguish it from a pagan burial. In all cases, the facts were noted in the burial register.

As a rule, the Indians of the mission area died from sheer age or from some illness. In rare cases they died from snake bite, were killed by wild animals or were injured in an accident such as falling from a tree or being crushed by a stone. Close research of the records discloses no death caused by murder. Some deaths of a sudden nature are recorded but not many. Indians buried in the mission cemetery through the years 1789-1854, number just a few short of 4,000. . . .

Labor and Mission Industries

The missionaries realized that their Indian charges could not be expected to be as industrious as a citizen of western Europe. The manner of life they were leading at the mission was a complete change from that of their aboriginal state. Consequently the work schedule was mild. Consideration was also given to age, sex and individual ability. The missionaries also knew that they could not hold up their countrymen as models of dynamic energy. In 1812 Fray Ramón Olbés complained of the *gente de razón*.

> The people known as the *gente de razón* who live in this province are so lazy and so given to idleness that they know nothing else but to ride horseback, and consider all work as dishonorable. To them it seems that only Indians ought to work. So it happens that even for the most necessary personal maintenance, they solicit the service of Indians for cooking, washing, working in the garden, minding a baby, etc. Generally, we missionary fathers allow the Indians to work for them.

The mission Indians rose at sunrise and started to work about two hours after that. Except for those who did piece-work at regularly assigned tasks, the daily labors were given out each morning in the mission patio. Such work beginning at eight or nine in the morning depending on the season, ended at 11:15 when the padres took their noonday meal. In the afternoon "it is most certain that the Indians never work more than an hour and a half." This work, except for those who were working in the field, terminated about 3:45 P.M.

Women were assigned to the task of grinding wheat and corn. Each one ground two *almuds* daily for *atole*. When these grains were used to bake bread eight or nine women ground seven *almuds* of soaked wheat. Pregnant women were never put to work at the *metate* to grind wheat for making *atole*, for mixing flour or to any kind of work considered too heavy. "These women take care to advise us when they become pregnant in order that we may place their names on the list of expectant mothers." Instead they washed wool and cleaned wheat on the threshing floor. At times they were engaged in pulling up weeds and grass from the orchard. Most of the time they spent in leisure or in taking walks.

After giving birth they stayed in their houses as long as they wished, presenting themselves to the missionaries when they felt they could return to work. At times, with older women they carried wood to the *pozolera* or ground the daily *almud* of wheat on the *metate*. The firewood was close at hand so that these women finished their chore in about two hours. When herbs had to be crushed for use in curing leather even the pregnant women helped. The Christian men laughed at the padres for the solicitude in behalf of the expectant mothers saying: "After all, do not the pagan women also bear children?" All able, employable women helped to carry adobes when the mission carts were not available, the bricks always being close to the site of the building to be erected.

Women also aided in transporting bricks and tiles. They very rarely carried stones and when they did it was the smaller type. . . used in laying foundations. Other material was transported by day laborers by means of oxen or by muleteers with their mules. Children over nine years of age were employed in combing wool and at looms assisting weavers. Others guarded freshly made tiles and adobes to prevent them being trampled upon by animals. "The majority are engaged in playing their youthful games."

The weaving of cloth was one of the principal mission industries which was already in full operation by 1796. It was based on piecework. When the allotted work was finished the Indians were free. Between March and October weavers wove ten *varas* of cloth for shirts, skirts and loin cloths. If they wove more they were paid for it at the rate of two *reales* (eight *reales* equaled a *peso*) for each additional ten *varas*. Pay was in kind. Often 100 *varas* were woven in five days. Those who made blankets had to finish three as a piecework assignment. Carders combed three pounds of wool which was woven into shirts, skirts and loin cloths and four pounds when the material was used for blankets.

Spinners spun a pound a day to the width of a foot for clothing and one and a half pounds a foot in width for blankets. From November to February this work was somewhat curtailed. "The greater number of those employed at the looms finish their piece-work before noon." Hence afternoons were free and in the evenings no one worked.

Olbés commented in 1812:

> In these missions the fathers take care to clothe the neophytes in a most decent yet withal humble manner, their clothes being a coarse cloth or sackcloth. To those who show greater effort in some labor or service we give clothes such as the *gente de razón* wear. We notice that they like to go about well dressed but not so the old men and women for occasionally we find it necessary to have recourse to threats to make them clothe themselves with what we give them for the sake of decency.

Another important mission industry, done on a piece-work basis, was the manufacture of tiles and adobes. Nine men made 360 adobe bricks a day, of the size two-thirds in length and one-third in width. "The nine who do this work never labor after eleven o'clock in the morning, never on Saturdays and often not on Fridays because on the previous days they have already finished their piece-work assigned for the week.

A group of sixteen men aided by two women who administered straw and sand, made 500 tiles a day. Troughs filled with clay were close at hand. These tile-makers "finish their work before ten o'clock and still they complete their assignment before Saturday when they are free to take a walk or to rest."

At the end of each year each neophyte without distinction was given a blanket. Every six months men received a new loin cloth, every seventh month a new shirt while the women received a new skirt. All this material was of a bluish wool unbleached. The mission had three looms at which sixty-five neophytes were employed. On May 26, 1800, the padres started keeping records of loom production. Between then and October 30, 800 *varas* of shirt and loin cloths, 700 *varas* of blanket cloth and 400 *varas* for skirt cloth were manufactured.

> From this account any disinterested person may infer that the neophytes of the mission can be clothed in the manner described. Moreover, we cover with shirts made of Puebla cloth the pagans who come to receive baptism. The old clothes they leave are not only collected but are burned in order that clothing that belonged to a sick person will not be used by one who is well.

When pagans brought their children to be baptized the padres gave them some clothing for their offspring. These children were taken back to their native *rancherias* and at a later age were brought back to the mission to be trained by the missionaries.

In the matter of housing in the beginning the neophytes built their own houses about the mission in the same manner in which they constructed them in their native villages in paganism.

. . .[I]n 1798 padres began an [attempt to avoid the danger of fire by building] houses of adobe with tile roofs. . . . These houses were six and a third *varas* long, four and a fourth *varas* wide. Each house had its door and window. The only reason they were not larger was because of the difficulty of hauling lumber by means of oxen over a bad road more than fourteen leagues. These houses were separated one from the other by partition walls and built along a straight street.

Construction of such houses continued until 1807 when they numbered 252. The Indians appear to have shown enthusiasm for these new homes. At first the missionaries asked the Indians if they wished this new type of housing and the majority were in favor. Larger ones would have been built if the padres had been able to obtain longer beams for the roofing. When the padres made known to the Indians these difficulties, they told the missionaries where the necessary pine lumber could be found and then they went out to seek it.

Though a stand of pine was found in the mountains at a great distance, the Indians were not discouraged. They offered to build a road to the place so that oxen could transport it. When volunteers were called for more men applied than could be used. Between thirty and forty were chosen to construct this road. No other overseer was placed in charge than an Indian who was better skilled than the rest. It took eight weeks to build this road which was so apt for the purpose that "the fathers who passed over it afterwards at times to visit sick pagans and Christians in the *rancherias* of the sierra, as well as the soldiers who accompanied them, were struck in admiration on seeing what mere Indians had accomplished."

As a result each year a number of houses were built until the village was completed. The padres then also planned to build a reservoir of stone, brick and mortar forty *varas* square. "The Indians already know about this and consequently, they realize that they will have to transport stone, make adobes, tiles, bricks and mortar. They also know the purpose we have in mind in doing these things; it is for their own comfort."

Leisure, Recreation, and Holiday

As pagans, the Chumash had their recreations and diversions in their dances, primitive music and certain simple games. When they entered mission life the element of recreation was neither forgotten nor minimized. During free time an Indian could do as he liked. Evenings and Sundays, and to a great extent Saturdays, were free. For many the afternoons on all week days were free. In those days too, there were many more ecclesiastical holy days when abstinence from work was obligatory as on Sundays. The Indians had a surprising number of non-work days and hours.

By 1800 a pattern of holidays had been worked out. Every Sunday after Mass one of the padres read out the names of one fifth of the neophytes, who received permission to go out on an excursion. The padres kept a notebook of all the Christians of the village who thus took their turn in revisiting their native village. Those who had come to the mission from nearby villages were allowed to return to them for a week, those who had been natives of more distant villages could remain for two weeks. Thus, except for the time when the harvest was gathered which was a community project, or when a week occurred wherein there was a holy day, one fifth of the Indians were away from the mission. Those who had to remain at the mission because of the holy day received permission to be away during the following week with a succeeding group. In that case two-fifths of the Indians were absent. After the harvest was gathered which took about a month, all the Indians left the mission in two distinct groups. It frequently happened that even during the four weeks they remained at the mission, some Indians asked for permission to leave and if they had a reason this was granted. Moreover, very many asked for a free day at times to go fishing, to visit the presidio or merely to take a walk along the beach. Again such permissions were granted. This freedom of association with their relatives had the good effect of bringing more pagans into the mission and had a good physical and psychological effect on the mission Indians themselves.

In September, after the harvest, the two groups who left the mission went into the mountains to gather *islay* or *tayiyas* (the wild cherry) for which they had a great relish. It contained a very bitter juice which was rendered more tasty after heated water was added. After the *islay* ripened, the acorns were ready for plucking. Only a few of the Indians, mostly older ones, chose to stay at home during this season. "During all this time the Christians live freely in the open country and on Saturday many come in to hear Mass (on Sunday) but not all."

During their stay in the mountains and on their excursions to their villages these Indians were not supervised by either missionary or soldier. The fact that most of them returned to the mission appears to be conclusive evidence that life at the mission for the majority, at least, was satisfactory. It is true there were some fugitives. This is understandable for there were always those who preferred their aboriginal freedom.

During free time at the mission the Indians could divert themselves with music, dancing and games. After the evening meal the young men, as a rule, stayed in the front patio until the bell was rung at 8:30.

> All are at liberty to go and sleep in their *ranchería*. But since every night they hold a dance in the *pozolera* or in the patio of the mission, or play the cello, violin or guitar, or entertain themselves at some game, the majority remain until the Poor Souls' bell is rung. At this hour many depart while others leave at nine o'clock which is the hour when the gate of the quadrangle is closed.

In a report made to the governor, Goycoechea had stated that the Indians enjoyed three types of games. Tapis concurred. One was a guessing game played by groups of twos or fours. These alternately guessed in which hand the opposite players held concealed a small stick. Another game called for considerably more exertion. An Indian threw a hoop of straw along a very smooth, clean plot of ground and while the hoop was in motion another tried to throw through it a long, thin pole. The third game Goycoechea forgot to mention. Tapis supplied the details.

The Indians were avid card players, though forbidden by royal decree to play simply because they could not control their gambling instincts. In such games they would sacrifice the very clothes they wore. These card games had become very common in Santa Barbara during the four years prior to 1800. Eight packs of cards were confiscated in 1800 alone. The Indians played not only among themselves but with the presidio soldiers from whom they learned the game in the first place....

Discipline, Restrictions, and Punishment

Part of the training of the mission neophytes consisted in the maintenance of discipline, the imposition of certain restrictions and in several types of chastisement considered proper in that age. Except in criminal offenses in which blood was shed, this discipline was relegated to the missionaries.

In accepting Christianity the Indian of the mission system was not coerced. He was encouraged to join, attracted by gifts and kindness but he was free to accept or reject it. As a matter of fact, many if not the greater majority of the Chumash around Santa Barbara did not become Christians. Once however, an Indian accepted his new mode of life he was not considered free to reject it. He was counted as a professed Christian and member of the Spanish commonwealth though without full citizenship. Until the time of his emancipation he was expected to undergo a gradual training in a Christian environment under Hispanic social and political influences.

On March 1, 1805, Fray Estevan Tapis wrote to Governor Arrillaga concerning his ideas on Indian freedom.

> I have observed that the pagans who are reduced (to mission life) gladly embrace baptism and with free choice. During the time they are being catechized which can be called a period of probation, they become acquainted with the maxims, laws and precepts of religion. They see the physical labors done by the neophytes and witness as well the punishments administered

to delinquents when mildness does not serve to correct them. In a word, from the time of their instruction they know what they will have to do and practice once they become Christians. With a knowledge of all this they ask for baptism when they can with full liberty return to their villages and remain in their pagan state.

Despite all this at Santa Barbara as well as at other missions certain Indians retained a hankering after their aboriginal form of life and fled from the mission. This, despite "the moderate work designed for their own well being." Tapis declared that these fugitives had no other reason for so acting than their own inconstancy.

I have observed that the means of holding them to their duty consists in soldiers going after them in pursuit. At this mission of Santa Barbara during the twelve years I have been in these parts we have inviolably adhered to the practice which its experienced founder, the Rev. Father Antonio Paterna, had established which substantially is the common practice at all the missions. As a result for the past few years there have been few who fled whereas before there were plenty who became fugitives at Santa Barbara.

It appears that in accepting the Catholic faith the Indians did not find too much difficulty nor did they show any particular aversion to it. The Chumash were not idolaters nor did they offer sacrifices. They worshiped neither sun nor moon. They acknowledged a certain *Sup* or *Chupu* but they did not know who he was nor did they have any images of him. In his honor they threw seeds or bird feathers about them in thanksgiving for favors received.

The fundamental Catholic beliefs were taught to the catechumens before baptism and these were reviewed for them daily in the *doctrina* at Mass. This was given both in Spanish and Chumash while additional instructions were given in sermons on Sundays and feast days as well as before marriage and before their annual confession. Morning and evening prayers were held in common in church. "The Indians," wrote Olbés, "continue to accept the beliefs and understand what the missionary fathers teach them in this particular matter concerning eternity, rewards, punishment, final judgment, heavenly glory, purgatory and hell."

Where serious breaches in the observance of the moral law occurred and when amendment could not be obtained by persuasion, a certain amount of external discipline was brought to bear on the matter. In a general way, the padres found the women more inclined to virtue and piety than the men. "We are laboring to imbue them with the principles of religion so that in time they will be able to give themselves over to the practice of virtue [without external aids]." The missionaries of course, had to be tolerant in overlooking certain superstitious practices and had to allow for an incomplete observance of Christian morals.

The dominant vices of both sexes, according to Olbés, were unchastity and theft. Lying was very common though in this matter the Indians had an amoral attitude. Married people showed proper love towards each other and they loved their children. "The missionary fathers are careful to educate both the parents and the children for the former have very little ability to do this by themselves for in this respect they are little more than children themselves."

To safeguard young, unmarried women from promiscuity, at every mission the fathers assigned them to special sleeping quarters called a *monjerio* outside the Christian village which was a section of the mission compound. Concerning this institution at Santa Barbara, Tapis wrote:

The single women are confined to a room at the mission where they sleep at night and it is a manifest deception to say that they live there continually during the day. For then they are permitted to dwell in the houses of their parents or relatives after they finish their work in the morning and afternoon. This room for the single women is seventeen *varas* long and seven wide and has a tile floor. In its upper portion it has a large window with its wooden grill, and four small

> windows to admit light and give ventilation. It also has its facilities for the night. A platform twenty *varas* long and two and a fourth *varas* wide with a stair case leading to it, made of tile and mortar, adjoins the walls for the benefit of those who desire to sleep a little higher up. At night there is a fire for warmth and every night a tallow candle is provided for illumination.

When the bell was rung in the morning and the door of the quadrangle opened, an Indian *alcalde* unlocked the *monjerio*. If he was not available the missionary supplied for him. The supervision of these girls as well as the rest of the Indians was under the *alcalde*. Tapis stated that these young girls did not go out walking as often as the married people or the bachelors not because they were not as privileged as other but because they asked for the permission less frequently. Such permission was denied them when walking became an occasion for causing ''mischief.''

The punishments in vogue at the mission, the manner of administering them and the reasons therefor were expressed by Tapis in great detail. Physical punishment was resorted to only when paternal correction and reproof went unheeded. The instruments of punishment were the shackles, the lash and the stocks. The mission had no jail. Women were rarely punished beyond being placed in the stocks.

If an Indian ran away or failed to return after his monthly excursion, other Christian neophytes were sent after him. On being returned he was reproached for failing to be at divine services on Sunday or holy day. He was warned that if he repeated the transgression he would be chastized. If he transgressed a second time he was put in the stocks or given the lash. In certain cases even this was insufficient to effect a reform. Then he was placed in shackles and at the same time given work to do. In case of a theft or fight where harm could arise, the parties were first chastized and then exhorted to abhor theft and to keep the peace. ''It has been observed that this is the most successful way of maintaining public and private tranquillity.'' At no time were rations ever diminished in punishment for a misdeed.

The stocks for the women were in the apartment used by the single women. As a rule, transgressions of women were punished by one, two or three days in stocks according to the gravity of the offense. If the woman proved obstinate or ran away she was chastized by the hand of another woman in the apartment of the women. Only rarely were women placed in shackles.

> We use the authority which Almighty God concedes to parents for the proper education of their children, now exhorting, now rebuking, now also chastizing when necessity demands it. For these chastisements generally the assistance of the commandant or of the guard is not solicited. Yet it has always been asked when it appeared expedient to us. The Indians feel that they are never punished because of some spirit of ill will or other as Goycoechea asserts. Hence it is that the neophytes accept with humility the chastisements and afterwards they remain as affectionate towards the fathers as before.

Tapis admitted that the pagans had more liberty than the Christians and that the former had not yet subjected themselves to Christianity ''but this greater liberty denied to the Christians for the very reason of their being such, is more than compensated for in the clothing and food which the mission gives them whether they are ill or in good health. . . .''

On the 14th June at sun rise, thirty-four foreigners, some of them Americans, took possession of the town of Sonoma, made prisoners of four of the principle men of the place, and under an escort sent them to New Helvetia, then took charge of the barracks containing eight pieces of cannon, three hundred stand of arms, and a large quantity of other munitions of war, and took likewise many of the horses belonging to the Commandant D. Guadalupe Vallejo, and forming themselves into a company under the command of William B. Ide of the United States, fortified the town. On the following day, Commander Ide issued a Proclamation to the people and hoisted a new flag, having a white field with a red border, and a Bear and a Star in the middle; they continued in possession until the 10th day of July (never having more than fifty or sixty men), when they lowered their flag and Lieutenant Revere U.S. Navy, having read the Commodore's Proclamation, hoisted the U.S. Flag under a salute in presence of a large concourse of people. **—Thomas Oliver Larkin, July 18, 1846.**[1]

An officer who will not go beyond out-of-date and insufficient orders in an emergency, who will not use his own discretion, is not worth his salt. **—Allan Nevins, historian**

That [Frémont's action in California in '46 and '47] was the career of a military adventurer, a filibuster, and an officer of the United States Army committing mutiny. **—Bernard De Voto, historian**

CHAPTER 3

...E BEAR FLAG REBELLION

...es or Villains?

...e flag be hauled down for good and given and honorable
...grizzly bear, five-pointed star and the enigmatic legend,
...or of something more suitable? The central question here
...lag is attractive, but whether the actions it commemorates
...symbolism is worthy of honor. The original "Bear Flag"
... Yankee rebels led by John C. Frémont, and it is their
...record—that is at stake.

...ess California sparked the Mexican War is hardly an issue
...ressive actions of the United States. Others will make con-
...in a address to hostile students in a foreign country some
...cted as the aggressor and imperialist with Mexico in 1846.
...California in the prelude to the fighting which ended with
...lk made no bones about wanting California or about a con-
...nother—by diplomacy or by war. For example, Americans
...ses and then abused (as in Texas in 1835), nor were Ameri-
...l well entrenched in the land (as in Oregon). No amount of
... Mexicans to sell California. For a while Polk kept the door

...*Business, and Official Correspondence of the Merchant and United States Consul in*
...1952-1955), V, 140-141.

open for local negotiations with the Californios. But since he felt frustrated in diplomacy, reasonably assured of a victory in warfare, and confident of the nation's backing, he finally behaved provocatively in Texas and brought on a war there instead.

One matter of dispute, however, is the way in which the Americans on the scene acted to convert California into a Yankee province. Even admitting that a slightly underripe California was about to fall into the Yankee basket, could there have been a friendlier harvest? The answer is yes, if you accept the notion that diplomatic negotiations instead of force would have persuaded the native Californians to come into the Union voluntarily; no, if you believe that the Mexican War made peaceful negotiations impossible. Did Frémont have any valid call to arms, that is, any justifiable reason to come back from Oregon in June of 1846 and encourage an armed rebellion? Yes, if one puts real credence in the Gillespie mission; no, if one thinks that the marine lieutenant had no critical intelligence to impart to Frémont. Did the Bear Flaggers have any genuine grievances? Yes, if you accept the idea that the rumors of impending assaults on the Yankees seemed quite real; no, if you think of the Americans as an impetuous lot of filibusters willing to seize on the flimsiest pretext to rebel.

As for the present-day flag, is it perpetuating a legend of heroism worth remembering, or is it keeping alive the deeds of hotheads and bunglers that had best be forgotten?

Allan Nevins, the first author to present his argument, generally looks with favor upon Frémont's actions at the time of the outbreak of hostilities in California. He finds Frémont "gallant, daring and useful" to the American cause. To the other agents of Manifest Destiny, the Bear Flag rebels, he is less complimentary; but he is more approving than not, and the net effect is a plus for all of them.

Bernard DeVoto seems to relish every opportunity to lampoon Frémont, calling him a "blunderer," "worse than a fool," and even a man whose actions verged on "treason." Nor has he much warmth in his heart for Frémont's companions, who created and sustained the "one-month one-town republic." *(Editor's note)*

5.
An Appreciation by Allan Nevins

John C. Frémont and his fellow rebels made countless enemies, but the first man to write an extended critique based on original research was Josiah Royce in his history, California, from the Conquest in 1846 to the Second Vigilance Committee in San Francisco *(1886). Royce started out with a certain inherent skepticism, and after plowing through a mountain of data and seeking out the retired General Frémont for an interview, he concluded that every rule of human decency and social responsibility had been violated by the Yankees in the 1846 episode. Many writers followed suit. The 1911 edition of the* Encyclopaedia Britannica *declared of the episode that it was "a very small, very disingenuous, inevitably an anomalous and in the variety of proclamations and other concomitant incidents rather a ridiculous affair."*

Allan Nevins' interpretation ran against this tide. Nevins' fascination with Frémont emerges in not one but two biographies about the man—a two-volume work and a one-volume condensation— plus several editions of Frémont's Narratives of Exploration and Adventure. *At nearly every turn where Frémont's actions were controversial—from his several Western treks in the 1840's to his falling out with Lincoln in the Civil War—Nevins has taken a friendly view. It is only fair to note, however, that thirty years of study have changed the author's mind. Nevins reduces Frémont from "Pathfinder" (1928) to the more mundane "Pathmarker" (1955), and in the preface to the 1956 edition of the* Narratives, *he says, "If I were to write the biography completely anew, it would be with a marked difference of approach." Whether the new biography would take a more critical view of the adventurer's military career, including the California episode, is not altogether clear; but it is certain that Nevins would not greatly downgrade Frémont's accomplishments as a topographer, the one area in which he seems to have earned a permanent place in history.*

The present selection is from the two-volume work, Frémont: The West's Greatest Adventurer.[2] *In it, Nevins deals with the justification for Frémont's belligerent return to California in 1846, his relationship to the rebellion already under way, and his overall contribution to the war effort. As the reader will discover, the biographer finds Frémont somewhat over ambitious and enigmatic, but Nevins feels that Frémont was operating on sound instincts.*

. . . Here we are confronted by one of the most baffling problems of Frémont's career. What were the instructions brought by [Lt. Archibald H.] Gillespie which caused Frémont to cut short his explorations, turn south, invade California, and begin in earnest the war which he had threatened a few weeks earlier? He knew that mere re-entrance upon California soil, from which he had been expelled with a warning to keep off, would be construed as a hostile act. Did he have genuine warrant for his course? Or did he, with his usual precipitancy, leap to conclusions and base a bold and stubborn policy upon inadequate authority?

Gillespie, a headlong, high-spirited young officer, had left Washington in November, 1845, and reached Monterey on April 17, 1846, on the ship *Cyane* by way of Hawaii. He brought Frémont a copy of an official dispatch from Buchanan at the head of the State Department, a packet of family missives from Senator Benton and Jessie, and some verbal explanations, as well as much news picked up en route. The family letters, of course, had no official weight. Frémont knew that the Senator's long experience, his position as chairman of the Senate Military Committee, and his great political prestige, made him powerful with the Administration. He knew that Benton would stand by him loyally in anything he did. But, as an army officer, Frémont also knew that nothing the Senator wrote could be used as warrant for any military step, and that to launch his force of sixty upon a warlike course he required some direct official authority, unless he were ready to take the risk of disavowal and punishment. The only really official document brought by Gillespie was Buchanan's dispatch. What policy did it warrant Frémont in pursuing?

The answer appears simple. The dispatch was directed, not to Frémont, but to the consul, Larkin, though Gillespie had been ordered to take it to Frémont. It contained nothing whatever that the explorer could construe as a suggestion that he employ armed force against the Californians. It instructed Larkin to carry on a peaceable intrigue for the secession of California from Mexico by the voluntary act of its inhabitants. He was requested to be discreet, cautious, and sleepless. He was to approach the California authorities, assure them of American good will in their disputes with Mexico, and encourage them to break loose with a promise of our "kind offices as a sister republic." Once they became a separate nation, such as Texas had been, they might look forward to annexation. "If the people should desire to unite their destiny with ours," wrote Buchanan, "they would be received as brethren."

One other injunction was laid upon Larkin with special emphasis. He was told that Washington had reason to fear British or French aggression in California; Larkin himself, in fact, had warned the Government of this. He must counteract foreign machinations by friendly appeals: "On all proper occasions you should not fail prudently to warn the government and people of California of the danger of such an interference to their peace and happiness; to inspire them with a jealousy of European dominion; and to arouse in their bosoms that love of liberty and independence so

[2]Allan Nevins, *Frémont: The West's Greatest Adventurer, Being a Biography from Certain Hitherto Unpublished Sources. . . and Some Accounts of the Period of Expansion Which Found a Brilliant Leader in the Pathfinder* (New York and London: Harper and Brothers. 1928), I, 273-322. Footnotes omitted here. The single volume edition is called *Frémont: Pathmaker of the West* (New York, London, Toronto: Longmans Green and Co., 1955).

natural to the American continent.'' Larkin, that is, was to do his best to detach California from Mexico for the United States, but he was to do so with the aid and good will of the Californians. Obviously, Frémont had here no authority for hostile action. . . .

So much for the official documents; but there remain the private letters and Gillespie's verbal information, upon which Frémont, as he stated later, unquestionably based his actions. Gillespie brought a budget of exciting news. He told Frémont that Sloat had heard of his encounter with Castro through the brig *Hannah*, and had promptly sent the sloop *Portsmouth* to San Francisco to protect the Americans, where it still lay. He told him that Mexico and the United States had now drifted to the very brink, if not beyond the brink, of war; and that Taylor had advanced to the Rio Grande, where fighting was expected at any time. He brought news that the Mexican authorities at Mazatlán, at last accounts, had expected Sloat to blockade the port at once, and had fled to Rosario with the archives. Finally, Gillespie showed Frémont a letter which Larkin had sent him, under date of April 23, to San Francisco, just as he was starting north to find the explorer. ''Capt. Montgomery (of the sloop *Portsmouth*) is of the opinion,'' wrote the consul, ''that Commodore Sloat may by the next mail (6 or 8 days) have a declaration on the part of the United States against Mexico, in which case we shall see him in a few days to take the country.'' He added that the Californians were much disturbed by the *Portsmouth*'s arrival. ''I have (as my opinion) said to Generals Castro, Carrillo, and Vallejo, that our flag may fly here in thirty days. The first says, for his own plans, war is preferable to peace.''

As a matter of fact, on the very days that Gillespie and Neal reached Frémont, May 8 and 9, 1846, the first sharp battles of the Mexican War occurred. Frémont felt almost certain that fighting was already under way. In the light of Gillespie's news of the imminence of war, the injunctions regarding peace and conciliation in the dispatch to Larkin seemed unreal and out of date. The explorer says as much in his *Memoirs*. ''This idea was no longer practicable as actual war was inevitable and immediate,'' he writes; ''moreover, it was in conflict with our own instructions. We dropped this idea from our minds, but falling on others less informed, it came near losing us California.'' He later adds that ''the rapid progress of affairs had already rendered'' conciliation impossible, and made it necessary to ''carry out the ultimate purpose of the government.''

But Gillespie also bore family letters, and verbal instructions from Secretary Bancroft. Upon the nature of the family letters, we have explicit statements from both Frémont and Jessie, and both agree that they warned Frémont to be ready to take a militant stand. Mrs. Frémont asserts that they might be said to be in a family cipher, for they were full of prearranged references to talks and agreements known only at home. Frémont states this more emphatically. Benton's letter, he says, ''while apparently of friendship and family detail, contained passages and suggestions which, read by the light of many conversations and discussions with himself and others at Washington, clearly indicated to me that I was required by the government to find out any foreign schemes in relation to California, and so far as it might be in my power, to counteract them.'' In a conversation long afterward with Josiah Royce, Frémont said that the letters were particularly clear upon the desirability ''of taking and holding possession of California in the event of any occurrence that would justify it, leaving it to my discretion to decide upon such an occurrence.'' He was warned of the British designs and told that Polk desired that he ''should not let the English get possession of California, but should use any means in his power, or any occasion that offered, to prevent such a thing.''

No doubt Frémont's recollection of the affair might be regarded as confused or colored; but it is in great measure corroborated by a letter, inaccurate in a few particulars but illuminating, which Secretary Bancroft wrote him in old age, where Royce's book had made the subject controversial. Bancroft speaks of verbal instructions:

> You as an officer of the army were made thoroughly acquainted with the state of things in California.
>
> My motive in sending so promptly the order to take possession was not from any fear that

England would resist, but from the apprehension that an English man of war in San Francisco harbor would have a certain degree of inconvenience, and that it was much better for us to be masters there before the ship should arrive; and my orders reached there very long before any English vessel was off California. The shameful delay of Sloat made a danger, but still he took possession of San Francisco before a British ship arrived.

Not having my papers here, all I can say is, that after your interview with Gillespie, you were absolved from any orders as an explorer, and became an officer of the American army, warned by your government of your new danger against which you became bound to defend yourself; and it was made known to you, on the authority of the Secretary of the Navy, that a great object of the President was to obtain possession of California. If I had been in your place, I should have considered myself bound to do what I could to promote the purpose of the President. You were alone, no Secretary of War to appeal to, he was thousands of miles off; and yet it was officially made known to you that your country was at war; and it was so made known expressly to guide your conduct. It was further made known to you, that the acquisition of California was become a chief object of the President. If you had letters to that effect from the Secretary of War, you had your warrant. If you were left without orders from the War Department, certainly you learned through the Secretary of the Navy (Bancroft himself) that the President's plan of war included the taking possession of California.

The truth is, that no officer of the government had anything to do with California but the Secretary of the Navy, so long as I was in the Cabinet. It had been my desire to acquire California by all honorable means much before that time. . . .

Of strict legal authority for re-entering Mexican territory and fomenting an insurrection by the American settlers along the Sacramento, Frémont had none; of moral authority, he had a great deal. He knew that the written message to Larkin, like that to Sloat, had to be guarded and harmless in tenor, for it might easily fall into Mexican hands. He would, therefore, give the greater weight to verbal communications. The very fact that Gillespie had been ordered without fail to find and talk with Frémont was full of significance. With the knowledge that immediate war was almost a certainty, which was he to do: push on north and homeward by way of the Oregon Trail, leaving the scene of action behind him, or return at once to California? No man of courage and patriotism could hesitate. It was impossible to stand still; it would have been a spiritless and craven act to turn his back on California; the only course was to retrace his steps. . . .

His sudden reappearance within forbidden bounds created a commotion among the American residents, and inevitably the malcontents and adventurers who longed for a conflict with Mexico responded most warmly to the excitement. Many came riding into Frémont's camp. During 1845, a large number of new emigrants had arrived, so that there were now fully 800 Americans, nearly all of them able-bodied men, in the province. Some were legal landowners who had gone through the necessary process of becoming citizens; the great majority, however, were simply squatters, or men who picked up a living by combining work as ranch hands with hunting and trapping. To understand Frémont's relations with them, it should be understood that they conformed to the rough frontier type. While a number showed sterling character and high ability, the gamut among the reckless sailors, ignorant, rugged frontier farmers, and buckskin-clad trappers ran to a low level. With the Anglo-Saxon's instinctive feeling of superiority, most of them looked down upon the gay, indolent, inefficient Californians, who loved gambling, guitars, and fandangos, and who made so little use of the rich country. They felt that California ought to be in the hands of their own virile, energetic race, and that it was only a question of time and opportunity till they should take it over.

These men brought Frémont a wild variety of rumors—that war between the United States and Mexico had begun; that it was about to begin; that Castro and his merciless greaser crew were planning to fall upon all foreign settlers and scatter them to the winds; that Castro and others were plotting to separate California from Mexico, but were unwilling to place it under American protection;

that the British were scheming to annex California forthwith. Samuel Hensley, one of the leading American settlers, and Neal, with whom Frémont had talked at length, agreed that the American residents would either have to leave the country soon, or fight for the homes they had made. Frémont lent an especially attentive ear to stories of aggression against the Americans and of plans of the California authorities to injure and restrict them. His own clash with the Government a few weeks earlier had prepared him to believe anything of Mexican treachery and bullying. . . .

[O]n April 31, 1846, while Frémont was still proceeding northward into Oregon, Castro had issued a proclamation warning the Americans again that they had no right whatever to hold land unless they became Mexican citizens. In this paper he instructed all the judges that they could not legally permit any sale or other transfer of realty to foreigners; while he gave brusque notice to Yankee squatters that not only would they forfeit any purchase they had made, but they would "be subject, unless they retire voluntarily from the country, to be expelled from it whenever the government may find it convenient." Castro, an ambitious, bombastic man, who liked to strut a bit, even made warlike preparations, and talked of bringing armed forces against the settlers. Reports of this, perhaps exaggerated, quickly reached the Sacramento.

There was really a vast deal of covert ill feeling and distrust between the majority of the American settlers and the general body of Californians. Josiah Royce, in his volume on California, writes as if Frémont's precipitation of the so-called Bear Flag War were the origin of the sullen hostility between the two peoples which followed the annexation of the province. Actually, the tension between the races was already painful. Not merely did the Americans tend to regard the natives as lazy, childlike, untruthful, and cowardly. The Californians, for their part, tended to look upon the immigrants as rough, overbearing, and grasping—as brutal fellows whose one aim was gain. In general, mutual understanding was impossible. Protestant against Catholic, Anglo-Saxon against Latin, strenuous pioneers against idlers—they were sundered by instinctive antipathies. The part which Americans had played in various California revolts had excited animosity and fear. Moreover, the Californians had sufficient racial pride to resent the American annexation of Texas, and had doubtless learned from Mexican writers that the Spanish-speaking people there had fared ill. A few liberal and informed Californians favored American control, but the predominant view was antagonistic.

Frémont was impressed by the reports of Castro's threatening attitude and of the danger of Indian attacks. It seemed altogether likely to him that the Mexican officials would try to incite the savages to an uprising. Some settlers who came into his camp declared that the half-civilized Indians working on the ranches were leaving their tasks and taking to the mountains, an indication of imminent hostilities. Sutter sent Frémont a courier with a message which the Captain interpreted as meaning that an Indian onslaught was in preparation. Inasmuch as California had never had a military force able to cope with the tribes, outlying farms had frequently been sacked, and it was only recently that Sutter himself had felt safe. The province between Lassen's ranch and the Mexican line contained perhaps 20,000 aborigines, of whom half had a smattering of civilization; but current reports exaggerated their numbers to 40,000 or more. They were lazy, unthrifty, and thievish; physically, they were greatly inferior to the best tribes of the plains, as for instance, the Sioux; but when aroused and collected in numbers, they were a real menace. Frémont shared the frontiersman's usual prejudice against savages, whom he regarded as uniformly treacherous, base, and cruel. Once he had seen a party of emigrants after a band of Indians had wreaked its worst upon them—and he had never forgotten it. He still felt a keen resentment over the death of his faithful Basil Lajeunesse. Telling the settlers that he would take precautions to protect them and their families, he kept close surveillance over such Indians as he could, and made ready for active operations. . . .

Many of the settlers had reached the conclusion that, no matter what Frémont did, the time had come for them to act. William Hargrave, who had settled in the Napa Valley two years earlier, tells us that his American neighbors there considered the outlook "very gloomy"; that they feared the Mexicans would try to eject them; and that "we foreigners were ready to fight for our new homes."

We have a similar account by William F. Sweasy, who was for a time Sutter's bookkeeper at the Fort. The settlers had heard, he states, that a large number of the native Californians had met at Monterey to discuss a plan for declaring the territory free and placing it under the protection of a foreign flag, and that a majority were in favor of a British protectorate. The arrival of the British warship *Collingwood* made English annexation seem, to some observers at least, a distinct danger. A spontaneous American revolt was on the point of breaking out when Frémont so fortuitously returned. According to Hargrave, he was one of a party of nine or ten men who came to Frémont's camp to seek assistance. "Kelsey acted as spokesman," he says, "and I do not recollect the language used, but my impression was at the time that Frémont, though very cautious and evidently averse to precipitate action, was willing enough to resume active operations, but he preferred to see for himself in how far the settlers of Napa and Sonoma Valley were ready to shake off the Mexican yoke. At any rate, he peremptorily refused to take any responsibility for sudden action on our part and endeavored to delay or frustrate our efforts. Whether Frémont expressed himself differently when he spoke to Kelsey alone, later in the day, I cannot say."

Frémont was playing a waiting game. He knew that the settlers were determined to act, he gave them at least partial encouragement, and he bided his time. The great object was to gain California for the United States, and this seemed to him the shrewdest course. "We made no secret of our intentions," Hargrave says of the settlers, "to keep up the agitation till the opportunity arrived for a bold stroke. On our return to the Napa Valley we found that the revolutionary movement had gained more ground, and steps were taken at once to organize a force sufficient for our first enterprise—the capture of Sonoma." He adds that a majority of the men on the north side of San Francisco Bay did not feel friendly toward Frémont at the beginning of the Bear Flag War, but became cordial later. The recollections of John Fowler of Napa County strongly corroborate Hargrave's account. He declares that the fear of the Mexicans was such that many settlers had been preparing to leave California for the States or for Oregon. Others wished to fight, and "I was in favor of acting at once independent of Col. Frémont and without consulting him." Swasey says simply that "the Americans and foreigners generally were called together in Sacramento, Napa and Sonoma Valleys for the purpose of resistance." It would seem that Swasey, who was close to Larkin at this time, thought he knew what were the confidential instructions of the Federal Government which Gillespie had brought to Frémont. "Their substance was," he states, "that the Colonel should be governed by circumstances, and if a movement appeared among the Americans to bring about an annexation to the United States, or to defeat the designs of another government (the object of the *Collingwood* being well understood), he should identify himself therewith, keeping near to California to be prepared for such emergency." This testimony is worth little as regards the supposed instructions; it is worth a good deal as to what was in Frémont's mind.

He did not need to rouse the settlers to fall upon the defenseless Californians whom Royce pities so much; the Americans had already been aroused by a fear, for which they had only too good grounds, of hostile action by the California authorities. He was glad to see their armed rising. It meant the swift end of Mexican authority, for he had no doubt that the settlers could defeat Castro. It meant the forestalling of any action which the British might contemplate. The settlers' action would be decisive as regarded the future American sovereignty in California, and yet the American Government would not be involved. If they were hard pressed, he might join them, leaving Washington free to disavow his step if it wished. If he heard of the commencement of war with Mexico, he would certainly join them. There can be little doubt that Frémont, speaking confidentially, promised the settlers that if worse came to worst he would come to their aid—though as a blind he still spoke of leaving shortly for the States. While he maintained great reticence as to the instructions he had received through Gillespie, everyone supposed that whatever he did was with the authority of the United States.

Frémont's waiting game was, if you will, the game of an opportunist; but it was precisely his duty to be an opportunist. Royce later criticized him for being bloody-minded and precipitate; the

American settlers at the time criticized him for being hesitant and careful. ''We left him,'' says Hargrave, ''most of us somewhat disgusted with the result of our interview.'' His course exposed him to misunderstanding, but any course he could possibly have taken would have done that. Under these circumstances, the first blow was struck.

It happened that Castro had sent a Lieutenant Arce to the north shore of San Francisco Bay to collect some scattered horses bearing the government brand. The officer collected about one hundred and fifty animals, and was taking them southward by way of Sutter's Fort and the San Joaquin Valley. Necessarily, the whole countryside knew of the movement: Arce, in the bright Mexican uniform of blue, red, and silver effects, supervising a dozen men, with their flashy serapes, high Mexican saddles, and lassoes, as they herded the mounts at a trot toward the fords of the Sacramento, the cavalcade raising a thick cloud of dust under the June sky. They reached Sutter's Fort, stayed overnight as Sutter's guests, and went on south the next day to the Cosumnes River, sixteen or eighteen miles distant, where they camped for the night. Here they were surprised by a party of a dozen settlers, under Ezekiel Merritt, who disarmed them, took away their horses, and insultingly told them to carry the news to Castro. Merritt was a tall, rawboned frontiersman, fearless, simple, and fond of risks, who was a natural chieftain for the rougher immigrants. He regarded Frémont with enormous respect, and later Frémont called him his field lieutenant.

. . . [The capture of Arce's horses helped raise in northern California the signal of war.] No one in this remote Mexican province yet knew that almost a month earlier (May 12, 1846) Congress had declared war; that in the battles of Palo Alto and Resaca de la Palma, Taylor had driven the Mexicans across the Rio Grande. The acts of Frémont and Merritt produced a feeling of consternation among the peace-loving Americans and friendly Californians. When Sutter heard that Arce had been attacked by a group of settlers, he expressed astonishment and indignation. Other Americans were immensely pleased. At last, they felt, California was to be brought quickly and decisively under the American flag. Many of high character welcomed the new turn of affairs. Long afterward an observer asked an estimable pioneer who had four sons under Frémont if he felt any compunction in attacking the Californians. ''He said he had Scripture example for it. The Israelites took the promised land of the East by arms, and the Americans must take the promised land of the West in the same way.''

Frémont now saw that he had aroused forces that could not easily be suppressed; that he had set in motion men of headlong temper, and made it certain that the Mexican authorities would strike back. The result was his decision, still keeping in the background, to instigate an attack upon the small military post of Sonoma, fifteen miles north of San Francisco Bay. Here were cannon, small arms, munitions, and horses, which Frémont needed; here lived General Vallejo, once commandant general of the province—a firm friend of American annexation—who might be used to influence the public. A quick stroke, with the raising of the American flag, would once for all end the danger that England, in collusion with Mexico, would occupy California. Frémont states that he sent Merritt, his field lieutenant, into the town ''instructed to surprise'' it. It is clear that he had planned all the steps beforehand, and anticipated little or no resistance.

The feat was quickly accomplished. Sonoma was an old mission establishment, now a dull and ruinous-looking place, infested by countless fleas. The chief buildings—the quartel, the residences of Vallejo, his brother, and his brother-in-law, Jacob Leese, and a few others—looked upon a large plaza, defigured after the careless California fashion by the skulls and skeletons of slaughtered beeves. At dead of night, some thirty-three or thirty-four armed settlers rode into the unsuspecting hamlet, or as they grandiloquently called it, the fortress, routed the astonished Californians out of bed, and took possession of the military equipment. These included eight fieldpieces, two hundred stands of arms, and almost a hundredweight of powder. Vallejo, protesting, was taken with the rest to Sutter's Fort, where Merritt and Frémont had planned to keep them. . . .

Events now moved rapidly. Some of the settlers who had taken Sonoma had ideas of their own as to how a revolt should be conducted. At such figures as William B. Ide, a shrewd, fussy, dogmatic

Jack-of-all-trades, who had wandered west from Vermont, successively a farmer, school-teacher, carpenter and rancher, or as Dr. Semple, an unbelievably long and lanky Kentuckian, who was quick on the trigger and loved an illiterate kind of rhetoric, it is easy to sneer. Josiah Royce has sneered at these typical frontier figures in the best Boston-Brahmin manner. They were not drawing-room ornaments. They did not have the horror which a philosophical pacifist like Dr. Royce felt for the rude acts of warfare which have usually accompanied the American conquest of new territory. But they did organize carefully their little uprising, thus touched off by Frémont, give it an orderly form, and attempt in the best Jeffersonian manner to justify it.

Sonoma was held by the settlers as a combination of fort and headquarters, and the little garrison there rapidly increased from fifteen or eighteen to forty men. On the very first day, June 14, 1846, the captors redeemed themselves from the charge of being a loose mob of marauders by declaring the "Republic of California." This scheme of an independent republic had been revolved by Americans for years. One recruit, William L. Todd, a nephew of Mrs. Abraham Lincoln, took a piece of whitish brown cloth a yard and a half in length and with either some paint or some poke-berry juice (the accounts are conflicting) placed upon it a large star in the upper right-hand corner, and facing this at the top the figure of a grizzly bear. Native Californians gazing contemptuously at this design were heard later to call it "the shoat." Across the middle of the flag were painted the words "California Republic." When it was hoisted on the empty Mexican staff, the Bear Flag Party and the Bear Flag War had found an imperishable name. This flag was a symbol to which the settlers attached the utmost importance. It meant order. Only one unruly fellow dared to suggest that Sonoma be sacked, and "a unanimous indignant frown made him shrink from the presence of honest men." It meant liberty; Dr. Semple was voluble in preaching the abstract principles of republicanism. It meant American rule forever replacing Mexican rule, as Ide formally asserted (in his proclamation of June 18, 1846)....

The raising of the Bear Flag, the circulation of Ide's proclamation of the "Republic," and the news of the occupation of Sonoma aroused the immediate anger of the Mexican officials. Castro replied with two proclamations on June 17. He had no forces beyond San Francisco Bay, but he promptly collected what troops he could farther south, and dispatched them under an officer named De la Torre to the relief of Sonoma. Their approach became known on June 23; the Bear Flag forces sent couriers to ask Frémont's help, and marched out under Lieutenant Ford to repulse the Californians. The result was a brisk engagement about a dozen miles from San Rafael, in which the Bear Flag men killed two Californians, wounded several more, and put the whole body to helter-skelter flight. While this happened, Frémont was casting off all disguise and taking the field. He was glad to have the call to arms. He had made up his mind that the crisis had come, and that it was "unsafe to leave events to mature under unfriendly, or mistaken, direction."

Frémont and his rescue party reached Sonoma on June 25, 1846, and with an augmented force of 160 men in all he at once took up the pursuit of De la Torre's retreating troops. The Captain had not acted without serious thought. He believed that his open entry into the struggle would prevent the Bear Flag settlers from being ultimately crushed by the stronger forces of Castro, and would deter any British agents from proclaiming a protectorate of California. If war had begun between the United States and Mexico, all would be well. On the other hand, if peace were maintained and it became necessary to disavow Frémont, little harm would have been done. The Captain took steps to make disavowal easy by drafting his resignation and laying it aside in an envelope to be sent to Senator Benton, who could transmit it to the War Department at his discretion.

It was only by great luck combined with an adroit ruse that De la Torre's crippled force escaped south of San Francisco Bay to a point of safety. The Californians had better horses than the Americans. De la Torre, having thus gained the head start, put a false message into the hands of an Indian, announcing an imminent attack upon Sonoma by Castro himself, and when the Indian was captured, Frémont hastily turned back from his pursuit to protect the threatened town; and De la Torre was then fortunate enough to find a large boat at Sausalito on the north shore of the Bay, and to make his way across. The anger and chagrin of the Americans at failing to crush their antagonists were extreme. They had as yet lost no men in open battle, but when Lieutenant Ford was marching to repulse De la Torre near San Rafael on the Bay, the settlers had come upon the bodies of two American immigrants, Tom Cowan, or Cowie, and a man named Fowler, murdered by the roadside. It was plain that they had been tortured to death, and their disemboweled and mutilated corpses presented a shocking spectacle. Cowan had been well-known and greatly liked, and the episode aroused a stern desire for revenge. A little later, when the Americans were in possession of San Rafael, some Californians landed from a boat, were intercepted by Kit Carson, who was on patrol duty, and when they offered resistance, were shot down. This appears to have been a cold-blooded murder. In excuse, it has been said that they were messengers bearing official Mexican orders, and that they tried to escape; and a long controversy has raged over the question whether the killing of the two—some say three—was defensible. There is little doubt that it was not.

Had Frémont foreseen how harshly a group of later historians would criticize his daring series of acts in turning back from his explorations, fomenting the Bear Flag uprising, and finally assuming its open leadership, he would have been dismayed and incredulous. Without partiality for Frémont, it is impossible to believe that this criticism, in the extreme terms in which Royce and Hittell state it, is justified. Frémont is accused of acting without specific authority, and of course that charge is true. He was six months' travel by a dangerous and difficult route from Washington; through Gillespie he had received news which made him feel it was his duty to assume a certain independent responsibility. He did just what a long line of officers of the English-speaking race have always done in emergencies. The British Empire owes half its territory to subalterns, generals, ship captains, and merchants who have acted without authority and been applauded later. Andrew Jackson had no authority in 1818 to invade the Spanish territory of Florida and seize Pensacola, but he did it. Commodore T. A. C. Jones had had no authority in 1842 for the occupation of Monterey, but he occupied it. An officer who will not go beyond out-of-date and insufficient orders in an emergency, who will not use his own discretion, is not worth his salt. Admiral Sloat was just such an officer, and the Administration in Washington regarded Sloat's timidity and vacillation on the Pacific Coast as a national misfortune, and made that fact clear to him.

Frémont has been accused, again, of taking action which, orders or no orders, was not justified by the facts of the California situation, or his knowledge of the general wishes of the Federal Government. But it is useless to deny that he left Washington with verbal instructions from the Administration; besides his own word, we have that of Senator Benton, Mrs. Frémont, and Secretary Bancroft for the fact, and they all had a high regard for the truth. It is useless to deny that the fear of an Indian attack was general; Sutter himself feared it. It cannot be denied, finally, that Castro was acting in a way which filled the American settlers with apprehension for their property and personal safety—his own orders and proclamations prove that—or that Frémont had good reason for fearing a sudden British proclamation of some form of protectorate. Royce is especially caustic in his treatment of the panic of the Bear Flag leaders regarding Castro. But of this one of our ablest historians writes:

> First, many of the settlers had ample reasons to feel alarmed: the illegality of their presence; Castro's sudden and cruel seizure of Americans in 1840; his attack upon Frémont in violation (the Americans believed) of a promise; official notices, issued about May 1, to the effect that a majority of the Americans were liable to be expelled at the convenience of the authorities; Castro's warlike preparations; his talk of moving against the immigrants with armed forces; and reports, more or less authentic, and reliable, from various persons regarding what he said or intended. Secondly, the contemporary testimony of Frémont, Gillespie, and other Americans—some of it given under oath—that alarm was actually felt is too strong to be rejected. Much has been made (by Royce) of Bidwell, a clerk of Sutter's, who tells us that alarm was not felt. But (1) his statement was made thirty years after the events; (2) he admits that

he was not on good terms with Frémont, and his statement aims to show that Frémont invented the story of alarm as an excuse for his conduct; (3) his statement is in other respects clearly inaccurate; (4) it assumes that he knew the sentiment of all the persons on the Sacramento, yet proves that an important fact may have been known to but few; (5) it shows that at the critical time he was absent in the mountains; (6) it says "Californians were always talking of expelling Americans," and therefore were talking of it in April, 1846; (7) his book mentions that in 1845 an attack upon New Helvetia was so confidently expected that he rode night and day to warn Sutter. . . .

Almost equally violent is Royce's attack upon the "legend" that the British had designs upon California; but the British archives show that these designs were well matured. The apprehension that England would forestall us was dwelt upon in the Senate early in 1846; it filled Secretary Bancroft's mind. "The expansive course of Great Britain," says the historian just quoted, "remarks dropped by English writers, repeated warnings dropped from our diplomatic and consular agents at Mexico, and the consensus of opinion in California, Mexico, France, and the United States were quite enough to warrant suspicions of England." Sloat, Stockton, and Larkin all feared Rear Admiral Sir George Seymour's intentions. British policy since 1815 has usually been extremely considerate of American susceptibilities, and it was so in this instance. But the English naval contingent on the Pacific coast would have been glad to secure a diplomatic foothold if it could be done without antagonizing the Americans. This was perceived with growing clarity in Washington. Frémont's activities along the coast, and his return at a critical juncture from the north, accentuated the feeling of the British officers that the United States was determined to obtain California, and that it would be impossible to act without coming into sharp collision with American aims and agents.

Above all, Frémont has been assailed as a mischief maker who spilt innocent blood, aroused a resentment among the native Californians which quadrupled the difficulties of the subsequent American occupation, and laid the foundations for a lasting animosity between these Californians and the Americans. Actually, the Bear Flag uprising did not cost a dozen lives all told. A more nearly bloodless conquest or revolution it would be hard to find. In weighing Josiah Royce's denunciation of it, we must recall that Royce was a thorough-going pacifist to whom any fighting of any character was abhorrent. An armed clash, in view of the outbreak of the Mexican War, was inevitable, and northern California could not have been secured with a shorter casualty list. As for the ill-feeling aroused by the Bear Flag uprising, much of it appears quickly to have evaporated. The Americans, after Frémont took full control, bore themselves for the most part in an exemplary manner. There were no outrages, no depredations, and few aberrations from the rule of strict obedience and orderliness; Alexander Godey tells us, truthfully, that Frémont's operations "were eminently characterized by a regard for the rights and interests of the inhabitants of the country through which his forces marched, which secured to him the kindest feelings of regard and respect of the entire California population." It is true that there was a sudden angry flare-up of the Californians against the Americans after Sloat raised his flag, and much semi-guerrilla warfare. But where did it occur? Not in northern California, where Frémont had acted, but in southern California. As for the legacy of ill feeling which the events of 1846 left, that was largely inevitable. Any historian who supposes that two races so alien in blood, could have lived together without sharp friction is very naive.

Frémont was not the liberator of California. It would in all probability have fallen safely and surely into American hands had he gone unambitiously north to the Oregon Trail in the spring of 1846. But he did play a gallant, daring, and useful role in expediting the American conquest, making it easy for the Navy to act, preventing the possible occurrence of complications with Great Britain, and enabling California to be almost wholly pacified before the first overland forces under General Kearny arrived.

6.
Bernard DeVoto's Biting Sarcasm

In range of scholarship and pungency of style on the Frémont question, no writer ever out did Bernard DeVoto in his The Year of Decision: 1846.[3] *For DeVoto, who died in 1947 after serving for 20 years as editor of* Harper's Magazine, *the West held a special fascination. He produced two other histories of the West,* The Course of Empire *and* Across the Wide Missouri. *He also edited the* Journals of Lewis and Clark.

Year of Decision *is a study of the amazing confluence of events that advanced the cause of American expansionism in the single year of 1846, including the Mormon migration to Utah, the Oregon Treaty, the tragedy of the Donner Party, the outbreak of the Mexican War, the Bear Flag revolution, and the fighting by American troops throughout the Southwest. The excerpt below leaves no possible doubt of the author's distaste for young Frémont and his fellow rebels, as DeVoto chronicles a comic-opera version of the "heroic events of the summer of 1846 in California.*

At the beginning of March [of 1846], Frémont was continuing his northward progress toward Oregon by moving west over the Santa Cruz Mountains and south toward Monterey in violation of his agreement and in defiance of the authorities. They now took action. On March 5, at Hartnell ranch near Salinas, an officer of the California militia rode into his camp and gave him letters from the prefect and the *comandante*. Both directed him to take his force out of the department at once. The hero worked on a hair trigger. He ordered the lieutenant out of camp with a red-fire message for his superiors, moved hastily into the hills, set up a breastwork of logs on the top of Gavilán Peak, nailed Old Glory to a pole, and prepared to be sacrificed. "If we are unjustly attacked," he wrote to Larkin, "we will fight to extremity and refuse quarter, trusting our country to avenge our death. . . . If we are hemmed in and assaulted here, we will die, every man of us, under the flag of our country . . ." He had been told to get out, on the ground that he had broken faith with the officials, lied about his instructions and intentions, broken the law, defied the courts, and condoned the misbehavior of his men. There had been no thought of killing him.

Nobody was ready to confer martyrdom on him, and though his mountain men were hot for a go with the greasers he got nothing for his brave words except an artist's pleasure in the style. Consul Larkin found so little intelligence in his actions that he supposed Frémont could not have understood the official orders and wrote explaining them—meanwhile asking Don José Castro not to get rough but to talk things over with the hero in simple language. Also, seeing his patient intrigue all but ruined by this dramaturgy, he hastily asked for a man-of-war at Monterey, to persuade all parties to dampen their powder. As for Don José, he mustered what militia he could, circularized an already agitated countryside with proclamations, and paraded his forces under the spyglasses trained on them from Gavilán Peak. That was the traditional way of using force in California.

It worked. In his lofty fortress Frémont reverberated with the most dramatic emotions but his position was impossible in both law and tactics, as he realized when the McGuffey phase had passed. He was here without the slightest authority of his government, which could only disavow him, and the Californians had ordered him out on sufficient grounds and altogether within their rights. They were unlikely to attack him on the Gavilán and, if they had attacked, his mountain men could have shot them to pieces. But they must eventually have starved him out and then ridden him down with the long lances that were to win them San Pascual. However stirring his compositions and however humiliating the retreat, no great deed was possible and he had to get out. After three days of Hollywood fantasy, his flagpole fell down and he told his men that this showed they had done enough for honor. He moved out, most slow and dignified.

---

[3]Bernard DeVoto, *The Year of Decision: 1846* (1st Ed., 1942: Boston: Houghton Mifflin Co., 1961), 11-472.

He went at last to the San Joaquin Valley, and from there moved to the Sacramento, reaching Sutter's Fort again on March 21. (On that day Jim Clyman wrote to him and, at Jalapa, Slidell was notified that Mexico would not receive a minister from Mr. Polk.) There was nothing to do but refit his party at Sutter's and carry out his original instructions. Heading toward Oregon, he got to Neal's ranch on Butte Creek, March 28 (Neal had come out as his blacksmith on the Second Expedition and had stayed), and on the thirtieth reached Peter Lassen's place on Deer Creek, some two hundred miles out from Sutter's. . . .

There were about eight hundred Americans in California. . . . This languorous society where no one worked hard, not even the Indian slaves, where no one set much value on wealth, industry, or sober righteousness, where the standard of living was far below the standard of manners, where progress was unheard of and the principles of *laissez faire* governed everything except the commerce to which they should apply only—in this society there was nothing whatever that the expansionist Yankees of the 1840's could admire. Furthermore they were committed to an implicit revolution; they were invaders and their land titles hung on the whim of a nation which had made an open move to dispossess them. They knew how brittle were the few remaining bonds that held the province to Mexico. They knew and freely assisted the vague apprehensions that one or another nation half the world away would hold out a hand to catch it as it fell. They knew that a sizable number of Californians, and those among the most substantial, hoped it would be an American hand and preferred that sovereignty to the grafters sent from Mexico to collect the revenue, the convicts sent to maintain them, and the native picaros who formally contended with both. . . . A mixed solution had reached the point of saturation; shake it ever so slightly and something must crystallize out.

. . .They [the Americans] had interpreted Frémont's arrival in the light of their hopes and holdings. With Frémont gone and the hope withdrawn, they were again at the mercy, if not of the greasers at least of the land system—and what had they come for if not for land? (Well, some for health, some for adventure, some as deserters or fugitives, some merely as flotsam.) They ought to do something about it.

Back in Monterey, the U.S. sloop *Cyane* dropped anchor on April 17 and Lieutenant Gillespie repeated to Consul Larkin the instructions he had memorized at Mexico City. He had been just short of six months on his way. Larkin presented him as an invalid traveling for his health, and he rode north to Yerba Buena and the vice consul. From there he set out to overtake Frémont. . . .

Some patches of snow still lingered round the sheltered roots of the great pines on the shore of Big Klamath Lake, and Benton, on the basis of what his son-in-law wrote about it, was to interpret that snow to the Senate as a fierce winter storm that endangered the Pathfinder's life and turned him back again to the settlements. Frémont could also have found ice in the bottoms of northward-sloping ravines.

It was a picturesque scene on the edge of Klamath Lake, in southern Oregon. The Pathfinder enjoyed the splash of firelight on the dark, the columns of enormous evergreens growing dim above it. "How Fate pursues a man!" he wrote. Fate, on horseback, had taken the persons of William Sigler and Frémont's former blacksmith, Sam Neal, riding hell-bent through the night. Hooves sounded afar off through the forest silence and, tumbling into the firelight, the messengers told Frémont that an officer of the marines with dispatches for him was on his trail—and they thought the Indians were following close behind him. . . .

So there was another, more important campfire at Klamath Lake, in "a glade or natural meadow, shut in by the forest, with a small stream and good grass." May 9, 1846. A hero's hour had struck.

All the accounts which Frémont later gave of this meeting are in the tone forbidden by Hamlet, "We could an we would," and they are contradictory. But only once, and that once flatly contradicted by many other passages, does he get altogether out of imitation and into assertion. "Now it was officially made known to me that my country was at war," he says in his *Memoirs*. His best biographer, Mr. Nevins, all but repeats the assertion when he says that Gillespie, having had on February 22 at Mazatlán information from Mexico City of about February 10, could tell Frémont "that Taylor had advanced to the Rio Grande, where fighting was expected at any time."

Both statements are wrong. As for Mr. Nevins': Taylor's orders to advance to the Rio Grande were issued at Washington on January 13, he received them on February 3, he moved out of Corpus Christi on March 8, he reached the Rio Grande on March 28, and nothing was known about his orders or his movements at Mexico City on February 10 or at Mazatlán on February 22. As for Frémont's: not only was there no unofficial information in Gillespie's possession that there was war between Mexico and the United States, not only was the "official" information in his dispatches based on Polk's October confidence that there would be no war, but the dispatch which he repeated to Frémont expressly stipulated that California was to be pacified.

The deliberate implication of Frémont's private and public testimony (in his court-martial and in the hearings on the claims of the California Battalion) is that, on May 9, he received orders to go back to California and produce an incident. The deliberate but more veiled implication of Gillespie's testimony and depositions is the same. But whenever either of them is brought to an unequivocal issue, each flatly declares that there were no such orders. The repeated insinuation that there were secret instructions invariably dissolves when facts are approached. There were no secret instructions from anyone. Frémont was lying.

Frémont ultimately rests on the private letters from his wife and from Benton (neither of them qualified to give him orders or in this instance even advice), which he says, were in a kind of family cipher. (This cipher, we are to understand, consisted of oblique allusions to earlier conversations.) It all boils down to the fact that Benton again advised him to watch out for foreign intervention in California if war with Mexico—which Benton did not favor and did not expect—should break out, or if the negotiations over Oregon should reach a crisis (as he did not think they would). Unquestionably the chairman of the Committee on Military Affairs wrote just that to his son-in-law. But it was not a solicitation to act, it was not official, and it was written at a time when Benton was shut out from the secretive Polk's confidence. The final bit of "official" evidence is a letter and memorandum furnished to Frémont forty years later by George Bancroft, then eighty-six years old. The two documents say nothing directly to the point, are at variance with the demonstrable facts, contain much ambiguity, and, in short, are the untrustworthy recollections of an old man who was remembering fierce controversy through the fiercer passions of the Civil War. . . .

. . . Frémont had no instructions from Polk to produce an incident or to begin a conquest.

From Polk's *Diary* for March 21, 1848:

> The Senate of the U.S. having passed a Resolution calling for a letter addressed by the Secretary of State to Mr. Larkin, U.S. consul at Monterey, in California, in October, 1845, it was a question submitted for consideration (in the Cabinet) today whether it was compatible with the public interest to comply with the call. The letter was read. It was confidential and had for its object the protection of American interests and the prevention of British and French interference in California. . . . A false impression is being attempted by the administration in Congress, to be made, to the effect that this letter to Mr. Larkin contained instructions to produce a revolution in California before Mexico commenced the War against the U.S. & that Col. Frémont had the authority to make the revolution. The publication of the letter will prove the falsehood of such an inference.

The Pathfinder reached a decision while he sat by the dying fire after all the others were asleep. To go back to California and do a great deed, for honor and glory. To seize California for the United States and wrap Old Glory 'round him, to give a deed to the greatness in him. To seize the hour, take fortune at the full, and make his cast. To trust that the war which was certain to come would transform an act of brigandage into an act of patriotism, would transform the actor from a military adventurer, a freebooter, a filibuster, into a hero.

He was a hero from that moment on until he died, but always with the lines just out of drawing. Time, circumstance, and destiny always co-operated with him for a while, and always betrayed him in the end.

ornia to initiate a movement which should seize it for the
xico or as a safeguard against Great Britain did not matter
as promptly surrounded by men who had long wanted to
and anxious because the expected war had not developed,
ice of his return. The expected was now going to happen
t was an instigator of it.
nent. If it could be arranged for some of the Americans
s attacked by Castro, then Frémont could come to their
attack him, then all the rest would follow in strict accor-
a shifty plan. It worked.
ont, in the course of which he angered some of them by
his counsel too long, a band of Americans rode out on
were acting on their own or they were acting under his
ome time back, had sent a requisition to General Maríano

the Cosumnes, they surprised and captured the general's
drove the horses back to Sutter's. Arce hurried to Castro
at his horses had been stolen by American highwaymen.
n which this raid appeared to confirm. He began to fight
and by raising troops.
ymen were delighted to find themselves a vanguard of
vas war. If it was war, then the laws of strategy required
of enemy troops. There were no troops but, at the
he California equivalent of troops, a general. This was
who in theory commanded the northern frontier for Cas-
custody. He was perhaps the most considerable citizen
rican annexation and had been suspected of conspiring

orders for the capture of Sonoma. He thereby outraged
of wanting to hog the glory after refusing to take the
now and including William Todd, the nephew of Mrs.
aries reached Sonoma before dawn on June 14. In the
reports which Senator Benton was to trumpet to an admiring nation the town figured as a fortified, garrisoned, and formidably armed presidio. That is what Old Bullion gathered about it from his son-in-law's letter, but Sonoma was a tiny little cluster of adobe houses and could have been captured by Tom Sawyer and Huck Finn. The conquerors found General Vallejo asleep.

They gathered in not only this general but a lieutenant colonel and a captain to boot. They told Vallejo that he was a prisoner of war. He had some difficulty understanding what war he was a prisoner of and set out brandy for his captors, so that they could talk it over. Conquerors and conquered wrote out a formal statement of terms, and by its third paragraph, the product of good native liquor, the California Republic was born.

To some of the army outside the house conquest began to look rather like a drunk. Others wanted to plunder the town. Still others, in cold morning air, began to wonder if high spirits had not carried them too far. The new republic nearly died of second thoughts, but it was saved by the Yankee school master, William Ide. He made a noble speech, and from then on was, for a brief but appealing time, chief of state.... There had to be a republic. Otherwise there was no sovereignty and the prisoners were being held simply by thugs; otherwise supplies seized for the army would just be stolen.

They sent the prisoners to Frémont, in camp near Sutter's Fort, and at Sonoma began mustering the Americans who rode in as the news traveled, scared or glad to be getting along with the revolution at last. President Commander Ide, calling upon his memory of speeches made from Yankee bandstands on Lexington and Concord Day, poured out his soul in a proclamation. He recited the grievances that a revolt must have if it is to gather in the shadow of Thomas Jefferson; there weren't any grievances but he made some good phrases. He summoned all native Californians of goodwill to rally to the free government now conferred on them at Sonoma. He sketched out the policies it would adopt. He closed with allusions to the bravery of his followers, all forty of them to the native American hatred of tyranny, and to the favor of heaven.

When Josiah Royce came to narrate these events, in the study that remains on the whole the best one, he would find no solemnity adequate to describe this scene of a handful of exceedingly tough customers brushing a varnish of classical American rhetoric over a mere foray by brigands. He alluded to the Hunting of the Snark and let it go at that. There is a neater allusion in the works of W. S. Gilbert but one is deterred from making the parallel. For another parallel comes to mind. Here were some American settlers in California, some of them legitimate immigrants and others just adventurers on the loose, announcing in the morning sunlight to some amiable, peaceful, and extremely bewildered Californians that they were creating a new Texas on the golden shore. Comic enough. But in a study in the White House, on the plane of international affairs, with all due circumstance of diplomatics and phrased in better English than Conquistador Ide used, a new Texas was precisely what the President of the United States had envisaged.

They had a Republic, California model, by proclamation, out of Lexington and Brook Farm. So while they went about giving it substance they ought also to set up a standard to which honest republicans might repair. William Todd obliged, women's patriotism assisting him. The wife of one revolutionist sacrificed a chemise and the wife of another one a petticoat, and Todd made a flag. Red flannel stripes across a white (or at least unbleached) field. He painted in red a crude five-pointed star in the left-hand corner and, facing it, an animal standing on its hind legs, doubtless remembered in emergency from the state seal of Missouri. A realist, or he may have been an adept of symbolism, described it as a hog, but Todd meant it for a bear. Underneath, in ink or pokeberry juice, he lettered in the legend: California Republic. He left the i out of the last syllable and made a blot painting it over again, but the one-village nation had the ensign that has come down to glory.

All California north of Monterey quivered with alarm or curiosity. The amazed Montgomery, of the navy's sloop *Portsmouth*, hurried to proclaim that neither he nor the United States had or wanted any part in the creation of this commonwealth. The one accredited representative of the United States, Consul Larkin, realized that if any hope of fulfilling his instructions had remained after Frémont's drama on Gavilán Peak, this gaudier drama had extinguished it. In resignation he also disavowed the Republic and told the California authorities that he would help them bring its proprietors to justice. More Americans rode in to join the founding fathers, others rode in the other direction to join Frémont, and the Californians rode in all directions, taking counsel....

A little order began to come out of the miscellaneous riding. Certain improvised bands came together and Castro made plans to recapture Sonoma, the capital of the Republic and so far its entire domain. Commander Ide, who now had a flag and a proclamation, was receiving volunteers, was offering a square league of his future conquest as a bonus for enlisting (thus repeating the leit motif), and had organized his forces into the First Artillery and the First Rifles. He had made prisoners of war of the town's *alcalde*, a simple-hearted and extremely bewildered young man, and thirty or forty other citizens. He invented a service of supply and information—and had to combat the foul rumor that he was a Mormon or a Mormon agent. A dispatch from Frémont arrived, to be forwarded to Montgomery at San Francisco Bay. Ide called on the versatile Todd to become a courier. Todd was valorous but unacquainted with the principles of military security. He ran into one of the bands of wandering horsemen and now the Californians in their turn had a prisoner of war. At once they had two more. For Ide sent a couple of his recruits, Fowler and Cowie, to procure a keg of powder for the Republic's army and they also met some horsemen on the public road. These were more excitable horsemen: if there was going to be a war, let it begin here. They shot Fowler and Cowie. Since they were enemy horsemen, this was clearly against the laws of war. (It was promptly, and erroneously, rumored that they had dismembered the bodies.)

Word of these captures, though not of the murders, reached the Republic, and Ide sent out his lieutenant, Ford, with a dozen and a half irregulars to retake the prisoners. On June 23 they met some horsemen at the hamlet of San Antonio and took four of them prisoner. The next morning they blundered into a party of fifty campaigning Californians who had stopped for breakfast at Olompali, halfway between Santa Rosa and Petaluma. This was the first of three detachments which Castro intended to send against Sonoma but the only one that got across the Bay. It was led by Captain Joaquin de la Torre, who was mightily surprised to find himself under fire. The Americans were equally startled but gamer. They took cover, killed one Californian, wounded another one, and presently had de la Torre riding hell for leather down the back trail to San Rafael. Ford went on to his original destination and recaptured William Todd, then rode back to Sonoma. . . . End of the military history of the California Republic.

Meanwhile Captain Frémont, commanding sixty American freebooters of his own and nearly as many irregular recruits, had become an open ally of the Republic. He was imprisoning at Sutter's Fort all peaceful wayfarers his men encountered— including certain Americans who could not understand that what they took to be a violation of the public peace was an honorable warfare to liberate the enslaved. Also he was in a literary phase, spouting letters of explanation, manifesto, and deception—to Montgomery, to Larkin, to Senator Benton—describing the purity of his intentions, the extreme peril of his situation, and the wakeful resolution of his heart. . . . No one could look ahead to the summer of 1864, to a time when history's stage manager would make him, for a while, a candidate for the Presidency against not only A. Lincoln but George B. McClellan as well. He had McClellan's talent for believing himself surrounded by irresistible hordes of enemies and for calculating his chances at something like one in ten thousand. So now he peoples the countryside with marching masses of murderous Mexicans—hundreds of them and all thirsting like the Indians of ten-cent fiction for the hero's gore. Moreover, he was somehow being insulted as well as hunted down, and one of his letters announced that, besides defeating the Californians, he intended to force an apology from them.

Word reached him at Sutter's of Castro's intention to attack Sonoma. The Republic was in danger! So gallop, gallop, Frémont *au secours*! Eighty miles he took his cavalry at full speed and at the end found himself in extreme danger—of being fired on by the garrison of Sonoma, who had been weakened by the dispatch of Ford's expedition but would nevertheless sell their lives dearly when hooves came pounding through the night. Good playwriting saved the Conquistador just as the lighted match was arching to the breech of Sonoma's cannon. Frémont, as senior officer of guerrillas, now took command of the Republic's military establishment, and the next day Ford got back with word that de la Torre had escaped. . . .

As the curtain falls on this act, the performance may seem below the standard of great drama. But if the hero's role has been trivial, let Hubert Howe Bancroft remind us what he had achieved. He had made himself, by his actions so far, Bancroft sums up, "a popular hero, a Senator of the United States, a candidate for the Presidency, a millionaire *ad interim*, [and] a major-general."

Bancroft adds that he was a lucky fellow. Right—so far. How lucky he was is apparent when one considers what would certainly have happened to Frémont and his guerrillas if, civil war having been precipitated in a California which was slow to act but could have annihilated the revolutionists, the news of the outbreak of the Mexican war had not now reached responsible men who had instructions to act. That news arrived at about the time when Frémont captured his empty fortress. The one-town California Republic ended its sovereignty and the conquest of California began....

Scared stiff that he might have exceeded his instructions, [Commodore] Sloat had nevertheless had the flag raised at Yerba Buena, Sonoma, Bodega, and elsewhere, and had issued a decent and proper proclamation. He had, remember, been told to occupy the California ports, proclaim the occupation a deliverance from tyranny, and invite the consent of the natives. Events, particularly the Bear Flag opera, had made his instructions obsolete, but consul Larkin still hoped that his own intrigue could succeed. To Larkin the Bear Flag incident seemed [a venture in outlawry: which is what it was,] and he yearned to get Frémont under control. So did Sloat, though he also hoped that Frémont was acting under orders, in which case he should feel much better about his own episode in imperialism. (He kept remembering Ap Catesby Jones.) Neither Pico nor Castro accepted his invitation to come in and collaborate with him, and Castro, who was moving south and losing troops by desertion as he went, inquired what he made of the Bear Flag filibuster. Sloat longed for Frémont, who was supposed to be pursuing Castro. Frémont, marching toward Monterey by routes which could not possibly have intercepted Castro, was eager to join Sloat.

For Sloat was the duly constituted commander of the United States forces in California and could legitimatize Frémont. When they met, Sloat asked what authority Frémont was acting under, and the Conqueror was forced to admit that he had no authority. The admission shocked the commodore and strengthened his determination to get out of here fast, letting others bear the responsibilities of empire. He was old, sick, irresolute, and a long way from Washington. But he refused to cooperate in Frémont's proposed march against Santa Barbara and Los Angeles, which was to complete the Conquest, and refused to muster Frémont's battalion into the service of the United States.

This was embarrassing. The Conquest remained illegitimate and the Conqueror's status was that of a thug. The sense of grievance burst into flame and Frémont would presently write to Senator Benton an account of these events....

But a different commodore arrived, to whom Sloat joyfully turned over command and responsibility. This was a d'Artagnan part, played by Robert Field Stockton, an energetic, imaginative personage cast as a sea dog. Commodore Stockton needed only to survey the situation in order to understand the cinematic requirements. He supplied them. He commissioned Frémont (it is hard to see by what authority) as a major in the army, made Gillespie a captain, and mustered in Frémont's irregulars as the Navy Battalion of Mounted Riflemen. That is, in strict accuracy, as the Horse Marines. He furiously prepared to conquer the rest of California and, be sure, issued a proclamation.

The touch of paranoia Frémont suffered from had magnified actual events, just as the desert mirage magnifies actual objects. Much of Frémont's career in California is explained by the fact that he was seeing mirages—delusions. But Stockton was not suffering delusions—he was lying.... If there had been hope of conciliating Castro, Pico, or the Californians in general, he destroyed it with his proclamation of July 29. Quite properly, the Californians had made some impromptu opposition to Frémont's filibuster but, so far, they had not at all opposed the forces of the United States. Nevertheless Stockton accused Castro of "lawless violence" and an intention to "with the aid of hostile Indians keep this beautiful country in a constant state of revolution and blood"—which was not only a lie but absurd as well....

Frémont's memoirs show that he was not happy in having to accept a superior commander, but as Major Jinks of the Horse Marines he was at last legitimate. Stockton embarked the Navy Battalion of Mounted Riflemen on the *Cyane*, July 26, and sent them off to occupy San Diego. Kit Carson's most poignant journey followed: he got seasick and so did his messmates, who had just finished a big drunk. Frémont raised the flag at San Diego on July 29, and after impressing horses started north to join Stockton on August 8. The Conqueror's record remained untarnished; he had not yet faced a hostile force in California. He never did.

Stockton made up a landing force of 360 marines and sailors and sailed in the *Congress* on August 1. He stopped to raise the flag at Santa Barbara and reached San Pedro on August 6. Larkin, who was with him and still hoped to abate the show of force, got in touch with Castro and Pico, whose pathetic efforts to raise a defensive army were failing. They would have been happy to declare a truce and meet Stockton for negotiations. A rout is more glorious than a treaty, however, and Stockton refused with a ruffle of drums which proved that the navy was as good as the army at soliloquy. So the governor and the *comandante*, oozing a rhetoric that is no less absurd in that it expressed the genuine emotions of conquered people, gave up the struggle for which they could rouse no popular support and abandoned their fragmentary forces. Castro rode away for Mexico and Pico, after hiding for a month near San Juan Capistrano, escaped to Lower California. There was now not even a mirage of opposition. On August 14 Frémont's command joined Stockton's and the land army of sailors occupied Los Angeles. This was five days before Kearny entered Santa Fe, and the Conquest of California, Major Frémont second in command, was completed. . . for a while.

Stockton sat down to write his report, or shooting script, to the Secretary of the Navy. (It would come into the hands of Mason, formerly Attorney General, who took the place when Polk made Bancroft Minister to England.) He told his chief that in less than a month he had "chased the Mexican army more than three hundred miles along the coast, pursued them thirty miles in the interior of their own country, routed and dispersed them and secured the Territory to the United States, ended the war, restored peace and harmony among the people, and put a civil government into successful operation.

What war? What army? What harmony? What civil government? But it was a practical treatment for the movies and the Secretary of the Navy was in Washington. . . .

Stockton's later career—in the United States Senate and in the Ku Klux Klan of the period, the American Party—contains nothing to weaken the judgment that he was a fool. He did not quite make the nomination for the Presidency. Frémont did, and in doing so jeopardized the Republican Party, as from then on he repeatedly jeopardized the United States. You cannot let him off so lightly as Stockton. He was worse than a fool, he was an opportunist, an adventurer, and a blunderer on a truly dangerous scale. He was foisted on the Republic in the hour of its peril by the power of publicity, the reputation erected on his career in California during '46 and '47. That was the career of a military adventurer, a filibuster, and officer of the United States Army committing mutiny. In the Civil War, as in California, he made a play for every opportunity that would serve John Charles Frémont, regardless of its effect on the United States. Then, as in California, he created spectacle but bungled what he had started out to do. Only, in the Civil War he came into the keeping of men with stronger intelligences and clearer understanding of the forces at work who could use the symbol of John Charles Frémont for their private purposes. Their purposes were not pretty and Frémont did nothing to inconvenience them. That they did not destroy the United States was not their fault. Neither was it Frémont's (It was in part the responsibility of a major general who in February of '47 arrived in California as a lieutenant of artillery, William Tecumseh Sherman.) Technically and in the light of his own conscience, he was not a traitor to the United States in 1864. That this was not for lack of the raw stuff out of which treason is made was clear in '64—and was clear in '47.

God and events were against Frémont. He tried to be a great man but something always happened. . . .

This frightful accident recalled the people to their senses, and they began to act a little less like madmen, than they had previously done. They elected a vigilance committee, and authorized persons to go to The Junction and arrest the suspected Spaniards.

The first act of the Committee was to try a Mexicana, who had been foremost in the fray. She has always worn male attire, and on this occasion, armed with a pair of pistols, she fought like a very fury. Luckily, inexperienced in the use of fire-arms, she wounded no one. She was sentenced to leave the Bar by day-light—a perfectly just decision, for there is no doubt she is a regular little demon. Some went so far as to say she ought to be hanged, for she was the indirect cause of the fight. You see always, it is the old, cowardly excuse of Adam in Paradise—the woman tempted me, and I did eat,—as if the poor frail head, once so pure and beautiful, had not sin enough of its own, dragging it forever downward, without being made to answer for the wrongdoing of a whole community of men.

The next day, the Committee tried five or six Spaniards, who were proven to have been the ringleaders in the sabbath-day riot. Two of them were sentenced to be whipped, the remainder to leave the Bar that evening, the property of all to be confiscated to the use of the wounded persons. Oh Mary! imagine my anguish when I heard the first blow fall upon those wretched men. —**"Dame Shirley," from Indian Bar, August 4, 1852.**[1]

CHAPTER 4

THE SAN FRANCISCO VIGILANTES OF 1856

Government "by laws or by men"?

Going onto the American frontier always made some Americans feel they had been thrust into a moral wilderness which would provide a torturous test of all their established values and institutions. Gold Rush diaries and letters are particularly rich in references to the temptations of the flesh, the threat of dissipation and crime among the youth, the general dangers to life and limb posed by brigands, and the possibility of the complete breakdown of morality, law, and order. In the Sierra as well as in the more established society of San Francisco in 1849 and in the early 1850's, the rapidity of physical and social mobility was unparalleled. Social standards based on respectability and wealth seemed to have vanished. The presence of tens of thousands of "foreigners," whose values and attitudes were unknown, intensified the anxiety. And while the need for social control increased, old systems of restraint seemed to wither away. All of this posed quite dramatically the eternal conflict between private desires and social responsibility. It was, as one miner imagined, as close as modern man could come to seeing himself in a State of Nature.

How people and institutions actually fared in this crucible has been the subject of a great deal of conjecture. Some have written that, in sum, the dangers were great but the people even greater, so that for each crisis new and exemplary popular government and popular justice were mere extensions of the disorder which had called them into being in the first place—that lynch law was never more depraved than in Gold Rush California. California was a case in which, to borrow the memorable phrase of Justice Marshall, it was difficult to know whether a government of men or of laws would prevail. In fact, it was sometimes hard to know where one left off and the other began.

---

[1]Louise Amelia Knapp Smith Clappe, *The Shirley Letters from the California Mines in 1851-52: Being a Series of Twenty-three Letters from Dame Shirley. . . to Her Sister in Massachusetts. . . Reprinted from the Pioneer Magazine of 1854-55*, Thomas C. Russell, ed. (San Francisco: Thomas C. Russell, 1922), 263- 264.

One phase of Gold Rush history lends itself particularly well to testing the mettle of government—the causes and consequences of vigilante justice in San Francisco. Following are three selections on this subject: two written by participants and one by a recent writer.

The most respectable of the vigilante groups in California was the San Francisco Committee of Vigilance formed in 1856. That group had leaders of the most impeccable reputation, a huge following, the most enduring results, and the best historical "image." Its legacy is unique in that even the staunchest enemies of vigilante justice elsewhere in California will make an exception in favor of the Committee of 1856.

The San Franciscans had attempted twice, in 1849 and 1851, to purge their civic sins by invoking "popular justice." But by 1856 it was a town in which major crimes were common, while justice was practically at a standstill. Hundreds of homicides had occurred—one source puts the figure at 1000—but only one man had been prosecuted. The underworld had high connections, and ballot-box stuffing and other forms of political corruption had made the municipal government a sham. Banking and business practices were suspect. Then on May 14, 1856, James King of William, editor of the San Francisco *Bulletin*, published a damaging screed on the checkered career of County Supervisor James P. Casey. That night Casey took revenge by shooting King as the editor left his office. Though some San Franciscans considered King a meddlesome fool with an axe to grind, most thought he was a courageous truth-teller. The next day the Committee of Vigilance, headed by William T. Coleman, was formed to produce justice outside the law. In rebuttal another group established a Law and Order Party, led by William Tecumseh Sherman, who was then a prominent San Francisco banker and commander of the California militia. The Committee set up its headquarters at "Ft. Gunnybags," a downtown office building surrounded by sandbags, and on May 18 sent its thousands of minions to remove Casey from the jail and to seize Charles Cora, a miscreant who had been formally tried and exonerated in court for killing a U.S. marshall. Both were "tried" and "convicted" by the Committee, operating in secret but using generally accepted practices of open court. A week after he was shot, King died; he was buried May 22, the day of the executions of Casey and Cora.

Meanwhile, the municipal government had capitulated, Sherman was unable to get arms for the militia, the President refused to help Governor Johnson, and the Committee, an extra-legal body with its own military force, took complete command of the most important city in the American West. On June 21, a Committee "policeman" was stabbed by David S. Terry, Justice of the California Supreme Court. Terry was imprisoned by the vigilantes but freed when his victim survived the assault. Had the policeman died, the Committee would have faced the prospect of having to execute a high public official and thereby creating the basis for an armed confrontation with the state militia or perhaps U.S. troops. The Committee kept at its self-appointed job of purification, exiling a number of evil-doers, and hanging two more confessed murderers, until it finally disbanded August 18. A sound municipal government took over that year and San Francisco was blessed by clean government for the next decade.

The question is, then, whether the end justifies the means: since the Committee was so "clean" and effectual, was its seizure of power morally justified? Or, despite the urbane quality of the Committee, was it an embryo police state with dangerous implications?

In what follows, two contemporary Protestant ministers assume the roles of moral advocates. Rev. R. P. Cutler speaks warmly for the necessity of the Committee and the restraint it exercised. Taking an opposite view, Rev. W. A. Scotta launches into a blistering attack on its work. The final statement is an ambivalent but mostly sympathetic opinion on the Committee by a recent author, Stanton A. Coblentz. *(Editor's note)*

7.
Rev. R. P. Cutler Defends the Committee

At noon, on May 22, 1856, while the Vigilantes took James P. Casey to the scaffold to be hanged for killing James King of William, the coffin of the dead man lay in the Unitarian Church on Stockton Street where the pastor delivered a sermon on the fallen "Purifier." "[King] has died a martyr to freedom of speech and the press," Rev. R. P. Cutler intoned, "a martyr to progress of society here, its progress upwards towards a higher moral plane. And by this it is chiefly that he won such distinguished and universal regard, and that his death, as well as the circumstances of his death, has made such an impression and so deeply touched the general sympathy. . . . Death sanctifies all his good deeds and worthy efforts."

On Thanksgiving Day that same year, Cutler gave another sermon reviewing the events of the recent season. As shown below, he saw every action of the Committee as having the purest of motives. He believed that citizens had an ultimate right of revolution against corrupt government and that the current situation called for the exercise of that right.[2]

. . . I know very well that the Committee of Vigilance has been the subject of severe and angry criticism on both sides of the continent. It has been condemned, on general principles, by some who knew, and many who did not know, whereof they affirmed. But I have tried to look at the whole movement as an impartial spectator. I have watched the causes from which it sprung, have seen the points at issue, and the character of the two parties which came into the conflict, and something of the motives which moved the opposition. I have not intentionally overlooked any fact or argument, or constitutional objection, which may have been urged against the Committee, or disregarded any hot and bitter denunciation that has been hurled upon them while in the midst of their work, or since it has been done. I must be allowed to say, for one, and I say it with an increasing conviction of its truth, that there has not been, in any portion of the land, a more needful, a more patriotic or wisely conducted demonstration for civil rights and the public good since the days of the Revolution. There was an extraordinary assumption of power, but there was an extraordinary occasion for its exercise. The Constitution of the State does not and cannot provide for such a state of things as existed. No law of man could reach the difficulty except the law of *force*. The people had neglected their duty to the government. The ballot-box was in the hands of hired ruffians, who maintained their usurpation by force, the combined force of revolvers, bowie knives and brandy. Some of the worst men on earth were in office, and could not be dislodged. The courts of law had become torpid, and the administration of justice exceedingly lax and corrupt; the public funds were robbed and wasted; the streets were broken and impassable, and the public affairs fast tending to utter ruin.

Now, I ask, where was the remedy for this, in a peculiar community like ours? Does the Constitution provide for wresting the ballot-box from such men as your McGowans, and Caseys, and Mulligans, and Kearneys, except by *armed force*? Were they men to give up their advantage by mere persuasion and argument, or ridicule? Were they to shamed out of their effrontery and political gambling? No, the supposition is absurd. Would time and patience cure the evil? No, time and patience made everything worse—gangrene sinks deeper by neglect. They did not die and never resigned. Would an indignant convention of the people, and spirited and caustic resolutions effect the desired change? This would be like painted lightning and harmless thunder, mere *brutum fulmen*. There was absolutely nothing that would reach the case but *force*. Our citizens were compelled to take their rights by main strength, *vi et armis*, or not have them at all. There was a plain necessity for a violent collision, for an illegal assumption of power, and the power was assumed against law, for

[2]Rev. R. P. Cutler, *A Thanksgiving Sermon: Delivered in the First Unitarian Church, Stockton Street, on Sunday Morning, November 23, 1856* (San Francisco: Commercial Book and Job Stream Printing Establishment, 1856), 16-21.

law and the enjoyment of civil rights. The choice was between civil revolution and civil ruin. Revolution was chosen, and revolution by force and the bayonet. A fatal disease was upon the body politic, and the case must be probed even at the most fearful risks and hazards. A cancer must not be tampered with, but must be cut from the system. The best citizens armed themselves without the sanctions of law, with the virtuous aim, not to overturn the Constitution, but to establish it and gain its protection; not to subvert law, but to render the laws effective; not to destroy order, but to bring order out of confusion, and to restore a solid peace.

Never was there an issue more false, and empty and delusive than that raised between the Committee and their opponents, by the opponents themselves. For every man knows, and every candid man will acknowledge, that the Vigilance Committee aimed, with a serious and honest purpose at heart, however illegal the manner, at the establishment of both *law* and *order*. This was their aim, and this was the immediate result of their action, and a result which every day renders more conspicuous. In *form*, their action was in contravention of law and order, but in *fact*, and under the existing necessity of the case, their action was the only means by which law and order could be secured. In an extraordinary condition, the best citizens of society armed and organized, assumed the authority of the courts, only that the courts might be awakened to a sense of their duty, and better fulfill their sacred function, and this has been the effect. The courts of this county, as everybody knows, have been endowed with new life, and justice is no longer a name. The necessity of the case, the purity of intention steadily shown throughout, the wise caution of their proceeding, together with the unquestionable and obvious good results secured, will form the Committee's triumphant defense with all candid men everywhere, and with impartial posterity. And where on earth was there ever such a civil demonstration as this? A whole city aroused and armed against corruption, villainy and crime. A self-supported army of five thousand men, in constant drill for the public service, for the banishment of outlaws, for the protection of life and for municipal reform. And under this martial array, never was a city better governed or more at peace. Under this rule, what act of injustice was done? Was any life taken which had not been forfeited by crime, or that the laws would not have taken could the laws have been enforced? Was any one banished whose presence was not an offense to the good morals of this community? And is it not honorable and noteworthy that five thousand men in arms, of different nations, and temperaments, and habits of life, could assume the complete control of this city and hold it for months without committing any serious acts of indiscretion? Did not these men, when all things are considered, act most nobly? Could the same thing be carried so wisely, and discreetly, and successfully through, anywhere else on earth? This city has had a bad name in former days. But this wisdom and moderation, in the exercise of power, by such numbers of her citizens combined, and armed, and exercised, too, for the public morals and the public security, against the worst men and the worst crimes, ought to do much to redeem her reputation, and to set her up in honor before the eyes of the world.

All honor, then I say, to the Committee of Vigilance. It is an institution well adapted to the present, passing needs of a community like this. It was, certainly, the only power on earth, nor was there any in Heaven, which bad men in this country so feared, and which struck such wholesome terror into hardened criminals and veterans in guilt. The power was assumed by responsible citizens, and exercised with the greatest wisdom, and for the public good. The occasion was most urgent. The public mind was ripe for action. Patience was exhausted. The cause most irritating, and the immediate appeal stirred deep every manly heart. The blood of the martyred King cried from the ground, and from this call there sprung a municipal reform, which has swept with wholesome effects through this entire locality, ending in the complete triumph of the people, at the ballot-box, over ruffian rule, robbery and misdirection. And there has been an auspicious inauguration of a new era and a better state of things. We ought to be thankful for every social step taken in the right direction. One fair and decent election at the polls has been achieved, let us be thankful for *that*, and hail it as a sign of that future political and social regeneration, which is to lift the name of this fair city from the dust, and render her worthy to be the seat and center of a great western empire on the Pacific coast...

8.
Rev. W. A. Scott Defends Law and Order

Perhaps the most eloquent minority opinion against the 1856 vigilantes and in favor of "law and order" was the one penned by Rev. W. A. Scott, a Presbyterian minister of San Francisco. After a letter of his got the silent treatment from the pro-Vigilante newspaper, the San Francisco Pacific, *Scott dispatched a copy of it to a Philadelphia religious journal which did publish it.*[3] *Eventually the Scott letter was the subject of heated discussions back in San Francisco, and he was hanged in effigy.*

As is plainly evident, Scott believed lawful reform possible and finds as many arguments against the vigilantes as his Unitarian counterpart, Cutler, found for them.

To the Editors of the *Pacific* of San Francisco:

Messrs. Editors—It is with the deepest grief and mortification that I have read your articles since the beginning of the present most unhappy excitement in San Francisco, and especially your article of the 12th of June, "The Church and the Crisis"...

...I have remonstrated with you; I have written private letters to the principal editor, but all in vain. The columns of the *Pacific*, which the friends of Christ here and in the East have been endeavoring to establish and sustain as an organ of Christianity, still teem with effusions in behalf of violence to our laws, and call for the banishment of citizens—a punishment unknown to our Constitution and fundamental laws—and still call for blood and for the progress of "the Revolution."

Under these circumstances nothing is left to me but to protest, and let my friends know that the *Pacific* does not represent the principles that I hold, and which I believe to be according to the Bible and the Constitution. You say, that "of all the ministers of this State, we know of only one or two who have not expressed themselves favorable, and nearly every one has preached upon the subject." "With scarcely a single exception in the whole State, the pastors have approved of the action of the Committee. Most of them have preached on the subject. They have animated the people to go forward in the reform, as the work of religion—the work of God." And again, you say, "it is not a new thing for the Church to be found in the van of great revolutions." "The Church throughout the State is with this movement," &c. Now,

1. I hope you are mistaken, and that it will be found that I am not left absolutely alone. There may not be seven thousand who have not bowed the knee to Baal, but I trust I am not alone. Other ministers, however, have the same privileges that I have, and are quite as able to speak for themselves. It happened that I was absent in the mountains when Mr. King was killed and the insurrection began. Casey and Cora were hanged before I returned home. I left the city in peace, and after an absence of two weeks I returned and found it in arms. On my return I was told the religious newspapers are in favor of the revolution; the clergy of the city are all, or nearly all, on the side of the Vigilance Committee. I was told that I must pray for the Committee, and preach in their behalf, and that if my sentiments against them were known, I should "lose my congre-

[3]Rev. W. A. Scott to *Philadelphia Presbyterian*, n.d., reprinted in Conrad Weigand (W. Carroll, pseud.), *Dr. Scott, the Vigilance Committee and the Church: A Lecture...Delivered in Music Hall, San Francisco, October 12, 1856* (San Francisco: Whitton, Towne & Co., 1856).

gation." All this, and much more of a like character, is true; but I cannot still believe that it is right to pledge the Church of Christ to any such proceedings.

2. Are you, gentlemen, correct when you assign the Church "the van of great revolutions?" Is it really a part of our holy religion to contravene our established laws and courts of justice? Does the Church teach us to defy the chief magistrate of the State, and mock at his proclamation, and to assume the administration of such power as executes the highest penalties, and to rule over the city by a secret, self-appointed, irresponsible, but armed and powerful association? If so, I have certainly failed altogether to apprehend the true nature and mission of the Christian Church. I thought its founder was the Prince of Peace, and that his kingdom was not this world—that it consisted of righteousness, peace, and joy in the Holy Ghost. Nor have I ever found a single text in the Bible authorizing disobedience to the civil magistrate. On the contrary we are commanded to obey our ruler, even when they are as wicked as Caligula or Nero. Nor can I find where the Church has any commission to put herself in the van of any other revolution than that of preaching peace to all nations, through the blood of Christ...

3. Are you not also mistaken in calling this "work of God" "a great revolution?" The wisest advocates of the Lynch law system now prevailing as far as I know, deny that there is any revolution. If we are in a revolution, what is it for? It is true, our city has been badly governed. Corruption, vice and bloodshedding have prevailed to an alarming extent. But still it is not contended that our fundamental laws must be altered or even amended. They are admitted to be good, but said to be badly administered. It is hardly true, however, that the officers of the law were more corrupt and unfaithful here than in other cities. And it is hard to reconcile the plea of necessity for the organization of the Vigilance Committee with the improvement that we have been constantly told has been made in society. What is the influence of our Lyceums, Mercantile Library, and Mechanical Associations, of our public schools and our *thirty-one* churches, with their Sabbath schools, if now the city cannot be governed without a Lynch law court? You may depend upon it, this kind of proceeding contradicts all our statements as to our improvement in morals and in religion. This is a terrible blow to California throughout all civilized nations. And to my mind it is perfectly preposterous to contend that the many thousands of men and money wielded by the Committee, could not have secured in a lawful manner the purity of our elections and the faithful execution of the laws as far as perfection in such things can be obtained in human courts. If they could not, then our republican institutions are a failure. Indeed, I have not yet seen a plea in justification of mob law that is not a blow at Republicanism.

4. But, reverend brethren, what is this "work of God" that you have so often advocated, and that you tell the world the Church and her ministers are carrying forward? Was it to call worshippers from the house of God on the Lord's day, and to march to the jail, and by the prestige of French soldiers, and other armed aliens, as well as of armed citizens, overawe the Sheriff, and take some of the prisoners out of his hands? Was it the "work of God" to condemn these prisoners to death, and then to hang them out of the windows of a warehouse, converted for the time into a fortress, with dungeons, and cells, and iron handcuffs, and all the direful enginery of death? Do you teach that it is the "work of God" to hold a military fortress in the heart of a peaceful commercial city, and to erect barricades in the street, and plant cannon so as to command the public thoroughfares and to fill the streets with armed men, infantry and cavalry, to visit the homes of our citizens in the dead hours of night, and drag fathers from their beds to dungeons, and to banish them from their country, and to do all this without any legal authority whatever? Nay, more; to do all this, and much more of the same sort, not only without lawful authority, but in direct violation of the proclamation of the Chief Magistrate of the State, and in violation of the sacred rights secured to us by the constitution and laws of the United States and of the State of California. I have been taught that ministers of Christ are ambassadors of peace, whose weapons of war were not carnal, but spiritual. If it were even so then, that I stand alone on this coast, I cannot help it. I cannot preach what the word of God forbids...

5. It is marvellous how you can find an analogy between some mere local corruption in San Francisco and the causes of the English revolution of 1688, or the American revolution of 1776, or of the wars of Great Britain in the days of Robert Hall. In 1668, and in 1776, and in the days of Cromwell, there was no way to obtain redress but by revolution. Fundamental laws had to be obtained. Great fundamental rights and principles, both as to civil liberty and religious, had to be secured by force. The government was not then,as now, in the hands of the people. They had not the right of making their own laws, and of electing their own officers. Nor was there then, as now with us, *a constitutional way to change or amend our laws, and to remove unfaithful officers.* There is no analogy or resemblance in the cases. With us, if the laws do not reach the evil, let the people, in a constitutional way, make laws that will reach it. The wrongs complained of in a popular government, cannot make it right or expedient to paralyze all law. *It is law, and not lawlessness*, we want. Our government, as Chief Justice Marshall has said, is ''one of laws, and not of men.'' It is the people, but the people embodied in a written constitution, and in written laws made in pursuance of that constitution. So ample and so specific is the method prescribed in our constitution, and in our laws, for amending or changing them, that it is the decision of the Supreme Court of the United States that *a revolution by force is impossible*. See decision in 7 Howard's Report, in the Rhode Island affair. It must be so; for if there is not a constitutional way of correcting the abuses of popular governments, they cannot stand. . . .

Finally, as to the great Robert Hall's preaching to soldiers, it were well for us to remember that they were not citizens armed to trample under foot the laws of the land—armed to arrest citizens, and haul them before a Lynch law court and try them in secret, and condemn them, and exile or hang them without a trial by jury, as the Constitution directs. They were, if I recollect correctly, soldiers armed to repel an expected invasion of England by Napoleon. I have not the vanity to compare myself to the great Briton, nor the ''most seraphic spirit of his age,'' Jonathan Edwards; nor with the eloquent President Dwight, whom you name; but I venture to say with a profound veneration for these great men, that there is nothing in their lives or works that is favorable to Lynch law or mob violence. And also, that though I have not preached in favor of the people taking the laws into their own hands, nor encouraged my congregation to do ''the work of God'' by disregarding all constitutional authority; yet I venture to say that I have preached according to my ability, more frequently before ''armed volunteers'' than either of them, and probably oftener than all of them ever did. And I am ready to do so again, when, as in their days, our volunteers shall be armed to go forth against the enemies of their country, and to repel invaders upon our soil. But the case is wholly ''changed'' when it is brother against brother, and an American city is in arms against the chief magistrate of the State. I cannot preach in favor of governing this fair city by the cannon's mouth. My platform is the *Bible* and the *Constitution* and the *Union* just as they are.

Very respectfully yours,
W. A. SCOTT

SAN FRANCISCO, Aug. 4, 1856

9.
A Summation by Stanton A. Coblentz

One of the more useful works on the 1856 episode is Stanton A. Coblentz, Villains and Vigilantes, *which focuses on the consequences of the Committee's activities.*[4] *In his concluding passages Coblentz asks, "Considering how soon the benefits of Vigilance were lost; considering that, in less than a quarter of a century, they had ceased to be visible, what was the net eventual gain from the entire movement?" What follows is the nub of his answer.*

. . . The entire record of the popular tribunals, from the affair of The Hounds* to the adjournment of the Committee of 1856, is the story of the rise of public indignation, is the story of mass revolt against vice and iniquity, is the story of the gradual rousing of a frontier community to a sense of public welfare and security. That a variety of motives played their part cannot be denied—personal fear and the lust of revenge, the passions and audacity of the mob no less than the idealism of the reformer; yet the framework of Vigilance was in the spirit of righteous wrath against organized wrongdoing, and the movement flourished precisely in proportion to the strength of that spirit. Eruptions of this wholesome feeling occurred both in 1849 and 1851, but were not powerful enough to leave any prolonged effects; and, only after the appearance of James King of William and his blasting editorials, was the popular mind stirred to such impatience with corruption that eight or nine thousand men could combine spontaneously in a Vigilance Committee, giving freely of their time and energy in the effort to sweep the city clean. That the results of such a movement could endure for even ten years is extraordinary, for it owed its efficacy solely to the flame of public virtue engendered in the minds of the citizens; and in a growing and changing community, with new members constantly being admitted from without, with a new generation growing up, and with no new measures in vogue for training the citizens in political morality, it was to be expected that the old spirit of corruption would gradually creep in again and the gains be eventually dissipated and lost.

One of the objections most frequently leveled against the San Francisco Committees of Vigilance is that they were lawless organizations, founded without any shadow of legal right, and operating in opposition to the duly established authorities. This argument, it appears to me, would have much more weight if there had been any "duly established authorities"; but in a community where most if not all the public officers owed their power to purchase, fraud or other means of usurpation, it would be difficult to stimulate any great amount of virtuous enthusiasm for the representatives of legality. Certainly Sheriff Scanell, paying for his election with a huge gift to the Democratic nominating committee and reimbursing himself while in office, was not in a moral position superior to that of the Vigilantes, even though the latter did not act under the hypocritical color of law; certainly, he was less the representative of the law's *intention* when he shielded the criminals such as Cora and Casey, than were the Committee members when they marched against the jail and illegally removed the prisoners. So far as San Francisco itself is concerned, it is unquestionable that the Vigilantes, acting without any shadow of constitutional right, came nearer to fulfilling the aims of justice and maintaining a rule of order, than did the set of office-holders they so vigorously opposed. Grim, sinister, and dictatorial as they were, and self-invested with martial authority, they yet accomplished the purpose for which they had organized; and the token of their sincerity is to be seen in the rapidity with which they disbanded once they had achieved the avowed ends for which they had worked.

There is, however, a larger phase of the question which must be considered—and one that

---

[4]Stanton A. Coblentz, *Villains and Vigilantes: The Story of James King of William and Pioneer Justice in California* (New York: Wilson-Erickson, 1936), 248-252.

*The expulsion from San Francisco of a terrorist band known as "The Hounds," or "The Regulators," by the first vigilante group, July 1849.

reaches beyond the boundaries of any single city or state. Even though the Vigilance Committee proved salutary for San Francisco, does that mean that it was beneficent in its wider influence, that it set a happy precedent for the country as a whole, and moved by the power of a blessed example? Here, unfortunately, our answer must be less favorable. It is manifest that they were not unmixed. In widely scattered sections of the country, but particularly in the West—in Idaho, in Montana, in Nevada, and other states—Vigilance organizations sprang into being; organizations which did not always follow the scrupulous methods of their San Francisco predecessor; which did not always keep written records, conduct cautious trials, or decide with discretion or impartiality. Sometimes, indeed, they capably filled a hiatus in the law, and rid the country of predatory gangs of ruffians; but at other times they succumbed to prejudices, sectional or racial animosities, and the brutal impulses of the mob. Thus the Vigilantes of Montana, though one of the best of the organizations, maintained strict secrecy of membership, and had a habit of trying and passing judgment on suspected criminals even *before* they were caught; thus, the committees in Oregon, Idaho and elsewhere tended to degrade themselves into the tools of ambitious or passionate individuals, and sometimes deservedly ended as objects of public denunciation; thus, in Texas, an abolitionist was as likely to fall victim to the committees as was a criminal, and in innumerable cases the prey of mob wrath was executed without more than the travesty of a trial. Worst still were the horrors perpetrated by the so-called Vigilantes of the night-riding variety: the Knights of the White Camelia, the Ghouls of the Klu Klux Klan, and the agents of other secret societies, who presented the spectacle of lynch law in some of its most shocking and outrageous forms.

Today, the term Vigilante is used to denote almost everything that the original Vigilantes were not. Whenever bands of hired thugs and bullies are employed to put down strikers at a mine, we hear them referred to as Vigilantes; whenever a gang of desperadoes set out to inflict punishment on alleged Reds or Communists, again the term Vigilante is used; whenever a mob of race-inflamed Southerners undertake to hang a negro without even the semblance of a trial, once more we hear mention of a Vigilance organization. And the perpetrators of a thousand and one diverse atrocities, while knowing nothing of the original Vigilance movement, use the name of Vigilance to justify them in their villianies. Ironically, it may be pointed out that the targets of the first pre-Vigilance organization—the rascally society of Hounds—would, in present-day parlance, be known as Vigilantes when staging their dastardly attack upon the Chilean quarters.

Thus it will appear that, beneficent as the San Francisco Committees may have been in the immediate results they attained, they have possibly done more damage than good in the long run. In common with many other groups of rebels and reformers, they have lent themselves to imitation in their worst features; or, rather, their worst tendencies have been exaggerated and perpetuated, while their better characteristics have been overlooked or forgotten. They were, unquestionably, composed in the main of sturdy and conscientious men, indignant at the spectacle of crime unleashed, and honestly trying to find a remedy for a flaw in the social structure; yet their successors, in too many cases, were neither sturdy nor conscientious, were dominated by personal bias or passion, and committed crimes that made the name Vigilante a reproach and a warning.

It will, accordingly, perhaps be forever impossible to determine whether the Vigilance movement was a success or failure; whether the cleansing of a single city or state for the period of a few years was compensation enough for the establishment of a precedent that too often has been viciously interpreted. . . .

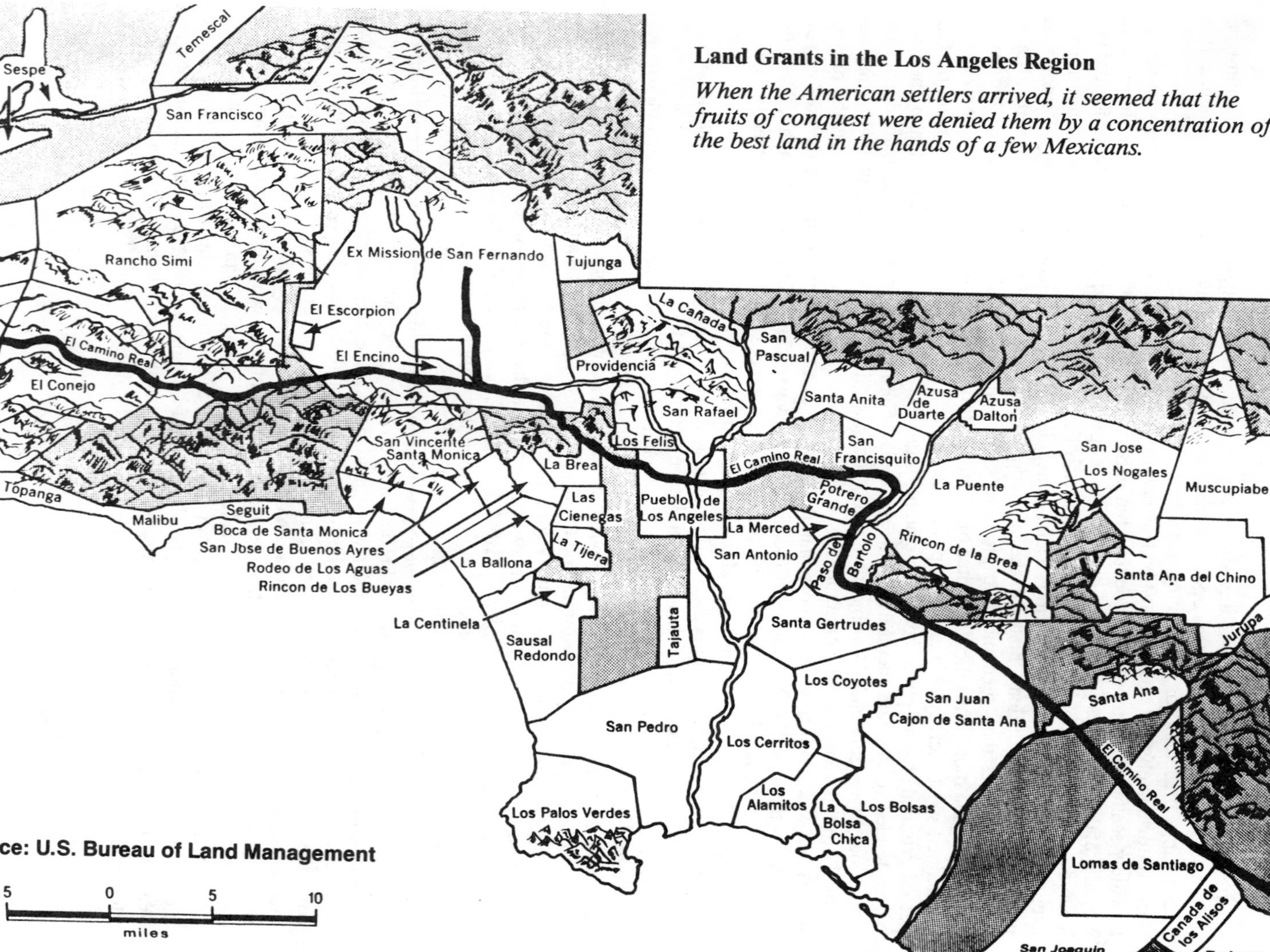

Land Grants in the Los Angeles Region

When the American settlers arrived, it seemed that the fruits of conquest were denied them by a concentration of the best land in the hands of a few Mexicans.

Were the titles to land in California today (1859) as clear as in Ohio or Iowa, nothing could check the impetus with which California would bound forward in a career of unparalleled thrift and growth. It were far better for the state and her people that those titles were wrongly settled, than that they should remain as now. I met today an intelligent farmer, who has had three different farms in this state, and has lost them successively by adjudication adverse to his title. I would earnestly implore grantees and squatters to avoid litigation wherever that is possible, and arrest it as soon as possible, eschewing appeals, save in flagrant cases, and meeting each other half-way in settlement as often as may be. The present cost of litigation, enormous as it is, is among the lesser evil consequences of this general anarchy as to land titles.

Should these ever be settled, it will probably be found advisable to legislate for the speedy breaking up and distribution of the great estates now held under good titles by a few individuals. —**Horace Greely, 1859.**[1]

CHAPTER **5**

THE DISPUTED MEXICAN LAND TITLES

Settlers vs. Rancheros?

By charting the evolution of land tenure alone, one might attempt to write the entire span of human history. The fact that land has been the source of food and thus of life itself is certainly central to this point. But, beyond its actual fertility, land has been treasured as the seat of family life, the foundation of social esteem, the basis of political power. Land takes endless shapes as wilderness, fiefdom, farm, urban real estate, commons; it has a complicated and variable legal status; it is frequently a commodity for speculation, a subject of litigation, a source of warfare and revolution. The desire of a people to hold land communally or in private parcels, or to break up large estates, or to reconstitute many small ones into fewer large ones, tells a great deal about that people's social values and ideology. So it is that much of California's history in the period from about 1850 to 1880 is reflected in her land policy.

For present purposes, the focus is on that part of the land question which embodies the clash of cultures between the native Californians, or Californios, and the Anglo-Americans. The decimation of the ranchos belonging to the original Spanish-Mexican claimants was both a cause and a consequence of the claimants' demise as an ethnic group and as a social class; for them the defeat was nothing less than revolutionary. And yet, ironically, to the Yankees who toppled the old landlords and acquired the land, the victory was a bitter one, for the ensuing land policies entailed all sorts of snares that kept most of them from making full and satisfactory use of the land.

"If the history of the Mexican grants of California is ever written," Henry George asserted in *Our Land and Land Policy* in 1871, "it will be a history of greed, of perjury, of corruption, of spoliation, and high-handed robbery, for which it will be difficult to find a parallel. . . ."[2] A century later nobody has yet undertaken to write that history, partly because of its enormous complexity, yet few would challenge Henry George's opinion. The sorry mess that passed for land policy in the newly opened California had the effect of discouraging immigration and farming and of

---

[1]Horace Greeley, *Overland Journey from New York to San Francisco in the Summer of 1859* (New York: C. M. Saxton, Barker & Co., 1860), 341- 342.

[2]Henry George, *Our Land and Land Policy, National and State* (San Francisco: White and Bauer, 1871), 14.

producing costly litigation, loss of property, and untold anguish—not to say loss of life particularly among the original claimants. The free-wheeling speculation in land, the rapid concentration of crop and grazing land into the hands of a few landlords, and the difficulties encountered by both the claimants and the Yankee settlers stemmed from the basic inadequacies of policy. The general verdict is that hardly anything good came from the land policy of the era 1850 to 1880.

Once having established what policy toward land was (a difficult feat in itself), the question to be faced is what caused the mess in the first place. Was it neglect or deliberate bad faith on the part of Yankees? If it was deliberate, to what extent can fault be attributed to the squatters, the lawyers, the politicians? Was there a conspiracy to defraud the rightful owners of their property, or was the property lost as a result of impersonal forces and inevitable population pressures? Or did the claimants themselves bring on their own defeat by ineptitude or greed or outmoded economics? What policies could have been tried in place of, or in addition to, the Land Law of 1851? These and other questions have received responses that vary according to two general viewpoints, "pro-settler" and "pro-claimant." Both are represented here. The article by John S. Hittell defends the claimants, and the second item, by Paul W. Gates, supports the Yankee settlers. *(Editor's note)*

10.
John S. Hittell Gives the Brief of the Original Claimants

Whether done through direct violence or legislation, the seizure of the ranchos from the Californios was a species of robbery, writes John S. Hittell in 1857 in a brief summary of the land question.[3]

Hittell as a young Forty-niner had walked to California; after a short stint in the diggings he joined the staff of the state's leading newspaper, the San Francisco Alta California, *an association that lasted 28 years. His best-known books are* The Resources of California *(1863) and* A History of the City of San Francisco, and Incidentally of the State of California *(1878). His brother, Theodore Henry Hittell, wrote a four-volume* History of California *(1885-1897).*

Although not himself a landowner, Hittell's interest in land matters was partially personal; he helped his friend José Limantour support a sensational claim to the San Francisco pueblo lands. When the courts threw out the Limantour claim as a wholesale fraud, Hittell himself also repudiated it. Yet he remained convinced that most of the original claims were sound and that Yankee land policies involved serious moral wrongs.

The establishment of the American dominion in California, made it necessary that the titles to land, owned in the State, under grants from Mexico, should be recognised and protected in accordance with the principles of American law. Protection was due to the land owners under the general principles of equity and the laws of nations, and had been expressly provided in the treaty of Guadalupe Hidalgo. It was necessary that the protection should be in accordance with the principles of American law, because the vast majority of the population soon came to be composed of Americans, who naturally introduced their own system of law—the only system suited to their method of conducting business.

But there was a question of much difficulty as to how this protection should be furnished. The Mexican titles were lacking in many of the conditions necessary to a perfect title under the American laws. The land systems of the two countries were constructed on entirely different principles and with different objects. The Mexican system was a good one for the purposes to be attained by it;

[3]John S. Hittell, "Mexican Land Claims in California," *Hutching's Illustrated California Magazine*, II (1857-1858), 442-448.

it was suited to the wants of the natives of California. They were stock-growers;—their only occupation, and wealth and staple food was furnished by their herds. They owned immense numbers of horses and horned cattle, and to furnish them with pasture, each ranchero required a large tract of land, which might be used by his own stock, exclusively. The public land in California was very extensive; it was worth nothing; there was little demand for it; no evils had been experienced, none were feared from the accumulation of great tracts, in the hands of a few owners; every grant was supposed to be a benefit to the State, by furnishing a home to a new citizen; and so, large grants were made without stint, on nearly every application. If the applicant could show that the land was public property, and unoccupied, he could obtain from 10,000 to 50,000 acres without expense, on condition that he would make the ranch his home, build a house on it, and place several hundred head of horned cattle upon it. These grants were usually made without any accurate description of the land; there never had been any government survey of any portion of the territory; there were no surveyors in the country to locate the boundaries; neither would the applicants have been willing in most cases to pay for surveys; nor was there any apparent need for them, land being very cheap and quarrels about boundaries very rare. Sometimes the land granted was described with certain fixed natural boundaries. In other cases, the grant might be described as lying in a narrow valley, between two ranges of mountains, and extending from a tree, rock, or clump of willows, up or down the valley far enough to include three, six or ten square leagues. The most common form of grant was for a certain number of square leagues, lying in a much larger district, bounded by well known landmarks. Thus the famous Mariposa grant of Frémont is for ten square leagues—44,386 acres, equivalent to a tract about nine miles square—in the district bounded by the San Joaquin river on the west, the Sierra Nevada mountains on the east, the Merced river on the north, and the Chowchillas on the south; which district includes nearly 100 square leagues. Under such a grant, the Mexican law allowed the grantee to select any place within the larger limits, and make it his home.

The grants made were not carefully registered. The law prescribed that the petitions for land should all be preserved, and a record of them kept, and that a registry should be made of all the lands granted; but the affairs of the Governor's office were loosely conducted; and in many cases where the claimants have been in possession for twenty years, and have an undoubted title, there is nothing in the archives or records of the former government to show for it. In many respects the California governor(s) had been very careless about granting lands. Sometimes they would grant the same lands to several persons; and there was one instance wherein Gov. Micheltorena ordered that every person in the Northern District of California, who had petitioned for land before a certain date, and whose petition had not been acted upon, should be the owner of the land asked for; provided the nearest Alcalde should certify that it belonged to the public domain. In these cases no title to the grantees was ever made by the Governor.

I have thus briefly mentioned the main peculiarities of the Mexican system of disposing of the public land in California, as distinguished from the American system. The Mexican government made no survey of the land; granted it away in immense tracts, without any fixed boundaries, leaving the grantee a wide discretion in regard to location, and keeping no careful registry of the grants.

When the great immigration of '49 filled the land with Americans, it became necessary to provide for the recognition and protection of the good Mexican titles by the American Courts. But how was this to be done? By the ordinary State Courts? The judges would not be sufficiently able, and would be ignorant of the laws under which the grants had been made; and the juries would be composed of Americans whose interests would lead them to do injustice to the large land owners. Besides, the lawmakers and judges elected by a deeply interested populace could not be depended upon to do justice under such circumstances.

Or should the protection be rendered by the appointment of a commission, instructed to make a summary examination of all claims, declare all those valid which had been in possession previous to the conquest, and of which some record might be found in the archives; leaving the other claims to be tried in the U.S. Courts? This was the policy which should have been pursued.

But that plan was not to prevail. Mr. Gwin's bill "to ascertain and settle the private land claims in the State of California," became a law, on the 30th of March 1851. This act provides for the appointment of a special Judicial Committee, (to be composed of three judges) before which all claimants to land, in the State, under Mexican titles, should bring suit against the Federal Government, within two years after the date of the act, under penalty of forfeiting their land. It provided further, that a law agent should be appointed, who should "superintend the interest of the United States in every case." It provided further, that appeals might be taken in these land cases, from the judgments of the Commission to the U.S. District Court, and from the latter, to the Supreme Court of the United States. It provided further, that in the trial of these cases, the Commission and the courts should "be governed by the treaty of Guadalupe Hidalgo, the law of nations, the laws, usages and customs of the country from which the claim is derived, the principles of equity, and the decisions of the Supreme Court of the United States."

This act provided that the owners of land should sue the Government or lose their land. But why be subjected to so severe a condition? The land owners had committed no offence, that they should be threatened with spoliation. It was not their fault that the Mexican land system differed from the American. The introduction of a new system by the Government did not justify the invalidation of titles, which had been good before, and the subjection of the owners to tedious and expensive litigation. When the American Government took California, it was in honor bound to leave the titles to property as secure as they were at the time of the transfer, and express provision to this effect was made in the treaty. Let us imagine that California were to be again transferred to some other power, whose land system is far more complex and strict than our own, and that all our present titles should be declared incomplete and insecure, and that every land owner should be taxed to one-fourth of the value of his land to pay for defending his title before a foreign and hostile Court, and if successful, should not get his title until six or eight years after the commencement of the litigation;— would we not exclaim against it as extremely unjust? But what is the difference between that supposed case and the actual one under consideration? There is no difference between the principles involved in the two cases; each supposes a great wrong —such a wrong as has been committed by the Federal Government of the United States upon holders of land in California under Mexican grants.

The Land Commission was opened in this city, January 1st, 1852, and in the ensuing fourteen months, 812 suits were brought, and these were all decided previous to the 3rd of March, 1855, at which time the Commission dissolved.

It was severe hardship for owners of land under grants from Mexico, that they should be required to sue the government of the United States, (which ought to have protected — not persecuted them,) or lose their land; but this hardship was rendered much more severe by the peculiar circumstances under which suits had to be tried. The trials were to be had in San Francisco at a time when the expenses of traveling and of living in San Francisco were very great, and the fees of lawyers enormous. The prosecution of the suits required a study of the laws of Mexico, in regard to the disposition of public lands, and this study had, of course, to be paid for by the clients. In many cases the claimants had to come to San Francisco from remote parts of the State; having three hundred miles to travel, bringing their witnesses with them at their own expense. The witnesses were nearly all native Californians, and it was necessary to employ interpreters at high prices.

Meanwhile the claimant could not dispose of his land, on account of the cloud there was on his title; neither could he have it surveyed by the U.S. Surveyor so as to give notice to the public where his land really lay. As he could not give a secure title, nor, in most cases, tell where his boundaries were, the Americans were not disposed to buy the land. Many squatters were, no doubt, glad of a pretext under which they might take other people's land and use [it] without paying rent; but the circumstances were often such that they were justified in refusing to buy. The number of settlers or squatters became large; they formed a decided majority of the voters in several of the counties; their political influence was great; politicians bowed down before them; all political parties courted them; and most of the U.S. Land Agents, and District Attorneys, appointed under the influence of the California Congressmen, became the representatives of the settler interest, and failed to represent the true interest of the United States. Every device known to the law was resorted to to defeat the claimant, or delay the confirmation of his grant, as though it were the interest of the Federal Government to defeat every claimant, or to postpone his success as long as possible.

Eight hundred and twelve important suits, to be tried according to the principles of strange laws, and on evidence given in a strange tongue, and where the testimony, in many of the cases, covered hundreds of pages of manuscript, were not to be disposed of in any brief period. In fact, the Commission did not clear its docket until more than three years after its organization. This delay, which would have been disastrous in any country, was doubly so in California. During the greater portion of this time, the titles to most of the good farming land in the settled districts of the State, were declared to be unsettled. The delay was an encouragement to dishonest, and often a justification of honest squatters. They wanted to cultivate the ground; they could not learn whether the land they wished to occupy was public or private property; they knew the question would not be decided soon, and therefore they might know, if dishonest, that they might make a profit by seizing land which they were morally certain would be, and should be, confirmed to the claimant; and if honest, they could not be expected to pay for property, to which, in many cases, the title was one in which they could place no confidence. The consequence of the system was, that a large portion of the most valuable farming land in the State was occupied by squatters. This occupation contributed greatly to injure the value of the property. The land owner could not sell his land, nor use it, and yet he was compelled to pay taxes. His ranch brought serious evils upon him. It was the seat of a multitude of squatters, who—as a necessary consequence of antagonistic pecuniary interest,—were his bitter enemies. Cases we know, where they fenced in his best land; laid their claims between his house and his garden; threatened to shoot him if he should trespass on their inclosure; killed his cattle if they broke through the sham fences; cut down his valuable shade and fruit trees, and sold them for fire-wood; made no permanent improvements, and acted generally as tho' they were determined to make all the immediate profit possible, out of the ranch. Such things were not rare: they are familiar to every person who knows the general course of events during the last five years in Sonoma, Napa, Solano, Contra Costa, Santa Clara, Santa Cruz and Monterey Counties. Blood was not unfrequently spilled in consequence of the feuds between the land holders and the squatters; the victims in nearly every case, belonging to the former class.

After the Federal Government had committed the error of compelling every California land owner to bring suit for his own land, which he had held in indisputable ownership under the Mexican dominion, and even before the independence of Mexico and Spain,—and after the Government stubbornly contested every case before a tribunal whose learning, ability, and honesty, was and is, universally admitted,—after all this, it is strange that those persons, whose claims were confirmed, and who had been in possession of their land before the American conquest, and in cases where there was no suspicion of fraud, were not allowed to take their own property once for all. But no; Uncle Sam told all the Californians who had gained their suits, that they could not take their land till they had sued him again; he would appeal every case; the claimant must make another fight for his property, or be despoiled.

Here, then, was the whole work to be gone over again in the Federal District Courts, of which there are two in the State; and in each district there are about four hundred claims, to be tried by a judge, much of whose time is occupied with the trial of admiralty cases. The land suits must all be defended, or attended to, by the United States District Attorney, much of whose time is occupied with criminal cases, and civil business in which the Federal Government is interested. The result is delay upon delay.

The first case was submitted to Judge Hoffman about July, 1853,; and now, after the lapse of nearly five years, there are still about one hundred and twenty cases in both districts undecided. Of all this number, only twenty-two have been rejected; and in almost every case where a decree of confirmation was entered in the Land Commission, the judgment has been affirmed in the District Court. The judges of both District Courts are men and lawyers of fair fame, and, so far as I am informed, are not accused, by any person worthy of regard, of having rendered dishonest decisions. It would seem that after a second confirmation, the General Government would in common decency permit such claimants as had possession of their lands in 1846, and could show some kind of title from Mexico, to take the land as of perfect title: but no; in every case where the judgment was [for] the claimant, an appeal was taken to the United States Supreme Court. It is true that not all the cases were forced to trial; the Government, after having had the cases placed on the docket, and having forced the claimants to prepare for trial, dismissed the appeals in some four hundred cases. But two hundred claims are now before the court of last resort, and the one hundred and twenty undecided must also go there, or most of them. The United States Supreme Court has decided about fifteen of the appealed claims within four years, and if they should make the same speed in the future, we may expect that their docket will be cleared of Californian land cases in seventy-five years, or thereabouts. The Government appeals from every decision of the District Court in favor of the claimant, but makes no provision to have the suit brought to a hearing in the Supreme Court. In appealed cases it is the recognized duty of the appealing party to pay for sending up the papers, so that the higher court can take some action in the matter. But the American Government violates this plain rule of right, and law, and custom, and tells the claimant that he must pay this expense out of his own pocket, or wait for an indefinite time before his title can be settled; and no provision is made that he shall be repaid, even when he advances the money.

Such legislation as should make all land titles insecure— declare all landed property confiscated, unless the owner should sue the Government and gain the suit, and should [in] appeal[s] to two higher courts, and. . . gain the suit in each tribunal—and provide that all titles should be unsettled for four years, most of them for six years, and many for ten or fifteen years, would fall very severely upon any people; but it has fallen with double severity upon the Californian. While his title has been denied by the Government, and he has consequently been unable to sell at a fair price, he has seen the "flush times" gradually disappear, land has rapidly fallen in price, and he can foresee that when his title shall be finally confirmed, his property will not be worth one fourth of what it was in 1851 and 1852.

The proclamation by the Government that there were not perfect land titles in the State, and the notoriety of the fact that every claim was to be closely contested, encouraged squatting upon the land in dispute. The State Government favored the squatters, and passed laws to protect them; providing that if the claim were confirmed to the Mexican grantee, he should sell the land, or buy the improvements; the value of the land and the improvements to be appraised by a jury, so constituted that it would do great injustice to the Mexican claimant, who would have to sell at one half of the value of his land, or buy at twice the value of the improvements.

It is not possible to obtain any accurate knowledge of the extent of the pecuniary losses to which the claimants have been subjected, by the injustice of the Federal Government, in thus rendering their titles insecure, and forcing them to go to law. I am informed by an intelligent gentleman from Los Angeles, that it is commonly estimated there that two fifths of the land has gone to pay the fees of the lawyers employed to prosecute the claims; and I suppose it may safely be said, that on an average the holders of Mexican grants paid away not less than one fourth of their land in defending their titles. More than one in ten of the victorious claimants have been ruined by the costliness of the litigation; and of those whose claims have been finally dismissed, a considerable portion have been lost to the claimants merely because they were unable to pay for the costly litigation necessary to defend their rights.

Only two pleas have been made to extenuate or justify the stubborn opposition made by the agents of the Government to the recognition of the Californian land holders. These pleas are, *first*, that many of the claims are fraudulent; and, *secondly*, that the Californians claim too much land.

It is not true that *many* of the claims are fraudulent. The Land Commission did not reject one claim, and the District Courts have rejected only two, on the ground of fraud. There may be twenty-five fraudulent claims in all; I believe not more. there may be many claims which would not have been valid under the Mexican law; but these are not fraudulent, and have been or will be rejected. But even if there were a hundred, that would be no reason why the Government should attempt to rob the holders of land under titles undoubtedly good in equity and under the Mexican law. A distinction might be made between the two classes, of the suspicious and the undoubtedly good claims. But the Federal Government made no distinction. The Peralta grant, which was made in the last century, and has been in constant possession ever since, under a perfect title according to the Mexican law, was subjected to the same litigation and vexatious delay, and was given over to the tender mercies of the squatters in the same manner with the most questionable title in all the land.

The other plea is still worse. It may be that the welfare of the people requires the land to be equally divided among them; but shall that justify the Government in robbing — directly by violence, or indirectly by litigation — the owners of large tracts? If it be wrong for me to rob my neighbor of his dollars, is it right for Uncle Sam to rob Peralta, or any other Californian, of his land? And let it be remembered that temporary dispossession is morally as wrong as entire and final spoliation. I admit that it were far better for the country that the Mexican grant-holders should not own so much land; I admit that it were better, looking at the question abstractly, that the settlers should own all the land they claim; I admit that the settlers are more active and industrious, and contribute vastly more, in proportion to their means, to the development and wealth of the State, than do the native holders of the large grants; but all this has nothing to do with the main question.

The question now naturally arises, whether, a great wrong having been done, there is no remedy? Are not the sufferers entitled to an indemnity from Congress? In justice they are; but there would be so many difficulties in the way of ascertaining the damage, and of apportioning the indemnifying fund among the losers, that probably any committee appointed by Congress to investigate the matter, would report against any indemnification.

The law prohibiting the official survey of Spanish claims previous to confirmation, has been productive of great evils to settlers and claimants. In most cases it is now too late to remedy these evils; in a few cases, perhaps, considerable benefits would be conferred by changing the law, and permitting all claimants to have United States surveys made of their ranches, so that the surveys, being recorded, may serve as notice of what land is not claimed. And if the grant holder be unwilling to pay for the survey of his land before final confirmation, the Government should pay in every case where there are many settlers, in justice to the latter. It would have been well if the law of 1851 had provided for the early survey of all the claims in possession at the time of the conquest, and had prohibited the maintenance of any ejectment suit until the recording of an official survey. Under the present law, the holder of a confirmed floating grant, to be located within certain boundaries, may eject settlers from any place within those boundaries, though they contain ten times the amount of land called for by the grant.

Not only has the system adopted by the Federal Government, in regard to Mexican grants, been most injurious and unjust to the claimants, but it has also been very injurious to the country at large. It has deprived the people in the most populous agricultural districts, of permanent titles; has prevented the erection of fine houses, valuable improvements, permanent homes; has contributed to make the population unsettled; to keep families from coming to the country; and, in fine, has been one of the chief causes of the present unsound condition of the social and business relations of California.

11. Paul W. Gates Presents the Settlers' Side

The longstanding need for a new look at the legislative and political side of the land question is partially met by this article by Paul W. Gates.[4]

Professor Gates' credentials for writing this study are impressive. Perhaps the leading historian of U.S. land policy, Professor Gates has published, among other works, The Illinois Central Railroad and Its Colonization Work *(1934),* The Wisconsin Pine Lands of Cornell University *(1944),* Fifty Million Acres: Conflicts over Kansas Land Policy, 1854-1890 *(1954), and* The Farmer's Age *(1961), as well as numerous articles in leading journals. He has been President of the Mississippi Valley Historical Association.*

Gates' article is well informed—distilled from newspaper items, legislative reports, court records, and correspondence of participants—and shows an unprecedented sympathy for the Yankee settler. It tells what the pioneer settler (too often maligned as a "squatter," Gates says) wanted in the way of legislation, and what he got or was denied, particularly as compared with legislation on frontiers other than California's. The discussion involves such technical terms from traditional American land policy as "pre-emption" and "occupancy rights" as they apply to the California problem.

Landseekers arriving in California after 1848—and after the first years of the gold rush most immigrants wanted land—found a most confused complex of seemingly insoluble problems facing them wherever they tried to obtain title to land. From San Diego to Shasta, in the coastal valleys, in the Sacramento and San Joaquin valleys, and in the Bay region, there were some eight hundred private land claims that called for between thirteen million and fourteen million acres of land. A heritage from the Spanish-Mexican period, these claims either had been granted or were alleged to have been granted to government officers, members of their families and supporters, for cattle ranches. Mostly they ranged in size from one to eleven leagues of 4,426 acres to the league. Accumulation of claims or grants had permitted individuals and families to acquire holdings of far greater size. More than half of the eight hundred claims were based on grants made in the years just preceding American control, eighty-seven of them being dated 1846, the year of the transfer. Most of those made in the forties had been given to intimates of officials in anticipation of the rise in land values expected to follow American control. War, the gold rush, and the withdrawal of laborers made improvements impossible for some time after 1846. When the backwash of population from the mines set in and disillusioned Californians turned to the land, not one of the claims had been surveyed—some had not even been located. Few had clearly established boundaries or extensive improvements, and on many there was no indication of use, save for the presence of small herds of cattle or sheep. It was to take years before the claims were adjudicated, their ownership clearly established, their boundaries located.

Settlers pouring into California found no fences, no surveyor's corners. Aware of two long held traditions fundamental to American land policies—the right of pre-emption and the right of occupants to their improvements—they felt safe in searching out vacant and undeveloped land, moving upon it and devoting months, even years, to its improvements. Involved in the right of pre-emption was the right of squatters who settled upon vacant and unimproved land on which there were no other private rights to buy their tracts at the minimum price before the public auction was held. A corollary to the right of pre-emption was the occupancy right of a settler, who had improved land to which he had an imperfect title and who later lost his land when ejectment proceedings were brought against him by someone having a better title, to recover from the successful

[4]Paul W. Gates, "California's Embattled Settlers," California Historical Society *Quarterly*, XLI, No. 2 (June 1962), 99-125. Footnotes omitted.

claimant the value of his improvements as assessed by a local jury, less deductions for damage to the land. Pre-emption is an ancient institution dating from colonial times and was early experimented with by the federal government in special acts. It was made general and prospective in 1841, and applied to unsurveyed land in certain areas in the early fifties. Similarly, occupancy rights were recognized by Virginia in the seventeenth century and despite a hostile Supreme Court decision in 1823 were firmly planted through the newer states by 1851. Rights that had been so generally recognized elsewhere would, American immigrants felt, surely be granted in California by state and federal legislation.

Land for investment and land for improvement into farms was the lodestone which drew immigrants westward, eager to emulate the life story of affluent men in their home communities whose wealth had come from the rise in the value of landed property which they had had the wisdom to acquire early. It was this scramble for land which sent values up and transformed almost worthless Mexican claims into valuable possessions, particularly in the Bay region and in Santa Clara, Napa, Solano, Sonoma, Sacramento, and San Joaquin counties. Here there were few signs of ownership in the way of improvements or fences; but, unfortunately, here also were concentrated many large claims. Some original owners were forced to dispose of their claims because of taxes, attorneys' and court fees, and their own extravagance. Other owners clung to their possessions, unwilling to break up the great ranchos, though the titles were becoming involved because of deaths, heirships, and wardships. In the Bay region the Mexican claimants seemed to be most persistent in refusing to sell, among them being the Peralta, Estudillo, Soto, Castro, Vallejo, De la Guerra, and Alviso families. They were only willing to lease, it was said. But leasing would not give the tenants a share in the rising land values that everyone expected. Tenancy was rarely a satisfactory position for an American brought up on the assumption that land in the United States was cheap and that everyone should have a piece of it and a share in the prosperity the future was sure to bring.

Settlers swarmed over the slightly used claims of northern California and not finding boundaries, corners, surveyors' posts, or other evidence of ownership, assumed that the land would ultimately be surveyed and opened to pre-emption. In the resulting conflict between the landlords attempting to maintain their titles and the settlers hopeful of gaining ownership, bitterness developed that frequently degenerated into outright warfare on a small scale.

By the time the settler issue became one of the most bitterly controverted questions in California politics, the land seekers consisted of two groups: those who had been quite ignorant at the time they made their settlements of any adverse claims; those who, knowing of the possible existence of adverse claims, nevertheless made their settlements willfully, assuming that the claims were either fraudulent or that the United States government would not confirm grants of such large size without improvements and that the land would therefore become public domain and subject to the public land laws.

Aggravating the problem of land rights was the fact that Congress moved slowly in establishing a board of land commissioners to investigate the claims, to reject those which did not conform to Mexican land law or were fraudulent, and to confirm those properly made and on which the conditions had been satisfied. The board in turn was tardy because of the frequent illness of its members, the turnover of the commissioners resulting from the Democratic victory in 1852, and the resignation of some of its members. Also, the frequent long absences of the judges of the district courts seriously slowed the work of adjudication. . . .

As the land commission and the district and Supreme courts of the United States slowly waded through the piles of documents presented in evidence to prove the validity of the claims, it became apparent that there was a tendency to favor confirming claims even when there were grave questions concerning them. This was particularly true of the two higher courts. Jeremiah S. Black, Attorney General of the United States, charged in 1858 that the rights of the government had been placed "in extreme jeopardy" by blatant fraud "so artfully got up" that the tribunals had been "induced to look upon them with a certain degree of allowance and even of favor." Not only did the district court appear to disregard or minimize evidence of fraud and perjury on occasion, but the federal Supreme Court abandoned well-established precedents which required that the utmost vigilance be exercised in determining whether the grantees of incomplete claims had conformed to all the requirements of the law of the governments making the grants.

Settlers learning that their improvements might be within the boundaries of claims became alarmed at the course the law was taking, and began a drumfire of condemnation of the grants. Taking an extreme legalistic position, it was possible for them to argue that the courts were acting too leniently, indeed unwisely, in leaning over backward to concede rights to claimants in dubious cases. They demanded strict interpretation of rights and rigid insistence on justice and the establishment of a concentration of land ownership not to be found elsewhere in the United States.

With the decisions going against the settlers on many of the claims, it was apparent that help was needed from Congress and from the California legislature, and more funds were essential to secure abler attorneys to combat the skillful defense of the claimants. There was also a question concerning the integrity of the law agents. At least one government attorney defended the government side unsuccessfully when he had a personal interest in securing an adverse decision, and another representative of the government was accused of being largely interested in a number of San Francisco claims.

To accomplish their objectives the settlers, through the few newspapers friendly to them and through representatives in the state legislature and Senator Gwin in Washington, slowly amassed their strength and expressed their will. They wanted settlers whose improvements were found to be on confirmed private claims to be given title to their improvements and the owners of the claims to be granted compensation elsewhere, or in lieu of that they wanted protective measures that would recognize their occupancy rights. Also, they wanted Congress to extend to them the same free land policy it had already given settlers in Oregon, and they wanted restriction written into the land laws that would reserve land suitable for agriculture for settlers only.

Senator William Gwin. . . and Governor John Bigler in California became the chief spokesmen of the settlers in their efforts to gain recognition of what they regarded as their rights. Gwin was much influenced by the 1849 report of Captain Henry W. Halleck on the land claims in which stress had been laid on the doubtful character of many of the claims, particularly those not specifically located and having no clearly established boundaries, no development, and which had been granted in the very closing days of the Mexican regime. Gwin suspected that many of the grants had been antedated or were otherwise based on fraudulent documents. His sympathies seemed to be for the time, whether solely for political reasons is not important, with the "hardy, industrious emigrants" who on their small tracts made intensive improvements which gave them superior equity to their land. . . . He had participated in drafting the Land Act of 1851 which provided for the establishment of the land commission and the procedure it was to follow in adjudicating the claims. In drafting the measure he had tried to make sure that care would be taken in judging the "incomplete cattle range concessions," with their "ill-defined, vagrant or floating limits," as he called the claims, to eliminate all that was fraudulent and incomplete. Though not entirely successful in 1851 in securing the protection he deemed necessary for the settlers' interests, for there was keen opposition to his settler oriented views from Benton and others more sympathetic to the claimants of large tracts, he had succeeded in including a provision in the act that confirmation by the commission would "not affect the interests of third parties." In this way he had saved settlers' rights for further adjudication. . . .

Two other settler-oriented bills sponsored by Gwin became law on March 3, 1853. The first extended pre-emption to settlers who were then upon, or who later took up, land on private claims which were subsequently declared invalid by the Supreme Court. This measure was to give hope unduly and unfortunately to settlers on many California claims. The second measure granted for one year the privilege of pre-emption to settlers on unsurveyed land in California. Subsequently, in the midst of excitement over the invalidation of the Occupancy Law in 1857, Gwin was attacked for including a provision in this act of March 3, 1853, barring pre-emption to settlers on land claimed under a foreign grant. Possibly the inclusion of this provision was a tactical error, but there was doubt that a grant of pre-emption on the claims would stand a court test.

The difficulty of surveying land in the vicinity of Mexican claims was so great owing to the unsettled boundaries and the slowness with which the claims were adjudicated and their surveys finally approved (many claims were not finally surveyed and patented until the 1870's and 1880's) that only through pre-emption could settlers be protected in their improvements. The special pre-emption act of 1853 and its extension in 1854 were approved without vocal opposition. . . .

. . . [I]n California advocates of occupancy laws were beginning their drive to protect settlers in the value of their improvements. The election of 1851 had shown the strength of the settlers, who had supported John Bigler and the Democratic party from which they expected aid—support that had counted significantly in Bigler's victory. A bill to grant occupancy rights was reported back from the Judiciary Committee by Archibald Peachy (member of the law firm of Halleck, Peachy, and Billings, which was to have a major share in the defense of the claims) with the recommendation that it not be passed on the ground that it was in conflict with common law, would be productive of litigation and infringement of the rights of property, and was unconstitutional. Notwithstanding this report the legislature adopted a possessory act, sometimes called a "state pre-emption law," to protect settlers on public lands who made two hundred dollars worth of improvements and filed an affidavit in the recorder's office after which they could be absent from the land for a year without losing their rights. In 1853 Governor Bigler declared his opposition to the inclusion of any mineral lands within private claims and recommended the prompt interposition of the state before the federal courts to prevent confirmation of a decision made by the land commission, presumably in the case of Frémont's claim to Mariposa. To speed up the adjudication of the claims he urged that the land commission be abolished and cases be taken directly into the federal courts. Free land to actual settlers he thought a major need, but he said nothing about an occupancy measure at this time. . . .

Rumblings of settler unrest broke out into bloodshed when claimants resorted to ejectment action to rid large holdings of "squatters." In 1853 a claimant was shot in Sonoma County; a sheriff with a posse and a large cannon was attacked by a group of settlers in Santa Barbara County, one man was killed and the sheriff was knifed; settlers in San Mateo County were angry with the commission for its confirmation of the Pulgas claim and threatened to resist any action to eject them; bitter clashes occurred on the Sutter claim next to Sacramento; and near open warfare developed between thirty-five masked settlers and the sheriff and his posse in Napa County. Elsewhere in Alameda and Santa Clara counties friction between settlers and claimants was common.

The settler movement was becoming a major political issue that no aspiring or incumbent office holder could afford to ignore, and in 1854 Governor Bigler found it desirable to declare in favor of an occupancy law similar to those most states had on their statute books. In line with this recommendation, an assemblyman from Santa Clara County introduced a bill that would concede occupancy rights to settlers claiming no more than 160 acres which, when they entered upon it, was wild and unimproved and appeared to have no title adverse to the government. If ejectment proceedings were brought against such settlers they would be entitled, if defeated, to have a jury determine the value of their improvements which the successful litigants were to pay and no man holding a Mexican title was to sit on the jury of evaluation. . . .

Delay in determining titles discouraged both owners and settlers from making improvements and seriously retarded the development of the state. *The California Farmer* declared that the entire country was suffering, "families are suffering; emigration is stayed (and what could be worse to a Californian) from our shores, and all stimulus is lost." Failure of the legislature to enact an occupancy law in 1854 and 1855 consequently led that journal to offer its own proposal to deal with title controversies and settlers' rights. *The Farmer* considered itself neutral, as between claimants and settlers, and thought its formula reflected that neutrality, but at the same time it encouraged the making of improvements. The plan called for the election of a board of reference to be composed of the best men of the state who could appraise the improvements made by the occupant in the event the title was confirmed to the claimant, and that the appraisal be paid by the claimant to the occupant. . . . Actually, the proposal differed little from the conventional occupancy laws in operation for two hundred years in the United States except that the appraisal of improvements was to be made by the board of reference which might not be a local body and might not therefore be as favorable to the occupants as would a local jury.

Governor Bigler continued to urge the need for legislation on occupancy rights, stressing that other public land states had long since adopted such measures. In 1856 he held that in California where there was "so much uncertainty as to *lines* and *titles*, errors in location must necessarily often occur, and there certainly should, therefore, be provision made for the security of the *bona fide* settler in such cases." A fully prepared and well-guarded act would produce a feeling of security, "settle existing disputes, and prevent future difficulties and controversies" respecting titles. Persons subject to swift ejectment would not make permanent improvements, and those who had made substantial improvements thinking they were on public land surely deserved to recover the value thereof in ejectment. Bigler took issue with the view advanced by the claimants, their lawyers, and the newspapers reflecting their position that settlers were a disorderly, lawless, rowdy and drunken people. He believed them to be "the most stable, enterprising and permanent of the population of a new State, and come hither with their families to surround themselves. . . with the manifold blessings and endearments of home.". . .

Excitement over settlers' rights reached a high point in 1855 and 1856. A settler convention met in Sacramento for two days in August 1855, at which threats were made to establish a settler party unless the Democrats and Whigs paid more attention to their needs. The convention resolved that all laws ought to favor the actual possessor who occupied land peaceably and without fraud, that claimants' and settlers' rights should be settled in the courts; and it demanded that settlers if ejected be allowed the value of their improvements. The resolutions were taken back by the members to their communities where signatures were to be secured, and were then to be forwarded to the legislature.

The action of the courts in their generous confirmation of claims, particularly the approval of five debatable claims (Frémont, Cruz Cervantes, Ritchie, Limantour, and Bolton and Barron) aroused great indignation and strengthened the feeling that the entire process of adjudicating the claims was working badly. Influential business men in San Francisco, badgered by intrusions upon their speculatively held lots by squatters whom they found it difficult to eject, looked down their noses at all settlers or squatters until they found themselves virtually in the same position by the decisions in the Bolton and Barron case involving ownership of 10,186 acres and in the Limantour case involving a four league claim, all in San Francisco County. On announcement of the confirmation of the Bolton and Barron claim, shares in it skyrocketed to $5,000, and persons having improvements on the claim were frightened at the prospect of having to buy their land a second time at the current inflated values. For the moment merchants in San Francisco and settlers on claims in rural areas saw eye to eye. A meeting of owners of improvements on the Bolton and Barron tract voted to raise funds with which to carry the case to the Supreme Court and to join with the Settlers' League throughout the state in elections to secure officers favorable to their position. . . .

Three of these debatable decisions were reversed by Ogden Hoffman, Federal District Judge for Northern California, to whom important questions concerning land claims were carried on appeal. Hoffman was held in high repute as a lawyer and judge, and settlers could take heart from these decisions, for they seemed to assure a more critical examination of the legal base of the claims than the commission was affording. Settlers hopes were soon dashed, for in 1855, the Supreme Court reversed Hoffman in the Frémont and Cruz Cervantes cases and upheld him in the Reading case, thereby establishing broadly liberal precedents that virtually rewrote Mexican law and applied this revision retroactively to California grants. The commission and the Supreme Court. . . were reversing long held precedents concerning the need for complete title papers in conformity with the laws of Spain, France, or England. To avoid further effects from this reversal and from the shocking weakness of the government defense, the legislature called for an amendment to the Act of 1851 that would prevent the location of all floating grants, such as Frémont's Mariposa claim, on occupied land and take from the United States surveyors discretion in locating the grants. The resolution also asked that additional and competent counsel be engaged by the government in the defense of its title where antedated, incomplete, spurious , and unimproved grants were up for consideration.

The settlers' agitation gained its major objective with the adoption of a bill on March 26, 1856, for the protection of settlers and to quiet titles. This measure had all the earmarks of occupancy laws which other states had been enacting and strengthening ever since 1797, when Kentucky wrote its first measure; and in addition it had some unique features caused by the chaotic title situation in California. Persons having better titles (Mexican grant) to land on which a settler was established if successful in an action of ejectment were liable for the value of the improvements the settler had made and for the growing crops on the land unless they could maintain that the grant in question had been surveyed, the boundaries distinctly marked, and the field notes of the survey filed in the recorder's office. Thus far the bill met the views of settlers....

The occupancy measure, even when shorn of its antimonopoly feature, was still a bitter dose for many members of the legislature to swallow. Objections were made that it was unconstitutional, and the conservative tendencies of many members were revealed by their efforts to weaken it by amendment. Settler influence was too strong, however, and members rushed to be recorded for it on the final vote, which was fifty-one to seventeen in the assembly and sixteen to nine in the senate. Leaders of the opposition were Pablo de la Guerra, whose family had 374,000 acres in claims confirmed to it, and José María Covarrubias, whose Castaic and Catalina Island claims, amounting to 68,000 acres, were confirmed.

The measure was immediately challenged in the state courts and reached the California supreme court in the January term of 1857. Chief Justice Murray, in his search for doctrine to justify striking down the act, reverted to an old, somewhat discredited, and generally abandoned decision of Justice Bushrod Washington of 1823, involving the occupancy laws of Kentucky....

The Chief Justice came to the nub of the case by showing that the principal difference between the California statute and those of other states was that most occupancy laws required that a settler should have a color of title in the form of a grant, deed, or tax title to enable him to recover damages in ejectment whereas the California statute assured him damages if the successful claimant had failed to survey and mark out his boundaries clearly and file the survey. The Chief Justice could not see that many California settlers, certainly not the "squatters" who rudely destroyed boundaries in San Francisco, had "entered innocently upon lands" and deserved the protection of the law. Murray was convinced that the California law authorized "one man to intrude upon the lands of another," and he appeared to think it offered "a premium to fraud and violence." He was troubled by the retrospective character of the law, though similar laws throughout American development would have had little significance if they had not been permitted to apply retrospectively. In striking down the measure, the Chief Justice referred sentimentally to the "early pioneers" whose health, welfare, and happiness he was deeply concerned about but made no effort to apply that concern to innocent settlers who had taken up unmarked, unimproved, unsurveyed land, and developed it with years of labor....

...[I]t might have been possible for Congress to have avoided the worst of the title conflicts in California by providing that only grants fulfilling all obligations of the Mexican land system should be confirmed, that all other claimants should have settlers' rights to land they had improved, and that all the balance of their claims should become public domain. If Congress had rigidly required a strict interpretation of the grants, many of them would have been rejected and at no loss to the owners, for they had made no improvements at all on the grants given in 1845 and 1856. As a further step toward adjusting the Mexican land system to the American economy, the government might have offered to buy the vacant and unimproved land in the claims with good titles at the going price of 1848 or 1850. Such an offer, if accepted, as doubtless it would have been by some of the always impecunious grantees, would have contracted to a small figure the area in confirmed and patented grants. Enlightened Congressional leadership combined with abler defense of the government title to the claims in the early fifties and more respect for precedent by the Supreme Court was needed. The worst injustice resulting from the involved California land litigation was not that some claimants were put to great expense in defending their rights and that many lost their inflated and undeveloped claims, but that some persons who *had* made considerable improvements on their claims, but had not succeeded in completing all those required before the final title under Mexican law, and who therefore could not prove title, lost all their improvements without a preemption or homestead right. In this respect and in this only the California Land Act of 1851 accorded less generous treatment to Californians than was given residents of other territories at the time they were transferred to American control. . . .

The attempted Luco and Limantour swindles, which involved 814,000 acres or enough to make 5,000 farms of 160 acres each, together with other doubtful claims as yet unsettled and the growing bitterness between the claimants and the settlers over the question of surveys, pushed the settler movement to greater extremes. Since the Mexican grants had not clearly specified boundaries, it proved possible for owners, when their claims were confirmed and the surveys were being run, to have the government surveyors so establish their lines as to exclude the barren, waste, and mountain land from the allowed acreage and to include the valley land on which their improvements and those of the settlers had long since been made. Thus settlers on the four-league Tzabaco Rancho in Sonoma County took violent exception to the way the surveyors were running jagged lines to include their claims instead of surveying the rancho in a compact form as their instructions were said to prescribe. The surveyors were charged with straddling a mountain to include in two valley tracts, not one, some of the choicest developed land in the Russian River valley. Excited by fears of the loss of their homes, settlers mobbed the surveyors, destroyed their field notes, and roughed up one of the agents of the claimants. When a federal marshal later appeared in the region to arrest the participants, it was reported they were all away hunting. There followed mass meetings, appeals to the land office to order new surveys, and angry denunciation of the "pestilential land thieves" who had no regard for settlers' interests. With five hundred settlers organized in four land leagues threatening to prevent the law officers from functioning as long as they appeared to be on the side of the claimants, further action by the state appeared essential. . . .

Settlers were correct in maintaining that many of the claims were fraudulent or incomplete and should be rejected, but their inclination was to maintain that all large claims were of this category. It was difficult for them to understand why a fully documented claim that had been through all the procedures for a good title and yet was undeveloped, save perhaps for a small improvement in one corner of the tract, should be confirmed. Improvements and use were conditions necessary for confirmation, settlers held. Whatever the conditions for confirmation, they felt that claimants who ejected settlers and later had their own claims voided deserved severe punishment. In line with their views Governor J. Neely Johnson recommended in 1858 that steps be taken to protect the rights of settlers which would avoid the objectionable features of the Occupancy Act of 1856 but would at the same time assure them some redress. The resulting law provided that persons ousted from Mexican claims which were later rejected or, if confirmed, did not include the land from which persons had been ejected, could recover possession of the land they had previously lost with the rents and profits from the time they were ejected until they were restored to possession together with all costs and damages they may have sustained. Such a measure might discourage holders of Mexican claims from resorting to the law to eject settlers until the courts had finally determined the validity of the claims and the surveys had been completed and approved. . . .

Meanwhile, greater attention was being given to the defense of government titles in California. . . .

. . . Improved presentation of the claims led to the rejection of the Cambuston claim of eleven leagues, the second of the Sutter claims of 22 leagues, the Luco and Limantour claims, and the immensely valuable Bolton and Barron claim. In 1859 claims containing close to two and one half million acres were rejected by the Supreme Court, mostly on the ground of fraud. . . .

Between 1860 and 1862 eleven additional claims containing 317,000 acres were rejected by the Supreme Court on most of which there had been sharp settler-claimant conflict. The reaction to the decisions of the Court on these claims and others on which boundary disputes were producing equally aggravating friction showed that a considerable number of Californians had come to regard large and undeveloped holdings of valley land as immoral, contrary to natural law, and therefore open to settlement by them. . . .

The decade of controversy over titles had wrought much havoc in California and left in its wake bitterness against the Land Act of 1851 which was incorrectly held responsible for the plight of landowners, and contempt for legal institutions which settlers felt leaned heavily on the side of the claimants. Many claim owners had exhausted their resources in litigation instead of using them to develop their properties, and their undeveloped land invited intrusion and settlement. Attorneys' fees, court costs, taxes, and interest on borrowed funds carrying interest rates as high as five and six percent a month, forced foreclosures and the breakup of many claims, undoubtedly a useful step, but it was achieved in the wrong way. It was far better to come to terms with settlers where possible and use the income from rents or sales to push titles to conclusion as rapidly as possible. Though some critics were coming to recognize the shortsightedness of the large owners in attempting to retain intact their immense holdings, many were to continue to fight to that end for a decade and more to come. The tragedy is that more vision was not displayed in foreseeing some of these difficulties and in devising a means by which all undeveloped and unused land in the claims were made at the outset public lands.

Major and measurable effects of the errors committed in the framing of the Land Act of 1851 that were shown in the Census of 1860 were the great concentration of ownership of agricultural land that had continued into the twentieth century, the high average size and consequent smaller number of farms, and the large number of farmers who owned no land.

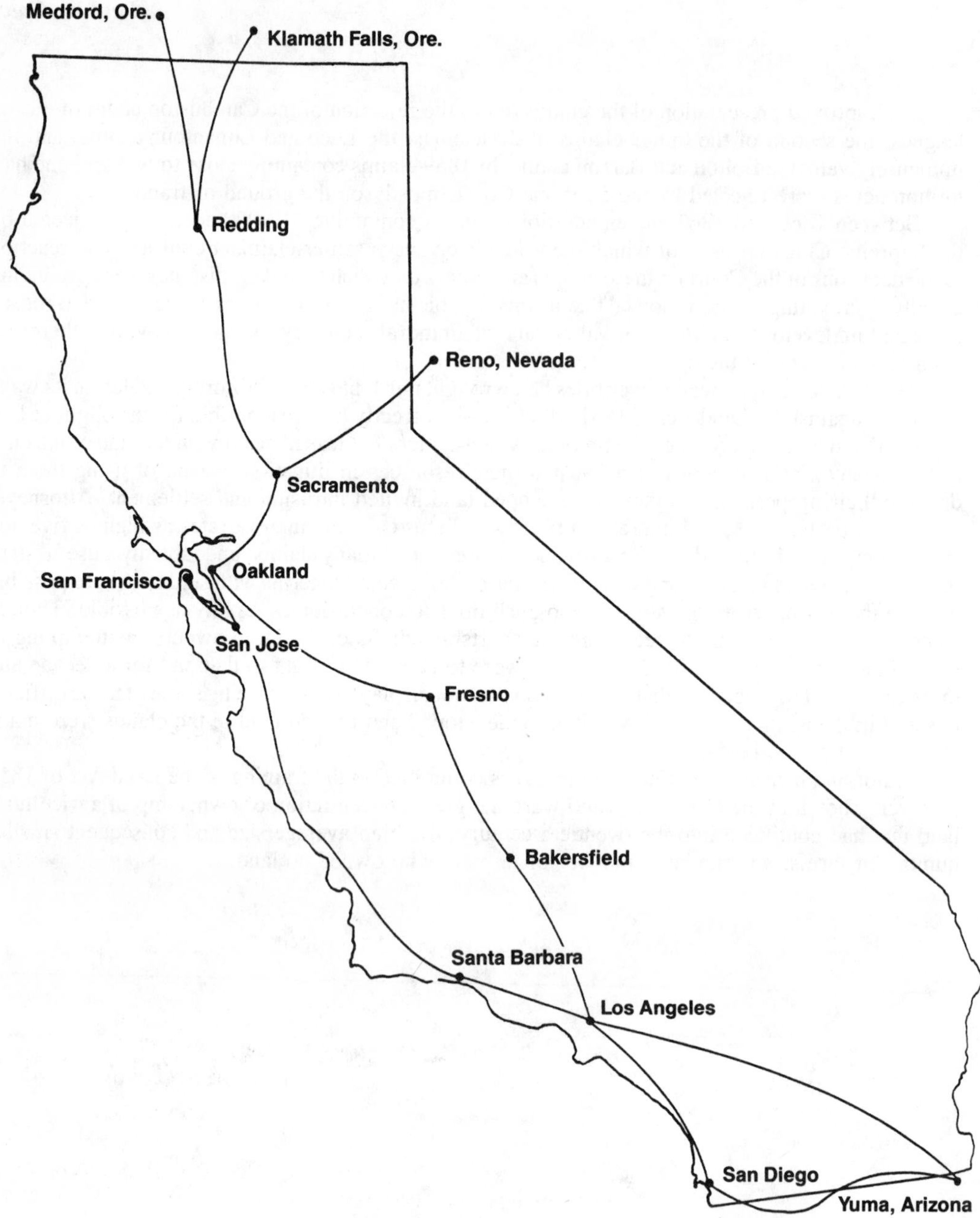

Main Lines of the Southern Pacific Railroad System

In the early years of California railroading, the Southern Pacific had an effective monopoly of shipping through the major agricultural regions, between the main cities, and from the state to all the major regions of the nation.

At half-past six a.m. we were seated in a car of the Central Pacific Railroad, bound on the long, long journey across the Continent. The morning was all that could be desired, and it promised a day wherein all the wonders and beauties of the route across the Sierra Nevada could be viewed to the greatest possible advantage. . . .

. . . We can't have perfection at once; time alone can make this gigantic enterprise equal to all the requirements of the age, but the Central Pacific has done wonders when we consider the few months it has taken to lay so vast an amount of track over a country of which so much is a wilderness and a desert. "Give the devil his due," and don't growl over this road for a year to come—not until the two have joined and time has been given to correct errors in construction that at first were unavoidable. Let us be proud that we have a railroad across the Continent; one that places New York within a week of San Francisco and that shows the world what American energy and enterprise can do when there is an object to be gained by it.

—Letter from a correspondent in the *New York Herald,* May 3, 1869.

CHAPTER 6

THE CONSTITUTIONAL CONVENTION OF 1879-1880 AND THE SOUTHERN PACIFIC RAILROAD

Grappling with the "Octopus"

In the 1870's, social strife erupted in California that was so intense it caught the eye of none other than Karl Marx. Marx reputedly saw the struggle as a new vindication of his theories in *Das Kapital* describing "monopoly concentration," capitalist exploitation, and class warfare. The 1870's was indeed a period of extended hard times in the Promised Land of California, and the dreams of many settlers were then completely crushed. California's economy had evolved in two short decades from a system of free-wheeling competition and relative social equality to one that was increasingly stratified, hedged in by powerful corporations, and subject to economic depression. Like the nation at large after 1875, California experienced a widespread unemployment, bank failures, business bankruptcies, mortgage defaults, and stock losses. But in California there were also droughts and poor harvests, and anti-Chinese riots. The grievances of labor against capital produced an unprecedented political movement, the Workingmen's Party. This group was led by the sand-lot orator Dennis Kearney, who espoused a peculiar brand of class and race warfare.

To many disaffected Californians, a basic source of evil was the Southern Pacific Railroad. Of course, back in May of 1869 the completion of the first cross-country rail hookup had conjured up visions of unlimited material progress in the Far West. Yet a short time later the "S.P." fell from grace and became the focus of bitter complaints and controversy. Caucasian workers inveighed against the railroad for hiring masses of Chinese construction hands. Farmers denounced the railroad's burdensome freight schedules and its duplicity in the sale of land. Small merchants alleged the existence of secret pacts that gave rebates to large shippers. Rival corporations complained of physical destruction to their equipment by agents of the Southern Pacific. Passengers murmured of poor service and stockholders of mismanagement. Meantime it had become the state policy of the Big Four—Leland Stanford, Collis P. Huntington, Charles Crocker, and Mark Hopkins—to seize control over *all* transportation facilities in the state, including ferries, stagecoaches, interurban lines, and feeder roads, and to brook no interference from the government or from rival companies. This strategy required the gradual construction of a ubiquitous political machine to select judges, rig the nominating conventions of both major parties (and some minor ones too), bribe municipal officials and legislators, silence the press, befuddle the voters, and in general meddle in governmental affairs at every turn. The Southern Pacific Railroad was well on its way to becoming Frank Norris' "Octopus."[1]

Under the prodding of those moderates and radicals who sought to curb the "interests" in California (banks, land syndicates, labor contractors, and other large corporations such as the Southern Pacific), a constitutional convention was authorized in 1879 to create a new framework of government. Reformers believed that the constitution of 1849 was hopelessly inadequate to insure the free flow of bank credit, free access to the public domain, and free competition, as well as the equitable taxation and control of foreign labor that they assumed to be essential to democracy. Thus the convention was charged with a herculean task of social reconstruction. It was a foregone conclusion that through all the debates there would shine the stark class, racial, and social animosities of the day. Of the 152 elected delegates, 77 were nonpartisan, 11 Republican, 10 Democratic, 3 Independent, and most significantly, 51 Workingmen; the Workingmen seized the limelight with their anti-Chinese, anti-monopoly, and anti-Railroad advocacy, and their vague hints of violence should the convention invoke their displeasure.

To say the least, 1878 was not a time for dispassionate discourse, and much of what was said at the convention was said in anger and fear. In the colorful language of the Workingmen, all issues, including the railroad issue, boiled down to a contest between "capital and labor." But it is more accurate to say that the fundamental divisions in the convention were three: the defenders of the new industrial order founded on corporate power (the "conservatives"), the moderate reformers (the "liberals"), and radical labor spokesmen who veered in the direction of drastic reform if not outright revolution. The Workingmen who had called for the convention were less than psychologically attuned to the constitutional process. "The Constitution of the United States is a political abortion. . . ." one frustrated Workingmen's delegate explained. "It has ever been construed in the interest of capital. . . . It has outlived its usefulness. . . . If to preserve the Constitution liberty must be suppressed, then abolish the Constitution." Yet there were in the chamber some 57 lawyers, many of them corporation lawyers and other natural defenders of the status quo. To them the U.S. Constitution and the ideas behind it seemed all but sanctified: they refused to yield to the "communists" and their ilk without a desperate fight. These conservatives feared that the moderates would give in to the radicals, allowing a general curtailment of property rights through taxation, regulatory commissions, and restrictions on the immigration of the Chinese. The moderates, of course got caught in the squeeze by looking for compromise and modest advance in an area charged with explosive energies.

Naturally the Southern Pacific was a major topic in the convention, and the discussion turned to the possibility of establishing a railroad commission with broad powers to control freight rates and shipping policies. A presentation of the reform viewpoint on the railroad issue was made by Morris M. Estee. Aside from hirelings of the Southern Pacific, there were those in the chamber with deep convictions about the blessings of *laissez faire.* Thomas B. McFarland was such a conservative spokesman. A railway commission was finally authorized, but without teeth. For all the efforts at reform in the conventions and afterward, it should be noted, the railroad continued to rule in solitary grandeur over one of the richest states in the Union. It was simply bigger, richer, and better staffed with attorneys, and thus more powerful than all of its enemies in and out of government combined. Indeed the net result in each of the major constitution disputes was either a change so modest as to be meaningless or a reaffirmation of the status quo. Not until the advent of Hiram Johnson and the Progressive legislature of 1911 was the Southern Pacific trimmed down to size. Meanwhile, other powerful utility corporations arose that posed similar dilemmas about public res-

---

[1]Frank Norris, *The Octopus* (1901); a novel depicting the farmers' contest with the S.P. in the Mussel Slough region of Tulare County in 1880.

traint over private enterprise; in this form the problem of corporate power and the public interest is still alive today.

California is still governed by the 1879 constitution—and by a loosely woven patchquilt of amendments. From 1963 to 1974 a commission of 60 citizens and 20 legislators proposed major revisions that were submitted to the legislature and eventually to the voters, who approved most of them. In the process many confusing and contradictory provisions were simplified, pruned out, or left to the legislature to convert into statutes. The sections were grouped in a more logical way, and the length of the entire document was shortened by one-third. However, many substantive issues were left unsettled. In addition, during the last decade the document has once more ballooned in size. Consequently, the shape and content of the constitution remains a policy issue for future Californians to deal with. *(Editor's note)*

12.
Morris M. Estee Proposes Stronger Restraints on Corporate Power

The chairman of the convention committee that recommended regulation of the railroads was San Francisco attorney Morris M. Estee, a former speaker of the California Assembly and a top official in the reform-minded Independent Party. He loathed Dennis Kearney but not the Workingmen, who liked him and helped elect him for his anti-monopoly, anti-corporation, anti-railroad views. He was temperamentally a moderate and capable of working with both the Kearneyites and conservatives, although each accused him of vacillating.

Taking the long view, his position in the speech of November 12, 1878, was that of the moderate reformer rather than a radical seeking the ruin of corporations of the new industrial society.[2] *His argument stems from a conservative doctrine about the responsibilities of public corporations, a view expressed by the U. S. Supreme Court in* Munn vs. Illinois *in 1877: railroads are monopolies "affected with a public interest" and subject to public control.*

Estee's innovation would be the establishment of an elective board of railroad commissioners with powers to regulate rates, prevent abuses and examine business records. Such a commission was eventually established, but it did not have the effect that Estee had envisioned.

. . . In opening the debate on the subject of the reports of the Committee on Corporations other than Municipal, I am reminded that the questions presented for our consideration are among the gravest that can come before this Convention.

For years the people of this State, and indeed all the Pacific States, nay, of most of the other States of the Union, have been brought face to face with these great questions. In some instances they have been settled by constitutional or statutory provisions; in others they are yet unsettled; in all instances they have inspired the most serious consideration of the leading statesmen of the country.

The result of the action of this Convention, if favorable to the report of your committee, will mark a new era in the history of this State; it will stamp upon the organic law of California that right of visitation and regulation of railroads necessary for the protection of the people. It will establish a tribunal whose officers are selected by the people, and before which the individual and the corporation may appear and demand justice.

[2] *Debates and Proceedings of the Constitutional Convention of the State of California Convened. . . September 28, 1878* (Sacramento: State Printing Office, 1881), I, 377-381.

It will take from the halls of legislation the corrupting influence of corporate power; and it will establish mutual confidence between the producer and common carrier, which nothing else thus far devised has.

It may be admitted that nearly all the great business enterprises of the country are in the hands of corporations.

The insurance business is conducted by corporations, the banking business is conducted by corporations, the mining business is in the hands of corporations, the entire carrying trade of the country, not only of the Pacific Coast but of the whole nation, is in the hands of corporations. Natural persons no longer control these great interests. The reasons, Mr. Chairman and gentlemen of the Convention, I attribute to three causes: First, the difficulty of one man controlling money sufficient to handle such great enterprises; second, the personal, financial, and moral irresponsibility of corporations; and lastly, "corporations never die."

Mr. Chairman, in rising to defend the report made by your committee, sir, I am prepared to say for one, and I think in this respect I echo the voice of your committee, that your committee had no desire to imperil any of these interests. They know, and we all know, that the dollar owned by a corporation has as much right to be protected, to be defended by the organic law of this state, as the dollar owned by the humblest individual in the country. They know, and we all know, that the whole republic, and especially this coast, has been largely indebted for its prosperity to the railroad corporations of the country. We are aware, sir, and every member on this floor must be aware, that it would be impossible now to carry on the great commercial interests of the country but for railroads....

The great services to the country of railroads in peace or war are beyond computation; they are widespread, reaching every interest, touching every individual. It being of such vast importance, the American people have come to think upon this question. The political and financial power of railroads in the United States are immense, and have become a grand *imperium in imperio*—a government within a government, a power within a power, greater than the mightiest, grander and more colossal than any other financial institution hitherto known in the history of civilization. Sir, it was originally the belief of most of us— it was the belief of the fathers of the republic—that monopolies in a free country could not and ought not to exist. On that proposition there was a warfare made many years ago against the National Bank, and after a long and most earnest contest, that institution was destroyed. That was not the sole reason, but it was one of the grand moving powers that controlled the public sentiment of the American people at that time, that monopolies must not be established in a free country. But, sir, monopolies do exist; monopolies will exist; in the very nature of things, they must exist. We cannot help it. You may talk to the winds and tell them not to blow, and they will still blow. So it is with monopolies. We have got to take facts as they are. The people will not put fifty, or a hundred, or two hundred millions of dollars, or any other vast sum, in a great enterprise like a railroad institution or the building or establishing of railroads, unless it is virtually a monopoly. It is true that when it was found out that monopolies did exist to a certain extent, it was believed the evil could be remedied, if it be an evil—which I will reach hereafter—by competition, and thereby avoid the effect of the monopoly. But, sir, now I lay down the doctrine adopted by George Stephenson, and by many of the most eminent men of the country, that where combination is possible, competition is impossible; that in truth and in fact there is no such thing as competition today in the great carrying trade of the country on land; that there cannot be....

...The great railroad questions of the nation, are of recent origin—nothing old, nothing historical. There are no precedents that are not of the living present; we can see it all around and about us. We don't go to any old musty tomes to find out what the opinions of our fathers were as to railroads, for they had none. The gentleman's reference to the past goes back too far. Many different remedies are presented in this article on corporations, each reaching, in some degree, a wrong complained of, and all touching the question of regulation. And about the first of them is the one relative to the establishment of a Commission.

I am aware, sir, that the question of adopting a section of that character, providing for a Railroad Commission, stuck many minds in this Convention as something unusual and extraordinary; that to provide for a Commission in a Constitution was too grave a matter, because it would take a long time to remedy the evil, if evil arises from it; that it would be better to leave this matter in the hands of the people, or, in other words, in the hands of the Legislature. On this point your committee—or a majority of them—agreed. And among the reasons—all of which I shall not attempt to give—they claimed, first, that a Commission was the fairest body that could be selected; the fairest to the companies and the fairest to the people. They claimed it was the fairest, sir, because no man can act justly and fairly upon any important question of that kind unless he comprehends the subject; and that a Commission elected for the term of four years can certainly so inform itself upon the questions as to be able to pass upon those questions that necessarily require the consideration of strong reasoning capacity; that a legislative body coming together once in two years, in session but a comparatively short time, could not give to this question such consideration as the magnitude of the subject demanded. Another of the chief reasons which was urged or discussed in that committee, sir, was that it got rid, to a large degree, of the great disgraces of the time—I will not say in California only— namely, the corrupting influences in legislative bodies. I am not saying, sir, that it always happens in legislative bodies, or that legislative bodies are always corrupt when handling these questions, but what I do say is that it is recognized everywhere throughout the Union among thoughtful men that when questions materially affecting the railroads come up for consideration before legislative bodies the bad men of the country swarm around the Legislature. They seem to know something that nobody else does. That money is freely used on such occasions is not and cannot be denied. . . .

. . . Your committee thought that the remedy rested in a Commission, and whether that section which has been framed by them will represent your ideas I am not here to argue. We believe that the principle is right; that a Commission elected by the people ought to control this matter; that while it is possible, sir, to buy three men—more possible to buy three men than to buy one hundred twenty—yet personal responsibility makes men honest; personal responsiblility makes men conservative; personal responsibility always makes men capable. When you throw the whole weight of this great question into a legislative body no one is responsible. All are, it is true, but there is no individual responsibility. But when you elect a constitutional officer whose duty it shall be [to] settle these questions; when he takes the oath of office it carries with it a solemnity and a realization of the duties which devolve upon him that in no case can rest upon the member of the Legislature. . . .

In every civilized country where railroads have been built, some form of regulation has been adopted. And why should it not be? They are established for a public use. They are common carriers. The people are all interested. Their money may be in it. But when they built that road, when they incorporated themselves to build it, they knew exactly in what direction they were going to build it, and over what line. They knew that they were going to perform a certain duty to the public, namely, transporting passengers and freight for a certain price, and the people had a right to regulate it just as much as they have a right to regulate a toll road. And it is really marvelous, when we come to think of it, that every gentleman will admit that everywhere in this nation the Boards of Supervisors in the various counties have always regulated the toll roads where the franchise has been given to them, but that it is wrong to regulate these matters of paramount interest on these great highways of the nation. It is because the railroads perform these great functions, and because they affect every interest and every want of the people, that they should be regulated by the people. I do not say that this company here has to be regulated. I am not saying that it has not. I have my own private opinion as to that. But what I do say is that this Constitutional Convention should provide a means whereby all railroad companies may be controlled. . . .

. . . The existence of the railroads depends upon the people, and the prosperity of people depends upon the fairness with which the railroads control their property. But for the people themselves these roads would not have existed. But for the roads we could not transport our grain, our freight, and our persons. We are entitled to that mutual relation occupied by persons holding great trusts, whereby they put money into an enterprise in which the public are interested. We say that the creature we shall not by any act of ours become greater than its creator. We say the creature made by the statute, created by the law, shall not under any state of circumstances be more potent, more powerful to control its affairs, than the State itself. . . .

13.
Thomas B. McFarland Warns of the Reform "Mania"

In the sort of modest reform proposed by Estee, other men foresaw the start of a revolutionary onslaught against property that would eventually topple civilization itself. One such anxious person was delegate Thomas B. McFarland of Sacramento. McFarland was a Republican and a corporation attorney who fiercely opposed everything the Workingmen and reformers favored and who sided with the conservative bloc on all the key issues of taxes, Chinese immigration, railroad and corporation regulation.

McFarland unburdened himself on December 3, 1878, in an address to the convention concerning the proposed railroad commission, a segment of which is excerpted below.[3]

. . . Now, sir, it is apparent to the unprejudiced mind that all this clamor about railroads and corporations originates in this house. It is a mania. It is evolved from the inner consciences of some men here, as spiders spin their webs. I say there is no popular demand for any such extraordinary legislation to-day. I say the people do not call for it. I insist that the relations between the railroads and the people are satisfactory— and, if it were not so, we should hear from the people upon the subject. . . . It seems to me, sir, that some gentlemen in the Convention, like some newspapers, are undertaking to build up public opinion upon which they may feed, and upon which they may ride to popularity. . . .

Sir, I have a great respect for Courts. I think Courts are generally right, and I know of no way in which civilized society can be conducted except through the instrumentality of Courts, which must have a final adjudication of rights; but I do not know any slavish doctrine that would prevent any man from expressing his opinion about a decision of a Court, and I pretend to say that the decision of the Supreme Court of the United States, in the case alluded to [*Munn* v. *Illinois*], is most destructive of the leading ideas of American government, the most ruinous to personal liberty, of any decision ever made in any Court in the United States or England. . . . If that be the law, then the Legislature can say what Booth & Company shall charge for groceries, what Holbrook, Merrill & Company shall charge for a bar of iron or a stove; what Lyon & Company shall charge for a sack of onions. . . . .

. . . Now, sir, the leading principle of the Democratic party, the one asserted by its greatest leaders, and built into its platforms, was this—and it is a good principle too—there are not many things in the Democratic party, connected with it, that I can indorse, but this I can, the gentleman knows it—"that government is the best that governs the least." And, sir, the converse of the propo-

[3]*Debates*, I, 547-549.

sition is true, that that government is the worst which to the greatest extent sticks the finger of inquisitorial power into private affairs, and keeps the eye of official espionage upon the daily walk and conduct of the citizen. And I say that that decision is a blow at this doctrine, and goes to the point that every citizen in his private business is at the mercy of the Legislature.....

But we do not deny the power to control. It stands on a better and firmer basis than that decision. "The Court awards it, and the law doth give it." So did the bard, apparently, give to Shylock power over the life of the unfortunate merchant of Venice; but can you cut the pound of flesh nearest the heart without the life-blood of your whole political and economic system following the knife? Does it follow that you must exercise the power because you have it? The Legislature of this State has immense power; it has all the power not taken away from it by the Constitution of the State and the United States. Shall it be exercised for bad purposes as well as good? That is the question, sir. Now, the point I make is this: that there never has been presented before this Convention any evidence to warrant any such extraordinary and revolutionary legislation as this section provides for. I say you propose to put into the Constitution a proposition almost unknown to the history of nations, and when you propose to do that it devolves upon you to show that an evil exists here as great as was ever known in the history of nations. I say you have not done it—it is all declamation.... Now, sir, I say this: that the judgment of men who have given the most attention to railroad matters, is that the best thing to do with them, as a general rule, is to let them alone; to hold over them the legislative power, so that it, at any moment, can, when a case of extortion comes, remedy it.... I do not deny the power of the Legislature to regulate freights and fares, when they choose to do so, or when they think the time has come that they ought to do it. They have done it already, to some extent, and they hold that power, and if exercised wrongly, and it is shown within a year, or within six months, that the law is wrong, the Legislature is ready to alter or repeal it. But here, sir, in the report of your committee, you have put in, already, dozens of sections, that are irrepealable, permanent, beyond the reach of the Legislature—that cannot be reached by any ordinary power—and you propose to give the remnant of the power to another Commission, over which neither the Legislature nor the people can have any control. That is what is proposed to be done....

....These men do not only propose to tinker with the vital organs of the State, but propose to take away a portion of them as a surgeon would cut away a portion of the heart, or liver, or lungs; and they propose to establish a Commission of three men to whom these several parts are to be given. Was such a proposition ever heard of in a free government—in a government that pretends to have a free Constitution? The proposition was never heard of before; certainly not in America, and never heard of in England after she commenced to become free. Why, this Commission is to be a Court. They are to hear and determine all complaints. I do not know in what manner, not according to the ordinary processes of law, I suppose. Everybody who has a complaint, whether frivolous or not, could come before a Commission and it would have to spend the most of its time in hearing complaints, and would not have time to examine into the question of freights and fares or pass laws upon that subject....

...Now, in regard to the railroad companies in this State, the statements are wonderfully wild and exaggerated.... It seems to me that every gentleman ought to understand that it is to the interests of California that the railroads of California should be under the control of California men. They have been so owned thus far. What has been the result? Why, sir, when you go as far as the Central Pacific runs eastward, to Ogden, you find that the trade to that point comes to California, and upon the other side it goes to the East. And I have been informed by a gentleman not connected with the railroad, that if the City of San Francisco had given her million of dollars, as she agreed to do, that the railroad would have been pushed one hundred miles further, and we would have had all the trade of Utah. Everybody knows that if the Southern Pacific is owned and controlled by California men, that the whole trade of that part of the country, almost to the Mississippi River, will come to California, and if it is owned by Eastern men it will go there. And yet you want to fill up your Constitution with burdens and provisions that will discourage any California man from putting a dollar into railroads. . . .

. . . Why, sir, a great deal has been said about the members of this railroad company getting rich. Well, sir, would you expect them in such a magnificent enterprise as that to get poor? Would you expect an enterprise costing the millions of money that the Central Pacific Railroad cost to be so nicely graduated at the start that the men who built it would neither lose a dollar nor be in a position where they could make more than legal interest? Why, sir, the mechanic, the carpenter, the contractor, in estimating the expense of a house consisting only a few thousand dollars, will sometimes make a mistake of several hundred, and yet you expect that a railroad can be commenced at the Pacific Ocean, run over almost inaccessible mountains, over deserts, through Indian countries, through undiscovered countries you might say, and that at the start you are going to calculate this thing down so nicely that the men who build it shall neither lose a dollar or make more than legal interest. Why, sir, would any man of common sense go into a hazardous business of that kind upon any such terms? Suppose some men were going to prospect for a mine. They find a hill which they think may contain a mine; they are willing to put their money in for the purpose of determining whether there is a mine there or not, and if they lose, they lose all. If there is no mine there, everything is lost. If there be a mine there, they make money. Suppose you say to them: "If you find a mine there you shall not make more than about ten per cent a year on your investment." Would any man of sense undertake to open a mine? Would any man in his senses undertake to go into a thing upon the condition that he might lose everything, but he should not make more than the man who loans money on mortgage?

The Government of the United States wanted to build a railroad from the East to the West. It was a national enterprise. They considered first whether they would build it themselves as a piece of government work, or whether they would help somebody else to build it. They said: "Instead of building it ourselves, we will offer a certain proposition to a company. We will give you so much land; we will guarantee your bonds for so much a mile. If upon that condition you will build this railroad, it is a contract." Well, sir, it was accepted,and after these subsidies had been granted there was not half a dozen men in the State of California that believed it could be done. It was called the Dutch Flat swindle, and it was said that they only intended to run it to Dutch Flat, so as to draw the trade of that section and of Virginia City. The certificates of stock were hawked around the City of San Francisco, and there was not a man to buy them. The City of San Francisco, after having subscribed one million dollars, after the land grants had been made, compromised by paying six hundred thousand dollars—a little more than one half—because she believed that it never could be a successful business operation. That is history. But because it turned out successful, and a few men got rich, gentlemen say, "Take it away from them." Is that sense? Is that justice? Is that in accordance with any rule or system of laws the world ever saw? . . . . Do gentlemen undertake to say that the State owns these railroads? I do not understand anybody to take such a position as that. Who owns the locomotives and the cars that run on them? Are they not private property? And yet you propose to hand over that property—every car, every locomotive, every station, every machine shop which that company has built— you propose to take it all and give it over to three men, with a strong hand, just as if you proposed to take from the gentleman his homestead and give it to me. Don't they own it practically under the bill? Can't they control it without any other governing power at all—without any restraint whatever? What could the railroad companies do under that bill except to say to them: "Gentlemen, upon what terms shall we be allowed to use our own property?" There is no restraint upon them; there is no limit to their powers. No man can point to the line where it stops. These three Commissioners can in the course of their four years control millions of property; property not their own; property that does no belong to the State which proposes to give it to them; property which belongs to private individuals; and yet they have the power to take that property and control it, and make it utterly worthless, if they choose. It seems to me the position is too monstrous to be entertained by any body of sensible men like this.

I have nothing further to say. I only say that I stand upon this principle: that the Legislature, under the decision of the Court, have the right to regulate fares and freights; that at the present time it is not policy to do it; that the people who are dealing with the railroad companies do not ask it to be done; and that the power it possesses should be left with the Legislature that comes fresh from the people every year—the Legislature which, if it happens to commit an error, can correct it.

The referendum works well and is a safe-guard against bad legislative practices. The initiative seems to me to work ill. I would prefer to see our laws changed so as to put the initiative of new laws, not at the disposition of any private individual or group of individuals who have a pet scheme, but at the disposition of public organs of governments. . . . The great difficulty of the popular initiative is that measures have to go to the voters without the advantage of discussion and amendment in the process of their framing and I believe that few legislative measures are satisfactory for final vote until they have had the advantage of criticism and amendment. . . . I am not in favor of the initiative as it now stands.

—David P. Burrows, former President of the University of California, to John Randolph Haynes; February 7, 1927.

For twenty years in my lectures I opposed the Initiative and Referendum, but I have seen the error of my ways and am now as strongly in favor of them as I was formerly opposed.

—Woodrow Wilson, on the letterhead of the League to Protect the Initiative; 1925.

CHAPTER 7

INITIATIVE, REFERENDUM AND NON-PARTISAN ELECTIONS

The Progressives' Legacy

One of the world's most highly respected commentators on governmental affairs, England's Lord Bryce, ridiculed the California Constitution of 1879 as an inept document, and he had ample reason to do so, yet he surely would have looked favorably on the reform in politics and government that swept the state after the election of 1910. Following a spirited campaign in which the Southern Pacific Railroad was the chief target of attack, Governor Hiram Johnson came to power on the Progressive Republican ticket and introduced a series of laws and constitutional amendments that had more far-reaching and enduring effects than most of the work produced at the 1879 constitutional convention. The legislature of 1911 was proclaimed one of the best seen anywhere in American life—perhaps the very best of all time, according to Theodore Roosevelt.

The California Progressives from about 1905 to 1920 operated on relatively simple assumptions: in their own terms, their chief objectives were to restore government to the people, diminish the authority of political bosses, and restrain monopolies from strangling free competition in the market place. To accomplish these ends the Progressives instituted a number of techniques, among them the initiative and referendum, the recall of elected officials, the direct primary to replace the party caucus, cross-filing, and the non-partisan ballot for state and local elections. Once in power, they swiftly wrote into law bills putting teeth into the railroad commission, curtailing the aggressive power of utility companies, preventing the incursion of private corporations into publicly owned natural preserves, extending to women the right to vote, and establishing a personal income tax, minimum wages for women and children, and a greatly improved civil service system. While a few of these reforms may be termed expedients to help prolong the Progressive Republican regime against a possible loss of power to the stand-patters within their party, most were long-range and long overdue efforts to bolster the popular will against machine politics. Never again, the liberals hoped, would the forces of greed and corruption make such headway in California; never again would people of good will have to undertake such strenuous efforts on behalf of popular rule.

It must be said to their everlasting praise that when the California Progressives "kicked the railroad out of politics" and went on to storm Sacramento, they refrained from creating a new corrupt political machine. They set high moral standards and, by and large, adhered to them. They never succeeded, however, in eliminating entrenched organization. On the contrary, they seem to have cleared the way for hundreds of new pressure groups—all of whom had been looking for a place in the sun and were grateful for the *new* opportunity to find it. Today, for example, Sacramento is host to more powerful and effective lobbies than any other state capital in the nation. Thus, in the long run many Progressive victories were compromised.

The dilemma faced by the Progressives may be stated in this way: How shall democratic government be perfected and grass roots influence be extended in an era in which corporate growth and organizational giantism are watch words? The question is as valid today as it was in 1910.

By way of an answer, it is appropriate to examine the functioning of some of the pet political techniques used by the Progressives. It hardly matters which one in particular is studied in detail: most contain food for thought about the operation of politics and government in California. The following selections provide the pros and cons on, first, direct legislation and, second, non-partisan ballots. The materials in both cases come from the records of the Commonwealth Club of California, perhaps the state's greatest public forum. A third and final segment is devoted to a brief historical survey of the implications of Progressivism, written by a leading political scientist.

Many questions have been raised over the years about direct legislation and also about non-partisan voting, or rather about the first cousin to non-partisan voting, cross-filing. Have the voters generally acted intelligently on direct legislative measures? Have initiatives and referendums broken or merely altered the power of pressure groups? As the "gun behind the door," does the system constitute a desirable or undesirable check on the authority of the legislature? Does it tend to educate voters to their responsibilities, as was intended back in 1911, or simply to confuse them when they are making weighty decisions? Would party discipline now cure the same ills for which the Progressives once prescribed the elimination of parties? Would a restoration of partisanship in local government have as salutary an influence as some claim it has had on state government? How *can* the "interests" be controlled, if not through the old Progressive devices? Any reasoned answers, however incomplete, would provide a test of the Progressives' assumptions about the possibility of true popular rule in an era of organization politics. *(Editor's note)*

14.
A Debate on Initiative and Referendum: Haynes in Favor, Adams Opposed

The liberal Republican legislature of 1911 gave California voters the option of voting for or against a constitutional amendment to permit direct legislation. One part of this measure, the part on initiatives, would allow the electorate to enact statutes and constitutional amendments quite independently of the legislature, and another part, on referendums, would reserve to the people the right to annul any act passed by the lawmakers. Both initiatives and referendums would originate through petitions bearing a number of signatures equal to a percentage of the vote cast in the preceding gubernatorial election—eight per cent for initiatives and five per cent for referendums. Also, signatures of five per cent of the voters could inaugurate an "indirect initiative," that is, could put a bill forcibly before the legislature for its consideration. In all direct legislation, a majority vote of the electorate would carry and the veto power of the governor would be nullified.

On the eve of the election of October 11, the Commonwealth Club of San Francisco sponsored a debate to review the issue of direct legislation.[1] *For the pro side the Club invited the best-qualified speaker in the country, Dr. John Randolph Haynes of Los Angeles, the pioneer advocate of the idea in California. The initiative, referendum, and recall provisions of the Los Angeles charter, the first such provisions of any city in the country, were personally drafted by Haynes in 1903. Trained as a physician and surgeon, Haynes arrived from Pennsylvania in 1887 and eventually held many posts in local and state government, from civil service commissioner to member of the state board of charities, from water commissioner of Los Angeles to regent of the University. He belonged to most of the leading social and service organizations, including the Commonwealth Club, and he wrote on many governmental problems.*

Haynes' opposite number in the 1911 debate was Edward Francis Adams, an articulate editorial writer for the San Francisco Chronicle *who was something of an expert on economics and who had been vice president and president of the Club in its first ten years. Adams wrote three books:* The Modern Farmer *(1899),* Critique of Socialism *(1905), and* The Inhumanity of Socialism *(1913).*

The direct legislation measure carried in 1911. By 1979 it had been invoked 434 times with varying results. To cite but a few instances, among the measures now considered most salutary are those concerning the form of the state budget, the powers of the attorney general, the selection of judges, and the funding of public education; among the ones defeated and still considered in most quarters as bizarre are the single tax (rejected six times), antivivisection (rejected three times), the "Ham and Eggs" retirement plan (rejected twice), and the licensing of "naturopaths" (rejected once).

Critics have contended all along that initiatives are an open invitation to small groups possessing sufficient zeal or money to qualify pet measures, sometimes year after year in the face of pronounced voter opposition. Also, the professionalism and big expenditures that have crept into the initiative campaigns have been termed antithetical to the democratic process; nearly five million dollars was spent on the "oil-and-gas initiative" of 1956. The tendency of many initiatives to try to limit the legislature's powers of taxation but not its responsibility to make expenditures has also been denounced as reckless and unfair. Increase the number of signatures required to qualify measures, critics suggest, or require electors to visit the registrar office to sign petitions, prohibit professional organizations from circulating petitions, prohibit measures defeated in one election from coming up again at the next, limit the subject matters to be dealt with, or, best of all, simply repeal the process of direct legislation outright. All of these ideas have been seriously suggested in the past decades.

Defenders of direct legislation have retorted that increasing the number of signatures would create an absolute field day for the professional organizations, while eliminating the professional organizations would mean that only a few well-financed initiatives could ever qualify. To cut out the "repeater" initiatives would be difficult because the sponsors could alter a few words and claim that they are introducing an altogether new proposal. Any attempt to limit the powers of the electorate (so that laws affecting taxation could not be introduced by the initiative or referendum, for instance) would be doomed to failure. Outright repeal would negate the healthy concern shown for government by the millions of voters who turn out to cast their ballots on direct legislation; and it would simply fail to carry.

In looking back over the basic arguments of the club meeting of August 9, 1911, it is well to ask whether the fears of the opponents or the hopes of the advocates came true, or whether neither set of prophecies were fulfilled.

Report by Dr. John Randolph Haynes

This amendment should be adopted by the people of California on the tenth day of October, next. The movement for direct popular government is not something by itself; it does not stand

[1]"Direct legislation," *Transactions of the Commonwealth Club of California*, VI (September, 1911), 286-296.

alone. It is part of a world-wide movement. The nations and peoples of the earth are rushing towards democracy at a pace that astounds the conservative mind and fills the heart of the radical with joy. Despotisms are giving way to constitutional monarchies; witness Russia, Turkey, Persia, and even China. Constitutional monarchies are giving way to republics; witness France and Portugal; Spain and Italy seem almost ready to follow suit. Republics are giving way in turn to democracies; witness Switzerland and the commonwealths of our own republic. England, nominally a constitutional monarchy, appears almost to have overleaped the intervening stage of a republic, and, under the forms and stage dress of royalty, is taking on many of the characteristics of a pure democracy. . . .

In our own republic of America we find the same evolution in progress. Eight States through the adoption of the initiative and referendum now reserve to the people the right to take the control of affairs out of the hands of their servants at such times and in such matters as they may see fit. Popular rule through the introduction of the initiative and referendum became an actuality in South Dakota in 1898, in Oregon in 1902, in Montana, 1906; in Oklahoma, 1907; Maine and Missouri, 1908; Arkansas and Colorado, 1910. Besides these eight States in which popular rule is in actual operation, the question has been submitted to the people and carried in three other States, Utah, North Dakota, and Arizona, but is not yet in operation. In six other States both party platforms promise the people an opportunity to vote upon the adoption of these measures of direct government; Wisconsin, Illinois, Kansas, and our own California. In still six other States, Ohio, Minnesota, Wyoming, Idaho, Washington, and Iowa, one of the two dominant parties has pledged itself to introduce the same measure. Municipalities are following the states in the adoption of direct government. Two hundred American cities have adopted the initiative and referendum.

Direct Legislation Is Not New

The measures are frequently spoken of as new, untried and experimental in character. Such is not the case. Both the initiative and referendum are older than our Federal Constitution. The people of Georgia as early as 1777 held the power to initiate constitutional amendments. For more than three hundred years the towns of New England have governed themselves under a system of pure democracy, differing little in principle from the direct legislation system coming into use in States and cities throughout the nation. The general court of Massachusetts in 1778 submitted to the people a constitution for a referendum vote. All of our States, Delaware excepted, submit their constitutions and constitutional amendments to the people; and in many States other measures concerning education, taxation, etc., are submitted to the referendary vote.

This amendment should be adopted in California for the following reasons:

A. Experience shows us that the happiness, wisdom and prosperity of a people bear a definite ratio to the extent of their power and participation in the business of government. Compare the conditions existing in Russia, for example, with those in Switzerland; one, an autocracy and the other a pure democracy.

B. The act of law making operates in the case of the individual voter as a great educator. Twenty per cent more newspapers are published in Switzerland in proportion to the population than in the United States. The Swiss voter feels that he personally bears the responsibility for the right conduct of his government. Hence his sense of responsibility is markedly developed.

C. The people are conservative and do not enact many, nor ultra radical laws. Switzerland and its political subdivisions enact fewer laws than any other political communities in the world. In the first quarter century after the adoption of the initiative in the Canton of Zurich, recourse was had to it in but three cases. In 1902 the people of Oregon, by a vote of ten to one, adopted a direct legislation amendment and since that time have voted upon sixty-four laws and constitutional amendments. They have by a vote varying greatly in the size of the majority adopted thirty and rejected thirty-four of the measures proposed. Maine voted upon and rejected three measures last election. South Dakota rejected woman's suffrage and Washington adopted it. On the fifteenth of November, last, San Francisco voted upon thirty-eight proposed charter amendments; adopted eighteen and rejected twenty. In looking over these amendments I must confess that they seem to have made very few mistakes in judgment. The people of Los Angeles have had the power to directly legislate for eight years and have had only one initiative election during that time and the measures submitted to the people at general elections have been few and have been voted upon with rare discrimination.

Do People Vote Intelligently Upon Measures?

D. They are better fitted to vote upon measures, the text of which is sent to them three months before election with arguments pro and con; than they are to vote for a long array of office holders of whom they know little or nothing. Surely they are better fitted to express an intelligent opinion on a few measures after three months' consideration, than a legislative body is to act upon two or three thousand measures during a session of sixty days.

Do the People Vote Upon Measures?

E. A surprisingly large number do so and the percentage increases with succeeding elections. In Maine, a few months ago, in the first election in which the people voted upon measures, fifty per cent of those voting for Governor voted upon the measures submitted. In Missouri sixty per cent of the people voted upon measures submitted. In San Francisco the vote cast upon measures exceeded forty-five thousand out of a total registration of sixty-three thousand; and in Oregon, where direct legislation has been longest in working order, the percentage varies from 61 to 87 per cent of the vote cast for candidates.

F. A writer in the March issue of the *Political Science Quarterly*, George Haynes of Worcester, Mass., in an article treating on "People's Rule in Oregon," although approaching his subject in a frankly unfriendly attitude, nevertheless feels called upon to admit that upon the whole, the people and people's rule have made good in Oregon. Referring to the election of last autumn, he says: "As the smoke of the contest clears away, it is evident that 'people's rule' has strengthened its position." In the first place slavish adherence to national party lines must have been very largely destroyed in an election where a State normally Republican by a 25,000 majority chose a Democratic Governor by a plurality of 6,000. In the second place, the conditions of the campaign were such that it "would have been difficult for any Oregon voter to have remained totally ignorant of the principal points involved in the more important measures on which he was to vote." In the third place, the conditions of the campaign brought out a very heavy vote. The State contains about 135,000 registered voters. The vote on these measures referred directly to the people for settlement reached the extraordinary total of 120,248. He concludes thus: "Considering the immense complexity of the task which was set before them, it must be acknowledged that the Oregon voters stood the test remarkably well." . . . There has been a vitality, a genuineness in Oregon politics sharply in contrast with the State campaigns in many of the eastern States. . . .

Bribery of the people's representatives by special interests is the great demoralizing factor in our unchecked representative system of government. The majority of the electorate are honest, and desire good government. If you wish to have a truly representative government, and an honest and efficient one, give to the honest majority the power to directly legislate and to veto the acts of their representatives. It is much easier to bribe a few representatives than to bribe the majority of the many electors.

The advocates of direct legislation point convincingly to the experience of political communities where it has been in operation many years. Opponents avoid reference to its actual workings, but theorize as to what dire things may happen under certain contingencies.

Its advocates do not desire the abolition of legislative bodies, but demand the right of final decision where the acts of their servants are unsatisfactory.

As appendices, I submit the record of:

1. All the votes cast by the people of Oregon on initiative and referendum measures from 1902 to 1910 inclusive.

2. All the referendary votes cast by the people of California from 1879 to 1910 inclusive.
3. Record of all measures voted upon by the people of Oklahoma from 1908 to 1910 inclusive.
4. Detailed vote of the people of San Francisco on their charter amendments of 1910.

A careful study of these tables demonstrates:

1. That the people vote upon measures as well as men, when given the opportunity.
2. That the largest vote is upon the measures that are of the greatest importance and best understood, thus making it plain that there is an automatic disfranchisement of those ignorant of the subject.
3. That the people vote most carefully and discriminatingly.
4. That legislation termed "rash" and "ill-advised" is not favored by the people. The body of the voters is conservative, being conservative on the side of the public welfare.

The fight for people's rule is already won. The demand has become universal and irresistible. Senator [Elihu] Root, himself for many years perhaps the most noted and best paid of the attorneys who serve the Wall Street interests, recently created dismay in the hearts of "stand-patters," by the declaration in his speech as chairman of the New York Republican Convention that the people of the whole country were dissatisfied with the present indirect, representative system; that they felt that their will was not being carried out, and that the demand for direct power through the initiative and referendum could no longer be denied. You may as well attempt to stem the ocean at its flood tide, as to try to stop this onward, world-wide sweep of democracy.

. . . .

Report by Edward Francis Adams

I am opposed to all direct legislation of any kind that can possibly be avoided, except on the question of incurring public debt. In man's primitive state, institutions are imposed at the point of the sword, by the strong man backed by retainers inspired by the hope of plunder. That is right, for in that state there is no alternative but anarchy. It is the rude working out of Nature's processes. In the dim future which a riotous imagination may picture as glorious, mankind may acquire the ability to legislate wisely, en masse, if they are then fed 4 with manna so that they have leisure to do it. But not now. But for the present I do, however, think this nation so far advanced that with due regard to our own welfare we may safely adopt a constitution prescribing a frame of government, if we stop there and leave all legislation to such legislators as we may be able to elect.

Instance of the Constitution of 1879

For a shocking example of the evils of the referendum we need only refer to the direct legislation embodied in our own constitution of 1879, glorified in that day as the ultimate word of perfect human wisdom, and whose blunders we have been trying to undo ever since. And yet the legislation of which it is full had been submitted to the scrutiny and earnest debate of a body of far abler men than we can ever hope to assemble in a Legislature. Under popular pressure they submitted laws which as a Legislature they would never have enacted, and which the people adopted with no comprehension of their results. The legislation in our constitution is responsible for the majority of our most costly litigation, for uncertainties of the law, for delays and denials of justice and for most of our great body of judge-made laws—judge-made, not because judges wish to make law, but because the poor devils are compelled to decide cases, and before they can do so must often make the law to decide them with. They cannot even guess what the people intended.

I believe in representative government. It is fashionable just now to glorify "the people," extol their wisdom and integrity and declare their infallibility. And if I were after an office that is what I should have to do to get it. What I am saying now would forever make my election to anything impossible and carry political damnation to any higher up who should appoint me. But I believe it useful for some one who does not want anything except respect as an honest man to stand out in the open and say what two-thirds of you think. As one of the people, and possessing average intelligence, I protest that we are a purblind and blundering lot, carried away by every wind of doctrine. I for one declare that I am utterly incapable of legislating for myself and desire to live under laws which have been enacted by a Legislature, which can amend or repeal them if mistakes are made, in the firm conviction that whether good or bad they will be better than any which I could make for myself without the assistance of the process of legislation. And I further affirm that in the main our legislators are honest and their legislation good.

Initiative Worse Than Referendum

If the referendum be bad the initiative is worse. It is the uncorking of all the bottles of crankiness, and it is one of the strongest arguments of the proponents of the initiative that the people will probably vote down most of the laws that are proposed. But why subject ourselves to the torment and expense? Any law that ought to be passed, and any law that the people really demand, whether it ought to be passed or not, will be passed by a Legislature; but in the process of legislation it will be licked into some kind of reasonable shape, and can be amended if not right, or repealed when we are tired of it. The more direct legislation you have, the greater and the more costly will be our litigation, and the greater the body of our judge-made law.

The recall is an abomination. It is evidence of almost inconceivable hysteria in the American people that they cannot wait to get rid of an official, whom in the fulness of their wisdom they have just elected, until the expiration of his brief term of office. What we seem to need is a dose of soothing syrup. The recall of judges would be an atrocity. The talk about the people being as competent to recall as to elect is nonsensical. Personally I do not believe the people more competent to elect judges than to elect railroad commissioners, and I heartily favor that change in the glorious constitution of 1879, which takes from us that power which we have shown our incompetence to use wisely, and place it in the hands of our good Governor and his successors forever. But when we do elect judges we elect them on their general reputation at the bar or on the bench, and if we ever recall them we shall do it not because of their general conduct on the bench, but because we are mad about some particular decision—which the recall will not change—just as some of the people in one of the judicial districts of Oregon are now trying to recall a judge whose charge to the jury on the Oregon law of self defense is assumed to have set free a murderer whom the recallers think should be hanged. What is wanted of the recall is that judges may be terrorized into deciding law points to produce the result which popular clamor demands, regardless of what the judge thinks the law really is. It would never be invoked in a single instance except as the result of popular clamor against some special decision, in which the judge is far more likely to be right than the people. It is as wicked to terrorize a judge as to bribe him, and far more dangerous to society.

No Protection Against Venality

If it be said that we elect venal legislators, I reply that for the most part we do not. Some of us do. I have helped to do it. We do elect many who are not very wise and who have a certain weakness of moral fiber that is common to most of us. But if we have not the capacity to choose faithful and capable representatives whom we know or can find out about, we certainly have not—at least I have not—the capacity to pass wisely upon laws whose effect we do not know and cannot find out about. . . .

Graft the Enemy of Society

Let us get down to business. What we really want is to get rid of graft and there I—possibly because I have no occasion to profit by graft—am with you. I believe that whoever gives or receives a bribe should be sent to the penitentiary, and be forever debarred from decent society. And the money paid to a political boss now in the penitentiary was a bribe, whether or not any Supervisor ever got a cent of it. It was paid to buy Supervisors' votes, and it did buy them, and in that was the crime. The distribution of the boodle was of no public consequence.

You will never by any contrivance stop graft until its exposure involves social ostracism. So long as known grafters are received into decent society, and known graftees are elected presidents of labor unions, grafting will go on, because those things are infallible signs that the people are willing that it shall go on. Anything which the people really hate carries social stigma. When former President Roosevelt refused to attend a public dinner if a certain public man was present, he made one of his good hits. It is known that he once made a similar requirement in this city. Good for Roosevelt.

But that sort of bribery is the least of our venality, although that permeates the community as all know who have occasion to deal with public officials or others in a fiduciary capacity. Commissions and presents are expected to be paid and are paid, which ought not to be paid and which improperly increase costs to buyers.

Bribes Paid by the Public

Our greatest curse is bribes paid by salaries from the public treasury. One may, in a certain sense, respect the robust rascality of one who takes his bribe money out of his own pocket or even from the treasury of the corporation whose affairs he administers, but to steal it out of the public treasury is sneaky and contemptible. And yet we do it right along and it is not considered a social sin.

Are not the workers for the purification of our politics as clamorous for the spoils as those whom they helped to displace, and do they not make the lives of those who have the appointing power as miserable? Is not yielding up a portion of one's pay virtually the price of public employment in this city today? And is not the division of the patronage if they get it the most vexing question among those who can influence elections for the bread and butter offices? Is not the hope of a job for oneself or his friends the mainspring of political effort among the rank and file? And is not that to say that the money of all shall be taken to advance the fortunes of the few?

Our grievance against corporations who debauch our politics is not that they have caused bad laws to be passed or even that they have prevented the passage of good laws, although they have done that; but that they have caused the nomination of known thieves to legislative positions, and of incompetent, venal or prejudiced men to administrative or judicial positions, and required as the price of their support to aspirants to high office that the salaries paid by the State shall be used to pay the wages of the contemptible beings who do their dirty work.

And yet we people, alleged to be all wise and certain to do right, have regularly elected the men whom we knew to have been selected by these means for the purpose of plundering the public, even if most of them are personally honest.

No Remedy in Direct Legislation

And we shall never cure any of these ills by the initiative, the referendum or recall. What we shall do is by ill-considered legislation, enacted under the spur of passion, to hamper and distress legitimate enterprise and industry, not intentionally but certainly, drive out capital and increase unemployment, increase litigation, arrest economic and social progress and keep the community in a ferment first for new fangled and drastic legislation, and later for repealing or changing it just as we are doing now.

The wave of emotional politics which is passing over the country comes from the failure to realize that the irresistible forces of nature act upon man as upon other forms of life; an exaggerated idea of our poser to change the direction of these forces; and apparently no conception whatever of the danger of too forcible interference. I have faith that mankind will work out its moral salvation, but that we shall do it sooner by working with nature rather than against her. There was direct legislation of all kinds in ancient Greece and that civilization perished in rottenness. There were direct primaries—doubtless preceded by "conferences"—when the warriors of the Germanic forests raised their chosen leaders upon their shields. But the progress of civilization evolved better methods and we ought not to revert to barbaric ways. . . .

The Real Remedies for Misgovernment

The remedy for our evils is not in direct legislation but in our own purification; in the creation of public sentiment which makes the giving or acceptance of public employment as wages for political service infamous, whether the patronage be dispensed by a President of the United States or a boss of San Francisco; in driving from decent society bribe givers and bribe takers; in giving honor, and not abuse, to faithful public service, no matter whether of our own party or not, thereby creating conditions which will not disgust men of character with public service, and turn it into the hands of those willing to peddle offices for power; in making political contributions by public servants, or their acceptance, a felony; in abstaining from the practice each of our own petty grafts in private as well as public life, thereby creating a habit of mind which abhors graft. . . .

. . . Reform is needed not in our social machinery but in our social character. . . . And so long as our habit of mind permits us to regard graft of any kind otherwise than with loathing and contempt, we shall find such superficial and fussy measures as the initiative, referendum and recall not even palliative, but inconsequential, tiresome, deceiving, foolish, puttering and useless.

15. A Debate on the Non-Partisan Ballot: Rowell in Favor, Shortridge Opposed

Cross-filing, the most problematical part of the Progressive heritage, developed in 1911 as a hybrid of the direct primary system and the tradition of nonpartisanship in local elections. As early as 1866 California parties were empowered to nominate candidates in direct primary elections instead of in the last democratic caucus or convention methods. The primary was made mandatory in 1909. It was also the custom in California to elect judges, city and county officials, and school district officers without assigning them any party labels. When Hiram Johnson was faced by a split of the GOP in 1911 and a possible loss of leadership, he succeeded in having the 1909 primary law modified so that the candidate of a party was not required to have supported that party in the previous election. When Johnson switched to the Progressive Party in 1912 he sought a second modification, one that expressly allowed a candidate to seek the nominations of two parties at once. This he sought, and secured, in anticipation of becoming both the Progressive and the GOP candidate for reelection. Thus cross-filing came about less as an article of Progressive faith than as a means of keeping power.

Finally, to carry the matter one step further, the Progressives proposed the non-partisan election of governors and members of the legislature. That came within an ace of victory. The legislature passed such an act and the governor signed it on April 28, 1915, but it was submitted to the voters as a referendum and overturned on October 26, 1915. In a sense the defeat made little difference because, as Carey McWilliams has written, cross-filing by itself "made a shambles of party regularity and party discipline in California."

In the following debate at the Commonwealth Club in 1915[2] *the first speaker at the rostrum was Chester Harvey Rowell, editor and publisher of the* Fresno Republican *from 1989 to 1920, one of the luminaries of California progressivism. Rowell had emigrated from Illinois, where he was born in 1867. He helped organize and he presided over the Lincoln-Roosevelt League from 1907 to 1911 when it spearheaded the Johnson victory, and thereafter he held several governmental posts. Rowell's opponent at the club, Samuel Morgan Shortridge, was an attorney and stalwart*

[2]"Non-Partisan Ballot Acts," *Transactions of the Commonwealth Club of California*, (1915), 463-486.

Republican who had supported Taft in 1911. He too was a midwesterner, having been born in Iowa in 1884. Shortridge was elected to the U.S. Senate in 1921 and served there until 1927.

While this debate is not specifically about cross-filing, the basic arguments on its behalf might be deduced from the discussion of nonpartisanship. In any event, the central theme, whether there should or should not be a party system in California, came very clearly to the fore.

Argument by Chester H. Rowell

Non-partisanship in the government of California is not a thing that is proposed as a novelty. It is a thing that is, and long has been. Some one has estimated that ninety-nine per cent of the elective officers in California are now chosen by the non-partisan system, and it is proposed merely to add the other one per cent. You held an election in San Francisco last week by the non-partisan system. You held last year a state election as to the office of State Superintendent of Public Instruction, Justices of the Supreme Court, and Justices of the District Court of Appeals by the non-partisan system. Two years ago in all the counties of California the election was held, as it had been held long before that in San Francisco, for choosing county officers by the non-partisan system. If the non-partisan system destroys parties, then parties have long since been destroyed. It is proposed now to complete that system by adding to it the nine offices that remain out of the thousands that have already been included in it. The importance of the proposition is, that among these nine offices are included the office of Governor and the office of member of the Legislature. . . .

The real issue is upon the two offices of Governor and member of the Legislature. As to those, we may say that non-partisanship is already the actual policy of the people of California, even with the awkward machinery of party nomination. Take the situation at the last election in regard to the State Controller, State Treasurer and Attorney General. In the party primaries all three of the parties, by the vote of the majority of the members of all three of the parties, nominated the same man. In other words, the people insisted on making non-partisan nominations, even with the awkward machinery of partisan primaries. If you have already established non-partisanship in substance, it is only an elementary matter of efficiency to provide tools that fit the job.

As to the Governor, there was no attempt on the part of any candidate for Governor to run for the nomination of any party except his own; but it happened that the nominee of a party which had about one-fourth of the registration received almost exactly half of all the votes. If the people of California had voted at the primary in the same way they did at the election, it is a mathematical fact that the Governor would have received the nomination of all three parties.

As to the Legislature: the members of the Assembly are eighty in number; and if I remember the figures rightly, they had between them 153 party nominations. Among them was a small minority of stubborn partisans who had rigidly refused to have more than one party nominations. As to the rest, the average member of the Legislature was the nominee of more than two parties; one of them was the nominee of five parties, and a considerable number of them were the nominees of three parties, and most of them of two. Hence, the people in the election of the last Legislature broke over the machinery of party nominations and made non-partisan nominations.

To sum up, we have already established by law non-partisan nominations for nearly all the offices in this state; and we merely propose to add to it the few more offices as to which the people, even without the machinery for it, have already insisted on making non-partisan nominations.

There is not, and there never was, any reason why you should select members of the Legislature by virtue of their opinions on the tariff question. The Constitution of the United States forbids them to have any official opinions on that subject. Logically there never was any relation between parties and state offices, any more than there was between parties and local offices. But formerly we used the machinery of parties for both state and local offices because we had not yet learned to devise any other; and when we devised other machinery for local offices, we used it for them, and found it worked. You used it in San Francisco last week so successfully that you got rid, by the first election, of nearly the whole ticket. You had nine offices to fill at the election last week, and you filled seven of them by majority vote and got rid of them. Suppose, instead of that, you had party primaries. You would have nominated candidates of five parties, and you would have at the next election, instead of three people to vote for, forty-five; and it is likely that among the forty-five would not have been the candidate for Mayor who did receive the majority of all the votes in the city, and who was thereby demonstrated to have been the choice of the majority. In other words, by actual test in this city, within a week you have found that the non-partisan system is more practical and more efficient many times over than the partisan system could possibly have been made.

You began that system in San Francisco and by gradual experience we have expanded that system from cities to counties. In the counties now we elect all the officials by non-partisan methods. A recent canvass of county officials has been made as to their opinion in regard to it. Not all the returns are in, but those that have come so far show that the county officials who have been through the mill are twelve to one in favor of the non-partisan system as to county officials. We have elected judges by the non-partisan system, and by actual test we have succeeded in electing eighty per cent of them at the first election. By the party system we would not have succeeded in electing any of them at the first election, and we would confuse the issue as to all of them at the final election.

So we have reached the time that we are practically able to do what logically we always should have done—elect the Governor and the members of the Legislature by the same method that we familiarly elect all our other officials.

There are only two logical and practical things to do: One of them is to go forward and finish the non-partisan system by including in it the very few offices which remain. The other is to go backward and abolish the non-partisan system by putting back into the party system all the offices that have up to now been taken out of it. A study of the arguments made on both sides shows that those who are protesting against this final extension of the non-partisan system, propose to take the first step in a campaign which shall go backward and backward until they have first applied the partisan system to all the offices that used to be included in it, and shall then abolish the direct primary, and restore the old convention system of party nominations. Logically, there is no choice except one or the other of these systems, and that logic is recognized by both sides.

The arguments made in favor of the partisan system are based almost exclusively on the fiction of party responsibility. It is a very plausible and pleasant theory. The only trouble with it is that there never was any such thing. There are no parties that are or ever were responsible for the officials of this state. In fact, the momentary situation is that there are no parties nationally that are responsible. But I hope we will get them. Is the Democratic party responsible for President Wilson? Everybody knows that President Wilson is responsible for the Democratic party. (Laughter.) That is an illogical situation, though at present it is an extremely practical and perhaps desirable situation. But that has always been the situation—that party responsibility did not exist.

It is also argued that we will substitute personal for party government. In the first place, we never had party government: and when we had the pretended machinery of party government in full operation over the entire state, what we did have then was personal government by persons who elected themselves. The worst we can get under the new system would be personal government by persons whom we elect. . . .

Argument by Samuel M. Shortridge

. . . .

I say that this proposed law is un-American in letter, spirit, and purpose. It is the most politically intolerant law ever proposed in California. When analyzed it is seen to be a species of political bigotry. It strikes at the liberty of the citizen in denying to him the right freely to organize and to act in concert in respect to matters political affecting the welfare of the state. . . .

A political party is simply an organization or association of citizens who believe in fundamental principles and seek, through proper governmental action, to carry those principles into operation.

Thus far I suppose that most aggressive reformer who mistakes change for progress will admit that we are upon sound and safe grounds. . . .

I plant myself on this proposition: The right to organize and maintain political parties or organizations is an inherent right of the people, a fundamental right, a constitutional right. Under the constitution of this state, by the provision which I have quoted, the duty is imposed upon the Legislature to guard and protect the people in the exercise of that right. But instead of enacting such a law, we have before us a proposed statute which directly and indirectly undermines and destroys that right, strikes down party organization, and denies the people any and all protection in the relation of this constitutional right.

Now, I trust it will not be offensive to my friend upon the other side—and, of course, in speech I have the utmost respect for my friend on my right—when I call his attention to decisions of our Supreme Court in respect to this fundamental right. . . . The thought of it is that any law which will seek to destroy that right, hamper the people, shackle the people, embarrass them in the exercise of their right to organize, and to act in unison, is violative of the organic law and cannot be upheld. . . .

The thought which has run through every primary law in this series was that when citizens organized themselves together they were entitled to declare their principles, and to seek to nominate men committed to those principles who, as their representatives, through legislation or executive action, would carry out those adopted principles; and they argued that the Democratic party, this historical Democratic party which has been controlling this government for half its life, and the Republican party which for half a century guided the destinies of the republic, or any other party, be it new-born or ancient, was entitled to shape its own policies and purposes, and not be intruded into or upon by interlopers who would seek to frustrate it and defeat its very purpose and its every plan. . . .

My friends here concede, as I understand it, that national parties are well and good, and that we may as citizens divide honorably as to national matters. They concede that party organization is wise in respect to matters affecting the republic. I contend that citizens may divide in respect to great political questions affecting the affairs of a state; and since they divide as to the problems affecting the welfare of the state, they should have a right to organize, and the laws should protect their organization—all to the end that they may seek thus by co-operation and by acting together to carry out their ideas or their principles.

My learned friend here argues that because forsooth we have adopted non-partisanship in local, domestic or municipal affairs, and extended it, as he says, to the judiciary, and possibly some other party administrative offices, therefore it shall go on. That assumes that what we have already done has been beneficial to California. It assumes that we have better government, better citizens, better men, and better women today than we have ever had before—that government is better. It assumes something I do not admit. I say that in municipal affairs, I say that in state affairs, the welfare of this state was guarded, its industries were advanced, its people multiplied, under systems existing before these new dispensations. I say that in municipal affairs, and in our state affairs, California has had splendid officials on bench and in executive chair. For one, I think that under the old system, Frederick Low, Governor Haight, Governor Bartlett, were as high and honorable and just and patriotic as any of their successors. I think that Pond and Bartlett and others in San Francisco were just as honorable and just as capable as any of their successors; and I think that Stephen M. White, with his poverty and his genius, unafraid to stand forth as a Democrat, was equal perhaps to one who now fills his place.

[Concluding Remarks]

MR. SHORTRIDGE: . . . . Now, gentlemen, if it be true—and I think they admit it—that national parties are essential, I am one who believes in state parties in order that the national parties may be furthered and strengthened. Any man knows little of the affairs of this state if he says that the destruction of state organizations will not affect national organizations; and if national organizations are essential, as is conceded, state organizations are needed in order to assist the national party.

Now, gentlemen, if this be so, if you believe in the people, if you think they have some right, why don't you let them exercise their right? Why seek to hamper them; why seek to shackle them; why prevent them from organizing in the way they have organized, and acting as in their judgment they think wise? National parties have been recognized from the beginning of this government. There has always been party government in this nation. The only man who perhaps was above and beyond all party considerations was the Father of his Country. But before his second term expired there were militant and aggressive political parties, the one led by the great Hamilton, and the other by the illustrious Jefferson; and from the Jeffersonian, then called the Democratic-Republican party, down to this hour, there has been the great cleavage between the American people upon great national questions, and there has been party government. Is there not party government today? Could there be anything in the nature of successful administration in Washington without organization? Congress would become a mob, and President Wilson could not carry out a policy at all. We have a great state, a thousand miles long, with millions of people dividing upon many matters; and yet we are told that we should act as though we were a little New England village gathered under a chestnut tree to consider the affairs of the town. We are a great state, and men will divide, and wisely divide.... I go further, and I ask you, gentlemen, and I ask others, if what you propose has resulted in better government? Has the millennium come? And how will you individually seek to accomplish anything except by organization?...

Let us be frank with one another. Honorable men, men of character, men of intelligence, men who look behind and forward, may differ upon these questions, and the very fact that they differ and seek to co-operate builds up organizations and parties.

Now, my friend Mr. Monroe suggests that independent of all laws the people may assemble together, and he is right. There is no Legislature that can deny the people that right. But since the government has taken over the instrumentalities of election, and the full control of elections, these proposed laws destroy our rights to thus assemble and to put forward candidates committed to certain definite policies. My contention has been and is, that the law should not make it impossible for men to carry out their matured plans.

In the State of California you tell me that we have an administration that has achieved great and splendid results. Why, gentlemen, if all you say be true, if all you claim be true, if you have worked great reforms, if you have removed all inequalities, if you have redeemed and regenerated and disenthralled California, if you have made us a happy people, why don't you let the laws alone? Under the present laws the present administration has come into power. True, some walk under half a dozen banners, but they are in power, and with a natural inclination of men possessed of power, seek to retain it. The present executive sought a Republican nomination in 1910. He was nominated by the Republican party, elected as such, and served his term. In 1912 he sought to abandon that party and form a new one. He had a perfect constitutional right to do so and the several gentlemen who serve us today had a right to seek office through multi-party nominations. They tell us they have wrought a great good. Heaven bless them if it all be true—and let us hope it is. And why now, having achieved all this—and I see some of my friends that we walked and fought and bled together with in other days (laughter) who are now in happy possession of office. May you have long life, but not long tenure. (Laughter.)...

MR. ROWELL: ...Mr. Shortridge has, with much eloquence, which I would not have power to emulate, even if I had the time, defended the right of public assembly, and has defined political parties. As to political parties let me, by Mr. Shortridge's definition, introduce to you one of the most important and certainly the wisest political party of California, because it is here assembled and is the Commonwealth Club; which, by his definition, is a political party, but which is not thereby entitled to have the State of California print its name on the political ballot, and does not need that privilege to exercise all the political power it wants to. . . .

You do now elect 16,000 officers in California by the non-partisan system, and it is proposed to add 131 more, and by all the arguments that have been made, the argument is against the 16,000 as well as the 131. . . .

As a matter of fact, there is only one argument against these non-partisan bills, and that is a tremendously powerful argument, one of the most powerful arguments in human nature or politics. It is the argument of inertia. People are against these bills because their habits of thought were established in another way and it is hard to change their habits of thought.

Permit me to call attention to an anomaly. You have heard the eloquence of Mr. Shortridge against the chaos of determining things by direct vote of the people. Therefore, because they believe in representative government, and do not believe in burdening the people with these things, those who believe with him appeal for the vote of the people against [these bills] by referendum. . . . [T]hose who have invoked the referendum are those who do not believe in it. . . .

There is in favor of these bills the presumption that comes from their passage by the Legislature, and the fact that the system is already in operation as to nearly everything. Those who oppose this slight extension of the system frankly say that they are opposed to it as to all the rest of the offices. Mr. Shortridge has himself so indicated, and so have all the others who have argued in print or otherwise. This means that if it is not extended, that if the attempt to extend it includes the little that is left and were to be defeated this time, you are to take a step going clear back to the old system. You are now to choose merely between adding the one per cent and finishing the system or going back to the old system. The choice presented to you frankly by both sides is between the two opposing systems.

We have the long record of party government given to us in the remarks of Mr. Sexton, and by our own historical knowledge we know how it has worked in California. As pointed out by Professor Plehn, we ought to have state parties, we ought to have municipal parties. At present we do. All of you who are Progressives, and most of you who are Republicans and Democrats, voted for Governor Johnson. The returns show it. That was a state party split up between our national parties. You had an election here last week, and you had three city parties in it. They did not have any name, but every one of you knew which one you belonged to and why. . . . [T]hose of you who were Republicans and Democrats last time had no chance to participate in the nomination of a Progressive Governor, because you were tremendously interested in the question who was to be the nominee for the United States Senator. You had to vote also as between the one or the other nominees for Governor when the returns show that you did not have the slightest interest in who was nominated, or the slightest intention to vote for either one. You had the situation where the very opportunity to exercise your party right to choose your candidate for United States Senator compelled you to exercise a right you did not want—to choose a candidate for Governor that you were not going to vote for. . . .

16. Dean E. McHenry Comments

On the occasion of the Gold Rush centennial, Prof. Dean E. McHenry set out to write a survey[3] *that would briefly answer the question, "What makes California politics tick?" Professor McHenry sees four basic tendencies in California: (1) weakness of political parties; (2) extraordinary influence of pressure groups; (3) marked independence of the electorate; and (4) "extreme and unique political movements." Then, under the heading "Historical Factors," he elaborates the background of these four tendencies.*

Professor McHenry became chancellor of the University of California, Santa Cruz, in 1961, after a distinguished academic career. Born in California in 1910, he attended U.C.L.A., Stanford, and Berkeley, where he received his Ph.D. in political science. He is author and co-author of articles and books that include the American Federal Government *(with J.H. Ferguson, in 1943),* State and Local Government in California, *with Winston Crouch and others (1952), and works on the British Labor Party and on the "third force" in Canada.*

In the course of McHenry's discussion one notices an antagonism not to Progressives as such, but to the long-range consequences of some of their stratagems, e.g., cross-filing. It was this very sort of criticism of cross-filing that led to its repeal in 1959 and a partial resurgence of partisanship in California. One should ask, however, whether other conclusions of his 1948 analysis may still be relevant.

Historical Factors

The transcontinental railroad was completed in 1869. It brought radical changes in California's political and economic conditions, and it remained the acknowledged political boss for some forty years. The methods of the company were revealed in the exhibits and testimony of a notable court case and of a congressional investigation. The railroad got into politics, national and state, in order to secure grants and concessions and to defend itself against discrimination and blackmail.

In the early nineties Leland Stanford retired from the presidency of the railroad and was succeeded by Huntington. William F. Herrin then was chosen legal counsel for the company whose political activities for the next two decades remained in Herrin's province. The machine he headed maintained a close control over local and state politics that was relatively unbroken until the progressive "revolution" of 1910. This control amounted to domination of the Republican party and, to some extent, of the Democratic party as well. There were Southern Pacific candidates, often on both tickets, at each election.

The machine yoke was thrown off by the victory of the progressive forces in the election of November, 1910, whose campaign was conducted by the Lincoln-Roosevelt League, which had been organized three years earlier. Progressive standard-bearer was Hiram W. Johnson, who was elected Governor and who remained leader of the reform movement until his resignation to enter the United States Senate in 1917. In that six-year period, California had one of the finest administrations any state has ever enjoyed, and much of California's reputation for "advanced" legislation dates back to this period. Johnson was succeeded by another progressive Governor and the progressive majority in the Legislature continued.

The conservative forces returned in the election of 1922. There was no turnover in party. As in states of the deep south, the real conflict occurred in the party primary, for California was a one party state. The Republican primary settled whether progressive or conservative factions should govern. In 1926 the progressives came back under the leadership of C. C. Young; four years later the pendulum swung back to the conservative side, led by James Rolph, Jr.

[3]Dean E. McHenry, "The Pattern of California Politics," *Western Political Quarterly*, I (March, 1948), 46-53.

By 1934 it began to look as if the Democrats might threaten the long spell of Republican rule. However, the nomination of Upton Sinclair proved too much for the voters to take in one dose, and a conservative Republican regime under Frank F. Merriam secured a victory. In 1938 a New Deal Democrat, Culbert L. Olson, won the governorship. He was the first and only Democratic Governor since 1889. For the first time since 1893, the Assembly, too, was Democratic. The Senate remained Republican, as it has been since 1889. In 1942 the Democratic tide was halted and turned back with the election of Republican Governor Earl Warren and the resurgency of Republican strength in both houses of the Legislature.

While any recent political history of California will mention frequently the term *Party*, it would be erroneous to assume that a truly responsible system of party government has been in operation. Thus, from 1910 to 1934 the important cleavage was not between parties but among factions of the Republican party. When, belatedly, the New Deal did come to state affairs, the Democratic administration was careless and soon lost public confidence. Since 1942 there has been a sort of ''era of good feeling,'' with party lines substantially obscured in the Legislature and in much of the state. . . .

Perversions of the Primary

When California adopted a direct primary law in 1909, the legislation contained the usual type of party test to be complied with by aspirants for nominations. In order to qualify, the candidate must declare that he had supported the party at the preceding general election. This test was modified in 1911. It was abolished outright in 1913 when candidates were given expressly the right to seek the nomination of more than one party. The practice that has grown up under this provision is called ''cross-filing.'' After thirty-five years of experience with it, cross-filing deserves the designation of one of the greatest barriers to party responsibility yet devised.

Cross-filing is in very general use by candidates for state executive, state legislative, and congressional offices. . . . The successful cross-filer manages to secure both major party nominations. Then, at the general election, his name appears on the ballot together with either the ''Republican-Democratic'' label, or with the ''Democratic-Republican'' label, his own party being named first. The final election becomes a mere formality for the successful cross-filer, who is spared the expense, energy, and worry of conducting a campaign. In the 1946 California general election the following offices were, in effect, filled in the primaries by one candidate's securing both major party nominations: Governor, Secretary of State, Controller, Treasurer, all four members of the Board of Equalization, one-half of the Representatives in Congress, and about three-fourths of the state legislators.

The basic objection to cross-filing is that it destroys party responsibility. No party can be held accountable to any extent for the actions of its nominee when that person is not even a member of the party. Another objection is that the system often produces a minority winner, a candidate who cross-files successfully, but in so doing, fails to poll a clear majority of the votes cast. If he has the largest number of votes for each party, then he is declared the nominee of each despite the fact that a real majority has not favored him. The average voter finds the cross-filing scheme highly deceptive, for he is confronted with a long primary ballot filled with names of candidates about whom he knows little, particularly those for minor offices. Consequently, although he wishes to have nominees who support the general program of his party, he may cast his ballot, without realizing it, for candidates of the opposing party. In the general election, then, the electorate receives a ballot that offers no real candidate alternatives for a large share of the partisan offices listed thereon. The results are capricious and it is obvious that such a system places a premium on deception and political irresponsibility.

Cross-filing is even more incomprehensible and illogical when other aspects of the primary law are examined. Thus, the latter provided since 1917 that a candidate is disqualified from holding another party's nomination unless he also secures his own. Nearly every primary election produces one or more disqualifications; the appropriate party committees are empowered to fill vacancies so created. The disqualification clause is a feeble gesture back toward some measure of party loyalty. It conflicts sharply with the principal argument for cross-filing, namely that voters should be allowed to choose the best candidates regardless of party lines. Another contradiction is found in the test of party affiliation required of voters but not of candidates. California has the closed primary. No voter may participate in a party primary unless he is registered on the rolls with that party. The voter is kept in the strait jacket of party regularity on the grounds that choosing party candidates is a party matter, and may not be participated in by outsiders. Yet, cross-filing gives the candidates license to trespass in the reservation of parties other than his own.

Other Influences

Initiative, referendum, and recall—have played a minor role in the pattern of California politics. Even during the Olson administration (1939-1943), when there was a revival of the idea of party government, actual party responsibility was interrupted by the use of the initiative and referendum. When the Democratic caucus agreed upon a course of action in the Legislature, its affirmative actions could be held up and defeated through the referendum, and its negative decisions reversed through the statutory or constitutional initiative. Moreover, the recall may be used to terminate the services of an office holder before the normal time, thus relieving a party of responsibility for an unpopular member of its team, and interfering either with the operation of the united front or with the collective responsibility of the party's office holders.

Likewise, the widespread use of the merit system in California state and local governments cuts off one of the more obvious ways of providing nutrition for deserving Democrats and reputable Republicans. The civil service is so influential as a pressure group in politics, and the public is so alert to the values of the merit basis of public employment that the system may be expected to be strengthened, rather than to diminish.

Finally, sectionalism both of the urban-rural and north-south varieties has proven a barrier to the unity necessary to build strong, state-wide parties. Since 1926 the state has been operating under a plan of representation in its senate that gives rural areas and small counties control over that body and minimizes urban representation. Los Angeles county, for example, contains 40 percent of the population of the state, yet receives only one-fortieth of the Senate representation. Two small counties together form a senatorial district that contains little more than one-tenth of one percent of the state's population, yet also gets one of the forty senatorships. So long as there is no agreement on the basis of representation, it is difficult to have cordial relations within parties.

North versus south and San Francisco versus Los Angeles controversies still exist, but are less violent than a generation ago. In the great reapportionment struggles of 1921 and 1931, party lines were torn asunder and the sectional groups grappled in a free-for-all fight of major proportions. Many sectional considerations enter into internal party arrangements today. By state law, the state chairmanship of each party must alternate yearly between north and south. The reapportionment proceedings of 1941 were relatively harmonious. Actually, for the first time since the turn of the century the really significant differences were more partisan than sectional.

Parties or No Parties

Nonpartisanship for local, judicial, and school offices is another potent cause of the weakness of parties. The reformers of 1910 and after blamed parties, at least in part, for corruption and venality in municipal and county affairs. They argued convincingly that there was no Republican way to pave a street or Democratic method of disposing of garbage, that local government was largely a matter of administration, and that the judicial bench as well as the school classroom must not be tainted by party influences. The effects of making many offices nonpartisan were devastating to party organization. They reduced the number of partisan elective offices of government within the state from several thousand to some hundred and fifty state and federal offices. Those remaining under the partisan plan were so far removed from the precinct and other local party leaders, that the difficult struggle to keep party machinery functioning on an active basis, finally was given up by these local units.

Today, in the great urban centers of California, the ballot has remained long, and the voter is faced with the impossible task of passing judgment on the stewardship in office of a host of individuals about whom he knows little or nothing. Deprived of party labels, he seeks help from the easiest sources. First, there is the local newspaper; the more obscure the office the greater the influence of press recommendations. Second, there are the channels of communication that can be commanded by those most able to pay. Napoleon found that divine aid was on the side with the strongest legions, and an American general argued for getting there "fustest with the mostest." He who enjoys press support and has the money to buy plenty of radio time, billboard space, and printing services has an inside track for winning the votes of the confused voter.

Of course, some party organization does exist in California, but it is largely window dressing. County central committees are the only ones elected by the voters of the party. Below this level are odds and ends of local and district clubs and associations with no clearly defined authority or relationship to the county committees. Above is the state central committee, a mammoth affair that is made up on an *ex officio* and appointive basis. The state convention, a biennial occasion, is composed of the party's nominees (or their appointees) for the elective state and federal offices in the state. In the current decade the central committees of the two major parties number over six hundred each, and the state conventions over one hundred fifty. The duties of both are nominal and vague.

Conclusion

California politics is different from other states more in terms of emphasis and degree than in any fundamental forces. Through a combination of historical factors, the nature of the population, and some unique legal devices, party has been relegated to a meager and nominal role—impotent, starved, ill organized, and dishonored. Into the vacuum created by the shrinking of party, the pressure groups have entered. Purposeful, well organized, and well financed, they have thrown their weight and influence around both in campaigns and in the Legislature.

Denied the "crutch" of party both through the adoption of nonpartisanship for all local, school, and judicial offices, and through the deceptive practice of cross-filing, the voter has been forced to grope through the excessively long ballot without proper aid. Since he is confronted with a task that staggers the most alert citizen, the average man must pick up his civic data on a hand-to-mouth basis. The newspapers thereby secure a great boost in political influence. So do they who can hire the principal media of information dissemination.

Although possessing many of the new fangled trappings of democracy, California falls far short of truly responsible politics. In every state and nation of any size, political parties have been found essential to the proper functioning of democratic politics in big government. Therefore, California should explore every avenue of strengthening parties. Reform ought to begin with the abolition of cross-filing, a most deceptive and pernicious practice. Party bodies should be given sufficient power to activate themselves. They should have freedom to adopt their own organizational forms. Party committees or pre-primary conventions might well be empowered to indicate preferred candidates on the primary ballot. The convention plan of nominating state-wide candidates, as is used in New York, should be given full consideration. The existing situation is unsatisfactory and untenable. Either parties ought to be abolished outright or they ought to be given conditions under which they can live and provide their services.

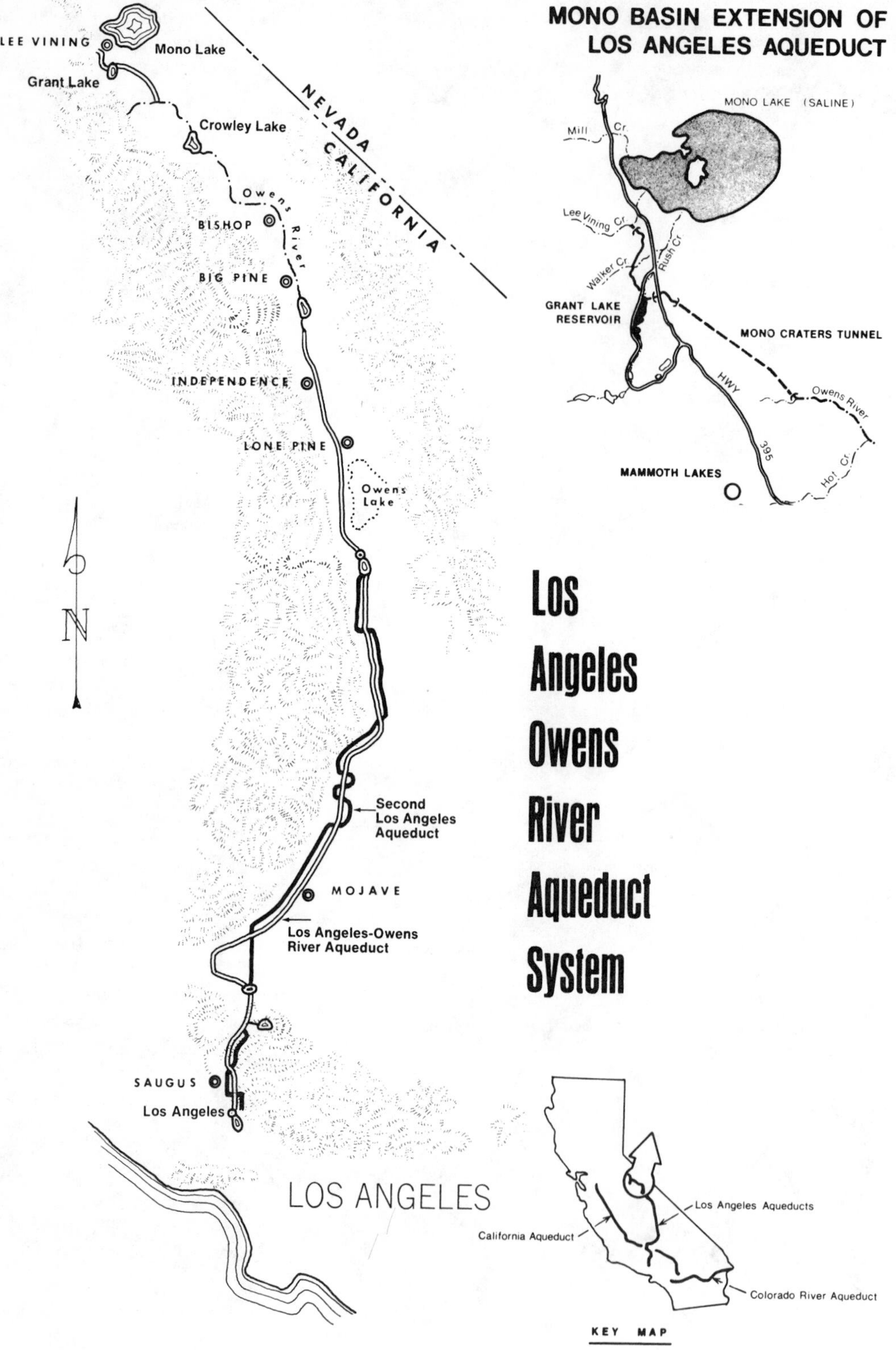

MONO BASIN EXTENSION OF LOS ANGELES AQUEDUCT
MONO LAKE (SALINE)
Mill Cr.
Lee Vining Cr.
Walker Cr.
Rush Cr.
GRANT LAKE RESERVOIR
MONO CRATERS TUNNEL
HWY 395
Owens River
Hot Cr.
MAMMOTH LAKES
LEE VINING
Mono Lake
Grant Lake
Crowley Lake
NEVADA
CALIFORNIA
Owens River
BISHOP
BIG PINE
INDEPENDENCE
LONE PINE
Owens Lake
N
Second Los Angeles Aqueduct
MOJAVE
Los Angeles-Owens River Aqueduct
SAUGUS
Los Angeles
LOS ANGELES
Los Angeles Owens River Aqueduct System
Los Angeles Aqueducts
California Aqueduct
Colorado River Aqueduct
KEY MAP

The Owens Valley struggle was not one of right against wrong. . . . There was justice on both sides, and chicanery on both sides. The valley people were motivated not just by a desire to maintain their homes, but by a desire to sell land at an inflated value. Personal profit motives spurred the activities of some city representatives. Eventually a fairly amicable agreement was reached, but not until after many had been badly hurt financially, and a lasting reservoir of ill will had been filled.

—**Raymond F. Dasmann, *The Destruction of California*, 1965.**[1]

CHAPTER 8

LOS ANGELES IN THE OWENS RIVER VALLEY
"Rape" or Enlightened Self-interest?

A. *Owens River Valley*
B. *Mono Lake*

When the first city arose in the Tigris-Euphrates Valley some thousands of years ago and its inhabitants began lording it over the rustics in the hinterlands, the stage was set for a contest between city and country whose drama would be played out in all civilizations. Indeed, it is likely to continue long into the future. City dwellers have always been susceptible to the charge of imperialism for their seemingly insatiable hunger for the territory and natural resources of the backlands. They, in turn, have always retorted that their acquisitions provide the basis for the world's material progress and civilization. In the United States, a nation with strong agrarian roots and a latter-day flowering of cities, the rivalry has from time to time reached classic proportions.

Nowhere in American history can one find a more dramatic instance of the urban-rural contest than in the effort of Los Angeles to siphon off water from the Owens River Valley, and in the resistance—at times forcible—of the Owensites. At best, Los Angeles' action represents the wise and foresighted policy of the city planners to ensure an adequate water supply for a potentially great metropolis; at worst, an intrusion into a peaceful agricultural valley for selfish motives and by unjust means. How interpreters have seen it has depended on their attitudes toward cities, farmers, businesspeople, or great feats of engineering. But most admit that the scheme was an amazingly ambitious one, involving the acquisition of water rights and land along the Owens River, the building of an aqueduct some 230 miles long, the negotiation with the federal government which owned some of the right of way, the annexation of the San Fernando Valley to the city of Los Angeles, and the voting of a bond issue to pay for the aqueduct.

Today, partly because of the entrepreneurs who brought off the scheme in the period 1904 to 1928, the Los Angeles water supply system is the envy of most other big cities in the nation. But those who look closely at the way it was developed may be puzzled as to some of the details—for instance, whether or not the negotiations of ex-Mayor Fred Eaton, of Los Angeles, were legitimate, and whether the federal government greased the skids for Los Angeles. Was an unethical syndicate in operation in the San Fernando Valley? Also, in subsequent efforts to enlarge the flow of water into the aqueduct, did Los Angeles behave in a conscionable manner? Did the financial machinations

[1]Raymond F. Dasmann, *The Destruction of California* (New York: The Macmillan Company, 1965), 145.

of the Watterson brothers of the Owens Valley invalidate their leadership of the resistance? Finally, we may ask whether alternatives to the aqueduct could have been found which would have kept the social peace.

As can be expected in any contest involving the disposition of commodities as precious as desert water and millions of dollars of real estate, the issue was supercharged with emotion. Of the torrent of items published on this subject over the years, the three that appear below manage to bring out most of the abrasive issues that make up the conflict. The selection by Don J. Kinsey says nearly everything nice that has been said about the city's water policy in the Owens Valley; by contrast Morrow Mayo's chapter is a collection of practically all of the ugly charges leveled against it, and Mayo's charges are expressed in the boldest possible terms. The third selection, a passage from a more recent book by Remi Nadeau, attempts to answer Mayo's chapter directly and to offer a cooler and better informed judgment on the topic.

While the first part of this chapter deals directly with the Owens River contest, the second part refers to a struggle that took place 100 miles further north along the Los Angeles aqueduct, at Mono Lake. The waters that feed the huge, 60 square-mile lake supply Angelenos with twenty percent of their drinking water. This diversion from Mono's tributary streams began in 1940 and has resulted in a reduction of the level of the ancient lake by some 40 feet and an increase in its salt content. In turn this has had an impact on the life-cycle of the brine shrimp who inhabit the lake, the numerous birds who visit it, and on the overall air quality of the Mono basin. The future of the delicate ecosystem of the unique lunar-like body of water is clouded. This is evident from a reading of the reprints concerning the square-off between the Mono Lake Committee and the Los Angeles Department of Water and Power (DWP).

All sorts of other noteworthy fights have flared up at California's far-flung water holes (see chapters 11 and 16). . . . In about 1907 San Francisco emulated Los Angeles by reaching far afield for a new water supply. The intrusion of the Bay City into the Hetch Hetchy Valley in the scenic Yosemite area provoked nearly as much furor as that of Los Angeles into the Owens Valley, except that the most vocal opposition came not from farmers but from conservationists. For years, beginning in the late nineteenth century, courts up and down the state were swamped with litigation involving the claims of riparian users versus the claims of users under the right of appropriation. This contest developed when the early legislatures gave equal weight to common law (including riparian claims) and to the far different claims laws established by the miners in the gold diggings. This dispute threatened the entire future of irrigation in California until the 1920's when the courts affirmed a rule of "reasonable use" on any stream of water in the state. Meanwhile, a bitter feud about river debris had developed between the hydraulic miners upstream and the farmers downstream in the Central Valley and has had repercussions in the present century. Also, a battle flared up in the Central Valley in the 1930's and in the Imperial Valley in the 1960's over the federal government's contention that *no* water diverted in a system constructed with federal funds could be delivered to holders of more than 160 acres of land.

Finally, there is the momentous dispute between California and Arizona over the distribution of Colorado River water. That contest came to a head in the U.S. Supreme Court case *Arizona* v. *California* (1953). *(Editor's note)*

A. *The Owens River Valley*

17.
A Benevolent Version, by the Los Angeles Department of Water and Power

As part of a continuous effort to answer criticism, the Los Angeles Department of Water and Power in 1928 published an illustrated booklet giving its side of the dispute with the Owens River Valley. By contrast with the critic's shrill cries of murder and "rape," the author of this public relations document, Don J. Kinsey, employed a soft tone of voice and tried to marshal every argument that would show the city as "statesmanlike" in its dealings with the residents of the Owens Valley.[2] *Kinsey minimizes the early period of possibly devious planning and emphasizes the period of violent reaction by valley residents. He also emphasizes the engineering genius of William Mulholland, the material benefits involved in the aqueduct, the "exhorbitant" demands of valley dwellers, and the personal interests of the Owens Valley leaders, especially the Watterson brothers. Kinsey's ultimate justification was that Los Angeles was a great city in the making, which was driven by necessity to go to Owens Valley in search of water.*

Los Angeles Goes to Inyo

Picture the Owens Valley of Inyo County in 1905.

A community of five thousand people residing in an isolated, mountain and desert bound valley, 4,000 feet above the level of the sea.

The Valley's gold and silver rush had subsided. Most of the mines had been worked out or abandoned.

Its commercial and farming development was hindered because of the Valley's isolation from the reminder of the state. Prior to the building of the Los Angeles Aqueduct, Owens Valley had no standard railroad contact with the outside world. Its nearest railroad connection with southern California markets was Mojave, 180 miles south of the town of Bishop. Between Mojave and the Valley was the Desert, crossed only by a winding, uncertain wagon trail.

By 1905, Los Angeles had become the metropolis of the Pacific Southwest—a city of 160,000 inhabitants situated in the midst of a semi-arid region and growing so rapidly as to be the object of nation-wide wonderment. The Los Angeles river and a few scattering wells constituted the city's only water supply sources. Although more dependable in its habits than many western streams, the Los Angeles river carried a limited supply of water. Even in normal years it was capable of supplying not more that 250,000 persons; in dry years its supply dropped down dangerously near the actual needs of the 160,000 people then living in the city. . . .

With a constantly increasing population and a water supply already taxed to its limit, Los Angeles faced the most vital problem of its history. To meet the necessities of its inhabitants, the city must secure a large additional supply of water. Exhaustive surveys disclosed that no such supply was available within Southern California. Seeking relief from a desperate situation, the people turned to William Mulholland, then, as now, chief engineer of the city's municipal water system.

Mulholland, who had come to America from his birthplace in Ireland when a youth of 14, had

[2]Don J. Kinsey, *The Water Trail: The Story of Owens Valley and the Controversy Surrounding the Efforts of a Great City to Secure the Water Required to Meet the Needs of an Evergrowing Population* (Los Angeles: Department of Water and Power, City of Los Angeles, 1928), 7-39.

won recognition as a hydraulic engineer of marked ability. Starting with the Los Angeles water system in 1878 and becoming its chief engineer in 1886, he already had raised these works from the status of a few haphazard open ditches to a modern and efficient supply and distributing system. This was the man destined to conceive and successfully complete the greatest and most daring aqueduct project the world had ever seen.

Having been told of the Owens River, 250 miles north of Los Angeles, Mulholland decided to investigate the possibilities of this stream.

Arriving in Owens Valley, Mulholland found a river fed by the melting snows of the Sierra Nevadas. A portion of the river's water was used upon the ranch lands of the Valley; the remainder, and the greater share, was wasted by the river as it emptied into Owens Lake—a salt-incrusted sink without an outlet.

After tramping for 40 days over the rugged peaks and blazing desert sands between Owens River and Los Angeles, Mulholland returned to the city and made his report. He stated that the water needed by the city was available in Owens River. To bring this water to Los Angeles would require the construction of an aqueduct 250 miles long. The project, he announced, was feasible; it would cost $24,500,000; it would meet the needs of 2,000,000 people; and, if the people were willing, he was ready to start the job at once.

It was the longest aqueduct ever projected by mind of man. Natural obstacles in the way of its route appeared to be well nigh insurmountable. But the people believed Mulholland could carry through, and by a ratio of 14 to 1 they approved the necessary bond issues. . . .

In the Spring of 1906 there was presented for adoption by Congress a bill authorizing the purchase by the City of Los Angeles of certain government lands in Owens Valley needed as right-of-way for the Aqueduct and as storage reservoir sites. Immediately, it became apparent that the Aqueduct project was faced with vigorous opposition. . . .

Although Los Angeles sought only to use the surplus waters of Owens River, after the needs of the ranchers had been fulfilled, there were those in Owens Valley who opposed the use of this water by the City. They had hopes that the government would build an irrigation project in Owens Valley.

It is true that the Reclamation Service had started a survey of the Owens Valley district in 1904. This region was one of the eleven sections investigated in California by the Reclamation Service, following the adoption of the Reclamation Act in 1902. In view of the fact that only three of the eleven original California tentative projects ever were authorized by the Reclamation Service, it is a matter of grave doubt whether the Government would ever have built an irrigation system for Owens Valley, even though there had been no Los Angeles Aqueduct. . . .

The Aqueduct and the Valley

William Mulholland, at the time he made his preliminary surveys in 1905, had reported that it would require five years and $24,500,000 to construct an aqueduct capable of carrying sufficient water from Owens River to supply the needs of 2,000,000 people in Los Angeles.

It was a tremendous task and a great vision of future growth to be submitted for approval before the citizens of a city whose population then numbered 160,000. Nevertheless, the plan was accepted and the necessary bonds voted by overwhelming majorities. . . .

In October, 1908, actual work on the Aqueduct was started, and just five years later, in October, 1913, the first water from Owens River, ending its 250 mile journey through the completed Aqueduct, came tumbling down the San Fernando Cascades into Los Angeles. When the last bill had been paid it was disclosed that the Aqueduct, including its rights-of-way, had cost $24,460,000 or just $40,000 less than Mulholland's original estimate.

The Los Angeles Aqueduct was hailed throughout the nation as the most spectacular and daring engineering accomplishment ever attempted by an American city. Five thousand men laboring through five blazing desert summers and freezing mountain winters, under the direction of William

Mulholland, had done what many declared was impossible.

When completed, the Aqueduct included 142 separate tunnels, aggregating 53 miles in length; 12 miles of inverted steel siphons, varying from 7 to 11 feet in diameter; 24 miles of open unlined conduit; 39 miles of open concrete-lined conduit, and 97 miles of covered conduit. Additional miles were taken up by three large reservoirs, the largest of these, the Haiwee reservoir, being capable of storing more than twenty billion gallons of water. . . .

Prior to the construction of the standard gauge railroad into Owens Valley, that section of California virtually had been isolated from the remainder of the state. The railroad brought the large and profitable markets of Southern California within easy and economic reach of the Valley farming centers. Hundreds of the Valley's residents were given steady employment during and following the building of the Aqueduct. At the present time the payroll of the City of Los Angeles in Owens Valley amounts approximately to $100,000 a month. . . .

Aqueduct Power

Conceived primarily as a water supply system for a great and growing city, the Aqueduct was destined to bestow upon both Owens Valley and Los Angeles the golden benefits of cheap hydro-electric power.

. . . With its intake on Owens River twelve miles north of the town of Independence and approximately 4,000 feet above sea level, the Aqueduct would drop in its course to Los Angeles to an elevation of 800 feet at its terminus. This fall of 3,200 feet, far more than was required to carry the water to Los Angeles by gravity, immediately suggested hydro-power possibilities to Aqueduct engineers.

The same surveys that disclosed the hydro-power opportunities along the route of the Aqueduct also indicated that the construction of the water line would necessitate the boring of many miles of hard rock tunnels and the excavation of millions of feet of earth for the huge conduits that were to carry the water to the southern city. . . . .

It was recognized that the cheapest and most efficient form of power for such purposes would be electricity. There was, however, no electricity developed and available for use in Owens Valley. Investigations soon disclosed that sufficient hydro-power to meet all Aqueduct construction needs could be developed from several of the mountain creeks that emptied into Owens River along the line of the project. . . .

When the Aqueduct was completed, power from the City's three hydro-electric plants in Owens Valley was released for use by the industries, mines, ranches and townspeople in the Valley. . . .

[Two more plants were installed.] From the five power plants now operated by the City of Los Angeles in Owens Valley a total of 13,000 horsepower is generated. Because it is not economically feasible to carry this quantity of power over a 250-mile transmission line to Los Angeles, the energy is all retained in Owens Valley and made available for the development of that region.

While building and operating the Owens Valley electric system, [Chief Engineer E. F.] Scattergood also gave his attention to the problem of utilizing the great power possibilities of the Aqueduct itself. In accordance with plans worked out by Mr. Scattergood, five power plants, generating a total of 118,000 horsepower of hydro-electric energy, have been placed in operation along the line of the water carrier. . . . .

It was the development of large quantities of cheap power along the Aqueduct that led to the organization, under the direction of Mr. Scattergood, of the Los Angeles Bureau of Power and Light, recognized today as the largest municipally-owned electric utility in the United States.

The Long Valley Dam

. . . Officials and engineers for the City of Los Angeles as early as 1914 attempted to negotiate with the Valley ranchers with the view of working out an agreement on water storage and regulation that would provide the ranchers with the water as they needed it, and also supply the requirements of the Aqueduct. Careful studies and surveys of the water run-off in the Owens Valley basin previously had been made by Los Angeles Water Bureau engineers under the direction of William Mulholland.

When the City's proposals were submitted, representatives of the Valley people declared that they would insist upon making their own studies of the River before entering into a water agreement. After a delay of seven years, representatives of the City and the Valley met and discussed the terms of the proposed agreement. It seemed that a settlement satisfactory to everyone concerned would follow without fail.

On its side, the City offered to construct a dam 100 feet high in Owens Gorge thus creating a reservoir in Long Valley some thirty miles north of the northern end of Owens Valley. Such a dam was not needed particularly so far as the City was concerned, since large storage capacity was already available along the line of the Aqueduct. In Haiwee reservoir, sixty miles below the Aqueduct intake, more than twenty billion gallons of water could be stored, and there were other storage basins along the waterway as it approached Los Angeles.

The principal beneficiaries of the Long Valley dam, it was shown, would be the Owens Valley irrigators who would be provided with a regulated water supply.

In 1921 preliminary work on the dam was started by the City, but in the midst of this work a group of Owens Valley residents headed by W.W. Watterson, a Bishop banker, filed suit enjoining the City from the construction of the Long Valley dam. The Watterson group declared that the City must build its Long Valley dam to a height of 150 feet to remove their objections. Los Angeles engineering authorities pointed out that a dam higher than 100 feet would not be feasible or practicable. Investigation had disclosed, they submitted, that because of the loose and porous formation of Owens Gorge above the 100-foot level, water even though raised beyond that height could not be held in storage but would leak out through the canyon walls back of the dam. . . .

The City of Los Angeles refused to build the Long Valley dam to a height which its engineers had found would be impracticable. Building of the lower structure was blocked by the Valley group's injunction. The first attempt at a settlement of the Owens Valley water problem had failed, and the Valley ranchers had lost an opportunity to secure, without cost, a regulated irrigation supply.

Land Purchases

Following the completion of the Aqueduct, eight long years were consumed by negotiations between representatives of the City of Los Angeles and Owens Valley with the view of arriving at an agreement that would provide for regulation and use of Owens River water in a manner mutually beneficial to the City and the Valley. All these negotiations were fruitless. In the meantime conditions were shaping themselves in a manner destined to force the situation to a sharp and bitter issue.

On the one hand, Los Angeles found itself growing in a manner that amazed the entire world. Its population was increasing by leaps and bounds. More and more water was required to supply the needs of its new residents numbered by the hundreds of thousands. To meet this need it was necessary constantly to increase the flow of the Aqueduct and to make proper provision for the future.

On the other hand, the entire Southwest, beginning in 1920, was slipping into a cycle of abnormally dry years. Even on the peaks of the Sierra Nevadas the winter snow falls were far below normal. By 1923, conditions had become serious.

Practically all of the Owens Valley ranch land irrigated from the River was above the Aqueduct intake. Consequently the irrigators had first call on the water from the river.

As the situation presented itself to officials of the City, there was only one course remaining open. Los Angeles must purchase ranch land having water rights on Owens River so that the water attaching to this land could be diverted into the Aqueduct should the need arise.

With the view of disturbing the situation in the Valley as little as possible, the Board of Water and Power Commissioners, in 1923, authorized the purchase of the ranches in what was known as the McNally Ditch area. These ranches, being situated on the east side of the river, were detached in a great measure from the remainder of the irrigated region in the Valley on the west side of the river.

Prices offered for the lands were believed to be liberal, since they amounted, on the average, to about twice the market value of the ranches. But in the midst of these purchases, a group of men from the town of Bishop organized the McNally land owners into a pool and demanded prices which the City regarded as unreasonable. In order to secure the water land urgently needed, the City was forced to cross the river and purchase lands on the west side of the stream. . . .

. . . Since 1923, the City has purchased approximately 80,000 acres of land in Owens Valley, and now owns about 90 per cent of all the Owens River water land. For this land the City paid Valley land owners more than $12,000,000.

The City's Methods

Faced with the grave responsibility of protecting the Aqueduct water supply, upon which depended the health and the very lives of a million people in Los Angeles, the City's Water and Power Commission in 1923 had authorized a program of water land purchases in Owens Valley. . . .

With the launching of these land purchases, the Los Angeles officials almost immediately found themselves violently attacked by an active and hostile group in Owens Valley. This group of ranchers and townsmen headed by W. W. and Mark Q. Watterson, operators of the Valley's five banks, declared that the City's land purchasing program was ruining the Valley.

It was charged by the hostile Valley group that the City was ''beating down'' the ranchers and forcing them to sell their holdings at sacrifice prices. It was further asserted that the City was ''drying up'' the Valley ranchers' lands, and destroying their crops. In answer to these declarations, the Los Angeles officials called attention to the actual prices being paid for Valley land and pointed out that these prices amounted to twice the previous market value of the holdings. Concerning the charge that the City was ''drying up'' the ranchers' lands, Los Angeles officials drew attention to the fact that the irrigators' holdings were all situated above the point on the river where water was diverted into the Aqueduct. Consequently, it was shown that it would be a physical impossibility for the City to take any water from Valley ranchers, since the ranchers had first call on the water. . . .

In January, 1925, after the Valley ranchers had refused to accept a plan of leaving 30,000 acres permanently under cultivation, the Water and Power Commission authorized a general land purchasing program.

The Commission retained three prominent Owens Valley residents to act as a board of appraisers with the duty of appraising every piece of property and recommending the price to be paid by the City. The men on the appraisal board were George Naylor, chairman of the Inyo County Board of Supervisors; Vivian Jones, Inyo County Assessor, and Grant Clark, former County Assessor. The records show that the prices recommended by this board invariably were paid by the City. . . .

Aqueduct Dynamitings

Charging that the City of Los Angeles was devastating Owens Valley, a group of Valley ranchers and townsmen, headed by W. W. and M. Q. Watterson, financial barons of the region, had launched a violent attack upon officials of the City's Department of Water and Power in 1923. . . .

''The Los Angeles water officials are forcing the Valley folk to sell their lands. Our people do not want to dispose of their homes; they want to be left alone.'' This, in substance, was the burden of the first charges that rose from the Watterson group. But when the City offered to purchase all of the less fertile water land and leave 30,000 acres of the best holdings permanently under private ownership with a guarantee of a 100 per cent irrigation supply, the same group rejected the offer and demanded that the City buy all the Valley land.

When the City, in response to these demands, resumed its land purchases, attempts were made to organize the Valley land owners into pools and to demand for these holdings prices amounting, in some instances, to ten times the assessed valuation of the property. On the City's refusal to pay such prices, charges of unfair dealings and ruinous tactics were hurled against the Los Angeles officials and spread broadcast throughout the state and nation.

The City's land purchases, the Watterson group next declared, were wrecking the Valley towns and undermining commercial activity. To recompense the merchants and townspeople for these asserted losses, the City was called upon to pay damages or "reparations."

Early in 1924, it occurred to the hostile Valley group to emphasize their demands and their charges by various acts of violence. It was at this point that there arose within the Valley a reign of terror that held that region in its grip for more than three years. Those responsible for the campaign of violence and terrorism first revealed their methods on the night of May 21, 1924, when a band of men, under cover of darkness, dynamited a section of the Aqueduct near the town of Lone Pine.

On November 16 of the same year a mob of Valley townsmen and ranchers, under the leadership of M. Q. Watterson, seized the Alabama Hills spillway gates of the Aqueduct, and for three days wasted the full flow of the Aqueduct upon the barren sands of the surrounding desert.

Following the seizure of the Aqueduct there was a period of comparative peace for almost a year and a half. On May 14, 1926, however, the dynamiters again resumed their activities. On that date a ten-foot section of a concrete-lined section of the Aqueduct was blown out one mile south of the Alabama Hills spillway gates.

Another year passed, and then, on the night of May 27, 1927, ten masked men overpowered the City's guards at the No Name Canyon siphon and destroyed by dynamite a 450-foot section of this gigantic siphon pipe. The following night the penstock of the City's Big Pine power house was dynamited, and on June 5 a section of the Aqueduct near the Cottonwood power house was partially destroyed by dynamite.

Then followed four more dynamite attacks on the Aqueduct on June 20, June 24, July 15 and July 16.

All of the Aqueduct dynamitings were perpetrated at night, and up to the present time not a single person has been arrested by Into County authorities as a result of these criminal acts.

Fortunately for the citizens of Los Angeles, none of the dynamitings seriously affected that city's water supply. Interruptions in the Aqueduct flow resulting from these nine attempts to destroy the great waterway were all brief and occurred at times when there was more than sufficient water in Los Angeles storage reservoirs to meet the people's needs.

It has been estimated, however, that more than $250,000 in damages were suffered by the City through these numerous thrusts at its Aqueduct.

Reparations

Appropriating a term that has become well known since the close of the World War, a group of Owens Valley townspeople in 1924 launched a campaign to secure "reparations" from the City of Los Angeles.

Speaking through organizations formed in the towns of Bishop and Big Pine, this group asserted that the residents of these two communities had suffered financial reverses through the purchase by Los Angeles of the adjacent ranch land. It was demanded that the City pay the townspeople reparations to compensate them for the losses which, it was alleged, had been suffered by business houses, property owners and the like.

During the 1925 session of the State Legislature, an Owens Valley group caused to be enacted a law under which it was proposed to enforce collection of reparations from Los Angeles. Following the enactment of the law, the City waited for the Valley claimants to file their suits for damages. Months passed by, however, and no such suits were filed. Instead the "reparationists" devoted themselves to a bitter attack upon the City through various newspaper mediums and through the circulation of pamphlets.

In response to the claims for reparations, officials of the City's Department of Water and Power made two answers.

First. They stated that they did not believe that the Valley towns had suffered any such losses as were claimed. The reparationists had declared that the Valley was being depopulated; Los Angeles officials produced records showing that 70 per cent of the purchased ranches had been leased to tenant operators, in many instances, the original owners. The claim that the City was permitting the Valley lands to go back to sagebrush was contradicted by the City when it revealed that it had expended more than $200,000 in one year in improving and modernizing the ranch houses in the purchased area. Assertions that the City was cutting down sources of revenue for the Valley towns was met by the showing that the City's Aqueduct payroll during the past several years has amounted to more than $75,000 a month and that this payroll, in a great measure, is spent in a region with a total population of about 7,000. The City further presented figures indicating that it was paying 43 per cent of the entire Into County tax bill.

Second. The Los Angeles officials stated that if the Valley towns possessed just grounds for damage claims they should file the proper action in the Courts and permit the cases to be decided on their merits, the same as any other person or group of persons seeking damages. The Water and Power Department officials pointed out that they had no legal right to authorize the payment of any public money for reparations until the legality of the claims had been established.....

The Wattersons

...Two men have stood out conspicuously and continuously as the leaders of those who have opposed the plans and policies of the City. These two men are Wilfred W. and Mark Q. Watterson....

Any man desiring to borrow money for business development or for any other purpose must look to these two men, since they operated the only banks in the Valley. A large proportion of the ranches in the Valley were mortgaged, and these mortgages, in almost every instance, were held by the Watterson brothers....

During the spring and early summer of 1927, the Wattersons were active leaders in a bitter fight on the part of Valley townspeople to force Los Angeles to pay them "reparations" for damages alleged to have resulted from the purchase of ranch land by the City. The amounts demanded totaled approximately $3,000,000, and of this total, the Wattersons claimed more than $400,000. As the summer progressed, the demands for payment were emphasized by numerous dynamite attacks on the Aqueduct. It was in the midst of this campaign for "reparations" that the Wattersons' banks, on August 4, closed their doors. In printed notices pasted on the closed doors of the Watterson Brothers' five banks, they declared that the banks had been forced to suspend business because of the "destructive operations" of the City of Los Angeles. When examiners from the State Banking Department had completed their investigations, however, they charged the Wattersons with embezzling $460,000 from their depositors in the Valley. Criminal charges were filed against the bankers. They were prosecuted by District Attorney Hession of Inyo County, and on November 10 were found guilty on 36 counts by a jury of Owens Valley residents. On November 14 they were sentenced to San Quentin penitentiary by Superior Judge Lambert....

Owens Valley Today

With the coming of spring and summer [1928], the Valley is well on its way toward better and happier conditions. With the Summer come the vacationists and the tourists. In fact, there are those who believe that the matchless scenic beauty of the High Sierras is destined to make Owens Valley a nationally famous resort center, with all the prosperity that accompanies such activity.

That a large percentage of the best agricultural land will be kept under cultivation by the City has been plainly indicated by officials of the Water Bureau. Already the City has expended a quarter of a million dollars in improving purchased ranch properties. It is now busily engaged in drilling wells to be used largely for the benefit of the irrigators.

The dominant economic force in Owens Valley today, of course, is the City of Los Angeles. . . . But the failure of the Watterson banks apparently has marked the passing of the night rider and the dynamiter. And now, perhaps, the time has arrived when the City and the Valley will be permitted to join hands in peace and mutual helpfulness.

18.
Morrow Mayo, on a "Ruthless, Stupid, Cruel and Crooked" Deal

The Department of Water and Power's fight to justify its presence in the Owens Valley was an uphill battle; for instance, Morrow Mayo's hostile book Los Angeles *was published in 1933, a full twenty years after the aqueduct was completed. Except for Willie A. Chalfant's* The Story of Inyo *which appeared in 1922, Mayo's chapter entitled "The Rape of Owens Valley" is probably the most savage attack on the action by Los Angeles that ever appeared in print. Mayo's criticism is all the more compelling considering that the rest of the book is largely appreciative of the people and events in the city's recent history. In the inflammatory excerpt that appears below,*[3] *Mayo declares that the negotiations over the Owens River water constituted a secret and illegal deal to line the pockets of a few greedy individuals, a merciless and unnecessary destruction of country life, a scheme that defrauded the people of Los Angeles as much as those of the Owens Valley. With greater honesty and forebearance on the part of the city fathers, he concludes, the citizens of both the Owens River Valley and Los Angeles could have benefited enormously from the development of the watershed of the eastern slope of the Sierra.*

Mayo was a well-known journalist. He wrote from the heart, and his version of the water story was long taken for gospel. Yet many of his chief assertions—for example, that a conspiratorial land syndicate was operating in the San Fernando Valley—were based on hearsay and conjecture. The hard evidence he needed to bolster the more touchy side of his story was carefully suppressed, if it ever existed in the first place. Thus his work must be taken as largely journalism instead of scholarship.

II

Two hundred and fifty miles northeast of Los Angeles, in Inyo County, near the Nevada line, there is a long, slender, arid region, about ten miles wide and one hundred miles long, known as Owens Valley. This is Mary Austin's original "Land of Little Rain." In its natural state the valley supports little life except cactus, sagebrush, and chaparral, tarantulas, horned toads and rattlesnakes. But this desert valley has one freakish, inexhaustible, priceless treasure. . . . Through the center of this arid valley runs Owens River, a life-giving, permanent stream, fed by the melted snows of the High Sierras—including the melted snows of Mount Whitney, towering twelve thousand feet above it—a permanent supply of pure, fresh water. This strange river terminates at the southern end of the valley in a saline lake which has no outlet. And this lake, though its water is

[3]Morrow Mayo, *Los Angeles* (New York: Alfred Knopf, 1933), 221- 246.

Unfit for irrigation, tempers the curse of the desert heat (like the Salt Lake of Utah) and serves as a cooling agent. Eleven months a year, except right along the banks of Owens River, the valley in its natural state would be as dry as the Mojave Desert.

But Owens Valley, until recently, has not been *in its natural state* for seventy years. Everyone who has traveled through the Southwest—indeed, everyone who has seen the orange groves of southern California—has seen what water can do to desert land. Hospitable to nothing in its natural state, the desert land, when irrigated, seems to be richer than any other soil. Thus seventy years ago homesteaders selected this region, because of its permanent river, as one of the potentially richest sections in California. It would take water and work and time to make something out of this God-forsaken country; but these struggling, pioneer men and women were not afraid to work. . . . The first settlers went, with no illusions, into this uninhabited, scorching valley in covered wagons in 1861, taking with them their children and all their earthly belongings; seed, live stock, and crude tools. . . . Slowly the desert bloomed-two narrow, cultivated strips on each side of the river—two strips gradually widening as the water was led out from the stream, acre by acre. Orchards began to bear; wheat, corn, and clover grew in the fields; cattle grazed in pasture-land. Farther and farther from the river homesteaders took up land. Finally, there were flood-diversion canals running down from the hills, and irrigation ditches running out five miles from the river, with homesteaders living near them, and all working to build up the country, to keep the canals open and clean, the water moving.

Gradually a part of this desert was transformed into a rich agricultural valley. Along the river a series of little towns sprang up and prospered—Bishop, Independence, Laws, Manzanar, Lone Pine, and others. Unproductive acres blossomed into prosperous ranches, desert shacks into fine farm-houses, flanked by barns, silos, shade trees, and flowers. Roads and schoolhouses were built. A railroad came up from Los Angeles. There were eight thousand people in Owens Valley. . . .

III

Two hundred and thirty miles south of Owens Valley, *twenty miles northwest of Los Angeles,* there was another arid valley of about a hundred and fifty thousand acres, San Fernando Valley, where the land got little water, and which, in its natural state, was virtually desert land.

Some time between 1899 and 1903, when Los Angeles was growing hand over fist—and the orange-growers were beginning to drain the Los Angeles River and the artesian wells—a select group of public-spirited Los Angeles business men, bankers, and real-estate operators hit upon a great idea. Just who conceived it I do not know, but he was a genius. It was a fantastic scheme, but they were Men of Vision. They decided to buy up the worthless San Fernando Valley land, acquire control of the Owens River, and then frighten the taxpayers of Los Angeles into paying for a huge aqueduct to bring water down two hundred and fifty miles over mountain and desert—to give Los Angeles an added water-supply and, incidentally, to use a great portion of the water to irrigate the San Fernando Valley and thus convert that desert region into a fertile farming section, just outside the city. It was a bold, tremendous enterprise, a piece of business in the grand manner. For several years the little group conspired secretly, and eventually they worked out and perfected their scheme.

In 1903 the United States Reclamation Service became suddenly interested in Owens Valley. J. B. Lippincott, chief engineer of the U.S. Reclamation Service in California, appeared on the scene and began to explain to the ranchers that a benevolent Government was working out a plan to place about two hundred thousand additional acres of their desert valley land under irrigation, for the purpose of further promoting settlement, prosperity, and development. The people of Owens Valley were overjoyed.

Meanwhile down in Los Angeles a small real-estate syndicate began buying up San Fernando Valley land at five, ten, twenty, fifty dollars an acre.

The U.S. Reclamation engineers working under Lippincott went into Owens Valley, "made extensive investigations, tested the soil, measured the area of farming lands, determined the duty of water in the soil and climate, surveyed sites of proposed storage dams," and otherwise went ahead with the Federal project. Lippincott told the farmers and mutual water companies that they should co-ordinate their forces with the Government in order to advance the Government's plans; that is, they should pool their interests, and turn over their rights and claims to the Government, so that Uncle Sam could get the whole thing in hand at once and go ahead. By doing this, he said, when the project was completed, they would be able to get the water-improved lands, most of which they already owned, for the actual cost of the development, estimated at twenty-three dollars an acre. If for any reason the Government should not go through with the project, their priority rights would of course be returned to them, the Government would restore all reservoir and power filings to their former status, and furthermore the Reclamation Service would turn over to the valley people all charts, maps, surveys, stream measurements, etc., so that in any case the farmers stood to gain by the transaction. The trusting citizens thereupon surrendered their claims and locations to the Federal Government, and every co-operation was given the National Reclamation Service by the people of Inyo County. . . .

In 1899-1900 Fred Eaton was Mayor of Los Angeles. In 1904 Mr. Eaton, representing himself as Lippincott's agent, went into Owens Valley and began taking options on land which was riparian to the Owens River. He was in possession of the United States Reclamation Service maps and surveys (the property of the Federal Government), and the ranchers believed that he was obtaining the lands for the Government. In obtaining these options Eaton followed what is known as the "checkerboard" or "spot-zone" system; that is, he followed the irrigation canals from the river, obtaining options, if possible, on every other ranch on each side. The following year Eaton returned to the valley, acquiring more land, and bringing with him William Mulholland, chief of the Los Angeles Water Department, and a group of Los Angeles bankers. The presence of these bankers aroused the suspicions of the Owens Valley ranchers for the first time; the presence of the bankers, plus vague rumors which now began to reach the valley, that somebody down in Los Angeles, two hundred and fifty miles southward, was after their water. At the same time Lippincott began to hint that the reclamation project might be abandoned.

On June 27, 1905, W. S. Austin, Land Registrar at Independence, wrote a letter to the United States Land Office at Washington, from which I quote a few excerpts: "In the spring of 1905 Mr. Eaton returned to the Valley, representing himself as Mr. Lippincott's agent in examining right-of-way applications for power purposes which had been filed by the government. He had then in his possession maps which had been prepared by the Reclamation Service. In April 1905 Mr. Eaton began to secure options on land and water rights in Owens Valley to the value of about a million dollars and shortly thereafter he brought a number of well known Los Angeles capitalists and bankers into the valley to look over these properties. . . . The well known friendship between him and Mr. Lippincott and the fact the Mr. Eaton had represented the supervising Engineer for the Government (Lippincott), made it easier for these rights to be secured, for the people were all generously inclined toward the government project, and believed Mr. Eaton to be the agent of the Reclamation Service. Mr. Eaton's own statement was that he had bought these lands for a cattle ranch. . . .

"An abandonment of the project by the Government at this time will make it appear that the extensive surveys and measurements of the past two years have all been made in the interest of a band of speculators, and it will result in inflicting a severe loss upon all settlers and owners of property in Owens Valley."

By this time Eaton had obtained options on considerable riparian land along the river and elsewhere. He thereupon exercised his options and bought the land. Lippincott then announced definitely that the reclamation project had been abandoned by the Government. He resigned from the United States Reclamation Service and took a job with the Los Angeles Water Department, an assistant to Mulholland, turning over to the city all maps, charts, field surveys, stream measurements, etc. This data told the story of what could be done and what had been planned for Owens Valley, *and gave also the ownership, value, and status of every piece of land in the valley.* At the same time this information was denied to the people of Owens Valley. It was subsequently proved, and very shortly, that Lippincott had been receiving a salary from the city of Los Angeles while still a government officer and while he was ostensibly promoting the mythical Federal reclamation project in the valley. . . .

Not a word of all this had appeared in the Los Angeles papers. For three years the people of Los Angeles were kept in ignorance while the scheme was being hatched. The city of Los Angeles was to get an aqueduct, but the city—even the City Council—was unaware of it. Only the little group of leading citizens and the newspapers (let in on the deal for fear that they might expose it) knew what was going on. For three years the newspapers suppressed the news. By July 1905, however, the time was ripe for printing it. Eaton now owned much of the land riparian to Owens River and was ready to deed it to the city. The syndicate now owned virtually all of near-by San Fernando Valley. Money was needed to pay Eaton, to gain control of the full flow of Owens River, and to bring the water down to Los Angeles. The papers agreed to break the story simultaneously, part in the morning and part in the afternoon papers. . . .

. . . The "poor downtrodden farmers" of Owens Valley did not have the slightest objection to the city of Los Angeles acquiring an additional water-supply from the High Sierras by impounding the melted snows, storing the flood-waters, and augmenting the flow of Owens River. There was not the slightest need for secrecy, not the slightest need for conspiracy. Enough water comes down from the High Sierras each year, ninety-nine per cent of it wasted, to supply the needs of half the people in the State of California. There was not the slightest reason why the people of Owens Valley, the Federal Government, and the Angel City should not have co-operated on the entire project. All that was necessary to give Owens Valley twice as much water as it was getting, and Los Angeles twice as much as it has ever received from its aqueduct, was to build a storage reservoir above Owens Valley.

But the San Fernando land-grabbers and the politicians of the Water Department, whom they controlled, had no time to waste upon such a public project. The city (that is, the small group who ran it) simply announced that it was going to stick an aqueduct into the Owens River and divert *all* that life-giving water to Los Angeles, two hundred and fifty miles away, and furthermore that it was out to buy, and proposed to acquire, some seventy thousand additional acres still owned by the ranchers in order to gain full control of the river. . . . .

Protest after protest rained upon Roosevelt, the Secretary of the Interior, and United States Senators, but without avail. The way had been greased. On the contrary, a bill was prepared granting to Los Angeles a free right of way for an aqueduct on government lands through Inyo, Kern, and Los Angeles counties.

At the same time Los Angeles, through the press, through pamphlets, and otherwise, began to impress upon its citizens, most of whom were newcomers, the need for an immediate supply of water. Unless they voted bonds for building an aqueduct and getting water from Owens River, they were told that the country would soon dry up. Water was run into the sewers—"for purposes of necessary sanitation, to flush the system"—decreasing the supply in the reservoirs. The people were forbidden to water their lawns and gardens. This drought, artificial or real, lasted throughout the dry summer months; lawns in the city turned brown and flowers died.

On election day the people of Los Angeles voted the aqueduct bonds—twenty-two and a half million dollars' worth—to build an aqueduct from Owens River to Los Angeles and to defray other expenses of the project to bring Los Angeles a domestic water-supply.

With this money in hand the city "acquired" all the land that Eaton had acquired in Owens Valley, and Mulholland started to build the longest aqueduct in the world. . . .

In 1906 the Honorable Gifford Pinchot (now Governor of Pennsylvania), at that time chief of the United States Forest Service under Roosevelt, issued an order transforming a great portion of the desert land of Owens Valley into a *Federal forest district*!—thereby withdrawing approximately two hundred thousand acres of land from its homestead status. . . .

. . . Pinchot's order immediately stopped all further settlement in Owens Valley and closed these government desert lands against homesteading. The land was closed for six years, during which time Los Angeles prepared, and filed in advance, applications for its use. In 1911 when President Taft rescinded Pinchot's order and returned the land to a homestead status, the claims of Los Angeles were accepted, and the city thereupon obtained possession of all this land.

Meanwhile the Los Angeles Aqueduct Bill was being rushed through Congress. In the presence of Secretary of the Interior Hitchcock, Chief Forester Pinchot, and Director Walcott of the Geological Survey, President Roosevelt dictated a letter to the Secretary of the Interior approving the bill. . . .

Accordingly, the Aqueduct Bill was passed by Congress and signed by Roosevelt. He had hardly signed it before the syndicate which owned San Fernando Valley began to advertise that the aqueduct would go through San Fernando Valley, and that early investors in the thousands of acres of dusty stubble fields there would make lots of money with the use of Owens River water on that land.

In the meantime, Los Angeles started devastating the ranches which it had acquired in Owens Valley, by withholding water from them; and also it began to force the other ranchers to sell out. This was accomplished by a deliberate process of ruination. The city not only permitted no water on its own land, but also placed hundreds of pumps on the edges of it, drawing the water from its own land and also from that near by. Owning much of the land along the irrigation ditches, it refused to do any work on them or pay any of the expense towards keeping them clean; in fact, it did everything possible to clog them up and stop the flow of water. The City of the Angels built dikes in front of these irrigation ditches, altered the course of the river, and even dynamited private storage reservoirs. Thus it forced the ranchers to sell their land to the city at condemnation prices and get out. Long before the city had acquired legal control of the flow of the river, it stuck the nose of the aqueduct into the stream and began taking the water by force, with armed men patrolling the aqueduct and the river day and night.

The great pipe-line was. . . built 233 miles, but not to Los Angeles. It was built to the San Fernando Valley, and there it stopped, and there a great part of the flow of the water was distributed. Members of the real-estate syndicate subdivided their land and sold it at from five hundred to a thousand dollars an acre, clearing profits estimated at one hundred million dollars on their elegant San Fernando subdivision. But, you will say, both the bond issue and the Aqueduct Bill called for the building of the aqueduct to Los Angeles. Well, the land speculators took care of that by the simple expedient of annexing 100,800 acres of agricultural San Fernando land to the city, thus *taking Los Angeles to the aqueduct.* San Fernando Valley is today a part of the City of the Angels, and that is another reason why this municipal monstrosity covers so much territory. In 1930, eighty-eight thousand acre feet of Owens River water, taken through the Los Angeles aqueduct, was used for irrigation in San Fernando Valley. It was enough water to provide each and every one of the 1,300,000 people in Los Angeles fifty gallons a day for one year. . . .

The whole project could have been accomplished to the advantage of everybody concerned (except perhaps the San Fernando land-grabbers) simply by building a storage reservoir in Long Valley, a natural reservoir above Owens Valley. Long Valley is one of the finest reservoir sites in America—a level stretch of meadow land, twenty square miles in extent. It is twenty-five miles above the highest diversion point in Owens Valley, at an altitude of about 6,500 feet, where the water is uncontaminated by human habitation.

As Mr. Faulkner wrote in the Sacramento *Union:* "On April 17, 1920, at a hearing before the Public Lands Committee of the United States Senate, W. B. Matthews, counsel for the city of Los Angeles, testified in response to a question by the late Congressman Raker regarding Long Valley:

'It is the largest and finest reservoir in the country.' In December 1906 a board of distinguished consulting engineers, John R. Freeman, Frederick B. Sterns, and James D. Schuyler, recommended the use of this storage reservoir in Long Valley. They found a foundation capable of supporting a dam of any construction. A dam 165 feet high and only 525 long at the top would store approximately 350,000 acre feet of water in Long Valley.

"If this storage facility had been developed, it would have provided an equated water flow of over nine hundred second cubic feet at the diversion point above the valley. Proper conservation of the water coming down from the various streams in the valley would have produced a total volume sufficient to have kept under cultivation the eighty thousand acres of first-class farming land in the valley, and still have given Los Angeles twice as much water every day in the year as has ever been in the aqueduct on any day since the aqueduct entered service. These are the facts of record from government engineers and the city's own engineers. . . ."

In short, the nose of the aqueduct was simply stuck into the Owens River, diverting the water, while pumps were installed in the ground to suck into the aqueduct water from all the surrounding farming land. In other words, the water was simply stolen from one valley, already under cultivation, and distributed upon another, uncultivated valley 233 miles away.

IV

It takes some time to destroy an agricultural section. It took Los Angeles fourteen years to ruin Owens Valley. The aqueduct was completed in 1913. In the early spring of 1927 there appeared a full-page advertisement in most of the large California papers beginning: *"We, the farming communities of Owens Valley, being about to die, salute you!"* The ranchers were giving up the ghost.

As I write, the New York *Times* of August 26, 1932 lies before me, containing one of Will Rogers's syndicated dispatches. I quote the first paragraph: "Bishop, Cal., Aug. 25—Ten years ago this was a wonderful valley with one-quarter of a million acres of fruit and alfalfa. But, Los Angeles had to have more water for the Chamber of Commerce to drink more toasts to its growth, more water to dilute its orange juice and more water for its geraniums to delight the tourists, while the giant cottonwoods here died. So, now, this is a valley of desolation.'. . . .

A few years ago the State of California decided to build a highway up from Los Angeles through Owens Valley to reach the scenery of the High Sierras. Los Angeles fought the building of this road in every possible manner, but nevertheless the road was built, a paved highway leading through Owens Valley to Lake Tahoe and on to Yosemite National Park. I surely do not need to say that ordinarily the Los Angeles boosters would have whooped this project up to the skies. Why was it opposed? The Angel City did not want the world to see its destruction of Owens Valley. It was cutting down the shade trees along the county road; poplars, locusts, and cottonwoods from twenty to sixty years old. "Treelover" Pinchot should have seen that "conservation."

But the State highway was built, right up through the valley, and as the tourist drives along it today, his eyes feast upon a picture of desolation—dying orchards, empty schoolhouses, and abandoned farms. It looks like a country devastated by war. . . .

There has been a great deal of violence in the valley. The aqueduct was dynamited nine times. In 1927 the spillway in the Alabama Hills was opened by three hundred enraged ranchers, who kept it open for four days to get some water on their land. Los Angeles, however, first introduced lawlessness and dynamite in Owens Valley. Agents of the city, officials and employees of the Public Service Commission, dynamited storage dams at Lake Mary, on Fishlake Creek, and Hot Springs Creek, to get water for the aqueduct. Working in the dead of night, they threw dikes around irrigation-canal intakes.

In rushing the water down to San Fernando Valley and controlling it at its terminus, instead of at its source, Mulholland built a series of dams all around Los Angeles, the largest at San Francisquito Canyon, near Saugus. This dam was condemned by engineers in high standing as a deathtrap. Two years after its construction, on the night of March 12, 1928, it fell apart, and waters rushed down through the valleys taking a toll of six hundred lives and millions of dollars' worth of property. . . .

. . . The City of the Angels moved through this [Owens] valley like a devastating plague. It was ruthless, stupid, cruel, and crooked. It deliberately ruined Owens Valley. It stole the waters of the Owens River. It drove the people of Owens Valley from their home, a home which they had built from the desert. It turned a rich, reclaimed, agricultural section of a thousand square miles back into primitive desert. For no sound reason, for no sane reason, it destroyed a helpless agricultural section and a dozen towns. It was an obscene enterprise from beginning to end.

Today there is a saying in California about this funeral ground, which may well remain as its epitaph:

''The Federal Government of the United States held Owens Valley while Los Angeles raped it.''

19.
The Water Seekers, by Remi A. Nadeau

Mayo and Chalfant were passionate defenders of a lost cause, who made up in conviction what they lacked in information. Now that the dust of battle has subsided, cooler analysis is possible; Remi Nadeau's The Water Seekers, *a book based on scholarly research but intended principally for laymen, fills that need. Nadeau does not think very highly of Mayo's overall interpretation. Moreover, he believes that the source of the controversy was not so much the original conquest over water rights in the Owens Valley before 1913 as the muddled negotiations over construction of a dam in Long Valley (which lay to the north of Owens Valley and had an enormous water potential). That trouble came in the 1920's.*[4]

Remi Nadeau, author, lecturer, and sometime publicity writer, has several popular history books to his credit: City-Makers: The Men Who Transformed Los Angeles from Village to Metropolis during the First Great Boom, 1868-76 *(1948);* Los Angeles: From Mission to Modern City *(1960); and* Ghost Towns and Mining Camps of California *(1965). His* California: The New Society *(1963) is intended as non-academic social criticism.*

. . . Through this period [the early 1930's] . . . , families were piling autos high with household belongings, taking a last look at the old farmhouse, and heading down the highway to Southern California or San Joaquin Valley. They had not been driven from their homes, as some have claimed. But with the sale of their property they had left behind a part of their lives in as beautiful a pastoral valley as California possesses. Their feelings at this uprooting process were expressed in a series of prose sketches appearing in the Inyo *Independent* during the early thirties.

''It is not the loss of the home, or the garden . . . or the growing business which has been the test,'' said one; ''it's the loss of the years, and the hope and the endeavor. . . .''

Stronger words than these were hurled at the city in a simultaneous outburst of critical writing. It seemed that all the pent-up feelings created by the Owens Valley war were suddenly released in a torrent of words. Willie Chalfant, unrelenting editor of the Inyo *Register,* turned out a revised edition of his *Story of Inyo* in 1933, unleashing a terrific diatribe against Los Angeles. . . .

---

[4]Remi A. Nadeau, *The Water Seekers* (Garden City, N.Y.: Doubleday and Company, Inc., 1950), 126-131.

> With adequate storage of flood waters [he declared], there would have been little occasion for interference with the streams that were the very life-blood of Owens Valley; there would have been no destruction of homes and farms; Owens Valley towns would have continued to grow; there would have been water for all; millions of dollars would have been saved to the city; and Los Angeles would not have created for itself a repute that generations may not forget.

At the same time outside writers were seizing the Owens Valley story and extracting from it the last drop of pathos and sensationalism. A Southern California newspaperman named Morrow Mayo far surpassed Chalfant's accusations in his history book, *Los Angeles.* Under the provocative chapter title, "The Rape of Owens Valley," he tackled his subject with obvious relish. Some of the legitimate complaints of valley people became the basis of wild charges and inaccurate history.

"The city of the Angels moved through this valley like a devastating plague," he charged. "It was ruthless, stupid, cruel, and crooked. It deliberately ruined Owens Valley. It stole the waters of the Owens River."

To refute his statements one by one would seem unnecessary if they had not been believed and repeated by later writers. He claimed, for example, that the Owens Valley project was conceived by the men who bought land in San Fernando Valley for the purpose of reaping huge profits at public expense; that Los Angeles "forced the ranchers to sell to the city at condemnation prices and get out"; that it took water from the river forcibly without a legal right, "with armed men patrolling the aqueduct and the river day and night."

Even the Owens Valley people made no such claims as these. Fred Eaton and no other conceived the Owens River scheme. In practically every case ranchers sold to the city because they were offered highly attractive prices. Los Angeles took extreme care to establish legal water rights from the beginning; for several years, in fact, it was prevented from exercising part of these rights because of forcible diversions by some of the ranchers. And the aqueduct guards were not mounted to take water from the river but to protect the ditch from dynamitings by some of the valley men.

Unfortunately Mr. Mayo's book has not been challenged. . . . Many an Angeleno believes that his city "robbed" Owens Valley of its water and used it for nothing else than to fatten San Fernando Valley.

Certainly the Owens Valley episode was bad enough without burdening Los Angeles with such imaginary crimes. It appears true that city officials used questionable political methods to kill federal development in Owens Valley, gain rights of way, and hold water filings; that they failed to build a reservoir at the head of the aqueduct which would have prevented the need of desolating Owens Valley; that for several years they had no settled land-buying policy, causing loss of confidence among valley citizens; and that they hurt business in the towns by purchase of farms, but refused to assume responsibility for such losses. These are the grievances of valley people.

Without these injustices there would have been ample reason for good feeling between city and valley. Los Angeles had shown examples of good will which in other circumstances would have earned the friendship of the settlers. Construction of the aqueduct had brought Owens Valley its long-sought rail connection with Southern California; city power plants provided electricity for Lone Pine and Independence; while exempted by law from paying taxes in Into County, Los Angeles voluntarily paid them anyway, and helped to push through a legislative bill legalizing the process; it exerted efforts to get a paved highway into the valley, and helped local towns to publicize the attractions of the eastern Sierra.

But the spirit of co-operation which might have been engendered by these neighborly deeds was turned into hatred and violence by the results of one tragic mistake. From the city's failure to build Long Valley Dam stem most of the other costly events; through it Los Angeles could have had enough storage capacity to tide itself through dry years and still leave surplus water for Owens Valley farmers. Without it the drought forced city purchases in the upper valley and loss of trade to its townspeople. When Los Angeles failed to heed protests from the settlers their answer was written in dynamite.

Ironically enough, Los Angeles tolerated this glaring mistake throughout the Owens Valley war. Only after the crisis had passed and the entire valley lay in its control did the city turn to remove the root of the trouble.

It had long been known that Los Angeles could acquire Long Valley whenever it would meet Fred Eaton's price, which was a million dollars or more. Mulholland, believing Eaton was attempting to hold up the city, had refused to deal. But by the middle 1920's, when drought was threatening their water supply, Los Angeles officials were ready to ignore Mulholland's feud with Eaton. Ed Leahey, the city's valley representative, had begun buying land in upper Owens Valley at extravagant prices, and believed the same liberality should be extended to Long Valley.

"Eaton has never been connected with the dynamitings," he told Mulholland. "We should give him as good a deal as the dynamiters."

The Chief agreed, and negotiations were opened with the man who ruled Long Valley. But Eaton was quick-tempered and stubborn; after trying for twenty years to get his price on the property, he would not compromise now. He knew Long Valley was far more valuable as a reservoir site than as a cattle ranch and believed that if the city resorted to condemnation it would have to pay a reservoir price. Leahey dickered and argued with him time after time, offering as high as $750,000. To Eaton the amount was unthinkable; he finally developed such a violent reaction at the mere mention of the figure that the Los Angeles agent had to forget it. . . .

But other events were crowding in upon Eaton to force a crisis on Long Valley. Though he owned a controlling share in the Eaton Land and Cattle Company, there were other interested parties who urged acceptance of the city's offer. About 1926, while Eaton was in Los Angeles, the Watterson bankers loaned $200,000 to the Eaton company through some of its other officers, and took a mortgage on Long Valley. The transaction should have been invalid without Eaton's knowledge, but before he could take necessary action the Wattersons sold the paper to the Pacific Southwest Trust and Savings Bank—a Los Angeles firm. Soon afterward the Watterson banks crashed. With them went the $200,000, which had supposedly been on deposit.

The loss was beginning of disaster for Fred Eaton. He was left with a mortgage on his Long Valley lands and no way to pay it off. For years he battled the Pacific Southwest Bank in the courts, claiming that he could not be held by a note he had not signed. But in 1932 the bank won its case and foreclosed the mortgage. Long Valley at last went under the hammer to satisfy the debt; Fred Eaton's twenty-seven-year fight had ended in calamity.

Los Angeles bought the property on December 8, 1932. It might have profited by Eaton's desperation, but paid an appraisal price of $650,000. Two thirds of this was absorbed by the bank note, interest, and fees. Eaton and his associates split the rest, and had little left after paying an accumulation of debts. It was bitter fruit after a million-dollar dream.

At last the city had bought Long Valley at its own price, but the few hundred thousand it had retained were a costly economy. Many millions in Owens Valley land purchases might have been saved and a farming community spared from desolation if Long Valley Reservoir had been bought and developed in the early twenties . . . .

B. *Mono Lake*

20.
The Mono Lake Committee: "Mono is an Endangered Oasis"

In 1978 a non-profit citizens group was formed to promote the cause of Mono Lake. The Mono Lake Committee advocates stabilizing the lake at a level that will ensure a healthy ecosystem, doing scientific research on the ecosystem, limiting water diversion to L.A., and establishing a Mono Lake National Park or Monument to aid in its protection. The committee has pursued its cause with some success in the courts and the legislature. The following selection is derived from a 1983 position paper issued by the Committee.[5] *(Editor's note)*

The Lake and Its Setting

The blue expanse of Mono Lake, with its black and white volcanic islands, occupies the bottom of the Mono Basin bathtub. It lies at an elevation of about 6,400 feet, over a mile below the Sierran peaks that spawn its tributary streams. Twice the size of San Francisco, it stretches 13 miles east-west by eight miles north-south. Although its average depth is only 50 feet, no other natural lake entirely within California holds a greater volume of water. . . .

FLUCTUATING LAKE LEVELS

"Half a dozen little mountain brooks flow into Mono Lake," exclaimed Mark Twain, "but not a stream of any kind flows out of it..[sic] What it does with its surplus water is a dark and bloody mystery." The answer is simple: it evaporates. Every year roughly 45 inches of water evaporate from Mono's surface. Before Rush, Lee Vining and other creeks were diverted, inflow from streams, springs, rain and snow balanced this evaporative loss. . . . Hence the lake level remained more or less constant from year to year.

Over long periods of time, however, a series of wet, dry, warm or cold years would cause the lake to rise or fall many feet. . . . Since diversions began in 1941, the lake has fallen another 40 feet. Today it is smaller than it has been for thousands of years. . . .

STRANGE WATER, STRANGE TUFA

The streams feeding Mono Lake pick up trace amounts of salts and minerals as they flow over rock and soil. Because the lake has no outlet, these substances collect in its water, where they are concentrated as freshwater evaporates. Over millennia, the lake has become saltier than seawater. . . .

Carbonates are also responsible for the strange but delicate mineral formations, called tufa, that grace Mono Lake's shores. These mushrooming rocks, knobby spires and pillared ruins, rivalled nowhere else on earth, look as if they belong on another planet. . . .

The Living Sea

FEW SPECIES, COUNTLESS INDIVIDUALS

Surprisingly few species dwell in Mono Lake. The unusual water chemistry precludes fish and

[5] "Mono Lake, Endangered Oasis: A Position Paper of the Mono Lake Committee," (Lee Vining, *California: The Mono Lake Committee*, 1983).

most other aquatic organisms. But salt-tolerant shrimp, insects and microscopic life thrive in phenomenal abundance.

You need not be a biologist to sense Mono's wealth of life. Just try to tally the lake's brine shrimp and brine flies. At peak densities over 55,000 brine shrimp crowd a cubic yard of lake water; the overall annual population exceeds four trillion individuals and weighs over six million pounds dry weight. Brine flies darken the shore for mile after mile; four thousand have been tallied in a square foot. "Their buzz," wrote J. Ross Browne in 1865, "sounds like the brewing of a distant storm." In comparison freshwater lakes are biological deserts....

The cornucopia of flies and shrimp attracts millions of birds.... Eighty species of water birds, just about every North American shorebird, duck, grebe and gull, visit Mono's shores.... For five species in particular the lake is of critical importance: nesting California Gulls and Snowy Plovers, and migrating Wilson's Phalaropes, Northern Phalaropes and Eared Grebes.

NESTING GULLS

California Gulls are lured by plentiful food and safe island nesting sanctuaries. About 50,000, 95 percent of the state's breeding population, nest at Mono Lake.... With hungry mouths to feed, abundant food is a necessity. The islands protect eggs and young from coyotes, raccoons and other mainland predators. Without such protection, the colonies would be annihilated—as recent events sadly prove....

AN AVIAN GAS STATION

Mono Lake is a vital link in a migratory bird flyway that stretches across the Americas. Phalaropes and other shorebirds stop at the lake en route to wintering areas in South America. So do most of North America's Eared Grebes.... As many as 800,000 grebes and 150,000 phalaropes have been tallied on its waters at one time....

The Water Seekers

To the men who backed and built the aqueduct, Mono was a worthless, saline "dead sea".... The water seekers planned to divert Rush, Lee Vining, Walker and Parker creeks, four of five major streams feeding Mono Lake, into the Owens River and the Los Angeles Aqueduct via an eleven-mile tunnel under the Mono Craters.... The City brought suits to condemn property and water rights, a maneuver calculated to force farmers to sell for lower prices.

...In 1941 the first water was diverted from the Mono Basin into the Owens River, thereby extending the aqueduct system to an intake 338 miles from Los Angeles, farther north than San Francisco, But for Mono Lake, worse was yet to come.

In 1963 the Los Angeles Department of Water and Power initiated construction of a second aqueduct to, as they put it, "salvage the water in Mono Basin being lost into the saline water of Mono Lake." Since its completion in 1970, diversions from Mono's tributary streams have increased approximately fifty percent to an average of about 100,000 acre-feet of water. (An acre-foot is enough water to flood one acre of land one foot deep.)

The two Los Angeles aqueducts are marvels of engineering efficiency. The water flows by gravity through tunnels and siphons all the way from Mono to Los Angeles, generating hydroelectric power en route. But it doesn't come for free. At the northern end of the pipe, Mono Lake is dying.

Paradise Into Alkali

THE DEADLY SALT BUILD-UP

Mono Lake is dropping at an average rate of 18 vertical inches each year. Since diversions began, it has fallen over 40 vertical feet, its volume has been halved, its salinity has doubled and

17,000 acres of lake bottom have been exposed to the sun and wind. An ugly bathtub ring of white alkali surrounds its shores. Where once there were meadows, now there is oozy mud.

At present diversion rates, Mono Lake is projected to drop another 50 feet before it stabilized at one-third its natural surface area and less than one-fifth its natural volume. . . . Before the end of the century, even Paoha Island will be a peninsula.

As Mono Lake shrinks, its carbonates, sulfates, chlorides and other solutes become ever more concentrated. Salinity has already doubled. Unless diversions are reduced, it will triple by the turn of the century and quadruple by the year 2015. . . . Mono's shrimp, flies, algae and birds can thrive in saline, alkaline water up to a critical point, but not beyond. That point will be passed long before the lake stabilizes at a salinity of approximately twenty-seven percent.

The collapse of Mono Lake's ecosystem may not be far off. Especially alarming is the drastic decline in spring brine shrimp, probably due to the failure of overwintering eggs to hatch normally. Between 1979 and 1981, the spring shrimp population plummeted by eighty-five-to ninety-five percent. . . . Undoubtedly this contributed to the death of 25,000 gull chicks in 1981, virtually the entire hatch. Heat stress, due to lack of shade on poorer habitat.

ALKALI SMOG

. . .During Mono's frequent windstorms, billowing alkali erupts from 17,000 acres of exposed lakebottom, rises thousands of feet in the air and travels hundreds of miles before being deposited on vegetation, wildlife and humans.

The Mono Lake dust contains sulfates and other substances suspected to be toxic to plants, animals and humans. The minute size of the dust particles aggravates the health hazard, for they can be drawn deep into the sensitive regions of the lower lungs. . . .

IT HAS HAPPENED BEFORE

One hundred twenty miles to the south, between Los Angeles and Mono Lake, lie a hundred square miles of glaring white alkali. Only old-timers recall the broad expanse of water that reflected Mt. Whitney and its neighboring Sierran summits in the days before the Owens River was shunted into the Los Angeles Aqueduct. Looking across the parched, barren depression that once was Owens Lake, it is difficult to imagine steamboats plying its waters or millions of birds feasting along its shores. By 1928 sixteen years after the completion of the aqueduct, Owens Lake has turned into dust. . . .

What Will Be Lost?

A PLACE OF NATIONAL PARK STATURE

Mono is one of America's most extraordinary bodies of water, a lake which people, not just birds, treasure and enjoy. Every year tens of thousands of visitors walk its beaches, boat and swim in its waters, marvel at its volcanoes and tufa spires, or just enjoy its pristine, spacious setting. What they find cannot be measured monetarily or put into words.

A WILDLIFE RESOURCE AND UNIQUE ECOSYSTEM

Mono's millions of birds are an integral part of a highly productive, unique community attuned to an ancient alkaline lake unlike any other on our planet. An entire ecosystem, not just a species, is threatened with extinction.

More is at stake than one lake's wildlife. Mono is a link in a flyway that stretches across the Americas. From British Columbia to Baja California gulls depart from beaches, towns and fields to rear their young on Mono's islands. Grebes and ducks born in Canada feed at the lake en route to Mexico. So do sandpipers and phalaropes migrating from the Arctic to South America. Most of these birds have nowhere else to go. Most of the links in the flyway have already dried to dust.

AN ECONOMIC RESOURCE

Over 250 tons of brine shrimp (over 20 billion individuals) are harvested each summer from Mono Lake—one of the few local industries other than tourism. The shrimp are marketed as fish food. In the future, they could be used to raise fish for human consumption. . . .

A SCIENTIFIC RESOURCE

Because of its relatively simple, yet highly productive biological community, Mono Lake is an ideal natural laboratory for ecological research. Such studies enlarge our understanding of the more complex ecosystems on which we directly depend. . . .

In response to public concern, the California Department of Water Resources convened the Task Force in December 1978. Representatives from Water Resources, Fish and Game, Bureau of Land Management, Forest Service, Fish and Wildlife Service, Mono County and Los Angeles Department of Water and Power were charged with developing "a plan of action to preserve and protect the natural resources of the Mono Basin, considering economic and social factors." One year later, after sixteen meetings, three public workshops and three public hearings, the Task Force released its recommendations: curtail diversions and raise the lake.

The Task Force Compromise

The Task Force plan is a compromise. It would not end diversions or restore Mono Lake to pristine conditions. It would raise the lake to its 1970 elevation of 6,388 feet—high enough to safeguard gull rookeries and reduce, but not eliminate, dust pollution. Until the lake attains that elevation, the plan would cut diversions by an average of 85,000 acre-feet per year.

But how would Los Angeles replace the water? While 85,000 is less than two percent (1/500th) of the total consumed by California annually, it still amounts to fourteen percent of Los Angeles' yearly thirst by more than the 85,000 acre-feet needed by the lake. How? Through water conservation and wastewater reclamation.

Ninety-five percent of all household water ends up in the sewer. The Task Force Plan would cut this waste with low-flush toilets, water-saving toilet devices, low-flow showerheads and flow restrictors. Estimated savings in Los Angeles: 41,000 acre-feet annually. . . .

But the Los Angeles Department of Water and Power (DWP) has fought the Task Force Plan. DWP claims that. . .the cost "in terms of water, energy and dollars is clearly unreasonable. . . ."

THE LESSON OF THE CALIFORNIA DROUGHT

During 1978 and 1977, Californians weathered the worst drought in the state's history. With rainfall a fraction of normal and reservoirs reduced to puddles, people had to conserve. In 1977 urban water consumption dropped by twenty percent, saving 434,000 acre-feet statewide. The people of Los Angles conserved sixteen percent (97,000 acre-feet), more than enough to save Mono Lake. . . .

By comparison the Task Force Plan is modest. According to California Water resources, common sense conservation could save not just 41,000 but at least 140,000 acre-feet of water per year by the turn of the century. Reclamation could recycle not just 56,000 but at least 100,000 acre-feet annually. In the City of Los Angeles alone! . . .

A WET YEAR/DRY YEAR APPROACH

Still there are times when humans do need a little of Mono's water. During the 1967-77 drought, for instance. For this reason the Task Force Plan provides for increasing diversions "during any period of extreme drought conditions," i.e. when alternative supplies are truly unavailable. The lake would not suffer if we let it rise when the rains returned.

But DWP rejects this "wet year/dry year" compromise. It wants all, every year, regardless of need. . . .

GREED NOT NEED

Why isn't DWP more generous? Because Mono Basin water costs DWP about one-third as much as other supplies.... In fact, alternative water supplies are readily available. Los Angeles taxpayers have paid about $400 million to maintain rights to over 600,000 acre-feet of Colorado River and State Project water, but DWP uses as little as possible from these sources.... Instead, to maximize profits, it squeezes all it can from the Owens Valley and Mono Basin. Since 1970, average purchases from other sources have declined from about 150,000 to only 25,000 acre-feet per year.

DWP is playing a shell game. By increasing Mono-Owens diversions, it frees an equivalent amount of Colorado River and State Project water. This water allows more of rural southern California to be subdivided, especially Orange and San Diego counties, Mono is being sacrificed, not to meet present needs, but to fuel future urban sprawl....

CRUCIAL COURT VICTORY FOR MONO LAKE

The California Supreme Court has come to the aid of Mono Lake with a landmark decision that reaffirms the public interest in protecting natural resources. In a 5-1 opinion handed down on February 17, 1983, the high court ruled that Mono Lake's defenders can "rely on the public trust doctrine in seeking reconsideration of the allocation of the waters of Mono Basin." Writing for the majority, Justice Allen E. Broussard called the lake a "scenic and ecological treasure of national significance" in danger of becoming " a desert wasteland." As a result of this decision, Los Angeles may have to relinquish at least some of the water it now diverts from Mono Lake's tributary streams.... The suit alleges the DWP's diversions violate the "public trust"....

With the Mono Lake ruling the public trust assumes new and greater potency. First, the high court extended the trust to the non-navigable tributaries of navigable waters. Second, it affirmed the state's power to invoke the trust to revoke previously granted rights, and to enforce the public trust against lands long thought free of its influence.

THE COMMITTEE POSITION

The Mono Lake Committee seeks a compromise between the needs of Mono Lake and the needs of the City of Los Angeles. To protect the Mono Basin environment, the Committee advocates the following measures:

1. Stabilization of Mono Lake at least ten feet above the minimum level required to support a healthy ecosystem and assure that alkali dust does not endanger vegetation or human health....
2. A research program that monitors Mono Lake's health and projects the short-and-long term impacts of lowering the lake level....
3. A "wet year/dry year" plan that limits diversions to dry years when Mono Basin water is really needed....
4. A statewide program of urban and agricultural water conservation and wastewater reclamation that will substantially reduce the need for Mono Basin water....
5. Establishment of a Mono Lake National Park or monument....

21.
DWP: "Mono's Water Supply is Very Important to Los Angeles"

In a briefing paper especially prepared for this book,[6] DWP acknowledges that it is lowering the level of Mono Lake, but denies that this is injuring the ecology of that body of water. Moreover, it asserts that the Mono Basin water supply is crucial to the people of Los Angeles, and can be replaced only at great cost.

The City of Los Angeles ("the City") has operated its water collection and aqueduct facilities in the Mono Basin, located 340 miles north of Los Angeles, since 1941 under water rights established in accordance with California State law. Today, the annual diversion of 100,000 acre-feet of water provides about one-sixth of the city's water supply, enough to serve 500,000 persons.

This water originates from diversion of four of the seven major freshwater streams tributary to saline Mono Lake. As the water flows by gravity along the 338-mile Los Angeles Aqueduct system, it also generates more than 300 million kilowatt-hours of clean hydroelectric energy in several power plants, equivalent to burning 500,000 barrels of oil annually at a conventional fossil-fueled power plant.

In 1940, to mitigate the effects of removing water from below the points of diversion in the Mono Basin and removing water from the stream bed in the Owens Gorge for power generation purposes, the City signed an agreement with the California Department of Fish and Game in which the City would donate the land, provide the water, and also provide $25,000 for a fish hatchery at Hot Creek, near the City's Crowley Lake reservoir. Hot Creek hatchery and three other Eastern Sierra fish hatcheries, produce 4 million trout for planting purposes annually.

In the Eastern Sierra, Mono Basin water is a valuable recreational resource enjoyed by visitors to Grant Lake and Crowley Lake Reservoirs, constructed by the City as part of the Mono Basin Project, and by fishermen along the Owens River.

The City has invested more than $100 million in the Mono Basin water and power facilities with no financial assistance from the State or Federal government. The commitment of these funds was based on specific State and Federal actions, including initial applications submitted to the State in 1923 and again in 1934; the granting, by the State, of initial permits to operate the Project in 1940; and the issuance of licenses, the highest form of State water right, in 1974. During this period, Congress also acted in support of the city's Mono Basin Project by passing two acts, a 1931 Act withdrawing lands for the City's project, and a 1936 Act granting the City rights of way over Federal lands for the project.

The Controversy

The City's Mono Basin diversions have been the subject of continuing controversy since the late 1970's. At the current 100,000 acre-feet per year diversion rate, Mono Lake level will decline until it stabilizes in 80 to 100 years with a surface area of about 38 square miles, about two-thirds its present size of 63 square miles.

In 1979, the National Audubon Society, Friends of the Earth, Mono Lake Committee and several individuals filed a lawsuit to challenge the City's Mono Basin water rights. On February 17, 1983, the California Supreme Court issued a major decision in this case, ruling a balancing trial must be held to weigh the water use benefits of Los Angeles residents against whatever adverse environmental impacts those diversions may have in the Mono Basin. Adverse impacts have been

[6]Department of Water and Power, "Los Angeles' Mono Basin Water Supply," 1985, ms.

alleged to include: 1) recent or impending peril to the ecosystem due to increased lake salinity; 2) decrease in California Gull productivity due to the unavailability of Mono Lake's second largest island, called Negit, for gull nesting; and 3) alkali dust storms.

MONO BASIN ENVIRONMENT

Overview

Over the last several years, the City of Los Angles has been the major source for funding of studies on the Mono Lake environment. These studies, performed to obtain better information upon which to base decisions on management of Mono Basin resources, are continuing. Through 1985, the City has committed almost $2 million to Mono Lake environmental research.

Despite allegations to the contrary, these comprehensive studies performed by the City and others have shown that the Mono Lake ecosystem is as productive as it has ever been. The studies indicate that *natural* variations in the Mono Lake ecosystem, especially the effect of two abnormally wet winters, have had a much greater impact on the Mono Lake environment in the 1980-1985 period than has water diversions and lake level. Natural variations will continue to be the cause of most of the significant changes in the foreseeable future.

Lake Levels and Research

Due to natural evaporative processes, Mono Lake has been saline for eons and uninhabitable for fish. As a result of the City's diversion of fresh water streams tributary to Mono Lake, the lake level is slowly declining. Today, Mono Lake has an area of about 65 square miles and is about 2.5 times saltier than the ocean.

How the declining lake level will affect the Mono Lake ecosystem is the subject of comprehensive environmental studies sponsored by the City. Since 1980. an expanded Mono Lake monitoring and research program has developed new information about the lake's California Gull and migratory bird populations, chemistry and life forms, springs, and air quality.

California Gulls

Substantial numbers of California Gulls continue to nest and raise their young on the numerous islets that have formed at Mono Lake. Occasional gull counts between 1916 and 1953 indicate that the number of nesting adult gulls were no more than 5,000 at the lake. However, the numbers have risen dramatically in recent years. Since 1976, approximately 40,000 to 50,000 adult California Gulls have been observed at the lake each year. The productivity of the gulls, measured by the number of gull chicks hatched and raised to maturity, has varied each year since 1980. These variations have been due to significant weather conditions such as abnormally high summer temperatures in 1981 causing heat stress, mild temperatures in 1982 which enhanced productivity and severe summer storms in 1983.

Negit Island, one of Mono Lake's two largest islands, had been a primary nesting area for the gulls until the late 1970's. However, Negit Island was connected to the mainland in 1979 due to the lowering lake level. By mid-1983, Negit Island was again surrounded by water due to abnormally high runoff during 1982 and 1983. During 1984, the gulls did not nest on the island although it was available and nesting area on other islets at the lake had been reduced by severe erosion.

In early 1985, habitat management measures, including the use of wooden gull decoys, were instituted by the Point Reyes Bird Observatory on Negit Island to attempt to lure gulls to nest. In May 1985, perhaps as a result of these management efforts, two small groups of gulls were found nesting on Negit for the first time since 1979.

Dr. Joseph R. Jehl, Jr., Associate Director of Hubbs Marine Research Institute in San Diego, is studying the Mono Lake gull colony. Dr. Jehl has found, in related research with Dr. Sheila Mahoney of Florida-Atlantic University, that the high salinity of the lake poses no problem for the gulls. These birds adapt behaviorally to the saline lake water by drinking large amounts of fresh water through the day and by shaking excess lake water from their prey, mainly brine shrimp.

Brine Shrimp

Brine shrimp living in Mono Lake form the most abundant food source used by California Gulls and other migratory birds. Continued monitoring of Mono Lake's brine shrimp population is being performed by researchers from the University of California at Santa Barbara, under a grant from the City. In addition, laboratory experiments on factors affecting the hatching of brine shrimp eggs, which may be a critical issue, will continue by staff of the University of California at Davis under another grant from the City.

Results of these studies are expected to develop a better understanding of the life cycle and productivity of brine shrimp. For example, this research will help explain why in 1984, after salinity was reduced by the heavy runoff of 1982 and 1983, peak brine shrimp numbers were down to less than one fifth of the peak recorded in 1980 when salinity was near the highest on record. It is becoming evident that fluctuations are part of natural cycles and that impacts due to salinities are not discernible when natural fluctuations are considered.

Migratory Birds

The major migratory birds to visit the Mono Basin are Eared Grebes, Wilson's Phalaropes, and Northern Phalaropes. The grebes are the commonest species, numbering about 750,000 each fall. The Wilson's Phalaropes number about 120,000 individuals and the Northern Phalaropes about 50,000 individuals.

The migratory birds use Mono Lake as a stopping point on their long migrations to their wintering grounds in the south. The birds feed on the tremendous amounts of brine shrimp and brine flies at the lake, to prepare them for the next step in their long migration.

Dr. Jehl has monitored the condition of these migrants since 1981, and reports that each year they have done exceptionally well at the lake, exhibiting negligible problems related to the declining lake level. In addition to regular monitoring, Dr. Jehl has performed research, together with Dr. Mahoney, on how the Eared Grebes and Wilson's Phalaropes adapt to Mono Lake's high salt content.

Air Quality

Studies in the Mono Basin indicate that the principally inhabited area on the west side of the lake has excellent air quality. Even east of the lake, downwind from exposed lake shoreline, air quality is excellent ninety percent of the time. The City is funding studies to develop reasonable measures to mitigate the amount of dust blown from exposed shoreline.

Need for Research

The Mono Basin water supply is very important to Los Angeles. It is a reliable resource that provides high quality water and clean renewable energy. Any decision that would take water away from Los Angeles should be made on the basis of clear scientific connection between water diversions and environmental harm. There is plenty of time, prior to making such decisions, for studies of the ecosystem to develop a better understanding of Mono Basin environmental conditions and any impacts caused by City water diversions.

WATER SUPPLY

Overview

To fully understand the importance of the City's Mono Basin supply, it is necessary to examine the Southern California water resource system. Southern Californians depend on water imported from three distant sources to make up for inadequate amounts of rainfall and groundwater. These sources include Colorado River water conveyed by the 242-mile Colorado River Aqueduct, California State Water Project water conveyed by the 444-mile California Aqueduct, and the Owens Valley and the Mono Basin water, delivered through the 338-mile Los Angeles Aqueduct System.

The Metropolitan Water District (MWD) of Southern California distributes the water imported through the Colorado River Aqueduct and the California Aqueduct to 27 member agencies serving more than 130 cities. Los Angeles distributes water from the Los Angeles Aqueducts to consumers within the City.

Los Angeles Water Supply

The Los Angeles Aqueduct System provides 78 percent of the City's water supply. Local groundwater basins provide 17 percent while the remaining five percent is purchased from MWD. The City has a legal entitlement to purchase about one third of MWD's supplies. However, because the City's usage has been less than its entitlement, the surplus has been supplied to other municipalities in Southern California.

The City's water supply from the Mono Basin averages 100,000 acre-feet per year, or one sixth of the total supply. This is enough water to meet the needs of about 500,000 persons, or a city approximately the size of San Francisco. Suggestions have been made that the Mono Basin water is unnecessary, and by employing a more aggressive water conservation program, the City could get by without this portion of its supply. The City already has a voluntary conservation program as comprehensive as any major California city. The program is long-range and includes metering, leak detection, school educational programs, commercial and industrial conservation awards programs, a residential irrigation program, and free commercial and residential conservation audits. In 1981, Los Angeles completed distribution of water conservation kits to each household within the City at a cost of nearly $1 million. This distribution continues to each new City residential water customer.

The City also has an ordinance which is activated during droughts to mandate appropriate levels of rationing, depending on the water supply conditions. This was in effect during the drought in 1977.

Even with all of these measures, the Los Angeles water consumption has returned to a level nearly as great as that experienced prior to the 1976-77 drought due to continuing growth in population and commercial development within the City. This increase in consumption has occurred not only in the City, but statewide use has also returned to, and in some cases exceeded, the pre-drought levels. For example, during the most severe portion of the drought in 1977, water use in Sacramento was 258 gallons per person per day (gpcd). In 1984, Sacramento water use had increased to 283 gpcd. In Los Angeles, the same trend occurred with water use of 149 gpcd in 1977 increasing to 185 gpcd by 1984.

During a drought or similar emergency, there is more motivation for customers to change their water use habits than during a time of water abundance. To maintain a one-sixth reduction of water use by the City's residents on a continuing basis would require permanent mandatory measures that could include rationing.

The replacement cost of the Mono Basin water supply is estimated at a minimum of $37 million annually. The cost of buying replacement water from imported water sources serving Southern California would be more than $22 million per year at prices that took effect July 1, 1985. Replacing the lost hydroelectric energy generated by this water could cost an additional $15 million per year. The 25-year cost of replacing the water and energy would exceed $1 billion.

Southern California

Regional water supply planning for Southern California is based on the City's continued supply from Mono Basin. At some future time, demand will exceed current supplies. If the Mono Basin supply is cut back, all those in Southern California who depend on imported water would be forced to curtail their use unless a replacement supply from some currently undeveloped water resource was available.

About fifty-five percent of Southern California's 1.2 million acre-foot legal entitlement of Colorado River water cannot be used after the Central Arizona Project begins operation in 1985 unless the Colorado River is in a surplus condition. The amount of cutback could be as much as sixty percent of this supply during dry periods, or the equivalent of roughly one fifth of the total water used by the 12 million residents of Southern California. It was the Colorado River supply that saved Southern California from widespread water shortages during the 1967-77 drought.

The only feasible replacement water supply is water collected and transported by California's State Water Project. This project is only a little more than fifty percent complete. Should a repeat of a seven-year dry period occur, California would experience serious water shortages with severity increasing with time. This is due to the fact that as the demand for SWP (State Water Project) water grows and upstream Sacramento-San Joaquin Delta uses increase, the yield of the project decreases.

Since population in Southern California will continue to increase, long-term and reliable water sources are needed to offset shortages that can occur in present dry years, or will occur during normal years beginning in the 1990's.

Conclusion

The Mono Basin is a state resource. If resources in the Mono Basin are at some time valued higher than the City's water rights and if the City through such action lost Mono Basin water and energy, the State should share in the resolution and restitution to Los Angeles. At a minimum this would involve replacement water and energy. It is anticipated that such resolution be made only after serious consideration of the facts on each side of the controversy.

Proposed Division of California

I haven't seen the measure [a proposed initiative constitutional amendment to reapportion the Senate on the basis of population] and do not care to comment expressly on its terms, but I will say I have always believed the rural counties are of much more significance in the life of our State than the population of those counties would represent.

And I also believe the principle of balanced representation in the two houses of the Legislature is in keeping with the Federal system of representation. **—Governor Earl Warren, 1947.**[1]

. . . [S]ocieties and civilizations change . . . [a] nation once primarily rural in character becomes predominantly urban. Representation schemes once fair and equitable become archaic and outdated. But the basic principle of representative government remains . . . the weight of a citizen's vote cannot . . . depend on where he lives . . . .

We hold that, as a basic constitutional standard, the Equal Protection Clause [of the Fourteenth Amendment] requires that the seats in both houses of a bicameral state legislature must be apportioned on a population basis. Simply stated, an individual's right to vote for state legislators is unconstitutionally impaired when its weight is in a substantial fashion diluted when compared with votes of citizens living in other parts of the State. **—Chief Justice Earl Warren, 1964.**[2]

San Francisco and Los Angeles are not just two cities. They represent two value structures. Indeed they are the capital of two different nations. **—Joel Garreau, *Nine Nations of North America*, 1981**

Personally, I think the two-state idea is ridiculous. It's wonderful to have two cities so far apart so close together—Californians all. **—Herb Caen, *San Francisco Chronicle*, Nov. 18, 1982.**

CHAPTER 9

REGIONAL RIVALRIES
How Many Californias?

A. *Reapportionment in 1926*
B. *Reapportionment in 1965*
C. *San Francisco vs. Los Angeles*

This topic deals with regional rivalries in California. There have been many such rivalries in history. The strongest ones are, first, the contest that has pitted the north against the south, and, second, the one between San Francisco and Los Angeles. The north south rivalry dates back to Spanish and Mexican days, and, therefore, is deeply etched in folklore. Sometimes north-south regionalism has been packed with political dynamite, as when it related to the apportionment of the state legislature, an issue that is highlighted in this chapter. Water development issues have also been laced with north-south rivalries (see Chapter XVI, on the peripheral canal). Serious political observers sometimes refer to the ''Two Californias''—witness a book with that title issued in 1983.[3] Often the contest is less than serious, but it never totally disappears.

[1]Quoted in the *Sacramento Bee*, November 24, 1947.
[2]Delivering the opinion of the U.S. Supreme Court in *Reynolds v. Sims*, 377 U.S. 533 (June 15, 1964).
[3]Michael DiLeo and Eleanor Smith, *Two Californias: The Truth About The Split State Movement* (Covelo, California: Island Press, 1933)

In 1965 Governor Edmund Brown signed a bill reapportioning the California legislature according to the new dictum of the U.S. Supreme Court—"one person, one vote"—and thereby closed the books on thirty years of bitter wrangling over the composition of the state senate. Starting in 1966, the old system of apportioning the Assembly by population and the Senate by counties was ended, and both houses were apportioned by population. Although in some states the high court's decision overturned a rural-urban balance going back to the founding of that nation, in California the decision restored the status quo that had existed from 1850 to 1926. The real puzzle is not that a drastic reapportionment came about in 1965, but that it came about in 1926. Since the number of agrarian voters in the 1920's was dropping sharply and the number of city voters was climbing, why were the cities unable to keep their power? Why, furthermore, did the cities then live with an unfavorable arrangement for forty years? To rephrase the question, why did urban California, especially booming Los Angeles, lose out to apparently weaker forces in 1926, and why in the 1940's, 1950's, and 1960's were powerful pressure groups in the cities unable to bring about an apportionment more favorable to themselves?

An abbreviated reply is possible. By a strange combination of forces that is perhaps typically Californian, there developed in the 1920's a general siding against Los Angeles by the agricultural hinterlands linked with San Francisco and Alameda counties. This resulted in the 1926 reduction of representation for all California cities. Before long some well-organized forces within the city of Los Angeles had joined with ideologically congenial groups elsewhere in opposing efforts to restore the original urban voting strength in the Senate. Thus the urban-rural contest that was a staple item in most states was twisted and shaped in California by a peculiar rivalry between the two largest cities in the state, a rivalry reinforced by regional tensions between the North and the South. Moreover, although the number of people in the agricultural areas declined, the overall power of "agribusiness" rose. This conservative group combined forces with urban groups that sought similar political ends, and the two resisted any attempts to change the new system of apportionment.

The election of 1926 brought the problem to a head. The following documents describe this contest and then discuss the reapportionment law of 1965. The major issues are explored in this manner, including the question of the effect of the newly redistricted Senate on the future course of legislation. *(Editor's note)*

A. *Reapportionment, 1926*

The constitutions of 1850 and 1879 had both stipulated that population should be used as the basis of representation in the two houses of the California legislature. The system caused no consternation until 1910, when the U.S. census revealed that Alameda, Los Angeles, and San Francisco counties then held 48 per cent of the state's population. With the less populous counties nervously anticipating the demise of their political influence, the legislature fell into a deadlock over the chore of redistricting and it took a special session in December of 1911 to hammer out the details. The work was not completed until San Francisco and Los Angeles were each docked one member in the Assembly, to compensate for their new found strength in the Senate. The issue grew even more critical when the 1920 census showed that the customary process of redistricting not only would give the urban parts of the state control over both houses of the legislature but also would give Los Angeles the decided edge over other California cities. As a result the rural interests in the legislature locked arms with supporters from San Francisco and Alameda counties and for the next five years simply refused to reapportion the legislature.

To compel the balky legislature to fulfill its constitutional duty, a group of petitioners from Los Angeles qualified an initiative amendment relating to apportionment. This appeared on the ballot in 1926 as Proposition 20. It was known as the "commission plan" because it stipulated that in the event of further delay in the Senate and Assembly, the Secretary of State, Attorney General, and Surveyor General should constitute themselves a commission to do the job of redistricting. To offset this move, a second group introduced an initiative constitutional amendment to change the Senate makeup from population representation to county representation. This they called the "federal plan" because of its resemblance to the U.S. Congress where the upper house represents areas, while the lower house represents people. Under the federal plan no county could have more than one senator, but the less populous counties could be grouped together so that one senator represented two or three counties at most.

Although the commission plan garnered a 65,000 vote majority in Southern California, it failed heavily in the north and went down to defeat. The federal plan was approved by 76,000 in the north, for a state-wide total of 405,000 in favor and 346,000 opposed. As a result, the federal plan went into effect and Los Angeles lost seven out of its eight seats in the Senate, San Francisco six of seven, and Alameda three of its original four. *(Editor's note)*

22.
Official Arguments on Proposition 20 and 28, 1926

"Taxation without representation" was the resounding (though hackneyed) battle cry for Proposition 20. It referred to the fact that the urban areas of the state were paying out more in revenue than the less populous districts but were less fully represented in the Senate. The advocates of Proposition 28 used the catch phrase "well balanced legislature" to characterize their plan to give the upper house to the rural parts of the state but to keep the lower house for the cities. These slogans from the 1926 election cropped up constantly for the next thirty years.

The chief sponsor of Proposition 20, Ralph Arnold, was by profession a geologist and petroleum engineer, and by avocation chairman of the Los Angeles County Republican Central Committee and editor of his party's journal, the California Republican. His chief opponent, Charles C. Teague, was a banker and agricultural marketing expert, who for thirty years headed one of the state's most successful agricultural enterprises, the California Fruit Growers Exchange. Although Proposition 28 was backed by leading farm organizations, the principal supporter named in its official pamphlet,[4] David P. Barrows, was not an agriculturist but a noted Berkeley professor of political science who from 1919 to 1923 had been President of the University of California.

20	REAPPORTIONMENT COMMISSION. Initiative measure adding Section 6 1/2 to Article IV of Constitution. Creates reapportionment commission composed of Secretary of State, Attorney General and Surveyor General. If Legislature fails, at first session after each census, to adjust senatorial and assembly districts and reapportion representation as provided by Constitution, requires said commission to make such adjustment and reapportionment, and file same with Secretary of State, within three months after adjournment of such legislative session. Declares said commission shall make and file such reapportionment on basis of 1920 census within three months after this amendment takes effect.	YES NO

Argument in Favor of Reapportionment Commission Initiative Measure.

The constitution of California—the paramount law of the state—provides, in effect, that for the purpose of choosing members of the legislature the state shall be divided into forty senatorial and

[4]Thomas M. Gannon, comp., *Amendments to Constitution. . . to be Submitted to the Electors of the State of California at the General Election on Tuesday, November 2, 1926* (Sacramento: State of California Printing Office, 1926), 24-35.

eighty assembly districts **as nearly equal in population as may be**, and that every ten years the legislature at its first regular session after each national census "**shall**" adjust such districts and reapportion the representation so as to preserve them "as nearly equal in population as may be."

This is the cornerstone of republican government such as ours. It assures to each individual, no matter what his race, creed, position in life or geographical location, an equal vote in the government under which he lives. No other method assures this equality of representation.

The constitution of the State of California makes it mandatory for the legislature to redistrict the state after each federal census. Since the census of 1920, the legislators, in three sessions of the legislature, have violated their oaths by refusing to redistrict as directed by the constitution. Such lack of action has worked great injustice in those communities within the state which grew rapidly in population between 1910 and 1920.

This has resulted in taxation without representation for these communities, and has developed in them the same spirit of righteous indignation and resentment which raised the cry of our forefathers, "Taxation without representation is tyranny!"

It is un-American for any group of men and women to work such an injustice on their fellow citizens as the last three sessions of the legislature has imposed on many of the communities of this state.

The proposed amendment leaves with the legislature the constitutional duty of reapportionment and, in the event of failure on the part of the legislature to act, as it has failed since 1920, it creates a commission, composed of the secretary of state, attorney general and surveyor general, whose duty it shall be to reapportion the state—but only in case the legislature continues to refuse to act.

Further provision is made that, if the commission thus created fails to act, the Supreme Court shall have power, by writ of mandate, to compel action, thus making compliance with the constitution absolutely certain.

This is not a sectional measure; it represents the best interest of the state from every section and from every point of view. The plain American principle of representation according to the population is provided for directly, effectively and easily under this amendment.

Protect your equal representative rights and preserve the spirit of American government by voting YES on proposition number 20, thus providing a means to compel your representatives to obey the constitution of California.

RALPH ARNOLD

Arguments Against Reapportionment Commission Initiative Measure.

This proposed constitutional amendment would compel the reforming of state senatorial and assembly districts in such a way as to place the great centers of population, comprising but 3 per cent of the state's area, in complete control of the state legislature, thus depriving the great rural sections of the state, comprising 97 per cent of the state's area, of any effective voice in the state law-making body.

It is sponsored by a group from Los Angeles city and placed on the ballot by initiative petition signed almost exclusively by citizens of Los Angeles, there being only a few signatures on the petition from one other county.

The legislature of California has repeatedly refused to place the centers of population in complete control of the state law-making body, even though urged by constitutional provision and the insistent demand of political interests benefiting thereby.

This amendment proposes to set up a commission directed to do the thing which the legislature, the members of which are peculiarly in touch with the issue involved, have repeatedly refused to do, because of the certain knowledge that to do so would be against the best interest of the state as a whole.

Taking advantage of a provision written into the California constitution in 1879 when the concentration of 60 or 70 per cent of the total population of the state in 3 per cent of its territory was not contemplated as a possibility, those sponsoring this measure are seeking to fasten irrevocably on California a condition permitting a part of the population to control the entire state, which is an intolerable situation.

The proposed amendment is against established practice in American representative government and seeks to establish in California a situation without precedent in any American commonwealth, a situation whereby a large part of the commonwealth would be heavily taxed to maintain the state government and yet would be denied any effective voice in that government.

Twenty-nine states in the United States have definitely provided against the possibility of virtual disfranchisement of any portion of their area by setting up a balanced legislature which neither city nor country can control, and California citizens should not adopt a provision such as this proposed amendment which is so manifestly against the public welfare, against the established and satisfactory practice in the federal government and in other states, and against all American tradition.

Vote NO on this amendment.

C.C. TEAGUE

28	LEGISLATIVE REAPPORTIONMENT. Initiative measure. Amends Constitution, Article IV, Section 6. For choosing legislators requires Legislature, immediately following each Federal census, and next Legislature using 1920 census, to divide State into forty senatorial and eighty assembly districts, comprising contiguous territory, with assembly districts as equal in population as possible, no county or city and county containing more than one senatorial district, and no senatorial district comprising more than three counties of small population; creates Reapportionment Commission, comprising Lieutenant Governor, Attorney General, Surveyor General, Secretary of State and State Superintendent of Public Instruction, to make apportionment if Legislature fails to act.	YES / NO

Argument in Favor of Legislative Reapportionment Initiative Measure.

"FEDERAL PLAN."

This proposed constitutional, amendment will take the place of section 6, article 4, of the constitution of California, which now provides that the state shall be divided into forty senatorial districts and eighty assembly districts "as nearly equal in population as may be, and composed of contiguous territory."

The growth of city population in California, and particularly the unprecedented development of the two great urban regions of the state, will have the effect, if representation is reapportioned according to present law, of consolidating political power in the inhabitants of 3 per cent of the area of the state to the prejudice of the representative rights of the balance of the population who inhabit 97 per cent of the area of the state. The state legislature, foreseeing disadvantages to the general interests of the state, has repeatedly declined, since the publication of the last federal census, to reapportion representation on the basis of existing law.

The present amendment would alter the constitution so as to enable the legislature to find a solution to the difficulty that will protect the right of the great bulk of the state to fair representation.

The plan is called the "Federal Plan" because its provisions resemble those of the federal constitution with respect to representation in the United States congress. It rests upon a principle widely recognized in American government and other governments that representation in a public assembly is equitably apportioned not according to population **alone** but according to two factors—**population** and **territory**.

The measure will preserve to rural California and the great agricultural producing areas which comprise it, the control of one house of the state legislature, namely: the senate. The measure makes no change in assembly districts. It does not increase the members of the legislature. It can not, in any way, add to state expense.

Under this plan no county or city and county has more than one senator. The small counties are grouped, but are given at least one senator to each three counties. There are fifty-eight counties in the state and forty senators. To illustrate the working of the plan, twenty-seven of these counties might, by reason of superior population, each elect one senator; sixteen counties grouped in twos might elect eight; and fifteen counties grouped in threes might elect five. Every large homogeneous geographical area of the state is assured one representative in the senate.

Twenty-nine states of the Union have based their legislative representation in some form upon this principle, and these states include, among others, New York, Pennsylvania, Massachusetts, Iowa, and Ohio. The principle was submitted to a popular election in Ohio in 1903, and was overwhelmingly adopted by 731,000 votes for it and only 26,479 votes against the principle. This amendment is sponsored by the California Farm Bureau Federation, the State Grange, the Farmers Union, and the Agricultural Legislative Committee. But it is also supported by chambers of commerce, women's clubs, and civic organizations generally throughout the state. It will create a well-balanced legislature in which neither the cities nor the countryside may predominate. It is a just and wholesome provision. It will give the state a better legislature than is possible under present law, and will be a fair determination of a controversy disturbing to the best interests of California.

Vote YES on this amendment.

DAVID P. BARROWS

Argument Against Legislative Reapportionment Initiative Measure.

The proposed amendment is unfair and impractical so far as it relates to senatorial districts.

The provision that no county or city and county shall contain more than one senatorial district would limit Alameda, Los Angeles and San Francisco to one senator each. These three combined have 200,000 more than half of the population of the state, so the result would be that the majority would have only three senators, and the minority would be represented by thirty-seven senators. There is no good reason for discrimination.

The agricultural and commercial interests are so closely allied and interwoven that neither one as such should have the greater power in legislation. The only fair way is to base the representation on population, in accordance with the fundamental principles of our government that the majority shall rule.

The amendment prescribes no method of determining how the senatorial districts shall be formed. It merely provides that counties of small population shall be grouped in districts of not more than three counties in one district. It is left to the legislature or reapportionment commission to determine arbitrarily and without restriction how it shall be done. Many of the counties of small population are contiguous, so it will follow that sparsely settled districts must be formed, and even the agricultural sections will not have equal representation in the senate as among themselves.

The populous counties pay the greater share of taxes, and should have the controlling voice in the expenditure of the state's funds.

If the citizens of these centers should vote for this amendment they would help to disfranchise themselves.

Vote NO and preserve American principles.

DANA R. WELLER

23.
The *Los Angeles Times* Finds "Extraordinary Divergence" between the North and the South, 1926

In evaluating the 1926 election, the Los Angeles Times *discovered that the north and the south were in diametric contradiction not merely on the two reapportionment propositions but on all of the important initiative measures, including prohibition, legalized gambling, Bible reading in the public schools, and highway appropriations.*[5] *The* Times *lauded Southern California for its temperate and conservative attitude toward liquor consumption, gambling at the races, and the use of the Scriptures in the schools, as well as for its enlightened self-interest regarding highway and reapportionment measures. Yet it did not relish the prospect of a widening political schism in California and advocated unity and mutual understanding.*

In any event, the legislative apportionment issue of 1926 should be seen against a background of regional conflict—something more than the simple urban-rural split that the proponents of the federal plan described in their campaign literature.

Two Sections of State Are Diametric

Vote-Analysis Shows Extraordinary Divergence on Most Important Measures on Ballot

At no election in the history of California have the two great natural divisions of the State been so widely split on fundamentals as in the balloting on State propositions last Tuesday.

As though the rugged ridge of the Tehachapi were actually a dividing wall between two peoples of opposite interests, opposite opinions and opposite faiths, Northern and Southern California voted as two separate and distinct groups, each homogeneous in itself but diametric to the other on the major propositions on the ballot.

For example:

The forty-six counties north of the Tehachapi voted to repeal the Wright Prohibition-Enforcement Act by a majority of nearly 60,000.

The twelve counties south of the Tehachapi voted to retain the Wright Act by a majority of 110,000, round numbers.

Northern California, the forty-six counties before mentioned, voted in favor of the added gasoline tax, Proposition No. 4 on the ballot, by a majority of 170,000.

Southern California rejected No. 4 by more than 220,000 majority.

Northern California rejected No. 8, the highway fund proposition, by a majority of 460,000.

Southern California favored No. 8 to the extent of 80,000 majority.

Northern California voted by a majority of 227,000 not to permit the Bible to be read in the public schools.

Southern California favored reading the Bible in the public schools by a majority of 68,000.

Northern California rejected constitutional reapportionment by a majority of more than 200,000.

Southern California favored constitutional reapportionment by a majority of 65,000.

Northern California voted for the Federal plan of reapportionment with a majority of 76,000.

Southern California rejected Federal reapportionment by a majority of 17,000. All these figures are approximated. The exact vote appears elsewhere.

The Reasons

In some of these cases there were good reasons for the divergence of opinion between the North and the South. Proposition No. 4, for example, was a northern measure calculated to perpetuate

[5] *Los Angeles Times*, November 6, 1926.

and enlarge the present system of State highway financing whereby the South pays two-thirds of the bills and gets one-third of the benefits and the North pays one-third of the bills and gets two-thirds of the benefits. Except for a group of highway contractors and material men who stood to make money if No. 4 carried, the only support the gasoline tax measure had in the South were the two Los Angeles Hearst papers, who fell in line with the North at the orders of John Francis Neylan of San Francisco, dictator of Hearst policies on the Pacific Coast.

On the other hand, Proposition No. 8 was a highway-financing measure sponsored by the Automobile Club of Southern California as a means of adjusting the present intolerable inequities of the California highway situation. It proposed to give to each section of the State its exact share of highway money and actually allocated to the northern counties a little over half of the funds to be appropriated from the general fund for highway building and maintenance. The North, so long accustomed to getting two-thirds of the highway money, declared this a frightful imposition, an attitude in which they were heartily supported by the Hearst papers both in San Francisco and Los Angeles.

Of the two reapportionment plans on the ballot, No. 20 provided for redistricting the State on a basis of population, as provided by the State constitution, for purposes of representation in the State Legislature. This would have given Southern California a majority in both houses by reason of its preponderance of population and would have taken away from the North the majorities in the Legislature by which it has so long been able to vote itself the lion's share of state benefits, notwithstanding that the South pays over half the taxes. The reason for the North's huge majority against constitutional reapportionment is readily to be perceived.

Proposition No. 28, on the other hand, presented a plan by which the northern counties will retain control of the Senate and, they hope, of the Assembly as well. It provides for representation on the Federal plan—that is, one Senator from each of the larger counties and one from each two or three of the smaller ones, with representation in the Assembly on a population basis. Consequently the North voted for No. 28 and the South against it, though not in sufficient numbers to overcome the northern majority. There was no well-crystallized opposition to No. 28 in the south.

Less obvious are the reasons for the differences between the two section on race-track gambling. Bible in the schools and prohibition enforcement. In general, the North took what is sometimes described as a "liberal" view on these questions. This phase of the election is discussed on the editorial page of today's *Times*.

In Unity There is Strength

. . . There has been slowly developing in California two divergent civic points of view, each definite, pronounced, supported by two great populous localities, one embracing the southern half and the other the northern half of this exceptionally favored State.

Two empires are in process of development here, each thriving, each facing a potential growth as amazing and as far beyond the present as the present is beyond the past.

The welfare and highest interests of one should harmonize—not conflict—with the other. California should fulfill its destiny through the achievement of the ideals and efforts of one people working in unison toward a common goal. Divided against itself, this State will invite and undoubtedly will experience the unfortunate results which such division entails.

Last Tuesday's general election in California did not in certain of its aspects create a situation satisfactory to the great body of citizens, north and south, which sincerely and earnestly desires the State to go forward in a spirit of cooperation and unity.

The nation at large must regard with bewilderment and uncertainty the spectacle presented here. The diametric opinions on great and vital issues expressed by the voters of Southern and Northern California will not and should not go unheeded or unremarked. And the conditions revealed by the results of the election do not call for criticism or recrimination, but for honest reflection and contemplation.

It may be conceded that an absence of adequate information or uncertainty as to the necessity for enactment of measures relating to policies of government may have caused a majority of the voters of Southern California to reach one decision and the voters of Northern California to render another verdict.

Far more significant was the sharp and unequivocal difference of view on questions relating to public morality and the maintenance of laws designed to protect the individual citizen and the State from evils fully demonstrated and readily understood.

The *Times* does not venture upon a criticism of the huge majority vote in Northern California for repeal of the Wright Act, which is a measure designed solely for the purpose of enabling State and municipal authorities to aid the Federal government in enforcing a part of the Constitution of the United States, but this newspaper is gratified that the overwhelming sentiment in Southern California for retention of this necessary and beneficial law has saved California as a whole from lawless consequence of repeal.

It is due largely to the great majority of voters in Southern California that the vicious evils of legalized gambling have not been invited into this State; for the sentiment of the majority of voters in the San Francisco district favored enactment of a measure that would have made gambling on horse races permissible under our State law. Beyond any doubt, tens of thousands of those voting for repeal of the Wright Act and for introduction of gambling in California were inspired by a feeling that ''liberalizing'' of the law is desirable.

But the real object of those responsible for submission of these proposals was not liberality or liberty. These already exist under our form of government. The object sought was license and many good citizens unwittingly gave this movement their sanction at the ballot box. Southern California, by a great majority, favored the reading of the Bible in the public schools—a function performed in all but few States of the Union and one followed in a majority of the schools of the nation since it foundation. In this issue, too, the northern half of the population demonstrated an opposite opinion.

Southern California should not fall into the error of indulging in any feeling of superior virtue by reason of the expression of a majority of its electorate; neither should Northern California resort to derision or sneers for the asserted pharisaical attitude of the people of this region. As a people this State is divided on issues which must be compared. There is a need for an exchange of ideas and for mutual observation.

The empire of Southern California is safe in the course its people have chosen. It is growing in material things, its people are happy. They have built their social structure on solid ground. As long as they continue so their future greatness in all things is assured. The evidence is indisputable that the people of Southern California have one conception of the obligations of citizenship and the people of Northern California another. The composing of these differences must be in the keeping of the thinking people of the whole State.

B. *Reapportionment in 1965*

The voters of the state stymied no less than five attempts to overturn the federal plan: Proposition 20 in 1926, a referendum in 1928 intended to resist the new apportionment (that simply reaffirmed it by a whopping 692,000 to 570,000) Proposition 13 in 1948, Proposition 15 in 1960, and Proposition 23 in 1961. Each time the proposal varied slightly and the opposing sides were composed differently, but each time the practical result was the same and the federal plan stood its ground. Meanwhile, in the Assembly an additional six constitutional amendments were introduced between 1948 and 1960, only to suffer the same fate as the initiative actions.

The changes sought by so many reformers for so long finally came from an unexpected quarter:

the U.S. Supreme Court, headed by Chief Justice Earl Warren who as governor of California had backed the federal plan and opposed reapportionment. The occasion was the high court's ruling in *Reynolds* vs. *Sims* (1964), which spelled the doom of all state legislative bodies composed on the basis of space instead of inhabitants.

The immediate result in the California Senate was an attempt to stall for time and to find a reorganization plan that might meet the rule of "one man, one vote" without completely smashing the status quo. At first the only suggestion approved by the upper house was a bill to divide the state in two. Later, however, under the threat of a court order, the legislature complied fully with the new dictum.

What long-range effects would come from the new redistricting: boss rule, union or city domination, destruction of agricultural interests and rural folkways, southern imperialism with control over the state's resources and revenues? Or, would the status quo be maintained after all? Perhaps the results would be something else entirely, something as yet unforeseen. The following article taken from a nationwide magazine and an evaluation by a political scientist are particularly illuminating on these questions. *(Editor's note)*

24. *U.S. News & World Report* Asks, "Should California be Chopped in Half?"

The above query—half serious and half mocking—has a history that reaches as far back as regional factionalism in Mexican California. In 1849 the first Constitutional Convention gave serious consideration to creating a state north of the Tehachapi Mountains and a territory in the south. In 1859 the voters in a special referendum actually authorized the legislature to split the state in two, although a fear that this might dovetail with the formation of the Confederacy soon stymied the move. Thereafter the idea of the "great divorce" gradually dwindled as a practical measure.

The scheme was revised in 1965, when State Senator Richard J. Dolwig suggested division to offset any increase in southern influence that might result from an extensive Senate reapportionment. Out of the 51 counties north of the Tehachapi, Dolwig would have created the state of "North California," and out of the remaining seven, "South California." The Senate took the Dolwig bill quite seriously and passed it by a vote of 22 to 16, although the Assembly, whose members called it at best "impractical" and at worst "hysterical," killed it. In what follows, U.S. News & World Report *investigates the pros and cons of state division.*[6]

It is California, home State of Chief Justice Earl Warren, where the Supreme Court's attempts to force legislative change appear heading for a showdown.

Here, conflict over legislative reapportionment could literally split America's biggest and fastest-growing State in two.

Under way now is a movement to divide the State into "South California" and "North California" as an escape from reapportionment which would give Los Angeles virtual rule over the entire State.

What would emerge would be two States entirely different in character.

"South California," built around Los Angeles County and six adjoining counties, would contain some citrus and truck-farming areas. But its biggest asset would be a vast and expanding indus-

[6] *U.S. New and World Report*, LVIII (February 8, 1965), 61-62.

trial complex, a key area for the nation's aerospace industries. On the basis of 1964 Census Bureau estimates, it would have a population of 10.3 million, still large enough to be fifth among States in the U.S.

''North California'' could boast the glittering metropolis of San Francisco as the center of an industrial and banking complex. But is over-all economy would be geared largely to agriculture, water and lumber. Consisting of 51 of California's present counties, it would have 7.8 million people and rank eighth among States in population.

Two proposals

A bill to split the State along these lines has been introduced by Senator Richard Dolwig, a Republican of San Mateo County, and 23 other members of the 40-man senate. It would divide the State along county lines near the Tehachapi Mountains—the traditional dividing line between northern and southern parts of the State.

Also in the works is a bill submitting the proposal to California voters and a resolution placing it before Congress for its approval, as required by law.

Before California's legislature at this time, too, is a bill to reapportion both houses strictly according to population under the Court's formula of ''one person, one vote.''

As matters now stand, that bill has about as little chance of passage as the one to split California into two States. Reason is that it would end a political system, hammered out by mutual consent 40 years ago, that most Californians apparently would like to keep as being best-suited to the peculiar problems of this State.

That system, designed to quiet the fear of Los Angeles held by the rest of the State, gave no county more than one seat in the senate. From time to time, Los Angeles political leaders have tried to change this—with no success.

What this has given California is a legislature based on a ''rolling consensus'' between the senate and the house, which has identical powers but is elected somewhat according to population. It has been the house which advanced free-spending legislation, often to the benefit of southern California, and the senate which has seen to it that the inhabitants of sparsely settled counties had their needs taken care of. Major issues usually were threshed out in conference between delegates from the two houses.

If reapportionment is carried out, the situation will be far different.

Los Angeles, already dominant in the house, would have a virtual stranglehold on that body. And the ''consensus'' system of legislation would be wiped out be a huge change in the senate, where Los Angeles and its surrounding counties would get at least 21 of the 40 seats, against the 7 they now have.

Northern Californians say they know what would come next.

One of the first moves that southern California legislators would make, it is charged, would be a grab for the State's water supplies. Two thirds of those supplies are found in northern counties, but it is the arid southern counties that provide two thirds of the demand for water. . . .

. . . Says Senator Dolwig: ''Years ago we got an example of how Los Angeles exercises its power whenever it can get away with it. Long before we had water laws in this State, Los Angeles moved in on Owens Valley. It took its water without any regard for the people living there—and Owens Valley today is a wasteland.''

There is fear also that southern California, once it controlled highway funds, would spend them on freeways in the Los Angeles area instead of maintaining and expanding highways in the mountains and valleys of the north.

On the other side of this argument, it is being pointed out that southern California now has 15 per cent of the vote in the senate, but pays 80 per cent of the State's taxes. Los Angles County, which in 1960 had 6 million persons, held one senate seat. This gave it parity with the senatorial district comprising three northern counties which together had 14,294 inhabitants.

Nevertheless, even in southern California it is being said that this big and powerful State is too diverse,and has too many feuds smoldering below the surface, to permit unchecked rule by the majority under the Supreme Court formula. Governor Edmund G. (''Pat'') Brown and others have criticized the scope of the Court's decisions on legislative apportionment as being excessive. Richard Carpenter, executive director of the League of California Cities, has said: ''When 85 to 90 per cent of a State's population can be concentrated on less than 2 per cent of its land area, the tyranny of the majority toward minority interests can be as devastating as any exercised by a single dictator.''

Troubles ahead

It is also being pointed out that the troubles now in sight for California go far beyond simple conflict between rural and urban interests, often seen as the only issue of real importance in the Court's orders to reapportion legislatures. What is being awakened here, at this time, is the feeling of many that two Californias already exist in fact, if not in law.

Over the years, it has been southern California that has given heaviest support to such ''radical'' ideas as the Townsend Plan, as well as to militant right-wing and other ''fringe'' groups.

Northern California, on the other hand, has looked down on ''fringe'' groups, and its ''liberalism'' has tended to be rather orthodox. San Franciscans regard Los Angeles as raw and uncultured—while in Los Angeles aspersions against northern ''cow counties'' are heard.

So deep are these differences that some authorities are saying that California has become too big and too complex to be governed effectively as one State, regardless of the outcome of the reapportionment fight. . . .[7]

25.
A Political Scientist Explains the Reapportionment of 1965

Professor Joseph P. Harris of the University of California at Berkeley, in his short survey, California Politics,[8] *provides among other things a useful summary of the legislative apportionment battle. Most important in the present context is his discussion of the probable future course of legislation now that the Senate is at last reconstituted. He gives a number of reasons why the results promise to be less than revolutionary.*

. . . On October 27, 1965, Governor Brown signed into law an act redistricting the state for the election of both houses of the legislature on the basis of population, thus ending a controversy which had lasted for more than thirty years. The reapportionment of the Senate by population was strongly opposed by the Senate, whose members sought in various ways to avoid compliance with the Reynolds v. Sims decision of the United States Supreme Court in 1964, which had held that both houses of the state legislature must be apportioned on the basis of population. Speaking for the Court, Chief Justice Warren had stated:

> Legislators represent people, not trees or acres. Legislators are elected by voters, not farms or cities or economic interest. . . Weighting the votes of citizens differently, by any method or means, merely because of where they happen to reside, hardly seems justifiable. . . . Full and

[7] Copyright 1965 U.S. News & World Report, Inc.

[8] Joseph P. Harris, *California Politics* (San Francisco: Chandler Publishing Co., 1967), 94-110.

> effective participation by all citizens in state government requires, therefore, that each citizen have an equally effective voice in the election of members of his state legislature. Modern and viable state government needs, and the Constitution demands, no less. . . . A citizen, a qualified voter, is no more nor no less so because he lives in the city or on the farm. . . . This is the clear and strong command of our Constitution's Equal Protection Clause. . . [which] demands no less than substantially equal state legislative representation for all citizens, of all places as well as all races.[9]

Relying on this decision, a United States District Court held that the apportionment of the state Senate was unconstitutional in 1964, but deferred any judicial action until after July 1, 1965, in order to give the legislature an opportunity to reapportion the Senate so as to meet the requirements of the federal Constitution.

Reapportionment was the first order of business when the California legislature met in January, 1965, but the Assembly and the Senate were unable to agree and adjourned without action. The legislature, however, passed a resolution memorializing Congress to submit a constitutional amendment to the states to permit apportionment of one house of a state legislature on a basis other than population, if approved by the voters of the state, and voted funds to send a delegation to visit other state legislatures to urge them to support such an amendment. The failure of the Dirksen constitutional amendment in 1965 to secure the required two-thirds vote in the United States Senate crushed any hope of securing an amendment to the United States Constitution in time to avoid reapportionment of the California Senate.

After the legislature adjourned in 1965 without reapportioning the Senate in compliance with the ruling of the United States Supreme Court, a citizen petition was filed with the California Supreme Court seeking a writ of mandate to require reapportionment of the Senate. The Court accepted jurisdiction and on September 1, 1965, handed down a decision requiring the legislature to reapportion both houses by not later than December 9, 1965. Reapportionment by this date was necessary if it was to become effective in the primary and general elections in 1966. Although the Assembly had supposedly been apportioned on the basis of population in 1961, the Court held that the differences in population of the districts were in some instances so great as to deny equal protection required by the federal Constitution. The largest district had a population of 306,191 in 1960, and that of the smallest was 72,105. . . .

The legislature could no longer delay reapportionment; if it failed to act the Supreme Court would put its own plan into effect. Meeting at the call of the governor in October, 1965, it moved promptly to reapportion both houses on the Assembly districts, but a complete revision of the Senate districts was necessary. As required by the California Supreme Court, the Senate apportionment of 1965 achieved substantial equality in the population of districts. The least populous district had 337,629 residents, while the most populous district had 441,482 (1960 Census statistics). This spread was in great contrast to that of the 1961 apportionment, in which one mountain district had a population of 14,196, and the most populous district, Los Angeles County, had over 6 million. . . .

. . . The rule of "one man—one vote" was put into effect by the 1965 apportionment. Los Angeles County, which formerly held only one seat, was allocated 14 and shared another with a part of adjoining Orange County; San Diego and Alameda each received 2 seats and shared a third; San Francisco, 2; Orange, Santa Clara, and Sacramento, 1 each and shared another; and 5 metropolitan counties—Marin, Solano, San Joaquin, Kern, and Santa Barbara—which did not have sufficient population to form a district, were combined with an adjoining county.

The Senate elected in 1966 from all 40 senatorial districts necessarily lost many of its former members from the rural, mountain, and less populous counties, many of whom had served long periods. Their places were taken by new members from Los Angeles and the other large metropoli-

[9] *Reynolds v. Sims*, 377 U.S. 533,562,563,565,568.

tan counties. Control passed from the northern counties to the south, from the less populous counties to the large metropolitan counties. . . . Twenty members of the Assembly ran for the Senate in the 1966 primaries, and 17 were nominated. The Senate in 1967, accordingly, has almost as many former members of the Assembly as former Senators, and the large majority of its members are experienced legislators.

How will these changes in the membership of the Senate affect its work and its role in state politics? . . .

The controversy over the apportionment of the Senate was not, in fact, a struggle for power between the rural and urban counties, as is often supposed. Nor was it primarily a struggle between the North and the South, though the northern counties, rural and urban, feared the dominance of the Senate by Los Angeles County, which they believed would result if the Senate was apportioned according to population. The other southern counties also feared the dominance of Los Angeles County and voted against several proposals to give it more seats in the Senate. The struggle was primarily a contest between conservatives and liberals. Conservatives wanted a Senate that would act as a restraint on liberal legislation passed by the Assembly, a majority of whose members were elected by the large cities. From 1931 to 1965 the Senate was strongly conservative, which attitude conservative groups attributed largely to the "federal plan" of apportionment. Business groups in the large cities opposed apportionment of the Senate according to population, which they believed would result in the election of a more liberal body. On the other hand, liberals favored apportionment by population because they desired a more liberal Senate. The Senators elected from sparsely settled counties were, as a rule, attorneys or businessmen whose outlooks on most public issues were similar to those held by businessmen, bankers, and industrialists in the large cities. As one acute observer has pointed out, for many years the Senate was ruled by a powerful clique of men who had long served in the legislature.

> Many had great wealth and commanded great respect in their own counties. They were vigorous minded, politically adroit, genuinely interested in government, and they relished their power and their prowess. . . . They came from such places as Newman, El Centro, Marysville, Angels Camp, and San Bernardino.[10]

This ruling group retired and the strongly conservative Senate came to an end in the 1950's. By 1959 the Democrats had a better than two-to-one majority in the Senate, stronger than their majority in the Assembly. The Senate was no longer a bastion of conservatism, though it was still ruled by a small group of senior members. . . .

. . . Whether the senators elected from the metropolitan counties, or those elected from the south, will vote as a bloc remains to be seen. Before reapportionment, members of the Senate rarely voted as a regional bloc, nor was there a north-south division except when there was a definite regional issue, as the transportation of water from the north to the south. Even when there was a definite regional issue, which was uncommon, it was usually resolved by a compromise. As a rule, conservatives from all parts of the state have voted together on controversial social and economic issues, and liberals have done the same. On the great majority of issues before the legislature, however, there is no conservative or liberal position, but like-minded members on each particular issue have joined together. It is unlikely that the change in the apportionment of the Senate will alter this practice.

Since the Senate will in all probability continue to be a more conservative body than the Assembly, the fears of conservatives may prove to be unfounded. Because of its greater prestige, power, and the opportunity which it affords its members to render distinguished public service, the Senate

[10]Mary Ellen Leary, "The Legislature," in *California State Government: Its Tasks and Organization* (New York: American Assembly, Columbia University, 1956), 22.

will continue to attract persons of greater maturity, experience, and standing in their own communities than those attracted to the Assembly. Conservatism in the late 1960's is strongest in the three large metropolitan counties in the south, which received fifteen additional members of the Senate—Los Angeles, Orange, and San Diego. It is likely that a majority of the new senators from these counties will be conservative in outlook, regardless of party label. . . .

Will the agricultural and rural interest of the state be adequately represented in the new Senate? Although the rural counties have lost roughly three-fourths of their seats in the Senate, it should be noted that seven of the metropolitan counties, including Los Angeles, are also leading agricultural counties. It is quite unlikely that the new Senate will ride roughshod over the rural and agricultural interests of the state. Probably smaller portions of state highway funds will be spent in the future in the rural counties of the north and more in the urban counties, especially in the south, but few if any other changes in state policies that can be attributed to the changed membership of the Senate are likely to occur.

Because of the shift from the north to the south, of population, political power, and a majority of the members of the Senate, it has been urged that the state be divided into two states—North and South. This proposal should not be taken seriously. The two sections of the state are interdependent and are united by many ties—historical, economic, political, cultural, and other. Dissolution, even were it possible (which it is not), would greatly harm both sections and destroy the greatness of California. For eighty years the northern part of the state had a large majority of the population and dominated both houses of the state legislature. During this period legislative members from the north and the south worked together cooperatively and harmoniously, and there is no reason to assume that they will not do so in the future.

C. *San Francisco vs. Los Angeles*

In many cases regionalism in California has expressed itself as a cultural contest between the two largest cities of the state, San Francisco and Los Angeles. Playfully or otherwise, the residents of those metropolises have sparred with one another over large and small matters—the quality of restaurants, baseball teams, theatre, opera, architecture, transportation, climate and newspapers. It is a perennial debate, with no final resolution in sight. *(Editor's note)*

26.
The *New York Times* Examines the Rivalry between Los Angeles and San Francisco, 1955

In 1955 the New York Times Magazine[11] *carried a piece comparing life in San Francisco and Los Angeles. The author R. L. Duffus, a member of the* Times *editorial board, was educated at Stanford University and started his newspaper career in San Francisco. Readers may wish to decide what, if anything, has changed in the last three decades and what is likely to change in the future.*

While the population of the United States increased about 20 per cent during the last decade, the population of California went up by about 50 percent. . . .

[11] "The Two States of California," vol. 1, 20, December 18, 1955.

A symbol of this phenomenon is perhaps that the Golden State, with what almost seems like a single stride, has assumed a majestic political importance. The Republicans have recognized this notable truth by selecting San Francisco as the scene of their 1956 nominating convention. Moreover, California, like Virginia in the old days and Ohio and New York in more recent times, is making an effort to be the mother of Presidents—or at least of Presidential candidates. Senator William F. Knowland had admitted that under certain circumstances he will declare himself in January. Vice President Richard M. Nixon has made no such declaration, but he is a potential candidate, at least for Vice President, and some of his friends have still higher ambitions for him. A third and even more distinguished Californian, Chief Justice Earl G. Warren, has been mentioned, although his stated position is that he is not and will not become a candidate.

. . . This is California a little over a century after the Gold Rush. California is no longer a place. It is an event. . . .

This is California. Two cities dominate it. What isn't in some way hooked up with San Francisco is hooked up in some way with Los Angeles. But there has been a change not only in size of its population but in the weight of its distribution. . . .

The old balance between north and south has changed. The forty-four counties of California which are generally considered as northern have a population of about 5,170,000, or 40.7 per cent of the whole state. The remaining fourteen, which include Los Angeles City and County, have the other 59.3 per cent—7,000,000 and up, always up.

The relative populations of the political cities are misleading because San Francisco is confined to a small county and cannot cross county lines, whereas Los Angeles has a big county to play around in. Thus, San Francisco has about 800,000 persons on a little over ninety-one square miles of which only about forty-five square miles, most of them dry, on which to house its 2,150,000 (and more) inhabitants.

The metropolitan areas, as defined by the Bureau of the Census, tell a more accurate story. For Los Angeles the Bureau allocates Los Angeles and Orange Counties and gets a total of 5,221,000 and up. For San Francisco the bureau allows six counties and achieves a total of about 2,500,000. If there were complete justice, and California cities did not have to stop at county lines, Los Angeles would still be about twice as populous as San Francisco.

The drift is south. Why, a San Franciscan doesn't know. A Los Angeleno knows but is too busy to find the words.

Los Angeles is California's runaway child. The old philosophers who used to sit around the parks, maybe playing a few games of horseshoes once in a while, the worshipers of the sun, the cultists: these have not disappeared from Los Angeles—not by any means—but they aren't news any more, or at most, they are what journalists call feature material. The news is the intrusion into sunny southern California of the spirit of Chicago and Detroit.

With this change has come, within California, a conflict of place and cultures. Californians stand as one in agreement that all sane persons would, if they could choose, live in California. But which California? This is the question.

It is impossible to be unbiased in this argument. All the observer can do is to state the facts with respect for the truth as he sees it. . . .

Los Angeles is warmer than San Francisco, but not so much warmer as most of us think—an annual mean temperature of 63, as compared with San Francisco's 56.5. It is less humid—there is an annual rainfall of 15.23 as compared with San Francisco's 22.18.

Los Angeles is not so dramatically hilly as San Francisco. Some who have examined it carelessly would say it is flat. This is not true—one point in the city is over 5,000 feet above the sea. You can see a lot of Los Angeles from Beverly Hills, which is inside it but not a part of it, or from a highly respectable ridge called The Strip, which is also inside but is believed to belong to the county. There are mountains to the north, east and south. You cross or go around one range of hills to get to a part of the city—the San Fernando Valley. There are hills in downtown Los Angeles that you can skid down on your two feet, just as you do on Mason and a few other streets in San Francisco.

But generally, in Los Angeles you think of valleys and plains. In San Francisco you think of hills and water. That is the topographical difference, and in spite of the inequalities in the Los Angeles terrain it is a big one. It is a psychological difference, too, and it is a tremendous one. The Los Angeles area is a basin. The San Francisco area, except for the part of it occupied by water, is a bulge.

Let us look more closely at each of these cities. San Francisco, which came into prominence at the time of the Gold Rush more than a century ago, was known around the world before anybody outside of the immediate neighborhood ever heard of Los Angeles. San Francisco crowns one of the lordliest sites on earth; a great harbor with a narrow approach; hills in the city itself and real mountains to the north, southwest and east; canyons that could be, and were, broadened and tamed.

Under the stimulus of gold, then of silver, then of the railway and the opening markets of the Pacific, it grew with tremendous vigor. It grew impulsively, without much planning. When the important part of it burned after the earthquake of 1906—and though it was fire that did the vast damage there really was an earthquake—it rebuilt gaily on its old foundations.

In recent years it has spread—across the bay on a mighty bridge, across the Golden Gate on another, down the peninsula. It continues to grow, inside and outside its political limits. It remains charged with vigor. It takes life joyfully, but not easily.

But, as a friendly critic said, it is a completed city; it is a city built on the older pattern; it is a city that will not within its political boundaries, much alter its character in the years to come. A recent visitor tested this observation; he saw vast developments all along the land periphery, but in ten years the inner nature of the city had not greatly changed. Why should it? It was already good.

San Francisco is the kind of city that will boast officially of all the material evidence of wealth and progress. They are there. Trade increases. Industries multiply and grow. Each dawn brings into the north new settlers from the East, to work and to buy.

But this is not so much a city as it is a way of life. What other metropolis would cherish the outmoded cable cars as San Francisco does. San Francisco loves them, San Francisco rides up and down Powell and California Streets in a kind of frantic delight, the city falling away and rising as though it were alive. . . .

. . . San Francisco is the ships coming and going in the mighty bay; it is the lights at night from Nob, Telegraph and Russian Hills; it is Golden Gate Park, a lovely monument forever to a man named McLaren, who nursed it for a long lifetime; it is the beach below the Cliff House; it is the restaurants where whole families go night after night; it is Fisherman's Wharf, Lone Mountain and the Twin Peaks; it is the hills down which you must not walk without rubber heels, if you value your bones; it is the sunset gleam on long rows of stucco-colored houses that used to be bleak, unpainted wood but have been beautified in late decades; it is joy and sin and colds in the head and fog stinging the throat like wine; it is the neighborhood pride that makes the Portrero distinguish itself from the near-by Mission District, and North Beach look down on both, and all of them, including the relatively new Marina, feel sorry for commuters and villagers.

This is San Francisco, and if you don't look out, if you listen to the returned exile, if you converse a little with the outwardly cynical, native-born and permanent inhabitants, you will be captured and never get away. . . .

Let us not distort the picture. San Francisco is one of the world's great ports. In value of cargo, its harbor surpasses Los Angeles. In any other part of the world the fact that it has quadrupled its manufacturing output since 1919 would be regarded as impressive. It is less so only because industrial Los Angeles has gone ahead so much faster that it has outrun San Francisco and the San Francisco area three to one.

San Francisco works, no doubt about that. But it isn't the work one thinks of in and around San Francisco, it is the play the work buys.

But in Los Angles one cannot help thinking it is the work that is the fun; it is the work that is the big game. The working and the playing cannot always be pulled apart.

For Los Angeles is building, some of its inhabitants believe, a new kind of city. It will be a kind of city without any recognizable center. Its important function will be scattered. Its energy will be felt far and wide.

Whereas San Francisco even with its immediate suburbs, is compact, Los Angeles sprawls. The old city that has made up, so the jest went, of country villages tacked together, has become an almost violently aggressive organism. It has acquired, as one young Los Angeles business man said, an explosive quality.

Its increasingly eager quest for water is a good illustration. Half a century ago it solved all its foreseeable water problems by running an aqueduct 254 miles down from the Owens River. Almost immediately it felt the need for still more water, and soon began the steps that brought part of the Colorado River into Southern California. The time is now forseeable when even this will not be enough, and the city has its eyes on the Feather River, far to the north and east.

The Easterner may think of motion pictures and oranges when he visualizes Los Angeles and its neighborhood. Motion pictures are indeed a bit element measured in prestige and in value of product. Yet early this year they were employing only about 33,000 persons. There were nearly 700,000 in various kinds of manufacturing and more than 458,000 in the service occupations.

Aircraft, petroleum and metal-working of various kinds do not appeal to some imaginations as do motion pictures and oranges, but they are the elements that keep Los Angles going and growing. They are the elements that make one think of Detroit and Chicago. They have sent a throb of energy through the plains and hills of Los Angeles and into the neighboring counties of Orange and San Bernardino.

This is no longer an area of rest and contemplation, if ever it was. The retired farmer may still find its outflung areas relaxing, but it is not the retired farmer or the retired anybody who has made Los Angeles grow and spread. The slice of population that has come into Los Angeles in the last few years is probably no older than that of the national population in general, and it may be younger. The old Plaza sleeps under its tattered palms and shabby oaks, but the Plaza belongs to another world.

In San Francisco the inhabitant who seeks recreation is likely to leave his home for a while. He may do this also in Los Angeles—and he may not. He may visit many miles of beaches without going outside the city. He has his theatres, his restaurants, his parks. He can go up to the mountains and find city-owned land up there. But this is not a city which one can grasp as a whole as he can grasp San Francisco. He can scarcely go downtown. Although there is a neighborhood called downtown, there is no center, there is no area in which people by common consent congregate in their lighter moments.

More and more, as it may seem to one who inspects some of the miles and miles of new housing, big and little, sprawling over Los Angeles, the people of this city try to get away from it all within the four walls and the patios of their homes. True, almost every reasonably expensive house has room for two or more cars in its garage or, more likely, its "car port."

But it also has a swimming pool. This luxury is not confined to the motion picture aristocracy. The bourgeoisie who engage in more prosaic occupations also have swimming pools as broad, as long and as deep as available income allows.

Whatever the statistics may show, the eye tells one that Los Angeles has taken to its heart the one-family home. These may be little and they may be big, but nowadays they all tend to be flat and they fit into the slopes on which they are built. The Mediterranean style of architecture is out of fashion. One does not live in a Florentine villa if he can afford something more modern and perhaps funnier.

If one seeks a final distinction it seems to be that the joy of life in San Francisco is external and visible, whereas in Los Angeles life tends to withdraw into groups and neighborhoods and even into the family circle. The joy of life is undoubtedly there, but it is a joy that is at once more fierce and more reserved than San Francisco's.

For the whole of Los Angeles is in a way a kind of workshop. Here the architect plays with his plans, but the bricks, the mortar, the steel of the city that is to be, are still strewn around. It takes a particular kind of person to endure this situation, much less to love it. It takes a kind of energy that used not to be associated with Los Angeles. It takes an eye and an imagination that can project lines into the future.

If California were Italy and the days of small wars were still with us, we might expect the people of California's Rome—that is to say, Los Angeles—to build their forum and their temples but also to form hard-marching legions. We might expect those legions to proceed with certain dourness and discipline, munching their dried olives and their wheat, northward and eastward.

We might expect a relative lack of color in this modern Rome and in the lives of its people. We might look for a cultivation of the things of this world, with an occasional turning toward the sibyls and prophetesses in moments of relaxation. We would take it for granted that the dream of empire was in the making and that decadence was far away.

As for San Francisco, one would expect always the glint of burnished steel and the flash of bright colors in the flags and raiment of its defenders. The energy is there, but it is an energy of reserving and enjoying and not of expanding. Expansion will happen, to be sure, but it will happen more or less by law and nature and not out of the feverish human spirit.

The spirit of San Francisco will never again be feverish. It lost that quality when the last of the ruins of 1906—of the earthquake and fire—were cleaned up. Now the city is dedicated to the love of life, whose indulgence it does not postpone until some later time.

Los Angeles may be the last of our great cities to grow dramatically beneath our eyes, to emerge some day stark and beautiful out of the present dust and rubble of its building. Some day it may solidify into a kind of form and pattern and create a new tradition.

But San Francisco is here already. Let Rome march. San Francisco rejoices still in being beautifully and impregnably Florence.

My case stands for the precedent that it can happen again. This is not only my case. This is not only a Japanese-American case.... This is an American case.

—Gordon Hirabayashi, in federal court, 1985 (Quoted in the *Los Angeles Times*, June 16, 1985).

...the Japanese in California should be under armed guard to the last man and woman right now and to hell with habeas corpus until the danger is over.

—Westbrook Pegler,political commentator, 1942.[1]

Never in the thousands of years of human history has a group of citizens been branded on so wholesale a scale as being treacherous to the land in which they live.

We question the motives and patriotism of men and leaders who intentionally fan racial animosity and hatred....

[But] we are going into exile as our duty to our country because the President and the military commander of this area have deemed it a necessity. We are gladly cooperating because this is one way of showing that our protestations of loyalty are sincere.

—President, Japanese-American Citizens League, March 8,1942.[2]

It was really cruel and harsh. To pack and evacuate in forty-eight hours was an impossibility. Seeing mothers completely bewildered with children crying from want....

The parents may be aliens but the children are all American citizens. Did the government.... intend to ignore their rights regardless of their citizenship?... "Evacuate!" Here my first doubt of American Democracy crept into the far corners of my heart with the sting that I could not forget.

—Joseph Kurihara, a Japanese-American born in Hawaii.[3]

CHAPTER 10

INTERNMENT OF THE JAPANESE-AMERICANS IN WORLD WAR II

Military Necessity, Group Pressure, or Mass Bigotry?

"The worst single wholesale violation of the civil rights of American citizens in our history"—that is the verdict of the American Civil Liberties Union on the evacuation of 110,000 persons of Japanese background from the Pacific Coast during the Second World War.

In 1942, the advocates of internment professed to see all manner of imminent dangers in not incarcerating the Japanese; sabotage, espionage, fifth column activities, and backlash vigilante activities by the non-Japanese. In the emotional atmosphere that followed the surprise attack on Pearl Harbor, it was held that the presence of a free-roaming Japanese population would reduce the morale on the homefront, and thus cripple the war effort. Many Americans believed that the Japanese emperor had a mystical command over Japanese emigres and even over their offspring born in America ("A Jap is a Jap," General De Witt, the man who guided the evacuation, is quoted as saying.) To this was coupled the image of a fanatical militarism rampant among persons of Japanese background, made all the more ominous by the fact that the Japanese normally

[1]*Los Angeles Times*, February 29, 1942.

[2]*Oakland Tribune*, February 16, 1942.

[3]Dorothy Swaine Thomas and Richard Nishimoto, *The Spoilage: Japanese-American Evacuation and Resettlement* (Berkeley and Los Angeles: University of California Press, 1946.) 367-368.

retained dual citizenship. It was supposed, even by California Attorney General Earl Warren, that Japanese farmers had deliberately taken up farms in strategic locations (such as on land located near power lines) so as to be in a position to create mischief in wartime. The wartime emergency dictated a suspension of constitutional guarantees, and all persons of Japanese background, citizens and aliens alike, would have to be incarcerated.

Aside from an occasional conscience-stricken individual (like former Progressive leader, Chester Rowell, see chapter 7), or organization, and aside from an outraged Japanese-American community, there was little opposition to the conviction that "The Japanese must go!"

Today, all known evidence is against the idea that in 1942 the Japanese-Americans were a clear and present danger to the nation's security. Not one act of sabotage or forcible defiance of the government was adduced against them before or after their incarceration. In Hawaii, where persons of Japanese background had constituted up to thirty-seven percent of the population and held many sensitive posts in industry and government, nobody—not even the military—saw a necessity for total evacuation or even for selective evacuation. The official policy of tolerance in Hawaii proved a stunning success. Finally, there is the thorough going dedication of the GI's of Japanese background who fought in the U.S. Army.

How did it happen that men of otherwise good judgment and good will, such as Earl Warren, came to urge the detention of citizens as well as non-citizens? Why did almost an entire state succumb overnight to a mass psychosis about which it would later feel regret? Of course, the interplay of human emotions and social conditions that produce xenophobia is always hard to pin down. The original concept of military necessity was quite obvious, of course, as developed by General De Witt in the following selection. Another widely accepted explanation of the 1942 episode is that the pressure of organized groups of growers, businessmen, service clubs, and veterans' organizations, together with the conduct of government leaders and politicians on all levels, brought on the evacuation. This theory is fully expounded by political scientist Morton Grodzins in the second selection. A counter theory, however, is developed in the third selection by Jacobus ten Broek and associates, who attribute the problem to a generalized hysterical prejudice on the part of the entire community of Caucasians.

The evacuees made a near-miraculous re-entry into postwar society, but the scars remain. Gordon Hirabayashi is one victim who refuses to forget the indignity and the violation of constitutional rights that he suffered in the spring of 1942. As a twenty-four year old college senior in Seattle he deliberately defied the 8 p.m. to 6 a.m. curfew on persons of Japanese background and refused to obey the evacuation deadline of May 12, 1942. An American citizen by birth and a Christian pacifist by religious conviction, he would not bow to the military orders. He was arrested and served a seven-month jail term. In 1943 his case went on appeal to the U.S. Supreme Court, but his conviction was upheld. He served another year in jail for refusing to answer Selective Service questions about his loyalty to the United States and the emperor of Japan. At the age of 67, he returned to court, armed with newly uncovered documents purporting to show that the government suppressed, altered, and destroyed evidence for his earlier trial and that the allegation of a danger of Japanese sabotage in 1942 was false.

Other Japanese-Americans have subsequently had similar convictions set aside, but always on narrow grounds. Mr. Hirabayashi, has gone to court seeking a thorough airing of the issue and a complete and final vindication, for the benefit not only of the victims but of the Constitution itself. His case serves as a vivid reminder of how easily civil liberties can be lost during wartime hysteria and how strong the tendency toward racism was in California. *(Editor's note)*

27.
Lt. Gen. J. L. De Witt Asserts the Military Viewpoint

The ranking army officer of the Western Defense Command in 1942 was Lt. General J. L. De Witt, who was to carry out the order to intern the Japanese. John Lesesne De Witt (1880-1951) first saw active duty in France in World War I; that service brought him the French Legion of Honor and assignment with the War Department General Staff. After serving on the General Staff from 1919 to 1928, he did a stint in the Philippines, was commandant of the Army War College from 1937 to 1938, and went finally to Fourth Army headquarters in San Francisco. He retired in 1947 with the Distinguished Service Medal and four oak leaf clusters.

The next item is the brief letter of transmittal accompanying De Witt's Final Report *to the War Department,*[4] *a massive compendium on the evacuation. The letter bespeaks De Witt's interest in doing the job assigned to him as painlessly as possible, but also his firm conviction that relocation was "impelled by military necessity."*

1. I transmit herewith my final report on the evacuation of Japanese from the Pacific Coast.

2. The evacuation was impelled by military necessity. The security of the Pacific Coast continues to require the exclusion of Japanese from the area now prohibited to them and will so continue as long as that military necessity exists. The surprise attack at Pearl Harbor by the enemy crippled a major portion of the Pacific Fleet and exposed the West Coast to an attack which could not have been substantially impeded by defensive fleet operations. More than 115,000 persons of Japanese ancestry resided along the coast and were significantly concentrated near many highly sensitive installations essential to the war effort. Intelligence services records reflected the existence of hundreds of Japanese organizations in California, Washington, Oregon and Arizona which, prior to December 7, 1941, were actively engaged in advancing Japanese war aims. These records also disclosed that thousands of American-born Japanese had gone to Japan to receive their education and indoctrination there and had become rabidly pro-Japanese and then had returned to the United States. Emperor-worshipping ceremonies were commonly held and millions of dollars had flowed into the Japanese imperial war chest from the contributions freely made by Japanese here. The continued presence of a large, unassimilated, tightly knit racial group, bound to an enemy nation by strong ties of race, culture, custom and religion along a frontier vulnerable to attack constituted a menace which had to be dealt with. Their loyalties were unknown and time was of the essence. The evident aspirations of the enemy emboldened by his recent successes made it worse than folly to have left any stone unturned in the building up of our defenses. It is better to have had this protection and not to have needed it than to have needed it and not to have had it—as we have learned to our sorrow.

3. On February 14, 1942, I recommended to the War Department that the military security of the Pacific Coast required the establishment of broad civil control, anti-sabotage and counter-espionage measures, including the evacuation therefrom of all persons of Japanese ancestry. In recognition of this situation, the President issued Executive Order No. 9066 on February 19, 1942, authorizing the accomplishment of these and any other necessary security measures. By letter dated February 20, 1942, the Secretary of War authorized me to effectuate my recommendations and to exercise all of the powers which the Executive Order conferred upon him and upon any military commander designated by him. A number of separate and distinct security measures have been instituted under the broad authority thus delegated, and future events may demand the initiation of

---

[4]Lt. Gen. J. L. DeWitt to Chief of Staff, U.S. Army, June 5, 1943, in U.S. Army Western Defense Command and Fourth Army, *Final Report, Japanese Evacuation from the West Coast, 1942*. (Washington, D.C. Government Printing Office, 1943), vii-x.

others. Among the steps taken was the evacuation of Japanese from western Washington and Oregon, California, and southern Arizona. Transmitted herewith is the final report of that evacuation. . . .

5. There was neither pattern nor precedent for an undertaking of this magnitude and character; yet over a period of less than ninety operating days, 110,442 persons of Japanese ancestry were evacuated from the West Coast. This compulsory organized mass migration was conducted under complete military supervision. It was effected without major incident in a time of extreme pressure and severe national stress, consummated at a time when the energies of the military were directed primarily toward the organization and training of an Army of sufficient size and equipment to fight a global war. The task was, nevertheless, completed without any appreciable divergence of military personnel. Comparatively few were used, and there was no interruption in a training program.

6. In the orderly accomplishment of the program, emphasis was placed upon the making of due provision against social and economic dislocation. Agricultural production was not reduced by the evacuation. Over ninety-nine per cent of all agricultural acreage in the affected area owned or operated by evacuees was successfully kept in production. Purchasers, lessees, or substitute operators were found who took over the acreage subject to relinquishment. The Los Angeles *Herald* and *Express* and the San Diego *Union*, on February 23, 1943, and the Tacoma *News-Tribune*, on February 25, 1943, reported increases not only in the value but also in the quantity of farm production in their respective areas.

7. So far as could be foreseen, everything essential was provided to minimize the impact of evacuation upon evacuees, as well as upon economy. Notwithstanding, exclusive of the costs of construction of facilities, the purchase of evacuee motor vehicles, the aggregate of agricultural crop loans made and the purchase of office equipment now in use for other government purposes, the entire cost was $1.46 per evacuee a day for the period of evacuation, Assembly Center residence and transfer operations. This cost includes financial assistance to evacuees who voluntarily migrated from the area before the controlled evacuation phase of the program. It also covers registration and processing costs; storage of evacuee property and all other aspects of the evacuee property protection program. It includes hospitalization and medical care of all evacuees from the date of evacuation; transportation of evacuees and their personal effects from their homes to Assembly Centers; complete care in Assembly Centers, including all subsistence, medical care and nominal compensation for work performed. It also reflects the cost of family allowances and clothing as well as transportation and meals during the transfer from Assembly to Relocation Centers.

8. Accomplishment of the program in the manner selected would have been impossible without the participation of the Federal civilian agencies so ably assisting throughout. . .

28. A Theory of Group Pressure

The gunfire had barely stopped in the Pacific when thousands of books and articles of every description began to be turned out, covering every possible aspect of the relocation episode. One of the most outstanding was Morton Grodzins' Americans Betrayed,[5] *a searching political analysis.*

Professor Grodzins (1917-1964) received a Ph.D. from the University of California, Berkeley (1945). He held the chairmanship of the Department of Political Science at the University of Chicago (1955 to 1958), and was a fellow of the Center for the Advanced Study of Behavioral Science at Stanford (1958 to 1959).

Searching for an explanation of the decision-making process in this affair, Grodzins examined the activity of pressure groups, congressional delegations, and state and local political leaders. A large part of his work detailed the formation of the policy by the Roosevelt Administration in Washington, including the activities of the War Department, Congress, and the judiciary. He amassed a great deal of information about the shaping of public opinion by the press and radio, and he presented what little information there was about the opposition to the evacuation. His research convinced him that the policy was not only irrational and unjust, but the result of organized and concerted effort.

. . . There is almost no end to the number and variety of groups that devoted attention, in a more or less organized fashion, to the alleged necessity for Japanese evacuation. Lions and Elks passed resolutions in common with the Supreme Pyramid of Sciots and a California Townsend Club. Several dozen labor unions acted in agreement with agricultural, manufacturing, and businessmen's associations, as well as with the Magnolia Study Club of Anaheim, California, and the University of Oregon Mothers. The resolutions of numerous civilian defense councils were echoed by a Palm Springs "Committee of the People," the Orosi Citizens Committee, the Lindsay Women's Club, and the North Hollywood Home Owners. American Legion activities were seconded by United Spanish War Veterans, Veterans of Foreign Wars, Disabled American Veterans of the World War, the Military Order of the Purple Heart, and the Puente Class in Christian Citizenship. An East Los Angeles Noon Club demanded evacuation in common with a West Los Angeles Breakfast Club.

The complete story of the attempts of various groups to foster the Japanese evacuation will probably never be told. The most active proponents of mass evacuation were certain agricultural and business groups, chambers of commerce, the American Legion, the California Joint Immigration Committee, and the Native Sons and Daughters of the Golden West.

The Western Growers Protective Association

The Western Growers Protective Association was a co-operative organization whose membership controlled approximately 85 per cent of the row-crop vegetables shipped from California. Members of the association were large producers, and their products went almost exclusively to canneries and to eastern markets. This is a type of farming into which American Japanese had made comparatively slight inroads, i.e., the Japanese of California were for the most part truck gardeners whose produce was sold in the metropolitan areas of the state. Nevertheless, some Japanese, particularly those holding acreages in the Imperial Valley and Salinas areas, were in direct competition with members of the association.

One of the earliest wartime statements produced with respect to the unimportance of American-Japanese in Pacific Coast agriculture was that of the [Western Growers] Protective Association [later the Western Growers Association]. An official of the group (*F. W. McNabb*) transmitted to

[5]Morton Grodzins *Americans Betrayed: Politics and the Japanese Evacuation* (Chicago: University of Illinois Press, 1949), 21-128. Footnotes omitted.

the chairman of the Monterey County Defense Council on January 3, 1942, data showing that some 1,200 Japanese Americans of California and Arizona controlled approximately 37,100 acres of vegetable land. Despite these "rather appalling figures," he wrote:

I feel that the danger of possible food shortage (vegetables) by reasons of elimination of Japanese growers has been unduly magnified, although the total as shown by these preliminary and possibly not entirely accurate figures is staggering, yet, I do not believe that any serious dislocation will occur if these alien Japanese growers are properly eliminated.

In the event that Japanese were removed from the land, the agricultural leaders explained, it was possible that there would be a shortage of "certain luxury commodities such as romaine, radishes, parsley, and possibly a few early tomatoes." The shortages would not be serious because the acreages operated by Japanese farmers were "choice" and would be readily taken up by the white farmers who had been unable to compete with the Japanese "due to their low standards of living and the long hours which the Japanese work, not only themselves, but their families." The contention that Japanese were an unimportant factor in the production of California vegetables was pursued consistently by the association during the subsequent weeks. . . .

Mr. McNabb forwarded a copy of one of his estimates of Japanese vegetable production to Attorney-General Earl Warren of California as early as January 3 [1942], commenting: "We trust that your office will make a sincere effort to eliminate as many of these undesirable aliens from the land of California as is possible at this time. Let me assure you that our entire organization. . . is behind you squarely in any action you see fit to take in this matter."

On January 10, *Mr. McNabb* wrote to William Cecil, director of the California Department of Agriculture, protesting the latter's statement to the effect that 40 per cent of the vegetables in California were grown by Japanese. The association leader had heard this statement "to my horror and amazement" quoted in a radio broadcast giving Mr. Cecil's reasons for doubting the feasibility of an evacuation program.

I can only hope that he [the radio broadcaster] misquoted you because a statement of that sort coming from the state Department of Agriculture, would be rather unfortunate for the vegetable industry of California, particularly as *the vegetable industry ever since December 7 has joined in every movement to eliminate Japanese growers from the vegetable picture and to move them at least 300 miles East from the Pacific coastline or preferably, in my opinion, 300 miles due West.* [italics supplied].

The interest of the Western Growers Protective Association also extended to federal officials. On January 22, 1942, Mr. Mc Nabb wrote Congressman John Z. Anderson to urge the following drastic program.

1. That all Japanese, whether national or native born, be required to register, producing birth certificates, and all those who cannot produce American birth certificates, immediately be placed in concentration camps at least 300 miles west [sic] of the Pacific Coast line.

2. That all American born Japanese be required to report to local police authorities at least once a week.

3. That no Japanese be permitted to leave the community where residing without a police permit, and no Japanese be permitted to work in defense industries.

4. That all Japanese be requested to move inland at least 300 miles, and no Japanese be permitted within 300 miles of the Pacific Coast line under death penalty.

5. That the possession of fire arms or ammunition of any kind by Japanese be prohibited under death penalty.

6. That all Japanese funds and properties be immediately frozen and placed under control of alien custodian. . . .

It was "not far-fetched or beyond the realm of possibility," the association officer wrote, that in the event of invasion at least twenty-five thousand Japanese would exchange civilian clothing for uniforms and appear as "full-fledged members of the Japanese armed forces...".

Chambers of Commerce

Perhaps the most politically sophisticated of the groups interested in the Japanese evacuation were the Los Angeles Chamber of Commerce and related chambers of the Pacific Coast. The Los Angeles group was one of the first organizations concerned with the wartime Japanese problem. As early as December 22, 1941, its 'Agricultural Committee recommended that all Japanese nationals in the United States be placed "under absolute federal control." In February, 1942, the Los Angeles Chamber as a whole went on record "favoring the movement of Japanese to an area beyond fifty miles from the Pacific Coast and the Mexican border, and the employment of Japanese thus removed to the fullest possible extent."

The Chamber of Commerce did not, like other groups, bombard either congressmen or newspapers with copies of their resolutions. Instead, the matter was given to the hands of *Thomas B. Drake*, friend of congressional representatives and representative, himself, of the Los Angeles Chamber in Washington. *Mr. Drake's* activities are described in detail in the chapter devoted to congressional activity, since he played a major role in that theater of operations. Here it may be summarized that the representative of the Los Angeles Chamber of Commerce (1) was instrumental in bringing Pacific Coast congressmen together for the first time in consideration of Japanese evacuation; (2) was actually the author of the first resolution demanding evacuation that was passed by the West Coast delegations as their own; (3) consistently supplied congressmen with data and recommendations, working particularly in close harmony with Congressman Costello of Los Angeles, who gave his name to at least one program supplied by the chamber; and (4) played an active role in the final formulation of the various committees of the western delegations and in the delegations' final recommendation for mass evacuation of both citizens and aliens....

The American Legion

...The national Legion's wartime attitude toward Japanese in America was not fully expressed until the national convention of August, 1942. However, the national commissions (on national defense, naval affairs, merchant marine, aeronautics and civil defense) met in Washington, D.C. on January 19, 1942, and unanimously adopted a resolution "calling for immediate action by the Government in evacuating and interning all enemy aliens and nationals in combat zones, such as the Pacific Coast." In later action on the West Coast, "enemy aliens and nationals" were freely translated as "Japanese, both aliens and American citizens." Little was said of any necessity for evacuating German and Italian aliens, and many Legion spokesmen favored treating these groups with leniency.

In California the War Council of the [American Legion] department met on January 5, 1942. One of seven resolutions passed was aimed at Japanese Americans. The action precisely followed the dual citizenship line of the California Joint Immigration Committee, represented in high Legion councils by State Adjutant James Fisk, who was also the chairman of the Joint Committee. This resolution noted the freedom being allowed enemy aliens and the fact that many of these aliens resided "in strategic locations where they could at a moment's notice commit very destructive acts of sabotage and espionage." The War Council therefore demanded that immediate steps be taken, "to see that all such enemy aliens be placed in concentration camps and that the land and/or property owned...by such aliens be placed under government supervision...; that all Japanese who are known to hold dual citizenship also be placed in concentration camps...."

The Native Sons of the Golden West

Historically, the Native Sons and Daughters of the Golden West based opposition to Japanese (and other orientals) in California on biological arguments. The advent of war with the Japanese Empire gave those arguments greater moment and a wider audience than they had ever enjoyed before. The first three postwar issues of the organization's official publication, the *Grizzly Bear*, illustrated the intensity of the racial animus as well as the auxiliary economic fear of losing the land of California to the Japanese.

In January, 1942, Clarence M. Hunt, deputy grand president of the Native Sons, and editor of the *Grizzly Bear*, reviewed the long history of the Native Sons' campaign against the Japanese.

> Had the warning been heeded—had the federal and state authorities been "on the alert" and rigidly enforced the Exclusion Law and the Alien Land Law; had the Jap propaganda agencies in this country been silenced; had the legislation been enacted. . .denying citizenship to offspring of all aliens ineligible to citizenship; had the Japs been prohibited from colonizing in strategic locations; had not Jap-dollars been so eagerly sought by White landowners and businessmen; had a dull ear been turned to the honeyed words of the Japs and the pro-Japs; had the yellow-Jap and the white-Jap "fifth columnists" been disposed of within the law; had Japan been denied the privilege of using California as a breeding ground for dual-citizens (nisei);—the treacherous Japs probably would not have attacked Pearl Harbor December 7, 1941, and this country would not today be at war with Japan.

In February an editorial titled "Save California" dealt with the laxities of enforcement of the Alien Land Act and declared: "The Japs must be dispossessed of every foot of California land they now hold, and the land must be escheated to the state! That course alone will eliminate the possibility of another 'Pearl Harbor incident.'" And in March the editorial read:

> Regardless of the United States' anticipated and hoped for complete victory over the Japs in the struggle now raging, California, as well as other Pacific Coast states, will in time be lost to the White race unless all Japs now here, alien and native born, be permanently routed from these shores. . . .
>
> Want to preserve California as a White man's paradise? Speechifying and resoluting will not do it. So, organize and prosecute a campaign along the course here suggested. . . .

In urging the evacuation itself, the Native Sons. . .demanded the immediate removal "of all Japs" from the coastal zone. . .[and] the incarceration of all Japanese "in concentration camps." Both groups specifically included American citizens of Japanese descent as well as aliens.

Miscellaneous Groups

Some idea of the great number and variety of organizations demanding evacuation was given at the beginning of this chapter. Of the businessmen's fraternal organizations, Elks and Lions clubs were most active, Eleven lodges of the Benevolent Protectorate and six local units of the Lions favored evacuation. So far as the present data indicate, only one West Coast Rotary (at Glendale, California) took similar action. A California Kiwanis Club (Shafter) circulated form letters urging the evacuation, and a resolution of the Seattle Downtown Kiwanis Club formally asked that "all enemy aliens and all Japanese. . .forthwith be removed from the Pacific slope."

Though considerably less active than the American Legion, other military groups displayed interest in the problem. Labor unions from Ketchikan, Alaska, to Los Angeles, California, joined in urging evacuation. Represented were fishermen, building-trades workers, carpenters, textile workers, cereal workers, meat-cutters, and butchers, retail clerks, stage employees, hotel and restaurant workers, electric employees, and general laborers. . . . A strong statement in opposition to evacuation was made by the secretary of the California State Industrial Union Council (affiliated with the Congress of Industrial Organization), but the C.I.O. Los Angeles Union Council passed a resolution in favor of the movement.

Employer's and businessmen's groups, in common with chambers of commerce and corporation agriculturists, expressed similar statements, the pro-evacuation action of the Metal Trades Manufacturing Association of southern California, the Pasadena Lake-Washington Business Men's Association, the Eastern Washington Beet Growers Association, and the Los Angles Realty Board being examples in point. . . .

Comment

. . . Not all organizations, by any means, were calling for evacuation. But opposition groups were far outnumbered and almost unpublicized. In contrast, virtually every one of the hundreds of resolutions in favor of evacuation was represented by newspaper headlines and by one or more letters to local and national political leaders and by similar communications to military officers. . . .

Officials of the Western Growers Protective Association stated many times that the removal of Japanese would not be a disruptive economic factor. At the same time, several invitations to profit as a result of evacuation were published in the association's own journal. Thus in February, 1942, it was noted that "the alien Japanese element are going out of the wholesale produce trade in Los Angeles, and many of the large firms are on the market for a few cents on the dollar." In April, 1942, a chart was published that showed Japanese Americans had controlled 31,000 of the 46,000 acres devoted to growing vegetables for the Los Angeles area. "Those looking toward the Los Angeles market as an outlet for their vegetables should . . . take into account the type of crop of which shortages probably exist," the article advised . . .

An even more direct evidence of the association's post-evacuation statements contradicting its pre-evacuation assertions (with proof that profit actually was made as the result of evacuation) was contained in a review of the 1942 activities of the association, written by its managing secretary. This revealing statement said:

> A very great dislocation of our industry occurred when the Japanese were evacuated from Military Zones one and two in the Pacific Coast Areas, and although as shipping groups these dislocations were not so severe the feeding of the cities in close proximity to large Japanese truck farm holdings was considerable and shortages in many commodities developed and prices skyrocketed to almost unheard of values. This, coupled with increased buying power in practically every district of the United States, also brought to the growers and shippers most satisfactory prices on almost every commodity shipped from California and Arizona. . . .

The stand of various Farm Bureau Federations, during the pre-evacuation months, that Japanese labor might be needed but that the state (to quote a county bureau secretary) could "certainly do without Japanese farm operators and supervisors" was still another evidence of the economic motive at work. For the Farm Bureau, too, this became even more clear after evacuation had taken place. In a meeting of the State Federation in November, 1942, it was reported that "California vegetable growers have no intention of inviting the banished Japanese back after the war to compete with them." The Japanese question became a prominent issue at the meeting. "The vegetable growers, more keenly appreciative of what they face in Japanese competition than other groups, appear to be unanimous in wanting the Nipponese kept out. A number of growers frankly admitted they prefer white competition."

Economic gain was not the only extraneous regional factor that was a part of the demand for evacuation. The Native Sons of the Golden West and the California Joint Immigration Committee viewed the removal of Japanese as a means of stamping out the threat they saw to California arising out of the alleged high birth rate and the alleged alien culture of resident Japanese. . . .

All this does not impute hypocrisy to those who urged evacuation as a measure of national defense but who simultaneously satisfied other desires. The war provided the unique situation whereby patriotism (i.e. a desire to protect the West Cost from the enemy) could become parallel with economic, racial, and political considerations. . . .

The evacuation proposals raised problems of fundamental importance to a democracy. It was demanded that more than 110,000 people, the largest portion of whom were citizens of the United States, be removed from their homes and businesses and incarcerated under military guard. Yet a consideration of the extreme gravity of this act in terms of democratic principles was conspicuously lacking in the efforts of the pressure groups to bring about evacuation. This was partly the result of the extraordinary wartime situation and of the deteriorating position of the Western allies in the South Pacific. It was also, however, a new manifestation of an old disregard for civil rights by certain California groups. On one hand, organizations typified by the Native Sons of the Golden West had never believed that even American citizens of oriental ancestry were entitled to American rights and privileges. On the other hand, virtually all the economic groups most active in urging evacuation had histories to interfere with the right of labor to organize. The La Follette committee's extensive investigation of deprivations of civil rights by California employers' associations severely criticized the very organizations most active in fostering the Japanese evacuation. These included the Western Growers Protective Association, the Grower-Shipper Vegetable Association, the Los Angeles Chamber of Commerce, the California Farm Bureau Federation, and the Merchants and Manufacturers Association.

The two sets of historical factors nicely complemented each other. Racial, economic, and political drives were abetted by the disregard for civil liberties and together were easily turned to the drastic program of mass evacuation. Evacuation was universally presented as a measure to protect the West Coast from sabotage, espionage, and fifth-column dangers. How far the regional demands frequently were from the issue of national defense was best illustrated *after* Japanese had been removed from the West Coast and incarcerated. Though further repressive measures against Japanese Americans had no direct relationship to the national safety, it was at this time that the greatest regional effort was made to have the group treated as one of special iniquity. Demands were made that Japanese not be ''coddled'' in their isolated barrack cities; that no Japanese be allowed to leave the barbed-wire enclosures to go anywhere in the United States; that Japanese be permanently barred from the Far Western States or (in alternative) prohibited from owning land and operating businesses; that the sexes be separated so that relocation centers would not become ''breeding farms''; that citizens of Japanese ancestry be deprived of their citizenship; that the entire minority group be deported at the end of the war. . . .

State and Local Political Leaders

. . . Immediately after Pearl Harbor there were official statements from California's governor and many others expressing faith and loyalty of resident Japanese and urging that tolerance be shown them. An apparent lack of interest followed, which,in turn, was ended by the most vehement expressions in favor of mass incarceration without respect to citizenship. As on the Washington level, there were at first wide variations of opinion with respect to the type of control measures necessary and the manner in which they should be administered; as on the Washington level, opposition to the forced, mass movement collapsed once the demands for that movement reached their full voice. Only one important local official, the mayor of Tacoma, Washington, went on record as opposed to the blanket imposition of restrictions on citizens and aliens alike. . . .

Attorney-General Earl Warren of California

Early in February, 1942, the California State Personnel Board issued an order barring from civil service positions all citizens who were ''descendants'' of alien enemies. Though covering all ''descendants'' of German, Italian, and Japanese aliens, the order was clearly aimed at American

Japanese and was applied only against them. But this action was taken in the face of the vigorous, formal dissent of Attorney-General Earl Warren of California. The ruling of the Personnel Board, he wrote, attempted to establish different degrees of loyalty and in so doing "discriminates against naturalized citizens and citizens by birth of the first generation, in favor of those citizens whose forebears have lived in this country for a greater number of generations." Such distinctions were neither recognized nor sanctioned by any provision of the Constitution nor by any law...

The attorney-general took a similar position when Governor Culbert Olson authorized the State Department of Agriculture to revoke licenses of enemy aliens handling produce. In an opinion addressed to the State Department of Professional and Vocational Standards, the attorney-general declared that such a wholesale revocation of licenses was unlawful.

On February 2, the positions of Governor Olson and Attorney-General Warren had been reversed. After meeting with army officers, the governor had announced that mass evacuation of Japanese aliens would not be necessary; on the same day, however, a meeting of district attorneys and sheriffs of California convened by the attorney-general produced a resolution urging that "all alien Japanese be forthwith evacuated from all areas in the State of California to some place in the interior...for the duration of the war."

Three days before this meeting Mr. Warren had for the first time publicly declared himself in favor of evacuation: "I have come to the conclusion that the Japanese situation as it exists in this state today, may well be the Achilles heel of the entire civilian defense effort. Unless something is done it may bring about a repetition of Pearl Harbor."

At the meeting itself the attorney-general spoke at length on the same theme...That no sabotage had yet occurred was an ominous fact:

> It seems to me that it is quite significant that in this great state of ours we have had no fifth-column activities and no sabotage reported. It looks very much to me as though it is a studied effort not to have any until the zero hour arrives...That was the history of Pearl Harbor. I can't help believing that the same thing is planned for us in California. It would be inconsistent with everything the Axis has ever done, if it was not planned for us in California.

The assembled law-enforcement officers were in complete sympathy with the desire to remove Japanese aliens from strategic areas...

Mr. Warren agreed "a hundred per cent" with the expressed desire "to get...these Japs off the land right away." Regardless, however, of his own views and those of the law-enforcement officers, the attorney-general pointed out that they possessed "no power of internment." "If we did, perhaps we could come to an agreement pretty quickly in this room as to what should be done." In the absence of internment power, the attorney-general argued, every effort should be bent to utilize the tools that did exist...

The attorney-general made it clear that he would transmit to federal authorities the mandate of the assembled district attorneys and sheriffs that it was essential to move Japanese en masse from coastal areas. The local law-enforcement officers were most insistent on this point...

Comment

Two points of special interest emerge from this overview of the activity of state and local political officials with respect to the Japanese evacuation.

First, the record demonstrates clearly that state and local officials, in effect, became powerful influences upon federal officials in fostering the evacuation. Their role here was analogous to that of the congressional delegations.

Secondly, the history provides an unusual insight into the wartime attitudes of California officials.

Attorney-General Warren's record is characterized, on one side, by a scrupulous regard for the legal status of resident Japanese and, on the other, by a determination to foster the evacuation by every possible lawful means.

Mayor Bowron of Los Angeles apparently found no inconsistency in asserting that "the form of internment" he advocated for Japanese was "not internment" within the usual meaning of the term; or in announcing that the "rights" of American citizens of Japanese ancestry "will be respected" on the day after he had approved the dismissal of a group of these citizens from their jobs in the city government; or in publicly asserting that the dangers of sabotage were so great "the Japanese, both alien and American born, must go" while privately writing that he would prefer to have all the Japanese remain in Los Angeles rather than have the city "greatly inconvenienced" or subjected to "some sort of martial law."

Governor Olson's position as a leader of liberal forces did not prevent him from taking three radically different stands on the evacuation issue within a period of five months.

California law-enforcement officers, whose primary responsibility was to control those taking extralegal action, did not scruple to argue that evacuation be carried out because of threats of such action.

Above all this there prevailed a basic distrust of the Japanese population as a group. . . . This view was asserted by officials of all degrees of importance and from each of the three western states.

The dismissal of California state employees was the most striking manifestation of this feeling. Initially, a resolution was passed condemning all racial discrimination. Then, in rapid succession, came a series of discriminatory events: a second legislative resolution asked for the "investigation" of the "descendants" of alien enemies employed by the state: eligibility lists were closed to Japanese Americans; questionaires were sent to employees whose names "sounded Japanese"; wholesale suspension and wholesale dismissal charges were then filed without reference to the questionnaires and without reference to individual merit.

One of the remarkable aspects of the whole proceeding was the fact that a number of the employees in question were innocent of even the charges made; i.e., they could not read Japanese and did not subscribe to Japanese newspapers; they did not attend the Buddhist church and had not studied at language schools; they did not belong to Japanese American organizations and they had renounced their Japanese citizenship.

The Personnel Board did not heed such facts. And the dismissals were enforced despite the attorney-general's ruling that they were unconstitutional. Not a single specific act of questionable conduct or disloyalty on the part of a Japanese American employee was brought before the board.

29. Both Explanations Discounted

It is the contention of the authors of the next passage,[6] *Jacobus ten Broek, Edward N. Barnhart, and Floyd W. Matson, that writers such as Grodzins have greatly overdrawn the picture of a well-drilled army of businessmen, community leaders, and nativist groups converging on the Japanese-Americans with fixed bayonets. Instead, they insist that the anti-Japanese prejudice was amorphous and widely scattered throughout the population, that remarkably few local government leaders acquiesced in the hysteria, and that De Witt's actual decision of February 14,1942, to put the Japanese into camps arose quite independently of the activities of any pressure group . . . the authors*

[6]Jacobus ten Broek, Edward N. Barnhart, and Floyd W. Matson, *Prejudice, War and the Constitution: Japanese American Evacuation and Resettlement* (Berkeley and Los Angeles: University of California Press, 1954), 85-334.

spend the bulk of their book laying the blame where they feel it belongs: with the state tradition of racism, with the people, with the military, with President Roosevelt, and, finally, with the Supreme Court, which cast over the entire affair a sanctimonious aura that was as repugnant as it was indelible.

The senior author of this work, Ten Broek, was born in Canada in 1911, but was educated and naturalized in this country. He holds a Harvard law degree and has been a lecturer and professor at various institutions; also, from 1959 to 1960 he was a fellow at the Center for Advanced Study in the Behavioral Sciences at Palo Alto. Another major work by Ten Broek is Anti-Slavery Origins of the Fourteenth Amendment *(1955).*

What prompted the responsible officials in the Army and the government to take the drastic step of uprooting the entire West Coast Japanese American population; removing them from their homes and confining them in camps?

In most discussions of the episode the official explanation of military necessity has been discounted. In its place various hypotheses have been advanced, of which by far the most frequently defended and widely accepted are two that may be called the "pressure group" and "politician" theories....

The Pressure Group Theory

Morton Grodzins in *Americans Betrayed*, presents the pressure-group theory in its most elaborate form...[but] examination of the evidence adduced...reveals a common defect which would seem to be fatal to the theory. None of its proponents has effectively correlated the activities of pressure groups with the policy decisions of the responsible military and government officials at the time when the decisions were made. The dates of the principal decisions are known; any theory of why the policy-makers acted as they did must therefore show, as a preliminary step, that the alleged influence was brought to bear before the policy was determined....

Among students of the evacuation episode, Grodzins alone has presented appreciable data on the activities of a wide variety of groups and interests to support the claim of their influence upon official policy. However, his allegiance to the pressure-group wavers...[still,] in the end Grodzins appears to attribute the decision to the unsound judgment of De Witt prior to February 14 to recommend the second program; exclusion of all Japanese from the coast? Is there convincing proof that all or many of the pressure groups were conspicuously active in bringing their views to the attention of the general? Specifically, as it is true that organized agricultural interest, the most commonly cited, insistently urged the banishment of the Japanese in the period after Pearl Harbor and before mid-February? Were their demands known to De Witt? From what is known of the activities of these and other groups, are we led to conclude that the general must have succumbed to their pressure—or is the evidence so nebulous as to indicate that the truth does not lie here?

Pressure Groups and Coastal Exclusion

Agricultural groups...Grodzins...does present a variety of material on the actions of agricultural groups to confirm his assertion of their impact on policy.... But Grodzins' evidence does not show that the agricultural community was uniformly or even substantially exercised over the Japanese issue. Only six of the hundreds of West Coast agricultural associations publicly expressed proevacuation opinions: i.e., four of the approximately one hundred food and agricultural trade associations in California, two of the many in Washington, and none of the one hundred and fifty or more in Oregon. Nor does Grodzins offer evidence to support his charge that "many smaller groups" beyond the few he specifically mentions were active. Furthermore, the "pressure" prior to February 14 was altogether trifling and was not even directed primarily at De Witt. It consisted of eight letters from officials of three associations to congressmen, a visit by the secretary of one organization to Washington early in December, the adoption of a resolution favoring evacuation by one association, and a telegram to a governor passed on to Attorney General Biddle. The activity of the two other associations occurred after February 14.

To Grodzins the rural villains of the piece were the Western Growers Protective Association and the Grower-Shipper Vegetable Association. Of the first he says that it "bent every effort to foster the evacuation"; yet its known activities before February 14 consisted of one letter by its president recommending evacuation to a congressman, and the passage by the board of directors of a resolution favoring evacuation which was not even published in the association's monthly publication. On such evidence the indictment of the association for powerful early agitation seems grossly unjustified. The activity of the Grower-Shipper Association, before February 14, consisted of a visit by an official to a congressman. The governing board of the group failed even to pass a resolution favoring evacuation....

Finally, the same author's claim that "growing and marketing organizations were uniformly in favor of evacuation" is not substantiated by the record. Agricultural and food associations did not present a united front. Two such groups are known to have gone on record *against* mass evacuation of the Japanese; the Washington Produce Shippers Association of Seattle, and the Olympia [Washington] Oyster Growers Association. The oyster growers complained that the removal of the Japanese would "practically paralyze the industry." The manager of the produce shippers, testifying before the Tolan Committee, not only did "not concur in the recommendation of a mass evacuation," but declared that "wholesale evacuation would be an economic waste and a stupid error...."

Business groups and service clubs.... Did this section of society raise the cry for Japanese exclusion in such strong and imperative tones that the Army must have been stirred by it? The available data would seem to indicate otherwise. Of the approximately 1,150 nonagricultural trade and business associations in California, exactly one officially advocated evacuation in the period before February 14; and of the many similar organizations in Oregon and Washington none is known to have so acted. Chambers of commerce were no more outstanding in their activity. The California State Chamber of Commerce and the Washington State Federation of Commercial Organizations passed no resolutions. Of the more than 600 city and county chambers in the three West Coast states, only six adopted resolutions prior to the decision of February 14. Only one of California's 36 county chambers is known to have passed a proevacuation resolution before that date; and of the approximately 350 city chambers in the state, a total of three were on record as approving resolution during the period. None of the 80 Oregon city and county chambers expressed an opinion before mid-February; of the many Washington chambers only two are known to have done so.

Service clubs are also accused by Grodzins, the Lions being said to have been among "the most active." But...the many hundreds of Lions, Rotary, and Kiwanis clubs in the West Coast states, only two are known to have expressed sentiment for evacuation before February 14. Not one of the three hundred Rotary clubs on the Pacific Coast was on record with a resolution favoring evacuation during the period of decision.

Nor can the case against the businessmen be upheld.... Historically, the role of big business groups had been one of consistent support of the Japanese and voluble opposition to the anti-Japanese agitation—even during periods when public prejudice was highest against the Orientals. In this role big business was indeed acting from motives of self-interest since its primary concern was with employment of Japanese labor and maintenance of favorable trade relations. It is not to be doubted that after Pearl Harbor numerous individual businessmen and some business groups became hostile to the Japanese Americans—but, far from sustaining any "devil theory," this proves only that they were private citizens and members of the general public, caught up with the rest of the populace in the mounting wave of indignation and fear that swept the Pacific Coast in the early months of war.

Military and patriotic societies.... The American legion was by far the most active in its campaign; but even Legion activity cannot be adjudged to have been so extensive that De Witt must beyond doubt have been stirred by it. Of the 873 posts and 50 area and district organizations of the Legion on the West Coast, 25 urged the removal either of enemy aliens in general, of Japanese nationals, or of all Japanese Americans, in the period before February 14.... Five resolutions came from California, all limited to urging internment of enemy aliens or dual citizens, or both....

As for the other military societies, of the many hundreds of posts of the VFW, the Order of the Purple Heart, the United Spanish War Veterans, and the Disabled Veterans of the World War, only one isolated post is known to have asked before mid-February for Japanese evacuation, although two called for removal or internment of all enemy aliens.

...Does it appear that [the agitation of] the Native Sons of the Golden West and the California Joint Immigration Committee after Pearl Harbor created significant pressure upon De Witt? The facts would seem to point to a negative answer. It was not until February 14—the day of the De Witt recommendation and two months and one week after Pearl Harbor—that the Board of Grand Officers of the Native Sons expressed an opinion in favor of evacuation. Before that date only four of the more than one hundred and fifty subordinate parlors and assemblies are known to have expressed the same opinion.... [T]he official journal, the *Grizzly Bear*, failed to express an editorial opinion in favor of evacuation through the first six months of 1942—although it did continue to voice its traditional demands for the permanent removal of Japanese from California.... The California Joint Immigration Committee was equally lethargic....

Social clubs and fraternal societies.—Can the pressure-group hypothesis be redeemed by the actions of the many social clubs and benevolent societies along the Pacific slope?... There may well have been "almost no end" to the variety of such groups; but there was a definite limit to the numbers. The impression conveyed by the above passage of hundreds of groups in frenzied activity is wholly unwarranted: the files of the Department of Justice contained the resolutions of only four West Coast social and civic clubs besides those specified by Grodzins. Moreover, only three of the thousands of such groups in the three coastal states, are known to have demanded evacuation *before* February 14....

...If De Witt had received copies of all known resolutions of the groups which advocated Japanese evacuation in the days before February 14—an unlikely supposition, as most of them were directed elsewhere—his mail would have contained a total of thirty-two such recommendations.... It seems unreasonable to suppose that these scattered expressions of opinion, from a handful of organizations for the most part obscure, would have been sufficient in themselves—even had the general known of them—to have commanded that decision....

The Politician Theory

The explanation that the evacuation was the result of interest-motivated efforts of politicians on the West Coast and in Congress is almost as frequently encountered as the pressure-group theory. The charge may be summarized briefly: In response to the growing apprehension of the public and its antagonism toward the Japanese Americans, and always alert to find ways of capitalizing on groundswells of opinions by acting with the appearance of leading them, politicians and office-holders on all levels of government raised their voices for the removal of the offending minority. So insistent was their pressure and so powerful their influence that the Army and the government were forced to capitulate.... "The mayors of Los Angeles, San Francisco, Portland and Seattle all favored mass evacuation; various grand juries and city councils and boards of supervisors presented similar demands; and law enforcement officials, in general, spoke in favor of the proposal." Grodzins is still more explicit. The subtitle of his book, "Politics and the Japanese Evacuation," suggests his commitment; and the text spells it out in elaborate detail. "State and local political leaders played no subsidiary role in the movement to bring about Japanese evacuation," he asserts. "Every prominent west coast political leader and virtually every local law-enforcement officer made known their belief in the necessity of evacuation...."

West Coast Politicians

[But] the activities of public officials on the West Coast before February 14, 1942, were relatively, if not absolutely, insignificant. State, county, and city officials were not uniformly or even prominently outspoken for evacuation at the time when their views might have swayed the commanding general.

The state level. At first, the governors of none of the three West Coast states were publicly on record in favor of mass evacuation. Governor Culbert L. Olson of California even sought to have an alternative plan of his own adopted calling for employment of Japanese Americans under supervision on California farms. In the period under discussion Olson's public statements were characterized by pleas for tolerance, concern for the safety of the Japanese and affirmations of their loyalty to the United States.

The lieutenant governors of California and Washington made no statements in favor of evacuation, nor did the secretaries of state. None of the attorney generals for the three states was a public advocate of the move. . . .

California's attorney general in 1942, Earl Warren, has been charged by several writers with great if not crucial influence in promoting evacuation. However, an examination of the evidence fails to sustain the many allegations against him; and in particular there remains no proof that Warren ever publicly declared himself in favor of mass evacuation prior to mid-February. His appearance before the Tolan Committee, of course, could not have influenced De Witt. His utterances at the meeting of the Joint Immigration Committee were not made known to the general (and indeed the extent of the committee's pressure seems to have been a press release of February 13, issued on the very eve of De Witt's "Final Recommendation"). Further, there is no evidence one way or the other as to what Warren's sentiment was on February 11 when he accompanied Mayor Bowron of Los Angeles in a personal call on De Witt.

The city level. . . . There is no evidence to show that more than one of the thousands of mayors of West Coast municipalities—Fletcher Bowron of Los Angeles—expressed an opinion publicly prior to mid-February in favor of security measures against the Japanese. Grodzins claims that "local elected officials of small California communities were very active," but the only evidence cited is an instance in Ventura where residents were reportedly urged " 'to add their voices to the cry for action by telegraphing their congressional representatives.' " (Examination of the newspaper story quoted by Grodzins shows that the officials were not urging mass evacuation but only seeking to have the Department of Justice declare Ventura a restricted area. This would not have excluded aliens but merely subjected them to curfew and travel controls.)

Bowron, alone among West Coast mayors, advocated placement of the Japanese at agricultural labor in supervised camps and urged action of some sort upon General De Witt before February 14. In a press release of February 6, he clarified his labor proposal: "I have not advocated the mass internment of all Japanese within the usual meaning of the term. . . . For alien Japanese residents, it would, in a sense, be a form of internment, but without the necessity of closely confined incarceration, there should be no need for breaking up families." In company with Earl Warren and Tom Clark, Bowron called on De Witt on February 11 to urge security measures against the Japanese. But, despite assertions to the contrary, there is no substantial evidence that De Witt was influenced in his policy decisions by this visit. Bowron himself did not claim it was causative; he said only that his comments "may have been the last straw. . . ."

. . . Unless further and stronger data are brought forth, therefore, the politician theory must be adjudged "not proven."

Conclusion

The pressure-group and politician theories of responsibility fall short of substantiation not only on the ground of activity, but also on that of influence. For why should General De Witt have heeded these scattered recommendations and petitions? Although politicians might be expected to respond to a show of pressure from the public or from important groups, the general was not a politician. He was a career officer with no interest in public office; his job and the regard of his superiors were not dependent on popular opinion. He was faced with a military problem: the defense of the coast. Why should he depart from his military estimate of the situation to undertake an extensive, unprecedented, and "unmilitary" program at the behest of a handful of private organizations and some minor officials?

To assert that De Witt contemplated the program of evacuation out of conviction that the military situation required it is not, of course, to concur in his judgment or to maintain that it was isolated from the surrounding community of opinion. It is a central contention of this book that the claim of "military necessity" was unjustified—but that the dereliction was one of folly, not of knavery. The racism exhibited by the general and his staff was blatant and unmistakable, and clearly corresponded to (if it did not surpass) that of articulate public opinion along the Pacific Coast in the early months of war. But this is additional reason for believing that the military did not need to be persuaded, rather than that it did.

The responsibility of the Army and the government for the decisions which led from curfew through evacuation to detention cannot be shifted. But it can be shared, in a lesser degree, by all who demanded, affirmed, or acquiesced in those decisions. These included politicians, Legionnaires, businessmen, laborers, farmers, Native Sons,—in fact, the "public" of the Pacific Coast. It was not in the self-interest of "powerful economic groups" generally to move against the Japanese Americans; indeed, many who opposed evacuation acted in a manner more consistent with economic motives. But the anti-Japanese demands of all these constituent elements of the public were clearly in harmony with the suspicion and distrust which the West Coast had nurtured for so many generations and which the fortunes of war brought so painfully to its consciousness. No theory of backstage machinations and skillfully organized agitation on the part of reactionary interests and corrupt officials is needed to explain the course of events which culminated in the confinement of an entire minority group on racial grounds.... That among the clamoring voices there were some who stood to profit is undeniable. Most undeniable of all is the the American people generally, and the people of the West Coast in particular, were anxious, angry, and afraid; that in this mood the familiar specter of the "yellow peril" appeared before them, and that they struck out blindly at its shadow—not knowing that by this blow they were to damage , not the enemy, but the constitutional safeguards of their own free way of life....

The responsibility for this flagrant breach of the nation's constitutional and moral ideas may be readily assigned.

It rests first and primarily with the people: the people of the nation in general; the people of the West Coast in particular. Popular feelings and attitudes were complex, but the two major forces which contributed to their development may be identified. First, of course, was the war itself....

The reaction of the American people to these catastrophic events [German and Japanese victories in 1941-1942] was not merely one of disbelief and incredulity; it was one of rising anger, fear, apprehension, and frustration. In this atmosphere few were heard to protest the removal from the western coastal area of those who had ancestral connections with Japan.

The second major force operating in the formation of popular attitudes, especially on the West Coast, was a long history of anti-Oriental and a specifically anti-Japanese agitation. The Japanese attack on Pearl Harbor activated, but did not begin, the Japanese American episode. The basis for the episode is to be found in the history of the Pacific frontier, when the first Japanese immigrants arrived to share the popular prejudice against the Chinese and eventually to inherit it.... Rising Japanese military and national strength, coupled with an aggressive policy of expansion following the Russo-Japanese War, gave seeming substance to the secret-agent element of the stereotype. The attack of Pearl Harbor provided, in the minds of the people, its complete substantiation. That Japanese immigrants and their descendants should now aid and support the ancestral government was all that was needed to bring about a total realization of the stereotype of the "yellow peril."

The primary responsibility of the people for the action taken against the Japanese Americans cannot be shifted to the shoulders of pressure groups and politicians. The activity of such organizations and individuals before the basic decision of mid-February, 1942 (and indeed after) has been greatly exaggerated both as to extent and influence. The pressure groups of all varieties, the politicians in Congress, the state legislatures, and the executive departments, did not so much lead as follow the people. Many of them, in fact, pulled in the opposite direction; still more took no public stand at all. Some who moved against the Japanese Americans were prompted by the hope of economic gain; others acted contrary to their own self-interest. In the scattered and spasmodic, not to say desultory, actions of these varied groups along the coast in the early months of war there is little sign of systematic organization or crafty connivance; all that can be said is that of a mountainous plot existed its labor brought forth a mouse. But although the voices raised in discordant chorus against the Japanese Americans had no common organization, they did have a common heritage and a common fear. For politicians, farmer, businessmen, and exalted rulers are also people, private citizens, and members of the general public, who share the prevailing attitudes, beliefs, and habits of their communities. Not only do they respond to and exploit the prejudices of their fellow, they also possess them. In early 1942, their expression of anti-Orientalism was basically neither premonitory nor self-serving. It was an illustration and reflection of public sentiment.

Responsibility for the episode rests, secondarily, with the military, particularly General De Witt and the Western Defense Command. To portray General De Witt as the sole or even the chief villain in this tragic drama, as has so often been done, is a much an injustice as to absolve him altogether. But his role, though subordinate, was important. The governmental activity which resulted in the establishment of the Japanese American program was initiated by General De Witt. He made the proposal to his superiors and requested authority to execute it. For having done so he must stand convicted by history of committing a military blunder—the perpetration of an outrage on citizen civilians which was not required by the emergency. The plea of military necessity cannot be sustained. Statements from General De Witt's Final Report make it plain that the proposal to evacuate and imprison the Japanese Americans was not the product of a military estimate of the military situation. That the program of exclusion and incarceration resulted from a proper and commendable concern about the security of the West Coast does not mean that the decision to inaugurate it was not based on palpable race prejudice in the Western Defense Command.

Even greater responsibility rests upon President Franklin D. Roosevelt and his civilian aides in the War Department, Secretary Henry L. Stimson and Assistant Secretary John J. McCloy, and upon the Congress of the United States. General De Witt did not order evacuation and incarceration independently and without prior authorization from his superiors. . . . He presented his plan and request for authority to the War Department, thence to the President, and eventually to Congress. In response, the President, as the President alone could, issued Executive Order 9066, fully empowering the Secretary of War to put the proposed plan into operation. Thereafter, and pursuant to this delegation of authority, Secretary Henry L. Stimson, the civilian head of the War Department, and John J. McCloy, his civilian assistant, first modified the plan by exempting German and Italian American citizens and aliens, then ordered it put into effect, and finally, continuously supervised its execution. Meanwhile, the Congress of the United States duly enacted Public Law 503, encompassing and providing civilian sanctions for Executive Order 9066 and the subdelegations under it. . . .

McCloy's apologetic statement that "military men made the decision—it was a military decision" may indicate the attitude of the Washington officials involved in the decision. It does not and it cannot, however, explain the failure of McCloy and of Secretary Stimson to perform the function implicit in the historic purpose behind the requirement that the War Department must have civilian heads. Responsibility rests, finally, with the courts, and especially with the Supreme Court of the United States. In many ways the failure of the Supreme Court was the greatest failure of all. For the military is preoccupied with war, not with the Constitution and men's rights. The President and

Congress, too, are "war-waging" branches of government. The primary action and affirmative decision was theirs; but they moved on the brink of the event when the general course and outcome of the war were altogether uncertain. In 1945 General Marshall pointed out that in "the black days of 1942 when the Japanese conquered all of Malaysia, occupied Burma, and threatened India while the German armies approached the Volga and the Suez. . . Germany and Japan came so close to complete domination of the world that we do not yet realize how thin the thread of Allied survival had been stretched."

Among the branches of government, the Supreme Court occupies a unique position. It is not so much an active as a reflective body. It decisions are made on the nether side of the event. Its job is not primary but secondary. It is the historian of events as much as it is their maker. It exerts only such constructive leadership as derives from the power to negate the policy of others. Its self-arrogated and perhaps inherent function is to strike the governmental balance between motion and stability, between new action and old doctrines, between the powers of the nation and men's rights.

If the court had struck down the program, the Japanese American episode would have lived in history as nothing worse than a military blunder. But the court approved the program as constitutional, a step with implications and consequences accurately described by Justice Jackson in his dissenting opinion on the *Korematsu* case:

> Much is said of the danger to liberty from the Army program for deporting and detaining these citizens of Japanese extraction. But a judicial construction of the due process clause that will sustain this order is a far more subtle blow to liberty than the promulgation of the order itself. A military order, however unconstitutional, is not apt to last longer than the military emergency. Even during that period a succeeding commander may revoke it all. But once a judicial opinion rationalizes such an order to show that it conforms to the Constitution, or rather rationalizes the Constitution to show that the Constitution sanctions such an order, the Court for all time has validated the principle of racial discrimination in criminal procedure and of transplanting American citizens. The principle then lies about like a loaded weapon ready for the hand of any authority that can bring forward a plausible claim of an urgent need. Every repetition imbeds that principle more deeply in our law and thinking and expands it to new purposes. All who observe the work of courts are familiar with what Judge Cardozo described as "the tendency of a principle to expand itself to the limit of its logic." A military commander may overstep the bounds of constitutionality, and it is an incident. But if we review and approve, that passing incident becomes the doctrine of the Constitution. There it has a generative power of its own, and all that it creates will be in its own image.

. . . The role of the court in the Japanese American episode of World War I was. . . one of the great failures in its history— comparable with its surrender to slavery in *Prigg* v. *Pennsylvania* and in *Dred Scott* v. *Sanford*. . . .

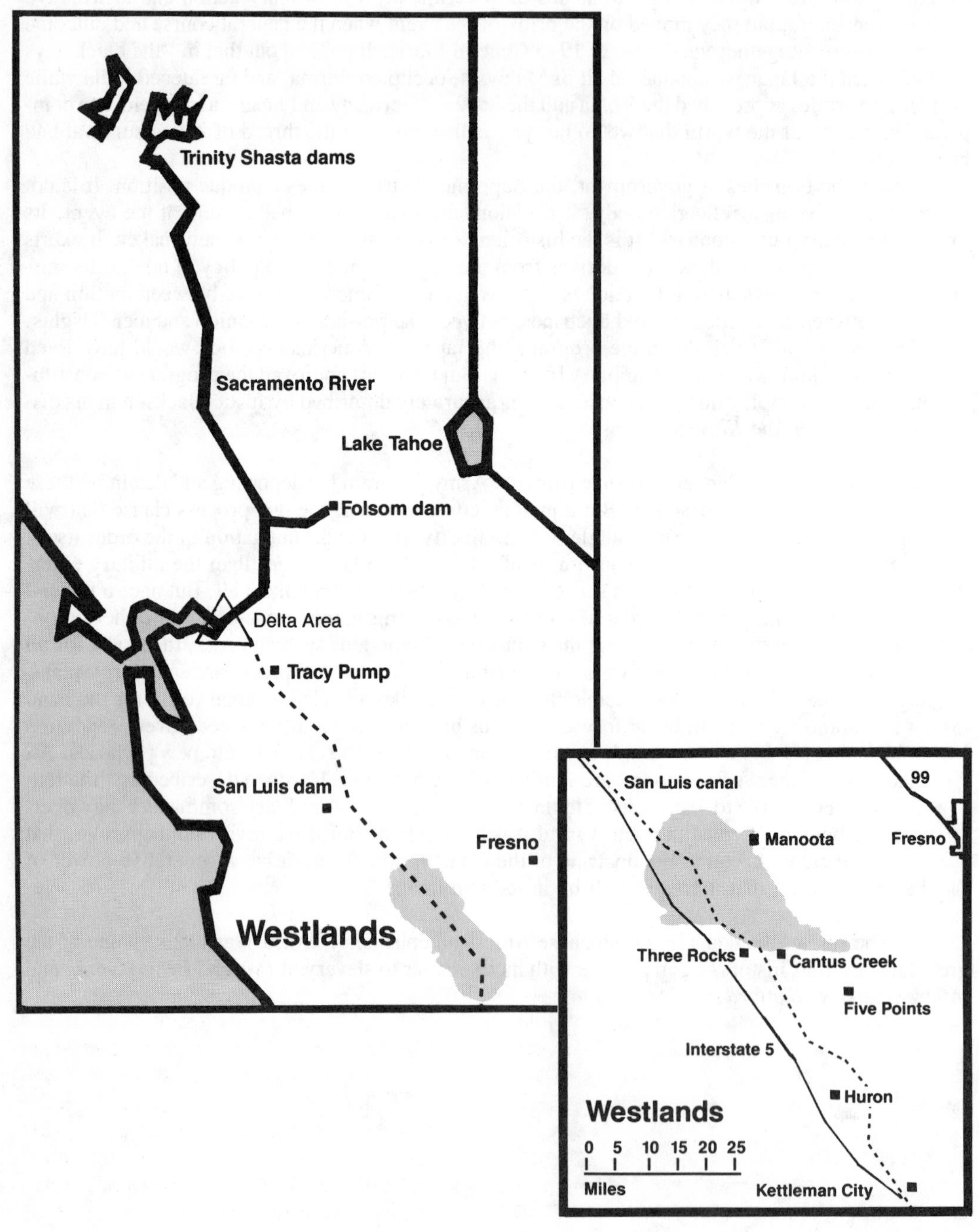
Trinity Shasta dams
Sacramento River
Lake Tahoe
Folsom dam
Delta Area
Tracy Pump
San Luis dam
Fresno
Westlands
San Luis canal
99
Manoota
Fresno
Three Rocks
Cantus Creek
Five Points
Interstate 5
Huron
Westlands
0 5 10 15 20 25
Miles
Kettleman City

I wish to save the very wealthy men of this country and their advocates and upholders from the ruin that they would bring upon themselves if they were permitted to have their way.

—Theodore Roosevelt, in a speech in San Francisco, explaining why he signed the original bill setting forth the 160-acre limitation.

I think I learned a long time ago that this issue [reclamation law] has deep roots. We're dealing with important skirmishes in a battle that's been going on for a hundred years and is going to go on for a lot more.

—Paul S. Taylor, U.S. Berkeley, Oral History Project.

As an agricultural community we had a settled way of life, in which the people on one side of the valley were knowledgeable of people on the other side of the valley, where one knew the history of families on the other side and [for] quite a ways around, where people shared the same experiences and were beset by the same problems. The same rainstorm ruined your crop as your neighbor's crop. You commiserated together. You had successes and failures together. Your children were born, raised, reared, married in the same area and you watched them go off and become in many cases farmers or farmer's wives.

—Yvonne Jacobson, *Passing Farms, Enduring Values: Santa Clara Valley*, 1984.

I think farm people are entitled to think about growing and expanding and bringing to their families all the advantages that other people have. And in this present time that means usually operating on a larger scale, adding a bigger investment and becoming in effect a businessman-farmer. And you don't have to be 40 acres and a mule in order to be classed as a family farm. That's an archaic concept.

—Henry Schacht, Vice President, California Canners and Growers.

CHAPTER 11

THE 160-ACRE LIMITATION
Archaic Remnant or Democratic Alternative

The key to farming in California has long been irrigated water. Those who have had access to reclamation water—by tapping into the vast network of canals, ditches, aqueducts, and artificial reservoirs—could share in the bounteous outpouring of farm goods that has typified California. Natural stream flow and underground sources can nurture only small amounts of the fertile soil of this state.

The basic law covering water development in Western America was the federal reclamation law of 1902. It not only set in motion the machinery to build dams and reservoirs, but established precise limits on those who were to receive the water. The policy issue in 1902 was how to unleash the riches of the soil for the benefit of family farmers and rather than giant speculators, absentee landlords or such corporate developers as railroads. To achieve this objective, Congress imposed a limit of 160 acres as the amount of land a farmer could own while drawing water from a federal reclamation project, and further provided that the farmer had to live on that land and not be an absentee landlord. In this way a Progressive Congress and a Progressive President (Theodore Roosevelt) affirmed their support for the family farm, a time-honored democratic institution which might otherwise suffer unfair competition.

Nevertheless, in the formative years between 1910 and 1945 California farming came to be best typified by agribusiness—agriculture dominated not by small farms but by large and medium-sized ones, many of them corporate farms. The movers and shakers of this agriculture were heavily capitalized enterprises, operating huge acres of irrigated land, employing a large migratory labor force, and vertically integrated to deal in everything from seed production to wholesale marketing. Farming estates in California were referred to as "factories in the field."

The reclamation law did not work as originally intended. The 160-acre limitation withstood many court tests, but was weakly enforced by federal officials. When. . .the big landowners charged the Bureau of Reclamation with trying to "rule the Valley," and unsuccessfully pleaded with Congress for an exemption (see also, Chapter 16, on the Peripheral Canal), they resorted to litigation. In 1958 the U.S. Supreme Court ruled in the *Ivanhoe* Case that the water was intended for people on the basis of the greatest good for the greatest number. The high court thus let stand the original law with its democratic principle intact.

California's powerful agribusiness interests now lobbied the legislature for a brand new, state-financed water reclamation project that would not be hindered by the 160-acre limit. Small farmers represented by the Grange organization and representatives for organized labor protested that this would be a giveaway for big farmers. But the legislature, persuaded that the future of industrial and municipal growth depended on new sources of water, voted to create the California Water Project, and Governor Pat Brown approved it. This support from urban industrial quarters and from the governor turned the trick. The electorate approved the $1.7 billion bond authorizations in 1959-1960, most of which went to create the Feather River Project. Water was delivered in the 1970's. One of the most amazing transformations occurred in the Westlands Water District, on the barren western side of the San Joaquin Valley. Much of the activity was at the hands of big corporate land owners.

The federal government allowed many administrative exemptions for the 160-acre limit. Thus a spouse and all the children in a family could each claim 160 acres and acquire a total well above 160 acres. Farm partnerships, corporations, trusts and joint tenancies could also assemble multiple claims. Lessees of farm land got major exemptions. Since natural flowing water was exempt by law, the definition of what constituted natural flowing water could sometimes be stretched. And while the 1902 law required a farmer to live on the land to avoid absentee landlordism, this part of the law was frequently ignored.

In the 1970's proponents of limitation filed several suits to enforce the original democratic concepts. One decision required new land-sale procedures to facilitate smaller scale farm purchases in the Westlands Water District. Another court decision required new regulations on water distribution in Imperial Valley, which drew on federal water from the Colorado. Interior Secretary Cecil Andrus in the administration of President Carter developed restrictive regulations. It was estimated that about 750,000 acres were held in portions larger than 160 acres and would face divestment. The regulations were, however, opposed by California Governor Jerry Brown's administration and set aside by Secretary of the Interior James Watt in the administration of President Reagan.

To some extent the issue turned on the viability of the family-sized farm in California. The findings of objective studies were inconclusive. One United States Department of Agriculture report in 1978 showed that a 160-acre farm in the Westlands District of the Central Valley would earn $25,000, while a 360-acre farm in the Imperial Valley would earn $21,000, both fair rates of return at a time when the median California income was $18,000. Critics replied that the report was based on a dubious hypothetical crop rotation, and neglected to take into account certain risks. Clearly, they said, larger farms were more flexible to operate than smaller ones.

Actually, the *number* of small or moderate-sized family farms in California was relatively large. In 1966 there were 98,000 farms. More than two-thirds of them were under 100 acres. But their numbers were shrinking and their market share was smaller than that of the big ones. Giant corporations had emerged. Tenneco West, the farm conglomerate headquartered in Bakersfield (which had bought out Kern County Land Company), operated 120,000 acres.

Reclamation water came to be highly subsidized in California. The growers were not forced to pay the full share of the cost of the water, nor were they ever charged for the interest on the costs of the irrigation facilities. Some of them, like cattle growers, simply never earned enough to pay their own way under any circumstances. The federal taxpayer made up the deficit. The subsidy in 1976 averaged from $500 to $1,000 an acre to all participants in the federal reclamation program in California.

The question became: was the 160-acre limit basically a sound idea that should be more strongly enforced or did it represent merely a nostalgic yearning for a bygone era? If it was still valid, if it still represented the essence of democracy and freedom of opportunity, how could it be enforced without destroying the efficiency of the large California agribusiness? If it was sentimental nonsense, if it was outmoded, how could it be modified, and what would take its place? Should the water subsidies be eliminated altogether?

Somehow there had to be a way to maintain the spirit, if not the letter, of the law. In the late 1970's Congress held hearings and subsequently passed the Reclamation Reform Act of 1982. This highly complex compromise legislation expanded water entitlements to some family farms or small corporate farms which owned up to 960 acres. But by the same token it ended the water subsidy in many categories, especially for the big growers and for the limited partnerships ("paper farmers") that had become active in agriculture. So, if it cost the government as much as $35 to $40 an acre-foot of water (the average was around $8), that would be the actual fee paid by the customer.

Meanwhile, in the 1980's farming entered a period of severe crisis. Even in California, where farming has been one of the great success stories, the headlines told of farm foreclosures, forced sales, soaring debts and bankruptcies, unstable banks and failing farm credit institutions. Even moderate sized and big agricultural units in California were experiencing severe stress.

The highly complex and far-reaching changes in the basic water reclamation law were scheduled to take full effect in the late 1980's. At that time, some observers predicted, it might not only reduce the number of big farms and of speculative "paper farms," but it might also have a devastating effect on small farmers who could not afford the water. The exact outcome of the reform on family farms could not be foretold. *(Editor's note)*

30.
Dr. Paul S. Taylor: Enforce the 160-Acre Limit to Bolster Democracy

For many years, Dr. Paul S. Taylor, a University of California, Berkeley, economist, waged a one-man crusade for stricter enforcement of the 160-acre limit. He gathered evidence, published articles and presented testimony to courts and before Congress hoping to prevent the emasculation of the reclamation law of 1902. He wanted to modernize it but not let it die. In 1970 he published the following brief item in an AFL-CIO publication.[1]

...The fight for water in the West is as old as the dreams of the 1870's to "make the desert bloom as a rose" through irrigation. At the center of the struggle is the limitation on the water any one individual may receive—the amount of water necessary to irrigate a "family-sized farm" of 160 acres.

Ironically, the westerners had to convince a skeptical nation that such a limitation would be

[1]"The Fight For Water," *AFL-CIO American Federationist,* December, 1970.

included when the dream of irrigating the Central Valley of California with public funds was proposed in the late 19th century. An eastern President and a southern-dominated Congress had to be reassured that the 160-acre limitation would work... [T]he proponents overcame the skeptics, won the vote of Congress and the signature of President Theodore Roosevelt and opened the flow of water through the Reclamation Act of 1902.

And the 160-acre limitation has been under constant attack ever since. The attack has taken every conceivable form—through legislation, the courts and the policies of the Department of the Interior.

By and large, the legislative attempts to circumvent the law have been unsuccessful...But the administration of the Reclamation Act has been quite a different matter. It is through a series of administrative dodges that wealthy landowners and corporations have successfully flouted the 160-acre law.

Attacks on the 160-acre limitation began as early as 1905, almost immediately after the basic law had been passed. And they have continued to today, from such sources as the Task Force on the Acreage Limitation Problem, a five-man panel appointed by Governor Ronald Reagan which reported in January 1968 that the 160-acre limitation was "archaic." And in late 1970, the Public Land Law Review Commission, chaired by Rep. Wayne Aspinall (D.Colo.), was recommending another massive corporate giveaway.

The trick of such forces has been to chip away at the 160-acre limitation through piecemeal exemptions for small projects. Such was done successfully for the Salt River Project in Arizona; the Colorado-Big Thompson project in 1938; the Nevada-Truckee and Humboldt projects in 1940.

Emboldened by these successes, further attempts were made to widen the exemptions through a full-scale legislative attack on the law in 1944, 1947 and through the 1950's....

The 1950's saw the birth of the Engle Formula, named after Sen. Clair Engle (D. Cal.), which is still embodied today in the recommendations of the Reagan Task Force and a bill introduced by Senator George Murphy. Basically, the Engle Formula enables owners of giant tracts to "buy their way out" of the 160-acre limitation by refunding a tiny portion of the generous subsidy given them. This circumvention of the law was held at bay throughout that era by the efforts of such as Sen. Paul Douglas (D. Ill.), who once vowed he would "fight on the beaches, in the fields, on the streets and from house to house to protect the people of the United States from one of the greatest landsteals that has ever been attempted...."

A later attempt is the scheme proposed by Murphy, one which was still pending at the time he was defeated for re-election. It would extend the Engle circumvention formula to all reclamation projects. Opponents of speculation control in California even created a State Water Project to receive federal water and money and at the same time gain exemption from federal acreage limitation. The plea for exemption was made that federal law ought not to apply, since the state was putting up money for its own project. The "catch" is that the state project uses federal facilities, to which acreage limitation does apply.

The stakes are tremendous in bringing irrigation water to these arid lands. Of the 25.3 million acres which have been reclaimed through irrigation in 17 western states, federal projects account for 6.5 million acres. This was done at a total construction cost of $10 billion, with $2 billion of that spent since 1958, primarily in the Colorado Basin and California's Central Valley.

The largesse which this public expense has produced is equally tremendous. In 1957, the value of crops on such lands was $928 million, bringing the cumulative total since 1906 to $13.3 billion. Astoundingly, it has doubled in the decade since then. In 1967 alone, the crop value for one year was $1.95 billion, twice the 1957 total. And the cumulative total was brought over $26 billion, also doubled since 1957.

The human stakes are also high. As long as the various methods of evading the 160-acre limitation are successful, wealthy and corporate land owners can continue their virtual feudal domination of the land. Observers 80 years apart have noted this. British Ambassador James Bryce, visiting

California in the 1880's, characterized it as a land of "enormous farms, in which the soil is cultivated by hired laborers many of whom are discharged after harvest—a phenomenon rare in the United States, which is elsewhere a country of moderately sized farms, owned by persons who do most of their labours by their own or their children's hands." Bryce attributed this to the history of the state, saying that when "California was ceded to the United States, land speculators bought up large tracts under Spanish titles and others subsequently acquired great domains by purchase, either from the railways which had received land grants or directly from the government."

Similarly, it was 80 years later, during one of the recurrent Senate battles over water rights that Sen. Douglas said. "There are strong forces in California which own enormous amounts of land, and they do not want to accept the 160-acre limitation. . . If we have that kind of concentration of ownership growing high value crops such as lettuce, oranges and citrus fruit, I will tell the Senate what kind of agricultural system we will have. We will have an agricultural system with a few owners and a great mass of Mexican-American laborers, living in hovels, receiving low wages and with a life of feudalism in the Central Valley of California, as indeed we now have in part. . . ."

The social and economic injustices which repeated violations of the 1902 law help perpetrate were mentioned by the AFL-CIO in 1966 when it testified against "any further appropriations for construction of the Westlands Water Delivery System until all excess land owners have signed recordable contracts to divest" themselves of their holdings over 160 acres. The language of today's marketplace reveals motivation for water development in the raw. An advertisement in the San Francisco Chronicle of April 21, 1970, makes the appeal to readers in advance of the coming of water:

"Make your money grow in the booming 'Antelope Valley in sunny Southern California'," the ad said. "Everyone knows about the tremendous growth in real estate values in Southern California. . . ."

Major Gen. Jackson Graham of the U.S. Army Corps of Engineers pithily challenged the right of uncontrolled private speculation to shape the course of water development when he asked: "Is a man entitled to buy up, settle or promote a chunk of desert and then demand that his government bring water to him from the general direction of the North Pole?"

These questions are critical: Who plans? Who develops and with what motivations? Who, if anyone, attends to the public interest? In 1964 Secretary of the Interior Stewart L. Udall confessed mildly that "on occasion" administrators, and even Congress itself, had "exhibited a degree of concern for the excess landowner which may be difficult to reconcile with the policies embraced by the excess land law."

The strength and persistence of large landholders' opposition to anti-monopoly measures on water development testifies to their conviction of a deep division between private and public interests. Their open opposition to the 160-acre law, which continues undiminished, has just received a stealthy "assist" from the Public Land Law Review Commission.

A few projects—two or three—were specifically exempted from acreage limitation by Congress. Interior Department approvals of these breaches of national policy were supplied by subordinates during absences of Secretary of the Interior Harold L. Ickes, staunch defender of the water limitation.

The generous public subsidies afforded by reclamation law to private landowners were steadily enlarged. By the later 1940's, for instance, Central Valley irrigators in California were allocated 63 percent of reimbursable project costs and required to repay only 17 percent. The public policy controls within the law were as steadily attacked and an elaborate assortment of tactics developed to undermine or eliminate them.

On May 13, 1944, *Business Week* magazine outlined four of the tactics. Two of these were defeated in Congress outright. One was to obtain an exemption of the Central Valley Project from the 160-acre law. The other was to make use of the Army Engineers who originally were outside the excess land law. Congress repaired this omission in 1944.

A third tactic was to pump groundwaters, hoping the excess land law would not be applied even though these waters were improved in quantity and quality by a reclamation project. Through lax administration which Udall called "difficult to reconcile with the policies embraced by the excess land laws," this tactic has persisted to this day. It is under challenge in the courts.

A fourth tactic described in 1944 was to "sidestep" the federal 160-acre law by having the State of California take over the project, "paying the entire bill." Erwin Cooper, for eight years an associate of the California Department of Water Resources, calls the state's Oroville reservoir a "political reservoir" to circumvent the 160-acre law in the interest of large land owners.

While resisting outright repeal of the 160-acre limitation, Congress shows signs of weakening if a face-saving device can be found. The "Engle formula" is such a device.

The spirit behind the Engle formula was well summarized by Engle himself, who told Congress: "I grant you, you start kicking the 160-acre limitation and it is like inspecting the rear end of a mule: You want to do it from a safe distance because you might get kicked through the side of the barn. But it can be done with circumspection, and I hope we can exercise circumspection."

The attack on the law through the administrative branch of government has been most successful of all. In practice the Interior Department ignores the law passed by Congress in 1914 that requires the secretary to obtain agreements from landholders to dispose of their excess lands "before any contract is let or work begun for the construction of any reclamation project."

In a legal opinion written in 1961 the Solicitor of Interior quoted and emphasized this 1914 law. Yet barely three years later he told Congress that an owner of excess lands "must volunteer" and "has an unlimited time" to sign—or not to sign. That "unlimited time" given an owner goes a long way in explaining how the law has been so successfully flouted.

Other laws which Interior has not enforced rigidly enough include the 1902 statute requiring that rights to the use of water may be sold only to "an actual bona fide resident on such land, or occupant thereof residing in the neighborhood" and the 1926 statute that bars owners from receiving water from a reclamation project if they refuse to agree to sale of their excess lands.

On the west side of the San Joaquin Valley the Interior Department is spending upwards of a half billion dollars on a project three-fourths of the lands of which are in excess, and whose holders fail to agree to their disposal as required by reclamation law. By delivering surface waters the project inevitably improves groundwaters of ineligible as well as eligible land. . . .

Turning his back on the Interior Department's widespread failure to observe the law, the Comptroller General invited the owner of "about 110,000 acres, of 20 percent of the irrigable land within the Westlands service area" to give its views. The views of the Southern Pacific, as may be surmised, are unfavorable to the 160-acre law.

While remaining silent on the Interior Departments failures to enforce the law, the Comptroller General suggests to Congress instead that it "may wish to consider the applicability" of the Murphy bill "to the San Luis service area." The effect of his suggestion, if followed, would be to remove public control over private speculation in the public water resource.

Greater concern over preservation of private speculation means diminished concern over preservation of environment. The San Luis-Westlands project is a clear example. The large landowners of that area have put down deep well pumps to mine the groundwaters as a tactic to escape the 160-acre law. They have avoided its application so far—with the help of cooperating administrators-but the physical effects on the environment are serious. The quality of the groundwaters is declining, crops are suffering, the water table is falling and the pump lift increasing.

Another example of environmental damage influenced by resistance to public policy as embodied in the 160-acre law is in the Sacramento Valley. There the Bureau of Reclamation gave diverters of water from the river 10.4 acre-feet per annum. This amount equals four times the average Central Valley water duty of 2.6 acre-feet per annum. Manipulation of this grossly excessive quantity of water enables large landowners to escape acreage limitation law—at the expense of water needed badly in the Delta and in San Francisco Bay.

Water is a public resource. The money that finances its development is public money. Public interest, not private pressures, should guide development. The time has come to modernize the 160-acre statute, but not to destroy it. . . .

The national interest, not just a regional interest, is at stake in western reclamation. The water is a national resource, and likewise the law, policy and money that guide and achieve development. . . .

The historic national tradition that guided our disposal of land furnishes clear precedent to guide our current disposal of public water and money to finance and subsidize that disposal. The subsidy is substantial, ranging from something like $600 to $2,000 an acre. This does not include the values that flow from public development of the public water resource. He who receives these receives an extremely generous gift.

When our nation gave away its public lands, it ear-marked a generous share for education. Between 1803 and 1966 more than 94 million of the 228 million acres given by the federal government to states were donated for educational purposes. Impetus was given to higher education by the Morrill Act signed by President Abraham Lincoln and is in addition to the rights made to common schools as well. This record shows the magnitude of what comparable "water grants for education" could achieve today.

Conservationists, like educators, recognize the need to modernize reclamation law. The Sierra Club supports "federal purchase" of reclaimed lands in excess of 160 acres per individual owner "with the understanding that lands so purchased would be sold or leased under open space regulations." The National Wildlife Federation states that it favors "a strong policy which will permit the government to acquire from landowners those properties in excess of 160 acres. We would support a program for federal purchase of excess lands divested by owners on reclamation projects, particularly if the funds accruing from re-sale are used for education and conservation."

The concept that government should purchase excess lands prior to construction of reclamation projects is well established. As early as 1892 Gov. Joseph Toole of Montana proposed that the public "first acquire title to" lands to be reclaimed. . . .

The technique of modernization is simple. Present law requires sale of excess lands at the pre-water, pre-project price. Government authorization to purchase will provide a ready market and in turn allow the government to sell or lease with appropriate land-use regulations that will preserve agricultural greenbelts and open spaces and check urban sprawl and slurb. Revenues from sale or lease can be assigned to such public purposes as education, the land and water conservation fund, or simply returned to the federal treasury.

The struggle continues to this day over the fruits of public investment to develop the public water resource—both financial and environmental fruits. . . .

The outcome is suspended in the balance. The stakes are gigantic, as both speculating private interests and informed citizens have known for a century. The question is whether the recent activity of educators and conservationists will be sufficient to tip the balance toward modernization of reclamation law to serve truly public purposes.

31.
California Farmer: The 160-Acre Limit is "Planned Poverty"

Many growers in recent decades opposed the proposals of the federal government to enforce the 160-acre water limit as being too restrictive. Negative arguments are capsulized in the following items from the influential farm journal, California Farmer. *The first is an editorial by Jack Pickert, while the second is a news article on hearings held in Sacramento and Fresno, late in 1977.*[2]

The 160-Acre Deal is a "Rip-Off" [an editorial]

. . . The Westlands was a huge desolate alluvial fan of land on the west side of the San Joaquin Valley. The people who pioneered it had a real rough time taming that land and had to go down to incredible depths for well water.

Then the Federal Government came along and said that since this was state water flowing from a Federal dam they would be subject to the 160-acre limitation.

Growers had to sign recordable contracts that after 10 years they must sell all land over the 160 acres for one person or 320 for husband and wife.

Out of 344,600 acres of land under recordable contract, some 93,728 acres have gone under forced-sale.

The do-gooders have had two Senate committees crawling all over the Westlands District in hopes they will bust the whole thing up into small farms.

Here is another case where a law 74 years old just doesn't fit the modern scene. There are a few people in this state that could possibly make a fair living on 320 acres in the Westlands area but they are few and far between.

First of all, it would cost close to a half a million dollars to buy the land and finance the equipment and pay pre-harvest and harvest costs. Unless you had the cash on hand, most of the money would go to the banker.

The person who is going to try and make a living on his small Westland tract must be thoroughly familiar with the area and just how it has to be farmed.

Senators Tunney and Cranston and Congressmen Sisk and Krebs are trying to get legislation through that would give loans to qualified farmers in excess land up to $150,000 for 160 acres. In our mind this is just compounding the felony.

One thing that we forgot to add: If they enforce the letter of the law one must live on the land. It's not the greatest place in the world to live. Also the way houses are selling around our area, the $150,000 the government loaned you at 5 percent would get pretty well wiped-out just building the house.

The whole 160-acre deal is a rip-off. From here it looks like planned poverty.

America Faces Agrarian Reform [a news report]

Angry California growers arrived in busloads to participate in the recent hearings on the 160-acre limitation conducted by the United States Department of the Interior. With protest signs waving, growers came to register their distaste for the proposed regulations concerning the Reclamation Act of 1922—regulations that many observers feel constitute blatant discrimination against agriculture.

The stage was set for this confrontation on August 13, 1976 when the United States District court for the District of Columbia ordered the Department of Interior to "forthwith initiate public rule-making proceedings respecting the criteria and procedures to be used by the Bureau of Recla-

[2]The editorial, "The 160-Acre Deal is a 'Rip-off'," appeared April 17, 1976; the news report, "America Faces Agrarian Reform," written by reporters Don Razee, Hart Porteous, Al Pryor, and Ron Leach, appeared January 7, 1978.

mation, Department of the Interior, to approve 'excess lands' sales under the federal Reclamation Laws.''

The resulting proposals would make several major changes affecting all future sales of excess land, including:

* Ownership would be limited to 160 acres per person.

* More than 160 acres in multiple ownership would only be approved when a family relationship exists among all owners.

* Owners would be required to live on the land or within 50 miles of it.

* The Secretary of Interior would approve prices on subsequent sales of excess lands for at least 10 years, and monitor sales for 20-25 years to prevent ''unreasonable profits.''

* Land leases would be limited to 160 acres for any person or corporation.

* Sellers would not be allowed to lease back land from the buyer.

* Disposal of excess land would be required in five years, rather than the present practice of 10 years.

* A lottery or other means would be established to elect buyers of excess lands....

Sacramento Hearing

Some 150 persons testified at the Sacramento hearing which ran from 9 a.m. to 10 p.m. Presiding at the two-day affair was Interior Department Solicitor Leo Krulitz. Also in attendance were Clifford Barrett, assistant commissioner of the Bureau of Reclamation, and Billy Martin, regional director of the bureau.

Congressman Robert Leggett, the first to testify, made it clear that farmers are not the only ones indignant about the proposed regulations. He charged that the Interior Department has, in essence, declared war on the family farmers of California....

Rominger's Opposition

State Director of Food and Agriculture Richard Rominger shocked politicians at the Sacramento hearing with his strong opposition to virtually all of the proposed regulations. In a statement cleared by Governor Brown, Rominger said, '' I believe the proposals go beyond what is required by the court order and are so restrictive as to make it unlikely that most family farmers could survive in these times of rapidly rising costs and uncertain water supplies....''

Implying that the proposed regulations are not suited to agriculture today, Rominger pointed out that ''Under today's conditions, farms need to be of sufficient size to permit them to generate enough income to stay financially secure and endure years of low prices or low production.''

The State Director of Food and Agriculture charged that the concept of limiting the farm family to lineal descendants is overally restrictive.

He explained that, while many family farms are operated by brothers and sisters and their children, some partnerships exist between unrelated farmers. ''It is unreasonable to rule that these farmers should not be permitted to sell to each other or to each others' children,'' Rominger insisted.

Rominger attacked the proposed leasing requirements, suggesting that they ''erect barriers unnecessary for the preservation of the family farm.'' He reminded that many people entering agriculture, especially young farmers, must begin by leasing land.

Rominger also criticized the use of a lottery. He said that ''In addition to family members, people previously associated with the land such as tenants and employees should have an opportunity to buy excess lands.

''The lottery should be reserved for those parcels where the Secretary takes power of attorney to sell the excess land,'' Rominger claimed.

Krulitz called a press conference to denounce Rominger's statements. When asked if he thought Rominger's remarks represented the views of the Brown Administration, Krulitz remarked, ''

When a person of cabinet rank makes a statement at a hearing such as this, it can be assumed that it is the official position of the administration.''

Administration Shift

Krulitz said he was baffled by the apparent shift in Brown's position because the Department of the Interior entered into an earlier agreement with the Brown Administration concerning the Westlands Water District which, according to Krulitz, contained much stronger restrictions than the program now suggested.

Secretary of Interior Andrus also registered disappointment with the California governor. Andrus claimed he was urged by Brown to adopt much stricter regulations than are now proposed.

Andrus implied that Brown is now playing politics with an eye toward the 1980 presidential election.

Ray Momboisse, attorney for the non-profit, public-interest law firm Pacific Legal Foundation, testified that enforcing the 160-acre limitation and imposing the residency requirement would have a catastrophic impact on agriculture across the nation, as well as in California.

The Pacific Legal Foundation attorney charged that the Interior Department has shown utter contempt for the National Environmental Policy Act by refusing to prepare an environmental impact statement before promulgating the rules....

Legal Action

The Pacific Legal Foundation filed one of several suits against the Interior Department, demanding that an environmental impact statement be prepared before any regulations are enforced. Momboisse suggested that the Interior Department is reluctant to issue environmental and economic impact statements because such statements would reveal a tremendous adverse impact on the agricultural community, employment, consumer prices, and the environment.

Another suit against the Secretary of the Interior and the U.S. Commissioner of the Bureau of Reclamation has been filed by the American Farm Bureau Federation and the California Farm Bureau. The suit, aimed at stopping proposed acreage limitation regulations on Bureau of Reclamation projects, seeks a ''declaratory judgment and injunctive relief.''

That suit charges that the defendants are violating the National Environmental Policy Act of 1969 by failure to prepare and circulate an environmental impact statement. Defendants are also charged with failure to comply with the guidelines of the Council on Environmental Quality and the departmental manual of the Department of Interior.

California Farm Bureau President Fred Heringer...charged that the people who formulated the proposed regulations had little understanding of western water development, western water law, or farming in general. ''Such proposals, formulated in Washington, are a dangerous fraud on the public,'' he blasted.

Delay Urged

Heringer urged a delay in implementing the proposed regulations until their economic and social impact can be determined.

Also suggesting a delay was Richard Brann, member of the Solano County Board of Supervisors. He asked, on behalf of the Board, that the proposals be set aside until:

* An economic and environmental impact statement is prepared covering the effect of implementation on each irrigation district in the Western states and on the economy of these states.

* Congress reviews the proposed regulations and addresses itself to the feasibility of applying the 1902 Reclamation Law to 1977 conditions.

* There is clarification on the issue of co-mingling federally financed water with state water projects and riparian entitlements. As presently interpreted by some water authorities, the pro-

posed regulations would pre-empt for the federal government 90 percent of the water in California. Riparian lands would be controlled by the proposed regulations.

C. W. Jones, president of the San Luis and Delta-Mendota Water Users Association, painted a grim picture of how the proposed regulations, if implemented, would affect his association's membership. Jones noted that some 50 percent of the ownership within his area would not comply with the 50-mile residency requirement.

"These owners," he warned, "would have to move within the limits for compliance, sell the interest in their property, or lose their water rights."

Jones added that if only 160 acres could be leased by an individual, "There would be insufficient qualified farmers for the leasing of agricultural lands, and production would suffer."

He explained that 50-60 percent of the land currently leased in the association area—420,000-500,000 acres—would be affected by the 160 acre limitation.

Only 16.5 percent of the landowners in the San Luis Water District could comply with the residency requirements proposed by Interior Secretary Andrus.

According to Cecil Carey, chief engineer and manager of the water district, there are land parcels in the district owned by 22 different people living in five different states of the U.S. as well as Taiwan. Only one of the owners resides within the 50 mile radius of the property that is proposed in the new rules.

Carey noted that the owners have a loan obligation of $760 per acre for their water distribution systems. He asked: "Will they be forced to sell their inheritance that has been within their family for over 50 years? As a practical matter, what will be accomplished by these residency requirements? Will the additional district and government costs be justified?"

He added, "If residency does become a requirement and it is retroactive, it will force over 80 percent of the owners within our district to either sell their lands, redesignate ownership, or to relocate within the residential limit."

Karen Lang articulated a point that was frequently reiterated at the two-day Sacramento hearing: namely, syblings are excluded in the definition of a family relationship. Lang, of West Sacramento, warned that brothers and sisters will lose their right to federal water if they are farming together. . . .

Growers Suggestions

How would growers modify the proposed regulations? Many who testified asked that all acreage and residency requirements be eliminated. Others suggested that the acreage limitation be increased to 640 acres per individual, plus another 640 acres for the wife and each child. . . .

Fresno Hearing

The story was much the same at the Interior Department hearing in Fresno. Over 800 persons attended the two-day affair, punctuated with pieces of agricultural equipment snaking some two miles through downtown.

Panel Chairman James A. Joseph, Under Secretary of the Interior, was criticized shortly after the hearing commenced for arbitrarily changing the published order of testimony and alternately selecting representatives for, or against, the proposed regulations.

As a result of Joseph's action, George Ballis of National Land for People (NLP) was able to testify before television cameras the first morning of the hearings, despite the fact that Ballis was listed as 52nd on the program.

It was the decision in the NLP v. Interior Department suit in 1976 that initially ordered the Secretary of the Interior to promulgate rules and regulations for the sale of excess lands.

Fresno lawyer Kendall Manock testified that Secretary of Interior Andrus is far exceeding the intent of this court order. "The court," Manock explained, "merely required the Secretary of the Interior to initiate formal rule making in conformance with the Administrative Procedure Act.

"The court said nothing regarding the substantive content of reclamation rules," he noted.

Rewriting The Law

The Fresno lawyer charged that rather than merely enforcing the reclamation laws, Secretary Andrus is seeking to rewrite the laws without congressional approval.

"There is nothing in federal reclamation laws, either as enacted by Congress or interpreted by the courts, which would justify the proposed regulations regarding restrictions on leasing excess or non-excess lands, sale of excess lands through the use of a lottery, limitations of sales and gifts or excess lands to lineal descendants, or applications of acreage limitations across project lines," according to Manock.

He added that no determination has been made that residency is a requirement of reclamation law. "Such proposals," the lawyer testified, "raise broad national public policy issues and should be the subject of congressional, rather than administrative consideration."

In a statement released prior to the Fresno hearing, Manock suggested that the proposed regulations and the associated definitions of the "lineal family" could cause major disturbances in the financing and business organization of western farms. He explained that under the new rules, any family farm would be prevented from obtaining long term bank loans unless a partnership agreement was made.

Size vs. Ownership

Manock added that reclamation law does not limit the size of the farm units. He noted that several federal court decisions on the reclamation law have specifically and favorably pointed to land leasing as a means of gaining a more workable farms size, despite the 160 acre ownership limitation.

"Reclamation law doesn't deal with the size of a farm at all," he maintained. "It only deals with the size of ownership."

In testimony at the Fresno hearing, Westlands Water District Manager Jerald Butchert claimed, "The draft report suffers from a fundamental misconception that the spirit and intent of reclamation law is violated by farm operations as contrasted with farm ownerships."

Butchert maintained that from the time of the enactment of the 1902 law to the present, farms exceeding 160 or 320 acres through leasing and multiple ownerships have been knowingly accepted as consistent with the law. He added that while Congress has made many reclamation law changes, it has never even proposed restrictions on the size of operations.

"To declare that large operations are contrary to the spirit and intent of the law," Butchert testified, "does not correctly reflect history.

32.
Lynn Ludlow and Will Hearst: Ignoring the Law Promotes Monopolies

The San Francisco Examiner *published a series of articles from January 11 to 18, 1976 entitled, "The Paper Farmers." It marshalled evidence and levelled heavy criticism at the way the water law was being enforced. A particular target was the Westlands Water District. The byline for the series went to reporters Lynn Ludlow and Will Hearst, grandson of the famous newspaper publisher, William Randolph Hearst.*

Landowners who control the big Westlands Water District want a new federal irrigation contract that amounts to a long term giveaway of an estimated $2 billion in taxpayer funds.

These are the same corporate farm operators who pumped out their underground water basin, then pleaded for government aid.

The 572,072-acre irrigation district was formed in 1952 on the arid west side of the San Joaquin Valley to contract for federally subsidized water from the San Luis Canal/California Aqueduct.

Investigation by the *Examiner* shows that the proposed 84-page contract includes direct subsidies, hidden benefits and unearned profits for paper farmers, absentee investors and big landowners.

These windfalls were predicated on an unkept promise of the National Reclamation Act. It says federal water can't irrigate more than 160 acres per farmer, who must live on or near the fields.

Under the 1902 law, federal irrigation was linked by Congress to land redistribution. The intent was to break up the huge ranches and railroad holdings of the West and allow settlers to share the benefits of public investment.

Instead, under the interim contract in effect, farm operations remain big while title to the 180-acre units is acquired by speculators, family trusts and buyer groups.

Westlands directors are elected by a system of one vote for every dollar of assessed valuation. The biggest landowners include Standard Oil, Bangor Punta Inc., the Boston Ranch of J.G. Boswell (a director of Safeway, Inc.), the Colt Ranch, Giffen Inc., Anderson, Clayton & Co. and the Southern Pacific Land Co. With 106,000 acres, the railroad controls 20 percent of the district's votes.

The proposed contract includes the same enforcement loopholes, plus new ones.

Enforcement is the job of the U.S. Bureau of Reclamation, which would rather build dams than get involved in land reform controversies.

The pending contract has been approved by the bureau, the Department of the Interior and directors of the district.

The new contract has been held up solely at the request of a U.S. Senate joint committee studying the family farm. It will conduct hearings in Fresno Feb. 16, 17.

The contract would guarantee at least 1.15 million acre feet of water per year for the district, which is as big as many emerging nations and richer than most.

In testifying before a congressional committee in 1956, the late J. E. O'Neill, a cattleman-cotton producer who put Westlands together, emphasized the desperation of landowners who had been pumping overdrafts from deep wells for 50 years.

"We would rather comply with the 160-acre limitation than to let the land go back to jackrabbits," O'Neill said.

For its part, the Bureau of Reclamation was promising to uphold the acreage limitation.

"It is the duty of the Bureau of Reclamation, as part of the executive branch of the government, to enforce the law of the land as it exists today," said Robert J. Plafford Jr., then regional director in Sacramento, at a Fresno meeting in 1967.

The government's promise was emphasized a year earlier, when the interim Westlands contracts were defended by Kenneth Holum, assistant secretary of the interior.

He told a Senate committee, "I should like to emphasize continuing and keen interest of the department in furthering the interests of the family farm concept in our irrigated agricultural programs. The reclamation program has traditionally sought to foster such family farm developments."

Today the district's farm operations, many of them fashioned from multiple ownerships by absentee investors, average about 2,000 acres each. Most owners, farm operators and field hands live somewhere else.

Federal water has been delivered in growing quantity for more than a decade to Westlands landowners.

Although more than 100,000 acres have been broken into 160-acre units, only two family farm operations exist in the district.

Clive Ririe, a former Bureau of Reclamation staffer in Fresno, offered one explanation in a statement to Congress. He said he resigned "because of the lack of any real desire on the part of the bureau administrator to enforce the provisions of the law."

Geoffrey Lanning, former assistant solicitor of the department of the Interior said last year:

"The Bureau of Reclamation deliberately violated or avoided the 160-acre limitation, doing so by failure to administer the law at all or, when pressed, by having its captive lawyers write crude loophole provisions that let the many big landowners ignore this public safeguard."

Edward Weinberg, former solicitor for the department in the Kennedy Administration, now concedes "less than a burning desire to provide the staffing and funds" necessary to fully enforce land reform goals.

Richard Dauber, assistant regional solicitor in Sacramento, ended a spirited defense of the government by saying, "I'm just a flunky. Policy comes from Washington."

In effect, that policy is built into the revised contract. It will be in force through the year 2008, by which time land ownership patterns will be well established.

Here are some questions raised about the new Westlands contract:

* Residency Rule—The new contract (like the existing one) does not mention one crucial provision built into the National Reclamation act of 1902.

The law says the recipient of federally subsidized water must be "an actual *bona fide* resident on such land or occupant thereof residing in the neighborhood."

"Long discarded" (in the words of legal spokesmen for the Interior Department), the residency rule was upheld in 1971 by U.S. District Judge William Murray in an Imperial Valley case that was argued by San Francisco attorney Arthur Brunwasser.

The Government promptly challenged Murray's ruling. It has been stayed, pending appeals.

Without the residency rule, breakup of the great landholdings of Westlands has meant little more than a complicated shuffle of deeds, agreements, mortgages and leaseback contracts.

* Acreage Limitation—Funds for the dams and canals come from the 1902 law, which Congress intended as a way to irrigate the arid valleys of the West while breaking up the vast holdings of railroads and cattle kings.

In addition to the residency rule, Congress declared in 1902 that federal water couldn't be delivered to more than 160 acres per farmer.

To receive irrigation, according to a rule of the Bureau of Reclamation, the owner must agree to dispose of excess land (everything over 160 acres) at pre-project prices within a 10-year period.

The new contract would permit sale of excess land to "any purchaser," including investors, farm brokers or other excess landowners, so long as the 10-year agreement remained in force.

The change would have the effect of encouraging speculation by wheeler dealers.

It isn't authorized by the law itself.

* Windfall Profits—Federal law forbids sale of excess lands at prices higher than the land value before irrigation came along.

In a provision upheld by the California Supreme Court in 1958, the law says excess lands must be appraised at the time the owner signs the agreement that gives him up to 10 years to sell.

The new contract doesn't include this requirement, which was upheld this month by a federal court in South Dakota. Current practice by the Bureau of Reclamation is to appraise land at the time of sale, not at the time of the agreement.

Pre-project land value in Westlands was estimated at $50 to $100 an acre in the 1950's, and those appraisals didn't take into account the rapidly sinking water table.

The bureau approves sale prices today of $500 to $700 an acre. This is about five times what prices would have been had appraisals taken place when the law says they should have.

At $100 an acre, 160 acres would cost $16,000. At $500, the cost is $80,000. For the landless, the difference is crucial.

Former Rep. Jerome Waldie has noted that growers and government officials argue that 160 acres isn't big enough to support a family farm.

"I cannot understand why an economic entity of 160 acres is so worthless it cannot be farmed," he testified, "but so expensive that you cannot purchase it."

* No Inflation Escalator—Money from water sales is supposed to pay district operating and maintenance costs. What's left over is to be allocated to the Westlands' unspecified share of federal construction costs for the San Luis Unit of the California Aqueduct and the Central Valley Project.

As district operating costs climb with inflation over the 40-year life of the contract, the allocation for loan repayment will shrink accordingly.

* Bargain Rates—The basic water charge is $7.50 per acre foot (enough water to cover an acre to the depth of one foot, or about 325,000 gallons). This is for water as it leaves the canal and enters the district distribution system.

The price is less than a third of the average cost to customers of the state-run California Water Project, which is supposed to be self-financing (but doesn't include an acreage limitation).

Pumping from deep wells costs as much as $17 an acre foot.

* Free Ride—Although they must pay the $7.50 per acre foot, landowners have 10 years or more before they must begin repayment of the district's 1,000-mile system of buried pipelines and 370-mile system of drain collectors.

According to the contract, the additional water use charge for these systems won't be levied until they are declared "substantially complete."

Completion has been delayed for various reasons, including lack of federal funds. The target date is 1982.

Then the additional charge on top of the $7.50 will probably be $14. give or take a couple of dollars.

This means an annual public subsidy of about $14 million to landowners until the system is completed.

* The $100 Million Extra—The original ceiling for the distribution/drain systems was $184.4 million. This was raised to $227.9 million in the new contract to provide for annexation of the West Plains Water Storage District.

The new ceiling is estimated at $370 million by the Department of the Interior. This higher figure, caused in part by inflation, isn't in the draft contract.

* The Public Interest—The new contract, like its predecessor, calls for no-interest loans over 40 years to repay federal construction costs of the Westlands venture.

The interest is donated as a public gift because of the land reform promises of federal reclamation projects.

Costs of unpaid interest aren't easy to figure.

Depending on what would be a fair interest rate and schedule, the cost of interest would at least equal the government's cash outlay.

Ralph M. Brody, the district manager, estimated that a loan with interest would double the cost of the project.

The outlay includes the distribution and drainage systems, which will cost about $370 million; the Westlands share of the San Luis Unit's state-federal dam and canal works, about $480 million, and the district's share of the construction costs of the Central Valley Project.

The CVP share can't be figured, according to the Bureau of Reclamation, until the system is complete. This may take another 25 to 50 years.

(Some CVP costs are repaid through sales of water and hydroelectric power, and it's all very, very complicated.)

Figuring the cost of unpaid interest as roughly the same as construction costs, the direct federal subsidy to Westlands farm operators would be at least a billion dollars.

* Power Structure—Under the new contract, like the old one, hydroelectric power will be delivered free or very cheaply from the Central Valley Project's dams to Westlands and the San Luis Unit.

They share a huge appetite for electricity because of the huge pumping plants that lift water from the Delta to the California Aqueduct and from the canal to the San Luis Reservoir and Coalinga Canal.

Westlands also needs power for its own system of wells.

The need is estimated at about 620 million kilowatt hours a year.

This is more, for example, than the entire annual power output expected from the Auburn Dam, a Bureau of Reclamation project being built for more that $600 million.

(The same dam will release only 318,000 acre feet of water a year, less than a third of that demanded by the Westlands contract. In effect, the Auburn Dam's price tag reflects the cost of building hydroelectric power facilities for the use of the Westlands project.)

The power subsidy will amount to about $12 million a year at PG&E rates or $2.5 million a year at the usual CVP sales price. Over 40 years, these direct subsidies would be $480 million or $100 million, respectively.

* Underground Freeloaders—The contract says replenishment of the underground water table is an "unavoidable result" of federal irrigation.

Landowners who have signed federal irrigation agreements have donated their costly wells to the Westlands district, which will continue pumping from them.

Those who refused federal irrigation (and are thus exempt from acreage limitation) can pump from an underground water basin replenished at public expense. The new contract appears to close the door on future legal efforts to remedy this situation.

When the Senate panel conducted hearings in Washington last summer, Reclamation Commissioner Gilbert Stamm testified his agency didn't have the power to carry out land redistribution to family farmers.

Sen. Gaylor Nelson, D-Wis, called Stamm's admission one of the most shocking things I have ever seen.

In an interview, Nelson said later, "It's a damned good law, and they have converted it to the service of economically established people."

Brody, manager and chief counsel for the Westlands district, argues forcefully that the new contract contains nothing new.

Dr. Paul S. Taylor, professor emeritus of economics at UC Berkeley and a critic of the contract, says it further weakens the original goals of Congress.

He quotes Fred Seaton, former secretary of the interior, who once said, "What I am concerned about is a process by which inferences are based on inferences and there is a whittling away at a principle until all that is left is a pile of shavings."

33.
Ralph M. Brody: The Reclamation Law is Being Properly Enforced and Works Well

The highest paid public official in California in the 1970's was Ralph M. Brody, manager and chief counsel of Westlands Water District, a major recipient of federal reclamation water. Brody made no apologies for any policy adopted in Westlands. He responded to critics by asserting that the 160-acre limit was being fully implemented. Testifying before a Senate subcommittee in 1972, he said that the big estates were being broken up, and sold off in small parcels—while the water was unleashing the fertility of the otherwise barren soil and thereby bolstering the state's economy. The following is Brody's testimony on February 17, 1976 before the Select Committee on Small Business and the Committee on Interior and Insular Affairs, U.S. Senate. The topic was, "Will the Family Farm Survive in America?"

. . . It is my purpose here today to demonstrate that the law is being rigidly complied with and that its objectives are being achieved in Westlands Water District. . . . Consistently with the chief objective of the law, land monopolies are being broken up. The land is being broken up into 160-acre or smaller ownerships never to be consolidated into larger ownerships again as long as the law remains in effect. Very large ownerships are being dismantled never to be reassembled. The ownership may become smaller, but they will never again be larger than 160 acres. The ownerships being thus broken up are being operated in dramatically smaller units than heretofore. Thus goes the trend—and rapidly. . . .

What is and has been the situation in Westlands Water District *vis-a-vis* the 160-acre limitation?

First, I would respectfully urge your Committees to bear in mind throughout your deliberations that the large ownerships now being broken up . . . were an existing fact a long time before and at the time the Project was authorized by the Congress. . . . They are now being dismantled and there is nothing to be accomplished by criticizing or discussing the size of those holdings now. Yet, such discussions persist.

The large land holdings came into existence because there was no other way by which the land could be developed. They grew as a result of the physical circumstance that the only available source of water was underground. Wells at that time cost from $50,000 to $75,000 and even then did not yield enough water during the peak of the irrigation season to irrigate all of the land. A portion of the land, then, had to remain fallow or be planted to lesser paying crops, with the result that the dollar yield per acre was low. This meant, in turn, that more acres had to be planted. It was on this basis that over 90% of the land had been developed at the time the Project came into being.

I would remind you that the matter of subsidy also was known to the Congress at the time the Project was authorized. It was the same subsidy that has been provided on every Reclamation project since 1902.

Of course, it was the subsidy that attracted the landowners to the Federally financed Project. But the subsidy did not come entirely free of conditions. If the subvention was to be made available to them, the owners had to accept acreage limitation. As a price, they had to agree that they would break up their holdings if they wanted the advantage of the subsidy during the period between the time when they first received water and until they sold the land. They chose to accept the conditions and the consequences of a Federal project.

With all of this in mind, they made commitments to the Congress of the United States, at the time they were soliciting authorization of the Project, that they *would* sign recordable contracts and they *would* dispose of their holdings. . . .

That the landowners have kept their pledge is demonstrable. In Westlands Water District more recordable contracts have been signed (1,147), more land has been placed under recordable contract

(350,000 acres) by more excess landowners (303), and more land under recordable contract has been sold into non-excess status (109,000 acres) than has occurred cumulatively in the 73 years of reclamation history. The accomplishments are shown on the maps accompanying this statement. . . .

At the end of December, 1975, 109,161 acres of the land under recordable contract had been sold to 928 eligible buyers at a price approved by the Department of the Interior and well before the ten-year period had expired. . . .

The next legitimate question that might be asked could well be—What happened to the 109,000 acres of land that were sold?

This acreage was sold by some 60 landowners. In addition to increasing the number of landowners, it increased the number of farm operators. What had been farmed theretofore by 28 farming entities is now being operated by 93—a more than threefold increase. What is more dramatic, however, is that 68,000 acres of the 109,000 that had previously been farmed by only two entities is now being operated by more than 65 farming operations, mostly families. What was formerly owned by two corporations is now owned by 557 individuals and, with respect to the entire 109,000 acres, what was owned by 60 individuals is now owned by 928 persons. . . .

Considerable talk has occurred here and elsewhere of residency and the lack of new homes in the District. Even if residency were required, living within 50 miles of the land qualified the owner so that the new residences would not necessarily show up in the District. It is interesting to note, nevertheless, that of the 928 purchasers of excess land sold pursuant to recordable contract, 63% or 588 live within 50 miles of Westlands Water District. It might be added here that if that requirement is found to be applicable by the courts, Westlands will, of course, comply with it by refusing to deliver water to lands owned by persons who would not qualify as a resident. . . .

And what is the makeup of the ownerships of the 109,000 acres purchased from the excess landowners?

A review of the sales and farm operations indicates the following which respect to the ownership and operating patterns of the 109,000 acres sold from excess status under recordable contract into a non-excess status:

1. All of the buyers own 160 acres or less per person in the District. Most of the buyers, are, however, members of a group of people who joined together to purchase lands located in the same general area with a view toward their lands being farmed together, at least during the initial years of their ownership. There were approximately 125 such groups.

2. With very few exceptions, the buyers, excluding housewives, minors and retirees, have as their principal business, farming or a job directly related to farming.

3. While all of the buyers own 160 acres or less, much of their land is, for economic reasons such as pooling of farming equipment, purchasing of supplies, etc., farmed in blocks larger than 160 acres. Not uncommon are family-run operations in which father, mother, children and their spouses own the land and are involved in various capacities in the farming operation. . . .

4. On the other hand, the number of individuals not related by family to the other buyers and leasing to an operator in which they have no interest is relatively small. Only about 10% of the groups of buyers, or about 35 of the 928 buyers, fall into this category. These buyers own only about 3-1/2% of the 109,000 acres sold into a non-excess status.

5. With few exceptions, the buyers of the land had no prior business or family relationship with the seller. . . .

6. In contrast, most buyers are related by family to one another and to the person or persons currently operating the farm. A typical arrangement involves one or more persons both owning and operating the farm.

7. Less than 5% of the buyers can be termed "professional people" (doctors, lawyers, dentists, school teachers, accountants) who might be investing for tax shelter.

8. In some instances, buyers living elsewhere in California find that they can manage their

Westlands land themselves by employing key personnel as foremen to oversee the day-to-day farm operations, but reserving to themselves the management decisions. Other purchasers continue to live in the immediate vicinity to conduct their farming. In addition, nonresident farming families continue to move into the area to farm land which they have purchased.

9. Since 1968, the number of landowners in the District has increased from 2,491 to 3,996 and that increase included an added 1,510 new owners of 160 acres or less. And the number of farm operations increased from 97 to 210. . . .

Where are the facts that support the statements that the large landowners are selling off most of their property to relatives and former employees? They [critics] cite as an example the sale of the property of Mr. Russell Giffen [who]. . . in keeping with his promise to the Congress, sold some 43,000 acres of land in 160-acre or smaller parcels. . . out of the 43,210 acres sold by Mr. Giffen, a total of about 1,800 acres was sold to members of his family and about 4,100 acres were sold to 9 former employees and their families. These lands were sold on the same terms and at the same price as the other 37,000 acres were sold to others.

This is not to concede that a sale to members of one's family or to employees or former employees requires defending. It is a well established fact and principle of our society and our law that we pass on to our descendants our land or other resources. . . .

Since when has it been wrong or disgraceful for a man to give his land to his heirs, let alone sell it to them as was done in this case? Since when has it become against public policy for a man to reward the loyalty of his present or former employees? Since when has it been against public policy for him to favor his employees over others in the disposition of his property? Will it next be contrary to public policy to grant stock options or pensions to employees?

Another matter that requires discussion is that regarding the price for which the land is sold. Often the remark has been made that the land must be sold at its "pre-water" or "pre-project" value. This is no basis in law for such a statement. . . .

Practically every point raised here by the objectors and raised in the press, accurately or inaccurately, insofar as acreage limitation enforcement is concerned, is predicated on one assumption. That assumption is that the residency requirement of the 1902 law applies. One may feel that too few buyers live on the land. One may feel that each parcel should be farmed by itself and not with others as part of a larger operation. One may believe, as those protesting here today seem to believe, apparently without investigation, that no new homes are being built on the land. One may bemoan family operations which exceed a few hundred acres. It makes no difference. Even if these are legitimate opinions, they are not legitimate criticisms. They are all predicated on the assumption that the 1902 provision as to residency still is in effect. If it were applicable, most of these situations could not exist. If it is not applicable, there is no issue of enforcement. The fact remains, however, the fundamental issue is residency.

Overlooked in this discussion and the reference to legislative history of the 1902 Act is the discussion concerning the equal, if not superior, purpose of the 1902 law in its anti-monopoly objective. When one reads the legislative history of the sections of the law with which we are concerned here, a persuasive argument can be made that an equal, if not predominant, concern of the Congress was land monopoly. It would appear that it first wanted to break up existing land monopolies and to preclude the accumulation of large land empires. Now the suggestion is being made that the sales of land which would achieve that objective, the breakup of monopoly, be stopped or delayed. At the same time, the same objectors are decrying the subsidies which are going to the large landowners who do not sell.

But there is a matter of equity that lies here also. One should not be beguiled by the emotional, and I might add, somewhat inaccurate remonstrations that all of the problems originated with Westlands Water District. The matter of nonenforcement of the residency requirement did not originate with Westlands or with this particular Commissioner of Reclamation or this Secretary of the Interior or with these landowners.

For over 60 years the provision has been considered as not being legally operable. . . . If the Court states that the law is as it has been construed for the past 60 years, that is, not being applicable, Westlands will deliver water to the land, if it is otherwise eligible to receive it under the law. If, on the other hand, the Court says that residency is required, we will not furnish water to the land and will comply with the law as to that part of it, as we have faithfully and completely done with respect to the excess land provisions of the law. But until the Congress or the Court tells us to do differently, we will comply with the law as it is; that is, as enacted by the Congress or interpreted by the courts. We will not comply with it as others might wish the law to be. If there is dissatisfaction, it must be with the law itself and, if that is the case, I respectfully suggest that the Congress is the place to change it. . . .

By way of summary, I would state that we have demonstrated that compliance with the law is being achieved—and rigorously so—and the objectives of the law are being achieved extensively. The facts belie the statements of those who refer to corporate holdings that existed when the Project was started and imply that the large corporate holdings are now being formed and developed. The facts belie their contention that there is a predominance of absentee owners or that the major group of buyers of excess lands are "paper farmers"—whatever that means. The law and the facts refute their contention that Project benefits are being included in approved land sales. The facts deny the accusation that the bulk of the land is being sold to relatives and employees of the large landowner. The facts destroy the implication that the seller is retaining control over the land sold.

The reality of the situation is that the actual buyers are eligible buyers under the law, but these objectors wish other buyers to be preferred. If such a preference is desired and desirable, the correction must be made by a change in the law. At no time has the point been proven, nor any proof been offered, that once land has been placed on the market, any potential purchaser of the type to whom the objectors would wish a preference to be given and who was financially able to acquire the land was rejected in favor of another.

I can only close by repeating what I stated earlier. Westlands Water District and the Bureau of Reclamation has had an outstanding record in compliance with and achieving the objectives of the excess land provisions of the Federal reclamation laws. And it has done so with its facilities for delivering water only 70% complete and within a very short period of time since the start of substantial deliveries of water to the District. It will continue to comply with the law religiously. We are willing to let the record speak for itself. That is what is important; it is not the distortions and twisting of it by those whose astuteness consists in their ability to find a difficulty for any solution.

34. Prof. E. Phillip LeVeen: All Water Subsidies Are Bad and Should Be Stopped

Agricultural economist E. Phillip LeVeen, of U.C. Berkeley, told Congress during the debate on a revision of the 1902 reclamation law that water subsidies were subverting the intent of the original reclamation law and should be ended at once.[3]

Introduction

This report analyzes a major issue in the current congressional debate over the future of Reclamation policy—the water subsidy. It will be argued that there is little justification for its continuation under either (1) the present policies of the U.S. Bureau of Reclamation (USBR) or (2) those contemplated by most of the proposed Reclamation Act amendments currently before Congress.

The subsidy no longer meets the original objectives of the Reclamation Act. Its elimination would restore fiscal stability to the Reclamation program, provide a measure of equity in the distribution of project benefits, and change the incentives that now encourage wasteful development and use of water, an increasingly scarce natural resource. The only justifiable way to continue the subsidy would involve a major revision of Reclamation policy to bring it into line with its original objectives. Few if any of the legislative proposals before Congress would effectively do this.

These arguments will be illustrated with examples drawn from the recent experience of the Westlands Water District, which contains the newest and most expensive of all Reclamation irrigation projects, and which demonstrates, in the extreme, many of the irrationalities of current Reclamation administration policy.

Brief Background to the Current Situation

In 1902 Congress established the Reclamation program to achieve two different policy goals. On one hand, it wished to encourage greater development of water resources and to bring apparently useless western land under cultivation and produce more food and fiber. On the other hand, Congress wanted to promote broad social and economic development, with widespread land ownership and a family farm system of production. To insure achievement of these broad social goals, Congress further stipulated that in order for a family to be eligible for project water, it must not own more than 160 acres within federal water projects, and must reside on or near its land. Congress also provided a small additional benefit to stimulate such economic development by permitting water users to repay the full cost of irrigation construction over a ten-year period, interest-free.

In the intervening 76 years, Congress has not amended the acreage or the residency requirements. It has, however, extended the original ten-year interest-free repayment period to 40 years, and has changed the repayment criteria so that water users are no longer liable for full repayment of all project costs. Since 1939, water users repay only the portion of irrigation costs they can "afford" to repay (measure by an ability-to-pay formula) and the remaining costs are paid from other project revenues, mainly from sales of hydroelectric power. The effect of these amendments has been to increase the water subsidy dramatically, although this was presumably not the intention of Congress. Instead, Congress amended the law to provide relief to hard-pressed farmers who could not pay the high costs of federal water during a period of extreme agricultural depression, and to stimulate the Reclamation program during the New Deal in order to provide massive public employment. . . .

The current crisis in Reclamation policy arises from a growing discrepancy between the state

---

[3]Phillip LeVeen's views were published under the title of "Reclamation Policy at a Crossroads," in *Public Affairs Report*, Bulletin of the Institute of Government Studies, U.C. Berkeley, Vol. 19, October, 1978.

goals of the Reclamation Act and the actual implementation of the program by the USBR. Through a variety of questionable administrative interpretations of the law, USBR has all but eliminated the effectiveness of the residency and acreage requirements, and has thereby disregarded the broad social and distributional goals that remain part of its legal mandate. These administrative procedures, in combination with the growing magnitude of the water subsidy, have led to the construction of increasingly expensive water projects that impose considerable costs on the taxpayer, misallocate water resources, and give highly concentrated benefits to a few landowners. . . . [A]t present about 30 pieces of legislation are before Congress, containing at least six major alternative approaches to modernization of the 1902 Reclamation law.

The Issues in the Congressional Debate

Much of the debate over the future administration of Reclamation projects centers on questions of efficiency and fairness. Large landowners have argued that a stricter interpretation of the Reclamation law, forcing a reduction in farm size, would be out of step with modern agricultural technology and would therefore increase production costs, reduce farmer welfare, and raise food prices. They further contend that any reversal of current administrative procedures constitutes an unfair use of public power since most project participants based their decisions to accept federal water on past practices and interpretations of the law.

Proponents of a stricter interpretation respond that smaller 160-to 320-acre farms are economically viable and efficient enough to produce food at current prices. This position has considerable academic support. They also contend that the broad social and economic development goals encouraged by the original Reclamation Act of 1902—widespread land ownership and family farms—remain important and relevant policy objectives today, and can be implemented only by returning to the strict enforcement of existing acreage and residency requirements.

Neither side of the debate has given the subsidy issue much attention, mainly because neither side wants the subsidy eliminated. In the final analysis, however, the most important question confronting Congress is whether or not to continue subsidizing water.

The Magnitude of the Water Subsidy

As noted above, the major subsidy to Reclamation Water users is the exemption from paying interest on the costs of irrigation facilities. . . .

In summary, an explicit subsidy in the form of the interest exemption and the use of hydroelectric revenues is granted to water users, which reduces their share of total construction costs to about 15 percent. Inflation adds an unintentional subsidy by further reducing this share to about 5 percent. Using conservative assumptions, these figures imply that the present value (1976 dollars) of the water subsidy throughout the Reclamation program averaged at least $500 per acre and was probably twice that figure. A more definite estimate for this subsidy is available for the Westlands, the newest of the irrigation projects, where water users repay all irrigation construction costs and receive no explicit subsidy from electricity revenues. Nevertheless, the estimated present value of the subsidy is between $1,800 and $2,200 per acre, depending on the outcome of water price negotiations between the government and the water district. This means that the total public cost of irrigating 160 acres averages $77,000 throughout the program and about $353,000 in the Westlands. . . .

The Nature and Magnitude of Project Benefits

As indicated earlier, there is no necessary relationship between the economic benefits created by irrigation and the overall costs of irrigation projects. Efficient resource development consists of funding only projects whose total economic benefits are greater than their costs. These were the kinds of projects that Congress originally envisioned in 1902 and that modern resource development policy guidelines are intended to foster. Under such conditions, water users would experience benefits from project development, even if they were required to repay full project costs. If such projects are subsidized, the water user simply earns an even greater benefit at someone else's expense.

As already implied, many Reclamation projects do not meet these efficiency criteria. Inefficient projects would not be built if water users were forced to repay their full costs (including interest) because the benefits received through increased land productivity would not compensate for the higher repayment obligations. But when water users are not required to repay a very significant portion of project costs, this means that highly inefficient projects will nevertheless provide landowners with substantial benefits. For example, as noted above, the Westlands subsidy amounts to $2,200 per acres. The writer's research shows that this expenditure creates benefits equal to about $1,000 (or less) per acre. If landowners were required to pay the full costs of irrigating this region, they would not have supported the project, since they would have been worse off with the project and better off without it, even though contending with declining ground water supplies. . . .

Subsidized irrigation has encouraged expanded crop production in the arid West, and has thereby imposed increasing costs on the taxpayer through the effects of expansion on the creation of surpluses, and on farmers in competing rain-fed agricultural regions who have lost their competitive position in some crops. For example, after the cotton quotas were eliminated in 1972, cotton production expanded rapidly in California, especially in the Westlands, to the detriment of smaller southern farmers and the related rural economies that lost a profitable market. This shift in location would have been much less pronounced without the public subsidy. Also, since 40 percent of Reclamation cropland is planted in crops subject to government commodity programs, the irrigation of the West has encouraged greater production of crops already in surplus supply. This in turn has helped force the government to impose price supports and supply controls throughout the nation (at considerable taxpayer expense) in order to maintain farm prices at politically acceptable levels. In short, the expansion of irrigation in the West has several invisible but nevertheless costly side-effects. If these were accurately estimated and incorporated into our cost-benefit analyses, the overall inefficiency of Reclamation would be seen as even greater than is generally understood. Briefly, subsidized water permits lands of lesser quality ("scrub lands") that would otherwise not be cultivated, to be put into production. But once they are in production with subsidized water, they have a "heritage" and as time goes by it is difficult if not impossible to stop the subsidy. Yet it is a wasteful use of good water, which is increasingly in short supply. Thus, the subsidy encourages putting good water on bad land, and on a long-term basis. . . .

In summary, the subsidy favors the selection and development of inefficient projects. It helps the USBR to maintain an ever-expanding program, although the efficient irrigation sites have long since been exhausted and the nation continues to face agricultural surpluses. It also encourages the inefficient use of water, which is in short supply. Moreover, since the inefficiencies are often substantial, once projects are in being any attempt to eliminate the water subsidy would lead to economic hardship and possible bankruptcy for many producers. In a sense, we are trapped by our past mistakes. . . .

Westlands' Benefits

The writer has investigated the distribution of project benefits in the Westlands Water District, finding that under the current administrative practices of the USBR, virtually all project benefits accrued to the original landowners of record at the time of water deliveries in 1968. This accrual of benefits to original owners has been facilitated by the USBR's administrative interpretation of the Reclamation law, which has led to several questionable practices.

The most important of these practices is the agency's failure to impose the residency requirement, allowing absentee owners to keep their land and lease it out. These actions have all but eliminated the incentives for owners of excess land to place their holdings on the market for new family farmers. Instead, owners can redistribute their holdings under new titles, using the names of family members, relatives, or corporations, in order to conform to the 160-acre restriction on ownership.

Next they can lease the land to large agricultural management firms that farm the land in major tracts, using hired managers and laborers. If residency were required, most of this reorganization of titles would be pointless, since the new ''owners'' do not live on the land, and could not qualify for water.

The second most important practice that allows the original owners to capture project benefits is the ten-year grace period for the sale of excess land, during which time the original owner is allowed to purchase subsidized project water for his entire holdings. In the Westlands, the total value of access to subsidized water and the additional income created over a ten-year period was estimated to be $950 per acre. In addition, when a landowner sells during the grace period, the USBR has permitted selling prices well in excess of the true ''non-project'' land price, thereby allowing the seller to capture additional project benefits. In the Westlands this has amounted to an additional benefit of about $400 per acre. Finally, the USBR has permitted land sales whereby all price controls were effectively avoided and the original owner captured the entire capitalized value of the subsidy.

In 1968, when water deliveries began, there were approximately 2,500 individuals and corporate landowners in the 545,000 acre Westlands Water District. About 84 percent of this land was held by 280 individuals or corporations, with an average holdings of 1,650 acres. The average benefit received by this group was therefore about $1.6 million per owner. On the other hand, the 2,200 other owners, with holdings averaging about 40 acres, received about $40,000 each in benefits from the subsidy.

In 1968 the Westlands was organized into 97 farms (with ''farms'' defined in terms of production units). Absentee landowners leased their holding in these farms, which are generally run by hired management and labor. Today, with only half of the land classified as ''excess'' and possibly available for subdivision into smaller farms, there are only about 216 farms (also mostly leased) averaging about 2,200 acres each. Even if the remaining excess land were subdivided in a similar manner the district would not have more than 350 to 400 farms when the last of the excess land had eventually been sold.

In short, under the current administration of the Reclamation Act, a project has been built whose costs exceed benefits by a ratio of two to one. The public will have spent over $1 billion to irrigate 545,000 acres and create about 300 new farms ($3.3 million per farm). Moreover these farms will be run mainly by hired managers and workers. The benefits of this project will have been captured by a small number of individuals and corporations, many of whom have little interest in or contact with farming, and certainly could not be called ''family farmers.''

The Westlands experience, though perhaps the most extreme of all Reclamation projects, helps demonstrate the irrationality of the way the Reclamation program has been administered. The large subsidy, never intended by Congress, is used to make an inefficient project politically desirable. USBR administrative practices give a major share of project benefits to the original landowners, helping insure their active support for the program. This arrangement allows the expansion of the Reclamation program, thereby satisfying the agency and select members of Congress, while giving large windfall benefits to those who are fortunate enough to own land in the right places at the right time.

On the other hand, the would-be family farmer in whose name this large expenditure is justified receives few benefits. The general public pays much of the bill, both through taxes and through the less visible costs of malallocated resources. . . .

Conclusion

Large water subsidies are the source of most of the problems in the current Reclamation program. Unfortunately, these effects are not well understood, and have been lost in the current congressional debate over acreage and residency requirements. The subsidy has created political incentives encouraging the construction of ''pork-barrel'' projects which, in turn, require the overdevelopment of rivers and streams and the overconsumption of water by agriculture at a very high public cost.

The subsidy was originated to facilitate the rural development goals of the Reclamation Act. But in fact the record shows that under the program's current administration the subsidy has increased the economic and political power of the original landowners. It has not promoted small family farms or rural development. Instead, the subsidy has contributed to inefficient water resource development and regressive social development.

What is to be done? The previous analysis suggests the following approaches.

First, the subsidy should be withdrawn from all future projects. Rural development no longer is the most pressing issue. Instead, the main concern is efficient resource development. No matter how widely distributed the subsidy might be, its benefits cannot justify the continued inefficient overdevelopment of irrigation facilities. Where rural development is desirable, other kinds of public policy can achieve these goals more efficiently. If the subsidy for new projects is withdrawn, it is unlikely that there will be any large-scale water development projects in the future, at lest until agricultural prices have risen to much higher levels than now prevail.

Secondly, with respect to projects already completed or under construction, the minimum appropriate reform would reduce the subsidy by requiring water users to repay their share of construction costs, plus cooperation and maintenance costs, within a reasonable time.

Third, with respect to restrictions on acreage and residency, appropriate reforms would depend on the extent of the subsidy and the age of the program.

(1) Future projects are considered first. If the subsidy were eliminated from future projects, the case for such restrictions would be weakened. Moreover strict acreage and residency requirements might prevent efficient projects from being built, because of landowner reluctance.

Even if the subsidy should be continued for future projects, however, strict requirements would still inhibit construction of water projects, both efficient and inefficient. Accordingly, removal of the subsidy seems clearly preferable to acreage and residency restraints, although the latter would be better than continuation of present practices.

(2) With respect to projects under construction or completed in the comparatively recent past, if participants are willing and able to make full repayment of costs plus interest, an exemption from acreage and residency requirements would seem appropriate. But the situation is different if a substantial subsidy continues indefinitely and the land remains in the hands of the original owners—as is true of Westlands. In these cases strict acreage and residency requirements—like those in the NLP bill-can appropriately be imposed without unduly penalizing such owners, who would already have benefitted from land-value appreciation.

(3) Finally, in older projects like those in the Imperial Valley, we must acknowledge that to impose acreage and residency restrictions would inflict large uncompensated losses on existing owners, who are not the original owners and beneficiaries from the initial land-value appreciation. Accordingly, such old projects should either be exempted, or if restrictions are imposed they should be accompanied by some form of compensation.

To sum up, the greatest opportunity for experimentation is with future projects yet unbuilt, where elimination of the subsidy seems the most appropriate policy. Substantial experimentation is also possible with projects under construction or recently completed—such as the Westlands—where strict acreage and residency requirements are appropriate policies, along with other measures to encourage rural development.

35.
Tristan E. G. Krogius: Large Corporate Farms are a "Non-Issue"

Tenneco West, Inc., which operates over one million acres of land in western United States, is one of the largest and most successful public corporations involved in agriculture. Its president, Tristan E. G. Krogius, defended corporate farming in an address entitled, "Role of the Corporate Grower in California Agriculture," delivered in Fresno, August 20, 1984.[4] *In it he claimed that there should be more, not fewer, big corporations in farming because they are more competitive than any other type of enterprise.*

. . . .To us, the importance of agriculture to our state and nation is clear. However, this is not clear to many voters, and the prospects for agriculture seem surprisingly uncertain! Special interest groups have for years been conducting attacks designed to discredit, demoralize and destroy agriculture. These attacks have included attempts to destroy modern farming by redistributing the land, by banning essential herbicides and insecticides, by government control of private agricultural lands, by denial of use of public lands for productive purposes, by stopping water development, and by government regulation of the marketplace.

A subject which has, from time to time in the past, been an emotionally-charged issue has been the perceived dominance of farming in California by big public corporations. In fact, however, this is a "non-issue" because large public corporations have never really been a major factor in California agriculture. At the peak, big public corporations have farmed only 5% of irrigated farmland in California and this figure could soon be less. With the sale of Getty Oil to Texaco and the sale of Superior Oil to Mobil Oil, there have been announced intentions by these major oil companies to spin off their newly-acquired farming interests. However, no other big companies really are buyers for the 80,000 plus acres involved or for substantial other acreage also on the market. The reason for this is that corporate farming has not been particularly profitable for many of those who have tried it and the outlook a currently is especially bleak with the strong U.S. dollar hindering exports, and oversupply dampening prices.

The problem in the future really is one of "too little" and not "too much" participation by large corporations in farming. In support of this position I offer the following argument:

The U.S. depends on being competitive in world markets. Successful competition requires capital and large U.S. corporations bring capital to farming. With this capital and with the resource of the large corporation it is in a unique position to bring *innovation* to farming. And, large corporations can bring marketing and management skills to agriculture. Furthermore, large corporations have the financial strength to compete with large co-ops who tend to hold down competition from independent processors. This all adds up to the fact that large public companies can provide the *competition* which is absolutely essential for innovation and for invigoration of a commodity industry. . . .

A company such as ours has resources in many foreign countries which gives us the opportunity to expand our worldwide markets. Large corporate farmers have an ongoing commitment to R&D and have been responsible for the development of new plants and varieties on their test farms which better meet the needs of the consumer. Finally, large companies have the capital and the resources to operate in a variety of micro climates to bring the food service operator the year around supply he needs in commodities such as grapes and tree fruit.

But having suggested that we should have more, not less, major corporations involved in agriculture I'm at a loss to suggest how to attract such companies to this arena which is characterized by big risks and small returns. . . . A most interesting view was recently propounded by Peter

[4]Reprinted in *Produce Marketing Almanac* (1985), 66-75.

Lewis, a New York investment banker with interest in farming. He deals with complaints that the government is subsidizing the U.S. farmer with the contradictory view that U.S. agriculture actually supports the state rather than the state supporting agriculture. First he point out that the ripple effect of agriculture on our economy is much greater than people realize. . .one estimate is that 22% of all jobs in the U.S. are traceable to agriculture even though less than 5% are directly employed on the farm. The U.S. consumer enjoys low food prices. Everyone in the food distribution chain except the farmer and shipper is earning a good return on his investment. The bankers, Jack-In-The-Box, motels, etc., operating in the farmers' areas all have healthy returns on their capital. Meanwhile, agriculture makes a much smaller return. . .so who's subsidizing whom? Our media, especially in California, are full of all the opportunities for increased employment being brought about through expansion of the electronics industry; an industry that is being locally subsidized. I can assure you that all the electronics expansion imaginable won't be able to offset agricultural losses if we as a nation cease to be competitive in world markets. California as well as many other farm states better get much more enlightened on such issues as the need for making water available at a reasonable cost!

. . .Over half of the water in California is wasted through run-off into the ocean. What we have is a serious water distribution problem. Elitists who want to stop California's growth, and social activists who find power and employment in environmental issues, have been trying to assert control over water. . .the lifeblood of the state. On last November's ballot these groups devised a clever initiative called The Water Initiative which would have crippled the state's water project and which would have had the effect of taking thousands of acres of land out of production. . . . [W]e brought our resources to bear against the water initiative and were largely responsible for creating and financing the campaign which trounced it by a vote of 2:1. Before this campaign we were losing 3:2 in the polls.

The disappearing farmland issue is another social activist phony issue. Clifton Lutrell writing in the Federal Reserve Board of St.Louis' prestigious *Review* notes that the number of acres from which crops were harvested in the U.S. actually increased from 286 million to 337 million in the decade of the 1970's. . .an 18% increase. To put it into perspective, that's about 50 million acres which is equal to the entire land area of the state of Nebraska. During the same period, yields increased about 20% This, then, totals an increase of almost 40% in total production which permitted growth in U.S. exports while consumers were spending a declining part of their disposable income on food. And, herein, also lies the problem farmers are facing. With the curtailment of exports, there is an oversupply of many commodities. . . .

While we may not be purely capitalistic society in the sense that our economic system incorporates pragmatic solutions which are to the left of the free market concept, we do believe that competition is the lifeblood of our system. I really don't see volume controls lessening competition so long as they are impartially administered.

We have a tremendous farm production, marketing and distribution system here in California. While it is suffering some dislocations and while there will be acreage going out of production in many commodities, the healthy competition between co-ops, independents, small farmers and corporate farmers has built this machine. . . .

In summary, then, my topic today was to discuss the role of the corporate grower in California agriculture. Tenneco West has been successful in what we do. We have a long-term commitment to the land. The driving goal of our company is to "enhance and realize the optimum value of our land base by maintaining a major presence in the real estate, food and agricultural related economies." We own about 1 million acres in the western U.S. and are the major urban developer in Kern County as well as being grower-shippers of fresh products and growers and/or processors of commodities such as dates, raisin, almonds and pistachios. We also lease almost 100,000 acres of irrigated farmland to independent farmers. We try to be good corporate citizens, believe we make a positive contribution to California agriculture, and our aim is to build our company on quality. . . .

UNIVERSITY OF CALIFORNIA CAMPUSES
CALIFORNIA STATE COLLEGE CAMPUSES
Humboldt State College, Arcata
Chico
Davis
Sacramento
Sonoma State College, Rohnert Park
Berkeley
San Francisco
Hayward
Stanislaus State College, Turlock
San Jose
Santa Cruz
Fresno
Polytechnic College, San Luis Obispo
San Fernando Valley State College, Northridge
Los Angeles
Polytechnic College, Pomona
San Bernardino
Riverside
Santa Barbara
Fullerton
Dominguez Hills
Irvine
Long Beach
San Diego

The California System of Higher Education

The University does not deserve a response of loyalty and allegiance from you. There is only one proper response to Berkeley from undergraduates: that you ORGANIZE AND SPLIT THIS CAMPUS WIDE OPEN!...

Go to the top. Make your demands to the Regents. If they refuse to give you an audience: start a program of agitation, petitioning, rallies, etc., in which the final resort will be CIVIL DISOBEDIENCE. In the long run, there is the possibility that you will find it necessary to perform civil disobedience at a couple of major University public ceremonies....

—Brad Cleveland, former Berkeley student, in a "Letter to Undergraduates," September 10, 1984.[1]

The University...has shown patience. This patience has been met with impatience and with violence of the law. The university has shown tolerance. This tolerance has been met with intolerance and distortion of the truth. The university has shown reasonableness. This reasonableness has been met with irrationality and intransigence. The university has shown decency. This decency has been met with indecency and ill-will.

—Clark Kerr, former University of California at Berkeley president, December 3, 1964.[2]

CHAPTER 12

THE UNIVERSITY UNDER FIRE
The Berkeley Free Speech Movement of 1964

The relationship between the academic world and its surrounding community has been a stormy one ever since the elders of Athens condemned Socrates for impiety and corruption of youth and forced him to drink the hemlock.

Of course, not many cases of academic conflict have had the same poignancy or tragedy as the trial of Socrates, although occasionally (as during the "town and gown" battles at medieval Oxford and Paris) they have led to armed combat and have produced memorable results. Usually the dispute has been over doctrine: the issue then becomes the right of the professor to teach disputed material, or of the student to learn unorthodox views, or both—a simple definition of academic freedom. Whether the dispute is over theological questions in the French medieval universities, or Darwinian evolution in the nineteenth-century American colleges, or even the right of students to climb flagpoles, the pressures of society have often been enormous. Total victory or defeat may be at stake, as the king, or bishop, or parliament, or legislature seeks to bring the recalcitrants into line. The resistance of the accused has been equally determined. At the very least such disputes lead to bitterness and rancor that last for years and to serious questionings and doubts about the very meaning of the university and the search for truth.

In the case of the American university, when it is a public institution and the people retain a vested interest in the financing of it, academic controversies will usually have political implications that are particularly hard to resolve. By the late 1940's the University of California, a state university, had come to be recognized as one of this country's great institutions of higher learning. At that juncture it witnessed the loyalty oath controversy of 1949-1952 and, with the scars of that battle

[1]Published in the Berkeley *Slate Supplement Report*, September 10, 1964.

[2]As quoted in Seymour Martin Lipset and Sheldon S. Wolin, eds., *The Berkeley Student Revolt* (Garden City, New York: Doubleday and Company, Inc., 1965), 245.

not quite healed, it passed through the Berkeley student revolt—in 1964, which was the most serious ordeal in its history.

Student life at Berkeley was never completely restful, but the school year opened at an unusually agitated pace in September 1964 and the tempo increased to a frenzy by December, when the institution ceased to function normally. It was a presidential election year and the statewide campaign for Proposition 14 to repeal the Rumford Housing Act, a campaign that evoked covert anti-Negro bias, added an element of bitterness. University students freshly returned from civil rights activities in the South were organizing sit-ins and other protests at off-campus locations, including the offices of the conservative Oakland *Tribune*.

Then the university unexpectedly revoked permission to distribute literature at Sather Gate. Students and faculty of widely differing political persuasions protested that this violated constitutionally protected rights of free speech and assembly.

This was followed by the emergence of the Free Speech Movement led by the Militant Mario Savio, a 22-year-old philosophy major who urged drastic liberalization of campus political regulations "or else...," and the sit-in at Sproul Hall which started September 30 and culminated in the entrapment of a police car on October 1. An eleventh-hour truce was signed which at first promised a rapprochement, including negotiations to change the rules, but in the following weeks relations between the students and the administration again deteriorated. At 3 A.M. on December 3, with batteries of press cameras focused on the entrance of Sproul Hall, over 600 uniformed police officers arrived to break up a sit-in involving 800 dissidents. This brought the faculty to its feet, and on December 8 it met to issue a series of resolutions.

Some factors that contributed to the revolt are the recent increase in the size of Berkeley campus to 27,000 students, the expansion of the University into a statewide system of eight campuses and the attendant centralization of the administration, the slow-burning irritation among the Berkeley faculty upon seeing its power relatively diminished within the statewide Academic Senate, and the decreasing attention to undergraduate instruction that was in counterpoint to the increasing moral fervor of the student body. The malaise of "multiversity" so ably diagnosed by President Kerr himself in 1963 had become critical within his own institution.

After a year or so of seemingly fruitful dialogue, campus relations deteriorated and a confrontation was in the making. On November 30, 1966, the radicals staged another sit-in on the campus that resulted—two years to the day after the grand finale of the 1964 revolt—in a full-scale student strike. Again the issue involved regulations concerning the use of campus facilities for off-campus organizations, but the mood was even more grim than before: the strikers could not make their demands stick; the faculty failed to please either the administration, the students, or itself; and the administration was dejected and dismayed at having to call upon the police again to end a disturbance. A chill fell over the campus. Meantime, the general public showed its displeasure with the Berkeley campus by defeating Governor Brown's bid for reelection in 1966, and the Regents did the same in early 1967 by firing President Kerr. The latter episode raised the specter of partisanship creeping into the government of the university, and a move was under way in the legislature to change the membership of the Board of Regents by eliminating the ex officio members—the governor, lieutenant governor, assembly speaker, superintendent of public instruction, and the head of the Alumni Association.

The FSM revolt made Berkeley one of the cradles of the nationwide student rebellion of the 1960s. The agitation there resumed during the increasing political polarization over the Vietnam War. And in May 1969 the campus was rocked by the ugly "People's Park" controversy, when the "street people" of Berkeley occupied a block of University-owned land and made it into a park. A riot ensued, the National Guard was called in and the campus tear-gassed. A young bystander was killed in the melee.

What sort of conduct can the people of California reasonably expect of the students and faculty in the state university and colleges supported by taxation? How free of outside pressure should scholars be to pursue their own ends? Where does the public interest end and academic freedom begin? How can partisanship be prevented in public higher education? Should the university serve as a public utility for the manufacture of professionals, a "multiversity" of disputing factions, a community of freewheeling scholars operating pretty much on their own rules, or none of these? As the FSM rebellion passed into history, these were some of the unsolved riddles involving public higher education in California.

One thing was certain—the Berkeley Revolt of 1964 was no mere wild episode dreamed up by "a bunch of California kooks." It was an expression of widespread ferment in higher education that was capable of shaking the ivy, if not the roots, of every college and university in the country.

After the shouting died down, the University instituted rules affecting campus political organizations that seemed to work. These regulations allowed public debate on even the most controversial of topics. Constitutionally protected rights of free expression, speech, assembly, worship, and distribution and sale of literature were to be allowed on campus. Demonstrations were also permitted as long as they did not interfere with the orderly operation of the University and were conducted in accordance with time, place and manner regulations.

In the spring of 1985, student activism suddenly hit many American campuses, including those of the U.C. system. There were heated debates on whether the University of California should continue its involvement with nuclear weapons testing; whether affirmative action policies were contributing to a shortage of minority students and faculty; whether fraternities should be allowed to hold theme parties that tended to demean ethnic groups; whether the University should use animals in medical research; and, most importantly, whether the University should continue to invest in U.S. companies doing business in South Africa. Demonstrations against South African apartheid erupted on many campuses. Scores of sit-in protestors, who were trying to convince the Regents to divest themselves of $2.4 billion in investments, were arrested at Sproul Hall. But, however animated the protests, and however numerous the arrests, the rules of discourse were not challenged. The demonstrations were non-violent and there was no recurrence of a "free speech" issue. *(Editor's note)*

36. The Position of the Free Speech Movement

"The issue," the Free Speech Movement declared time and again, "is free speech." Yet this was too narrow a construction, for as the struggle widened the rebels complained not only that they had been deprived of their constitutional rights under the First Amendment, but also that the entire university was shot through with weaknesses. The issue became alienation—that is, an indictment of over-large classes, remoteness on the part of professors, the cold efficiency of the administration, and a host of other factors that left the student with a sense of anomie. These charges struck a responsive chord even among those students who were by nature disinclined to rebellion or were politically conservative.

In 1965 the FSM tried to regroup as a more stable and legitimate political coalition, but by 1966 it had virtually disappeared as a center of student activity. Many of its major charges had become clouded by cries that it was a "filthy speech movement" and by such questions as whether nonstudents had the right to participate in campus affairs.

There can hardly be any question about the public reaction to the rebellion. In mid-January the California Poll *directed by Mervin D. Field interviewed a cross section of the state's population and found "that 92 per cent of the adult public had heard or read something about the demon-*

strations and that 74 per cent of the public takes a disapproving attitude toward them." As many as 55 per cent disapproved strongly; only 4 per cent approved strongly.

Of the innumerable fliers and statements issued by the FSM, the following two are selected for their brevity and clarity.[3]

The Position of the Free Speech Movement on Speech and Political Activity

1. Regulation of Advocacy Under the First Amendment

Civil liberties and political freedoms which are constitutionally protected off campus must be equally protected on campus for all persons. Similarly, illegal speech or conduct should receive no greater protection on campus than off campus. The administration, like any other agency of government, may not regulate the content of speech and political conduct. Regulations governing the time, place and manner of exercising constitutional rights are necessary for the maintenance and proper operation of university functions, but they must not interfere with the opportunity to speak or the content of speech.

In contrast, the university regulations adopted by the Regents on November 20, 1964 and interpreted by the chancellor, read as follows:

> The Regents adopt the policy . . . that certain campus facilities carefully selected and properly regulated, may be used by students and staff for planning, implementing, raising funds or recruiting participants for lawful off-campus action, not for unlawful off-campus action.

By making the distinction between advocating "lawful" and "unlawful" action, the Regents propose to regulate the content of speech on campus. It is this distinction that is at the heart of FSM opposition to these regulations. . . .

2. Impropriety of Nonjudicial Forums for Punishing Political Activity

Under the November 20th regulations, if the chancellor accuses a student of advocating an unlawful act, the student and his sponsoring organization are liable to punishment by the university. A student so accused may appear before the Faculty Committee on Student Conduct, whose members are appointed by the chancellor, and whose opinions are only advisory to him.

The Free Speech Movement considers this to be unconstitutional and unwise for the following two reasons.

(1) Since such a procedure allows the chancellor to assume the role of prosecutor, judge and jury simultaneously, the students have no confidence that the final verdict will be fair. In fact, the history of the treatment of civil liberties cases by the campus administration reveals an insensitivity to safeguarding such liberties.

Further, the fact that the administration is peculiarly vulnerable to pressures originating outside the university should remove it from consideration as the proper authority for determining guilt or innocence in the extremely sensitive area of speech, assembly and protest within the First Amendment. It must be emphasized that the current crisis has not developed in a vacuum. These rules work a grave hardship on the civil-rights movement in Northern California. Organizations in this movement rely heavily on negotiations, demonstrations, picketing and other such legal tactics. It is true, however, that in order to focus attention on a serious injustice and to bring pressure to bear for its correction, civil-rights workers sometimes employ tactics which result in violation of law. Without passing on the propriety of such acts, the Free Speech Movement insists that the question whether their *advocacy* is legal or illegal must be left to the courts, which are institutionally independent of the shifting pressures of the community. . . .

[3]As quoted in Seymour Martin Lipset and Sheldon S. Wolin, eds., *The Berkeley Student Revolt* (Garden City, New York: Doubleday and Company, Inc., 1965), 201-215.

(2) Even if complete mutual trust existed between the administration and the student body, and even if the university attempted to observe the requirements of due process, it would be impossible for it to provide all of the safeguards of our judicial system, or otherwise to fulfill the functions of a court. The points in controversy, relating to the degree of responsibility of an act of advocacy for an act advocated, are of such a delicate and complex nature that even the courts have not built up wholly adequate precedents. Certainly, then, a nonjudicial body should be considered incompetent in this area.

On the other hand, the students' position that the courts alone have jurisdiction does not in any way imply the creation of a haven for illegal activity on the campus. On the contrary, it involves just the opposite of this—the *removal* of any special protection the university may now afford, as well as any extra-legal punishment. The student becomes subject to the same process of trial and punishment for illegal acts that all other citizens must accept.

3. On-Campus Regulation of the Form of Free Expression

The Free Speech Movement recognizes the necessity for regulations ensuring that political activity and speech do not interfere with the formal educational functions of the university. Rallies must not be held so as to disturb classes, block traffic, damage university property, conflict with other scheduled public meetings or rallies, etc. Such regulation is purely formal; no discretion to regulate the *content* of speech can constitutionally be permitted the controlling authority. Further, the regulations must be carefully tailored to protect or promote these state interests without unduly burdening the opportunity to speak, hear, or engage in political activity on the campus.

At the present time, university regulations governing the *form* of expression on the campus are promulgated by the administration, while other segments of the university community are limited to a purely advisory capacity. It is the general position of the Free Speech Movement that those persons and organizations subject to regulations must have a part in their final enactment. It is especially important as a safeguard against abuse or factual error that students share the responsibility for promulgating regulations over the form of speech. The administration has demonstrated many times its propensity to plead the necessity to regulate form as an excuse for regulating content. For example, the administration has until recently designated a place removed from the area of normal student traffic as the sole ''Hyde Park area,'' thus seriously hampering access to listeners. As the local ACLU [American Civil Liberties Union] has pointed out,

> a denial of certain avenues of such access (such as the open areas of the campus) with the claim that there are others, which though perhaps not as desirable are nonetheless available, will not avoid violation of the First Amendment unless the government entity. . . can demonstrate that there are no available alternative means of achieving its purposes, and that the purposes in question are so necessary as to be, in the language of the Court, ''compelling.''

Because of such past experience, and because of the important principle of democratic self-government involved, the Free Speech Movement has taken the position that final regulation of the form of exercise of speech should be by a tripartite committee, consisting of representatives chosen independently by the students, faculty and administration.

The Administration: Bungling Friend or Deliberate Enemy? (Leaflet)

The issue is free speech.

Early this semester we were confronted with administrative rulings drastically reducing political activity on campus. The rights to solicit members, to collect funds, to advocate action in off-campus projects, rights students have always had at Cal, were abolished by administrative fiat. The rulings were the response of a single individual, Chancellor Strong, to right-wing political pressure. They had absolutely no basis in law, reason, tradition, or general Regents' policy.

Administration officials frustrated all our attempts to explain that these ruling were unacceptable restrictions on our freedom of speech. Rights unexercised are lost, so we finally disregarded the new restrictions and continued normal campus political activity. In retaliation, the administration singled out eight participating students and suspended them. When Chancellor Strong ordered Jack Weinberg's arrest, our protest spontaneously grew to a massive sit-in around the police car. Under pressure of this demonstration, Clark Kerr finally agreed to meet with student representatives, and thirty-three and one-half hours after Jack's arrest an agreement was signed. . . .

Since the administration could not lose face, the agreement had to be worded to allow intermediate agencies to make the concessions we demanded. Thus the cases of the eight students were to be turned over to the Student Conduct Committee of the Academic Senate and acted on within a week, Jack was to be booked but then released, and a joint faculty-student-administration committee was to be set up to review the new restrictions and make recommendations to the administration. President Kerr assured us that he would consider carefully our recommendations for members to sit on this committee and told us that we had to have some trust in the administration.

Now, what has happened to this agreement? The cases of the suspended students were supposed to be referred to the Student Conduct Committee of the Academic Senate, but no such committee of the Academic Senate exists. In fact, the cases were referred to a committee appointed by Chancellor Strong. The duration of the suspensions was to be decided within a week. Almost two weeks have passed and the students have not had a hearing before any committee at all. President Kerr promised to consider student recommendations for the joint faculty-student-administration committee, yet when the Free Speech Movement tried to contact him during the weekend with its recommendations, he was consistently unavailable. Monday morning the names of the committee members appeared in the newspapers.

President Kerr had demonstrated bad faith even before this. As the students, in compliance with the agreement, dispersed from around the police car, Kerr was holding a press conference. He smeared and red-baited the entire Free Speech Movement. He said the students used "Communist tactics," whatever those are. Forty per cent of the leadership, Kerr said, were non-students (they were, of course, students suspended by the administration). He even was quoted in the *Examiner* of October 3 as saying that 49 per cent of the students "followed the Mao-Castro line"!

President Kerr told us that we should trust the administration. His statements and actions, from the moment the agreement was signed, have betrayed our trust.

The agreement is broken, but our demands remain. . . . The issue is free speech.

Why Are UC Students Still Not Satisfied?!!

The Regents' meeting of November 20 resulted in surprisingly harsh rulings concerning the dispute over political activity on the Berkeley campus.

I. Although the Heyman Committee recommended that six of the eight students suspended on September 30 *should not have been suspended at all*, the Regents voted to confirm their suspensions; in addition, while voting to reinstate all eight, the Regents decided that Mario Savio and Art Goldberg should be placed on probation for the rest of this semester. Such probation could easily result in expulsion for both, because they have been in repeated violation of university regulations since September 30.

II. The Regents voted to allow the administration to take disciplinary action against students, staff, and organizations who advocate illegal off-campus actions. The wording of the resolution is ambiguous, and the responsibility for interpreting it is given to Chancellor Strong. The Regents rejected without consideration the proposals concerning political freedom made by various faculty members, the ASUC Senate, and the FSM. . . .

. . . Up until today the faculty has played the role of mediator in the dispute between the administration and the students. In so doing, the faculty has seriously compromised the principles of the First and Fourteenth Amendments. The faculty by its compromising proposals, has allowed the administration to becloud the principles involved.

Let the faculty now stand up and unequivocally support the students of this campus in their just demands for full political freedom.

We urge all students to attend the Academic Senate meeting today—place as yet undetermined.

We Want a University (Dedicated to the 800)
By the Free Speech Movement

. . .

FSM: Moral Impetus, the Factory, and the Society

I. The Moral Impetus

. . .The Berkeley campus has become a new place since the beginning of the semester. Many are trying to tell us that what we are trying to do may destroy the university. We are fully aware that we are doing something which has implicit proportions so immense as to be frightening. We are frightened of our power as a movement; but it is a healthy fear. We must not allow our fear to lead us into believing that we are being destructive. We are beginning to *build* a great university. So long as the students stand united in firmness and dignity, and the faculty stands behind us, the university cannot be destroyed. . . .

. . .Sadly there is reason to believe that even after all of the suffering which has occurred in our community, the overwhelming majority of faculty members have not been permanently changed, have not joined our community, *have not really listened to our voices*—at this late date. For a moment of December 8th, eight hundred and twenty-four professors gave us all a glimpse—a brief, glorious vision—of the university as a loving community. If only the Free Speech Movement could have ended that day! . . . . After December 8th most faculty members moved quickly to rebuild their justifications for years of barren compromise.

We challenge the faculty to be courageous. A university is a community of students and scholars: be equal to the position of dignity you should hold!! . . . Too many people underestimate the resilience of a community fighting for a principle. Internally, the health of the university is improving. Communication, spirit, moral and intellectual curiosity, all have increased. The faculty has been forced to take the studentbody more seriously; it has begun to respect students. Furthermore, it has gained the opportunity to achieve a profound respect from the students. Those professors at Cal and other universities who love to teach, should be looking to Berkeley as the nation's greatest reservoir of students who embody the vital balance of moral integrity and high intellectual calibre. . . . Those who fearfully warn that we are destroying the university, are unwittingly weakening the FSM and the university. In the final analysis, only fear destroys!

II. Free Speech and the Factory

In our fight for free speech we said the "machine" must stop. We said that we must put our bodies on the line, on the machinery, in the wheels and gears, and that the "knowledge factory" must be brought to a halt. Now we must begin to clarify, for ourselves, what we mean by "factory."

We need to clarify this because the issues of free speech and the factory, of politics and education on the campus, are in danger of becoming separated. For example, the press has had the tendency to assert this separation when they insist that we return to our studies; that we are not in a center for political activity, but a center for education. Likewise, the faculty betrays the same tendency in its desire to settle the free speech issue as quickly and quietly as possible in order that we may return to the "normal conduct" of our "great university."

In contrast to this tendency to separate the issues, many thousands of *us*, the Free Speech Movement, have asserted that politics and education are inseparable, that the *political* issue of the First and Fourteenth Amendments and the *educational issue* cannot be separated. In place of "great university," we have said "impersonal bureaucracy," "machine," or "knowledge factory." If we emerge as victors from our long and still hard-to-be-won battle for free speech, will we then be returning to *less* than a factory? Is this a great university? If we are to take *ourselves* seriously we must define precisely what we meant when we said "knowledge factory."

The best way to identify the parts of our multiversity machinery is simply observe it "stripped down" to the bare essentials. In the context of a dazzling circus of "bait," which obscures our vision of the machinery, we get a four-year-long series of sharp staccatos: eight semesters, forty courses, one hundred twenty or more "units," ten to fifteen impersonal lectures per week, one to three oversized discussion meeting per week led by poorly paid graduate student "teachers." Over a period of four years the student-cog receives close to forty bibliographies; evaluation amounts to little more than pushing the test button, which results in over one hundred regurgitations in four years; and the writing of twenty to thirty-five "papers" in four years, in this context means that they are of necessity technically and substantially poor due to a lack of time for thought. The course-grade-unit system structure, resting on the foundation of departmentalization, produces knowledge for the student-cog, which has been exploded into thousands of bits and is force-fed, by the coercion of grades. We all know what happens when we really get "turned on" by a great idea, a great man, or a great book: we pursue that interest at the risk of flunking out. The pursuit of thought, a painful but highly exhilarating process, requires, above all, the element of time. . . .

III. The Factory and the Society

. . . The university has become grotesquely distorted into a "multiversity"; a public utility serving the purely technical needs of a society. In Clark Kerr's words, it is a factory for the production of knowledge and technicians to service society's many bureaucracies. . . .

Research and training replace scholarship and learning. In this system even during the first two years, the student is pressured to specialize or endure huge, impersonal lecture courses. He loses contact with his professors as they turn more to research and publishing, and away from teaching. His professors lose contact with one another as they serve a discipline and turn away from dialogue. Forms and structures stifle humane learning.

The student is powerless even to affect those aspects of the university supposedly closest to him. His student "government" by political castrates is a fraud permitted to operate only within limits imposed autocratically by the administration. Thus it is constitutionally mandated to serve the status quo. Likewise, the student has no power over the social regulations which affect his privacy, and little influence in shaping the character of the dormitories in which he lives. The university assumes the role of the parent.

As a human being seeking to enrich himself, the student has no place in the multiversity. Instead he becomes a mercenary, paid off in grades, status, and degrees, all of which can eventually be cashed in for hard currency on the job market. His education is not valued for its enlightenment and the freedom it should enable him to enjoy, but for the amount of money it will enable him to make. Credits for courses are subtly transformed into credit cards as the multiversity inculcates the values of the acquisitive society.

It has been written that "The main concern of the university should not be with the publishing of books, getting money from legislators, lobbying for federal aid, wooing the rich, producing bombs and deadly bacteria," Nor should it be with passing along the morality of the middle class, nor the morality of the white man, nor even the morality of the potpourri we call "western society." Nor should it be with acting as a second household or church for the young man away from home, nor as a playground for twisters, neophyte drinkers, and pledge classes. . . . Paul Goodman poignantly comments upon the plight of the modern student: "The labor of intelligent youth is needed and they are accordingly subjected to tight scheduling, speedup and other factory exploitative methods. Then it is not surprising if they organize their CIO. It is frivolous to tell them to go elsewhere if they don't like the rules; for they have no choice but to go to college, and one factory is like another."

In saying these things it is important to avoid a certain misunderstanding. . . that we have a fundamental bias against institutions as such; that we wish to destroy the structure altogether. . . . [On the contrary, we believe that] popular government cannot survive without education for the people. The people are more and more in the schools. But the pressure of the logistics of mass popular education combined with excessive greed has resulted in the machinery of the educational process having displaced the freedom to learn. We must now begin the demand of the right to know; to know the realities of the present world-in-revolution, and to have an opportunity to learn how to think clearly in an extended manner about that world. It is ours to demand meaning; we must insist upon meaning!

37. President Kerr States the Administration Viewpoint

As president of the University of California, Clark Kerr was an ironic figure—a brilliant professional mediator whose powers failed him at the most difficult moment of his career, a liberal who ultimately defended the status quo, a foe of radicals who was discharged by conservatives, a prophet of trouble who was unable to cope with the prophecy when it came true.

By Kerr's own admission his administration was flustered by the "intensity of student reaction" to the political ban at Sather Gate and by the eruption of civil disobedience on campus. And yet Kerr takes strong exception to the charge that administration incompetence was the major factor.[4] *He also flatly denies that free speech was ever the issue, for he kept the avenues to discussion wide open from start to finish. While allowing for the inevitable excitement of the political campaign and for the electricity added by the civil rights movement, and granting that the "multiversity" had its structural defects, President Kerr asserts that the student revolt arose because of a band of willful rebels. In his eyes the final responsibility lies with the arrogant and intransigent left-wing minority who, influenced by Communists and communist doctrine, foolishly tried to destroy the system rather than to correct its flaws.*

Clark Kerr will be remembered for other things besides his handling of the student rebellion. He was a distinguished professor of industrial relations, and a former Chancellor of the Berkeley campus. As president he was responsible for liberalizing the stringent political regulations that governed the university during the 1950's. He was also instrumental in the creation of the Master Plan for Higher Education and in overseeing the vast expansion of the university onto eight different campuses. An author of note, his book on Uses of the University *is considered a significant analysis of higher education.*

Statement by President Clark Kerr
(December 3, 1964)

Governor Brown last night decided that the unlawful sit-in in Sproul Hall must be ended

[4]As quoted in Seymour Martin Lipset and Sheldon S. Wolin, eds., *The Berkeley Student Revolt* (Garden City, New York: Doubleday and Company, Inc., 1965), 245-251. President Kerr's message to the alumni is reprinted with the permission of the *California Monthly*.

immediately. He has the final responsibility for the maintenance of law and order in California. The university, which has always stood for democratic principles, including observance of the law, expects faculty, staff and students to carry on the orderly processes of the university and to reject what has become an FSM attempt at anarchy.

The FSM issued an ultimatum which had nothing to do with free speech and which it knew, and publicly stated, the university could not possibly accept. This ultimatum called for the abdication by the university of its responsibilities. The ultimatum was not accepted. The FSM then again seized Sproul Hall, as it had done before, and stated it planned to bring the university to a "grinding halt."

The FSM and its leaders from the start declared the police would have to haul them out. They are now finding that, in their efforts to escape the gentle discipline of the university, they have thrown themselves into the arms of the less understanding discipline of the community at large. They have asked that they be subject only to external law and external courts. They are learning that the community is no more sympathetic with anarchy than the university they so violently condemn.

The students at the start of this affair in September had an understandable concern. Certain practices in the "Sather Gate tradition," which lay outside university policy, had been allowed by the Berkeley campus to take place at Telegraph and Bancroft. The campus administration ended these practices on September 14 and student protest boiled up. After wide consultation within the university, the Telegraph and Bancroft area has again been made available for the earlier practices. The Regents at their November meeting went beyond this. They changed a general university policy of many years standing to permit on-campus planning, recruiting and fund raising for lawful off-campus action. They did this in response to student requests and faculty proposals, and also in light of changing court decisions. The chancellor immediately after the Regents' meeting made a number of other adjustments, which lay within his authority, in keeping with faculty and ASUC suggestions.

This protest has never been over "free speech." There has been and is freedom of speech in the University of California. The protest has been over organizing political action on campus. This is now allowed with the one qualification that unlawful action cannot be mounted on the campus. . . .

This protest has had the slogan of "free speech"; . . . but it has now become an instrument of anarchy and of personal aggrandizement.

For two months the university has encouraged discussion, emphasized the facts, examined and implemented new policies. It has counted on this process to yield better policies and more understanding. It has counted on this process to separate the well-intentioned students from the hard-core recalcitrants. This process had had some constructive results. However, passion and irrationality and rumor have still held sway in some quarters.

The university is an institution whose primary obligation is to educate its students. It has shown patience. This patience has been met with impatience and with violation of the law. The university has shown tolerance. This tolerance has been met with intolerance and distortion of the truth. . . .

When patience and tolerance and reasonableness and decency have been tried, yet democratic processes continue to be forsaken by the FSM in favor of anarchy, then the process of law enforcement takes over. This nation is devoted to freedom under the law, not to anarchy under a willful minority. . . .

The rule of law must be honored in California. Faculty, staff and students honor it by their conduct of the regular affairs of the university at the level of distinction for which this university has been noted. The Associated Students and other student groups have shown a great sense of responsibility, and many faculty members have contributed much in the way of helpful suggestions and calm good judgment. These efforts of the large majority of students and faculty deserve public recognition and the support of the citizens of California.

A Message to Alumni
By President Clark Kerr

The Sather Gate tradition, with its soap-boxes, was moved to Telegraph and Bancroft after the Student Union was built and when the north end of Telegraph Avenue, beyond Bancroft, was dedicated by the City to the University. In September 1959, I suggested that a twenty-six foot strip be returned to the City of Berkeley. The Regents approved this by a vote of 15 to 2; but the transfer was never formally made, although many of us thought it had been. It was on this twenty-six foot strip that political action became more and more intense until in September, 1964, the Berkeley campus felt it necessary to ban such activity. . . .

1. The intensity of student reaction took the Berkeley campus and university-wide administration by surprise. In retrospect, some of the factors explaining how it all boiled up into such a head of steam, so quickly, appear to be these:

> There was a hotly contested presidential campaign which aroused the emotions of many people, students included. Also Proposition 14 on the California ballot was loaded with passion.
>
> Civil rights constitute a great moral issue for the student generation of today. Some Cal students were just back from Mississippi and Alabama; others had lived there in spirit all summer. University and college campuses have been a primary recruiting ground for civil rights workers and demonstrators. Some students returned to Berkeley with their plans all made for election and civil rights activity only to find the "Sather Gate tradition" seriously curtailed. They reacted immediately. The Berkeley and university-wide administrations took prompt action to respond to student protests. . . . On September 16, Chancellor Strong, Vice Chancellor Sherriffs, Dean Towle and I met to discuss the problem. Several adjustments were shortly made, such as: Sproul Hall steps were designated as a temporary open discussion area, and a specified number of tables were allowed back on the Bancroft strip. But these adjustments were not taken, as they were intended, as evidence that the administration was listening and responding favorably to student requests. They did not lead to willingness to talk and be reasonable, but rather to greater and greater demands and to more and more direct action. They have a new technique—civil disobedience. Some of them really believe that illegal methods are the only effective ones available to gain the ends they desire. It was very difficult, on October 2, 1964, to persuade some leaders of the demonstrators to agree to "desist from. . . their illegal protest against university regulations." They agreed most reluctantly; several saying that such methods were their only hope of success. Civil disobedience is very difficult to handle on a university campus. The administration is faced with two equally intolerable possibilities—countenancing greater and greater flouting of the rules or attempting to enforce the rules against massive group violations. The activists gained support from non-activists. The presence of large numbers of police on campus on October 2 and December 3 antagonized many students. The Berkeley campus is big and somewhat impersonal, particularly for the new undergraduate, and there has been growing dissatisfaction with the quality of undergraduate life. Many students found friendships and excitement in the mass demonstrations. The campus activists had support and some leadership from the substantial numbers of "non-students" who now live around the Berkeley campus using certain of its facilities and participating in selected aspects of its activities. Some of these are ex-students. The person in the police car on October 1 was a non-student, as was the first person to lie down in front of the car. . .
>
> The United States is now a nation of young people; about 46 per cent of the population is under 25 years of age. Nearly 5 million of these young people are now in college. This leads a few of the activists to have a sense of potential power and a desire for actual power—power certainly against the college or university administration; potentially against the faculty, and

particularly against society at large. There is a new drive in the minds of some student activists; they see themselves as new men of power working in a nerve center of society.

2. The students were not the only actors on the stage:

The courts have been changing their interpretations of the law quite substantially in recent years. The university has liberalized its rules in many ways in recent years also—sufficiently so to be given the Alexander Meiklejohn Award for contributions to academic freedom by the American Association of University Professors in the spring of 1964. But, by the fall of 1964, certain of the university's rules had become of doubtful legal enforceability. The university did not permit on-campus recruitment of participants for political action off campus or on-campus organization of such action. Stanford University, in May, 1964, after reviewing the changing character of the law and of student interests had quietly revised its rules. The administration underestimated the intensity of student reaction to the impairment of the ''Sather Gate tradition,'' and had no experience in coping with mass civil disobedience on campus. The faculty, except for the very small group consistently identified with the FSM, became involved rather slowly and tentatively at first. The cry of freedom always strikes a responsive chord in faculty hearts. The sight of police on campus is anathema. Faculty members face their students daily in class and have a bond of sympathy with them. In the end, the great majority of the faculty did become involved and came to play a constructive role. The Regents acted in a sensible fashion from the beginning. They remained united around a policy of reasonable changes in the rules and maintenance of law and order on campus. Their unity was a great source of strength to the university.

3. Some claims have been made repeatedly by the FSM which have doubtful substance:

That freedom of speech was the issue. There was and is great freedom of speech. There were limitations on direct political activity organized on campus. That no channels of communication were open. In fact, the chancellor, members of his staff, and university-wide officials talked with FSM leaders in person and by telephone at numerous times during October and November. Furthermore, exchanges of written statements between student groups and the administration are a matter of record. The renewal of direct action in November was because the tri-partite committee, which had made great progress, was moving too slowly for the FSM and was not moving in the exact direction the FSM desired. Many channels were open in addition to these—including the ASUC—but few were used. That there was police brutality. This has not been proved. That the administration engaged in making improper charges. I did say in October that, among the outsiders who turned up, some had been sympathetic with Communist causes. I consider this a statement of fact. That the strike was an overwhelming success. As a matter of fact, it hardly touched any school or college except Letters and Science and here there was very little effect in the sciences. Most of the students most of the time went about their regular affairs.

4. . . . The Berkeley campus is one of the great university campuses of the nation. It must rise to even greater heights for its own sake and for the sake of the whole university and the State of California. It can do so and it will. The alumni can help greatly as they have so often and in so many ways throughout the history of the university.

First, we need to understand what happened, and this may be the most difficult task of all. Among other things, we need to realize that only a small percentage of students enrolled at Berkeley was involved in violation of the law or of university regulations. Second, we need to approach our problems in a constructive fashion. We need reasonable rules, reasonably enforced. We need improvements in the quality of undergraduate life. We need respect for democratic processes and the rights of others, exercised by all members of the university community. Third, we need to avoid, to the greatest extent possible, new acts of retribution beyond what the law will require in the cases now before the courts, for such acts will only serve to impede the process of reconciliation. This need not be a Greek tragedy with disastrous consequences for all the actors. We can write our own happier ending if we write it with tolerance and reason and confidence in the future.

The University of California is one of the great experiments in all higher education—an experiment in combining quantity and quality, an experiment in freedom within a public context, an experiment in cooperation among campuses and with other segments of higher education, an experiment in using knowledge and training on an unprecedented scale for the benefit of all mankind. The failures in this single episode, regrettable as these failures are, are far outweighed by the successes of the great experiment.

38.
Some Faculty Observations on the Revolt

The appearance of uniformed police on the campus jolted a somewhat irresolute faculty into forthright action, and though the teaching staff tried to take an intermediate position between that of the administration and that of the FSM, it generally supported the latter. On December 8, 1964, the Berkeley Division of the Academic Senate passed a series of resolutions by a vote of 824 to 115. These said in essence that the University officials should declare an amnesty for all rebels previously accused of misconduct; that the "time, place, and manner" of political activity should be reasonably controlled, but that "the content of speech or advocacy should not be restricted by the University"; and that the Academic Senate should take part in any future efforts to discipline students accused of improper political activity. Predictably, this pleased the FSM but was not received with enthusiasm by the administration or the Board of Regents.

The commentary on the December 8 resolutions by Herbert McClosky, professor of political science (taken from the Berkeley Daily Gazette, *December 15, 1964), supports the Senate's actions. The second commentary, by Professor Henry Stapp of the Lawrence Radiation Laboratory at Berkeley, is more nearly neutral,[5] somewhat reminiscent of the discussion that occurred during the days of the San Francisco vigilante trials in the previous century (see Chapter 4). A dissenting minority at the December 8 meeting took exception to the idea that students should be allowed to advocate illegal actions.*

Statement on Academic Senate Resolution of December 8,1964
By Herbert McClosky, Professor of Political Science, Berkeley

On December 8, the Berkeley Division of the Academic Senate adopted a five point resolution designed to end the current controversy over student political rights and to return the campus to its normal academic pursuits. . . .

[5]As quoted in Seymour Martin Lipset and Sheldon S. Wolin, eds., *The Berkeley Student Revolt* (Garden City, New York: Doubleday and Company, Inc. 1965), 257-267.

General Observations

Two concerns, I believe, lay uppermost in the minds of the resolution's proponents: the survival of the university as one of the world's most distinguished educational institutions; and the conviction that academic freedom obligates us to extend to students the widest possible latitude for political expression and advocacy. . . .

What began in a small way with the imposition of new restrictions on student freedom to support political candidates, to collect funds, to recruit members, and to man tables at certain locations on the campus had "escalated" into mass demonstrations, sit-ins, and strikes by the students, and suspensions, mass arrests, threatened dismissals of teaching assistants, and new restrictions on advocacy by the administration.

The crisis, in short, had become intolerable. Had it continued in its rampant form—and the senate's resolution or one like it not been adopted—we would now be facing a series of clearly predictable and potentially disastrous events. Among these events; a continuation of mass demonstrations and possible new sit-ins and arrests; sympathy strikes by hundreds of teaching assistants; the dismissal of these assistants, as promised by the administration; and, as an inevitable consequence, the resignation of large numbers of faculty members.

With the decline of faculty quality, it would become even more difficult than it is now to attract gifted students. The competition for qualified graduate students is, if anything, as intense as is the competition for outstanding faculty members. . . . No one would gain if the crisis were to continue and the tragic consequences I have sketched were to occur. The students would suffer an immense loss by having to attend a university of diminished intellectual quality. The administration, the Regents, and the people of California would suffer immeasurably from the loss of gifted teachers, scientists, poets, engineers, and social scientists whose contribution to the intellectual and material welfare of the state has been incalculable. The faculty, of course, would suffer from a loss of *elan* and of pride of membership in the university community.

None of these losses need be suffered if the controversy is soon resolved, if differences are negotiated and long-range solutions are evolved. The resolution of December 8 may be imperfect in some respects, but it offers a focal point around which all parties can reasonable converge. For the time being, at least, it has diminished the sense of emergency and has temporarily alleviated the most pressing grievances. In this respect, it has been successful.

The resolution was not intended to assign blame or responsibility. Some of its supporters felt that the administration had contributed disproportionately to the crisis by hasty and ill-conceived actions, by failure to consult students on prospective changes in the rules, and by violations of the spirit, if not the letter, of previous agreements concerning discipline. Many also felt that the administration had meddled needlessly in the regulation of student political activity and had thereby provoked the subsequent outbreak.

Other faculty members who supported the resolution placed primary responsibility upon the students, blaming them for their impatience, for their withdrawal from the administration-faculty-student committee established to negotiate differences, and for their tactics of civil disobedience in a context in which such tactics were unjustified.

The resolution does not align the faculty with one side or the other. It was conceived in the spirit of mediation, and in the desire to do justice to the legitimate student claims to freedom of political speech and advocacy. At the same time, however, it seeks to safeguard the authority of the university to regulate the "time, place, and manner of conducting political activity on the campus." No license is granted to either students or non-students to behave on campus in any way they please. Despite the intemperate accusations of certain editorial writers, the control of the university has not been vested by this resolution in "irresponsible hands of student troublemakers. . . ." Nor have "acts of anarchic defiance" been "condoned."

Lifting of Penalties

. . . Although some faculty members believed that all violations of university discipline must be severely punished, others felt that the students had been provoked needlessly. Most important, however, they felt that the granting of immunity from university discipline for all acts prior to December 8 was a *sine qua non* of any settlement. Without it, we would be hopelessly mired and unable to extricate ourselves.

The adoption of this view was a sign not of weakness or capitulation but of realism and charity. There is a time to punish and a time to forgive. There are occasions when forgiveness for disobedience of the rules does more to strengthen the rules and the legitimate authority of the rule makers than the strict enforcement of the rules and the exacting of retribution for failure to obey them.

We should also keep in mind who the offenders were. In our distress, many of us have forgotten that the so-called "rebels" and dissenters are our own students-young men and women of quality and intelligence, the future doctors, lawyers, professors, writers, scientists, and political leaders of the society. Some have disobeyed the law, but they are not "criminals." A few are passing through youthful flirtations with revolutionary political movements (from which, as the experience of their predecessors attests, they will soon emerge), while a great many have shown themselves superior in courage and moral conscience by their activities on behalf of civil rights.

They are not without blame. . . . But like the administration whom they oppose, the vast majority of students who participated in the protests are decent and civilized, liberal and tolerant, sincere and responsible. To have taken a punitive, righteous, or sanctimonius attitude toward them would have been unworthy of a great university and damaging to the settlement of this unfortunate affair. . . .

Nothing in the resolution jeopardizes in any way its authority to determine the "time, place and manner" by which the political activities of students and non-students shall be regulated. Point 2 of the resolution explicitly provides for this. Not only can the university impose intramural penalties for breaches of discipline in this area, but it possesses the power granted to it by the state of California to prosecute individuals or groups who violate the law when on university property. . . .

Just as the university can regulate the use of university facilities by students, so a *a fortiori* can it control the use of those facilities by non-students. Regulations governing such uses are now being considered by the committee on Academic Freedom, a highly respected group of faculty members who can be expected to evolve a plan of regulation that will satisfy both the normal teaching and research functions of the university as well as the rights of students to assemble, associate, and discuss in a manner befitting the requirements of a free society. . . .

The faculty has asked that the content of speech or advocacy on the campus shall not be restricted by the university, and that the political activities of students when they are away from the campus shall not be subject to university regulations.

The provisions asks the university, therefore, to relinquish the burden of imposing intramural punishments on the content of political speech.

Apart from the First Amendment, there are many reasons of realism and prudence for adopting this recommendation. For the university to regulate these matters would involve it in a complex. technical, and rapidly changing jurisprudence. It would need to constitute itself a court, with all the attendant paraphernalia, of judges, lawyers, prosecutors, witnesses, verbatim transcripts, rules of evidence, and numerous other elements of accepted judicial procedure. The university has neither the competence nor the facilities for undertaking this role. It would require the policing of political speeches by every student and visitor on the campus. It would also require the surveillance of 60,000 students as they engage in political activities in other parts of the community.

The political difficulties, of course, would arise whenever the university rendered a decision that was repugnant to some interest or political action group that favored, or opposed, the content of what had been advocated.

By imposing university punishments for alleged illegal advocacy or for advocacy leading to illegal acts beyond the campus, the university would open itself to an interminable series of litigations, student and faculty protests, petitions, unfavorable press notices, and pressures from organized interest groups. Furthermore, with the civil rights movement now at its height, it would be impossible for the university to escape the appearance (and the charge) of having interfered with the effort to achieve the rights of an oppressed minority. . . .

Careful investigation of this matter I am certain, will persuade all parties to the controversy that the differences that have developed around this question are more shadow than substance. I trust they will also be persuaded that in matters of free speech, the university must be "more royalist than the king." The freedom to think and to express one's thoughts is the indispensable ingredient of the search for truth and the instruction of the young. Unless it is applied in fullest measure, a university is impossible.

As a center of learning and enlightenment, moreover, the university bears an obligation to the community to set a standard and to uphold the great values of the American democratic tradition against every challenge and temptation.

Some of my colleagues fear that by refusing to intervene in the regulation of speech, we shall somehow reduce the university's autonomy and its freedom from civil interference. Others, however, voice precisely the opposite charge. The resolution, they assert, seeks to convert the university into a fortress from which students can mount political activity against the society with impunity. Both charges, in my opinion, are without substance. In practice, the university will be neither more autonomous nor less autonomous for having put this provision into effect.

Academic Senate Committee

The last of the major points dealt with in the resolution calls for the establishment of a faculty disciplinary committee that would be appointed by and responsible to the Berkeley Division of the Academic Senate. Although the senate has on various occasions in the past exercised this power, the regulation of discipline has in recent years fallen primarily upon the chancellor and other administrative officers, with the advice and assistance of appointed faculty members.

If I assess correctly the opinions of most faculty members on this question, there is no great enthusiasm for reassuming the burden of enforcing discipline in the area of student political conduct. Why then have they adopted this provision?

I believe they have done so for two reasons essentially: a great number of students appear to have lost confidence in the old agencies by which political activities have been regulated and disciplined. The second reason is that many faculty members hope that with the content of advocacy freed from the burdens of regulation, and with the liberalization of the rules governing political conduct already achieved or in the making, the relatively minor matters of enforcing the time, place, and manner of conducting political activity on the campus will not prove a heavy burden. In short, many expect that this committee will have little to do. . . .

In summary, then, the resolution expresses no principle that is fundamentally at variance with previous university practice or professed policy. All of its provisions could easily be absorbed into existing university framework with little or no difficulty.

Reflections on the Crisis at Berkeley
By Henry Stapp, Lawrence Radiation Laboratory, Berkeley

The events at the University of California must be recognized as a critical point in the nation's history; the issues involve basic questions of political rights and social obligations, and the outcome is likely to set a pattern for expressing grievances that will profoundly affect the entire land. . . .

The conflict at Berkeley is only incidentally a matter of university regulations. The central issue is the challenge to the nation's traditional precept of respect for law inevitably posed by the civil disobedience demonstrations in the South. . . .

The direct immediate question is under what circumstances civil disobedience is a morally acceptable method of expressing grievances in a society where democratic principles prevail. A proposed answer is that if a person is willing to face legal punishment to dramatize his grievances, then this is a moral right that should always be respected.

The proposal is in direct conflict with the traditional view that in a society in which democratic principles prevail it is the moral and social obligation of the responsible citizen to support and obey a law regardless of his personal feelings. He does this not from fear of punishment but from respect for the rights of others as defined by majority opinion. This tradition of respect for democratic law is commonly regarded as the bedrock upon which our society is built; that without this abiding commitment by responsible citizens to a respect for law, our society would surely crumble.

The issue raised, therefore, is whether this tradition of respect for laws, regardless of opposing conviction, should be modified to give respectability to nonviolent civil disobedience as a method for expressing grievance even in a society where democratic principles prevail.

An example of the new morality is the Berkeley sit-in. There the specific cause was a university move to discipline student leaders. . . . But aroused by the disciplinary move the students invoked the sit-in method used in the South by their leaders. . . . If a move to discipline four students leads to massive civil disobedience, what is to be expected in serious situations?

A much debated point in the Berkeley dispute is whether the university is abridging a constitutional right by prohibiting the mounting of illegal actions from its premises. . . . [But], separate from the legal question is one of policy: assuming the university has the legal rights to forbid the mounting of illegal actions on its premises, should these rights be exercised? The faculty said an emphatic no.

The manner in which the faculty expressed themselves has placed the Regents in the position of having to oppose the Academic Senate resolution, thereby jeopardizing the university, or in effect, to repudiate the traditional basis for social and political morality in this country. The traditional moral position calls not only for submission to the laws of democratic society but for an active commitment on their behalf, the responsible citizen not only obeys the laws but exercises the legal means within his power to prevent illegal action. . . .

Now among the many points raised by the students is the point that a university education should provide more than book-learning; there is also the education for citizenship provided by involvement in political discussion and action. This could not be more true. That is one reason why university policy in this matter is so important. Should not the university policy itself be an example of the type of moral commitment to legality that one expects from responsible citizens? If the university abdicates the position of positive commitment to the support of law on the grounds of academic freedom, will this not be an example and precedent for the abdication of this responsibility by other groups and individuals on the basis of their own special interests?

What such questions signalize, and what every citizen must face, is that this nation is entering a genuine moral crisis; some of its most basic precepts are under serious attack from important quarters. . . . The conscientious citizen must, therefore, carefully weigh whether progress in California today toward the elimination of injustice is sufficiently unsatisfactory to warrant the desertion of our traditional principles. . . .

The tragedy of the Berkeley situation is that we are faced on the one hand with the perilous course of inviting chaos by officially repudiating at the outset the traditional precepts upon which this country has been based, with no clear guideline for the future, or, on the other hand, with the destruction of one of the nation's greatest universities. . . .

The essential source of disagreement in Berkeley is that one side is concerned mainly with a large number of grievances that are individually rather insignificant, particularly on the national scale. They are essentially grievances against administration handling of various problems. In expressing these grievances the students used methods not sanctioned by traditional morality. And in the proposed solution the traditional morality is directly repudiated. The forces opposing student demands take the perspective of the nation as a whole. They do not see that student grievances at a school administration can warrant jeopardizing the stability of the nation by a repudiation of our traditional moral structure.

The hope and good fortune in the Berkeley situation lie in the fact that the clash occurred in Berkeley. For in Berkeley is gathered one of the nation's most illustrious faculties, at a university presided over by one of the nation's most liberal presidents. The Regents are distinguished and dedicated representatives of the people of California, and the students and graduate students are among the nation's brightest. Since the challenge was inevitable we can be thankful that an important first phase of the conflict can be acted upon by the best products of American culture in the Berkeley environment of goodwill. If toleration and understanding cannot be found in Berkeley, then the nation's fate is dark.

There are no words to express the shock, the sick horror that a civilized city feels at a moment like this. . . . Decent citizens everywhere, regardless of color, can only pray that this anarchy will soon end.
—*Los Angeles Times* editorial, August 15, 1965.

I think the positives outweighed the negatives. For once, the city listened. It made them realize that the people here had the same desires and needs as anybody else.
—Grace Payne, Watts resident and booster, *Los Angeles Times*, August 11, 1965.

That so-called rebellion didn't do nothing but put us back another 50 years trying to deal [with problems]. . . . It was ugly then, it's still ugly.
—J. R. Hill, 45 years of age, quoted in *Los Angeles Times*, August 11, 1985.

CHAPTER 13

THE WATTS RIOTS OF 1965
Riot and Rebellion

On August 11, 1965 some ten thousand black people took to the streets in South Central Los Angeles and put the torch to their ghetto. For six days Americans sat at their TV screens watching the unprecedented looting, burning, killing that resulted in thirty-four deaths, over one thousand injured, about four thousand arrests, and $40 million in property damage. Wearing full combat gear and armed with fixed bayonets, the California National Guard finally managed on August 17 to re-establish something approaching law and order.

Watts turned out to be a world-class urban disturbance. Widely observed and searchingly studied, it became—and remains— a symbol of what was wrong with black-white relations throughout the United States. Was it riot or rebellion or both? Commentators advanced various theories. Conservatives thought it was a descent into barbarism, and some blamed the civil rights movement for stirring up deep passions. Liberals said it was brought on by the ''revolution of rising expectations,'' an allusion to the long-overdue promises to minorities of social justice, contrasted by the painfully weak process of achieving those idealistic goals. One social scientist called Watts a ''commodity riot,'' an allusion to the looting of retail establishments. Still other viewers believed it was a spontaneous street disturbance with no leaders, no special pattern, and no long range objectives other than releasing a momentary expression of rage and powerlessness. Some participants recalled feeling that throwing rocks against the police gave them a momentary surge of power that was exhilarating and unforgettable. To this day there is no unanimity of opinion as to the causes, although almost everyone alludes to the underlying problems of poverty, joblessness, and of strained police-community relations.

The dismay over Watts, one of the ugliest domestic disturbances in recent American history, was profound. Why did it hit Los Angeles, a city reputed to have some of the ''best'' slums in the nation? Could it have been prevented? Had civil rights activities incited the rioters? Where was black leadership in the moment of crisis? How did the quality of police-community relations affect the outcome? Had the chief of police, the mayor, the governor and the lieutenant governor exercised proper authority? What role did the administration of federal welfare programs play? Did the passage of an anti-fair housing measure at the previous general election (Proposition 14) have much to do with inciting trouble? Was it possible to repair the damage so as to preclude a recurrence?

In order to arrive at some conclusions, Governor Edmund G. ''Pat'' Brown appointed a blue-ribbon commission with broad investigative powers to review the evidence and come forward with specific recommendations. The result was the McCone Report, one of the most widely publicized official documents of recent California history. As might be expected the report itself became a subject of controversy. A state civil rights commission reacted negatively to it.

Two decades later Angelenos still wondered whether the riot of 1965 had achieved anything worthwhile. Was life in the black ghetto any different—any better—than it had been in the 1960's? These questions prompted the local human relations commissions to hold hearing in 1984 to review the situation. The following selections—from the historic McCone report, from a critical commentary by a state civil rights commission, and from the findings of a local human relations commission twenty years later—probe the meaning of the Watts riots from different perspectives. *(Editor's note)*

39. The McCone Report

The eight-member commission appointed by the Governor to investigate the Watts disturbances was headed by John A. McCone, former head of the Central Intelligence Agency. The other commissioners were Warren M. Christopher (Vice Chairman), Judge Earl C. Broady, Asa V. Call, The Very Rev. Charles S. Casassa, the Rev. James Edward Jones, Dr. Sherman M. Mellinkoff, and Mrs Robert G. Neumann. After 64 meetings in which it heard the testimony of a great many community leaders, government officials, academicians, and welfare specialists, the commission prepared a report. The McCone Commission Report,[1] *some 100 pages in length, provided a description of the precipitating incident and a brief overview of the deadly events that followed; however, the report dwelt mainly on underlying causes of discontent in Watts. Conditions in the job market, welfare, housing, schooling, and, to a lesser extent, such aspects as bus and travel facilities in the Watts area are named as contributing factors. The Report was generally well received by the press, the mayor, and the chief of police.*

Much of the increase came through migration from Southern states and many arrived with the anticipation that this dynamic city would somehow spell the end of life's endless problems. To those who have come with high hopes and great expectations and see the success of others so close at hand, failure brings a special measure of frustration and disillusionment. Moreover, the fundamental problems, which are the same here as in the cities which were racked by the 1964 riots, are intensified by what may well be the least adequate network of public transportation in any major city in America.

Looking back, we can also see that there was a series of aggravating events in the twelve months prior to the riots.

—Publicity given to the glowing promise of the Federal poverty program was paralleled by reports of controversy and bickering over the mechanism to handle the program here in Los Angeles, and when the projects did arrive, they did not live up to their press notices.

[1]State of California, Governor's Commission on the Los Angeles Riots, ''Violence in the City—An Ending or a Beginning?'' (Los Angeles: The author), 1965, 4-88.

—Throughout the nation, unpunished violence and disobedience to law were widely reported, and almost daily there were exhortations, here and elsewhere, to take the most extreme and even illegal remedies to right a wide variety of wrongs, real and supposed.

—In addition, many Negroes here felt and were encouraged to feel that they had been affronted by the passage of Proposition 14—an initiative measure passed by two-thirds of the voters in November 1964 which repealed the Rumford Fair Housing Act and unless modified by the voters or invalidated by the courts will bar any attempt by state or local governments to enact similar laws. . . .

Nor was the rioting exclusively a projection of the Negro problem. It is part of an American problem which involves Negroes but which equally concerns other disadvantaged groups. In this report, our major conclusions and recommendations regarding the Negro problem in Los Angeles apply with equal force to the Mexican-Americans, a community which is almost equal in size to the Negro community and whose circumstances are similarly disadvantageous and demand equally urgent treatment. That the Mexican-American community did not riot is to its credit; it should not be to its disadvantage.

The Dull Devastating Spiral of Failure

In examining the sickness in the center of our city, what has depressed and stunned us most is the dull, devastating spiral of failure that awaits the average disadvantaged child in the urban core. His home life all too often fails to give him the incentive and the elementary experience with words and ideas which prepares most children for school. Unprepared and unready, he may not learn to read or write at all; and because he shares his problem with 30 or more in the same classroom, even the efforts of the most dedicated teachers are unavailing. Age, not achievement, passes him on to higher grades, but in most cases he is unable to cope with courses in the upper grades because they demand basic skills which he does not possess. . . .

Frustrated and disillusioned, the child becomes a discipline problem. Often he leaves school, sometimes before the end of junior high school. (About two-thirds of those who enter the three high schools in the center of the curfew area do not graduate.) He slips into the ranks of the permanent jobless, illiterate and untrained, unemployed and unemployable. . . .

Reflecting this spiral of failure, unemployment in the disadvantaged areas runs two to three times the county average, and the employment available is too often intermittent. A family whose breadwinner is chronically out of work is almost invariable a disintegrating family. Crime rates soar and welfare rolls increase, even faster than the population.

This spiral of failure has a most damaging side effect. Because of the low standard of achievement in the schools in the urban core and adjacent areas, parents of the better students from advantaged backgrounds remove them from these schools, either by changing the location of the family home or by sending the children to private school. In turn, the average achievement level of the schools in the disadvantaged area sinks lower and lower. The evidence is that this chain reaction is one of the principal factors in maintaining de facto school segregation in the urban core and producing it in the adjacent areas where the Negro population is expanding. From our study, we are persuaded that there is a reasonable possibility that raising the achievement levels of the disadvantaged Negro child will materially lessen the tendency towards de facto segregation in education, and that this might possibly also make a substantial contribution to ending all de facto segregation.

All Segments of Society

Perhaps for the first time our report will bring into clear focus, for all the citizens to see, the economic and sociological conditions in our city that underlay the gathering anger which impelled the rioters to escalate the routine arrest of a drunken driver into six days of violence. Yet, however powerful their grievances, the rioters had no legal or moral justification for the wounds they inflicted. Many crimes, a great many felonies, were committed. Even more dismaying, as we studied the record, was the large number of brutal exhortations to violence which were uttered by some Negroes. Rather than making proposals, they laid down ultimatums with the alternative being violence. All this nullified the admirable efforts of hundreds, if not thousands, both Negro and white, to quiet the situation and restore order.

What can be done to prevent a recurrence of the nightmare of August? It stands to reason that what we and other cities have been doing, costly as it all has been, is not enough. Improving the conditions of Negro life will demand adjustments on a large scale unknown to any great society. The programs that we are recommending will be expensive and burdensome. And the burden, along with the expense, will fall on all segments of our society—on the public and private sectors, on industry and labor, on company presidents and hourly employees, and most indispensably, upon the members and leaders of the Negro community. For unless the disadvantaged are resolved to help themselves, whatever else is done by others is bound to fail.

The consequences of inaction, indifference, and inadequacy, we can all be sure now, would be far costlier in the long run than the cost of correction. If the city were to elect to stand aside, the walls of segregation would rise even higher. The disadvantaged community would become more and more estranged and the risk of violence would rise. The cost of police protection would increase, and yet would never be adequate. Unemployment would climb; welfare costs would mount apace. And the preachers of division and demagoguery would have a matchless opportunity to tear our nation asunder.

Of Fundamental and Durable Import

As a Commission, we are seriously concerned that the existing breach, if allowed to persist, could in time split our society irretrievably. So serious and so explosive is the situation that, unless it is checked, the August riots may seem by comparison to be only a curtain-riser for what could blow up one day in the future. . . .

The Problem—Deep and Serious

The conduct of law enforcement agencies, most particularly the Los Angeles Police Department, has been subject to severe criticism by many Negroes who have appeared before the Commission as witnesses. . . . "Police brutality" has been the recurring charge. One witness after another has recounted instances in which, in their opinion, the police have used excessive force or have been disrespectful and abusive in their language or manner.

(The more than seventy cases of alleged police brutality which were submitted to the Commission contributed to our understanding of the depths of the feelings of a segment of the Negro community toward the Police Department. Because our responsibility has been to review the general policy and procedure for handling citizen complaints rather than to review individuals cases, we have referred all of the cases to the appropriate and responsible agencies.)

On the other hand, the police have explained to us the extent to which the conduct of some Negroes when apprehended has required the use of force in making arrests. Example after example has been recited of arrestees, both men and women, becoming violent, struggling to resist arrest, and thus requiring removal by physical force. Other actions, each provocative to the police and each requiring more than normal action by the police in order to make an arrest or to perform other duties, have been described to us.

Chief of Police Parker appears to be the focal point of the criticism within the Negro community. He is the man distrusted by most Negroes and they carefully analyze for possible anti-Negro meaning almost every action he takes and every statement he makes. . . . Despite the depth of the feeling against Chief Parker expressed to us by so many witnesses, he is recognized, even by many of his most vocal critics, as a capable Chief who directs an efficient police force that serves well this entire community.

With respect to the Los Angeles County Sheriff's Department, the situation is somewhat different. Generally speaking, the Negro community does not harbor the same angry feeling toward the Sheriff or his staff as it does toward the Los Angeles police. Nevertheless, witnesses recited to us instances of alleged brutality and excessive use of force by deputy sheriffs on duty.

The reasons for the feeling that law enforcement officers are the enemy of the Negro are manifold and it is well to reflect on them before they are accepted. An examination of seven riots in northern cities of the United States in 1964 reveals that each one was started over a police incident, just as the Los Angeles riot started with the arrest of Marquette Frye. In each of the 1964 riots, "police brutality" was an issue, as it was here, and, indeed, as it has been in riots and insurrections elsewhere in the world. The fact that this charge is repeatedly made must not go unnoticed, for there is a real danger that persistent criticism will reduce and perhaps destroy the effectiveness of law enforcement.

Our society is held together by respect for law. A group of officers who represent a tiny fraction of one percent of the population is the thin thread that enforces observance of law by those few who would do otherwise. If police authority is destroyed, if their effectiveness is impaired, and if their determination to use the authority vested in them to preserve a law abiding community is frustrated, all of society will suffer because groups would feel free to disobey the law and inevitably their number would increase. Chaos might easily result. So, while we must examine carefully the claim of police brutality and must see that justice is done to all groups within our society, we must, at the same time, be sure that law enforcement agencies, upon which so much depends, are not rendered impotent. . . .

More Negroes and Mexican-Americans Must Enter Careers in Law Enforcement

Finally, the Commission expresses its concern over the relatively few sworn officer personnel in the Police Department and the Sheriff's Department who are Negroes or Mexican-Americans. Only four percent of the sworn personnel of the Police Department and six percent of the Sheriff's Department are Negroes and an even smaller percentage are Mexican-Americans. . . .

We believe it essential that the number of sworn officers of each minority group should be increased substantially. To bring this about, more active recruitment by the Police and Sheriff's Departments and the civil service must be undertaken. Furthermore, educational and private institutions and organizations, and political leaders as well, should encourage members of the minority groups to enter careers in law enforcement. Finally, budget support for extensive efforts in recruitment, which should perhaps include pre-employment preparatory training, should be provided by both the City Council and the Board of Supervisors.

To implement our conclusions, we offer the following recommendations:

1) The Board of Police Commissioners should be strengthened.

2) Investigations of all citizen complaints should be conducted by an independent Inspector General under the authority of the Chief of Police in the implementation of procedures established by the Board of Police Commissioners.

3) The Police Department should institute expanded community relations programs.

4) The Sheriff's Department should effectuate these recommendations to the extent that they are applicable to it.

Employment—Key to Independence

Unemployment—The Immediate Problem

The most serious immediate problem that faces the Negro in our community is employment—securing and holding a job that provides him an opportunity for livelihood, a chance to earn the means to support himself and his family, a dignity, and a reason to feel that he is a member of our community in a true and a very real sense. Unemployment and the consequent idleness are at the root of many of the problems we discuss in this report. Many witnesses have described to us, dramatically and we believe honestly, the overwhelming hopelessness that comes when a man's efforts to find a job come to naught. Inevitably, there is despair and a deep resentment of a society which he feels has turned its back upon him. Welfare does not change this. It provides the necessities of life, but adds nothing to a man's stature, nor relieves the frustrations that grow. In short, the price for public assistance is loss of human dignity.

The welfare program that provides for his children is administered so that it injures his position as the head of his household, because aid is supplied with less restraint to a family headed by a woman, married or unmarried. Thus, the unemployed male often finds it to his family's advantage to drift away and leave the family to fend for itself. Once he goes, the family unit is broken and is seldom restored. Changes in welfare administration designed to hold together rather than break apart the family have not been wholly successful.

From unemployment, other problems develop. In a discouraged frame of mind, the unemployed is driven toward anti-social behavior. Even if he remains at home, he neither serves as a worthy example to his children nor does he actively motivate them to go to school and study. Thus, a chain reaction takes place. The despair and disillusionment of the unemployed parent is passed down to the children. The example of failure is vividly present and the parent's frustrations and habits become the children's. ("Go to school for what?" one youngster said to us.)

There is no immediate total solution to this problem, but it is our opinion that far more can be done than is now being done by government, by the private business sector, by organized labor, and by the Negro community, individually and jointly, to find jobs in the short range and in the long range to train Negroes so that a high proportion of them will not remain out of work.

Government Job Efforts

Government authorities have recognized the problem and have moved to solve it. City, county, state and federal governments have helped to siphon off some of the distress by hiring high proportions of Negroes. For example, 25% of all new Los Angeles county employees in 1964 were Negro.

Other government programs have been initiated and more have been proposed. These are designed to provide immediate full time and part time employment of the qualified plus training for the unqualified. As examples, under the War on Poverty Program, the Job Corps has provided a full-time work-training program for 363 youths. The Neighborhood Youth Corps has provided part time work for over 1500 youths from the south central area. Also, the Neighborhood Adult Participation Project has constructively employed over 400 in Los Angeles and this number is scheduled to double in the near future.

More recently, and perhaps belatedly, the State Department of Employment, using funds provided by the U.S. Department of Labor, has opened Youth Opportunity Centers to counsel youths in disadvantaged areas and assist them in finding employment. Also, the State Employment Service has recently opened an office in Watts to provide more convenient job placement service to nearby residents.

No law forbids the employer or labor union from maintaining records of the ethnic background of their work force or membership. Some employers have complained that they do not keep such records because they fear the information will, in some way, be used against them. The FEPC [Fair Employment Practices Commission] must make a special effort to dispel the fear held by some employers that it would attempt to force the employment of specified percentages of minority workers irrespective of qualifications. Since the employer lives in a competitive environment, the FEPC and its administrators must hold to the principle of equality in opportunity based upon the ability of the individual rather than merely on numbers of minority workers employed.

In making this recommendation, we believe that if the maximum degree of cooperation from employers and labor unions is to be achieved, FEPC and other agencies dealing with discriminatory employment practices must continue to rely heavily on persuasion and education in the affirmative action programs. These are the techniques that have been most successful in the past.

Arrest Records

Evidence gathered by the Commission's staff indicates that a job applicant with an arrest record faces an additional burden in finding employment. While security considerations sometimes preclude hiring an applicant with an arrest record, blanket rejection of such persons without regard for the nature of the arrest or whether there has been a conviction should be discouraged. We urge employers to re-assess job qualifications with a view to considering whether it is feasible to increase employment opportunities for persons with arrest records.

In light of the foregoing considerations, we recommend:

1. There should immediately be developed in the affected area a job training and placement center through the combined efforts of Negroes, employers, labor unions, and government.

2. Federal and state governments should seek to insure, through the development of new facilities and additional means of communications, that maximum advantage is taken of government and private training programs and employment opportunities in our disadvantaged communities.

3. Legislation should be enacted requiring employers with more than 250 employees and all labor unions to report annually to the State Fair Employment Practices Commission the racial composition of their work force and membership.

Education—Our Fundamental Resource

. . . [W]e launched an in-depth study to determine the quality of education offered in the public schools in the riot area and in other areas of the city. A comparison was made between schools in the riot area (and other disadvantaged areas of the city) and schools in other sections of the city (citywide, and in an advantaged area). Five study areas were selected within the Los Angeles City Unified School District. Four of these are disadvantaged areas: Watts and Avalon (predominantly Negro and within the riot area), and Boyle Heights and East Los Angeles (predominantly Mexican-American and outside the riot area). The other study area included Pacific Palisades, Westwood, and Brentwood, which are, by comparison, advantaged areas. Citywide data were also compiled. . . .

It is our belief that raising the level of scholastic achievement will lessen the trend towards *de facto* segregation in the schools in the areas into which the Negroes are expanding and, indeed, will tend to reduce all *de facto* segregation. It is our conclusion that the very low level of scholastic achievement we observe in the predominately Negro schools contributes to *de facto* segregation in the schools. In turn school segregation apparently contributes importantly to all *de facto* segregation. We reason, therefore, that raising the scholastic achievement might reverse the entire trend of *de facto* segregation. There is no proof of this and therefore we cannot demonstrate by specific example that success of the school program we propose will have the effect of *de facto* segregation within the schools or elsewhere we indicate as a possibility.

Accordingly, our major recommendations are:

1. Elementary and junior high schools in the disadvantaged areas which have achievement levels substantially below the city average should be designated as "Emergency Schools." In each of these schools, an "Emergency Literacy Program" should be established consisting of a drastic reduction in class size to a maximum of 22 students and additional supportive personnel to provide special services. It is estimated that this program will cost at least $250 per year per student in addition to present per student costs and exclusive of capital expenditures, and that it must be continued for a minimum of six years for the elementary schools and three years for the junior high schools.

2. A permanent pre-school program should be established throughout the school year to provide education beginning at age three. Efforts should be focused on the development of language skills essential to prepare children to learn to read and write.

A recent survey indicates that 90% of the AFDC [Aid to Families with Dependent Children] families are Negro. In nine out of 10 of these homes, the father is absent. Over 70% of the parents involved were born in the South or Southwest. Seven out of 10 families on AFDC receive aid for one or more illegitimate children.

In Los Angeles County as a whole, expenditures for the AFDC program have been increasing dramatically, far outrunning the population trends. Between 1960 and 1964, when county population increased 13%, expenditures for the AFDC program rose by 73%. Between 1963 and 1964, when county population increased 2.5%, AFDC expenditures increased over 14% from $69.4 million to $79.5 million annually. Expenditures for the new AFDC-U program, which amounted to $10.2 million in 1964, are not included in the foregoing computation and, therefore, do not explain the rapid increases.

We have no intention of opposing the humanitarian purposes of the welfare program. Nevertheless, we are profoundly disturbed by the accelerating trend of expenditure. Our concern is heightened by the fact that this is occurring, not at a time of economic downturn or depression, but during the present period of unparalleled prosperity for our nation and state. A portion of the rapid increase may be explained by the fact that the Negro and Mexican-American population in Los Angeles is estimated to have increased approximately 40% in the last five years, compared with the general population increase of 13 percent in the same period. Moreover, the high unemployment in this area, referred to early in this report, no doubt has contributed to the increase. However, the increase in AFDC expenditures, coupled with the increase in population, raises a question in the minds of some whether the generosity of the California welfare program compared with those in the southern and southwestern states is not one of the factors causing the heavy immigration of disadvantaged people to Los Angeles.

We are making recommendations in other fields which can assist in lightening the welfare load. The program we are recommending in the field of education will, we believe, have a major impact on unemployment over the long term. We hope our recommendations in the field of employment will have a similar effect in the shorter run. In an important sense, the cost of these programs is justified by their potential for reducing welfare expenses.

However, to be successful in doing so, these programs must be accompanied with a recognition that a truly successful welfare program must, wherever feasible, create an initiative and an incentive on the part of the recipients to become independent of state assistance. Otherwise, the welfare program promotes an attitude of hopelessness and permanent dependence. . . .

Similarly, welfare agencies should be cognizant of the many available training programs. From our study of the matter, we believe that there is much room for improvement here. We also believe that the use of child care centers to free heads of families for employment or training should be emphasized. . . .

Health Problems

Statistics indicate that health conditions of the residents of south central Los Angeles are relatively poor and facilities to provide medical care are insufficient. Infant mortality, for example, is about one and one-half times greater than the city-wide average. Life expectancies are considerably shorter. A far lower percentage of the children are immunized against diphtheria, whooping cough, tetanus, smallpox, and poliomyelitis than in the rest of the county.

As established by the comprehensive reports of consultants to the Commission, the number of doctors in the southeastern part of Los Angeles is grossly inadequate as compared with other parts of the city. It is reported that there are 106 physicians for some 252,000 people, whereas the county ratio is three times higher. The hospitals readily accessible to the citizens in southeastern Los Angeles are also grossly inadequate in quality and in numbers of beds. Of the eight proprietary hospitals, which have a total capacity of 454 beds, only two meet minimum standards of professional quality. The two large public hospitals, County General and Harbor General, are both distant and difficult to reach. . . .

In light of the information presented to it, the Commission believes that immediate and favorable consideration should be given to a new, comprehensively-equipped hospital in this area, which is now under study by various public agencies. . . .

The Negro and the Leader

Finally, we come to the role of the Negro leader and his responsibility to his own people and to the community in which he lives. The signing of the Voting Rights Act By President Johnson in the spring of 1965 climaxed a long and bitter fight over civil rights. To be sure, the civil rights controversy has never been the issue in our community that it has been in the South. However, the accusations of the leaders of the national movement have been picked up by many local voices and have been echoed throughout the Negro community here. As we have said in the opening chapter of this report, the angry exhortations and the resulting disobedience to law in many parts of our nation appear to have contributed importantly to the feeling of rage which made the Los Angeles riots possible. Although the commission received much thoughtful and constructive testimony from Negro witnesses, we also heard statements of the most extreme and emotional nature. For the most part, our study fails to support—indeed the evidence disproves—most of the statements made by the extremists. We firmly believe that progress towards ameliorating the current wrongs is difficult in an atmosphere pervaded by these extreme statements.

If the recommendations we make are to succeed, the constructive assistance of all negro leaders is absolutely essential. No amount of money, no amount of effort, no amount of training will raise the disadvantaged negro to the position he seeks and should have within this community—a position of equality—unless he himself shoulders a full share of the responsibility for his own well being. The efforts of the Negro leaders, and there are many able and dedicated ones among us, should be directed toward urging and exhorting their followers to this end. (A comment regarding this by the Rev. James Edward Jones is set forth below.)

The Commission recognizes that much of what it has to say about causes and remedies is not new, although it is backed up by fresh additional evidence coming out of the investigation of the Los Angeles riots. At the same time, the Commission believes that there is an urgency in solving the problems, old or new, and that all Americans, whatever their color, must become aware of this urgency. Among the many steps which should be taken to improve the present situation, the commission affirms again that the three fundamental issues in the urban problems of disadvantaged minorities are: employment, education and police-community relations. Accordingly, the Commission looks upon its recommendations in these three ares as as the heart of its plea and the City's best hope.

As we have said earlier in this report, there is no immediate remedy for the problems of the Negro and other disadvantaged in our community. The problems are deep and the remedies are costly and will take time. However, through the implementation of the programs we propose, with the dedication we discuss, and with the leadership we call for from all, our Commission states without dissent, that the tragic violence that occurred during the six days of August will not be repeated.

Comments of the Rev. James Edward Jones

1. There is the observation at the top of page 11 that the generosity of California welfare programs encourage heavy immigration of disadvantaged peoples to the Los Angeles area. I have

been unable to find statistics to justify this statement and violently disagree with this unjustifiable projection. The report has also stated that Negroes like other disadvantaged peoples have come to Los Angeles to seek the better opportunities offered in an urban area. Welfare programs discourage immigration to receive public assistance because new arrivals cannot qualify for aid with less than one year of residence. Have other immigrants come to Los Angeles to get on welfare rolls or rather to find job opportunities? I am sure that statistics bear out my observation rather than that which appears in the report.

2. I do not believe it is the function of this Commission to put a lid on protest registered by those sweltering in ghettos of the urban areas of our country. We speak of the malaise in our cities and in our society in general. We also recognize in our report that "The Negro found that he entered the competitive life of the city with very real handicaps: he lacked education, training, and experience, and his handicaps were aggravated by racial barriers which were more traditional than legal. He found himself, for reasons for which he had no responsibility and over which he had no control, in a situation in which providing a livelihood for himself and his family was most difficult and at times desperate. Thus, with the passage of time, altogether too often the rural Negro who has come to the city sinks into despair." Yet the report concludes that all of the ameliorating efforts—such as education and other governmental programs—will be of no avail unless he helps himself. It is true that you cannot make a musician out of a child who is unwilling to learn, even though you provide the best teachers and the best instruments. But it must be remembered in dealing with the member of a disadvantaged minority who has never heard music or seen a musical instrument that he must be motivated to help himself. Therefore, he has a right to protest when circumstances do not allow him to participate in the mainstream of American society. Protest against forces which reduce individuals to second-class citizens, political, cultural, and psychological nonentities, are part of the celebrated American tradition. As long as an individual "stands outside looking in" he is not part of that society; that society cannot say that he does not have a right to protest, nor can it say that he must shoulder a responsibility which he has never been given an opportunity to assume.

40.
The California Advisory Committee is "Sorely Disappointed"

However warmly received in certain quarters, the McCone Report did arouse the ire of civil rights leaders, welfare workers and certain government officials like Lieutenant Governor Glenn Anderson, whom it had criticized for negligence. But the closest thing to a full-scale refutation came from the California Advisory Committee to the United States Commission on Civil Rights, headed by the controversial and outspoken Episcopal Bishop, Rt. Rev. James A. Pike of San Francisco.

The Committee consisted of Bishop Pike, Hon. Robert J. Drewes, Northern Vice-Chairman, Stephen Reinhardt, Southern Vice-Chairman, Ira M. Heyman, Rabbi Morton A. Bauman, William Becker, Mrs. Marjorie Benedict, Renaldo Carreon, Jr., M.D., Bert N. Corona, Mervyn M. Dymally, Mrs. Carl Kuchman, Hon. Loren Miller, Alpha L. Montgomery, and Dr. Hubert Phillips. Like its counterparts in the other 49 states, the Committee was charged by the 1957 U.S. Civil Rights Act with advising the parent body concerning federal policy on the state level. Thus when the McCone group adjourned, the Committee went into action on its own, probing the causes of the Watts disturbances, the validity of the Report, and the operation of federal programs in the city's distressed area. "We are sorely disappointed by the McCone Commission Report" is the opening salvo leveled by the Committee.[2] *From there the "Analysis of the McCone Commission Report" goes on to accuse the Report of superficiality, unoriginality, and lack of vision, and for heaping as much unfair abuse upon the the Blacks of Los Angeles as it heaps praise upon the police. Intermittently the analysis makes its own recommendations for remedial action; these recommendations vary drastically from those of the Report.*

When originally issued, the "Analysis of the McCone Commission Report" was snubbed by the major daily newspapers as well as by the mayor and chief of police. "I would question the competency of this Committee and its bias," Chief Parker told the Los Angeles Times, *"since two of its members [Judge Loren Miller and Assemblyman Mervyn Dymally] have been involved in the civil rights movement subjectively."*

For that very reason it deserves a reading. It is reprinted here, along with a postscript by a dissenting Committee member.

The McCone Commission Report—A Bitter Disappointment

We are sorely disappointed by the McCone Commission Report. Although there are a number of constructive suggestions which the Commission proposed, we feel the report falls far short of even the Commission's own view of its role. Certainly, it does not begin to deal adequately with the underlying problems. It prescribes aspirin where surgery is required.

The McCone Commission states, "Perhaps for the first time our report will bring into clear focus for all the citizens to see, the economic and sociological conditions in our city that underlay the gathering anger. . . ." With a budget of approximately $250,000.00 a professional staff of 30, a secretarial staff of 15, and the services of 26 consultants, this might not have been too much to ask. Yet, the McCone Commission fails in this assignment. The report is elementary, superficial, unoriginal and unimaginative. It offers little, if anything, in the way of a study of economic and sociological conditions not previously available in published reports of public agencies such as the Los Angeles County Commission on Human Relations. In fact, we believe that a recently printed series of articles on southeast Los Angeles in the *Los Angeles Times*, at no expense to the public, provides a far better and more well-informed picture of the economic and sociological conditions in our city.

Further, the report demonstrates a surprising ignorance of studies conducted by other groups. It fails to note the warnings of potential trouble in Los Angeles—warnings which our public officials chose to ignore or scoff at. We are particularly mindful of the excellent report to the Attorney-General of California prepared by Assistant Attorney-General Howard Jewell, May 25, 1964, in which he specifically and unmistakably warned that the bitter conflict between the Chief of Police, William H. Parker, and the civil rights movement might well lead to riots and violence in the streets of Los Angeles. Jewell noted, "The evidence from Los Angeles is ominous." He pleaded for immediate action, saying, "I think it is truly a situation in which a stitch in time would save nine." In his report Jewell quoted the perceptive warning of a member of this Advisory Committee, Judge Loren Miller. The Jewell report quotes Judge Miller as follows: "Violence in Los Angeles is inevitable. Nothing can or will be done about it until after the fact. Then there will be the appointment of a commission which will damn the civil rights leaders and the Chief alike." Judge Miller's prediction was in error only to the extent that the McCone Commission failed to levy the criticism against Chief Parker which was so obviously called for.

In view of the Jewell report and other similar studies, we cannot help but feel that the absence of constructive steps to avert a riot, and the lack of preparation for dealing with one when it occurred, constituted acts of gross negligence on the part of local officials, including Mayor Yorty and Chief of Police Parker. The McCone Commission says, in an unconvincing manner, "Perhaps

[2]California State Advisory Committee to the United States Commission on Civil Rights, "An Analysis of the McCone Commission Report" (January 1966), mimeographed, 2-13.

the people of Los Angeles should have seen trouble gathering under the surface calm.'' This observation misses the point completely. The officials of Los Angeles were expressly warned of the possibility of riots, failed to act, and instead chose to label those who cried out for reform as troublemakers or rabble-rousers.

We also find running through the McCone Commission Report a marked and surprising lack of understanding of the civil rights movement and a tendency to criticize those who ask for a redress of grievances rather than those who deprive citizens of their constitutional rights. For example, the McCone Commission attributes the riot in part to those who in the year preceding its occurrence urged action ''to right a wide variety of wrongs, real and supposed.'' We think this conclusion readily lends itself to misinterpretation and plays into the hands of those who seek to stifle the civil rights movement....

We believe that the passage of Proposition 14 contributed to the tensions and resentment in the Negro community. That it would do so was obvious. Yet, the McCone Commission has no comment to make concerning Proposition 14 itself. The McCone Commission fails to mention that Proposition 14 dealt a serious blow to the cause of equal rights and equal opportunities. Instead of considering the primary issue (Proposition 14), the McCone Commission appears to cluck regretfully over the fact of Negro reaction to an injustice. We are not certain why the McCone Commission felt compelled to observe that Negroes were ''encouraged'' to feel affronted, or who the McCone Commission believes encouraged Negroes to do so. Although the McCone Commission apparently failed to appreciate the significance of Proposition 14, the Negro community did not. It needed no encouragement....

[T]he McCone Commission failed totally to make any findings concerning the existence or nonexistence of police malpractices, or the justification, or lack thereof, of the almost universal feeling on the part of Negroes that such malpractices exist to a significant degree.

We consider the portion of the McCone Commission Report which deals with police-community relations to be a step backward. The Negro community assumed justifiably, based on Governor Brown's charge to the Commission, that it would provide a forum for the determination of its complaints against the Police Department. A large number of specific cases were presented to the McCone Commission, but the Commission failed to consider them. This we regret deeply.

Although the McCone Commission expressly refused to pass judgment on the validity of complaints of police malpractice, it did not allow its failure to resolve this essential issue to inhibit it from warning against the grave dangers inherent in criticizing the Police Department. In effect, it called for an end to criticism of Chief Parker and the Department. How it could do so, after confessing its unwillingness to determine whether such criticism is meritorious, escapes us. Nevertheless, in its section on police-community relations the McCone Commission again engaged in one of its exercises in reverse logic, in which the people who protest injustice are found to be jeopardizing our society, rather than those whose acts give rise to the criticism. We are particularly struck by the following sentence. ''The fact that this charge (police brutality) is repeatedly made must not go unnoticed, for there is a real danger that persistent criticism will reduce and perhaps destroy the effectiveness of law enforcement'' While we too are concerned over criticism of the police, we believe that this criticism is not only proper, but necessary, if Negro citizens are not receiving equal treatment under the law. We call not for an end to criticism, but for an impartial investigation which will determine whether Negro citizens in Los Angeles are receiving the rights to which they are entitled under our Constitution.

We also consider that the McCone Commission failed in its treatment of the subject of police attitudes and particularly those of the administration of the Police Department. Although the commission recommended the institution of an Inspector General system, increased efforts in the area of police-community relations, and more frequent meetings of the Police Commission, these recommendations fall far short of a serious treatment of the problem. We conclude, regretfully, that the ...Commission in effect whitewashed Chief Parker and the administration of the Police....

For years, police officials, and particularly Chief Parker, have turned a deaf ear to the complaints of Negro citizens of Los Angeles. Chief Parker had constantly refused to meet with Negro leaders, has challenged their right to represent their community, and has disparaged the civil rights movement. His refusal to recognize the very existence of the problem of police-community relations is exemplified by his statement to our California Advisory Committee in the Fall of 1962. "Basically, I do not believe that there is any difficult problem existing in the relationship between the Los Angeles Police Department and the Negro community." The extent to which these attitudes on the part of the police administration contributed to the tension in August 1965, is immeasurable. . . .

Other Official Attitudes and Actions

We do not believe that any report can be effective if it seeks to avoid fixing responsibility for basic failures. While criticism's sake serves no useful purpose, the failure to criticize where criticism is justified can only encourage those whose action contributed to the problems which existed in Los Angeles in August of 1965, and exist today. Official attitudes towards the Negro community are of major importance in determining whether harmonious relations between majority and minority groups will exist. Where such official attitudes are unresponsive to the needs of the Negro community, it may be expected that the community will be restless and dissatisfied. We believe that the attitudes and actions of Mayor Yorty prior to and during the riot contributed substantially to its existence and duration. In fact, throughout the City administration there has been a demonstrable lack of understanding and concern for the Negro community. This fact must be recognized if official attitudes are to be changed.

The Mayor of Los Angeles, Samuel Yorty, has apparently been more interested in travels, national and international, than he has in visiting the Negro community. During the riots he absented himself from Los Angeles; one day he visited San Diego and on another day spoke to a group of business leaders at the Commonwealth Club in San Francisco. Since the riot, he has shown far less interest in resolving the issues in Southeast Los Angeles than he has in traveling to South Viet Nam. Although our peripatetic Mayor appears to consider himself under a duty to advise the President concerning foreign policy, in the opinion of the Committee he has shown little interest in, or capacity for, resolving issues of race relations in Los Angeles.

The McCone Commission's failure to recognize the need for a change in the attitudes on the part of City officials constitutes a positive disservice to the ostensible objectives of the Commission. We might point out that the failure to criticize does not appear to stem from a desire on the part of the McCone Commission to limit itself to constructive suggestions. It did not hesitate to criticize Negro spokesmen and civil rights leaders, though not by name, in various portions of its report. Nor, did it hesitate to criticize an individual by name when it appeared a scapegoat was needed.

The individual the McCone Commission chose to criticize was Lieutenant-Governor of California, Glenn M. Anderson. This criticism we find wholly unwarranted.

The criticism of Lieutenant-Governor Anderson stemmed from the fact that he called out the National Guard shortly before 4:00 p.m. on Friday, August 13. The McCone Commission notes that Chief Parker's request that the Guard be called out was made around 11:00 a.m. that day. The McCone Commission also notes, however, that at 1:00 p.m. after consultation with Guard officers and civilian officials, Lieutenant-Governor Anderson ordered that the Guard be assembled at the armories at 5:00 p.m. General Hill, Adjutant General and Commander of the Guard, had advised Anderson that 5:00 p.m. was the earliest hour at which the troops could be assembled. The delay which the Commission appears to criticize is the two-hour period between 11:00 a.m. and 1:00 p.m. This "delay" was occasioned by the fact that Anderson, who was in Berkeley attending a meeting of the Board of Regents of the much troubled University of California, desired to consult with Guard officers and civilian officials before committing the Guard to action. He flew to Sacramento to meet with General Hill immediately upon being advised of Chief Parker's request.

We have several comments on the above facts. First, Lieutenant-Governor Anderson left Los Angeles for Berkeley on Friday the 13th because he was assured on that morning by the Los Angeles Police Department that "the situation was rather well in hand," which advice subsequently proved to be erroneous. Second, we do not agree that the Lieutenant-Governor should have called out the Guard merely on the basis of telephone reports. We think that a decision to send the Guard into a ghetto area to quell racial troubles should be made only after careful and analysis and consideration. We do not believe that a two-hour period in which to determine this grave question is unreasonable. Nor do we believe that a desire to consult personally with responsible officials is unwarranted.

We note, though the McCone Commission did not, that the Guard was probably mobilized more rapidly and more efficiently in this instance than on any other occasion in the history of this country on which the Guard has been requested to quell civil disobedience. We also note that no deaths had occurred prior to the calling out of the Guard. While property destruction was severe and even disastrous, we can well understand the reluctance of the Lieutenant-Governor to order armed troops into action without adequate consultation with Guard officials. The fact is that following the calling out of the Guard, 34 human beings were killed—almost all Negroes. These deaths may well have been inevitable, but they help us understand the desire of the Lieutenant-Governor for careful deliberation before ordering troops into action. . . .

Areas of Possible Federal Implementation of McCone Commission Report

General Observations

The remainder of this report will be devoted to a consideration of those areas in which direct Federal action, particularly the expenditure of Federal funds, is required. The McCone Commission made a number of specific recommendations in the fields of education, employment and housing. In each of these areas we believe that the recommendations made by the McCone Commission are wholly inadequate. In some of these areas we think that the inadequacy of the McCone Commission's recommendations stems from a basic failure to comprehend the nature or significance of the underlying problem.

Nevertheless, we believe that the specific recommendations if enacted would constitute a step forward. The very fact that the recommendations were made is of great significance, for a number of proposals which previously lacked sufficient public support may now find a climate of public acceptance. In this respect the McCone Commission has rendered a worthwhile public service.

Preliminarily, we should note our endorsement of the specific steps proposed by the McCone Commission in the areas of education, employment and housing. We are concerned, however, that consideration of these proposals may blind state and local officials to the need for continued efforts to find more basic solutions to the underlying problems. If the specific steps suggested by the McCone Commission are treated as essential preliminaries to a more serious treatment of the issues, they will prove of substantial value. If they are treated as a solution to the problem, more harm than good will have been accomplished. In this respect it is our impression that the McCone Commission realized the limitations of its report. We believe it attempted to suggest only programs which it thought would find ready acceptance. However, we also believe that the McCone Commission underestimated the willingness of governmental agencies, Federal and State, to devote their resources and efforts to providing a solution to problems which must at all costs be solved. In our opinion, it set its sights too low.

Even the limited specific proposals made by the McCone Commission require the participation of the Federal Government if they are to be realized. Governor Brown and Mayor Yorty have met to discuss the financing of the programs suggested by the McCone Commission Report. They each have announced separately that substantial Federal funds will be necessary if effective action is to be taken. The State and City have established a committee to work on joint implementation of the McCone Commission recommendations. In view of the request for Federal assistance already made by the Governor and the Mayor, we believe that the Federal Government should assign a full-time official to participate in the implementation of the recommendations of the McCone Commission. This assignment should be made immediately.

Housing

We believe that the portion of the McCone Commission Report which deals with housing fails completely to deal with the essential issues. The report leaves the impression that the fact that Los Angeles is a segregated community is a result primarily of the voluntary actions of Negroes, compounded by the existence of segregated communities, we are concerned that the McCone Commission failed to recognize the adverse effect of past governmental actions as a major force contributing to the creation of segregated communities. Although the McCone Commission was fully advised of the extent to which location of subsidized low-cost housing projects in ghetto areas contributed to the present pattern of discrimination in Los Angeles, it failed to acknowledge this fact. We believe that the pattern of government-sponsored segregated housing must be reversed by affirmative governmental action. Deliberate efforts must be made to create integrated low-cost housing developments, and to locate housing projects in areas where integration is practical. We do not underestimate the extent to which the Federal Government can, when it desires to do so, influence the actions of private sectors of the economy, particularly where the use of Federal funds or guarantees is involved.

We are disturbed by the McCone Commission's failure to treat the existence of segregated communities as a major issue. The section of the report dealing with housing consists mainly of an historical discussion and a few minor suggestions for improving life in the ghetto. In our view, most of the evils discussed in other sections of the McCone Commission Report stem from the very existence of the ghetto system. Unless this fact is recognized, all of the recommendations offered by the McCone Commission will, in the long run, be meaningless. We think a frontal assault of segregated communities is essential. Immediate attention should be given by the Federal Government to developing methods of breaking up the ghettos. We would suggest that this issue be given priority by the new Department of Housing and Urban Development and that the housing problem in Los Angeles receive first attention.

Certain steps, in our opinion, should be taken immediately. Among these we would include the expansion of the Executive Order 11063 regarding discrimination in housing which covers only a small proportion of present housing. We would also include the adoption of regulations governing savings and loan institutions and banks subject to the jurisdiction of agencies such as the Federal Home Loan Bank Board and the Federal Deposit Insurance Corporation or which are otherwise subject to such regulation. The Executive Order and regulations should require as a condition to the lending of funds for housing construction the execution of nondiscrimination covenants.

Education

With respect to education, we also believe that the McCone Commission recommendations misconceive the basic issue. While we endorse the specific proposals for reduction in class size and the institution of pre-school programs, we do not agree with the premise that an end to *de facto* segregation can be accomplished by improving the level of education in minority areas. We find that the McCone Commission's recommendations are deficient as a result of the failure of the Commission to focus on the primary goal of eliminating *de facto* segregation and a failure to note the relationship between segregated education and segregated housing.

The McCone Commission devotes most of the section of the report on education to seeking to find methods of improving facilities in the ghetto areas. We find this approach to be strikingly reminiscent of the Southern solution to educational problems prior to the 1954 Supreme Court decisions in the school segregation cases. The Southern solution, whenever complaints were made concerning educational opportunities for Negroes, was to urge the improvement of Negro facilities so as to make them equal to those which existed in white areas. We agree that the facilities in Negro areas should be improved, but we do not believe that such improvement will add materially to solving the problem of *de facto* segregation. Nor do we think that separate but equal "or even better" is enough in Los Angeles in 1965. The problem of our segregated school system must be recognized and met head-on without further delay.

We believe that *de facto* segregation can best be ended by a frontal attack on the system of segregated communities. We think, however, that at the same time an effort must be made directly in the area of education. This can be accomplished in several ways. One is to insist that new schools be constructed in locations which will draw students from both white and Negro communities. Another is to modify the doctrine that attendance in all schools must be based solely on neighborhood patterns. These are problems which the McCone Commission ignored. They also ignored the ruling of the California Supreme Court that because *de facto* segregation denies a pupil equal protection of the laws and due process of law, school officials must not only refrain from intentionally causing segregated schooling but are under a duty to take affirmative steps to end it. . . .

Employment

We feel that the McCone Commission recommendations with respect to employment are also inadequate. Again, we agree that the specific proposals contained in the McCone Commission Report should be adopted. We find two basic shortcomings, however, in the approach of the McCone Commission. First, we strongly disagree with the McCone Commission's rejection of Governor Brown's suggestion for an immediate Federally financed program to create additional jobs. With respect to the Governor's suggestion, the McCone Commission comments, "Since we are somewhat skeptical about the feasibility of this program (especially as to the capacity of the unemployed in the disadvantaged areas to fulfill the jobs specified), we feel it should be tested on a pilot basis before a massive program is launched."

We believe that there is an urgent need for a massive program to create additional jobs and that it should be launched immediately. We think that job training for presently existing jobs does not provide an answer to our problem—particularly in view of the increasing rate of automation. We favor the enactment of a substantial program of public works which offer immediate employment to a large number of those currently unemployed and at the same time will permit the construction of much needed facilities, particularly in minority areas. We do not believe that a public works program constitutes a utopian concept in our "great society." To the contrary, we feel that job training for unemployed Negroes can only give rise to false hopes and produce additional bitterness unless a substantial number of additional jobs are created by Federal action.

We also believe that the McCone Commission did not recognize the failure of present programs to concentrate sufficiently on the problem of unemployment of those who are presently heads of families. We believe that while youth training and youth counseling are essential in order to avoid a new generation of unemployed, we cannot afford to abandon the older unemployed. We do not single out the McCone Commission for criticism in this respect. It is our feeling, however, that the Commission did not give sufficient attention to the need for concentrated efforts to solve the immediate problem of unemployment for so many heads of Negro families.

Public Welfare

The McCone Commission Report was quite critical of the administration of welfare programs. Its criticisms were made, however, by way of raising questions rather than answering them. The questions raised are disturbing and they create implications which, if untrue, do a serious disservice to the entire system of public welfare. We note, for example, the following three sentences in the McCone Commission Report: "However, the increase in AFDC [Aid to Families with Dependent Children] expenditures, coupled with the increase in population, raises a question in the minds of some whether the generosity of the California welfare program compared with those in the southern and southwestern states is not one of the factors causing the heavy immigration of disadvantaged people to Los Angeles. . . . We are assured that many of the present recipients would rather have work than welfare, but the simple arithmetic of the matter makes us uncertain. . . . Indeed, we were told that the 18 year old girl who is no longer eligible for assistance when living with her mother may have considerable incentive to become a mother herself so as to be eligible again as the head of a new family group.''

With respect to the statements quoted above, we find it regrettable that the McCone Commission felt it necessary to raise such important questions but was incapable of answering them. Nevertheless, in view of the substantial contributions of the Federal Government to the Public Welfare program in Los Angeles County (42 percent according to the McCone Commission), we believe that the questions raised by the McCone Commission require an answer. We note that one of the two Negro members of the McCone Commission vigorously dissented from this portion of the report. However, we believe that the report itself cannot help but undermine public confidence in the public welfare program. In view of the McCone Commission's unwillingness to reach conclusions concerning the basic questions raised by it, we see no alternative to an immediate Federal study which will either justify the newly-created lack of public confidence or restore that confidence and lay the McCone Commission's insinuations to rest.

Coordination of Federal Programs

We also note the McCone Commission finding with respect to the dispersal and lack of coordination of Federal programs for administering funds in minority areas. Here, we believe the McCone Commission's Report points up an area where positive action is required. We believe that the Federal Government should give immediate consideration to consolidation and integration of Federally administered or supported programs, and to improving the channels of disseminating information concerning the availability of Federal assistance.

Dissenting Statement

Submitted by Member R. J. Carreon, Jr.

As a member of the Southern California Advisory Committee to your honorable body, I respectfully, though emphatically, wish to express my disagreement with some of the findings and conclusions arrived at by our group which met during the past weekend to evaluate the report of the McCone Commission recommendations concerning the August riots in Los Angeles. I did not attend said meeting because I was not available until two days after it was held.

I am in agreement with the Advisory Committee Report except for the portion which deals with law enforcement, particularly as it relates to the Los Angeles Police Department. My reasons for disagreeing with that portion of the Advisory Committee Report are set forth below.

Because of my years of devotion to the cause of equality in civil and human rights and being a member of a deeply affected minority, shortly after the Watts Riots I accepted reappointment to the (Civilian) Police Commission of Los Angeles. As I expected, this position afforded me an inside view to the accusations and counter-accusations which followed the tragic events. Based on my long experience with the Mexican-American minority problems, my advantageous observation position and my sense of fair play, I have the following impressions regarding our report to you.

1. Generally, it is expertly presented with the specific purpose of erroneously placing all the blame for the rioting, looting, killing and arson on the law enforcement agencies in general, and the Los Angeles Police Department in particular. Chief William H. Parker, a national symbol of police honesty, discipline and integrity has been made the principal target of senseless tirades. His surrender to the forces of evil and civil disobedience, under any pretense, is impossible.

2. The McCone Commission, which rightfully requested specific complaints of Police malpractice, was ''swamped'' with seventy such grievances. Of these, 55% were against the Sheriff's Departments, and some against the California Highway Patrol. Of the less than 30 complaints

against the local police, some are over a year old, but all are being carefully investigated, as are all complaints customarily, and the guilty, I know, will be punished.

3. The McCone Commission Report, which I have studied from the day it was first available, is the result of intensive study and evaluation of facts by a blue ribbon cross section of devoted public-minded individuals. These experts have analyzed the symptoms and recommended treatments which may fall short, but a cure-all should not be expected, as our Committee would want and presumes to have.

4. Certainly civil rights, as well as police-community relations problems exist in this area as elsewhere. We also have housing, equality of opportunity and employment deficiencies to alleviate. I for one certainly welcome a U.S. Commission on Civil Rights meeting here anytime but fail to see how it can create a utopia which would summarily appease all of us interested in the civil rights image of our country and the genuine welfare of all our fellow citizens.

Finally, I wish to assure you that the Police Department, as well as other City, County and State agencies are already implementing some of the recommendations contained in the material of the McCone Commission report to our Governor.

41.
L.A. County and L.A. City Human Relations Commissions: Many Problems Remain Unresolved

Almost two decades after the burning stopped. the human relations commissions of the city and the county of Los Angeles held joint hearing to assess the progress, or lack of it, in South-Central Los Angeles since the riot of 1965. Eighteen presenters gave testimony. The findings and recommendations, reprinted in their entirety, present a mixed bag on conditions in the black ghetto.[3]

Findings

The following finding of the Los Angeles County and Los Angeles City Human Relations Commissions are based on the testimony presented at this hearing and in supporting documents. In some cases, specific and detailed information was presented to support assertions and conclusions of the speakers. In other cases, the presentations were anecdotal or summarized the opinions and feelings of limited segments of the South Central Los Angeles community. The Commissions have found that perceptions are often as important as facts, however, and they have been treated as such in the assessment below.

1. We find that the greatest progress since 1965 has been made in Transportation.

   A. The McCone Commission called for a public subsidy to give Southern California Rapid Transit District (SCRTD) financial ability to provide an adequate and reasonable bus transportation system. SCRTD now receives Federal, State, and local subsidies.

   B. The Commission also urged SCRTD to acquire the existing small transportation companies. SCRTD has done so, and only eight municipal operators continue to provide fixed-route services today.

[3]Los Angeles County Commission on Human Relations, and Los Angeles City Human Relations Commission, "McCone Revisited: A Focus on Solutions to Continuing Problems in South Central Los Angeles. Report on a Public Hearing . . ." (the authors, January 1985), 11-16.

C. The third McCone suggestion, to establish transfer agreements between the various operators within the region, was accomplished in 1974,

D. The McCone Commission also called for the immediate establishment of an adequate east-west cross town service to permit efficient transportation to and from the area. In 1974 the system was designed into a grid in two sections, South Central and San Fernando Valley. This reduced the need to transfer when making intercommunity trips.

E. The proposed Metrorail system, while not necessarily having an immediate service impact on south Central Los Angeles, is perceived to be a potential source of jobs for South Central Los Angeles residents during construction.

2. We find that significant progress has been made in Health, although many critical problems remain.

A. The McCone Commission urged that a new, comprehensively equipped hospital be built in the South Central Los Angeles area. The Martin Luther King Jr. Hospital and Drew Post-Graduate Medical School were completed in 1972.

B. The Commission also urged the Los Angeles County Departments of Health and Mental Health to increase the number of facilities and services in South Central Los Angeles. The Hubert H. Humphrey Health Center was completed in 1976, and other improvements in health care delivery have been reported.

C. Despite the progress noted, South Central Los Angeles still has the highest infant mortality rate, the lowest rate of immunization, the highest incidence of communicable disease, an alarming rate of drug abuse, and the fewest doctors per capita in the County. The area leads the County in morbidity and mortality rates. The number of Black teenage pregnancies increases each year. Homicide is the primary cause of mortality among Black males in South Central Los Angeles.

3. We find that despite substantial progress Police-Community Relations and the issue of equitable law enforcement continues to be one of the most contentious and serious problems for residents of South Central Los Angeles.

A. The Board of Police Commissioners has been strengthened: it now assumes a more active role in Department management, meets once a week, and determines policy governing use of deadly force, retention of intelligence files on private citizens, review of disciplinary cases, and arrest of undocumented workers. The position of Inspector, Administration of Discipline was established in 1967, and in 1977 it was replaced by a Commission Services Coordinator to assist the Board of Police Commissioners, and sentiment for a Citizens Police Review Board still exists.

B. The Los Angeles Police Department has developed a number of programs since 1965 to address the need for non-punitive police-citizen communication: Community Relations Officers, the Police Role in Government programs, and programs to involve the community actively in crime prevention, such as the Basic Car Plan and the Neighborhood Watch Program. In 1971 the Department decentralized, placing top command physically closer to the community. The Department indicates that human relations training is emphasized at all levels, and in 1983 a formal Community Orientation Program was initiated in the

Southeast area. Despite these efforts, however, criticism of the Department in regard to communication remains.

C. The Department has made a serious effort to recruit Black and Latino sworn personnel, and there has been a significant increase since 1965. The issue of how sworn personnel are assigned throughout the City has become a matter of substantial controversy, however, with organizations such as the Los Angeles Branch of NAACP, Southern Christian Leadership Conference, and South Central Organizing Committee, among others, contending that the allocation formula fails to make a sufficient distinction between crimes against property and crimes against people, to the detriment of South Central Los Angeles. The allocation formula is a source of considerable discontent.

4. We find that problems of Employment in South Central Los Angeles remain critical.

A. Despite efforts of organizations such as Chad McClellan's Chamber of Commerce Committee, the Watts Labor Community Action Committee, the Los Angeles Urban League, and the Westminster Neighborhood Association there now appears to be no comprehensive job training and placement center or program in the area, and coordination of existing programs is described as poor.

B. Plant closures and the disappearance of jobs in heavy manufacturing have made a major impact on South Central Los Angeles, whose residents are least able to avail themselves of the high tech, light manufacturing, defense, and service jobs that may replace many of the low-skilled and semi-skilled jobs previously available.

C. The California State Department of Fair Employment and Housing ensures employers' adherence to non-discrimination regulations, but they no longer maintain an office in South Central Los Angeles, and the effectiveness of their work in promoting affirmative minority hiring is unclear.

5. We find that problems of Welfare and Social Services remain critical.

Poverty is becoming increasingly feminized: nearly one-third of all households with children in South Central Los Angeles are headed by women. The Federal program for Targeted Jobs, Tax Credits, which is designed to offer private sector employers a tax credit for hiring welfare recipients, does not appear to be working. Reduction in Federal funds for welfare and social services has had a disproportionate negative impact on the level and quality of life in the South Central area.

6. We find that problems of Education remain critical and may be growing worse.

A. The McCone Commission recommended that elementary and junior high schools with achievement levels below the average for the Los Angeles Unified School District be designated "Emergency Schools," but this was not done. The Commission recommended establishment of a permanent pre-school program beginning at age three to focus on development of language skills, but this was not done.

B. Schools in South Central Los Angeles are as racially isolated today as in 1965, perhaps more so. Achievement scores remain among the poorest in the District. Parent participation is extremely low throughout the area.

C. Problems stemming from teacher shortages in the area and the use of year-round schools primarily for Blacks and Latino pupils did not exist in 1965 and were not cited by the McCone Commission.

D. The expansion of the Permits With Transportation Program (PWT) is perceived to have a deleterious effect on the schools of South Central Los Angeles, pulling needed teachers, students, and resources away from the area without having a substantial impact on district-wide desegregation.

E. The School Based Quality Assured Instructional Delivery System, developed and implemented in Region C of the District, appears to be effective but has not been utilized throughout the South Central area.

7. We find that Housing remains one of the most critical problems in South Central Los Angeles.

A. The McCone Commission urged implementation of a continuing urban rehabilitation and renewal program for South Central Los Angeles. This has not been done, and clear public housing policy for the area—Federal, State, and local—is still lacking. Affordable and desirable low-density units for lower and middle income households are not being constructed, exacerbating the continuing shortage.

B. Redlining, although declared unlawful, is still perceived as a substantial problem, as are high interest rates, rising material and labor costs, speculation, and the absence of information and education regarding available housing services.

Recommendations

Some problems reported 19 years ago by the McCone Commission have been resolved. Many have not. In some cases, the problems are complex and difficult. In some cases, cooperation and coordination among the groups and organizations which are essential for the development of solutions have been lacking. Responsibility, accountability, and will, and their absence, seem to be at the root of many problems described in this report. The recommendations that follow attempt to overcome this difficulty. While realizing that involvement of other agencies is critical, we have focused on one key agency in each problem area.

The Los Angeles County Human Relations Commission and the Los Angeles City Human Relations Commission recommend:

1. In each area where the Commissions have found serious problems in South Central Los Angeles, a key agency should be designated by the appropriate authority to review the McCone Commission Report, the Report of the Joint Task Force on South Central Los Angeles, and this hearing report on McCone Revisited in order to develop specific solutions to the problems identified, ways to implement those solutions, resources required, and a timetable for implementation, however long-range. These agencies should be designated as quickly as possible and should report back to the appointing authority by July 1985.

a. The Los Angeles County Board of Supervisors should direct the County Health Department to develop a plan to reduce infant mortality, increase the rate of immunization, reduce communicable disease, reduce drug abuse, increase the number of physicians, and otherwise address the health problems of South Central Los Angeles.

b. The Mayor of Los Angeles and the Los Angeles City Council should request the Board of Police Commissioners to develop a plan, in cooperation with the Chief of Police, to improve police-community relations, police-community communication, and the current allocation or deployment formula in South Central Los Angeles. The plan should also address the issues of drug traffic and homicide in South Central Los Angeles.

c. The Board of Supervisors, Mayor, and City Council should request the Governor to direct the California State Employment Development Department to develop a plan, including legislation if necessary, to address the critical employment problems of South Central Los Angeles.

d. The Board of Supervisors should direct the County Department of Public Social Services to develop a plan, including legislation if necessary, to address the critical welfare and social services problems of South Central Los Angeles.

e. The Los Angeles Unified School District Board of Education should direct the Superintendent of Schools to develop a plan to decrease racial isolation, increase achievement scores, increase parent participation, reduce teacher shortages, improve year-round schools, and otherwise address the education problems of South Central Los Angeles.

f. The Mayor and City Council should request the City Planning Commission to develop a plan, including legislation if necessary, to address the critical housing problems of South Central Los Angeles.

2. A Blue Ribbon Task Force composed of elected officials and leaders from private industry, religious institutions, and the community, should be appointed by the Governor by January 1986. This Task Force, acting with the same sense of responsibility and urgency as the McCone Commission, would evaluate responses to the preceding recommendations and the effectiveness of solutions offered, making a report to the Governor and the public.

We cannot emphasize too strongly the critical nature of the problems described in this report and the implications of continued inaction. We should not have to wait for a second Los Angeles riot to erupt to bring these problems to serious public attention.

It is scarcely necessary to dwell on the crime involved in the destruction of the oldest trees on earth. The cutting of a sequoia for grape stakes or railroad ties is like breaking up one's grandfather's clock for kindling to save the trouble of splitting logs at the woodpile.

—Madison Grant, quoted by Francois Leydet, *The Last Redwoods and the Parkland of Redwood Creek.*

I appeal to you...to protect these mighty trees, these wonderful monuments of beauty.... There is nothing more practical in the end than the preservation of anything that appeals to the higher emotions in mankind.

—President Theodore Roosevelt.

So, all in all, while I am sorry I shall not be here to see it, I very much look forward to the time when towns or companies in the Redwood Region will be celebrating their 600th year of tree farming and manufacturing of redwood forest products and at the same time hosting citizens who want to enjoy themselves in these woods. Only a major take-over by government—and commitment of otherwise productive forests to the single use of recreation— will prevent this happy dream from coming true.

—Philip T. Farnsworth, executive vice president, California Redwood Association address, June 8, 1966.

CHAPTER 14

SAVING THE COASTAL REDWOODS, 1966-1978

Park Land and the Lumber Industry

A. *The Creation of Redwood National Park, 1966-1968*
B. *The Park Expansion Battle, 1977-1978*

"A tree is a tree," Governor Ronald Reagan supposedly told a cheering meeting of the Western Wood Products Association in 1966. "How many more do you need to look at?" Though he later denied making this remark,[1] it has come to represent the essence of the anti-environmentalist attitude about forests.

At that time there was a major political storm brewing in California over the coastal redwoods. The lumber companies of the North Coast wanted to cut trees on private land adjacent to protected state park land. Conservation groups protested that this would threaten both protected and unprotected redwood trees, and proposed that a national park be established in the endangered area. Since the state lacked the funds, or the will, to buy any substantial park land and a national forest offered no absolute protection, environmentalists proposed that a large redwoods national park be established to protect all of the endangered trees. Conflict over the redwood forests of northern California erupted twice, first over the establishment of the park in the late 1960's, and again over the enlargement of its boundaries in the 1970's.

The original stand of coastal redwoods—*Sequoia sempervirens*, as distinguished from the Big Trees, or *Sequoia giganteum*, that grow in the Sierra Nevada—once stretched from Monterey County on the south to the Oregon border on the north. Some specimens tower overhead as high as 350 feet. As the redwoods are all but impervious to fire and insect pests, some of them live to

[1]Quoted in *Sacramento Bee*, September 12, 1966; denial, ibid., September 14, 1966. He also is quoted as saying, "I'm the guy who bleeds every time a tree is cut down," *Fresno Bee*, April 28, 1966.

be two thousand years old. They are among the oldest living things on earth, and they are direct descendants of a species that inhabited North America fifty million years ago.

Since the 1870's there has been a measure of protection for forest lands in the U.S. But along the California coast, where a center for redwood cutting came into being during the gold rush era, very little land was protected. Redwood was used extensively for home building in San Francisco, and for other industries, as well. The grape stake is still a favorite in the extensive vineyards of California. A major timber industry developed around Humboldt Bay that worked the thick stands of trees in Humboldt and Del Norte counties. Before the 1960's about 95 percent of the original stand of these trees had already been cut down commercially.

The coastal redwoods were more vulnerable to the logger's axe than the Big Trees because they were more useful commercially. Excessive cutting by loggers, who loved to pit their muscles and axes against the awesome trees, caused repeated outcry among conservationists even before the end of the century. The first successful campaign of the conservationists resulted in the establishment of Big Basin state park in the Santa Cruz mountains in 1901. Further efforts languished until 1918, when the Save-the-Redwoods League was formed. For sixty years this organization "pitted [its] vigor as fund raisers, negotiators, politicians, and publicists against the enterprise of the loggers in a race for the old trees."[2] The League's main stratagem was to raise private funds, purchase forest land and turn it over to the state for permanent protection. In the 1960's the League was joined by the Sierra Club.

Conservation themes are, of course, major themes in California history and John Muir's work to save Yosemite is legendary. Regarding forests there have been two main trends within this movement: (1) *conservation*, which encourages sustained lumber yield for commercial use, and (2) *preservation*, which involves the permanent protection of wild areas and discourages all cutting or other development. Both have been exemplified in the state's history, sometimes with jarring effect. The Hetch Hetchy controversy that culminated in 1913 comes immediately to mind. To some extent both issues also were present in the redwood controversy in that the policy objective was how to find a balance between the needs for sustained growth in the privately owned forests, while still preserving the virgin timber in adjacent park land for aesthetic and scientific value. The lumber companies professed a deep interest in both; and on this they were challenged by their political opponents.

The redwood industry argued in the 1960's that there were already enough redwoods under protection, particularly in the state parks and that the industry's own future was at stake if more forest land was withdrawn from cutting. Industry opponents argued that the state parks were inadequate; and that even the old-growth trees in these parks were threatened by the actions of timber companies on private land. The traditional selective method of redwood cutting required a large area to be opened up for felling the fragile giants. Increasingly at issue was "clearcutting," a method of harvesting that levelled all trees and stumps to the ground on a given site. The lumber companies claimed that this extreme method actually promoted efficient cutting as well as healthy regrowth. But it left an area as visibly devastated as a war zone and sometimes resulted in erosion that was harmful to nearby uncut areas.

After a bitter congressional contest from 1965 to 1968, a compromise was struck that established a national park of about fifty-eight thousand acres. It allowed both clearcutting and wilderness recreation in a narrow river valley. Even Governor Reagan approved of this measure.

But the redwood park with its compromise boundaries pleased no one, and frustrated everyone. Clearcutting just outside the park's boundaries continued, with harmful effect to protected watersheds. So the battle was rejoined from 1969 to 1978. The Sierra Club led the way with nationwide publicity, legal action and lobbying to enlarge the park boundaries before it was too late. The

[2]Susan R. Schrepfer, *The Fight to Save the Redwoods: A History of Environmental Reform, 1917-1978*, Madison: The University of Wisconsin Press, 1983, xiv.

moderate Progressive reform movement of the early part of the century had evolved into a militant protest movement in the 1960's and 1970's.

The contest in the 1970's was doubly bitter because the redwood industry, the mainstay of Humboldt County's economy, was more depressed than ever. Not only was there much at stake for the industry—the major companies were Georgia-Pacific Co., Simpson Lumber Co., Louisiana-Pacific and Arcata Lumber—but also for the forest and mill workers, and for the local businesses of the North Coast.

After 1977 the question was whether timber cutting was a permanent enterprise, as the lumber companies vehemently professed, or whether it was destined to be eliminated in the foreseeable future, as conservationists alleged. Theoretically the lumber industry was supposed to be using a policy of sustained yield. At first the labor unions were convinced that timbering was here to stay, and they allied themselves strongly with the lumber companies. Later, when the companies lost credibility on this score, the unions broke ranks. Instead, they sought a job phase-out program from Congress that would compensate the workers in the declining industry.

Different plans were debated. At a heated congressional hearing in Eureka loggers pounded their axe handles on the floor and swung wedge blades overhead. The net result was a law expanding the park from 58,000 to 132,000 acres. About $350 million was appropriated to purchase private land. A protection zone was established where the national government could acquire even more land, if necessary. In consequence, an almost continuous stretch of forested coastland from Redwood Creek in the south to the Smith River on the north was placed under the protection of the state or national government and was closed to timber cutting. In addition, at the insistence of Congressional Representative Phil Burton, the law included salary and layoff benefits to the affected workers.

The race to save the redwoods ended with about five percent of the pure redwood grove preserved. Some of the new growth forests were quite extensive and impressive. The redwood industry was greatly curtailed, though not driven to extinction. The controversy of late has been whether or not to turn over the state parks to the federal government so as to allow the National Park Service to manage them more efficiently. The timber industry and local business leaders declare that since the establishment of the Redwood National Park, their worst fears about economic stagnation have come true. They document the contraction of local businesses, the chronically high rate of unemployment (over 14 percent), the low rate of Park attendance, and the overall sluggishness of tourism.[3]

But the questions raised by the redwood controversy have wide ramifications that will recur inevitably in other forms: When should environmental considerations take precedence over the demands of private enterprise? When should economic growth be restricted, especially in areas that are economically depressed? What compensation should be given to those who lose their jobs in a program of environmental protection? Is there a future for a forest industry run on the basis of moderate, sustained, long- term yield? And finally what should be the extent and limits of government rules and prohibitions in the area of environmental protection? *(Editor's note)*

[3]Richard A. Good, public relations dept., Georgia-Pacific, Atlanta, Georgia.

A. *The Creation of a Redwoods National Park, 1966-1968*

42.
Sierra Club: How to Really Save the Redwoods

In an open letter in December of 1965 the Sierra Club urged President Lyndon B. Johnson to establish a national park along Redwood Creek, in the Klamath River area. The Club and other environmental groups backed Plan I submitted by the National Park Service, and opposed other plans that would provide for a smaller and less comprehensive park.[4]

December 15, 1965

The President
The White House
Washington, D.C.

Dear Mr. President:

The last chance for the Redwood National Park that this country needs and can still set aside is rapidly slipping away. Nothing less than boldness on your part—supported by foresighted citizens everywhere—will rescue the unique coastal redwoods it is this generation's unique obligation to save.

Secretary Udall, in his foreword to the book we published to serve a vital cause, wrote, ". . .it will surprise no conservationist that John Muir's Sierra Club should raise a banner and lead the fight for a Redwood National Park. Such a wilderness park will surely be established if the eloquent words and pictures of this book arouse enough lovers of the land before it is too late.

They were aroused. You yourself have seen the book and know from it the shocking story it tells of unprecedented abuse of land. You met with the leading conservation organizations a year ago June, and we were honored to be there. You directed that the Secretary conduct a study to determine where the park should be. He did.

We like the park the study singled out—the last chance to save almost enough of the most remarkable trees, the last of the unprotected virgin redwood forest still intact enough to deserve the name national park. The park would rescue from destruction —when combined with the stands earlier boldness saved in a few small California state parks—5 to 6 per cent of the original redwood-producing lands (20 per cent no longer produce timber).

The Park Service Plan (Plan I) was a plan for a real park. We like it. So does the National Parks Association, the Wilderness Society, the National Audubon Society, Trustees for Conservation, the Citizens Committee on Natural Resources, the Federation of Western Outdoor Clubs, and—right in the heart of the Redwood country—the Citizens for a Redwood National Park.

Others do not like it—particularly those who could be intimidated by a powerful industry and its extensive public-relations program. Some leaders in the industry have been public-spirited. Others, and those they could influence, would let the park be destroyed. They would settle for a false-front redwood national park—a thin line of trees shielding the highway traveler from the destruction beyond. Or for an existing state park, relabeled as a national park. Some voices, too, are now calling for an easy, bargain-basement national park that would cost little and save little in an area no longer of national park caliber—an area the state is capable of caring for if imaginatively

[4] It appeared in many newspapers, December 17, 1965.

led. Still others would prefer redwoods lying down, converted to fences, panels and siding, poling, posts, pulp, and picnic tables.

We, and we think the generations on down into the future, would like to see our last virgin redwoods vertical, not prone. We believe that you, the man who presides in this hour of decision for the redwoods, will have the imagination, the inspiration, and the courage to put before the next session of Congress and to urge the enactment of legislation that will create the real Redwood National Park.

All signs point to Redwood Creek, up near the Klamath. The last intact watersheds are here, the ecological integrity, the variety of climate and terrain, the unique habitat of the Roosevelt elk, the wild Gold Bluffs Beach and Prairie Creek redwoods in the adjoining state park. This is the comprehensive opportunity, the plan with boldness to excite the public imagination, the battle worth the bruises and bleeding—and the rewards for centuries to come.

Pilot bills have already been introduced by Congressmen Jeffrey Cohelan and Phillip Burton of California, Henry Reuss of Wisconsin, and John P. Saylor of Pennsylvania—bills that provide for an adequate park, and adequate safeguards for the local people while the transition is made from an economy that forecloses on virgin redwoods to an economy that perpetuates them, that respects them for the unique national scenic resource they are and can always be.

Saving them won't be easy. Industries, like people, would rather die than change their habits.

The price will be high, but not out of reach when you consider what the stakes are. It is worth a substantial indebtedness if that is what it takes to get an adequate national park.

We think that future generations will welcome the chance to pay their share. The alternative—a fragmented, decimated, hollow shell of what there once was—will be a vestigial bit of forest that "reminds you of the places on your face you missed when you shaved."

The great forests of the Klamath River are gone. Below Jedediah Smith Park, the forests of the Smith River are gone. On the upper reaches of Redwood Creek itself, on the headwaters of Mill Creek, on the Mad, the Trinity, the Van Duzen, the Eel, on the Ten Mile, the Noyo, the Big, the Navarro, the Russian, the Garcia, down the line to Muir Woods, and to the Big Sur country —in all these places the redwoods have fallen, have been trucked or floated or railroaded out, and have never been adequately replaced. Mill Valley doesn't remember the forests that once sustained the mill that gave it its name. Of the redwood heritage of a century ago, the virgin redwood forest that has been felled would extend from San Francisco to Washington and never be less than a mile wide. It was a good thing at the time perhaps; but good things came to an end.

What we ask now is that you support, and give Americans a chance to support, a Redwood National Park one-twenty-fifth the size of Yellowstone, costing at today's prices 75 cents to one dollar per American—a priceless opportunity, never to be known again if we miss it now.

There are a thousand conservation needs, but few with this urgency. Within two years, if industry continues to cut at its present rate in the area singled out on Redwood Creek by the National Park Service for the national park, there will be nothing worthy of the name left to save.

We urge you to act with all vigor and all speed on the one plan that will truly serve America—a Redwood National Park, boldly delineated, on Redwood Creek.

Sincerely,
William E. Siri, President
Edgar Wayburn, Vice-President
David Brower, Executive Director
Michael McCloskey, Conservation Director
and, most of our 35,000 members
all over the country

P.S. There is nothing in this for us or for the club itself except work—and the satisfaction of helping save the important parts of America's natural beauty.

43.
Georgia-Pacific Co.: "Yes, America's Majestic Redwoods Have Already been Saved!"

While awaiting congressional action on a park bill in the winter of 1967-1968, Georgia-Pacific Co. decided to cut timber on land that some environmentalists hoped would be protected in a future park. Georgia-Pacific did not oppose the formation of a national park, but held that it should be formed by turning existing state parks over to the federal government without adding any new acreage. An accompanying photo showed part of a magnificent grove of climax redwood, worth $6 million dollars, that it had donated to the Nature Conservancy. The giant corporation defended its action and attacked the environmentalist opposition in a full-page ad that appeared in 11 newspapers in January 1968.[5]

Recently, there has been a great hue and cry to the effect that California's coastal redwoods (*Sequoia sempervirens*) are vanishing. The implication is that the last of these trees are in danger of falling before chain saws. Trumpets have sounded for a redwood national park—"before the redwoods have vanished."

These allegations are simply not true! Knowledgeable individuals have deplored the methods used by small pressure groups to influence the public and the Congress. Professor Emeritus Emmanuel Fritz of the University of California, and probably the world's leading authority on redwoods, wrote:

> "There has never been a time when the privilege of viewing redwoods at their best was more secure for future generations."

He further stated:

> "In brief, the methods used by leading organized proponents (of a redwood national park) include distortions and innuendo."

"Distortions and innuendo." Strong but accurate words. The following statements are leading arguments put forth by pressure groups in support of their position on redwoods. After each statement is an analysis of the situation as it *actually* exists.

INNUENDO:
"The last majestic coastal redwood trees are in danger of being cut and destroyed forever."

FACT:
Right now, today, over 180,000 acres of coastal redwoods have been saved—set aside never to be cut. This land supports virtually all existing cathedral-like groves. This land is already in state, county and municipal parks or forests.

To give some idea of the magnitude of the giant trees already in parks, right now, sufficient numbers of these coastal redwoods are permanently protected to form a continuous row of trees, side by side, 8 feet or larger in diameter, from San Francisco to New York City. . . over 1 3/4 million giant trees in all.

---

[5]See *Wall Street Journal*, January 26, 1968.

INNUENDO:

"There were once 2-million acres of giant coastal redwoods; now there are less than 250,000 acres."

FACT:

Less than one-hundred thousand of these 2-million acres ever contained the giant cathedral-like redwood groves which everyone reads about and wants saved. Cathedral-like groves grow mostly on rich alluvial benches and flats. Most "redwood forests" contain many other species. These redwoods are found on steep hills and ridgetops and are intermixed with other species—often only 5% of the forest is redwood. The fact is, virtually all of the majestic redwoods standing today have *already* been saved.

INNUENDO:

"The forest products industry is denuding the forest, leaving destruction in its wake."

FACT:

The forest products industry manages its commercial redwood timberlands on a sustained yield basis. The truth is that of the 2-million acres which originally contained some redwoods, an estimated 1,900,000 acres still grow redwood trees in nature, usually reaching full maturity in 80 to 100 years and usually starting to die at 350 or 400 years. Sustained yield tree farming means growing trees to replace harvested ones as quickly as possible on a continuous basis. This Georgia-Pacific policy assures us of a never-ending crop of timber. The fact is, virtually all of the land which ever grew coastal redwoods is still growing redwoods and will continue to do so.

INNUENDO:

"More redwoods are needed for recreational purposes."

FACT:

The best redwoods are *already* in park status. The 130,000 acres of redwoods already set aside need recreational development, not wholesale additions. Less than 7% of the recreation potential of the large existing redwood parks has been developed, the other 93% has yet to be tapped. In addition, forest products companies have designated 365,000 acres of timberlands containing redwoods for hunting, fishing, camping and other recreational activities. The fact is, the giant redwoods have *already* been saved, and there is plenty of land *already* available for recreational development.

INNUENDO:

"Additional upstream lands are needed to protect watersheds and save the cathedral-like groves from destruction by flooding."

FACT:

Cathedral-like redwood groves have withstood floods from the beginning of time. In fact, deposits of rich alluvial soil which settled on flatlands and benches from floods are responsible for the size and purity of the groves which are in park status. Today, the idea that land is left denuded and subject to wholesale erosion after timber harvest, is simply not true. Young redwood growth is either planted, seeded or springs up in nature, maintaining sufficient soil stability and watershed control. The fact is, the giant redwood groves have *already* been saved and are *already* safe from wholesale flood damage.

INNUENDO:

"The only majestic Sequoias in California are the coastal redwoods."

FACT:

The National Park Service says:

"The coast redwoods (*Sequoia sempervirens*) are often confused with their cousin the giant sequoia (*Sequoia gigantea*), which grows along the western slopes of the Sierra Nevada between elevations of 4,000 and 8,000 feet. Magnificent groves of this species are preserved in Yosemite, Sequoia and Kings Canyon National Parks. The giant sequoias are undoubtedly the largest living things on the face of the earth."

The fact is that California *already has three* national parks containing redwoods in an area much larger than Delaware. These have huge groves of the larger, older Sequoia, some so large you can drive a car through the tree trunk. Nearly 98.6% of these trees are completely protected in parks.

Georgia-Pacific's position with regard to a redwood national park:

Georgia-Pacific does not oppose the formation of a coastal redwoods national park, but we believe such a park must be created out of one or more of the state parks because that's where the truly magnificent redwoods now stand. We object to the attempt, through vicious attack and innuendo by pressure groups, to stampede the Congress and the American people into a costly addition of aesthetically inferior land to meet a non-existent need. Wholesale locking up of this land could cost American taxpayers an estimated two-hundred million dollars, or more. It is our contention, supported by fact, that such a move is prohibitively expensive, and would do nothing to serve the national interest.

Georgia-Pacific/the growth company
421 S.W. Sixth Ave., Portland, Oregon 97204

44.
Sierra Club: Stop "Legislation by Chainsaw"

The Sierra Club responded to the move by Georgia-Pacific with a full-page ad that also appeared in major newspapers.[6] *It is reproduced in full below, minus a dramatic photo of a clearcut area, and coupons that could be clipped and sent to congressional representatives and corporate officials. The photo caption complimented Arcata Redwood Co. for behaving more responsibly than Georgia-Pacific by withholding further cutting in critical areas until final park boundaries would be determined by Congress, indicating corporations "*can *behave responsibly."*

While Congress has been considering the exact boundaries for a great Redwood National Park, Georgia-Pacific Corp. has begun logging within two spectacular regions which should be selected. The company says it is doing this (potentially reducing the park's size and quality with its chainsaws) ". . .in the interests of our stockholders." QUESTION: how many G-P stockholders disapprove of such behavior in their names? (The coupons below offer them and everyone else an opportunity to help delay the logging, so that Congress, not Georgia-Pacific, may define the optimum park borders.)

1. In November, the Senate passed a bill (S.2515) which would establish a redwood national

[6]*Wall Street Journal*, January 24, 1968. In some newspapers this ad appeared *before* the one by Georgia-Pacific.

park. It is a small park— narrow enough to walk across in a few hours—but as a compromise plan it represents a gain. Conservation minded people support it, and hope it may be improved.

2. The bill permits 2,346 acres to be added to the park by the Secretary of the Interior. The House of Representatives has this option as well, and the many park supporters in the House have made clear their intention of fighting for this addition. But this can happen only if, a) the bill moves through quickly and, b) if Georgia-Pacific does not cut the trees down meanwhile.

3. Georgia-Pacific began cutting in the McArthur-Elam Creek area in late October, and then, about December 11, in the Emerald Mile. (See map.) The first logging there is for access roads, landings, and other clearing operations preliminary to full scale clear-cut logging.

4. Georgia-Pacific, in committing these acts, may not be violating any laws. Nor is it violating the wording of promises it has made. To explain:

> A year ago, after tremendous public pressure, G-P and three other logging concerns agreed to halt logging within redwood areas proposed as parks, until the Senate had acted to define the boundaries. Now the Senate has done so. But *the House has not*. G-P , therefore (unlike the other three redwood companies) feels it may now quickly cut down everything beyond the Senate lines. Then, you see, there will be no point in having the House, or Secretary Udall add the Emerald Mile or the McArthur-Elam Creek area, or others. The trees will already have become patio furniture.

5. On Dec. 4, Rep. Jeffery Cohelan reported, with outrage, his exchange with G-P on this question. (From the *Congressional Record*):

> Cohelan: Adjacent to the Senate park boundaries are virgin redwoods lovely enough to grace the best redwood national park. . . . These trees are now being fed to the sawmills of the Georgia-Pacific Corp., forever blocking the opportunity for us to choose them to dignify a park worthy of its name . . . . We thus wrote the following letter to Georgia-Pacific (signed by Cohelan and 34 other congressmen):
>
> ". . . Since the entire question of the precise lines and acreage of the proposed park should be finally determined some time next spring, we hope that this request to suspend further logging [in some 3,000 acres adjacent to the Senate boundary] will be favorably considered."
>
> Georgia-Pacific answered:
>
> ". . . it is necessary for us to do some harvesting in this area in order to run our plants on an economically sound basis. For the above reason and in the interest of our employees, our stock holders and good forest management and indeed as a corporate citizen, we respectfully must decline your request."

6. Mr. Cohelan then said, "The second largest lumbering concern in the world says it cannot accord the House the same concern it voluntarily gave the Senate . . . . I deplore this indifference to the public interest."

7. It is important to place G-P's urgent desire to proceed into the proper context:

The company's profits last year were 50 million dollars. This year, by all reports, prospects are better still. The redwood land it says it must cut represents *less than one one-thousandth of G-P's holdings*. It's not as though there are no other trees to cut for a few months, so Congress can do its work. We are speaking of 3,000 acres among three and one-half million.

8. Can anyone believe that by briefly refraining from logging one one-thousandth of its acreage Georgia-Pacific will be doing a disservice to its employees and its stockholders?

As we've shown, this is not a company whose profits are perceptibly dependent on 3,000 acres. But what if it were, and a few cents per share *could* be realized at year's end? Do most G-P stockholders believe it worth the price all *other* Americans would pay? We suspect not.

9. What can be done?

If you are a G-P shareholder, let your management know what you think of its actions, which if not in formal contempt of Congress, are by any standard, contemptuous of it.

Or, if you are just a concerned citizen, write G-P; write your Congressmen; write the President. . . and let them know you consider that a redwood national park worthy of your children should not be sacrificed for one company's few pennies of profit per share. Thank you.

B. *The Park Expansion Battle, 1977-1978*

45.
The Redwood Industry: "There is Neither Need Nor Reason" to Expand the Park

Responding to environmentalist pressures for park expansion, the redwood lumber companies and unions issued a pamphlet in April 1975 on the "Proposed Expansion of the Redwood National Park: The Industry's View." An excerpt appears below. The document was jointly produced by three AFL-CIO affiliates—Western Council of Lumber Production and Industrial Workers, Redwood District Council of Lumber and Sawmill Workers, and Local 2592 Lumber and Sawmill Workers—as well as Arcata Redwood Company, Louisiana-Pacific Corporation, and Simpson Timber Company. This coalition also issued public appeals under the name of the "Save-Our-Jobs Committee."

INTRODUCTION

The world's tallest trees seem to attract controversy like giant, evergreen lightning rods. For more than a century, they inspired proposals for a national park in the coast redwoods, though the first serious effort was not made until 1879. Other attempts followed in 1911, 1920, and 1946. Meanwhile the State of California and citizen groups began their redwood park acquisition programs as early as 1901.

Finally, in 1968, the present National Park was established by a legislative taking of 28,000 acres, most of which had been owned by four timber products companies. The balance of the authorized 58,000 acres was to be rounded out by acquisition of miscellaneous governmental holdings and the anticipated inclusion of 27,500 acres of adjacent parklands owned by the State of California.

A ceiling cost of $92 million was authorized. In partial compensation to former landowners, 13,000 acres of the U.S. Forest Service's Northern Redwood Purchase Unit was made available in trade. Most of the remaining Federal obligation for compensation was left to be worked out by negotiations or by proceedings in the U.S. Court of Claims. In early 1975 these proceedings still had not been completed.

Also still in contention is the donation of three state parks considered in the 1968 Act. By 1975, not one acre of these State-owned redwoods had yet been transferred to Federal jurisdiction.

The ink was hardly dry on the Redwood National Park Act when those preservationist groups which had pressed so hard for its establishment gave notice that they would not accept the compromise represented by enabling legislation. They continued to agitate for their conception of a park twice as large as Congress believed it should be. With the aid of a body of misinformation and distorted facts, they now claim that enlargement of the Park is needed for recreation and sightseeing; that not enough *Sequoia sempervirens* has been preserved; that logging on higher watersheds endangers portions of the Park. None of these claims has received the support of the National Park Service or any Federal or State Administration—and with good reason, because the facts do not support the claims.

THE ISSUES

The present Park has cost far more than Congress believed it would cost.

Redwood National Park can be called a park of superlatives. It features the tallest trees in the world, the largest coast redwood tree, the longest stretch of park beach front on the Pacific Coast, and was the first to be acquired entirely by legislative taking—the instant seizure of private land to prevent escalating prices.

After more than a half-dozen years, the Park's potential is unrealized, and it has assumed other, less-pleasant superlatives. Among these is its cost. From the beginning, the authorized expenditure was higher than any other national park in history and was more expensive than all others combined. To date, acquisition costs of private land have been $167 million, including interest payments. This already is 81% above the originally authorized ceiling. Further payments of principal totaling at least $15 million, plus interest, are in contention and unsettled. Severance damage claims of up to $100 million, plus interest are an additional unsettled cost. In the size of its cost over-run alone, Redwood National Park has already surpassed the total amount of approximately $72 million available in fiscal 1975 from the Land and Water Conservation Fund for all National Park Service acquisitions nationwide.

Costs of enlarging the Park would be enormous.

Recent opinion surveys show two issues to be of paramount interest to the public: inflation and unemployment.[7] Redwood National Park extension proposals would aggravate both concerns.

It is now proposed that approximately 70,000 acres of timberlands and 4,000 acres of prairies and unstocked land be added to the Park. About 93% of the forested portion is rated as high-site land, capable of growing a large volume of continuous tree crops. Redwood type accounts for 83%. This combination indicates that the lands proposed for addition to the Park are among the most valuable and productive commercial forest lands in the country. Acquisition costs would be accordingly high.

> The immediate harvest value of sawtimber in the area, according to 1974 figures used by the county assessor, averages $135 per thousand board feet. Total volume of sawtimber (12 inches in diameter and larger) in the area proposed for addition is estimated at a minimum of 2.1 billion board feet. At 1974 values, the sawtimber alone is worth $275 million or more before application of any discount factor.
>
> The $275 million estimate does not consider the value of the land or young trees smaller than 12 inches in diameter. It does not include the value of improvements, consisting primarily of 340 miles of private roads. Nor are present unknowns such as loss of milling capacity and other severance costs included in the estimate.
>
> Park extension would cause the immediate withdrawal of enough timber to build about 200,000 homes, which would provide housing for more than half-a-million people.
>
> According to U.S. Forest Service estimates, each dollar of value represented by standing timber generates $25 in the nation's economy after harvest. On this basis, the gross loss from

[7]In the 1960s Georgia-Pacific employed about 1500 workers in the affected area, and in 1986 about 800.

a 74,000-acre Park expansion would eventually be more than $7 billion—spread across the land in lost payrolls, taxes, profits, jobs and homes.

These same timber lands under young-growth forest management are capable of producing new timber growth worth (at 1974 values) about $10 million each year. Using the $1-to-$25 multiplier, the increment loss would amount to $250 million a year—every year.

The National Park Service is now faced with a backlog of authorized, but unfunded parkland acquisitions across the country amounting to $572 million. Annual allocations for this purpose amount to about $70 million. Without increased appropriations, it would take at least eight years at this level to pay for commitments already made.

The Park Service contends with a staggering backlog of $2.3 billion in unfunded development needs. At the present level of funding, it would take more than two generations just to meet this deficit.

The Redwoods are saved.

Even if people have shown little interest in visiting their North Coast redwood parks, it is of no matter, say some advocates of Park extension; the objective is to protect a disappearing species and save the last of the redwoods.

Preservation of the best examples of coast redwoods began at the turn of the century. Today there are more than 181,000 acres of redwood parks and reserves in governmental ownership. They contain the tallest and largest specimens, the most northerly and southerly groves, and what loggers and preservationists alike agree are the finest forests. In land area, the redwood parklands are equivalent to a mile-wide forest stretching from Washington, D.C. to Youngstown, Ohio.

In a unique cooperative program combining public funds and private donations, more than one-third of all the superlative redwoods known to have existed and more than nine-tenths of those that exist today have been preserved in public ownership.

Governmental parks and reserves are the equivalent of 23% of the entire redwood commercial forest acreage.

In California and Oregon, about 75,000 acres of old-growth or virgin coast redwoods are found in more than 100 parks, reserves, campgrounds, wilderness areas and natural study areas administered by governmental agencies. This makes the coast redwood, qualitatively as well as quantitatively, the best protected species of tree in the United States.

According to ecologists who have studied the coast redwood, the species may well be overprotected. The unanimous concern of these scientists is that by artificially curtailing natural disturbances of fire, flood and siltation, park status will allow the law of plant succession to prevail. Robbed of its natural competitive advantages, the redwood in those parks is doomed to be replaced by lesser trees. One specialist states that ''Hemlock National Park'' may be our gift to later generations unless artificial manipulation of park vegetation is practiced in the future, or unless some redwood lands are left under management.

In Humboldt County, where the proposed Park additions would be made, there are already 82,669 acres of redwood reserves. If the virgin or old-growth redwood timber in these governmental ownerships were to be spaced in a line of standing trees five feet apart, they would form a forested wall reaching from San Francisco to New York City. . . .

Some proponents claim that extension of National Park boundaries is necessary to preserve more prairies, entire watersheds and other examples of the redwood spectrum. But ''most of the redwood province is already represented in parks,'' according to the California Department of Parks and Recreation. ''There is no need to acquire additional lands.''

Within the authorized boundaries of Redwood National Park, visitors may see three natural prairies, a scenic river mouth, a scenic river valley, a significant waterway, the entire watersheds of eight streams, a geologic fault, rugged coastal associates of inland form features, a characteristic waterway, lake and lagoon. . . .

Essentially all of the best redwood groves in the watersheds of Redwood Creek are already located within the boundaries of Redwood National Park.

"There aren't any last redwoods," concluded a former president of the Save-the-Redwoods League. "The redwoods are saved."

Areas proposed for enlargement of the present Park are remote and rugged. Even the annexation of 74,000 acres would add less than half of the privately owned watershed lands of Redwood Creek. About 90% of the drainage, according to a 1973 report of the Department of the Interior, has been harvested and reforested at some time during the last four decades. These proposed additions not only fail to meet national park standards of quality, but would add nothing to make the Park more attractive to the public.

Park watersheds are protected.

The proposed extension of Redwood National Park boundaries is often rationalized by the contention that public acquisition of upstream lands is necessary to provide downstream protection from the effects of erosion.

Usually cited in support of this contention is the case of Bull Creek in Humboldt Redwoods State Park, where flooding two decades ago caused damage to trees in Rockefeller Forest. There could hardly be a less valid example. One-tenth the size of Redwood Creek drainage, and located 60 miles away, Bull Creek is appreciably different—as are all other watersheds—in soil composition, topography, rainfall, vegetative cover, aspect, fire history, human influences and floodproneness. A major difference is that the forests of the 27 square-mile Bull Creek basin are Douglas fir type, with a small percentage of redwoods concentrated in the 690-acre Rockefeller Grove of the lower valley. Firs and other conifers differ from redwoods in being unable to regrow naturally as quickly after logging to green the land and provide cover. Nor can any other commercial species match the redwood stump's wide-ranging, shallow root system that remains alive after logging to help keep the soil in place.

The Bull Creek flood of 1955 came with record "thousand-year" rains, and followed a decade of disastrous forest fires, land-clearing for agriculture, over-grazing, and logging practices on the watershed that would not meet today's state forest practice rules. None of these man-caused effects has occurred in areas adjacent to Redwood National Park. The Bull Creek damage was caused by a series of accidentally formed debris dams that suddenly released walls of water to undercut streambanks and topple trees. By contrast, the tremendous "2,000-year" floods of 1964-65 on the North Coast caused no additional damage to the large redwoods in Rockefeller Forest. Though the entire Bull Creek basin has been acquired by the State, periodic flooding continues, just as soil samples show it has for at least 35 centuries. . . .

After more than a century of harvesting operations, there exists no example where *redwood* logging has caused unnatural damage to downstream park resources.

During recent years, thorough studies of Redwood National Park watersheds in Humboldt County have been made by the Department of the Interior (1973), the U.S. Department of Agriculture in cooperation with the California Department of Water Resources (1970), the National Park Service (1964, 1967), the California Resources Agency (1966), Humboldt State University (1963), and several private consultants (1966, 1969). Not one of these professional surveys recommended public acquisition of lands beyond the authorized boundaries as a means of protecting the Park from the effects of erosion or possible flooding.

Authorities concur that Park-related drainages, in common with most others in the Redwood Region, are subject to periodic erosion, flooding and siltation. They further point out that these natural forces are an essential element in maintaining the groves of huge trees found on parkland flats and benches. The interagency North Coast watershed study of 1970 found that 80% to 90% of stream sediment in the area is attributable to natural conditions and not connected with logging.

"Most of the streambank erosion in Redwood Creek appears to be a natural occurrence," the analysis concluded.

The Conference Report accompanying the Redwood National Park Act authorized the Secretary of the Interior to make agreements with owners of Park watershed areas which will assure land management practices affording "as full protection as is reasonably possible" to Park resources. "No acquisition (beyond the specified 58,000 acres) shall be effectuated other than by donation."

Following analysis of the watershed surveys made in the 278 square-mile Redwood Creek drainage, the Park Service and industrial owners of commercial forests in watersheds above the Park in 1974 cooperated in drafting an elaborate set of timber-harvesting guidelines. These agreements cover essentially all of the concerns about Park protection that have been expressed by the Park Service, its watershed consultants and by conservationists. The guidelines are the most restrictive ever applied to private timberlands. They are effective not only in a 21 square-mile "buffer zone" surrounding Park boundaries in the Redwood Creek area, but also cover specified critical areas and road-building in much of the rest of the watershed. The harvesting guidelines, unprecedented in the history of either park or forest management, are now in effect. . . .

Concurrently, the rules and regulations of California's Forest Practice Act of 1973 have become effective. With the force of law, the rules prescribe stringent requirements—area by area, based on soil types—which must be met before, during and after a harvesting-reforestation operation. The Act's conditions governing watershed safeguards and productivity standards are considered by the Sierra Club to be "far and away the nation's toughest."

Forestlands adjacent to the Park are subject to many other laws and regulations governing scenic values, water quality, fish habitat and watershed protection. These are administered by the California Department of Fish and Game, the Coastal Zone Conservation Commission and the Water Quality Control Board. Not one of these agencies has recorded a violation of the laws and regulations entrusted to its jurisdiction in areas adjacent to Redwood National Park.

The primary assurance of watershed protection on industrial forestland is often overlooked. That is the business philosophy and performance record of the companies having responsibility for stewardship of the land. In Humboldt County, these firms are permanent. Their basic asset is the land and its ability to produce crops of timber in perpetuity. The land is managed accordingly.

The park has failed to meet promises and expectations.

Three years of controversy preceding establishment of the Park culminated in governmental promises and predictions that it would satisfy the esthetic, economic and recreational expectations of those interested in or affected by the Park.

Citizens of the North Coast area were assured a new era of prosperity. Timber products operators were given hopes of Federal income tax relief and accelerated harvest of timber on the nearby Six Rivers National Forest. Displaced workers would receive job retraining, employment in new public works programs, and family financial assistance. The citizens of America were promised a park that would be "the crown jewel of the National Park System," providing a million annual visits by the end of the fifth year. None of the promises have come true. . . . In its first five years of operation—the chronological benchmark optimistically set by the Department of the Interior—the Park has produced the following record:

Humboldt County, where two-thirds of the Federally acquired land is located, suffered a 7% drop in timber industry employment while similar employment state-wide climbed 8%.

The County's population gained at a rate less than half that of the rest of California.

Annual timber production in the County dropped more than 9% while state-wide timber production rose 2%. About three-quarters of all old-growth timber in Humboldt County is government-owned and exempt from property taxation. Taxes on remaining private timber have more than doubled. Per capita assessed valuation has risen 31%.

Though starting at zero, attendance at Redwood National Park in combination with its three adjacent redwood state parks increased at a rate below the average of other national parks.[8]

The annual timber cut on the Six Rivers National Forest, which was supposed to be increased, actually declined by 18%. During the same period, average annual cut on other national forests rose 3%.

Though not entirely attributable to establishment of the Park, unemployment in Humboldt County has been classed by the State as ''persistent,'' and during the first five years of the Park's existence reached an average annual rate nearly twice as high as the national jobless rate.

Some of the defaulted promises and predictions can be traced to lack of funds for Park development and visitor facilities. Appropriations for capital improvements have been made at an average rate of about $200,000 a year—6% of the $3.1 million recognized as needed and once promised by Ex-Secretary of the Interior Stewart H. Udall.

The assumption in the 1968 Act that the State of California would donate its three adjacent redwood parks to complete the 58,000-acre total has not been realized. If the Federal government were to purchase these State lands at current value, the cost would approach several hundred million dollars.

Among the reasons sometimes advanced for extending Redwood National Park boundaries is the presumed need for more recreational land to accommodate more hikers, campers, boaters and picnickers, and to make more superlative redwoods available for sightseers.

The facts and the disappointing five-year record fail to support these conclusions.

In 1973, the total of visitor hours spent at the Park was less than 7% of the average of all of the 298 other units in the National Park System; it was less than 3% of the combined annual average for the 74 other units in the ''natural'' category.

Proposals for Park expansion center in Humboldt County, where 68% of the Park's Federal ownership is located but where only 8% of the total visits are recorded.

The Redwood Creek area, where most of the proposed additions would be made, and which includes the grove of tallest trees in the world, has proved to be among the Park's least popular attractions. Only 2,863 visits were recorded in 1973 in any part of the entire 10 mile-long portion of the valley in Federal ownership.

The average visitor spends less than one hour in the Park, costing American taxpayers more than $3 per visitor-hour for operating and maintenance expenses alone. The sum does not include costs of acquisition, costs of interest payments, costs of severance damages, or costs of capital improvements and visitor facilities.

Indicators such as highway traffic counts and taxes on hotel/motel rooms show that the Redwood National Park area lags behind increases in state-wide averages.

There has been no gain in hotel/motel capacity in the gateway communities of Orick and Crescent City since the Park was established. No camping spaces have been developed by the National Park Service.

Secretary of the Interior Udall stated during hearings which considered establishment of the Park that it would, after five years, provide an increase of 950,000 visitor days per year over the present visitation to the state parks within the proposed Park's boundaries. But according to Park Service figures, visits in 1973 totaled 210,491. The visitor-*hour* total of 204,333 indicates that the average visit was less than one hour long. . . .

Visitor attendance at the three adjacent state parks increased at a rate no faster than that recorded at other coast redwood parks in the State Park System.

[8]Attendance in 1980 was 539,000 visitors, well below the 2.5 million once predicted by the Park Service for 1983.

Recreational activities available to Park visitors in the Redwood Creek area are already offered on the adjacent private lands without taxpayer cost. Seasonal hunting for deer and other game, prohibited within the Park, is an added attraction on adjacent tree farms.

More than half of California's 100 million acres is government-owned and available for public recreation. The state has more acreage in the National Park System than any other and possesses 15.5% of the country's total national park acreage. No need has been demonstrated in California for additions to its national parks, certainly not at Redwood National Park, which is located in one of the least accessible portions of the state.

Additions to the Park would cause severe economic impacts.

Unlike most acquisitions of private land for park purposes, the withdrawal of productive timberland, and especially high-value redwoods, produces economic and social effects reaching far into the future.

Among these consequences is the crippling or forced abandonment of carefully prepared harvesting programs intended to assure continuing productivity of the land and an ongoing source of raw materials to local wood-processing plants.

Before Redwood National Park was established, the Park Service reported that the redwood industry would reach a point of balance between annual cubic-foot growth of timber (five inches in diameter and larger) and annual average cut of timber in 1975. The one-to-one ratio of sawtimber growth (12 inches and larger) and annual cut would not be reached until 1983, when the industry could sustain its current level of production into the future.

The 1968 legislative taking of 26,500 acres of industrial forestland for the Park not only removed many years' production from the carefully tended inventory of old-growth timber, but upset the critical age-class distribution of trees upon which the redwood industry was relying for future stability.

Humboldt County is timber-producing country. Attractive as it may seem to concrete-bound residents of metropolitan areas, California's remote north-western corner is destined to remain timber-producing country. Its economy is about 80% dependent on timber and the land that grows it.

The contributions of the travel business, meetings, conventions and recreation-tourism combined represent only 8% of Humboldt County's economic base. A large proportion of this is generated by local residents. In this rainiest area of the state, about 85% of all tourist travel occurs during a three-month period. There is little realistic expectation that the area's economic base can expand much beyond dependence on timber, and there is no good reason why it should if timber production and wood processing is not disrupted. In the case of agriculture, there is little potential for expansion beyond its present contribution of 6%, simply because the climate and rugged topography of the area is unsuitable. Commercial fisheries are approaching maximum limitations and account for slightly less than 6%. Any hoped-for expansion of the economy rests with the timber industry. In turn, economic expansion would require a dependable supply of raw material.

Among other adverse effects on the local economic base which might reasonably be expected from expansion of the existing Park are:

> Loss of jobs would eventually exceed 750 in the timber products industry. An additional 1,100 jobs would eventually be lost among those indirectly dependent on utilization of the timber resource on the affected acreage.
>
> Annual growth capacity of new timber on the lands which would be taken by Park expansion averages 1,843 board feet per acre. This ranks the area among the most productive timberland in the world. If left in private management, the land will grow an average of 130 million board feet of wood annually. Converted to lumber and plywood, this is enough to build 10,000 or more homes a year—every year.
>
> As a by-product of the area's annual growth capacity, the left-overs from this logging

and manufacturing are expected to provide raw material for manufacturing 120 tons of pulp a day in perpetuity.

In Humboldt County, where more than one-quarter of the land is government-owned, private timber and timberland provided 31% of the assessed value (real property) tax base in 1974. Under the proposal for adding 74,000 acres to the existing Park, the County would lose 12% of its remaining taxable timber land acreage and 10% of the total assessed value of all real property within the County. Such losses would be permanent, penalizing local government and schools on an ongoing basis. The tax burden would necessarily be shifted to remaining sources of revenue.

> In the last decade, more than $125 million has been invested in three Humboldt County pulp and particle board mills. These year-round plants rely on chips made from once-wasted residues of lumber and plywood manufacture. A predictable supply of raw material—in delicate balance since 1968—obviously is vital.

CONCLUSIONS

Much remains to be done before a Redwood National Park as constituted by the enabling legislation of 1968 becomes a reality which was then envisioned. These imperatives include (1) the adoption of a master plan to determine the extent and timing of visitor facility development within the Park; (2) implementation of that plan; (3) completion of payments to former owners of what are now parkland; and (4) the fair testing of cooperative watershed protection measures recommended by the Act of 1968 as well as by subsequent investigations.

The exorbitant costs of adding to the Park would be in no way justifiable. Expenditure of hundreds of millions of tax dollars would add no more superlative redwoods, no more tourist attractions, and no more visitor facilities. It would provide no more protection to the surrounding watersheds than can be assured with present state forest practice legislation and national park harvesting guidelines. In addition to local economic and social disruptions, Park enlargement would divert huge sums which might he better expended in part on development of the existing Park and in part on acquisition and development of national parklands needed elsewhere.

The watersheds adjacent to the Park are now as well-protected as technology, human reason and skill will permit.

There is no demonstrable need for additional acreage to accommodate public recreation in the northern Redwood Region. Large areas of the present parks remain undeveloped and inaccessible.

While America's housing goals go largely unfilled, the need for new housing continues to grow. To satisfy this pressing socio-economic objective, it has become public policy and a national need to apply intensified management practices on the remaining commercial timberlands to meet the rising demand for renewable wood building materials.

With these national needs unmet, and amidst reports that curtailment of existing visitor facilities at other national parks may become necessary for lack of funds, the expenditure of large sums for such questionable acquisitions as proposed enlargement of Redwood National Park would be denying recreational opportunities elsewhere. Park Service professionals have testified that there is no longer a need for additional acreage in the "natural" category, such as Redwood National Park. The demand is, instead, for recreational type parks located where people can use and enjoy them.

America needs both its parks and its productive land base. Responsible stewardship requires decisions based on thoughtful planning and a balancing of values, rather than misguided emotionalism, if all the public's needs are to be satisfied.

46. Peggy Wayburn (The Sierra Club): "Time Has All But Run Out for the Virgin Redwoods"

In the course of this battle the Sierra Club became the most militant and effective national environmental group. Peggy Wayburn, a free-lance writer and Club activist (her husband was a vice president of the Club), wrote two articles on the topic— ''The Short Sorry History of Redwood National Park,'' and, ''The Redwoods: An Era Dying''—which are excerpted below.[9] *In them she tried to address directly some of the charges levelled in ''The Industry's View'' (excerpted above), including the job-loss problem.*

From ''The Short Sorry History of Redwood National Park''

On July 16, 1975, U.S. District Court Judge William T. Sweigert ruled in a case brought by the Sierra Club that the U.S. Department of the Interior had ''unreasonably and arbitrarily. . . refused and neglected'' to perform its duties in protecting the Redwood National Park in California from damage caused by logging on lands adjacent to the park. Sweigert ordered the department to take ''reasonable'' action by December 15th to gain protection for the park under terms of the National Park System Act, and especially the Redwood National Park Act, and to turn to Congress for additional funding if necessary. This decision was a vindication for conservationists, a major victory for the Sierra Club Legal Defense Fund, and a landmark in the field of environmental law as well, defining a trust concept which may set a highly useful precedent for public-lands management.

Judge Sweigert's decision also wrote another chapter in the sad, curious history of the Redwood National Park. Whether or not it will alter the course of that history, however, is another question, considering what has happened to this park in the seven years of its existence.

Here are the highlights of the sorry record:

1968

Having given away California's coastal redwoods (along with the other public lands of the West) a century earlier, Congress decides at long last to ''save'' them. After decades of logging, there are only fragments—totally about 200,000 acres—left of the once great two-million-acre primeval forest. Caught between enormous public pressure to establish a Redwood National Park and an outraged timber industry, which must sell back some of its remaining forests for such a park, Congress compromises. ''To preserve significant examples of the primeval coastal redwood (*Sequoia sempervirens*) forests and the streams and seashore with which they are associated for purposes of public inspiration, enjoyment, and scientific study,'' Congress puts together a park which is a hodgepodge of diverse areas totaling 56,205 acres in all. It includes three of California's finest state parks— Prairie Creek, Jedediah Smith, and Del Norte Redwoods—whose 28,000 acres are not included in the record $92,000,000 purchase price authorized. It takes in a thirty-three-mile strip of beach and coast, with the Redwood Highway running through it. It contains about two-thirds of the small, superb Lost Man Creek watershed in Humboldt County. The park's most controversial feature, however, is a seven-mile long, one-half-mile wide ''worm'' of primeval forest snaking up Redwood Creek to form an exceptionally vulnerable appendage to a meager, sprawling body. The reason for this curious corridor, which lies in the middle of extensive and active logging operations, is simple: it includes the little river flat where grows the tallest tree on earth, 367 feet high.

The Congress is aware, at least in part, of the precarious nature of this park design. Taking

[9] The first article appeared in the *Sierra Club Bulletin* (October 1975), 52-55, and the second in *Cry California*, XIII (Winter 1977), 19-23.

cognizance of the threat posed by logging adjacent to the park, the park act directs the Secretary of the Interior to take action "with particular attention to minimizing the siltation of the streams, damage to the timber, and assuring the preservation of the scenery within the boundaries of the National Park." Furthermore, the Congress states its intent "that clearcutting will not occur immediately around the Park." The Secretary of the Interior is therefore authorized to: (1) enlarge the boundaries of the park by adding approximately 2,000 acres at strategic places; (2) acquire a scenic corridor along specified sections of the Redwood Highway to screen unsightly, devastated, logged areas from park visitors' eyes; and (3) enter into management agreements with the timber companies logging adjacent to the park boundaries and to acquire less-than-fee interests—or an in-fee interest, if necessary—in buffer areas essential to "protect the timber, soil and streams" inside the park.

While not ideal, the powers accorded to the secretary are significant: using them, he can round out the park's 11,000 acres of previously unprotected old-growth forest to 13,000 acres, an increase of nearly twenty percent. He can also negotiate effectively with the timber industry—which intends to log right up to every park boundary—to establish adequate buffer zones. He can, in short, hold damage to the park to a minimum while new efforts are mounted to gain a more rational Redwood National Park. Conservationists who have fought long and hard for a "Pyrrhic victory" are not entirely discouraged. As soon as President Lyndon Johnson signs the Redwood National Park Act in early October, 1968, the Sierra Club importunes Interior Secretary Stewart Udall to exercise his authority promptly to enlarge the new park and give it maximum protection. . . . Mr. Udall fails to act.

1969

Endless studies of the Redwood National Park commence. A twelve-man Redwood National Park Master Planning Team is appointed to consider the park's problems and make recommendations for development: two of the team members are from the Save the Redwoods League, another from the Sierra Club.

Dr. Edward Stone of the University of California, Berkeley, heads an official study which documents what everyone already knows: the new park has major problems. It lacks watershed protection. It is situated in highly erosive and unstable terrain. ". . .the fate of critical portions of the Park lies in the hands of private landowners in the watersheds tributary to the Park." Stone recommends a substantial buffer zone and controlled cutting around the park. The next decade, he notes, will be critical to its future.

While the Park Service is studying the situation, the Bureau of Outdoor Recreation is negotiating with timber companies, Georgia Pacific (later Louisiana Pacific), Simpson, and Arcata, to acquire the lands authorized for park purchase. The Bureau of Land Management (BLM) is surveying the park boundaries. The Forest Service is evaluating its forest holdings which will be used in exchange. The industry is clearcutting the slopes of Redwood Creek.

Gordon Robinson, Sierra Club forester, responds to the Stone report by proposing specific, stringent regulations for logging in areas adjacent to the park. He declares that "clearcutting the Redwood Creek slopes is intolerable." National Park Service forester Ted Hatzimanolis rebuts Robinson: clearcutting of Redwood Creek is not intolerable, he states, if clearcut areas are no larger than fifteen acres.

In November, the National Park Service produces a new "study." Called a "Concept Paper for Proposed Buffer and Watershed Management," it rejects the Stone report, the Robinson rebuttal, the Hatzimanolis surrebuttal, and industry's practices. It proposes instead to "Continue and Expand Coordinated Management and Research Objectives Heading Toward Elimination or Control of All Potentially Destructive Inputs Within the Entire Watershed of Redwood Creek."

The Sierra Club writes Undersecretary of the Interior Russell Train that "Time is running out quickly [for the Redwood National Park]. . . once again we face legislation by chainsaw. . . the logging companies are moving in to define the character of the land before park boundary surveys are even completed.'' Mr. Train takes no action.

1970

Minority members of the Redwood National Park Master Plan Team urge action, but get none. The studies continue.

The Sierra Club urges the new Secretary of the Interior, Rogers Morton, to intercede for the Redwood Park. Mr. Morton does not act.

The National Park Service makes a first feeble attempt to set up a buffer management plan with one timber company, Georgia Pacific. The proposed agreement gets nowhere. Another set of guidelines is drafted, but no action results. The Bureau of Outdoor Recreation goes on negotiating costs with the timber companies. The Bureau of Outdoor Recreation goes on negotiating costs with the timber companies. The BLM goes on surveying. The timber companies go on cutting.

Boundaries of the national park are irrevocably defined by logging in Bridge Creek, McArthur-Elam Creek, and Lost Man Creek. Clearcutting increasingly mutilates the small, exquisite watershed of Skunk Cabbage Creek, an area of prime park potential.

1971

Frustrated by inaction in the Department of the Interior and the National Park Service, the Sierra Club calls for and gets Senate oversight hearings on the Redwood national Park. Only one witness—representing the Sierra Club—calls the situation deplorable, even desperate. The National Park Service and the Bureau of Outdoor Recreation say they have no problems. . . . No action results.

The ''Preliminary Draft Master Plan'' is released. It deals almost entirely in concepts for interpretation of the new park. A minority report points out the need for an optimum park, asks for ways to gain better boundaries and protection, and for strict land-use controls in adjacent areas. . . . No action is taken.

The Sierra Club legally petitions Secretary of the Interior Morton to meet his obligations to protect the Redwood Park. . . . No action results. But secretly, the National Park Service does at last offer specific suggestions to the secretary of ways to enlarge boundaries, to establish scenic corridors, and to acquire management easements as well as in-fee lands along key tributary streams. . . . The recommendations, however, are not implemented.

The Redwood National Park superintendent and the three logging companies in Redwood Creek ''agree in principle'' that buffer-zone management is possible. Negotiations for ''harvesting guidelines'' continue.

A Park Service spokesman notes that the buffer-zone issue is ''extremely volatile,'' and that the ''timber companies have been sensitive. . . to any overview that would inhibit their freedom of action on their lands.''

Another 10,000 acres of primeval redwoods are liquidated in the redwood region, much of them in the Redwood Creek watershed. The old-growth redwood resource is being rapidly depleted.

Park visitors wishing to view the Tall Trees Grove must walk eight miles up Redwood Creek (and back), or trespass on lumber company property to get there.

1972

Assistant Secretary of the Interior Nathaniel Reed pays his first visit to the Redwood National Park, and appoints an interdisciplinary Redwood Task Force under Dr. Richard Curry of the

Interior Department to study the situation. Members of the task force include experts in geology, geomorphology, hydrology, forestry, aquatic biology, and a representative of the Earth Satellite Corporation. The Sierra Club requests a copy of the Curry task force report.

A revised Preliminary Draft Master Plan for the Redwood Park is issued. It is virtually the same as the earlier version, but the minority report has been deleted.

Another 10,000 acres of primeval redwoods are liquidated. Park visitors continue to dodge logging trucks on roads through the park.

The photograhic survey of the Redwood Creek watershed prepared by the Earth Satellite Corporation documents gravely increased damage caused by tractors, clearcutting, roads carved out of steep slopes, too-small or poorly located culverts, and year-round logging.

1973

In January, the Sierra Club sues Secretary of the Interior Morton under the Freedom of Information Act to obtain release of the Curry task force report. The court rules in the club's favor. The report contains frightening information: masses of soil and debris loosed by logging are moving across the terrain and down the watercourses of the Redwood National Park. There is accelerated landslide activity and windthrow. Raised stream beds and changing stream currents, along with streamborne sediments, are undercutting banks and threatening the "unique redwood vegetation community" inside the park. The "wormlike appendage" of the park is especially threatened. Protection is impossible without strict land-use controls outside the park boundary. Ninety percent of the primeval forest in Redwood Creek has now been logged.

The Curry report recommends (1) no logging on slide-prone areas, (2) a two-year moratorium on logging within seventy-five feet of critical tributary streams, and (3) in-fee acquisition, costing $15 million to $16 million, of an 800 -foot buffer zone. The Office of Management and Budget flatly refuses to approve release of the Curry report to the public without deleting the recommendations for in-fee acquisition.

Based on the findings in the Curry report, the Sierra Club initiates new legal action against the Secretary of the Interior to force protective action for the beleaguered park.

The park superintendent reopens negotiations with the timber industry on "harvesting guidelines," making new and major concessions. The three companies respond that, since each is different, each needs a special agreement. Negotiations continue; so does logging.

The sound of the chainsaws now whines loudly along the edge of many areas of the park. Logs so huge they must be halved to fit on truck beds keep rolling out of Redwood Creek and down the park roads. The waters of Redwood Creek are heavy and grey with sediment.

The National Park Service initiates a new study to get "hard technical data." Richard Janda of the United States Geological Survey heads the three-year study which is to monitor the park's condition and evaluate the buffer management proposals made to date.

1974

California Congressmen Phillip Burton and John Burton introduce a bill to enlarge the Redwood National Park. The House has its mind on other matters and takes no action.

All three logging companies are now operating in one place or another inside what might have been the 800-foot buffer zone: Louisiana Pacific clearcuts a forty-one-acre patch inside it.

The three sets of "harvest guidelines" proposed by the National Park Service are again being negotiated with the individual companies. The guidelines are weaker than before, shot though with "exceptions" and "deviations." They allow for twenty-acre clearcut patches. There are no provisions for enforcement. There has been no public input into their development.

The banks along Redwood Creek at the Tall Trees Grove are being visibly undercut. One of the larger trees in the grove falls across Redwood Creek. Around the base of the world's tallest tree the silt is piling higher and higher.

California passes strict new logging regulations, which apply throughout the state.

1975

In the redwood region, inflation and the shortage of mortgage money for housing are taking their toll. The industry blames the conservationists and the Redwood Park for the region's ills. Two huge trees are felled by vandals in the Ladybird Johnson Grove.

The state of California attempts to enforce restrictive forestry requirements, then partly backs down; logging resumes full tilt, though perhaps under slightly better regulations than before. The state recommends new studies in the Redwood National Park watershed.

Congressman Phillip Burton again introduces a bill to enlarge the Redwood National Park. This one is cosponsored by fifty-one of his colleagues.

Two lumber companies sign "harvesting guideline" agreements, but must wait official confirmation in Washington, D.C. Meanwhile, the guidelines have been so weakened that they are essentially meaningless: they will allow the entire "buffer zone" to be clearcut up to park boundaries within seven years.

As a new effort to protect the park gains momentum, the timber companies logging in Redwood Creek join with AFL-CIO members to produce an expensive brochure entitled "The Industry's View." This repeats old, familiar anti-park arguments. It fails to mention the depressed housing market or the national recession, and again blames the present park for the redwood region's economic woes, present and future.

It is reliably estimated that only six or seven years supply of old-growth redwood remains to be cut, well under 100,000 acres. When this is gone, so will be the redwood industry as it presently exists.

California's leading newspapers begin to headline the news that the world's tallest tree is threatened by encroaching logging. One states that $163 million—not $92 million—has already been spent for the park, which may be almost literally going down the drain. Figures from the Department of the Interior put land acquisition costs at $117,082,147.88, including interest charges.

Richard Janda, in a deposition for the Sierra Club suit, admits that he may be conducting a "post mortem" of the Redwood National Park rather than monitoring a study.

District Judge William T. Sweigert rules for the Sierra Club and directs the Secretary of the Interior to take "reasonable steps within a reasonable time" to protect the Redwood National Park.

The redwoods keep on falling, falling, falling. . . .

Thus the hard fact emerges that court victory or no, time has all but run out for the virgin redwoods. The great primeval forests are now nearly gone. The best chance we have to rescue the Redwood National Park lies in passage of the Burton bill. Under the bill's terms, another 11,000 acres of primeval redwoods would be spared the axe, and the present park would be enlarged by 73,470 acres of desperately needed, although cutover, watershed terrain. With careful management, this wounded land perhaps can recover. In any case, acquisition of the watershed offers the only opportunity there will ever be to gain real protection for the Redwood National Park we have, and for a species that survived for 165 million years—until we found it.

From "The Redwoods: An Era Dying"

. . .Most of California's North Coast region is, in fact, hurting economically more than any other region in the state. And while this is nothing new, for economic problems have been chronic in this area, the present situation is different. After more than 125 years of intensive operation, the logging industry here is finally reaching the end of its old-growth forest resource. An era is dying.

CHOOSING UP SIDES

The scenario of the last days of this era is noteworthy. The timber industry is determined to log on as it always has, to the last of its great trees. Environmentalists are determined to gain expansion of the hard-won Redwood National Park in Humboldt County while there is still a chance. In a curious alliance, organized labor is not only siding with an industry that has a violently anti-union history (there are still no woodworkers' unions in the redwood region), it is providing shock troops for industry's battle against park expansion. A good segment of the local community is joining enthusiastically in the fray, on the side of what it likes to call "Big Timber." Thus, while the last of the old-growth forests are falling, the issue of jobs versus environment has moved onto center stage and into the spotlight. Furthermore, everyone in the cast of characters is convinced that God is on his side, and emotions are at fever heat.

"What ever happened to private ownership of land and the Bill of Rights?" members of the industry ask plaintively. "This was our land, our forests and our home long before the environmentalists came. We are fighting to preserve what is ours." LOGGER IS NOT A DIRTY WORD, proclaimed a recent ad in Humboldt County. (By inference, *environmentalist* is.) "Most residents of our county fear we will be swallowed alive in continual grabs for parklands. The environmentalists want to force us out of work, off our land, and out of the county."

Organized labor was hardly less vehement in the recent hearings on Congressman Phillip Burton's bill to expand Redwood National Park, and spokesmen for the AFL-CIO accused environmentalists of being cold-hearted zealots who care nothing for the working man. Environmentalists, in turn, insist that they are as humanitarian as labor leaders and that the future economy of the North Coast region is going to suffer irrevocable losses with or without expansion of the park.

Who is right? What are the realities of the economic situation in the North Coast counties, present and future? What will happen if the park is expanded? Is the issue *really* jobs versus environment, or is it more complex?

In looking for answers to these questions, it is useful to review briefly some of the economic background of the region.

Unfortunately, some of the facts are not and never will be known. For example, the millions of dollars that have flowed out of the forests of Humboldt, Del Norte and Mendocino counties cannot be accurately tallied, for logging began so long ago. It is even difficult to determine how many millions of dollars are currently flowing out to these counties, but it may be significant that Arcata Redwood Company, one of the principal companies now in action, just reported the best quarter in its history.

How will jobs be affected?

Since jobs have become the crux of the present crisis, let us start with the employment picture. As noted, it has historically been highly unstable. The job force in all three counties has expanded and contracted like an accordion, responding to the pressures of the timber market. Since the mid-fifties, however, when the Douglas-fir bonanza brought the last of the great good times, the accordion has been squeezing ever slimmer. Employment has gone steadily downhill.

Not only have there been fewer jobs every year, but the rate of increase in unemployment has been exceptionally high, especially since 1970. The unemployment rate stood at 11 percent in Del Norte County in 1970; by 1975 it had almost doubled to 20 percent. During the same five-year period, unemployment in Humboldt County moved up from 10 to 15 percent, and in Mendocino County it zoomed from 8 to 15 percent. (By contrast, unemployment in the state as a whole averaged 10 percent in 1975.)

Coinciding with the increase in unemployment, there has been a steady erosion of jobs in the timber industry. Since 1955, the decline of both traditional jobs and workers in the woods and in the mills has been striking: from nearly 13,000 people employed in timber and related wood industries in Humboldt County in 1955, the number dropped to a little over 6,000 in 1975. In Mendocino county, the number has declined by one half from more than 6,000 to 3,000. In Del Norte county, the industry job market has declined most dramatically of all, from around 3,000 in 1955 to about 1,000 twenty years later.

Adding perspective to these statistics is the fact that in the 1950's, approximately half the job force in Humboldt and Mendocino counties was directly involved with logging or associated wood-products industry. Today, the percentage of workers in this category in the two counties has shrunk to 25 percent. In Del Norte County, the figure is just 30 percent.

Along with the loss of traditional jobs in the North Coast country in recent years, there has also been an increase in seasonal layoffs. Workers in the woods—sawyers, buckers, fallers and so forth—customarily worked six to eight months a year, the length of employment being dictated by the weather. At the same time, most mill workers had been steadily employed.

In the early 1960's, however, a trend of seasonal layoffs emerged in the mills as well as in the woods. Now many mill workers are laid off after six or eight months of work. Other mill employees work only every other week. Conservative statistics estimate that at least 25 percent of timber industry employees were hit with seasonal unemployment in 1975.

Depletion of the forests

Several obvious factors have influenced the job picture in the North Coast counties. There has been the steady depletion of the resource, the old-growth redwood and Douglas-fir forests. As the trees have been cut down, countless small operators—the little mills, and the "gyppo" or independent loggers, who contract with owners to cut trees and deliver them to mills the loggers do not own—have lost their supplies and simply gone out of business. At the same time, the traditionally family-owned and independent larger companies have—with one or two notable exceptions—become part of multinational corporations such as Georgia Pacific (now Louisiana Pacific).

Automation has been increasing in the woods as well as in the mills. Older equipment, scaled to handle the enormous old-growth trees, has not only been wearing out, it has become ever more obsolete. Virtually all new equipment, much of it designed for anticipated second-growth operations, is more and more automated. As a recent study of regional unemployment puts it: "Technological development results in diminishing labor requirements to accomplish each of the steps needed to convert standing trees to finished products."

National and international demands for timber for housing starts and other building have also, of course, played roles in the North Coast job market. The redwood and Douglas-fir logs formerly milled and used locally or nationally have flowed increasingly out of the state and out of the country, a large percentage going to Japan. As old-growth redwood and Douglas-fir become ever scarcer, however, the demand is increasing inexorably and the price per board foot is skyrocketing (as anyone buying wood products well knows). But while supply and demand have directly affected employment in the past, today's increasing scarcity of old-growth wood is swelling industry profits rather than boosting the local job market.

The industry, plainly, would like to log on to the end without interference. Estimates as to how long that might take vary. Some suggest that the supply of saw timber in the North Coast counties will be exhausted in a matter of five years. Daniel D. Oswald of the U.S. Forest Service's Pacific Northwest Forest and Range Experimental Station predicts that the supply will be generally depleted by 1990, with or without expansion of Redwood National Park. (About 9,000 acres of old-growth forest lands—approximately one year's logging supply—would be removed from commercial production by park expansion.)

When the old growth is gone

A few conclusions can be drawn from the foregoing. Not only has industry-related employment in the North Coast area declined during past decades, it will inevitably continue to decline as automation increases and old-growth supplies disappear. Once the old-growth forests are gone, there will be a wrenching readjustment. And clearly, the local economy of the area must have another base if it is to survive.

The industry contends that its second-growth operations will be ready to supply this base when the time comes *if*, but only *if*, it is allowed to cut all its present old-growth holdings. The truth of this argument has not been demonstrated, and many experts state flatly that it is impossible for the industry to develop a viable large-scale, second-growth operation in time to take up the anticipated slack in employment. (Serious widespread efforts to regenerate forests in the North Coast counties date only from the 1960's, when national attention was focused onto redwood logging practices. As efforts to establish Redwood National Park escalated, tree-farms signs popped up like mushrooms on industry properties.)

Since it takes coastal redwoods about 200 years to gain maturity (and closer to 500 years to approximate most of the old growth now being logged), future logging in the region will necessarily depend upon immature redwood timber or other faster-growing species of trees such as native Douglas fir and the Monterey pine, which is being introduced to replace the redwood in many places. (A recent Humboldt County guidebook tells the tourist that emphasis in the logging industry has already shifted from redwood to Douglas fir.)

Under any circumstances, second-growth logging operations, whenever they do get under way on a major scale and whatever species they consume, will be totally different from the old-growth operations now winding down. They will require few of the customary skills and they will be highly automated, which will result in an even more greatly reduced labor force.

Is there another natural resource base, then, to which the counties can turn? Unfortunately, the impact of more than a century and a quarter of logging has greatly altered the environment. Many have been damaged or destroyed. For example, such anadromous fish as steelhead and salmon, which might have provided the basis for a large-scale commercial fishery, have been radically reduced in number during the last century. A major factor in this reduction has been the thousands of miles of North Coast rivers and streams devastated by atrocious logging practices. Now choked with slash, their shade removed, their gravels seriously disturbed or eroded away, former spawning grounds have been rendered useless.

Loss of water quality is another result of logging activities. The silt burden carried by the Eel River, for instance, is now greater than that of the Mississippi, which drains half a continent. As another example, the loss of topsoil and the dislocation of soil structure occasioned by the use of massive logging equipment on unstable soils have altered the water table in parts of the region, thus affecting water supplies to agricultural lands, homes and communities. Naturally productive forestlands have also been damaged severely and in some places, made sterile. Jobs and business opportunities that would stem from a productive natural environment are nonexistent.

What about the tourists?

Tourism, the second largest industry in the North Coast counties, does promise a somewhat diversified economic base in the future, but much needs to be done to develop it. Recreational opportunities are limited: as the fishery has been altered, both sport and commercial fishing have suffered. The cool and foggy northern climate discourages sun-worshippers (although it can be delightfully warm a short distance inland), and while the beaches are magnificent, the swimming asks for wetsuits. (It has been proposed, half seriously, that certain North Coast rivers—the Eel, the Mad, the Van Dusen—might be dammed to provide water-based recreational facilities, but the present cost, according to an experienced construction engineer, would be "out of sight.")

The California state redwood parks as well as Redwood National Park have provided the major tourist attractions to the region in the past. There is serious concern that Redwood National Park may be injured beyond recovery by the increasingly intense logging going on in areas directly surrounding it. Protection of the park is a primary goal of those who seek its enlargement, for the quality of the park experience suffers simply from the sound of logging trucks and falling trees.

But the development of tourism will require a considerable change in attitude on the part of a sizable portion of the community. Many of the local business people appear to be wedded to the idea that "Big Timber is our way of life. . .and it always will be." It is interesting that in many handouts to tourists, little or no mention is made of Redwood National Park. A "towering creature named Bigfoot" gets equal billing with the "towering redwoods." Visits to mills and tree farms are recommended above visits to state parks. Rock and fossil hunting and viewing Victorian mansions are featured as major recreational opportunities.

Where does the proposed expansion of Redwood National Park fit into the future economy of the North Coast counties? Opponents of park expansion, both in the industry and in organized labor, argue that the present park has already produced a serious setback in the local economy and that its expansion would bring certain doomsday.

In light of certain facts, it is hard to understand the basis for this argument. Since establishment of the park in 1968, the three major mills affected have actually increased their annual lumber output. Louisiana Pacific's Samoa mill, for example, produced 623 million board feet in 1965 and 83 million in 1976; their Big Lagoon mill produced 34 million board feet in 1965 as compared with 46 million in 1976. Furthermore, owing to the exchange of federally owned old-growth timberlands (primarily in Del Norte County) for those in private hands, the available supply of old-growth timber was scarcely diminished by establishment of the national park. (It is noteworthy that the two counties with the most serious recent unemployment, Del Norte and Mendocino, are outside the principal park area.) The industry also received millions of dollars in compensation for land acquired for the park, and will receive millions more if expansion proceeds. It is paradoxical that the lumber industry should be booming while unemployment is increasing so alarmingly.

The hope of restoration

Proponents of park expansion believe that by insuring a major recreation resource, an enlarged and protected park would provide the base for a greatly expanded and more stable tourist industry. Moreover, legislation now before Congress to enlarge Redwood National Park contains an interesting and promising new approach to the jobs problem. Incorporated in the bill introduced by Senator Alan Cranston is an imaginative and practical plan to rehabilitate and restore logged-over areas in the park around Redwood Creek. According to Meca Wawona, author of a report recently issued by the Center for Education and Manpower Resources in Ukiah, this program could employ an estimated 2,100 to 2,500 workers in the first year of operation. The jobs would be directed toward erosion control, restoration of natural drainages, stabilization of gullies, slash disposal, recontouring of hillsides, and other rehabilitation. Eventually, the restored areas could support improved timber production, renewed fisheries, and improved recreational opportunities.

This proposal has unique advantages. For instance, the program of intensive labor has been designed to insure year-round employment. The skills required for the work would include many used in logging. (A principal objection to earlier job programs has been the fact that they would require massive retraining.) Chain-sawyers and choke setters could be employed in removing slash; operators of such heavy equipment as tractors and graders would be needed for realigning slopes, removing logging roads, and so on. Dumptruck operators would be employed in hauling and redistributing gravels and other disturbed soils. Wawona foresees other types of work, such as "splitting of small old-growth logs [frequently left on the site of logging in the past] into usable construction materials. . . fuelbreak construction, control burning and mechanical slash-disposal to reduce fire hazard, wildlife habitat improvement, trail engineering and construction, wattling [landslide control], reforestation, and thinning and maintenance of nearly all of the above." Wawona believes that workers on these projects would not only be able to exercise old skills but would acquire new ones such as engineering, carpentry, surveying, and small-equipment operation for certain specific jobs.

A project such as this in the Redwood Creek watershed area would more than provide jobs for workers displaced by park expansion. Further, and more significant, it could serve as a model for rehabilitation efforts in other areas. The precise acreage in the North Coast counties that would benefit from rehabilitation and restoration to productivity has not been determined, but Huey Johnson, recently appointed director of natural resources for California, estimates that at least one million acres of forestland in the state are currently nonproductive. He equates this with 20,000 potential jobs that could be filled. Johnson is developing rehabilitation plans to be implemented by the state and it is to be hoped that state and national efforts can be coordinated. In any event, rehabilitation and reforestation programs not only promise an immediate increase in jobs, they also offer the long-run possibility of expanded timber operation, more logs, more supplies for construction, more work for union members all over the country.

Here in California's North Coast counties, then, the real issue appears to be not jobs *versus* environment, but a dual issue of jobs *and* environment. The two are not natural enemies, indeed they can be of benefit to one another. For forest renewal, more so here than urban renewal, promises employment, a more stable economy, and a healthier and more livable environment. The present opportunity offers a challenge, and something that has been notably missing in much of the region—hope.

The measure of a truly progressive society, Governor Jerry Brown recently stated, is its ability to find new alternatives and to develop new approaches to meet its problems. In the North Coast country there is a unique chance to do just that. Change is inevitable in the very near future, and it can be change for the better. . . .

These days, more of the persons who enter the U.S. have different colors and languages. They come with the same dreams held by the Pilgrims. They just dream in another language. Freedom is not a concept owned exclusively by the English language. . . . We need to move from the mentality of tying language to loyalty. . . . Skills are taught. Loyalty is earned. People will be loyal if we give them the freedom to obtain and retain a variety of skills without pronouncing which skills are "official."

—Herman Sillas, Jr., attorney, Long Beach *Press Telegram*, January 19,1985.

I think this [bill to make English the official state language] will be an important signal to the "biculturists" in this state, the people who have decided we really need to have a separate culture and a separate identity for different ethnic groups, that we're no longer going to allow them to systematically chip away at the English language in the state of California.

—Assembly representative Frank Hill (R-Whittier) author of bill, quoted in San Francisco *Examiner*, January 9, 1985.

CHAPTER 15

Bilingual Education
Learning Tool or Crutch?

A. *The Case For Bilingual Education*
B. *The Case Against Bilingual Education*
C. *Related Language Issues*

Should California encourage bilingualism in the schools, in government agencies, on ballots, and elsewhere in public life? Or, should the state insist on the sole use of English in these areas?

The controversy arises from the fact that California has both a heterogeneous ethnic mixture and a long tradition of favoring a homogeneous use of English. Some people have demanded bilingualism as a fair and useful adjustment for newcomers. Others have opposed it as disruptive to the entire society and even to those whom it is supposed to help. Because bilingualism has implications for education, immigration, and politics—three subjects often hotly argued in public and private—it is an issue which stirs the blood.

The demand for bilingual education arose during the politically charged atmosphere of the 1960's. It was favored especially by Chicano activists who, inspired by black civil rights leaders, sought to reduce the school drop-out rate, increase ethnic pride, and overcome political isolation. It satisfied those Americans who were throwing off the old melting-pot theory of assimilation and were embracing cultural pluralism. But it displeased others, especially people of Anglo-Saxon background who still believed in the tradition of the melting-pot and were forced into a defensive posture.

The advocates of bilingualism had liberal allies in the Congress and the White House. Together they produced in 1968 an amendment to the Elementary and Secondary Education Act of 1965 called the Bilingual Education Act (or, Title VII). No one could predict at that time how many students would be involved or what might be the right method of instruction. The program had experimental objectives, limited funding, and was to be locally administered. It was aimed primarily at "economically disadvantaged" pupils.

Allowing for many local variations, bilingualism came to be defined as a program for teaching youngsters key subjects in their native language while bringing them toward full competency in English, rather than having them wait to learn English before teaching them other subjects like math, history, or reading. Two conflicting objectives emerged among the advocates. The more militant demanded that bilingualism become a permanent part of a student's educational experience from kindergarten through high school, and provide not only language instruction, but the history and culture of the mother country, as well. This was called "maintenance" bilingualism, or "bilingual/bicultural" education. The moderates wanted bilingualism merely in the lower grades, to bridge a temporary cultural gap until the youngster became proficient in English and could shift into the mainstream of the public school curriculum. This came to be called "transitional" bilingualism.

However defined, bilingualism soon impacted heavily on schools throughout the nation. By 1974 it involved an annual budget of over $58 million and covered more than 300,000 pupils.

That year the reform program was bolstered by a U.S. Supreme Court case, *Lau* v. *Nichols*, which had originated in San Francisco's Chinatown. In a class-action suit brought on behalf of 1,800 Chinese families, it was charged that non-English-speaking children were being denied equal educational opportunity by not receiving special education courses in their own language. The high court agreed with the parents. While the court said nothing about bilingualism as such, the decision caused Congress to expand the Bilingual Education Act.

Also in 1974 liberal Democratic senators Edward Kennedy of Massachusetts and Alan Cranston of California authored a new amendment to the Bilingual Act. Using the Lau decision to expand the allocations, it removed the poverty clause that had limited the program to economically disadvantaged students and expanded it to pupils without regard to their social status. It took for granted the efficacy of the program—although few studies had as yet been done to determine whether or not it worked. The amendment provided measures to prevent undue segregation for students in the program, and it established an Office of Bilingual Education to oversee it.

A year later Congress mandated bilingual ballots in some voting jurisdictions in answer to serious charges of discrimination against potential Mexican voters in west Texas. It amended the Civil Rights Act of 1964 so as to encourage the use of multilingual ballots to overcome disabilities at the polls. Although no one levelled the same charges of overt discrimination in California, major urban counties in the state chose to print ballots in Spanish and English.

In its first decade of operation bilingualism achieved a central position in educational policy. The idea was incorporated into federal and state laws dealing with vocational, adult and higher education, as well as programs for migratory workers, library construction, Indian education, and the like. California was one of scores of states that mandated their own programs to supplement federal aid.

The Bilingual Education Act was renewed in 1978. For the first time, Congress heard a serious debate on the efficacy of bilingual instruction. A massive study by an independent testing agency contracted by the Office of Education pointed out serious flaws in the system, and questioned its effectiveness. Nevertheless, because bilingualism had become institutionalized in the schools and had strong political support even among some Anglos and white ethnics, it survived the ordeal.

In the 1980's, however, the growing mood of political conservatism in the nation favored those who held onto the old melting-pot ideal. In California and elsewhere defenders of this theory of assimilation questioned bilingual assumptions. Why, they asked, should ballots be printed in any language other than English, since naturalized voters were legally required to be competent about the constitution in English? Indeed, why should not English be declared the official language of the state and of the nation?

The move to make English the official language of the U.S. was inspired by California's Republican senator, S.I. Hayakawa. A Canadian immigrant of Japanese ancestry, a former college president, a professor of semantics, and a political conservative, Hayakawa carried weight nationally even after he retired from the Senate. He helped form a movement to support an English Language

Amendment, or "ELA." The intention of its supporters was to restrict bilingual education programs, as well as limit the use of languages other than English by public agencies.

The California-based organization sparked by Hayakawa qualified a ballot initiative measure in 1984 known as Proposition 38. It mandated the California governor to inform the U.S. president of the popular sentiment against multilingual ballots. The voters approved the measure by a wide margin, and the letter was sent.

The materials on bilingualism presented below deal primarily with the controversy over education. The first section states the case for bilingual instruction; the second states the case against it; a third section touches on related issues, such as multilingual ballots and the campaign to make English the official language of the country.

While reviewing this controversy a great many questions come to mind. If all groups asserted their right to cultural self-determination would this weaken or strengthen society? How do the educational problems of Chicanos compare with those of blacks, Asians and other ethnic groups? Are English as a Second Language, and total immersion into English, alternatives to bilingual instruction? In the opinion of teachers—as opposed to that of theoreticians or politicians—precisely how has bilingual instruction operated in the classroom? If and when Congress again amends the Education Act, what new reforms should it institute? If ELA were approved how would it affect bilingual education programs and other aspects of our culture? Is English already so deeply ingrained that a forced change would make little difference, or could the measure have widespread ramifications? *(Editor's note)*

A. *The Case For Bilingual Education*

47. Marcos de Leon Seeks a "New Educational Philosophy"

A pioneer advocate of bilingual education in California was Marcos de Leon, a Van Nuys public school teacher who, as early as the 1940's, believed that it would answer the special educational needs of Hispanic youngsters. De Leon summarized his beliefs in the following article dating from 1959.[1]

Today the Mexican-American is faced with three areas which demand of him continual adjustment: (1) the community to which he has been relegated and in which he has surrounded himself with those ancestral cultural elements rendering optimum security; (2) the total community which in spite of himself will not accept him as a bona fide citizen; and (3) the school, which ignores the fact that his life is molded by living in two worlds: a cultural dichotomy not touched by the curriculum.

One premise is certain. We can no longer accept the school's usual education program, teaching methods, and evaluation techniques developed for the English-speaking student as a valid educational approach with the Mexican-American without considering: (1) the bicultural community in which he lives; (2) the lack of his complete and total acceptability by "American" society ; (3) the consequent isolation and segregation, which produces unassimilated social units; (4) the socio-

[1]Marcos de Leon: "Wanted: A New Educational Philosophy for the Mexican-American," *California Journal of Secondary Education*, xxxiv (January 1959), 398-402.

economic status peculiar to this unacceptability; and, (5) the inherent cultural lag brought on by barriers which prohibit normal participation in community living and thereby affects maximum personality growth.

Efforts to identify himself with the representative culture have been attempted in various degrees, depending on the social level of the person and the community in which he resides. Yet, in spite of it all, he still remains a foreigner, a stranger, and for all intents and purposes a "Mexican" with the common stereotyped connotations brought on by some one hundred years of cultural conflict.

Moreover, the partial disintegration of the parent culture and the fact he has been taught through social pressure to be ashamed of and even to disown his ethnic ancestry, has made the Mexican-American a victim of confusion, frustration, and insecurity.

A very practical teaching of mental hygiene is that one cannot run away from himself, or what he is, or from that in which he believes. To do so is to invite disaster. Somewhere along the way, the Mexican-American must make a stand and recognize the fact that if there is to be progress against those barriers which prevent and obstruct a more functional citizenship, he must above all retrieve his dignity and worth as a person with a specific ethnic antecedent, having a positive contribution to make to civilization. No man can find a true expression for living who is ashamed of himself or his people.

Whatever progress in education and community consciousness has been achieved by Mexican-Americans can be attributed to (1) becoming realistically aware of their nonacceptance by American society; (2) finding personal dignity and worth in their ethnical and cultural background; and (3) sacrificing immediate ethnic integration and assimilation by excelling in education and the professions, thereby making a greater contribution to American democracy.

Educational practice and community organization should be directed toward creating conditions which contribute to the security and well being of all its members. Where two basic cultures such as the English and Spanish have come to throw circles of influence over one another, the method whereby this takes place and its relation to the growth of youngsters should be a matter of concern for administrators and teachers.

It is, therefore, strongly recommended that educational theory and practice, in order to guide and direct Mexican-American youth and fulfill the complex needs arising from a bicultural life, should: (1) incorporate intelligently the sociological processes of acculturation, diffusion, and assimilation; (2) embrace a functional theory of culture and its relation to the growth of human personality; and (3) establish within the existing educational objectives a means for making the Mexican-American's social integration and cultural assimilation in American society a smoother and more stable process.

A dire need is recognized for studies in the dynamics of acculturation, diffusion, and assimilation...

The problem is somewhat clarified by Herskovitz with his definition of acculturation: "Acculturation," he says, "comprehends those phenomena which result when groups of individuals having different cultures come into continuous firsthand contact with a subsequent change in the original cultural patterns of either or both groups." Acculturation, therefore, as defined, permits a two-way process of cultural exchange and influence, permeating and molding every phase of man's social life. Such an uninhibited relationship between two cultures can be directed with definite goals and objectives, or left to chance.

Throughout the Southwest, elements of the cultures peculiar to the United States and Mexico have thrown constant and continuous circles of influence over one another for over a century. In every village and city this rubbing of elbows of the two cultures, involving food, art, music, religion, architecture, clothing, language, ideas, and attitudes, is actually occurring, albeit undirected, but serving the only purpose that culture was meant to fulfill: adjustment and security to its members.

Those cultural traits representative of the Mexican area found in the curriculum of the school are varied and sporadic, depending on the interest of the administrator and teaching personnel, as well as the experience and preparation of the latter: (1) Spanish is offered in some school systems at every possible level of instruction or included as an academic requirement, or not at all; (2) social studies units and courses in art, music, and home economics touch upon some of these elements in keeping with the conditions expressed above.

By and large, however, school administrators have failed utterly to implement the acculturation process by developing a more dynamic and functional curriculum for the Mexican-American student.

If we are to utilize the community and its needs to strengthen the school's program, elements of food, art, clothing, music, language, and history, peculiar to the Mexican area, should certainly be included in the curriculum of those schools serving large numbers of Mexican-Americans. In the average school program, however, one finds almost exclusively those cultural elements peculiar to the American scene composing the curriculum. This not only violates the best recommended procedures and methods for setting up the curriculum for a bicultural community, but prevents the school from assuming its role as an educational institution for the total community and leaves very little leeway for anything but a frustrating and sometimes sterile learning situation. . . .

In the past, the process of acculturation apparently was left unguided and without direction. The idea that the United States is the "melting pot" of the world does not necessarily hold true. The frustration and insecurity brought on by a "melting" process, carried on at random and conditioned by cultural conflicts, are too great to permit this "catch as catch can" philosophy to reign over and control the life of the Mexican-American any longer. The school cannot continue to function as an isolated unit, or continue to carry on practices based on tradition for the bicultural community, under the present "all or none" concept as an educational philosophy.

48. Prof. Dolores Escobar Litsinger Describes Basic Underlying Assumptions

What are the underlying assumptions of a program of bilingualism, and how would it work in the classroom? A capsulized answer to this question was given by Professor Dolores Escobar Litsinger, of California State University, Northridge, in a book that she published in 1973. A portion of it appears here.[2]

The concept of bilingual-bicultural education includes several basic ideas which could provide the stimulus for some of the most exciting educational innovations in recent years. Presently, bilingual education programs within the United States are found largely in elite private schools, parochial schools, or as special programs for linguistically-disadvantaged students. Illustrating the last category, Mexican-American students are being exposed to bilingual education in an attempt to reverse the statistics of academic failure which characterize them. In the broadest context, however, experiments in bilingual education may provide teaching models which could enrich the education of all american youth.

[2]*The Challenge of Teaching Mexican-American Students* (New York, American Book Company, 1973), 141-146. Footnotes deleted.

THE ASSETS OF BILINGUALISM

The first assumption fundamental to bilingual education is that an individual who can communicate through speaking, reading, and writing more than one language possesses an intellectual advantage and is an asset to society. He can, for example, enjoy a richer personal life because of his ability to enter more fully into the literary, philosophic, or social community to two cultures. At the same time, the bilingual individual possesses practical competencies needed in a variety of jobs and professions.

Related to this assumption is the idea that the more than six million Spanish-speaking persons within the United States provide a valuable source of existing and potential bilinguals. Rather than being considered a national liability with large numbers unemployed and undereducated, they might become a national asset, if their potential were developed.

THE CONTROVERSY OVER BILINGUAL-BICULTURAL EDUCATION

Though the advantages of bilingualism have long been recognized, the question as to whether the development of bilinguals should be a *major* goal of public education has not been resolved. Whether the public schools should encourage cultural pluralism is even more controversial. Arguments against a comprehensive bilingual-bicultural program of instruction vary from concerns about practicality and learning interference to those involving the effect of bilingualism upon national security....

In spite of growing acceptance of the concept of bilingual programs of instruction in public schools, the issues surrounding bilingual-bicultural education will draw supporters and opponents within any given community.

Some of the most complex and relevant questions about bilingual-bicultural education are raised by educators, themselves. Does bilingual instruction impede the development of creativity and high thought processes? Does bilingual instruction hinder the acquisition of English language skills? Could instructional time be better spent teaching English since most Mexican-Americans lack fluency in Spanish, as well as English.

The complete answer to these questions, and others, will depend upon continued and thoughtful research; however, there is currently some indication that bilingualism *per se* does not produce learning handicaps.

> The evidence seems to be that the problems of bilingual children arise not from the fact of their speaking two languages, but from educational policy affecting the two languages, and from other factors, sociological and economic outside the school. The fact is that bilingualism is eagerly sought world wide, both by the elite and by the middle and lower classes, for the intellectual and economic advantages it can bring...

The same report goes on to state that review of "scores of studies of bilingualism reveal that where bilingualism has been found to be a problem is commonly in situations where child-speakers of a home language which is different from the school language are given no formal education in and through their home language."

The point of view that instruction in Spanish is time wasted because the children speak inferior Spanish can be challenged from a variety of sources....

Making a value judgment upon the type of Spanish spoken by Mexican-American students is intellectually unsound. Linguistic scholars place the language characteristics of any group within a theoretical framework without attaching positive or negative connotations. The Spanish spoken by Mexican Americans can be considered a dialect of Spanish and in some localities almost a Creole language drawn from both Spanish and English.

Theories which attempt to classify types of bilingualism also do so without value judgments. For example, a common classification system distinguishes the "compound bilingual" from the "coordinate bilingual." The coordinate bilingual develops two sets of language systems which are culturally, temporally separated in time, or functionally separate. The compound bilingual develops a bilingual language system within a single context in which the symbols of two languages are interchangeable alternatives with the same meaning. The Mexican-American often falls into the latter category; he uses the linguistic symbols of both languages mixed in a single utterance regardless of whether English or Spanish syntax is used. Though this classification system may have significant implications for teaching and learning, it does not imply that either type of bilingual is superior culturally or intellectually.

In the classroom situation it is difficult to make an accurate assessment of the amount of Spanish spoken by the student, much less make a judgment about the quality spoken. Many Mexican-American students hide their Spanish linguistic ability in the schoolroom. For example, in one bilingual education program observed by the author, investigators attempting to determine the students' dominant language complained that many students systematically tried to "cover-up" their Spanish language skills.

A similar situation occurred in a kindergarten room visited regularly. English speakers were matched with Spanish speakers to give each practice in hearing the second language. A child from each group was placed in the play corner for forty-five minutes and observed. After the first few minutes, the dialogue continued completely in Spanish in spite of the fact that *none* of the supposedly English speakers previously demonstrated any facility in Spanish. Serious questions should be raised about a learning environment in which children so quickly learn to hide their abilities.

Perhaps the research most significant to bilingual programs of education will deal with areas involving student attitudes about language and the culture it represents. Pedagogically, investigation is needed to clarify questions concerning the timing of introducing the second language, the sequence and pacing of teaching both the native* language and second language, the effects of culture and poverty in relation to teaching techniques, and the effects of bilingualism upon thought processes and creativity.

(*The term "native" as used in this chapter is synonymous with "first" language, but is to be distinguished from dominant language. Dominant language is defined as the language *most* used by the individual.)

A majority of studies, to date, encourage the development of the native language until the learner is able to engage in abstract thinking. However, there is also adequate indication that the second language is best introduced between the ages of six and eleven years before the native language is completely developed and the learner develops self-consciousness about a "foreign" language. This evidence places great responsibility upon the elementary school for not only maintaining the native language, but also for effectively introducing the second language.

In the case of the Mexican-American student, the school must reevaluate the importance of the Spanish language not only as a medium of instruction, but as a foundation for learning English. It is reasonable to assume that when we curtail native language development, at its beginning levels (oral language with limited vocabulary and syntax), we may be violating developmental thought processes. . . .

The curtailment of native language development, combined with the school's insistence that non-English speaking students learn a "foreign language" (English) before concepts are taught in science, social science, mathematics, literature, etc., could well account for much of the academic retardation experienced by a high percentage of Mexican-American students. It is not unusual for students who are recent arrivals from Mexico and who have well developed Spanish language skills to learn English quickly and to achieve academically more rapidly than Mexican Americans born in the United States.

THE NEED FOR REFORM

Bilingual-bicultural instruction arises out of the need for reform in the education of Mexican-

American students. Regardless of the doubts and controversies surrounding bilingual-bicultural education, many educators feel that the failure of overwhelming numbers of Spanish speaking students in traditional programs of education demand experimentation with school organization and instructional procedures. Proponents of bilingual education look to bilingual instruction in other countries and during other eras as proof that bilingual education can and does work. As a final argument, they propose that bilingual education offers a likely solution to the academic failure of Mexican-Americans, and they feel certain that it could do no worse than existing instructional programs. In any case, most educators involved in bilingual-bicultural education exhibit a willingness to evaluate the results of their programs.

EXPERIMENTAL PROGRAMS

Bilingual-bicultural education is still experimental and embraces many programs at various stages of development. While some bilingual-bicultural programs are currently being developed and implemented, others are already entering a period of rigorous evaluation. Therefore, any discussion of the area must assume that continued experiments and validation will result in the expansion of certain practices and the discontinuation of others. Furthermore, there is every indication that the development of substantive bilingual-bicultural programs of instruction will involve experts from many disciplines because of the complexity of bilingualism and the widespread interest such programs arouse. Interdisciplinary development and evaluation may prove to be one of the most valuable aspects of present and forthcoming experiments in bilingual-bicultural education. . . .

EMPHASIS ON THE IMPORTANCE OF MINORITY CULTURE

Bilingual-bicultural education recognizes the importance of the minority student's culture. As the name implies, these programs assume that language is an important aspect of culture. Language is considered more than a tool for learning, a medium of instruction or communication. Language is seen as an intricate part of personality, an expression of culture significant to the self-image, an essential part of ethnic identification and cultural preservation. Hence, the term bilingual-bicultural emerges; it signifies a conscious effort to retain the cultural milieu from which language develops. To many members of the Mexican-American community, the Spanish language is symbolic of their culture, and bilingual-bicultural education programs are tangible evidence of the majority's willingness to legitimatize that culture.

There is concern, however, that bilingual-bicultural programs of education proliferate because of political expediency rather than because of educational value. For that reason, it is essential that educators interested in Mexican-American students become acquainted with the problems, teaching strategies, and contributions of promising bilingual-bicultural education programs.

49.
Maria M. Swanson: Bilingualism is "A Valuable Learning Tool"

Simply stated, bilingual instruction is a vital educational tool. So states Maria Medina Swanson, chair of the National Advisory Council for Bilingual Education, as part of an exchange of ideas printed in the San Jose Mercury, *January 3, 1979.*

Would anyone ever question the need for reading? Math? Social studies? Of course not! Education, no matter how much we criticize it, continues to be our hope for a better world.

But what if the student doesn't speak or understand English? The U.S. Supreme Court stated in 1974 in *Lau* v. *Nichols*, "There is no equality of treatment merely by providing students with the same facilities, textbooks, teachers and curriculum, for students who do not understand English are effectively foreclosed from any meaningful education."

In order to provide a meaningful education to millions of language minority children, schools are using a common sense approach bilingual education. The purpose of bilingual education is to move the student as efficiently and effectively as possible into the mainstream of English language curriculum. While students develop their skills in specialized English as a Second Language (ESL) classes, they receive subject matter instruction in the native language.

When English language skills have increased enough to enable success in all-English instruction, the student leaves the bilingual program. He is not kept back in grade level nor trapped in communication difficulties nor made to feel ashamed of his language, his family his culture. He is on his way to becoming a productive American.

Why not just teach them English? It may take two weeks, two months, or two years to learn a language. Waiting until the student learns enough English to understand subjects is a waste of the student's time and a denial of his knowledge and potential.

We've come a long way since then technologically and humanistically. Our children cannot survive unless they receive an adequate education. Bilingual education is a step in that direction.

B. *The Case Against Bilingual Education*

50.
Philip W. Quig: Bilingual Instruction is "Highly Undesirable"

The reply to Ms. Swanson's statement in the San Jose Mercury *(above) was delivered by Philip W. Quig, former editor of* Foreign Affairs, *an influential journal of opinion.*

If teaching in a foreign language achieved what its proponents claim, it would be hard to fault. But bilingual education has not proved to be a "powerful learning tool;" rather it is a crutch permitting minorities to postpone the day of reckoning when they must—for their good and ours—be equipped to handle English. It reduces the incentive to learn English, generally at the very age when acquisition of a new language is easiest.

Bilingual education is not only unnecessary. It is highly undesirable. It invites the fearsome dissension born of linguistic dualism. Bilingual education is "separate but equal" in a new guise. Where a minority constitutes a substantial proportion of a school district, bilingual education tends to perpetrate cultural separatism.

The notion that minorities have linguistic rights which the state must preserve seems totally alien to the spirit of the Constitution (*Lau* v *Nichols* notwithstanding). Bilingual education and the requirement that public documents and notices be printed in minority languages are the first steps in a process by which we are becoming a bilingual society.

As Hispanic Americans acquire political influence comparable to their numbers, it is only to be expected that they will try to make it more convenient for Latinos to live and work without knowledge of English. We have only to observe our northern neighbor to see how difficult it is for two languages and cultures to co-exist amicably. There can be no doubt that tensions are already acute in those parts of the U.S. heavily populated with Latinos, some of whom show no desire to learn English.

Our nation has been vastly enriched by its variety of cultural traditions, but the preservation of cultural identity is properly the responsibility of each ethnic group, not of the state.

Let us spare no effort in helping Latinos (or any other minority) to learn English, and let many more North Americans learn Spanish by choice not compulsion. But let us not run the risk of endangering national unity and permitting ignorance of a common language to be added to the difficulties of communicating with one another.

51.
Prof. Richard Rodriguez: Bilingual Instruction is Wrong-Headed

Few Hispanics have voiced public objection to bilingual education. For this reason alone the following critical commentary of Richard Rodriguez, a California Chicano and a professor of English, is of particular interest. His words are also intensely personal and evocative, as he describes how language affects both the public *and the* private *person. He asserts that cultural assimilation and cultural separation both contain gains and losses for the individual. This selection is taken from an autobiographical essay that appeared in* The American Scholar.[3]

An accident of geography sent me to a school where all my classmates were white and many were the children of doctors and lawyers and business executives. On that first day of school, my classmates must certainly have been uneasy to find themselves apart from their families, in the first institution of their lives. But I was astonished. I was fated to be the "problem student" in class.

The nun said, in a friendly but oddly impersonal voice: "Boys and girls, this is Richard Rodriguez." (I heard her sound it out: Rich-heard Road-ree-guess.) It was the first time I had heard anyone say my name in English. "Richard," the nun repeated more slowly, writing my name down in her book. Quickly I turned to see my mother's face dissolve in a watery blur behind the pebbled-glass door.

Now, many years later, I hear of something called "bilingual education"—a scheme proposed in the late 1960's by Hispanic-American social activists, later endorsed by a congressional vote. It is a program that seeks to permit non-English-speaking children (many from lower class homes) to use their "family language" as the language of school. Such, at least, is the aim its supporters announce. I hear them, and am forced to say no: It is not possible for a child, any child, ever to use his family's language in school. Not to understand this is to misunderstand the public uses of schooling and to trivialize the nature of intimate life.

Memory teaches me what I know of these matters. The boy reminds the adult. I was a bilingual

[3] "Aria: A Memoir of a Bilingual Childhood," *The American Scholar*, (Winter, 1980-81).

child, but of a certain kind: "socially disadvantaged," the son of working-class parents, both Mexican immigrants. . . .

I grew up in a house where the only regular guests were my relations. . . . Our house stood apart—gaudy yellow in a row of white bungalows. We were the people with the noisy dog, the people who raised chickens. We were the foreigners on the block. . . .

In public, my father and mother spoke a hesitant, accented, and not always grammatical English. And then they would have to strain, their bodies tense, to catch the sense of what was rapidly said by *los gringos*. At home, they returned to Spanish. The language of their Mexican past sounded in counterpoint to the English spoken in public. The words would come quickly, with ease. Conveyed through those sounds was the pleasing, soothing, consoling reminder that one was at home.

During those years when I was first learning to speak, my mother and father addressed me only in Spanish; in Spanish I learned to reply. By contrast, English (*ingles*) was the language I came to associate with *gringos*, rarely heard in the house. I learned my first words of English overhearing my parents speaking to strangers. At six years of age, I knew just enough words for my mother to trust me on errands to stores one block away—but no more. . . .

My own sounds I was unable to hear, but I knew that I spoke English poorly. My words could not extend to form complete thoughts. . . in a way, it didn't matter very much that my parents could not speak English with ease. Their linguistic difficulties had no serious consequences. My mother and father made themselves understood at the county hospital clinic and at government offices. And yet, in another way, it mattered very much. It was unsettling to hear my parents struggle with English. Hearing them, I'd grow nervous, and my clutching trust in their protection and power would be weakened. . . .

But then there was Spanish: *español*, the language rarely heard away from the house; *español*, the language which seemed to me therefore a private language, my family's language. To hear its sounds was to feel myself specially recognized as one of the family, apart from *los otros*. A simple remark, an inconsequential comment could convey that assurance. My parents would say something to me and I would feel embraced by the sounds of their words. Those sounds said: *I am speaking with ease in Spanish. I am addressing you in words I never use with los gringos. I recognize you as someone special, close, like no one outside. You belong with us. In the family. Ricardo.*

At the age of six, well past the time when most middle-class children no longer notice the difference between sounds uttered at home and words spoken in public, I had a different experience. I lived in a world compounded of sounds. . . . I shared with my family a language enchantingly private—different from that used in the city around us.

Just opening or closing the screen door behind me was an important experience. I'd rarely leave home all alone or without feeling reluctance. Walking down the sidewalk, under the canopy of tall trees, I'd warily notice the (suddenly) silent neighborhood kids who stood warily watching me. Nervously, I'd arrive at the grocery store to hear there the sound of the gringo, reminding me that in this so-big world I was a foreigner. But if leaving home was never routine, neither was coming back. Walking toward our house, climbing the steps from the sidewalk, in summer when the front door was open, I'd hear voices beyond the screen door talking in Spanish. For a second or two I'd stay, linger there listening. Smiling, I'd hear my mother call out, saying in Spanish, "Is that you, Richard?" Those were her words, but all the while her sounds would assure me: *You are home now. Come closer inside. With us. "Si,"* I'd reply. . . .

Plainly it is not healthy to hear such sounds so often. It is not healthy to distinguish public from private sounds so easily. I remained cloistered by sound, timid and shy in public, too dependent on the voices at home. And yet I was a very happy child when I was at home. I remember many nights when my father would come back from work, and I'd hear him call out to my mother in Spanish, sounding relieved. In Spanish, his voice would sound the light and free notes that he never could manage in English. Some nights I'd jump up just hearing his voice. My brother and I would come running into the room where he was with our mother. Our laughing (so deep was the pleasure!) became screaming. Like others who feel the pain of public alienation, we transformed the knowledge of our public separateness into a consoling reminder of our intimacy. Excited, our voices joined in a celebration of sounds. *We are speaking now the way we never speak out in public—we are together*, the sounds told me. . . .

Supporters of bilingual education imply today that students like me miss a great deal by not being taught in their family's language. What they seem not to recognize is that, as a socially disadvantaged child, I regarded Spanish as a private language. It was a ghetto language that deepened and strengthened my feeling of public separateness. What I needed to learn in school was that I had the right, and the obligation, to speak the public language. . . .

Without question, it would have pleased me to have heard my teachers address me in Spanish when I entered the classroom. I would have felt much less afraid. I would have imagined that my instructors were somehow "related" to me; I would indeed have heard their Spanish as my family's language. I would have trusted them and responded with ease. But I would have delayed— postponed for how long?—having to learn the language of public society. I would have evaded—and for how long?—learning the great lesson of school: that I had a public identity.

Fortunately, my teachers were unsentimental about their responsibility. What they understood was that I needed to speak public English. So their voices would search me out, asking me questions. . . . But I couldn't believe English could be my language to use. (In part, I did not want to believe it.) I continued to mumble. I resisted the teacher's demands. (Did I somehow suspect that once I learned this public language my family life would be changed?) Silent, waiting for the bell to sound, I remained dazed, diffident, afraid. . . .

Three months passed. Five. A half year. Unsmiling, ever watchful, my teachers . . . began to connect my behavior with the slow progress my brother and sisters were making . . . one Saturday morning, three nuns arrived at the house to talk to our parents. . . . "Do your children speak only Spanish at home, Mrs. Rodriguez?" . . . . With great tact, the visitors continued, "Is it possible for you and your husband to encourage your children to practice their English when they are at home?" Of course my parents complied. What would they not do for their children's well-being? And how could they question the church's authority which those women represented? In an instant they agreed to give up the language (the sounds) which had revealed and accentuated our family's closeness. The moment after the visitors left, the change was observed. "*Ahora*, speak to us only *en ingles*," my father and mother told us.

At first, it seemed a kind of game. After dinner each night, the family gathered together to practice "our" English. It was still then *ingles*, a language foreign to us, so we felt drawn to it as strangers. Laughing, we would try to define words we could not pronounce. We played with strange English sounds, often over-anglicizing our pronunciations. And we filled the smiling gaps of our sentences with familiar Spanish sounds. But that was cheating, somebody shouted, and everyone laughed.

In school, meanwhile, like my brother and sisters, I was required to attend a daily tutoring session. I needed a full year of this special work. . . . Most of all, I needed to hear my mother and father speak to me in a moment of seriousness in "broken"—suddenly heartbreaking—English. This scene was inevitable. One Saturday morning I entered the kitchen where my parents were talking, but I did not realize that they were talking in Spanish until, the moment they saw me, their voices changed and they began speaking English. The *gringo* sounds they uttered startled me. Pushing me away. In that moment of trivial misunderstanding and profound insight, I felt my throat twisted by unsounded grief. I simply turned and left the room. But I had no place to escape to where I could grieve in Spanish. My brother and sisters were speaking English in another part of the house.

Again and again in the days following, as I grew increasingly angry, I was obliged to hear my mother and father encouraging me: "Speak to us *en ingles*." Only then did I determine to learn classroom English. Thus, sometime afterward it happened: one day in school, I raised my hand to volunteer an answer to a question. I spoke out in a loud voice and I did not think it remarkable when the entire class understood. That day I moved very far from being the disadvantaged child I had been only days earlier. Taken hold at last was the belief, the calming assurance, that I *belonged* in public.

Shortly after, I stopped hearing the high, troubling sounds of *los gringos*. A more and more confident speaker of English, I didn't listen to how strangers sounded when they talked to me.... Conversations quickened.... Sound and word were thus tightly wedded.... An eight-year-old boy, I finally came to accept what had been technically true since my birth: I was an American citizen.

But diminished by then was the special feeling of closeness at home.... Our family remained a loving family, but one greatly changed. We were no longer so close, no longer bound tightly together by the knowledge of our separateness from *los gringos*. Neither my older brother nor my sisters rushed home after school any more. Nor did I. When I arrived home, often there would be neighborhood kids in the house. Or the house would be empty of sounds....

There was a new silence at home. As we children learned more and more English, we shared fewer and fewer words with our parents. Sentences needed to be spoken slowly when one of us addressed our mother or father. Often the parent wouldn't understand. The child would need to repeat himself. Still the parent misunderstood. The young voice, frustrated, would end up saying, "Never mind"—the subject was closed....

My mother! My father! After English became my primary language, I no longer knew what words to use in addressing my parents. The old spanish words (those tender accents of sound) I had earlier used—*mama* and *papa*—I couldn't use any more.... Whenever I'd speak to my parents, I would try to get their attention by looking at them. In public conversations, I'd refer to them as my "parents" or my "mother" and "father."

My mother and father, for their part, responded differently, as their children spoke to them less. My mother grew restless, seemed troubled and anxious at the scarceness of words exchanged in the house.... She'd join conversations she overheard, but her intrusions often stopped her children's talking. By contrast, my father seemed to grow reconciled to the new quiet. Though his English somewhat improved, he tended more and more to retire into silence....

The silence at home, however, was not simply the result of fewer words passing between parents and children. More profound for me was the silence created by my inattention to sounds. At about the time I no longer bothered to listen with care to the sounds of English in public, I grew careless about listening to the sounds made by the family when they spoke. Most of the time I would hear someone speaking at home and didn't distinguish his sounds from the words people uttered in public. I didn't even pay much attention to my parents' accented and ungrammatical speech—at least not at home. Only when I was with them in public would I become alert to their accents but even then their sounds caused me less and less concern. For I was growing increasingly confident of my own public identity....

Bilingual educators say today that children lose a degree of "individuality" by becoming assimilated into public society.... But the bilingualists oversimplify when they scorn the value and necessity of assimilation. They do not seem to realize that a person is individualized in two ways. So they do not realize that, while one suffers a diminished sense of *private* individuality by being assimilated into public society, such assimilation makes possible the achievement of *public* individuality.

Simplistically again, the bilingualists insist that a student should be reminded of his difference from others in mass society, of his "heritage." But they equate mere separateness with individuality. The fact is that only in private—with intimates—is separateness from the crowd a prerequisite for individuality; an intimate "tells" me that I am unique, unlike all others, apart from the crowd. In public, by contrast, full individuality is achieved, paradoxically, by those who are able to consider themselves members of the crowd. Thus it happened to me. Only when I was able to think of myself as an American, no longer an alien in *gringo* society, could I seek the rights and opportunities necessary for full public individuality. . . . Those middle-class ethnics who scorn assimilation seem to me filled with decadent self-pity, obsessed by the burden of public life. Dangerously, they romanticize public separateness and trivialize the dilemma of those who are truly socially disadvantaged.

If I rehearse here the changes in my private life after my Americanization, it is finally to emphasize a public gain. The loss implies the gain. The house I returned to each afternoon was quiet. Intimate sounds no longer greeted me at the door. Inside there were other noises. The telephone rang. Neighborhood kids ran past the door of the bedroom where I was reading my schoolbooks—covered with brown shopping-bag paper. Once I learned the public language, it would never again be easy for me to hear intimate family voices. More and more of my day was spent hearing words, not sounds. But that may only be a way of saying that on the day I raised my hand in class and spoke loudly to an entire roomful of faces, my childhood started to end.

I grew up the victim of a disconcerting confusion. As I became fluent in English, I could no longer speak Spanish with confidence. I continued to understand spoken Spanish, and in high school I learned how to read and write Spanish. But for many years I could not pronounce it. A powerful guilt blocked my spoken words; an essential glue was missing whenever I would try to connect words to form sentences. I would be unable to break a barrier of sound, to speak freely. I would speak, or try to speak, Spanish, and I would manage to utter halting, hiccuping sounds which betrayed my unease. (Even today I speak Spanish very slowly, at best.). . . .

Embarrassed, my parents would often need to explain their children's inability to speak fluent Spanish during those years. My mother encountered the wrath of her brother, her only brother, when he came up from Mexico one summer with his family and saw his nieces and nephews for the very first time. After listening to me, he looked away and said what a disgrace it was that my siblings and I couldn't speak Spanish, "*su propria idioma*," He made that remark to my mother, but I noticed that he stared at my father. . . .

I recount such incidents only because they suggest the fierce power that Spanish had over many people I met at home, how strongly Spanish was associated with closeness. Most of those people. . .could have spoken English to me, but many wouldn't. They seemed to think that Spanish was the only language we could use among ourselves, that Spanish alone permitted our association. (Such persons are always vulnerable to the ghetto merchant and the politician who have learned the value of speaking their clients' "family language" so as to gain immediate trust.) For my part, I felt that by learning English I had somehow. . .betrayed my immediate family. I knew that my parents had encouraged me to learn English. I knew that I had turned to English with angry reluctance. But once I spoke English with ease, I came to feel guilty. I sensed that I had broken the spell of intimacy which had once held the family so close together. It was this original sin against my family that I recalled whenever anyone addressed me in Spanish and I responded confounded.

Yet even during those years of guilt, I was coming to grasp certain consoling truths about language and intimacy—truths that I learned gradually. . . . *Intimacy is not created by a particular language; it is created by intimates.* Thus the great change in my life was not linguistic but social. If, after becoming a successful student, I no longer heard intimate voices as often as I had earlier, it was not because I spoke English instead of Spanish. It was because I spoke public language for most of my day. I moved easily at last, a citizen in a crowded city of words.

. . .I think of the black political activists who lately have argued in favor of using black English in public schools—an argument that varies only slightly from that of foreign-language bilingualists. I have heard "radical" linguists make the point that black English is a complex and intricate version of English. And I do not doubt it. But neither do I think that black English should be a language of public instruction. What makes it inappropriate in classrooms is not something in the language itself but, rather, what lower-class speakers make of it. Just as Spanish would have been a dangerous language for me to have used at the start of my education, so black English would be a dangerous language to use in the schooling of teenagers for whom it reinforces feelings of public separateness.

This seems to me an obvious point to make, and yet it must be said. In recent years there have been many attempts to make the language of the alien a public language. "Bilingual education, two ways to understand. . ." television and radio commercials glibly announce. Proponents of bilingual education are careful to say that above all they want every student to acquire a good education. Their argument goes something like this: Children permitted to use their family language will not be so alienated and will be better able to match the progress of English-speaking students in the crucial first months of schooling. Increasingly confident of their ability, such children will be more inclined to apply themselves to their studies in the future. But then the bilingualists also claim another very different goal. They say that children who use their family language in school will retain a sense of their ethnic heritage and their family ties. Thus the supporters of bilingual education want it both ways. They propose bilingual schooling as a way of helping students acquire the classroom skills crucial for public success. But they likewise insist that bilingual instruction will give students a sense of their identity apart from the English-speaking public.

Behind this scheme gleams a bright promise for the alien child: one can become a public person while still remaining a private person. Who would not want to believe such an appealing idea? Who can be surprised that the scheme has the support of so many middle-class ethnic Americans? If the barrio or ghetto child can retain his separateness even while being publicly educated, then it is almost possible to believe that no private cost need be paid for public success. . . . Middle-class supporters of public bilingualism toy with the confusion of those Americans who cannot speak standard English as well as they do. Moreover, bilingual enthusiasts sin against intimacy. A Hispanic-American tells me, "I will never give up my family language," and he clutches a group of words as though they were the source of his family ties. He credits to language what he should credit to family members. This is a convenient mistake, for as long as he holds on to certain familiar words, he can ignore how much else has actually changed in his life. . . .

C. *Related Language Issues*

52.
Bill Press: Preserve Bilingual Ballots, Vote No on Prop. 38

In the 1984 general election, backers of Proposition 38 attempted to abolish the use of bilingual ballots in California and to compel the use of English ballots only. KABC-TV political commentator Bill Press wrote the following opinion piece in the Los Angeles Times *opposing Proposition 38.*[4]

There are few things on the California ballot that most voters are likely to agree on—save one. Proposition 38.

This is the initiative that wants all future ballots written in English only. With no organized opposition, it probably will succeed in this age of born-again patriotism. But it will not be, as some pretend, democracy's finest hour. It may be, instead, democracy's meanest hour.

There are no compelling economic or political arguments for English-only ballots. The only thing that Proposition 38 seems to have going for it is the gut feeling that "real Americans don't speak Spanish."

[4]"Proposition 38: An Exercise in Degrading Democracy," *Los Angeles Times*, October 18, 1984.

So blinded by patriotism or pride, most Californians are unaware of the basic facts about this initiative:

—Proposition 38 would have no direct effect. The law requires bilingual ballots only in... counties where more than 5% of the population are minorities who don't speak English well enough to participate in the electoral process. But that law is a federal statute. So even if Proposition 38 passed with 90% of the vote, it would merely require the governor to write Congress and the President a letter asking for the federal policy to be overturned. (In response to... a 1980 initiative, Gov. Edmund G. Brown, Jr. wrote President Reagan a letter urging a nuclear freeze. We're still waiting.)

—Even indirectly, Proposition 38 affects but few counties. When the 1975 Voting Rights Act was passed, 39 California counties, including Los Angeles and San Francisco, were required to print bilingual (Spanish or Chinese) voting materials. The law was amended this year, and now only 10 California counties must provide ballots in Spanish and English: Fresno, Imperial, Kern, Kings, Madera, Merced, Monterey, San Benito, Tulare and Yuba. In those 10 counties, with 914,513 registered voters, only 9,362 bilingual ballots had to be printed for Nov. 6.

—Proposition 38 would not save taxpayers much money. For the 10 counties affected, the cost of printing 9,362 ballots was $71,000. The cost to the state of printing and mailing 50,000 bilingual voter pamphlets was $50,000. So the total cost of California's bilingual ballot program for this election was only $121,000. By contrast, the English-only Committee spent $200,000 qualifying Proposition 38 for the ballot.

—Proposition 38 would not "save" the English language, nor would it force anyone to learn English—the goals of the English-Only Committee. "For over 200 years," warns the committee's California chairman, Stanley Diamond, "our unifying force in this country with millions of immigrants has been the English language. We think it is under threat."

The English-Only Committee's founder, John Tanton of Potoskey, Mich., argues that only by forcing Latino citizens to vote in English can we force Latinos to learn English, thereby "doing what is best for the minorities themselves."

Even assuming that Tanton can dictate "what is best for minorities," his major premise is wrong. It is indeed vital for immigrants to learn and master English. They will. They already do. But it is not English-language ballots that persuade them. It is something much more basic to survival: the need to find a job, support a family, get an education, integrate into American society, move up the ladder.

—Proposition 38 would discourage voting, not encourage it.

The goal, the noble goal, of the Voting Rights Act is to make voting easier for those Americans who still have difficulty with the English language. Experience shows that they fall into two groups.

First, new senior citizens. By law, immigrants over 50 years of age who have been in this country more than 20 years are exempt from the English-language test for citizenship. They may be fiercely proud Americans. They simply have not mastered English. Nor are they required to by law.

The second group that would be affected is new citizens who have passed the basic citizenship test—written at a 5th grade level of English—but are not yet comfortable enough with English to follow the complexities of some ballot measures. Hardly surprising in California, where ballot arguments are often written in English so obtuse they confound even an American-born, English-speaking college graduate.

For both groups, the bilingual ballot was designed as a temporary measure to facilitate their participation in government *of* and *by* the people. Without it, those hesitant in English will not run out for a crash course in legalese. They will simply not vote.

And so Proposition 38.

A sure thing. A bad thing.

Its passage would tell us only one thing: whether we are secure enough in our Americanism to allow 9,300 elderly Latinos to read voting materials in their own language.

I hope so.

53.
A Student Exchange on Bilingual Ballots

The San Jose State University student newspaper, the Spartan, *carried an exchange between two students, Wendy Stitt and Amy Yannello that appears next.*

At issue: Should ballots be bilingual?

PRO: A necessity for new Americans
By Wendy Stitt

Our country encourages all people to actively participate in our government. There was never any doubt that this goal would be difficult to achieve and maintain.

A method used to try to pique the interest of those people who are new to our country is to make the ballots understandable and readable. There are large groups of people who are forced to leave their own country for one reason or another. These people choose to immigrate to the United States. Often due to circumstances beyond their control they are put into this new country with no knowledge of how our government is run.

We should encourage these immigrants to meld and become active participants in our republic. We in America stress the importance of voting. Many immigrants who want to integrate and become active citizens soon realize the only way to really express their ideas to our representatives is to vote.

Our country is a melting pot. Therefore Americans are not all one nationality. At one time or another our ancestors came from a different country.

The United States of America is made up of immigrants; that is what is special about us. We should offer people coming into our country who care enough to vote the opportunity to do just that—vote. The only way these people can do that is if we offer them bilingual ballots.

Bilingual ballots enable the people who are interested in contributing to and becoming a part of the electorate now and in future years to do so immediately. Their interest then is passed on to the next generation. Hopefully this attitude will be carried through to future generations.

People who are unable to express themselves become frustrated and soon are apathetic to the problems around them.

Our system encourages people to vote, to have their say. There are places to register to vote all over the country, yet if bilingual ballots are not offered to non-English-speaking citizens, many of those people we are encouraging to vote would be unable to vote.

Many people argue that it's the duty of every American to register to vote, and not enough people who are eligible to vote do indeed vote. If bilingual ballots were not offered to the non-English citizens, there would be even fewer registered voters.

The United States of America is a free and democratic country. Every person who is a citizen and over 18, whether they are men or women, black or white, etc. are offered the opportunity to vote. Not only is it not fair, it is also undemocratic to deny non-English-speaking citizens of the United States the privilege every United States citizen has—to vote. Bilingual television as well as bilingual radio stations are offered to the non-English-speaking public, bilingual ballots should also be offered to those citizens of the United States.

Good results from having bilingual ballots far outweigh the bad. Offering bilingual ballots encourages our new citizens to vote and to have their say in their government.

Bilingual ballots allow people the right of freedom of choice. They allow non-English-speaking citizens of the United States the freedom to decide whether or not to vote. If bilingual ballots are not offered, then we essentially are denying many people that right, the freedom of choice.

By not allowing citizens to vote because they do not speak the language, we are denying people one of the most basic rights in our constitution: the right of its citizens to have a say in how their government is run.

CON: Knowledge of English is a Must
by Amy Yannello

Bilingual elections are the product of good intentions gone awry.

While arguing that the right to vote belongs to everyone, and indeed it does, supporters of bilingual ballots have gone to the extreme by suggesting that this right be provided regardless of the consequences.

Proponents of the program maintain that English-only ballots exclude a large block of the voting population—namely Hispanics.

It's not unlikely to hear them cite the Voting Rights Act of 1965, which recognized that blacks had been unjustly denied their right to vote.

To group the two together is to confuse the issue.

Discrimination on the basis of color, over which someone has no control, is wrong. Asking a block of citizens to accommodate themselves to a common language only makes good sense.

Of course everyone should have the right to vote.

But for all of our cultural heritage and diversity we have to remember that English is the working language of the land. And, while voting is a right, we have got to be able to exercise this right intelligently.

This seems an impossibility if we apply a "Tower of Babel" logic to a democratic process.

Why not provide ballots for the Vietnamese, Italian, or Iranian communities? The argument here is that these groups have not shown "sufficient need." This is correct. They have learned the language, so where's the need?

Most would agree that if one were to move to another country, it would be expected of them to learn the language that is most frequently used there. So why should it be any different for people living in America?

How will it help to have Spanish ballots when such a large majority of the news is in English? Granted, there are Spanish newspapers and newscasts, but by and large, the fact remains— most information comes to us in English.

Providing ballots which are written in both Spanish and English only serves to segregate the Hispanic community by not providing an incentive to master the English language.

Bilingual ballots are not a help, but a crutch because while they may allow more of the Hispanic community to participate in the voting process, it also further perpetuates the handicap by making the segregation more pronounced.

An important fact the supporters would like us to forget is that there are a large group of Spanish citizens who realize that while it is important to maintain their cultural customs and beliefs, it is necessary to learn a second language if they are to participate in government effectively.

Bilingual ballots are a slap in the face to those citizens who have worked so hard to integrate themselves into the English-speaking society of which they are now apart.

To oppose bilingual ballots is not to oppose or disregard the Hispanic community. On the contrary, it is believed that Hispanics, especially those in California, make up a viable block of voters. It is also believed they want to be actively involved.

But to be involved, and to be taken seriously, requires more than the ability to punch a ballot.

It requires knowledge.

A knowledge that will only come when we stop dividing communities, and start unifying them.

54.
Governor Deukmejian: "We the People of California Do Hereby Find. . ."

After the voters approved Proposition 38, Governor George Deukmejian dispatched the following official letter to President Ronald Reagan.

November 21,1984

The Honorable Ronald Reagan
President
The White House
Washington, D.C. 20500

Dear Mr. President:

On November 6, 1984, California voters approved a ballot measure which states:

''We the People of the State of California do hereby find and declare that:

''The United States has been and will continue to be enriched by the cultural contributions of immigrants from many countries with many different traditions.

''A common language, English, unites our immigrant residents, fosters harmony among our people, promotes political stability, permits interchange of ideas at many levels and encourages societal integration.

''The United States Government should foster similarities that unite our people, and the most important of which is the use of the English language.

''Multilingual ballots are divisive, costly and often delay or prevent our immigrant citizens from moving into the economic, political, educational and social mainstream of our country.

''Multilingual ballots are unnecessary since immigrants seeking citizenship must pass an examination for literacy and proficiency in English.''

The measure further directs me to send the following message to the President of the United States:

''The People of the State of California recognizing the importance of a common language in unifying our diverse nation hereby urge that Federal law be amended so that ballots, voters' pamphlets and all other official voting materials shall be printed in English only.''

Most cordially,
/s/
George Deukmejian

55.
Sen. Sam Hayakawa: A Constitutional Amendment is Needed

In 1981 California Senator S.I. Hayakawa, who was trained as a semanticist and language specialist, introduced an amendment to the U.S. Constitution that would make English the official language of the United States. The new article would state:

"Section 1. The English language shall be the official language of the United States.
"Section 2. The Congress shall have the power to enforce this article by appropriate legislation."

Hayakawa sparked a nationwide campaign to back the proposal. The following remarks by him were quoted in a speech by Senator Symms and appeared in the Congressional Record, *January 22, 1985.*

Mr. Hayakawa: Mr. President, language is a powerful tool. A common language can unify, separate languages can fracture and fragment a society. The American "melting pot" has succeeded in creating a vibrant new culture among peoples of many different cultural backgrounds largely because of the widespread use of common language, English.

Learning English has been the primary task of every immigrant group for two centuries. Participation in the common language has rapidly made available to each new group the political and economic benefits of American society. Those who have mastered English have overcome the major hurdle to full participation in our democracy.

A constitutional. . .amendment is needed to clarify the confusing signals we have given in recent years to immigrant groups. For example, the requirements for naturalization as a U.S. citizen say you must be able to "read, write, and speak words in ordinary usage in the English language." And though you must be a citizen to vote, some recent legislation has required bilingual ballots in some areas. This amendment would end that contradictory, logically conflicting situation.

Bilingual education programs were originally designed to help non-English speaking children learn English quickly so they could join the mainstream of education and of our society. The Carter administration attempted to substantially broaden this mandate by proposing requirements for schools to teach other academic subjects entirely in students' native language.

I believe that we are being dishonest with linguistic minority groups if we tell them they can take full part in American life without learning the English language. We may wish it were otherwise, but it simply is not so. As the son of an immigrant to an English-speaking country, I know this from personal experience. If I spoke no English, my world would be limited to the Japanese-speaking community, and no matter how talented I was, I could never do business, seek employment, or take part in public affairs outside that community.

Let me explain what the amendment will do, upon its passage by Congress and ratification by three-fourths of the States:

It will establish English as the official language of State, Federal, and local government business;

It will abolish requirements for bilingual election materials;

It will allow transition instruction in English for non-English speaking students, but do away with requirements for foreign-language instruction in other academic subjects;

It will end the false promise being made to new immigrants that English is unnecessary. . . .

On the other hand, and this is important, there are things the amendments will not do:

It will not prevent the use of any other language within communities, churches, or cultural schools.

That is, Yiddish schools, Hispanic schools, Japanese, and Chinese schools are perfectly all right insofar as their support by local communities, but not by the taxpayer.

It will not prevent the use of second languages for the purpose of public convenience and safety, for example on signs in public places, but it will not allow governments to require multilingual postings or publications.

I am thinking, Mr. President, of such signs as you see in the street sometimes, "Danger, construction area." If this sign is put up in a building lot in Chinatown, let us say, there is certainly no objection whatsoever to putting signs to that effect in Chinese or any other language that is appropriate for the passerby. So, for purposes of public convenience and safety, other languages may be used wherever necessary. I think that what we have, in Washington, Los Angeles, and San Francisco, street signs in Chinese or Japanese, are perfectly acceptable, because they are also accompanied by street signs in English. They are also acceptable because they give a cosmopolitan flavor to those cities that have them and we are proud of the fact that we are a cosmopolitan culture.

My amendment, Mr. President, will not prevent public schools from offering instruction in other languages, nor will it prevent schools and colleges from requiring some study of a foreign language.

Incidentally, Mr. President, we are crippled in international relations because of our imperfect command not only of the well known languages like Spanish, French, German, or Italian, but we have very few speakers of Chinese, Japanese, Russian, Hungarian, Arabic, Thai—some languages some people here ought to know so they can serve our Nation intelligently in diplomatic service or in trade. If we have a huge trade deficit *vis-a-vis* Japan, for example, it is because they have some Japanese salesmen speaking English in New York, Chicago, Los Angeles, and elsewhere, but we have very, very few Japanese-speaking Americans doing a selling job in Tokyo or Osaka.

So, at the same time that I declare English to be the official language of the United States, I am not trying to discourage foreign language studies.

The ability to forge unity from diversity makes our society strong. We need all the elements, Germans, Hispanics, Hellenes, Italians, Chinese, all the cultures that make our Nation unique. Unless we have a common basis for communicating and sharing ideas, we all lose. The purpose of this proposal is to insure that American democracy always strives to include in its mainstream everyone who aspires to citizenship.

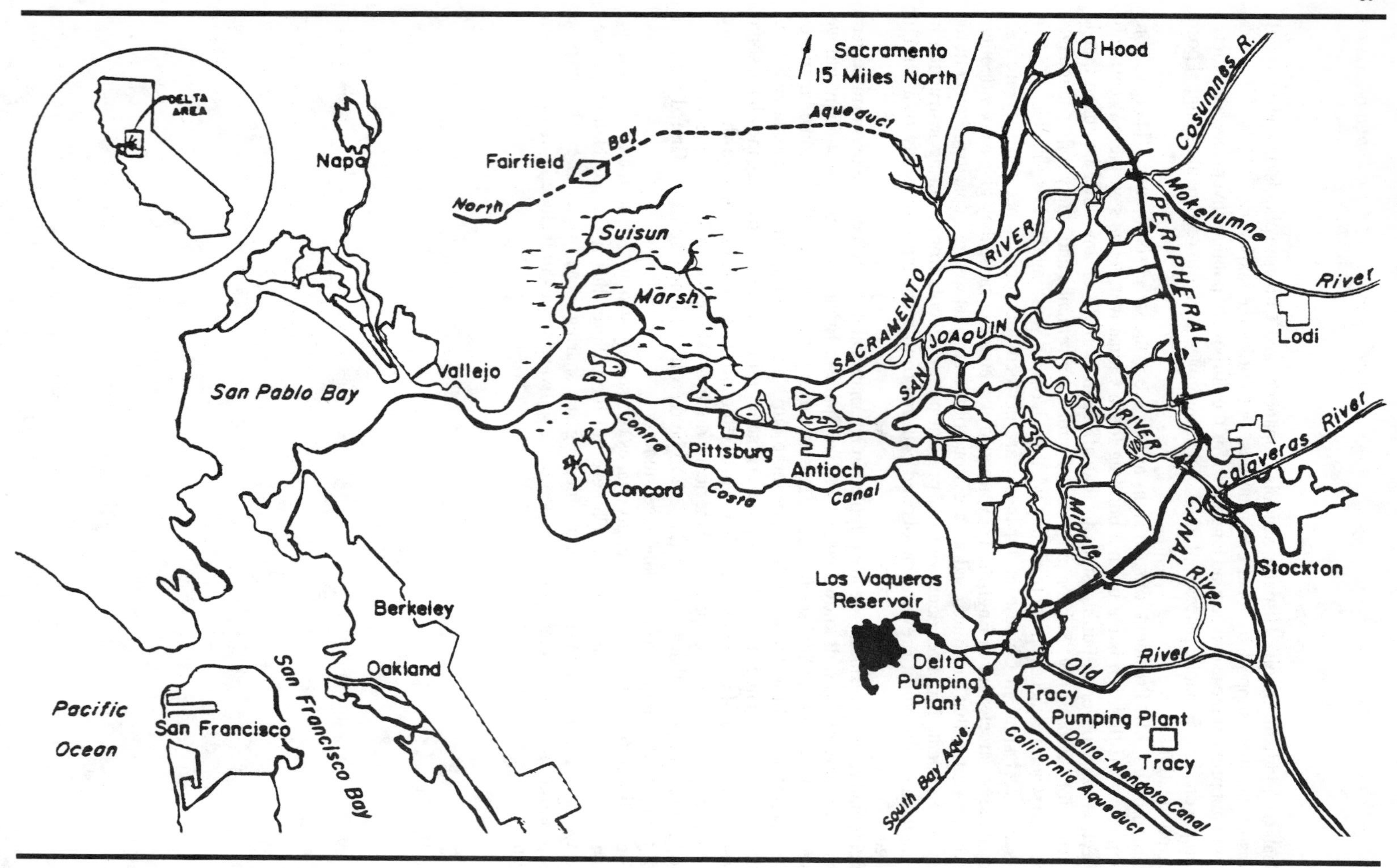

The Peripheral Canal

You see, Mr. Gittes, either you bring the water to LA, or you bring LA to the water.

—John Houston to Jack Nicholson in "Chinatown," cited in Michael Di Leo and Eleanor Smith, *Two Californias*.

We don't want to give the Metropolitan Water district the plumbing to suck us dry in a drought year.

—Dante Nomellini, Delta attorney, *New West*, Sept. 10, 1979, cited in Di Leo and Smith, *Two Californias*.

There's enough water in Northern California, right? And Southern California needs water, right? So what's the problem? I don't know why the north resents the south taking their water. It's only drainage to them and lifeblood to us.

—Malibu hotel developer, *San Francisco Chronicle*, May 11, 1982, cited in Di Leo and Smith, *Two Californias*.

Even if they understood all the complex political, environmental and economic issues involved in the canal debate, northerners would still feel they were being cheated by a peripheral canal that [would] divert up to 80 percent of the flow of the Sacramento River [and ship it south]. What was the north getting in return? Kern County vegetables.

—Spencer Michels, producer of the 1981 KQED documentary, "Two Californias," quoted in *California Living*, April 11, 1982.

The history of California in the twentieth century is the story of a state inventing itself with water.

—William Kahrl, Water and Power, quoted in *California Living*, April 11, 1982.

CHAPTER 16

THE PERIPHERAL CANAL
Expensive Boondoggle or Absolute Necessity?

A. *The Case for a Canal*
B. *The Case Against a Canal*
C. *What Next?*

Nothing is more controversial in California than water—who has it, who wants it, and how much it costs to deliver. In recent years much controversy has centered on the Sacramento-San Joaquin Delta region (see accompanying map), which is the hub for the transfer of enormous quantities of water from one part of the state to the other. By examining that area one can learn a great deal about water development issues in California.

Basically the question has been whether, and how, to complete the existing State Water Project so as to increase the flow of Northern California waters to Southern California. If the project is to continue growing then probably some form of canal would have to be dug to direct the northern waters through or around the delta. The following materials focus specifically on the public referendum that was held in 1980-1982 on Senate Bill 200, which called for the building of a peripheral canal.

SB 200 involved the future supply of water for Southern California and the future of the delta region, where the waters of the San Joaquin and Sacramento rivers, and their tributaries, converge. It is the largest inland estuary in the United States. It teems with fish and bird life and its shores comprise one of the richest agricultural regions in the state. The $9 billion-a-year agriculture industry and the city dwellers of Southern California both had a tremendous stake in that water.

Proponents of the canal—led by the Metropolitan Water District of Southern California and many agribusinesses—asserted that the facility was essential to the future of the California Water Project and to the delta, as well as to the well-being of Southern California. The big ditch was needed not only to alleviate pending shortages of water south of the Tehachapi Mountains, but also to cleanse and improve the water flowing through the delta.

Opponents of the canal—a coalition of conservationists and, unexpectedly, even some growers who wanted the law to guarantee water development on the rivers of the north coast—refuted the arguments for a new canal. In the words of one of them, "California's water system is out of control, growing where it is not needed, driving up taxes, wrecking rivers and lakes—and wasting millions of acres-feet of water each year." Foes of the canal contended that other alternatives were available, including better conservation methods, especially in agriculture.

In the end California voters resoundingly rejected the peripheral canal proposal. While a majority of Southern California voters favored it, northern opposition was strong enough to defeat it.

Predicting the future course of water development is a notoriously difficult task. No one planning the water future of California in the 1950's could have imagined the impact that energy costs would have on costs of water delivery systems in the 1970's. Similarly, no one is now in a position to anticipate the controlling forces of the next generation. But, clearly, demand for more water was likely to increase in Southern California, especially since the U.S. Supreme Court had ruled that California's share from the Colorado River will have to diminish. And clearly the State Water Project would be the most likely system to replenish any deficiency in Southern California's water supply.

Thus, despite the outcome of the 1982 referendum, the canal idea continued to percolate in all serious discussions of water development. Water was the source of endless debate in a variety of other ways, as well. Problems of increasing chemical pollution and deteriorating water quality presented headaches for city dwellers and rural interests alike. Much depended on the question of water subsidy to agriculture. (Chapter XI, which deals with the 160-acre limitation, touches on the water-subsidy question.) In this chapter the materials are divided into three parts—first, arguments favoring the canal, second, those opposed, and third, opinion hinting at the next phase of development.

While assessing the readings (as well as basic textbook information) the reader should keep in mind the following questions: Why is the Delta region pivotal for water development in California? Who are the vested interests in determining water policy? What is at stake for urban, industrial and agricultural water users, and for recreational and environmental concerns? The demands of Southern California may be real or imagined but they are heavy. How do they impact on the overall water-development discussion? Regarding SB 200, what arguments were advanced as an alternative to the canal? SB 200 was a compromise package. Who backed it and who opposed it, and why, in the final analysis, did the voters reject it? Again, while it is impossible to predict future water development, it is clear that Southern California's demand for more water will continue. If so, what is the next step? *(Editor's note)*

A. *The Case For The Canal*

56.
California Water Commission: SB 200 is the Only Viable Solution

Proposition 8 backing SB 200 and a peripheral canal was actively supported by the California Water Commission, a body appointed by the governor to advise the California Water Resources Agency. The Commission's reasons are spelled out in the following position paper.[1]

In June 1982, the voters of California will either approve or reject Senate Bill 200—and by that action they will also ratify or nullify Proposition 8. Although the public will be voting to approve or reject the SB 200 statute, the central issue is the Peripheral Canal.

Countless words have been written about this issue. Even a cursory examination of material related to the Peripheral Canal (and SB 200 and Proposition 8) reveals the following statements:

—The Peripheral Canal is an environmental and water supply necessity.
—The Peripheral Canal is not needed.
—The Canal will save the delta.
—The Canal will ruin the delta.
—The Canal will cost $680 million. . . 1 billion. . . 7 billion. . . 10 billion. . . 23 billion.
—The Canal costs will be paid by water users.
—The Canal costs will be paid by the taxpaying public.
—The San Joaquin Valley and Southern California need the water.
—The San Joaquin Valley and Southern California do not need the water.
—California has sufficient water for all the State.
—The Peripheral Canal will suck the north State dry.
—Oil Companies and the Corporate giants will reap unjust profits from subsidized water.
—If the Peripheral Canal is built, there will be power blackouts all over Northern California.
—There are many preferable alternatives and the Canal is the worst possible choice.

The above statements, all purporting to be factual—and all obviously glaring contradictions—briefly summarize some of the major points of contention regarding the Canal. While the possible list of similar contradictory statements is almost endless, the above statements tend to cover the key issues.

This paper will briefly examine the above statements, discuss the source and rationale for them, and attempt to put the issues in proper perspective.

Since the 1860's, California has been conducting studies and developing its capability to manage and distribute its total water resources. Over 30 years ago, the State Water Project (SWP) was conceived as the next logical step in the water management and distribution process. Approved by the electorate in 1960, the SWP was designed and sized to provide additional supplies to areas of the San Joaquin Valley, the San Francisco Bay area, and Southern California. Thirty-one Water Supply Contractors (now 30 contractors because of consolidation) in these areas, having identified existing and future water supply needs, signed contracts beginning in 1961 to pay the cost of con-

[1]California Water Commission, "Proposition Paper on SB 200, Proposition 8 and the Peripheral Canal" (Sacramento, 1981).

structing and operating the SWP. The validity of their need was implied by their willingness to immediately begin payments for water to be received at a later date.

The basic concept of the SWP is to develop 4.23 million acre-feet (MAF) of firm annual water supply and transport it to areas of need in the 30 contract service areas—including the San Francisco Bay area, the San Joaquin Valley and Southern California. The most practical, effective, economical, and ecologically desirable way to do this was felt by the planners to be by developing a source (principally the Feather River/Oroville Dam), moving the water across the delta with a delta transfer facility, and thence to areas of use via the California Aqueduct.

The firm delivery yield from present project facilities is about 2.3 MAF per year. Moving even this quantity of water across the delta through natural channels has caused stress on the delta—particularly the fish population. However, 30 Water Supply Contractors expect (by virtue of signed contracts with the State) to receive increasing quantities of water from the SWP. To meet contractual obligations, the State must identify the additional yield required, and identify a way to move this greater quantity of water across the delta. It is apparent that the State has little choice on whether or not to develop and move the water—only a choice of how. SB 200, with Proposition 8, is currently that choice.

SB 200 does not purport to solve all of the many inequities and unsolved political and socio-economic problems involved in California's water resource management. However, it does attack the immediate need for improved delta and support facilities.

The Delta: Salvation or Disaster with the Canal?

The current favorable delta salinity conditions exist primarily because of upstream development (Shasta, Oroville, and Folsom Dams). Under pre-project conditions (1920-1944) sea water moved upstream and into the delta when fresh water flows decreased in late spring and through the summer. While delta salinity in recent years (especially dry years) is significantly better than under pre-project conditions, the fishery is not. the problem for the State then, is how to move several million acre-feet of water annually across, around, or through the delta and at the same time control salinity and improve the fishery.

Opponents of the Canal say it is an immense 43-mile-long ditch, ''big enough to float an oil tanker,'' which ''will divert more than 70 percent of the flow of the Sacramento River'' and thus ruin the delta.

It is a well documented fact that the export capacity of the Canal is 18,250 cubic-feet-per-second (CFS)—which is therefore the maximum flow that can be diverted. The capacity of the Sacramento River and its adjacent flood bypass is over 500,000 cfs in the vicinity of the proposed Canal intake. Winter flows of 50,000 cfs to 100,000 cfs in the Sacramento are typical and higher flood flows are not uncommon.

Opponents of the Canal say it will destroy the delta fishery—the wildlife will disappear—and native vegetation will wither away. However, SB 200 was specifically worded to protect and enhance the delta including: the requirement that the SWP be operated to restore fisheries to historic levels; the requirement that the canal be constructed in stages with testing of fish screens for adequacy before Canal completion; the provision that these be limitations on exports to ensure maintenance of historic levels of fish and wildlife; compliance with delta water quality standards and water right limitations to protect the delta and San Francisco Bay; and assurance of water necessary for agricultural production in the delta. Both the California Department of Fish and Game, and the U.S. Fish and Wildlife Service strongly endorse early construction of the Canal.

Costs

A wide range of numbers, including $680 million, $1 billion, $7 billion, and $23 billion have been identified as being ''the cost of the Peripheral Canal.'' Each of these numbers has some relationship to the SWP but most of them are completely out of context when associated with the Canal alone. The explanation and derivation of these figures (borne out by various technical reports of the Department of Water Resources (DWR) is as follows:

—$680 million is the estimated cost of the Canal at 1981 prices.

—$1 billion is the estimated cost of construction the Canal over a 10-year period from 1984-1994, allowing for inflation at 9 percent per year.

—$7 billion (7.23 billion) was the estimated cost (1977) of all facilities provided for under SB 346 (predecessor to SB 200) and included escalation due to inflation to the year 2000. Over one half of these estimated costs of SB 346 were assumed to be federal Central Valley Project costs.

—$10 billion ($10.1 billion) was a revised estimate (published in DWR's Bulletin 132-80) of the total cost of the SWP at the year 2000 including all expenditures dating back to 1952. $23 billion (23.3 billion) was an estimate of total SWP costs from 1952 out to the year 2035, including escalation due to inflation and including facilities to be built beyond the year 2000.

Water Supply

Canal opponents (particularly in Northern California) fear there is not enough water to satisfy the entire State—and that Southern California will overwhelm the north State and take the water.

It should be noted that the reservoir storage capacity on the major streams of the Sacramento Valley is about 10 MAF—that in an average year, flow in these streams is about 17 MAF,—and that in the comparatively wet year 1977-78, it was over 25 MAF. The additional firm yield needed for the SWP is only 1.9 MAF—with 700,000 a.f. of this to be provided by the Peripheral Canal. Even in the year 2000, and with the Canal in operation, delta outflow in excess of minimum requirements would be 6.9 MAF in an average year. 16.5 MAF in a typical wet year, and 1.0 MAF in a typical dry year. SB 200 (with the Canal) provides for offstream storage (Los Vaqueros) and ground water storage programs in the south San Francisco Bay area, the San Joaquin Valley, and Southern California to take advantage of excess flows in wet years. From a water supply standpoint, when the 1.9 MAF new yield provided by SB 200 is taken in the context of total flow of Sacramento Valley streams and excess delta outflows, the fears that the north could be hurt are totally unrealistic.

Who Pays?

Canal opponents state or imply that the cost of SB 200, including the Canal, will be paid by the taxpaying public.

This is not true. As a contractual obligation, the 30 Water Service Contractors pay all of the capital, and operating, maintenance and replacement costs of the Project allocated to water supply. The financial arrangements for the SWP are a matter of public record which is updated and published periodically by DWR in its Bulletin 132 series and verified by the Water Service Contractor auditors.

Unjust Profits

Canal opponents on the one hand say that huge oil companies and other agribusiness entities will be the principal beneficiaries of cheap water from the Canal. On the other hand, opponents also say the price of water will be so high that people in Los Angeles will not be able to afford it. These contradictory remarks can be refuted by reiterating the aforementioned fact that all State contractors pay all the costs of water delivered to their respective service area.

Power Blackouts

One of the most widely misunderstood factors in the State Water Project operation is the power required to deliver the water. It must be understood that the Project consumes and generates vast quantities of power; the critical factor is the new amount consumed, not the total. Careful studies indicate that by the year 2000, the net consumption of the Project will be about 3.1% of the total power consumption in California, with or without the Peripheral Canal. The Canal itself will create a difference of only .02%

Long-term power contracts and already-planned new power sources, (for example: in-stream hydropower recovery plants, hydroplants to be built at existing dams, geothermal sources, and other energy alternatives) will assure that the Project, and most certainly the Peripheral Canal, will not "cause blackouts" anywhere. The cost of the additional power to fulfill the ultimate delivery requirements will be borne by the Project contractors just as are all other operating costs.

Alternatives

Some opponents suggest an all-out effort in water conservation and waste water reclamation; other groups recommend against approval of SB 200 "at this time"—but for totally opposite reasons. These alternatives will be discussed below.

Conservation and Reclamation

Conservation and waste water reclamation play important roles in California's water management program. The Governor, coincident with signing SB 200, issued an Executive Order which included the following three salient points:

(1) The Department of Water Resources is directed to prepare a plan of water conservation, reclamation and management for the State Water Project to be submitted to the State Water Resources Control Board, such plan to recommend actions that could be undertaken by the State and its water service contractors to reduce the demand for water, to reclaim urban and agricultural waste water, to store water underground in order to provide for dry years, and to provide for consideration of pricing changes, water exchanges, and other methods of reducing the demand for new water facilities.

(2) The Department of Water Resources is hereby directed to implement as quickly as possible a program to desalt 400,000 acre-feet of agricultural waste water.

(3) And finally, the State Water Resources Control Board is urged to require water conservation plans in the exercise of their water rights authority.

The fact that this Executive Order, when taken in the context of SB 200, is considered by some SB 200 detractors to place inadequate emphasis on conservation and reclamation and considered by other SB 200 detractors to place too much emphasis on conservation and reclamation, suggests that perhaps the emphasis is just what it should be, an important part (but only a part) of the comprehensive new water supply program provided by SB 200.

Ground Water Management

Some well-informed proponents who see the Peripheral Canal as an environmental necessity, oppose SB 200 at this time because it does not include mandatory ground water controls to prevent overdrafts. There is substantial statewide agreement on the need for ground water management. However, the realities of the political process were such that including ground water controls in SB 200 would have resulted in defeating the entire legislative package. Eventually (but perhaps well into the futures) a practical ground water law probably will be adopted. However, to wait for this possibility to occur, as a condition before proceeding with the SB 200 program, will deny the delta the increased protection of features included in the SB 200 program.

Wait for "A Better Deal"?

Some groups of agriculturally oriented interests are opposing SB 200 at this time—not because they do not see a need for the Canal, but because of their concerns about the increased protections of North Coast streams included in Proposition 8. Ironically, these same groups have perhaps the most to lose if the Canal is not available in time to meet their needs, particularly in dry years.

Astute observers of California's water and environmental politics in recent years agree that any development of the North Coast streams will be the last resort effort; something that would occur only if and when all other sources have failed to keep pace with needs. To "wait for a better deal" in the belief that such development will be "easy" in the 1980's, (or anytime in the future) as a result of power politics, ignores the established viewpoint of the California voting public.

Conclusion

The Peripheral Canal (and its alternatives) is probably the most thoroughly studied water project in the world. From a statewide perspective, balancing the needs and attainable goals with environmental and economic constraints, the choice in 1982 seems clear. To provide adequate water supplies for all of California, to improve water quality, restore the delta fishery, and to provide environmental and other protections, the only viable solution is the Peripheral Canal as provided in SB 200 and Proposition 8.

57.
Metropolitan Water District: The Canal Will Protect the Delta and Help Southern California

As one of the state's largest water contractors, Metropolitan Water District (MWD) strongly favored the Peripheral Canal measure. Bulletins issued by its speakers bureau indicate why. One of the major arguments propounded for the canal involved Southern California's pending loss of water from the Colorado River.

BULLETIN #1

There are four major interrelated environmental problems in the delta that would be corrected by the Peripheral Canal. They are:

A. Reverse Flows;
B. Saltwater intrusion;
C. Degraded water quality; and
D. Reduced fish populations.

Reverse flows are caused by operation of the State Water Project and Federal Central Valley Project export pumps and are of two types. First, in preproject conditions, the flows in the southern delta channels were generally from south to north. With the project operating under low delta outflow conditions, flows in the southern delta channels are reversed and move from north to south toward the pumps. Second, as exports increase, reverse flows in the extreme western delta also occur under low delta outflow conditions. Under this condition, Sacramento River water flows around the western end of Sherman Island, causing water to flow upstream in portions of the San Joaquin River. These reverse flows adversely affect the migrating anadromous fish seeking their spawning areas. This results in a reduction in fish population. The Peripheral Canal will eliminate these reverse flows.

Saltwater intrusion is caused by insufficient freshwater delta outflow. The delta, being at sea level, is subject to the ocean tides. When there is insufficient outflow, saltwater from San Francisco Bay intrudes into the delta. This is most common during the summer months and drought periods. Under such conditions, this problem can also be caused by operation of the export pumps. The Peripheral Canal will eliminate the reverse flow problem and subsequent drawing in of salt water as discussed in Paragraph 2.

Water Quality problems in the delta result primarily from two factors. Water quality is degraded because of saltwater intrusion and from agricultural return flows from farming operations in the delta and the San Joaquin Valley. Release points along the Peripheral Canal will allow introduction of high quality Sacramento River water into the interior delta. This will restore the natural direction of flows in the delta channels and will flush out the agricultural return flows.

Declining fish populations have resulted from operation of the export pumps which pull fry (small fish) and their food supply out of the delta. The pumps also cause flow reversals in the southern delta channels. Currently, the export pumps draw water from the fishery nursery area, which is in the western delta, to the pumps in the south delta. Fish screens are incorporated in these facilities, but they cannot effectively screen the small fish or their food supply. The intake to the Peripheral Canal, which will remove the effect of the export pumps on the nursery area. The canal will include an extensive fish screen facility at Hood, 43 miles north of the existing pumps, where the fish are larger and able to be screened out.

SB 200 and Proposition 8, along with existing State laws, assure that the problems in the delta discussed above will be corrected. Additional facilities to be constructed in the delta and Suisun Marsh will maintain the environmental integrity of these areas.

BULLETIN #16

Summary

The Total cost of building the Peripheral Canal is $680 million in 1981 dollars. Because construction will take more than a decade, inflation is expected to push the price to $1.3 billion.

No state taxes will be used. The state will build the canal and the project contractors will reimburse the state. The primary sources of financing are revenue bonds that are repaid with project revenues, and the California Water Fund, which gets money from state tidelands oil and gas royalties and from contractors' payments that are in excess of project operating costs and annual bond debt service costs. The tidelands royalties account for a small portion of the total financing. Money will also come from miscellaneous receipts. Bonds will be sold only on an as-needed basis.

This financing mechanism has made the SWP one of the most financially sound major public works projects in the country.

BULLETIN #17

The reliability of an area's imported water supply depends upon three conditions: (1) adequate reservoir storage in the area where the water originates to provide a full and dependable supply during the most critical runoff years; (2) water conveyance facilities capable of transporting the water from the origin to the area of use; (3) assured rights to the water necessary to serve future demands.

A case in point is the Metropolitan Water District's water supply from the State Water Project. In this case, Metropolitan has firm contractual rights for 2.0 million acre-feet of the State project water by the year 1990. However, the project's dependable yield is insufficient to meet even the existing demands of its water service contractors. Metropolitan's share of the State Water Project yield, based on the adverse water condition experienced in 1976-77, would leave Metropolitan about 750,000 acre-feet short of meeting its 1990 projected demands. Furthermore, even in years of normal water supply, the project has insufficient conveyance facilities to meet its contractors' future demands. Without the Peripheral Canal, it will not be possible to fully serve Metropolitan's 1990 projected demands. And not only is the Peripheral Canal necessary for conveyance purposes, but it also increases the dependable yield of the State Water Project. This increased yield is the result of the greater amounts of winter flood flows that can be captured with the canal, and the decrease in the amount of Delta outflow required to keep sea water out of the Delta.

Another case in point is Metropolitan's Colorado River water supply. Some 60 million acre feet of storage capacity—more than four times the annual runoff of the river—could result in a highly dependable water supply. And Metropolitan's Colorado River Aqueduct is capable of transporting 1.2 million acre-feet per year to Metropolitan's service area. However, Metropolitan's future rights to Colorado River water are severely limited. The Law of the River—a collection of compacts, treaties, laws, and court decisions which determines Metropolitan's rights to Colorado River water—is discussed in Speakers Bureau Bulletin 18.

BULLETIN #18

The Colorado River Compact of 1922 apportioned the waters of the river between the Upper and Lower Basin states. The Lower Basin states—Arizona, California, and Nevada—were apportioned 7.5 million acre-feet per year for their consumptive use.

Subsequently, contracts with the Federal government for water deliveries from Lake Mead were executed by seven California water agencies. These agencies consisted of two groups: the agricultural agencies (Palo Verde Irrigation District, Yuma Project, Imperial Irrigation District, and Coachella Valley Water District) and the Metropolitan Water District (which includes the City of Los Angeles and the City and/or County of San Diego). The contracts were in accordance with the terms of a Seven-Party Agreement the agencies had executed among themselves. The Seven-Party Agreement allocated 5,362,000 acre-feet per year of water among the agencies and set priorities for use of the water. The division of water and priorities of the two groups were as follows:

Priority	Agency	1,000 AF
1-3	Agricultural Agencies	3,850
4	Metropolitan Water District	550
5	Metropolitan Water District	662
6	Agricultural Agencies	300
	Total	5,362

In 1964, the U. S. Supreme Court Decree in *Arizona* vs. *California* apportioned the Lower Basin's 7.5 million acre-feet among the states. The apportionment limited California's annual rights to Colorado River water to 4.4 million acre-feet. The decree also apportioned 2.8 million acre-feet per year to Arizona and 0.3 million acre-feet per year to Nevada.

Under operating criteria promulgated by the Secretary of the Interior, the limitation on California's use of Colorado River water will become effective when the Central Arizona Project commences delivery of water. At that time, presently estimated to be in 1985, California's annual rights to Colorado River water will be reduced to 4.4 million acre-feet, and only enough water will be available to meet the first four priorities. Indian and other miscellaneous water rights will be included in the fourth priority and will take precedence over Metropolitan's rights.

Recent annual use of Colorado River water in California is about 5.0 million acre-feet. Of this total, Metropolitan normally uses about 0.8 million acre-feet and the agricultural agencies and others about 4.2 million acre-feet. Based on the recent recommendation of the special master appointed by the U.S. Supreme Court to determine Indian rights to Colorado River water, as much as 172,000 acre-feet per year could be awarded to the lower Colorado River Indians. If these Indian water rights are all included in the fourth priority, after California's apportionment is reduced to 4.4 million acre-feet per year, the amounts of Colorado River water available for Metropolitan's service area could be as low as 325,000 acre-feet per year after conveyance losses are deducted.

Under the Supreme Court decree, California is entitled to one-half of any surplus Colorado River water available. First call on any such surplus would go to Metropolitan under its fifth priority right. However, the probability of surplus water being available will begin to decline after the Central Arizona Project begins diversions, and will be remote in the mid-1990's. Surplus water cannot be counted on as a dependable water supply.

BULLETIN #19

As discussed in Speakers Bureau Bulletin 18, after the Central Arizona Project commences operation, estimated to be in 1985, not only will Metropolitan's water rights be reduced but the water rights of California's agricultural agencies will be reduced as well. They will be limited to the first three priorities of 3.85 million acre-feet per year. Since their present use is about 4.2 million acre-feet per year, the agricultural agencies will also have to reduce their use of Colorado River water.

The recent lining of 49 miles of the Coachella Canal has saved an estimated 132,000 acre-feet per year of water. It has been suggested that lining the 37-mile reach of the All-American Canal from Pilot Knob to the East Highline Canal could save an additional 70,000 acre-feet per year. However, the cost of the water salvaged by lining the canal would be high by the agricultural agencies standards. It would cost about $155 per acre-foot—similar to costs of future water supplies available to the Metropolitan Water District. For these reasons, it has been suggested that Metropolitan pay for the canal lining in exchange for the rights to the salvaged water.

The principal problem with this suggestion is that the agricultural agencies have a number of potential uses for the salvaged water. These use include: maintaining current lands in production after the agricultural agencies Colorado River water rights are reduced; meeting the variations in water demand from one year to the next which result from changes in weather and crops; putting additional lands into production; and providing water for increased leaching needs because of increased salinity of the irrigation water and the improved land drainage. Because of these future water uses, and because of the agricultural agencies rights to the water, it does not appear that Metropolitan could receive any of the salvaged water.

Under existing California water law, Metropolitan cannot use water that is part of a water right belonging to another party. Metropolitan could no more use the agricultural agencies unused water than it could use San Francisco's or the East Bay Municipal Utility District's unused water supplies from the Tuolumne or Mokelumne rivers. These unused supplies provide for the growth in future water demands in these areas. Metropolitan's future water supplies must come from areas where surplus water, not needed by local residents, is available.

B. *The Case Against A Canal*

58.
Friends of the Earth: The Big Ditch Unnecessary and Will Harm the Environment

The case against the canal was argued cogently in a pamphlet written by Harry Dennis and issued by Friends of the Earth,[2] one of the environmental groups which opposed SB 200.

CHAPTER I

With Governor Brown's signature, State Senate Bill 200 became law in July 1980, authorizing the Peripheral Canal and other additions to California's State Water Project. Passage of SB 200

[2]*Water & Power: The Peripheral Canal and Its Alternatives* (1981). The excerpts come from Chapts. I, "The Water Choice," 9-15, II, "California's Waterscape," 16-44, and VII, "What We Can Do Instead," 133-135. Mr Dennis is now a medical student and works on environmental issues as a volunteer.

brought to a close nearly two decades of legislative debate over expansion of the State Water Project. But the issue is far from settled.

Opponents of SB 200 gathered 850,000 signatures, more than twice the number needed to put a bill up for a public vote. California's next statewide election—in November 1981 or June 1982—will include a referendum on SB 200. The water lobby is working overtime to convince the public that we need this enormously expensive project to bring water from northern California to the farms and cities of the south.

In the south, the message is, "When Arizona takes its water, we'll run dry." The Metropolitan Water District (MWD) is going all out on this campaign, even sending employees to a drama coach to help them carry this doomsday cry more effectively. Some 40 to 80 speeches are being given each month by MWD officials—and they will speak before any group that will listen. The California Association of Car Washers, the Fullerton Rotary Club, and the Coalition of Southern California Business Interests are among those who have been warned of the impending water shortages.

People in northern California are being broadcast a different message.

The Peripheral Canal, they are told, is needed to restore the fish and wildlife of the Sacramento-San Joaquin Delta. Those who don't believe that—and there are quite a few—are warned that SB 200 is the best bill they will get. If the Peripheral Canal is rejected by the voters on this round, the agribusiness and land development lobbyists will be back in Sacramento, pushing for other ways to move the water south—and when they succeed, the new projects will be unencumbered by the constitutional guarantees that California voters granted to the Delta and the north coast rivers when they passed Proposition 8 in November of 1980.

Why all the hullabaloo over a 42-mile ditch?

—Farmers in the Delta fear that the Canal will mean poorer quality water flowing through the sloughs that border their farms.

—Some people in southern California realize that there are cheaper ways to meet their water needs, and fear that expanding the State Water Project now will make city people continue to spend millions of their property tax dollars to subsidize Kern County farmers.

Environmentalists fear that, constitutional guarantees notwithstanding, the U.S. Fish and Wildlife Service chief for California and Nevada was right when he wrote, "On the day that construction is started for a Peripheral Canal, you can say goodbye to the upper Sacramento and Eel Rivers (and perhaps other north coast streams) as we know them today."

—Many wildlife lovers fear that the Peripheral Canal, by allowing increased water exports, threatens the fish and wildlife that live in the Sacramento-San Joaquin Delta.

—Energy conservation advocates are concerned about the huge amounts of energy that the project consumes. The A.D. Edmonston pumping plant, which drives water 2,000 feet up the Tehachapis, uses as much electricity as did the entire city of Los Angeles in 1965. An expanded State Water Project is projected to use 10 billion kilowatt hours of electricity in the year 2000—about as much power as is used in 2 million homes. The SB 200 facilities will cost five billion dollars—a big enough sum to start with, but the state Department of Water Resources has calculated that once the canal is begun, completion of the State Water Project, including pumping stations and all, will cost some *twenty-three* billion dollars.

Contracts and Efficiencies

Water development planning in California, as practiced in 1980-1, is not based on need. It is based on contracts that water districts signed with the state in the early 1960's, and on the customers' ability to pay. It ignores how water is used, and where, and the consequences of "developing" it and moving it from place to place.

This approach leaves out—in fact, it precludes—efficient water use, and is not suitable for modern-day California. *Efficient Water Use in California,* a study completed by the Rand Corporation in 1978, concluded that "There is no general state policy to encourage efficient use of water within California, and in fact there are substantial impediments to efficient use embodied in state water law, administrative decisions, and organizational behavior within the water industry.

We are considering spending up to $23 billion to expand the State Water Project, yet farmers who find that they have extra water *now* are unable to sell it to someone who might be able to use it.

Evidence abounds for far better approaches to solving California's water needs:

—The state's Advisory Panel on Agricultural Water Conservation concluded that "Statewide implementation of water conservation measures will help reduce the water shortages forecast for the near future, without curtailing the present level of agricultural production or economic activity."

—The Governor's Commission to Review Water Rights Law recommended changes that could improve the efficiency of water use in California and halt the further destruction of our already overdrawn groundwater basins.

—The southern district office of the Department of Water Resources has produced several reports that confirm that cheaper and less environmentally destructive ways exist to meet southern California's demand for water over the next two decades. DWR reports have concluded that state-mandated water conservation measures will cut demand in the area significantly, and they show that moderate, voluntary conservation efforts by the area's residents will more than make up for the shortfall in supply that MWD predicts. Other reports prove MWD to be underestimating the potential of wastewater conservation and find that large amounts of water are wasted in the agricultural Imperial Valley; some of the savings could go to MWD. (Now, excess water in the Imperial Valley is simply dumped into the Salton Sea, which is rising and flooding out farmers who are unlucky enough to own land on its shores.

—An internal MWD memorandum allows that if these facilities are built, the district would have a surplus of "perhaps as much as 750,000 acre-feet in 1990." Since MWD customers pay nearly all the costs of the water, whether they use it or not, that surplus will prove tremendously expensive to southern Californians in the years to come.

Three Arguments, Pro-Canal

When forced to admit that there might be less expensive ways to meet southern California's needs through the year 2000, state officials invariably fall back on three arguments:

—the law binds them to honor the contracts signed 20 years ago;
—the Peripheral Canal is needed to save the Delta from further degradation, and
—the San Joaquin Valley needs more water so farmers there can stop relying on overexploited groundwater.

The first argument ignores the fact that California's Constitution requires "reasonable and beneficial use" of water. Since making our use of water more efficient could take care of the state's needs for at least the next twenty years, the state could argue, if it chose, that expanding the State Water Project now constitutes an *un*reasonable use of our state's water.

On the second and third arguments, the officials have good points: The Delta *is* now in bad shape, and overdraft in the San Joaquin Valley *is* a problem. These are real and serious concerns.

But would the Peripheral Canal solve them? The U.S. Fish and Wildlife Service, for one, and the National Marine and Fisheries Service, for another, believe that the Peripheral Canal will not halt the Delta's decline. Concerning groundwater, the Rand Report authors concluded, "Massive application of surface imports will not solve the groundwater problem, particularly if the surface imports are subsidized (sold at less than marginal cost)." Water from an expanded State Water Project would sometimes be sold at far below its marginal cost, since the cost of new facilities is averaged in with the cost of existing, cheaper facilities.

So why the push to expand the State Water Project? There are two big player on the Pro-Canal side. Agribusiness, California's most potent lobby, benefits from an overbuilt water supply system.

When there is extra water sloshing around, farmers can pick up irrigation water cheaply. Agribusiness is willing to spend huge amounts of money on political candidates and "public education" campaigns to ensure a continued supply of cheap water.

MWD's motives for working so hard to waste their customers' money are probably mixed. It would be easy to chalk it up to a conspiracy: several MWD board members own land or are associated with companies that own land in the Central Valley. This land benefits from cheap surplus water. Others' business interests are in the home building or financing industries, for whom new water means more development and more business.

But Mike Bradley, a visiting professor at UCLA's Department of Urban Planning, has been following the activities of MWD and was forced to the conclusion that "It's not a conspiracy—it's a religion." MWD has reached out to grab more and more of California's water so steadily over the last half century that growth has become the nature of the beast. Perhaps MWD officials figure that southern California will need a Peripheral Canal someday (as it might if agricultural water policy is not reformed substantially in the next few decades) and figure the time is ripe; they can get it now and had better get it while they can.

The Opposition

Arrayed against the Big Two is a phalanx of coalitions, including environmentalists; Delta and Sacramento Valley farmers; wilderness advocates who want to protect the north coast rivers; groups and people who are working on reforming the way water is allotted to big farms in this state; tax-cutters; and those agglomerations of fishermen, hunters, boaters, bird-watchers—and the merchants who service them—that are called "recreationists."

Underlying it all is the fact that expanding the State Water Project now would be a tremendous waste of money, energy, and wildlife. There are cheaper, more benign paths available—several unbiased studies have pointed them out.

An informed public has a golden opportunity, in the referendum on the Peripheral Canal, to turn the situation around. This will take a detailed understanding of the water systems of California, both the natural ones and those that engineers and politicians have constructed. It will take a knowledge of water economics, and an involvement in politics—though this need go no further than voting against the Canal.

A majority vote against the Canal could signal the start of a new water age for America's richest agricultural state, and for its most populous cities. It could start us on a path toward using the amounts of water we really have, to do the tasks we really need done, in balance with the supplies nature gives us and the needs of our environment. . . .

CHAPTER 2

The Delta: The Central Issue

The Sacramento-San Joaquin Delta remains the biggest obstacle to a smoothly running State Water Project. it was once an enormous marshland, with beaver, bear, and elk. Mississippi-style river boats carried miners and travellers from the Suisun area to Sacramento and Stockton.

The Delta soil is very rich; over the last century, dikes and levies have been built, and now the Delta consists of some 60 intensively farmed islands surrounded by more than 700 miles of waterways. It is the largest inland estuarine system in the U.S. The Delta is at (or below) sea level, so water shortages are no problem. Generally, the sloughs and rivers in the Delta are filled with fresh water, fed by the Sacramento and San Joaquin, and the other rivers of the Central Valley. When fresh water flows slacken, though, salt water from San Francisco Bay creeps into the Delta with the high tides, damaging the farms and industries in the Delta region that depend on a high-quality water supply. . . .

While the projects have successfully kept the salt water from intruding so deeply into the Delta at the end of the dry season, the lower average flow out of the Delta means that fresh water and salt water meet farther up the Delta than they once did. The effects of this shift are not clearly understood; they are only now beginning to be studied. This is but one indication of our poor understanding of the hydraulics and biology of the Delta. It is on this partial knowledge that the state's Delta water quality standards rest. These standards are periodically changed—but slowly and in politically charged proceedings—as new information becomes available.

When Rivers Run Backward

The projects, as now operating, have had one clearly damaging effect on the hydraulics of the Delta. When the pumps at the south side of the Delta are working near full capacity, water does not really flow *through* the Delta; rather, it flows *around* the Delta.

The bulk of the water reaching the pumps has been drawn down the main channel of the Sacramento River, around Sherman Island at the western edge of the Delta—where it mixes with the more salty water from the Bay—and back up the south side of the Delta. This effect, called "reverse flow," is a serious problem in the late summer, when low natural flows coincide with peak water demand in the south.

The farmers and communities of the Delta draw their water directly out of the sloughs. Farmers and townspeople are rightfully concerned that reverse flow can bring them poor quality water. Farmers in the southern Delta especially have to contend with the possibility that the project will induce water quality problems. If the water gets too salty, production on their farms will drop. . . .

Delta Fish and Game

The state and federal projects, as now operated, have substantially harmed the fish and wildlife of the Delta region. There haven's yet been enough studies to outline the major effects fully, but several facts are clear:

—Fish are confused by abnormal flows in the Delta, and their spawning is disrupted.

—Substantial numbers of fish are drawn to the pumps and many eggs and young fish are exported with the water.

—Stripped bass populations dropped to about 60 percent of their previous levels after the projects started exporting water (and have recently dropped further).

—The Suisun Marsh, which supports a wide range of waterfowl, has been degraded by increasing salinity. The state Fish and Game Department considers Suisun Marsh California's most important wetland, and we are losing it.

—More is *not* known about the dynamics of the Delta ecosystem than *is* known. . . .

To the extent that fish in the San Francisco Bay and nearby coastal waters travel into the Delta to spawn, the health of San Francisco's regional fishery is tied to the health of the Delta. Scientists with the National Marine Fisheries Service at Tiburon, on the north edge of San Francisco Bay, have postulated that the coastal waters off San Francisco's Golden Gate are supported in good measure by the nutrients that flow out of the Delta. Cutting back on Delta outflow could be affecting the offshore fishery. There haven't been enough studies to demonstrate whether or not this is so.

Preliminary studies conducted by NMFS indicate that striped bass may be suffering from pollutants in the water. . . .

Where do the pollutants come from? Agricultural runoff from the San Joaquin Valley, industrial wastes from the shores of the lower Sacramento River, and wastes from San Francisco Bay communities have all entered the estuary. Since total flows out of the Delta are now approximately half of historical levels (15 million acre-feet in an average year versus 30 million acre feet), what pollution does enter the Bay-Delta ecosystem is not flushed out as effectively as it might have been.

(During the great flood of 1862, which put most of Sacramento under water, a steady torrent of fresh water flowed through the Golden Gate for ten days, reportedly displacing salt water clear out to the Farallon Islands, twenty miles off the coast.)

Farming in the Delta

Another type of problem has plagued Delta farmers thanks to the State Water Project. Farmers whose tracts are adjacent to the higher-velocity currents flowing to the pumps have complained that their levees are eroding unusually quickly. If true, then the project is exacerbating an already very serious problem. The levees in the Delta are now a century or more old. They are expensive to maintain and many aren't maintained well. Levee breaks have occurred with increasing frequency, resulting in lost crops and expensive reclamation efforts, or if the land is not reclaimed, the loss of productive farmland. . . .

Water Mining in the San Joaquin

San Joaquin Valley, a tremendously productive agricultural region, also has serious water problems. Farmers, perhaps anticipating that they will get more water from the State Water Project in the next few years, perhaps paying attention to their short term interests only, or perhaps just getting the cheapest water they can, have been "mining" the San Joaquin Valley's groundwater. They are pumping water out of the ground faster than it is replaced by rainfall or seepage from surface water. Groundwater is now being depleted by 2.2 million acre-feet per year in California; most of it is being pumped in the San Joaquin Valley.

When groundwater is mined too severely, not only is water lost, but the ground's ability to hold water can be permanently diminished. Soil sinks or compresses when too much water is removed. In some parts of the San Joaquin Valley, the land has sunk as much as 30 feet because so much groundwater has been withdrawn. The Department of Water Resources is considering storing water in groundwater basins to reduce the need for new dams—"charging" the basins in wet years for use in drier years. As we abuse our groundwater supplies, though, the underground basins' capacity for easing our long-term water supply problems is diminished.

The San Joaquin Valley's other big problem is salt buildup in the soil. To maintain productivity, farmers must continually wash salts out of the root zone of their crops. This is done by giving the crops more water than will be taken up by the roots, so that the excess water will percolate below the root zone, carrying the salts down with it.

Along the east side of the San Joaquin Valley, subsurface drainage is good, so farmers have no trouble getting rid of the salts. On the west side of the valley, though, many of the farms have only about eight feet of soil; under that there is a solid clay barrier. Water carries salts through this barrier only slowly, if at all. Briny groundwater collect above this layer; after several years, this groundwater can build up enough to reach the root zone of the crops. At that point, flushing does no good. For a while, the farmer can grow crops that are more salt resistant, but eventually the groundwater will be of such poor quality that commercial crops cannot be grown.

If the land is to be farmed, a means of drainage must be found.

This constellation of problems and expectations—perhaps most importantly the demands of contractors for their full entitlement of water under the agreements reached in the 1960s— has led planners to call for an expansion of the State Water Project. What was needed, and what the state government struggled for twenty years to find, was a plan that would fill diverse demands:

* the demands of the south, both in the San Joaquin Valley and over the Tehachapis, for more water.
* the demands of Delta farmers for guaranteed high quality water; and
* the demands of many Californians for the least environmentally damaging solution.

The Peripheral Canal, a bold engineering move to bring clean water completely *around* the Delta, emerged as a possible solution. The Legislators liked it, the water industry loved and lobbied for it, and it seemed to offer most things to most interests, so the Legislature mandated it. But it ran into immediate and tough political opposition. There were just too many questions; we've been asking a few. Let us now turn to the Canal itself. . . .

CHAPTER 7

Until the institutions that guide our water management are reformed to promote efficient use of the resource, no new facilities should be built.

Water is ultimately a limited resource: expanding the State Water Project now will only delay us in successfully coming to grips with that fact. Energy, too, is a limited resource, and the large scale, energy-intensive, technical rescues of water mis-management will make less and less sense as the price of energy continues to climb.

This is not to say that ambitious projects, such as those authorized by SB 200, will not or should not be approved sometime in the future. Even with complete reform of our water system, we may someday find the need to increase the interbasin transfers of water in California. But the current system so clouds both supply and demand that reasonable judgments of the necessity of new water facilities are impossible.

As discussed in chapter four, the major steps to reform should be:

* Clarify water rights through stream-by-stream adjudication: this was recommended by Governor's Commission on Water Rights Law.
* Wherever practicable (and it is practicable for most agricultural users) transfer the rights to water from the water district to the water user.
* Remove state and district-level impediments to trading excess water. Do not allow trade of water *rights*, though.
* Oversee water transfers to ensure that they remain temporary and voluntary: monitor them to ensure that public interest is not harmed.
* Phase out property taxes as a way to support water district operations.
* Amend State Water Project contracts to require marginal cost pricing for all Project facilities. The state should support efforts to reform federal water project pricing.
* Eliminate property-based voting in the water districts.
* Establish locally directed groundwater management programs to meet statewide groundwater management goals.

The Sacramento-San Joaquin Delta is in bad shape and needs help. Construction of the Peripheral Canal promises to do more harm than good. As long as exports increase, it is probable that the fishery will decline even if fish hatcheries plant massive numbers of fish. (The Bureau of Reclamation's failure to maintain the Trinity River fishery provides a grim lesson.)

Therefore the state should:

* Follow the National Marine Fisheries Service's advice to the federal government, and place a clear limit on Delta exports, preferably at current entitlement levels.
* Require the Department of Fish and Game's agreement with the Department of Water Resources to provide for the restoration of fish and wildlife in the Delta, without regard to federal cooperation.

These reforms will not come easily. Some excellent people, notably Dr. Paul S. Taylor, have been trying to reform various aspects of California's water system for decades. There has been, and will continue to be, tremendous amounts of money poured into efforts to block reform.

But there is reason to hope.

Californians have long worried about the environmental damage caused by the State Water Project. Many southern Californians are questioning the need for additional, expensive water from north of the Tehachapis when cheaper water is available. And the new administration in Washington, DC, believing that that government is best that hands out the least subsidies, may see fit to end the tremendous subsidies that federal water projects offer to agribusiness.

Maybe the time for reform has come.

C. *What Next?*

59. Supervisor Sunne McPeak: Let's Form a New "Consensus"

Despite the resounding defeat suffered by the canal proposal at the polls, the issue would not die. It continued to appear in stories and opinion pieces in various newspapers, including the Oakland Tribune *of January 25, 1985, which reported on the efforts of a Contra Costa county supervisor to develop a new statewide consensus on water.*

SAN FRANCISCO—Contra Costa County Supervisor Sunne McPeak yesterday called for lasting peace in the water wars between Northern and Southern California and offered an ambitious plan to achieve it.

Her proposal includes constitutional guarantees for San Francisco Bay and the Delta, coordination of state and federal water programs, massive new reservoirs south of the Delta and conservation measures in Southern California.

McPeak, long a leader in the effort to protect Northern California water from wholesale shipment south, heads an unusual public-private group called the Committee for Water Policy Consensus.

Membership includes public officials from 12 Northern California counties and representatives of industry, public utilities, conservationist, sportsmen and farmers.

It is the proposals hammered out by this coalition, one of six ad hoc water policy committees around the state, which McPeak introduced yesterday at a Commonwealth Club workshop.

She said she intends to campaign vigorously to develop a statewide consensus for the plan that the governor and Legislature will be unable to ignore.

"There is a more rational approach to managing our water resources in an environmentally safe and economically sound manner," McPeak said. "No region of the state can be benefited at the expense of another."

Deukmejian, who failed last year to win legislative support for his own billion-dollar Delta water transfer proposal, said last week that he does not intend to introduce any new water plans this year. He said he would listen, however, if the Legislature came up with its own water development measure.

McPeak outlined three keys to "a new water ethic" for California:

* Establishing legal protection within the state constitution "so the entire Bay and Delta system will have first call" on Northern California's water before any greater quantities are shipped south.

"Policy before plumbing," she called it.

Besides constitutional guarantees and new water quality standards sufficient to control salt water intrusion into the Delta, an agreement requiring the state Water Project and the federal Central Valley Project to abide by such standards would be necessary, she said.

* Conservation and construction, including storage facilities south of the Delta to store surplus rainwater, rather than allowing it to pass through the Delta and Bay into the Pacific.

"We physically do not have the ability to capture that surplus today," she said, suggesting that reservoirs could be built in Merced County near Los Banos and in Contra Costa County near the Clifton Court Forebay.

Such storage facilities could be used as the source of increased water when it is needed in Southern California, she said.

In addition, conservation measures including reclamation of waste water could provide the south with between 1 million and 2.5 million acre feet annually, McPeak said.

* The final key, she said, is a process which will build a broad-based, bi-partisan, state-wide consensus on water issues which can set aside "politics as usual" and bring together the governor, the Legislature and key interest groups.

Members of McPeak's committee will be attempting to create that consensus by presenting their proposals to local governments and civic groups for endorsement, another committee spokesman said.

60.
San Diego Evening Tribune: Thunderheads on the Horizon

Swimming against the tide of Northern opposition, Senator Ruben Ayala (Democrat of Chino) introduced new legislation in 1985 to complete the State Water Project. The San Diego Evening Tribune *was not too optimistic about its passage and looked with greater interest on plans to conserve water in the Imperial Valley.*[3]

There are thunderheads on the horizon—not only the kind that bring rains, but the kind that mean the next salvo in the North-South water battle is about to be fired.

True to this word, state Sen. Ruben Ayala, D-Chino, already has introduced a new water bill for consideration in the 1985 legislative session. The bill would authorize completion of the half-finished State Water Project.

Ayala deserves praise for his prompt effort to find some compromise that would allow more surplus Northern California water to flow south. A less determined legislator might have given up under the withering political pressures from Northern California with an irrational fear that Southern California will spoil their rivers and deprive them of water.

Ayala's new bill offers a strong assurance that the water quality in Northern California and the Sacramento-San Joaquin River Delta won't suffer. And it would only require a majority vote for passage in the Legislature.

But San Diegans can't be optimistic.

For two decades, those who oppose finishing the State Water Project have managed to bottle up proposals designed to let more northern water flow to Southern California. Many of these same opponents already have tolled the bell for Ayala's latest plan.

Technically, Gov. Deukmejian could move ahead with his water plans without legislative approval—an option he threatened at one point, but with his re-election race looming in 1986, it's not realistic to think he'll risk Northern California's wrath.

If politics is holding back Northern California's waters as surely as any concrete dam, San

[3] "Fighting to Finish State Water Project," December 18, 1984.

Diegans must look elsewhere. With more than 90 percent of the water supply pumped in from Northern California and the Colorado River, we can't afford to stand by idly. Our best prospect for increasing our imported water supply lies in the plan to save as much as 438,000 acre-feet (an acre-foot is enough to serve a family of five for a year) through conservation in Imperial Valley.

The Metropolitan Water District of Southern California has hammered out a tentative agreement with the Imperial Irrigation District for lining canals and installing other water-saving devices. The water saved could then be sold to MWD's customers, including the San Diego County Water Authority.

We must not be lulled by the rains now greening our yards and filling San Diego's reservoirs. The specter of drought is always present in Southern California. And we know with certainty that Arizona will soon be taking a portion of the Colorado River that once went to Southern California.

Let's hope for the best in Sacramento—but move with urgency on any water project that promises fewer political pitfalls.

61.
Southern California Water Committee: Ready for a New War

In the never-ending struggle to slake the thirst of Southern California, government agencies, water contractors and private interest groups formed a new committee to educate and promote further expansion of the State Water Project. Details of the new campaign were described in the Gannet newspaper chain in December 1984.[4]

SACRAMENTO—After years of blistering defeats in water wars, populous and thirsty Southern California—from Ventura to San Diego—is positioning itself for another major campaign to capture more water.

Battle plans are being drawn by the newly formed Southern California Water committee, a partnership of governments, businesses, water agencies and special interest groups.

By involving these four sectors, which "didn't even know each other, let alone work together," the committee, holding its first board meeting this week, will become a viable force in Southern California water politics, said founder Harriet Wieder, chairwoman of the Orange County Board of Supervisors.

"This committee is the first serious step that Southern California as a region has taken on the issue of water," she said.

The new strategy is prompting mixed reaction among Northern California water partisans.

Assemblyman Patrick Johnston, D-Stockton, says the move should be stopped.

Water lawyer John Dante Nomellini thinks the situation calls for caution but believes it could be the opening to a north/south armistice.

And San Joaquin County Supervisor Douglass Wilhoit is saying I told you so.

They are among local and Northern California officials waiting to see what will develop from the coalition. To date, all eight Southern California counties have joined the committee, each appointing a local county supervisor to the panel.

All but one southern county—Imperial—have tossed in the annual $10,000 membership fee. Faced with a fiscal crunch, Imperial County is soliciting that fee from its business community.

By chipping in smaller dues, four cities, including Grand Terrace, also have joined, along with

---

[4] "California Ready for New War on Water," *Sacramento Recorder*, December 16, 1985.

water agencies, special interest groups, chambers of commerce and major businesses like Atlantic Richfield, Arthur Young and Co., Pacific Bell Telephone, Mission Viejo Co. and the Irvine Co.

At least 10 water agencies have signed on, including Metropolitan Water District, Municipal Water District of Orange County, Los Angeles City Department of Water and Power, and the Upper San Gabriel Valley Municipal Water District.

The committee is quietly attracting—and rejuvenating— Southern California heavy-weights whose political clout took a beating in recent water flights. Calling itself a non-profit, non-lobbying educational group, the Irvine based committee was incorporated in September and plans to appoint an executive director next week.

The aim of its $397,000 annual budget: To ''educate'' Southern Californians who helped vote down the 1982 Peripheral Canal and idly watched Republican Gov. George Deukmejian's ''Through-Delta'' water plan die in the Legislature this year.

Both proposals, carried by Sen. Ruben Ayala, D-Chino, would have increased shipments of Northern California water from the Stockton-Sacramento Delta to Southern California, thus completing the controversial state water project.

The projects evaporated, Ayala said, because Southern Californians are too laid back and complacent about water, which Ayala admits ''is not a very sexy issue.''

On Friday he unveiled a new plan. The project would cost $500 million to $600 million and would ship another 400,000 acre-feet of Northern California water to the south. It is nearly identical to Deukmejian's ill-fated through-Delta proposal.

''We should not let one-third of the population (which lives in Northern California) dictate to the other two-thirds what ought to be done in terms of water issues,'' said Ayala, chairman of the powerful Senate Agriculture and Water Resources Committee and supporter of Wieder's group.

Those are fighting words to Northern Californians who say southerners should conserve water before they go plundering northward.

Johnston, whose campaign against Republican challenger Wilhoit in this year's Assembly campaign turned into a virtual referendum on the defeated Deukmejian plan, said he agrees with the notion of ''educating'' voters and not formulating water policy by emotion.

''But they should not start with the premise that the south will go dry if we don't significantly expand the water delivery system in the north,'' Johnston said.

Johnston opposes any increased export of Northern California water to the south and said he hopes the new committee doesn't consider such a plan. Johnston thinks the state water project, adopted nearly 25 years ago, is sorely outdated and not longer addresses current California water needs.

He mentioned an oft repeated theme of Assemblyman Phil Isenberg, D-Sacramento: ''We need to have policy before plumbing.''

62. Sen. John Doolittle: Northern California Will Not Be Tricked

State Senator John Doolittle (Republican of Citrus Heights) went on record in January 1985 as saying that Northern California would remain on its guard in the continuing water war with Southern California, and would not be tricked into giving away its "most precious resource to special interest groups."[5]

The most dominant and controversial issue in the recent political campaigns was again "northern water." The campaigns are over now but the water issue rolls on. I recently noted the reintroduction of Peripheral Canal-type legislation by a southern California legislator.

That's why I'm warning those northern Californians who oppose such north to south water transfer schemes that we can expect another one in the immediate future.

It is not appropriate yet for northerners to ship their water southward. We do not have adequate safeguards to protect our area-of-origin rights. Currently, a simple majority (51 percent) vote in the Legislature can change existing water law. The state may build a canal pledged only to take "excess" run-off water from the north. That can be easily changed from "excess" water to "all the water we want" because the Legislature is dominated by representatives from the heavily populated southland. That is a reality with which we must live.

Legislation was introduced this past year which tied a canal to a well-publicized constitutional amendment "protecting" northern water rights. This amendment would have required a tougher, two-thirds Legislative vote to change existing water law. While that is a step in the right direction, it is not sufficient to guard against a pro-south, legislative power play to change the intended use of the canal facilities, once built. More than 70 percent of California's population resides south of Sacramento. There are already enough southern legislative votes to override even a two-thirds protection.

THE ORIGINAL Peripheral Canal (1982) and this year's through-Delta Canal both would have transported about 500,000 acre feet (AF) of water southward each year. Theoretically, this water would have been only the excess water which currently leaves northern California, moves through the Delta and into the Ocean. There are a series of pumps, however, which can easily be directed to pull more water southward through the California Aqueduct. Not all the pumps are now in use, more can easily be installed and the aqueduct widened and deepened whenever Southern California desires so.

Several ways have been identified that southern and central California can save 400,000 to 500,000 acre feet of water annually. One way is to line with concrete the hundreds of miles of dirt irrigation canals in the Imperial Valley. That alone would save enough to eliminate need for a northern canal to take our water. The one-time expenditure for the lining would pay for itself quickly in water savings.

More efficient agricultural practices in the south would also help. Approximately one-third of all irrigation water used in the San Joaquin Valley is wasted. Why? Because it is more cost effective to waste water than to impose strict conservation measures.

How can that be? Because water for the southern agribusinessmen is so heavily subsidized, they pay $4-10 per AF for water for which many urban consumers elsewhere are paying hundreds of dollars per AF.

It is also a simple matter of supply and demand. The southern mega-farmers do not need the water, but if they increase supply relative to demand, the price per unit drops. That is why they want northern water—the whole state would help pay for it.

---

[5]"Protection from Water Schemes," *Sacramento Recorder*, January 3, 1985.

DURING THE DROUGHT a few years back, the supply of water available to southern agribusiness firms dropped sharply. They had to conserve their water because conservation had temporarily become more cost-efficient than wasting the surplus. As a result, they saved tremendous amounts of water. You see, they can operate with far less than they say they need.

If we cut out the subsidies and let the natural balance created by freemarket supply and demand take over, the south would pay a fair price for water and not try to buy more than they need.

I urge all northern Californians to watch the activities at their State Capitol this upcoming two-year session,. We are not selfish, water-hoarding zealots in the north. But we will not let ourselves be tricked into giving away our most precious resource to special interest groups who want it—not because they need it, but because they can widen their profit margins at our expense.

U.F.W. is not a union. It's a political movement in which Chavez has latched on to the workers of the "ag" community and confiscated their resources to get political power.

—**Michael Payne, Bruce Church, Inc. executive, New York *Times*, July 31, 1983.**

The growers and their allies can say that Cesar Chavez is losing ground; that the UFW is on the decline. What I saw in 1984 [California election campaigning by UFW members] convinced me that Cesar Chavez is the undisputed leader of California farm workers and that he, and the union he leads, symbolizes hope and faith for millions of Hispanics and other good people who will never work on a farm.

—**Willie Brown, speaker, California Assembly.**

CHAPTER 17

AGRICULTURAL LABOR RELATIONS

The Stormy Legacy of Collective Bargaining

A. *The Role of the United Farm Workers (AFL-CIO)*
B. *The Role of the Agricultural Labor Relations Board*

Since the turn of the century an army of migrant workers has marched up and down the state's rich agricultural valleys, following the seasons, planting and harvesting the crops. California growers have depended for the most part on a supply of labor that is large, cheap, and mobile, which means that most of the workers have been foreign-born Chinese, Japanese, Hindus, Filipinos, and lately and most notably, Mexicans. Anglo field hands started entering the picture during the Great Depression of the 1930s, with the migration from the Dust Bowl. Living conditions in the labor camps were notoriously bad. The plight of the migrants was captured by two literary classics, John Steinbeck's novel, *The Grapes of Wrath* (1939), and Carey McWilliams' social history, *Factories in the Field* (1939). In the 1950s a famous CBS television documentary by Edward R. Murrow was aptly titled "Harvest of Shame."

From time to time these farm laborers tried to form unions to bring about better wages and working conditions. The growers—who were themselves highly organized—strongly resisted attempts at organization. They asserted that a farm was not a factory whose assembly line could survive being turned on and off by work stoppages, but rather a precarious enterprise and a way of life that could be destroyed by excessive labor demands plotted by outside agitators.

When Congress passed the National Labor Relations Act in the 1930s it specifically exempted farm workers, who therefore were not accorded the right to bargain collectively with their employers. They were not covered by laws regulating wages, hours, and conditions, or restricting child labor; nor did they receive unemployment benefits or assurances of decent housing or living conditions. Wages remained relatively low. Efforts by farm workers to form unions and demand improvements remained sporadic and ineffectual, and were sometimes met with ferocious resistance by growers and local police authorities.

Agricultural labor relations in California took a dramatic turn in the 1960s with the emergence of Cesar Chavez and the farm workers movement. Chavez was born into an Arizona migrant family that had lost its farm during the Great Depression, and had joined the procession of migrants to California "where the grapes of wrath were stored." He started organizing in Delano in 1962 by passing out cards to farm workers, asking them what they earned, and what they thought they should earn. Patiently wending his way through eighty-six towns between Arvin and Stockton, he picked up considerable support, although he had not yet received organized labor's blessings.

Chavez formed the National Farm Worker Association, an independent welfare-cooperative union. Its members paid modest dues and received various benefits, including access to a co-op food store, pharmacy, service station, burial insurance, and legal services. NFWA claimed a membership of 50,000 in 1964.

The union and its allies achieved one major legislative victory in 1964 when Congress let the bracero program lapse. These contract workers had competed with American labor and their departure made union organizing somewhat easier.

But the union's main test was whether it could force employers to sit down and bargain collectively with it on behalf of the workers. In 1965 NFWA backed a strike at Delano that was organized by a union of Filipino grape workers, the Agricultural Workers Organizing Committee, an affiliate of the AFL-CIO. Most of the strikers were skilled hands employed on big vineyards and earning around $1.20 an hour—the same pay as the braceros—plus incentive pay of twenty-five cents a box, and union recognition. The growers, especially the big ones, resisted vigorously.

The continuous flow of Mexican immigrants, green-card workers, and "wetbacks" posed a central problem for the striking union. These nonstriking workers—"scabs" in union parlance—were easily trucked onto farms and ranches by growers to replace the strikers. Borrowing a page from the civil rights movement, Chavez espoused a policy of non-violence. "La Huelga"—the strike—won the support of the AFL-CIO, and of liberal Democrats like Mayor Daley of Chicago and Sen. Robert Kennedy of New York. Other unions refused to handle grapes, but the strike continued without letup.

To increase the pressure on the grape growers the union devised a new stratagem—a nationwide consumer boycott. Schenley Industries, a major wine and liquor producer, and Di Giorgio, a major distributor of food (under the familiar S & W label) feared consumer rejection of their full product lines and settled with the union in 1966. But the table-grape producers were less vulnerable to consumer resistance and refused to bow as readily. Eventually the union won a few big contracts. The victory was dramatic for "La Causa" (as the Union called its struggle) and its allies, but was less than sweeping.

The farm workers soon joined the ranks of the AFL-CIO, and eventually became known as the United Farm Workers. UFW immediately faced a new challenge, when the independent Teamsters union decided to try organizing farm workers. The AFL-CIO poured millions of dollars into the task of backing the UFW. Many employers preferred to settle with the less militant Teamsters. The Teamsters concluded that the task of organizing the farm workers was too costly and in 1977 withdrew from the fray, leaving the field to the UFW.

Even more important, in 1975 Gov. Edmund G. Brown, Jr., a strong friend of UFW, signed a bill creating the Agricultural Labor Relations Act which gave farm laborers the right to choose their bargaining agent through democratic elections. It created a five-member Agricultural Labor Relations Board, a quasi-judicial body, which oversaw the elections and investigated and settled charges of unfair labor practices. Within three years some six hundred farm elections had been held.

Over the years UFW continued its struggle for survival against many obstacles. By 1982 it represented approximately 25,000 out of 250,000 agricultural workers in California. Their contracts succeeded in raising the wages of the workers and even introduced pensions in some farming operations. But great structural changes have been under way in agriculture in the past decade. Increased mechanization steadily reduced the numbers of field hands. Farmers in the 1980's were suffering a serious depression. Deeply in debt, undercapitalized, and experiencing increased competition, some growers took their operations to Mexico to take advantage of a cheaper labor source. This has reduced the number of employer targets available to the union. Rising operational costs stiffened the growers' resistance to union demands. Internal conflict has sapped UFW energy.

Still floating in and out of the picture and undermining further unionization efforts were the illegal immigrants from Mexico and elsewhere. Sometimes as many as 50,000 undocumented workers were said to be in the fields. They worked for lower wages, and, lacking the rights of citizens, remained reluctant to join a union.

In the decade since its establishment, ALRB has lived in a swirl of controversy. During the Jerry Brown administration the union generally approved of ALRB's operation, while detractors charged that the board was little more than a tool of Chavez and the UFW. The increasing climate of political conservatism in the 1980's favored the growers. They found in Republican governor George Deukmejian a strong ally. By the same token, UFW complained bitterly about the governor's open hostility to the ALRB. They believed that Deukmejian would eventually appoint a conservative majority, starve it of funds, reduce its clout, and perhaps even try to kill it altogether.

Two questions are addressed in this chapter. First, what has been the historical legacy of the United Farm Workers in California and has it earned a lasting place in the structure of agriculture? Second, what has been the impact of the Agricultural Labor Relations Board? Either it has served the people of California well by reducing strife and stabilizing the industry, and therefore deserves to be strengthened; or, it has worked poorly and should be modified.

A. *The United Farm Workers (AFL-CIO)*

In 1985 the UFW had been in existence for over two decades. This subsection begins with a general review article by the *Sacramento Bee* dealing with the problems of farm workers and the experience of the union. It includes several items from Cesar Chavez and the UFW, and ends with an article that is severely critical of the union president. *(Editor's note)*

63.
Rick Rodriguez: In a 20-year Fight, Little is Reaped

The Sacramento Bee *ran a series of articles from March 31 to April 4, 1985 called "Farm Labor: A Lean Harvest." Selections from the first of the series, entitled, "20-Year Fight: Little is Reaped," written by Mr. Rodriguez, lead off this chapter.*

Twenty years ago, a small group of grape workers in Delano threw down their tools and screamed, "Enough."

They said they had suffered enough of poverty and exploitation, of back-breaking physical work and lack of medical care. These strikers were the farm workers whose "harvest of shame" roused the conscience of America in the 1960s. Within months, what began as a strike over a few cents an hour became "la causa," a movement to improve the lives of farm workers led by a community organizer turned labor leader, Cesar Chavez.

Through years of mass marches, bitter and costly strikes and consumer boycotts, farm laborers eventually won some of the basic rights that most American workers had gained decades earlier.

But now, despite significant pockets of progress, they are still a society apart. The question then is, what has become of the farm worker?

...Three of every four farm worker families in California still live in poverty, according to a new state-commissioned study.

. . . Eighteen years after the federal government adopted a migrant education program to help children of farm workers, half of California's migrant students quit school before ninth grade and nine of 10 never graduate.

. . . Despite California's stringent field safety laws, farm laborers have the highest rate of work-related illnesses of any industry.

. . . Illegal aliens pushed north by economic and political realities in Mexico and Central America often find themselves living in overcrowded houses, trailers and shacks. Or in the brush. . . .

The majority continue to be illiterate even in their first language. They receive poor medical care. They are poorly housed, ill fed and relegated to the shadows of California society. . . .

The farm workers are a people all but forsaken even by the bureaucracies established to serve them. Much of the basic research on their needs comes from studies that have accumulated 10 to 20 years of dust on shelves.

Although no two government agencies agree on how many farm workers there are in the Golden State, the average estimate is about 250,000.

Farm workers even stand to lose some of the gains they've made as the state's $14 billion agriculture industry undergoes its worst economic crisis since the Great Depression.

In the past, California farmers have dodged downturns, largely because of the diversity of their crops. But this time they are caught in a nationwide crisis caused by low commodity prices, a weak export market and huge debts incurred during the expansion and inflationary years of the 1970's

Economists estimate that about one-third of the state's 50,000 commercial growers are distressed, and about 10 percent are expected to fail by the end of the year. For the survivors, cost-cutting has become essential, and farm workers already have felt the impact.

In Fresno County, the state's agricultural center, wages and benefits have been slashed by as much as 30 percent, said Galen Johnson, a Caruthers grape grower who was recently forced to sell his 140-acre farm.

"In 1983, we paid 16 cents a tray (for grapes) and other growers paid 18 cents," he said. "But last year, we all paid 12 cents.". . . .

There are other trends taking root. Mechanical harvesters and other forms of labor-saving technology are playing an increasing role in the planting, harvesting and irrigating of many of the state's 260 commercial crops. Mechanization has resulted in huge job losses in some crops.

Winter lettuce growers in the Imperial Valley have been shifting thousands of acres 60 miles to the east to Arizona, a right-to-work state where lower wages are paid and there are fewer pesticide regulations to enforce. It's meant a loss of jobs for a region that traditionally has the state's highest unemployment rate, over 30 percent. . . .

That isn't to say that workers in California's No. 1 industry haven't progressed.

—Gone from California's vegetable fields is "el cortito," the short-handled hoe. Its banishment, according to one medical study, reduced back injuries by 34 percent.

—Ten years ago, California farm workers won the same right to union membership that other workers had enjoyed since 1935. Since then, almost 100,000 have cast secret ballots in elections conducted by the state Agricultural Labor Relations Board. In addition, workers have collected nearly $3.5 million in back wages for discriminatory practices.

—Medical and dental benefits and pensions were unheard of 20 years ago. Now they're enjoyed by gradually increasing numbers, albeit a fraction of the total. A recent survey of 578 San Joaquin Valley growers, for example, showed that 12 percent were paying for medical benefits for their workers.

—Unemployment insurance, extended to farm workers nine years ago, has cut the need for some to follow crops.

—Wages have increased, most dramatically in the vegetable industry where unions like Chavez's United Farm Workers have made their presence felt. Hundreds of growers have adopted professional management techniques, spurred by the threat of unionization.

But the progress comes crop-by-crop and region-by region.

While up to 20,000 vegetable workers earn a minimum of $7 an hour and up to $20 on piece-rates, harvesters of many crops are being paid the $3.35 state minimum wage. The average wage is about $4.50 an hour.

Among farm workers, other gains are measured in the most basic of terms.

"What pleases me most is the way the attitude of the growers changed," said Felicisimo Abad, a 73-year-old retired grape worker from Delano. "They give us a little more respect now."

"Before the strike in '65 there was only one tin can for the crew, for everyone to drink out of. When we won contracts, we had paper cups and toilets."

Chavez said, "There's no question there's been progress if you take in the union's sphere of influence. But in areas like northern San Diego county workers are living beneath trees. A lot of poor people are still very bad off."

The UFW, which grew to 80,000 members, is now down to 30,000 by its own count and rival unions say the count is more like 15,000.

A significant change in 20 years has been the demographics of the agricultural work force: Most are Mexican or of Mexican descent.

Although Mexican nationals made up half the workers in 1965, there remained substantial numbers of white and black farm workers, remnants of the 1930s Dust Bowl migrations from the Midwest. A new study by Richard Mines, agricultural economist, shows now that nearly three-fourths of the state's farm workers were born in Mexico. And a large portion of the remainder are Texans of Mexican descent and California-born children of Mexican immigrants.

Almost three-fourths of the farm workers are married and there is a much higher percentage of women than in 1965.

State Sen. Art Torres believes the progress of 20 years has failed to make an impact on the overall quality of farm workers' lives. . . .

Gov. Deukmejian, who counts growers among his chief supporters, decreased the state Agricultural Labor Relations Board budget by more than a quarter. Budgets for health and housing programs for farm workers have been cut slightly or have stagnated without increases for inflation.

"We don't have a hospitable environment to say the least," said Marcus Brown, a lobbyist specializing in housing issues for California Rural Legal Assistance.

President Reagan's proposals to cut back farm-related programs also could have a backlash on farm workers.

Brown said a proposal by Reagan to shut down the Farmers Home Administration would wipe out $130 million in federal aid for farm worker and rural housing projects in California.

The Reagan administration is trying to administratively change immigration regulations to make it easier for California growers to bring in workers from Mexico for specified periods to harvest perishable crops.

Some researchers have suggested that a return to a guest-worker program will increase dependency on foreign labor and slow progress in wages and working conditions.

To Gloria Hernandez, a Fresno community worker, the changing political and economic climate adds up to one conclusion: "We're not moving ahead anymore. In fact, I think we are going backwards."

64.
Cesar Chavez: "Our Influence Will Grow, Not Diminish."

Foes claimed in 1985 that the UFW was in decline. A conservative governor was standing firm against the union, they said, ALRB was becoming less of a "union tool," internal dissension was sapping the union's strength, Chavez was succumbing to autocracy and nepotism, employers were fleeing to Mexico, workers were being displaced by machines, illegals were undermining organizing efforts, and, as a consequence, the union's membership and influence were declining. Even the new UFW grape boycott announced in 1984 seemed to some a sign of weakness. Amid this chorus of negativism, Cesar Chavez accepted an invitation to address the prestigious Commonwealth Club in San Francisco on November 9, 1985.[1] Scattered among his audience of three hundred listeners were some Central Valley growers. They heard him totally reject the negativism, affirm his union's positive legacy, and predict for it a victorious future.

Twenty-one years ago last September, on a lonely stretch of railroad track paralleling U.S. Highway 101 near Salinas, 32 bracero farm workers lost their lives in a tragic accident. The braceros had been imported from Mexico to work on California farms. They died when their bus, which was converted from a flatbed truck, drove in front of a freight train. Conversion of the bus had not been approved by any government agency. The driver had tunnel vision. Most of the bodies lay unidentified for days. No one, including the grower who employed the workers, even knew their names.

Today, thousands of farm workers live under savage conditions beneath trees and amid garbage and human excrement near tomato fields in San Diego County, tomato fields which use the most modern farm technology. Vicious rats gnaw on them as they sleep. They walk miles to buy food at inflated prices and they carry in water from irrigation pumps.

Child labor is still common in many farm areas. As much as 30% of Northern California's garlic harvesters are under-aged children. Kids as young as six years old have voted in state-conducted union elections since they qualified as workers.

Some 800,000 underaged children work with their families harvesting crops across America.

Babies born to migrant workers suffer 25 percent higher infant mortality than the rest of the population.

Malnutrition of migrant worker children is 10 times higher than the national rate.

Farm workers' average life expectancy is still 49 years, compared to 73 years for the average American.

All my life, I have been driven by one dream, one goal, one vision: To overthrow a farm labor system in this nation that treats farm workers as if they were not important human beings. Farm workers are not agricultural implements—they are not beasts of burden—to be used and discarded.

That dream was born in my youth. It was nurtured in my early days of organizing. It has flourished. It has been attacked.

That vision grew from my own experience with racism, with hope, with the desire to be treated fairly and to see my people treated as human beings and not as chattel. It grew from anger and rage—emotions I felt 40 years ago when people of my color were denied the right to see a movie or eat at a restaurant in many parts of California. It grew from the humiliation I felt as a boy who couldn't understand how the growers could abuse and exploit farm workers when there were so many of us and so few of them.

All Hispanics—urban and rural, young and old—are connected to the farm workers' experience. We had all lived through the fields or our parents had. We shared that common humiliation.

---

[1]Excerpts are taken from a manuscript version of the full speech and from an abridged version, published as, "Farm Workers Respond to Immoral Attack by Affirming UFW's Legacy," in *Food and Justice*, a new publication (January 1985), 24-27.

How could our people believe that their children could become lawyers and doctors and business people while this shame, this injustice was permitted to continue?

More than a Union

Those who attack our cause often say, "It's not really a union. It's something else: a social movement, a civil rights movement. It's something dangerous."

They're half right.

The United Farm Workers is first and foremost a union. But the UFW has always been something more than a union, although it's never been dangerous if you believe in the Bill of Rights.

We attacked that historical source of shame and infamy that our people in this country lived with. We attacked that injustice not by complaining; not by seeking hand-outs; not by becoming soldiers in the War on Poverty.

We organized! Farm workers acknowledged we had allowed ourselves to become victims in a democratic society, a society where majority rule and collective bargaining are supposed to be more than academic theories or political rhetoric. And by addressing this historical problem, we created confidence and pride and hope in an entire people's ability to create the future.

The UFW's survival, its very existence, sent out a signal to all Hispanics that we were fighting for our dignity; that we were challenging and overcoming injustice; that we were empowering the least educated among us, the poorest among us.

The message was clear: If it could happen in the fields, it could happen anywhere—in cities, in the courts, in the city councils, in the state legislatures.

Empowering People

From time to time you will hear our opponents declare that the UFW is weak; that the UFW has no support; that the UFW has not grown fast enough. Our obituary has been written many times.

How ironic it is that the same forces that argue so passionately that we are not influential are the same forces that continue to fight us so hard. The UFW's power in agriculture has nothing to do with the number of farm workers under contract. . . or even the farm worker's ability to conduct successful boycotts.

The very fact of our existence forces an entire industry—unionized and nonunionized—to spend millions of dollars year after year on increased wages, improved working conditions,and benefits for workers.

If we're so weak and unsuccessful, why do the growers continue to fight us with such passion? Because as long as we continue to exist, farm workers will benefit from our existence even if they don't work under union contract. In that sense, it doesn't really matter whether we have 100,000 members or 500,000 members. In truth, hundreds of thousands of farm workers are better off today because of our work. And Hispanics who don't work in agriculture are better off today because of what the farm workers taught people about organization, about pride and strength, about seizing control over their own lives.

Our union will forever exist as an empowering force among people. That means our influence will grow and not diminish.

Two major trends give us hope.

New Grape Boycott

First, we have returned to a tried and tested weapon in the farm workers' nonviolent arsenal—the boycott!

After the Agricultural Labor Relations Act became law in 1975, we dismantled our boycott to work with the law. The law helped farm workers make progress in overcoming poverty and injustice. But under Republican Governor George Deukmejian, the law that guarantees our right to organize no longer protects farm workers.

Farm workers were forced to declare a new international boycott of California grapes (except the 3% of grapes produced under UFW contract). The Harris poll showed that 17 million Americans boycotted grapes. We are convinced that those people and that good will have not disappeared. They are responding again not to picketlines and leafletting alone, but to the high-tech boycott of today—a boycott that uses computers and direct mail and advertising techniques which have revolutionized business and politics in recent years. We achieved more success with the boycott in 1984 than we achieved in the 14 years since 1970.

The other trend which gives us hope is the monumental growth of Hispanic influence in this country. South of the Sacramento River in California, Hispanics make up more than 25% of the population. That figure will top 30% by the year 2000. There are 1.1 million Hispanic voters in California.

In light of these trends, it is absurd to believe or suggest that we are going to go back in time as an organization or as a people!

History On Our Side

I am told why farm workers should be discouraged and pessimistic: Republicans control the Governor's Office and the White House. There is a conservative trend in the nation.

Yet we are filled with hope and encouragement.

We have looked into the future and the future is ours! History and inevitability are on our side. The farm workers and their children—and the Hispanics and their children—are the future in California! And corporate growers are the past!

These trends are part of the forces of history which cannot be stopped! No person and no organization can resist them for very long. They are inevitable!

Once social change begins, it cannot be reversed. You cannot uneducate the person who has learned to read. You cannot humiliate the person who feels pride. You cannot oppress the people who are not afraid anymore.

Our opponents must understand that it's not just a union we have built. For nearly 20 years our movement has been on the cutting edge of a people's cause. And you cannot do away with an entire people; You cannot stamp out a people's cause.

Like the other immigrant groups, the day will come when we win the economic and political rewards which are in keeping with our numbers in society. The day will come when the politicians will do the right thing by our people out of political necessity and not out of charity or idealism.

That day may not come this year. That day may not come during this decade. But it will come, someday!

And when that day comes, we shall see the fulfillment of that passage from the Book of Matthew in the New Testament, "That the last shall be first and the first shall be last."

And on that day, our nation shall fulfill its creed. And that fulfillment shall enrich us all.

65.
UFW: "Going Back to Where We Left Off in 1975"

Unions cannot legally engage in secondary boycotts—attempting to influence workers to strike in sympathy at business establishments where there is no labor dispute. But economic boycotts pitched at consumers are legal. By relying on innovative direct-marketing techniques that involve computerized mailing lists and demographic analysis, UFW began to achieve success in its new grape boycott in 1984.[2]

The United Farm Workers' boycott of California grapes became a rallying cry during the 1960s and '70s. It symbolized the farm workers' hopes for a better life . And it worked.

Over 17 million Americans boycotted grapes. As a result, farm workers won better wages and working conditions, and protections from dangerous pesticides and other abuses.

During the early 1970s, when most grape workers were covered by UFW contracts, they were the best paid and protected farm workers in the nation. But that changed. In 1973, growers gave the contracts to the Teamsters Union and most grape workers have been unprotected ever since.

Now, because few vineyard workers have union contracts, wages and benefits have fallen far behind what farm workers who labor in other crops receive.

Many grape workers have tried to bring back the UFW by voting for the union in elections held under California's pioneering farm labor law. But most growers won't sign contracts. Under Republican Governor George Deukmejian, the nine year old law which requires growers to bargain in good faith with their workers has stopped working.

So the UFW has returned to the non-violent tactic that served farm workers so well. On July 11, UFW President Cesar Chavez declared a new boycott of California grapes (except the 3% of grapes produced under union contract) with a news conference in Fresno and a large rally with grape workers in Delano.

"Today we are going back to where we left off in 1975," Chavez said, referring to the year the UFW dismantled its last grape boycott after the Agricultural Labor Relations Act became law. "We take this action because, under Deukmejian, the law that guarantees our right to organize has been shut down. It doesn't work anymore!"

The farm labor leader said Deukmejian's failure to enforce the law has taken a "terrible toll in human tragedy (among) thousands of farm worker families that are already poor during the best of times. Families whose hopes for a better life have been destroyed" by the governor's actions.

More than 36,000 farm workers are waiting for growers to sign contracts after the workers voted in secret ballot elections to be represented by the UFW, he added, "Many have been fired for supporting the union. Many others have lost their jobs because growers illegally changed the names of their companies to avoid signing union contracts."

---

[2]*Food and Justice*, a UFW publication (January, 1985), 33-34.

66.
C. C. Bruno: "I Refuse to Bow to the UFW Union"

The UFW and its president have evoked bitter attacks over the years. Interestingly enough, the growers rarely make frontal attacks on Chavez, who enjoys personal popularity, preferring instead to attack the ALRB. Serious attacks come from the media, though, sometimes even from moderate or liberal sources. Such was the case when The Humanist, *a journal of liberal opinion, published the following article. It is reprinted along with a reply by the labor leader.*[3]

A friend has urged me to speak out. I am dumbfounded by what I read in the newspapers. Many reporters and ministers are championing Cesar Chavez and the United Farm Workers Union as if they were apple pie and motherhood, when right now we farmworkers are losing our freedom and basic rights to this union's abusive control. It is not clear to enough Americans that whoever controls the food on our table can control our country.

Maybe nobody will want to hear what I have to say. I am for labor, good wages, job security, and for people. And I am aware that there are those who twist the truth and will try to silence anyone who risks speaking up. But I want to tell it like it is.

Monday morning, June 11, I was packing lettuce on one of the five wrapping machines moving down a field in southern Monterey County, California. Felipe, the foreman yelled: "It's them!" I looked up and saw strikers get out of their cars at the entrance of the access road. They ran over to the government inspector's car and began rocking it. The inspector, an older fellow, tried to stop them. But they busted out the car windows and turned it over. Cars of more strikers pulled up. From a bullhorn in Spanish and English they shouted: "Scab! Strike-breaker! Come out and join us!" At least fifty strikers came toward the machine I was on. Some carried red flags with the black eagle. For a moment I thought of the flags that ran me across the rice paddies of Korea for eleven months and twenty-three days. Other strikers were waving jack handles.

I shouted to the women wrappers to drop the rolls of paper off the pipes. We could use the pipes to defend ourselves. The strikers who faced us threatened: "Come out on strike or we'll get you!" They stayed out of range of our pipes. "Scab! We'll see you tonight. We'll burn your camp!" Three carloads of sheriff's deputies appeared. When the deputies threatened to use gas, the strikers ran back to their cars. Afterwards, my stomach was in knots. It was as bad as any day I spent in six years in the Marines. I could hardly open my hand to let go of the pipe. Even seeing the sheriff's deputies did not relieve the tension.

What is this all about? Some of us in my crew have worked together for several months. Some of the strikers have never worked for my company at all. In fact, some of them have just arrived from Mexico.

My barracks was quiet. We expected the strikers to show up during the night. Each of us got hold of a pipe. None of us played cards and we kept our radios low. I noticed that the Mexicans did not talk about their wives, to whom they send their money and return south of the border several months a year. We told each other what we would do if attacked, and tried to understand how outsiders could call us scabs and strike-breakers. You don't like to be called a scab when your family depends on you. These outsiders are trying to make us feel like intruders on our own ground.

The next few days I kept thinking of my boyhood in West Virginia. I saw my parents and brothers and sisters loading our belongings into someone else's car and moving to Boone County and into another shack. That is my only memory of my father.

My mother could find little paying work in those hills. She had no schooling, but could write

---

[3]The article appeared in the issue of November-December 1979; the reply in March-April 1980. An even more wide-ranging attack appeared in the *Village Voice* (New York), August 14 and 21, 1984, and was widely disseminated in California by the grower Bruce Church,Inc. In November of that year, Chavez filed a multi-million dollar libel suit against both the *Village Voice* and Bruce Church, Inc.

her name—I think. To support us she had to have a husband, and each husband wanted some children of his own. Finally there were thirteen of us.

When I was about nine, I often walked along the railroad tracks picking up coal to take home. Sometimes I met a miner on his way from work. One day he asked what I would like for my birthday. "Shoes," I said. Later on he gave my mother some money and we hitchhiked all the way to Charleston. I saw a pair of red boots with black trim. That was it. The sales man gave me a pair of socks. I still remember how proud I was of my first pair of shoes.

After we moved to Logan County, I wanted to help my mom. A coalminer, who got three dollars a ton for loading coal, let me go into the mine and help him. At eleven, it felt good to take home some money.

At sixteen, I managed to get into the Marines. I had new clothes, outdoor activity, learned new things, knew pretty well what I would be doing from day to day, and had a regular income. There was good food, lots of it. And above all, I belonged to something. I had my own identity.

For twenty years now I've worked in the fields and orchards up and down California and southern Oregon. Now life is changed. Guards protect our barracks at night and in the daytime deputy sheriffs are standing by in the fields. We're all on edge. Strikers can now come into the camp parking lot legally. Their leaflets are only in Spanish. Anglos don't count. They warn us that if we don't walk off our jobs we will regret it. No longer do I feel free to follow the peak harvests and choose where I want to work.

My friends, Mexican and Anglos alike, agree we're paid more than we've ever been paid in our lives. We get more than some warehouse and office workers downtown. My base rate is $4.35 an hour, and I make some additional through piecework incentives. Last week, after deductions for social security and disability—we are given free medical plan and life insurance—I got a check for $268. I pay $7.50 a day for my bunk and three meals. A hot lunch is brought to us wherever we are at noon. Complaints? Just normal griping.

We live in fear now. There's violence throughout the Valley. They've been destroying tractors and equipment. I know of workers they've beaten who are no longer around. The worst threat is when they tell us we'll be laid off when the UFW forces our employers to sign.

As the son of a coalminer whose work didn't pay him a living wage and as a labor man all my life, I can't figure out how this eight-month-old strike has anything to do with labor's cause. The large vegetable growers and farmers pay decent wages. The Teamster's Union has signed up some growers and probably has gotten the best contracts. They've signed Bud Antle, the world's largest lettuce grower, and I think general labor now gets a base of $5 an hour. Anyhow, the Teamsters charge their members straight dues rather than a percentage of earnings, as the UFW does. There's talk that when Chavez gets complete control he will increase the percentage from our wages and take thirty cents a box from the growers. For what? And what is he doing for the Mexicans he is forcing into dependency?

A kind of brooding sickness is engulfing us. There's little radio music or laughter. Some of us are scared to be out alone at night. It looks to me like we will soon be pawns of a system set up by outsiders. Most of us—Mexicans, Anglos, and blacks—don't want any part of a union for Mexicans only.

The United Farm Workers is a far cry from a union of the people, by the people, for the people. I know what it means to be turned down for membership in the UFW. It happened to me in 1963, 1967, and 1978. It seemed to me the only reason was my race. To encourage Anglos and blacks already in the union to drop out, the Mexican dispatcher in the hiring hall gives the best jobs to his own people and leaves the Anglos and blacks to the last. You can understand my frustration at what is happening in this country.

It's wrong for ministers who have not actually worked in the fields to talk only to strikers and not to us. They pretend that harassment, violence, and racism don't exist. They imagine that by supporting the United Farm Workers they are helping us. Not me. Not anyone I work with.

At times some of us in the barracks talk this over. One fellow expressed what I believe. I am partially accepted by the Mexicans, because my wife was Mexican and I spent three months working on a garbanzo and cattle farm in Sinaloa. My friend put it this way: "The Mexican Revolution freed us from peonage to the large landowners. Now what is happening? We are about to become peons again. If you don't go along with the UFW, you don't work. The union takes our money and tells us where to work, how many hours, how much we'll get, and how we have to spend some of our free time. I didn't come to the States to become a peon again."

Not many people know about the "good-standing" law for agricultural workers in California that goes against their basic human rights. In this state, agricultural workers come under the Agricultural Labor Relations Act. Here the UFW is permitted to have contracts requiring an employee to remain in good standing in the Union.

Who judges this good standing? In the union-grower contracts it says: "The union shall be the sole judge of good standing." The UFW decides and forces the employer to fire anyone it wishes. Members have to accept certain political, social, and economic views. If we don't participate in political fundraising, demonstrations, strikes, and other disruptions, the union can have us fired. Just like that. And it's all done legally. But why should the UFW have the sole power to fire me?

Thousands of workers who left the fields in August to join Chavez's march had to do so to remain in good standing with the union. Otherwise they could have lost their jobs. If you were in their situation, what would you do? Believe me, there was no love or compassion behind his march.

Not long ago Senate Bill 504 was introduced in the California legislature to amend the ALRA to protect us from union excesses. At the same time, the bill keeps our rights to bargain collectively or to strike or to choose whatever union we want. The Senate and the Assembly passed it, but Governor Jerry Brown vetoed it. What kind of a person is Governor Brown?

Most farmworkers have to knuckle under to the UFW. Your family has to eat. It's a matter of survival. The Chavistas, the ministers, and politicians are reducing Mexicans to subservience. Chavez's talk about liberation doesn't make any more sense than his opposition to machines in the fields. What will the ministers say a few years from now when one union controls the production and price of food that goes across the tables of rich and poor alike? Now is the time to preserve human rights.

My way of life will be destroyed if I have to work through a hiring hall. The know-how I've acquired through twenty years in agriculture will then mean nothing. I take pride in my work. In June my company's lettuce-loading team won first place in the Salinas agricultural competition. If effort and ability become meaningless, what becomes of me? I won't be able to travel from harvest to harvest, to see old friends and make new ones, to be free.

I suppose that later on I will be forced to adjust to the hiring hall, to being told where to work and when and how and what else to do. That is, if they let me join. But I'm not ready for that now. I can't face the prospect of doors being closed just because I want a free lifestyle, like to work hard, and want to accomplish something. You see, I didn't get much schooling or formal training and I'm not licensed to do anything. For me the UFW is the end of a dream, maybe the American dream.

Some of my ancestors came to America to lead independent lives. They wanted, I guess, to be free from the heavy hand of government and church. I am sad to think that my own daughter and son will grow up the victims of what is happening now. Too many people go by what they are told instead of asking those who are doing the work. Within me, I know I have to do something. But what?

If even lawyers and doctors are taken in by a union leader and his public-relations assistants, what hope is there for us? The issue for me is not wages and working conditions. It's freedom of the individual. What we are seeing is a union gaining control over its members and perhaps eventually of the food that goes onto everyone's table. Maybe whoever controls our food can control our country.

One day the field supervisor overheard some of us talking. He asked: "Would you speak up?"

I said: ''Anywhere, any time, to anybody.'' The next day I was on a plane to Sacramento. You should have seen it. Just six of us. Some big shots and me. They were busy with papers and I watched out the window.

There were reporters in Sacramento. They wanted to know why I talked the way I was talking. One of them asked who was paying me. All kinds of things. It was hard to believe. There they are supposed to be reporting the truth and all that reporter could think about was that you speak up only if you're paid to do so. What's happening to make him think like that?

I was glad to leave Sacramento. One of the men on the plane handed me a card and said: ''Look me up some time for coffee.'' What does he think? Coffee where? When? I'm in the fields. He's not there. I didn't keep his card. Usually I believe everything I hear, but I believe it in my own way. I don't like to argue.

I know I should fight back harder. The UFW has the money, the public relations, the lies, the ministerial associations, the politicians. Even the growers are scared of them. But finally the growers can up their prices and people down the line will have to pay more. But what can I up? It's my life. I have to work. It's farmwork I know and can do well at. It's a good life. The best I've known. And now they are trying to take it away from me. And, maybe they will succeed.

Chavez response to Bruno

We want to critically examine a few points made by C. C. Bruno in *The Humanist.*

In his lead paragraph, Mr. Bruno claims he is ''dumbfounded'' because ''reporters and ministers are championing'' the farmworkers' cause as if it were ''apple pie and motherhood.'' By that we interpret him to mean that the union has ''pulled the wool over the eyes'' of not only the nation's press but the countless priests, sisters, ministers, and rabbis who have aided the UFW over the years. Not to mention the National Council of Churches, the U.S. Catholic Bishops, and Central Conference of American Rabbis, and other groups which have steadfastly supported the farmworkers.

After disposing of that charge matter of factly, Mr. Bruno moves on to the real point he wants to make—or whoever is speaking through him wants to make (I wonder who that is): ''It is not clear to enough Americans that whoever controls the food on our tables can control our country.'' Later he wrote, ''The issue for me is not wages and working conditions. It's freedom of the individual.'' (We already know who controls the food system—agribusiness which Mr. Bruno works for; so what's the issue?)

Unless I'm dreaming when I read those lines in *The Humanist* I could have sworn the quotes came word for word from the right-wing propaganda issued by the National Right-to-Work Committee. Perhaps someone has pulled the wool over *The Humanist's* eyes.

Who is C. C. Bruno? We were first exposed to Mr. Bruno last spring when he was the star attraction at a grower press conference in Sacramento. You see, agribusiness has no credibility with the American people. So it tries to get workers like C. C. Bruno to do its dirty work for it in public.

When the lettuce strike began in January 1979, the growers hired the Dolphin Group, a seductive Los Angeles public relations-advertising agency, to polish their public image. The agency is headed by Bill Roberts, who successfully handled Reagan and Ford, and does PR for the John Connally presidential campaign. Through expensive full-page ads in major newspapers and carefully staged press conferences in California, the PR men tried to portray growers as advocates for farmworkers' human rights and the United Farm Workers as a threat to worker liberty.

Mr. Bruno was to have been a potent weapon in this new PR strategy. But after the news conference, attended by much of the Sacramento press corps, the growers and the PR men dropped him from their arsenal because of his embarrassing references to ''those damn Mexicans who are taking our jobs'' and his comparison of striking farmworkers to the ''gooks'' and ''Viet Cong'' he had fought in Korea and opposed in Vietnam. Some reporters sarcastically dubbed him as ''the growers'

Bruno.'' Perhaps that accounts for his low opinion of the press. Or could it have been that Mr. Bruno—or whoever speaks through him—was angered that reporters saw through the masquerade.

Well, that was the last we saw or heard of Mr. Bruno until he popped up in *The Humanist.*

Mr. Bruno talks of violence, of damage to tractors and equipment. He speaks in general terms of alleged beatings of strikebreakers by strikers, although he offers no documentation. Why doesn't he talk of the brutal murder February 10, 1979, of UFW striker Rufino Contreras by three armed foremen employed by lettuce grower Marlo Saikhon? Rufino, 28 and the father of two young children, was shot in the face with a .38 caliber bullet by the grower gunmen (Anthony San Diego, Leonardo Barriga, and Froilan Mendoza) and then left face-down in the lettuce field as the gunmen kept Rufino's co-workers from coming to his aid with continuing gunfire at the ranch in Southern California's Imperial Valley.

Why doesn't Mr. Bruno speak of Juan del Campo, who was savagely beaten about the head on November 1, 1979, by fifteen scabs employed by Growers Exchange Company near El Centro. [Ed. note: This occurred after Mr. Bruno wrote his article.] The strikebreakers ran Juan and four other strikers he was riding with off the road with their cars and administered the attack while Imperial County sheriff's deputies looked on from their patrol car. And why doesn't Mr. Bruno talk about the hundreds of strikers—men, women, and children—who were beaten and brutalized by heavily armed private security guards and other grower agents—some members of the Ku Klux Klan—who were brought in by Mr. Bruno's employers and other growers. (Early in the strike the Klan's grand dragon in Southern California acknowledged to reporters that the KKK had stationed members in the growers' camp.)

Time does not permit us to respond point for point to Mr. Bruno's charges—or charges levelled by those who speak through Mr. Bruno. (For one of the three years he claims to have been denied membership in the UFW, we had no membership because we had no contracts with growers. In another we had one agreement, but we had not even begun organizing in the vegetable industry that year. Mr. Bruno admits in print that his Sacramento press conference—his ''speaking out''—was orchestrated by the growers.)

Who would be interested in such an article appearing in *The Humanist*? The National Right-to-Work Committee wanted to reprint the Bruno article. A coincidence? Or is it?

B. *The Agricultural Labor Relations Board*

The stated purpose of the Agricultural Labor Relations Act of 1975 was to ''. . .ensure peace in the agricultural fields by guaranteeing justice for all agricultural workers and stability in labor relations.'' It gave workers the right to act together to help themselves, to engage in union organizational activity and to select their own representatives for purposes of collective bargaining. It prohibited employers from interfering with worker rights, protected workers against the coercion of both employers and unions and prohibited unions from engaging in certain types of strikes and picketing. It established an enforcement agency—the Agricultural Labor Relations Board.

After ten years of ALRB operation, Californians were asking whether that agency had achieved its purpose. Growers said that it had shown unmistakable bias in favor of the union and demanded that its powers be trimmed. With equal vigor the union said that ALRB had been just—until the advent of Governor Deukmejian. Below are the opinions of two growers, the union president and a labor writer. *(Editor's note)*

67. Mats Murata: ALRB is Biased Toward the Union

The following piece by the president of the San Joaquin Nisei Farmers League is fairly typical of grower opinion.[4]

Much is being written about the Agricultural Labor Relations Board (ALRB) and changes, both budgetary and personnel, it is undergoing. Questions are being raised with respect to the impact such changes will have on the farmer and the agricultural worker in California. This will attempt to analyze the reasons for, nature of and impact of such changes.

Historically, the ALRB came into being because Gov. Edmund G. Brown Jr. represented to various growers associations and agricultural leaders in the state that he would appoint an impartial board to administer the program. As soon as the Agricultural Labor Relations Act (ALRA) was enacted, Brown reneged on this promise and appointed four out of five labor—oriented board members, with the first chairman being a man who had marched with Cesar Chavez.

This act is experimental and nearly 10 years after its enactment in California, California remains the only state to have such an act. Impartiality in appointments was critical, and Brown's failure to live up to his promises started the board off on a note of extreme controversy. As with any experimental piece of legislation, changes are needed once the law is put into practice. Brown continued to make the ALRB a focus of controversy by vetoing all changes which had been passed by the Legislature during his administration.

The result of this lack of impartiality in initial appointments and the protective cloak of Brown under which the ALRB operated, was compounded in the supporting staff appointments which largely reflected the bias of the governor. Living in the rarefied atmosphere of this protective cloak from Brown's Office, and supported by staff persons who reflected the bias existing on the board, the board made a number of legally unsound decisions which have subsequently been overturned in the courts, but only after years of litigation at costs of hundreds of thousands of dollars to the taxpayers and similar amounts to the farmers. Examples of this type of action by the ALRB can be found in the Carian Farms case. Here, in 1977 the majority of the farm workers voting in this election rejected the union. The board not only threw out the election in 1980, but ordered Carian Farms to bargain with the UFW. The Fourth District Court of Appeals annulled the ALRB decision in 1984, stating that the law provides the only way a farmer can be ordered to bargain with the union is where the majority of the workers vote for a union through the election process. Other examples of these types of decisions are found in the ALRB telling farmers what crops they must plant, or risk penalties for reducing their labor requirements by planting less labor intensive crops, and the Triple E case in Stockton where the California Supreme Court overturned a board decision upholding a UFW won election in spite of misconduct on the part of UFW. This process lasted over seven years and cost the taxpayers and the farmer in excess of $100,000.

Brown's overzealousness in protecting this law which history now shows was enacted by the Legislature at Brown's urging, has done this experimental legislation another disservice. His administration repeatedly blocked efforts to bring the Agricultural Labor Relations Act into compliance with the National Labor Relations Act. Increasingly, farm workers, farmers and legislators have realized that this compliance feature is important to eliminate some of the injustices resulting from practical application of the experimental ALRA. The ALRA has a "make whole" remedy which is not found in the NLRA. This provision gives the ALRB the power to impose penalties on farmers for standing up to their rights in the hearing process. Under its "make whole" powers, the ALRB may order a farmer to give workers a large pay raise, including back pay, for time spent

[4] "ALRB: Broken Promises," *Stockton Record*, April 1, 1984.

in litigation, even if workers had been on strike or had no contract. In the Abatti case, the ALRB ordered the company to pay as estimated $18.5 million in "make whole" settlements. This type of ALRB advocacy on behalf of the United Farm Workers will result in approximately 2,500 Imperial Valley residents being out of work when Abatti shuts its doors on June 30. This is an example of an abuse of power by the ALRB which is damaging to the farm worker. In other examples of this type, third generation farmers have elected to go out of business rather than continue to farm under the type of environment the ALRA is providing.

The ALRA permits the United Farm Workers (UFW) to require a farm worker member to contribute a portion of his wages to a political action committee to remain in "good standing" with the UFW. This collection device of the UFW is called "Citizen Participation Day." Such monies are then contributed by the political action arm of the UFW to politicians being supported by the UFW and who may not be the ones who would be supported by the farm worker given a voluntary choice. Where else in this "free country" must a worker contribute to a political fund to be doled out by his boss as a condition of keeping his job? Brown saw fit to veto legislation enacted by the Legislature to remedy this defect in the original ALRA.

With the loss of the UFW's protector in the form of Brown, the focus of the UFW has now shifted to the Legislature. Through the "Citizen's Participation Day" mandatory collection program, the UFW PAC collected and contributed nearly $600,000 to state legislative races in the last campaign. This figure included a $250,000 contribution to speaker Willie Brown's campaign committee and $126,000 to Senate Leader David Roberti's campaign committee. Monies from these two leaders' funds were then used to elect legislators, who despite their statements to the contrary, are politically indebted to these two leaders, who are, in turn, politically indebted to the UFW.

This shift of focus to the Legislature was evidenced by a one-year delay in the Legislature's confirmation of Governor Deukmejian's appointment, David Stirling, as general counsel to the ALRB. Due to Brown's appointment policies prior to his departure as governor, no vacancies will occur on the ALRB until approximately two years after the end of Brown's term. After years of a decision making process which reflected Brown's political philosophy of supporting the UFW, Stirling was appointed by Deukmejian to the general counsel's office in an attempt to restore some of the balance that is needed in the decision making process. In this capacity, Stirling screens cases, and unlike his predecessors, has stated that he will require proof of union complaints before filing charges which cost the taxpayers money to prosecute and the farmers money to defend. Since this procedure represents a departure from the Brown days of using the ALRB to economically beat growers into UFW contracts, by inundating them with charges, the Legislature held up the confirmation of Stirling for one year. It is hoped that the appointment of Stirling will result in the elimination of such abuses as filing false claims to harass farmers as was done in the Patterson Farms case in Stanislaus County.

In the Patterson Farms case the UFW filed a claim in behalf of a worker that he had been wrongfully discharged. The worker, in fact, had voluntarily quit his job some two weeks earlier than the discharge was alleged to have occurred. The ALRB agents investigated the case and were furnished with information showing the worker voluntarily terminated. The ALRB issued a complaint and took the matter up to the day of trial, at considerable expense to the taxpayers and Patterson Farms to defend the case, before voluntarily dismissing a case which never should have been filed had the ALRB required proof and done a thorough job of investigation. It appears that what Stirling is proposing is to run the general counsel's office of the ALRB in the same manner that every district attorney in this state runs his office: that is to require proof of a claim before you spend the taxpayer's money filing a complaint. For this he is being criticized by Brown's appointments on the ALRB and by the UFW.

The next battle involving the ALRB is that of the budget. Opponents claim that while Deukmejian cut other state agencies 4 percent to make up the deficit he inherited from Brown, he cut the ALRB budget 27 percent. What such opponents fail to disclose is that the ALRB budget grew from $5,299,000 in 1975-76 to $9,355,000 in 1982-83 under Brown. By making deeper cuts in the ALRB budget Deukmejian held the ALRB budget increase over this time period to 29 percent, rather than the 57 percent increase it had enjoyed under Brown.

For any decision-making system to work and to have the confidence and acceptance of those who are regulated by it, it must have appointments and staffing which represent balanced viewpoints and render decisions based on a balancing of the competing viewpoints. This is how our two-party legislative system works, our judicial system works, and the NLRB works. The Legislature is elected by the people and the latter two systems have been staffed by appointments reflecting both Democratic and Republican philosophies over the years. The result of this is that we have a mixture, or balance, of both viewpoints at the decision making and staff levels.

To make the ALRA work, it must be staffed by board and staff members who represent both viewpoints, not just one, and it must have changes in its law to bring it into compliance with the National Labor Relations Act which has worked for nearly 50 years. These changes are overdue and should not be held hostage by the Legislature.

68. Daryl Arnold: "All of Agriculture Suffers" by the ALRB Bias

The president of the Western Growers Association proposes changes in the ALRA.[5]

For eight years the Western Growers Association and other agricultural groups in California have made no secret of their dissatisfaction with the Agricultural Labor Relations Act.

Industry has sponsored amendments to the law, and has opposed the appointment of individuals to the farm labor board who demonstrate a bias against industry.

For the most part, success stories for agriculture in farm labor have been few and far between.

The reason for agriculture's lack of success until now has been the United Farm Workers union's close ties to former Gov. Jerry Brown. He believed the UFW needed its own law to help organize farm workers in the state. Once established he blocked any attempts to change it.

In 1979, 1980 and 1981, Brown vetoed bills which would have limited UFW membership "goodstanding" requirements to payment of customary dues and initiation fees, as is the case with unions operating under the NLRA.

He also consistently appointed individuals to serve on the board which industry believed demonstrated a bias for the UFW and against agriculture.

But there appears to be a change in farm politics in the state developing these days. Last year, with the impending departure of Gov. Brown from office, the UFW apparently felt it needed to change its tactics to maintain its strong influence on farm labor matters in the state. It reportedly poured $661,000 into legislative campaigns in 1982, ranking it second to none among political action committees in the state. Recipients of its contributions can be found in heavy numbers on virtually every standing committee of the Legislature. Any organization with that kind of political muscle doesn't need the protection of a state agency.

Another tactic used by the UFW has been to charge the Western Growers Association and other groups with using what the union calls their "new-found-clout" with the new administration to "illicitly influence" administrative decisions at the ALRB. WGA has not illicitly sought favorable

[5]*Bakersfield Californian*, May 29, 1983.

decisions from any legislative or appointed governing body or person as UFW President Cesar Chavez claims.

In fact, with the UFW's history of influence with Brown, and its enormous campaign spending, this allegation is nothing more than the pot calling the kettle black.

The net effect of all this on farm labor politics remains to be seen. The one thing that hasn't changed is the law itself, the bias of the board and its agents, and the genuine lack of agricultural knowledge which permeates the agency. All of agriculture suffers—not just employers, but workers as well.

No decisions in the board's history reflects this more than the Bertuccio crop change ruling. The board ruled that grower Paul Bertuccio was guilty of bad-faith bargaining when he failed to negotiate a decision to sell a 40-acre section of his garlic crop for seed rather than for fresh market consumption.

According to the ALRB, workers must be given the opportunity to bargain over decisions regarding what to grow, how to harvest it, and how many acres will be planted if the decision could have a significant impact on employees.

To place the UFW, or any union, in a position to bargain over crop decisions could fundamentally alter California's farm industry. What sort of "give and take" required in the collective bargaining process realistically could occur with respect to crop changes? Wouldn't the union's position be the same every time—that is to maintain the status quo unless another crop would require more workers? How could an urgent decision be reached swiftly?

These are some of the questions which will be raised in the appeal of the ruling in the courts.

Perhaps the most punitive aspect of California's farm labor law is the "make-whole" remedy, and how it is applied by the board.

Make-whole exists to penalize employers whom the ALRB finds to have bargained in bad faith, or engaged in surface bargaining. If found guilty, the employer may be required to "make-whole" its workers for wages lost as a result of the employer's actions. Past awards by the ALRB have often been in the millions of dollars.

This provision puts employers at an immediate disadvantage at the bargaining table. It forces them to enter into contracts to which they might not otherwise agree. This unfairness is compounded by the fact there is no equal punishment for the union within the law when it is found guilty of similar violations.

The make-whole provision, the Bertuccio ruling and other pro-union provisions of the law such as the good standing issue and strike access, all combine to create an environment that seriously jeopardizes the well-being of California agriculture and the jobs of thousands of farm workers in the state.

If the industry is to remain a strong and viable element of California's economy, change must take place. The law must be amended to provide a fair environment for both employers and employees. Fair and impartial individuals must be appointed to board positions. And everyone at the ALRB—from members of the board on down to field agents—must make a concerted effort to educate themselves about the industry they regulate.

69.
Chavez: The Bias Charge is "Phony"

Union head Chavez asserts in a letter to the Los Angeles Times[6] *that the bias charge is completely disproven by an independent government source.*

Since George Deukmejian became governor, he and his political appointees have argued that their changes in the Agricultural Labor Relations Board were necessary to correct "an easily perceived bias towards" farm workers and our union.

That premise mirrored an avalanche of similar charges by growers from almost the moment the law took effect in 1975. These stories have been given broad circulation in the press and the Legislature.

We always knew Gov. Deukmejian would cripple the ALRB because agribusiness special interests are his biggest ally and contributor; growers gave him $1 million to run for governor in 1982—and nearly as much last year for his reapportionment initiative. The phony bias accusation created the political camouflage Deukmejian needed to pay back his debt to agribusiness.

The bias charge was repeated so often that even some of our friends accepted it as fact. That's why we supported an independent performance audit of the ALRB's 10-year record.

That investigation was conducted by the prestigious office of the Auditor General of California. As you know, the auditor general works under the direction of a bipartisan, bicameral committee of the Legislature—the Joint Legislative Audit Committee. Its chairman is Assemblyman Art Agnos (D-San Francisco). Its vice chairman is Sen. Ken Maddy. (Maddy, a Fresno Republican, is one of agriculture's leading champions.) The audit took many months and $63,000 to complete.

Auditor General Thomas Hayes stated his conclusions at a legislative hearing on May 29:

—Based upon a statistical analysis and court review of ALRB decisions, "we didn't find any direct evidence of bias. It appears as though the legal system is upholding the board's decisions in a great majority of cases."

An examination of the 153 appellate court cases that reviewed board rulings showed: 119 ALRB decisions upheld and another 19 modified and upheld. The ALRB was reversed in only 15 cases. Since "the courts looked at (ALRB) cases in great detail," the board's appeals court record is an important measure of whether its decisions are legally correct and supported by the evidence.

—Even Sen. Maddy conceded that "if the board were biased it would be reflected in an overwhelming number of rebuttals" of the decisions by the appellate courts.

—Another key finding was a major increase in the number of charges filed by farm workers against growers that are dismissed by Deukmejian's ALRB appointees. "There has been a higher rate of dismissal of charges. . .especially in this fiscal year," Hayes testified.

The auditor general's testimony exposed Deukmejian naked to the truth that the assault on the ALRB was designed to pay back his debt to corporate agribusiness:

—A massive 30% cut in the ALRB's budget targeting the investigators, prosecutors, and hearing judges who enforce the law on a daily basis.

—A huge rise in the backlog of uninvestigated farm worker charges against growers, which jumped from 392 in 1982 to more than 1,000 in 1984. (There was a massive dismissal of

[6] *Los Angeles Times*, June 29, 1985.

farm worker charges in late 1984 so Deukmejian could claim, in a Feb. 8, 1985 speech, that "this year, we've nearly eliminated the backlog we inherited.")

—Closing off the process of forcing growers to pay farm workers tens of millions of dollars they are owed in back pay due to employer violations. Not a single court or ALRB-ordered back-pay case has been processed since the governor took office in January, 1983.

—Deukmejian appointees have unilaterally tried to settle farm worker cases with growers for as little as 10 cents on the dollar. Federal policy is that worker back-pay cases can never be resolved for less than 90% of what they are worth.

—Farm workers who cooperated with ALRB investigators on the promise of confidentiality find Deukmejian agents are turning their names over to the growers—growers who have been found guilty of coercing and retaliating against their workers.

—Deukmejian's appointees have conducted a systematic purge of ALRB Civil Service employees who don't share the governor's pro-grower philosophy. In a petition, nearly all the staff from the ALRB's Salinas office said, "We are punished for our efforts to carry out the law since such efforts are seen as signs of 'philosophical differences.'" When a Deukmejian political appointee saw the petition he threatened to fire those who signed it.

70. Dick Meister: Deukmejian's Farm Labor Policies are Regressive

San Francisco labor writer Dick Meister, co-author of Long Time Coming: The Struggle to Unionize America's Farm Workers, *predicts that the governor's policies may bring back cries of "boycott" and "strike."*[7]

Remember? The red banners of the United Farm Workers Union waving high above demonstrators everywhere. The chants of "boycott!" The cries of "strike!" The demand of UFW President Cesar Chavez and other farmworker advocates for union rights.

Thanks to Gov. Deukmejian and his grower allies, those scenes are about to be repeated. For the governor has just about voided the Agricultural Labor Relations Act that finally granted the demand of the UFW and its supporters in 1975.

The nine-year-old law remains on the books, certainly, as still the only law in the country to grant farm workers the collective bargaining rights granted most non-farm workers 40 years before through federal law. But the state law's effectiveness has been virtually destroyed by Deukmejian's cuts in the budget of the agency that administers it, the Agricultural Labor Relations Board, and by his appointment of an anti-labor general counsel to run the ALRB.

The trouble began with the governor's austerity budget of last year. Although cutting other state agency budgets by an average of 4 percent, Deukmejian slashed 27 percent—$2.6 million—from the already sparse ALRB budget.

That forced the board to reduce its staff of 190 by almost one-fourth. Since then, says a veteran board staffer, "We've barely been functioning at all."

That may be an understatement. The agency has been taking an average of almost five months to rule on complaints and almost as long to set up union representation elections and certify the results.

Most of the complaints involve growers who refuse to bargain or reach contract agreements

[7] Los Angeles *Herald Examiner*, April 1, 1984.

with the UFW despite their employees' votes for UFW representation, who fire union sympathizers, deny union organizers access to their workers and otherwise violate the law.

The overwhelmed farm labor board has a backlog of more than 1,100 such complaints—a number that has been growing steadily since Deukmejian imposed the budget cut.

Growers, who contributed more than $1 million to the governor's election campaign, naturally were ''thrilled'' by Deukmejian's action, as lobbyist Ray Gabriel of the California Farm Bureau Federation declared.

They are as pleased by Deukmejian's refusal to propose any increase in this year's ALRB budget, despite the board's worsening problems, the $950 million reserve in the governor's overall budget and his proposals for increasing the budgets of most other agencies.

But probably the growers' greatest pleasure has come from Deukmejian's appointment of David Stirling as the ALRB's general counsel. That made Stirling in effect the chief prosecutor, with the power to decide whether a complaint will be dismissed, delayed, settled administratively by regional officials or his headquarters staff, or brought to the board for decision.

Growers hardly could have asked for more. Stirling voted against labor's position 80 percent of the time during his six years in the Assembly, supported the governor's ALRB budget cut and is openly hostile to the board's members and much of its staff for what he attacks as their pro-union ''bias.''

Most of the members and staff see the Agricultural Labor Relations Act as purposely ''biased'' in favor of farm unionization, just as the National Labor Relations Act of 1935, which excludes farm workers, clearly was ''biased'' in favor of industrial unionization. But Stirling—like Deukmejian and the growers—doesn't agree, even though the ''bias'' was obvious in the debate preceding enactment of the farm labor law.

The law was envisioned as a device to grant the protection of unionization to the state's severely exploited farm workers and to end the conflict that was occurring because of the worker attempts to win union rights in the absence of legal procedures.

Stirling nevertheless maintains that the law must be carried out in the ''balanced'' manner favored by the governor and growers. In practice, that has meant actions which have stymied the ALRB at least as much as the budget cut.

During the 14 months as general counsel, Stirling has:

—Ordered his own staff in Sacramento to review all rulings made against growers in the board's regional offices. In many cases, that has delayed action beyond the short harvest seasons common in farming, so that workers whose rights had been violated were gone by the time a ruling was issued. It also has subjected workers to hostility from employers, who know that workers' complaints will not be ruled on for a long time—if ever.

—Unilaterally withdrawn at least three complaints issued previously against growers and moved to lessen the penalties levied against some other violators. In one case in Bakersfield, Stirling ordered an ALRB lawyer to settle for less than even the grower acknowledged owing employees in back pay for his five-year-old refusal to bargain with their union. During settlement talks with a regional board official, who charged the grower with owing $400,000, the grower admitted owing $314,000. But after talking with a lawyer for the Western Growers Association, Stirling ordered the penalty cut to $200,000.

—Transferred to other regions staff members whose conduct had been criticized by growers in the regions where they had been working.

Since Stirling began taking such actions, the average wait between the filing and resolution of complaints has increased by 1 1/2 months, and the number of complaints outstanding at any time has more than doubled.

Stirling blames that on ''extremely biased'' board and staff members who insist on granting

"100 percent of what the union wants" in settling complaints, rather than compromising—being "more businesslike," in the words of growers lobbyist Gabriel.

Courts, however have rejected 95 percent of the grower appeals of the ALRB's supposedly biased rulings. It's much more likely that the delays—and Stirling's actions—stem from an attempt by Deukmejian to greatly weaken the farm labor law.

"He's trying to dismantle the agency," notes board member Jerome Waldie, a former congressman from Contra Costa County.

Deukmejian won't have the power to implement his plans fully until 1986, when the staggered four-year terms of a majority of incumbent board members will have expired and the governor will be able to replace them with appointees who share his views.

The UFW can't expect much help from the board in the meantime, however—not with Stirling running the show. Nor can the union expect much from the Legislature. After all, the Senate confirmed Stirling as general counsel—despite the UFW's intensive lobbying, despite the professed ideological support for the union by most members of the Legislature's Democratic majority, even despite the UFW's $750,000 in contributions to the Democrats' 1982 election campaigns.

That will mean, says Cesar Chavez, that the century-long struggle between California's farm workers and growers will move once more from Sacramento "out to the streets and into the fields."

"Now that we no longer have access to the law," says Chavez, much of the money and effort that previously went into political activities aimed at guaranteeing and furthering the UFW's rights under the law will go into direct actions.

Instead of complaining to the ALRB about growers who refused to sign union contracts, the UFW will wage strikes and "high-tech boycotts" against the growers' produce and the stores selling the produce, using computers and high-speed presses for extensive direct-mail and telephone campaigns.

The UFW's concentration on legal and political activity since enactment of the farm labor law and the slowdown in enforcement of the law has caused great problems for the union. But the UFW has not forgotten how to wage the boycotts that were the key to winning the law. In January, for instance, the union's boycott pressures forced Lucky Stores to pull off the shelves of 182 markets in four states lettuce from Salinas grower Bruce Church, a primary UFW target who had been selling fully 10 percent of his lettuce to the supermarket chain.

"Sure, Gov. Deukmejian has eliminated the effectiveness of the law," says Democrat Richard Floyd of Hawthorne, chairman of the Assembly's Labor Committee. "But Cesar Chavez and the United Farm Workers will do very well without it. The ALRB did not create the UFW. We're going to see a lot of heavy-duty action from now on." Chavez agrees: "Unions aren't controlled by governments. They are very hard to destroy."

There are villages in which men fish and women weave and ones in which women fish and men weave, in either village the work done by men is valued higher than the work done by the women.

—Margaret Mead, anthropologist.

I really think the comparable worth advocates are looking for a restructuring of our society and they're trying to wrap their really radical notions in jargon, by telling women they're discriminated against and making [men] feel guilty. . . . What they really want is federal wage controls. . . .

I think most of them are socialists at heart. [They are] an elite class who think they know better how to run our lives than the rest of us. . . .

I don't think that it is discrimination and an unjust society that has guided women into clerical jobs and men into firefighter and police jobs. . . . I think the majority of women want to be wives and mothers and they do not look at life as a full time dedication to the work force. No, when you're a part time or sometime worker, you simply aren't as valuable to your employer. That differential between men and women has to be taken into consideration.

—Phyllis Schlafly, founder and president of the Eagle Forum, quoted in *Common Cause*, March/April 1983, p. 39.

How can you say that a man who collects garbage is worth more than a woman who teaches kids in a nursery school, or a nurse who keeps a patient alive? [Schlafly is] insulting every woman in this society. . . if she doesn't think that women should be paid [decent salaries] if they're nursery school teachers or if they're secretaries, and that because women are doing [a certain job] it's worth nothing. That's so obscene it simply clarifies that Phyllis Schlafly is a traitor to her own sex. The work women do is essential to society, and it has not been valued for what it's worth because women have done it.

—Betty Freidan, founder and former president of the National Organization for Women (NOW), quoted in *Common Cause*, March/April 1983, p.39.

CHAPTER 18

COMPARABLE WORTH IN SAN JOSE
Social Necessity or Enemy of Free Enterprise

In July, 1981 a public employees union in San Jose went on strike for "comparable worth" for women. The walkout by Local 101 of the American Federation of State, County and Municipal Employees (AFSCME) was the first of its kind on this issue anywhere in the nation. Librarians, mechanics, janitors and clerical workers—men and women—stayed on the picket line for nine days. The job action resulted in a compromise settlement on the question of pay equity for women that both sides hailed as historic. The city agreed to spend $1.5 million to equalize the gender gap. In the next two years it would give equity adjustments of five percent to fifteen percent for workers in sixty-two underpaid female-dominated classifications. "The strike was a total success," declared a business agent for Local 101. "We won dignity, justice, and pay equity for our members. Now everyone in the country knows 'the way to San Jose.'"

The origin of the strike occurred two years earlier when two hundred women employees at San Jose had left work in a "sickout." As part of a settlement the city agreed to hire an independent management consultant to study the issue. This resulted in the Hay Study (1979), an explosive report made by Hay Associates, which generally confirmed the charges of sex discrimination in city wages.

San Jose Mayor Janet Gray Hayes declared that the pact signed July 14, 1981 was "the first giant step toward fairness in the workplace for women. Today will go down in history as the day so-called 'women's work' was recognized for its inherent value to society."

Not everyone was as ecstatic. The *Wall Street Journal* editorialized: "When the nine day strike by municipal workers in San Jose, California was settled Tuesday, the lid was removed from Pandora's box, and a new approach for setting pay for women has made its escape. Under the innocuous name of 'comparable worth,' it would abolish the labor market and have everyone's pay set by bureaucrats."

In the face of rising controversy everyone agreed on one basic point—a great gulf separated the wages of men and women. In 1955 American women earned sixty-four cents for every dollar earned by men. Thirty years later they earned barely sixty cents to the man's dollar. In fact, in California the California Commission on the Status of Women reported in 1981 that women earned only forty-nine cents on the dollar.

Generally women's wages were not lower because they were being paid less than men for doing the same job—an illegal practice since the Equal Pay Act of 1963 and Title VII of the 1964 Civil Rights Act. Their pay was lower because they worked in job categories that historically have paid less. About half of all working women were office clerical workers, sales clerks, teachers, and nurses, all traditionally low-paying occupations often labelled "women's work."

Women's rights advocates, labor leaders, and a variety of policy makers and political leaders—mostly liberals—stressed the inequity of this situation. The issue surfaced during the administration of Gov. Jerry Brown. Why should nurses earn less than truck drivers, or women with college educations average less than men who had only finished the eighth grade? These critics have asserted that jobs requiring similar education, responsibility, or skill should be paid the same. In effect they were asking business and government to use a new economic and social calculus to bring women's wages up to those of men. The called this policy "comparable worth," or, "pay equity."

Opponents of comparable worth asserted that the market place was the best way to determine a job's worth. Artificially raising women's wages would destroy free enterprise and would be too costly to the economy. Cutting across job lines to set pay scales was comparing eggs and oranges. The best solution, according to these market-place economists, was for women to seek out better-paying jobs. In the meantime, government should stay out of the picture.

Equity issues began to emerge in the 1970's when corporations and government agencies throughout the nation ordered job evaluation studies to learn whether they were conforming to federal laws outlawing job discrimination on the basis of sex. The surveys documented wide disparities. Pay equity soon became the subject of collective bargaining negotiations, law suits and legislative debate.

Who is to say what a job is worth? Isn't the market place the best mechanism to determine pay scales? If not the market place, won't the government have to step in and dictate wages and hours, as in the socialist nations? Are women in fact the victims of conscious discrimination, or simply subject to the same natural market forces that determine all wages? And, assuming that society really wanted comparable worth, was it ready to foot the bill for the resulting higher costs of consumer goods, as well as the higher taxes needed for government employee wages?

The problem involved a disagreement over causes and remedies. Wages seemed to decline in a given category when the proportion of women workers in it increased. In the United States in 1870, 97.5% of all clerical workers were men; they earned twice as much as blue collar workers. Currently, when 80% of clerical workers were women, they earned considerably less. Why did this happen? And why were women drawn to these low paying occupations? Did women choose low paying jobs because of cultural conditioning and lack of skills? Or were these jobs low paying simply because they were occupied by women?

What could those concerned do about pay inequity? They could go to court. They could make it a subject for collective bargaining negotiation. Or they could make it an issue for legislative bodies.

Regardless of the arena where it came up, much hinged on whether one believed that an objective value could be assigned to a job and, additionally, that all similar jobs should receive the same pay. Those who favored comparable worth said that jobs had their own value, apart from the market place. They asserted that the worth of a job could be measured objectively. Regardless of the particular job title under discussion, qualified persons could compare degree of skill, years of schooling and training, physical effort, extent of responsibility, and difficulty of working conditions.

By contrast, the California Chamber of Commerce, speaking for a large segment of private employers, asserted that such classification could not be done objectively or fairly. It would cause economic havoc throughout the state, sacrificing existing jobs and losing new businesses.

Even before the strike made headlines in San Jose, the pay equity issue had surfaced at all levels of government in California. The state tried in vain (at least, as of 1985) to resolve the issue for its own employees. It balked at ordering a full job survey, although the state senate completed one that indicated great disparities. In 1985 Governor Deukmejian vetoed a $76.6 million bill allotted by the state legislature to correct pay inequities based on gender. Unions documented obvious inequities among the employees of the University of California and the California State University system.

Small and large municipal governments alike grappled with the problem. A rare success was achieved by tiny Pismo Beach, which, by equalizing the pay of fourteen women and thirty-six men in 1984, became the first town in the nation to fully implement comparable worth. By contrast, Los Angeles County, after refusing to acknowledge the problem officially, was slapped with a suit in 1985 by a service employees union representing thirty to forty thousand workers. Generally the pace of change has been slow.

The San Jose strike in 1981, destined to be remembered as the first labor contest in American history involving comparable worth or pay equity for women, highlighted a problem which may take many years to solve. The battles will doubtless be fought in the federal courts and in state and local legislatures, and at bargaining tables. For California as well as the nation it may well become "the most explosive job issue of the 80s." *(Editor's note)*

71.
Commission on the Status of Women: A Survey of the Issue, 1981

In 1981, the California Commission on the Status of Women appointed by Gov. Jerry Brown held fact-finding hearings. Just before doing so it released a brief statement entitled, "Comparability: An Issue for the 80s," describing the purpose of the hearings. It is reprinted here in full and serves to delineate the issue as it then stood.

It is illegal to use the paycheck as a tool of discrimination. So say the Federal Equal Pay Act of 1963 and Title VII of the 1964 Civil Rights Act. For 17 years, the law has required that men and women performing the same work receive the same wage. For 16 years, it has been against the law to deny a woman a job—particularly in a traditionally male field—simply on the basis of sex.

Yet women in this country today continue to earn less money than men—much less. The wage gap between men and women actually has been growing. In 1955, a working woman took home 64 cents for every dollar earned by a man. Today, the paycheck of the average working woman contains only 59 cents for every dollar earned by her male counterpart.

We now realize that the wage gap between men and women persists because of a phenomenon known as occupational segregation. When men and women perform identical work, they receive, in most cases, identical pay. But the vast majority of working women do not hold the same jobs as men. They are employed in occupations that are predominantly female, occupations that are historically low in pay and low in status. Roughly half of all adult women in this country are working outside the home; nearly 80 percent of them are segregated into clerical, service, unskilled industrial, and retail occupations. A number of experts claim that many of these jobs are undervalued and consequently undercompensated because they are held by women.

There are some colorful examples which illustrate this point. For hundreds of years, a secretarial position was respectable, responsible, well-paid, and occupied by a man. The flowing and readable handwriting of a good clerk was prized by businessmen and attorneys. Then the typewriter was invented, and clerical work became menial drudgery. It was then that the field opened to the women who were moving into the labor force. Now more than 90 percent of all clericals are women, and they are paid considerably less than the equivalent salaries of their male predecessors.

In today's business world, a good secretary must have a high school education, the ability to understand complex instructions and complicated technical material, a command of sophisticated office machinery, and excellent communication skills. Yet in the majority of organizations, the wage rate for secretaries does not match that for parking lot attendants, stock room clerks, and custodians. Is the work of the secretary any less valuable to the organization than that of other employee classifications? More often than not, the answer lies not in the value of the work, but in the gender of the person who performs it. In Denver, the city and county pay the nurses on its payroll less than they pay tree trimmers and painters. The University of Washington in Seattle pays its experienced secretaries anywhere from one hundred to several hundred dollars a month less than starting truck drivers.

According to the United States Equal Employment Opportunity Commission (EEOC), pay differentials based solely on sex (and race) constitute wage discrimination. In the winter of 1979, the EEOC held hearings to investigate "whether wage rates of jobs in which women and minorities have been historically segregated are likely to be depressed because those jobs are occupied by these groups. . . . There is evidence that the low rates of pay associated with such segregated jobs constitute the major explanation for the 'earnings gap' between minority and female workers on the one hand and white males on the other."

What can be done to close the wage gap between men and women? If men and women were evenly distributed among all occupations, the gap would narrow considerably. We have seen some movement in this direction in recent years, but it will be a long, long time before occupational segregation is worn away.

Another approach to the problem lies in the concept of equal pay for work of comparable worth. Comparability, as it is known, holds that jobs which require comparable skills, responsibility, and effort should earn comparable compensation. A cogent explanation of comparability is offered by Mary Helen Doherty in her paper, "Equal Pay for Work of Comparable Worth: The Issue of Wage Comparability." "Comparability steps beyond the equal pay for equal work concept by delving into comparisons of the pay differentials between 'men's' jobs and 'women's' jobs. The management tool utilized in making such comparisons is the long-standing system of job evaluation. Dating back to the days of Frederick W. Taylor in 1881, measurements of job worth were utilized for the purpose of setting pay rates on the assumption that it is the job, not the worker, that is evaluated and rated. In order to develop an effective solution to the problem of sex segregation of occupations and sex bias in pay rates, job evaluation systems can be effectively employed to determine the worth of jobs independently of the job market and to demonstrate that wages assigned by the market do not always reflect worth."

In short, the crux of comparable worth is the job evaluation system by which one determines the relative value of jobs in an office, an organization, or an industry. The proponents of comparability believe that bias-free job evaluation systems are possible. In fact, the EEOC has contracted with the National Academy of Sciences to study existing systems of job analysis and evaluation.

The Academy's Committee on Occupational Classification and Analysis has already sent an interim report to the EEOC which analyzes the most common systems of job evaluation. While the interim report draws no conclusions, it does state that "three features of formal job evaluation procedures render problematic their utility for job worth assessment in a labor force highly segregated by sex." These include a propensity to weight evaluation factors by pegging them to current discriminatory wage rates; the subjectivity inherent in job stereotyping; and the tendency for employers to use a different job evaluation plan for each sector of the organization, making it impossible to compare the worth of jobs from one sector to another.

The interim report implies that the final report could go either way. That is, "the utility of these procedures may more than outweigh any shortcomings," or the problems may be so great that existing job evaluation procedures may prove useless in resolving wage discrimination disputes. Once the EEOC receives the final report, it is expected to eventually issue guidelines on comparable worth.

Enthusiasm for comparable worth is far from universal. By and large, the arguments against comparability fall under three headings: logic, economics, and legality. The essence of the opposition to comparability is contained in an article in the Winter, 1980 issue of the *University of Michigan Journal of Law Reform*, "Wage Discrimination and the 'Comparable Worth' Theory in Perspective," by Bruce A. Nelson, Edward M. Option, Jr., and Thomas E. Wilson. The authors argue that while job segregation is a statistically provable fact of life, there is no logically demonstrable proof of the linkage between job segregation and wage discrimination. A wholesale assumption of wage discrimination such as that made by the EEOC does not differentiate among employers who discriminate and those who do not, nor does it specify exactly how much an employee or group of employees is underpaid. Of the three methods of evaluating the worth of a given job—market value, job evaluation systems, and marginal productivity analysis—only the latter has some validity in measuring wage discrimination, and even then, the analysis is only indirect and inferential.

The economic opposition to comparability relates in part to the projected cost of implementing the theory. Two years ago, it was estimated conservatively that to raise the aggregate pay of the country's full-time working women so that the median pay for women equalled that for men would add $150 billion a year to civilian payrolls. Today the cost would be even greater.

Many opponents of comparability believe that the most valid means of determining job worth is the law of supply and demand in a free marketplace. Thus, if there is a dire shortage of secretaries, wages would rise to lure more workers into the field until the need is met. The reason secretarial wages remain depressed is because there has never been a shortage of women willing to meet the demand. Mandated pay structures would throw the natural balance completely out of alignment.

Perhaps most critical to comparability is the question of whether there is legal basis for enforcing it. The EEOC is looking to Title VII of the Civil Rights Act of 1964 as the legal foundation for its eventual guidelines on comparability. A number of experts feel that Title VII does not provide the necessary justification, and with two notable exceptions, the courts have agreed.

The nurses of Denver, mentioned earlier, filed suit against the city and county for sex discrimination. The U.S. District Court judge who found against the plaintiffs said, "This is a case which is pregnant with the possibility of disrupting the entire economic system of the United States of America. . . . I'm not going to restructure the entire economy of the U.S." At the University of Northern Iowa, a study placed secretaries and maintenance workers in the same labor grade or salary classification. Nonetheless, the university persisted in paying the secretaries less. When the women sued the university, the court upheld the school, saying in part, "We find nothing in the text and history of Title VII suggesting that Congress intended to abrogate the laws of supply and demand or other economic principles that determine wage rates for various kinds of work."

In only two of the several discrimination suits filed citing Title VII as the legal basis for challenging pay inequity in a comparable worth situation has the court accepted its applicability. The most widely known case involved a suit brought against Westinghouse by the International Union of Electrical, Radio and Machine Workers. In August 1980, the Third Circuit Court of Appeals in Philadelphia overturned a lower court ruling and found that the 1964 Civil Rights Act did provide that women doing work comparable to men in the same company should receive equal pay. In some circles, this decision is seen as the signal the EEOC has been waiting for to issue its guidelines on comparable worth or to file its own suit. . . .

Obviously, equal pay for work of comparable worth is a concept of tremendous significance for women in the labor force, and also the subject of heated and growing controversy. In this matter, as in others affecting the women of California, the State Commission on the Status of Women will be looked to as a source of objective information. Therefore, the Commission has scheduled a series of hearings to examine the issue of comparability from all sides. The Commission will use the information gathered in written and oral testimony and taken from research conducted by the staff to assess the significance of comparability for the women of California.

72.
AFSCME: "No Dignity Without Equality"

Council 57 of the American Federation of State, County and Municipal Employees presented its position on the San Jose bargaining fight at a hearing of the California Commission on the Status of Women held in San Francisco in May 1981. While reviewing the history of the conflict AFSCME briefly summarized the methodology of the Hay Study, a "quantitative" job analysis of public employee jobs in San Jose completed in December 1980. It is in this way that comparable worth advocates hoped to measure "eggs and oranges."

There can be no dignity in work
until workers have dignity
No dignity without equality

Although women have made substantial gains in terms of life expectancy, education, and employment since the turn of the century, the income gap between men and women continues to widen.

While in 1955 the average working women made 64 cents for every dollar of a man's income, in 1980, it's dropped to 59 cents. Women with four years of college have lower incomes than men who have completed only eight years of school. . . .

From the report of the California Commission on the Status of Women comes the following: . . . . The fact that women predominate in a job classification tends to depress the wage scale for that category. The use of the prevailing wage system approach to the setting of salaries perpetrates the effects of the sexually depressed wage." Again, from the report of the California Commission on the Status of Women, the report of the 1975 Commission.

AFSCME, the largest public employee union representing over 1 1/2 million workers, has fought long, hard, and loud to remove discrimination in whatever form, from the lives of our members. Members who are attorneys, librarians, chemists, recreation specialists, instructional aides, gardeners, food service workers, custodians, planners, secretaries, data processing personnel, account clerks, school crossing guards, nurses, assessors, appraisers, correctional officers, teachers, doctors, technologists, how farmers, predatory animal trappers, workers with every level of education, professional, technical, clerical and maintenance workers....

We have made significant gains through negotiated programs...and have been, at times, somewhat successful through the courts. Yet the courts tend to be slow if not *deaf* in recognizing this *cry* of discrimination; *deaf* to the cry of eight nurses in Denver who allege sex discrimination as the City of Denver is paying more for tree trimmers, painters, and tire service men than for nurses; *deaf* when the U.S. District Court Judge rules against the Denver eight stating not that they weren't worth more but ruling that their claim was "pregnant with the possibility of disrupting the entire economic system of the United States."

A most inappropriate choice of words in a most unconscionable statement of denial. AFSCME views the collective bargaining process in the absence of legislation or judicial recognition of pay disparity as the means to resolve our members concerns.

Collective bargaining remains the single most effective force for workers on a local basis to promote change, whether it be change in working conditions to provide a safe, pleasant, and healthful work environment or changes to improve their lives which, in turn, acts to change the structure of our societies, and so to San Jose.

In the City of San Jose, AFSCME represents approximately 2,000 full and part time workers through two chapters of Local 101. They are the Municipal Employees Federation which represents professional, technical, clerical and custodial employees, the largest city union, and the Confidential Chapter, one of the few, if not the only in the State, Union represented group of confidential employees. The Unit is made up of workers such as City Council Secretaries, Legal Secretaries, the Mayor's Secretary, Personnel Analysts, and other employees being privy to the inner workings of government.

SOME HISTORY:

In 1977, after experiencing another year of paternalistic bargaining practices by the City Administration, concerned union activists organized the women's affirmative action committee of the Municipal Employees Federation, Local 101. The committee determined to change the City's employment relationship as it applied to women. Many months were spent in the development of specific issues. Surveys were circulated to Union members asking for input; site meetings were conducted; strategy sessions ran far into the night; the result was an exhaustive position paper and affirmative action proposal entitled *Women Working*. The proposal addressed the issue of eliminating sex discrimination from the pay and personnel practices of the City of San Jose and covered such areas as career ladders, bi-lingual pay, job sharing, flexible work schedules, child care and of course, pay equity.

The proposal was submitted to the City in May, 1978, as part of a comprehensive contract package.

With the passage in June of 1978 of Prop 13 and the resultant legislative, boondoggled SB 154 and 2212, the wage freeze for all government workers, as a condition of receipt of "State bail-out aid," bargaining between the City and the Union necessarily was stretched out into the Spring of 1979. With the California Supreme Court's decision invalidating the wage freeze provisions bargaining resumed. The City, however, continued to deny to the Union the issue of pay equity, nor would they seriously address the rest of the Union's proposals. On April 6, 1979, almost 200 City women phoned in sick or left work that day due to illness. The Union packed the next Council meeting protesting the lack of "good faith" bargaining and demanding that the City put the issue of pay parity up for study. Less than a week later, the contract was signed; the City Manager acceded to the Union's demands. Specifically, the City would contract with Hay Associates, a nationally known Personnel Consultant firm, to do a comparable worth study of non-management classes to show the wage relationship of predominately male versus predominately female workers.

The Union made it clear that our position would remain one of internal equity based on the "comparable worth" of City classes and that we would *not tolerate* the use of the *discriminatory market place* as it relates to predominately female classifications.

So the Study began.

In order to establish an objective basis of job comparison, it was first necessary to do a total analysis of presently performed duties within the non-management classes and to create new or revise existing job specifications. This was done through questionnaires and interviews (where necessary). Throughout this process the Union watch-dogged the Study, constantly communicating with workers, explaining what to do, how to do it, meeting with management, objecting when necessary, making sure that this phase was done, as we saw it, appropriately. After review by employees, an appeal process was used to resolve any employee concerns.

Phase II consisted of an analysis of job classes and the allocation to each class of specific points by a committee based on the system utilized by Hay Associates in their so-called method of "quantitative" job evaluation.

The committee was a key element determining, as the Union saw it, the creditability of the Study. As such, we made sure that *our* representatives were on the committee and throughout this phase, as in Phase I, monitored the Study. We advised our committee members as to possible problems with the consultants or City management and asked them to demand as much consistent objectivity as possible be maintained throughout [sic] this critical phase.

The committee was comprised of 10 City workers representing the major occupational groups. Out of the 10, one was management, 6 were AFSCME members, and the remainder were representatives of other units such as the Blue Collar maintenance groups and the Architect & Engineers. The Union demanded, through extensive lobbying, the specific individuals selected for the committee.

The committee met for almost 5 months utilizing the Hay methodology in analyzing over 280 separate and distinct job classifications.

WHAT IS THE HAY METHODOLOGY AND HOW DOES IT WORK?

The Hay Study is called a "quantitative" job evaluation system because it attempts to measure exact amounts of base elements found in all jobs.

The Hay System conceives of jobs as being composed of aspects related to each other in the following order:

Know-how: How much and what kind of knowledge is required to solve problems and meet the accountabilities. (Accountabilities are the end result of the job itself, according to Hay jargon.)

Problem Solving: What will be the quality and quantity of problems faced by the job's incumbent as he/she attempts to meet these accountabilities?

Accountability: What are the results this job is expected to produce?

Measuring the Jobs: In measuring the worth of a job in relation to other jobs in the same organization, the Hay System claims to employ a "refined understanding" of the three basic elements. This "refinement" will lead to a concrete scale of measurement for use in evaluation.

It is assumed by the Hay System that there exists a *spectrum*, or *continuum* of know-how, problem solving and accountability,and that a determination can be made concerning the exact quality of each basic element involved in the job.

The three basic elements are each considered to comprise a separate spectrum which moves from the simplest measurable factor to the most complex. The basic elements then are broken down as follows:

Know-how:

1. *Practical procedures, specialized techniques, and scientific disciplines.* These terms provide the basis for a scale of functional knowledge running from the simple to the highly complex and represent the depth of knowledge needed for the job.

2. *Managerial Know-how:* This dimension provides for a continuum of those skills involved in the areas of organizing, planning, executing, controlling and evaluating and covers the breadth of knowledge needed for management.

3. *Human Relations Skills:* This type of know-how measures the degree of knowledge concerning people and their motivation necessary to get a job done. These skills are those involved in direct, active contact with others.

Problem Solving:

1. *Thinking Environment.* Is your job guided by simple rules and detailed instructions or by "general policies and ultimate goals," or somewhere between?

2. *Thinking Challenge.* On your job, do you make "simple choices of learned things," or do you handle novel situations requiring the development of new concepts.

Accountability:

1. *Freedom to Act*—This refers to the organizational restrictions upon, and impediments to, an individual's freedom to take independent action.

2. *Impact*—The kind of effect the job has upon the attainment of an important corporate objective.

3. *Magnitude*—Refers to the dollar size of the area most affected by the job.

A separate, fourth factor, working conditions, will be considered, but will be the least significant factor, unless the job is especially hazardous. Working conditions are measured by observing (1) physical effort requirements and (2) environmental hazards.

What's Most Important?

Wherever the Hay System has been used, it has been observed that the percentage of specialized know-how decreases with the higher level positions. The real pay-off factors are apparently problem solving and accountability.

After considerably sore thumbing to assure consistent application, the committee's task was completed. All that remained was for the consultants to take the committee's findings and combine them with other data, current salaries, predominance of sex by class and such in order to determine if the Union's original allegations were correct.

In late December of 1980, the Hay consultants presented their completed study to the City. The results dramatically affirmed the Union's allegations of sex discrimination in the pay practices of the non-management classes of the city of San Jose. The Study summary states that the predominately female classes are paid 2 to 10% below the overall trend and predominately male classes are paid 8 to 15% above the overall trend.

That, however, does not represent the disparity, the pay disparity on the basis of comparable worth.

If two classes have the same comparable worth value, or number of Study points, they should be paid the same. The disparity is the difference between the wages of two classes, one predominately male the other predominately female, such as a Nurse (predominately female) and an Assistant Fire Master Mechanic (predominately male) both having the same relative value with wage differences being $684 a month or $9,120 a year. Another example: a Legal Secretary (predominately female) and an Instrument Repair Technician (predominately male) both having again the same relative value, the wage difference is $780 a month or $9,432 a year.

This is pay disparity and as far as we're concerned, this is the result of sex discrimination. Discrimination fostered and perpetrated by the employer's reliance on the traditional *market place* approach to salary setting. A market place that most effectively establishes appropriate wages (subject to collective bargaining) for predominately male classes, but one that carries for predominately female classes an established practice of salary fixing on the basis of sex to get more by paying less.

We contend not that the male classes are overpaid and therefore wages should be adjusted somehow downward, but that predominately female classes have been underpaid, and, therefore, should have these class wages adjusted upwards.

The Prospects for Implementation

The Union had anticipated that the Study would be completed prior to the beginning of contract bargaining this past Spring, however, because of delays for one reason or another we found ourselves at the bargaining table absent the Study data. So we attempted to negotiate a provision allowing for the re-opening of our contract after the Study was completed. However, the City's negotiator balked at this saying (1) that the City would not commit to even giving us a copy of the Study and (2) that the City would not agree to a re-opener, well. . . after asking for a clarification, were we actually hearing what we thought we were hearing? Yes, the City, through their negotiator, was backing down. We got up, said stuff it, and walked out. For the next 2 1/2 weeks, we lobbied the Council and Administration, picketed City buildings and generally raised Hell! Early one morning I opened the San Jose *Mercury* to a glaring article—City Manager Gets 25% Pay Increase—after a brief scream, I went to the City, walked into the Manager's Office dropped the paper on his desk and informed him that this was a very big mistake. . .5 minutes later we had a signed, written contract to (1) get a complete copy of the Study and (2) to bargain on implementation.

We received the Study on December 18, 1980, just two weeks before the new expanded 11 member council (previously 7) would take office. Our immediate concern was to start the process of bargaining. We presented the City with a demand to bargain and two days before Christmas we met for the first time. *A very important meeting establishing, at last, the legal obligation to collectively bargain comparable worth in the City of San Jose.*

How We Are Bargaining the Issue:

We recognize that in order to actually make adjustments in wages to resolve pay disparity, it is first necessary that the employer accept the concept of comparable worth. The City of San Jose, we believe, has accepted the concept and has, in fact, wholly implemented internal equity adjustments for the management staff in May of 1980, adjustments that, in some cases, amounted to more than a 30% raise and with the Study taking almost two years to complete at a cost of around $500,000, we feel the commitment is still there, somewhere.

In the development of a bargaining strategy three major components were recognized:

1. Internal support—membership education through a Steward system. The regular use of flyers, newsletters, site meetings, and bargaining alerts to keep the membership actively involved in the bargaining process.

2. External support—the creation of an outside advocacy group consisting of national, state, and local organizations concerned with the issue. Their role is to provide political, and community support through direct action lobbying such as personal visits, phone calls, telegrams, letters, etc.

And finally, the process of collective bargaining itself or the presentation of proposals and counter proposals by the two parties. However, the issue of pay parity and our reliance on the Hay Study cannot be bargained in the traditional sense—come in high, City in low, and through a process of dialogue and discourse, move toward settlement, a compromise settlement. If we rely on the Study then we are necessarily limited by the Study results.

Where Are We?

We, again, began bargaining in December, there have been 14 sessions, 8 of which have been after the Union declared that an impasse existed and a State Mediator entered the process.

The inability to reach agreement is based on the two parties differing interpretations of the Study as to adverse impact and degree of resolution necessary.

As a result of this current impasse, a number of events have occurred or are about to occur.

1. On Tuesday, March 24th, a rally was held in the lobby of City Hall, a large rally where the membership affirmed its commitment to pay parity and with very loud and clear voices sent that message echoing through the building even into a luncheon being hosted by the Mayor.

2. The following Friday, March 27, a mysterious epidemic of what has been called "Hay Fever" dropped into the City around noon. City workers both male and female walked off their jobs protesting the apparent "bad faith" bargaining posture the City had adopted. The walkout affected all services including shutting down all but 1 of the 17 branch libraries. The Police Department support services, Airport and Recreation Departments, as well as City Hall were all basically shutdown.

3. The following Tuesday, March 31st, the Union packed the Council Chambers with City workers. Pinned to their clothes were buttons stating that they were tired of getting only 59 cents and that they, as workers are a *budget priority*.

Lacking any reasonable progress the Union has sought and obtained strike sanction. Sanction that undoubtedly will be used if the City continues to deny the reasonable demands of the Union, demands based on the following consideration:

1. That California government in general and the City of San Jose in particular will be facing reduced revenues in the 1981/82 fiscal year, therefore the Union's proposal is to defer the first year adjustments from the 1980/81 fiscal year to the 1981/82 fiscal year.

2. That the Union's proposal provides for a first-year cost of less than 2% of payroll.

3. That the Union's proposal will provide for the orderly phase-in of adjustments that will resolve pay disparity.

4. That upon full implementation of the Union's proposal the parties will review the wage structure to determine if the issue of pay parity has been resolved.

5. That the City management classes were adjusted in 1980 on the basis of internal equity at a first-year cost of 5.3% of payroll.

6. That the current spread between management classes and their immediate non-management subordinates is, in some cases, more than 60%.

7. That within the City of San Jose non-management classifications, women working in female dominated areas (clerical, library, recreation services, etc.) make on the average 15% less than comparable jobs in male dominated areas (15% means $3,000 a year disparity).

8. That the City has spent over $500,000 in consultant fees and staff time to complete the Hay Study.

9. That the City and the Union have publicly committed themselves to provide, on the basis of comparable worth, internal equity in the wage compensation of City employees. . . .

73.
AFSCME: We Did It In San Jose!

With good reason, the newspaper of the international AFSCME claimed a major victory in August 1981.

Now the whole nation knows the way to San Jose.

That's because the determined members of AFSCME Local 101's San Jose Municipal Employees Federation (MEF) recently won and ratified an historic pay equity package.

"Comparable worth is the economic issue of the '80's. The tremendous strength and determination shown by our members during the strike and negotiations is impressive," sums up AFSCME Pres. Jerry Wurf.

The win follows a three-year struggle culminating in an eight-day strike last month. The new settlement provides some $1.4 million to upgrade wages for jobs that have been traditionally undervalued and held by women.

The two-year pact—believed to be the first in the nation to move towards equal pay for jobs of comparable worth—also provides general wage increases. They total 7.5% the first year and 8% the second for the 2,000 AFSCME represented city workers.

"We all feel terrific and we're proud of Local 101, Council 57, the International Union and of each other," says a beaming Council 57 Business Agent Prudence Slaathaug.

"The city council had the correct perception that they weren't only facing us, but AFSCME's million members as well," adds Slaathaug.

The $1.4 million in pay equity adjustments will mean—notes Local 101 MEF Vice Pres. Nancy Clifford—additional raises averaging better than 9.6% over two years for workers in traditionally female jobs.

"The principle of pay equity has been established in San Jose and it's going to spread all across America," declares AFSCME Women's Activities Coordinator Cathy Collette.

That principle—and the victory—were fought for by determined members like account clerks Larry and Charlene Keeton, who walked the picket line with their 9 1/2 month-old son and another child on the way.

"One hundred percent of our income stood right there on the picket line, but we were determined to stand up for the issue of pay equity," notes Charlene Keeton.

Though San Jose's mayor has sought to take credit for the progress towards pay equity, "everything that has been won in San Jose has been won by the union and resisted by the mayor and the city council," notes Council 57 Director George Popyack.

"We've shown," adds MEF Pres. Mike Ferrero, "that pay equity is not just an issue for women. Over 500 city workers—men and women—have signed up with AFSCME in the course of this three-year struggle."

The struggle isn't over yet, adds MEF Vice Pres. Clifford, whose recreation department job was shown to be undervalued by $12,000. She notes that the historic gains still fall short of complete pay equity.

"We did quite well, given the economic situation out here, but it's just the beginning," sums up Clifford. "We won't rest until we've won full pay equity for all of our people."

74.
Council Member Claude Fletcher: Equal Pay, Yes! Comparable Worth, No!

Not everyone connected with the settlement approved of it. At least one city official, Council member Claude Fletcher, took strong exception to it, as he explained in a guest column in the San Jose Mercury News *July 15, 1981.*

San Jose is the first city in the nation to become embroiled in a labor dispute over the concept of comparable worth. I do not disagree with the reason and motive behind comparable worth, that many female-dominated jobs should be paid more. However, I strongly object to the method used in the comparable worth concept to address this inequity. The comparable worth approach is simply inappropriate in our democratic free-enterprise system.

The monetary worth of a job in our economic system is what an employer must pay to attract and keep a qualified work force. The comparable worth concept would replace this market value definition of job worth with an artificial determination of worth made by a committee on the basis of subjective ratings of various aspects of each job. This approach, although well-intentioned, flies in the face of the very basis of our free-enterprise system.

This elusive artificial definition of job worth advocated by the proponents of comparable worth is a very shaky foundation upon which to attempt a total restructuring of the nation's entire wage system. The true monetary value of a job has virtually no meaning outside the labor market. If an employer pays wages that are too low, he will not keep his employees. If an employer pays wages that are too high, the business will become unprofitable and will fail. On the other hand, if government pays wages that are above the market rate it will not go out of business. Rather, a greater burden will be placed on the taxpayer either in the form of higher taxes or lower service levels.

I believe government should pay wages competitive with those in private industry, both to attract qualified employees and to avoid the inefficiencies of a high turnover rate. However, especially in view of the Civil Service protections enjoyed by public employees, I do not believe public employees should be paid wages higher than those paid in private industry. This would occur if government were to take the lead in implementing the comparable worth concept. I could not in good conscience place this additional burden on the taxpayers.

Even assuming that this comparable worth approach was appropriate, I would have difficulty accepting these artificial job worth determinations as gospel. Either conscious or unconscious bias of one sort or another is not only likely, but probably inevitable in any such job evaluation system. In examining the job comparisons resulting from the Hay study, it seems that apparent inequities are created as well as resolved by this subjective approach.

If San Jose is indeed taking the lead in what could become a national trend, I believe it is appropriate to look at the national consequences of accepting the comparable worth concept. The proponents of comparable worth do not argue that jobs that are overpaid according to their artificial determinations should have their pay lowered, only that underpaid jobs should have their pay raised. The net result of such a massive wage increase with no increase in productivity would obviously be massive increases in inflation. These higher wages would also result in greater unemployment due to business cutbacks or job exportation.

I could accept these consequences if I felt that fully implementing this comparable worth approach was the right thing to do. However, I believe that replacing market forces with artificial determinations of worth is contrary to our free-enterprise system and goes against the very essence of our free democratic society. Historically, the imposition of artificial controls or standards on the marketplace has proven to be ineffective and often counterproductive.

I strongly support equal pay for equal work, and I believe that any individual regardless of sex or race should have equal opportunity to compete for employment at any level of any occupation. I simply do not support the concept of government interfering in our economy by setting artificial wage levels.

75.
California Chamber of Commerce: "Comparable Worth is Socialism"[1]

Once the state government began adjusting pay scales to achieve comparable worth, how are private employers supposed to behave, if government was adjusting its pay scales? Should they too be forced to consider pay adjustments for women in labor negotiations, or face penalties for ''unfair labor practice''? The California Chamber of Commerce vigorously opposed comparable worth in both the public and private sectors. No doubt it spoke for many employers and political conservatives. The following items are drawn from its newsletter, Alert, *March 20, 1981, April 10, 1981.*

March 20, 1981

Comparable worth is a concept that is being promoted by the state's Commission on the Status of Women. They see it as the answer to increasing the income of working women in California. It means that each person in the work force, public or private, would be paid according to the relationship that his or her job has with all other jobs in that work force.

Comparable worth would be very costly. It would cost private industry billions of dollars. Public testimony indicates that if the salaries of all state employees were adjusted according to comparable worth, it would cost California taxpayers $125 million the first year.

AB 129 (Lockyer), the legislative vehicle for the concept, is heavily supported by women's groups and some unions. Comparable worth is not only broadly misunderstood, but is fatally flawed. For example, a horizontal comparison for the position of secretary could possibly encompass gardeners, airline hostesses or laboratory technicians. Comparable worth would also relate all jobs vertically. Those higher or lower than secretaries would be positioned, such as file clerks, executive secretaries, or administrative assistants. The object is to give each job in the workforce a relationship to all other jobs.

What sort of criteria is used to compare one job with all other jobs in this grand design? Lockyer's bill would require each job to be carefully reviewed for comparability of skills, education, experience, knowledge, responsibility, accountability, and physical effort. There is no requirement to evaluate a person's marketability according to the demands of the marketplace. The creators of comparable worth believe that their plan will eliminate the so-called inequities between school teachers ($20,000 per year), San Francisco garbage collectors ($20,000 per year), truck drivers

[1]Chamber of Commerce *Alert*, April 10, 1981.

($30,000 per year), electricians ($25,000 to $30,000 per year) or university professors earning about the same.

The fatal flaws are these: 1) Comparable worth eliminates the marketplace as the economic force behind the value of the worker and places the power into the hands of a small committee; 2) It freezes all salaries by creating a master plan of salaries, thus one job's money value could not be changed without upsetting all other jobs. One would think that unions would oppose such a prospect. The market place reflects a continuous and immediate consensus of millions of people. It is an old socialistic practice to replace the decision-making of the many with a committee of a few.

The statutes currently contain laws requiring equal pay for equal work. They require female workers to be treated the same as male workers. These laws should be given a chance to operate because the concept of comparable worth would irreparably destroy natural market forces. Those that support comparable worth as a tool to equalize salaries between men and women may be well motivated but they are pursuing the wrong remedy. The Chamber is opposed to AB 129.

April 10, 1981

Background

The comparable worth concept assumes that each job has an intrinsic "true" worth that can be measured independently of actual wage and salary scales which would lock that skill into position above, below or on par with all other skills. This twentieth century caste system also assumes that each job in the work force has a relative value to every other job in the work force; also that these relationships would be expressed as a master plan of jobs. Each worker's job would have a value expressed in earnings. Once this master plan is established, no changes could be made without disturbing or re-evaluating all other jobs. In effect, the relationship between jobs becomes fixed.

Each job would be evaluated by a committee according to a point system which is devised by yet another committee. Such a system would eliminate the natural economic forces of the marketplace where many people are bidding for the services of the worker. Comparable worth would replace the decision of the many in the marketplace with the decision of a few on a committee.

The increased cost of labor, a consequence of switching to the comparable worth concept, would probably be enormous to government and industry. Testimony before public hearings recently held by the California Commission on the Status of Women revealed that if the state set salary schedules according to the theory of comparable worth, it would increase the state budget about $140 million in the first year. It is assumed that to make current market values adjust to synthetic values under a comparable worth system, the only monetary adjustments would be upwards, even though the more honest, fair approach would require meeting on middle ground. Meeting on middle ground would include *equal pay cuts* and, therefore, be closer to a "wash" on costs.

Beyond that, however, comparable worth is unworkable. How could a committee of people evaluate creative talents or the factors of leadership, sales ability, loyalty or dozens of other abilities be judged. Can a select committee of people, each with a bias, make better judgments than the whole market place? Finally, the judgment process would become so complex and cumbersome that confidence in the final master plan would be extremely low, individual dissatisfaction very high, probably universally unacceptable.

Position

The California Chamber opposes comparable worth as a basis for establishing wages for any job.

Reasons

1) *Comparable worth would be very costly.* Increasing the cost of labor without increasing productivity increases the cost of a product, making California products non-competitive with those produced outside its borders.

2) *California will lose jobs.* States offering a labor force that would reduce the cost of doing business will attract industry.

3) *The concept is unfair and unworkable.*

4) *The marketplace would be destroyed.* Comparable worth bypasses the marketplace and ignores the natural economic forces at work.

5) *Comparable worth is socialism.* When the decisions of the many (the market place) are replaced or overridden by a committee of the few, it is in essence, socialism at work.

6) *Existing laws will work if given time.* It is the law in California that men and women must be paid the same wage for the same work. It is the law that employers cannot discriminate between men and women when recruiting, firing, employing or promoting employees.

Opposing views

1) Comparable worth would correct alleged economic disparities between female-dominated jobs and male-dominated jobs.

2) Existing laws haven't corrected alleged disparities and stronger remedies are required.

3) Comparable pay would correct job segregation that often locks women in predominately low-paying occupations.

4) Comparable worth means more money for employees.

Status or action needed

AB 129 (Lockyer) adopts the concept of comparable worth for public employees. The measure is moving through the legislative process. Every person is asked to call or write his state assemblyman or senator urging them to oppose this legislation.

Staff contact: John Yewell, director, Industrial Safety & Health Department.

76.
David Kirp: Comparable Worth is About as Scientific as Alchemy

The associate editor of the Sacramento Bee[2] *doubts that comparable worth deserves to become a rule of law.*

THE "COMPARABLE worth" train is leaving the station, and progressive-minded politicians had better clamber aboard. That's the national message: All three Democratic presidential candidates have endorsed the notion that jobs for which responsibilities, skills and working conditions are comparable overall should be similarly paid.

It's also the message being heard loud and clear in Sacramento. The Legislature has tucked nearly $80 million into the state's budget for raises that would go to those female-dominated jobs—which, it is said, are unfairly compensated—and there will be a new commission figuring out how to divide those funds....

The argument for comparable worth is straightforward and not without intuitive appeal. Women earn considerable less than men, partly because they tend to cluster in female-dominated fields like teaching, office work and nursing that pay relatively little. Comparable-worth advocates go further, and claim that the jobs women do pay less *because* they're regarded as women's work.

[2]June 25, (1984).

Take the argument that far, and the remedy is plain: Make salaries in comparable "men's and women's" jobs comparable, the wage gap will close, and—*voila*—equity.

BUT HOW IS THIS to be accomplished? It's one thing to say, as the Supreme Court did some years back, that day watchmen, who were mostly women, and night watchmen, mostly men, perform essentially the same job and so should be paid the same amount; equal pay for equal work has been the law of the land for two decades. It's much more complicated to make comparisons between supposedly comparable jobs. Likening legal secretaries to carpenters is, as the saying goes, like comparing apples and oranges.

Yet that's precisely what's done. Various job factors are weighed, points toted up, and a composite "score" produced. One personnel administrator regards these efforts as an "infant science," but that's being generous. Comparable-worth calculations seem about as scientific as alchemy.

"Why does a mental health technician earn $6,552 a year less than an auto mechanic?" the invitation to a state Senate forum on comparable worth asks. The right answer, according to the invitation, is "because women's jobs are undervalued."

THAT MAY BE true, but there is another, and at least equally plausible, possibility. Maybe the wages paid to mechanics are relatively high because their work is gritty and unpleasant to many people; keeping mechanics' pay high makes the job seem more attractive. Maybe, in other words, the law of supply and demand that is conventionally supposed to govern the marketplace actually works.

That's unlikely, the comparable-worth advocates counter, noting the many imperfections in how the market matches people and jobs. Besides, they add, the laws of supply and demand aren't to be confused with the Ten Commandments, to be tampered with at one's peril. Government tampers all the time—in fixing minimum wages, for instance, or setting the ground rules for collective bargaining—in order to accomplish something more important than purity of the marketplace. Why not intervene to promote pay equity for women?

Why not, indeed? Despite the difficulties in calibrating what equity means, there's no reason why employees and employers shouldn't negotiate over the issue; that way, both sides know what they're getting into. But comparable worth ought not be imposed from on high in the name of justice, for its adverse impacts just may fall most heavily on those whom the policy aims to assist; women making unconventional career choices and poor women.

SINCE THE PASSAGE of the 1964 Civil Rights Act, concern about sex discrimination in the work force has aimed at breaking down the barriers that keep men and women in their respective places. Those obstacles haven't vanished, of course—it's no easy life being a female coal miner—but most jobs are far more open to both sexes than they were even a decade ago.

Ironically, a wage scheme that boosted the salaries of traditionally female jobs, in the name of comparable worth, could perpetuate job segregation. Women have become lawyers rather than teachers, technicians rather than secretaries, partly because of the wage gap. A world run according to comparable-worth principles would alter those calculations. That would leave women free to continue in their familiar jobs, as clerks and librarians, at pleasantly unfamiliar wages, while men carried on, undisturbed, in the "man's world." This may not happen, of course—wages aren't the only reason for career choices—but it's not the happiest of outcomes to contemplate.

Worse are the possible consequences of comparable worth for poor women, who are supposed to be its biggest beneficiaries. In the short run, their wages would be raised most—all the comparable-worth formulas show this—but that might conceivably price them out of the market. Since these workers would become better paid, without at the same time becoming more productive, their employers would be tempted to look elsewhere to get the job done. That means contracting out work to firms, here or abroad, that pay lower wages; substituting machines for no-longer-affordable labor; or hiring fewer and better-trained workers, who would now seem relatively cheaper because their wages hadn't increased so dramatically.

THE ARGUMENT that increasing wages in the name of equity hurts poor people has been used whenever the least-well-off press their cause; it's a staple in the opposition to the minimum wage, for instance. In the comparable-worth context, however, the sacrifice may just be too great, the gains to workers too small, and the justness too speculative to be worth the sacrifice.

It's this speculative quality that argues for slowing down the comparable-worth train. The Legislature should allow bargaining over the issue, by all means, and keep an eye on what happens as particular localities—or particular firms—turn pay equity into their operating slogan. But now isn't the time to turn this notion, at once appealing and profoundly disquieting in its implications, into a rule of law.

77.
Joanne Jacobs: "Comparable Worth" is Artificial and Unworkable

This opinion piece published in San Jose is interesting because its author uses some feminist arguments to oppose comparable worth schemes.[3]

From the ivied quadrangles of Yale to the rusted tower of Santa Clara County government, and a lot of places in between, women are demanding "equal pay for comparable worth."

It's a nice idea, but a bad one.

Yale's clerical and technical workers, 82 percent female, are striking over the issue, protesting that they average $13,000 a year while predominantly male truck drivers for the university make $18,000.

Last month, the Women's Concerns Task Force urged Santa Clara County to set aside $2 million beginning next year to equalize the pay of clerks and librarians with park rangers and planners.

Profit-making employers don't order "comparable-worth" studies, since they have no intention of paying any employee more than the going rate. But governments, from Uncle Sam down to your local high school district, are fascinated with the seemingly hard numbers of "comparable worth" studies.

The theory is that the "worth" of any job can be determined by a consultant with a calculator and a scale of "knowledge and skills," "mental demands," "accountability" and "working conditions" or similar categories. This is supposed to be fairer than the market system, which may pay a skilled secretary less than a manual laborer or a registered nurse less than an electrician.

Certainly, women's work is never done for a big salary. Feminists blame socialization (Mom didn't raise me to be a plumber) or discrimination (If a woman does it, it must not be worth much) or economics (Women crowd into a few job categories, creating an oversupply of willing, exploitable workers) or biology (Dropping in and out of the labor force to have children depresses women's earnings) or marriage (Wives earn much less than never-married women, who earn as much as never-married men).

Low-paying pink-collar jobs put 35.7 percent of female-headed households below the poverty line. The feminization of poverty is a real problem, but I just don't think comparable worth is the solution.

As a woman, I'm angered that pink-collar women don't earn a living wage. As a taxpayer, I dread the prospect of paying government workers more than the market rate, on the advice of an overpaid consultant.

When the experts are finished adding up their point rankings, female-dominated jobs are usually

[3] San Jose *Mercury News* October 12, 1884.

found to pay 5-25 percent less than "comparable" male-dominated jobs, and the women have powerful support for claim to higher wages. Nobody ever suggests paying the men less. . . .

If the pay gap between men, whose median income is $20,683, and women, $12,172, were closed, poverty could be cut almost in half. But where would the money come from? Washington state taxpayers will have to come up with as much as $1 billion in raises and back pay for female state employees, who won a "comparable worth" lawsuit in December 1983. Nationwide, it would cost employers $250 billion to close the gap.

And who's to say whether the "knowledge and skills" required to sort laundry is comparable to the demands of petunia planting, or to compare the nastiness of guarding prisoners to the "mental demands" of ordering library books. Consultants are just ordinary mortals who have acquired a few initials and a stack of business cards. Well-educated themselves, they tend to value schooling and credentials they may underestimate what it takes to heft garbage cans for a living. Their numbers look objective and scientific; they represent a series of guesses, prejudices and judgment calls.

The economic worth of very different jobs can only be judged accurately by the market: What are employers willing to pay? What are employees willing to take?

Unfortunately, women persist in accepting jobs at wages men won't touch. They let employers undervalue their efforts by undervaluing themselves. And they stay in their clean and comfortable offices, keeping their fingernails clean and their paychecks small.

The growing number who are supporting themselves and a couple of kids—often with little help from the departed dad—need more than "pin money" to pay for the peanut butter, but their salaries reflect long-gone days when most working women were supplementing a husband's income.

Women ought to make more. They ought to organize and demand more—not by virtue of a consultant's study or by arguments about "equality" and "worth" and "fairness," but by the old-fashioned take-this-job-and-shove-it method.

Sex stereotypes are fading; most of the old barriers are down. Women don't have to be senior clerk-typists if park rangering pays better. Very few jobs require substantial physical strength these days. Women can go where the money is, and destroy the pink-collar ghetto in the process.

"Comparable worth" is an artificial, unworkable, bureaucratic route to Lake Woebegone, where all the women are strong, all the men are good looking and all the children are above average.

Selected Bibliography
by Richard H. Peterson

This brief bibliographical guide is meant to be selective rather than comprehensive. Students should also refer to Professor Pitt's footnotes for additional references pertinent to the eighteen major issues contained in his *California Controversies, Second Edition.* The major California history and government texts also contain useful bibliographies. Articles in such journals as *California History*, the *Southern California Quarterly*, *The Californians*, the *Pacific Historical Review*, the *Pacific Historian*, and the *California Journal* will serve further to illuminate the controversies.

Chapter 1: California's Uniqueness

Baur, John E., *The Health Seekers of Southern California, 1870–1900* (Huntington Library, 1959).
"California, The Nation within a Nation," special edition of the *Saturday Review*, September 23, 1967.
Hornbeck, David, *California Patterns: A Geographical and Historical Atlas* (Mayfield, 1983).
McEntire, Davis, *The Population of California* (Commonwealth Club of California, 1946).
McWilliams, Carey, *California: The Great Exception* (Peregrine Smith, 1976; originally published, 1949).
Miller, Crane B. and Richard S. Hyslop, *California: The Geography of Diversity* (Mayfield, 1983).
Rawls, James J. and Claudia K. Jurmain, eds., *California: A Place, A People, A Dream* (Chronicle Books, 1986).
Starr, Kevin, *Americans and the California Dream, 1850–1915* (Oxford University Press, 1973).
______, *Inventing the Dream: California through the Progressive Era* (Oxford University Press, 1985).
Wright, Doris M., "The Making of Cosmopolitan California–An Analysis of Immigration, 1848–1870," *California Historical Society Quarterly* (now *California History*), XIX (December, 1940), 323–343, and XX (March 1941), 65–79.

Chapter 2: Franciscan Missionaries

Archibald, Robert, "Indian Labor at the California Missions: Slavery or Salvation?," *Journal of San Diego History*, XXIV (Spring 1978), 172–182.
______, *The Economic Aspects of the California Missions* (Academy of American Franciscan History, 1978).
Bolton, Herbert E., "The Mission as a Frontier Institution in the Spanish American Colonies," *American Historical Review*, XXIII (October 1917), 42–61.
Cook, Sherburne F., *Population Trends among the California Mission Indians* (University of California Press, 1940).
______, *The Conflict between the California Indian and White Civilization: The Indian versus the Spanish Mission* (University of California Press, 1943).
Guest, Florian F., "An Examination of the Thesis of S. F. Cook on the Forced Conversion of Indians in the California Missions," *Southern California Quarterly*, LXI (Spring 1979), 1–78.

______, "The Indian Policy under Fermin Francisco de Lasuen, California's Second Father President," *California History* XLV (September 1966), 195–224.

Heizer, Robert, "Impact of Colonization on the Native California Societies," *Journal of San Diego History*, XXIV (Winter 1978), 121–139.

Meighan, Clement W., "Indians and California Missions," *Southern California Quarterly*, LXIX (Fall 1987), 187–201.

Phillips, George H., "Indians and the Breakdown of the Spanish Mission System in California," *Ethnohistory*, XXI (Fall 1974), 291–302.

Chapter 3: Frémont and the Bear Flag Rebellion

Bigelow, John, *Memoir of the Life and Public Services of John Charles Frémont (Derby and Jackson, 1856).*

Egan, Ferol, *Frémont, Explorer for a Restless Nation* (Doubleday, 1977).

Frémont, John C., *Memoirs of my Life* (Belford, Clarke and Co., 1887).

Hagwood, John A., "John C. Frémont and the Bear Flag Rebellion: A Reappraisal," *Southern California Quarterly*, XLIX (June 1962), 67–96.

Harlow, Neal, *California Conquered: War and Peace on the Pacific, 1846–1850* (University of California Press, 1982).

Hussey, John A., "The United States and the Bear Flag Revolt," Ph.D. diss., University of California, Berkeley, 1941.

Jackson, Donald and Mary Lee Spence, eds., *The Expeditions of John Charles Frémont*, 3 vols. (University of Illinois Press, 1970–1984).

Marti, Werner H., *Messenger of Destiny: The California Adventures, 1846–1847, of Archibald H. Gillespie, U.S. Marine Corps* (J. Howell, 1960).

Rogers, Fred B., *William Brown Ide, Bear Flagger* (J. Howell, 1962).

Rolle, Andrew, "Exploring an Explorer: Psychohistory and John Charles Frémont," *Pacific Historical Review*, LI (May 1982), 135–164.

Chapter 4: The San Francisco Vigilantes of 1856

Bancroft, Hubert H., *Popular Tribunals*, 2 vols. (The History Co., 1887), especially vol. II.

Brown, Richard Maxwell, "Pivot of American Vigilantism: The San Francisco Vigilance Committee of 1856," in John A. Carroll, ed., *Reflections of Western Historians* (University of Arizona Press, 1969), 105–119.

Caughey, John W., *Their Majesties the Mob* (University of Chicago Press, 1960).

Coleman, William T., "San Francisco Vigilance Committees," *Century Magazine*, XLIII (November 1891), 133–150.

Ellison, William H., *A Self-Governing Dominion: California, 1849–1860* (University of California Press, 1950).

Lotchin, Roger W., *San Francisco, 1846–1856: From Hamlet to City* (Oxford University Press, 1974).

Royce, Josiah, *California from the Conquest in 1846 to the Second Vigilance Committee in San Francisco: A Study of American Character* (Peregrine Smith, 1970; reprint of the original 1886 edition).

Senkewicz, Robert M., S. J., *Vigilantes in Gold Rush San Francisco* (Stanford University Press, 1985).

Tinneman, Ethel M., "The Opposition to the San Francisco Vigilance Committee in 1856," M.A. thesis, University of California, Berkeley, 1941.

U.S. Senate Executive Documents, 34th Congress, 1st and 2nd sessions, vol. 15 (U.S. Government Printing Office, 1857).

Chapter 5: The Disputed Mexican Land Titles

Baker, Charles C., "Mexican Land Grants in California," Historical Society of Southern California *Annual Publications*, IX (1914), 236–244.

Becker, Robert H., *Designs on the Land: Diseños of California Ranchos and their Makers* (Book Club of California, 1969).

Cleland, Robert G., *The Cattle on a Thousand Hills: Southern California, 1850–1880* (Huntington Library, 1951).

Field, Alston G., "Attorney General Black and the California Land Claims," *Pacific Historical Review*, IV (1935), 235–245.

Gates, Paul W., "Adjudication of Spanish-Mexican Land Claims in California," *Huntington Library Quarterly* XXI (May 1958), 213–236.

______, "Pre-Henry George Land Warfare in California," *California History*, XLVI (June 1967), 121–148.

______, "The California Land Act of 1851," *California History,* L (December 1971), 395–430.

Hoffman, Ogden, *Reports of Land Cases Determined in the United States District Court of the Northern District of California... 1853–1958*, vol. 1 (Numa Hubert, 1862).

Pitt, Leonard, *The Decline of the Californios: A Social History of the Spanish-Speaking Californians, 1846–1890* (University of California Press, 1966).

Robinson, W. W., *Land in California: The Story of Mission Lands, Ranchos, Squatters, Mining Claims, Railroad Grants, Land Script, Homesteads* (University of California Press, 1948).

Chapter 6: The Constitutional Convention of 1879–1880 and the Southern Pacific Railroad

Davis, Winfield S., *History of Political Conventions in California, 1849–1892* (California State Library, 1892).

George, Henry, "The Kearney Agitation in California," *Popular Science Monthly*, XVII (August 1880), 433–453.

Johnson, David A., "The Legacy of 1849 and the Constitution of 1879," paper delivered at a symposium honoring Earl Warren, University of California, San Diego, November 1979.

Kauer, Ralph, "The Workingmen's Party of California," *Pacific Historical Review*, XIII (September 1944), 278–291.

Lewis, Oscar, *The Big Four: The Story of Huntington, Stanford, Hopkins, and Crocker and the Building of the Central Pacific* (Alfred Knopf, 1939).

Mc Afee, Ward, *California's Railroad Era, 1850–1911* (Golden West Books, 1973).

Moorehead, Dudley T., "Sectionalism and the California Constitution of 1879," *Pacific Historical Review*, XII (September 1943), 287–294.

Nash, Gerald D., "The California Railroad Commission, 1876–1911," *Southern California Quarterly*, XLIV (December 1962), 287–306.

Swisher, Carl B., *Motivation and Political Technique in the California Constitutional Convention, 1878–1879* (Da Capo Press, 1969; originally published, 1930).

Williams, R. Hal, *The Democratic Party and California Politics, 1880–1896* (Stanford University Press, 1973).

Chapter 7: Initiative, Referendum, and Non-Partisan Elections

Brestoff, Nick, "The California Initiative Process: A Suggestion for Reform," *Southern California Law Review*, XLVIII (1975), 922–958.

California League of Women Voters, *Initiative and Referendum in California: A Legacy Lost?* (League of Women Voters, 1983).

Crouch, Winston S., *The Initiative and Referendum in California* (The Haynes Foundation, 1950).

Findley, James C., "Cross-filing and the Progressive Movement in California Politics," *Western Political Quarterly*, XII (September 1958), 699–711.

Georges, Joseph, "Undertaking the Tough Task of Bouncing a Local Official," *California Journal*, IX, 3 (March 1979), 104–106.

Lee, Eugene, "California," in David Butler and A. Ranney, eds., *Referendums: A Comparative Study of Practice and Theory* (American Enterprise Institute for Public Policy Research, 1978).

______, *The Politics of Nonpartisanship* (University of California Press, 1960).

Mowry, George E., *The California Progressives* (University of California Press, 1951).

Olin, Spencer C., Jr., *California's Prodigal Sons: Hiram Johnson and the Progressives, 1911–1917* (University of California Press, 1968).

Quinn, Tony, "The Proliferation of Recalls in our Single-Issue Society," *California Journal*, X, 11 (November 1979), 400–401.

Chapter 8: Los Angeles in the Owens River Valley

Bass, Ron, "The Troubled Waters of Mono Lake: Unique Ecological Resource or Wasteful Brine Sink?," *California Journal*, X, 10 (October 1979), 349–350.

Chalfant, Willie A., *The Story of Inyo* (Chalfant Press, 1933).

Chasan, Daniel J., "Mono Lake vs. L.A.: A Tug of War for Precious Water," *Smithsonian Magazine*, XI, 11 (February 1981), 42–51.

Hoffman, Abraham, *Vision or Villainy: Origins of the Owens Valley-Los Angeles Water Controversy* (Texas A & M University Press, 1980).

Kahrl, William L., "The Politics of California Water: Owens Valley and the Los Angeles Aqueduct, 1900–1927," *California Historical Quarterly*, LV (Spring 1976), 2–25 and (Summer 1976), 98–120.

______, *Water and Power: The Conflict over Los Angeles' Water Supply in the Owens Valley* (University of California Press, 1982).

Ostrom, Vincent, *Water and Politics: A Study of Water Policies and Administration in the Development of Los Angeles* (The Haynes Foundation, 1953).

Robinson, W. W., "Myth Making in the Los Angeles Area," *Southern California Quarterly*, XLV (March 1963), 83–94.

Walton, John, "Picnic at Alabama Gates: The Owens Valley Rebellion, 1904–1927," *California History*, LXV (September 1986), 192–206, 230–231.

Young, Gordon, "The Troubled Waters of Mono Lake," *National Geographic*, CLX, 4 (October 1981), 504–519.

Chapter 9: Regional Rivalries

Baker, Gordon E., *The Reapportionment Revolution: Representation, Political Power, and the Supreme Court* (Random House, 1966).

Barclay, Thomas S., "Reapportionment in California," *Pacific Historical Review*, V (June 1936), 93–129.

Bemis, George W., "Sectionalism and Representation in the California State Legislature, 1911–1931," Ph.D. diss., University. of California, Berkeley, 1935.

Burdick, Eugene, "The Three Californias," *Holiday*, XXXVII (October 1965), 60–74.

Cherny, Robert W. and William Issel, *San Francisco: Presidio, Port and Pacific Metropolis* (Boyd and Fraser, 1981).

Fairbanks, Robert, "Reapportionment, 1982," *California Journal*, XIV, 3 (March 1983), 104–121.

Hinderaker, Ivan, "Politics of Reapportionment," in Eugene P. Dvorin and Arthur J. Misner, eds., *California Politics and Policies* (Addison-Wesley, 1966), 131–164.

Rolle, Andrew, *Los Angeles: From Pueblo to City of the Future* (Boyd and Fraser, 1981).

Salzman, Ed, "Reapportionment 1981," *California Journal*, XII, 11 (November 1981), 382–389.

Wolfinger, Raymond E. and Fred I. Greenstein, "Regional Political Differences in California," in Eugene Lee and Willis Hawley, eds., *The Challenge of California* (Little, Brown and Co., 1970), 89–99. (Reprinted from the *American Political Science Review*, LXIII (March 1969), 74–85.)

Chapter 10: Internment of the Japanese-Americans in World War II

Daniels, Roger, *Concentration Camps, USA: Japanese Americans and World War II* (Holt, Rinehart and Winston, 1971).

______, *The Decision to Relocate the Japanese Americans* (J. P. Lippincott, 1975).

Girdner, Audrie and Anne Loftis, *The Great Betrayal: The Evacuation of the Japanese-Americans during World War II* (Macmillan, 1969).

Hata, Donald T., Jr., and Nadine I. Hata, *Japanese Americans and World War II* (Forum Press, 1974).

Irons, Peter, *Justice at War: The Story of the Japanese American Internment* (Oxford University Press, 1983).

Modell, John, *The Economics and Politics of Racial Accommodation: The Japanese of Los Angeles, 1900–1942* (University of Illinois Press, 1977).

Rostow, Eugene V., "The Japanese American Cases–A Disaster," *Yale Law Journal*, LIV (June 1945), 489–453.

U.S. Congress, House of Representatives, *Hearings before the Select Committee Investigating National Defense Migration,* Part 29, San Francisco Hearings, February 21, 1942 (U.S. Government Printing Office, 1942), 11009–11021, includes the testimony of California's Attorney General, Earl Warren.

Wakatsuki, Jeanne and James Houston, *Farewell to Manzanar* (Houghton Mifflin, 1973).

Weglyn, Michi, *Years of Infamy: The Untold Story of America's Concentration Camps* (William Morrow, 1976).

Chapter 11: The 160-Acre Limitation

Coate, Charles E., "Water, Power, and Politics in the Central Valley Project," Ph.D. diss., University of California, Berkeley, 1969.

Davis, Alten B., "The Excess Law in the Central Valley of California," Ph.D. diss., University of California, Berkeley, 1962.

Downey, Sheridan, *They Would Rule the Valley* (Irrigation Districts Association of California, 1947).

Koppes, Clayton R., "Public Water, Private Land: Origins of the Acreage Limitation Controversy, 1933–1953," *Pacific Historical Review*, XLVII (November 1978), 607–636.
Pisani, Donald J., *From the Family Farm to Agribusiness: The Irrigation Crusade in California and the West* (University of California Press, 1984).
Taylor, Paul S., "Destruction of Federal Reclamation Policy? The *Ivanhoe* Case," *Stanford Law Review*, X (1957), 76–111.
———, "Excess Land Law: Calculated Circumvention," *California Law Review*, LII (December 1964), 978–1014.
———, "Excess Land Law: Pressure versus Principle," *California Law Review*, XLVII (August 1959), 499–541.
U.S. Congress, Senate, Select Committee on Small Business and the Committee on Interior and Insular Affairs, "Will the Family Farm Survive in America?," *Hearings*, 94 Congress, 1st sess. (1975), Part 1 and Part 1A–1C, includes a discussion of reclamation policy in the Westlands Water District of California.
U.S. Department of Agriculture, Economics, Statistics, and Cooperative Service, "The U.S. Department of the Interior's Proposed Rules for Enforcement of the Reclamation Act of 1902: An Economic Impact Analysis," *A Staff Report* (U.S. Government Printing Office, February 1978), especially 11–32.

Chapter 12: The University Under Fire

Draper, Hal, *Berkeley: The New Student Revolt* (Grove Press, 1965).
Heirich, Max A., *The Spiral of Conflict* (Columbia University Press, 1971).
Kerr, Clark, *The Uses of the University* (Harvard University Press, 1963).
Miller, Michael V. and Susan Gilmore, eds., *Revolution at Berkeley* (Dell Publishing Co., 1965).
Payne, Bruce, David Walls, and Jerry Berman, "The Philosophy of Clark Kerr," in Dennis Hale and Jonathan Eisen, eds., *The California Dream* (Collier Books, 1968), 142–151.
Rorabaugh, W. J., "The Berkeley Free Speech Movement," in James J. Rawls, ed., *New Directions in California History: A Book of Readings* (McGraw-Hill, 1988), 333–347. (The essay is from a larger work in progress, a history of Berkeley in the 1960s.)
Sampson, Edward E., Jacob P. Siegel, and Alan N. Schoonmaker, "The FSM and the Berkeley Campus," paper delivered at the Western Psychological Association meeting, June 1965.
Stadtman, Verne A., *The University of California, 1868–1968* (McGraw-Hill, 1970).
"The FSM–1964," *California Monthly*, VC (December 1984), 16–22. (Published by the California Alumni Association, this article includes the recollections of former student radicals Mario Savio and Bettina Aptheker as well as those of University of California faculty and administrators from the 1960s.)
Wolin, Sheldon S. and John H. Schaar, "Berkeley and the University Revolution," *New York Review of Books*, February 9, 1967.

Chapter 13: The Watts Riots of 1965

Boskin, Joseph and Victor Pilson, "The Los Angeles Riot of 1965: A Medical Profile of an Urban Crisis," *Pacific Historical Review*, XXXIX (August 1970), 353–365.
Button, James W., *Black Violence: Political Impact of the 1960s Riots* (Princeton University Press, 1978).
Cohen, Nathan, ed., *The Los Angeles Riots: A Socio-Psychological Study* (Praeger, 1970).
Conot, Robert, *Rivers of Blood, Years of Darkness* (Bantam, 1967).

De Graaf, Lawrence B., "Negro Migration to Los Angeles, 1930–1950," Ph.D. diss., University of California, Los Angeles, 1962. (This work is also available from R. and E. Research Associates, 1974).

______, "The City of Black Angels: Emergence of the Los Angeles Ghetto, 1890–1930," *Pacific Historical Review*, XXXIX (August 1970), 323–352.

Feagin, Joe R. and Harlan Hahn, *Ghetto Revolts: The Politics of Violence in American Cities* (Macmillan, 1973).

Fogelson, Robert M., comp., *The Los Angeles Riots* (Arno, 1969).

Hacker, Frederick J., "What the McCone Commission Didn't See," *Frontier*, XVII (March 1966), 10–15.

Sears, David O. and John B. McConahay, *The Politics of Violence: The New Urban Blacks and the Watts Riot* (Houghton Mifflin, 1973).

Chapter 14: Saving the Coastal Redwoods, 1966–1978

Burgess, Sherwood D., "The Forgotten Redwoods of the East Bay," *California Historical Society Quarterly*, XXX (March 1951), 1–14.

Fritz, Emanuel, *California Coast Redwood: An Annotated Bibliography* (Foundation for American Resource Management, 1957).

Hutchinson, William H., *California Heritage: A History of Northern California Lumbering* (Forest History Society, 1974).

Melendy, Howard B., "One Hundred Years of the Redwood Lumber Industry, 1850–1950," Ph.D. diss., Stanford University, 1953.

National Park Service, *The Redwoods* (U.S. Dept. of the Interior, 1964).

Runte, Alfred, *National Parks: The American Experience* (University of Nebraska Press, 1979).

Schrepfer, Susan R., "A Conservative Reform: Saving the Redwoods, 1917 to 1940," Ph.D. diss., University of California, Riverside, 1971.

______, "Conflict in Preservation: The Sierra Club, Save-the-Redwoods League, and Redwood National Park," *Journal of Forest History*, XXIV (April 1980), 60–77.

Stanger, Frank M., *Sawmills in the Redwoods: Logging on the San Francisco Peninsula, 1949–1967* (San Mateo County Historical Society, California, 1967).

Wayburn, Edgar, "The Redwood National Park–a Forest of Stumps?," *Sierra Club Bulletin*, L, 7 (October 1965), 10–11.

Chapter 15: Bilingual Education

Carter, Thomas P., *Mexican Americans in School: A History of Educational Neglect* (College Entrance Examination Board, 1970).

Epstein, N., *Language, Ethnicity, and the Schools: Policy Alternatives for Bilingual-Bicultural Education* (George Washington University, Institute for Educational Leadership, 1977).

Gann, L. H. and Peter J. Duignan, *The Hispanics in the United States: A History* (Westview Press, 1986), 232–252, includes an analysis of the case for and against bilingual education.

Guerra, Manuel H., "Bilingualism and Biculturalism: Assets for Chicanos," in Arnulfo D. Trejo, ed., *The Chicanos: As We See Ourselves* (University of Arizona Press, 1980), 121–132.

Henderson, Keith J., "Bilingual Educational Programs Spawning Flood of Questions," *Albuquerque Journal*, June 11, 1978.

Ridge, Martin, "Bilingualism, Biculturalism: California's New Past," *Southern California Quarterly* LXVI (Spring 1984), 47–60.

Rossiter, Robert E., "Bilingual Education: Training for the Ghetto," *Policy Review*, XXV (Summer 1983), 36–45.

Washburn, David E., *Ethnic Studies, Bilingual/Bicultural Education and Multicultural Teacher Education in the United States* (Inquiry International, 1979).

Weinberg, Myer, *Minority Students: A Research Appraisal* (U.S. Department of Health, Education, and Welfare, 1977).

Ylisea, James, "Bilingual Bellwether at Bay," *Christian Science Monitor*, October 18, 1982, includes a critique of Ronald Reagan's policy.

Chapter 16: The Peripheral Canal

Blackburn, Daniel J., "The Farm Bureau's Big Switch on the Big Ditch," *California Journal*, XII, 3 (March 1981), 88–92.

Clark, Cheryl, "Breaking the Faith: Southern California Dissidents: We Don't Need Northern Water Now," *California Journal*, XVI, 5 (May 1985), 194–198.

Di Leo, Michael and Eleanor Smith, *Two Californias: The Truth about the Split-State Movement* (Island Press, 1983).

Dourgarian, James M., "The Peripheral Canal: Environmental Concerns Catch up with Southern Thirst," *California Journal*, VI, 7 (July 1975), 249–250.

Jackson, W. Turrentine and Alan M. Paterson, *The Sacramento-San Joaquin Delta: The Evolution and Implementation of Water Policy: An Historical Perspective* (California Water Resources Center, 1977).

Johnson, Elizabeth, "The Delta Canal, Anything but a Peripheral Issue: Get Ready for the Water War of the 80s," *California Journal*, XI, 10 (October 1980), 376–378.

Kahrl, William, ed., *The California Water Atlas* (The Governor's Office of Planning and Research, distributed by William Kaufmann, 1979).

Metropolitan Water District of Southern California, *Overview of Future Water Supply Available to Metropolitan* (Metropolitan Water District, 1979).

Rossman, Antonio, "Water: Where Do We Go From Here?," *California Journal*, XIII, 9 (September 1982), 349–350.

Walters, Dan, "The Evaporation of Consensus on Brown's $7 Billion Water Plan," *California Journal*, X, 4 (April 1979), 140–142.

Chapter 17: Agricultural Labor Relations

Brazil, Eric, "Why the ALRB is under Constant Attack," *California Journal*, X, 6 (June 1979), 194–196.

Cottle, Rex L., et al., *Labor and Property Rights in California Agriculture* (Texas A & M University Press, 1982), provides a highly critical view of the ALRB.

Daniel, Cletus E., *Bitter Harvest–A History of California Farmworkers, 1870–1941* (University of California Press, 1982).

Galarza, Ernesto, *Farm Workers and Agri-Business in California, 1947–1960* (University of Notre Dame Press, 1977).

Gonzales, Ray, "A Surprise Chicano View of Cesar Chavez," *California Journal*, VIII, 4 (April 1977), 110.

Kushner, Sam, *The Long Road to Delano* (International Publishers, 1975).

Levy, Jacques, *Cesar Chavez: Autobiography of La Causa* (W. W. Norton, 1975).

Majka, Linda and Theodore, *Farm Workers, Agribusiness, and the State* (Temple University Press, 1982), includes a legislative history of the ALRB.
Meister, Dick and Ann Loftis, *A Long Time Coming: The Struggle to Unionize American Farm Workers* (Macmillan, 1977).
Taylor, Ronald B., *Chavez and the Farm Workers* (Beacon Press, 1975).

Chapter 18: Comparable Worth in San Jose

Aaron, Henry J., *The Comparable Worth Controversy* (Brookings Institution, 1986).
California Commission on the Status of Women, *Pay Inequities for Women: Comparable Worth and other Solutions* (Commission on the Status of Women, 1983). Also, see *California Women*, a monthly bulletin published by the Commission.
California Employment Development Department, *Women at Work in California* (State Printing Office, 1978).
Fogel, Walter A., *The Equal Pay Act: Implications for Comparable Worth* (Praeger, 1984).
Hamilton, Mildred, "Pay Equity–Most Explosive Job Issue of the 80s," *San Francisco Examiner*, (April 22, 1984).
Hunter, Frances C., *Equal Pay for Comparable Worth* (Praeger, 1986).
Jonisch, Terri E. and Sherry B. Jeffe, "Issue for the 80s: Pay Equity between Men and Women," *California Journal*, XVI, 1 (January 1985), 27–29.
Miller, Margaret I. and Helene Linker, "Equal Rights Campaigns in California and Utah," *Society*, VI (May/June, 1974), 40–53.
Moore, Marian E., "Comparable Worth: Factors that Affect its Implementation," M.A. thesis, San Diego State University, 1983.
U.S. Department of Labor, *The Earnings Gap between Women and Men* (U.S. Government Printing Office, 1979).

Reactions at Supports and Connections for a Three-Dimensional Structure

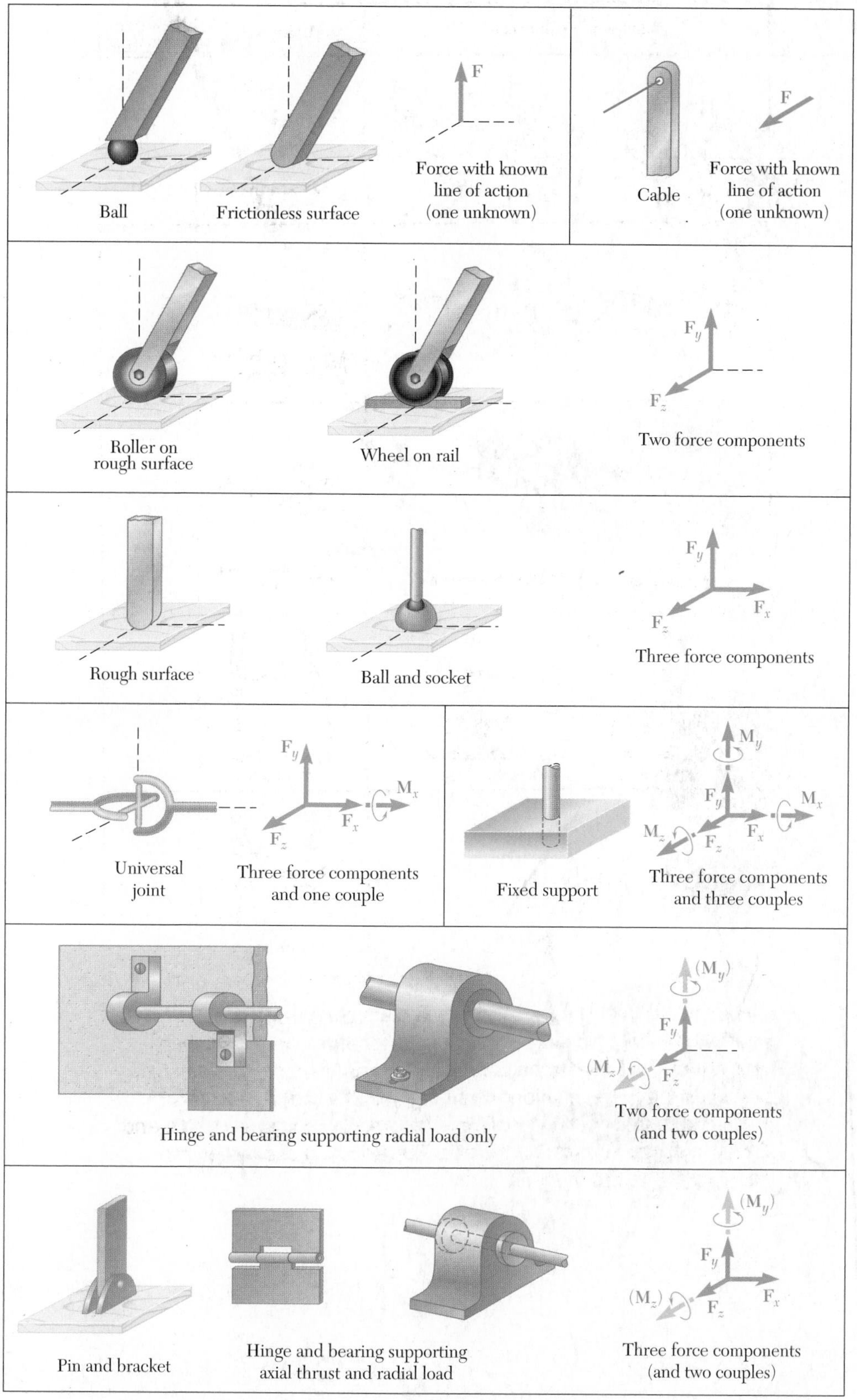

Ball

Frictionless surface

F

Force with known line of action (one unknown)

Cable

F

Force with known line of action (one unknown)

Roller on rough surface

Wheel on rail

F_y

F_z

Two force components

Rough surface

Ball and socket

F_y

F_x

F_z

Three force components

Universal joint

F_y

M_x

F_x

F_z

Three force components and one couple

Fixed support

M_y

F_y

M_x

M_z

F_x

F_z

Three force components and three couples

Hinge and bearing supporting radial load only

(M_y)

F_y

(M_z)

F_z

Two force components (and two couples)

Pin and bracket

Hinge and bearing supporting axial thrust and radial load

(M_y)

F_y

(M_z)

F_z

F_x

Three force components (and two couples)

Eighth Edition

VECTOR MECHANICS FOR ENGINEERS

Statics

(SI Units)

FERDINAND P. BEER
Late of Lehigh University

E. RUSSELL JOHNSTON, JR.
University of Connecticut

ELLIOT R. EISENBERG
The Pennsylvania State University

With the collaboration of
David F. Mazurek
U.S. Coast Guard Academy

Adapted by
Nilanjan Malik
Dept. of Mechanical Engineering
Institute of Technology
Banaras Hindu University

Singapore • Boston • Burr Ridge, IL • Dubuque, IA • Madison, WI • New York • San Francisco
St. Louis • Bangkok • Kuala Lumpur • Lisbon • London • Madrid • Mexico City
Milan • Montreal • New Delhi • Seoul • Sydney • Taipei • Toronto

The McGraw-Hill Companies

VECTOR MECHANICS FOR ENGINEERS: STATICS
Eighth Edition in SI Units

10 09 08 07 06 05 04 03 02 01
20 09 08
CTP MPM

When ordering this title, use ISBN: 978-007-127359-6 or MHID: 007-127359-X

Printed in Singapore

About the Authors

As publishers of the books by Ferd Beer and Russ Johnston we are often asked how they happened to write their books together with one of them at Lehigh and the other at the University of Connecticut.

The answer to this question is simple. Russ Johnston's first teaching appointment was in the Department of Civil Engineering and Mechanics at Lehigh University. There he met Ferd Beer, who had joined that department two years earlier and was in charge of the courses in mechanics.

Ferd was delighted to discover that the young man who had been hired chiefly to teach graduate structural engineering courses was not only willing but eager to help him reorganize the mechanics courses. Both believed that these courses should be taught from a few basic principles and that the various concepts involved would be best understood and remembered by the students if they were presented to them in a graphic way. Together they wrote lecture notes in statics and dynamics, to which they later added problems they felt would appeal to future engineers, and soon they produced the manuscript of the first edition of *Mechanics for Engineers* that was published in June 1956.

The second edition of *Mechanics for Engineers* and the first edition of *Vector Mechanics for Engineers* found Russ Johnston at Worcester Polytechnic Institute and the next editions at the University of Connecticut. In the meantime, both Ferd and Russ assumed administrative responsibilities in their departments, and both were involved in research, consulting, and supervising graduate students—Ferd in the area of stochastic processes and random vibrations and Russ in the area of elastic stability and structural analysis and design. However, their interest in improving the teaching of the basic mechanics courses had not subsided, and they both taught sections of these courses as they kept revising their texts and began writing the manuscript of the first edition of their *Mechanics of Materials* text.

Their collaboration spanned more than half a century and many successful revisions of all of their textbooks, and Ferd's and Russ's contributions to engineering education have earned them a number of honors and awards. They were presented with the Western Electric Fund Award for excellence in the instruction of engineering students by their respective regional sections of the American Society for Engineering Education, and they both received the Distinguished Educator Award from the Mechanics Division of the same society. Starting in 2001, the New Mechanics Educator Award of the Mechanics Division has been named in honor of the Beer and Johnston author team.

Ferdinand P. Beer. Born in France and educated in France and Switzerland, Ferd received an M.S. degree from the Sorbonne and an Sc.D. degree in theoretical mechanics from the University of Geneva. He came to the United States after serving in the French army during the early part of World War II and taught for four years at Williams College in the Williams-MIT joint arts and engineering program. Following his service at Williams College, Ferd joined the faculty of Lehigh University where he taught for thirty-seven years. He held several positions, including University Distinguished Professor and chairman of the Department of Mechanical Engineering and Mechanics, and in 1995 Ferd was awarded an honorary Doctor of Engineering degree by Lehigh University.

E. Russell Johnston, Jr. Born in Philadelphia, Russ holds a B.S. degree in civil engineering from the University of Delaware and an Sc.D. degree in the field of structural engineering from the Massachusetts Institute of Technology. He taught at Lehigh University and Worcester Polytechnic Institute before joining the faculty of the University of Connecticut where he held the position of Chairman of the Civil Engineering Department and taught for twenty-six years. In 1991 Russ received the Outstanding Civil Engineer Award from the Connecticut Section of the American Society of Civil Engineers.

Elliot R. Eisenberg. Elliot holds a B.S. degree in engineering and an M.E. degree, both from Cornell University. He has focused his scholarly activities on professional service and teaching, and he was recognized for this work in 1992 when the American Society of Mechanical Engineers awarded him the Ben C. Sparks Medal for his contributions to mechanical engineering and mechanical engineering technology education and for service to the American Society for Engineering Education. Elliot taught for thirty-two years, including twenty-nine years at Penn State where he was recognized with award for both teaching and advising.

David F. Mazurek. David holds a B.S. degree in ocean engineering and an M.S. degree in civil engineering from the Florida Institute of Technology and a Ph.D. degree in civil engineering from the University of Connecticut. He was employed by the Electric Boat Division of General Dynamics Corporation and taught at Lafayette College prior to joining the U.S. Coast Guard Academy, where he has been since 1990. He has served on the American Railway Engineering and Maintenance of Way Association's Committee 15—Steel Structures for the past fourteen years. His professional interests include bridge engineering, tall towers, structural forensics, and blast-resistant design.

Contents

3
RIGID BODIES: EQUIVALENT SYSTEMS OF FORCES
73

4
EQUILIBRIUM OF RIGID BODIES
157

5
DISTRIBUTED FORCES: CENTROIDS AND CENTERS OF GRAVITY

219

6
ANALYSIS OF STRUCTURES

284

7
FORCES IN BEAMS AND CABLES
353

8
FRICTION
411

9
DISTRIBUTED FORCES: MOMENTS OF INERTIA
471

Preface

OBJECTIVES

The main objective of a first course in mechanics should be to develop in the engineering student the ability to analyze any problem in a simple and logical manner and to apply to its solution a few, well-understood, basic principles. This text is designed for the first courses in statics and dynamics offered in the sophomore or junior year, and it is hoped that this text, as well as the following volume, *Vector Mechanics for Engineers: Dynamics*, will help the instructor achieve this goal.†

GENERAL APPROACH

Vector analysis is introduced early in the text and is used throughout the presentation of statics and dynamics. This approach leads to more concise derivations of the fundamental principles of mechanics. It also results in simpler solutions of three-dimensional problems in statics and makes it possible to analyze many advanced problems in kinematics and kinetics, which could not be solved by scalar methods. The emphasis in this text, however, remains on the correct understanding of the principles of mechanics and on their application to the solution of engineering problems, and vector analysis is presented chiefly as a convenient tool.‡

Practical Applications Are Introduced Early. One of the characteristics of the approach used in this book is that mechanics of *particles* is clearly separated from the mechanics of *rigid bodies*. This approach makes it possible to consider simple practical applications at an early stage and to postpone the introduction of the more

†This text and its companion title, *Vector Mechanics for Engineers: Dynamics,* is available in a single volume, *Vector Mechanics for Engineers: Statics and Dynamics,* eighth edition.

‡In a parallel text, *Mechanics for Engineers,* fourth edition, the use of vector algebra is limited to the addition and subtraction of vectors.

difficult concepts. For example, the statics of particles is treated first (Chap. 2); after the rules of addition and subtraction of vectors are introduced, the principle of equilibrium of a particle is immediately applied to practical situations involving only concurrent forces. The statics of rigid bodies is considered in Chaps. 3 and 4. In Chap. 3, the vector and scalar products of two vectors are introduced and used to define the moment of a force about a point and about an axis. The presentation of these new concepts is followed by a thorough and rigorous discussion of equivalent systems of forces leading, in Chap. 4, to many practical applications involving the equilibrium of rigid bodies under general force systems.

New Concepts Are Introduced in Simple Terms. Since this text is designed for the first course in statics and dynamics, new concepts are presented in simple terms and every step is explained in detail. On the other hand, by discussing the broader aspects of the problems considered, and by stressing methods of general applicability, a definite maturity of approach is achieved. For example, the concepts of partial constraints and statical indeterminacy are introduced early and are used throughout.

Fundamental Principles Are Placed in the Context of Simple Applications. The fact that mechanics is essentially a *deductive* science based on a few fundamental principles is stressed. Derivations have been presented in their logical sequence and with all the rigor warranted at this level. However, the learning process being largely *inductive*, simple applications are considered first. For example:

- The statics of particles precedes the statics of rigid bodies, and problems involving internal forces are postponed until Chap. 6.
- In Chap. 4, equilibrium problems involving only coplanar forces are considered first and solved by ordinary algebra, while problems involving three-dimensional forces and requiring the full use of vector algebra are discussed in the second part of the chapter.

Free-Body Diagrams Are Used Both to Solve Equilibrium Problems and to Express the Equivalence of Force Systems. Free-body diagrams are introduced early, and their importance is emphasized throughout the text. They are used not only to solve equilibrium problems but also to express the equivalence of two systems of forces or, more generally, of two systems of vectors. The advantage of this approach becomes apparent in the study of the dynamics of rigid bodies, where it is used to solve three-dimensional as well as two-dimensional problems. By placing the emphasis on "free-body-diagram equations" rather than on the standard algebraic equations of motion, a more intuitive and more complete understanding of the fundamental principles of dynamics can be achieved. This approach, which was first introduced in 1962 in the first edition of *Vector Mechanics for Engineers*, has now gained wide acceptance among mechanics teachers in this country. It is, therefore, used in preference to the method of dynamic equilibrium and to the equations of motion in the solution of all sample problems in this book.

A Four-Color Presentation Uses Color to Distinguish Vectors. Color has been used, not only to enhance the quality of the illustrations, but also to help students distinguish among the various types of vectors they will encounter. While there is no intention to "color code" this text, the same color is used in any given chapter to represent vectors of the same type. Throughout *Statics*, for example, red is used exclusively to represent forces and couples, while position vectors are shown in blue and dimensions in black. This makes it easier for the students to identify the forces acting on a given particle or rigid body and to follow the discussion of sample problems and other examples given in the text.

Optional Sections Offer Advanced or Speciality Topics. A large number of optional sections have been included. These sections are indicated by asterisks and thus are easily distinguished from those which form the core of the basic mechanics course. They may be omitted without prejudice to the understanding of the rest of the text.

The topics covered in the optional sections in *Statics* include the reduction of a system of forces to a wrench, applications to hydrostatics, shear and bending-moment diagrams for beams, equilibrium of cables, products of inertia and Mohr's circle, mass products of inertia and principal axes of inertia for three-dimensional bodies, and the method of virtual work. An optional section on the determination of the principal axes and the mass moments of inertia of a body of arbitrary shape is included (Sec. 9.18). The sections on beams are especially useful when the course in statics is immediately followed by a course in mechanics of materials, while the sections on the inertia properties of three-dimensional bodies are primarily intended for the students who will later study in dynamics the three-dimensional motion of rigid bodies.

The material presented in the text and most of the problems require no previous mathematical knowledge beyond algebra, trigonometry, and elementary calculus; all the elements of vector algebra necessary to the understanding of the text are carefully presented in Chaps. 2 and 3. In general, a greater emphasis is placed on the correct understanding and application of the concepts of differentiation and integration than on the nimble manipulation of mathematical formulas. In this connection, it should be mentioned that the determination of the centroids of composite areas precedes the calculation of centroids by integration, thus making it possible to establish the concept of moment of area firmly before introducing the use of integration.

CHAPTER ORGANIZATION AND PEDAGOGICAL FEATURES

Chapter Introduction. Each chapter begins with an introductory section setting the purpose and goals of the chapter and describing in simple terms the material to be covered and its application to the solution of engineering problems. Chapter outlines provide students with a preview of chapter topics.

Chapter Lessons. The body of the text is divided into units, each consisting of one or several theory sections, one or several sample problems, and a large number of problems to be assigned. Each unit corresponds to a well-defined topic and generally can be covered in one lesson. In a number of cases, however, the instructor will find it desirable to devote more than one lesson to a given topic. The *Instructor's and Solutions Manual* contains suggestions on the coverage of each lesson.

Sample Problems. The sample problems are set up in much the same form that students will use when solving the assigned problems. They thus serve the double purpose of amplifying the text and demonstrating the type of neat, orderly work that students should cultivate in their own solutions.

Solving Problems on Your Own. A section entitled *Solving Problems on Your Own* is included for each lesson, between the sample problems and the problems to be assigned. The purpose of these sections is to help students organize in their own minds the preceding theory of the text and the solution methods of the sample problems so that they can more successfully solve the homework problems. Also included in these sections are specific suggestions and strategies which will enable students to more efficiently attack any assigned problems.

Homework Problem Sets. Most of the problems are of a practical nature and should appeal to engineering students. They are primarily designed, however, to illustrate the material presented in the text and to help students understand the principles of mechanics. The problems are grouped according to the portions of material they illustrate and are arranged in order of increasing difficulty. Problems requiring special attention are indicated by asterisks. Answers to 70 percent of the problems are given at the end of the book. Problems for which the answers are given are set in straight type in the text, while problems for which no answer is given are set in italic.

Chapter Review and Summary. Each chapter ends with a review and summary of the material covered in that chapter. Marginal notes are used to help students organize their review work, and cross-references have been included to help them find the portions of material requiring their special attention.

Review Problems. A set of review problems is included at the end of each chapter. These problems provide students further opportunity to apply the most important concepts introduced in the chapter.

Computer Problems. Each chapter includes a set of problems designed to be solved with computational software. Many of these problems provide an introduction to the design process. In *Statics*, for example, they may involve the analysis of a structure for various configurations and loadings of the structure or the determination of the equilibrium positions of a mechanism which may require an iterative method of solution. Developing the algorithm required to solve a given mechanics problem will benefit the students in two different ways: (1) it will help them gain a better understanding of the mechanics principles involved; (2) it will provide them with an opportunity to apply their computer skills to the solution of a meaningful engineering problem.

SUPPLEMENTS

An extensive supplements package for both instructors and students is available with the text.

Instructor's Solutions Manual. An *Instructor's Solutions Manual* is available to instructors who are adopting this book for the course they are teaching. Instructors are encouraged to contact the local sales representatives in their respective countries.

McGraw-Hill's ARIS—Assessment, Review and Instruction System. ARIS is a complete homework and course management system for *Vector Mechanics for Engineers: Statics and Dynamics*. Instructors can create and share course materials and assignments with other instructors, edit questions and algorithms, import their own content, and create announcements and due dates for assignments. ARIS has automatic grading and reporting of easy-to-assign algorithmically generated homework, quizzes, and tests. Other resources available on ARIS include S.M.A.R.T. tutorials, a homework problem bank, Lecture PowerPoints, and images from the text. Visit www.mhhe.com/ beerjohnston8 for more information on the supplements available with this text.

Hands-on Mechanics. Hands-on Mechanics is a website designed for instructors who are interested in incorporating three-dimensional, hands-on teaching aids into their lectures. Developed through a partnership between the McGraw-Hill Engineering Team and the Department of Civil and Mechanical Engineering at the United States Military Academy at West Point, this website not only provides detailed instructions for how to build 3-D teaching tools using materials found in any lab or local hardware store but also provides a community where educators can share ideas, trade best practices, and submit their own demonstrations for posting on the site. Visit www.handsonmechanics.com.

ACKNOWLEDGEMENTS

The authors wish to acknowledge the collaboration of David Mazurek and Phillip Cornwell to this eighth edition of *Vector Mechanics for Engineers* and thank them especially for their crucial role in making the extensive problem set revision possible.

A special thanks go to our colleagues who thoroughly checked the solutions and answers of all problems in this edition and then prepared the solutions for the accompanying *Instructor's Solutions*

Manual: Yohannes Ketema of University of Minnesota; Amy Mazurek of Williams Memorial Institute; David Oglesby of University of Missouri-Rolla; Gerald Rehkugler of Cornell University; Dean Updike of Lehigh University; and Daniel W. Yannitell of Louisiana State University.

We are pleased to recognize Dennis Ormond and Michael Haughey of Fine Line Illustrations of Farmingdale, New York, for the artful illustrations which contribute so much to the effectiveness of the text.

The authors thank the many companies that provided photographs for this edition. We also wish to recognize the determined efforts and patience of our photo researcher Sabina Dowell.

The authors also thank the members of the staff at McGraw-Hill for their support and dedication during the preparation of this new edition. We particularly wish to acknowledge the contributions of Sponsoring Editor Michael Hackett, Developmental Editor Katie White, and Senior Project Manager Kay Brimeyer.

The authors gratefully acknowledge the many helpful comments and suggestions offered by users of the previous editions of *Vector Mechanics for Engineers.*

E. Russell Johnston, Jr.
Elliot R. Eisenberg
William E. Clausen

List of Symbols

$\mathbf{a}$, a	Acceleration
a	Constant; radius; distance; semimajor axis of ellipse
$\overline{\mathbf{a}}$, $\overline{a}$	Acceleration of mass center
$\mathbf{a}_{B/A}$	Acceleration of B relative to frame in translation with A
$\mathbf{a}_{P/\mathcal{F}}$	Acceleration of P relative to rotating frame $\mathcal{F}$
$\mathbf{a}_c$	Coriolis acceleration
$\mathbf{A}, \mathbf{B}, \mathbf{C}, \ldots$	Reactions at supports and connections
$A, B, C, \ldots$	Points
A	Area
b	Width; distance; semiminor axis of ellipse
c	Constant; coefficient of viscous damping
C	Centroid; instantaneous center of rotation; capacitance
d	Distance
$\mathbf{e}_n$, $\mathbf{e}_t$	Unit vectors along normal and tangent
$\mathbf{e}_r$, $\mathbf{e}_\theta$	Unit vectors in radial and transverse directions
e	Coefficient of restitution; base of natural logarithms
E	Total mechanical energy; voltage
f	Scalar function
f_f	Frequency of forced vibration
f_n	Natural frequency
$\mathbf{F}$	Force; friction force
g	Acceleration of gravity
G	Center of gravity; mass center; constant of gravitation
h	Height; sag of cable; angular momenntum per unit mass
$\mathbf{H}_O$	Angular momentum about point O
$\dot{\mathbf{H}}_G$	Rate of change of angular momentum $\mathbf{H}_G$ with respect to frame of fixed orientation
$(\dot{\mathbf{H}}_G)_{Gxyz}$	Rate of change of angular momentum $\mathbf{H}_G$ with respect to rotating frame $Gxyz$
$\mathbf{i}, \mathbf{j}, \mathbf{k}$	Unit vectors along coordinate axes
i	Current
$I, I_x, \ldots$	Moments of inertia

$\bar{I}$	Centroidal moment of inertia
$I_{xy}, \ldots$	Products of inertia
J	Polar moment of inertia
k	Spring constant
k_x, k_y, k_O	Radii of gyration
$\bar{k}$	Centroidal radius of gyration
l	Length
$\mathbf{L}$	Linear momentum
L	Length; span; inductance
m	Mass
m'	Mass per unit length
$\mathbf{M}$	Couple; moment
$\mathbf{M}_O$	Moment about point O
$\mathbf{M}_O^R$	Moment resultant about point O
M	Magnitude of couple or moment; mass of earth
M_{OL}	Moment about axis OL
n	Normal direction
$\mathbf{N}$	Normal component of reaction
O	Origin of coordinates
$\mathbf{P}$	Force; vector
$\dot{\mathbf{P}}$	Rate of change of vector $\mathbf{P}$ with respect to frame of fixed orientation
q	Mass rate of flow; electric charge
$\mathbf{Q}$	Force; vector
$\dot{\mathbf{Q}}$	Rate of change of vector $\mathbf{Q}$ with respect to frame of fixed orientation
$(\dot{\mathbf{Q}})_{Oxyz}$	Rate of change of vector $\mathbf{Q}$ with respect to frame $Oxyz$
$\mathbf{r}$	Position vector
$\mathbf{r}_{B/A}$	Position vector of B relative to A
r	Radius; distance; polar coordinate
$\mathbf{R}$	Resultant force; resultant vector; reaction
R	Radius of earth; resistance
$\mathbf{s}$	Position vector
s	Length of arc; length of cable
$\mathbf{S}$	Force; vector
t	Time; thickness; tangential direction
$\mathbf{T}$	Force
T	Tension; kinetic energy
$\mathbf{u}$	Velocity
u	Variable
U	Work
$\mathbf{v}, v$	Velocity
v	Speed
$\bar{\mathbf{v}}, \bar{v}$	Velocity of mass center
$\mathbf{v}_{B/A}$	Velocity of B relative to frame in translation with A
$\mathbf{v}_{P/\mathcal{F}}$	Velocity of P relative to rotating frame $\mathcal{F}$
$\mathbf{V}$	Vector product; shearing force
V	Volume; potential energy; shear
w	Load per unit length

$\mathbf{W}$, W	Weight; load
x, y, z	Rectangular coordinates; distances
$\dot{x}, \dot{y}, \dot{z}$	Time derivatives of coordinates x, y, z
$\overline{x}, \overline{y}, \overline{z}$	Rectangular coordinates of centroid, center of gravity, or mass center
$\boldsymbol{\alpha}$, α	Angular acceleration
α, β, γ	Angles
γ	Specific weight
δ	Elongation
$\delta\mathbf{r}$	Virtual displacement
δU	Virtual work
ε	Eccentricity of conic section or of orbit
$\boldsymbol{\lambda}$	Unit vector along a line
η	Efficiency
θ	Angular coordinate; Eulerian angle; angle; polar coordinate
μ	Coefficient of friction
ρ	Density; radius of curvature
τ	Periodic time
τ_n	Period of free vibration
ϕ	Angle of friction; Eulerian angle; phase angle; angle
φ	Phase difference
ψ	Eulerian angle
$\boldsymbol{\omega}$, ω	Angular velocity
ω_f	Circular frequency of forced vibration
ω_n	Natural circular frequency
$\boldsymbol{\Omega}$	Angular velocity of frame of reference

CHAPTER 1

Introduction

The fundamental principles of mechanics, which were formulated by Sir Isaac Newton in the latter part of the seventeenth century, are the foundation of much of today's engineering. The design and analysis of almost all devices and systems requires a knowledge of these principles.

INTRODUCTION

1.1. WHAT IS MECHANICS?

Mechanics can be defined as that science which describes and predicts the conditions of rest or motion of bodies under the action of forces. It is divided into three parts: mechanics of *rigid bodies,* mechanics of *deformable bodies,* and mechanics of *fluids.*

The mechanics of rigid bodies is subdivided into *statics* and *dynamics,* the former dealing with bodies at rest, the latter with bodies in motion. In this part of the study of mechanics, bodies are assumed to be perfectly rigid. Actual structures and machines, however, are never absolutely rigid and deform under the loads to which they are subjected. But these deformations are usually small and do not appreciably affect the conditions of equilibrium or motion of the structure under consideration. They are important, though, as far as the resistance of the structure to failure is concerned and are studied in mechanics of materials, which is a part of the mechanics of deformable bodies. The third division of mechanics, the mechanics of fluids, is subdivided into the study of *incompressible fluids* and of *compressible fluids.* An important subdivision of the study of incompressible fluids is *hydraulics,* which deals with problems involving water.

Mechanics is a physical science, since it deals with the study of physical phenomena. However, some associate mechanics with mathematics, while many consider it as an engineering subject. Both these views are justified in part. Mechanics is the foundation of most engineering sciences and is an indispensable prerequisite to their study. However, it does not have the *empiricism* found in some engineering sciences, that is, it does not rely on experience or observation alone; by its rigor and the emphasis it places on deductive reasoning it resembles mathematics. But, again, it is not an *abstract* or even a *pure* science; mechanics is an *applied* science. The purpose of mechanics is to explain and predict physical phenomena and thus to lay the foundations for engineering applications.

Photo 1.1 Sir Isaac Newton

1.2. FUNDAMENTAL CONCEPTS AND PRINCIPLES

Although the study of mechanics goes back to the time of Aristotle (384–322 B.C.) and Archimedes (287–212 B.C.), one has to wait until Newton (1642–1727) to find a satisfactory formulation of its fundamental principles. These principles were later expressed in a modified form by d'Alembert, Lagrange, and Hamilton. Their validity remained unchallenged, however, until Einstein formulated his *theory of relativity* (1905). While its limitations have now been recognized, *newtonian mechanics* still remains the basis of today's engineering sciences.

The basic concepts used in mechanics are *space, time, mass,* and *force.* These concepts cannot be truly defined; they should be accepted on the basis of our intuition and experience and used as a mental frame of reference for our study of mechanics.

The concept of *space* is associated with the notion of the position of a point P. The position of P can be defined by three lengths measured from a certain reference point, or *origin,* in three given directions. These lengths are known as the *coordinates* of P.

To define an event, it is not sufficient to indicate its position in space. The *time* of the event should also be given.

The concept of *mass* is used to characterize and compare bodies on the basis of certain fundamental mechanical experiments. Two bodies of the same mass, for example, will be attracted by the earth in the same manner; they will also offer the same resistance to a change in translational motion.

A *force* represents the action of one body on another. It can be exerted by actual contact or at a distance, as in the case of gravitational forces and magnetic forces. A force is characterized by its *point of application*, its *magnitude*, and its *direction;* a force is represented by a *vector* (Sec. 2.3).

In newtonian mechanics, space, time, and mass are absolute concepts, independent of each other. (This is not true in *relativistic mechanics,* where the time of an event depends upon its position, and where the mass of a body varies with its velocity.) On the other hand, the concept of force is not independent of the other three. Indeed, one of the fundamental principles of newtonian mechanics listed below indicates that the resultant force acting on a body is related to the mass of the body and to the manner in which its velocity varies with time.

You will study the conditions of rest or motion of particles and rigid bodies in terms of the four basic concepts we have introduced. By *particle* we mean a very small amount of matter which may be assumed to occupy a single point in space. A *rigid body* is a combination of a large number of particles occupying fixed positions with respect to each other. The study of the mechanics of particles is obviously a prerequisite to that of rigid bodies. Besides, the results obtained for a particle can be used directly in a large number of problems dealing with the conditions of rest or motion of actual bodies.

The study of elementary mechanics rests on six fundamental principles based on experimental evidence.

The Parallelogram Law for the Addition of Forces. This states that two forces acting on a particle may be replaced by a single force, called their *resultant,* obtained by drawing the diagonal of the parallelogram which has sides equal to the given forces (Sec. 2.2).

The Principle of Transmissibility. This states that the conditions of equilibrium or of motion of a rigid body will remain unchanged if a force acting at a given point of the rigid body is replaced by a force of the same magnitude and same direction, but acting at a different point, provided that the two forces have the same line of action (Sec. 3.3).

Newton's Three Fundamental Laws. Formulated by Sir Isaac Newton in the latter part of the seventeenth century, these laws can be stated as follows:

FIRST LAW. If the resultant force acting on a particle is zero, the particle will remain at rest (if originally at rest) or will move with constant speed in a straight line (if originally in motion) (Sec. 2.10).

SECOND LAW. If the resultant force acting on a particle is not zero, the particle will have an acceleration proportional to the magnitude of the resultant and in the direction of this resultant force.

As you will see in Sec. 12.2, this law can be stated as

$$\mathbf{F} = m\mathbf{a} \tag{1.1}$$

where $\mathbf{F}$, m, and $\mathbf{a}$ represent, respectively, the resultant force acting on the particle, the mass of the particle, and the acceleration of the particle, expressed in a consistent system of units.

THIRD LAW. The forces of action and reaction between bodies in contact have the same magnitude, same line of action, and opposite sense (Sec. 6.1).

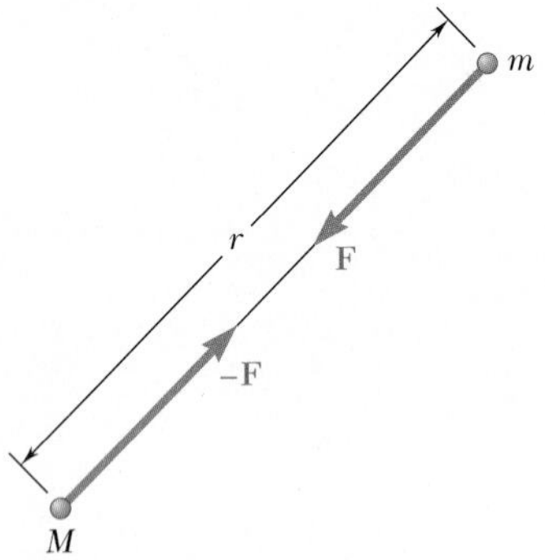

Fig. 1.1

Newton's Law of Gravitation. This states that two particles of mass M and m are mutually attracted with equal and opposite forces $\mathbf{F}$ and $-\mathbf{F}$ (Fig. 1.1) of magnitude F given by the formula

$$F = G\frac{Mm}{r^2} \tag{1.2}$$

where r = distance between the two particles
G = universal constant called the *constant of gravitation*

Newton's law of gravitation introduces the idea of an action exerted at a distance and extends the range of application of Newton's third law: the action $\mathbf{F}$ and the reaction $-\mathbf{F}$ in Fig. 1.1 are equal and opposite, and they have the same line of action.

Photo 1.2 When in earth orbit, people and objects are said to be *weightless* even though the gravitational force acting is approximately 90% of that experienced on the surface of the earth. This apparent contradiction will be resolved in Chapter 12 when we apply Newton's second law to the motion of particles.

A particular case of great importance is that of the attraction of the earth on a particle located on its surface. The force $\mathbf{F}$ exerted by the earth on the particle is then defined as the *weight* $\mathbf{W}$ of the particle. Taking M equal to the mass of the earth, m equal to the mass of the particle, and r equal to the radius R of the earth, and introducing the constant

$$g = \frac{GM}{R^2} \tag{1.3}$$

the magnitude W of the weight of a particle of mass m may be expressed as†

$$W = mg \tag{1.4}$$

The value of R in formula (1.3) depends upon the elevation of the point considered; it also depends upon its latitude, since the earth is not truly spherical. The value of g therefore varies with the position of the point considered. As long as the point actually remains on the surface of the earth, it is sufficiently accurate in most engineering computations to assume that g equals 9.81 m/s^2 or 32.2 ft/s^2.

†A more accurate definition of the weight $\mathbf{W}$ should take into account the rotation of the earth.

The principles we have just listed will be introduced in the course of our study of mechanics as they are needed. The study of the statics of particles carried out in Chap. 2 will be based on the parallelogram law of addition and on Newton's first law alone. The principle of transmissibility will be introduced in Chap. 3 as we begin the study of the statics of rigid bodies, and Newton's third law in Chap. 6 as we analyze the forces exerted on each other by the various members forming a structure. In the study of dynamics, Newton's second law and Newton's law of gravitation will be introduced. It will then be shown that Newton's first law is a particular case of Newton's second law (Sec. 12.2) and that the principle of transmissibility could be derived from the other principles and thus eliminated (Sec. 16.5). In the meantime, however, Newton's first and third laws, the parallelogram law of addition, and the principle of transmissibility will provide us with the necessary and sufficient foundation for the entire study of the statics of particles, rigid bodies, and systems of rigid bodies.

As noted earlier, the six fundamental principles listed above are based on experimental evidence. Except for Newton's first law and the principle of transmissibility, they are independent principles which cannot be derived mathematically from each other or from any other elementary physical principle. On these principles rests most of the intricate structure of newtonian mechanics. For more than two centuries a tremendous number of problems dealing with the conditions of rest and motion of rigid bodies, deformable bodies, and fluids were solved by applying these fundamental principles. Many of the solutions obtained could be checked experimentally, thus providing a further verification of the principles from which they were derived. It was only in the last century that Newton's mechanics was found at fault, in the study of the motion of atoms and in the study of the motion of certain planets, where it must be supplemented by the theory of relativity. But on the human or engineering scale, where velocities are small compared with the speed of light, Newton's mechanics has yet to be disproved.

1.3. SYSTEMS OF UNITS

Associated with the four fundamental concepts introduced in the preceding section are the so-called *kinetic units,* that is, the units of *length, time, mass,* and *force.* These units cannot be chosen independently if Eq. (1.1) is to be satisfied. Three of the units may be defined arbitrarily; they are then referred to as *base units.* The fourth unit, however, must be chosen in accordance with Eq. (1.1) and is referred to as a *derived unit.* Kinetic units selected in this way are said to form a *consistent system of units.*

International System of Units (SI Units†). In this system, which will be in universal use when the United States completes its conversion to SI units, the base units are the units of length, mass, and time, and they are called, respectively, the *meter* (m), the *kilogram* (kg), and the *second* (s). All three are arbitrarily defined. The second, which was originally chosen to represent 1/86 400 of the mean

†SI stands for *Système International d'Unités* (French).

solar day, is now defined as the duration of 9 192 631 770 cycles of the radiation corresponding to the transition between two levels of the fundamental state of the cesium-133 atom. The meter, originally defined as one ten-millionth of the distance from the equator to either pole, is now defined as 1 650 763.73 wavelengths of the orange-red light corresponding to a certain transition in an atom of krypton-86. The kilogram, which is approximately equal to the mass of 0.001 m^3 of water, is defined as the mass of a platinum-iridium standard kept at the International Bureau of Weights and Measures at Sèvres, near Paris, France. The unit of force is a derived unit. It is called the *newton* (N) and is defined as the force which gives an acceleration of 1 m/s^2 to a mass of 1 kg (Fig. 1.2). From Eq. (1.1) we write

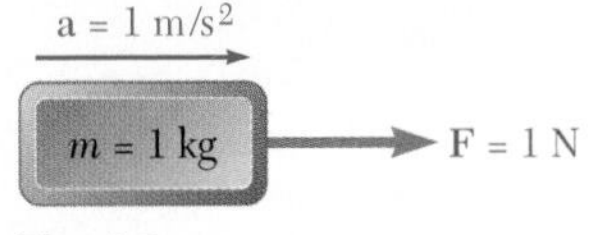

Fig. 1.2

$$1 \text{ N} = (1 \text{ kg})(1 \text{ m/s}^2) = 1 \text{ kg} \cdot \text{m/s}^2 \tag{1.5}$$

The SI units are said to form an *absolute* system of units. This means that the three base units chosen are independent of the location where measurements are made. The meter, the kilogram, and the second may be used anywhere on the earth; they may even be used on another planet. They will always have the same significance.

The *weight* of a body, or the *force of gravity* exerted on that body, should, like any other force, be expressed in newtons. From Eq. (1.4) it follows that the weight of a body of mass 1 kg (Fig. 1.3) is

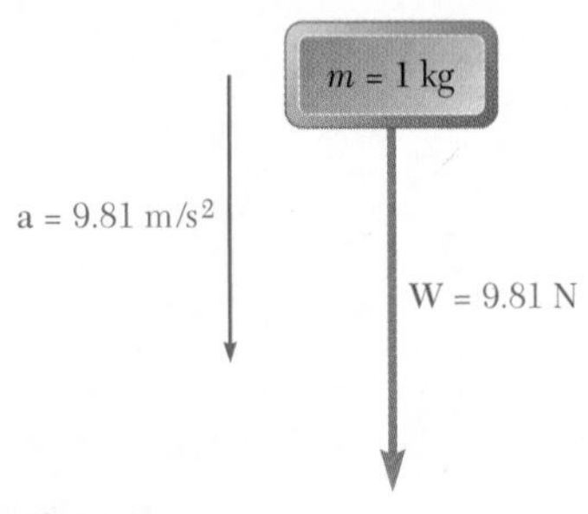

Fig. 1.3

$$\begin{aligned} W &= mg \\ &= (1 \text{ kg})(9.81 \text{ m/s}^2) \\ &= 9.81 \text{ N} \end{aligned}$$

Multiples and submultiples of the fundamental SI units may be obtained through the use of the prefixes defined in Table 1.1. The multiples and submultiples of the units of length, mass, and force most frequently used in engineering are, respectively, the *kilometer* (km) and the *millimeter* (mm); the *megagram*† (Mg) and the *gram* (g); and the *kilonewton* (kN). According to Table 1.1, we have

$$1 \text{ km} = 1000 \text{ m} \qquad 1 \text{ mm} = 0.001 \text{ m}$$
$$1 \text{ Mg} = 1000 \text{ kg} \qquad 1 \text{ g} = 0.001 \text{ kg}$$
$$1 \text{ kN} = 1000 \text{ N}$$

The conversion of these units into meters, kilograms, and newtons, respectively, can be effected by simply moving the decimal point three places to the right or to the left. For example, to convert 3.82 km into meters, one moves the decimal point three places to the right:

$$3.82 \text{ km} = 3820 \text{ m}$$

Similarly, 47.2 mm is converted into meters by moving the decimal point three places to the left:

$$47.2 \text{ mm} = 0.0472 \text{ m}$$

†Also known as a *metric ton*.

Table 1.1. SI Prefixes

Multiplication Factor	Prefix†	Symbol
1 000 000 000 000 = 10^{12}	tera	T
1 000 000 000 = 10^9	giga	G
1 000 000 = 10^6	mega	M
1 000 = 10^3	kilo	k
100 = 10^2	hecto‡	h
10 = 10^1	deka‡	da
0.1 = 10^{-1}	deci‡	d
0.01 = 10^{-2}	centi‡	c
0.001 = 10^{-3}	milli	m
0.000 001 = 10^{-6}	micro	μ
0.000 000 001 = 10^{-9}	nano	n
0.000 000 000 001 = 10^{-12}	pico	p
0.000 000 000 000 001 = 10^{-15}	femto	f
0.000 000 000 000 000 001 = 10^{-18}	atto	a

†The first syllable of every prefix is accented so that the prefix will retain its identity. Thus, the preferred pronunciation of kilometer places the accent on the first syllable, not the second.

‡The use of these prefixes should be avoided, except for the measurement of areas and volumes and for the nontechnical use of centimeter, as for body and clothing measurements.

Using scientific notation, one may also write

$$3.82 \text{ km} = 3.82 \times 10^3 \text{ m}$$
$$47.2 \text{ mm} = 47.2 \times 10^{-3} \text{ m}$$

The multiples of the unit of time are the *minute* (min) and the *hour* (h). Since 1 min = 60 s and 1 h = 60 min = 3600 s, these multiples cannot be converted as readily as the others.

By using the appropriate multiple or submultiple of a given unit, one can avoid writing very large or very small numbers. For example, one usually writes 427.2 km rather than 427 200 m, and 2.16 mm rather than 0.002 16 m.†

Units of Area and Volume. The unit of area is the *square meter* (m^2), which represents the area of a square of side 1 m; the unit of volume is the *cubic meter* (m^3), equal to the volume of a cube of side 1 m. In order to avoid exceedingly small or large numerical values in the computation of areas and volumes, one uses systems of subunits obtained by respectively squaring and cubing not only the millimeter but also two intermediate submultiples of the meter, namely, the *decimeter* (dm) and the *centimeter* (cm). Since, by definition,

$$1 \text{ dm} = 0.1 \text{ m} = 10^{-1} \text{ m}$$
$$1 \text{ cm} = 0.01 \text{ m} = 10^{-2} \text{ m}$$
$$1 \text{ mm} = 0.001 \text{ m} = 10^{-3} \text{ m}$$

†It should be noted that when more than four digits are used on either side of the decimal point to express a quantity in SI units—as in 427 200 m or 0.002 16 m—spaces, never commas, should be used to separate the digits into groups of three. This is to avoid confusion with the comma used in place of a decimal point, which is the convention in many countries.

the submultiples of the unit of area are

$$1\ \text{dm}^2 = (1\ \text{dm})^2 = (10^{-1}\ \text{m})^2 = 10^{-2}\ \text{m}^2$$
$$1\ \text{cm}^2 = (1\ \text{cm})^2 = (10^{-2}\ \text{m})^2 = 10^{-4}\ \text{m}^2$$
$$1\ \text{mm}^2 = (1\ \text{mm})^2 = (10^{-3}\ \text{m})^2 = 10^{-6}\ \text{m}^2$$

and the submultiples of the unit of volume are

$$1\ \text{dm}^3 = (1\ \text{dm})^3 = (10^{-1}\ \text{m})^3 = 10^{-3}\ \text{m}^3$$
$$1\ \text{cm}^3 = (1\ \text{cm})^3 = (10^{-2}\ \text{m})^3 = 10^{-6}\ \text{m}^3$$
$$1\ \text{mm}^3 = (1\ \text{mm})^3 = (10^{-3}\ \text{m})^3 = 10^{-9}\ \text{m}^3$$

It should be noted that when the volume of a liquid is being measured, the cubic decimeter (dm^3) is usually referred to as a *liter* (L).

Other derived SI units used to measure the moment of a force, the work of a force, etc., are shown in Table 1.2. While these units will be introduced in later chapters as they are needed, we should note an important rule at this time: When a derived unit is obtained by dividing a base unit by another base unit, a prefix may be used in the numerator of the derived unit but not in its denominator. For example, the constant k of a spring which stretches 20 mm under a load of 100 N will be expressed as

$$k = \frac{100\ \text{N}}{20\ \text{mm}} = \frac{100\ \text{N}}{0.020\ \text{m}} = 5000\ \text{N/m} \qquad \text{or} \qquad k = 5\ \text{kN/m}$$

but never as $k = 5$ N/mm.

Table 1.2. Principal SI Units Used in Mechanics

Quantity	Unit	Symbol	Formula
Acceleration	Meter per second squared	. . .	m/s^2
Angle	Radian	rad	†
Angular acceleration	Radian per second squared	. . .	rad/s^2
Angular velocity	Radian per second	. . .	rad/s
Area	Square meter	. . .	m^2
Density	Kilogram per cubic meter	. . .	kg/m^3
Energy	Joule	J	$\text{N} \cdot \text{m}$
Force	Newton	N	$\text{kg} \cdot \text{m/s}^2$
Frequency	Hertz	Hz	s^{-1}
Impulse	Newton-second	. . .	$\text{kg} \cdot \text{m/s}$
Length	Meter	m	‡
Mass	Kilogram	kg	‡
Moment of a force	Newton-meter	. . .	$\text{N} \cdot \text{m}$
Power	Watt	W	J/s
Pressure	Pascal	Pa	N/m^2
Stress	Pascal	Pa	N/m^2
Time	Second	s	‡
Velocity	Meter per second	. . .	m/s
Volume			
Solids	Cubic meter	. . .	m^3
Liquids	Liter	L	$10^{-3}\ \text{m}^3$
Work	Joule	J	$\text{N} \cdot \text{m}$

†Supplementary unit (1 revolution $= 2\pi$ rad $= 360°$).

‡Base unit.

U.S. Customary Units. Most practicing American engineers still commonly use a system in which the base units are the units of length, force, and time. These units are, respectively, the *foot* (ft), the *pound* (lb), and the *second* (s). The second is the same as the corresponding SI unit. The foot is defined as 0.3048 m. The pound is defined as the *weight* of a platinum standard, called the *standard pound*, which is kept at the National Institute of Standards and Technology outside Washington, the mass of which is 0.453 592 43 kg. Since the weight of a body depends upon the earth's gravitational attraction, which varies with location, it is specified that the standard pound should be placed at sea level and at a latitude of 45° to properly define a force of 1 lb. Clearly the U.S. customary units do not form an absolute system of units. Because of their dependence upon the gravitational attraction of the earth, they form a *gravitational* system of units.

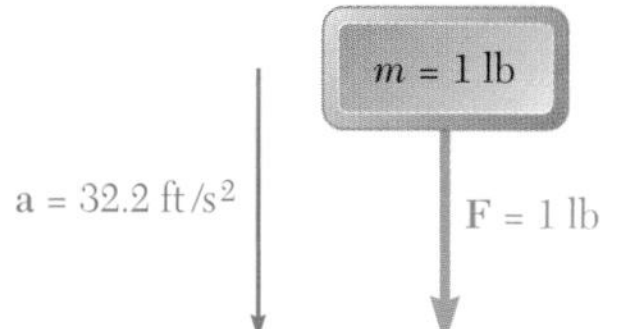

Fig. 1.4

While the standard pound also serves as the unit of mass in commercial transactions in the United States, it cannot be so used in engineering mechanics computations, since such a unit would not be consistent with the base units defined in the preceding paragraph. Indeed, when acted upon by a force of 1 lb, that is, when subjected to the force of gravity, the standard pound receives the acceleration of gravity, $g = 32.2 \text{ ft/s}^2$ (Fig. 1.4), not the unit acceleration required by Eq. (1.1). The unit of mass consistent with the foot, the pound, and the second is the mass which receives an acceleration of 1 ft/s² when a force of 1 lb is applied to it (Fig. 1.5). This unit, sometimes called a *slug*, can be derived from the equation $F = ma$ after substituting 1 lb and 1 ft/s² for F and a, respectively. We write

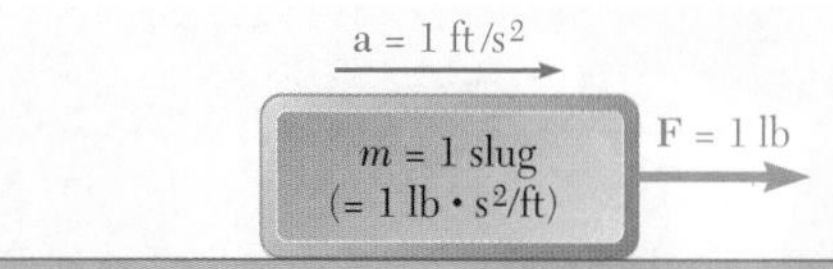

Fig. 1.5

$$F = ma \qquad 1 \text{ lb} = (1 \text{ slug})(1 \text{ ft/s}^2)$$

and obtain

$$1 \text{ slug} = \frac{1 \text{ lb}}{1 \text{ ft/s}^2} = 1 \text{ lb} \cdot \text{s}^2/\text{ft} \tag{1.6}$$

Comparing Figs. 1.4 and 1.5, we conclude that the slug is a mass 32.2 times larger than the mass of the standard pound.

The fact that in the U.S. customary system of units bodies are characterized by their weight in pounds rather than by their mass in slugs will be a convenience in the study of statics, where one constantly deals with weights and other forces and only seldom with masses. However, in the study of dynamics, where forces, masses, and accelerations are involved, the mass m of a body will be expressed in slugs when its weight W is given in pounds. Recalling Eq. (1.4), we write

$$m = \frac{W}{g} \tag{1.7}$$

where g is the acceleration of gravity ($g = 32.2 \text{ ft/s}^2$).

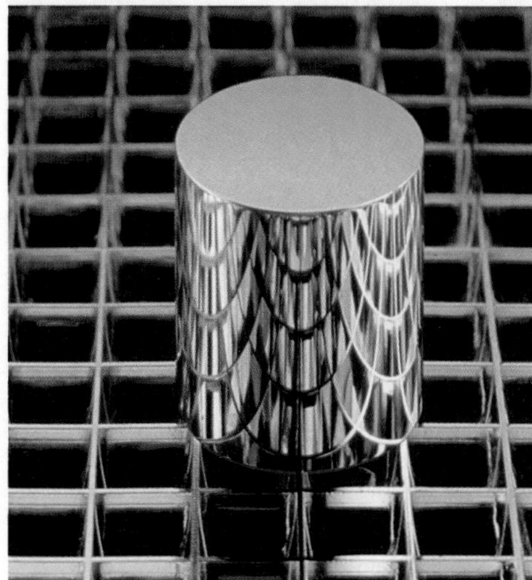

Photo 1.3 The unit of mass is the only basic unit still based on a physical standard. Work is in progress to replace this standard with one based on unchanging natural phenomena.

Other U.S. customary units frequently encountered in engineering problems are the *mile* (mi), equal to 5280 ft; the *inch* (in.), equal to $\frac{1}{12}$ ft; and the *kilopound* (kip), equal to a force of 1000 lb. The *ton* is often used to represent a mass of 2000 lb but, like the pound, must be converted into slugs in engineering computations.

The conversion into feet, pounds, and seconds of quantities expressed in other U.S. customary units is generally more involved and requires greater attention than the corresponding operation in SI units. If, for example, the magnitude of a velocity is given as $v =$ 30 mi/h, we convert it to ft/s as follows. First we write

$$v = 30\frac{\text{mi}}{\text{h}}$$

Since we want to get rid of the unit miles and introduce instead the unit feet, we should multiply the right-hand member of the equation by an expression containing miles in the denominator and feet in the numerator. But, since we do not want to change the value of the right-hand member, the expression used should have a value equal to unity. The quotient (5280 ft)/(1 mi) is such an expression. Operating in a similar way to transform the unit hour into seconds, we write

$$v = \left(30\frac{\text{mi}}{\text{h}}\right)\left(\frac{5280\text{ ft}}{1\text{ mi}}\right)\left(\frac{1\text{ h}}{3600\text{ s}}\right)$$

Carrying out the numerical computations and canceling out units which appear in both the numerator and the denominator, we obtain

$$v = 44\,\frac{\text{ft}}{\text{s}} = 44\text{ ft/s}$$

Photo 1.4 The importance of including units in all calculations cannot be over emphasized. It was found that the $125 million *Mars Climate Orbiter* failed to go into orbit around Mars because the prime contractor had provided the navigation team with operating data based on U.S. units rather than the specified SI units.

1.4. CONVERSION FROM ONE SYSTEM OF UNITS TO ANOTHER

There are many instances when an engineer wishes to convert into SI units a numerical result obtained in U.S. customary units or vice versa. Because the unit of time is the same in both systems, only two kinetic base units need be converted. Thus, since all other kinetic units can be derived from these base units, only two conversion factors need be remembered.

Units of Length. By definition the U.S. customary unit of length is

$$1\text{ ft} = 0.3048\text{ m} \tag{1.8}$$

It follows that

$$1\text{ mi} = 5280\text{ ft} = 5280(0.3048\text{ m}) = 1609\text{ m}$$

or

$$1\text{ mi} = 1.609\text{ km} \tag{1.9}$$

Also

$$1\text{ in.} = \tfrac{1}{12}\text{ ft} = \tfrac{1}{12}(0.3048\text{ m}) = 0.0254\text{ m}$$

or

$$1\text{ in.} = 25.4\text{ mm} \tag{1.10}$$

Units of Force. Recalling that the U.S. customary unit of force (pound) is defined as the weight of the standard pound (of mass 0.4536 kg) at sea level and at a latitude of 45° (where $g = 9.807\text{ m/s}^2$) and using Eq. (1.4), we write

$$W = mg$$
$$1 \text{ lb} = (0.4536 \text{ kg})(9.807 \text{ m/s}^2) = 4.448 \text{ kg} \cdot \text{m/s}^2$$

or, recalling Eq. (1.5),

$$1 \text{ lb} = 4.448 \text{ N} \tag{1.11}$$

Units of Mass. The U.S. customary unit of mass (slug) is a derived unit. Thus, using Eqs. (1.6), (1.8), and (1.11), we write

$$1 \text{ slug} = 1 \text{ lb} \cdot \text{s}^2/\text{ft} = \frac{1 \text{ lb}}{1 \text{ ft/s}^2} = \frac{4.448 \text{ N}}{0.3048 \text{ m/s}^2} = 14.59 \text{ N} \cdot \text{s}^2/\text{m}$$

and, recalling Eq. (1.5),

$$1 \text{ slug} = 1 \text{ lb} \cdot \text{s}^2/\text{ft} = 14.59 \text{ kg} \tag{1.12}$$

Although it cannot be used as a consistent unit of mass, we recall that the mass of the standard pound is, by definition,

$$1 \text{ pound mass} = 0.4536 \text{ kg} \tag{1.13}$$

This constant may be used to determine the *mass* in SI units (kilograms) of a body which has been characterized by its *weight* in U.S. customary units (pounds).

To convert a derived U.S. customary unit into SI units, one simply multiplies or divides by the appropriate conversion factors. For example, to convert the moment of a force which was found to be $M = 47 \text{ lb} \cdot \text{in.}$ into SI units, we use formulas (1.10) and (1.11) and write

$$\begin{aligned} M = 47 \text{ lb} \cdot \text{in.} &= 47(4.448 \text{ N})(25.4 \text{ mm}) \\ &= 5310 \text{ N} \cdot \text{mm} = 5.31 \text{ N} \cdot \text{m} \end{aligned}$$

The conversion factors given in this section may also be used to convert a numerical result obtained in SI units into U.S. customary units. For example, if the moment of a force was found to be $M = 40 \text{ N} \cdot \text{m}$, we write, following the procedure used in the last paragraph of Sec. 1.3,

$$M = 40 \text{ N} \cdot \text{m} = (40 \text{ N} \cdot \text{m})\left(\frac{1 \text{ lb}}{4.448 \text{ N}}\right)\left(\frac{1 \text{ ft}}{0.3048 \text{ m}}\right)$$

Carrying out the numerical computations and canceling out units which appear in both the numerator and the denominator, we obtain

$$M = 29.5 \text{ lb} \cdot \text{ft}$$

The U.S. customary units most frequently used in mechanics are listed in Table 1.3 with their SI equivalents.

1.5. METHOD OF PROBLEM SOLUTION

You should approach a problem in mechanics as you would approach an actual engineering situation. By drawing on your own experience and intuition, you will find it easier to understand and formulate the problem. Once the problem has been clearly stated, however, there is

Table 1.3. U.S. Customary Units and Their SI Equivalents

Quantity	U.S. Customary Unit	SI Equivalent
Acceleration	ft/s^2	$0.3048\ m/s^2$
	$in./s^2$	$0.0254\ m/s^2$
Area	ft^2	$0.0929\ m^2$
	in^2	$645.2\ mm^2$
Energy	$ft \cdot lb$	1.356 J
Force	kip	4.448 kN
	lb	4.448 N
	oz	0.2780 N
Impulse	$lb \cdot s$	$4.448\ N \cdot s$
Length	ft	0.3048 m
	in.	25.40 mm
	mi	1.609 km
Mass	oz mass	28.35 g
	lb mass	0.4536 kg
	slug	14.59 kg
	ton	907.2 kg
Moment of a force	$lb \cdot ft$	$1.356\ N \cdot m$
	$lb \cdot in.$	$0.1130\ N \cdot m$
Moment of inertia		
Of an area	in^4	$0.4162 \times 10^6\ mm^4$
Of a mass	$lb \cdot ft \cdot s^2$	$1.356\ kg \cdot m^2$
Momentum	$lb \cdot s$	$4.448\ kg \cdot m/s$
Power	$ft \cdot lb/s$	1.356 W
	hp	745.7 W
Pressure or stress	lb/ft^2	47.88 Pa
	lb/in^2 (psi)	6.895 kPa
Velocity	ft/s	0.3048 m/s
	in./s	0.0254 m/s
	mi/h (mph)	0.4470 m/s
	mi/h (mph)	1.609 km/h
Volume	ft^3	$0.02832\ m^3$
	in^3	$16.39\ cm^3$
Liquids	gal	3.785 L
	qt	0.9464 L
Work	$ft \cdot lb$	1.356 J

no place in its solution for your particular fancy. *The solution must be based on the six fundamental principles stated in Sec. 1.2 or on theorems derived from them.* Every step taken must be justified on that basis. Strict rules must be followed, which lead to the solution in an almost automatic fashion, leaving no room for your intuition or "feeling." After an answer has been obtained, it should be checked. Here again, you may call upon your common sense and personal experience. If not completely satisfied with the result obtained, you should carefully check your formulation of the problem, the validity of the methods used for its solution, and the accuracy of your computations.

The *statement* of a problem should be clear and precise. It should contain the given data and indicate what information is required. A neat drawing showing all quantities involved should be included. Separate diagrams should be drawn for all bodies involved, indicating clearly the forces acting on each body. These diagrams are known as *free-body diagrams* and are described in detail in Secs. 2.11 and 4.2.

The *fundamental principles* of mechanics listed in Sec. 1.2 *will be used to write equations* expressing the conditions of rest or motion of the bodies considered. Each equation should be clearly related to one of the free-body diagrams. You will then proceed to solve the problem, observing strictly the usual rules of algebra and recording neatly the various steps taken.

After the answer has been obtained, it should be *carefully checked.* Mistakes in *reasoning* can often be detected by checking the units. For example, to determine the moment of a force of 50 N about a point 0.60 m from its line of action, we would have written (Sec. 3.12)

$$M = Fd = (50 \text{ N})(0.60 \text{ m}) = 30 \text{ N} \cdot \text{m}$$

The unit N · m obtained by multiplying newtons by meters is the correct unit for the moment of a force; if another unit had been obtained, we would have known that some mistake had been made.

Errors in *computation* will usually be found by substituting the numerical values obtained into an equation which has not yet been used and verifying that the equation is satisfied. The importance of correct computations in engineering cannot be overemphasized.

1.6. NUMERICAL ACCURACY

The accuracy of the solution of a problem depends upon two items: (1) the accuracy of the given data and (2) the accuracy of the computations performed.

The solution cannot be more accurate than the less accurate of these two items. For example, if the loading of a bridge is known to be 75,000 lb with a possible error of 100 lb either way, the relative error which measures the degree of accuracy of the data is

$$\frac{100 \text{ lb}}{75{,}000 \text{ lb}} = 0.0013 = 0.13 \text{ percent}$$

In computing the reaction at one of the bridge supports, it would then be meaningless to record it as 14,322 lb. The accuracy of the solution cannot be greater than 0.13 percent, no matter how accurate the computations are, and the possible error in the answer may be as large as $(0.13/100)(14{,}322 \text{ lb}) \approx 20 \text{ lb}$. The answer should be properly recorded as $14{,}320 \pm 20$ lb.

In engineering problems, the data are seldom known with an accuracy greater than 0.2 percent. It is therefore seldom justified to write the answers to such problems with an accuracy greater than 0.2 percent. A practical rule is to use 4 figures to record numbers beginning with a "1" and 3 figures in all other cases. Unless otherwise indicated, the data given in a problem should be assumed known with a comparable degree of accuracy. A force of 40 lb, for example, should be read 40.0 lb, and a force of 15 lb should be read 15.00 lb.

Pocket electronic calculators are widely used by practicing engineers and engineering students. The speed and accuracy of these calculators facilitate the numerical computations in the solution of many problems. However, students should not record more significant figures than can be justified merely because they are easily obtained. As noted above, an accuracy greater than 0.2 percent is seldom necessary or meaningful in the solution of practical engineering problems.

CHAPTER 2

Statics of Particles

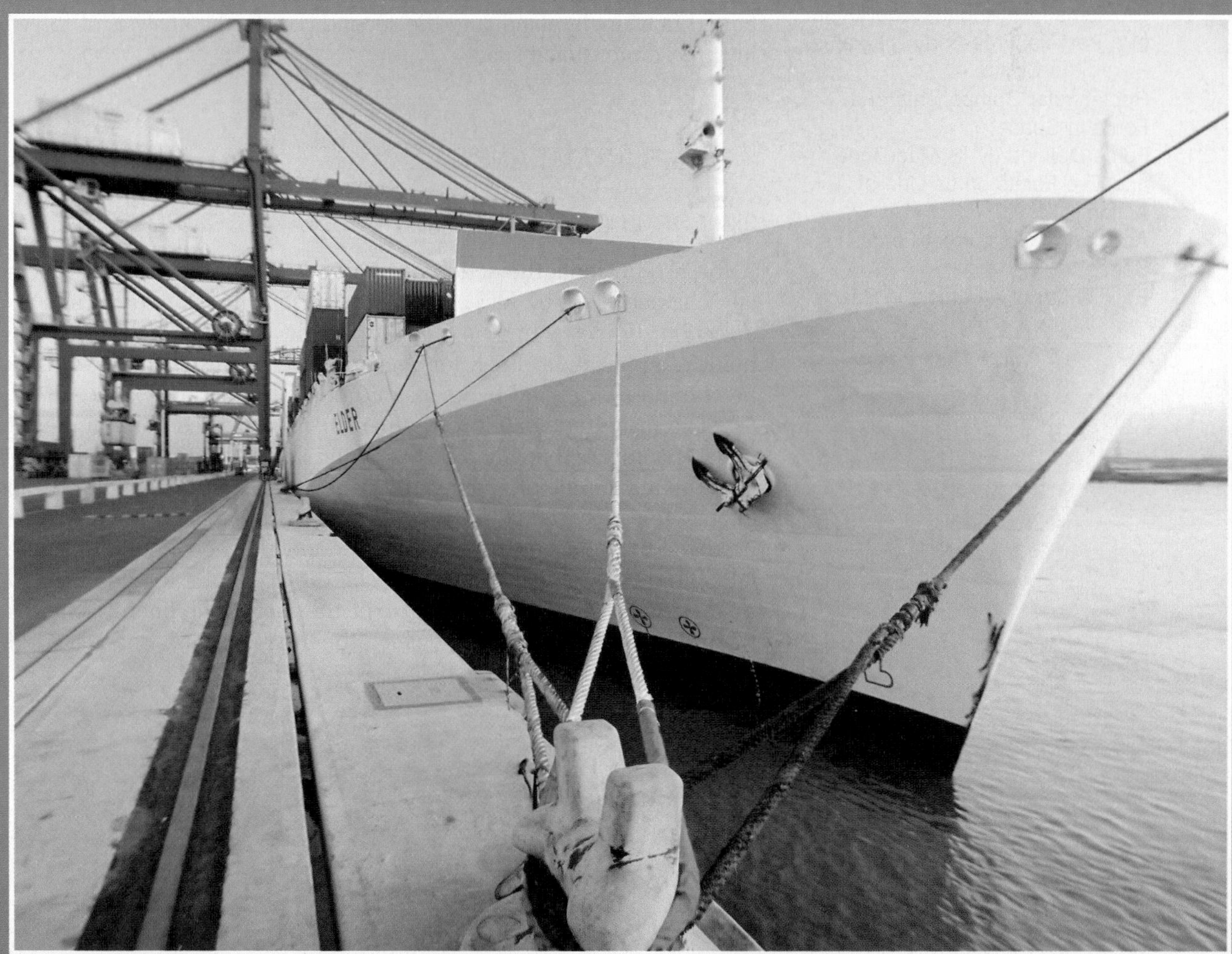

Many engineering problems can be solved by considering the *equilibrium* of a *particle.* In this chapter you will learn that by treating the bollard as a particle, the relation among the tensions in the ropes can be obtained.

STATICS OF PARTICLES

2.1. INTRODUCTION

In this chapter you will study the effect of forces acting on particles. First you will learn how to replace two or more forces acting on a given particle by a single force having the same effect as the original forces. This single equivalent force is the *resultant* of the original forces acting on the particle. Later the relations which exist among the various forces acting on a particle in a state of *equilibrium* will be derived and used to determine some of the forces acting on the particle.

The use of the word *particle* does not imply that our study will be limited to that of small corpuscles. What it means is that the size and shape of the bodies under consideration will not significantly affect the solution of the problems treated in this chapter and that all the forces acting on a given body will be assumed to be applied at the same point. Since such an assumption is verified in many practical applications, you will be able to solve a number of engineering problems in this chapter.

The first part of the chapter is devoted to the study of forces contained in a single plane, and the second part to the analysis of forces in three-dimensional space.

FORCES IN A PLANE

2.2. FORCE ON A PARTICLE. RESULTANT OF TWO FORCES

A force represents the action of one body on another and is generally characterized by its *point of application,* its *magnitude,* and its *direction.* Forces acting on a given particle, however, have the same point of application. Each force considered in this chapter will thus be completely defined by its magnitude and direction.

The magnitude of a force is characterized by a certain number of units. As indicated in Chap. 1, the SI units used by engineers to measure the magnitude of a force are the newton (N) and its multiple the kilonewton (kN), equal to 1000 N, while the U.S. customary units used for the same purpose are the pound (lb) and its multiple the kilopound (kip), equal to 1000 lb. The direction of a force is defined by the *line of action* and the *sense* of the force. The line of action is the infinite straight line along which the force acts; it is characterized by the angle it forms with some fixed axis (Fig. 2.1).

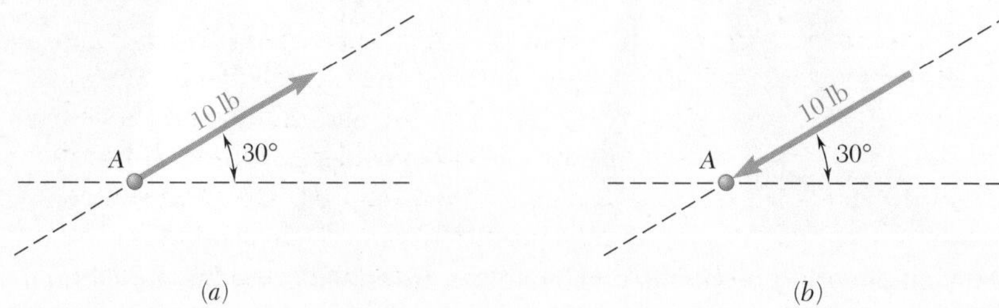

Fig. 2.1

The force itself is represented by a segment of that line; through the use of an appropriate scale, the length of this segment may be chosen to represent the magnitude of the force. Finally, the sense of the force should be indicated by an arrowhead. It is important in defining a force to indicate its sense. Two forces having the same magnitude and the same line of action but different sense, such as the forces shown in Fig. 2.1*a* and *b*, will have directly opposite effects on a particle.

Experimental evidence shows that two forces **P** and **Q** acting on a particle *A* (Fig. 2.2*a*) can be replaced by a single force **R** which has the same effect on the particle (Fig. 2.2*c*). This force is called the *resultant* of the forces **P** and **Q** and can be obtained, as shown in Fig. 2.2*b*, by constructing a parallelogram, using **P** and **Q** as two adjacent sides of the parallelogram. *The diagonal that passes through A represents the resultant.* This method for finding the resultant is known as the *parallelogram law* for the addition of two forces. This law is based on experimental evidence; it cannot be proved or derived mathematically.

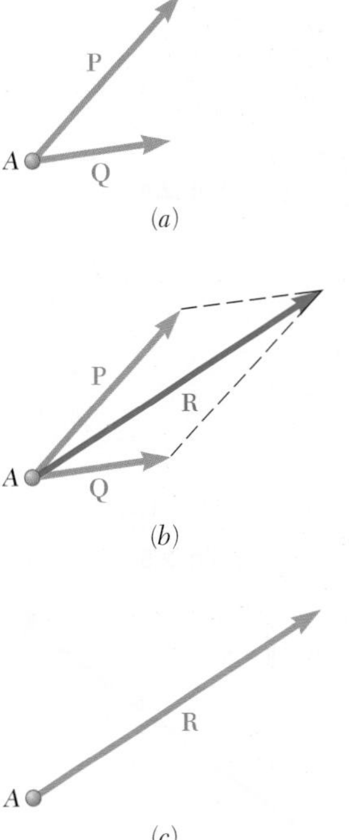

Fig. 2.2

2.3. VECTORS

It appears from the above that forces do not obey the rules of addition defined in ordinary arithmetic or algebra. For example, two forces acting at a right angle to each other, one of 4 lb and the other of 3 lb, add up to a force of 5 lb, *not* to a force of 7 lb. Forces are not the only quantities which follow the parallelogram law of addition. As you will see later, *displacements, velocities, accelerations,* and *momenta* are other examples of physical quantities possessing magnitude and direction that are added according to the parallelogram law. All these quantities can be represented mathematically by *vectors,* while those physical quantities which have magnitude but not direction, such as *volume, mass,* or *energy,* are represented by plain numbers or *scalars.*

Vectors are defined as *mathematical expressions possessing magnitude and direction, which add according to the parallelogram law.* Vectors are represented by arrows in the illustrations and will be distinguished from scalar quantities in this text through the use of boldface type (**P**). In longhand writing, a vector may be denoted by drawing a short arrow above the letter used to represent it ($\vec{P}$) or by underlining the letter ($\underline{P}$). The magnitude of a vector defines the length of the arrow used to represent the vector. In this text, italic type will be used to denote the magnitude of a vector. Thus, the magnitude of the vector **P** will be denoted by *P*.

A vector used to represent a force acting on a given particle has a well-defined point of application, namely, the particle itself. Such a vector is said to be a *fixed,* or *bound,* vector and cannot be moved without modifying the conditions of the problem. Other physical quantities, however, such as couples (see Chap. 3), are represented by vectors which may be freely moved in space; these vectors are called *free* vectors. Still other physical quantities, such as forces

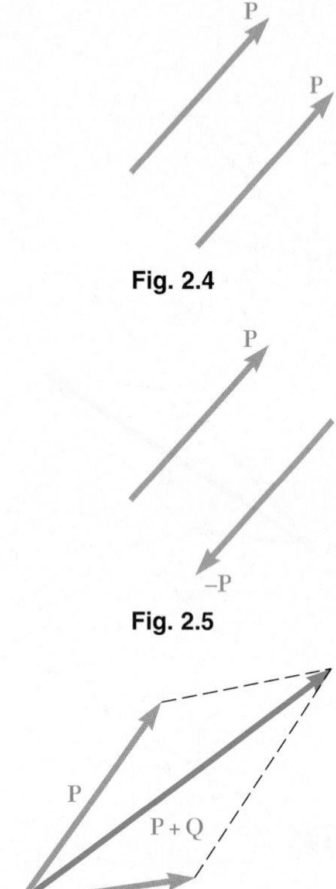

Fig. 2.4

Fig. 2.5

Fig. 2.6

acting on a rigid body (see Chap. 3), are represented by vectors which can be moved, or slid, along their lines of action; they are known as *sliding* vectors.†

Two vectors which have the same magnitude and the same direction are said to be *equal,* whether or not they also have the same point of application (Fig. 2.4); equal vectors may be denoted by the same letter.

The *negative vector* of a given vector **P** is defined as a vector having the same magnitude as **P** and a direction opposite to that of **P** (Fig. 2.5); the negative of the vector **P** is denoted by $-\mathbf{P}$. The vectors **P** and $-\mathbf{P}$ are commonly referred to as *equal and opposite* vectors. Clearly, we have

$$\mathbf{P} + (-\mathbf{P}) = 0$$

2.4. ADDITION OF VECTORS

We saw in the preceding section that, by definition, vectors add according to the parallelogram law. Thus, the sum of two vectors **P** and **Q** is obtained by attaching the two vectors to the same point A and constructing a parallelogram, using **P** and **Q** as two sides of the parallelogram (Fig. 2.6). The diagonal that passes through A represents the sum of the vectors **P** and **Q**, and this sum is denoted by $\mathbf{P} + \mathbf{Q}$. The fact that the sign + is used to denote both vector and scalar addition should not cause any confusion if vector and scalar quantities are always carefully distinguished. Thus, we should note that the magnitude of the vector $\mathbf{P} + \mathbf{Q}$ is *not,* in general, equal to the sum $P + Q$ of the magnitudes of the vectors **P** and **Q**.

Since the parallelogram constructed on the vectors **P** and **Q** does not depend upon the order in which **P** and **Q** are selected, we conclude that the addition of two vectors is *commutative,* and we write

$$\mathbf{P} + \mathbf{Q} = \mathbf{Q} + \mathbf{P} \tag{2.1}$$

†Some expressions have magnitude and direction, but do not add according to the parallelogram law. While these expressions may be represented by arrows, they *cannot* be considered as vectors.

A group of such expressions is the finite rotations of a rigid body. Place a closed book on a table in front of you, so that it lies in the usual fashion, with its front cover up and its binding to the left. Now rotate it through 180° about an axis parallel to the binding (Fig. 2.3*a*); this rotation may be represented by an arrow of length equal to 180 units and oriented as shown. Picking up the book as it lies in its new position, rotate it now through

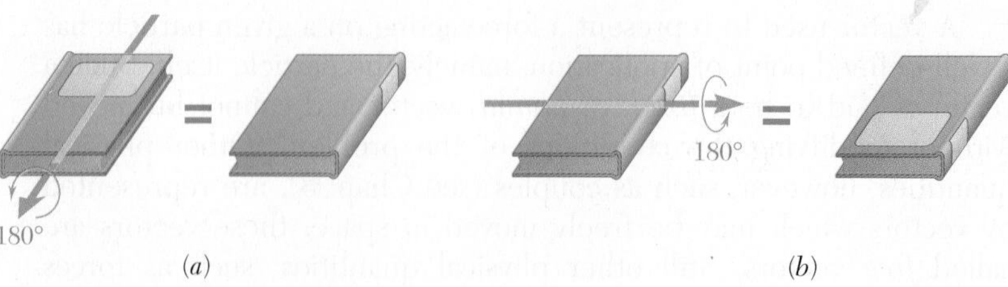

Fig. 2.3 Finite rotations of rigid body

From the parallelogram law, we can derive an alternative method for determining the sum of two vectors. This method, known as the *triangle rule,* is derived as follows. Consider Fig. 2.6, where the sum of the vectors **P** and **Q** has been determined by the parallelogram law. Since the side of the parallelogram opposite **Q** is equal to **Q** in magnitude and direction, we could draw only half of the parallelogram (Fig. 2.7*a*). The sum of the two vectors can thus be found by *arranging* **P** *and* **Q** *in tip-to-tail fashion and then connecting the tail of* **P** *with the tip of* **Q**. In Fig. 2.7*b*, the other half of the parallelogram is considered, and the same result is obtained. This confirms the fact that vector addition is commutative.

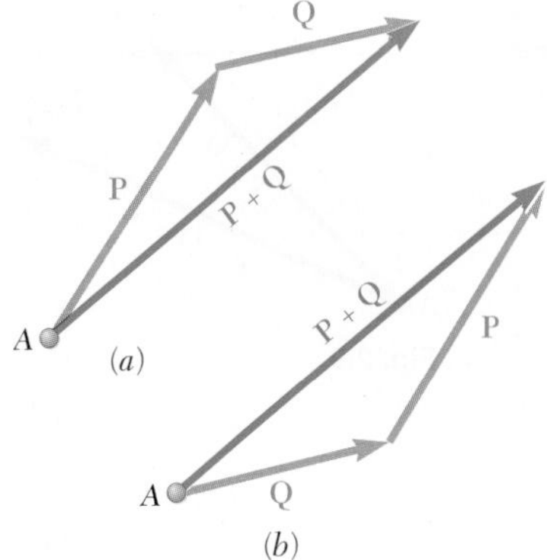

Fig. 2.7

The *subtraction* of a vector is defined as the addition of the corresponding negative vector. Thus, the vector $\mathbf{P} - \mathbf{Q}$ representing the difference between the vectors **P** and **Q** is obtained by adding to **P** the negative vector $-\mathbf{Q}$ (Fig. 2.8). We write

$$\mathbf{P} - \mathbf{Q} = \mathbf{P} + (-\mathbf{Q}) \tag{2.2}$$

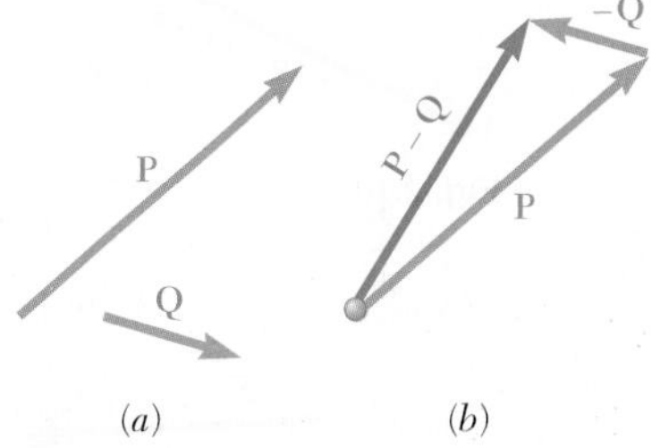

Fig. 2.8

Here again we should observe that, while the same sign is used to denote both vector and scalar subtraction, confusion will be avoided if care is taken to distinguish between vector and scalar quantities.

We will now consider the *sum of three or more vectors.* The sum of three vectors **P**, **Q**, and **S** will, *by definition,* be obtained by first adding the vectors **P** and **Q** and then adding the vector **S** to the vector $\mathbf{P} + \mathbf{Q}$. We thus write

$$\mathbf{P} + \mathbf{Q} + \mathbf{S} = (\mathbf{P} + \mathbf{Q}) + \mathbf{S} \tag{2.3}$$

Similarly, the sum of four vectors will be obtained by adding the fourth vector to the sum of the first three. It follows that the sum of any number of vectors can be obtained by applying repeatedly the parallelogram law to successive pairs of vectors until all the given vectors are replaced by a single vector.

180° about a horizontal axis perpendicular to the binding (Fig. 2.3*b*); this second rotation may be represented by an arrow 180 units long and oriented as shown. But the book could have been placed in this final position through a single 180° rotation about a vertical axis (Fig. 2.3*c*). We conclude that the sum of the two 180° rotations represented by arrows directed respectively along the z and x axes is a 180° rotation represented by an arrow directed along the y axis (Fig. 2.3*d*). Clearly, the finite rotations of a rigid body *do not* obey the parallelogram law of addition; therefore, they *cannot* be represented by vectors.

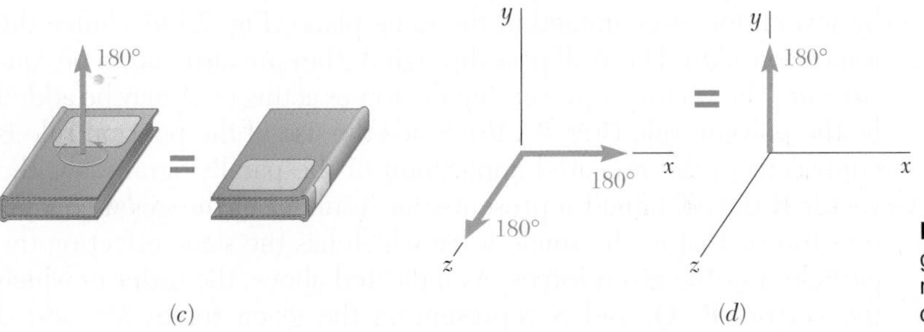

Photo 2.1 As we have shown, either the parallelogram law or the triangle rule can be used to determine the resultant force exerted by the two long cables on the hook.

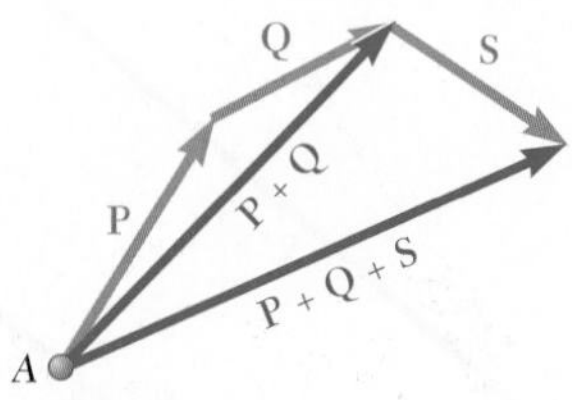

Fig. 2.9

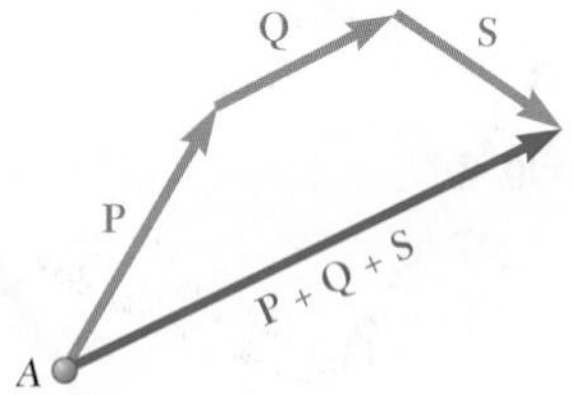

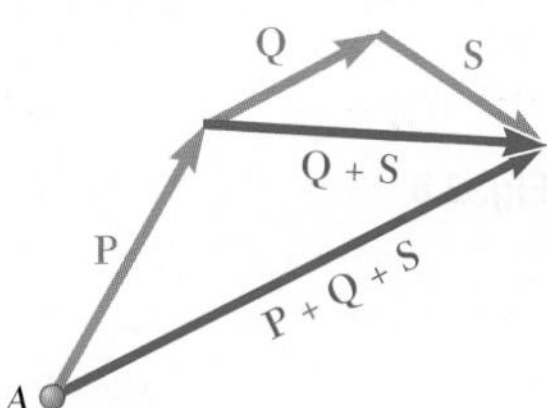

Fig. 2.10

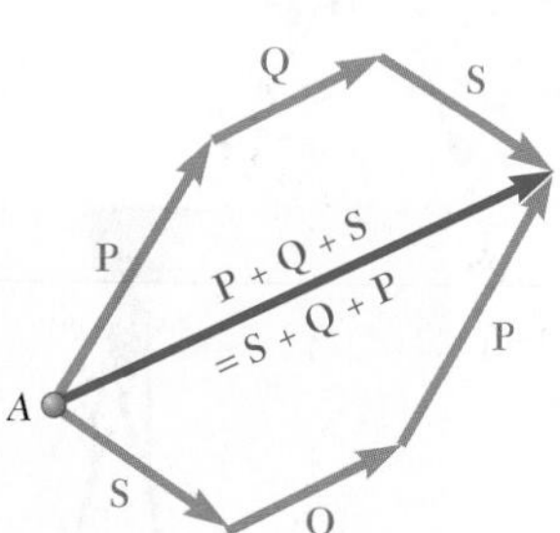

Fig. 2.11

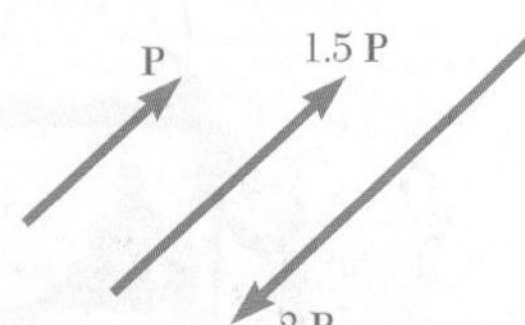

Fig. 2.12

Fig. 2.13

If the given vectors are *coplanar,* that is, if they are contained in the same plane, their sum can be easily obtained graphically. For this case, the repeated application of the triangle rule is preferred to the application of the parallelogram law. In Fig. 2.9 the sum of three vectors **P**, **Q**, and **S** was obtained in that manner. The triangle rule was first applied to obtain the sum **P** + **Q** of the vectors **P** and **Q**; it was applied again to obtain the sum of the vectors **P** + **Q** and **S**. The determination of the vector **P** + **Q**, however, could have been omitted and the sum of the three vectors could have been obtained directly, as shown in Fig. 2.10, by *arranging the given vectors in tip-to-tail fashion and connecting the tail of the first vector with the tip of the last one.* This is known as the *polygon rule* for the addition of vectors.

We observe that the result obtained would have been unchanged if, as shown in Fig. 2.11, the vectors **Q** and **S** had been replaced by their sum **Q** + **S**. We may thus write

$$\mathbf{P} + \mathbf{Q} + \mathbf{S} = (\mathbf{P} + \mathbf{Q}) + \mathbf{S} = \mathbf{P} + (\mathbf{Q} + \mathbf{S}) \tag{2.4}$$

which expresses the fact that vector addition is *associative.* Recalling that vector addition has also been shown, in the case of two vectors, to be commutative, we write

$$\begin{aligned} \mathbf{P} + \mathbf{Q} + \mathbf{S} &= (\mathbf{P} + \mathbf{Q}) + \mathbf{S} = \mathbf{S} + (\mathbf{P} + \mathbf{Q}) \\ &= \mathbf{S} + (\mathbf{Q} + \mathbf{P}) = \mathbf{S} + \mathbf{Q} + \mathbf{P} \end{aligned} \tag{2.5}$$

This expression, as well as others which may be obtained in the same way, shows that the order in which several vectors are added together is immaterial (Fig. 2.12).

Product of a Scalar and a Vector. Since it is convenient to denote the sum **P** + **P** by 2**P**, the sum **P** + **P** + **P** by 3**P**, and, in general, the sum of n equal vectors **P** by the product n**P**, we will define the product n**P** of a positive integer n and a vector **P** as a vector having the same direction as **P** and the magnitude nP. Extending this definition to include all scalars, and recalling the definition of a negative vector given in Sec. 2.3, we define the product k**P** of a scalar k and a vector **P** as a vector having the same direction as **P** (if k is positive), or a direction opposite to that of **P** (if k is negative), and a magnitude equal to the product of P and of the absolute value of k (Fig. 2.13).

2.5. RESULTANT OF SEVERAL CONCURRENT FORCES

Consider a particle A acted upon by several coplanar forces, that is, by several forces contained in the same plane (Fig. 2.14*a*). Since the forces considered here all pass through A, they are also said to be *concurrent.* The vectors representing the forces acting on A may be added by the polygon rule (Fig. 2.14*b*). Since the use of the polygon rule is equivalent to the repeated application of the parallelogram law, the vector **R** thus obtained represents the resultant of the given concurrent forces, that is, the single force which has the same effect on the particle A as the given forces. As indicated above, the order in which the vectors **P**, **Q**, and **S** representing the given forces are added together is immaterial.

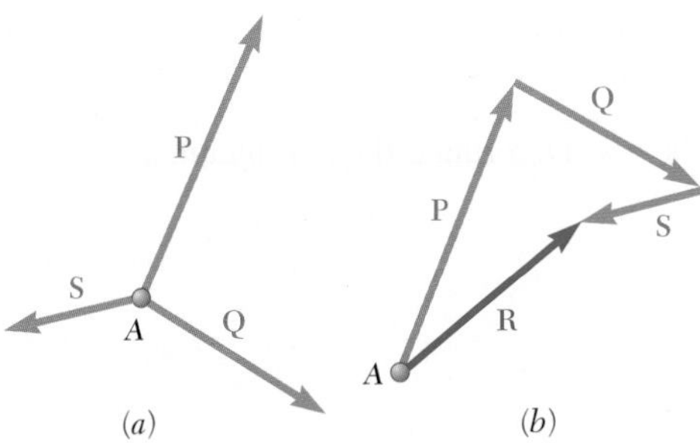

Fig. 2.14

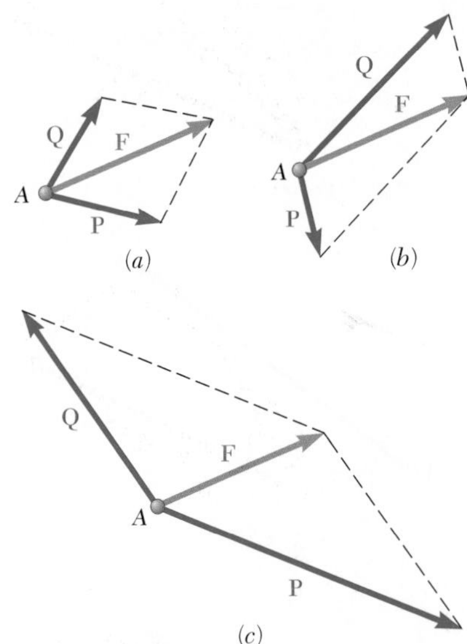

Fig. 2.15

2.6. RESOLUTION OF A FORCE INTO COMPONENTS

We have seen that two or more forces acting on a particle may be replaced by a single force which has the same effect on the particle. Conversely, a single force **F** acting on a particle may be replaced by two or more forces which, together, have the same effect on the particle. These forces are called the *components* of the original force **F**, and the process of substituting them for **F** is called *resolving the force* **F** *into components.*

Clearly, for each force **F** there exist an infinite number of possible sets of components. Sets of *two components* **P** *and* **Q** are the most important as far as practical applications are concerned. But, even then, the number of ways in which a given force **F** may be resolved into two components is unlimited (Fig. 2.15). Two cases are of particular interest:

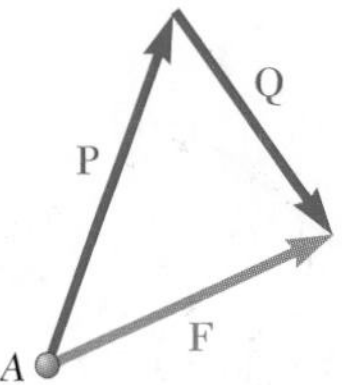

Fig. 2.16

1. *One of the Two Components,* **P**, *Is Known.* The second component, **Q**, is obtained by applying the triangle rule and joining the tip of **P** to the tip of **F** (Fig. 2.16); the magnitude and direction of **Q** are determined graphically or by trigonometry. Once **Q** has been determined, both components **P** and **Q** should be applied at *A*.
2. *The Line of Action of Each Component Is Known.* The magnitude and sense of the components are obtained by applying the parallelogram law and drawing lines, through the tip of **F**, parallel to the given lines of action (Fig. 2.17). This process leads to two well-defined components, **P** and **Q**, which can be determined graphically or computed trigonometrically by applying the law of sines.

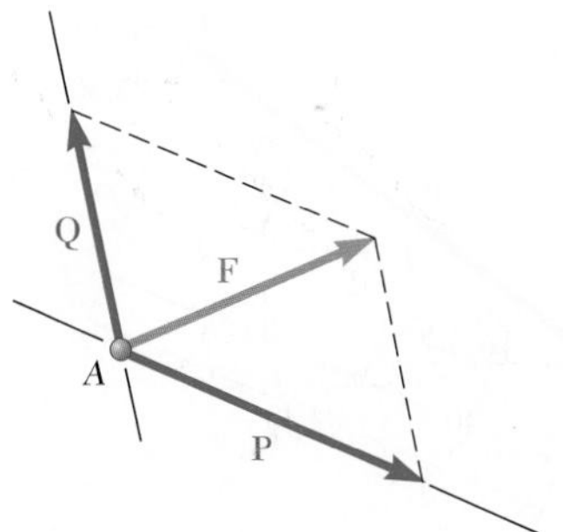

Fig. 2.17

Many other cases can be encountered; for example, the direction of one component may be known, while the magnitude of the other component is to be as small as possible (see Sample Prob. 2.2). In all cases the appropriate triangle or parallelogram which satisfies the given conditions is drawn.

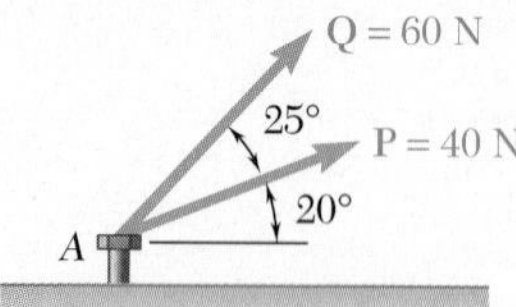

SAMPLE PROBLEM 2.1

The two forces **P** and **Q** act on a bolt A. Determine their resultant.

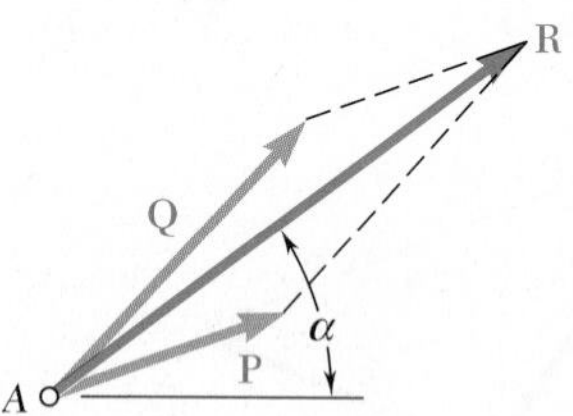

SOLUTION

Graphical Solution. A parallelogram with sides equal to **P** and **Q** is drawn to scale. The magnitude and direction of the resultant are measured and found to be

$$R = 98 \text{ N} \qquad \alpha = 35° \qquad \mathbf{R} = 98 \text{ N} \measuredangle 35° \blacktriangleleft$$

The triangle rule may also be used. Forces **P** and **Q** are drawn in tip-to-tail fashion. Again the magnitude and direction of the resultant are measured.

$$R = 98 \text{ N} \qquad \alpha = 35° \qquad \mathbf{R} = 98 \text{ N} \measuredangle 35° \blacktriangleleft$$

Trigonometric Solution. The triangle rule is again used; two sides and the included angle are known. We apply the law of cosines.

$$R^2 = P^2 + Q^2 - 2PQ \cos B$$
$$R^2 = (40 \text{ N})^2 + (60 \text{ N})^2 - 2(40 \text{ N})(60 \text{ N}) \cos 155°$$
$$R = 97.73 \text{ N}$$

Now, applying the law of sines, we write

$$\frac{\sin A}{Q} = \frac{\sin B}{R} \qquad \frac{\sin A}{60 \text{ N}} = \frac{\sin 155°}{97.73 \text{ N}} \tag{1}$$

Solving Eq. (1) for sin A, we have

$$\sin A = \frac{(60 \text{ N}) \sin 155°}{97.73 \text{ N}}$$

Using a calculator, we first compute the quotient, then its arc sine, and obtain

$$A = 15.04° \qquad \alpha = 20° + A = 35.04°$$

We use 3 significant figures to record the answer (see Sec. 1.6):

$$\mathbf{R} = 97.7 \text{ N} \measuredangle 35.0° \blacktriangleleft$$

Alternative Trigonometric Solution. We construct the right triangle BCD and compute

$$CD = (60 \text{ N}) \sin 25° = 25.36 \text{ N}$$
$$BD = (60 \text{ N}) \cos 25° = 54.38 \text{ N}$$

Then, using triangle ACD, we obtain

$$\tan A = \frac{25.36 \text{ N}}{94.38 \text{ N}} \qquad A = 15.04°$$

$$R = \frac{25.36}{\sin A} \qquad R = 97.73 \text{ N}$$

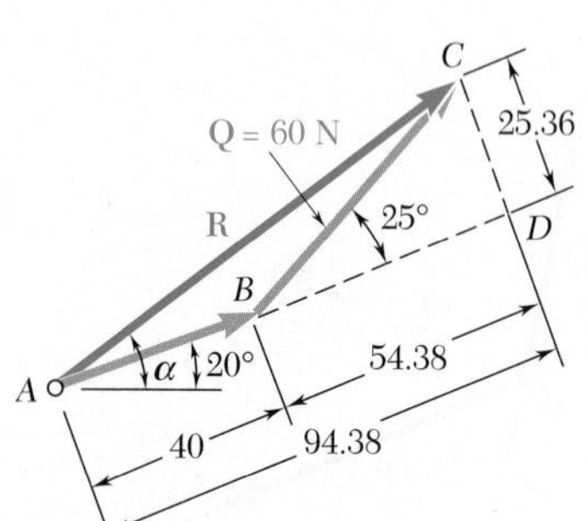

Again, $\alpha = 20° + A = 35.04° \qquad \mathbf{R} = 97.7 \text{ N} \measuredangle 35.0° \blacktriangleleft$

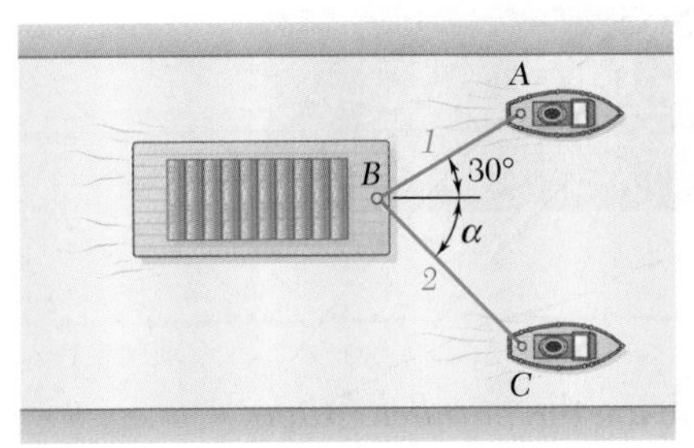

SAMPLE PROBLEM 2.2

A barge is pulled by two tugboats. If the resultant of the forces exerted by the tugboats is a 5000-N force directed along the axis of the barge, determine (*a*) the tension in each of the ropes knowing that $\alpha = 45°$, (*b*) the value of α for which the tension in rope 2 is minimum.

SOLUTION

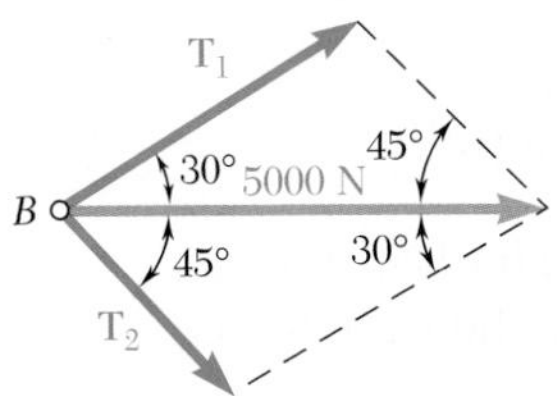

a. Tension for $\alpha = 45°$. ***Graphical Solution.*** The parallelogram law is used; the diagonal (resultant) is known to be equal to 5000 lb and to be directed to the right. The sides are drawn parallel to the ropes. If the drawing is done to scale, we measure

$$T_1 = 3700 \text{ N} \qquad T_2 = 2600 \text{ N} \quad ◀$$

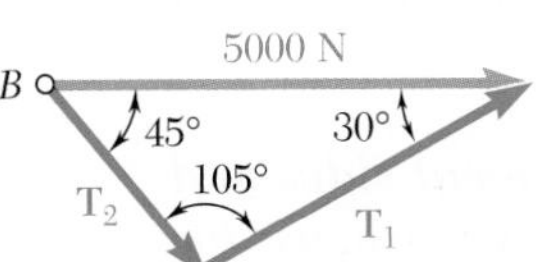

Trigonometric Solution. The triangle rule can be used. We note that the triangle shown represents half of the parallelogram shown above. Using the law of sines. we write

$$\frac{T_1}{\sin 45°} = \frac{T_2}{\sin 30°} = \frac{5000 \text{ N}}{\sin 105°}$$

With a calculator, we first compute and store the value of the last quotient. Multiplying this value successively by sin 45° and sin 30°, we obtain

$$T_1 = 3660 \text{ N} \qquad T_2 = 2590 \text{ N} \quad ◀$$

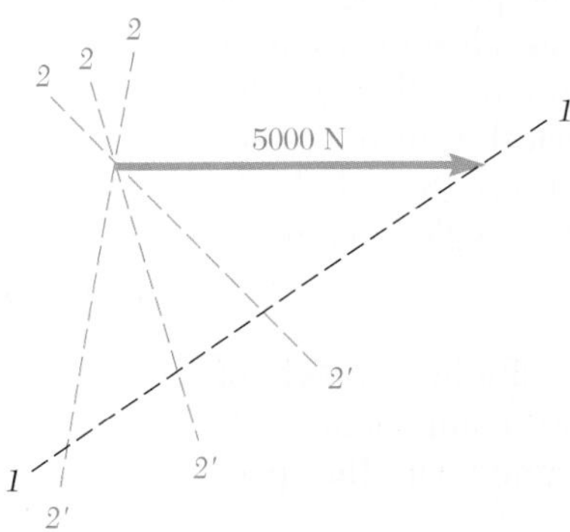

b. Value of α for Minimum T_2. To determine the value of α for which the tension in rope 2 is minimum, the triangle rule is again used. In the sketch shown, line *1-1'* is the known direction of $\mathbf{T}_1$. Several possible directions of $\mathbf{T}_2$ are shown by the lines 2-2′. We note that the minimum value of T_2 occurs when $\mathbf{T}_1$ and $\mathbf{T}_2$ are perpendicular. The minimum value of T_2 is

$$T_2 = (5000 \text{ N}) \sin 30° = 2500 \text{ N}$$

Corresponding values of T_1 and α are

$$T_1 = (5000 \text{ N}) \cos 30° = 4330 \text{ N}$$
$$\alpha = 90° - 30° \qquad\qquad \alpha = 60° \quad ◀$$

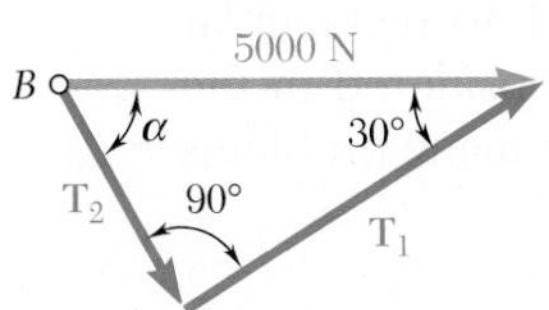

SOLVING PROBLEMS ON YOUR OWN

The preceding sections were devoted to introducing and applying the *parallelogram law* for the addition of vectors.

You will now be asked to solve problems on your own. Some may resemble one of the sample problems; others may not. What all problems and sample problems in this section have in common is that they can be solved by the direct application of the parallelogram law.

Your solution of a given problem should consist of the following steps:

1. Identify which of the forces are the applied forces and which is the resultant. It is often helpful to write the vector equation which shows how the forces are related. For example, in Sample Prob. 2.1 we would have

$$\mathbf{R} = \mathbf{P} + \mathbf{Q}$$

You should keep that relation in mind as you formulate the next part of your solution.

2. Draw a parallelogram with the applied forces as two adjacent sides and the resultant as the included diagonal (Fig. 2.2). Alternatively, you can *use the triangle rule,* with the applied forces drawn in tip-to-tail fashion and the resultant extending from the tail of the first vector to the tip of the second (Fig. 2.7).

3. Indicate all dimensions. Using one of the triangles of the parallelogram, or the triangle constructed according to the triangle rule, indicate all dimensions—whether sides or angles—and determine the unknown dimensions either graphically or by trigonometry. If you use trigonometry, remember that the law of cosines should be applied first if two sides and the included angle are known [Sample Prob. 2.1], and the law of sines should be applied first if one side and all angles are known [Sample Prob. 2.2].

As is evident from the figures of Sec. 2.6, the two components of a force need not be perpendicular. Thus, when asked to resolve a force into two components, it is essential that you align the two adjacent sides of your parallelogram with the specified lines of action of the components.

If you have had prior exposure to mechanics, you might be tempted to ignore the solution techniques of this lesson in favor of resolving the forces into rectangular components. While this latter method is important and will be considered in the next section, use of the parallelogram law simplifies the solution of many problems and should be mastered at this time.

Problems†

2.1 Two forces **P** and **Q** are applied as shown at point A of a hook support. Knowing that $P = 15$ N and $Q = 25$ N, determine graphically the magnitude and direction of their resultant using (*a*) the parallelogram law, (*b*) the triangle rule.

2.2 Two forces **P** and **Q** are applied as shown at point A of a hook support. Knowing that $P = 45$ N and $Q = 15$ N, determine graphically the magnitude and direction of their resultant using (*a*) the parallelogram law, (*b*) the triangle rule.

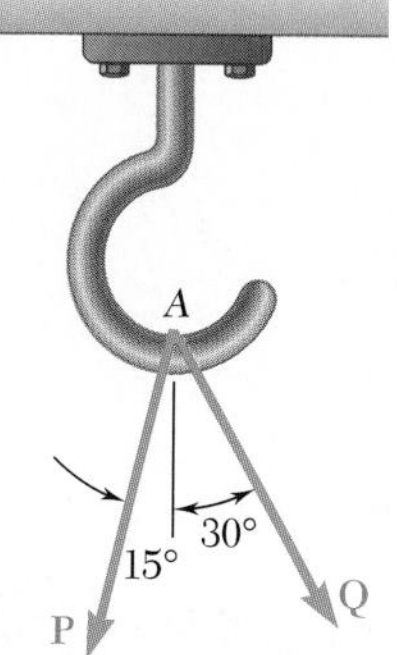

Fig. P2.1 and P2.2

2.3 Two forces are applied to an eye bolt fastened to a beam. Determine graphically the magnitude and direction of their resultant using (*a*) the parallelogram law, (*b*) the triangle rule.

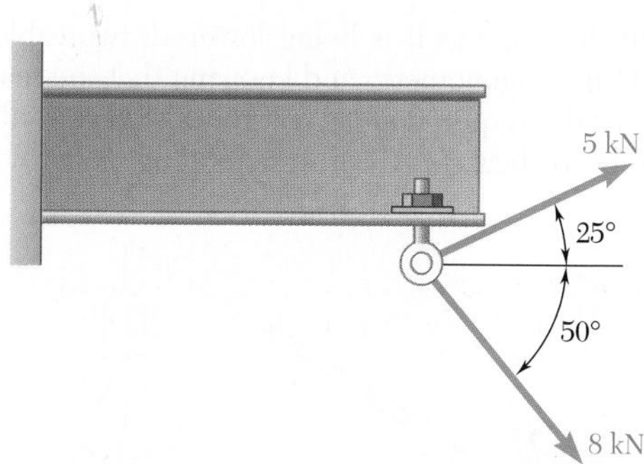

Fig. *P2.3*

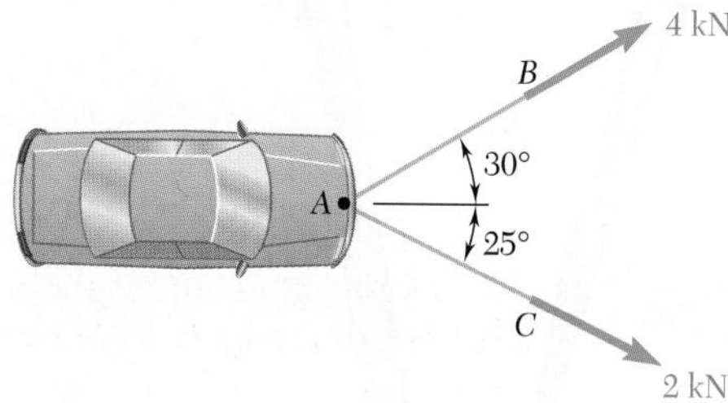

Fig. P2.4

2.4 A disabled automobile is pulled by means of ropes subjected to the two forces as shown. Determine graphically the magnitude and direction of their resultant using (*a*) the parallelogram law, (*b*) the triangle rule.

2.5 The 200-N force is to be resolved into components along lines *a-a′* and *b-b′*. (*a*) Determine the angle α using trigonometry knowing that the component along *a-a′* is to be 150 N. (*b*) What is the corresponding value of the component along *b-b′*?

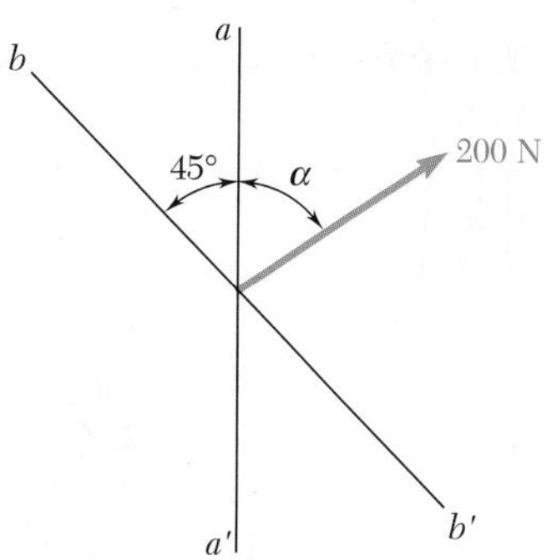

Fig. P2.5 and P2.6

2.6 The 200-N force is to be resolved into components along lines *a-a′* and *b-b′*. (*a*) Determine the angle α using trigonometry knowing that the component along *b-b′* is to be 120 N. (*b*) What is the corresponding value of the component along *a-a′*?

2.7 Two forces are applied as shown to a hook support. Using trigonometry and knowing that the magnitude of **P** is 600 N, determine (*a*) the required angle α if the resultant **R** of the two forces applied to the support is to be vertical, (*b*) the corresponding magnitude of **R**.

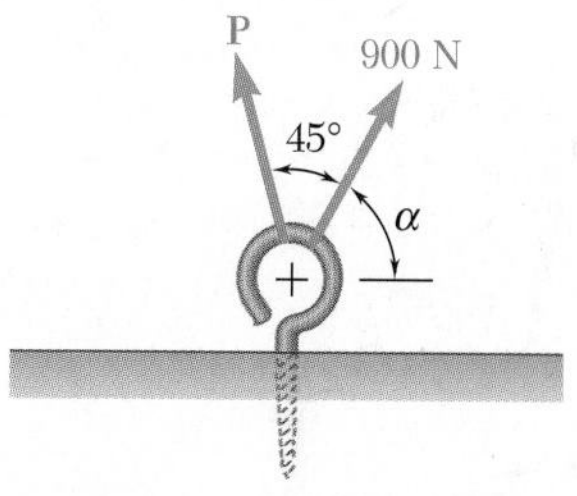

Fig. P2.7

†Answers to all problems set in straight type (such as **2.1**) are given at the end of the book. Answers to problems with a number set in italic type (such as ***2.3***) are not given.

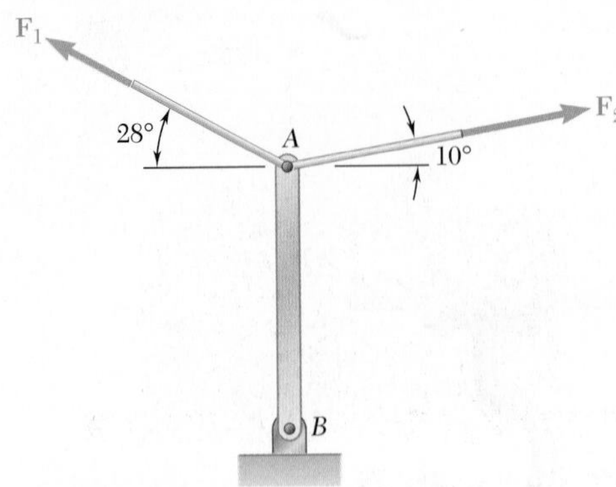

Fig. P2.8 and *P2.9*

2.8 Two control rods are attached at *A* to lever *AB*. Using trigonometry and knowing that the force in the left-hand rod is $F_1 = 30$ N, determine (*a*) the required force F_2 in the right-hand rod if the resultant **R** of the forces exerted by the rods on the lever is to be vertical, (*b*) the corresponding magnitude of **R**.

2.9 Two control rods are attached at *A* to lever *AB*. Using trigonometry and knowing that the force in the right-hand rod is $F_2 = 20$ N, determine (*a*) the required force F_1 in the left-hand rod if the resultant **R** of the forces exerted by the rods on the lever is to be vertical, (*b*) the corresponding magnitude of **R**.

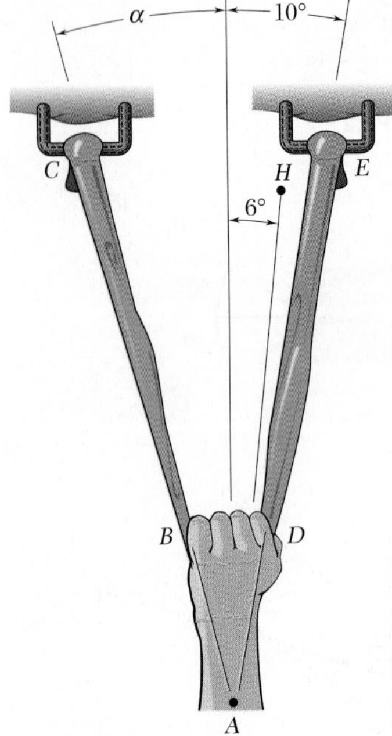

Fig. P2.10

2.10 An elastic exercise band is grasped and then is stretched as shown. Knowing that the tensions in portions *BC* and *DE* of the band are 80 N and 60 N, respectively, determine, using trigonometry, (*a*) the required angle α if the resultant **R** of the two forces exerted on the hand at *A* is to be vertical, (*b*) the corresponding magnitude of **R**.

2.11 To steady a sign as it is being lowered, two cables are attached to the sign at *A*. Using trigonometry and knowing that $\alpha = 25°$, determine (*a*) the required magnitude of the force **P** if the resultant **R** of the two forces applied at *A* is to be vertical, (*b*) the corresponding magnitude of **R**.

2.12 To steady a sign as it is being lowered, two cables are attached to the sign at *A*. Using trigonometry and knowing that the magnitude of **P** is 70 N, determine (*a*) the required angle α if the resultant **R** of the two forces applied at *A* is to be vertical, (*b*) the corresponding magnitude of **R**.

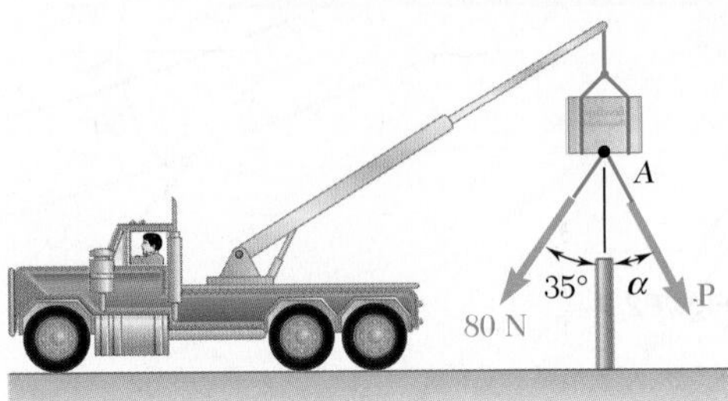

Fig. P2.11 and *P2.12*

2.13 As shown in Fig. P2.11, two cables are attached to a sign at *A* to steady the sign as it is being lowered. Using trigonometry, determine (*a*) the magnitude and direction of the smallest force **P** for which the resultant **R** of the two forces applied at *A* is vertical, (*b*) the corresponding magnitude of **R**.

2.14 As shown in Fig. P2.10, an elastic exercise band is grasped and then is stretched. Knowing that the tension in portion *DE* of the band is 70 N, determine, using trigonometry, (*a*) the magnitude and direction of the smallest force in portion *BC* of the band for which the resultant **R** of the two forces exerted on the hand at *A* is directed along a line joining points *A* and *H*, (*b*) the corresponding magnitude of **R**.

2.15 Solve Prob. 2.1 using trigonometry.

2.16 Solve Prob. 2.2 using trigonometry.

2.17 Solve Prob. 2.3 using trigonometry.

2.18 For the hook support of Prob. 2.7, determine, using trigonometry, the magnitude and direction of the resultant of the two forces applied to the support knowing that $P = 500$ N and $\alpha = 60°$.

2.19 Two structural members A and B are bolted to a bracket as shown. Knowing that both members are in compression and that the force is 30 kN in member A and 20 kN in member B, determine, using trigonometry, the magnitude and direction of the resultant of the forces applied to the bracket by members A and B.

2.20 Two structural members A and B are bolted to a bracket as shown. Knowing that both members are in compression and that the force is 20 kN in member A and 30 kN in member B, determine, using trigonometry, the magnitude and direction of the resultant of the forces applied to the bracket by members A and B.

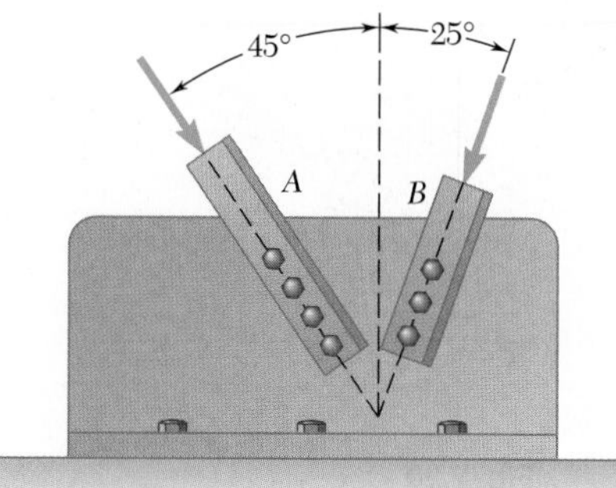

Fig. P2.19 and *P2.20*

2.7. RECTANGULAR COMPONENTS OF A FORCE. UNIT VECTORS†

In many problems it will be found desirable to resolve a force into two components which are perpendicular to each other. In Fig. 2.18, the force **F** has been resolved into a component $\mathbf{F}_x$ along the x axis and a component $\mathbf{F}_y$ along the y axis. The parallelogram drawn to obtain the two components is a *rectangle,* and $\mathbf{F}_x$ and $\mathbf{F}_y$ are called *rectangular components.*

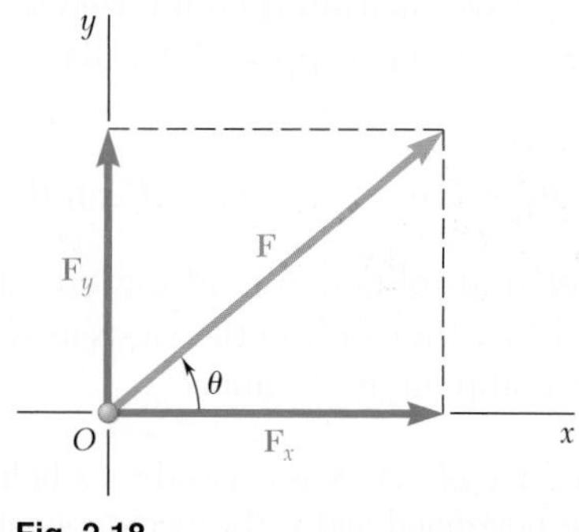

Fig. 2.18

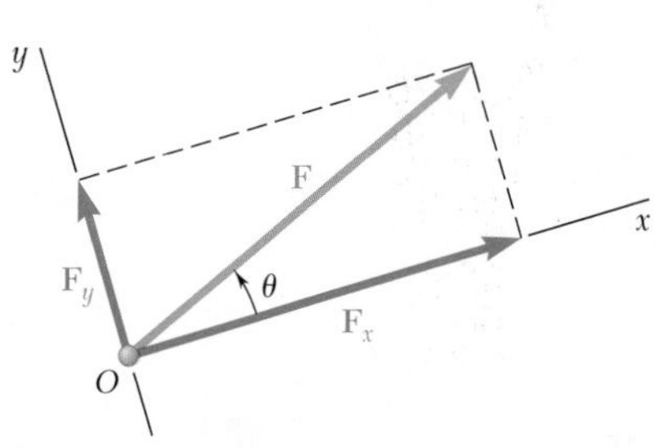

Fig. 2.19

The x and y axes are usually chosen horizontal and vertical, respectively, as in Fig. 2.18; they may, however, be chosen in any two perpendicular directions, as shown in Fig. 2.19. In determining the rectangular components of a force, the student should think of the construction lines shown in Figs. 2.18 and 2.19 as being *parallel* to the x and y axes, rather than *perpendicular* to these axes. This practice will help avoid mistakes in determining *oblique* components as in Sec. 2.6.

†The properties established in Secs. 2.7 and 2.8 may be readily extended to the rectangular components of any vector quantity.

Two vectors of unit magnitude, directed respectively along the positive x and y axes, will be introduced at this point. These vectors are called *unit vectors* and are denoted by **i** and **j**, respectively (Fig. 2.20). Recalling the definition of the product of a scalar and a vector given in Sec. 2.4, we note that the rectangular components $\mathbf{F}_x$ and $\mathbf{F}_y$ of a force **F** may be obtained by multiplying respectively the unit vectors **i** and **j** by appropriate scalars (Fig. 2.21). We write

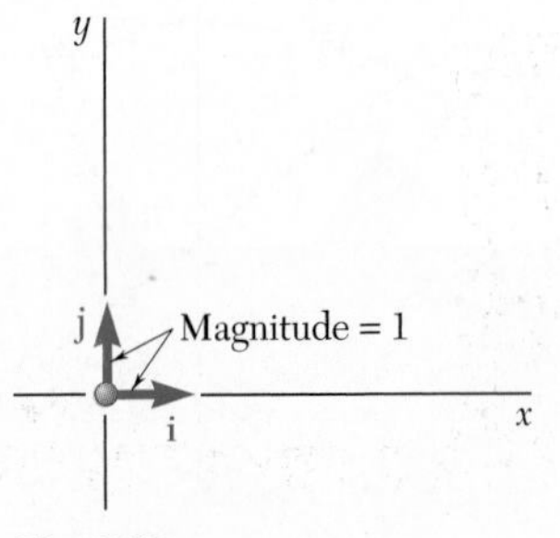

Fig. 2.20

$$\mathbf{F}_x = F_x\mathbf{i} \qquad \mathbf{F}_y = F_y\mathbf{j} \tag{2.6}$$

and

$$\mathbf{F} = F_x\mathbf{i} + F_y\mathbf{j} \tag{2.7}$$

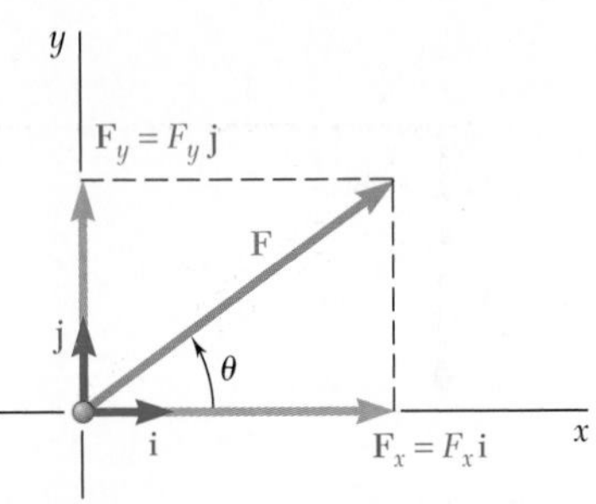

Fig. 2.21

While the scalars F_x and F_y may be positive or negative, depending upon the sense of $\mathbf{F}_x$ and of $\mathbf{F}_y$, their absolute values are respectively equal to the magnitudes of the component forces $\mathbf{F}_x$ and $\mathbf{F}_y$. The scalars F_x and F_y are called the *scalar components* of the force **F**, while the actual component forces $\mathbf{F}_x$ and $\mathbf{F}_y$ should be referred to as the *vector components* of **F**. However, when there exists no possibility of confusion, the vector as well as the scalar components of **F** may be referred to simply as the *components* of **F**. We note that the scalar component F_x is positive when the vector component $\mathbf{F}_x$ has the same sense as the unit vector **i** (that is, the same sense as the positive x axis) and is negative when $\mathbf{F}_x$ has the opposite sense. A similar conclusion may be drawn regarding the sign of the scalar component F_y.

Denoting by F the magnitude of the force **F** and by θ the angle between **F** and the x axis, measured counterclockwise from the positive x axis (Fig. 2.21), we may express the scalar components of **F** as follows:

$$F_x = F\cos\theta \qquad F_y = F\sin\theta \tag{2.8}$$

We note that the relations obtained hold for any value of the angle θ from 0° to 360° and that they define the signs as well as the absolute values of the scalar components F_x and F_y.

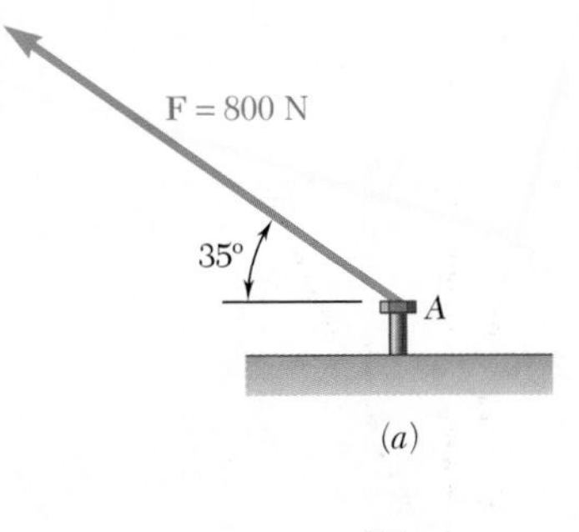

Example 1. A force of 800 N is exerted on a bolt A as shown in Fig. 2.22*a*. Determine the horizontal and vertical components of the force.

In order to obtain the correct sign for the scalar components F_x and F_y, the value $180° - 35° = 145°$ should be substituted for θ in Eqs. (2.8). However, it will be found more practical to determine by inspection the signs of F_x and F_y (Fig. 2.22*b*) and to use the trigonometric functions of the angle $\alpha = 35°$. We write, therefore,

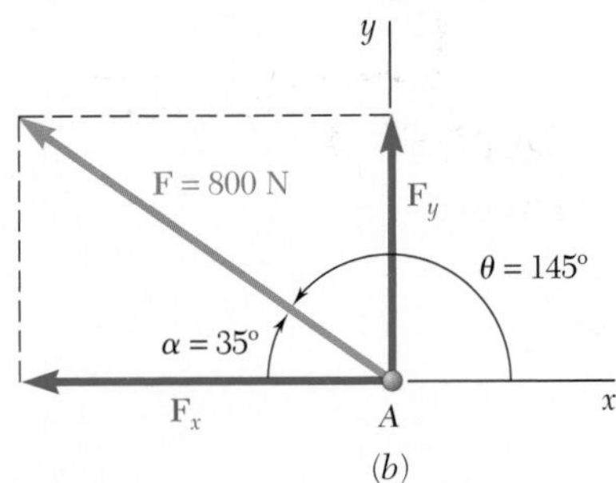

Fig. 2.22

$$F_x = -F\cos\alpha = -(800\text{ N})\cos 35° = -655\text{ N}$$
$$F_y = +F\sin\alpha = +(800\text{ N})\sin 35° = +459\text{ N}$$

The vector components of **F** are thus

$$\mathbf{F}_x = -(655\text{ N})\mathbf{i} \qquad \mathbf{F}_y = +(459\text{ N})\mathbf{j}$$

and we may write **F** in the form

$$\mathbf{F} = -(655\text{ N})\mathbf{i} + (459\text{ N})\mathbf{j}$$

Example 2. A man pulls with a force of 300 N on a rope attached to a building, as shown in Fig. 2.23*a*. What are the horizontal and vertical components of the force exerted by the rope at point *A*?

It is seen from Fig. 2.23*b* that

$$F_x = +(300\text{ N})\cos\alpha \qquad F_y = -(300\text{ N})\sin\alpha$$

Observing that $AB = 10$ m, we find from Fig. 2.23*a*

$$\cos\alpha = \frac{8\text{ m}}{AB} = \frac{8\text{ m}}{10\text{ m}} = \frac{4}{5} \qquad \sin\alpha = \frac{6\text{ m}}{AB} = \frac{6\text{ m}}{10\text{ m}} = \frac{3}{5}$$

We thus obtain

$$F_x = +(300\text{ N})\tfrac{4}{5} = +240\text{ N} \qquad F_y = -(300\text{ N})\tfrac{3}{5} = -180\text{ N}$$

and write

$$\mathbf{F} = (240\text{ N})\mathbf{i} - (180\text{ N})\mathbf{j}$$

When a force **F** is defined by its rectangular components F_x and F_y (see Fig. 2.21), the angle θ defining its direction can be obtained by writing

$$\tan\theta = \frac{F_y}{F_x} \tag{2.9}$$

The magnitude *F* of the force can be obtained by applying the Pythagorean theorem and writing

$$F = \sqrt{F_x^2 + F_y^2} \tag{2.10}$$

or by solving for *F* one of the Eqs. (2.8).

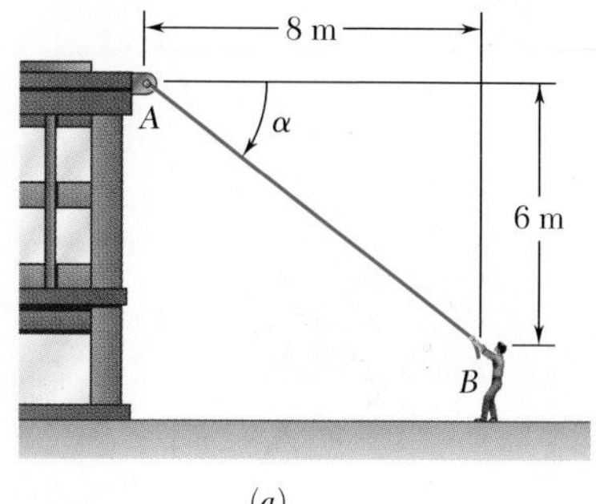

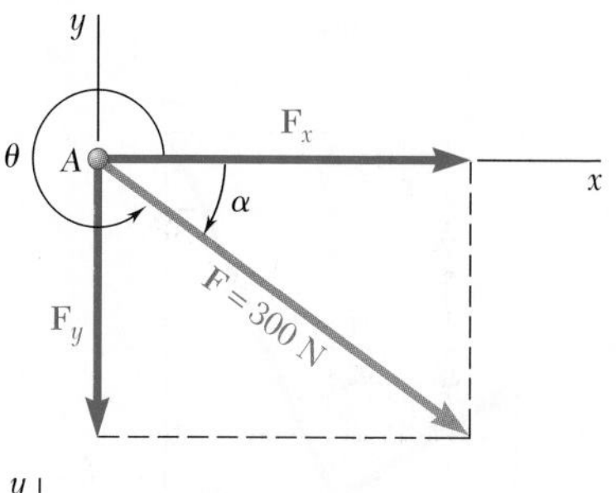

Fig. 2.23

Example 3. A force $\mathbf{F} = (700\text{ N})\mathbf{i} + (1500\text{ N})\mathbf{j}$ is applied to a bolt *A*. Determine the magnitude of the force and the angle θ it forms with the horizontal.

First we draw a diagram showing the two rectangular components of the force and the angle θ (Fig. 2.24). From Eq. (2.9), we write

$$\tan\theta = \frac{F_y}{F_x} = \frac{1500\text{ N}}{700\text{ N}}$$

Using a calculator,† we enter 1500 N and divide by 700 N; computing the arc tangent of the quotient, we obtain $\theta = 65.0°$. Solving the second of Eqs. (2.8) for *F*, we have

$$F = \frac{F_y}{\sin\theta} = \frac{1500\text{ N}}{\sin 65.0°} = 1655\text{ N}$$

The last calculation is facilitated if the value of F_y is stored when originally entered; it may then be recalled to be divided by $\sin\theta$.

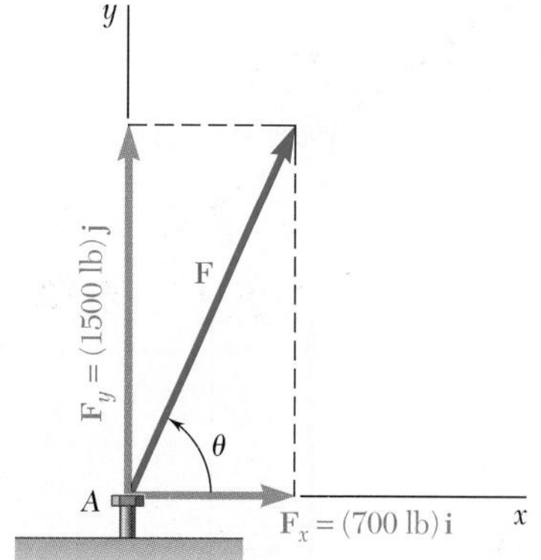

Fig. 2.24

†It is assumed that the calculator used has keys for the computation of trigonometric and inverse trigonometric functions. Some calculators also have keys for the direct conversion of rectangular coordinates into polar coordinates, and vice versa. Such calculators eliminate the need for the computation of trigonometric functions in Examples 1, 2, and 3 and in problems of the same type.

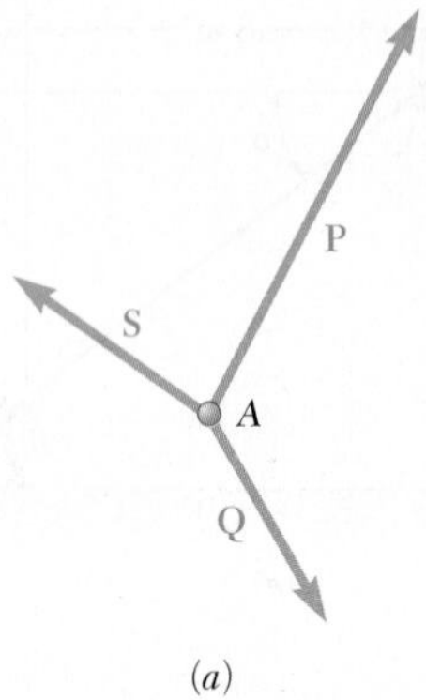

(a)

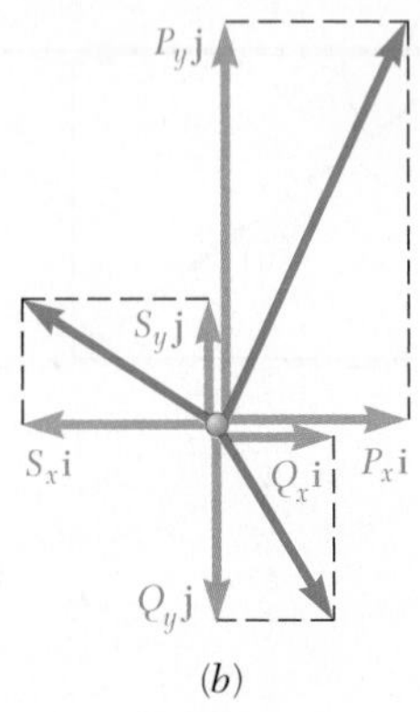

(b)

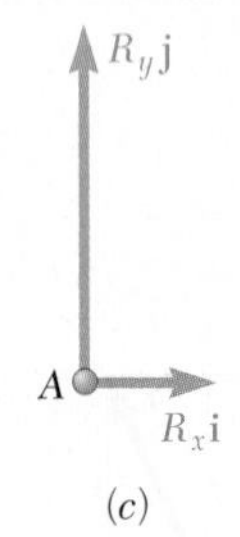

(c)

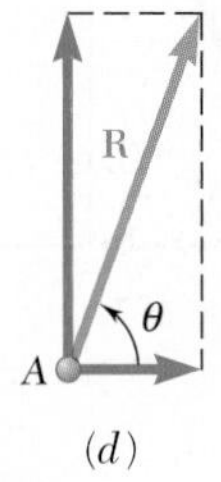

(d)

Fig. 2.25

2.8. ADDITION OF FORCES BY SUMMING *X* AND *Y* COMPONENTS

It was seen in Sec. 2.2 that forces should be added according to the parallelogram law. From this law, two other methods, more readily applicable to the *graphical* solution of problems, were derived in Secs. 2.4 and 2.5: the triangle rule for the addition of two forces and the polygon rule for the addition of three or more forces. It was also seen that the force triangle used to define the resultant of two forces could be used to obtain a *trigonometric* solution.

When three or more forces are to be added, no practical trigonometric solution can be obtained from the force polygon which defines the resultant of the forces. In this case, an *analytic* solution of the problem can be obtained by resolving each force into two rectangular components. Consider, for instance, three forces **P**, **Q**, and **S** acting on a particle A (Fig. 2.25*a*). Their resultant **R** is defined by the relation

$$\mathbf{R} = \mathbf{P} + \mathbf{Q} + \mathbf{S} \tag{2.11}$$

Resolving each force into its rectangular components, we write

$$\begin{aligned} R_x\mathbf{i} + R_y\mathbf{j} &= P_x\mathbf{i} + P_y\mathbf{j} + Q_x\mathbf{i} + Q_y\mathbf{j} + S_x\mathbf{i} + S_y\mathbf{j} \\ &= (P_x + Q_x + S_x)\mathbf{i} + (P_y + Q_y + S_y)\mathbf{j} \end{aligned}$$

from which it follows that

$$R_x = P_x + Q_x + S_x \qquad R_y = P_y + Q_y + S_y \tag{2.12}$$

or, for short,

$$R_x = \Sigma F_x \qquad R_y = \Sigma F_y \tag{2.13}$$

We thus conclude that *the scalar components R_x and R_y of the resultant* **R** *of several forces acting on a particle are obtained by adding algebraically the corresponding scalar components of the given forces.*†

In practice, the determination of the resultant **R** is carried out in three steps as illustrated in Fig. 2.25. First the given forces shown in Fig. 2.25*a* are resolved into their x and y components (Fig. 2.25*b*). Adding these components, we obtain the x and y components of **R** (Fig. 2.25*c*). Finally, the resultant $\mathbf{R} = R_x\mathbf{i} + R_y\mathbf{j}$ is determined by applying the parallelogram law (Fig. 2.25*d*). The procedure just described will be carried out most efficiently if the computations are arranged in a table. While it is the only practical analytic method for adding three or more forces, it is also often preferred to the trigonometric solution in the case of the addition of two forces.

†Clearly, this result also applies to the addition of other vector quantities, such as velocities, accelerations, or momenta.

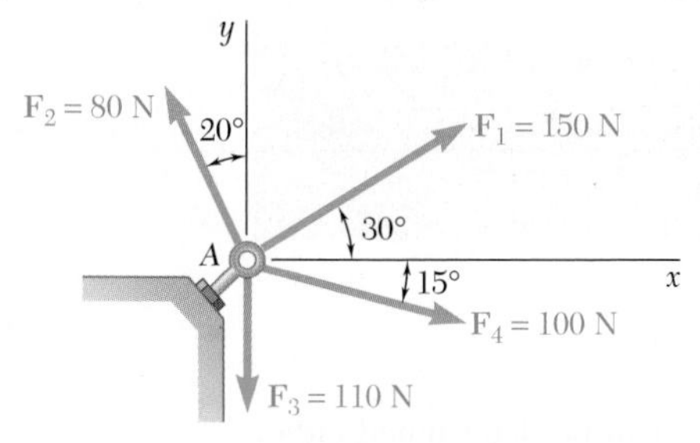

SAMPLE PROBLEM 2.3

Four forces act on bolt A as shown. Determine the resultant of the forces on the bolt.

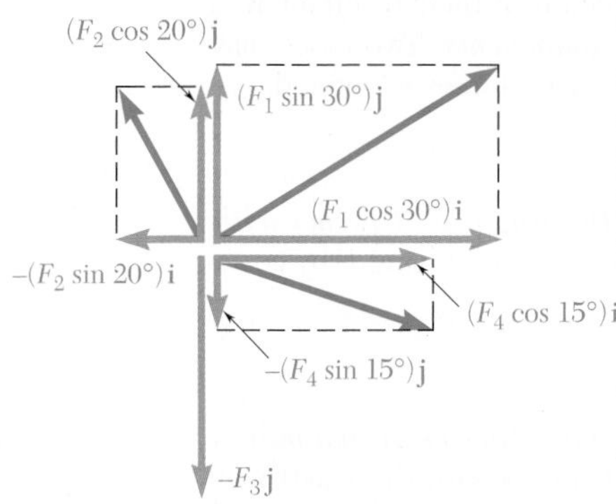

SOLUTION

The x and y components of each force are determined by trigonometry as shown and are entered in the table below. According to the convention adopted in Sec. 2.7, the scalar number representing a force component is positive if the force component has the same sense as the corresponding coordinate axis. Thus, x components acting to the right and y components acting upward are represented by positive numbers.

Force	Magnitude, N	x Component, N	y Component, N
$\mathbf{F}_1$	150	+129.9	+75.0
$\mathbf{F}_2$	80	−27.4	+75.2
$\mathbf{F}_3$	110	0	−110.0
$\mathbf{F}_4$	100	+96.6	−25.9
		$R_x = +199.1$	$R_y = +14.3$

Thus, the resultant $\mathbf{R}$ of the four forces is

$$\mathbf{R} = R_x\mathbf{i} + R_y\mathbf{j} \qquad \mathbf{R} = (199.1 \text{ N})\mathbf{i} + (14.3 \text{ N})\mathbf{j} \quad \blacktriangleleft$$

The magnitude and direction of the resultant may now be determined. From the triangle shown, we have

R
α
$R_y = (14.3 \text{ N})\mathbf{j}$
$R_x = (199.1 \text{ N})\mathbf{i}$

$$\tan \alpha = \frac{R_y}{R_x} = \frac{14.3 \text{ N}}{199.1 \text{ N}} \qquad \alpha = 4.1°$$

$$R = \frac{14.3 \text{ N}}{\sin \alpha} = 199.6 \text{ N} \qquad \mathbf{R} = 199.6 \text{ N} \measuredangle 4.1° \quad \blacktriangleleft$$

With a calculator, the last computation may be facilitated if the value of R_y is stored when originally entered; it may then be recalled to be divided by $\sin \alpha$. (Also see the footnote on p. 29.)

SOLVING PROBLEMS ON YOUR OWN

You saw in the preceding lesson that the resultant of two forces can be determined either graphically or from the trigonometry of an oblique triangle.

A. ***When three or more forces are involved,*** the determination of their resultant **R** is best carried out by first resolving each force into *rectangular components.* Two cases may be encountered, depending upon the way in which each of the given forces is defined:

Case 1. ***The force* F *is defined by its magnitude F and the angle α it forms with the x axis.*** The x and y components of the force can be obtained by multiplying F by $\cos \alpha$ and $\sin \alpha$, respectively [Example 1].

Case 2. ***The force* F *is defined by its magnitude F and the coordinates of two points A and B on its line of action*** (Fig. 2.23). The angle α that **F** forms with the x axis may first be determined by trigonometry. However, the components of **F** may also be obtained directly from proportions among the various dimensions involved, without actually determining α [Example 2].

B. ***Rectangular components of the resultant.*** The components R_x and R_y of the resultant can be obtained by adding algebraically the corresponding components of the given forces [Sample Prob. 2.3].

You can express the resultant in *vectorial form* using the unit vectors **i** and **j**, which are directed along the x and y axes, respectively:

$$\mathbf{R} = R_x\mathbf{i} + R_y\mathbf{j}$$

Alternatively, you can determine the *magnitude and direction* of the resultant by solving the right triangle of sides R_x and R_y for R and for the angle that **R** forms with the x axis.

In the examples and sample problem of this lesson, the x and y axes were horizontal and vertical, respectively. You should remember, however, that for some problems it will be more efficient to rotate the axes to align them with one or more of the applied forces.

Problems

2.21 Determine the x and y components of each of the forces shown.

2.22 Determine the x and y components of each of the forces shown.

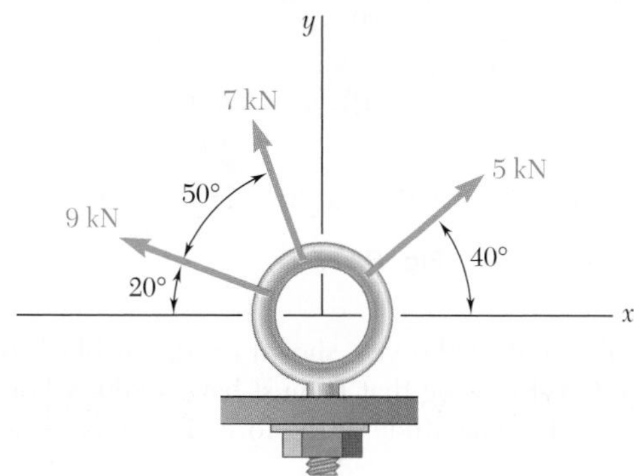

Fig. P2.22

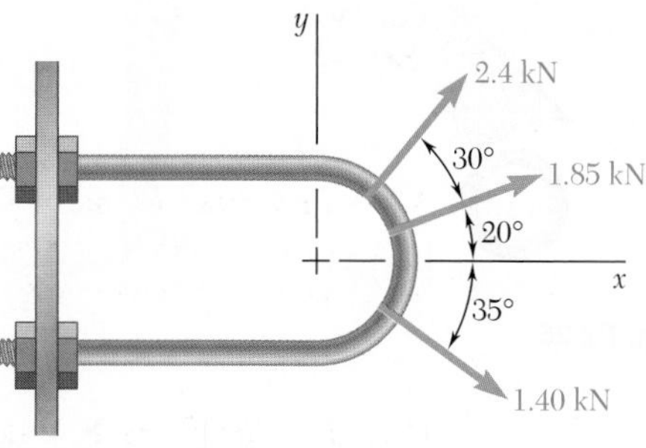

Fig. P2.21

2.23 and 2.24 Determine the x and y components of each of the forces shown.

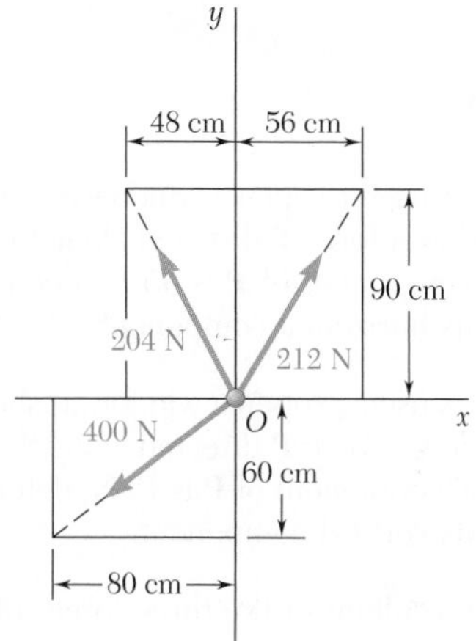

Fig. P2.24

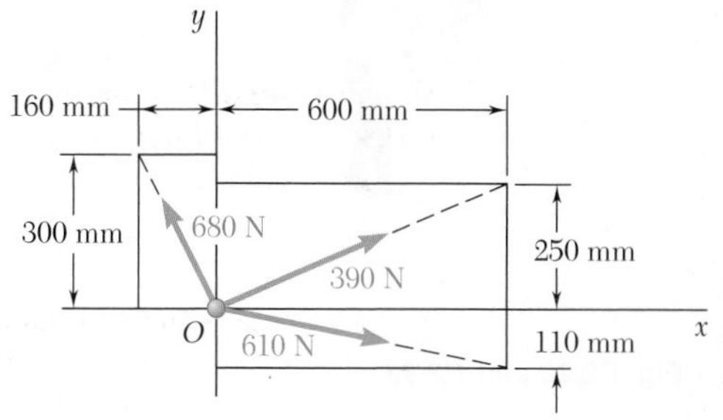

Fig. P2.23

2.25 Member BD exerts on member ABC a force $\mathbf{P}$ directed along line BD. Knowing that $\mathbf{P}$ must have a 960-N vertical component, determine (a) the magnitude of the force $\mathbf{P}$, (b) its horizontal component.

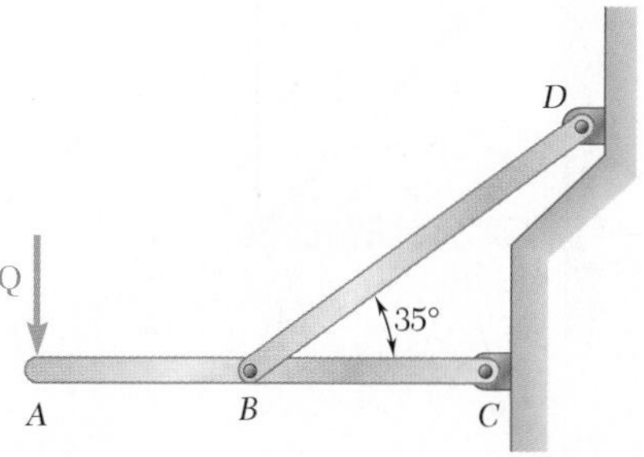

Fig. P2.25

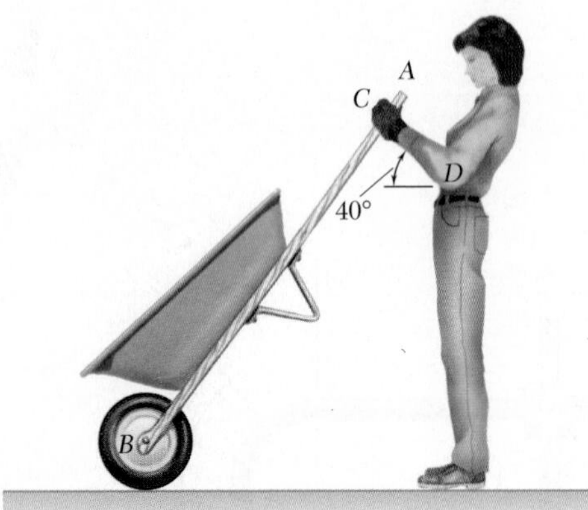

Fig. P2.26

2.26 While emptying a wheelbarrow, a gardener exerts on each handle AB a force $\mathbf{P}$ directed along line CD. Knowing that $\mathbf{P}$ must have a 30-N horizontal component, determine (*a*) the magnitude of the force $\mathbf{P}$, (*b*) its vertical component.

2.27 Activator rod AB exerts on crank BCD a force $\mathbf{P}$ directed along line AB. Knowing that $\mathbf{P}$ must have a 100-N component perpendicular to arm BC of the crank, determine (*a*) the magnitude of the force $\mathbf{P}$, (*b*) its component along line BC.

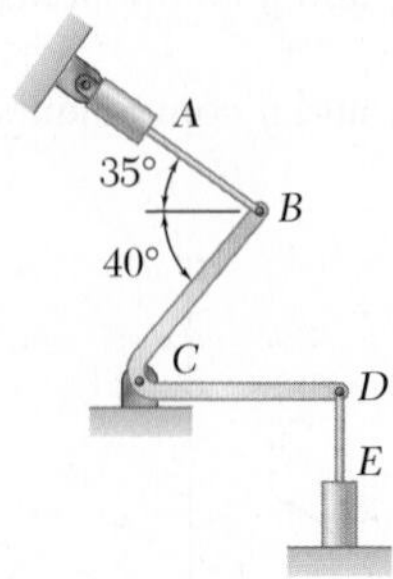

Fig. *P2.27*

2.28 Member CB of the vise shown exerts on block B a force $\mathbf{P}$ directed along line CB. Knowing that $\mathbf{P}$ must have a 260-N horizontal component, determine (*a*) the magnitude of the force $\mathbf{P}$, (*b*) its vertical component.

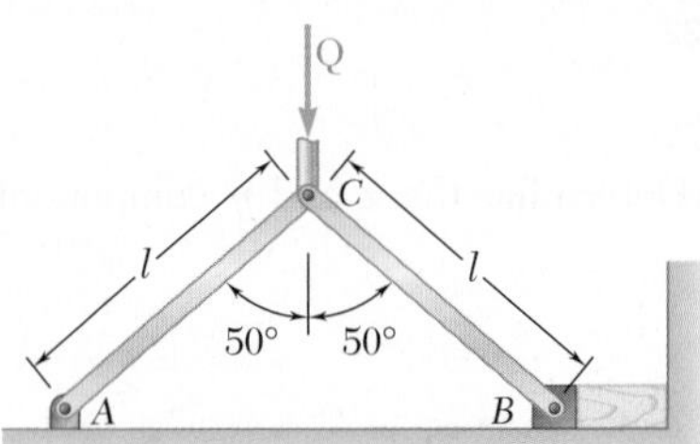

Fig. P2.28

Fig. P2.29 and *P2.30*

2.29 A window pole is used to open a window as shown. Knowing that the pole exerts on the window a force $\mathbf{P}$ directed along the pole and that the magnitude of the vertical component of $\mathbf{P}$ is 45 N, determine (*a*) the magnitude of the force $\mathbf{P}$, (*b*) its horizontal component.

2.30 A window pole is used to open a window as shown. Knowing that the pole exerts on the window a force $\mathbf{P}$ directed along the pole and that the magnitude of the horizontal component of $\mathbf{P}$ is 18 N, determine (*a*) the magnitude of the force $\mathbf{P}$, (*b*) its vertical component.

2.31 Determine the resultant of the three forces of Prob. 2.21.

2.32 Determine the resultant of the three forces of Prob. 2.22.

2.33 Determine the resultant of the three forces of Prob. 2.24.

2.34 Determine the resultant of the three forces of Prob. 2.23.

2.35 Knowing that the tension in cable BC is 145 N, determine the resultant of the three forces exerted at point B of beam AB.

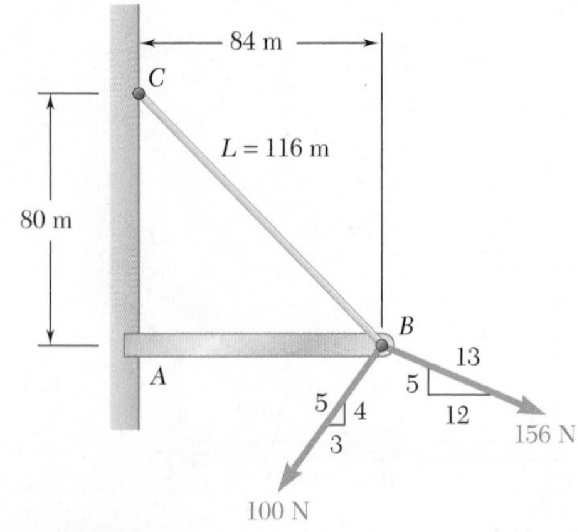

Fig. P2.35

2.36 A collar that can slide on a vertical rod is subjected to the three forces shown. Determine (*a*) the value of the angle α for which the resultant of the three forces is horizontal, (*b*) the corresponding magnitude of the resultant.

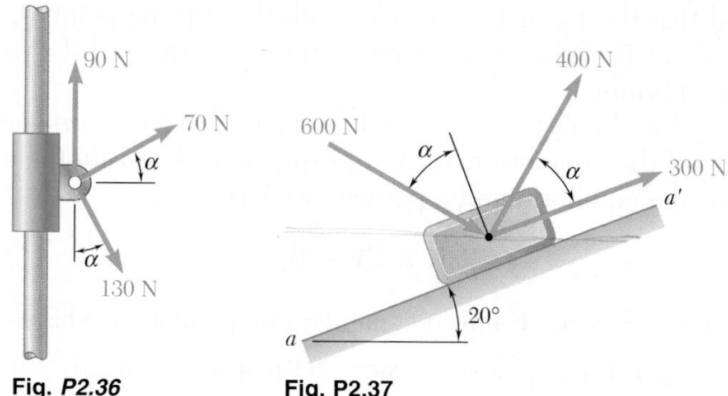

Fig. *P2.36* **Fig. P2.37**

2.37 Knowing that $\alpha = 65°$, determine the resultant of the three forces shown.

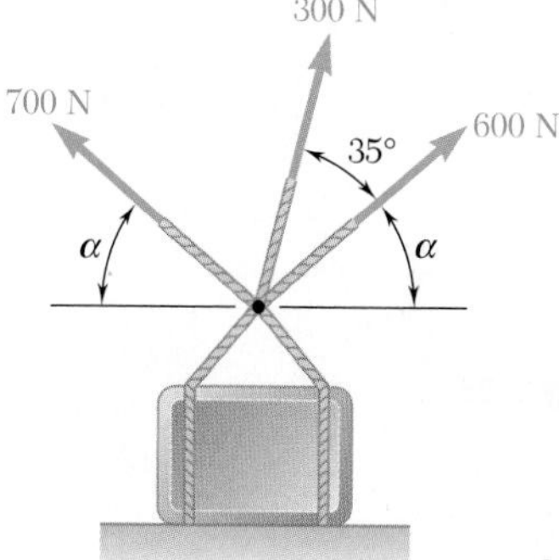

Fig. P2.38

2.38 Knowing that $\alpha = 50°$, determine the resultant of the three forces shown.

2.39 For the beam of Prob. 2.35, determine (*a*) the required tension in cable *BC* if the resultant of the three forces exerted at point *B* is to be vertical, (*b*) the corresponding magnitude of the resultant.

2.40 For the three forces of Prob. 2.38, determine (*a*) the required value of α if the resultant is to be vertical, (*b*) the corresponding magnitude of the resultant.

2.41 For the block of Prob. 2.37, determine (*a*) the required value of α if the resultant of the three forces shown is to be parallel to the incline, (*b*) the corresponding magnitude of the resultant.

2.42 Boom *AB* is held in the position shown by three cables. Knowing that the tensions in cables *AC* and *AD* are 900 N and 1200 N, respectively, determine (*a*) the tension in cable *AE* if the resultant of the tensions exerted at point *A* of the boom must be directed along *AB*, (*b*) the corresponding magnitude of the resultant.

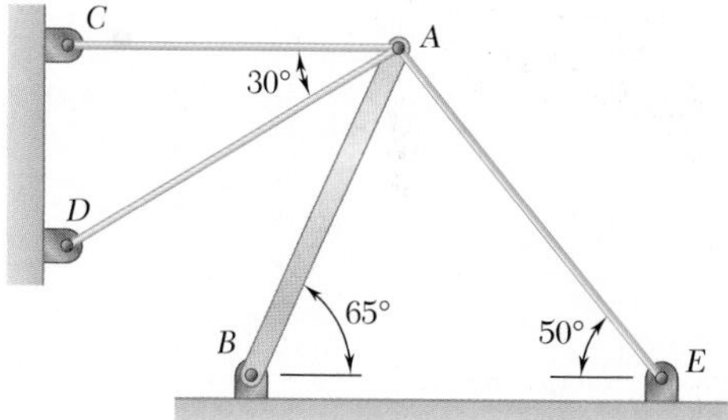

Fig. *P2.42*

2.9. EQUILIBRIUM OF A PARTICLE

In the preceding sections, we discussed the methods for determining the resultant of several forces acting on a particle. Although it has not occurred in any of the problems considered so far, it is quite possible for the resultant to be zero. In such a case, the net effect of the given forces is zero, and the particle is said to be in equilibrium. We thus have the following definition: *When the resultant of all the forces acting on a particle is zero, the particle is in equilibrium.*

A particle which is acted upon by two forces will be in equilibrium if the two forces have the same magnitude and the same line of action but opposite sense. The resultant of the two forces is then zero. Such a case is shown in Fig. 2.26.

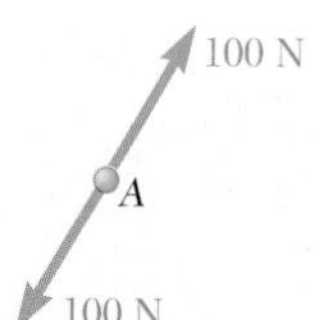

Fig. 2.26

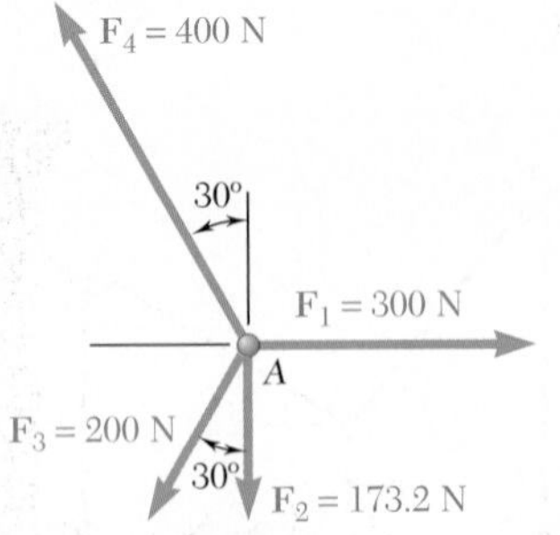

Fig. 2.27

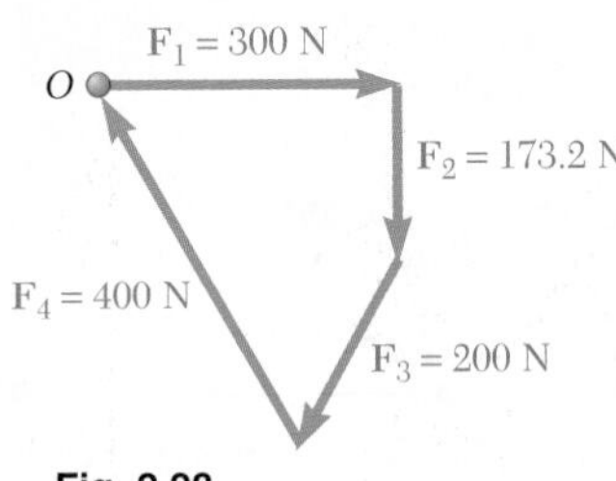

Fig. 2.28

Another case of equilibrium of a particle is represented in Fig. 2.27, where four forces are shown acting on A. In Fig. 2.28, the resultant of the given forces is determined by the polygon rule. Starting from point O with $\mathbf{F}_1$ and arranging the forces in tip-to-tail fashion, we find that the tip of $\mathbf{F}_4$ coincides with the starting point O. Thus the resultant **R** of the given system of forces is zero, and the particle is in equilibrium.

The closed polygon drawn in Fig. 2.28 provides a *graphical* expression of the equilibrium of A. To express *algebraically* the conditions for the equilibrium of a particle, we write

$$\mathbf{R} = \Sigma\mathbf{F} = 0 \tag{2.14}$$

Resolving each force **F** into rectangular components, we have

$$\Sigma(F_x\mathbf{i} + F_y\mathbf{j}) = 0 \qquad \text{or} \qquad (\Sigma F_x)\mathbf{i} + (\Sigma F_y)\mathbf{j} = 0$$

We conclude that the necessary and sufficient conditions for the equilibrium of a particle are

$$\Sigma F_x = 0 \qquad \Sigma F_y = 0 \tag{2.15}$$

Returning to the particle shown in Fig. 2.27, we check that the equilibrium conditions are satisfied. We write

$$\begin{aligned}\Sigma F_x &= 300\text{ N} - (200\text{ N})\sin 30° - (400\text{ N})\sin 30° \\ &= 300\text{ N} - 100\text{ N} - 200\text{ N} = 0 \\ \Sigma F_y &= -173.2\text{ N} - (200\text{ N})\cos 30° + (400\text{ N})\cos 30° \\ &= -173.2\text{ N} - 173.2\text{ N} + 346.4\text{ N} = 0\end{aligned}$$

2.10. NEWTON'S FIRST LAW OF MOTION

In the latter part of the seventeenth century, Sir Isaac Newton formulated three fundamental laws upon which the science of mechanics is based. The first of these laws can be stated as follows:

If the resultant force acting on a particle is zero, the particle will remain at rest (if originally at rest) or will move with constant speed in a straight line (if originally in motion).

From this law and from the definition of equilibrium given in Sec. 2.9, it is seen that a particle in equilibrium either is at rest or is moving in a straight line with constant speed. In the following section, various problems concerning the equilibrium of a particle will be considered.

2.11. PROBLEMS INVOLVING THE EQUILIBRIUM OF A PARTICLE. FREE-BODY DIAGRAMS

In practice, a problem in engineering mechanics is derived from an actual physical situation. A sketch showing the physical conditions of the problem is known as a *space diagram.*

The methods of analysis discussed in the preceding sections apply to a system of forces acting on a particle. A large number of problems involving actual structures, however, can be reduced to problems concerning the equilibrium of a particle. This is done by choosing a significant particle and drawing a separate diagram showing this particle and all the forces acting on it. Such a diagram is called a *free-body diagram.*

As an example, consider the 75-kg crate shown in the space diagram of Fig. 2.29*a*. This crate was lying between two buildings, and it is now being lifted onto a truck, which will remove it. The crate is supported by a vertical cable, which is joined at *A* to two ropes which pass over pulleys attached to the buildings at *B* and *C*. It is desired to determine the tension in each of the ropes *AB* and *AC*.

In order to solve this problem, a free-body diagram showing a particle in equilibrium must be drawn. Since we are interested in the rope tensions, the free-body diagram should include at least one of these tensions or, if possible, both tensions. Point *A* is seen to be a good free body for this problem. The free-body diagram of point *A* is shown in Fig. 2.29*b*. It shows point *A* and the forces exerted on *A* by the vertical cable and the two ropes. The force exerted by the cable is directed downward, and its magnitude is equal to the weight *W* of the crate. Recalling Eq. (1.4), we write

$$W = mg = (75 \text{ kg})(9.81 \text{ m/s}^2) = 736 \text{ N}$$

and indicate this value in the free-body diagram. The forces exerted by the two ropes are not known. Since they are respectively equal in magnitude to the tensions in rope *AB* and rope *AC*, we denote them by $\mathbf{T}_{AB}$ and $\mathbf{T}_{AC}$ and draw them away from *A* in the directions shown in the space diagram. No other detail is included in the free-body diagram.

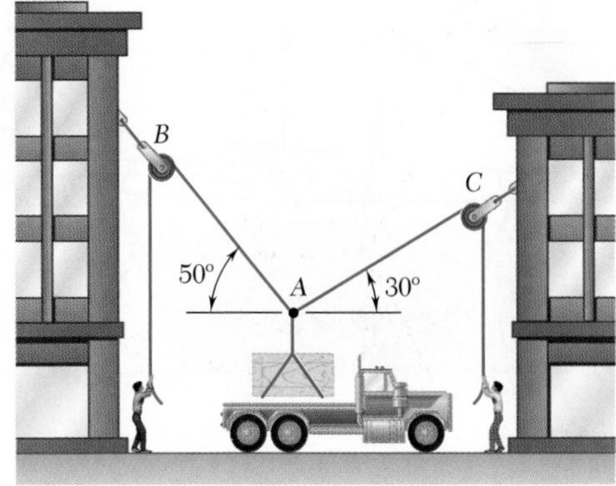

(*a*) Space diagram

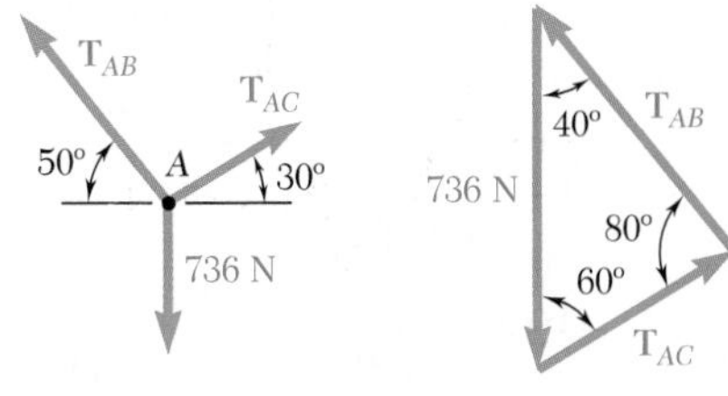

(*b*) Free-body diagram (*c*) Force triangle

Fig. 2.29

Since point *A* is in equilibrium, the three forces acting on it must form a closed triangle when drawn in tip-to-tail fashion. This *force triangle* has been drawn in Fig. 2.29*c*. The values T_{AB} and T_{AC} of the tension in the ropes may be found graphically if the triangle is drawn to scale, or they may be found by trigonometry. If the latter method of solution is chosen, we use the law of sines and write

$$\frac{T_{AB}}{\sin 60°} = \frac{T_{AC}}{\sin 40°} = \frac{736 \text{ N}}{\sin 80°}$$

$$T_{AB} = 647 \text{ N} \qquad T_{AC} = 480 \text{ N}$$

When a particle is in *equilibrium under three forces,* the problem can be solved by drawing a force triangle. When a particle is in *equilibrium under more than three forces,* the problem can be solved graphically by drawing a force polygon. If an analytic solution is desired, the *equations of equilibrium* given in Sec. 2.9 should be solved:

$$\Sigma F_x = 0 \qquad \Sigma F_y = 0 \tag{2.15}$$

These equations can be solved for no more than *two unknowns;* similarly, the force triangle used in the case of equilibrium under three forces can be solved for two unknowns.

The more common types of problems are those in which the two unknowns represent (1) the two components (or the magnitude and direction) of a single force, (2) the magnitudes of two forces, each of known direction. Problems involving the determination of the maximum or minimum value of the magnitude of a force are also encountered (for example, see Probs. 2.59 through 2.63).

Photo 2.2 As illustrated in the above example, it is possible to determine the tensions in the cables supporting the shaft shown by treating the hook as a particle and then applying the equations of equilibrium to the forces acting on the hook.

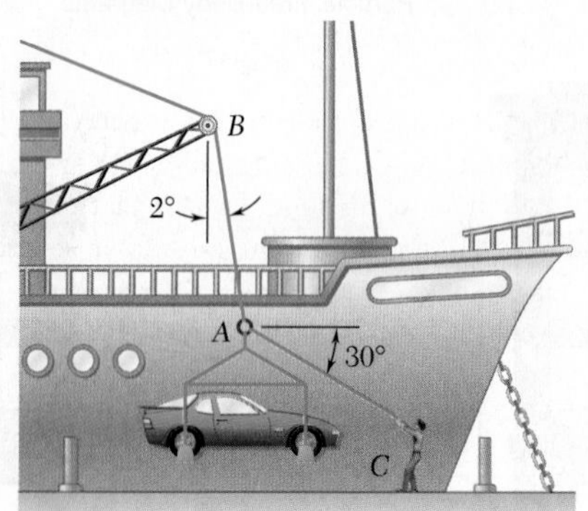

SAMPLE PROBLEM 2.4

In a ship-unloading operation, a 3500-N automobile is supported by a cable. A rope is tied to the cable at A and pulled in order to center the automobile over its intended position. The angle between the cable and the vertical is 2°, while the angle between the rope and the horizontal is 30°. What is the tension in the rope?

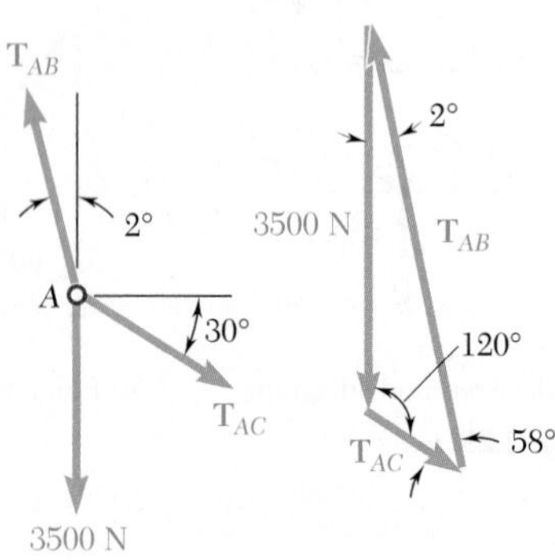

SOLUTION

Free-Body Diagram. Point A is chosen as a free body, and the complete free-body diagram is drawn. T_{AB} is the tension in the cable AB, and T_{AC} is the tension in the rope.

Equilibrium Condition. Since only three forces act on the free body, we draw a force triangle to express that it is in equilibrium. Using the law of sines, we write

$$\frac{T_{AB}}{\sin 120°} = \frac{T_{AC}}{\sin 2°} = \frac{3500 \text{ N}}{\sin 58°}$$

With a calculator, we first compute and store the value of the last quotient. Multiplying this value successively by sin 120° and sin 2°, we obtain

$$T_{AB} = 3570 \text{ N} \qquad T_{AC} = 144 \text{ N} \blacktriangleleft$$

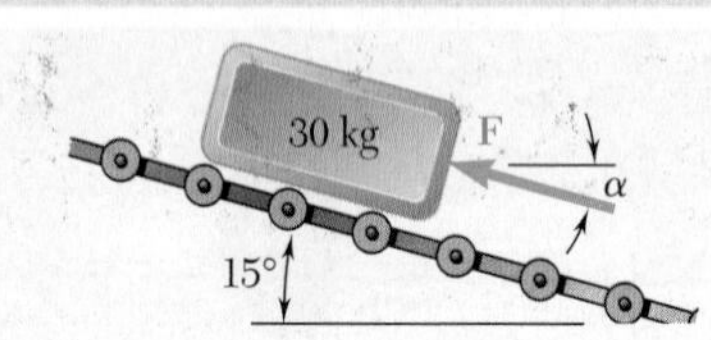

SAMPLE PROBLEM 2.5

Determine the magnitude and direction of the smallest force **F** which will maintain the package shown in equilibrium. Note that the force exerted by the rollers on the package is perpendicular to the incline.

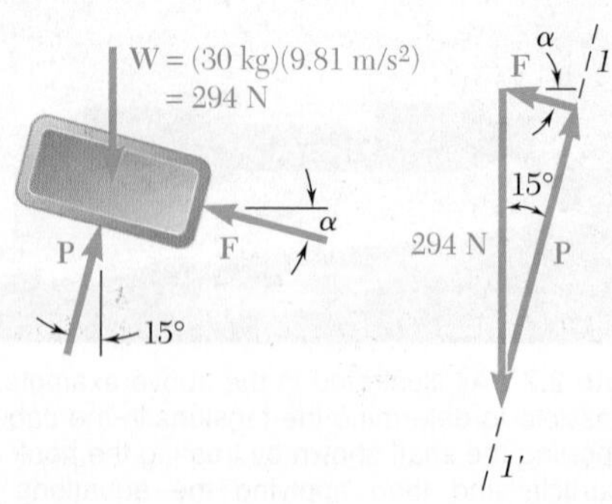

SOLUTION

Free-Body Diagram. We choose the package as a free body, assuming that it can be treated as a particle. We draw the corresponding free-body diagram.

Equilibrium Condition. Since only three forces act on the free body, we draw a force triangle to express that it is in equilibrium. Line *1-1'* represents the known direction of **P**. In order to obtain the minimum value of the force **F**, we choose the direction of **F** perpendicular to that of **P**. From the geometry of the triangle obtained, we find

$$F = (294 \text{ N}) \sin 15° = 76.1 \text{ N} \qquad \alpha = 15°$$

$$\mathbf{F} = 76.1 \text{ N} ⦪15° \blacktriangleleft$$

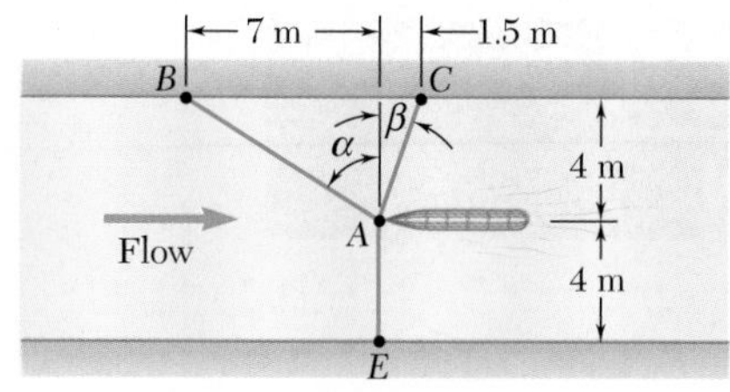

SAMPLE PROBLEM 2.6

As part of the design of a new sailboat, it is desired to determine the drag force which may be expected at a given speed. To do so, a model of the proposed hull is placed in a test channel and three cables are used to keep its bow on the centerline of the channel. Dynamometer readings indicate that for a given speed, the tension is 40 N in cable *AB* and 60 N in cable *AE*. Determine the drag force exerted on the hull and the tension in cable *AC*.

SOLUTION

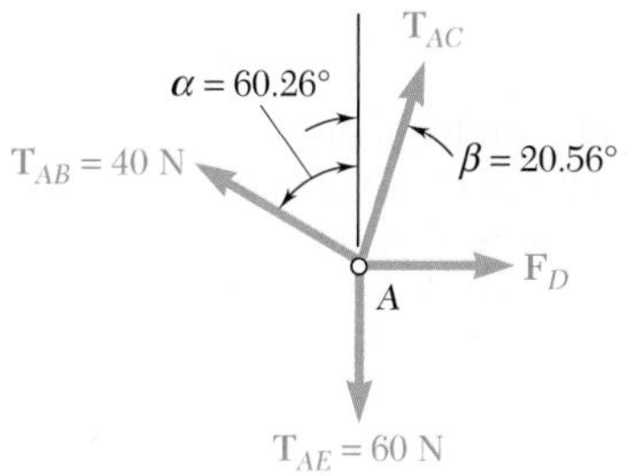

Determination of the Angles. First, the angles α and β defining the direction of cables *AB* and *AC* are determined. We write

$$\tan \alpha = \frac{7\text{ m}}{4\text{ m}} = 1.75 \qquad \tan \beta = \frac{1.5\text{ m}}{4\text{ m}} = 0.375$$

$$\alpha = 60.26^\circ \qquad \beta = 20.56^\circ$$

Free-Body Diagram. Choosing the hull as a free body, we draw the free-body diagram shown. It includes the forces exerted by the three cables on the hull, as well as the drag force $\mathbf{F}_D$ exerted by the flow.

Equilibrium Condition. We express that the hull is in equilibrium by writing that the resultant of all forces is zero:

$$\mathbf{R} = \mathbf{T}_{AB} + \mathbf{T}_{AC} + \mathbf{T}_{AE} + \mathbf{F}_D = 0 \tag{1}$$

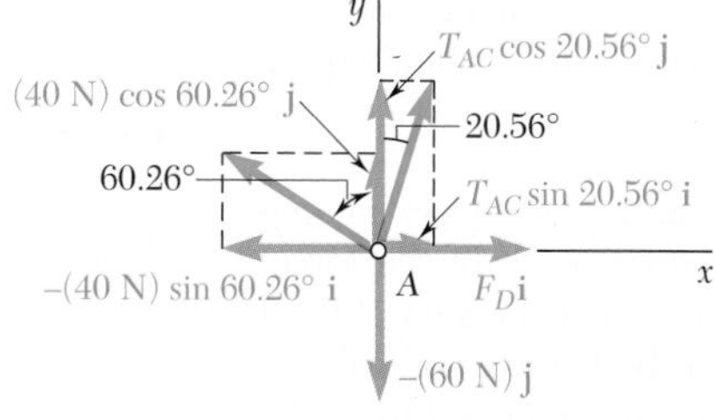

Since more than three forces are involved, we resolve the forces into x and y components:

$$\begin{aligned}
\mathbf{T}_{AB} &= -(40\text{ N}) \sin 60.26^\circ\mathbf{i} + (40\text{ N}) \cos 60.26^\circ\mathbf{j} \\
&= -(34.73\text{ N})\mathbf{i} + (19.84\text{ N})\mathbf{j} \\
\mathbf{T}_{AC} &= T_{AC} \sin 20.56^\circ\mathbf{i} + T_{AC} \cos 20.56^\circ\mathbf{j} \\
&= 0.3512T_{AC}\mathbf{i} + 0.9363T_{AC}\mathbf{j} \\
\mathbf{T}_{AE} &= -(60\text{ N})\mathbf{j} \\
\mathbf{F}_D &= F_D\mathbf{i}
\end{aligned}$$

Substituting the expressions obtained into Eq. (1) and factoring the unit vectors **i** and **j**, we have

$$(-34.73\text{ N} + 0.3512T_{AC} + F_D)\mathbf{i} + (19.84\text{ N} + 0.9363T_{AC} - 60\text{ N})\mathbf{j} = 0$$

This equation will be satisfied if, and only if, the coefficients of **i** and **j** are equal to zero. We thus obtain the following two equilibrium equations, which express, respectively, that the sum of the x components and the sum of the y components of the given forces must be zero.

$$\Sigma F_x = 0: \qquad -34.73\text{ N} + 0.3512T_{AC} + F_D = 0 \tag{2}$$

$$\Sigma F_y = 0: \qquad 19.84\text{ N} + 0.9363T_{AC} - 60\text{ N} = 0 \tag{3}$$

From Eq. (3) we find $\qquad T_{AC} = +42.9\text{ lb}$ ◀

and, substituting this value into Eq. (2), $\qquad F_D = +19.66\text{ lb}$ ◀

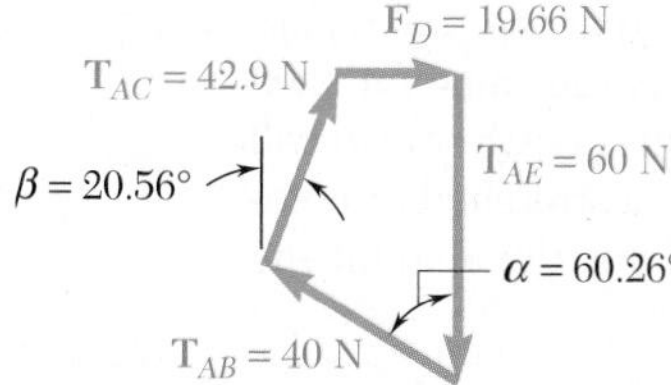

In drawing the free-body diagram, we assumed a sense for each unknown force. A positive sign in the answer indicates that the assumed sense is correct. The complete force polygon may be drawn to check the results.

SOLVING PROBLEMS ON YOUR OWN

When a particle is in *equilibrium,* the resultant of the forces acting on the particle must be zero. Expressing this fact in the case of a particle under *coplanar forces* will provide you with two relations among these forces. As you saw in the preceding sample problems, these relations can be used to determine two unknowns—such as the magnitude and direction of one force or the magnitudes of two forces.

Drawing a free-body diagram is the first step in the solution of a problem involving the equilibrium of a particle. This diagram shows the particle and all the forces acting on it. Indicate on your free-body diagram the magnitudes of known forces as well as any angle or dimensions that define the direction of a force. Any unknown magnitude or angle should be denoted by an appropriate symbol. Nothing else should be included on the free-body diagram.

Drawing a clear and accurate free-body diagram is a must in the solution of any equilibrium problem. Skipping this step might save you pencil and paper, but is very likely to lead you to a wrong solution.

Case 1. If only three forces are involved in the free-body diagram, the rest of the solution is best carried out by drawing these forces in tip-to-tail fashion to form a *force triangle.* This triangle can be solved graphically or using trigonometry for no more than two unknowns [Sample Probs. 2.4 and 2.5].

Case 2. If more than three forces are involved, it is to your advantage to use an *analytic solution.* Begin by selecting appropriate x and y axes and resolve each of the forces shown in the free-body diagram into x and y components. Expressing that the sum of the x components and the sum of the y components of all the forces are both zero, you will obtain two equations which you can solve for no more than two unknowns [Sample Prob. 2.6].

It is strongly recommended that when using an analytic solution the equations of equilibrium be written in the same form as Eqs. (2) and (3) of Sample Prob. 2.6. The practice adopted by some students of initially placing the unknowns on the left side of the equation and the known quantities on the right side may lead to confusion in assigning the appropriate sign to each term.

We have noted that regardless of the method used to solve a two-dimensional equilibrium problem we can determine at most two unknowns. If a two-dimensional problem involves more than two unknowns, one or more additional relations must be obtained from the information contained in the statement of the problem.

Some of the following problems contain small pulleys. We will assume that the pulleys are frictionless, so the tension in the rope or cable passing over a pulley is the same on each side of the pulley. In Chap. 4 we will discuss why the tension is the same. Lastly, as we will discuss in Chap. 10, the magnitude of the force **F** exerted on a body by a stretched or compressed spring is given by $F = kx$, where k is the spring constant and x is the amount the spring is stretched or compressed from its undeformed length.

Problems

2.43 Knowing that $\alpha = 50°$ and that boom AC exerts on pin C a force directed along line AC, determine (*a*) the magnitude of that force, (*b*) the tension in cable BC.

2.44 Two cables are tied together at C and are loaded as shown. Determine the tension (*a*) in cable AC, (*b*) in cable BC.

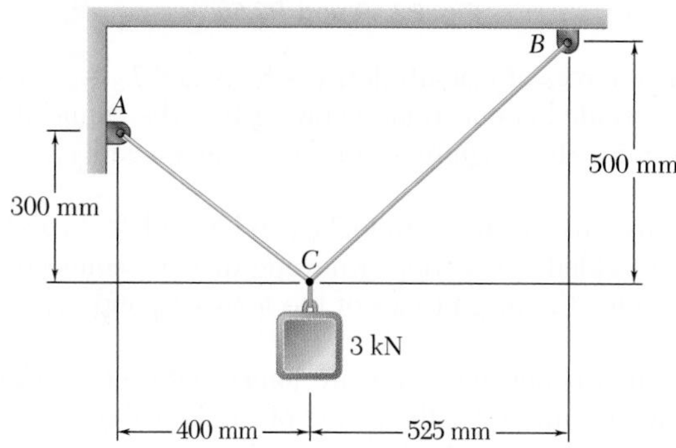

Fig. P2.44

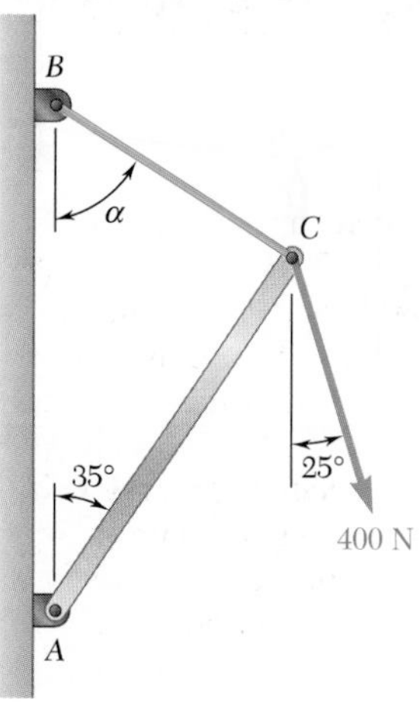

Fig. P2.43

2.46 An irregularly shaped machine component is held in the position shown by three clamps. Knowing that $F_A = 940$ N, determine the magnitudes of the forces F_B and F_C exerted by the other two clamps.

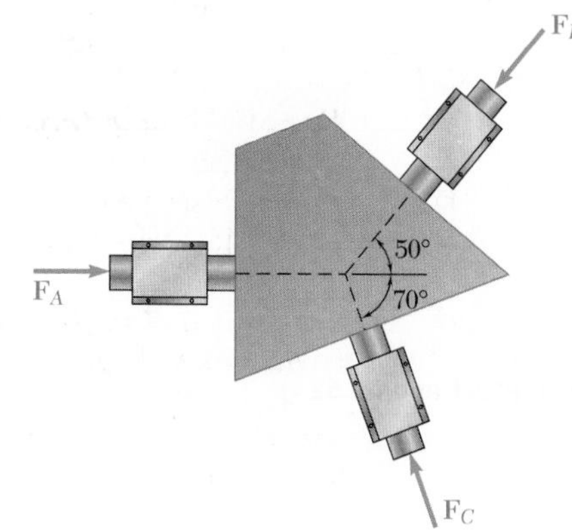

Fig. *P2.45*

2.46 Ropes AB and AC are thrown to a boater whose canoe had capsized. Knowing that $\alpha = 25°$ and that the magnitude of the force $\mathbf{F}_R$ exerted by the river on the boater is 70 N, determine the tension (*a*) in rope AB, (*b*) in rope AC.

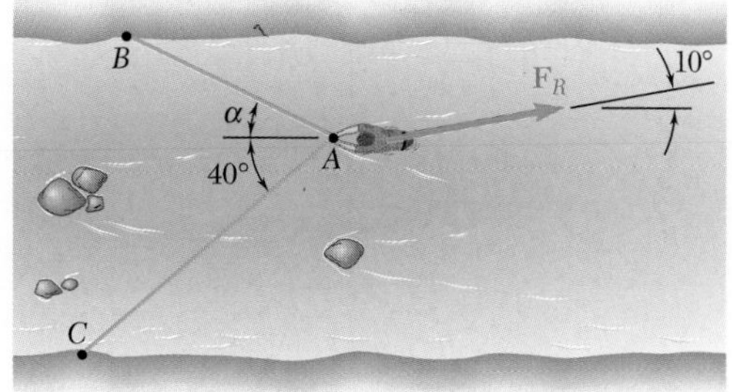

Fig. P2.46

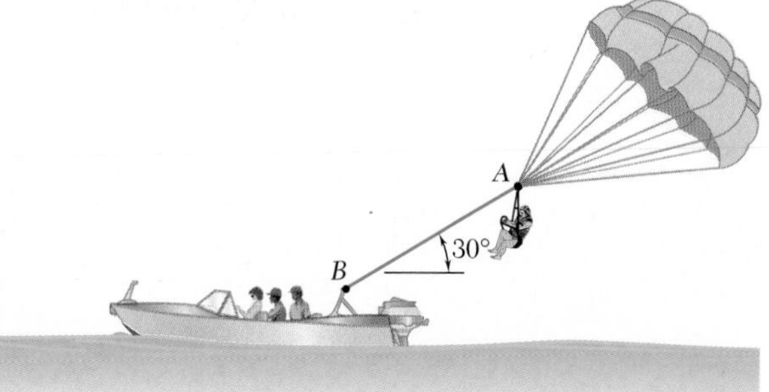

Fig. P2.47

2.47 A boat is pulling a parasail and rider at a constant speed. Knowing that the rider weighs 550 N and that the resultant force $\mathbf{R}$ exerted by the parasail on the towing yoke A forms an angle of 65° with the horizontal, determine (*a*) the tension in the tow rope AB, (*b*) the magnitude of $\mathbf{R}$.

2.48 Two traffic signals are temporarily suspended from a cable as shown. Knowing that the signal at B weighs 300 N, determine the weight of the signal at C.

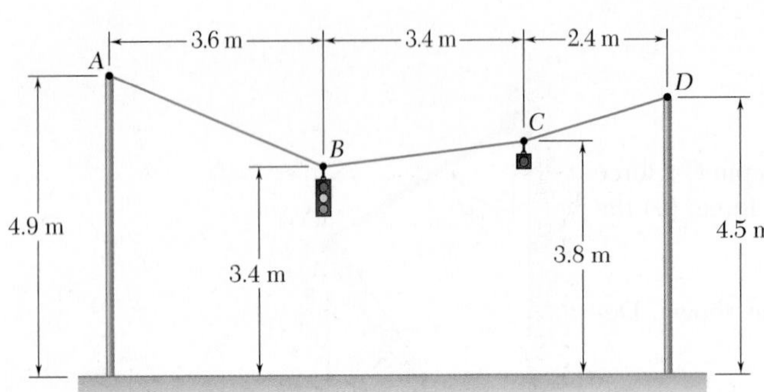

Fig. P2.48

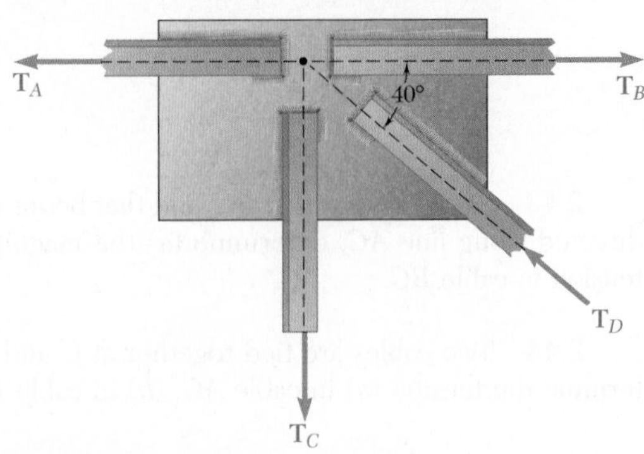

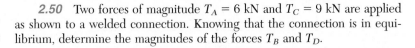

Fig. P2.49 and P2.50

2.49 Two forces of magnitude $T_A = 8$ kN and $T_B = 15$ kN are applied as shown to a welded connection. Knowing that the connection is in equilibrium, determine the magnitudes of the forces T_C and T_D.

2.50 Two forces of magnitude $T_A = 6$ kN and $T_C = 9$ kN are applied as shown to a welded connection. Knowing that the connection is in equilibrium, determine the magnitudes of the forces T_B and T_D.

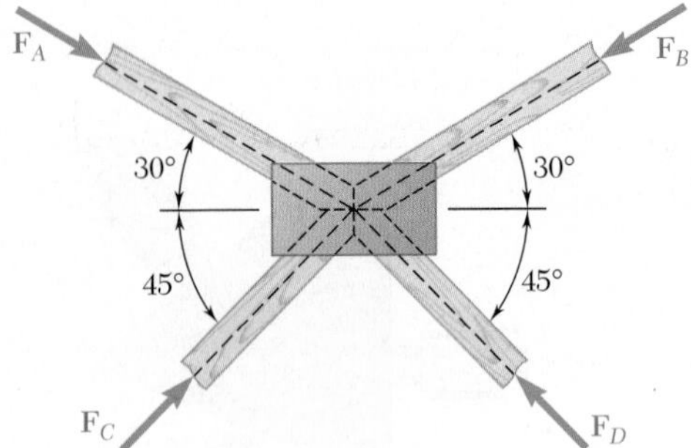

Fig. P2.51 and P2.52

2.51 Four wooden members are joined with metal plate connectors and are in equilibrium under the action of the four forces shown. Knowing that $F_A = 2.3$ kN and $F_B = 2.1$ kN, determine the magnitudes of the other two forces.

2.52 Four wooden members are joined with metal plate connectors and are in equilibrium under the action of the four forces shown. Knowing that $F_A = 1.9$ kN and $F_C = 2.4$ kN, determine the magnitudes of the other two forces.

2.53 In a circus act, an aerialist performs a handstand on a wheel while being pulled across a high wire ABC of length 8 m by another performer as shown. Knowing that the tension in rope DE is 35 N when the aerialist is held in equilibrium at $a = 2.5$ m, determine (*a*) the weight of the aerialist, (*b*) the tension in the wire.

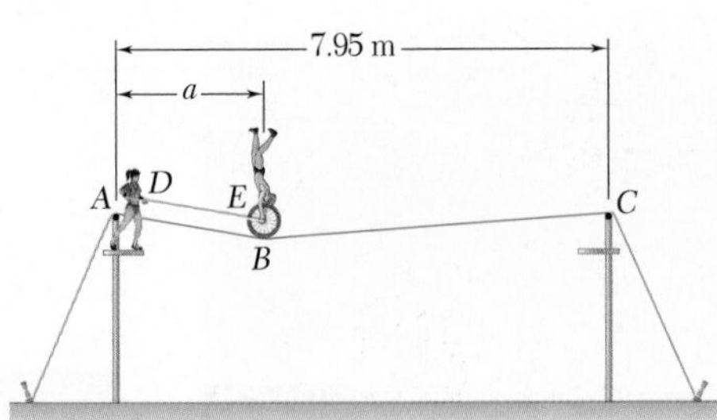

Fig. P2.53 and P2.54

2.54 In a circus act, an aerialist performs a handstand on a wheel while being pulled across a high wire ABC of length 8 m by another performer as shown. Knowing that the aerialist weighs 720 N and is being held in equilibrium at $a = 3$ m, determine (*a*) the tension in the wire, (*b*) the tension in rope DE.

2.55 Two cables tied together at C are loaded as shown. Knowing that $W = 190$ N, determine the tension (*a*) in cable AC, (*b*) in cable BC.

2.56 Two cables tied together at C are loaded as shown. Determine the range of values of W for which the tension will not exceed 240 N in either cable.

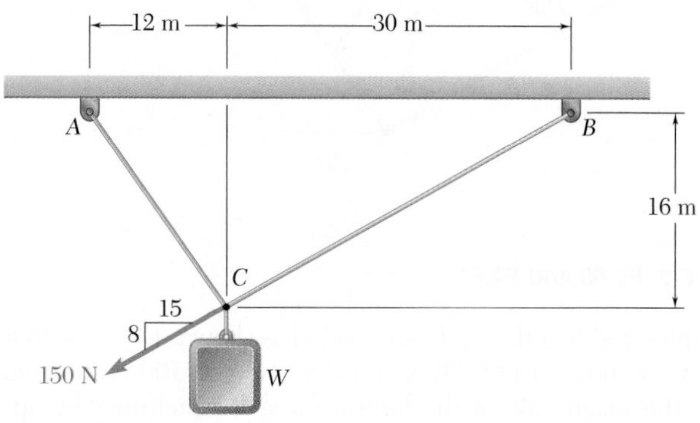

Fig. P2.55 and *P2.56*

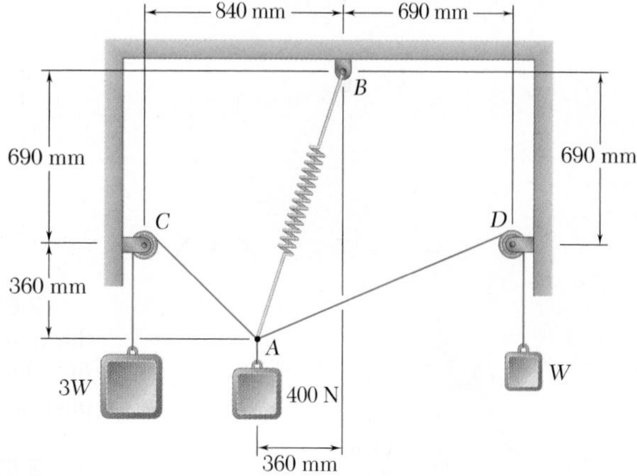

Fig. P2.57

2.57 A load of weight 400 N is suspended from a spring and two cords that are attached to blocks of weights $3W$ and W as shown. Knowing that the constant of the spring is 800 N/m, determine (*a*) the value of W, (*b*) the unstretched length of the spring.

2.58 A block of weight W is suspended from a 25-cm-long cord and two springs of which the unstretched lengths are 22.5 cm. Knowing that the constants of the springs are $k_{AB} = 9$ N/cm and $k_{AD} = 3$ N/cm, determine (*a*) the tension in the cord, (*b*) the weight of the block.

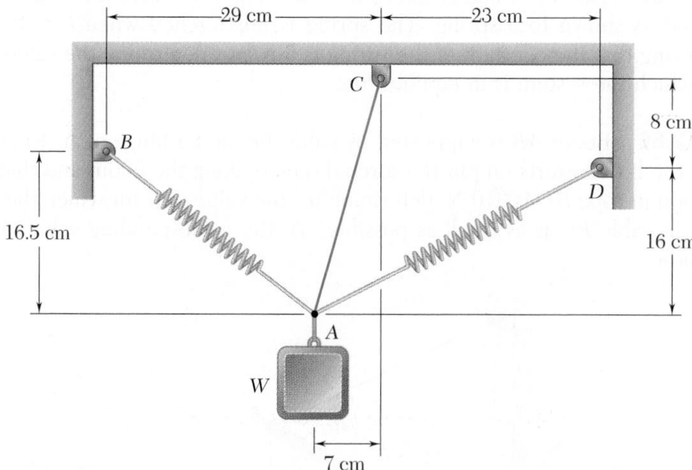

Fig. P2.58

2.59 For the ropes and force of the river of Prob. 2.46, determine (*a*) the value of α for which the tension in rope AB is as small as possible, (*b*) the corresponding value of the tension.

2.60 Two cables tied together at C are loaded as shown. Knowing that the maximum allowable tension in each cable is 900 N, determine (a) the magnitude of the largest force $\mathbf{P}$ which may be applied at C, (b) the corresponding value of α.

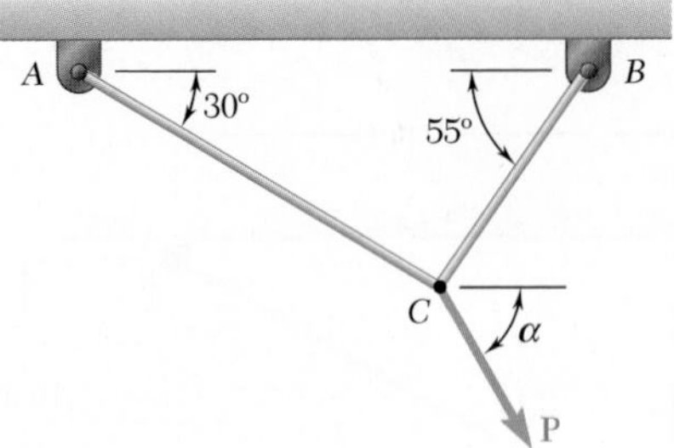

Fig. P2.60 and P2.61

2.61 Two cables tied together at C are loaded as shown. Knowing that the maximum allowable tension is 1400 N in cable AC and 700 N in cable BC, determine (a) the magnitude of the largest force $\mathbf{P}$ which may be applied at C, (b) the corresponding value of α.

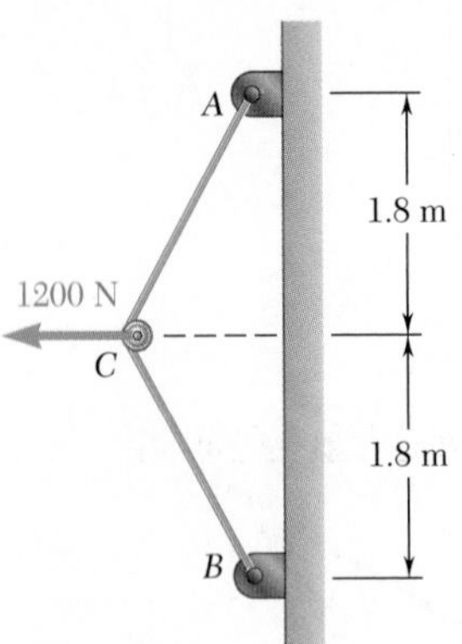

Fig. P2.62

2.62 Knowing that portions AC and BC of cable ACB must be equal, determine the shortest length of cable that can be used to support the load shown if the tension in the cable is not to exceed 870 N.

2.63 For the structure and loading of Prob. 2.43, determine (a) the value of α for which the tension in cable BC is as small as possible, (b) the corresponding value of the tension.

2.64 Collar A can slide on a frictionless vertical rod and is attached as shown to a spring. The constant of the spring is 4 N/cm, and the spring is unstretched when h = 12 cm. Knowing that the system is in equilibrium when h = 16 cm, determine the weight of the collar.

2.65 The 9-N collar A can slide on a frictionless vertical rod and is attached as shown to a spring. The spring is unstretched when h = 12 cm. Knowing that the constant of the spring is 3 N/cm, determine the value of h for which the system is in equilibrium.

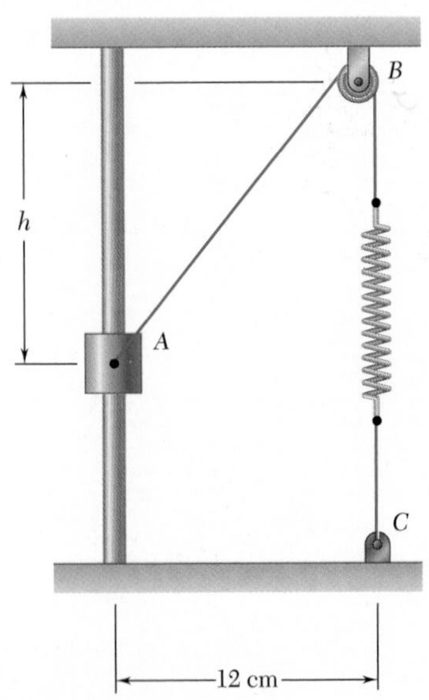

Fig. ***P2.64*** and P2.65

2.66 Boom AB is supported by cable BC and a hinge at A. Knowing that the boom exerts on pin B a force directed along the boom and that the tension in rope BD is 310 N, determine (a) the value of α for which the tension in cable BC is as small as possible, (b) the corresponding value of the tension.

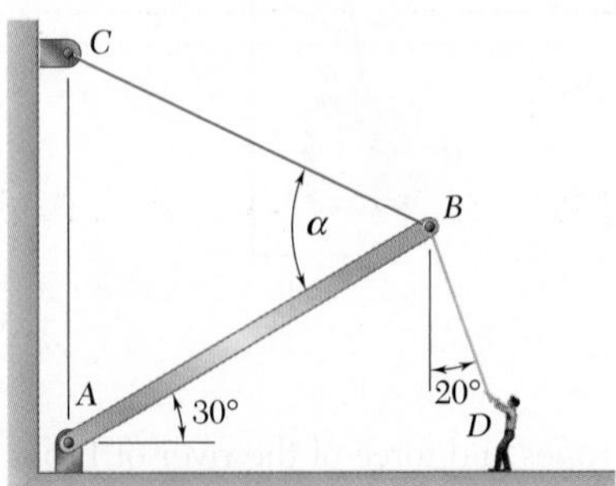

Fig. P2.66

2.67 The force **P** is applied to a small wheel that rolls on the cable *ACB*. Knowing that the tension in both parts of the cable is 140 N, determine the magnitude and direction of **P**.

Fig. P2.67

2.68 A 280-kg crate is supported by several rope-and-pulley arrangements as shown. Determine for each arrangement the tension in the rope. (*Hint:* The tension in the rope is the same on each side of a simple pulley. This can be proved by the methods of Chap. 4.)

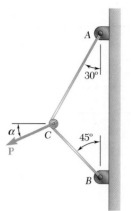

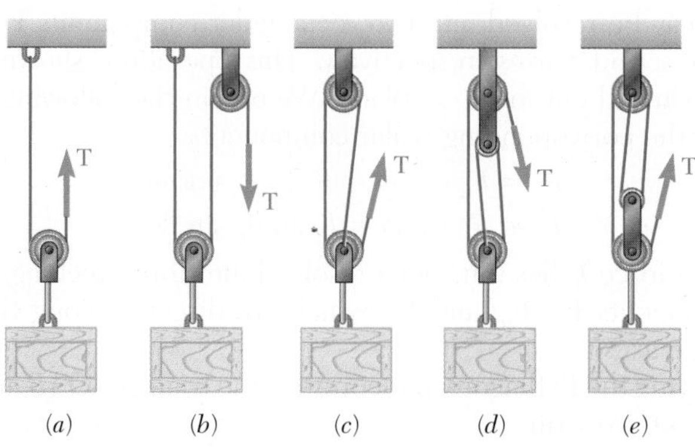

Fig. ***P2.68***

2.69 Solve parts *b* and *d* of Prob. 2.68 assuming that the free end of the rope is attached to the crate.

2.70 A load **Q** is applied to the pulley *C*, which can roll on the cable *ACB*. The pulley is held in the position shown by a second cable *CAD*, which passes over the pulley *A* and supports a load **P**. Knowing that $P = 800$ N, determine (*a*) the tension in cable *ACB*, (*b*) the magnitude of load **Q**.

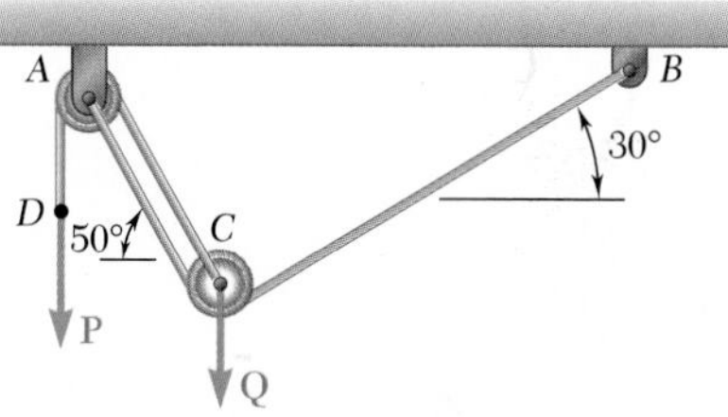

Fig. P2.70 and ***P2.71***

2.71 A 2000-N load **Q** is applied to the pulley *C*, which can roll on the cable *ACB*. The pulley is held in the position shown by a second cable *CAD*, which passes over the pulley *A* and supports a load **P**. Determine (*a*) the tension in cable *ACB*, (*b*) the magnitude of load **P**.

2.72 Three forces are applied to a bracket. The directions of the two 30-N forces can vary, but the angle between these forces is always 50°. Determine the range of values of α for which the magnitude of the resultant of the forces applied to the bracket is less than 120 N.

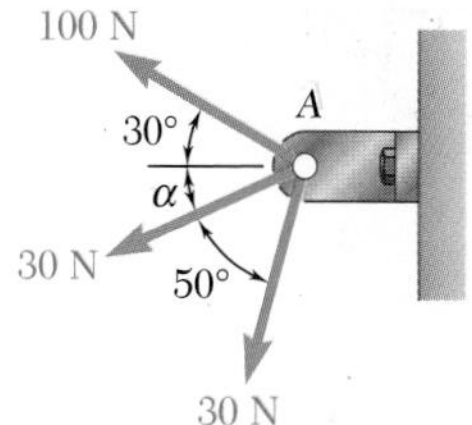

Fig. P2.72

FORCES IN SPACE

2.12. RECTANGULAR COMPONENTS OF A FORCE IN SPACE

The problems considered in the first part of this chapter involved only two dimensions; they could be formulated and solved in a single plane. In this section and in the remaining sections of the chapter, we will discuss problems involving the three dimensions of space.

Consider a force **F** acting at the origin *O* of the system of rectangular coordinates *x*, *y*, *z*. To define the direction of **F**, we draw the

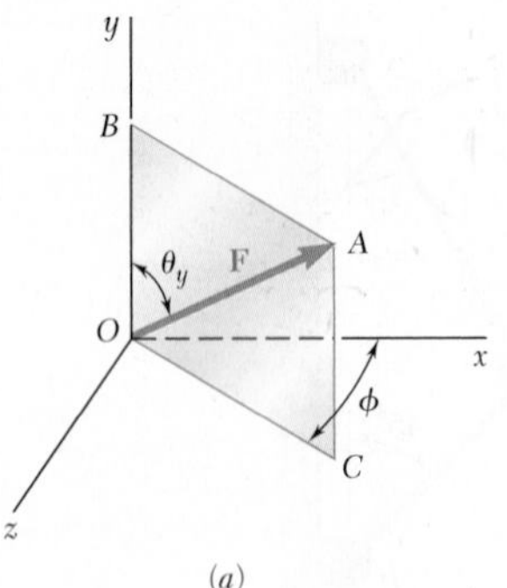

(a)

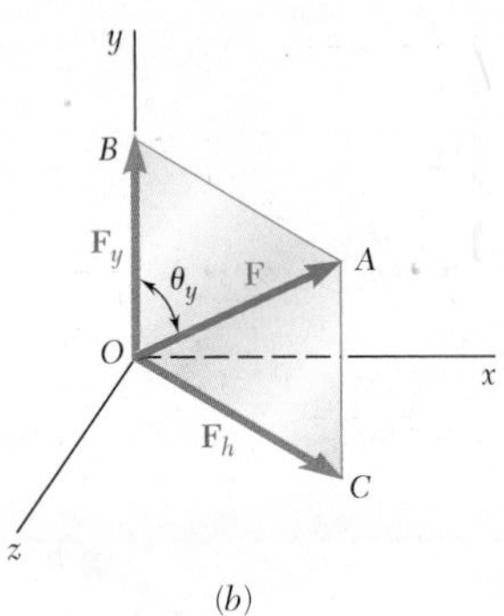

(b)

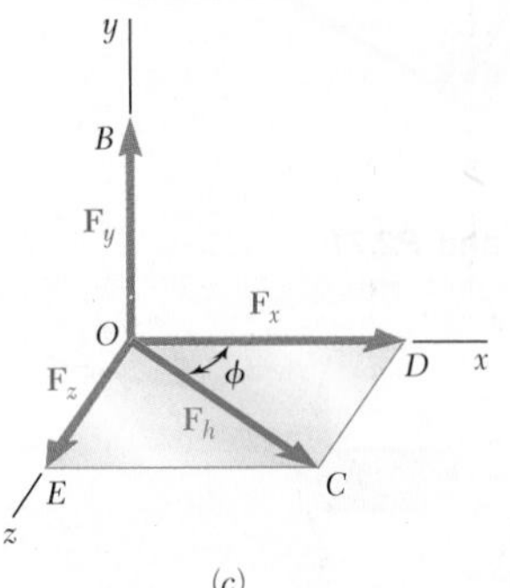

(c)

Fig. 2.30

vertical plane $OBAC$ containing $\mathbf{F}$ (Fig. 2.30*a*). This plane passes through the vertical y axis; its orientation is defined by the angle ϕ it forms with the xy plane. The direction of $\mathbf{F}$ within the plane is defined by the angle θ_y that $\mathbf{F}$ forms with the y axis. The force $\mathbf{F}$ may be resolved into a vertical component $\mathbf{F}_y$ and a horizontal component $\mathbf{F}_h$; this operation, shown in Fig. 2.30*b*, is carried out in plane $OBAC$ according to the rules developed in the first part of the chapter. The corresponding scalar components are

$$F_y = F \cos \theta_y \qquad F_h = F \sin \theta_y \tag{2.16}$$

But $\mathbf{F}_h$ may be resolved into two rectangular components $\mathbf{F}_x$ and $\mathbf{F}_z$ along the x and z axes, respectively. This operation, shown in Fig. 2.30*c*, is carried out in the xz plane. We obtain the following expressions for the corresponding scalar components:

$$\begin{aligned} F_x &= F_h \cos \phi = F \sin \theta_y \cos \phi \\ F_z &= F_h \sin \phi = F \sin \theta_y \sin \phi \end{aligned} \tag{2.17}$$

The given force $\mathbf{F}$ has thus been resolved into three rectangular vector components $\mathbf{F}_x$, $\mathbf{F}_y$, and $\mathbf{F}_z$, which are directed along the three coordinate axes.

Applying the Pythagorean theorem to the triangles OAB and OCD of Fig. 2.30, we write

$$\begin{aligned} F^2 &= (OA)^2 = (OB)^2 + (BA)^2 = F_y^2 + F_h^2 \\ F_h^2 &= (OC)^2 = (OD)^2 + (DC)^2 = F_x^2 + F_z^2 \end{aligned}$$

Eliminating F_h^2 from these two equations and solving for F, we obtain the following relation between the magnitude of $\mathbf{F}$ and its rectangular scalar components:

$$F = \sqrt{F_x^2 + F_y^2 + F_z^2} \tag{2.18}$$

The relationship existing between the force $\mathbf{F}$ and its three components $\mathbf{F}_x$, $\mathbf{F}_y$, and $\mathbf{F}_z$ is more easily visualized if a "box" having $\mathbf{F}_x$, $\mathbf{F}_y$, and $\mathbf{F}_z$ for edges is drawn as shown in Fig. 2.31. The force $\mathbf{F}$ is then represented by the diagonal OA of this box. Figure 2.31*b* shows the right triangle OAB used to derive the first of the formulas (2.16): $F_y = F \cos \theta_y$. In Fig. 2.31*a* and *c*, two other right triangles have also been drawn: OAD and OAE. These triangles are seen to occupy in the box positions comparable with that of triangle OAB. Denoting by θ_x and θ_z, respectively, the angles that $\mathbf{F}$ forms with the x and z axes, we can derive two formulas similar to $F_y = F \cos \theta_y$. We thus write

$$F_x = F \cos \theta_x \qquad F_y = F \cos \theta_y \qquad F_z = F \cos \theta_z \tag{2.19}$$

The three angles θ_x, θ_y, and θ_z define the direction of the force $\mathbf{F}$; they are more commonly used for this purpose than the angles θ_y and ϕ introduced at the beginning of this section. The cosines of θ_x, θ_y, and θ_z are known as the *direction cosines* of the force $\mathbf{F}$.

Introducing the unit vectors $\mathbf{i}$, $\mathbf{j}$, and $\mathbf{k}$, directed respectively along the x, y, and z axes (Fig. 2.32), we can express $\mathbf{F}$ in the form

$$\mathbf{F} = F_x\mathbf{i} + F_y\mathbf{j} + F_z\mathbf{k} \tag{2.20}$$

where the scalar components F_x, F_y, F_z are defined by the relations (2.19).

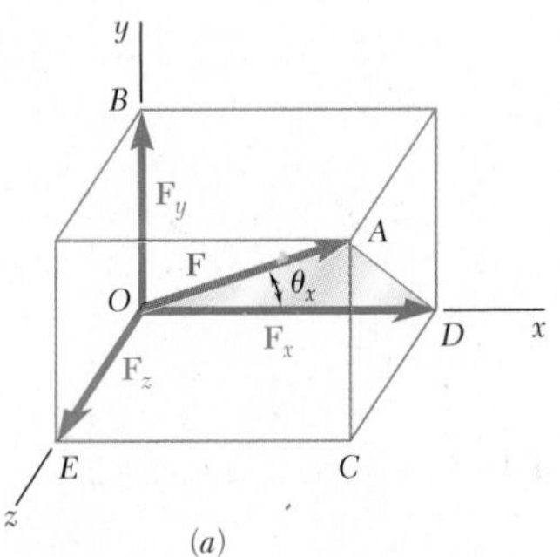

(a)

Fig. 2.31

Example 1. A force of 500 N forms angles of 60°, 45°, and 120°, respectively, with the x, y, and z axes. Find the components F_x, F_y, and F_z of the force.

Substituting $F = 500$ N, $\theta_x = 60°$, $\theta_y = 45°$, $\theta_z = 120°$ into formulas (2.19), we write

$$F_x = (500 \text{ N}) \cos 60° = +250 \text{ N}$$
$$F_y = (500 \text{ N}) \cos 45° = +354 \text{ N}$$
$$F_z = (500 \text{ N}) \cos 120° = -250 \text{ N}$$

Carrying into Eq. (2.20) the values obtained for the scalar components of **F**, we have

$$\mathbf{F} = (250 \text{ N})\mathbf{i} + (354 \text{ N})\mathbf{j} - (250 \text{ N})\mathbf{k}$$

As in the case of two-dimensional problems, a plus sign indicates that the component has the same sense as the corresponding axis, and a minus sign indicates that it has the opposite sense.

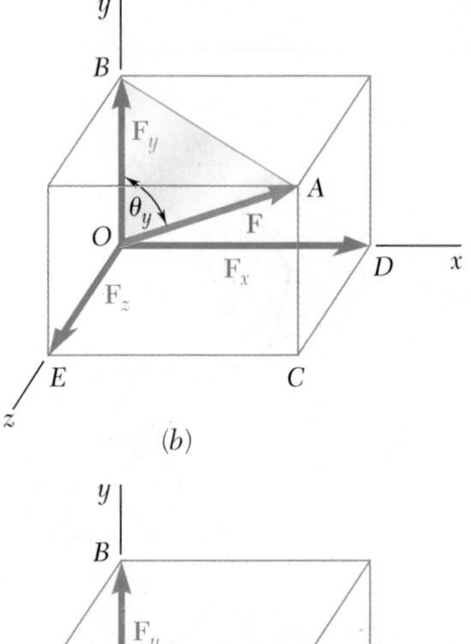

The angle a force **F** forms with an axis should be measured from the positive side of the axis and will always be between 0 and 180°. An angle θ_x smaller than 90° (acute) indicates that **F** (assumed attached to O) is on the same side of the yz plane as the positive x axis; $\cos \theta_x$ and F_x will then be positive. An angle θ_x larger than 90° (obtuse) indicates that **F** is on the other side of the yz plane; $\cos \theta_x$ and F_x will then be negative. In Example 1 the angles θ_x and θ_y are acute, while θ_z is obtuse; consequently, F_x and F_y are positive, while F_z is negative.

Substituting into (2.20) the expressions obtained for F_x, F_y, and F_z in (2.19), we write

$$\mathbf{F} = F(\cos \theta_x \mathbf{i} + \cos \theta_y \mathbf{j} + \cos \theta_z \mathbf{k}) \qquad (2.21)$$

which shows that the force **F** can be expressed as the product of the scalar F and the vector

$$\boldsymbol{\lambda} = \cos \theta_x \mathbf{i} + \cos \theta_y \mathbf{j} + \cos \theta_z \mathbf{k} \qquad (2.22)$$

Clearly, the vector $\boldsymbol{\lambda}$ is a vector whose magnitude is equal to 1 and whose direction is the same as that of **F** (Fig. 2.33). The vector $\boldsymbol{\lambda}$ is referred to as the *unit vector* along the line of action of **F**. It follows from (2.22) that the components of the unit vector $\boldsymbol{\lambda}$ are respectively equal to the direction cosines of the line of action of **F**:

$$\lambda_x = \cos \theta_x \qquad \lambda_y = \cos \theta_y \qquad \lambda_z = \cos \theta_z \qquad (2.23)$$

We should observe that the values of the three angles θ_x, θ_y, and θ_z are not independent. Recalling that the sum of the squares of the components of a vector is equal to the square of its magnitude, we write

$$\lambda_x^2 + \lambda_y^2 + \lambda_z^2 = 1$$

or, substituting for λ_x, λ_y, and λ_z from (2.23),

$$\cos^2 \theta_x + \cos^2 \theta_y + \cos^2 \theta_z = 1 \qquad (2.24)$$

In Example 1, for instance, once the values $\theta_x = 60°$ and $\theta_y = 45°$ have been selected, the value of θ_z *must* be equal to 60° or 120° in order to satisfy identity (2.24).

When the components F_x, F_y, and F_z of a force **F** are given, the magnitude F of the force is obtained from (2.18). The relations (2.19) can then be solved for the direction cosines,

$$\cos \theta_x = \frac{F_x}{F} \qquad \cos \theta_y = \frac{F_y}{F} \qquad \cos \theta_z = \frac{F_z}{F} \qquad (2.25)$$

and the angles θ_x, θ_y, θ_z characterizing the direction of **F** can be found.

Fig. 2.31

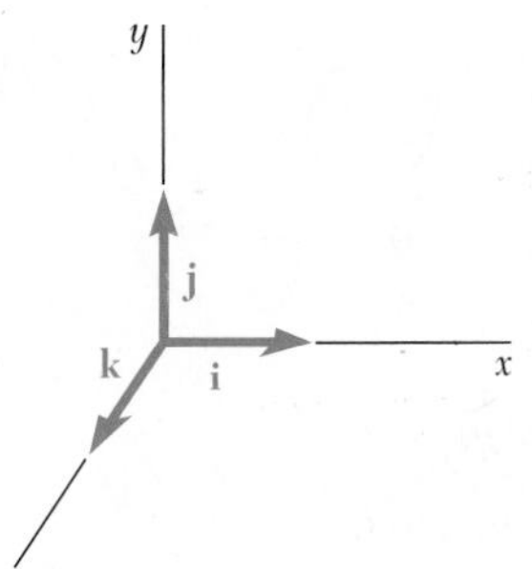

Fig. 2.32

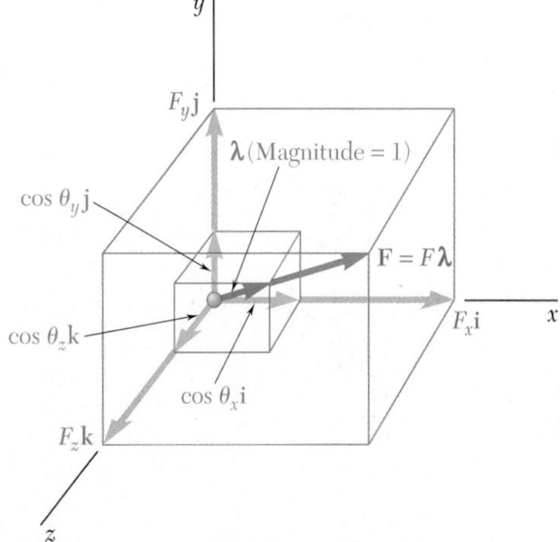

Fig. 2.33

Example 2. A force **F** has the components $F_x = 20$ N, $F_y = -30$ N, $F_z = 60$ N. Determine its magnitude F and the angles θ_x, θ_y, and θ_z it forms with the coordinate axes.

From formula (2.18) we obtain†

$$\begin{aligned} F &= \sqrt{F_x^2 + F_y^2 + F_z^2} \\ &= \sqrt{(20 \text{ N})^2 + (-30 \text{ N})^2 + (60 \text{ N})^2} \\ &= \sqrt{4900} \text{ N} = 70 \text{ N} \end{aligned}$$

Substituting the values of the components and magnitude of **F** into Eqs. (2.25), we write

$$\cos\theta_x = \frac{F_x}{F} = \frac{20 \text{ N}}{70 \text{ N}} \qquad \cos\theta_y = \frac{F_y}{F} = \frac{-30 \text{ N}}{70 \text{ N}} \qquad \cos\theta_z = \frac{F_z}{F} = \frac{60 \text{ N}}{70 \text{ N}}$$

Calculating successively each quotient and its arc cosine, we obtain

$$\theta_x = 73.4° \qquad \theta_y = 115.4° \qquad \theta_z = 31.0°$$

These computations can be carried out easily with a calculator.

2.13. FORCE DEFINED BY ITS MAGNITUDE AND TWO POINTS ON ITS LINE OF ACTION

In many applications, the direction of a force **F** is defined by the coordinates of two points, $M(x_1, y_1, z_1)$ and $N(x_2, y_2, z_2)$, located on its line of action (Fig. 2.34). Consider the vector $\overrightarrow{MN}$ joining M and N

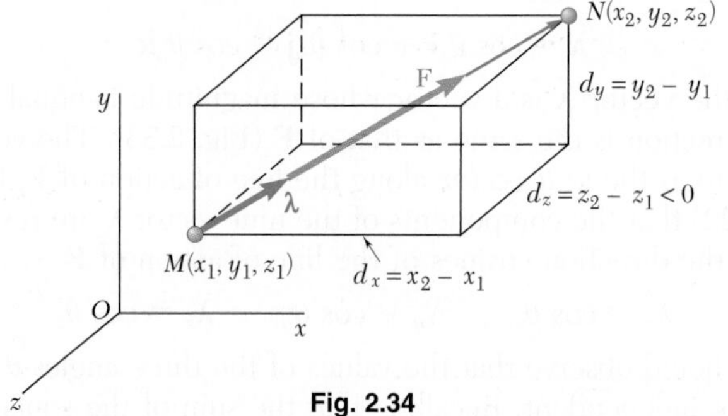

Fig. 2.34

and of the same sense as **F**. Denoting its scalar components by d_x, d_y, and d_z, respectively, we write

$$\overrightarrow{MN} = d_x\mathbf{i} + d_y\mathbf{j} + d_z\mathbf{k} \tag{2.26}$$

The unit vector $\boldsymbol{\lambda}$ along the line of action of **F** (i.e., along the line MN) can be obtained by dividing the vector $\overrightarrow{MN}$ by its magnitude MN. Substituting for $\overrightarrow{MN}$ from (2.26) and observing that MN is equal to the distance d from M to N, we write

$$\boldsymbol{\lambda} = \frac{\overrightarrow{MN}}{MN} = \frac{1}{d}(d_x\mathbf{i} + d_y\mathbf{j} + d_z\mathbf{k}) \tag{2.27}$$

†With a calculator programmed to convert rectangular coordinates into polar coordinates, the following procedure will be found more expeditious for computing F: First determine F_h from its two rectangular components F_x and F_z (Fig. 2.30c), then determine F from its two rectangular components F_h and F_y (Fig. 2.30b). The actual order in which the three components F_x, F_y, and F_z are entered is immaterial.

Recalling that **F** is equal to the product of F and λ, we have

$$\mathbf{F} = F\boldsymbol{\lambda} = \frac{F}{d}(d_x\mathbf{i} + d_y\mathbf{j} + d_z\mathbf{k}) \tag{2.28}$$

from which it follows that the scalar components of **F** are, respectively,

$$F_x = \frac{Fd_x}{d} \qquad F_y = \frac{Fd_y}{d} \qquad F_z = \frac{Fd_z}{d} \tag{2.29}$$

The relations (2.29) considerably simplify the determination of the components of a force **F** of given magnitude F when the line of action of **F** is defined by two points M and N. Subtracting the coordinates of M from those of N, we first determine the components of the vector $\overrightarrow{MN}$ and the distance d from M to N:

$$d_x = x_2 - x_1 \qquad d_y = y_2 - y_1 \qquad d_z = z_2 - z_1$$

$$d = \sqrt{d_x^2 + d_y^2 + d_z^2}$$

Substituting for F and for d_x, d_y, d_z, and d into the relations (2.29), we obtain the components F_x, F_y, and F_z of the force.

The angles θ_x, θ_y, and θ_z that **F** forms with the coordinate axes can then be obtained from Eqs. (2.25). Comparing Eqs. (2.22) and (2.27), we can also write

$$\cos\theta_x = \frac{d_x}{d} \qquad \cos\theta_y = \frac{d_y}{d} \qquad \cos\theta_z = \frac{d_z}{d} \tag{2.30}$$

and determine the angles θ_x, θ_y, and θ_z directly from the components and magnitude of the vector $\overrightarrow{MN}$.

2.14. ADDITION OF CONCURRENT FORCES IN SPACE

The resultant **R** of two or more forces in space will be determined by summing their rectangular components. Graphical or trigonometric methods are generally not practical in the case of forces in space.

The method followed here is similar to that used in Sec. 2.8 with coplanar forces. Setting

$$\mathbf{R} = \Sigma\mathbf{F}$$

we resolve each force into its rectangular components and write

$$\begin{aligned} R_x\mathbf{i} + R_y\mathbf{j} + R_z\mathbf{k} &= \Sigma(F_x\mathbf{i} + F_y\mathbf{j} + F_z\mathbf{k}) \\ &= (\Sigma F_x)\mathbf{i} + (\Sigma F_y)\mathbf{j} + (\Sigma F_z)\mathbf{k} \end{aligned}$$

from which it follows that

$$R_x = \Sigma F_x \qquad R_y = \Sigma F_y \qquad R_z = \Sigma F_z \tag{2.31}$$

The magnitude of the resultant and the angles θ_x, θ_y, and θ_z that the resultant forms with the coordinate axes are obtained using the method discussed in Sec. 2.12. We write

$$R = \sqrt{R_x^2 + R_y^2 + R_z^2} \tag{2.32}$$

$$\cos\theta_x = \frac{R_x}{R} \qquad \cos\theta_y = \frac{R_y}{R} \qquad \cos\theta_z = \frac{R_z}{R} \tag{2.33}$$

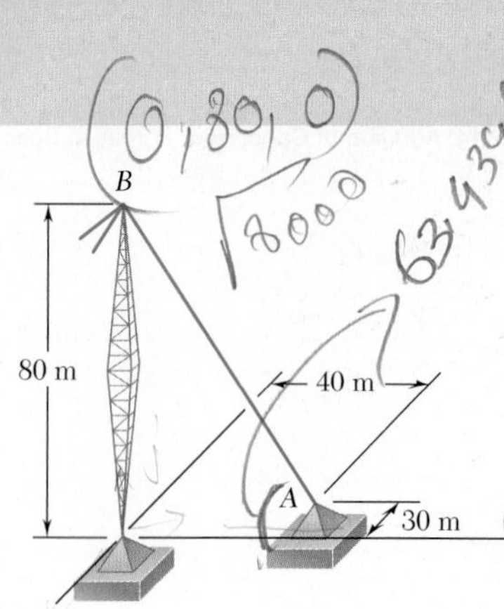

SAMPLE PROBLEM 2.7

A tower guy wire is anchored by means of a bolt at A. The tension in the wire is 2500 N. Determine (*a*) the components F_x, F_y, and F_z of the force acting on the bolt, (*b*) the angles θ_x, θ_y, and θ_z defining the direction of the force.

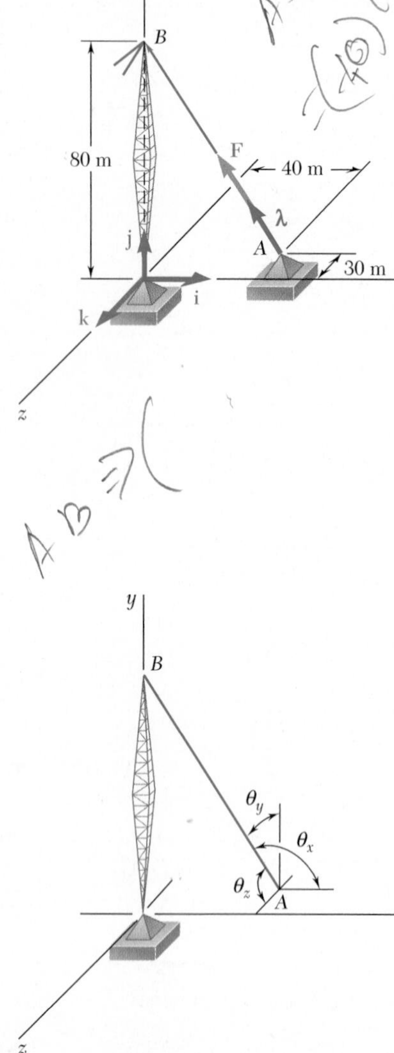

SOLUTION

***a.* Components of the Force.** The line of action of the force acting on the bolt passes through A and B, and the force is directed from A to B. The components of the vector $\overrightarrow{AB}$, which has the same direction as the force, are

$$d_x = -40 \text{ m} \qquad d_y = +80 \text{ m} \qquad d_z = +30 \text{ m}$$

The total distance from A to B is

$$AB = d = \sqrt{d_x^2 + d_y^2 + d_z^2} = 94.3 \text{ m}$$

Denoting by **i**, **j**, and **k** the unit vectors along the coordinate axes, we have

$$\overrightarrow{AB} = -(40 \text{ m})\mathbf{i} + (80 \text{ m})\mathbf{j} + (30 \text{ m})\mathbf{k}$$

Introducing the unit vector $\boldsymbol{\lambda} = \overrightarrow{AB}/AB$, we write

$$\mathbf{F} = F\boldsymbol{\lambda} = F\frac{\overrightarrow{AB}}{AB} = \frac{2500 \text{ N}}{94.3 \text{ m}}\overrightarrow{AB}$$

Substituting the expression found for $\overrightarrow{AB}$, we obtain

$$\mathbf{F} = \frac{2500 \text{ N}}{94.3 \text{ m}}[-(40 \text{ m})\mathbf{i} + (80 \text{ m})\mathbf{j} + (30 \text{ m})\mathbf{k}]$$

$$\mathbf{F} = -(1060 \text{ N})\mathbf{i} + (2120 \text{ N})\mathbf{j} + (795 \text{ N})\mathbf{k}$$

The components of **F**, therefore, are

$$F_x = -1060 \text{ N} \qquad F_y = +2120 \text{ N} \qquad F_z = +795 \text{ N} \blacktriangleleft$$

***b.* Direction of the Force.** Using Eqs. (2.25), we write

$$\cos\theta_x = \frac{F_x}{F} = \frac{-1060 \text{ N}}{2500 \text{ N}} \qquad \cos\theta_y = \frac{F_y}{F} = \frac{+2120 \text{ N}}{2500 \text{ N}}$$

$$\cos\theta_z = \frac{F_z}{F} = \frac{+795 \text{ N}}{2500 \text{ N}}$$

Calculating successively each quotient and its arc cosine, we obtain

$$\theta_x = 115.1° \qquad \theta_y = 32.0° \qquad \theta_z = 71.5° \blacktriangleleft$$

(*Note:* This result could have been obtained by using the components and magnitude of the vector $\overrightarrow{AB}$ rather than those of the force **F**.)

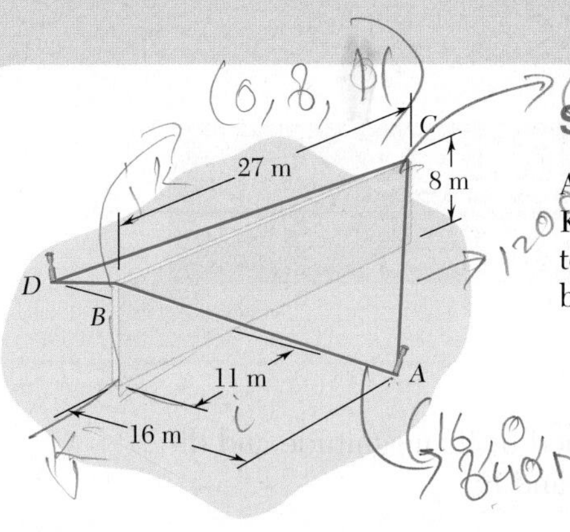

SAMPLE PROBLEM 2.8

A wall section of precast concrete is temporarily held by the cables shown. Knowing that the tension is 840 N in cable *AB* and 1200 N in cable *AC*, determine the magnitude and direction of the resultant of the forces exerted by cables *AB* and *AC* on stake *A*.

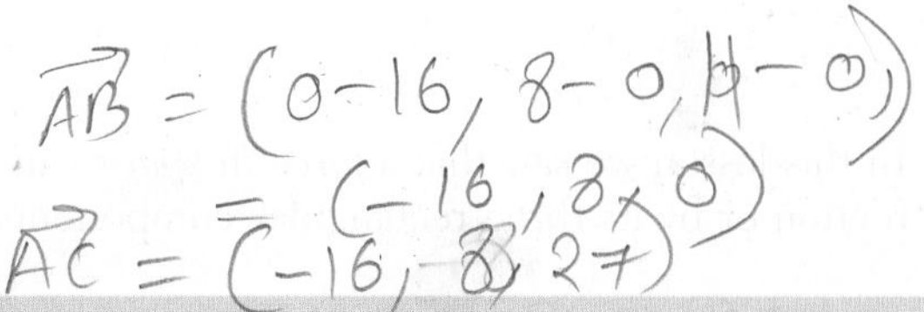

SOLUTION

Components of the Forces. The force exerted by each cable on stake *A* will be resolved into *x*, *y*, and *z* components. We first determine the components and magnitude of the vectors $\overrightarrow{AB}$ and $\overrightarrow{AC}$, measuring them from *A* toward the wall section. Denoting by **i**, **j**, and **k** the unit vectors along the coordinate axes, we write

$$\overrightarrow{AB} = -(16 \text{ m})\mathbf{i} + (8 \text{ m})\mathbf{j} + (11 \text{ m})\mathbf{k} \qquad AB = 21 \text{ m}$$
$$\overrightarrow{AC} = -(16 \text{ m})\mathbf{i} + (8 \text{ m})\mathbf{j} - (16 \text{ m})\mathbf{k} \qquad AC = 24 \text{ m}$$

Denoting by $\boldsymbol{\lambda}_{AB}$ the unit vector along *AB*, we have

$$\mathbf{T}_{AB} = T_{AB}\boldsymbol{\lambda}_{AB} = T_{AB}\frac{\overrightarrow{AB}}{AB} = \frac{840 \text{ N}}{21 \text{ m}}\overrightarrow{AB}$$

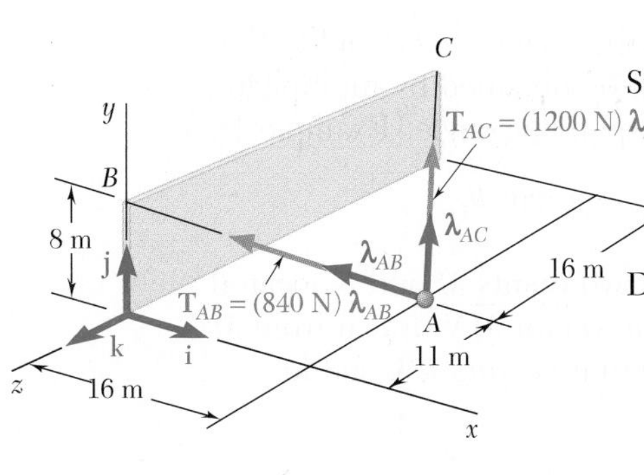

Substituting the expression found for $\overrightarrow{AB}$, we obtain

$$\mathbf{T}_{AB} = \frac{840 \text{ N}}{21 \text{ m}}[-(16 \text{ m})\mathbf{i} + (8 \text{ m})\mathbf{j} + (11 \text{ m})\mathbf{k}]$$
$$\mathbf{T}_{AB} = -(640 \text{ N})\mathbf{i} + (320 \text{ N})\mathbf{j} + (440 \text{ N})\mathbf{k}$$

Denoting by $\boldsymbol{\lambda}_{AC}$ the unit vector along *AC*, we obtain in a similar way

$$\mathbf{T}_{AC} = T_{AC}\boldsymbol{\lambda}_{AC} = T_{AC}\frac{\overrightarrow{AC}}{AC} = \frac{1200 \text{ N}}{24 \text{ m}}\overrightarrow{AC}$$
$$\mathbf{T}_{AC} = -(800 \text{ N})\mathbf{i} + (400 \text{ N})\mathbf{j} - (800 \text{ N})\mathbf{k}$$

Resultant of the Forces. The resultant **R** of the forces exerted by the two cables is

$$\mathbf{R} = \mathbf{T}_{AB} + \mathbf{T}_{AC} = -(1440 \text{ N})\mathbf{i} + (720 \text{ N})\mathbf{j} - (360 \text{ N})\mathbf{k}$$

The magnitude and direction of the resultant are now determined:

$$R = \sqrt{R_x^2 + R_y^2 + R_z^2} = \sqrt{(-1440)^2 + (720)^2 + (-360)^2}$$

$R = 1650 \text{ N}$ ◀

From Eqs. (2.33) we obtain

$$\cos\theta_x = \frac{R_x}{R} = \frac{-1440 \text{ N}}{1650 \text{ N}} \qquad \cos\theta_y = \frac{R_y}{R} = \frac{+720 \text{ N}}{1650 \text{ N}}$$
$$\cos\theta_z = \frac{R_z}{R} = \frac{-360 \text{ N}}{1650 \text{ N}}$$

Calculating successively each quotient and its arc cosine, we have

$\theta_x = 150.8°$ $\quad\theta_y = 64.1°$ $\quad\theta_z = 102.6°$ ◀

SOLVING PROBLEMS ON YOUR OWN

In this lesson we saw that a *force in space* can be defined by its magnitude and direction or by its three rectangular components F_x, F_y, and F_z.

A. ***When a force is defined by its magnitude and direction,*** its rectangular components F_x, F_y, and F_z can be found as follows:

Case 1. If the direction of the force $\mathbf{F}$ is defined by the angles θ_y and ϕ shown in Fig. 2.30, projections of $\mathbf{F}$ through these angles or their complements will yield the components of $\mathbf{F}$ [Eqs. (2.17)]. Note that the x and z components of $\mathbf{F}$ are found by first projecting $\mathbf{F}$ onto the horizontal plane; the projection $\mathbf{F}_h$ obtained in this way is then resolved into the components $\mathbf{F}_x$ and $\mathbf{F}_z$ (Fig. 2.30*c*).

When solving problems of this type, we strongly encourage you first to sketch the force $\mathbf{F}$ and then its projection $\mathbf{F}_h$ and components F_x, F_y, and F_z before beginning the mathematical part of the solution.

Case 2. If the direction of the force $\mathbf{F}$ is defined by the angles θ_x, θ_y, and θ_z that $\mathbf{F}$ forms with the coordinate axes, each component can be obtained by multiplying the magnitude F of the force by the cosine of the corresponding angle [Example 1]:

$$F_x = F\cos\theta_x \qquad F_y = F\cos\theta_y \qquad F_z = F\cos\theta_z$$

Case 3. If the direction of the force $\mathbf{F}$ is defined by two points M and N located on its line of action (Fig. 2.34), you will first express the vector $\overrightarrow{MN}$ drawn from M to N in terms of its components d_x, d_y, and d_z and the unit vectors $\mathbf{i}$, $\mathbf{j}$, and $\mathbf{k}$:

$$\overrightarrow{MN} = d_x\mathbf{i} + d_y\mathbf{j} + d_z\mathbf{k}$$

Next, you will determine the unit vector $\boldsymbol{\lambda}$ along the line of action of $\mathbf{F}$ by dividing the vector $\overrightarrow{MN}$ by its magnitude MN. Multiplying $\boldsymbol{\lambda}$ by the magnitude of $\mathbf{F}$, you will obtain the desired expression for $\mathbf{F}$ in terms of its rectangular components [Sample Prob. 2.7]:

$$\mathbf{F} = F\boldsymbol{\lambda} = \frac{F}{d}(d_x\mathbf{i} + d_y\mathbf{j} + d_z\mathbf{k})$$

It is advantageous to use a consistent and meaningful system of notation when determining the rectangular components of a force. The method used in this text is illustrated in Sample Prob. 2.8 where, for example, the force $\mathbf{T}_{AB}$ acts from stake A toward point B. Note that the subscripts have been ordered to agree with the direction of the force. It is recommended that you adopt the same notation, as it will help you identify point 1 (the first subscript) and point 2 (the second subscript).

When forming the vector defining the line of action of a force, you may think of its scalar components as the number of steps you must take in each coordinate direction to go from point 1 to point 2. It is essential that you always remember to assign the correct sign to each of the components.

B. ***When a force is defined by its rectangular components F_x, F_y, and F_z,*** you can obtain its magnitude F by writing

$$F = \sqrt{F_x^2 + F_y^2 + F_z^2}$$

You can determine the direction cosines of the line of action of **F** by dividing the components of the force by F:

$$\cos \theta_x = \frac{F_x}{F} \qquad \cos \theta_y = \frac{F_y}{F} \qquad \cos \theta_z = \frac{F_z}{F}$$

From the direction cosines you can obtain the angles θ_x, θ_y, and θ_z that **F** forms with the coordinate axes [Example 2].

C. ***To determine the resultant* R *of two or more forces*** in three-dimensional space, first determine the rectangular components of each force by one of the procedures described above. Adding these components will yield the components R_x, R_y, and R_z of the resultant. The magnitude and direction of the resultant can then be obtained as indicated above for the force **F** [Sample Prob. 2.8].

Problems

Fig. P2.73 and *P2.74*

2.73 To stabilize a tree partially uprooted in a storm, cables *AB* and *AC* are attached to the upper trunk of the tree and then are fastened to steel rods anchored in the ground. Knowing that the tension in cable *AB* is 950 N, determine (*a*) the components of the force exerted by this cable on the tree, (*b*) the angles θ_x, θ_y, and θ_z that the force forms with axes at *A* which are parallel to the coordinate axes.

2.74 To stabilize a tree partially uprooted in a storm, cables *AB* and *AC* are attached to the upper trunk of the tree and then are fastened to steel rods anchored in the ground. Knowing that the tension in cable *AC* is 810 N, determine (*a*) the components of the force exerted by this cable on the tree, (*b*) the angles θ_x, θ_y, and θ_z that the force forms with axes at *A* which are parallel to the coordinate axes.

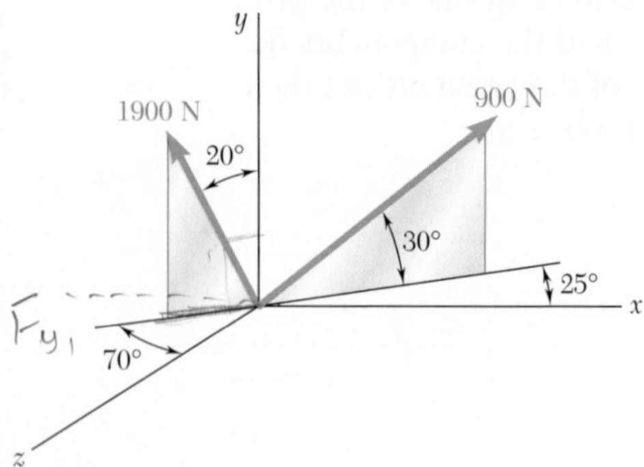

Fig. P2.75 and P2.76

2.75 Determine (*a*) the *x*, *y*, and *z* components of the 900-N force, (*b*) the angles θ_x, θ_y, and θ_z that the force forms with the coordinate axes.

2.76 Determine (*a*) the *x*, *y*, and *z* components of the 1900-N force, (*b*) the angles θ_x, θ_y, and θ_z that the force forms with the coordinate axes.

2.77 A gun is aimed at a point *A* located 20° west of north. Knowing that the barrel of the gun forms an angle of 35° with the horizontal and that the maximum recoil force is 180 N, determine (*a*) the *x*, *y*, and *z* components of that force, (*b*) the values of the angles θ_x, θ_y, and θ_z that define the direction of the recoil force. (Assume that the *x*, *y*, and *z* axes are directed, respectively, east, up, and south.)

2.78 Solve Prob. 2.77 assuming that point *A* is located 25° north of west and that the barrel of the gun forms an angle of 30° with the horizontal.

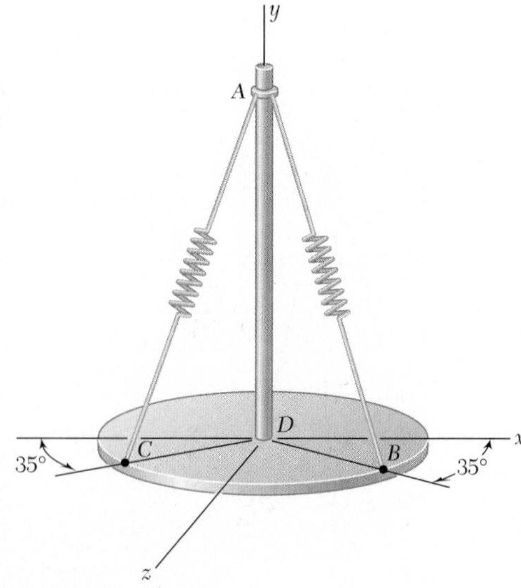

Fig. P2.79 and P2.80

2.79 The angle between the spring *AB* and the post *DA* is 30°. Knowing that the tension in the spring is 220 N, determine (*a*) the *x*, *y*, and *z* components of the force exerted by this spring on the plate, (*b*) the angles θ_x, θ_y, and θ_z that the force forms with the coordinate axes.

2.80 The angle between the spring *AC* and the post *DA* is 30°. Knowing that the *x* component of the force exerted by spring *AC* on the plate is 180 N, determine (*a*) the tension in spring *AC*, (*b*) the angles θ_x, θ_y, and θ_z that the force exerted at *C* forms with the coordinate axes.

2.81 Determine the magnitude and direction of the force $\mathbf{F} = (65\text{ N})\mathbf{i} - (80\text{ N})\mathbf{j} - (200\text{ N})\mathbf{k}$.

2.82 Determine the magnitude and direction of the force $\mathbf{F} = (450\text{ N})\mathbf{i} + (600\text{ N})\mathbf{j} - (1800\text{ N})\mathbf{k}$.

2.83 A force acts at the origin of a coordinate system in a direction defined by the angles $\theta_x = 43.2°$ and $\theta_z = 83.8°$. Knowing that the y component of the force is -50 N, determine (a) the angle θ_y, (b) the other components and the magnitude of the force.

2.84 A force acts at the origin of a coordinate system in a direction defined by the angles $\theta_x = 113.2°$ and $\theta_y = 78.4°$. Knowing that the z component of the force is -35 N, determine (a) the angle θ_z, (b) the other components and the magnitude of the force.

2.85 A force **F** of magnitude 250 N acts at the origin of a coordinate system. Knowing that $F_x = 80$ N, $\theta_y = 72.4°$, and $F_z > 0$, determine (a) the components F_y and F_z, (b) the angles θ_x and θ_z.

2.86 A force **F** of magnitude 320 N acts at the origin of a coordinate system. Knowing that $\theta_x = 104.5°$, $F_z = -120$ N, and $F_y < 0$, determine (a) the components F_x and F_y, (b) the angles θ_y and θ_z.

2.87 A steel rod is bent into a semicircular ring of radius 36 cm and is supported in part by cables BD and BE which are attached to the ring at B. Knowing that the tension in cable BD is 55 N, determine the components of the force exerted by the cable on the support at D.

2.88 A steel rod is bent into a semicircular ring of radius 36 cm and is supported in part by cables BD and BE which are attached to the ring at B. Knowing that the tension in cable BE is 60 N, determine the components of the force exerted by the cable on the support at E.

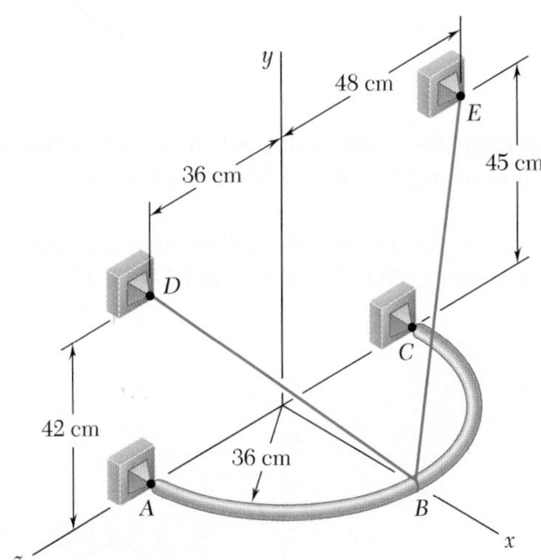

Fig. P2.87 and P2.88

2.89 A transmission tower is held by three guy wires anchored by bolts at B, C, and D. If the tension in wire AB is 2100 N, determine the components of the force exerted by the wire on the bolt at B.

2.90 A transmission tower is held by three guy wires anchored by bolts at B, C, and D. If the tension in wire AD is 1260 N, determine the components of the force exerted by the wire on the bolt at D.

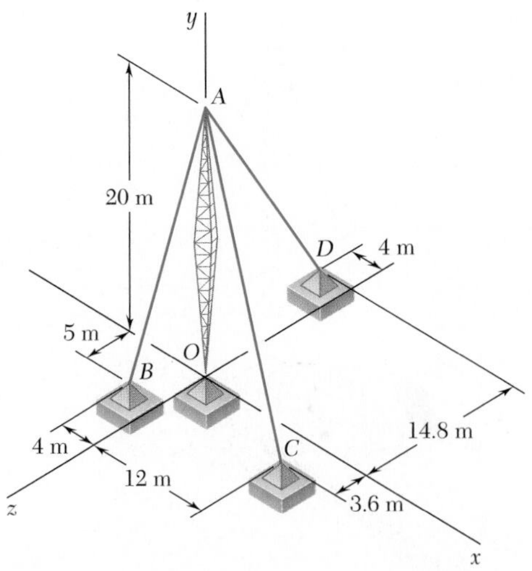

Fig. *P2.89* and P2.90

2.91 Two cables BG and BH are attached to the frame ACD as shown. Knowing that the tension in cable BG is 450 N, determine the components of the force exerted by cable BG on the frame at B.

2.92 Two cables BG and BH are attached to the frame ACD as shown. Knowing that the tension in cable BH is 600 N, determine the components of the force exerted by cable BH on the frame at B.

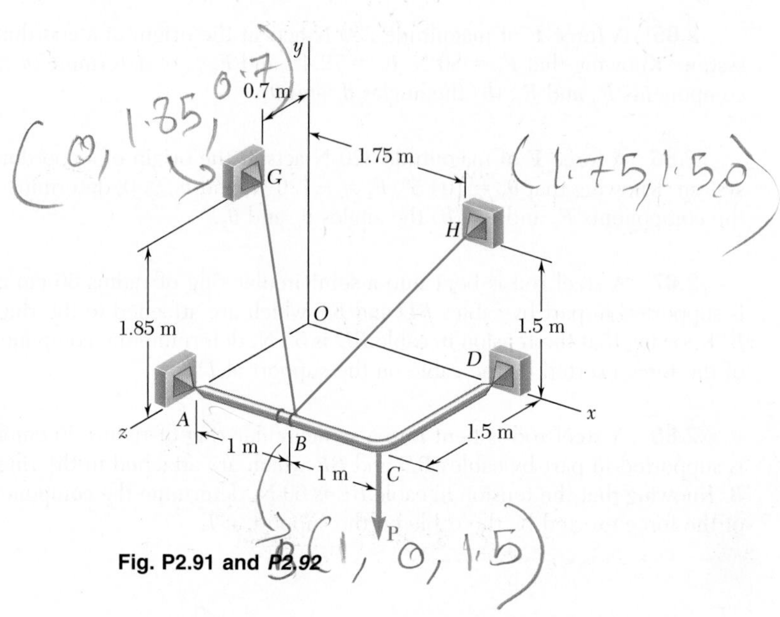

Fig. P2.91 and *P2.92*

2.93 Determine the magnitude and direction of the resultant of the two forces shown knowing that $P = 4$ kN and $Q = 8$ kN.

2.94 Determine the magnitude and direction of the resultant of the two forces shown knowing that $P = 6$ kN and $Q = 7$ kN.

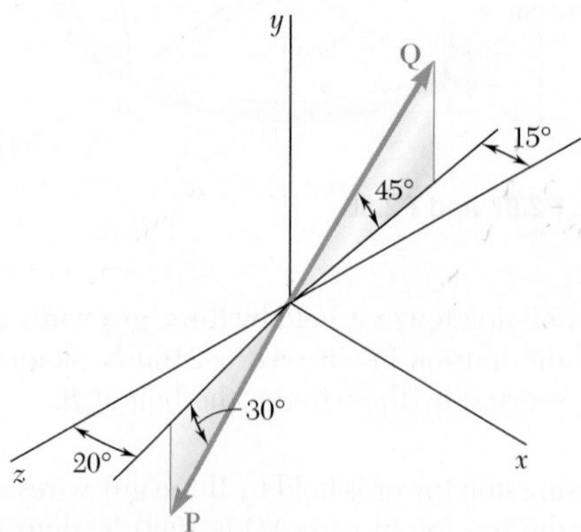

Fig. P2.93 and *P2.94*

2.95 The boom OA carries a load $\mathbf{P}$ and is supported by two cables as shown. Knowing that the tension is 510 N in cable AB and 765 N in cable AC, determine the magnitude and direction of the resultant of the forces exerted at A by the two cables.

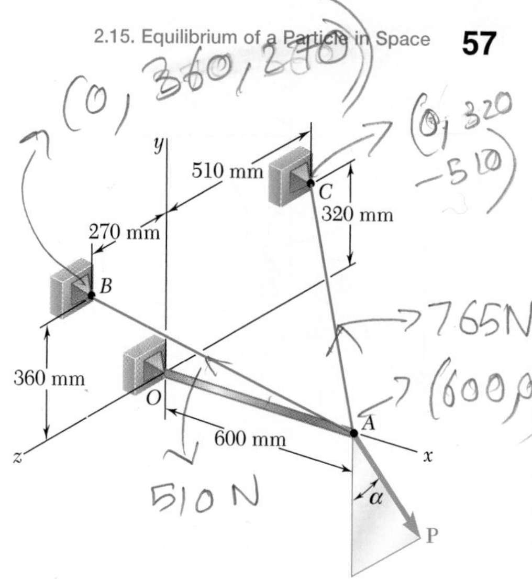

Fig. P2.95

2.96 Assuming that in Prob. 2.95 the tension is 765 N in cable AB and 510 N in cable AC, determine the magnitude and direction of the resultant of the forces exerted at A by the two cables.

2.97 For the tree of Prob. 2.73, knowing that the tension in cable AB is 760 N and that the resultant of the forces exerted at A by cables AB and AC lies in the yz plane, determine (*a*) the tension in AC, (*b*) the magnitude and direction of the resultant of the two forces.

2.98 For the tree of Prob. 2.73, knowing that the tension in cable AC is 980 N and that the resultant of the forces exerted at A by cables AB and AC lies in the yz plane, determine (*a*) the tension in AB, (*b*) the magnitude and direction of the resultant of the two forces.

2.99 For the boom of Prob. 2.95, knowing that $\alpha = 0°$, the tension in cable AB is 600 N, and the resultant of the load $\mathbf{P}$ and the forces exerted at A by the two cables is directed along OA, determine (*a*) the tension in cable AC, (*b*) the magnitude of the load $\mathbf{P}$.

2.100 For the transmission tower of Prob. 2.89, determine the tensions in cables AB and AD knowing that the tension in cable AC is 1770 N and that the resultant of the forces exerted by the three cables at A must be vertical.

2.15. EQUILIBRIUM OF A PARTICLE IN SPACE

According to the definition given in Sec. 2.9, a particle A is in equilibrium if the resultant of all the forces acting on A is zero. The components R_x, R_y, and R_z of the resultant are given by the relations (2.31); expressing that the components of the resultant are zero, we write

$$\Sigma F_x = 0 \qquad \Sigma F_y = 0 \qquad \Sigma F_z = 0 \tag{2.34}$$

Equations (2.34) represent the necessary and sufficient conditions for the equilibrium of a particle in space. They can be used to solve problems dealing with the equilibrium of a particle involving no more than three unknowns.

To solve such problems, you first should draw a free-body diagram showing the particle in equilibrium and *all* the forces acting on it. You can then write the equations of equilibrium (2.34) and solve them for three unknowns. In the more common types of problems, these unknowns will represent (1) the three components of a single force or (2) the magnitude of three forces, each of known direction.

Photo 2.3 While the tension in the *four* cables supporting the shipping container cannot be found using the *three* equations of (2.34), a relation between the tensions can be obtained by considering the equilibrium of the hook.

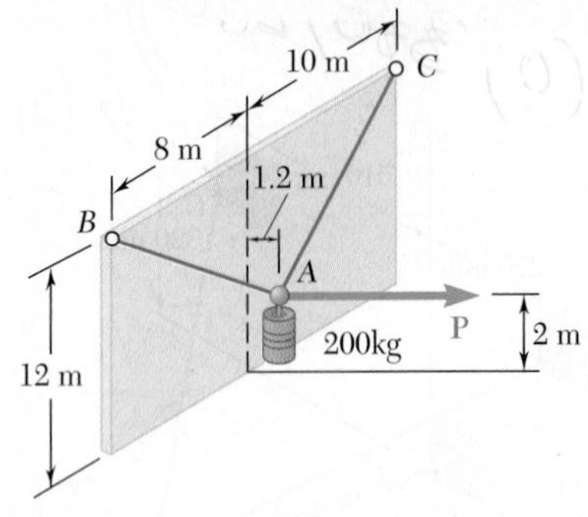

SAMPLE PROBLEM 2.9

A 200-kg cylinder is hung by means of two cables AB and AC, which are attached to the top of a vertical wall. A horizontal force **P** perpendicular to the wall holds the cylinder in the position shown. Determine the magnitude of **P** and the tension in each cable.

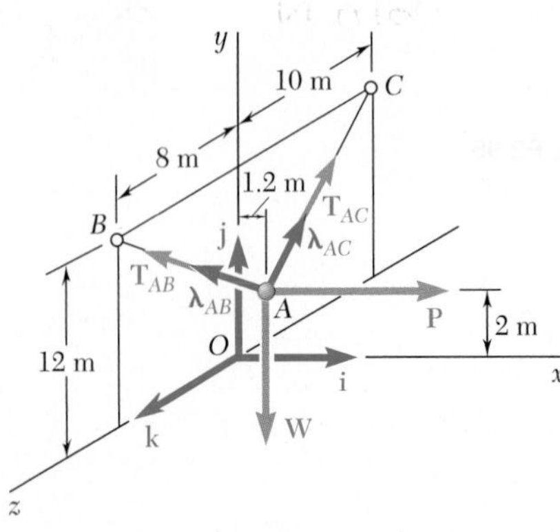

SOLUTION

Free-body Diagram. Point A is chosen as a free body; this point is subjected to four forces, three of which are of unknown magnitude.

Introducing the unit vectors **i**, **j**, and **k**, we resolve each force into rectangular components.

$$\mathbf{P} = P\mathbf{i}$$
$$\mathbf{W} = -mg\mathbf{j} = -(200 \text{ kg})(9.81 \text{ m/s}^2)\mathbf{j} = -(1962 \text{ N})\mathbf{j} \qquad (1)$$

In the case of $\mathbf{T}_{AB}$ and $\mathbf{T}_{AC}$, it is necessary first to determine the components and magnitudes of the vectors $\overrightarrow{AB}$ and $\overrightarrow{AC}$. Denoting by $\boldsymbol{\lambda}_{AB}$ the unit vector along AB, we write

$$\overrightarrow{AB} = -(1.2 \text{ m})\mathbf{i} + (10 \text{ m})\mathbf{j} + (8 \text{ m})\mathbf{k} \qquad AB = 12.862 \text{ m}$$
$$\boldsymbol{\lambda}_{AB} = \frac{\overrightarrow{AB}}{12.862 \text{ m}} = -0.09330\mathbf{i} + 0.7775\mathbf{j} + 0.6220\mathbf{k}$$
$$\mathbf{T}_{AB} = T_{AB}\boldsymbol{\lambda}_{AB} = -0.09330T_{AB}\mathbf{i} + 0.7775T_{AB}\mathbf{j} + 0.6220T_{AB}\mathbf{k} \qquad (2)$$

Denoting by $\boldsymbol{\lambda}_{AC}$ the unit vector along AC, we write in a similar way

$$\overrightarrow{AC} = -(1.2 \text{ m})\mathbf{i} + (10 \text{ m})\mathbf{j} - (10 \text{ m})\mathbf{k} \qquad AC = 14.193 \text{ m}$$
$$\boldsymbol{\lambda}_{AC} = \frac{\overrightarrow{AC}}{14.193 \text{ m}} = -0.08455\mathbf{i} + 0.7046\mathbf{j} - 0.7046\mathbf{k}$$
$$\mathbf{T}_{AC} = T_{AC}\boldsymbol{\lambda}_{AC} = -0.08455T_{AC}\mathbf{i} + 0.7046T_{AC}\mathbf{j} - 0.7046T_{AC}\mathbf{k} \qquad (3)$$

Equilibrium Condition. Since A is in equilibrium, we must have

$$\Sigma\mathbf{F} = 0: \qquad \mathbf{T}_{AB} + \mathbf{T}_{AC} + \mathbf{P} + \mathbf{W} = 0$$

or, substituting from (1), (2), and (3) for the forces and factoring **i**, **j**, and **k**,

$$(-0.09330T_{AB} - 0.08455T_{AC} + P)\mathbf{i} + (0.7775T_{AB} + 0.7046T_{AC} - 1962 \text{ N})\mathbf{j} + (0.6220T_{AB} - 0.7046T_{AC})\mathbf{k} = 0$$

Setting the coefficients of **i**, **j**, and **k** equal to zero, we write three scalar equations, which express that the sums of the x, y, and z components of the forces are respectively equal to zero.

$$\Sigma F_x = 0: \qquad -0.09330T_{AB} - 0.08455T_{AC} + P = 0$$
$$\Sigma F_y = 0: \qquad +0.7775T_{AB} + 0.7046T_{AC} - 1962 \text{ N} = 0$$
$$\Sigma F_z = 0: \qquad +0.6220T_{AB} - 0.7046T_{AC} = 0$$

Solving these equations, we obtain

$P = 235$ N $\quad T_{AB} = 1402$ N $\quad T_{AC} = 1238$ N ◀

SOLVING PROBLEMS ON YOUR OWN

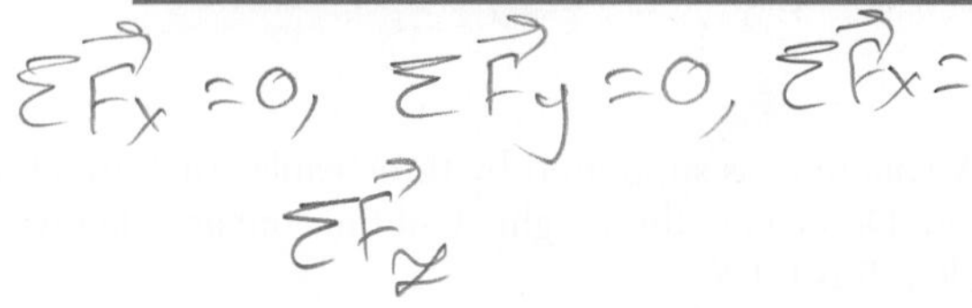

We saw earlier that when a particle is in *equilibrium*, the resultant of the forces acting on the particle must be zero. Expressing this fact in the case of the equilibrium of a *particle in three-dimensional space* will provide you with three relations among the forces acting on the particle. These relations can be used to determine three unknowns—usually the magnitudes of three forces.

Your solution will consist of the following steps:

1. Draw a free-body diagram of the particle. This diagram shows the particle and all the forces acting on it. Indicate on the diagram the magnitudes of known forces, as well as any angles or dimensions that define the direction of a force. Any unknown magnitude or angle should be denoted by an appropriate symbol. Nothing else should be included on your free-body diagram.

2. Resolve each of the forces into rectangular components. Following the method used in the preceding lesson, you will determine for each force **F** the unit vector $\boldsymbol{\lambda}$ defining the direction of that force and express **F** as the product of its magnitude F and the unit vector $\boldsymbol{\lambda}$. When two points on the line of action of **F** are known, you will obtain an expression of the form

$$\mathbf{F} = F\boldsymbol{\lambda} = \frac{F}{d}(d_x\mathbf{i} + d_y\mathbf{j} + d_z\mathbf{k})$$

where d, d_x, d_y, and d_z are dimensions obtained from the free-body diagram of the particle. We also showed the direction of **F** can be defined in terms of the angles θ_y and ϕ. If a force is known in magnitude as well as in direction, then F is known and the expression obtained for **F** is completely defined; otherwise F is one of the three unknowns that should be determined.

3. Set the resultant, or sum, of the forces exerted on the particle equal to zero. You will obtain a vectorial equation consisting of terms containing the unit vectors **i**, **j**, or **k**. You will group the terms containing the same unit vector and factor that vector. For the vectorial equation to be satisfied, the coefficient of each of the unit vectors must be equal to zero. Thus, setting each coefficient equal to zero will yield three scalar equations that you can solve for no more than three unknowns [Sample Prob. 2.9].

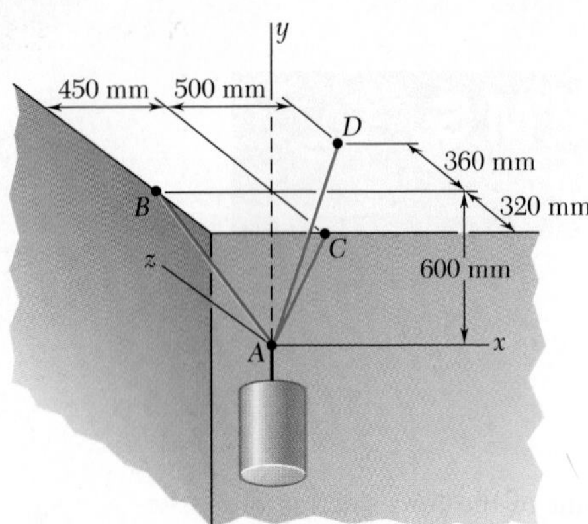

Fig. *P2.101* and P2.102

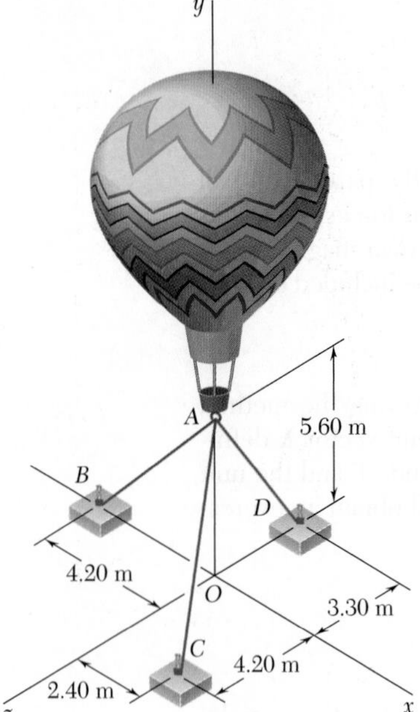

Fig. P2.103 and *P2.104*

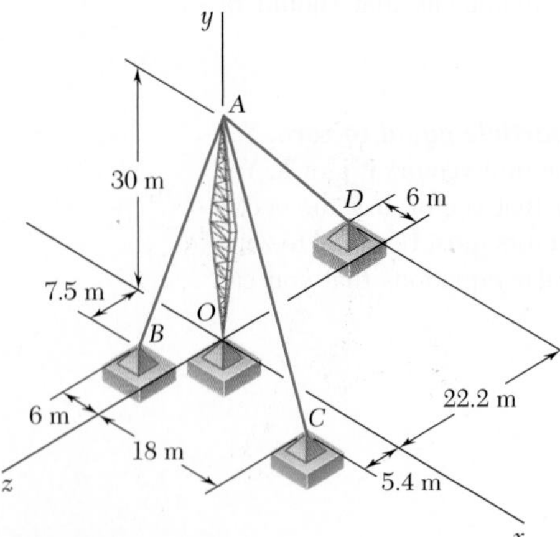

Fig. P2.107 and P2.108

Problems

2.101 A container is supported by three cables that are attached to a ceiling as shown. Determine the weight *W* of the container knowing that the tension in cable *AB* is 6 kN.

2.102 A container is supported by three cables that are attached to a ceiling as shown. Determine the weight *W* of the container knowing that the tension in cable *AD* is 4.3 kN.

2.103 Three cables are used to tether a balloon as shown. Determine the vertical force **P** exerted by the balloon at *A* knowing that the tension in cable *AB* is 259 N.

2.104 Three cables are used to tether a balloon as shown. Determine the vertical force **P** exerted by the balloon at *A* knowing that the tension in cable *AC* is 444 N.

2.105 The support assembly shown is bolted in place at *B*, *C*, and *D* and supports a downward force **P** at *A*. Knowing that the forces in members *AB*, *AC*, and *AD* are directed along the respective members and that the force in member *AB* is 29.2 N, determine the magnitude of **P**.

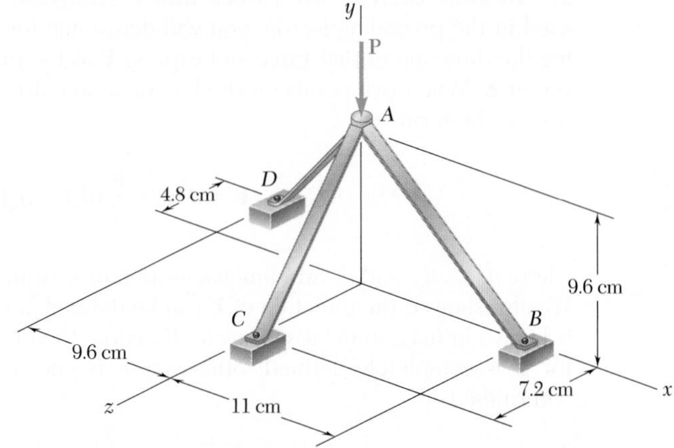

Fig. P2.105 and P2.106

2.106 The support assembly shown is bolted in place at *B*, *C*, and *D* and supports a downward force **P** at *A*. Knowing that the forces in members *AB*, *AC*, and *AD* are directed along the respective members and that $P = 45$ N, determine the forces in the members.

2.107 A transmission tower is held by three guy wires attached to a pin at *A* and anchored by bolts at *B*, *C*, and *D*. If the tension in wire *AB* is 3.6 kN, determine the vertical force **P** exerted by the tower on the pin at *A*.

2.108 A transmission tower is held by three guy wires attached to a pin at *A* and anchored by bolts at *B*, *C*, and *D*. If the tension in wire *AC* is 2.6 kN, determine the vertical force **P** exerted by the tower on the pin at *A*.

2.109 A 320 N load of lumber is lifted using a triple leg sling. Knowing that at the instant shown the lumber is at rest, determine the tension in each leg of the sling.

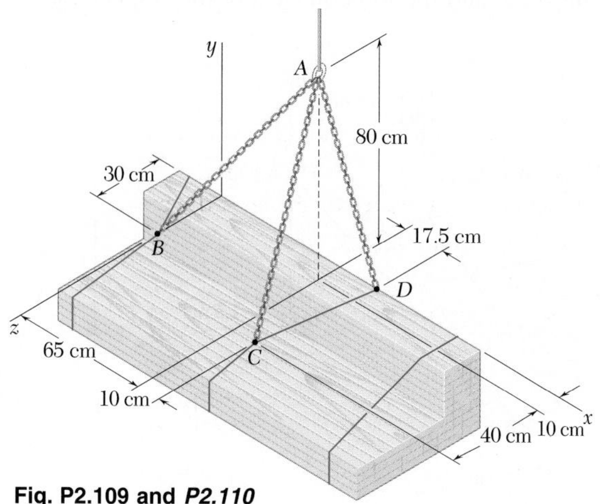

Fig. P2.109 and *P2.110*

2.110 A load of lumber is lifted using a triple leg sling. Knowing that at the instant shown the lumber is at rest and that the tension in leg AD is 220 N, determine the weight of the lumber.

2.111 A force **P** is applied as shown to a uniform cone which is supported by three cords, where the lines of action of the cords pass through the vertex A of the cone. Knowing that $P = 0$ and that the tension in cord BE is 0.2 N, determine the weight W of the cone.

2.112 A force **P** is applied as shown to a uniform cone which is supported by three cords, where the lines of action of the cords pass through the vertex A of the cone. Knowing that the cone weighs 1.6 N, determine the range of values of P for which cord CF is taut.

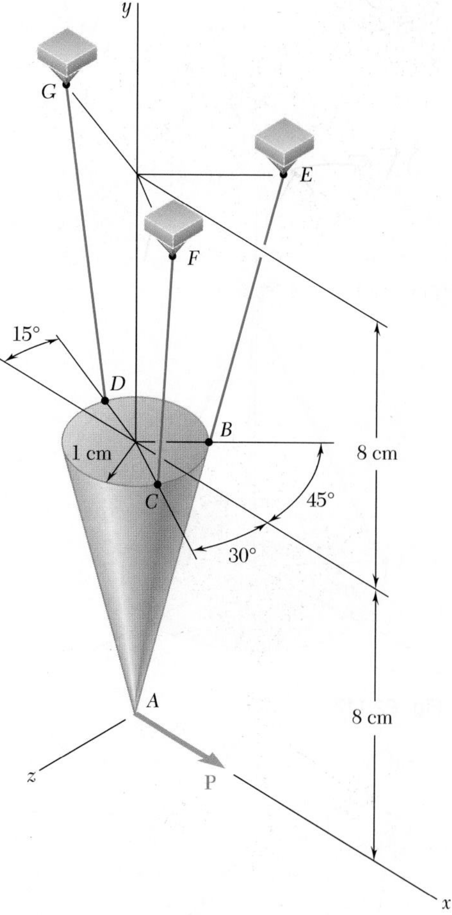

Fig. *P2.111* and P2.112

2.113 A 16-kg triangular plate is supported by three wires as shown. Knowing that $a = 150$ mm, determine the tension in each wire.

2.114 A 16-kg triangular plate is supported by three wires as shown. Knowing that $a = 200$ mm, determine the tension in each wire.

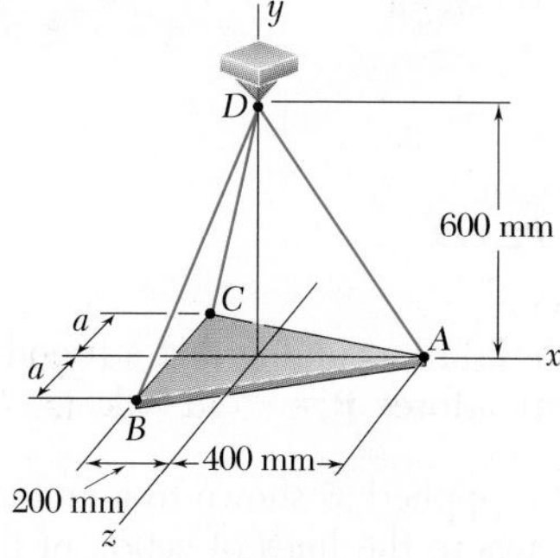

Fig. P2.113 and P2.114

2.115 A transmission tower is held by three guy wires attached to a pin at A and anchored by bolts at B, C, and D. Knowing that the tower exerts on the pin at A an upward vertical force of 8 kN, determine the tension in each wire.

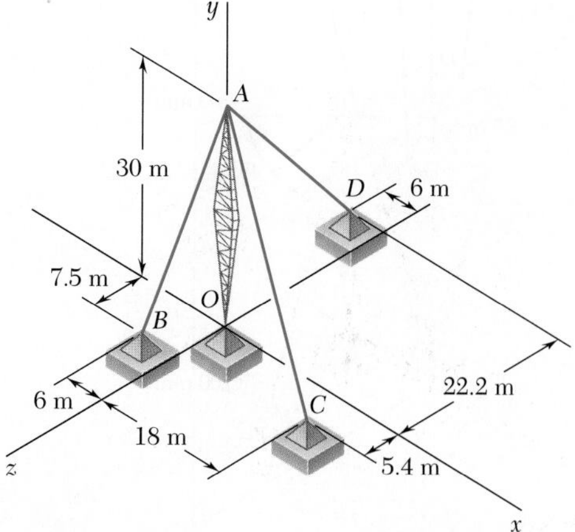

Fig. P2.115

2.116 A derrick boom is guyed by cables AC and AD. A worker is lifting a 20-kg block by pulling on a rope that passes through the pulley at A. Knowing that the boom AB exerts a force at A that is directed from B to A, determine this force and the force in each of the two cables.

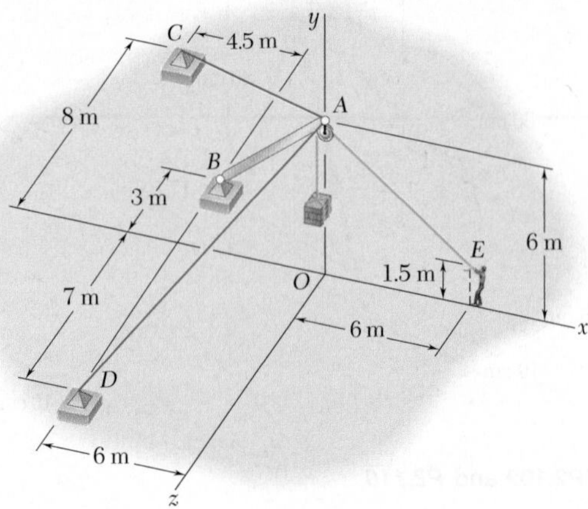

Fig. P2.116

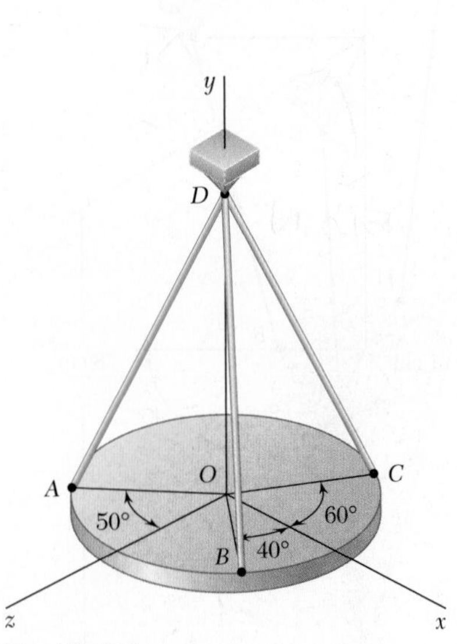

Fig. *P2.117*

2.117 A horizontal circular plate weighing 62 N is suspended as shown from three wires that are attached to a support D and that form 30° angles with the vertical. Determine the tension in each wire.

2.118 For the cone of Prob. 2.112, determine the range of values of P for which cord DG is taut if $\mathbf{P}$ is directed in the $-x$ direction.

2.119 In trying to move across a slippery icy surface, a 175-N man uses two ropes AB and AC. Knowing that the force exerted on the man by the icy surface is perpendicular to that surface, determine the tension in each rope.

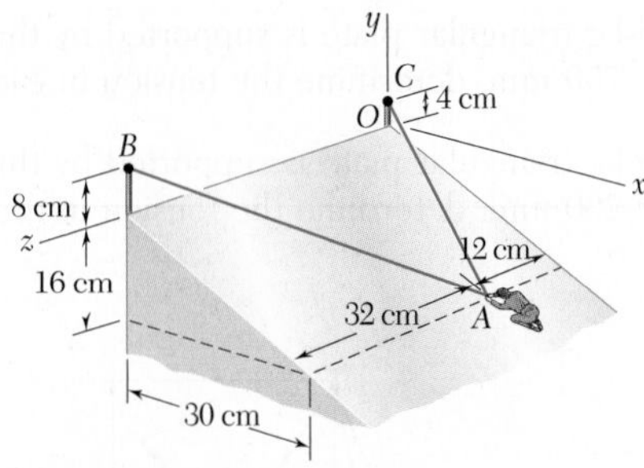

Fig. *P2.119*

2.120 Solve Prob. 2.119 assuming that a friend is helping the man at A by pulling on him with a force $\mathbf{P} = -(45\text{ N})\mathbf{k}$.

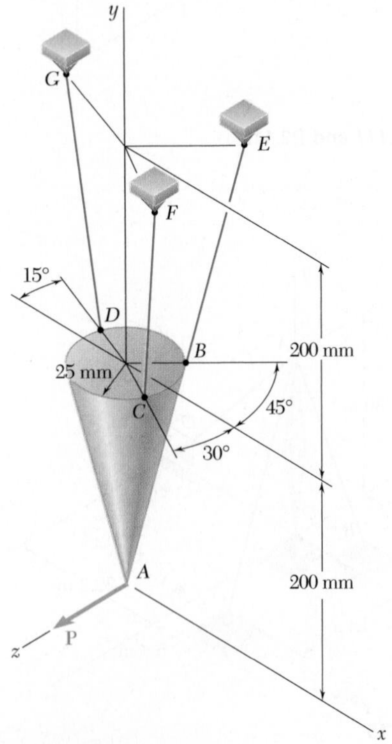

2.121 A force $\mathbf{P}$ is applied as shown to a uniform cone which is supported by three cords, where the lines of action of the cords pass through the vertex A of the cone. Knowing that the cone weighs 10.5 N and that $P = 0$, determine the tension in each cord.

2.122 A force $\mathbf{P}$ is applied as shown to a uniform cone which is supported by three cords, where the lines of action of the cords pass through the vertex A of the cone. Knowing that the cone weighs 10.5 N and that $P = 0.5$ N, determine the tension in each cord.

Fig. P2.121 and P2.122

2.123 To lower a pack of weight W to the hiker at C, the hikers at A and B have passed a rope ADB through a ring attached to the pack at D. The hiker at C is 64 m below A and guides the pack using rope CD. Knowing that at the instant shown the pack is at rest and that the tension in rope CD is 17 N, determine the tension in rope ADB and the weight of the pack. (*Hint:* The tension is the same in both portions of rope ADB.)

2.124 To lower a pack of weight W to the hiker at C, the hikers at A and B have passed a rope ADB through a ring attached to the pack at D. The hiker at C is 64 m below A and guides the pack using rope CD. Knowing that $W = 120$ N and that at the instant shown the pack is at rest, determine the tension in each rope. (*Hint:* The tension is the same in both portions of rope ADB.)

2.125 A piece of machinery of weight W is temporarily supported by cables AB, AC, and ADE. Cable ADE is attached to the ring at A, passes over the pulley at D and back through the ring, and is attached to the support at E. Knowing that $W = 1400$ N, determine the tension in each cable. (*Hint:* The tension is the same in all portions of cable ADE.)

2.126 A piece of machinery of weight W is temporarily supported by cables AB, AC, and ADE. Cable ADE is attached to the ring at A, passes over the pulley at D and back through the ring, and is attached to the support at E. Knowing that the tension in cable AB is 300 N, determine (*a*) the tension in AC, (*b*) the tension in ADE, (*c*) the weight W. (*Hint:* The tension is the same in all portions of cable ADE.)

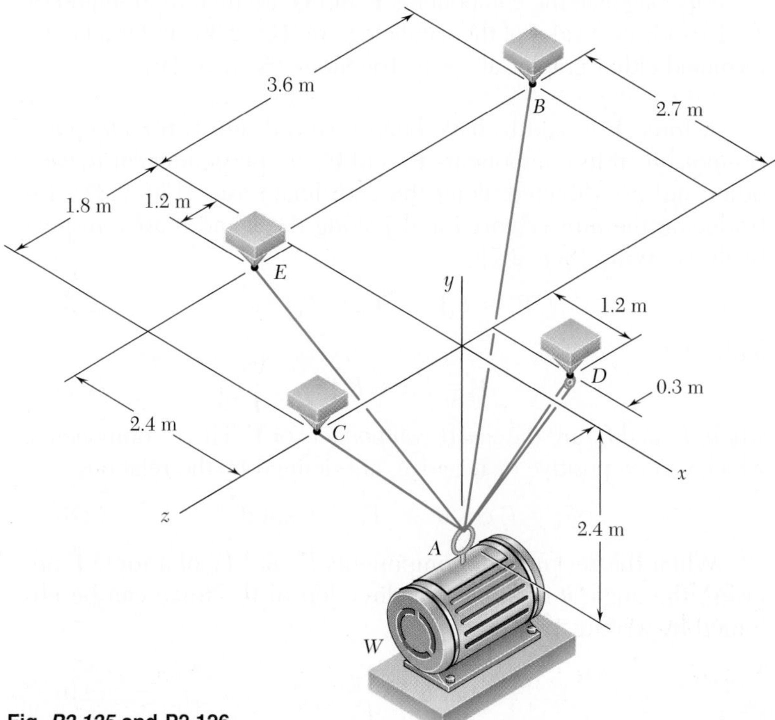

Fig. *P2.125* and P2.126

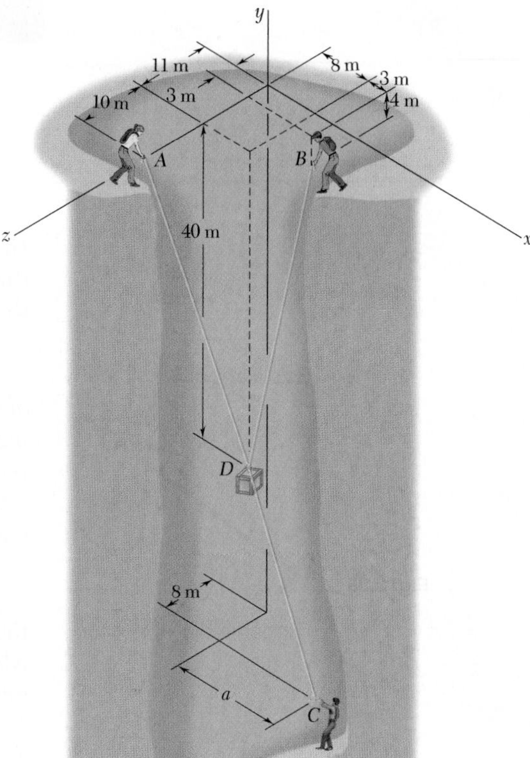

Fig. P2.123 and P2.124

2.127 Collars A and B are connected by a 1-m-long wire and can slide freely on frictionless rods. If a force $\mathbf{P} = (680\text{ N})\mathbf{j}$ is applied at A, determine (*a*) the tension in the wire when $y = 300$ mm, (*b*) the magnitude of the force $\mathbf{Q}$ required to maintain the equilibrium of the system.

2.128 Solve Prob. 2.127 assuming $y = 550$ mm.

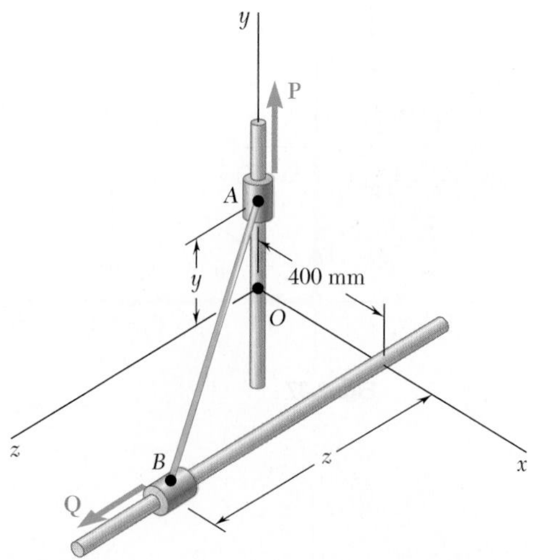

Fig. P2.127

REVIEW AND SUMMARY FOR CHAPTER 2

In this chapter we have studied the effect of forces on particles, that is, on bodies of such shape and size that all forces acting on them may be assumed applied at the same point.

Resultant of two forces

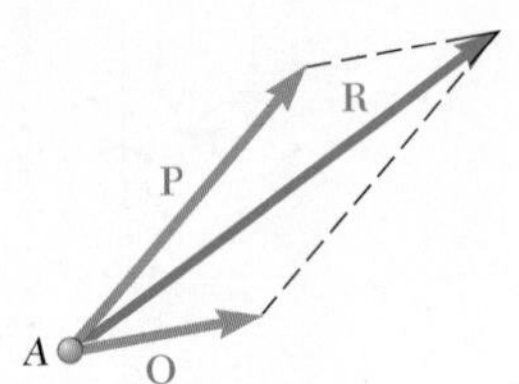

Fig. 2.35

Forces are *vector quantities*; they are characterized by a *point of application*, a *magnitude*, and a *direction*, and they add according to the *parallelogram law* (Fig. 2.35). The magnitude and direction of the resultant **R** of two forces **P** and **Q** can be determined either graphically or by trigonometry, using successively the law of cosines and the law of sines [Sample Prob. 2.1].

Components of a force

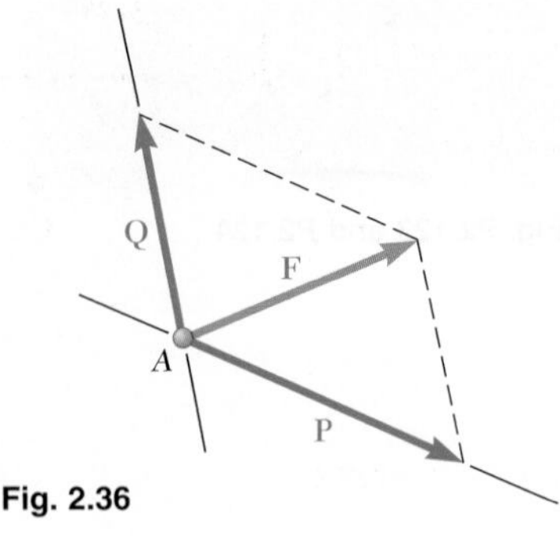

Fig. 2.36

Any given force acting on a particle can be resolved into two or more *components*, that is, it can be replaced by two or more forces which have the same effect on the particle. A force **F** can be resolved into two components **P** and **Q** by drawing a parallelogram which has **F** for its diagonal; the components **P** and **Q** are then represented by the two adjacent sides of the parallelogram (Fig. 2.36) and can be determined either graphically or by trigonometry [Sec. 2.6].

Rectangular components
Unit vectors

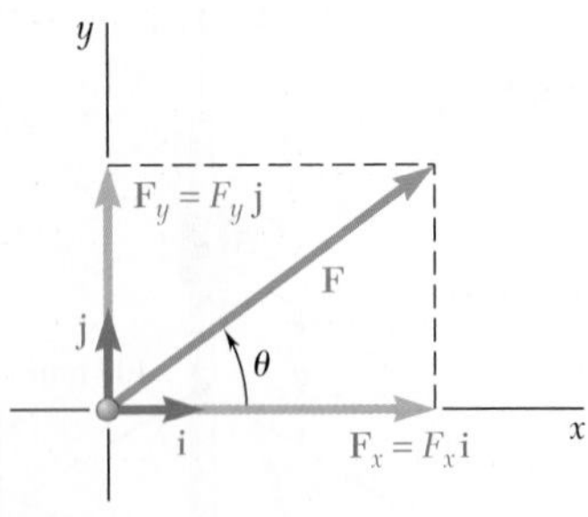

Fig. 2.37

A force **F** is said to have been resolved into two *rectangular components* if its components $\mathbf{F}_x$ and $\mathbf{F}_y$ are perpendicular to each other and are directed along the coordinate axes (Fig. 2.37). Introducing the *unit vectors* **i** and **j** along the x and y axes, respectively, we write [Sec. 2.7]

$$\mathbf{F}_x = F_x\mathbf{i} \qquad \mathbf{F}_y = F_y\mathbf{j} \tag{2.6}$$

and

$$\mathbf{F} = F_x\mathbf{i} + F_y\mathbf{j} \tag{2.7}$$

where F_x and F_y are the *scalar components* of **F**. These components, which can be positive or negative, are defined by the relations

$$F_x = F\cos\theta \qquad F_y = F\sin\theta \tag{2.8}$$

When the rectangular components F_x and F_y of a force **F** are given, the angle θ defining the direction of the force can be obtained by writing

$$\tan\theta = \frac{F_y}{F_x} \tag{2.9}$$

The magnitude F of the force can then be obtained by solving one of the equations (2.8) for F or by applying the Pythagorean theorem and writing

$$F = \sqrt{F_x^2 + F_y^2} \tag{2.10}$$

Resultant of several coplanar forces

When *three or more coplanar forces* act on a particle, the rectangular components of their resultant **R** can be obtained by adding algebraically the corresponding components of the given forces [Sec. 2.8]. We have

$$R_x = \Sigma F_x \qquad R_y = \Sigma F_y \qquad (2.13)$$

The magnitude and direction of **R** can then be determined from relations similar to Eqs. (2.9) and (2.10) [Sample Prob. 2.3].

Forces in space

A force **F** in *three-dimensional space* can be resolved into rectangular components $\mathbf{F}_x$, $\mathbf{F}_y$, and $\mathbf{F}_z$ [Sec. 2.12]. Denoting by θ_x, θ_y, and θ_z, respectively, the angles that **F** forms with the x, y, and z axes (Fig. 2.38), we have

$$F_x = F \cos \theta_x \qquad F_y = F \cos \theta_y \qquad F_z = F \cos \theta_z \quad (2.19)$$

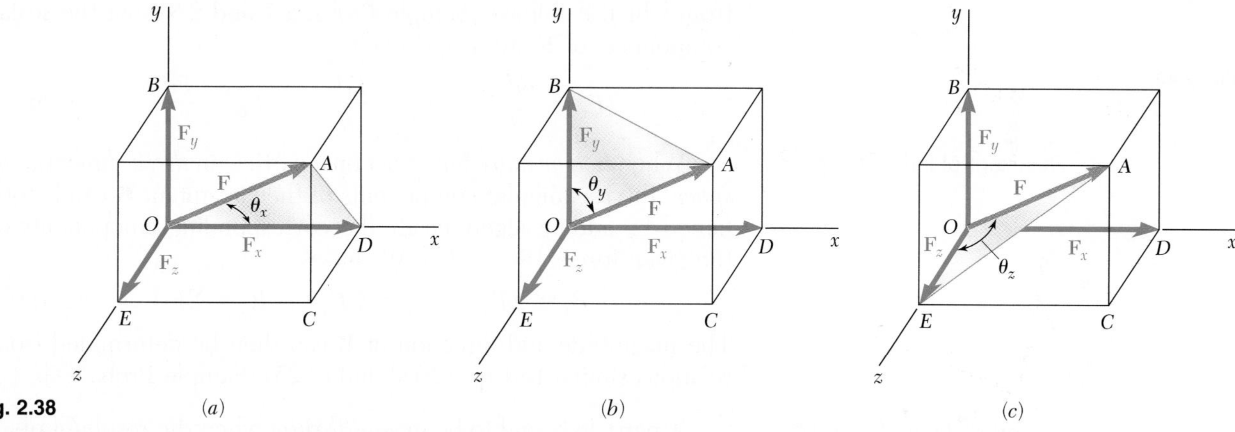

Fig. 2.38 (a) (b) (c)

Direction cosines

The cosines of θ_x, θ_y, and θ_z are known as the *direction cosines* of the force **F**. Introducing the unit vectors **i**, **j**, and **k** along the coordinate axes, we write

$$\mathbf{F} = F_x\mathbf{i} + F_y\mathbf{j} + F_z\mathbf{k} \qquad (2.20)$$

or

$$\mathbf{F} = F(\cos \theta_x\mathbf{i} + \cos \theta_y\mathbf{j} + \cos \theta_z\mathbf{k}) \qquad (2.21)$$

which shows (Fig. 2.39) that **F** is the product of its magnitude F and the unit vector

$$\boldsymbol{\lambda} = \cos \theta_x\mathbf{i} + \cos \theta_y\mathbf{j} + \cos \theta_z\mathbf{k}$$

Since the magnitude of $\boldsymbol{\lambda}$ is equal to unity, we must have

$$\cos^2 \theta_x + \cos^2 \theta_y + \cos^2 \theta_z = 1 \qquad (2.24)$$

When the rectangular components F_x, F_y, and F_z of a force **F** are given, the magnitude F of the force is found by writing

$$F = \sqrt{F_x^2 + F_y^2 + F_z^2} \qquad (2.18)$$

and the direction cosines of **F** are obtained from Eqs. (2.19). We have

$$\cos \theta_x = \frac{F_x}{F} \qquad \cos \theta_y = \frac{F_y}{F} \qquad \cos \theta_z = \frac{F_z}{F} \quad (2.25)$$

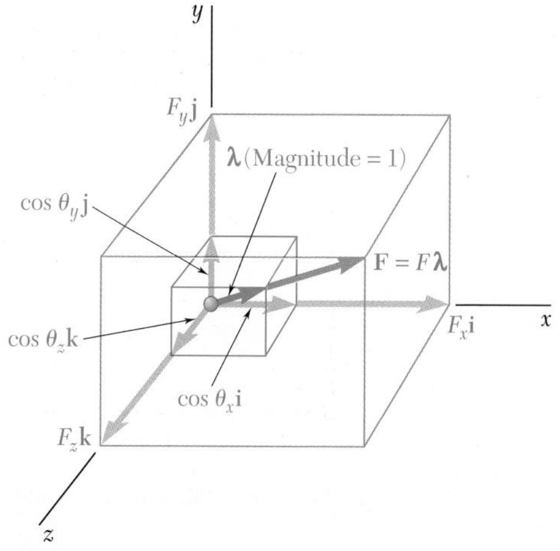

Fig. 2.39

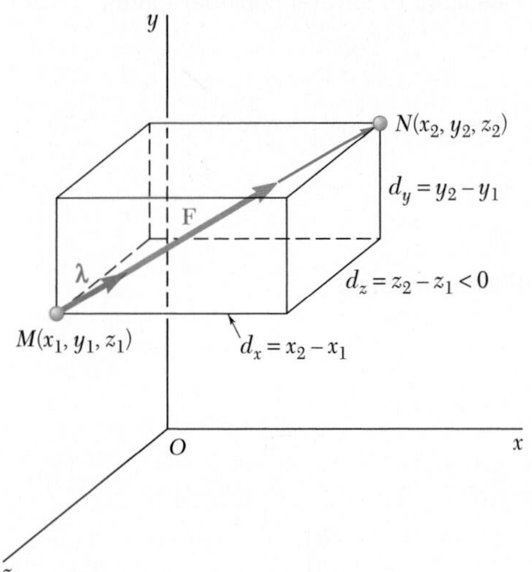

Fig. 2.40

When a force **F** is defined in three-dimensional space by its magnitude F and two points M and N on its line of action [Sec. 2.13], its rectangular components can be obtained as follows. We first express the vector $\overrightarrow{MN}$ joining points M and N in terms of its components d_x, d_y, and d_z (Fig. 2.40); we write

$$\overrightarrow{MN} = d_x\mathbf{i} + d_y\mathbf{j} + d_z\mathbf{k} \tag{2.26}$$

We next determine the unit vector $\boldsymbol{\lambda}$ along the line of action of **F** by dividing $\overrightarrow{MN}$ by its magnitude $MN = d$:

$$\boldsymbol{\lambda} = \frac{\overrightarrow{MN}}{MN} = \frac{1}{d}(d_x\mathbf{i} + d_y\mathbf{j} + d_z\mathbf{k}) \tag{2.27}$$

Recalling that **F** is equal to the product of F and $\boldsymbol{\lambda}$, we have

$$\mathbf{F} = F\boldsymbol{\lambda} = \frac{F}{d}(d_x\mathbf{i} + d_y\mathbf{j} + d_z\mathbf{k}) \tag{2.28}$$

from which it follows [Sample Probs. 2.7 and 2.8] that the scalar components of **F** are, respectively,

$$F_x = \frac{Fd_x}{d} \qquad F_y = \frac{Fd_y}{d} \qquad F_z = \frac{Fd_z}{d} \tag{2.29}$$

Resultant of forces in space

When *two or more forces* act on a particle in *three-dimensional space,* the rectangular components of their resultant **R** can be obtained by adding algebraically the corresponding components of the given forces [Sec. 2.14]. We have

$$R_x = \Sigma F_x \qquad R_y = \Sigma F_y \qquad R_z = \Sigma F_z \tag{2.31}$$

The magnitude and direction of **R** can then be determined from relations similar to Eqs. (2.18) and (2.25) [Sample Prob. 2.8].

Equilibrium of a particle

A particle is said to be in *equilibrium* when the resultant of all the forces acting on it is zero [Sec. 2.9]. The particle will then remain at rest (if originally at rest) or move with constant speed in a straight line (if originally in motion) [Sec. 2.10].

Free-body diagram

To solve a problem involving a particle in equilibrium, one first should draw a *free-body diagram* of the particle showing all the forces acting on it [Sec. 2.11]. If *only three coplanar forces* act on the particle, a *force triangle* may be drawn to express that the particle is in equilibrium. Using graphical methods or trigonometry, this triangle can be solved for no more than two unknowns [Sample Prob. 2.4]. If *more than three coplanar forces* are involved, the equations of equilibrium

$$\Sigma F_x = 0 \qquad \Sigma F_y = 0 \tag{2.15}$$

should be used. These equations can be solved for no more than two unknowns [Sample Prob. 2.6].

Equilibrium in space

When a particle is in *equilibrium in three-dimensional space* [Sec. 2.15], the three equations of equilibrium

$$\Sigma F_x = 0 \qquad \Sigma F_y = 0 \qquad \Sigma F_z = 0 \tag{2.34}$$

should be used. These equations can be solved for no more than three unknowns [Sample Prob. 2.9].

Review Problems

2.129 Two forces are applied as shown to a hook support. Using trigonometry and knowing that the magnitude of **P** is 14 N, determine (*a*) the required angle α if the resultant **R** of the two forces applied to the support is to be horizontal, (*b*) the corresponding magnitude of **R**.

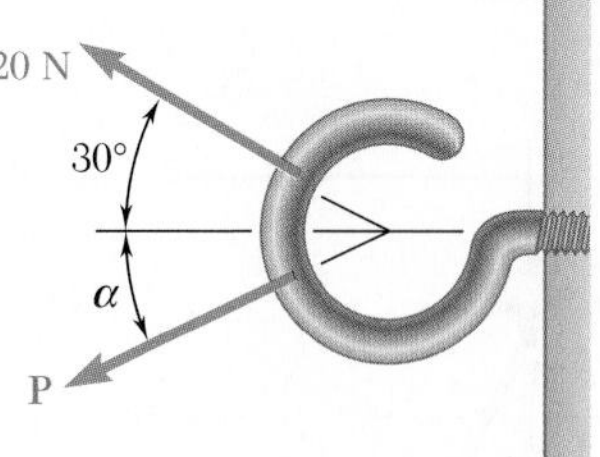

Fig. P2.129

2.130 Determine the x and y components of each of the forces shown.

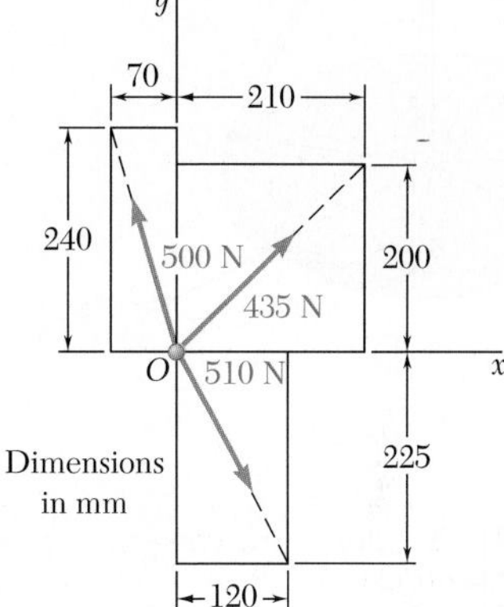

Fig. *P2.130*

2.131 The guy wire BD exerts on the telephone pole AC a force **P** directed along BD. Knowing that **P** has a 450-N component along line AC, determine (*a*) the magnitude of the force **P**, (*b*) its component in a direction perpendicular to AC.

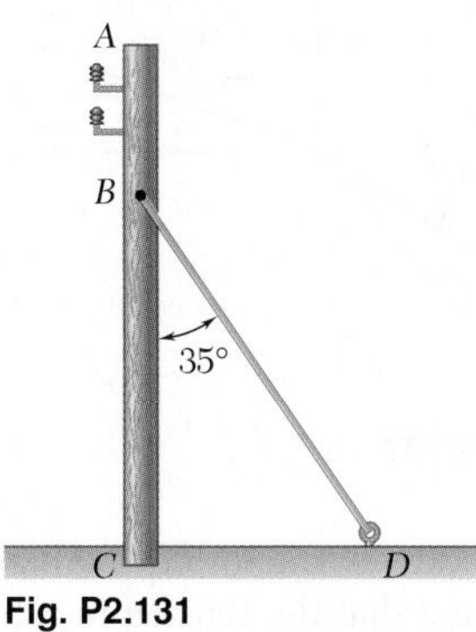

Fig. P2.131

2.132 Knowing that $\alpha = 25°$, determine the tension (*a*) in cable AC, (*b*) in rope BC.

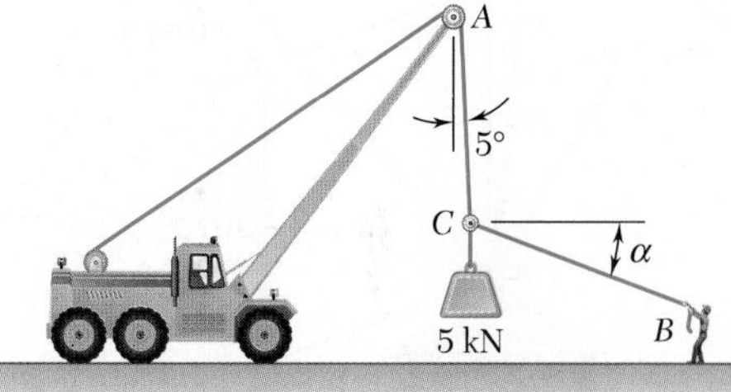

Fig. P2.132

2.133 The cabin of an aerial tramway is suspended from a set of wheels that can roll freely on the support cable ACB and is being pulled at a constant speed by cable DE. Knowing that $\alpha = 42°$ and $\beta = 32°$, that the tension in cable DE is 20 kN, and assuming the tension in cable DF to be negligible, determine (*a*) the combined weight of the cabin, its support system, and its passengers, (*b*) the tension in the support cable ACB.

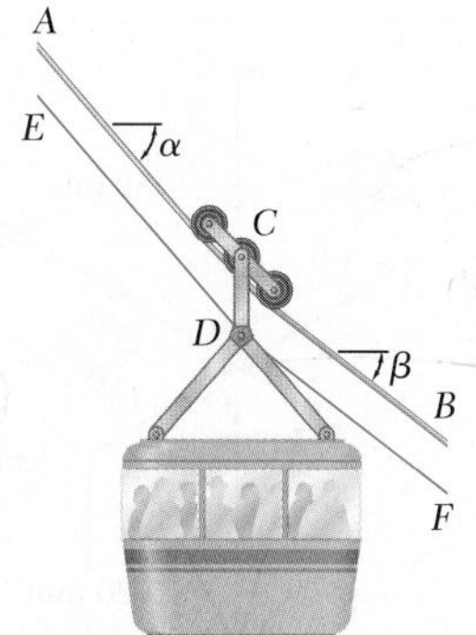

Fig. *P2.133*

2.134 A 350-N load is supported by the rope-and-pulley arrangement shown. Knowing that $\beta = 25°$, determine the magnitude and direction of the force **P** which should be exerted on the free end of the rope to maintain equilibrium. (See the hint of Prob. 2.68.)

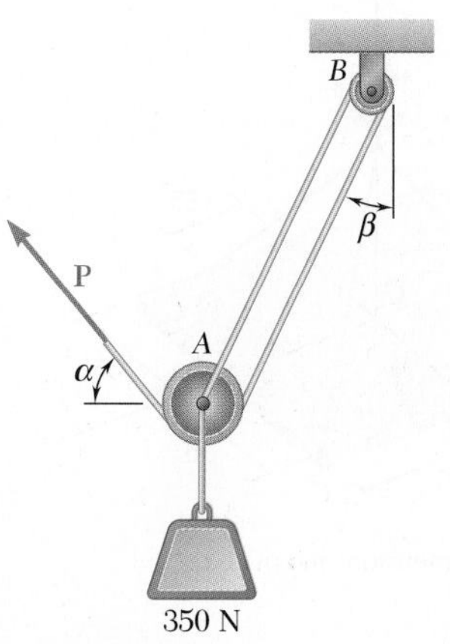

Fig. P2.134

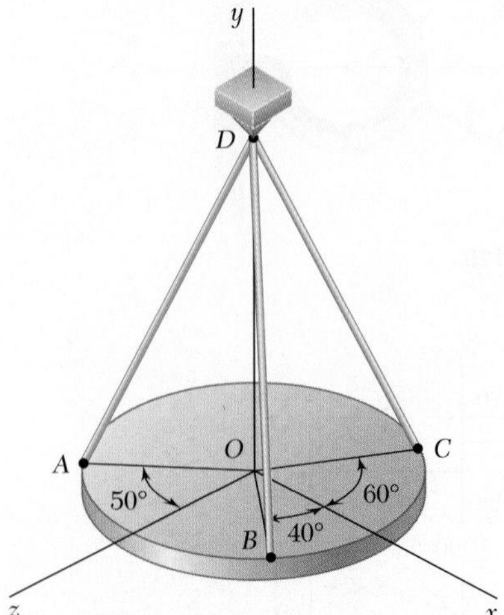

Fig. P2.135

2.135 A horizontal circular plate is suspended as shown from three wires that are attached to a support at D and that form 30° angles with the vertical. Knowing that the x component of the force exerted by wire AD on the plate is 220.6 N, determine (*a*) the tension in wire AD, (*b*) the angles θ_x, θ_y, and θ_z that the force exerted at A forms with the coordinate axes.

2.136 A force **F** of magnitude 600 N acts at the origin of a coordinate system. Knowing that $F_x = 200$ N, $\theta_z = 136.8°$, and $F_y < 0$, determine (*a*) the components F_y and F_z, (*b*) the angles θ_x and θ_y.

2.137 Find the magnitude and direction of the resultant of the two forces shown knowing that $P = 500$ N and $Q = 600$ N.

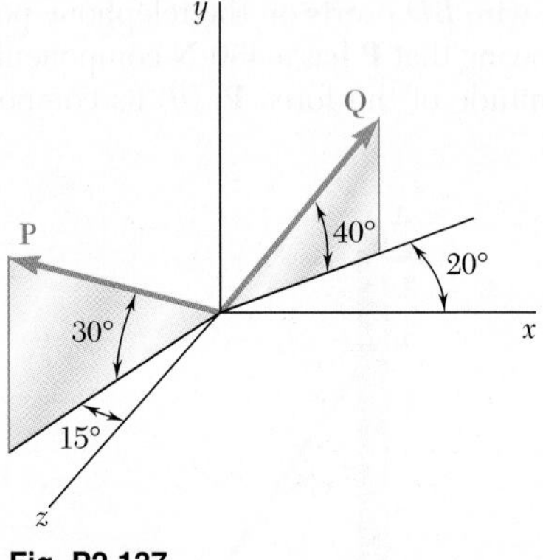

Fig. P2.137

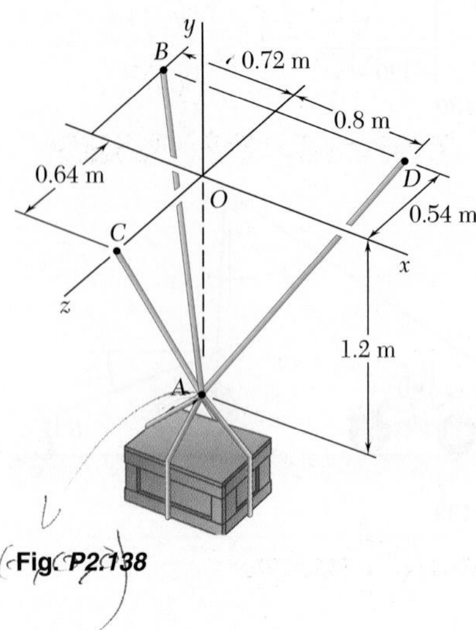

Fig. P2.138

2.138 The crate shown is supported by three cables. Determine the weight of the crate knowing that the tension in cable AB is 3 kN.

2.139 A rectangular plate is supported by three cables as shown. Knowing that the tension in cable AD is 120 N, determine the weight of the plate.

2.140 A container of weight W is suspended from ring A. Cable BAC passes through the ring and is attached to fixed supports at B and C. Two forces $\mathbf{P} = P\mathbf{i}$ and $\mathbf{Q} = Q\mathbf{k}$ are applied to the ring to maintain the container in the position shown. Knowing that $W = 1200$ N, determine P and Q. (*Hint:* The tension is the same in both portions of cable BAC.)

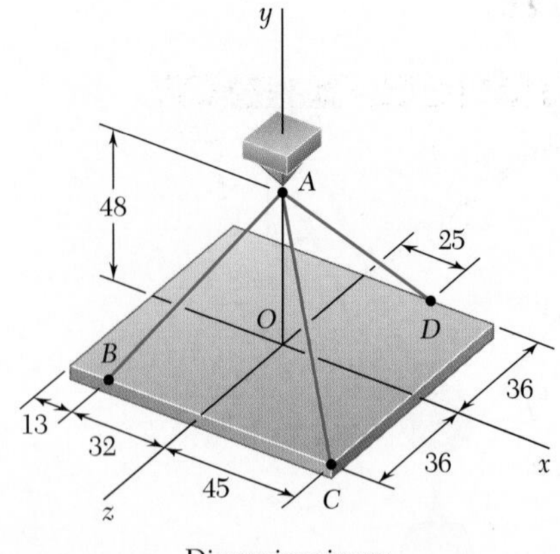

Fig. P2.139

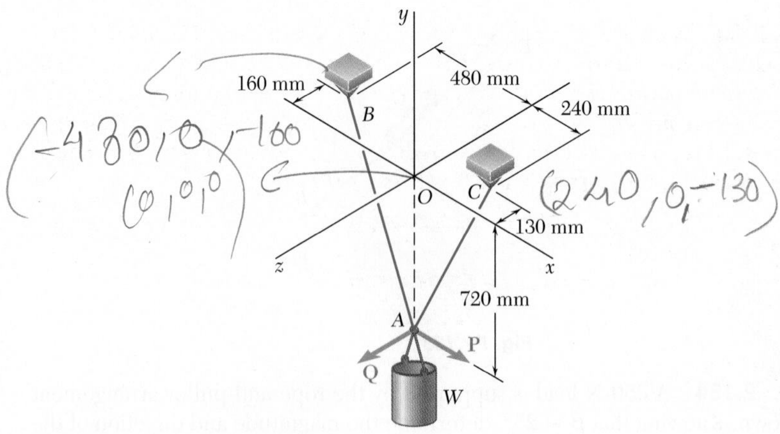

Fig. *P2.140*

Computer Problems

2.C1 Using computational software, determine the magnitude and direction of the resultant of n coplanar forces applied at a point A. Use this software to solve Probs. 2.31, 2.32, 2.33, and 2.34.

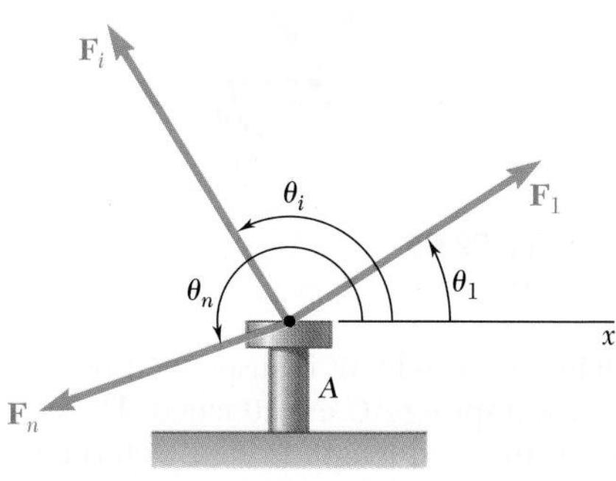

Fig. P2.C1

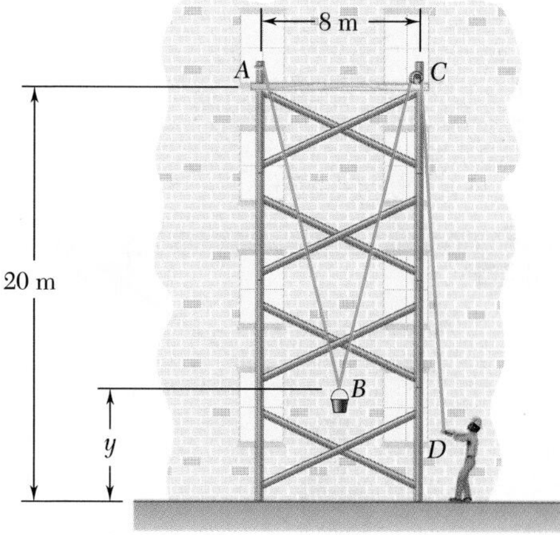

Fig. P2.C2

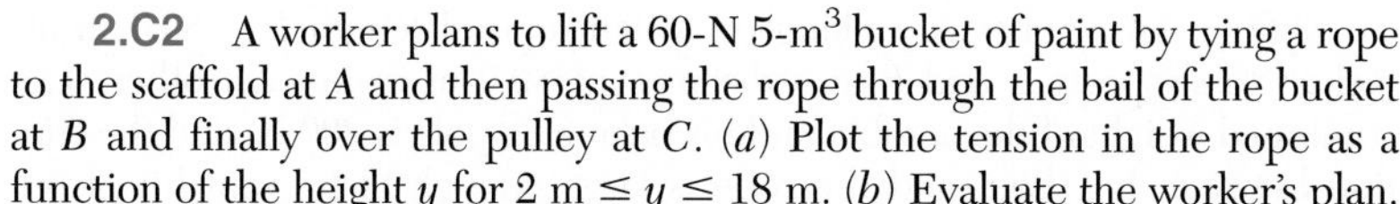

2.C2 A worker plans to lift a 60-N 5-m^3 bucket of paint by tying a rope to the scaffold at A and then passing the rope through the bail of the bucket at B and finally over the pulley at C. (*a*) Plot the tension in the rope as a function of the height y for $2 \text{ m} \leq y \leq 18 \text{ m}$. (*b*) Evaluate the worker's plan.

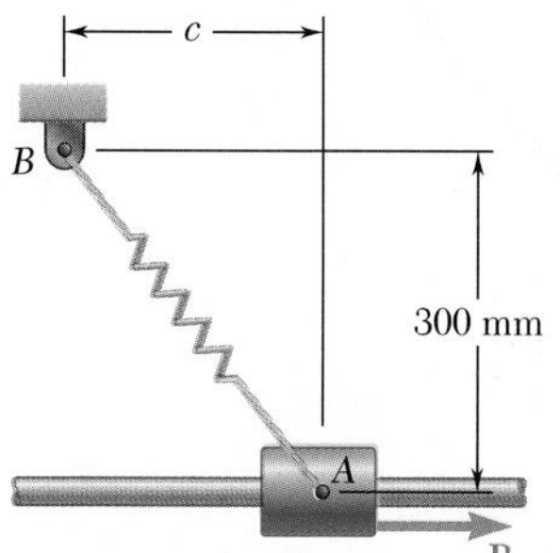

Fig. P2.C3

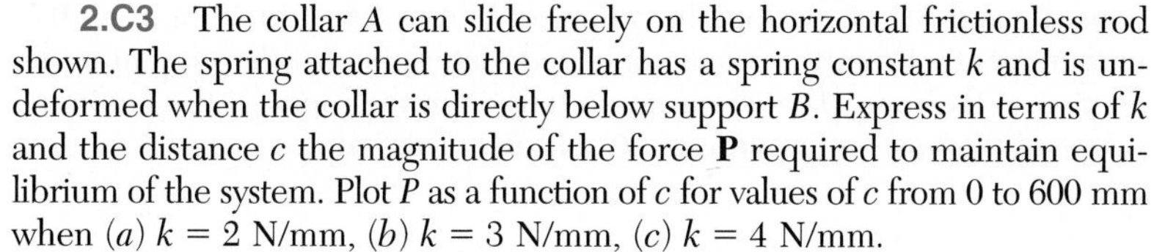

2.C3 The collar A can slide freely on the horizontal frictionless rod shown. The spring attached to the collar has a spring constant k and is undeformed when the collar is directly below support B. Express in terms of k and the distance c the magnitude of the force **P** required to maintain equilibrium of the system. Plot P as a function of c for values of c from 0 to 600 mm when (*a*) $k = 2$ N/mm, (*b*) $k = 3$ N/mm, (*c*) $k = 4$ N/mm.

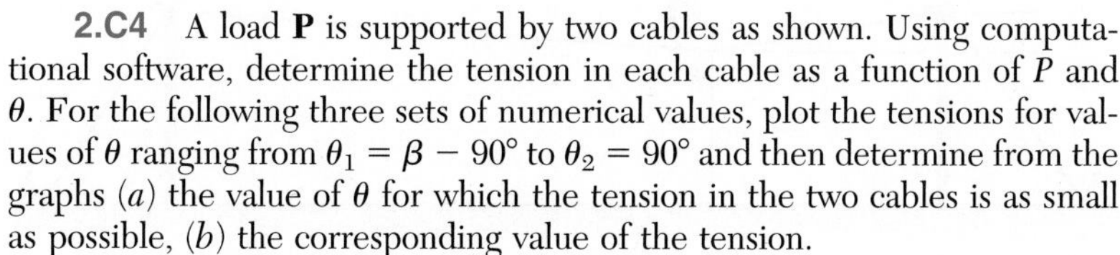

2.C4 A load **P** is supported by two cables as shown. Using computational software, determine the tension in each cable as a function of P and θ. For the following three sets of numerical values, plot the tensions for values of θ ranging from $\theta_1 = \beta - 90°$ to $\theta_2 = 90°$ and then determine from the graphs (*a*) the value of θ for which the tension in the two cables is as small as possible, (*b*) the corresponding value of the tension.

(1) $\alpha = 35°, \beta = 75°, P = 1.6$ kN
(2) $\alpha = 50°, \beta = 30°, P = 2.4$ kN
(3) $\alpha = 40°, \beta = 60°, P = 1.0$ kN

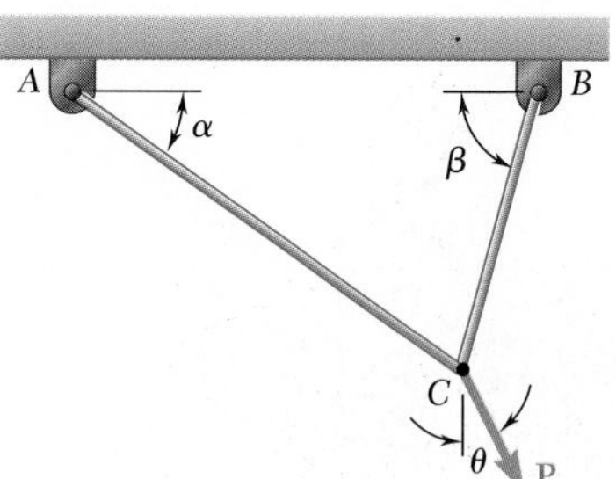

Fig. P2.C4

2.C5 Cables AC and BC are tied together at C and are loaded as shown. Knowing that $P = 100$ N, (*a*) express the tension in each cable as a function of θ. (*b*) Plot the tension in each cable for $0 \leq \theta \leq 90°$. (*c*) From the graph obtained in part *a*, determine the smallest value of θ for which both cables are in tension.

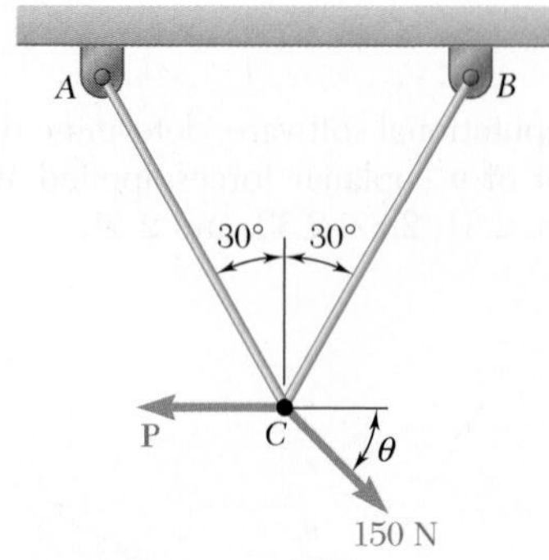

Fig. P2.C5

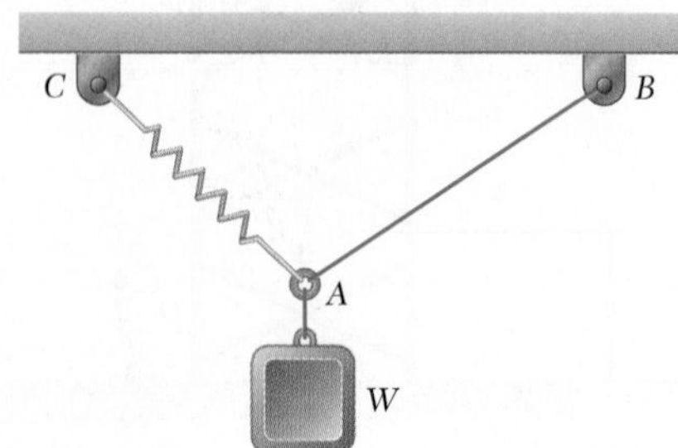

Fig. P2.C6

2.C6 A container of weight W is suspended from ring A to which cable AB of length 5 m and spring AC are attached. The constant of the spring is 100 N/m, and its unstretched length is 3 m. Determine the tension in the cable when (*a*) $W = 120$ N, (*b*) $W = 160$ N.

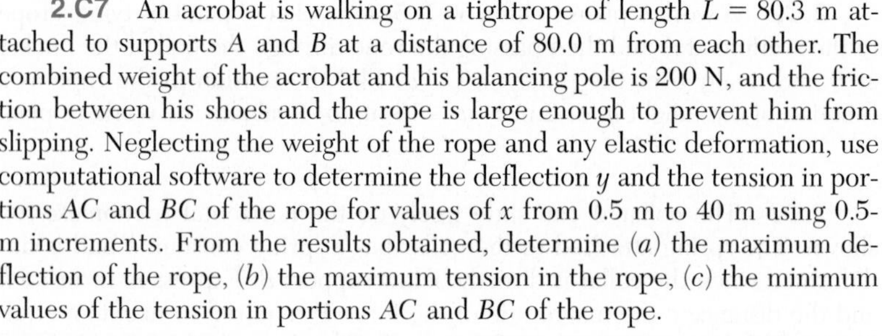

2.C7 An acrobat is walking on a tightrope of length $L = 80.3$ m attached to supports A and B at a distance of 80.0 m from each other. The combined weight of the acrobat and his balancing pole is 200 N, and the friction between his shoes and the rope is large enough to prevent him from slipping. Neglecting the weight of the rope and any elastic deformation, use computational software to determine the deflection y and the tension in portions AC and BC of the rope for values of x from 0.5 m to 40 m using 0.5-m increments. From the results obtained, determine (*a*) the maximum deflection of the rope, (*b*) the maximum tension in the rope, (*c*) the minimum values of the tension in portions AC and BC of the rope.

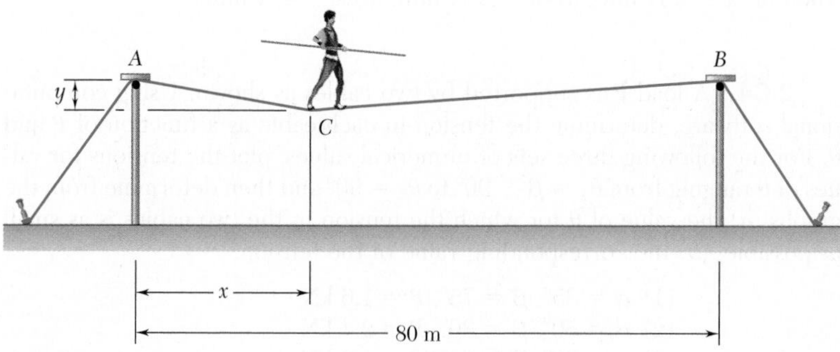

Fig. P2.C7

2.C8 The transmission tower shown is guyed by three cables attached to a pin at *A* and anchored at points *B*, *C*, and *D*. Cable *AD* is 21 m long and the tension in that cable is 20 kN. (*a*) Express the *x*, *y*, and *z* components of the force exerted by cable *AD* on the anchor at *D* and the corresponding angles θ_x, θ_y, and θ_z in terms of α. (*b*) Plot the components of the force and the angles θ_x, θ_y, and θ_z for $0 \leq \alpha \leq 60°$.

2.C9 A tower is guyed by cables *AB* and *AC*. A worker ties a rope of length 12 m to the tower at *A* and exerts a constant force of 160 N on the rope. (*a*) Express the tension in each cable as a function of θ knowing that the resultant of the tensions in the cables and the rope is directed downward. (*b*) Plot the tension in each cable as a function of θ for $0 \leq \theta \leq 180°$, and determine from the graph the range of values of θ for which both cables are taut.

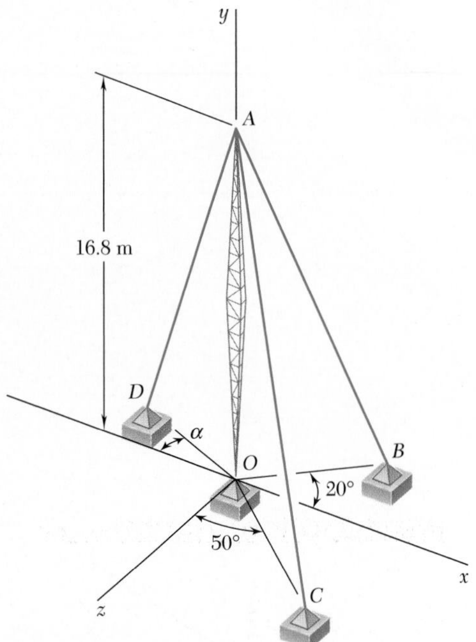

Fig. P2.C8

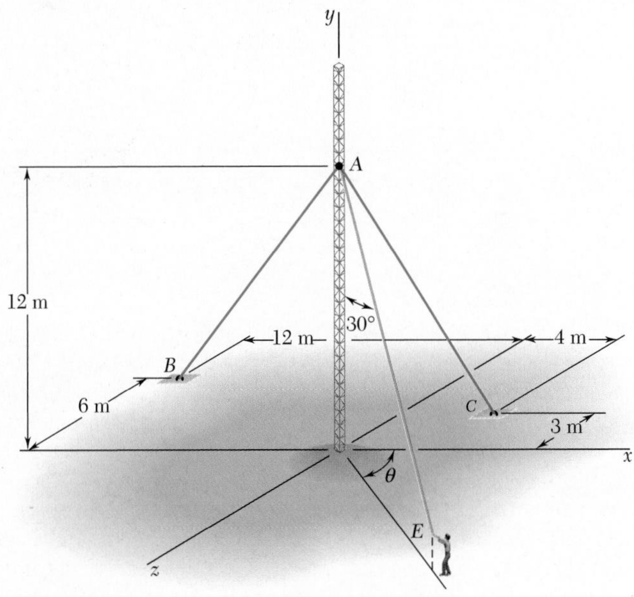

Fig. P2.C9

2.C10 Collars *A* and *B* are connected by a 10-m-long wire and can slide freely on frictionless rods. If a force **Q** of magnitude 25 N is applied to collar *B* as shown, determine the tension in the wire and the corresponding magnitude of the force **P** required to maintain equilibrium. Plot the tension in the wire and the magnitude of the force **P** for $0 \leq x \leq 5$ m.

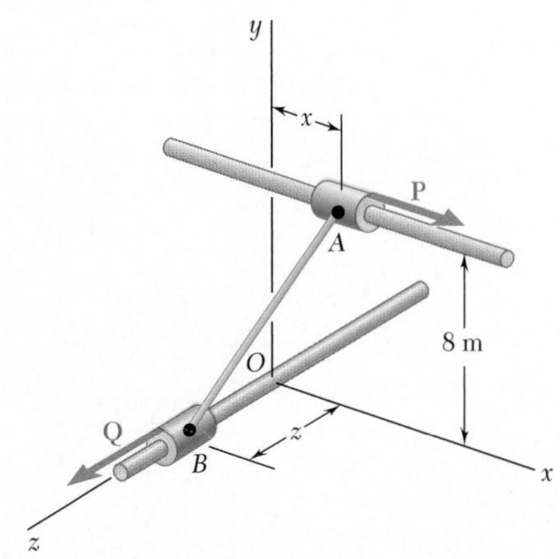

Fig. P2.C10

CHAPTER 3

Rigid Bodies: Equivalent Systems of Forces

It will be shown in this chapter that the system of nonconcurrent forces acting on the harness of the parasail can be replaced with a simpler equivalent system.

RIGID BODIES: EQUIVALENT SYSTEMS OF FORCES

3.1. INTRODUCTION

In the preceding chapter it was assumed that each of the bodies considered could be treated as a single particle. Such a view, however, is not always possible, and a body, in general, should be treated as a combination of a large number of particles. The size of the body will have to be taken into consideration, as well as the fact that forces will act on different particles and thus will have different points of application.

Most of the bodies considered in elementary mechanics are assumed to be *rigid*, a *rigid body* being defined as one which does not deform. Actual structures and machines, however, are never absolutely rigid and deform under the loads to which they are subjected. But these deformations are usually small and do not appreciably affect the conditions of equilibrium or motion of the structure under consideration. They are important, though, as far as the resistance of the structure to failure is concerned and are considered in the study of mechanics of materials.

In this chapter you will study the effect of forces exerted on a rigid body, and you will learn how to replace a given system of forces by a simpler equivalent system. This analysis will rest on the fundamental assumption that the effect of a given force on a rigid body remains unchanged if that force is moved along its line of action (*principle of transmissibility*). It follows that forces acting on a rigid body can be represented by *sliding vectors*, as indicated earlier in Sec. 2.3.

Two important concepts associated with the effect of a force on a rigid body are the *moment of a force about a point* (Sec. 3.6) and the *moment of a force about an axis* (Sec. 3.11). Since the determination of these quantities involves the computation of vector products and scalar products of two vectors, the fundamentals of vector algebra will be introduced in this chapter and applied to the solution of problems involving forces acting on rigid bodies.

Another concept introduced in this chapter is that of a *couple*, that is, the combination of two forces which have the same magnitude, parallel lines of action, and opposite sense (Sec. 3.12). As you will see, any system of forces acting on a rigid body can be replaced by an equivalent system consisting of one force acting at a given point and one couple. This basic system is called a *force-couple system*. In the case of concurrent, coplanar, or parallel forces, the equivalent force-couple system can be further reduced to a single force, called the *resultant* of the system, or to a single couple, called the *resultant couple* of the system.

3.2. EXTERNAL AND INTERNAL FORCES

Forces acting on rigid bodies can be separated into two groups: (1) *external forces* and (2) *internal forces*.

1. The *external forces* represent the action of other bodies on the rigid body under consideration. They are entirely responsible for the external behavior of the rigid body. They will either cause it to move or ensure that it remains at rest. We shall be concerned only with external forces in this chapter and in Chaps. 4 and 5.

2. The *internal forces* are the forces which hold together the particles forming the rigid body. If the rigid body is structurally composed of several parts, the forces holding the component parts together are also defined as internal forces. Internal forces will be considered in Chaps. 6 and 7.

As an example of external forces, let us consider the forces acting on a disabled truck that three people are pulling forward by means of a rope attached to the front bumper (Fig. 3.1). The external forces acting on the truck are shown in a *free-body diagram* (Fig. 3.2). Let us first consider the *weight* of the truck. Although it embodies the effect of the earth's pull on each of the particles forming the truck, the weight can be represented by the single force **W**. The *point of application* of this force, that is, the point at which the force acts, is defined as the *center of gravity* of the truck. It will be seen in Chap. 5 how centers of gravity can be determined. The weight **W** tends to make the truck move vertically downward. In fact, it would actually cause the truck to move downward, that is, to fall, if it were not for the presence of the ground. The ground opposes the downward motion of the truck by means of the reactions $\mathbf{R}_1$ and $\mathbf{R}_2$. These forces are exerted *by* the ground *on* the truck and must therefore be included among the external forces acting on the truck.

Fig. 3.1

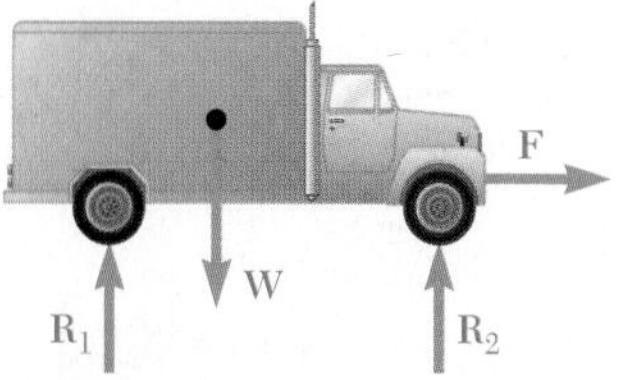

Fig. 3.2

The people pulling on the rope exert the force **F**. The point of application of **F** is on the front bumper. The force **F** tends to make the truck move forward in a straight line and does actually make it move, since no external force opposes this motion. (Rolling resistance has been neglected here for simplicity.) This forward motion of the truck, during which each straight line keeps its original orientation (the floor of the truck remains horizontal, and the walls remain vertical), is known as a *translation*. Other forces might cause the truck to move differently. For example, the force exerted by a jack placed under the front axle would cause the truck to pivot about its rear axle. Such a motion is a *rotation*. It can be concluded, therefore, that each of the *external forces* acting on a *rigid body* can, if unopposed, impart to the rigid body a motion of translation or rotation, or both.

3.3. PRINCIPLE OF TRANSMISSIBILITY. EQUIVALENT FORCES

The *principle of transmissibility* states that the conditions of equilibrium or motion of a rigid body will remain unchanged if a force **F** acting at a given point of the rigid body is replaced by a force **F′** of the same magnitude and same direction, but acting at a different point, *provided that the two forces have the same line of action* (Fig. 3.3). The two forces **F** and **F′** have the same effect on the rigid body and are said to be *equivalent*. This principle, which states that the action of a force may be *transmitted* along its line of action, is based on experimental evidence. It *cannot* be derived from the properties established so far in this text and must therefore be accepted as an experimental law. However, as you will see in Sec. 16.5, the principle of transmissibility can be derived from the study of the dynamics of rigid bodies, but this study requires the introduction of Newton's

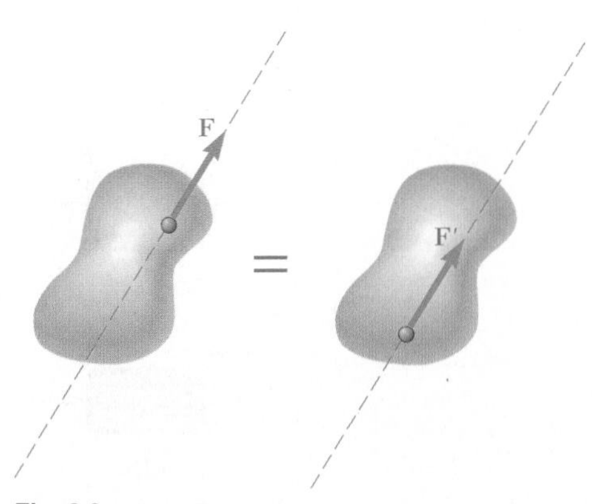

Fig. 3.3

second and third laws and of a number of other concepts as well. Therefore, our study of the statics of rigid bodies will be based on the three principles introduced so far, that is, the parallelogram law of addition, Newton's first law, and the principle of transmissibility.

It was indicated in Chap. 2 that the forces acting on a particle could be represented by vectors. These vectors had a well-defined point of application, namely, the particle itself, and were therefore fixed, or bound, vectors. In the case of forces acting on a rigid body, however, the point of application of the force does not matter, as long as the line of action remains unchanged. Thus, forces acting on a rigid body must be represented by a different kind of vector, known as a *sliding vector,* since forces may be allowed to slide along their lines of action. We should note that all the properties which will be derived in the following sections for the forces acting on a rigid body will be valid more generally for any system of sliding vectors. In order to keep our presentation more intuitive, however, we will carry it out in terms of physical forces rather than in terms of mathematical sliding vectors.

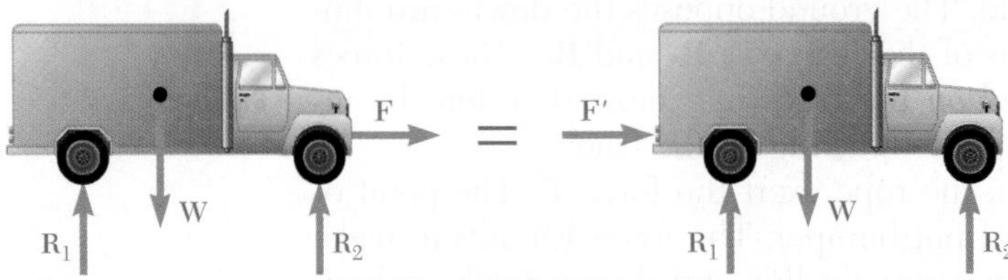

Fig. 3.4

Returning to the example of the truck, we first observe that the line of action of the force **F** is a horizontal line passing through both the front and the rear bumpers of the truck (Fig. 3.4). Using the principle of transmissibility, we can therefore replace **F** by an *equivalent force* **F**′ acting on the rear bumper. In other words, the conditions of motion are unaffected, and all the other external forces acting on the truck (**W**, $\mathbf{R}_1$, $\mathbf{R}_2$) remain unchanged if the people push on the rear bumper instead of pulling on the front bumper.

The principle of transmissibility and the concept of equivalent forces have limitations, however. Consider, for example, a short bar *AB* acted upon by equal and opposite axial forces $\mathbf{P}_1$ and $\mathbf{P}_2$, as shown in Fig. 3.5*a*. According to the principle of transmissibility, the force $\mathbf{P}_2$ can be replaced by a force $\mathbf{P}_2'$ having the same magnitude, the same direction, and the same line of action but acting at *A* instead of *B* (Fig. 3.5*b*). The forces $\mathbf{P}_1$ and $\mathbf{P}_2'$ acting on the same particle can

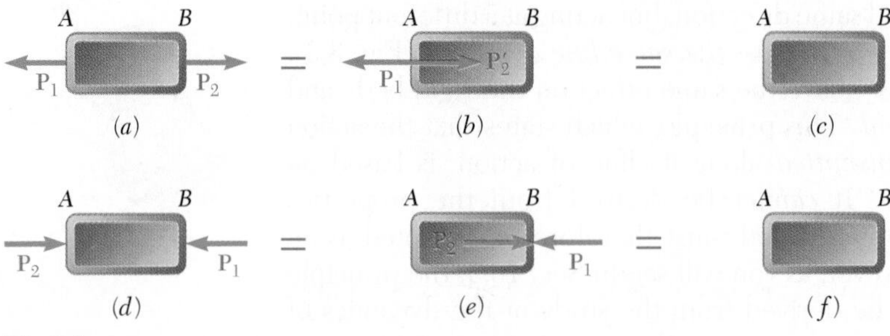

Fig. 3.5

be added according to the rules of Chap. 2, and, as these forces are equal and opposite, their sum is equal to zero. Thus, in terms of the external behavior of the bar, the original system of forces shown in Fig. 3.5*a* is equivalent to no force at all (Fig. 3.5*c*).

Consider now the two equal and opposite forces $\mathbf{P}_1$ and $\mathbf{P}_2$ acting on the bar *AB* as shown in Fig. 3.5*d*. The force $\mathbf{P}_2$ can be replaced by a force $\mathbf{P}'_2$ having the same magnitude, the same direction, and the same line of action but acting at *B* instead of at *A* (Fig. 3.5*e*). The forces $\mathbf{P}_1$ and $\mathbf{P}'_2$ can then be added, and their sum is again zero (Fig. 3.5*f*). From the point of view of the mechanics of rigid bodies, the systems shown in Fig. 3.5*a* and *d* are thus equivalent. But the *internal forces* and *deformations* produced by the two systems are clearly different. The bar of Fig. 3.5*a* is in *tension* and, if not absolutely rigid, will increase in length slightly; the bar of Fig. 3.5*d* is in *compression* and, if not absolutely rigid, will decrease in length slightly. Thus, while the principle of transmissibility may be used freely to determine the conditions of motion or equilibrium of rigid bodies and to compute the external forces acting on these bodies, it should be avoided, or at least used with care, in determining internal forces and deformations.

3.4. VECTOR PRODUCT OF TWO VECTORS

In order to gain a better understanding of the effect of a force on a rigid body, a new concept, the concept of *a moment of a force about a point,* will be introduced at this time. This concept will be more clearly understood, and applied more effectively, if we first add to the mathematical tools at our disposal the *vector product* of two vectors.

The vector product of two vectors **P** and **Q** is defined as the vector **V** which satisfies the following conditions.

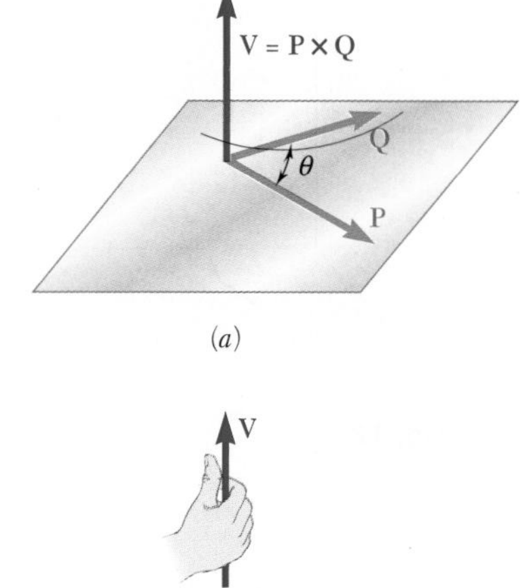

(*a*)

(*b*)

Fig. 3.6

1. The line of action of **V** is perpendicular to the plane containing **P** and **Q** (Fig. 3.6*a*).
2. The magnitude of **V** is the product of the magnitudes of **P** and **Q** and of the sine of the angle θ formed by **P** and **Q** (the measure of which will always be 180° or less); we thus have

$$V = PQ \sin \theta \qquad (3.1)$$

3. The direction of **V** is obtained from the *right-hand rule*. Close your right hand and hold it so that your fingers are curled in the same sense as the rotation through θ which brings the vector **P** in line with the vector **Q**; your thumb will then indicate the direction of the vector **V** (Fig. 3.6*b*). Note that if **P** and **Q** do not have a common point of application, they should first be redrawn from the same point. The three vectors **P**, **Q**, and **V**—taken in that order—are said to form a *right-handed triad*.†

†We should note that the x, y, and z axes used in Chap. 2 form a right-handed system of orthogonal axes and that the unit vectors **i**, **j**, **k** defined in Sec. 2.12 form a right-handed orthogonal triad.

As stated above, the vector **V** satisfying these three conditions (which define it uniquely) is referred to as the vector product of **P** and **Q**; it is represented by the mathematical expression

$$\mathbf{V} = \mathbf{P} \times \mathbf{Q} \tag{3.2}$$

Because of the notation used, the vector product of two vectors **P** and **Q** is also referred to as the *cross product* of **P** and **Q**.

It follows from Eq. (3.1) that, when two vectors **P** and **Q** have either the same direction or opposite directions, their vector product is zero. In the general case when the angle θ formed by the two vectors is neither 0° nor 180°, Eq. (3.1) can be given a simple geometric interpretation: The magnitude V of the vector product of **P** and **Q** is equal to the area of the parallelogram which has **P** and **Q** for sides (Fig. 3.7). The vector product **P** × **Q** will therefore remain unchanged if we replace **Q** by a vector **Q′** which is coplanar with **P** and **Q** and such that the line joining the tips of **Q** and **Q′** is parallel to **P**. We write

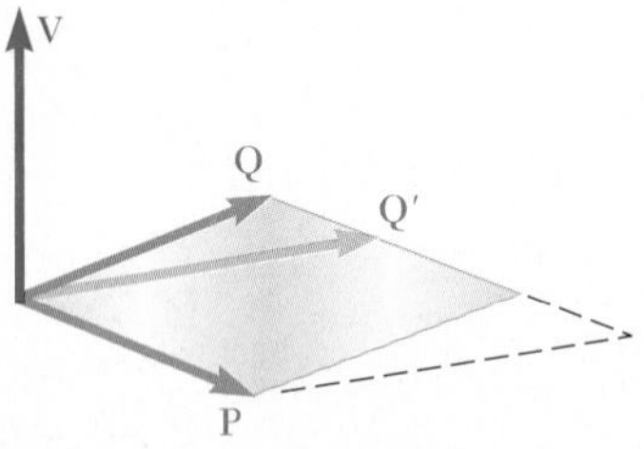

Fig. 3.7

$$\mathbf{V} = \mathbf{P} \times \mathbf{Q} = \mathbf{P} \times \mathbf{Q}' \tag{3.3}$$

From the third condition used to define the vector product **V** of **P** and **Q**, namely, the condition stating that **P**, **Q**, and **V** must form a right-handed triad, it follows that vector products *are not commutative*, that is, **Q** × **P** is not equal to **P** × **Q**. Indeed, we can easily check that **Q** × **P** is represented by the vector −**V**, which is equal and opposite to **V**. We thus write

$$\mathbf{Q} \times \mathbf{P} = -(\mathbf{P} \times \mathbf{Q}) \tag{3.4}$$

Example. Let us compute the vector product **V** = **P** × **Q** where the vector **P** is of magnitude 6 and lies in the zx plane at an angle of 30° with the x axis, and where the vector **Q** is of magnitude 4 and lies along the x axis (Fig. 3.8).

It follows immediately from the definition of the vector product that the vector **V** must lie along the y axis, have the magnitude

$$V = PQ \sin \theta = (6)(4) \sin 30° = 12$$

and be directed upward.

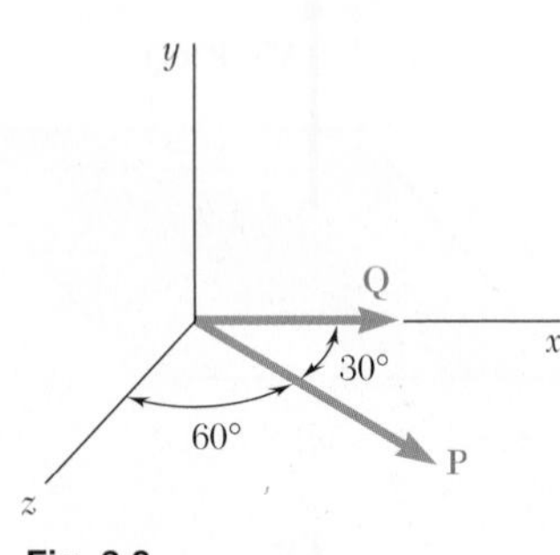

Fig. 3.8

We saw that the commutative property does not apply to vector products. We may wonder whether the *distributive* property holds, that is, whether the relation

$$\mathbf{P} \times (\mathbf{Q}_1 + \mathbf{Q}_2) = \mathbf{P} \times \mathbf{Q}_1 + \mathbf{P} \times \mathbf{Q}_2 \tag{3.5}$$

is valid. The answer is *yes*. Many readers are probably willing to accept without formal proof an answer which they intuitively feel is correct. However, since the entire structure of both vector algebra and statics depends upon the relation (3.5), we should take time out to derive it.

We can, without any loss of generality, assume that **P** is directed along the y axis (Fig. 3.9a). Denoting by **Q** the sum of $\mathbf{Q}_1$ and $\mathbf{Q}_2$, we drop perpendiculars from the tips of **Q**, $\mathbf{Q}_1$, and $\mathbf{Q}_2$ onto the zx plane, defining in this way the vectors $\mathbf{Q}'$, $\mathbf{Q}_1'$, and $\mathbf{Q}_2'$. These vectors will be referred to, respectively, as the *projections* of **Q**, $\mathbf{Q}_1$, and $\mathbf{Q}_2$ on the zx plane. Recalling the property expressed by Eq. (3.3), we note that the left-hand member of Eq. (3.5) can be replaced by $\mathbf{P} \times \mathbf{Q}'$ and that, similarly, the vector products $\mathbf{P} \times \mathbf{Q}_1$ and $\mathbf{P} \times \mathbf{Q}_2$ can respectively be replaced by $\mathbf{P} \times \mathbf{Q}'_1$ and $\mathbf{P} \times \mathbf{Q}'_2$. Thus, the relation to be proved can be written in the form

$$\mathbf{P} \times \mathbf{Q}' = \mathbf{P} \times \mathbf{Q}'_1 + \mathbf{P} \times \mathbf{Q}'_2 \tag{3.5'}$$

We now observe that $\mathbf{P} \times \mathbf{Q}'$ can be obtained from $\mathbf{Q}'$ by multiplying this vector by the scalar P and rotating it counterclockwise through 90° in the zx plane (Fig. 3.9b); the other two vector products

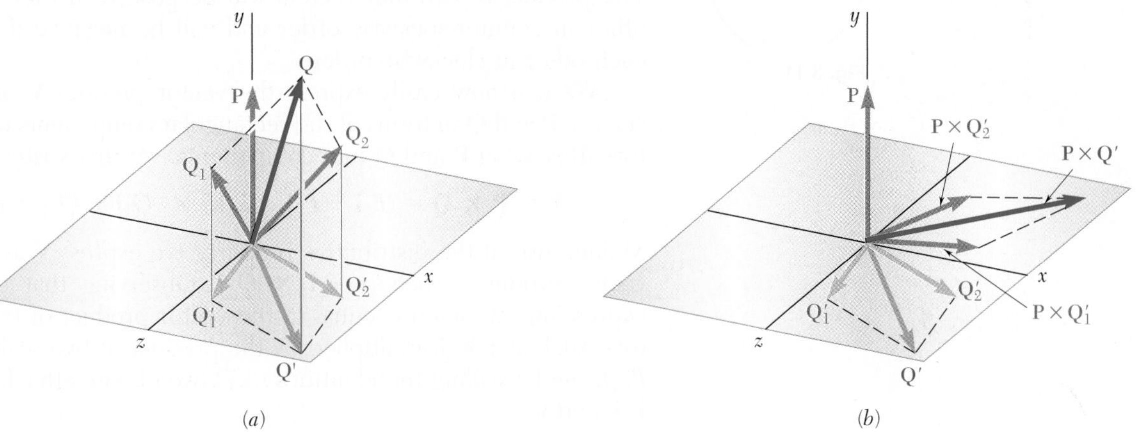

Fig. 3.9

in (3.5′) can be obtained in the same manner from $\mathbf{Q}'_1$ and $\mathbf{Q}'_2$, respectively. Now, since the projection of a parallelogram onto an arbitrary plane is a parallelogram, the projection $\mathbf{Q}'$ of the sum $\mathbf{Q}$ of $\mathbf{Q}_1$ and $\mathbf{Q}_2$ must be the sum of the projections $\mathbf{Q}'_1$ and $\mathbf{Q}'_2$ of $\mathbf{Q}_1$ and $\mathbf{Q}_2$ on the same plane (Fig. 3.9a). This relation between the vectors $\mathbf{Q}'$, $\mathbf{Q}'_1$, and $\mathbf{Q}'_2$ will still hold after the three vectors have been multiplied by the scalar P and rotated through 90° (Fig. 3.9b). Thus, the relation (3.5′) has been proved, and we can now be sure that the distributive property holds for vector products.

A third property, the associative property, does not apply to vector products; we have in general

$$(\mathbf{P} \times \mathbf{Q}) \times \mathbf{S} \neq \mathbf{P} \times (\mathbf{Q} \times \mathbf{S}) \tag{3.6}$$

3.5. VECTOR PRODUCTS EXPRESSED IN TERMS OF RECTANGULAR COMPONENTS

Let us now determine the vector product of any two of the unit vectors $\mathbf{i}$, $\mathbf{j}$, and $\mathbf{k}$, which were defined in Chap. 2. Consider first the product $\mathbf{i} \times \mathbf{j}$ (Fig. 3.10a). Since both vectors have a magnitude equal to 1 and since they are at a right angle to each other, their vector product will also be a unit vector. This unit vector must be $\mathbf{k}$, since the vectors $\mathbf{i}$, $\mathbf{j}$, and $\mathbf{k}$ are mutually perpendicular and form a right-handed triad. On the other hand, it follows from the right-hand rule given on page 77 that the product $\mathbf{j} \times \mathbf{i}$ will be equal to $-\mathbf{k}$ (Fig. 3.10b). Finally, it should be observed that the vector product of a unit

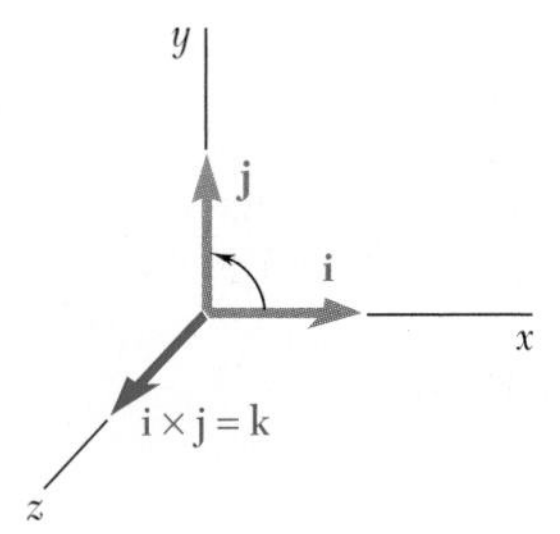

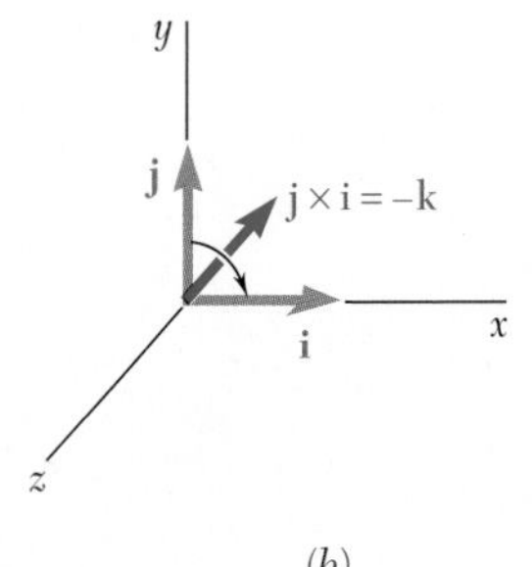

Fig. 3.10

vector with itself, such as $\mathbf{i} \times \mathbf{i}$, is equal to zero, since both vectors have the same direction. The vector products of the various possible pairs of unit vectors are

$$\begin{array}{lll} \mathbf{i} \times \mathbf{i} = \mathbf{0} & \mathbf{j} \times \mathbf{i} = -\mathbf{k} & \mathbf{k} \times \mathbf{i} = \mathbf{j} \\ \mathbf{i} \times \mathbf{j} = \mathbf{k} & \mathbf{j} \times \mathbf{j} = \mathbf{0} & \mathbf{k} \times \mathbf{j} = -\mathbf{i} \\ \mathbf{i} \times \mathbf{k} = -\mathbf{j} & \mathbf{j} \times \mathbf{k} = \mathbf{i} & \mathbf{k} \times \mathbf{k} = \mathbf{0} \end{array} \tag{3.7}$$

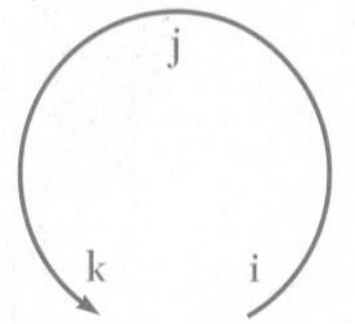

Fig. 3.11

By arranging in a circle and in counterclockwise order the three letters representing the unit vectors (Fig. 3.11), we can simplify the determination of the sign of the vector product of two unit vectors: The product of two unit vectors will be positive if they follow each other in counterclockwise order and will be negative if they follow each other in clockwise order.

We can now easily express the vector product $\mathbf{V}$ of two given vectors $\mathbf{P}$ and $\mathbf{Q}$ in terms of the rectangular components of these vectors. Resolving $\mathbf{P}$ and $\mathbf{Q}$ into components, we first write

$$\mathbf{V} = \mathbf{P} \times \mathbf{Q} = (P_x\mathbf{i} + P_y\mathbf{j} + P_z\mathbf{k}) \times (Q_x\mathbf{i} + Q_y\mathbf{j} + Q_z\mathbf{k})$$

Making use of the distributive property, we express $\mathbf{V}$ as the sum of vector products, such as $P_x\mathbf{i} \times Q_y\mathbf{j}$. Observing that each of the expressions obtained is equal to the vector product of two unit vectors, such as $\mathbf{i} \times \mathbf{j}$, multiplied by the product of two scalars, such as P_xQ_y, and recalling the identities (3.7), we obtain, after factoring out $\mathbf{i}$, $\mathbf{j}$, and $\mathbf{k}$,

$$\mathbf{V} = (P_yQ_z - P_zQ_y)\mathbf{i} + (P_zQ_x - P_xQ_z)\mathbf{j} + (P_xQ_y - P_yQ_x)\mathbf{k} \tag{3.8}$$

The rectangular components of the vector product $\mathbf{V}$ are thus found to be

$$\begin{aligned} V_x &= P_yQ_z - P_zQ_y \\ V_y &= P_zQ_x - P_xQ_z \\ V_z &= P_xQ_y - P_yQ_x \end{aligned} \tag{3.9}$$

Returning to Eq. (3.8), we observe that its right-hand member represents the expansion of a determinant. The vector product $\mathbf{V}$ can thus be expressed in the following form, which is more easily memorized:†

$$\mathbf{V} = \begin{vmatrix} \mathbf{i} & \mathbf{j} & \mathbf{k} \\ P_x & P_y & P_z \\ Q_x & Q_y & Q_z \end{vmatrix} \tag{3.10}$$

†Any determinant consisting of three rows and three columns can be evaluated by repeating the first and second columns and forming products along each diagonal line. The sum of the products obtained along the red lines is then subtracted from the sum of the products obtained along the black lines.

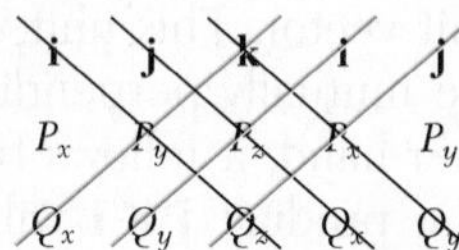

3.6. MOMENT OF A FORCE ABOUT A POINT

Let us now consider a force **F** acting on a rigid body (Fig. 3.12*a*). As we know, the force **F** is represented by a vector which defines its magnitude and direction. However, the effect of the force on the rigid body depends also upon its point of application *A*. The position of *A* can be conveniently defined by the vector **r** which joins the fixed reference point *O* with *A*; this vector is known as the *position vector* of *A*.† The position vector **r** and the force **F** define the plane shown in Fig. 3.12*a*.

We will define the *moment of* **F** *about O* as the vector product of **r** and **F**:

$$\mathbf{M}_O = \mathbf{r} \times \mathbf{F} \tag{3.11}$$

According to the definition of the vector product given in Sec. 3.4, the moment $\mathbf{M}_O$ must be perpendicular to the plane containing *O* and the force **F**. The sense of $\mathbf{M}_O$ is defined by the sense of the rotation which will bring the vector **r** in line with the vector **F**; this rotation will be observed as *counterclockwise* by an observer located at the tip of $\mathbf{M}_O$. Another way of defining the sense of $\mathbf{M}_O$ is furnished by a variation of the right-hand rule: Close your right hand and hold it so that your fingers are curled in the sense of the rotation that **F** would impart to the rigid body about a fixed axis directed along the line of action of $\mathbf{M}_O$; your thumb will indicate the sense of the moment $\mathbf{M}_O$ (Fig. 3.12*b*).

Finally, denoting by θ the angle between the lines of action of the position vector **r** and the force **F**, we find that the magnitude of the moment of **F** about *O* is

$$M_O = rF \sin \theta = Fd \tag{3.12}$$

where *d* represents the perpendicular distance from *O* to the line of action of **F**. Since the tendency of a force **F** to make a rigid body rotate about a fixed axis perpendicular to the force depends upon the distance of **F** from that axis as well as upon the magnitude of **F**, we note that *the magnitude of* $\mathbf{M}_O$ *measures the tendency of the force* **F** *to make the rigid body rotate about a fixed axis directed along* $\mathbf{M}_O$.

In the SI system of units, where a force is expressed in newtons (N) and a distance in meters (m), the moment of a force is expressed in newton-meters (N · m). In the U.S. customary system of units, where a force is expressed in pounds and a distance in feet or inches, the moment of a force is expressed in lb · ft or lb · in.

We can observe that although the moment $\mathbf{M}_O$ of a force about a point depends upon the magnitude, the line of action, and the sense of the force, it does *not* depend upon the actual position of the point of application of the force along its line of action. Conversely, the moment $\mathbf{M}_O$ of a force **F** does not characterize the position of the point of application of **F**.

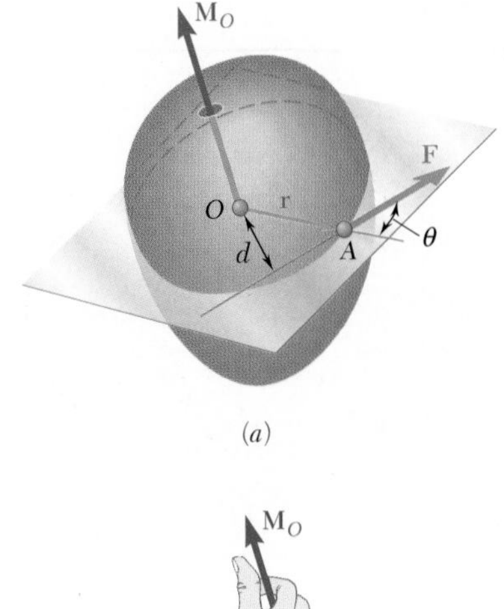

(*a*)

$\mathbf{M}_O$

(*b*)

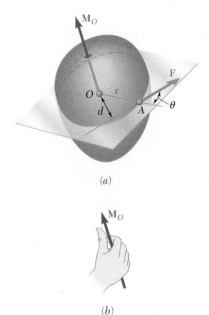

Fig. 3.12

†We can easily verify that position vectors obey the law of vector addition and, thus, are truly vectors. Consider, for example, the position vectors **r** and **r′** of *A* with respect to two reference points *O* and *O′* and the position vector **s** of *O* with respect to *O′* (Fig. 3.40*a*, Sec. 3.16). We verify that the position vector $\mathbf{r}' = \overrightarrow{O'A}$ can be obtained from the position vectors $\mathbf{s} = \overrightarrow{O'O}$ and $\mathbf{r} = \overrightarrow{OA}$ by applying the triangle rule for the addition of vectors.

However, as it will be seen presently, the moment $\mathbf{M}_O$ of a force $\mathbf{F}$ of given magnitude and direction *completely defines the line of action of* $\mathbf{F}$. Indeed, the line of action of $\mathbf{F}$ must lie in a plane through O perpendicular to the moment $\mathbf{M}_O$; its distance d from O must be equal to the quotient M_O/F of the magnitudes of $\mathbf{M}_O$ and $\mathbf{F}$; and the sense of $\mathbf{M}_O$ determines whether the line of action of $\mathbf{F}$ is to be drawn on one side or the other of the point O.

We recall from Sec. 3.3 that the principle of transmissibility states that two forces $\mathbf{F}$ and $\mathbf{F}'$ are equivalent (that is, have the same effect on a rigid body) if they have the same magnitude, same direction, and same line of action. This principle can now be restated as follows: *Two forces* $\mathbf{F}$ *and* $\mathbf{F}'$ *are equivalent if, and only if, they are equal* (that is, have the same magnitude and same direction) *and have equal moments about a given point O*. The necessary and sufficient conditions for two forces $\mathbf{F}$ and $\mathbf{F}'$ to be equivalent are thus

$$\mathbf{F} = \mathbf{F}' \quad \text{and} \quad \mathbf{M}_O = \mathbf{M}'_O \tag{3.13}$$

We should observe that it follows from this statement that if the relations (3.13) hold for a given point O, they will hold for any other point.

Problems Involving Only Two Dimensions. Many applications deal with two-dimensional structures, that is, structures which have length and breadth but only negligible depth and which are subjected to forces contained in the plane of the structure. Two-dimensional structures and the forces acting on them can be readily represented on a sheet of paper or on a blackboard. Their analysis is therefore considerably simpler than that of three-dimensional structures and forces.

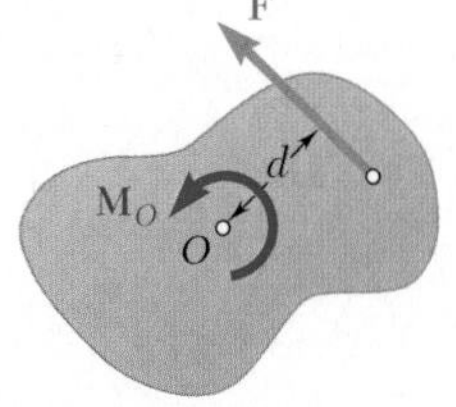

(a) $M_O = +Fd$

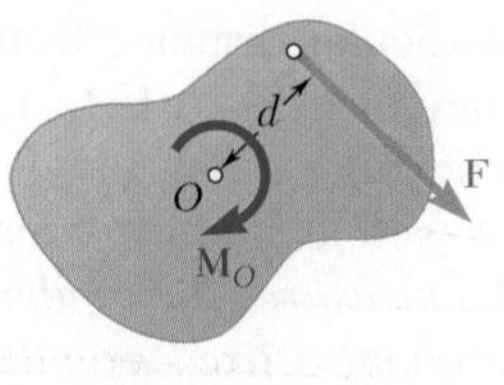

(b) $M_O = -Fd$

Fig. 3.13

Consider, for example, a rigid slab acted upon by a force $\mathbf{F}$ (Fig. 3.13). The moment of $\mathbf{F}$ about a point O chosen in the plane of the figure is represented by a vector $\mathbf{M}_O$ perpendicular to that plane and of magnitude Fd. In the case of Fig. 3.13*a* the vector $\mathbf{M}_O$ points *out of* the paper, while in the case of Fig. 3.13*b* it points *into* the paper. As we look at the figure, we observe in the first case that $\mathbf{F}$ tends to rotate the slab counterclockwise and in the second case that it tends to rotate the slab clockwise. Therefore, it is natural to refer to the sense of the moment of $\mathbf{F}$ about O in Fig. 3.13*a* as counterclockwise ↺, and in Fig. 3.13*b* as clockwise ↻.

Since the moment of a force $\mathbf{F}$ acting in the plane of the figure must be perpendicular to that plane, we need only specify the *magnitude* and the *sense* of the moment of $\mathbf{F}$ about O. This can be done by assigning to the magnitude M_O of the moment a positive or negative sign according to whether the vector $\mathbf{M}_O$ points out of or into the paper.

3.7. VARIGNON'S THEOREM

The distributive property of vector products can be used to determine the moment of the resultant of several *concurrent forces*. If several forces $\mathbf{F}_1$, $\mathbf{F}_2$, . . . are applied at the same point A (Fig. 3.14), and if we denote by $\mathbf{r}$ the position vector of A, it follows immediately from Eq. (3.5) of Sec. 3.4 that

$$\mathbf{r} \times (\mathbf{F}_1 + \mathbf{F}_2 + \cdots) = \mathbf{r} \times \mathbf{F}_1 + \mathbf{r} \times \mathbf{F}_2 + \cdots \tag{3.14}$$

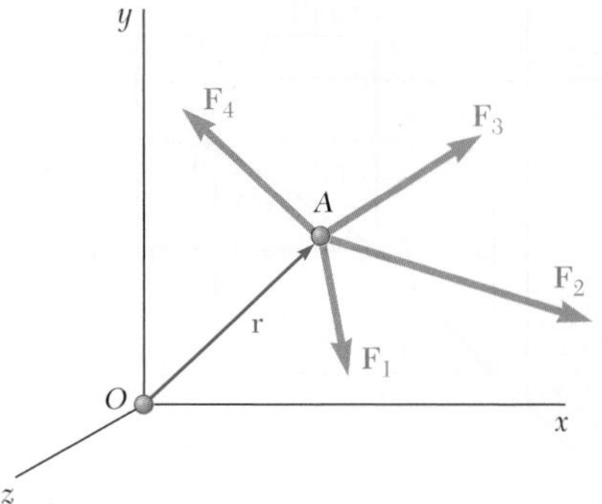

Fig. 3.14

In words, *the moment about a given point O of the resultant of several concurrent forces is equal to the sum of the moments of the various forces about the same point O*. This property, which was originally established by the French mathematician Pierre Varignon (1654–1722) long before the introduction of vector algebra, is known as *Varignon's theorem*.

The relation (3.14) makes it possible to replace the direct determination of the moment of a force $\mathbf{F}$ by the determination of the moments of two or more component forces. As you will see in the next section, $\mathbf{F}$ will generally be resolved into components parallel to the coordinate axes. However, it may be more expeditious in some instances to resolve $\mathbf{F}$ into components which are not parallel to the coordinate axes (see Sample Prob. 3.3).

3.8. RECTANGULAR COMPONENTS OF THE MOMENT OF A FORCE

In general, the determination of the moment of a force in space will be considerably simplified if the force and the position vector of its point of application are resolved into rectangular x, y, and z components. Consider, for example, the moment $\mathbf{M}_O$ about O of a force $\mathbf{F}$ whose components are F_x, F_y, and F_z and which is applied at a point A of coordinates x, y, and z (Fig. 3.15). Observing that the components of the position vector $\mathbf{r}$ are respectively equal to the coordinates x, y, and z of the point A, we write

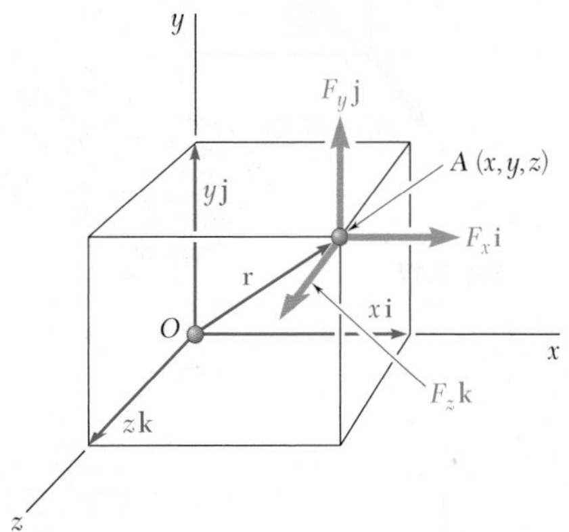

Fig. 3.15

$$\mathbf{r} = x\mathbf{i} + y\mathbf{j} + z\mathbf{k} \tag{3.15}$$
$$\mathbf{F} = F_x\mathbf{i} + F_y\mathbf{j} + F_z\mathbf{k} \tag{3.16}$$

Substituting for $\mathbf{r}$ and $\mathbf{F}$ from (3.15) and (3.16) into

$$\mathbf{M}_O = \mathbf{r} \times \mathbf{F} \tag{3.11}$$

and recalling the results obtained in Sec. 3.5, we write the moment $\mathbf{M}_O$ of $\mathbf{F}$ about O in the form

$$\mathbf{M}_O = M_x\mathbf{i} + M_y\mathbf{j} + M_z\mathbf{k} \tag{3.17}$$

where the components M_x, M_y, and M_z are defined by the relations

$$\begin{aligned} M_x &= yF_z - zF_y \\ M_y &= zF_x - xF_z \\ M_z &= xF_y - yF_x \end{aligned} \tag{3.18}$$

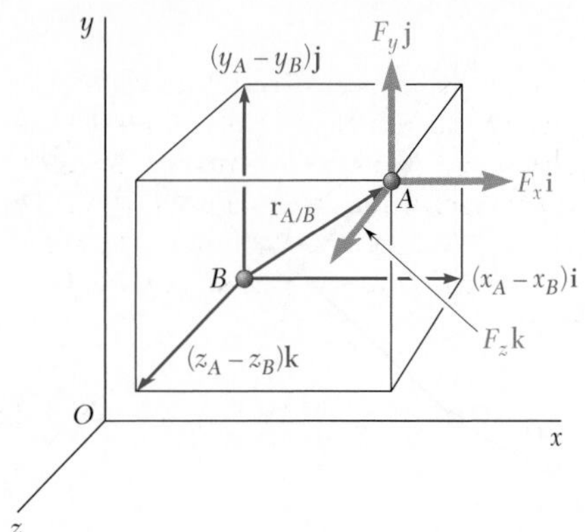

Fig 3.16

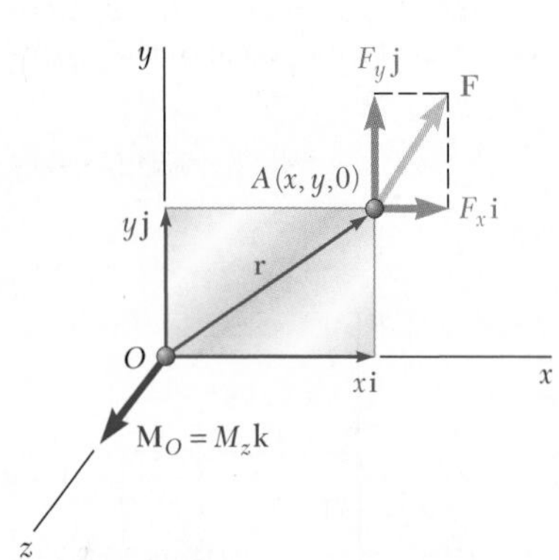

Fig. 3.17

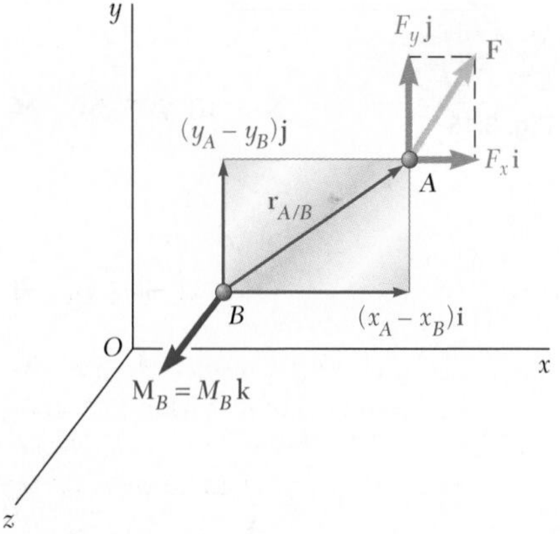

Fig. 3.18

As you will see in Sec. 3.11, the scalar components M_x, M_y, and M_z of the moment $\mathbf{M}_O$ measure the tendency of the force $\mathbf{F}$ to impart to a rigid body a motion of rotation about the x, y, and z axes, respectively. Substituting from (3.18) into (3.17), we can also write $\mathbf{M}_O$ in the form of the determinant

$$\mathbf{M}_O = \begin{vmatrix} \mathbf{i} & \mathbf{j} & \mathbf{k} \\ x & y & z \\ F_x & F_y & F_z \end{vmatrix} \tag{3.19}$$

To compute the moment $\mathbf{M}_B$ about an arbitrary point B of a force $\mathbf{F}$ applied at A (Fig. 3.16), we must replace the position vector $\mathbf{r}$ in Eq. (3.11) by a vector drawn from B to A. This vector is the *position vector of A relative to B* and will be denoted by $\mathbf{r}_{A/B}$. Observing that $\mathbf{r}_{A/B}$ can be obtained by subtracting $\mathbf{r}_B$ from $\mathbf{r}_A$, we write

$$\mathbf{M}_B = \mathbf{r}_{A/B} \times \mathbf{F} = (\mathbf{r}_A - \mathbf{r}_B) \times \mathbf{F} \tag{3.20}$$

or, using the determinant form,

$$\mathbf{M}_B = \begin{vmatrix} \mathbf{i} & \mathbf{j} & \mathbf{k} \\ x_{A/B} & y_{A/B} & z_{A/B} \\ F_x & F_y & F_z \end{vmatrix} \tag{3.21}$$

where $x_{A/B}$, $y_{A/B}$, and $z_{A/B}$ denote the components of the vector $\mathbf{r}_{A/B}$:

$$x_{A/B} = x_A - x_B \qquad y_{A/B} = y_A - y_B \qquad z_{A/B} = z_A - z_B$$

In the case of *problems involving only two dimensions*, the force $\mathbf{F}$ can be assumed to lie in the xy plane (Fig. 3.17). Setting $z = 0$ and $F_z = 0$ in Eq. (3.19), we obtain

$$\mathbf{M}_O = (xF_y - yF_x)\mathbf{k}$$

We verify that the moment of $\mathbf{F}$ about O is perpendicular to the plane of the figure and that it is completely defined by the scalar

$$M_O = M_z = xF_y - yF_x \tag{3.22}$$

As noted earlier, a positive value for M_O indicates that the vector $\mathbf{M}_O$ points out of the paper (the force $\mathbf{F}$ tends to rotate the body counterclockwise about O), and a negative value indicates that the vector $\mathbf{M}_O$ points into the paper (the force $\mathbf{F}$ tends to rotate the body clockwise about O).

To compute the moment about $B(x_B, y_B)$ of a force lying in the xy plane and applied at $A(x_A, y_A)$ (Fig. 3.18), we set $z_{A/B} = 0$ and $F_z = 0$ in the relations (3.21) and note that the vector $\mathbf{M}_B$ is perpendicular to the xy plane and is defined in magnitude and sense by the scalar

$$M_B = (x_A - x_B)F_y - (y_A - y_B)F_x \tag{3.23}$$

SAMPLE PROBLEM 3.1

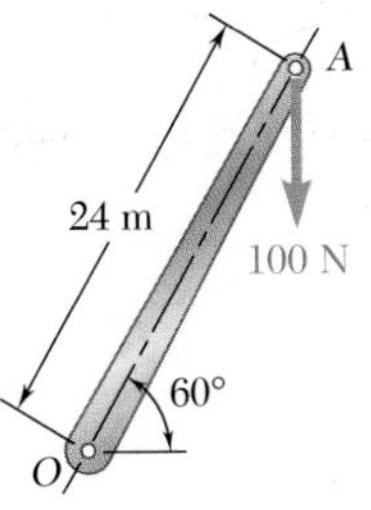

A 100-N vertical force is applied to the end of a lever which is attached to a shaft at O. Determine (*a*) the moment of the 100-N force about O; (*b*) the horizontal force applied at A which creates the same moment about O; (*c*) the smallest force applied at A which creates the same moment about O; (*d*) how far from the shaft a 240-N vertical force must act to create the same moment about O; (*e*) whether any one of the forces obtained in parts *b*, *c*, and *d* is equivalent to the original force.

SOLUTION

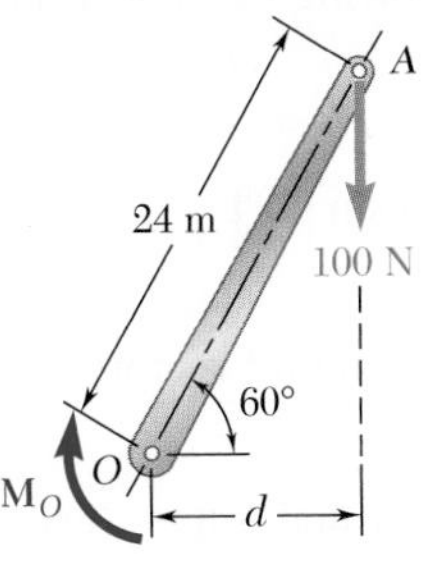

***a.* Moment about *O*.** The perpendicular distance from O to the line of action of the 100-N force is

$$d = (24 \text{ m}) \cos 60° = 12 \text{ m}$$

The magnitude of the moment about O of the 100-N force is

$$M_O = Fd = (100 \text{ N})(12 \text{ m}) = 1200 \text{ N} \cdot \text{m}$$

Since the force tends to rotate the lever clockwise about O, the moment will be represented by a vector $\mathbf{M}_O$ perpendicular to the plane of the figure and pointing *into* the paper. We express this fact by writing

$$\mathbf{M}_O = 1200 \text{ N} \cdot \text{m} \circlearrowright \quad ◀$$

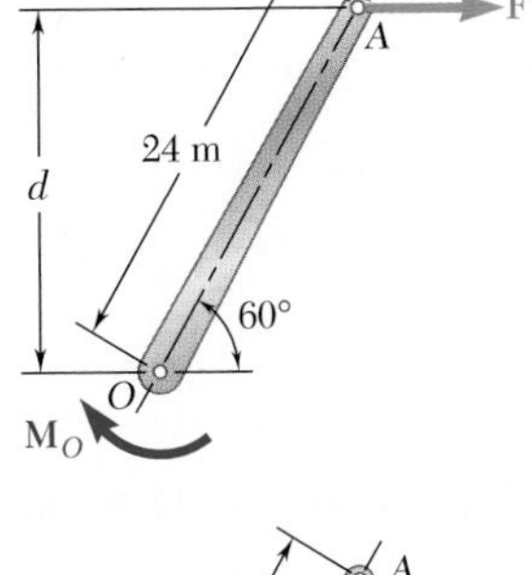

***b.* Horizontal Force.** In this case, we have

$$d = (24 \text{ m}) \sin 60° = 20.8 \text{ m}$$

Since the moment about O must be 1200 N · m, we write

$$M_O = Fd$$
$$1200 \text{ N} \cdot \text{m} = F(20.8 \text{ m})$$
$$F = 57.7 \text{ N} \qquad \mathbf{F} = 57.7 \text{ N} \rightarrow \quad ◀$$

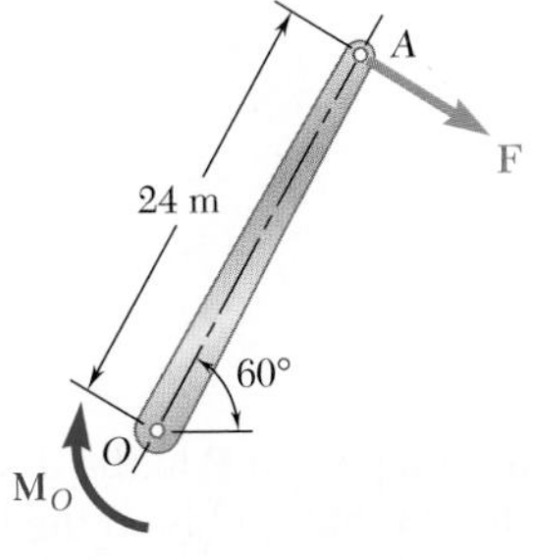

***c.* Smallest Force.** Since $M_O = Fd$, the smallest value of F occurs when d is maximum. We choose the force perpendicular to OA and note that $d = 24$ m; thus

$$M_O = Fd$$
$$1200 \text{ N} \cdot \text{m} = F(24 \text{ m})$$
$$F = 50 \text{ N} \qquad \mathbf{F} = 50 \text{ N} \measuredangle 30° \quad ◀$$

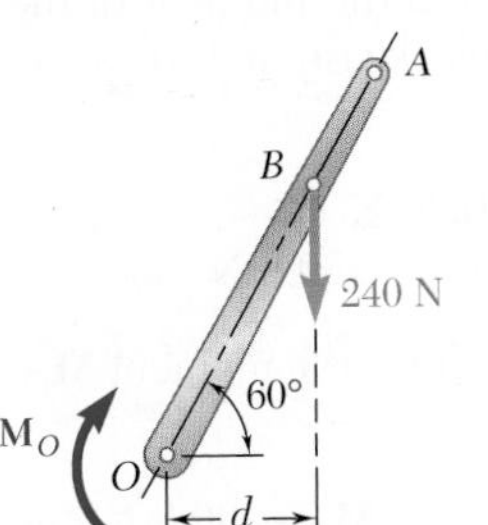

***d.* 240-lb Vertical Force.** In this case $M_O = Fd$ yields

$$1200 \text{ N} \cdot \text{m} = (240 \text{ N})d \qquad d = 5 \text{ m}$$

but $\quad OB \cos 60° = d \qquad OB = 10 \text{ m} \quad ◀$

e. None of the forces considered in parts *b*, *c*, and *d* is equivalent to the original 100-N force. Although they have the same moment about O, they have different x and y components. In other words, although each force tends to rotate the shaft in the same manner, each causes the lever to pull on the shaft in a different way.

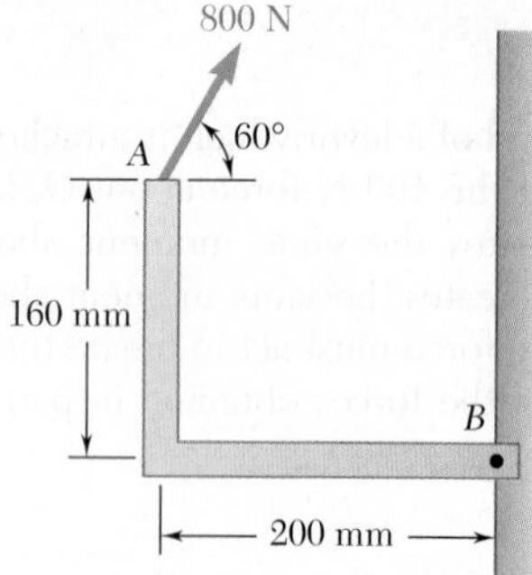

SAMPLE PROBLEM 3.2

A force of 800 N acts on a bracket as shown. Determine the moment of the force about B.

SOLUTION

The moment $\mathbf{M}_B$ of the force $\mathbf{F}$ about B is obtained by forming the vector product

$$\mathbf{M}_B = \mathbf{r}_{A/B} \times \mathbf{F}$$

where $\mathbf{r}_{A/B}$ is the vector drawn from B to A. Resolving $\mathbf{r}_{A/B}$ and $\mathbf{F}$ into rectangular components, we have

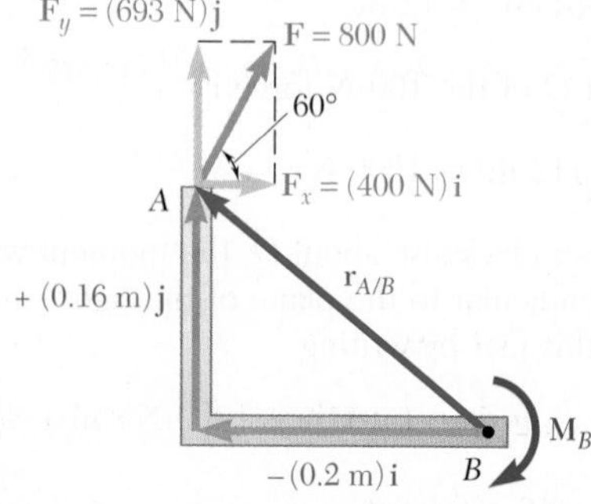

$$\mathbf{r}_{A/B} = -(0.2\text{ m})\mathbf{i} + (0.16\text{ m})\mathbf{j}$$
$$\mathbf{F} = (800\text{ N})\cos 60°\mathbf{i} + (800\text{ N})\sin 60°\mathbf{j}$$
$$= (400\text{ N})\mathbf{i} + (693\text{ N})\mathbf{j}$$

Recalling the relations (3.7) for the vector products of unit vectors (Sec. 3.5), we obtain

$$\mathbf{M}_B = \mathbf{r}_{A/B} \times \mathbf{F} = [-(0.2\text{ m})\mathbf{i} + (0.16\text{ m})\mathbf{j}] \times [(400\text{ N})\mathbf{i} + (693\text{ N})\mathbf{j}]$$
$$= -(138.6\text{ N}\cdot\text{m})\mathbf{k} - (64.0\text{ N}\cdot\text{m})\mathbf{k}$$
$$= -(202.6\text{ N}\cdot\text{m})\mathbf{k} \qquad \mathbf{M}_B = 203\text{ N}\cdot\text{m} \circlearrowright \blacktriangleleft$$

The moment $\mathbf{M}_B$ is a vector perpendicular to the plane of the figure and pointing *into* the paper.

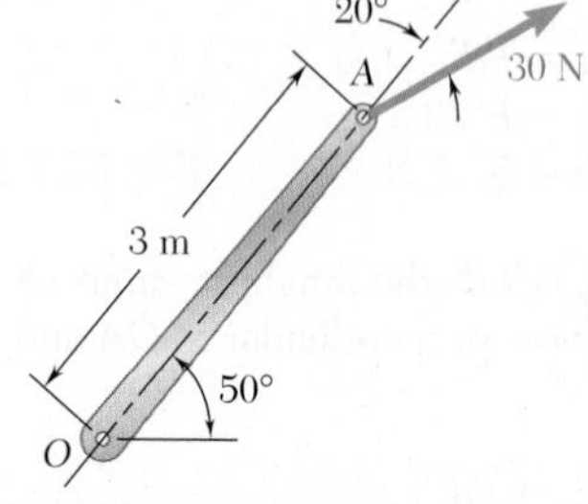

SAMPLE PROBLEM 3.3

A 30-N force acts on the end of the 3-m lever as shown. Determine the moment of the force about O.

SOLUTION

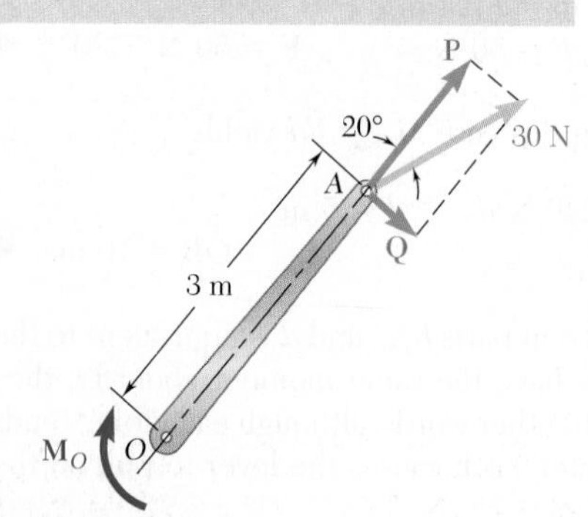

The force is replaced by two components, one component $\mathbf{P}$ in the direction of OA and one component $\mathbf{Q}$ perpendicular to OA. Since O is on the line of action of $\mathbf{P}$, the moment of $\mathbf{P}$ about O is zero and the moment of the 30-N force reduces to the moment of $\mathbf{Q}$, which is clockwise and, thus, is represented by a negative scalar.

$$Q = (30\text{ N})\sin 20° = 10.26\text{ N}$$
$$M_O = -Q(3\text{ m}) = -(10.26\text{ N})(3\text{ m}) = -30.8\text{ N}\cdot\text{m}$$

Since the value obtained for the scalar M_O is negative, the moment $\mathbf{M}_O$ points *into* the paper. We write

$$\mathbf{M}_O = 30.8\text{ N}\cdot\text{m} \circlearrowright \blacktriangleleft$$

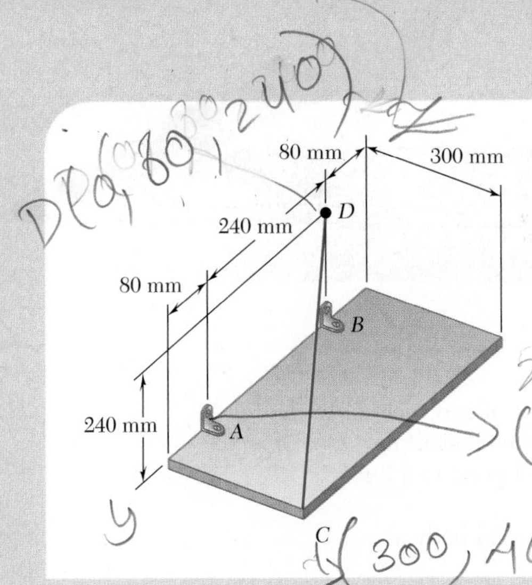

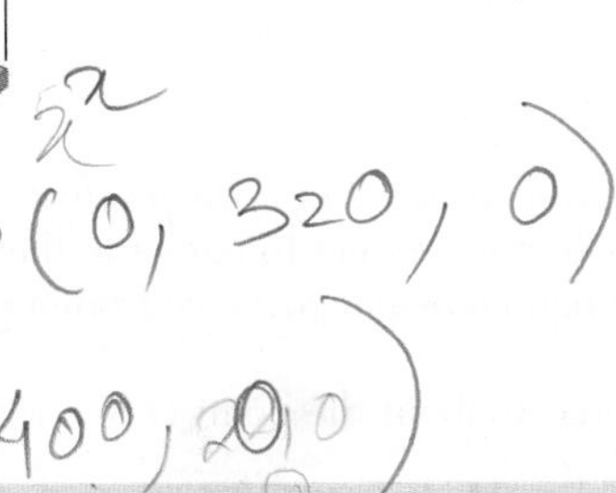

SAMPLE PROBLEM 3.4

A rectangular plate is supported by brackets at *A* and *B* and by a wire *CD*. Knowing that the tension in the wire is 200 N, determine the moment about *A* of the force exerted by the wire on point *C*.

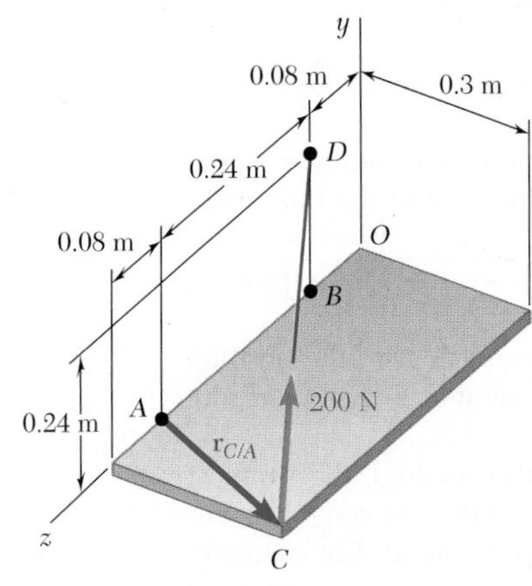

SOLUTION

The moment $\mathbf{M}_A$ about *A* of the force **F** exerted by the wire on point *C* is obtained by forming the vector product

$$\mathbf{M}_A = \mathbf{r}_{C/A} \times \mathbf{F} \qquad (1)$$

where $\mathbf{r}_{C/A}$ is the vector drawn from *A* to *C*,

$$\mathbf{r}_{C/A} = \overrightarrow{AC} = (0.3 \text{ m})\mathbf{i} + (0.08 \text{ m})\mathbf{k} \qquad (2)$$

and **F** is the 200-N force directed along *CD*. Introducing the unit vector $\boldsymbol{\lambda} = \overrightarrow{CD}/CD$, we write

$$\mathbf{F} = F\boldsymbol{\lambda} = (200 \text{ N})\frac{\overrightarrow{CD}}{CD} \qquad (3)$$

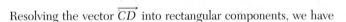

Resolving the vector $\overrightarrow{CD}$ into rectangular components, we have

$$\overrightarrow{CD} = -(0.3 \text{ m})\mathbf{i} + (0.24 \text{ m})\mathbf{j} - (0.32 \text{ m})\mathbf{k} \qquad CD = 0.50 \text{ m}$$

Substituting into (3), we obtain

$$\mathbf{F} = \frac{200 \text{ N}}{0.50 \text{ m}}[-(0.3 \text{ m})\mathbf{i} + (0.24 \text{ m})\mathbf{j} - (0.32 \text{ m})\mathbf{k}]$$

$$= -(120 \text{ N})\mathbf{i} + (96 \text{ N})\mathbf{j} - (128 \text{ N})\mathbf{k} \qquad (4)$$

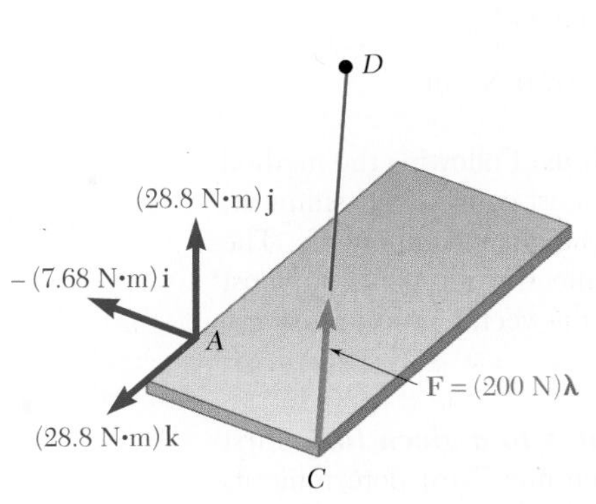

Substituting for $\mathbf{r}_{C/A}$ and **F** from (2) and (4) into (1) and recalling the relations (3.7) of Sec. 3.5, we obtain

$$\mathbf{M}_A = \mathbf{r}_{C/A} \times \mathbf{F} = (0.3\mathbf{i} + 0.08\mathbf{k}) \times (-120\mathbf{i} + 96\mathbf{j} - 128\mathbf{k})$$

$$= (0.3)(96)\mathbf{k} + (0.3)(-128)(-\mathbf{j}) + (0.08)(-120)\mathbf{j} + (0.08)(96)(-\mathbf{i})$$

$$\mathbf{M}_A = -(7.68 \text{ N}\cdot\text{m})\mathbf{i} + (28.8 \text{ N}\cdot\text{m})\mathbf{j} + (28.8 \text{ N}\cdot\text{m})\mathbf{k} \quad \blacktriangleleft$$

Alternative Solution. As indicated in Sec. 3.8, the moment $\mathbf{M}_A$ can be expressed in the form of a determinant:

$$\mathbf{M}_A = \begin{vmatrix} \mathbf{i} & \mathbf{j} & \mathbf{k} \\ x_C - x_A & y_C - y_A & z_C - z_A \\ F_x & F_y & F_z \end{vmatrix} = \begin{vmatrix} \mathbf{i} & \mathbf{j} & \mathbf{k} \\ 0.3 & 0 & 0.08 \\ -120 & 96 & -128 \end{vmatrix}$$

$$\mathbf{M}_A = -(7.68 \text{ N}\cdot\text{m})\mathbf{i} + (28.8 \text{ N}\cdot\text{m})\mathbf{j} + (28.8 \text{ N}\cdot\text{m})\mathbf{k} \quad \blacktriangleleft$$

SOLVING PROBLEMS ON YOUR OWN

In this lesson we introduced the *vector product* or *cross product* of two vectors. In the following problems, you will use the vector product to compute the *moment of a force about a point* and also to determine the *perpendicular distance* from a point to a line.

We defined the moment of the force **F** about the point O of a rigid body as

$$\mathbf{M}_O = \mathbf{r} \times \mathbf{F} \tag{3.11}$$

where **r** is the position vector *from O to any point* on the line of action of **F**. Since the vector product is not commutative, it is absolutely necessary when computing such a product that you place the vectors in the proper order and that each vector have the correct sense. The moment $\mathbf{M}_O$ is important because its magnitude is a measure of the tendency of the force **F** to cause the rigid body to rotate about an axis directed along $\mathbf{M}_O$.

1. ***Computing the moment*** $\mathbf{M}_O$ ***of a force in two dimensions.*** You can use one of the following procedures:

a. Use Eq. (3.12), $M_O = Fd$, which expresses the magnitude of the moment as the product of the magnitude of **F** and the *perpendicular distance* d from O to the line of action of **F** [Sample Prob. 3.1].

b. Express **r** and **F** in component form and formally evaluate the vector product $\mathbf{M}_O = \mathbf{r} \times \mathbf{F}$ [Sample Prob. 3.2].

c. Resolve **F** into components respectively parallel and perpendicular to the position vector **r**. Only the perpendicular component contributes to the moment of **F** [Sample Prob. 3.3].

d. Use Eq. (3.22), $M_O = M_z = xF_y - yF_x$. When applying this method, the simplest approach is to treat the scalar components of **r** and **F** as positive and then to assign, by observation, the proper sign to the moment produced by each force component. For example, applying this method to solve Sample Prob. 3.2, we observe that both force components tend to produce a clockwise rotation about B. Therefore, the moment of each force about B should be represented by a negative scalar. We then have for the total moment

$$M_B = -(0.16 \text{ m})(400 \text{ N}) - (0.20 \text{ m})(693 \text{ N}) = -202.6 \text{ N} \cdot \text{m}$$

2. ***Computing the moment*** $\mathbf{M}_O$ ***of a force*** **F** ***in three dimensions.*** Following the method of Sample Prob. 3.4, the first step in the process is to select the most convenient (simplest) position vector **r**. You should next express **F** in terms of its rectangular components. The final step is to evaluate the vector product $\mathbf{r} \times \mathbf{F}$ to determine the moment. In most three-dimensional problems you will find it easiest to calculate the vector product using a determinant.

3. ***Determining the perpendicular distance d from a point A to a given line.*** First assume that a force **F** of known magnitude F lies along the given line. Next determine its moment about A by forming the vector product $\mathbf{M}_A = \mathbf{r} \times \mathbf{F}$, and calculate this product as indicated above. Then compute its magnitude M_A. Finally, substitute the values of F and M_A into the equation $M_A = Fd$ and solve for d.

Problems

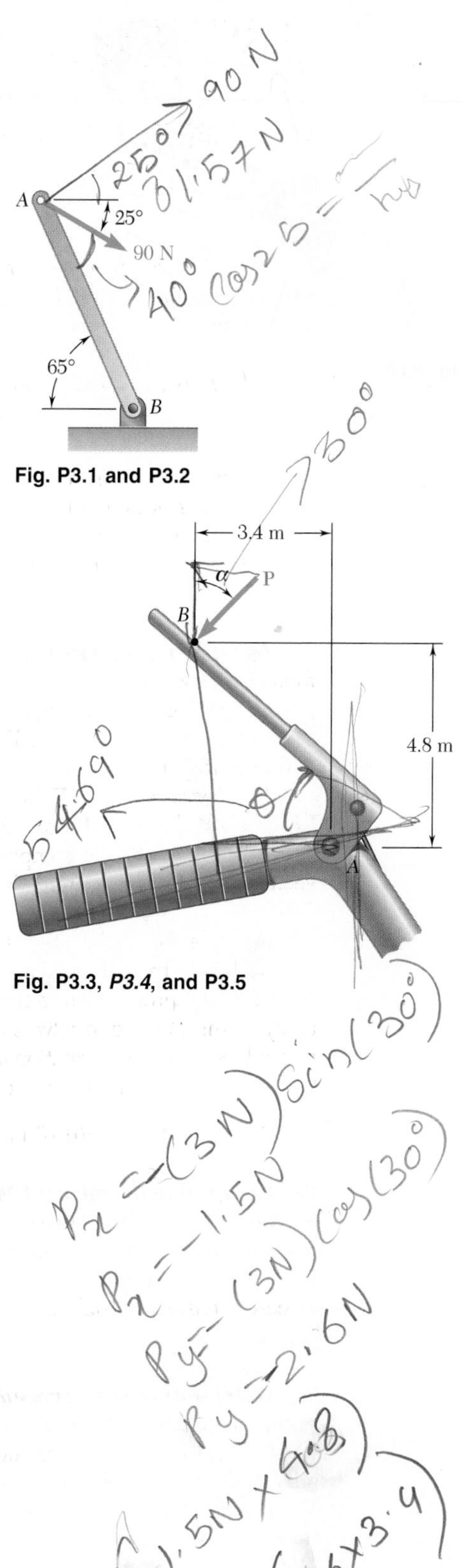

Fig. P3.1 and P3.2

Fig. P3.3, *P3.4*, and P3.5

3.1 A 90-N force is applied to the control rod AB as shown. Knowing that the length of the rod is 225 mm, determine the moment of the force about point B by resolving the force into components along AB and in a direction perpendicular to AB.

3.2 A 90-N force is applied to the control rod AB as shown. Knowing that the length of the rod is 225 mm, determine the moment of the force about point B by resolving the force into horizontal and vertical components.

3.3 A 3-N force **P** is applied to the lever which controls the auger of a snowblower. Determine the moment of **P** about A when α is equal to 30°.

3.4 The force **P** is applied to the lever which controls the auger of a snowblower. Determine the magnitude and the direction of the smallest force **P** which has a 19.5-N · m counterclockwise moment about A.

3.5 A 2.9-N force **P** is applied to the lever which controls the auger of a snowblower. Determine the value of α knowing that the moment of **P** about A is counterclockwise and has a magnitude of 17 N · m.

3.6 A sign is suspended from two chains AE and BF. Knowing that the tension in BF is 200 N, determine (*a*) the moment about A of the force exerted by the chain at B, (*b*) the smallest force applied at C which creates the same moment about A.

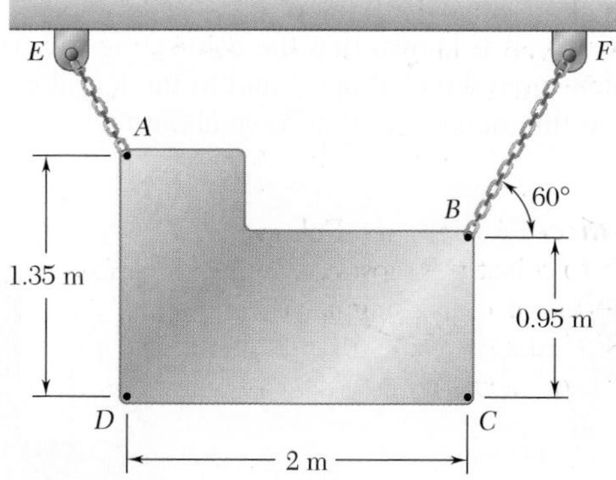

Fig. P3.6 and P3.7

3.7 A sign is suspended from two chains AE and BF. Knowing that the tension in BF is 200 N, determine (*a*) the moment about A of the force exerted by the chain at B, (*b*) the magnitude and sense of the vertical force applied at C which creates the same moment about A, (*c*) the smallest force applied at B which creates the same moment about A.

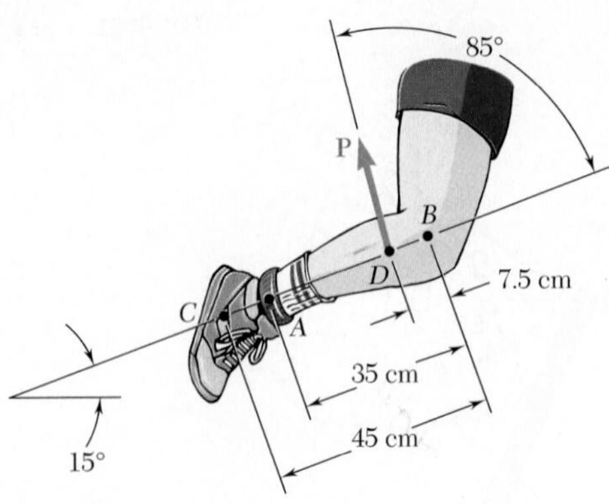

Fig. *P3.8*

3.8 An athlete is exercising while wearing a 5-kg ankle weight at A as shown. Determine (a) the moment of the weight about the knee joint at B, (b) the magnitude of the muscular force **P** which creates a moment of equal magnitude about B, (c) the smallest force **F** applied at C which creates the same moment about B as the weight.

3.9 A winch puller AB is used to straighten a fence post. Knowing that the tension in cable BC is 260 N, length a is 8 cm, length b is 35 cm, and length d is 76 cm, determine the moment about D of the force exerted by the cable at C by resolving that force into horizontal and vertical components applied (a) at point C, (b) at point E.

3.10 It is known that a force with a moment of 7840 N · cm about D is required to straighten the fence post CD. If $a = 8$ cm, $b = 35$ cm, and $d = 112$ cm, determine the tension that must be developed in the cable of winch puller AB to create the required moment about point D.

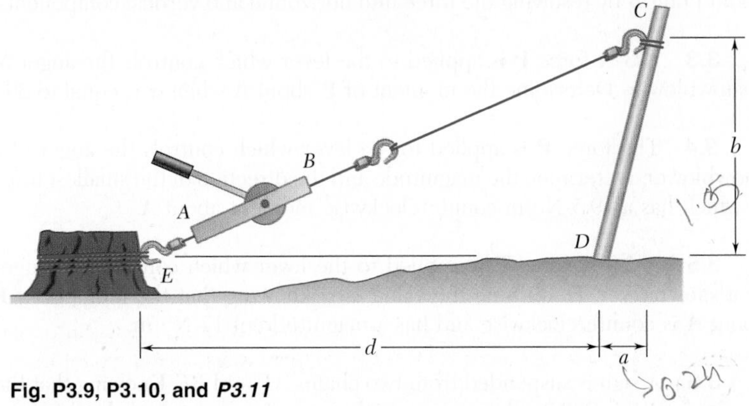

Fig. P3.9, P3.10, and *P3.11*

3.11 It is known that a force with a moment of 1152 N · m about D is required to straighten the fence post CD. If the capacity of the winch puller AB is 2880 N, determine the minimum value of distance d to create the specified moment about point D knowing that $a = 0.24$ m and $b = 1.05$ m.

3.12 and *3.13* It is known that the connecting rod AB exerts on the crank BC a 2.5-kN force directed down and to the left along the centerline of AB. Determine the moment of that force about C.

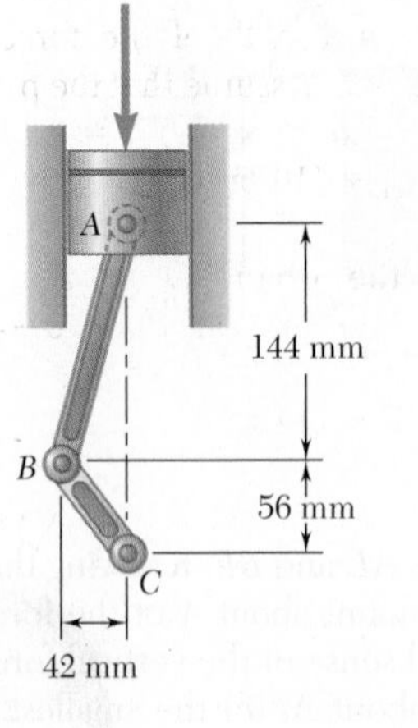

Fig. P3.12

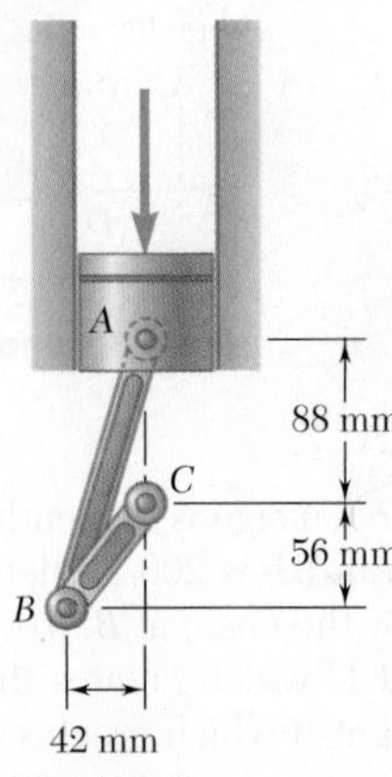

Fig. *P3.13*

3.14 A 64-mm-diameter circular follower B is held against cam A as shown. Knowing that the cam exerts on the follower a force of magnitude 80 N directed along the common normal BC, determine the moment of the force about the pin at D.

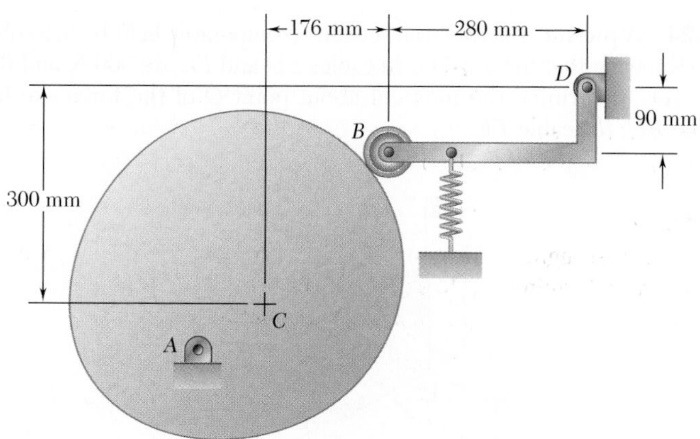

Fig. P3.14

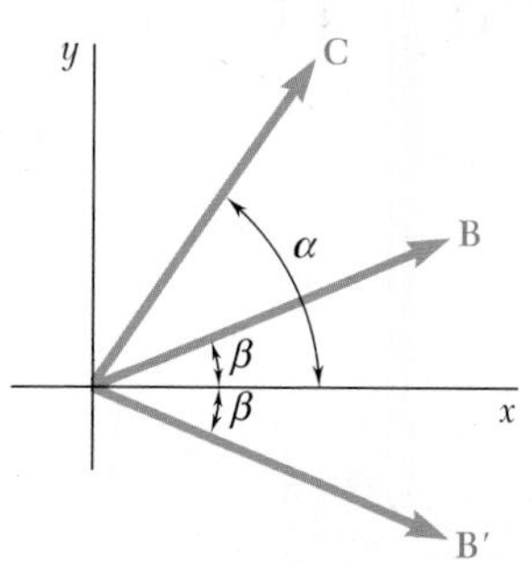

Fig. P3.15

3.15 Form the vector products $\mathbf{B} \times \mathbf{C}$ and $\mathbf{B}' \times \mathbf{C}$, where $B = B'$, and use the results obtained to prove the identity

$$\sin \alpha \cos \beta = \tfrac{1}{2} \sin (\alpha + \beta) + \tfrac{1}{2} \sin (\alpha - \beta).$$

3.16 A line passes through the points (630 mm, −225 mm) and (−210 mm, 270 mm). Determine the perpendicular distance d from the line to the origin O of the system of coordinates.

3.17 A plane contains the vectors **A** and **B**. Determine the unit vector normal to the plane when **A** and **B** are equal to, respectively, (*a*) $12\mathbf{i} - 6\mathbf{j} + 9\mathbf{k}$ and $-3\mathbf{i} + 9\mathbf{j} - 7.5\mathbf{k}$, (*b*) $-14\mathbf{i} - 2\mathbf{j} + 8\mathbf{k}$ and $3\mathbf{i} + 1.5\mathbf{j} - \mathbf{k}$.

3.18 The vectors **P** and **Q** are two adjacent sides of a parallelogram. Determine the area of the parallelogram when (*a*) $\mathbf{P} = (3 \text{ cm})\mathbf{i} + (7 \text{ cm})\mathbf{j} - (2 \text{ cm})\mathbf{k}$ and $\mathbf{Q} = -(5 \text{ cm})\mathbf{i} + (1 \text{ cm})\mathbf{j} + (3 \text{ cm})\mathbf{k}$, (*b*) $\mathbf{P} = (2 \text{ cm})\mathbf{i} - (4 \text{ cm})\mathbf{j} - (3 \text{ cm})\mathbf{k}$ and $\mathbf{Q} = (6 \text{ cm})\mathbf{i} - (1 \text{ cm})\mathbf{j} + (5 \text{ cm})\mathbf{k}$.

3.19 Determine the moment about the origin O of the force $\mathbf{F} = (7.5 \text{ N})\mathbf{i} + (3 \text{ N})\mathbf{j} - (4.5 \text{ N})\mathbf{k}$ which acts at a point A. Assume that the position vector of A is (*a*) $\mathbf{r} = -(6 \text{ m})\mathbf{i} + (3 \text{ m})\mathbf{j} + (1.5 \text{ m})\mathbf{k}$, (*b*) $\mathbf{r} = (2 \text{ m})\mathbf{i} - (0.75 \text{ m})\mathbf{j} - (1 \text{ m})\mathbf{k}$, (*c*) $\mathbf{r} = -(2.5 \text{ m})\mathbf{i} - (1 \text{ m})\mathbf{j} + (1.5 \text{ m})\mathbf{k}$.

3.20 Determine the moment about the origin O of the force $\mathbf{F} = (3 \text{ N})\mathbf{i} - (6 \text{ N})\mathbf{j} + (4 \text{ N})\mathbf{k}$ which acts at a point A. Assume that the position vector of A is (*a*) $\mathbf{r} = -(7.5 \text{ m})\mathbf{i} + (3 \text{ m})\mathbf{j} - (6 \text{ m})\mathbf{k}$, (*b*) $\mathbf{r} = -(0.75 \text{ m})\mathbf{i} + (1.5 \text{ m})\mathbf{j} - (1 \text{ m})\mathbf{k}$, (*c*) $\mathbf{r} = -(8 \text{ m})\mathbf{i} + (2 \text{ m})\mathbf{j} - (14 \text{ m})\mathbf{k}$.

3.21 A small boat hangs from two davits, one of which is shown in the figure. The tension in line $ABAD$ is 369 N. Determine the moment about C of the resultant force $\mathbf{R}_A$ exerted on the davit at A.

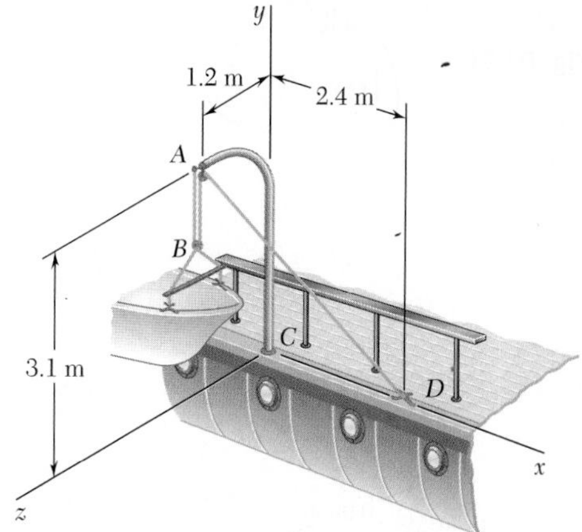

Fig. P3.21

3.22 A 36-N force is applied to a wrench to tighten a showerhead. Knowing that the centerline of the wrench is parallel to the x axis, determine the moment of the force about A.

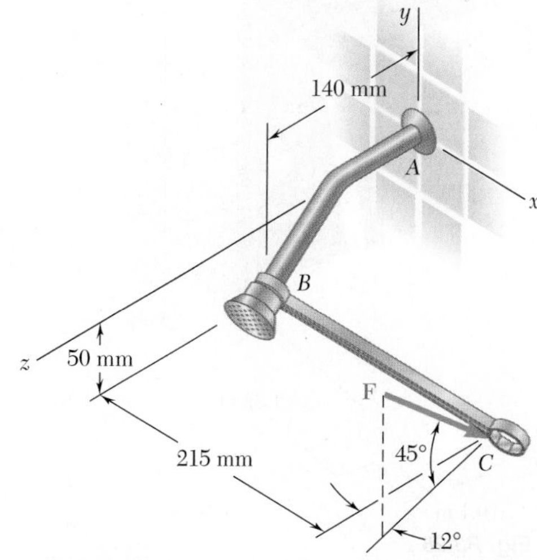

Fig. *P3.22*

3.23 Before a telephone cable is strung, rope *BAC* is tied to a stake at *B* and is passed over a pulley at *A*. Knowing that portion *AC* of the rope lies in a plane parallel to the *xy* plane and that the magnitude of the tension **T** in the rope is 62 N, determine the moment about *O* of the resultant force exerted on the pulley by the rope.

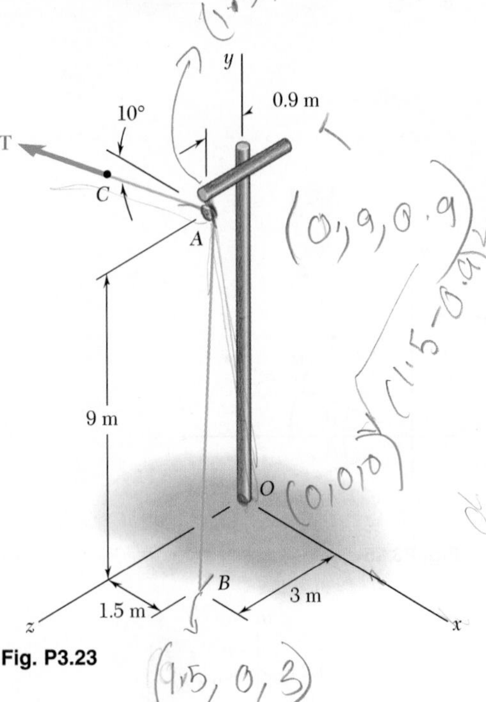

Fig. P3.23

3.24 A precast concrete wall section is temporarily held by two cables as shown. Knowing that the tensions in cables *BD* and *FE* are 900 N and 675 N, respectively, determine the moment about point *O* of the force exerted by (*a*) cable *BD*, (*b*) cable *FE*.

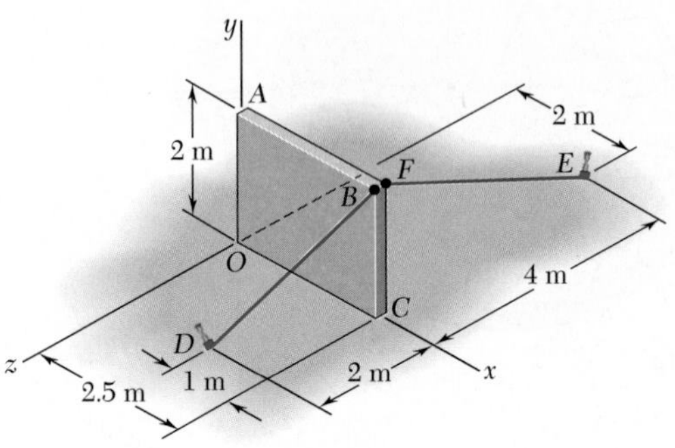

Fig. P3.24

3.25 In an arm wrestling contest, a 150-N force **P** is applied to the hand of one of the contestants by his opponent. Knowing that *AB* = 15.2 cm and *BC* = 16 cm, determine the moment of the force about *C*.

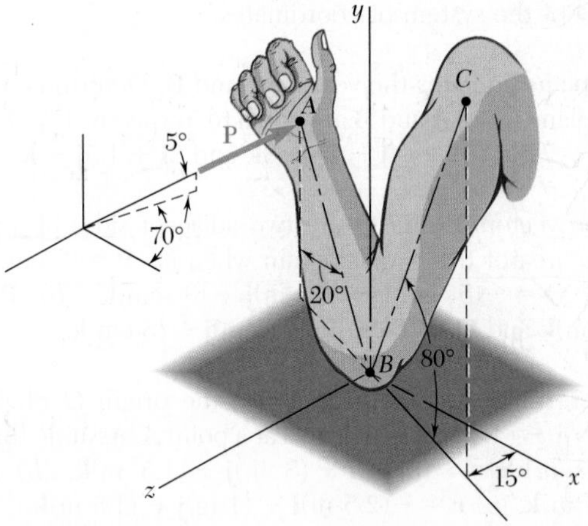

Fig. P3.25

3.26 A wooden board *AB*, which is used as a temporary prop to support a small roof, exerts at point *A* of the roof a 228-N force directed along *BA*. Determine the moment about *C* of that force.

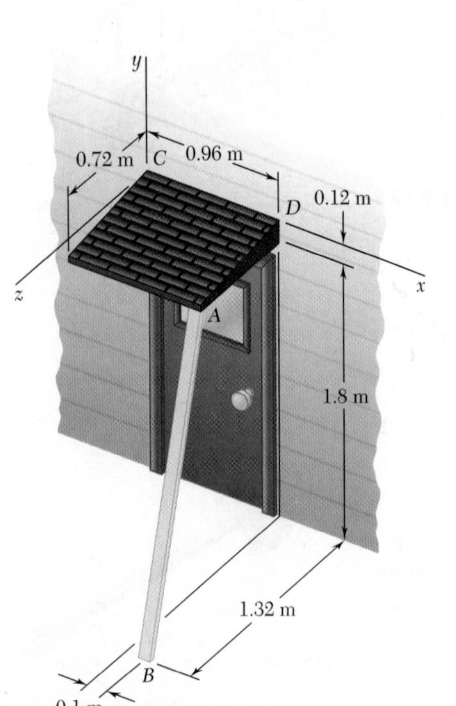

Fig. P3.26

3.27 In Prob. 3.21, determine the perpendicular distance from point *C* to portion *AD* of the line *ABAD*.

3.28 In Prob. 3.23, determine the perpendicular distance from point *O* to portion *AC* of rope *BAC*.

3.29 In Prob. 3.23, determine the perpendicular distance from point O to portion AB of rope BAC.

3.30 In Prob. 3.24, determine the perpendicular distance from point C to cable BD.

3.31 In Prob. 3.25, determine the perpendicular distance from point C to the line of action of force **P**.

3.32 In Prob. 3.26, determine the perpendicular distance from point D to a line drawn through points A and B.

3.33 In Prob. 3.26, determine the perpendicular distance from point C to a line drawn through points A and B.

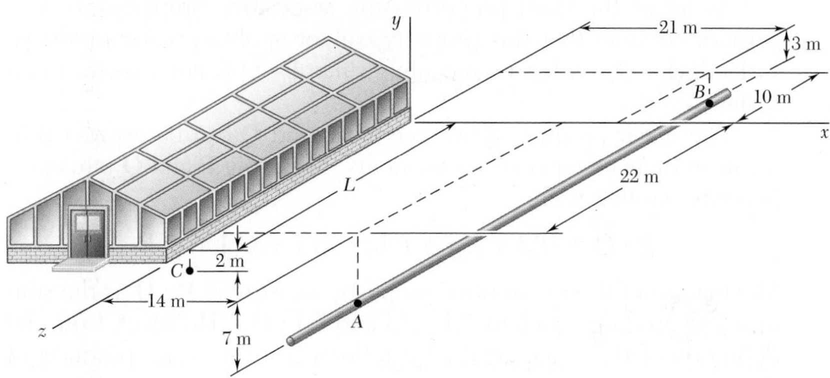

Fig. *P3.34*

3.34 A gardener wishes to connect a water supply pipe from point C on the foundation of a 30-m-long greenhouse to a water main that passes through points A and B. Determine (a) the value of L which minimizes the length of supply pipe needed, (b) the length of pipe needed.

3.9. SCALAR PRODUCT OF TWO VECTORS

The *scalar product* of two vectors **P** and **Q** is defined as the product of the magnitudes of **P** and **Q** and of the cosine of the angle θ formed by **P** and **Q** (Fig. 3.19). The scalar product of **P** and **Q** is denoted by $\mathbf{P} \cdot \mathbf{Q}$. We write therefore

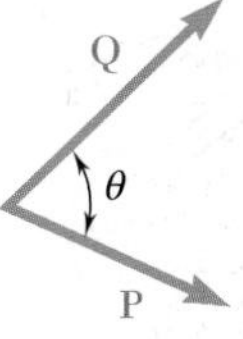

Fig. 3.19

$$\mathbf{P} \cdot \mathbf{Q} = PQ \cos \theta \tag{3.24}$$

Note that the expression just defined is not a vector but a *scalar*, which explains the name *scalar product*; because of the notation used, $\mathbf{P} \cdot \mathbf{Q}$ is also referred to as the *dot product* of the vectors **P** and **Q**.

It follows from its very definition that the scalar product of two vectors is *commutative*, that is, that

$$\mathbf{P} \cdot \mathbf{Q} = \mathbf{Q} \cdot \mathbf{P} \tag{3.25}$$

To prove that the scalar product is also *distributive*, we must prove the relation

$$\mathbf{P} \cdot (\mathbf{Q}_1 + \mathbf{Q}_2) = \mathbf{P} \cdot \mathbf{Q}_1 + \mathbf{P} \cdot \mathbf{Q}_2 \tag{3.26}$$

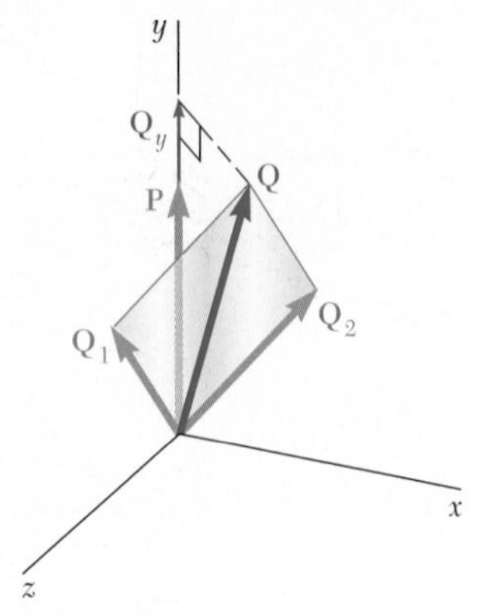

Fig. 3.20

We can, without any loss of generality, assume that **P** is directed along the y axis (Fig. 3.20). Denoting by **Q** the sum of $\mathbf{Q}_1$ and $\mathbf{Q}_2$ and by θ_y the angle **Q** forms with the y axis, we express the left-hand member of (3.26) as follows:

$$\mathbf{P} \cdot (\mathbf{Q}_1 + \mathbf{Q}_2) = \mathbf{P} \cdot \mathbf{Q} = PQ \cos \theta_y = PQ_y \qquad (3.27)$$

where Q_y is the y component of **Q**. We can, in a similar way, express the right-hand member of (3.26) as

$$\mathbf{P} \cdot \mathbf{Q}_1 + \mathbf{P} \cdot \mathbf{Q}_2 = P(Q_1)_y + P(Q_2)_y \qquad (3.28)$$

Since **Q** is the sum of $\mathbf{Q}_1$ and $\mathbf{Q}_2$, its y component must be equal to the sum of the y components of $\mathbf{Q}_1$ and $\mathbf{Q}_2$. Thus, the expressions obtained in (3.27) and (3.28) are equal, and the relation (3.26) has been proved.

As far as the third property—the associative property—is concerned, we note that this property cannot apply to scalar products. Indeed, $(\mathbf{P} \cdot \mathbf{Q}) \cdot \mathbf{S}$ has no meaning, since $\mathbf{P} \cdot \mathbf{Q}$ is not a vector but a scalar.

The scalar product of two vectors **P** and **Q** can be expressed in terms of their rectangular components. Resolving **P** and **Q** into components, we first write

$$\mathbf{P} \cdot \mathbf{Q} = (P_x\mathbf{i} + P_y\mathbf{j} + P_z\mathbf{k}) \cdot (Q_x\mathbf{i} + Q_y\mathbf{j} + Q_z\mathbf{k})$$

Making use of the distributive property, we express $\mathbf{P} \cdot \mathbf{Q}$ as the sum of scalar products, such as $P_x\mathbf{i} \cdot Q_x\mathbf{i}$ and $P_x\mathbf{i} \cdot Q_y\mathbf{j}$. However, from the definition of the scalar product it follows that the scalar products of the unit vectors are either zero or one.

$$\begin{array}{lll} \mathbf{i} \cdot \mathbf{i} = 1 & \mathbf{j} \cdot \mathbf{j} = 1 & \mathbf{k} \cdot \mathbf{k} = 1 \\ \mathbf{i} \cdot \mathbf{j} = 0 & \mathbf{j} \cdot \mathbf{k} = 0 & \mathbf{k} \cdot \mathbf{i} = 0 \end{array} \qquad (3.29)$$

Thus, the expression obtained for $\mathbf{P} \cdot \mathbf{Q}$ reduces to

$$\mathbf{P} \cdot \mathbf{Q} = P_xQ_x + P_yQ_y + P_zQ_z \qquad (3.30)$$

In the particular case when **P** and **Q** are equal, we note that

$$\mathbf{P} \cdot \mathbf{P} = P_x^2 + P_y^2 + P_z^2 = P^2 \qquad (3.31)$$

Applications

1. ***Angle formed by two given vectors.*** Let two vectors be given in terms of their components:

$$\mathbf{P} = P_x\mathbf{i} + P_y\mathbf{j} + P_z\mathbf{k}$$
$$\mathbf{Q} = Q_x\mathbf{i} + Q_y\mathbf{j} + Q_z\mathbf{k}$$

To determine the angle formed by the two vectors, we equate the expressions obtained in (3.24) and (3.30) for their scalar product and write

$$PQ \cos \theta = P_xQ_x + P_yQ_y + P_zQ_z$$

Solving for $\cos \theta$, we have

$$\cos \theta = \frac{P_xQ_x + P_yQ_y + P_zQ_z}{PQ} \qquad (3.32)$$

2. *Projection of a vector on a given axis.* Consider a vector **P** forming an angle θ with an axis, or directed line, OL (Fig. 3.21). The *projection of* **P** *on the axis* OL is defined as the scalar

$$P_{OL} = P \cos \theta \tag{3.33}$$

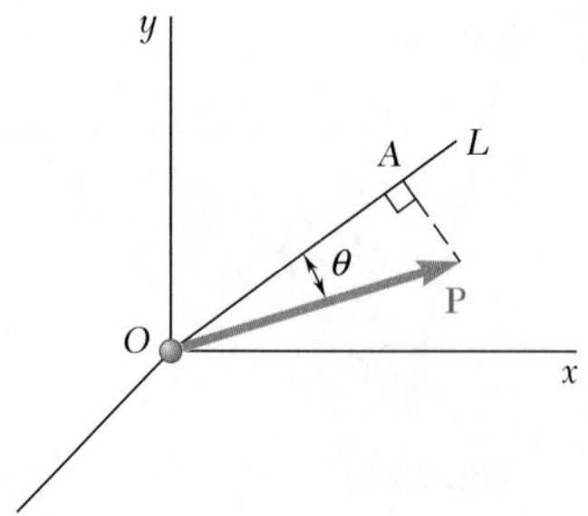

Fig. 3.21

We note that the projection P_{OL} is equal in absolute value to the length of the segment OA; it will be positive if OA has the same sense as the axis OL, that is, if θ is acute, and negative otherwise. If **P** and OL are at a right angle, the projection of **P** on OL is zero.

Consider now a vector **Q** directed along OL and of the same sense as OL (Fig. 3.22). The scalar product of **P** and **Q** can be expressed as

$$\mathbf{P} \cdot \mathbf{Q} = PQ \cos \theta = P_{OL}Q \tag{3.34}$$

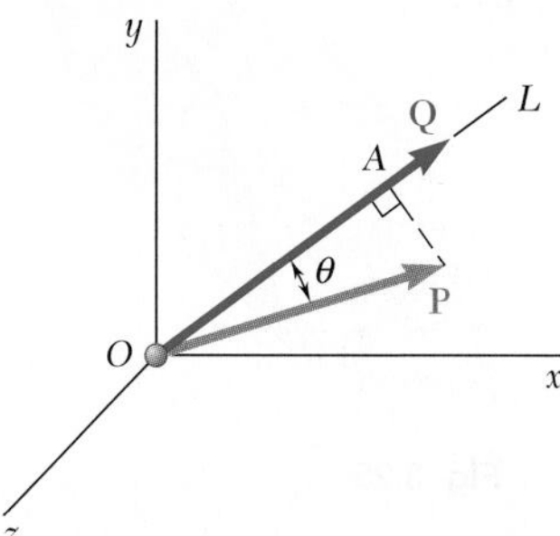

Fig. 3.22

from which it follows that

$$P_{OL} = \frac{\mathbf{P} \cdot \mathbf{Q}}{Q} = \frac{P_xQ_x + P_yQ_y + P_zQ_z}{Q} \tag{3.35}$$

In the particular case when the vector selected along OL is the unit vector $\boldsymbol{\lambda}$ (Fig. 3.23), we write

$$P_{OL} = \mathbf{P} \cdot \boldsymbol{\lambda} \tag{3.36}$$

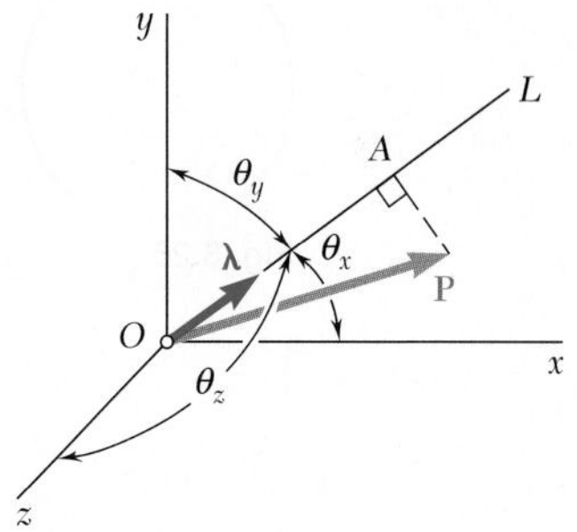

Fig. 3.23

Resolving **P** and $\boldsymbol{\lambda}$ into rectangular components and recalling from Sec. 2.12 that the components of $\boldsymbol{\lambda}$ along the coordinate axes are respectively equal to the direction cosines of OL, we express the projection of **P** on OL as

$$P_{OL} = P_x \cos \theta_x + P_y \cos \theta_y + P_z \cos \theta_z \tag{3.37}$$

where θ_x, θ_y, and θ_z denote the angles that the axis OL forms with the coordinate axes.

3.10. MIXED TRIPLE PRODUCT OF THREE VECTORS

We define the *mixed triple product* of the three vectors **S**, **P**, and **Q** as the scalar expression

$$\mathbf{S} \cdot (\mathbf{P} \times \mathbf{Q}) \tag{3.38}$$

obtained by forming the scalar product of **S** with the vector product of **P** and **Q**.†

†Another kind of triple product will be introduced later (Chap. 15): the *vector triple product* $\mathbf{S} \times (\mathbf{P} \times \mathbf{Q})$.

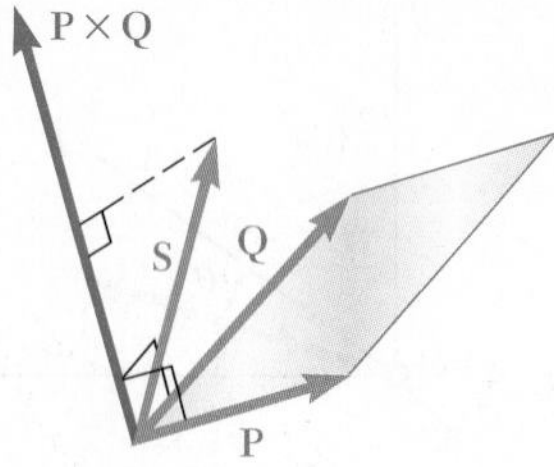

Fig. 3.24

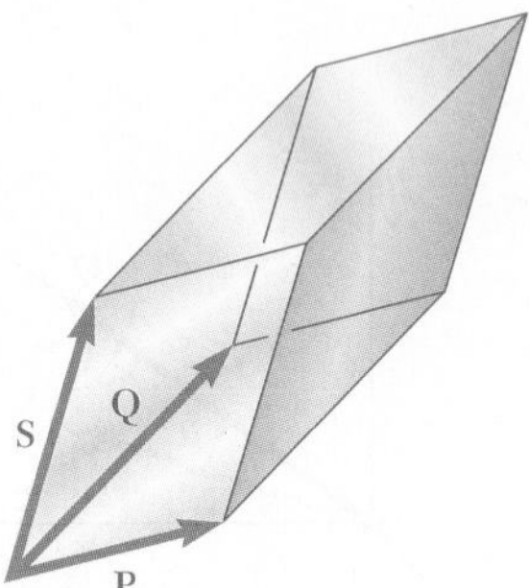

Fig. 3.25

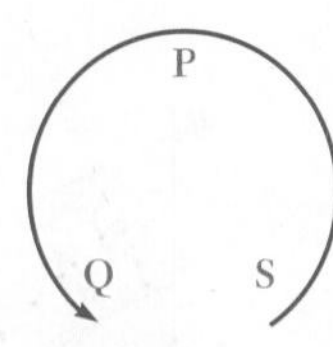

Fig. 3.26

A simple geometrical interpretation can be given for the mixed triple product of **S**, **P**, and **Q** (Fig. 3.24). We first recall from Sec. 3.4 that the vector **P** × **Q** is perpendicular to the plane containing **P** and **Q** and that its magnitude is equal to the area of the parallelogram which has **P** and **Q** for sides. On the other hand, Eq. (3.34) indicates that the scalar product of **S** and **P** × **Q** can be obtained by multiplying the magnitude of **P** × **Q** (that is, the area of the parallelogram defined by **P** and **Q**) by the projection of **S** on the vector **P** × **Q** (that is, by the projection of **S** on the normal to the plane containing the parallelogram). The mixed triple product is thus equal, in absolute value, to the volume of the parallelepiped having the vectors **S**, **P**, and **Q** for sides (Fig. 3.25). We note that the sign of the mixed triple product will be positive if **S**, **P**, and **Q** form a right-handed triad and negative if they form a left-handed triad [that is, $\mathbf{S} \cdot (\mathbf{P} \times \mathbf{Q})$ will be negative if the rotation which brings **P** into line with **Q** is observed as clockwise from the tip of **S**]. The mixed triple product will be zero if **S**, **P**, and **Q** are coplanar.

Since the parallelepiped defined in the preceding paragraph is independent of the order in which the three vectors are taken, the six mixed triple products which can be formed with **S**, **P**, and **Q** will all have the same absolute value, although not the same sign. It is easily shown that

$$\begin{aligned}\mathbf{S} \cdot (\mathbf{P} \times \mathbf{Q}) &= \mathbf{P} \cdot (\mathbf{Q} \times \mathbf{S}) = \mathbf{Q} \cdot (\mathbf{S} \times \mathbf{P}) \\ &= -\mathbf{S} \cdot (\mathbf{Q} \times \mathbf{P}) = -\mathbf{P} \cdot (\mathbf{S} \times \mathbf{Q}) = -\mathbf{Q} \cdot (\mathbf{P} \times \mathbf{S})\end{aligned} \tag{3.39}$$

Arranging in a circle and in counterclockwise order the letters representing the three vectors (Fig. 3.26), we observe that the sign of the mixed triple product remains unchanged if the vectors are permuted in such a way that they are still read in counterclockwise order. Such a permutation is said to be a *circular permutation*. It also follows from Eq. (3.39) and from the commutative property of scalar products that the mixed triple product of **S**, **P**, and **Q** can be defined equally well as $\mathbf{S} \cdot (\mathbf{P} \times \mathbf{Q})$ or $(\mathbf{S} \times \mathbf{P}) \cdot \mathbf{Q}$.

The mixed triple product of the vectors **S**, **P**, and **Q** can be expressed in terms of the rectangular components of these vectors. Denoting **P** × **Q** by **V** and using formula (3.30) to express the scalar product of **S** and **V**, we write

$$\mathbf{S} \cdot (\mathbf{P} \times \mathbf{Q}) = \mathbf{S} \cdot \mathbf{V} = S_x V_x + S_y V_y + S_z V_z$$

Substituting from the relations (3.9) for the components of **V**, we obtain

$$\begin{aligned}\mathbf{S} \cdot (\mathbf{P} \times \mathbf{Q}) = S_x(P_y Q_z - P_z Q_y) &+ S_y(P_z Q_x - P_x Q_z) \\ &+ S_z(P_x Q_y - P_y Q_x)\end{aligned} \tag{3.40}$$

This expression can be written in a more compact form if we observe that it represents the expansion of a determinant:

$$\mathbf{S} \cdot (\mathbf{P} \times \mathbf{Q}) = \begin{vmatrix} S_x & S_y & S_z \\ P_x & P_y & P_z \\ Q_x & Q_y & Q_z \end{vmatrix} \tag{3.41}$$

By applying the rules governing the permutation of rows in a determinant, we could easily verify the relations (3.39) which were derived earlier from geometrical considerations.

3.11. MOMENT OF A FORCE ABOUT A GIVEN AXIS

Now that we have further increased our knowledge of vector algebra, we can introduce a new concept, the concept of *moment of a force about an axis.* Consider again a force **F** acting on a rigid body and the moment $\mathbf{M}_O$ of that force about O (Fig. 3.27). Let OL be an axis through O; *we define the moment M_{OL} of* **F** *about OL as the projection OC of the moment $\mathbf{M}_O$ onto the axis OL.* Denoting by $\boldsymbol{\lambda}$ the unit vector along OL and recalling from Secs. 3.9 and 3.6, respectively, the expressions (3.36) and (3.11) obtained for the projection of a vector on a given axis and for the moment $\mathbf{M}_O$ of a force **F**, we write

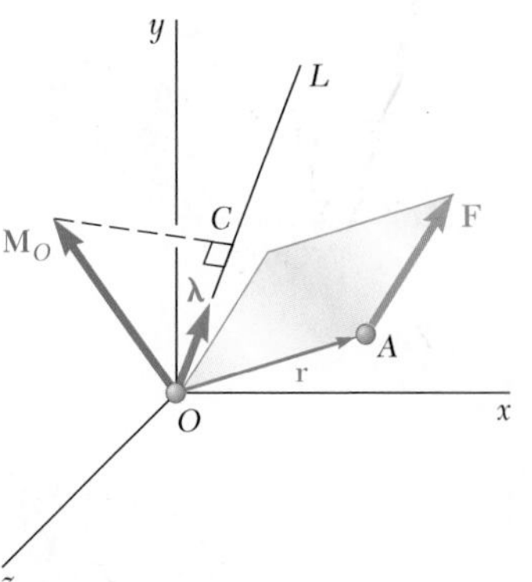

Fig. 3.27

$$M_{OL} = \boldsymbol{\lambda} \cdot \mathbf{M}_O = \boldsymbol{\lambda} \cdot (\mathbf{r} \times \mathbf{F}) \tag{3.42}$$

which shows that the moment M_{OL} of **F** about the axis OL is the scalar obtained by forming the mixed triple product of $\boldsymbol{\lambda}$, **r**, and **F**. Expressing M_{OL} in the form of a determinant, we write

$$M_{OL} = \begin{vmatrix} \lambda_x & \lambda_y & \lambda_z \\ x & y & z \\ F_x & F_y & F_z \end{vmatrix} \tag{3.43}$$

where $\lambda_x, \lambda_y, \lambda_z$ = direction cosines of axis OL
x, y, z = coordinates of point of application of **F**
F_x, F_y, F_z = components of force **F**

The physical significance of the moment M_{OL} of a force **F** about a fixed axis OL becomes more apparent if we resolve **F** into two rectangular components $\mathbf{F}_1$ and $\mathbf{F}_2$, with $\mathbf{F}_1$ parallel to OL and $\mathbf{F}_2$ lying in a plane P perpendicular to OL (Fig. 3.28). Resolving **r** similarly into two components $\mathbf{r}_1$ and $\mathbf{r}_2$ and substituting for **F** and **r** into (3.42), we write

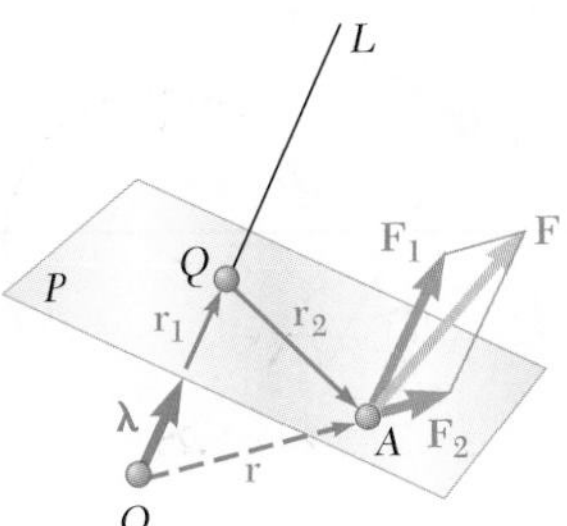

Fig. 3.28

$$\begin{aligned} M_{OL} &= \boldsymbol{\lambda} \cdot [(\mathbf{r}_1 + \mathbf{r}_2) \times (\mathbf{F}_1 + \mathbf{F}_2)] \\ &= \boldsymbol{\lambda} \cdot (\mathbf{r}_1 \times \mathbf{F}_1) + \boldsymbol{\lambda} \cdot (\mathbf{r}_1 \times \mathbf{F}_2) + \boldsymbol{\lambda} \cdot (\mathbf{r}_2 \times \mathbf{F}_1) + \boldsymbol{\lambda} \cdot (\mathbf{r}_2 \times \mathbf{F}_2) \end{aligned}$$

Noting that all of the mixed triple products except the last one are equal to zero, since they involve vectors which are coplanar when drawn from a common origin (Sec. 3.10), we have

$$M_{OL} = \boldsymbol{\lambda} \cdot (\mathbf{r}_2 \times \mathbf{F}_2) \tag{3.44}$$

The vector product $\mathbf{r}_2 \times \mathbf{F}_2$ is perpendicular to the plane P and represents the moment of the component $\mathbf{F}_2$ of **F** about the point Q where OL intersects P. Therefore, the scalar M_{OL}, which will be positive if $\mathbf{r}_2 \times \mathbf{F}_2$ and OL have the same sense and negative otherwise, measures the tendency of $\mathbf{F}_2$ to make the rigid body rotate about the fixed axis OL. Since the other component $\mathbf{F}_1$ of **F** does not tend to make the body rotate about OL, we conclude that *the moment M_{OL} of* **F** *about OL measures the tendency of the force* **F** *to impart to the rigid body a motion of rotation about the fixed axis OL.*

It follows from the definition of the moment of a force about an axis that the moment of **F** about a coordinate axis is equal to the component of $\mathbf{M}_O$ along that axis. Substituting successively each of the unit vectors **i**, **j**, and **k** for $\boldsymbol{\lambda}$ in (3.42), we observe that the expressions thus obtained for the *moments of* **F** *about the coordinate axes* are respectively equal to the expressions obtained in Sec. 3.8 for the components of the moment $\mathbf{M}_O$ of **F** about O:

$$\begin{aligned} M_x &= yF_z - zF_y \\ M_y &= zF_x - xF_z \\ M_z &= xF_y - yF_x \end{aligned} \tag{3.18}$$

We observe that just as the components F_x, F_y, and F_z of a force **F** acting on a rigid body measure, respectively, the tendency of **F** to move the rigid body in the x, y, and z directions, the moments M_x, M_y, and M_z of **F** about the coordinate axes measure the tendency of **F** to impart to the rigid body a motion of rotation about the x, y, and z axes, respectively.

More generally, the moment of a force **F** applied at A about an axis which does not pass through the origin is obtained by choosing an arbitrary point B on the axis (Fig. 3.29) and determining the projection on the axis BL of the moment $\mathbf{M}_B$ of **F** about B. We write

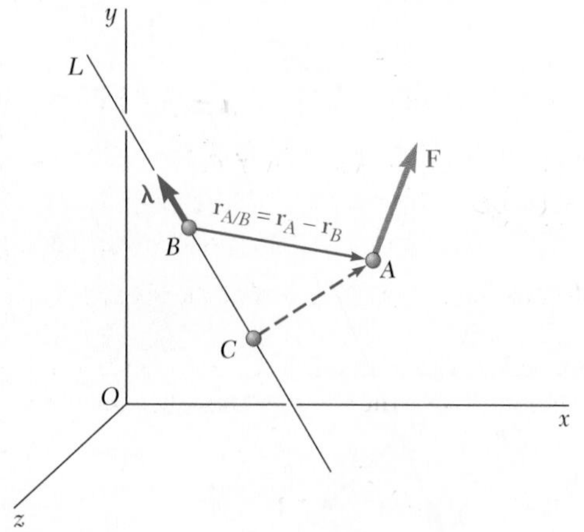

Fig. 3.29

$$M_{BL} = \boldsymbol{\lambda} \cdot \mathbf{M}_B = \boldsymbol{\lambda} \cdot (\mathbf{r}_{A/B} \times \mathbf{F}) \tag{3.45}$$

where $\mathbf{r}_{A/B} = \mathbf{r}_A - \mathbf{r}_B$ represents the vector drawn from B to A. Expressing M_{BL} in the form of a determinant, we have

$$M_{BL} = \begin{vmatrix} \lambda_x & \lambda_y & \lambda_z \\ x_{A/B} & y_{A/B} & z_{A/B} \\ F_x & F_y & F_z \end{vmatrix} \tag{3.46}$$

where $\lambda_x, \lambda_y, \lambda_z$ = direction cosines of axis BL

$x_{A/B} = x_A - x_B \qquad y_{A/B} = y_A - y_B \qquad z_{A/B} = z_A - z_B$

F_x, F_y, F_z = components of force **F**

It should be noted that the result obtained is independent of the choice of the point B on the given axis. Indeed, denoting by M_{CL} the result obtained with a different point C, we have

$$\begin{aligned} M_{CL} &= \boldsymbol{\lambda} \cdot [(\mathbf{r}_A - \mathbf{r}_C) \times \mathbf{F}] \\ &= \boldsymbol{\lambda} \cdot [(\mathbf{r}_A - \mathbf{r}_B) \times \mathbf{F}] + \boldsymbol{\lambda} \cdot [(\mathbf{r}_B - \mathbf{r}_C) \times \mathbf{F}] \end{aligned}$$

But, since the vectors $\boldsymbol{\lambda}$ and $\mathbf{r}_B - \mathbf{r}_C$ lie in the same line, the volume of the parallelepiped having the vectors $\boldsymbol{\lambda}$, $\mathbf{r}_B - \mathbf{r}_C$, and **F** for sides is zero, as is the mixed triple product of these three vectors (Sec. 3.10). The expression obtained for M_{CL} thus reduces to its first term, which is the expression used earlier to define M_{BL}. In addition, it follows from Sec. 3.6 that, when computing the moment of **F** about the given axis, A can be any point on the line of action of **F**.

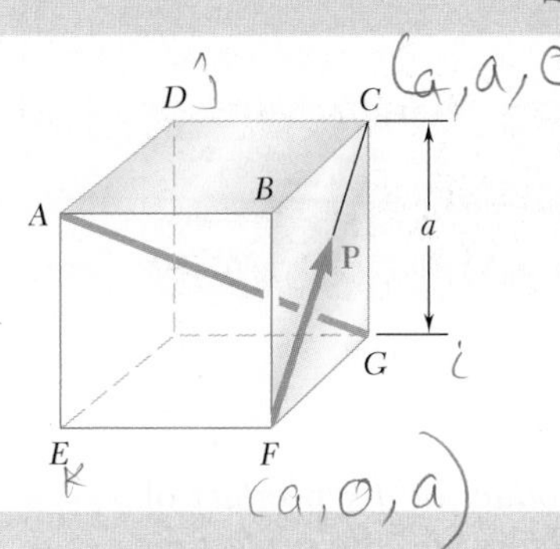

SAMPLE PROBLEM 3.5

A cube of side a is acted upon by a force **P** as shown. Determine the moment of **P** (*a*) about A, (*b*) about the edge AB, (*c*) about the diagonal AG of the cube. (*d*) Using the result of part *c*, determine the perpendicular distance between AG and FC.

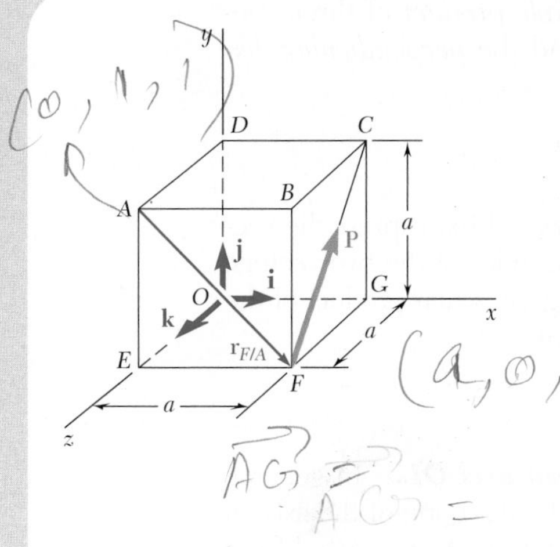

SOLUTION

***a.* Moment about A.** Choosing x, y, and z axes as shown, we resolve into rectangular components the force **P** and the vector $\mathbf{r}_{F/A} = \overrightarrow{AF}$ drawn from A to the point of application F of **P**.

$$\mathbf{r}_{F/A} = a\mathbf{i} - a\mathbf{j} = a(\mathbf{i} - \mathbf{j})$$
$$\mathbf{P} = (P/\sqrt{2})\mathbf{j} - (P/\sqrt{2})\mathbf{k} = (P/\sqrt{2})(\mathbf{j} - \mathbf{k})$$

The moment of **P** about A is

$$\mathbf{M}_A = \mathbf{r}_{F/A} \times \mathbf{P} = a(\mathbf{i} - \mathbf{j}) \times (P/\sqrt{2})(\mathbf{j} - \mathbf{k})$$
$$\mathbf{M}_A = (aP/\sqrt{2})(\mathbf{i} + \mathbf{j} + \mathbf{k}) \quad ◀$$

***b.* Moment about AB.** Projecting $\mathbf{M}_A$ on AB, we write

$$M_{AB} = \mathbf{i} \cdot \mathbf{M}_A = \mathbf{i} \cdot (aP/\sqrt{2})(\mathbf{i} + \mathbf{j} + \mathbf{k})$$
$$M_{AB} = aP/\sqrt{2} \quad ◀$$

We verify that, since AB is parallel to the x axis, M_{AB} is also the x component of the moment $\mathbf{M}_A$.

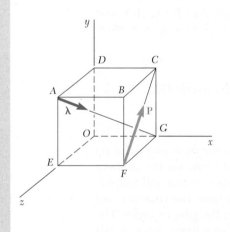

***c.* Moment about Diagonal AG.** The moment of **P** about AG is obtained by projecting $\mathbf{M}_A$ on AG. Denoting by $\boldsymbol{\lambda}$ the unit vector along AG, we have

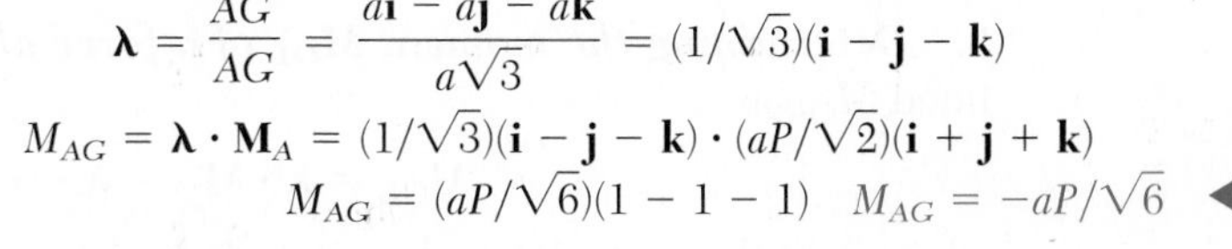

$$\boldsymbol{\lambda} = \frac{\overrightarrow{AG}}{AG} = \frac{a\mathbf{i} - a\mathbf{j} - a\mathbf{k}}{a\sqrt{3}} = (1/\sqrt{3})(\mathbf{i} - \mathbf{j} - \mathbf{k})$$
$$M_{AG} = \boldsymbol{\lambda} \cdot \mathbf{M}_A = (1/\sqrt{3})(\mathbf{i} - \mathbf{j} - \mathbf{k}) \cdot (aP/\sqrt{2})(\mathbf{i} + \mathbf{j} + \mathbf{k})$$
$$M_{AG} = (aP/\sqrt{6})(1 - 1 - 1) \qquad M_{AG} = -aP/\sqrt{6} \quad ◀$$

Alternative Method. The moment of **P** about AG can also be expressed in the form of a determinant:

$$M_{AG} = \begin{vmatrix} \lambda_x & \lambda_y & \lambda_z \\ x_{F/A} & y_{F/A} & z_{F/A} \\ F_x & F_y & F_z \end{vmatrix} = \begin{vmatrix} 1/\sqrt{3} & -1/\sqrt{3} & -1/\sqrt{3} \\ a & -a & 0 \\ 0 & P/\sqrt{2} & -P/\sqrt{2} \end{vmatrix} = -aP/\sqrt{6}$$

***d.* Perpendicular Distance between AG and FC.** We first observe that **P** is perpendicular to the diagonal AG. This can be checked by forming the scalar product $\mathbf{P} \cdot \boldsymbol{\lambda}$ and verifying that it is zero:

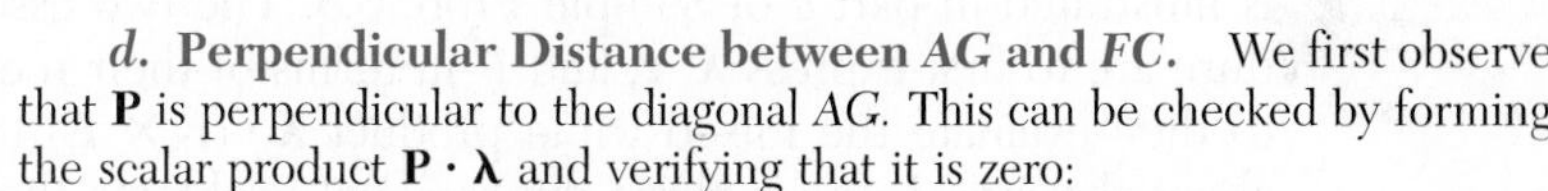

$$\mathbf{P} \cdot \boldsymbol{\lambda} = (P/\sqrt{2})(\mathbf{j} - \mathbf{k}) \cdot (1/\sqrt{3})(\mathbf{i} - \mathbf{j} - \mathbf{k}) = (P\sqrt{6})(0 - 1 + 1) = 0$$

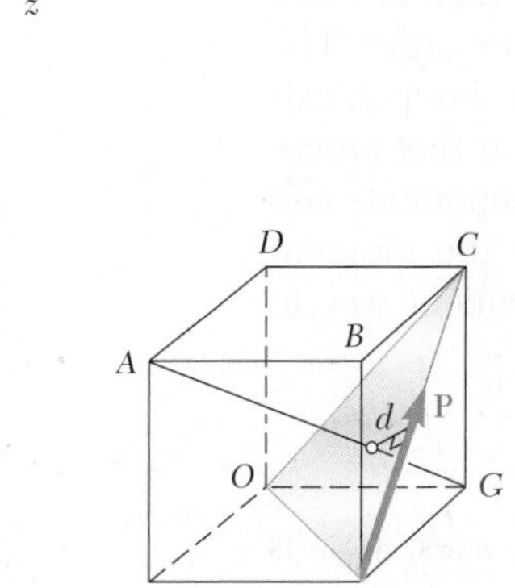

The moment M_{AG} can then be expressed as $-Pd$, where d is the perpendicular distance from AG to FC. (The negative sign is used since the rotation imparted to the cube by **P** appears as clockwise to an observer at G.) Recalling the value found for M_{AG} in part *c*,

$$M_{AG} = -Pd = -aP/\sqrt{6} \qquad d = a/\sqrt{6} \quad ◀$$

SOLVING PROBLEMS ON YOUR OWN

In the problems for this lesson you will apply the *scalar product* or *dot product* of two vectors to determine the *angle formed by two given vectors* and the *projection of a force on a given axis.* You will also use the *mixed triple product* of three vectors to find the *moment of a force about a given axis* and the *perpendicular distance between two lines.*

1. ***Calculating the angle formed by two given vectors.*** First express the vectors in terms of their components and determine the magnitudes of the two vectors. The cosine of the desired angle is then obtained by dividing the scalar product of the two vectors by the product of their magnitudes [Eq. (3.32)].

2. ***Computing the projection of a vector P on a given axis OL.*** In general, begin by expressing **P** and the unit vector $\boldsymbol{\lambda}$, that defines the direction of the axis, in component form. Take care that $\boldsymbol{\lambda}$ has the correct sense (that is, $\boldsymbol{\lambda}$ is directed from O to L). The required projection is then equal to the scalar product $\mathbf{P} \cdot \boldsymbol{\lambda}$. However, if you know the angle θ formed by **P** and $\boldsymbol{\lambda}$, the projection is also given by $P \cos \theta$.

3. ***Determining the moment M_{OL} of a force about a given axis OL.*** We defined M_{OL} as

$$M_{OL} = \boldsymbol{\lambda} \cdot \mathbf{M}_O = \boldsymbol{\lambda} \cdot (\mathbf{r} \times \mathbf{F}) \tag{3.42}$$

where $\boldsymbol{\lambda}$ is the unit vector along OL and **r** is a position vector *from any point* on the line OL *to any point* on the line of action of **F**. As was the case for the moment of a force about a point, choosing the most convenient position vector will simplify your calculations. Also, recall the warning of the previous lesson: the vectors **r** and **F** must have the correct sense, and they must be placed in the proper order. The procedure you should follow when computing the moment of a force about an axis is illustrated in part *c* of Sample Prob. 3.5. The two essential steps in this procedure are to first express $\boldsymbol{\lambda}$, **r**, and **F** in terms of their rectangular components and to then evaluate the mixed triple product $\boldsymbol{\lambda} \cdot (\mathbf{r} \times \mathbf{F})$ to determine the moment about the axis. In most three-dimensional problems the most convenient way to compute the mixed triple product is by using a determinant.

As noted in the text, when $\boldsymbol{\lambda}$ is directed along one of the coordinate axes, M_{OL} is equal to the scalar component of $\mathbf{M}_O$ along that axis.

4. Determining the perpendicular distance between two lines. You should remember that it is the perpendicular component $\mathbf{F}_2$ of the force $\mathbf{F}$ that tends to make a body rotate about a given axis OL (Fig. 3.28). It then follows that

$$M_{OL} = F_2 d$$

where M_{OL} is the moment of $\mathbf{F}$ about axis OL and d is the perpendicular distance between OL and the line of action of $\mathbf{F}$. This last equation gives us a simple technique for determining d. First assume that a force $\mathbf{F}$ of known magnitude F lies along one of the given lines and that the unit vector $\boldsymbol{\lambda}$ lies along the other line. Next compute the moment M_{OL} of the force $\mathbf{F}$ about the second line using the method discussed above. The magnitude of the parallel component, F_1, of $\mathbf{F}$ is obtained using the scalar product:

$$F_1 = \mathbf{F} \cdot \boldsymbol{\lambda}$$

The value of F_2 is then determined from

$$F_2 = \sqrt{F^2 - F_1^2}$$

Finally, substitute the values of M_{OL} and F_2 into the equation $M_{OL} = F_2 d$ and solve for d.

You should now realize that the calculation of the perpendicular distance in part d of Sample Prob. 3.5 was simplified by $\mathbf{P}$ being perpendicular to the diagonal AG. In general, the two given lines will not be perpendicular, so that the technique just outlined will have to be used when determining the perpendicular distance between them.

Problems

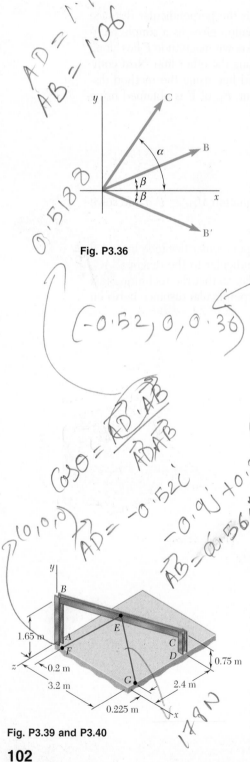

3.35 Given the vectors $\mathbf{P} = -4\mathbf{i} + 8\mathbf{j} - 3\mathbf{k}$, $\mathbf{Q} = 9\mathbf{i} - \mathbf{j} - 7\mathbf{k}$, and $\mathbf{S} = 5\mathbf{i} - 6\mathbf{j} + 2\mathbf{k}$, compute the scalar products $\mathbf{P} \cdot \mathbf{Q}$, $\mathbf{P} \cdot \mathbf{S}$, and $\mathbf{Q} \cdot \mathbf{S}$.

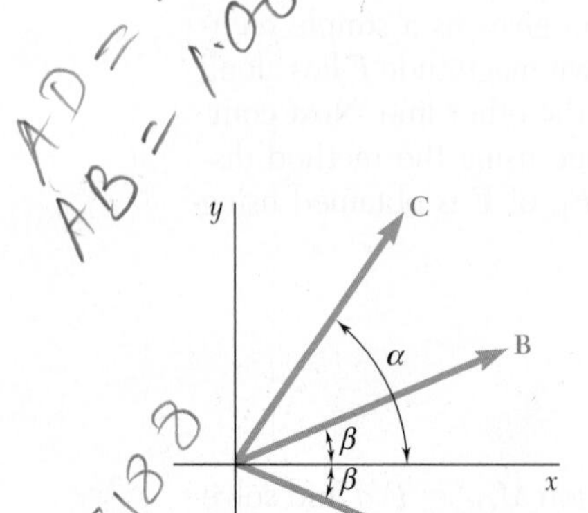

Fig. P3.36

3.36 Form the scalar products $\mathbf{B} \cdot \mathbf{C}$ and $\mathbf{B}' \cdot \mathbf{C}$, where $B = B'$, and use the results obtained to prove the identity

$$\cos \alpha \cos \beta = \tfrac{1}{2} \cos (\alpha + \beta) + \tfrac{1}{2} \cos (\alpha - \beta).$$

3.37 Three cables are used to support a container as shown. Determine the angle formed by cables *AB* and *AD*.

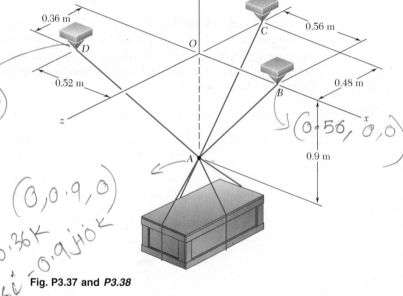

Fig. P3.37 and *P3.38*

3.38 Three cables are used to support a container as shown. Determine the angle formed by cables *AC* and *AD*.

Fig. P3.39 and P3.40

3.39 Steel framing members *AB*, *BC*, and *CD* are joined at *B* and *C* and are braced using cables *EF* and *EG*. Knowing that *E* is at the midpoint of *BC* and that the tension in cable *EF* is 110 N, determine (*a*) the angle between *EF* and member *BC*, (*b*) the projection on *BC* of the force exerted by cable *EF* at point *E*.

3.40 Steel framing members *AB*, *BC*, and *CD* are joined at *B* and *C* and are braced using cables *EF* and *EG*. Knowing that *E* is at the midpoint of *BC* and that the tension in cable *EG* is 178 N, determine (*a*) the angle between *EG* and member *BC*, (*b*) the projection on *BC* of the force exerted by cable *EG* at point *E*.

3.41 Shown are a mast and a portion of the rigging of a schooner. Members CD and EF lie in the same plane, and CD is of length 7.5 m and forms an angle of 45° with a vertical line drawn through C. Knowing that when $\theta = 15°$ the tension in rope AB is 230 N, determine (*a*) the angle between ropes AB and BD, (*b*) the projection on BD of the force exerted by rope AB at point B.

3.42 Shown are a mast and a portion of the rigging of a schooner. Members CD and EF lie in the same plane, and CD is of length 7.5 m and forms an angle of 45° with a vertical line drawn through C. Knowing that when $\theta = 10°$ the tension in rope BD is 250 N, determine (*a*) the angle between rope BD and gaff CD, (*b*) the projection on CD of the force exerted by rope BD at point D.

3.43 Determine the volume of the parallelopiped of Fig. 3.25 when (*a*) $\mathbf{P} = (3 \text{ m})\mathbf{i} - (4 \text{ m})\mathbf{j} + (1 \text{ m})\mathbf{k}$, $\mathbf{Q} = -(7 \text{ m})\mathbf{i} + (6 \text{ m})\mathbf{j} - (8 \text{ m})\mathbf{k}$, $\mathbf{S} = (9 \text{ m})\mathbf{i} - (2 \text{ m})\mathbf{j} - (3 \text{ m})\mathbf{k}$, (*b*) $\mathbf{P} = -(5 \text{ m})\mathbf{i} - (7 \text{ m})\mathbf{j} + (4 \text{ m})\mathbf{k}$, $\mathbf{Q} = (6 \text{ m})\mathbf{i} - (2 \text{ m})\mathbf{j} + (5 \text{ m})\mathbf{k}$, $\mathbf{S} = -(4 \text{ m})\mathbf{i} + (8 \text{ m})\mathbf{j} - (9 \text{ m})\mathbf{k}$.

3.44 Given the vectors $\mathbf{P} = -3\mathbf{i} - 7\mathbf{j} + 5\mathbf{k}$, $\mathbf{Q} = -2\mathbf{i} + \mathbf{j} - 4\mathbf{k}$, and $\mathbf{S} = 8\mathbf{i} + S_y\mathbf{j} - 6\mathbf{k}$, determine the value of S_y for which the three vectors are coplanar.

3.45 The rectangular platform is hinged at A and B and is supported by a cable that passes over a frictionless hook at E. Knowing that the tension in the cable is 1349 N, determine the moment about each of the coordinate axes of the force exerted by the cable at C.

3.46 The rectangular platform is hinged at A and B and is supported by a cable that passes over a frictionless hook at E. Knowing that the tension in the cable is 1349 N, determine the moment about each of the coordinate axes of the force exerted by the cable at D.

3.47 A fence consists of wooden posts and a steel cable fastened to each post and anchored in the ground at A and D. Knowing that the sum of the moments about the z axis of the forces exerted by the cable on the posts at B and C is -48 N · m, determine the magnitude of $\mathbf{T}_{CD}$ when $T_{BA} = 14$ N.

3.48 A fence consists of wooden posts and a steel cable fastened to each post and anchored in the ground at A and D. Knowing that the sum of the moments about the y axis of the forces exerted by the cable on the posts at B and C is 156 N · m, determine the magnitude of $\mathbf{T}_{BA}$ when $T_{CD} = 7.5$ N.

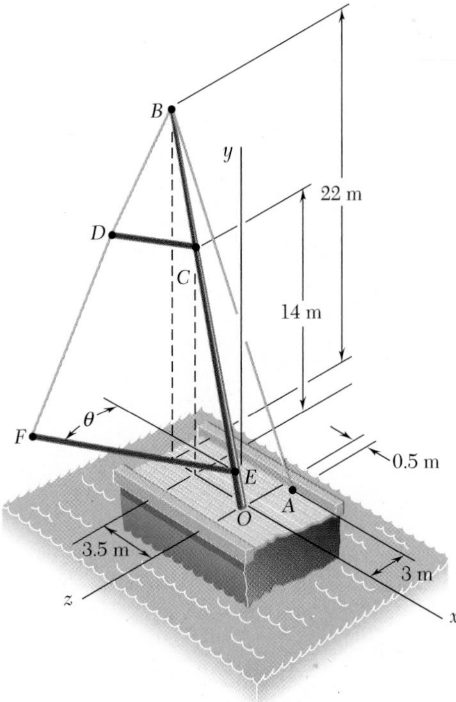

Fig. P3.41 and P3.42

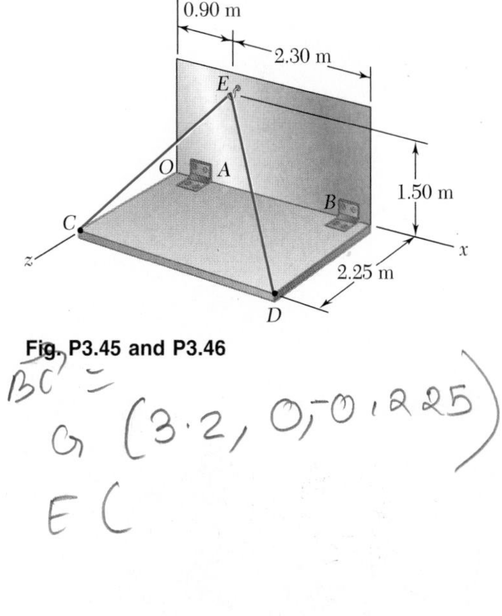

Fig. P3.45 and P3.46

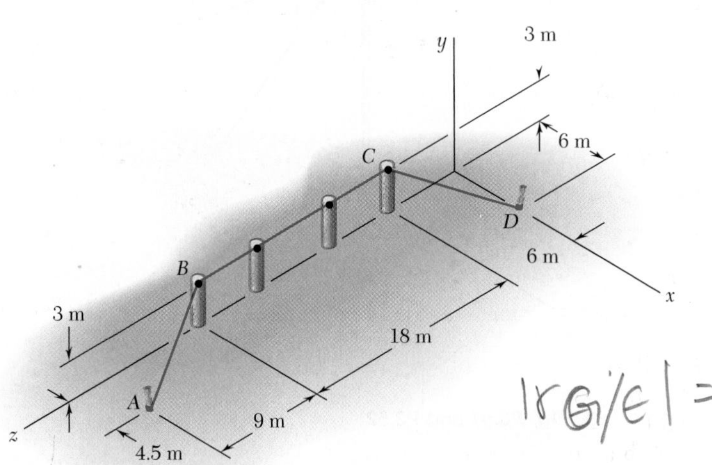

Fig. P3.47 and P3.48

3.49 A force **P** is applied to the lever of an arbor press. Knowing that **P** lies in a plane parallel to the yz plane and that $M_x = 26\ \mathrm{N \cdot m}$, $M_y = -23\ \mathrm{N \cdot m}$, and $M_z = -4\ \mathrm{N \cdot m}$, determine the magnitude of **P** and the values of ϕ and θ.

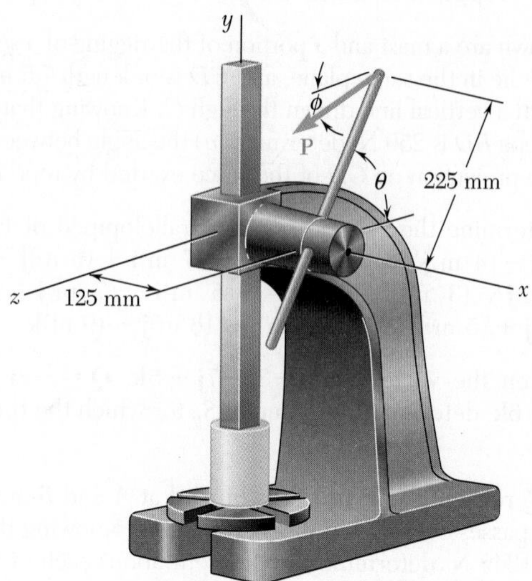

Fig. P3.49 and P3.50

3.50 A force **P** is applied to the lever of an arbor press. Knowing that **P** lies in a plane parallel to the yz plane and that $M_y = -20\ \mathrm{N \cdot m}$ and $M_z = -3.5\ \mathrm{N \cdot m}$, determine the moment M_x of **P** about the x axis when $\theta = 60°$.

3.51 Utility pole BC is guyed by cable AB as shown. Knowing that the magnitude of the force exerted by the cable at B is 70 N and that the moment of that force about the x axis is $-763\ \mathrm{N \cdot m}$, determine the length of the pole.

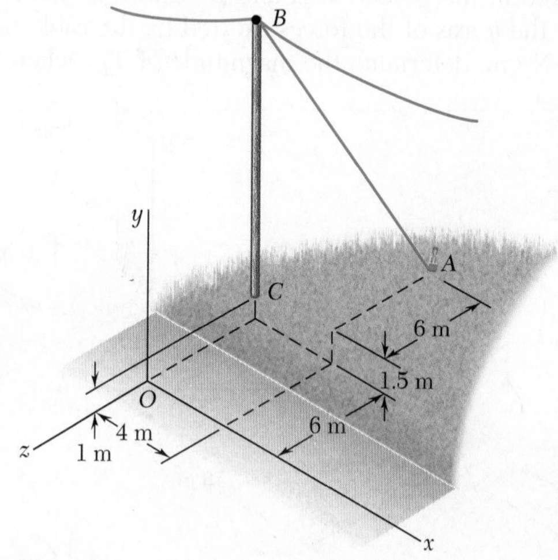

Fig. *P3.51* and P3.52

3.52 Utility pole BC is guyed by cable AB as shown. Knowing that the moments about the x and z axes of the force exerted by the cable at B are $-900\ \mathrm{N \cdot m}$ and $-315\ \mathrm{N \cdot m}$, respectively, determine the length of the pole.

3.53 The frame ACD is hinged at A and D and is supported by a cable that passes through a ring at B and is attached to hooks at G and H. Knowing that the tension in the cable is 1125 N, determine the moment about the diagonal AD of the force exerted on the frame by portion BH of the cable.

3.54 The frame ACD is hinged at A and D and is supported by a cable that passes through a ring at B and is attached to hooks at G and H. Knowing that the tension in the cable is 1125 N, determine the moment about the diagonal AD of the force exerted on the frame by portion BG of the cable.

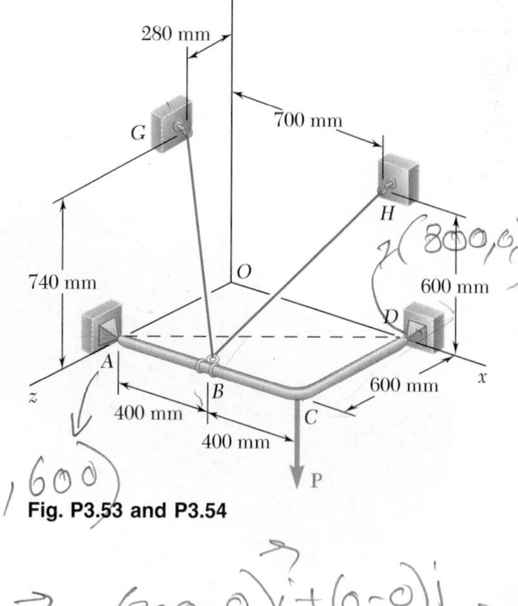

Fig. P3.53 and P3.54

3.55 The 2.4-m-wide portion $ABCD$ of an inclined, cantilevered walkway is partially supported by members EF and GH. Knowing that the compressive force exerted by member EF on the walkway at F is 24.3 kN, determine the moment of that force about edge AD of the walkway.

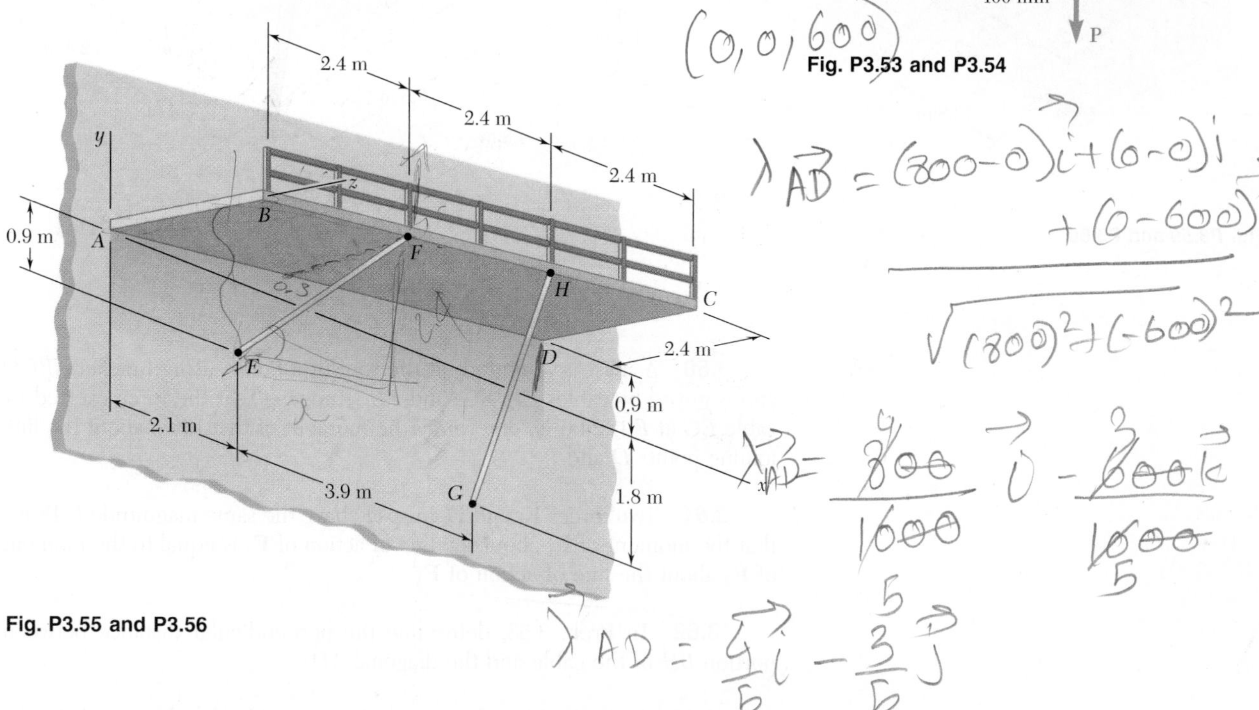

Fig. P3.55 and P3.56

3.56 The 2.4-m-wide portion $ABCD$ of an inclined, cantilevered walkway is partially supported by members EF and GH. Knowing that the compressive force exerted by member GH on the walkway at H is 21.3 kN, determine the moment of that force about edge AD of the walkway.

3.57 A rectangular tetrahedron has six edges of length a. A force $\mathbf{P}$ is directed as shown along edge BC. Determine the moment of $\mathbf{P}$ about edge OA.

3.58 A rectangular tetrahedron has six edges of length a. (*a*) Show that two opposite edges, such as OA and BC, are perpendicular to each other. (*b*) Use this property and the result obtained in Prob. 3.57 to determine the perpendicular distance between edges OA and BC.

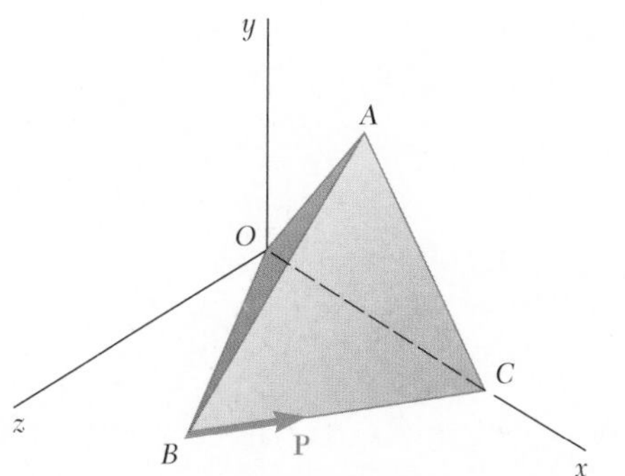

Fig. P3.57 and P3.58

3.59 A mast is mounted on the roof of a house using bracket *ABCD* and is guyed by cables *EF*, *EG*, and *EH*. Knowing that the force exerted by cable *EF* at *E* is 29.7 N, determine the moment of that force about the line joining points *D* and *I*.

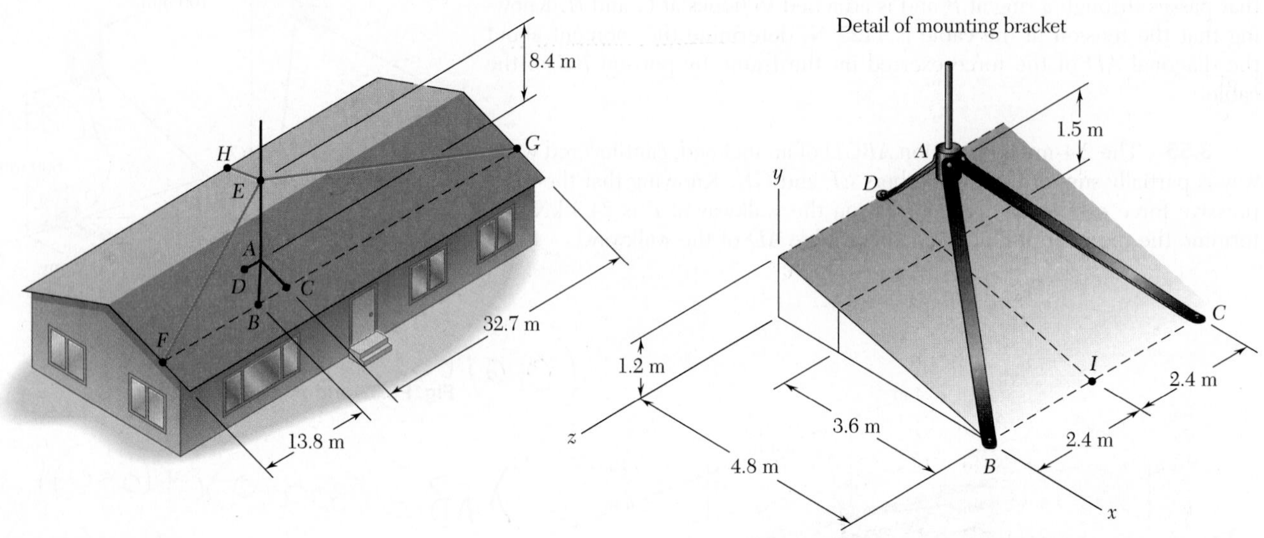

Fig. *P3.59* and P3.60

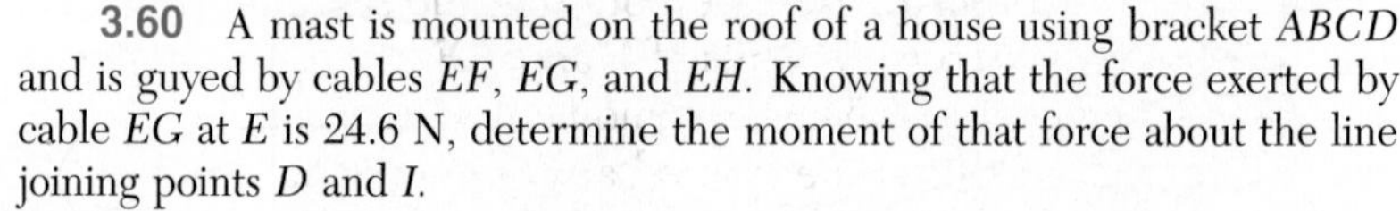

3.60 A mast is mounted on the roof of a house using bracket *ABCD* and is guyed by cables *EF*, *EG*, and *EH*. Knowing that the force exerted by cable *EG* at *E* is 24.6 N, determine the moment of that force about the line joining points *D* and *I*.

3.61 Two forces $\mathbf{F}_1$ and $\mathbf{F}_2$ in space have the same magnitude *F*. Prove that the moment of $\mathbf{F}_1$ about the line of action of $\mathbf{F}_2$ is equal to the moment of $\mathbf{F}_2$ about the line of action of $\mathbf{F}_1$.

***3.62** In Prob. 3.53, determine the perpendicular distance between portion *BH* of the cable and the diagonal *AD*.

****3.63*** In Prob. 3.54, determine the perpendicular distance between portion *BG* of the cable and the diagonal *AD*.

***3.64** In Prob. 3.59, determine the perpendicular distance between cable *EF* and the line joining points *D* and *I*.

***3.65** In Prob. 3.60, determine the perpendicular distance between cable *EG* and the line joining points *D* and *I*.

****3.66*** In Prob. 3.55, determine the perpendicular distance between member *EF* and edge *AD* of the walkway.

***3.67** In Prob. 3.56, determine the perpendicular distance between member *GH* and edge *AD* of the walkway.

3.12. MOMENT OF A COUPLE

Two forces **F** *and* −**F** *having the same magnitude, parallel lines of action, and opposite sense are said to form a couple.* (Fig. 3.30). Clearly, the sum of the components of the two forces in any direction is zero. The sum of the moments of the two forces about a given point, however, is not zero. While the two forces will not translate the body on which they act, they will tend to make it rotate.

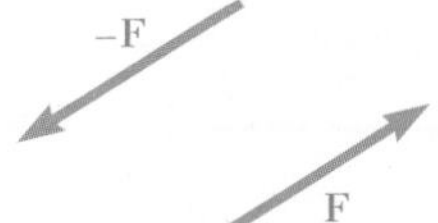

Fig. 3.30

Denoting by $\mathbf{r}_A$ and $\mathbf{r}_B$, respectively, the position vectors of the points of application of **F** and −**F** (Fig. 3.31), we find that the sum of the moments of the two forces about O is

$$\mathbf{r}_A \times \mathbf{F} + \mathbf{r}_B \times (-\mathbf{F}) = (\mathbf{r}_A - \mathbf{r}_B) \times \mathbf{F}$$

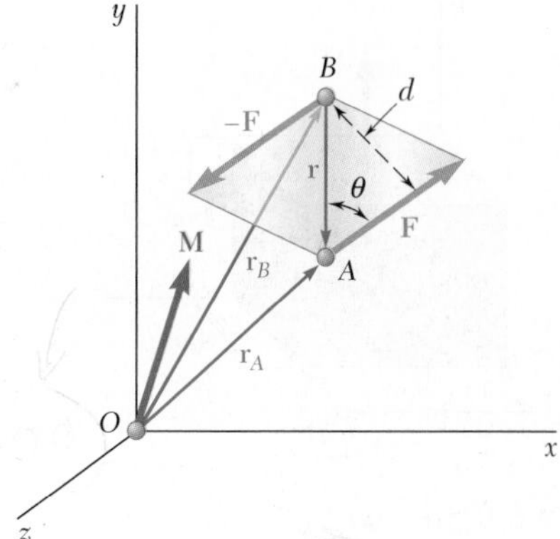

Fig. 3.31

Setting $\mathbf{r}_A - \mathbf{r}_B = \mathbf{r}$, where **r** is the vector joining the points of application of the two forces, we conclude that the sum of the moments of **F** and −**F** about O is represented by the vector

$$\mathbf{M} = \mathbf{r} \times \mathbf{F} \tag{3.47}$$

The vector **M** is called the *moment of the couple;* it is a vector perpendicular to the plane containing the two forces, and its magnitude is

$$M = rF \sin \theta = Fd \tag{3.48}$$

where d is the perpendicular distance between the lines of action of **F** and −**F**. The sense of **M** is defined by the right-hand rule.

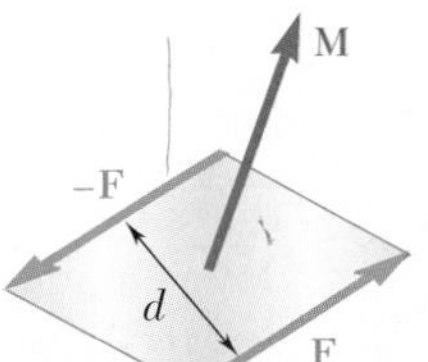

Fig. 3.32

Since the vector **r** in (3.47) is independent of the choice of the origin O of the coordinate axes, we note that the same result would have been obtained if the moments of **F** and −**F** had been computed about a different point O'. Thus, the moment **M** of a couple is a *free vector* (Sec. 2.3) which can be applied at any point (Fig. 3.32).

From the definition of the moment of a couple, it also follows that two couples, one consisting of the forces $\mathbf{F}_1$ and $-\mathbf{F}_1$, the other of the forces $\mathbf{F}_2$ and $-\mathbf{F}_2$ (Fig. 3.33), will have equal moments if

$$F_1 d_1 = F_2 d_2 \tag{3.49}$$

and if the two couples lie in parallel planes (or in the same plane) and have the same sense.

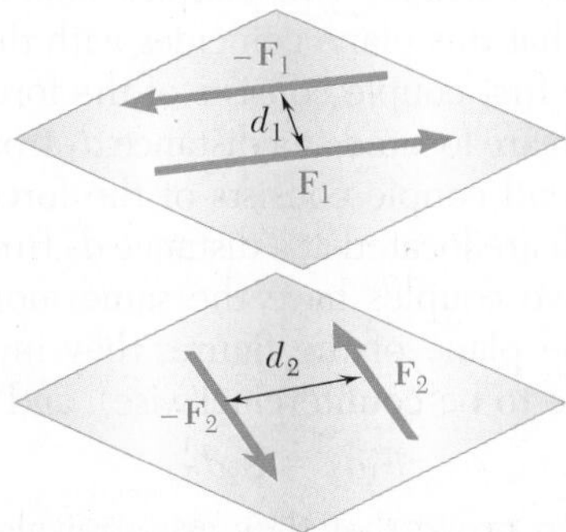

Fig. 3.33

Photo 3.1 The parallel upward and downward forces of equal magnitude exerted on the arms of the lug nut wrench are an example of a couple.

3.13. EQUIVALENT COUPLES

Figure 3.34 shows three couples which act successively on the same rectangular box. As seen in the preceding section, the only motion a couple can impart to a rigid body is a rotation. Since each of the three couples shown has the same moment **M** (same direction and same magnitude $M = 120 \text{ N} \cdot \text{m}$), we can expect the three couples to have the same effect on the box.

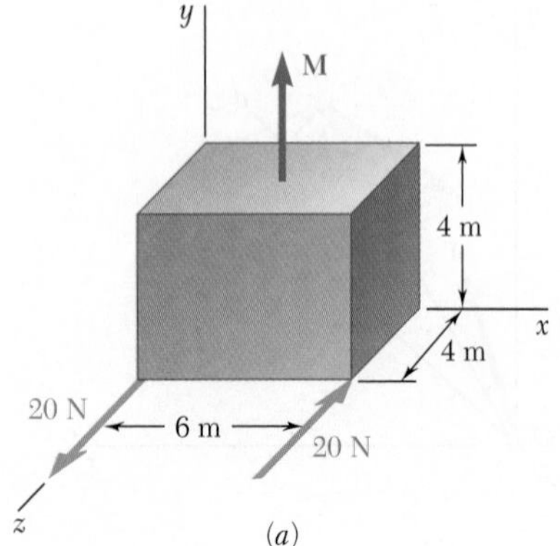

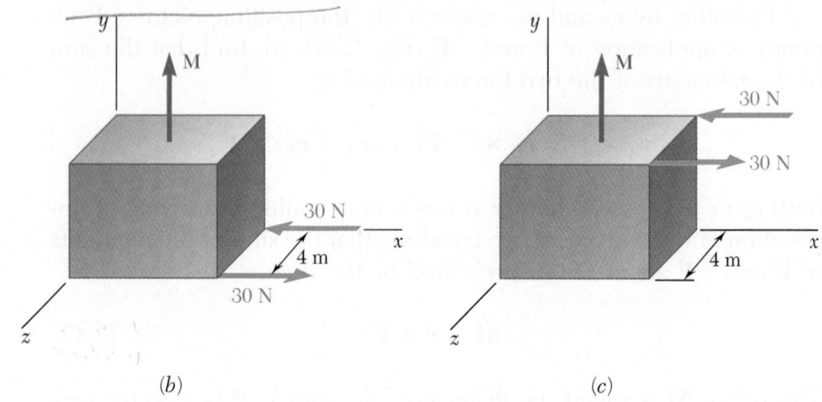

Fig. 3.34

As reasonable as this conclusion appears, we should not accept it hastily. While intuitive feeling is of great help in the study of mechanics, it should not be accepted as a substitute for logical reasoning. Before stating that two systems (or groups) of forces have the same effect on a rigid body, we should prove that fact on the basis of the experimental evidence introduced so far. This evidence consists of the parallelogram law for the addition of two forces (Sec. 2.2) and the principle of transmissibility (Sec. 3.3). Therefore, we will state that *two systems of forces are equivalent* (that is, they have the same effect on a rigid body) *if we can transform one of them into the other by means of one or several of the following operations:* (1) replacing two forces acting on the same particle by their resultant; (2) resolving a force into two components; (3) canceling two equal and opposite forces acting on the same particle; (4) attaching to the same particle two equal and opposite forces; (5) moving a force along its line of action. Each of these operations is easily justified on the basis of the parallelogram law or the principle of transmissibility.

Let us now prove that *two couples having the same moment* **M** *are equivalent*. First consider two couples contained in the same plane, and assume that this plane coincides with the plane of the figure (Fig. 3.35). The first couple consists of the forces $\mathbf{F}_1$ and $-\mathbf{F}_1$ of magnitude F_1, which are located at a distance d_1 from each other (Fig. 3.35*a*), and the second couple consists of the forces $\mathbf{F}_2$ and $-\mathbf{F}_2$ of magnitude F_2, which are located at a distance d_2 from each other (Fig. 3.35*d*). Since the two couples have the same moment **M**, which is perpendicular to the plane of the figure, they must have the same sense (assumed here to be counterclockwise), and the relation

$$F_1 d_1 = F_2 d_2 \tag{3.49}$$

must be satisfied. To prove that they are equivalent, we shall show that the first couple can be transformed into the second by means of the operations listed above.

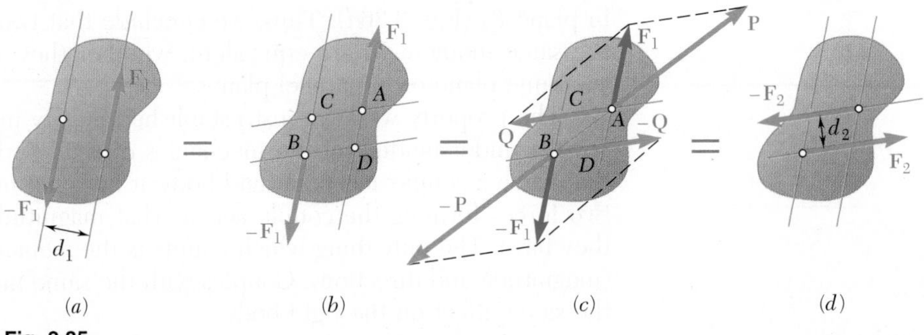

Fig. 3.35

Denoting by A, B, C, D the points of intersection of the lines of action of the two couples, we first slide the forces $\mathbf{F}_1$ and $-\mathbf{F}_1$ until they are attached, respectively, at A and B, as shown in Fig. 3.35*b*. The force $\mathbf{F}_1$ is then resolved into a component $\mathbf{P}$ along line AB and a component $\mathbf{Q}$ along AC (Fig. 3.35*c*); similarly, the force $-\mathbf{F}_1$ is resolved into $-\mathbf{P}$ along AB and $-\mathbf{Q}$ along BD. The forces $\mathbf{P}$ and $-\mathbf{P}$ have the same magnitude, the same line of action, and opposite sense; they can be moved along their common line of action until they are applied at the same point and may then be canceled. Thus the couple formed by $\mathbf{F}_1$ and $-\mathbf{F}_1$ reduces to a couple consisting of $\mathbf{Q}$ and $-\mathbf{Q}$.

We will now show that the forces $\mathbf{Q}$ and $-\mathbf{Q}$ are respectively equal to the forces $-\mathbf{F}_2$ and $\mathbf{F}_2$. The moment of the couple formed by $\mathbf{Q}$ and $-\mathbf{Q}$ can be obtained by computing the moment of $\mathbf{Q}$ about B; similarly, the moment of the couple formed by $\mathbf{F}_1$ and $-\mathbf{F}_1$ is the moment of $\mathbf{F}_1$ about B. But, by Varignon's theorem, the moment of $\mathbf{F}_1$ is equal to the sum of the moments of its components $\mathbf{P}$ and $\mathbf{Q}$. Since the moment of $\mathbf{P}$ about B is zero, the moment of the couple formed by $\mathbf{Q}$ and $-\mathbf{Q}$ must be equal to the moment of the couple formed by $\mathbf{F}_1$ and $-\mathbf{F}_1$. Recalling (3.49), we write

$$Qd_2 = F_1 d_1 = F_2 d_2 \qquad \text{and} \qquad Q = F_2$$

Thus the forces $\mathbf{Q}$ and $-\mathbf{Q}$ are respectively equal to the forces $-\mathbf{F}_2$ and $\mathbf{F}_2$, and the couple of Fig. 3.35*a* is equivalent to the couple of Fig. 3.35*d*.

Next consider two couples contained in parallel planes P_1 and P_2; we will prove that they are equivalent if they have the same moment. In view of the foregoing, we can assume that the couples consist of forces of the same magnitude F acting along parallel lines (Fig. 3.36*a* and *d*). We propose to show that the couple contained in plane P_1 can be transformed into the couple contained in plane P_2 by means of the standard operations listed above.

Let us consider the two planes defined respectively by the lines of action of $\mathbf{F}_1$ and $-\mathbf{F}_2$ and by those of $-\mathbf{F}_1$ and $\mathbf{F}_2$ (Fig. 3.36*b*). At a point on their line of intersection we attach two forces $\mathbf{F}_3$ and $-\mathbf{F}_3$, respectively equal to $\mathbf{F}_1$ and $-\mathbf{F}_1$. The couple formed by $\mathbf{F}_1$ and $-\mathbf{F}_3$ can be replaced by a couple consisting of $\mathbf{F}_3$ and $-\mathbf{F}_2$ (Fig. 3.36*c*), since both couples clearly have the same moment and are contained in the same plane. Similarly, the couple formed by $-\mathbf{F}_1$ and $\mathbf{F}_3$ can be replaced by a couple consisting of $-\mathbf{F}_3$ and $\mathbf{F}_2$. Canceling the two

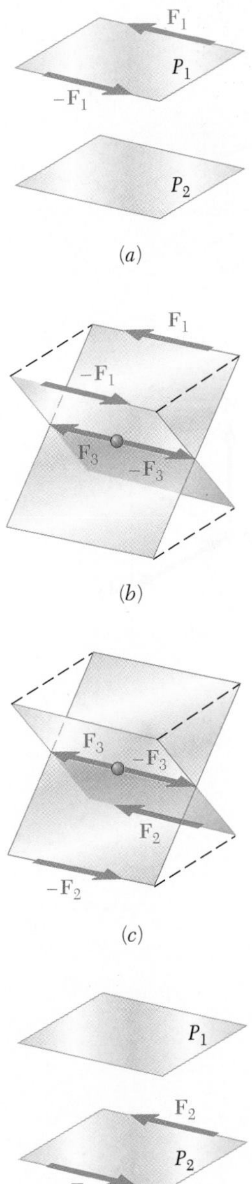

Fig. 3.36

equal and opposite forces $\mathbf{F}_3$ and $-\mathbf{F}_3$, we obtain the desired couple in plane P_2 (Fig. 3.36*d*). Thus, we conclude that two couples having the same moment **M** are equivalent, whether they are contained in the same plane or in parallel planes.

The property we have just established is very important for the correct understanding of the mechanics of rigid bodies. It indicates that when a couple acts on a rigid body, it does not matter where the two forces forming the couple act or what magnitude and direction they have. The only thing which counts is the *moment* of the couple (magnitude and direction). Couples with the same moment will have the same effect on the rigid body.

3.14. ADDITION OF COUPLES

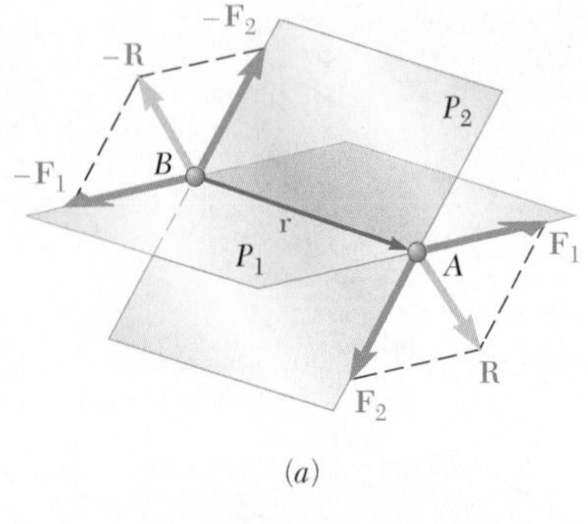

(*a*)

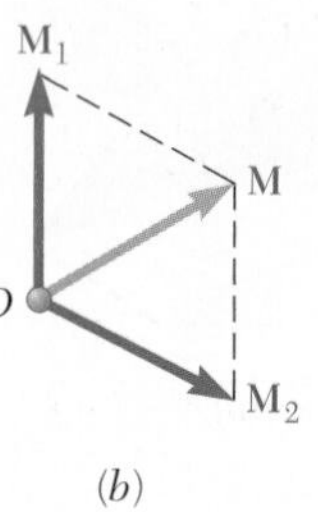

(*b*)

Fig. 3.37

Consider two intersecting planes P_1 and P_2 and two couples acting respectively in P_1 and P_2. We can, without any loss of generality, assume that the couple in P_1 consists of two forces $\mathbf{F}_1$ and $-\mathbf{F}_1$ perpendicular to the line of intersection of the two planes and acting respectively at A and B (Fig. 3.37*a*). Similarly, we assume that the couple in P_2 consists of two forces $\mathbf{F}_2$ and $-\mathbf{F}_2$ perpendicular to AB and acting respectively at A and B. It is clear that the resultant $\mathbf{R}$ of $\mathbf{F}_1$ and $\mathbf{F}_2$ and the resultant $-\mathbf{R}$ of $-\mathbf{F}_1$ and $-\mathbf{F}_2$ form a couple. Denoting by $\mathbf{r}$ the vector joining B to A and recalling the definition of the moment of a couple (Sec. 3.12), we express the moment $\mathbf{M}$ of the resulting couple as follows:

$$\mathbf{M} = \mathbf{r} \times \mathbf{R} = \mathbf{r} \times (\mathbf{F}_1 + \mathbf{F}_2)$$

and, by Varignon's theorem,

$$\mathbf{M} = \mathbf{r} \times \mathbf{F}_1 + \mathbf{r} \times \mathbf{F}_2$$

But the first term in the expression obtained represents the moment $\mathbf{M}_1$ of the couple in P_1, and the second term represents the moment $\mathbf{M}_2$ of the couple in P_2. We have

$$\mathbf{M} = \mathbf{M}_1 + \mathbf{M}_2 \tag{3.50}$$

and we conclude that the sum of two couples of moments $\mathbf{M}_1$ and $\mathbf{M}_2$ is a couple of moment $\mathbf{M}$ equal to the vector sum of $\mathbf{M}_1$ and $\mathbf{M}_2$ (Fig. 3.37*b*).

3.15. COUPLES CAN BE REPRESENTED BY VECTORS

As we saw in Sec. 3.13, couples which have the same moment, whether they act in the same plane or in parallel planes, are equivalent. There is therefore no need to draw the actual forces forming a given couple in order to define its effect on a rigid body (Fig. 3.38*a*). It is sufficient to draw an arrow equal in magnitude and direction to the moment **M** of the couple (Fig. 3.38*b*). On the other hand, we saw in Sec. 3.14 that the sum of two couples is itself a couple and that the moment **M** of the resultant couple can be obtained by forming the vector sum of the moments $\mathbf{M}_1$ and $\mathbf{M}_2$ of the given couples. Thus, couples obey the law of addition of vectors, and the arrow used in Fig. 3.38*b* to represent the couple defined in Fig. 3.38*a* can truly be considered a vector.

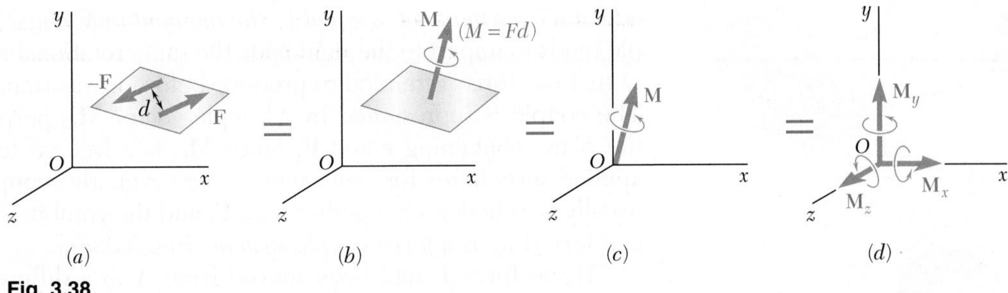

Fig. 3.38

The vector representing a couple is called a *couple vector.* Note that, in Fig. 3.38, a red arrow is used to distinguish the couple vector, *which represents the couple itself,* from the *moment* of the couple, which was represented by a green arrow in earlier figures. Also note that the symbol ↰ is added to this red arrow to avoid any confusion with vectors representing forces. A couple vector, like the moment of a couple, is a free vector. Its point of application, therefore, can be chosen at the origin of the system of coordinates, if so desired (Fig. 3.38*c*). Furthermore, the couple vector **M** can be resolved into component vectors $\mathbf{M}_x$, $\mathbf{M}_y$, and $\mathbf{M}_z$, which are directed along the coordinate axes (Fig. 3.38*d*). These component vectors represent couples acting, respectively, in the *yz*, *zx*, and *xy* planes.

3.16. RESOLUTION OF A GIVEN FORCE INTO A FORCE AT *O* AND A COUPLE

Consider a force **F** acting on a rigid body at a point *A* defined by the position vector **r** (Fig. 3.39*a*). Suppose that for some reason we would rather have the force act at point *O*. While we can move **F** along its line of action (principle of transmissibility), we cannot move it to a point *O* which does not lie on the original line of action without modifying the action of **F** on the rigid body.

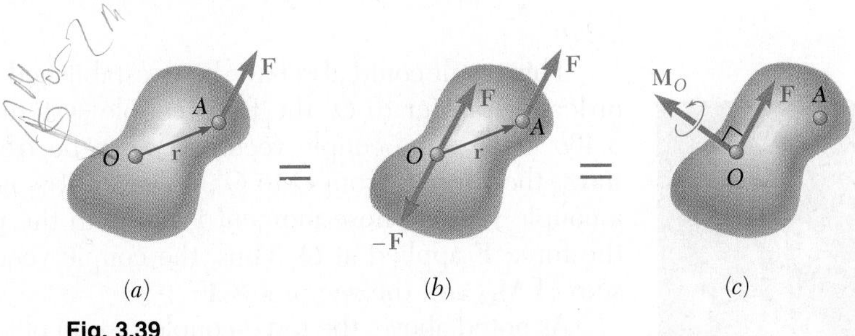

Fig. 3.39

We can, however, attach two forces at point *O*, one equal to **F** and the other equal to −**F**, without modifying the action of the original force on the rigid body (Fig. 3.39*b*). As a result of this transformation, a force **F** is now applied at *O*; the other two forces form a

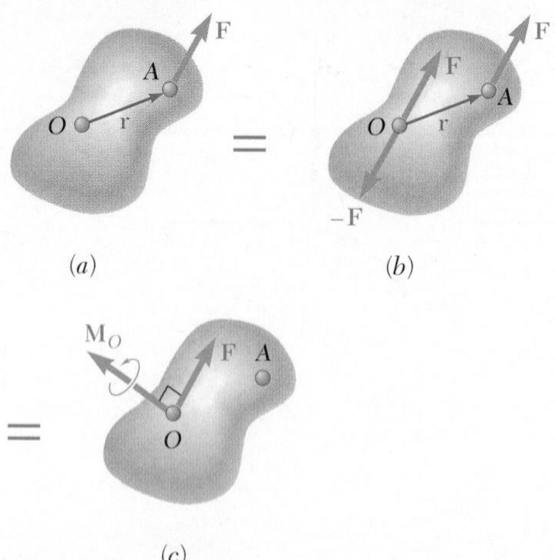

Fig. 3.39 (*repeated*)

couple of moment $\mathbf{M}_O = \mathbf{r} \times \mathbf{F}$. Thus, *any force* **F** *acting on a rigid body can be moved to an arbitrary point O provided that a couple is added whose moment is equal to the moment of* **F** *about O.* The couple tends to impart to the rigid body the same rotational motion about O that the force **F** tended to produce before it was transferred to O. The couple is represented by a couple vector $\mathbf{M}_O$ perpendicular to the plane containing **r** and **F**. Since $\mathbf{M}_O$ is a free vector, it may be applied anywhere; for convenience, however, the couple vector is usually attached at O, together with **F**, and the combination obtained is referred to as a *force-couple system* (Fig. 3.39*c*).

If the force **F** had been moved from A to a different point O' (Fig. 3.40*a* and *c*), the moment $\mathbf{M}_{O'} = \mathbf{r}' \times \mathbf{F}$ of **F** about O' should have been computed, and a new force-couple system, consisting of **F** and of the couple vector $\mathbf{M}_{O'}$, would have been attached at O'. The relation existing between the moments of **F** about O and O' is obtained by writing

$$\mathbf{M}_{O'} = \mathbf{r}' \times \mathbf{F} = (\mathbf{r} + \mathbf{s}) \times \mathbf{F} = \mathbf{r} \times \mathbf{F} + \mathbf{s} \times \mathbf{F}$$

$$\mathbf{M}_{O'} = \mathbf{M}_O + \mathbf{s} \times \mathbf{F} \tag{3.51}$$

where **s** is the vector joining O' to O. Thus, the moment $\mathbf{M}_{O'}$ of **F** about O' is obtained by adding to the moment $\mathbf{M}_O$ of **F** about O the vector product $\mathbf{s} \times \mathbf{F}$ representing the moment about O' of the force **F** applied at O.

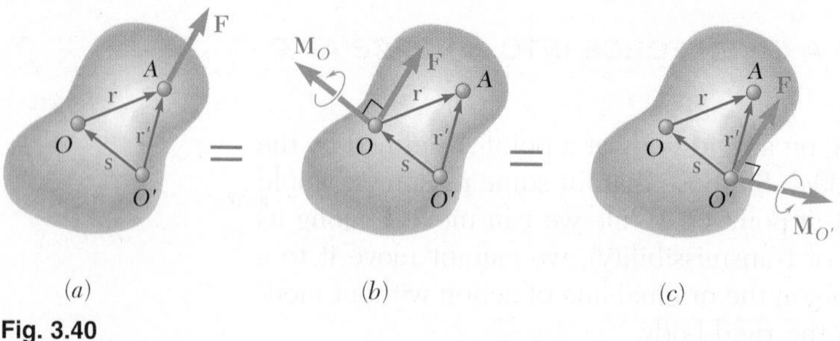

Fig. 3.40

This result could also have been established by observing that, in order to transfer to O' the force-couple system attached at O (Fig. 3.40*b* and *c*), the couple vector $\mathbf{M}_O$ can be freely moved to O'; to move the force **F** from O to O', however, it is necessary to add to **F** a couple vector whose moment is equal to the moment about O' of the force **F** applied at O. Thus, the couple vector $\mathbf{M}_{O'}$ must be the sum of $\mathbf{M}_O$ and the vector $\mathbf{s} \times \mathbf{F}$.

As noted above, the force-couple system obtained by transferring a force **F** from a point A to a point O consists of **F** and a couple vector $\mathbf{M}_O$ perpendicular to **F**. Conversely, any force-couple system consisting of a force **F** and a couple vector $\mathbf{M}_O$ which are *mutually perpendicular* can be replaced by a single equivalent force. This is done by moving the force **F** in the plane perpendicular to $\mathbf{M}_O$ until its moment about O is equal to the moment of the couple to be eliminated.

Photo 3.2 The force exerted by each hand on the wrench could be replaced with an equivalent force-couple system acting on the nut.

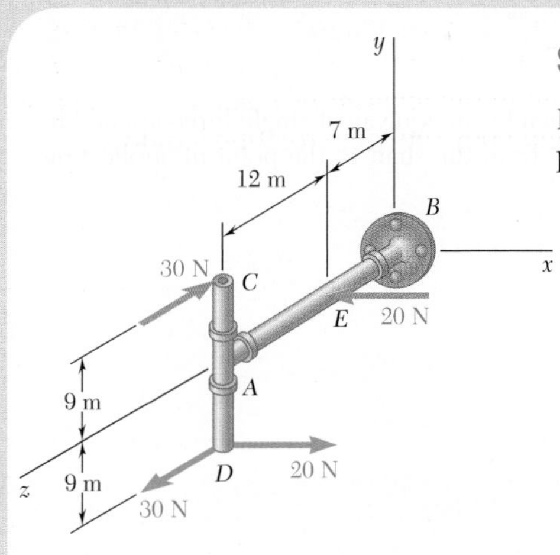

SAMPLE PROBLEM 3.6

Determine the components of the single couple equivalent to the two couples shown.

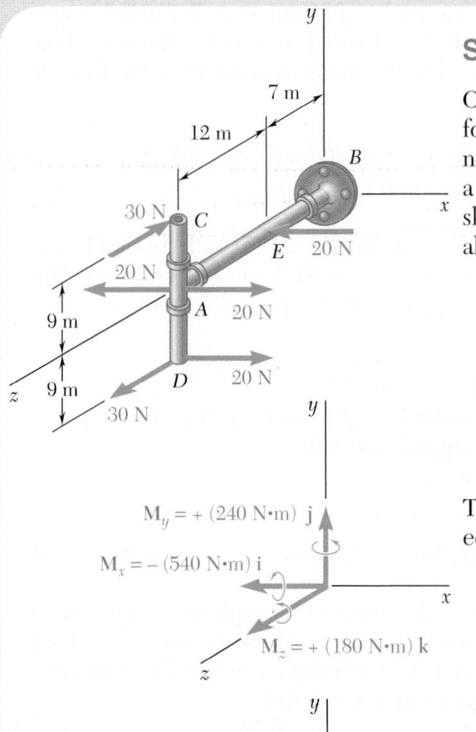

SOLUTION

Our computations will be simplified if we attach two equal and opposite 20-N forces at A. This enables us to replace the original 20-N-force couple by two new 20-N-force couples, one of which lies in the zx plane and the other in a plane parallel to the xy plane. The three couples shown in the adjoining sketch can be represented by three couple vectors $\mathbf{M}_x$, $\mathbf{M}_y$, and $\mathbf{M}_z$ directed along the coordinate axes. The corresponding moments are

$$M_x = -(30\text{ N})(18\text{ m}) = -540\text{ N}\cdot\text{m}$$
$$M_y = +(20\text{ N})(12\text{ m}) = +240\text{ N}\cdot\text{m}$$
$$M_z = +(20\text{ N})(9\text{ m}) = +180\text{ N}\cdot\text{m}$$

These three moments represent the components of the single couple **M** equivalent to the two given couples. We write

$$\mathbf{M} = -(540\text{ N}\cdot\text{m})\mathbf{i} + (240\text{ N}\cdot\text{m})\mathbf{j} + (180\text{ N}\cdot\text{m})\mathbf{k} \quad ◀$$

Alternative Solution. The components of the equivalent single couple **M** can also be obtained by computing the sum of the moments of the four given forces about an arbitrary point. Selecting point D, we write

$$\mathbf{M} = \mathbf{M}_D = (18\text{ m})\mathbf{j} \times (-30\text{ N})\mathbf{k} + [(9\text{ m})\mathbf{j} - (12\text{ m})\mathbf{k}] \times (-20\text{ N})\mathbf{i}$$

and, after computing the various vector products,

$$\mathbf{M} = -(540\text{ N}\cdot\text{m})\mathbf{i} + (240\text{ N}\cdot\text{m})\mathbf{j} + (180\text{ N}\cdot\text{m})\mathbf{k} \quad ◀$$

SAMPLE PROBLEM 3.7

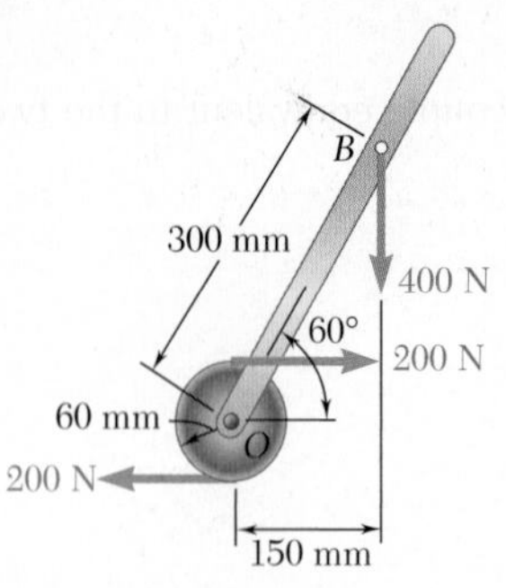

Replace the couple and force shown by an equivalent single force applied to the lever. Determine the distance from the shaft to the point of application of this equivalent force.

SOLUTION

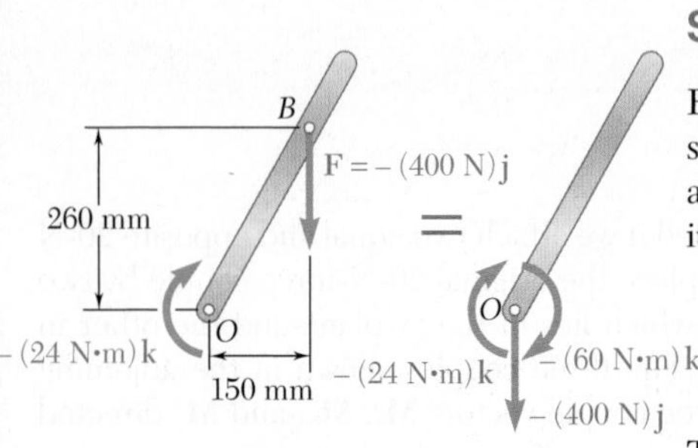

First the given force and couple are replaced by an equivalent force-couple system at O. We move the force $\mathbf{F} = -(400 \text{ N})\mathbf{j}$ to O and at the same time add a couple of moment $\mathbf{M}_O$ equal to the moment about O of the force in its original position.

$$\mathbf{M}_O = \overrightarrow{OB} \times \mathbf{F} = [(0.150 \text{ m})\mathbf{i} + (0.260 \text{ m})\mathbf{j}] \times (-400 \text{ N})\mathbf{j}$$
$$= -(60 \text{ N} \cdot \text{m})\mathbf{k}$$

This couple is added to the couple of moment $-(24 \text{ N} \cdot \text{m})\mathbf{k}$ formed by the two 200-N forces, and a couple of moment $-(84 \text{ N} \cdot \text{m})\mathbf{k}$ is obtained. This last couple can be eliminated by applying $\mathbf{F}$ at a point C chosen in such a way that

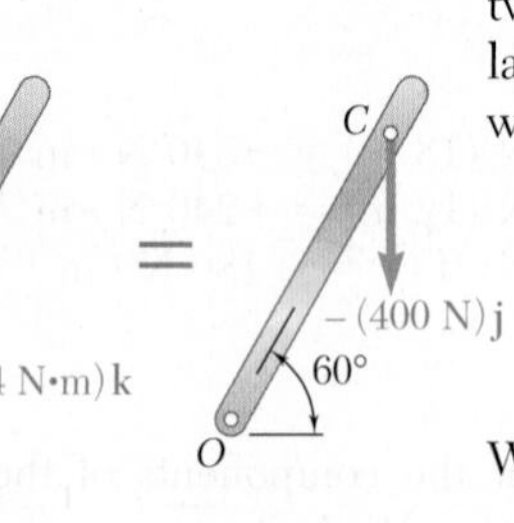

$$-(84 \text{ N} \cdot \text{m})\mathbf{k} = \overrightarrow{OC} \times \mathbf{F}$$
$$= [(OC) \cos 60°\mathbf{i} + (OC) \sin 60°\mathbf{j}] \times (-400 \text{ N})\mathbf{j}$$
$$= -(OC) \cos 60°(400 \text{ N})\mathbf{k}$$

We conclude that

$$(OC) \cos 60° = 0.210 \text{ m} = 210 \text{ mm} \qquad OC = 420 \text{ mm} \blacktriangleleft$$

Alternative Solution. Since the effect of a couple does not depend on its location, the couple of moment $-(24 \text{ N} \cdot \text{m})\mathbf{k}$ can be moved to B; we thus obtain a force-couple system at B. The couple can now be eliminated by applying $\mathbf{F}$ at a point C chosen in such a way that

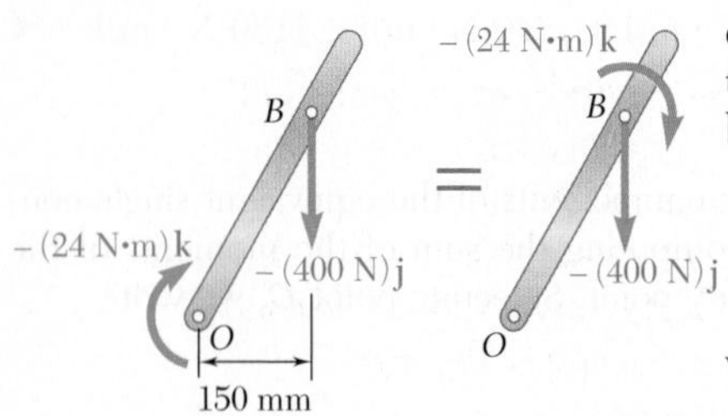

$$-(24 \text{ N} \cdot \text{m})\mathbf{k} = \overrightarrow{BC} \times \mathbf{F}$$
$$= -(BC) \cos 60°(400 \text{ N})\mathbf{k}$$

We conclude that

$$(BC) \cos 60° = 0.060 \text{ m} = 60 \text{ mm} \qquad BC = 120 \text{ mm}$$
$$OC = OB + BC = 300 \text{ mm} + 120 \text{ mm} \qquad OC = 420 \text{ mm} \blacktriangleleft$$

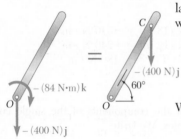

SOLVING PROBLEMS ON YOUR OWN

In this lesson we discussed the properties of *couples.* To solve the problems which follow, you will need to remember that the net effect of a couple is to produce a moment **M**. Since this moment is independent of the point about which it is computed, **M** is a *free vector* and thus remains unchanged as it is moved from point to point. Also, two couples are *equivalent* (that is, they have the same effect on a given rigid body) if they produce the same moment.

When determining the moment of a couple, all previous techniques for computing moments apply. Also, since the moment of a couple is a free vector, it should be computed relative to the most convenient point.

Because the only effect of a couple is to produce a moment, it is possible to represent a couple with a vector, the *couple vector,* which is equal to the moment of the couple. The couple vector is a free vector and will be represented by a special symbol, ↗, to distinguish it from force vectors.

In solving the problems in this lesson, you will be called upon to perform the following operations:

1. Adding two or more couples. This results in a new couple, the moment of which is obtained by adding vectorially the moments of the given couples [Sample Prob. 3.6].

2. Replacing a force with an equivalent force-couple system at a specified point. As explained in Sec. 3.16, the force of the force-couple system is equal to the original force, while the required couple vector is equal to the moment of the original force about the given point. In addition, it is important to observe that the force and the couple vector are perpendicular to each other. Conversely, it follows that a force-couple system can be reduced to a single force only if the force and couple vector are mutually perpendicular (see the next paragraph).

3. Replacing a force-couple system (with **F** *perpendicular to* **M***) with a single equivalent force.* Note that the requirement that **F** and **M** be mutually perpendicular will be satisfied in all two-dimensional problems. The single equivalent force is equal to **F** and is applied in such a way that its moment about the original point of application is equal to **M** [Sample Prob. 3.7].

Problems

3.68 A steel plate is acted upon by two couples as shown. Determine (*a*) the moment of the couple formed by the two 40-N forces, (*b*) the value of α if the resultant of the two couples is 8 N · m counterclockwise and d = 820 mm, (*c*) the perpendicular distance between the two 24-N forces if the resultant of the two couples is zero.

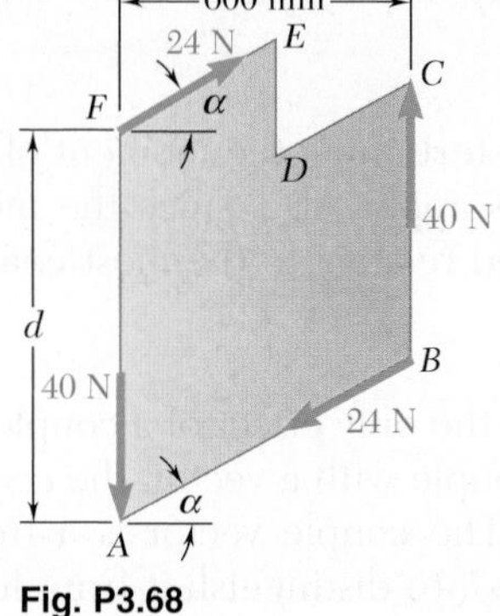

Fig. P3.68

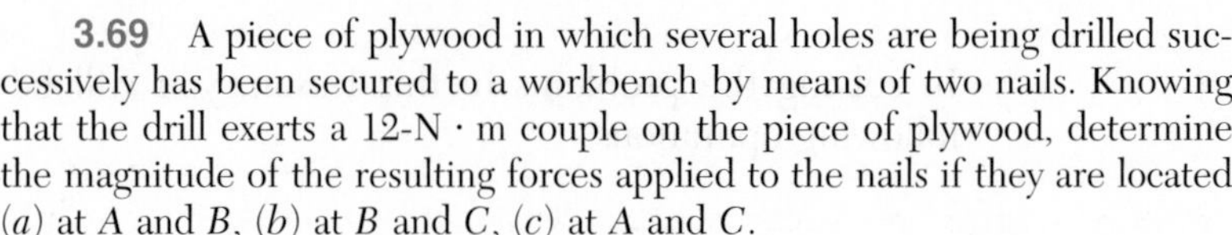
3.69 A piece of plywood in which several holes are being drilled successively has been secured to a workbench by means of two nails. Knowing that the drill exerts a 12-N · m couple on the piece of plywood, determine the magnitude of the resulting forces applied to the nails if they are located (*a*) at *A* and *B*, (*b*) at *B* and *C*, (*c*) at *A* and *C*.

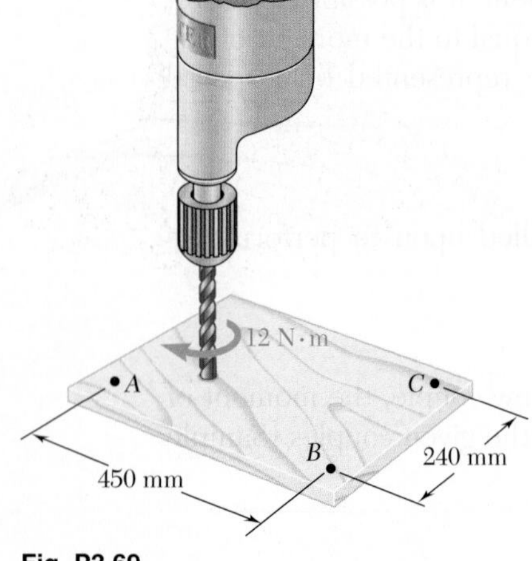

Fig. P3.69

3.70 The steel plate shown supports six 2-cm-radius idler rollers mounted on the plate as shown. Two flat belts pass around the rollers, and rollers *A* and *D* are adjusted so that the tension in each belt is 10 N. Determine (*a*) the resultant couple acting on the plate if a = 8 cm, (*b*) the value of a so that the resultant couple acting on the plate is 480 N · m clockwise.

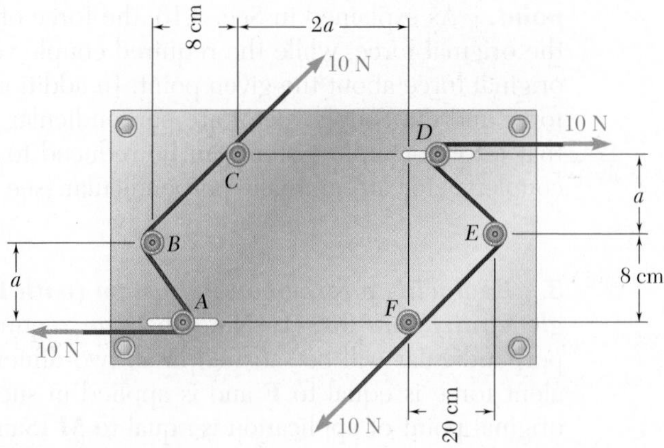

Fig. P3.70

3.71 Two 2.4-cm-diameter pegs are mounted on a steel plate at A and C, and two rods are attached to the plate at B and D. A cord is passed around the pegs and pulled as shown, while the rods exert on the plate 2.5-N forces as indicated. (*a*) Determine the resulting couple acting on the plate when $T = 9$ N. (*b*) If only the cord is used, in what direction should it be pulled to create the same couple with the minimum tension in the cord? (*c*) Determine the value of that minimum tension.

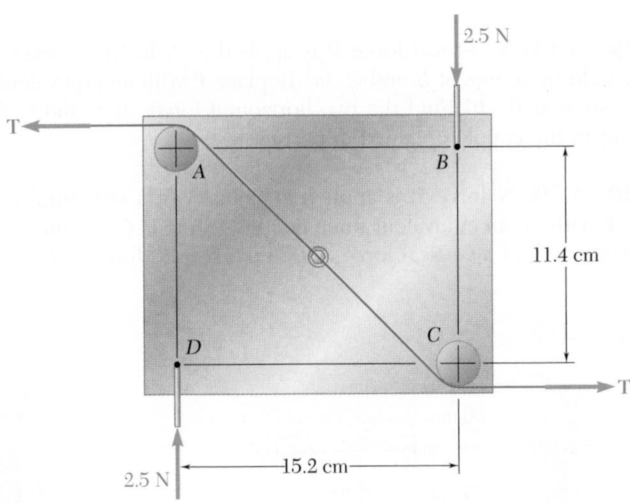

Fig. P3.71

3.72 The two shafts of a speed-reducer unit are subjected to couples of magnitude $M_1 = 18$ N · m and $M_2 = 7.5$ N · m, respectively. Replace the two couples with a single equivalent couple, specifying its magnitude and the direction of its axis.

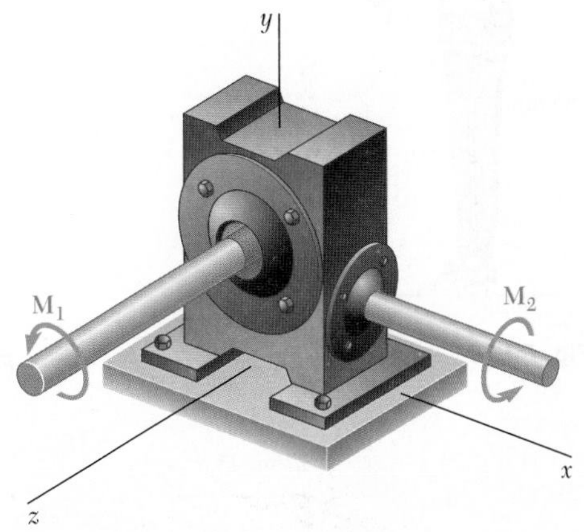

Fig. P3.72

***3.73* and 3.74** Knowing that $P = 0$, replace the two remaining couples with a single equivalent couple, specifying its magnitude and the direction of its axis.

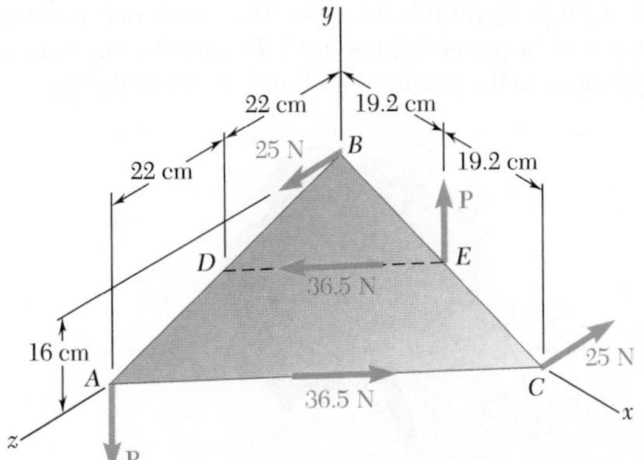

Fig. *P3.73* and P3.76

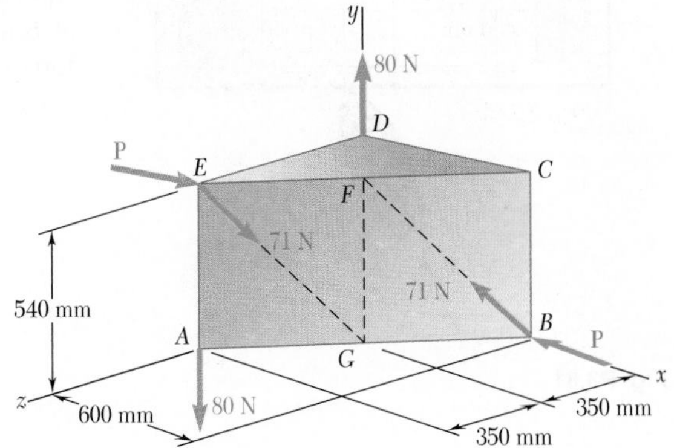

Fig. P3.74 and P3.75

3.75 Knowing that $P = 90$ N, replace the three couples with a single equivalent couple, specifying its magnitude and the direction of its axis.

3.76 Knowing that $P = 52.5$ N, replace the three couples with a single equivalent couple, specifying its magnitude and the direction of its axis.

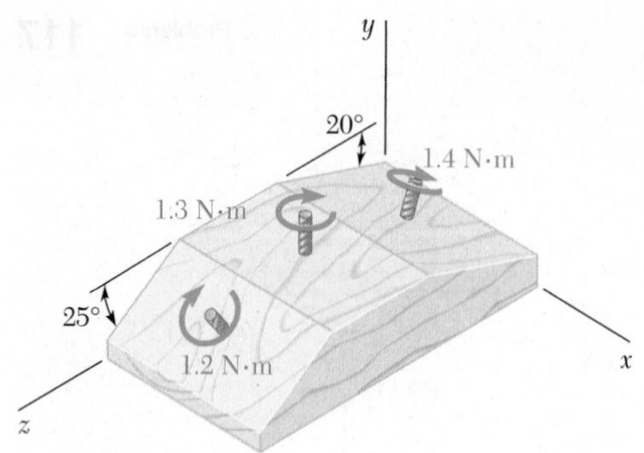

Fig. P3.77

3.77 In a manufacturing operation, three holes are drilled simultaneously in a workpiece. Knowing that the holes are perpendicular to the surfaces of the workpiece, replace the couples applied to the drills with a single equivalent couple, specifying its magnitude and the direction of its axis.

3.78 A force **P** of magnitude 160 N is applied to a man's hand as shown. Replace **P** with an equivalent force-couple system (*a*) at the elbow *B*, (*b*) at the shoulder *C*.

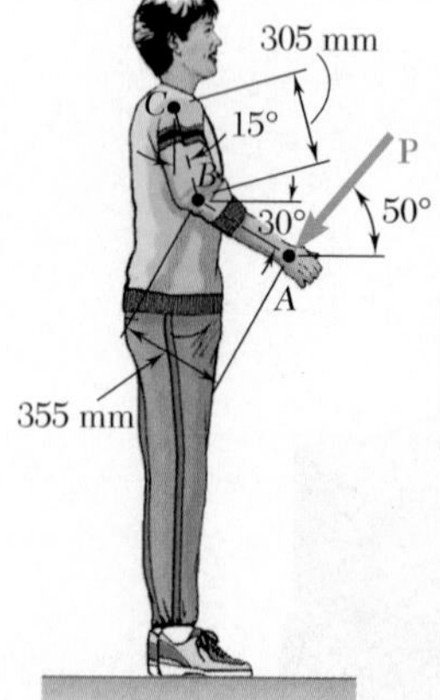

Fig. P3.78

3.79 A 135-N vertical force **P** is applied at *A* to the bracket shown, which is held by screws at *B* and *C*. (*a*) Replace **P** with an equivalent force-couple system at *B*. (*b*) Find the two horizontal forces at *B* and *C* that are equivalent to the couple obtained in part *a*.

3.80 A 700-N force **P** is applied at point *A* of a structural member. Replace **P** with (*a*) an equivalent force-couple system at *C*, (*b*) an equivalent system consisting of a vertical force at *B* and a second force at *D*.

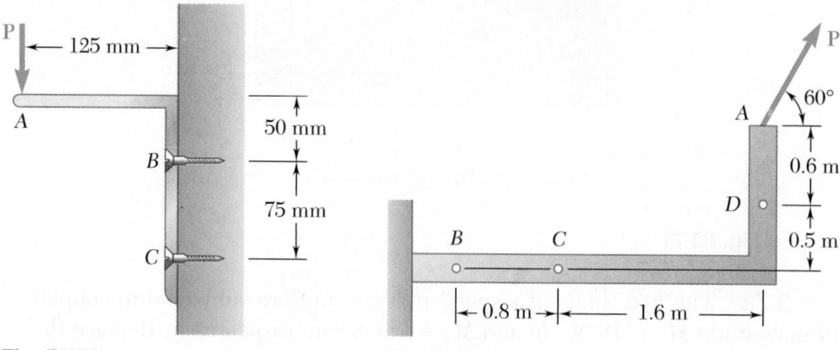

Fig. P3.79

Fig. P3.80

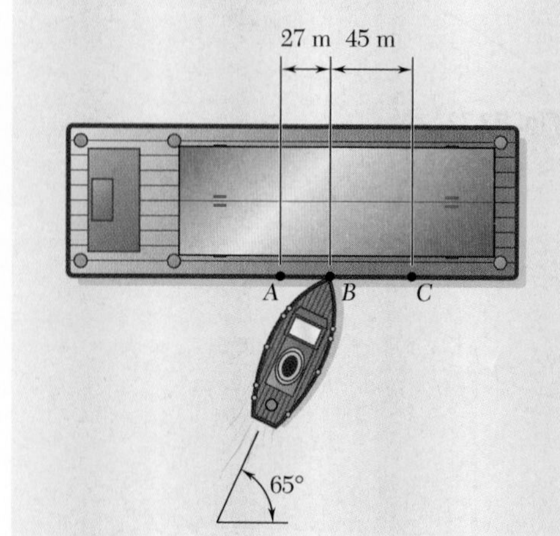

Fig. P3.81

3.81 A tugboat exerts a 2.8-kN force along its axis on a barge at point *B*. Replace the force applied at *B* with an equivalent system formed by two parallel forces applied at *A* and *C*.

3.82 A landscaper tries to plumb a tree by applying a 54-N force as shown. Two helpers then attempt to plumb the same tree, with one pulling at *B* and the other pushing with a parallel force at *C*. Determine these two forces so that they are equivalent to the single 54-N force shown in the figure.

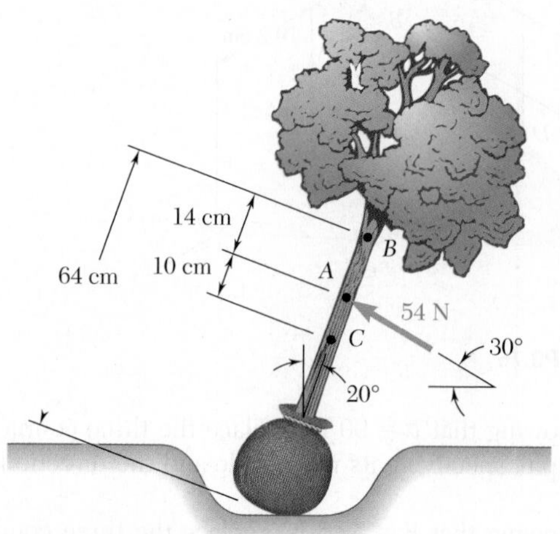

Fig. P3.82

3.83 A landscaper tries to plumb the tree shown in Fig. P3.82 by applying a 54-N force. (*a*) Replace that force with an equivalent force-couple system at *C*. (*b*) Two helpers attempt to plumb the same tree, with one applying a horizontal force at *C* and the other pulling at *B*. Determine these two forces if they are to be equivalent to the single force of part *a*.

3.84 A force and a couple are applied to a beam. (*a*) Replace this system with a single force **F** applied at point *G*, and determine the distance *d*. (*b*) Solve part *a* assuming that the directions of the two 150-N forces are reversed.

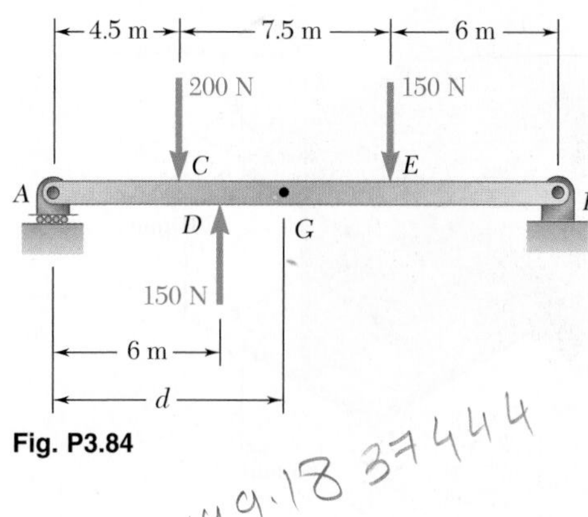

Fig. P3.84

3.85 Three workers trying to move a 1 × 1 × 1.2-m crate apply to the crate the three horizontal forces shown. (*a*) If *P* = 240 N, replace the three forces with an equivalent force-couple system at *A*. (*b*) Replace the force-couple system of part *a* with a single force, and determine where it should be applied to side *AB*. (*c*) Determine the magnitude of **P** so that the three forces can be replaced with a single equivalent force applied at *B*.

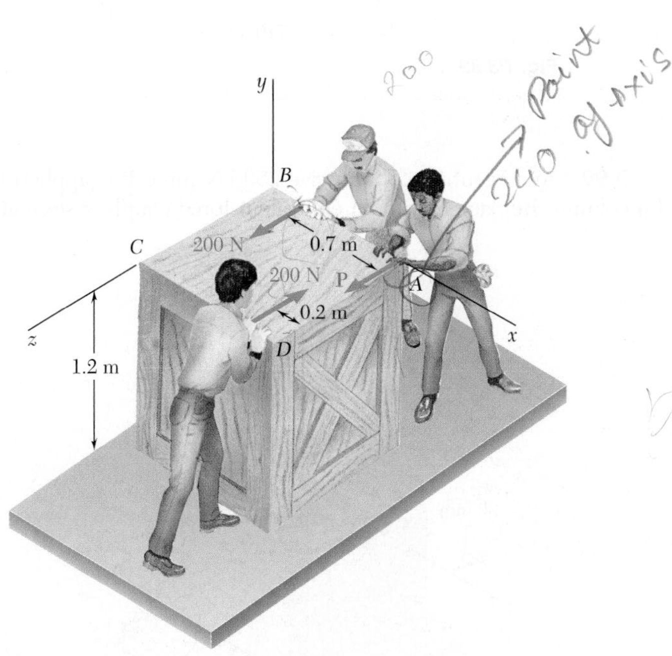

Fig. *P3.85*

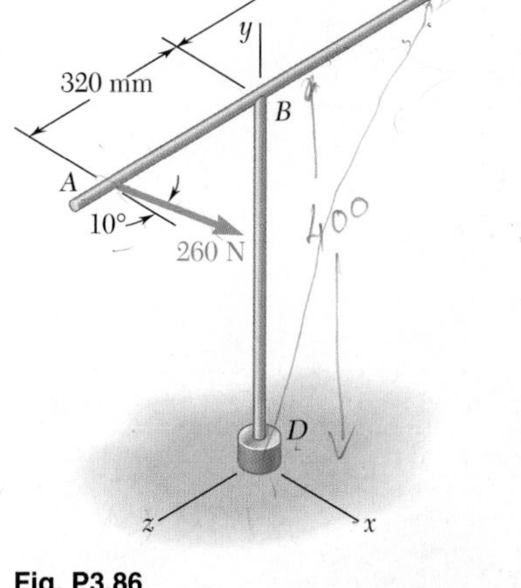

Fig. P3.86

3.86 To open an in-ground water valve, two workers apply the two horizontal forces shown to the handle of a valve wrench. Show that these forces are equivalent to a single force and specify, if possible, the point of application of the single force on handle *ABC*.

3.87 Three cables attached to a disk exert on it the forces shown. (*a*) Replace the three forces with an equivalent force-couple system at *A*. (*b*) Determine the single force which is equivalent to the force-couple system obtained in part *a*, and specify its point of application on a line drawn through points *A* and *D*.

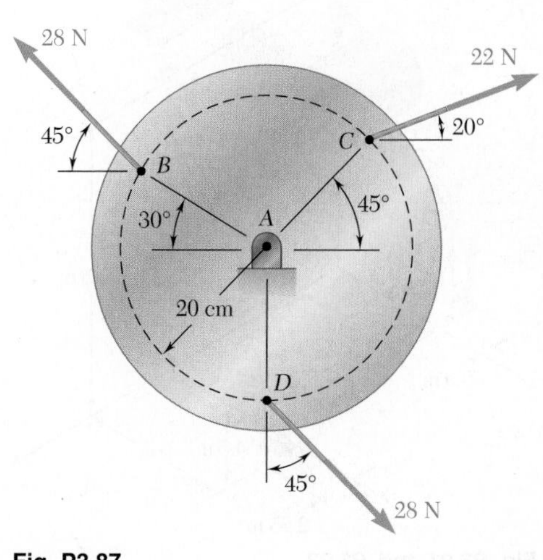

Fig. P3.87

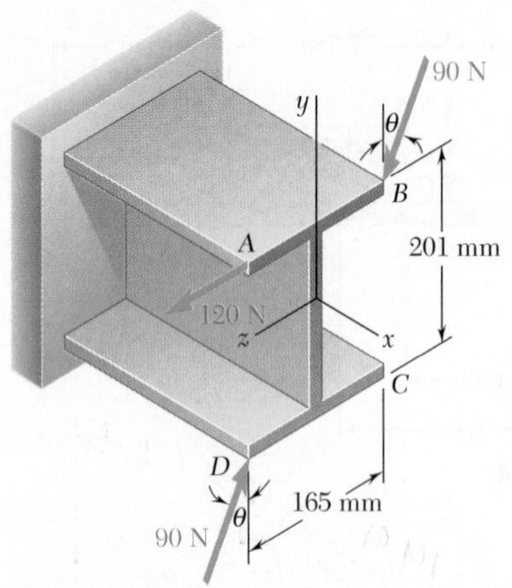

Fig. P3.88

3.88 A force and a couple lying in the yz plane are applied to the end of a cantilevered wide-flange beam. This system is to be replaced with a single equivalent force. (*a*) For $\theta = 15°$, determine the magnitude and the line of action of the equivalent force. (*b*) Determine the value of θ if the line of action of the equivalent force intersects a line drawn through points B and C 40 mm above C.

3.89 A trapezoidal plate is acted upon by the force **P** and the couple shown. Determine (*a*) the point of application on the plate of the smallest force **F** that is equivalent to the given system, (*b*) the magnitude and direction of **F**.

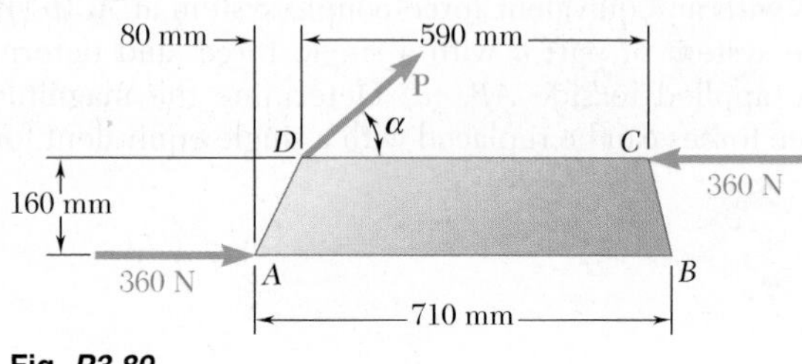

Fig. *P3.89*

3.90 An eccentric, compressive 250-kN force **P** is applied to the end of a column. Replace **P** with an equivalent force-couple system at G.

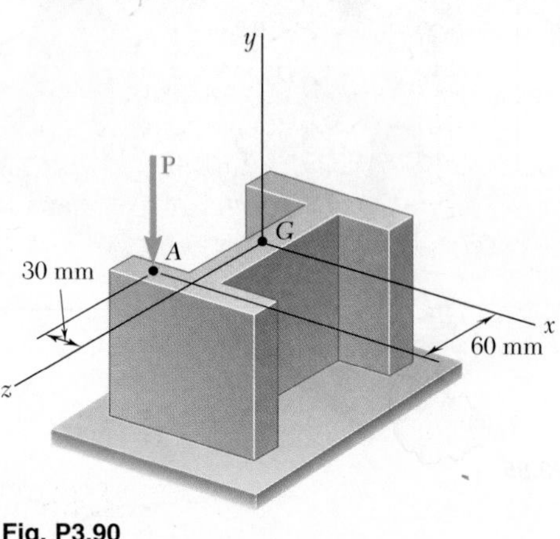

Fig. P3.90

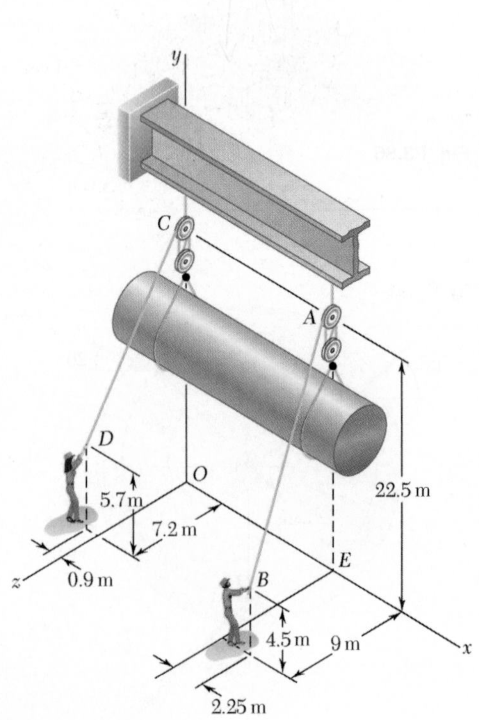

Fig. P3.91 and *P3.92*

3.91 Two workers use blocks and tackles attached to the bottom of an I-beam to lift a large cylindrical tank. Knowing that the tension in rope AB is 54 N, replace the force exerted at A by rope AB with an equivalent force-couple system at E.

3.92 Two workers use blocks and tackles attached to the bottom of an I-beam to lift a large cylindrical tank. Knowing that the tension in rope CD is 61 N, replace the force exerted at C by rope CD with an equivalent force-couple system at O.

3.93 The jib crane shown is oriented so that its boom AD is parallel to the x axis and is used to move a heavy crate. Knowing that the tension in cable AB is 10.5 kN, replace the force exerted by the cable at A with an equivalent force-couple system at the center O of the base of the crane.

3.94 A plumber applies a 220-N force to the handle of a wrench as she removes a coupling from the end of a pipe. Knowing that the wrench and the force lie in a vertical plane parallel to the yz plane, replace the force with an equivalent force-couple system at the origin of the coordinate system.

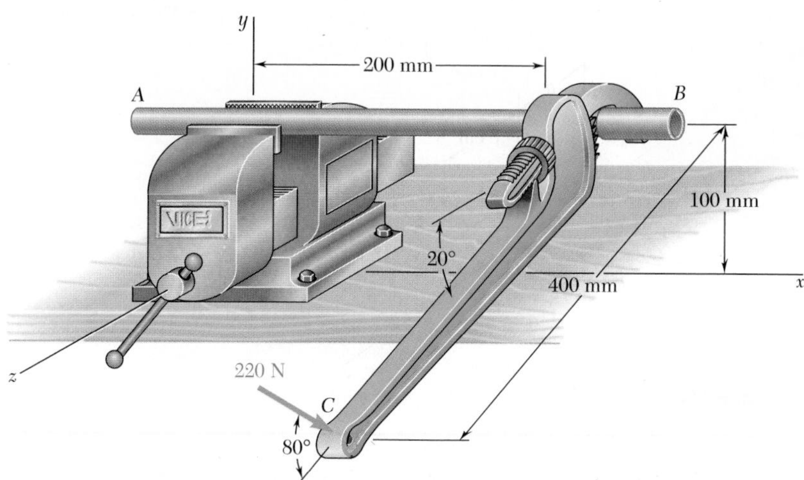

Fig. P3.94

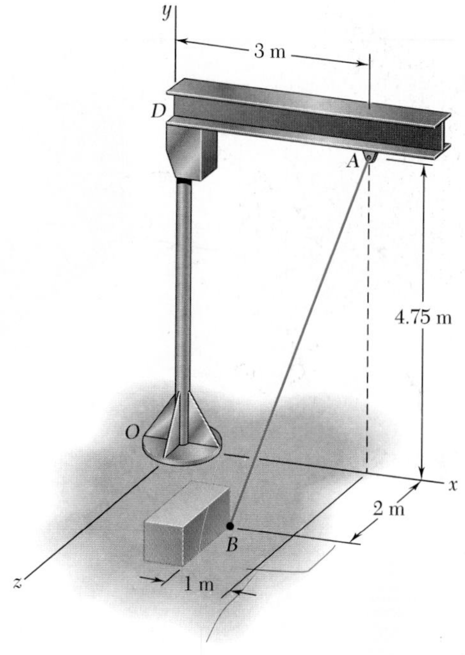

Fig. P3.93

3.95 A 63-N force **F** and 560-N · cm couple **M** are applied to corner A of the block shown. Replace the given force-couple system with an equivalent force-couple system at corner D.

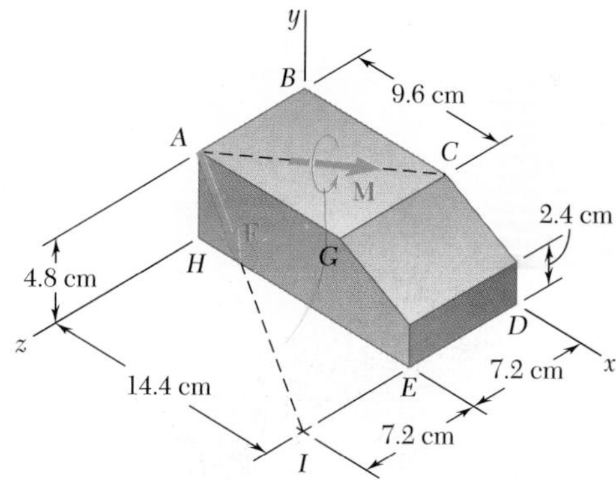

Fig. P3.95

3.96 The handpiece of a miniature industrial grinder weighs 2.4 N, and its center of gravity is located on the y axis. The head of the handpiece is offset in the xz plane in such a way that line BC forms an angle of 25° with the x direction. Show that the weight of the handpiece and the two couples $\mathbf{M}_1$ and $\mathbf{M}_2$ can be replaced with a single equivalent force. Further assuming that $M_1 = 0.068$ N · m and $M_2 = 0.065$ N · m, determine (*a*) the magnitude and the direction of the equivalent force, (*b*) the point where its line of action intersects the xz plane.

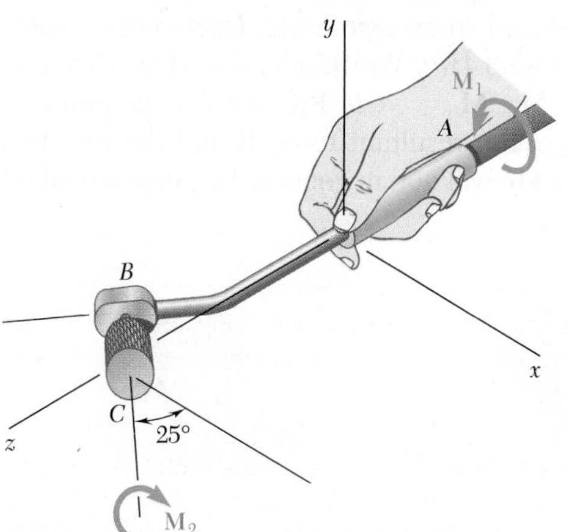

Fig. P3.96

3.97 A 20-N force $\mathbf{F}_1$ and a 40-N · cm couple $\mathbf{M}_1$ are applied to corner E of the bent plate shown. If $\mathbf{F}_1$ and $\mathbf{M}_1$ are to be replaced with an equivalent force-couple system ($\mathbf{F}_2$, $\mathbf{M}_2$) at corner B and if $(M_2)_z = 0$, determine (*a*) the distance d, (*b*) $\mathbf{F}_2$ and $\mathbf{M}_2$.

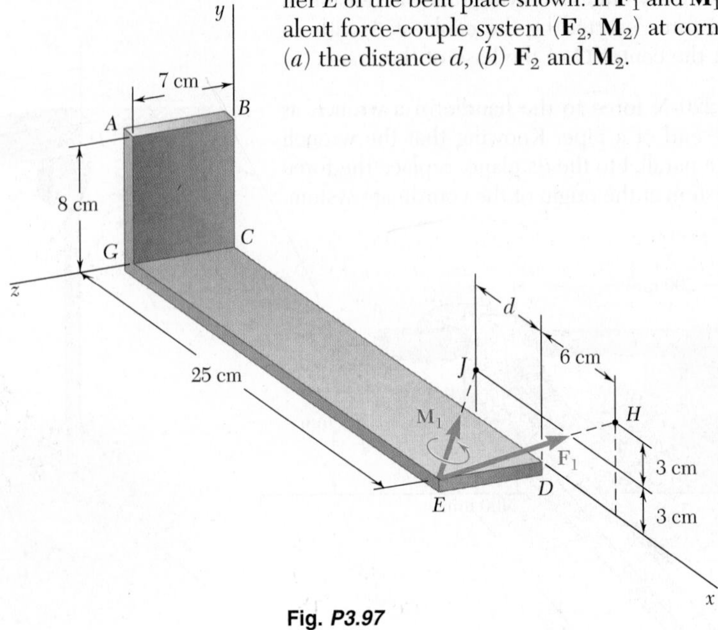

Fig. *P3.97*

3.17. REDUCTION OF A SYSTEM OF FORCES TO ONE FORCE AND ONE COUPLE

Consider a system of forces $\mathbf{F}_1$, $\mathbf{F}_2$, $\mathbf{F}_3$, . . . acting on a rigid body at the points A_1, A_2, A_3, . . . *defined by the position vectors* $\mathbf{r}_1$, $\mathbf{r}_2$, $\mathbf{r}_3$, *etc.* (Fig. 3.41*a*). As seen in the preceding section, $\mathbf{F}_1$ can be moved from A_1 to a given point O if a couple of moment $\mathbf{M}_1$ equal to the moment $\mathbf{r}_1 \times \mathbf{F}_1$ of $\mathbf{F}_1$ about O is added to the original system of forces. Repeating this procedure with $\mathbf{F}_2$, $\mathbf{F}_3$, . . . , we obtain the system shown in Fig. 3.41*b*, which consists of the original forces, now acting at O, and the added couple vectors. Since the forces are now concurrent, they can be added vectorially and replaced by their resultant $\mathbf{R}$. Similarly, the couple vectors $\mathbf{M}_1$, $\mathbf{M}_2$, $\mathbf{M}_3$, . . . can be added vectorially and replaced by a single couple vector $\mathbf{M}_O^R$. Any system of forces, however complex, can thus be reduced to an *equivalent force-couple system acting at a given point* O (Fig. 3.41*c*). We should note that while each of the couple vectors $\mathbf{M}_1$, $\mathbf{M}_2$, $\mathbf{M}_3$, . . . in Fig. 3.41*b* is perpendicular to its corresponding force, the resultant force $\mathbf{R}$ and the resultant couple vector $\mathbf{M}_O^R$ in Fig. 3.41*c* will not, in general, be perpendicular to each other.

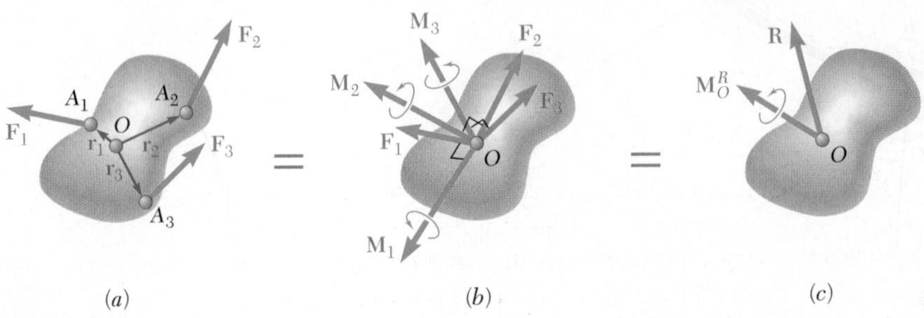

Fig. 3.41

The equivalent force-couple system is defined by the equations

$$\mathbf{R} = \Sigma\mathbf{F} \qquad \mathbf{M}_O^R = \Sigma\mathbf{M}_O = \Sigma(\mathbf{r} \times \mathbf{F}) \tag{3.52}$$

which express that the force **R** is obtained by adding all the forces of the system, while the moment of the resultant couple vector $\mathbf{M}_O^R$, called the *moment resultant* of the system, is obtained by adding the moments about O of all the forces of the system.

Once a given system of forces has been reduced to a force and a couple at a point O, it can easily be reduced to a force and a couple at another point O'. While the resultant force **R** will remain unchanged, the new moment resultant $\mathbf{M}_{O'}^R$ will be equal to the sum of $\mathbf{M}_O^R$ and the moment about O' of the force **R** attached at O (Fig. 3.42). We have

$$\mathbf{M}_{O'}^R = \mathbf{M}_O^R + \mathbf{s} \times \mathbf{R} \tag{3.53}$$

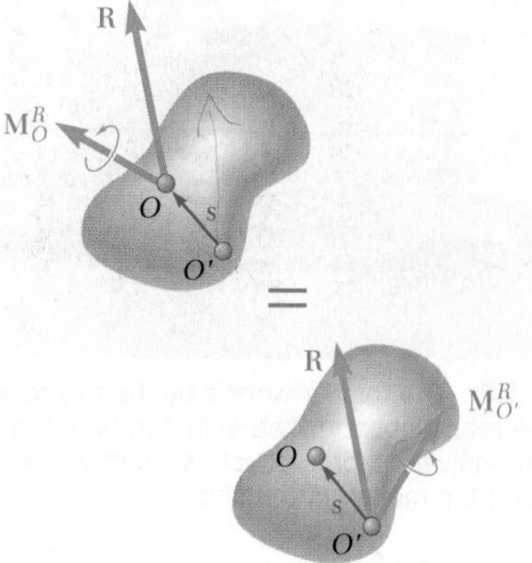

Fig. 3.42

In practice, the reduction of a given system of forces to a single force **R** at O and a couple vector $\mathbf{M}_O^R$ will be carried out in terms of components. Resolving each position vector **r** and each force **F** of the system into rectangular components, we write

$$\mathbf{r} = x\mathbf{i} + y\mathbf{j} + z\mathbf{k} \tag{3.54}$$
$$\mathbf{F} = F_x\mathbf{i} + F_y\mathbf{j} + F_z\mathbf{k} \tag{3.55}$$

Substituting for **r** and **F** in (3.52) and factoring out the unit vectors **i**, **j**, **k**, we obtain **R** and $\mathbf{M}_O^R$ in the form

$$\mathbf{R} = R_x\mathbf{i} + R_y\mathbf{j} + R_z\mathbf{k} \qquad \mathbf{M}_O^R = M_x^R\mathbf{i} + M_y^R\mathbf{j} + M_z^R\mathbf{k} \tag{3.56}$$

The components R_x, R_y, R_z represent, respectively, the sums of the x, y, and z components of the given forces and measure the tendency of the system to impart to the rigid body a motion of translation in the x, y, or z direction. Similarly, the components M_x^R, M_y^R, M_z^R represent, respectively, the sum of the moments of the given forces about the x, y, and z axes and measure the tendency of the system to impart to the rigid body a motion of rotation about the x, y, or z axis.

If the magnitude and direction of the force **R** are desired, they can be obtained from the components R_x, R_y, R_z by means of the relations (2.18) and (2.19) of Sec. 2.12; similar computations will yield the magnitude and direction of the couple vector $\mathbf{M}_O^R$.

3.18. EQUIVALENT SYSTEMS OF FORCES

We saw in the preceding section that any system of forces acting on a rigid body can be reduced to a force-couple system at a given point O. This equivalent force-couple system characterizes completely the effect of the given force system on the rigid body. *Two systems of forces are equivalent, therefore, if they can be reduced to the same*

Photo 3.3 The forces exerted by the tow rope and the rear tugboat on the ship can be replaced with an equivalent force-couple system when analyzing the motion of the ship.

force-couple system at a given point O. Recalling that the force-couple system at O is defined by the relations (3.52), we state that *two systems of forces*, $\mathbf{F}_1$, $\mathbf{F}_2$, $\mathbf{F}_3$, . . . and $\mathbf{F}'_1$, $\mathbf{F}'_2$, $\mathbf{F}'_3$, . . . , *which act on the same rigid body are equivalent if, and only if, the sums of the forces and the sums of the moments about a given point O of the forces of the two systems are, respectively, equal.* Expressed mathematically, the necessary and sufficient conditions for the two systems of forces to be equivalent are

$$\Sigma \mathbf{F} = \Sigma \mathbf{F}' \quad \text{and} \quad \Sigma \mathbf{M}_O = \Sigma \mathbf{M}'_O \tag{3.57}$$

Note that to prove that two systems of forces are equivalent, the second of the relations (3.57) must be established with respect to *only one point O*. It will hold, however, with respect to *any point* if the two systems are equivalent.

Resolving the forces and moments in (3.57) into their rectangular components, we can express the necessary and sufficient conditions for the equivalence of two systems of forces acting on a rigid body as follows:

$$\begin{array}{lll} \Sigma F_x = \Sigma F'_x & \Sigma F_y = \Sigma F'_y & \Sigma F_z = \Sigma F'_z \\ \Sigma M_x = \Sigma M'_x & \Sigma M_y = \Sigma M'_y & \Sigma M_z = \Sigma M'_z \end{array} \tag{3.58}$$

These equations have a simple physical significance. They express that two systems of forces are equivalent if they tend to impart to the rigid body (1) the same translation in the x, y, and z directions, respectively, and (2) the same rotation about the x, y, and z axes, respectively.

3.19. EQUIPOLLENT SYSTEMS OF VECTORS

In general, when two systems of vectors satisfy Eqs. (3.57) or (3.58), that is, when their resultants and their moment resultants about an arbitrary point O are respectively equal, the two systems are said to be *equipollent*. The result established in the preceding section can thus be restated as follows: *If two systems of forces acting on a rigid body are equipollent, they are also equivalent.*

It is important to note that this statement does not apply to *any* system of vectors. Consider, for example, a system of forces acting on a set of independent particles which do *not* form a rigid body. A different system of forces acting on the same particles may happen to be equipollent to the first one; that is, it may have the same resultant and the same moment resultant. Yet, since different forces will now act on the various particles, their effects on these particles will be different; the two systems of forces, while equipollent, are *not equivalent*.

3.20. FURTHER REDUCTION OF A SYSTEM OF FORCES

We saw in Sec. 3.17 that any given system of forces acting on a rigid body can be reduced to an equivalent force-couple system at O consisting of a force $\mathbf{R}$ equal to the sum of the forces of the system and a couple vector $\mathbf{M}_O^R$ of moment equal to the moment resultant of the system.

When $\mathbf{R} = 0$, the force-couple system reduces to the couple vector $\mathbf{M}_O^R$. The given system of forces can then be reduced to a single couple, called the *resultant couple* of the system.

Let us now investigate the conditions under which a given system of forces can be reduced to a single force. It follows from Sec. 3.16 that the force-couple system at O can be replaced by a single force $\mathbf{R}$ acting along a new line of action if $\mathbf{R}$ and $\mathbf{M}_O^R$ are mutually perpendicular. The systems of forces which can be reduced to a single force, or *resultant,* are therefore the systems for which the force $\mathbf{R}$ and the couple vector $\mathbf{M}_O^R$ are mutually perpendicular. While this condition *is generally not satisfied* by systems of forces in space, it *will be satisfied* by systems consisting of (1) concurrent forces, (2) coplanar forces, or (3) parallel forces. These three cases will be discussed separately.

1. *Concurrent forces* are applied at the same point and can therefore be added directly to obtain their resultant $\mathbf{R}$. Thus, they always reduce to a single force. Concurrent forces were discussed in detail in Chap. 2.
2. *Coplanar forces* act in the same plane, which may be assumed to be the plane of the figure (Fig. 3.43*a*). The sum $\mathbf{R}$ of the forces of the system will also lie in the plane of the figure, while the moment of each force about O, and thus the moment resultant $\mathbf{M}_O^R$, will be perpendicular to that plane. The force-couple system at O consists, therefore, of a force $\mathbf{R}$ and a couple vector $\mathbf{M}_O^R$ which are mutually perpendicular (Fig. 3.43*b*).† They can be reduced to a single force $\mathbf{R}$ by moving $\mathbf{R}$ in the plane of the figure until its moment about O becomes equal to $\mathbf{M}_O^R$. The distance from O to the line of action of $\mathbf{R}$ is $d = M_O^R/R$ (Fig. 3.43*c*).

Photo 3.4 The coplanar forces exerted by the four tugboats on the USS *Pasadena* could be replaced with a single equivalent force exerted by one tugboat.

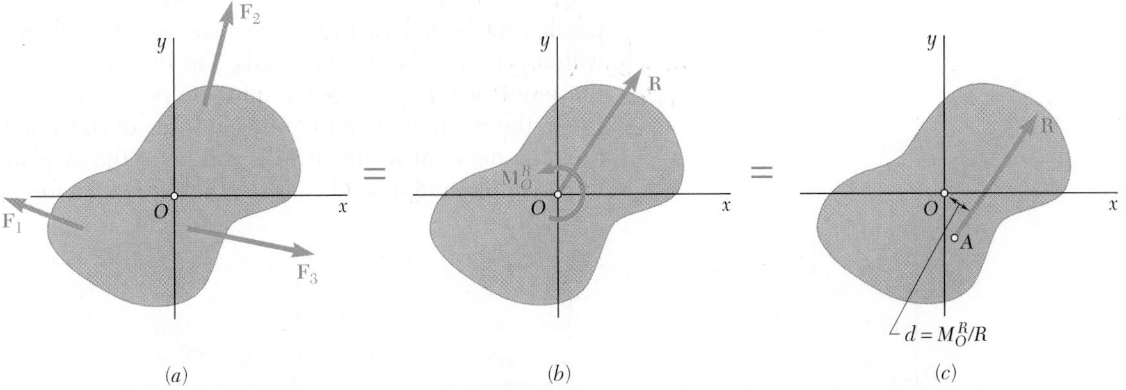

Fig. 3.43

†Since the couple vector $\mathbf{M}_O^R$ is perpendicular to the plane of the figure, it has been represented by the symbol ↺. A counterclockwise couple ↺ represents a vector pointing out of the paper, and a clockwise couple ↻ represents a vector pointing into the paper.

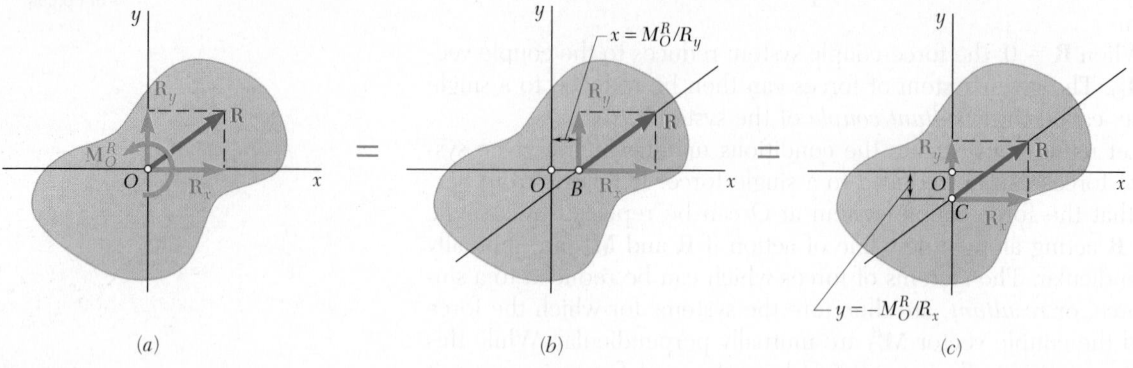

Fig. 3.44

As noted in Sec. 3.17, the reduction of a system of forces is considerably simplified if the forces are resolved into rectangular components. The force-couple system at O is then characterized by the components (Fig. 3.44a)

$$R_x = \Sigma F_x \qquad R_y = \Sigma F_y \qquad M_z^R = M_O^R = \Sigma M_O \tag{3.59}$$

To reduce the system to a single force $\mathbf{R}$, we express that the moment of $\mathbf{R}$ about O must be equal to $\mathbf{M}_O^R$. Denoting by x and y the coordinates of the point of application of the resultant and recalling formula (3.22) of Sec. 3.8, we write

$$xR_y - yR_x = M_O^R$$

which represents the equation of the line of action of $\mathbf{R}$. We can also determine directly the x and y intercepts of the line of action of the resultant by noting that $\mathbf{M}_O^R$ must be equal to the moment about O of the y component of $\mathbf{R}$ when $\mathbf{R}$ is attached at B (Fig. 3.44b) and to the moment of its x component when $\mathbf{R}$ is attached at C (Fig. 3.44c).

3. *Parallel forces* have parallel lines of action and may or may not have the same sense. Assuming here that the forces are parallel to the y axis (Fig. 3.45a), we note that their sum $\mathbf{R}$ will also be parallel to the y axis. On the other hand, since the moment of a given force must be perpendicular to that force, the moment about O of each force of the system, and thus the moment resultant $\mathbf{M}_O^R$, will lie in the zx plane. The force-couple system at O consists, therefore, of a force $\mathbf{R}$ and

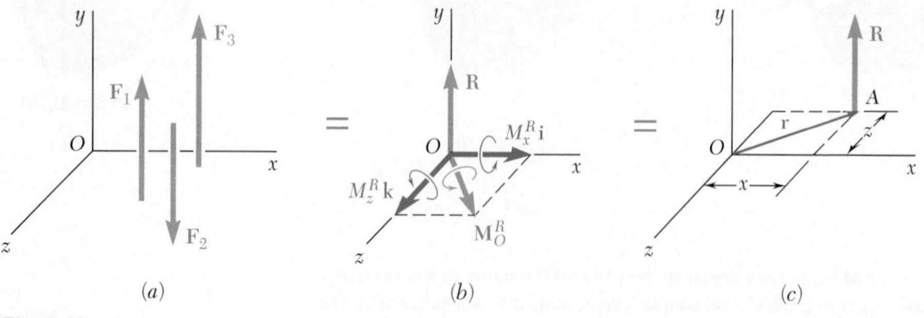

Fig. 3.45

a couple vector $\mathbf{M}_O^R$ which are mutually perpendicular (Fig. 3.45*b*). They can be reduced to a single force $\mathbf{R}$ (Fig. 3.45*c*) or, if $\mathbf{R} = 0$, to a single couple of moment $\mathbf{M}_O^R$.

In practice, the force-couple system at O will be characterized by the components

$$R_y = \Sigma F_y \qquad M_x^R = \Sigma M_x \qquad M_z^R = \Sigma M_z \tag{3.60}$$

The reduction of the system to a single force can be carried out by moving $\mathbf{R}$ to a new point of application $A(x, 0, z)$ chosen so that the moment of $\mathbf{R}$ about O is equal to $\mathbf{M}_O^R$. We write

$$\mathbf{r} \times \mathbf{R} = \mathbf{M}_O^R$$
$$(x\mathbf{i} + z\mathbf{k}) \times R_y\mathbf{j} = M_x^R\mathbf{i} + M_z^R\mathbf{k}$$

By computing the vector products and equating the coefficients of the corresponding unit vectors in both members of the equation, we obtain two scalar equations which define the coordinates of A:

$$-zR_y = M_x^R \qquad xR_y = M_z^R$$

These equations express that the moments of $\mathbf{R}$ about the x and z axes must, respectively, be equal to M_x^R and M_z^R.

Photo 3.5 The parallel wind forces acting on the highway signs can be reduced to a single equivalent force. Determining this force can simplify the calculation of the forces acting on the supports of the frame to which the signs are attached.

*3.21. REDUCTION OF A SYSTEM OF FORCES TO A WRENCH

In the general case of a system of forces in space, the equivalent force-couple system at O consists of a force $\mathbf{R}$ and a couple vector $\mathbf{M}_O^R$ which are not perpendicular, and neither of which is zero (Fig. 3.46*a*). Thus, the system of forces *cannot* be reduced to a single force or to a single couple. The couple vector, however, can be replaced by two other couple vectors obtained by resolving $\mathbf{M}_O^R$ into a component $\mathbf{M}_1$ along $\mathbf{R}$ and a component $\mathbf{M}_2$ in a plane perpendicular to $\mathbf{R}$ (Fig. 3.46*b*). The couple vector $\mathbf{M}_2$ and the force $\mathbf{R}$ can then be replaced by a single force $\mathbf{R}$ acting along a new line of action. The original system of forces thus reduces to $\mathbf{R}$ and to the couple vector $\mathbf{M}_1$ (Fig. 3.46*c*), that is, to $\mathbf{R}$ and a couple acting in the plane perpendicular to $\mathbf{R}$. This particular force-couple system is called a *wrench,* and the resulting combination of push and twist is found in drilling and tapping operations

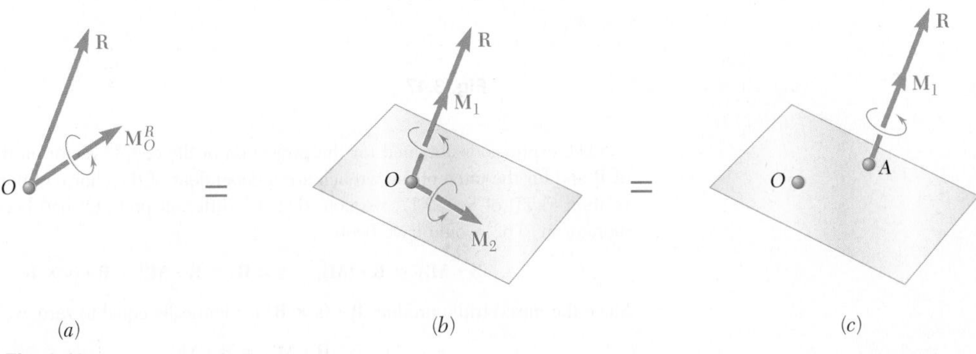

Fig. 3.46

and in the tightening and the loosening of screws. The line of action of **R** is known as the *axis of the wrench*, and the ratio $p = M_1/R$ is called the *pitch* of the wrench. A wrench, therefore, consists of two collinear vectors, namely, a force **R** and a couple vector

$$\mathbf{M}_1 = p\mathbf{R} \tag{3.61}$$

Recalling the expression (3.35) obtained in Sec. 3.9 for the projection of a vector on the line of action of another vector, we note that the projection of $\mathbf{M}_O^R$ on the line of action of **R** is

$$M_1 = \frac{\mathbf{R} \cdot \mathbf{M}_O^R}{R}$$

Thus, the pitch of the wrench can be expressed as†

$$p = \frac{M_1}{R} = \frac{\mathbf{R} \cdot \mathbf{M}_O^R}{R^2} \tag{3.62}$$

Photo 3.6 The pushing-turning action associated with the tightening of a screw illustrates the collinear lines of action of the force and couple vector that constitute a wrench.

To define the axis of the wrench, we can write a relation involving the position vector **r** of an arbitrary point P located on that axis. Attaching the resultant force **R** and couple vector $\mathbf{M}_1$ at P (Fig. 3.47) and expressing that the moment about O of this force-couple system is equal to the moment resultant $\mathbf{M}_O^R$ of the original force system, we write

$$\mathbf{M}_1 + \mathbf{r} \times \mathbf{R} = \mathbf{M}_O^R \tag{3.63}$$

or, recalling Eq. (3.61),

$$p\mathbf{R} + \mathbf{r} \times \mathbf{R} = \mathbf{M}_O^R \tag{3.64}$$

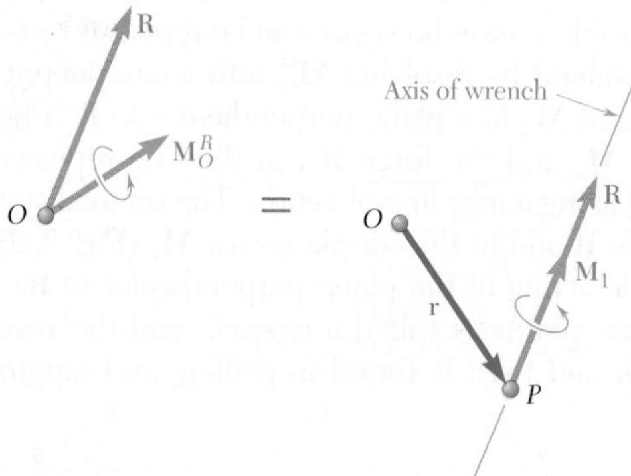

Fig. 3.47

†The expressions obtained for the projection of the couple vector on the line of action of **R** and for the pitch of the wrench are independent of the choice of point O. Using the relation (3.53) of Sec. 3.17, we note that if a different point O' had been used, the numerator in (3.62) would have been

$$\mathbf{R} \cdot \mathbf{M}_{O'}^R = \mathbf{R} \cdot (\mathbf{M}_O^R + \mathbf{s} \times \mathbf{R}) = \mathbf{R} \cdot \mathbf{M}_O^R + \mathbf{R} \cdot (\mathbf{s} \times \mathbf{R})$$

Since the mixed triple product $\mathbf{R} \cdot (\mathbf{s} \times \mathbf{R})$ is identically equal to zero, we have

$$\mathbf{R} \cdot \mathbf{M}_{O'}^R = \mathbf{R} \cdot \mathbf{M}_O^R$$

Thus, the scalar product $\mathbf{R} \cdot \mathbf{M}_O^R$ is independent of the choice of point O.

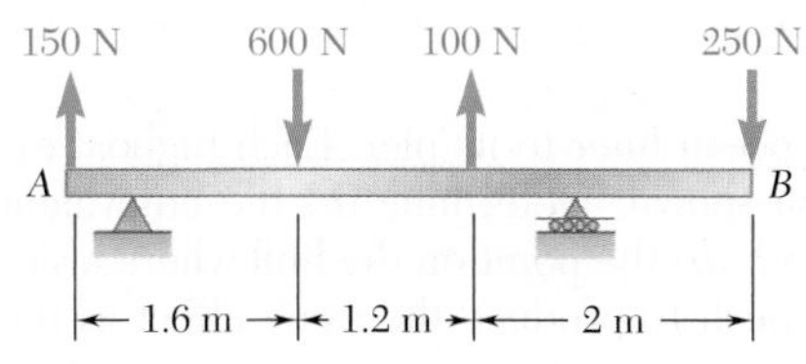

SAMPLE PROBLEM 3.8

A 4.80-m-long beam is subjected to the forces shown. Reduce the given system of forces to (*a*) an equivalent force-couple system at *A*, (*b*) an equivalent force-couple system at *B*, (*c*) a single force or resultant.

Note. Since the reactions at the supports are not included in the given system of forces, the given system will not maintain the beam in equilibrium.

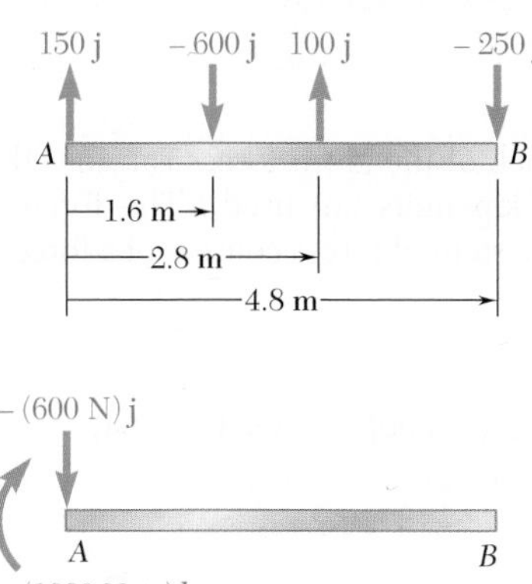

SOLUTION

***a.* Force-Couple System at *A*.** The force-couple system at *A* equivalent to the given system of forces consists of a force $\mathbf{R}$ and a couple $\mathbf{M}_A^R$ defined as follows:

$$\begin{aligned}\mathbf{R} &= \Sigma\mathbf{F}\\ &= (150\text{ N})\mathbf{j} - (600\text{ N})\mathbf{j} + (100\text{ N})\mathbf{j} - (250\text{ N})\mathbf{j} = -(600\text{ N})\mathbf{j}\\ \mathbf{M}_A^R &= \Sigma(\mathbf{r}\times\mathbf{F})\\ &= (1.6\mathbf{i})\times(-600\mathbf{j}) + (2.8\mathbf{i})\times(100\mathbf{j}) + (4.8\mathbf{i})\times(-250\mathbf{j})\\ &= -(1880\text{ N}\cdot\text{m})\mathbf{k}\end{aligned}$$

The equivalent force-couple system at *A* is thus

$$\mathbf{R} = 600\text{ N}\downarrow \qquad \mathbf{M}_A^R = 1880\text{ N}\cdot\text{m}\ ⤸ \quad ◀$$

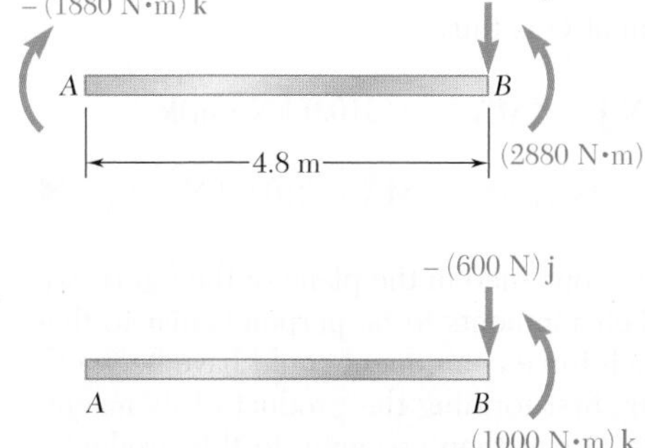

***b.* Force-Couple System at *B*.** We propose to find a force-couple system at *B* equivalent to the force-couple system at *A* determined in part *a*. The force $\mathbf{R}$ is unchanged, but a new couple $\mathbf{M}_B^R$ must be determined, the moment of which is equal to the moment about *B* of the force-couple system determined in part *a*. Thus, we have

$$\begin{aligned}\mathbf{M}_B^R &= \mathbf{M}_A^R + \overrightarrow{BA}\times\mathbf{R}\\ &= -(1880\text{ N}\cdot\text{m})\mathbf{k} + (-4.8\text{ m})\mathbf{i}\times(-600\text{ N})\mathbf{j}\\ &= -(1880\text{ N}\cdot\text{m})\mathbf{k} + (2880\text{ N}\cdot\text{m})\mathbf{k} = +(1000\text{ N}\cdot\text{m})\mathbf{k}\end{aligned}$$

The equivalent force-couple system at *B* is thus

$$\mathbf{R} = 600\text{ N}\downarrow \qquad \mathbf{M}_B^R = 1000\text{ N}\cdot\text{m}\ ⤺ \quad ◀$$

***c.* Single Force or Resultant.** The resultant of the given system of forces is equal to $\mathbf{R}$, and its point of application must be such that the moment of $\mathbf{R}$ about *A* is equal to $\mathbf{M}_A^R$. We write

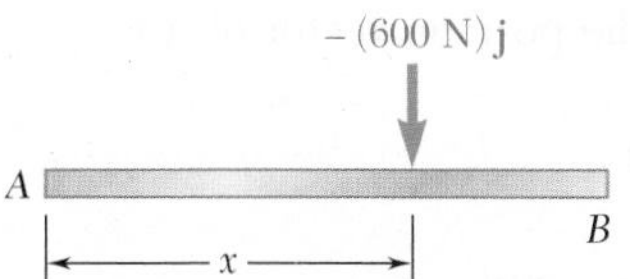

$$\begin{aligned}\mathbf{r}\times\mathbf{R} &= \mathbf{M}_A^R\\ x\mathbf{i}\times(-600\text{ N})\mathbf{j} &= -(1880\text{ N}\cdot\text{m})\mathbf{k}\\ -x(600\text{ N})\mathbf{k} &= -(1880\text{ N}\cdot\text{m})\mathbf{k}\end{aligned}$$

and conclude that $x = 3.13$ m. Thus, the single force equivalent to the given system is defined as

$$\mathbf{R} = 600\text{ N}\downarrow \qquad x = 3.13\text{ m} \quad ◀$$

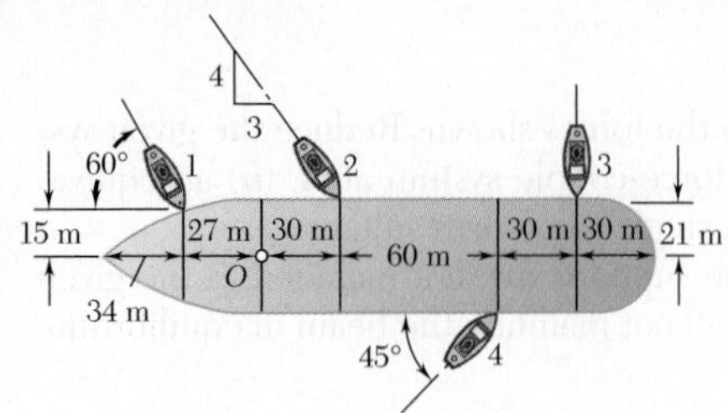

SAMPLE PROBLEM 3.9

Four tugboats are used to bring an ocean liner to its pier. Each tugboat exerts a 5000-N force in the direction shown. Determine (*a*) the equivalent force-couple system at the foremast *O*, (*b*) the point on the hull where a single, more powerful tugboat should push to produce the same effect as the original four tugboats.

SOLUTION

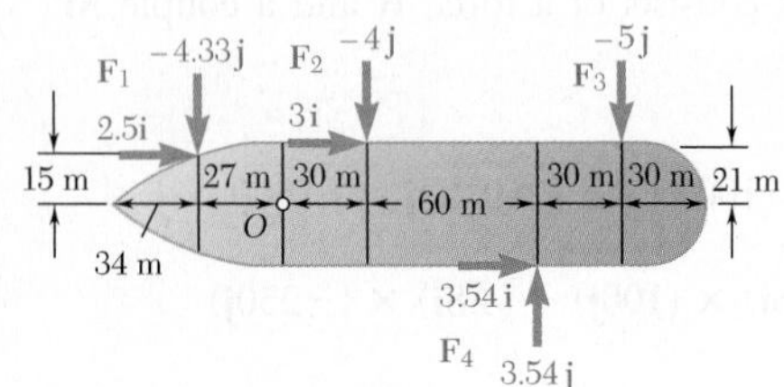

***a.* Force-Couple System at *O*.** Each of the given forces is resolved into components in the diagram shown (kip units are used). The force-couple system at *O* equivalent to the given system of forces consists of a force **R** and a couple $\mathbf{M}_O^R$ defined as follows:

$$\begin{aligned}\mathbf{R} &= \Sigma\mathbf{F}\\ &= (2.50\mathbf{i} - 4.33\mathbf{j}) + (3.00\mathbf{i} - 4.00\mathbf{j}) + (-5.00\mathbf{j}) + (3.54\mathbf{i} + 3.54\mathbf{j})\\ &= 9.04\mathbf{i} - 9.79\mathbf{j}\end{aligned}$$

$$\begin{aligned}\mathbf{M}_O^R &= \Sigma(\mathbf{r} \times \mathbf{F})\\ &= (-27\mathbf{i} + 15\mathbf{j}) \times (2.50\mathbf{i} - 4.33\mathbf{j})\\ &\quad + (30\mathbf{i} + 21\mathbf{j}) \times (3.00\mathbf{i} - 4.00\mathbf{j})\\ &\quad + (120\mathbf{i} + 21\mathbf{j}) \times (-5.00\mathbf{j})\\ &\quad + (90\mathbf{i} - 21\mathbf{j}) \times (3.54\mathbf{i} + 3.54\mathbf{j})\\ &= (117 - 37.5 - 120 - 63 - 600 + 318.6 + 74)\mathbf{k}\\ &= -310.9\mathbf{k}\end{aligned}$$

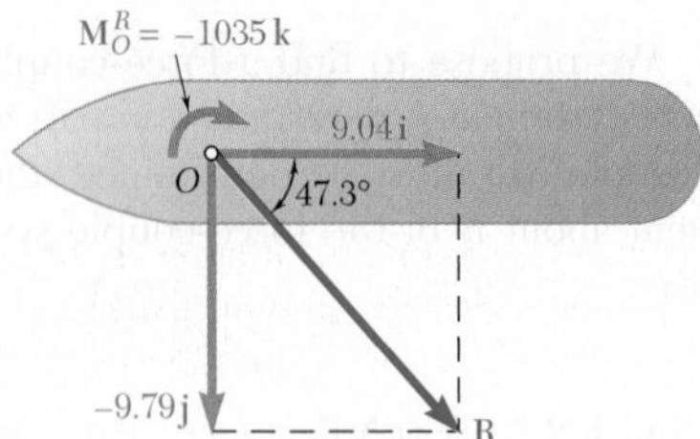

The equivalent force-couple system at *O* is thus

$$\mathbf{R} = (9.04 \text{ kN})\mathbf{i} - (9.79 \text{ kN})\mathbf{j} \qquad \mathbf{M}_O^R = -(310.9 \text{ kN} \cdot \text{m})\mathbf{k}$$

or $\quad \mathbf{R} = 13.33 \text{ kN} \measuredangle 47.3° \qquad \mathbf{M}_O^R = 310.9 \text{ kN} \cdot \text{m} \circlearrowright$ ◀

Remark. Since all the forces are contained in the plane of the figure, we could have expected the sum of their moments to be perpendicular to that plane. Note that the moment of each force component could have been obtained directly from the diagram by first forming the product of its magnitude and perpendicular distance to *O* and then assigning to this product a positive or a negative sign depending upon the sense of the moment.

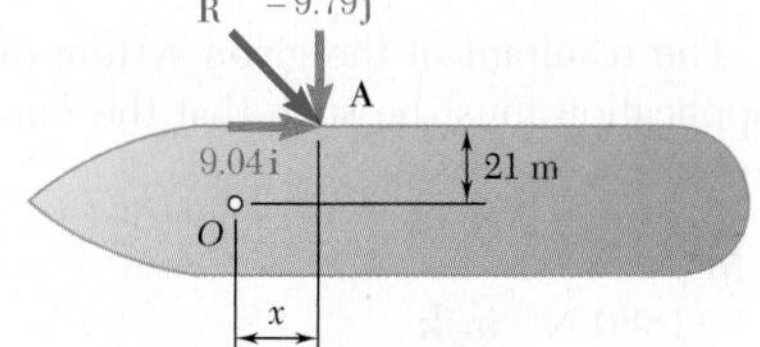

***b.* Single Tugboat.** The force exerted by a single tugboat must be equal to **R**, and its point of application *A* must be such that the moment of **R** about *O* is equal to $\mathbf{M}_O^R$. Observing that the position vector of *A* is

$$\mathbf{r} = x\mathbf{i} + 70\mathbf{j}$$

we write

$$\begin{aligned}\mathbf{r} \times \mathbf{R} &= \mathbf{M}_O^R\\ (x\mathbf{i} + 21\mathbf{j}) \times (9.04\mathbf{i} - 9.79\mathbf{j}) &= -310.9\mathbf{k}\\ -x(9.79)\mathbf{k} - 189.8\mathbf{k} &= -310.9\mathbf{k} \qquad x = 12.4 \text{ m}\end{aligned}$$ ◀

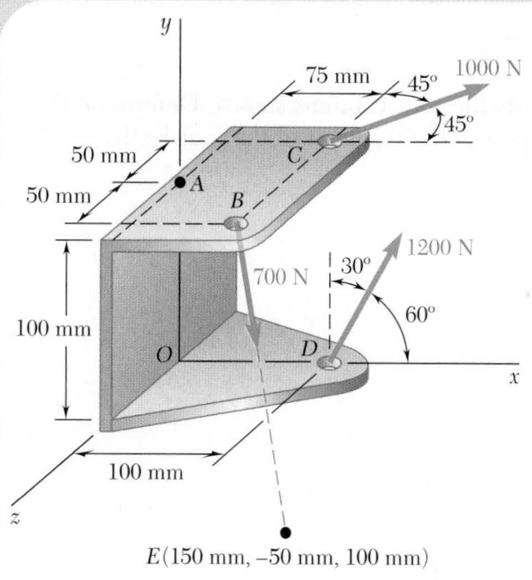

SAMPLE PROBLEM 3.10

Three cables are attached to a bracket as shown. Replace the forces exerted by the cables with an equivalent force-couple system at *A*.

SOLUTION

We first determine the relative position vectors drawn from point *A* to the points of application of the various forces and resolve the forces into rectangular components. Observing that $\mathbf{F}_B = (700\ \text{N})\boldsymbol{\lambda}_{BE}$ where

$$\boldsymbol{\lambda}_{BE} = \frac{\overrightarrow{BE}}{BE} = \frac{75\mathbf{i} - 150\mathbf{j} + 50\mathbf{k}}{175}$$

we have, using meters and newtons,

$$\mathbf{r}_{B/A} = \overrightarrow{AB} = 0.075\mathbf{i} + 0.050\mathbf{k} \qquad \mathbf{F}_B = 300\mathbf{i} - 600\mathbf{j} + 200\mathbf{k}$$
$$\mathbf{r}_{C/A} = \overrightarrow{AC} = 0.075\mathbf{i} - 0.050\mathbf{k} \qquad \mathbf{F}_C = 707\mathbf{i} - 707\mathbf{k}$$
$$\mathbf{r}_{D/A} = \overrightarrow{AD} = 0.100\mathbf{i} - 0.100\mathbf{j} \qquad \mathbf{F}_D = 600\mathbf{i} + 1039\mathbf{j}$$

The force-couple system at *A* equivalent to the given forces consists of a force $\mathbf{R} = \Sigma\mathbf{F}$ and a couple $\mathbf{M}_A^R = \Sigma(\mathbf{r} \times \mathbf{F})$. The force $\mathbf{R}$ is readily obtained by adding respectively the *x*, *y*, and *z* components of the forces:

$$\mathbf{R} = \Sigma\mathbf{F} = (1607\ \text{N})\mathbf{i} + (439\ \text{N})\mathbf{j} - (507\ \text{N})\mathbf{k} \quad \blacktriangleleft$$

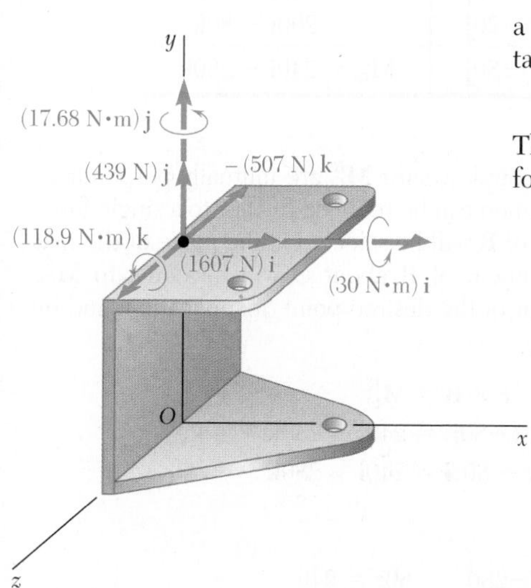

The computation of $\mathbf{M}_A^R$ will be facilitated if we express the moments of the forces in the form of determinants (Sec. 3.8):

$$\mathbf{r}_{B/A} \times \mathbf{F}_B = \begin{vmatrix} \mathbf{i} & \mathbf{j} & \mathbf{k} \\ 0.075 & 0 & 0.050 \\ 300 & -600 & 200 \end{vmatrix} = 30\mathbf{i} \qquad -45\mathbf{k}$$

$$\mathbf{r}_{C/A} \times \mathbf{F}_C = \begin{vmatrix} \mathbf{i} & \mathbf{j} & \mathbf{k} \\ 0.075 & 0 & -0.050 \\ 707 & 0 & -707 \end{vmatrix} = \qquad 17.68\mathbf{j}$$

$$\mathbf{r}_{D/A} \times \mathbf{F}_D = \begin{vmatrix} \mathbf{i} & \mathbf{j} & \mathbf{k} \\ 0.100 & -0.100 & 0 \\ 600 & 1039 & 0 \end{vmatrix} = \qquad 163.9\mathbf{k}$$

Adding the expressions obtained, we have

$$\mathbf{M}_A^R = \Sigma(\mathbf{r} \times \mathbf{F}) = (30\ \text{N}\cdot\text{m})\mathbf{i} + (17.68\ \text{N}\cdot\text{m})\mathbf{j} + (118.9\ \text{N}\cdot\text{m})\mathbf{k} \quad \blacktriangleleft$$

The rectangular components of the force $\mathbf{R}$ and the couple $\mathbf{M}_A^R$ are shown in the adjoining sketch.

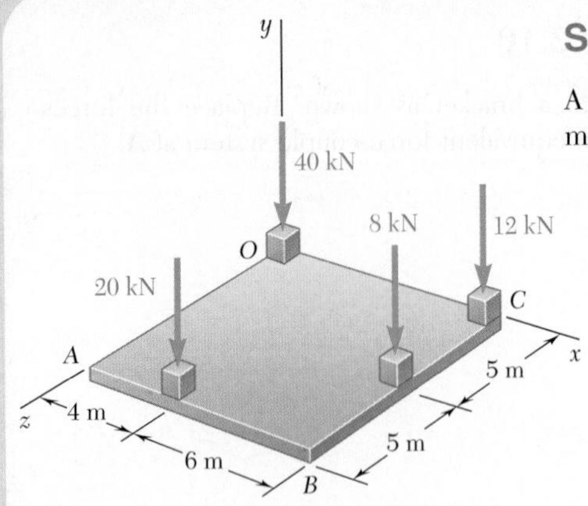

SAMPLE PROBLEM 3.11

A square foundation mat supports the four columns shown. Determine the magnitude and point of application of the resultant of the four loads.

SOLUTION

We first reduce the given system of forces to a force-couple system at the origin *O* of the coordinate system. This force-couple system consists of a force **R** and a couple vector $\mathbf{M}_O^R$ defined as follows:

$$\mathbf{R} = \Sigma\mathbf{F} \qquad \mathbf{M}_O^R = \Sigma(\mathbf{r} \times \mathbf{F})$$

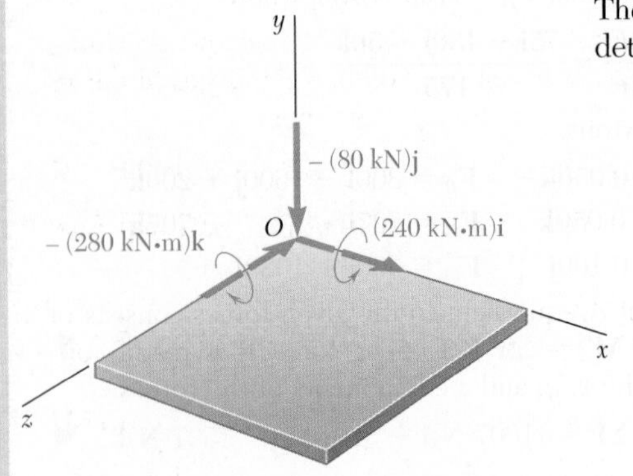

The position vectors of the points of application of the various forces are determined, and the computations are arranged in tabular form.

r, m	**F**, kN	**r** × **F**, kN · m
0	$-40\mathbf{j}$	0
$10\mathbf{i}$	$-12\mathbf{j}$	$-120\mathbf{k}$
$10\mathbf{i} + 5\mathbf{k}$	$-8\mathbf{j}$	$40\mathbf{i} - 80\mathbf{k}$
$4\mathbf{i} + 10\mathbf{k}$	$-20\mathbf{j}$	$200\mathbf{i} - 80\mathbf{k}$
	$\mathbf{R} = -80\mathbf{j}$	$\mathbf{M}_O^R = 240\mathbf{i} - 280\mathbf{k}$

Since the force **R** and the couple vector $\mathbf{M}_O^R$ are mutually perpendicular, the force-couple system obtained can be reduced further to a single force **R**. The new point of application of **R** will be selected in the plane of the mat and in such a way that the moment of **R** about *O* will be equal to $\mathbf{M}_O^R$. Denoting by **r** the position vector of the desired point of application, and by *x* and *z* its coordinates, we write

$$\mathbf{r} \times \mathbf{R} = \mathbf{M}_O^R$$
$$(x\mathbf{i} + z\mathbf{k}) \times (-80\mathbf{j}) = 240\mathbf{i} - 280\mathbf{k}$$
$$-80x\mathbf{k} + 80z\mathbf{i} = 240\mathbf{i} - 280\mathbf{k}$$

from which it follows that

$$-80x = -280 \qquad 80z = 240$$
$$x = 3.50 \text{ m} \qquad z = 3.00 \text{ m}$$

We conclude that the resultant of the given system of forces is

$$\mathbf{R} = 80 \text{ kN} \downarrow \qquad \text{at } x = 3.50 \text{ m}, z = 3.00 \text{ m} \quad ◀$$

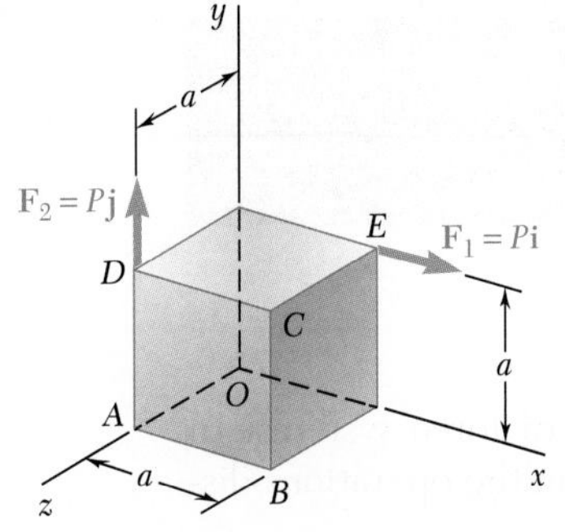

SAMPLE PROBLEM 3.12

Two forces of the same magnitude P act on a cube of side a as shown. Replace the two forces by an equivalent wrench, and determine (a) the magnitude and direction of the resultant force $\mathbf{R}$, (b) the pitch of the wrench, (c) the point where the axis of the wrench intersects the yz plane.

SOLUTION

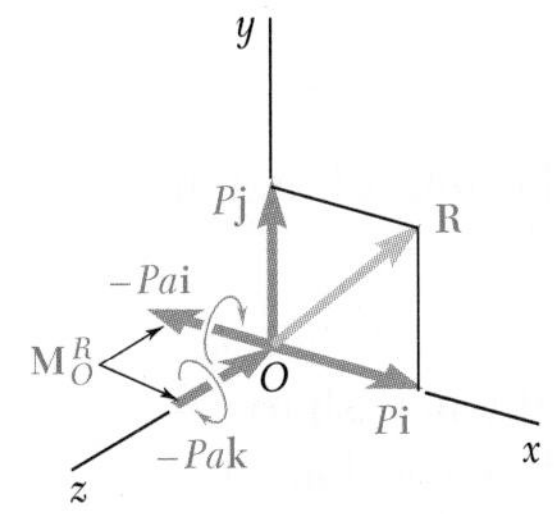

Equivalent Force-Couple System at *O*. We first determine the equivalent force-couple system at the origin O. We observe that the position vectors of the points of application E and D of the two given forces are $\mathbf{r}_E = a\mathbf{i} + a\mathbf{j}$ and $\mathbf{r}_D = a\mathbf{j} + a\mathbf{k}$. The resultant $\mathbf{R}$ of the two forces and their moment resultant $\mathbf{M}_O^R$ about O are

$$\mathbf{R} = \mathbf{F}_1 + \mathbf{F}_2 = P\mathbf{i} + P\mathbf{j} = P(\mathbf{i} + \mathbf{j}) \qquad (1)$$

$$\mathbf{M}_O^R = \mathbf{r}_E \times \mathbf{F}_1 + \mathbf{r}_D \times \mathbf{F}_2 = (a\mathbf{i} + a\mathbf{j}) \times P\mathbf{i} + (a\mathbf{j} + a\mathbf{k}) \times P\mathbf{j}$$

$$= -Pa\mathbf{k} - Pa\mathbf{i} = -Pa(\mathbf{i} + \mathbf{k}) \qquad (2)$$

a. Resultant Force R. It follows from Eq. (1) and the adjoining sketch that the resultant force $\mathbf{R}$ has the magnitude $R = P\sqrt{2}$, lies in the xy plane, and forms angles of 45° with the x and y axes. Thus

$$R = P\sqrt{2} \qquad \theta_x = \theta_y = 45° \qquad \theta_z = 90° \quad ◀$$

b. Pitch of Wrench. Recalling formula (3.62) of Sec. 3.21 and Eqs. (1) and (2) above, we write

$$p = \frac{\mathbf{R} \cdot \mathbf{M}_O^R}{R^2} = \frac{P(\mathbf{i} + \mathbf{j}) \cdot (-Pa)(\mathbf{i} + \mathbf{k})}{(P\sqrt{2})^2} = \frac{-P^2a(1 + 0 + 0)}{2P^2} \qquad p = -\frac{a}{2} \quad ◀$$

c. Axis of Wrench. It follows from the above and from Eq. (3.61) that the wrench consists of the force $\mathbf{R}$ found in (1) and the couple vector

$$\mathbf{M}_1 = p\mathbf{R} = -\frac{a}{2}P(\mathbf{i} + \mathbf{j}) = -\frac{Pa}{2}(\mathbf{i} + \mathbf{j}) \qquad (3)$$

To find the point where the axis of the wrench intersects the yz plane, we express that the moment of the wrench about O is equal to the moment resultant $\mathbf{M}_O^R$ of the original system:

$$\mathbf{M}_1 + \mathbf{r} \times \mathbf{R} = \mathbf{M}_O^R$$

or, noting that $\mathbf{r} = y\mathbf{j} + z\mathbf{k}$ and substituting for $\mathbf{R}$, $\mathbf{M}_O^R$, and $\mathbf{M}_1$ from Eqs. (1), (2), and (3),

$$-\frac{Pa}{2}(\mathbf{i} + \mathbf{j}) + (y\mathbf{j} + z\mathbf{k}) \times P(\mathbf{i} + \mathbf{j}) = -Pa(\mathbf{i} + \mathbf{k})$$

$$-\frac{Pa}{2}\mathbf{i} - \frac{Pa}{2}\mathbf{j} - Py\mathbf{k} + Pz\mathbf{j} - Pz\mathbf{i} = -Pa\mathbf{i} - Pa\mathbf{k}$$

Equating the coefficients of $\mathbf{k}$, and then the coefficients of $\mathbf{j}$, we find

$$y = a \qquad z = a/2 \quad ◀$$

SOLVING PROBLEMS ON YOUR OWN

This lesson was devoted to the reduction and simplification of force systems. In solving the problems which follow, you will be asked to perform the operations discussed below.

1. ***Reducing a force system to a force and a couple at a given point A.*** The force is the *resultant* **R** of the system and is obtained by adding the various forces; the moment of the couple is the *moment resultant* of the system and is obtained by adding the moments about *A* of the various forces. We have

$$\mathbf{R} = \Sigma\mathbf{F} \qquad \mathbf{M}_A^R = \Sigma(\mathbf{r} \times \mathbf{F})$$

where the position vector **r** is drawn from *A* to *any point* on the line of action of **F**.

2. ***Moving a force-couple system from point A to point B.*** If you wish to reduce a given force system to a force-couple system at point *B* after you have reduced it to a force-couple system at point *A*, you need not recompute the moments of the forces about *B*. The resultant **R** remains unchanged, and the new moment resultant $\mathbf{M}_B^R$ can be obtained by adding to $\mathbf{M}_A^R$ the moment about *B* of the force **R** applied at *A* [Sample Prob. 3.8]. Denoting by **s** the vector drawn from *B* to *A*, you can write

$$\mathbf{M}_B^R = \mathbf{M}_A^R + \mathbf{s} \times \mathbf{R}$$

3. ***Checking whether two force systems are equivalent.*** First reduce each force system to a force-couple system *at the same, but arbitrary, point A* (as explained in paragraph 1). The two systems are equivalent (that is, they have the same effect on the given rigid body) if the two force-couple systems you have obtained are identical, that is, if

$$\Sigma\mathbf{F} = \Sigma\mathbf{F}' \qquad \text{and} \qquad \Sigma\mathbf{M}_A = \Sigma\mathbf{M}'_A$$

You should recognize that if the first of these equations is not satisfied, that is, if the two systems do not have the same resultant **R**, the two systems cannot be equivalent and there is then no need to check whether or not the second equation is satisfied.

4. ***Reducing a given force system to a single force.*** First reduce the given system to a force-couple system consisting of the resultant **R** and the couple vector $\mathbf{M}_A^R$ at some convenient point *A* (as explained in paragraph 1). You will recall from

the previous lesson that further reduction to a single force is possible *only if the force* **R** *and the couple vector* $\mathbf{M}_A^R$ *are mutually perpendicular*. This will certainly be the case for systems of forces which are either *concurrent, coplanar,* or *parallel*. The required single force can then be obtained by moving **R** until its moment about A is equal to $\mathbf{M}_A^R$, as you did in several problems of the preceding lesson. More formally, you can write that the position vector **r** drawn from A to any point on the line of action of the single force **R** must satisfy the equation

$$\mathbf{r} \times \mathbf{R} = \mathbf{M}_A^R$$

This procedure was used in Sample Probs. 3.8, 3.9, and 3.11.

5. ***Reducing a given force system to a wrench.*** If the given system is comprised of forces which are not concurrent, coplanar, or parallel, the equivalent force-couple system at a point A will consist of a force **R** and a couple vector $\mathbf{M}_A^R$ which, in general, *are not mutually perpendicular*. (To check whether **R** and $\mathbf{M}_A^R$ are mutually perpendicular, form their scalar product. If this product is zero, they are mutually perpendicular; otherwise, they are not.) If **R** and $\mathbf{M}_A^R$ are not mutually perpendicular, the force-couple system (and thus the given system of forces) *cannot be reduced to a single force*. However, the system can be reduced to a *wrench*—the combination of a force **R** and a couple vector $\mathbf{M}_1$ directed along a common line of action called the *axis of the wrench* (Fig. 3.47). The ratio $p = M_1/R$ is called the *pitch* of the wrench.

To reduce a given force system to a wrench, you should follow these steps:

a. Reduce the given system to an equivalent force-couple system ($\mathbf{R}$, $\mathbf{M}_O^R$), typically located at the origin O.

b. Determine the pitch p from Eq. (3.62)

$$p = \frac{M_1}{R} = \frac{\mathbf{R} \cdot \mathbf{M}_O^R}{R^2} \qquad (3.62)$$

and the couple vector from $\mathbf{M}_1 = p\mathbf{R}$.

c. Express that the moment about O of the wrench is equal to the moment resultant $\mathbf{M}_O^R$ of the force-couple system at O:

$$\mathbf{M}_1 + \mathbf{r} \times \mathbf{R} = \mathbf{M}_O^R \qquad (3.63)$$

This equation allows you to determine the point where the line of action of the wrench intersects a specified plane, since the position vector **r** is directed from O to that point.

These steps are illustrated in Sample Prob. 3.12. Although the determination of a wrench and the point where its axis intersects a plane may appear difficult, the process is simply the application of several of the ideas and techniques developed in this chapter. Thus, once you have mastered the wrench, you can feel confident that you understand much of Chap. 3.

Problems

3.98 A 5-m-long beam is subjected to a variety of loadings. (*a*) Replace each loading with an equivalent force-couple system at end *B* of the beam. (*b*) Which of the loadings are equivalent?

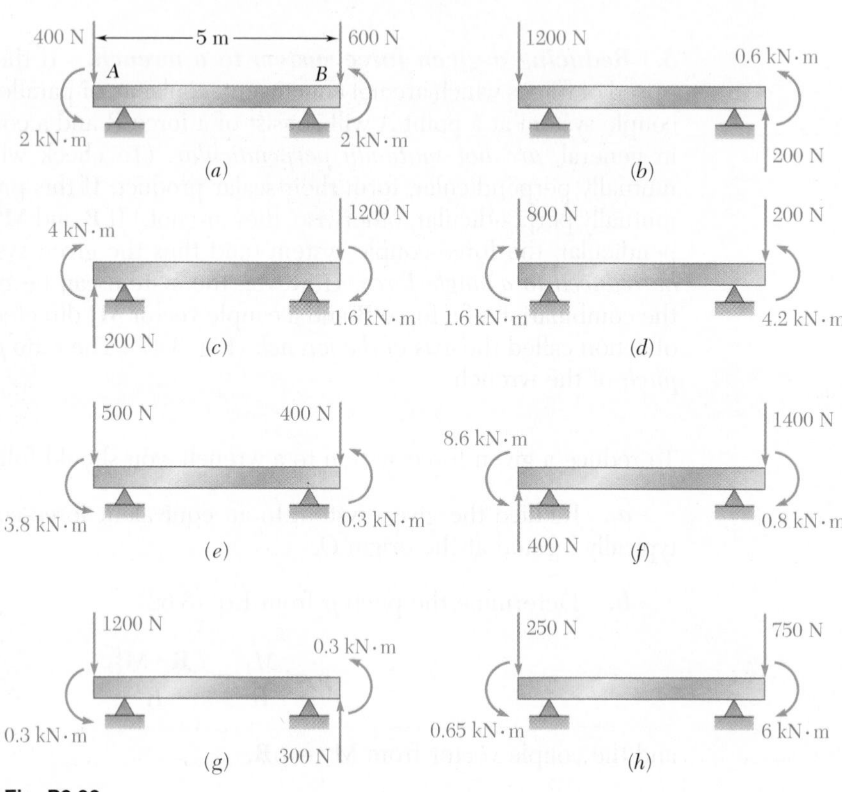

Fig. P3.98

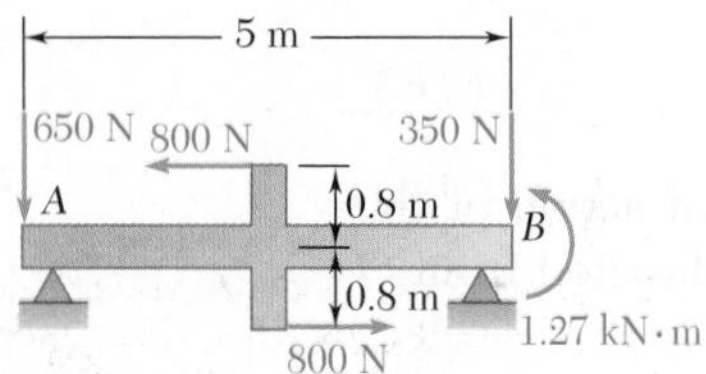

Fig. P3.99

3.99 A 5-m-long beam is loaded as shown. Determine the loading of Prob. 3.98 that is equivalent to this loading.

3.100 Determine the single equivalent force and the distance from end *A* to its line of action for the beam and loading shown when (*a*) $\mathbf{F}_B = 200\ \text{N} \downarrow$, $M_B = 100\ \text{N} \cdot \text{m}$, (*b*) $\mathbf{F}_B = 100\ \text{N} \uparrow$, $M_B = -600\ \text{N} \cdot \text{m}$, (*c*) $\mathbf{F}_B = 100\ \text{N} \downarrow$, $M_B = -200\ \text{N} \cdot \text{m}$.

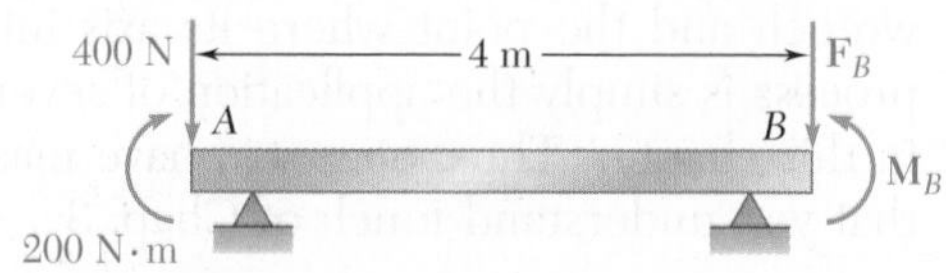

Fig. P3.100

3.101 Five separate force-couple systems act at the corners of a metal block, which has been machined into the shape shown. Determine which of these systems is equivalent to a force $\mathbf{F} = (2\ \text{N})\mathbf{j}$ and a couple of moment $\mathbf{M} = (48\ \text{N} \cdot \text{cm})\mathbf{i} + (32\ \text{N} \cdot \text{cm})\mathbf{k}$ located at point A.

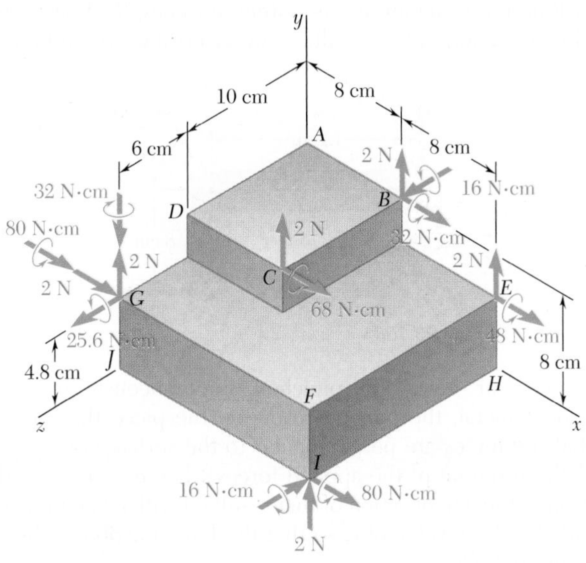

Fig. P3.101

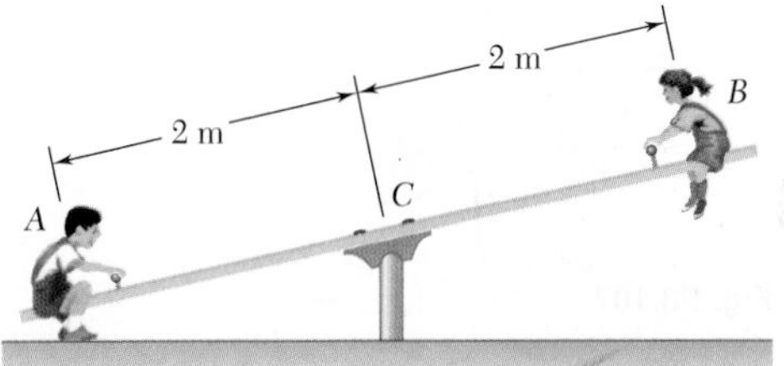

Fig. *P3.102*

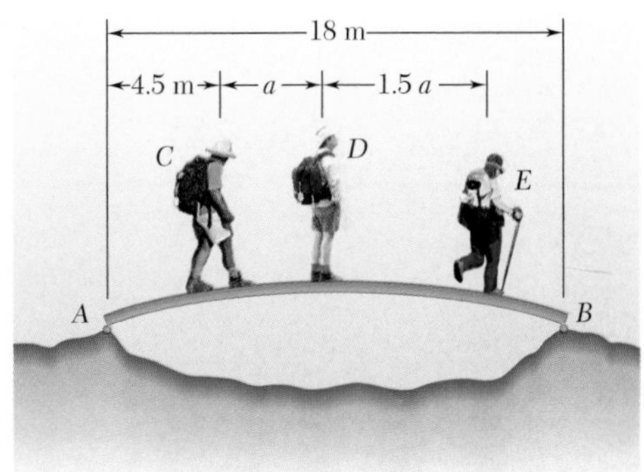

Fig. P3.103

3.102 The masses of two children sitting at ends A and B of a seesaw are 38 kg and 29 kg, respectively. Determine where a third child should sit so that the resultant of the weights of the three children will pass through C if she has a mass of (*a*) 27 kg, (*b*) 24 kg.

3.103 Three hikers are shown crossing a footbridge. Knowing that the weights of the hikers at points C, D, and E are 200 N, 175 N, and 135 N, respectively, determine (*a*) the horizontal distance from A to the line of action of the resultant of the three weights when $a = 3.3$ m, (*b*) the value of a so that the loads on the bridge supports at A and B are equal.

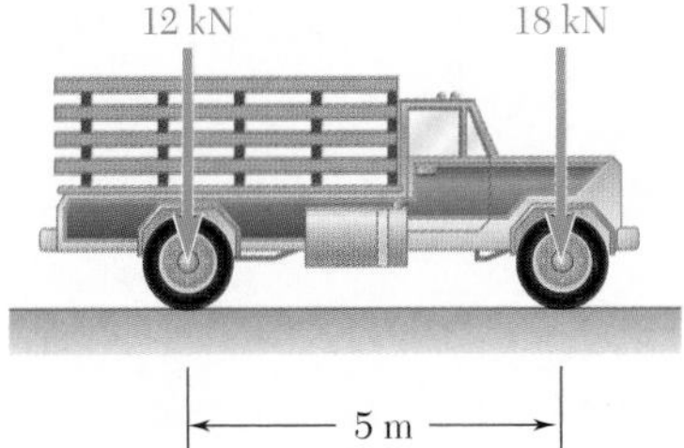

Fig. *P3.104*

3.104 By driving a truck over a scale, it was determined that the loads on the front and rear axles are 18 kN and 12 kN, respectively, when the truck is empty. Determine the weight and the location of the heaviest load that the truck can carry if the load on each axle is not to exceed 40 kN.

3.105 Fixture $ABCD$ is used to apply forces to photoelastic models of mechanical components. For the model and forces shown, determine when $\alpha = 50°$ (*a*) the resultant of the applied forces, (*b*) the point where the line of action of the resultant intersects a line drawn through points F and G.

3.106 Fixture $ABCD$ is used to apply forces to photoelastic models of mechanical components. For the model and forces shown, determine (*a*) the value of α so that the line of action of the resultant of the applied forces passes through the model 100 mm to the right of the 40-N force, (*b*) the resultant of the applied forces.

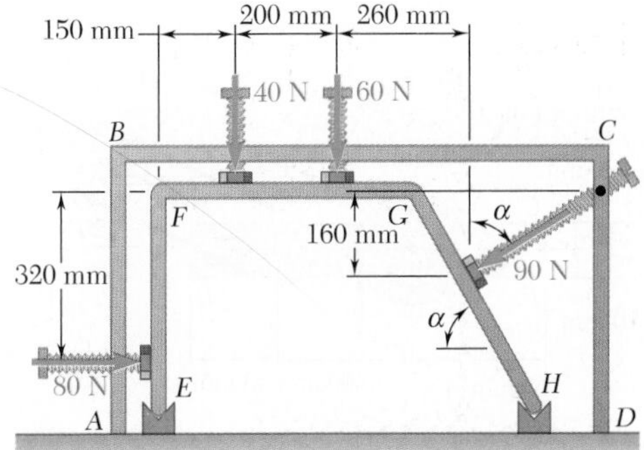

Fig. P3.105 and P3.106

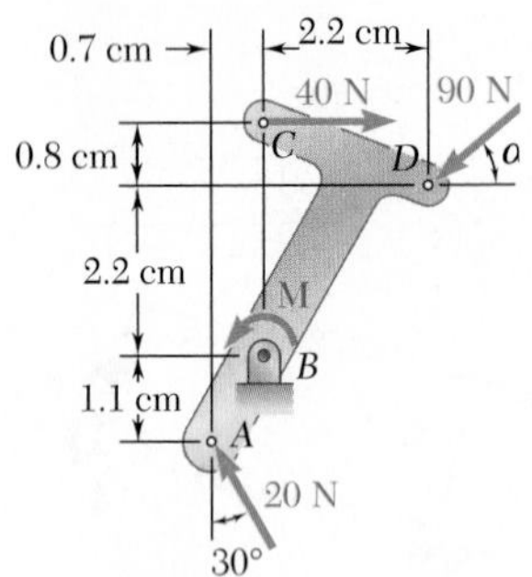

Fig. P3.107

3.107 When the couple **M** is applied to the link in a mechanism, the resulting forces exerted on the link from a guide and the connecting links are as shown. Determine (*a*) the values of **M** and α so that the applied forces and couple can be reduced to a single equivalent force whose line of action passes through points *B* and *D*, (*b*) the equivalent force.

3.108 The three forces and a couple shown are applied to an angle bracket. (*a*) Find the resultant of this system of forces. (*b*) Locate the points where the line of action of the resultant intersects line *AB* and line *BC*.

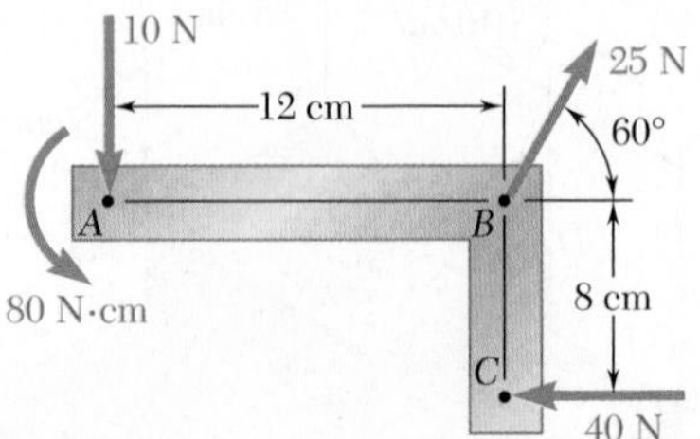

Fig. *P3.108*

3.109 As four holes are punched simultaneously in a piece of aluminum sheet metal, the punches exert on the piece the forces shown. Knowing that the forces are perpendicular to the surfaces of the piece, determine (*a*) the resultant of the applied forces when $\alpha = 45°$ and the point of intersection of the line of action of that resultant with a line drawn through points A and B, (*b*) the value of α so that the line of action of the resultant passes through fold *EF*.

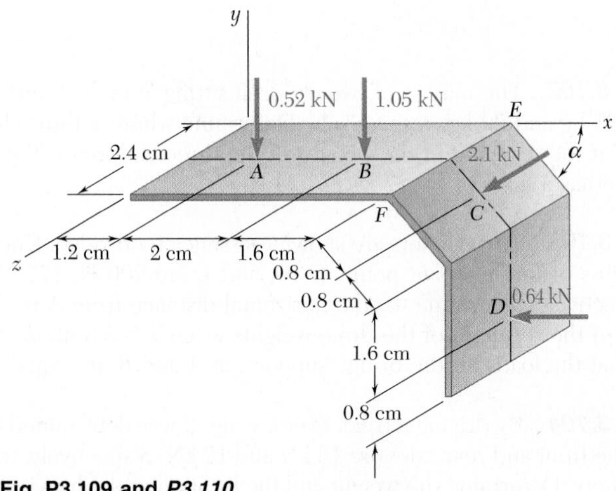

Fig. P3.109 and *P3.110*

3.110 As four holes are punched simultaneously in a piece of aluminum sheet metal, the punches exert on the piece the forces shown. Knowing that the forces are perpendicular to the surfaces of the piece, determine (*a*) the value of α so that the resultant of the applied forces is parallel to the 2.1-kN force, (*b*) the corresponding resultant of the applied forces and the point of intersection of its line of action with a line drawn through points *A* and *B*.

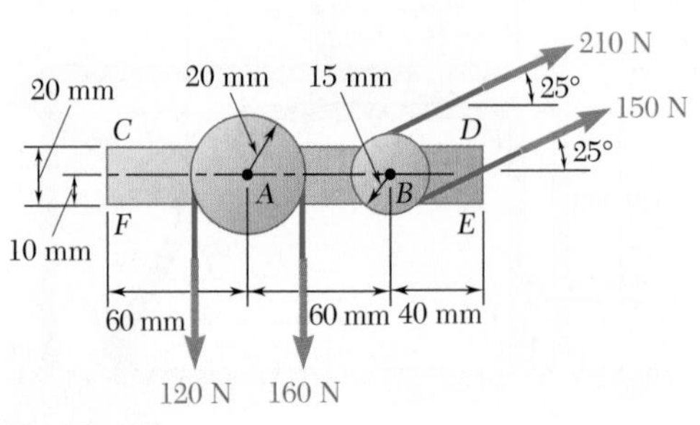

Fig. P3.111

3.111 Pulleys *A* and *B* are mounted on bracket *CDEF*. The tension on each side of the two belts is as shown. Replace the four forces with a single equivalent force, and determine where its line of action intersects the bottom edge of the bracket.

3.112 Three forces and a couple act on crank *ABC*. For $P = 25$ N and $\alpha = 40°$, (*a*) determine the resultant of the given system of forces, (*b*) locate the point where the line of action of the resultant intersects a line drawn through points *B* and *C*, (*c*) locate the point where the line of action of the resultant intersects a line drawn through points *A* and *B*.

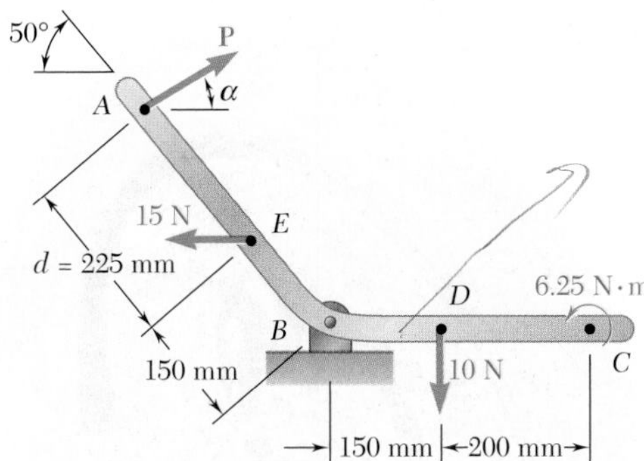

Fig. P3.112 and P3.113

3.113 Three forces and a couple act on crank *ABC*. Determine the value of *d* so that the given system of forces is equivalent to zero at (*a*) point *B*, (*b*) point *D*.

3.114 As follower *AB* rolls along the surface of member *C*, it exerts a constant force **F** perpendicular to the surface. (*a*) Replace **F** with an equivalent force-couple system at the point *D*. (*b*) For $b = 30$ cm and $h = 60$ cm, determine the value of *x* for which the moment of the equivalent force-couple system at *D* is maximum.

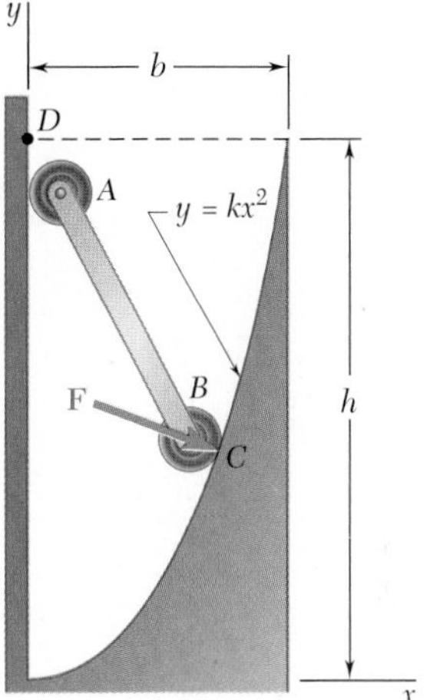

Fig. P3.114

3.115 A machine component is subjected to the forces shown, each of which is parallel to one of the coordinate axes. Replace these forces with an equivalent force-couple system at *A*.

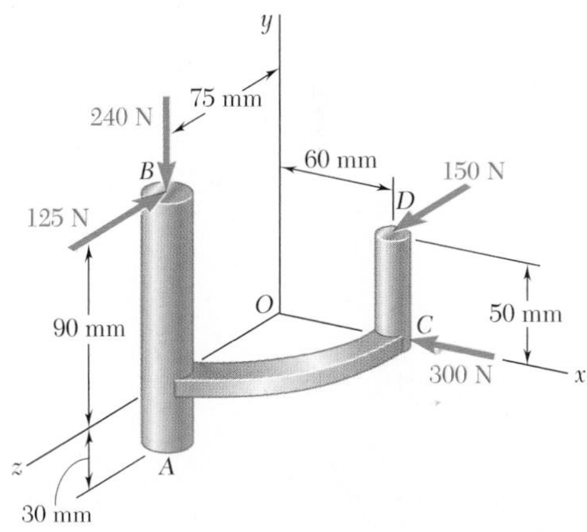

Fig. P3.115

3.116 As a block of wood is sanded, it exerts on the disk of the sander a force **F** of magnitude 1.8 N. Knowing that the belt forces exerted on the 5-cm-diameter pulley lie in a plane parallel to *yz* plane, replace **F** and the belt forces with an equivalent force-couple system at *O*.

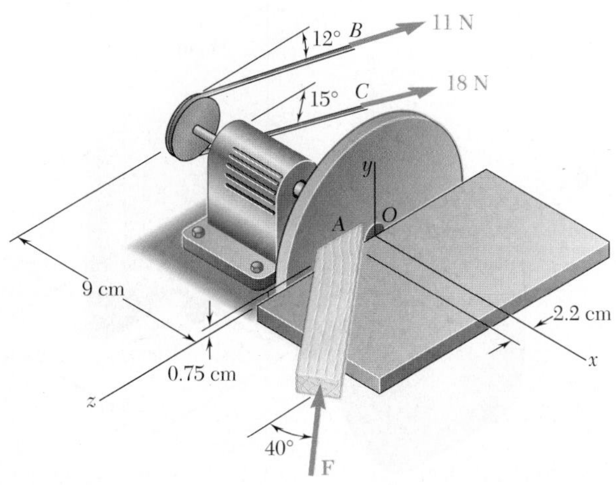

Fig. *P3.116*

3.117 A car owner uses wrench ABC to loosen the lug nut at C. The length of the handle AB is 372 mm, and the owner applies forces **A** and **B** to the wrench. Knowing that these forces are equivalent to a force-couple system at O consisting of the force $\mathbf{R} = -(10\text{ N})\mathbf{i} + (6\text{ N})\mathbf{k}$ and the couple $\mathbf{M}_O = (60\text{ N}\cdot\text{m})\mathbf{i} + (0.05\text{ N}\cdot\text{m})\mathbf{j} - (10\text{ N}\cdot\text{m})\mathbf{k}$, determine the forces applied at A and B when $A_z = 2$ N.

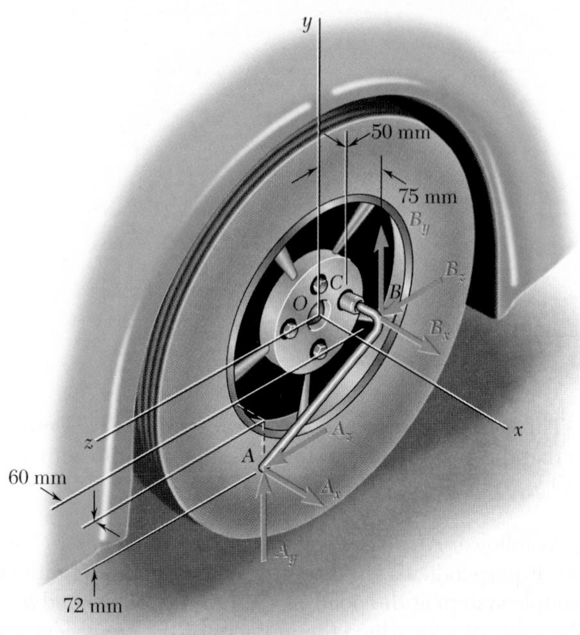

Fig. P3.117

3.118 While using a pencil sharpener, a student applies the forces and couple shown. (*a*) Determine the forces exerted at B and C knowing that these forces and the couple are equivalent to a force-couple system at A consisting of the force $\mathbf{R} = (3.9\text{ N})\mathbf{i} + R_y\mathbf{j} - (1.1\text{ N})\mathbf{k}$ and the couple $\mathbf{M}_A^R = M_x\mathbf{i} + (1.5\text{ N}\cdot\text{cm})\mathbf{j} - (1.1\text{ N}\cdot\text{cm})\mathbf{k}$. (*b*) Find the corresponding values of R_y and M_x.

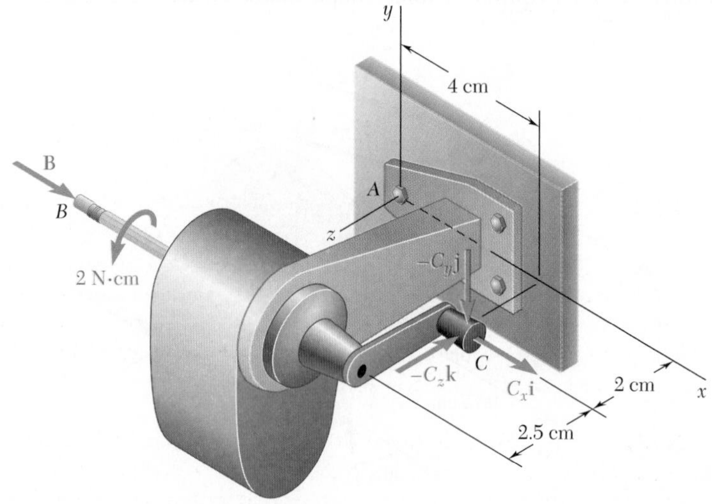

Fig. P3.118

3.119 A portion of the flue for a furnace is attached to the ceiling at A. While supporting the free end of the flue at F, a worker pushes in at E and pulls out at F to align end E with the furnace. Knowing that the 50-N force at F lies in a plane parallel to the yz plane, determine (*a*) the angle α the force at F should form with the horizontal if duct AB is not to tend to rotate about the vertical, (*b*) the force-couple system at B equivalent to the given force system when this condition is satisfied.

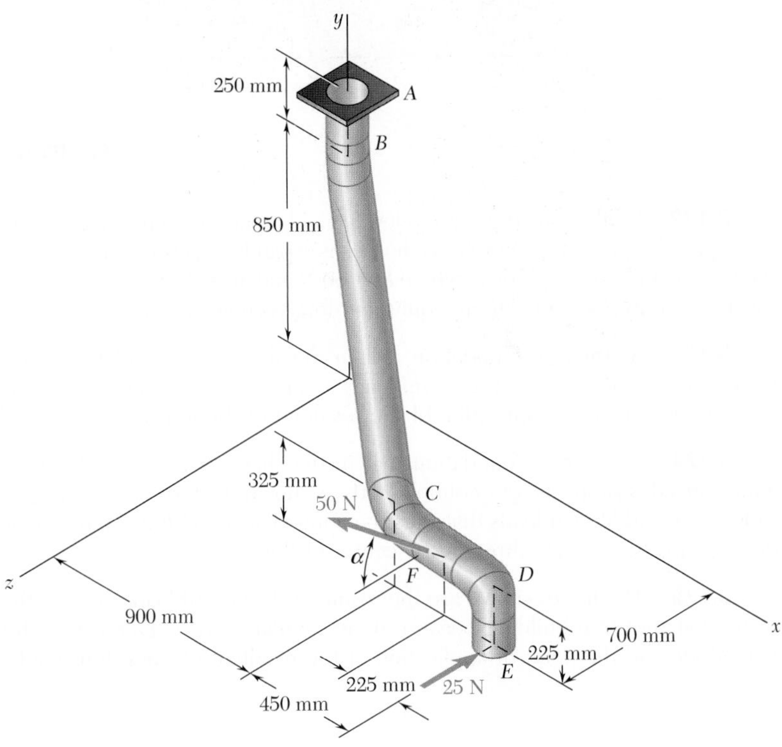

Fig. P3.119 and P3.120

3.120 A portion of the flue for a furnace is attached to the ceiling at A. While supporting the free end of the flue at F, a worker pushes in at E and pulls out at F to align end E with the furnace. Knowing that the 50-N force at F lies in a plane parallel to the yz plane and that $\alpha = 60°$, (*a*) replace the given force system with an equivalent force-couple system at C, (*b*) determine whether duct CD will tend to rotate clockwise or counterclockwise relative to elbow C, as viewed from D to C.

3.121 As an adjustable brace BC is used to bring a wall into plumb, the force-couple system shown is exerted on the wall. Replace this force-couple system with an equivalent force-couple system at A knowing that $R = 21.2$ N and $M = 13.25$ N · m.

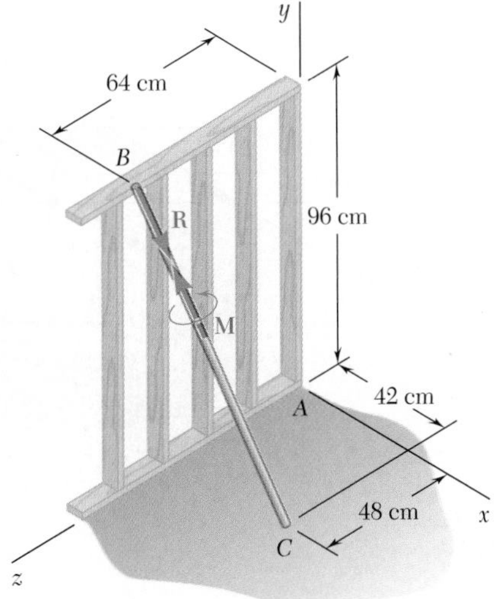

Fig. *P3.121*

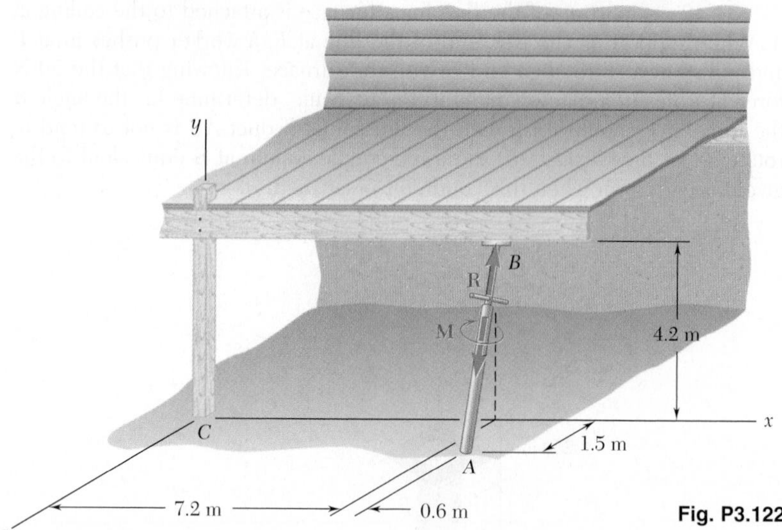

Fig. P3.122

3.122 While a sagging porch is leveled and repaired, a screw jack is used to support the front of the porch. As the jack is expanded, it exerts on the porch the force-couple system shown, where $R = 60$ N and $M = 22.5$ N · m. Replace this force-couple system with an equivalent force-couple system at C.

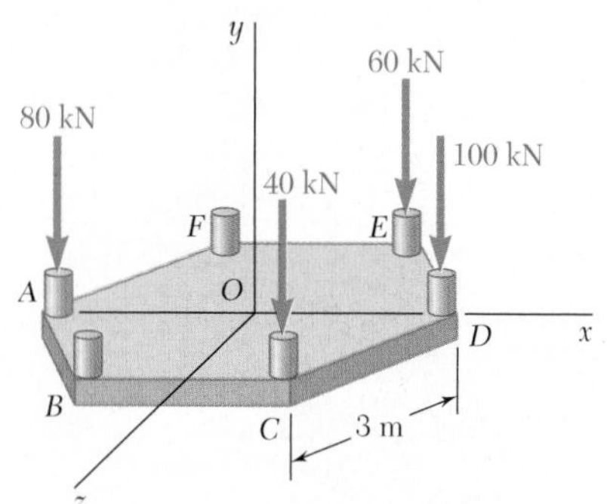

Fig. P3.123 and P3.124

3.123 A concrete foundation mat in the shape of a regular hexagon with 3-m sides supports four column loads as shown. Determine the magnitude and the point of application of the resultant of the four loads.

3.124 A concrete foundation mat in the shape of a regular hexagon with 3-m sides supports four column loads as shown. Determine the magnitudes of the additional loads that must be applied at B and F if the resultant of all six loads is to pass through the center of the mat.

3.125 The forces shown are the resultant downward loads on sections of the flat roof of a building because of accumulated snow. Determine the magnitude and the point of application of the resultant of these four loads.

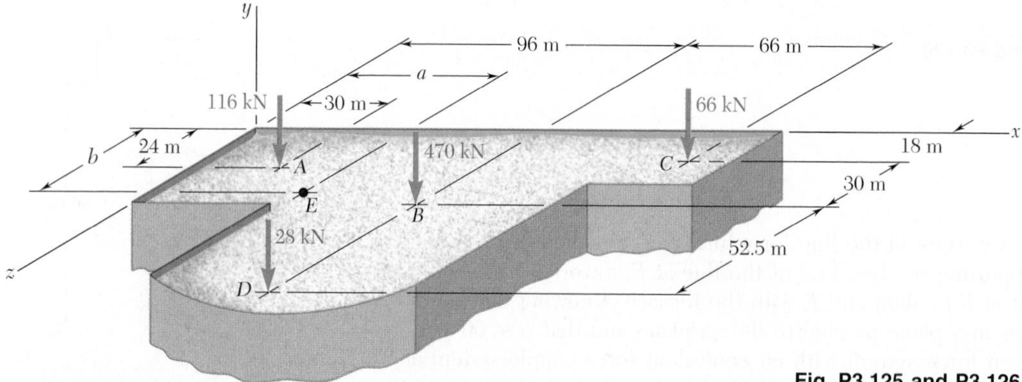

Fig. P3.125 and P3.126

3.126 The forces shown are the resultant downward loads on sections of the flat roof of a building because of accumulated snow. If the snow represented by the 116-kN force is shoveled so that this load acts at E, determine a and b knowing that the point of application of the resultant of the four loads is then at B.

*3.127 A group of students loads a 2 × 4-m flatbed trailer with two 0.6 × 0.6 × 0.6-m boxes and one 0.6 × 0.6 × 1.2-m box. Each of the boxes at the rear of the trailer is positioned so that it is aligned with both the back and a side of the trailer. Determine the smallest load the students should place in a second 0.6 × 0.6 × 1.2-m box and where on the trailer they should secure it, without any part of the box overhanging the sides of the trailer, if each box is uniformly loaded and the line of action of the resultant of the weights of the four boxes is to pass through the point of intersection of the centerlines of the trailer and the axle. (*Hint:* Keep in mind that the box may be placed either on its side or on its end.)

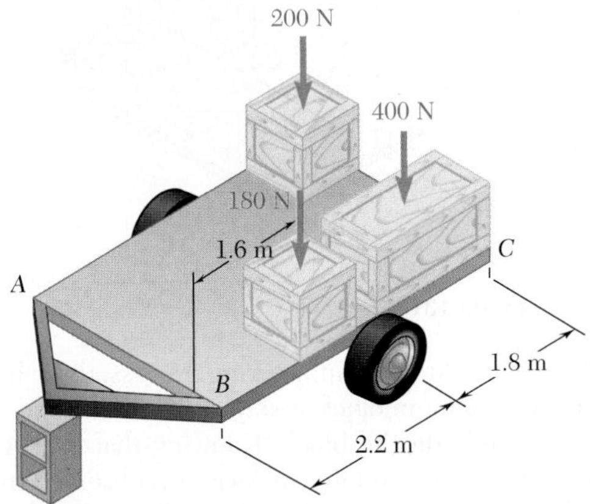

Fig. *P3.127*

*3.128 Solve Prob. 3.127 if the students want to place as much weight as possible in the fourth box and that at least one side of the box must coincide with a side of the trailer.

*3.129 A piece of sheet metal is bent into the shape shown and is acted upon by three forces. Replace the three forces with an equivalent wrench and determine (*a*) the magnitude and direction of the resultant **R**, (*b*) the pitch of the wrench, (*c*) the point where the axis of the wrench intersects the *yz* plane.

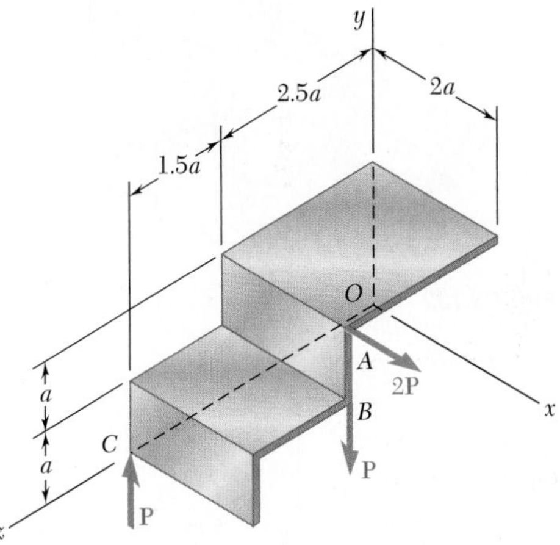

Fig. P3.129

*3.130 A block of wood is acted upon by three forces of the same magnitude *P* and having the directions shown. Replace the three forces with an equivalent wrench and determine (*a*) the magnitude and direction of the resultant **R**, (*b*) the pitch of the wrench, (*c*) the point where the axis of the wrench intersects the *xy* plane.

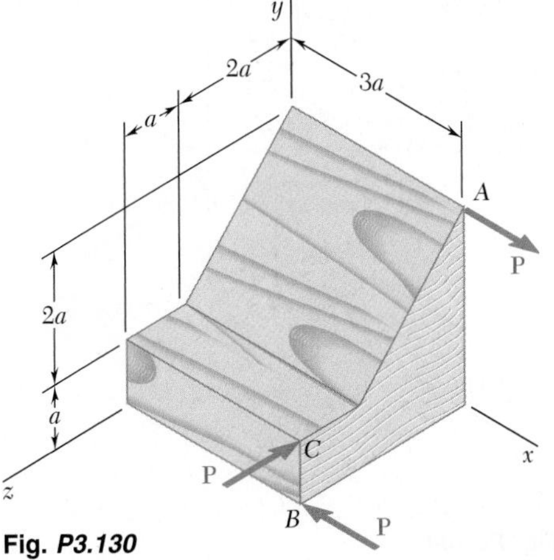

Fig. *P3.130*

*3.131 The forces and couples shown are applied to two screws as a piece of sheet metal is fastened to a block of wood. Reduce the forces and the couples to an equivalent wrench and determine (*a*) the resultant force **R**, (*b*) the pitch of the wrench, (*c*) the point where the axis of the wrench intersects the *xz* plane.

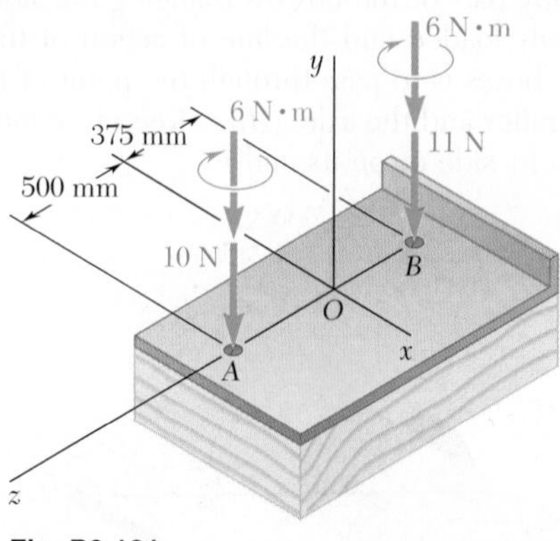

Fig. P3.131

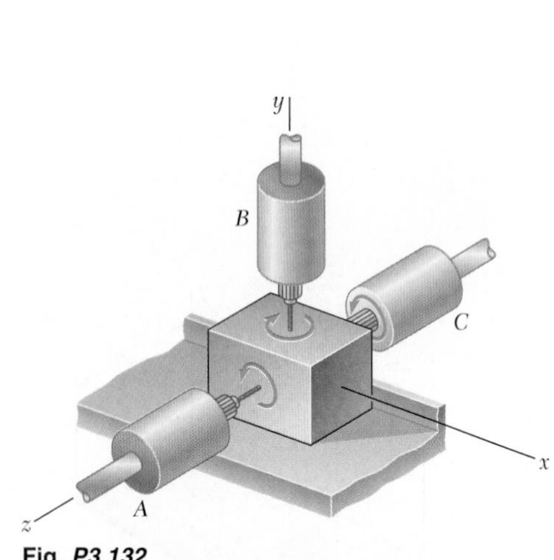

Fig. *P3.132*

*3.132 In an automated manufacturing process, three holes are drilled simultaneously in an aluminum block as shown. Each drill exerts a 50-N force and a 0.100-N · m couple on the block. Knowing that drill *A* rotates counterclockwise and drills *B* and *C* rotate clockwise (as observed from each drill), reduce the forces and couples exerted by the drills on the block to an equivalent wrench and determine (*a*) the resultant force **R**, (*b*) the pitch of the wrench, (*c*) the point where the wrench intersects the *xz* plane.

*3.133 Two bolts *A* and *B* are tightened by applying the forces and couples shown. Replace the two wrenches with a single equivalent wrench and determine (*a*) the resultant **R**, (*b*) the pitch of the single equivalent wrench, (*c*) the point where the axis of the wrench intersects the *yz* plane.

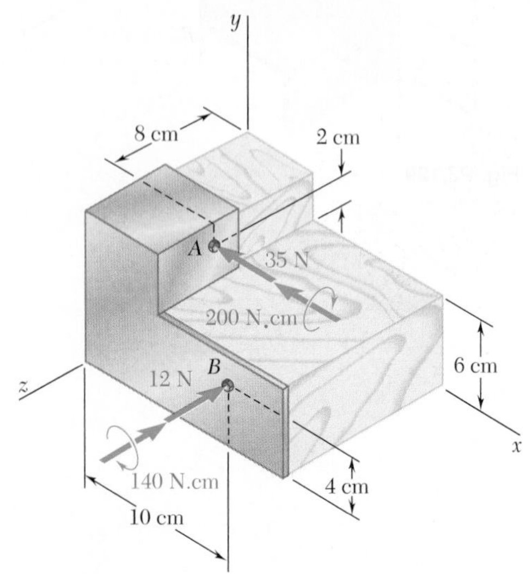

Fig. P3.133

*3.134 Two bolts *A* and *B* are tightened by applying the forces and couple shown. Replace the two wrenches with a single equivalent wrench and determine (*a*) the resultant **R**, (*b*) the pitch of the single equivalent wrench, (*c*) the point where the axis of the wrench intersects the *xz* plane.

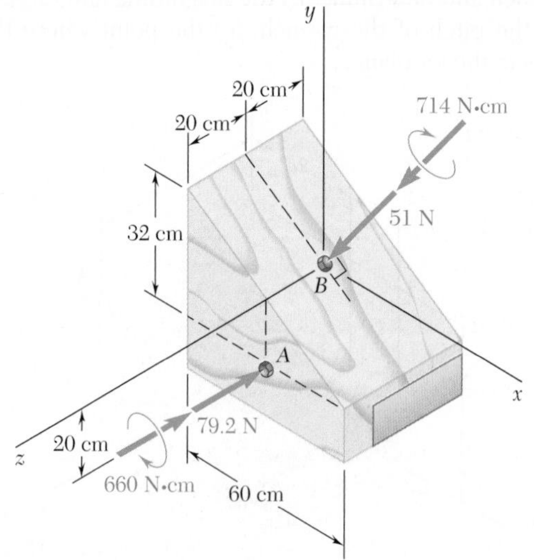

Fig. *P3.134*

***3.135** A flagpole is guyed by three cables. If the tensions in the cables have the same magnitude P, replace the forces exerted on the pole with an equivalent wrench and determine (*a*) the resultant force **R**, (*b*) the pitch of the wrench, (*c*) the point where the axis of the wrench intersects the xz plane.

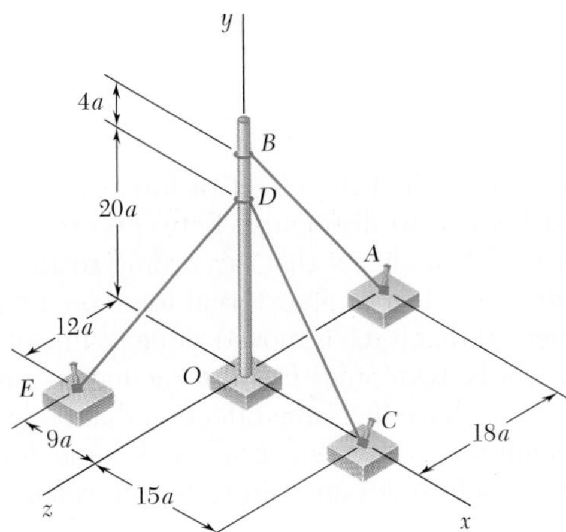

Fig. P3.135

***3.136* and *3.137** Determine whether the force-and-couple system shown can be reduced to a single equivalent force **R**. If it can, determine **R** and the point where the line of action of **R** intersects the yz plane. If it cannot be so reduced, replace the given system with an equivalent wrench and determine its resultant, its pitch, and the point where its axis intersects the yz plane.

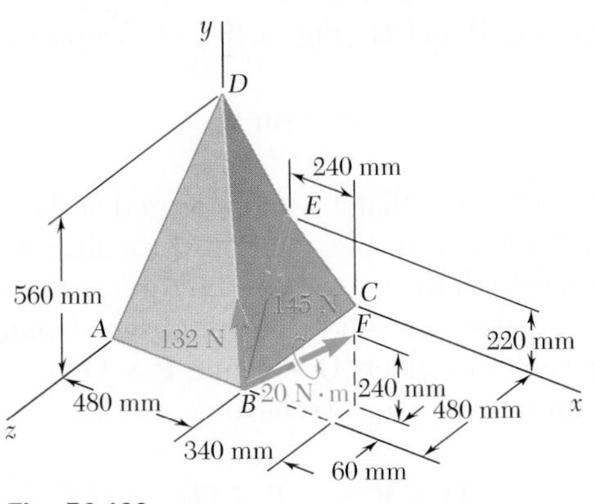

Fig. P3.136

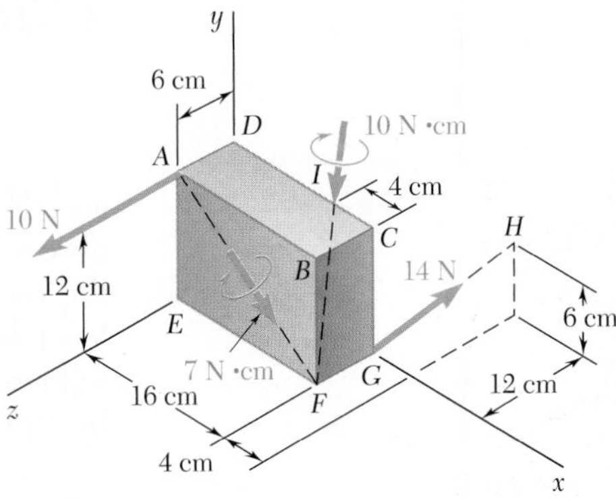

Fig. P3.137

***3.138** Replace the wrench shown with an equivalent system consisting of two forces perpendicular to the z axis and applied respectively at A and B.

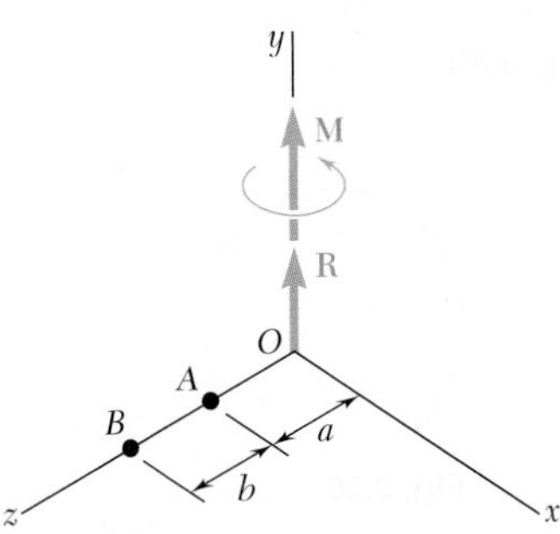

Fig. P3.138

***3.139** Show that, in general, a wrench can be replaced with two forces chosen in such a way that one force passes through a given point while the other force lies in a given plane.

***3.140** Show that a wrench can be replaced with two perpendicular forces one of which is applied at a given point.

***3.141** Show that a wrench can be replaced with two forces one of which has a prescribed line of action.

REVIEW AND SUMMARY FOR CHAPTER 3

Principle of transmissibility

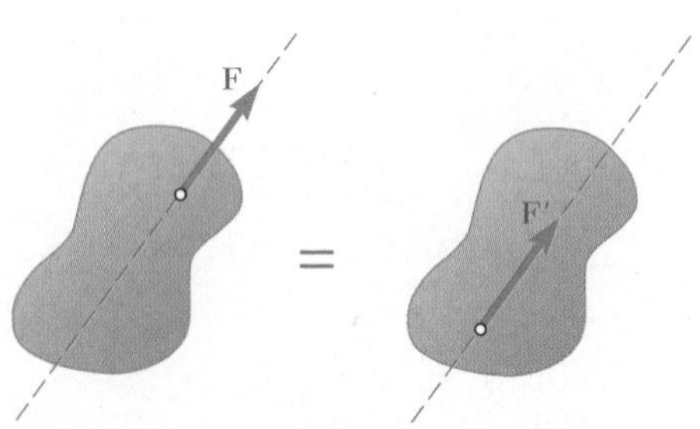

Fig. 3.48

In this chapter we studied the effect of forces exerted on a rigid body. We first learned to distinguish between *external* and *internal* forces [Sec. 3.2] and saw that, according to the *principle of transmissibility,* the effect of an external force on a rigid body remains unchanged if that force is moved along its line of action [Sec. 3.3]. In other words, two forces **F** and **F′** acting on a rigid body at two different points have the same effect on that body if they have the same magnitude, same direction, and same line of action (Fig. 3.48). Two such forces are said to be *equivalent*.

Vector product of two vectors

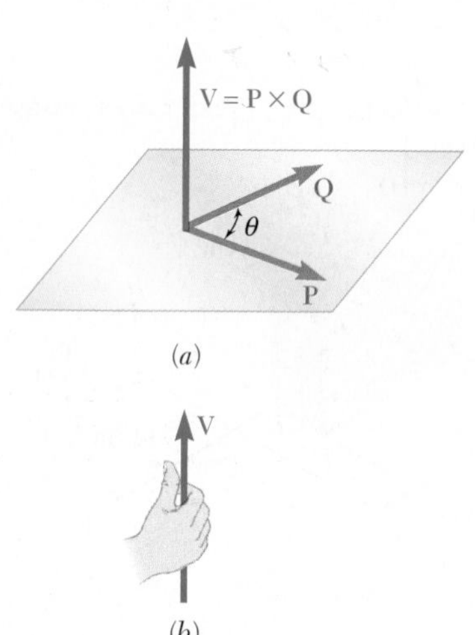

Fig. 3.49

Before proceeding with the discussion of *equivalent systems of forces,* we introduced the concept of the *vector product of two vectors* [Sec. 3.4]. The vector product

$$\mathbf{V} = \mathbf{P} \times \mathbf{Q}$$

of the vectors **P** and **Q** was defined as a vector perpendicular to the plane containing **P** and **Q** (Fig. 3.49), of magnitude

$$V = PQ \sin \theta \tag{3.1}$$

and directed in such a way that a person located at the tip of **V** will observe as counterclockwise the rotation through θ which brings the vector **P** in line with the vector **Q**. The three vectors **P**, **Q**, and **V**—taken in that order—are said to form a *right-handed triad.* It follows that the vector products **Q × P** and **P × Q** are represented by equal and opposite vectors. We have

$$\mathbf{Q} \times \mathbf{P} = -(\mathbf{P} \times \mathbf{Q}) \tag{3.4}$$

It also follows from the definition of the vector product of two vectors that the vector products of the unit vectors **i**, **j**, and **k** are

$$\mathbf{i} \times \mathbf{i} = 0 \qquad \mathbf{i} \times \mathbf{j} = \mathbf{k} \qquad \mathbf{j} \times \mathbf{i} = -\mathbf{k}$$

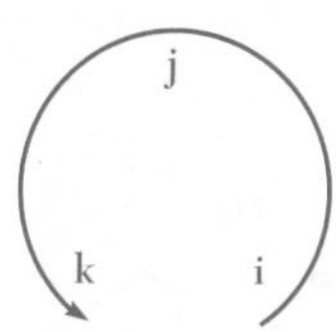

Fig. 3.50

and so on. The sign of the vector product of two unit vectors can be obtained by arranging in a circle and in counterclockwise order the three letters representing the unit vectors (Fig. 3.50): The vector product of two unit vectors will be positive if they follow each other in counterclockwise order and negative if they follow each other in clockwise order.

Rectangular components of vector product

The *rectangular components of the vector product* **V** of two vectors **P** and **Q** were expressed [Sec. 3.5] as

$$\begin{aligned} V_x &= P_yQ_z - P_zQ_y \\ V_y &= P_zQ_x - P_xQ_z \\ V_z &= P_xQ_y - P_yQ_x \end{aligned} \tag{3.9}$$

Using a determinant, we also wrote

$$\mathbf{V} = \begin{vmatrix} \mathbf{i} & \mathbf{j} & \mathbf{k} \\ P_x & P_y & P_z \\ Q_x & Q_y & Q_z \end{vmatrix} \tag{3.10}$$

Moment of a force about a point

The *moment of a force* **F** *about a point* O was defined [Sec. 3.6] as the vector product

$$\mathbf{M}_O = \mathbf{r} \times \mathbf{F} \tag{3.11}$$

where **r** is the *position vector* drawn from O to the point of application A of the force **F** (Fig. 3.51). Denoting by θ the angle between the lines of action of **r** and **F**, we found that the magnitude of the moment of **F** about O can be expressed as

$$M_O = rF \sin \theta = Fd \tag{3.12}$$

where d represents the perpendicular distance from O to the line of action of **F**.

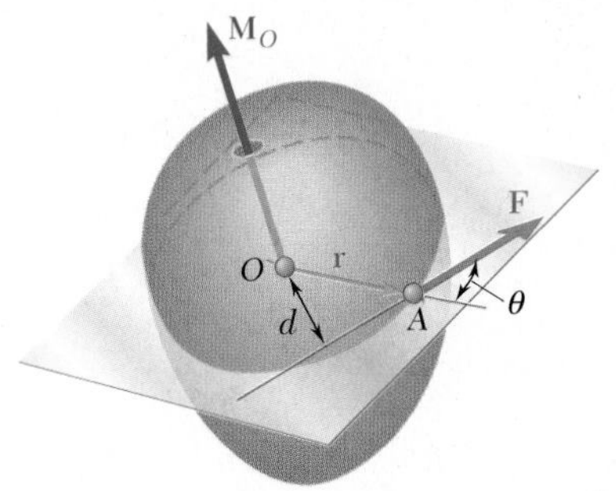

Fig. 3.51

Rectangular components of moment

The *rectangular components of the moment* $\mathbf{M}_O$ *of a force* **F** were expressed [Sec. 3.8] as

$$\begin{aligned} M_x &= yF_z - zF_y \\ M_y &= zF_x - xF_z \\ M_z &= xF_y - yF_x \end{aligned} \tag{3.18}$$

where x, y, and z are the components of the position vector **r** (Fig. 3.52). Using a determinant form, we also wrote

$$\mathbf{M}_O = \begin{vmatrix} \mathbf{i} & \mathbf{j} & \mathbf{k} \\ x & y & z \\ F_x & F_y & F_z \end{vmatrix} \tag{3.19}$$

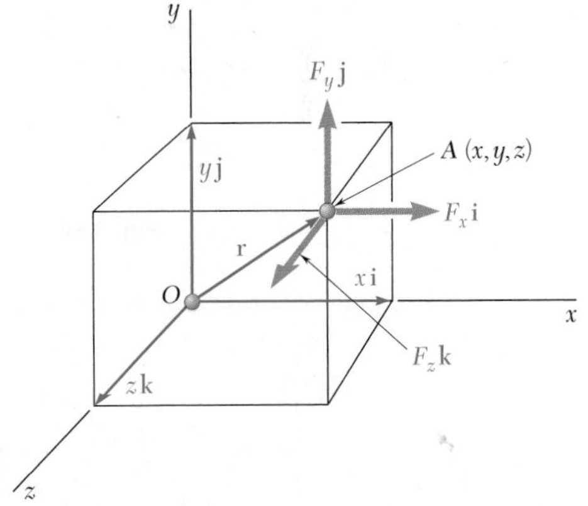

Fig. 3.52

In the more general case of the moment about an arbitrary point B of a force **F** applied at A, we had

$$\mathbf{M}_B = \begin{vmatrix} \mathbf{i} & \mathbf{j} & \mathbf{k} \\ x_{A/B} & y_{A/B} & z_{A/B} \\ F_x & F_y & F_z \end{vmatrix} \tag{3.21}$$

where $x_{A/B}$, $y_{A/B}$, and $z_{A/B}$ denote the components of the vector $\mathbf{r}_{A/B}$:

$$x_{A/B} = x_A - x_B \qquad y_{A/B} = y_A - y_B \qquad z_{A/B} = z_A - z_B$$

In the case of *problems involving only two dimensions*, the force **F** can be assumed to lie in the *xy* plane. Its moment $\mathbf{M}_B$ about a point *B* in the same plane is perpendicular to that plane (Fig. 3.53) and is completely defined by the scalar

$$M_B = (x_A - x_B)F_y - (y_A - y_B)F_x \qquad (3.23)$$

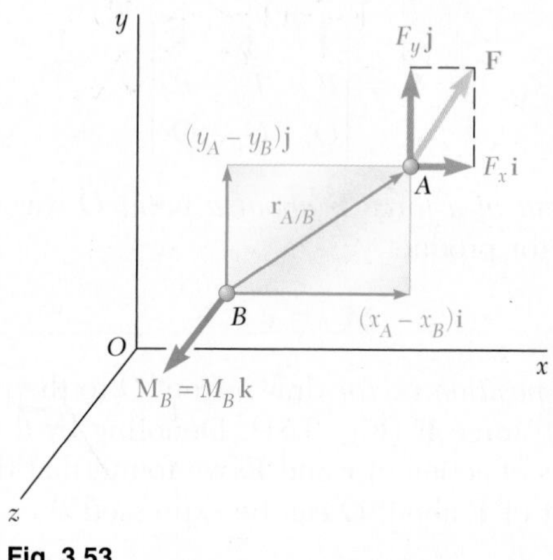

Fig. 3.53

Various methods for the computation of the moment of a force about a point were illustrated in Sample Probs. 3.1 through 3.4.

Scalar product of two vectors

The *scalar product* of two vectors **P** and **Q** [Sec. 3.9] was denoted by $\mathbf{P} \cdot \mathbf{Q}$ and was defined as the scalar quantity

$$\mathbf{P} \cdot \mathbf{Q} = PQ \cos \theta \qquad (3.24)$$

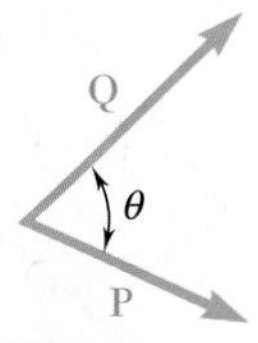

Fig. 3.54

where θ is the angle between **P** and **Q** (Fig. 3.54). By expressing the scalar product of **P** and **Q** in terms of the rectangular components of the two vectors, we determined that

$$\mathbf{P} \cdot \mathbf{Q} = P_xQ_x + P_yQ_y + P_zQ_z \qquad (3.30)$$

Projection of a vector on an axis

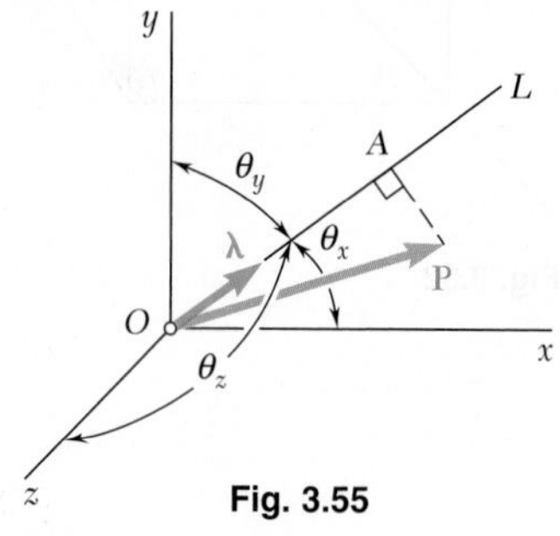

Fig. 3.55

The *projection of a vector* **P** *on an axis OL* (Fig. 3.55) can be obtained by forming the scalar product of **P** and the unit vector $\boldsymbol{\lambda}$ along *OL*. We have

$$P_{OL} = \mathbf{P} \cdot \boldsymbol{\lambda} \qquad (3.36)$$

or, using rectangular components,

$$P_{OL} = P_x \cos \theta_x + P_y \cos \theta_y + P_z \cos \theta_z \qquad (3.37)$$

where θ_x, θ_y, and θ_z denote the angles that the axis *OL* forms with the coordinate axes.

Mixed triple product of three vectors

The *mixed triple product* of the three vectors **S**, **P**, and **Q** was defined as the scalar expression

$$\mathbf{S} \cdot (\mathbf{P} \times \mathbf{Q}) \qquad (3.38)$$

obtained by forming the scalar product of **S** with the vector product of **P** and **Q** [Sec. 3.10]. It was shown that

$$\mathbf{S}\cdot(\mathbf{P}\times\mathbf{Q}) = \begin{vmatrix} S_x & S_y & S_z \\ P_x & P_y & P_z \\ Q_x & Q_y & Q_z \end{vmatrix} \qquad (3.41)$$

where the elements of the determinant are the rectangular components of the three vectors.

Moment of a force about an axis

The *moment of a force* **F** *about an axis OL* [Sec. 3.11] was defined as the projection OC on OL of the moment $\mathbf{M}_O$ of the force **F** (Fig. 3.56), that is, as the mixed triple product of the unit vector $\boldsymbol{\lambda}$, the position vector **r**, and the force **F**:

$$M_{OL} = \boldsymbol{\lambda}\cdot\mathbf{M}_O = \boldsymbol{\lambda}\cdot(\mathbf{r}\times\mathbf{F}) \qquad (3.42)$$

Using the determinant form for the mixed triple product, we have

$$M_{OL} = \begin{vmatrix} \lambda_x & \lambda_y & \lambda_z \\ x & y & z \\ F_x & F_y & F_z \end{vmatrix} \qquad (3.43)$$

where $\lambda_x, \lambda_y, \lambda_z$ = direction cosines of axis OL
x, y, z = components of **r**
F_x, F_y, F_z = components of **F**

An example of the determination of the moment of a force about a skew axis was given in Sample Prob. 3.5.

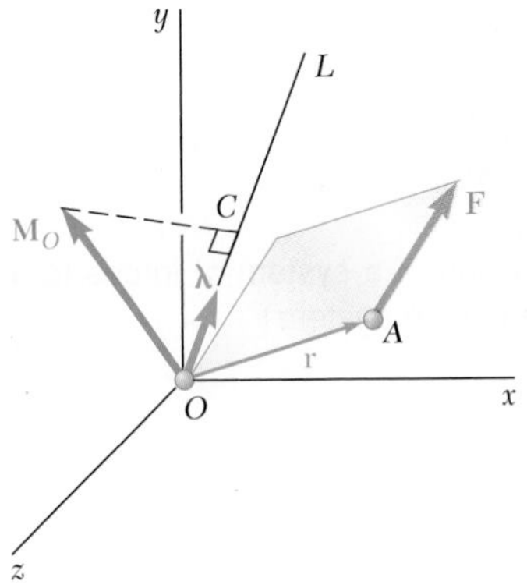

Fig. 3.56

Couples

Two forces **F** *and* −**F** *having the same magnitude, parallel lines of action, and opposite sense are said to form a couple* [Sec. 3.12]. It was shown that the moment of a couple is independent of the point about which it is computed; it is a vector **M** perpendicular to the plane of the couple and equal in magnitude to the product of the common magnitude F of the forces and the perpendicular distance d between their lines of action (Fig. 3.57).

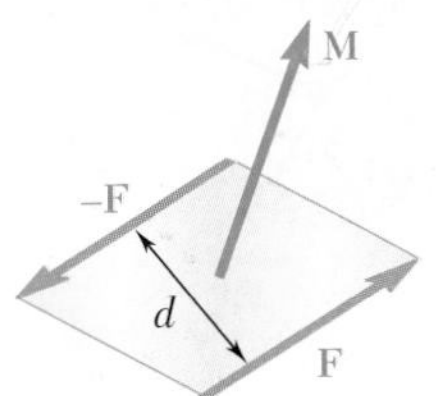

Fig. 3.57

Two couples having the same moment **M** are *equivalent,* that is, they have the same effect on a given rigid body [Sec. 3.13]. The sum of two couples is itself a couple [Sec. 3.14], and the moment **M** of the resultant couple can be obtained by adding vectorially the moments $\mathbf{M}_1$ and $\mathbf{M}_2$ of the original couples [Sample Prob. 3.6]. It follows that a couple can be represented by a vector, called a *couple vector,* equal in magnitude and direction to the moment **M** of the couple [Sec. 3.15]. A couple vector is a *free vector* which can be attached to the origin O if so desired and resolved into components (Fig. 3.58).

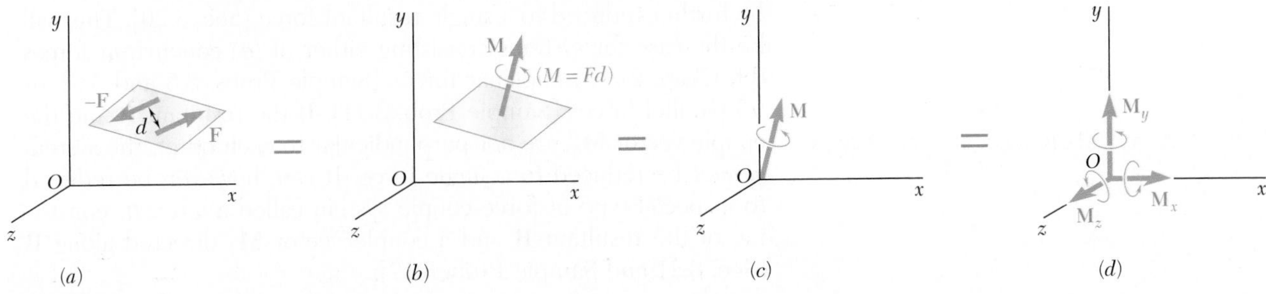

Fig. 3.58

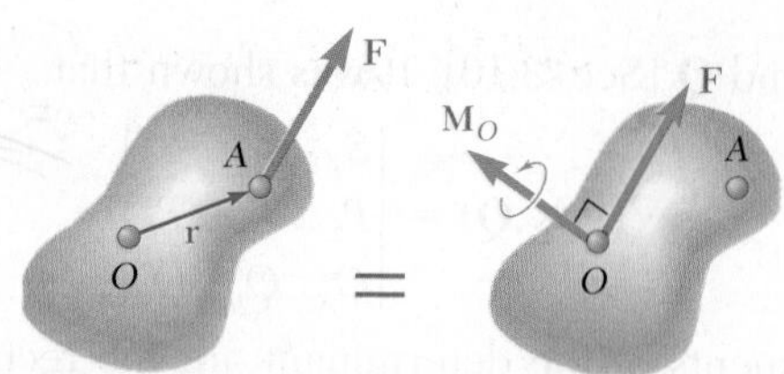

Fig. 3.59

Force-couple system

Any force $\mathbf{F}$ acting at a point A of a rigid body can be replaced by a *force-couple system* at an arbitrary point O, consisting of the force $\mathbf{F}$ applied at O and a couple of moment $\mathbf{M}_O$ equal to the moment about O of the force $\mathbf{F}$ in its original position [Sec. 3.16]; it should be noted that the force $\mathbf{F}$ and the couple vector $\mathbf{M}_O$ are always perpendicular to each other (Fig. 3.59).

Reduction of a system of forces to a force-couple system

It follows [Sec. 3.17] that *any system of forces can be reduced to a force-couple system at a given point O* by first replacing each of the forces of the system by an equivalent force-couple system at O (Fig. 3.60) and then adding all the forces and all the couples determined in this manner to obtain a resultant force $\mathbf{R}$ and a resultant couple vector $\mathbf{M}_O^R$ [Sample Probs. 3.8 through 3.11]. Note that, in general, the resultant $\mathbf{R}$ and the couple vector $\mathbf{M}_O^R$ will not be perpendicular to each other.

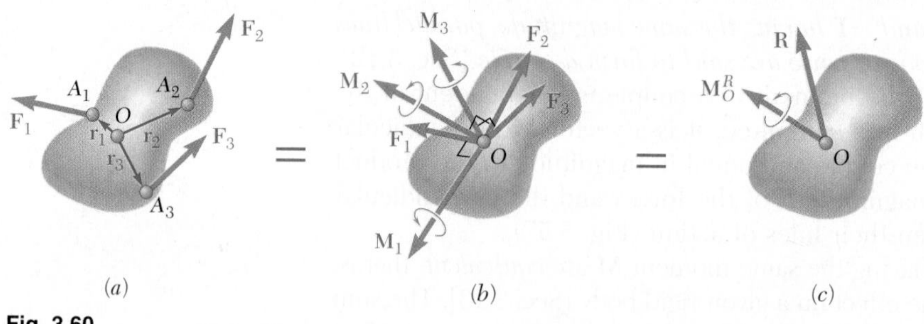

Fig. 3.60

Equivalent systems of forces

We concluded from the above [Sec. 3.18] that, as far as a rigid body is concerned, *two systems of forces,* $\mathbf{F}_1, \mathbf{F}_2, \mathbf{F}_3, \ldots$ *and* $\mathbf{F}'_1, \mathbf{F}'_2, \mathbf{F}'_3, \ldots$, *are equivalent if, and only if,*

$$\Sigma\mathbf{F} = \Sigma\mathbf{F}' \quad \text{and} \quad \Sigma\mathbf{M}_O = \Sigma\mathbf{M}'_O \qquad (3.57)$$

Further reduction of a system of forces

If the resultant force $\mathbf{R}$ and the resultant couple vector $\mathbf{M}_O^R$ are perpendicular to each other, the force-couple system at O can be further reduced to a single resultant force [Sec. 3.20]. This will be the case for systems consisting either of (*a*) concurrent forces (cf. Chap. 2), (*b*) coplanar forces [Sample Probs. 3.8 and 3.9], or (*c*) parallel forces [Sample Prob. 3.11]. If the resultant $\mathbf{R}$ and the couple vector $\mathbf{M}_O^R$ are *not* perpendicular to each other, the system *cannot* be reduced to a single force. It can, however, be reduced to a special type of force-couple system called a *wrench,* consisting of the resultant $\mathbf{R}$ and a couple vector $\mathbf{M}_1$ directed along $\mathbf{R}$ [Sec. 3.21 and Sample Prob. 3.12].

Review Problems

3.142 It is known that a vertical force of 800 N is required to remove the nail at C from the board. As the nail first starts moving, determine (*a*) the moment about B of the force exerted on the nail, (*b*) the magnitude of the force **P** which creates the same moment about B if $\alpha = 10°$, (*c*) the smallest force **P** which creates the same moment about B.

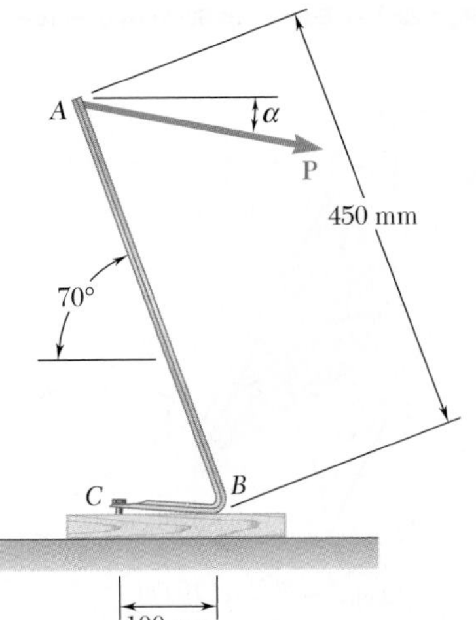

Fig. P3.142

3.143 A mechanic uses a piece of pipe AB as a lever when tightening an alternator belt. When he pushes down at A, a force of 580 N is exerted on the alternator B. Determine the moment of that force about bolt C if its line of action passes through O.

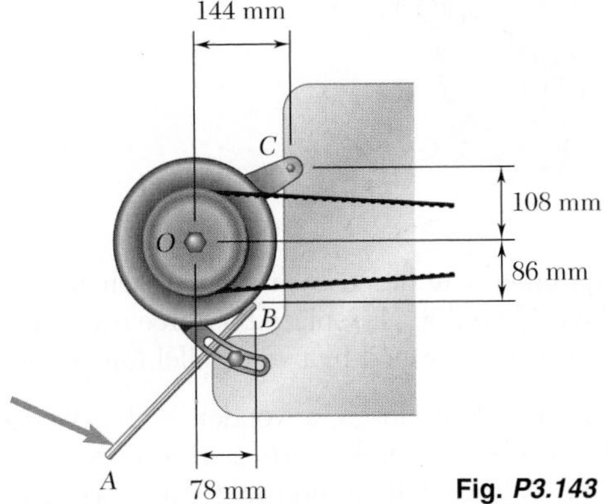

Fig. *P3.143*

3.144 The ramp $ABCD$ is supported by cables at corners C and D. The tension in each of the cables is 360 N. Determine the moment about A of the force exerted by (*a*) the cable at D, (*b*) the cable at C.

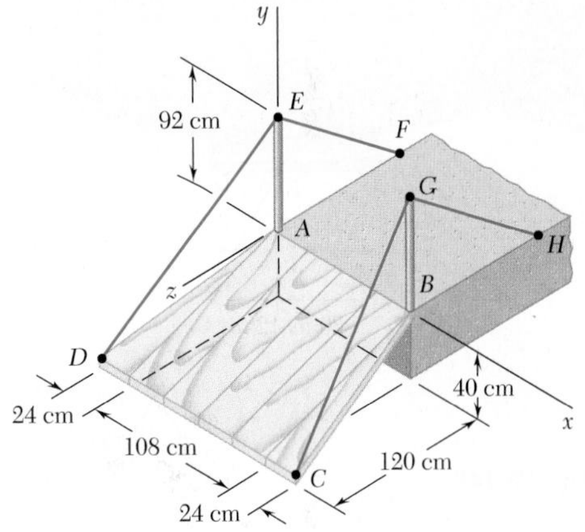

Fig. P3.144

3.145 Consider the volleyball net shown. Determine the angle formed by guy wires AC and AD.

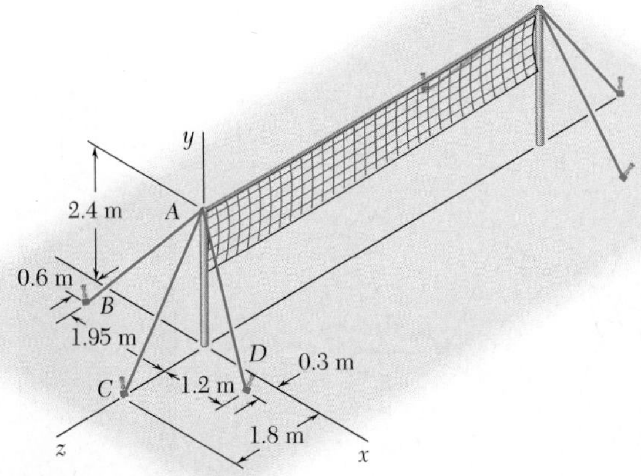

Fig. P3.145

3.146 To lift a heavy crate, a man uses a block and tackle attached to the bottom of an I-beam at hook B. Knowing that the moments about the y and z axes of the force exerted at B by portion AB of the rope are, respectively, 100 N · m and −400 N · m, determine the distance a.

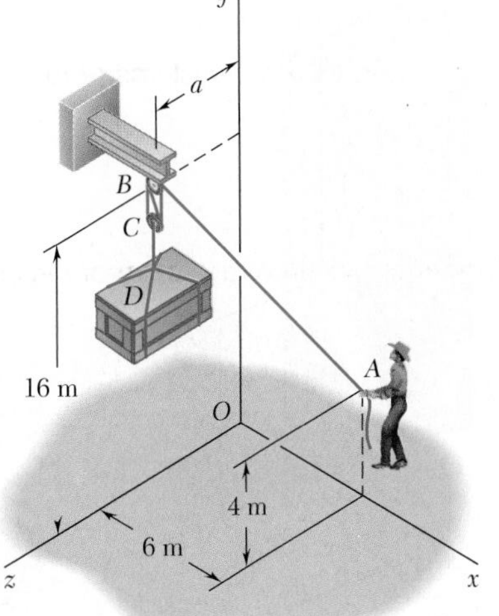

Fig. P3.146

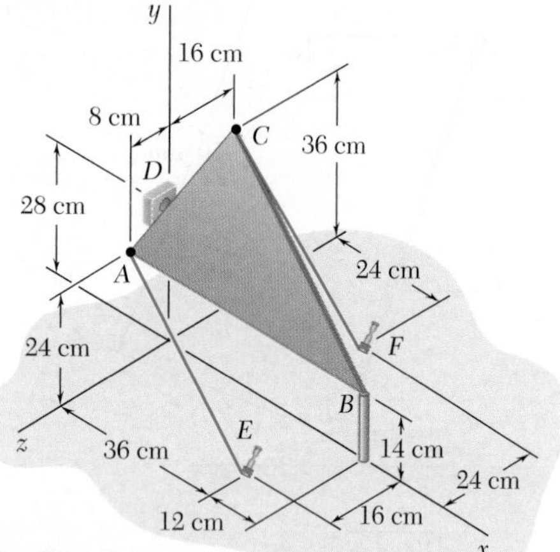

Fig. P3.147

3.147 The triangular plate ABC is supported by ball-and-socket joints at B and D and is held in the position shown by cables AE and CF. If the force exerted by cable CF at C is 132 N, determine the moment of that force about the line joining points D and B.

3.148 The tension in the cable attached to the end C of an adjustable boom ABC is 1000 N. Replace the force exerted by the cable at C with an equivalent force-couple system (*a*) at A, (*b*) at B.

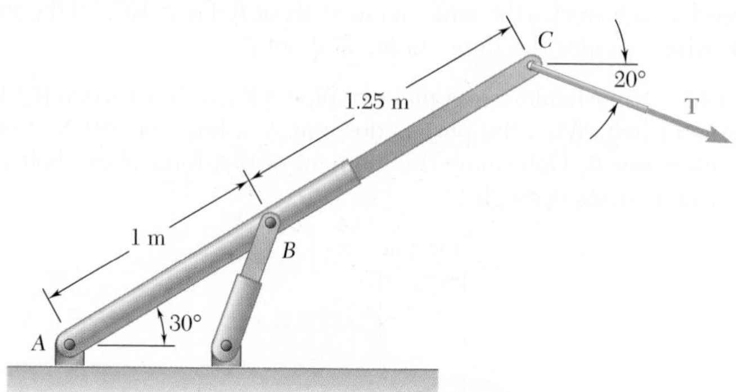

Fig. P3.148

3.149 A dirigible is tethered by a cable attached to its cabin at B. If the tension in the cable is 250 N, replace the force exerted by the cable at B with an equivalent system formed by two parallel forces applied at A and C.

3.150 To keep a door closed, a wooden stick is wedged between the floor and the doorknob. The stick exerts at B a 45-N force directed along line AB. Replace that force with an equivalent force-couple system at C.

3.151 Gear C is rigidly attached to arm AB. If the forces and couple shown can be reduced to a single equivalent force at A, determine the equivalent force and the magnitude of the couple **M**.

3.152 As plastic bushings are inserted into a 3-cm-diameter cylindrical sheet metal container, the insertion tool exerts the forces shown on the enclosure. Each of the forces is parallel to one of the coordinate axes. Replace these forces with an equivalent force-couple system at C.

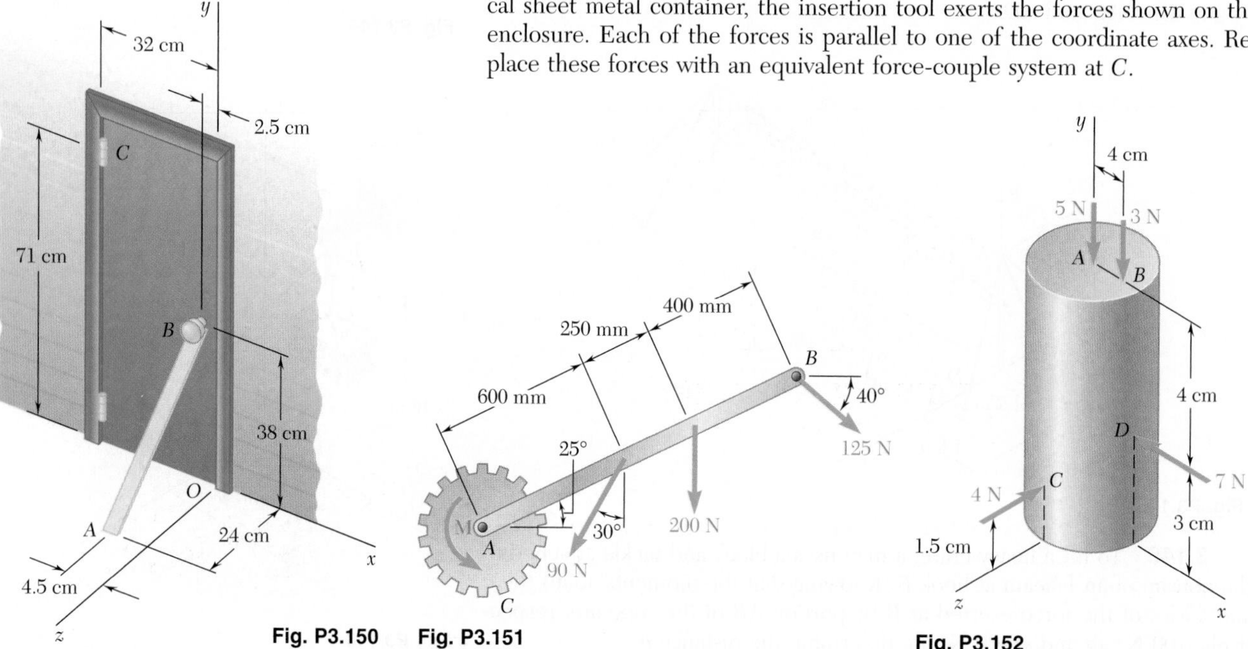

Fig. P3.149

Fig. P3.150

Fig. P3.151

Fig. P3.152

3.153 Three children are standing on a 15 × 15-m raft. The weights of the children at points *A*, *B*, and *C* are 85 kg, 60 kg, and 90 kg, respectively. If a fourth child of weight 95 kg climbs onto the raft, determine where she should stand if the other children remain in the positions shown and the line of action of the resultant of the four weights is to pass through the center of the raft.

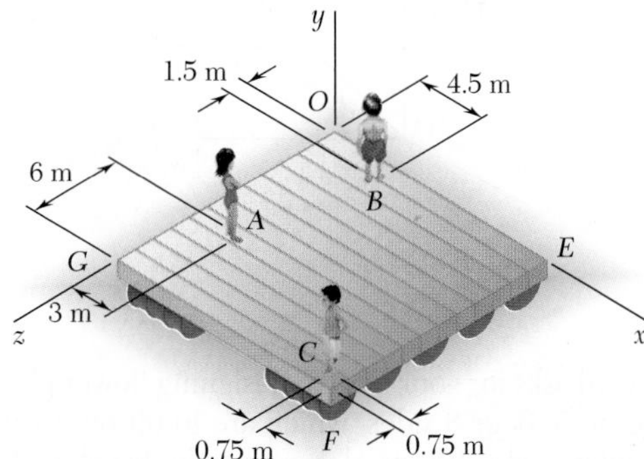

Fig. ***P3.153***

Computer Problems

3.C1 Rod *AB* is held in place by a cord *AC* that has a tension *T*. Using computational software, determine the moment about *B* of the force exerted by the cord at point *A* in terms of the tension *T* and the distance *c*. Plot the moment about *B* for 320 mm $\leq c \leq$ 960 mm when (*a*) $T = 50$ N, (*b*) $T = 75$ N, (*c*) $T = 100$ N.

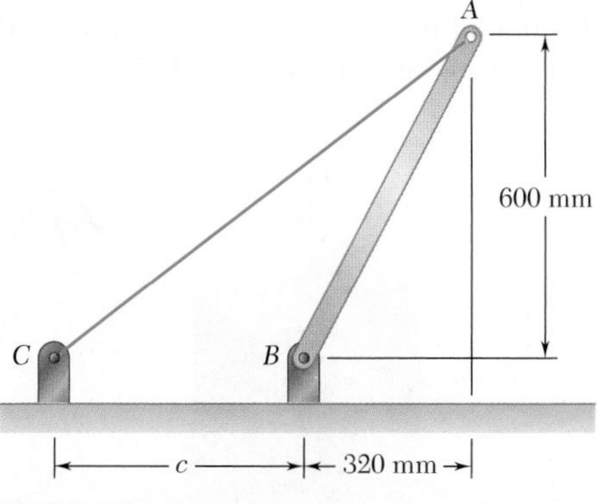

Fig. P3.C1

3.C2 A 400-mm tube *AB* can slide freely along a horizontal rod. The ends *A* and *B* of the tube are connected by elastic cords fixed to point *C*. (*a*) Determine the angle θ between the two cords *AC* and *BC* as a function of *x*. (*b*) Plot the angle θ between the cords *AC* and *BC* as a function of *x* for -400 mm $\leq x \leq$ 400 mm.

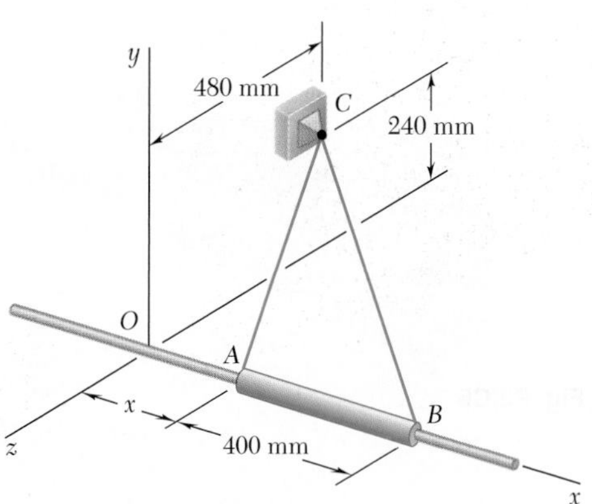

Fig. P3.C2

3.C3 Using computational software, determine the perpendicular distance between the line of action of a force **F** and the line OL. Use this software to solve (*a*) Prob. 3.62, (*b*) Prob. 3.63, (*c*) Prob. 3.65.

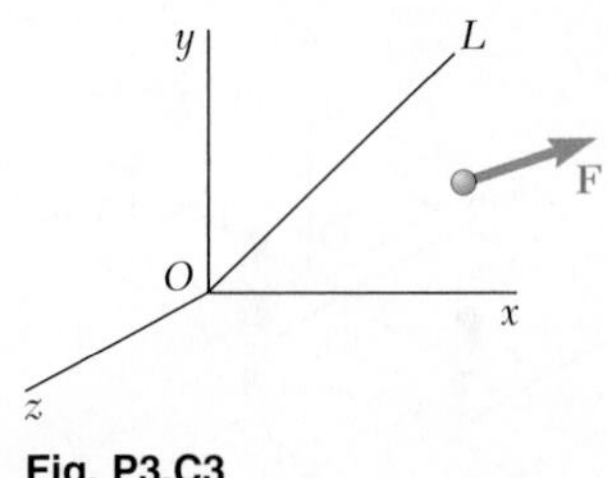

Fig. P3.C3

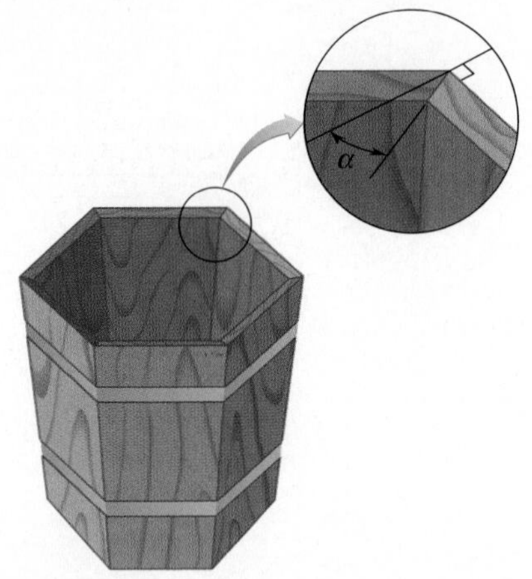

Fig. P3.C4

3.C4 A friend asks for your help in designing flower planter boxes. The boxes are to have 4, 5, 6, or 8 sides, which are to tilt outward at 10°, 20°, or 30°. Using computational software, determine the bevel angle α for each of the twelve planter designs. (*Hint:* The bevel angle α is equal to one-half of the angle formed by the inward normals of two adjacent sides.)

3.C5 A crane is oriented so that the end of the 15.24-m boom OA lies in the yz plane as shown. The tension in cable AB is 875 N. Determine the moment about each of the coordinate axes of the force exerted on A by cable AB as a function of x. Plot each moment as a function of x for $-4.6 \text{ m} \leq x \leq 4.6 \text{ m}$.

Fig. P3.C5

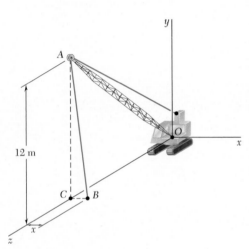

3.C6 A physical therapy patient lying on her right side holds a 1.5-kg dumbbell A in her left hand and slowly raises it along a circular path. Knowing that the center of the path is at B and that the path lies in the xy plane, plot the scalar components of the moment about C of the weight of the dumbbell as functions of θ for $-70° \leq \theta \leq 40°$.

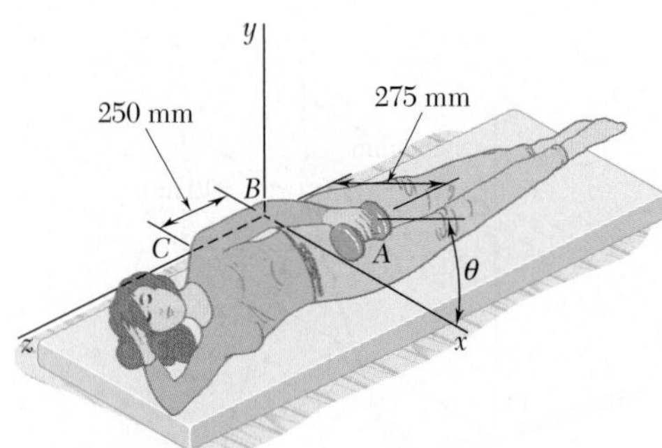

Fig. P3.C6

3.C7 The right angle horizontal speed-reducer shown weighs 40 N, and its center of gravity is located on the y axis. Knowing that $M_1 = An^2$ and $M_2 = An^3$, determine the single force that is equivalent to the weight of the unit and the two couples acting on it and the point of coordinates $(x, 0, z)$ where the line of action of the single force intersects the floor. Plot x and z as functions of n for $2 \leq n \leq 6$ when (*a*) $A = 0.75 \text{ N} \cdot \text{m}$, (*b*) $A = 1.5 \text{ N} \cdot \text{m}$, (*c*) $A = 2 \text{ N} \cdot \text{m}$.

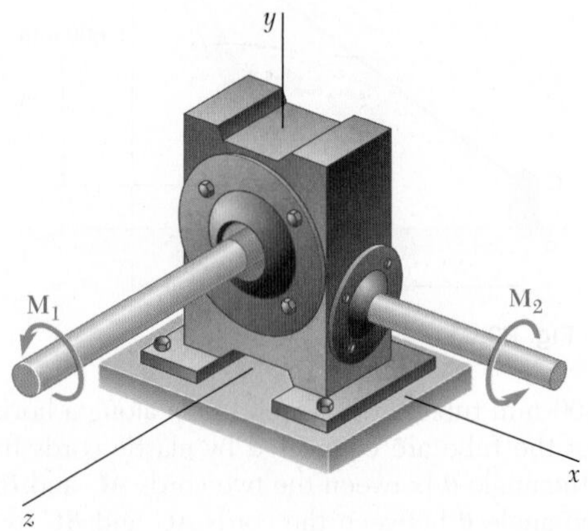

Fig. P3.C7

3.C8 A beam AB is subjected to several vertical forces as shown. Using computational software, determine the magnitude of the resultant of the forces and the distance x_C to point C, the point where the line of action of the resultant intersects AB. Use this software to solve Prob. 3.103*a*.

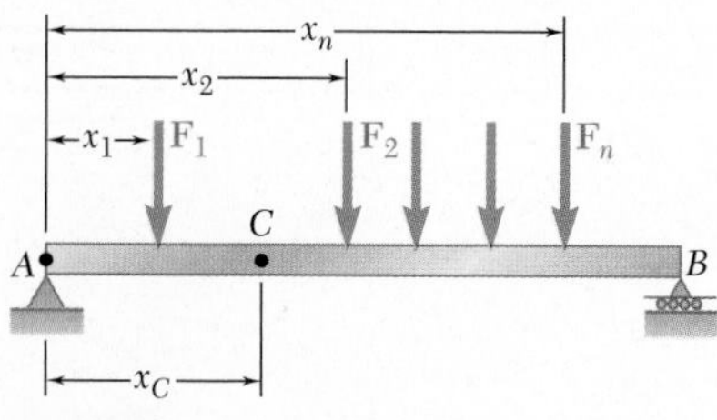

Fig. P3.C8

3.C9 Using computational software, determine the magnitude and the point of application of the resultant of the vertical forces $\mathbf{P}_1, \mathbf{P}_2, \ldots, \mathbf{P}_n$ which act at points $\mathbf{A}_1, \mathbf{A}_2, \ldots, \mathbf{A}_n$ that are located in the xz plane. Use this software to solve (*a*) Prob. 3.123, (*b*) Prob. 3.125.

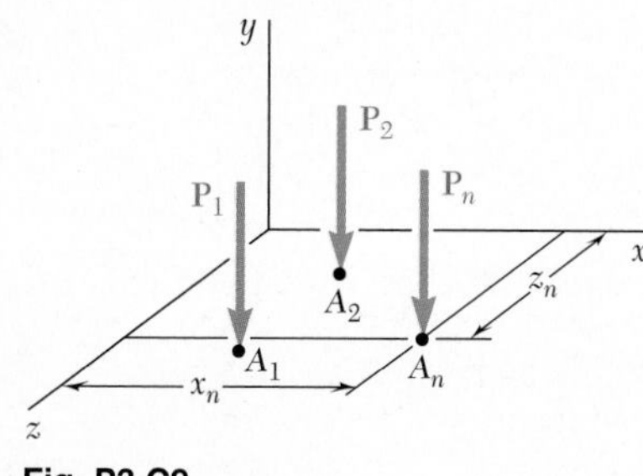

Fig. P3.C9

3.C10 Using computational software, determine whether a system of forces and couples can be reduced to a single equivalent force $\mathbf{R}$, and if it can, determine $\mathbf{R}$ and the point where the line of action of $\mathbf{R}$ intersects the yz plane. Use this software to solve (*a*) Prob. 3.136, (*b*) Prob. 3.137.

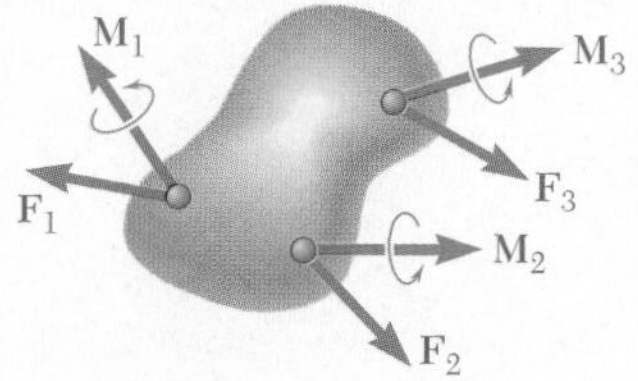

Fig. P3.C10

CHAPTER 4

Equilibrium of Rigid Bodies

For each of the wind turbines shown, the sum of the moments of the static and dynamic loads about the base of the tower must be computed to ensure that the couple of the reaction at the base does not cause failure of the tower.

EQUILIBRIUM OF RIGID BODIES

4.1. INTRODUCTION

We saw in the preceding chapter that the external forces acting on a rigid body can be reduced to a force-couple system at some arbitrary point O. When the force and the couple are both equal to zero, the external forces form a system equivalent to zero, and the rigid body is said to be in *equilibrium*.

The necessary and sufficient conditions for the equilibrium of a rigid body, therefore, can be obtained by setting $\mathbf{R}$ and $\mathbf{M}_O^R$ equal to zero in the relations (3.52) of Sec. 3.17:

$$\Sigma \mathbf{F} = 0 \qquad \Sigma \mathbf{M}_O = \Sigma(\mathbf{r} \times \mathbf{F}) = 0 \tag{4.1}$$

Resolving each force and each moment into its rectangular components, we can express the necessary and sufficient conditions for the equilibrium of a rigid body with the following six scalar equations:

$$\Sigma F_x = 0 \qquad \Sigma F_y = 0 \qquad \Sigma F_z = 0 \tag{4.2}$$

$$\Sigma M_x = 0 \qquad \Sigma M_y = 0 \qquad \Sigma M_z = 0 \tag{4.3}$$

The equations obtained can be used to determine unknown forces applied to the rigid body or unknown reactions exerted on it by its supports. We note that Eqs. (4.2) express the fact that the components of the external forces in the x, y, and z directions are balanced; Eqs. (4.3) express the fact that the moments of the external forces about the x, y, and z axes are balanced. Therefore, for a rigid body in equilibrium, the system of the external forces will impart no translational or rotational motion to the body considered.

In order to write the equations of equilibrium for a rigid body, it is essential to first identify all of the forces acting on that body and then to draw the corresponding *free-body diagram*. In this chapter we first consider the equilibrium of *two-dimensional structures* subjected to forces contained in their planes and learn how to draw their free-body diagrams. In addition to the forces *applied* to a structure, the *reactions* exerted on the structure by its supports will be considered. A specific reaction will be associated with each type of support. You will learn how to determine whether the structure is properly supported, so that you can know in advance whether the equations of equilibrium can be solved for the unknown forces and reactions.

Later in the chapter, the equilibrium of three-dimensional structures will be considered, and the same kind of analysis will be given to these structures and their supports.

4.2. FREE-BODY DIAGRAM

In solving a problem concerning the equilibrium of a rigid body, it is essential to consider *all* of the forces acting on the body; it is equally important to exclude any force which is not directly applied to the body. Omitting a force or adding an extraneous one would destroy the conditions of equilibrium. Therefore, the first step in the solution of the problem should be to draw a *free-body diagram* of the rigid body under consideration. Free-body diagrams have already been used on many occasions in Chap. 2. However, in view of their importance to the solution of equilibrium problems, we summarize here the various steps which must be followed in drawing a free-body diagram.

1. A clear decision should be made regarding the choice of the free body to be used. This body is then detached from the ground and is separated from all other bodies. The contour of the body thus isolated is sketched.

2. All external forces should be indicated on the free-body diagram. These forces represent the actions exerted *on* the free body *by* the ground and *by* the bodies which have been detached; they should be applied at the various points where the free body was supported by the ground or was connected to the other bodies. The *weight* of the free body should also be included among the external forces, since it represents the attraction exerted by the earth on the various particles forming the free body. As will be seen in Chap. 5, the weight should be applied at the center of gravity of the body. When the free body is made of several parts, the forces the various parts exert on each other should *not* be included among the external forces. These forces are internal forces as far as the free body is concerned.

3. The magnitudes and directions of the *known external forces* should be clearly marked on the free-body diagram. When indicating the directions of these forces, it must be remembered that the forces shown on the free-body diagram must be those which are exerted *on*, and not *by*, the free body. Known external forces generally include the *weight* of the free body and *forces applied* for a given purpose.

4. *Unknown external forces* usually consist of the *reactions*, through which the ground and other bodies oppose a possible motion of the free body. The reactions constrain the free body to remain in the same position and, for that reason, are sometimes called *constraining forces.* Reactions are exerted at the points where the free body is *supported by* or *connected to* other bodies and should be clearly indicated. Reactions are discussed in detail in Secs. 4.3 and 4.8.

5. The free-body diagram should also include dimensions, since these may be needed in the computation of moments of forces. Any other detail, however, should be omitted.

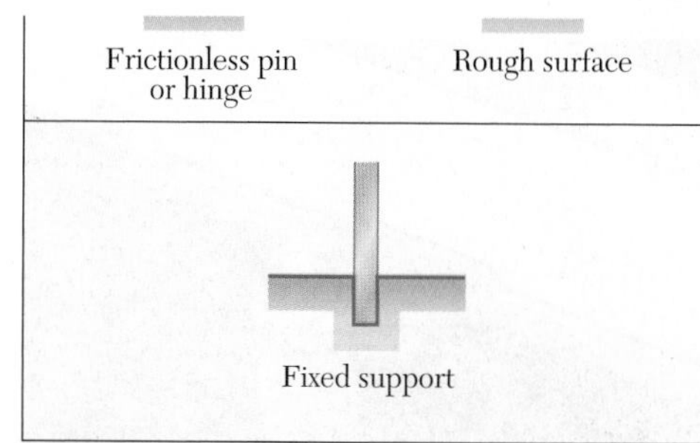

Photo 4.1 A free-body diagram of the tractor shown would include all of the external forces acting on the tractor: the weight of the tractor, the weight of the load in the bucket, and the forces exerted by the ground on the tires.

Photo 4.2 In Chap. 6, we will discuss how to determine the internal forces in structures made of several connected pieces, such as the forces in the members that support the bucket of the tractor of Photo 4.1.

EQUILIBRIUM IN TWO DIMENSIONS

4.3. REACTIONS AT SUPPORTS AND CONNECTIONS FOR A TWO-DIMENSIONAL STRUCTURE

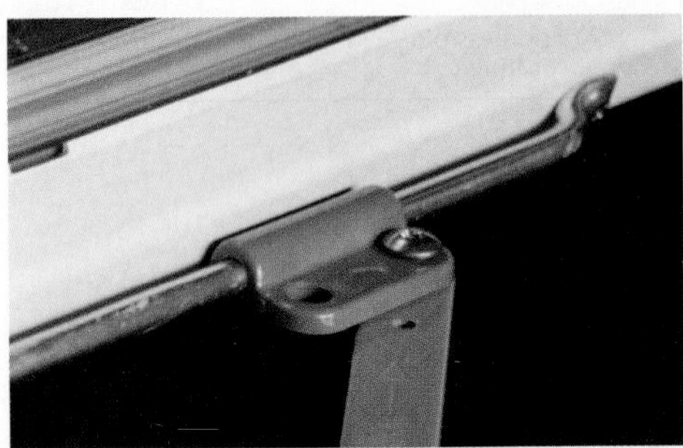

Photo 4.3 As the link of the awning window opening mechanism is extended, the force it exerts on the slider results in a normal force being applied to the rod, which causes the window to open.

Photo 4.4 The abutment-mounted rocker bearing shown is used to support the roadway of a bridge.

Photo 4.5 Shown is the rocker expansion bearing of a plate girder bridge. The convex surface of the rocker allows the support of the girder to move horizontally.

In the first part of this chapter, the equilibrium of a two-dimensional structure is considered; that is, it is assumed that the structure being analyzed and the forces applied to it are contained in the same plane. Clearly, the reactions needed to maintain the structure in the same position will also be contained in this plane.

The reactions exerted on a two-dimensional structure can be divided into three groups corresponding to three types of *supports,* or *connections:*

1. *Reactions Equivalent to a Force with Known Line of Action.* Supports and connections causing reactions of this type include *rollers, rockers, frictionless surfaces, short links and cables, collars on frictionless rods,* and *frictionless pins in slots.* Each of these supports and connections can prevent motion in one direction only. They are shown in Fig. 4.1, together with the reactions they produce. Each of these reactions involves *one unknown,* namely, the magnitude of the reaction; this magnitude should be denoted by an appropriate letter. The line of action of the reaction is known and should be indicated clearly in the free-body diagram. The sense of the reaction must be as shown in Fig. 4.1 for the cases of a frictionless surface (toward the free body) or a cable (away from the free body). The reaction can be directed either way in the case of double-track rollers, links, collars on rods, and pins in slots. Single-track rollers and rockers are generally assumed to be reversible, and thus the corresponding reactions can also be directed either way.

2. *Reactions Equivalent to a Force of Unknown Direction and Magnitude.* Supports and connections causing reactions of this type include *frictionless pins in fitted holes, hinges,* and *rough surfaces.* They can prevent translation of the free body in all directions, but they cannot prevent the body from rotating about the connection. Reactions of this group involve *two unknowns* and are usually represented by their x and y components. In the case of a rough surface, the component normal to the surface must be directed away from the surface, and thus is directed toward the free body.

3. *Reactions Equivalent to a Force and a Couple.* These reactions are caused by *fixed supports,* which oppose any motion of the free body and thus constrain it completely. Fixed supports actually produce forces over the entire surface of contact; these forces, however, form a system which can be reduced to a force and a couple. Reactions of this group involve *three unknowns,* consisting usually of the two components of the force and the moment of the couple.

Support or Connection	Reaction	Number of Unknowns
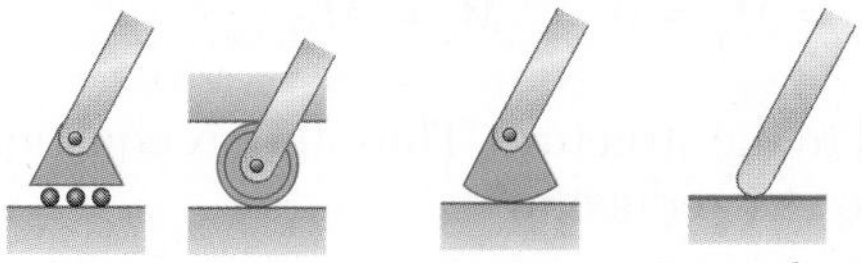 Rollers; Rocker; Frictionless surface	 Force with known line of action	1
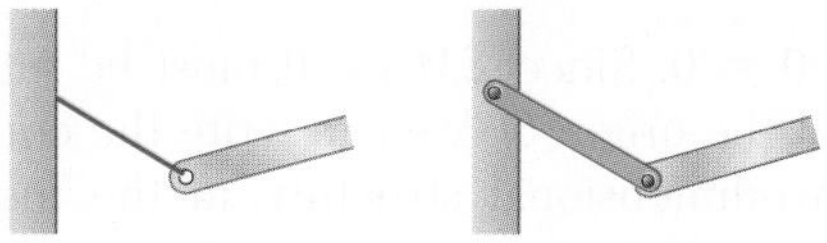 Short cable; Short link	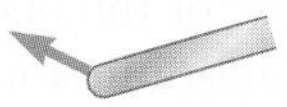 Force with known line of action	1
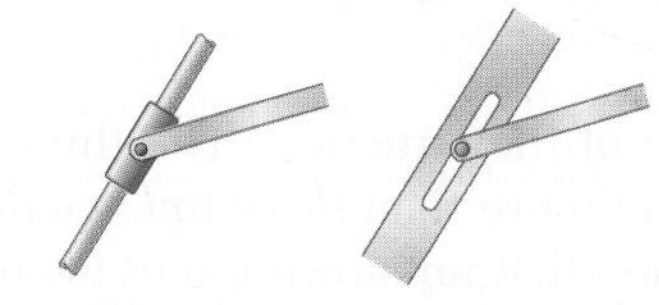 Collar on frictionless rod; Frictionless pin in slot	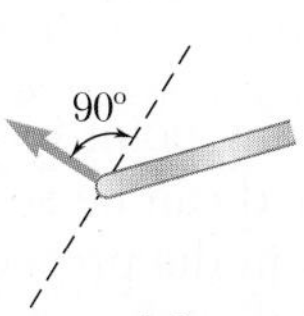 90° Force with known line of action	1
Frictionless pin or hinge; Rough surface	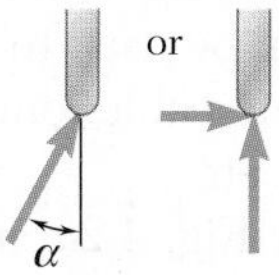 or α Force of unknown direction	2
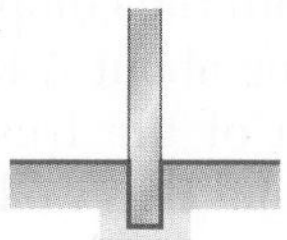 Fixed support	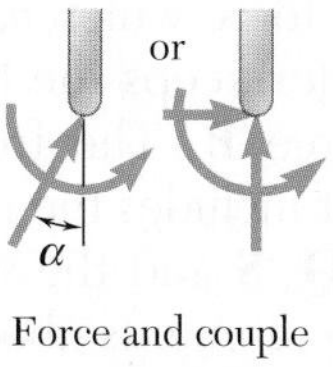 or α Force and couple	3

Fig. 4.1 Reactions at supports and connections.

When the sense of an unknown force or couple is not readily apparent, no attempt should be made to determine it. Instead, the sense of the force or couple should be arbitrarily assumed; the sign of the answer obtained will indicate whether the assumption is correct or not.

4.4. EQUILIBRIUM OF A RIGID BODY IN TWO DIMENSIONS

The conditions stated in Sec. 4.1 for the equilibrium of a rigid body become considerably simpler for the case of a two-dimensional structure. Choosing the x and y axes to be in the plane of the structure, we have

$$F_z = 0 \qquad M_x = M_y = 0 \qquad M_z = M_O$$

for each of the forces applied to the structure. Thus, the six equations of equilibrium derived in Sec. 4.1 reduce to

$$\Sigma F_x = 0 \qquad \Sigma F_y = 0 \qquad \Sigma M_O = 0 \tag{4.4}$$

and to three trivial identities, $0 = 0$. Since $\Sigma M_O = 0$ must be satisfied regardless of the choice of the origin O, we can write the equations of equilibrium for a two-dimensional structure in the more general form

$$\Sigma F_x = 0 \qquad \Sigma F_y = 0 \qquad \Sigma M_A = 0 \tag{4.5}$$

where A is any point in the plane of the structure. The three equations obtained can be solved for no more than *three unknowns.*

We saw in the preceding section that unknown forces include reactions and that the number of unknowns corresponding to a given reaction depends upon the type of support or connection causing that reaction. Referring to Sec. 4.3, we observe that the equilibrium equations (4.5) can be used to determine the reactions associated with two rollers and one cable, one fixed support, or one roller and one pin in a fitted hole, etc.

Consider Fig. 4.2*a*, in which the truss shown is subjected to the given forces **P**, **Q**, and **S**. The truss is held in place by a pin at A and a roller at B. The pin prevents point A from moving by exerting on the truss a force which can be resolved into the components $\mathbf{A}_x$ and $\mathbf{A}_y$; the roller keeps the truss from rotating about A by exerting the vertical force **B**. The free-body diagram of the truss is shown in Fig. 4.2*b*; it includes the reactions $\mathbf{A}_x$, $\mathbf{A}_y$, and **B** as well as the applied forces **P**, **Q**, **S** and the weight **W** of the truss. Expressing that the sum of the moments about A of all of the forces shown in Fig. 4.2*b* is zero, we write the equation $\Sigma M_A = 0$, which can be used to determine the magnitude B since it does not contain A_x or A_y. Next, expressing that the sum of the x components and the sum of the y components of the forces are zero, we write the equations $\Sigma F_x = 0$ and $\Sigma F_y = 0$, from which we can obtain the components A_x and A_y, respectively.

An additional equation could be obtained by expressing that the sum of the moments of the external forces about a point other than A is zero. We could write, for instance, $\Sigma M_B = 0$. Such a statement, however, does not contain any new information, since it has already been established that the system of the forces shown in Fig. 4.2*b* is equivalent to zero. The additional equation *is not independent* and cannot be used to determine a fourth unknown. It will be useful,

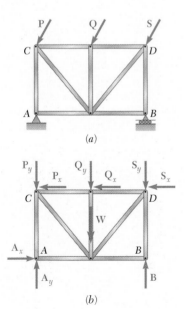

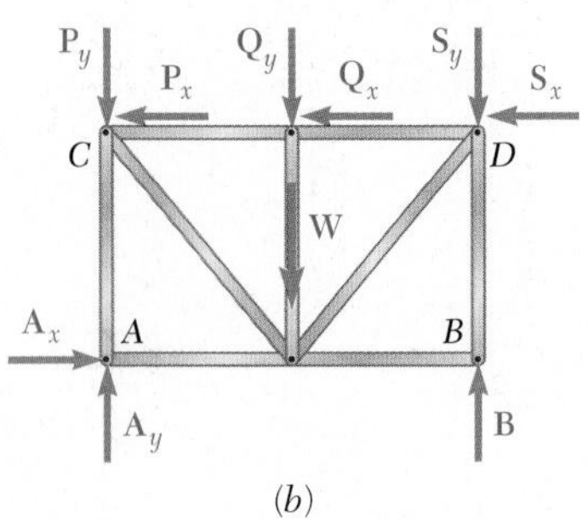

Fig. 4.2

however, for checking the solution obtained from the original three equations of equilibrium.

While the three equations of equilibrium cannot be *augmented* by additional equations, any of them can be *replaced* by another equation. Therefore, an alternative system of equations of equilibrium is

$$\Sigma F_x = 0 \qquad \Sigma M_A = 0 \qquad \Sigma M_B = 0 \tag{4.6}$$

where the second point about which the moments are summed (in this case, point B) cannot lie on the line parallel to the y axis that passes through point A (Fig. 4.2*b*). These equations are sufficient conditions for the equilibrium of the truss. The first two equations indicate that the external forces must reduce to a single vertical force at A. Since the third equation requires that the moment of this force be zero about a point B which is not on its line of action, the force must be zero, and the rigid body is in equilibrium.

A third possible set of equations of equilibrium is

$$\Sigma M_A = 0 \qquad \Sigma M_B = 0 \qquad \Sigma M_C = 0 \tag{4.7}$$

where the points A, B, and C do not lie in a straight line (Fig. 4.2*b*). The first equation requires that the external forces reduce to a single force at A; the second equation requires that this force pass through B; and the third equation requires that it pass through C. Since the points A, B, and C do not lie in a straight line, the force must be zero, and the rigid body is in equilibrium.

The equation $\Sigma M_A = 0$, which expresses that the sum of the moments of the forces about pin A is zero, possesses a more definite physical meaning than either of the other two equations (4.7). These two equations express a similar idea of balance, but with respect to points about which the rigid body is not actually hinged. They are, however, as useful as the first equation, and our choice of equilibrium equations should not be unduly influenced by the physical meaning of these equations. Indeed, it will be desirable in practice to choose equations of equilibrium containing only one unknown, since this eliminates the necessity of solving simultaneous equations. Equations containing only one unknown can be obtained by summing moments about the point of intersection of the lines of action of two unknown forces or, if these forces are parallel, by summing components in a direction perpendicular to their common direction. For example, in Fig. 4.3, in which the truss shown is held by rollers at A and B and a short link at D, the reactions at A and B can be eliminated by summing x components. The reactions at A and D will be eliminated by summing moments about C, and the reactions at B and D by summing moments about D. The equations obtained are

$$\Sigma F_x = 0 \qquad \Sigma M_C = 0 \qquad \Sigma M_D = 0$$

Each of these equations contains only one unknown.

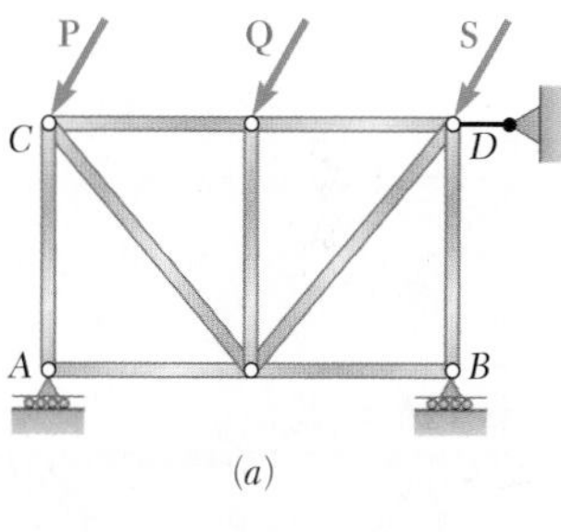

(*a*)

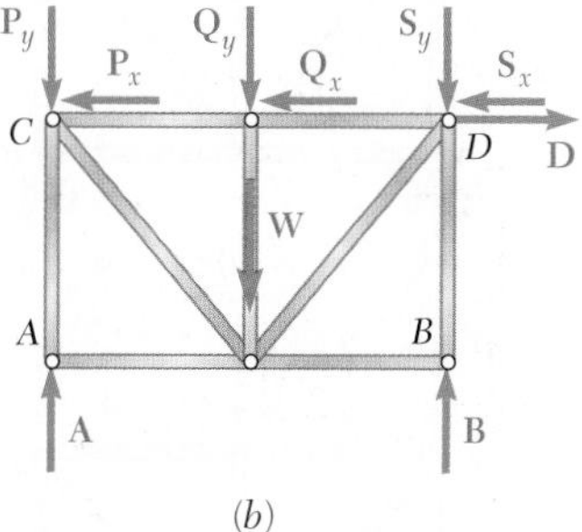

(*b*)

Fig. 4.3

4.5. STATICALLY INDETERMINATE REACTIONS. PARTIAL CONSTRAINTS

In the two examples considered in the preceding section (Figs. 4.2 and 4.3), the types of supports used were such that the rigid body could not possibly move under the given loads or under any other loading conditions. In such cases, the rigid body is said to be *completely constrained.* We also recall that the reactions corresponding to these supports involved *three unknowns* and could be determined by solving the three equations of equilibrium. When such a situation exists, the reactions are said to be *statically determinate.*

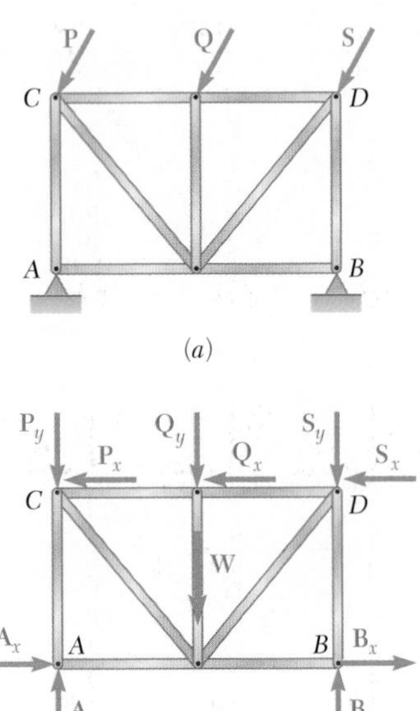

Fig. 4.4 Statically indeterminate reactions.

Consider Fig. 4.4*a*, in which the truss shown is held by pins at *A* and *B*. These supports provide more constraints than are necessary to keep the truss from moving under the given loads or under any other loading conditions. We also note from the free-body diagram of Fig. 4.4*b* that the corresponding reactions involve *four unknowns.* Since, as was pointed out in Sec. 4.4, only three independent equilibrium equations are available, there are *more unknowns than equations;* thus, all of the unknowns cannot be determined. While the equations $\Sigma M_A = 0$ and $\Sigma M_B = 0$ yield the vertical components B_y and A_y, respectively, the equation $\Sigma F_x = 0$ gives only the sum $A_x + B_x$ of the horizontal components of the reactions at *A* and *B*. The components A_x and B_x are said to be *statically indeterminate.* They could be determined by considering the deformations produced in the truss by the given loading, but this method is beyond the scope of statics and belongs to the study of mechanics of materials.

The supports used to hold the truss shown in Fig. 4.5*a* consist of rollers at *A* and *B*. Clearly, the constraints provided by these supports are not sufficient to keep the truss from moving. While any vertical motion is prevented, the truss is free to move horizontally. The truss is said to be *partially constrained.*† Turning our attention to Fig. 4.5*b*, we note that the reactions at *A* and *B* involve only *two unknowns.* Since three equations of equilibrium must still be satisfied, there are *fewer unknowns than equations,* and, in general, one of the equilibrium equations will not be satisfied. While the equations $\Sigma M_A = 0$ and $\Sigma M_B = 0$ can be satisfied by a proper choice of reactions at *A* and *B*, the equation $\Sigma F_x = 0$ will not be satisfied unless the sum of the horizontal components of the applied forces happens to be zero. We thus observe that the equlibrium of the truss of Fig. 4.5 cannot be maintained under general loading conditions.

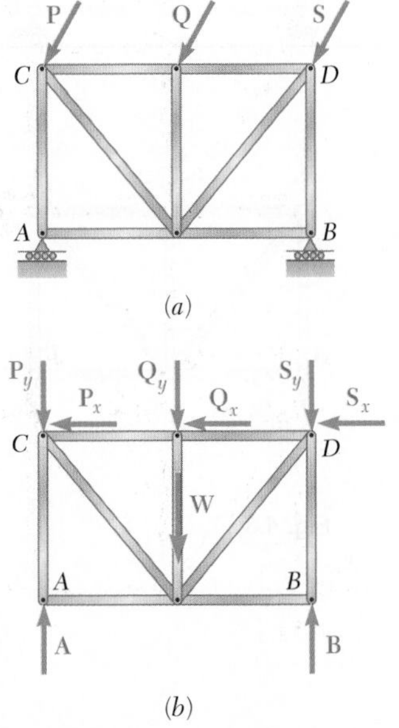

Fig. 4.5 Partial constraints.

It appears from the above that if a rigid body is to be completely constrained and if the reactions at its supports are to be statically determinate, *there must be as many unknowns as there are equations of equilibrium.* When this condition is *not* satisfied, we can be certain either that the rigid body is not completely constrained or that the reactions at its supports are not statically determinate; it is also possible that the rigid body is not completely constrained *and* that the reactions are statically indeterminate.

We should note, however, that, while *necessary,* the above condition is *not sufficient.* In other words, the fact that the number of

†Partially constrained bodies are often referred to as *unstable.* However, to avoid confusion between this type of instability, due to insufficient constraints, and the type of instability considered in Chap. 10, which relates to the behavior of a rigid body when its equilibrium is disturbed, we will restrict the use of the words *stable* and *unstable* to the latter case.

unknowns is equal to the number of equations is no guarantee that the body is completely constrained or that the reactions at its supports are statically determinate. Consider Fig. 4.6*a*, in which the truss shown is held by rollers at *A*, *B*, and *E*. While there are three unknown reactions, **A**, **B**, and **E** (Fig. 4.6*b*), the equation $\Sigma F_x = 0$ will not be satisfied unless the sum of the horizontal components of the applied forces happens to be zero. Although there are a sufficient number of constraints, these constraints are not properly arranged, and the truss is free to move horizontally. We say that the truss is *improperly constrained.* Since only two equilibrium equations are left for determining three unknowns, the reactions will be statically indeterminate. Thus, improper constraints also produce static indeterminacy.

Another example of improper constraints—and of static indeterminacy—is provided by the truss shown in Fig. 4.7. This truss is held by a pin at *A* and by rollers at *B* and *C*, which altogether involve four unknowns. Since only three independent equilibrium equations are available, the reactions at the supports are statically indeterminate. On the other hand, we note that the equation $\Sigma M_A = 0$ cannot be satisfied under general loading conditions, since the lines of action of the reactions **B** and **C** pass through *A*. We conclude that the truss can rotate about *A* and that it is improperly constrained.†

The examples of Figs. 4.6 and 4.7 lead us to conclude that *a rigid body is improperly constrained whenever the supports,* even though they may provide a sufficient number of reactions, *are arranged in such a way that the reactions must be either concurrent or parallel.*‡

In summary, to be sure that a two-dimensional rigid body is completely constrained and that the reactions at its supports are statically determinate, we should verify that the reactions involve three—and only three—unknowns and that the supports are arranged in such a way that they do not require the reactions to be either concurrent or parallel.

Supports involving statically indeterminate reactions should be used with care in the *design* of structures and only with a full knowledge of the problems they may cause. On the other hand, the *analysis* of structures possessing statically indeterminate reactions often can be partially carried out by the methods of statics. In the case of the truss of Fig. 4.4, for example, the vertical components of the reactions at *A* and *B* were obtained from the equilibrium equations.

For obvious reasons, supports producing partial or improper constraints should be avoided in the design of stationary structures. However, a partially or improperly constrained structure will not necessarily collapse; under particular loading conditions, equilibrium can be maintained. For example, the trusses of Figs. 4.5 and 4.6 will be in equilibrium if the applied forces **P**, **Q**, and **S** are vertical. Besides, structures which are designed to move *should* be only partially constrained. A railroad car, for instance, would be of little use if it were completely constrained by having its brakes applied permanently.

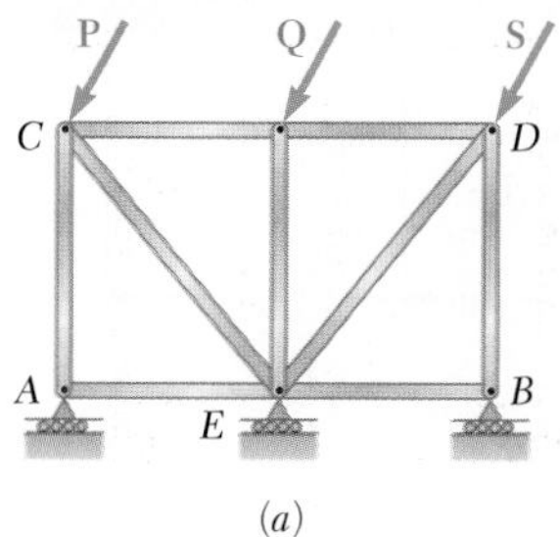

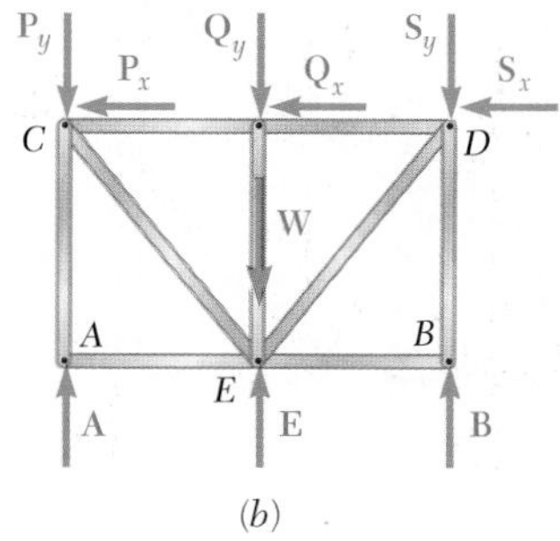

Fig. 4.6 Improper constraints.

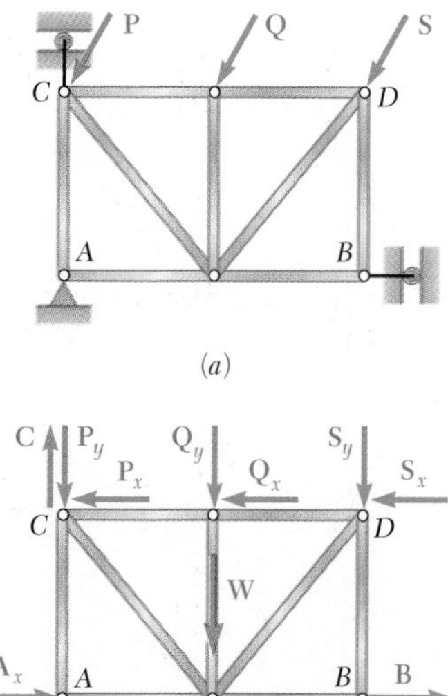

Fig. 4.7 Improper constraints.

†Rotation of the truss about *A* requires some "play" in the supports at *B* and *C*. In practice, such play will always exist. In addition, we note that if the play is kept small, the displacements of the rollers *B* and *C* and, thus, the distances from *A* to the lines of action of the reactions **B** and **C** will also be small. The equation $\Sigma M_A = 0$ then requires that **B** and **C** be very large, a situation which can result in the failure of the supports at *B* and *C*.

‡Because this situation arises from an inadequate arrangement or *geometry* of the supports, it is often referred to as *geometric instability*.

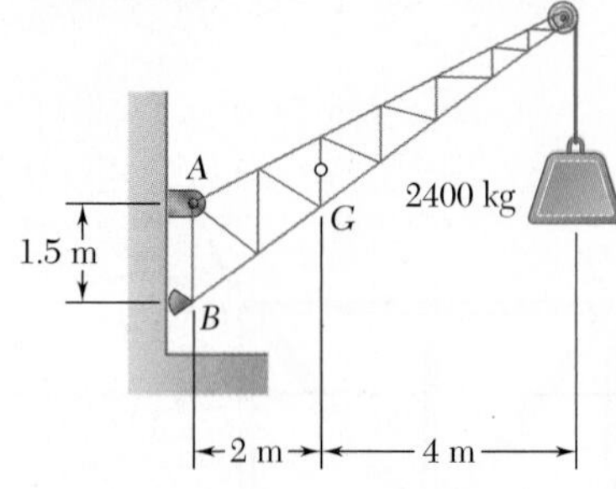

SAMPLE PROBLEM 4.1

A fixed crane has a mass of 1000 kg and is used to lift a 2400-kg crate. It is held in place by a pin at A and a rocker at B. The center of gravity of the crane is located at G. Determine the components of the reactions at A and B.

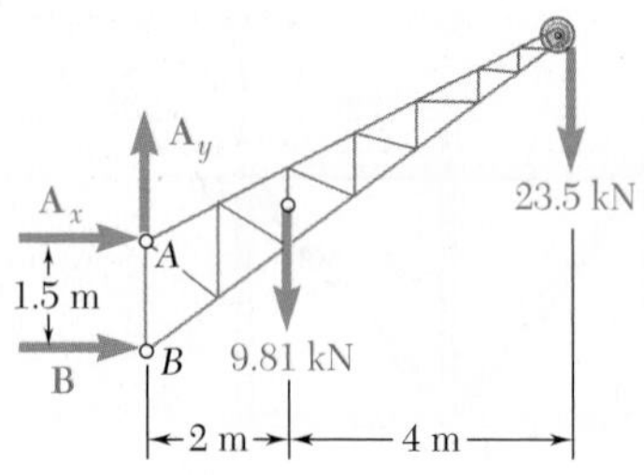

SOLUTION

Free-Body Diagram. A free-body diagram of the crane is drawn. By multiplying the masses of the crane and of the crate by $g = 9.81 \text{ m/s}^2$, we obtain the corresponding weights, that is, 9810 N or 9.81 kN, and 23 500 N or 23.5 kN. The reaction at pin A is a force of unknown direction; it is represented by its components $\mathbf{A}_x$ and $\mathbf{A}_y$. The reaction at the rocker B is perpendicular to the rocker surface; thus, it is horizontal. We assume that $\mathbf{A}_x$, $\mathbf{A}_y$, and $\mathbf{B}$ act in the directions shown.

Determination of *B*. We express that the sum of the moments of all external forces about point A is zero. The equation obtained will contain neither A_x nor A_y, since the moments of $\mathbf{A}_x$ and $\mathbf{A}_y$ about A are zero. Multiplying the magnitude of each force by its perpendicular distance from A, we write

$$+\circlearrowleft \Sigma M_A = 0: \quad B(1.5 \text{ m}) - (9.81 \text{ kN})(2 \text{ m}) - (23.5 \text{ kN})(6 \text{ m}) = 0$$
$$B = +107.1 \text{ kN} \qquad \mathbf{B} = 107.1 \text{ kN} \rightarrow \blacktriangleleft$$

Since the result is positive, the reaction is directed as assumed.

Determination of $\mathbf{A}_x$. The magnitude of $\mathbf{A}_x$ is determined by expressing that the sum of the horizontal components of all external forces is zero.

$$\xrightarrow{+} \Sigma F_x = 0: \quad A_x + B = 0$$
$$A_x + 107.1 \text{ kN} = 0$$
$$A_x = -107.1 \text{ kN} \qquad \mathbf{A}_x = 107.1 \text{ kN} \leftarrow \blacktriangleleft$$

Since the result is negative, the sense of $\mathbf{A}_x$ is opposite to that assumed originally.

Determination of $\mathbf{A}_y$. The sum of the vertical components must also equal zero.

$$+\uparrow \Sigma F_y = 0: \quad A_y - 9.81 \text{ kN} - 23.5 \text{ kN} = 0$$
$$A_y = +33.3 \text{ kN} \qquad \mathbf{A}_y = 33.3 \text{ kN} \uparrow \blacktriangleleft$$

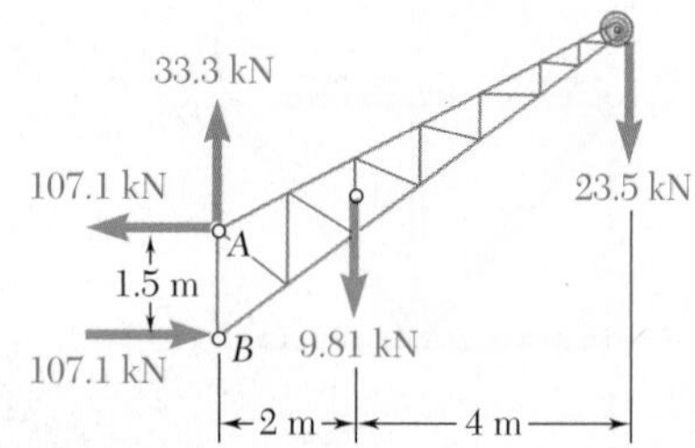

Adding vectorially the components $\mathbf{A}_x$ and $\mathbf{A}_y$, we find that the reaction at A is 112.2 kN $\nwarrow$17.3°.

Check. The values obtained for the reactions can be checked by recalling that the sum of the moments of all of the external forces about any point must be zero. For example, considering point B, we write

$$+\circlearrowleft \Sigma M_B = -(9.81 \text{ kN})(2 \text{ m}) - (23.5 \text{ kN})(6 \text{ m}) + (107.1 \text{ kN})(1.5 \text{ m}) = 0$$

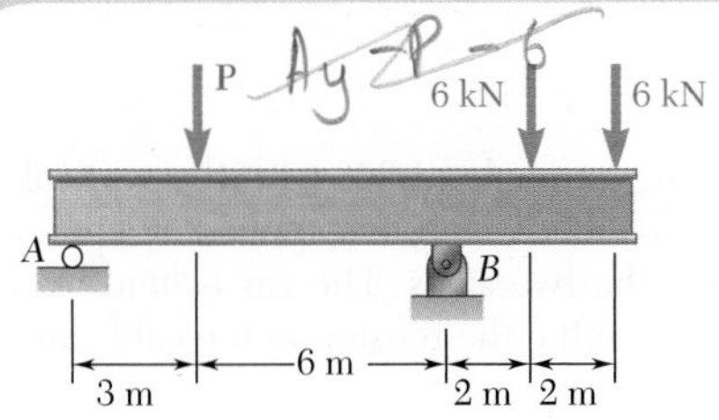

SAMPLE PROBLEM 4.2

Three loads are applied to a beam as shown. The beam is supported by a roller at A and by a pin at B. Neglecting the weight of the beam, determine the reactions at A and B when $P = 15$ kN.

SOLUTION

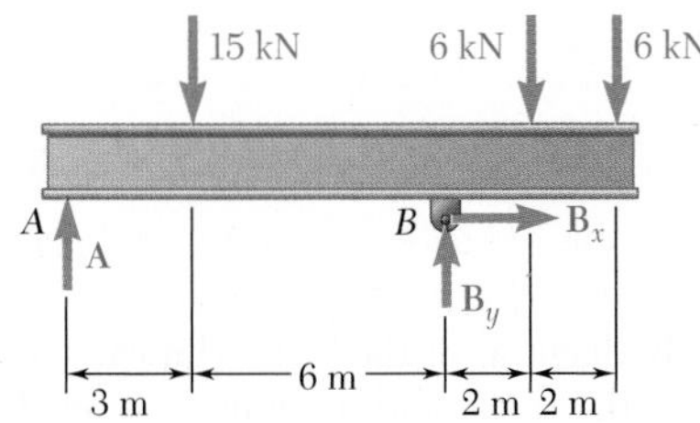

Free-Body Diagram. A free-body diagram of the beam is drawn. The reaction at A is vertical and is denoted by **A**. The reaction at B is represented by components $\mathbf{B}_x$ and $\mathbf{B}_y$. Each component is assumed to act in the direction shown.

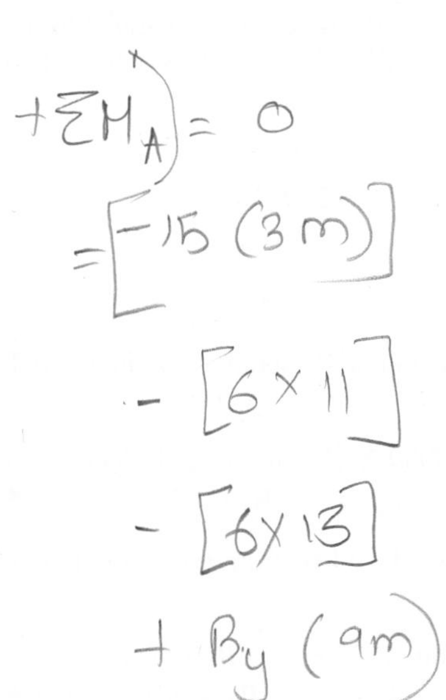

Equilibrium Equations. We write the following three equilibrium equations and solve for the reactions indicated:

$\xrightarrow{+}\Sigma F_x = 0$: $\qquad B_x = 0 \qquad \mathbf{B}_x = 0$ ◀

$+\circlearrowleft\Sigma M_A = 0$:

$$-(15 \text{ kN})(3 \text{ m}) + B_y(9 \text{ m}) - (6 \text{ kN})(11 \text{ m}) - (6 \text{ kN})(13 \text{ m}) = 0$$

$$B_y = +21.0 \text{ kN} \qquad \mathbf{B}_y = 21.0 \text{ kN} \uparrow$$ ◀

$+\circlearrowleft\Sigma M_B = 0$:

$$-A(9 \text{ m}) + (15 \text{ kN})(6 \text{ m}) - (6 \text{ kN})(2 \text{ m}) - (6 \text{ kN})(4 \text{ m}) = 0$$

$$A = +6.00 \text{ kN} \qquad \mathbf{A} = 6.00 \text{ kN} \uparrow$$ ◀

Check. The results are checked by adding the vertical components of all of the external forces:

$$+\uparrow\Sigma F_y = +6.00 \text{ kN} - 15 \text{ kN} + 21.0 \text{ kN} - 6 \text{ kN} - 6 \text{ kN} = 0$$

Remark. In this problem the reactions at both A and B are vertical; however, these reactions are vertical for different reasons. At A, the beam is supported by a roller; hence the reaction cannot have a horizontal component. At B, the horizontal component of the reaction is zero because it must satisfy the equilibrium equation $\Sigma F_x = 0$ and because none of the other forces acting on the beam has a horizontal component.

We could have noticed at first glance that the reaction at B was vertical and dispensed with the horizontal component $\mathbf{B}_x$. This, however, is a bad practice. In following it, we would run the risk of forgetting the component $\mathbf{B}_x$ when the loading conditions require such a component (that is, when a horizontal load is included). Also, the component $\mathbf{B}_x$ was found to be zero by using and solving an equilibrium equation, $\Sigma F_x = 0$. By setting $\mathbf{B}_x$ equal to zero immediately, we might not realize that we actually made use of this equation and thus might lose track of the number of equations available for solving the problem.

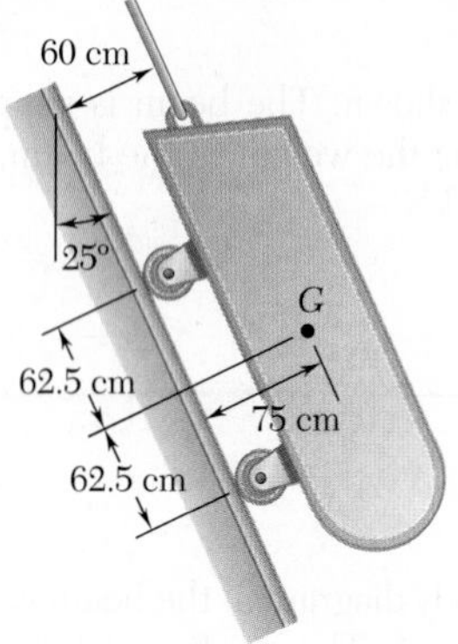

SAMPLE PROBLEM 4.3

A loading car is at rest on a track forming an angle of 25° with the vertical. The gross weight of the car and its load is 5500 N, and it is applied at a point 7.5 cm from the track, halfway between the two axles. The car is held by a cable attached 60 cm from the track. Determine the tension in the cable and the reaction at each pair of wheels.

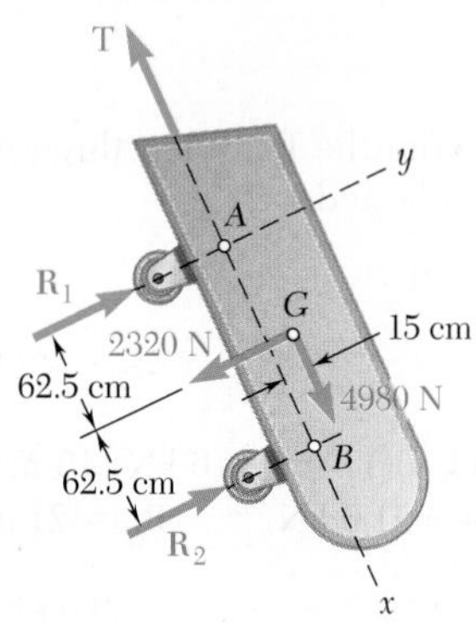

SOLUTION

Free-Body Diagram. A free-body diagram of the car is drawn. The reaction at each wheel is perpendicular to the track, and the tension force **T** is parallel to the track. For convenience, we choose the x axis parallel to the track and the y axis perpendicular to the track. The 5500-N weight is then resolved into x and y components.

$$W_x = +(5500 \text{ N}) \cos 25° = +4980 \text{ N}$$
$$W_y = -(5500 \text{ N}) \sin 25° = -2320 \text{ N}$$

Equilibrium Equations. We take moments about A to eliminate **T** and $\mathbf{R}_1$ from the computation.

$$+\circlearrowleft \Sigma M_A = 0: \quad -(2320 \text{ N})(62.5 \text{ cm}) - (4980 \text{ N})(15 \text{ cm}) + R_2(12.5 \text{ cm}) = 0$$
$$R_2 = +1757.6 \text{ N} \qquad \mathbf{R}_2 = 1757.6 \text{ N} \nearrow \blacktriangleleft$$

Now, taking moments about B to eliminate **T** and $\mathbf{R}_2$ from the computation, we write

$$+\circlearrowleft \Sigma M_B = 0: \quad (2320 \text{ N})(62.5 \text{ cm}) - (4980 \text{ N})(15 \text{ cm}) - R_1(125 \text{ cm}) = 0$$
$$R_1 = +562.4 \text{ N} \qquad \mathbf{R}_1 = 562.4 \text{ N} \nearrow \blacktriangleleft$$

The value of T is found by writing

$$\searrow + \Sigma F_x = 0: \quad 4980 \text{ N} - T = 0$$
$$T = +4980 \text{ N} \qquad \mathbf{T} = 4980 \text{ N} \nwarrow \blacktriangleleft$$

The computed values of the reactions are shown in the adjacent sketch.

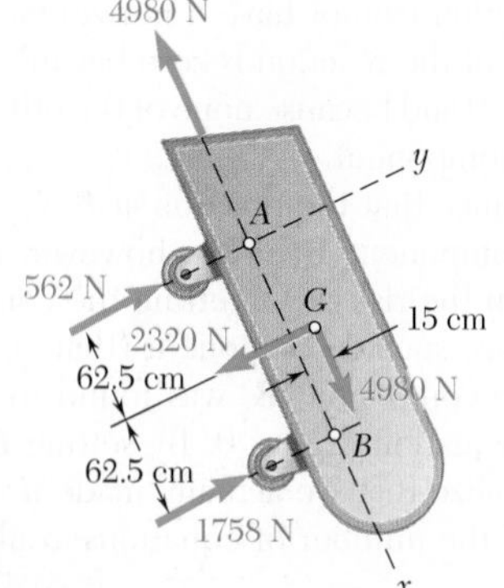

Check. The computations are verified by writing

$$\nearrow + \Sigma F_y = +562 \text{ N} + 1758 \text{ N} - 2320 \text{ N} = 0$$

The solution could also have been checked by computing moments about any point other than A or B.

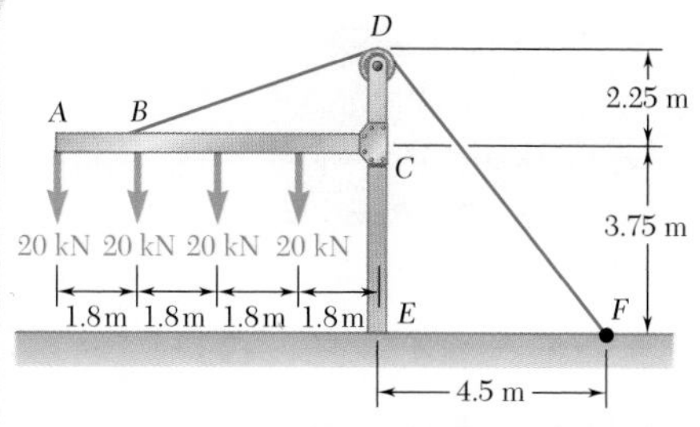

SAMPLE PROBLEM 4.4

The frame shown supports part of the roof of a small building. Knowing that the tension in the cable is 150 kN, determine the reaction at the fixed end E.

SOLUTION

Free-Body Diagram. A free-body diagram of the frame and of the cable BDF is drawn. The reaction at the fixed end E is represented by the force components $\mathbf{E}_x$ and $\mathbf{E}_y$ and the couple $\mathbf{M}_E$. The other forces acting on the free body are the four 20-kN loads and the 150-kN force exerted at end F of the cable.

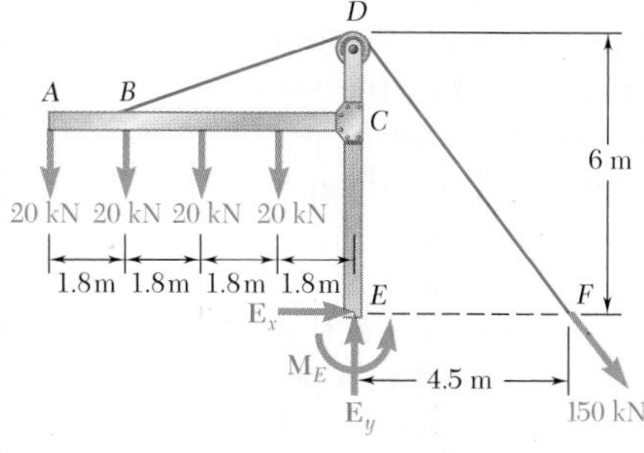

Equilibrium Equations. Noting that $DF = \sqrt{(4.5\text{ m})^2 + (6\text{ m})^2} = 7.5$ m, we write

$$\overset{+}{\rightarrow}\Sigma F_x = 0: \qquad E_x + \frac{4.5}{7.5}(150\text{ kN}) = 0$$

$$E_x = -90.0\text{ kN} \qquad \mathbf{E}_x = 90.0\text{ kN} \leftarrow \blacktriangleleft$$

$$+\uparrow\Sigma F_y = 0: \qquad E_y - 4(20\text{ kN}) - \frac{6}{7.5}(150\text{ kN}) = 0$$

$$E_y = +200\text{ kN} \qquad \mathbf{E}_y = 200\text{ kN} \uparrow \blacktriangleleft$$

$$+\circlearrowleft\Sigma M_E = 0: \qquad (20\text{ kN})(7.2\text{ m}) + (20\text{ kN})(5.4\text{ m}) + (20\text{ kN})(3.6\text{ m})$$

$$+ (20\text{ kN})(1.8\text{ m}) - \frac{6}{7.5}(150\text{ kN})(4.5\text{ m}) + M_E = 0$$

$$M_E = +180.0\text{ kN}\cdot\text{m} \qquad \mathbf{M}_E = 180.0\text{ kN}\cdot\text{m}\ \circlearrowleft \blacktriangleleft$$

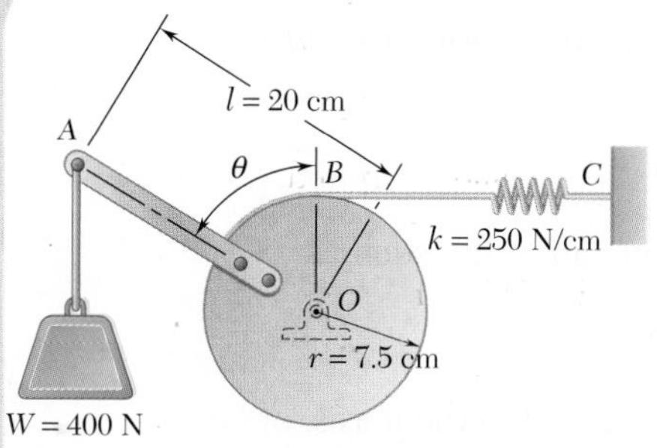

SAMPLE PROBLEM 4.5

A 800-N weight is attached at A to the lever shown. The constant of the spring BC is $k = 250$ N/cm, and the spring is unstretched when $\theta = 0$. Determine the position of equilibrium.

SOLUTION

Free-Body Diagram. We draw a free-body diagram of the lever and cylinder. Denoting by s the deflection of the spring from its undeformed position, and noting that $s = r\theta$, we have $F = ks = kr\theta$.

Equilibrium Equation. Summing the moments of $\mathbf{W}$ and $\mathbf{F}$ about O, we write

$$+\circlearrowleft\Sigma M_O = 0: \qquad Wl\sin\theta - r(kr\theta) = 0 \qquad \sin\theta = \frac{kr^2}{Wl}\theta$$

Substituting the given data, we obtain

$$\sin\theta = \frac{(250\text{ N/cm})(7.5\text{ cm})^2}{(800\text{ N})(20\text{ cm})}\theta \qquad \sin\theta = 0.8789\theta$$

Solving numerically, we find $\qquad \theta = 0 \qquad \theta = 49.8° \blacktriangleleft$

SOLVING PROBLEMS ON YOUR OWN

You saw that the external forces acting on a rigid body in equilibrium form a system equivalent to zero. To solve an equilibrium problem your first task is to draw a neat, reasonably large *free-body diagram* on which you will show all external forces and relevant dimensions. Both known and unknown forces must be included.

For a two-dimensional rigid body, the reactions at the supports can involve one, two, or three unknowns depending on the type of support (Fig. 4.1). For the successful solution of a problem, a correct free-body diagram is essential. Never proceed with the solution of a problem until you are sure that your free-body diagram includes all loads, all reactions, and the weight of the body (if appropriate).

As you construct your free-body diagrams, it will be necessary to assign directions to the unknown reactions. We suggest you always assume these forces act in a positive direction, so that positive answers always imply forces acting in a positive direction, while negative answers always imply forces acting in a negative direction. Similarly, we recommend you always assume the unknown force in a rod or cable is tensile, so that a positive result always means a tensile reaction. While a negative or comprehensive reaction is possible for a rod, a negative answer for a cable is impossible and, therefore, implies that there is an error in your solution.

1. ***You can write three equilibrium equations*** and solve them for *three unknowns.* The three equations might be

$$\Sigma F_x = 0 \qquad \Sigma F_y = 0 \qquad \Sigma M_O = 0$$

However, there are usually several sets of equations that you can write, such as

$$\Sigma F_x = 0 \qquad \Sigma M_A = 0 \qquad \Sigma M_B = 0$$

where point B is chosen in such a way that the line AB is not parallel to the y axis, or

$$\Sigma M_A = 0 \qquad \Sigma M_B = 0 \qquad \Sigma M_C = 0$$

where the points A, B, and C do not lie in a straight line.

2. ***To simplify your solution,*** it may be helpful to use one of the following solution techniques if applicable.

   a. ***By summing moments about the point of intersection*** of the lines of action of two unknown forces, you will obtain an equation in a single unknown.

b. By summing components in a direction perpendicular to two unknown parallel forces, you will obtain an equation in a single unknown.

In some of the following problems you will be asked to determine the *allowable range of values* of the applied load for a given set of constraints, such as the maximum reaction at a support or the maximum force in one or more cables or rods. For problems of this type, you first assume a *maximum* loading situation (for example, the maximum allowed force in a rod), and then apply the equations of equilibrium to determine the corresponding unknown reactions and applied load. If the reactions satisfy the constraints, then the applied load is either the maximum or minimum value of the allowable range. However, if the solution violates a constraint (for example, the force in a cable is compressive), the initial assumption is wrong and another loading condition must be assumed (for the previous example, you would assume the force in the cable is zero, the *minimum* allowed reaction). The solution process is then repeated for another possible *maximum* loading to complete the determination of the allowable range of values of the applied load.

As in Chap. 2, we strongly recommend you always write the equations of equilibrium in the same form that we have used in the preceding sample problems. That is, both the known and unknown quantities are placed on the left side of the equation, and their sum is set equal to zero.

Problems

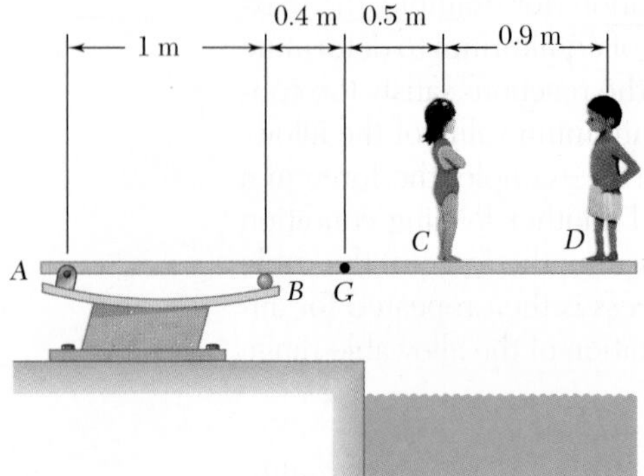

Fig. P4.1

4.1 Two children are standing on a diving board that weighs 300 N. Knowing that the weights of the children at C and D are 120 N and 180 N, respectively, determine (*a*) the reaction at A, (*b*) the reaction at B.

4.2 The boom on a 19000-N truck is used to unload a pallet of shingles of weight 7000 N. Determine the reaction at each of the two (*a*) rear wheels B, (*b*) front wheels C.

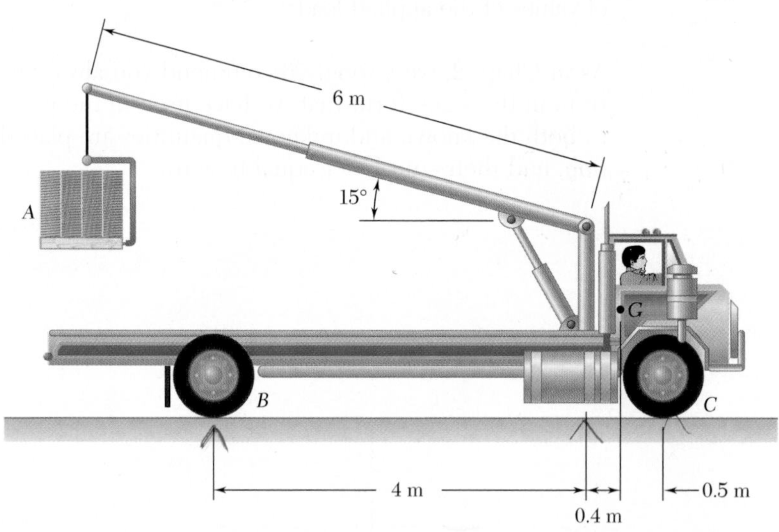

Fig. P4.2

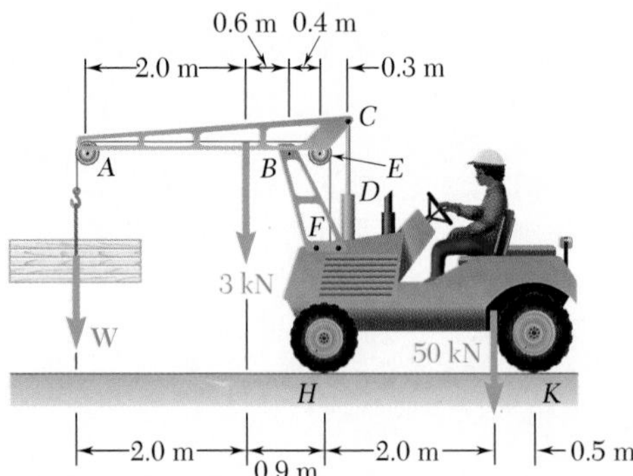

Fig. P4.3 and P4.4

4.3 A load of lumber weighing $W = 25$ kN is being raised by a mobile crane. The weight of the boom ABC and the combined weight of the truck and driver are as shown. Determine the reaction at each of the two (*a*) front wheels H, (*b*) rear wheels K.

4.4 A load of lumber weighing $W = 25$ kN is being raised as shown by a mobile crane. Knowing that the tension is 25 kN in all portions of cable AEF and that the weight of boom ABC is 3 kN, determine (*a*) the tension in rod CD, (*b*) the reaction at pin B.

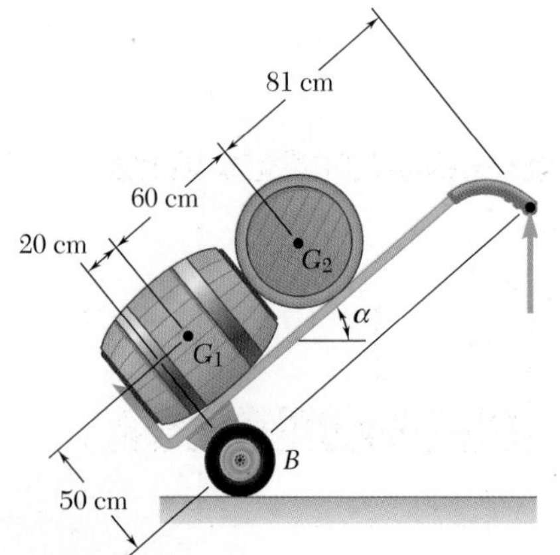

Fig. *P4.5*

4.5 A hand truck is used to move two barrels each weighing 160 N. Neglecting the weight of the hand truck, determine (*a*) the vertical force **P** which should be applied to the handle to maintain equilibrium when $\alpha = 35°$, (*b*) the corresponding reaction at each of the two wheels.

4.6 Solve Prob. 4.5 when $\alpha = 40°$.

4.7 When cars C and D stop on a two-lane bridge, the forces exerted by their tires on the bridge are as shown. Determine the total reactions at A and B when (*a*) $a = 2.9$ m, (*b*) $a = 8.1$ m.

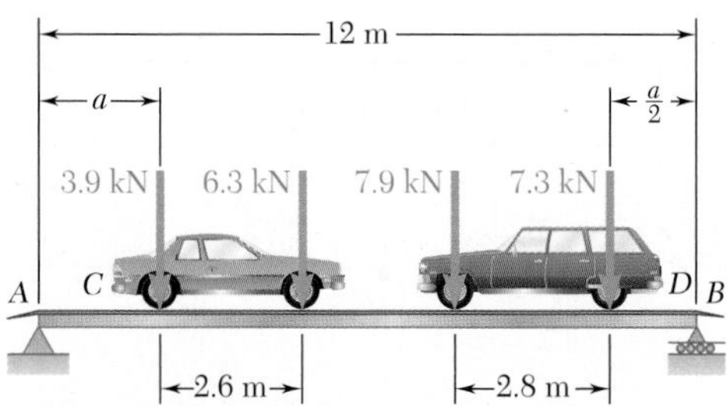

Fig. P4.7 and P4.8

4.8 When cars C and D stop on a two-lane bridge, the forces exerted by their tires on the bridge are as shown. When both cars are on the bridge, determine (*a*) the value of a for which the total reaction at A is maximum, (*b*) the corresponding total reactions at A and B.

4.9 A control rod is attached to a crank at A and cords are attached at B and C. For the given force in the rod, determine the range of values of the tension in the cord at C knowing that the cords must remain taut and that the maximum allowed tension in a cord is 70 N.

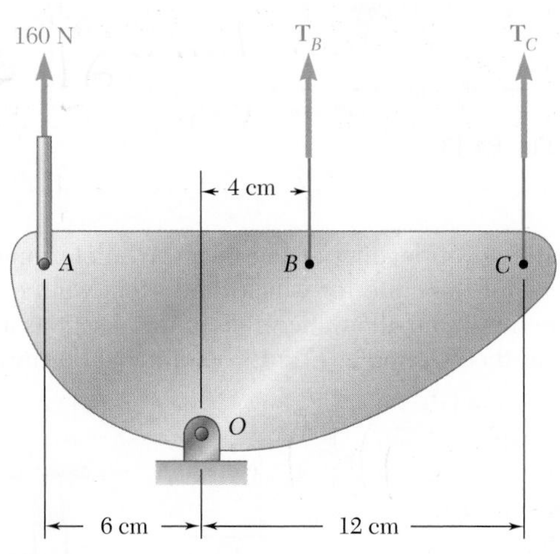

Fig. P4.9

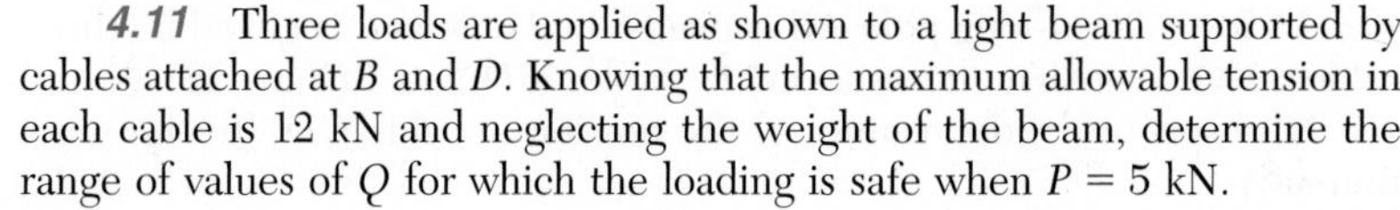

4.10 Three loads are applied as shown to a light beam supported by cables attached at B and D. Neglecting the weight of the beam, determine the range of values of Q for which neither cable becomes slack when $P = 0$.

4.11 Three loads are applied as shown to a light beam supported by cables attached at B and D. Knowing that the maximum allowable tension in each cable is 12 kN and neglecting the weight of the beam, determine the range of values of Q for which the loading is safe when $P = 5$ kN.

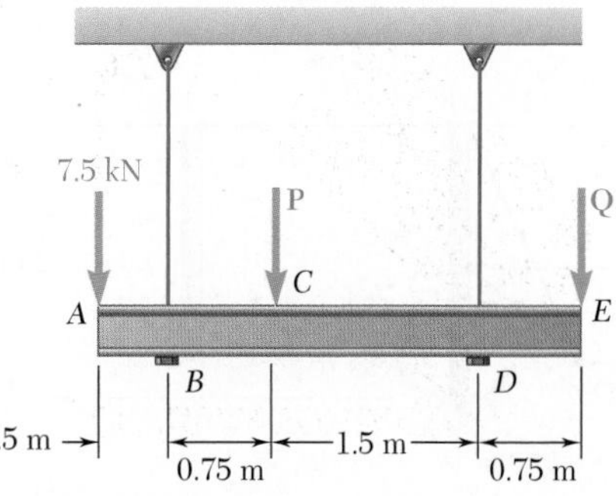

Fig. P4.10 and *P4.11*

4.12 Four boxes are placed on a uniform 28 N wooden plank which rests on two sawhorses. Knowing that the weights of boxes B and D are 9 N and 90 N, respectively, determine the range of values of the weight of box A so that the plank remains in equilibrium when box C is removed.

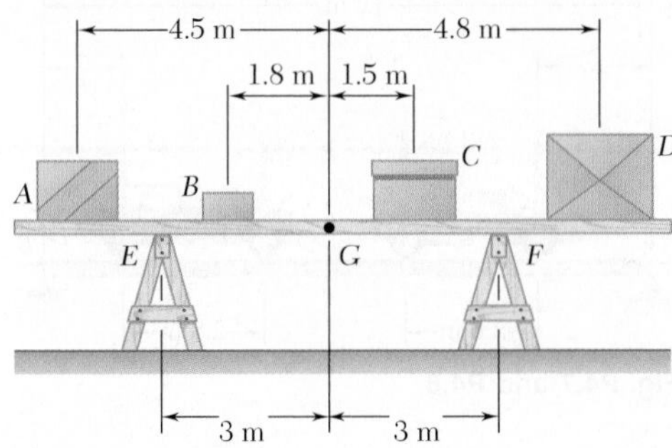

Fig. P4.12

4.13 For the beam and loading shown, determine the range of values of the distance a for which the reaction at B does not exceed 250 N downward or 500 N upward.

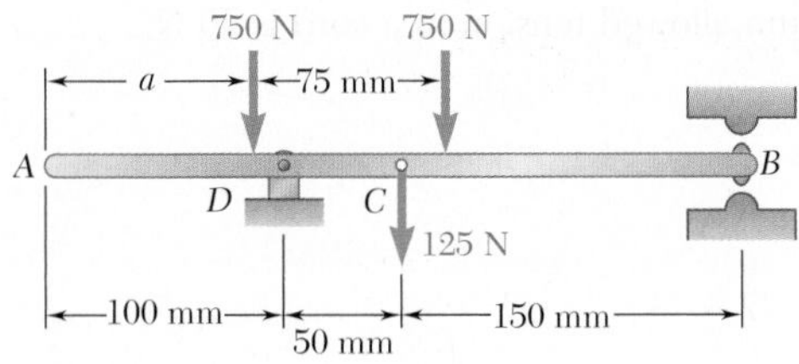

Fig. P4.13

4.14 For the given loading of the beam AB, determine the range of values of the mass of the crate for which the system will be in equilibrium knowing that the maximum allowable value of the reactions at each support is 2.5 kN and that the reaction at E must be directed downward.

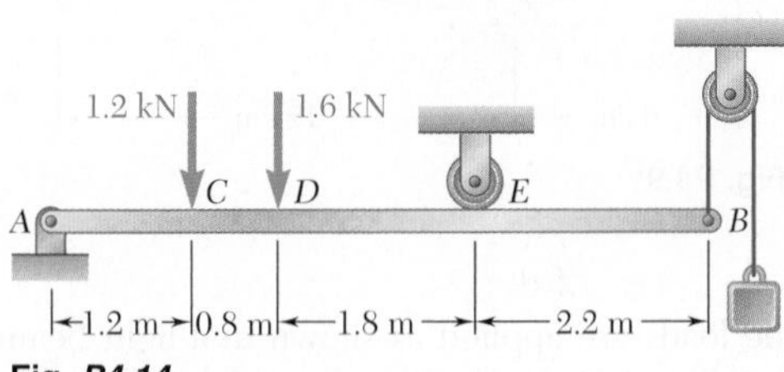

Fig. P4.14

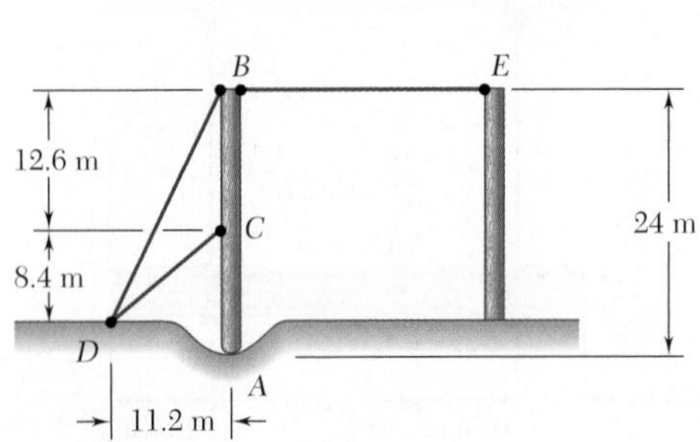

Fig. P4.15

4.15 A 24-m-long pole AB is placed in a hole and is guyed by three cables. Knowing that the tensions in cables BD and BE are 221 N and 161 N, respectively, determine (a) the tension in cable CD, (b) the reaction at A.

4.16 A follower $ABCD$ is held against a circular cam by a stretched spring which exerts a force of 12 N for the position shown. Knowing that the tension in rod BE is 8 N, determine (*a*) the force exerted on the roller at A, (*b*) the reaction at bearing C.

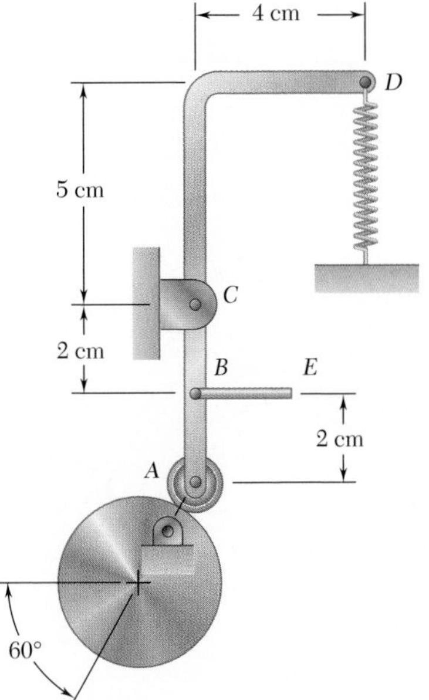

Fig. P4.16

4.17 Determine the reactions at A and B when (*a*) $\alpha = 0$, (*b*) $\alpha = 90°$, (*c*) $\alpha = 30°$.

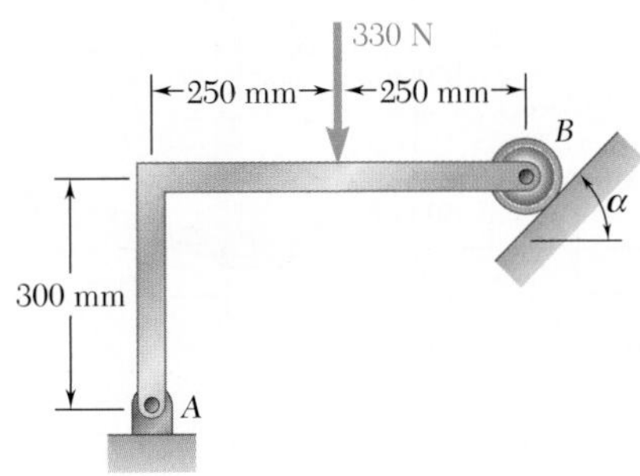

Fig. *P4.17*

4.18 Solve Prob. 4.17 assuming that the 330-N force is replaced with an 82.5-N · m clockwise couple.

4.19 The lever BCD is hinged at C and is attached to a control rod at B. If $P = 200$ N, determine (*a*) the tension in rod AB, (*b*) the reaction at C.

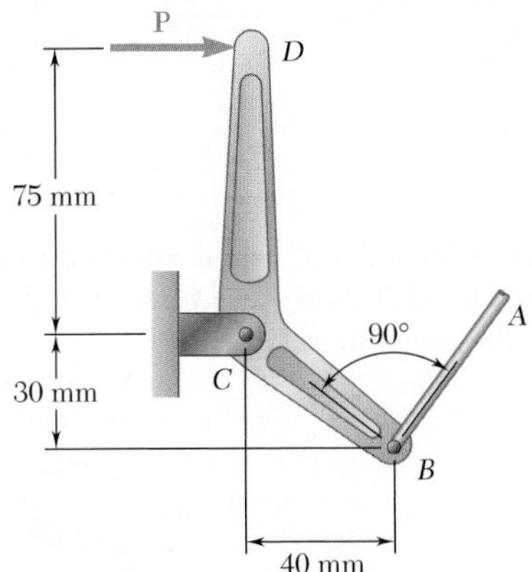

Fig. P4.19 and *P4.20*

4.20 The lever BCD is hinged at C and is attached to a control rod at B. Determine the maximum force **P** which can be safely applied at D if the maximum allowable value of the reaction at C is 500 N.

4.21 The required force to be exerted at A by lever ABC is 6 N. Knowing that $\alpha = 30°$ and that the spring has been stretched 3 cm, determine (*a*) the constant k of the spring, (*b*) the reaction at B.

4.22 The required force to be exerted at A by lever ABC is 8 N. Knowing that the stretched spring exerts a 24-N force at C, determine (*a*) the value of α, (*b*) the reaction at B.

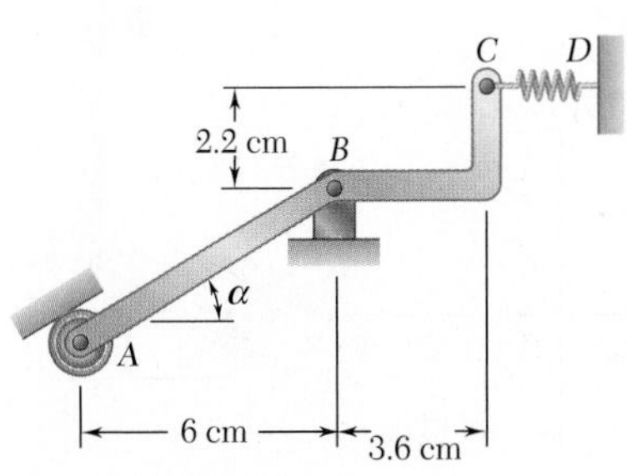

Fig. P4.21 and *P4.22*

4.23 and 4.24 A steel rod is bent to form a mounting bracket. For each of the mounting brackets and loadings shown, determine the reactions at A and B.

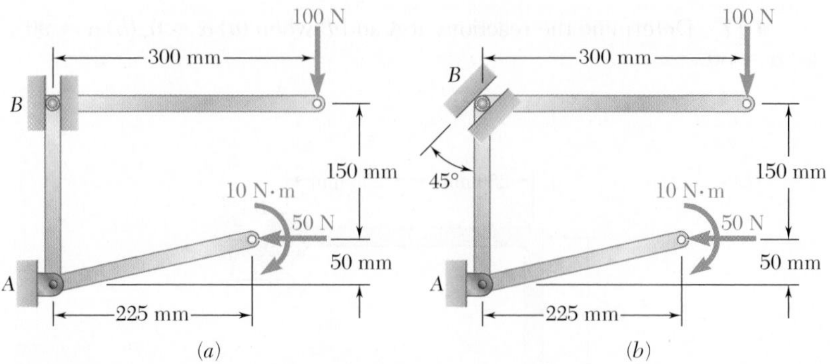

Fig. P4.23

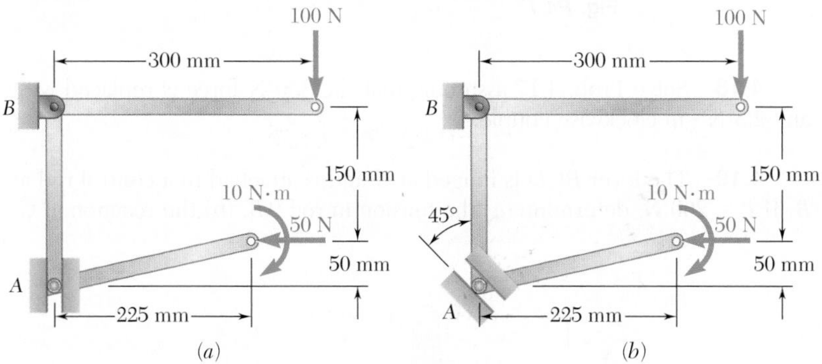

Fig. P4.24

4.25 A lever AB is hinged at C and is attached to a control cable at A. If the lever is subjected to a 120-N vertical force at B, determine (a) the tension in the cable, (b) the reaction at C.

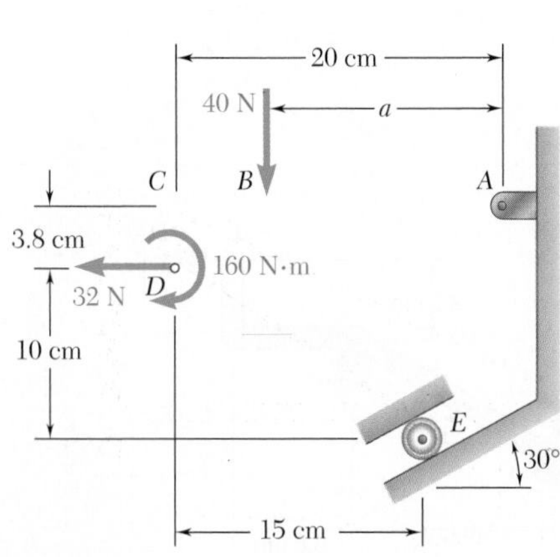

Fig. P4.26

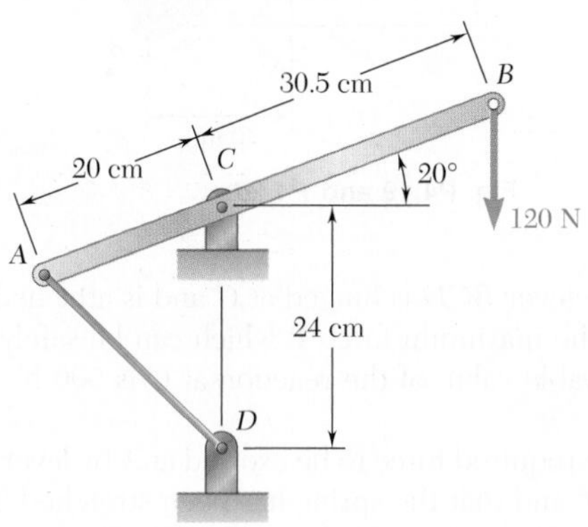

Fig. *P4.25*

4.26 For the frame and loading shown, determine the reactions at A and E when (a) $a = 5$ cm, (b) $a = 19$ cm.

4.27 A sign is hung by two chains from mast *AB*. The mast is hinged at *A* and is supported by cable *BC*. Knowing that the tensions in chains *DE* and *FH* are 225 N and 135 N, respectively, and that $d = 0.39$ m, determine (*a*) the tension in cable *BC*, (*b*) the reaction at *A*.

4.28 A sign is hung by two chains from mast *AB*. The mast is hinged at *A* and is supported by cable *BC*. Knowing that the tensions in chains *DE* and *FH* are 135 N and 90 N, respectively, and that $d = 0.462$ m, determine (*a*) the tension in cable *BC*, (*b*) the reaction at *A*.

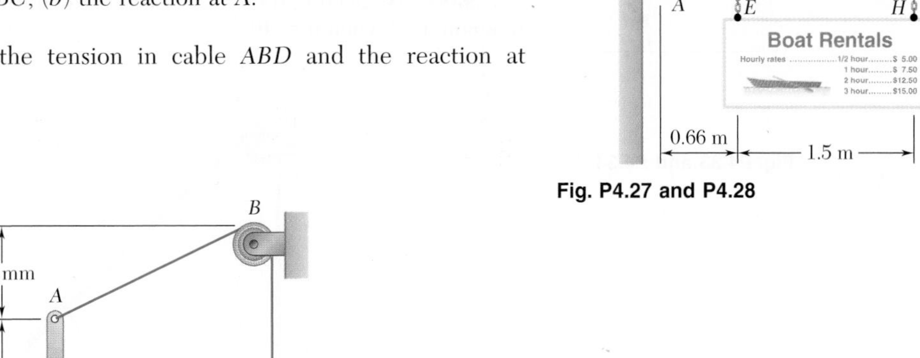

Fig. P4.27 and P4.28

4.29 Determine the tension in cable *ABD* and the reaction at support *C*.

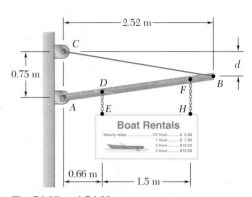

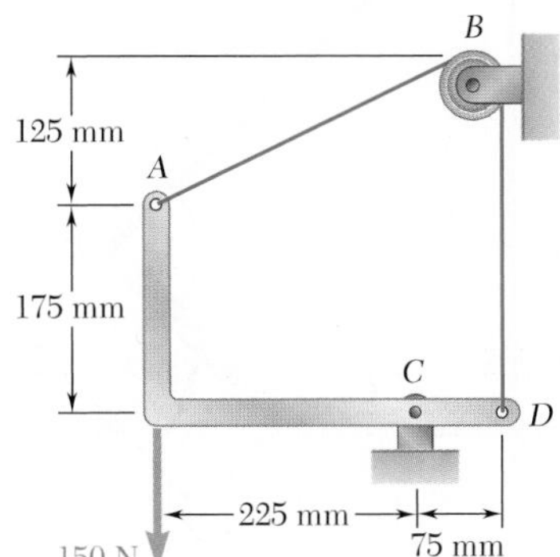

Fig. P4.29

4.30 Neglecting friction and the radius of the pulley, determine the tension in cable *BCD* and the reaction at support *A* when $d = 10$ cm.

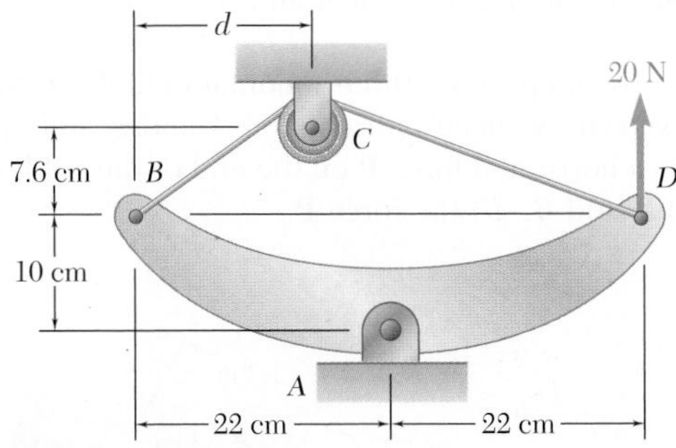

Fig. P4.30 and P4.31

4.31 Neglecting friction and the radius of the pulley, determine the tension in cable *BCD* and the reaction at support *A* when $d = 18$ cm.

4.32 Neglecting friction and the radius of the pulley, determine (*a*) the tension in cable *ADB*, (*b*) the reaction at *C*.

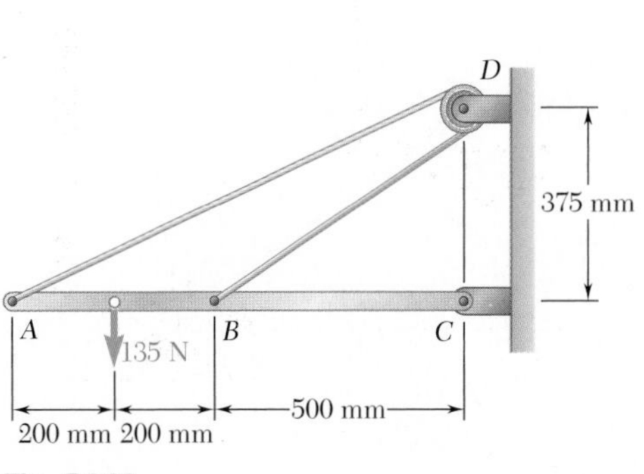

Fig. *P4.32*

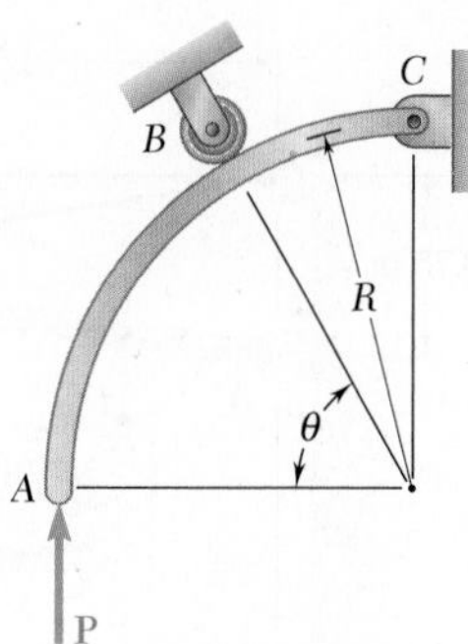

Fig. P4.33 and P4.34

4.33 Rod ABC is bent in the shape of a circular arc of radius R. Determine (*a*) the value of θ so that the magnitudes of the reactions at B and C are equal, (*b*) the corresponding reactions at B and C.

4.34 Rod ABC is bent in the shape of a circular arc of radius R. Determine (*a*) the value of θ which minimizes the magnitude of the reaction at C, (*b*) the corresponding reactions at B and C.

4.35 Neglecting friction, determine the tension in cable ABD and the reaction at C when $\theta = 40°$.

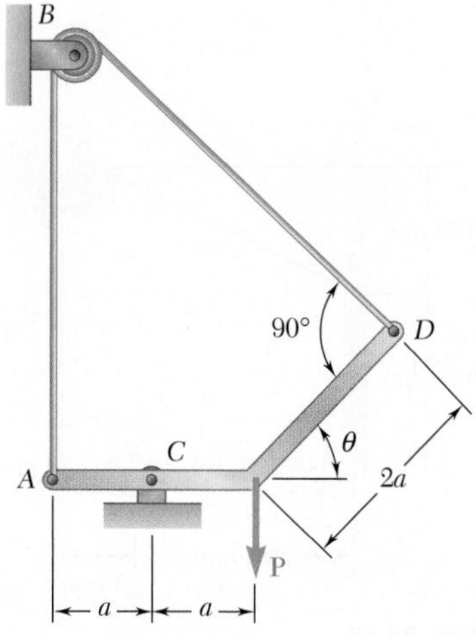

Fig. P4.35 and *P4.36*

4.36 Neglecting friction, determine (*a*) the value of θ for which the tension in cable ABD is $3P/4$, (*b*) the corresponding reaction at C.

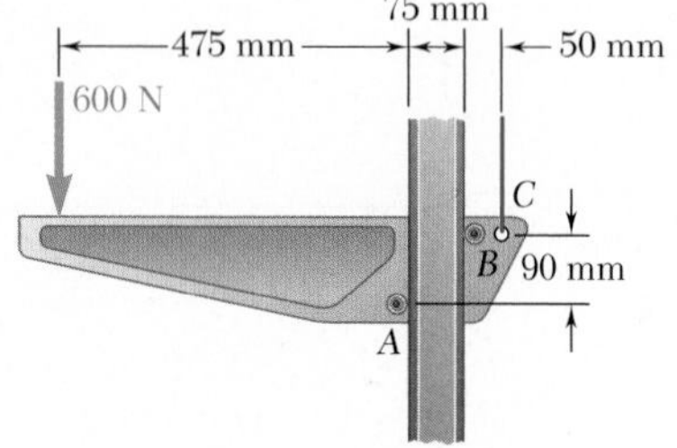

Fig. P4.37

4.37 A movable bracket is held at rest by a cable attached at C and by frictionless rollers at A and B. For the loading shown, determine (*a*) the tension in the cable, (*b*) the reactions at A and B.

4.38 To cross a crevasse, three mountain climbers position a 3.5-m-long ladder as shown. Neglecting friction at A and B and knowing that the hiker at A exerts a horizontal force **P** on the end of the ladder, determine (*a*) the reactions at A and B, (*b*) the force **P**.

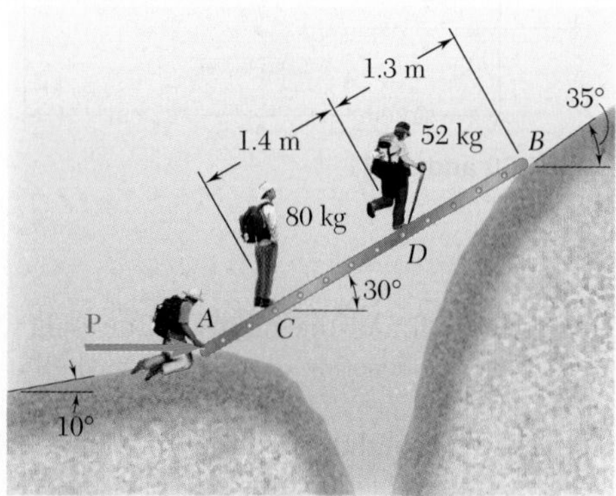

Fig. P4.38

4.39 Rod $ABCD$ is bent in the shape of a circular arc of radius 4 cm and rests against frictionless surfaces at A and D. Knowing that the collar at B can move freely on the rod and that $\theta = 45°$, determine (*a*) the tension in cord OB, (*b*) the reactions at A and D.

4.40 Rod $ABCD$ is bent in the shape of a circular arc of radius 4 cm and rests against frictionless surfaces at A and D. Knowing that the collar at B can move freely on the rod, determine (*a*) the value of θ for which the tension in cord OB is as small as possible, (*b*) the corresponding value of the tension, (*c*) the reactions at A and D.

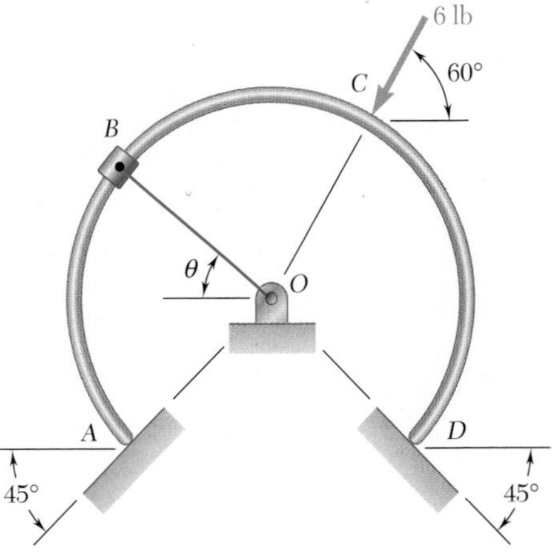

Fig. P4.39 and P4.40

4.41 A movable bracket is held at rest by a cable attached at E and by frictionless rollers. Knowing that the width of post FG is slightly less than the distance between the rollers, determine the force exerted on the post by each roller when $\alpha = 20°$.

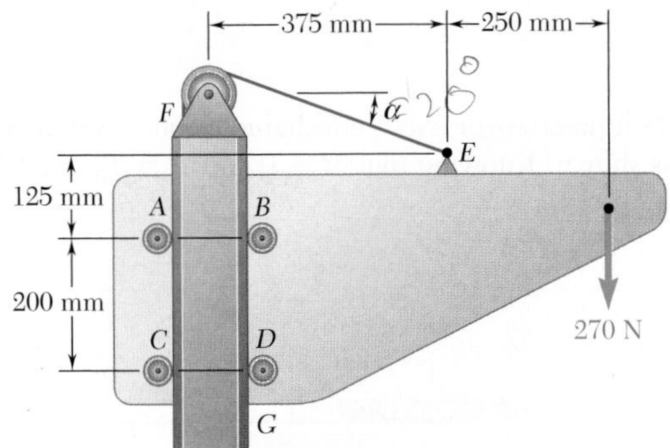

Fig. P4.41

4.42 Solve Prob. 4.41 when $\alpha = 30°$.

4.43 A parabolic slot has been cut in plate AD, and the plate has been placed so that the slot fits two fixed, frictionless pins B and C. The equation of the slot is $y = x^2/4$, where x and y are expressed in cm. Knowing that the input force $P = 2$ N, determine (*a*) the force each pin exerts on the plate, (*b*) the output force **Q**.

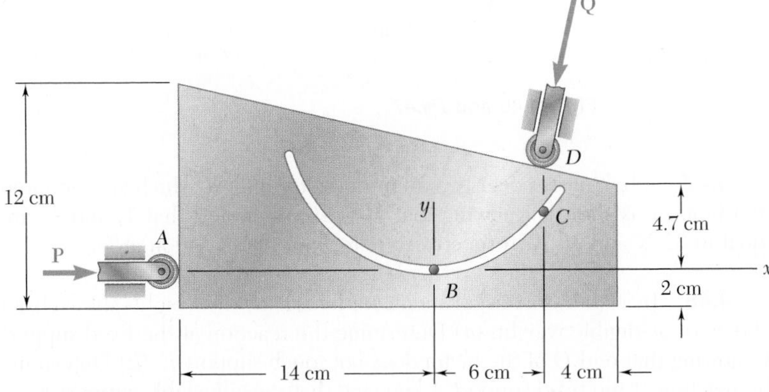

Fig. *P4.43* and *P4.44*

4.44 A parabolic slot has been cut in plate AD, and the plate has been placed so that the slot fits two fixed, frictionless pins B and C. The equation of the slot is $y = x^2/4$, where x and y are expressed in inches. Knowing that the maximum allowable force exerted on the roller at D is 4 N, determine (*a*) the corresponding magnitude of the input force **P**, (*b*) the force each pin exerts on the plate.

4.45 A 10-kg block can be supported in the three different ways shown. Knowing that the pulleys have a 100-mm radius, determine the reaction at A in each case.

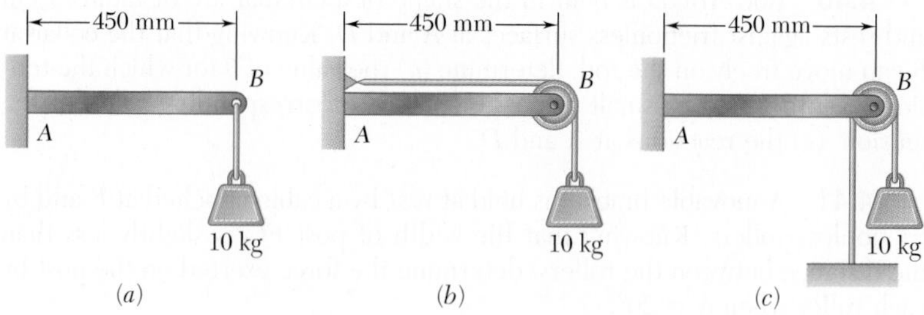

Fig. P4.45

4.46 A belt passes over two 5-cm-diameter pulleys which are mounted on a bracket as shown. Knowing that $M = 0$ and $T_i = T_o = 24$ N, determine the reaction at C.

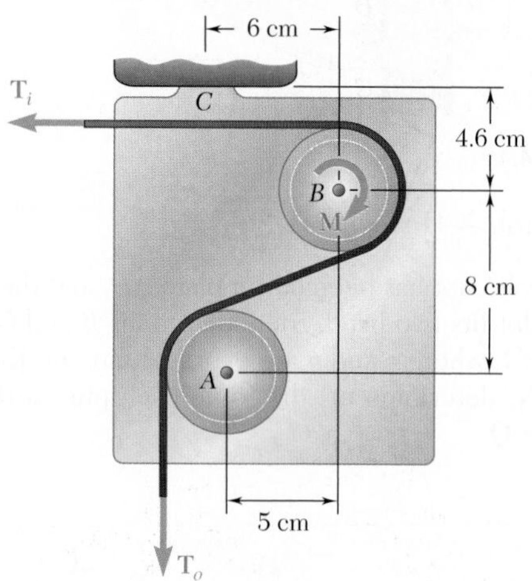

Fig. P4.46 and *P4.47*

4.47 A belt passes over two 5-cm-diameter pulleys which are mounted on a bracket as shown. Knowing that $M = 16$ N · m and that T_i and T_o are equal to 32 N and 16 N, respectively, determine the reaction at C.

4.48 In a laboratory experiment, students hang the weights shown from a beam of negligible weight. (*a*) Determine the reaction at the fixed support A knowing that end D of the beam does not touch support E. (*b*) Determine the reaction at the fixed support A knowing that the adjustable support E exerts an upward force of 2.4 N on the beam.

4.49 In a laboratory experiment, students hang the weights shown from a beam of negligible weight. Determine the range of values of the force exerted on the beam by the adjustable support E for which the magnitude of the couple at A does not exceed 40 N · m.

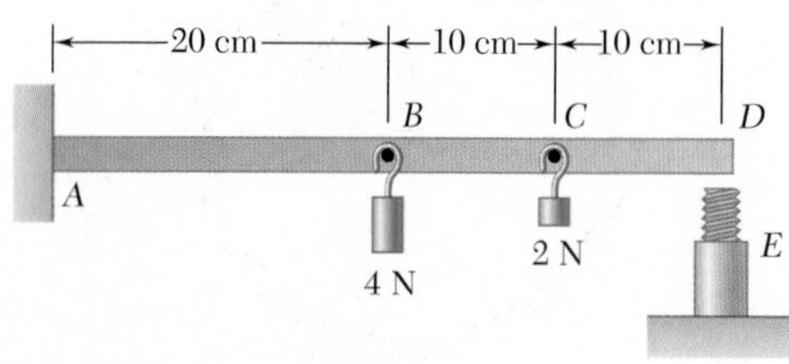

Fig. P4.48 and *P4.49*

4.50 The rig shown consists of a 5.4-kN horizontal member *ABC* and a vertical member *DBE* welded together at *B*. The rig is being used to raise a 16.2-kN crate at a distance $x = 4.8$ m from the vertical member *DBE*. If the tension in the cable is 18 kN, determine the reaction at *E* assuming that the cable is (*a*) anchored at *F* as shown in the figure, (*b*) attached to the vertical member at a point located 0.4 m above *E*.

4.51 The rig shown consists of a 5.4-kN horizontal member *ABC* and a vertical member *DBE* welded together at *B* and is used to raise a 16.2-kN crate. Determine (*a*) the required tension in cable *ADCF* if the maximum value of the couple at *E* is to be as small as possible as *x* varies from 0.6 m to 7 m, (*b*) the corresponding maximum value of the couple.

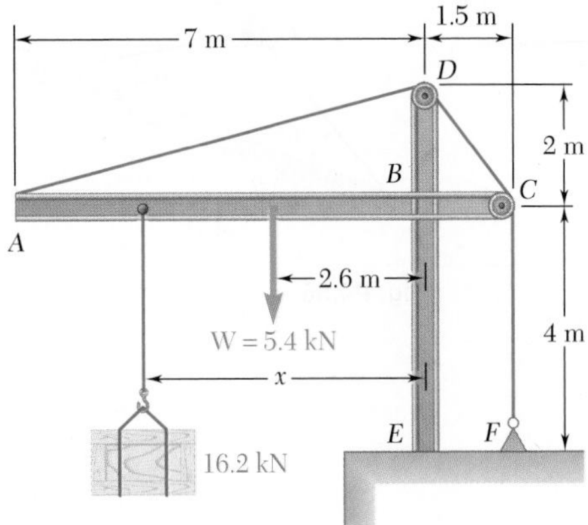

Fig. P4.50 and P4.51

4.52 A 160-kg utility pole is used to support at *C* the end of an electric wire. The tension in the wire is 540 N, and the wire forms an angle of 15° with the horizontal at *C*. Determine the largest and smallest allowable tensions in the guy cable *BD* if the magnitude of the couple at *A* can not exceed 360 N · m.

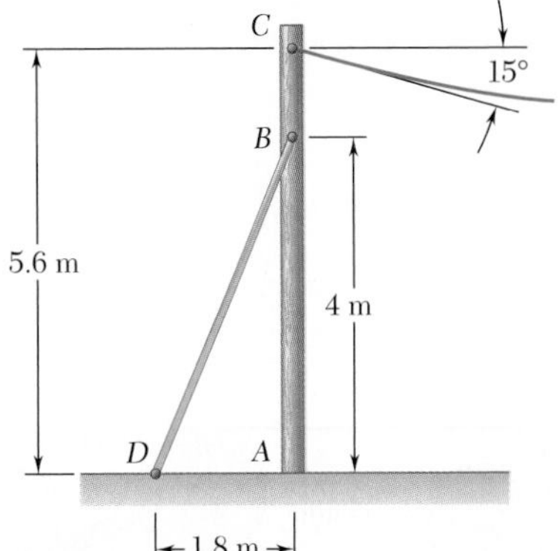

Fig. P4.52

4.53 Uniform rod *AB* of length l and mass m lies in a vertical plane and is acted upon by a couple **M**. The ends of the rod are connected to small rollers which rest against frictionless surfaces. (*a*) Express the angle θ corresponding to equilibrium in terms of M, m, g, and l. (*b*) Determine the value of θ corresponding to equilibrium when $M = 2.7$ N · m, $m = 2$ kg, and $l = 0.8$ m.

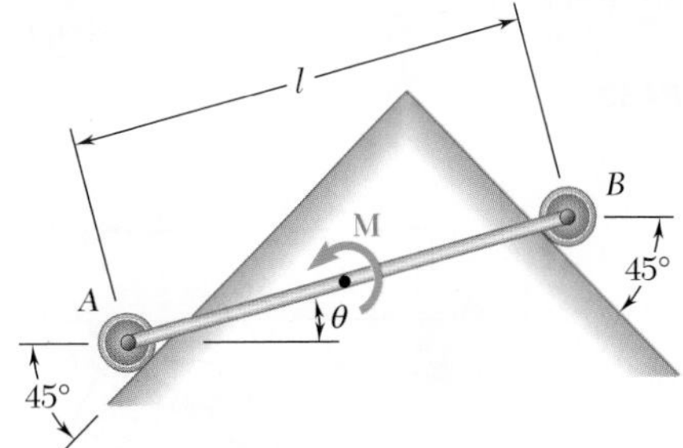

Fig. P4.53

4.54 Rod *AB* of length l and negligible weight lies in a vertical plane and is pinned to blocks *A* and *B*. The weight of each block is *W*, and the blocks are connected by an elastic cord which passes over a pulley at *C*. Neglecting friction between the blocks and the guides, determine the value of θ for which the tension in the cord is equal to (*a*) zero, (*b*) *W*.

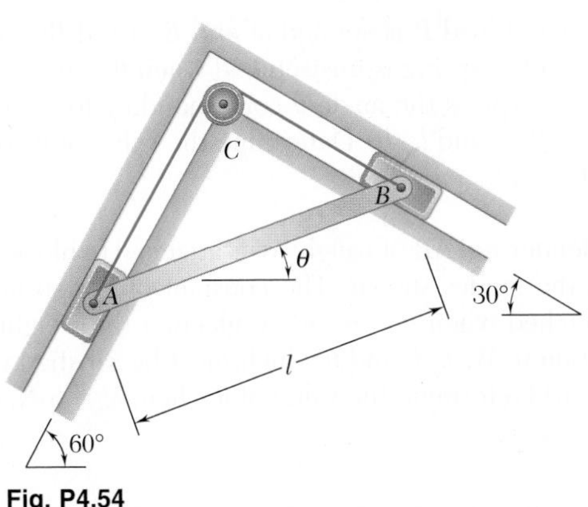

Fig. P4.54

4.55 A thin, uniform ring of mass m and radius R is attached by a frictionless pin to a collar at *A* and rests against a small roller at *B*. The ring lies in a vertical plane, and the collar can move freely on a horizontal rod and is acted upon by a horizontal force **P**. (*a*) Express the angle θ corresponding to equilibrium in terms of m, g, and P. (*b*) Determine the value of θ corresponding to equilibrium when $m = 700$ g and $P = 3$ N.

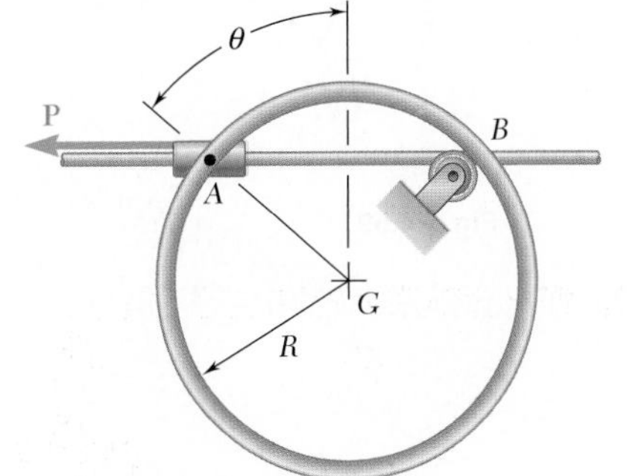

Fig. *P4.55*

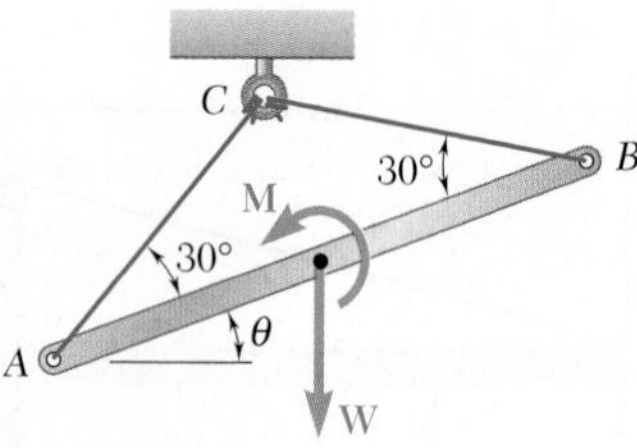

Fig. P4.56

4.56 A uniform rod having a length of 1 m and mass of 2 kg is suspended from two cords AC and BC. Determine the angle θ corresponding to the equilibrium position when a couple $\mathbf{M}$ of magnitude 3 N · m is applied to the rod.

4.57 A vertical load $\mathbf{P}$ is applied at end B of rod BC. The constant of the spring is k, and the spring is unstretched when $\theta = 90°$. (*a*) Neglecting the weight of the rod, express the angle θ corresponding to equilibrium in terms of P, k, and l. (*b*) Determine the value of θ corresponding to equilibrium when $P = \frac{1}{4}kl$.

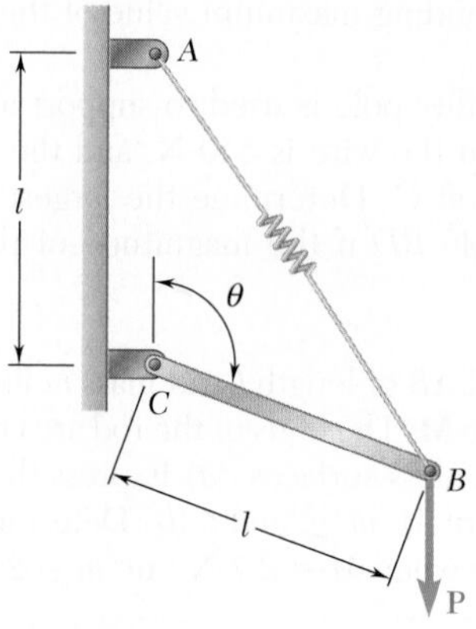

Fig. P4.57

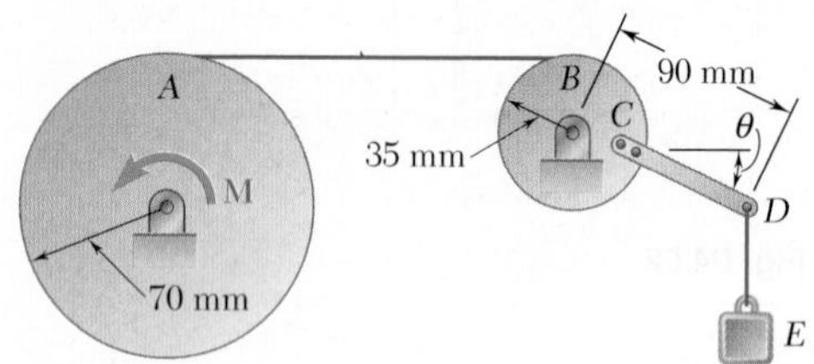

Fig. *P4.58*

4.58 Cable AB is wrapped around two drums as shown. Attached to drum A is a torsion spring for which $M = k\phi$, where $k = 58$ N · m/rad and ϕ is the angle of rotation in radians of the drum. Knowing that the mass of block E is 10 kg and that the torsion spring is unstretched when $\theta = 0$, determine the value of θ corresponding to equilibrium.

4.59 A vertical load $\mathbf{P}$ is applied at end B of rod BC. The constant of the spring is k and the spring is unstretched when $\theta = 0$. (*a*) Neglecting the weight of the rod, express the angle θ corresponding to the equilibrium position in terms of P, k, and l. (*b*) Determine the value of θ corresponding to equilibrium if $P = 2kl$.

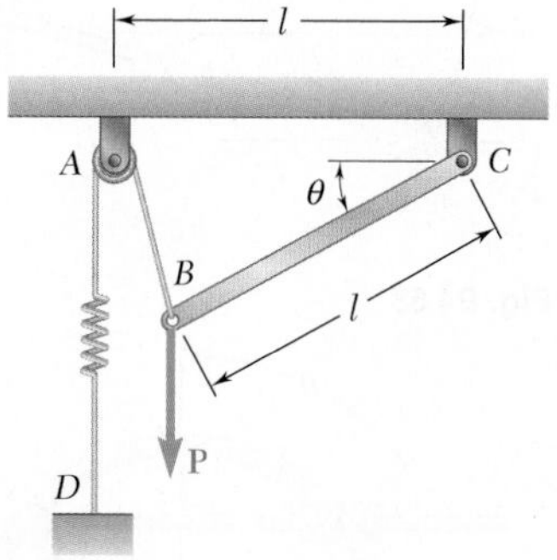

Fig. P4.59

4.60 A slender rod AB of weight W is attached to blocks A and B which move freely in the guides shown. The constant of the spring is k, and the spring is unstretched when $\theta = 0$. (*a*) Neglecting the weight of the blocks, derive an equation in W, k, l, and θ which must be satisfied when the rod is in equilibrium. (*b*) Determine the value of θ when $W = 8$ N, $l = 76$ cm, and $k = 1.8$ N/m.

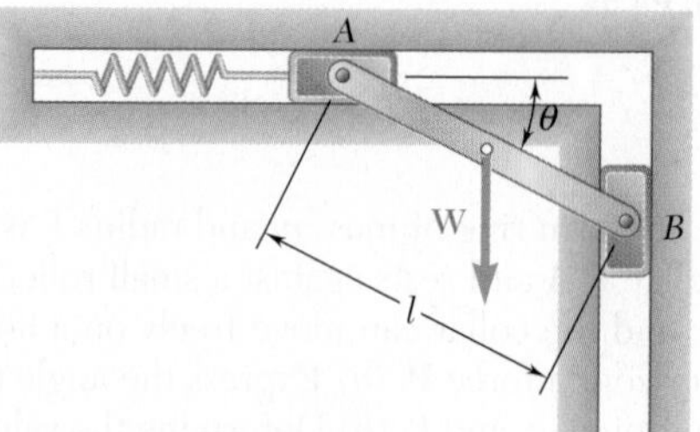

Fig. P4.60

4.61 The bracket ABC can be supported in the eight different ways shown. All connections consist of frictionless pins, rollers, or short links. In each case, determine whether (*a*) the plate is completely, partially, or improperly constrained, (*b*) the reactions are statically determinate or indeterminate, (*c*) the equilibrium of the plate is maintained in the position shown. Also wherever possible, compute the reactions assuming that the magnitude of the force **P** is 100 N.

4.62 Eight identical 50 × 76-cm rectangular plates each weighing 100 N are held in a vertical plane as shown. All connections consist of frictionless pins, rollers, or short links. For each case, answer the questions listed in Prob. 4.61, and wherever possible, compute the reactions.

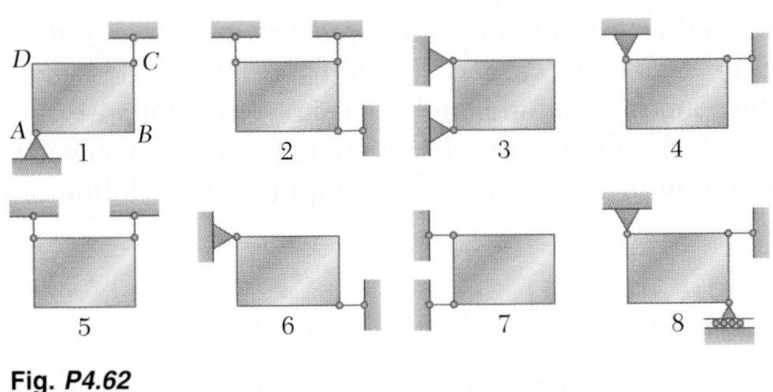

Fig. *P4.62*

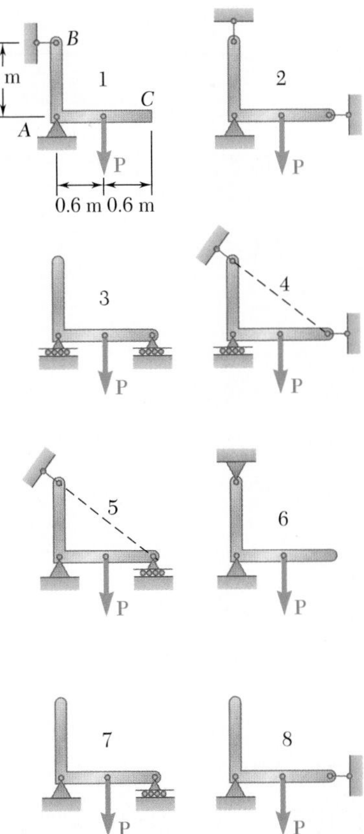

Fig. P4.61

4.6. EQUILIBRIUM OF A TWO-FORCE BODY

A particular case of equilibrium which is of considerable interest is that of a rigid body subjected to two forces. Such a body is commonly called a *two-force body*. It will be shown that *if a two-force body is in equilibrium, the two forces must have the same magnitude, the same line of action, and opposite sense.*

Consider a corner plate subjected to two forces $\mathbf{F}_1$ and $\mathbf{F}_2$ acting at A and B, respectively (Fig. 4.8*a*). If the plate is to be in equilibrium, the sum of the moments of $\mathbf{F}_1$ and $\mathbf{F}_2$ about any point must be zero. First, we sum moments about A. Since the moment of $\mathbf{F}_1$ is obviously zero, the moment of $\mathbf{F}_2$ must also be zero and the line of action of $\mathbf{F}_2$ must pass through A (Fig. 4.8*b*). Summing moments about B, we prove similarly that the line of action of $\mathbf{F}_1$ must pass through B (Fig. 4.8*c*). Therefore, both forces have the same line of action (line AB). From either of the equations $\Sigma F_x = 0$ and $\Sigma F_y = 0$ it is seen that they must also have the same magnitude but opposite sense.

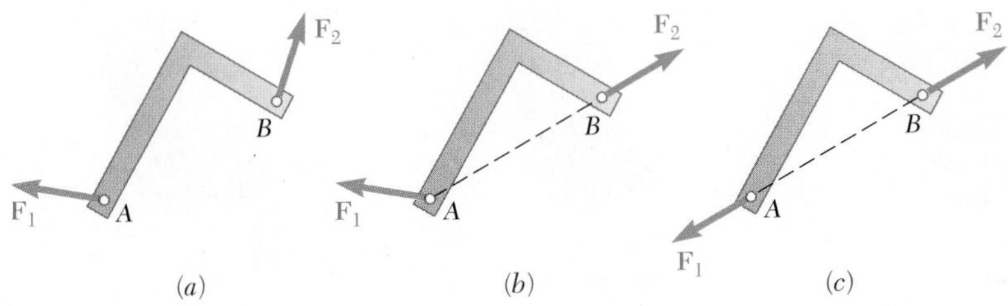

Fig. 4.8

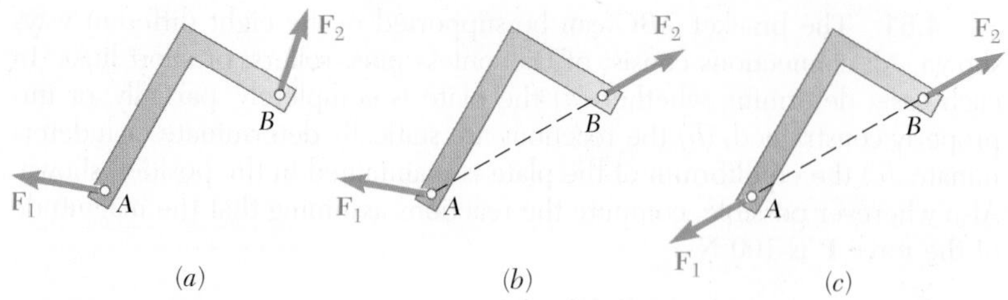

Fig. 4.8 *(repeated)*

If several forces act at two points A and B, the forces acting at A can be replaced by their resultant $\mathbf{F}_1$ and those acting at B can be replaced by their resultant $\mathbf{F}_2$. Thus a two-force body can be more generally defined as *a rigid body subjected to forces acting at only two points*. The resultants $\mathbf{F}_1$ and $\mathbf{F}_2$ then must have the same line of action, the same magnitude, and opposite sense (Fig. 4.8).

In the study of structures, frames, and machines, you will see how the recognition of two-force bodies simplifies the solution of certain problems.

4.7. EQUILIBRIUM OF A THREE-FORCE BODY

Another case of equilibrium that is of great interest is that of a *three-force body*, that is, a rigid body subjected to three forces or, more generally, *a rigid body subjected to forces acting at only three points*. Consider a rigid body subjected to a system of forces which can be reduced to three forces $\mathbf{F}_1$, $\mathbf{F}_2$, and $\mathbf{F}_3$ acting at A, B, and C, respectively (Fig. 4.9*a*). It will be shown that if the body is in equilibrium, *the lines of action of the three forces must be either concurrent or parallel.*

Since the rigid body is in equilibrium, the sum of the moments of $\mathbf{F}_1$, $\mathbf{F}_2$, and $\mathbf{F}_3$ about any point must be zero. Assuming that the lines of action of $\mathbf{F}_1$ and $\mathbf{F}_2$ intersect and denoting their point of intersection by D, we sum moments about D (Fig. 4.9*b*). Since the moments of $\mathbf{F}_1$ and $\mathbf{F}_2$ about D are zero, the moment of $\mathbf{F}_3$ about D must also be zero, and the line of action of $\mathbf{F}_3$ must pass through D (Fig. 4.9*c*). Therefore, the three lines of action are concurrent. The only exception occurs when none of the lines intersect; the lines of action are then parallel.

Although problems concerning three-force bodies can be solved by the general methods of Secs. 4.3 to 4.5, the property just established can be used to solve them either graphically or mathematically from simple trigonometric or geometric relations.

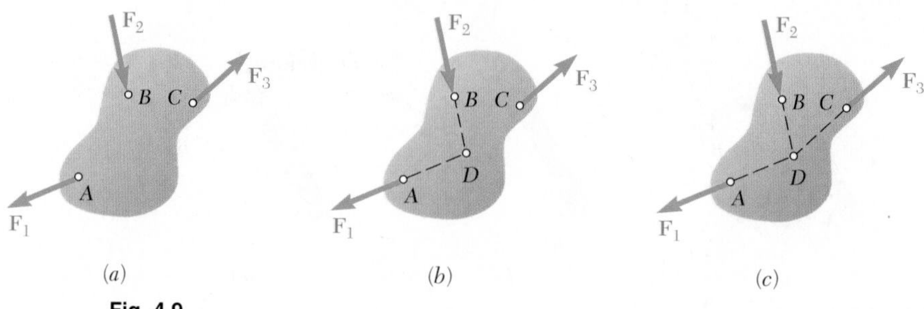

Fig. 4.9

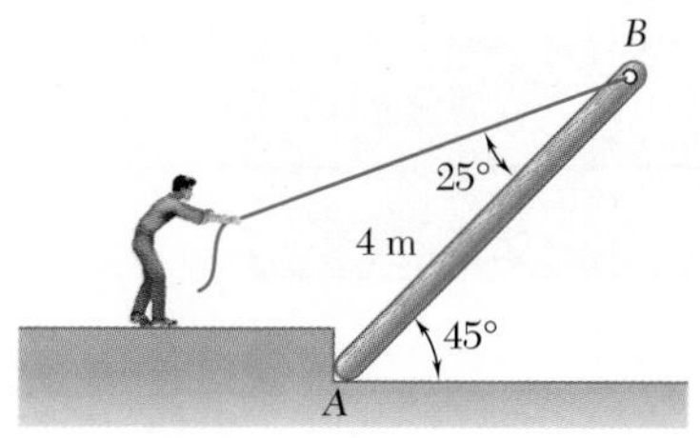

SAMPLE PROBLEM 4.6

A man raises a 10-kg joist, of length 4 m, by pulling on a rope. Find the tension T in the rope and the reaction at A.

SOLUTION

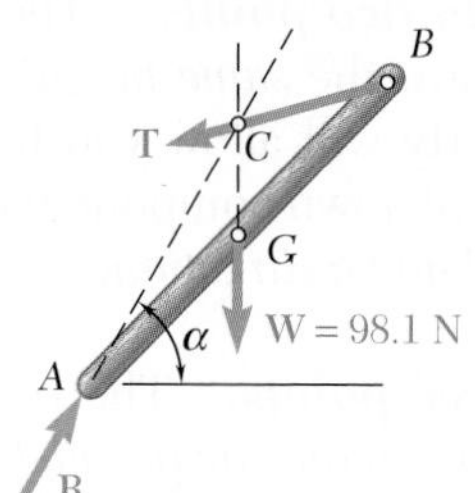

Free-Body Diagram. The joist is a three-force body, since it is acted upon by three forces: its weight **W**, the force **T** exerted by the rope, and the reaction **R** of the ground at A. We note that

$$W = mg = (10 \text{ kg})(9.81 \text{ m/s}^2) = 98.1 \text{ N}$$

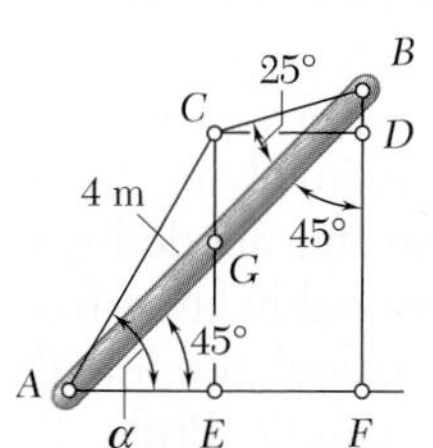

Three-Force Body. Since the joist is a three-force body, the forces acting on it must be concurrent. The reaction **R**, therefore, will pass through the point of intersection C of the lines of action of the weight **W** and the tension force **T**. This fact will be used to determine the angle α that **R** forms with the horizontal.

Drawing the vertical BF through B and the horizontal CD through C, we note that

$$AF = BF = (AB) \cos 45° = (4 \text{ m}) \cos 45° = 2.828 \text{ m}$$
$$CD = EF = AE = \tfrac{1}{2}(AF) = 1.414 \text{ m}$$
$$BD = (CD) \cot (45° + 25°) = (1.414 \text{ m}) \tan 20° = 0.515 \text{ m}$$
$$CE = DF = BF - BD = 2.828 \text{ m} - 0.515 \text{ m} = 2.313 \text{ m}$$

We write

$$\tan \alpha = \frac{CE}{AE} = \frac{2.313 \text{ m}}{1.414 \text{ m}} = 1.636$$

$\alpha = 58.6°$ ◀

We now know the direction of all the forces acting on the joist.

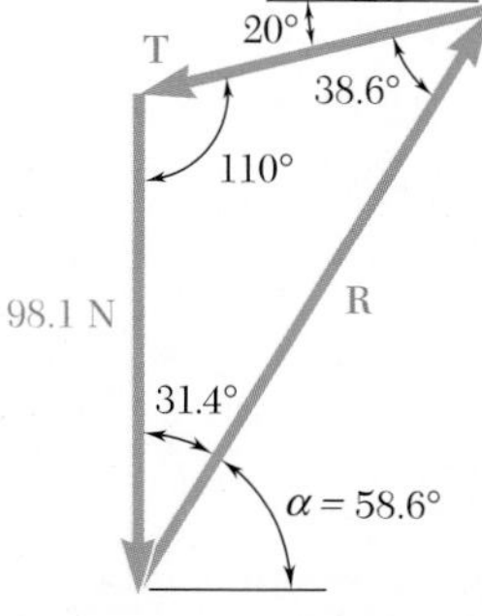

Force Triangle. A force triangle is drawn as shown, and its interior angles are computed from the known directions of the forces. Using the law of sines, we write

$$\frac{T}{\sin 31.4°} = \frac{R}{\sin 110°} = \frac{98.1 \text{ N}}{\sin 38.6°}$$

$T = 81.9 \text{ N}$ ◀

$\mathbf{R} = 147.8 \text{ N} \measuredangle 58.6°$ ◀

SOLVING PROBLEMS ON YOUR OWN

The preceding sections covered two particular cases of equilibrium of a rigid body.

1. *A two-force body is a body subjected to forces at only two points.* The resultants of the forces acting at each of these points must have the *same magnitude, the same line of action, and opposite sense.* This property will allow you to simplify the solutions of some problems by replacing the two unknown components of a reaction by a single force of unknown magnitude but of *known direction*.

2. *A three-force body is subjected to forces at only three points.* The resultants of the forces acting at each of these points must be *concurrent or parallel.* To solve a problem involving a three-force body with concurrent forces, draw your free-body diagram showing that the lines of action of these three forces pass through the same point. The use of geometry will then allow you to complete the solution using a force triangle [Sample Prob. 4.6].

Although the principle noted above for the solution of problems involving three-force bodies is easily understood, it can be difficult to determine the needed geometric constructions. If you encounter difficulty, first draw a reasonably large free-body diagram and then seek a relation between known or easily calculated lengths and a dimension that involves an unknown. This was done in Sample Prob. 4.6, where the easily calculated dimensions AE and CE were used to determine the angle α.

Problems

4.63 Horizontal and vertical links are hinged to a wheel, and forces are applied to the links as shown. Knowing that $a = 75$ mm, determine the value of P and the reaction at A.

4.64 Horizontal and vertical links are hinged to a wheel, and forces are applied to the links as shown. Determine the range of values of the distance a for which the magnitude of the reaction at A does not exceed 180 N.

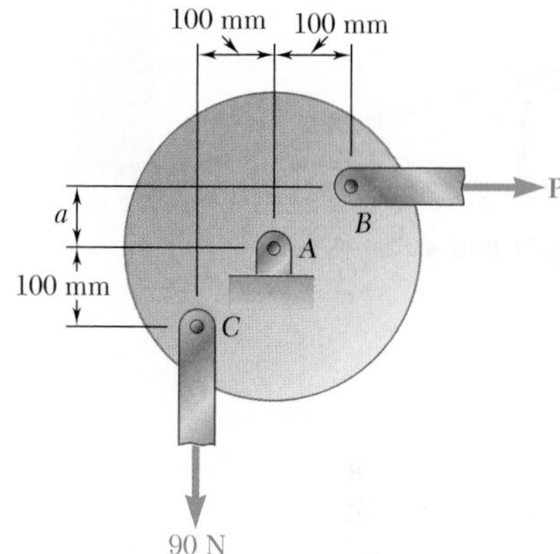

Fig. P4.63 and P4.64

4.65 Using the method of Sec. 4.7, solve Prob. 4.21.

4.66 Using the method of Sec. 4.7, solve Prob. 4.33.

4.67 A T-shaped bracket supports a 150-N load as shown. Determine the reactions at A and C when (*a*) $\alpha = 90°$, (*b*) $\alpha = 45°$.

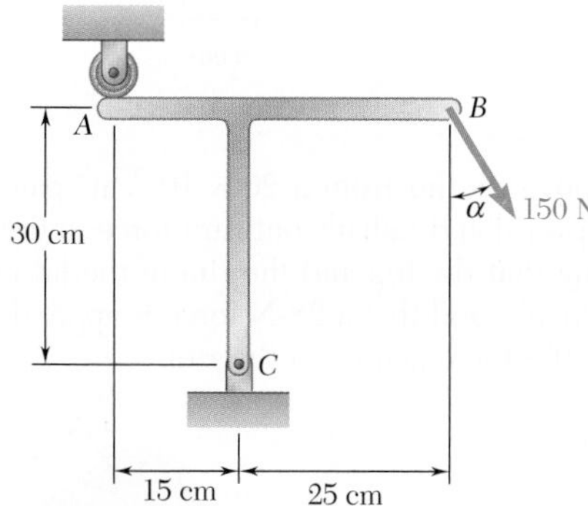

Fig. P4.67

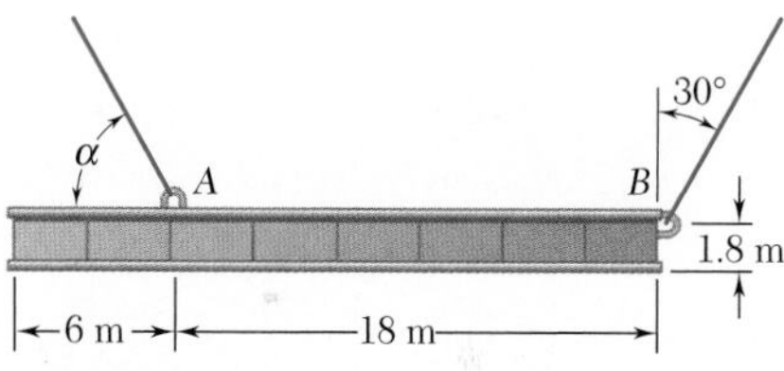

Fig. *P4.68*

4.68 A uniform plate girder weighing 12 kN is held in a horizontal position by two crane cables. Determine the angle α and the tension in each cable.

4.69 To remove a nail, a small block of wood is placed under a crowbar, and a horizontal force **P** is applied as shown. Knowing that $l = 88$ mm and $P = 130$ N, determine the vertical force exerted on the nail and the reaction at B.

4.70 To remove a nail, a small block of wood is placed under a crowbar, and a horizontal force **P** is applied as shown. Knowing that the maximum vertical force needed to extract the nail is 2600 N and that the horizontal force **P** is not to exceed 290 N, determine the largest acceptable value of distance l.

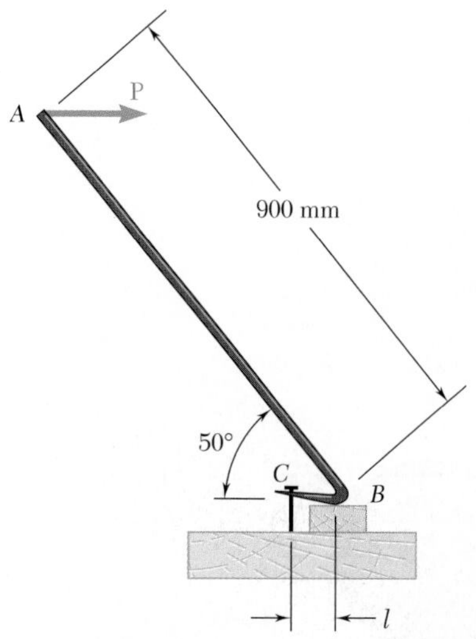

Fig. P4.69 and 4.70

4.71 A worker is raising a 9.2-m-long ladder of mass 53 kg as shown. Knowing that $a = 1.8$ m and that the force exerted by the worker is perpendicular to the ladder, determine (*a*) the force exerted by the worker, (*b*) the reaction at *B*.

4.72 A worker is raising a 9.2-m-long ladder of mass 53 kg as shown. Knowing that the force exerted by the worker is perpendicular to the ladder, determine (*a*) the smallest value of *a* for which the vertical component of the reaction at *B* is zero, (*b*) the corresponding force exerted by the worker.

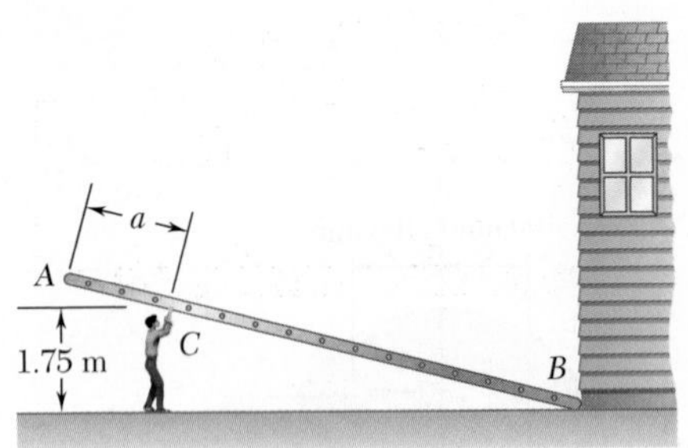

Fig. P4.71 and *4.72*

4.73 To remove the lid from a 20×10^{-3} m^3 can, the tool shown is used to apply an upward and radially outward force to the bottom inside rim of the lid. Assuming that the rim rests against the tool at *A* and that a 40-N force is applied as indicated to the handle, determine the force acting on the rim.

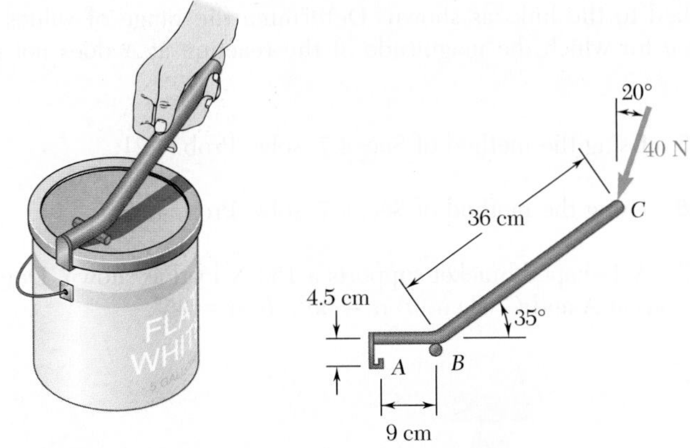

Fig. P4.73

4.74 To remove the lid from a 20×10^{-3} m^3 pail, the tool shown is used to apply an upward and radially outward force to the bottom inside rim of the lid. Assuming that the top and the rim of the lid rest against the tool at *A* and *B*, respectively, and that a 28-N force is applied as indicated to the handle, determine the force acting on the rim.

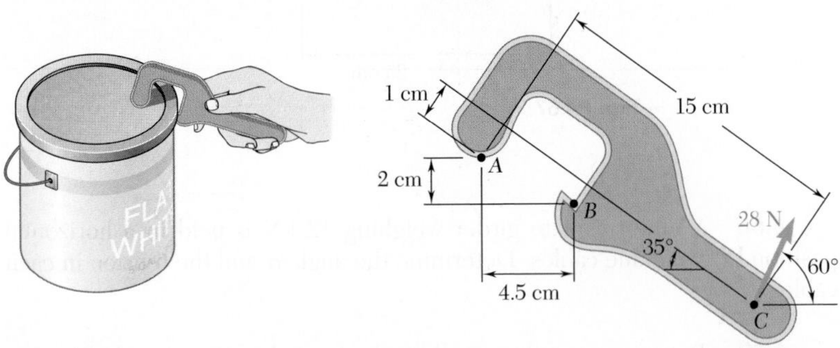

Fig. P4.74

4.75 A 20-kg roller of diameter 200 mm, which is to be used on a tile floor, is resting directly on the subflooring as shown. Knowing that the thickness of each tile is 8 mm, determine the force **P** required to move the roller onto the tiles if the roller is pushed to the left.

4.76 A 20-kg roller of diameter 200 mm, which is to be used on a tile floor, is resting directly on the subflooring as shown. Knowing that the thickness of each tile is 8 mm, determine the force **P** required to move the roller onto the tiles if the roller is pulled to the right.

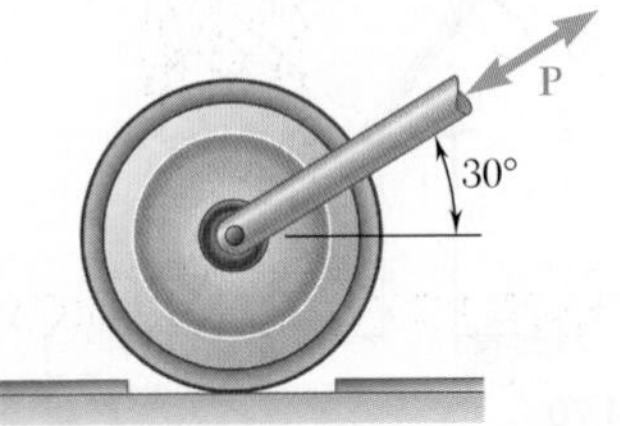

Fig. *P4.75* and P4.76

4.77 The clamp shown is used to hold the rough workpiece C. Knowing that the maximum allowable compressive force on the workpiece is 80 N and neglecting the effect of friction at A, determine the corresponding (a) reaction at B, (b) reaction at A, (c) tension in the bolt.

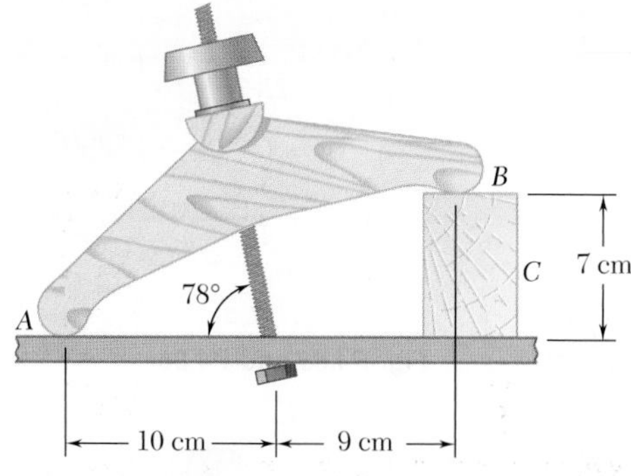

Fig. P4.77

4.78 A small hoist is mounted on the back of a pickup truck and is used to lift a 500-N crate. Determine (a) the force exerted on the hoist by the hydraulic cylinder BC, (b) the reaction at A.

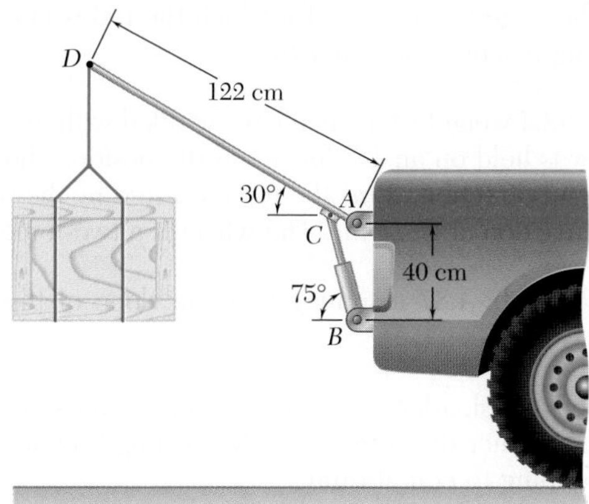

Fig. P4.78

4.79 The L-shaped member ACB is supported by a pin and bracket at C and by an inextensible cord attached at A and B and passing over a frictionless pulley at D. Determine (a) the tension in the cord, (b) the reaction at C.

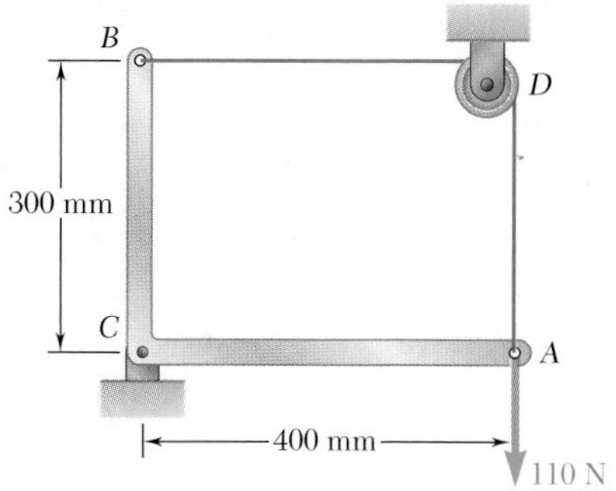

4.80 Member $ABCD$ is supported by a pin and bracket at C and by an inextensible cord attached at A and D and passing over frictionless pulleys at B and E. Neglecting the size of the pulleys, determine the tension in the cord and the reaction at C.

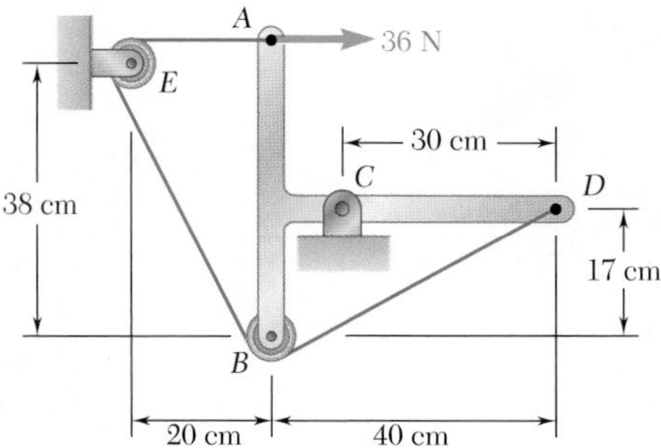

Fig. P4.80

Fig. P4.79

4.81 A modified peavey is used to lift a 20-cm-diameter log weighing 160 N. Knowing that $\theta = 45°$ and that the force exerted at C by the worker is perpendicular to the handle of the peavey, determine (a) the force exerted at C, (b) the reaction at A.

*4.82 A modified peavey is used to lift a 20-cm-diameter log weighing 160 N. Knowing that $\theta = 60°$ and that the force exerted at C by the worker is perpendicular to the handle of the peavey, determine (a) the force exerted at C, (b) the reaction at A.

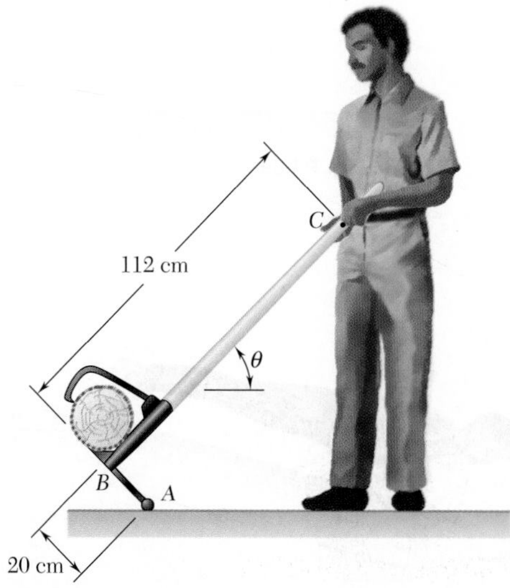

Fig. P4.81 and P4.82

4.83 Using the method of Sec. 4.7, solve Prob. 4.17c.

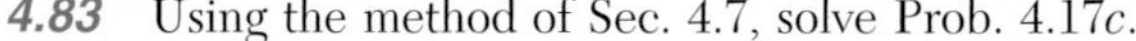

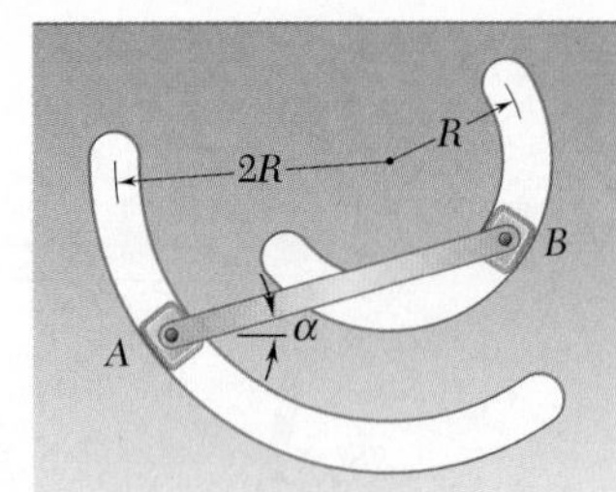

Fig. *P4.85* and P4.86

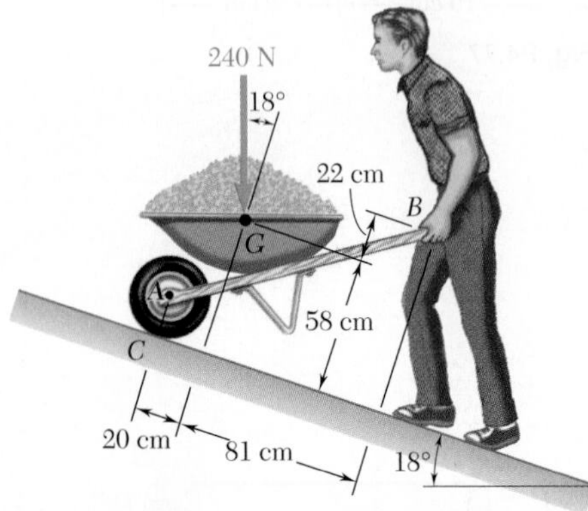

Fig. P4.87

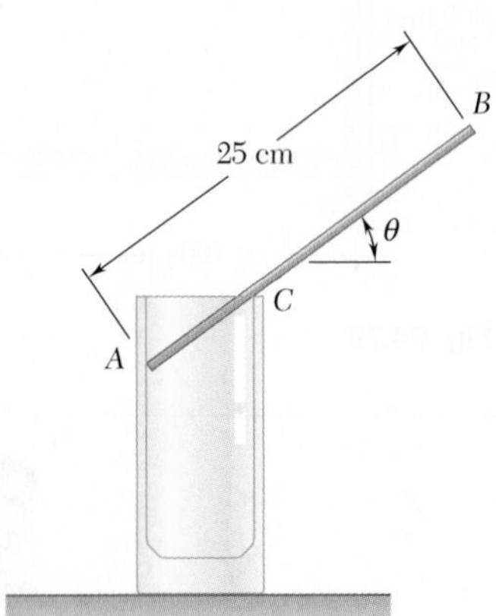

Fig. P4.89

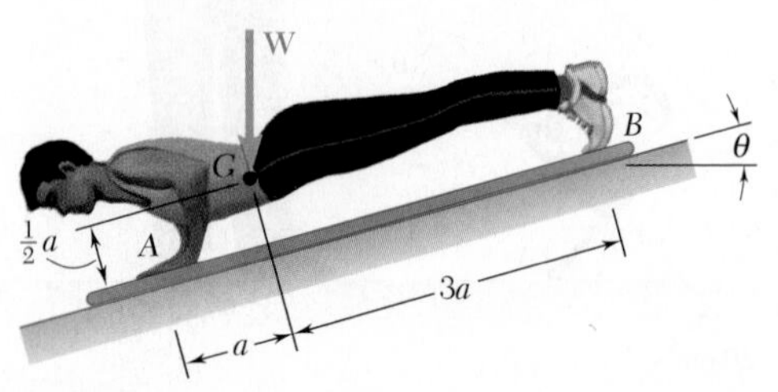

Fig. P4.93

4.84 Using the method of Sec. 4.7, solve Prob. 4.25.

4.85 The uniform rod AB of mass m and length L is attached to two blocks which slide freely in circular slots as shown. Knowing that the rod is in equilibrium and that $L = 2R$, determine (*a*) the angle α that the rod forms with the horizontal, (*b*) the reactions at A and B.

***4.86** The uniform rod AB of mass m and length L is attached to two blocks which slide freely in circular slots as shown. Knowing that $\alpha = 45°$, determine (*a*) the largest value of L for which the rod is in equilibrium, (*b*) the corresponding reactions at A and B.

4.87 The total weight of a wheelbarrow filled with gravel is 240 N. If the wheelbarrow is held on an 18° incline in the position shown, determine the magnitude and direction of (*a*) the force exerted by the worker on each handle, (*b*) the reaction at C. (*Hint.* The wheel is a two-force body.)

4.88 Solve Prob. 4.87 assuming that the slope of the incline is 18° downward.

4.89 A uniform slender rod 25 cm long and weighing 0.02 N is balanced on a glass of inner diameter 7 cm. Neglecting friction, determine the angle θ corresponding to equilibrium.

4.90 A slender rod of length L and weight W is attached to collars which can slide freely along the guides shown. Knowing that the rod is in equilibrium, derive an expression for the angle θ in terms of the angle β.

4.91 A 10-kg slender rod of length L is attached to collars which can slide freely along the guides shown. Knowing that the rod is in equilibrium and that $\beta = 25°$, determine (*a*) the angle θ that the rod forms with the vertical, (*b*) the reactions at A and B.

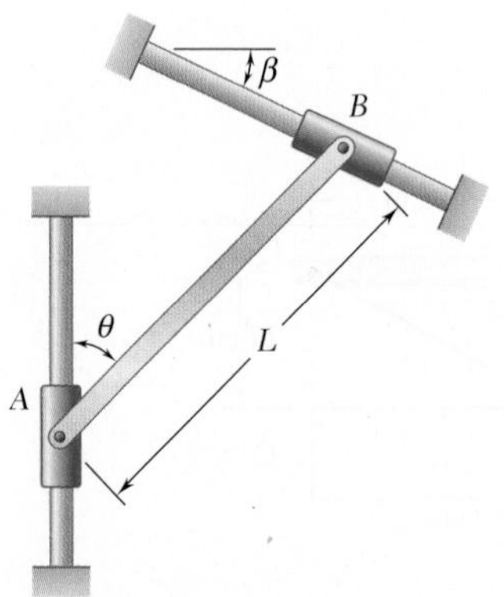

Fig. P4.90 and P4.91

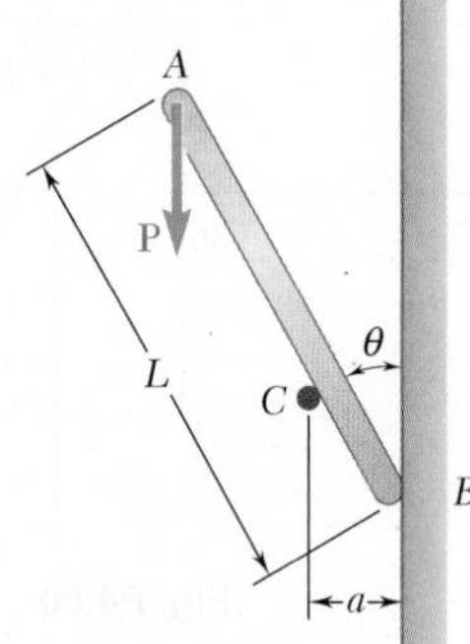

Fig. P4.92

4.92 A slender rod of length L is lodged between peg C and the vertical wall. It supports a load $\mathbf{P}$ at end A. Neglecting friction and the weight of the rod, determine the angle θ corresponding to equilibrium.

4.93 An athlete is doing push-ups on an inclined board. Neglecting friction between his shoes and the board, determine the value of θ if he wants to limit the magnitude of the total force exerted on his hands to 80 percent of his weight.

4.94 A uniform slender rod of length $2L$ and weight W rests against a roller at D and is held in the equilibrium position shown by a cord of length a. Knowing that $L = 20$ cm, determine (*a*) the angle θ, (*b*) the length a.

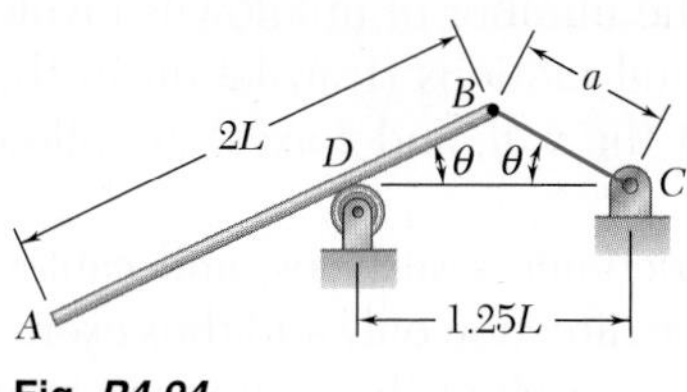

Fig. *P4.94*

4.95 A uniform slender rod of mass m and length $4r$ rests on the surface shown and is held in the given equilibrium position by the force **P**. Neglecting the effect of friction at A and C, (*a*) determine the angle θ, (*b*) derive an expression for P in terms of m and g.

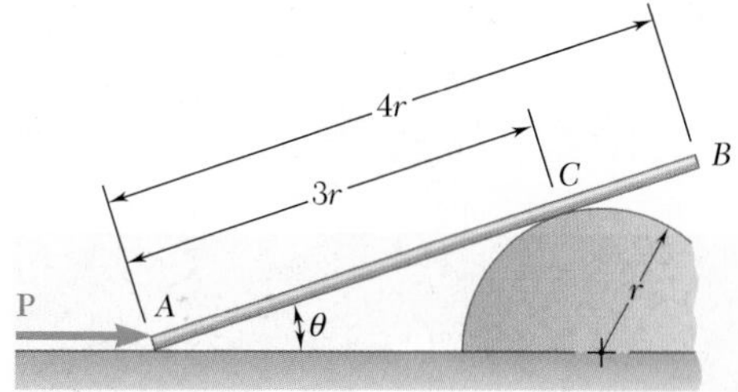

Fig. P4.95

EQUILIBRIUM IN THREE DIMENSIONS

4.8. EQUILIBRIUM OF A RIGID BODY IN THREE DIMENSIONS

We saw in Sec. 4.1 that six scalar equations are required to express the conditions for the equilibrium of a rigid body in the general three-dimensional case:

$$\Sigma F_x = 0 \qquad \Sigma F_y = 0 \qquad \Sigma F_z = 0 \tag{4.2}$$
$$\Sigma M_x = 0 \qquad \Sigma M_y = 0 \qquad \Sigma M_z = 0 \tag{4.3}$$

These equations can be solved for no more than *six unknowns*, which generally will represent reactions at supports or connections.

In most problems the scalar equations (4.2) and (4.3) will be more conveniently obtained if we first express in vector form the conditions for the equilibrium of the rigid body considered. We write

$$\Sigma \mathbf{F} = 0 \qquad \Sigma \mathbf{M}_O = \Sigma(\mathbf{r} \times \mathbf{F}) = 0 \tag{4.1}$$

and express the forces **F** and position vectors **r** in terms of scalar components and unit vectors. Next, we compute all vector products, either by direct calculation or by means of determinants (see Sec. 3.8). We observe that as many as three unknown reaction components may be eliminated from these computations through a judicious choice of the point O. By equating to zero the coefficients of the unit vectors in each of the two relations (4.1), we obtain the desired scalar equations.†

4.9. REACTIONS AT SUPPORTS AND CONNECTIONS FOR A THREE-DIMENSIONAL STRUCTURE

The reactions on a three-dimensional structure range from the single force of known direction exerted by a frictionless surface to the force-couple system exerted by a fixed support. Consequently, in problems involving the equilibrium of a three-dimensional structure, there can be between one and six unknowns associated with the reaction at each

†In some problems, it will be found convenient to eliminate the reactions at two points A and B from the solution by writing the equilibrium equation $\Sigma M_{AB} = 0$, which involves the determination of the moments of the forces about the axis AB joining points A and B (see Sample Prob. 4.10).

support or connection. Various types of supports and connections are shown in Fig. 4.10 with their corresponding reactions. A simple way of determining the type of reaction corresponding to a given support or connection and the number of unknowns involved is to find which of the six fundamental motions (translation in the x, y, and z directions, rotation about the x, y, and z axes) are allowed and which motions are prevented.

Ball supports, frictionless surfaces, and cables, for example, prevent translation in one direction only and thus exert a single force whose line of action is known; each of these supports involves one unknown, namely, the magnitude of the reaction. Rollers on rough surfaces and wheels on rails prevent translation in two directions; the corresponding reactions consist of two unknown force components. Rough surfaces in direct contact and ball-and-socket supports prevent translation in three directions; these supports involve three unknown force components.

Photo 4.6 Universal joints, easily seen on the drive shafts of rear-wheel-drive cars and trucks, allow rotational motion to be transferred between two noncollinear shafts.

Some supports and connections can prevent rotation as well as translation; the corresponding reactions include couples as well as forces. For example, the reaction at a fixed support, which prevents any motion (rotation as well as translation), consists of three unknown forces and three unknown couples. A universal joint, which is designed to allow rotation about two axes, will exert a reaction consisting of three unknown force components and one unknown couple.

Other supports and connections are primarily intended to prevent translation; their design, however, is such that they also prevent some rotations. The corresponding reactions consist essentially of force components but *may* also include couples. One group of supports of this type includes hinges and bearings designed to support radial loads only (for example, journal bearings, roller bearings). The corresponding reactions consist of two force components but may also include two couples. Another group includes pin-and-bracket supports, hinges, and bearings designed to support an axial thrust as well as a radial load (for example, ball bearings). The corresponding reactions consist of three force components but may include two couples. However, these supports will not exert any appreciable couples under normal conditions of use. Therefore, *only* force components should be included in their analysis *unless* it is found that couples are necessary to maintain the equilibrium of the rigid body, or unless the support is known to have been specifically designed to exert a couple (see Probs. 4.128 through 4.131).

Photo 4.7 The pillow block bearing shown supports the shaft of a fan used to ventilate a foundry.

If the reactions involve more than six unknowns, there are more unknowns than equations, and some of the reactions are *statically indeterminate*. If the reactions involve fewer than six unknowns, there are more equations than unknowns, and some of the equations of equilibrium cannot be satisfied under general loading conditions; the rigid body is only *partially constrained.* Under the particular loading conditions corresponding to a given problem, however, the extra equations often reduce to trivial identities, such as $0 = 0$, and can be disregarded; although only partially constrained, the rigid body remains in equilibrium (see Sample Probs. 4.7 and 4.8). Even with six or more unknowns, it is possible that some equations of equilibrium will not be satisfied. This can occur when the reactions associated with the given supports either are parallel or intersect the same line; the rigid body is then *improperly constrained.*

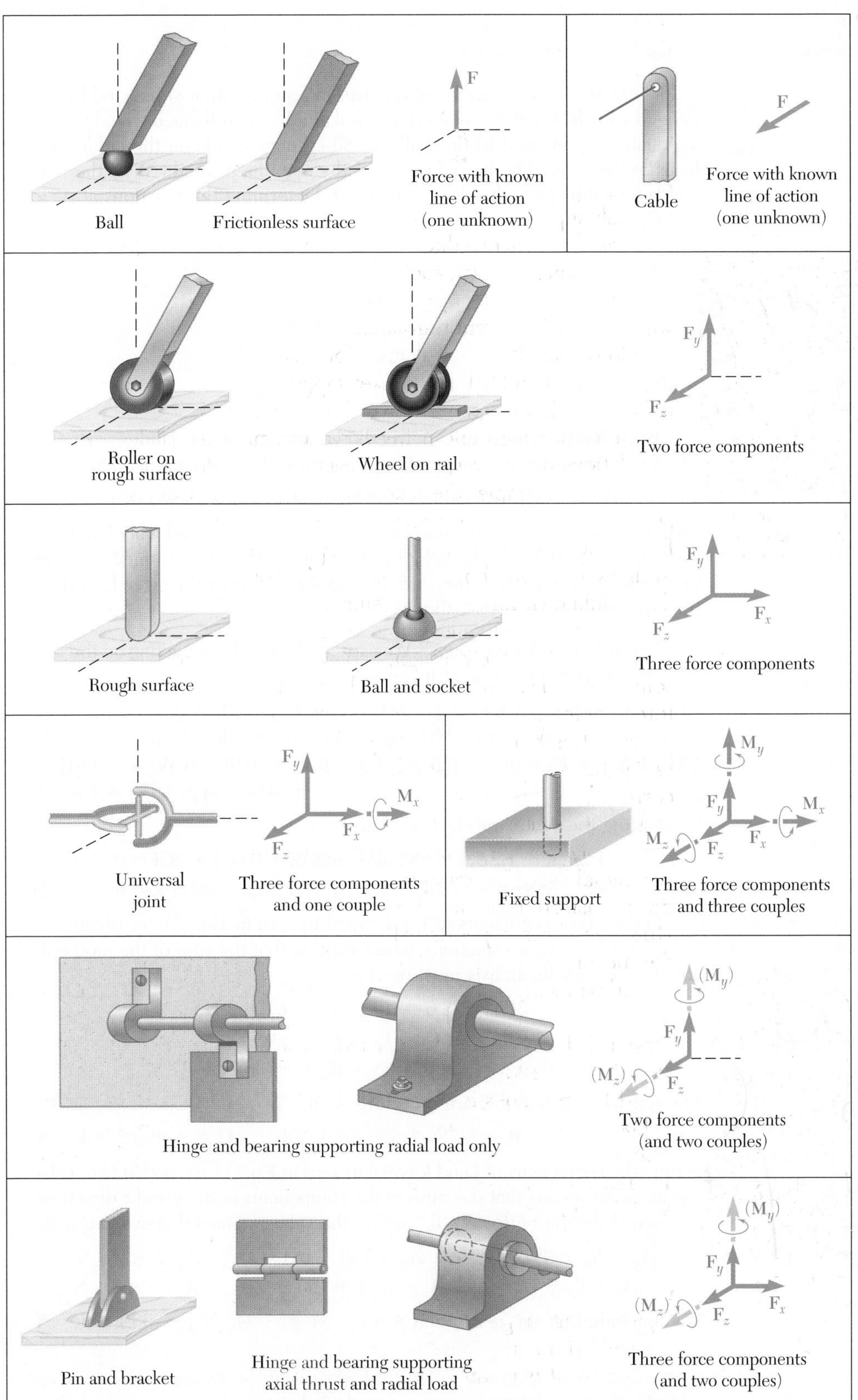

Fig. 4.10 Reactions at supports and connections.

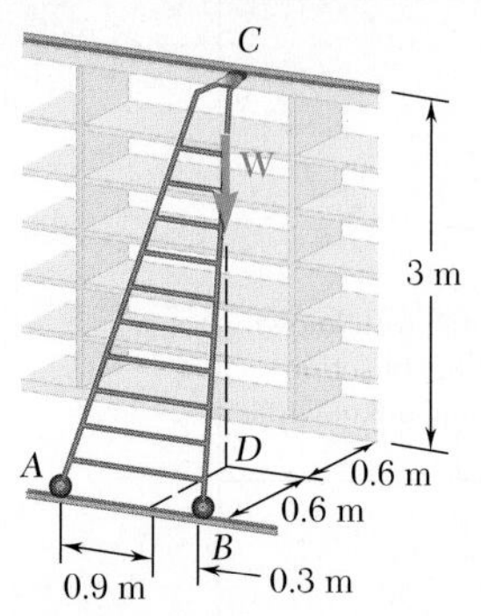

SAMPLE PROBLEM 4.7

A 20-kg ladder used to reach high shelves in a storeroom is supported by two flanged wheels A and B mounted on a rail and by an unflanged wheel C resting against a rail fixed to the wall. An 80-kg man stands on the ladder and leans to the right. The line of action of the combined weight $\mathbf{W}$ of the man and ladder intersects the floor at point D. Determine the reactions at A, B, and C.

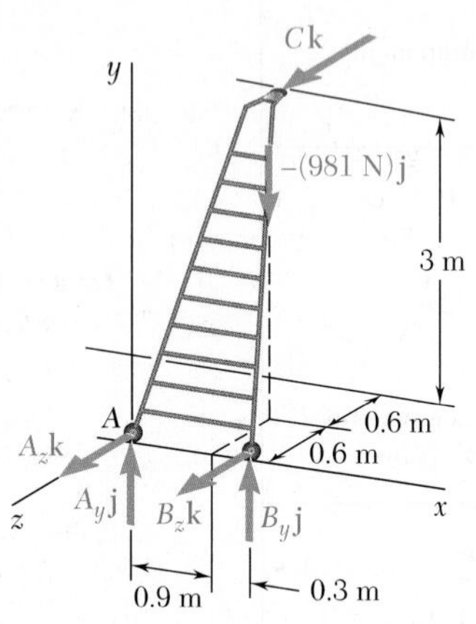

SOLUTION

Free-Body Diagram. A free-body diagram of the ladder is drawn. The forces involved are the combined weight of the man and ladder.

$$\mathbf{W} = -mg\mathbf{j} = -(80 \text{ kg} + 20 \text{ kg})(9.81 \text{ m/s}^2)\mathbf{j} = -(981 \text{ N})\mathbf{j}$$

and five unknown reaction components, two at each flanged wheel and one at the unflanged wheel. The ladder is thus only partially constrained; it is free to roll along the rails. It is, however, in equilibrium under the given load since the equation $\Sigma F_x = 0$ is satisfied.

Equilibrium Equations. We express that the forces acting on the ladder form a system equivalent to zero:

$$\Sigma\mathbf{F} = 0: \quad A_y\mathbf{j} + A_z\mathbf{k} + B_y\mathbf{j} + B_z\mathbf{k} - (981 \text{ N})\mathbf{j} + C\mathbf{k} = 0$$

$$(A_y + B_y - 981 \text{ N})\mathbf{j} + (A_z + B_z + C)\mathbf{k} = 0 \qquad (1)$$

$$\Sigma\mathbf{M}_A = \Sigma(\mathbf{r} \times \mathbf{F}) = 0: \quad 1.2\mathbf{i} \times (B_y\mathbf{j} + B_z\mathbf{k}) + (0.9\mathbf{i} - 0.6\mathbf{k}) \times (-981\mathbf{j}) + (0.6\mathbf{i} + 3\mathbf{j} - 1.2\mathbf{k}) \times C\mathbf{k} = 0$$

Computing the vector product, we have†

$$1.2B_y\mathbf{k} - 1.2B_z\mathbf{j} - 882.9\mathbf{k} - 588.6\mathbf{i} - 0.6C\mathbf{j} + 3C\mathbf{i} = 0$$

$$(3C - 588.6)\mathbf{i} - (1.2B_z + 0.6C)\mathbf{j} + (1.2B_y - 882.9)\mathbf{k} = 0 \qquad (2)$$

Setting the coefficients of **i**, **j**, **k** equal to zero in Eq. (2), we obtain the following three scalar equations, which express that the sum of the moments about each coordinate axis must be zero:

$$3C - 588.6 = 0 \qquad C = +196.2 \text{ N}$$

$$1.2B_z + 0.6C = 0 \qquad B_z = -98.1 \text{ N}$$

$$1.2B_y - 882.9 = 0 \qquad B_y = +736 \text{ N}$$

The reactions at B and C are therefore

$$\mathbf{B} = +(736 \text{ N})\mathbf{j} - (98.1 \text{ N})\mathbf{k} \qquad \mathbf{C} = +(196.2 \text{ N})\mathbf{k} \quad ◀$$

Setting the coefficients of **j** and **k** equal to zero in Eq. (1), we obtain two scalar equations expressing that the sums of the components in the y and z directions are zero. Substituting for B_y, B_z, and C the values obtained above, we write

$$A_y + B_y - 981 = 0 \qquad A_y + 736 - 981 = 0 \qquad A_y = +245 \text{ N}$$

$$A_z + B_z + C = 0 \qquad A_z - 98.1 + 196.2 = 0 \qquad A_z = -98.1 \text{ N}$$

We conclude that the reaction at A is $\quad \mathbf{A} = +(245 \text{ N})\mathbf{j} - (98.1 \text{ N})\mathbf{k} \quad ◀$

†The moments in this sample problem and in Sample Probs. 4.8 and 4.9 can also be expressed in the form of determinants (see Sample Prob. 3.10).

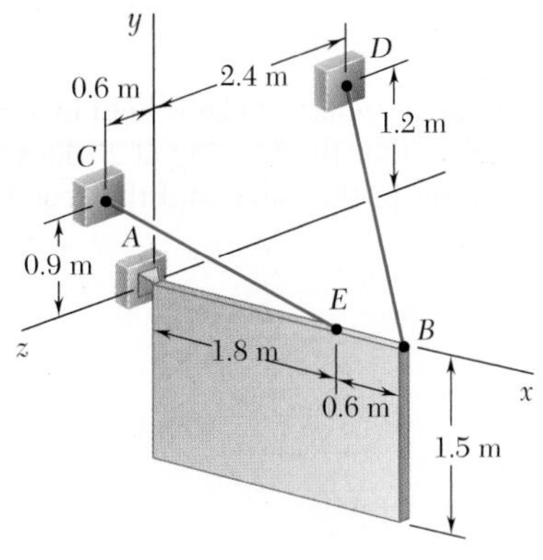

SAMPLE PROBLEM 4.8

A 1.5 × 2.4-m sign of uniform density weighs 540 N and is supported by a ball-and-socket joint at A and by two cables. Determine the tension in each cable and the reaction at A.

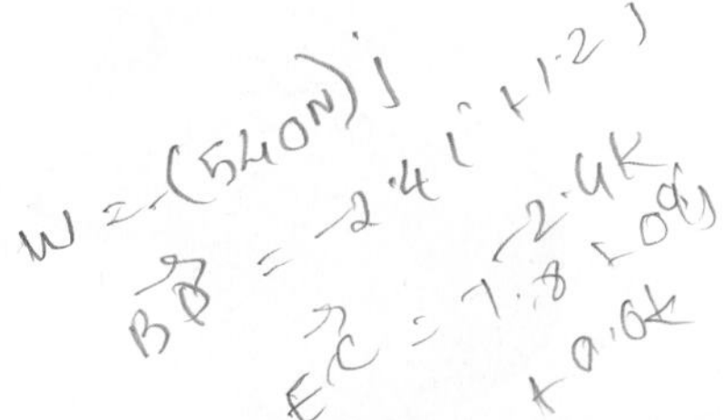

SOLUTION

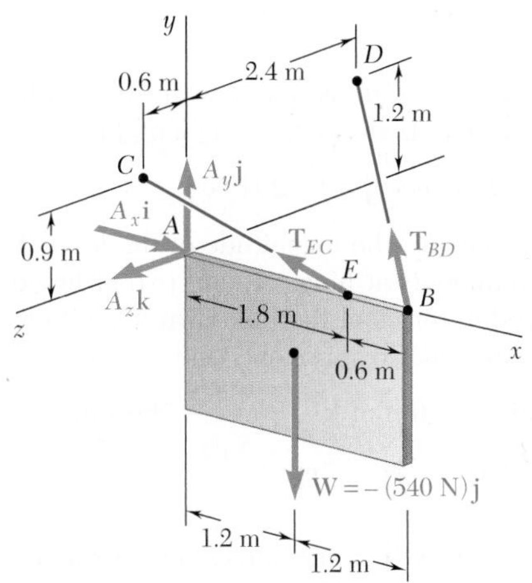

Free-Body Diagram. A free-body diagram of the sign is drawn. The forces acting on the free body are the weight $\mathbf{W} = -(540 \text{ N})\mathbf{j}$ and the reactions at A, B, and E. The reaction at A is a force of unknown direction and is represented by three unknown components. Since the directions of the forces exerted by the cables are known, these forces involve only one unknown each, namely, the magnitudes T_{BD} and T_{EC}. Since there are only five unknowns, the sign is partially constrained. It can rotate freely about the x axis; it is, however, in equilibrium under the given loading, since the equation $\Sigma M_x = 0$ is satisfied.

The components of the forces $\mathbf{T}_{BD}$ and $\mathbf{T}_{EC}$ can be expressed in terms of the unknown magnitudes T_{BD} and T_{EC} by writing

$$\overrightarrow{BD} = -(2.4 \text{ m})\mathbf{i} + (1.2 \text{ m})\mathbf{j} - (2.4 \text{ m})\mathbf{k} \qquad BD = 3.6 \text{ m}$$

$$\overrightarrow{EC} = -(1.8 \text{ m})\mathbf{i} + (0.9 \text{ m})\mathbf{j} + (0.6 \text{ m})\mathbf{k} \qquad EC = 2.1 \text{ m}$$

$$\mathbf{T}_{BD} = T_{BD}\left(\frac{\overrightarrow{BD}}{BD}\right) = T_{BD}(-\tfrac{2}{3}\mathbf{i} + \tfrac{1}{3}\mathbf{j} - \tfrac{2}{3}\mathbf{k})$$

$$\mathbf{T}_{EC} = T_{EC}\left(\frac{\overrightarrow{EC}}{EC}\right) = T_{EC}(-\tfrac{6}{7}\mathbf{i} + \tfrac{3}{7}\mathbf{j} + \tfrac{2}{7}\mathbf{k})$$

Equilibrium Equations. We express that the forces acting on the sign form a system equivalent to zero:

$$\Sigma\mathbf{F} = 0: \qquad A_x\mathbf{i} + A_y\mathbf{j} + A_z\mathbf{k} + \mathbf{T}_{BD} + \mathbf{T}_{EC} - (540 \text{ N})\mathbf{j} = 0$$

$$(A_x - \tfrac{2}{3}T_{BD} - \tfrac{6}{7}T_{EC})\mathbf{i} + (A_y + \tfrac{1}{3}T_{BD} + \tfrac{3}{7}T_{EC} - 540 \text{ N})\mathbf{j} + (A_z - \tfrac{2}{3}T_{BD} + \tfrac{2}{7}T_{EC})\mathbf{k} = 0 \qquad (1)$$

$$\Sigma\mathbf{M}_A = \Sigma(\mathbf{r} \times \mathbf{F}) = 0:$$

$$(2.4 \text{ m})\mathbf{i} \times T_{BD}(-\tfrac{2}{3}\mathbf{i} + \tfrac{1}{3}\mathbf{j} - \tfrac{2}{3}\mathbf{k}) + (1.8 \text{ m})\mathbf{i} \times T_{EC}(-\tfrac{6}{7}\mathbf{i} + \tfrac{3}{7}\mathbf{j} + \tfrac{2}{7}\mathbf{k}) + (1.2 \text{ m})\mathbf{i} \times (-540 \text{ N})\mathbf{j} = 0$$

$$(0.8T_{BD} + 0.771T_{EC} - 648 \text{ N})\mathbf{k} + (1.6T_{BD} - 0.5143T_{EC})\mathbf{j} = 0 \qquad (2)$$

Setting the coefficients of $\mathbf{j}$ and $\mathbf{k}$ equal to zero in Eq. (2), we obtain two scalar equations which can be solved for T_{BD} and T_{EC}:

$$T_{BD} = 202.6 \text{ N} \qquad T_{EC} = 630.3 \text{ N} \quad ◀$$

Setting the coefficients of $\mathbf{i}$, $\mathbf{j}$, and $\mathbf{k}$ equal to zero in Eq. (1), we obtain three more equations, which yield the components of $\mathbf{A}$. We have

$$\mathbf{A} = +(675.3 \text{ N})\mathbf{i} + (202.3 \text{ N})\mathbf{j} - (45.02 \text{ N})\mathbf{k} \quad ◀$$

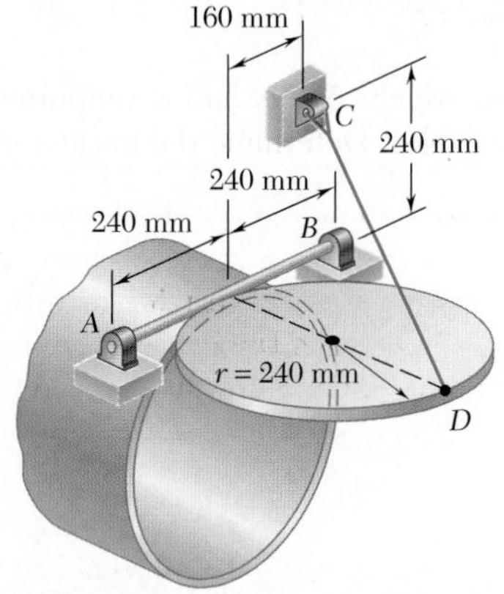

SAMPLE PROBLEM 4.9

A uniform pipe cover of radius $r = 240$ mm and mass 30 kg is held in a horizontal position by the cable CD. Assuming that the bearing at B does not exert any axial thrust, determine the tension in the cable and the reactions at A and B.

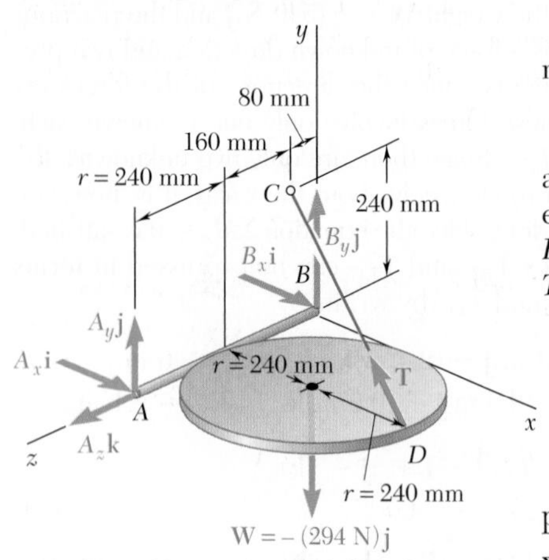

SOLUTION

Free-Body Diagram. A free-body diagram is drawn with the coordinate axes shown. The forces acting on the free body are the weight of the cover,

$$\mathbf{W} = -mg\mathbf{j} = -(30 \text{ kg})(9.81 \text{ m/s}^2)\mathbf{j} = -(294 \text{ N})\mathbf{j}$$

and reactions involving six unknowns, namely, the magnitude of the force $\mathbf{T}$ exerted by the cable, three force components at hinge A, and two at hinge B. The components of $\mathbf{T}$ are expressed in terms of the unknown magnitude T by resolving the vector $\overrightarrow{DC}$ into rectangular components and writing

$$\overrightarrow{DC} = -(480 \text{ mm})\mathbf{i} + (240 \text{ mm})\mathbf{j} - (160 \text{ mm})\mathbf{k} \qquad DC = 560 \text{ mm}$$

$$\mathbf{T} = T\frac{\overrightarrow{DC}}{DC} = -\tfrac{6}{7}T\mathbf{i} + \tfrac{3}{7}T\mathbf{j} - \tfrac{2}{7}T\mathbf{k}$$

Equilibrium Equations. We express that the forces acting on the pipe cover form a system equivalent to zero:

$$\Sigma\mathbf{F} = 0: \quad A_x\mathbf{i} + A_y\mathbf{j} + A_z\mathbf{k} + B_x\mathbf{i} + B_y\mathbf{j} + \mathbf{T} - (294 \text{ N})\mathbf{j} = 0$$

$$(A_x + B_x - \tfrac{6}{7}T)\mathbf{i} + (A_y + B_y + \tfrac{3}{7}T - 294 \text{ N})\mathbf{j} + (A_z - \tfrac{2}{7}T)\mathbf{k} = 0 \quad (1)$$

$$\Sigma\mathbf{M}_B = \Sigma(\mathbf{r} \times \mathbf{F}) = 0:$$

$$2r\mathbf{k} \times (A_x\mathbf{i} + A_y\mathbf{j} + A_z\mathbf{k}) + (2r\mathbf{i} + r\mathbf{k}) \times (-\tfrac{6}{7}T\mathbf{i} + \tfrac{3}{7}T\mathbf{j} - \tfrac{2}{7}T\mathbf{k}) + (r\mathbf{i} + r\mathbf{k}) \times (-294 \text{ N})\mathbf{j} = 0$$

$$(-2A_y - \tfrac{3}{7}T + 294 \text{ N})r\mathbf{i} + (2A_x - \tfrac{2}{7}T)r\mathbf{j} + (\tfrac{6}{7}T - 294 \text{ N})r\mathbf{k} = 0 \quad (2)$$

Setting the coefficients of the unit vectors equal to zero in Eq. (2), we write three scalar equations, which yield

$$A_x = +49.0 \text{ N} \qquad A_y = +73.5 \text{ N} \qquad T = 343 \text{ N} \blacktriangleleft$$

Setting the coefficients of the unit vectors equal to zero in Eq. (1), we obtain three more scalar equations. After substituting the values of T, A_x, and A_y into these equations, we obtain

$$A_z = +98.0 \text{ N} \qquad B_x = +245 \text{ N} \qquad B_y = +73.5 \text{ N}$$

The reactions at A and B are therefore

$$\mathbf{A} = +(49.0 \text{ N})\mathbf{i} + (73.5 \text{ N})\mathbf{j} + (98.0 \text{ N})\mathbf{k} \blacktriangleleft$$

$$\mathbf{B} = +(245 \text{ N})\mathbf{i} + (73.5 \text{ N})\mathbf{j} \blacktriangleleft$$

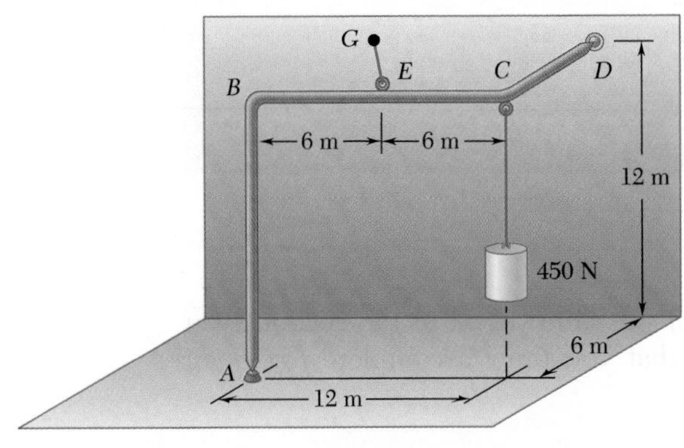

SAMPLE PROBLEM 4.10

A 450-N load hangs from the corner C of a rigid piece of pipe $ABCD$ which has been bent as shown. The pipe is supported by the ball-and-socket joints A and D, which are fastened, respectively, to the floor and to a vertical wall, and by a cable attached at the midpoint E of the portion BC of the pipe and at a point G on the wall. Determine (*a*) where G should be located if the tension in the cable is to be minimum, (*b*) the corresponding minimum value of the tension.

SOLUTION

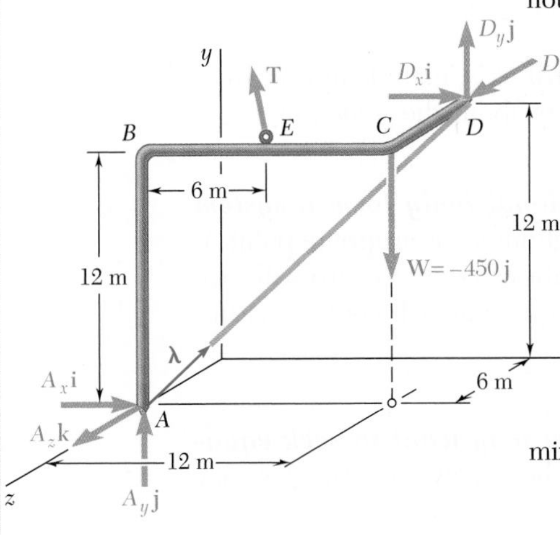

Free-Body Diagram. The free-body diagram of the pipe includes the load $\mathbf{W} = (-450 \text{ N})\mathbf{j}$, the reactions at A and D, and the force $\mathbf{T}$ exerted by the cable. To eliminate the reactions at A and D from the computations, we express that the sum of the moments of the forces about AD is zero. Denoting by $\boldsymbol{\lambda}$ the unit vector along AD, we write

$$\Sigma M_{AD} = 0: \qquad \boldsymbol{\lambda} \cdot (\overrightarrow{AE} \times \mathbf{T}) + \boldsymbol{\lambda} \cdot (\overrightarrow{AC} \times \mathbf{W}) = 0 \tag{1}$$

The second term in Eq. (1) can be computed as follows:

$$\overrightarrow{AC} \times \mathbf{W} = (12\mathbf{i} + 12\mathbf{j}) \times (-450\mathbf{j}) = -5400\mathbf{k}$$

$$\boldsymbol{\lambda} = \frac{\overrightarrow{AD}}{AD} = \frac{12\mathbf{i} + 12\mathbf{j} - 6\mathbf{k}}{18} = \tfrac{2}{3}\mathbf{i} + \tfrac{2}{3}\mathbf{j} - \tfrac{1}{3}\mathbf{k}$$

$$\boldsymbol{\lambda} \cdot (\overrightarrow{AC} \times \mathbf{W}) = (\tfrac{2}{3}\mathbf{i} + \tfrac{2}{3}\mathbf{j} - \tfrac{1}{3}\mathbf{k}) \cdot (-5400\mathbf{k}) = +1800$$

Substituting the value obtained into Eq. (1), we write

$$\boldsymbol{\lambda} \cdot (\overrightarrow{AE} \times \mathbf{T}) = -1800 \text{ N} \cdot \text{m} \tag{2}$$

Minimum Value of Tension. Recalling the commutative property for mixed triple products, we rewrite Eq. (2) in the form

$$\mathbf{T} \cdot (\boldsymbol{\lambda} \times \overrightarrow{AE}) = -1800 \text{ N} \cdot \text{m} \tag{3}$$

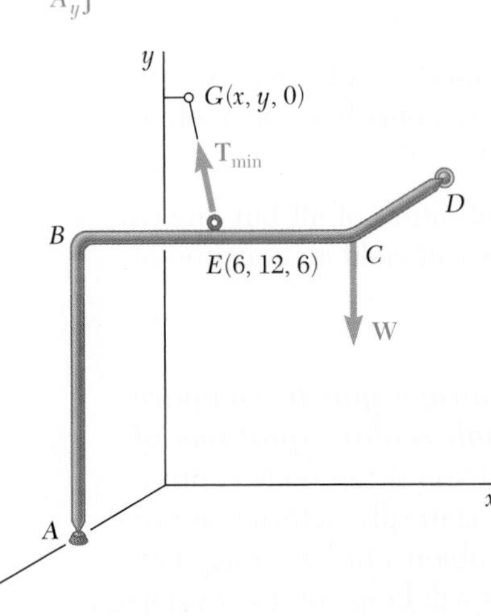

which shows that the projection of $\mathbf{T}$ on the vector $\boldsymbol{\lambda} \times \overrightarrow{AE}$ is a constant. It follows that $\mathbf{T}$ is minimum when parallel to the vector

$$\boldsymbol{\lambda} \times \overrightarrow{AE} = (\tfrac{2}{3}\mathbf{i} + \tfrac{2}{3}\mathbf{j} - \tfrac{1}{3}\mathbf{k}) \times (6\mathbf{i} + 12\mathbf{j}) = 4\mathbf{i} - 2\mathbf{j} + 4\mathbf{k}$$

Since the corresponding unit vector is $\tfrac{2}{3}\mathbf{i} - \tfrac{1}{3}\mathbf{j} + \tfrac{2}{3}\mathbf{k}$, we write

$$\mathbf{T}_{\text{min}} = T(\tfrac{2}{3}\mathbf{i} - \tfrac{1}{3}\mathbf{j} + \tfrac{2}{3}\mathbf{k}) \tag{4}$$

Substituting for $\mathbf{T}$ and $\boldsymbol{\lambda} \times \overrightarrow{AE}$ in Eq. (3) and computing the dot products, we obtain $6T = -1800$ and, thus, $T = -300$. Carrying this value into (4), we obtain

$$T_{\text{min}} = -200\mathbf{i} + 100\mathbf{j} - 200\mathbf{k} \qquad T_{\text{min}} = 300 \text{ N} \blacktriangleleft$$

Location of G. Since the vector $\overrightarrow{EG}$ and the force $\mathbf{T}_{\text{min}}$ have the same direction, their components must be proportional. Denoting the coordinates of G by x, y, 0, we write

$$\frac{x-6}{-200} = \frac{y-12}{+100} = \frac{0-6}{-200} \qquad x = 0 \quad y = 15 \text{ m} \blacktriangleleft$$

SOLVING PROBLEMS ON YOUR OWN

The equilibrium of a *three-dimensional body* was considered in the sections you just completed. It is again most important that you draw a complete *free-body diagram* as the first step of your solution.

1. As you draw the free-body diagram, pay particular attention to the reactions at the supports. The number of unknowns at a support can range from one to six (Fig. 4.10). To decide whether an unknown reaction or reaction component exists at a support, ask yourself whether the support prevents motion of the body in a certain direction or about a certain axis.

a. If motion is prevented in a certain direction, include in your free-body diagram an unknown reaction or *reaction component* that acts in the *same direction.*

b. If a support prevents rotation about a certain axis, include in your free-body diagram a *couple* of unknown magnitude that acts about the *same* axis.

2. The external forces acting on a three-dimensional body form a system equivalent to zero. Writing $\Sigma\mathbf{F} = 0$ and $\Sigma\mathbf{M}_A = 0$ about an appropriate point A, and setting the coefficients of $\mathbf{i}$, $\mathbf{j}$, and $\mathbf{k}$ in both equations equal to zero will provide you with six scalar equations. In general, these equations will contain six unknowns and can be solved for these unknowns.

3. After completing your free-body diagram, you may want to seek equations involving as few unknowns as possible. The following strategies may help you.

a. By summing moments about a ball-and-socket support or a hinge, you will obtain equations from which three unknown reaction components have been eliminated [Sample Probs. 4.8 and 4.9].

b. If you can draw an axis through the points of application of all but one of the unknown reactions, summing moments about that axis will yield an equation in a single unknown [Sample Prob. 4.10].

4. After drawing your free-body diagram, we encourage you to compare the number of unknowns to the number of nontrivial, scalar equations of equilibrium for the given problem. Doing so will tell you if the body is properly or partially constrained and whether the problem is statically determinate or indeterminate. Further, as we consider more complex problems in later chapters, keeping track of the numbers of unknowns and equations will help you to develop correct solutions.

Problems

4.96 Two transmission belts pass over a double-sheaved pulley that is attached to an axle supported by bearings at *A* and *D*. The radius of the inner sheave is 125 mm and the radius of the outer sheave is 250 mm. Knowing that when the system is at rest the tension is 90 N in both portions of belt *B* and 150 N in both portions of belt *C*, determine the reactions at *A* and *D*. Assume that the bearing at *D* does not exert any axial thrust.

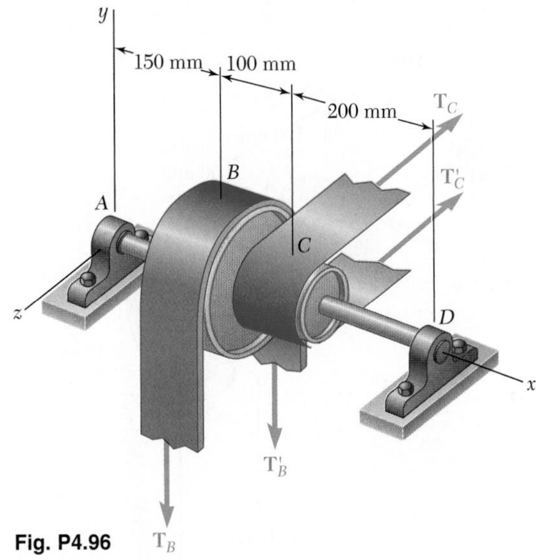

Fig. P4.96

4.97 Gears *A* and *B* are attached to a shaft supported by bearings at *C* and *D*. The diameters of gears *A* and *B* are 15 cm and 7.6 cm, respectively, and the tangential and radial forces acting on the gears are as shown. Knowing that the system rotates at a constant rate, determine the reactions at *C* and *D*. Assume that the bearing at *C* does not exert any axial force, and neglect the weights of the gears and the shaft.

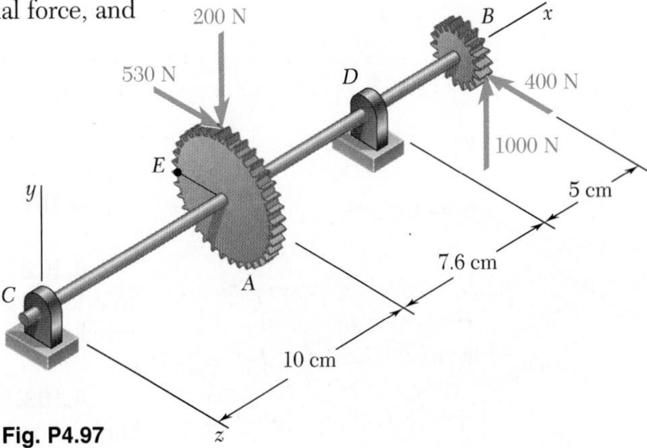

Fig. P4.97

4.98 Solve Prob. 4.97 assuming that for gear *A* the tangential and radial forces are acting at *E*, so that $\mathbf{F}_A = (530\text{ N})\mathbf{j} + (200\text{ N})\mathbf{k}$.

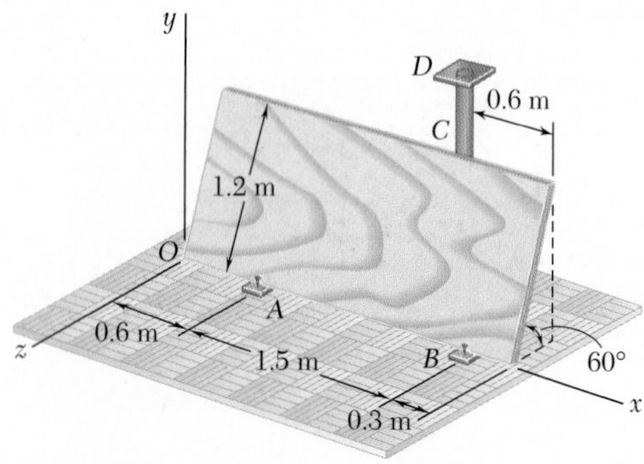

Fig. P4.99

4.99 A 1.2×2.4-m sheet of plywood having a mass of 18 kg has been temporarily propped against column CD. It rests at A and B on small wooden blocks and against protruding nails. Neglecting friction at all surfaces of contact, determine the reactions at A, B, and C.

4.100 For the portion of a machine shown, the 100-mm-diameter pulley A and wheel B are fixed to a shaft supported by bearings at C and D. The spring of constant 366 N/m is unstretched when $\theta = 0$, and the bearing at C does not exert any axial force. Knowing that $\theta = 180°$ and that the machine is at rest and in equilibrium, determine (*a*) the tension T, (*b*) the reactions at C and D. Neglect the masses of the shaft, pulley, and wheel.

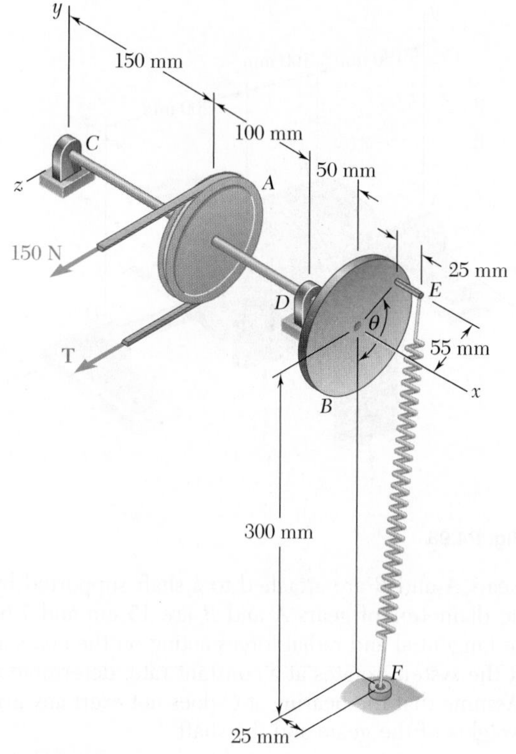

Fig. P4.100

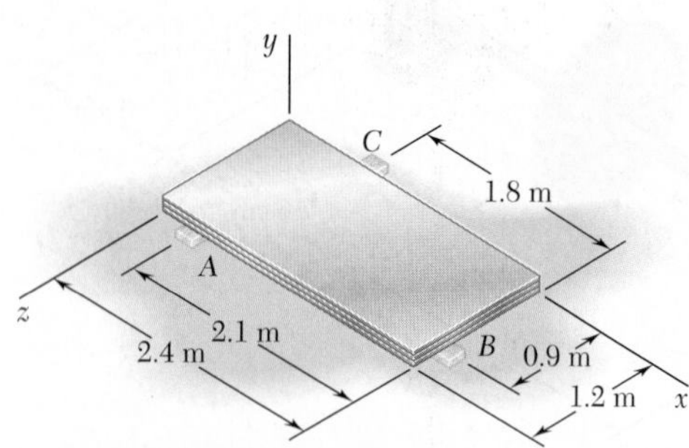

Fig. P4.102 and P4.103

4.101 Solve Prob. 4.100 for $\theta = 90°$.

4.102 A stack of several sheets of drywall of mass 170 kg rests on three wooden blocks placed under the edges of the stack. Determine the force exerted on each block.

4.103 A stack of several sheets of drywall of mass 170 kg rests on three wooden blocks placed under the edges of the stack. Determine the mass and the location of the lightest bucket of sand so that when placed on the top sheet of drywall the forces exerted on the three blocks are equal.

4.104 Two steel pipes AB and BC each having a weight per unit length of 30 N/m are welded together at B and are supported by three wires. Knowing that $a = 0.4$ m, determine the tension in each wire.

4.105 For the pipe assembly of Prob. 4.104, determine (*a*) the largest permissible value of a if the assembly is not to tip, (*b*) the corresponding tension in each wire.

4.106 A camera weighing 1 N is mounted on a small tripod weighing 0.8 N. Assuming that the weight of the camera is uniformly distributed and that the line of action of the weight of the tripod passes through D, determine (*a*) the vertical components of the reactions at A, B, and C when $\theta = 0$, (*b*) the maximum value of θ if the tripod is not to tip over.

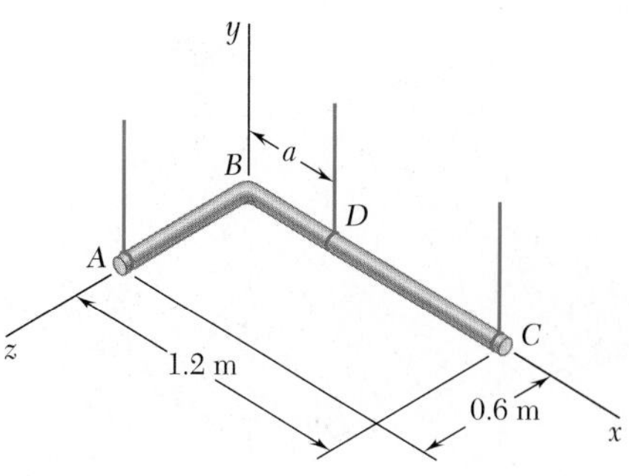

Fig. P4.104

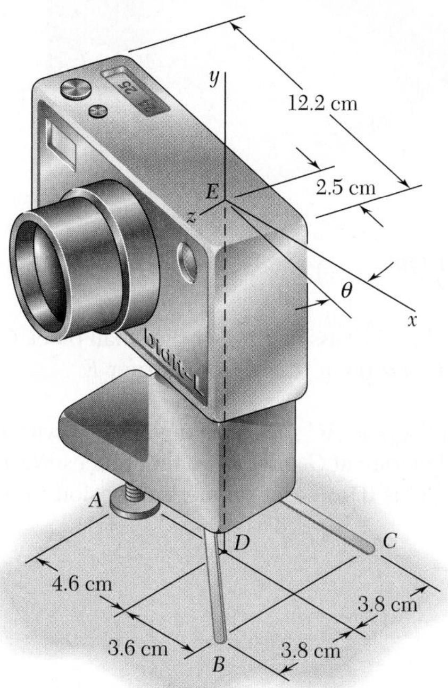

Fig. P4.106

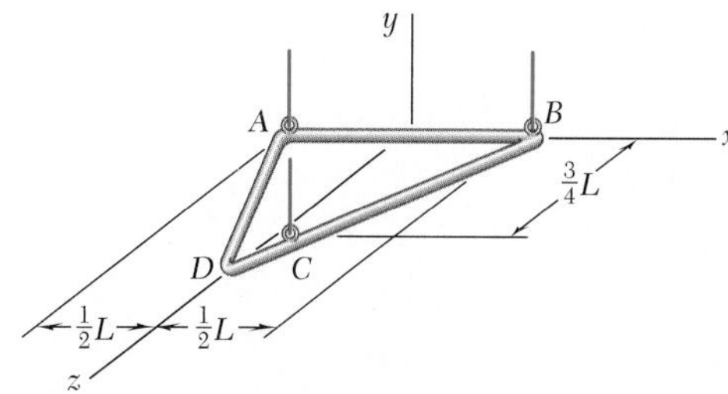

Fig. P4.107 and P4.108

4.107 A uniform brass rod of weight W and length $3L$ is bent into an equilateral triangle and then is hung from three wires as shown. Determine the tension in each wire.

4.108 A uniform brass rod of weight W and length $3L$ is bent into an equilateral triangle and then is hung from three wires as shown. A small collar of weight W is placed on side BD of the triangle and is positioned so that the tensions in the wires at A and B are equal. Determine (*a*) the tensions in the wires, (*b*) the position of the collar.

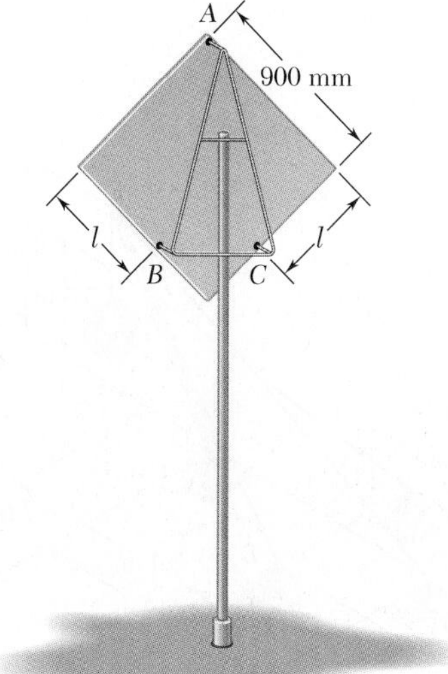

Fig. P4.109

4.109 A square steel sign is attached to frame ABC as shown. Knowing that the direction of the wind is perpendicular to the sign and that the wind exerts a force $\mathbf{F}_W$ of magnitude 135 N at the center of the front of the sign, determine (*a*) the value of l for which the horizontal components of the reactions at the three supports are equal, (*b*) the values of the horizontal components when $l = 500$ mm.

4.110 An opening in a floor is covered by a 1.4×1.8-m sheet of plywood weighing 54 N. The sheet is hinged at A and B and is maintained in a position slightly above the floor by a small block C. Determine the vertical component of the reaction (*a*) at A, (*b*) at B, (*c*) at C.

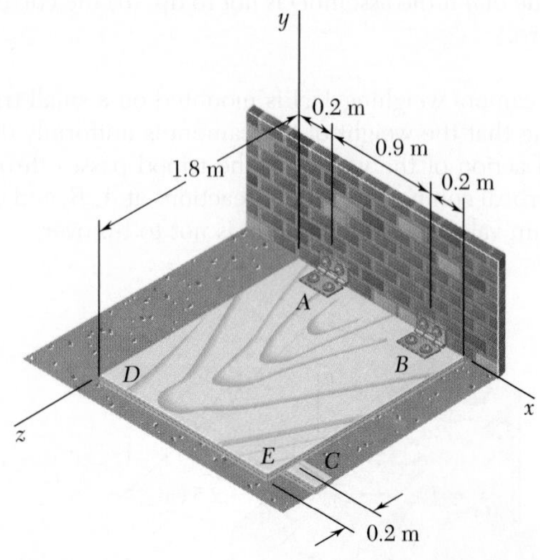

Fig. *P4.110*

4.111 Solve Prob. 4.110 assuming that the small block C is moved and placed under edge DE at a point 0.2 m from corner E.

4.112 The 3-m flagpole AC forms an angle of 30° with the z axis. It is held by a ball-and-socket joint at C and by two thin braces BD and BE. Knowing that the distance BC is 0.9 m, determine the tension in each brace and the reaction at C.

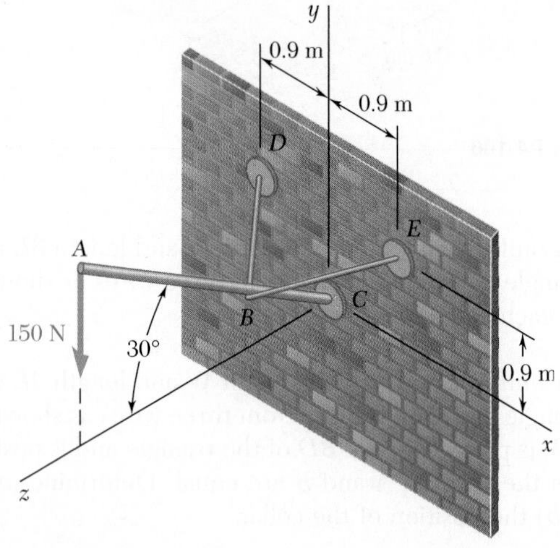

Fig. P4.112

4.113 A 5500-N piece of machinery hangs from a cable which passes over a pulley at E and is attached to a support at D. The boom AE is supported by a ball-and-socket joint at A and by two cables BF and CF. Determine (*a*) the tensions in cables BF and CF, (*b*) the reaction at A.

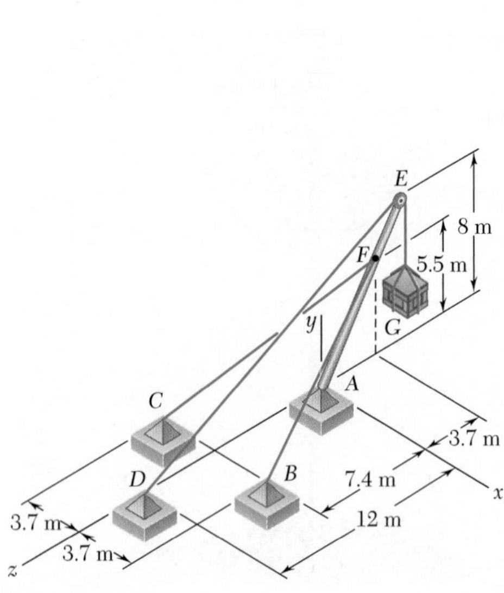

Fig. *P4.113*

4.114 Cable CD is attached to the 10-m mast ABC as shown. The base A of the mast is supported by a ball-and-socket joint, and the mast is guyed by cables BE and BF. Knowing that $\theta = 30°$ and $\phi = 10°$ and that the tension in cable CD is 600 N, determine (*a*) the tensions in cables BE and BF, (*b*) the reaction at A.

4.115 Cable CD is attached to the 10-m mast ABC as shown. The base A of the mast is supported by a ball-and-socket joint, and the mast is guyed by cables BE and BF. Knowing that $\phi = 8°$ and that the tensions in cables BE and BF are 840 N and 450 N, respectively, determine (*a*) the value of θ, (*b*) the tension in cable CD, (*c*) the reaction at A.

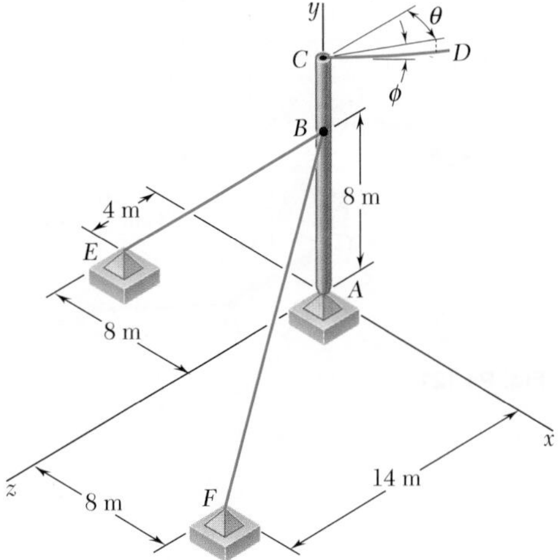

Fig. P4.114 and P4.115

4.116 A 2.4-m-long boom is held by a ball-and-socket joint at C and by two cables AD and BE. Determine the tension in each cable and the reaction at C.

4.117 Solve Prob. 4.116 assuming that the given 880-N load is replaced with two 440-N loads applied at A and B.

4.118 Two steel pipes $ABCD$ and EBF are welded together at B to form the boom shown. The boom is held by a ball-and-socket joint at D and by two cables EG and $ICFH$; cable $ICFH$ passes around frictionless pulleys at C and F. For the loading shown, determine the tension in each cable and the reaction at D.

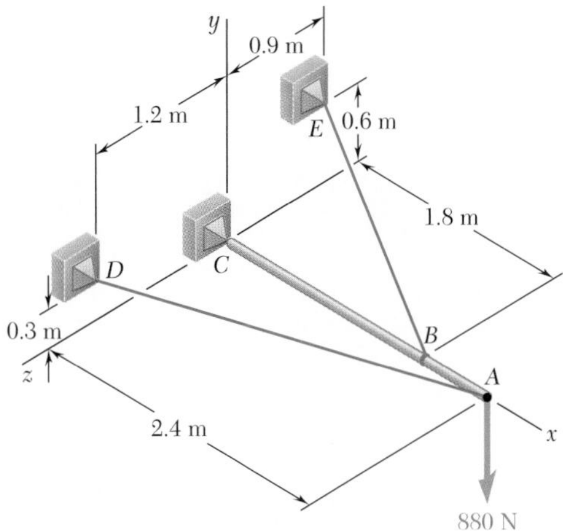

Fig. P4.116

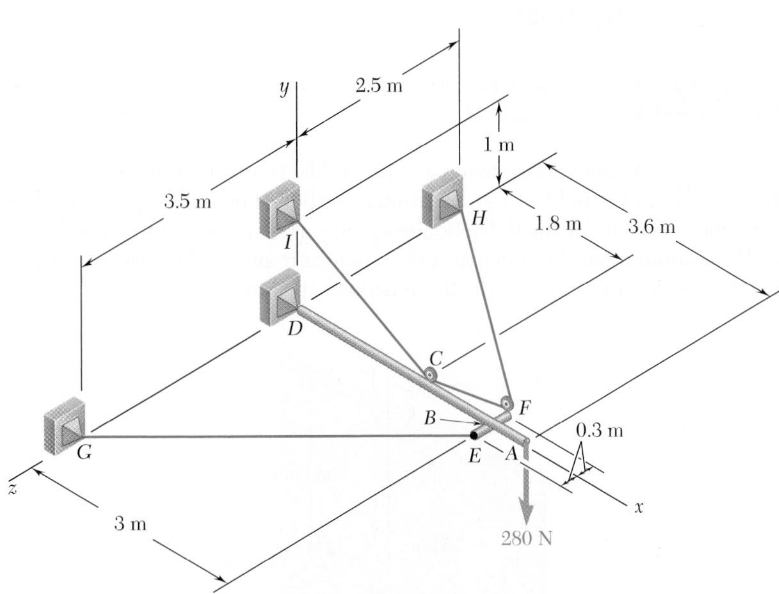

Fig. P4.118

4.119 Solve Prob. 4.118 assuming that the 280-N load is applied at B.

4.120 The lid of a roof scuttle weighs 150 N. It is hinged at corners A and B and maintained in the desired position by a rod CD pivoted at C; a pin at end D of the rod fits into one of several holes drilled in the edge of the lid. For the position shown, determine (*a*) the magnitude of the force exerted by rod CD, (*b*) the reactions at the hinges. Assume that the hinge at B does not exert any axial thrust.

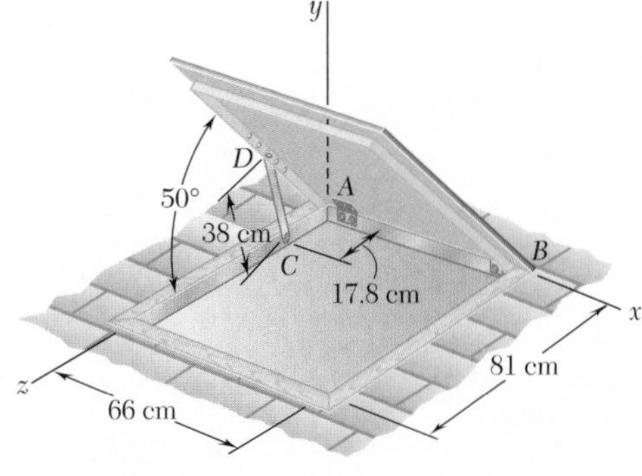

Fig. P4.120

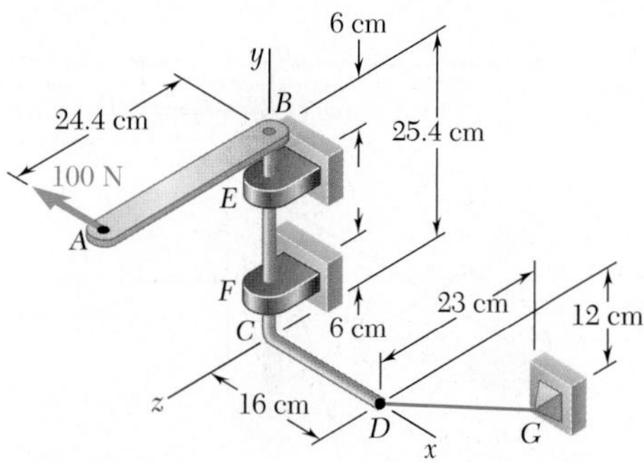

Fig. P4.121

4.121 The lever AB is welded to the bent rod BCD which is supported by bearings at E and F and by cable DG. Knowing that the bearing at E does not exert any axial thrust, determine (*a*) the tension in cable DG, (*b*) the reactions at E and F.

4.122 The rectangular plate shown has a mass of 15 kg and is held in the position shown by hinges A and B and cable EF. Assuming that the hinge at B does not exert any axial thrust, determine (*a*) the tension in the cable, (*b*) the reactions at A and B.

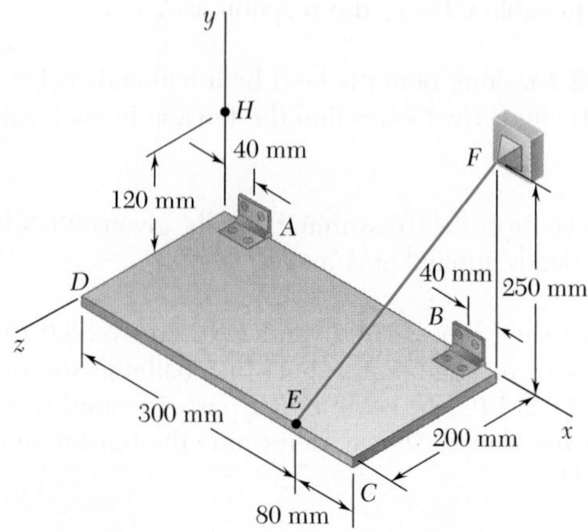

Fig. P4.122

4.123 Solve Prob. 4.122 assuming that cable EF is replaced by a cable attached at points E and H.

4.124 A small door having a mass of 7 kg is attached by hinges A and B to a wall and is held in the horizontal position shown by rope EFH. The rope passes around a small, frictionless pulley at F and is tied to a fixed cleat at H. Assuming that the hinge at A does not exert any axial thrust, determine (*a*) the tension in the rope, (*b*) the reactions at A and B.

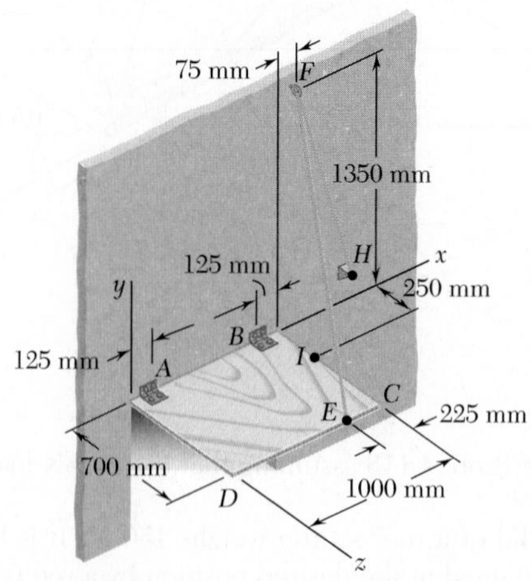

Fig. *P4.124*

4.125 Solve Prob. 4.124 assuming that the rope is attached to the door at I.

4.126 The horizontal platform $ABCD$ weighs 120 N and supports a 480-N load at its center. The platform is normally held in position by hinges at A and B and by braces CE and DE. If brace DE is removed, determine the reactions at the hinges and the force exerted by the remaining brace CE. The hinge at A does not exert any axial thrust.

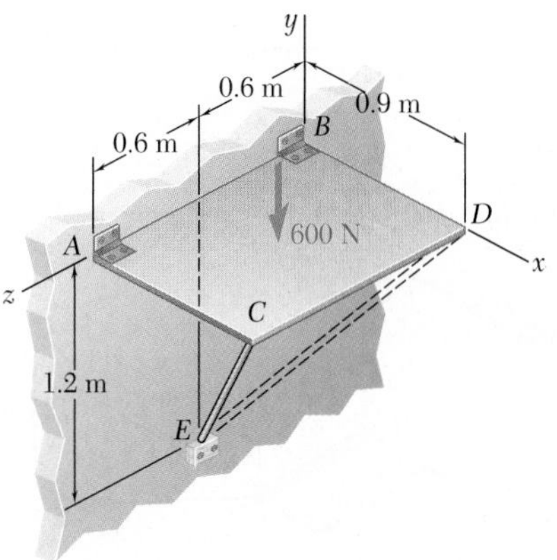

Fig. P4.126

4.127 A 1.2 × 2.4-m sheet of plywood is temporarily held by nails at D and E and by two wooden braces nailed at A, B, and C. Wind is blowing on the hidden face of the plywood sheet, and it is assumed that its effect can be represented by a force $P\mathbf{k}$ applied at the center of the sheet. Knowing that each brace becomes unsafe with respect to buckling when subjected to a 1.8-kN axial force, determine (*a*) the maximum allowable value of the magnitude P of the wind force, (*b*) the corresponding value of the z component of the reaction at E. Assume that the nails are loose and do not exert any couples.

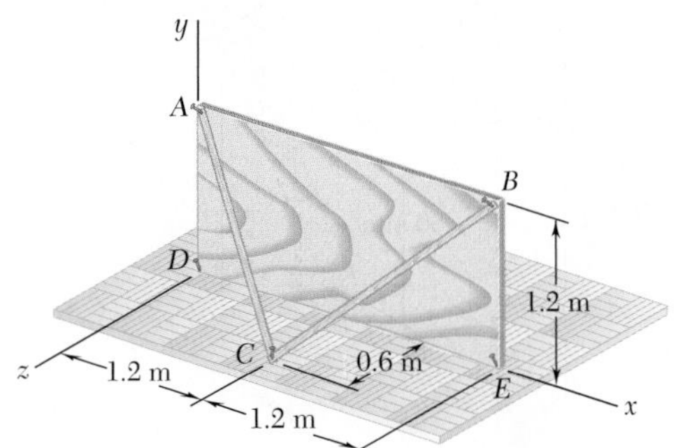

Fig. *P4.127*

4.128 The tensioning mechanism of a belt drive consists of frictionless pulley A, mounting plate B, and spring C. Attached below the mounting plate is slider block D which is free to move in the frictionless slot of bracket E. Knowing that the pulley and the belt lie in a horizontal plane, with portion F of the belt parallel to the x axis and portion G forming an angle of 30° with the x axis, determine (*a*) the force in the spring, (*b*) the reaction at D.

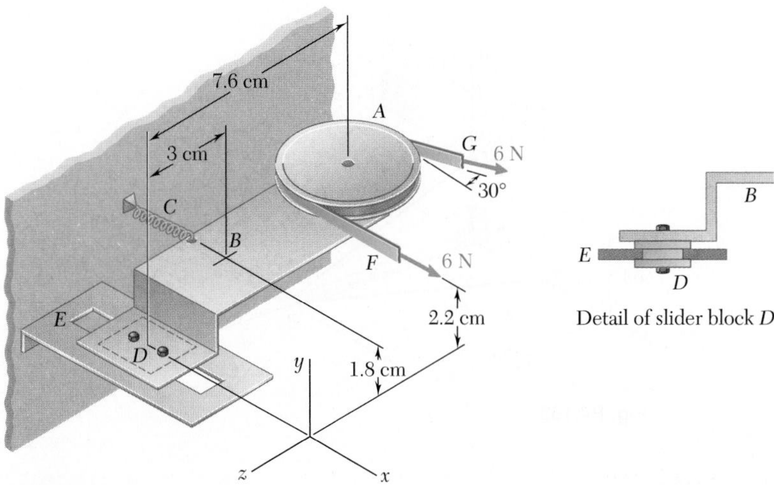

Fig. P4.128

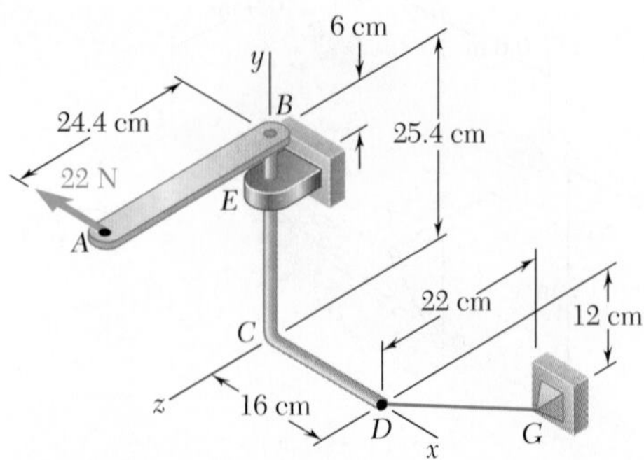

Fig. *P4.129*

4.129 The lever AB is welded to the bent rod BCD which is supported by bearing E and by cable DG. Assuming that the bearing can exert an axial thrust and couples about axes parallel to the x and z axes, determine (*a*) the tension in cable DG, (*b*) the reaction at E.

4.130 The bearing of lever ABD is free to slide along and to rotate about the horizontal pin at B. Knowing that the 24-N force lies in a plane parallel to the xy plane and that the bearing can exert couples about the y and z axes, determine (*a*) the forces in the stretched springs CF and DE, (*b*) the reaction at B.

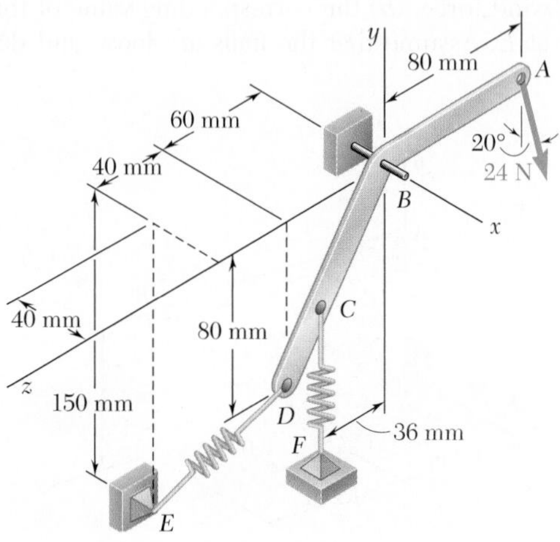

Fig. P4.130

4.131 Solve Prob. 4.124 assuming that the hinge at A is removed and that the hinge at B can exert couples about the y and z axes.

4.132 The rigid L-shaped member ABC is supported by a ball-and-socket joint at A and by three cables. Determine the tension in each cable and the reaction at A caused by the 1-kN load applied at G.

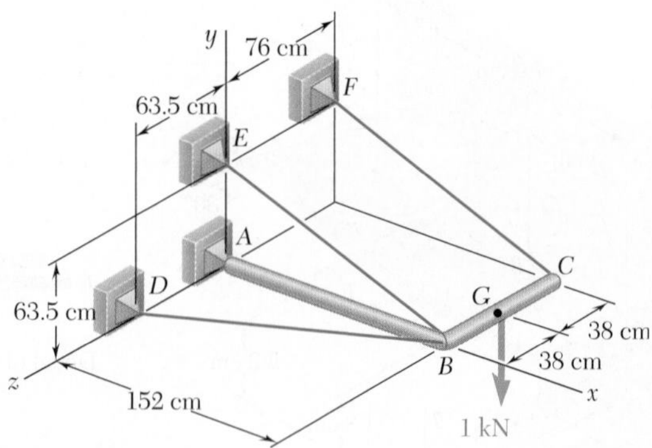

Fig. P4.132

4.133 Solve Prob. 4.132 assuming that an additional downward load of 1600 N is applied at C.

4.134 The frame shown is supported by three cables and a ball-and-socket joint at A. For $\mathbf{P} = 0$, determine the tension in each cable and the reaction at A.

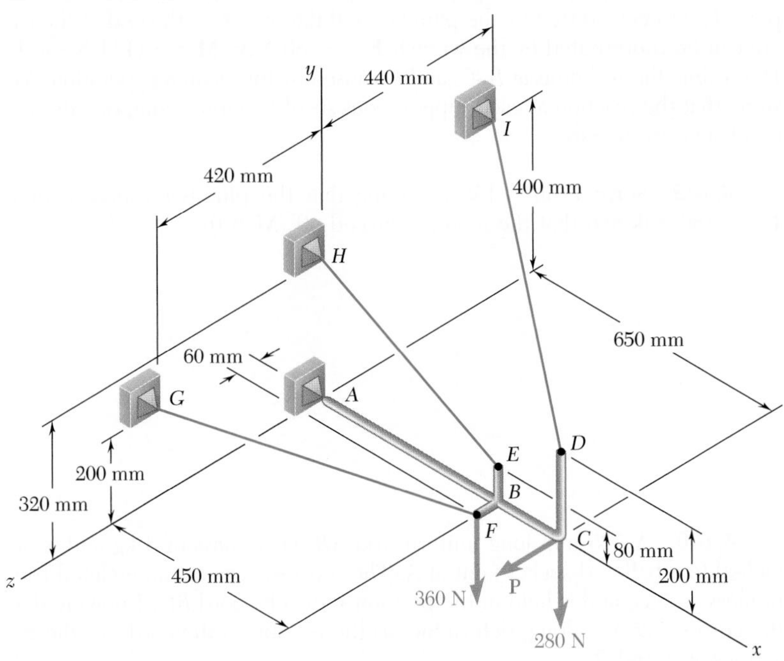

Fig. P4.134 and P4.135

4.135 The frame shown is supported by three cables and a ball-and-socket joint at A. For $P = 50$ N, determine the tension in each cable and the reaction at A.

4.136 Three rods of lengths $a = 23$ cm, $b = 15$ cm, and $c = 30.5$ cm are welded together to form the component shown. The component is supported by eyebolts at A and C and by a shallow slot cut in a block at B. Neglecting friction, determine the reactions at A, B, and C when $P = 80$ N, $M_A = 30$ N · m, and $M_C = 0$.

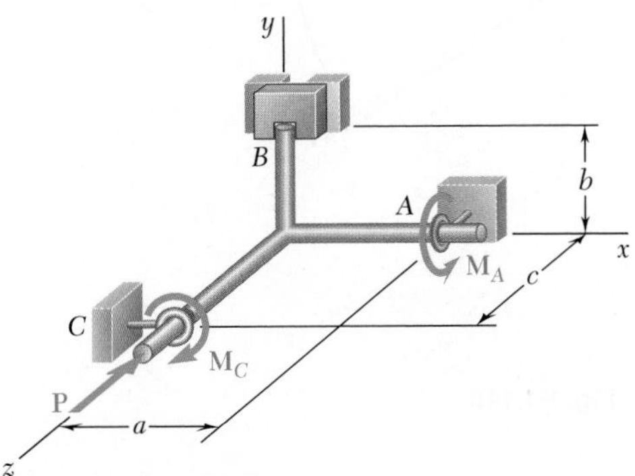

Fig. P4.136 and *P4.137*

4.137 Three rods of lengths $a = 240$ mm, $b = 200$ mm, and $c = 180$ mm are welded together to form the component shown. The component is supported by eyebolts at A and C and by a shallow slot cut in a block at B. Neglecting friction, determine the reactions at A, B, and C when $P = 60$ N, $M_A = 6.3$ N · m, and $M_C = 13$ N · m.

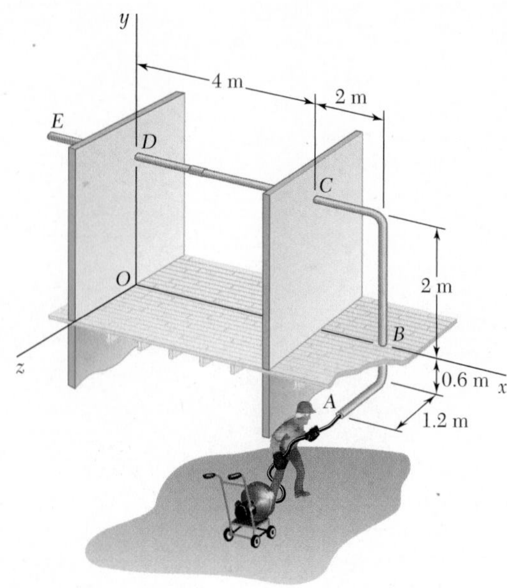

Fig. P4.138

4.138 To clean the clogged drainpipe AE, a plumber disconnected both ends of the pipe and inserted a power snake through the opening at A. The cutting head of the snake is connected by a heavy cable to an electric motor which rotates at a constant speed as the plumber forces the cable into the pipe. The forces exerted by the plumber and the motor on the end of the cable can be represented by the wrench $\mathbf{F} = -(80\text{ N})\mathbf{k}$, $\mathbf{M} = -(144\text{ N}\cdot\text{m})\mathbf{k}$. Determine the reactions at B, C, and D caused by the cleaning operation. Assume that the reaction at each support consists of two force components perpendicular to the pipe.

4.139 Solve Prob. 4.138 assuming that the plumber exerts a force $\mathbf{F} = -(80\text{ N})\mathbf{k}$ and that the motor is turned off ($\mathbf{M} = 0$).

4.140 A 525-mm-long uniform rod AB has a mass of 3 kg and is attached to a ball-and-socket joint at A. The rod rests against an inclined frictionless surface and is held in the position shown by cord BC. Knowing that the cord is 525 mm long, determine (*a*) the tension in the cord, (*b*) the reactions at A and B.

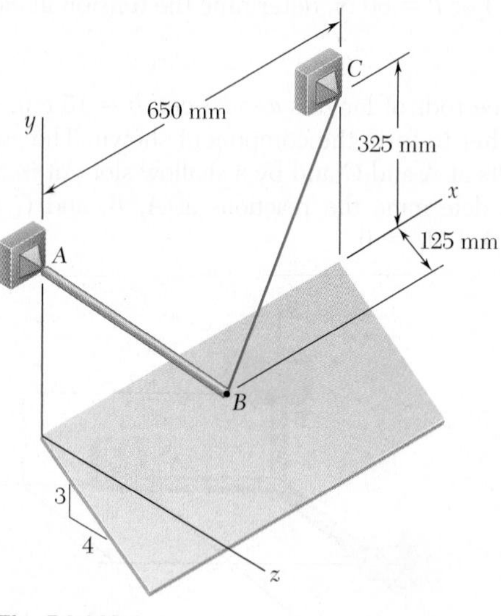

Fig. P4.140

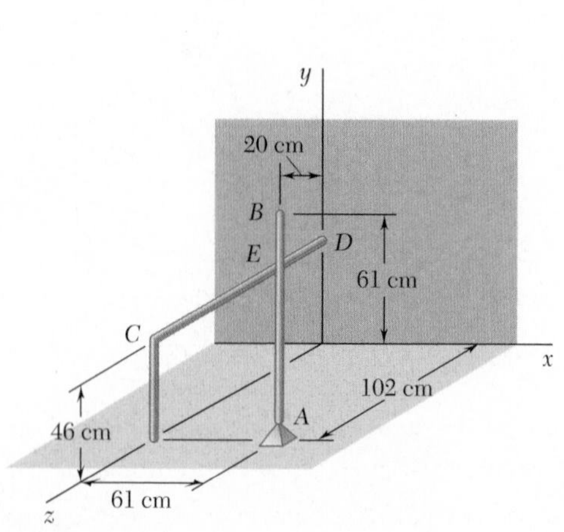

Fig. P4.141

4.141 The uniform 20-N rod AB is supported by a ball-and-socket joint at A and leans against both the rod CD and the vertical wall. Neglecting the effects of friction, determine (*a*) the force which rod CD exerts on AB, (*b*) the reactions at A and B. (*Hint:* The force exerted by CD on AB must be perpendicular to both rods.)

4.142 While being installed, the 25-kg chute $ABCD$ is attached to a wall with brackets E and F and is braced with props GH and IJ at its outer edge. Assuming that the weight of the chute is uniformly distributed, determine the magnitude of the force exerted on the chute by prop GH if prop IJ is removed.

4.143 While being installed, the 25-kg chute $ABCD$ is attached to a wall with brackets E and F and is braced with props GH and IJ at its outer edge. Assuming that the weight of the chute is uniformly distributed, determine the magnitude of the force exerted on the chute by prop IJ if prop GH is removed.

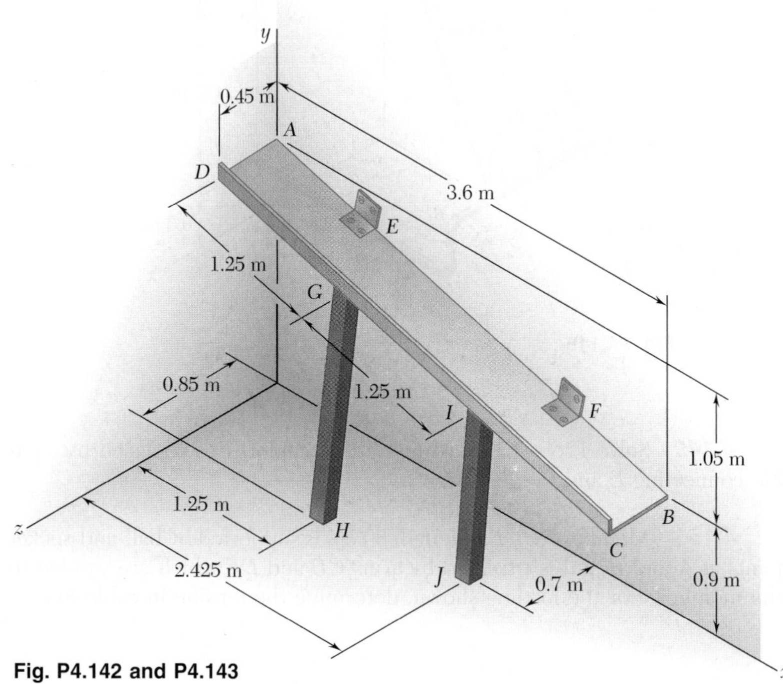

Fig. P4.142 and P4.143

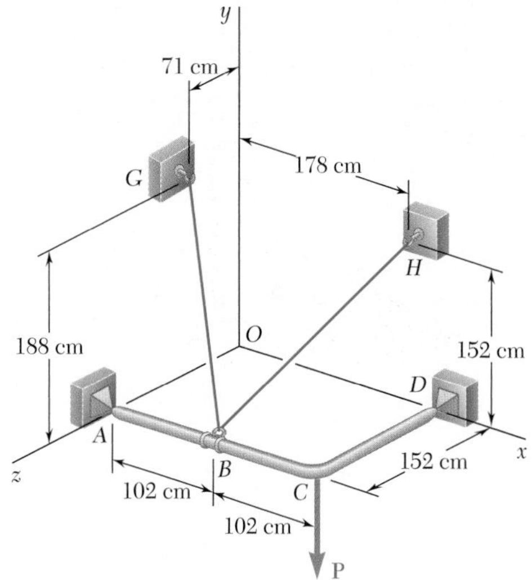

Fig. P4.144

4.144 The frame ACD is supported by ball-and-socket joints at A and D and by a cable that passes through a ring at B and is attached to hooks at G and H. Knowing that the frame supports at point C a load of magnitude $P = 150$ N, determine the tension in the cable.

4.145 Solve Prob. 4.144 assuming that the cable GBH is replaced by a cable GB attached at G and B.

4.146 Two 0.9×1.8-m plywood panels each weighing 60 N are nailed together as shown. The panels are supported by ball-and-socket joints at A and F and by the wire BH. Determine (*a*) the location of H in the xy plane if the tension in the wire is to be minimum, (*b*) the corresponding minimum tension.

4.147 Solve Prob. 4.146 subject to the restriction that H must lie on the y axis.

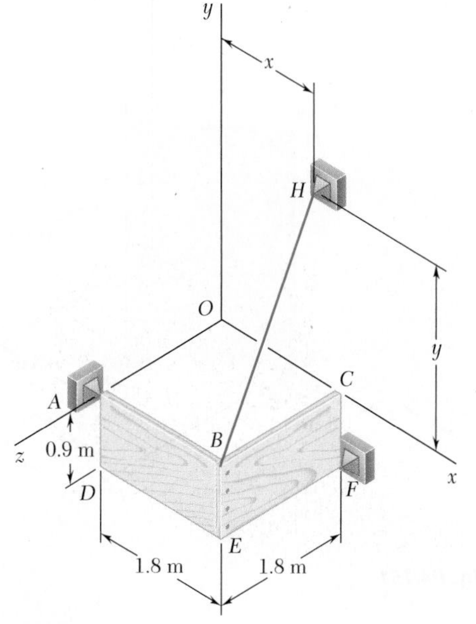

Fig. P4.146

4.148 To water seedlings, a gardener joins three lengths of pipe, AB, BC, and CD, fitted with spray nozzles and suspends the assembly using hinged supports at A and D and cable EF. Knowing that the pipe has a mass per unit length of 1.25 kg/m, determine the tension in the cable.

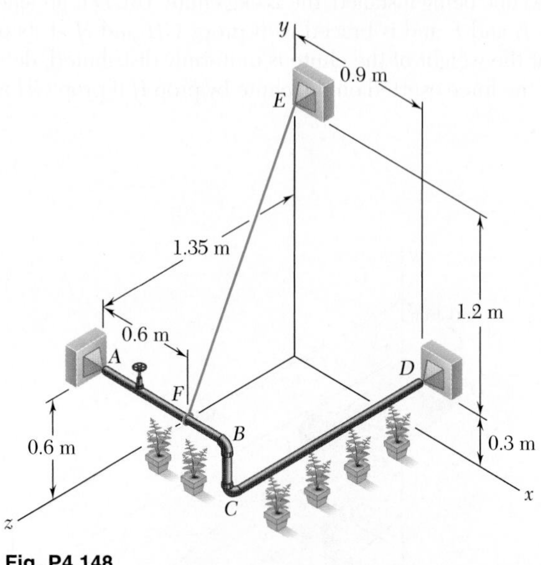

Fig. P4.148

4.149 Solve Prob. 4.148 assuming that cable EF is replaced by a cable connecting E and C.

4.150 Member $ACDB$ of length 80 cm is supported by ball-and-socket joints at A and B and is trisected by arms CE and DF which are welded to the member. For the loading shown, determine the tension in cable FG.

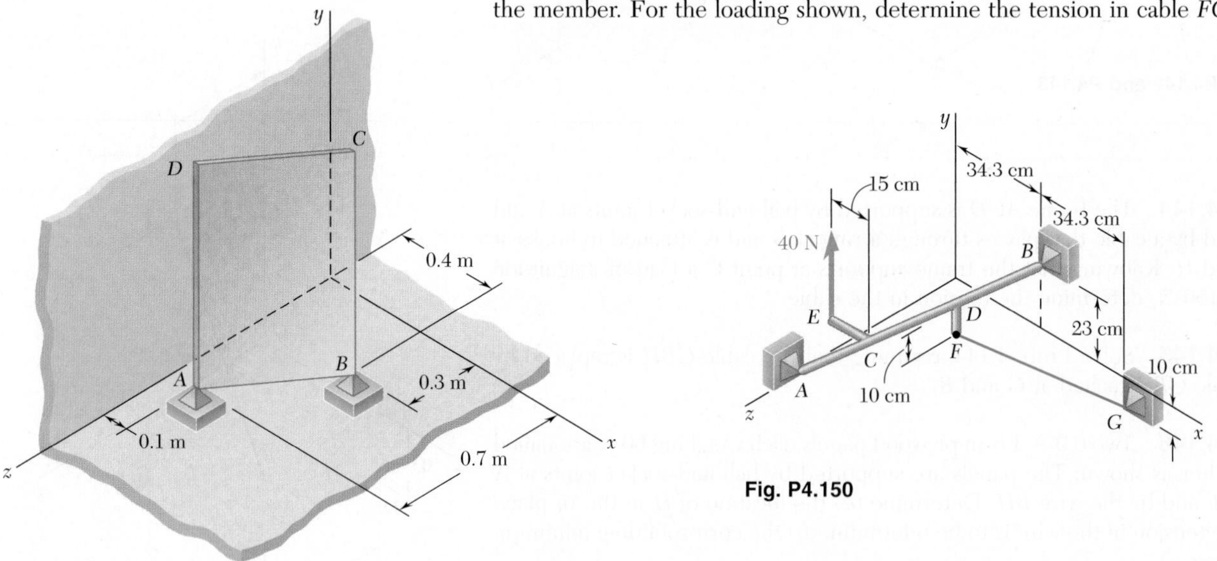

Fig. P4.150

Fig. *P4.151*

4.151 A uniform 0.5 × 0.75-m steel plate $ABCD$ has a mass of 40 kg and is attached to ball-and-socket joints at A and B. Knowing that the plate leans against a frictionless vertical wall at D, determine (*a*) the location of D, (*b*) the reaction at D.

REVIEW AND SUMMARY FOR CHAPTER 4

Equilibrium equations

This chapter was devoted to the study of the *equilibrium of rigid bodies,* that is, to the situation when the external forces acting on a rigid body *form a system equivalent to zero* [Sec. 4.1]. We then have

$$\Sigma \mathbf{F} = 0 \qquad \Sigma \mathbf{M}_O = \Sigma(\mathbf{r} \times \mathbf{F}) = 0 \qquad (4.1)$$

Resolving each force and each moment into its rectangular components, we can express the necessary and sufficient conditions for the equilibrium of a rigid body with the following six scalar equations:

$$\Sigma F_x = 0 \qquad \Sigma F_y = 0 \qquad \Sigma F_z = 0 \qquad (4.2)$$
$$\Sigma M_x = 0 \qquad \Sigma M_y = 0 \qquad \Sigma M_z = 0 \qquad (4.3)$$

These equations can be used to determine unknown forces applied to the rigid body or unknown reactions exerted by its supports.

Free-body diagram

When solving a problem involving the equilibrium of a rigid body, it is essential to consider *all* of the forces acting on the body. Therefore, the first step in the solution of the problem should be to draw a *free-body diagram* showing the body under consideration and all of the unknown as well as known forces acting on it [Sec. 4.2].

Equilibrium of a two-dimensional structure

In the first part of the chapter, we considered the *equilibrium of a two-dimensional structure;* that is, we assumed that the structure considered and the forces applied to it were contained in the same plane. We saw that each of the reactions exerted on the structure by its supports could involve one, two, or three unknowns, depending upon the type of support [Sec. 4.3].

In the case of a two-dimensional structure, Eqs. (4.1), or Eqs. (4.2) and (4.3), reduce to *three equilibrium equations,* namely

$$\Sigma F_x = 0 \qquad \Sigma F_y = 0 \qquad \Sigma M_A = 0 \qquad (4.5)$$

where A is an arbitrary point in the plane of the structure [Sec. 4.4]. These equations can be used to solve for three unknowns. While the three equilibrium equations (4.5) cannot be *augmented* with additional equations, any of them can be *replaced* by another equation. Therefore, we can write alternative sets of equilibrium equations, such as

$$\Sigma F_x = 0 \qquad \Sigma M_A = 0 \qquad \Sigma M_B = 0 \qquad (4.6)$$

where point B is chosen in such a way that the line AB is not parallel to the y axis, or

$$\Sigma M_A = 0 \qquad \Sigma M_B = 0 \qquad \Sigma M_C = 0 \qquad (4.7)$$

where the points A, B, and C do not lie in a straight line.

Since any set of equilibrium equations can be solved for only three unknowns, the reactions at the supports of a rigid two-dimensional structure cannot be completely determined if they involve *more than three unknowns;* they are said to be *statically indeterminate* [Sec. 4.5]. On the other hand, if the reactions involve *fewer than three unknowns*, equilibrium will not be maintained under general loading conditions; the structure is said to be *partially constrained.* The fact that the reactions involve exactly three unknowns is no guarantee that the equilibrium equations can be solved for all three unknowns. If the supports are arranged in such a way that the reactions are *either concurrent or parallel,* the reactions are statically indeterminate, and the structure is said to be *improperly constrained.*

Statical indeterminacy

Partial constraints

Improper constraints

Two particular cases of equilibrium of a rigid body were given special attention. In Sec. 4.6, a *two-force body* was defined as a rigid body subjected to forces at only two points, and it was shown that the resultants $\mathbf{F}_1$ and $\mathbf{F}_2$ of these forces must have the *same magnitude, the same line of action, and opposite sense* (Fig. 4.11), a property which will simplify the solution of certain problems in later chapters. In Sec. 4.7, a *three-force body* was defined as a rigid body subjected to forces at only three points, and it was shown that the resultants $\mathbf{F}_1$, $\mathbf{F}_2$, and $\mathbf{F}_3$ of these forces must be *either concurrent* (Fig. 4.12) *or parallel.* This properly provides us with an alternative approach to the solution of problems involving a three-force body [Sample Prob. 4.6].

Two-force body

Three-force body

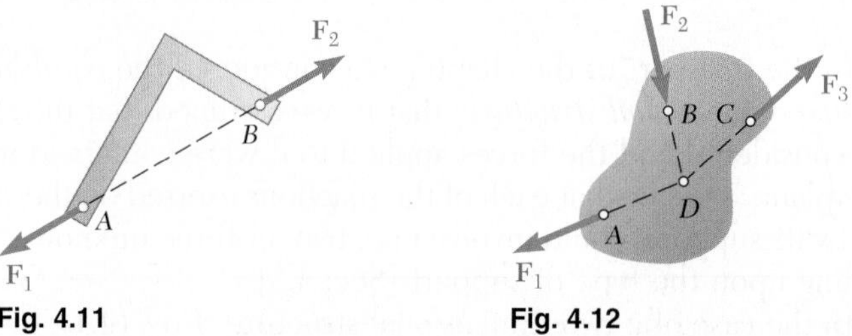

Fig. 4.11

Fig. 4.12

Equilibrium of a three-dimensional body

In the second part of the chapter, we considered the *equilibrium of a three-dimensional body* and saw that each of the reactions exerted on the body by its supports could involve between one and six unknowns, depending upon the type of support [Sec. 4.8].

In the general case of the equilibrium of a three-dimensional body, all of the six scalar equilibrium equations (4.2) and (4.3) listed at the beginning of this review should be used and solved for *six unknowns* [Sec. 4.9]. In most problems, however, these equations will be more conveniently obtained if we first write

$$\Sigma\mathbf{F} = 0 \qquad \Sigma\mathbf{M}_O = \Sigma(\mathbf{r} \times \mathbf{F}) = 0 \tag{4.1}$$

and express the forces $\mathbf{F}$ and position vectors $\mathbf{r}$ in terms of scalar components and unit vectors. The vector products can then be computed either directly or by means of determinants, and the desired scalar equations obtained by equating to zero the coefficients of the unit vectors [Sample Probs. 4.7 through 4.9].

We noted that as many as three unknown reaction components may be eliminated from the computation of $\Sigma \mathbf{M}_O$ in the second of the relations (4.1) through a judicious choice of point O. Also, the reactions at two points A and B can be eliminated from the solution of some problems by writing the equation $\Sigma M_{AB} = 0$, which involves the computation of the moments of the forces about an axis AB joining points A and B [Sample Prob. 4.10].

If the reactions involve more than six unknowns, some of the reactions are *statically indeterminate;* if they involve fewer than six unknowns, the rigid body is only *partially constrained.* Even with six or more unknowns, the rigid body will be *improperly constrained* if the reactions associated with the given supports either are parallel or intersect the same line.

Review Problems

4.152 The maximum allowable value of each of the reactions is 360 N. Neglecting the weight of the beam, determine the range of values of the distance d for which the beam is safe.

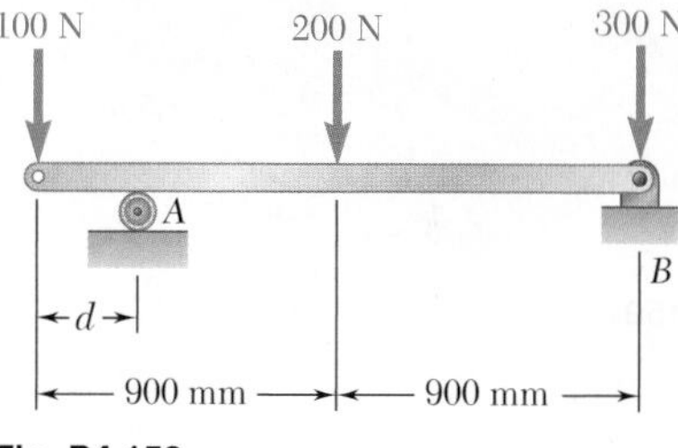

Fig. P4.152

4.153 Determine the maximum tension which can be developed in cable AB if the maximum allowable value of the reaction at C is 1000 N.

4.154 Neglecting friction, determine the tension in cable ABD and the reaction at support C.

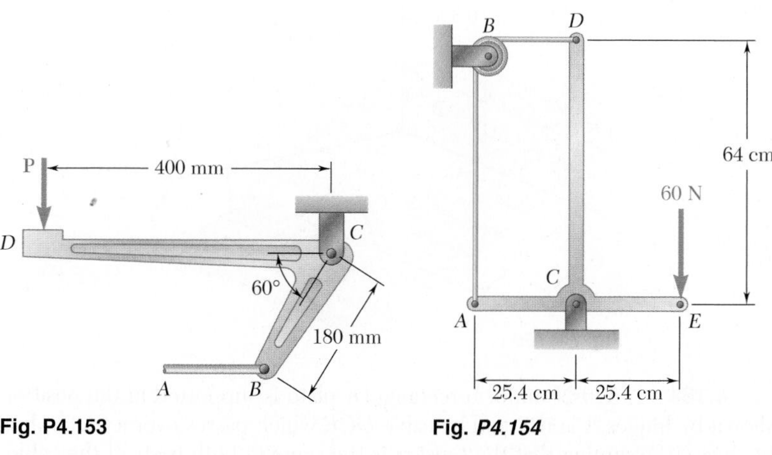

Fig. P4.153

Fig. P4.154

4.155 Knowing that the tension in wire BD is 600 N, determine the reaction at fixed support C for the frame shown.

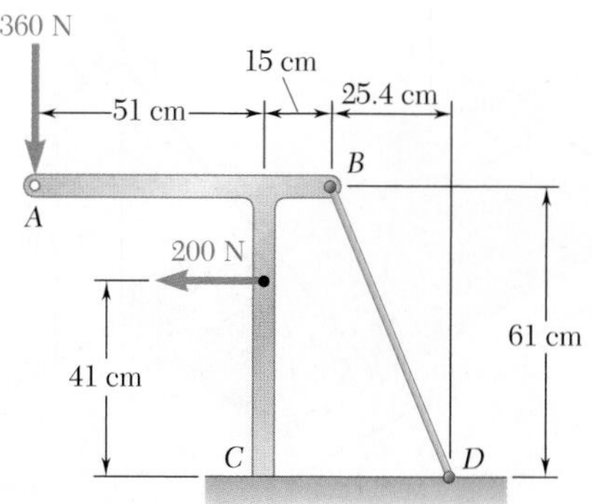

Fig. P4.155

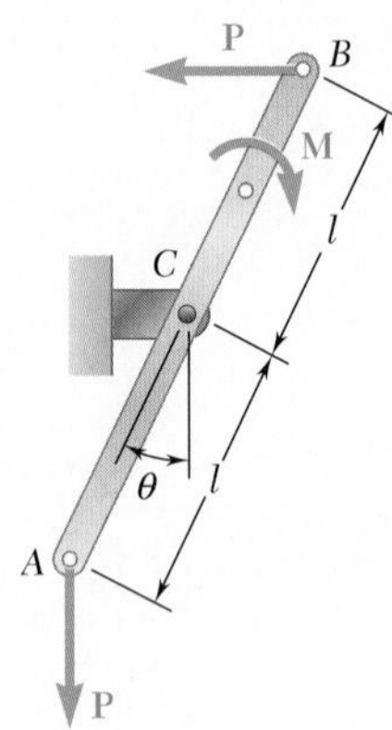

Fig. *P4.156*

4.156 Rod AB is acted upon by a couple $\mathbf{M}$ and two forces, each of magnitude P. (a) Derive an equation in terms of θ, P, M, and l which is satisfied when the rod is in equilibrium. (b) Determine the value of θ corresponding to equilibrium when $M = 650$ N · cm, $P = 40$ N, and $l = 15$ cm.

4.157 A 400-N crate is attached to the trolley-beam system shown. Knowing that $a = 0.5$ m, determine (a) the tension in cable CD, (b) the reaction at B.

4.158 Rod AB is bent into the shape of a circular arc and is lodged between two pegs D and E. It supports a load $\mathbf{P}$ at end B. Neglecting friction and the weight of the rod, determine the distance c corresponding to equilibrium when $a = 25$ mm and $R = 125$ mm.

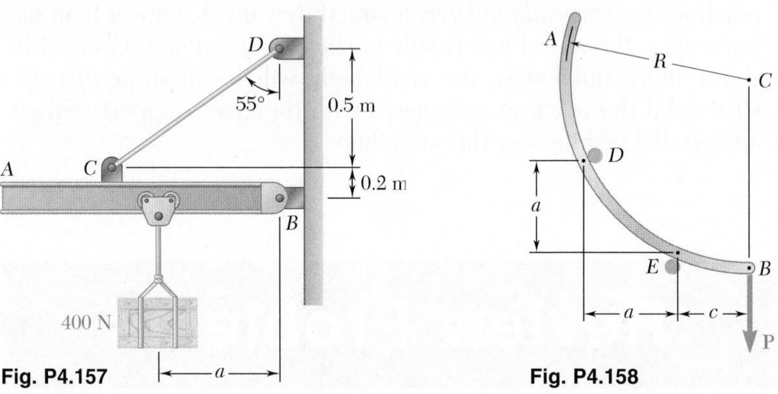

Fig. P4.157

Fig. P4.158

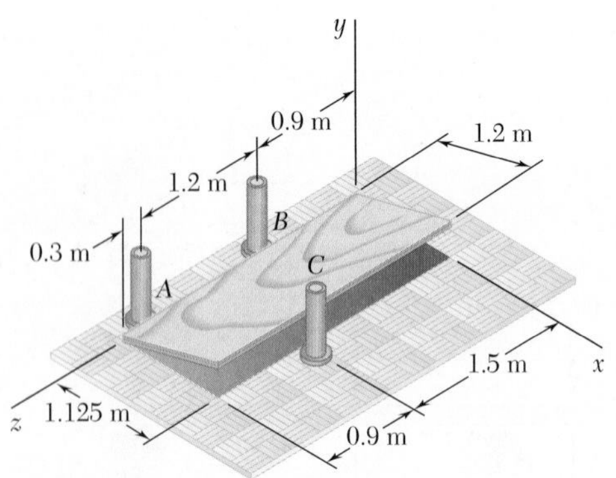

Fig. P4.159

4.159 A 1.2 × 2.4-m sheet of plywood having a mass of 17 kg has been temporarily placed among three pipe supports. The lower edge of the sheet rests on small collars A and B and its upper edge leans against pipe C. Neglecting friction at all surfaces, determine the reactions at A, B, and C.

4.160 A 30-kg cover for a roof opening is hinged at corners A and B. The roof forms an angle of 30° with the horizontal, and the cover is maintained in a horizontal position by the brace CE. Determine (a) the magnitude of the force exerted by the brace, (b) the reactions at the hinges. Assume that the hinge at A does not exert any axial thrust.

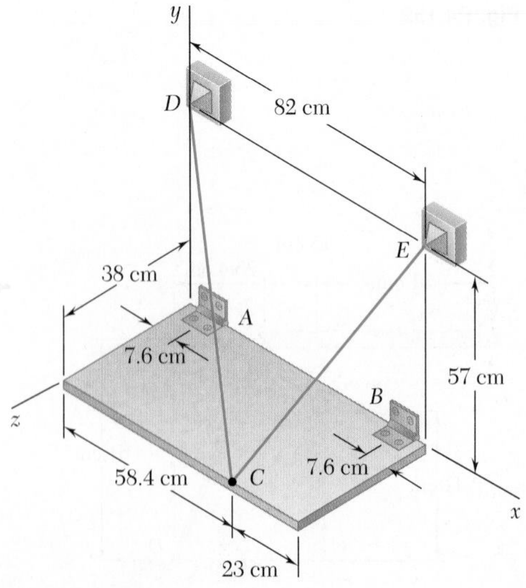

Fig. P4.161

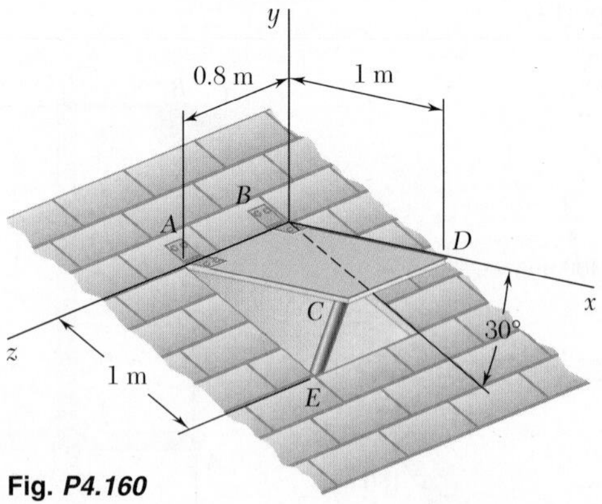

Fig. *P4.160*

4.161 A 570-N uniform rectangular plate is supported in the position shown by hinges A and B and by cable DCE which passes over a frictionless hook at C. Assuming that the tension is the same in both parts of the cable, determine (a) the tension in the cable, (b) the reactions at A and B. Assume that the hinge at B does not exert any axial thrust.

4.162 The rigid L-shaped member *ABF* is supported by a ball-and-socket joint at *A* and by three cables. For the loading shown, determine the tension in each cable and the reaction at *A*.

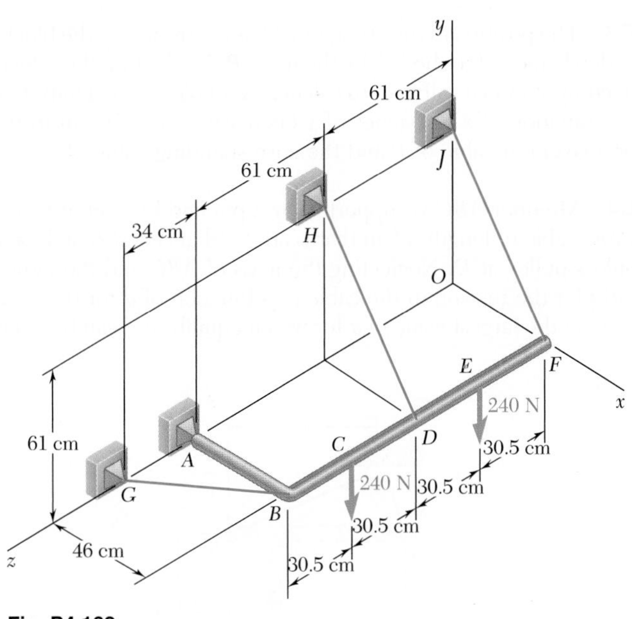

Fig. P4.162

63640

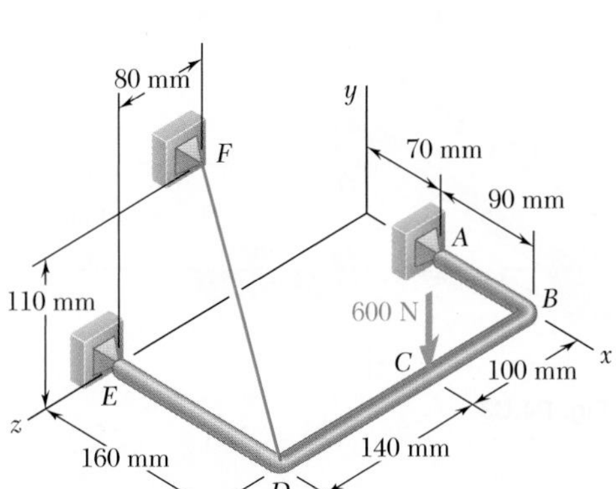

Fig. ***P4.163***

4.163 The bent rod *ABDE* is supported by ball-and-socket joints at *A* and *E* and by the cable *DF*. If a 600-N load is applied at *C* as shown, determine the tension in the cable.

Computer Problems

4.C1 A slender rod *AB* of weight *W* is attached to blocks at *A* and *B* which can move freely in the guides shown. The constant of the spring is *k*, and the spring is unstretched when the rod is horizontal. Neglecting the weight of the blocks, derive an equation in terms of θ, *W*, *l*, and *k* which must be satisfied when the rod is in equilibrium. Knowing that $W = 5$ kg and $l = 102$ cm, (*a*) calculate and plot the value of the spring constant *k* as a function of the angle θ for $15° \leq \theta \leq 40°$, (*b*) determine the two values of the angle θ corresponding to equilibrium when $k = 0.24$ N/cm.

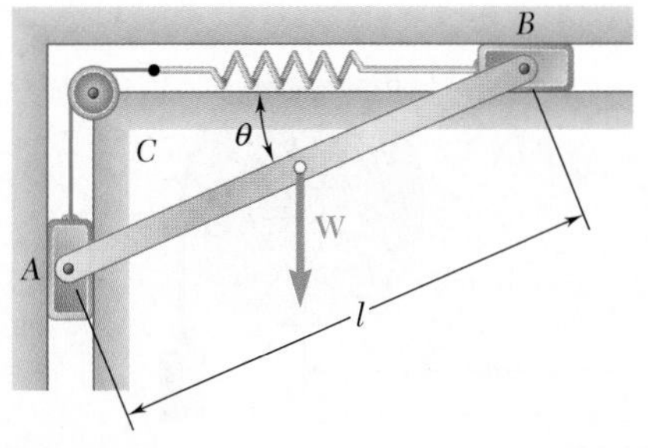

Fig. P4.C1

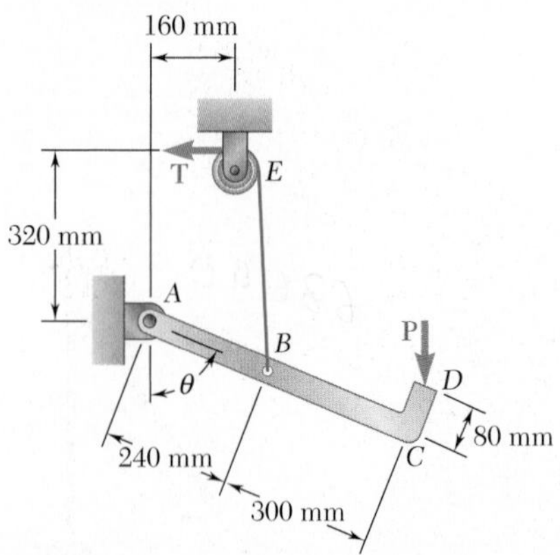

Fig. P4.C2

4.C2 The position of the L-shaped rod shown is controlled by a cable attached at point B. Knowing that the rod supports a load of magnitude $P = 200$ N, use computational software to calculate and plot the tension T in the cable as a function of θ for values of θ from 0 to 120°. Determine the maximum tension T_{max} and the corresponding value of θ.

4.C3 The position of the 10-kg rod AB is controlled by the block shown, which is slowly moved to the left by the force **P**. Neglecting the effect of friction, use computational software to calculate and plot the magnitude P of the force as a function of x for values of x decreasing from 76 cm to 0. Determine the maximum value of P and the corresponding value of x.

***4.C4** Member ABC is supported by a pin and bracket at C and by an inextensible cable of length 3.5 m that is attached at A and B and passes over a frictionless pulley at D. Neglecting the mass of ABC and the radius of the pulley, (*a*) plot the tension in the cable as a function of a for $0 \le a \le 2.4$ m, (*b*) determine the largest value of a for which equilibrium can be maintained.

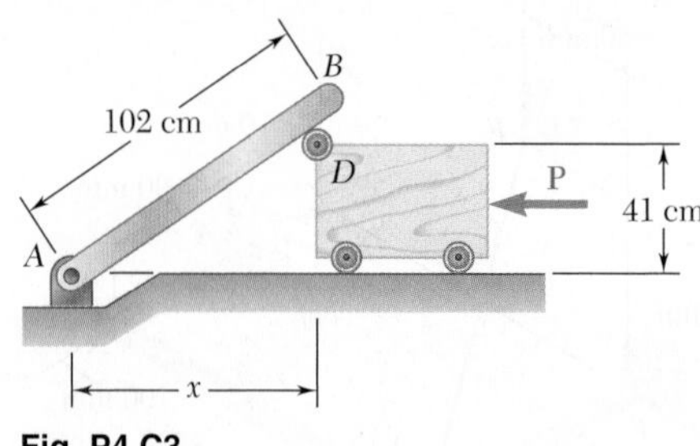

Fig. P4.C3

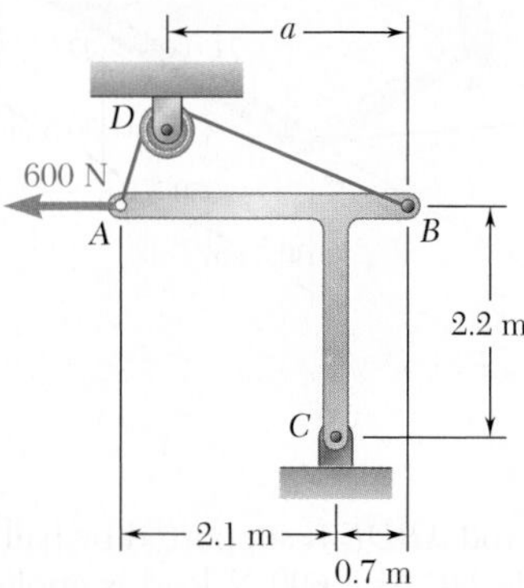

Fig. P4.C4

4.C5 and 4.C6 The constant of spring AB is k, and the spring is unstretched when $\theta = 0$. Knowing that $R = 200$ mm, $a = 400$ mm, and $k = 1$ kN/m, use computational software to calculate and plot the mass m corresponding to equilibrium as a function of θ for values of θ from 0 to 90°. Determine the value of θ corresponding to equilibrium when $m = 2$ kg.

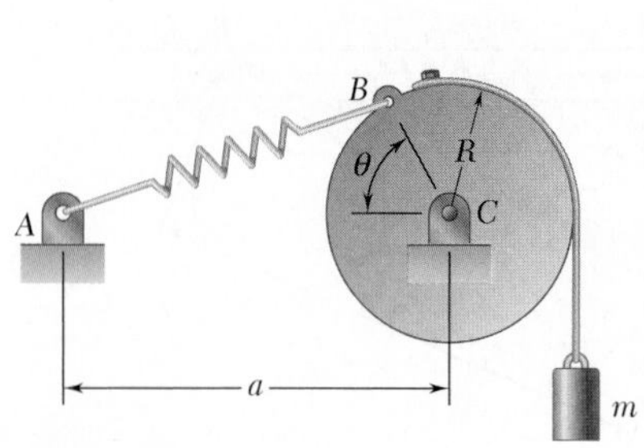

Fig. P4.C5

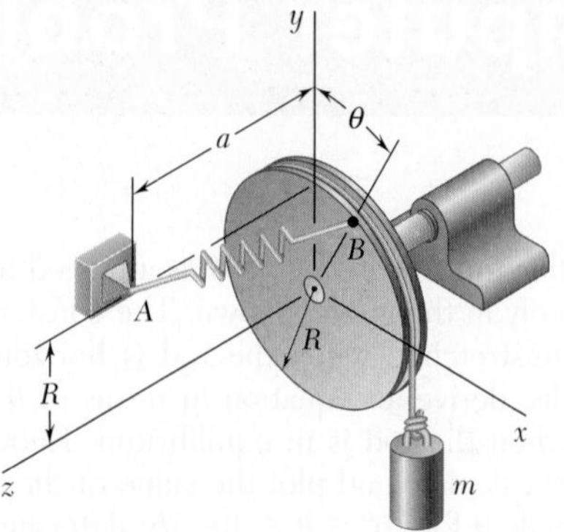

Fig. P4.C6

4.C7 An 20 × 25.4-cm panel of weight $W = 20$ kg is supported by hinges along edge AB. Cable CDE is attached to the panel at point C, passes over a small pulley at D, and supports a cylinder of weight W. Neglecting the effect of friction, use computational software to calculate and plot the weight of the cylinder corresponding to equilibrium as a function of θ for values of θ from 0 to 90°. Determine the value of θ corresponding to equilibrium when $W = 10$ kg.

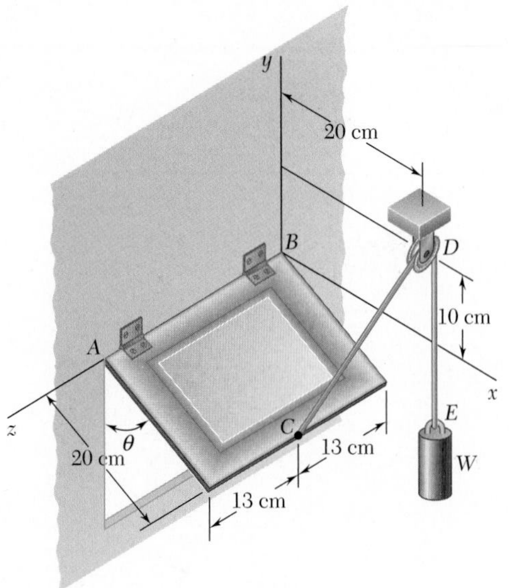

Fig. P4.C7

4.C8 A uniform circular plate of radius 300 mm and mass 26 kg is supported by three vertical wires that are equally spaced around its edge. A small 3-kg block E is placed on the plate at D and is then slowly moved along diameter CD until it reaches C. (*a*) Plot the tension in wires A and C as functions of a, where a is the distance of the block from D. (*b*) Determine the value of a for which the tension in wires A and C is minimum.

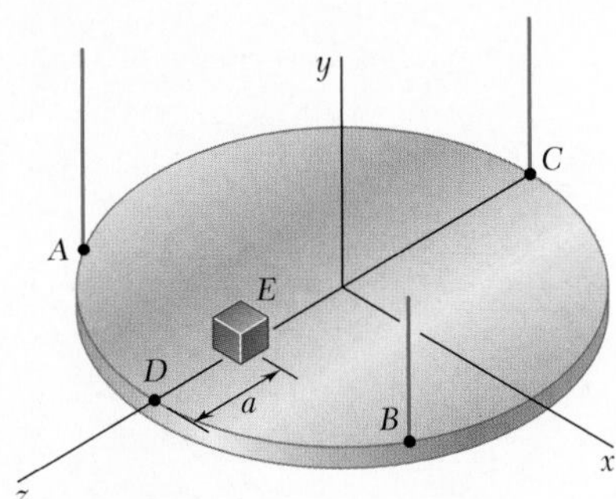

Fig. P4.C8

4.C9 The derrick shown supports a 2000-kg crate. It is held by a ball-and-socket joint at point A and by two cables attached at points D and E. Knowing that the derrick lies in a vertical plane forming an angle ϕ with the xy plane, use computational software to calculate and plot the tension in each cable as a function of ϕ for values of ϕ from 0 to 40°. Determine the value of ϕ for which the tension in cable BE is maximum.

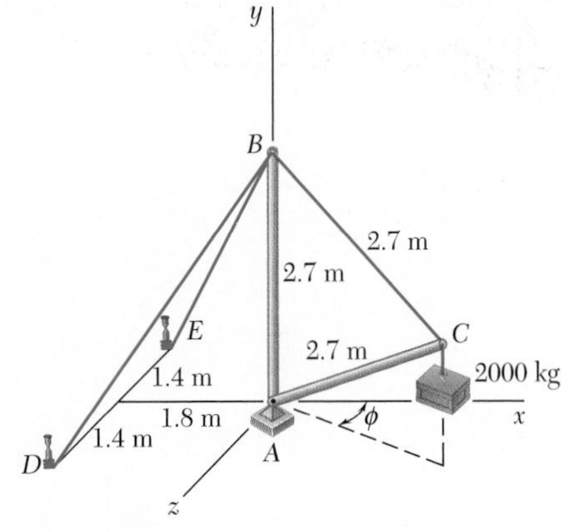

Fig. P4.C9

4.C10 The 70-kg uniform steel plate $ABCD$ is welded to shaft EF and is maintained in the position shown by the couple **M**. Knowing that collars prevent the shaft from sliding in the bearings and that the shaft lies in the yz plane, plot the magnitude M of the couple as a function of θ for $0 \leq \theta \leq 90°$.

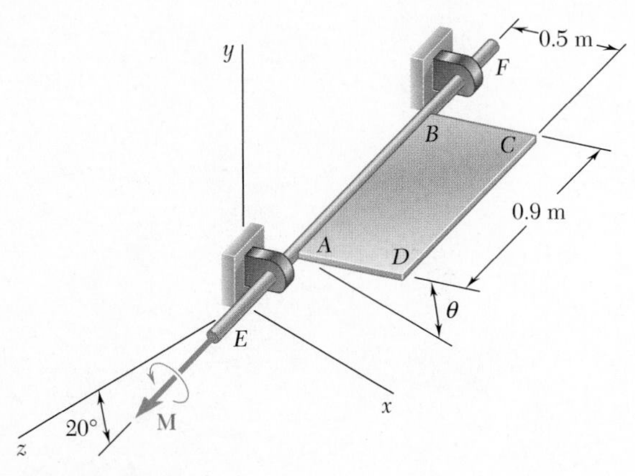

Fig. P4.C10

CHAPTER 5

Distributed Forces: Centroids and Centers of Gravity

Shown is a portion of the Skyway viaduct being constructed across the bay between San Francisco and Oakland. In this chapter we will introduce the concept of the centroid of an area; in subsequent courses the relation between the location of the centroid and the behavior of the roadway of the viaduct will be established.

DISTRIBUTED FORCES: CENTROIDS AND CENTERS OF GRAVITY

Photo 5.1 The precise balancing of the components of a mobile requires an understanding of centers of gravity and centroids, the main topics of this chapter.

5.1. INTRODUCTION

We have assumed so far that the attraction exerted by the earth on a rigid body could be represented by a single force **W**. This force, called the force of gravity or the weight of the body, was to be applied at the *center of gravity* of the body (Sec. 3.2). Actually, the earth exerts a force on each of the particles forming the body. The action of the earth on a rigid body should thus be represented by a large number of small forces distributed over the entire body. You will learn in this chapter, however, that all of these small forces can be replaced by a single equivalent force **W**. You will also learn how to determine the center of gravity, that is, the point of application of the resultant **W**, for bodies of various shapes.

In the first part of the chapter, two-dimensional bodies, such as flat plates and wires contained in a given plane, are considered. Two concepts closely associated with the determination of the center of gravity of a plate or a wire are introduced: the concept of the *centroid* of an area or a line and the concept of the *first moment* of an area or a line with respect to a given axis.

You will also learn that the computation of the area of a surface of revolution or of the volume of a body of revolution is directly related to the determination of the centroid of the line or area used to generate that surface or body of revolution (Theorems of Pappus-Guldinus). And, as is shown in Secs. 5.8 and 5.9, the determination of the centroid of an area simplifies the analysis of beams subjected to distributed loads and the computation of the forces exerted on submerged rectangular surfaces, such as hydraulic gates and portions of dams.

In the last part of the chapter, you will learn how to determine the center of gravity of a three-dimensional body as well as the centroid of a volume and the first moments of that volume with respect to the coordinate planes.

AREAS AND LINES

5.2. CENTER OF GRAVITY OF A TWO-DIMENSIONAL BODY

Let us first consider a flat horizontal plate (Fig. 5.1). We can divide the plate into n small elements. The coordinates of the first element

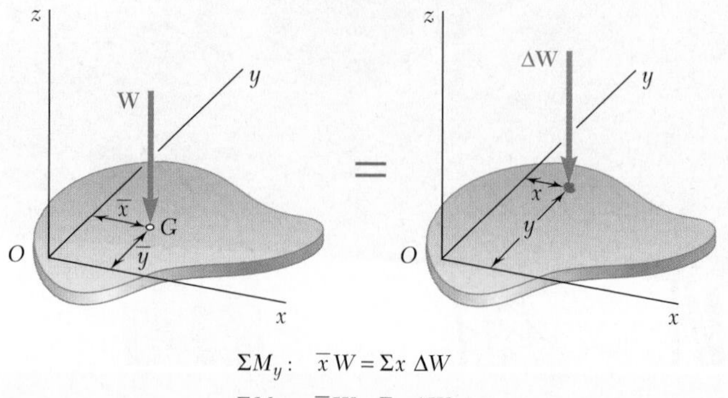

$$\Sigma M_y: \quad \bar{x}W = \Sigma x\,\Delta W$$

$$\Sigma M_x: \quad \bar{y}W = \Sigma y\,\Delta W$$

Fig. 5.1 Center of gravity of a plate.

are denoted by x_1 and y_1, those of the second element by x_2 and y_2, etc. The forces exerted by the earth on the elements of a plate will be denoted, respectively, by $\Delta\mathbf{W}_1, \Delta\mathbf{W}_2, \ldots, \Delta\mathbf{W}_n$. These forces or weights are directed toward the center of the earth; however, for all practical purposes they can be assumed to be parallel. Their resultant is therefore a single force in the same direction. The magnitude W of this force is obtained by adding the magnitudes of the elemental weights:

$$\Sigma F_z: \qquad W = \Delta W_1 + \Delta W_2 + \cdots + \Delta W_n$$

To obtain the coordinates $\bar{x}$ and $\bar{y}$ of the point G where the resultant $\mathbf{W}$ should be applied, we write that the moments of $\mathbf{W}$ about the y and x axes are equal to the sum of the corresponding moments of the elemental weights,

$$\begin{aligned} \Sigma M_y: &\quad \bar{x}W = x_1\,\Delta W_1 + x_2\,\Delta W_2 + \cdots + x_n\,\Delta W_n \\ \Sigma M_x: &\quad \bar{y}W = y_1\,\Delta W_1 + y_2\,\Delta W_2 + \cdots + y_n\,\Delta W_n \end{aligned} \tag{5.1}$$

If we now increase the number of elements into which the plate is divided and simultaneously decrease the size of each element, we obtain in the limit the following expressions:

$$W = \int dW \qquad \bar{x}W = \int x\,dW \qquad \bar{y}W = \int y\,dW \tag{5.2}$$

These equations define the weight $\mathbf{W}$ and the coordinates $\bar{x}$ and $\bar{y}$ of the center of gravity G of a flat plate. The same equations can be derived for a wire lying in the xy plane (Fig. 5.2). We note that the center of gravity G of a wire is usually not located on the wire.

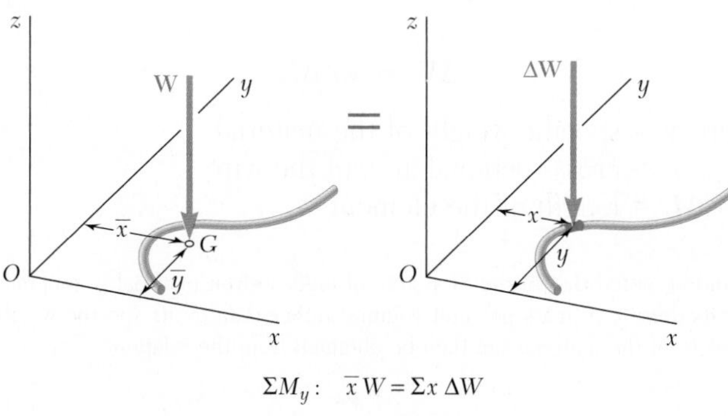

Fig. 5.2 Center of gravity of a wire.

5.3. CENTROIDS OF AREAS AND LINES

In the case of a flat homogeneous plate of uniform thickness, the magnitude ΔW of the weight of an element of the plate can be expressed as

$$\Delta W = \gamma t \, \Delta A$$

where γ = specific weight (weight per unit volume) of the material
t = thickness of the plate
ΔA = area of the element

Similarly, we can express the magnitude W of the weight of the entire plate as

$$W = \gamma t A$$

where A is the total area of the plate.

If U.S. customary units are used, the specific weight γ should be expressed in lb/ft^3, the thickness t in feet, and the areas ΔA and A in square feet. We observe that ΔW and W will then be expressed in pounds. If SI units are used, γ should be expressed in N/m^3, t in meters, and the areas ΔA and A in square meters; the weights ΔW and W will then be expressed in newtons.†

Substituting for ΔW and W in the moment equations (5.1) and dividing throughout by γt, we obtain

$$\begin{aligned} \Sigma M_y: \quad & \bar{x}A = x_1 \, \Delta A_1 + x_2 \, \Delta A_2 + \cdots + x_n \, \Delta A_n \\ \Sigma M_x: \quad & \bar{y}A = y_1 \, \Delta A_1 + y_2 \, \Delta A_2 + \cdots + y_n \, \Delta A_n \end{aligned}$$

If we increase the number of elements into which the area A is divided and simultaneously decrease the size of each element, we obtain in the limit

$$\bar{x}A = \int x \, dA \qquad \bar{y}A = \int y \, dA \tag{5.3}$$

These equations define the coordinates $\bar{x}$ and $\bar{y}$ of the center of gravity of a homogeneous plate. The point whose coordinates are $\bar{x}$ and $\bar{y}$ is also known as the *centroid C of the area* A of the plate (Fig. 5.3). If the plate is not homogeneous, these equations cannot be used to determine the center of gravity of the plate; they still define, however, the centroid of the area.

In the case of a homogeneous wire of uniform cross section, the magnitude ΔW of the weight of an element of wire can be expressed as

$$\Delta W = \gamma a \, \Delta L$$

where γ = specific weight of the material
a = cross-sectional area of the wire
ΔL = length of the element

†It should be noted that in the SI system of units a given material is generally characterized by its density ρ (mass per unit volume) rather than by its specific weight γ. The specific weight of the material can then be obtained from the relation

$$\gamma = \rho g$$

where $g = 9.81$ m/s^2. Since ρ is expressed in kg/m^3, we observe that γ will be expressed in (kg/m^3)(m/s^2), that is, in N/m^3.

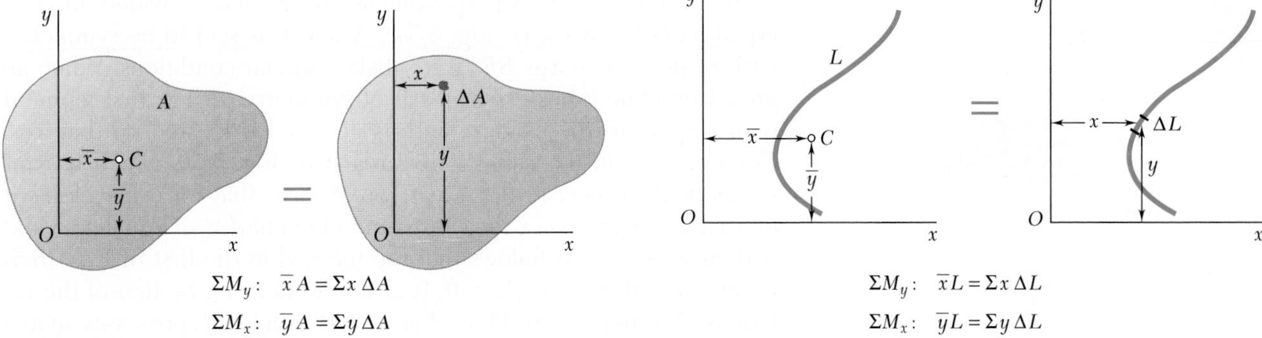

Fig. 5.3 Centroid of an area.

Fig. 5.4 Centroid of a line.

The center of gravity of the wire then coincides with the *centroid C of the line L* defining the shape of the wire (Fig. 5.4). The coordinates $\bar{x}$ and $\bar{y}$ of the centroid of the line L are obtained from the equations

$$\bar{x}L = \int x\,dL \qquad \bar{y}L = \int y\,dL \tag{5.4}$$

5.4. FIRST MOMENTS OF AREAS AND LINES

The integral $\int x\,dA$ in Eqs. (5.3) of the preceding section is known as the *first moment of the area A with respect to the y axis* and is denoted by Q_y. Similarly, the integral $\int y\,dA$ defines the *first moment of A with respect to the x axis* and is denoted by Q_x. We write

$$Q_y = \int x\,dA \qquad Q_x = \int y\,dA \tag{5.5}$$

Comparing Eqs. (5.3) with Eqs. (5.5), we note that the first moments of the area A can be expressed as the products of the area and the coordinates of its centroid:

$$Q_y = \bar{x}A \qquad Q_x = \bar{y}A \tag{5.6}$$

It follows from Eqs. (5.6) that the coordinates of the centroid of an area can be obtained by dividing the first moments of that area by the area itself. The first moments of the area are also useful in mechanics of materials for determining the shearing stresses in beams under transverse loadings. Finally, we observe from Eqs. (5.6) that if the centroid of an area is located on a coordinate axis, the first moment of the area with respect to that axis is zero. Conversely, if the first moment of an area with respect to a coordinate axis is zero, then the centroid of the area is located on that axis.

Relations similar to Eqs. (5.5) and (5.6) can be used to define the first moments of a line with respect to the coordinate axes and to express these moments as the products of the length L of the line and the coordinates $\bar{x}$ and $\bar{y}$ of its centroid.

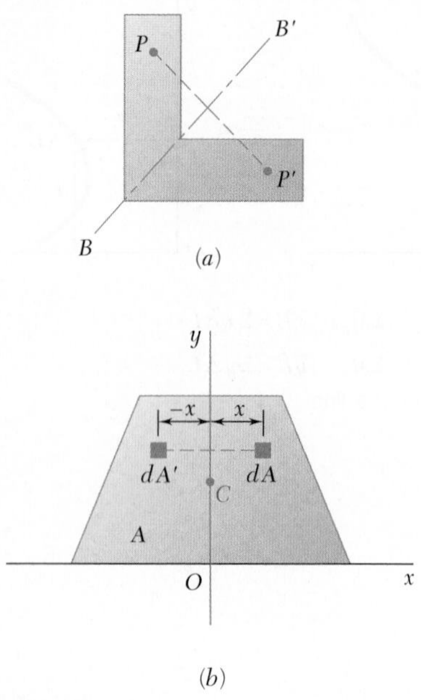

Fig. 5.5

An area A is said to be *symmetric with respect to an axis BB'* if for every point P of the area there exists a point P' of the same area such that the line PP' is perpendicular to BB' and is divided into two equal parts by that axis (Fig. 5.5*a*). A line L is said to be symmetric with respect to an axis BB' if it satisfies similar conditions. When an area A or a line L possesses an axis of symmetry BB', its first moment with respect to BB' is zero, and its centroid is located on that axis. For example, in the case of the area A of Fig. 5.5*b*, which is symmetric with respect to the y axis, we observe that for every element of area dA of abscissa x there exists an element dA' of equal area and with abscissa $-x$. It follows that the integral in the first of Eqs. (5.5) is zero and, thus, that $Q_y = 0$. It also follows from the first of the relations (5.3) that $\bar{x} = 0$. Thus, if an area A or a line L possesses an axis of symmetry, its centroid C is located on that axis.

We further note that if an area or line possesses two axes of symmetry, its centroid C must be located at the intersection of the two axes (Fig. 5.6). This property enables us to determine immediately the centroid of areas such as circles, ellipses, squares, rectangles, equilateral triangles, or other symmetric figures as well as the centroid of lines in the shape of the circumference of a circle, the perimeter of a square, etc.

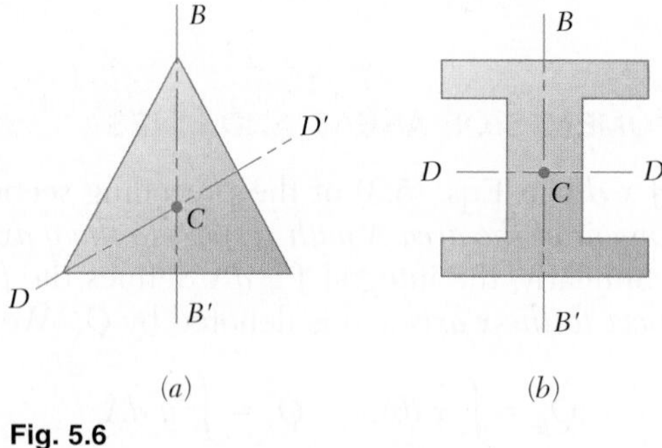

Fig. 5.6

An area A is said to be *symmetric with respect to a center O* if for every element of area dA of coordinates x and y there exists an element dA' of equal area with coordinates $-x$ and $-y$ (Fig. 5.7). It then follows that the integrals in Eqs. (5.5) are both zero and that $Q_x = Q_y = 0$. It also follows from Eqs. (5.3) that $\bar{x} = \bar{y} = 0$, that is, that the centroid of the area coincides with its center of symmetry O. Similarly, if a line possesses a center of symmetry O, the centroid of the line will coincide with the center O.

It should be noted that a figure possessing a center of symmetry does not necessarily possess an axis of symmetry (Fig. 5.7), while a figure possessing two axes of symmetry does not necessarily possess a center of symmetry (Fig. 5.6*a*). However, if a figure possesses two axes of symmetry at a right angle to each other, the point of intersection of these axes is a center of symmetry (Fig. 5.6*b*).

Determining the centroids of unsymmetrical areas and lines and of areas and lines possessing only one axis of symmetry will be discussed in Secs. 5.6 and 5.7. Centroids of common shapes of areas and lines are shown in Fig. 5.8A and B.

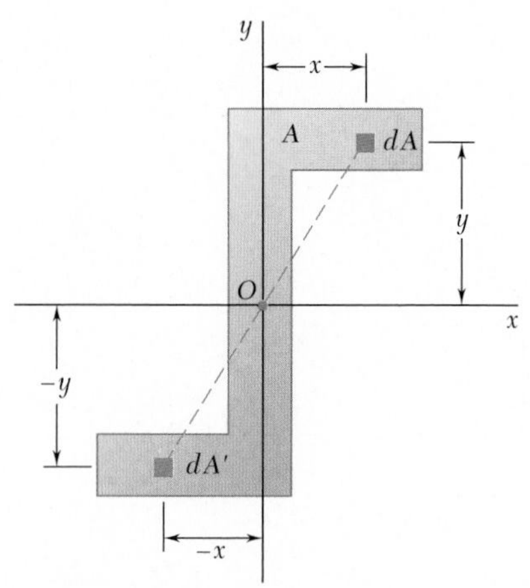

Fig. 5.7

Shape		$\bar{x}$	$\bar{y}$	Area
Triangular area	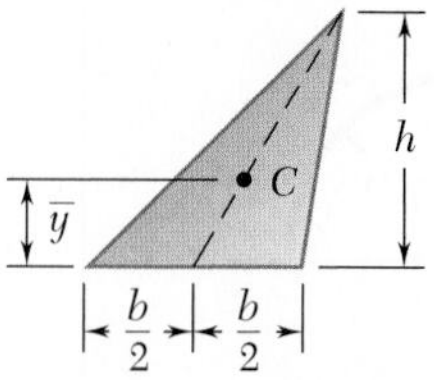		$\frac{h}{3}$	$\frac{bh}{2}$
Quarter-circular area	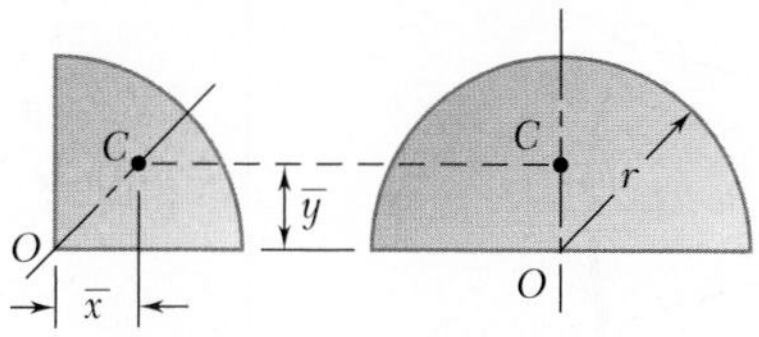	$\frac{4r}{3\pi}$	$\frac{4r}{3\pi}$	$\frac{\pi r^2}{4}$
Semicircular area		0	$\frac{4r}{3\pi}$	$\frac{\pi r^2}{2}$
Quarter-elliptical area	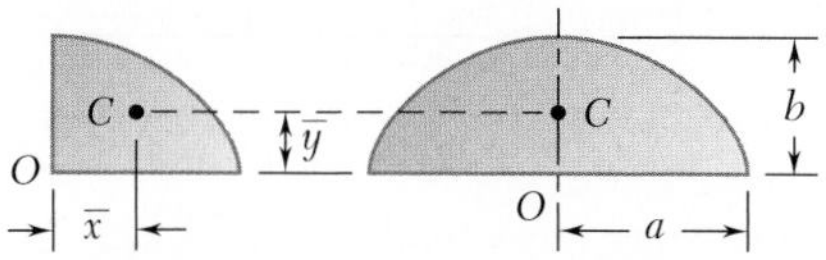	$\frac{4a}{3\pi}$	$\frac{4b}{3\pi}$	$\frac{\pi ab}{4}$
Semielliptical area		0	$\frac{4b}{3\pi}$	$\frac{\pi ab}{2}$
Semiparabolic area	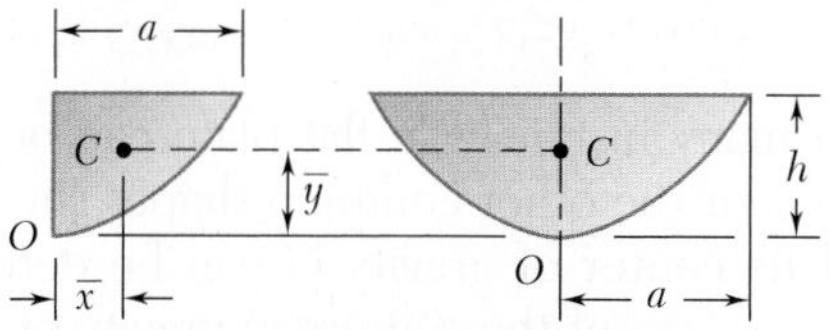	$\frac{3a}{8}$	$\frac{3h}{5}$	$\frac{2ah}{3}$
Parabolic area		0	$\frac{3h}{5}$	$\frac{4ah}{3}$
Parabolic spandrel	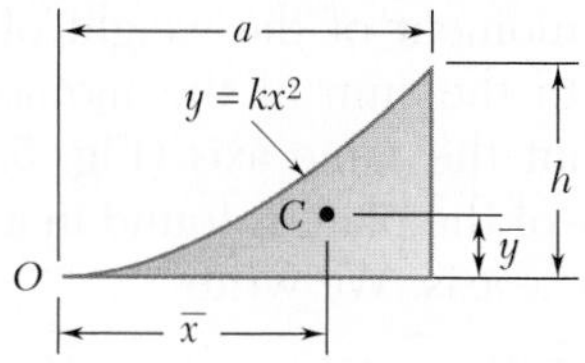 $y = kx^2$	$\frac{3a}{4}$	$\frac{3h}{10}$	$\frac{ah}{3}$
General spandrel	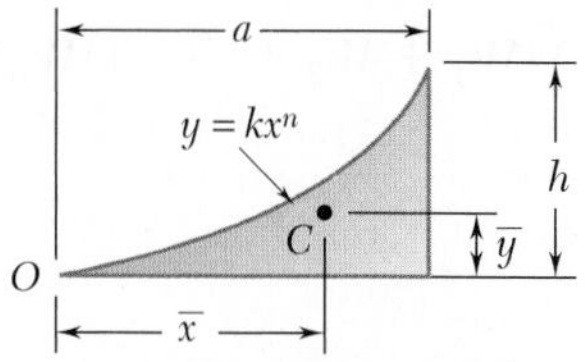 $y = kx^n$	$\frac{n+1}{n+2}a$	$\frac{n+1}{4n+2}h$	$\frac{ah}{n+1}$
Circular sector	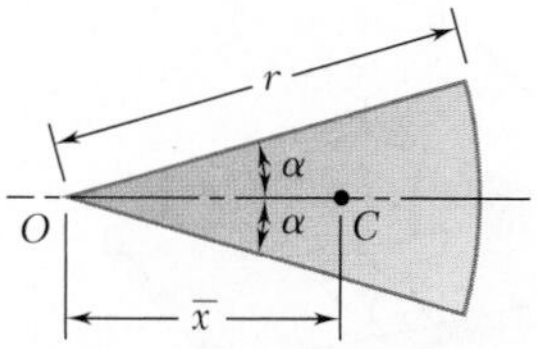	$\frac{2r \sin \alpha}{3\alpha}$	0	αr^2

Fig. 5.8A Centroids of common shapes of areas.

Shape		$\bar{x}$	$\bar{y}$	Length
Quarter-circular arc	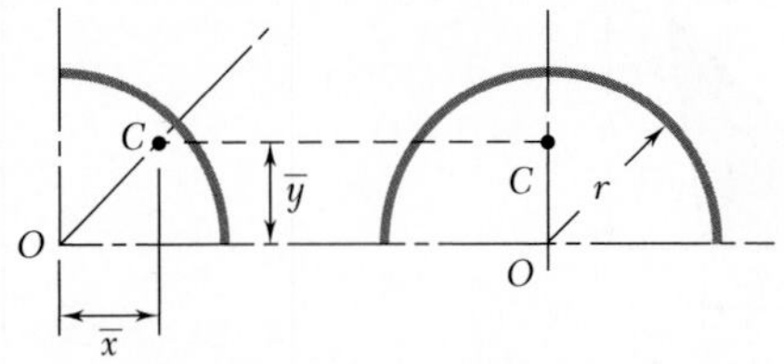	$\frac{2r}{\pi}$	$\frac{2r}{\pi}$	$\frac{\pi r}{2}$
Semicircular arc		0	$\frac{2r}{\pi}$	πr
Arc of circle	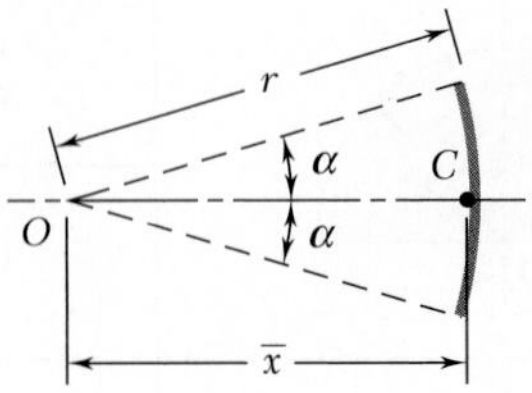	$\frac{r \sin \alpha}{\alpha}$	0	$2\alpha r$

Fig. 5.8B Centroids of common shapes of lines.

5.5. COMPOSITE PLATES AND WIRES

In many instances, a flat plate can be divided into rectangles, triangles, or the other common shapes shown in Fig. 5.8A. The abscissa $\overline{X}$ of its center of gravity G can be determined from the abscissas $\bar{x}_1$, $\bar{x}_2, \ldots, \bar{x}_n$ of the centers of gravity of the various parts by expressing that the moment of the weight of the whole plate about the y axis is equal to the sum of the moments of the weights of the various parts about the same axis (Fig. 5.9). The ordinate $\overline{Y}$ of the center of gravity of the plate is found in a similar way by equating moments about the x axis. We write

$$\Sigma M_y: \quad \overline{X}(W_1 + W_2 + \cdots + W_n) = \bar{x}_1 W_1 + \bar{x}_2 W_2 + \cdots + \bar{x}_n W_n$$

$$\Sigma M_x: \quad \overline{Y}(W_1 + W_2 + \cdots + W_n) = \bar{y}_1 W_1 + \bar{y}_2 W_2 + \cdots + \bar{y}_n W_n$$

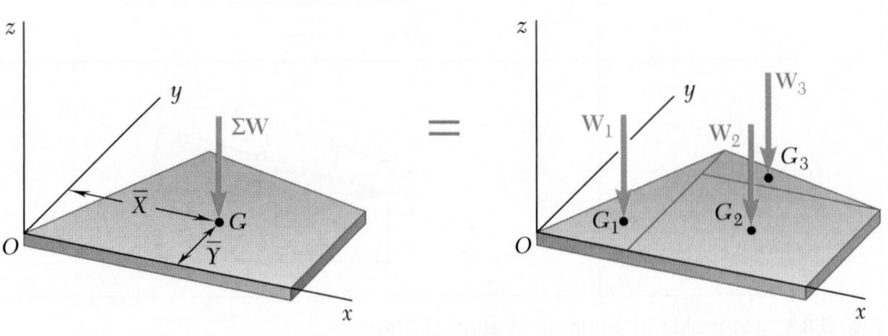

$$\Sigma M_y: \quad \overline{X}\,\Sigma W = \Sigma \bar{x} W$$

$$\Sigma M_x: \quad \overline{Y}\,\Sigma W = \Sigma \bar{y} W$$

Fig. 5.9 Center of gravity of a composite plate.

or, for short,

$$\bar{X}\Sigma W = \Sigma\bar{x}W \qquad \bar{Y}\Sigma W = \Sigma\bar{y}W \tag{5.7}$$

These equations can be solved for the coordinates $\bar{X}$ and $\bar{Y}$ of the center of gravity of the plate.

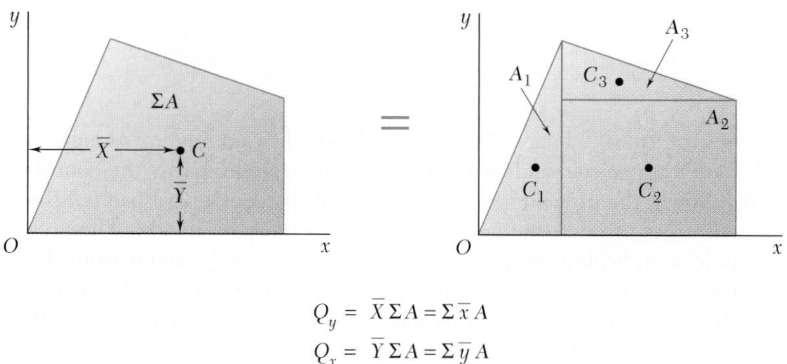

Fig. 5.10 Centroid of a composite area.

If the plate is homogeneous and of uniform thickness, the center of gravity coincides with the centroid C of its area. The abscissa $\bar{X}$ of the centroid of the area can be determined by noting that the first moment Q_y of the composite area with respect to the y axis can be expressed both as the product of $\bar{X}$ and the total area and as the sum of the first moments of the elementary areas with respect to the y axis (Fig. 5.10). The ordinate $\bar{Y}$ of the centroid is found in a similar way by considering the first moment Q_x of the composite area. We have

$$Q_y = \bar{X}(A_1 + A_2 + \cdots + A_n) = \bar{x}_1A_1 + \bar{x}_2A_2 + \cdots + \bar{x}_nA_n$$
$$Q_x = \bar{Y}(A_1 + A_2 + \cdots + A_n) = \bar{y}_1A_1 + \bar{y}_2A_2 + \cdots + \bar{y}_nA_n$$

or, for short,

$$Q_y = \bar{X}\Sigma A = \Sigma\bar{x}A \qquad Q_x = \bar{Y}\Sigma A = \Sigma\bar{y}A \tag{5.8}$$

These equations yield the first moments of the composite area, or they can be used to obtain the coordinates $\bar{X}$ and $\bar{Y}$ of its centroid.

Care should be taken to assign the appropriate sign to the moment of each area. First moments of areas, like moments of forces, can be positive or negative. For example, an area whose centroid is located to the left of the y axis will have a negative first moment with respect to that axis. Also, the area of a hole should be assigned a negative sign (Fig. 5.11).

Similarly, it is possible in many cases to determine the center of gravity of a composite wire or the centroid of a composite line by dividing the wire or line into simpler elements (see Sample Prob. 5.2).

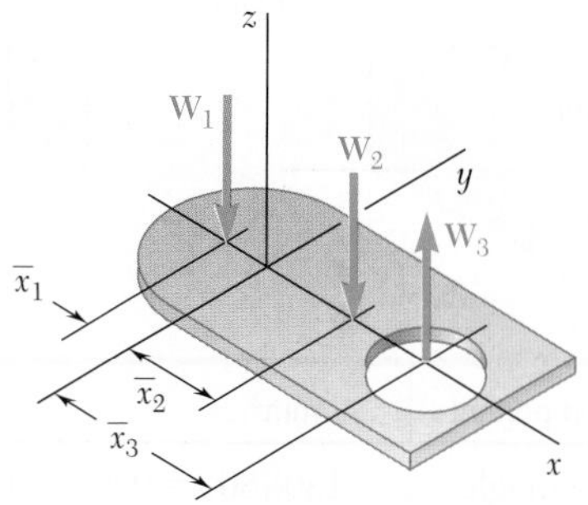

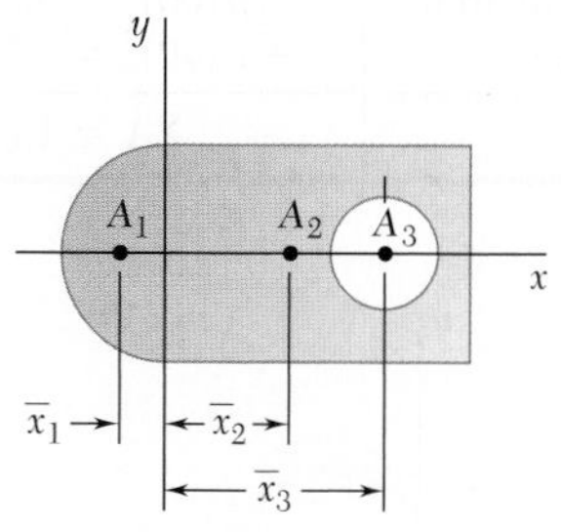

	$\bar{x}$	A	$\bar{x}A$
A_1 Semicircle	–	+	–
A_2 Full rectangle	+	+	+
A_3 Circular hole	+	–	–

Fig. 5.11

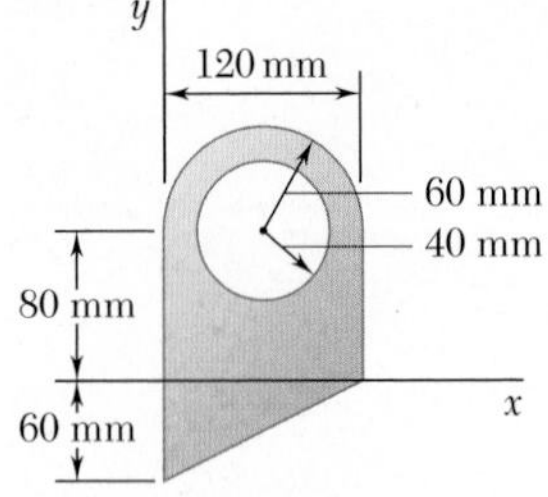

SAMPLE PROBLEM 5.1

For the plane area shown, determine (*a*) the first moments with respect to the *x* and *y* axes, (*b*) the location of the centroid.

SOLUTION

Components of Area. The area is obtained by adding a rectangle, a triangle, and a semicircle and by then subtracting a circle. Using the coordinate axes shown, the area and the coordinates of the centroid of each of the component areas are determined and entered in the table below. The area of the circle is indicated as negative, since it is to be subtracted from the other areas. We note that the coordinate $\bar{y}$ of the centroid of the triangle is negative for the axes shown. The first moments of the component areas with respect to the coordinate axes are computed and entered in the table.

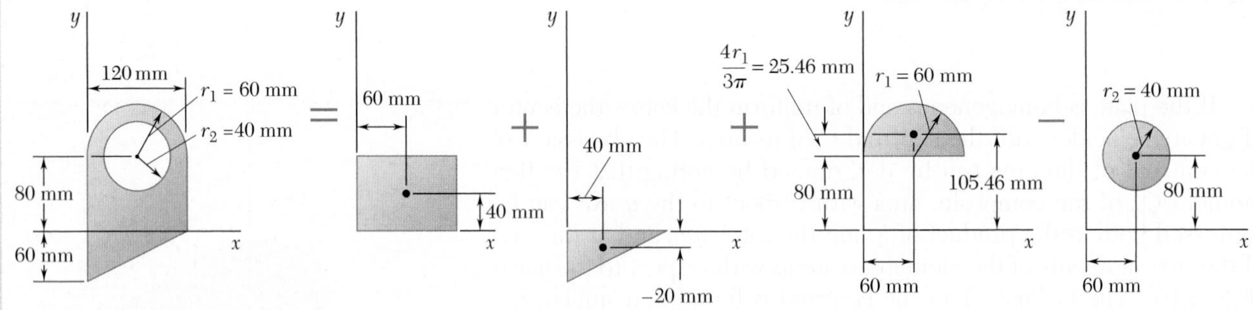

Component	A, mm²	$\bar{x}$, mm	$\bar{y}$, mm	$\bar{x}A$, mm³	$\bar{y}A$, mm³
Rectangle	$(120)(80) = 9.6 \times 10^3$	60	40	$+576 \times 10^3$	$+384 \times 10^3$
Triangle	$\frac{1}{2}(120)(60) = 3.6 \times 10^3$	40	-20	$+144 \times 10^3$	-72×10^3
Semicircle	$\frac{1}{2}\pi(60)^2 = 5.655 \times 10^3$	60	105.46	$+339.3 \times 10^3$	$+596.4 \times 10^3$
Circle	$-\pi(40)^2 = -5.027 \times 10^3$	60	80	-301.6×10^3	-402.2×10^3
	$\Sigma A = 13.828 \times 10^3$			$\Sigma\bar{x}A = +757.7 \times 10^3$	$\Sigma\bar{y}A = +506.2 \times 10^3$

***a.* First Moments of the Area.** Using Eqs. (5.8), we write

$$Q_x = \Sigma\bar{y}A = 506.2 \times 10^3 \text{ mm}^3 \qquad Q_x = 506 \times 10^3 \text{ mm}^3 \blacktriangleleft$$
$$Q_y = \Sigma\bar{x}A = 757.7 \times 10^3 \text{ mm}^3 \qquad Q_y = 758 \times 10^3 \text{ mm}^3 \blacktriangleleft$$

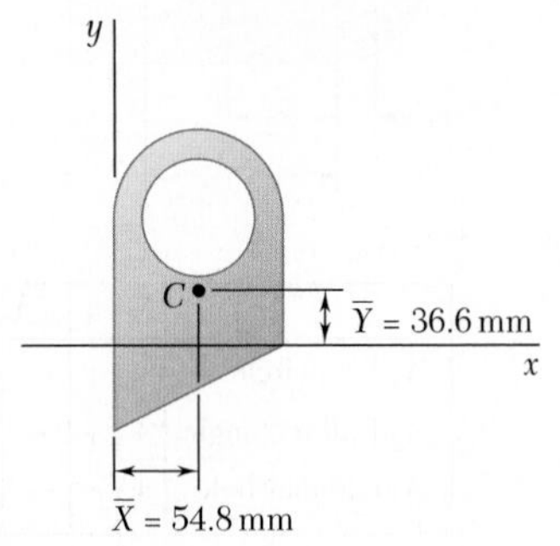

***b.* Location of Centroid.** Substituting the values given in the table into the equations defining the centroid of a composite area, we obtain

$$\bar{X}\Sigma A = \Sigma\bar{x}A: \qquad \bar{X}(13.828 \times 10^3 \text{ mm}^2) = 757.7 \times 10^3 \text{ mm}^3$$
$$\bar{X} = 54.8 \text{ mm} \blacktriangleleft$$

$$\bar{Y}\Sigma A = \Sigma\bar{y}A: \qquad \bar{Y}(13.828 \times 10^3 \text{ mm}^2) = 506.2 \times 10^3 \text{ mm}^3$$
$$\bar{Y} = 36.6 \text{ mm} \blacktriangleleft$$

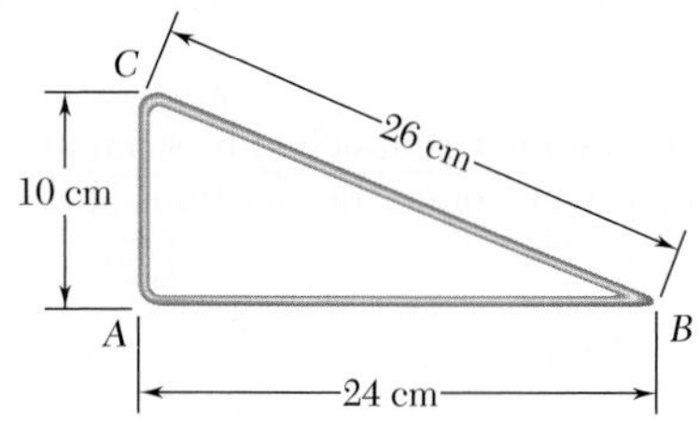

SAMPLE PROBLEM 5.2

The figure shown is made from a piece of thin, homogeneous wire. Determine the location of its center of gravity.

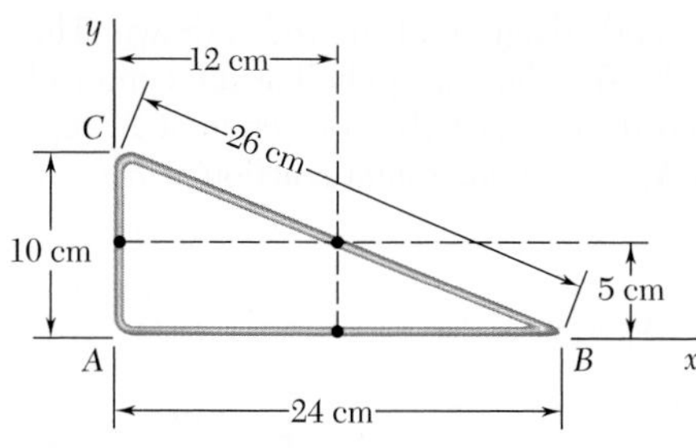

SOLUTION

Since the figure is formed of homogeneous wire, its center of gravity coincides with the centroid of the corresponding line. Therefore, that centroid will be determined. Choosing the coordinate axes shown, with origin at A, we determine the coordinates of the centroid of each line segment and compute the first moments with respect to the coordinate axes.

Segment	L, cm	$\bar{x}$, cm.	$\bar{y}$, cm	$\bar{x}L$, cm^2	$\bar{y}L$, cm^2
AB	24	12	0	288	0
BC	26	12	5	312	130
CA	10	0	5	0	50
	$\Sigma L = 60$			$\Sigma \bar{x}L = 600$	$\Sigma \bar{y}L = 180$

Substituting the values obtained from the table into the equations defining the centroid of a composite line, we obtain

$\bar{X}\Sigma L = \Sigma \bar{x}L$: $\quad \bar{X}(60 \text{ cm}) = 600 \text{ cm}^2$ $\quad \bar{X} = 10 \text{ cm}$ ◀

$\bar{Y}\Sigma L = \Sigma \bar{y}L$: $\quad \bar{Y}(60 \text{ cm}) = 180 \text{ cm}^2$ $\quad \bar{Y} = 3 \text{ cm}$ ◀

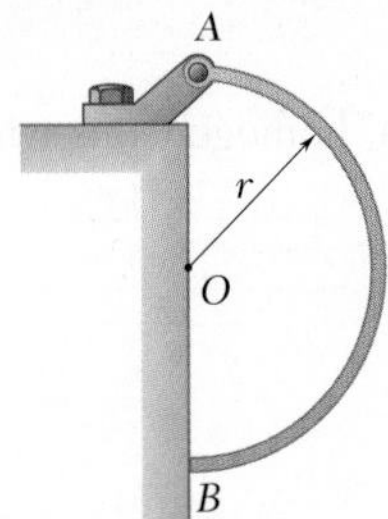

SAMPLE PROBLEM 5.3

A uniform semicircular rod of weight W and radius r is attached to a pin at A and rests against a frictionless surface at B. Determine the reactions at A and B.

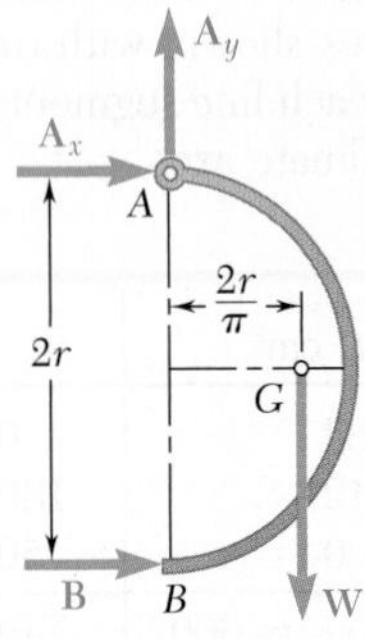

SOLUTION

Free-Body Diagram. A free-body diagram of the rod is drawn. The forces acting on the rod are its weight $\mathbf{W}$, which is applied at the center of gravity G (whose position is obtained from Fig. 5.8B); a reaction at A, represented by its components $\mathbf{A}_x$ and $\mathbf{A}_y$; and a horizontal reaction at B.

Equilibrium Equations

$$+\circlearrowleft \Sigma M_A = 0: \qquad B(2r) - W\left(\frac{2r}{\pi}\right) = 0$$

$$B = +\frac{W}{\pi} \qquad\qquad \mathbf{B} = \frac{W}{\pi} \rightarrow \blacktriangleleft$$

$$\xrightarrow{+} \Sigma F_x = 0: \qquad A_x + B = 0$$

$$A_x = -B = -\frac{W}{\pi} \qquad \mathbf{A}_x = \frac{W}{\pi} \leftarrow$$

$$+\uparrow \Sigma F_y = 0: \qquad A_y - W = 0 \qquad\qquad \mathbf{A}_y = W\uparrow$$

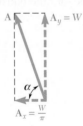

Adding the two components of the reaction at A:

$$A = \left[W^2 + \left(\frac{W}{\pi}\right)^2\right]^{1/2} \qquad\qquad A = W\left(1 + \frac{1}{\pi^2}\right)^{1/2} \blacktriangleleft$$

$$\tan \alpha = \frac{W}{W/\pi} = \pi \qquad\qquad \alpha = \tan^{-1} \pi \blacktriangleleft$$

The answers can also be expressed as follows:

$$\mathbf{A} = 1.049W \measuredangle 72.3° \qquad \mathbf{B} = 0.318W \rightarrow \blacktriangleleft$$

SOLVING PROBLEMS ON YOUR OWN

In this lesson we developed the general equations for locating the centers of gravity of two-dimensional bodies and wires [Eqs. (5.2)] and the centroids of plane areas [Eqs. (5.3)] and lines [Eqs. (5.4)]. In the following problems, you will have to locate the centroids of composite areas and lines or determine the first moments of the area for composite plates [Eqs. (5.8)].

1. ***Locating the centroids of composite areas and lines.*** Sample Problems 5.1 and 5.2 illustrate the procedure you should follow when solving problems of this type. There are, however, several points that should be emphasized.

a. The first step in your solution should be to decide how to construct the given area or line from the common shapes of Fig. 5.8. You should recognize that for plane areas it is often possible to construct a particular shape in more than one way. Also, showing the different components (as is done in Sample Prob. 5.1) will help you to correctly establish their centroids and areas or lengths. Do not forget that you can subtract areas as well as add them to obtain a desired shape.

b. We strongly recommend that for each problem you construct a table containing the areas or lengths and the respective coordinates of the centroids. It is essential for you to remember that areas which are "removed" (for example, holes) are treated as negative. Also, the sign of negative coordinates must be included. Therefore, you should always carefully note the location of the origin of the coordinate axes.

c. When possible, use symmetry [Sec. 5.4] to help you determine the location of a centroid.

d. In the formulas for the circular sector and for the arc of a circle in Fig. 5.8, the angle α must always be expressed in radians.

2. ***Calculating the first moments of an area.*** The procedures for locating the centroid of an area and for determining the first moments of an area are similar; however, for the latter it is not necessary to compute the total area. Also, as noted in Sec. 5.4, you should recognize that the first moment of an area relative to a centroidal axis is zero.

3. ***Solving problems involving the center of gravity.*** The bodies considered in the following problems are homogeneous; thus, their centers of gravity and centroids coincide. In addition, when a body that is suspended from a single pin is in equilibrium, the pin and the body's center of gravity must lie on the same vertical line.

It may appear that many of the problems in this lesson have little to do with the study of mechanics. However, being able to locate the centroid of composite shapes will be essential in several topics that you will soon encounter.

Problems

5.1 through 5.8 Locate the centroid of the plane area shown.

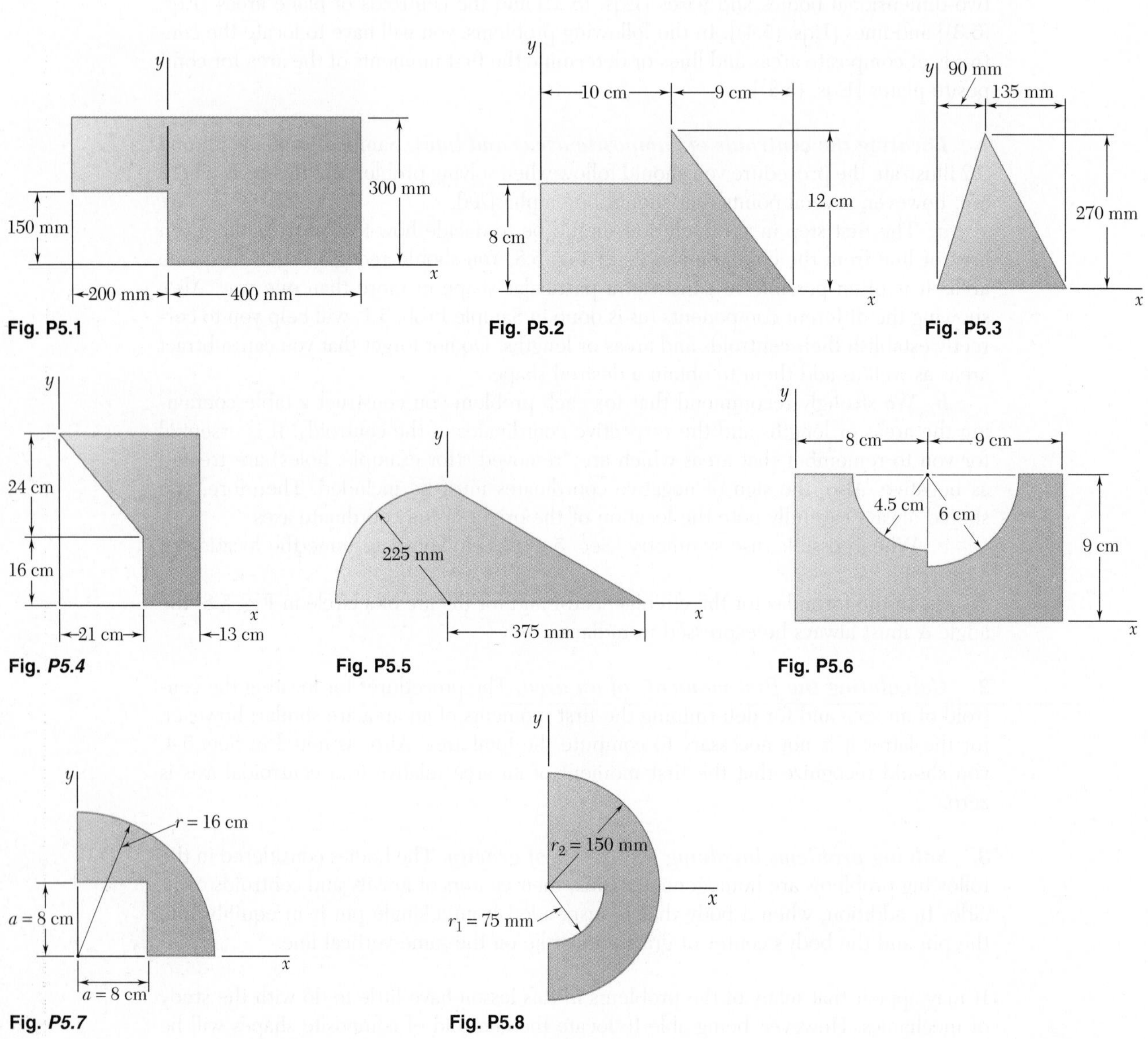

Fig. P5.1 **Fig. P5.2** **Fig. P5.3** **Fig. *P5.4*** **Fig. P5.5** **Fig. P5.6** **Fig. *P5.7*** **Fig. P5.8**

5.9 For the area of Prob. 5.8, determine the ratio r_2/r_1 so that $\bar{x} = 4r_1/3$.

5.10 Show that as r_1 approaches r_2, the location of the centroid approaches that of a circular arc of radius $(r_1 + r_2)/2$.

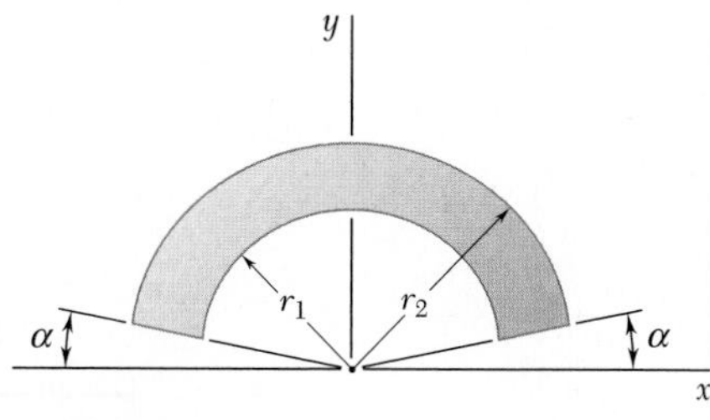

Fig. P5.10

5.11 through 5.16 Locate the centroid of the plane area shown.

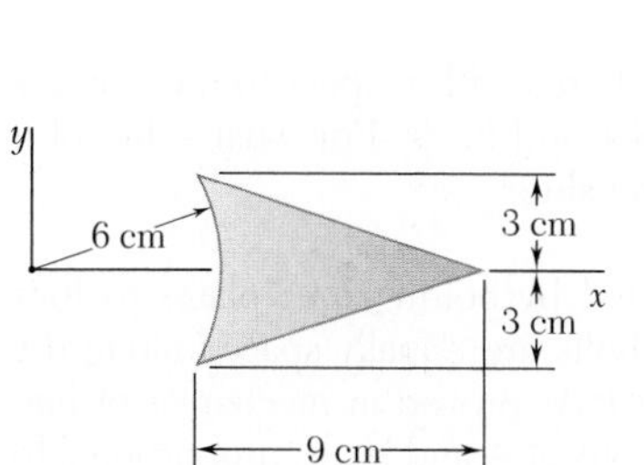

Fig. P5.11

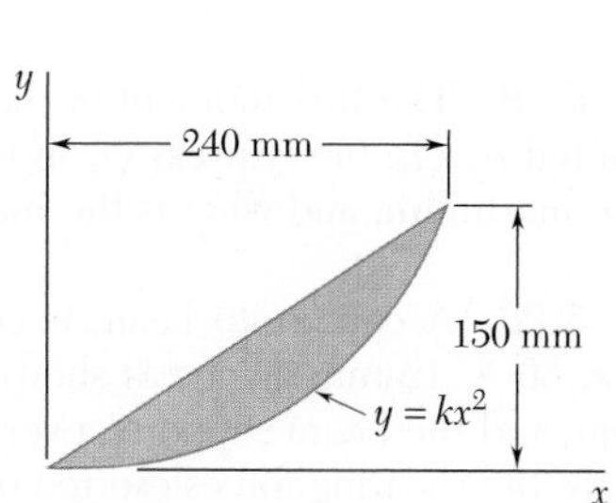

Fig. *P5.12*

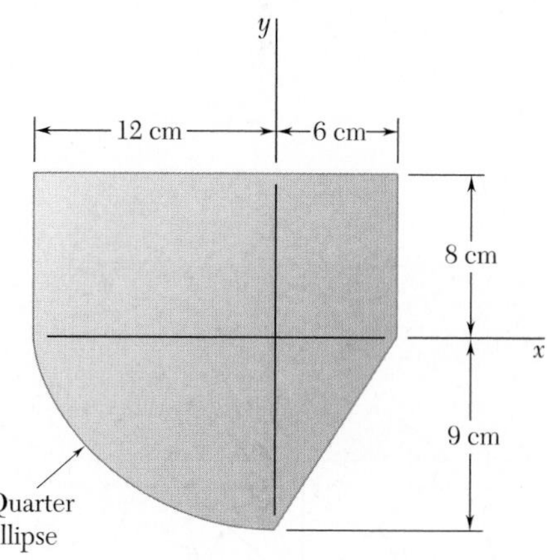

Fig. P5.13

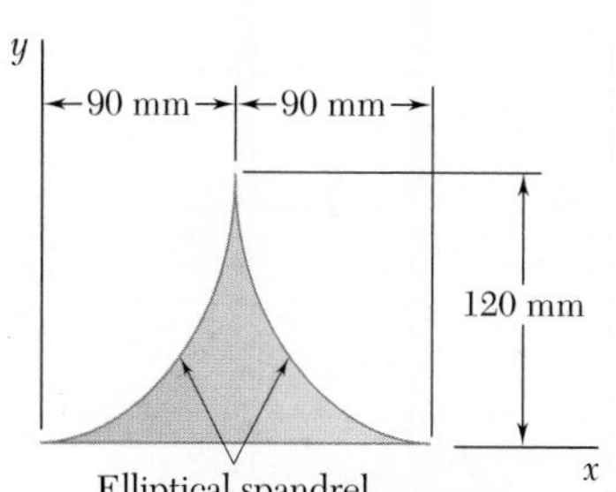

Fig. P5.14

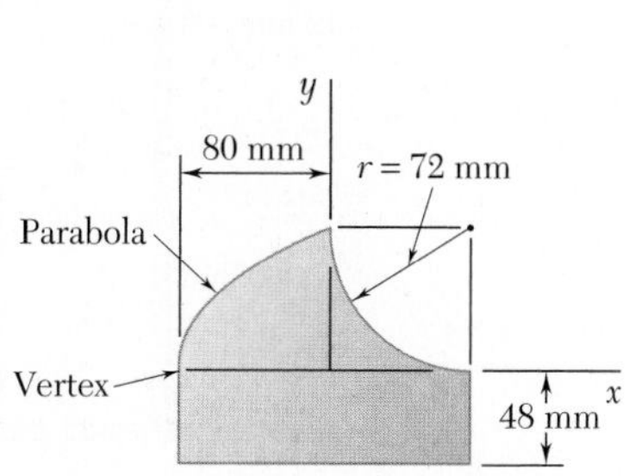

Fig. *P5.15*

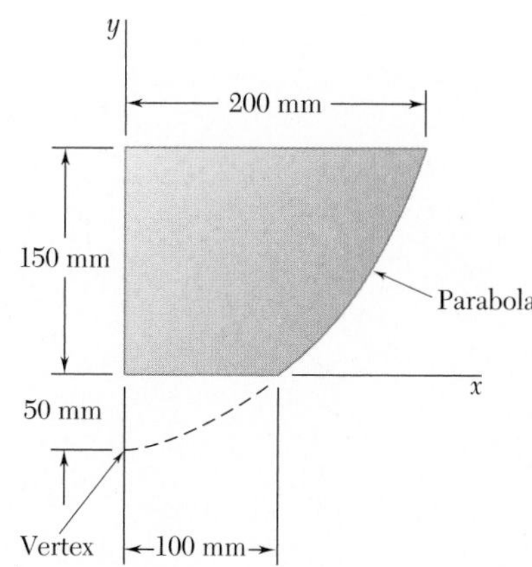

Fig. P5.16

5.17 and 5.18 The horizontal x axis is drawn through the centroid C of the area shown and divides the area into two component areas A_1 and A_2. Determine the first moment of each component area with respect to the x axis, and explain the results obtained.

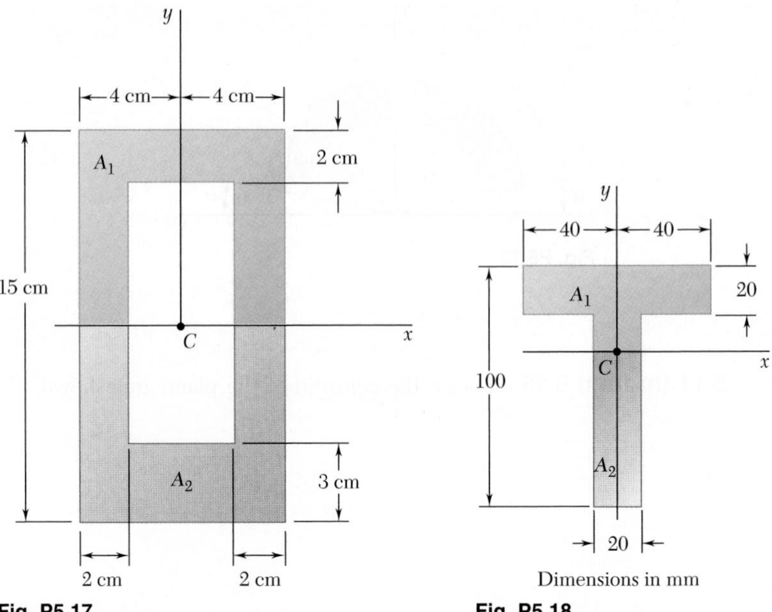

Fig. P5.17

Fig. P5.18

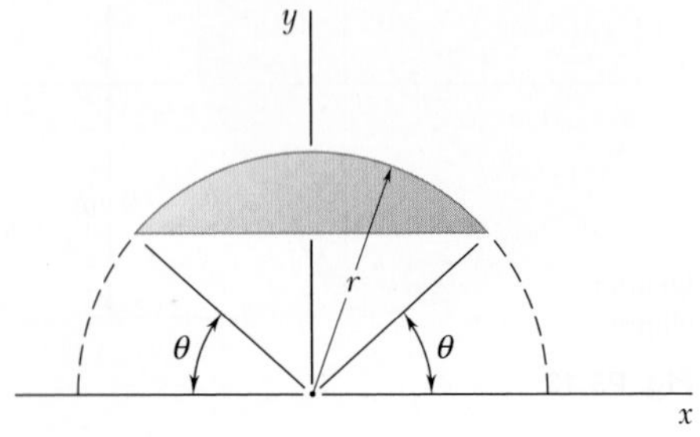

Fig. *P5.19*

5.19 The first moment of the shaded area with respect to the x axis is denoted by Q_x. (*a*) Express Q_x in terms of r and θ. (*b*) For what value of θ is Q_x maximum, and what is the maximum value?

5.20 A composite beam is constructed by bolting four plates to four $60 \times 60 \times 12$-mm angles as shown. The bolts are equally spaced along the beam, and the beam supports a vertical load. As proved in mechanics of materials, the shearing forces exerted on the bolts at A and B are proportional to the first moments with respect to the centroidal x axis of the red shaded areas shown, respectively, in parts a and b of the figure. Knowing that the force exerted on the bolt at A is 280 N, determine the force exerted on the bolt at B.

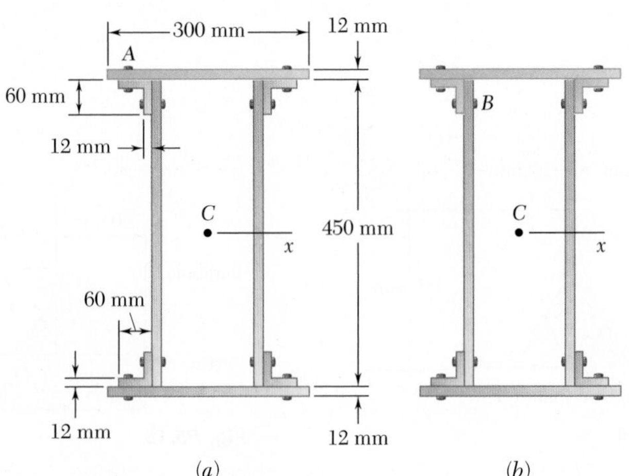

Fig. *P5.20*

5.21 through 5.24 A thin, homogeneous wire is bent to form the perimeter of the figure indicated. Locate the center of gravity of the wire figure thus formed.

5.21 Fig. P5.1.
5.22 Fig. P5.2.
5.23 Fig. P5.5.
5.24 Fig. P5.8.

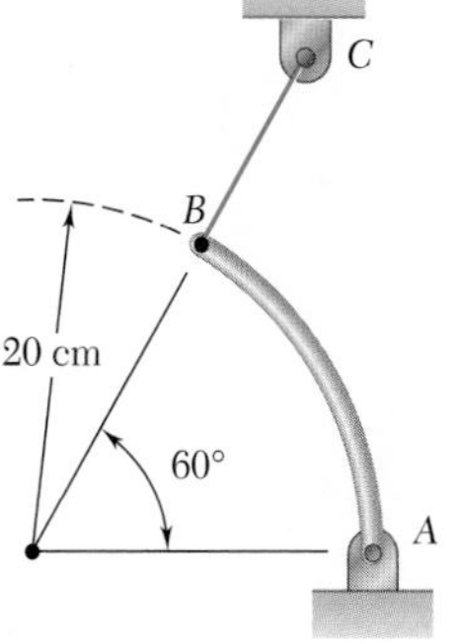

Fig. P5.25

5.25 A 0.8-kg uniform steel rod is bent into a circular arc of radius 20 cm as shown. The rod is supported by a pin at *A* and the cord *BC*. Determine (*a*) the tension in the cord, (*b*) the reaction at *A*.

5.26 The homogeneous wire *ABCD* is bent as shown and is supported by a pin at *B*. Knowing that $l = 200$ mm, determine the angle θ for which portion *BC* of the wire is horizontal.

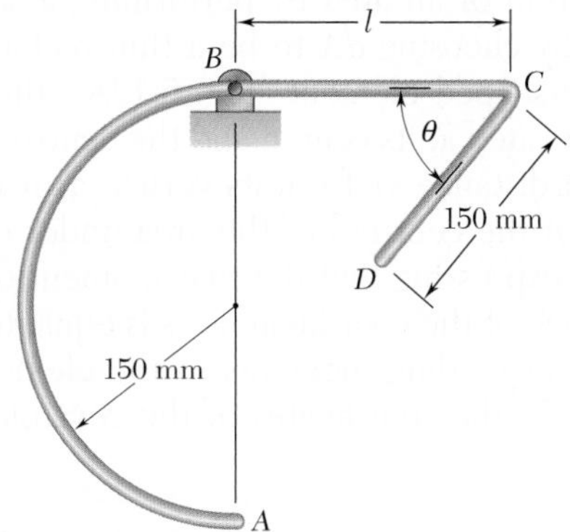

Fig. P5.26 and P5.27

5.27 The homogeneous wire *ABCD* is bent as shown and is supported by a pin at *B*. Knowing that $\theta = 30°$, determine the length l for which portion *CD* of the wire is horizontal.

5.28 Knowing that the figure shown is formed from a thin homogeneous wire, determine the length l of portion *CE* of the wire for which the center of gravity of the figure is located at point *C* when (*a*) $\theta = 15°$, (*b*) $\theta = 60°$.

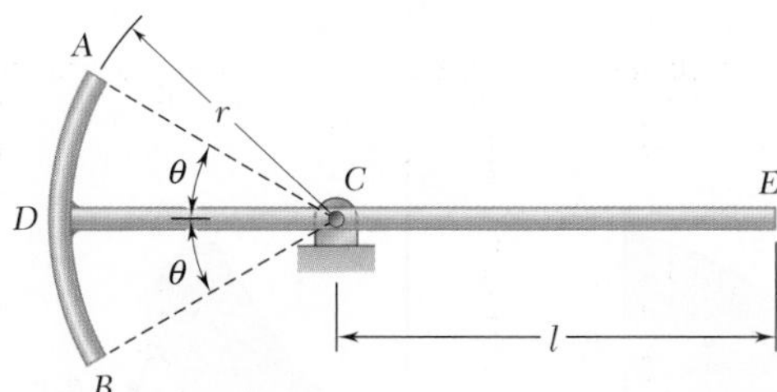

Fig. P5.28

5.29 Determine the distance h so that the centroid of the shaded area is as close to line BB' as possible when (*a*) $k = 0.2$, (*b*) $k = 0.6$.

5.30 Show when the distance h is selected to minimize the distance $\bar{y}$ from line BB' to the centroid of the shaded area that $\bar{y} = h$.

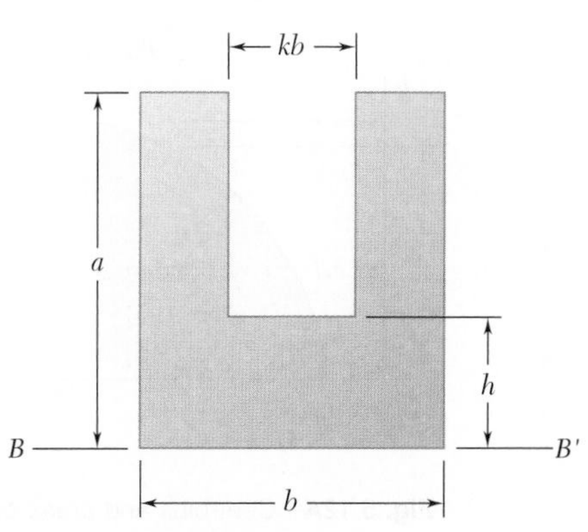

Fig. *P5.29* and *P5.30*

5.6. DETERMINATION OF CENTROIDS BY INTEGRATION

The centroid of an area bounded by analytical curves (that is, curves defined by algebraic equations) is usually determined by evaluating the integrals in Eqs. (5.3) of Sec. 5.3:

$$\bar{x}A = \int x\,dA \qquad \bar{y}A = \int y\,dA \tag{5.3}$$

If the element of area dA is a small rectangle of sides dx and dy, the evaluation of each of these integrals requires a *double integration* with respect to x and y. A double integration is also necessary if polar coordinates are used for which dA is a small element of sides dr and $r\,d\theta$.

In most cases, however, it is possible to determine the coordinates of the centroid of an area by performing a single integration. This is achieved by choosing dA to be a thin rectangle or strip or a thin sector or pie-shaped element (Fig. 5.12A); the centroid of the thin rectangle is located at its center, and the centroid of the thin sector is located at a distance $\frac{2}{3}r$ from its vertex (as it is for a triangle). The coordinates of the centroid of the area under consideration are then obtained by expressing that the first moment of the entire area with respect to each of the coordinate axes is equal to the sum (or integral) of the corresponding moments of the elements of area. Denoting by $\bar{x}_{el}$ and $\bar{y}_{el}$ the coordinates of the centroid of the element dA, we write

$$\begin{aligned} Q_y &= \bar{x}A = \int \bar{x}_{el}\,dA \\ Q_x &= \bar{y}A = \int \bar{y}_{el}\,dA \end{aligned} \tag{5.9}$$

If the area A is not already known, it can also be computed from these elements.

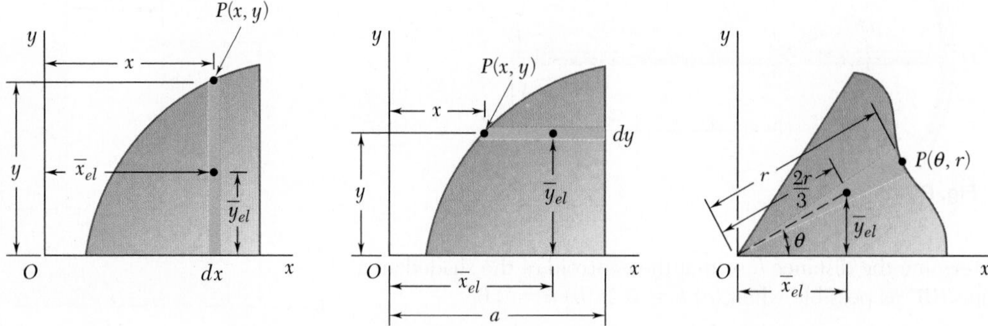

Fig. 5.12A Centroids and areas of differential elements.

The coordinates $\bar{x}_{el}$ and $\bar{y}_{el}$ of the centroid of the element of area dA should be expressed in terms of the coordinates of a point located on the curve bounding the area under consideration. Also, the area of the element dA should be expressed in terms of the coordinates of that point and the appropriate differentials. This has been done in Fig. 5.12B for three common types of elements; the pie-shaped element of part *c* should be used when the equation of the curve bounding the area is given in polar coordinates. The appropriate expressions

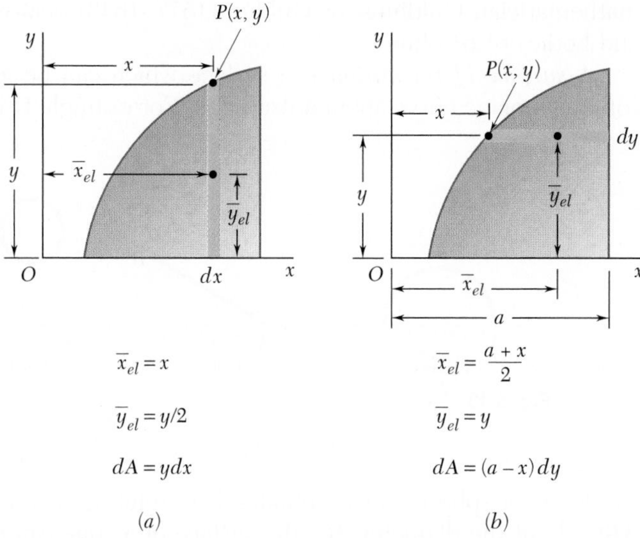

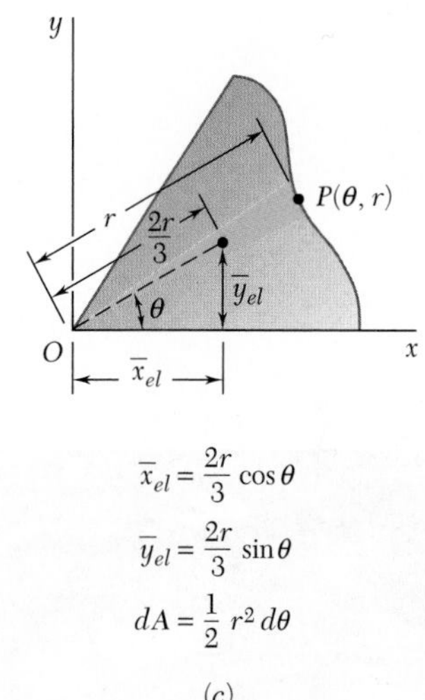

Fig. 5.12B Centroids and areas of differential elements.

should be substituted into formulas (5.9), and the equation of the bounding curve should be used to express one of the coordinates in terms of the other. The integration is thus reduced to a single integration. Once the area has been determined and the integrals in Eqs. (5.9) have been evaluated, these equations can be solved for the coordinates $\bar{x}$ and $\bar{y}$ of the centroid of the area.

When a line is defined by an algebraic equation, its centroid can be determined by evaluating the integrals in Eqs. (5.4) of Sec. 5.3:

$$\bar{x}L = \int x\,dL \qquad \bar{y}L = \int y\,dL \tag{5.4}$$

The differential length dL should be replaced by one of the following expressions, depending upon which coordinate, x, y, or θ, is chosen as the independent variable in the equation used to define the line (these expressions can be derived using the Pythagorean theorem):

$$dL = \sqrt{1 + \left(\frac{dy}{dx}\right)^2}\,dx \qquad dL = \sqrt{1 + \left(\frac{dx}{dy}\right)^2}\,dy$$

$$dL = \sqrt{r^2 + \left(\frac{dr}{d\theta}\right)^2}\,d\theta$$

After the equation of the line has been used to express one of the coordinates in terms of the other, the integration can be performed, and Eqs. (5.4) can be solved for the coordinates $\bar{x}$ and $\bar{y}$ of the centroid of the line.

5.7. THEOREMS OF PAPPUS-GULDINUS

These theorems, which were first formulated by the Greek geometer Pappus during the third century A.D. and later restated by the Swiss mathematician Guldinus, or Guldin, (1577–1643) deal with surfaces and bodies of revolution.

A *surface of revolution* is a surface which can be generated by rotating a plane curve about a fixed axis. For example (Fig. 5.13), the surface of a sphere can be obtained by rotating a semicircular arc ABC about the diameter AC, the surface of a cone can be produced by rotating a straight line AB about an axis AC, and the surface of a torus or ring can be generated by rotating the circumference of a circle about a nonintersecting axis. A *body of revolution* is a body which can be generated by rotating a plane area about a fixed axis. As shown in Fig. 5.14, a sphere, a cone, and a torus can each be generated by rotating the appropriate shape about the indicated axis.

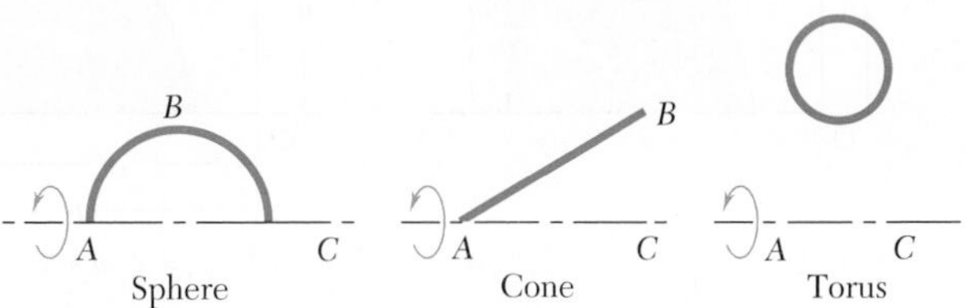

Fig. 5.13

Photo 5.2 The storage tanks shown are all bodies of revolution. Thus, their surface areas and volumes can be determined using the theorems of Pappus-Guldinus.

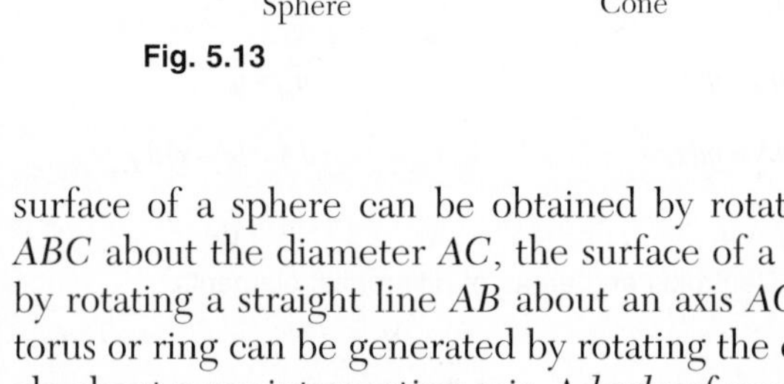

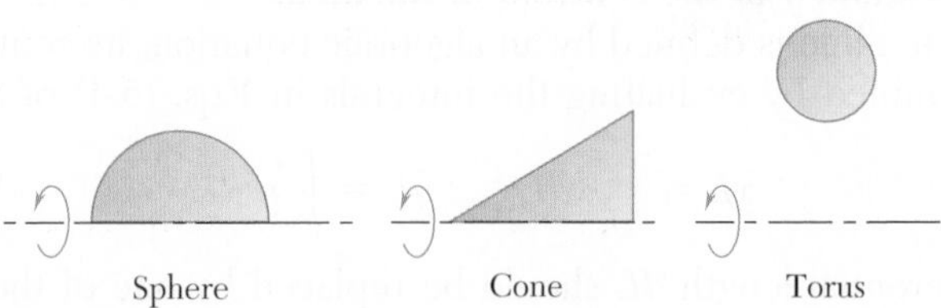

Fig. 5.14

THEOREM I. *The area of a surface of revolution is equal to the length of the generating curve times the distance traveled by the centroid of the curve while the surface is being generated.*

Proof. Consider an element dL of the line L (Fig. 5.15), which is revolved about the x axis. The area dA generated by the element dL is equal to $2\pi y\ dL$. Thus, the entire area generated by L is $A = \int 2\pi y\ dL$. Recalling that we found in Sec. 5.3 that the integral $\int y\ dL$

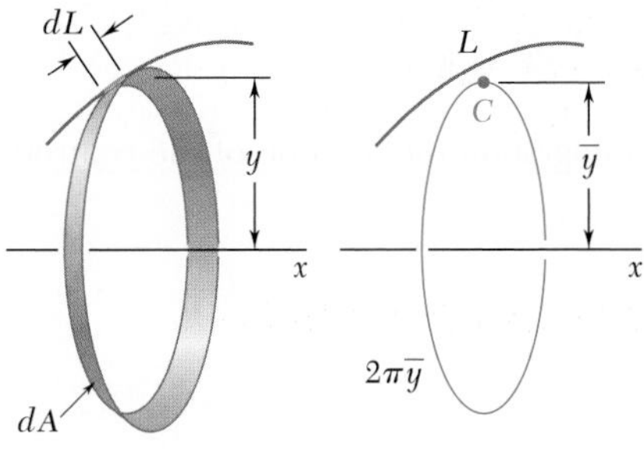

Fig. 5.15

is equal to $\bar{y}L$, we therefore have

$$A = 2\pi\bar{y}L \tag{5.10}$$

where $2\pi\bar{y}$ is the distance traveled by the centroid of L (Fig. 5.15). It should be noted that the generating curve must not cross the axis about which it is rotated; if it did, the two sections on either side of the axis would generate areas having opposite signs, and the theorem would not apply.

THEOREM II. *The volume of a body of revolution is equal to the generating area times the distance traveled by the centroid of the area while the body is being generated.*

Proof. Consider an element dA of the area A which is revolved about the x axis (Fig. 5.16). The volume dV generated by the element

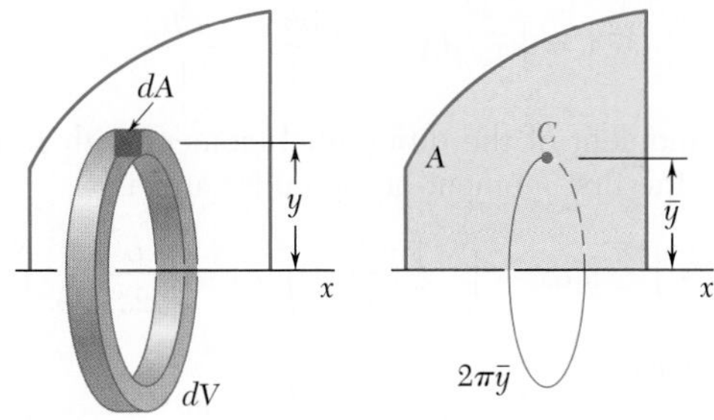

Fig. 5.16

dA is equal to $2\pi y\, dA$. Thus, the entire volume generated by A is $V = \int 2\pi y\, dA$, and since the integral $\int y\, dA$ is equal to $\bar{y}A$ (Sec. 5.3), we have

$$V = 2\pi\bar{y}A \tag{5.11}$$

where $2\pi\bar{y}$ is the distance traveled by the centroid of A. Again, it should be noted that the theorem does not apply if the axis of rotation intersects the generating area.

The theorems of Pappus-Guldinus offer a simple way to compute the areas of surfaces of revolution and the volumes of bodies of revolution. Conversely, they can also be used to determine the centroid of a plane curve when the area of the surface generated by the curve is known or to determine the centroid of a plane area when the volume of the body generated by the area is known (see Sample Prob. 5.8).

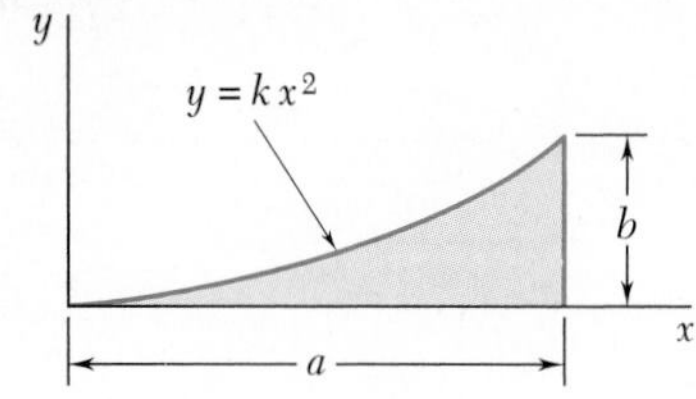

SAMPLE PROBLEM 5.4

Determine by direct integration the location of the centroid of a parabolic spandrel.

SOLUTION

Determination of the Constant k. The value of k is determined by substituting $x = a$ and $y = b$ into the given equation. We have $b = ka^2$ or $k = b/a^2$. The equation of the curve is thus

$$y = \frac{b}{a^2}x^2 \quad \text{or} \quad x = \frac{a}{b^{1/2}}y^{1/2}$$

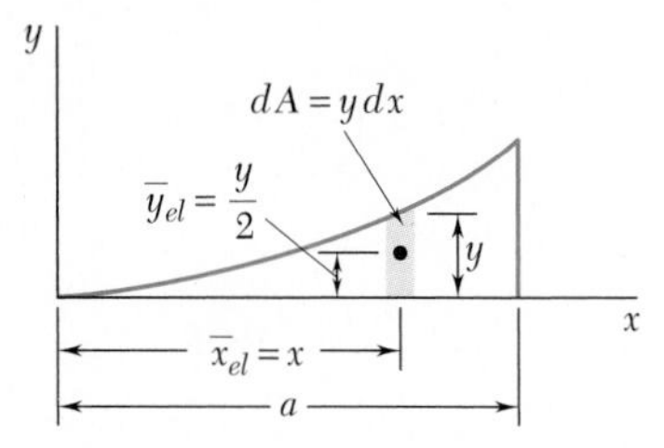

Vertical Differential Element. We choose the differential element shown and find the total area of the figure.

$$A = \int dA = \int y\,dx = \int_0^a \frac{b}{a^2}x^2\,dx = \left[\frac{b}{a^2}\frac{x^3}{3}\right]_0^a = \frac{ab}{3}$$

The first moment of the differential element with respect to the y axis is $\bar{x}_{el}\,dA$; hence, the first moment of the entire area with respect to this axis is

$$Q_y = \int \bar{x}_{el}\,dA = \int xy\,dx = \int_0^a x\left(\frac{b}{a^2}x^2\right)dx = \left[\frac{b}{a^2}\frac{x^4}{4}\right]_0^a = \frac{a^2b}{4}$$

Since $Q_y = \bar{x}A$, we have

$$\bar{x}A = \int \bar{x}_{el}\,dA \qquad \bar{x}\frac{ab}{3} = \frac{a^2b}{4} \qquad \bar{x} = \tfrac{3}{4}a \blacktriangleleft$$

Likewise, the first moment of the differential element with respect to the x axis is $\bar{y}_{el}\,dA$, and the first moment of the entire area is

$$Q_x = \int \bar{y}_{el}\,dA = \int \frac{y}{2}y\,dx = \int_0^a \frac{1}{2}\left(\frac{b}{a^2}x^2\right)^2 dx = \left[\frac{b^2}{2a^4}\frac{x^5}{5}\right]_0^a = \frac{ab^2}{10}$$

Since $Q_x = \bar{y}A$, we have

$$\bar{y}A = \int \bar{y}_{el}\,dA \qquad \bar{y}\frac{ab}{3} = \frac{ab^2}{10} \qquad \bar{y} = \tfrac{3}{10}b \blacktriangleleft$$

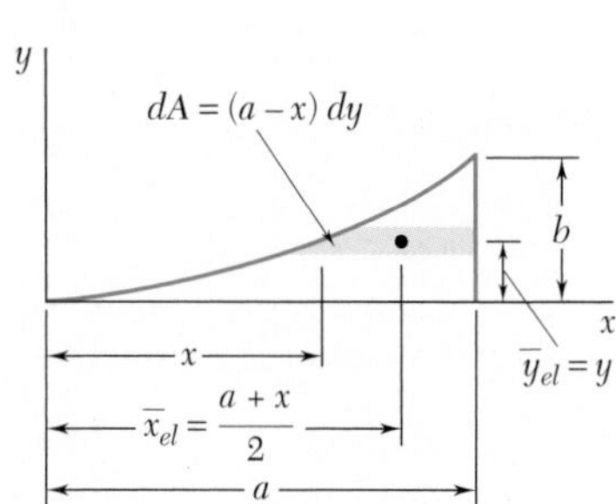

Horizontal Differential Element. The same results can be obtained by considering a horizontal element. The first moments of the area are

$$Q_y = \int \bar{x}_{el}\,dA = \int \frac{a+x}{2}(a-x)\,dy = \int_0^b \frac{a^2-x^2}{2}\,dy$$

$$= \frac{1}{2}\int_0^b \left(a^2 - \frac{a^2}{b}y\right)dy = \frac{a^2b}{4}$$

$$Q_x = \int \bar{y}_{el}\,dA = \int y(a-x)\,dy = \int y\left(a - \frac{a}{b^{1/2}}y^{1/2}\right)dy$$

$$= \int_0^b \left(ay - \frac{a}{b^{1/2}}y^{3/2}\right)dy = \frac{ab^2}{10}$$

To determine $\bar{x}$ and $\bar{y}$, the expressions obtained are again substituted into the equations defining the centroid of the area.

SAMPLE PROBLEM 5.5

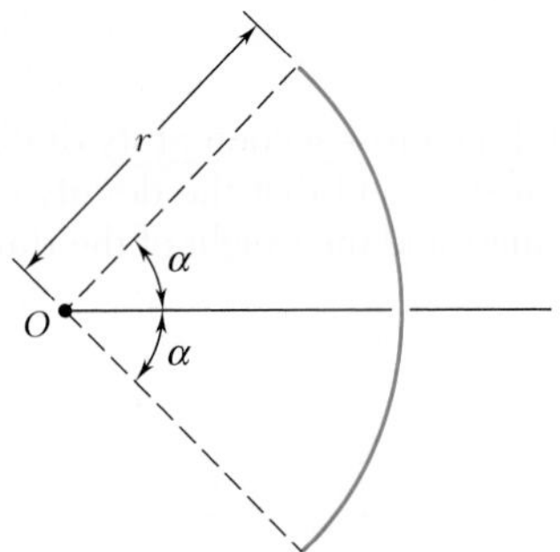

Determine the location of the centroid of the circular arc shown.

SOLUTION

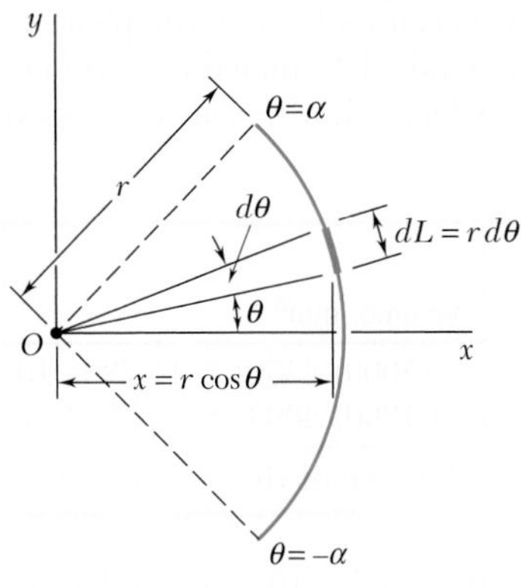

Since the arc is symmetrical with respect to the x axis, $\bar{y} = 0$. A differential element is chosen as shown, and the length of the arc is determined by integration.

$$L = \int dL = \int_{-\alpha}^{\alpha} r\, d\theta = r \int_{-\alpha}^{\alpha} d\theta = 2r\alpha$$

The first moment of the arc with respect to the y axis is

$$Q_y = \int x\, dL = \int_{-\alpha}^{\alpha} (r \cos \theta)(r\, d\theta) = r^2 \int_{-\alpha}^{\alpha} \cos \theta\, d\theta$$
$$= r^2[\sin \theta]_{-\alpha}^{\alpha} = 2r^2 \sin \alpha$$

Since $Q_y = \bar{x}L$, we write

$$\bar{x}(2r\alpha) = 2r^2 \sin \alpha \qquad \bar{x} = \frac{r \sin \alpha}{\alpha} \blacktriangleleft$$

SAMPLE PROBLEM 5.6

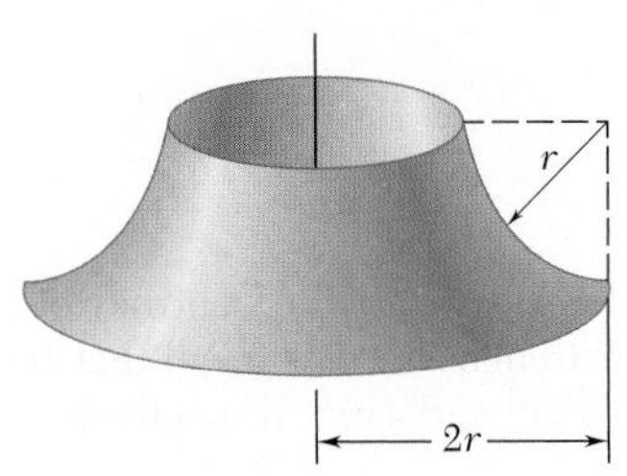

Determine the area of the surface of revolution shown, which is obtained by rotating a quarter-circular arc about a vertical axis.

SOLUTION

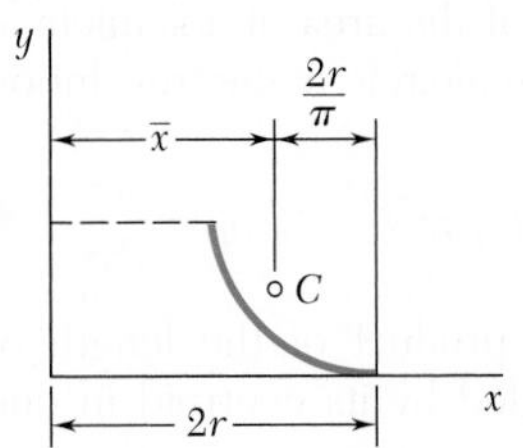

According to Theorem I of Pappus-Guldinus, the area generated is equal to the product of the length of the arc and the distance traveled by its centroid. Referring to Fig. 5.8B, we have

$$\bar{x} = 2r - \frac{2r}{\pi} = 2r\left(1 - \frac{1}{\pi}\right)$$

$$A = 2\pi\bar{x}L = 2\pi\left[2r\left(1 - \frac{1}{\pi}\right)\right]\left(\frac{\pi r}{2}\right)$$

$$A = 2\pi r^2(\pi - 1) \blacktriangleleft$$

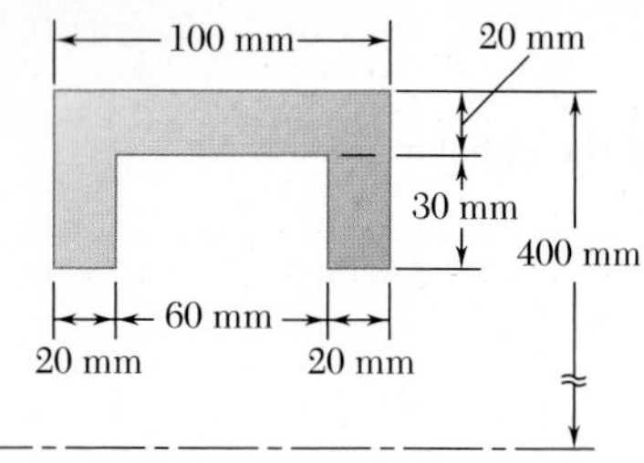

SAMPLE PROBLEM 5.7

The outside diameter of a pulley is 0.8 m, and the cross section of its rim is as shown. Knowing that the pulley is made of steel and that the density of steel is $\rho = 7.85 \times 10^3$ kg/m^3, determine the mass and the weight of the rim.

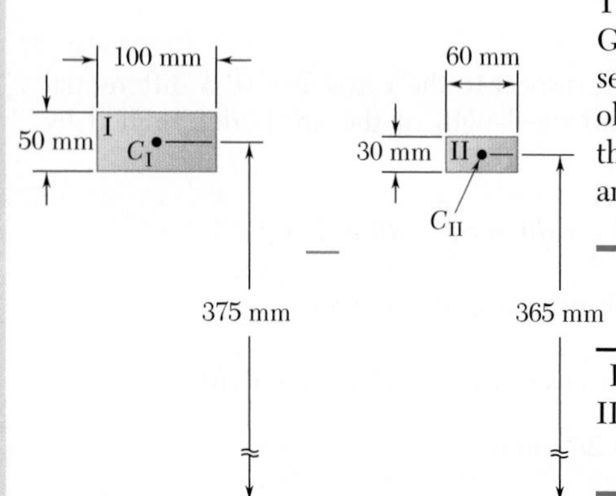

SOLUTION

The volume of the rim can be found by applying Theorem II of Pappus-Guldinus, which states that the volume equals the product of the given cross-sectional area and the distance traveled by its centroid in one complete revolution. However, the volume can be more easily determined if we observe that the cross section can be formed from rectangle I, whose area is positive, and rectangle II, whose area is negative.

	Area, mm^2	$\bar{y}$, mm	Distance Traveled by *C*, mm	Volume, mm^3
I	+5000	375	$2\pi(375) = 2356$	$(5000)(2356) = 11.78 \times 10^6$
II	−1800	365	$2\pi(365) = 2293$	$(-1800)(2293) = -4.13 \times 10^6$
				Volume of rim $= 7.65 \times 10^6$

Since 1 mm $= 10^{-3}$ m, we have 1 mm$^3 = (10^{-3}\text{ m})^3 = 10^{-9}$ m^3, and we obtain $V = 7.65 \times 10^6 \text{ mm}^3 = (7.65 \times 10^6)(10^{-9} \text{ m}^3) = 7.65 \times 10^{-3} \text{ m}^3$.

$$m = \rho V = (7.85 \times 10^3 \text{ kg/m}^3)(7.65 \times 10^{-3} \text{ m}^3) \qquad m = 60.0 \text{ kg} \blacktriangleleft$$

$$W = mg = (60.0 \text{ kg})(9.81 \text{ m/s}^2) = 589 \text{ kg} \cdot \text{m/s}^2 \qquad W = 589 \text{ N} \blacktriangleleft$$

SAMPLE PROBLEM 5.8

Using the theorems of Pappus-Guldinus, determine (*a*) the centroid of a semicircular area, (*b*) the centroid of a semicircular arc. We recall that the volume and the surface area of a sphere are $\frac{4}{3}\pi r^3$ and $4\pi r^2$, respectively.

SOLUTION

The volume of a sphere is equal to the product of the area of a semicircle and the distance traveled by the centroid of the semicircle in one revolution about the *x* axis.

$$V = 2\pi\bar{y}A \qquad \tfrac{4}{3}\pi r^3 = 2\pi\bar{y}(\tfrac{1}{2}\pi r^2) \qquad \bar{y} = \frac{4r}{3\pi} \blacktriangleleft$$

Likewise, the area of a sphere is equal to the product of the length of the generating semicircle and the distance traveled by its centroid in one revolution.

$$A = 2\pi\bar{y}L \qquad 4\pi r^2 = 2\pi\bar{y}(\pi r) \qquad \bar{y} = \frac{2r}{\pi} \blacktriangleleft$$

SOLVING PROBLEMS ON YOUR OWN

In the problems for this lesson, you will use the equations

$$\bar{x}A = \int x\,dA \qquad \bar{y}A = \int y\,dA \tag{5.3}$$

$$\bar{x}L = \int x\,dL \qquad \bar{y}L = \int y\,dL \tag{5.4}$$

to locate the centroids of plane areas and lines, respectively. You will also apply the theorems of Pappus-Guldinus (Sec. 5.7) to determine the areas of surfaces of revolution and the volumes of bodies of revolution.

1. *Determining by direct integration the centroids of areas and lines.* When solving problems of this type, you should follow the method of solution shown in Sample Probs. 5.4 and 5.5: compute A or L, determine the first moments of the area or the line, and solve Eqs. (5.3) or (5.4) for the coordinates of the centroid. In addition, you should pay particular attention to the following points.

a. Begin your solution by carefully defining or determining each term in the applicable integral formulas. We strongly encourage you to show on your sketch of the given area or line your choice for dA or dL and the distances to its centroid.

b. As explained in Sec. 5.6, the x and the y in the above equations represent the *coordinates of the centroid* of the differential elements dA and dL. It is important to recognize that the coordinates of the centroid of dA are not equal to the coordinates of a point located on the curve bounding the area under consideration. You should carefully study Fig. 5.12 until you fully understand this important point.

c. To possibly simplify or minimize your computations, always examine the shape of the given area or line before defining the differential element that you will use. For example, sometimes it may be preferable to use horizontal rectangular elements instead of vertical ones. Also, it will usually be advantageous to use polar coordinates when a line or an area has circular symmetry.

d. Although most of the integrations in this lesson are straightforward, at times it may be necessary to use more advanced techniques, such as trigonometric substitution or integration by parts. Of course, using a table of integrals is the fastest method to evaluate difficult integrals.

2. *Applying the theorems of Pappus-Guldinus.* As shown in Sample Probs. 5.6 through 5.8, these simple, yet very useful theorems allow you to apply your knowledge of centroids to the computation of areas and volumes. Although the theorems refer to the distance traveled by the centroid and to the length of the generating curve or to the generating area, the resulting equations [Eqs. (5.10) and (5.11)] contain the products of these quantities, which are simply the first moments of a line ($\bar{y}L$) and an area ($\bar{y}A$), respectively. Thus, for those problems for which the generating line or area consists of more than one common shape, you need only determine $\bar{y}L$ or $\bar{y}A$; you do not have to calculate the length of the generating curve or the generating area.

Problems

5.31 through 5.33 Determine by direct integration the centroid of the area shown. Express your answer in terms of a and h.

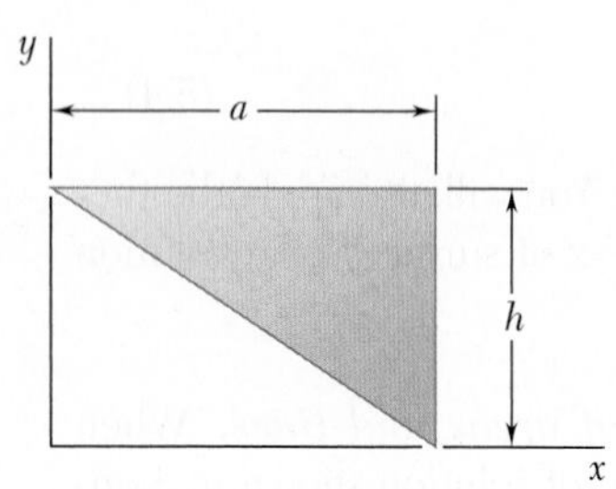

Fig. P5.31

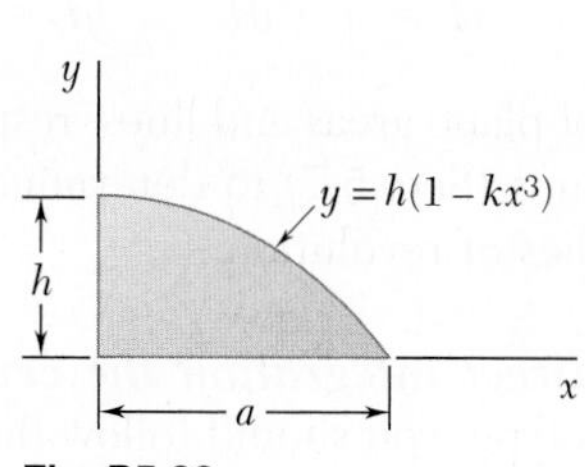

Fig. P5.32

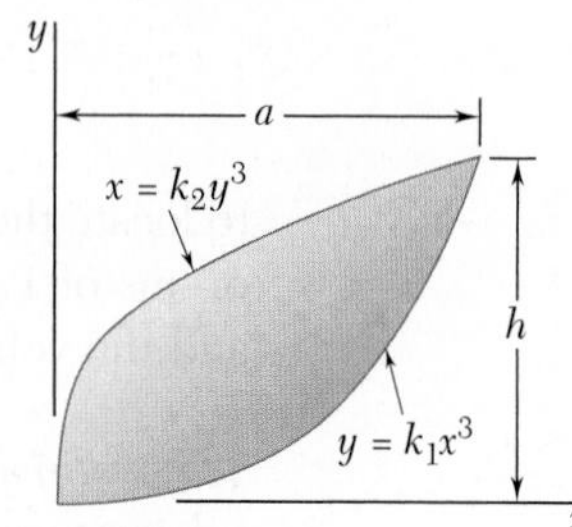

Fig. *P5.33*

5.34 through 5.36 Determine by direct integration the centroid of the area shown.

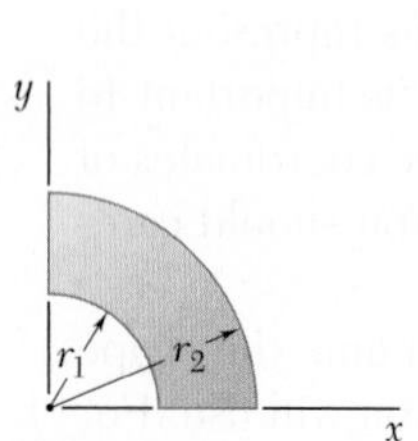

Fig. *P5.34*

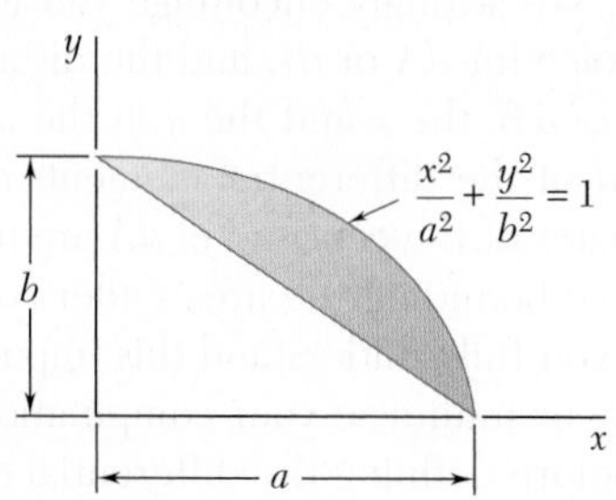

Fig. P5.35

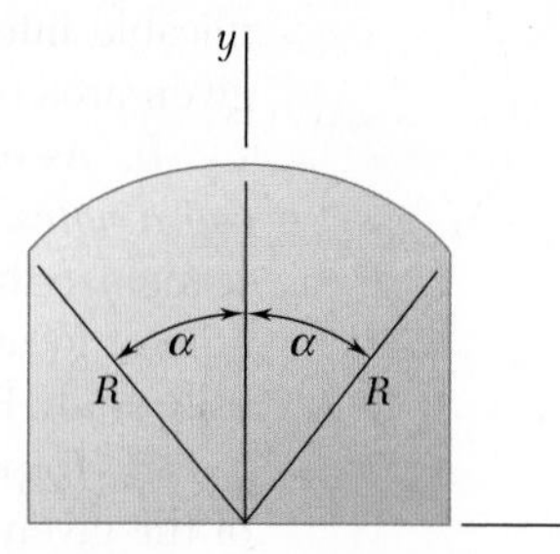

Fig. P5.36

5.37 and 5.38 Determine by direct integration the centroid of the area shown. Express your answer in terms of a and b.

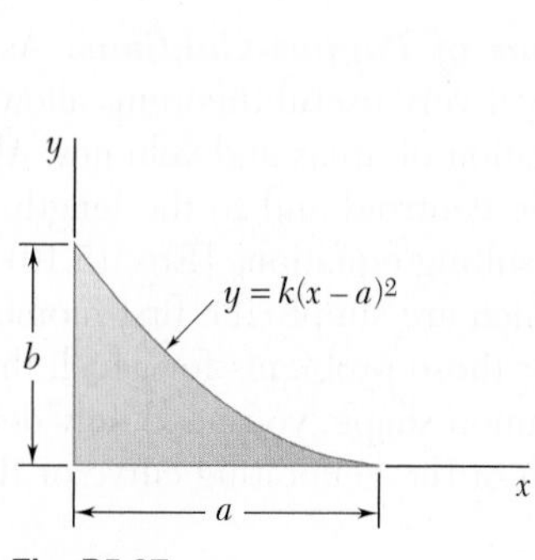

Fig. P5.37

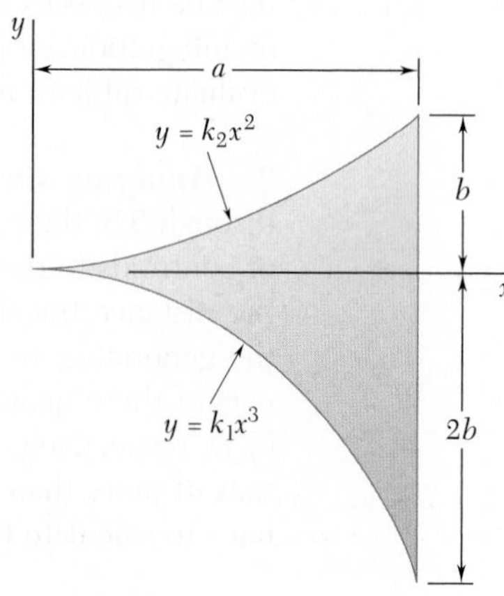

Fig. P5.38

5.39 Determine by direct integration the centroid of the area shown.

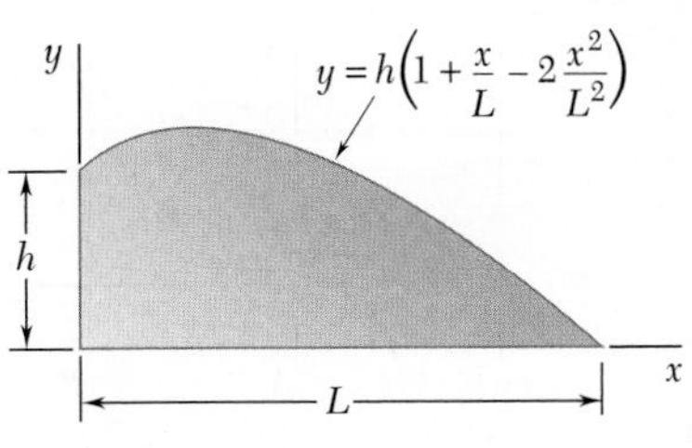

Fig. P5.39

5.40 and *5.41* Determine by direct integration the centroid of the area shown. Express your answer in terms of a and b.

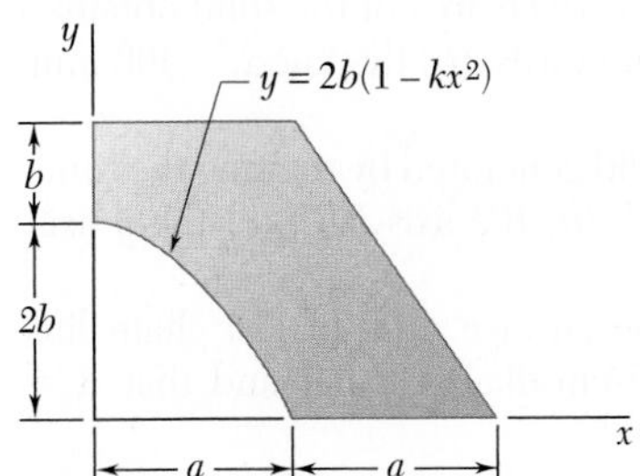

Fig. P5.40

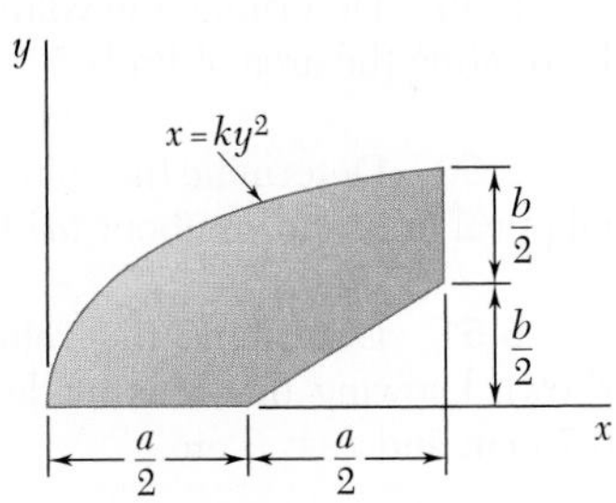

Fig. *P5.41*

5.42 and 5.43 A homogeneous wire is bent into the shape shown. Determine by direct integration the x coordinate of its centroid.

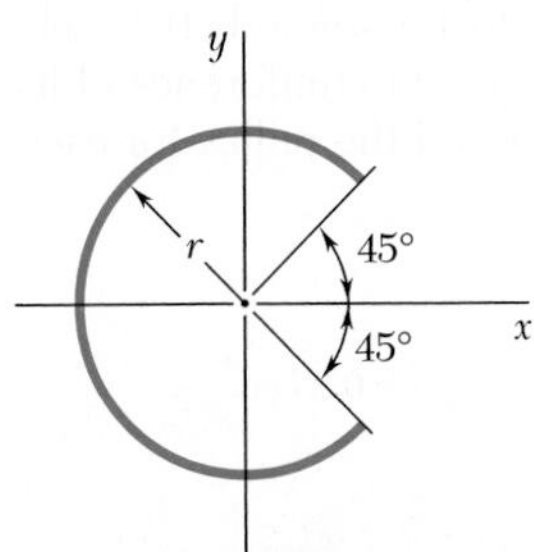

Fig. P5.42

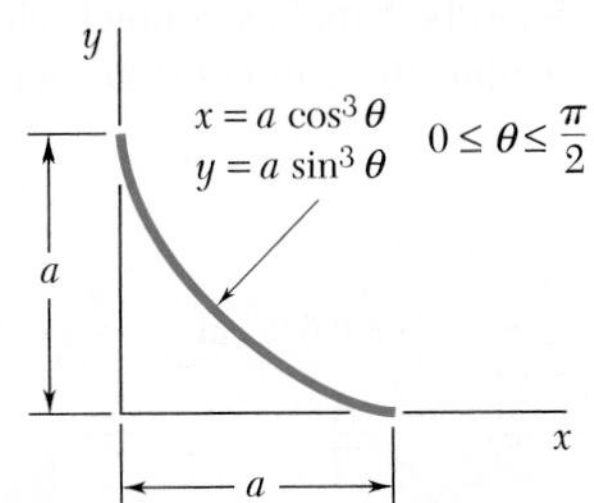

Fig. P5.43

**5.44* A homogeneous wire is bent into the shape shown. Determine by direct integration the x coordinate of its centroid. Express your answer in terms of a.

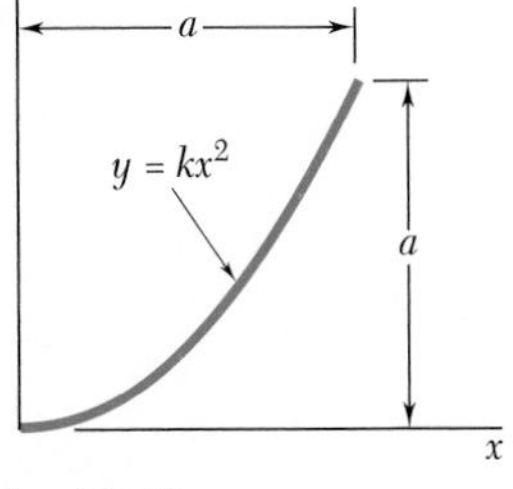

Fig. *P5.44*

*5.45 and *5.46 Determine by direct integration the centroid of the area shown.

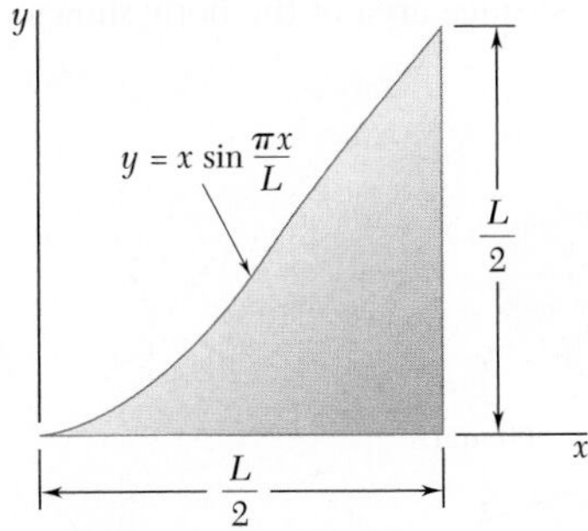

Fig. P5.45

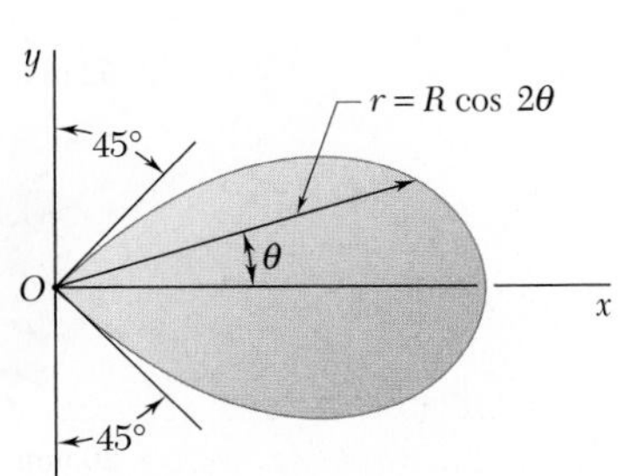

Fig. P5.46

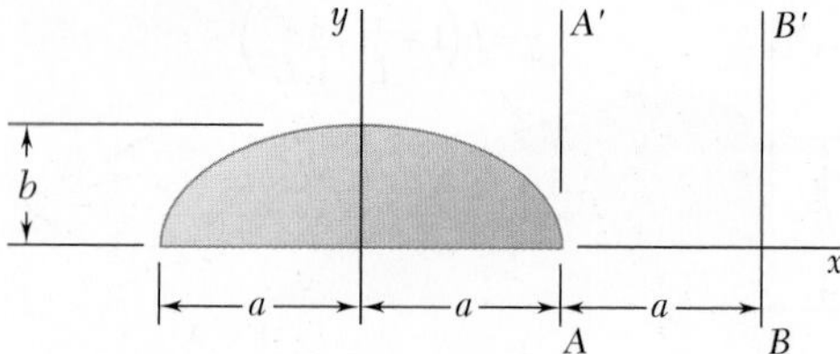

Fig. P5.50

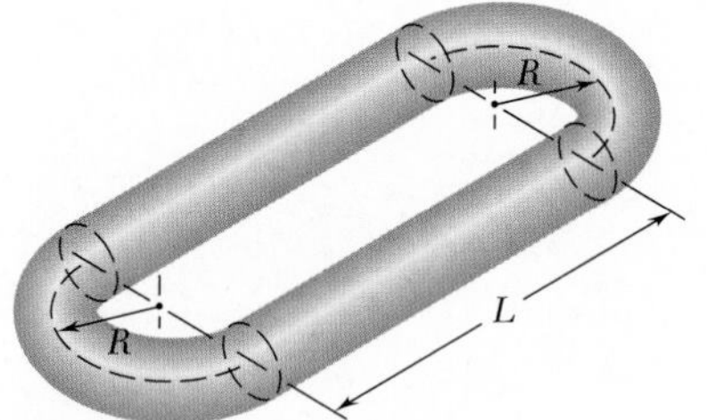

Fig. P5.51

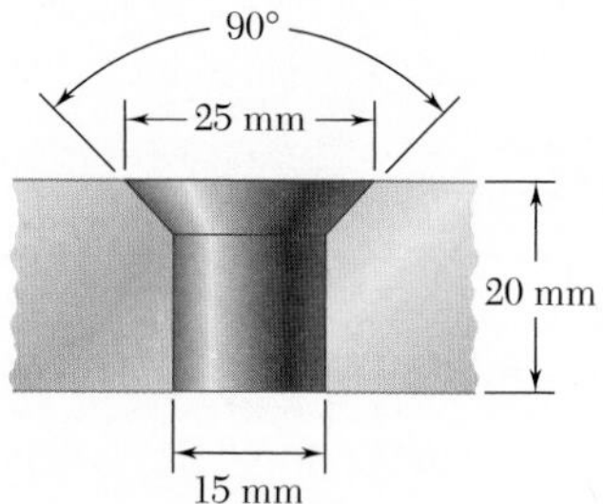

Fig. P5.53

5.47 Determine the volume and the surface area of the solid obtained by rotating the area of Prob. 5.2 about (*a*) the x axis, (*b*) the line $x = 19$ cm.

5.48 Determine the volume and the surface area of the solid obtained by rotating the area of Prob. 5.4 about (*a*) the y axis, (*b*) the line $y = 40$ cm.

5.49 Determine the volume and the surface area of the solid obtained by rotating the area of Prob. 5.1 about (*a*) the x axis, (*b*) the line $x = 400$ mm.

5.50 Determine the volume of the solid generated by rotating the semi-elliptical area shown about (*a*) the axis AA', (*b*) the axis BB', (*c*) the y axis.

5.51 Determine the volume and the surface area of the chain link shown knowing that it is made from a 0.5-cm-diameter bar and that $R = 0.75$ cm and $L = 3$ cm.

5.52 Verify that the expressions for the volumes of the first four shapes in Fig. 5.21 on page 261 are correct.

5.53 A 15-mm-diameter hole is drilled in a piece of 20-mm-thick steel; the hole is then countersunk as shown. Determine the volume of steel removed during the countersinking process.

5.54 Three different drive belt profiles are to be studied. If at any given time each belt makes contact with one-half of the circumference of its pulley, determine the *contact area* between the belt and the pulley for each design.

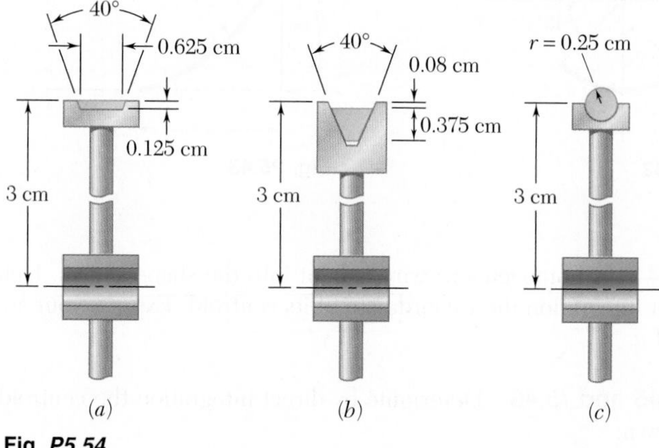

Fig. *P5.54*

5.55 Determine the volume and total surface area of the body shown.

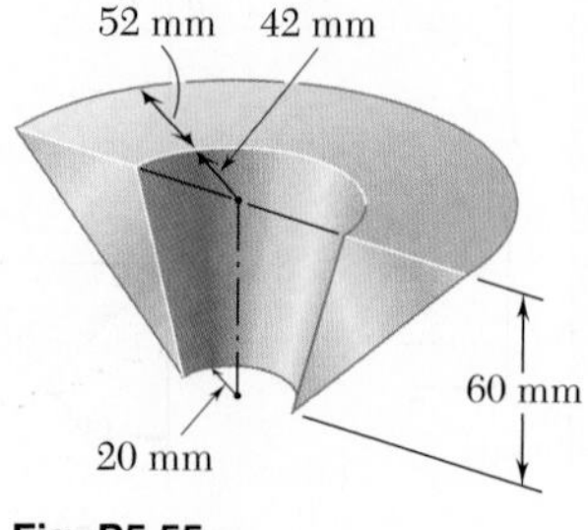

Fig. P5.55

5.56 The escutcheon (a decorative plate placed on a pipe where the pipe exits from a wall) shown is cast from yellow brass. Knowing that the density of yellow brass is 8470 kg/m^3, determine the mass of the escutcheon.

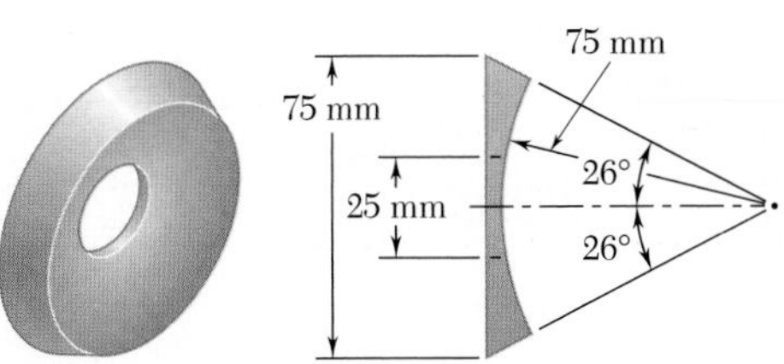

Fig. *P5.56*

5.57 The top of a round wooden table has the edge profile shown. Knowing that the diameter of the top is 44 cm before shaping and that the specific weight of the wood is 6789 N/m^3, determine the weight of the waste wood resulting from the production of 5000 tops.

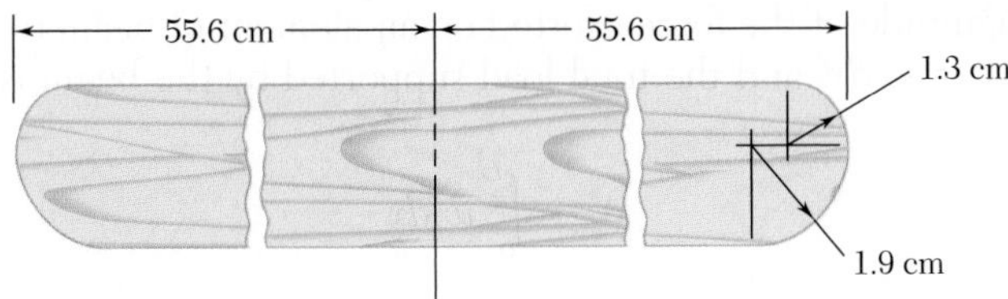

Fig. P5.57 and P5.58

5.58 The top of a round wooden table has the shape shown. Determine how many litres of lacquer are required to finish 5000 tops knowing that each top is given three coats of lacquer and that 1 litre of lacquer covers 46.5 m^2.

5.59 The aluminum shade for a small high-intensity lamp has a uniform thickness of 1 mm. Knowing that the density of aluminum is 2800 kg/m^3, determine the mass of the shade.

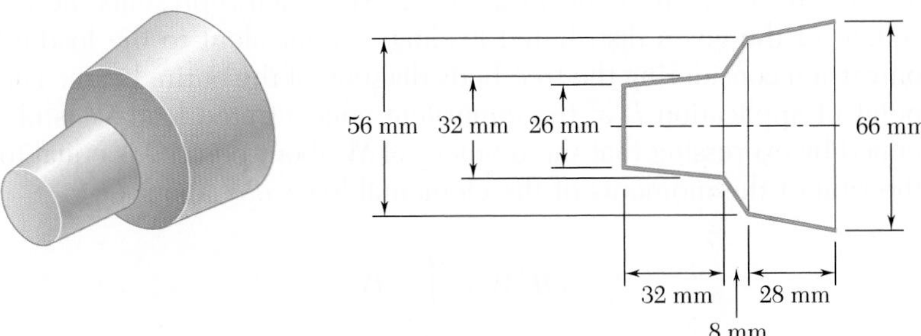

Fig. P5.59

**5.60* The reflector of a small flashlight has the parabolic shape shown. Determine the surface area of the inside of the reflector.

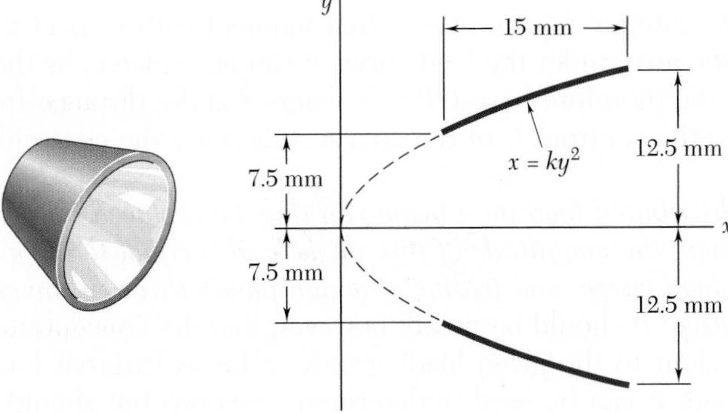

Fig. *P5.60*

*5.8. DISTRIBUTED LOADS ON BEAMS

The concept of the centroid of an area can be used to solve other problems besides those dealing with the weights of flat plates. Consider, for example, a beam supporting a *distributed load;* this load may consist of the weight of materials supported directly or indirectly by the beam, or it may be caused by wind or hydrostatic pressure. The distributed load can be represented by plotting the load w supported per unit length (Fig. 5.17); this load is expressed in N/m or in lb/ft. The magnitude of the force exerted on an element of beam of length dx is $dW = w\,dx$, and the total load supported by the beam is

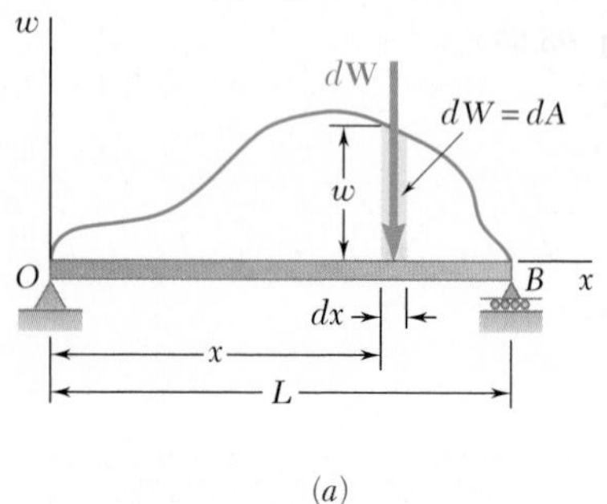

(a)

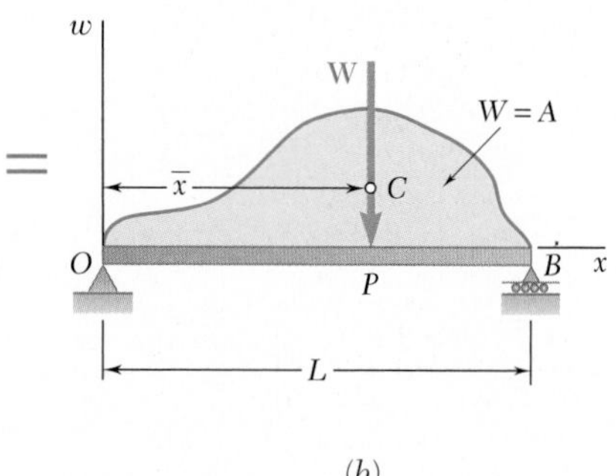

(b)

Fig. 5.17

$$W = \int_0^L w\,dx$$

We observe that the product $w\,dx$ is equal in magnitude to the element of area dA shown in Fig. 5.17*a*. The load W is thus equal in magnitude to the total area A under the load curve:

$$W = \int dA = A$$

We now determine where a *single concentrated load* **W**, of the same magnitude W as the total distributed load, should be applied on the beam if it is to produce the same reactions at the supports (Fig. 5.17*b*). However, this concentrated load **W**, which represents the resultant of the given distributed loading, is equivalent to the loading only when considering the free-body diagram of the entire beam. The point of application P of the equivalent concentrated load **W** is obtained by expressing that the moment of **W** about point O is equal to the sum of the moments of the elemental loads $d\mathbf{W}$ about O:

$$(OP)W = \int x\,dW$$

or, since $dW = w\,dx = dA$ and $W = A$,

$$(OP)A = \int_0^L x\,dA \qquad (5.12)$$

Since the integral represents the first moment with respect to the w axis of the area under the load curve, it can be replaced by the product $\bar{x}A$. We therefore have $OP = \bar{x}$, where $\bar{x}$ is the distance from the w axis to the centroid C of the area A (this is *not* the centroid of the beam).

A distributed load on a beam can thus be replaced by a concentrated load; the magnitude of this single load is equal to the area under the load curve, and its line of action passes through the centroid of that area. It should be noted, however, that the concentrated load is equivalent to the given loading only as far as external forces are concerned. It can be used to determine reactions but should not be used to compute internal forces and deflections.

Photo 5.3 The roofs of the buildings shown must be able to support not only the total weight of the snow but also the nonsymmetric distributed loads resulting from drifting of the snow.

*5.9. FORCES ON SUBMERGED SURFACES

The approach used in the preceding section can be used to determine the resultant of the hydrostatic pressure forces exerted on a *rectangular surface* submerged in a liquid. Consider the rectangular plate shown in Fig. 5.18, which is of length L and width b, where b is measured perpendicular to the plane of the figure. As noted in Sec. 5.8, the load exerted on an element of the plate of length dx is $w\,dx$, where w is the load per unit length. However, this load can also be expressed as $p\,dA = pb\,dx$, where p is the gage pressure in the liquid† and b is the width of the plate; thus, $w = bp$. Since the gage pressure in a liquid is $p = \gamma h$, where γ is the specific weight of the liquid and h is the vertical distance from the free surface, it follows that

$$w = bp = b\gamma h \tag{5.13}$$

which shows that the load per unit length w is proportional to h and, thus, varies linearly with x.

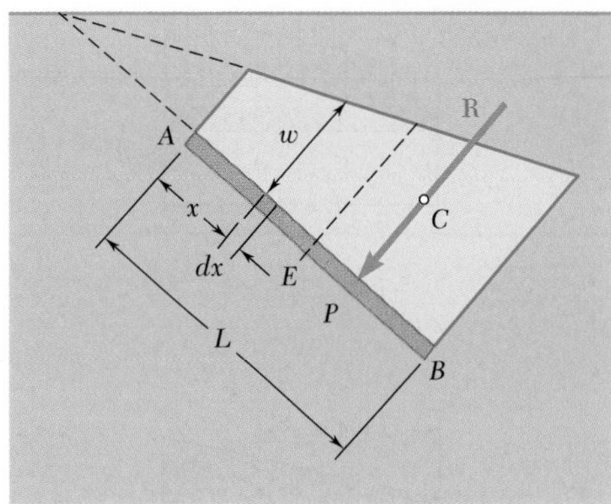

Fig. 5.18

Recalling the results of Sec. 5.8, we observe that the resultant **R** of the hydrostatic forces exerted on one side of the plate is equal in magnitude to the trapezoidal area under the load curve and that its line of action passes through the centroid C of that area. The point P of the plate where **R** is applied is known as the *center of pressure.*‡

Next, we consider the forces exerted by a liquid on a curved surface of constant width (Fig. 5.19*a*). Since the determination of the resultant **R** of these forces by direct integration would not be easy, we consider the free body obtained by detaching the volume of liquid ABD bounded by the curved surface AB and by the two plane surfaces AD and DB shown in Fig. 5.19*b*. The forces acting on the free body ABD are the weight **W** of the detached volume of liquid, the resultant $\mathbf{R}_1$ of the forces exerted on AD, the resultant $\mathbf{R}_2$ of the forces exerted on BD, and the resultant $-\mathbf{R}$ of the forces exerted *by the curved surface on the liquid.* The resultant $-\mathbf{R}$ is equal and opposite to, and has the same line of action as, the resultant **R** of the forces exerted *by the liquid on the curved surface.* The forces **W**, $\mathbf{R}_1$, and $\mathbf{R}_2$ can be determined by standard methods; after their values have been found, the force $-\mathbf{R}$ is obtained by solving the equations of equilibrium for the free body of Fig. 5.19*b*. The resultant **R** of the hydrostatic forces exerted on the curved surface is then obtained by reversing the sense of $-\mathbf{R}$.

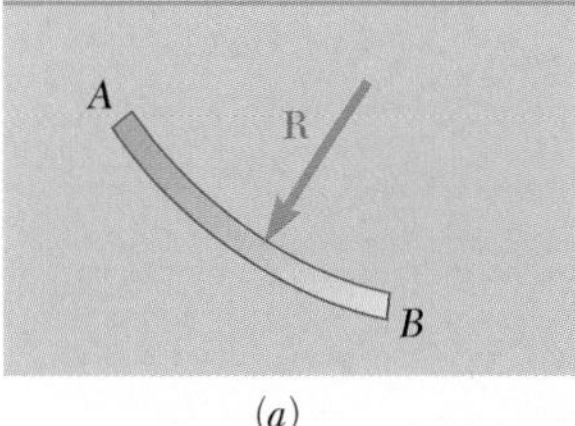

(*a*)

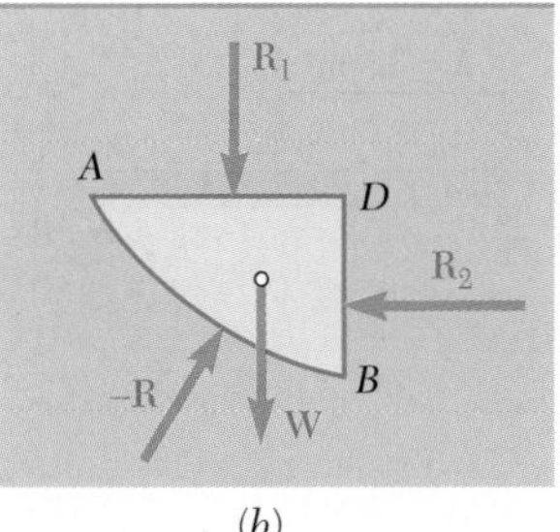

(*b*)

Fig. 5.19

The methods outlined in this section can be used to determine the resultant of the hydrostatic forces exerted on the surfaces of dams and rectangular gates and vanes. The resultants of forces on submerged surfaces of variable width will be determined in Chap. 9.

Photo 5.4 As discussed in this section, the Grand Coulee Dam supports three different kinds of distributed forces: the weights of its constitutive elements, the pressure forces exerted by the water on its submerged face, and the pressure forces exerted by the ground on its base.

†The pressure p, which represents a load per unit area, is expressed in N/m^2 or in lb/ft^2. The derived SI unit N/m^2 is called a *pascal* (Pa).

‡Noting that the area under the load curve is equal to $w_E L$, where w_E is the load per unit length at the center E of the plate, and recalling Eq. (5.13), we can write

$$R = w_E L = (bp_E)L = p_E(bL) = p_E A$$

where A denotes the area of the *plate.* Thus, the magnitude of **R** can be obtained by multiplying the area of the plate by the pressure at its center E. The resultant **R**, however, *should be applied at P, not at E.*

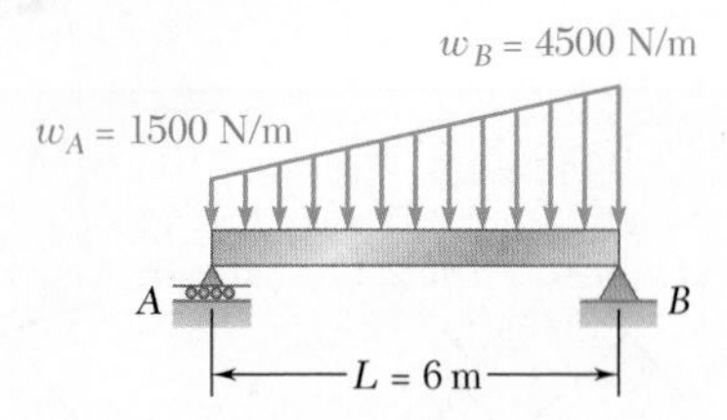

SAMPLE PROBLEM 5.9

A beam supports a distributed load as shown. (*a*) Determine the equivalent concentrated load. (*b*) Determine the reactions at the supports.

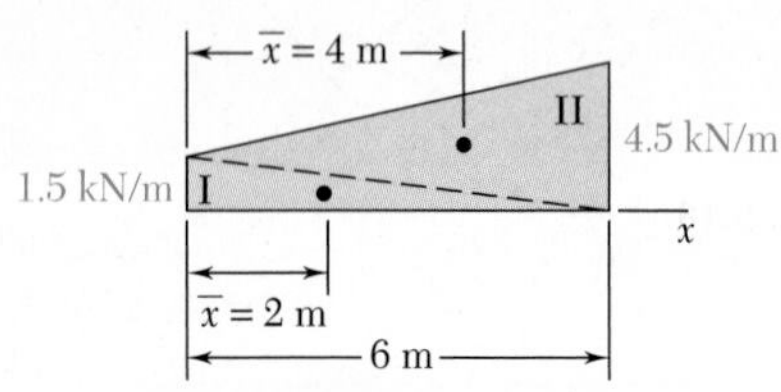

SOLUTION

***a.* Equivalent Concentrated Load.** The magnitude of the resultant of the load is equal to the area under the load curve, and the line of action of the resultant passes through the centroid of the same area. We divide the area under the load curve into two triangles and construct the table below. To simplify the computations and tabulation, the given loads per unit length have been converted into kN/m.

Component	*A*, kN	$\bar{x}$, m	$\bar{x}A$, kN · m
Triangle I	4.5	2	9
Triangle II	13.5	4	54
	$\Sigma A = 18.0$		$\Sigma \bar{x}A = 63$

Thus, $\bar{X}\Sigma A = \Sigma \bar{x}A$: $\quad \bar{X}(18 \text{ kN}) = 63 \text{ kN} \cdot \text{m} \quad \bar{X} = 3.5 \text{ m}$

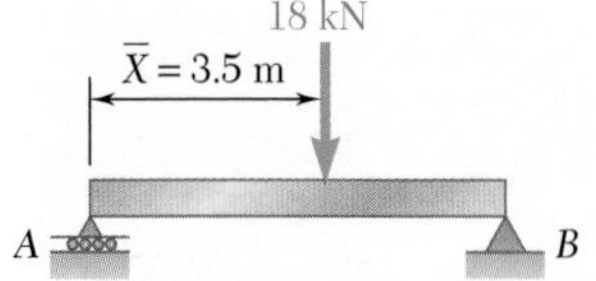

The equivalent concentrated load is

$$\mathbf{W} = 18 \text{ kN} \downarrow \quad ◀$$

and its line of action is located at a distance

$$\bar{X} = 3.5 \text{ m to the right of } A \quad ◀$$

***b.* Reactions.** The reaction at *A* is vertical and is denoted by **A**; the reaction at *B* is represented by its components $\mathbf{B}_x$ and $\mathbf{B}_y$. The given load can be considered to be the sum of two triangular loads as shown. The resultant of each triangular load is equal to the area of the triangle and acts at its centroid. We write the following equilibrium equations for the free body shown:

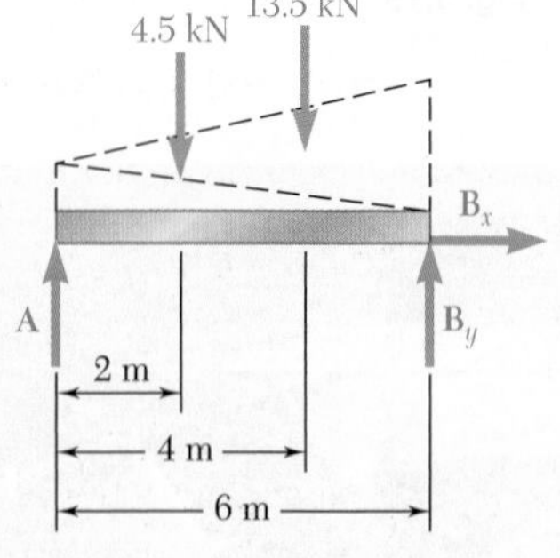

$\overset{+}{\rightarrow}\Sigma F_x = 0$: $\qquad \mathbf{B}_x = 0 \quad ◀$

$+\circlearrowleft \Sigma M_A = 0$: $\qquad -(4.5 \text{ kN})(2 \text{ m}) - (13.5 \text{ kN})(4 \text{ m}) + B_y(6 \text{ m}) = 0$

$$\mathbf{B}_y = 10.5 \text{ kN} \uparrow \quad ◀$$

$+\circlearrowleft \Sigma M_B = 0$: $\qquad +(4.5 \text{ kN})(4 \text{ m}) + (13.5 \text{ kN})(2 \text{ m}) - A(6 \text{ m}) = 0$

$$\mathbf{A} = 7.5 \text{ kN} \uparrow \quad ◀$$

Alternative Solution. The given distributed load can be replaced by its resultant, which was found in part *a*. The reactions can be determined by writing the equilibrium equations $\Sigma F_x = 0$, $\Sigma M_A = 0$, and $\Sigma M_B = 0$. We again obtain

$$\mathbf{B}_x = 0 \qquad \mathbf{B}_y = 10.5 \text{ kN} \uparrow \qquad \mathbf{A} = 7.5 \text{ kN} \uparrow \quad ◀$$

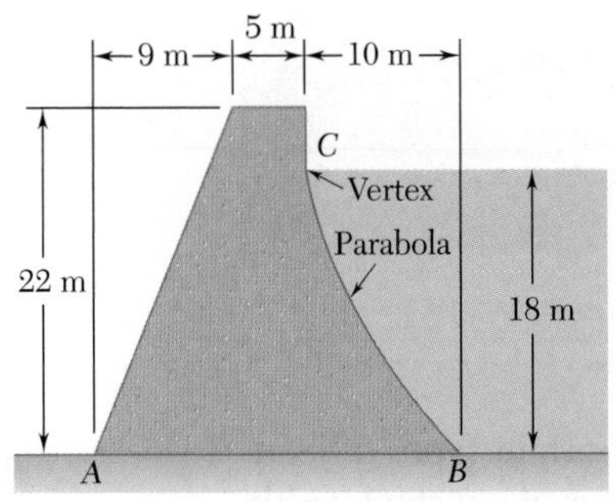

SAMPLE PROBLEM 5.10

The cross section of a concrete dam is as shown. Consider a 1-m-thick section of the dam, and determine (*a*) the resultant of the reaction forces exerted by the ground on the base *AB* of the dam, (*b*) the resultant of the pressure forces exerted by the water on the face *BC* of the dam. The specific weights of concrete and water are 2330 kg/m^3 and 970 kg/m^3, respectively.

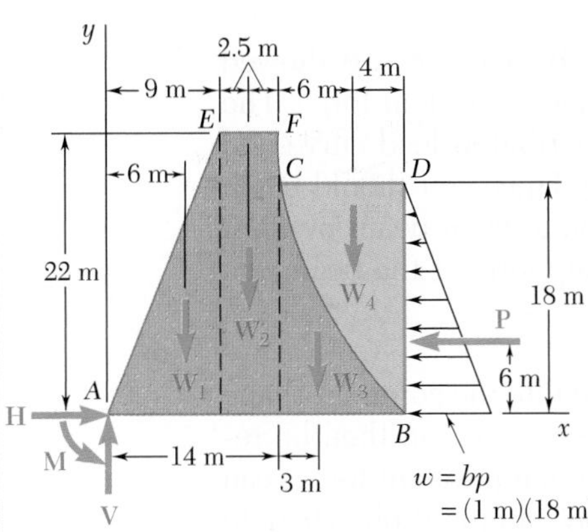

SOLUTION

a. Ground Reaction. We choose as a free body the 1-m-thick section *AEFCDB* of the dam and water. The reaction forces exerted by the ground on the base *AB* are represented by an equivalent force-couple system at *A*. Other forces acting on the free body are the weight of the dam, represented by the weights of its components $\mathbf{W}_1$, $\mathbf{W}_2$, and $\mathbf{W}_3$; the weight of the water $\mathbf{W}_4$; and the resultant **P** of the pressure forces exerted on section *BD* by the water to the right of section *BD*. We have

$$W_1 = \tfrac{1}{2}(9 \text{ m})(22 \text{ m})(1 \text{ m})(2330 \text{ kg/m}^3) = 2260566 \text{ N}$$
$$W_2 = (5 \text{ m})(22 \text{ m})(1 \text{ m})(2330 \text{ kg/m}^3) = 2511740 \text{ N}$$
$$W_3 = \tfrac{1}{3}(10 \text{ m})(18 \text{ m})(1 \text{ m})(2330 \text{ kg/m}^3) = 1370040 \text{ N}$$
$$W_4 = \tfrac{2}{3}(10 \text{ m})(18 \text{ m})(1 \text{ m})(970 \text{ kg/m}^3) = 1140720 \text{ N}$$
$$P = \tfrac{1}{2}(18 \text{ m})(1 \text{ m})(18 \text{ m})(970 \text{ kg/m}^3) = 1539972 \text{ N}$$

Equilibrium Equations

$\overset{+}{\rightarrow}\Sigma F_x = 0$: $\quad H - 1539972 \text{ N} = 0 \qquad \mathbf{H} = 1539972 \text{ N} \rightarrow$ ◀

$+\uparrow\Sigma F_y = 0$: $\quad V - 2260566 \text{ N} - 2511740 \text{ N} - 1370040 \text{ N} - 1140720 \text{ N} = 0$

$\mathbf{V} = 7283066 \text{ N}\uparrow$ ◀

$+\circlearrowleft\Sigma M_A = 0$: $\quad -(2260566 \text{ N})(6 \text{ m}) - (2511740 \text{ N})(11.5 \text{ m}) - (1370040 \text{ N})(17 \text{ m}) - (1140720 \text{ N})(20 \text{ m}) + (1539972 \text{ N})(6 \text{ m}) + M = 0$

$\mathbf{M} = 79313654 \text{ N} \cdot \text{m} \circlearrowleft$ ◀

We can replace the force-couple system obtained by a single force acting at a distance *d* to the right of *A*, where

$$d = \frac{79313654 \text{ N} \cdot \text{m}}{7283066 \text{ N}} = 10.89 \text{ m}$$

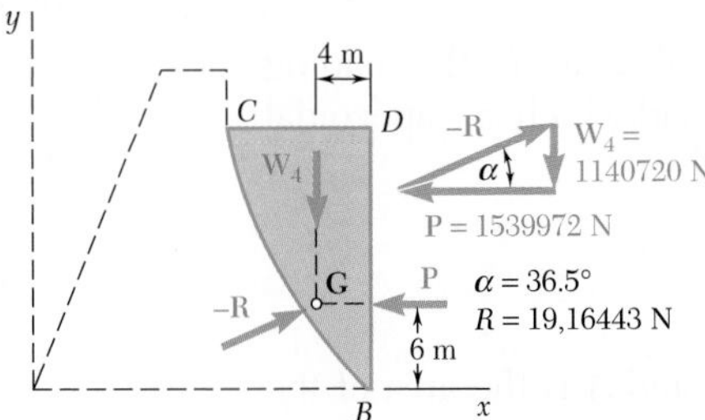

b. Resultant R of Water Forces. The parabolic section of water *BCD* is chosen as a free body. The forces involved are the resultant $-\mathbf{R}$ of the forces exerted by the dam on the water, the weight $\mathbf{W}_4$, and the force **P**. Since these forces must be concurrent, $-\mathbf{R}$ passes through the point of intersection *G* of $\mathbf{W}_4$ and **P**. A force triangle is drawn from which the magnitude and direction of $-\mathbf{R}$ are determined. The resultant **R** of the forces exerted by the water on the face *BC* is equal and opposite:

$\mathbf{R} = 1916443 \text{ N} \measuredangle 36.5°$ ◀

SOLVING PROBLEMS ON YOUR OWN

The problems in this lesson involve two common and very important types of loading: distributed loads on beams and forces on submerged surfaces of constant width. As we discussed in Secs. 5.8 and 5.9 and illustrated in Sample Probs. 5.9 and 5.10, determining the single equivalent force for each of these loadings requires a knowledge of centroids.

1. *Analyzing beams subjected to distributed loads.* In Sec. 5.8, we showed that a distributed load on a beam can be replaced by a single equivalent force. The magnitude of this force is equal to the area under the distributed load curve and its line of action passes through the centroid of that area. Thus, you should begin your solution by replacing the various distributed loads on a given beam by their respective single equivalent forces. The reactions at the supports of the beam can then be determined by using the methods of Chap. 4.

When possible, complex distributed loads should be divided into the common-shape areas shown in Fig. 5.8A [Sample Prob. 5.9]. Each of these areas can then be replaced by a single equivalent force. If required, the system of equivalent forces can be reduced further to a single equivalent force. As you study Sample Prob. 5.9, note how we have used the analogy between force and area and the techniques for locating the centroid of a composite area to analyze a beam subjected to a distributed load.

2. *Solving problems involving forces on submerged bodies.* The following points and techniques should be remembered when solving problems of this type.

a. The pressure p at a depth h below the free surface of a liquid is equal to γh or ρgh, where γ and ρ are the specific weight and the density of the liquid, respectively. The load per unit length w acting on a submerged surface of constant width b is then

$$w = bp = b\gamma h = b\rho gh$$

b. The line of action of the resultant force **R** acting on a submerged plane surface is perpendicular to the surface.

c. For a vertical or inclined plane rectangular surface of width b, the loading on the surface can be represented by a linearly distributed load which is trapezoidal in shape (Fig. 5.18). Further, the magnitude of **R** is given by

$$R = \gamma h_E A$$

where h_E is the vertical distance to the center of the surface and A is the area of the surface.

d. The load curve will be triangular (rather than trapezoidal) when the top edge of a plane rectangular surface coincides with the free surface of the liquid, since the pressure of the liquid at the free surface is zero. For this case, the line of action of **R** is easily determined, for it passes through the centroid of a *triangular* distributed load.

e. For the general case, rather than analyzing a trapezoid, we suggest that you use the method indicated in part *b* of Sample Prob. 5.9. First divide the trapezoidal distributed load into two triangles, and then compute the magnitude of the resultant of each triangular load. (The magnitude is equal to the area of the triangle times the width of the plate.) Note that the line of action of each resultant force passes through the centroid of the corresponding triangle and that the sum of these forces is equivalent to **R**. Thus, rather than using **R**, you can use the two equivalent resultant forces, whose points of application are easily calculated. Of course, the equation given for R in paragraph *c* should be used when only the magnitude of **R** is needed.

f. When the submerged surface of constant width is curved, the resultant force acting on the surface is obtained by considering the equilibrium of the volume of liquid bounded by the curved surface and by horizontal and vertical planes (Fig. 5.19). Observe that the force $\mathbf{R}_1$ of Fig. 5.19 is equal to the weight of the liquid lying above the plane AD. The method of solution for problems involving curved surfaces is shown in part *b* of Sample Prob. 5.10.

In subsequent mechanics courses (in particular, mechanics of materials and fluid mechanics), you will have ample opportunity to use the ideas introduced in this lesson.

Problems

5.61 and 5.62 For the beam and loading shown, determine (*a*) the magnitude and location of the resultant of the distributed load, (*b*) the reactions at the beam supports.

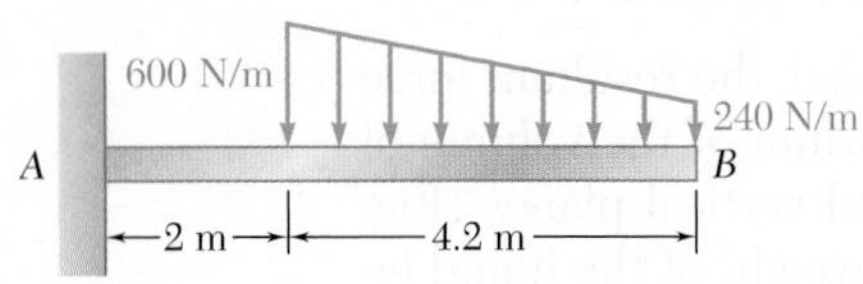

Fig. P5.61

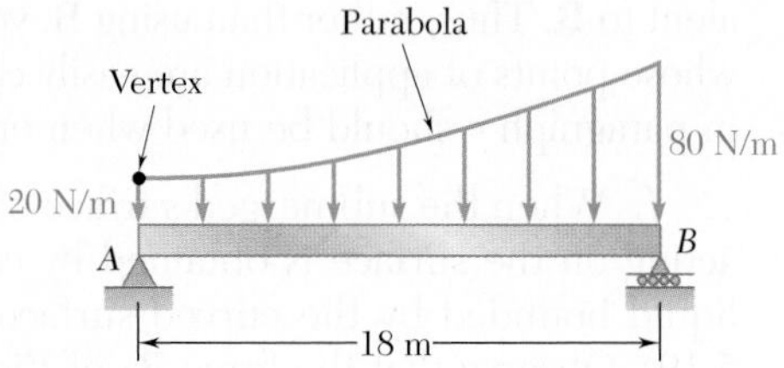

Fig. P5.62

5.63 through 5.68 Determine the reactions at the beam supports for the given loading.

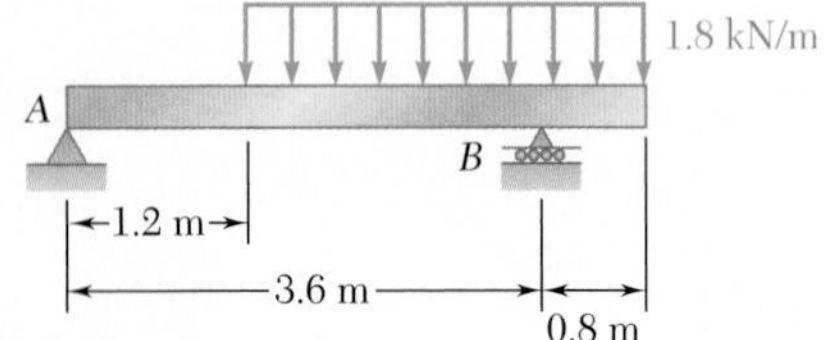

Fig. P5.63

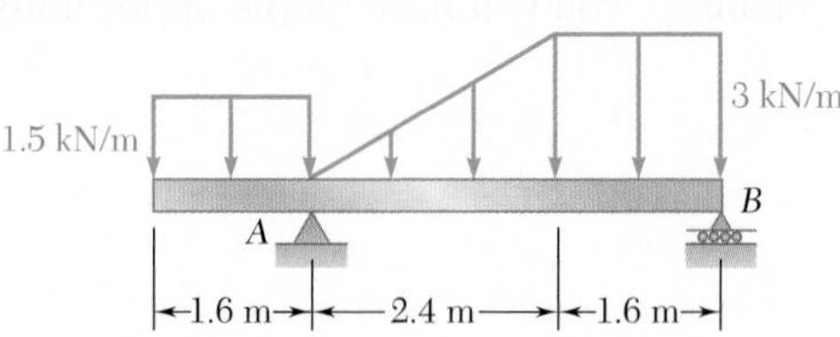

Fig. P5.64

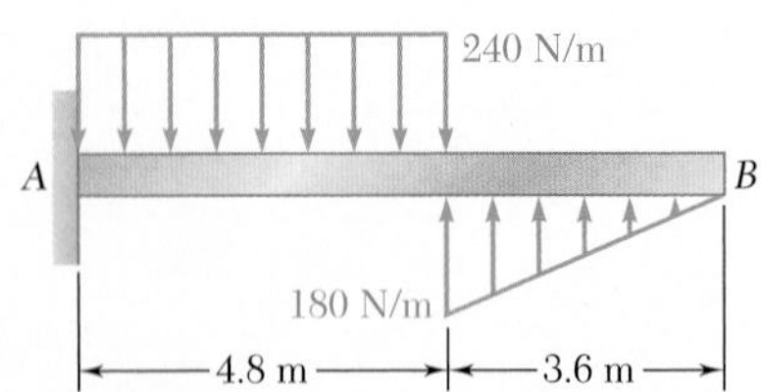

Fig. *P5.65*

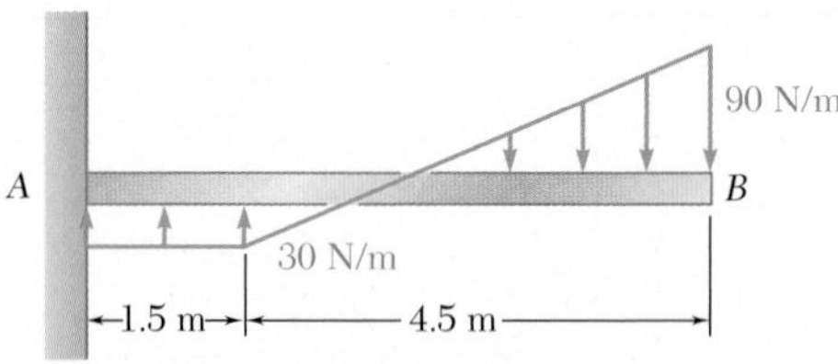

Fig. P5.66

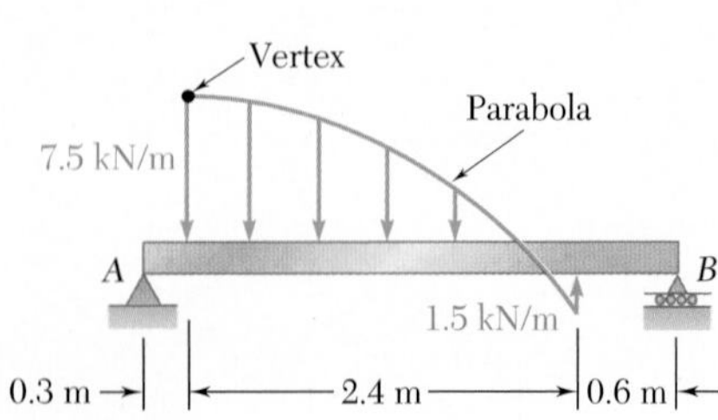

Fig. P5.67

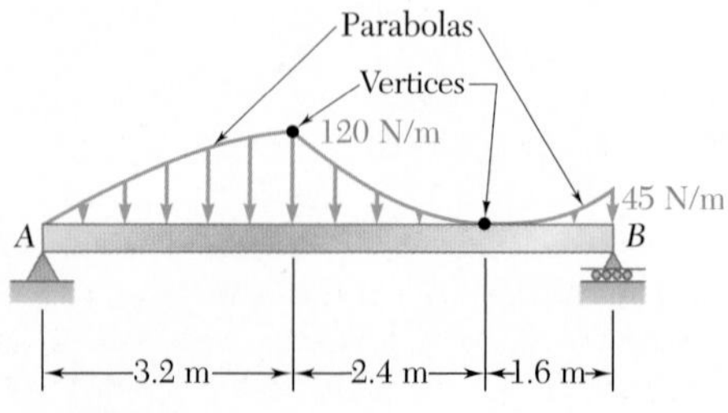

Fig. *P5.68*

5.69 Determine the reactions at the beam supports for the given loading when $w_0 = 1.5$ kN/m.

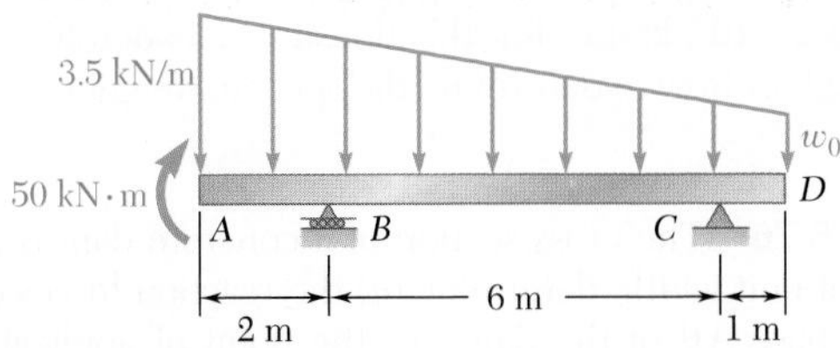

Fig. P5.69 and *P5.70*

5.70 Determine (*a*) the distributed load w_0 at the end D of the beam $ABCD$ for which the reaction at B is zero, (*b*) the corresponding reaction at C.

5.71 Knowing that $w = 300$ N/m, determine (*a*) the smallest distance a for which the vertical reaction at support B is twice that at A, (*b*) the corresponding reactions at the supports.

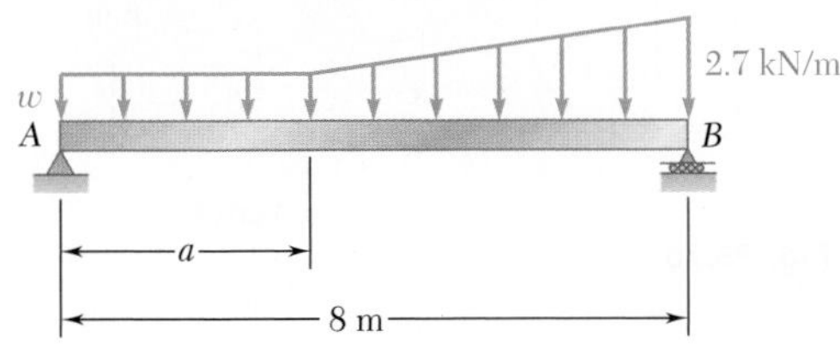

Fig. P5.71 and *P5.72*

5.72 Knowing that $w = 300$ N/m, determine (*a*) the distance a for which the ratio of the vertical reaction at support B to the vertical reaction at support A is maximum, (*b*) the corresponding reactions at the supports.

5.73 A grade beam AB supports three concentrated loads and rests on soil and the top of a large rock. The soil exerts an upward distributed load, and the rock exerts a concentrated load $\mathbf{R}_R$ as shown. Knowing that $P =$ 1 kN and $w_B = \frac{1}{2} w_A$, determine the values of w_A and R_R corresponding to equilibrium.

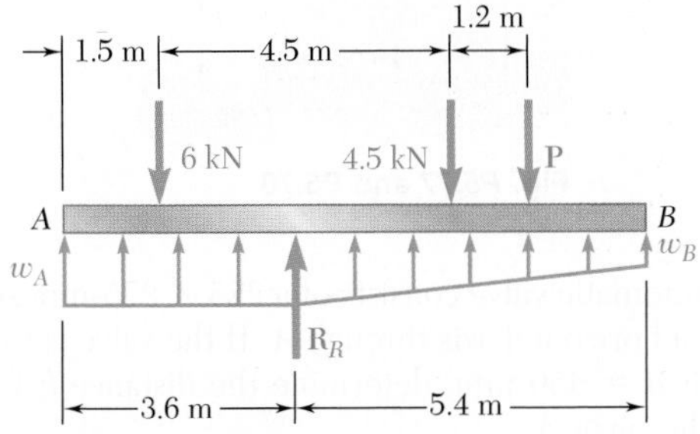

Fig. P5.73 and P5.74

5.74 A grade beam AB supports three concentrated loads and rests on soil and the top of a large rock. The soil exerts an upward distributed load, and the rock exerts a concentrated load $\mathbf{R}_R$ as shown. Knowing that $w_B =$ $0.4w_A$, determine (*a*) the largest value of $\mathbf{P}$ for which the beam is in equilibrium, (*b*) the corresponding value of w_A.

In the following problems, use $\gamma = 62.4$ lb/ft^3 for the specific weight of fresh water and $\gamma_c = 150$ lb/ft^3 for the specific weight of concrete if U.S. customary units are used. With SI units, use $\rho = 10^3$ kg/m^3 for the density of fresh water and $\rho_c = 2.40 \times 10^3$ kg/m^3 for the density of concrete. (See the footnote on page 222 for how to determine the specific weight of a material given its density.)

5.75 and 5.76 The cross section of a concrete dam is as shown. For a dam section of unit width, determine (*a*) the reaction forces exerted by the ground on the base *AB* of the dam, (*b*) the point of application of the resultant of the reaction forces of part *a*, (*c*) the resultant of the pressure forces exerted by the water on the face *BD* of the dam.

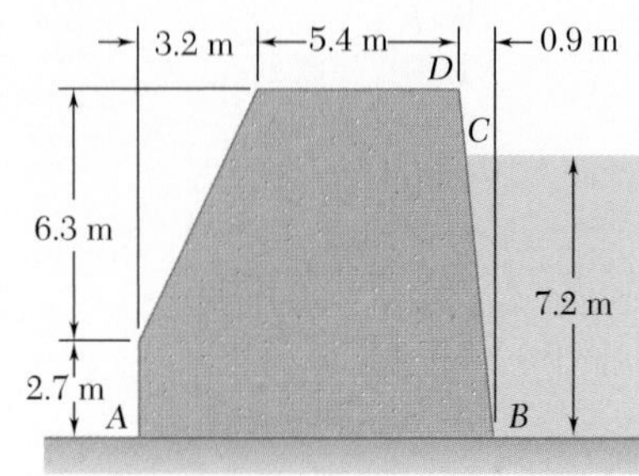

Fig. P5.75

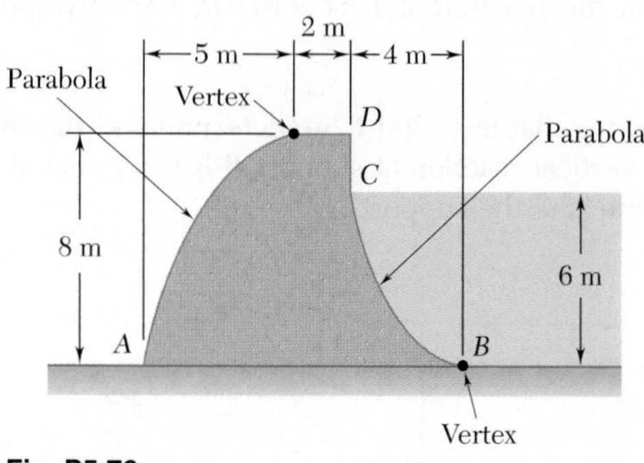

Fig. P5.76

5.77 An automatic valve consists of a 225 × 225-mm square plate that is pivoted about a horizontal axis through *A* located at a distance $h = 90$ mm above the lower edge. Determine the depth of water *d* for which the valve will open.

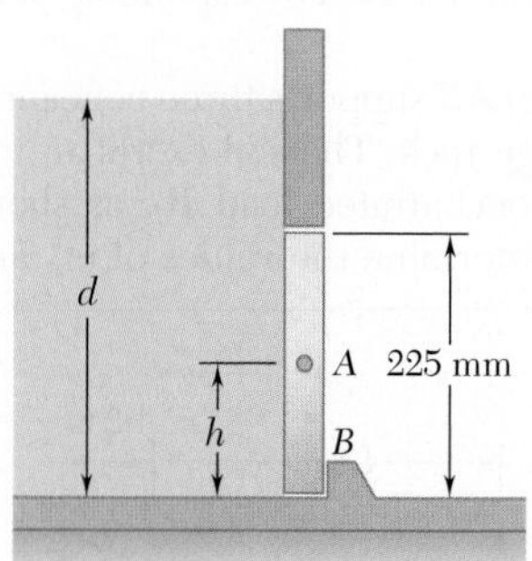

Fig. *P5.77* and P5.78

5.78 An automatic valve consists of a 225 × 225-mm square plate that is pivoted about a horizontal axis through *A*. If the valve is to open when the depth of water is $d = 450$ mm, determine the distance *h* from the bottom of the valve to the pivot *A*.

5.79 A freshwater marsh is drained to the ocean through an automatic tide gate that is 1.2 m wide and 2.7 high. The gate is held by hinges located along its top edge at *A* and bears on a sill at *B*. At a given time, the water levels in the marsh and in the ocean are $h = 1.8$ m and $d = 2.7$ m, respectively. Determine the force exerted by the sill on the gate at *B* and the hinge reaction at *A*. (Specific weight of salt water = 10^3 kg/m^3.)

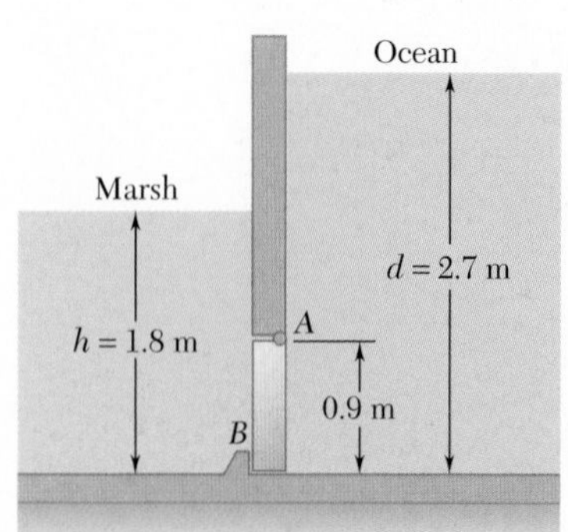

Fig. P5.79

5.80 The dam for a lake is designed to withstand the additional force caused by silt which has settled on the lake bottom. Assuming that silt is equivalent to a liquid of density $\rho_s = 1.76 \times 10^3$ kg/m^3 and considering a 1-m-wide section of dam, determine the percentage increase in the force acting on the dam face for a silt accumulation of depth 1.5 m.

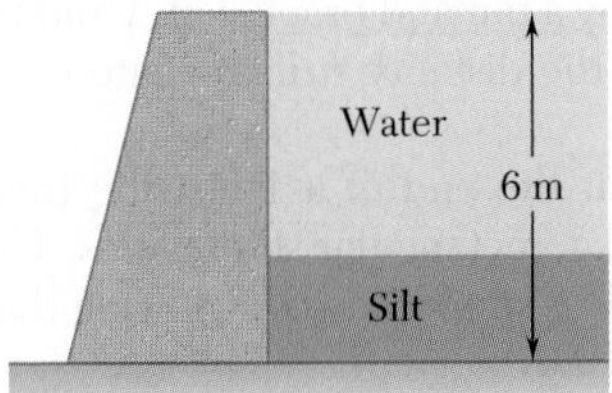

Fig. P5.80 and *P5.81*

5.81 The base of a dam for a lake is designed to resist up to 150 percent of the horizontal force of the water. After construction, it is found that silt (which is equivalent to a liquid of density $\rho_s = 1.76 \times 10^3$ kg/m^3) is settling on the lake bottom at a rate of 20 mm/yr. Considering a 1-m-wide section of dam, determine the number of years until the dam becomes unsafe.

5.82 A temporary dam is constructed in a 1.5-m-wide freshwater channel by nailing two boards to pilings located at the sides of the channel and propping a third board *AB* against the pilings and the floor of the channel. When rope *BC* is slack and neglecting friction, determine (*a*) the horizontal force exerted on board *AB* by each of the pilings, (*b*) the vertical force exerted on the top edge of board *AB*, (*c*) the reaction at *B*.

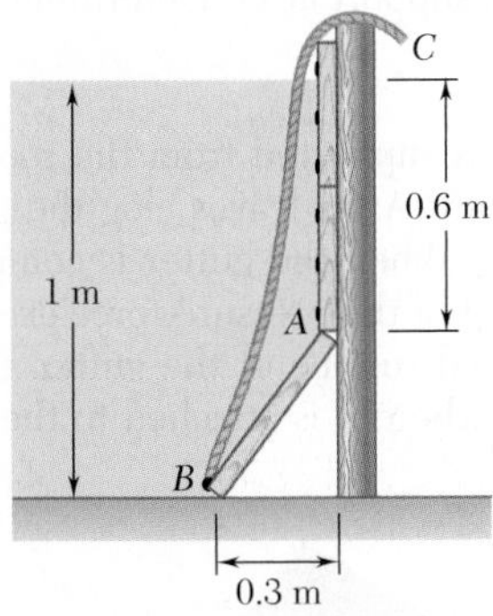

Fig. P5.82 and P5.83

5.83 A temporary dam is constructed in a 1.5-m-wide freshwater channel by nailing two boards to pilings located at the sides of the channel and propping a third board *AB* against the pilings and the floor of the channel. Neglecting friction, determine the magnitude and direction of the minimum tension required in rope *BC* to move board *AB*.

5.84 The gate *AB* is located at the end of a 1.8-m-wide water channel and is supported by hinges along its top edge *A*. Knowing that the floor of the channel is frictionless, determine the reactions at *A* and *B*.

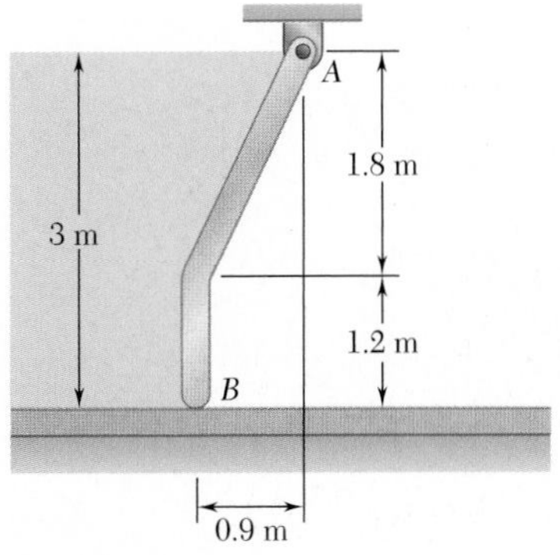

Fig. P5.84

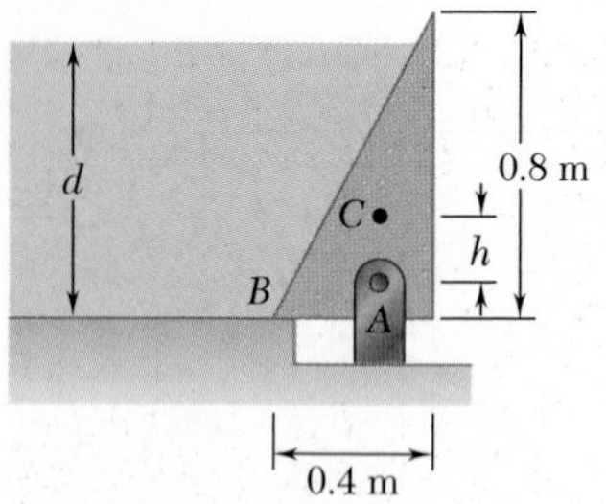

Fig. P5.85 and *P5.86*

5.85 A prismatically shaped gate placed at the end of a freshwater channel is supported by a pin and bracket at A and rests on a frictionless support at B. The pin is located at a distance $h = 0.1$ m below the center of gravity C of the gate. Determine the depth of water d for which the gate will open.

5.86 A prismatically shaped gate placed at the end of a freshwater channel is supported by a pin and bracket at A and rests on a frictionless support at B. Determine the distance h if the gate is to open when $d = 0.8$ m.

5.87 The gate at the end of a 1-m-wide freshwater channel is fabricated from three 125-kg, rectangular steel plates. The gate is hinged at A and rests against a frictionless support at D. Knowing that $d = 0.75$ m, determine the reactions at A and D.

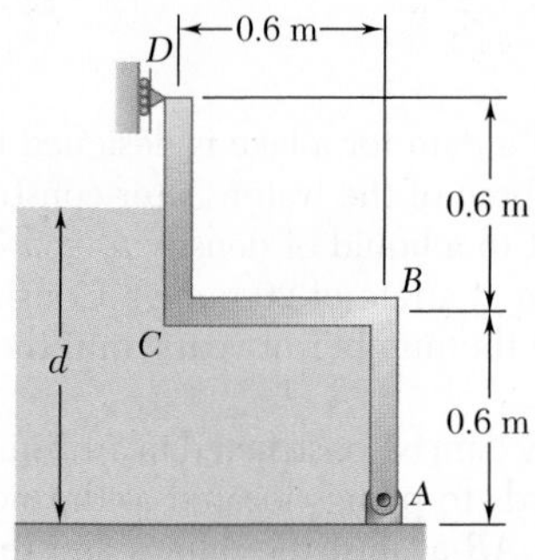

Fig. P5.87 and P5.88

5.88 The gate at the end of a 1-m-wide freshwater channel is fabricated from three 125-kg, rectangular steel plates. The gate is hinged at A and rests against a frictionless support at D. Determine the depth of water d for which the gate will open.

5.89 A rain gutter is supported from the roof of a house by hangers that are spaced 0.6 m apart. After leaves clog the gutter's drain, the gutter slowly fills with rainwater. When the gutter is completely filled with water, determine (*a*) the resultant of the pressure force exerted by the water on the 0.6-m section of the curved surface of the gutter, (*b*) the force-couple system exerted on a hanger where it is attached to the gutter.

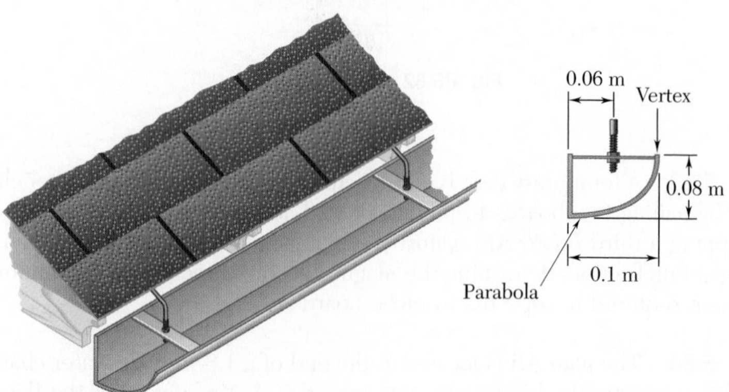

Fig. *P5.89*

5.10. CENTER OF GRAVITY OF A THREE-DIMENSIONAL BODY. CENTROID OF A VOLUME

The *center of gravity* G of a three-dimensional body is obtained by dividing the body into small elements and by then expressing that the weight $\mathbf{W}$ of the body acting at G is equivalent to the system of distributed forces $\Delta\mathbf{W}$ representing the weights of the small elements. Choosing the y axis to be vertical with positive sense upward (Fig. 5.20) and denoting by $\bar{\mathbf{r}}$ the position vector of G, we write that

Photo 5.5 To predict the flight characteristics of the modified Boeing 747 when used to transport a space shuttle, the center of gravity of each craft had to be determined.

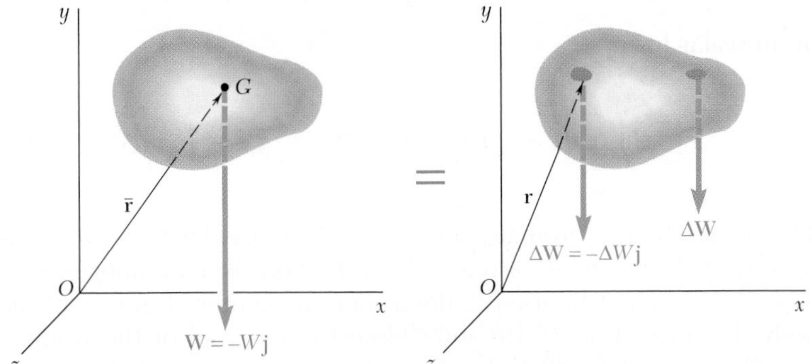

Fig. 5.20

$\mathbf{W}$ is equal to the sum of the elemental weights $\Delta\mathbf{W}$ and that its moment about O is equal to the sum of the moments about O of the elemental weights:

$$\begin{aligned} \Sigma\mathbf{F}: \qquad & -W\mathbf{j} = \Sigma(-\Delta W\mathbf{j}) \\ \Sigma\mathbf{M}_O: \qquad & \bar{\mathbf{r}} \times (-W\mathbf{j}) = \Sigma[\mathbf{r} \times (-\Delta W\mathbf{j})] \end{aligned} \tag{5.13}$$

Rewriting the last equation in the form

$$\bar{\mathbf{r}}W \times (-\mathbf{j}) = (\Sigma\mathbf{r}\,\Delta W) \times (-\mathbf{j}) \tag{5.14}$$

we observe that the weight $\mathbf{W}$ of the body is equivalent to the system of the elemental weights $\Delta\mathbf{W}$ if the following conditions are satisfied:

$$W = \Sigma\,\Delta W \qquad \bar{\mathbf{r}}W = \Sigma\mathbf{r}\,\Delta W$$

Increasing the number of elements and simultaneously decreasing the size of each element, we obtain in the limit

$$W = \int dW \qquad \bar{\mathbf{r}}W = \int \mathbf{r}\,dW \tag{5.15}$$

We note that the relations obtained are independent of the orientation of the body. For example, if the body and the coordinate axes were rotated so that the z axis pointed upward, the unit vector $-\mathbf{j}$ would be replaced by $-\mathbf{k}$ in Eqs. (5.13) and (5.14), but the relations (5.15) would remain unchanged. Resolving the vectors $\bar{\mathbf{r}}$ and $\mathbf{r}$ into rectangular components, we note that the second of the relations (5.15) is equivalent to the three scalar equations

$$\bar{x}W = \int x\,dW \qquad \bar{y}W = \int y\,dW \qquad \bar{z}W = \int z\,dW \tag{5.16}$$

If the body is made of a homogeneous material of specific weight γ, the magnitude dW of the weight of an infinitesimal element can be expressed in terms of the volume dV of the element, and the magnitude W of the total weight can be expressed in terms of the total volume V. We write

$$dW = \gamma\, dV \qquad W = \gamma V$$

Substituting for dW and W in the second of the relations (5.15), we write

$$\bar{\mathbf{r}}V = \int \mathbf{r}\, dV \tag{5.17}$$

or, in scalar form,

$$\bar{x}V = \int x\, dV \qquad \bar{y}V = \int y\, dV \qquad \bar{z}V = \int z\, dV \tag{5.18}$$

The point whose coordinates are $\bar{x}$, $\bar{y}$, and $\bar{z}$ is also known as the *centroid C of the volume V* of the body. If the body is not homogeneous, Eqs. (5.18) cannot be used to determine the center of gravity of the body; however, Eqs. (5.18) still define the centroid of the volume.

The integral $\int x\, dV$ is known as the *first moment of the volume with respect to the yz plane.* Similarly, the integrals $\int y\, dV$ and $\int z\, dV$ define the first moments of the volume with respect to the zx plane and the xy plane, respectively. It is seen from Eqs. (5.18) that if the centroid of a volume is located in a coordinate plane, the first moment of the volume with respect to that plane is zero.

A volume is said to be symmetrical with respect to a given plane if for every point P of the volume there exists a point P' of the same volume, such that the line PP' is perpendicular to the given plane and is bisected by that plane. The plane is said to be a *plane of symmetry* for the given volume. When a volume V possesses a plane of symmetry, the first moment of V with respect to that plane is zero, and the centroid of the volume is located in the plane of symmetry. When a volume possesses two planes of symmetry, the centroid of the volume is located on the line of intersection of the two planes. Finally, when a volume possesses three planes of symmetry which intersect at a well-defined point (that is, not along a common line), the point of intersection of the three planes coincides with the centroid of the volume. This property enables us to determine immediately the locations of the centroids of spheres, ellipsoids, cubes, rectangular parallelepipeds, etc.

The centroids of unsymmetrical volumes or of volumes possessing only one or two planes of symmetry should be determined by integration (Sec. 5.12). The centroids of several common volumes are shown in Fig. 5.21. It should be observed that in general the centroid of a volume of revolution *does not coincide* with the centroid of its cross section. Thus, the centroid of a hemisphere is different from that of a semicircular area, and the centroid of a cone is different from that of a triangle.

Shape		$\bar{x}$	Volume
Hemisphere	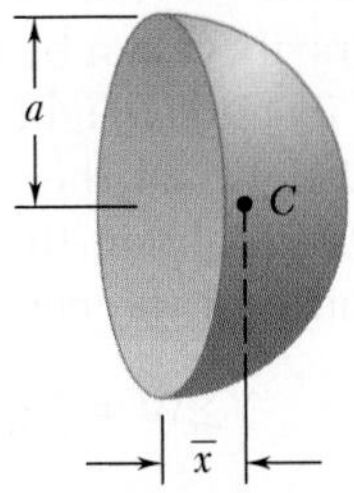	$\frac{3a}{8}$	$\frac{2}{3}\pi a^3$
Semiellipsoid of revolution	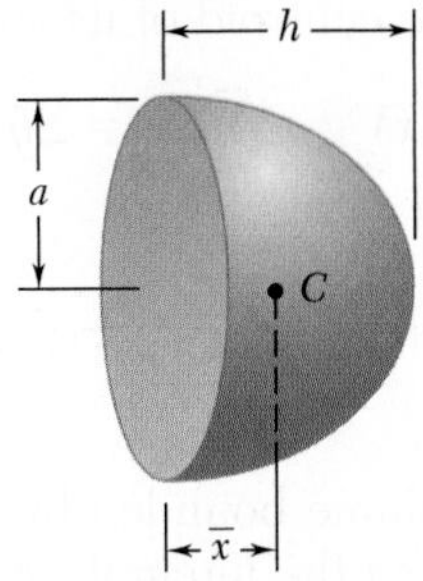	$\frac{3h}{8}$	$\frac{2}{3}\pi a^2 h$
Paraboloid of revolution	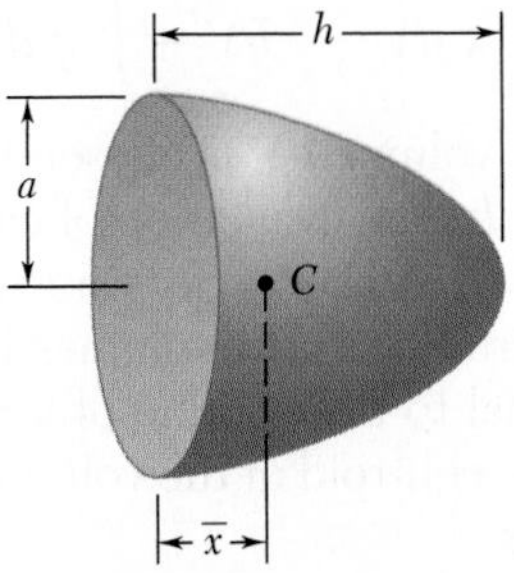	$\frac{h}{3}$	$\frac{1}{2}\pi a^2 h$
Cone	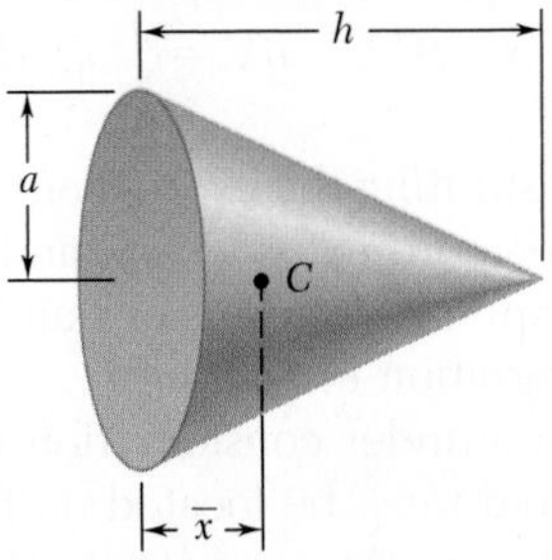	$\frac{h}{4}$	$\frac{1}{3}\pi a^2 h$
Pyramid	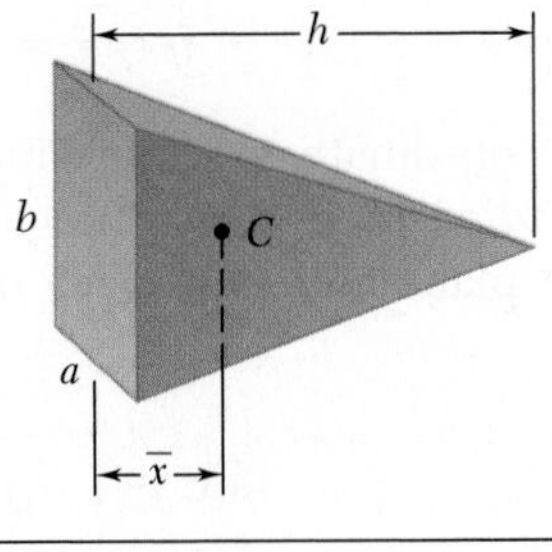	$\frac{h}{4}$	$\frac{1}{3}abh$

Fig. 5.21 Centroids of common shapes and volumes.

5.11. COMPOSITE BODIES

If a body can be divided into several of the common shapes shown in Fig. 5.21, its center of gravity G can be determined by expressing that the moment about O of its total weight is equal to the sum of the moments about O of the weights of the various component parts. Proceeding as in Sec. 5.10, we obtain the following equations defining the coordinates $\bar{X}$, $\bar{Y}$, and $\bar{Z}$ of the center of gravity G:

$$\bar{X}\Sigma W = \Sigma \bar{x} W \qquad \bar{Y}\Sigma W = \Sigma \bar{y} W \qquad \bar{Z}\Sigma W = \Sigma \bar{z} W \tag{5.19}$$

If the body is made of a homogeneous material, its center of gravity coincides with the centroid of its volume, and we obtain

$$\bar{X}\Sigma V = \Sigma \bar{x} V \qquad \bar{Y}\Sigma V = \Sigma \bar{y} V \qquad \bar{Z}\Sigma V = \Sigma \bar{z} V \tag{5.20}$$

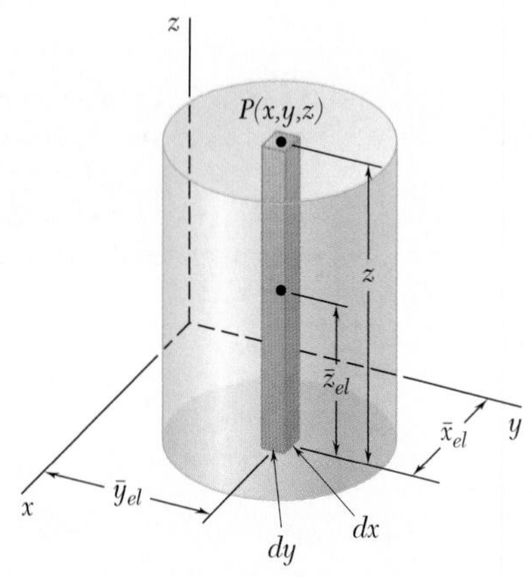

Fig. 5.22 Determination of the centroid of a volume by double integration.

5.12. DETERMINATION OF CENTROIDS OF VOLUMES BY INTEGRATION

The centroid of a volume bounded by analytical surfaces can be determined by evaluating the integrals given in Sec. 5.10:

$$\bar{x}V = \int x\,dV \qquad \bar{y}V = \int y\,dV \qquad \bar{z}V = \int z\,dV \tag{5.21}$$

If the element of volume dV is chosen to be equal to a small cube of sides dx, dy, and dz, the evaluation of each of these integrals requires a *triple integration.* However, it is possible to determine the coordinates of the centroid of most volumes by *double integration* if dV is chosen to be equal to the volume of a thin filament (Fig. 5.22). The coordinates of the centroid of the volume are then obtained by rewriting Eqs. (5.21) as

$$\bar{x}V = \int \bar{x}_{el}\,dV \qquad \bar{y}V = \int \bar{y}_{el}\,dV \qquad \bar{z}V = \int \bar{z}_{el}\,dV \tag{5.22}$$

and by then substituting the expressions given in Fig. 5.22 for the volume dV and the coordinates $\bar{x}_{el}$, $\bar{y}_{el}$, and $\bar{z}_{el}$. By using the equation of the surface to express z in terms of x and y, the integration is reduced to a double integration in x and y.

If the volume under consideration possesses *two planes of symmetry,* its centroid must be located on the line of intersection of the two planes. Choosing the x axis to lie along this line, we have

$$\bar{y} = \bar{z} = 0$$

and the only coordinate to determine is $\bar{x}$. This can be done with a *single integration* by dividing the given volume into thin slabs parallel to the yz plane and expressing dV in terms of x and dx in the equation

$$\bar{x}V = \int \bar{x}_{el}\,dV \tag{5.23}$$

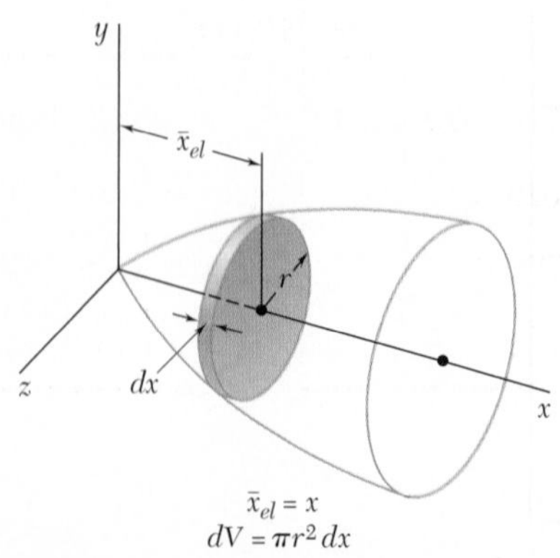

Fig. 5.23 Determination of the centroid of a body of revolution.

For a body of revolution, the slabs are circular and their volume is given in Fig. 5.23.

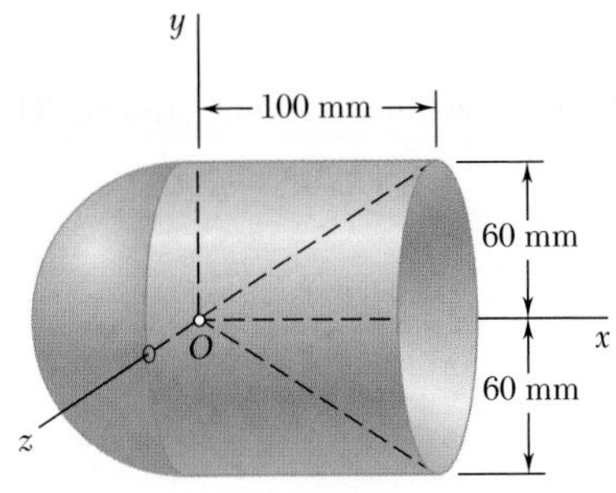

SAMPLE PROBLEM 5.11

Determine the location of the center of gravity of the homogeneous body of revolution shown, which was obtained by joining a hemisphere and a cylinder and carving out a cone.

SOLUTION

Because of symmetry, the center of gravity lies on the x axis. As shown in the figure below, the body can be obtained by adding a hemisphere to a cylinder and then subtracting a cone. The volume and the abscissa of the centroid of each of these components are obtained from Fig. 5.21 and are entered in the table below. The total volume of the body and the first moment of its volume with respect to the yz plane are then determined.

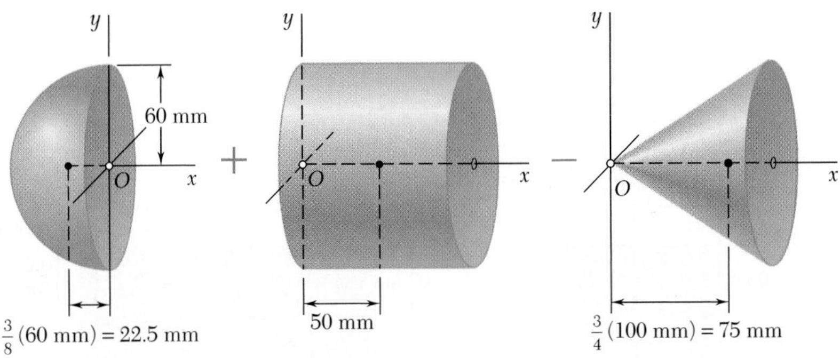

Component	Volume, mm^3	$\bar{x}$, mm	$\bar{x}V$, mm^4
Hemisphere	$\frac{1}{2}\frac{4\pi}{3}(60)^3 = \quad 0.4524 \times 10^6$	-22.5	-10.18×10^6
Cylinder	$\pi(60)^2(100) = \quad 1.1310 \times 10^6$	$+50$	$+56.55 \times 10^6$
Cone	$-\frac{\pi}{3}(60)^2(100) = -0.3770 \times 10^6$	$+75$	-28.28×10^6
	$\Sigma V = \quad 1.206 \times 10^6$		$\Sigma \bar{x} V = +18.09 \times 10^6$

Thus,

$\bar{X}\Sigma V = \Sigma \bar{x} V$: $\quad \bar{X}(1.206 \times 10^6 \text{ mm}^3) = 18.09 \times 10^6 \text{ mm}^4$

$$\bar{X} = 15 \text{ mm} \quad ◀$$

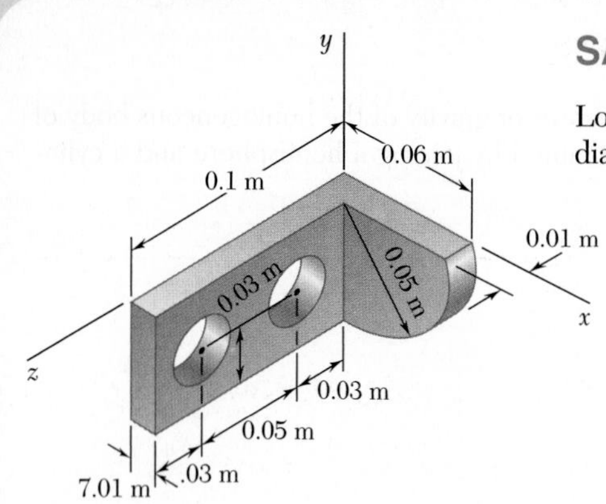

SAMPLE PROBLEM 5.12

Locate the center of gravity of the steel machine element shown. The diameter of each hole is 0.03 m.

SOLUTION

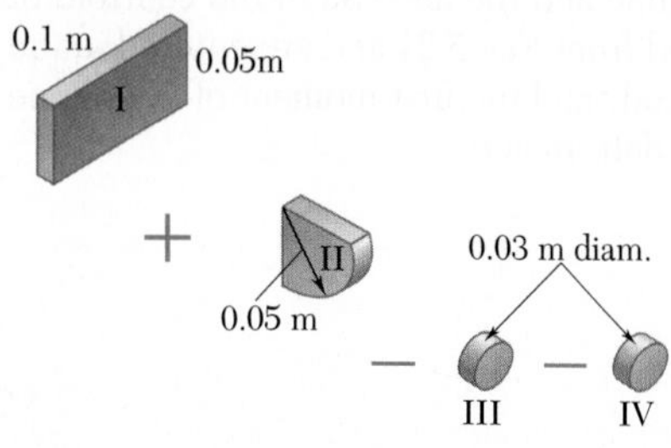

The machine element can be obtained by adding a rectangular parallelepiped (I) to a quarter cylinder (II) and then subtracting two 0.03-m-diameter cylinders (III and IV). The volume and the coordinates of the centroid of each component are determined and are entered in the table below. Using the data in the table, we then determine the total volume and the moments of the volume with respect to each of the coordinate planes.

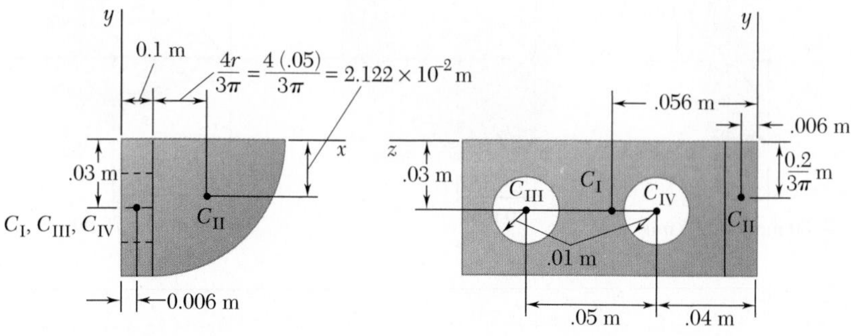

	V, m^3	$\bar{x}$, m	$\bar{y}$, m	$\bar{z}$, m	$\bar{x}V$, m^4	$\bar{y}V$, m^4	$\bar{z}V$, m^4
I	$(0.1)(0.05)(0.01) = 5 \times 10^{-5}$	.006	$-.03$	.056	3×10^{-7}	-15×10^{-7}	28×10^{-7}
II	$\frac{1}{4}\pi(0.05)^2(0.01) = 1.963 \times 10^{-5}$	.012	$-.002$	.006	2.4×10^{-7}	-0.4×10^{-7}	1.18×10^{-7}
III	$-\pi(0.01)^2(0.01) = -3.1415 \times 10^{-6}$	.006	$-.03$	.086	-0.188×10^{-7}	0.94×10^{-7}	-2.7×10^{-7}
IV	$-\pi(0.01)^2(0.01) = -3.1415 \times 10^{-6}$	.006	$-.03$	.04	-0.188×10^{-7}	0.94×10^{-7}	-1.26×10^{-7}
	$\Sigma V = 63.347 \times 10^{-6}$				$\Sigma\bar{x}V = 5.024 \times 10^{-7}$	$\Sigma\bar{y}V = -13.52 \times 10^{-7}$	$\Sigma\bar{z}V = 25.22 \times 10^{-7}$

Thus,

$\bar{X}\Sigma V = \Sigma\bar{x}V$: $\quad \bar{X} = 8 \times 10^{-3}$ m ◀

$\bar{Y}\Sigma V = \Sigma\bar{y}V$: $\quad \bar{Y} = -2.1 \times 10^{-2}$ m ◀

$\bar{Z}\Sigma V = \Sigma\bar{z}V$: $\quad \bar{Z} = 4 \times 10^{-2}$ m ◀

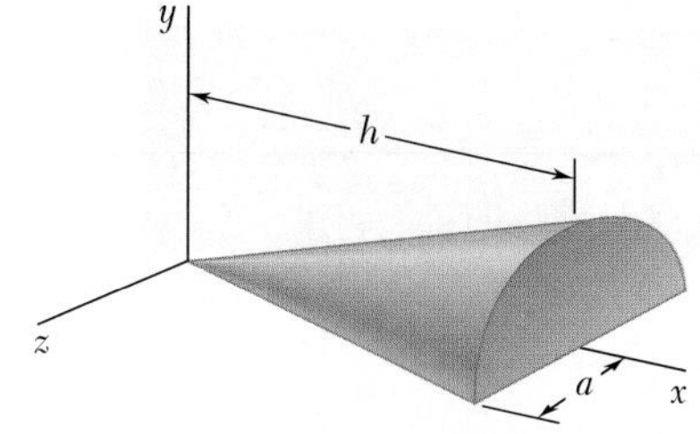

SAMPLE PROBLEM 5.13

Determine the location of the centroid of the half right circular cone shown.

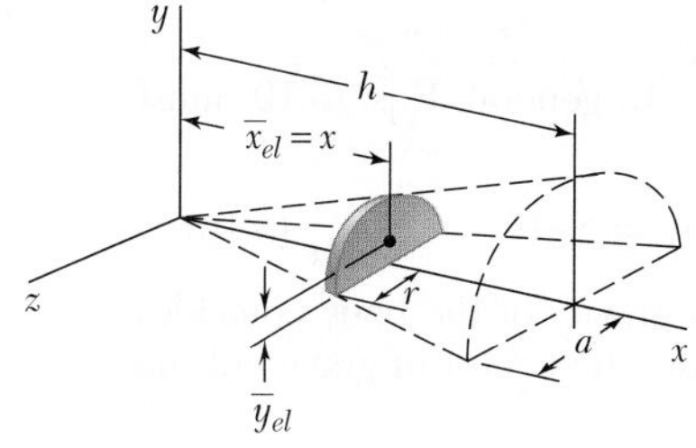

SOLUTION

Since the xy plane is a plane of symmetry, the centroid lies in this plane and $\bar{z} = 0$. A slab of thickness dx is chosen as a differential element. The volume of this element is

$$dV = \tfrac{1}{2}\pi r^2\, dx$$

The coordinates $\bar{x}_{el}$ and $\bar{y}_{el}$ of the centroid of the element are

$$\bar{x}_{el} = x \qquad \bar{y}_{el} = \frac{4r}{3\pi}$$

where $\bar{y}_{el}$ is obtained from Fig. 5.8 (semicircular area).

We observe that r is proportional to x and write

$$\frac{r}{x} = \frac{a}{h} \qquad r = \frac{a}{h}x$$

The volume of the body is

$$V = \int dV = \int_0^h \tfrac{1}{2}\pi r^2\, dx = \int_0^h \tfrac{1}{2}\pi\left(\frac{a}{h}x\right)^2 dx = \frac{\pi a^2 h}{6}$$

The moment of the differential element with respect to the yz plane is $\bar{x}_{el}\, dV$; the total moment of the body with respect to this plane is

$$\int \bar{x}_{el}\, dV = \int_0^h x(\tfrac{1}{2}\pi r^2)\, dx = \int_0^h x(\tfrac{1}{2}\pi)\left(\frac{a}{h}x\right)^2 dx = \frac{\pi a^2 h^2}{8}$$

Thus,

$$\bar{x}V = \int \bar{x}_{el}\, dV \qquad \bar{x}\frac{\pi a^2 h}{6} = \frac{\pi a^2 h^2}{8} \qquad \bar{x} = \tfrac{3}{4}h \blacktriangleleft$$

Likewise, the moment of the differential element with respect to the zx plane is $\bar{y}_{el}\, dV$; the total moment is

$$\int \bar{y}_{el}\, dV = \int_0^h \frac{4r}{3\pi}(\tfrac{1}{2}\pi r^2)\, dx = \frac{2}{3}\int_0^h \left(\frac{a}{h}x\right)^3 dx = \frac{a^3 h}{6}$$

Thus,

$$\bar{y}V = \int \bar{y}_{el}\, dV \qquad \bar{y}\frac{\pi a^2 h}{6} = \frac{a^3 h}{6} \qquad \bar{y} = \frac{a}{\pi} \blacktriangleleft$$

SOLVING PROBLEMS ON YOUR OWN

In the problems for this lesson, you will be asked to locate the centers of gravity of three-dimensional bodies or the centroids of their volumes. All of the techniques we previously discussed for two-dimensional bodies—using symmetry, dividing the body into common shapes, choosing the most efficient differential element, etc.—may also be applied to the general three-dimensional case.

1. ***Locating the centers of gravity of composite bodies.*** In general, Eqs. (5.19) must be used:

$$\bar{X}\Sigma W = \Sigma \bar{x} W \qquad \bar{Y}\Sigma W = \Sigma \bar{y} W \qquad \bar{Z}\Sigma W = \Sigma \bar{z} W \tag{5.19}$$

However, for the case of a *homogeneous body,* the center of gravity of the body coincides with the *centroid of its volume*. Therefore, for this special case, the center of gravity of the body can also be located using Eqs. (5.20):

$$\bar{X}\Sigma V = \Sigma \bar{x} V \qquad \bar{Y}\Sigma V = \Sigma \bar{y} V \qquad \bar{Z}\Sigma V = \Sigma \bar{z} V \tag{5.20}$$

You should realize that these equations are simply an extension of the equations used for the two-dimensional problems considered earlier in the chapter. As the solutions of Sample Probs. 5.11 and 5.12 illustrate, the methods of solution for two- and three-dimensional problems are identical. Thus, we once again strongly encourage you to construct appropriate diagrams and tables when analyzing composite bodies. Also, as you study Sample Prob. 5.12, observe how the x and y coordinates of the centroid of the quarter cylinder were obtained using the equations for the centroid of a quarter circle.

We note that *two special cases* of interest occur when the given body consists of either uniform wires or uniform plates made of the same material.

a. For a body made of *several wire elements* of the *same uniform cross section,* the cross-sectional area A of the wire elements will factor out of Eqs. (5.20) when V is replaced with the product AL, where L is the length of a given element. Equations (5.20) thus reduce in this case to

$$\bar{X}\Sigma L = \Sigma \bar{x} L \qquad \bar{Y}\Sigma L = \Sigma \bar{y} L \qquad \bar{Z}\Sigma L = \Sigma \bar{z} L$$

b. For a body made of *several plates* of the *same uniform thickness,* the thickness t of the plates will factor out of Eqs. (5.20) when V is replaced with the product tA, where A is the area of a given plate. Equations (5.20) thus reduce in this case to

$$\bar{X}\Sigma A = \Sigma \bar{x} A \qquad \bar{Y}\Sigma A = \Sigma \bar{y} A \qquad \bar{Z}\Sigma A = \Sigma \bar{z} A$$

2. ***Locating the centroids of volumes by direct integration.*** As explained in Sec. 5.11, evaluating the integrals of Eqs. (5.21) can be simplified by choosing either a thin filament (Fig. 5.22) or a thin slab (Fig. 5.23) for the element of volume dV. Thus, you should begin your solution by identifying, if possible, the dV which produces the single or double integrals that are the easiest to compute. For bodies of revolution, this may be a thin slab (as in Sample Prob. 5.13) or a thin cylindrical shell. However, it is important to remember that the relationship that you establish among the variables (like the relationship between r and x in Sample Prob. 5.13) will directly affect the complexity of the integrals you will have to compute. Finally, we again remind you that $\bar{x}_{el}$, $\bar{y}_{el}$, and $\bar{z}_{el}$ in Eqs. (5.22) are the coordinates of the centroid of dV.

Problems

5.90 The composite body shown is formed by removing a hemisphere of radius r from a cylinder of radius R and height $2R$. Determine (*a*) the y coordinate of the centroid when $r = 3R/4$, (*b*) the ratio r/R for which $\bar{y} = -1.2R$.

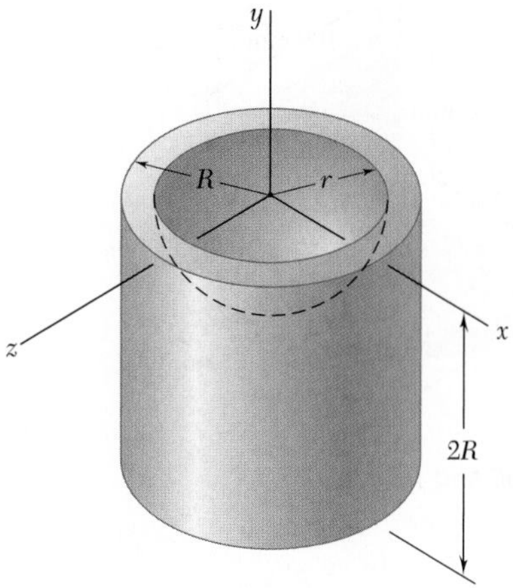

Fig. P5.90

5.91 Determine the y coordinate of the centroid of the body shown.

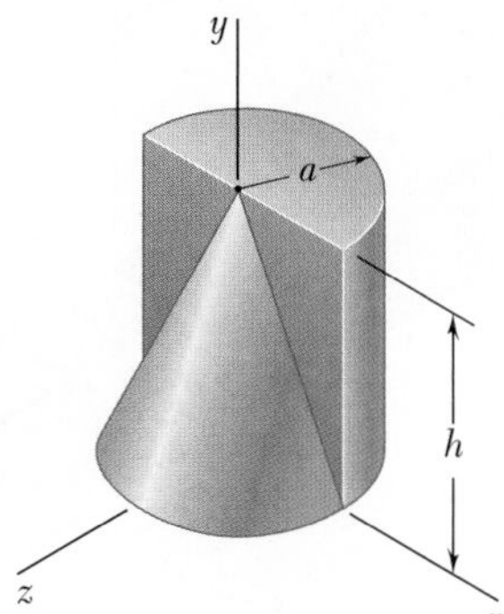

Fig. P5.91 and P5.92

5.92 Determine the z coordinate of the centroid of the body shown. (*Hint:* Use the result of Sample Prob. 5.13.)

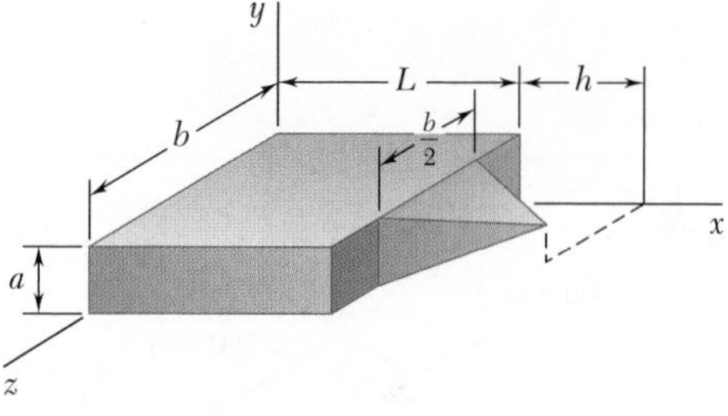

Fig. P5.93

5.93 Consider the composite body shown. Determine (*a*) the value of $\bar{x}$ when $h = L/2$, (*b*) the ratio h/L for which $\bar{x} = L$.

5.94 For the machine element shown, locate the y coordinate of the center of gravity.

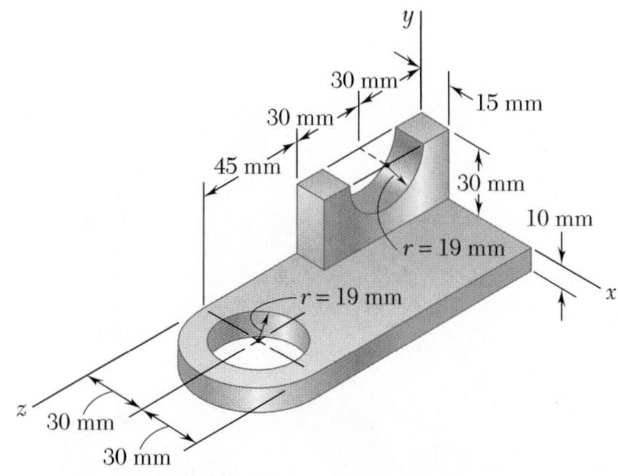

Fig. P5.94 and P5.95

5.95 For the machine element shown, locate the z coordinate of the center of gravity.

5.96 For the stop bracket shown, locate the x coordinate of the center of gravity.

5.97 For the stop bracket shown, locate the z coordinate of the center of gravity.

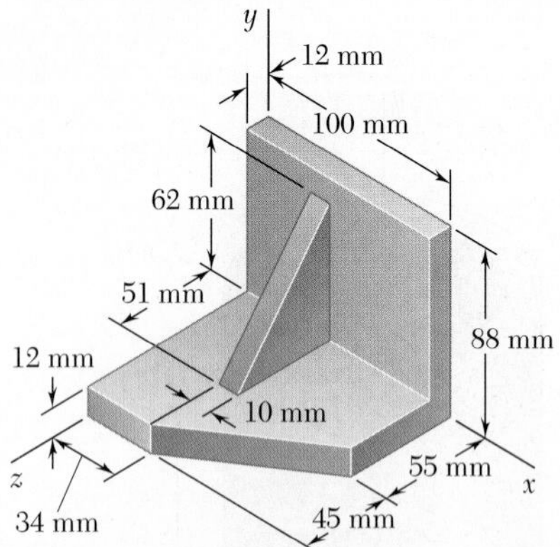

Fig. *P5.96* and *P5.97*

5.98 For the machine element shown, locate the x coordinate of the center of gravity.

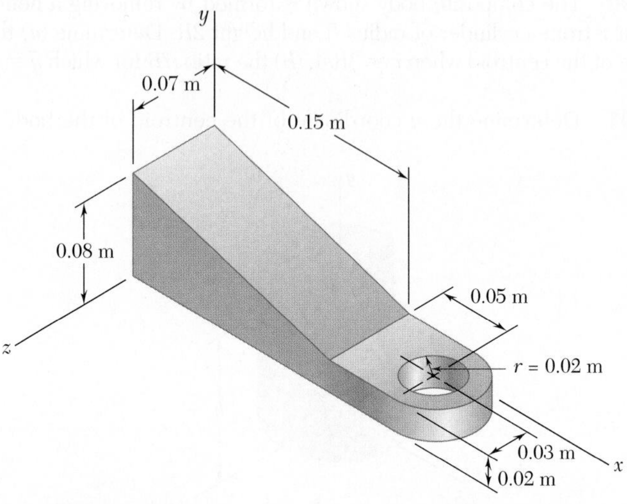

Fig. P5.98 and P5.99

5.99 For the machine element shown, locate the y coordinate of the center of gravity.

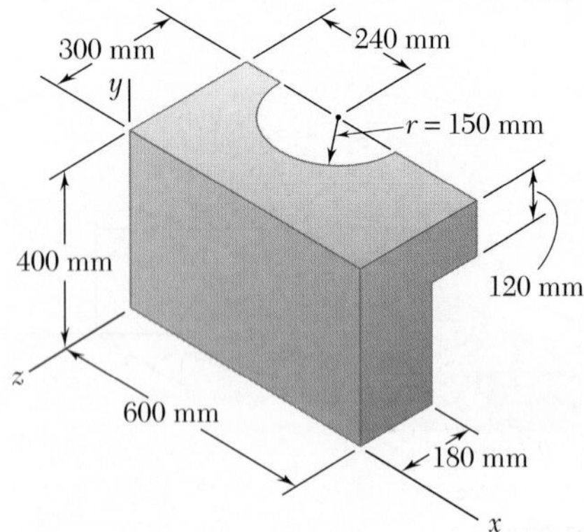

Fig. P5.100

5.100 Sheet metal of uniform thickness is used to fabricate a portion of the flashing for a roof. Locate the center of gravity of the flashing knowing that it is composed of the three elements shown.

5.101 Locate the center of gravity of the sheet-metal form shown.

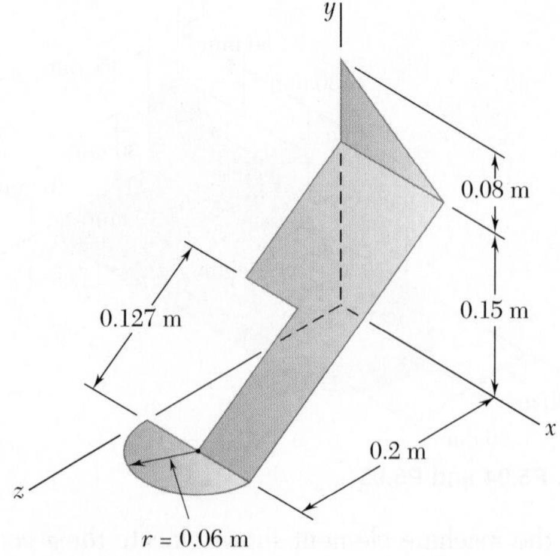

Fig. P5.101

5.102 Locate the center of gravity of the sheet-metal form shown.

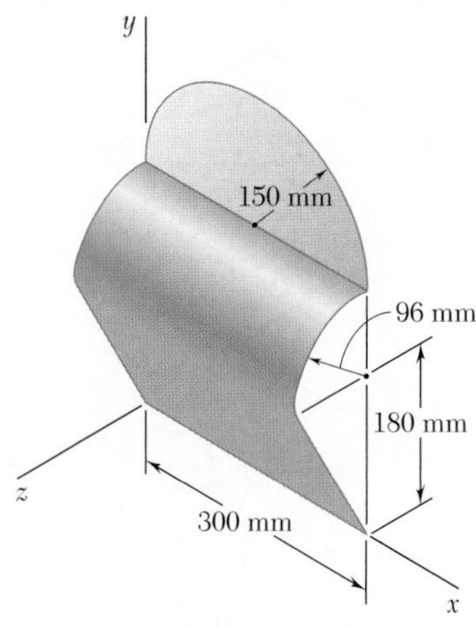

Fig. P5.102

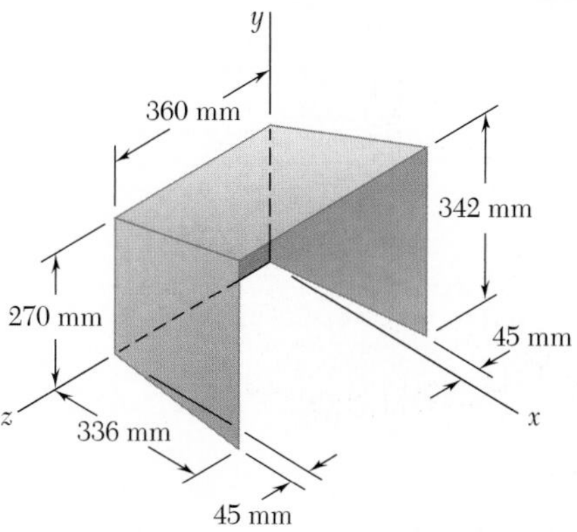

Fig. P5.103

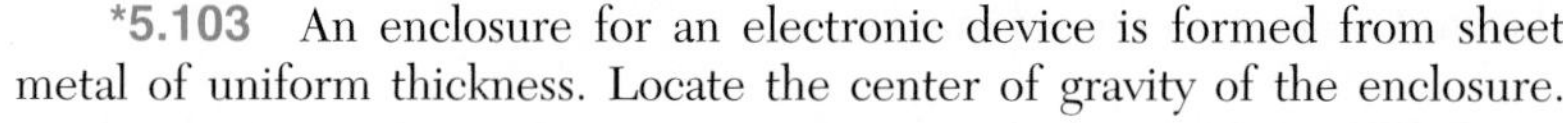

***5.103** An enclosure for an electronic device is formed from sheet metal of uniform thickness. Locate the center of gravity of the enclosure.

5.104 A chute is made from sheet metal of uniform thickness. Locate the center of gravity of the chute.

5.105 An 0.2-m-diameter cylindrical duct and a 0.1 × 0.2-m rectangular duct are to be joined as indicated. Knowing that the ducts are fabricated from the same sheet metal, which is of uniform thickness, locate the center of gravity of the assembly.

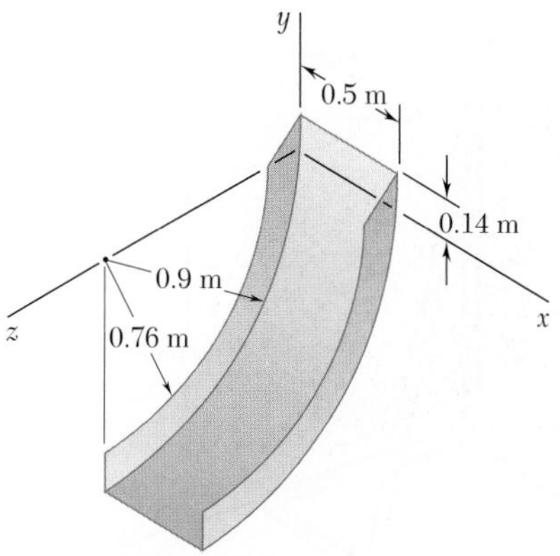

Fig. P5.104

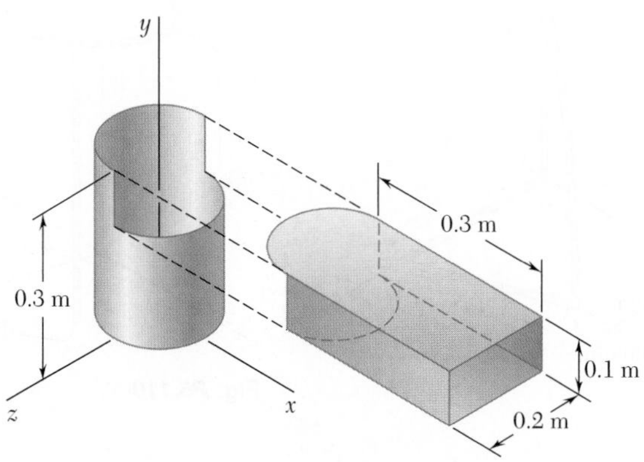

Fig. *P5.105*

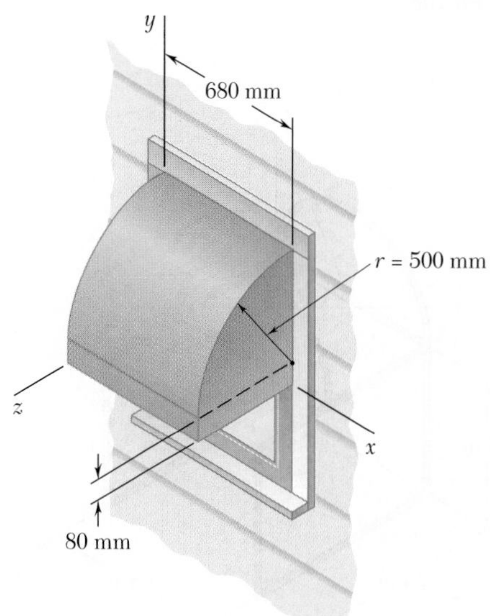

5.106 A window awning is fabricated from sheet metal of uniform thickness. Locate the center of gravity of the awning.

Fig. P5.106

5.107 The thin, plastic front cover of a wall clock is of uniform thickness. Locate the center of gravity of the cover.

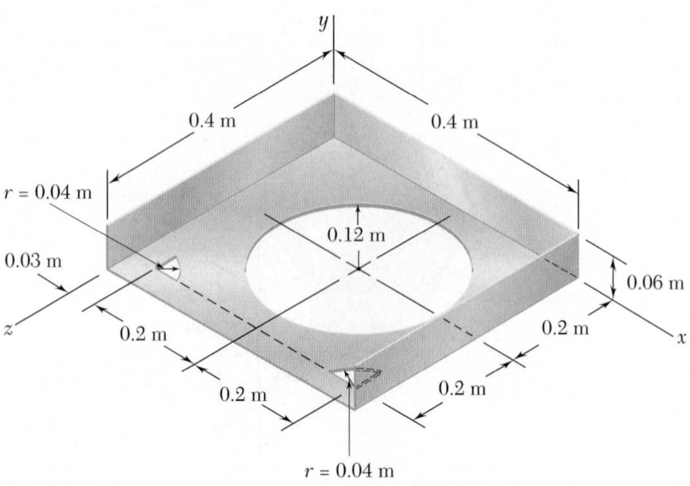

Fig. ***P5.107***

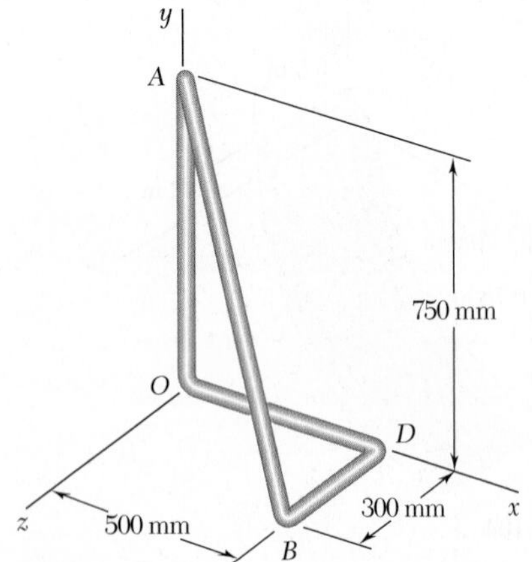

Fig. P5.108

5.108 A thin brass rod of uniform cross section is bent into the shape shown. Locate its center of gravity.

5.109 A thin steel wire of uniform cross section is bent into the shape shown, where arc BC is a quarter circle of radius R. Locate its center of gravity.

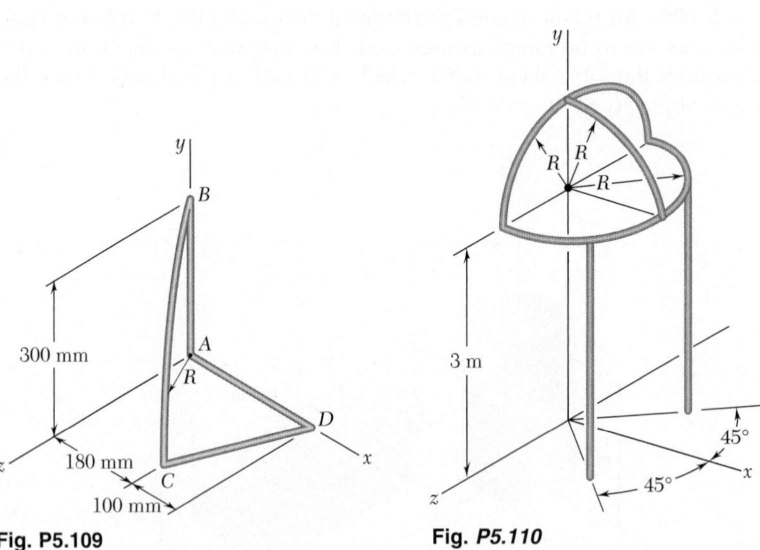

Fig. P5.109

Fig. ***P5.110***

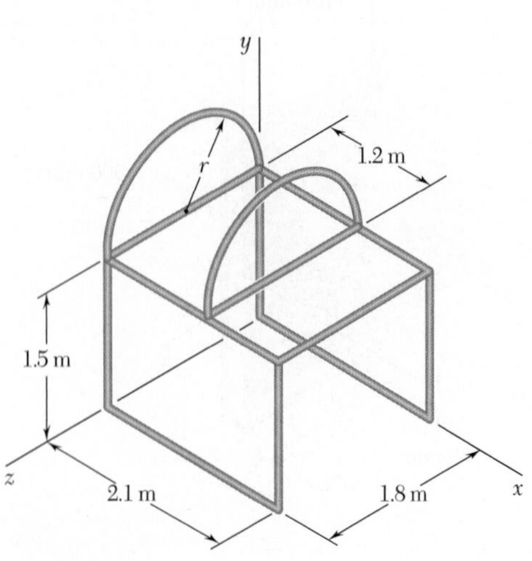

Fig. P5.111

5.110 The decorative metalwork at the entrance of a store is fabricated from uniform steel structural tubing. Knowing that $R = 1.2$ m, locate the center of gravity of the metalwork.

5.111 The frame of a portable equipment cover is fabricated from steel pipe of uniform diameter. Locate the center of gravity of the frame.

5.112 A scratch awl has a plastic handle and a steel blade and shank. Knowing that the specific weight of plastic is 10^3 kg/m^3 and that of steel is 8×10^3 kg/m^3, locate the center of gravity of the awl.

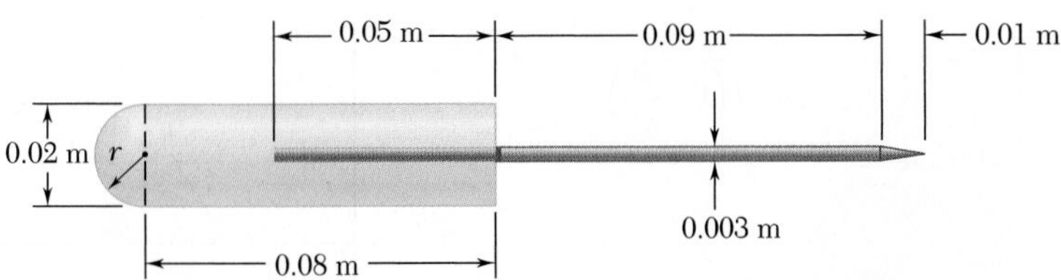

Fig. ***P5.112***

5.113 A flat-belt idler pulley is molded from polycarbonate and has a bronze bushing. Knowing that the densities of polycarbonate and bronze are 1250 kg/m^3 and 8800 kg/m^3, respectively, determine the x coordinate of the center of gravity of the pulley.

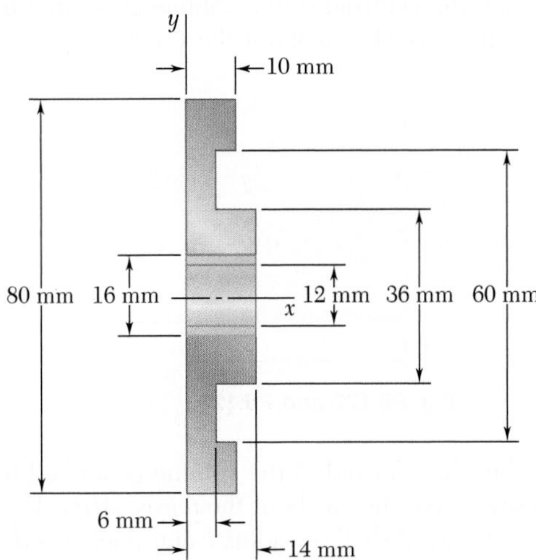

Fig. P5.113

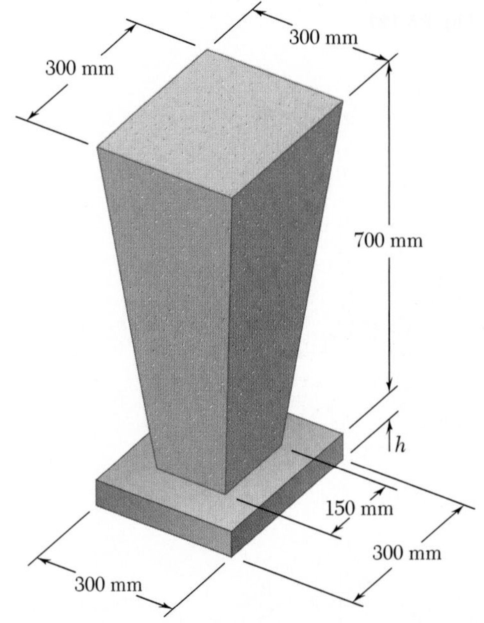

Fig. P5.114

5.114 A marker for a garden path consists of a truncated regular pyramid carved from stone of density 2570 kg/m^3. The pyramid is mounted on a steel base of thickness h. Knowing that the density of steel is 7860 kg/m^3 and that steel plate is available in 5-mm increments, specify the minimum thickness h for which the center of gravity of the marker is approximately 300 mm above the top of the base.

5.115 Three brass plates are brazed to a steel pipe to form the flagpole base shown. Knowing that the pipe has a wall thickness of 0.006 m and that each plate is 0.005 m thick, determine the location of the center of gravity of the base. (Specific weights: brass = 9×10^3 kg/m^3, steel = 8×10^3 kg/m^3.)

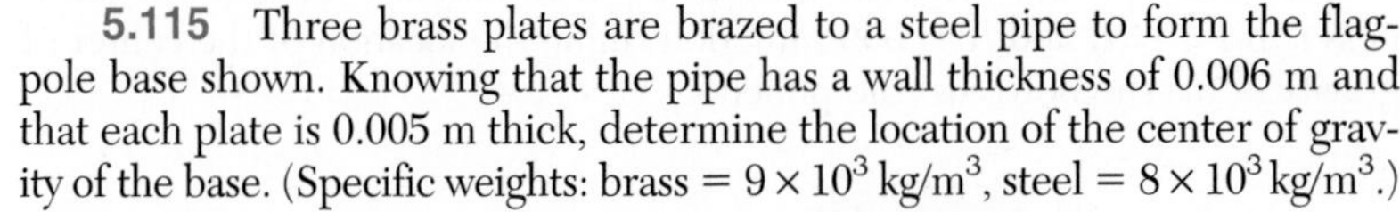

5.116 through 5.118 Determine by direct integration the values of $\bar{x}$ for the two volumes obtained by passing a vertical cutting plane through the given shape of Fig. 5.21. The cutting plane is parallel to the base of the given shape and divides the shape into two volumes of equal height.

5.116 A hemisphere.
5.117 A semiellipsoid of revolution.
5.118 A paraboloid of revolution.

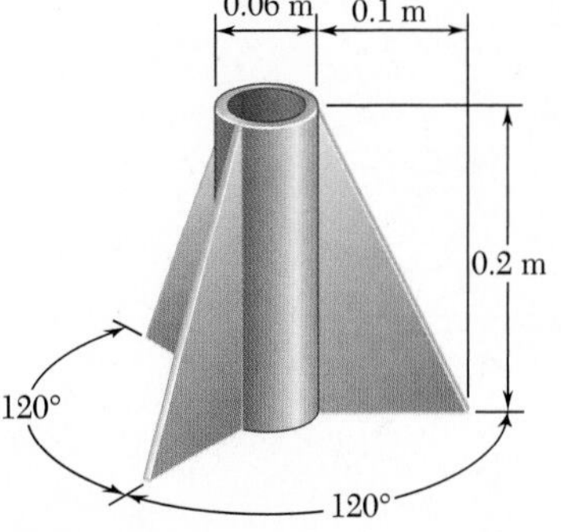

Fig. P5.115

5.119 and *5.120* Locate the centroid of the volume obtained by rotating the shaded area about the x axis.

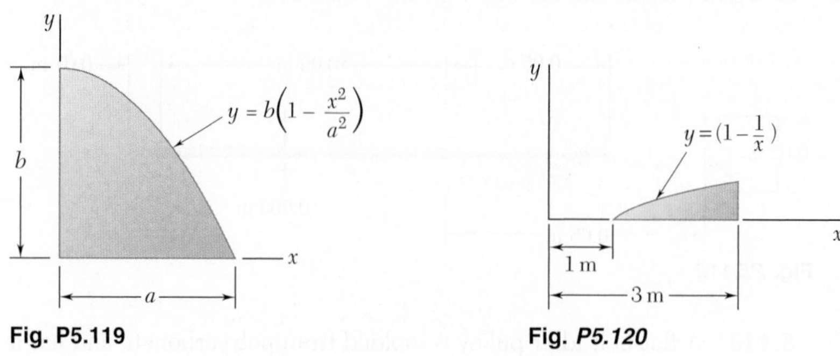

Fig. P5.119

Fig. *P5.120*

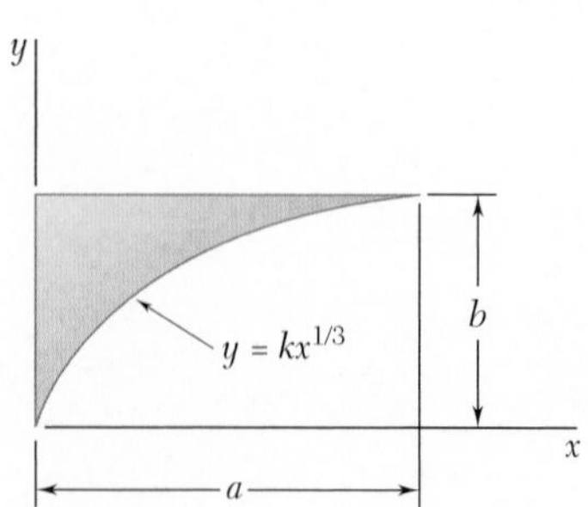

Fig. P5.121

5.121 Locate the centroid of the volume obtained by rotating the shaded area about the line $x = a$.

***5.122** Locate the centroid of the volume generated by revolving the portion of the cosine curve shown about the x axis.

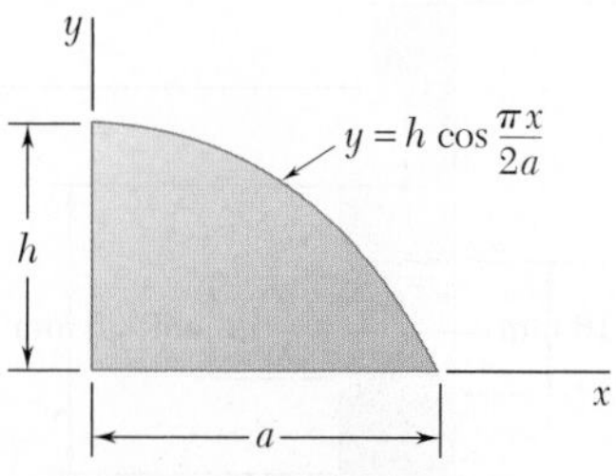

Fig. P5.122 and P5.123

***5.123** Locate the centroid of the volume generated by revolving the portion of the cosine curve shown about the y axis. (*Hint:* Use as an element of volume a thin cylindrical shell of radius r and thickness dr.)

***5.124** Show that for a regular pyramid of height h and n sides (n = 3, 4, . . .) the centroid of the volume of the pyramid is located at a distance $h/4$ above the base.

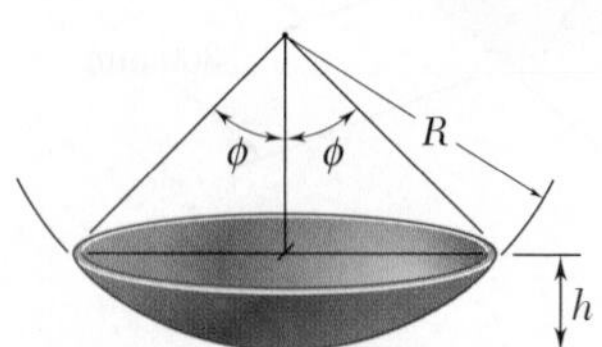

Fig. P5.125

***5.125** A thin spherical cup has a radius R and a uniform thickness t. Show by direct integration that the center of gravity of the cup is located at a distance $h/2$ above the base of the cup.

5.126 The sides and the base of a punch bowl are of uniform thickness t. If $t << R$ and R = 350 mm, determine the location of the center of gravity of (a) the bowl, (b) the punch.

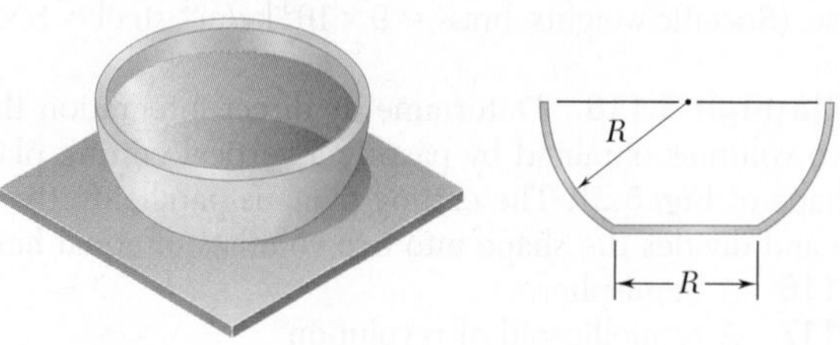

Fig. *P5.126*

5.127 After grading a lot, a builder places four stakes to designate the corners of the slab for a house. To provide a firm, level base for the slab, the builder places a minimum of 0.08 m of gravel beneath the slab. Determine the volume of gravel needed and the x coordinate of the centroid of the volume of the gravel. (*Hint:* The bottom of the gravel is an oblique plane, which can be represented by the equation $y = a + bx + cz$.)

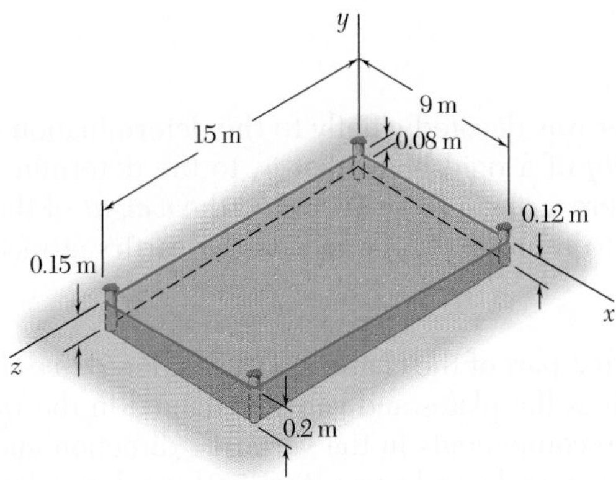

Fig. *P5.127*

5.128 Determine by direct integration the z coordinate of the centroid of the volume shown, which was cut from a rectangular prism by an oblique plane given by the equation $y = y_0 - y_1(x/a) - y_2(z/b)$.

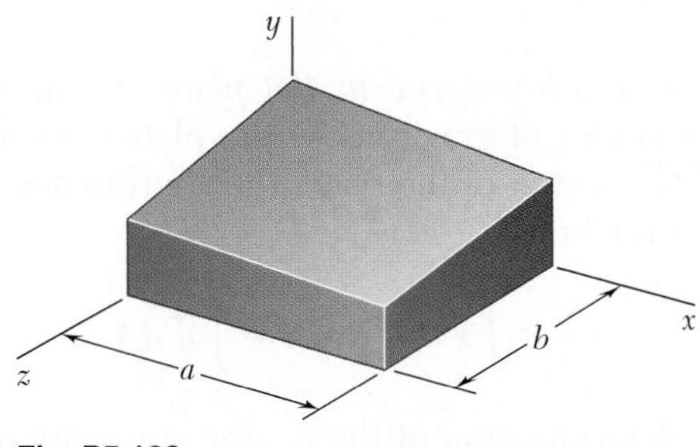

Fig. P5.128

5.129 Locate the centroid of the section shown, which was cut from a circular cylinder by an inclined plane.

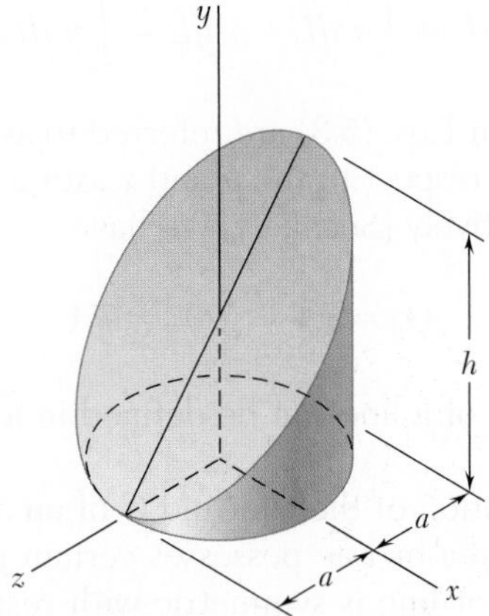

Fig. P5.129

REVIEW AND SUMMARY FOR CHAPTER 5

This chapter was devoted chiefly to the determination of the *center of gravity* of a rigid body, that is, to the determination of the point G where a single force $\mathbf{W}$, called the *weight* of the body, can be applied to represent the effect of the earth's attraction on the body.

Center of gravity of a two-dimensional body

In the first part of the chapter, we considered *two-dimensional bodies,* such as flat plates and wires contained in the xy plane. By adding force components in the vertical z direction and moments about the horizontal y and x axes [Sec. 5.2], we derived the relations

$$W = \int dW \qquad \bar{x}W = \int x\,dW \qquad \bar{y}W = \int y\,dW \tag{5.2}$$

which define the weight of the body and the coordinates $\bar{x}$ and $\bar{y}$ of its center of gravity.

Centroid of an area or line

In the case of a *homogeneous flat plate of uniform thickness* [Sec. 5.3], the center of gravity G of the plate coincides with the *centroid C of the area A* of the plate, the coordinates of which are defined by the relations

$$\bar{x}A = \int x\,dA \qquad \bar{y}A = \int y\,dA \tag{5.3}$$

Similarly, the determination of the center of gravity of a *homogeneous wire of uniform cross section* contained in a plane reduces to the determination of the *centroid C of the line L* representing the wire; we have

$$\bar{x}L = \int x\,dL \qquad \bar{y}L = \int y\,dL \tag{5.4}$$

First moments

The integrals in Eqs. (5.3) are referred to as the *first moments* of the area A with respect to the y and x axes and are denoted by Q_y and Q_x, respectively [Sec. 5.4]. We have

$$Q_y = \bar{x}A \qquad Q_x = \bar{y}A \tag{5.6}$$

The first moments of a line can be defined in a similar way.

Properties of symmetry

The determination of the centroid C of an area or line is simplified when the area or line possesses certain *properties of symmetry.* If the area or line is symmetric with respect to an axis, its centroid C lies on that axis; if it is symmetric with respect to two axes, C is located at the intersection of the two axes; if it is symmetric with respect to a center O, C coincides with O.

Center of gravity of a composite body

The *areas and the centroids of various common shapes* are tabulated in Fig. 5.8. When a flat plate can be divided into several of these shapes, the coordinates $\overline{X}$ and $\overline{Y}$ of its center of gravity G can be determined from the coordinates $\bar{x}_1, \bar{x}_2, \ldots$ and $\bar{y}_1, \bar{y}_2, \ldots$ of the centers of gravity $G_1, G_2, \ldots$ of the various parts [Sec. 5.5]. Equating moments about the y and x axes, respectively (Fig. 5.24), we have

$$\overline{X}\Sigma W = \Sigma \bar{x} W \qquad \overline{Y}\Sigma W = \Sigma \bar{y} W \tag{5.7}$$

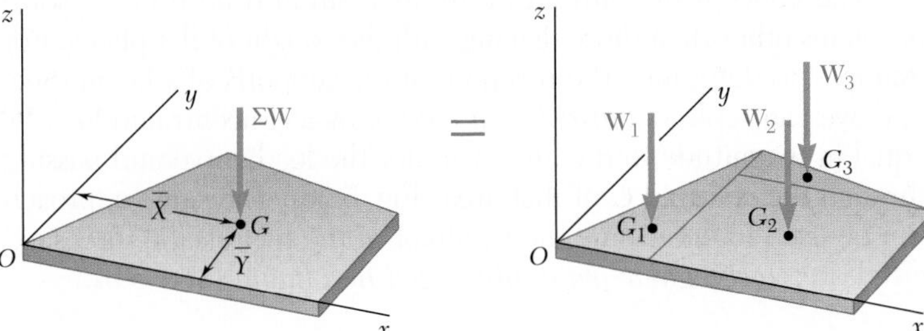

Fig. 5.24

If the plate is homogeneous and of uniform thickness, its center of gravity coincides with the centroid C of the area of the plate, and Eqs. (5.7) reduce to

$$Q_y = \overline{X}\Sigma A = \Sigma \bar{x} A \qquad Q_x = \overline{Y}\Sigma A = \Sigma \bar{y} A \tag{5.8}$$

These equations yield the first moments of the composite area, or they can be solved for the coordinates $\overline{X}$ and $\overline{Y}$ of its centroid [Sample Prob. 5.1]. The determination of the center of gravity of a composite wire is carried out in a similar fashion [Sample Prob. 5.2].

Determination of centroid by integration

When an area is bounded by analytical curves, the coordinates of its centroid can be determined by *integration* [Sec. 5.6]. This can be done by evaluating either the double integrals in Eqs. (5.3) or a *single integral* which uses one of the thin rectangular or pie-shaped elements of area shown in Fig. 5.12. Denoting by $\bar{x}_{el}$ and $\bar{y}_{el}$ the coordinates of the centroid of the element dA, we have

$$Q_y = \bar{x}A = \int \bar{x}_{el}\, dA \qquad Q_x = \bar{y}A = \int \bar{y}_{el}\, dA \tag{5.9}$$

It is advantageous to use the same element of area to compute both of the first moments Q_y and Q_x; the same element can also be used to determine the area A [Sample Prob. 5.4].

Theorems of Pappus-Guldinus

The *theorems of Pappus-Guldinus* relate the determination of the area of a surface of revolution or the volume of a body of revolution to the determination of the centroid of the generating curve or area [Sec. 5.7]. The area A of the surface generated by rotating a curve of length L about a fixed axis (Fig. 5.25*a*) is

$$A = 2\pi\bar{y}L \tag{5.10}$$

where $\bar{y}$ represents the distance from the centroid C of the curve to the fixed axis. Similarly, the volume V of the body generated by rotating an area A about a fixed axis (Fig. 5.25*b*) is

$$V = 2\pi\bar{y}A \tag{5.11}$$

where $\bar{y}$ represents the distance from the centroid C of the area to the fixed axis.

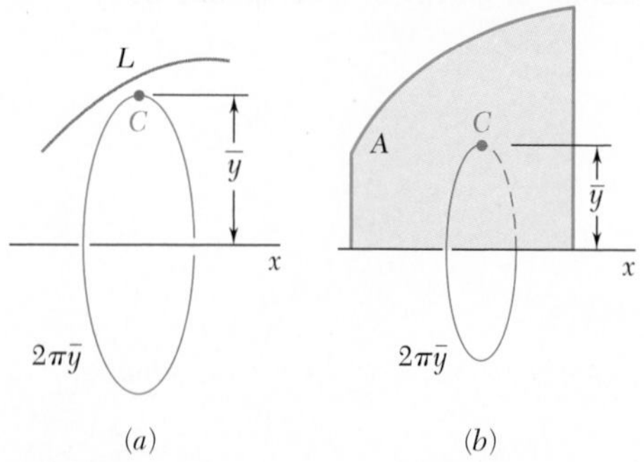

Fig. 5.25

Distributed loads

The concept of centroid of an area can also be used to solve problems other than those dealing with the weight of flat plates. For example, to determine the reactions at the supports of a beam [Sec. 5.8], we can replace a *distributed load* w by a concentrated load **W** equal in magnitude to the area A under the load curve and passing through the centroid C of that area (Fig. 5.26). The same approach can be used to determine the resultant of the hydrostatic forces exerted on a *rectangular plate submerged in a liquid* [Sec. 5.9].

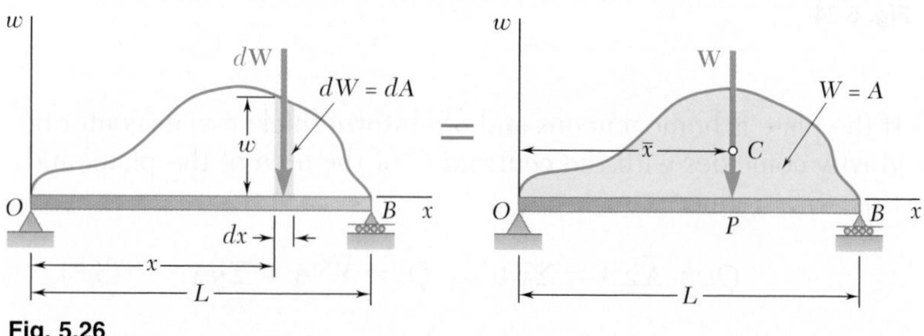

Fig. 5.26

Center of gravity of a three-dimensional body

The last part of the chapter was devoted to the determination of the *center of gravity G of a three-dimensional body*. The coordinates $\bar{x}$, $\bar{y}$, and $\bar{z}$ of G were defined by the relations

$$\bar{x}W = \int x\,dW \qquad \bar{y}W = \int y\,dW \qquad \bar{z}W = \int z\,dW \tag{5.16}$$

Centroid of a volume

In the case of a *homogeneous body*, the center of gravity G coincides with the *centroid C of the volume V* of the body; the coordinates of C are defined by the relations

$$\bar{x}V = \int x\,dV \qquad \bar{y}V = \int y\,dV \qquad \bar{z}V = \int z\,dV \tag{5.18}$$

If the volume possesses a *plane of symmetry*, its centroid C will lie in that plane; if it possesses two planes of symmetry, C will be located on the line of intersection of the two planes; if it possesses three planes of symmetry which intersect at only one point, C will coincide with that point [Sec. 5.10].

Center of gravity of a composite body

The *volumes and centroids of various common three-dimensional shapes* are tabulated in Fig. 5.21. When a body can be divided into several of these shapes, the coordinates $\overline{X}$, $\overline{Y}$, and $\overline{Z}$ of its center of gravity G can be determined from the corresponding coordinates of the centers of gravity of its various parts [Sec. 5.11]. We have

$$\overline{X}\Sigma W = \Sigma \bar{x} W \qquad \overline{Y}\Sigma W = \Sigma \bar{y} W \qquad \overline{Z}\Sigma W = \Sigma \bar{z} W \quad (5.19)$$

If the body is made of a homogeneous material, its center of gravity coincides with the centroid C of its volume, and we write [Sample Probs. 5.11 and 5.12]

$$\overline{X}\Sigma V = \Sigma \bar{x} V \qquad \overline{Y}\Sigma V = \Sigma \bar{y} V \qquad \overline{Z}\Sigma V = \Sigma \bar{z} V \qquad (5.20)$$

Determination of centroid by integration

When a volume is bounded by analytical surfaces, the coordinates of its centroid can be determined by *integration* [Sec. 5.12]. To avoid the computation of the triple integrals in Eqs. (5.18), we can use elements of volume in the shape of thin filaments, as shown in Fig. 5.27. Denoting by $\bar{x}_{el}$, $\bar{y}_{el}$, and $\bar{z}_{el}$ the coordinates of the centroid of the element dV, we rewrite Eqs. (5.18) as

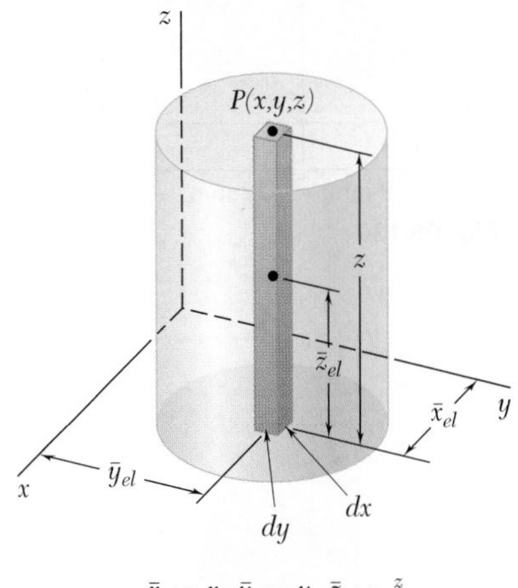

$\bar{x}_{el} = x, \ \bar{y}_{el} = y, \ \bar{z}_{el} = \frac{z}{2}$
$dV = z\,dx\,dy$

Fig. 5.27

$$\bar{x}V = \int \bar{x}_{el}\,dV \qquad \bar{y}V = \int \bar{y}_{el}\,dV \qquad \bar{z}V = \int \bar{z}_{el}\,dV \qquad (5.22)$$

which involve only double integrals. If the volume possesses *two planes of symmetry,* its centroid C is located on their line of intersection. Choosing the x axis to lie along that line and dividing the volume into thin slabs parallel to the yz plane, we can determine C from the relation

$$\bar{x}V = \int \bar{x}_{el}\,dV \qquad (5.23)$$

with a *single integration* [Sample Prob. 5.13]. For a body of revolution, these slabs are circular and their volume is given in Fig. 5.28.

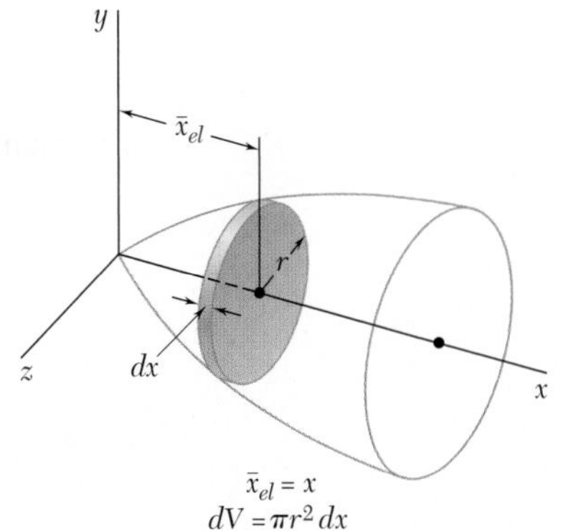

$\bar{x}_{el} = x$
$dV = \pi r^2\,dx$

Fig. 5.28

Review Problems

5.130 and 5.131 Locate the centroid of the plane area shown.

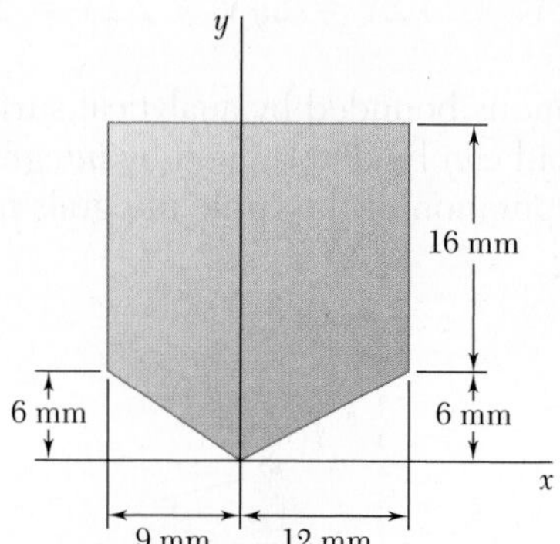

Fig. P5.130

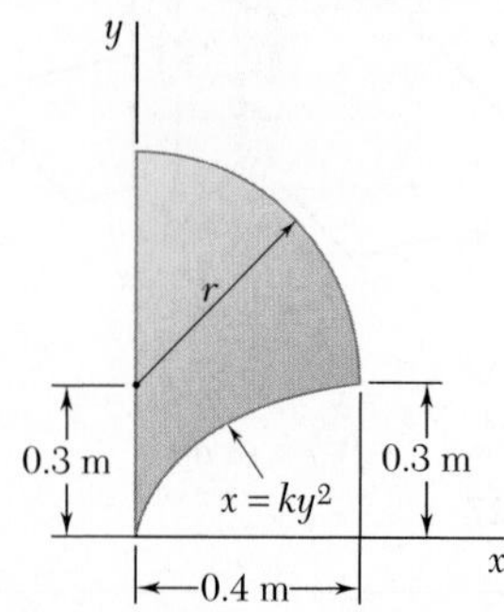

Fig. P5.131

5.132 A thin, homogeneous wire is bent to form the perimeter of Fig. P5.130. Locate the center of gravity of the wire figure thus formed.

5.133 The homogeneous wire $ABCD$ is bent as shown and is attached to a hinge at C. Determine the length L for which the portion BCD of the wire is horizontal.

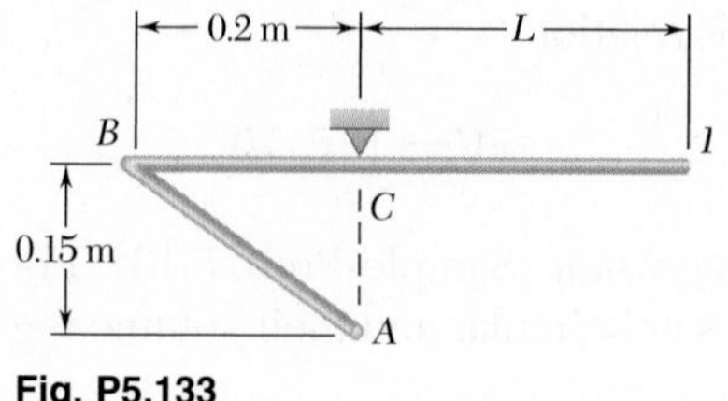

Fig. P5.133

5.134 Determine by direct integration the centroid of the area shown. Express your answer in terms of a and h.

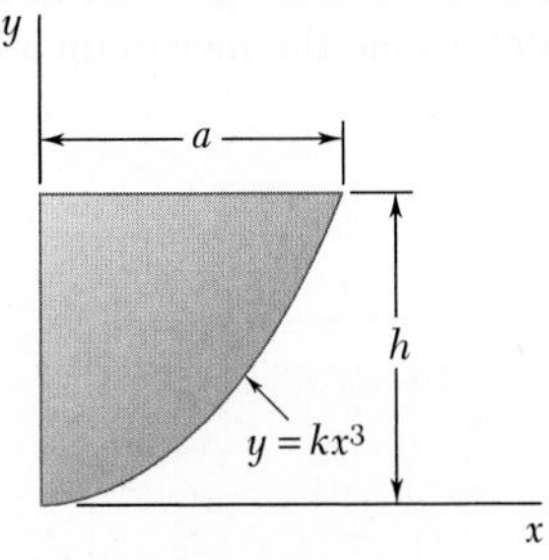

Fig. P5.134

5.135 Determine by direct integration the centroid of the area shown. Express your answer in terms of a and b.

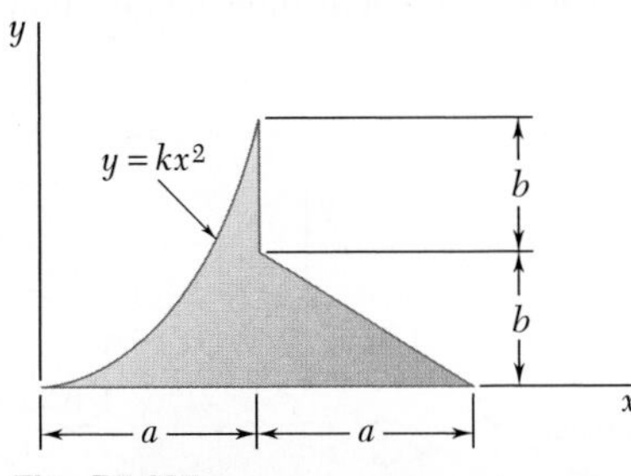

Fig. *P5.135*

5.136 Determine the capacity of the punch bowl shown if $R = 30.48$ cm.

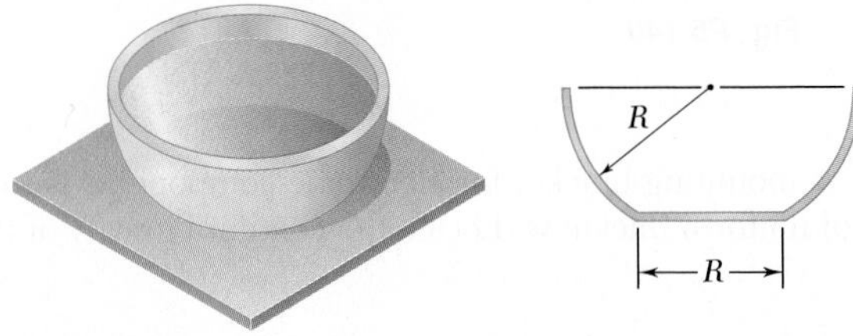

Fig. P5.136

***5.137* and 5.138** Determine the reactions at the beam supports for the given loading.

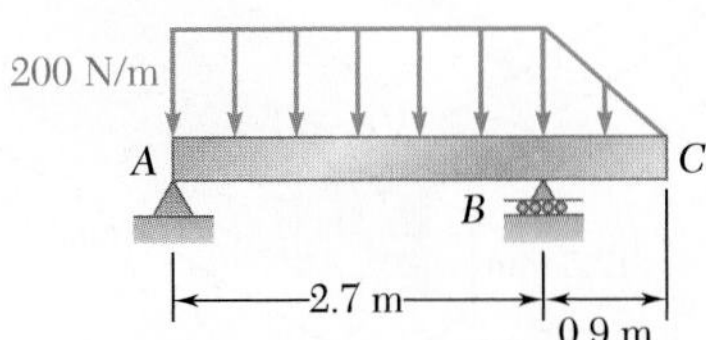

Fig. *P5.137*

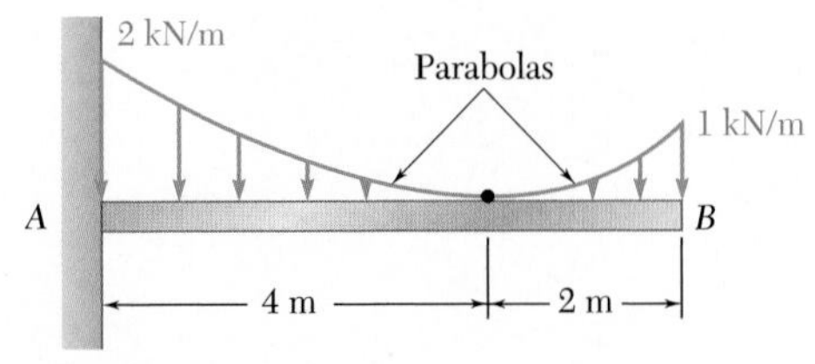

Fig. P5.138

5.139 The 2.7 × 3.6-m side AB of a tank is hinged at its bottom A and is held in place by a thin rod BC. The maximum tensile force the rod can withstand without breaking is 40 kN, and the design specifications require the force in the rod not to exceed 20 percent of this value. If the tank is slowly filled with water, determine the maximum allowable depth of water d in the tank.

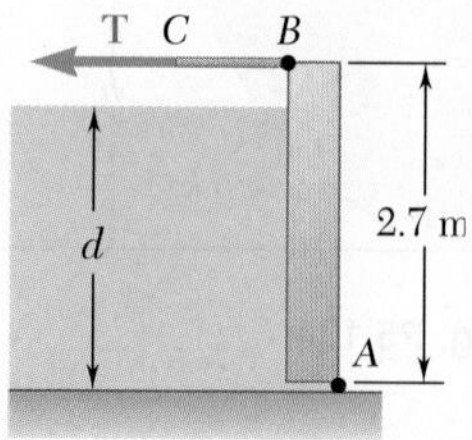

Fig. P5.139

5.140 For the machine element shown, determine the x coordinate of the center of gravity.

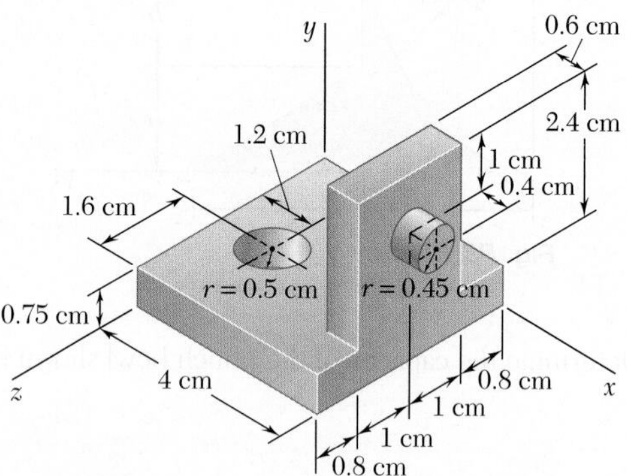

Fig. *P5.140*

5.141 A mounting bracket for electronic components is formed from sheet metal of uniform thickness. Locate the center of gravity of the bracket.

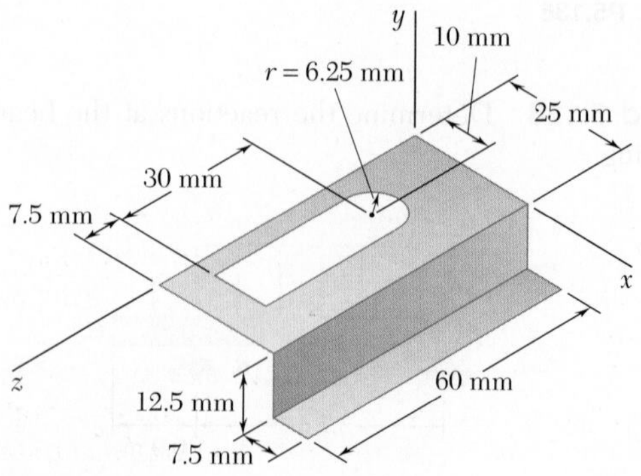

Fig. P5.141

Computer Problems

5.C1 For the trapezoid shown, determine the x and y coordinates of the centroid knowing that $h_1 = a/n^2$ and $h_2 = a/n$. Plot the values of $\bar{x}$ and $\bar{y}$ for $1 \leq n \leq 4$ and $a = 0.15$ m.

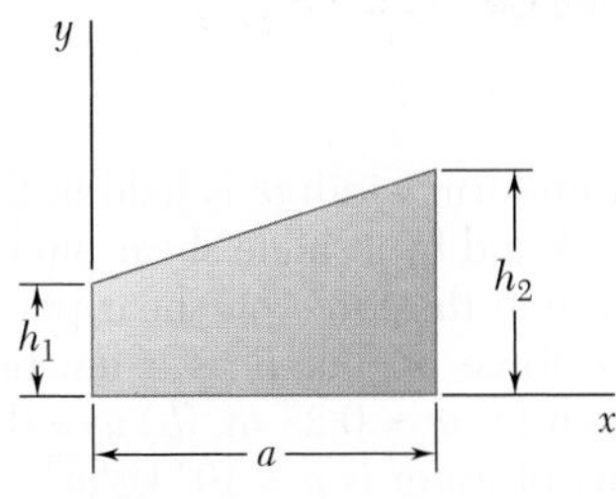

Fig. P5.C1

5.C2 Determine the distance h for which the centroid of the shaded area is as high above BB' as possible. Plot the ratio h/b as a function of k for $0.125 \leq k \leq 0.875$.

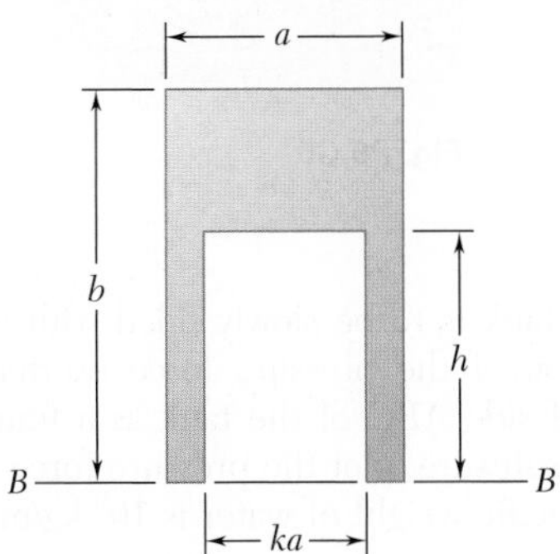

Fig. P5.C2

5.C3 Approximate the general spandrel shown using a series of n rectangles, each of width Δa and of the form $bcc'b'$, and then use computational software to calculate the coordinates of the centroid of the area. Locate the centroid when (*a*) $m = 2$, $a = 0.1$ m, $h = 0.1$ m; (*b*) $m = 2$, $a = 0.1$ m, $h = 0.6$ m; (*c*) $m = 5$, $a = 0.1$ m, $h = 0.1$ m; (*d*) $m = 5$, $a = 0.1$ m, $h = 0.6$ m. In each case compare the answers obtained to the exact values of $\bar{x}$ and $\bar{y}$ computed from the formulas given in Fig. 5.8A and determine the percentage error.

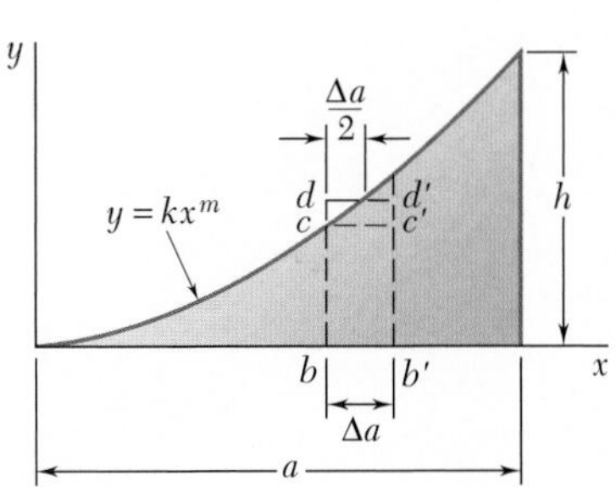

Fig. P5.C3

5.C4 Determine the volume and the surface area of the solid obtained by rotating the area shown about the y axis when $a = 80$ mm and (*a*) $n = 1$, (*b*) $n = 2$, (*c*) $n = 3$.

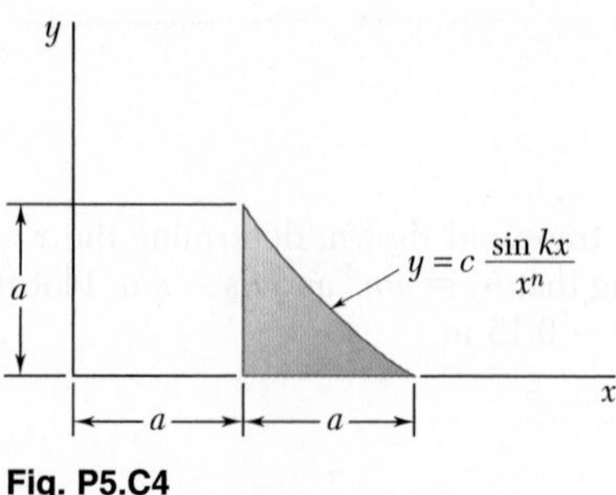

Fig. P5.C4

5.C5 Gate AB of uniform width w is held in the position shown by a hinge along its top edge A and by a single shear pin located at the center of its lower edge B. Determine the force on shear pin B as a function of the water depth d. Plot the force on pin B as a function of water depth for $0.54 \text{ m} \leq d \leq 1.5 \text{ m}$ when (*a*) $w = 0.25$ m, (*b*) $w = 0.50$ m, (*c*) $w = 0.75$ m, (*d*) $w = 1$ m. The density of water is $\rho = 10^3 \text{ kg/m}^3$.

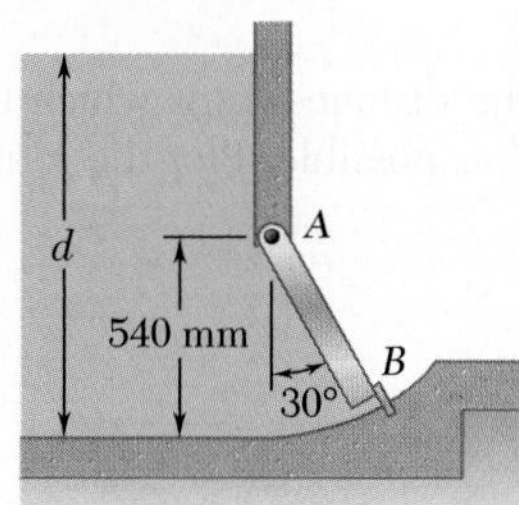

Fig. P5.C5

5.C6 An open tank is to be slowly filled with water. Determine the resultant and direction of the pressure force exerted by the water on a 1.2-m-wide section of side ABC of the tank as a function of the depth d. Using computational software, plot the pressure force as a function of d for $0 \leq d \leq 3$ m. The specific weight of water is 10^3 kg/m^3.

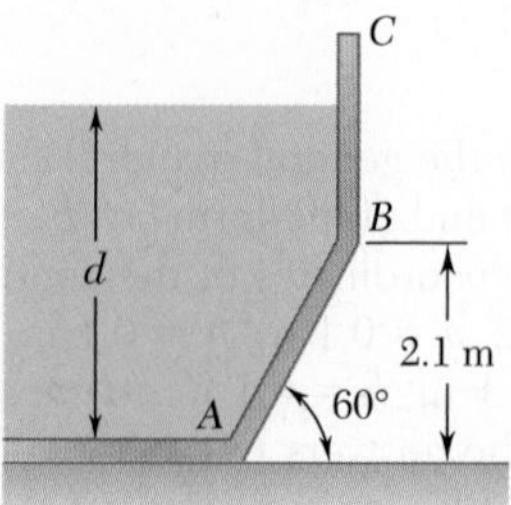

Fig. P5.C6

5.C7 The cross section of a concrete dam is as shown. For a dam section of 1-m width, plot the magnitude of the resultant of the reaction forces exerted by the ground on the base AB of the dam and the resultant of the pressure forces exerted by the water on the face BC of the dam as functions of the depth d of the water for $0 \le d \le 16$ m. The densities of concrete and water are 2.40×10^3 kg/m^3 and 10^3 kg/m^3, respectively.

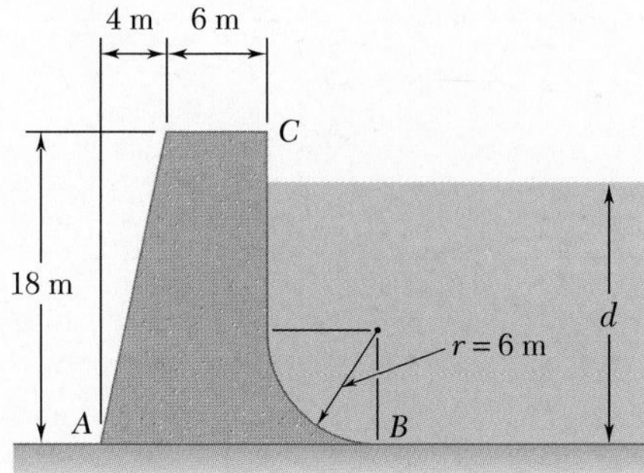

Fig. P5.C7

5.C8 A beam is subjected to the loading shown. Plot the magnitude of the vertical reactions at supports A and B as functions of distance a for $0 \le a \le 3$ m.

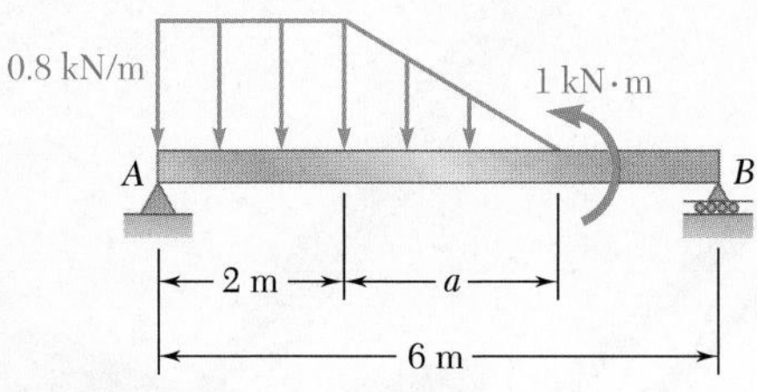

Fig. P5.C8

5.C9 The three-dimensional structure shown is fabricated from five thin steel rods of equal diameter. Using computational software, determine the coordinates of the center of gravity of the structure. Locate the coordinates of the center of gravity when (*a*) $h = 12$ m, $R = 4.5$ m, $\alpha = 90°$; (*b*) $h = 0.6$ m, $R = 0.8$ m, $\alpha = 30°$; (*c*) $h = 21$ m, $R = 19.5$ m, $\alpha = 135°$.

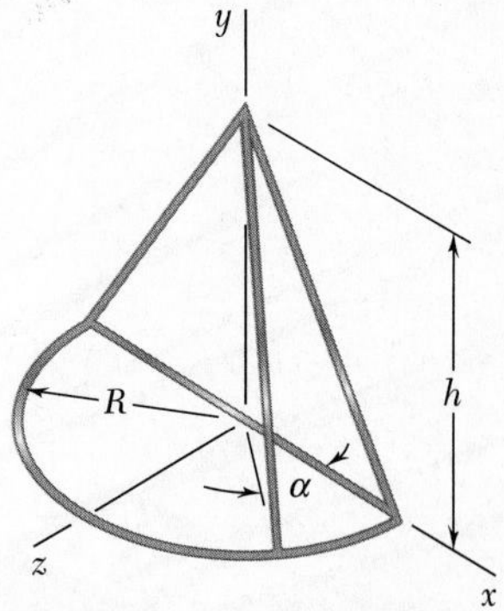

Fig. P5.C9

5.C10 Determine the y coordinate of the centroid of the body shown when $h = nb$ and $h = n^2b$. Plot $\overline{y}$ as a function of n for both cases using $1 \le n \le 10$ and (*a*) $b = 0.1$ m, (*b*) $b = 0.15$ m, (*c*) $b = 0.2$ m.

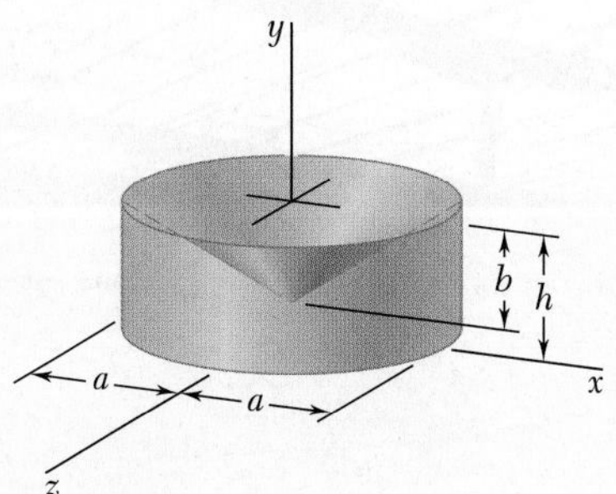

Fig. P5.C10

CHAPTER 6

Analysis of Structures

Trusses, such as the light-gauge steel trusses being used for the roof of the building shown, provide both a practical and an economical solution to many engineering problems.

ANALYSIS OF STRUCTURES

6.1. INTRODUCTION

The problems considered in the preceding chapters concerned the equilibrium of a single rigid body, and all forces involved were external to the rigid body. We now consider problems dealing with the equilibrium of structures made of several connected parts. These problems call for the determination not only of the external forces acting on the structure but also of the forces which hold together the various parts of the structure. From the point of view of the structure as a whole, these forces are *internal forces.*

Consider, for example, the crane shown in Fig. 6.1*a*, which carries a load *W*. The crane consists of three beams *AD*, *CF*, and *BE* connected by frictionless pins; it is supported by a pin at *A* and by a cable *DG*. The free-body diagram of the crane has been drawn in Fig. 6.1*b*. The external forces, which are shown in the diagram, include the weight $\mathbf{W}$, the two components $\mathbf{A}_x$ and $\mathbf{A}_y$ of the reaction at *A*, and the force $\mathbf{T}$ exerted by the cable at *D*. The internal forces holding the various parts of the crane together do not appear in the diagram. If, however, the crane is dismembered and if a free-body diagram is drawn for each of its component parts, the forces holding the three beams together will also be represented, since these forces are external forces from the point of view of each component part (Fig. 6.1*c*).

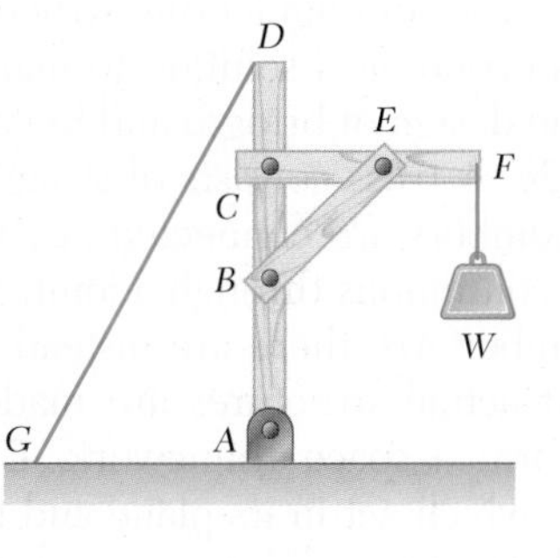

(*a*)

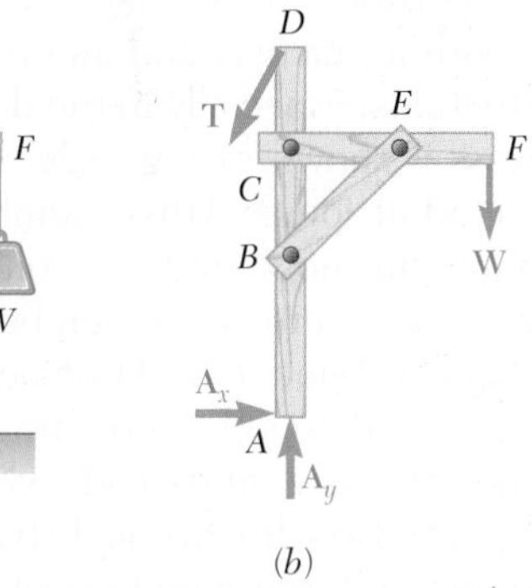

(*b*)

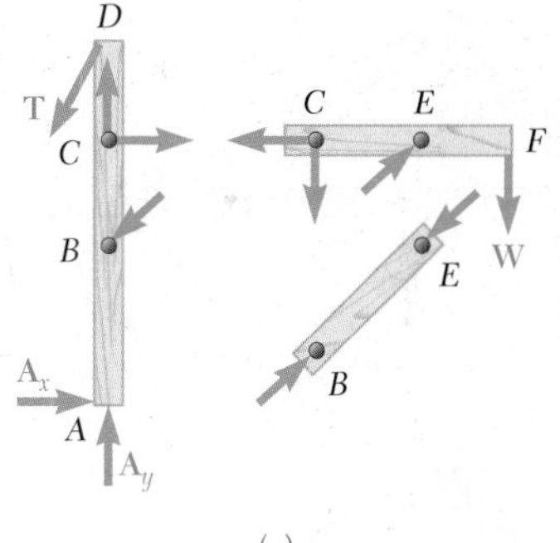

(*c*)

Fig. 6.1

It will be noted that the force exerted at *B* by member *BE* on member *AD* has been represented as equal and opposite to the force exerted at the same point by member *AD* on member *BE*; the force exerted at *E* by *BE* on *CF* is shown equal and opposite to the force exerted by *CF* on *BE*; and the components of the force exerted at *C* by *CF* on *AD* are shown equal and opposite to the components of the force exerted by *AD* on *CF*. This is in conformity with Newton's third law, which states that *the forces of action and reaction between bodies in contact have the same magnitude, same line of action, and opposite sense.* As pointed out in Chap. 1, this law, which is based on experimental evidence, is one of the six fundamental principles of elementary mechanics, and its application is essential to the solution of problems involving connected bodies.

Photo 6.1 Shown is a pin-jointed connection on the approach span to the San Francisco–Oakland Bay Bridge.

In this chapter, three broad categories of engineering structures will be considered:

1. *Trusses,* which are designed to support loads and are usually stationary, fully constrained structures. Trusses consist exclusively of straight members connected at joints located at the ends of each member. Members of a truss, therefore, are *two-force members,* that is, members each acted upon by two equal and opposite forces directed along the member.
2. *Frames,* which are also designed to support loads and are also usually stationary, fully constrained structures. However, like the crane of Fig. 6.1, frames always contain at least one *multiforce member,* that is, a member acted upon by three or more forces which, in general, are not directed along the member.
3. *Machines,* which are designed to transmit and modify forces and are structures containing moving parts. Machines, like frames, always contain at least one multiforce member.

TRUSSES

6.2. DEFINITION OF A TRUSS

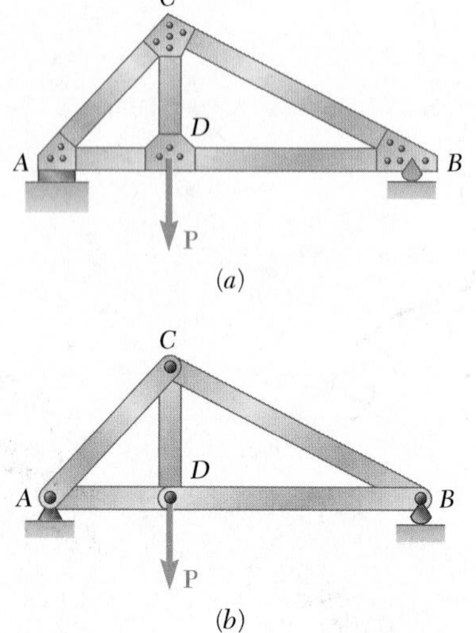

Fig. 6.2

The truss is one of the major types of engineering structures. It provides both a practical and an economical solution to many engineering situations, especially in the design of bridges and buildings. A typical truss is shown in Fig. 6.2*a*. A truss consists of straight members connected at joints. Truss members are connected at their extremities only; thus no member is continuous through a joint. In Fig. 6.2*a*, for example, there is no member *AB*; there are instead two distinct members *AD* and *DB*. Most actual structures are made of several trusses joined together to form a space framework. Each truss is designed to carry those loads which act in its plane and thus may be treated as a two-dimensional structure.

In general, the members of a truss are slender and can support little lateral load; all loads, therefore, must be applied to the various joints, and not to the members themselves. When a concentrated load is to be applied between two joints, or when a distributed load is to be supported by the truss, as in the case of a bridge truss, a floor system must be provided which, through the use of stringers and floor beams, transmits the load to the joints (Fig. 6.3).

The weights of the members of the truss are also assumed to be applied to the joints, half of the weight of each member being applied to each of the two joints the member connects. Although the members are actually joined together by means of bolted or welded connections, it is customary to assume that the members are pinned together; therefore, the forces acting at each end of a member reduce to a single force and no couple. Thus, the only forces assumed to be applied to a truss member are a single force at each end of the

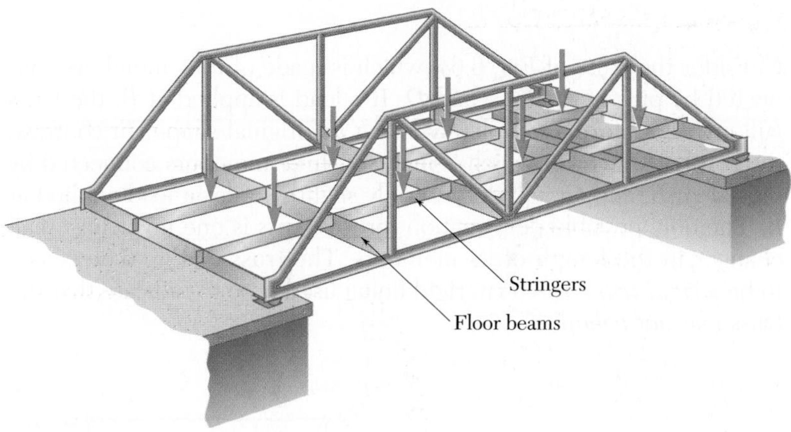

Fig. 6.3

member. Each member can then be treated as a two-force member, and the entire truss can be considered as a group of pins and two-force members (Fig. 6.2*b*). An individual member can be acted upon as shown in either of the two sketches of Fig. 6.4. In Fig. 6.4*a*, the forces tend to pull the member apart, and the member is in tension; in Fig. 6.4*b*, the forces tend to compress the member, and the member is in compression. A number of typical trusses are shown in Fig. 6.5.

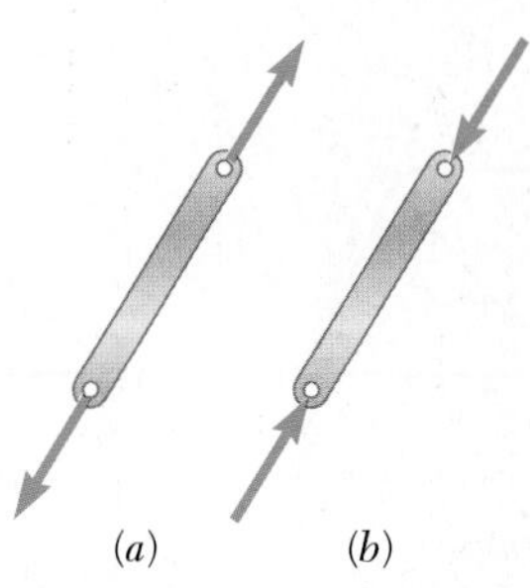

Fig. 6.4

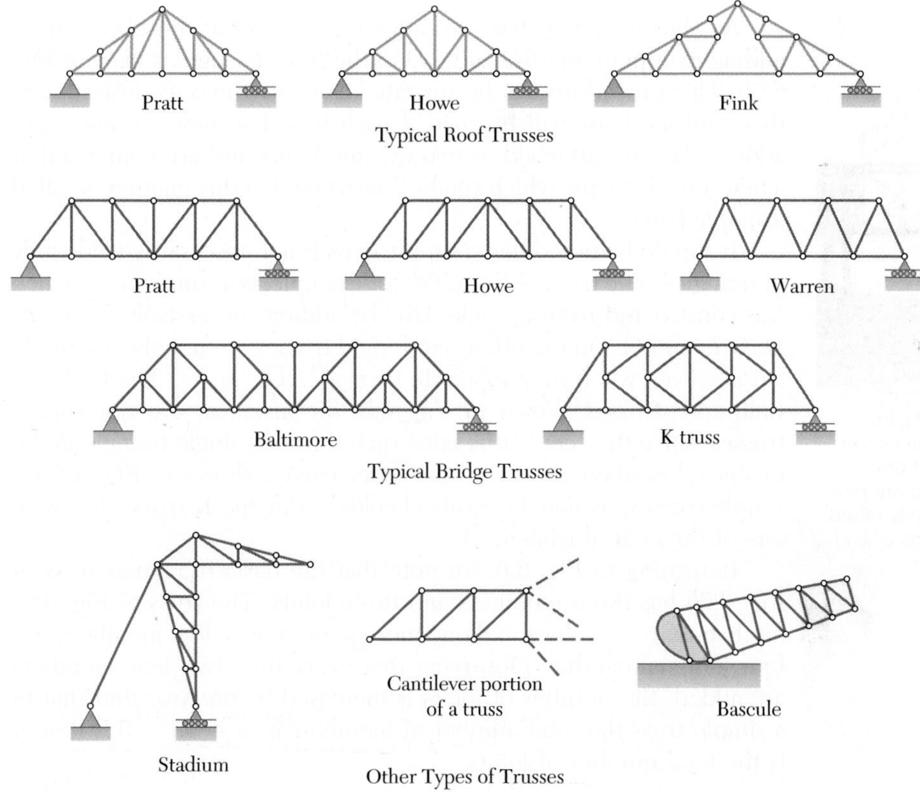

Fig. 6.5

6.3. SIMPLE TRUSSES

Consider the truss of Fig. 6.6*a*, which is made of four members connected by pins at *A*, *B*, *C*, and *D*. If a load is applied at *B*, the truss will greatly deform, completely losing its original shape. In contrast, the truss of Fig. 6.6*b*, which is made of three members connected by pins at *A*, *B*, and *C*, will deform only slightly under a load applied at *B*. The only possible deformation for this truss is one involving small changes in the length of its members. The truss of Fig. 6.6*b* is said to be a *rigid truss*, the term rigid being used here to indicate that the truss *will not collapse*.

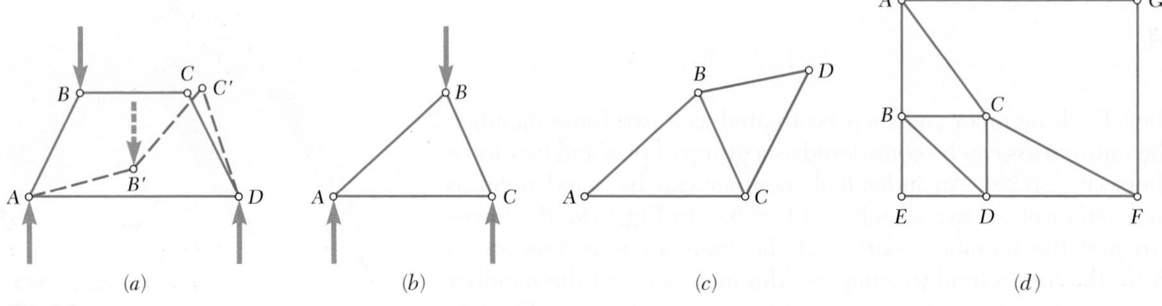

Fig. 6.6

As shown in Fig. 6.6*c*, a larger rigid truss can be obtained by adding two members *BD* and *CD* to the basic triangular truss of Fig. 6.6*b*. This procedure can be repeated as many times as desired, and the resulting truss will be rigid if each time two new members are added, they are attached to two existing joints and are connected at a new joint.† A truss which can be constructed in this manner is called a *simple truss*.

Photo 6.2 Two K-trusses were used as the main components of the movable bridge shown which moved above a large stockpile of ore. The bucket below the trusses picked up ore and redeposited it until the ore was thoroughly mixed. The ore was then sent to the mill for processing into steel.

It should be noted that a simple truss is not necessarily made only of triangles. The truss of Fig. 6.6*d*, for example, is a simple truss which was constructed from triangle *ABC* by adding successively the joints *D*, *E*, *F*, and *G*. On the other hand, rigid trusses are not always simple trusses, even when they appear to be made of triangles. The Fink and Baltimore trusses shown in Fig. 6.5, for instance, are not simple trusses, since they cannot be constructed from a single triangle in the manner described above. All the other trusses shown in Fig. 6.5 are simple trusses, as may be easily checked. (For the K truss, start with one of the central triangles.)

Returning to Fig. 6.6, we note that the basic triangular truss of Fig. 6.6*b* has three members and three joints. The truss of Fig. 6.6*c* has two more members and one more joint, that is, five members and four joints altogether. Observing that every time two new members are added, the number of joints is increased by one, we find that in a simple truss the total number of members is $m = 2n - 3$, where n is the total number of joints.

†The three joints must not be in a straight line.

6.4. ANALYSIS OF TRUSSES BY THE METHOD OF JOINTS

We saw in Sec. 6.2 that a truss can be considered as a group of pins and two-force members. The truss of Fig. 6.2, whose free-body diagram is shown in Fig. 6.7*a*, can thus be dismembered, and a free-body diagram can be drawn for each pin and each member (Fig. 6.7*b*). Each member is acted upon by two forces, one at each end; these forces have the same magnitude, same line of action, and opposite sense (Sec. 4.6). Furthermore, Newton's third law indicates that the forces of action and reaction between a member and a pin are equal and opposite. Therefore, the forces exerted by a member on the two pins it connects must be directed along that member and be equal and opposite. The common magnitude of the forces exerted by a member on the two pins it connects is commonly referred to as the *force in the member* considered, even though this quantity is actually a scalar. Since the lines of action of all the internal forces in a truss are known, the analysis of a truss reduces to computing the forces in its various members and to determining whether each of its members is in tension or in compression.

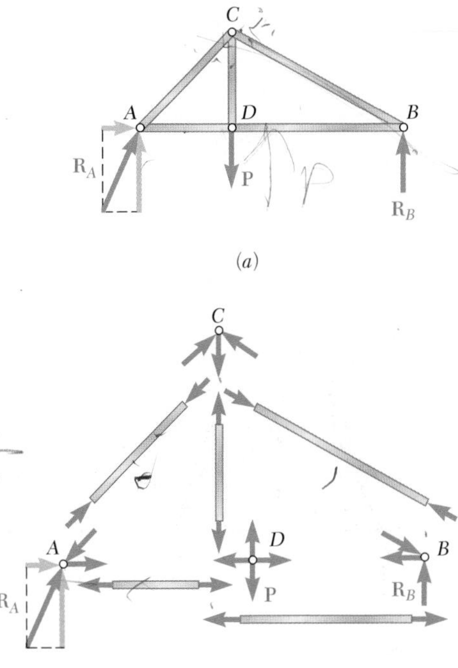

Fig. 6.7

Since the entire truss is in equilibrium, each pin must be in equilibrium. The fact that a pin is in equilibrium can be expressed by drawing its free-body diagram and writing two equilibrium equations (Sec. 2.9). If the truss contains n pins, there will, therefore, be $2n$ equations available, which can be solved for $2n$ unknowns. In the case of a simple truss, we have $m = 2n - 3$, that is, $2n = m + 3$, and the number of unknowns which can be determined from the free-body diagrams of the pins is thus $m + 3$. This means that the forces in all the members, the two components of the reaction $\mathbf{R}_A$, and the reaction $\mathbf{R}_B$ can be found by considering the free-body diagrams of the pins.

The fact that the entire truss is a rigid body in equilibrium can be used to write three more equations involving the forces shown in the free-body diagram of Fig. 6.7*a*. Since they do not contain any new information, these equations are not independent of the equations associated with the free-body diagrams of the pins. Nevertheless, they can be used to determine the components of the reactions at the supports. The arrangement of pins and members in a simple truss is such that it will then always be possible to find a joint involving only two unknown forces. These forces can be determined by the methods of Sec. 2.11 and their values transferred to the adjacent joints and treated as known quantities at these joints. This procedure can be repeated until all unknown forces have been determined.

Photo 6.3 Because roof trusses, such as those shown, require support only at their ends, it is possible to construct buildings with large, unobstructed floor areas.

As an example, the truss of Fig. 6.7 will be analyzed by considering the equilibrium of each pin successively, starting with a joint at which only two forces are unknown. In the truss considered, all pins are subjected to at least three unknown forces. Therefore, the reactions at the supports must first be determined by considering the entire truss as a free body and using the equations of equilibrium of a rigid body. We find in this way that $\mathbf{R}_A$ is vertical and determine the magnitudes of $\mathbf{R}_A$ and $\mathbf{R}_B$.

The number of unknown forces at joint A is thus reduced to two, and these forces can be determined by considering the equilibrium of pin A. The reaction $\mathbf{R}_A$ and the forces $\mathbf{F}_{AC}$ and $\mathbf{F}_{AD}$ exerted on pin

A by members AC and AD, respectively, must form a force triangle. First we draw $\mathbf{R}_A$ (Fig. 6.8); noting that $\mathbf{F}_{AC}$ and $\mathbf{F}_{AD}$ are directed along AC and AD, respectively, we complete the triangle and determine the magnitude and sense of $\mathbf{F}_{AC}$ and $\mathbf{F}_{AD}$. The magnitudes F_{AC} and F_{AD} represent the forces in members AC and AD. Since $\mathbf{F}_{AC}$ is directed down and to the left, that is, *toward* joint A, member AC pushes on pin A and is in compression. Since $\mathbf{F}_{AD}$ is directed *away* from joint A, member AD pulls on pin A and is in tension.

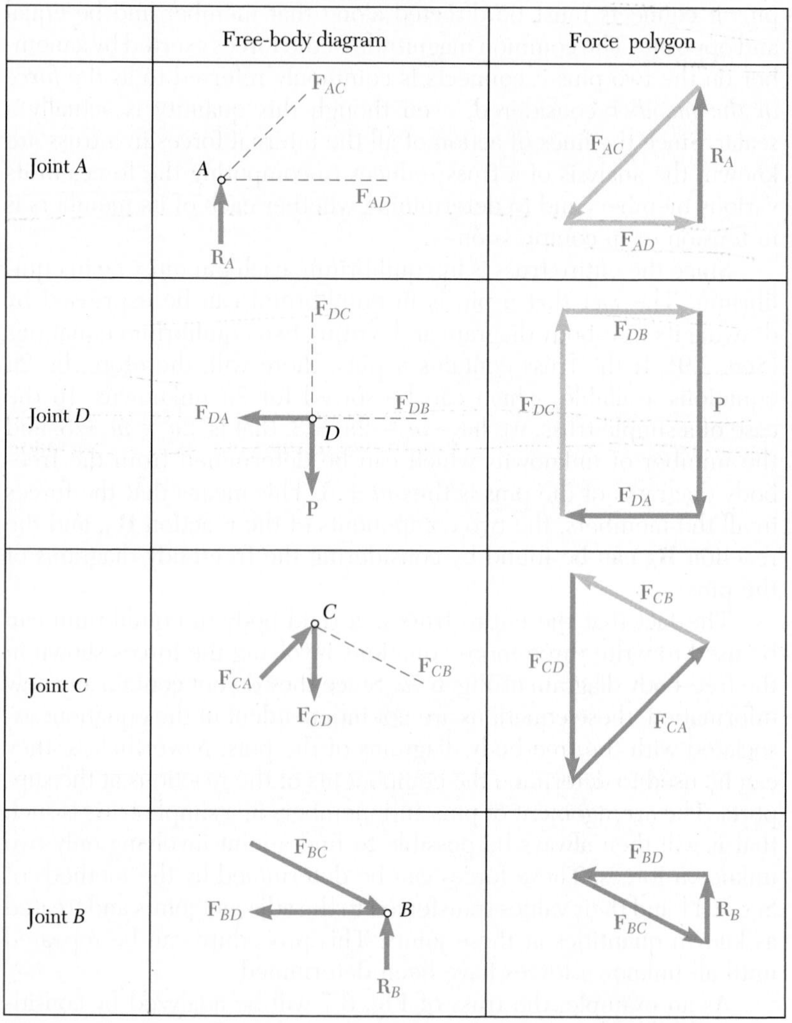

	Free-body diagram	Force polygon
Joint A	A, $\mathbf{F}_{AC}$, $\mathbf{F}_{AD}$, $\mathbf{R}_A$	$\mathbf{F}_{AC}$, $\mathbf{R}_A$, $\mathbf{F}_{AD}$
Joint D	$\mathbf{F}_{DC}$, $\mathbf{F}_{DA}$, $\mathbf{F}_{DB}$, D, $\mathbf{P}$	$\mathbf{F}_{DB}$, $\mathbf{F}_{DC}$, $\mathbf{P}$, $\mathbf{F}_{DA}$
Joint C	C, $\mathbf{F}_{CA}$, $\mathbf{F}_{CB}$, $\mathbf{F}_{CD}$	$\mathbf{F}_{CB}$, $\mathbf{F}_{CD}$, $\mathbf{F}_{CA}$
Joint B	$\mathbf{F}_{BC}$, $\mathbf{F}_{BD}$, B, $\mathbf{R}_B$	$\mathbf{F}_{BD}$, $\mathbf{R}_B$, $\mathbf{F}_{BC}$

Fig. 6.8

We can now proceed to joint D, where only two forces, $\mathbf{F}_{DC}$ and $\mathbf{F}_{DB}$, are still unknown. The other forces are the load $\mathbf{P}$, which is given, and the force $\mathbf{F}_{DA}$ exerted on the pin by member AD. As indicated above, this force is equal and opposite to the force $\mathbf{F}_{AD}$ exerted by the same member on pin A. We can draw the force polygon corresponding to joint D, as shown in Fig. 6.8, and determine the forces

$\mathbf{F}_{DC}$ and $\mathbf{F}_{DB}$ from that polygon. However, when more than three forces are involved, it is usually more convenient to solve the equations of equilibrium $\Sigma F_x = 0$ and $\Sigma F_y = 0$ for the two unknown forces. Since both of these forces are found to be directed away from joint D, members DC and DB pull on the pin and are in tension.

Next, joint C is considered; its free-body diagram is shown in Fig. 6.8. It is noted that both $\mathbf{F}_{CD}$ and $\mathbf{F}_{CA}$ are known from the analysis of the preceding joints and that only $\mathbf{F}_{CB}$ is unknown. Since the equilibrium of each pin provides sufficient information to determine two unknowns, a check of our analysis is obtained at this joint. The force triangle is drawn, and the magnitude and sense of $\mathbf{F}_{CB}$ are determined. Since $\mathbf{F}_{CB}$ is directed toward joint C, member CB pushes on pin C and is in compression. The check is obtained by verifying that the force $\mathbf{F}_{CB}$ and member CB are parallel.

At joint B, all of the forces are known. Since the corresponding pin is in equilibrium, the force triangle must close and an additional check of the analysis is obtained.

It should be noted that the force polygons shown in Fig. 6.8 are not unique. Each of them could be replaced by an alternative configuration. For example, the force triangle corresponding to joint A could be drawn as shown in Fig. 6.9. The triangle actually shown in Fig. 6.8 was obtained by drawing the three forces $\mathbf{R}_A$, $\mathbf{F}_{AC}$, and $\mathbf{F}_{AD}$ in tip-to-tail fashion in the order in which their lines of action are encountered when moving clockwise around joint A. The other force polygons in Fig. 6.8, having been drawn in the same way, can be made to fit into a single diagram, as shown in Fig. 6.10. Such a diagram, known as *Maxwell's diagram,* greatly facilitates the *graphical analysis* of truss problems.

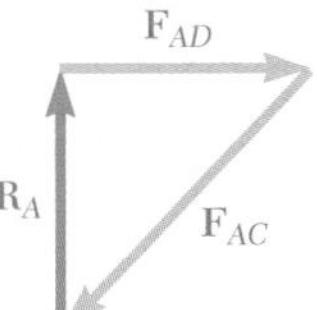

Fig. 6.9

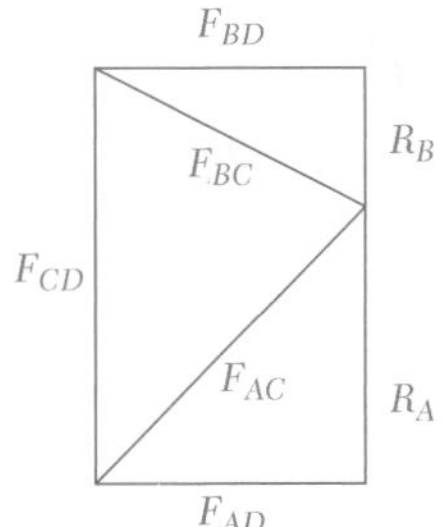

Fig. 6.10

*6.5. JOINTS UNDER SPECIAL LOADING CONDITIONS

Consider Fig. 6.11*a*, in which the joint shown connects four members lying in two intersecting straight lines. The free-body diagram of Fig. 6.11*b* shows that pin A is subjected to two pairs of directly opposite forces. The corresponding force polygon, therefore, must be a parallelogram (Fig. 6.11*c*), and *the forces in opposite members must be equal.*

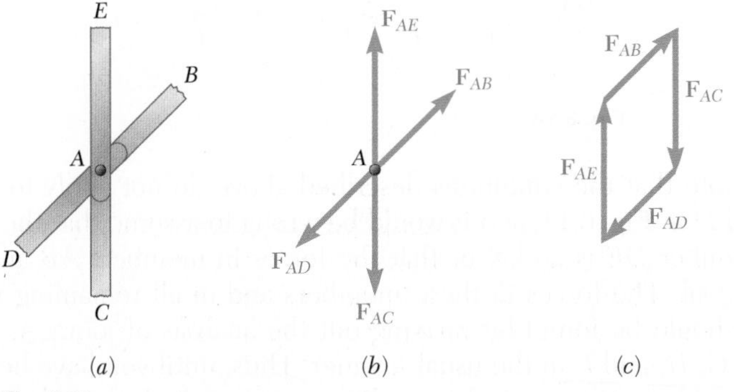

Fig. 6.11

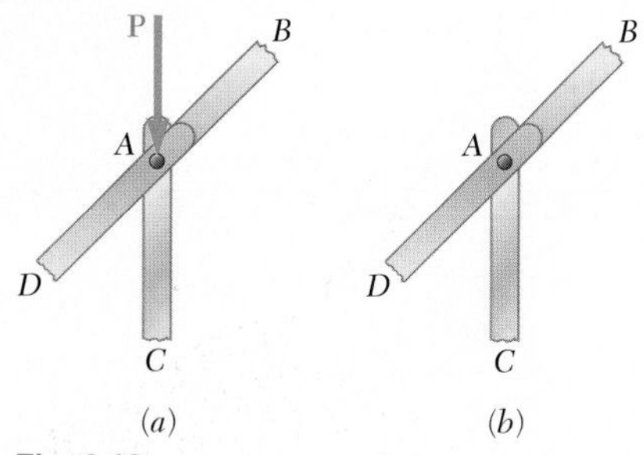

Fig. 6.12

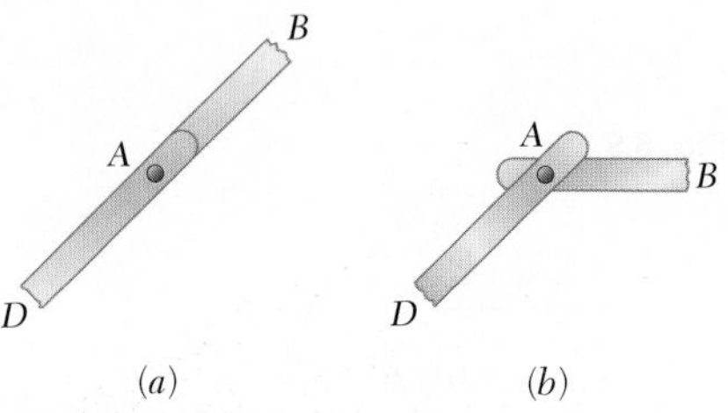

Fig. 6.13

Consider next Fig. 6.12*a*, in which the joint shown connects three members and supports a load **P**. Two of the members lie in the same line, and the load **P** acts along the third member. The free-body diagram of pin *A* and the corresponding force polygon will be as shown in Fig. 6.11*b* and *c*, with $\mathbf{F}_{AE}$ replaced by the load **P**. Thus, *the forces in the two opposite members must be equal, and the force in the other member must equal P.* A particular case of special interest is shown in Fig. 6.12*b*. Since, in this case, no external load is applied to the joint, we have $P = 0$, and the force in member *AC* is zero. Member *AC* is said to be a *zero-force member.*

Consider now a joint connecting two members only. From Sec. 2.9, we know that a particle which is acted upon by two forces will be in equilibrium if the two forces have the same magnitude, same line of action, and opposite sense. In the case of the joint of Fig. 6.13*a*, which connects two members *AB* and *AD* lying in the same line, *the forces in the two members must be equal* for pin *A* to be in equilibrium. In the case of the joint of Fig. 6.13*b*, pin *A* cannot be in equilibrium unless the forces in both members are zero. Members connected as shown in Fig. 6.13*b*, therefore, must be *zero-force members.*

Spotting the joints which are under the special loading conditions listed above will expedite the analysis of a truss. Consider, for example, a Howe truss loaded as shown in Fig. 6.14. All of the members represented by green lines will be recognized as zero-force members. Joint *C* connects three members, two of which lie in the same line, and is not subjected to any external load; member *BC* is thus a zero-force member. Applying the same reasoning to joint *K*, we find that member *JK* is also a zero-force member. But joint *J* is now in the same situation as joints *C* and *K*, and member *IJ* must be a zero-force member. The examination of joints *C*, *J*, and *K* also shows that the forces in members *AC* and *CE* are equal, that the forces in members *HJ* and *JL* are equal, and that the forces in members *IK* and *KL* are equal. Turning our attention to joint *I*, where the 20-kN load and member *HI* are collinear, we note that the force in member *HI* is 20 kN (tension) and that the forces in members *GI* and *IK* are equal. Hence, the forces in members *GI*, *IK*, and *KL* are equal.

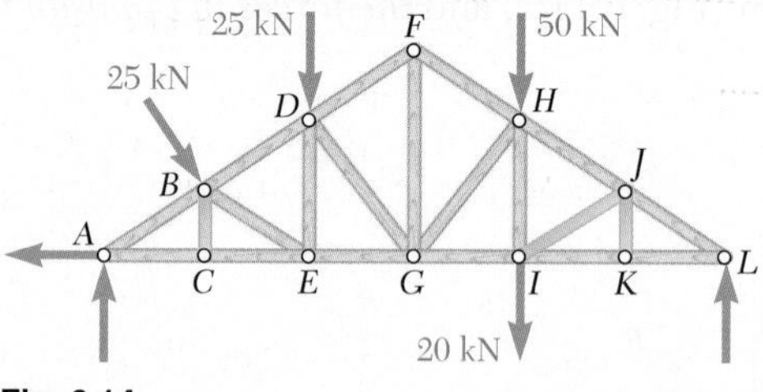

Fig. 6.14

Note that the conditions described above do not apply to joints *B* and *D* in Fig. 6.14, and it would be wrong to assume that the force in member *DE* is 25 kN or that the forces in members *AB* and *BD* are equal. The forces in these members and in all remaining members should be found by carrying out the analysis of joints *A*, *B*, *D*, *E*, *F*, *G*, *H*, and *L* in the usual manner. Thus, until you have become thoroughly familiar with the conditions under which the rules established in this section can be applied, you should draw the free-body diagrams of all pins and write the corresponding equilibrium equations (or draw the corresponding force polygons) whether or not the joints being considered are under one of the special loading conditions described above.

A final remark concerning zero-force members: These members are not useless. For example, although the zero-force members of Fig. 6.14 do not carry any loads under the loading conditions shown, the same members would probably carry loads if the loading conditions were changed. Besides, even in the case considered, these members are needed to support the weight of the truss and to maintain the truss in the desired shape.

*6.6. SPACE TRUSSES

When several straight members are joined together at their extremities to form a three-dimensional configuration, the structure obtained is called a *space truss.*

We recall from Sec. 6.3 that the most elementary two-dimensional rigid truss consisted of three members joined at their extremities to form the sides of a triangle; by adding two members at a time to this basic configuration, and connecting them at a new joint, it was possible to obtain a larger rigid structure which was defined as a simple truss. Similarly, the most elementary rigid space truss consists of six members joined at their extremities to form the edges of a tetrahedron $ABCD$ (Fig. 6.15*a*). By adding three members at a time to this basic configuration, such as AE, BE, and CE, attaching them to three existing joints, and connecting them at a new joint,† we can obtain a larger rigid structure which is defined as a *simple space truss* (Fig. 6.15*b*). Observing that the basic tetrahedron has six members and four joints and that every time three members are added, the number of joints is increased by one, we conclude that in a simple space truss the total number of members is $m = 3n - 6$, where n is the total number of joints.

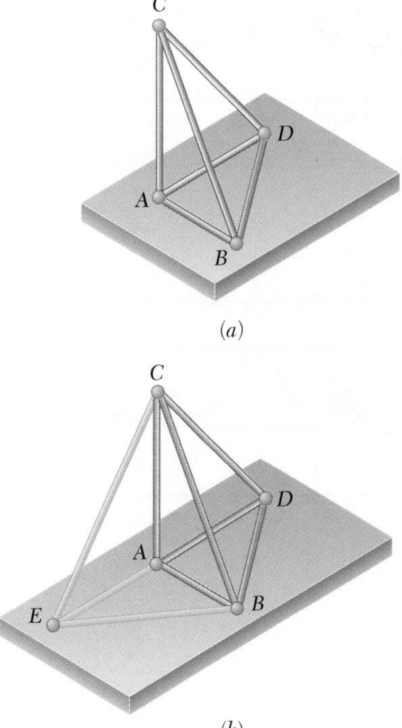

Fig. 6.15

If a space truss is to be completely constrained and if the reactions at its supports are to be statically determinate, the supports should consist of a combination of balls, rollers, and balls and sockets which provides six unknown reactions (see Sec. 4.9). These unknown reactions may be readily determined by solving the six equations expressing that the three-dimensional truss is in equilibrium.

Although the members of a space truss are actually joined together by means of bolted or welded connections, it is assumed that each joint consists of a ball-and-socket connection. Thus, no couple will be applied to the members of the truss, and each member can be treated as a two-force member. The conditions of equilibrium for each joint will be expressed by the three equations $\Sigma F_x = 0$, $\Sigma F_y = 0$, and $\Sigma F_z = 0$. In the case of a simple space truss containing n joints, writing the conditions of equilibrium for each joint will thus yield $3n$ equations. Since $m = 3n - 6$, these equations suffice to determine all unknown forces (forces in m members and six reactions at the supports). However, to avoid the necessity of solving simultaneous equations, care should be taken to select joints in such an order that no selected joint will involve more than three unknown forces.

Photo 6.4 Three-dimensional or space trusses are used for broadcast and power transmission line towers, roof framing, and spacecraft applications, such as components of the *International Space Station.*

†The four joints must not lie in a plane.

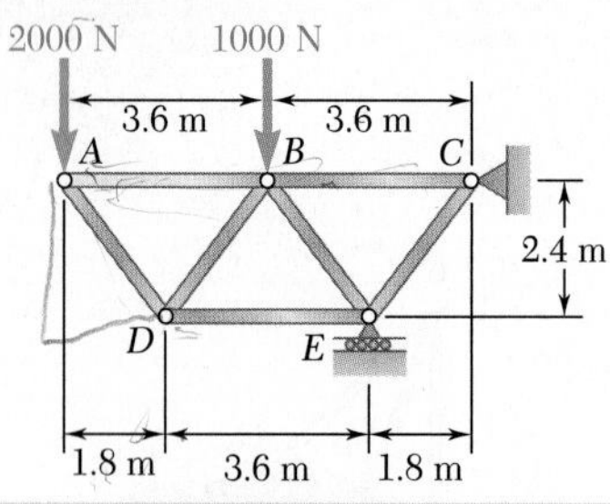

SAMPLE PROBLEM 6.1

Using the method of joints, determine the force in each member of the truss shown.

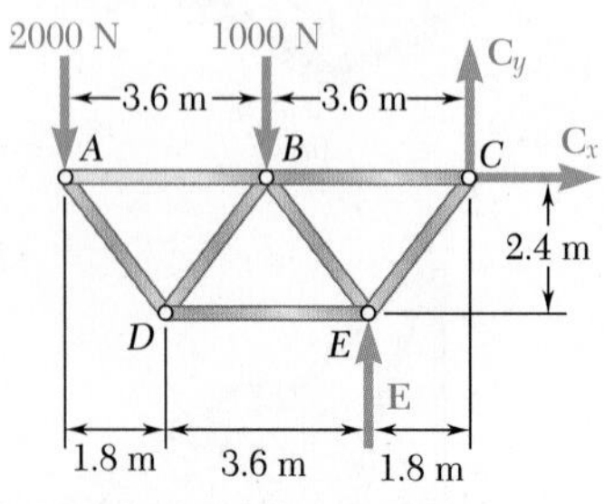

SOLUTION

Free Body: Entire Truss. A free-body diagram of the entire truss is drawn; external forces acting on this free body consist of the applied loads and the reactions at C and E. We write the following equilibrium equations.

$$+\circlearrowleft \Sigma M_C = 0: \quad (2000 \text{ N})(7.2 \text{ m}) + (1000 \text{ N})(3.6 \text{ m}) - E(1.8 \text{ m}) = 0$$

$$E = +10{,}000 \text{ N} \qquad \mathbf{E} = 10{,}000 \text{ N} \uparrow$$

$$\overset{+}{\rightarrow} \Sigma F_x = 0: \qquad \mathbf{C}_x = 0$$

$$+\uparrow \Sigma F_y = 0: \quad -2000 \text{ N} - 1000 \text{ N} + 10{,}000 \text{ N} + C_y = 0$$

$$C_y = -7000 \text{ N} \qquad \mathbf{C}_y = 7000 \text{ N} \downarrow$$

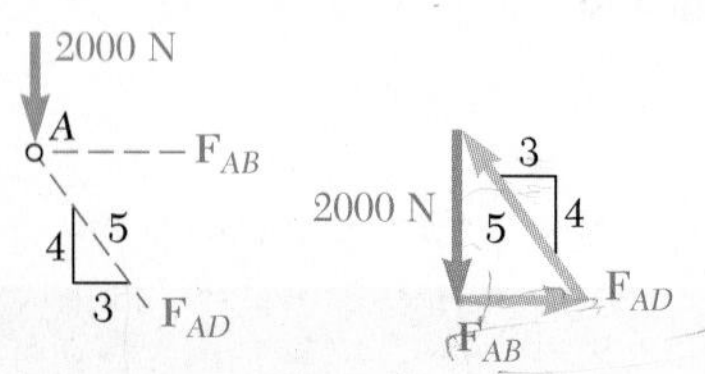

Free Body: Joint A. This joint is subjected to only two unknown forces, namely, the forces exerted by members AB and AD. A force triangle is used to determine $\mathbf{F}_{AB}$ and $\mathbf{F}_{AD}$. We note that member AB pulls on the joint and thus is in tension and that member AD pushes on the joint and thus is in compression. The magnitudes of the two forces are obtained from the proportion

$$\frac{2000 \text{ N}}{4} = \frac{F_{AB}}{3} = \frac{F_{AD}}{5}$$

$$F_{AB} = 1500 \text{ N } T \quad ◀$$
$$F_{AD} = 2500 \text{ N } C \quad ◀$$

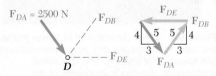

Free Body: Joint D. Since the force exerted by member AD has been determined, only two unknown forces are now involved at this joint. Again, a force triangle is used to determine the unknown forces in members DB and DE.

$$F_{DB} = F_{DA} \qquad F_{DB} = 2500 \text{ N } T \quad ◀$$
$$F_{DE} = 2(\tfrac{3}{5})F_{DA} \qquad F_{DE} = 3000 \text{ N } C \quad ◀$$

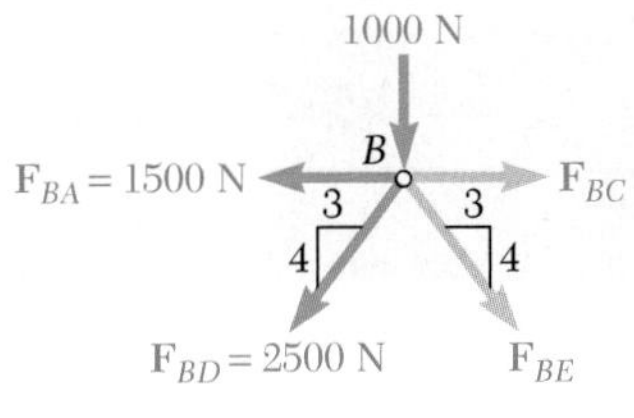

Free Body: Joint B. Since more than three forces act at this joint, we determine the two unknown forces $\mathbf{F}_{BC}$ and $\mathbf{F}_{BE}$ by solving the equilibrium equations $\Sigma F_x = 0$ and $\Sigma F_y = 0$. We arbitrarily assume that both unknown forces act away from the joint, that is, that the members are in tension. The positive value obtained for F_{BC} indicates that our assumption was correct; member BC is in tension. The negative value of F_{BE} indicates that our assumption was wrong; member BE is in compression.

$$+\uparrow\Sigma F_y = 0: \quad -1000 - \tfrac{4}{5}(2500) - \tfrac{4}{5}F_{BE} = 0$$
$$F_{BE} = -3750 \text{ N} \qquad F_{BE} = 3750 \text{ N } C \blacktriangleleft$$

$$\xrightarrow{+}\Sigma F_x = 0: \quad F_{BC} - 1500 - \tfrac{3}{5}(2500) - \tfrac{3}{5}(3750) = 0$$
$$F_{BC} = +5250 \text{ N} \qquad F_{BC} = 5250 \text{ N } T \blacktriangleleft$$

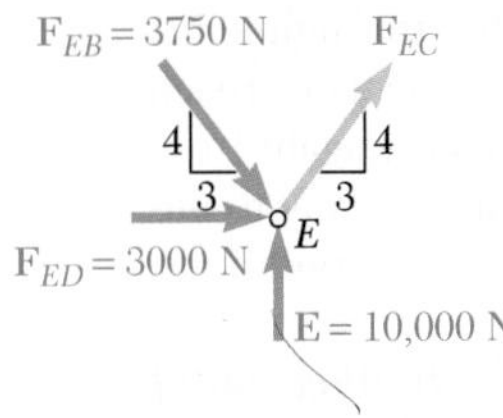

Free Body: Joint E. The unknown force $\mathbf{F}_{EC}$ is assumed to act away from the joint. Summing x components, we write

$$\xrightarrow{+}\Sigma F_x = 0: \quad \tfrac{3}{5}F_{EC} + 3000 + \tfrac{3}{5}(3750) = 0$$
$$F_{EC} = -8750 \text{ N} \qquad F_{EC} = 8750 \text{ N } C \blacktriangleleft$$

Summing y components, we obtain a check of our computations:

$$\begin{aligned} +\uparrow\Sigma F_y &= 10{,}000 - \tfrac{4}{5}(3750) - \tfrac{4}{5}(8750) \\ &= 10{,}000 - 3000 - 7000 = 0 \end{aligned} \qquad \text{(checks)}$$

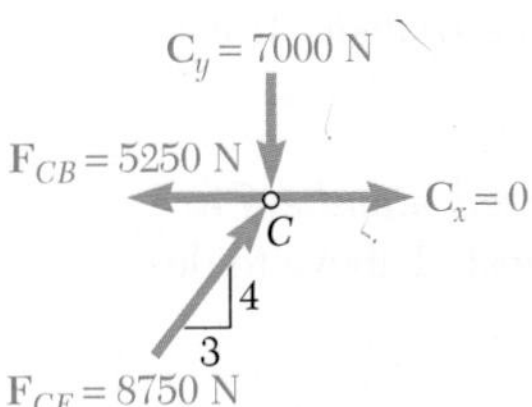

Free Body: Joint C. Using the computed values of $\mathbf{F}_{CB}$ and $\mathbf{F}_{CE}$, we can determine the reactions $\mathbf{C}_x$ and $\mathbf{C}_y$ by considering the equilibrium of this joint. Since these reactions have already been determined from the equilibrium of the entire truss, we will obtain two checks of our computations. We can also simply use the computed values of all forces acting on the joint (forces in members and reactions) and check that the joint is in equilibrium:

$$\xrightarrow{+}\Sigma F_x = -5250 + \tfrac{3}{5}(8750) = -5250 + 5250 = 0 \qquad \text{(checks)}$$
$$+\uparrow\Sigma F_y = -7000 + \tfrac{4}{5}(8750) = -7000 + 7000 = 0 \qquad \text{(checks)}$$

SOLVING PROBLEMS ON YOUR OWN

In this lesson you learned to use the *method of joints* to determine the forces in the members of a *simple truss*, that is, a truss that can be constructed from a basic triangular truss by adding to it two new members at a time and connecting them at a new joint. We note that the analysis of a *simple* truss can always be carried out by the method of joints.

Your solution will consist of the following steps:

1. ***Draw a free-body diagram of the entire truss,*** and use this diagram to determine the reactions at the supports.

2. ***Note that the choice of the first joint is not unique.*** Once you have determined the reactions at the supports of the truss, you can choose either of two joints as a starting point for your analysis. In Sample Prob. 6.1, we started at joint A and proceeded through joints D, B, E, and C, but we could also have started at joint C and proceeded through joints E, B, D, and A. On the other hand, having selected a first joint, you may in some cases reach a point in your analysis beyond which you cannot proceed. You must then start again from another joint to complete your solution. Because there is usually more than one way to analyze a truss, we encourage you to outline your solution *before* starting any computations.

3. ***Locate a joint connecting only two members, and draw the free-body diagram of its pin.*** Use this free-body diagram to determine the unknown force in each of the two members. If only three forces are involved (the two unknown forces and a known one), you will probably find it more convenient to draw and solve the corresponding force triangle. If more than three forces are involved, you should write and solve the equilibrium equations for the pin, $\Sigma F_x = 0$ and $\Sigma F_y = 0$, assuming that the members are in tension. A positive answer means that the member is in tension, a negative answer that the member is in compression. Once the forces have been found, enter their values on a sketch of the truss, with T for tension and C for compression.

In Sec. 6.4, we discussed how to use a force triangle to determine the unknown forces at a joint, and in Sample Prob. 6.1 we applied this technique to joints A and D. In each of these cases, the directions of the unknown forces at a joint were not specified in the associated free-body diagram—only their lines of action were shown. Thus, when you construct a force triangle, draw the known force first and then add the lines of action of the unknown forces, remembering that the forces must be arranged tip to tail to form a triangle. It is in this last step that the directions of the unknown forces are established.

4. ***Next, locate a joint where the forces in only two of the connected members are still unknown.*** Draw the free-body diagram of the pin and use it as indicated above to determine the two unknown forces.

5. ***Repeat this procedure until the forces in all the members of the truss have been found.*** Since you previously used the three equilibrium equations associated with the free-body diagram of the entire truss to determine the reactions at the supports, you will end up with three extra equations. These equations can be used to check your computations.

Problems

6.1 through 6.8 Using the method of joints, determine the force in each member of the truss shown. State whether each member is in tension or compression.

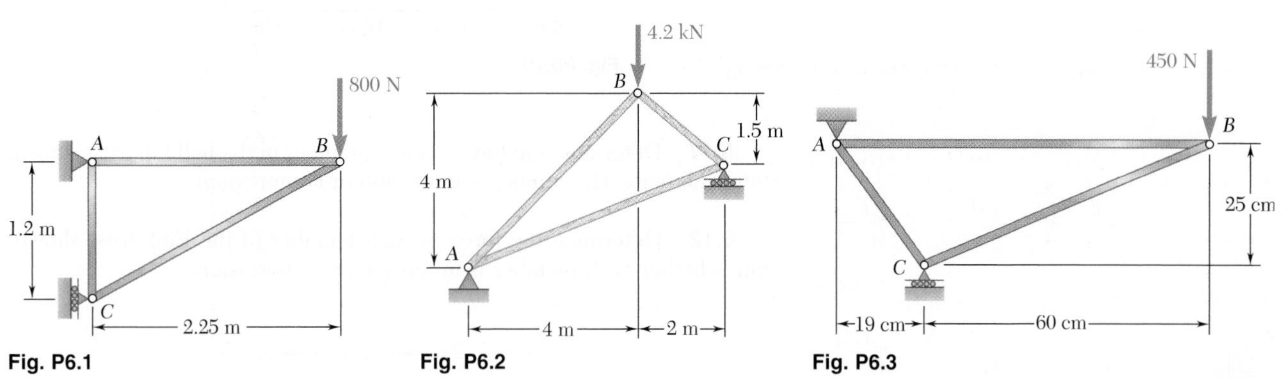

Fig. P6.1

Fig. P6.2

Fig. P6.3

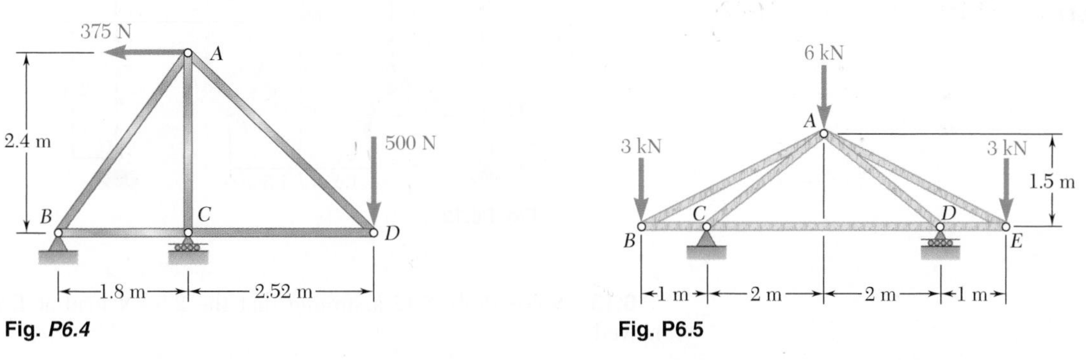

Fig. *P6.4*

Fig. P6.5

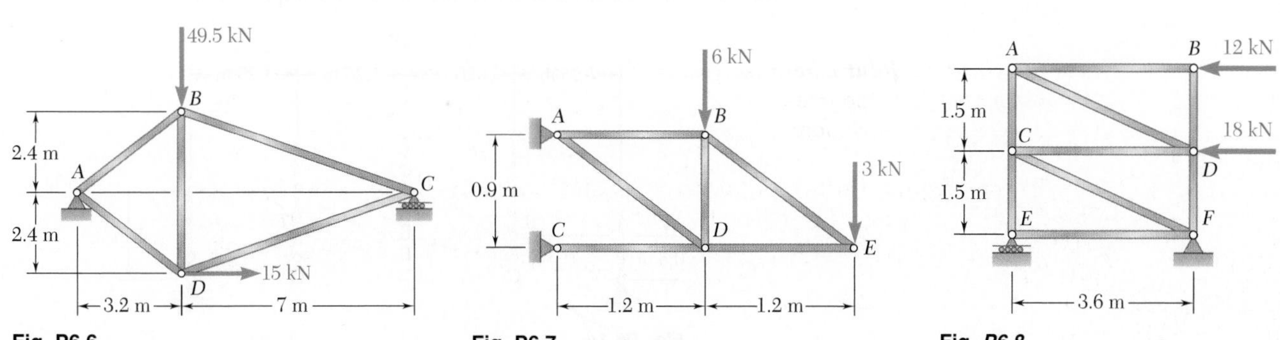

Fig. P6.6

Fig. P6.7

Fig. *P6.8*

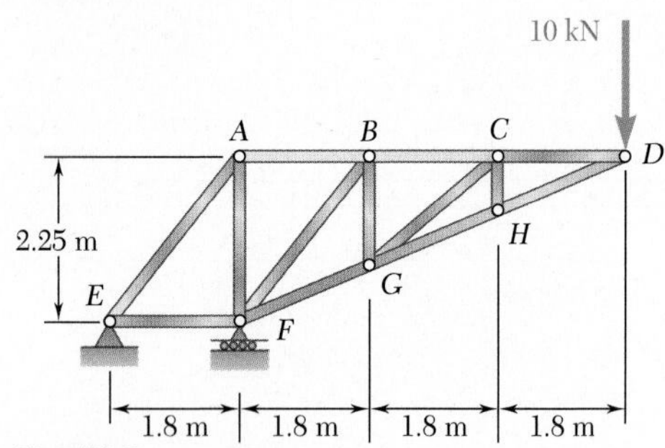

Fig. P6.9

6.9 Determine the force in each member of the truss shown. State whether each member is in tension or compression.

6.10 Determine the force in each member of the Gambrel roof truss shown. State whether each member is in tension or compression.

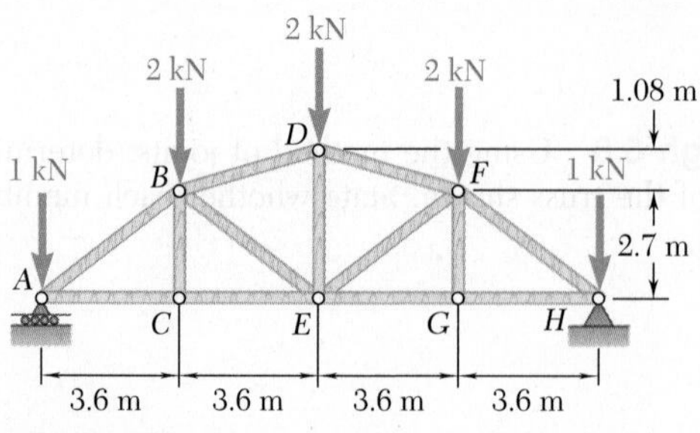

Fig. P6.10

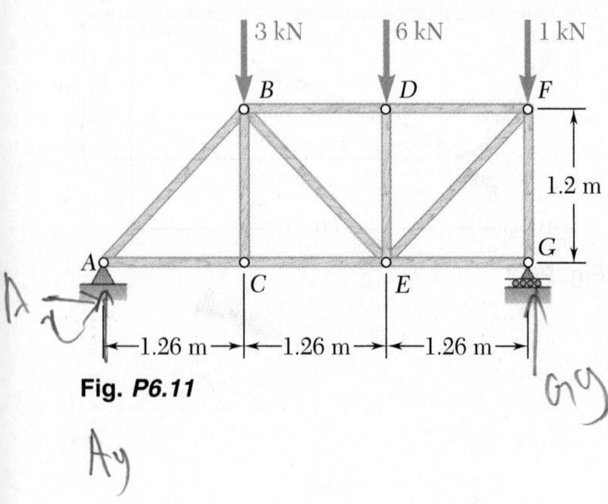

Fig. P6.11

6.11 Determine the force in each member of the half hip truss shown. State whether each member is in tension or compression.

6.12 Determine the force in each member of the Fink truss shown. State whether each member is in tension or compression.

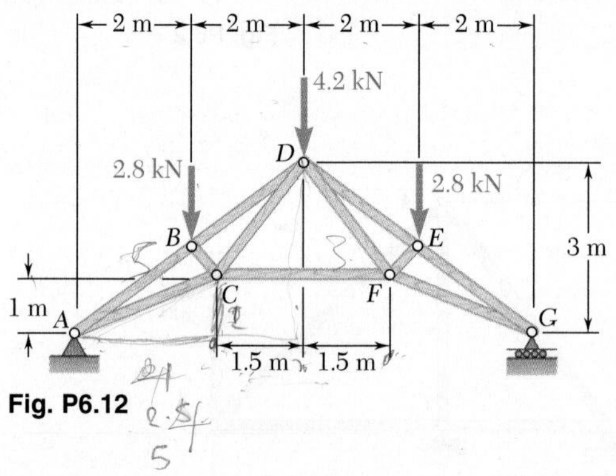

Fig. P6.12

6.13 Solve Prob. 6.12 assuming that the 2.8-kN load at E has been removed.

6.14 Determine the force in each member of the roof truss shown. State whether each member is in tension or compression.

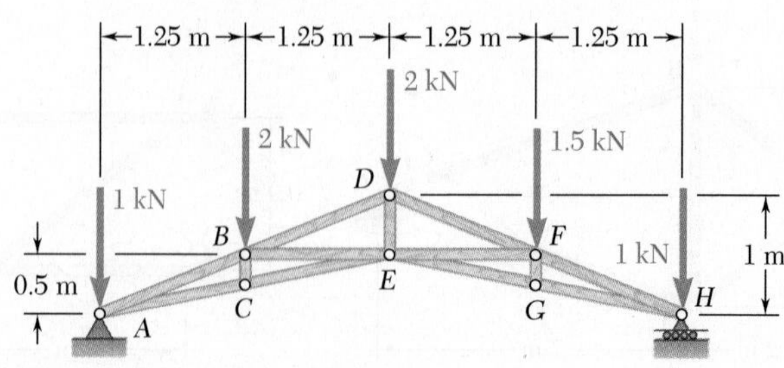

Fig. P6.14

6.15 For the Gambrel roof truss shown, determine the force in members *CG* and *CI* and in each of the members located to the left of the centerline of the truss. State whether each member is in tension or compression.

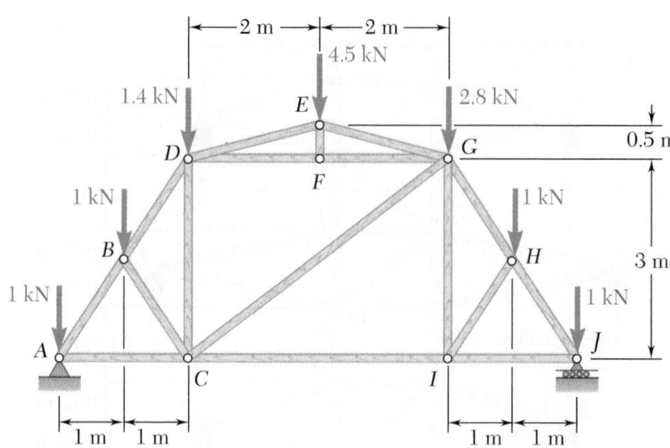

Fig. P6.15 and P6.16

6.16 For the Gambrel roof truss shown, determine the force in members *CG* and *CI* and in each of the members located to the right of the centerline of the truss. State whether each member is in tension or compression.

6.17 Determine the force in member *DE* and in each of the members located to the left of member *DE* for the inverted Howe roof truss shown. State whether each member is in tension or compression.

6.18 Determine the force in each of the members located to the right of member *DE* for the inverted Howe roof truss shown. State whether each member is in tension or compression.

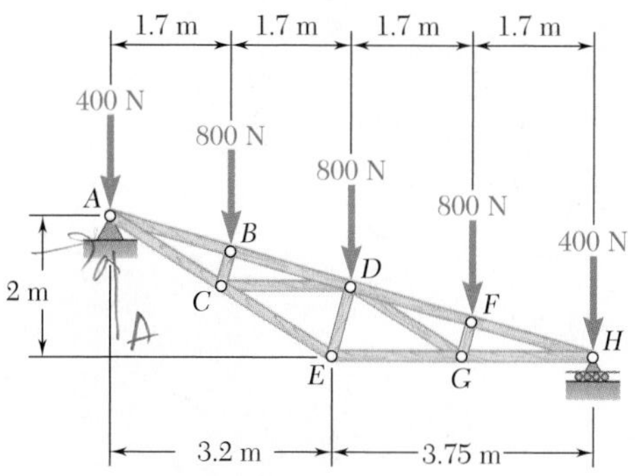

Fig. P6.17 and P6.18

6.19 Determine the force in each of the members located to the left of member *FG* for the roof truss shown. State whether each member is in tension or compression.

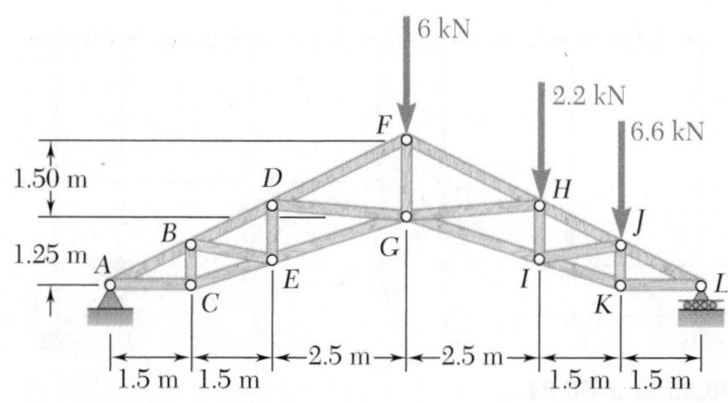

Fig. P6.19 and *P6.20*

6.20 Determine the force in member *FG* and in each of the members located to the right of member *FG* for the roof truss shown. State whether each member is in tension or compression.

6.21 The portion of truss shown represents the upper part of a power transmission line tower. For the given loading, determine the force in each of the members located above member *HJ*. State whether each member is in tension or compression.

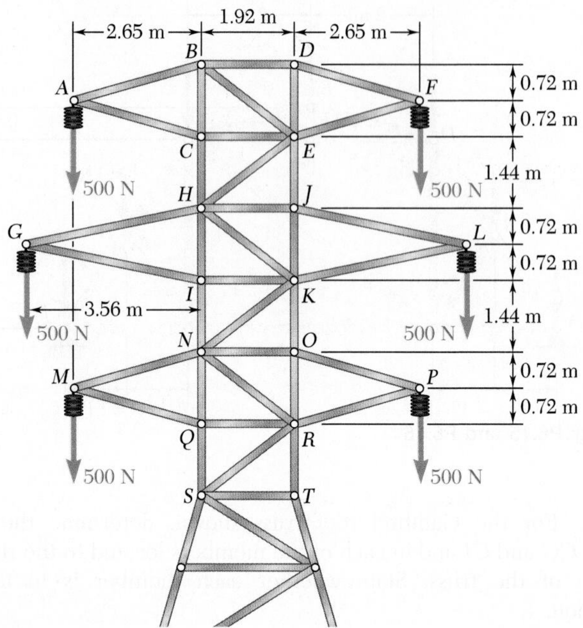

Fig. *P6.21*

6.22 For the tower and loading of Prob. 6.21 and knowing that $F_{CH} = F_{EJ} = 500$ N *C* and $F_{EH} = 0$, determine the force in member *HJ* and in each of the members located between members *HJ* and *NO*. State whether each member is in tension or compression.

6.23 For the roof truss shown, determine the force in each of the members located to the left of member *GH*. State whether each member is in tension or compression.

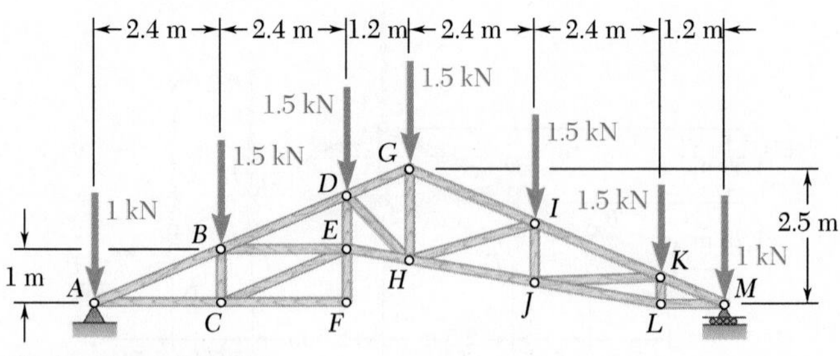

Fig. P6.23 and *P6.24*

6.24 Determine the force in member *GH* and in each of the members located to the right of member *GH* for the roof truss shown. State whether each member is in tension or compression.

6.25 Determine the force in each member of the truss shown. State whether each member is in tension or compression.

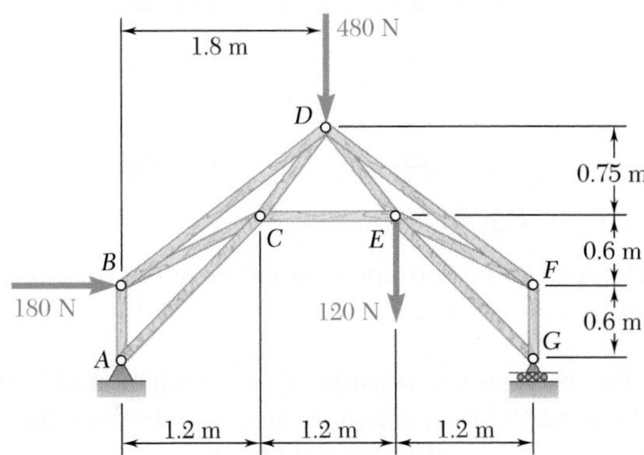

Fig. P6.25

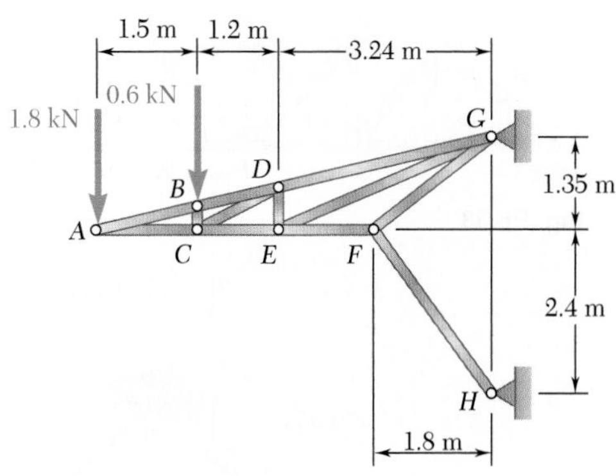

Fig. P6.26

6.26 Determine the force in each member of the truss shown. State whether each member is in tension or compression.

6.27 Determine whether the trusses of Probs. 6.14, 6.15, and 6.23 are simple trusses.

6.28 Determine whether the trusses of Probs. 6.21, 6.25, and 6.29 are simple trusses.

6.29 and 6.30 For the given loading, determine the zero-force members in the truss shown.

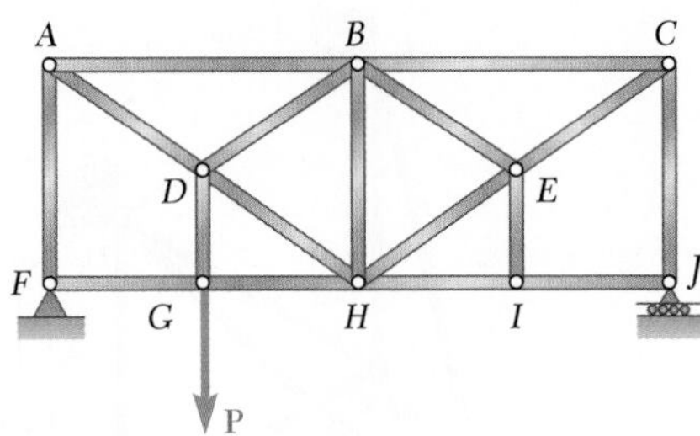

Fig. P6.29

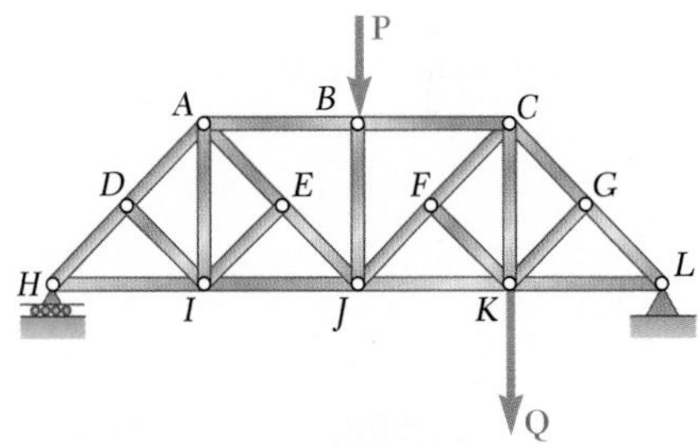

Fig. P6.30

6.31 and *6.32* For the given loading, determine the zero-force members in the truss shown.

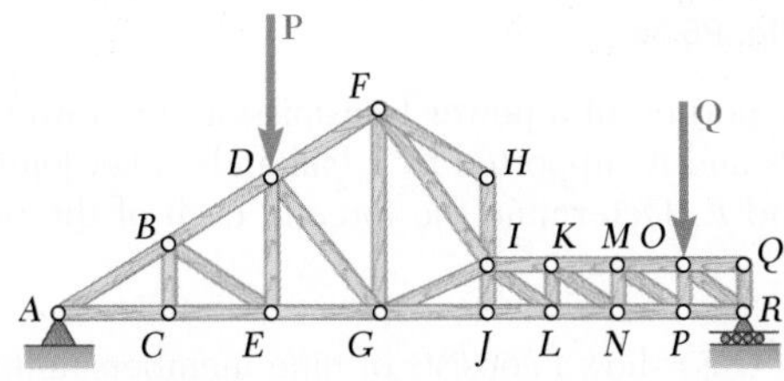

Fig. P6.31

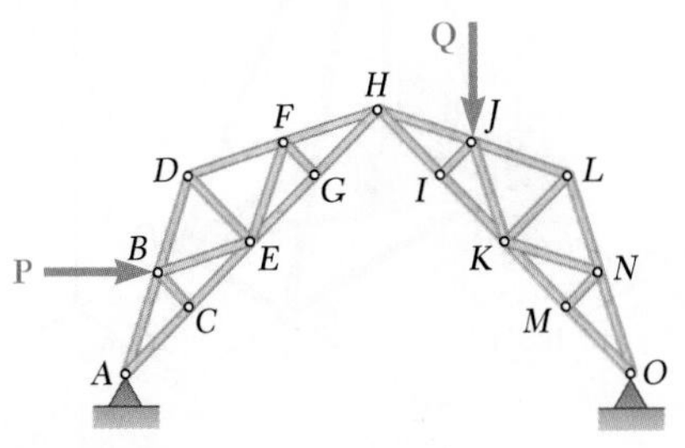

Fig. *P6.32*

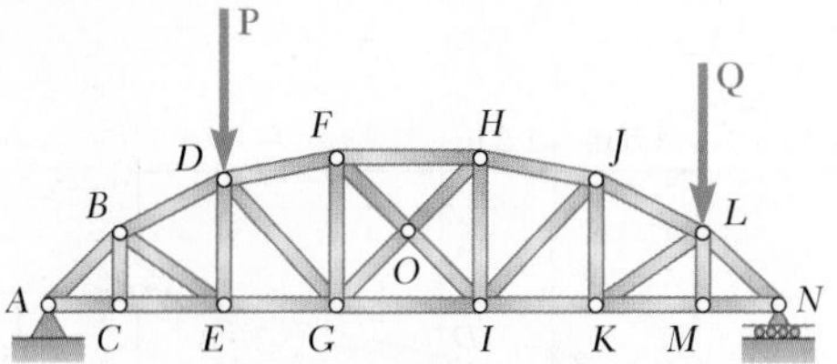

Fig. P6.33

6.33 and *6.34* For the given loading, determine the zero-force members in the truss shown.

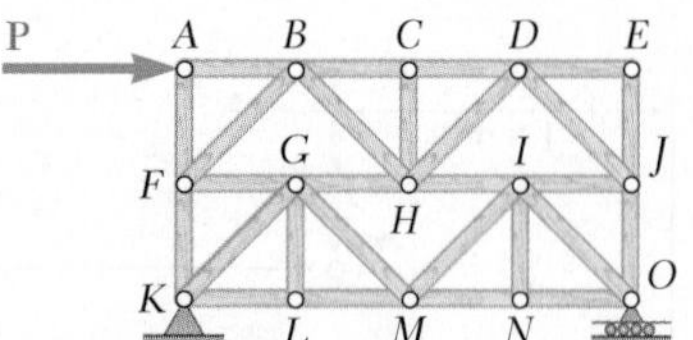

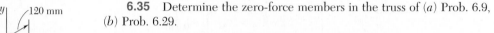

Fig. *P6.34*

6.35 Determine the zero-force members in the truss of (*a*) Prob. 6.9, (*b*) Prob. 6.29.

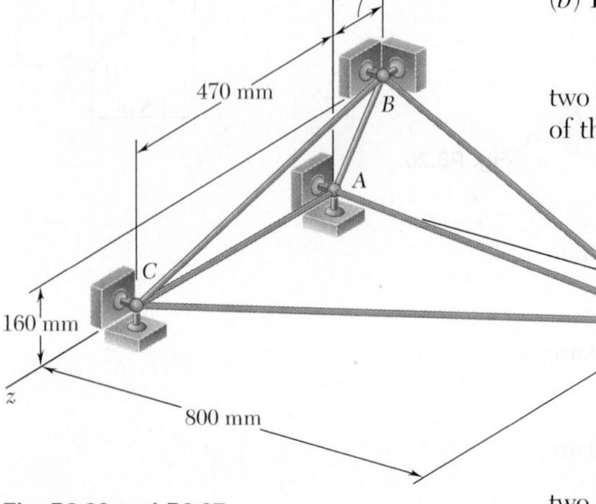

Fig. P6.36 and P6.37

***6.36** The truss shown consists of six members and is supported by two short links at each of the joints *A*, *B*, and *C*. Determine the force in each of the members for $\mathbf{P} = -(940 \text{ N})\mathbf{j}$ and $\mathbf{Q} = 0$.

***6.37** The truss shown consists of six members and is supported by two short links at each of the joints *A*, *B*, and *C*. Determine the force in each of the members for $\mathbf{P} = -(940 \text{ N})\mathbf{j}$ and $\mathbf{Q} = (987 \text{ N})\mathbf{k}$.

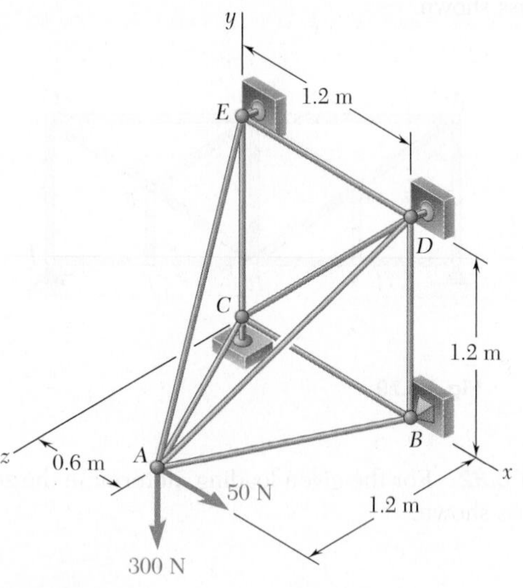

Fig. P6.38

***6.38** The portion of a power transmission line tower shown consists of nine members and is supported by a ball-and-socket joint at *B* and short links at *C*, *D*, and *E*. Determine the force in each of the members for the given loading.

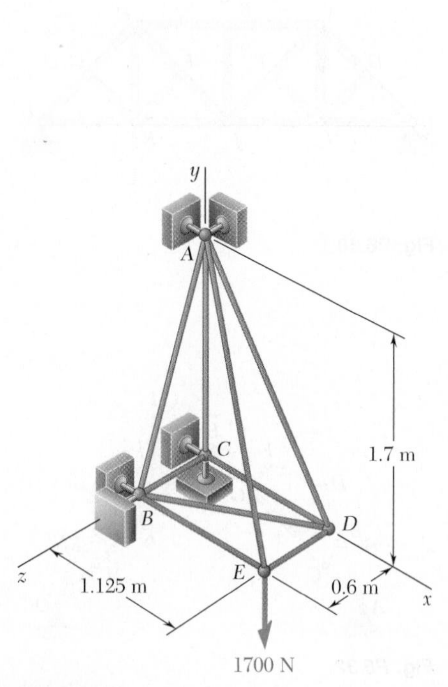

Fig. P6.39

***6.39** The truss shown consists of nine members and is supported by two short links at each of the joints *A*, *B*, and *C*. Determine the force in each of the members for the given loading.

***6.40** The truss shown consists of 18 members and is supported by a ball-and-socket joint at A, two short links at B, and one short link at G. (a) Check that this truss is a simple truss, that it is completely constrained, and that the reactions at its supports are statically determinate. (b) For the given loading, determine the force in each of the six members joined at E.

***6.41** The truss shown consists of 18 members and is supported by a ball-and-socket joint at A, two short links at B, and one short link at G. (a) Check that this truss is a simple truss, that it is completely constrained, and that the reactions at its supports are statically determinate. (b) For the given loading, determine the force in each of the six members joined at G.

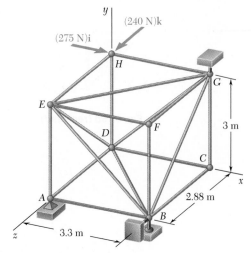

Fig. P6.40 and P6.41

6.7. ANALYSIS OF TRUSSES BY THE METHOD OF SECTIONS

The method of joints is most effective when the forces in all the members of a truss are to be determined. If, however, the force in only one member or the forces in a very few members are desired, another method, the method of sections, is more efficient.

Assume, for example, that we want to determine the force in member BD of the truss shown in Fig. 6.16a. To do this, we must determine the force with which member BD acts on either joint B or joint D. If we were to use the method of joints, we would choose either joint B or joint D as a free body. However, we can also choose as a free body a larger portion of the truss, composed of several joints and members, provided that the desired force is one of the external forces acting on that portion. If, in addition, the portion of the truss is chosen so that there is a total of only three unknown forces acting upon it, the desired force can be obtained by solving the equations of equilibrium for this portion of the truss. In practice, the portion of the truss to be utilized is obtained by *passing a section* through three members of the truss, one of which is the desired member, that is, by drawing a line which divides the truss into two completely separate parts but does not intersect more than three members. Either of the two portions of the truss obtained after the intersected members have been removed can then be used as a free body.†

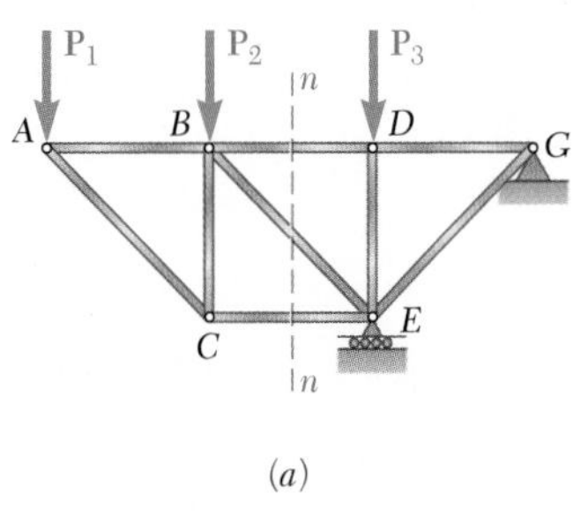

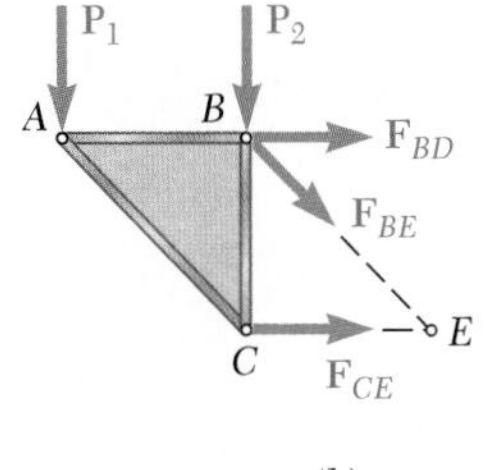

Fig. 6.16

In Fig. 6.16a, the section nn has been passed through members BD, BE, and CE, and the portion ABC of the truss is chosen as the free body (Fig. 6.16b). The forces acting on the free body are the loads $\mathbf{P}_1$ and $\mathbf{P}_2$ at points A and B and the three unknown forces $\mathbf{F}_{BD}$, $\mathbf{F}_{BE}$, and $\mathbf{F}_{CE}$. Since it is not known whether the members removed were in tension or compression, the three forces have been arbitrarily drawn away from the free body as if the members were in tension.

†In the analysis of certain trusses, sections are passed which intersect more than three members; the forces in one, or possibly two, of the intersected members can be obtained if equilibrium equations can be found where each involves only one unknown (see Probs. 6.60 through 6.63).

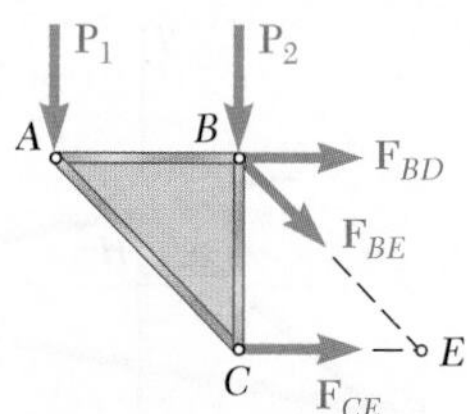

Fig. 6.16b (repeated)

The fact that the rigid body ABC is in equilibrium can be expressed by writing three equations which can be solved for the three unknown forces. If only the force $\mathbf{F}_{BD}$ is desired, we need write only one equation, provided that the equation does not contain the other unknowns. Thus the equation $\Sigma M_E = 0$ yields the value of the magnitude F_{BD} of the force $\mathbf{F}_{BD}$ (Fig. 6.16*b*). A positive sign in the answer will indicate that our original assumption regarding the sense of $\mathbf{F}_{BD}$ was correct and that member BD is in tension; a negative sign will indicate that our assumption was incorrect and that BD is in compression.

On the other hand, if only the force $\mathbf{F}_{CE}$ is desired, an equation which does not involve $\mathbf{F}_{BD}$ or $\mathbf{F}_{BE}$ should be written; the appropriate equation is $\Sigma M_B = 0$. Again a positive sign for the magnitude F_{CE} of the desired force indicates a correct assumption, that is, tension; and a negative sign indicates an incorrect assumption, that is, compression.

If only the force $\mathbf{F}_{BE}$ is desired, the appropriate equation is $\Sigma F_y = 0$. Whether the member is in tension or compression is again determined from the sign of the answer.

When the force in only one member is determined, no independent check of the computation is available. However, when all the unknown forces acting on the free body are determined, the computations can be checked by writing an additional equation. For instance, if $\mathbf{F}_{BD}$, $\mathbf{F}_{BE}$, and $\mathbf{F}_{CE}$ are determined as indicated above, the computation can be checked by verifying that $\Sigma F_x = 0$.

*6.8. TRUSSES MADE OF SEVERAL SIMPLE TRUSSES

Consider two simple trusses ABC and DEF. If they are connected by three bars BD, BE, and CE as shown in Fig. 6.17*a*, they will form together a rigid truss $ABDF$. The trusses ABC and DEF can also be combined into a single rigid truss by joining joints B and D into a single joint B and by connecting joints C and E by a bar CE (Fig. 6.17*b*). The truss thus obtained is known as a *Fink truss*. It should be noted that the trusses of Fig. 6.17*a* and *b* are *not* simple trusses; they cannot be constructed from a triangular truss by adding successive pairs of members as prescribed in Sec. 6.3. They are rigid trusses, however, as we can check by comparing the systems of connections used to hold the simple trusses ABC and DEF together (three bars in Fig. 6.17*a*, one pin and one bar in Fig. 6.17*b*) with the systems of supports discussed in Secs. 4.4 and 4.5. Trusses made of several simple trusses rigidly connected are known as *compound trusses*.

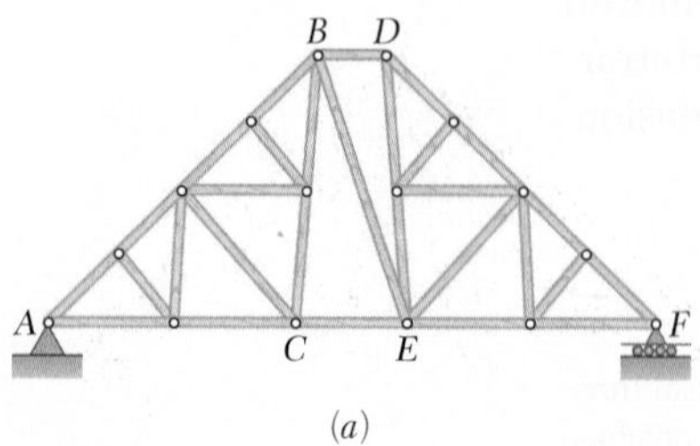

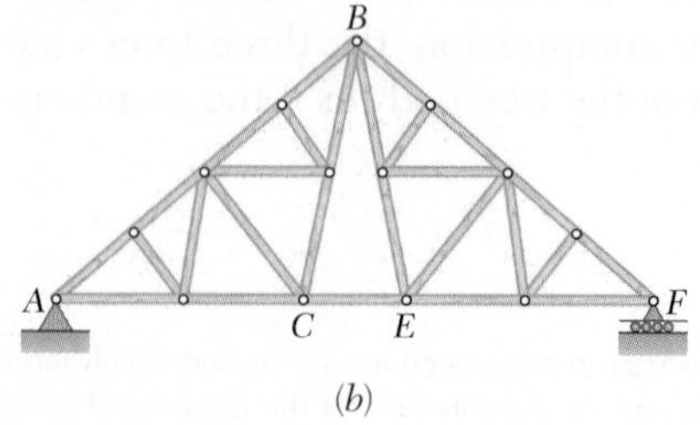

Fig. 6.17

In a compound truss the number of members m and the number of joints n are still related by the formula $m = 2n - 3$. This can be verified by observing that, if a compound truss is supported by a frictionless pin and a roller (involving three unknown reactions), the total number of unknowns is $m + 3$, and this number must be equal to the number $2n$ of equations obtained by expressing that the n pins are in equilibrium; it follows that $m = 2n - 3$. Compound trusses supported by a pin and a roller, or by an equivalent system of supports, are *statically determinate, rigid,* and *completely constrained.* This means that all of the unknown reactions and the forces in all the members can be determined by the methods of statics, and that the truss will neither collapse nor move. The forces in the members, however, cannot all be determined by the method of joints, except by solving a large number of simultaneous equations. In the case of the compound truss of Fig. 6.17*a*, for example, it is more efficient to pass a section through members *BD*, *BE*, and *CE* to determine the forces in these members.

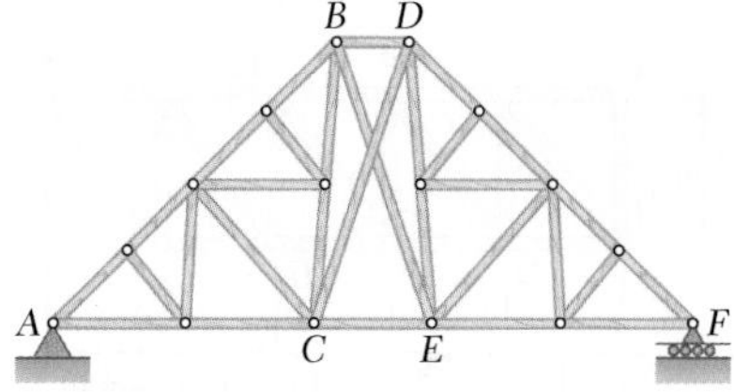

Fig. 6.18

Suppose, now, that the simple trusses *ABC* and *DEF* are connected by *four* bars *BD*, *BE*, *CD*, and *CE* (Fig. 6.18). The number of members m is now larger than $2n - 3$; the truss obtained is *overrigid,* and one of the four members *BD*, *BE*, *CD*, or *CE* is said to be *redundant.* If the truss is supported by a pin at *A* and a roller at *F*, the total number of unknowns is $m + 3$. Since $m > 2n - 3$, the number $m + 3$ of unknowns is now larger than the number $2n$ of available independent equations; the truss is *statically indeterminate.*

Finally, let us assume that the two simple trusses *ABC* and *DEF* are joined by a pin as shown in Fig. 6.19*a*. The number of members m is smaller than $2n - 3$. If the truss is supported by a pin at *A* and a roller at *F*, the total number of unknowns is $m + 3$. Since $m < 2n - 3$, the number $m + 3$ of unknowns is now smaller than the number $2n$ of equilibrium equations which should be satisfied; the truss is *nonrigid* and will collapse under its own weight. However, if two pins are used to support it, the truss becomes *rigid* and will not collapse (Fig. 6.19*b*). We note that the total number of unknowns is now $m + 4$ and is equal to the number $2n$ of equations. More generally, if the reactions at the supports involve r unknowns, the condition for a compound truss to be statically determinate, rigid, and completely constrained is $m + r = 2n$. However, while necessary, this condition is not sufficient for the equilibrium of a structure which ceases to be rigid when detached from its supports (see Sec. 6.11).

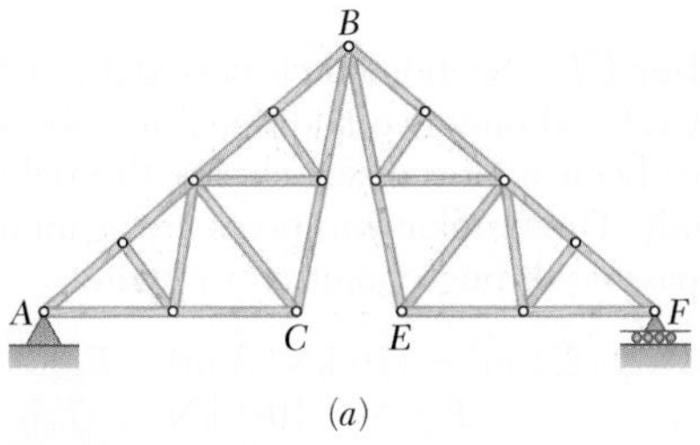

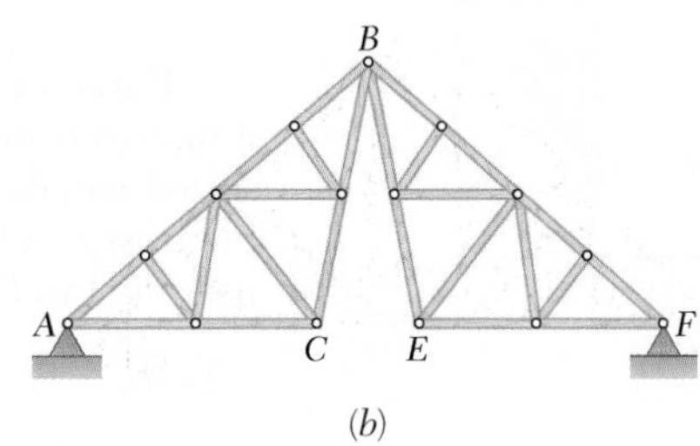

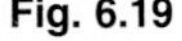
Fig. 6.19

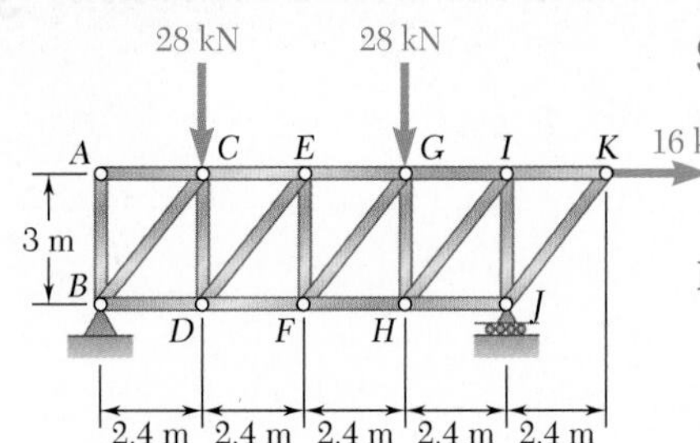

SAMPLE PROBLEM 6.2

Determine the force in members EF and GI of the truss shown.

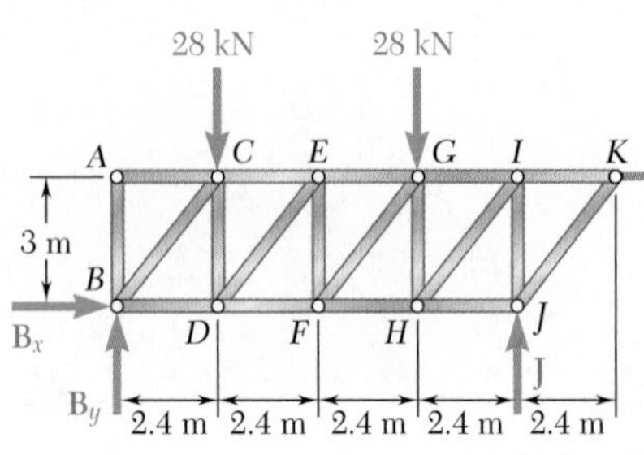

SOLUTION

Free Body: Entire Truss. A free-body diagram of the entire truss is drawn; external forces acting on this free body consist of the applied loads and the reactions at B and J. We write the following equilibrium equations.

$+\circlearrowleft \Sigma M_B = 0$:

$$-(28 \text{ kN})(2.4 \text{ m}) - (28 \text{ kN})(7.2 \text{ m}) - (16 \text{ kN})(3 \text{ m}) + J(9.6 \text{ m}) = 0$$

$$J = +33 \text{ kN} \qquad \mathbf{J} = 33 \text{ kN} \uparrow$$

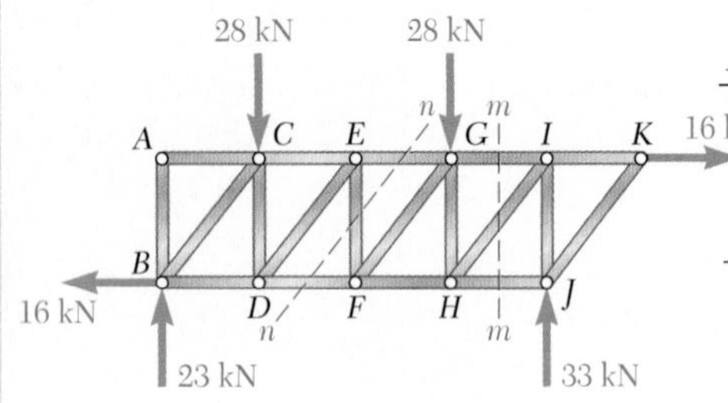

$\xrightarrow{+} \Sigma F_x = 0$: $\qquad B_x + 16 \text{ kN} = 0$

$$B_x = -16 \text{ kN} \qquad \mathbf{B}_x = 16 \text{ kN} \leftarrow$$

$+\circlearrowleft \Sigma M_J = 0$:

$$(28 \text{ kN})(7.2 \text{ m}) + (28 \text{ kN})(2.4 \text{ m}) - (16 \text{ kN})(3 \text{ m}) - B_y(9.6 \text{ m}) = 0$$

$$B_y = +23 \text{ kN} \qquad \mathbf{B}_y = 23 \text{ kN} \uparrow$$

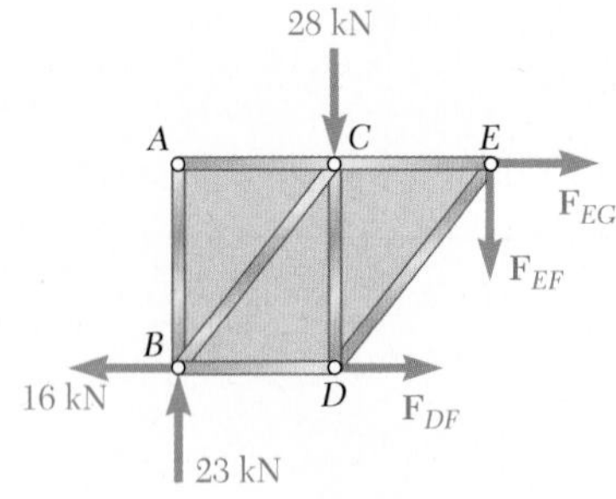

Force in Member EF. Section nn is passed through the truss so that it intersects member EF and only two additional members. After the intersected members have been removed, the left-hand portion of the truss is chosen as a free body. Three unknowns are involved; to eliminate the two horizontal forces, we write

$+\uparrow \Sigma F_y = 0$: $\qquad +23 \text{ kN} - 28 \text{ kN} - F_{EF} = 0$

$$F_{EF} = -5 \text{ kN}$$

The sense of $\mathbf{F}_{EF}$ was chosen assuming member EF to be in tension; the negative sign obtained indicates that the member is in compression.

$$F_{EF} = 5 \text{ kN } C \blacktriangleleft$$

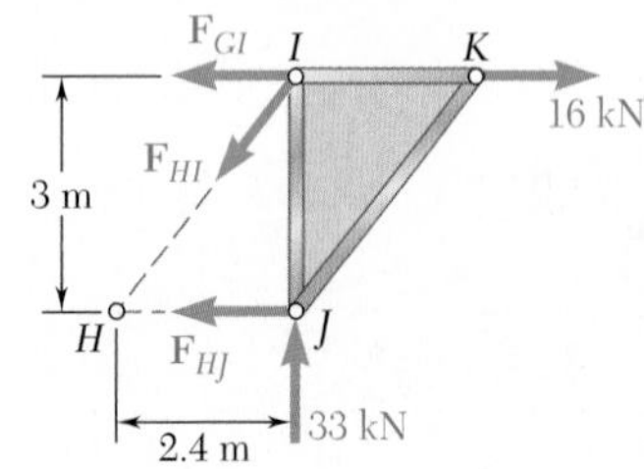

Force in Member GI. Section mm is passed through the truss so that it intersects member GI and only two additional members. After the intersected members have been removed, we choose the right-hand portion of the truss as a free body. Three unknown forces are again involved; to eliminate the two forces passing through point H, we write

$+\circlearrowleft \Sigma M_H = 0$: $\qquad (33 \text{ kN})(2.4 \text{ m}) - (16 \text{ kN})(3 \text{ m}) + F_{GI}(3 \text{ m}) = 0$

$$F_{GI} = -10.4 \text{ kN} \qquad F_{GI} = 10.4 \text{ kN } C \blacktriangleleft$$

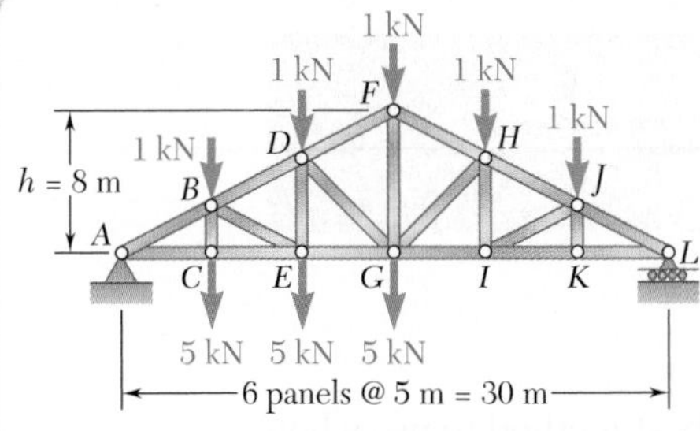

SAMPLE PROBLEM 6.3

Determine the force in members *FH*, *GH*, and *GI* of the roof truss shown.

SOLUTION

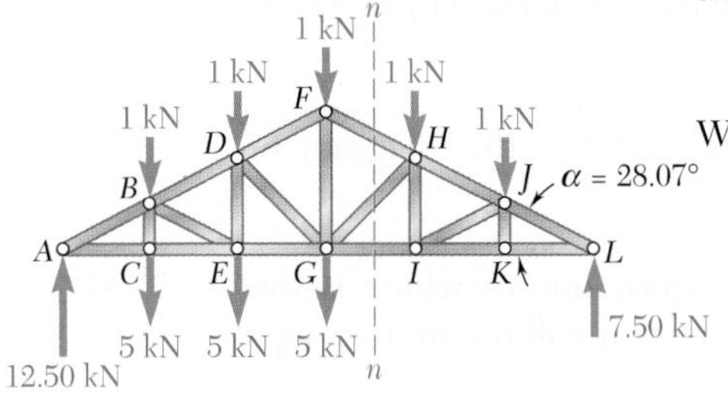

Free Body: Entire Truss. From the free-body diagram of the entire truss, we find the reactions at *A* and *L*:

$$\mathbf{A} = 12.50 \text{ kN}\uparrow \qquad \mathbf{L} = 7.50 \text{ kN}\uparrow$$

We note that

$$\tan \alpha = \frac{FG}{GL} = \frac{8 \text{ m}}{15 \text{ m}} = 0.5333 \qquad \alpha = 28.07°$$

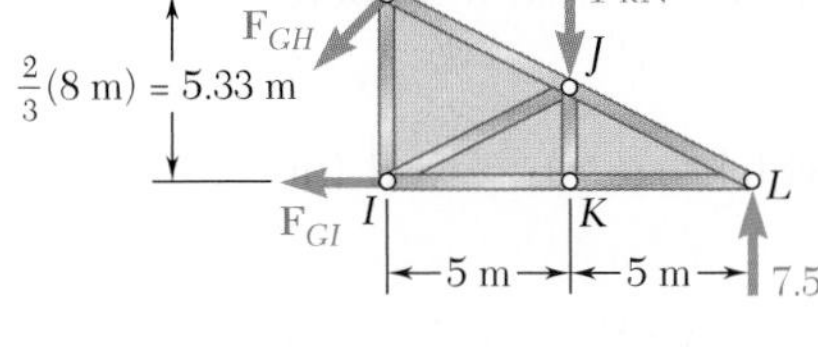

Force in Member *GI*. Section *nn* is passed through the truss as shown. Using the portion *HLI* of the truss as a free body, the value of F_{GI} is obtained by writing

$$+\circlearrowleft\Sigma M_H = 0: \qquad (7.50 \text{ kN})(10 \text{ m}) - (1 \text{ kN})(5 \text{ m}) - F_{GI}(5.33 \text{ m}) = 0$$
$$F_{GI} = +13.13 \text{ kN} \qquad F_{GI} = 13.13 \text{ kN } T \quad ◀$$

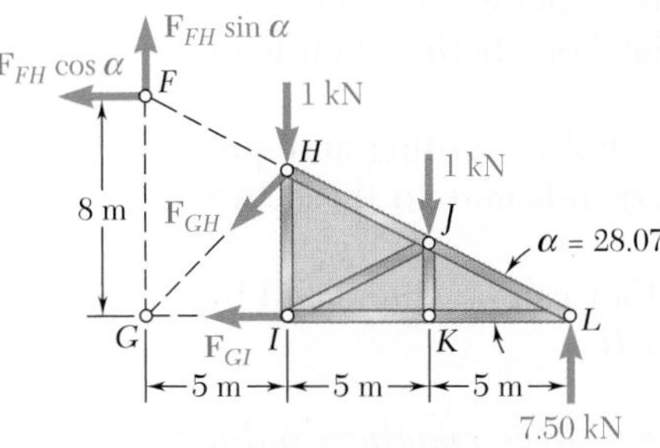

Force in Member *FH*. The value of F_{FH} is obtained from the equation $\Sigma M_G = 0$. We move $\mathbf{F}_{FH}$ along its line of action until it acts at point *F*, where it is resolved into its *x* and *y* components. The moment of $\mathbf{F}_{FH}$ with respect to point *G* is now equal to $(F_{FH} \cos \alpha)(8 \text{ m})$.

$$+\circlearrowleft\Sigma M_G = 0:$$
$$(7.50 \text{ kN})(15 \text{ m}) - (1 \text{ kN})(10 \text{ m}) - (1 \text{ kN})(5 \text{ m}) + (F_{FH} \cos \alpha)(8 \text{ m}) = 0$$
$$F_{FH} = -13.81 \text{ kN} \qquad F_{FH} = 13.81 \text{ kN } C \quad ◀$$

Force in Member *GH*. We first note that

$$\tan \beta = \frac{GI}{HI} = \frac{5 \text{ m}}{\frac{2}{3}(8 \text{ m})} = 0.9375 \qquad \beta = 43.15°$$

1 kN
F_{FH}
H
1 kN
β = 43.15°
J
F_{GH} sin β
L
G
F_{GI}
I
K
F_{GH} cos β
7.50 kN
5 m
5 m
5 m

The value of F_{GH} is then determined by resolving the force $\mathbf{F}_{GH}$ into *x* and *y* components at point *G* and solving the equation $\Sigma M_L = 0$.

$$+\circlearrowleft\Sigma M_L = 0: \qquad (1 \text{ kN})(10 \text{ m}) + (1 \text{ kN})(5 \text{ m}) + (F_{GH} \cos \beta)(15 \text{ m}) = 0$$
$$F_{GH} = -1.371 \text{ kN} \qquad F_{GH} = 1.371 \text{ kN } C \quad ◀$$

SOLVING PROBLEMS ON YOUR OWN

The *method of joints* that you studied earlier is usually the best method to use when the forces *in all the members* of a simple truss are to be found. However, the method of sections, which was covered in this lesson, is more effective when the force *in only one member* or the forces *in a very few members* of a simple truss are desired. The method of sections must also be used when the truss *is not a simple truss.*

A. ***To determine the force in a given truss member*** by the method of sections, you should follow these steps.

1. ***Draw a free-body diagram of the entire truss,*** and use this diagram to determine the reactions at the supports.

2. ***Pass a section through three members of the truss,*** one of which is the desired member. After you have removed these members, you will obtain two separate portions of the truss.

3. ***Select one of the two portions of the truss you have obtained, and draw its free-body diagram.*** This diagram should include the external forces applied to the selected portion as well as the forces exerted on it by the intersected members before these members were removed.

4. ***You can now write three equilibrium equations*** which can be solved for the forces in the three intersected members.

5. ***An alternative approach is to write a single equation,*** which can be solved for the force in the desired member. To do so, first observe whether the forces exerted by the other two members on the free body are parallel or whether their lines of action intersect.

   a. ***If these forces are parallel,*** they can be eliminated by writing an equilibrium equation involving *components in a direction perpendicular* to these two forces.

   b. ***If their lines of action intersect at a point H,*** they can be eliminated by writing an equilibrium equation involving *moments about H.*

6. ***Keep in mind that the section you use must intersect three members only.*** This is because the equilibrium equations in step 4 can be solved for three unknowns only. However, you can pass a section through more than three members to find the force in one of those members if you can write an equilibrium equation containing only that force as an unknown. Examples of such special situations are found in Probs. 6.60 through 6.63. Also, although we have considered separately the method of joints and the method of sections, you should recognize that these two techniques can be used sequentially to determine the force in a given member of a truss when the force cannot be found using a single section.

B. In Probs. 6.64–6.67 you will be asked to determine the tensile forces in the active counters of trusses (the forces in the other counters are zero). To determine the forces in each pair of counters, begin by determining the reactions at the supports and then pass a section through the truss which passes through the pair of counters. After selecting the portion of the truss to be analyzed and drawing its free-body diagram, next *assume* which counter is acting and use an equilibrium equation to determine the force in that counter. If the force is tensile, your assumption was correct; if not, you must repeat the analysis using the other counter of the pair as the active counter. However, you can often deduce which is the active counter by examining the free-body diagram, as a mental summation of forces of the external forces (loads and reactions at the supports) will imply which counter must act for equilibrium to exist (remembering that the force in a counter can only be tensile).

C. About completely constrained and statically determinate trusses:

1. First note that any simple truss which is simply supported is a completely constrained and statically determinate truss.

2. To determine whether any other truss is or is not completely constrained and statically determinate, you first count the number m of its members, the number n of its joints, and the number r of the reaction components at its supports. You then compare the sum $m + r$ representing the number of unknowns and the product $2n$ representing the number of available independent equilibrium equations.

a. If $m + r < 2n$, there are fewer unknowns than equations. Thus, some of the equations cannot be satisfied; the truss is only *partially constrained.*

b. If $m + r > 2n$, there are more unknowns than equations. Thus, some of the unknowns cannot be determined; the truss is *statically indeterminate.*

c. If $m + r = 2n$, there are as many unknowns as there are equations. This, however, does not mean that all the unknowns can be determined and that all the equations can be satisfied. To find out whether the truss is *completely* or *improperly constrained,* you should try to determine the reactions at its supports and the forces in its members. If all can be found, the truss is *completely constrained and statically determinate.*

Problems

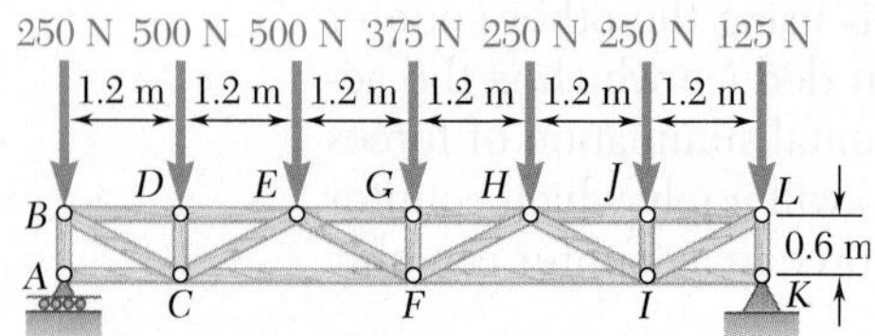

Fig. P6.42 and P6.43

6.42 A floor truss is loaded as shown. Determine the force in members *CF*, *EF*, and *EG*.

6.43 A floor truss is loaded as shown. Determine the force in members *FI*, *HI*, and *HJ*.

6.44 A vaulted roof truss is loaded as shown. Determine the force in members *BD*, *BE*, and *CE*.

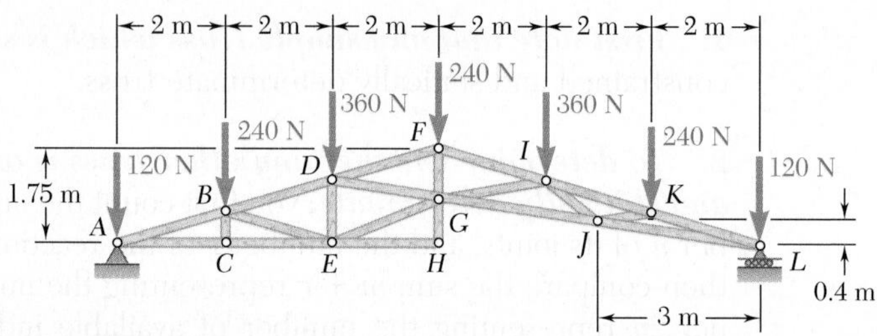

Fig. P6.44 and *P6.45*

6.45 A vaulted roof truss is loaded as shown. Determine the force in members *GJ*, *IJ*, and *IK*.

6.46 A parallel chord Pratt truss is loaded as shown. Determine the force in members *CE*, *DE*, and *DF*.

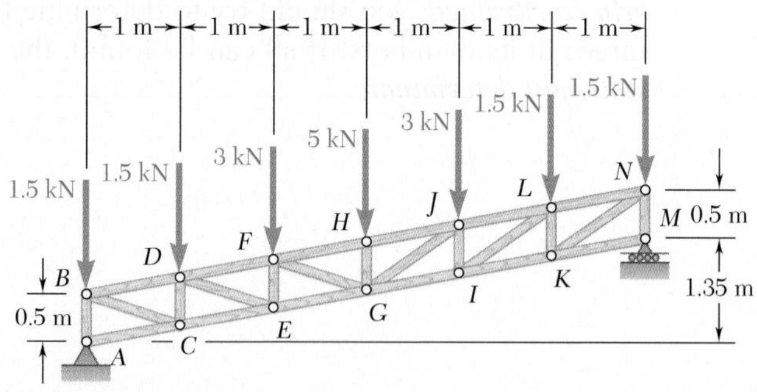

Fig. P6.46 and *P6.47*

6.47 A parallel chord Pratt truss is loaded as shown. Determine the force in members *GI*, *GJ*, and *HJ*.

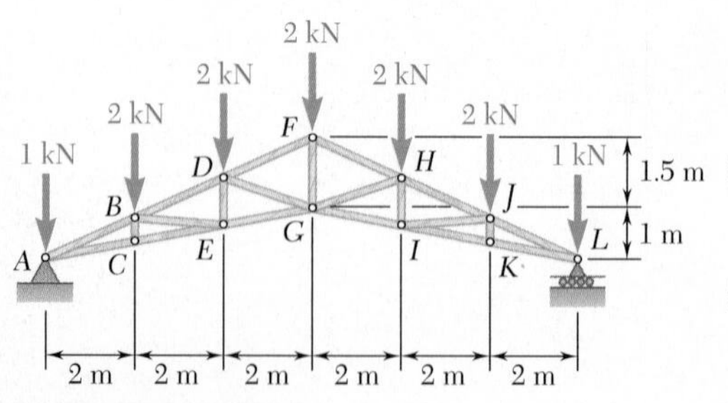

Fig. P6.48 and P6.49

6.48 A Howe scissors roof truss is loaded as shown. Determine the force in members *DF*, *DG*, and *EG*.

6.49 A Howe scissors roof truss is loaded as shown. Determine the force in members *GI*, *HI*, and *HJ*.

6.50 A Fink roof truss is loaded as shown. Determine the force in members *BD*, *CD*, and *CE*.

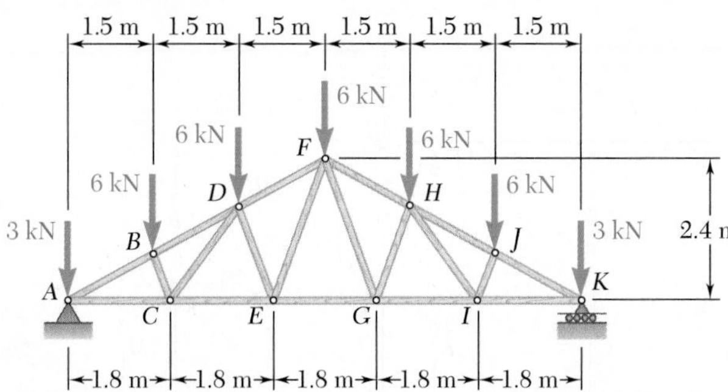

Fig. P6.50 and P6.51

6.51 A Fink roof truss is loaded as shown. Determine the force in members *FH*, *FG*, and *EG*.

6.52 A roof truss is loaded as shown. Determine the force in members *CE*, *DE*, and *EF*.

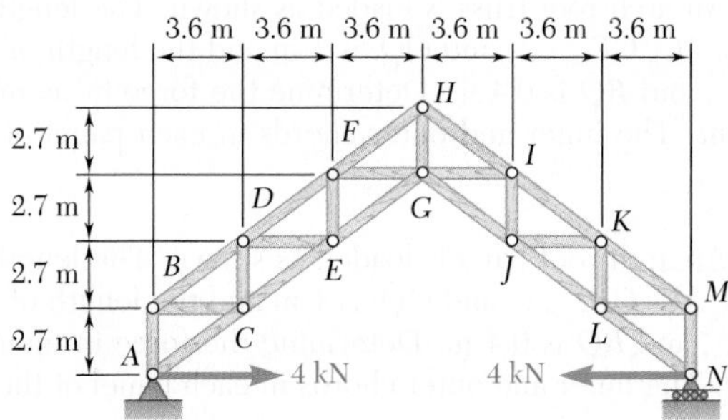

Fig. P6.52 and P6.53

6.53 A roof truss is loaded as shown. Determine the force in members *GI*, *HI*, and *IJ*.

6.54 A roof truss is loaded as shown. Determine the force in members *FH*, *GJ*, and *GI*.

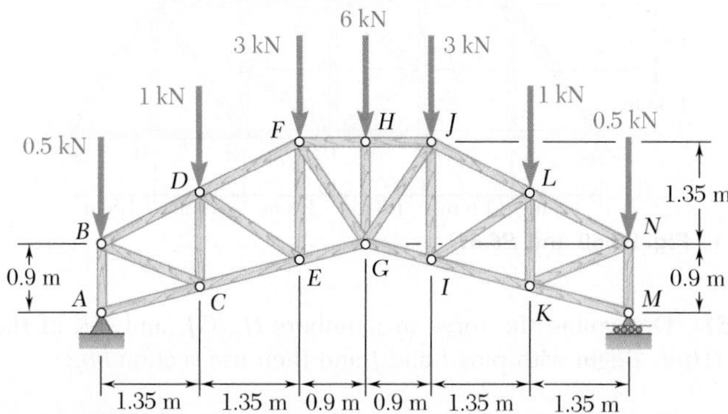

Fig. *P6.54*

6.55 A barrel vault truss is loaded as shown. Knowing that the length of the bottom chords *DF*, *FH*, . . . , and *QS* is 0.9 m, determine the force in members *IK*, *JL*, and *JM*.

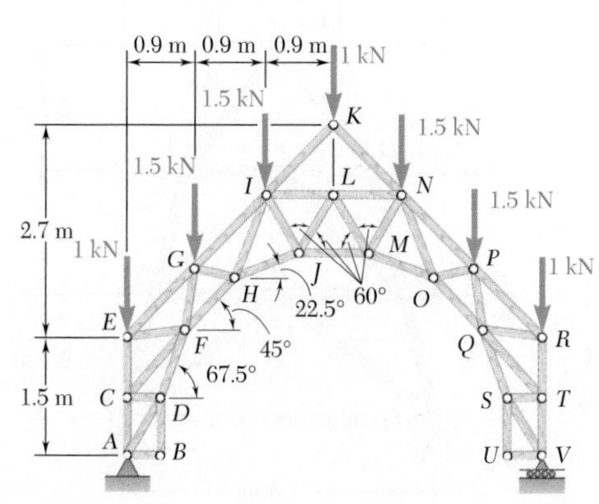

Fig. P6.55

6.56 A vaulted roof truss is loaded as shown. Determine the force in members *BE*, *CE*, and *DF*.

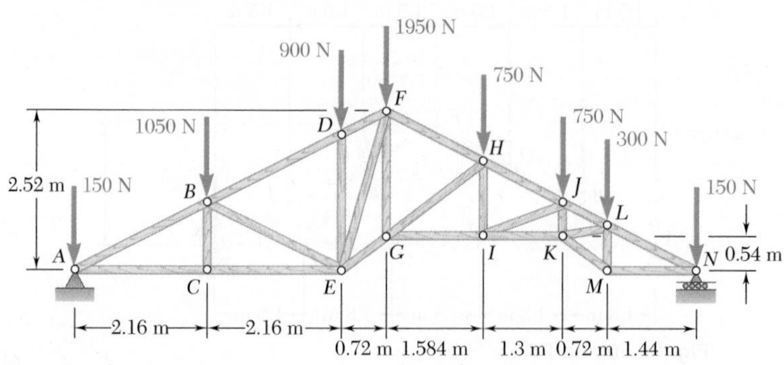

Fig. *P6.56* and P6.57

6.57 A vaulted roof truss is loaded as shown. Determine the force in members *HJ*, *IJ*, and *GI*.

***6.58** An arch roof truss is loaded as shown. The length of all of the outer chords, *AC*, *CE*, . . . , and *OQ*, is 1 m and the length of the webs *AB*, *CD*, *EF*, . . . , and *RQ* is 0.4 m. Determine the force in members *CE*, *CF*, and *DF*. (*Hint:* The inner and outer chords in each panel of the truss are not parallel.)

****6.59*** An arch roof truss is loaded as shown. The length of all of the outer chords, *AC*, *CE*, . . . , and *OQ*, is 1 m and the length of the webs *AB*, *CD*, *EF*, . . . , and *RQ* is 0.4 m. Determine the force in members *GI*, *GJ*, and *IJ*. (*Hint:* The inner and outer chords in each panel of the truss are not parallel.)

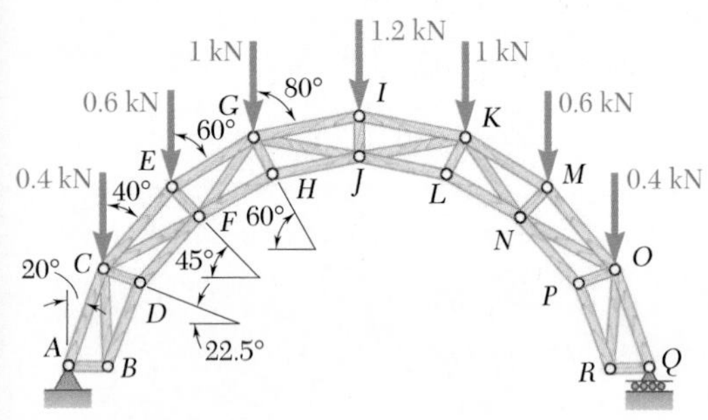

Fig. P6.58 and *P6.59*

6.60 Determine the force in members *DG* and *FH* of the truss shown. (*Hint:* Use section *aa*.)

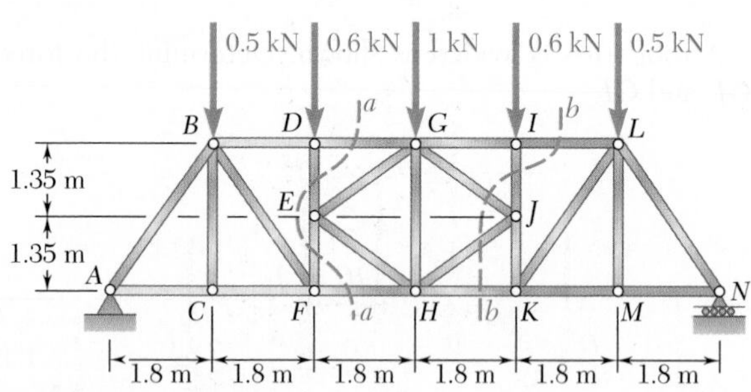

Fig. P6.60 and *P6.61*

6.61 Determine the force in members *IL*, *GJ*, and *HK* of the truss shown. (*Hint:* Begin with pins *I* and *J* and then use section *bb*.)

6.62 Determine the force in members *IK* and *HK* of the truss shown. (*Hint:* Use section *aa*.)

6.63 Determine the force in members *FI* and *EG* of the truss shown. (*Hint:* Use section *bb*.)

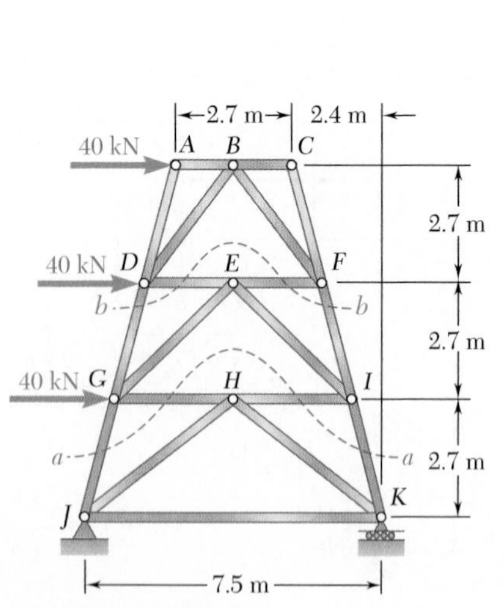

Fig. P6.62 and P6.63

6.64 The diagonal members in the center panel of the truss shown are very slender and can act only in tension; such members are known as *counters.* Determine the force in members BD and CE and in the counter which is acting when $P = 12$ kN.

6.65 Solve Prob. 6.64 when $P = 6$ kN.

***6.66* and 6.67** The diagonal members in the center panels of the truss shown are very slender and can act only in tension; such members are known as *counters*. Determine the force in member DE and in the counters which are acting under the given loading.

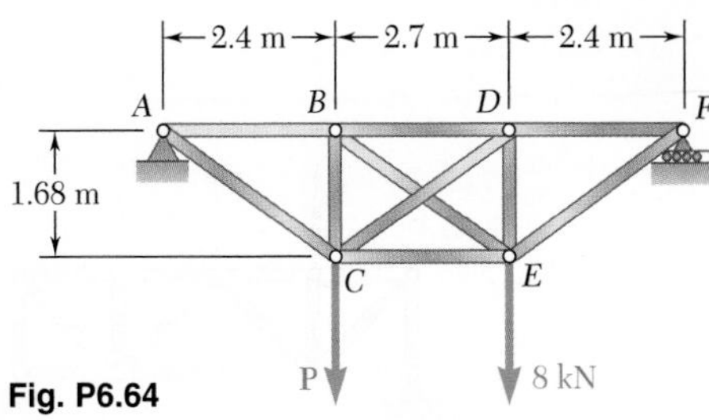

Fig. P6.64

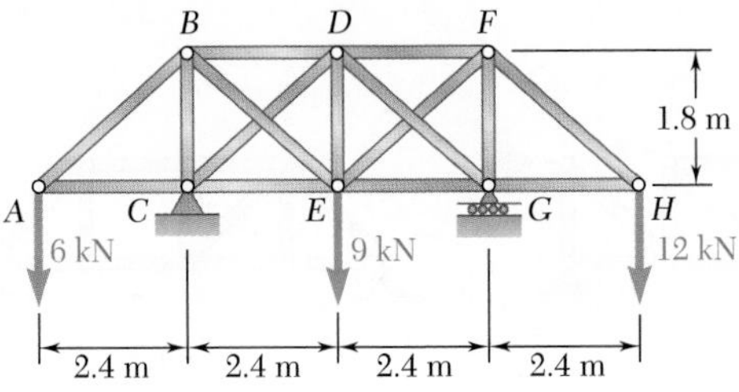

Fig. *P6.66*

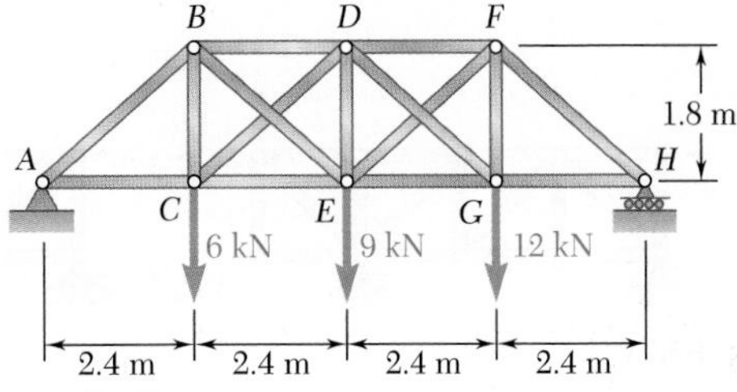

Fig. P6.67

6.68 The diagonal members CF and DE of the truss shown are very slender and can act only in tension; such members are known as *counters*. Determine the force in members CE and DF and in the counter which is acting when $P = 0$.

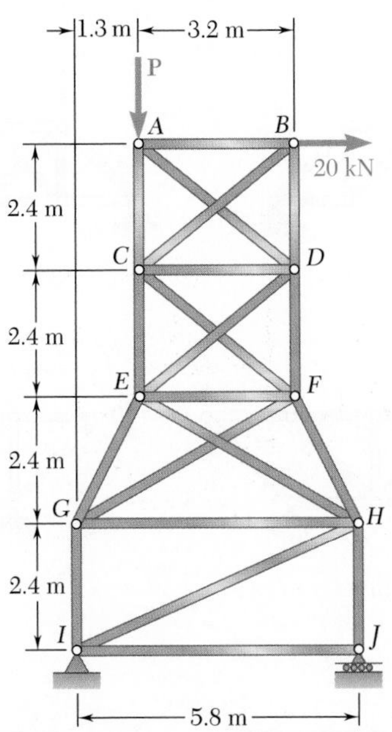

Fig. P6.68 and *P6.69*

6.69 The diagonal members EH and FG of the truss shown are very slender and can act only in tension; such members are known as *counters*. Determine the force in members EG and FH and in the counter which is acting when $P = 40$ kN.

6.70 through 6.75 Classify each of the structures shown as completely, partially, or improperly constrained; if completely constrained, further classify it as statically determinate or indeterminate. (All members can act both in tension and in compression.)

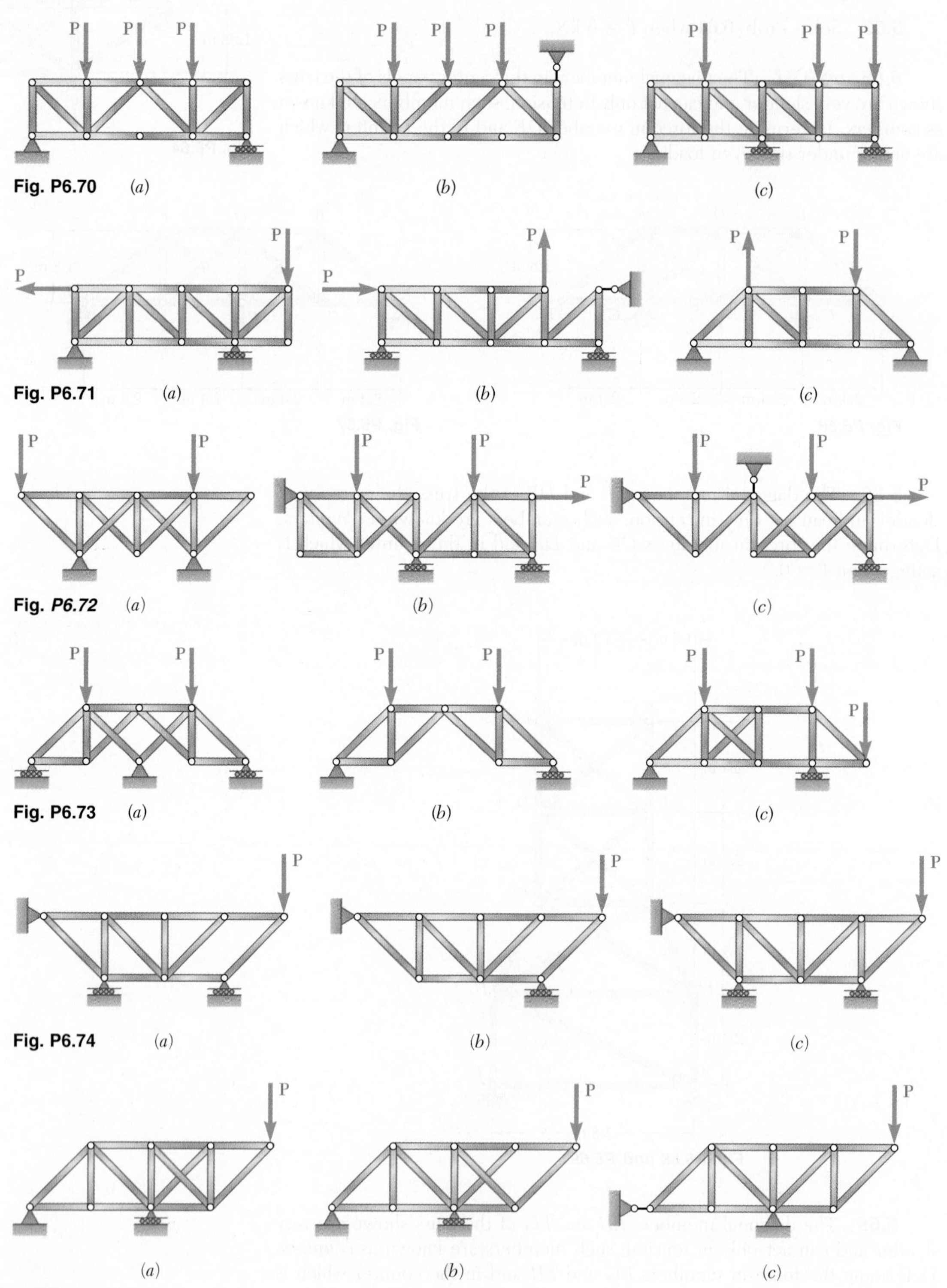

Fig. P6.70 (a) (b) (c)

Fig. P6.71 (a) (b) (c)

Fig. P6.72 (a) (b) (c)

Fig. P6.73 (a) (b) (c)

Fig. P6.74 (a) (b) (c)

(a) (b) (c)

Fig. P6.75

FRAMES AND MACHINES

6.9. STRUCTURES CONTAINING MULTIFORCE MEMBERS

Under trusses, we have considered structures consisting entirely of pins and straight two-force members. The forces acting on the two-force members were known to be directed along the members themselves. We now consider structures in which at least one of the members is a *multiforce* member, that is, a member acted upon by three or more forces. These forces will generally not be directed along the members on which they act; their direction is unknown, and they should be represented therefore by two unknown components.

Frames and machines are structures containing multiforce members. *Frames* are designed to support loads and are usually stationary, fully constrained structures. *Machines* are designed to transmit and modify forces; they may or may not be stationary and will always contain moving parts.

6.10. ANALYSIS OF A FRAME

As a first example of analysis of a frame, the crane described in Sec. 6.1, which carries a given load W (Fig. 6.20*a*), will again be considered. The free-body diagram of the entire frame is shown in Fig. 6.20*b*. This diagram can be used to determine the external forces acting on the frame. Summing moments about A, we first determine the force $\mathbf{T}$ exerted by the cable; summing x and y components, we then determine the components $\mathbf{A}_x$ and $\mathbf{A}_y$ of the reaction at the pin A.

In order to determine the internal forces holding the various parts of a frame together, we must dismember the frame and draw a free-body diagram for each of its component parts (Fig. 6.20*c*). First, the two-force members should be considered. In this frame, member BE is the only two-force member. The forces acting at each end of this member must have the same magnitude, same line of action, and opposite sense (Sec. 4.6). They are therefore directed along BE and will be denoted, respectively, by $\mathbf{F}_{BE}$ and $-\mathbf{F}_{BE}$. Their sense will be arbitrarily assumed as shown in Fig. 6.20*c*; later the sign obtained for the common magnitude F_{BE} of the two forces will confirm or deny this assumption.

Next, we consider the multiforce members, that is, the members which are acted upon by three or more forces. According to Newton's third law, the force exerted at B by member BE on member AD must be equal and opposite to the force $\mathbf{F}_{BE}$ exerted by AD on BE. Similarly, the force exerted at E by member BE on member CF must be equal and opposite to the force $-\mathbf{F}_{BE}$ exerted by CF on BE. Thus the forces that the two-force member BE exerts on AD and CF are, respectively, equal to $-\mathbf{F}_{BE}$ and $\mathbf{F}_{BE}$; they have the same magnitude F_{BE} and opposite sense, and should be directed as shown in Fig. 6.20*c*.

At C two multiforce members are connected. Since neither the direction nor the magnitude of the forces acting at C is known, these forces will be represented by their x and y components. The components $\mathbf{C}_x$ and $\mathbf{C}_y$ of the force acting on member AD will be arbitrarily directed to the right and upward. Since, according to Newton's third law, the forces exerted by member CF on AD and by member AD on

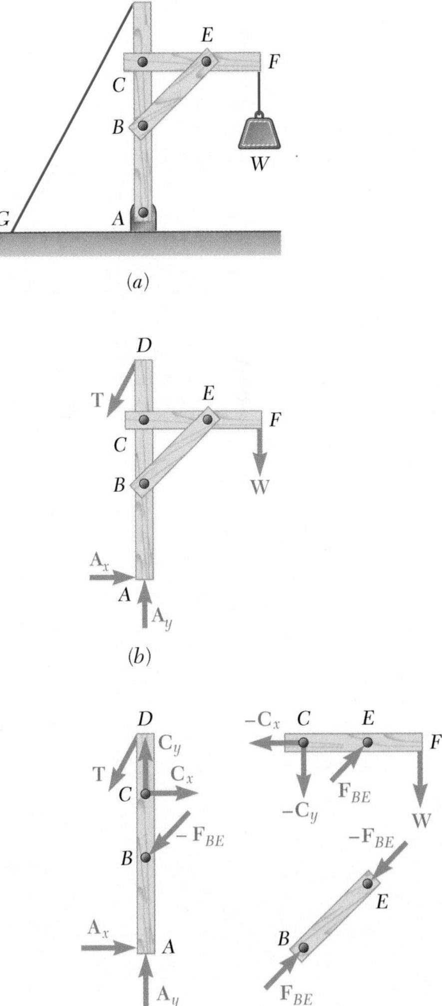

Fig. 6.20

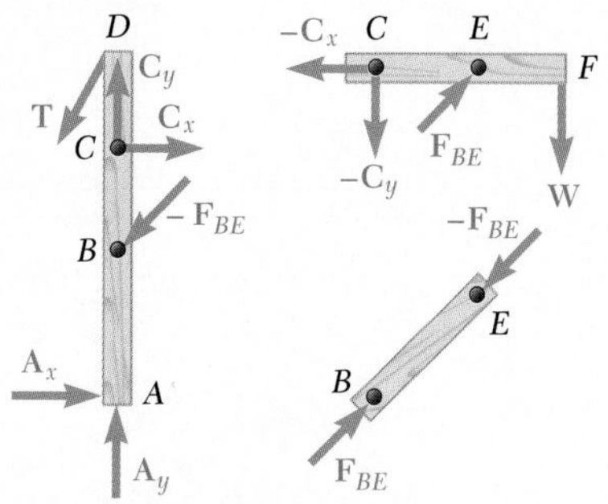

Fig. 6.20*c* (*repeated*)

CF are equal and opposite, the components of the force acting on member *CF* *must* be directed to the left and downward; they will be denoted, respectively, by $-\mathbf{C}_x$ and $-\mathbf{C}_y$. Whether the force $\mathbf{C}_x$ is actually directed to the right and the force $-\mathbf{C}_x$ is actually directed to the left will be determined later from the sign of their common magnitude C_x, a plus sign indicating that the assumption made was correct, and a minus sign that it was wrong. The free-body diagrams of the multiforce members are completed by showing the external forces acting at *A*, *D*, and *F*.†

The internal forces can now be determined by considering the free-body diagram of either of the two multiforce members. Choosing the free-body diagram of *CF*, for example, we write the equations $\Sigma M_C = 0$, $\Sigma M_E = 0$, and $\Sigma F_x = 0$, which yield the values of the magnitudes F_{BE}, C_y, and C_x, respectively. These values can be checked by verifying that member *AD* is also in equilibrium.

It should be noted that the pins in Fig. 6.20 were assumed to form an integral part of one of the two members they connected and so it was not necessary to show their free-body diagrams. This assumption can always be used to simplify the analysis of frames and machines. When a pin connects three or more members, however, or when a pin connects a support and two or more members, or when a load is applied to a pin, a clear decision must be made in choosing the member to which the pin will be assumed to belong. (If multiforce members are involved, the pin should be attached to one of these members.) The various forces exerted on the pin should then be clearly identified. This is illustrated in Sample Prob. 6.6.

6.11. FRAMES WHICH CEASE TO BE RIGID WHEN DETACHED FROM THEIR SUPPORTS

The crane analyzed in Sec. 6.10 was so constructed that it could keep the same shape without the help of its supports; it was therefore considered as a rigid body. Many frames, however, will collapse if detached from their supports; such frames cannot be considered as rigid bodies. Consider, for example, the frame shown in Fig. 6.21*a*, which consists of two members *AC* and *CB* carrying loads **P** and **Q** at their midpoints; the members are supported by pins at *A* and *B* and are connected by a pin at *C*. If detached from its supports, this frame will not maintain its shape; it should therefore be considered as made of *two distinct rigid parts AC* and *CB*.

†It is not strictly necessary to use a minus sign to distinguish the force exerted by one member on another from the equal and opposite force exerted by the second member on the first, since the two forces belong to different free-body diagrams and thus cannot easily be confused. In the Sample Problems, the same symbol is used to represent equal and opposite forces which are applied to different free bodies. It should be noted that, under these conditions, the sign obtained for a given force component will not directly relate the sense of that component to the sense of the corresponding coordinate axis. Rather, a positive sign will indicate that *the sense assumed for that component in the free-body diagram* is correct, and a negative sign will indicate that it is wrong.

The equations $\Sigma F_x = 0$, $\Sigma F_y = 0$, and $\Sigma M = 0$ (about any given point) express the conditions for the *equilibrium of a rigid body* (Chap. 4); we should use them, therefore, in connection with the free-body diagrams of rigid bodies, namely, the free-body diagrams of members AC and CB (Fig. 6.21*b*). Since these members are multiforce members, and since pins are used at the supports and at the connection, the reactions at A and B and the forces at C will each be represented by two components. In accordance with Newton's third law, the components of the force exerted by CB on AC and the components of the force exerted by AC on CB will be represented by vectors of the same magnitude and opposite sense; thus, if the first pair of components consists of $\mathbf{C}_x$ and $\mathbf{C}_y$, the second pair will be represented by $-\mathbf{C}_x$ and $-\mathbf{C}_y$. We note that four unknown force components act on free body AC, while only three independent equations can be used to express that the body is in equilibrium; similarly, four unknowns, but only three equations, are associated with CB. However, only six different unknowns are involved in the analysis of the two members, and altogether six equations are available to express that the members are in equilibrium. Writing $\Sigma M_A = 0$ for free body AC and $\Sigma M_B = 0$ for CB, we obtain two simultaneous equations which may be solved for the common magnitude C_x of the components $\mathbf{C}_x$ and $-\mathbf{C}_x$ and for the common magnitude C_y of the components $\mathbf{C}_y$ and $-\mathbf{C}_y$. We then write $\Sigma F_x = 0$ and $\Sigma F_y = 0$ for each of the two free bodies, obtaining, successively, the magnitudes A_x, A_y, B_x, and B_y.

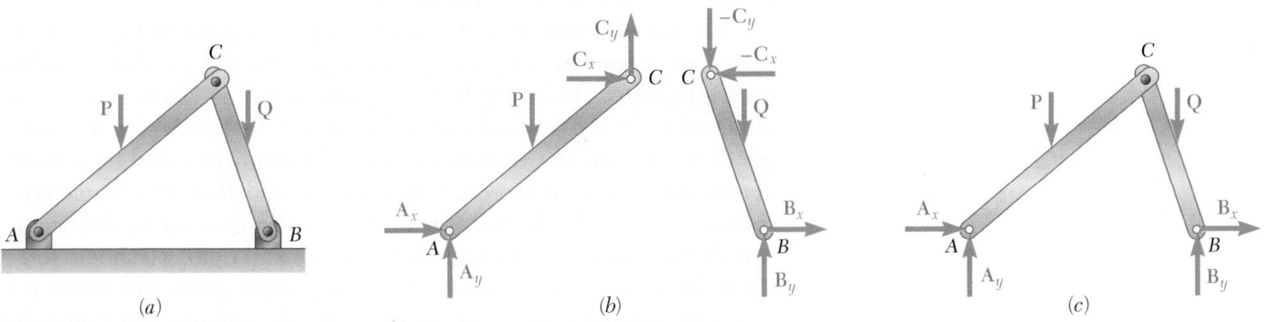

Fig. 6.21

It can now be observed that since the equations of equilibrium $\Sigma F_x = 0$, $\Sigma F_y = 0$, and $\Sigma M = 0$ (about any given point) are satisfied by the forces acting on free body AC, and since they are also satisfied by the forces acting on free body CB, they must be satisfied when the forces acting on the two free bodies are considered simultaneously. Since the internal forces at C cancel each other, we find that the equations of equilibrium must be satisfied by the external forces shown on the free-body diagram of the frame ACB itself (Fig. 6.21*c*), although the frame is not a rigid body. These equations can be used to determine some of the components of the reactions at A and B. We will also find, however, that *the reactions cannot be completely determined from the free-body diagram of the whole frame*. It is thus

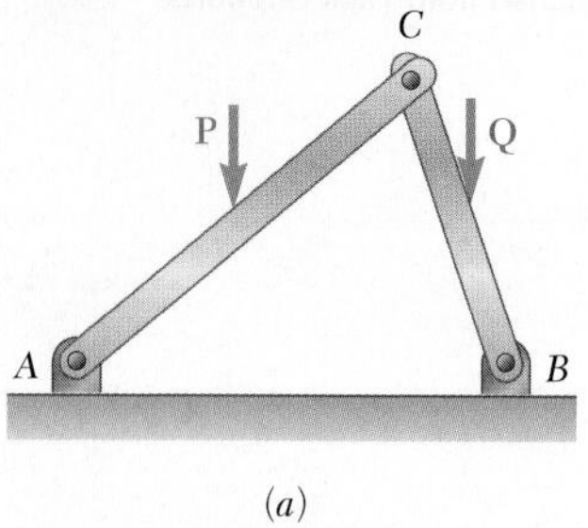

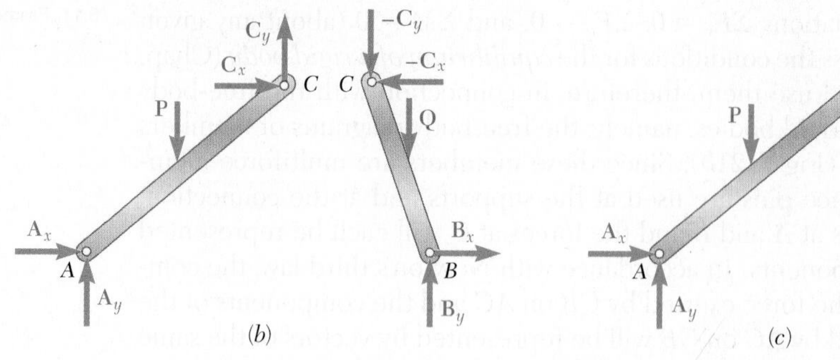

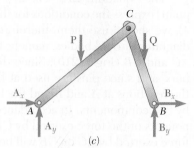

Fig. 6.21 (*repeated*)

necessary to dismember the frame and to consider the free-body diagrams of its component parts (Fig. 6.21*b*), even when we are interested in determining external reactions only. This is because the equilibrium equations obtained for free body *ACB are necessary conditions* for the equilibrium of a nonrigid structure, *but are not sufficient conditions.*

The method of solution outlined in the second paragraph of this section involved simultaneous equations. A more efficient method is now presented, which utilizes the free body *ACB* as well as the free bodies *AC* and *CB*. Writing $\Sigma M_A = 0$ and $\Sigma M_B = 0$ for free body *ACB*, we obtain B_y and A_y. Writing $\Sigma M_C = 0$, $\Sigma F_x = 0$, and $\Sigma F_y = 0$ for free body *AC*, we obtain, successively, A_x, C_x, and C_y. Finally, writing $\Sigma F_x = 0$ for *ACB*, we obtain B_x.

We noted above that the analysis of the frame of Fig. 6.21 involves six unknown force components and six independent equilibrium equations. (The equilibrium equations for the whole frame were obtained from the original six equations and, therefore, are not independent.) Moreover, we checked that all unknowns could be actually determined and that all equations could be satisfied. The frame considered is *statically determinate and rigid.*† In general, to determine whether a structure is statically determinate and rigid, we should draw a free-body diagram for each of its component parts and count the reactions and internal forces involved. We should also determine the number of independent equilibrium equations (excluding equations expressing the equilibrium of the whole structure or of groups of component parts already analyzed). If there are more unknowns than equations, the structure is *statically indeterminate*. If there are fewer unknowns than equations, the structure is *nonrigid*. If there are as many unknowns as equations, *and if all unknowns can be determined and all equations satisfied* under general loading conditions, the structure is *statically determinate and rigid*. If, however, due to an *improper arrangement* of members and supports, all unknowns cannot be determined and all equations cannot be satisfied, the structure is *statically indeterminate and nonrigid.*

†The word *rigid* is used here to indicate that the frame will maintain its shape as long as it remains attached to its supports.

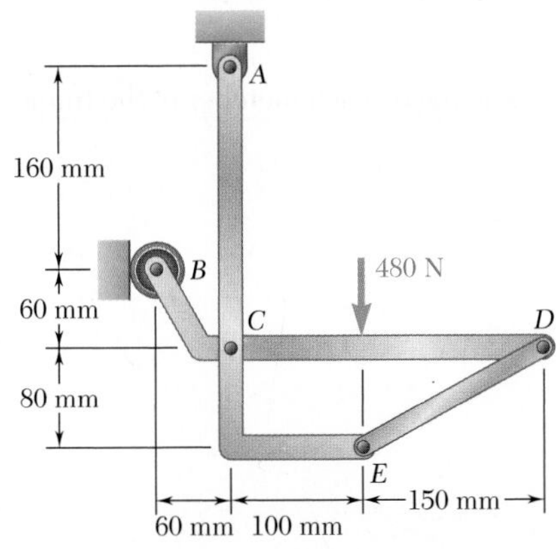

SAMPLE PROBLEM 6.4

In the frame shown, members ACE and BCD are connected by a pin at C and by the link DE. For the loading shown, determine the force in link DE and the components of the force exerted at C on member BCD.

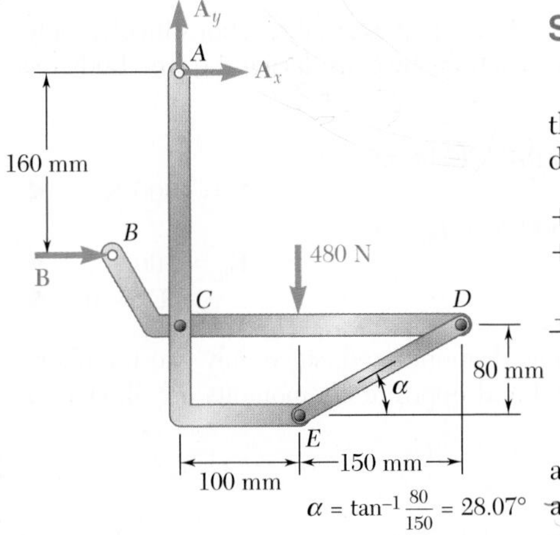

SOLUTION

Free Body: Entire Frame. Since the external reactions involve only three unknowns, we compute the reactions by considering the free-body diagram of the entire frame.

$+\uparrow\Sigma F_y = 0$: $\quad A_y - 480\text{ N} = 0 \quad A_y = +480\text{ N} \quad \mathbf{A}_y = 480\text{ N}\uparrow$

$+\circlearrowleft\Sigma M_A = 0$: $\quad -(480\text{ N})(100\text{ mm}) + B(160\text{ mm}) = 0$

$B = +300\text{ N} \quad \mathbf{B} = 300\text{ N}\rightarrow$

$\xrightarrow{+}\Sigma F_x = 0$: $\quad B + A_x = 0$

$300\text{ N} + A_x = 0 \quad A_x = -300\text{ N} \quad \mathbf{A}_x = 300\text{ N}\leftarrow$

Members. We now dismember the frame. Since only two members are connected at C, the components of the unknown forces acting on ACE and BCD are, respectively, equal and opposite and are assumed directed as shown. We assume that link DE is in tension and exerts equal and opposite forces at D and E, directed as shown.

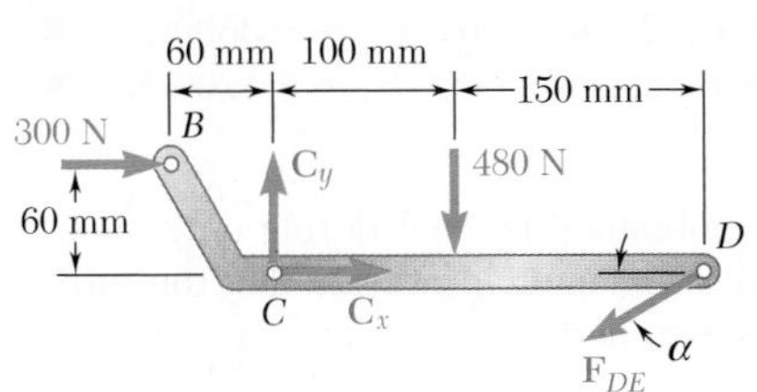

Free Body: Member BCD. Using the free body BCD, we write

$+\circlearrowleft\Sigma M_C = 0$:

$$-(F_{DE}\sin\alpha)(250\text{ mm}) - (300\text{ N})(80\text{ mm}) - (480\text{ N})(100\text{ mm}) = 0$$

$$F_{DE} = -561\text{ N} \qquad F_{DE} = 561\text{ N } C \quad ◀$$

$\xrightarrow{+}\Sigma F_x = 0$: $\quad C_x - F_{DE}\cos\alpha + 300\text{ N} = 0$

$C_x - (-561\text{ N})\cos 28.07° + 300\text{ N} = 0 \qquad C_x = -795\text{ N}$

$+\uparrow\Sigma F_y = 0$: $\quad C_y - F_{DE}\sin\alpha - 480\text{ N} = 0$

$C_y - (-561\text{ N})\sin 28.07° - 480\text{ N} = 0 \qquad C_y = +216\text{ N}$

From the signs obtained for C_x and C_y we conclude that the force components $\mathbf{C}_x$ and $\mathbf{C}_y$ exerted on member BCD are directed, respectively, to the left and up. We have

$$\mathbf{C}_x = 795\text{ N}\leftarrow,\ \mathbf{C}_y = 216\text{ N}\uparrow \quad ◀$$

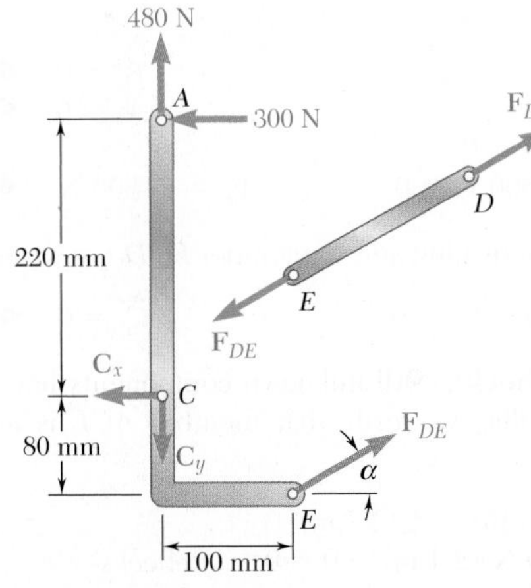

Free Body: Member ACE **(Check).** The computations are checked by considering the free body ACE. For example,

$$+\circlearrowleft\Sigma M_A = (F_{DE}\cos\alpha)(300\text{ mm}) + (F_{DE}\sin\alpha)(100\text{ mm}) - C_x(220\text{ mm})$$
$$= (-561\cos\alpha)(300) + (-561\sin\alpha)(100) - (-795)(220) = 0$$

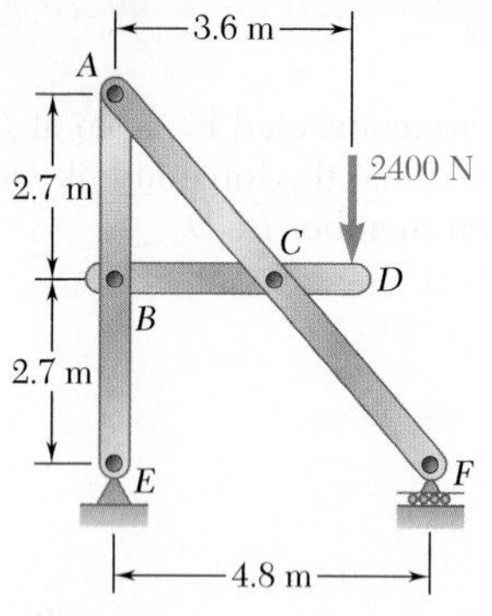

SAMPLE PROBLEM 6.5

Determine the components of the forces acting on each member of the frame shown.

SOLUTION

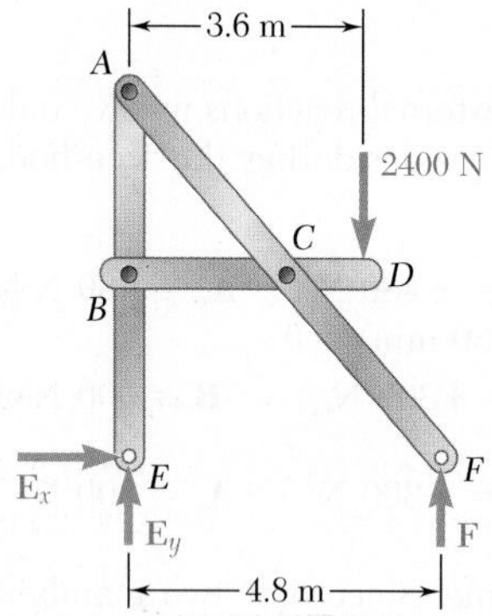

Free Body: Entire Frame. Since the external reactions involve only three unknowns, we compute the reactions by considering the free-body diagram of the entire frame.

$+\circlearrowleft\Sigma M_E = 0$: $\quad -(2400 \text{ N})(3.6 \text{ m}) + F(4.8 \text{ m}) = 0$
$F = +1800 \text{ N}$ $\qquad$ $\mathbf{F} = 1800 \text{ N}\uparrow$ ◀

$+\uparrow\Sigma F_y = 0$: $\quad -2400 \text{ N} + 1800 \text{ N} + E_y = 0$
$E_y = +600 \text{ N}$ $\qquad$ $\mathbf{E}_y = 600 \text{ N}\uparrow$ ◀

$\overset{+}{\rightarrow}\Sigma F_x = 0$: $\quad E_x = 0$ $\qquad$ $\mathbf{E}_x = 0$ ◀

Members. The frame is now dismembered; since only two members are connected at each joint, equal and opposite components are shown on each member at each joint.

Free Body: Member BCD

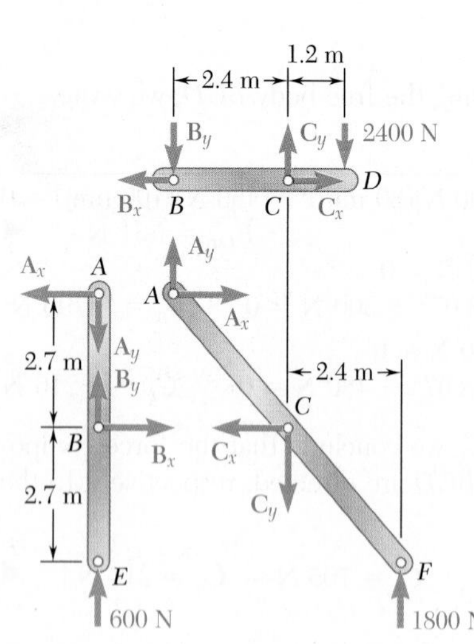

$+\circlearrowleft\Sigma M_B = 0$: $\quad -(2400 \text{ N})(3.6 \text{ m}) + C_y(2.4 \text{ m}) = 0$ $\qquad C_y = +3600 \text{ N}$ ◀
$+\circlearrowleft\Sigma M_C = 0$: $\quad -(2400 \text{ N})(1.2 \text{ m}) + B_y(2.4 \text{ m}) = 0$ $\qquad B_y = +1200 \text{ N}$ ◀
$\overset{+}{\rightarrow}\Sigma F_x = 0$: $\quad -B_x + C_x = 0$

We note that neither B_x nor C_x can be obtained by considering only member *BCD*. The positive values obtained for B_y and C_y indicate that the force components $\mathbf{B}_y$ and $\mathbf{C}_y$ are directed as assumed.

Free Body: Member ABE

$+\circlearrowleft\Sigma M_A = 0$: $\quad B_x(2.7 \text{ m}) = 0$ $\qquad B_x = 0$ ◀
$\overset{+}{\rightarrow}\Sigma F_x = 0$: $\quad +B_x - A_x = 0$ $\qquad A_x = 0$ ◀
$+\uparrow\Sigma F_y = 0$: $\quad -A_y + B_y + 600 \text{ N} = 0$
$-A_y + 1200 \text{ N} + 600 \text{ N} = 0$ $\qquad A_y = +1800 \text{ N}$ ◀

Free Body: Member BCD. Returning now to member *BCD*, we write

$\overset{+}{\rightarrow}\Sigma F_x = 0$: $\quad -B_x + C_x = 0 \qquad 0 + C_x = 0$ $\qquad C_x = 0$ ◀

Free Body: Member ACF (Check). All unknown components have now been found; to check the results, we verify that member *ACF* is in equilibrium.

$$+\circlearrowleft\Sigma M_C = (1800 \text{ N})(2.4 \text{ m}) - A_y(2.4 \text{ m}) - A_x(2.7 \text{ m})$$
$$= (1800 \text{ N})(2.4 \text{ m}) - (1800 \text{ N})(2.4 \text{ m}) - 0 = 0 \qquad \text{(checks)}$$

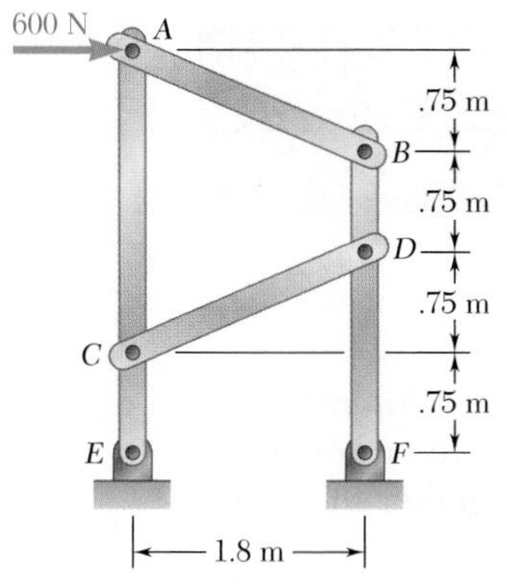

SAMPLE PROBLEM 6.6

A 600-N horizontal force is applied to pin A of the frame shown. Determine the forces acting on the two vertical members of the frame.

SOLUTION

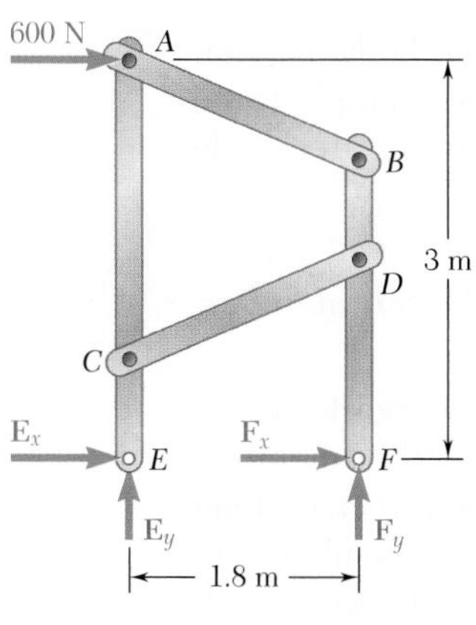

Free Body: Entire Frame. The entire frame is chosen as a free body; although the reactions involve four unknowns, $\mathbf{E}_y$ and $\mathbf{F}_y$ may be determined by writing

$$+\circlearrowleft\Sigma M_E = 0: \quad -(600 \text{ N})(3 \text{ m}) + F_y(1.8 \text{ m}) = 0$$
$$F_y = +1000 \text{ N} \qquad \mathbf{F}_y = 1000 \text{ N} \uparrow \blacktriangleleft$$
$$+\uparrow\Sigma F_y = 0: \quad E_y + F_y = 0$$
$$E_y = -1000 \text{ N} \qquad \mathbf{E}_y = 1000 \text{ N} \downarrow \blacktriangleleft$$

Members. The equations of equilibrium of the entire frame are not sufficient to determine $\mathbf{E}_x$ and $\mathbf{F}_x$. The free-body diagrams of the various members must now be considered in order to proceed with the solution. In dismembering the frame we will assume that pin A is attached to the multi-force member ACE and, thus, that the 600-N force is applied to that member. We also note that AB and CD are two-force members.

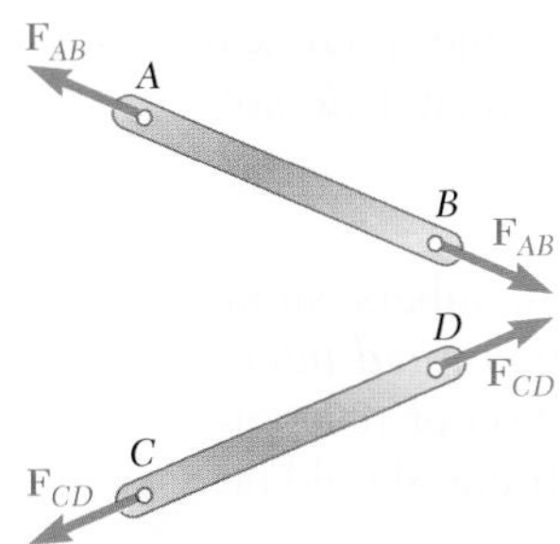

Free Body: Member ACE

$$+\uparrow\Sigma F_y = 0: \quad -\tfrac{5}{13}F_{AB} + \tfrac{5}{13}F_{CD} - 1000 \text{ N} = 0$$
$$+\circlearrowleft\Sigma M_E = 0: \quad -(600 \text{ N})(3 \text{ m}) - (\tfrac{12}{13}F_{AB})(3 \text{ m}) - (\tfrac{12}{13}F_{CD})(.75 \text{ m}) = 0$$

Solving these equations simultaneously, we find

$$F_{AB} = -1040 \text{ N} \qquad F_{CD} = +1560 \text{ N} \blacktriangleleft$$

The signs obtained indicate that the sense assumed for F_{CD} was correct and the sense for F_{AB} was incorrect. Summing now x components,

$$\xrightarrow{+}\Sigma F_x = 0: \quad 600 \text{ N} + \tfrac{12}{13}(-1040 \text{ N}) + \tfrac{12}{13}(+1560 \text{ N}) + E_x = 0$$
$$E_x = -1080 \text{ N} \qquad \mathbf{E}_x = 1080 \text{ N} \leftarrow \blacktriangleleft$$

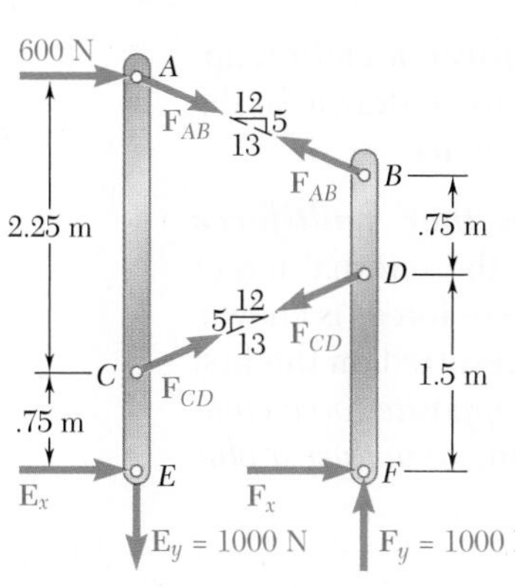

Free Body: Entire Frame. Since $\mathbf{E}_x$ has been determined, we can return to the free-body diagram of the entire frame and write

$$\xrightarrow{+}\Sigma F_x = 0: \quad 600 \text{ N} - 1080 \text{ N} + F_x = 0$$
$$F_x = +480 \text{ N} \qquad \mathbf{F}_x = 480 \text{ N} \rightarrow \blacktriangleleft$$

Free Body: Member BDF **(Check).** We can check our computations by verifying that the equation $\Sigma M_B = 0$ is satisfied by the forces acting on member BDF.

$$\begin{aligned}+\circlearrowleft\Sigma M_B &= -\left(\tfrac{12}{13}F_{CD}\right)(.75 \text{ m}) + (F_x)(2.25 \text{ m})\\ &= -\tfrac{12}{13}(1560 \text{ N})(.75 \text{ m}) + (480 \text{ N})(2.25 \text{ m})\\ &= -1080 \text{ N}\cdot\text{m} + 1080 \text{ N}\cdot\text{m} = 0 \qquad \text{(checks)}\end{aligned}$$

SOLVING PROBLEMS ON YOUR OWN

In this lesson you learned to analyze *frames containing one or more multiforce members*. In the problems that follow you will be asked to determine the external reactions exerted on the frame and the internal forces that hold together the members of the frame.

In solving problems involving frames containing one or more multiforce members, follow these steps:

1. ***Draw a free-body diagram of the entire frame.*** Use this free-body diagram to calculate, to the extent possible, the reactions at the supports. (In Sample Prob. 6.6 only two of the four reaction components could be found from the free body of the entire frame.)

2. ***Dismember the frame, and draw a free-body diagram of each member.***

3. ***Considering first the two-force members,*** apply equal and opposite forces to each two-force member at the points where it is connected to another member. If the two-force member is a straight member, these forces will be directed along the axis of the member. If you cannot tell at this point whether the member is in tension or compression, just *assume* that the member is in tension and *direct both of the forces away from the member*. Since these forces have the same unknown magnitude, give them both the *same name* and, to avoid any confusion later, *do not use a plus sign or a minus sign*.

4. ***Next, consider the multiforce members.*** For each of these members, show all the forces acting on the member, including *applied loads, reactions, and internal forces at connections*. The magnitude and direction of any reaction or reaction component found earlier from the free-body diagram of the entire frame should be clearly indicated.

   a. Where a multiforce member is connected to a two-force member, apply to the multiforce member a force *equal and opposite* to the force drawn on the free-body diagram of the two-force member, *giving it the same name*.

   b. Where a multiforce member is connected to another multiforce member, use *horizontal and vertical components* to represent the internal forces at that point, since neither the direction nor the magnitude of these forces is known. The direction you choose for each of the two force components exerted on the first multiforce member is arbitrary, but *you must apply equal and opposite force components of the same name* to the other multiforce member. Again, *do not use a plus sign or a minus sign.*

5. ***The internal forces may now be determined,*** as well as any *reactions* that you have not already found.

a. The free-body diagram of each of the multiforce members can provide you with *three equilibrium equations.*

b. To simplify your solution, you should seek a way to write an equation involving a single unknown. If you can locate *a point where all but one of the unknown force components intersect,* you will obtain an equation in a single unknown by summing moments about that point. *If all unknown forces except one are parallel,* you will obtain an equation in a single unknown by summing force components in a direction perpendicular to the parallel forces.

c. Since you arbitrarily chose the direction of each of the unknown forces, you cannot determine until the solution is completed whether your guess was correct. To do that, consider the *sign* of the value found for each of the unknowns: a *positive* sign means that the direction you selected was *correct;* a *negative* sign means that the direction is *opposite* to the direction you assumed.

6. ***To be more effective and efficient*** as you proceed through your solution, observe the following rules:

a. If an equation involving only one unknown can be found, write that equation and *solve it for that unknown.* Immediately *replace* that unknown wherever it appears on other free-body diagrams *by the value you have found.* Repeat this process by seeking equilibrium equations involving only one unknown until you have found all of the internal forces and unknown reactions.

b. If an equation involving only one unknown cannot be found, you may have to *solve a pair of simultaneous equations.* Before doing so, check that you have shown the values of all of the reactions that were obtained from the free-body diagram of the entire frame.

c. The total number of equations of equilibrium for the entire frame and for the individual members *will be larger than the number of unknown forces and reactions.* After you have found all the reactions and all the internal forces, you can use the remaining dependent equations to check the accuracy of your solution.

Problems

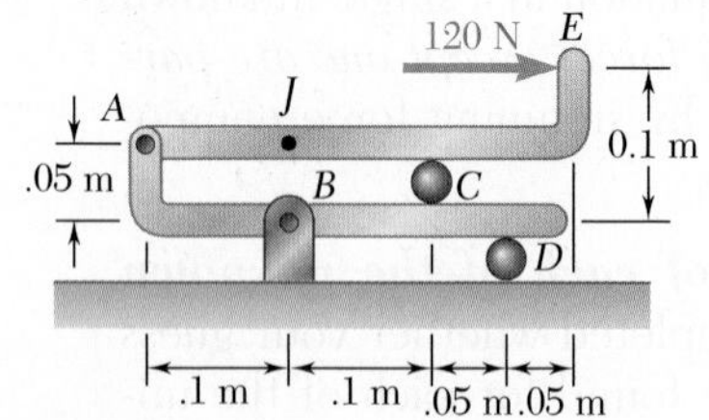

Fig. P6.76

6.76 Determine the components of all forces acting on member *ABCD* of the assembly shown.

6.77 For the frame and loading shown, determine the force acting on member *ABC* (*a*) at *B*, (*b*) at *C*.

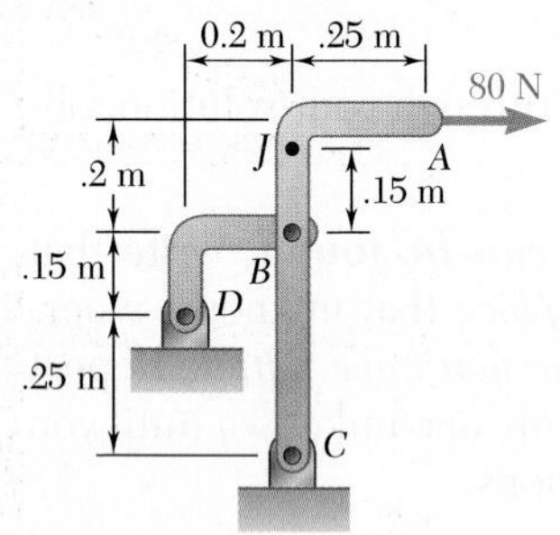

Fig. *P6.77*

6.78 For the frame and loading shown, determine the components of all forces acting on member *DECF*.

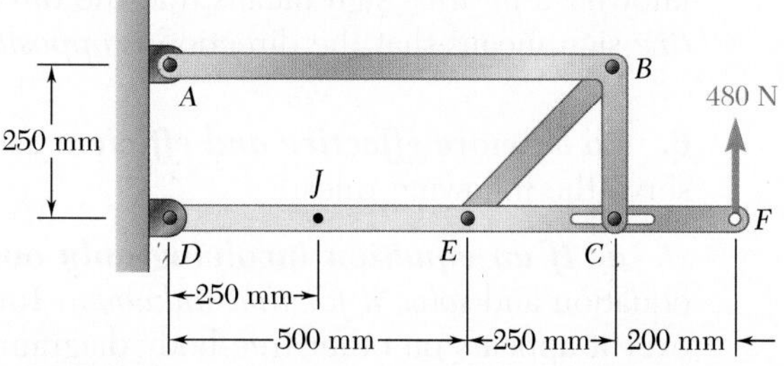

Fig. P6.78

6.79 Solve Prob. 6.78 assuming that the 480-N load is replaced with a clockwise couple of magnitude 400 N · m applied to member *DECF* at point *F*.

6.80 A circular ring of radius .2 m is pinned at *A* and is supported by rod *BC*, which is fitted with a collar at *C* that can be moved along the ring. For the position when $\theta = 35°$, determine (*a*) the force in rod *BC*, (*b*) the reaction at *A*.

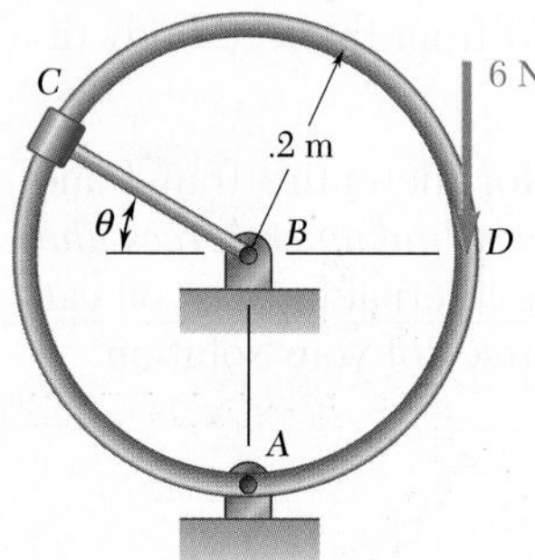

Fig. P6.80

6.81 Solve Prob. 6.80 when $\theta = -20°$.

6.82 For the frame and loading shown, determine the components of all forces acting on member *ABCD*.

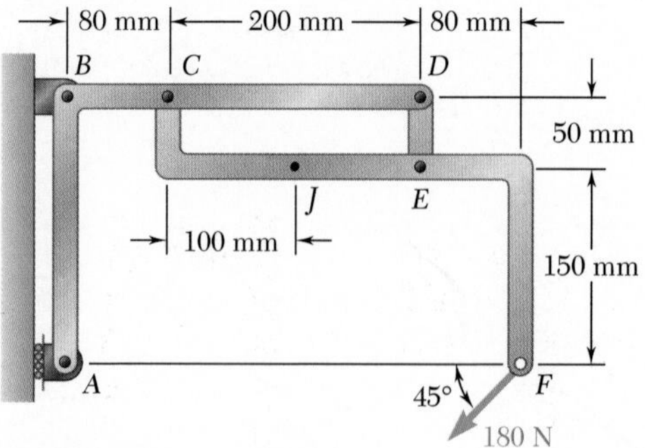

Fig. P6.82

6.83 Solve Prob. 6.82 assuming that the 180-N load is replaced with a clockwise couple of magnitude 60 N · m applied to member *CEF* at point *F*.

6.84 Determine the components of the reactions at A and E when a 24-N force directed vertically downward is applied (*a*) at B, (*b*) at D.

6.85 Determine the components of the reactions at A and E when a 320-N force directed vertically downward is applied (*a*) at B, (*b*) at D.

6.86 Determine the components of the reactions at A and E when a counterclockwise couple of magnitude 192 N · m is applied to the frame (*a*) at B, (*b*) at D.

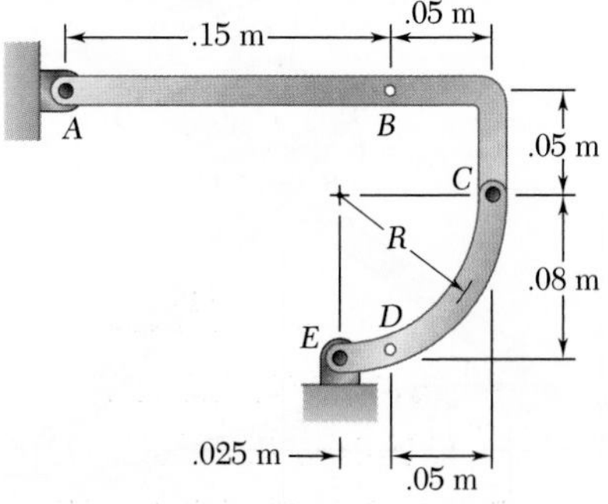

Fig. P6.84 and P6.86

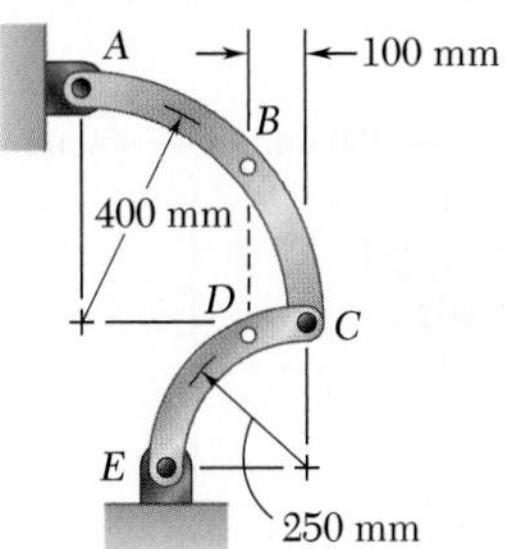

Fig. P6.85 and *P6.87*

6.87 Determine the components of the reactions at A and E when a counterclockwise couple of magnitude 120 N · m is applied to the frame (*a*) at B, (*b*) at D.

6.88 Determine all the forces exerted on member AI when a clockwise couple of magnitude 180 N · m is applied to the frame (*a*) at point D, (*b*) at point E.

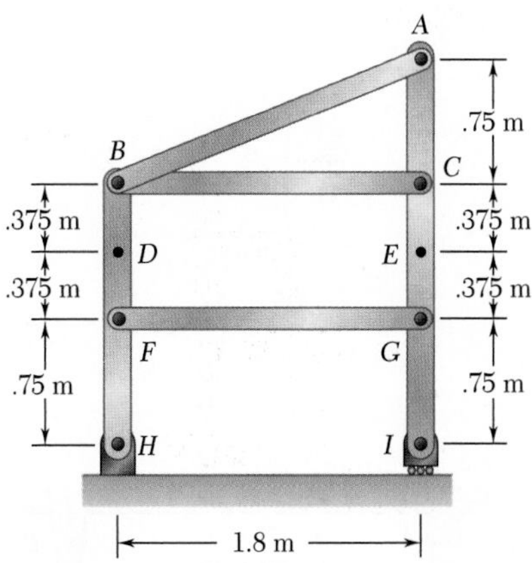

Fig. P6.88

6.89 The 120-N load can be moved along the line of action shown and can be applied at A, D, or E. Determine the components of the reactions at B and F when the 120-N load is applied (*a*) at A, (*b*) at D, (*c*) at E.

6.90 The 120-N load is removed and a 48-N · m clockwise couple is applied successively at A, D, and E. Determine the components of the reactions at B and F when the couple is applied (*a*) at A, (*b*) at D, (*c*) at E.

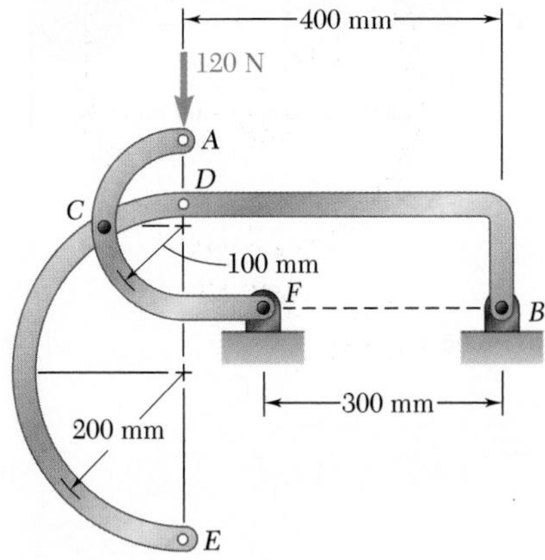

Fig. P6.89 and *P6.90*

6.91 (*a*) Show that when a frame supports a pulley at A, an equivalent loading of the frame and of each of its component parts can be obtained by removing the pulley and applying at A two forces equal and parallel to the forces that the cable exerted on the pulley. (*b*) Show that if one end of the cable is attached to the frame at point B, a force of magnitude equal to the tension in the cable should also be applied at B.

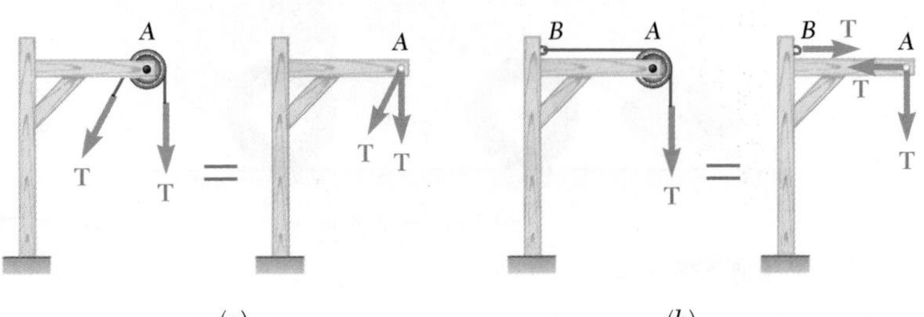

Fig. P6.91

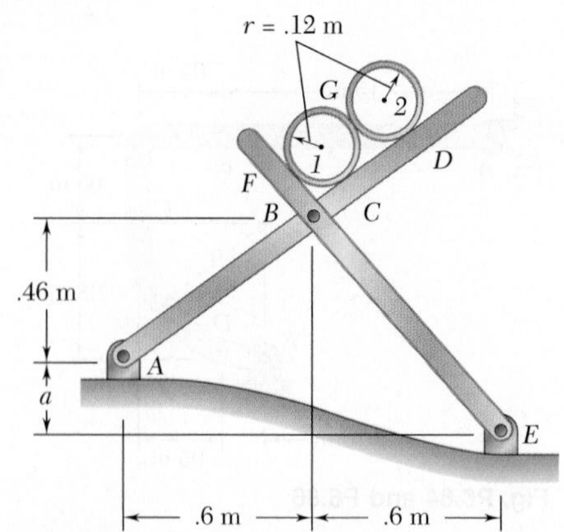

Fig. P6.92

6.92 Two .25-m-diameter pipes (pipe *1* and pipe *2*) are supported every 3 m by a small frame like the one shown. Knowing that the combined weight per unit length of each pipe and its contents is 35 kg/m and assuming frictionless surfaces, determine the components of the reactions at A and E when $a = 0$.

6.93 Solve Prob. 6.92 when $a = 0.36$ m

6.94 Knowing that the pulley has a radius of 60 mm, determine the components of the reactions at A and E.

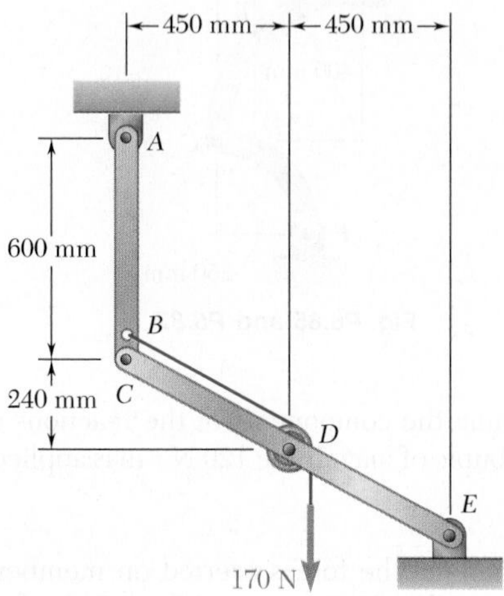

Fig. P6.94

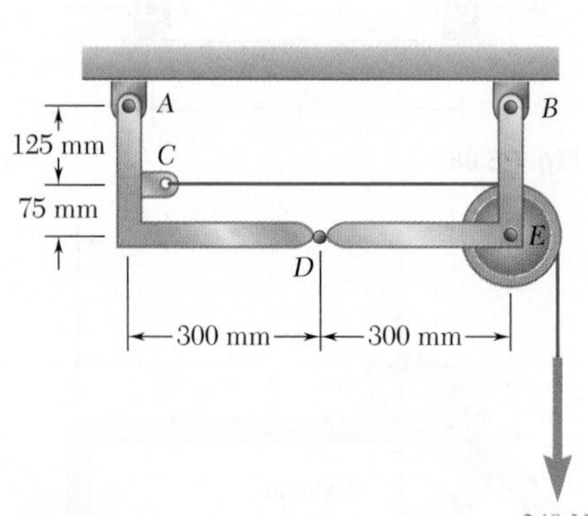

Fig. P6.95

6.95 Knowing that the pulley has a radius of 75 mm, determine the components of the reactions at A and B.

6.96 The cab and motor units of the front-end loader shown are connected by a vertical pin located 1.5 m behind the cab wheels. The distance from C to D is .75 m. The center of gravity of the 50-kN motor unit is located at G_m, while the centers of gravity of the 18-kN cab and 16-kN load are located, respectively, at G_c and G_l. Knowing that the machine is at rest with its brakes released, determine (*a*) the reactions at each of the four wheels, (*b*) the forces exerted on the motor unit at C and D.

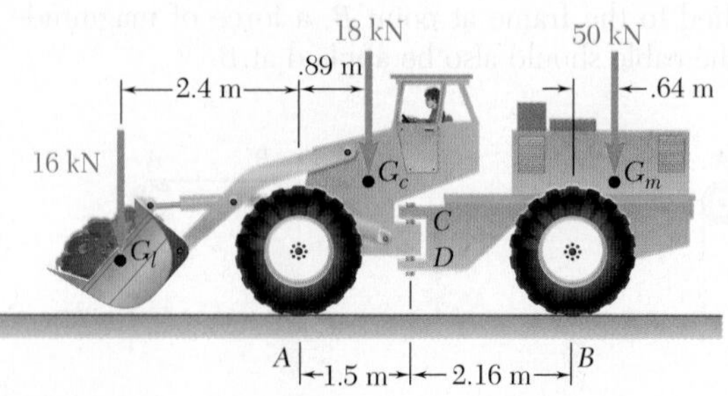

Fig. P6.96

6.97 Solve Prob. 6.96 assuming that the 16-kN load has been removed.

6.98 For the frame and loading shown, determine the components of all forces acting on member *ABD*.

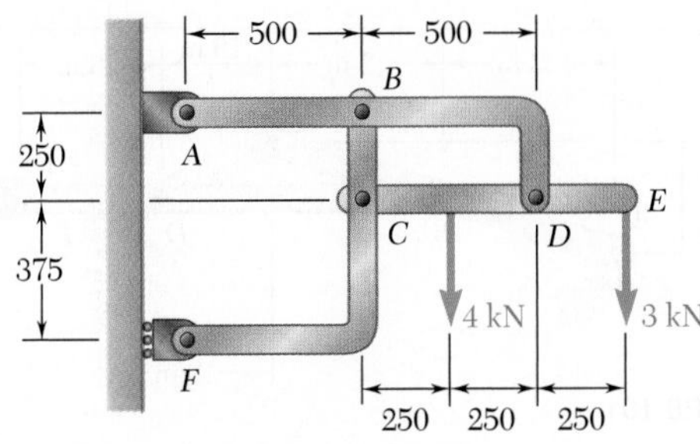

Fig. P6.98

6.99 For the frame and loading shown, determine the components of all forces acting on member *GBEH*.

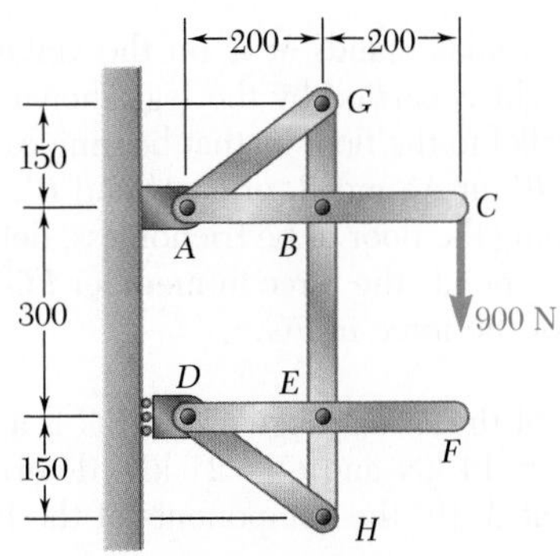

Fig. *P6.99*

6.100 For the frame and loading shown, determine the components of the forces acting on member *ABC* at *B* and *C*.

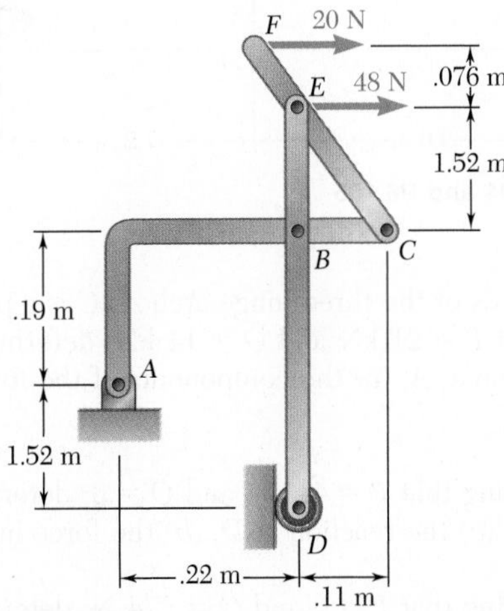

Fig. P6.100

6.101 For the frame and loading shown, determine the components of the forces acting on member *ABC* at *B* and *C*.

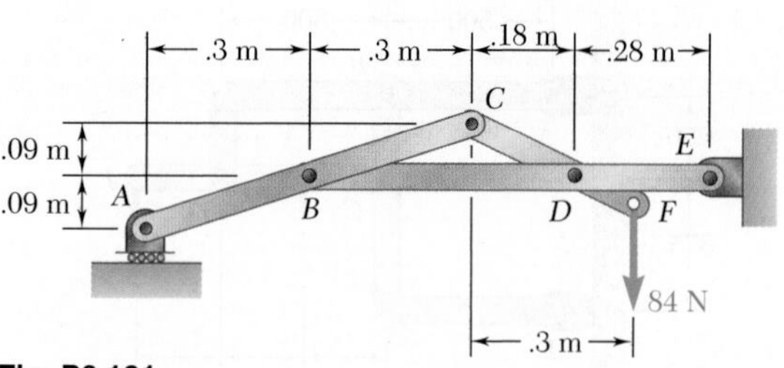

Fig. P6.101

6.102 A 56-kg woman stands at *C* on the vintage step stool shown. Half the woman's weight is carried by the legs shown. Determine the components of the force exerted at *E* on leg *BE* assuming that the bottom of each leg is not quite parallel to the floor so that bearing occurs at points *A* and *B*. Neglect the mass of the stool, and assume the floor to be frictionless.

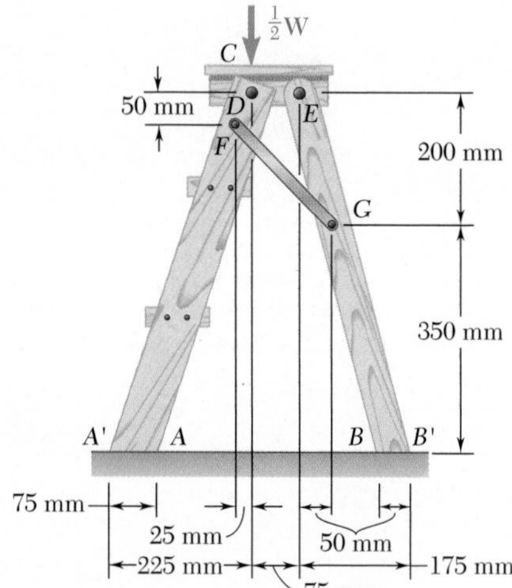

Fig. *P6.102* and P6.103

6.103 A 56-kg woman stands at *C* on the vintage step stool shown. Half the woman's weight is carried by the legs shown. The bottoms of the legs are not quite parallel to the floor so that bearing can occur in four ways: at *A* and *B*, at *A* and *B′*, at *A′* and *B*, or at *A′* and *B′*. Neglecting the mass of the stool and assuming the floor to be frictionless, determine (*a*) for which combination of bearing points the force in member *FG* is maximum, (*b*) the corresponding value of the force in *FG*.

6.104 The axis of the three-hinge arch *ABC* is a parabola with vertex at *B*. Knowing that $P = 14$ kN and $Q = 21$ kN, determine (*a*) the components of the reaction at *A*, (*b*) the components of the force exerted at *B* on segment *AB*.

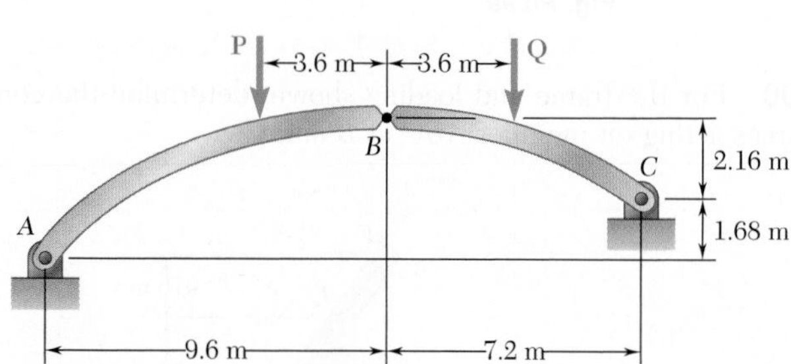

Fig. P6.104 and P6.105

6.105 The axis of the three-hinge arch *ABC* is a parabola with vertex at *B*. Knowing that $P = 21$ kN and $Q = 14$ kN, determine (*a*) the components of the reaction at *A*, (*b*) the components of the force exerted at *B* on segment *AB*.

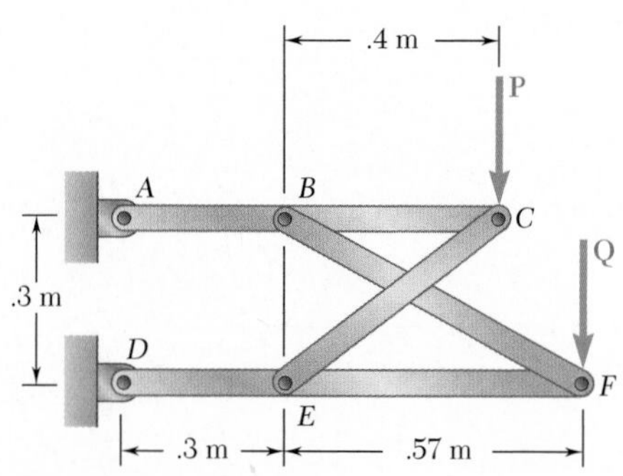

Fig. P6.106 and *P6.107*

6.106 Knowing that $P = 411$ N and $Q = 0$, determine for the frame and loading shown (*a*) the reaction at *D*, (*b*) the force in member *BF*.

6.107 Knowing that $P = 0$ and $Q = 274$ N, determine for the frame and loading shown (*a*) the reaction at *D*, (*b*) the force in member *BF*.

6.108 Two parallel members ABC and DEF are placed between two walls and are connected by link BE. Neglecting friction between the members and the walls, determine the range of values of the distance a for which the load **P** can be supported.

Fig. P6.108

6.109 through 6.111 The frame shown consists of members $ABCD$ and $EFGH$ and two links that connect the two members. Determine the force in each link for the given loading.

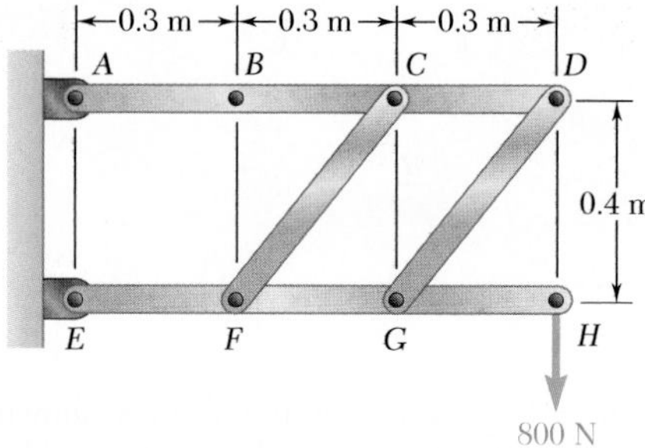
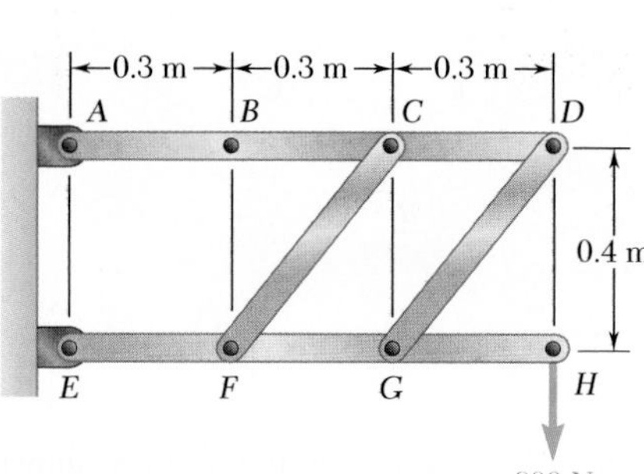

Fig. P6.109

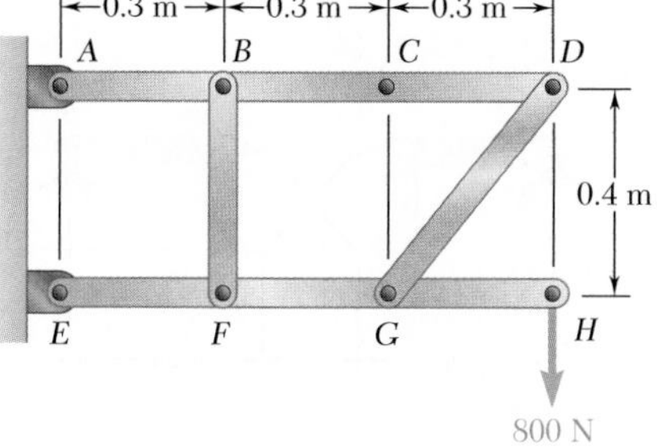

Fig. P6.110

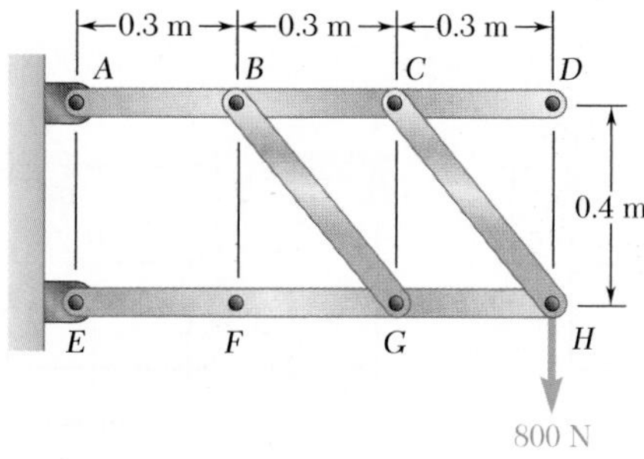

Fig. P6.111

6.112 Members ABC and CDE are pin-connected at C and are supported by the four links AF, BG, GD, and EH. For the loading shown, determine the force in each link.

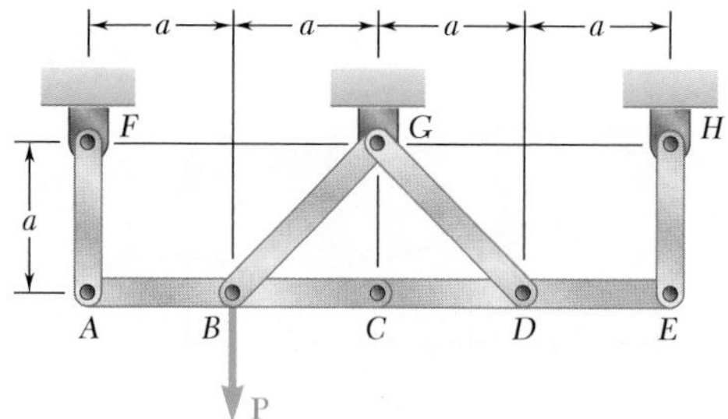

Fig. P6.112

6.113 Three wooden beams, each of length $3a$, are nailed together to form the support system shown. Assuming that only vertical forces are exerted at the connections, determine the vertical reactions at A, D, and F.

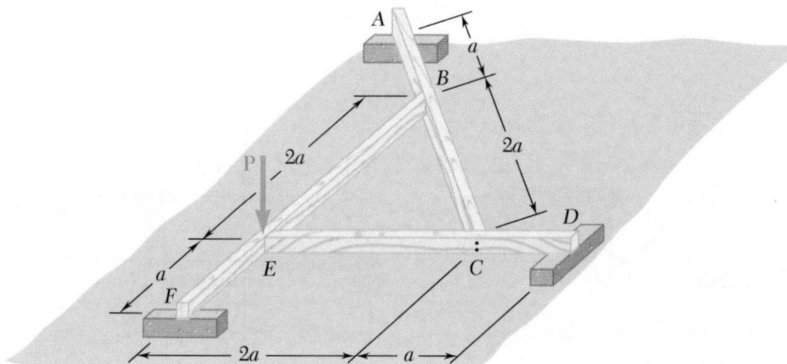

Fig. P6.113

6.114 Four wooden beams each of length $2a$ are nailed together at their midpoints to form the support system shown. Assuming that only vertical forces are exerted at the connections, determine the vertical reactions at A, D, E, and H.

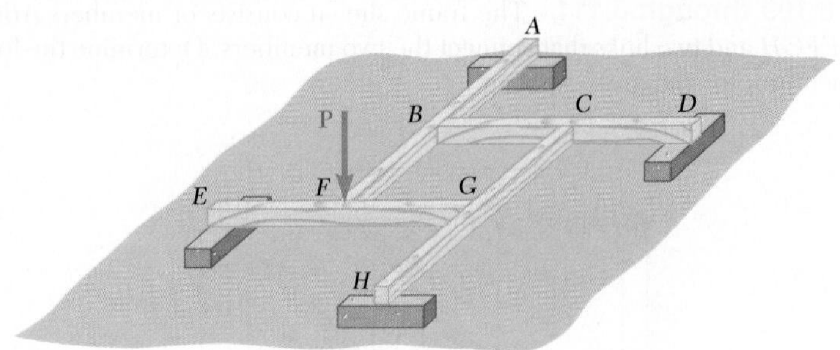

Fig. P6.114

6.115 through 6.117 Each of the frames shown consists of two L-shaped members connected by two rigid links. For each frame, determine the reactions at the supports and indicate whether the frame is rigid.

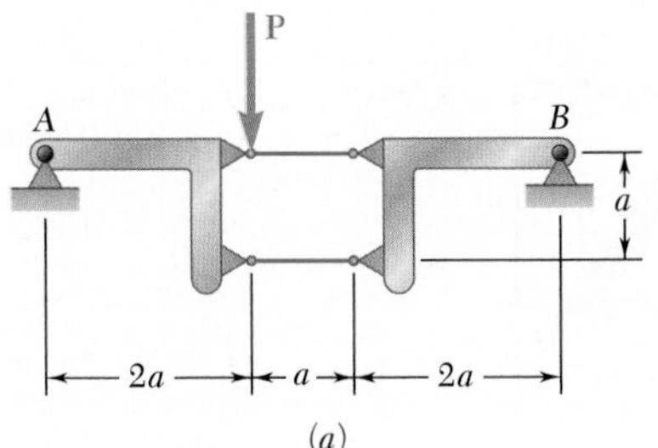

(a)

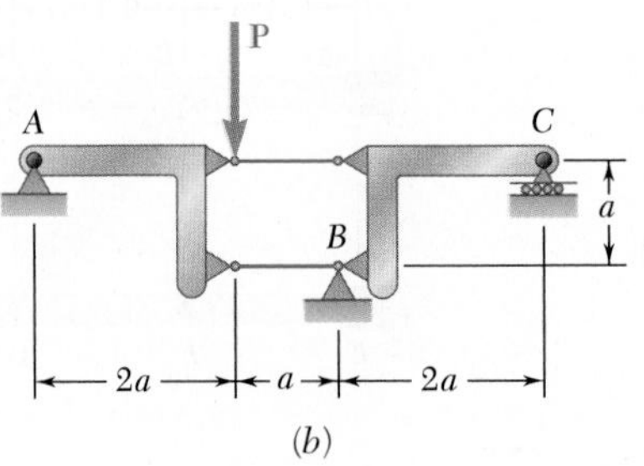

(b)

(c)

Fig. P6.115

(a)

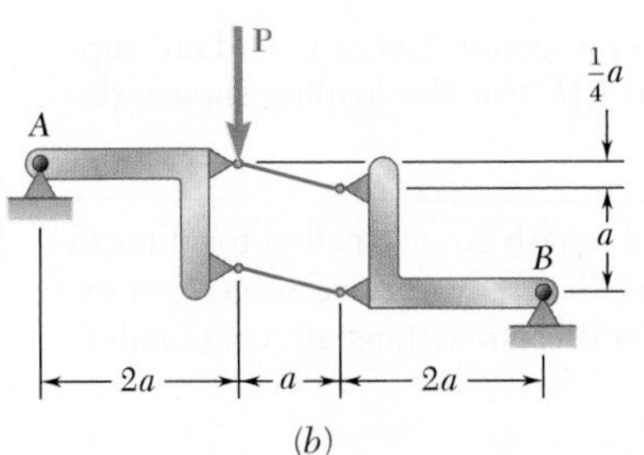

(b)

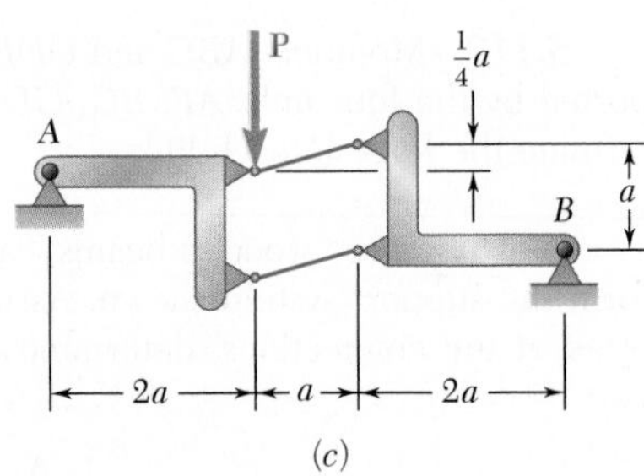

(c)

Fig. P6.116

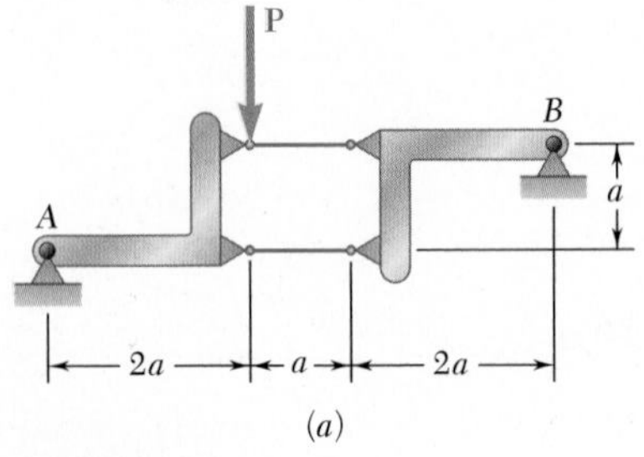

(a)

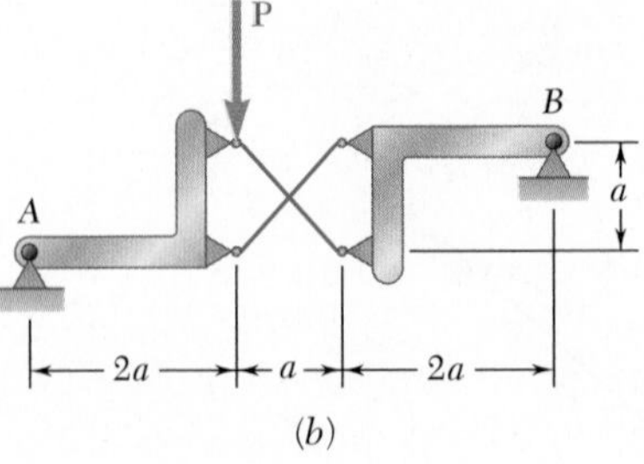

(b)

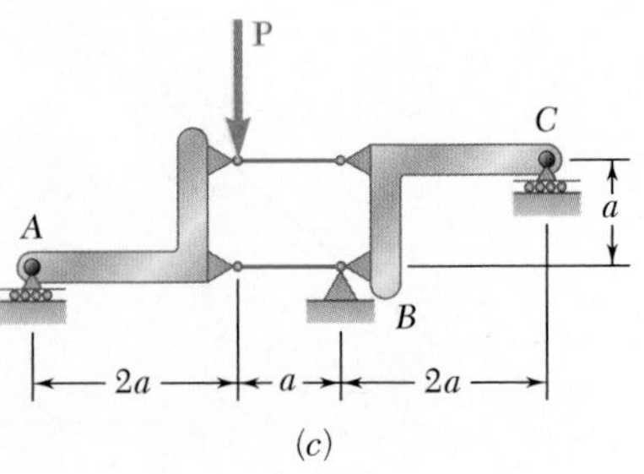

(c)

Fig. P6.117

6.12. MACHINES

Machines are structures designed to transmit and modify forces. Whether they are simple tools or include complicated mechanisms, their main purpose is to transform *input forces* into *output forces*. Consider, for example, a pair of cutting pliers used to cut a wire (Fig. 6.22*a*). If we apply two equal and opposite forces **P** and −**P** on their handles, they will exert two equal and opposite forces **Q** and −**Q** on the wire (Fig. 6.22*b*).

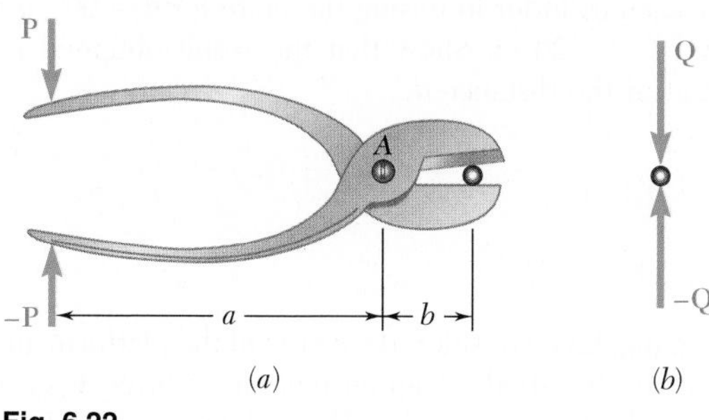

Fig. 6.22

Photo 6.5 The lamp shown can be placed in many positions. By considering various free bodies, the force in the springs and the internal forces at the joints can be determined.

To determine the magnitude Q of the output forces when the magnitude P of the input forces is known (or, conversely, to determine P when Q is known), we draw a free-body diagram of the pliers *alone*, showing the input forces **P** and −**P** and the *reactions* −**Q** and **Q** that the wire exerts on the pliers (Fig. 6.23). However, since

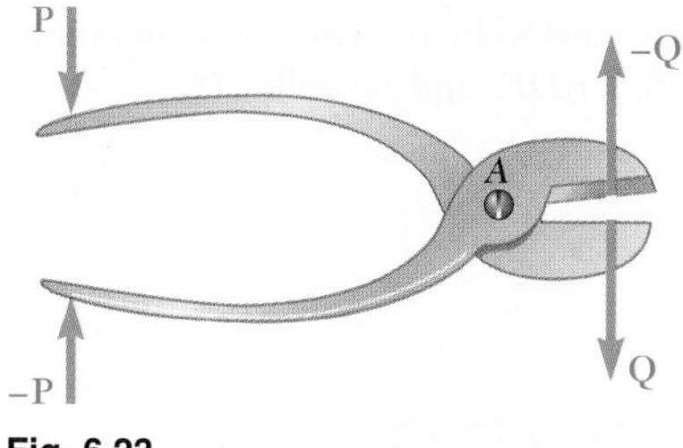

Fig. 6.23

a pair of pliers forms a nonrigid structure, we must use one of the component parts as a free body in order to determine the unknown forces. Considering Fig. 6.24*a*, for example, and taking moments about A, we obtain the relation $Pa = Qb$, which defines the magnitude Q in terms of P or P in terms of Q. The same free-body diagram can be used to determine the components of the internal force at A; we find $A_x = 0$ and $A_y = P + Q$.

In the case of more complicated machines, it generally will be necessary to use several free-body diagrams and, possibly, to solve simultaneous equations involving various internal forces. The free bodies should be chosen to include the input forces and the reactions to the output forces, and the total number of unknown force components involved should not exceed the number of available independent equations. It is advisable, before attempting to solve a problem, to determine whether the structure considered is determinate. There is no point, however, in discussing the rigidity of a machine, since a machine includes moving parts and thus *must* be nonrigid.

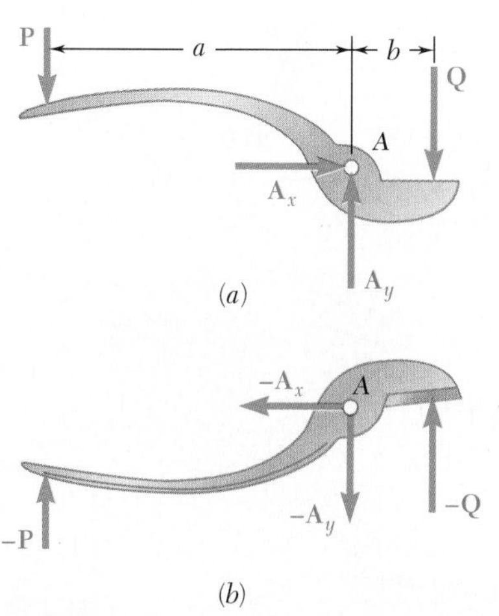

Fig. 6.24

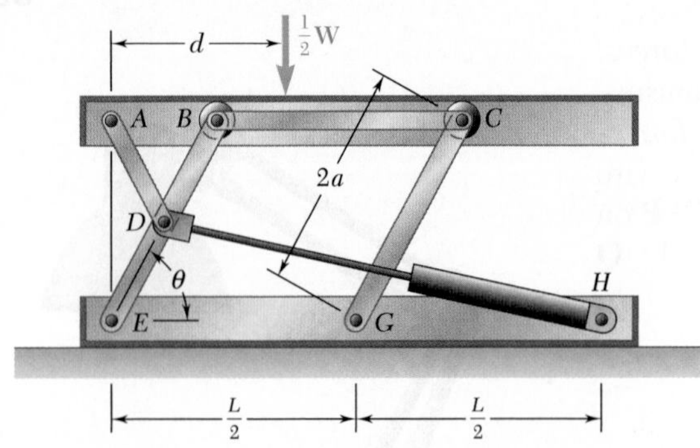

SAMPLE PROBLEM 6.7

A hydraulic-lift table is used to raise a 1000-kg crate. It consists of a platform and two identical linkages on which hydraulic cylinders exert equal forces. (Only one linkage and one cylinder are shown.) Members *EDB* and *CG* are each of length $2a$, and member *AD* is pinned to the midpoint of *EDB*. If the crate is placed on the table, so that half of its weight is supported by the system shown, determine the force exerted by each cylinder in raising the crate for $\theta = 60°$, $a = 0.70$ m, and $L = 3.20$ m. Show that the result obtained is independent of the distance d.

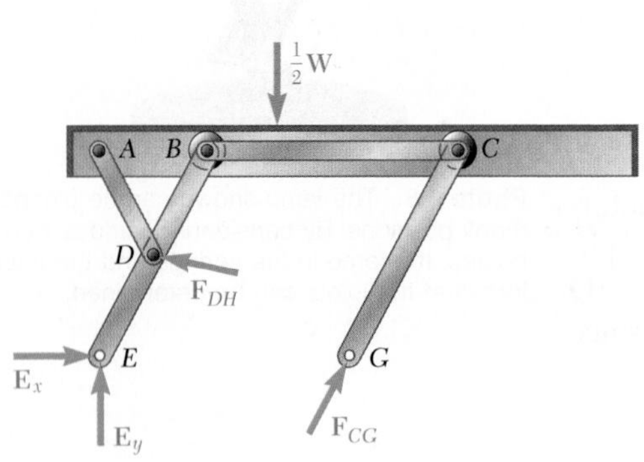

SOLUTION

The machine considered consists of the platform and the linkage. Its free-body diagram includes a force $\mathbf{F}_{DH}$ exerted by the cylinder, the weight $\frac{1}{2}\mathbf{W}$, and reactions at E and G that we assume to be directed as shown. Since more than three unknowns are involved, this diagram will not be used. The mechanism is dismembered and a free-body diagram is drawn for each of its component parts. We note that *AD*, *BC*, and *CG* are two-force members. We already assumed member *CG* to be in compression. We now assume that *AD* and *BC* are in tension; the forces exerted on them are then directed as shown. Equal and opposite vectors will be used to represent the forces exerted by the two-force members on the platform, on member *BDE*, and on roller *C*.

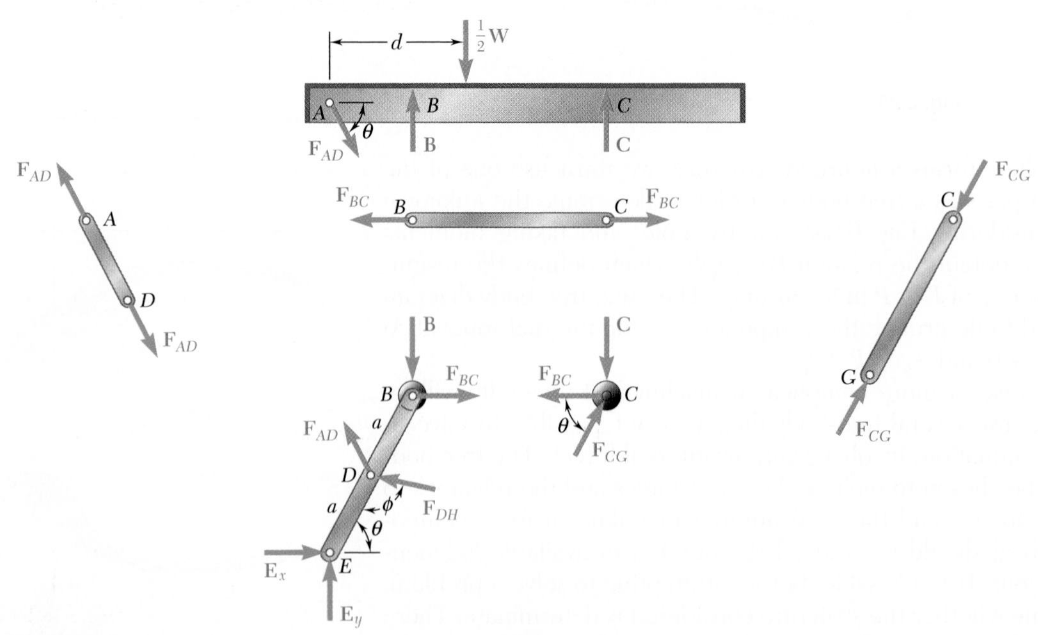

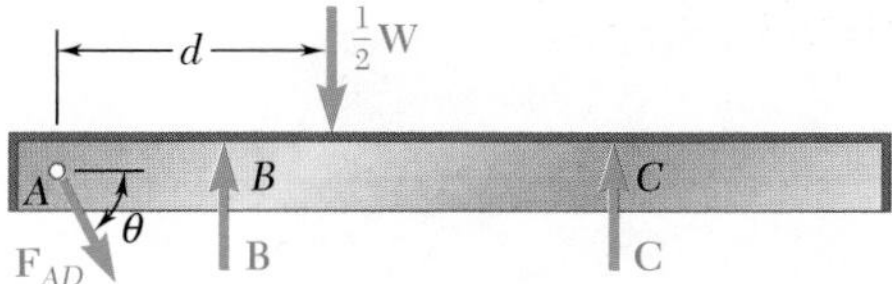

Free Body: Platform *ABC*.

$$\xrightarrow{+}\Sigma F_x = 0: \qquad F_{AD}\cos\theta = 0 \qquad F_{AD} = 0$$
$$+\uparrow\Sigma F_y = 0: \qquad B + C - \tfrac{1}{2}W = 0 \qquad B + C = \tfrac{1}{2}W \tag{1}$$

Free Body: Roller *C*. We draw a force triangle and obtain $F_{BC} = C\cot\theta$.

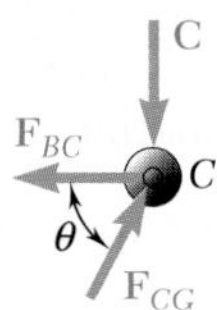

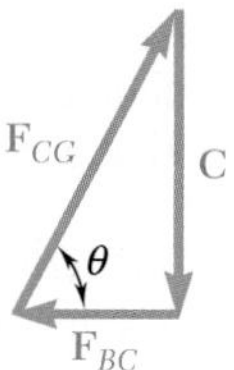

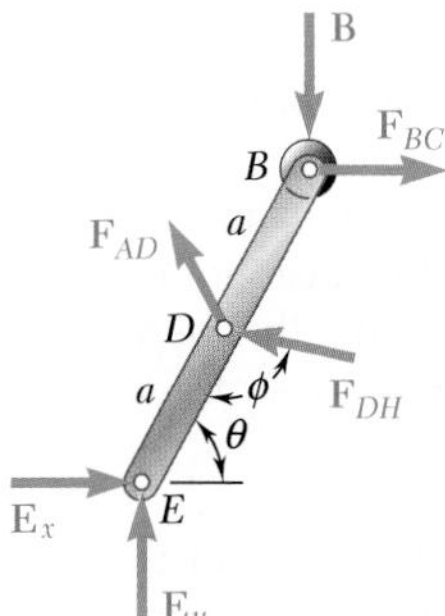

Free Body: Member *BDE*. Recalling that $F_{AD} = 0$,

$$+\circlearrowleft\Sigma M_E = 0: \qquad F_{DH}\cos(\phi - 90°)a - B(2a\cos\theta) - F_{BC}(2a\sin\theta) = 0$$
$$F_{DH}a\sin\phi - B(2a\cos\theta) - (C\cot\theta)(2a\sin\theta) = 0$$
$$F_{DH}\sin\phi - 2(B + C)\cos\theta = 0$$

Recalling Eq. (1), we have

$$F_{DH} = W\frac{\cos\theta}{\sin\phi} \tag{2}$$

and we observe that *the result obtained is independent of d.* ◀

Applying first the law of sines to triangle *EDH*, we write

$$\frac{\sin\phi}{EH} = \frac{\sin\theta}{DH} \qquad \sin\phi = \frac{EH}{DH}\sin\theta \tag{3}$$

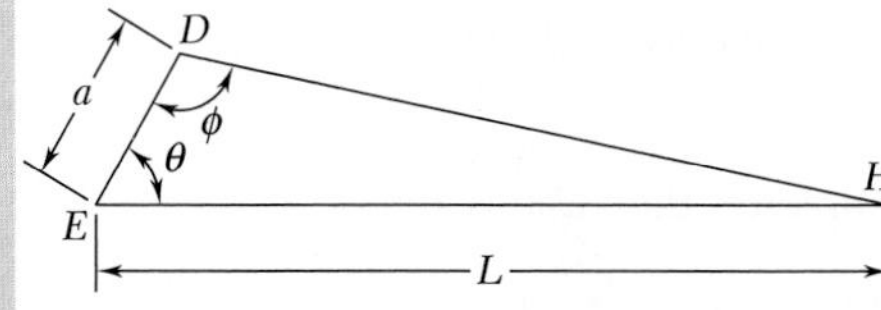

Using now the law of cosines, we have

$$(DH)^2 = a^2 + L^2 - 2aL\cos\theta$$
$$= (0.70)^2 + (3.20)^2 - 2(0.70)(3.20)\cos 60°$$
$$(DH)^2 = 8.49 \qquad DH = 2.91\text{ m}$$

We also note that

$$W = mg = (1000\text{ kg})(9.81\text{ m/s}^2) = 9810\text{ N} = 9.81\text{ kN}$$

Substituting for $\sin\phi$ from (3) into (2) and using the numerical data, we write

$$F_{DH} = W\frac{DH}{EH}\cot\theta = (9.81\text{ kN})\frac{2.91\text{ m}}{3.20\text{ m}}\cot 60°$$

$F_{DH} = 5.15$ kN ◀

SOLVING PROBLEMS ON YOUR OWN

This lesson was devoted to the analysis of *machines*. Since machines are designed to transmit or modify forces, they always contain moving parts. However, the machines considered here will always be at rest, and you will be working with the set of *forces required to maintain the equilibrium of the machine*.

Known forces that act on a machine are called *input forces. A machine transforms the input forces into output forces,* such as the cutting forces applied by the pliers of Fig. 6.22. You will determine the output forces by finding the forces equal and opposite to the output forces that should be applied to the machine to maintain its equilibrium.

In the preceding lesson you analyzed frames; you will now use almost the same procedure to analyze machines:

1. ***Draw a free-body diagram of the whole machine,*** and use it to determine as many as possible of the unknown forces exerted on the machine.

2. ***Dismember the machine, and draw a free-body diagram of each member.***

3. ***Considering first the two-force members,*** apply equal and opposite forces to each two-force member at the points where it is connected to another member. If you cannot tell at this point whether the member is in tension or in compression just *assume* that the member is in tension and *direct both of the forces away from the member*. Since these forces have the same unknown magnitude, *give them both the same name*.

4. ***Next consider the multiforce members.*** For each of these members, show all the forces acting on the member, including applied loads and forces, reactions, and internal forces at connections.

   a. ***Where a multiforce member is connected to a two-force member,*** apply to the multiforce member a force *equal and opposite* to the force drawn on the free-body diagram of the two-force member, *giving it the same name*.

   b. ***Where a multiforce member is connected to another multiforce member,*** use *horizontal and vertical components* to represent the internal forces at that point. The directions you choose for each of the two force components exerted on the first multiforce member are arbitrary, but *you must apply equal and opposite force components of the same name* to the other multiforce member.

5. ***Equilibrium equations can be written*** after you have completed the various free-body diagrams.

   a. ***To simplify your solution,*** you should, whenever possible, write and solve equilibrium equations involving single unknowns.

   b. ***Since you arbitrarily chose the direction of each of the unknown forces,*** you must determine at the end of the solution whether your guess was correct. To that effect, *consider the sign* of the value found for each of the unknowns. A *positive* sign indicates that your guess was correct, and a *negative* sign indicates that it was not.

6. ***Finally, you should check your solution*** by substituting the results obtained into an equilibrium equation that you have not previously used.

Problems

6.118 The shear shown is used to trim electronic-circuit-board laminates. Knowing that $P = 400$ N, determine (*a*) the vertical component of the force exerted on the shearing blade at D, (*b*) the reaction at C.

6.119 The shear shown is used to trim electronic-circuit-board laminates. Neglecting the thickness of the shearing blade and knowing that a vertical 3-kN shearing force at E is required to cut the laminate, determine (*a*) the magnitude of the applied force **P**, (*b*) the reaction at C.

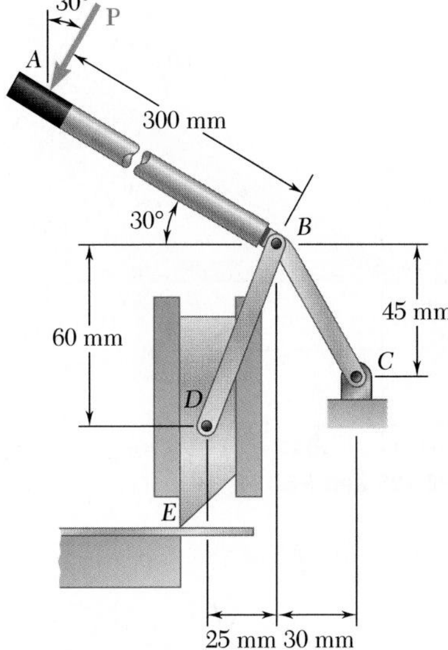

Fig. P6.118 and P6.119

6.120 The press shown is used to emboss a small seal at E. Knowing that $P = 250$ N, determine (*a*) the vertical component of the force exerted on the seal, (*b*) the reaction at A.

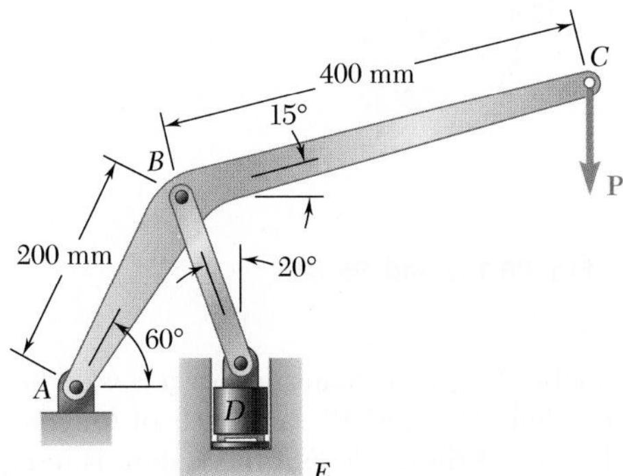

Fig. *P6.120* and *P6.121*

6.121 The press shown is used to emboss a small seal at E. Knowing that the vertical component of the force exerted on the seal must be 900 N, determine (*a*) the required vertical force **P**, (*b*) the corresponding reaction at A.

6.122 The control rod CE passes through a horizontal hole in the body of the toggle clamp shown. Determine (*a*) the force **Q** required to hold the clamp in equilibrium, (*b*) the corresponding force in link BD.

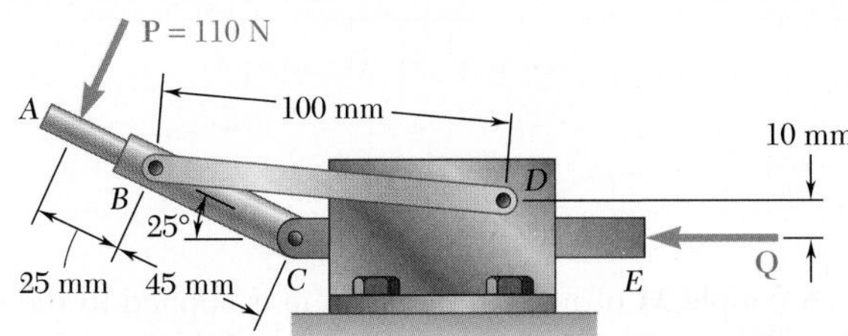

Fig. P6.122

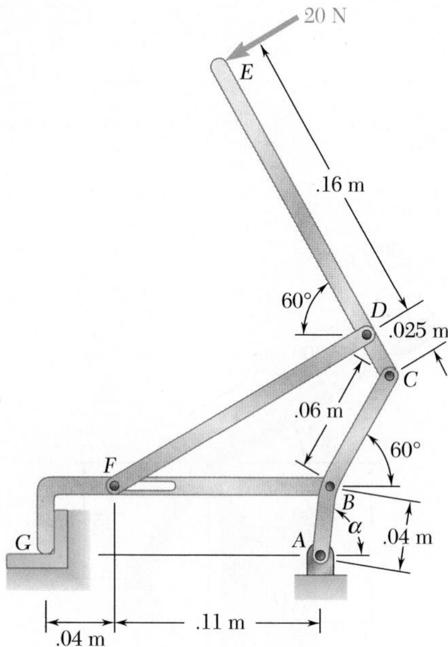

Fig. P6.123 and P6.124

6.123 The double-toggle latching mechanism shown is used to hold member G against the support. Knowing that $\alpha = 60°$, determine the force exerted on G.

6.124 The double-toggle latching mechanism shown is used to hold member G against the support. Knowing that $\alpha = 75°$, determine the force exerted on G.

6.125 The double-toggle mechanism shown is used in a punching machine. Knowing that links AB and BC are each of length .15 m, determine the couple **M** required to hold the system in equilibrium when $\phi = 20°$.

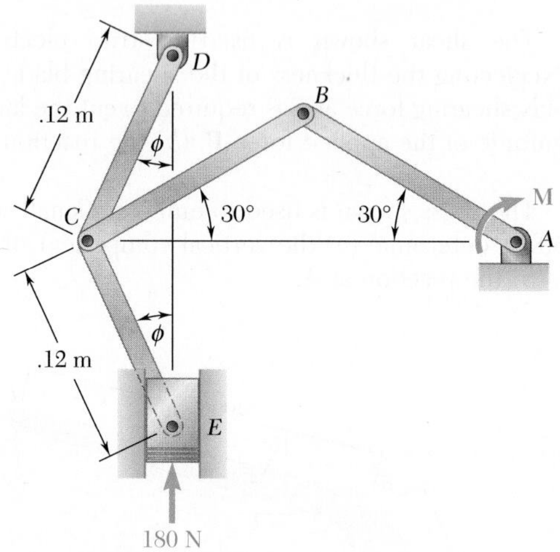

Fig. P6.125 and *P6.126*

6.126 The double-toggle mechanism shown is used in a punching machine. Knowing that links AB and BC are each of length .15 m and that $M = 660$ N · m, determine the angle ϕ if the system is in equilibrium.

6.127 A force **P** of magnitude 160 N is applied to the slider of the four-bar slider mechanism shown. For each of the two given positions, determine the couple **M** required to hold the system in equilibrium.

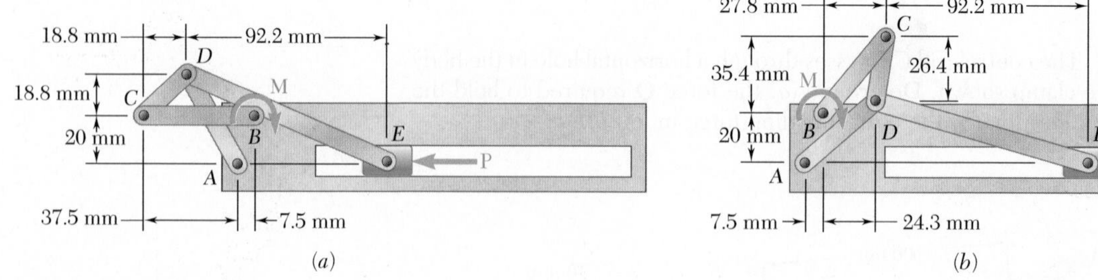

Fig. P6.127 and P6.128

6.128 A couple **M** of magnitude 6 N · m is applied to the input link of the four-bar slider mechanism shown. For each of the two given positions, determine the force **P** required to hold the system in equilibrium.

6.129 Arm BCD is connected by pins to crank AB at B and to a collar at C. Neglecting the effect of friction, determine the couple $\mathbf{M}$ required to hold the system in equilibrium when $\theta = 0$.

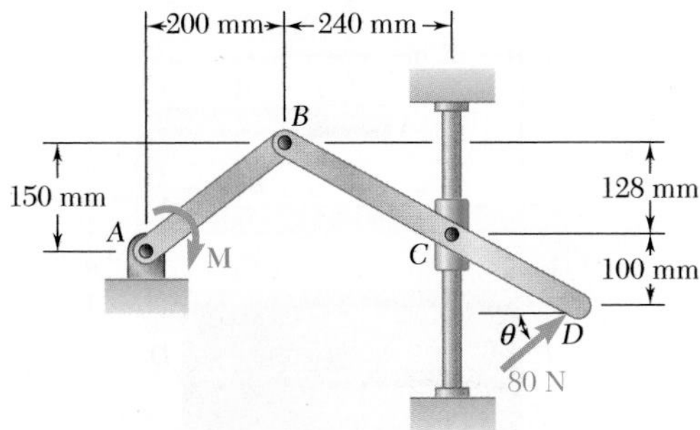

Fig. P6.129 and P6.130

6.130 Arm BCD is connected by pins to crank AB at B and to a collar at C. Neglecting the effect of friction, determine the couple $\mathbf{M}$ required to hold the system in equilibrium when $\theta = 45°$.

6.131 and 6.132 Two rods are connected by a slider block as shown. Neglecting the effect of friction, determine the couple $\mathbf{M}_A$ required to hold the system in equilibrium.

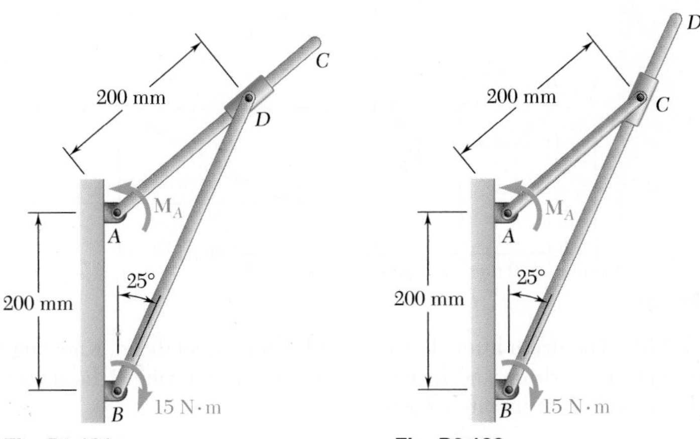

Fig. P6.131 **Fig. P6.132**

6.133 and *6.134* Rod CD is attached to the collar D and passes through a collar welded to end B of lever AB. Neglecting the effect of friction, determine the couple $\mathbf{M}$ required to hold the system in equilibrium when $\theta = 30°$.

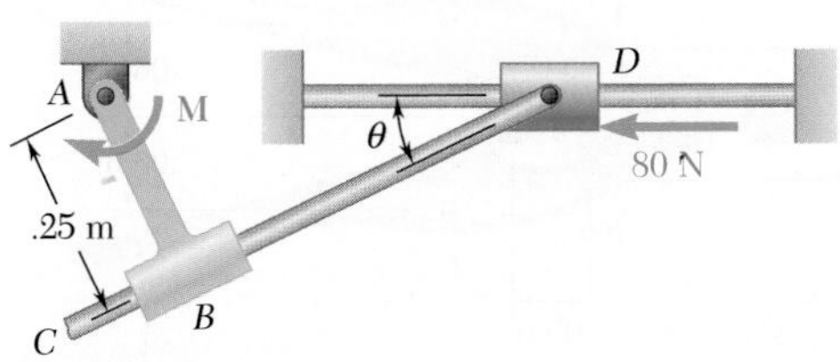

Fig. P6.133

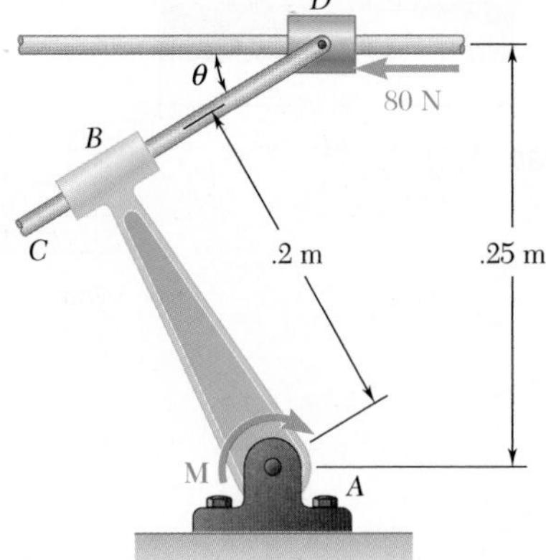

Fig. *P6.134*

6.135 A small barrel having a weight of 250 N is lifted by a pair of tongs as shown. Knowing that a = .127 m, determine the forces exerted at B and D on tong ABD.

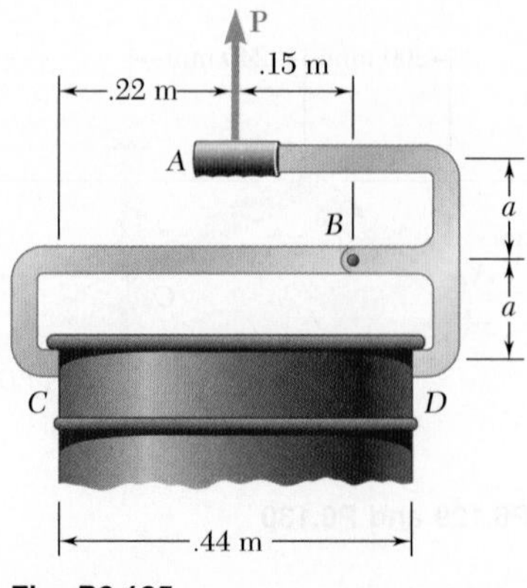

Fig. *P6.135*

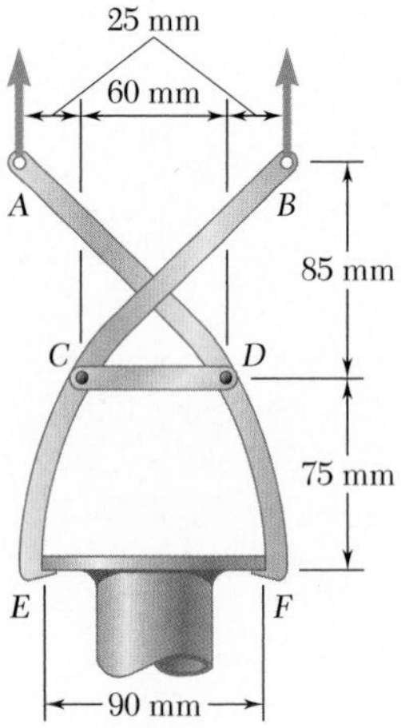

25 mm
60 mm
A
B
85 mm
C
D
75 mm
E
F
90 mm

Fig. P6.136

6.136 The tongs shown are used to apply a total upward force of 45 kN on a pipe cap. Determine the forces exerted at D and F on tong ADF.

6.137 The pallet puller shown is used to pull a loaded pallet to the rear of a truck. Knowing that P = 2.1 kN, determine the forces exerted at G and H on tong FGH.

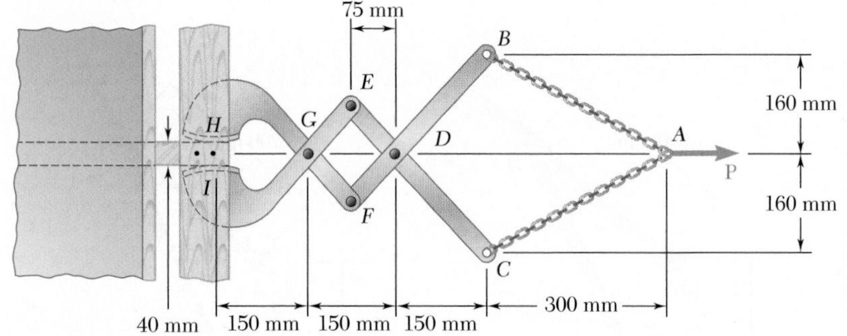

Fig. P6.137

6.138 The drum lifter shown is used to lift a steel drum. Knowing that the weight of the drum and its contents is 110 N, determine the forces exerted at F and H on member DFH.

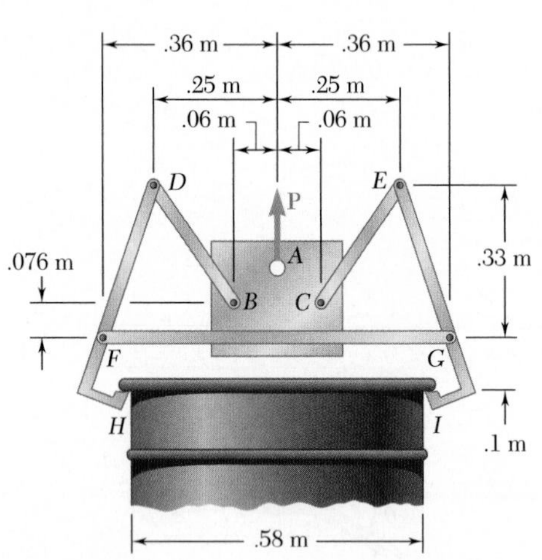

Fig. *P6.138*

6.139 A hand-operated hydraulic cylinder has been designed for use where space is severely limited. Determine the magnitude of the force exerted on the piston at D when two 90-N forces are applied as shown.

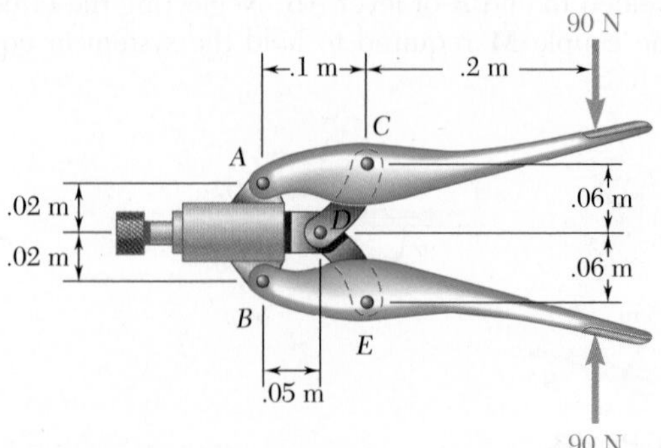

Fig. P6.139

6.140 The tool shown is used to crimp terminals onto electric wires. Knowing that a worker applies forces of magnitude $P = 135$ N to the handles, determine the magnitude of the crimping forces that are exerted on the terminal.

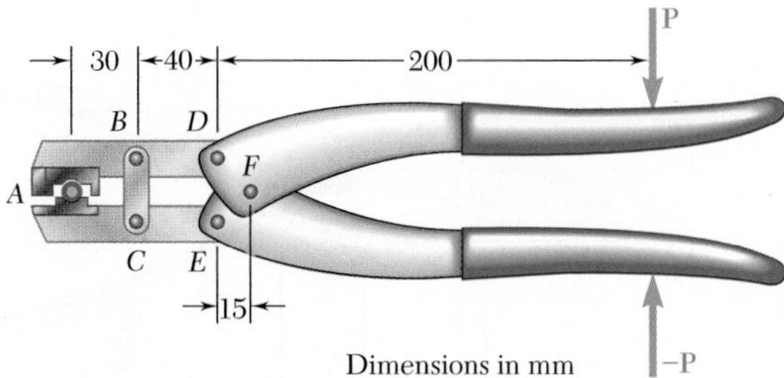

Fig. P6.140

6.141 The compound-lever pruning shears shown can be adjusted by placing pin A at various ratchet positions on blade ACE. Knowing that 1.5-kN vertical forces are required to complete the pruning of a small branch, determine the magnitude P of the forces that must be applied to the handles when the shears are adjusted as shown.

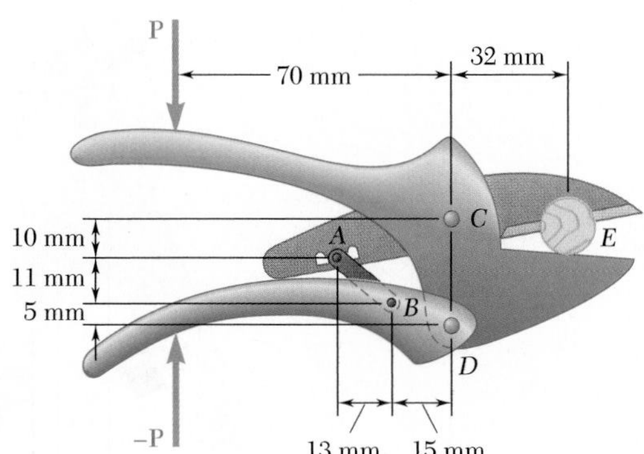

Fig. P6.141

6.142 A locking C-clamp is used to clamp two pieces of .006-m steel plate. Determine the magnitude of the gripping forces produced when two 30-N forces are applied as shown.

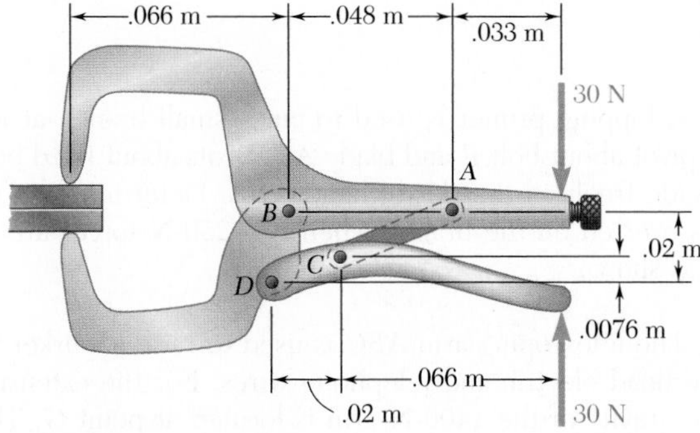

Fig. P6.142

6.143 Determine the force **P** which must be applied to the toggle BCD to maintain equilibrium in the position shown.

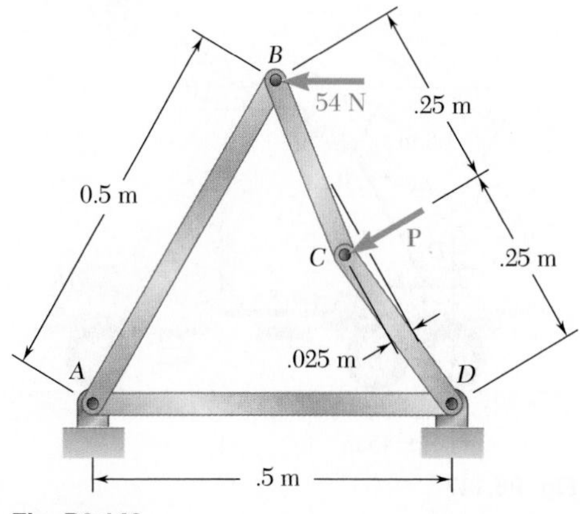

Fig. P6.143

6.144 In the locked position shown, the toggle clamp exerts at A a vertical 270-N force on the wooden block, and handle CF rests against the stop at G. Determine the force $\mathbf{P}$ required to release the clamp. (*Hint:* To release the clamp, the forces of contact at G must be zero.)

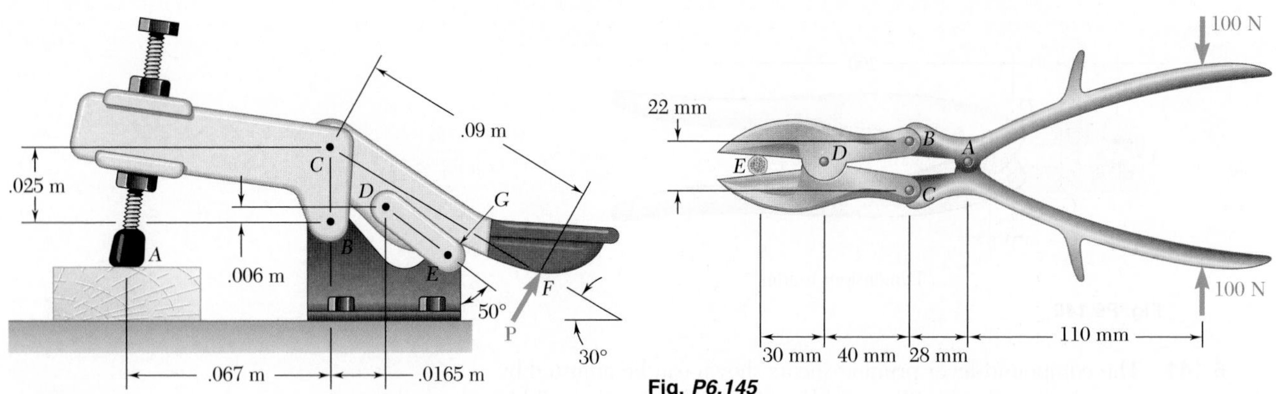

Fig. P6.144

Fig. *P6.145*

6.145 The bone rongeur shown is used in surgical procedures to cut small bones. Determine the magnitude of the forces exerted on the bone at E when two 100-N forces are applied as shown.

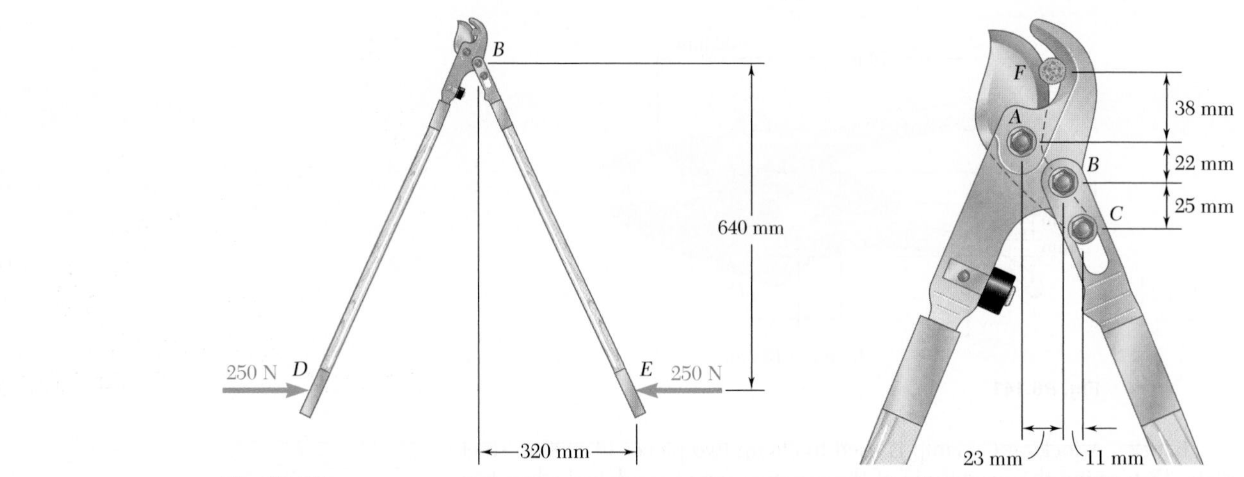

Fig. P6.146

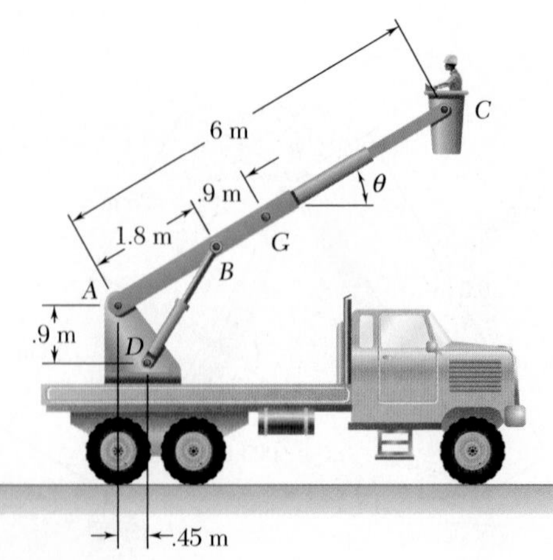

Fig. P6.147

6.146 A lopping pruner is used to cut a small branch at F. Handles AD and BE pivot about bolt B and blade AC pivots about fixed bolt A while bolt C can slide freely in the slot of handle BE. Determine the magnitude of the forces exerted on the branch when two 250-N forces are applied to the handles as shown.

6.147 The telescoping arm ABC is used to raise a worker to the elevation of overhead electric and telephone wires. For the extension shown, the center of gravity of the 1400-N arm is located at point G. The worker, the bucket, and equipment attached to the bucket together weigh 450 N and have a combined center of gravity at C. Determine the force exerted at B by the hydraulic cylinder BD when $\theta = 35°$.

6.148 The position of the spindle DE of a lift truck is partially controlled by two identical linkage-and-hydraulic-cylinder systems, only one of which is shown. A 3000-N spool of electric cable is held by the spindle in the position shown. Knowing that the load supported by the one system shown is 1500 N, determine (*a*) the force exerted by the hydraulic cylinder on point G, (*b*) the components of the force exerted on member BCF at point C.

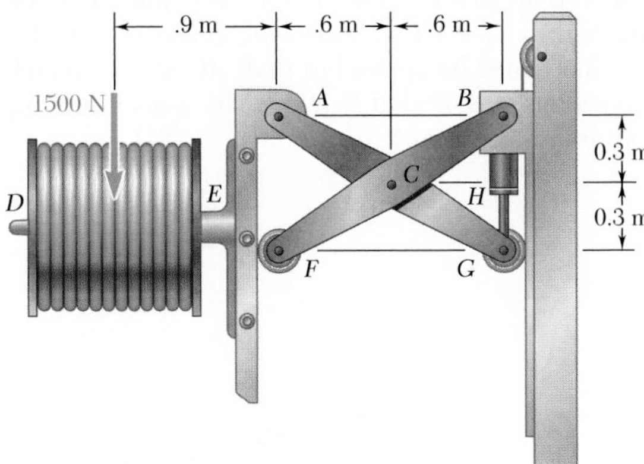

Fig. P6.148

6.149 The telescoping arm ABC is used to provide an elevated platform for construction workers. The workers and the platform together have a mass of 240 kg and have a combined center of gravity located directly above C. For the position when $\theta = 24°$, determine (*a*) the force exerted at B by the hydraulic cylinder BD, (*b*) the force exerted on the supporting carriage at A.

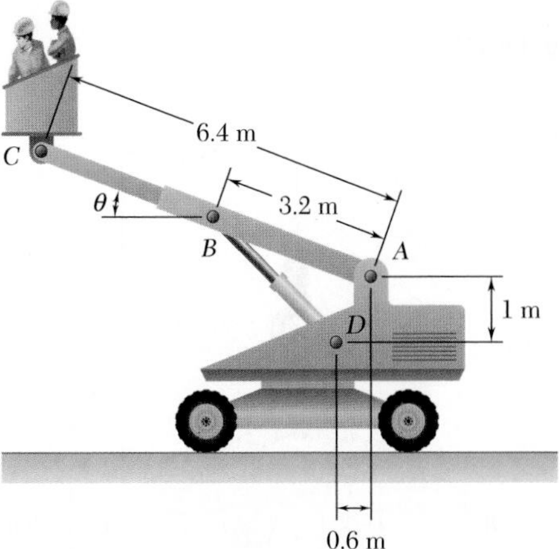

Fig. P6.149

6.150 A 500-kg concrete slab is supported by a chain and sling attached to the bucket of the front-end loader shown. The action of the bucket is controlled by two identical mechanisms, only one of which is shown. Knowing that the mechanism shown supports half of the 500-kg slab, determine the force (*a*) in cylinder CD, (*b*) in cylinder FH.

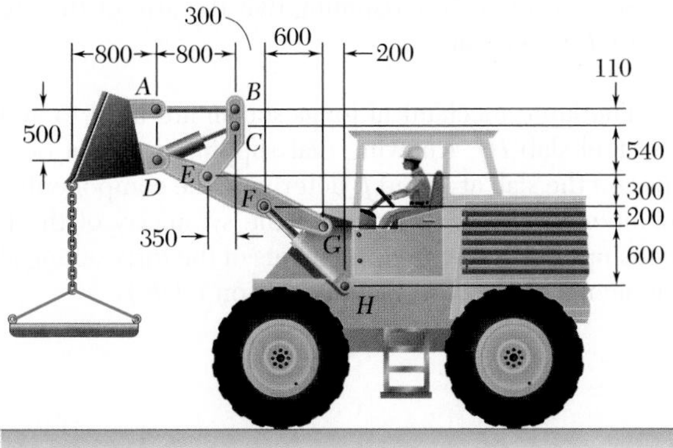

Fig. P6.150

6.151 In the planetary gear system shown, the radius of the central gear A is $a = 24$ mm, the radius of the planetary gears is b, and the radius of the outer gear E is $(a + 2b)$. A clockwise couple of magnitude $M_A = 15$ N · m is applied to the central gear A, and a counterclockwise couple of magnitude $M_S = 75$ N · m is applied to the spider BCD. If the system is to be in equilibrium, determine (*a*) the required radius b of the planetary gears, (*b*) the couple $\mathbf{M}_E$ that must be applied to the outer gear E.

Fig. P6.151

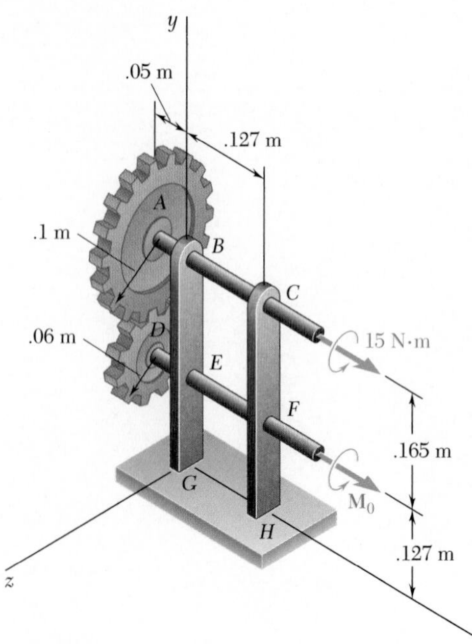

Fig. P6.152

6.152 Gears A and D are rigidly attached to horizontal shafts that are held by frictionless bearings. Determine (*a*) the couple $\mathbf{M}_0$ that must be applied to shaft DEF to maintain equilibrium, (*b*) the reactions at G and H.

***6.153** Two shafts AC and CF lie in the vertical xy plane and are connected by a universal joint at C. The bearings at B and D do not exert any axial forces. A couple of magnitude 50 N · m (clockwise when viewed from the positive x axis) is applied to shaft CF at F. At a time when the arm of the crosspiece attached to shaft CF is horizontal, determine (*a*) the magnitude of the couple which must be applied to shaft AC at A to maintain equilibrium, (*b*) the reactions at B, D, and E. (*Hint:* The sum of the couples exerted on the crosspiece must be zero.)

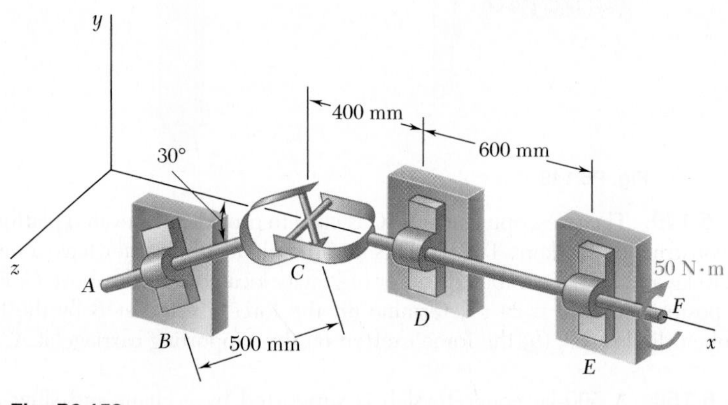

Fig. *P6.153*

***6.154** Solve Prob. 6.153 assuming that the arm of the crosspiece attached to shaft CF is vertical.

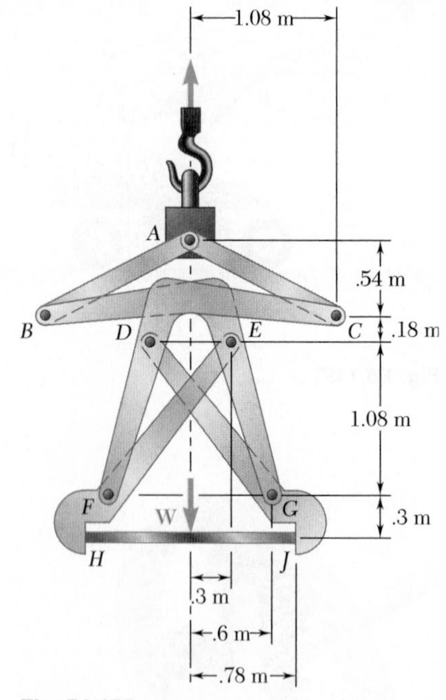

Fig. P6.155

***6.155** The large mechanical tongs shown are used to grab and lift a thick 1500-N steel slab HJ. Knowing that slipping does not occur between the tong grips and the slab at H and J, determine the components of all forces acting on member EFH. (*Hint:* Consider the symmetry of the tongs to establish relationships between the components of the force acting at E on EFH and the components of the force acting at D on CDF.)

REVIEW AND SUMMARY FOR CHAPTER 6

In this chapter you learned to determine the *internal forces* holding together the various parts of a structure.

Analysis of trusses

The first half of the chapter was devoted to the analysis of *trusses,* that is, to the analysis of structures consisting of *straight members connected at their extremities only*. The members being slender and unable to support lateral loads, all the loads must be applied at the joints; a truss may thus be assumed to consist of *pins and two-force members* [Sec. 6.2].

Simple trusses

A truss is said to be *rigid* if it is designed in such a way that it will not greatly deform or collapse under a small load. A triangular truss consisting of three members connected at three joints is clearly a rigid truss (Fig. 6.25*a*) and so will be the truss obtained by adding two new members to the first one and connecting them at a new joint (Fig. 6.25*b*). Trusses obtained by repeating this procedure are called *simple trusses*. We may check that in a simple truss the total number of members is $m = 2n - 3$, where n is the total number of joints [Sec. 6.3].

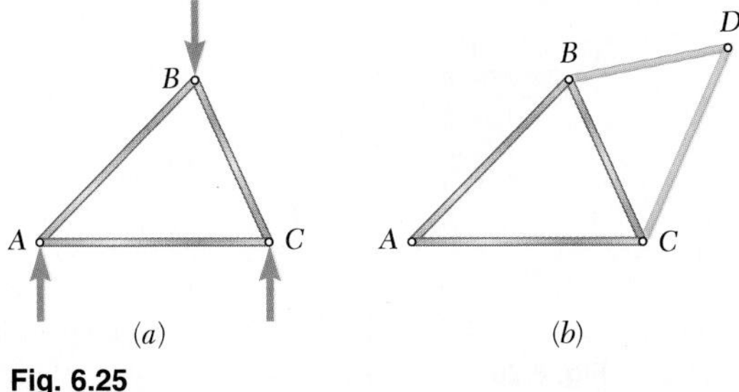

Fig. 6.25

Method of joints

The forces in the various members of a simple truss can be determined by the *method of joints* [Sec. 6.4]. First, the reactions at the supports can be obtained by considering the entire truss as a free body. The free-body diagram of each pin is then drawn, showing the forces exerted on the pin by the members or supports it connects. Since the members are straight two-force members, the force exerted by a member on the pin is directed along that member, and only the magnitude of the force is unknown. It is always possible in the case of a simple truss to draw the free-body diagrams of the pins in such an order that only two unknown forces are included in each diagram. These forces can be obtained from the corresponding two equilibrium equations or—if only three forces are involved—from the corresponding force triangle. If the force exerted by a member on a pin is directed toward that pin, the member is in *compression;* if it is directed away from the pin, the member is in *tension* [Sample Prob. 6.1]. The analysis of a truss is sometimes expedited by first recognizing *joints under special loading conditions* [Sec. 6.5]. The method of joints can also be extended to the analysis of three-dimensional or *space trusses* [Sec. 6.6].

Method of sections

The *method of sections* is usually preferred to the method of joints when the force in only one member—or very few members—of a truss is desired [Sec. 6.7]. To determine the force in member BD of the truss of Fig. 6.26*a*, for example, we *pass a section* through members BD, BE, and CE, remove these members, and use the portion ABC of the truss as a free body (Fig. 6.26*b*). Writing $\Sigma M_E = 0$, we determine the magnitude of the force $\mathbf{F}_{BD}$, which represents the force in member BD. A positive sign indicates that the member is in *tension;* a negative sign indicates that it is in *compression* [Sample Probs. 6.2 and 6.3].

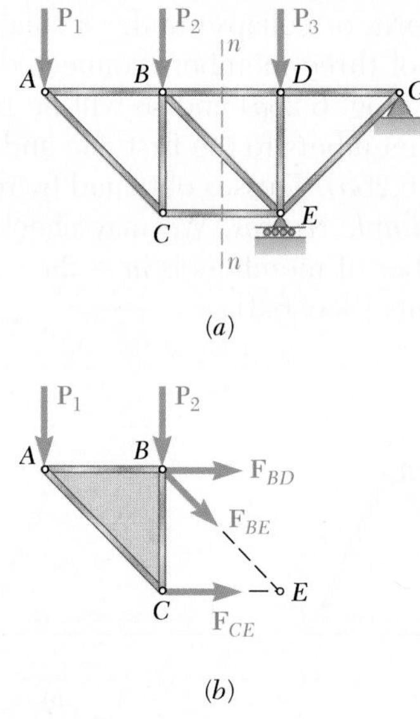

Fig. 6.26

Compound trusses

The method of sections is particularly useful in the analysis of *compound trusses,* that is, trusses which cannot be constructed from the basic triangular truss of Fig. 6.25*a* but which can be obtained by rigidly connecting several simple trusses [Sec. 6.8]. If the component trusses have been properly connected (for example, one pin and one link, or three nonconcurrent and nonparallel links) and if the resulting structure is properly supported (for example, one pin and one roller), the compound truss is *statically determinate, rigid, and completely constrained.* The following necessary—but not sufficient—condition is then satisfied: $m + r = 2n$, where m is the number of members, r is the number of unknowns representing the reactions at the supports, and n is the number of joints.

Frames and machines

The second part of the chapter was devoted to the analysis of *frames and machines*. Frames and machines are structures which contain *multiforce members,* that is, members acted upon by three or more forces. Frames are designed to support loads and are usually stationary, fully constrained structures. Machines are designed to transmit or modify forces and always contain moving parts [Sec. 6.9].

Analysis of a frame

To *analyze a frame,* we first consider the *entire frame as a free body* and write three equilibrium equations [Sec. 6.10]. If the frame remains rigid when detached from its supports, the reactions involve only three unknowns and may be determined from these equations [Sample Probs. 6.4 and 6.5]. On the other hand, if the frame ceases to be rigid when detached from its supports, the reactions involve more than three unknowns and cannot be completely determined from the equilibrium equations of the frame [Sec. 6.11; Sample Prob. 6.6].

Multiforce members

We then *dismember the frame* and identify the various members as either two-force members or multiforce members; pins are assumed to form an integral part of one of the members they connect. We draw the free-body diagram of each of the multiforce members, noting that when two multiforce members are connected to the same two-force member, they are acted upon by that member with *equal and opposite forces of unknown magnitude but known direction*. When two multiforce members are connected by a pin, they exert on each other *equal and opposite forces of unknown direction,* which should be represented by *two unknown components*. The equilibrium equations obtained from the free-body diagrams of the multiforce members can then be solved for the various internal forces [Sample Probs. 6.4 and 6.5]. The equilibrium equations can also be used to complete the determination of the reactions at the supports [Sample Prob. 6.6]. Actually, if the frame is *statically determinate and rigid,* the free-body diagrams of the multiforce members could provide as many equations as there are unknown forces (including the reactions) [Sec. 6.11]. However, as suggested above, it is advisable to first consider the free-body diagram of the entire frame to minimize the number of equations that must be solved simultaneously.

Analysis of a machine

To *analyze a machine,* we dismember it and, following the same procedure as for a frame, draw the free-body diagram of each of the multiforce members. The corresponding equilibrium equations yield the *output forces* exerted by the machine in terms of the *input forces* applied to it, as well as the *internal forces* at the various connections [Sec. 6.12; Sample Prob. 6.7].

Review Problems

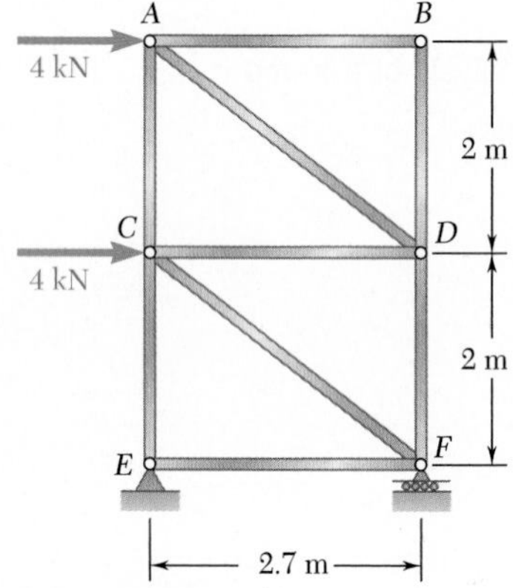

Fig. P6.156

6.156 Using the method of joints, determine the force in each member of the truss shown. State whether each member is in tension or compression.

6.157 Determine the force in member FG and in each of the members located to the right of member FG for the scissor roof truss shown. State whether each member is in tension or compression.

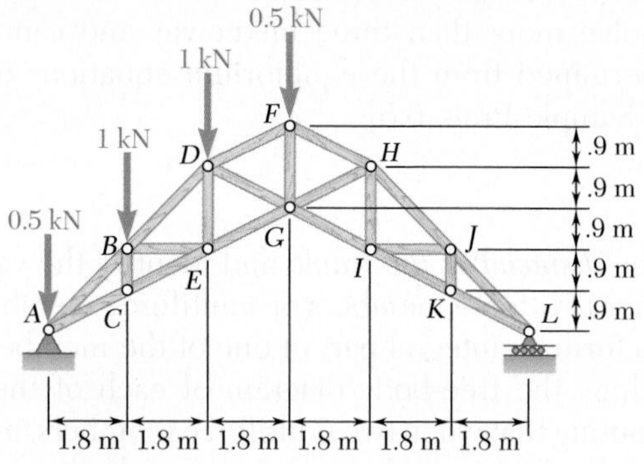

Fig. P6.157

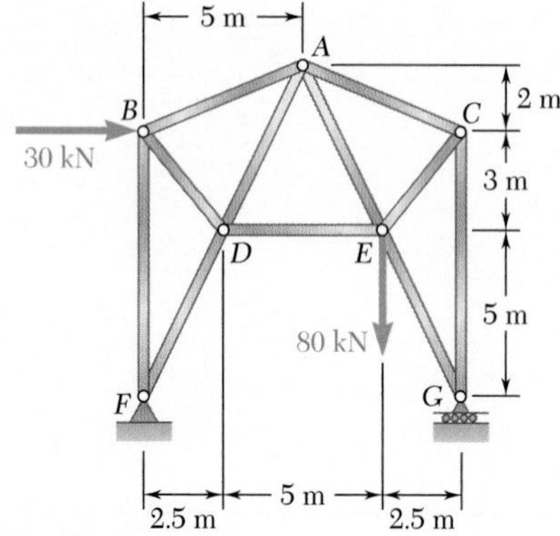

Fig. P6.158

6.158 Determine the force in each member of the truss shown. State whether each member is in tension or compression.

6.159 A pitched flat roof truss is loaded as shown. Determine the force in members CE, DE, and DF.

6.160 A stadium roof truss is loaded as shown. Determine the force in members AB, AG, and FG.

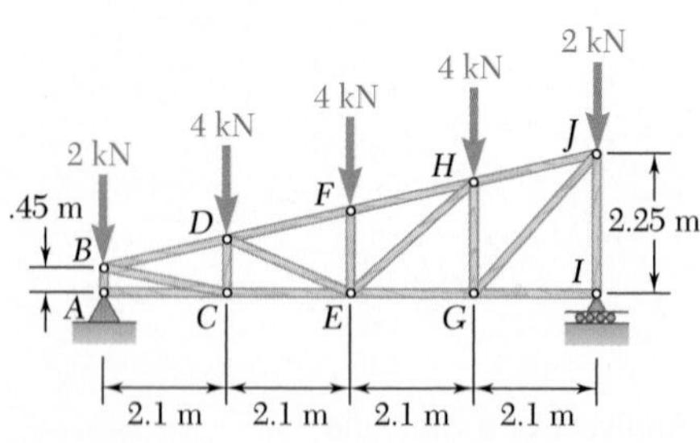

Fig. *P6.159*

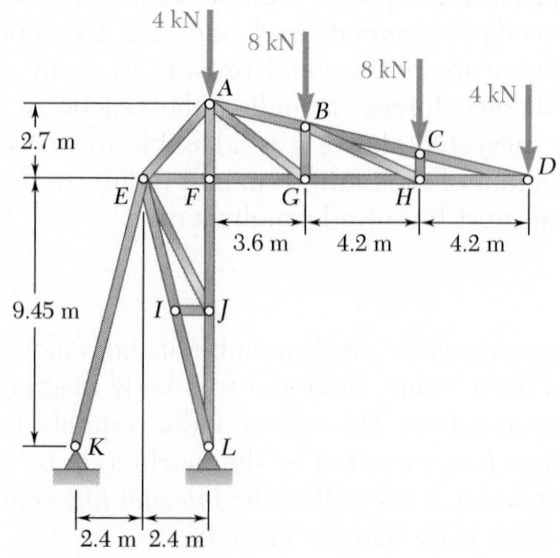

Fig. P6.160

6.161 Determine the force in members *AF* and *EJ* of the truss shown when $P = Q = 2$ kN. (*Hint:* Use section *aa*.)

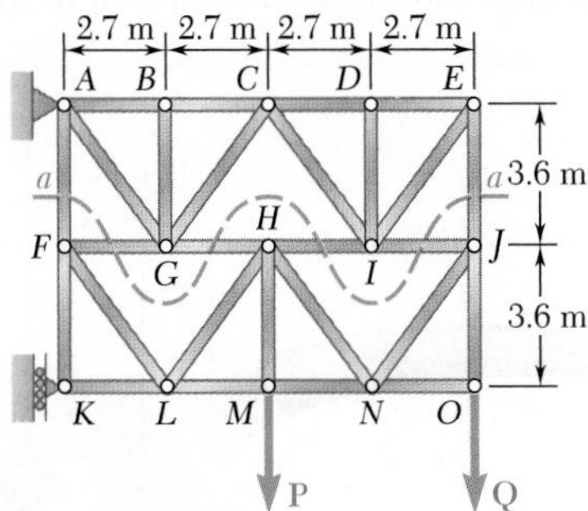

Fig. *P6.161*

6.162 For the frame and loading shown, determine the components of all forces acting on member *ABC*.

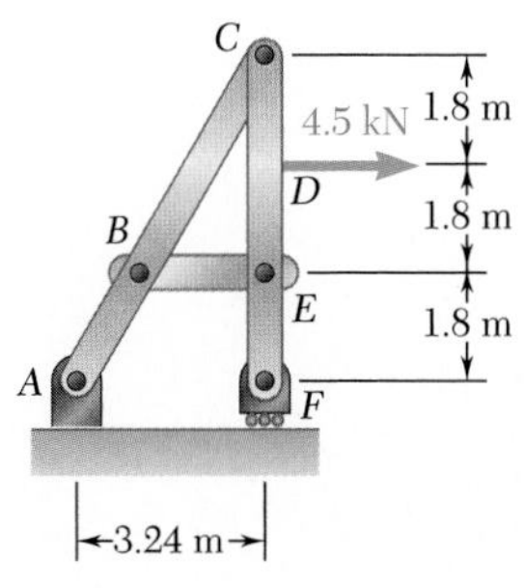

Fig. P6.162

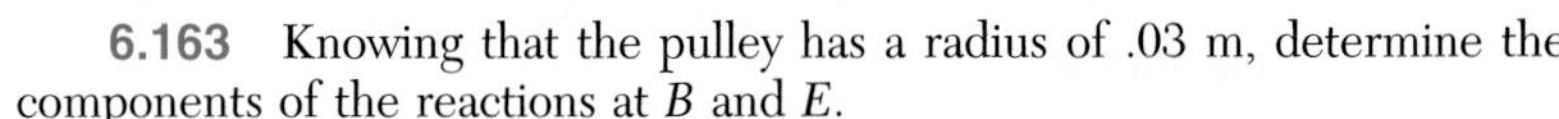

6.163 Knowing that the pulley has a radius of .03 m, determine the components of the reactions at *B* and *E*.

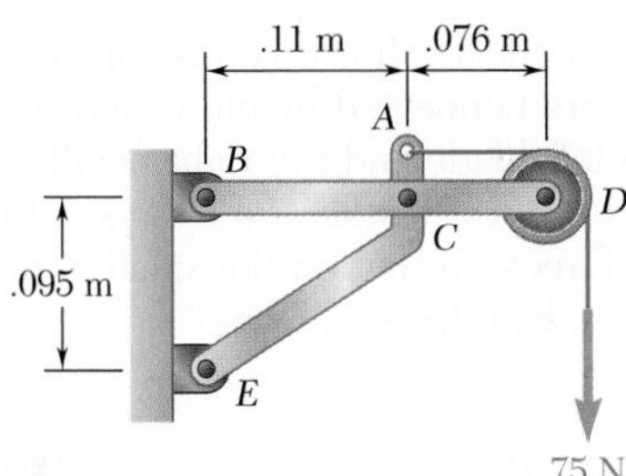

Fig. P6.163

6.164 Knowing that $P = 15$ N and $Q = 65$ N, determine the components of the forces exerted (*a*) on member *BCDF* at *C* and *D*, (*b*) on member *ACEG* at *E*.

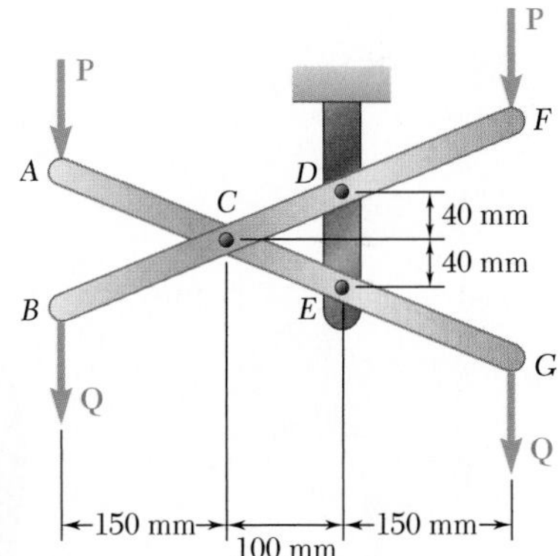

Fig. *P6.164*

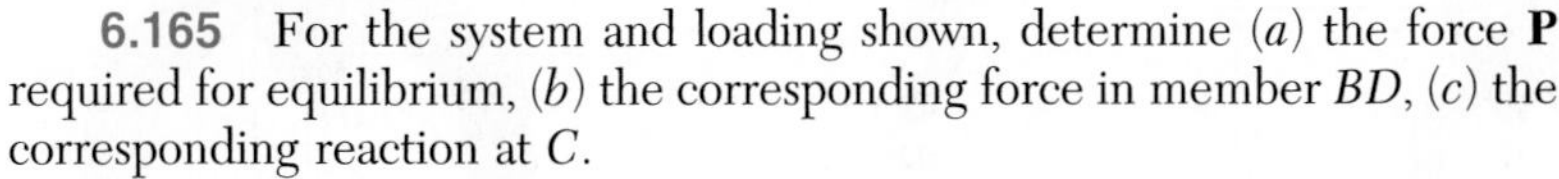

6.165 For the system and loading shown, determine (*a*) the force **P** required for equilibrium, (*b*) the corresponding force in member *BD*, (*c*) the corresponding reaction at *C*.

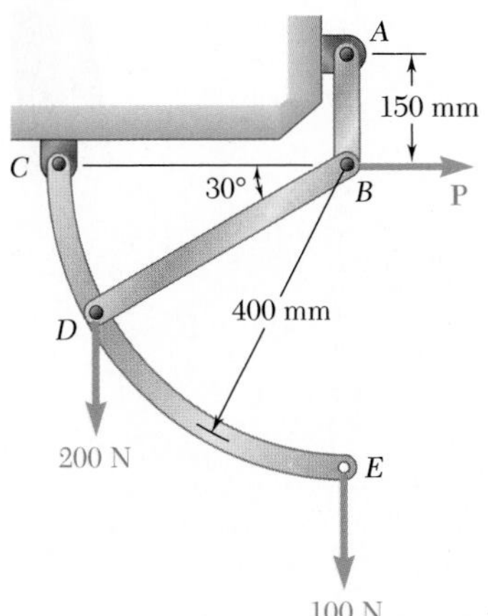

Fig. P6.165

6.166 Determine the magnitude of the gripping forces exerted along line *aa* on the nut when two 240-N forces are applied to the handles as shown. Assume that pins *A* and *D* slide freely in slots cut in the jaws.

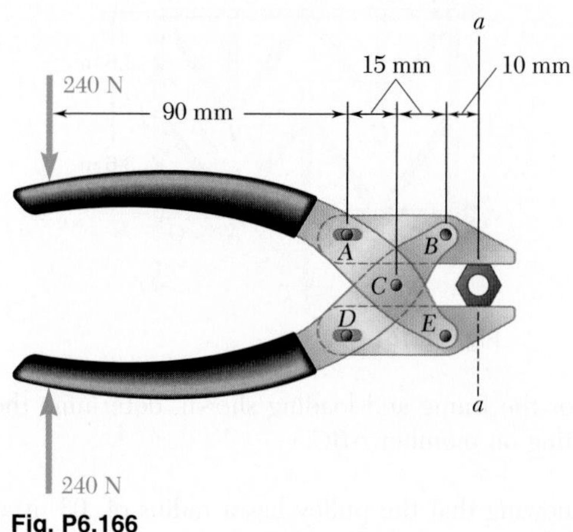

Fig. P6.166

6.167 The garden shears shown consist of two blades and two handles. The two handles are connected by pin *C* and the two blades are connected by pin *D*. The left blade and the right handle are connected by pin *A*; the right blade and the left handle are connected by pin *B*. Determine the magnitude of the forces exerted on the small branch *E* when two 20-N forces are applied to the handles as shown.

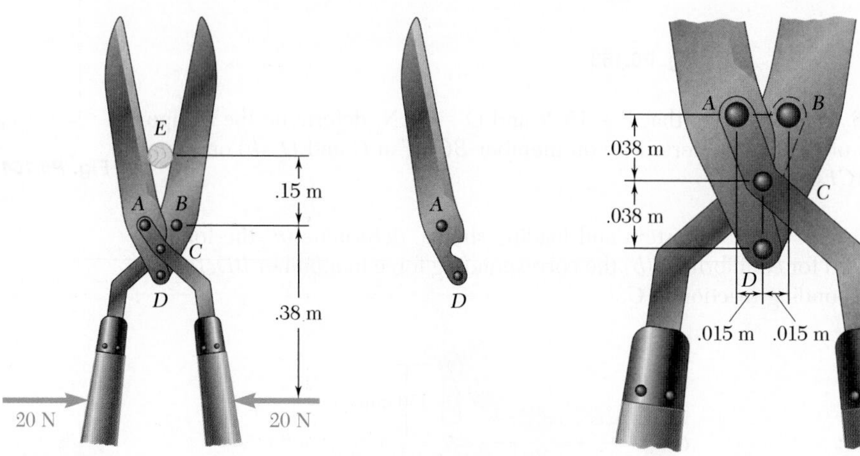

Fig. *P6.167*

Computer Problems

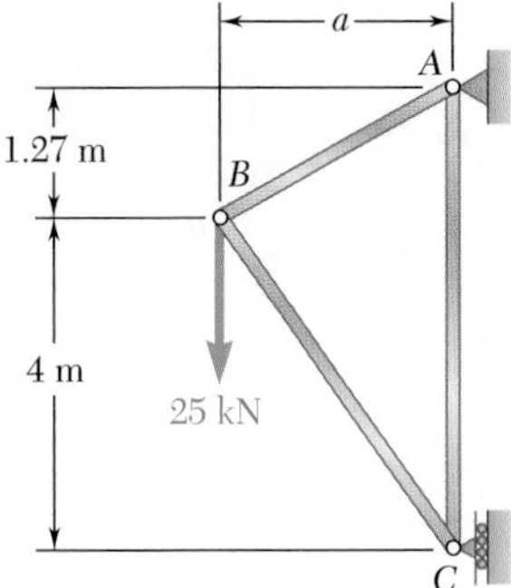

Fig. P6.C1

6.C1 For the loading shown, determine the force in each member of the truss as a function of the dimension a. Plot the force in each member for 40 in. $\leq a \leq 6$ m, with tensile forces plotted as positive and compressive forces as negative.

6.C2 In the Fink truss shown, a single 3.75-kN load is to be applied to the top chord of the truss at one of the numbered joints. Calculate the force in member CD as the load is successively applied at joints 1, 2, . . . , 9.

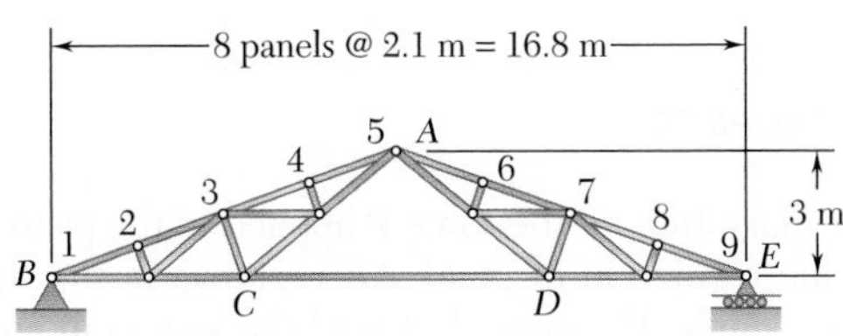

Fig. P6.C2

6.C3 The floor of a bridge will rest on stringers that will be simply supported by transverse floor beams, as in Fig 6.3. The ends of the beams will be connected to the upper joints of two trusses, one of which is shown in Fig. P6.C3. As part of the design of the bridge, it is desired to simulate the effect on this truss of driving a 3-kN truck over the bridge. Knowing that the distance between the truck's axles is $b = 2.25$ m and assuming that the weight of the truck is equally distributed over its four wheels, use computational software to calculate and plot the forces created by the truck in members BH and GH as a function of x for $0 \leq x \leq 17.25$ m. From the results obtained, determine (a) the maximum tensile force in BH, (b) the maximum compressive force in BH, (c) the maximum tensile force in GH. Indicate in each case the corresponding value of x.

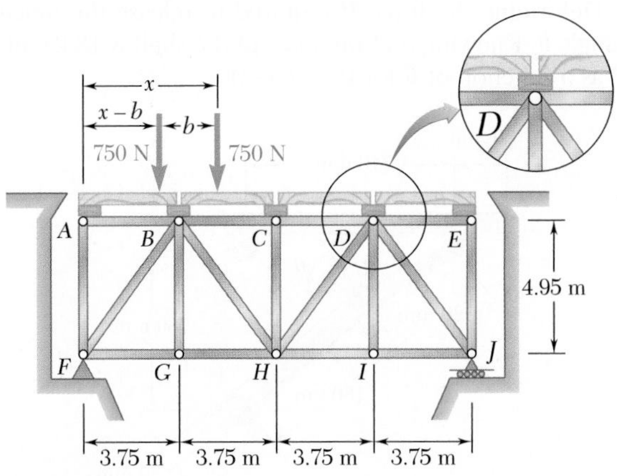

Fig. P6.C3

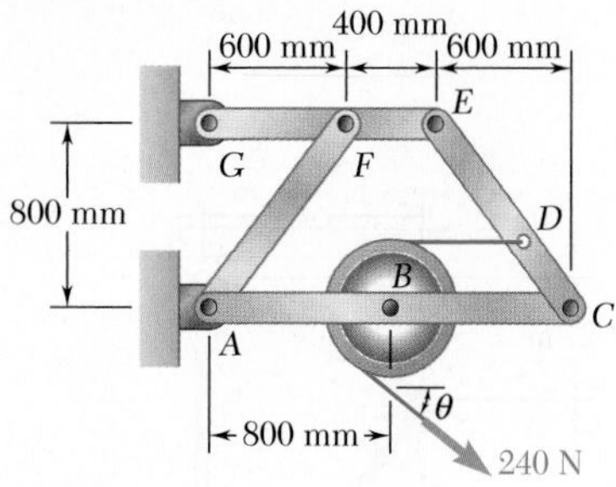

Fig. P6.C4

6.C4 Knowing that the radius of the pulley is 300 mm, plot the magnitude of the reactions at A and G as functions of θ for $0 \leq \theta \leq 90°$.

6.C5 The design of a robotic system calls for the two-rod mechanism shown. Rods AC and BD are connected by a slider block D as shown. Neglecting the effect of friction, calculate and plot the couple $\mathbf{M}_A$ required to hold the rods in equilibrium for values of θ from 0 to 120°. For the same values of θ, calculate and plot the magnitude of the force $\mathbf{F}$ exerted by rod AC on the slider block.

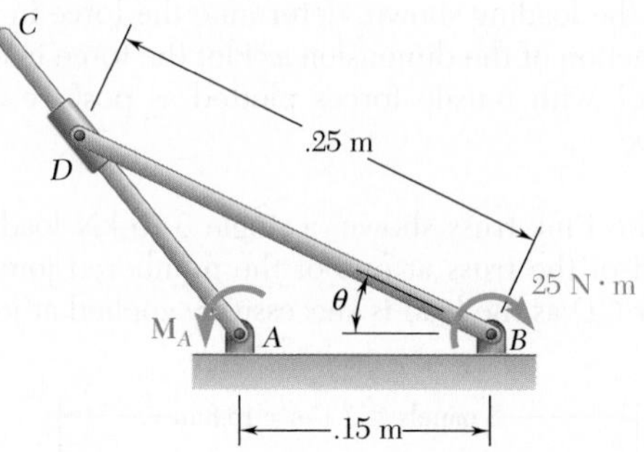

Fig. P6.C5

6.C6 The magnitude of the force $\mathbf{P}$ applied to the piston of an engine system during one revolution of crank AB is shown in the figure. Plot the magnitude of the couple $\mathbf{M}$ required to hold the system in equilibrium as a function of θ for $0 \leq \theta \leq 2\pi$.

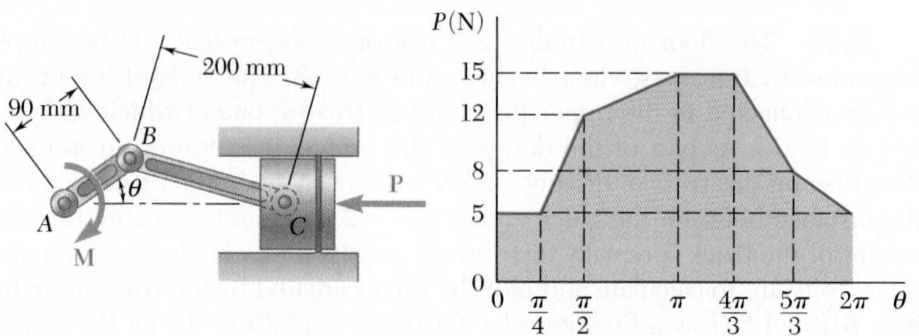

Fig. P6.C6

6.C7 The shelf ABC is held horizontally by a self-locking brace that consists of two parts BDE and EDF hinged at E and bearing against each other at D. Determine the force $\mathbf{P}$ required to release the brace as a function of the angle θ. Knowing that the mass of the shelf is 18 kg, plot the magnitude of $\mathbf{P}$ as a function of θ for $0° \leq \theta \leq 90°$.

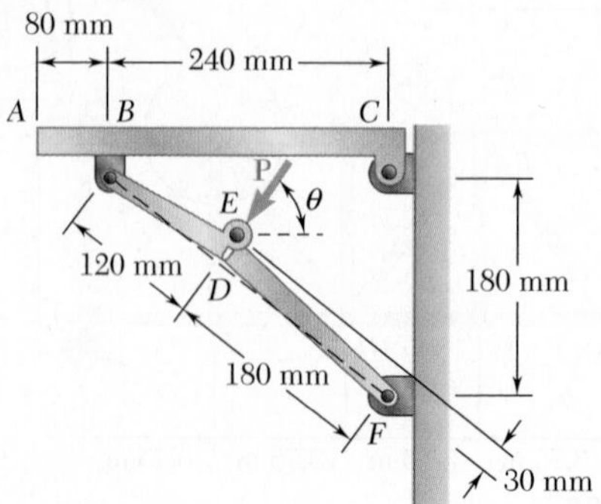

Fig. P6.C7

6.C8 In the mechanism shown, the position of boom AC is controlled by arm BD. For the loading shown, calculate and plot the reaction at A and the couple $\mathbf{M}$ required to hold the system in equilibrium as functions of θ for $-30° \leq \theta \leq 90°$. As part of the design process of the mechanism, determine (*a*) the value of θ for which M is maximum and the corresponding value of M, (*b*) the value of θ for which the reaction at A is maximum and the corresponding magnitude of this reaction.

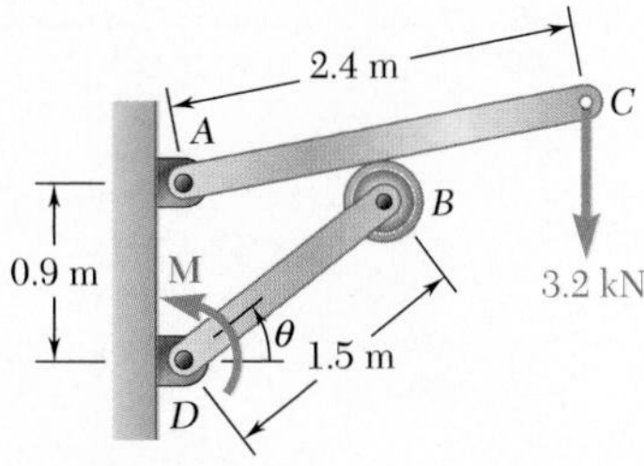

Fig. P6.C8

6.C9 Rod CD is attached to collar D and passes through a collar welded to end B of lever AB. As an initial step in the design of lever AB, use computational software to calculate and plot the magnitude M of the couple required to hold the system in equilibrium as a function of θ for $15° \leq \theta \leq 90°$. Determine the value of θ for which M is minimum and the corresponding value of M.

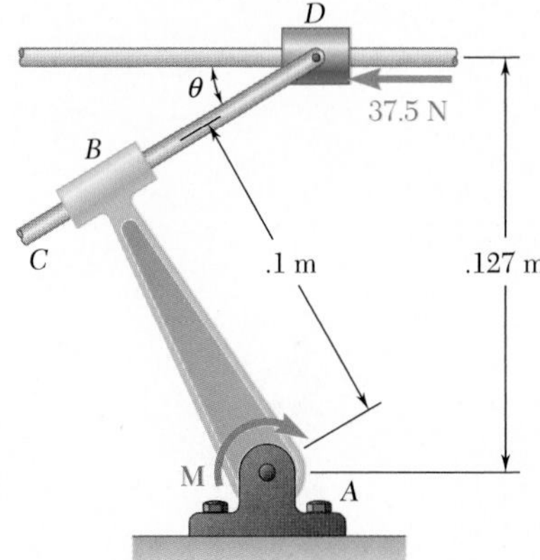

Fig. P6.C9

***6.C10** The tree trimmer shown is used to prune a 25-mm-diameter branch. Knowing that the tension in the rope is 70 N and neglecting the radii of the pulleys, plot the magnitude of the force exerted on the branch by blade BC as a function of θ for $0 \leq \theta \leq 90°$, where the cutting edge of the blade is vertical and just contacts the branch when $\theta = 0$. (*Hint:* Assume that the line of action of the force acting on the branch passes through the center of the branch and is perpendicular to the blade and that portions AD and AE of the rope are parallel to a line drawn through points A and E.)

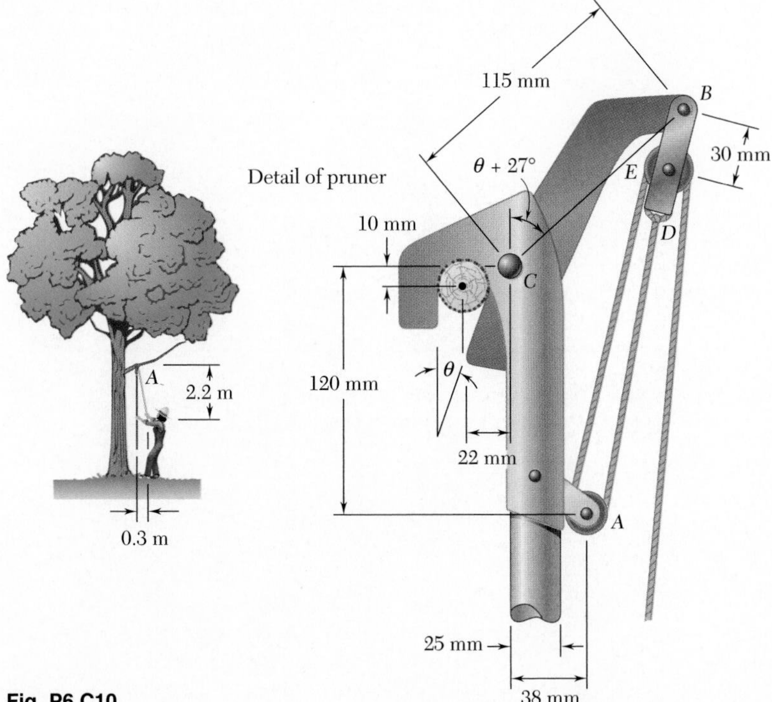

Fig. P6.C10

CHAPTER 7

Forces in Beams and Cables

The Grand Viaduc de Millau, completed in 2005, spans the Tarn River Gorge in southern France and is part of a new route between Paris and Barcelona. The 2.46-km-long, cable-stayed bridge and its tallest pier rise 245 m and 335 m, respectively, above the River Tarn.

*7.1. INTRODUCTION

In preceding chapters, two basic problems involving structures were considered: (1) determining the external forces acting on a structure (Chap. 4) and (2) determining the forces which hold together the various members forming a structure (Chap. 6). The problem of determining the internal forces which hold together the various parts of a given member will now be considered.

We will first analyze the internal forces in the members of a frame, such as the crane considered in Secs. 6.1 and 6.10, noting that whereas the internal forces in a straight two-force member can produce only *tension* or *compression* in that member, the internal forces in any other type of member usually produce *shear* and *bending* as well.

Most of this chapter will be devoted to the analysis of the internal forces in two important types of engineering structures, namely,

1. *Beams,* which are usually long, straight prismatic members designed to support loads applied at various points along the member.
2. *Cables,* which are flexible members capable of withstanding only tension and are designed to support either concentrated or distributed loads. Cables are used in many engineering applications, such as suspension bridges and transmission lines.

*7.2. INTERNAL FORCES IN MEMBERS

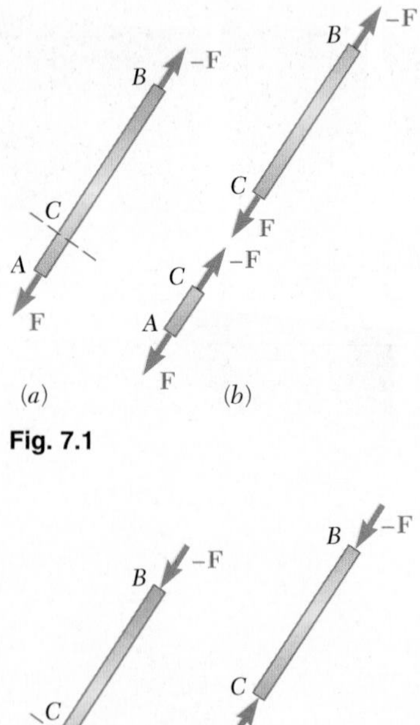

(*a*) (*b*)

Fig. 7.1

Let us first consider a *straight two-force member AB* (Fig. 7.1*a*). From Sec. 4.6, we know that the forces **F** and $-$**F** acting at A and B, respectively, must be directed along AB in opposite sense and have the same magnitude F. Now, let us cut the member at C. To maintain the equilibrium of the free bodies AC and CB thus obtained, we must apply to AC a force $-$**F** equal and opposite to **F**, and to CB a force **F** equal and opposite to $-$**F** (Fig. 7.1*b*). These new forces are directed along AB in opposite sense and have the same magnitude F. Since the two parts AC and CB were in equilibrium before the member was cut, *internal forces* equivalent to these new forces must have existed in the member itself. We conclude that in the case of a straight two-force member, the internal forces that the two portions of the member exert on each other are equivalent to *axial forces.* The common magnitude F of these forces does not depend upon the location of the section C and is referred to as the *force in member AB.* In the case considered, the member is in tension and will elongate under the action of the internal forces. In the case represented in Fig. 7.2, the member is in compression and will decrease in length under the action of the internal forces.

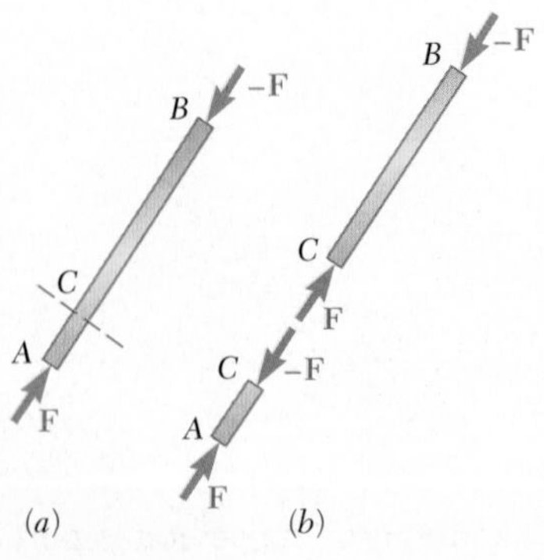

Fig. 7.2

Next, let us consider a *multiforce member.* Take, for instance, member AD of the crane analyzed in Sec. 6.10. This crane is shown again in Fig. 7.3*a*, and the free-body diagram of member AD is drawn in Fig. 7.3*b*. We now cut member AD at J and draw a free-body diagram for each of the portions JD and AJ of the member (Fig. 7.3*c* and *d*). Considering the free body JD, we find that its equilibrium will

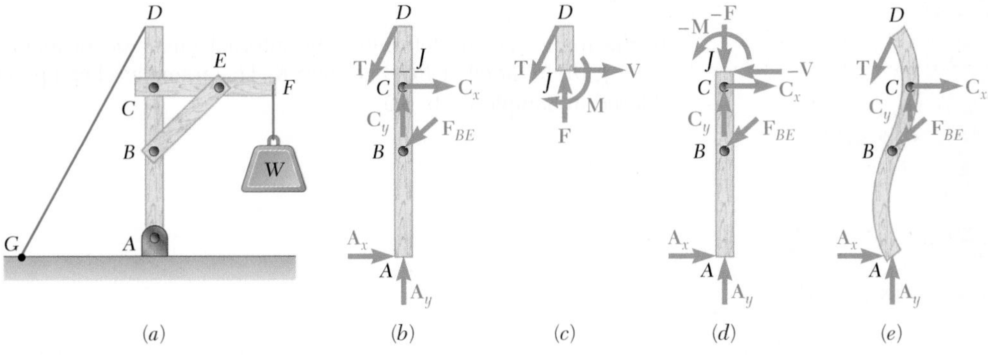

Fig. 7.3

be maintained if we apply at *J* a force **F** to balance the vertical component of **T**, a force **V** to balance the horizontal component of **T**, and a couple **M** to balance the moment of **T** about *J*. Again we conclude that internal forces must have existed at *J* before member *AD* was cut. The internal forces acting on the portion *JD* of member *AD* are equivalent to the force-couple system shown in Fig. 7.3*c*. According to Newton's third law, the internal forces acting on *AJ* must be equivalent to an equal and opposite force-couple system, as shown in Fig. 7.3*d*. It is clear that the action of the internal forces in member *AD* *is not limited to producing tension or compression* as in the case of straight two-force members; the internal forces *also produce shear and bending*. The force **F** is an *axial force;* the force **V** is called a *shearing force;* and the moment **M** of the couple is known as the *bending moment at J*. We note that when determining internal forces in a member, we should clearly indicate on which portion of the member the forces are supposed to act. The deformation which will occur in member *AD* is sketched in Fig. 7.3*e*. The actual analysis of such a deformation is part of the study of mechanics of materials.

It should be noted that in a *two-force member which is not straight,* the internal forces are also equivalent to a force-couple system. This is shown in Fig. 7.4, where the two-force member *ABC* has been cut at *D*.

Photo 7.1 The design of the shaft of a circular saw must account for the internal forces resulting from the forces applied to the teeth of the blade. At a given point in the shaft, these internal forces are equivalent to a force-couple system consisting of axial and shearing forces and a couple representing the bending and torsional moments.

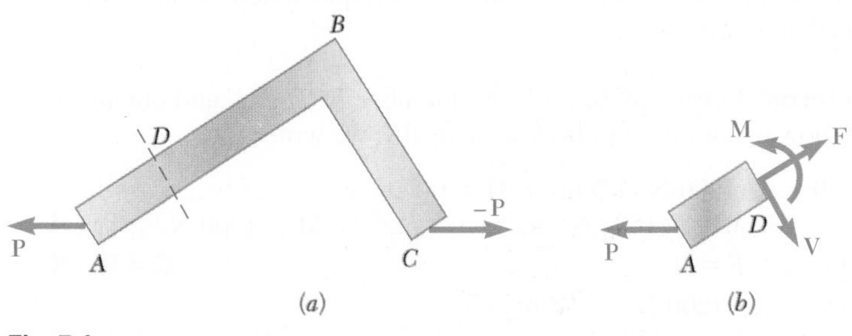

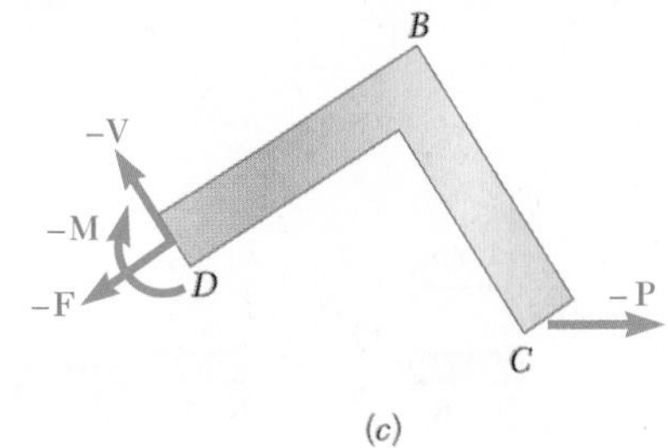

Fig. 7.4

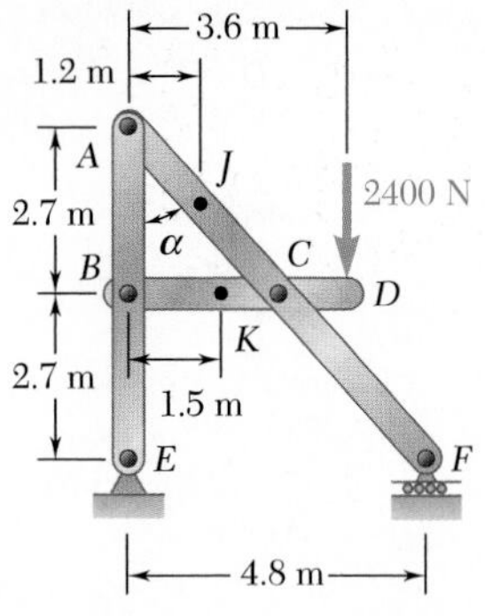

SAMPLE PROBLEM 7.1

In the frame shown, determine the internal forces (*a*) in member *ACF* at point *J*, (*b*) in member *BCD* at point *K*. This frame has been previously considered in Sample Prob. 6.5.

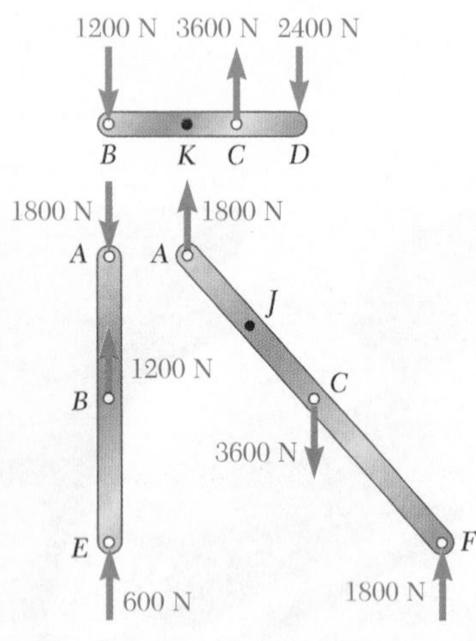

SOLUTION

Reactions and Forces at Connections. The reactions and the forces acting on each member of the frame are determined; this has been previously done in Sample Prob. 6.5, and the results are repeated here.

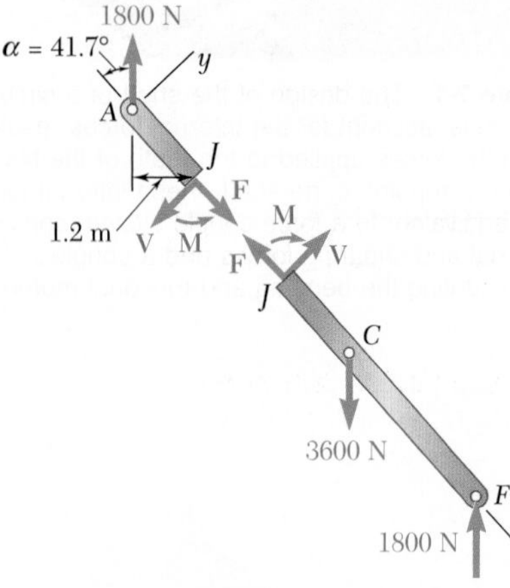

***a.* Internal Forces at *J*.** Member *ACF* is cut at point *J*, and the two parts shown are obtained. The internal forces at *J* are represented by an equivalent force-couple system and can be determined by considering the equilibrium of either part. Considering the *free body AJ*, we write

$+\circlearrowleft\Sigma M_J = 0$: $\quad -(1800 \text{ N})(1.2 \text{ m}) + M = 0$

$M = +2160 \text{ N} \cdot \text{m}$ $\qquad \mathbf{M} = 2160 \text{ N} \cdot \text{m} \circlearrowleft$ ◀

$+\searrow\Sigma F_x = 0$: $\quad F - (1800 \text{ N}) \cos 41.7° = 0$

$F = +1344 \text{ N}$ $\qquad \mathbf{F} = 1344 \text{ N} \searrow$ ◀

$+\nearrow\Sigma F_y = 0$: $\quad -V + (1800 \text{ N}) \sin 41.7° = 0$

$V = +1197 \text{ N}$ $\qquad \mathbf{V} = 1197 \text{ N} \swarrow$ ◀

The internal forces at *J* are therefore equivalent to a couple **M**, an axial force **F**, and a shearing force **V**. The internal force-couple system acting on part *JCF* is equal and opposite.

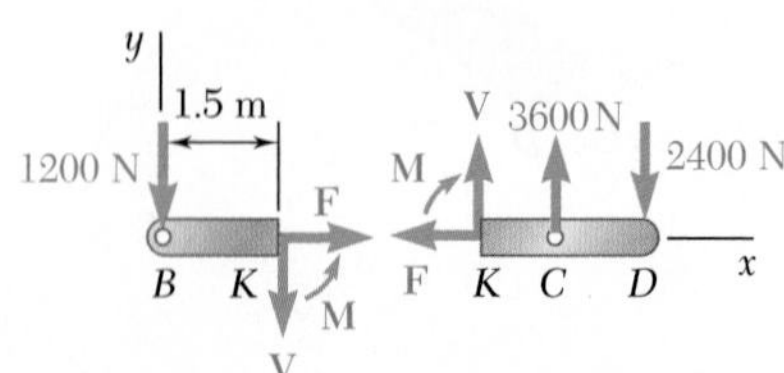

***b.* Internal Forces at *K*.** We cut member *BCD* at *K* and obtain the two parts shown. Considering the *free body BK*, we write

$+\circlearrowleft\Sigma M_K = 0$: $\quad (1200 \text{ N})(1.5 \text{ m}) + M = 0$

$M = -1800 \text{ N} \cdot \text{m}$ $\qquad \mathbf{M} = 1800 \text{ N} \cdot \text{m} \circlearrowright$ ◀

$\xrightarrow{+}\Sigma F_x = 0$: $\quad F = 0$ $\qquad \mathbf{F} = 0$ ◀

$+\uparrow\Sigma F_y = 0$: $\quad -1200 \text{ N} - V = 0$

$V = -1200 \text{ N}$ $\qquad \mathbf{V} = 1200 \text{ N} \uparrow$ ◀

SOLVING PROBLEMS ON YOUR OWN

In this lesson you learned to determine the internal forces in the member of a frame. The internal forces at a given point in a *straight two-force member* reduce to an axial force, but in all other cases, they are equivalent to a *force-couple system* consisting of an *axial force* **F**, a *shearing force* **V**, and a couple **M** representing the *bending moment* at that point.

To determine the internal forces at a given point *J* of the member of a frame, you should take the following steps.

1. ***Draw a free-body diagram of the entire frame,*** and use it to determine as many of the reactions at the supports as you can.

2. ***Dismember the frame, and draw a free-body diagram of each of its members.*** Write as many equilibrium equations as are necessary to find all the forces acting on the member on which point *J* is located.

3. ***Cut the member at point J, and draw a free-body diagram of each of the two portions*** of the member that you have obtained, applying to each portion at point *J* the force components and couple representing the internal forces exerted by the other portion. Note that these force components and couples are equal in magnitude and opposite in sense.

4. ***Select one of the two free-body diagrams*** you have drawn, and use it to write three equilibrium equations for the corresponding portion of the member.

   a. ***Summing moments about J*** and equating them to zero will yield the bending moment at point *J*.

   b. ***Summing components in directions parallel and perpendicular*** to the member at *J* and equating them to zero will yield, respectively, the axial and shearing force.

5. ***When recording your answers, be sure to specify the portion of the member*** you have used, since the forces and couples acting on the two portions have opposite senses.

Since the solutions of the problems in this lesson require the determination of the forces exerted on each other by the various members of a frame, be sure to review the methods used in Chap. 6 to solve this type of problem. When frames involve pulleys and cables, for instance, remember that the forces exerted by a pulley on the member of the frame to which it is attached have the same magnitude and direction as the forces exerted by the cable on the pulley [Prob. 6.91].

Problems

7.1 For the frame and loading of Prob. 6.99, determine the internal forces at a point J located halfway between points B and E.

7.2 For the frame and loading of Prob. 6.78, determine the internal forces at point J.

7.3 For the frame and loading of Prob. 6.82, determine the internal forces at point J.

7.4 For the frame and loading of Prob. 6.85*b*, determine the internal forces at point B.

7.5 Determine the internal forces at point J of the structure shown.

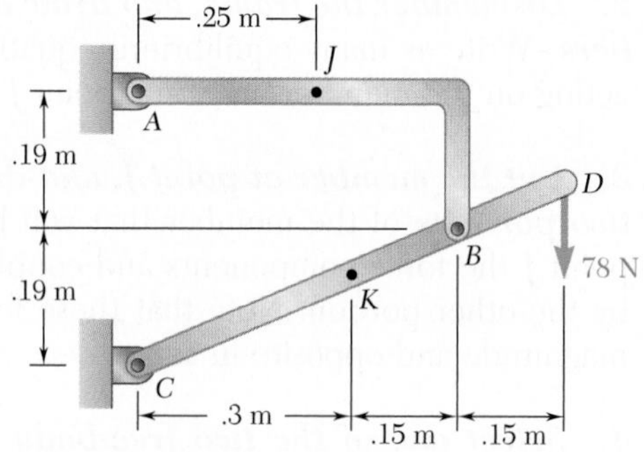

Fig. P7.5 and P7.6

7.6 Determine the internal forces at point K of the structure shown.

7.7 and 7.8 A half section of pipe rests on a horizontal surface as shown. Knowing that the half section of the pipe has a mass of 9 kg and neglecting friction between the pipe and the surface, determine the internal forces at point J.

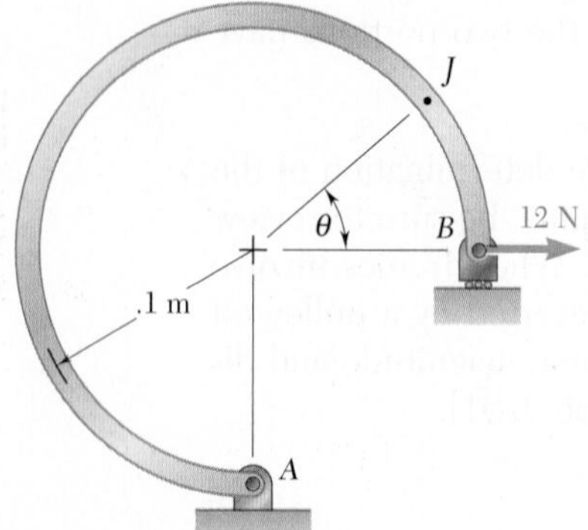

Fig. P7.9 and *P7.10*

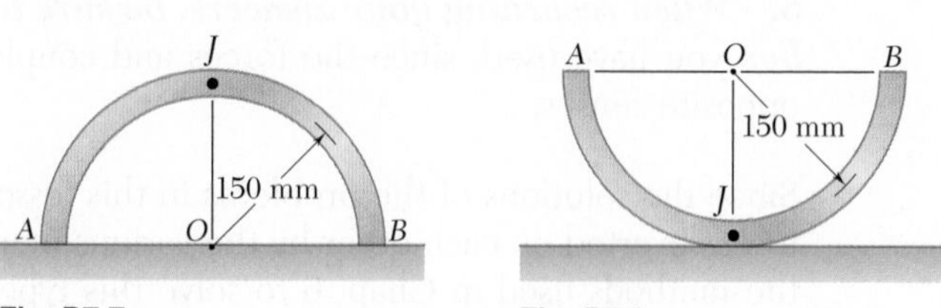

Fig. P7.7 **Fig. P7.8**

7.9 A rod is bent into a circular arc of radius .1 m as shown. For the given loading, determine the internal forces at point J when $\theta = 30°$.

7.10 A rod is bent into a circular arc of radius .1 m as shown. For the given loading, determine (*a*) the location at which the value of the bending moment is maximum, (*b*) the internal forces at that point.

7.11 Two members each consisting of straight and .2-m-radius quarter-circle portions are connected as shown and support a 120-N load at D. Determine the internal forces at point J.

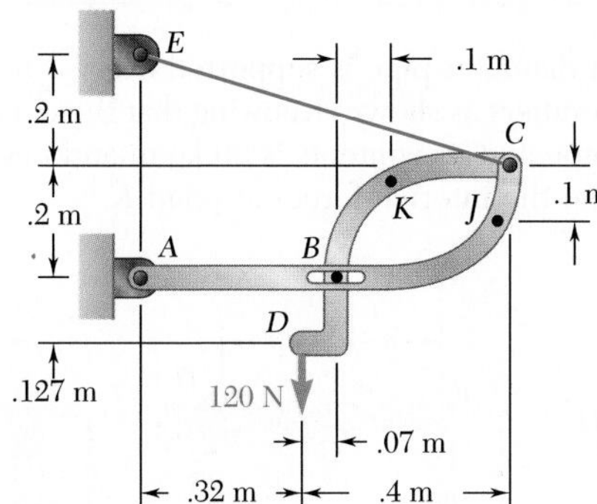

Fig. P7.11 and *P7.12*

7.12 Two members each consisting of straight and .2-m-radius quarter-circle portions are connected as shown and support a 120-N load at D. Determine the internal forces at point K.

7.13 The axis of the curved member AB is a parabola with its vertex at A. If a vertical load **P** of magnitude 1.8 kN is applied at A, determine the internal forces at J when $h = 240$ mm, $L = 800$ mm, and $a = 480$ mm.

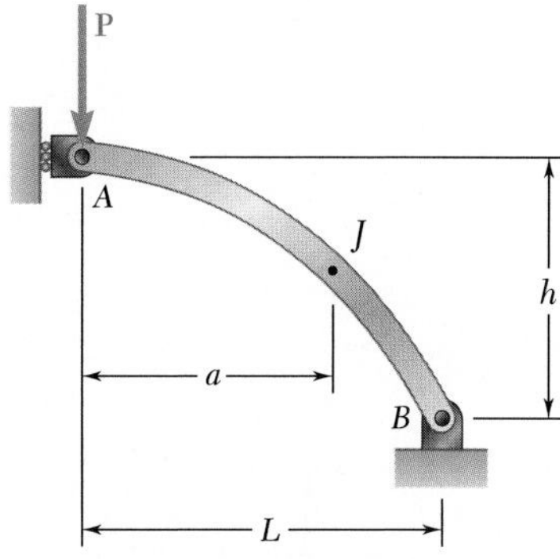

Fig. P7.13 and P7.14

7.14 Knowing that the axis of the curved member AB is a parabola with its vertex at A, determine the magnitude and location of the maximum bending moment.

7.15 Knowing that the radius of each pulley is 200 mm and neglecting friction, determine the internal forces at point J of the frame shown.

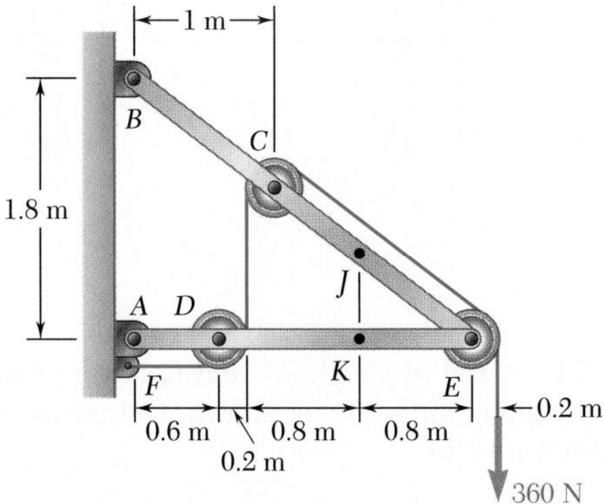

Fig. P7.15 and P7.16

7.16 Knowing that the radius of each pulley is 200 mm and neglecting friction, determine the internal forces at point K of the frame shown.

7.17 Knowing that the radius of each pulley is 125 mm and neglecting friction, determine the internal forces at point J of the frame shown.

7.18 Knowing that the radius of each pulley is 125 mm and neglecting friction, determine the internal forces at point K of the frame shown.

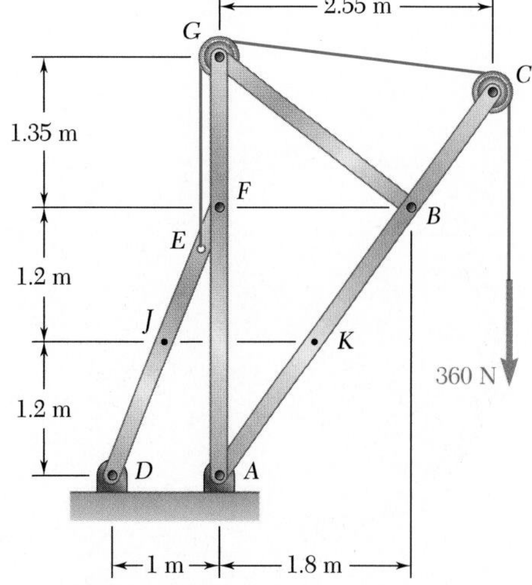

Fig. P7.17 and P7.18

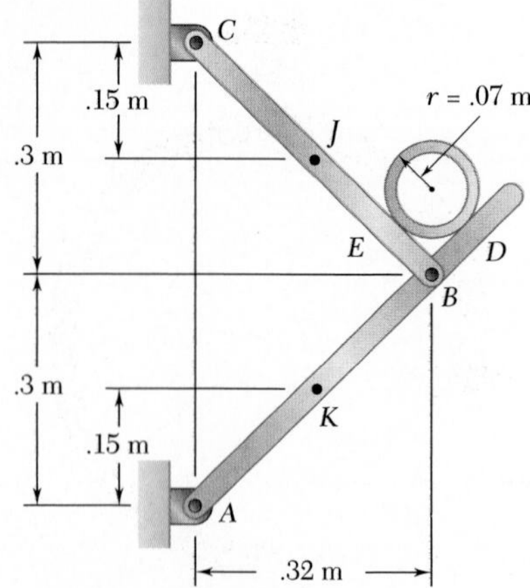

Fig. P7.19 and *P7.20*

7.19 A .14-m-diameter pipe is supported every 3 m by a small frame consisting of two members as shown. Knowing that the combined weight per unit length of the pipe and its contents is 30 kg/m and neglecting the effect of friction, determine the internal forces at point *J*.

7.20 A .14-m-diameter pipe is supported every 3 m by a small frame consisting of two members as shown. Knowing that the combined weight per unit length of the pipe and its contents is 30 kg/m and neglecting the effect of friction, determine the internal forces at point *K*.

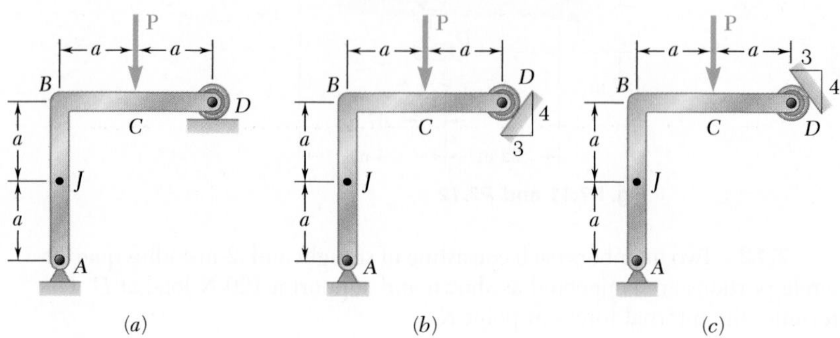

Fig. P7.21

7.21 and *7.22* A force **P** is applied to a bent rod which is supported by a roller and a pin and bracket. For each of the three cases shown, determine the internal forces at point *J*.

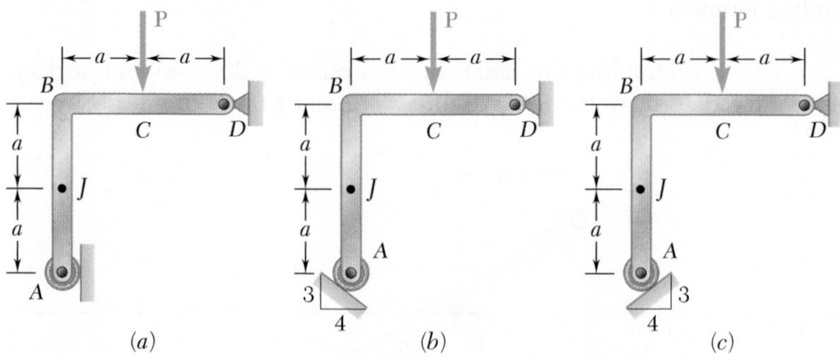

Fig. *P7.22*

7.23 and 7.24 A rod of weight *W* and uniform cross section is bent into a quarter circle and is supported as shown. Determine the bending moment at point *J* when $\theta = 30°$.

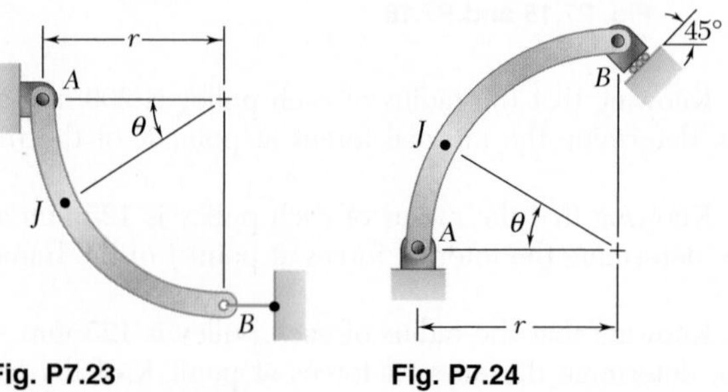

Fig. P7.23 Fig. P7.24

7.25 For the rod of Prob. 7.23, determine the location and magnitude of the maximum bending moment.

7.26 For the rod of Prob. 7.24, determine the location and magnitude of the maximum bending moment.

7.27 A rod of weight W and uniform cross section is bent into the circular arc of radius r shown. Determine the bending moment at point J when $\theta = 30°$.

7.28 A rod of weight W and uniform cross section is bent into the circular arc of radius r shown. Determine the bending moment at point J when $\theta = 120°$.

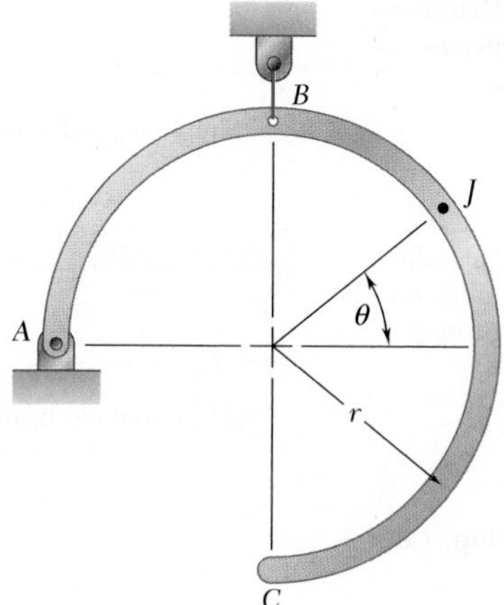

Fig. *P7.27* and *P7.28*

BEAMS

*7.3. VARIOUS TYPES OF LOADING AND SUPPORT

A structural member designed to support loads applied at various points along the member is known as a *beam*. In most cases, the loads are perpendicular to the axis of the beam and will cause only shear and bending in the beam. When the loads are not at a right angle to the beam, they will also produce axial forces in the beam.

Beams are usually long, straight prismatic bars. Designing a beam for the most effective support of the applied loads is a two-part process: (1) determining the shearing forces and bending moments produced by the loads and (2) selecting the cross section best suited to resist the shearing forces and bending moments determined in the first part. Here we are concerned with the first part of the problem of beam design. The second part belongs to the study of mechanics of materials.

A beam can be subjected to *concentrated loads* $\mathbf{P}_1$, $\mathbf{P}_2$, . . . , expressed in newtons, pounds, or their multiples kilonewtons and kips (Fig. 7.5*a*), to a *distributed load* w, expressed in N/m, kN/m, lb/ft, or kips/ft (Fig. 7.5*b*), or to a combination of both. When the load w per unit length has a constant value over part of the beam (as between A and B in Fig. 7.5*b*), the load is said to be *uniformly distributed* over that part of the beam. The determination of the reactions at the supports is considerably simplified if distributed loads are replaced by equivalent concentrated loads, as explained in Sec. 5.8. This substitution, however, should not be performed, or at least should be performed with care, when internal forces are being computed (see Sample Prob. 7.3).

Beams are classified according to the way in which they are supported. Several types of beams frequently used are shown in

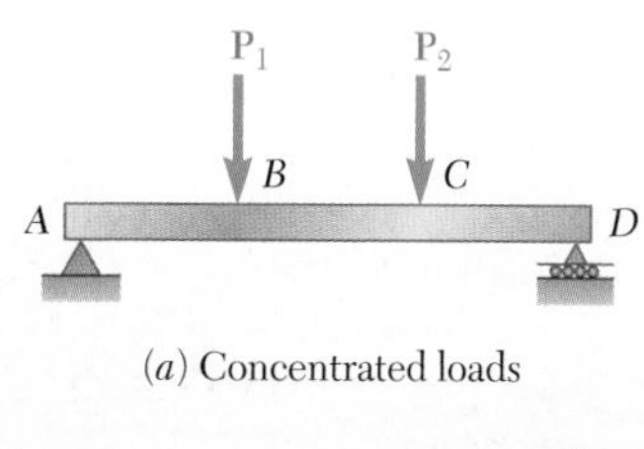

(*a*) Concentrated loads

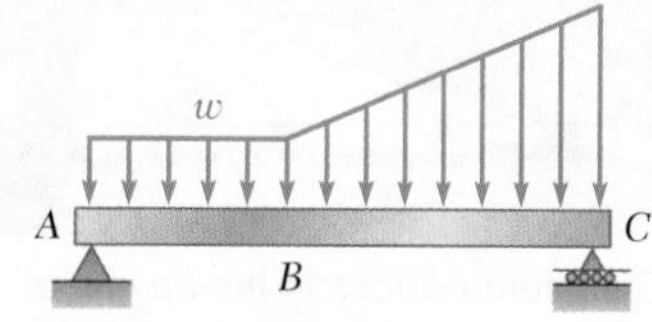

(*b*) Distributed load

Fig. 7.5

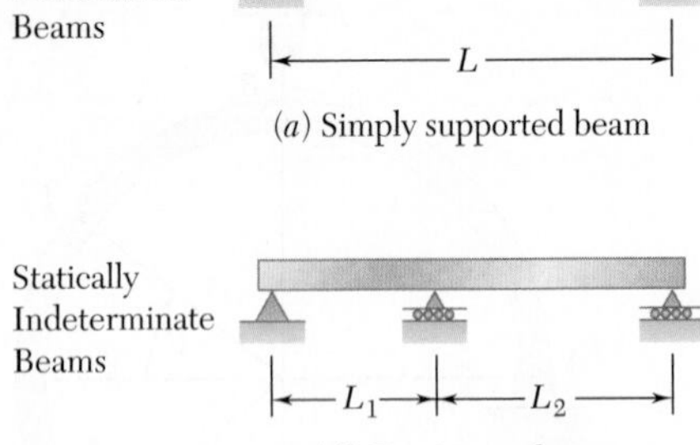

(a) Simply supported beam

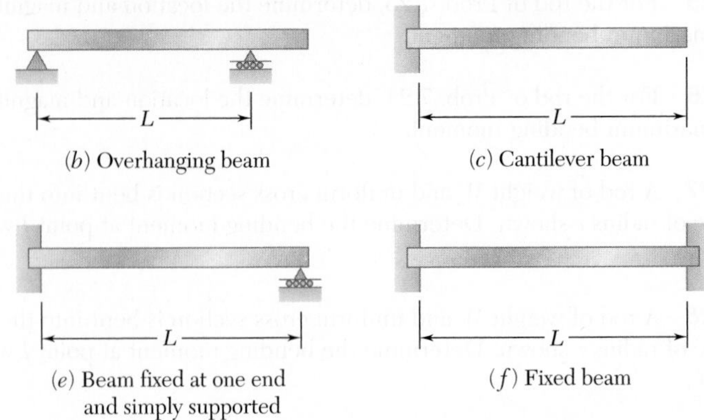

(b) Overhanging beam

(c) Cantilever beam

Statically Indeterminate Beams

(d) Continuous beam

(e) Beam fixed at one end and simply supported at the other end

(f) Fixed beam

Fig. 7.6

Fig. 7.6. The distance L between supports is called the *span*. It should be noted that the reactions will be statically determinate if the supports involve only three unknowns. If more unknowns are involved, the reactions will be statically indeterminate and the methods of statics will not be sufficient to determine the reactions; the properties of the beam with regard to its resistance to bending must then be taken into consideration. Beams supported by two rollers are not shown here; they are only partially constrained and will move under certain loadings.

Sometimes two or more beams are connected by hinges to form a single continuous structure. Two examples of beams hinged at a point H are shown in Fig. 7.7. It will be noted that the reactions at the supports involve four unknowns and cannot be determined from the free-body diagram of the two-beam system. They can be determined, however, by considering the free-body diagram of each beam separately; six unknowns are involved (including two force components at the hinge), and six equations are available.

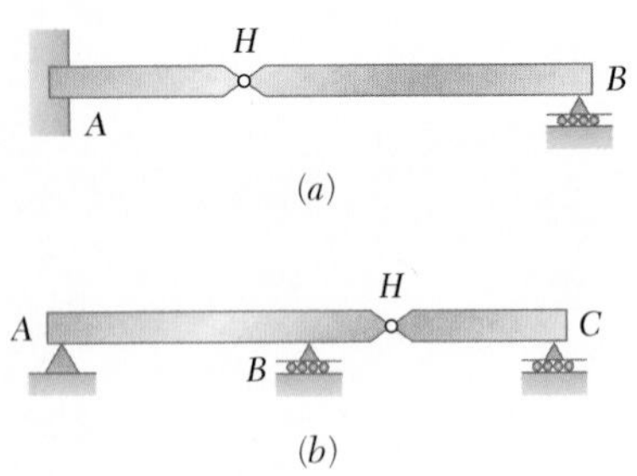

Fig. 7.7

*7.4. SHEAR AND BENDING MOMENT IN A BEAM

Consider a beam AB subjected to various concentrated and distributed loads (Fig. 7.8a). We propose to determine the shearing force and bending moment at any point of the beam. In the example considered here, the beam is simply supported, but the method used could be applied to any type of statically determinate beam.

First we determine the reactions at A and B by choosing the entire beam as a free body (Fig. 7.8b); writing $\Sigma M_A = 0$ and $\Sigma M_B = 0$, we obtain, respectively, $\mathbf{R}_B$ and $\mathbf{R}_A$.

To determine the internal forces at C, we cut the beam at C and draw the free-body diagrams of the portions AC and CB of the beam (Fig. 7.8c). Using the free-body diagram of AC, we can determine the shearing force $\mathbf{V}$ at C by equating to zero the sum of the vertical components of all forces acting on AC. Similarly, the bending moment $\mathbf{M}$ at C can be found by equating to zero the sum of the moments about C of all forces and couples acting on AC. Alternatively, we could use the free-body diagram of CB† and determine the shearing force $\mathbf{V}'$ and the bending moment $\mathbf{M}'$ by equating to zero the sum of the

Photo 7.2 The internal forces in the beams of the overpass shown vary as the truck crosses the overpass.

†The force and couple representing the internal forces acting on CB will now be denoted by $\mathbf{V}'$ and $\mathbf{M}'$, rather than by $-\mathbf{V}$ and $-\mathbf{M}$ as done earlier, in order to avoid confusion when applying the sign convention which we are about to introduce.

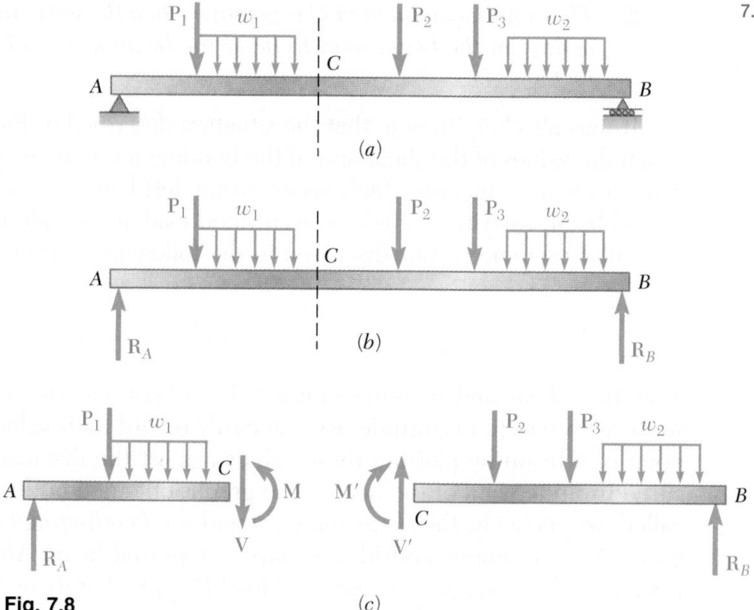

Fig. 7.8

vertical components and the sum of the moments about C of all forces and couples acting on CB. While this choice of free bodies may facilitate the computation of the numerical values of the shearing force and bending moment, it makes it necessary to indicate on which portion of the beam the internal forces considered are acting. If the shearing force and bending moment are to be computed at every point of the beam and efficiently recorded, we must find a way to avoid having to specify every time which portion of the beam is used as a free body. We shall adopt, therefore, the following conventions:

In determining the shearing force in a beam, *it will always be assumed* that the internal forces $\mathbf{V}$ and $\mathbf{V}'$ are directed as shown in Fig. 7.8*c*. A positive value obtained for their common magnitude V will indicate that this assumption was correct and that the shearing forces are actually directed as shown. A negative value obtained for V will indicate that the assumption was wrong and that the shearing forces are directed in the opposite way. Thus, only the magnitude V, together with a plus or minus sign, needs to be recorded to define completely the shearing forces at a given point of the beam. The scalar V is commonly referred to as the *shear* at the given point of the beam.

Similarly, *it will always be assumed* that the internal couples $\mathbf{M}$ and $\mathbf{M}'$ are directed as shown in Fig. 7.8*c*. A positive value obtained for their magnitude M, commonly referred to as the bending moment, will indicate that this assumption was correct, and a negative value will indicate that it was wrong. Summarizing the sign conventions we have presented, we state:

The shear V and the bending moment M at a given point of a beam are said to be positive when the internal forces and couples acting on each portion of the beam are directed as shown in Fig. 7.9a.

These conventions can be more easily remembered if we note that:

1. *The shear at C is positive when the* **external** *forces (loads and reactions) acting on the beam tend to shear off the beam at C as indicated in Fig. 7.9b.*

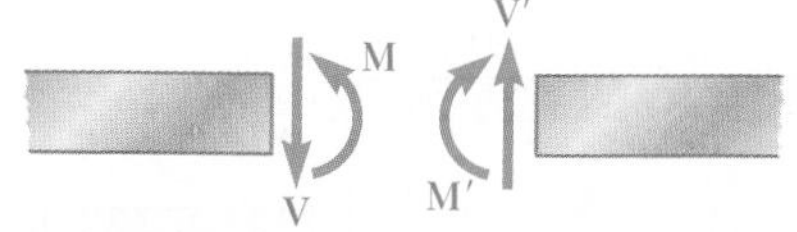

(*a*) Internal forces at section (positive shear and positive bending moment)

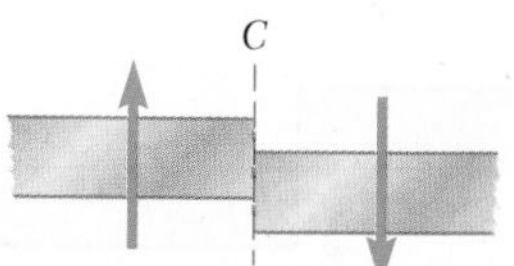

(*b*) Effect of external forces (positive shear)

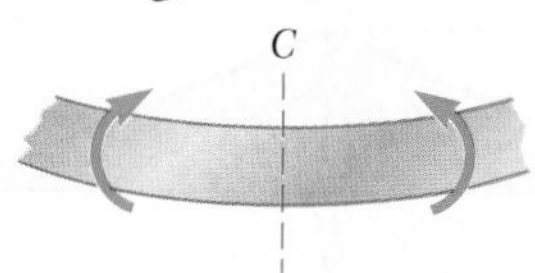

(*c*) Effect of external forces (positive bending moment)

Fig. 7.9

2. *The bending moment at C is positive when the* **external** *forces acting on the beam tend to bend the beam at C as indicated in Fig. 7.9c.*

It may also help to note that the situation described in Fig. 7.9, in which the values of the shear and of the bending moment are positive, is precisely the situation which occurs in the left half of a simply supported beam carrying a single concentrated load at its midpoint. This particular example is fully discussed in the following section.

*7.5. SHEAR AND BENDING-MOMENT DIAGRAMS

Now that shear and bending moment have been clearly defined in sense as well as in magnitude, we can easily record their values at any point of a beam by plotting these values against the distance x measured from one end of the beam. The graphs obtained in this way are called, respectively, the *shear diagram* and the *bending-moment diagram*. As an example, consider a simply supported beam AB of span L subjected to a single concentrated load $\mathbf{P}$ applied at its midpoint D (Fig. 7.10*a*). We first determine the reactions at the supports from the free-body diagram of the entire beam (Fig. 7.10*b*); we find that the magnitude of each reaction is equal to $P/2$.

Next we cut the beam at a point C between A and D and draw the free-body diagrams of AC and CB (Fig. 7.10*c*). *Assuming that shear and bending moment are positive,* we direct the internal forces $\mathbf{V}$ and $\mathbf{V}'$ and the internal couples $\mathbf{M}$ and $\mathbf{M}'$ as indicated in Fig. 7.9*a*. Considering the free body AC and writing that the sum of the vertical components and the sum of the moments about C of the forces acting on the free body are zero, we find $V = +P/2$ and $M = +Px/2$. Both shear and bending moment are therefore positive; this can be checked by observing that the reaction at A tends to shear off and to bend the beam at C as indicated in Fig. 7.9*b* and *c*. We can plot V and M between A and D (Fig. 7.10*e* and *f*); the shear has a constant value $V = P/2$, while the bending moment increases linearly from $M = 0$ at $x = 0$ to $M = PL/4$ at $x = L/2$.

Cutting, now, the beam at a point E between D and B and considering the free body EB (Fig. 7.10*d*), we write that the sum of the vertical components and the sum of the moments about E of the forces acting on the free body are zero. We obtain $V = -P/2$ and $M = P(L - x)/2$. The shear is therefore negative and the bending moment positive; this can be checked by observing that the reaction at B bends the beam at E as indicated in Fig. 7.9*c* but tends to shear it off in a manner opposite to that shown in Fig. 7.9*b*. We can complete, now, the shear and bending-moment diagrams of Fig. 7.10*e* and *f*; the shear has a constant value $V = -P/2$ between D and B, while the bending moment decreases linearly from $M = PL/4$ at $x = L/2$ to $M = 0$ at $x = L$.

It should be noted that when a beam is subjected to concentrated loads only, the shear is of constant value between loads and the bending moment varies linearly between loads, but when a beam is subjected to distributed loads, the shear and bending moment vary quite differently (see Sample Prob. 7.3).

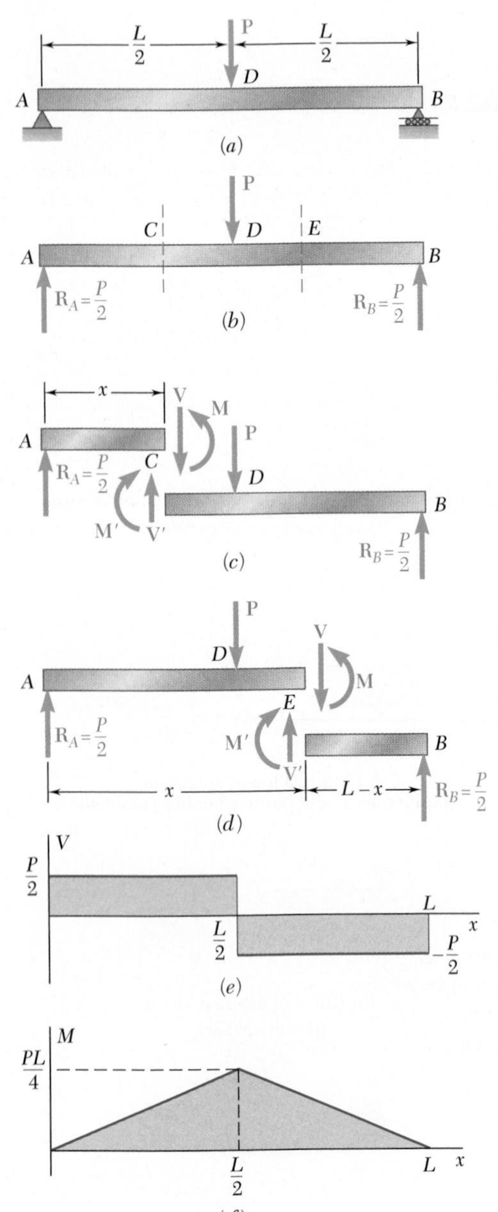

Fig. 7.10

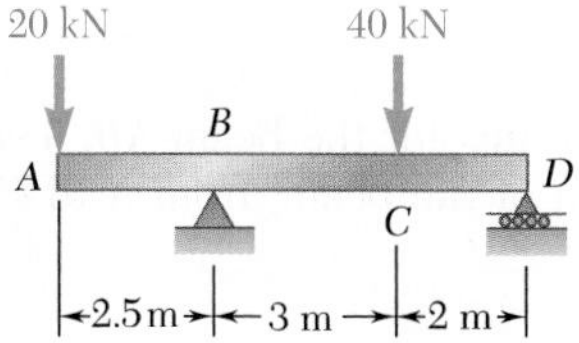

SAMPLE PROBLEM 7.2

Draw the shear and bending-moment diagrams for the beam and loading shown.

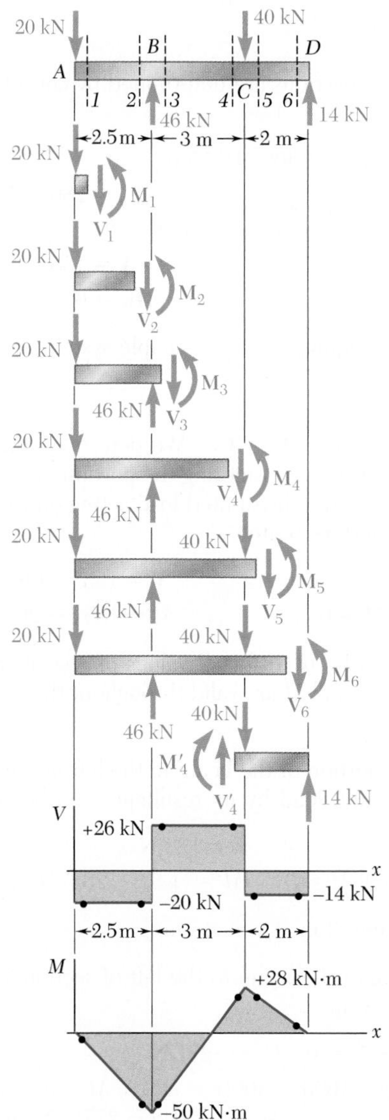

SOLUTION

Free-Body: Entire Beam. From the free-body diagram of the entire beam, we find the reactions at B and D:

$$\mathbf{R}_B = 46\ \text{kN}\uparrow \qquad \mathbf{R}_D = 14\ \text{kN}\uparrow$$

Shear and Bending Moment. We first determine the internal forces just to the right of the 20-kN load at A. Considering the stub of the beam to the left of section *1* as a free body and assuming V and M to be positive (according to the standard convention), we write

$$+\uparrow\Sigma F_y = 0: \quad -20\ \text{kN} - V_1 = 0 \qquad V_1 = -20\ \text{kN}$$
$$+\circlearrowleft\Sigma M_1 = 0: \quad (20\ \text{kN})(0\ \text{m}) + M_1 = 0 \qquad M_1 = 0$$

We next consider as a free body the portion of the beam to the left of section *2* and write

$$+\uparrow\Sigma F_y = 0: \quad -20\ \text{kN} - V_2 = 0 \qquad V_2 = -20\ \text{kN}$$
$$+\circlearrowleft\Sigma M_2 = 0: \quad (20\ \text{kN})(2.5\ \text{m}) + M_2 = 0 \qquad M_2 = -50\ \text{kN}\cdot\text{m}$$

The shear and bending moment at sections *3*, *4*, *5*, and *6* are determined in a similar way from the free-body diagrams shown. We obtain

$$V_3 = +26\ \text{kN} \qquad M_3 = -50\ \text{kN}\cdot\text{m}$$
$$V_4 = +26\ \text{kN} \qquad M_4 = +28\ \text{kN}\cdot\text{m}$$
$$V_5 = -14\ \text{kN} \qquad M_5 = +28\ \text{kN}\cdot\text{m}$$
$$V_6 = -14\ \text{kN} \qquad M_6 = 0$$

For several of the latter sections, the results are more easily obtained by considering as a free body the portion of the beam to the right of the section. For example, considering the portion of the beam to the right of section *4*, we write

$$+\uparrow\Sigma F_y = 0: \quad V_4 - 40\ \text{kN} + 14\ \text{kN} = 0 \qquad V_4 = +26\ \text{kN}$$
$$+\circlearrowleft\Sigma M_4 = 0: \quad -M_4 + (14\ \text{kN})(2\ \text{m}) = 0 \qquad M_4 = +28\ \text{kN}\cdot\text{m}$$

Shear and Bending-Moment Diagrams. We can now plot the six points shown on the shear and bending-moment diagrams. As indicated in Sec. 7.5, the shear is of constant value between concentrated loads, and the bending moment varies linearly; we therefore obtain the shear and bending-moment diagrams shown.

SAMPLE PROBLEM 7.3

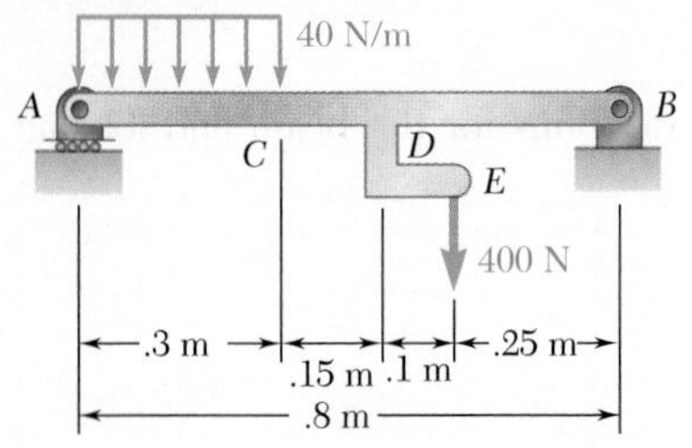

Draw the shear and bending-moment diagrams for the beam AB. The distributed load of 40 N/m extends over .3 m of the beam, from A to C, and the 400-N load is applied at E.

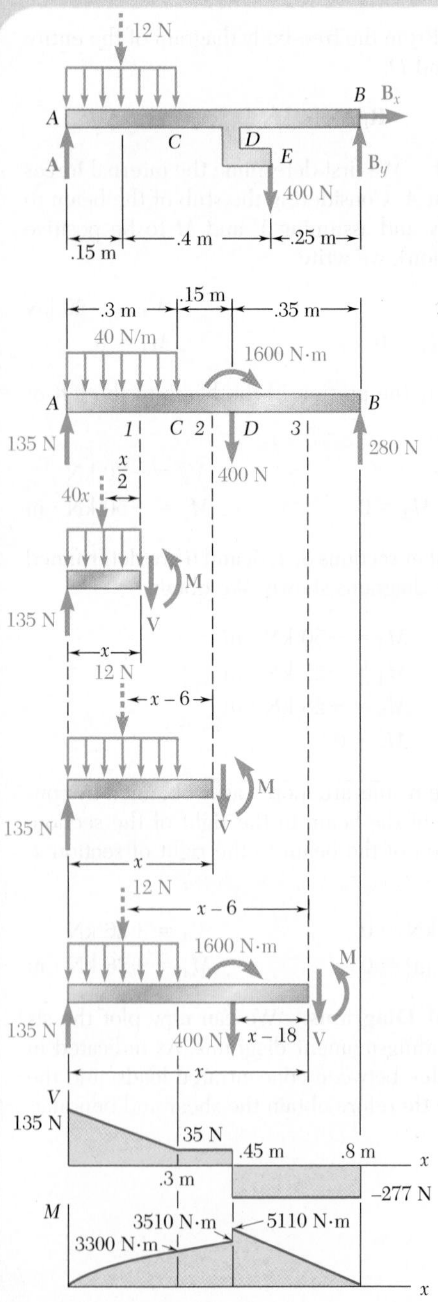

SOLUTION

Free-Body: Entire Beam. The reactions are determined by considering the entire beam as a free body.

$+\curvearrowleft\Sigma M_A = 0$: $\quad B_y(.8\text{ m}) - (12\text{ N})(.3\text{ m}) - (400\text{ N})(.55\text{ m}) = 0$

$B_y = +280\text{ N} \qquad \mathbf{B}_y = 280\text{ N}\uparrow$

$+\curvearrowleft\Sigma M_B = 0$: $\quad (12\text{ N})(.65\text{ m}) + (400\text{ N})(.25\text{ m}) - A(.8\text{ m}) = 0$

$A = +135\text{ N} \qquad \mathbf{A} = 135\text{ N}\uparrow$

$\xrightarrow{+}\Sigma F_x = 0$: $\quad B_x = 0 \qquad \mathbf{B}_x = 0$

The 400-N load is now replaced by an equivalent force-couple system acting on the beam at point D.

Shear and Bending Moment. ***From A to C.*** We determine the internal forces at a distance x from point A by considering the portion of the beam to the left of section *1*. That part of the distributed load acting on the free body is replaced by its resultant, and we write

$+\uparrow\Sigma F_y = 0$: $\quad 135 - 40x - V = 0 \qquad V = 135 - 40x$

$+\curvearrowleft\Sigma M_1 = 0$: $\quad -135x + 40x(\frac{1}{2}x) + M = 0 \qquad M = 135x - 20x^2$

Since the free-body diagram shown can be used for all values of x smaller than .3 m, the expressions obtained for V and M are valid throughout the region $0 < x < 3$ m.

From C to D. Considering the portion of the beam to the left of section *2* and again replacing the distributed load by its resultant, we obtain

$+\uparrow\Sigma F_y = 0$: $\quad 135 - 12 - V = 0 \qquad V = 123\text{ N}$

$+\curvearrowleft\Sigma M_2 = 0$: $\quad -135x + 12(x - .15) + M = 0 \qquad M = (1.8 + 123x)\text{ N}\cdot\text{m}$

These expressions are valid in the region $.3\text{ m} < x < .45\text{ m}$.

From D to B. Using the portion of the beam to the left of section *3*, we obtain for the region $.45\text{ m} < x < .8\text{ m}$.

$+\uparrow\Sigma F_y = 0$: $\quad 135 - .45\text{ m} - 400 - V = 0 \quad V = -277\text{ N}$

$+\curvearrowleft\Sigma M_3 = 0$: $\quad -135x + 12(x - .15) - 1600 + 400(x - .45) + M = 0$

$M = (1781.8 - 277x)\text{ N}\cdot\text{m}$

Shear and Bending-Moment Diagrams. The shear and bending-moment diagrams for the entire beam can be plotted. We note that the couple of moment 1600 N · m applied at point D introduces a discontinuity into the bending-moment diagram.

SOLVING PROBLEMS ON YOUR OWN

In this lesson you learned to determine the *shear* V and the *bending moment* M at any point in a beam. You also learned to draw the *shear diagram* and the *bending-moment diagram* for the beam by plotting, respectively, V and M against the distance x measured along the beam.

A. *Determining the shear and bending moment in a beam.* To determine the shear V and the bending moment M at a given point C of a beam, you should take the following steps.

1. *Draw a free-body diagram of the entire beam,* and use it to determine the reactions at the beam supports.

2. *Cut the beam at point C,* and, using the original loading, select one of the two portions of the beam you have obtained.

3. *Draw the free-body diagram of the portion of the beam you have selected,* showing:

a. *The loads and the reaction* exerted on that portion of the beam, replacing each distributed load by an equivalent concentrated load as explained earlier in Sec. 5.8.

b. *The shearing force and the bending couple representing the internal forces at C.* To facilitate recording the shear V and the bending moment M after they have been determined, follow the convention indicated in Figs. 7.8 and 7.9. Thus, if you are using the portion of the beam located to the *left of C,* apply at C a *shearing force* $\mathbf{V}$ *directed downward* and a *bending moment* $\mathbf{M}$ *directed counterclockwise.* If you are using the portion of the beam located to the *right of C,* apply at C a *shearing force* $\mathbf{V}'$ *directed upward* and a *bending moment* $\mathbf{M}'$ *directed clockwise* [Sample Prob. 7.2].

4. *Write the equilibrium equations for the portion of the beam you have selected.* Solve the equation $\Sigma F_y = 0$ for V and the equation $\Sigma M_C = 0$ for M.

5. *Record the values of V and M with the sign obtained for each of them.* A positive sign for V means that the shearing forces exerted at C on each of the two portions of the beam are directed as shown in Figs. 7.8 and 7.9; a negative sign means that they have the opposite sense. Similarly, a positive sign for M means that the bending couples at C are directed as shown in these figures, and a negative sign means that they have the opposite sense. In addition, a positive sign for M means that the concavity of the beam at C is directed upward, and a negative sign means that it is directed downward.

(continued)

B. Drawing the shear and bending-moment diagrams for a beam. These diagrams are obtained by plotting, respectively, V and M against the distance x measured along the beam. However, in most cases the values of V and M need to be computed only at a few points.

1. ***For a beam supporting only concentrated loads,*** we note [Sample Prob. 7.2] that

a. ***The shear diagram consists of segments of horizontal lines.*** Thus, to draw the shear diagram of the beam you will need to compute V only just to the left or just to the right of the points where the loads or the reactions are applied.

b. ***The bending-moment diagram consists of segments of oblique straight lines.*** Thus, to draw the bending-moment diagram of the beam you will need to compute M only at the points where the loads or the reactions are applied.

2. ***For a beam supporting uniformly distributed loads,*** we note [Sample Prob. 7.3] that under each of the distributed loads:

a. ***The shear diagram consists of a segment of an oblique straight line.*** Thus, you will need to compute V only where the distributed load begins and where it ends.

b. ***The bending-moment diagram consists of a parabolic arc.*** In most cases you will need to compute M only where the distributed load begins and where it ends.

3. ***For a beam with a more complicated loading,*** it is necessary to consider the free-body diagram of a portion of the beam of arbitrary length x and determine V and M as functions of x. This procedure may have to be repeated several times, since V and M are often represented by different functions in various parts of the beam [Sample Prob. 7.3].

4. ***When a couple is applied to a beam,*** the shear has the same value on both sides of the point of application of the couple, but the bending-moment diagram will show a discontinuity at that point, rising or falling by an amount equal to the magnitude of the couple. Note that a couple can either be applied directly to the beam, or result from the application of a load to a member rigidly attached to the beam [Sample Prob. 7.3].

Problems

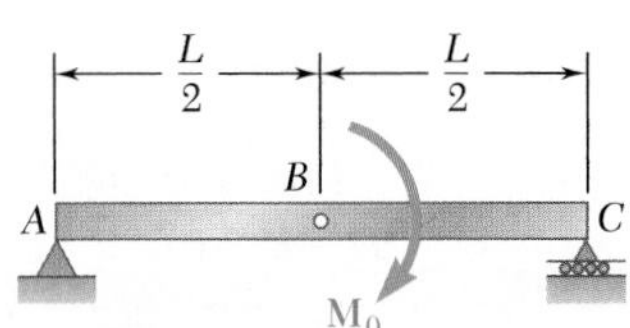

Fig. P7.29

7.29 through 7.32 For the beam and loading shown, (*a*) draw the shear and bending-moment diagrams, (*b*) determine the maximum absolute values of the shear and bending moment.

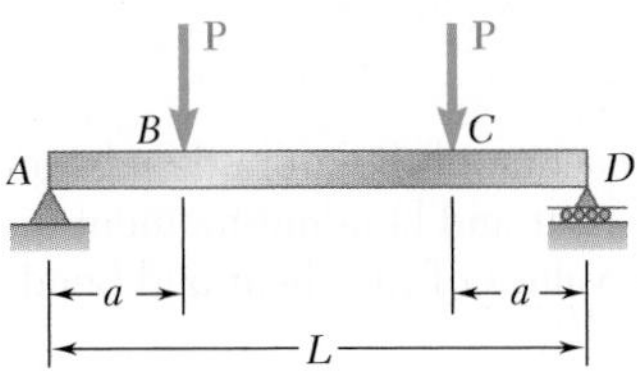

Fig. P7.30

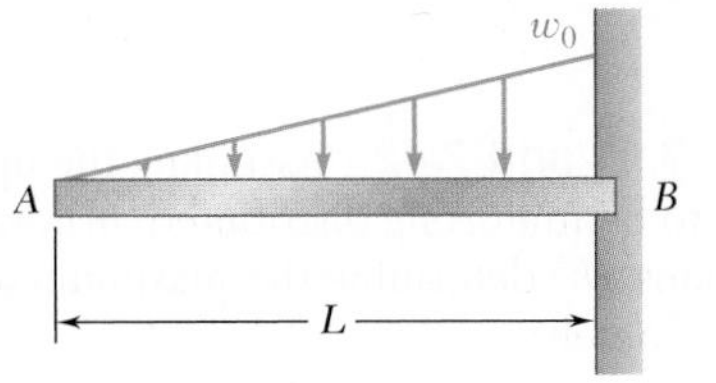

Fig. P7.31

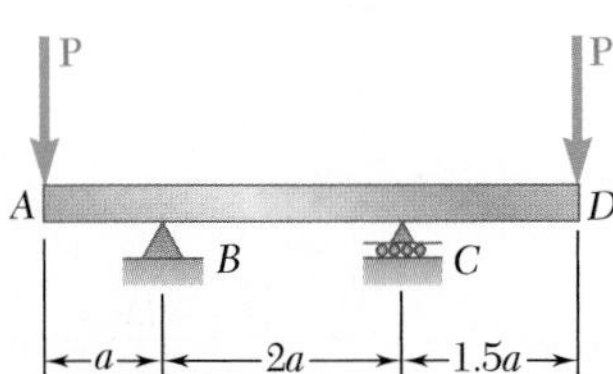

Fig. P7.32

***7.33* and 7.34** For the beam and loading shown, (*a*) draw the shear and bending-moment diagrams, (*b*) determine the maximum absolute values of the shear and bending moment.

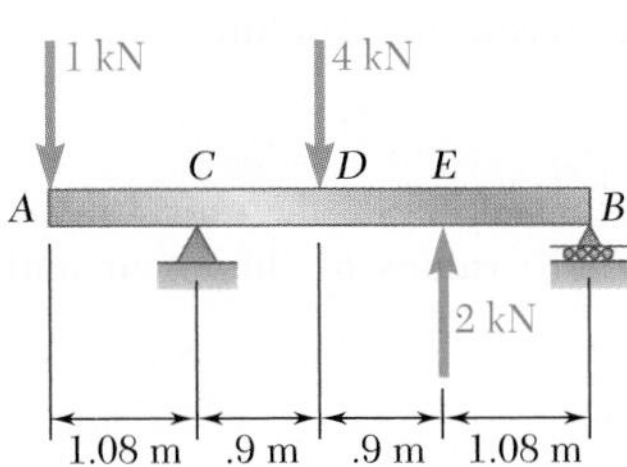

Fig. *P7.33*

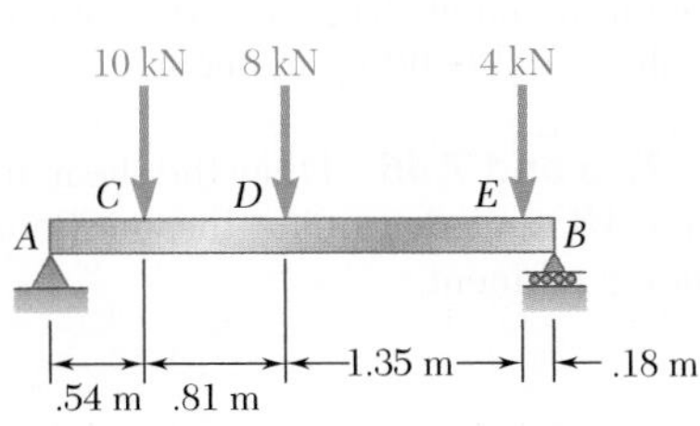

Fig. P7.34

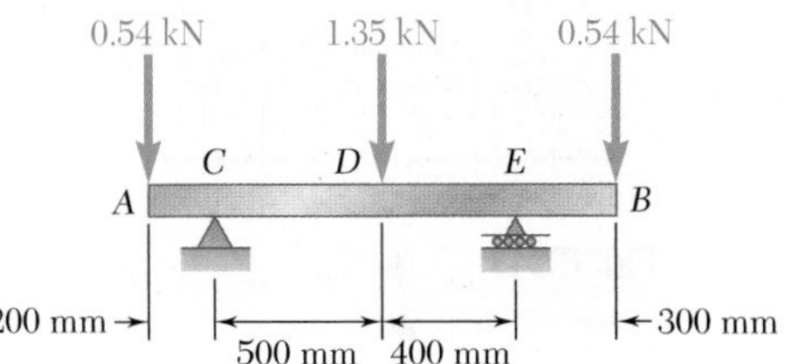

Fig. *P7.35*

***7.35* and 7.36** For the beam and loading shown, (*a*) draw the shear and bending-moment diagrams, (*b*) determine the maximum absolute values of the shear and bending moment.

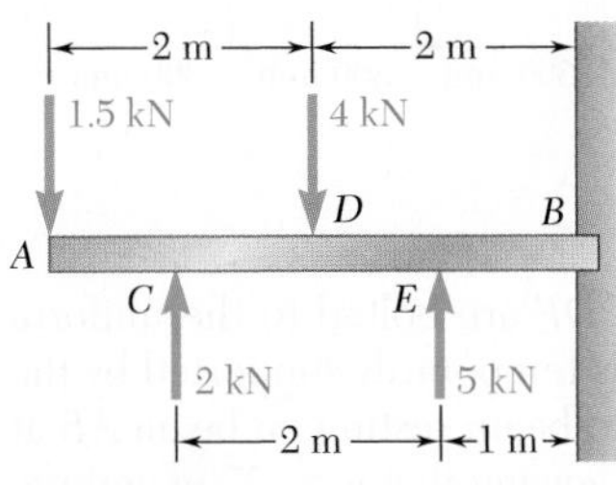

Fig. P7.36

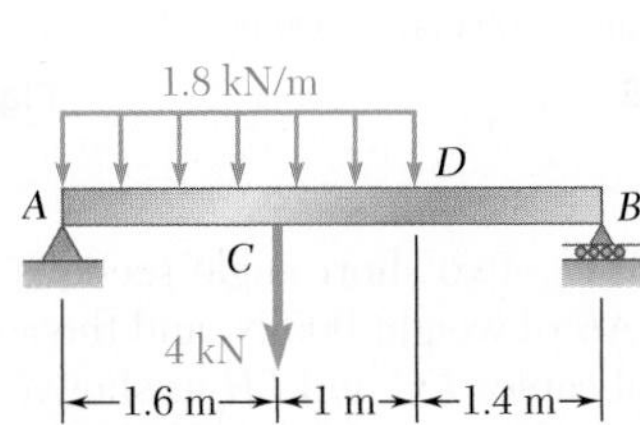

Fig. P7.37

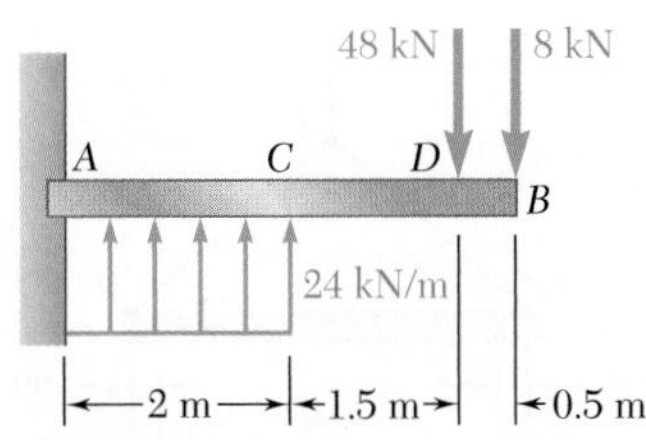

Fig. *P7.38*

7.37 and *7.38* For the beam and loading shown, (*a*) draw the shear and bending-moment diagrams, (*b*) determine the maximum absolute values of the shear and bending moment.

7.39 and 7.40 For the beam and loading shown, (*a*) draw the shear and bending-moment diagrams, (*b*) determine the maximum absolute values of the shear and bending moment.

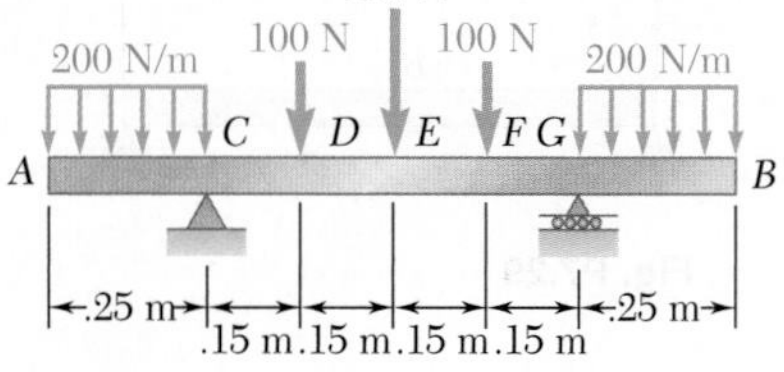

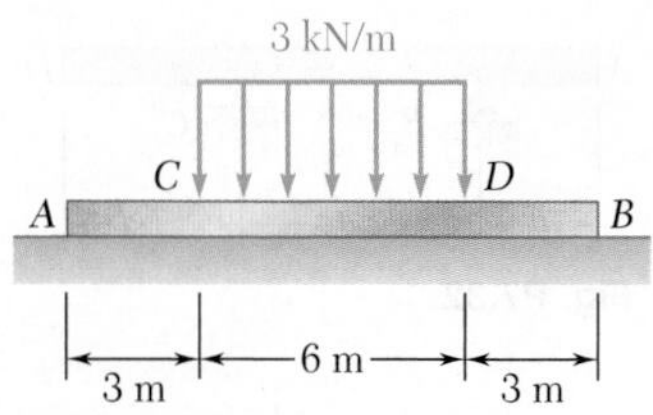

Fig. P7.39

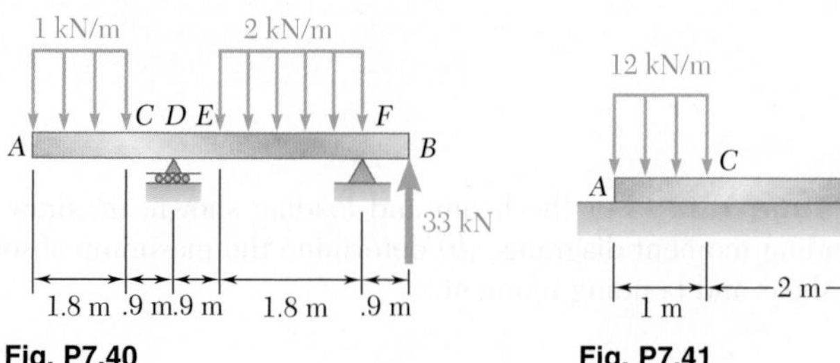

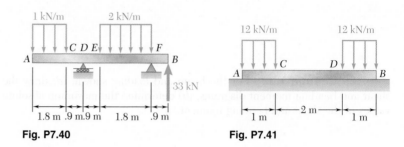

Fig. P7.40

Fig. P7.41

7.41 and *7.42* Assuming the upward reaction of the ground on beam *AB* to be uniformly distributed, (*a*) draw the shear and bending-moment diagrams, (*b*) determine the maximum absolute values of the shear and bending moment.

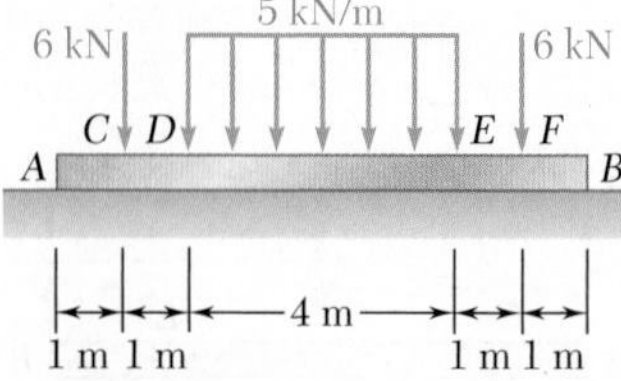

Fig. *P7.42*

7.43 Assuming the upward reaction of the ground on beam *AB* to be uniformly distributed, (*a*) draw the shear and bending-moment diagrams, (*b*) determine the maximum absolute values of the shear and bending moment.

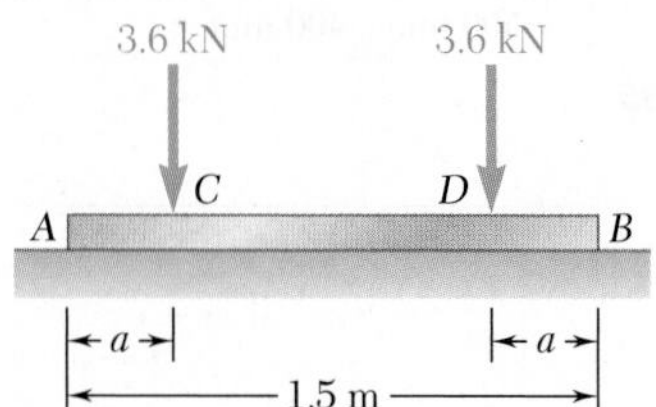

Fig. P7.43

7.44 Assuming the upward reaction of the ground on beam *AB* to be uniformly distributed and knowing that $a = 0.3$ m, (*a*) draw the shear and bending-moment diagrams, (*b*) determine the maximum absolute values of the shear and bending moment.

7.45 and *7.46* Draw the shear and bending-moment diagrams for the beam *AB*, and determine the maximum absolute values of the shear and bending moment.

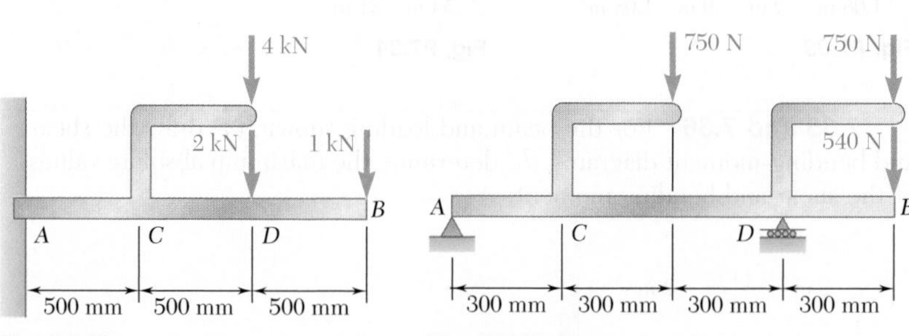

Fig. P7.45

Fig. *P7.46*

Fig. *P7.44*

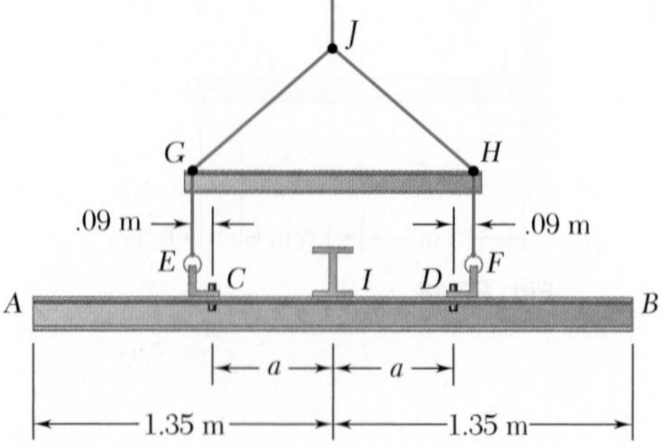

Fig. P7.47

7.47 Two short angle sections *CE* and *DF* are bolted to the uniform beam *AB* of weight 900 N, and the assembly is temporarily supported by the vertical cables *EG* and *FH* as shown. A second beam resting on beam *AB* at *I* exerts a downward force of 810 N on *AB*. Knowing that $a = .27$ m and neglecting the weight of the angle sections, (*a*) draw the shear and bending-moment diagrams for beam *AB*, (*b*) determine the maximum absolute values of the shear and bending moment in the beam.

7.48 Solve Prob. 7.47 when $a = .54$ m.

7.49 Draw the shear and bending-moment diagrams for the beam AB, and determine the maximum absolute values of the shear and bending moment.

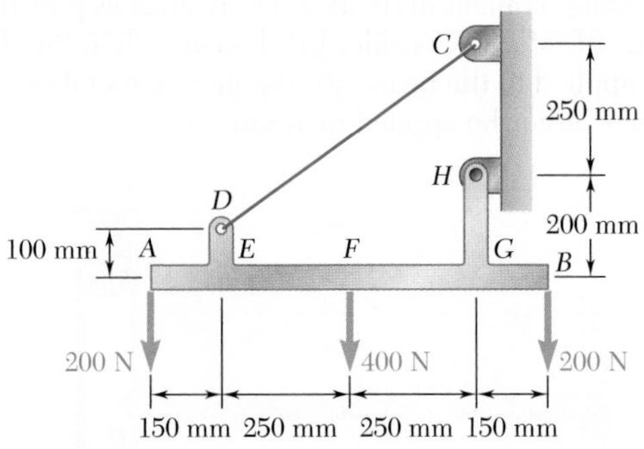

Fig. P7.49

7.50 Neglecting the size of the pulley at G, (*a*) draw the shear and bending-moment diagrams for the beam AB, (*b*) determine the maximum absolute values of the shear and bending moment.

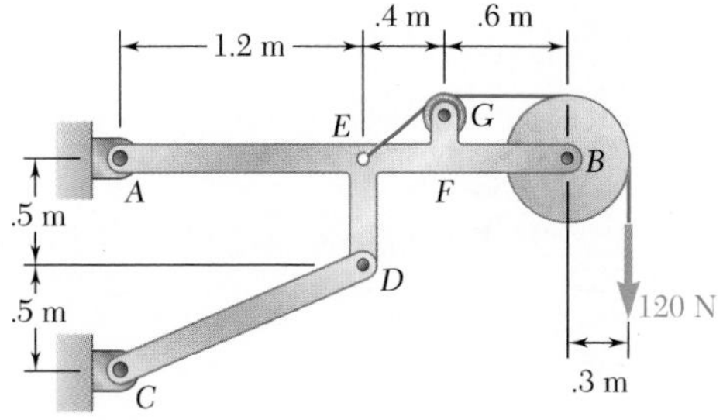

Fig. P7.50

7.51 For the beam of Prob. 7.44, determine (*a*) the distance a for which the maximum absolute value of the bending moment in the beam is as small as possible, (*b*) the corresponding value of $|M|_{max}$. (*Hint:* Draw the bending-moment diagram and then equate the absolute values of the largest positive and negative bending moments obtained.)

7.52 For the assembly of Prob. 7.47, determine (*a*) the distance a for which the maximum absolute value of the bending moment in beam AB is as small as possible, (*b*) the corresponding value of $|M|_{max}$. (See hint for Prob. 7.51.)

7.53 For the beam shown, determine (*a*) the magnitude P for which the maximum value of the bending moment is as small as possible, (*b*) the corresponding value of $|M|_{max}$. (See hint for Prob. 7.51.)

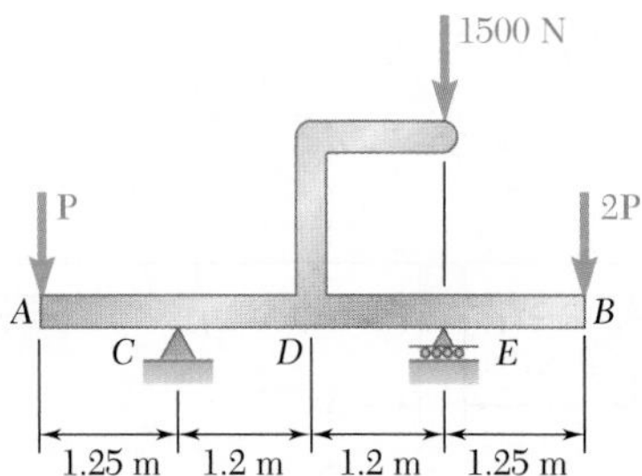

Fig. P7.53

7.54 For the beam and loading shown, determine (*a*) the distance a for which the maximum absolute value of the bending moment in the beam is as small as possible, (*b*) the corresponding value of $|M|_{max}$. (See hint for Prob. 7.51.)

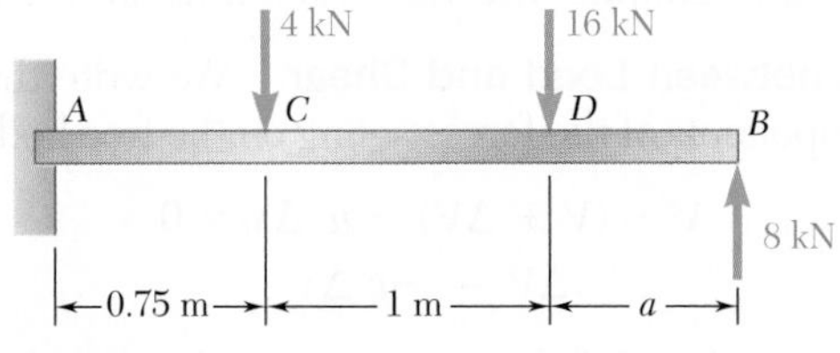

Fig. P7.54

7.55 Knowing that $P = Q = 500$ N, determine (*a*) the distance a for which the maximum absolute value of the bending moment in beam AB is as small as possible, (*b*) the corresponding value of $|M|_{max}$. (See hint for Prob. 7.51.)

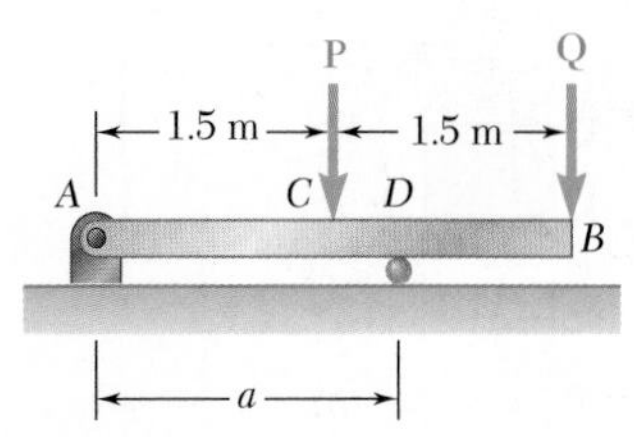

Fig. P7.55

7.56 Solve Prob. 7.55 assuming that $P = 250$ N and $Q = 500$ N.

***7.57** In order to reduce the bending moment in the cantilever beam AB, a cable and counterweight are permanently attached at end B. Determine the magnitude of the counterweight for which the maximum absolute value of the bending moment in the beam is as small as possible and the corresponding value of $|M|_{max}$. Consider (*a*) the case when the distributed load is permanently applied to the beam, (*b*) the more general case when the distributed load may either be applied or removed.

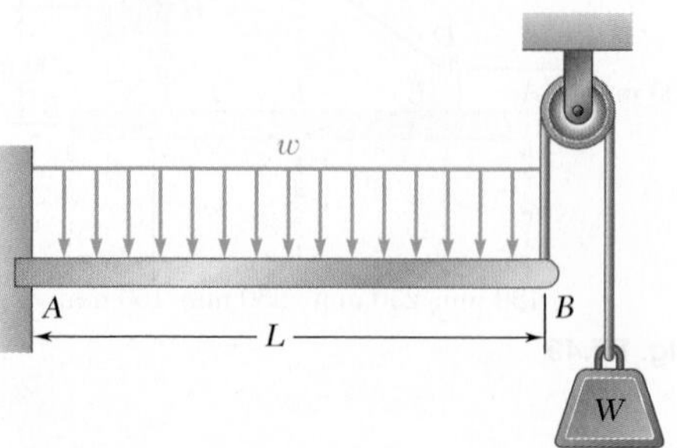

Fig. P7.57

---

*7.6. RELATIONS AMONG LOAD, SHEAR, AND BENDING MOMENT

When a beam carries more than two or three concentrated loads, or when it carries distributed loads, the method outlined in Sec. 7.5 for plotting shear and bending moment is likely to be quite cumbersome. The construction of the shear diagram and, especially, of the bending-moment diagram will be greatly facilitated if certain relations existing among load, shear, and bending moment are taken into consideration.

Let us consider a simply supported beam AB carrying a distributed load w per unit length (Fig. 7.11*a*), and let C and C' be two points of the beam at a distance Δx from each other. The shear and bending moment at C will be denoted by V and M, respectively, and will be assumed positive; the shear and bending moment at C' will be denoted by $V + \Delta V$ and $M + \Delta M$.

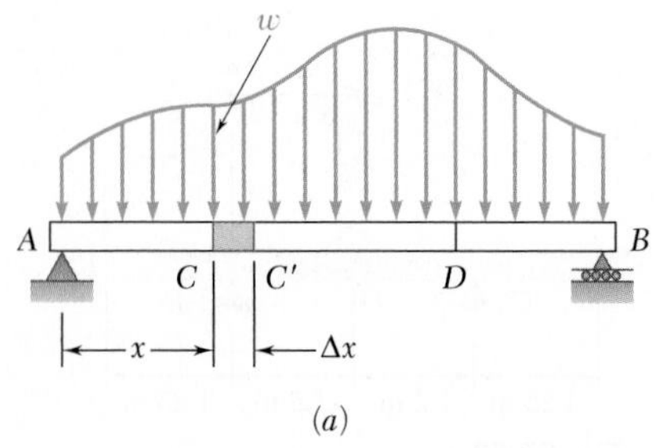

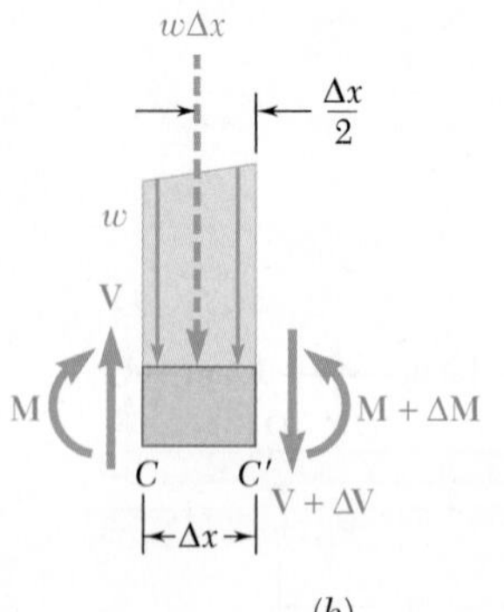

Fig. 7.11

Let us now detach the portion of beam CC' and draw its free-body diagram (Fig. 7.11*b*). The forces exerted on the free body include a load of magnitude $w\,\Delta x$ and internal forces and couples at C and C'. Since shear and bending moment have been assumed positive, the forces and couples will be directed as shown in the figure.

Relations between Load and Shear. We write that the sum of the vertical components of the forces acting on the free body CC' is zero:

$$V - (V + \Delta V) - w\,\Delta x = 0$$
$$\Delta V = -w\,\Delta x$$

Dividing both members of the equation by Δx and then letting Δx approach zero, we obtain

$$\frac{dV}{dx} = -w \tag{7.1}$$

Formula (7.1) indicates that for a beam loaded as shown in Fig. 7.11*a*, the slope dV/dx of the shear curve is negative; the absolute value of the slope at any point is equal to the load per unit length at that point. Integrating formula (7.1) between points C and D, we obtain

$$V_D - V_C = -\int_{x_C}^{x_D} w\, dx \tag{7.2}$$

$$V_D - V_C = -(\text{area under load curve between } C \text{ and } D) \tag{7.2$'$}$$

Note that this result could also have been obtained by considering the equilibrium of the portion of beam CD, since the area under the load curve represents the total load applied between C and D.

It should be observed that formula (7.1) *is not valid* at a point where a concentrated load is applied; the shear curve is discontinuous at such a point, as seen in Sec. 7.5. Similarly, formulas (7.2) and (7.2′) cease to be valid when concentrated loads are applied between C and D, since they do not take into account the sudden change in shear caused by a concentrated load. Formulas (7.2) and (7.2′), therefore, should be applied only between successive concentrated loads.

Relations between Shear and Bending Moment. Returning to the free-body diagram of Fig. 7.11*b*, and writing now that the sum of the moments about C' is zero, we obtain

$$(M + \Delta M) - M - V\,\Delta x + w\,\Delta x\frac{\Delta x}{2} = 0$$

$$\Delta M = V\,\Delta x - \tfrac{1}{2}w(\Delta x)^2$$

Dividing both members of the equation by Δx and then letting Δx approach zero, we obtain

$$\frac{dM}{dx} = V \tag{7.3}$$

Formula (7.3) indicates that the slope dM/dx of the bending-moment curve is equal to the value of the shear. This is true at any point where the shear has a well-defined value, that is, at any point where no concentrated load is applied. Formula (7.3) also shows that the shear is zero at points where the bending moment is maximum. This property facilitates the determination of the points where the beam is likely to fail under bending.

Integrating formula (7.3) between points C and D, we obtain

$$M_D - M_C = \int_{x_C}^{x_D} V\, dx \tag{7.4}$$

$$M_D - M_C = \text{area under shear curve between } C \text{ and } D \tag{7.4$'$}$$

Note that the area under the shear curve should be considered positive where the shear is positive and negative where the shear is negative. Formulas (7.4) and (7.4′) are valid even when concentrated loads are applied between C and D, as long as the shear curve has been correctly drawn. The formulas cease to be valid, however, if a *couple* is applied at a point between C and D, since they do not take into account the sudden change in bending moment caused by a couple (see Sample Prob. 7.7).

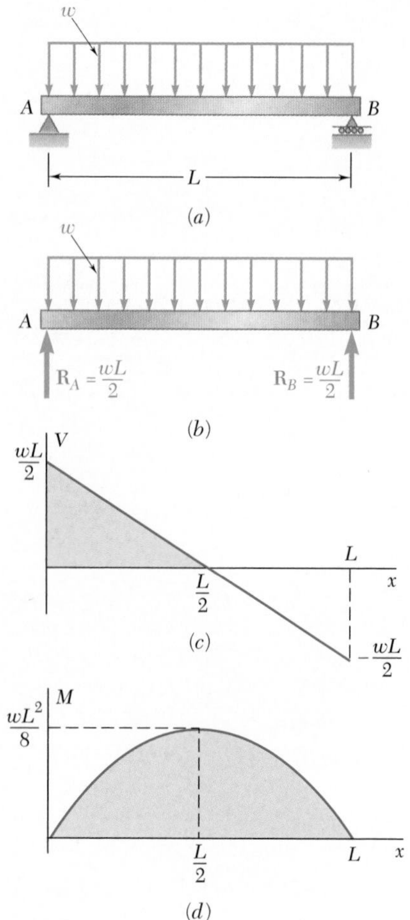

Fig. 7.12

Example. Let us consider a simply supported beam AB of span L carrying a uniformly distributed load w (Fig. 7.12*a*). From the free-body diagram of the entire beam we determine the magnitude of the reactions at the supports: $R_A = R_B = wL/2$ (Fig. 7.12*b*). Next, we draw the shear diagram. Close to the end A of the beam, the shear is equal to R_A, that is, to $wL/2$, as we can check by considering a very small portion of the beam as a free body. Using formula (7.2), we can then determine the shear V at any distance x from A. We write

$$V - V_A = -\int_0^x w\, dx = -wx$$

$$V = V_A - wx = \frac{wL}{2} - wx = w\left(\frac{L}{2} - x\right)$$

The shear curve is thus an oblique straight line which crosses the x axis at $x = L/2$ (Fig. 7.12*c*). Considering, now, the bending moment, we first observe that $M_A = 0$. The value M of the bending moment at any distance x from A can then be obtained from formula (7.4); we have

$$M - M_A = \int_0^x V dx$$

$$M = \int_0^x w\left(\frac{L}{2} - x\right) dx = \frac{w}{2}(Lx - x^2)$$

The bending-moment curve is a parabola. The maximum value of the bending moment occurs when $x = L/2$, since V (and thus dM/dx) is zero for that value of x. Substituting $x = L/2$ in the last equation, we obtain $M_{max} = wL^2/8$.

In most engineering applications, the value of the bending moment needs to be known only at a few specific points. Once the shear diagram has been drawn, and after M has been determined at one of the ends of the beam, the value of the bending moment can then be obtained at any given point by computing the area under the shear curve and using formula (7.4′). For instance, since $M_A = 0$ for the beam of Fig. 7.12, the maximum value of the bending moment for that beam can be obtained simply by calculating the area of the shaded triangle in the shear diagram:

$$M_{max} = \frac{1}{2}\frac{L}{2}\frac{wL}{2} = \frac{wL^2}{8}$$

In this example, the load curve is a horizontal straight line, the shear curve is an oblique straight line, and the bending-moment curve is a parabola. If the load curve had been an oblique straight line (first degree), the shear curve would have been a parabola (second degree), and the bending-moment curve would have been a cubic (third degree). The shear and bending-moment curves will always be, respectively, one and two degrees higher than the load curve. Thus, once a few values of the shear and bending moment have been computed, we should be able to sketch the shear and bending-moment diagrams without actually determining the functions $V(x)$ and $M(x)$. The sketches obtained will be more accurate if we make use of the fact that at any point where the curves are continuous, the slope of the shear curve is equal to $-w$ and the slope of the bending-moment curve is equal to V.

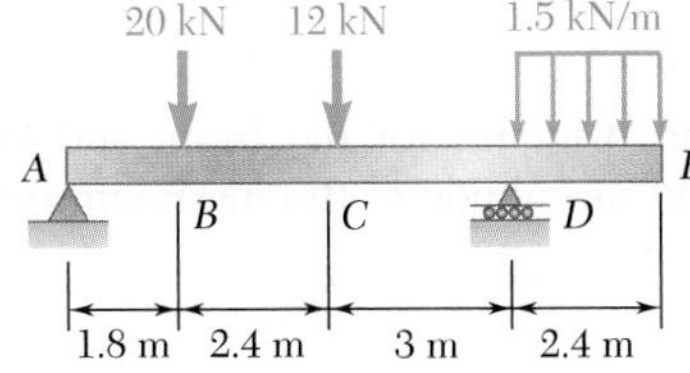

SAMPLE PROBLEM 7.4

Draw the shear and bending-moment diagrams for the beam and loading shown.

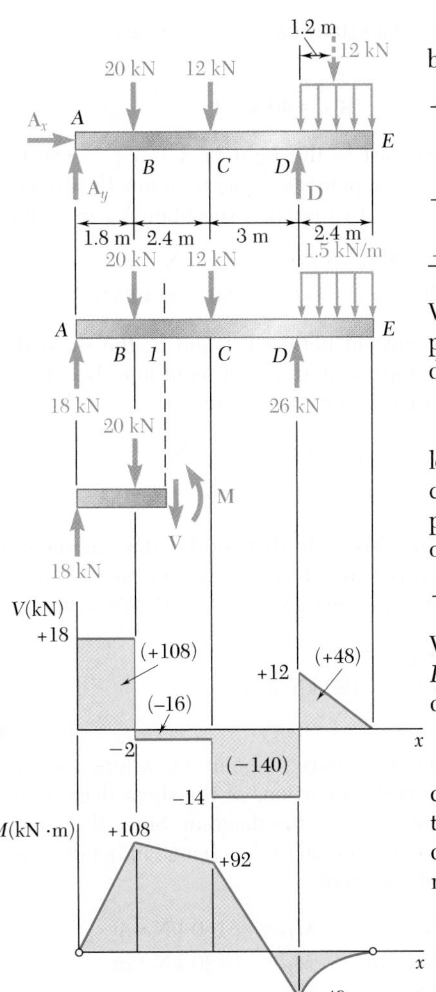

SOLUTION

Free-Body: Entire Beam. Considering the entire beam as a free body, we determine the reactions:

$+\circlearrowleft \Sigma M_A = 0$:

$$D(7.2 \text{ m}) - (20 \text{ kN})(1.8 \text{ m}) - (12 \text{ kN})(4.2 \text{ m}) - (12 \text{ kN})(8.4 \text{ m}) = 0$$

$$D = +26 \text{ kN} \qquad \mathbf{D} = 26 \text{ kN} \uparrow$$

$+\uparrow \Sigma F_y = 0$: $\quad A_y - 20 \text{ kN} - 12 \text{ kN} + 26 \text{ kN} - 12 \text{ kN} = 0$

$$A_y = +18 \text{ kN} \qquad \mathbf{A}_y = 18 \text{ kN} \uparrow$$

$\xrightarrow{+} \Sigma F_x = 0$: $\quad A_x = 0 \qquad \mathbf{A}_x = 0$

We also note that at both A and E the bending moment is zero; thus two points (indicated by small circles) are obtained on the bending-moment diagram.

Shear Diagram. Since $dV/dx = -w$, we find that between concentrated loads and reactions the slope of the shear diagram is zero (that is, the shear is constant). The shear at any point is determined by dividing the beam into two parts and considering either part as a free body. For example, using the portion of beam to the left of section *1*, we obtain the shear between B and C:

$+\uparrow \Sigma F_y = 0$: $\quad +18 \text{ kN} - 20 \text{ kN} - V = 0 \qquad V = -2 \text{ kN}$

We also find that the shear is +12 kN just to the right of D and zero at end E. Since the slope $dV/dx = -w$ is constant between D and E, the shear diagram between these two points is a straight line.

Bending-Moment Diagram. We recall that the area under the shear curve between two points is equal to the change in bending moment between the same two points. For convenience, the area of each portion of the shear diagram is computed and is indicated on the diagram. Since the bending moment M_A at the left end is known to be zero, we write

$$\begin{aligned} M_B - M_A &= +108 & M_B &= +108 \text{ kN} \cdot \text{m} \\ M_C - M_B &= -\ 16 & M_C &= +\ 92 \text{ kN} \cdot \text{m} \\ M_D - M_C &= -140 & M_D &= -\ 48 \text{ kN} \cdot \text{m} \\ M_E - M_D &= +\ 48 & M_E &= 0 \end{aligned}$$

Since M_E is known to be zero, a check of the computations is obtained.

Between the concentrated loads and reactions the shear is constant; thus the slope dM/dx is constant, and the bending-moment diagram is drawn by connecting the known points with straight lines. Between D and E, where the shear diagram is an oblique straight line, the bending-moment diagram is a parabola.

From the V and M diagrams we note that $V_{max} = 18$ kN and $M_{max} = 108$ kN · m.

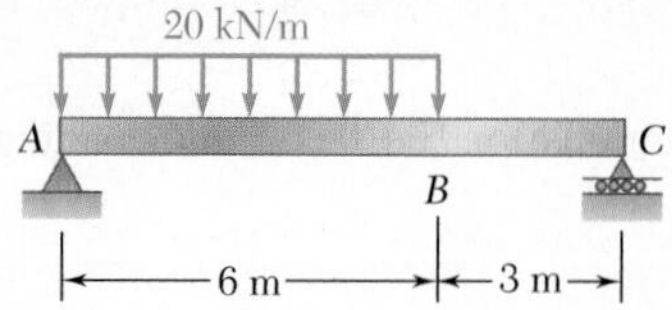

SAMPLE PROBLEM 7.5

Draw the shear and bending-moment diagrams for the beam and loading shown, and determine the location and magnitude of the maximum bending moment.

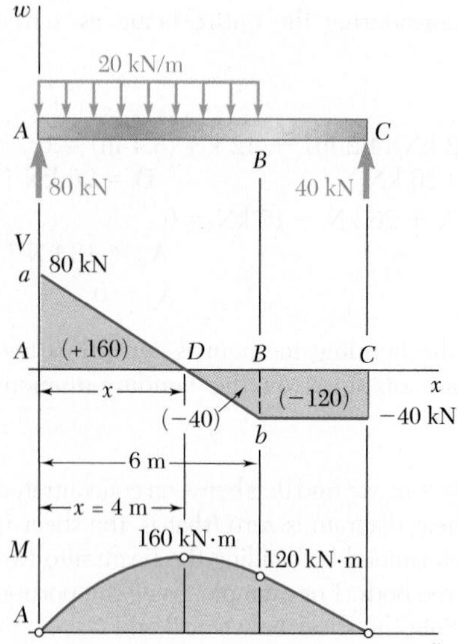

SOLUTION

Free-Body: Entire Beam. Considering the entire beam as a free body, we obtain the reactions

$$\mathbf{R}_A = 80 \text{ kN} \uparrow \qquad \mathbf{R}_C = 40 \text{ kN} \uparrow$$

Shear Diagram. The shear just to the right of A is $V_A = +80$ kN. Since the change in shear between two points is equal to *minus* the area under the load curve between the same two points, we obtain V_B by writing

$$V_B - V_A = -(20 \text{ kN/m})(6 \text{ m}) = -120 \text{ kN}$$
$$V_B = -120 + V_A = -120 + 80 = -40 \text{ kN}$$

Since the slope $dV/dx = -w$ is constant between A and B, the shear diagram between these two points is represented by a straight line. Between B and C, the area under the load curve is zero; therefore,

$$V_C - V_B = 0 \qquad V_C = V_B = -40 \text{ kN}$$

and the shear is constant between B and C.

Bending-Moment Diagram. We note that the bending moment at each end of the beam is zero. In order to determine the maximum bending moment, we locate the section D of the beam where $V = 0$. We write

$$V_D - V_A = -wx$$
$$0 - 80 \text{ kN} = -(20 \text{ kN/m})x$$

and, solving for x: $x = 4$ m ◀

The maximum bending moment occurs at point D, where we have $dM/dx = V = 0$. The areas of the various portions of the shear diagram are computed and are given (in parentheses) on the diagram. Since the area of the shear diagram between two points is equal to the change in bending moment between the same two points, we write

$$M_D - M_A = +160 \text{ kN} \cdot \text{m} \qquad M_D = +160 \text{ kN} \cdot \text{m}$$
$$M_B - M_D = -\ \ 40 \text{ kN} \cdot \text{m} \qquad M_B = +120 \text{ kN} \cdot \text{m}$$
$$M_C - M_B = -120 \text{ kN} \cdot \text{m} \qquad M_C = 0$$

The bending-moment diagram consists of a parabolic arc followed by a segment of a straight line; the slope of the parabola at A is equal to the value of V at that point.

The maximum bending moment is

$$M_{\text{max}} = M_D = +160 \text{ kN} \cdot \text{m} \quad ◀$$

SAMPLE PROBLEM 7.6

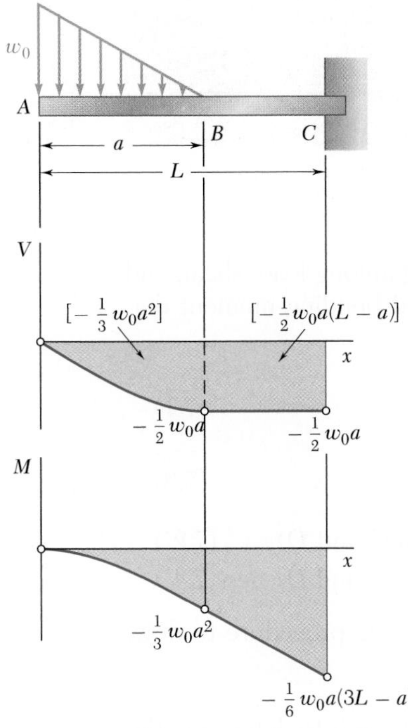

Sketch the shear and bending-moment diagrams for the cantilever beam shown.

SOLUTION

Shear Diagram. At the free end of the beam, we find $V_A = 0$. Between A and B, the area under the load curve is $\frac{1}{2}w_0a$; we find V_B by writing

$$V_B - V_A = -\tfrac{1}{2}w_0a \qquad V_B = -\tfrac{1}{2}w_0a$$

Between B and C, the beam is not loaded; thus $V_C = V_B$. At A, we have $w = w_0$, and, according to Eq. (7.1), the slope of the shear curve is $dV/dx = -w_0$, while at B the slope is $dV/dx = 0$. Between A and B, the loading decreases linearly, and the shear diagram is parabolic. Between B and C, $w = 0$, and the shear diagram is a horizontal line.

Bending-Moment Diagram. We note that $M_A = 0$ at the free end of the beam. We compute the area under the shear curve and write

$$M_B - M_A = -\tfrac{1}{3}w_0a^2 \qquad M_B = -\tfrac{1}{3}w_0a^2$$
$$M_C - M_B = -\tfrac{1}{2}w_0a(L-a)$$
$$M_C = -\tfrac{1}{6}w_0a(3L-a)$$

The sketch of the bending-moment diagram is completed by recalling that $dM/dx = V$. We find that between A and B the diagram is represented by a cubic curve with zero slope at A, and between B and C the diagram is represented by a straight line.

SAMPLE PROBLEM 7.7

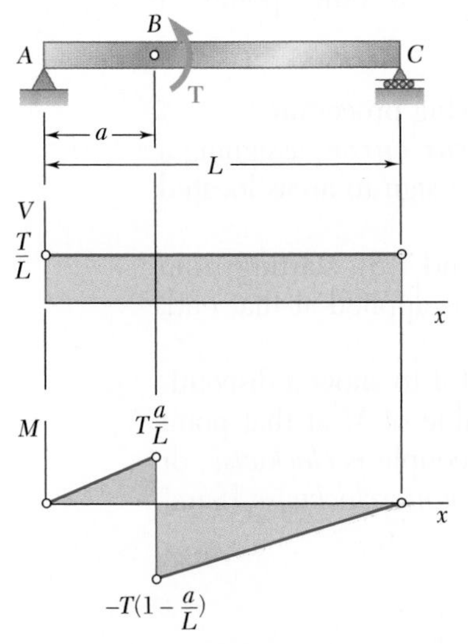

The simple beam AC is loaded by a couple of magnitude T applied at point B. Draw the shear and bending-moment diagrams for the beam.

SOLUTION

Free Body: Entire Beam. The entire beam is taken as a free body, and we obtain

$$\mathbf{R}_A = \frac{T}{L}\uparrow \qquad \mathbf{R}_C = \frac{T}{L}\downarrow$$

Shear and Bending-Moment Diagrams. The shear at any section is constant and equal to T/L. Since a couple is applied at B, the bending-moment diagram is discontinuous at B; the bending moment decreases suddenly by an amount equal to T.

SOLVING PROBLEMS ON YOUR OWN

In this lesson you learned how to use the relations existing among load, shear, and bending moment to simplify the drawing of the shear and bending-moment diagrams. These relations are

$$\frac{dV}{dx} = -w \qquad (7.1)$$

$$\frac{dM}{dx} = V \qquad (7.3)$$

$$V_D - V_C = -(\text{area under load curve between } C \text{ and } D) \qquad (7.2')$$

$$M_D - M_C = (\text{area under shear curve between } C \text{ and } D) \qquad (7.4')$$

Taking into account these relations, you can use the following procedure to draw the shear and bending-moment diagrams for a beam.

1. ***Draw a free-body diagram of the entire beam,*** and use it to determine the reactions at the beam supports.

2. ***Draw the shear diagram.*** This can be done as in the preceding lesson by cutting the beam at various points and considering the free-body diagram of one of the two portions of the beam that you have obtained [Sample Prob. 7.3]. You can, however, consider one of the following alternative procedures.

a. The shear V at any point of the beam is the sum of the reactions and loads to the left of that point; an upward force is counted as positive, and a downward force is counted as negative.

b. For a beam carrying a distributed load, you can start from a point where you know V and use Eq. (7.2′) repeatedly to find V at all the other points of interest.

3. ***Draw the bending-moment diagram,*** using the following procedure.

a. Compute the area under each portion of the shear curve, assigning a positive sign to areas located above the x axis and a negative sign to areas located below the x axis.

b. Apply Eq. (7.4′) repeatedly [Sample Probs. 7.4 and 7.5], starting from the left end of the beam, where $M = 0$ (except if a couple is applied at that end, or if the beam is a cantilever beam with a fixed left end).

c. Where a couple is applied to the beam, be careful to show a discontinuity in the bending-moment diagram by *increasing* the value of M at that point by an amount equal to the magnitude of the couple if the couple is *clockwise,* or *decreasing* the value of M by that amount if the couple is *counterclockwise* [Sample Prob. 7.7].

4. *Determine the location and magnitude of $|M|_{max}$.* The maximum absolute value of the bending moment occurs at one of the points where $dM/dx = 0$, that is, according to Eq. (7.3), at a point where V is equal to zero or changes sign. You should, therefore:

a. Determine the values of $|M|$, using the area under the shear curve, at the points where V changes sign; these points will occur under concentrated loads [Sample Prob. 7.4].

b. Determine the points where $V = 0$ and the corresponding values of $|M|$; these points will occur under a distributed load. To find the distance x between point C, where the distributed load starts, and point D, where the shear is zero, use Eq. (7.2′); for V_C use the known value of the shear at point C, for V_D use zero, and express the area under the load curve as a function of x [Sample Prob. 7.5].

5. *You can improve the quality of your drawings* by keeping in mind that at any given point, according to Eqs. (7.1) and (7.3), the slope of the V curve is equal to $-w$ and the slope of the M curve is equal to V. In particular, your drawings should clearly show where the slope of the curves is zero.

6. *Finally, for beams supporting a distributed load expressed as a function $w(x)$,* remember that the shear V can be obtained by integrating the function $-w(x)$, and the bending moment M can be obtained by integrating $V(x)$ [Eqs. (7.3) and (7.4)].

Problems

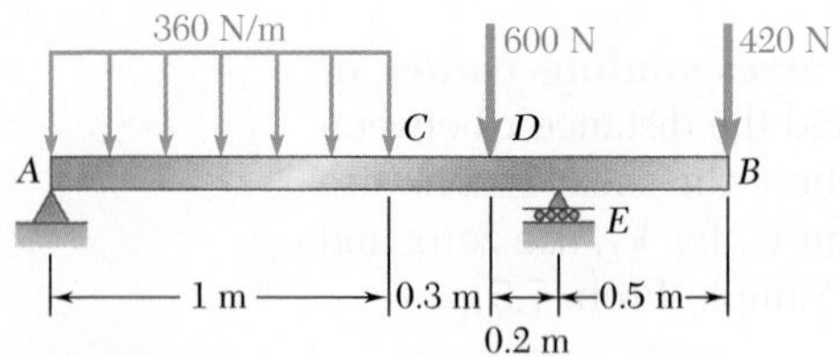

Fig. P7.64

7.58 Using the method of Sec. 7.6, solve Prob. 7.29.

7.59 Using the method of Sec. 7.6, solve Prob. 7.30.

7.60 Using the method of Sec. 7.6, solve Prob. 7.31.

7.61 Using the method of Sec. 7.6, solve Prob. 7.32.

7.62 Using the method of Sec. 7.6, solve Prob. 7.34.

7.63 Using the method of Sec. 7.6, solve Prob. 7.35.

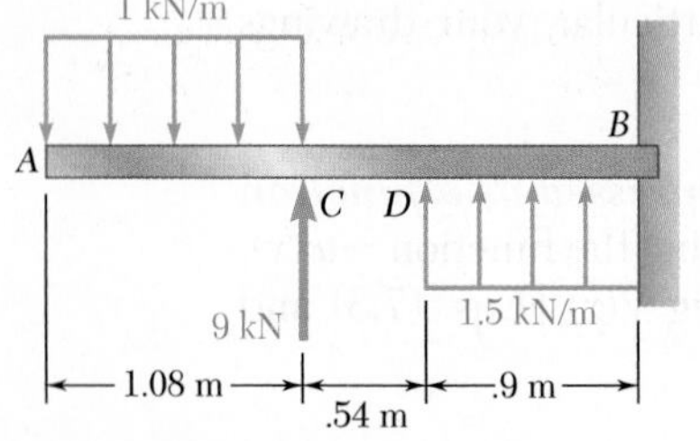

Fig. P7.65

7.64 and 7.65 For the beam and loading shown, (*a*) draw the shear and bending-moment diagrams, (*b*) determine the maximum absolute values of the shear and bending moment.

7.66 Using the method of Sec. 7.6, solve Prob. 7.37.

7.67 Using the method of Sec. 7.6, solve Prob. 7.38.

7.68 Using the method of Sec. 7.6, solve Prob. 7.39.

7.69 Using the method of Sec. 7.6, solve Prob. 7.40.

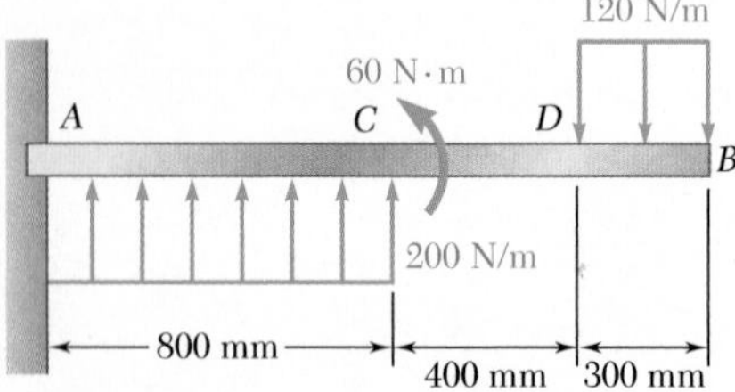

Fig. P7.70

7.70 and *7.71* For the beam and loading shown, (*a*) draw the shear and bending-moment diagrams, (*b*) determine the maximum absolute values of the shear and bending moment.

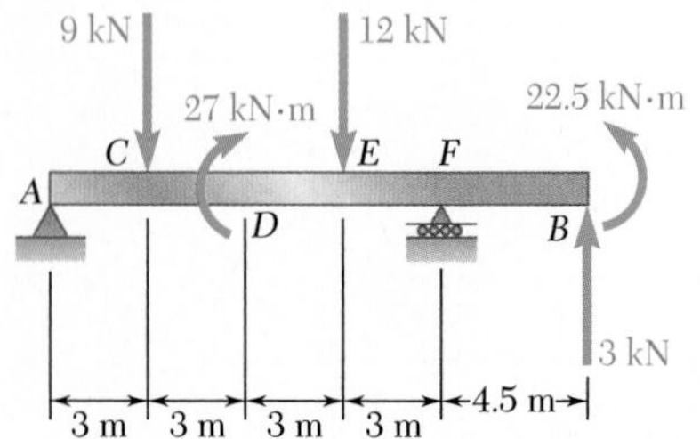

Fig. *P7.71*

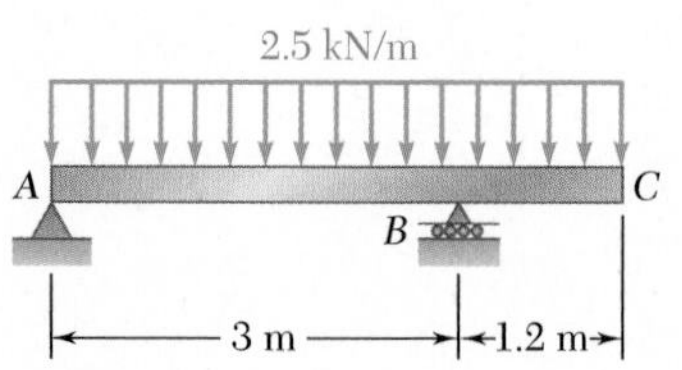

Fig. P7.72

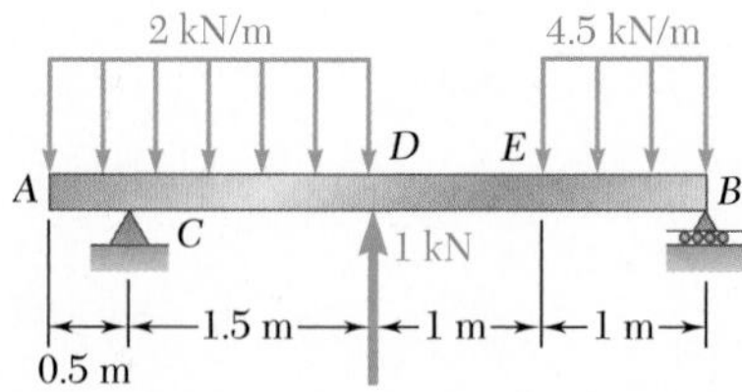

Fig. *P7.73*

7.72 and *7.73* For the beam and loading shown, (*a*) draw the shear and bending-moment diagrams, (*b*) determine the location and magnitude of the maximum bending moment.

7.74 For the beam shown, draw the shear and bending-moment diagrams, and determine the maximum absolute value of the bending moment knowing that (*a*) $P = 7$ kN, (*b*) $P = 10$ kN.

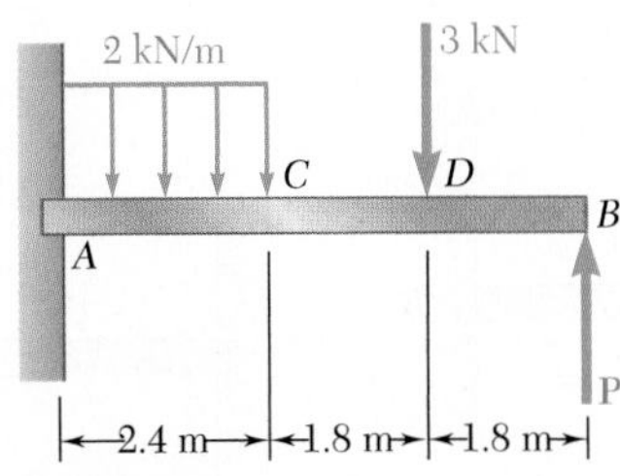

Fig. P7.74

7.75 For the beam shown, draw the shear and bending-moment diagrams, and determine the location and magnitude of the maximum absolute value of the bending moment.

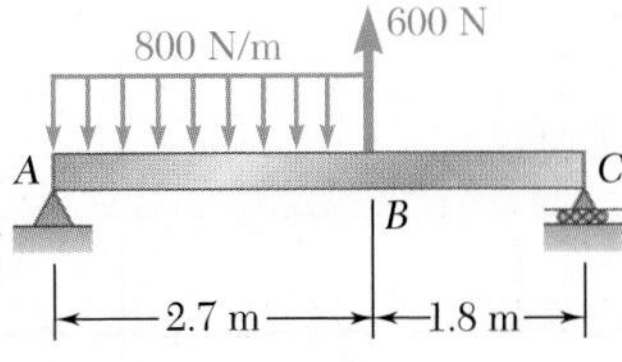

Fig. P7.75

7.76 For the beam and loading shown, (*a*) draw the shear and bending-moment diagrams, (*b*) determine the location and magnitude of the maximum absolute value of the bending moment.

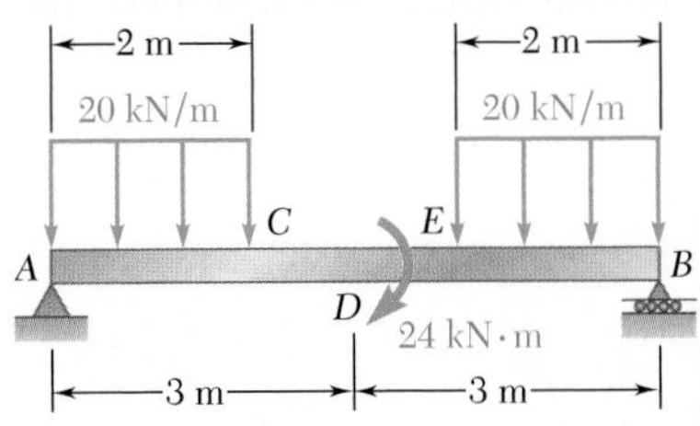

Fig. P7.76

7.77 Solve Prob. 7.76 assuming that the 24-kN · m couple applied at *D* is counterclockwise.

7.78 For beam *AB*, (*a*) draw the shear and bending-moment diagrams, (*b*) determine the location and magnitude of the maximum absolute value of the bending moment.

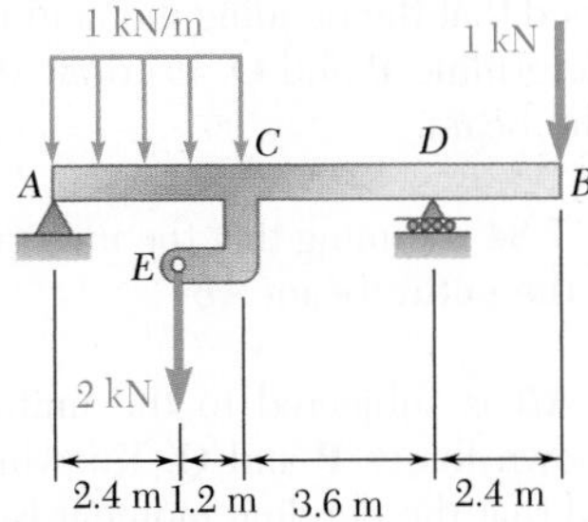

Fig. P7.78

7.79 Solve Prob. 7.78 assuming that the 2-kN force applied at *E* is directed upward.

7.80 and 7.81 For the beam and loading shown, (*a*) derive the equations of the shear and bending-moment curves, (*b*) draw the shear and bending-moment diagrams, (*c*) determine the location and magnitude of the maximum bending moment.

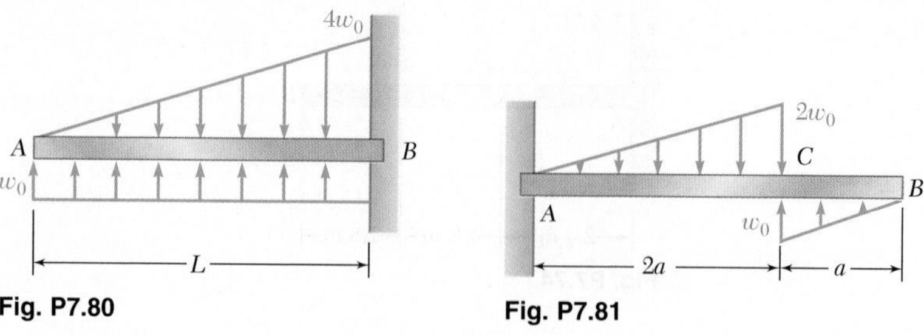

Fig. P7.80 **Fig. P7.81**

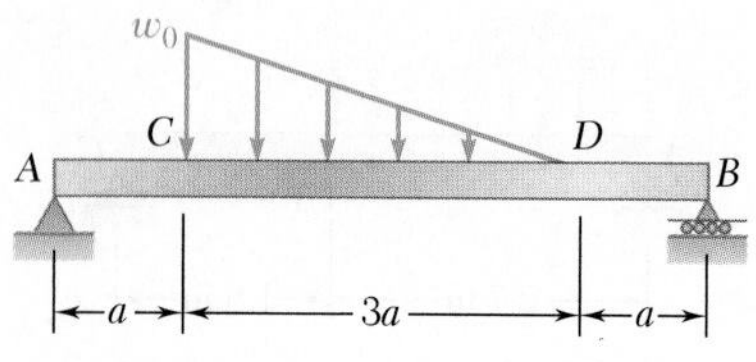

Fig. P7.82

7.82 For the beam shown, (*a*) draw the shear and bending-moment diagrams, (*b*) determine the location and magnitude of the maximum bending moment. (*Hint:* Derive the equations of the shear and bending-moment curves for portion *CD* of the beam.)

7.83 The distributed load on a deck caused by drifted snow can be approximated by the cubic load curve shown. Derive the equations of the shear and bending-moment curves, and determine the maximum bending moment.

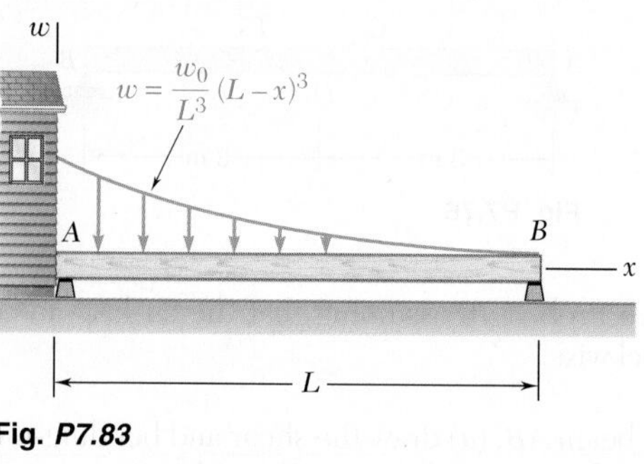

Fig. *P7.83*

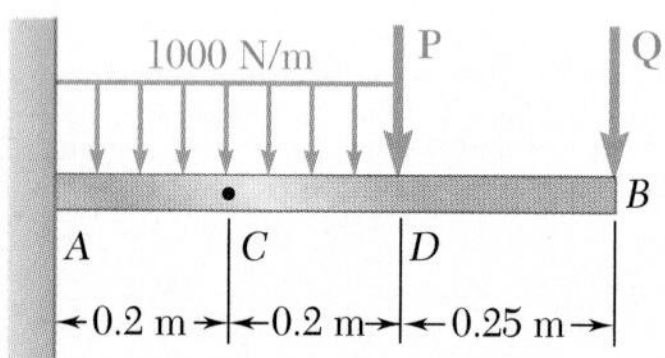

Fig. *P7.84*

***7.84* The beam *AB* supports the uniformly distributed load of 1000 N/m and two unknown forces **P** and **Q**. Knowing that it has been experimentally determined that the bending moment is −395 N · m at *A* and −215 N · m at *C*, (*a*) determine **P** and **Q**, (*b*) draw the shear and bending-moment diagrams for the beam.

***7.85** Solve Prob. 7.84 assuming that the uniformly distributed load of 1000 N/m extends over the entire beam *AB*.

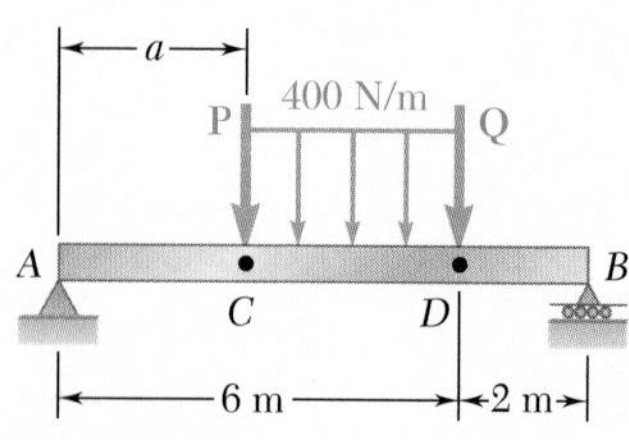

Fig. P7.86

***7.86** The beam *AB* is subjected to the uniformly distributed load shown and to two unknown forces **P** and **Q**. Knowing that it has been experimentally determined that the bending moment is +2.7 kN · m at *C* and +2.5 kN · m at *D* when $a = 2$ m, (*a*) determine **P** and **Q**, (*b*) draw the shear and bending-moment diagrams for the beam.

***7.87** Solve Prob. 7.86 when $a = 1.35$ m.

*7.7. CABLES WITH CONCENTRATED LOADS

Cables are used in many engineering applications, such as suspension bridges, transmission lines, aerial tramways, guy wires for high towers, etc. Cables may be divided into two categories according to their loading: (1) cables supporting concentrated loads, (2) cables supporting distributed loads. In this section, cables of the first category are examined.

Consider a cable attached to two fixed points A and B and supporting n vertical concentrated loads $\mathbf{P}_1, \mathbf{P}_2, \ldots, \mathbf{P}_n$ (Fig. 7.13a). We assume that the cable is *flexible,* that is, that its resistance to bending is small and can be neglected. We further assume that the *weight of the cable is negligible* compared with the loads supported by the cable. Any portion of cable between successive loads can therefore be considered as a two-force member, and the internal forces at any point in the cable reduce to a *force of tension directed along the cable.*

We assume that each of the loads lies in a given vertical line, that is, that the horizontal distance from support A to each of the loads is known; we also assume that the horizontal and vertical distances between the supports are known. We propose to determine the shape of the cable, that is, the vertical distance from support A to each of the points $C_1, C_2, \ldots, C_n$, and also the tension T in each portion of the cable.

Photo 7.3 Since the weight of the cable of the chairlift shown is negligible compared to the weights of the chairs and skiers, the methods of this section can be used to determine the force at any point in the cable.

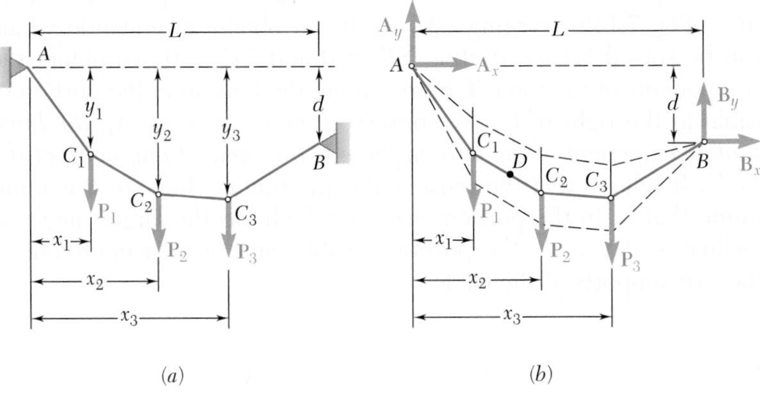

Fig. 7.13

We first draw the free-body diagram of the entire cable (Fig. 7.13b). Since the slope of the portions of cable attached at A and B is not known, the reactions at A and B must be represented by two components each. Thus, four unknowns are involved, and the three equations of equilibrium are not sufficient to determine the reactions at A and B.† We must therefore obtain an additional equation by considering the equilibrium of a portion of the cable. This is possible if

†Clearly, the cable is not a rigid body; the equilibrium equations represent, therefore, *necessary but not sufficient conditions* (see Sec. 6.11).

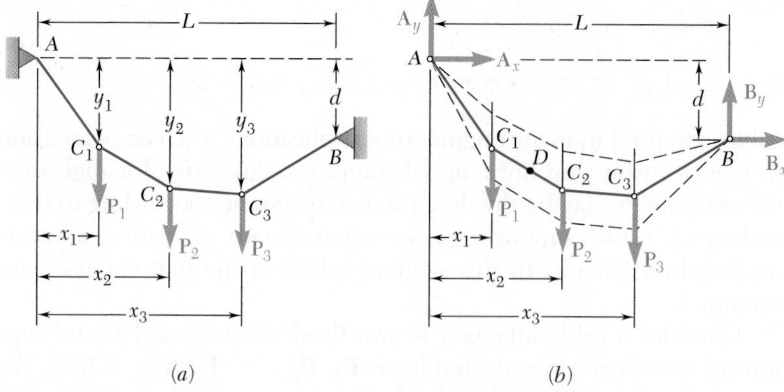

Fig. 7.13 *(repeated)*

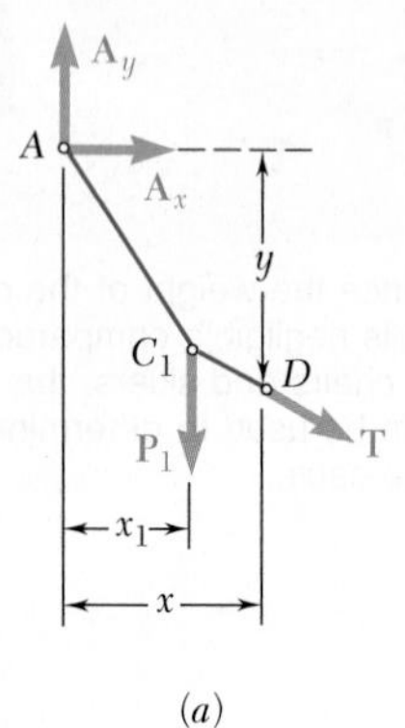

(a)

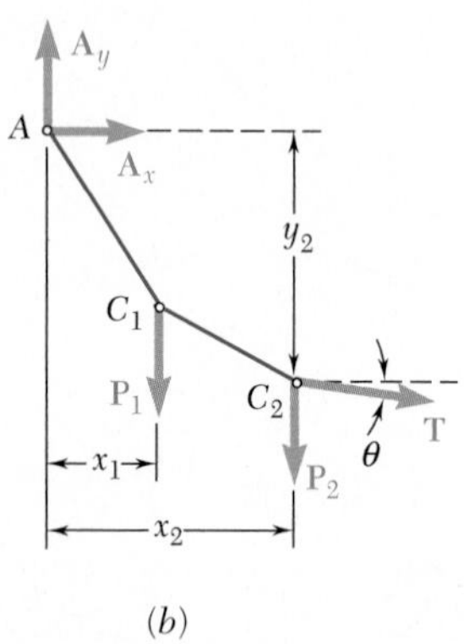

(b)

Fig. 7.14

we know the coordinates x and y of a point D of the cable. Drawing the free-body diagram of the portion of cable AD (Fig. 7.14*a*) and writing $\Sigma M_D = 0$, we obtain an additional relation between the scalar components A_x and A_y and can determine the reactions at A and B. The problem would remain indeterminate, however, if we did not know the coordinates of D, unless some other relation between A_x and A_y (or between B_x and B_y) were given. The cable might hang in any of various possible ways, as indicated by the dashed lines in Fig. 7.13*b*.

Once A_x and A_y have been determined, the vertical distance from A to any point of the cable can easily be found. Considering point C_2, for example, we draw the free-body diagram of the portion of cable AC_2 (Fig. 7.14*b*). Writing $\Sigma M_{C_2} = 0$, we obtain an equation which can be solved for y_2. Writing $\Sigma F_x = 0$ and $\Sigma F_y = 0$, we obtain the components of the force $\mathbf{T}$ representing the tension in the portion of cable to the right of C_2. We observe that $T \cos \theta = -A_x$; *the horizontal component of the tension force is the same at any point of the cable*. It follows that the tension T is maximum when $\cos \theta$ is minimum, that is, in the portion of cable which has the largest angle of inclination θ. Clearly, this portion of cable must be adjacent to one of the two supports of the cable.

*7.8. CABLES WITH DISTRIBUTED LOADS

Consider a cable attached to two fixed points A and B and carrying a *distributed load* (Fig. 7.15*a*). We saw in the preceding section that for a cable supporting concentrated loads, the internal force at any point is a force of tension directed along the cable. In the case of a cable carrying a distributed load, the cable hangs in the shape of a curve, and the internal force at a point D is a force of tension $\mathbf{T}$ *directed along the tangent to the curve*. In this section, you will learn to determine the tension at any point of a cable supporting a given distributed load. In the following sections, the shape of the cable will be determined for two particular types of distributed loads.

Considering the most general case of distributed load, we draw the free-body diagram of the portion of cable extending from the lowest point C to a given point D of the cable (Fig. 7.15*b*). The forces

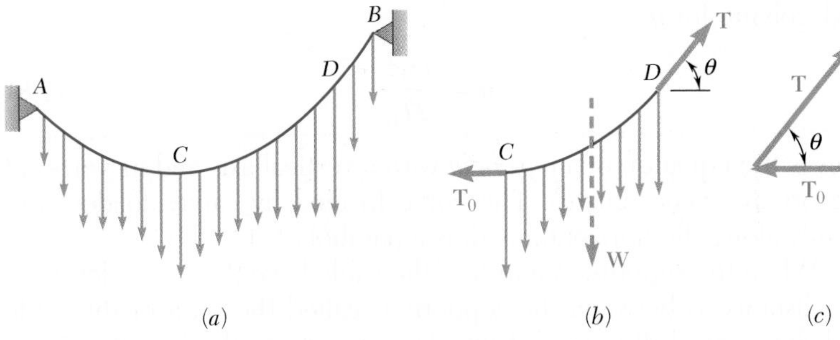

Fig. 7.15

acting on the free body are the tension force $\mathbf{T}_0$ at C, which is horizontal, the tension force $\mathbf{T}$ at D, directed along the tangent to the cable at D, and the resultant $\mathbf{W}$ of the distributed load supported by the portion of cable CD. Drawing the corresponding force triangle (Fig. 7.15c), we obtain the following relations:

$$T \cos \theta = T_0 \qquad T \sin \theta = W \tag{7.5}$$

$$T = \sqrt{T_0^2 + W^2} \qquad \tan \theta = \frac{W}{T_0} \tag{7.6}$$

From the relations (7.5), it appears that the horizontal component of the tension force $\mathbf{T}$ is the same at any point and that the vertical component of $\mathbf{T}$ is equal to the magnitude W of the load measured from the lowest point. Relations (7.6) show that the tension T is minimum at the lowest point and maximum at one of the two points of support.

*7.9. PARABOLIC CABLE

Let us assume, now, that the cable AB carries a load *uniformly distributed along the horizontal* (Fig. 7.16a). Cables of suspension bridges may be assumed loaded in this way, since the weight of the cables is small compared with the weight of the roadway. We denote by w the load per unit length (*measured horizontally*) and express it in N/m or in lb/ft. Choosing coordinate axes with origin at the lowest point C of the cable, we find that the magnitude W of the total load carried by the portion of cable extending from C to the point D of coordinates x and y is $W = wx$. The relations (7.6) defining the magnitude and direction of the tension force at D become

$$T = \sqrt{T_0^2 + w^2x^2} \qquad \tan \theta = \frac{wx}{T_0} \tag{7.7}$$

Moreover, the distance from D to the line of action of the resultant $\mathbf{W}$ is equal to half the horizontal distance from C to D (Fig. 7.16b). Summing moments about D, we write

$$+\circlearrowleft \Sigma M_D = 0: \qquad wx\frac{x}{2} - T_0 y = 0$$

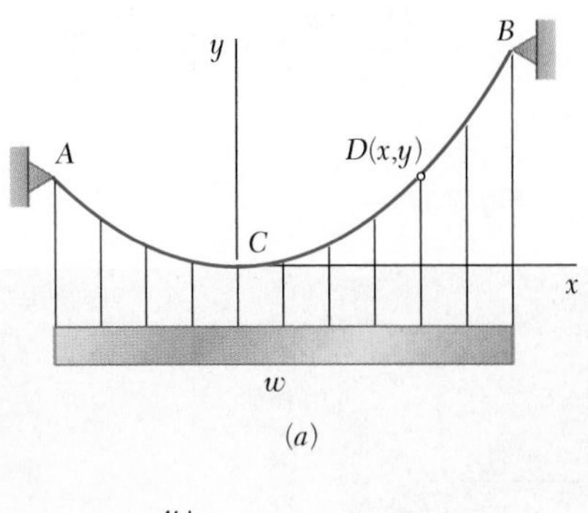

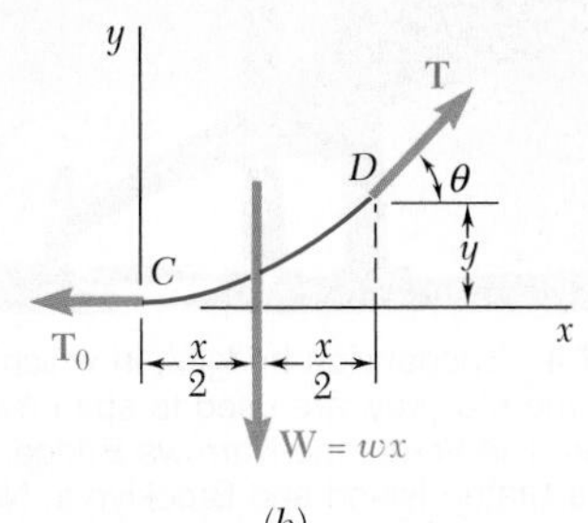

Fig. 7.16

and, solving for y,

$$y = \frac{wx^2}{2T_0} \tag{7.8}$$

This is the equation of a *parabola* with a vertical axis and its vertex at the origin of coordinates. The curve formed by cables loaded uniformly along the horizontal is thus a parabola.†

When the supports A and B of the cable have the same elevation, the distance L between the supports is called the *span* of the cable and the vertical distance h from the supports to the lowest point is called the *sag* of the cable (Fig. 7.17*a*). If the span and sag of a cable are known, and if the load w per unit horizontal length is given, the minimum tension T_0 may be found by substituting $x = L/2$ and $y = h$ in Eq. (7.8). Equations (7.7) will then yield the tension and the slope at any point of the cable, and Eq. (7.8) will define the shape of the cable.

When the supports have different elevations, the position of the lowest point of the cable is not known and the coordinates x_A, y_A and x_B, y_B of the supports must be determined. To this effect, we express that the coordinates of A and B satisfy Eq. (7.8) and that $x_B - x_A = L$ and $y_B - y_A = d$, where L and d denote, respectively, the horizontal and vertical distances between the two supports (Fig. 7.17*b* and *c*).

The length of the cable from its lowest point C to its support B can be obtained from the formula

$$s_B = \int_0^{x_B} \sqrt{1 + \left(\frac{dy}{dx}\right)^2}\, dx \tag{7.9}$$

Differentiating Eq. (7.8), we obtain the derivative $dy/dx = wx/T_0$; substituting into Eq. (7.9) and using the binomial theorem to expand the radical in an infinite series, we have

$$s_B = \int_0^{x_B} \sqrt{1 + \frac{w^2x^2}{T_0^2}}\, dx = \int_0^{x_B} \left(1 + \frac{w^2x^2}{2T_0^2} - \frac{w^4x^4}{8T_0^4} + \cdots\right) dx$$

$$s_B = x_B\left(1 + \frac{w^2x_B^2}{6T_0^2} - \frac{w^4x_B^4}{40T_0^4} + \cdots\right)$$

and, since $wx_B^2/2T_0 = y_B$,

$$s_B = x_B\left[1 + \frac{2}{3}\left(\frac{y_B}{x_B}\right)^2 - \frac{2}{5}\left(\frac{y_B}{x_B}\right)^4 + \cdots\right] \tag{7.10}$$

The series converges for values of the ratio y_B/x_B less than 0.5; in most cases, this ratio is much smaller, and only the first two terms of the series need be computed.

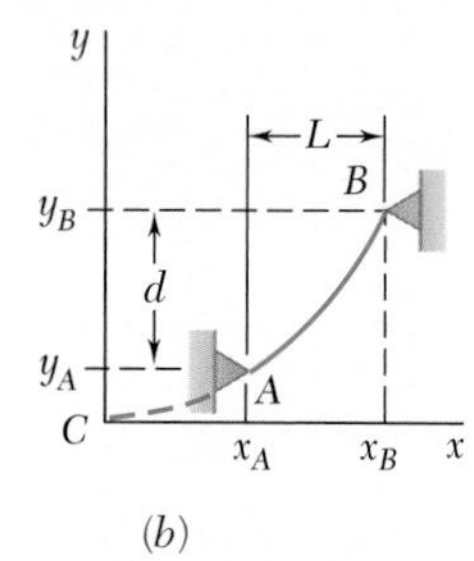

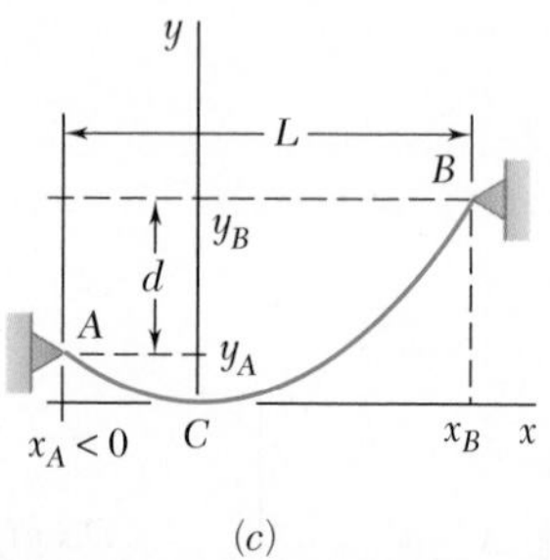

Fig. 7.17

Photo 7.4 Suspension bridges, in which cables support the roadway, are used to span rivers and estuaries. The Verrazano-Narrows Bridge, which connects Staten Island and Brooklyn in New York City, has the longest span of all bridges in the United States.

†Cables hanging under their own weight are not loaded uniformly along the horizontal, and they do not form a parabola. The error introduced by assuming a parabolic shape for cables hanging under their weight, however, is small when the cable is sufficiently taut. A complete discussion of cables hanging under their own weight is given in the next section.

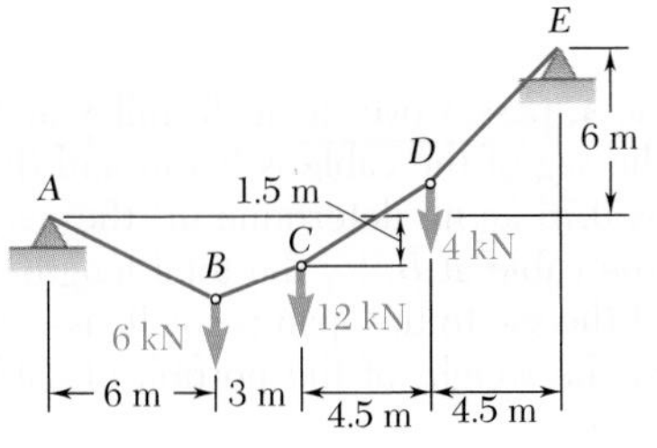

SAMPLE PROBLEM 7.8

The cable AE supports three vertical loads from the points indicated. If point C is 1.5 m below the left support, determine (*a*) the elevation of points B and D, (*b*) the maximum slope and the maximum tension in the cable.

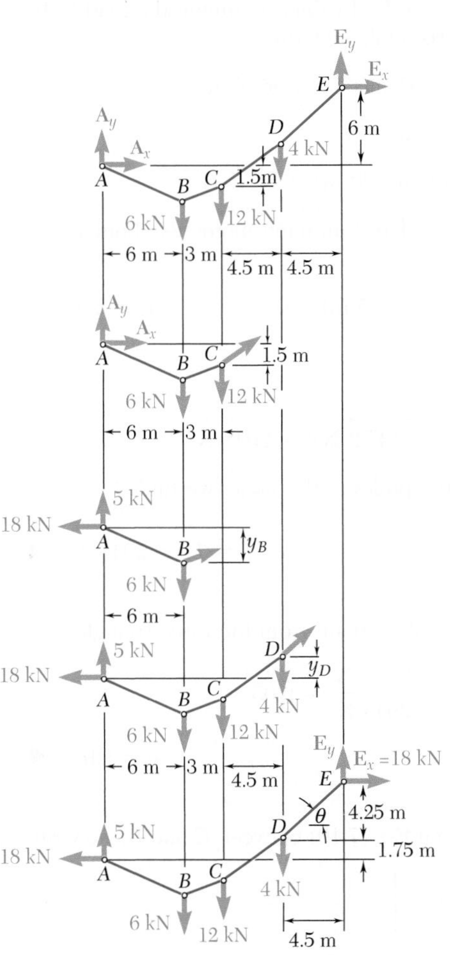

SOLUTION

Reactions at Supports. The reaction components $\mathbf{A}_x$ and $\mathbf{A}_y$ are determined as follows:

Free Body: Entire Cable

$$+\circlearrowleft \Sigma M_E = 0:$$

$$A_x(6 \text{ m}) - A_y(18 \text{ m}) + (6 \text{ kN})(12 \text{ m}) + (12 \text{ kN})(9 \text{ m}) + (4 \text{ kN})(4.5 \text{ m}) = 0$$

$$6A_x - 18A_y + 198 = 0$$

Free Body: ABC

$$+\circlearrowleft \Sigma M_C = 0: \qquad -A_x(1.5 \text{ m}) - A_y(9 \text{ m}) + (6 \text{ kN})(3 \text{ m}) = 0$$

$$-1.5A_x - 9A_y + 18 = 0$$

Solving the two equations simultaneously, we obtain

$$A_x = -18 \text{ kN} \qquad \mathbf{A}_x = 18 \text{ kN} \leftarrow$$

$$A_y = +5 \text{ kN} \qquad \mathbf{A}_y = 5 \text{ kN} \uparrow$$

***a.* Elevation of Points *B* and *D*.**

Free Body: AB Considering the portion of cable AB as a free body, we write

$$+\circlearrowleft \Sigma M_B = 0: \qquad (18 \text{ kN})y_B - (5 \text{ kN})(6 \text{ m}) = 0$$

$$y_B = 1.67 \text{ m below A} \quad \blacktriangleleft$$

Free Body: ABCD. Using the portion of cable $ABCD$ as a free body, we write

$$+\circlearrowleft \Sigma M_D = 0:$$

$$-(18 \text{ kN})y_D - (5 \text{ kN})(13.5 \text{ m}) + (6 \text{ kN})(7.5 \text{ m}) + (12 \text{ kN})(4.5 \text{ m}) = 0$$

$$y_D = 1.75 \text{ m above A} \quad \blacktriangleleft$$

***b.* Maximum Slope and Maximum Tension.** We observe that the maximum slope occurs in portion DE. Since the horizontal component of the tension is constant and equal to 18 kN, we write

$$\tan\theta = \frac{4.25 \text{ m}}{4.5 \text{ m}} \qquad \theta = 43.4° \quad \blacktriangleleft$$

$$T_{\max} = \frac{18 \text{ kN}}{\cos\theta} \qquad T_{\max} = 24.8 \text{ kN} \quad \blacktriangleleft$$

SAMPLE PROBLEM 7.9

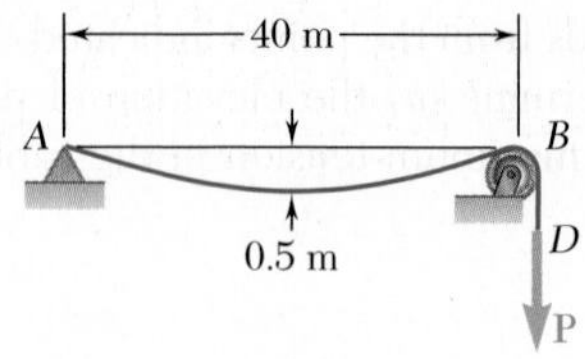

A light cable is attached to a support at A, passes over a small pulley at B, and supports a load $\mathbf{P}$. Knowing that the sag of the cable is 0.5 m and that the mass per unit length of the cable is 0.75 kg/m, determine (*a*) the magnitude of the load $\mathbf{P}$, (*b*) the slope of the cable at B, (*c*) the total length of the cable from A to B. Since the ratio of the sag to the span is small, assume the cable to be parabolic. Also, neglect the weight of the portion of cable from B to D.

SOLUTION

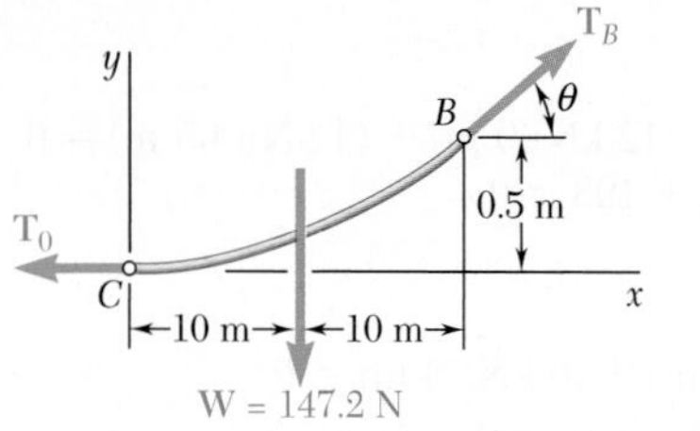

a. Load P. We denote by C the lowest point of the cable and draw the free-body diagram of the portion CB of cable. Assuming the load to be uniformly distributed along the horizontal, we write

$$w = (0.75 \text{ kg/m})(9.81 \text{ m/s}^2) = 7.36 \text{ N/m}$$

The total load for the portion CB of cable is

$$W = wx_B = (7.36 \text{ N/m})(20 \text{ m}) = 147.2 \text{ N}$$

and is applied halfway between C and B. Summing moments about B, we write

$$+\circlearrowleft \Sigma M_B = 0: \quad (147.2 \text{ N})(10 \text{ m}) - T_0(0.5 \text{ m}) = 0 \qquad T_0 = 2944 \text{ N}$$

From the force triangle we obtain

$$T_B = \sqrt{T_0^2 + W^2}$$
$$= \sqrt{(2944 \text{ N})^2 + (147.2 \text{ N})^2} = 2948 \text{ N}$$

Since the tension on each side of the pulley is the same, we find

$$P = T_B = 2948 \text{ N} \quad \blacktriangleleft$$

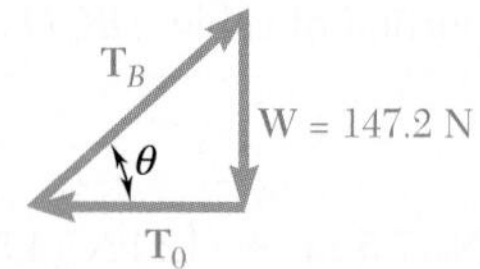

b. Slope of Cable at B. We also obtain from the force triangle

$$\tan \theta = \frac{W}{T_0} = \frac{147.2 \text{ N}}{2944 \text{ N}} = 0.05$$

$$\theta = 2.9° \quad \blacktriangleleft$$

c. Length of Cable. Applying Eq. (7.10) between C and B, we write

$$s_B = x_B\left[1 + \frac{2}{3}\left(\frac{y_B}{x_B}\right)^2 + \cdots\right]$$

$$= (20 \text{ m})\left[1 + \frac{2}{3}\left(\frac{0.5 \text{ m}}{20 \text{ m}}\right)^2 + \cdots\right] = 20.00833 \text{ m}$$

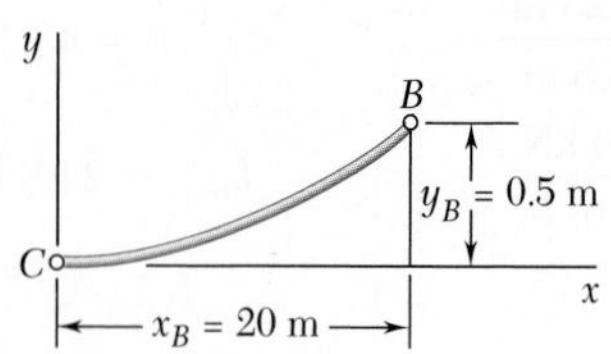

The total length of the cable between A and B is twice this value,

$$\text{Length} = 2s_B = 40.0167 \text{ m} \quad \blacktriangleleft$$

SOLVING PROBLEMS ON YOUR OWN

In the problems of this section you will apply the equations of equilibrium to *cables that lie in a vertical plane.* We assume that a cable cannot resist bending, so that the force of tension in the cable is always directed along the cable.

A. ***In the first part of this lesson we considered cables subjected to concentrated loads.*** Since the weight of the cable is neglected, the cable is straight between loads.

Your solution will consist of the following steps:

1. ***Draw a free-body diagram of the entire cable*** showing the loads and the horizontal and vertical components of the reaction at each support. Use this free-body diagram to write the corresponding equilibrium equations.

2. ***You will be confronted with four unknown components and only three equations of equilibrium*** (see Fig. 7.13). You must therefore find an additional piece of information, such as the *position* of a point on the cable or the *slope* of the cable at a given point.

3. ***After you have identified the point of the cable where the additional information exists,*** cut the cable at that point, and draw a free-body diagram of one of the two portions of the cable you have obtained.

   a. If you know the position of the point where you have cut the cable, writing $\Sigma M = 0$ about that point for the new free body will yield the additional equation required to solve for the four unknown components of the reactions. [Sample Prob. 7.8].

   b. If you know the slope of the portion of the cable you have cut, writing $\Sigma F_x = 0$ and $\Sigma F_y = 0$ for the new free body will yield two equilibrium equations which, together with the original three, can be solved for the four reaction components and for the tension in the cable where it has been cut.

4. ***To find the elevation of a given point of the cable and the slope and tension at that point*** once the reactions at the supports have been found, you should cut the cable at that point and draw a free-body diagram of one of the two portions of the cable you have obtained. Writing $\Sigma M = 0$ about the given point yields its elevation. Writing $\Sigma F_x = 0$ and $\Sigma F_y = 0$ yields the components of the tension force, from which its magnitude and direction can easily be found.

(continued)

5. ***For a cable supporting vertical loads only,*** you will observe that *the horizontal component of the tension force is the same at any point.* It follows that, for such a cable, the *maximum tension occurs in the steepest portion of the cable.*

B. ***In the second portion of this lesson we considered cables carrying a load uniformly distributed along the horizontal.*** The shape of the cable is then parabolic.

Your solution will use one or more of the following concepts:

1. ***Placing the origin of coordinates at the lowest point of the cable*** and directing the x and y axes to the right and upward, respectively, we find that *the equation of the parabola* is

$$y = \frac{wx^2}{2T_0} \tag{7.8}$$

The minimum cable tension occurs at the origin, where the cable is horizontal, and the maximum tension is at the support where the slope is maximum.

2. ***If the supports of the cable have the same elevation,*** the sag h of the cable is the vertical distance from the lowest point of the cable to the horizontal line joining the supports. To solve a problem involving such a parabolic cable, you should write Eq. (7.8) for one of the supports; this equation can be solved for one unknown.

3. ***If the supports of the cable have different elevations,*** you will have to write Eq. (7.8) for each of the supports (see Fig. 7.17).

4. ***To find the length of the cable*** from the lowest point to one of the supports, you can use Eq. (7.10). In most cases, you will need to compute only the first two terms of the series.

In Sample Prob. 7.9 we considered a cable hanging under its own weight. We observe that for taut cables their weights per unit length in the horizontal direction are approximately constant. This was the external loading condition of the cables analyzed in Sec. 7.9. Thus, we are able to apply the results obtained for this type of external loading to the special case of *taut* cables hanging under their own weights if w is now taken as the weight per unit length of the cables.

Problems

7.88 Two loads are suspended as shown from cable *ABCD*. Knowing that $d_C = 0.75$ m, determine (*a*) the distance d_B, (*b*) the components of the reaction at *A*, (*c*) the maximum tension in the cable.

7.89 Two loads are suspended as shown from cable *ABCD*. Knowing that the maximum tension in the cable is 3.6 kN, determine (*a*) the distance d_B, (*b*) the distance d_C.

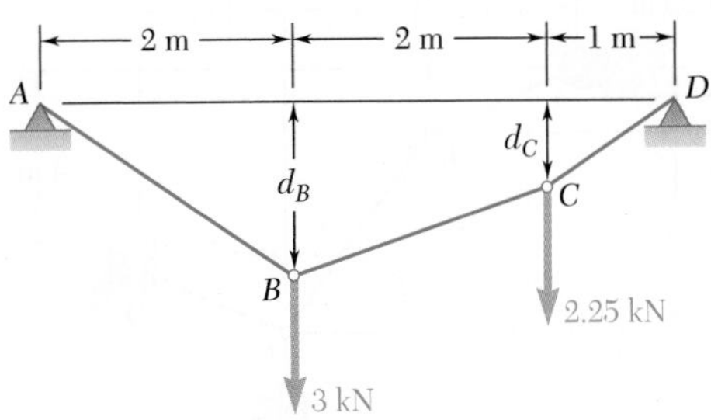

Fig. P7.88 and P7.89

7.90 Three loads are suspended as shown from cable *ABCDE*. Knowing that $d_C = 3.6$ m, determine (*a*) the components of the reaction at *E*, (*b*) the maximum tension in the cable.

7.91 Three loads are suspended from cable *ABCDE*. Determine distance d_C knowing that the maximum tension in the cable is 5 kN.

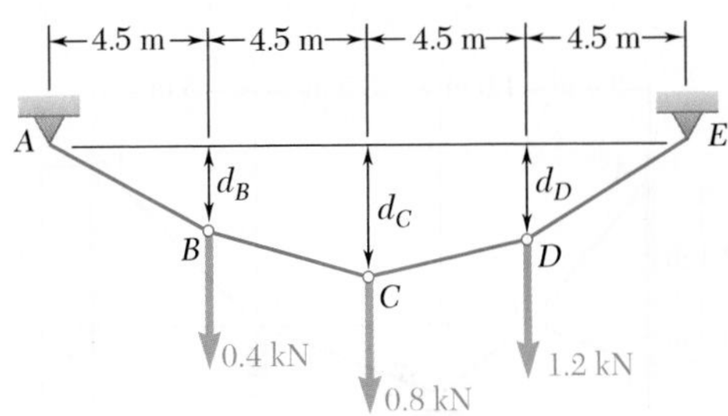

Fig. *P7.90* and P7.91

7.92 Cable *ABCDE* supports three loads as shown. Knowing that $d_C = 1.8$ m, determine (*a*) the reaction at *E*, (*b*) the distances d_B and d_D.

7.93 Cable *ABCDE* supports three loads as shown. Determine (*a*) the distance d_C for which portion *CD* of the cable is horizontal, (*b*) the corresponding reactions at the supports.

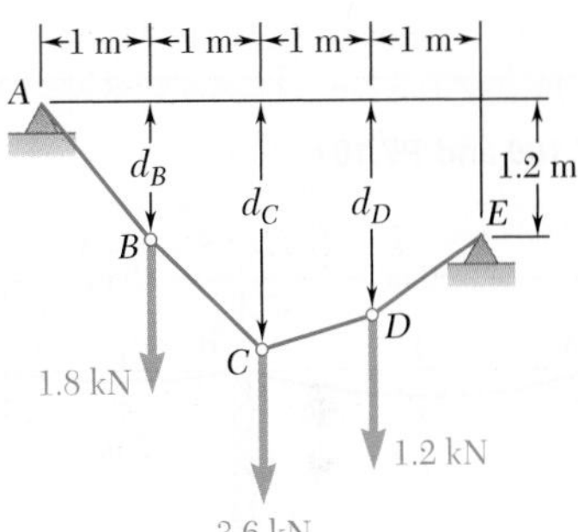

Fig. P7.92 and P7.93

7.94 An oil pipeline is supported at 1.8-m intervals by vertical hangers attached to the cable shown. Due to the combined weight of the pipe and its contents, the tension in each hanger is 400 N. Knowing that $d_C = 3.6$ m, determine (*a*) the maximum tension in the cable, (*b*) the distance d_D.

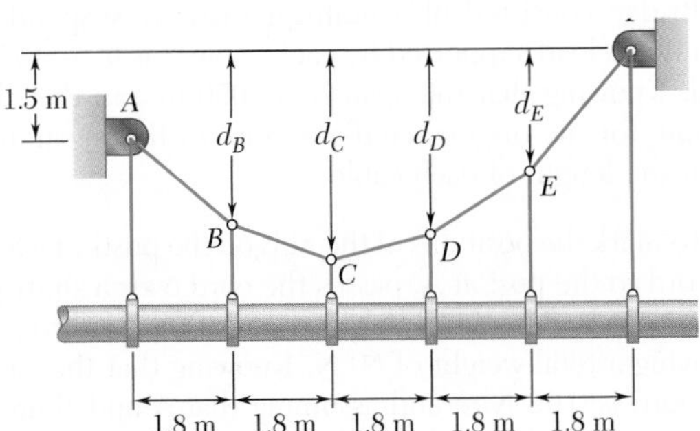

Fig. P7.94

7.95 Solve Prob. 7.94 assuming that $d_C = 2.7$ m.

7.96 Cable *ABC* supports two boxes as shown. Knowing that $b = 2.7$ m, determine (*a*) the required magnitude of the horizontal force **P**, (*b*) the corresponding distance *a*.

7.97 Cable *ABC* supports two boxes as shown. Determine the distances *a* and *b* when a horizontal force **P** of magnitude 25 N is applied at *C*.

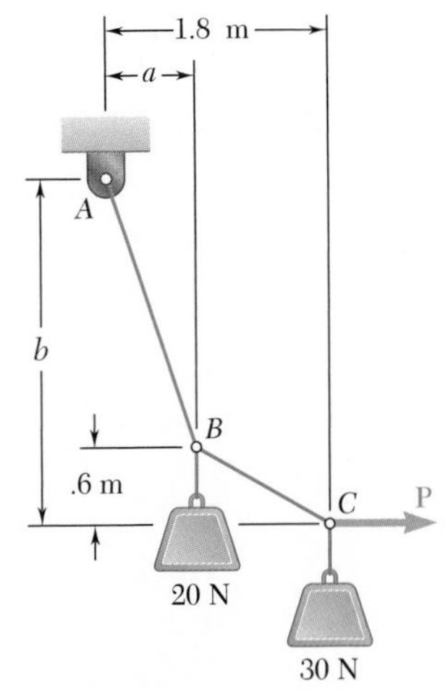

Fig. P7.96 and P7.97

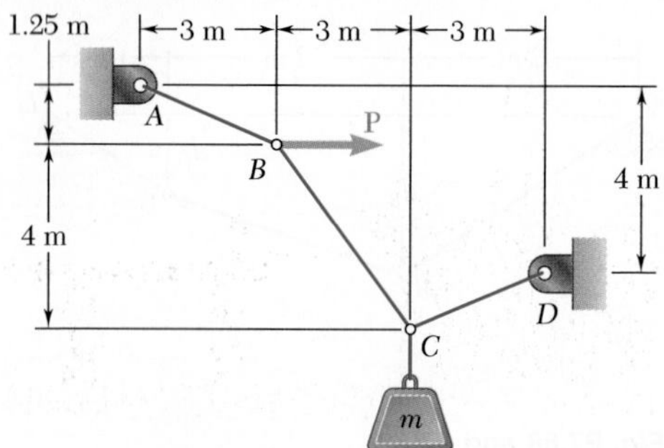

Fig. P7.98 and *P7.99*

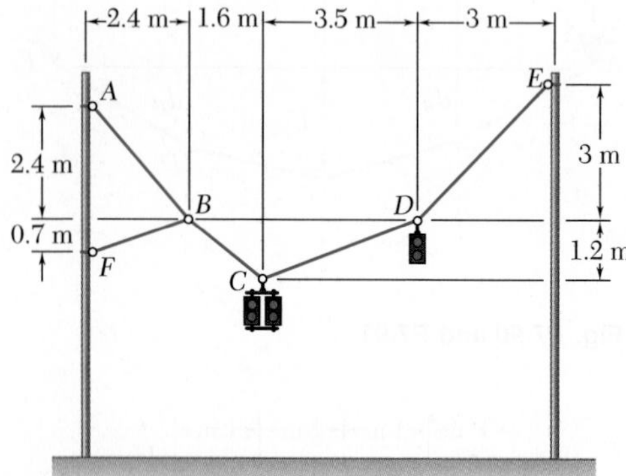

Fig. *P7.100* and P7.101

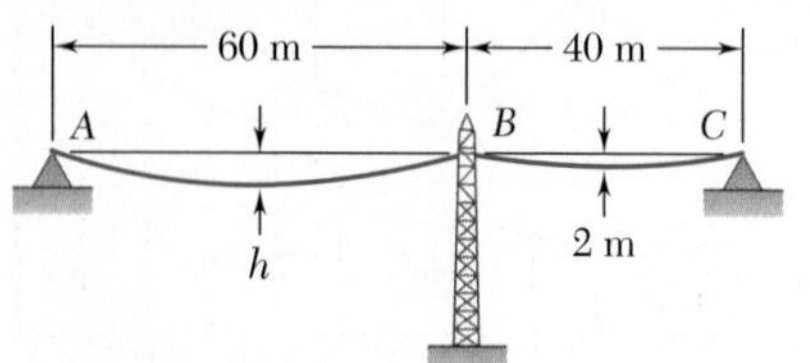

Fig. P7.103

7.98 A force **P** applied at B and a block attached at C maintain cable $ABCD$ in the position shown. Knowing that the force **P** has a magnitude of 1.32 kN, determine (*a*) the reaction at A, (*b*) the required mass m of the block, (*c*) the tension in each portion of the cable.

7.99 A force **P** applied at B and a block attached at C maintain cable $ABCD$ in the position shown. Knowing that the mass m of the block is 150 kg, determine (*a*) the reaction at D, (*b*) the required force **P**, (*c*) the tension in each portion of the cable.

7.100 Two traffic signals are temporarily suspended from cable $ABCDE$. Knowing that the mass of the signal at D is 34 kg, determine (*a*) the mass of the signal at C, (*b*) the tension in cable BF required to maintain the system in the position shown.

7.101 Two traffic signals are temporarily suspended from cable $ABCDE$. Knowing that the mass of the signal at C is 55 kg, determine (*a*) the mass of the signal at D, (*b*) the tension in cable BF required to maintain the system in the position shown.

7.102 An electric wire having a mass per unit length of 0.6 kg/m is strung between two insulators at the same elevation that are 60 m apart. Knowing that the sag of the wire is 1.5 m, determine (*a*) the maximum tension in the wire, (*b*) the length of the wire.

7.103 Two cables of the same diameter are attached to a transmission tower at B. Since the tower is slender, the horizontal component of the resultant of the forces exerted by the cables at B is to be zero. Knowing that the mass per unit length of the cables is 0.4 kg/m, determine (*a*) the required sag h, (*b*) the maximum tension in each cable.

7.104 Each cable of the Golden Gate Bridge supports a load $w = 11.1$ kN/m along the horizontal. Knowing that the span L is 1245 m and that the sag h is 139 m, determine (*a*) the maximum tension in each cable, (*b*) the length of each cable.

7.105 As originally constructed, the center span of the George Washington Bridge consisted of a uniform roadway suspended from four cables. The uniform load supported by each cable was $w = 9.75$ kN/m along the horizontal. Knowing that the span L is 1050 m and that the sag h was 95 m, determine for the original configuration (*a*) the maximum tension in each cable, (*b*) the length of each cable.

7.106 To mark the positions of the rails on the posts of a fence, a homeowner ties a cord to the post at A, passes the cord over a short piece of pipe attached to the post at B, and ties the free end of the cord to a bucket filled with bricks having a total weight of 60 N. Knowing that the weight per unit length of the cord is 0.02 N/m and assuming that A and B are at the same elevation, determine (*a*) the sag h, (*b*) the slope of the cord at B. Neglect the effect of friction.

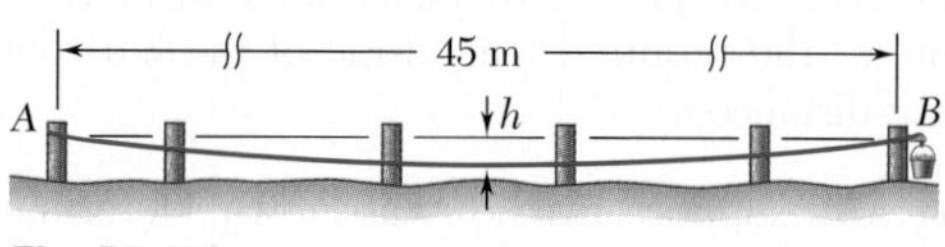

Fig. P7.106

7.107 A small ship is tied to a pier with a 5-m length of rope as shown. Knowing that the current exerts on the hull of the ship a 300-N force directed from the bow to the stern and that the mass per unit length of the rope is 2.2 kg/m, determine (*a*) the maximum tension in the rope, (*b*) the sag *h*. [*Hint:* Use only the first two terms of Eq. (7.10).]

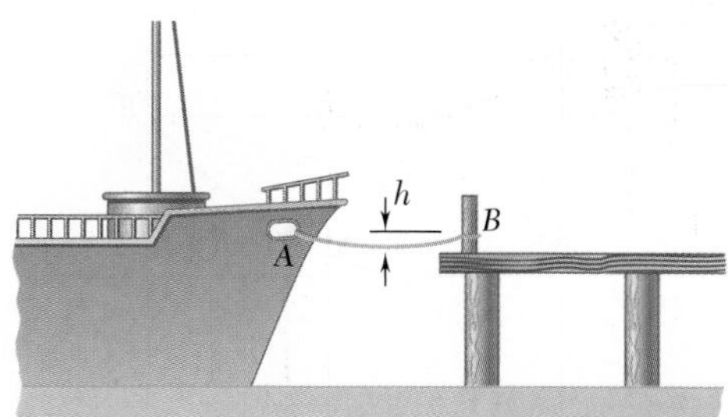

Fig. *P7.107*

7.108 The center span of the Verrazano-Narrows Bridge consists of two uniform roadways suspended from four cables. The design of the bridge allows for the effect of extreme temperature changes which cause the sag of the center span to vary from $h_w = 116$ m in winter to $h_s = 118$ m in summer. Knowing that the span is $L = 1278$ m, determine the change in length of the cables due to extreme temperature changes.

7.109 The total mass of cable *ACB* is 10 kg. Assuming that the mass of the cable is distributed uniformly along the horizontal, determine (*a*) the sag *h*, (*b*) the slope of the cable at *A*.

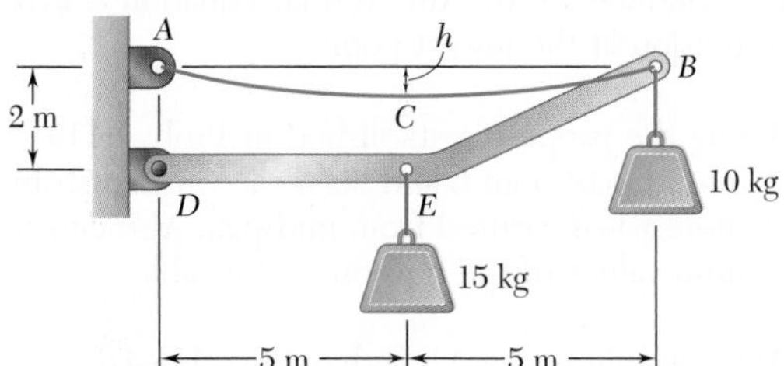

Fig. *P7.109*

7.110 Each cable of the side spans of the Golden Gate Bridge supports a load $w = 10.2$ N/m along the horizontal. Knowing that for the side spans the maximum vertical distance *h* from each cable to the chord *AB* is 9 m and occurs at midspan, determine (*a*) the maximum tension in each cable, (*b*) the slope at *B*.

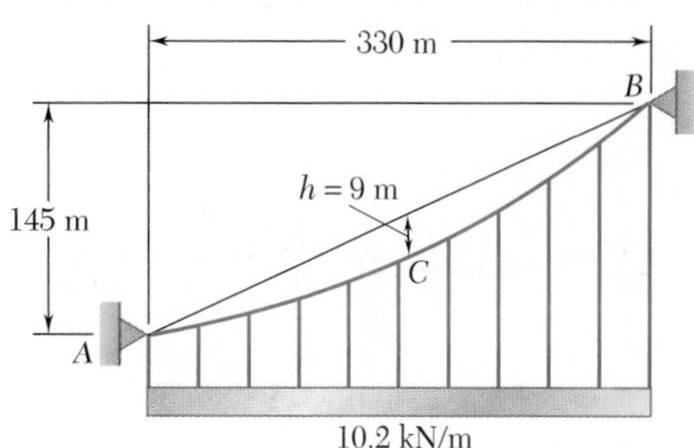

Fig. P7.110

7.111 Before being fed into a printing press located to the right of *D*, a continuous sheet of paper having a weight per unit length of 0.18 N/m passes over rollers at *A* and *B*. Assuming that the curve formed by the sheet is parabolic, determine (*a*) the location of the lowest point *C*, (*b*) the maximum tension in the sheet.

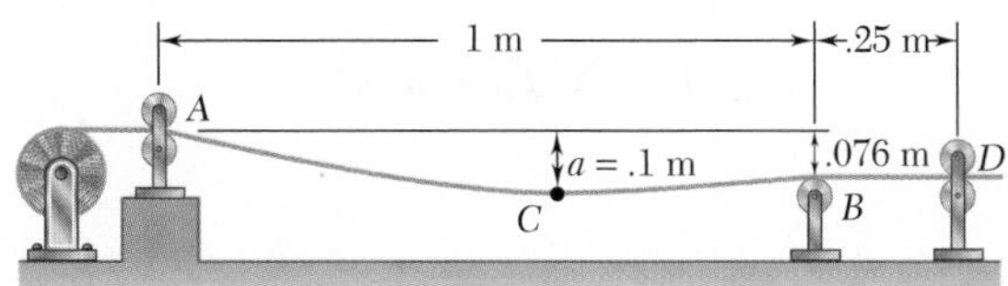

Fig. P7.111

7.112 Chain *AB* supports a horizontal, uniform steel beam having a mass per unit length of 85 kg/m. If the maximum tension in the chain is not to exceed 8 kN, determine (*a*) the horizontal distance *a* from A to the lowest point *C* of the chain, (*b*) the approximate length of the chain.

7.113 Chain *AB* of length 6.4 m supports a horizontal, uniform steel beam having a mass per unit length of 85 kg/m. Determine (*a*) the horizontal distance *a* from *A* to the lowest point *C* of the chain, (*b*) the maximum tension in the chain.

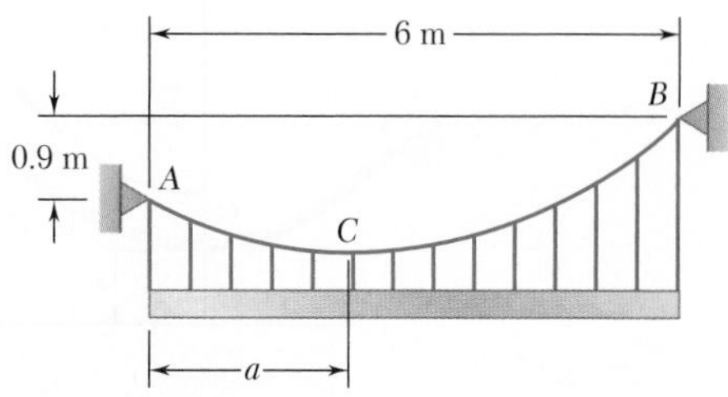

Fig. P7.112 and P7.113

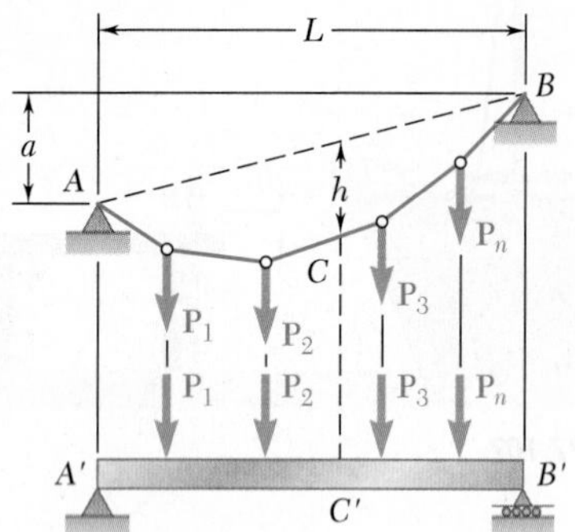

Fig. P7.114

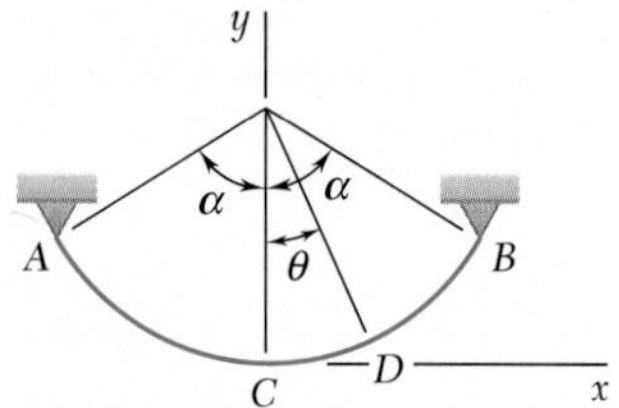

Fig. P7.121

***7.114** A cable AB of span L and a simple beam $A'B'$ of the same span are subjected to identical vertical loadings as shown. Show that the magnitude of the bending moment at a point C' in the beam is equal to the product T_0h, where T_0 is the magnitude of the horizontal component of the tension force in the cable and h is the vertical distance between point C and the chord joining the points of support A and B.

7.115 through 7.118 Making use of the property established in Prob. 7.114, solve the problem indicated by first solving the corresponding beam problem.

7.115 Prob. 7.89*a*.
7.116 Prob. 7.92*b*.
7.117 Prob. 7.94*b*.
7.118 Prob. 7.95*b*.

***7.119** Show that the curve assumed by a cable that carries a distributed load $w(x)$ is defined by the differential equation $d^2y/dx^2 = w(x)/T_0$, where T_0 is the tension at the lowest point.

***7.120** Using the property established in Prob. 7.119, determine the curve assumed by a cable of span L and sag h carrying a distributed load $w = w_0 \cos(\pi x/L)$, where x is measured from midspan. Also determine the maximum and minimum values of the tension in the cable.

***7.121** If the weight per unit length of the cable AB is $w_0/\cos^2\theta$, prove that the curve formed by the cable is a circular arc. (*Hint:* Use the property established in Prob. 7.119.)

*7.10. CATENARY

Let us now consider a cable AB carrying a load *uniformly distributed along the cable itself* (Fig. 7.18*a*). Cables hanging under their own weight are loaded in this way. We denote by w the load per unit length (*measured along the cable*) and express it in N/m or in lb/ft. The magnitude W of the total load carried by a portion of cable of length s extending from the lowest point C to a point D is $W = ws$. Substituting this value for W in formula (7.6), we obtain the tension at D:

$$T = \sqrt{T_0^2 + w^2s^2}$$

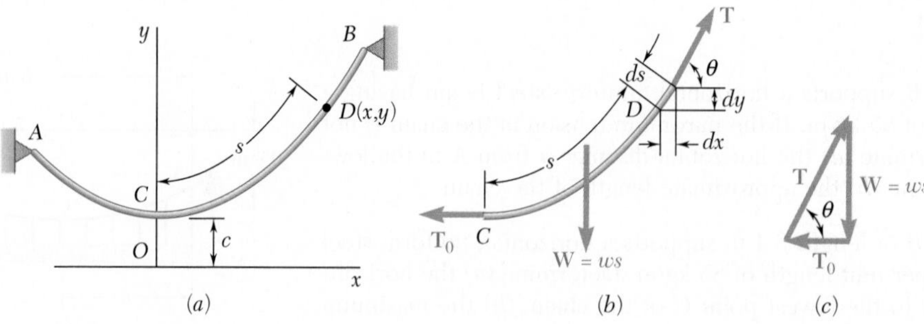

Fig. 7.18

In order to simplify the subsequent computations, we introduce the constant $c = T_0/w$. We thus write

$$T_0 = wc \qquad W = ws \qquad T = w\sqrt{c^2 + s^2} \tag{7.11}$$

The free-body diagram of the portion of cable CD is shown in Fig. 7.18*b*. This diagram, however, cannot be used to obtain directly the equation of the curve assumed by the cable, since we do not know the horizontal distance from D to the line of action of the resultant $\mathbf{W}$ of the load. To obtain this equation, we first write that the horizontal projection of a small element of cable of length ds is $dx = ds \cos \theta$. Observing from Fig. 7.18*c* that $\cos \theta = T_0/T$ and using Eqs. (7.11), we write

$$dx = ds \cos \theta = \frac{T_0}{T} ds = \frac{wc\, ds}{w\sqrt{c^2 + s^2}} = \frac{ds}{\sqrt{1 + s^2/c^2}}$$

Photo 7.5 The forces on the supports and the internal forces in the cables of the power line shown are discussed in this section.

Selecting the origin O of the coordinates at a distance c directly below C (Fig. 7.18*a*) and integrating from $C(0, c)$ to $D(x, y)$, we obtain†

$$x = \int_0^s \frac{ds}{\sqrt{1 + s^2/c^2}} = c\left[\sinh^{-1} \frac{s}{c}\right]_0^s = c \sinh^{-1} \frac{s}{c}$$

This equation, which relates the length s of the portion of cable CD and the horizontal distance x, can be written in the form

$$s = c \sinh \frac{x}{c} \tag{7.15}$$

The relation between the coordinates x and y can now be obtained by writing $dy = dx \tan \theta$. Observing from Fig. 7.18*c* that $\tan \theta = W/T_0$ and using (7.11) and (7.15), we write

$$dy = dx \tan \theta = \frac{W}{T_0} dx = \frac{s}{c} dx = \sinh \frac{x}{c} dx$$

†This integral can be found in all standard integral tables. The function

$$z = \sinh^{-1} u$$

(read "arc hyperbolic sine u") is the *inverse* of the function $u = \sinh z$ (read "hyperbolic sine z"). This function and the function $v = \cosh z$ (read "hyperbolic cosine z") are defined as follows:

$$u = \sinh z = \tfrac{1}{2}(e^z - e^{-z}) \qquad v = \cosh z = \tfrac{1}{2}(e^z + e^{-z})$$

Numerical values of the functions $\sinh z$ and $\cosh z$ are found in *tables of hyperbolic functions*. They may also be computed on most calculators either directly or from the above definitions. The student is referred to any calculus text for a complete description of the properties of these functions. In this section, we use only the following properties, which are easily derived from the above definitions:

$$\frac{d \sinh z}{dz} = \cosh z \qquad \frac{d \cosh z}{dz} = \sinh z \tag{7.12}$$

$$\sinh 0 = 0 \qquad \cosh 0 = 1 \tag{7.13}$$

$$\cosh^2 z - \sinh^2 z = 1 \tag{7.14}$$

Integrating from $C(0, c)$ to $D(x, y)$ and using Eqs. (7.12) and (7.13), we obtain

$$y - c = \int_0^x \sinh \frac{x}{c}\, dx = c\left[\cosh \frac{x}{c}\right]_0^x = c\left(\cosh \frac{x}{c} - 1\right)$$

$$y - c = c \cosh \frac{x}{c} - c$$

which reduces to

$$y = c \cosh \frac{x}{c} \tag{7.16}$$

This is the equation of a *catenary* with a vertical axis. The ordinate c of the lowest point C is called the *parameter* of the catenary. Squaring both sides of Eqs. (7.15) and (7.16), subtracting, and taking Eq. (7.14) into account, we obtain the following relation between y and s:

$$y^2 - s^2 = c^2 \tag{7.17}$$

Solving (7.17) for s^2 and carrying into the last of the relations (7.11), we write these relations as follows:

$$T_0 = wc \qquad W = ws \qquad T = wy \tag{7.18}$$

The last relation indicates that the tension at any point D of the cable is proportional to the vertical distance from D to the horizontal line representing the x axis.

When the supports A and B of the cable have the same elevation, the distance L between the supports is called the *span* of the cable and the vertical distance h from the supports to the lowest point C is called the *sag* of the cable. These definitions are the same as those given in the case of parabolic cables, but it should be noted that because of our choice of coordinate axes, the sag h is now

$$h = y_A - c \tag{7.19}$$

It should also be observed that certain catenary problems involve transcendental equations which must be solved by successive approximations (see Sample Prob. 7.10). When the cable is fairly taut, however, the load can be assumed uniformly distributed *along the horizontal* and the catenary can be replaced by a parabola. This greatly simplifies the solution of the problem, and the error introduced is small.

When the supports A and B have different elevations, the position of the lowest point of the cable is not known. The problem can then be solved in a manner similar to that indicated for parabolic cables, by expressing that the cable must pass through the supports and that $x_B - x_A = L$ and $y_B - y_A = d$, where L and d denote, respectively, the horizontal and vertical distances between the two supports.

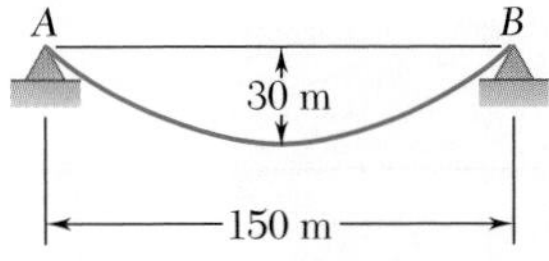

SAMPLE PROBLEM 7.10

A uniform cable weighing 3 N/m is suspended between two points *A* and *B* as shown. Determine (*a*) the maximum and minimum values of the tension in the cable, (*b*) the length of the cable.

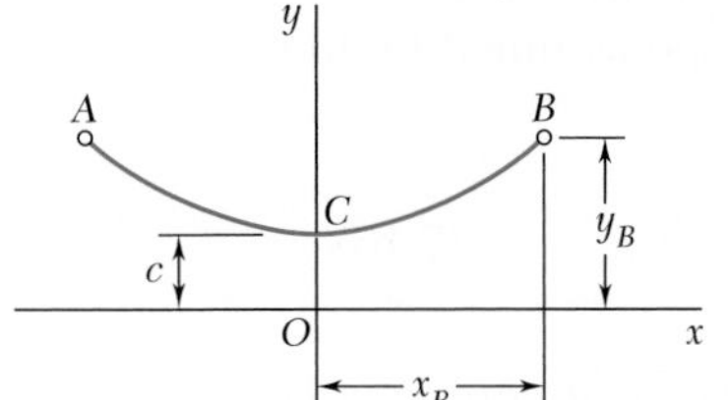

SOLUTION

Equation of Cable. The origin of coordinates is placed at a distance *c* below the lowest point of the cable. The equation of the cable is given by Eq. (7.16),

$$y = c \cosh \frac{x}{c}$$

The coordinates of point *B* are

$$x_B = 75 \text{ m} \qquad y_B = 30 + c$$

Substituting these coordinates into the equation of the cable, we obtain

$$30 + c = c \cosh \frac{75}{c}$$

$$\frac{30}{c} + 1 = \cosh \frac{75}{c}$$

The value of *c* is determined by assuming successive trial values, as shown in the following table:

c	$\frac{75}{c}$	$\frac{30}{c}$	$\frac{30}{c} + 1$	$\cosh \frac{75}{c}$
90	0.833	0.333	1.333	1.367
105	0.714	0.286	1.286	1.266
99	0.758	0.303	1.303	1.301
98.4	0.762	0.305	1.305	1.305

Taking $c = 98.4$, we have

$$y_B = 30 + c = 128.4 \text{ m}$$

***a.* Maximum and Minimum Values of the Tension.** Using Eqs. (7.18), we obtain

$$T_{min} = T_0 = wc = (3 \text{ N/m})(98.4 \text{ m}) \qquad T_{min} = 295.2 \text{ N} \blacktriangleleft$$

$$T_{max} = T_B = wy_B = (3 \text{ N/m})(128.4 \text{ m}) \qquad T_{max} = 385.2 \text{ N} \blacktriangleleft$$

***b.* Length of Cable.** One-half the length of the cable is found by solving Eq. (7.17):

$$y_B^2 - s_{CB}^2 = c^2 \qquad s_{CB}^2 = y_B^2 - c^2 = (128.9)^2 - (98.9)^2 \qquad s_{CB} = 82.5 \text{ m}$$

The total length of the cable is therefore

$$s_{AB} = 2s_{CB} = 2(82.5 \text{ m}) \qquad s_{AB} = 165 \text{ m} \blacktriangleleft$$

SOLVING PROBLEMS ON YOUR OWN

In the last section of this chapter you learned to solve problems involving a *cable carrying a load uniformly distributed along the cable*. The shape assumed by the cable is a catenary and is defined by the equation:

$$y = c \cosh \frac{x}{c} \tag{7.16}$$

1. *You should keep in mind that the origin of coordinates for a catenary is located at a distance c directly below the lowest point of the catenary.* The length of the cable from the origin to any point is expressed as

$$s = c \sinh \frac{x}{c} \tag{7.15}$$

2. *You should first identify all of the known and unknown quantities.* Then consider each of the equations listed in the text (Eqs. 7.15 through 7.19), and solve an equation that contains only one unknown. Substitute the value found into another equation, and solve that equation for another unknown.

3. *If the sag h is given,* use Eq. (7.19) to replace y by $h + c$ in Eq. (7.16) if x is known [Sample Prob. 7.10], or in Eq. (7.17) if s is known, and solve the equation obtained for the constant c.

4. *Many of the problems that you will encounter will involve the solution by trial and error* of an equation involving a hyperbolic sine or cosine. You can make your work easier by keeping track of your calculations in a table, as in Sample Prob. 7.10. Of course, you also can use a computer- or calculator-based numerical solution technique.

5. *It is important to recognize that the defining equation may have more than one solution.* To help you visualize this possibility, we encourage you first to graph the equation and then to solve for the root(s). If there is more than one root, you must determine which of the roots correspond to physically possible situations.

Problems

7.122 Two hikers are standing 10 m apart and are holding the ends of a 12-m length of rope as shown. Knowing that the mass per unit length of the rope is 0.07 kg/m, determine (*a*) the sag h, (*b*) the magnitude of the force exerted on the hand of a hiker.

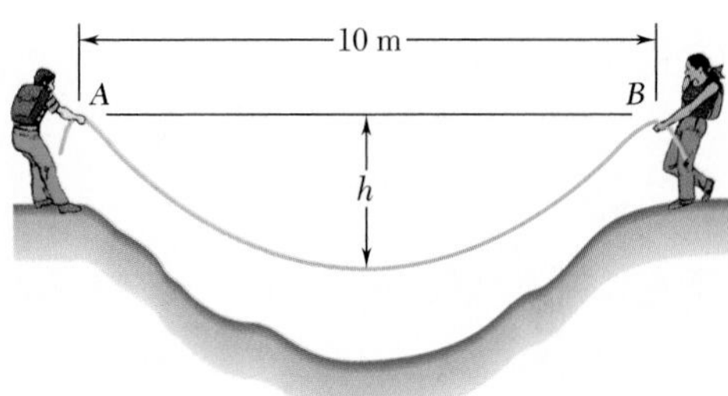

Fig. P7.122

7.123 A 18-m chain weighing 120 N is suspended between two points at the same elevation. Knowing that the sag is 7.2 m, determine (*a*) the distance between the supports, (*b*) the maximum tension in the chain.

7.124 An aerial tramway cable of length 150 m and weighing 2.8 N/m is suspended between two points at the same elevation. Knowing that the sag is 37.5 m, determine (*a*) the horizontal distance between the supports, (*b*) the maximum tension in the cable.

7.125 An electric transmission cable of length 130 m and mass per unit length of 3.4 kg/m is suspended between two points at the same elevation. Knowing that the sag is 30 m, determine the horizontal distance between the supports and the maximum tension in the cable.

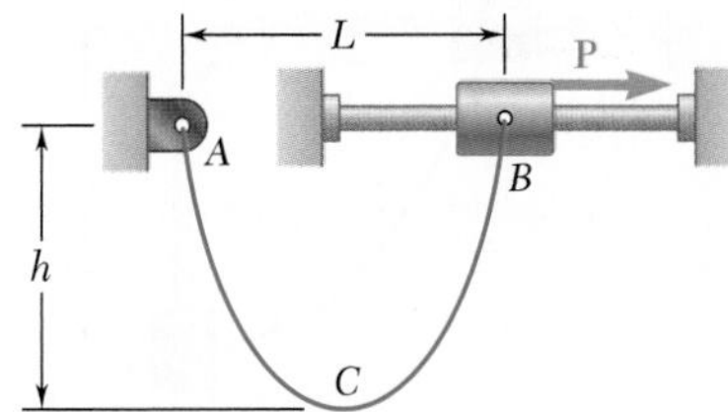

Fig. *P7.126* and P7.127

7.126 A 30-m length of wire having a mass per unit length of 0.3 kg/m is attached to a fixed support at A and to a collar at B. Neglecting the effect of friction, determine (*a*) the force **P** for which $h = 12$ m, (*b*) the corresponding span L.

7.127 A 30-m length of wire having a mass per unit length of 0.3 kg/m is attached to a fixed support at A and to a collar at B. Knowing that the magnitude of the horizontal force applied to the collar is $P = 30$ N, determine (*a*) the sag h, (*b*) the corresponding span L.

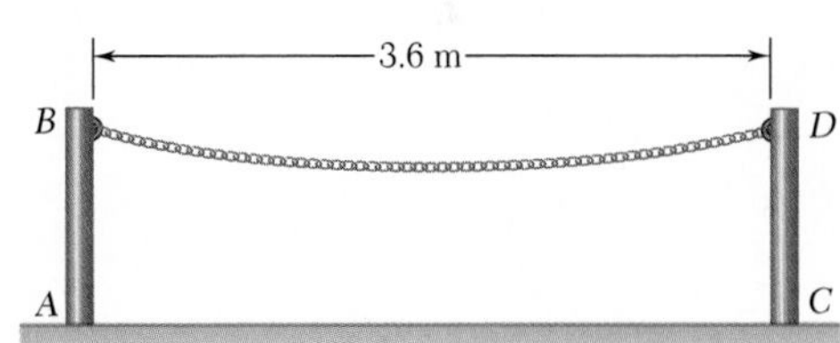

Fig. P7.128

7.128 An access road is closed by hanging a chain of length 3.8 m across the road. Knowing that the mass per unit length of the chain is 3.72 kg/m, determine (*a*) the sag h, (*b*) the magnitude of the horizontal component of the force exerted on post AB by the chain.

7.129 A 90-m length of wire is suspended from two points at the same elevation that are 60 m apart. Knowing that the maximum tension in the wire is 300 N, determine (*a*) the sag h, (*b*) the total mass of the wire.

7.130 Determine the sag of a 13.5-m length of chain which is attached to two points at the same elevation that are 6 m apart.

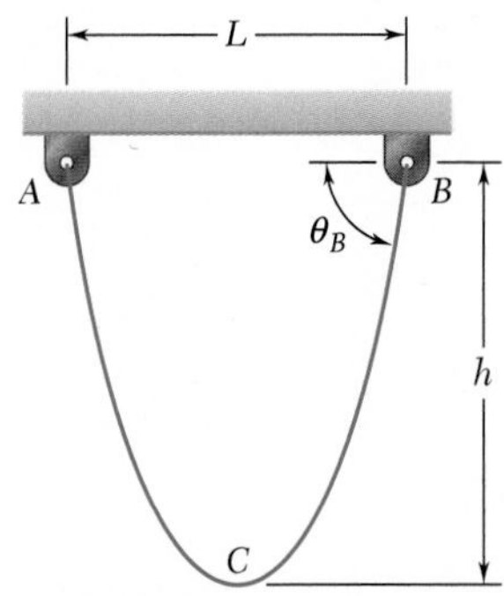

Fig. P7.131

7.131 A 3-m length of rope is attached to two supports A and B as shown. Determine (*a*) the span of the rope for which the span is equal to the sag, (*b*) the corresponding angle θ_B.

7.132 A cable having a mass per unit length of 3 kg/m is suspended between two points at the same elevation that are 48 m apart. Determine the smallest allowable sag of the cable if the maximum tension is not to exceed 1800 N.

7.133 A 7.2-m length of chain having a weight per unit length of 2.73 N/m is attached to a beam at A and passes over a small pulley at B as shown. Neglecting the effect of friction, determine the values of distance a for which the chain is in equilibrium.

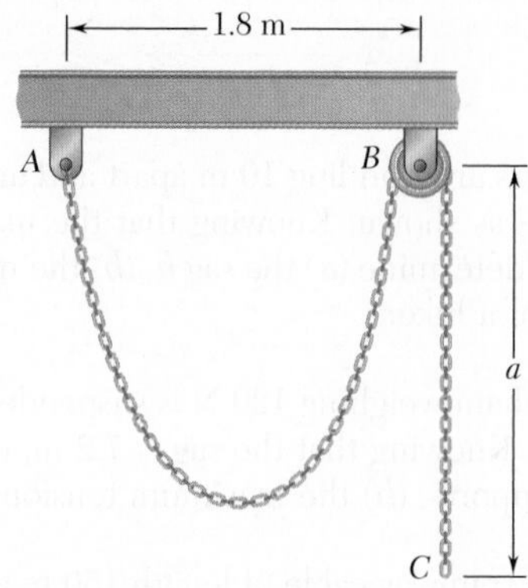

Fig. P7.133

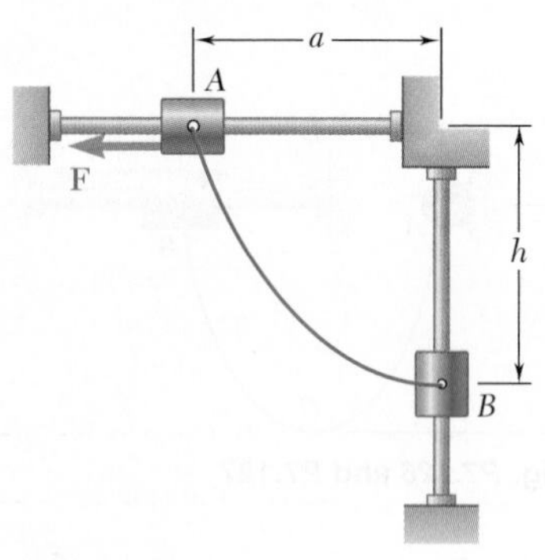

Fig. *P7.134*

7.134 The 3-m-long cable AB weighs 20 N and is attached to collars at A and B that can slide freely on the rods shown. Neglecting the weight of the collars, determine (*a*) the magnitude of the horizontal force **F** so that $h = a$, (*b*) the corresponding value of h and a, (*c*) the maximum tension in the cable.

7.135 A counterweight D of mass 40 kg is attached to a cable that passes over a small pulley at A and that is attached to a support at B. Knowing that $L = 15$ m and $h = 5$ m, determine (*a*) the length of the cable from A to B, (*b*) the mass per unit length of the cable. Neglect the mass of the cable from A to D.

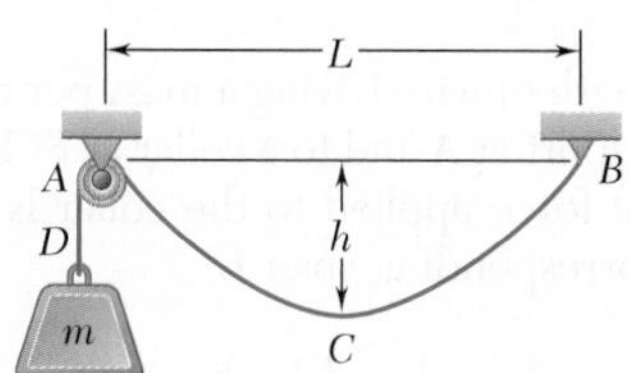

Fig. P7.135

7.136 To the left of point B, the long cable $ABDE$ rests on the rough horizontal surface shown. Knowing that the weight per unit length of the cable is 1.5 N/m, determine the force **F** when $a = 3.24$ m.

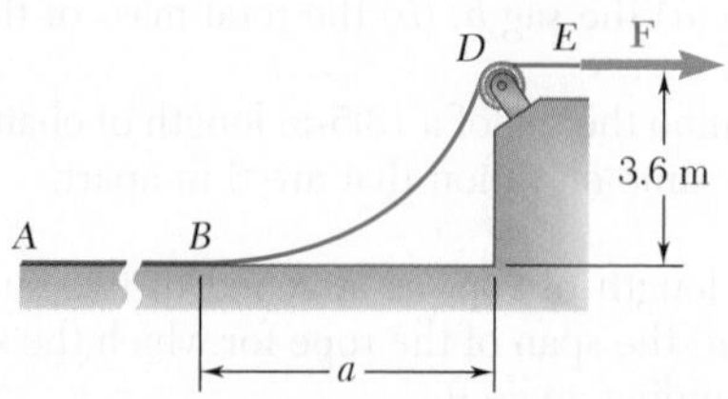

Fig. P7.136 and P7.137

7.137 To the left of point B, the long cable $ABDE$ rests on the rough horizontal surface shown. Knowing that the weight per unit length of the cable is 1.5 N/m, determine the force **F** when $a = 5.4$ m.

7.138 A uniform cable having a mass per unit length of 4 kg/m is held in the position shown by a horizontal force **P** applied at B. Knowing that $P = 800$ N and $\theta_A = 60°$, determine (*a*) the location of point B, (*b*) the length of the cable.

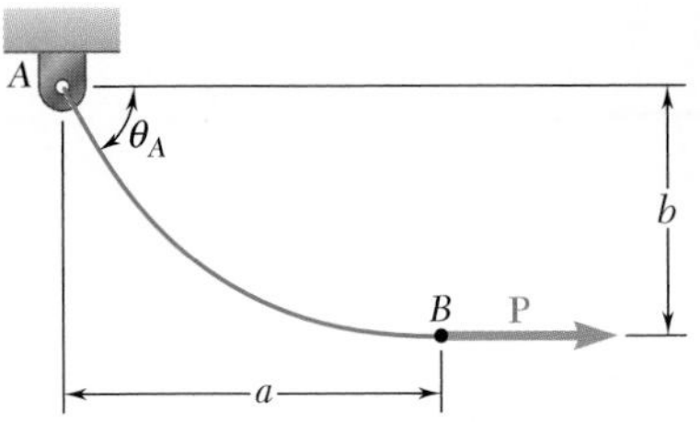

Fig. P7.138 and P7.139

7.139 A uniform cable having a mass per unit length of 4 kg/m is held in the position shown by a horizontal force **P** applied at B. Knowing that $P = 600$ N and $\theta_A = 60°$, determine (*a*) the location of point B, (*b*) the length of the cable.

7.140 An electric cable is hung between a utility pole and a house. Knowing that the mass per unit length of the cable is 2.1 kg/m, determine, (*a*) the distance from the house to the lowest point C of the cable, (*b*) the maximum tension in the cable.

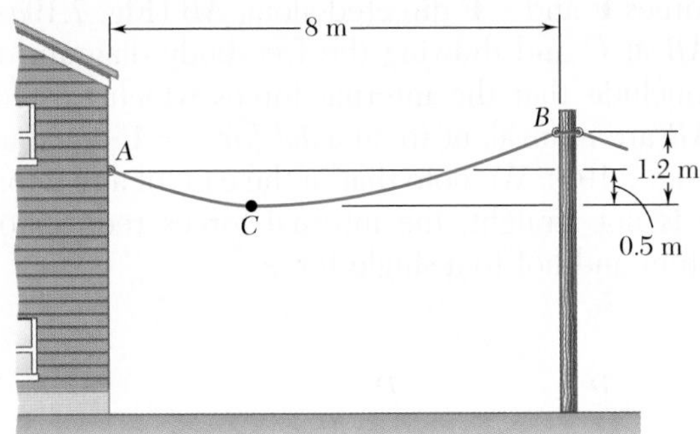

Fig. P7.140

7.141 The cable ACB weighs 0.3 N/m. Knowing that the lowest point of the cable is located at a distance $a = 1.8$ m below the support A, determine (*a*) the location of the lowest point C, (*b*) the maximum tension in the cable.

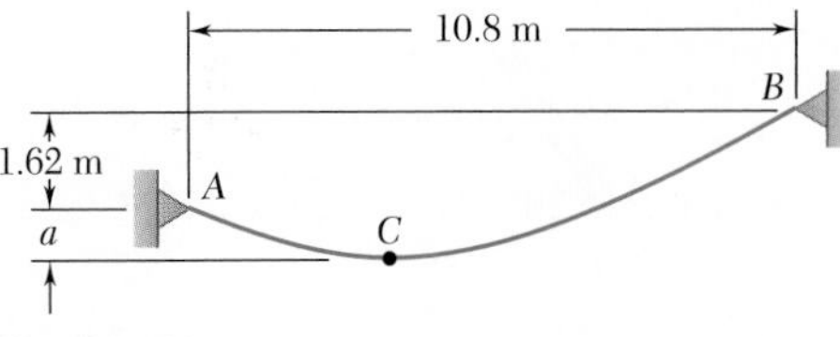

Fig. P7.141

7.142 Denoting by θ the angle formed by a uniform cable and the horizontal, show that at any point (*a*) $s = c \tan \theta$, (*b*) $y = c \sec \theta$.

7.143 (*a*) Determine the maximum allowable horizontal span for a uniform cable of mass per unit length m' if the tension in the cable is not to exceed a given value T_m. (*b*) Using the result of part *a*, determine the maximum span of a steel wire for which $m' = 0.34$ kg/m and $T_m = 32$ kN.

***7.144** A cable has a weight per unit length of 2 N/m and is supported as shown. Knowing that the span L is 5.4 m, determine the two values of the sag h for which the maximum tension is 80 N.

***7.145** Determine the sag-to-span ratio for which the maximum tension in cable AB is equal to the total weight of the cable.

***7.146** A cable of weight per unit length w is suspended between two points at the same elevation that are a distance L apart. Determine (*a*) the sag-to-span ratio for which the maximum tension T_{max} in the cable is as small as possible, (*b*) the corresponding values of θ_B and T_{max}.

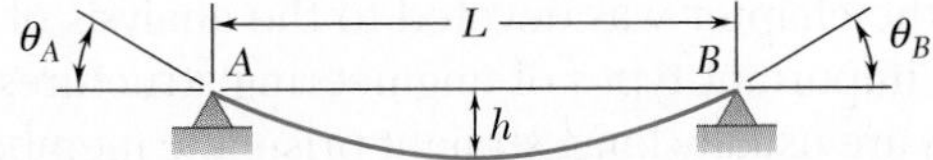

Fig. *P7.144*, *P7.145*, and P7.146

REVIEW AND SUMMARY FOR CHAPTER 7

In this chapter you learned to determine the internal forces which hold together the various parts of a given member in a structure.

Forces in straight two-force members

Considering first a *straight two-force member AB* [Sec. 7.2], we recall that such a member is subjected at A and B to equal and opposite forces $\mathbf{F}$ and $-\mathbf{F}$ directed along AB (Fig. 7.19*a*). Cutting member AB at C and drawing the free-body diagram of portion AC, we conclude that the internal forces which existed at C in member AB are equivalent to an *axial force* $-\mathbf{F}$ equal and opposite to $\mathbf{F}$ (Fig. 7.19*b*). We note that in the case of a two-force member which is not straight, the internal forces reduce to a force-couple system and not to a single force.

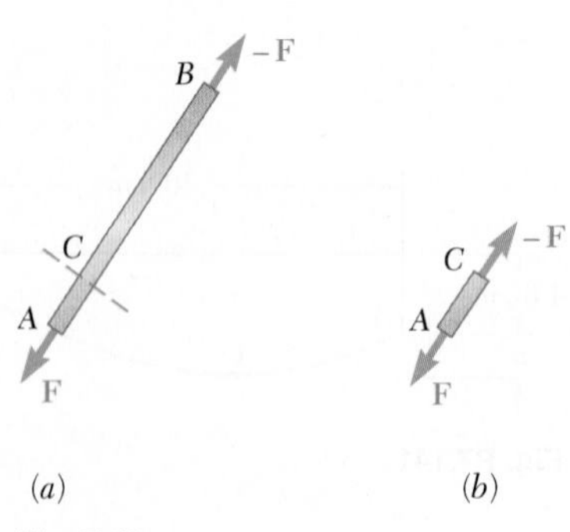

Fig. 7.19

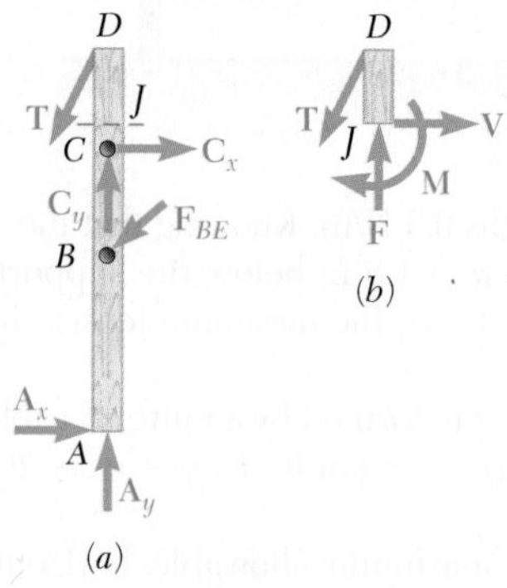

(a)

(b)

Fig. 7.20

Forces in multiforce members

Considering next a *multiforce member AD* (Fig. 7.20*a*), cutting it at J, and drawing the free-body diagram of portion JD, we conclude that the internal forces at J are equivalent to a force-couple system consisting of the *axial force* $\mathbf{F}$, the *shearing force* $\mathbf{V}$, and a couple $\mathbf{M}$ (Fig. 7.20*b*). The magnitude of the shearing force measures the *shear* at point J, and the moment of the couple is referred to as the *bending moment* at J. Since an equal and opposite force-couple system would have been obtained by considering the free-body diagram of portion AJ, it is necessary to specify which portion of member AD was used when recording the answers [Sample Prob. 7.1].

Forces in beams

Most of the chapter was devoted to the analysis of the internal forces in two important types of engineering structures: *beams* and *cables*. *Beams* are usually long, straight prismatic members designed to support loads applied at various points along the member. In general the loads are perpendicular to the axis of the beam and produce only *shear and bending* in the beam. The loads may be either *concentrated* at specific points, or *distributed* along the entire length or a portion of the beam. The beam itself may be supported in various ways; since only statically determinate beams are considered in this text, we limited our analysis to that of *simply supported beams, overhanging beams*, and *cantilever beams* [Sec. 7.3].

Shear and bending moment in a beam

To obtain the *shear* V and *bending moment* M at a given point C of a beam, we first determine the reactions at the supports by considering the entire beam as a free body. We then cut the beam at C and use the free-body diagram of one of the two portions obtained in this fashion to determine V and M. In order to avoid any confusion regarding the sense of the shearing force **V** and couple **M** (which act in opposite directions on the two portions of the beam), the sign convention illustrated in Fig. 7.21 was adopted [Sec. 7.4]. Once the values of the shear and bending moment have been determined at a few selected points of the beam, it is usually possible to draw a *shear diagram* and a *bending-moment diagram* representing, respectively, the shear and bending moment at any point of the beam [Sec. 7.5]. When a beam is subjected to concentrated loads only, the shear is of constant value between loads and the bending moment varies linearly between loads [Sample Prob. 7.2]. On the other hand, when a beam is subjected to distributed loads, the shear and bending moment vary quite differently [Sample Prob. 7.3].

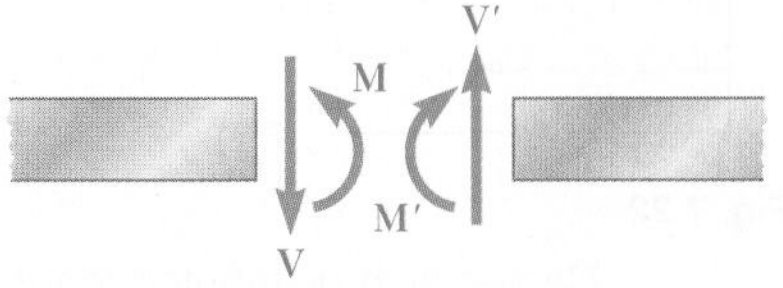

Internal forces at section
(positive shear and positive bending moment)

Fig. 7.21

Relations among load, shear, and bending moment

The construction of the shear and bending-moment diagrams is facilitated if the following relations are taken into account. Denoting by w the distributed load per unit length (assumed positive if directed downward), we have [Sec. 7.5]:

$$\frac{dV}{dx} = -w \qquad (7.1)$$

$$\frac{dM}{dx} = V \qquad (7.3)$$

or, in integrated form,

$$V_D - V_C = -(\text{area under load curve between } C \text{ and } D) \qquad (7.2')$$

$$M_D - M_C = \text{area under shear curve between } C \text{ and } D \qquad (7.4')$$

Equation (7.2′) makes it possible to draw the shear diagram of a beam from the curve representing the distributed load on that beam and the value of V at one end of the beam. Similarly, Eq. (7.4′) makes it possible to draw the bending-moment diagram from the shear diagram and the value of M at one end of the beam. However, concentrated loads introduce discontinuities in the shear diagram and concentrated couples introduce discontinuities in the bending-moment diagram, none of which are accounted for in these equations [Sample Probs. 7.4 and 7.7]. Finally, we note from Eq. (7.3) that the points of the beam where the bending moment is maximum or minimum are also the points where the shear is zero [Sample Prob. 7.5].

Cables with concentrated loads

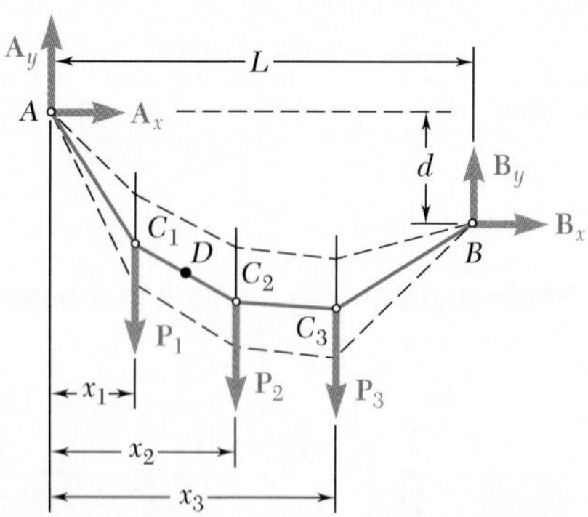

Fig. 7.22

Cables with distributed loads

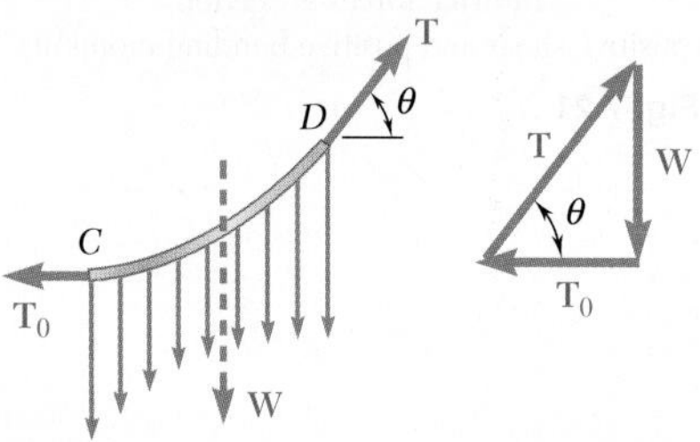

Fig. 7.23

Parabolic cable

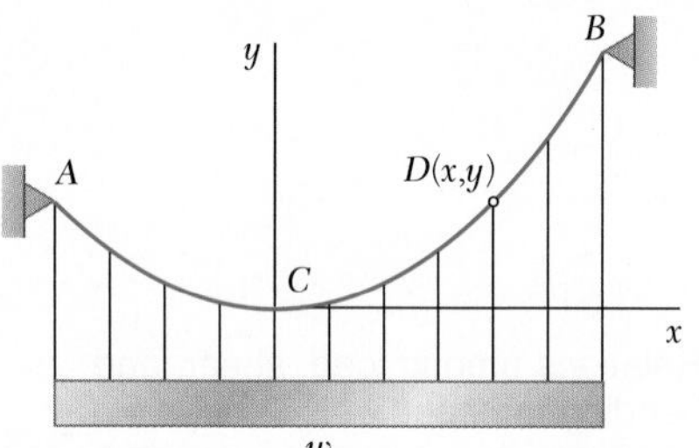

Fig. 7.24

Catenary

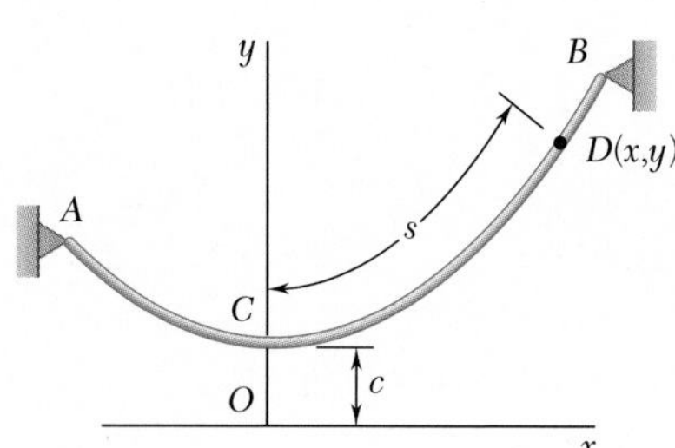

Fig. 7.25

The second half of the chapter was devoted to the analysis of *flexible cables*. We first considered a cable of negligible weight supporting *concentrated loads* [Sec. 7.7]. Using the entire cable AB as a free body (Fig. 7.22), we noted that the three available equilibrium equations were not sufficient to determine the four unknowns representing the reactions at the supports A and B. However, if the coordinates of a point D of the cable are known, an additional equation can be obtained by considering the free-body diagram of the portion AD or DB of the cable. Once the reactions at the supports have been determined, the elevation of any point of the cable and the tension in any portion of the cable can be found from the appropriate free-body diagram [Sample Prob. 7.8]. It was noted that the horizontal component of the force **T** representing the tension is the same at any point of the cable.

We next considered cables carrying *distributed loads* [Sec. 7.8]. Using as a free body a portion of cable CD extending from the lowest point C to an arbitrary point D of the cable (Fig. 7.23), we observed that the horizontal component of the tension force **T** at D is constant and equal to the tension T_0 at C, while its vertical component is equal to the weight W of the portion of cable CD. The magnitude and direction of **T** were obtained from the force triangle:

$$T = \sqrt{T_0^2 + W^2} \qquad \tan\theta = \frac{W}{T_0} \tag{7.6}$$

In the case of a load *uniformly distributed along the horizontal*—as in a suspension bridge (Fig. 7.24)—the load supported by portion CD is $W = wx$, where w is the constant load per unit horizontal length [Sec. 7.9]. We also found that the curve formed by the cable is a *parabola* of equation

$$y = \frac{wx^2}{2T_0} \tag{7.8}$$

and that the length of the cable can be found by using the expansion in series given in Eq. (7.10) [Sample Prob. 7.9].

In the case of a load *uniformly distributed along the cable itself* [for example, a cable hanging under its own weight (Fig. 7.25)] the load supported by portion CD is $W = ws$, where s is the length measured along the cable and w is the constant load per unit length [Sec. 7.10]. Choosing the origin O of the coordinate axes at a distance $c = T_0/w$ below C, we derived the relations

$$s = c \sinh \frac{x}{c} \tag{7.15}$$

$$y = c \cosh \frac{x}{c} \tag{7.16}$$

$$y^2 - s^2 = c^2 \tag{7.17}$$

$$T_0 = wc \qquad W = ws \qquad T = wy \tag{7.18}$$

which can be used to solve problems involving cables hanging under their own weight [Sample Prob. 7.10]. Equation (7.16), which defines the shape of the cable, is the equation of a *catenary*.

Review Problems

7.147 A semicircular rod is loaded as shown. Determine the internal forces at point J knowing that $\theta = 30°$.

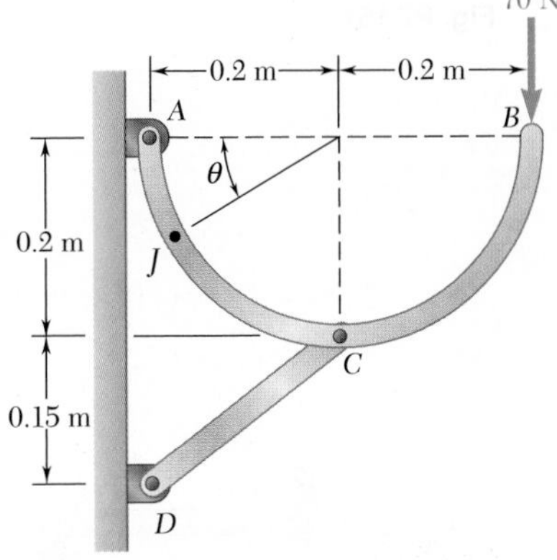

Fig. P7.147

7.148 Knowing that the radius of each pulley is .18 m and neglecting friction, determine the internal forces at point J of the frame shown.

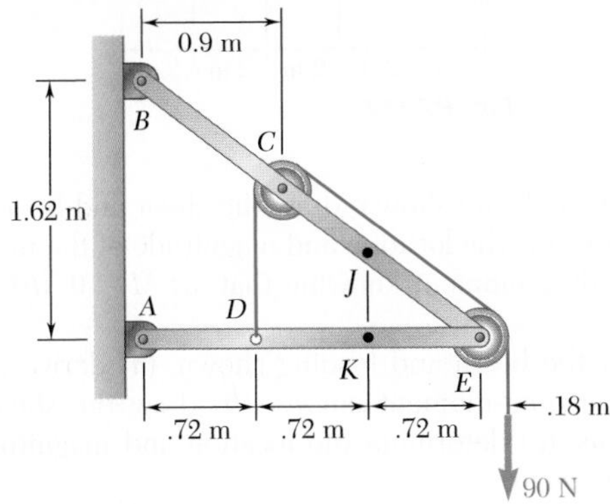

Fig. P7.148

7.149 A quarter-circular rod of weight W and uniform cross section is supported as shown. Determine the bending moment at point J when $\theta = 30°$.

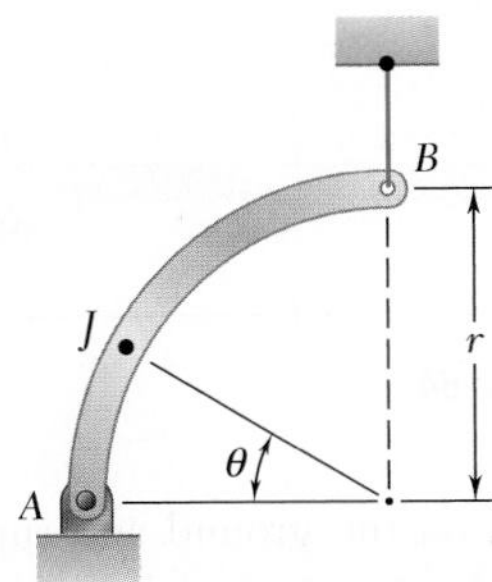

Fig. *P7.149*

7.150 For the beam and loading shown, (*a*) draw the shear and bending-moment diagrams, (*b*) determine the maximum absolute values of the shear and bending moment.

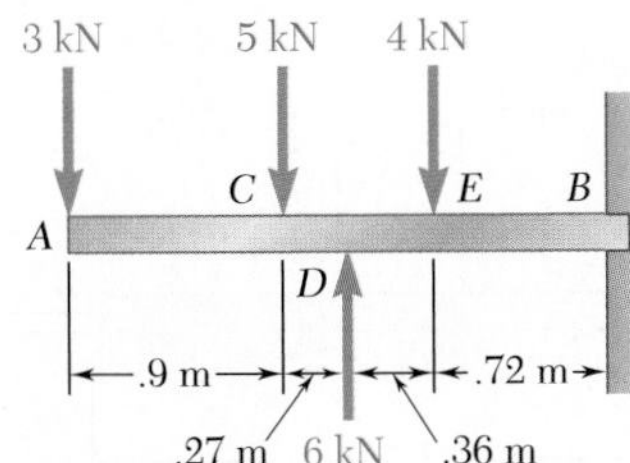

Fig. P7.150

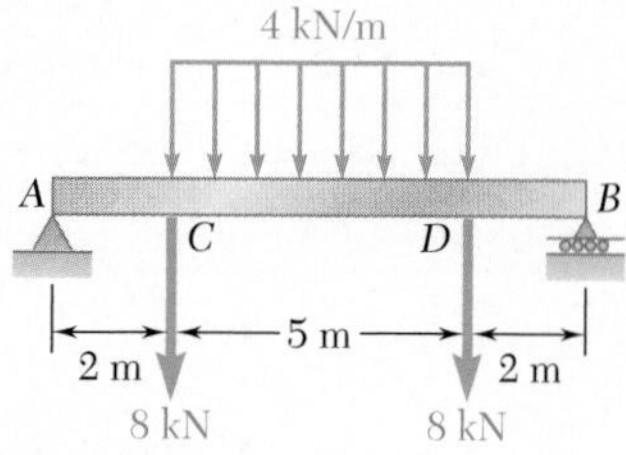

Fig. P7.151

7.151 For the beam and loading shown, (*a*) draw the shear and bending-moment diagrams, (*b*) determine the maximum absolute values of the shear and bending moment.

7.152 For the beam shown, determine (*a*) the magnitude *P* of the two upward forces for which the maximum absolute value of the bending moment is as small as possible, (*b*) the corresponding value of $|M|_{max}$. (See hint for Prob. 7.51.)

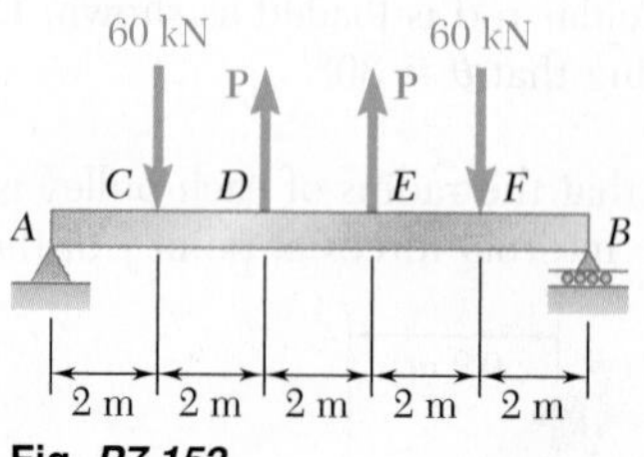

Fig. *P7.152*

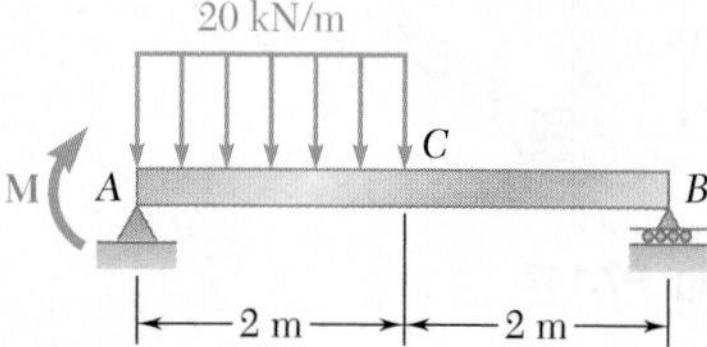

Fig. P7.153

7.153 For the beam shown, draw the shear and bending-moment diagrams, and determine the location and magnitude of the maximum absolute value of the bending moment knowing that (*a*) $M = 0$, (*b*) $M = 12$ kN · m.

7.154 For the beam and loading shown, (*a*) derive the equations of the shear and bending-moment curves, (*b*) draw the shear and bending-moment diagrams, (*c*) determine the location and magnitude of the maximum bending moment.

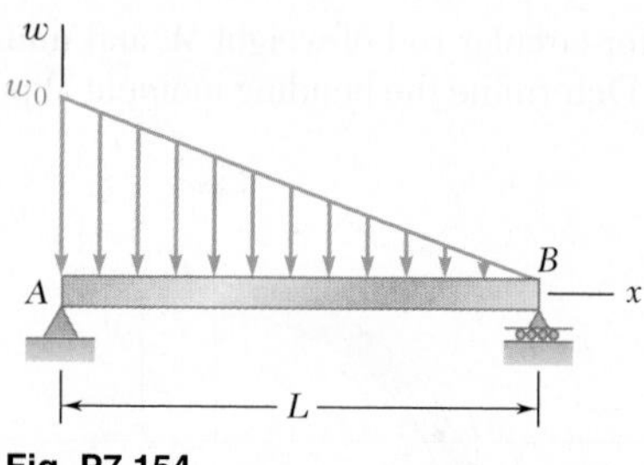

Fig. P7.154

7.155 Beam *AB* lies on the ground and supports the parabolic load shown. Assuming the upward reaction of the ground to be uniformly distributed, (*a*) derive the equations of the shear and bending-moment curves, (*b*) determine the maximum bending moment.

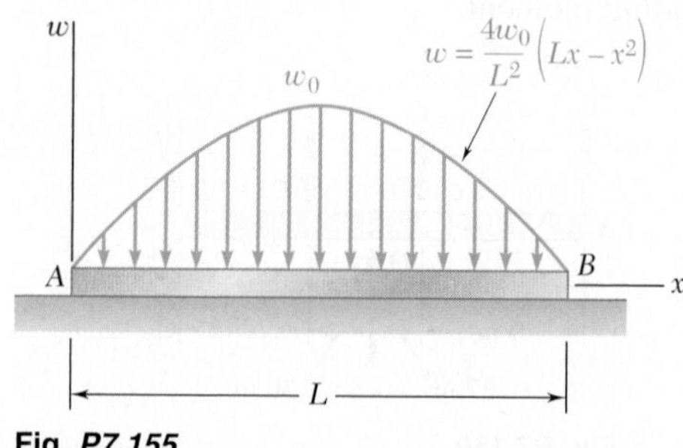

Fig. *P7.155*

7.156 Knowing that $d_C = 4$ m, determine (*a*) the reaction at *A*, (*b*) the reaction at *E*.

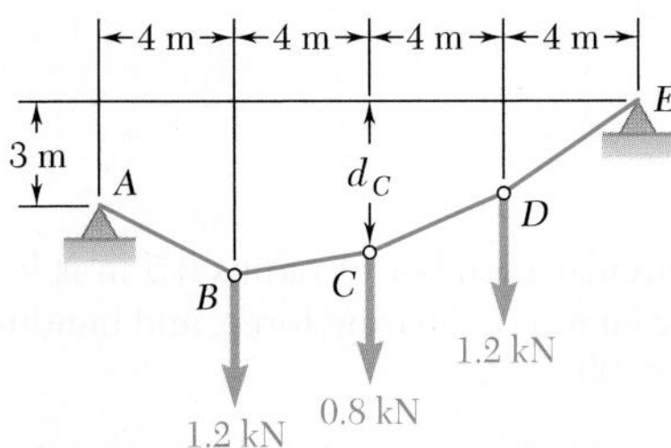

Fig. P7.156

7.157 A steam pipe weighing 50 N/m passes between two buildings 18 m apart and is supported by a system of cables as shown. Assuming that the weight of the cable is equivalent to a uniformly distributed loading of 7.5 N/m, determine (*a*) the location of the lowest point *C* of the cable, (*b*) the maximum tension in the cable.

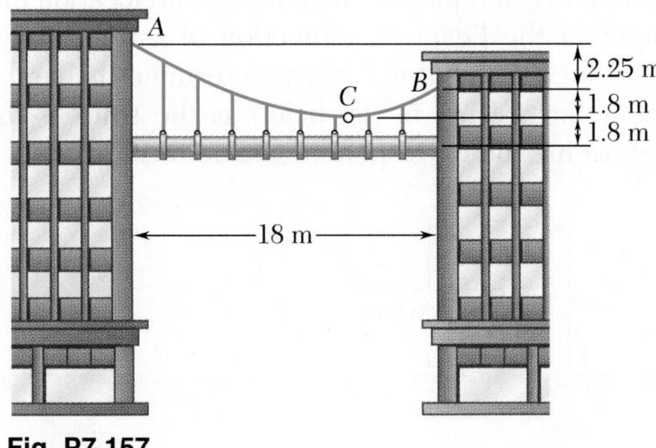

Fig. P7.157

7.158 A 60-m steel surveying tape weighs 4 N. If the tape is stretched between two points at the same elevation and pulled until the tension at each end is 16 N, determine the horizontal distance between the ends of the tape. Neglect the elongation of the tape due to the tension.

Computer Problems

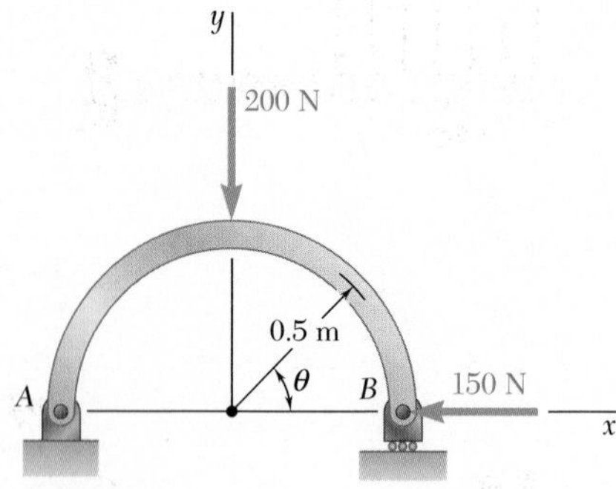

Fig. P7.C1

7.C1 A semicircular member of radius 0.5 m is loaded as shown. Plot the internal forces (axial force, shearing force, and bending moment) as functions of θ for $0 < \theta < 90°$.

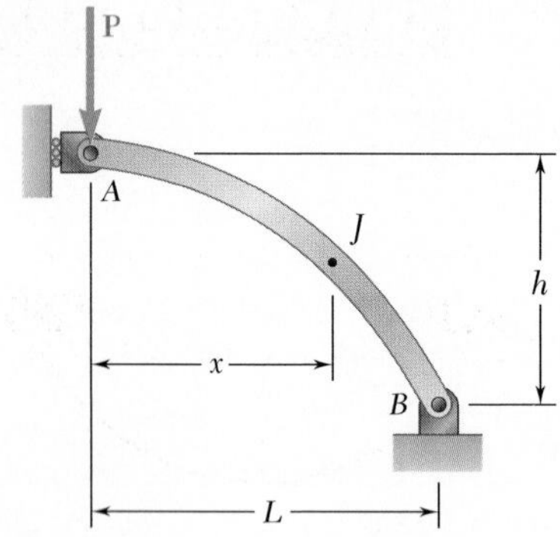

Fig. P7.C2

7.C2 The axis of the curved member AB is a parabola for which the vertex is at A and $L = nh$. Knowing that a vertical load **P** of magnitude 1.2 kN is applied at A, determine the internal forces and bending moment at an arbitrary point J. Plot the internal forces and bending moment as functions of x for $0.25L \leq x \leq 0.75L$ when $L = 400$ mm and (*a*) $n = 2$, (*b*) $n = 3$, (*c*) $n = 4$.

7.C3 The floor of a bridge will consist of narrow planks resting on two simply supported beams, one of which is shown in the figure. As part of the design of the bridge, it is desired to simulate the effect that driving a 12-kN truck over the bridge will have on this beam. The distance between the truck's axles is 1.8 m, and it is assumed that the weight of the truck is equally distributed over its four wheels. (*a*) Using computational software, calculate, using 0.15-m increments, and plot the magnitude and location of the maximum bending moment in the beam as a function of x for $-0.9 \text{ m} \leq x \leq 3 \text{ m}$. (*b*) Using smaller increments if necessary, determine the largest value of the bending moment that occurs in the beam as the truck is driven over the bridge, and determine the corresponding value of x.

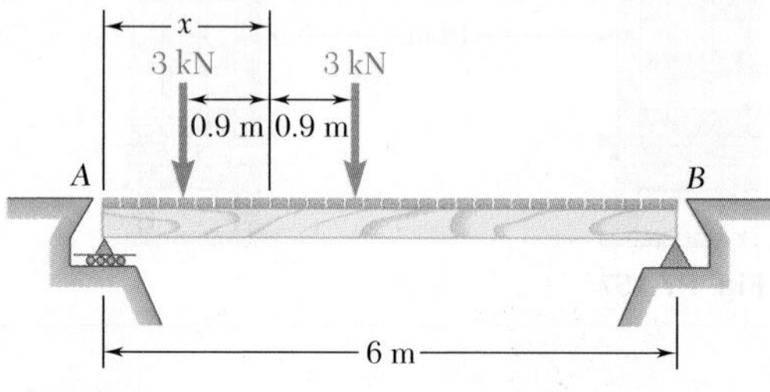

Fig. P7.C3

7.C4 Determine the equations for the shear and bending moment curves for beams 1 and 2 shown assuming that $w_0 = 15$ kN/m and $L = 3$ m. Plot the shear and bending moment diagrams for each beam.

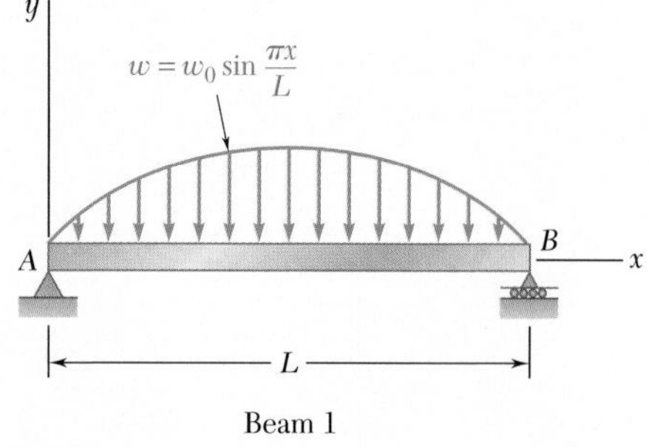

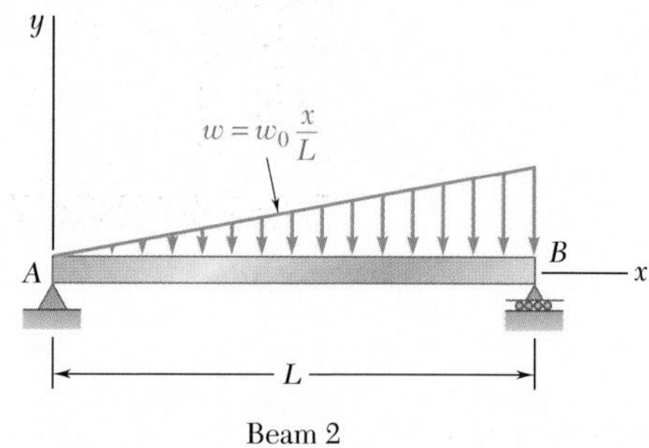

Fig. P7.C4

7.C5 A beam AB hinged at B and supported by a roller at D is to be designed to carry a load uniformly distributed from its end A to its midpoint C with maximum efficiency. As part of the design process, use computational software to determine the distance a from end A to the point D where the roller should be placed to minimize the absolute value of the bending moment M in the beam. (*Hint:* A short preliminary analysis will show that the roller should be placed under the load and that the largest negative value of M will occur at D, while its largest positive value will occur somewhere between D and C. Thus, you should draw the bending-moment diagram and then equate the absolute values of the largest positive and negative bending moments obtained.)

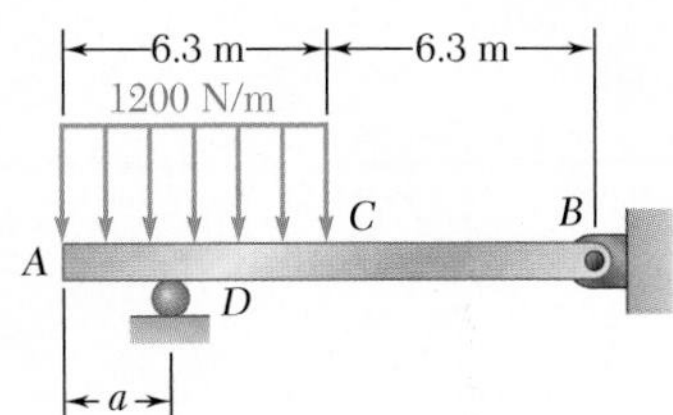

Fig. P7.C5

7.C6 Cable AB supports a load distributed uniformly along the horizontal as shown. The lowest portion of the cable is located at a distance a = 3.6 m below support A, and support B is located a distance $b = na$ above A. (*a*) Determine the maximum tension in the cable as a function of n. (*b*) Plot the maximum tension in the cable for $2 \leq n \leq 6$.

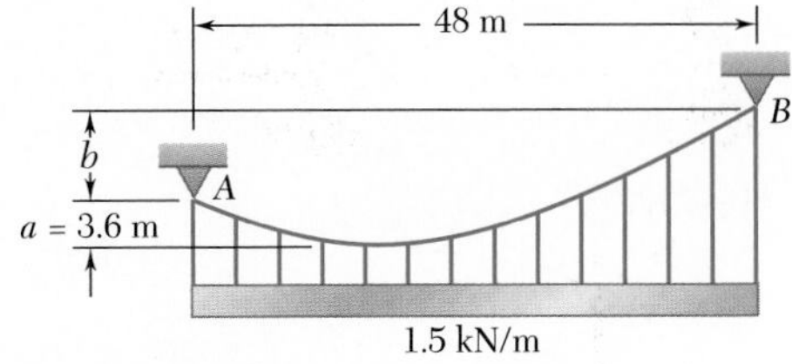

Fig. P7.C6

7.C7 Using computational software, solve Prob. 7.127 for values of P from 0 to 75 N using 5-N increments.

7.C8 A typical transmission-line installation consists of a cable of length s_{AB} and mass per unit length m' suspended as shown between two points at the same elevation. Using computational software, construct a table that can be used in the design of future installations. The table should present the dimensionless quantities h/L, s_{AB}/L, $T_0/m'gL$ and $T_{max}/m'gL$ for values of c/L from 0.2 to 0.5 using 0.025 increments and from 1 to 4 using 0.5 increments.

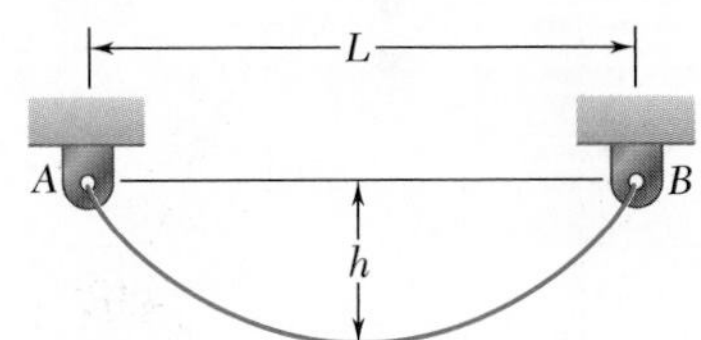

Fig. P7.C8

7.C9 The electrician shown is installing an electric cable weighing 0.2 N/m. As the electrician slowly climbs the ladder, the cable unwinds from the spool so that the tension T_B in the cable at B is 1.2 N. Knowing that h = 1.2 m when the electrician is standing on the ground, plot the magnitude of the force exerted on the hand of the electrician by the cable as a function of h for 1.2 m $\leq h \leq$ 4.8 m.

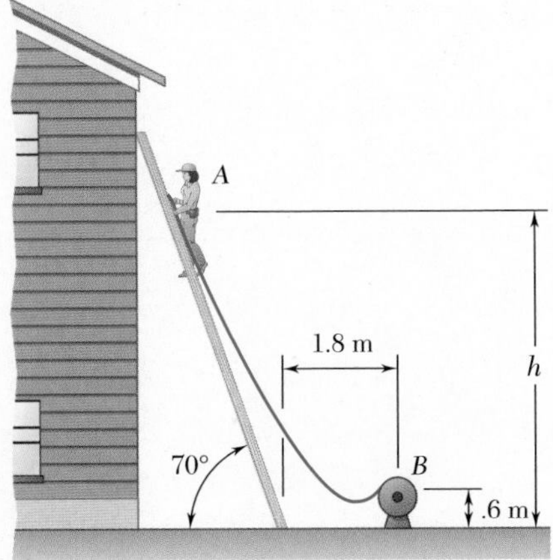

Fig. P7.C9

CHAPTER 8

Friction

The pegs used to tighten the strings of a violin rely on static-friction forces to keep them from rotating because of the moments about their axes of the tensile forces exerted by the strings. The vibrations of the strings create the sound emanating from the violin and are produced by kinetic-friction forces between the horsehair bow and the strings. The horsehair is coated with rosin to increase these frictional forces.

FRICTION

8.1. INTRODUCTION

In the preceding chapters, it was assumed that surfaces in contact were either *frictionless* or *rough*. If they were frictionless, the force each surface exerted on the other was normal to the surfaces and the two surfaces could move freely with respect to each other. If they were rough, it was assumed that tangential forces could develop to prevent the motion of one surface with respect to the other.

This view was a simplified one. Actually, no perfectly frictionless surface exists. When two surfaces are in contact, tangential forces, called *friction forces,* will always develop if one attempts to move one surface with respect to the other. On the other hand, these friction forces are limited in magnitude and will not prevent motion if sufficiently large forces are applied. The distinction between frictionless and rough surfaces is thus a matter of degree. This will be seen more clearly in the present chapter, which is devoted to the study of friction and of its applications to common engineering situations.

There are two types of friction: *dry friction,* sometimes called *Coulomb friction,* and *fluid friction*. Fluid friction develops between layers of fluid moving at different velocities. Fluid friction is of great importance in problems involving the flow of fluids through pipes and orifices or dealing with bodies immersed in moving fluids. It is also basic in the analysis of the motion of *lubricated mechanisms*. Such problems are considered in texts on fluid mechanics. The present study is limited to dry friction, that is, to problems involving rigid bodies which are in contact along *nonlubricated* surfaces.

In the first part of this chapter, the equilibrium of various rigid bodies and structures, assuming dry friction at the surfaces of contact, is analyzed. Later a number of specific engineering applications where dry friction plays an important role are considered: wedges, square-threaded screws, journal bearings, thrust bearings, rolling resistance, and belt friction.

8.2. THE LAWS OF DRY FRICTION. COEFFICIENTS OF FRICTION

The laws of dry friction are exemplified by the following experiment. A block of weight **W** is placed on a horizontal plane surface (Fig. 8.1*a*). The forces acting on the block are its weight **W** and the reaction of the surface. Since the weight has no horizontal component, the reaction of the surface also has no horizontal component; the reaction is therefore *normal* to the surface and is represented by **N** in Fig. 8.1*a*. Suppose, now, that a horizontal force **P** is applied to the block (Fig. 8.1*b*). If **P** is small, the block will not move; some other horizontal force must therefore exist, which balances **P**. This other force is the *static-friction force* **F**, which is actually the resultant of a great number of forces acting over the entire surface of contact between the block and the plane. The nature of these forces is not known exactly, but it is generally assumed that these forces are due to the irregularities of the surfaces in contact and, to a certain extent, to molecular attraction.

If the force **P** is increased, the friction force **F** also increases, continuing to oppose **P**, until its magnitude reaches a certain *maximum value* F_m (Fig. 8.1*c*). If **P** is further increased, the friction

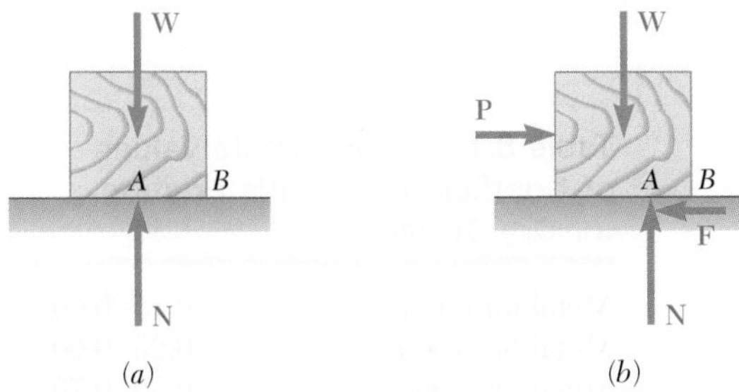

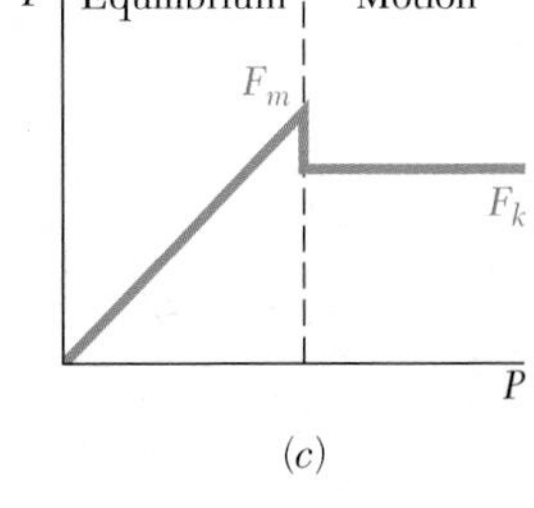

Fig. 8.1

force cannot balance it any more and the block starts sliding.† As soon as the block has been set in motion, the magnitude of **F** drops from F_m to a lower value F_k. This is because there is less interpenetration between the irregularities of the surfaces in contact when these surfaces move with respect to each other. From then on, the block keeps sliding with increasing velocity while the friction force, denoted by $\mathbf{F}_k$ and called the *kinetic-friction force,* remains approximately constant.

Experimental evidence shows that the maximum value F_m of the static-friction force is proportional to the normal component N of the reaction of the surface. We have

$$F_m = \mu_s N \tag{8.1}$$

where μ_s is a constant called the *coefficient of static friction.* Similarly, the magnitude F_k of the kinetic-friction force may be put in the form

$$F_k = \mu_k N \tag{8.2}$$

where μ_k is a constant called the *coefficient of kinetic friction.* The coefficients of friction μ_s and μ_k do not depend upon the area of the surfaces in contact. Both coefficients, however, depend strongly on the *nature* of the surfaces in contact. Since they also depend upon the exact condition of the surfaces, their value is seldom known with an accuracy greater than 5 percent. Approximate values of coefficients

†It should be noted that, as the magnitude F of the friction force increases from 0 to F_m, the point of application A of the resultant **N** of the normal forces of contact moves to the right, so that the couples formed, respectively, by **P** and **F** and by **W** and **N** remain balanced. If **N** reaches B before F reaches its maximum value F_m, the block will tip about B before it can start sliding (see Probs. 8.15 and 8.16).

of static friction for various dry surfaces are given in Table 8.1. The corresponding values of the coefficient of kinetic friction would be about 25 percent smaller. Since coefficients of friction are dimensionless quantities, the values given in Table 8.1 can be used with both SI units and U.S. customary units.

Table 8.1. Approximate Values of Coefficient of Static Friction for Dry Surfaces

Metal on metal	0.15–0.60
Metal on wood	0.20–0.60
Metal on stone	0.30–0.70
Metal on leather	0.30–0.60
Wood on wood	0.25–0.50
Wood on leather	0.25–0.50
Stone on stone	0.40–0.70
Earth on earth	0.20–1.00
Rubber on concrete	0.60–0.90

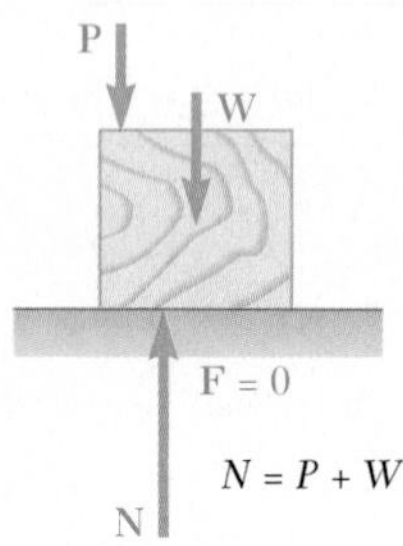

(*a*) No friction ($P_x = 0$)

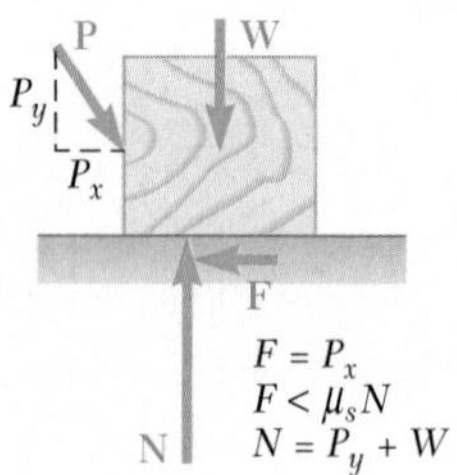

(*b*) No motion ($P_x < F_m$)

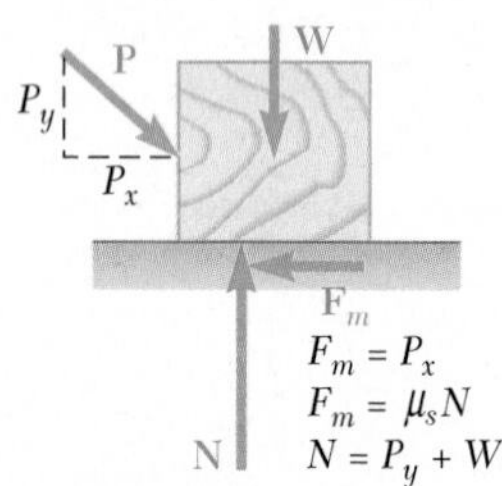

(*c*) Motion impending ⟶ ($P_x = F_m$)

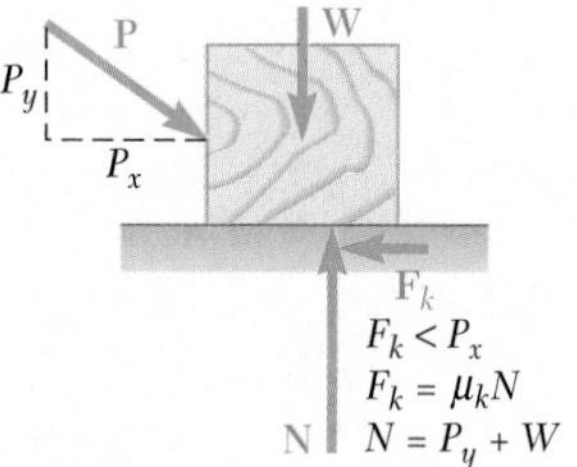

(*d*) Motion ⟶ ($P_x > F_m$)

Fig. 8.2

From the description given above, it appears that four different situations can occur when a rigid body is in contact with a horizontal surface:

1. The forces applied to the body do not tend to move it along the surface of contact; there is no friction force (Fig. 8.2*a*).

2. The applied forces tend to move the body along the surface of contact but are not large enough to set it in motion. The friction force **F** which has developed can be found by solving the equations of equilibrium for the body. Since there is no evidence that **F** has reached its maximum value, the equation $F_m = \mu_s N$ *cannot be used* to determine the friction force (Fig. 8.2*b*).

3. The applied forces are such that the body is just about to slide. We say that *motion is impending*. The friction force **F** has reached its maximum value F_m and, together with the normal force **N**, balances the applied forces. Both the equations of equilibrium and the equation $F_m = \mu_s N$ *can be used*. We also note that the friction force has a sense opposite to the sense of impending motion (Fig. 8.2*c*).

4. The body is sliding under the action of the applied forces, and the equations of equilibrium do not apply any more. However, **F** is now equal to $\mathbf{F}_k$ and the equation $F_k = \mu_k N$ may be used. The sense of $\mathbf{F}_k$ is opposite to the sense of motion (Fig. 8.2*d*).

8.3. ANGLES OF FRICTION

It is sometimes convenient to replace the normal force **N** and the friction force **F** by their resultant **R**. Let us consider again a block of weight **W** resting on a horizontal plane surface. If no horizontal force is applied to the block, the resultant **R** reduces to the normal force **N** (Fig. 8.3*a*). However, if the applied force **P** has a horizontal component $\mathbf{P}_x$ which tends to move the block, the force **R** will have a horizontal component **F** and, thus, will form an angle ϕ with the normal to the surface (Fig. 8.3*b*). If $\mathbf{P}_x$ is increased until motion becomes impending, the angle between **R** and the vertical grows and reaches a maximum value (Fig. 8.3*c*). This value is called the *angle of static friction* and is denoted by ϕ_s. From the geometry of Fig. 8.3*c*, we note that

$$\tan \phi_s = \frac{F_m}{N} = \frac{\mu_s N}{N}$$

$$\tan \phi_s = \mu_s \tag{8.3}$$

If motion actually takes place, the magnitude of the friction force drops to F_k; similarly, the angle ϕ between **R** and **N** drops to a lower value ϕ_k, called the *angle of kinetic friction* (Fig. 8.3*d*). From the geometry of Fig. 8.3*d*, we write

$$\tan \phi_k = \frac{F_k}{N} = \frac{\mu_k N}{N}$$

$$\tan \phi_k = \mu_k \tag{8.4}$$

Another example will show how the angle of friction can be used to advantage in the analysis of certain types of problems. Consider a block resting on a board and subjected to no other force than its weight **W** and the reaction **R** of the board. The board can be given any desired inclination. If the board is horizontal, the force **R** exerted by the board on the block is perpendicular to the board and balances the weight **W** (Fig. 8.4*a*). If the board is given a small angle of inclina-

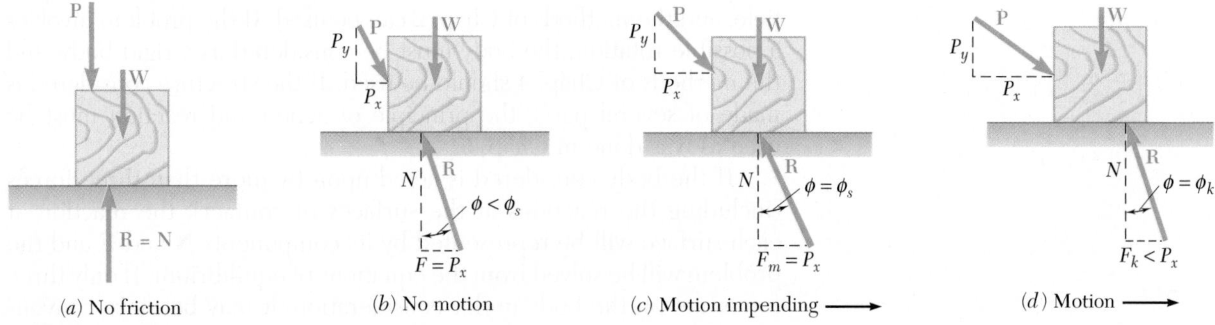

Fig. 8.3

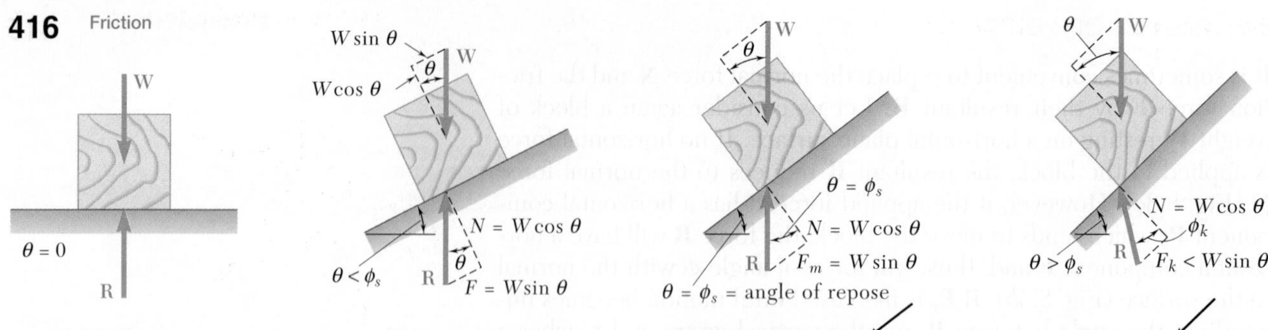

(*a*) No friction (*b*) No motion (*c*) Motion impending (*d*) Motion

Fig. 8.4

Photo 8.1 The coefficient of static friction between a package and the inclined conveyer belt must be sufficiently large to enable the package to be transported without slipping.

tion θ, the force **R** will deviate from the perpendicular to the board by the angle θ and will keep balancing **W** (Fig. 8.4*b*); it will then have a normal component **N** of magnitude $N = W \cos \theta$ and a tangential component **F** of magnitude $F = W \sin \theta$.

If we keep increasing the angle of inclination, motion will soon become impending. At that time, the angle between **R** and the normal will have reached its maximum value ϕ_s (Fig. 8.4*c*). The value of the angle of inclination corresponding to impending motion is called the *angle of repose.* Clearly, the angle of repose is equal to the angle of static friction ϕ_s. If the angle of inclination θ is further increased, motion starts and the angle between **R** and the normal drops to the lower value ϕ_k (Fig. 8.4*d*). The reaction **R** is not vertical any more, and the forces acting on the block are unbalanced.

8.4. PROBLEMS INVOLVING DRY FRICTION

Problems involving dry friction are found in many engineering applications. Some deal with simple situations such as the block sliding on a plane described in the preceding sections. Others involve more complicated situations as in Sample Prob. 8.3; many deal with the stability of rigid bodies in accelerated motion and will be studied in dynamics. Also, a number of common machines and mechanisms can be analyzed by applying the laws of dry friction. These include wedges, screws, journal and thrust bearings, and belt transmissions. They will be studied in the following sections.

The *methods* which should be used to solve problems involving dry friction are the same that were used in the preceding chapters. If a problem involves only a motion of translation, with no possible rotation, the body under consideration can usually be treated as a particle, and the methods of Chap. 2 can be used. If the problem involves a possible rotation, the body must be considered as a rigid body, and the methods of Chap. 4 should be used. If the structure considered is made of several parts, the principle of action and reaction must be used as was done in Chap. 6.

If the body considered is acted upon by more than three forces (including the reactions at the surfaces of contact), the reaction at each surface will be represented by its components **N** and **F** and the problem will be solved from the equations of equilibrium. If only three forces act on the body under consideration, it may be more convenient to represent each reaction by a single force **R** and to solve the problem by drawing a force triangle.

Most problems involving friction fall into one of the following *three groups:* In the *first group* of problems, all applied forces are given and the coefficients of friction are known; we are to determine whether the body considered will remain at rest or slide. The friction force **F** *required to maintain equilibrium* is unknown (its magnitude is *not* equal to $\mu_s N$) and should be determined, together with the normal force **N**, by drawing a free-body diagram and *solving the equations of equilibrium* (Fig. 8.5*a*). The value found for the magnitude F of the friction force is then compared with the maximum value $F_m = \mu_s N$. If F is smaller than or equal to F_m, the body remains at rest. If the value found for F is larger than F_m, equilibrium cannot be maintained and motion takes place; the actual magnitude of the friction force is then $F_k = \mu_k N$.

In problems of the *second group,* all applied forces are given and the motion is known to be impending; we are to determine the value of the coefficient of static friction. Here again, we determine the friction force and the normal force by drawing a free-body diagram and solving the equations of equilibrium (Fig. 8.5*b*). Since we know that the value found for F is the maximum value F_m, the coefficient of friction may be found by writing and solving the equation $F_m = \mu_s N$.

In problems of the *third group,* the coefficient of static friction is given, and it is known that the motion is impending in a given direction; we are to determine the magnitude or the direction of one of the applied forces. The friction force should be shown in the free-body diagram with a *sense opposite to that of the impending motion* and with a magnitude $F_m = \mu_s N$ (Fig. 8.5*c*). The equations of equilibrium can then be written, and the desired force determined.

As noted above, when only three forces are involved it may be more convenient to represent the reaction of the surface by a single force **R** and to solve the problem by drawing a force triangle. Such a solution is used in Sample Prob. 8.2.

When two bodies A and B are in contact (Fig. 8.6*a*), the forces of friction exerted, respectively, by A on B and by B on A are equal and opposite (Newton's third law). In drawing the free-body diagram of one of the bodies, it is important to include the appropriate friction force with its correct sense. The following rule should then be observed: *The sense of the friction force acting on A is opposite to that of the motion (or impending motion) of A as observed from B* (Fig. 8.6*b*).† The sense of the friction force acting on B is determined in a similar way (Fig. 8.6*c*). Note that the motion of A as observed from B is a *relative motion.* For example, if body A is fixed and body B moves, body A will have a relative motion with respect to B. Also, if both B and A are moving down but B is moving faster than A, body A will be observed, from B, to be moving up.

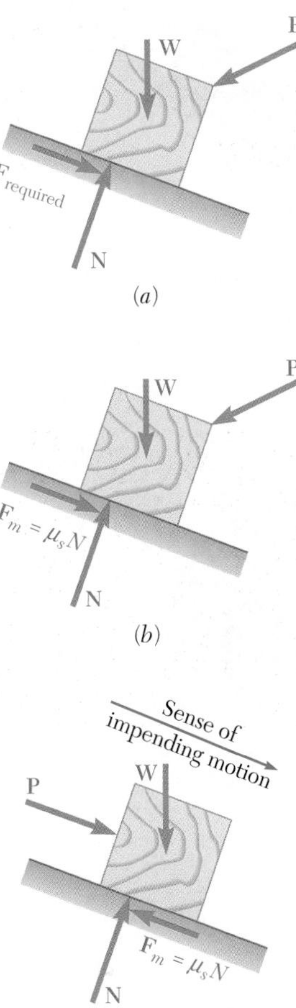

Fig. 8.5

†It is therefore *the same as that of the motion of B as observed from A.*

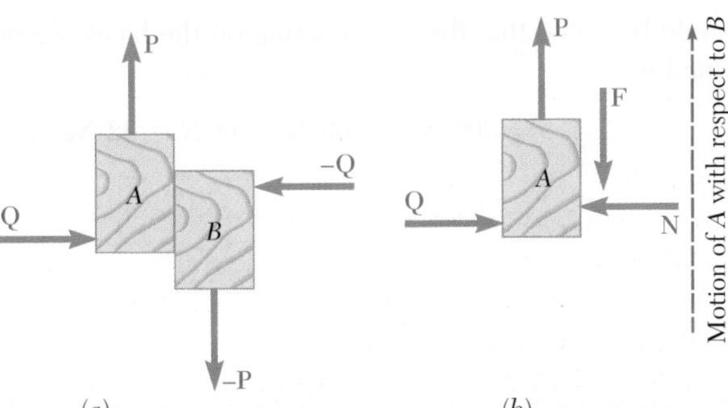

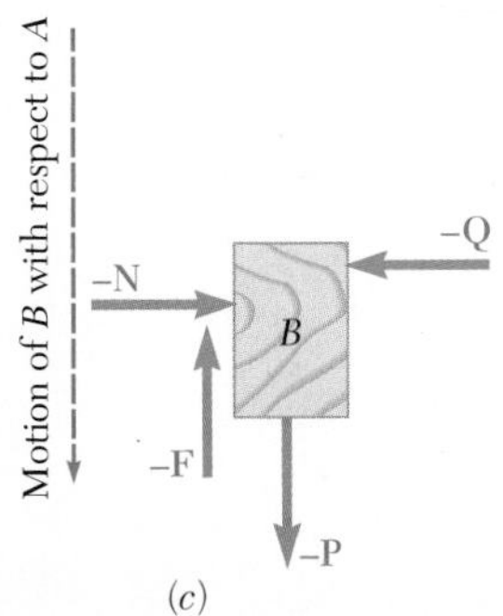

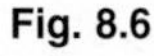
Fig. 8.6

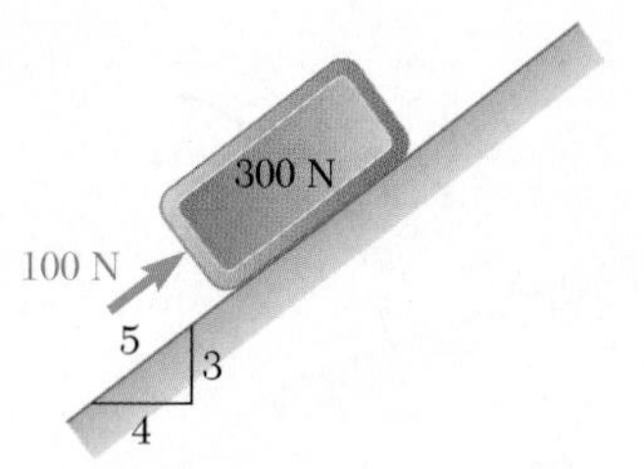

SAMPLE PROBLEM 8.1

A 100-N force acts as shown on a 300-N block placed on an inclined plane. The coefficients of friction between the block and the plane are $\mu_s = 0.25$ and $\mu_k = 0.20$. Determine whether the block is in equilibrium, and find the value of the friction force.

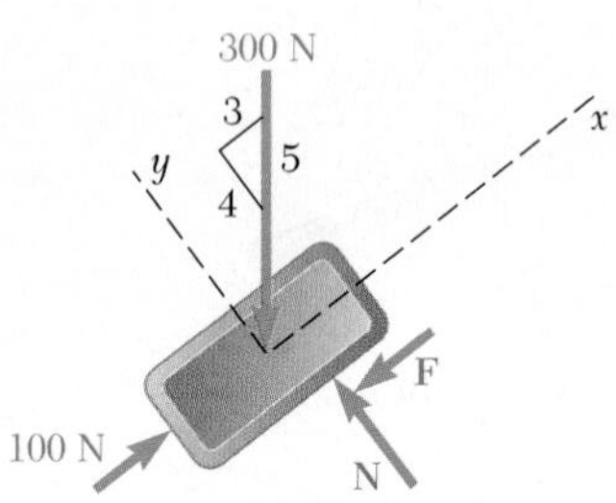

SOLUTION

Force Required for Equilibrium. We first determine the value of the friction force *required to maintain equilibrium.* Assuming that **F** is directed down and to the left, we draw the free-body diagram of the block and write

$$+\nearrow \Sigma F_x = 0: \qquad 100\text{ N} - \tfrac{3}{5}(300\text{ N}) - F = 0$$
$$F = -80\text{ N} \qquad \mathbf{F} = 80\text{ N}\nearrow$$

$$+\nwarrow \Sigma F_y = 0: \qquad N - \tfrac{4}{5}(300\text{ N}) = 0$$
$$N = +240\text{ N} \qquad \mathbf{N} = 240\text{ N}\nwarrow$$

The force **F** required to maintain equilibrium is an 80-N force directed up and to the right; the tendency of the block is thus to move down the plane.

Maximum Friction Force. The magnitude of the maximum friction force which can be developed is

$$F_m = \mu_s N \qquad F_m = 0.25(240\text{ N}) = 60\text{ N}$$

Since the value of the force required to maintain equilibrium (80 N) is larger than the maximum value which can be obtained (60 N), equilibrium will not be maintained and *the block will slide down the plane.*

Actual Value of Friction Force. The magnitude of the actual friction force is obtained as follows:

300 N

Motion

100 N

F = 48 N

N = 240 N

$$F_{\text{actual}} = F_k = \mu_k N$$
$$= 0.20(240\text{ N}) = 48\text{ N}$$

The sense of this force is opposite to the sense of motion; the force is thus directed up and to the right:

$$\mathbf{F}_{\text{actual}} = 48\text{ N}\nearrow \blacktriangleleft$$

It should be noted that the forces acting on the block are not balanced; the resultant is

$$\tfrac{3}{5}(300\text{ N}) - 100\text{ N} - 48\text{ N} = 32\text{ N}\swarrow$$

SAMPLE PROBLEM 8.2

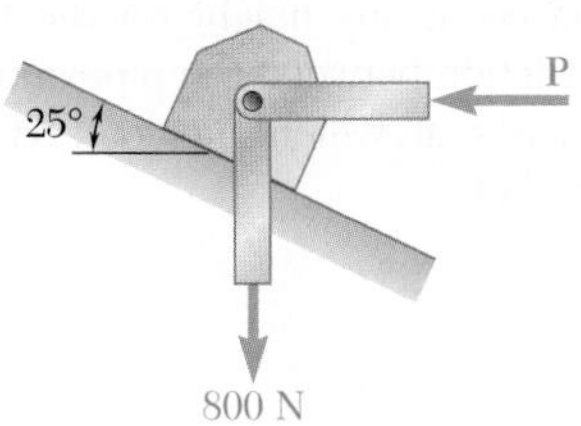

A support block is acted upon by two forces as shown. Knowing that the coefficients of friction between the block and the incline are $\mu_s = 0.35$ and $\mu_k = 0.25$, determine (*a*) the force **P** for which motion of the block up the incline is impending, (*b*) the friction force when the block is moving up, (*c*) the smallest force **P** required to prevent the block from sliding down.

SOLUTION

Free-Body Diagram. For each part of the problem we draw a free-body diagram of the block and a force triangle including the 800-N vertical force, the horizontal force **P**, and the force **R** exerted on the block by the incline. The direction of **R** must be determined in each separate case. We note that since **P** is perpendicular to the 800-N force, the force triangle is a right triangle, which can easily be solved for **P**. In most other problems, however, the force triangle will be an oblique triangle and should be solved by applying the law of sines.

a. Force* P *for Impending Motion of the Block Up the Incline

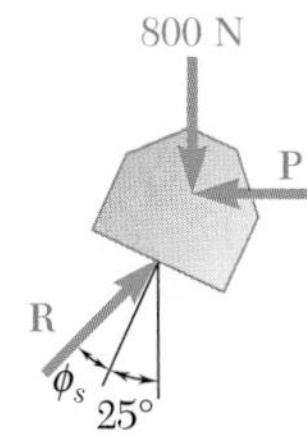

$\tan \phi_s = \mu_s$
$= 0.35$
$\phi_s = 19.29°$
$25° + 19.29° = 44.29°$

800 N P R

$$P = (800\text{ N}) \tan 44.29° \qquad \mathbf{P} = 780\text{ N} \leftarrow \blacktriangleleft$$

b. Friction Force* F *when the Block Moves Up the Incline

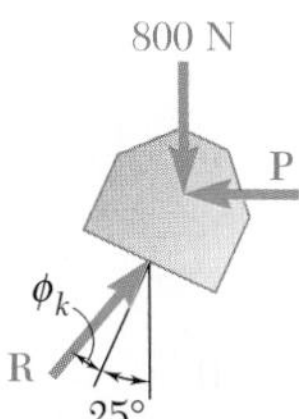

$\tan \phi_k = \mu_k$
$= 0.25$
$\phi_k = 14.04°$
$25° + 14.04° = 39.04°$

800 N P R

$$R = (800\text{ N})/\cos 39.04° = 1029.9\text{ N}$$

$$F = R \sin \phi_k = (1029.9\text{ N}) \sin 14.04°$$

$$\mathbf{F} = 250\text{ N} \searrow \blacktriangleleft$$

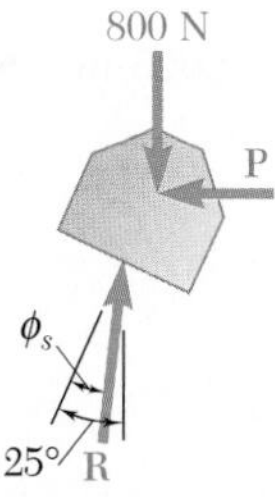

$\phi_s = 19.29°$
$25° - 19.29° = 5.71°$

P 800 N R

c. Force* P *for Impending Motion of the Block Down the Incline

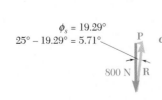

$$P = (800\text{ N}) \tan 5.71° \qquad \mathbf{P} = 80.0\text{ N} \leftarrow \blacktriangleleft$$

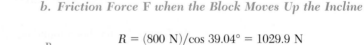

SAMPLE PROBLEM 8.3

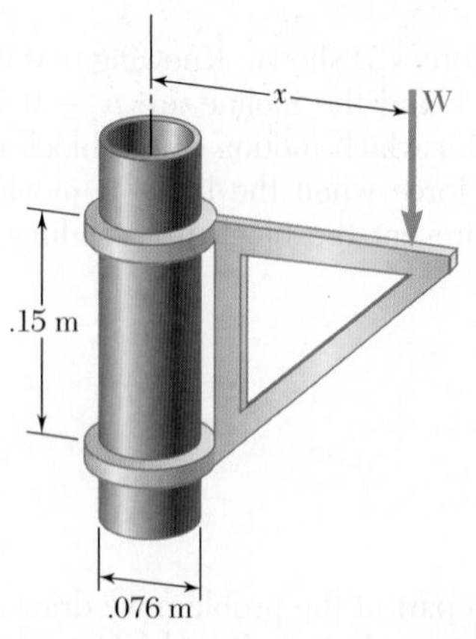

The movable bracket shown may be placed at any height on the 0.076-m-diameter pipe. If the coefficient of static friction between the pipe and bracket is 0.25, determine the minimum distance x at which the load **W** can be supported. Neglect the weight of the bracket.

SOLUTION

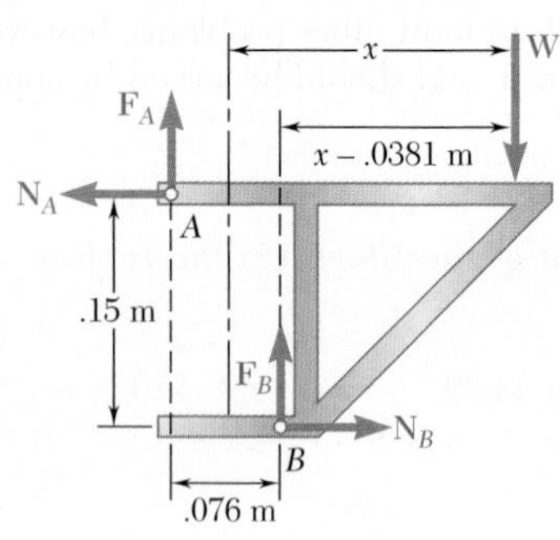

Free-Body Diagram. We draw the free-body diagram of the bracket. When **W** is placed at the minimum distance x from the axis of the pipe, the bracket is just about to slip, and the forces of friction at A and B have reached their maximum values:

$$F_A = \mu_s N_A = 0.25N_A$$
$$F_B = \mu_s N_B = 0.25N_B$$

Equilibrium Equations

$\overset{+}{\rightarrow}\Sigma F_x = 0$: $\quad N_B - N_A = 0$

$$N_B = N_A$$

$+\uparrow\Sigma F_y = 0$: $\quad F_A + F_B - W = 0$

$$0.25N_A + 0.25N_B = W$$

And, since N_B has been found equal to N_A,

$$0.50N_A = W$$
$$N_A = 2W$$

$+\circlearrowleft\Sigma M_B = 0$: $\quad N_A(.15 \text{ m}) - F_A(.076 \text{ m}) - W(x - .0381 \text{ m}) = 0$

$$.15N_A - .0228N_A - Wx + .0381W = 0$$
$$.3W - .0456W - Wx + .0381W = 0$$

Dividing through by W and solving for x,

$$x = .2925 \text{ m} \quad ◀$$

SOLVING PROBLEMS ON YOUR OWN

In this lesson you studied and applied the *laws of dry friction.* Previously you had encountered only (*a*) frictionless surfaces that could move freely with respect to each other, (*b*) rough surfaces that allowed no motion relative to each other.

A. *In solving problems involving dry friction,* you should keep the following in mind.

1. *The reaction* R *exerted by a surface on a free body* can be resolved into a normal component **N** and a tangential component **F**. The tangential component is known as the *friction force.* When a body is in contact with a fixed surface the direction of the friction force **F** is opposite to that of the actual or impending motion of the body.

a. No motion will occur as long as F does not exceed the maximum value $F_m = \mu_s N$, where μ_s is the *coefficient of static friction.*

b. Motion will occur if a value of F larger than F_m is required to maintain equilibrium. As motion takes place, the actual value of F drops to $F_k = \mu_k N$, where μ_k is the *coefficient of kinetic friction* [Sample Prob. 8.1].

2. *When only three forces are involved* an alternative approach to the analysis of friction may be preferred [Sample Prob. 8.2]. The reaction **R** is defined by its magnitude R and the angle ϕ it forms with the normal to the surface. No motion will occur as long as ϕ does not exceed the maximum value ϕ_s, where $\tan \phi_s = \mu_s$. Motion will occur if a value of ϕ larger than ϕ_s is required to maintain equilibrium, and the actual value of ϕ will drop to ϕ_k, where $\tan \phi_k = \mu_k$.

3. *When two bodies are in contact* the sense of the actual or impending relative motion at the point of contact must be determined. On each of the two bodies a friction force **F** should be shown in a direction opposite to that of the actual or impending motion of the body as seen from the other body.

B. *Methods of solution.* The first step in your solution is to *draw a free-body diagram* of the body under consideration, resolving the force exerted on each surface where friction exists into a normal component **N** and a friction force **F**. If several bodies are involved, draw a free-body diagram of each of them, labeling and directing the forces at each surface of contact as you learned to do when analyzing frames in Chap. 6.

The problem you have to solve may fall into one of the following five categories:

1. *All the applied forces and the coefficients of friction are known, and you must determine whether equilibrium is maintained.* Note that in this situation the friction force is unknown and *cannot be assumed to be equal* to $\mu_s N$.

a. Write the equations of equilibrium to determine N and F.

b. Calculate the maximum allowable friction force, $F_m = \mu_s N$. If $F \le F_m$, equilibrium is maintained. If $F > F_m$, motion occurs, and the magnitude of the friction force is $F_k = \mu_k N$ [Sample Prob. 8.1].

2. *All the applied forces are known, and you must find the smallest allowable value of μ_s for which equilibrium is maintained.* You will assume that motion is impending and determine the corresponding value of μ_s.

a. Write the equations of equilibrium to determine N and F.

b. Since motion is impending, $F = F_m$. Substitute the values found for N and F into the equation $F_m = \mu_s N$ and solve for μ_s.

3. ***The motion of the body is impending and μ_s is known; you must find some unknown quantity,*** such as a distance, an angle, the magnitude of a force, or the direction of a force.

a. Assume a possible impending motion of the body and, on the free-body diagram, draw the friction force in a direction opposite to that of the assumed motion.

b. Since motion is impending, $F = F_m = \mu_s N$. Substituting for μ_s its known value, you can express F in terms of N on the free-body diagram, thus eliminating one unknown.

c. Write and solve the equilibrium equations for the unknown you seek [Sample Prob. 8.3].

4. ***The system consists of several bodies and more than one state of impending motion is possible; you must determine a force, a distance, or a coefficient of friction for which motion is impending.***

a. Count the number of unknowns (forces, angles, etc.) and the total number of independent equations of equilibrium; the difference is equal to the number of surfaces at which motion can be impending.

b. Assume where motion is impending, and on the free-body diagrams of the bodies, draw the friction forces in directions opposite to the assumed motion.

c. At those surfaces where motion is assumed to be impending, $F = F_m = \mu_s N$.

d. Write and solve the equations of equilibrium for all unknowns.

e. Check your assumption by computing F and F_m for the surfaces where motion was assumed not to be impending. If $F < F_m$, your assumption was correct; however, if $F > F_m$, your assumption was incorrect, and it is then necessary to make a new assumption as to where motion impends and to repeat the solution process. You should always include a statement of your assumption and the associated check.

5. ***The impending motion of the body can be either sliding or tipping about a given point; you must find a force, a distance, or a coefficient of friction.***

a. Assume a possible impending sliding motion of the body and, on the free-body diagram, draw the friction force or forces in the direction opposite to that of the assumed motion.

b. Separately consider impending sliding and impending tipping.

i. For impending sliding, $F = F_m = \mu_s N$. Write the equations of equilibrium, and solve for the required unknown.

ii. For impending tipping, assume that the external reactions go to zero at all supports except for the reactions at the point about which tipping is assumed to be impending. Note for this case that $F \neq F_m$ and that the required unknown is determined from the equations of equilibrium.

The problems in this section require careful analysis, for they are some of the most difficult problems you will encounter in your statics course. You must always carefully draw free-body diagrams, paying particular attention to the directions of the friction forces. When it is necessary to assume the direction of the friction force, a positive answer implies a correct assumption, while a negative answer implies the friction force is directed opposite to the assumed direction. Also, the solutions of some problems are simplified using either the property of three-force bodies [Sec. 4.7] or the geometry of the system (for example, Prob. 8.23).

Problems

8.1 Knowing that $W_A = 25$ N and $\theta = 30°$, determine (*a*) the smallest value of W_B for which the system is in equilibrium, (*b*) the largest value of W_B for which the system is in equilibrium.

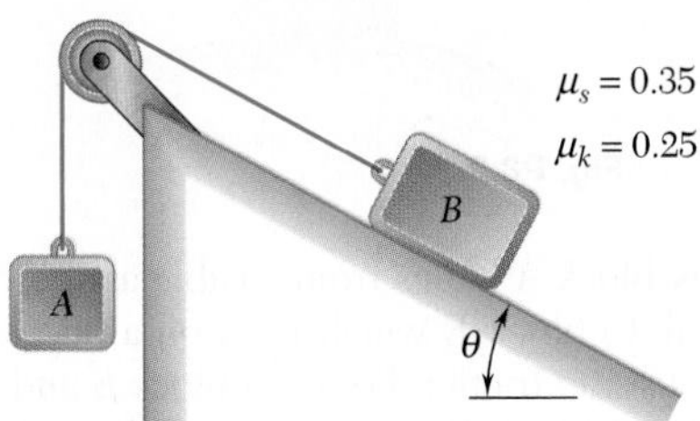

Fig. P8.1 and *P8.2*

8.2 Knowing that $W_A = 40$ N, $W_B = 52$ N, and $\theta = 25°$, determine (*a*) whether the system is in equilibrium, (*b*) the magnitude and direction of the friction force.

8.3 Determine whether the 10-kg block shown is in equilibrium, and find the magnitude and direction of the friction force when $P = 40$ N and $\theta = 20°$.

8.4 Determine whether the 10-kg block shown is in equilibrium, and find the magnitude and direction of the friction force when $P = 62.5$ N and $\theta = 15°$.

8.5 Knowing that $\theta = 25°$, determine the range of values of P for which equilibrium is maintained.

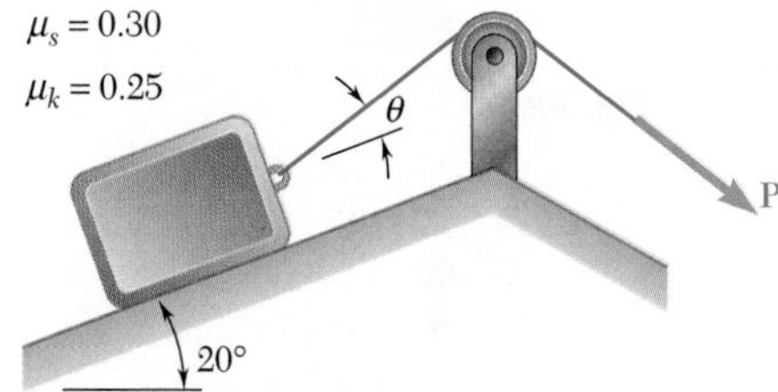

Fig. P8.3, *P8.4*, and P8.5

8.6 Knowing that the coefficient of static friction between the 20-kg block and the incline is 0.30, determine the smallest value of θ for which the block is in equilibrium.

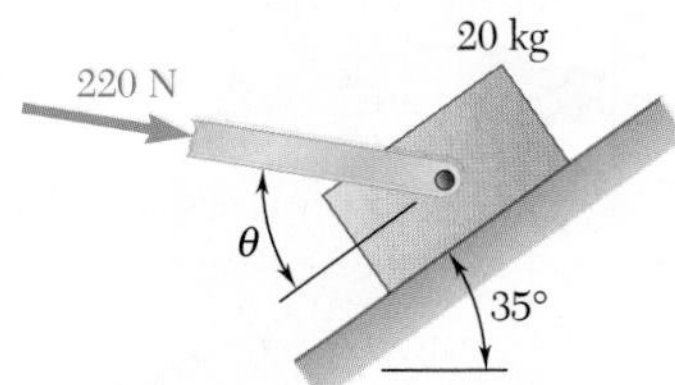

Fig. P8.6

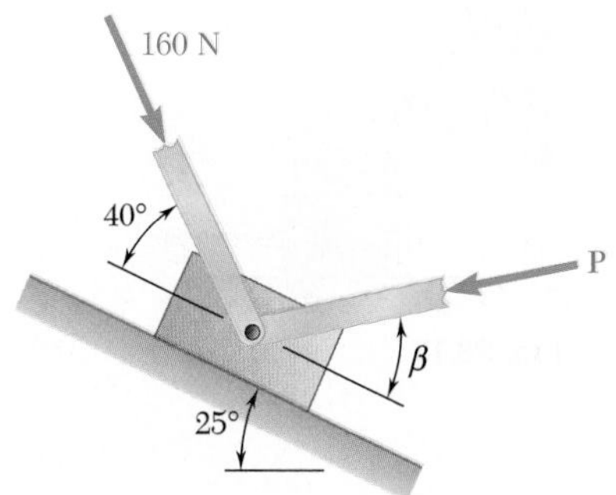

Fig. P8.7

8.7 Neglecting the mass of the block and knowing that the coefficient of static friction between the block and the incline is 0.35, determine (*a*) the smallest value of P for which the block is in equilibrium, (*b*) the corresponding value of β.

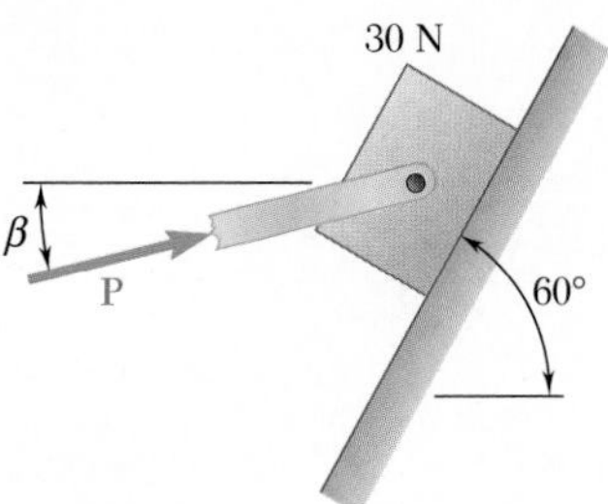

Fig. P8.8

8.8 Knowing that the coefficient of static friction between the 30-N block and the incline is $\mu_s = 0.25$, determine (*a*) the smallest value of P required to maintain the block in equilibrium, (*b*) the corresponding value of β.

8.9 A 15-N block is at rest as shown. Determine the positive range of values of θ for which the block is in equilibrium if (*a*) θ is less than 90°, (*b*) θ is between 90° and 180°.

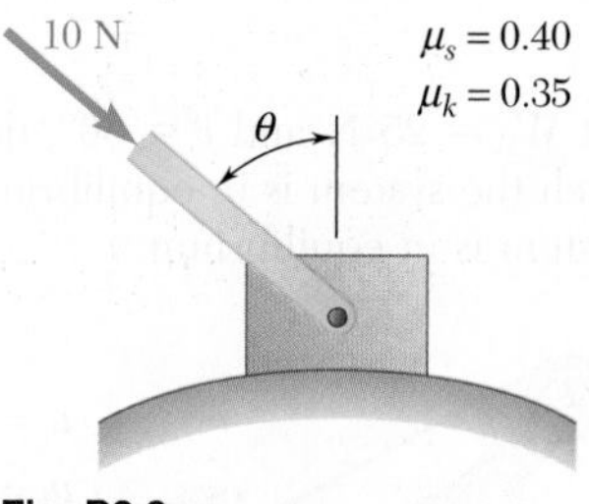

Fig. P8.9

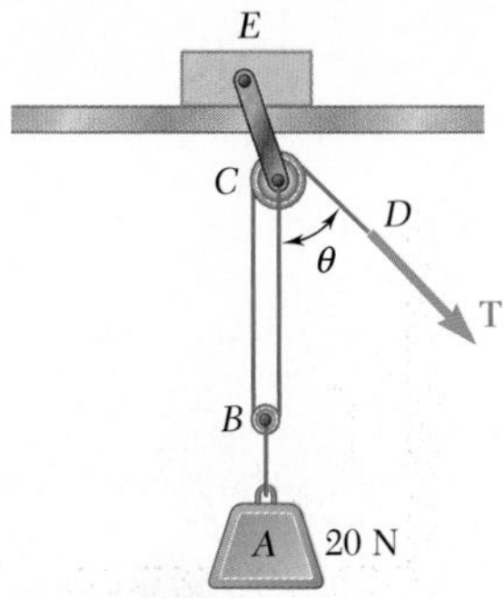

Fig. P8.10

8.10 The 20-N block A hangs from a cable as shown. Pulley C is connected by a short link to block E which rests on a horizontal rail. Knowing that the coefficient of static friction between block E and the rail is 0.35 and neglecting the weight of block E and friction in the pulleys, determine the maximum allowable value of θ if the system is to remain in equilibrium.

8.11 and 8.12 The coefficients of friction are $\mu_s = 0.40$ and $\mu_k = 0.30$ between all surfaces of contact. Determine the force **P** for which motion of the 30-kg block is impending if cable AB (*a*) is attached as shown, (*b*) is removed.

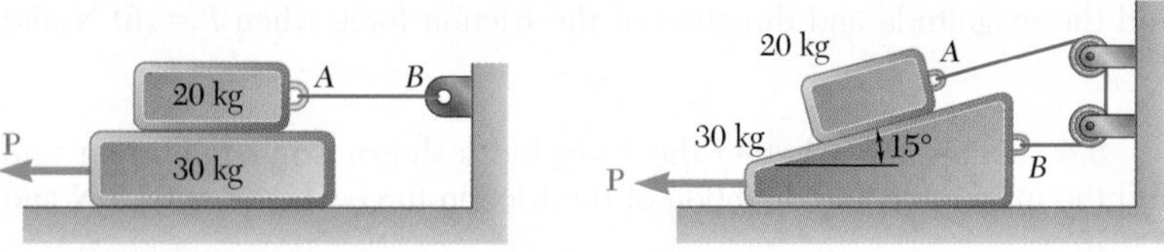

Fig. P8.11 Fig. P8.12

8.13 The 16-N block A is attached to link AC and rests on the 24-N block B. Knowing that the coefficient of static friction is 0.20 between all surfaces of contact and neglecting the weight of the link, determine the value of θ for which motion of block B is impending.

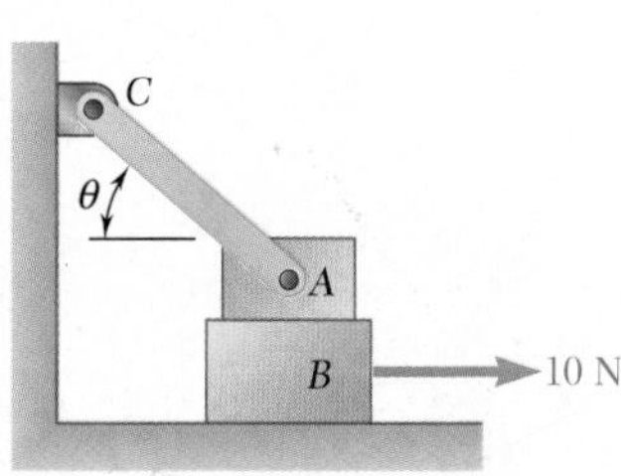

Fig. P8.13

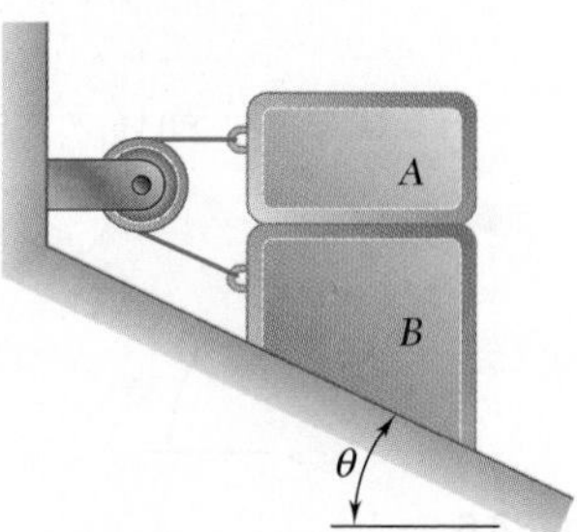

Fig. P8.14

8.14 The 20-N block A and the 40-N block B are at rest on an incline as shown. Knowing that the coefficient of static friction is 0.25 between all surfaces of contact, determine the value of θ for which motion is impending.

8.15 A packing crate of mass 40 kg must be moved to the left along the floor without tipping. Knowing that the coefficient of static friction between the crate and the floor is 0.35, determine (*a*) the largest allowable value of α, (*b*) the corresponding magnitude of the force **P**.

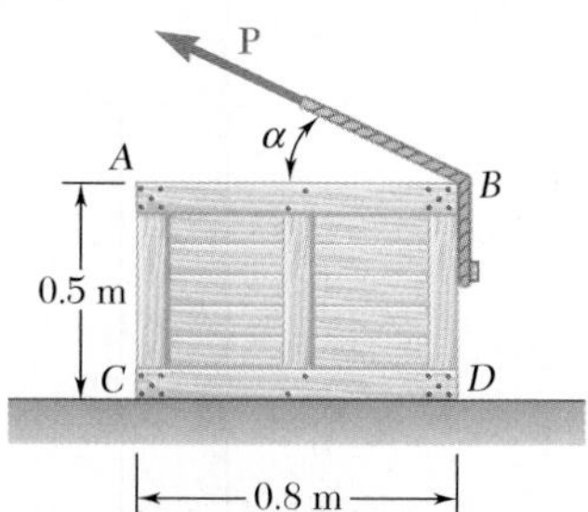

Fig. P8.15 and *P8.16*

8.16 A packing crate of mass 40 kg is pulled by a rope as shown. The coefficient of static friction between the crate and the floor is 0.35. If $\alpha = 40°$, determine (*a*) the magnitude of the force **P** required for impending motion of the crate, (*b*) whether sliding or tipping is impending.

8.17 The cylinder shown is of weight W and radius r. Express in terms of W and r the magnitude of the largest couple **M** which can be applied to the cylinder if it is not to rotate assuming that the coefficient of static friction is (*a*) zero at A and 0.36 at B, (*b*) 0.30 at A and 0.36 at B.

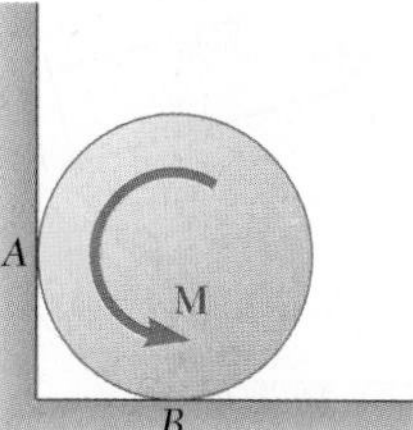

Fig. P8.17

8.18 A couple of magnitude 50 N · m is applied to the drum. Determine the smallest force that must be exerted by the hydraulic cylinder if the drum is not to rotate when the applied couple is directed (*a*) clockwise, (*b*) counterclockwise.

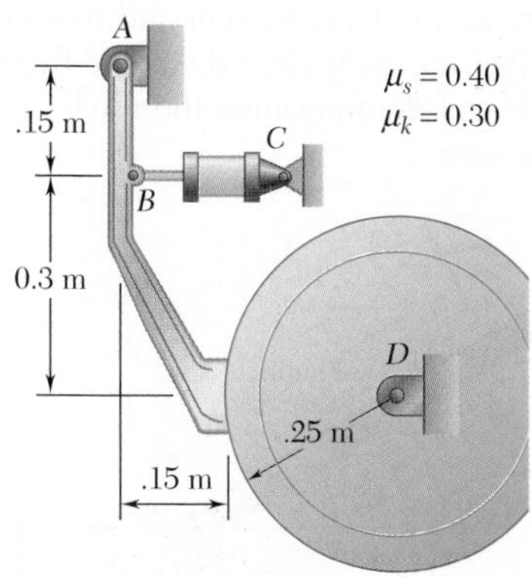

Fig. P8.18 and *P8.19*

8.19 The hydraulic cylinder exerts on pin B a force of 600 N directed to the right. Determine the moment of the friction force about the axle of the drum when the drum is rotating (*a*) clockwise, (*b*) counterclockwise.

***8.20** A cord is attached to and partially wound around a cylinder of weight W and radius r that rests on an incline as shown. Knowing that the coefficient of static friction between the cylinder and the incline is 0.35, find (*a*) the smallest allowable value of θ if the cylinder is to remain in equilibrium, (*b*) the corresponding value of the tension in the cord.

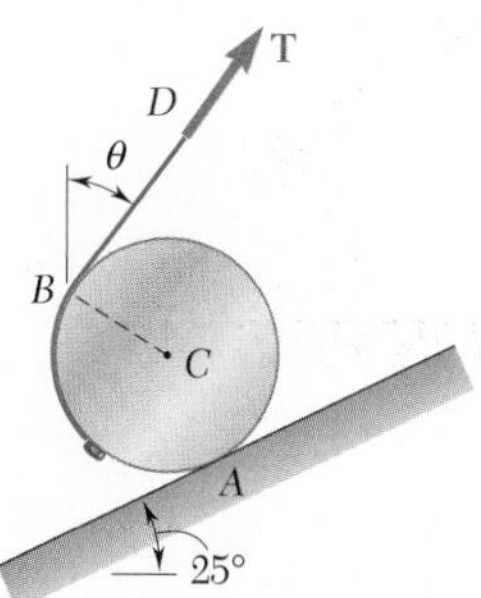

Fig. P8.20

8.21 and *8.22* A 6.5-m ladder AB of mass 10 kg leans against a wall as shown. Assuming that the coefficient of static friction μ_s is the same at both surfaces of contact, determine the smallest value of μ_s for which equilibrium can be maintained.

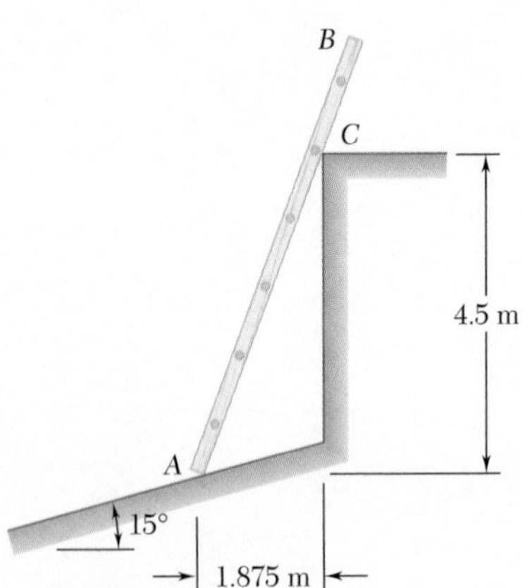

Fig. P8.21

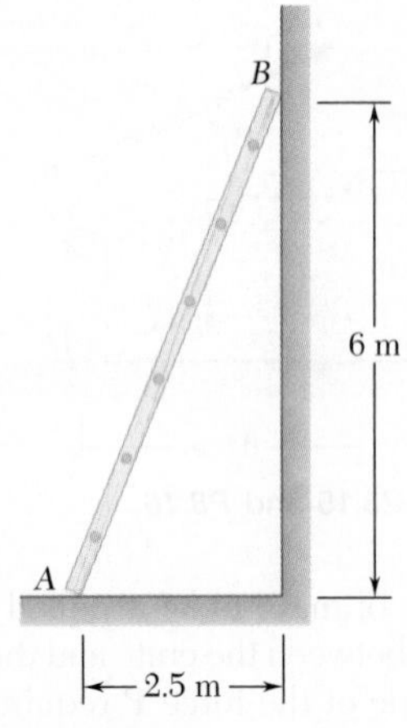

Fig. *P8.22*

8.23 End A of a slender, uniform rod of weight W and length L bears on a horizontal surface as shown, while end B is supported by a cord BC of length L. Knowing that the coefficient of static friction is 0.40, determine (a) the value of θ for which motion is impending, (b) the corresponding value of the tension in the cord.

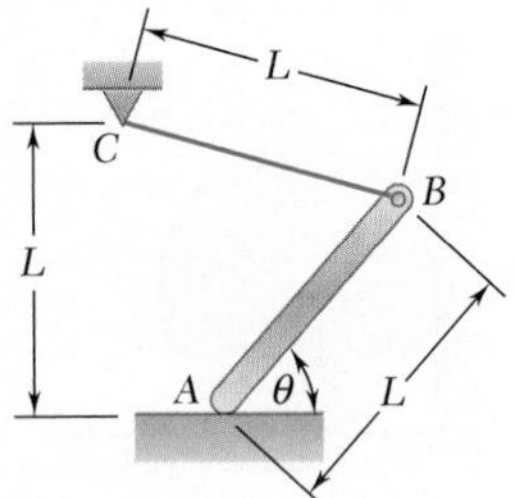

Fig. P8.23

8.24 A slender rod of length L is lodged between peg C and the vertical wall and supports a load $\mathbf{P}$ at end A. Knowing that $\theta = 35°$ and that the coefficient of static friction is 0.20 at both B and C, determine the range of values of the ratio L/a for which equilibrium is maintained.

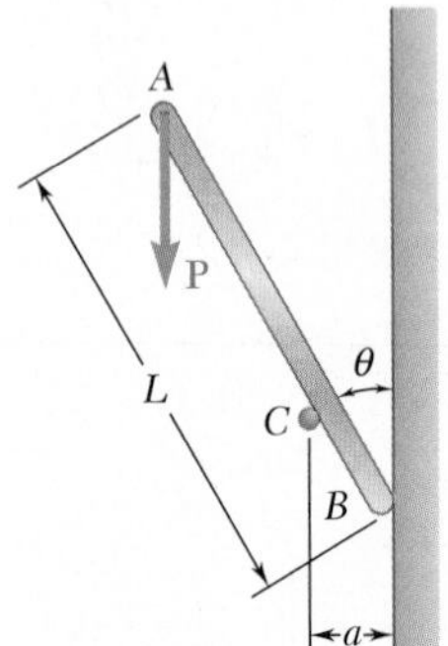

Fig. P8.24

8.25 The shear shown is used to cut and trim electronic-circuit-board laminates. Knowing that the coefficient of kinetic friction between the blade and the vertical guide is 0.20, determine the force exerted by the edge E of the blade on the laminate.

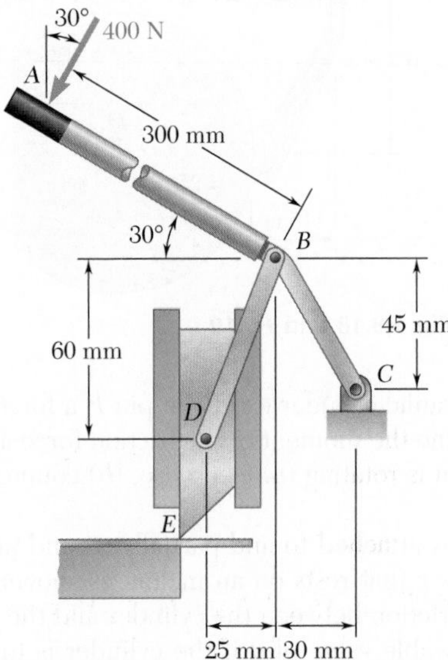

Fig. P8.25

8.26 The basic components of a clamping device are bar AB, locking plate CD, and lever EFG; the dimensions of the slot in CD are slightly larger than those of the cross section of AB. To engage the clamp, AB is pushed against the workpiece, and then force **P** is applied. Knowing that $P = 40$ N and neglecting the friction force between the lever and the plate, determine the smallest allowable value of the coefficient of static friction between the bar and the plate.

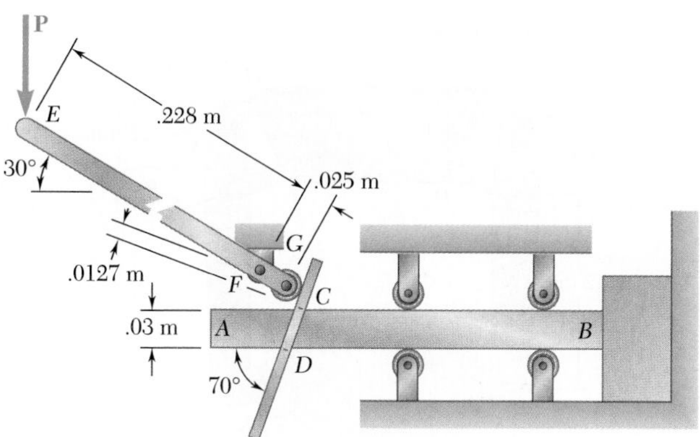

Fig. P8.26

8.27 The friction tongs shown are used to lift a 750-N casting. Knowing that $h = .9$ m, determine the smallest allowable value of the coefficient of static friction between the casting and blocks D and D'.

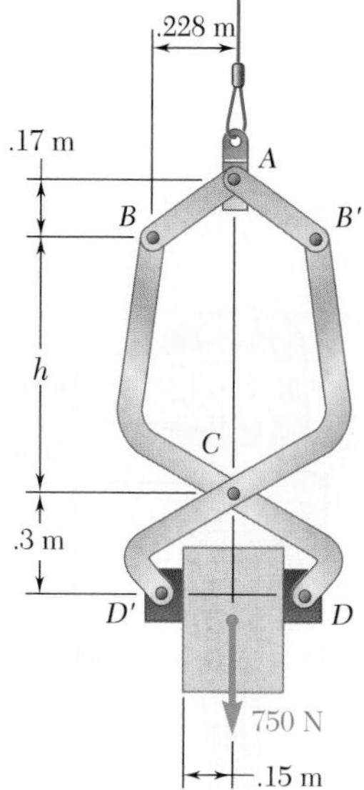

Fig. P8.27

8.28 The steel-plate clamp shown is used to lift a steel plate H weighing 550 N. Knowing that the normal force exerted on steel cam EG by pin D forms an angle of 40° with the horizontal and neglecting the friction force between the cam and the pin, determine the smallest allowable value of the coefficient of static friction between the cam and the plate.

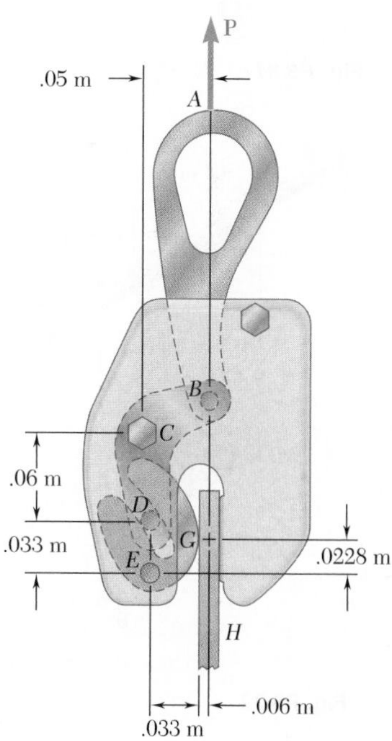

Fig. P8.28

8.29 A child having a mass of 18 kg is seated halfway between the ends of a small, 16-kg table as shown. The coefficient of static friction is 0.20 between the ends of the table and the floor. If a second child pushes on edge B of the table top at a point directly opposite to the first child with a force **P** lying in a vertical plane parallel to the ends of the table and having a magnitude of 66 N, determine the range of values of θ for which the table will (*a*) tip, (*b*) slide.

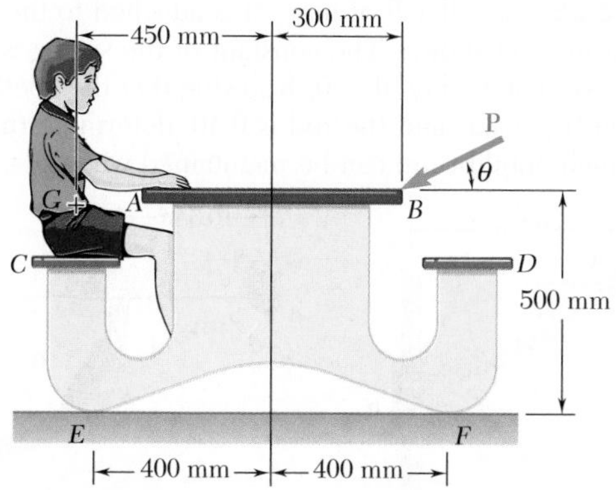

Fig. *P8.29*

*8.30 The lift-tong mechanism shown consists of twin four-bar linkages and is used to lift a 40-kg machine component. Knowing that L_{AB} = 36 mm, determine the smallest allowable value of the coefficient of static friction between the component and the gripping pads when (*a*) $\alpha = 0$, (*b*) $\alpha = 30°$. (*Hint:* Assume that lines drawn through pins *A* and *C* and *G* and *I* are vertical for all values of α.)

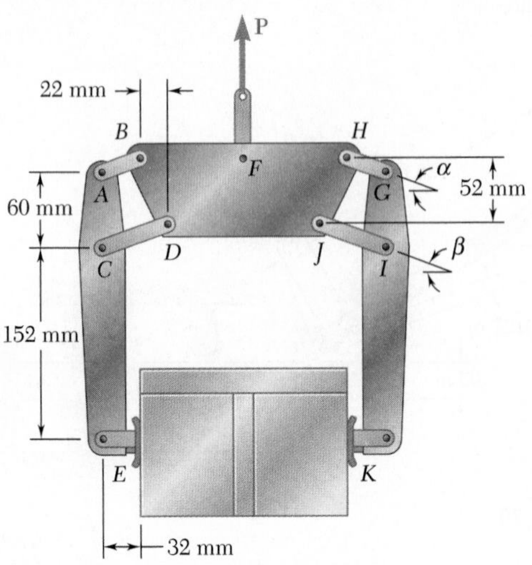

Fig. P8.30

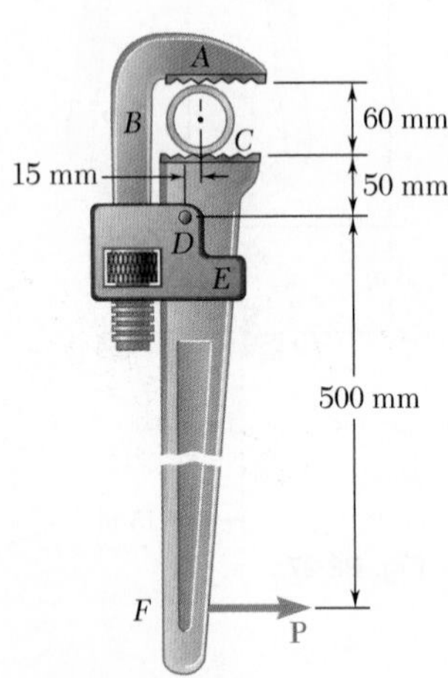

Fig. *P8.31*

8.31 A pipe of diameter 60 mm is gripped by the Stillson wrench shown. Portions *AB* and *DE* of the wrench are rigidly attached to each other, and portion *CF* is connected by a pin at *D*. If the wrench is to grip the pipe and be self-locking, determine the required minimum coefficients of friction at *A* and *C*.

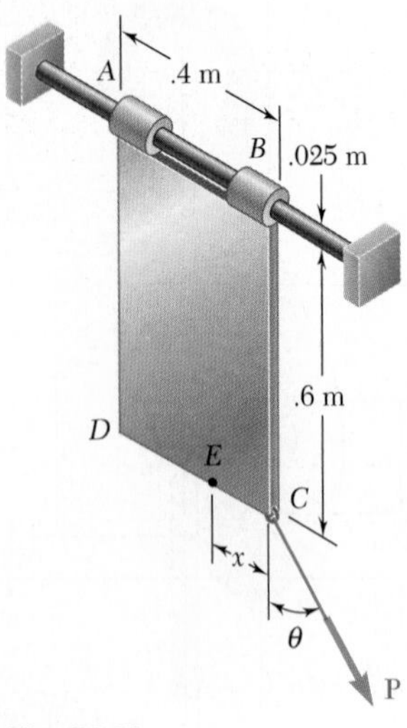

Fig. P8.32

8.32 A light metal panel is welded to two short sleeves of .025-m inside diameter that can slide on a horizontal rod. The coefficients of friction between the sleeves and the rod are $\mu_s = 0.40$ and $\mu_k = 0.30$. A cord attached to corner *C* is used to move the panel along the rod. Knowing that the cord lies in the same vertical plane as the panel, determine the range of values of θ for which the panel will be in impending motion to the right.

8.33 (*a*) Solve Prob. 8.32 assuming that the cord is attached at point *E* at a distance $x = .1$ m from corner *C*. (*b*) Determine the largest value of x for which the panel can be moved to the right.

8.34 and 8.35 A collar *B* of mass *m* is attached to the spring *AB* and can move along the rod shown. The constant of the spring is 1.5 kN/m and the spring is unstretched when $\theta = 0$. Knowing that the coefficient of static friction between the collar and the rod is 0.40, determine the range of values of *m* for which equilibrium can be maintained when $\theta = 30°$.

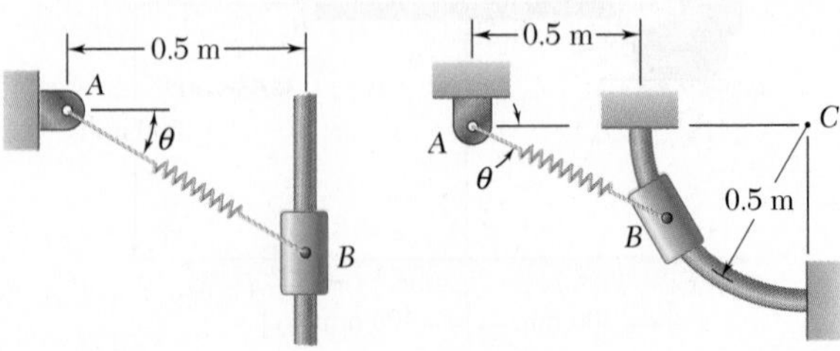

Fig. P8.34

Fig. P8.35

8.36 Denoting by μ_s the coefficient of static friction between the collar C and the horizontal rod, determine the largest magnitude of the couple **M** for which equilibrium is maintained. Explain what happens if $\mu_s \geq \tan\theta$.

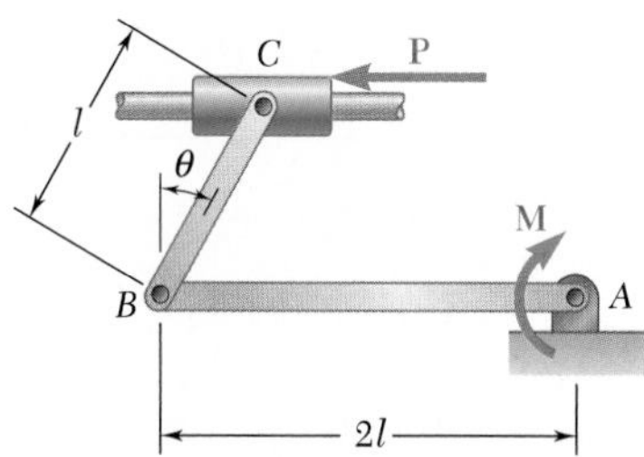

Fig. P8.36

8.37 Bar AB rests on the two quarter-circle surfaces shown. A force **P** is applied at point C, which is located at a distance a from end A. Neglecting the weight of the bar and knowing that the coefficient of static friction between the bar and each of the surfaces is 0.35, determine the smallest value of the ratio a/L for which the bar is in equilibrium.

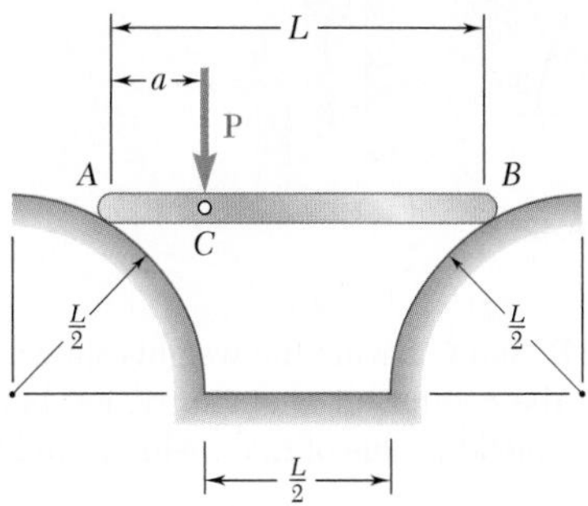

Fig. P8.37

8.38 The 90-N block A and the 60-N block B are connected by a slender rod of negligible weight. The coefficient of static friction is 0.40 between all surfaces of contact. Knowing that for the position shown the rod is horizontal, determine the range of values of P for which equilibrium is maintained.

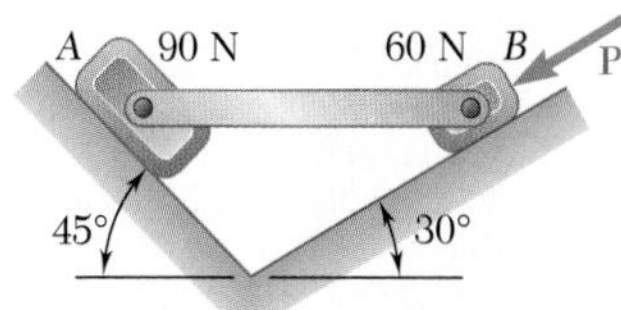

Fig. *P8.38*

8.39 Two rods are connected by a collar at B. A couple $\mathbf{M}_A$ of magnitude 12 N · m is applied to rod AB. Knowing that $\mu_s = 0.30$ between the collar and rod AB, determine the largest couple $\mathbf{M}_C$ for which equilibrium can be maintained.

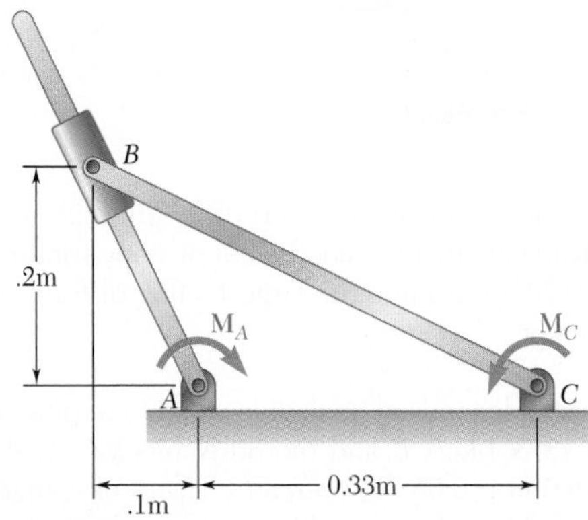

Fig. *P8.39*

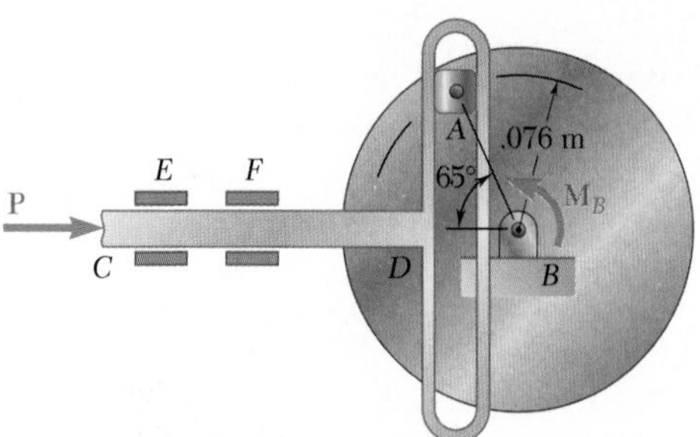

Fig. P8.40

8.40 Slider A is pinned to flywheel B and slides in the slot of yoke CD. Neglecting friction in bearings E and F and knowing that $P = 8$ N and $\mu_s = 0.25$ between the slider and the yoke, determine (*a*) the largest couple $\mathbf{M}_B$ for which equilibrium can be maintained, (*b*) the smallest couple $\mathbf{M}_B$ for which equilibrium can be maintained.

8.41 The 12-N slender rod AB is pinned at A and rests on the 36-N cylinder C. Knowing that the diameter of the cylinder is 0.3 m and that the coefficient of static friction is 0.35 between all surfaces of contact, determine the largest magnitude of the force **P** for which equilibrium is maintained.

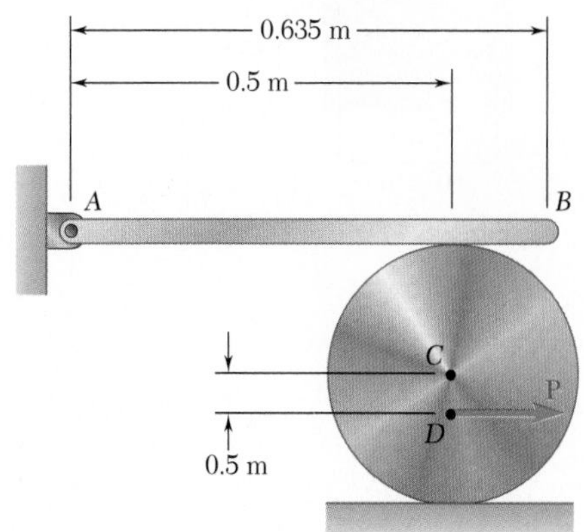

Fig. P8.41

8.42 The masses of blocks A and C are 2.4 kg and 6 kg, respectively. Knowing that $\mu_s = 0.50$ between block A and the incline and $\mu_s = 0.30$ between block C and the horizontal surface, determine (a) the smallest value of the mass of block B for which the blocks are in equilibrium, (b) the largest value of the mass of block B for which the blocks are in equilibrium.

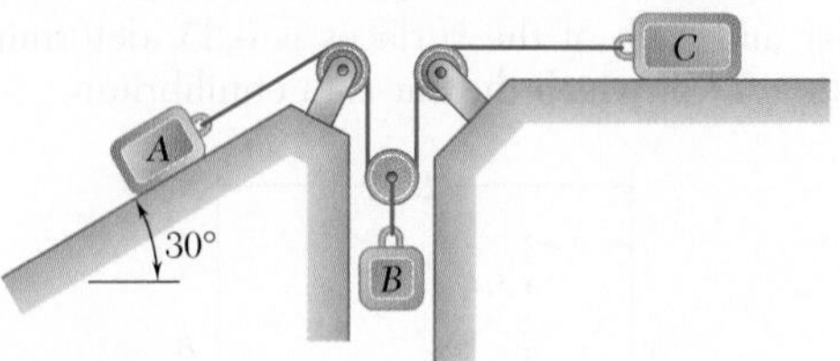

Fig. P8.42

8.43 Blocks A, B, and C having the weights shown are at rest on an incline. Denoting by μ_s the coefficient of static friction between all surfaces of contact, determine the smallest value of μ_s for which equilibrium is maintained.

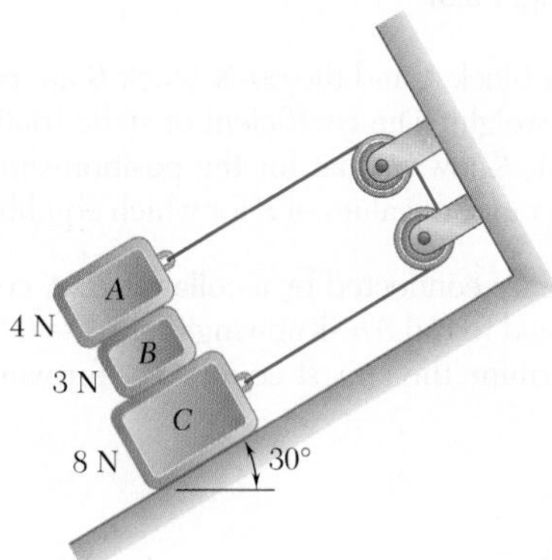

Fig. P8.43

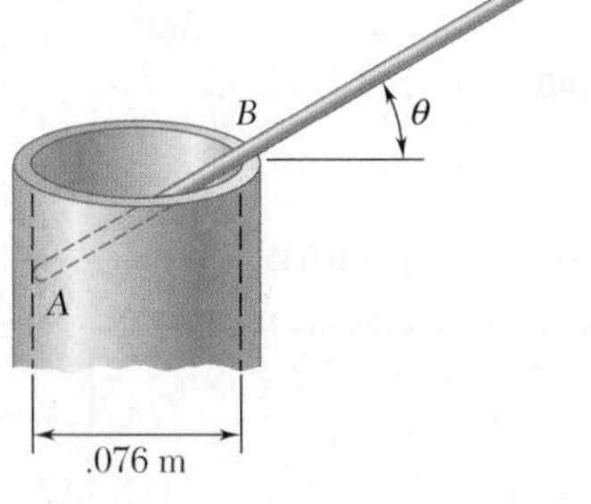

Fig. *P8.44*

8.44 A slender, uniform steel rod of length .228 m is placed inside a pipe as shown. Knowing that the coefficient of static friction between the rod and the pipe is 0.20, determine the largest value of θ for which the rod will not fall into the pipe.

8.45 Two slender rods of negligible weight are pin-connected at A and attached to the 18-N block B and the 80-N block C as shown. The coefficient of static friction is 0.55 between all surfaces of contact. Determine the range of values of P for which equilibrium is maintained.

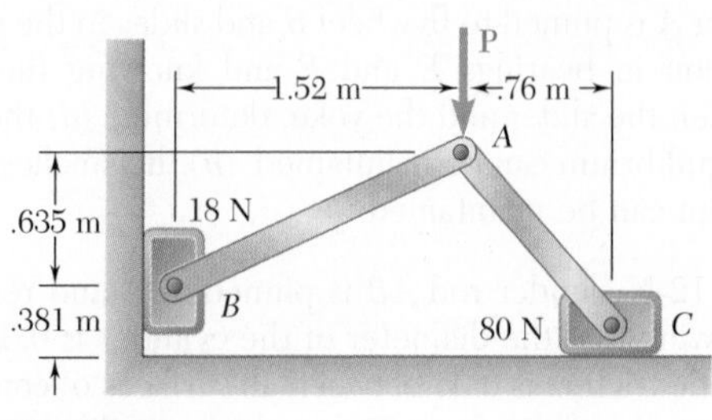

Fig. P8.45

8.5. WEDGES

Wedges are simple machines used to raise large stone blocks and other heavy loads. These loads can be raised by applying to the wedge a force usually considerably smaller than the weight of the load. In addition, because of the friction between the surfaces in contact, a properly shaped wedge will remain in place after being forced under the load. Wedges can thus be used advantageously to make small adjustments in the position of heavy pieces of machinery.

Consider the block A shown in Fig. 8.7a. This block rests against a vertical wall B and is to be raised slightly by forcing a wedge C between block A and a second wedge D. We want to find the minimum value of the force $\mathbf{P}$ which must be applied to the wedge C to move the block. It will be assumed that the weight $\mathbf{W}$ of the block is known, either given in pounds or determined in newtons from the mass of the block expressed in kilograms.

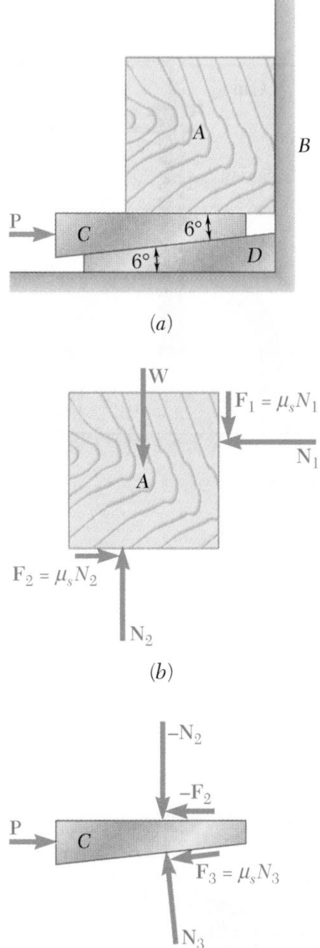

Fig. 8.7

The free-body diagrams of block A and of wedge C have been drawn in Fig. 8.7b and c. The forces acting on the block include its weight and the normal and friction forces at the surfaces of contact with wall B and wedge C. The magnitudes of the friction forces $\mathbf{F}_1$ and $\mathbf{F}_2$ are equal, respectively, to $\mu_s N_1$ and $\mu_s N_2$ since the motion of the block is impending. It is important to show the friction forces with their correct sense. Since the block will move upward, the force $\mathbf{F}_1$ exerted by the wall on the block must be directed downward. On the other hand, since the wedge C will move to the right, the relative motion of A with respect to C is to the left and the force $\mathbf{F}_2$ exerted by C on A must be directed to the right.

Considering now the free body C in Fig. 8.7c, we note that the forces acting on C include the applied force $\mathbf{P}$ and the normal and friction forces at the surfaces of contact with A and D. The weight of the wedge is small compared with the other forces involved and can be neglected. The forces exerted by A on C are equal and opposite to the forces $\mathbf{N}_2$ and $\mathbf{F}_2$ exerted by C on A and are denoted, respectively, by $-\mathbf{N}_2$ and $-\mathbf{F}_2$; the friction force $-\mathbf{F}_2$ must therefore be directed to the left. We check that the force $\mathbf{F}_3$ exerted by D is also directed to the left.

The total number of unknowns involved in the two free-body diagrams can be reduced to four if the friction forces are expressed in terms of the normal forces. Expressing that block A and wedge C are in equilibrium will provide four equations which can be solved to obtain the magnitude of $\mathbf{P}$. It should be noted that in the example considered here, it will be more convenient to replace each pair of normal and friction forces by their resultant. Each free body is then subjected to only three forces, and the problem can be solved by drawing the corresponding force triangles (see Sample Prob. 8.4).

Photo 8.2 Wedges are used as shown to split tree trunks because the normal forces exerted by the wedges on the wood are much larger than the forces required to insert the wedges.

8.6. SQUARE-THREADED SCREWS

Square-threaded screws are frequently used in jacks, presses, and other mechanisms. Their analysis is similar to the analysis of a block sliding along an inclined plane.

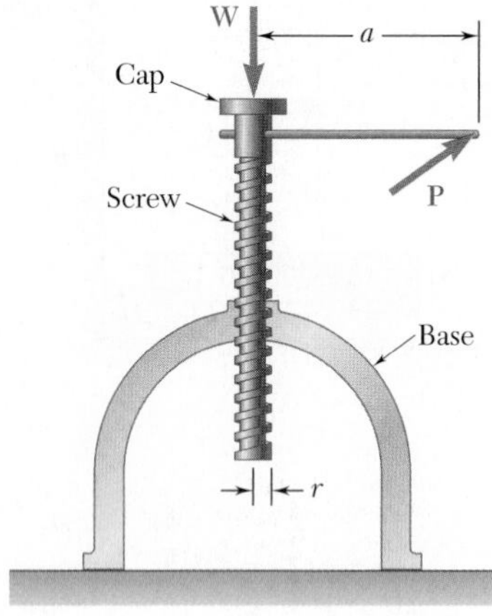

Fig. 8.8

Consider the jack shown in Fig. 8.8. The screw carries a load **W** and is supported by the base of the jack. Contact between the screw and the base takes place along a portion of their threads. By applying a force **P** on the handle, the screw can be made to turn and to raise the load **W**.

The thread of the base has been unwrapped and shown as a straight line in Fig. 8.9*a*. The correct slope was obtained by plotting horizontally the product $2\pi r$, where r is the mean radius of the thread, and vertically the *lead* L of the screw, that is, the distance through which the screw advances in one turn. The angle θ this line forms with the horizontal is the *lead angle*. Since the force of friction between two surfaces in contact does not depend upon the area of contact, a much smaller than actual area of contact between the two threads can be assumed, and the screw can be represented by the block shown in Fig. 8.9*a*. It should be noted, however, that in this analysis of the jack, the friction between the cap and the screw is neglected.

The free-body diagram of the block should include the load **W**, the reaction **R** of the base thread, and a horizontal force **Q** having the same effect as the force **P** exerted on the handle. The force **Q** should have the same moment as **P** about the axis of the screw and its magnitude should thus be $Q = Pa/r$. The force **Q**, and thus the force **P** required to raise the load **W**, can be obtained from the free-body diagram shown in Fig. 8.9*a*. The friction angle is taken equal to ϕ_s since the load will presumably be raised through a succession of short strokes. In mechanisms providing for the continuous rotation of a screw, it may be desirable to distinguish between the force required for impending motion (using ϕ_s) and that required to maintain motion (using ϕ_k).

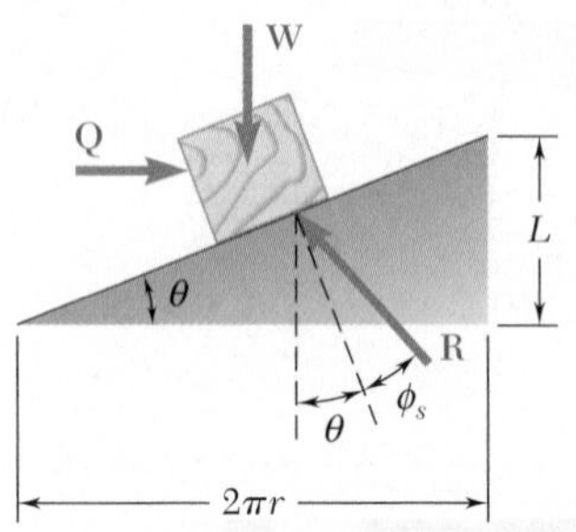

(*a*) Impending motion upward

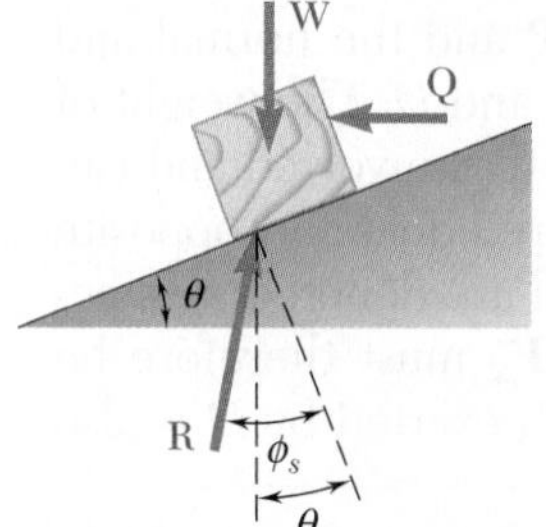

(*b*) Impending motion downward with $\phi_s > \theta$

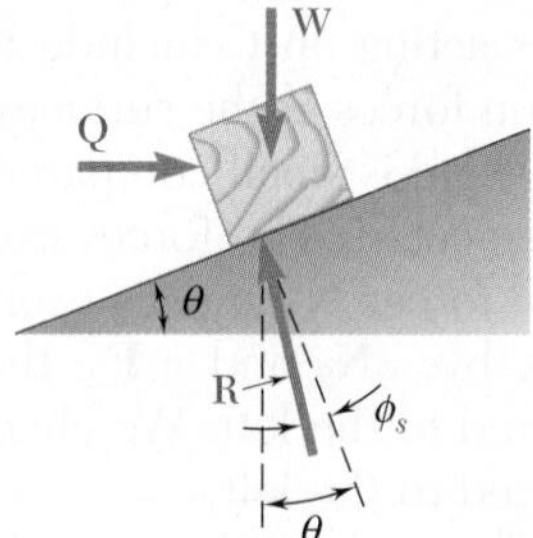

(*c*) Impending motion downward with $\phi_s < \theta$

Fig. 8.9 Block-and-incline analysis of a screw.

If the friction angle ϕ_s is larger than the lead angle θ, the screw is said to be *self-locking;* it will remain in place under the load. To lower the load, we must then apply the force shown in Fig. 8.9*b*. If ϕ_s is smaller than θ, the screw will unwind under the load; it is then necessary to apply the force shown in Fig. 8.9*c* to maintain equilibrium.

The lead of a screw should not be confused with its *pitch*. The lead was defined as the distance through which the screw advances in one turn; the pitch is the distance measured between two consecutive threads. While lead and pitch are equal in the case of *single-threaded* screws, they are different in the case of *multiple-threaded* screws, that is, screws having several independent threads. It is easily verified that for double-threaded screws, the lead is twice as large as the pitch; for triple-threaded screws, it is three times as large as the pitch; etc.

SAMPLE PROBLEM 8.4

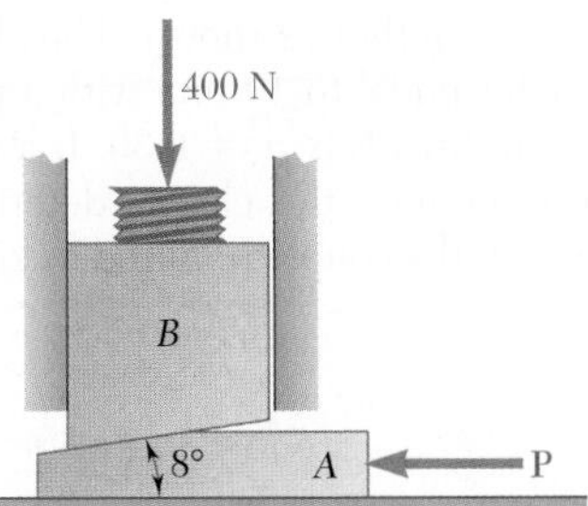

The position of the machine block B is adjusted by moving the wedge A. Knowing that the coefficient of static friction is 0.35 between all surfaces of contact, determine the force $\mathbf{P}$ for which motion of block B (*a*) is impending upward, (*b*) is impending downward.

SOLUTION

For each part, the free-body diagrams of block B and wedge A are drawn, together with the corresponding force triangles, and the law of sines is used to find the desired forces. We note that since $\mu_s = 0.35$, the angle of friction is

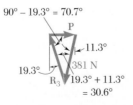

$$\phi_s = \tan^{-1} 0.35 = 19.3°$$

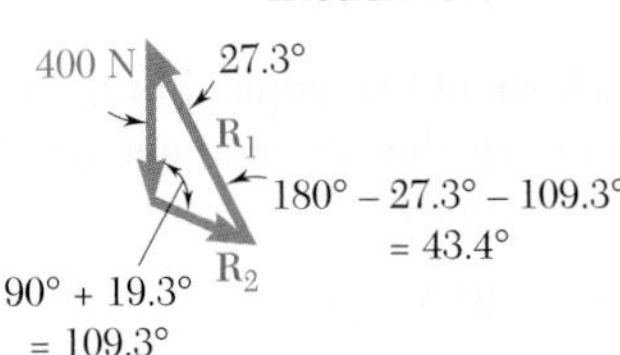

a. Force P for Impending Motion of Block Upward

Free Body: Block B

$$\frac{R_1}{\sin 109.3°} = \frac{400\text{ N}}{\sin 43.4°}$$

$$R_1 = 549\text{ N}$$

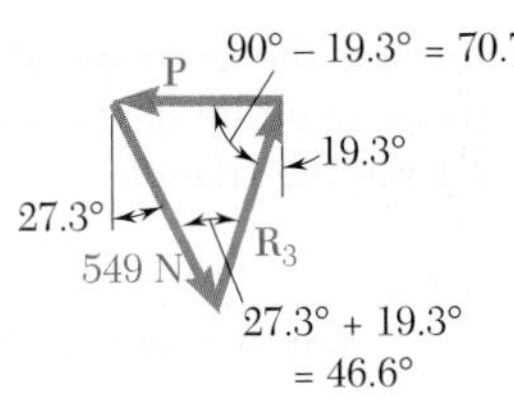

Free Body: Wedge A

$$\frac{P}{\sin 46.6°} = \frac{549\text{ N}}{\sin 70.7°}$$

$$P = 423\text{ N} \qquad \mathbf{P} = 423\text{ N} \leftarrow \blacktriangleleft$$

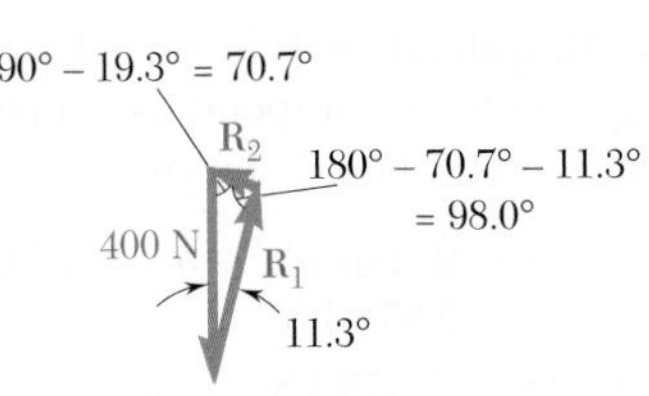

b. Force P for Impending Motion of Block Downward

Free Body: Block B

$$\frac{R_1}{\sin 70.7°} = \frac{400\text{ N}}{\sin 98.0°}$$

$$R_1 = 381\text{ N}$$

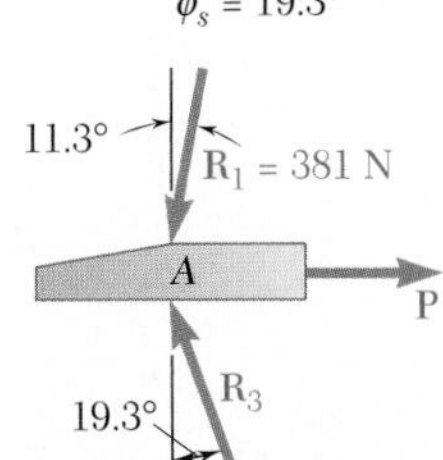

Free Body: Wedge A

$$\frac{P}{\sin 30.6°} = \frac{381\text{ N}}{\sin 70.7°}$$

$$P = 206\text{ N} \qquad \mathbf{P} = 206\text{ N} \rightarrow \blacktriangleleft$$

SAMPLE PROBLEM 8.5

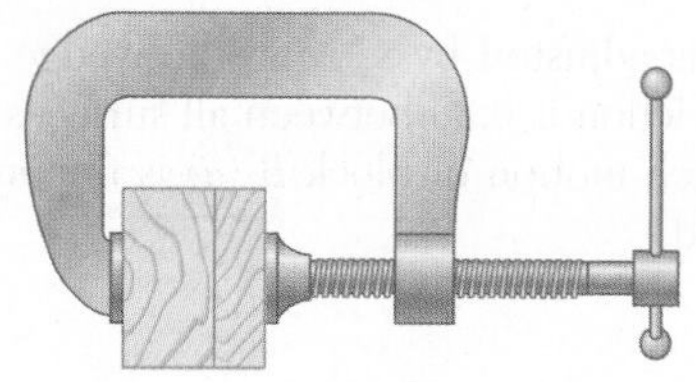

A clamp is used to hold two pieces of wood together as shown. The clamp has a double square thread of mean diameter equal to 10 mm with a pitch of 2 mm. The coefficient of friction between threads is $\mu_s = 0.30$. If a maximum couple of 40 N · m is applied in tightening the clamp, determine (*a*) the force exerted on the pieces of wood, (*b*) the couple required to loosen the clamp.

SOLUTION

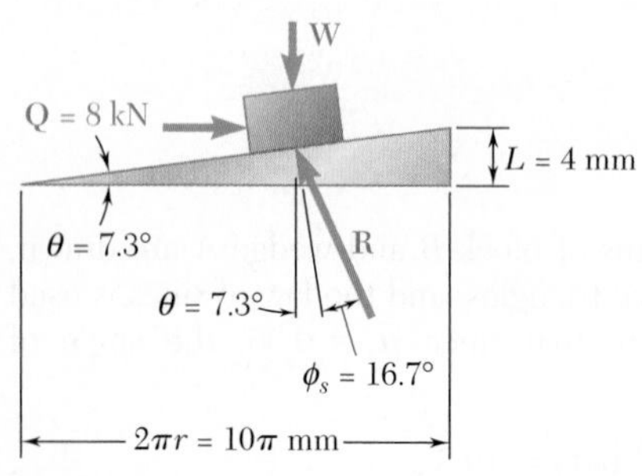

***a.* Force Exerted by Clamp.** The mean radius of the screw is $r = 5$ mm. Since the screw is double-threaded, the lead L is equal to twice the pitch: $L = 2(2 \text{ mm}) = 4$ mm. The lead angle θ and the friction angle ϕ_s are obtained by writing

$$\tan \theta = \frac{L}{2\pi r} = \frac{4 \text{ mm}}{10\pi \text{ mm}} = 0.1273 \qquad \theta = 7.3^\circ$$

$$\tan \phi_s = \mu_s = 0.30 \qquad \phi_s = 16.7^\circ$$

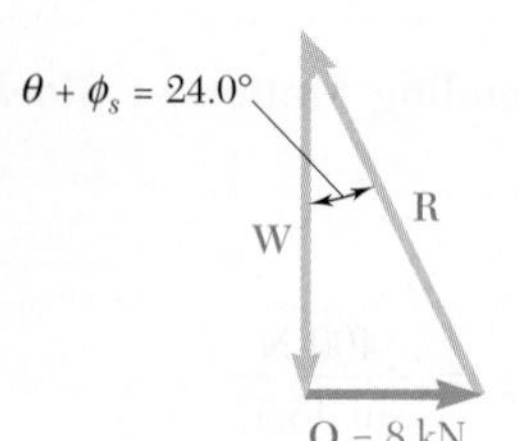

The force **Q** which should be applied to the block representing the screw is obtained by expressing that its moment Qr about the axis of the screw is equal to the applied couple.

$$Q(5 \text{ mm}) = 40 \text{ N} \cdot \text{m}$$

$$Q = \frac{40 \text{ N} \cdot \text{m}}{5 \text{ mm}} = \frac{40 \text{ N} \cdot \text{m}}{5 \times 10^{-3} \text{ m}} = 8000 \text{ N} = 8 \text{ kN}$$

The free-body diagram and the corresponding force triangle can now be drawn for the block; the magnitude of the force **W** exerted on the pieces of wood is obtained by solving the triangle.

$$W = \frac{Q}{\tan(\theta + \phi_s)} = \frac{8 \text{ kN}}{\tan 24.0^\circ}$$

$W = 17.97$ kN ◀

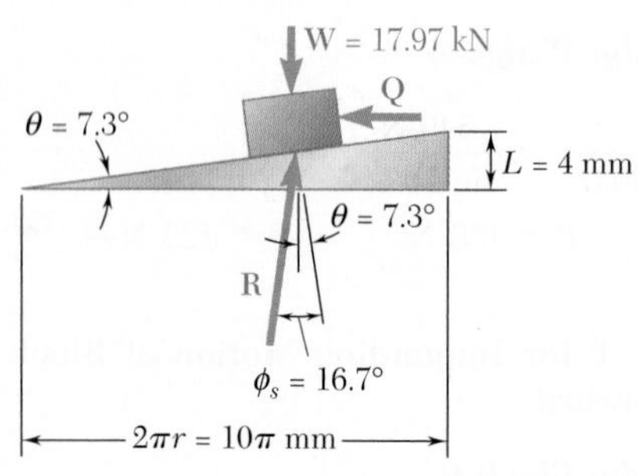

***b.* Couple Required to Loosen Clamp.** The force **Q** required to loosen the clamp and the corresponding couple are obtained from the free-body diagram and force triangle shown.

$$Q = W \tan(\phi_s - \theta) = (17.97 \text{ kN}) \tan 9.4^\circ$$
$$= 2.975 \text{ kN}$$

$$\text{Couple} = Qr = (2.975 \text{ kN})(5 \text{ mm})$$
$$= (2.975 \times 10^3 \text{ N})(5 \times 10^{-3} \text{ m}) = 14.87 \text{ N} \cdot \text{m}$$

Couple = 14.87 N · m ◀

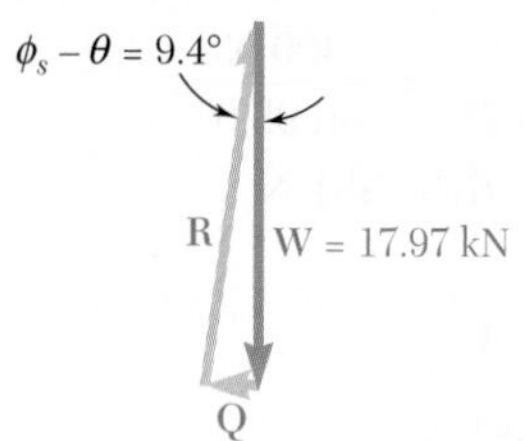

SOLVING PROBLEMS ON YOUR OWN

In this lesson you learned to apply the laws of friction to the solution of problems involving *wedges* and *square-threaded screws*.

1. ***Wedges.*** Keep the following in mind when solving a problem involving a wedge:

a. First draw a free-body diagram of the wedge and of all the other bodies involved. Carefully note the sense of the relative motion of all surfaces of contact and show each friction force acting in *a direction opposite* to the direction of that relative motion.

b. Show the maximum static friction force $\mathbf{F}_m$ at each surface if the wedge is to be inserted or removed, *since motion will be impending in each of these cases.*

c. The reaction R and the angle of friction, rather than the normal force and the friction force, can be used in many applications. You can then draw one or more force triangles and determine the unknown quantities either graphically or trigonometrically [Sample Prob. 8.4].

2. ***Square-Threaded Screws.*** The analysis of a square-threaded screw is equivalent to the analysis of a block sliding on an incline. To draw the appropriate incline, you should unwrap the thread of the screw and represent it by a straight line [Sample Prob. 8.5]. When solving a problem involving a square-threaded screw, keep the following in mind:

a. Do not confuse the pitch of a screw with the lead of a screw. The *pitch* of a screw is the distance between two consecutive threads, while the *lead* of a screw is the distance the screw advances in one full turn. The lead and the pitch are equal only in single-threaded screws. In a double-threaded screw, the lead is twice the pitch.

b. The couple required to tighten a screw is different from the couple required to loosen it. Also, screws used in jacks and clamps are usually *self-locking;* that is, the screw will remain stationary as long as no couple is applied to it, and a couple must be applied to the screw to loosen it [Sample Prob. 8.5].

Problems

8.46 and 8.47 Two 8° wedges of negligible weight are used to move and position a 530-N block. Knowing that the coefficient of static friction is 0.40 at all surfaces of contact, determine the magnitude of the force **P** for which motion of the block is impending.

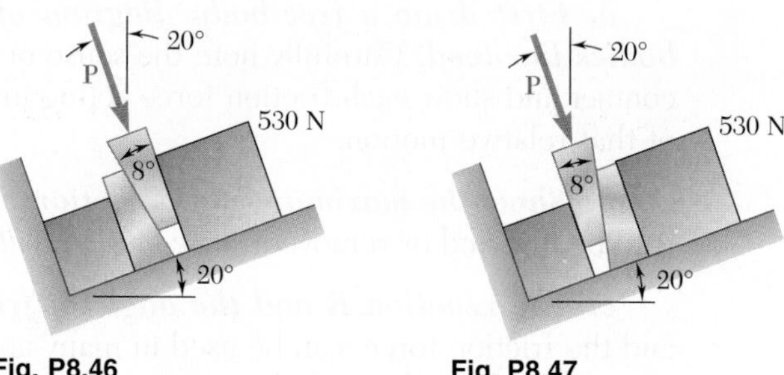

Fig. P8.46 Fig. P8.47

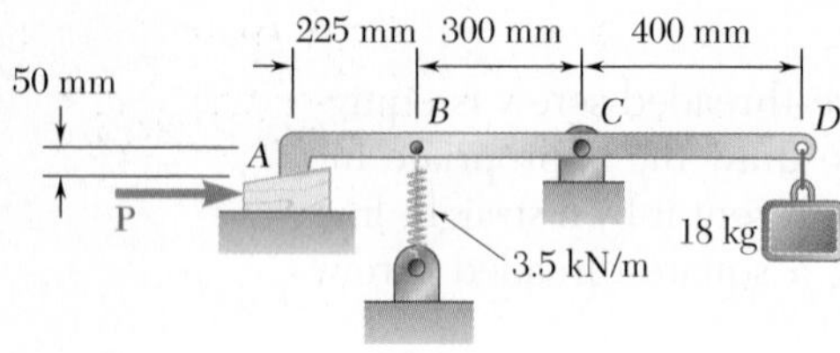

Fig. *P8.48*

8.48 An 18-kg mass is hung from a lever which rests against a 10° wedge at *A* and is supported by a frictionless pin at *C*. Knowing that the coefficient of static friction is 0.25 at both surfaces of the wedge and that for the position shown the spring is stretched 100 mm, determine (*a*) the magnitude of the force **P** for which motion of the wedge is impending, (*b*) the components of the corresponding reaction at *C*.

8.49 Solve Prob. 8.48 assuming that force **P** is directed to the left.

8.50 and 8.51 The elevation of the end of a steel beam supported by a concrete floor is adjusted by means of the steel wedges *E* and *F*. The base plate *CD* has been welded to the lower flange of the beam, and the end reaction of the beam is known to be 90 kN. The coefficient of static friction is 0.30 between the two steel surfaces and 0.60 between the steel and the concrete. If horizontal motion of the beam is prevented by the force **Q**, determine (*a*) the force **P** required for impending upward motion of the beam, (*b*) the corresponding force **Q**.

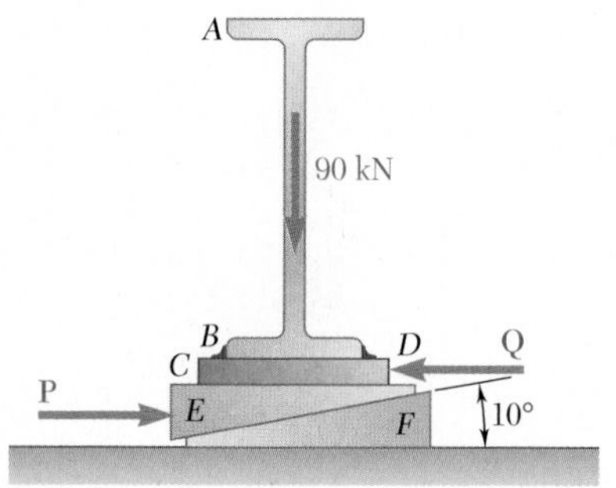

Fig. P8.50

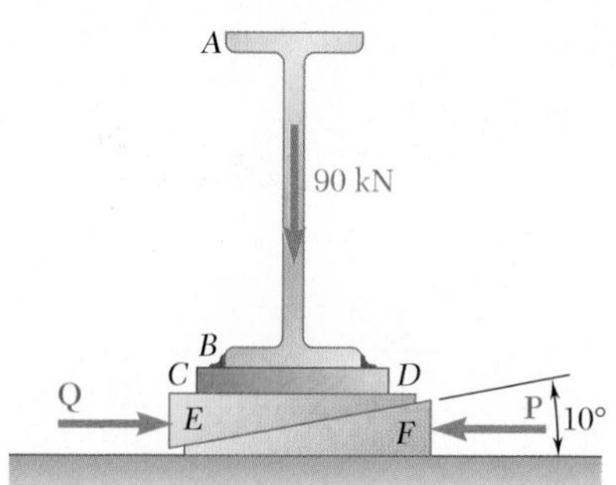

Fig. P8.51

8.52 and *8.53* A 16° wedge A of negligible weight is placed between two 175-N blocks B and C which are at rest on inclined surfaces as shown. The coefficient of static friction is 0.40 between both the wedge and the blocks and block C and the incline. Determine the magnitude of the force **P** for which motion of the wedge is impending when the coefficient of static friction between block B and the incline is (*a*) 0.40, (*b*) 0.60.

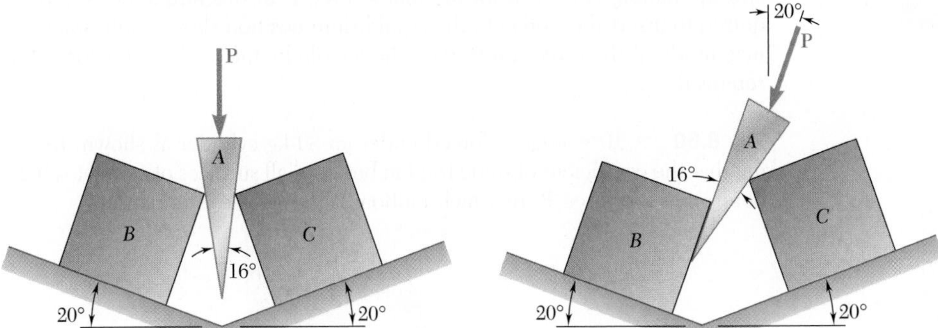

Fig. P8.52 **Fig. *P8.53***

8.54 To level a wood deck, wood wedges A and B are placed under a corner of the deck. Wedge B rests on a wood board as shown, and a bar clamp is used to apply equal and opposite forces to the wedges. Knowing that $\theta = 18°$ and that the coefficient of static friction is 0.35 between all wood surfaces and is 0.60 between the board and the ground, determine the magnitude P of the clamping forces for which upward motion of the deck is impending.

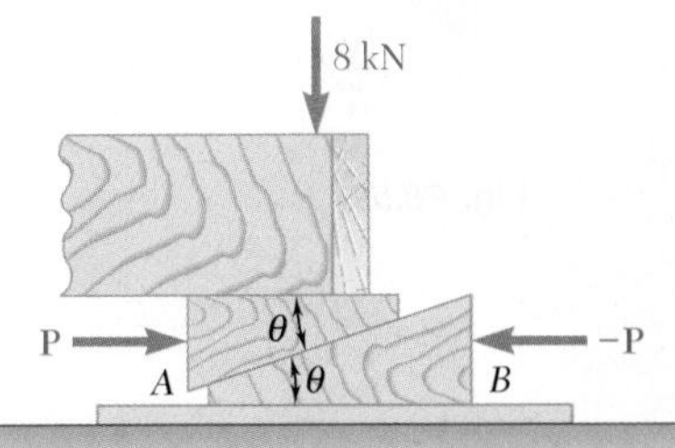

Fig. P8.54 and P8.55

8.55 To level a wood deck, wood wedges A and B are placed under a corner of the deck, and wedge B rests on a wood board as shown. Knowing that the coefficient of static friction is 0.35 between all wood surfaces and is 0.60 between the board and the ground, determine the maximum value of the wedge angle θ for which the system will remain in equilibrium after the clamping forces **P** and $-$**P** are removed.

8.56 A 12° wedge is to be forced under the corner B of the 250-N quarter cylinder shown. Knowing that the coefficient of static friction between the cylinder and the wedge is 0.35 and 0.50 between the wedge and the floor, determine the magnitude of the force **P** required for impending motion of the wedge.

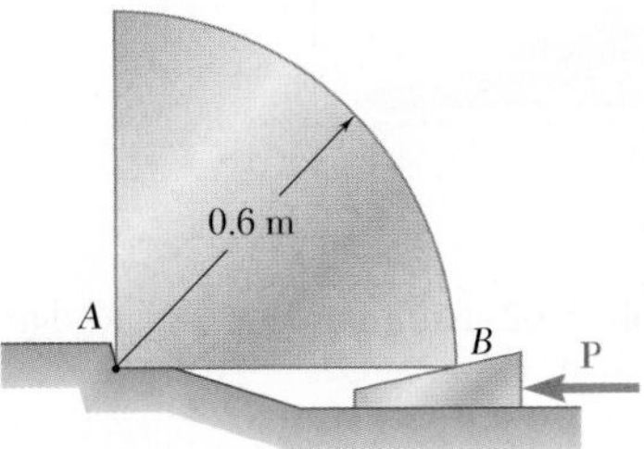

Fig. P8.56

8.57 A small screwdriver is used to pry apart the two coils of a circular key ring. The wedge angle of the screwdriver blade is 16° and the coefficient of static friction is 0.12 between the coils and the blade. Knowing that a force **P** of magnitude 3.5 N was required to insert the screwdriver to the equilibrium position shown, determine the magnitude of the forces exerted on the ring by the screwdriver immediately after force **P** is removed.

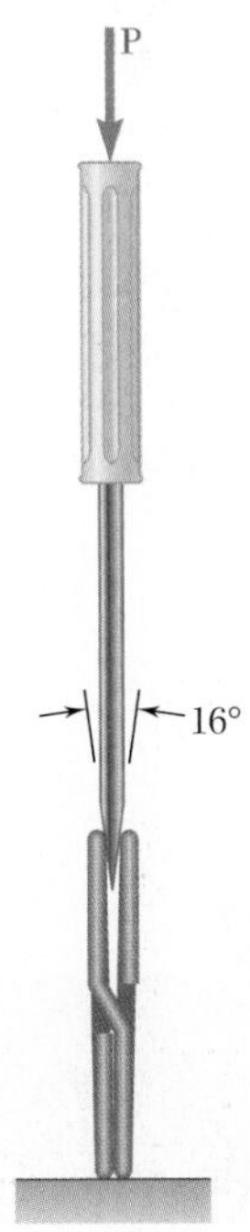

Fig. P8.57

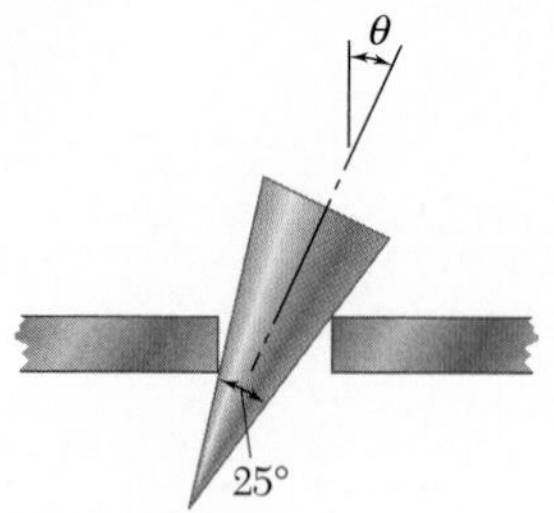

Fig. P8.58

8.58 A conical wedge is placed between two horizontal plates that are then slowly moved toward each other. Indicate what will happen to the wedge (*a*) if $\mu_s = 0.20$, (*b*) if $\mu_s = 0.30$.

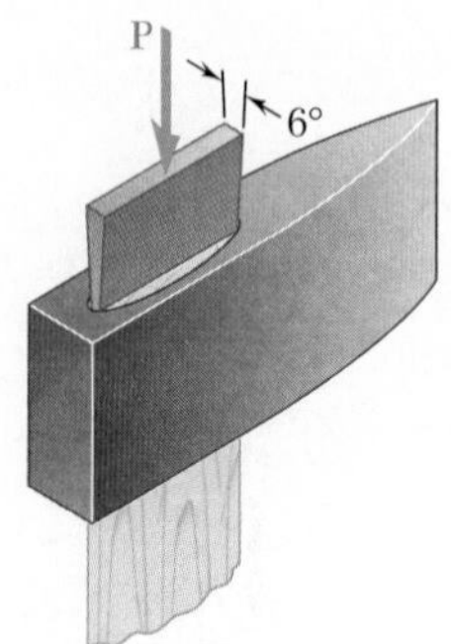

Fig. *P8.59*

8.59 A 6° steel wedge is driven into the end of an ax handle to lock the handle to the ax head. The coefficient of static friction between the wedge and the handle is 0.35. Knowing that a force **P** of magnitude 60 N was required to insert the wedge to the equilibrium position shown, determine the magnitude of the forces exerted on the handle by the wedge after force **P** is removed.

8.60 A 10° wedge is forced under an 80-kg cylinder as shown. Knowing that the coefficient of static friction between all surfaces of contact is 0.25, determine the force **P** for which motion of the wedge is impending.

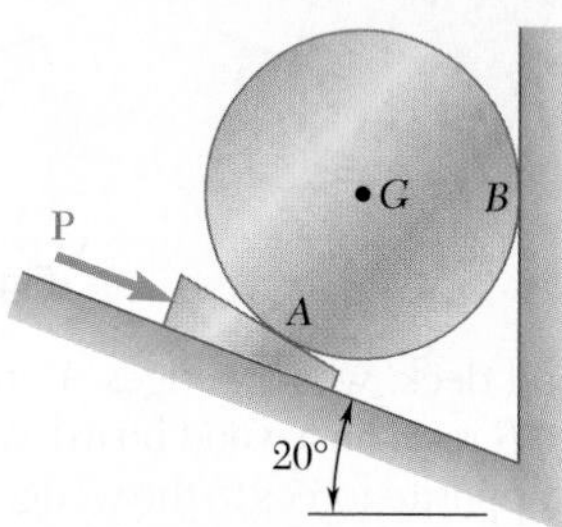

Fig. P8.60 and P8.61

8.61 A 10° wedge is forced under an 80-kg cylinder as shown. Knowing that the coefficient of static friction between the cylinder and the vertical wall is 0.30, determine the smallest coefficient of static friction between the wedge and the cylinder for which slipping can be impending at *B*.

8.62 Bags of grass seed are stored on a wooden plank as shown. To move the plank, a 9° wedge is driven under end *A*. Knowing that the weight of the grass seed can be represented by the distributed load shown and that the coefficient of static friction is 0.45 between all surfaces of contact, (*a*) determine the force **P** for which motion of the wedge is impending, (*b*) indicate whether the plank will slide on the floor.

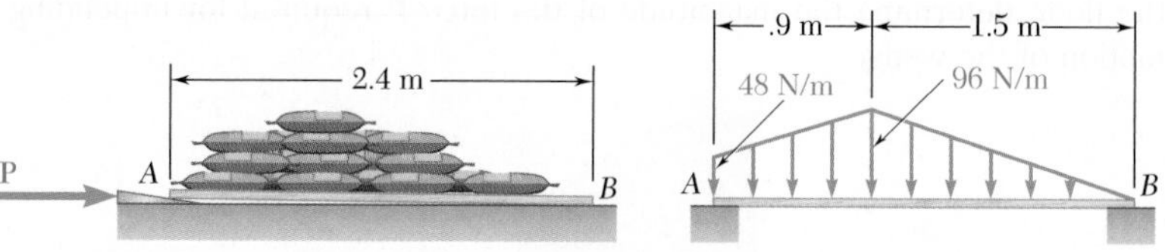

Fig. P8.62

8.63 Solve Prob. 8.62 assuming that the wedge is driven under the plank at *B* instead of at *A*.

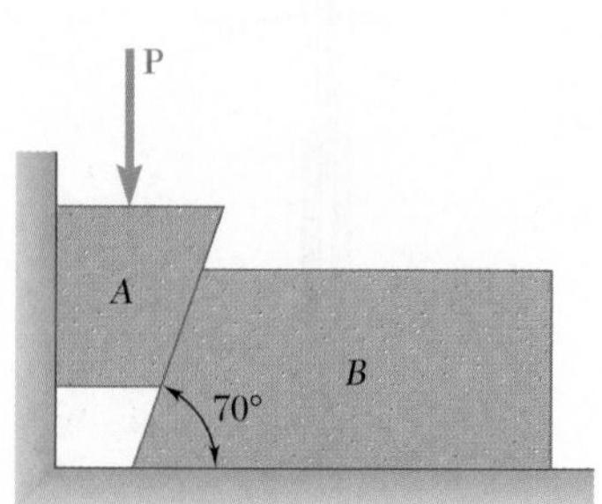

Fig. P8.64

***8.64** The 10-kg block *A* is at rest against the 50-kg block *B* as shown. The coefficient of static friction μ_s is the same between blocks *A* and *B* and between block *B* and the floor, while friction between block *A* and the wall may be neglected. Knowing that $P = 150$ N, determine the value of μ_s for which motion is impending.

***8.65** Solve Prob. 8.64 assuming that μ_s is the coefficient of static friction between all surfaces of contact.

8.66 Derive the following formulas relating the load **W** and the force **P** exerted on the handle of the jack discussed in Sec. 8.6. (*a*) $P = (Wr/a) \tan (\theta + \phi_s)$, to raise the load; (*b*) $P = (Wr/a) \tan (\phi_s - \theta)$, to lower the load if the screw is self-locking; (*c*) $P = (Wr/a) \tan (\theta - \phi_s)$, to hold the load if the screw is not self-locking.

8.67 The square-threaded worm gear shown has a mean radius of .0381 m and a lead of .009 m. The larger gear is subjected to a constant clockwise couple of 7.2 KN · m. Knowing that the coefficient of static friction between the two gears is 0.12, determine the couple that must be applied to shaft *AB* to rotate the large gear counterclockwise. Neglect friction in the bearings at *A*, *B*, and *C*.

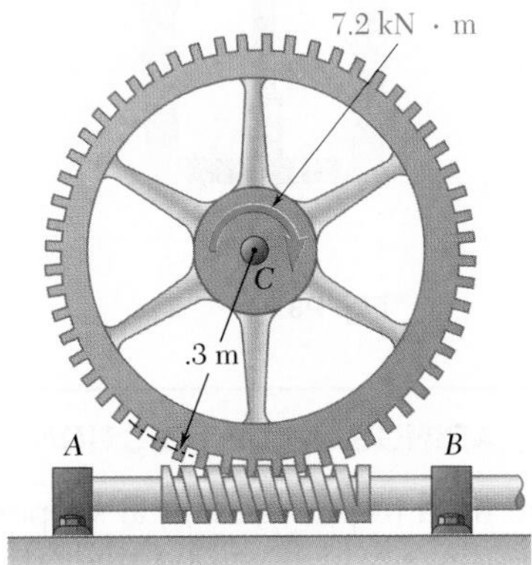

Fig. ***P8.67***

8.68 In Prob. 8.67, determine the couple that must be applied to shaft *AB* to rotate the gear clockwise.

8.69 High-strength bolts are used in the construction of many steel structures. For a .025-m-nominal-diameter bolt the required minimum bolt tension is 47.25 kN. Assuming the coefficient of friction to be 0.35, determine the required couple that should be applied to the bolt and nut. The mean diameter of the thread is 0.024 m, and the lead is .003 m. Neglect friction between the nut and washer, and assume the bolt to be square-threaded.

Fig. P8.69

8.70 The position of the automobile jack shown is controlled by a screw *ABC* that is single-threaded at each end (right-handed thread at *A*, left-handed thread at *C*). Each thread has a pitch of 2 mm and a mean diameter of 7.5 mm. If the coefficient of static friction is 0.15, determine the magnitude of the couple **M** that must be applied to raise the automobile.

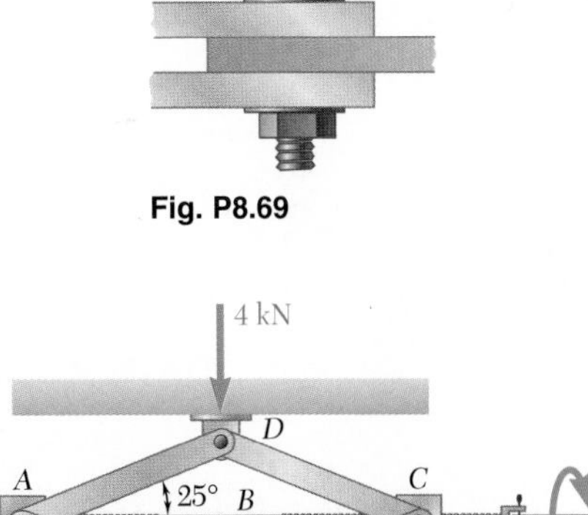

Fig. ***P8.70***

8.71 For the jack of Prob. 8.70, determine the magnitude of the couple **M** that must be applied to lower the automobile.

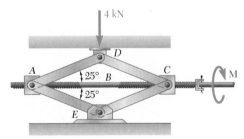

8.72 The vise shown consists of two members connected by two double-threaded screws of mean radius 6 mm and pitch 2 mm. The lower member is threaded at *A* and *B* ($\mu_s = 0.35$), but the upper member is not threaded. It is desired to apply two equal and opposite forces of 540 N on the blocks held between the jaws. Determine (*a*) which screw should be adjusted first, (*b*) the maximum couple applied in tightening the second screw.

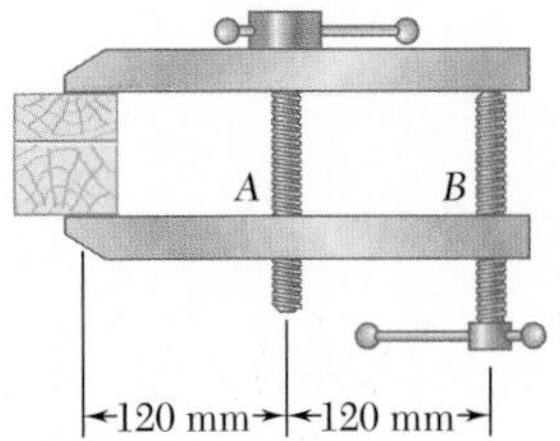

Fig. P8.72

8.73 Solve part *b* of Prob. 8.72 assuming that the wrong screw is adjusted first.

8.74 In the gear-pulling assembly shown, the square-threaded screw AB has a mean radius of .0234 m and a lead of .006 m. Knowing that the coefficient of static friction is 0.10, determine the couple which must be applied to the screw to produce a force of 1000 N on the gear. Neglect friction at end A of the screw.

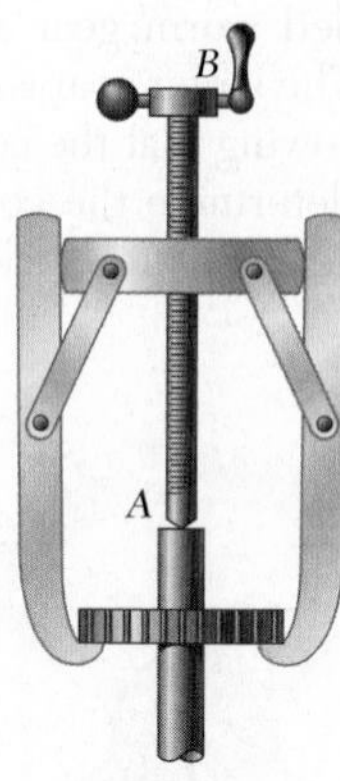

Fig. P8.74

*8.7. JOURNAL BEARINGS. AXLE FRICTION

Journal bearings are used to provide lateral support to rotating shafts and axles. Thrust bearings, which will be studied in the next section, are used to provide axial support to shafts and axles. If the journal bearing is fully lubricated, the frictional resistance depends upon the speed of rotation, the clearance between the axle and the bearing, and the viscosity of the lubricant. As indicated in Sec. 8.1, such problems are studied in fluid mechanics. The methods of this chapter, however, can be applied to the study of axle friction when the bearing is not lubricated or is only partially lubricated. It can then be assumed that the axle and the bearing are in direct contact along a single straight line.

Consider two wheels, each of weight **W**, rigidly mounted on an axle supported symmetrically by two journal bearings (Fig. 8.10*a*). If the wheels rotate, we find that to keep them rotating at constant speed, it is necessary to apply to each of them a couple **M**. The free-body diagram in Fig. 8.10*c* represents one of the wheels and the corresponding half axle in projection on a plane perpendicular to the axle. The forces acting on the free body include the weight **W** of the wheel, the couple **M** required to maintain its motion, and a force **R** representing the reaction of the bearing. This force is vertical, equal, and opposite to **W** but does not pass through the center O of the axle; **R** is located to the right of O at a distance such that its moment about O balances the moment **M** of the couple. Therefore, contact between the axle and bearing does not take place at the lowest point A when the axle rotates. It takes place at point B (Fig. 8.10*b*) or, rather, along a straight line intersecting the plane of the figure at B. Physically, this is explained by the fact that when the wheels are set in motion, the axle "climbs" in the bearings until slippage occurs. After sliding back slightly, the axle settles more or less in the position shown. This position is such that the angle between the reaction **R** and the normal to the surface of the bearing is equal to the angle of kinetic friction ϕ_k.

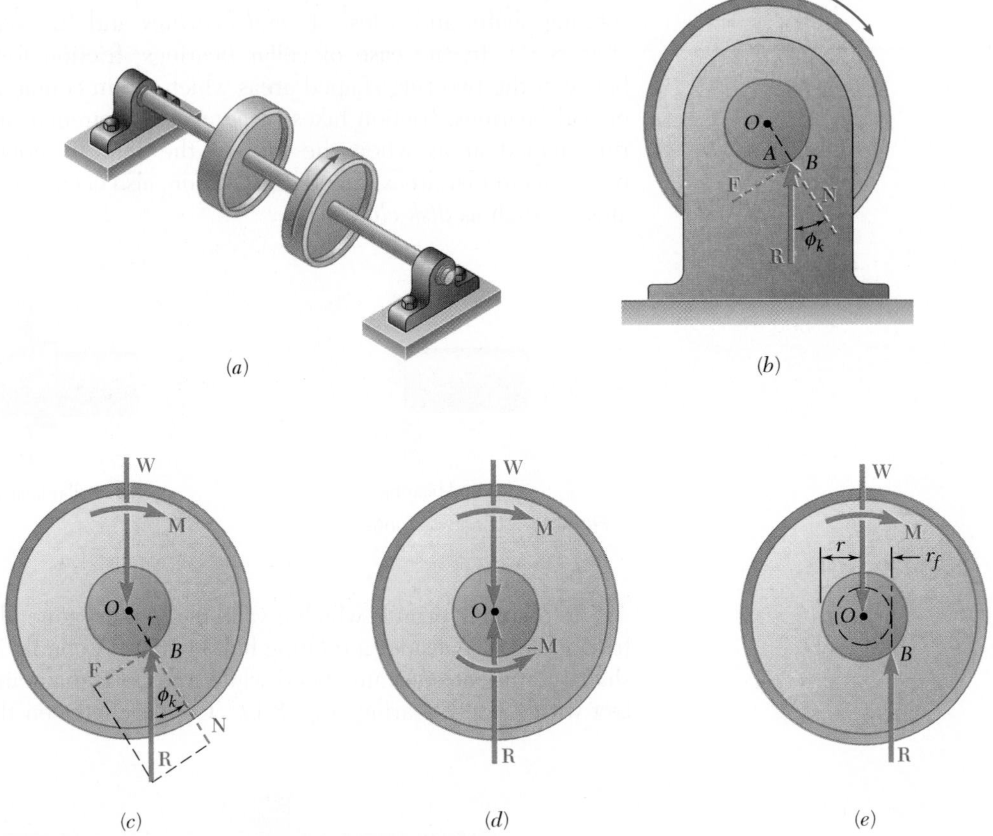

Fig. 8.10

The distance from O to the line of action of **R** is thus $r \sin \phi_k$, where r is the radius of the axle. Writing that $\Sigma M_O = 0$ for the forces acting on the free body considered, we obtain the magnitude of the couple **M** required to overcome the frictional resistance of one of the bearings:

$$M = Rr \sin \phi_k \tag{8.5}$$

Observing that, for small values of the angle of friction, $\sin \phi_k$ can be replaced by $\tan \phi_k$, that is, by μ_k, we write the approximate formula

$$M \approx Rr\mu_k \tag{8.6}$$

In the solution of certain problems, it may be more convenient to let the line of action of **R** pass through O, as it does when the axle does not rotate. A couple $-\mathbf{M}$ of the same magnitude as the couple **M** but of opposite sense must then be added to the reaction **R** (Fig. 8.10*d*). This couple represents the frictional resistance of the bearing.

In case a graphical solution is preferred, the line of action of **R** can be readily drawn (Fig. 8.10*e*) if we note that it must be tangent to a circle centered at O and of radius

$$r_f = r \sin \phi_k \approx r\mu_k \tag{8.7}$$

This circle is called the *circle of friction* of the axle and bearing and is independent of the loading conditions of the axle.

*8.8. THRUST BEARINGS. DISK FRICTION

Two types of thrust bearings are used to provide axial support to rotating shafts and axles: (1) *end bearings* and (2) *collar bearings* (Fig. 8.11). In the case of collar bearings, friction forces develop between the two ring-shaped areas which are in contact. In the case of end bearings, friction takes place over full circular areas, or over ring-shaped areas when the end of the shaft is hollow. Friction between circular areas, called *disk friction,* also occurs in other mechanisms, such as *disk clutches*.

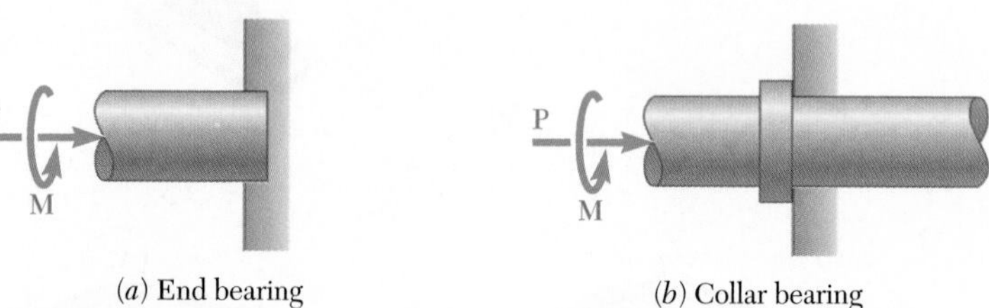

Fig. 8.11 Thrust bearings.

To obtain a formula which is valid in the most general case of disk friction, let us consider a rotating hollow shaft. A couple **M** keeps the shaft rotating at constant speed while a force **P** maintains it in contact with a fixed bearing (Fig. 8.12). Contact between the shaft and

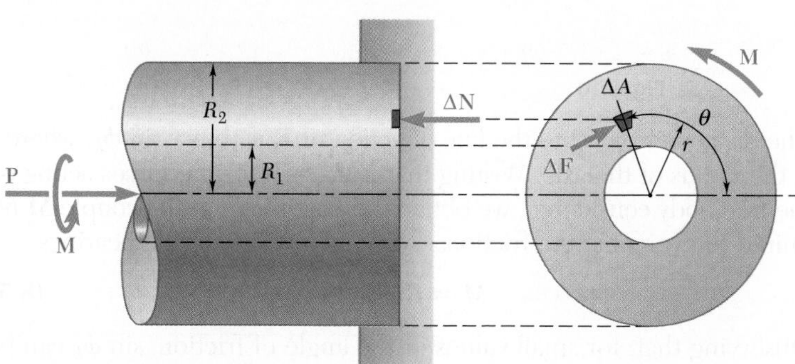

Fig. 8.12

the bearing takes place over a ring-shaped area of inner radius R_1 and outer radius R_2. Assuming that the pressure between the two surfaces in contact is uniform, we find that the magnitude of the normal force $\Delta\mathbf{N}$ exerted on an element of area ΔA is $\Delta N = P\,\Delta A/A$, where $A = \pi(R_2^2 - R_1^2)$, and that the magnitude of the friction force $\Delta\mathbf{F}$ acting on ΔA is $\Delta F = \mu_k\,\Delta N$. Denoting by r the distance from the axis of the shaft to the element of area ΔA, we express the magnitude ΔM of the moment of $\Delta\mathbf{F}$ about the axis of the shaft as follows:

$$\Delta M = r\,\Delta F = \frac{r\mu_k P\,\Delta A}{\pi(R_2^2 - R_1^2)}$$

The equilibrium of the shaft requires that the moment **M** of the couple applied to the shaft be equal in magnitude to the sum of the moments of the friction forces $\Delta\mathbf{F}$. Replacing ΔA by the infinitesimal element $dA = r\,d\theta\,dr$ used with polar coordinates, and integrating over the area of contact, we thus obtain the following expression for the magnitude of the couple **M** required to overcome the frictional resistance of the bearing:

$$M = \frac{\mu_k P}{\pi(R_2^2 - R_1^2)} \int_0^{2\pi} \int_{R_1}^{R_2} r^2\,dr\,d\theta$$

$$= \frac{\mu_k P}{\pi(R_2^2 - R_1^2)} \int_0^{2\pi} \tfrac{1}{3}(R_2^3 - R_1^3)\,d\theta$$

$$M = \tfrac{2}{3}\mu_k P \frac{R_2^3 - R_1^3}{R_2^2 - R_1^2} \qquad (8.8)$$

When contact takes place over a full circle of radius R, formula (8.8) reduces to

$$M = \tfrac{2}{3}\mu_k PR \qquad (8.9)$$

The value of M is then the same as would be obtained if contact between the shaft and the bearing took place at a single point located at a distance $2R/3$ from the axis of the shaft.

The largest torque which can be transmitted by a disk clutch without causing slippage is given by a formula similar to Eq. (8.9), where μ_k is replaced by the coefficient of static friction μ_s.

*8.9. WHEEL FRICTION. ROLLING RESISTANCE

The wheel is one of the most important inventions of our civilization. Its use makes it possible to move heavy loads with relatively little effort. Because the point of the wheel in contact with the ground at any given instant has no relative motion with respect to the ground, the wheel eliminates the large friction forces which would arise if the load were in direct contact with the ground. However, some resistance to the wheel's motion exists. This resistance has two distinct causes. It is due (1) to a combined effect of axle friction and friction at the rim and (2) to the fact that the wheel and the ground deform, with the result that contact between the wheel and the ground takes place over a certain area, rather than at a single point.

To understand better the first cause of resistance to the motion of a wheel, let us consider a railroad car supported by eight wheels mounted on axles and bearings. The car is assumed to be moving to the right at constant speed along a straight horizontal track. The

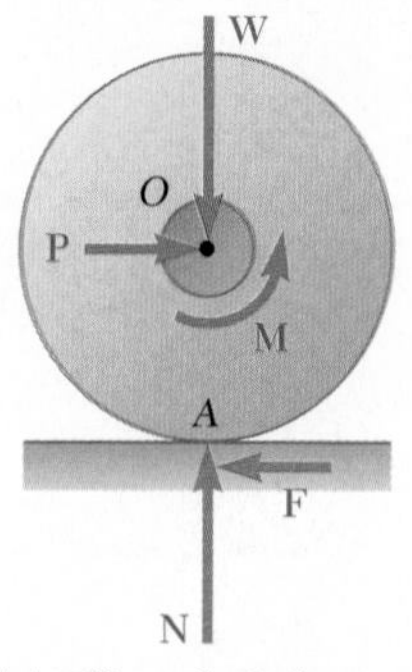

(*a*) Effect of axle friction

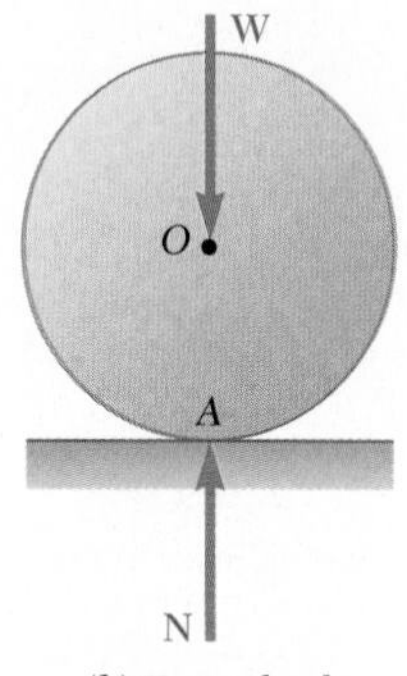

(*b*) Free wheel

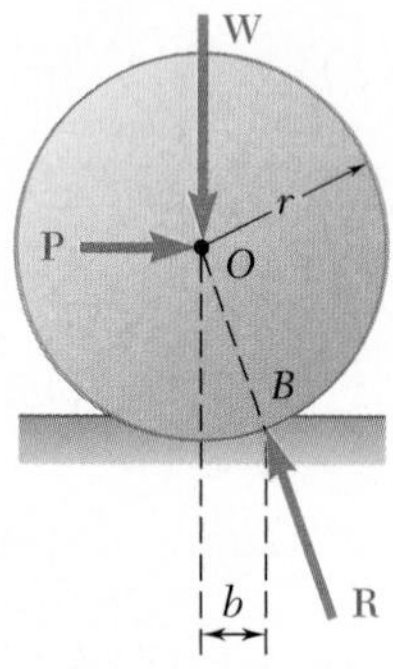

(*c*) Rolling resistance

Fig. 8.13

free-body diagram of one of the wheels is shown in Fig. 8.13*a*. The forces acting on the free body include the load **W** supported by the wheel and the normal reaction **N** of the track. Since **W** is drawn through the center *O* of the axle, the frictional resistance of the bearing should be represented by a counterclockwise couple **M** (see Sec. 8.7). To keep the free body in equilibrium, we must add two equal and opposite forces **P** and **F**, forming a clockwise couple of moment $-\mathbf{M}$. The force **F** is the friction force exerted by the track on the wheel, and **P** represents the force which should be applied to the wheel to keep it rolling at constant speed. Note that the forces **P** and **F** would not exist if there were no friction between the wheel and the track. The couple **M** representing the axle friction would then be zero; thus, the wheel would slide on the track without turning in its bearing.

The couple **M** and the forces **P** and **F** also reduce to zero when there is no axle friction. For example, a wheel which is not held in bearings and rolls freely and at constant speed on horizontal ground (Fig. 8.13*b*) will be subjected to only two forces: its own weight **W** and the normal reaction **N** of the ground. Regardless of the value of the coefficient of friction between the wheel and the ground, no friction force will act on the wheel. A wheel rolling freely on horizontal ground should thus keep rolling indefinitely.

Experience, however, indicates that the wheel will slow down and eventually come to rest. This is due to the second type of resistance mentioned at the beginning of this section, known as the *rolling resistance*. Under the load **W**, both the wheel and the ground deform slightly, causing the contact between the wheel and the ground to take place over a certain area. Experimental evidence shows that the resultant of the forces exerted by the ground on the wheel over this area is a force **R** applied at a point *B*, which is not located directly under the center *O* of the wheel but slightly in front of it (Fig. 8.13*c*). To balance the moment of **W** about *B* and to keep the wheel rolling at constant speed, it is necessary to apply a horizontal force **P** at the center of the wheel. Writing $\Sigma M_B = 0$, we obtain

$$Pr = Wb \tag{8.10}$$

where r = radius of wheel
b = horizontal distance between O and B

The distance b is commonly called the *coefficient of rolling resistance*. It should be noted that b is not a dimensionless coefficient since it represents a length; b is usually expressed in inches or in millimeters. The value of b depends upon several parameters in a manner which has not yet been clearly established. Values of the coefficient of rolling resistance vary from about 0.01 in. or 0.25 mm for a steel wheel on a steel rail to 5.0 in. or 125 mm for the same wheel on soft ground.

SAMPLE PROBLEM 8.6

A pulley of diameter .1 m can rotate about a fixed shaft of diameter .05 m. The coefficient of static friction between the pulley and shaft is 0.20. Determine (*a*) the smallest vertical force **P** required to start raising a 500-N load, (*b*) the smallest vertical force **P** required to hold the load, (*c*) the smallest horizontal force **P** required to start raising the same load.

SOLUTION

***a.* Vertical Force P Required to Start Raising the Load.** When the forces in both parts of the rope are equal, contact between the pulley and shaft takes place at *A*. When **P** is increased, the pulley rolls around the shaft slightly and contact takes place at *B*. The free-body diagram of the pulley when motion is impending is drawn. The perpendicular distance from the center *O* of the pulley to the line of action of **R** is

$$r_f = r \sin \phi_s \approx r\mu_s \qquad r_f \approx (.025 \text{ m})0.20 = .005 \text{ m}.$$

Summing moments about *B*, we write

$$+\circlearrowleft \Sigma M_B = 0: \qquad (.055 \text{ m})(500 \text{ N}) - (.045 \text{ m})P = 0$$
$$P = 611 \text{ N} \qquad\qquad \mathbf{P} = 611 \text{ N}\downarrow \quad ◀$$

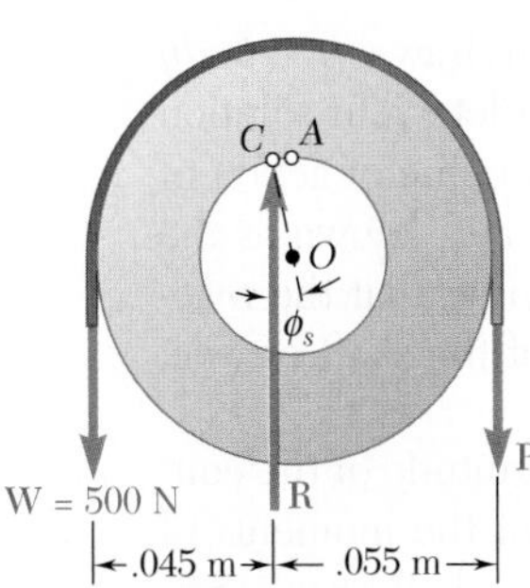

***b.* Vertical Force P to Hold the Load.** As the force **P** is decreased, the pulley rolls around the shaft and contact takes place at *C*. Considering the pulley as a free body and summing moments about *C*, we write

$$+\circlearrowleft \Sigma M_C = 0: \qquad (.045 \text{ m})(500 \text{ N}) - (.055 \text{ m})P = 0$$
$$P = 409 \text{ N} \qquad\qquad \mathbf{P} = 409 \text{ N}\downarrow \quad ◀$$

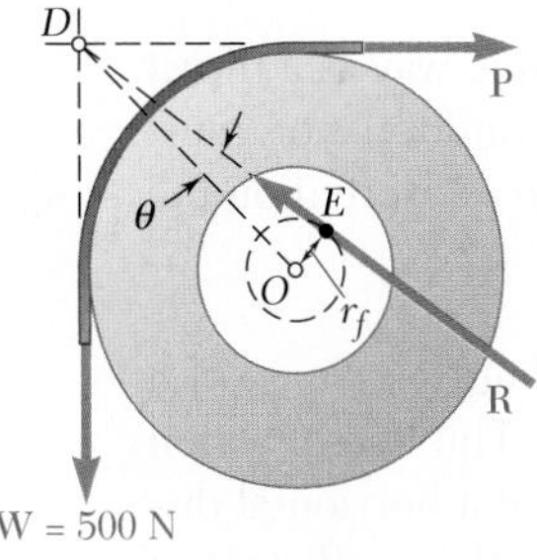

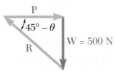

***c.* Horizontal Force P to Start Raising the Load.** Since the three forces **W**, **P**, and **R** are not parallel, they must be concurrent. The direction of **R** is thus determined from the fact that its line of action must pass through the point of intersection *D* of **W** and **P** and must be tangent to the circle of friction. Recalling that the radius of the circle of friction is $r_f = .005$ m, we write

$$\sin \theta = \frac{OE}{OD} = \frac{.005 \text{ m}}{(.05 \text{ m})\sqrt{2}} = 0.0707 \qquad \theta = 4.1°$$

From the force triangle, we obtain

$$P = W \cot (45° - \theta) = (500 \text{ N}) \cot 40.9°$$
$$= 577 \text{ N} \qquad\qquad \mathbf{P} = 577 \text{ N}\rightarrow \quad ◀$$

SOLVING PROBLEMS ON YOUR OWN

In this lesson you learned about several additional engineering applications of the laws of friction.

1. ***Journal bearings and axle friction.*** In journal bearings, the *reaction does not pass through the center of the shaft or axle* which is being supported. The distance from the center of the shaft or axle to the line of action of the reaction (Fig. 8.10) is defined by the equation

$$r_f = r \sin \phi_k \approx r\mu_k$$

if motion is actually taking place, and by the equation

$$r_f = r \sin \phi_s \approx r\mu_s$$

if the motion is impending.

Once you have determined the line of action of the reaction, you can draw a *free-body diagram* and use the corresponding equations of equilibrium to complete your solution [Sample Prob. 8.6]. In some problems, it is useful to observe that the line of action of the reaction must be tangent to a circle of radius $r_f \approx r\mu_k$, or $r_f \approx r\mu_s$, known as the *circle of friction* [Sample Prob. 8.6, part *c*]. It is important to remember that the reaction is always directed to oppose the actual or impending rotation of the shaft or axle.

2. ***Thrust bearings and disk friction.*** In a *thrust bearing* the magnitude of the couple required to overcome frictional resistance is equal to the sum of the moments of the *kinetic friction forces* exerted on the elements of the end of the shaft [Eqs. (8.8) and (8.9)].

An example of disk friction is the *disk clutch.* It is analyzed in the same way as a thrust bearing, except that to determine the largest couple that can be transmitted, you must compute the sum of the moments of the *maximum static friction forces* exerted on the disk.

3. ***Wheel friction and rolling resistance.*** You saw that the rolling resistance of a wheel is caused by deformations of both the wheel and the ground. The line of action of the reaction **R** of the ground on the wheel intersects the ground at a horizontal distance b from the center of the wheel. The distance b is known as the *coefficient of rolling resistance* and is expressed in inches or millimeters.

4. ***In problems involving both rolling resistance and axle friction,*** your free-body diagram should show that the line of action of the reaction **R** of the ground on the wheel is tangent to the friction circle of the axle and intersects the ground at a horizontal distance from the center of the wheel equal to the coefficient of rolling resistance.

Problems

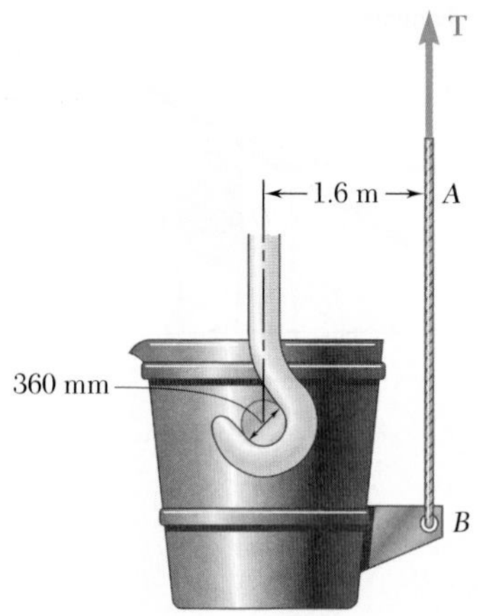

Fig. P8.75

8.75 A hot-metal ladle and its contents have a mass of 50 Mg. Knowing that the coefficient of static friction between the hooks and the pinion is 0.30, determine the tension in cable AB required to start tipping the ladle.

8.76 and *8.77* A windlass of .254-m diameter is used to raise or lower a 160-N load. The windlass is supported by two poorly lubricated bearings of .076-m diameter. Knowing that the coefficient of static friction between the shaft and the bearings is 0.50, determine the magnitude of the force **P** required for impending raising of the load.

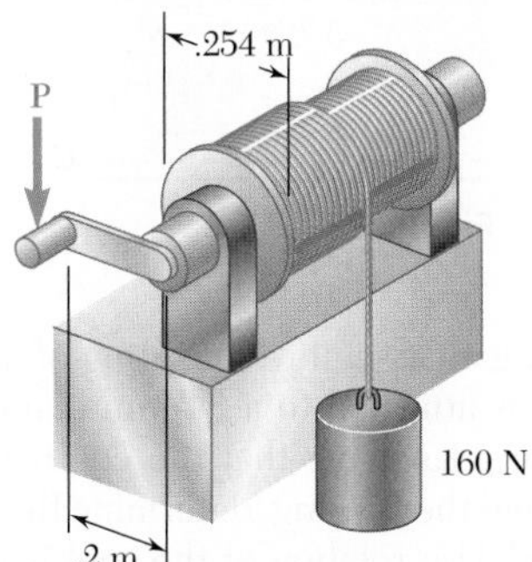

Fig. P8.76 and P8.78

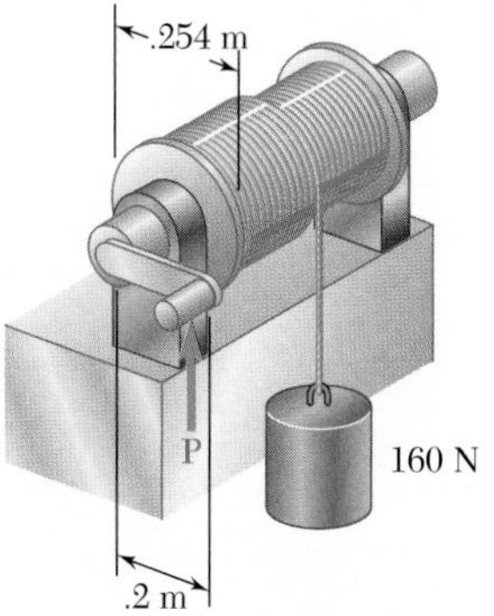

Fig. *P8.77* and *P8.79*

8.78 and *8.79* A windlass of .254-m diameter is used to raise or lower a 160-N load. The windlass is supported by two poorly lubricated bearings of .076-m diameter. Knowing that the coefficient of static friction between the shaft and the bearings is 0.50, determine the magnitude of the smallest force **P** required to maintain equilibrium.

8.80 Control lever ABC fits loosely on an 18-mm-diameter shaft at support B. Knowing that $P = 130$ N for impending clockwise rotation of the lever, determine (*a*) the coefficient of static friction between the shaft and the lever, (*b*) the magnitude of the force **P** for which counterclockwise rotation of the lever is impending.

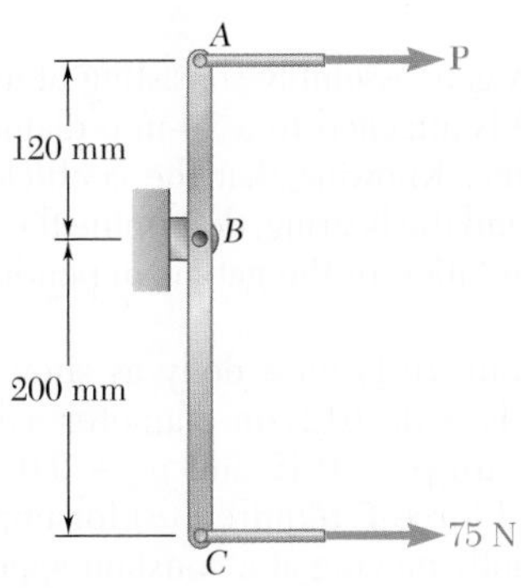

Fig. P8.80

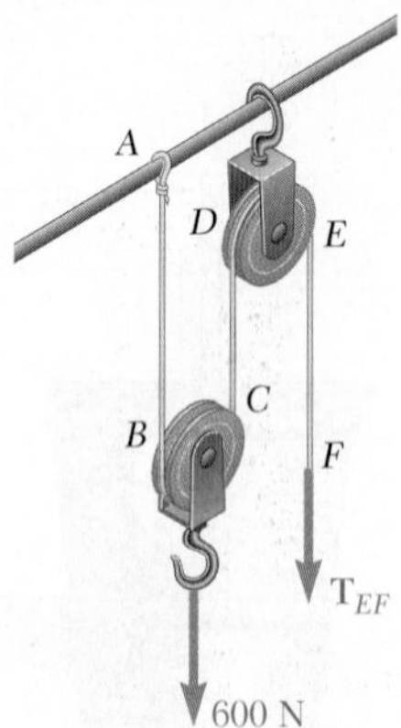

Fig. P8.81 and P8.82

8.81 The block and tackle shown are used to raise a 600-N load. Each of the 60-mm-diameter pulleys rotates on a 10-mm-diameter axle. Knowing that the coefficient of kinetic friction is 0.20, determine the tension in each portion of the rope as the load is slowly raised.

8.82 The block and tackle shown are used to lower a 600-N load. Each of the 60 mm-diameter pulleys rotates on a 10-mm-diameter axle. Knowing that the coefficient of kinetic friction is 0.20, determine the tension in each portion of the rope as the load is slowly lowered.

8.83 The link arrangement shown is frequently used in highway bridge construction to allow for expansion due to changes in temperature. At each of the .076-m-diameter pins A and B the coefficient of static friction is 0.20. Knowing that the vertical component of the force exerted by BC on the link is 50 kN, determine (*a*) the horizontal force which should be exerted on beam BC for impending motion of the link, (*b*) the angle that the resulting force exerted by beam BC on the link will form with the vertical.

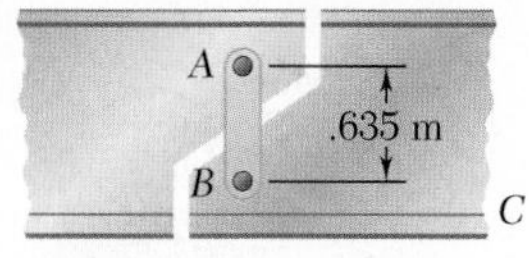

Fig. P8.83

8.84 and 8.85 A gate assembly consisting of a 24-kg gate ABC and a 66-kg counterweight D is attached to a 24-mm-diameter shaft B which fits loosely in a fixed bearing. Knowing that the coefficient of static friction is 0.20 between the shaft and the bearing, determine the magnitude of the force **P** for which counterclockwise rotation of the gate is impending.

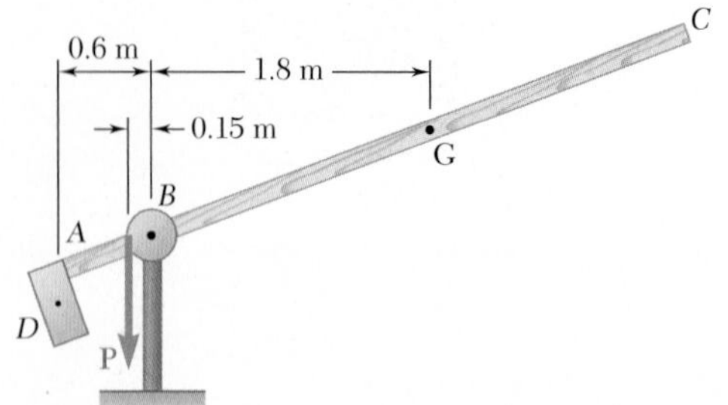

Fig. P8.84 and *P8.86*

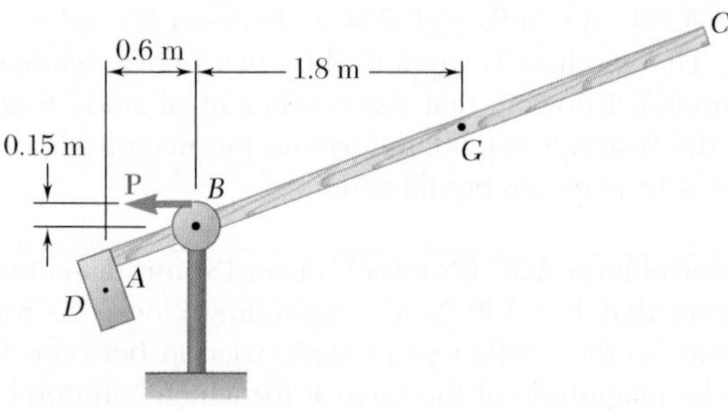

Fig. P8.85 and *P8.87*

8.86* and *8.87 A gate assembly consisting of a 24-kg gate ABC and a 66-kg counterweight D is attached to a 24-mm-diameter shaft B which fits loosely in a fixed bearing. Knowing that the coefficient of static friction is 0.20 between the shaft and the bearing, determine the magnitude of the force **P** for which clockwise rotation of the gate is impending.

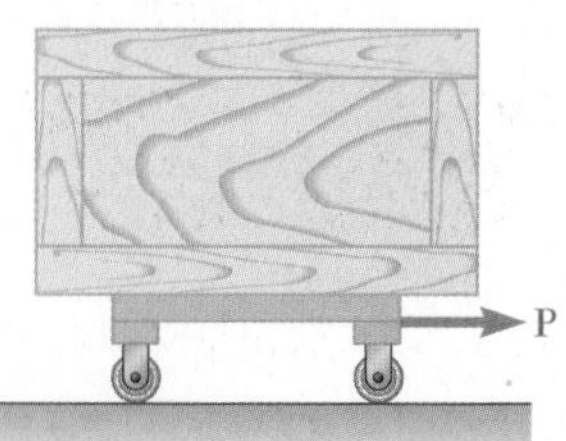

Fig. P8.88

8.88 A 500-N crate rests on a dolly as shown. The dolly has four .127-m-diameter wheels with .0127-m-diameter axles. Knowing that the coefficients of friction are $\mu_s = 0.12$ and $\mu_k = 0.08$, determine the magnitude of the horizontal force **P** required (*a*) for impending motion of the dolly, (*b*) to keep the dolly moving at a constant speed. Neglect rolling resistance between the wheels and the floor.

8.89 A scooter is designed to roll down a 3-percent slope at a constant speed. Assuming that the coefficient of kinetic friction between the 25-mm-diameter axles and the bearing is 0.12, determine the required diameter of the wheels. Neglect the rolling resistance between the wheels and the ground.

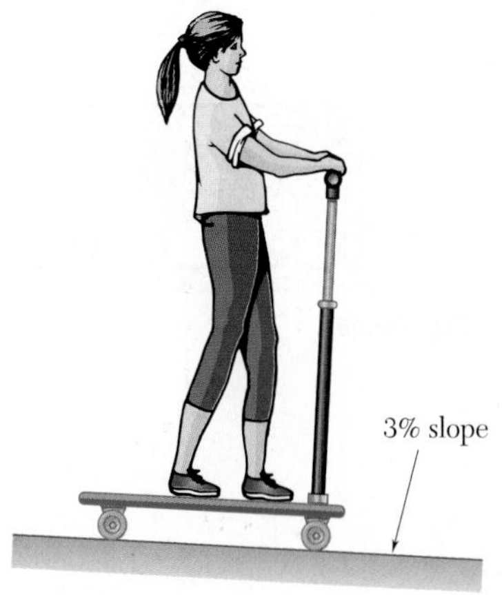

Fig. P8.89

8.90 A .178-m-diameter buffer weighs 10.1 N. The coefficient of kinetic friction between the buffing pad and the surface being polished is 0.60. Assuming that the normal force per unit area between the pad and the surface is uniformly distributed, determine the magnitude Q of the horizontal forces required to prevent motion of the buffer.

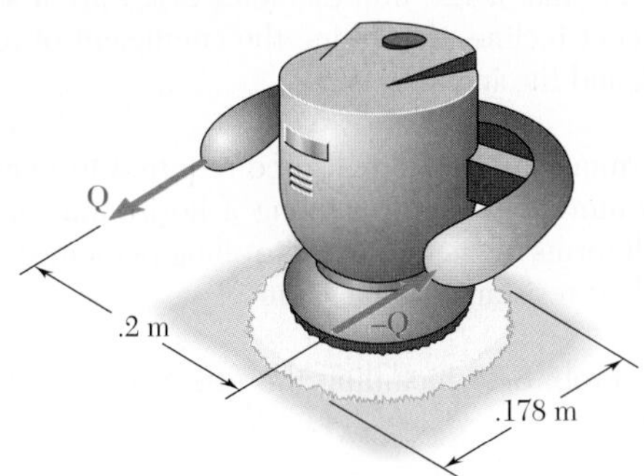

Fig. P8.90

8.91 The pivot for the seat of a desk chair consists of the steel plate A, which supports the seat, the solid steel shaft B which is welded to A and which turns freely in the tubular member C, and the nylon bearing D. If the weight **W** of a seated 80-kg person acts directly above the pivot, determine the magnitude of the couple **M** for which rotation of the seat is impending knowing that the coefficient of static friction is 0.15 between the tubular member and the bearing.

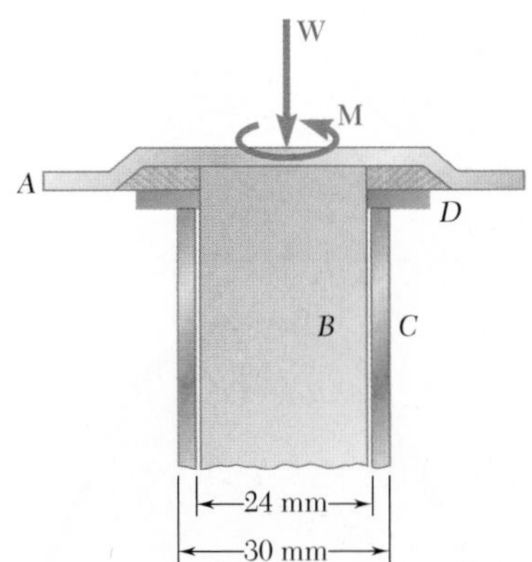

Fig. P8.91

***8.92** As the surfaces of a shaft and a bearing wear out, the frictional resistance of a thrust bearing decreases. It is generally assumed that the wear is directly proportional to the distance traveled by any given point of the shaft and thus to the distance r from the point to the axis of the shaft. Assuming then that the normal force per unit is inversely proportional to r, show that the magnitude M of the couple required to overcome the frictional resistance of a worn-out end bearing (with contact over the full circular area) is equal to 75 percent of the value given by formula (8.9) for a new bearing.

****8.93*** Assuming that bearings wear out as indicated in Prob. 8.92, show that the magnitude M of the couple required to overcome the frictional resistance of a worn-out collar bearing is

$$M = \frac{1}{2}\mu_k P(R_1 + R_2)$$

where P = magnitude of the total axial force
R_1, R_2 = inner and outer radii of collar

****8.94*** Assuming that the pressure between the surfaces of contact of the conical bearing shown is uniform, show that the magnitude M of the couple required to overcome frictional resistance is

$$M = \frac{2}{3}\frac{\mu_k P}{\sin\theta}\frac{R_2^3 - R_1^3}{R_2^2 - R_1^2}$$

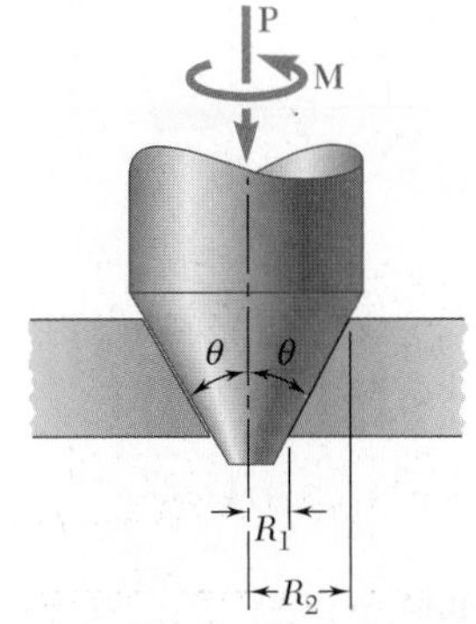

Fig. *P8.94*

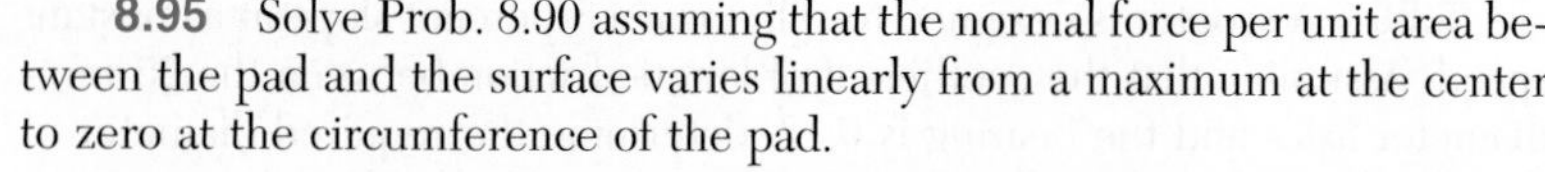

8.95 Solve Prob. 8.90 assuming that the normal force per unit area between the pad and the surface varies linearly from a maximum at the center to zero at the circumference of the pad.

Fig. *P8.96*

8.96 A 1000-N machine base is rolled along a concrete floor using a series of steel pipes with outside diameters of .127 m. Knowing that the coefficient of rolling resistance is .0006 m between the pipes and the base and .0015 m between the pipes and the concrete floor, determine the magnitude of the force **P** required to slowly move the base along the floor.

8.97 Knowing that a 120-mm-diameter disk rolls at a constant velocity down a 2-percent incline, determine the coefficient of rolling resistance between the disk and the incline.

8.98 Determine the horizontal force required to move a 1-Mg automobile with 460-mm-diameter tires along a horizontal road at a constant speed. Neglect all forms of friction except rolling resistance, and assume the coefficient of rolling resistance to be 1 mm.

8.99 Solve Prob. 8.88 including the effect of a coefficient of rolling resistance of .006 m.

8.100 Solve Prob. 8.89 including the effect of a coefficient of rolling resistance of 1.75 mm.

8.10. BELT FRICTION

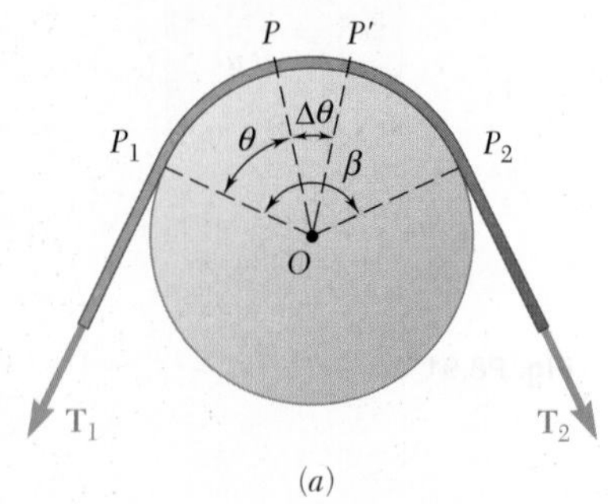

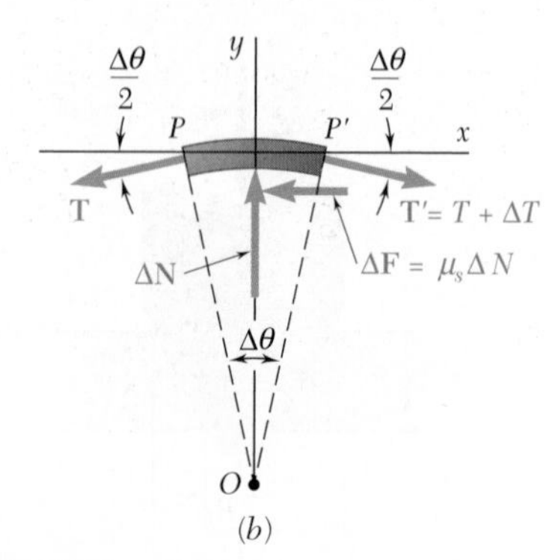

Fig. 8.14

Consider a flat belt passing over a fixed cylindrical drum (Fig. 8.14*a*). We propose to determine the relation existing between the values T_1 and T_2 of the tension in the two parts of the belt when the belt is just about to slide toward the right.

Let us detach from the belt a small element PP' subtending an angle $\Delta\theta$. Denoting by T the tension at P and by $T + \Delta T$ the tension at P', we draw the free-body diagram of the element of the belt (Fig. 8.14*b*). Besides the two forces of tension, the forces acting on the free body are the normal component $\Delta\mathbf{N}$ of the reaction of the drum and the friction force $\Delta\mathbf{F}$. Since motion is assumed to be impending, we have $\Delta F = \mu_s \Delta N$. It should be noted that if $\Delta\theta$ is made to approach zero, the magnitudes ΔN and ΔF, and the *difference* ΔT between the tension at P and the tension at P', will also approach zero; the value T of the tension at P, however, will remain unchanged. This observation helps in understanding our choice of notation.

Choosing the coordinate axes shown in Fig. 8.14*b*, we write the equations of equilibrium for the element PP':

$$\Sigma F_x = 0: \quad (T + \Delta T)\cos\frac{\Delta\theta}{2} - T\cos\frac{\Delta\theta}{2} - \mu_s \Delta N = 0 \qquad (8.11)$$

$$\Sigma F_y = 0: \quad \Delta N - (T + \Delta T)\sin\frac{\Delta\theta}{2} - T\sin\frac{\Delta\theta}{2} = 0 \qquad (8.12)$$

Solving Eq. (8.12) for ΔN and substituting into Eq. (8.11), we obtain after reductions

$$\Delta T \cos \frac{\Delta\theta}{2} - \mu_s(2T + \Delta T) \sin \frac{\Delta\theta}{2} = 0$$

Both terms are now divided by $\Delta\theta$. For the first term, this is done simply by dividing ΔT by $\Delta\theta$. The division of the second term is carried out by dividing the terms in the parentheses by 2 and the sine by $\Delta\theta/2$. We write

$$\frac{\Delta T}{\Delta\theta} \cos \frac{\Delta\theta}{2} - \mu_s\left(T + \frac{\Delta T}{2}\right) \frac{\sin(\Delta\theta/2)}{\Delta\theta/2} = 0$$

If we now let $\Delta\theta$ approach 0, the cosine approaches 1 and $\Delta T/2$ approaches zero, as noted above. The quotient of $\sin(\Delta\theta/2)$ over $\Delta\theta/2$ approaches 1, according to a lemma derived in all calculus textbooks. Since the limit of $\Delta T/\Delta\theta$ is by definition equal to the derivative $dT/d\theta$, we write

$$\frac{dT}{d\theta} - \mu_s T = 0 \qquad \frac{dT}{T} = \mu_s d\theta$$

Both members of the last equation (Fig. 8.14*a*) will now be integrated from P_1 to P_2. At P_1, we have $\theta = 0$ and $T = T_1$; at P_2, we have $\theta = \beta$ and $T = T_2$. Integrating between these limits, we write

$$\int_{T_1}^{T_2} \frac{dT}{T} = \int_0^{\beta} \mu_s \, d\theta$$

$$\ln T_2 - \ln T_1 = \mu_s\beta$$

or, noting that the left-hand member is equal to the natural logarithm of the quotient of T_2 and T_1,

$$\ln \frac{T_2}{T_1} = \mu_s\beta \qquad (8.13)$$

This relation can also be written in the form

$$\frac{T_2}{T_1} = e^{\mu_s\beta} \qquad (8.14)$$

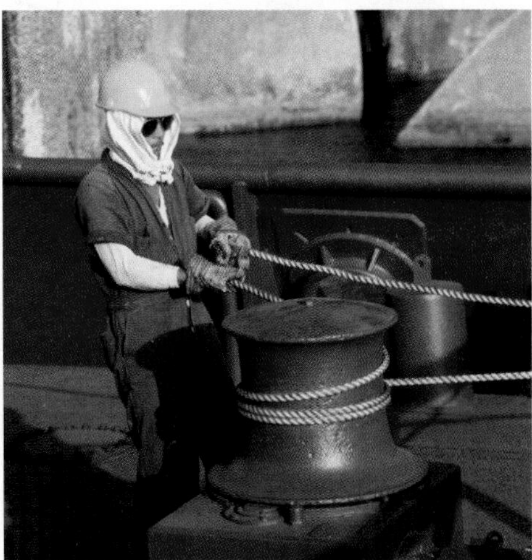
Photo 8.3 By wrapping the rope around the bollard, the force exerted by the worker to control the rope is much smaller than the tension in the taut portion of the rope.

The formulas we have derived apply equally well to problems involving flat belts passing over fixed cylindrical drums and to problems involving ropes wrapped around a post or capstan. They can also be used to solve problems involving band brakes. In such problems, it is the drum which is about to rotate, while the band remains fixed. The formulas can also be applied to problems involving belt drives. In these problems, both the pulley and the belt rotate; our concern is then to find whether the belt will slip, that is, whether it will move *with respect* to the pulley.

Formulas (8.13) and (8.14) should be used only if the belt, rope, or brake is *about to slip*. Formula (8.14) will be used if T_1 or T_2 is desired; formula (8.13) will be preferred if either μ_s or the angle of contact β is desired. We should note that T_2 is always larger than T_1; T_2 therefore represents the tension in that part of the belt or rope which *pulls*, while T_1 is the tension in the part which *resists*. We should also observe that the angle of contact β must be expressed in *radians*. The angle β may be larger than 2π; for example, if a rope is wrapped n times around a post, β is equal to $2\pi n$.

If the belt, rope, or brake is actually slipping, formulas similar to (8.13) and (8.14), but involving the coefficient of kinetic friction μ_k, should be used. If the belt, rope, or brake is not slipping and is not about to slip, none of these formulas can be used.

The belts used in belt drives are often V-shaped. In the V belt shown in Fig. 8.15*a* contact between the belt and the pulley takes

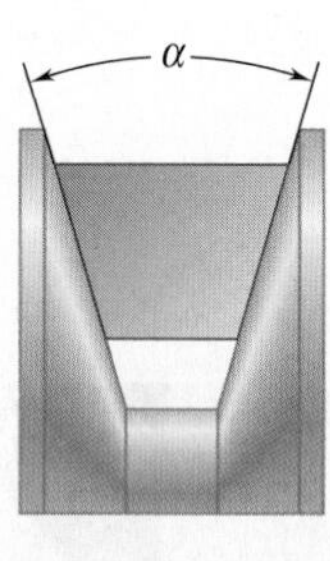

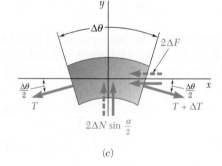

(*a*)

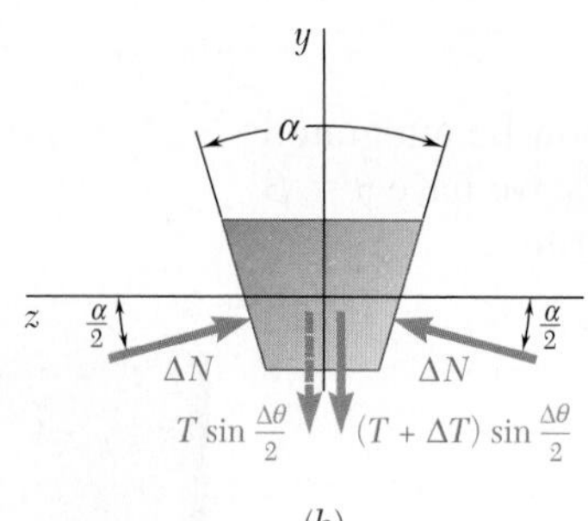

(*b*) (*c*)

Fig. 8.15

Photo 8.4 Large normal and friction forces on the sloping sides of the V belt increase the power that can be transmitted before slipping occurs.

place along the sides of the groove. The relation existing between the values T_1 and T_2 of the tension in the two parts of the belt when the belt is just about to slip can again be obtained by drawing the free-body diagram of an element of belt (Fig. 8.15*b* and *c*). Equations similar to (8.11) and (8.12) are derived, but the magnitude of the total friction force acting on the element is now 2 ΔF, and the sum of the y components of the normal forces is 2 ΔN sin $(\alpha/2)$. Proceeding as above, we obtain

$$\ln \frac{T_2}{T_1} = \frac{\mu_s \beta}{\sin (\alpha/2)} \tag{8.15}$$

or,

$$\frac{T_2}{T_1} = e^{\mu_s \beta / \sin (\alpha/2)} \tag{8.16}$$

SAMPLE PROBLEM 8.7

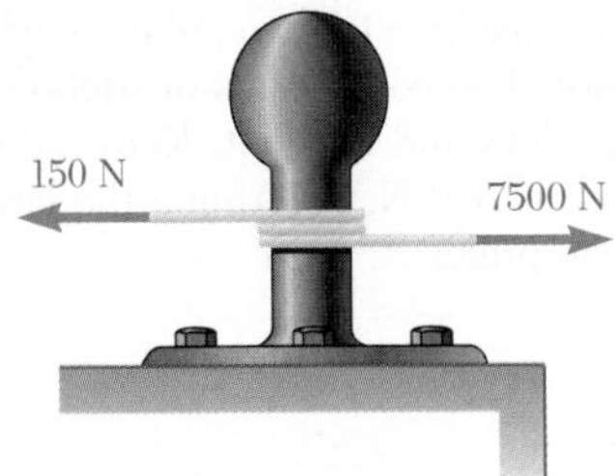

A hawser thrown from a ship to a pier is wrapped two full turns around a bollard. The tension in the hawser is 7500 N; by exerting a force of 150 N on its free end, a dockworker can just keep the hawser from slipping. (*a*) Determine the coefficient of friction between the hawser and the bollard. (*b*) Determine the tension in the hawser that could be resisted by the 150-N force if the hawser were wrapped three full turns around the bollard.

SOLUTION

a. Coefficient of Friction. Since slipping of the hawser is impending, we use Eq. (8.13):

$$\ln \frac{T_2}{T_1} = \mu_s \beta$$

Since the hawser is wrapped two full turns around the bollard, we have

$$\beta = 2(2\pi \text{ rad}) = 12.57 \text{ rad}$$
$$T_1 = 150 \text{ N} \qquad T_2 = 7500 \text{ N}$$

Therefore,

$$\mu_s \beta = \ln \frac{T_2}{T_1}$$

$$\mu_s(12.57 \text{ rad}) = \ln \frac{7500 \text{ N}}{150 \text{ N}} = \ln 50 = 3.91$$

$$\mu_s = 0.311 \qquad\qquad \mu_s = 0.311 \blacktriangleleft$$

b. Hawser Wrapped Three Turns around Bollard. Using the value of μ_s obtained in part a, we now have

$$\beta = 3(2\pi \text{ rad}) = 18.85 \text{ rad}$$
$$T_1 = 150 \text{ N} \qquad \mu_s = 0.311$$

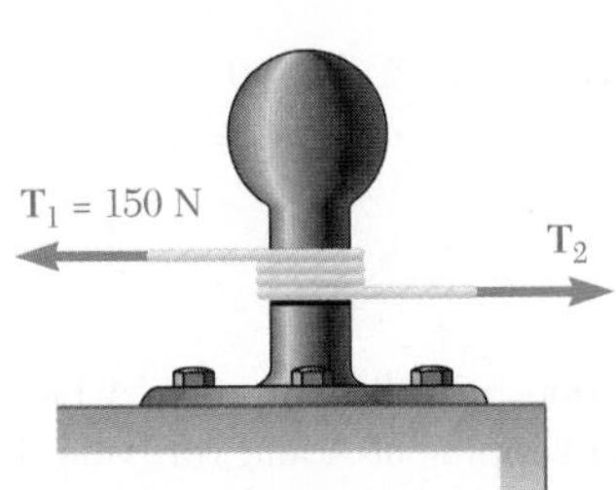

Substituting these values into Eq. (8.14), we obtain

$$\frac{T_2}{T_1} = e^{\mu_s \beta}$$

$$\frac{T_2}{150 \text{ N}} = e^{(0.311)(18.85)} = e^{5.862} = 351.5$$

$$T_2 = 52\,725 \text{ N}$$

$T_2 = 52.7 \text{ kN}$ ◀

SAMPLE PROBLEM 8.8

A flat belt connects pulley A, which drives a machine tool, to pulley B, which is attached to the shaft of an electric motor. The coefficients of friction are $\mu_s = 0.25$ and $\mu_k = 0.20$ between both pulleys and the belt. Knowing that the maximum allowable tension in the belt is 600 N, determine the largest couple which can be exerted by the belt on pulley A.

SOLUTION

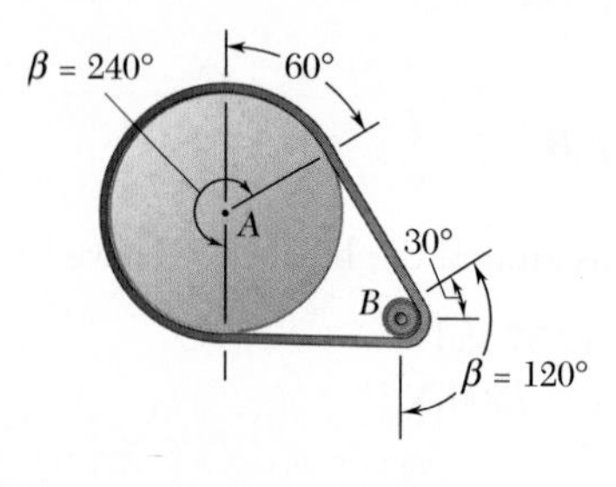

Since the resistance to slippage depends upon the angle of contact β between pulley and belt, as well as upon the coefficient of static friction μ_s, and since μ_s is the same for both pulleys, slippage will occur first on pulley B, for which β is smaller.

Pulley *B*. Using Eq. (8.14) with $T_2 = 600$ N, $\mu_s = 0.25$, and $\beta = 120° = 2\pi/3$ rad, we write

$$\frac{T_2}{T_1} = e^{\mu_s \beta} \qquad \frac{600\,\text{N}}{T_1} = e^{0.25(2\pi/3)} = 1.688$$

$$T_1 = \frac{600\,\text{N}}{1.688} = 355.4 \text{ N}$$

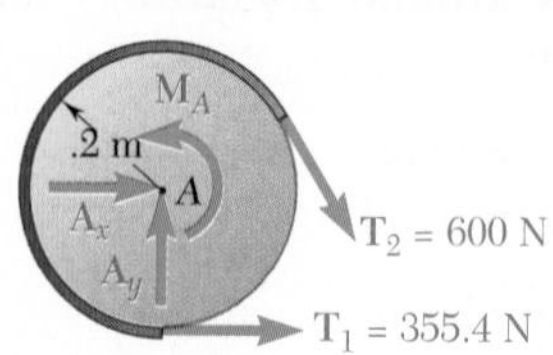

Pulley *A*. We draw the free-body diagram of pulley A. The couple $\mathbf{M}_A$ is applied to the pulley by the machine tool to which it is attached and is equal and opposite to the torque exerted by the belt. We write

$$+\circlearrowleft \Sigma M_A = 0: \quad M_A - (600 \text{ N})(.2 \text{ m}) + (355.4 \text{ N})(.2 \text{ m}) = 0$$

$$M_A = 48.9 \text{ N} \cdot \text{m} \qquad\qquad M_A = 49 \text{ N} \cdot \text{m} \blacktriangleleft$$

Note. We may check that the belt does not slip on pulley A by computing the value of μ_s required to prevent slipping at A and verifying that it is smaller than the actual value of μ_s. From Eq. (8.13) we have

$$\mu_s \beta = \ln \frac{T_2}{T_1} = \ln \frac{600 \text{ N}}{355.4 \text{ N}} = 0.524$$

and, since $\beta = 240° = 4\pi/3$ rad,

$$\frac{4\pi}{3} \mu_s = 0.524 \qquad \mu_s = 0.125 < 0.25$$

SOLVING PROBLEMS ON YOUR OWN

In the preceding section you learned about *belt friction*. The problems you will have to solve include belts passing over fixed drums, band brakes in which the drum rotates while the band remains fixed, and belt drives.

1. ***Problems involving belt friction*** fall into one of the following two categories:

a. Problems in which slipping is impending. One of the following formulas, involving the *coefficient of static friction* μ_s, may then be used:

$$\ln \frac{T_2}{T_1} = \mu_s \beta \qquad (8.13)$$

or

$$\frac{T_2}{T_1} = e^{\mu_s \beta} \qquad (8.14)$$

b. Problems in which slipping is occurring. The formulas to be used can be obtained from Eqs. (8.13) and (8.14) by replacing μ_s with the *coefficient of kinetic friction* μ_k.

2. ***As you start solving a belt-friction problem,*** be sure to remember the following:

a. The angle β must be expressed in radians. In a belt-and-drum problem, this is the angle subtending the arc of the drum on which the belt is wrapped.

b. The larger tension is always denoted by T_2, and the smaller tension is denoted by T_1.

c. The larger tension occurs at the end of the belt which is in the direction of the motion, or impending motion, of the belt relative to the drum. You can also determine the direction of the larger tension by remembering that the friction force acting on the belt and the larger tension are always opposed.

3. ***In each of the problems you will be asked to solve,*** three of the four quantities T_1, T_2, β, and μ_s (or μ_k) will either be given or readily found, and you will then solve the appropriate equation for the fourth quantity. There are two kinds of problems that you will encounter:

a. Find μ_s between the belt and the drum knowing that slipping is impending. From the given data, determine T_1, T_2, and β; substitute these values into Eq. (8.13) and solve for μ_s [Sample Prob. 8.7, part *a*]. Follow the same procedure to find the *smallest value* of μ_s for which slipping will not occur.

b. Find the magnitude of a force or couple applied to the belt or drum knowing that slipping is impending. The given data should include μ_s and β. If it also includes T_1 or T_2, use Eq. (8.14) to find the other tension. If neither T_1 nor T_2 is known but some other data is given, use the free-body diagram of the belt-drum system to write an equilibrium equation that you will solve simultaneously with Eq. (8.14) for T_1 and T_2. You will then be able to find the magnitude of the specified force or couple from the free-body diagram of the system. Follow the same procedure to determine the *largest value* of a force or couple which can be applied to the belt or drum if no slipping is to occur [Sample Prob. 8.8].

Problems

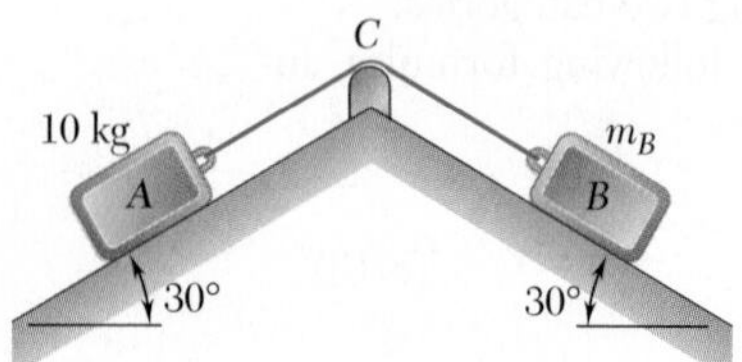

Fig. *P8.102* and *P8.103*

8.101 A hawser is wrapped two full turns around a bollard. By exerting a 320-N force on the free end of the hawser, a dockworker can resist a force of 20 kN on the other end of the hawser. Determine (*a*) the coefficient of static friction between the hawser and the bollard, (*b*) the number of times the hawser should be wrapped around the bollard if an 80-kN force is to be resisted by the same 320-N force.

8.102 Blocks *A* and *B* are connected by a cable that passes over support *C*. Friction between the blocks and the inclined surfaces may be neglected. Knowing that motion of block *B* up the incline is impending when $m_B = 8$ kg, determine (*a*) the coefficient of static friction between the rope and the support, (*b*) the largest value of m_B for which equilibrium is maintained. (*Hint:* See Prob. 8.128.)

8.103 Blocks *A* and *B* are connected by a cable that passes over support *C*. Friction between the blocks and the inclined surfaces may be neglected. Knowing that the coefficient of static friction between the rope and the support is 0.50, determine the range of values of m_B for which equilibrium is maintained. (*Hint:* See Prob. 8.128.)

8.104 A 120-kg block is supported by a rope which is wrapped $1\frac{1}{2}$ times around a horizontal rod. Knowing that the coefficient of static friction between the rope and the rod is 0.15, determine the range of values of *P* for which equilibrium is maintained.

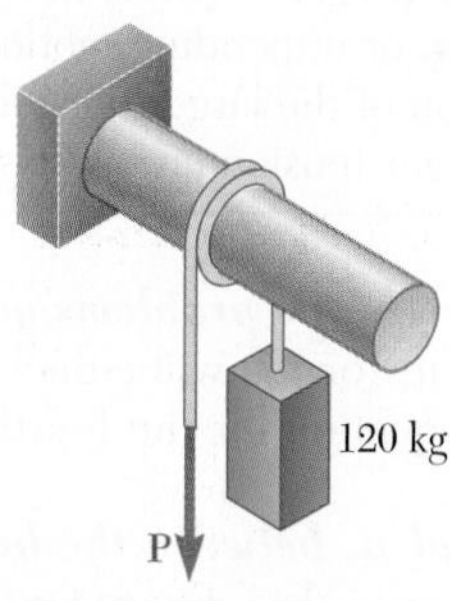

Fig. P8.104

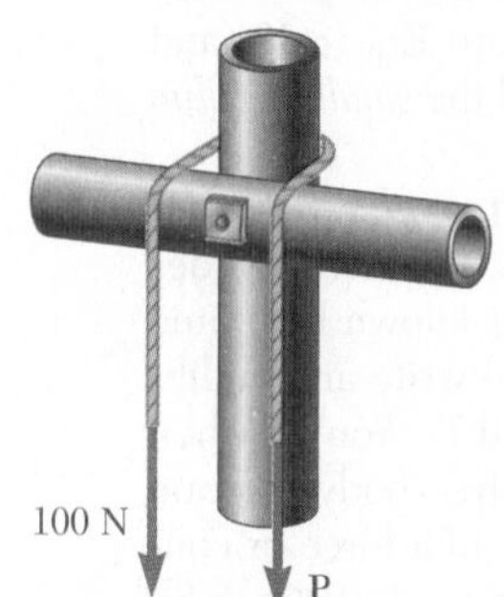

Fig. P8.105 and P8.106

8.105 Knowing that the coefficient of static friction is 0.25 between the rope and the horizontal pipe and 0.20 between the rope and the vertical pipe, determine the range of values of *P* for which equilibrium is maintained.

8.106 Knowing that the coefficient of static friction is 0.30 between the rope and the horizontal pipe and that the smallest value of *P* for which equilibrium is maintained is 20 N, determine (*a*) the largest value of *P* for which equilibrium is maintained, (*b*) the coefficient of static friction between the rope and the vertical pipe.

8.107 In the pivoted motor mount shown, the weight **W** of the 175-N motor is used to maintain tension in the drive belt. Knowing that the coefficient of static friction between the flat belt and drums A and B is 0.40 and neglecting the weight of platform CD, determine the largest couple which can be transmitted to drum B when the drive drum A is rotating clockwise.

8.108 Solve Prob. 8.107 assuming that the drive drum A is rotating counterclockwise.

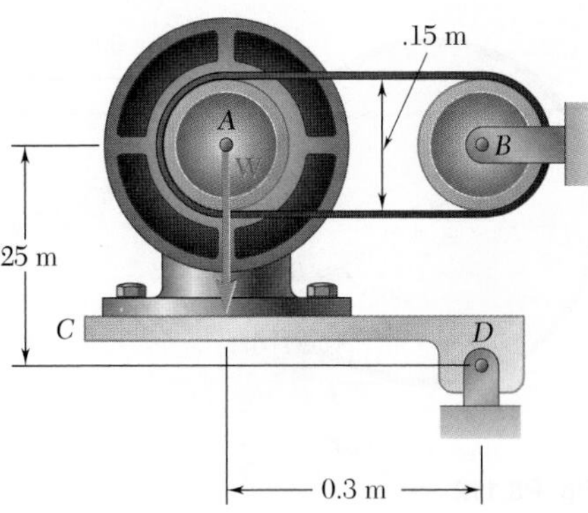

Fig. P8.107

8.109 A couple $\mathbf{M}_B$ of magnitude 2.4 N · m is applied to the drive drum B of a portable belt sander to maintain the sanding belt C at a constant speed. The total downward force exerted on the wooden workpiece E is 48 N, and $\mu_k = 0.10$ between the belt and the sanding platen D. Knowing that $\mu_s = 0.35$ between the belt and the drive drum and that the radii of drums A and B are 25 mm, determine (*a*) the minimum tension in the lower portion of the belt if no slipping is to occur between the belt and the drive drum, (*b*) the value of the coefficient of kinetic friction between the belt and the workpiece.

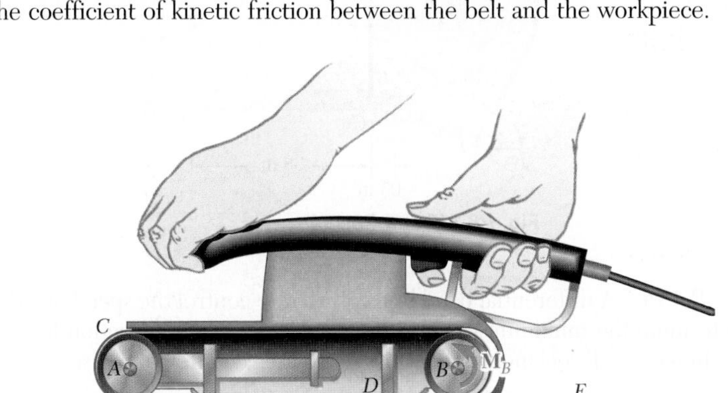

Fig. P8.109

8.110 The setup shown is used to measure the output of a small turbine. When the flywheel is at rest, the reading of each spring scale is 70 N. If a 12.60-N · m couple must be applied to the flywheel to keep it rotating clockwise at a constant speed, determine (*a*) the reading of each scale at that time, (*b*) the coefficient of kinetic friction. Assume that the length of the belt does not change.

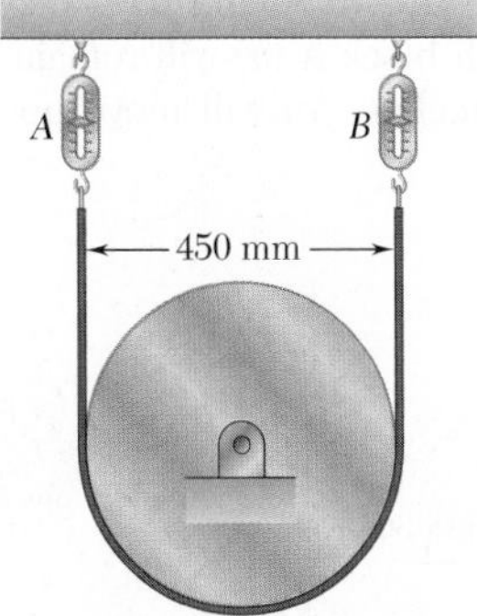

Fig. P8.110 and P8.111

8.111 The setup shown is used to measure the output of a small turbine. The coefficient of kinetic friction is 0.20, and the reading of each spring scale is 80 N when the flywheel is at rest. Determine (*a*) the reading of each scale when the flywheel is rotating clockwise at a constant speed, (*b*) the couple which must be applied to the flywheel. Assume that the length of the belt does not change.

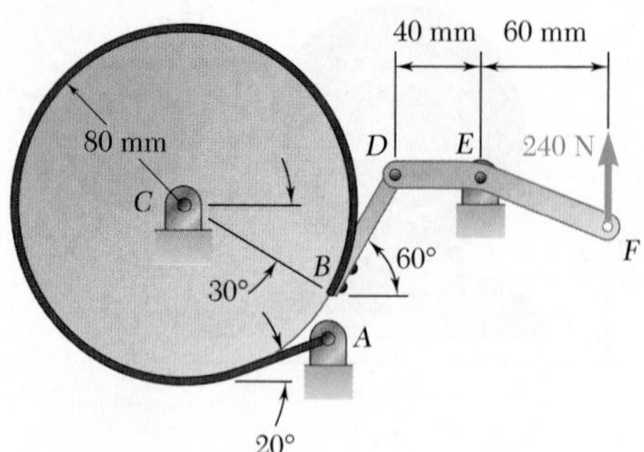

Fig. P8.112

8.112 The band brake shown is used to control the speed of a rotating drum. Determine the magnitude of the couple being applied to the drum knowing that the coefficient of kinetic friction between the belt and the drum is 0.25 and that the drum is rotating clockwise at a constant speed.

8.113 A differential band brake is used to control the speed of a drum which rotates at a constant speed. Knowing that the coefficient of kinetic friction between the belt and the drum is 0.30 and that a couple of magnitude 125 N · m is applied to the drum, determine the corresponding magnitude of the force **P** that is exerted on end D of the lever when the drum is rotating (*a*) clockwise, (*b*) counterclockwise.

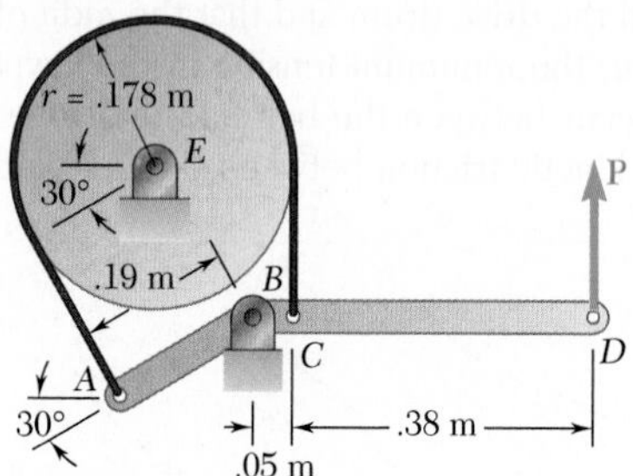

Fig. *P8.113* and P8.114

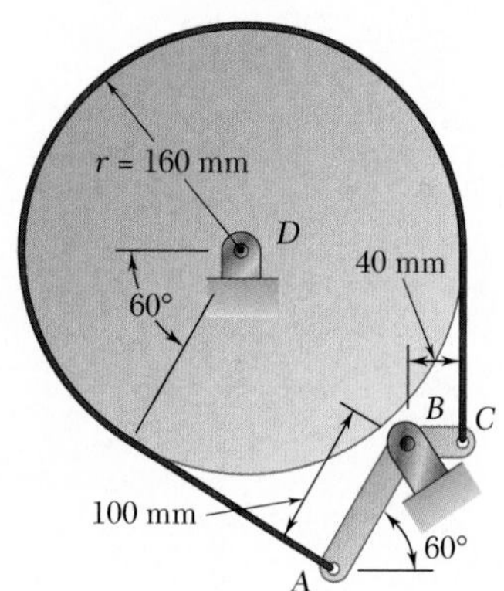

Fig. P8.115

8.114 A differential band brake is used to control the speed of a drum. Determine the minimum value of the coefficient of static friction for which the brake is self-locking when the drum rotates counterclockwise.

8.115 The drum brake shown permits clockwise rotation of the drum but prevents rotation in the counterclockwise direction. Knowing that the maximum allowed tension in the belt is 4.5 kN, determine (*a*) the magnitude of the largest counterclockwise couple that can be applied to the drum, (*b*) the smallest value of the coefficient of static friction between the belt and the drum for which the drum will not rotate counterclockwise.

8.116 Blocks A and C are connected by a rope that passes over drum B. Knowing that the drum rotates slowly clockwise and that the coefficients of friction at all surfaces are $\mu_s = 0.30$ and $\mu_k = 0.20$, determine the smallest mass of block C for which block A (*a*) will remain at rest, (*b*) will be in impending motion up the incline, (*c*) will move up the incline at a constant speed.

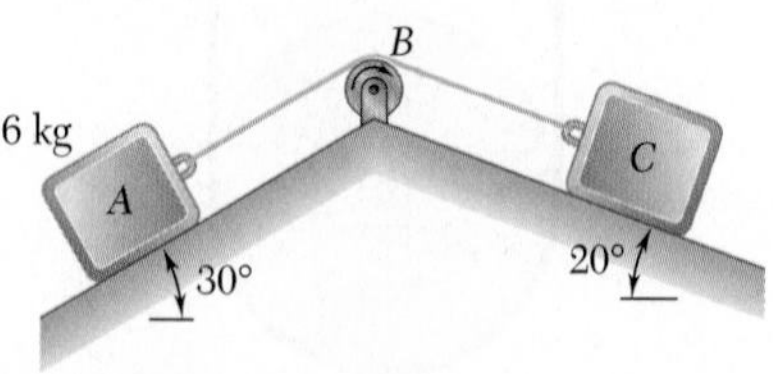

Fig. P8.116

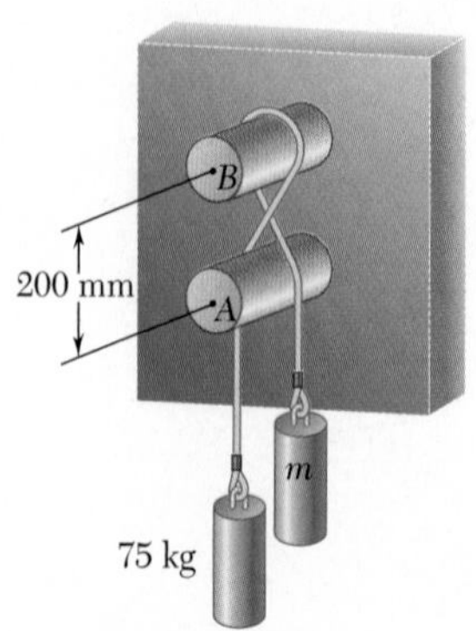

Fig. P8.117

8.117 A cord is placed over two 100-mm-diameter cylinders. Knowing that the coefficients of friction are $\mu_s = 0.30$ and $\mu_k = 0.25$, determine the largest mass m that can be raised when cylinder B is rotated slowly and cylinder A is kept fixed.

8.118 and 8.120 A cable passes around three .05-m-radius pulleys and supports two blocks as shown. Pulleys C and E are locked to prevent rotation, and the coefficients of friction between the cable and the pulleys are $\mu_s = 0.20$ and $\mu_k = 0.15$. Determine the range of values of the weight of block A for which equilibrium is maintained (*a*) if pulley D is locked, (*b*) if pulley D is free to rotate.

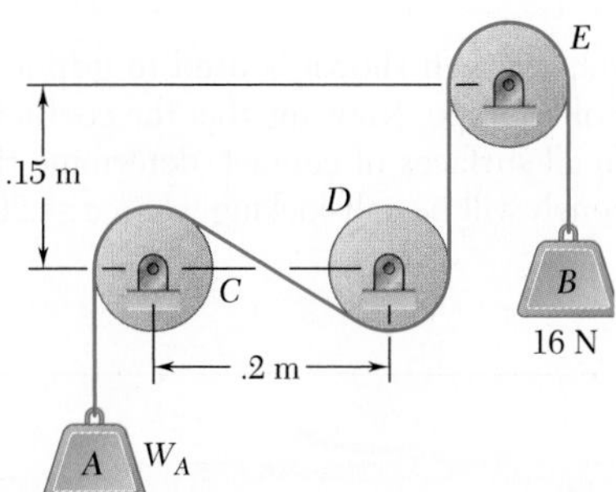

Fig. P8.118 and *P8.119*

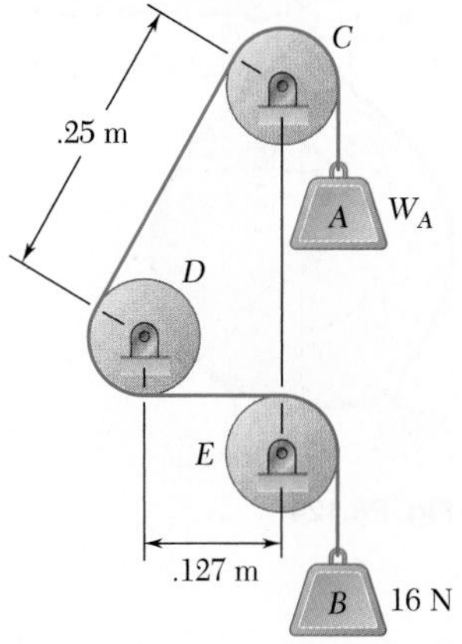

Fig. P8.120 and *P8.121*

8.119* and *8.121 A cable passes around three .05-m-radius pulleys and supports two blocks as shown. Two of the pulleys are locked to prevent rotation, while the third pulley is rotated slowly at a constant speed. Knowing that the coefficients of friction between the cable and the pulleys are $\mu_s = 0.20$ and $\mu_k = 0.15$, determine the largest weight W_A which can be raised (*a*) if pulley C is rotated, (*b*) if pulley E is rotated.

8.122 A recording tape passes over the 20-mm-radius drive drum B and under the idler drum C. Knowing that the coefficients of friction between the tape and the drums are $\mu_s = 0.40$ and $\mu_k = 0.30$ and that drum C is free to rotate, determine the smallest allowable value of P if slipping of the tape on drum B is not to occur.

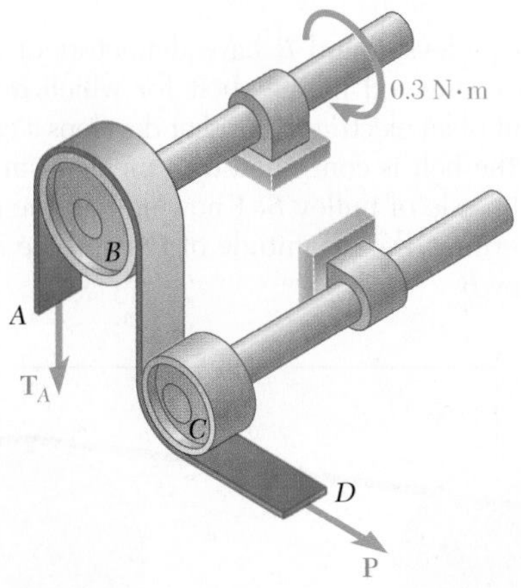

Fig. P8.122

8.123 Solve Prob. 8.122 assuming that the idler drum C is frozen and cannot rotate.

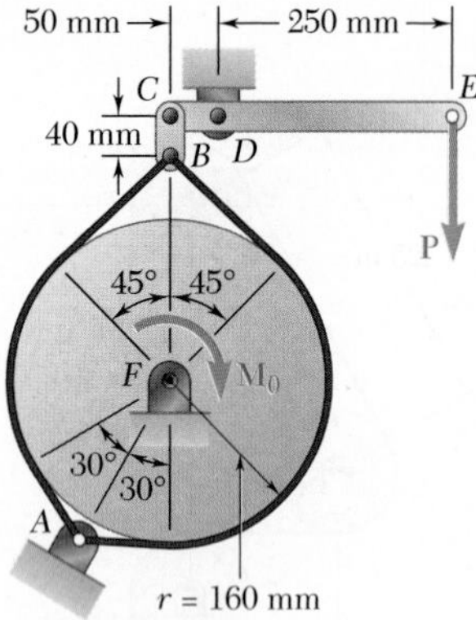

Fig. P8.124

8.124 For the band brake shown, the maximum allowed tension in either belt is 5.6 kN. Knowing that the coefficient of static friction between the belt and the 160-mm-radius drum is 0.25, determine (*a*) the largest clockwise moment $\mathbf{M}_0$ that can be applied to the drum if slipping is not to occur, (*b*) the corresponding force **P** exerted on end *E* of the lever.

8.125 Solve Prob. 8.124 assuming that a counterclockwise moment is applied to the drum.

8.126 The strap wrench shown is used to grip a pipe firmly without marring the surface of the pipe. Knowing that the coefficient of static friction is the same between all surfaces of contact, determine the smallest value of μ_s for which the wrench will be self-locking when $a = 200$ mm, $r = 30$ mm, and $\theta = 65°$.

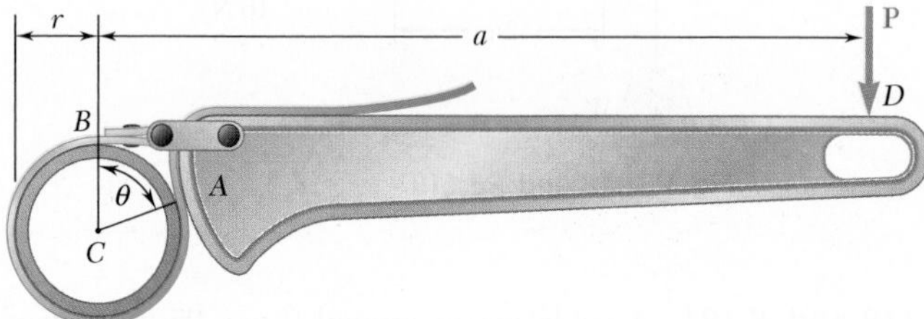

Fig. P8.126

8.127 Solve Prob. 8.126 assuming that $\theta = 75°$.

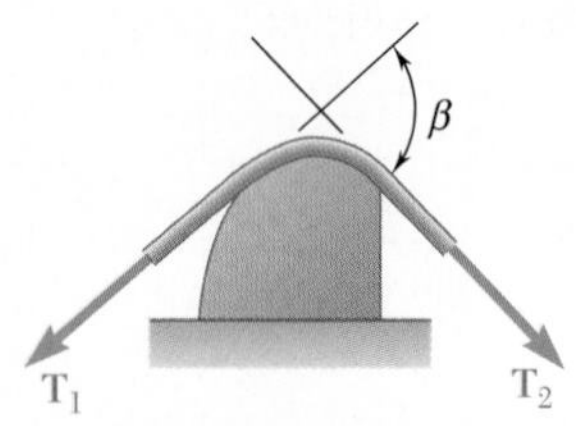

Fig. P8.128

8.128 Prove that Eqs. (8.13) and (8.14) are valid for any shape of surface provided that the coefficient of friction is the same at all points of contact.

8.129 Complete the derivation of Eq. (8.15), which relates the tension in both parts of a V belt.

8.130 Solve Prob. 8.107 assuming that the flat belt and drums are replaced with a V belt and V pulleys for which $\alpha = 36°$. (The angle α is as shown in Fig. 8.15*a*.)

8.131 The V pulleys *A* and *B* have diameters of .1 m and .2 m, respectively, and are connected by a V belt for which $\alpha = 36°$. Pulley *A* is mounted on the shaft of an electric motor that develops a couple $M = 5$ N · m, and the tension in the belt is controlled by a mechanism that applies a horizontal force **P** to the axle of pulley *B*. Knowing that the coefficient of static friction is 0.35, determine the magnitude of **P** when the maximum couple is transmitted to pulley *B*.

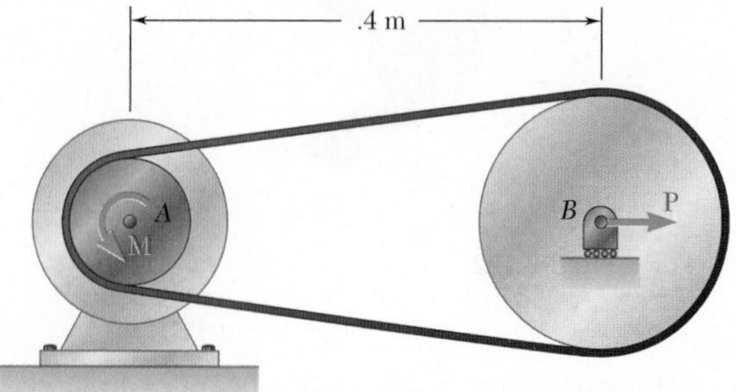

Fig. P8.131

REVIEW AND SUMMARY FOR CHAPTER 8

This chapter was devoted to the study of *dry friction,* that is, to problems involving rigid bodies which are in contact along *nonlubricated surfaces*.

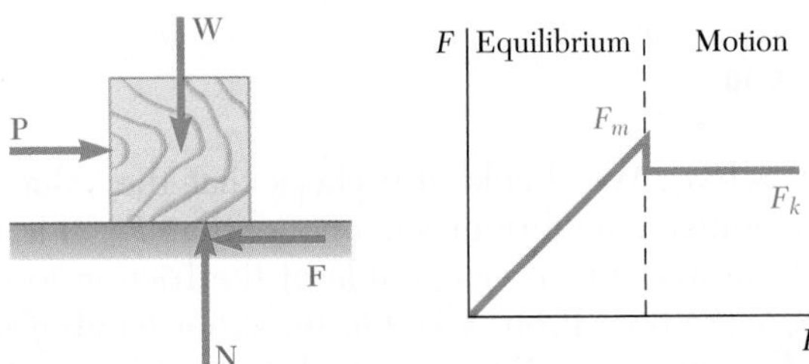

Fig. 8.16

Static and kinetic friction

Applying a horizontal force **P** to a block resting on a horizontal surface [Sec. 8.2], we note that the block at first does not move. This shows that a *friction force* **F** must have developed to balance **P** (Fig. 8.16). As the magnitude of **P** is increased, the magnitude of **F** also increases until it reaches a maximum value F_m. If **P** is further increased, the block starts sliding and the magnitude of **F** drops from F_m to a lower value F_k. Experimental evidence shows that F_m and F_k are proportional to the normal component N of the reaction of the surface. We have

$$F_m = \mu_s N \qquad F_k = \mu_k N \qquad (8.1, 8.2)$$

where μ_s and μ_k are called, respectively, the *coefficient of static friction* and the *coefficient of kinetic friction*. These coefficients depend on the nature and the condition of the surfaces in contact. Approximate values of the coefficients of static friction were given in Table 8.1.

Angles of friction

It is sometimes convenient to replace the normal force **N** and the friction force **F** by their resultant **R** (Fig. 8.17). As the friction force increases and reaches its maximum value $F_m = \mu_s N$, the angle ϕ that **R** forms with the normal to the surface increases and reaches a maximum value ϕ_s, called the *angle of static friction*. If motion actually takes place, the magnitude of **F** drops to F_k; similarly the angle ϕ drops to a lower value ϕ_k, called the *angle of kinetic friction*. As shown in Sec. 8.3, we have

$$\tan \phi_s = \mu_s \qquad \tan \phi_k = \mu_k \qquad (8.3, 8.4)$$

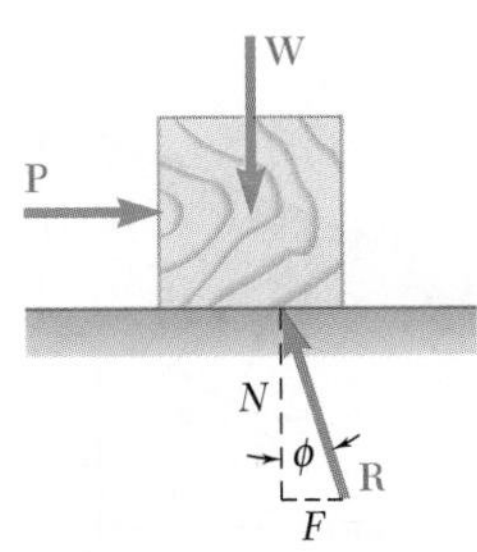

Fig. 8.17

Problems involving friction

When solving equilibrium problems involving friction, we should keep in mind that the magnitude F of the friction force is equal to $F_m = \mu_s N$ *only if the body is about to slide* [Sec. 8.4]. *If motion is not impending,* F and N should be considered as *independent unknowns* to be determined from the equilibrium equations (Fig. 8.18*a*). We should also check that the value of F required to maintain equilibrium is not larger than F_m; if it were, the body would move and the magnitude of the friction force would be $F_k = \mu_k N$ [Sample Prob. 8.1]. On the other hand, *if motion is known to be impending,* F has reached its maximum value $F_m = \mu_s N$ (Fig. 8.18*b*), and this expression may be substituted for F in the equilibrium equations [Sample Prob. 8.3]. When only three forces are involved in a free-body diagram, including the reaction **R** of the surface in contact with the body, it is usually more convenient to solve the problem by drawing a force triangle [Sample Prob. 8.2].

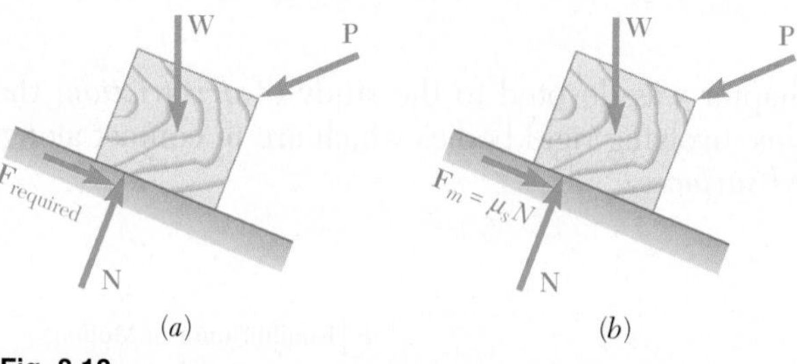

Fig. 8.18

When a problem involves the analysis of the forces exerted on each other by *two bodies A and B,* it is important to show the friction forces with their correct sense. The correct sense for the friction force exerted by B on A, for instance, is opposite to that of the *relative motion* (or impending motion) of A with respect to B [Fig. 8.6].

Wedges and screws

In the second part of the chapter we considered a number of specific engineering applications where dry friction plays an important role. In the case of *wedges,* which are simple machines used to raise heavy loads [Sec. 8.5], two or more free-body diagrams were drawn and care was taken to show each friction force with its correct sense [Sample Prob. 8.4]. The analysis of *square-threaded screws,* which are frequently used in jacks, presses, and other mechanisms, was reduced to the analysis of a block sliding on an incline by unwrapping the thread of the screw and showing it as a straight line [Sec. 8.6]. This is done again in Fig. 8.19, where r denotes the *mean radius* of the thread, L is the *lead* of the screw, that is, the distance through which the screw advances in one turn, **W** is the load, and Qr is equal to the couple exerted on the screw. It was noted that in the case of multiple-threaded screws the lead L of the screw is *not* equal to its pitch, which is the distance measured between two consecutive threads.

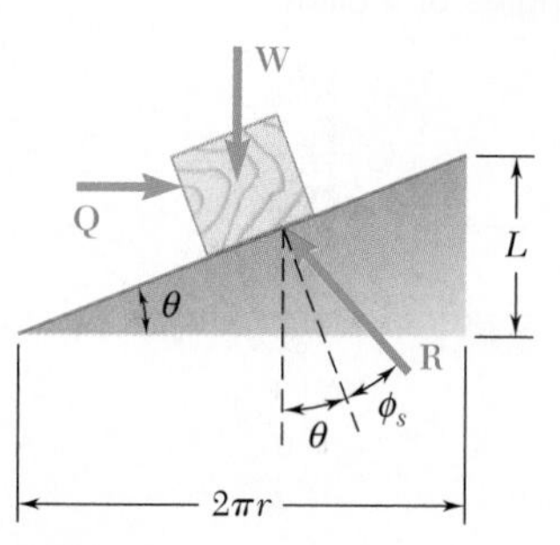

Fig. 8.19

Other engineering applications considered in this chapter were *journal bearings* and *axle friction* [Sec. 8.7], *thrust bearings* and *disk friction* [Sec. 8.8], *wheel friction* and *rolling resistance* [Sec. 8.9], and *belt friction* [Sec. 8.10].

Belt friction

In solving a problem involving a *flat belt* passing over a fixed cylinder, it is important to first determine the direction in which the belt slips or is about to slip. If the drum is rotating, the motion or impending motion of the belt should be determined *relative* to the rotating drum. For instance, if the belt shown in Fig. 8.20 is

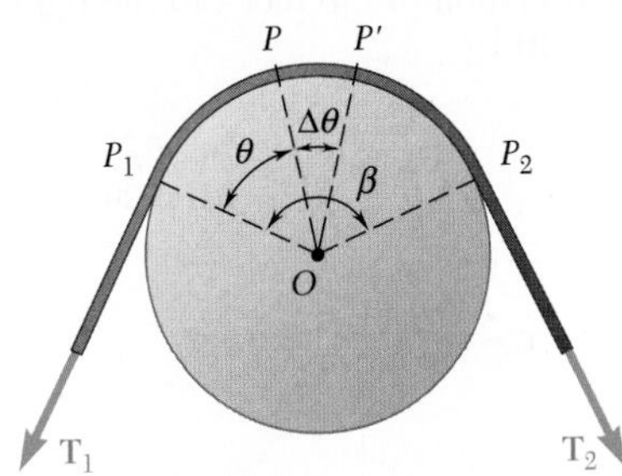

Fig. 8.20

about to slip to the right relative to the drum, the friction forces exerted by the drum on the belt will be directed to the left and the tension will be larger in the right-hand portion of the belt than in the left-hand portion. Denoting the larger tension by T_2, the smaller tension by T_1, the coefficient of static friction by μ_s, and the angle (in radians) subtended by the belt by β, we derived in Sec. 8.10 the formulas

$$\ln \frac{T_2}{T_1} = \mu_s \beta \tag{8.13}$$

$$\frac{T_2}{T_1} = e^{\mu_s \beta} \tag{8.14}$$

which were used in solving Sample Probs. 8.7 and 8.8. If the belt actually slips on the drum, the coefficient of static friction μ_s should be replaced by the coefficient of kinetic friction μ_k in both of these formulas.

Review Problems

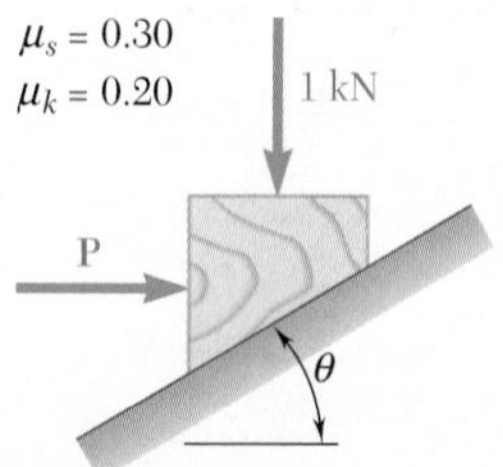

Fig. P8.132

8.132 Determine whether the block shown is in equilibrium, and find the magnitude and direction of the friction force when $\theta = 30°$ and $P = 200$ N.

8.133 Considering only values of θ less than 90°, determine the smallest value of θ for which motion of the block to the right is impending when (*a*) $m = 30$ kg, (*b*) $m = 40$ kg.

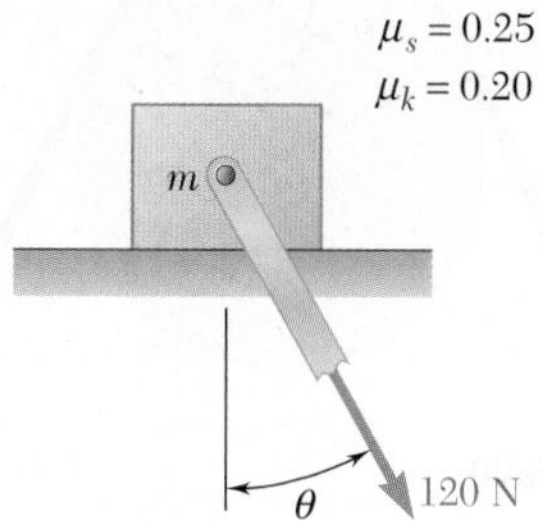

Fig. P8.133

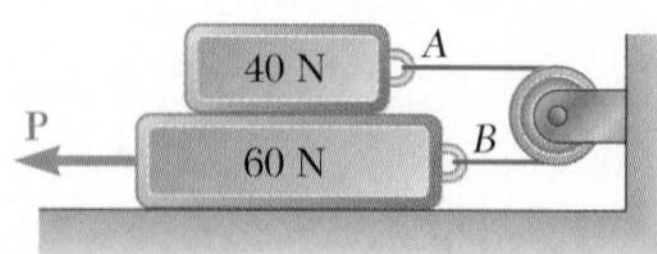

Fig. *P8.134*

8.134 The coefficients of friction are $\mu_s = 0.40$ and $\mu_k = 0.30$ between all surfaces of contact. Determine the force **P** for which motion of the 60-N block is impending if cable *AB* (*a*) is attached as shown, (*b*) is removed.

8.135 A 5.85-m ladder *AB* leans against a wall as shown. Assuming that the coefficient of static friction μ_s is the same at *A* and *B*, determine the smallest value of μ_s for which equilibrium is maintained.

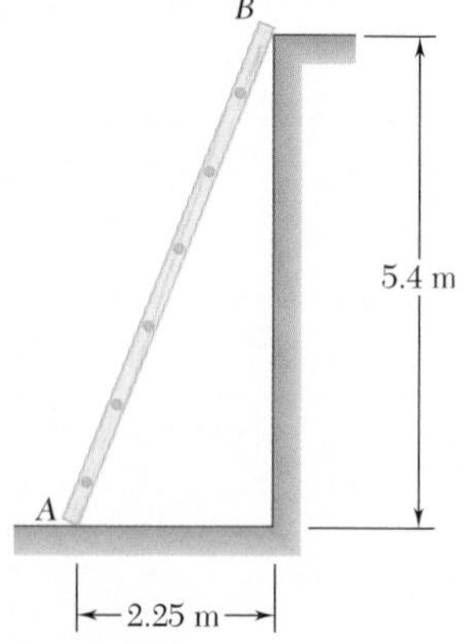

Fig. P8.135

8.136 A window sash having a mass of 4 kg is normally supported by two 2-kg sash weights. Knowing that the window remains open after one sash cord has broken, determine the smallest possible value of the coefficient of static friction. (Assume that the sash is slightly smaller than the frame and will bind only at points *A* and *D*.)

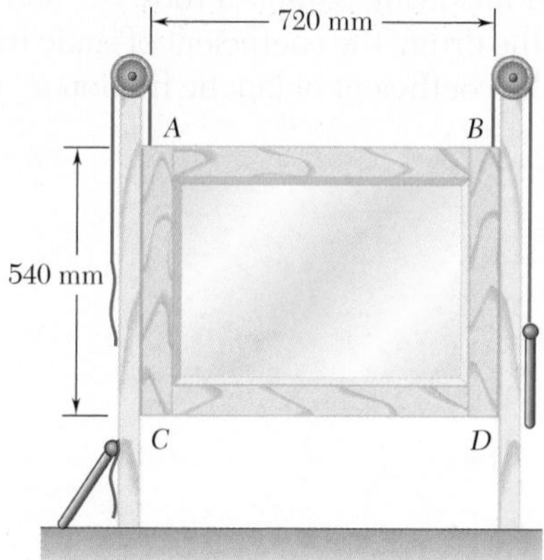

Fig. P8.136

8.137 A collar B of weight W is attached to the spring AB and can move along the rod shown. The constant of the spring is 1.5 kN/m and the spring is unstretched when $\theta = 0$. Knowing that the coefficient of static friction between the collar and the rod is 0.40, determine the range of values of W for which equilibrium is maintained when (*a*) $\theta = 20°$, (*b*) $\theta = 30°$.

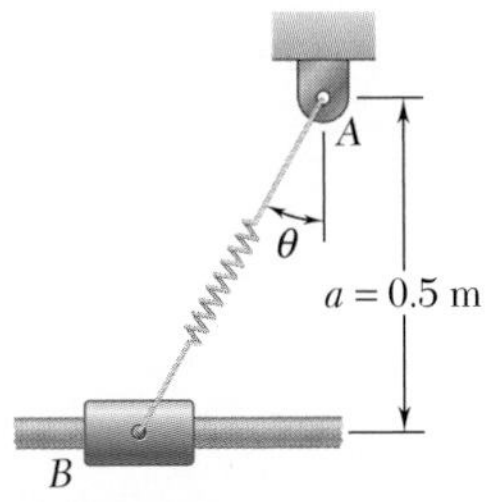

Fig. P8.137

8.137 Two slender rods of negligible weight are pin-connected at C and attached to blocks A and B each of weight W. Knowing that $\theta = 70°$ and that the coefficient of static friction between the blocks and the horizontal surface is 0.30, determine the largest value of P for which equilibrium is maintained.

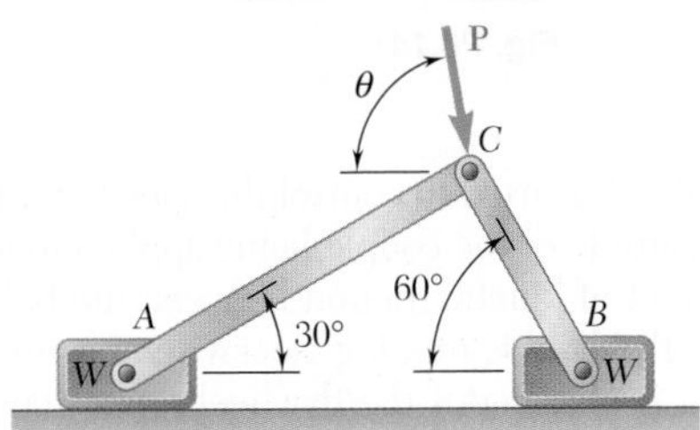

Fig. *P8.138*

8.139 Block A supports a pipe column and rests as shown on wedge B. Knowing that the coefficient of static friction at all surfaces of contact is 0.25 and that $\theta = 45°$, determine the smallest force $\mathbf{P}$ required to raise block A.

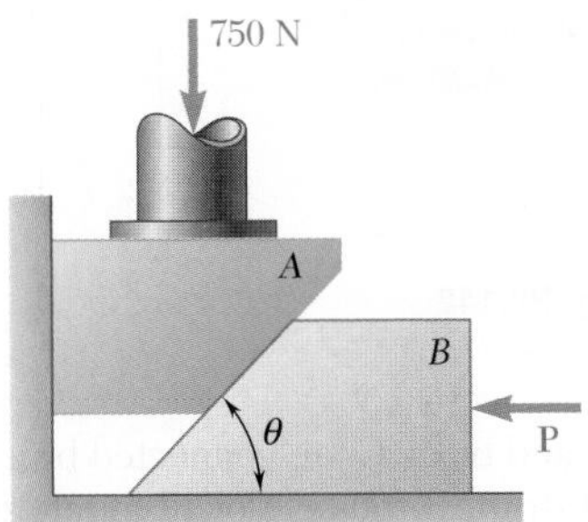

Fig. P8.139

8.140 The ends of two fixed rods A and B are single-threaded screws of mean radius .0076 m and pitch .0025 m. Rod A has a right-handed thread, and rod B has a left-handed thread. The coefficient of static friction between the rods and the threaded sleeve is 0.12. Determine the magnitude of the couple that must be applied to the sleeve to draw the rods closer together.

Fig. *P8.140*

8.141 A 120-mm-radius pulley of mass 5 kg is attached to a 30-mm-radius shaft which fits loosely in a fixed bearing. It is observed that motion of the pulley is impending if a 0.5-kg mass is added to block *A*. Determine the coefficient of static friction between the shaft and the bearing.

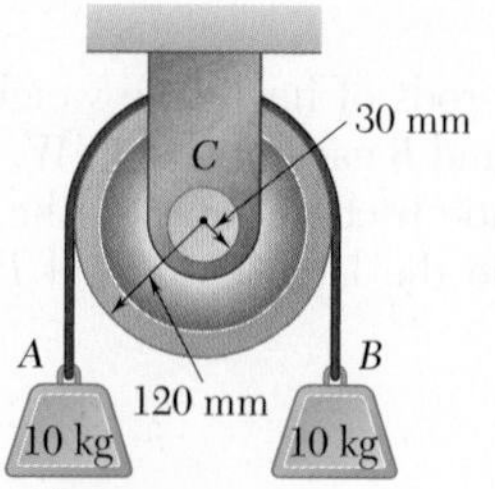

Fig. P8.141

8.142 A band belt is used to control the speed of a flywheel as shown. Determine the magnitude of the couple being applied to the flywheel knowing that the coefficient of kinetic friction between the belt and the flywheel is 0.25 and that the flywheel is rotating clockwise at a constant speed. Show that the same result is obtained if the flywheel rotates counterclockwise.

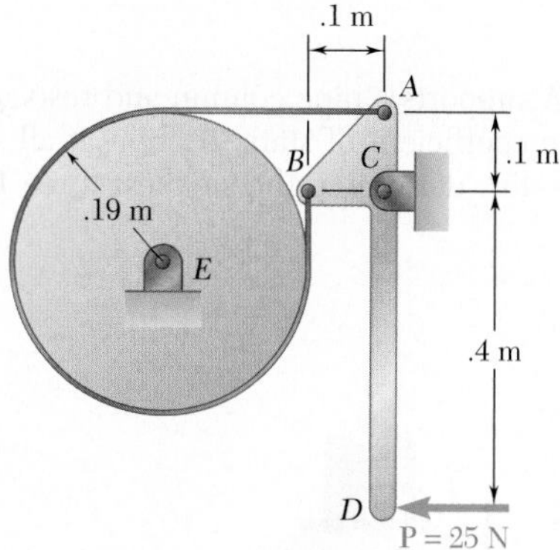

Fig. P8.142

8.143 Bucket *A* and block *C* are connected by a cable that passes over drum *B*. Knowing that drum *B* rotates slowly counterclockwise and that the coefficients of friction at all surfaces are $\mu_s = 0.35$ and $\mu_k = 0.25$, determine the smallest combined weight *W* of the bucket and its contents for which block *C* will (*a*) remain at rest, (*b*) be about to move up the incline, (*c*) continue moving up the incline at a constant speed.

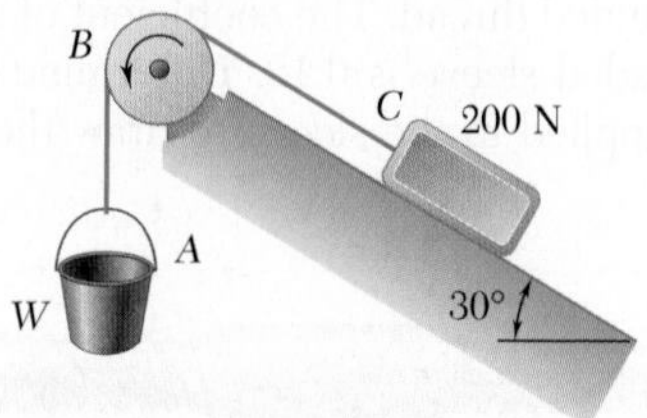

Fig. *P8.143*

Computer Problems

8.C1 Two blocks are connected by a cable as shown. Knowing that the coefficient of static friction between block A and the horizontal surface varies between 0 and 0.6, determine the values of θ for which motion is impending and plot these values as a function of the coefficient of static friction.

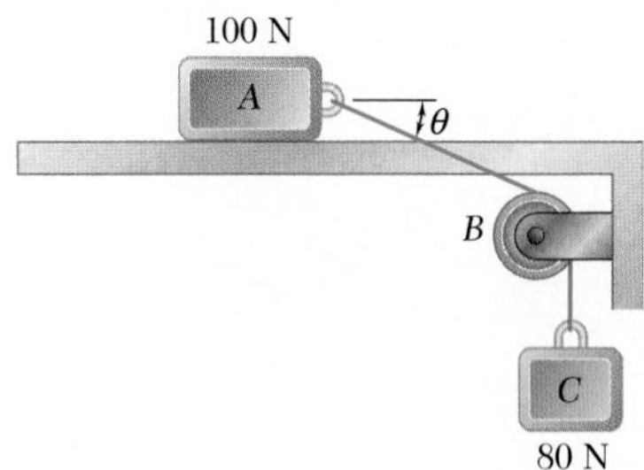

Fig. P8.C1

8.C2 The slender rod AB of length l = .38 m is attached to a collar A and rests on a wheel located at a vertical distance a = .0635 m from the horizontal rod on which the collar slides. Neglecting friction at C, use computational software to determine the range of values of the magnitude of **Q** for which equilibrium is maintained. Plot the maximum and minimum values of **Q** as functions of the coefficient of static friction for $0.10 \leq \mu_s \leq 0.55$ when P = 15 N and θ = 20°.

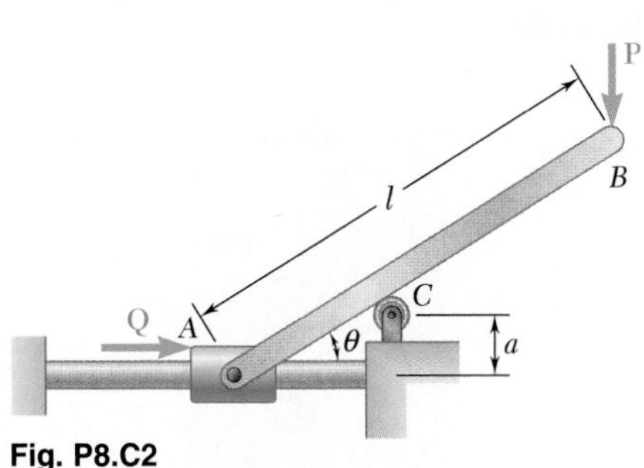

Fig. P8.C2

8.C3 Blocks A and B are supported by an incline which is held in the position shown. Knowing that the mass of block A is 10 kg and that the coefficient of static friction between all surfaces of contact is 0.15, use computational software to determine the value of θ for which motion is impending for values of the mass of block B from 0 to 50 kg using 5-kg increments.

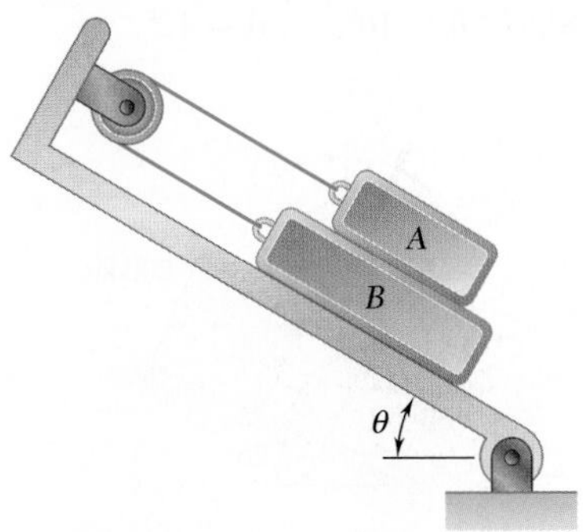

Fig. P8.C3

8.C4 The position of the 20-N rod AB is controlled by the 4-N block shown, which is slowly moved to the left by the force **P**. Knowing that the coefficient of kinetic friction between all surfaces of contact is 0.25, use computational software to plot the magnitude P of the force as a function of x for values of x from 1.14 m to 0.13 m. Determine the maximum value of P and the corresponding value of x.

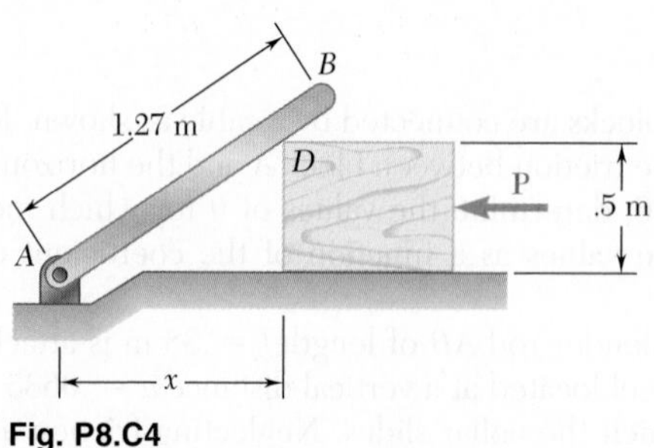

Fig. P8.C4

8.C5 A 0.6-N cylinder C rests on cylinder D as shown. Knowing that the coefficient of static friction μ_s is the same at A and B, use computational software to determine, for values of μ_s from 0 to 0.40 and using 0.05 increments, the largest counterclockwise couple **M** which can be applied to cylinder D if it is not to rotate.

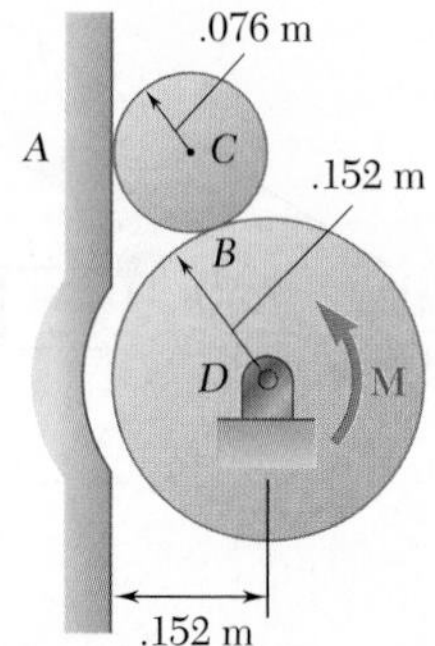

Fig. P8.C5

8.C6 Two identical wedges of negligible mass are used to move and position a 200-kg block. Knowing that the coefficient of static friction μ_s is the same between all surfaces of contact, plot the magnitude of the force **P** for which motion of the block is impending as a function of μ_s for $0.2 \leq \mu_s \leq 0.8$ when (*a*) $\theta = 8°$, (*b*) $\theta = 10°$, (*c*) $\theta = 12°$.

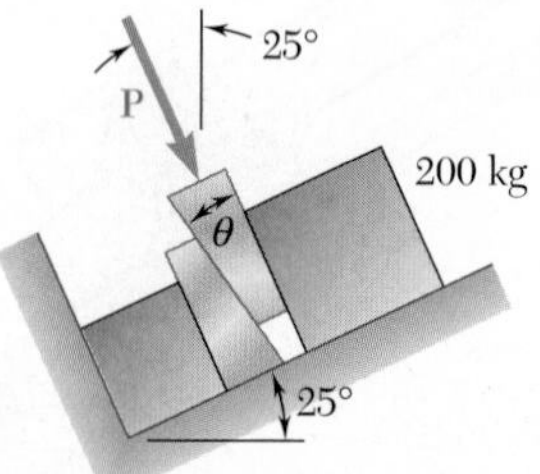

Fig. P8.C6

8.C7 The axle of the pulley shown is frozen and cannot rotate with respect to the block. Knowing that the coefficient of static friction between cable *ABCD* and the pulley varies between 0 and 0.55, determine (*a*) the corresponding values of θ for the system to remain in equilibrium, (*b*) the corresponding reactions at *A* and *D*, and (*c*) plot the values of θ as a function of the coefficient of friction.

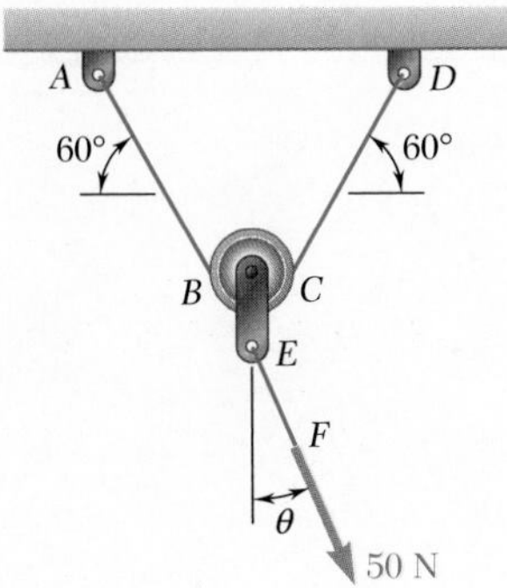

Fig. P8.C7

8.C8 A cable passes around two 50-mm-radius pulleys and supports two blocks as shown. Pulley *B* can only rotate clockwise and pulley *C* can only rotate counterclockwise. Knowing that the coefficient of static friction between the cable and the pulleys is 0.25, plot the minimum and maximum values of the mass of block *D* for which equilibrium is maintained as functions of θ for $15° \leq \theta \leq 40°$.

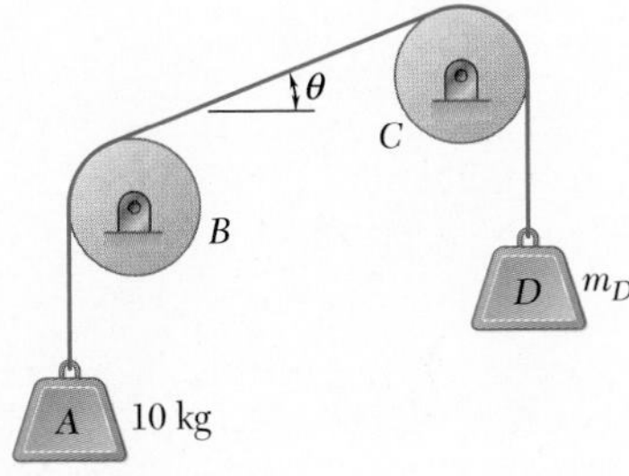

Fig. P8.C8

8.C9 A flat belt is used to transmit a couple from drum *A* to drum *B*. The radius of each drum is .1 m, and the system is fitted with an idler wheel *C* that is used to increase the contact between the belt and the drums. The allowable belt tension is 50 N, and the coefficient of static friction between the belt and the drums is 0.30. Using computational software, calculate and plot the largest couple that can be transmitted as a function of θ for $0 \leq \theta \leq 30°$.

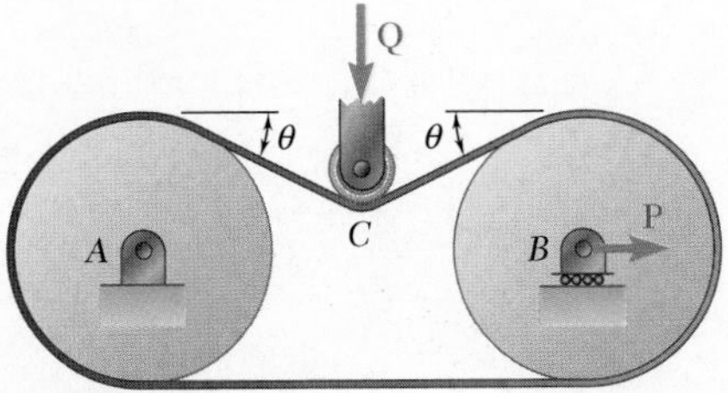

Fig. P8.C9

CHAPTER 9

Distributed Forces: Moments of Inertia

The strength of structural members depends to a large extent on the properties of their cross sections, particularly on the second moments—or moments of inertia—of their areas.

DISTRIBUTED FORCES: MOMENTS OF INERTIA

9.1. INTRODUCTION

In Chap. 5, we analyzed various systems of forces distributed over an area or volume. The three main types of forces considered were (1) weights of homogeneous plates of uniform thickness (Secs. 5.3 through 5.6), (2) distributed loads on beams (Sec. 5.8) and hydrostatic forces (Sec. 5.9), and (3) weights of homogeneous three-dimensional bodies (Secs. 5.10 and 5.11). In the case of homogeneous plates, the magnitude ΔW of the weight of an element of a plate was proportional to the area ΔA of the element. For distributed loads on beams, the magnitude ΔW of each elemental weight was represented by an element of area $\Delta A = \Delta W$ under the load curve; in the case of hydrostatic forces on submerged rectangular surfaces, a similar procedure was followed. In the case of homogeneous three-dimensional bodies, the magnitude ΔW of the weight of an element of the body was proportional to the volume ΔV of the element. Thus, in all cases considered in Chap. 5, the distributed forces were proportional to the elemental areas or volumes associated with them. The resultant of these forces, therefore, could be obtained by summing the corresponding areas or volumes, and the moment of the resultant about any given axis could be determined by computing the first moments of the areas or volumes about that axis.

In the first part of this chapter, we consider distributed forces $\Delta\mathbf{F}$ whose magnitudes depend not only upon the elements of area ΔA on which these forces act but also upon the distance from ΔA to some given axis. More precisely, the magnitude of the force per unit area $\Delta F/\Delta A$ is assumed to vary linearly with the distance to the axis. As indicated in the next section, forces of this type are found in the study of the bending of beams and in problems involving submerged nonrectangular surfaces. Assuming that the elemental forces involved are distributed over an area A and vary linearly with the distance y to the x axis, it will be shown that while the magnitude of their resultant $\mathbf{R}$ depends upon the first moment $Q_x = \int y\, dA$ of the area A, the location of the point where $\mathbf{R}$ is applied depends upon the *second moment*, or *moment of inertia*, $I_x = \int y^2\, dA$ of the same area with respect to the x axis. You will learn to compute the moments of inertia of various areas with respect to given x and y axes. Also introduced in the first part of this chapter is the *polar moment of inertia* $J_O = \int r^2\, dA$ of an area, where r is the distance from the element of area dA to the point O. To facilitate your computations, a relation will be established between the moment of inertia I_x of an area A with respect to a given x axis and the moment of inertia $I_{x'}$ of the same area with respect to the parallel centroidal x' axis (parallel-axis theorem). You will also study the transformation of the moments of inertia of a given area when the coordinate axes are rotated (Secs. 9.9 and 9.10).

In the second part of the chapter, you will learn how to determine the moments of inertia of various *masses* with respect to a given axis. As you will see in Sec. 9.11, the moment of inertia of a given mass about an axis AA' is defined as $I = \int r^2\, dm$, where r is the distance from the axis AA' to the element of mass dm. Moments of inertia of masses are encountered in dynamics in problems involving the rotation of a rigid body about an axis. To facilitate the computation of mass moments of inertia, the parallel-axis theorem will be introduced (Sec. 9.12). Finally, you will learn to analyze the transformation of moments of inertia of masses when the coordinate axes are rotated (Secs. 9.16 through 9.18).

9.2. SECOND MOMENT, OR MOMENT OF INERTIA, OF AN AREA

In the first part of this chapter, we consider distributed forces $\mathbf{\Delta F}$ whose magnitudes ΔF are proportional to the elements of area ΔA on which the forces act and at the same time vary linearly with the distance from ΔA to a given axis.

Consider, for example, a beam of uniform cross section which is subjected to two equal and opposite couples applied at each end of the beam. Such a beam is said to be in *pure bending*, and it is shown in mechanics of materials that the internal forces in any section of the beam are distributed forces whose magnitudes $\Delta F = ky\ \Delta A$ vary linearly with the distance y between the element of area ΔA and an axis passing through the centroid of the section. This axis, represented by the x axis in Fig. 9.1, is known as the *neutral axis* of the section. The forces on one side of the neutral axis are forces of compression, while those on the other side are forces of tension; on the neutral axis itself the forces are zero.

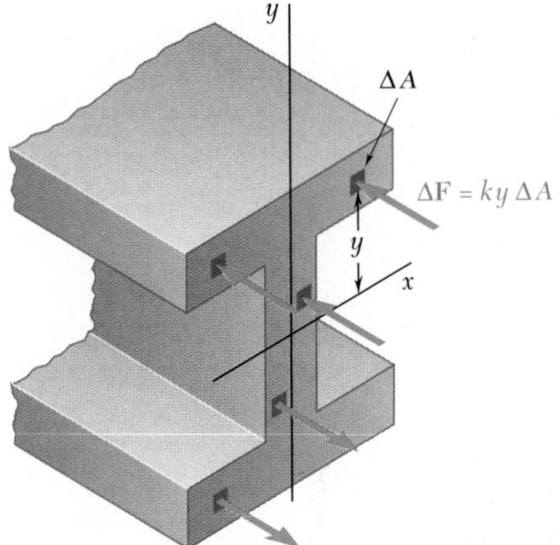

Fig. 9.1

The magnitude of the resultant $\mathbf{R}$ of the elemental forces $\mathbf{\Delta F}$ which act over the entire section is

$$R = \int ky\ dA = k \int y\ dA$$

The last integral obtained is recognized as the *first moment* Q_x of the section about the x axis; it is equal to $\bar{y}A$ and is thus equal to zero, since the centroid of the section is located on the x axis. The system of the forces $\mathbf{\Delta F}$ thus reduces to a couple. The magnitude M of this couple (bending moment) must be equal to the sum of the moments $\Delta M_x = y\ \Delta F = ky^2\ \Delta A$ of the elemental forces. Integrating over the entire section, we obtain

$$M = \int ky^2\ dA = k \int y^2\ dA$$

The last integral is known as the *second moment*, or *moment of inertia*,† of the beam section with respect to the x axis and is denoted by I_x. It is obtained by multiplying each element of area dA by the *square of its distance* from the x axis and integrating over the beam section. Since each product $y^2\ dA$ is positive, regardless of the sign of y, or zero (if y is zero), the integral I_x will always be positive.

Another example of a second moment, or moment of inertia, of an area is provided by the following problem from hydrostatics: A vertical circular gate used to close the outlet of a large reservoir is submerged under water as shown in Fig. 9.2. What is the resultant of the forces exerted by the water on the gate, and what is the moment of the resultant about the line of intersection of the plane of the gate and the water surface (x axis)?

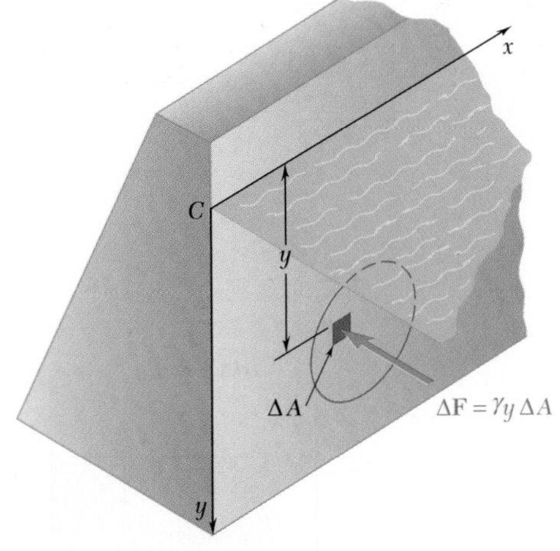

Fig. 9.2

†The term *second moment* is more proper than the term *moment of inertia*, since, logically, the latter should be used only to denote integrals of mass (see Sec. 9.11). In engineering practice, however, moment of inertia is used in connection with areas as well as masses.

If the gate were rectangular, the resultant of the forces of pressure could be determined from the pressure curve, as was done in Sec. 5.9. Since the gate is circular, however, a more general method must be used. Denoting by y the depth of an element of area ΔA and by γ the specific weight of water, the pressure at the element is $p = \gamma y$, and the magnitude of the elemental force exerted on ΔA is $\Delta F = p\,\Delta A = \gamma y\,\Delta A$. The magnitude of the resultant of the elemental forces is thus

$$R = \int \gamma y\, dA = \gamma \int y\, dA$$

and can be obtained by computing the first moment $Q_x = \int y\, dA$ of the area of the gate with respect to the x axis. The moment M_x of the resultant must be equal to the sum of the moments $\Delta M_x = y\,\Delta F = \gamma y^2\,\Delta A$ of the elemental forces. Integrating over the area of the gate, we have

$$M_x = \int \gamma y^2\, dA = \gamma \int y^2\, dA$$

Here again, the integral obtained represents the second moment, or moment of inertia, I_x of the area with respect to the x axis.

9.3. DETERMINATION OF THE MOMENT OF INERTIA OF AN AREA BY INTEGRATION

We defined in the preceding section the second moment, or moment of inertia, of an area A with respect to the x axis. Defining in a similar way the moment of inertia I_y of the area A with respect to the y axis, we write (Fig. 9.3*a*)

$$I_x = \int y^2\, dA \qquad I_y = \int x^2\, dA \tag{9.1}$$

These integrals, known as the *rectangular moments of inertia* of the area A, can be more easily evaluated if we choose dA to be a thin strip parallel to one of the coordinate axes. To compute I_x, the strip is chosen parallel to the x axis, so that all of the points of the strip are at the same distance y from the x axis (Fig. 9.3*b*); the moment of inertia dI_x of the strip is then obtained by multiplying the area dA of the strip by y^2. To compute I_y, the strip is chosen parallel to the y axis so that all of the points of the strip are at the same distance x from the y axis (Fig. 9.3*c*); the moment of inertia dI_y of the strip is $x^2\, dA$.

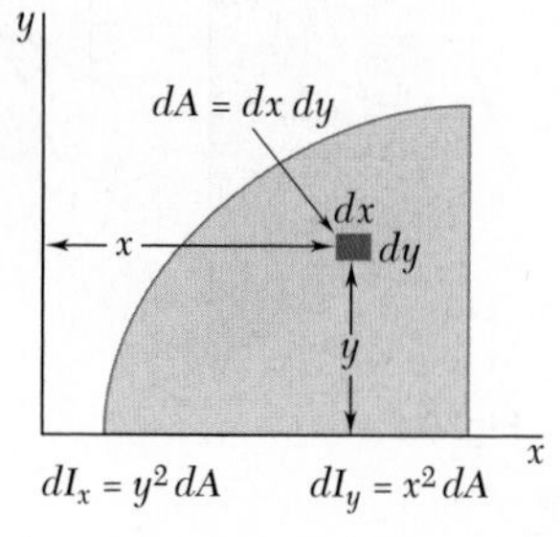

(*a*)

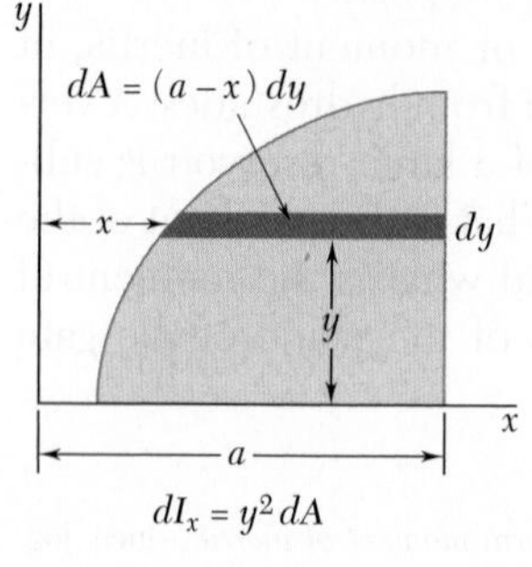

(*b*)

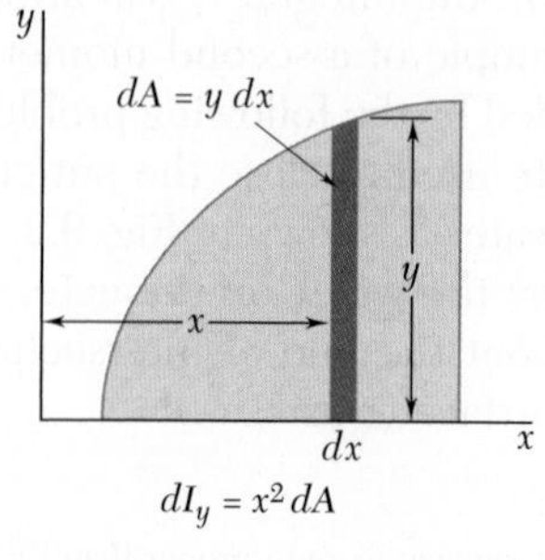

(*c*)

Fig. 9.3

Moment of Inertia of a Rectangular Area. As an example, let us determine the moment of inertia of a rectangle with respect to its base (Fig. 9.4). Dividing the rectangle into strips parallel to the x axis, we obtain

$$dA = b\,dy \qquad dI_x = y^2 b\,dy$$

$$I_x = \int_0^h by^2\,dy = \tfrac{1}{3}bh^3 \tag{9.2}$$

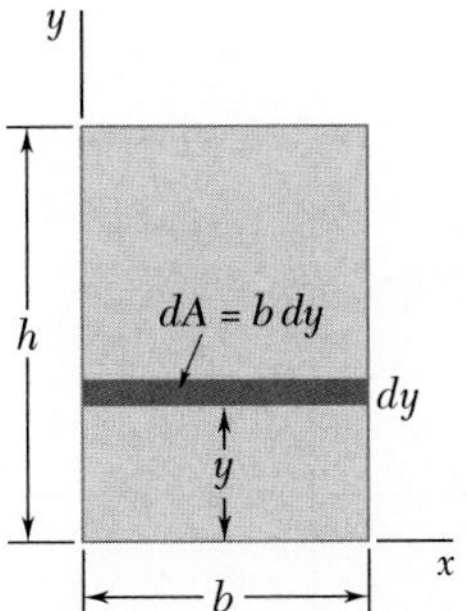

Fig. 9.4

Computing I_x and I_y Using the Same Elemental Strip. The formula just derived can be used to determine the moment of inertia dI_x with respect to the x axis of a rectangular strip which is parallel to the y axis, such as the strip shown in Fig. 9.3*c*. Setting $b = dx$ and $h = y$ in formula (9.2), we write

$$dI_x = \tfrac{1}{3}y^3\,dx$$

On the other hand, we have

$$dI_y = x^2\,dA = x^2 y\,dx$$

The same element can thus be used to compute the moments of inertia I_x and I_y of a given area (Fig. 9.5*a*). The analogous results for the area of Fig. 9.3*b* are shown in Fig. 9.5*b*.

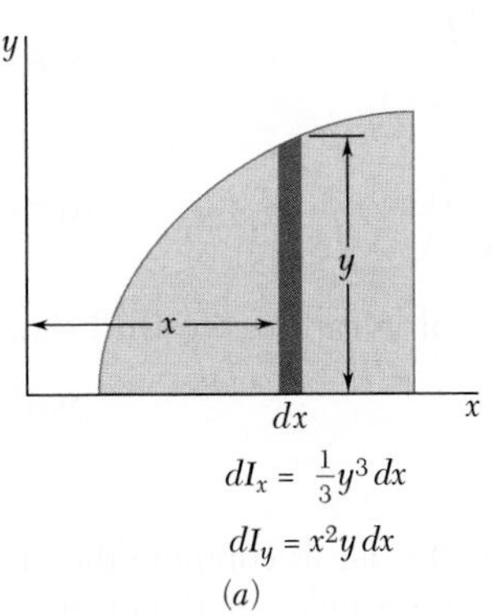

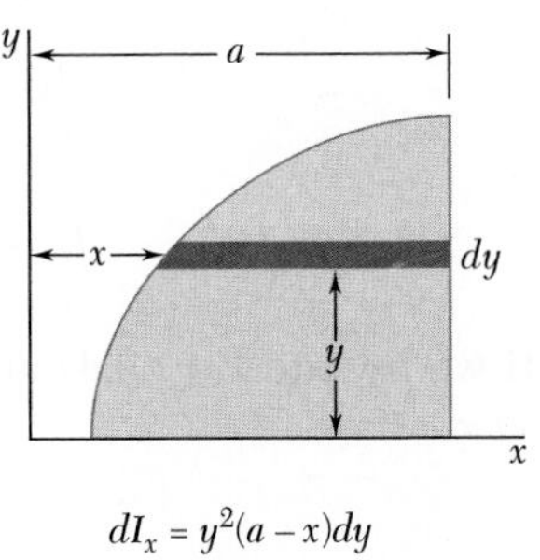

Fig. 9.5

9.4. POLAR MOMENT OF INERTIA

An integral of great importance in problems concerning the torsion of cylindrical shafts and in problems dealing with the rotation of slabs is

$$J_O = \int r^2\,dA \tag{9.3}$$

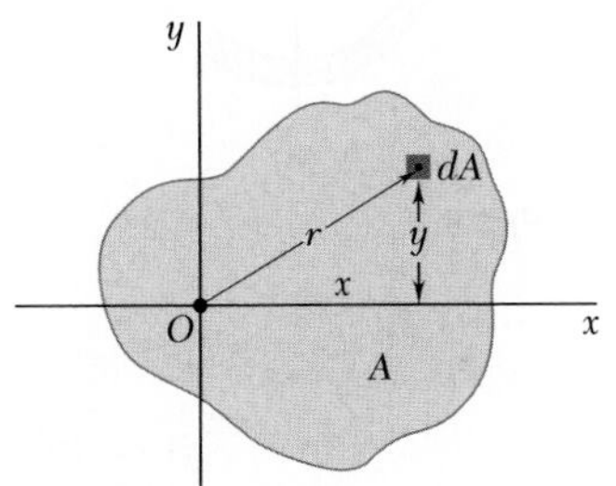

Fig. 9.6

where r is the distance from O to the element of area dA (Fig. 9.6). This integral is the *polar moment of inertia* of the area A with respect to *the "pole"* O.

The polar moment of inertia of a given area can be computed from the rectangular moments of inertia I_x and I_y of the area if these quantities are already known. Indeed, noting that $r^2 = x^2 + y^2$, we write

$$J_O = \int r^2\,dA = \int (x^2 + y^2)\,dA = \int y^2\,dA + \int x^2\,dA$$

that is,

$$J_O = I_x + I_y \tag{9.4}$$

9.5. RADIUS OF GYRATION OF AN AREA

Consider an area A which has a moment of inertia I_x with respect to the x axis (Fig. 9.7a). Let us imagine that we concentrate this area into a thin strip parallel to the x axis (Fig. 9.7b). If the area A, thus concentrated, is to have the same moment of inertia with respect to the x axis, the strip should be placed at a distance k_x from the x axis, where k_x is defined by the relation

$$I_x = k_x^2 A$$

Solving for k_x, we write

$$k_x = \sqrt{\frac{I_x}{A}} \tag{9.5}$$

The distance k_x is referred to as the *radius of gyration* of the area with respect to the x axis. In a similar way, we can define the radii of gyration k_y and k_O (Fig. 9.7c and d); we write

$$I_y = k_y^2 A \qquad k_y = \sqrt{\frac{I_y}{A}} \tag{9.6}$$

$$J_O = k_O^2 A \qquad k_O = \sqrt{\frac{J_O}{A}} \tag{9.7}$$

If we rewrite Eq. (9.4) in terms of the radii of gyration, we find that

$$k_O^2 = k_x^2 + k_y^2 \tag{9.8}$$

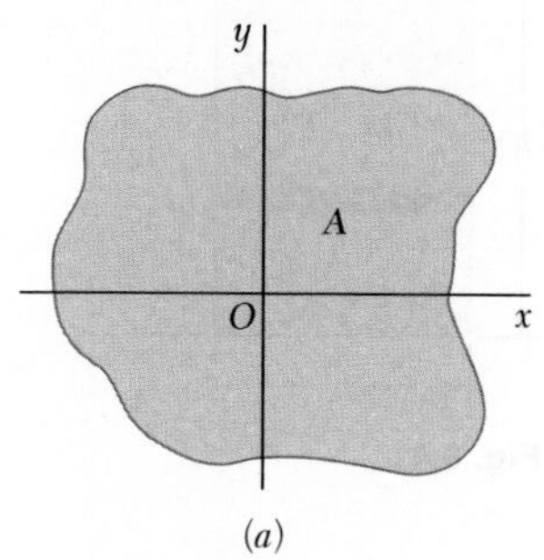

(a)

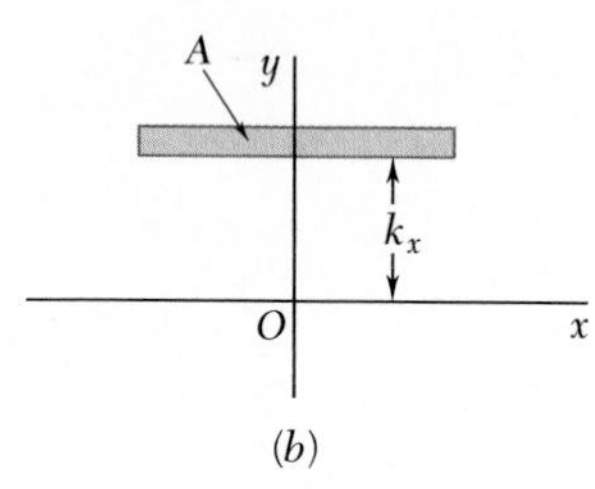

(b)

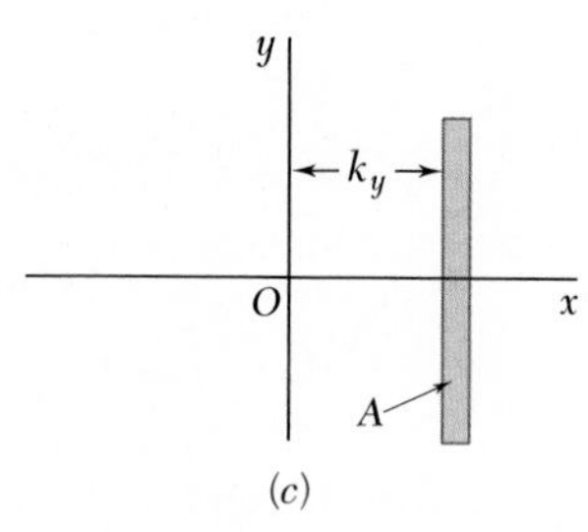

(c)

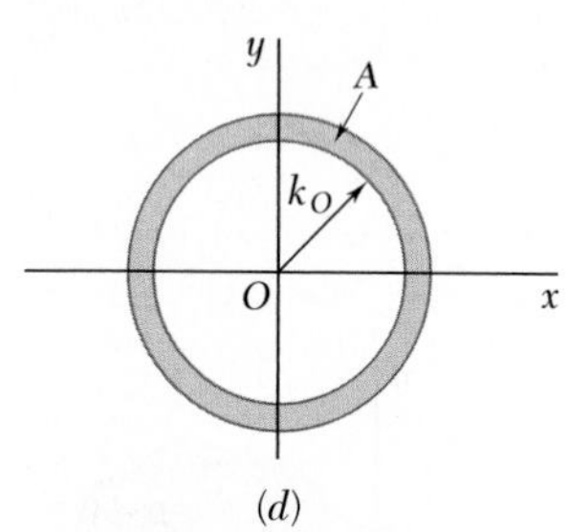

(d)

Fig. 9.7

Example. For the rectangle shown in Fig. 9.8, let us compute the radius of gyration k_x with respect to its base. Using formulas (9.5) and (9.2), we write

$$k_x^2 = \frac{I_x}{A} = \frac{\frac{1}{3}bh^3}{bh} = \frac{h^2}{3} \qquad k_x = \frac{h}{\sqrt{3}}$$

The radius of gyration k_x of the rectangle is shown in Fig. 9.8. It should not be confused with the ordinate $\bar{y} = h/2$ of the centroid of the area. While k_x depends upon the *second moment,* or moment of inertia, of the area, the ordinate $\bar{y}$ is related to the *first moment* of the area.

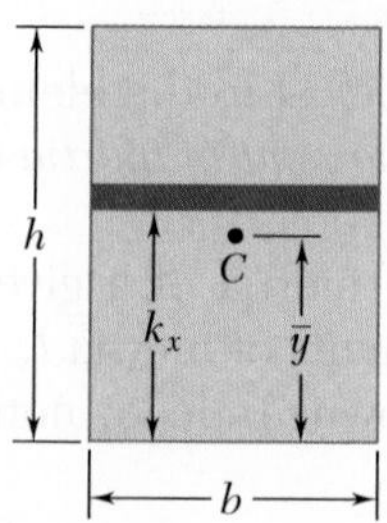

Fig. 9.8

SAMPLE PROBLEM 9.1

Determine the moment of inertia of a triangle with respect to its base.

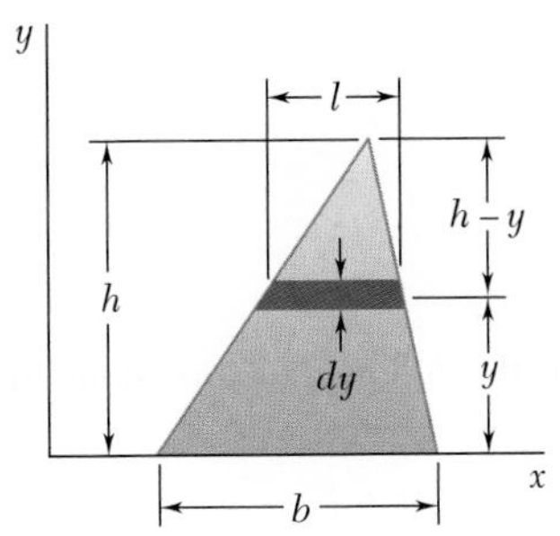

SOLUTION

A triangle of base b and height h is drawn; the x axis is chosen to coincide with the base. A differential strip parallel to the x axis is chosen to be dA. Since all portions of the strip are at the same distance from the x axis, we write

$$dI_x = y^2\,dA \qquad dA = l\,dy$$

Using similar triangles, we have

$$\frac{l}{b} = \frac{h-y}{h} \qquad l = b\frac{h-y}{h} \qquad dA = b\frac{h-y}{h}\,dy$$

Integrating dI_x from $y = 0$ to $y = h$, we obtain

$$I_x = \int y^2\,dA = \int_0^h y^2 b\frac{h-y}{h}\,dy = \frac{b}{h}\int_0^h (hy^2 - y^3)\,dy$$

$$= \frac{b}{h}\left[h\frac{y^3}{3} - \frac{y^4}{4}\right]_0^h \qquad I_x = \frac{bh^3}{12} \blacktriangleleft$$

SAMPLE PROBLEM 9.2

(*a*) Determine the centroidal polar moment of inertia of a circular area by direct integration. (*b*) Using the result of part *a*, determine the moment of inertia of a circular area with respect to a diameter.

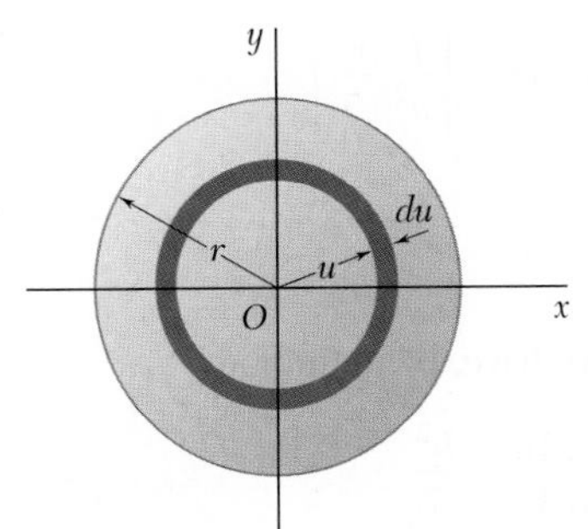

SOLUTION

***a.* Polar Moment of Inertia.** An annular differential element of area is chosen to be dA. Since all portions of the differential area are at the same distance from the origin, we write

$$dJ_O = u^2\,dA \qquad dA = 2\pi u\,du$$

$$J_O = \int dJ_O = \int_0^r u^2(2\pi u\,du) = 2\pi\int_0^r u^3\,du$$

$$J_O = \frac{\pi}{2}r^4 \blacktriangleleft$$

***b.* Moment of Inertia with Respect to a Diameter.** Because of the symmetry of the circular area, we have $I_x = I_y$. We then write

$$J_O = I_x + I_y = 2I_x \qquad \frac{\pi}{2}r^4 = 2I_x \qquad I_{\text{diameter}} = I_x = \frac{\pi}{4}r^4 \blacktriangleleft$$

SAMPLE PROBLEM 9.3

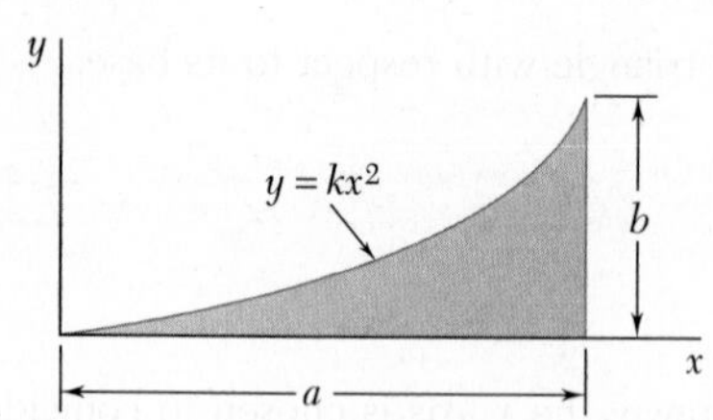

(*a*) Determine the moment of inertia of the shaded area shown with respect to each of the coordinate axes. (Properties of this area were considered in Sample Prob. 5.4.) (*b*) Using the results of part *a*, determine the radius of gyration of the shaded area with respect to each of the coordinate axes.

SOLUTION

Referring to Sample Prob. 5.4, we obtain the following expressions for the equation of the curve and the total area:

$$y = \frac{b}{a^2}x^2 \qquad A = \tfrac{1}{3}ab$$

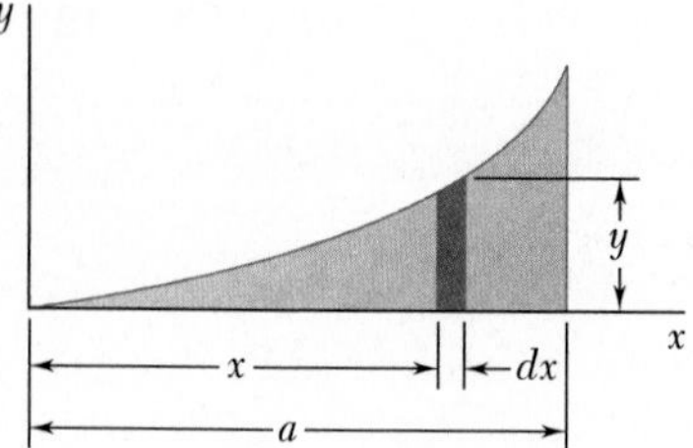

Moment of Inertia I_x. A vertical differential element of area is chosen to be dA. Since all portions of this element are *not* at the same distance from the x axis, we must treat the element as a thin rectangle. The moment of inertia of the element with respect to the x axis is then

$$dI_x = \tfrac{1}{3}y^3\,dx = \frac{1}{3}\left(\frac{b}{a^2}x^2\right)^3 dx = \frac{1}{3}\frac{b^3}{a^6}x^6\,dx$$

$$I_x = \int dI_x = \int_0^a \frac{1}{3}\frac{b^3}{a^6}x^6\,dx = \left[\frac{1}{3}\frac{b^3}{a^6}\frac{x^7}{7}\right]_0^a$$

$$I_x = \frac{ab^3}{21} \quad ◀$$

Moment of Inertia I_y. The same vertical differential element of area is used. Since all portions of the element are at the same distance from the y axis, we write

$$dI_y = x^2\,dA = x^2(y\,dx) = x^2\left(\frac{b}{a^2}x^2\right)dx = \frac{b}{a^2}x^4\,dx$$

$$I_y = \int dI_y = \int_0^a \frac{b}{a^2}x^4\,dx = \left[\frac{b}{a^2}\frac{x^5}{5}\right]_0^a$$

$$I_y = \frac{a^3b}{5} \quad ◀$$

Radii of Gyration k_x and k_y. We have, by definition,

$$k_x^2 = \frac{I_x}{A} = \frac{ab^3/21}{ab/3} = \frac{b^2}{7} \qquad k_x = \sqrt{\tfrac{1}{7}}\,b \quad ◀$$

and

$$k_y^2 = \frac{I_y}{A} = \frac{a^3b/5}{ab/3} = \tfrac{3}{5}a^2 \qquad k_y = \sqrt{\tfrac{3}{5}}\,a \quad ◀$$

SOLVING PROBLEMS ON YOUR OWN

The purpose of this lesson was to introduce the *rectangular and polar moments of inertia of areas* and the corresponding *radii of gyration*. Although the problems you are about to solve may appear to be more appropriate for a calculus class than for one in mechanics, we hope that our introductory comments have convinced you of the relevance of the moments of inertia to your study of a variety of engineering topics.

1. *Calculating the rectangular moments of inertia I_x and I_y.* We defined these quantities as

$$I_x = \int y^2\, dA \qquad I_y = \int x^2\, dA \tag{9.1}$$

where dA is a differential element of area $dx\, dy$. The moments of inertia are *the second moments of the area;* it is for that reason that I_x, for example, depends on the perpendicular distance y to the area dA. As you study Sec. 9.3, you should recognize the importance of carefully defining the shape and the orientation of dA. Further, you should note the following points.

a. The moments of inertia of most areas can be obtained by means of a single integration. The expressions given in Figs. 9.3*b* and *c* and Fig. 9.5 can be used to calculate I_x and I_y. Regardless of whether you use a single or a double integration, be sure to show on your sketch the element dA that you have chosen.

b. The moment of inertia of an area is always positive, regardless of the location of the area with respect to the coordinate axes. This is because it is obtained by integrating the product of dA and the *square* of a distance. (Note how this differs from the results for the first moment of the area.) Only when an area is *removed* (as in the case for a hole) will its moment of inertia be entered in your computations with a minus sign.

c. As a partial check of your work, observe that the moments of inertia are equal to an area times the square of a length. Thus, every term in an expression for a moment of inertia must be a *length to the fourth power*.

2. *Computing the polar moment of inertia J_O.* We defined J_O as

$$J_O = \int r^2\, dA \tag{9.3}$$

where $r^2 = x^2 + y^2$. If the given area has circular symmetry (as in Sample Prob. 9.2), it is possible to express dA as a function of r and to compute J_O with a single integration. When the area lacks circular symmetry, it is usually easier first to calculate I_x and I_y and then to determine J_O from

$$J_O = I_x + I_y \tag{9.4}$$

Lastly, if the equation of the curve that bounds the given area is expressed in polar coordinates, then $dA = r\, dr\, d\theta$ and a double integration is required to compute the integral for J_O [see Prob. 9.27].

3. *Determining the radii of gyration k_x and k_y and the polar radius of gyration k_O.* These quantities were defined in Sec. 9.5, and you should realize that they can be determined only after the area and the appropriate moments of inertia have been computed. It is important to remember that k_x is measured in the y direction, while k_y is measured in the x direction; you should carefully study Sec. 9.5 until you understand this point.

Problems

9.1 through 9.4 Determine by direct integration the moment of inertia of the shaded area with respect to the y axis.

9.5 through 9.8 Determine by direct integration the moment of inertia of the shaded area with respect to the x axis.

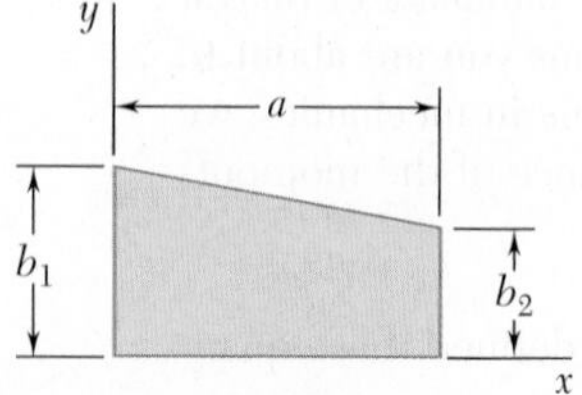

Fig. P9.1 and P9.5

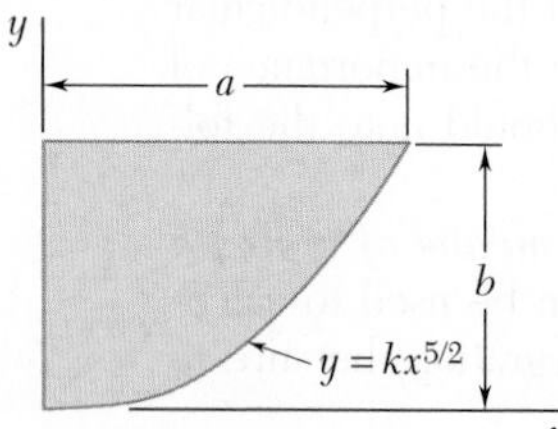

Fig. P9.2 and P9.6

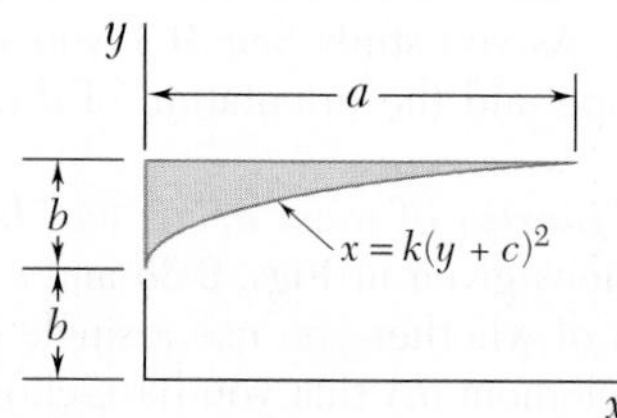

Fig. P9.3 and P9.7

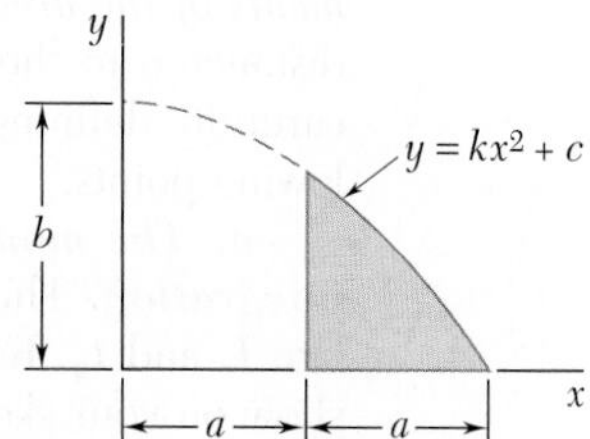

Fig. *P9.4* and *P9.8*

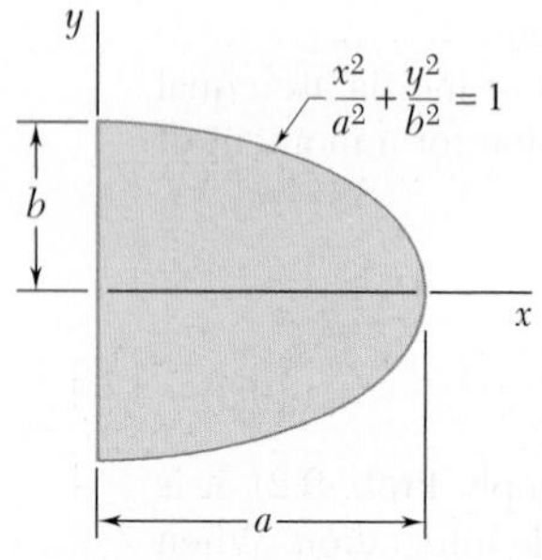

Fig. P9.9 and P9.12

9.9 through 9.11 Determine by direct integration the moment of inertia of the shaded area with respect to the x axis.

9.12 through 9.14 Determine by direct integration the moment of inertia of the shaded area with respect to the y axis.

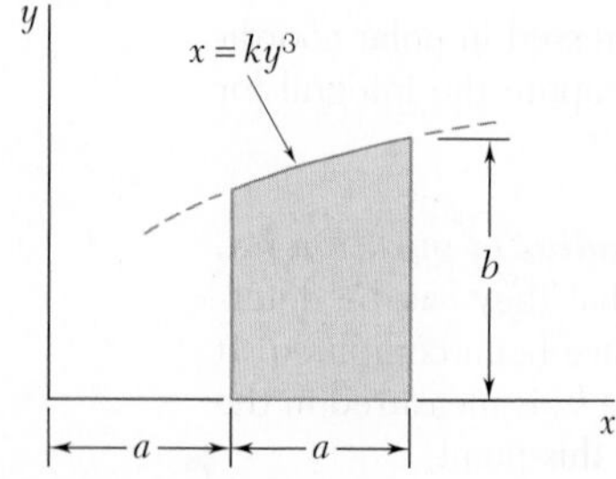

Fig. *P9.10* and *P9.13*

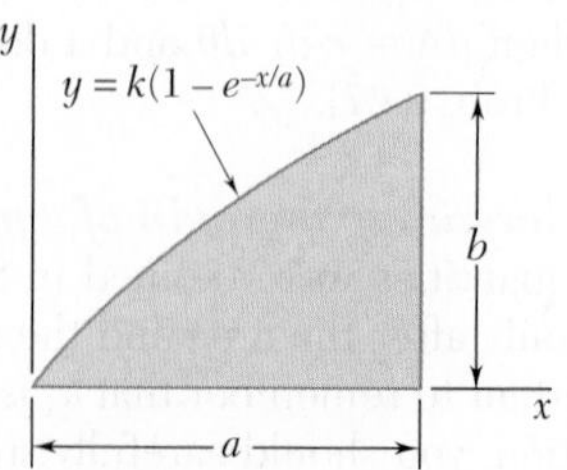

Fig. P9.11 and P9.14

9.15 and 9.16 Determine the moment of inertia and the radius of gyration of the shaded area shown with respect to the x axis.

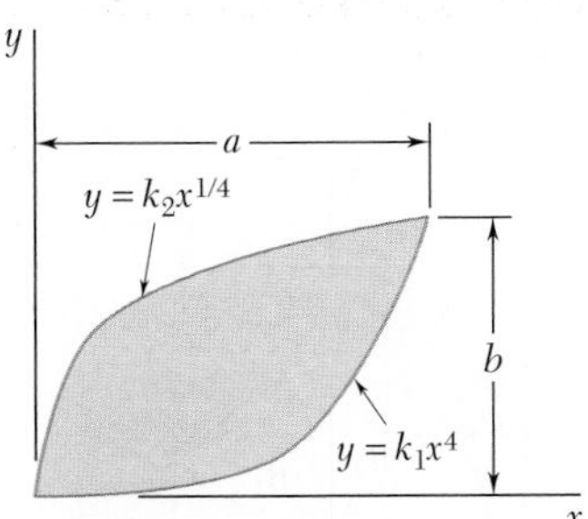

Fig. *P9.15* and *P9.17*

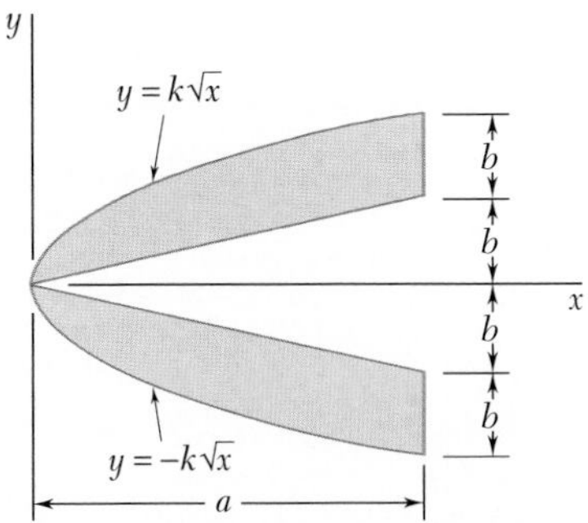

Fig. P9.16 and P9.18

9.17 and 9.18 Determine the moment of inertia and the radius of gyration of the shaded area shown with respect to the y axis.

9.19 Determine the moment of inertia and the radius of gyration of the shaded area shown with respect to the x axis.

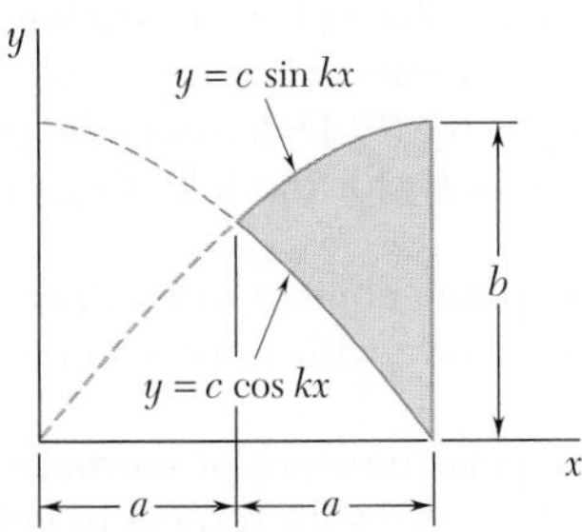

Fig. P9.19 and P9.20

9.20 Determine the moment of inertia and the radius of gyration of the shaded area shown with respect to the y axis.

9.21 Determine the polar moment of inertia and the polar radius of gyration of the rectangle shown with respect to the midpoint of one of its (*a*) longer sides, (*b*) shorter sides.

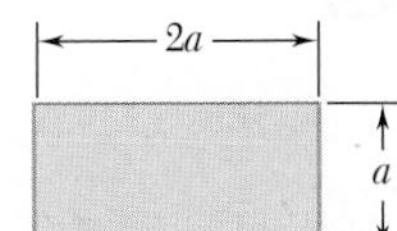

Fig. P9.21

9.22 Determine the polar moment of inertia and the polar radius of gyration of the shaded area shown with respect to point P.

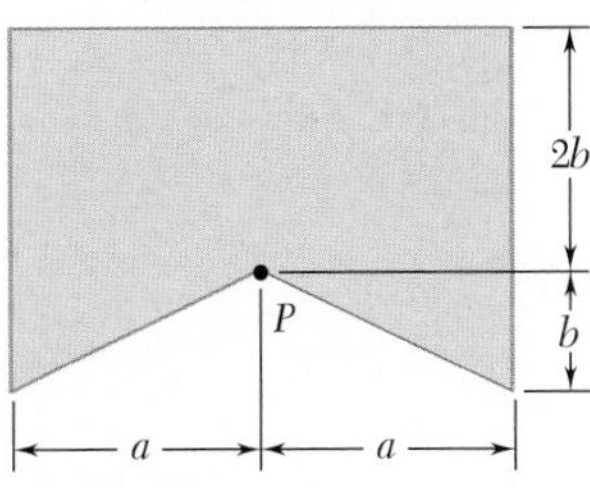

Fig. P9.22

9.23 and 9.24 Determine the polar moment of inertia and the polar radius of gyration of the shaded area shown with respect to point P.

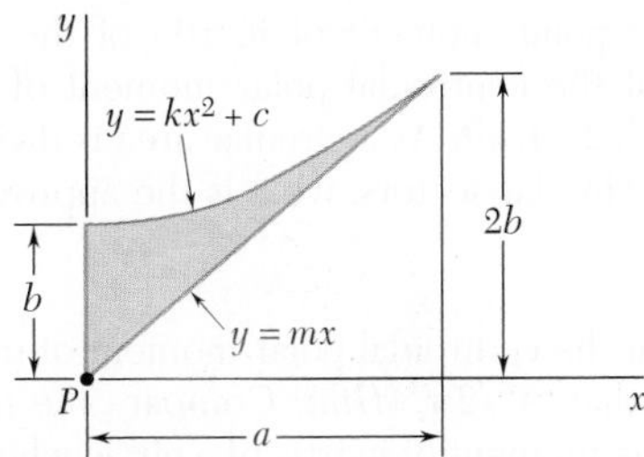

Fig. *P9.23*

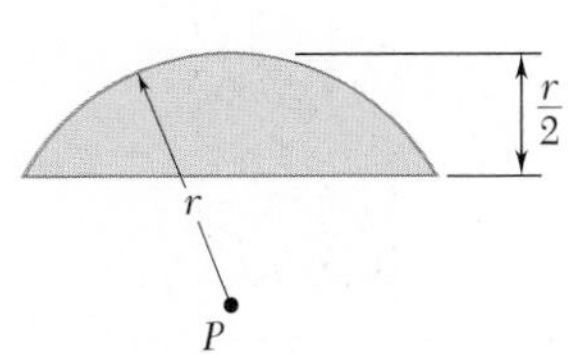

Fig. P9.24

9.25 (*a*) Determine by direct integration the polar moment of inertia of the area shown with respect to point O. (*b*) Using the result of part *a*, determine the moments of inertia of the given area with respect to the x and y axes.

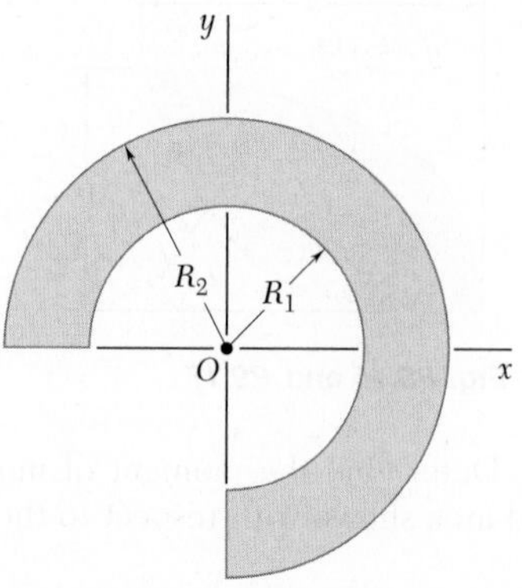

Fig. P9.25 and P9.26

9.26 (*a*) Show that the polar radius of gyration k_O of the area shown is approximately equal to the mean radius $R_m = (R_1 + R_2)/2$ for small values of the thickness $t = R_2 - R_1$. (*b*) Determine the percentage error introduced by using R_m in place of k_O for the following values of t/R_m: 1, $\frac{1}{4}$, $\frac{1}{16}$.

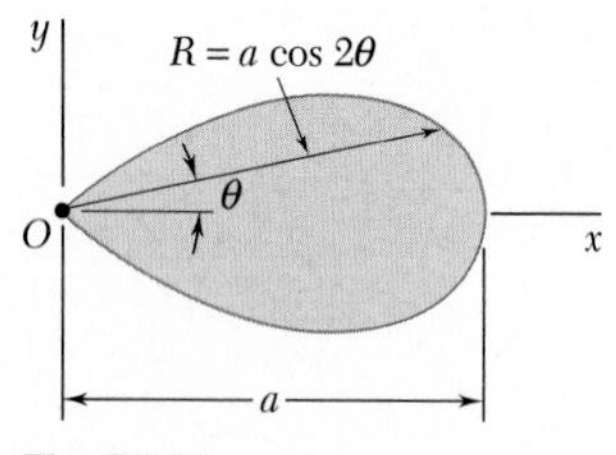

Fig. P9.27

9.27 Determine the polar moment of inertia and the polar radius of gyration of the shaded area shown with respect to point O.

9.28 Determine the polar moment of inertia and the radius of gyration of the isosceles triangle shown with respect to point O.

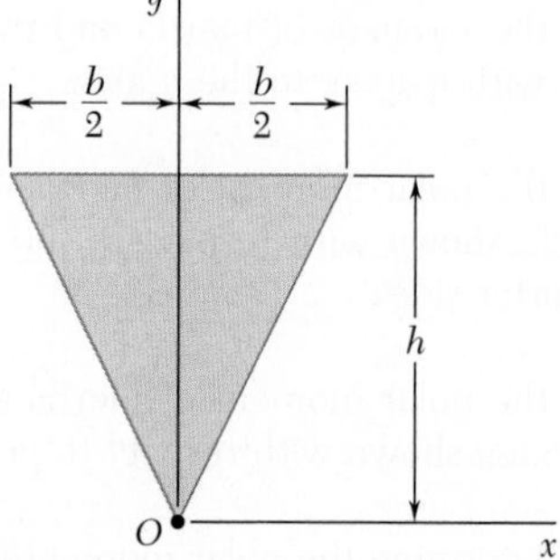

Fig. P9.28

***9.29** Using the polar moment of inertia of the isosceles triangle of Prob. 9.28, show that the centroidal polar moment of inertia of a circular area of radius r is $\pi r^4/2$. (*Hint:* As a circular area is divided into an increasing number of equal circular sectors, what is the approximate shape of each circular sector?)

***9.30** Prove that the centroidal polar moment of inertia of a given area A cannot be smaller than $A^2/2\pi$. (*Hint:* Compare the moment of inertia of the given area with the moment of inertia of a circle which has the same area and the same centroid.)

9.6. PARALLEL-AXIS THEOREM

Consider the moment of inertia I of an area A with respect to an axis AA' (Fig. 9.9). Denoting by y the distance from an element of area dA to AA', we write

$$I = \int y^2 \, dA$$

Let us now draw through the centroid C of the area an axis BB' parallel to AA'; this axis is called a *centroidal axis*. Denoting by y' the

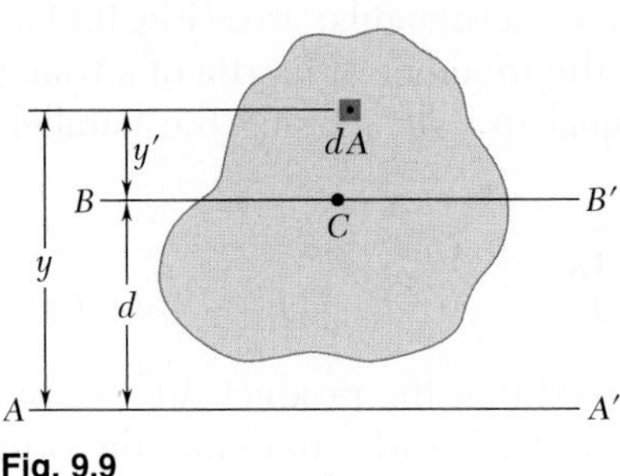

Fig. 9.9

distance from the element dA to BB', we write $y = y' + d$, where d is the distance between the axes AA' and BB'. Substituting for y in the above integral, we write

$$\begin{aligned} I &= \int y^2 \, dA = \int (y' + d)^2 \, dA \\ &= \int y'^2 \, dA + 2d \int y' \, dA + d^2 \int dA \end{aligned}$$

The first integral represents the moment of inertia $\bar{I}$ of the area with respect to the centroidal axis BB'. The second integral represents the first moment of the area with respect to BB'; since the centroid C of the area is located on that axis, the second integral must be zero. Finally, we observe that the last integral is equal to the total area A. Therefore, we have

$$I = \bar{I} + Ad^2 \tag{9.9}$$

This formula expresses that the moment of inertia I of an area with respect to any given axis AA' is equal to the moment of inertia $\bar{I}$ of the area with respect to the centroidal axis BB' parallel to AA' *plus* the product of the area A and the square of the distance d between the two axes. This theorem is known as the *parallel-axis theorem*. Substituting k^2A for I and $\bar{k}^2A$ for $\bar{I}$, the theorem can also be expressed as

$$k^2 = \bar{k}^2 + d^2 \tag{9.10}$$

A similar theorem can be used to relate the polar moment of inertia J_O of an area about a point O to the polar moment of inertia $\bar{J}_C$ of the same area about its centroid C. Denoting by d the distance between O and C, we write

$$J_O = \bar{J}_C + Ad^2 \qquad \text{or} \qquad k_O^2 = \bar{k}_C^2 + d^2 \tag{9.11}$$

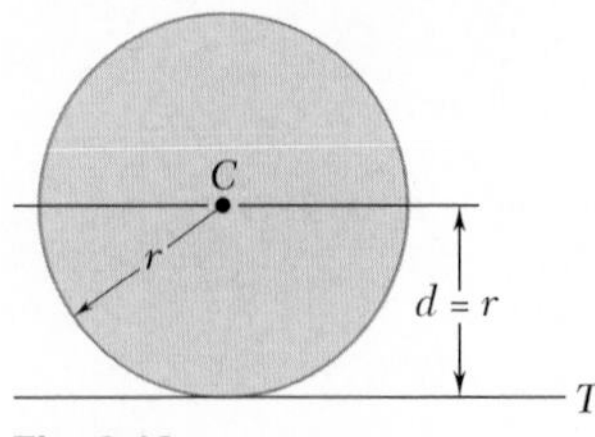

Fig. 9.10

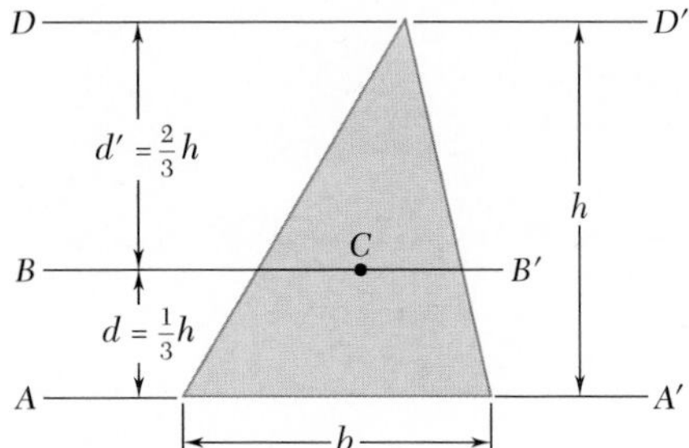

Fig. 9.11

Example 1. As an application of the parallel-axis theorem, let us determine the moment of inertia I_T of a circular area with respect to a line tangent to the circle (Fig. 9.10). We found in Sample Prob. 9.2 that the moment of inertia of a circular area about a centroidal axis is $\bar{I} = \frac{1}{4}\pi r^4$. We can write, therefore,

$$I_T = \bar{I} + Ad^2 = \tfrac{1}{4}\pi r^4 + (\pi r^2)r^2 = \tfrac{5}{4}\pi r^4$$

Example 2. The parallel-axis theorem can also be used to determine the centroidal moment of inertia of an area when the moment of inertia of the area with respect to a parallel axis is known. Consider, for instance, a triangular area (Fig. 9.11). We found in Sample Prob. 9.1 that the moment of inertia of a triangle with respect to its base AA' is equal to $\frac{1}{12}bh^3$. Using the parallel-axis theorem, we write

$$I_{AA'} = \bar{I}_{BB'} + Ad^2$$
$$\bar{I}_{BB'} = I_{AA'} - Ad^2 = \tfrac{1}{12}bh^3 - \tfrac{1}{2}bh(\tfrac{1}{3}h)^2 = \tfrac{1}{36}bh^3$$

It should be observed that the product Ad^2 was *subtracted* from the given moment of inertia in order to obtain the centroidal moment of inertia of the triangle. Note that this product is *added* when transferring *from* a centroidal axis to a parallel axis, but it should be *subtracted* when transferring *to* a centroidal axis. In other words, the moment of inertia of an area is always smaller with respect to a centroidal axis than with respect to any parallel axis.

Returning to Fig. 9.11, we observe that the moment of inertia of the triangle with respect to the line DD' (which is drawn through a vertex) can be obtained by writing

$$I_{DD'} = \bar{I}_{BB'} + Ad'^2 = \tfrac{1}{36}bh^3 + \tfrac{1}{2}bh(\tfrac{2}{3}h)^2 = \tfrac{1}{4}bh^3$$

Note that $I_{DD'}$ could not have been obtained directly from $I_{AA'}$. The parallel-axis theorem can be applied only if one of the two parallel axes passes through the centroid of the area.

9.7. MOMENTS OF INERTIA OF COMPOSITE AREAS

Consider a composite area A made of several component areas A_1, A_2, A_3, . . . Since the integral representing the moment of inertia of A can be subdivided into integrals evaluated over A_1, A_2, A_3, . . . , the moment of inertia of A with respect to a given axis is obtained by adding the moments of inertia of the areas A_1, A_2, A_3, . . . with respect to the same axis. The moment of inertia of an area consisting of several of the common shapes shown in Fig. 9.12 can thus be obtained by using the formulas given in that figure. Before adding the moments of inertia of the component areas, however, the parallel-axis theorem may have to be used to transfer each moment of inertia to the desired axis. This is shown in Sample Probs. 9.4 and 9.5.

The properties of the cross sections of various structural shapes are given in Fig. 9.13. As noted in Sec. 9.2, the moment of inertia of a beam section about its neutral axis is closely related to the computation of the bending moment in that section of the beam. The determination of moments of inertia is thus a prerequisite to the analysis and design of structural members.

Photo 9.1 Figure 9.13 tabulates data for a small sample of the rolled-steel shapes that are readily available. Shown above are two examples of wide-flange shapes that are commonly used in the construction of buildings.

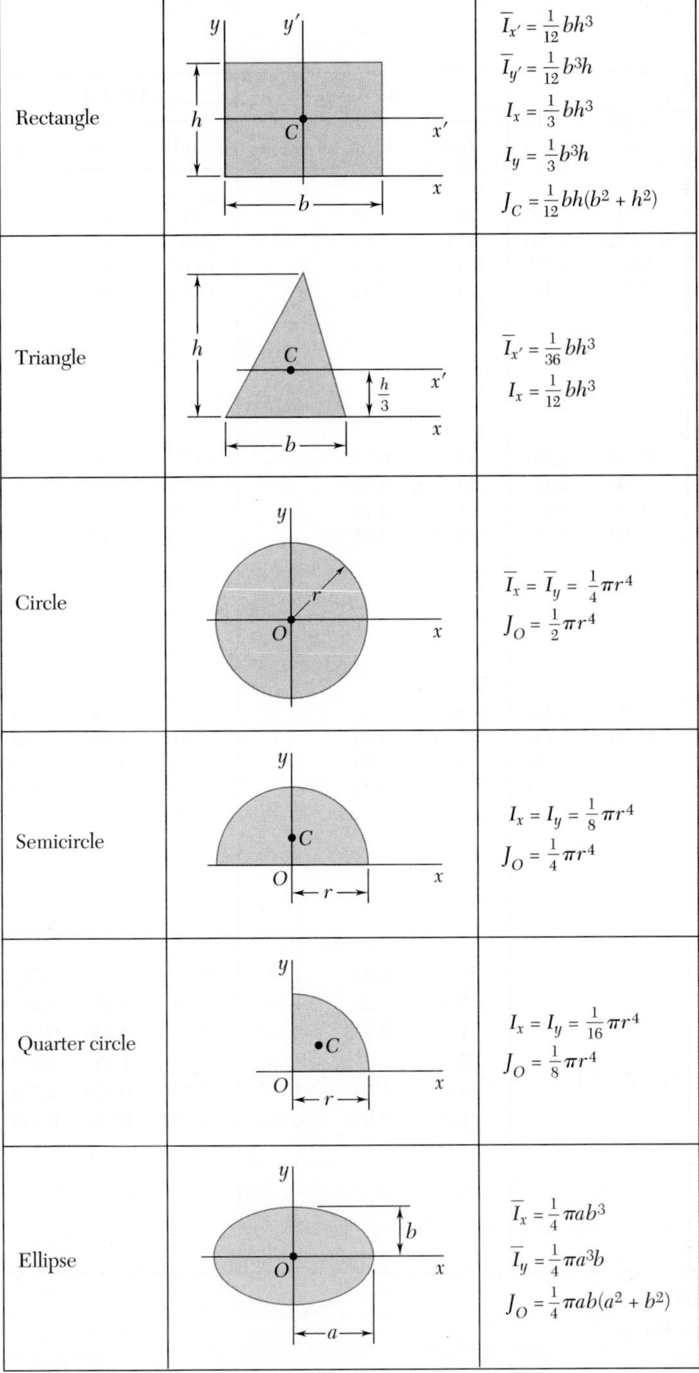

Rectangle
$\bar{I}_{x'} = \frac{1}{12}bh^3$
$\bar{I}_{y'} = \frac{1}{12}b^3h$
$I_x = \frac{1}{3}bh^3$
$I_y = \frac{1}{3}b^3h$
$J_C = \frac{1}{12}bh(b^2 + h^2)$
Triangle
$\bar{I}_{x'} = \frac{1}{36}bh^3$
$I_x = \frac{1}{12}bh^3$
Circle
$\bar{I}_x = \bar{I}_y = \frac{1}{4}\pi r^4$
$J_O = \frac{1}{2}\pi r^4$
Semicircle
$I_x = I_y = \frac{1}{8}\pi r^4$
$J_O = \frac{1}{4}\pi r^4$
Quarter circle
$I_x = I_y = \frac{1}{16}\pi r^4$
$J_O = \frac{1}{8}\pi r^4$
Ellipse
$\bar{I}_x = \frac{1}{4}\pi ab^3$
$\bar{I}_y = \frac{1}{4}\pi a^3b$
$J_O = \frac{1}{4}\pi ab(a^2 + b^2)$

Fig. 9.12 Moments of inertia of common geometric shapes.

It should be noted that the radius of gyration of a composite area is *not* equal to the sum of the radii of gyration of the component areas. In order to determine the radius of gyration of a composite area, it is first necessary to compute the moment of inertia of the area.

	Designation	Area, in²	Depth, in.	Width, in.	Axis X-X			Axis Y-Y		
					$\bar{I}_x$, in⁴	$\bar{k}_x$, in.	$\bar{y}$, in.	$\bar{I}_y$, in⁴	$\bar{k}_y$, in.	$\bar{x}$, in.
W Shapes (Wide-Flange Shapes)	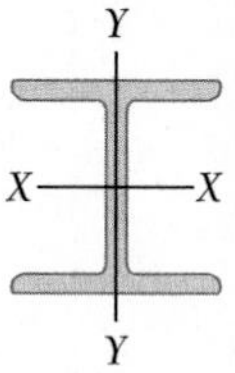 W18 × 50†	14.7	17.99	7.495	800	7.38		40.1	1.65	
	W16 × 40	11.8	16.01	6.995	518	6.63		28.9	1.57	
	W14 × 30	8.85	13.84	6.730	291	5.73		19.6	1.49	
	W8 × 24	7.08	7.93	6.495	82.8	3.42		18.3	1.61	
S Shapes (American Standard Shapes)	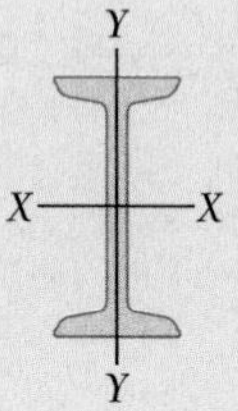 S18 × 70†	20.6	18.00	6.251	926	6.71		24.1	1.08	
	S12 × 50	14.7	12.00	5.477	305	4.55		15.7	1.03	
	S10 × 35	10.3	10.00	4.944	147	3.78		8.36	0.901	
	S6 × 17.25	5.07	6.00	3.565	26.3	2.28		2.31	0.675	
C Shapes (American Standard Channels)	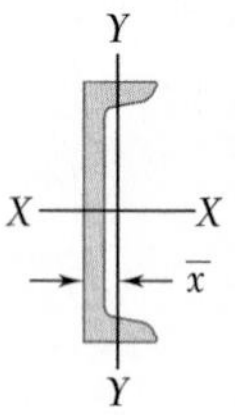 C12 × 25†	7.35	12.00	3.047	144	4.43		4.47	0.780	0.674
	C10 × 20	5.88	10.00	2.739	78.9	3.66		2.81	0.692	0.606
	C8 × 13.75	4.04	8.00	2.343	36.1	2.99		1.53	0.615	0.553
	C6 × 10.5	3.09	6.00	2.034	15.2	2.22		0.866	0.529	0.499
Angles	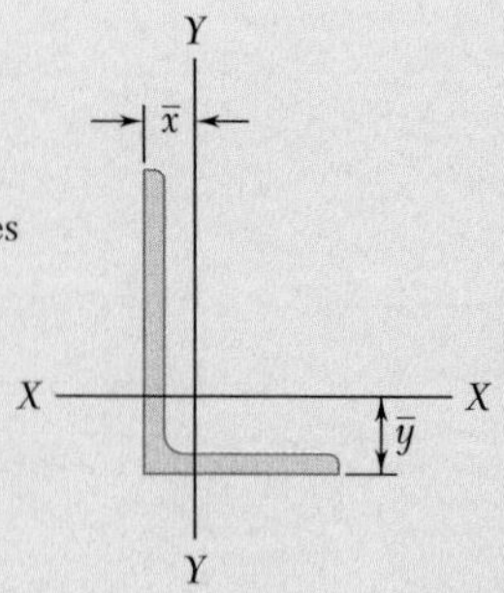 L6 × 6 × $\frac{3}{4}$‡	8.44			28.2	1.83	1.78	28.2	1.83	1.78
	L4 × 4 × $\frac{1}{2}$	3.75			5.56	1.22	1.18	5.56	1.22	1.18
	L3 × 3 × $\frac{1}{4}$	1.44			1.24	0.930	0.842	1.24	0.930	0.842
	L6 × 4 × $\frac{1}{2}$	4.75			17.4	1.91	1.99	6.27	1.15	0.987
	L5 × 3 × $\frac{1}{2}$	3.75			9.45	1.59	1.75	2.58	0.829	0.750
	L3 × 2 × $\frac{1}{4}$	1.19			1.09	0.957	0.993	0.392	0.574	0.493

Fig. 9.13A Properties of Rolled-Steel Shapes (U.S. Customary Units).*

*Courtesy of the American Institute of Steel Construction, Chicago, Illinois

†Nominal depth in inches and weight in pounds per foot

‡Depth, width, and thickness in inches

	Designation	Area mm^2	Depth mm	Width mm	Axis X-X $\bar{I}_x$ 10^6 mm^4	$\bar{k}_x$ mm	$\bar{y}$ mm	Axis Y-Y $\bar{I}_y$ 10^6 mm^4	$\bar{k}_y$ mm	$\bar{x}$ mm
W Shapes (Wide-Flange Shapes) 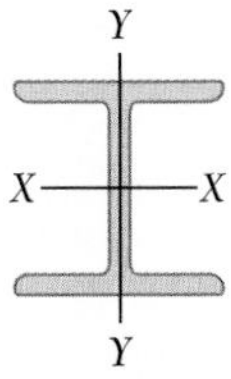	W460 × 74†	9450	457	190	333	188		16.6	41.9	
	W410 × 60	7580	407	178	216	169		12.1	40.0	
	W360 × 44	5730	352	171	122	146		8.18	37.8	
	W200 × 35.9	4580	201	165	34.4	86.7		7.64	40.8	
S Shapes (American Standard Shapes) 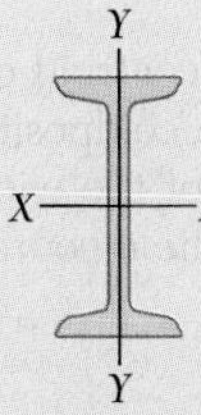	S460 × 104†	13300	457	159	385	170		10.4	27.5	
	S310 × 74	9480	305	139	126	115		6.69	26.1	
	S250 × 52	6670	254	126	61.2	95.8		3.59	22.9	
	S150 × 25.7	3270	152	91	10.8	57.5		1.00	17.2	
C Shapes (American Standard Channels) 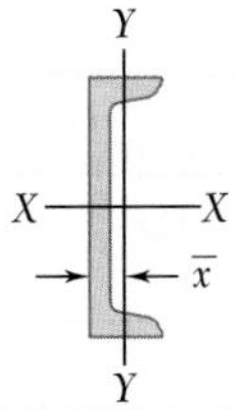	C310 × 37†	5690	305	77	59.7	112		1.83	19.7	17.0
	C250 × 30	3780	254	69	32.6	92.9		1.14	17.4	15.3
	C200 × 27.9	3560	203	64	18.2	71.5		0.817	15.1	14.3
	C150 × 15.6	1980	152	51	6.21	56.0		0.347	13.2	12.5
Angles 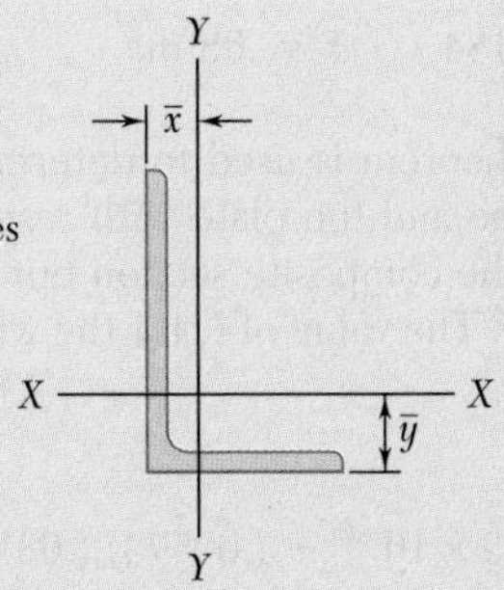	L152 × 152 × 19.0‡	5420			11.6	46.3	44.9	11.6	46.3	44.9
	L102 × 102 × 12.7	2430			2.34	31.0	30.2	2.34	31.0	30.2
	L76 × 76 × 6.4	932			0.517	23.6	21.4	0.517	23.6	21.4
	L152 × 102 × 12.7	3060			7.20	48.5	50.3	2.64	29.4	25.3
	L127 × 76 × 12.7	2420			3.93	40.3	44.4	1.06	20.9	19.0
	L76 × 51 × 6.4	772			0.453	24.2	25.1	0.166	14.7	12.6

Fig. 9.13B Properties of Rolled-Steel Shapes (SI Units).

†Nominal depth in millimeters and mass in kilograms per meter

‡Depth, width, and thickness in millimeters

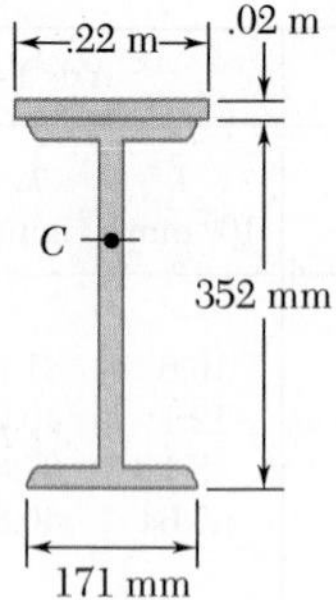

SAMPLE PROBLEM 9.4

The strength of a W360 × 44 rolled-steel beam is increased by attaching a .22 × .02-m plate to its upper flange as shown. Determine the moment of inertia and the radius of gyration of the composite section with respect to an axis which is parallel to the plate and passes through the centroid C of the section.

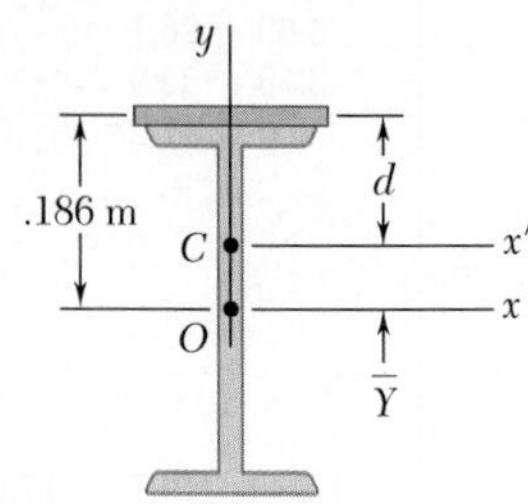

SOLUTION

The origin O of the coordinates is placed at the centroid of the wide-flange shape, and the distance $\overline{Y}$ to the centroid of the composite section is computed using the methods of Chap. 5. The area of the wide-flange shape is found by referring to Fig. 9.13A. The area and the y coordinate of the centroid of the plate are

$$A = (.22\text{ m})(.02\text{ m}) = .0044\text{ m}^2$$
$$\bar{y} = \tfrac{1}{2}(.352\text{ m}) + \tfrac{1}{2}(.02\text{ m}) = .186\text{ m}$$

Section	Area, m^2	$\bar{y}$, m	$\bar{y}A$, m^3
Plate	.0044	.186	.0008184
Wide-flange shape	.00573	0	0
	$\Sigma A = .01013$		$\Sigma\bar{y}A = .0008184$

$$\overline{Y}\Sigma A = \Sigma\bar{y}A \qquad \overline{Y}(.01013) = .0008184 \qquad \overline{Y} = .08\text{ m}$$

Moment of Inertia. The parallel-axis theorem is used to determine the moments of inertia of the wide-flange shape and the plate with respect to the x' axis. This axis is a centroidal axis for the composite section but *not* for either of the elements considered separately. The value of $\bar{I}_x$ for the wide-flange shape is obtained from Fig. 9.13A.

For the wide-flange shape,

$$I_{x'} = \bar{I}_x + A\overline{Y}^2 = 122 + (.00573)(.08)^2 = 122 \times 10^{-6} + (.00573)\,(.08)$$
$$= 2158.67 \times 10^6\text{ m}^4$$

For the plate,

$$I_{x'} = \bar{I}_x + Ad^2 = \tfrac{1}{12}(.22)(.02)^3 + (.0044)(.186 - .08)^2 = 4.95 \times 10^{-5}\text{ m}^4$$

For the composite area,

$$I_{x'} = 208.17 \times 10^{-6}\text{ m}^4 \quad ◀$$

Radius of Gyration. We have

$$k_{x'}^2 = \frac{I_{x'}}{A} = \frac{208.17 \times 10^{-6}\text{ m}^4}{0.01013\text{ m}^2} = .143\text{ m} \quad ◀$$

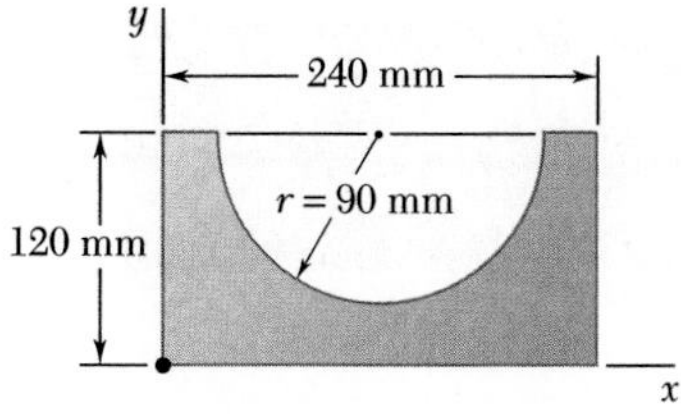

SAMPLE PROBLEM 9.5

Determine the moment of inertia of the shaded area with respect to the x axis.

SOLUTION

The given area can be obtained by subtracting a half circle from a rectangle. The moments of inertia of the rectangle and the half circle will be computed separately.

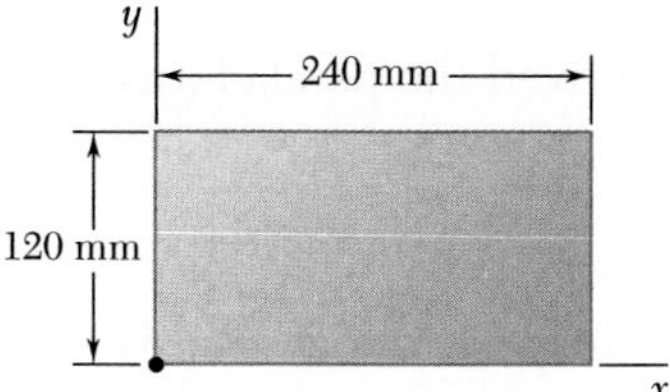

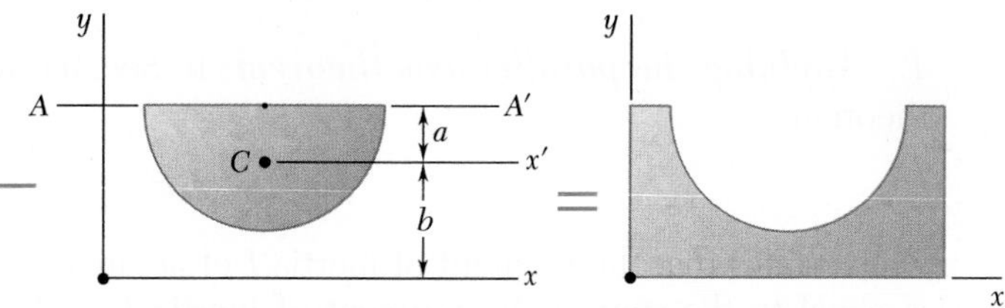

Moment of Inertia of Rectangle. Referring to Fig. 9.12, we obtain

$$I_x = \tfrac{1}{3}bh^3 = \tfrac{1}{3}(240 \text{ mm})(120 \text{ mm})^3 = 138.2 \times 10^6 \text{ mm}^4$$

Moment of Inertia of Half Circle. Referring to Fig. 5.8, we determine the location of the centroid C of the half circle with respect to diameter AA'.

$$a = \frac{4r}{3\pi} = \frac{(4)(90 \text{ mm})}{3\pi} = 38.2 \text{ mm}$$

The distance b from the centroid C to the x axis is

$$b = 120 \text{ mm} - a = 120 \text{ mm} - 38.2 \text{ mm} = 81.8 \text{ mm}$$

Referring now to Fig. 9.12, we compute the moment of inertia of the half circle with respect to diameter AA'; we also compute the area of the half circle.

$$I_{AA'} = \tfrac{1}{8}\pi r^4 = \tfrac{1}{8}\pi(90 \text{ mm})^4 = 25.76 \times 10^6 \text{ mm}^4$$
$$A = \tfrac{1}{2}\pi r^2 = \tfrac{1}{2}\pi(90 \text{ mm})^2 = 12.72 \times 10^3 \text{ mm}^2$$

Using the parallel-axis theorem, we obtain the value of $\bar{I}_{x'}$:

$$I_{AA'} = \bar{I}_{x'} + Aa^2$$
$$25.76 \times 10^6 \text{ mm}^4 = \bar{I}_{x'} + (12.72 \times 10^3 \text{ mm}^2)(38.2 \text{ mm})^2$$
$$\bar{I}_{x'} = 7.20 \times 10^6 \text{ mm}^4$$

Again using the parallel-axis theorem, we obtain the value of I_x:

$$I_x = \bar{I}_{x'} + Ab^2 = 7.20 \times 10^6 \text{ mm}^4 + (12.72 \times 10^3 \text{ mm}^2)(81.8 \text{ mm})^2$$
$$= 92.3 \times 10^6 \text{ mm}^4$$

Moment of Inertia of Given Area. Subtracting the moment of inertia of the half circle from that of the rectangle, we obtain

$$I_x = 138.2 \times 10^6 \text{ mm}^4 - 92.3 \times 10^6 \text{ mm}^4$$

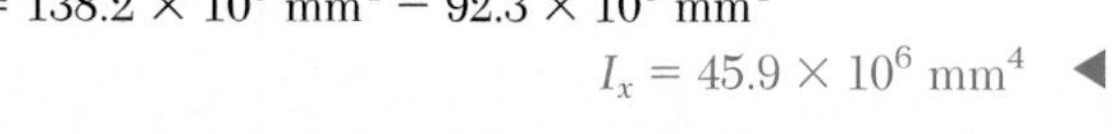
$I_x = 45.9 \times 10^6 \text{ mm}^4$ 

SOLVING PROBLEMS ON YOUR OWN

In this lesson we introduced the *parallel-axis theorem* and illustrated how it can be used to simplify the computation of moments and polar moments of inertia of composite areas. The areas that you will consider in the following problems will consist of common shapes and rolled-steel shapes. You will also use the parallel-axis theorem to locate the point of application (the center of pressure) of the resultant of the hydrostatic forces acting on a submerged plane area.

1. ***Applying the parallel-axis theorem.*** In Sec. 9.6 we derived the parallel-axis theorem

$$I = \bar{I} + Ad^2 \qquad (9.9)$$

which states that the moment of inertia I of an area A with respect to a given axis is equal to the sum of the moment of inertia $\bar{I}$ of that area with respect to the *parallel centroidal axis* and the product Ad^2, where d is the distance between the two axes. It is important that you remember the following points as you use the parallel-axis theorem.

a. The centroidal moment of inertia $\bar{I}$ of an area A can be obtained by subtracting the product Ad^2 from the moment of inertia I of the area with respect to a parallel axis. Therefore, as we noted in Example 2 and illustrated in Sample Prob. 9.5, it follows that the moment of inertia $\bar{I}$ is *smaller* than the moment of inertia I of the same area with respect to any parallel axis.

b. The parallel-axis theorem can be applied only if one of the two axes involved is a centroidal axis. Therefore, as we noted in Example 2, to compute the moment of inertia of an area with respect to a *noncentroidal axis* when the moment of inertia of the area is known with respect to *another noncentroidal axis,* it is necessary to *first compute* the moment of inertia of the area with respect to the *centroidal axis parallel to the two given axes.*

2. ***Computing the moments and polar moments of inertia of composite areas.*** Sample Probs. 9.4 and 9.5 illustrate the steps you should follow to solve problems of this type. As with all composite-area problems, you should show on your sketch the common shapes or rolled-steel shapes that constitute the various elements of the given area, as well as the distances between the centroidal axes of the elements and the axes about which the moments of inertia are to be computed. In addition, it is important that the following points be noted.

a. The moment of inertia of an area is always positive, regardless of the location of the axis with respect to which it is computed. As pointed out in the comments for the preceding lesson, it is only when an area is *removed* (as in the case of a hole) that its moment of inertia should be entered in your computations with a minus sign.

b. The moments of inertia of a semiellipse and a quarter ellipse can be determined by dividing the moment of inertia of an ellipse by 2 and 4, respectively. It should be noted, however, that the moments of inertia obtained in this manner are *with respect to the axes of symmetry of the ellipse*. To obtain the *centroidal* moments of inertia of these shapes, the parallel-axis theorem should be used. Note that this remark also applies to a semicircle and to a quarter circle and that the expressions given for these shapes in Fig. 9.12 are *not* centroidal moments of inertia.

c. To calculate the polar moment of inertia of a composite area, you can use either the expressions given in Fig. 9.12 for J_O or the relationship

$$J_O = I_x + I_y \tag{9.4}$$

depending on the shape of the given area.

d. Before computing the centroidal moments of inertia of a given area, you may find it necessary to first locate the centroid of the area using the methods of Chap. 5.

3. ***Locating the point of application of the resultant of a system of hydrostatic forces.*** In Sec. 9.2 we found that

$$R = \gamma \int y \, dA = \gamma \bar{y} A$$

$$M_x = \gamma \int y^2 \, dA = \gamma I_x$$

where $\bar{y}$ is the distance from the x axis to the centroid of the submerged plane area. Since $\mathbf{R}$ is equivalent to the system of elemental hydrostatic forces, it follows that

$$\Sigma M_x: \qquad y_P R = M_x$$

where y_P is the depth of the point of application of $\mathbf{R}$. Then

$$y_P(\gamma \bar{y} A) = \gamma I_x \qquad \text{or} \qquad y_P = \frac{I_x}{\bar{y} A}$$

In closing, we encourage you to carefully study the notation used in Fig. 9.13 for the rolled-steel shapes, as you will likely encounter it again in subsequent engineering courses.

Problems

9.31 and 9.32 Determine the moment of inertia and the radius of gyration of the shaded area with respect to the x axis.

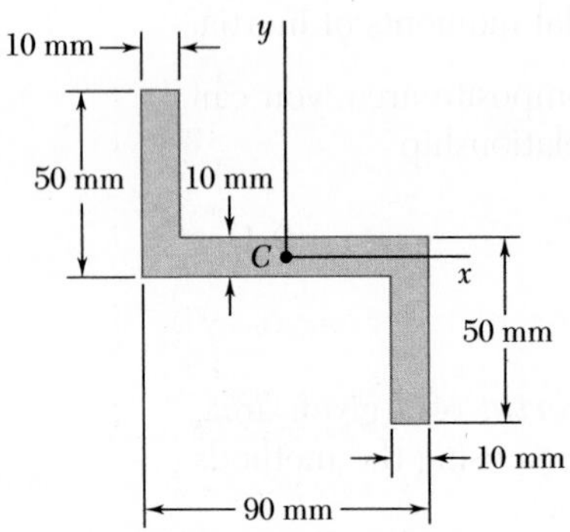

Fig. P9.31 and P9.33

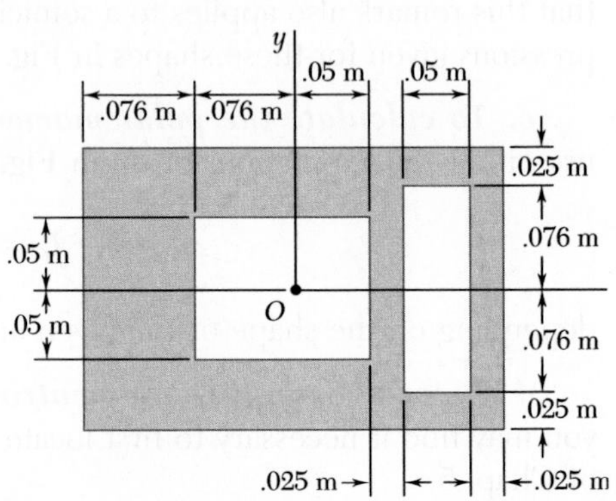

Fig. P9.32 and P9.34

9.33 and 9.34 Determine the moment of inertia and the radius of gyration of the shaded area with respect to the y axis.

9.35* and *9.36 Determine the moments of inertia of the shaded area shown with respect to the x and y axes.

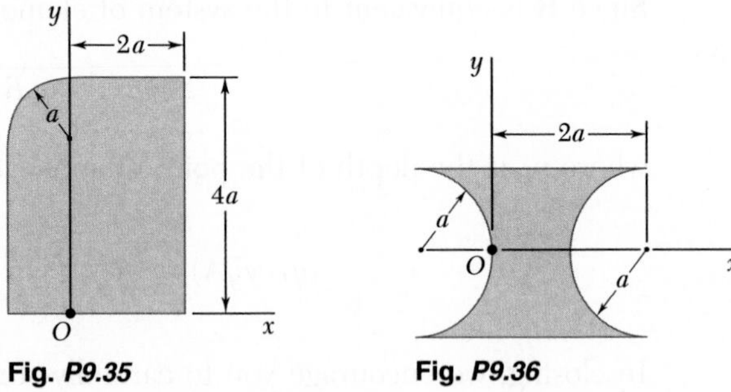

Fig. *P9.35*

Fig. *P9.36*

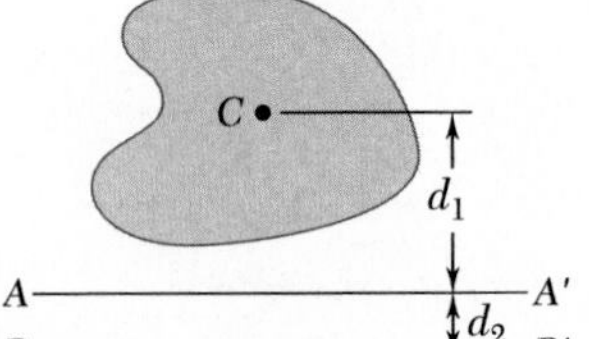

Fig. P9.37 and P9.38

9.37 Determine the shaded area and its moment of inertia with respect to a centroidal axis parallel to AA' knowing that its moments of inertia with respect to AA' and BB' are 2.2×10^6 mm^4 and 4×10^6 mm^4, respectively, and that $d_1 = 25$ mm and $d_2 = 10$ mm.

9.38 Knowing that the shaded area is equal to 6000 mm^2 and that its moment of inertia with respect to AA' is 18×10^6 mm^4, determine its moment of inertia with respect to BB' for $d_1 = 50$ mm and $d_2 = 10$ mm.

9.39 If $d_1 = 2a$, determine the distance a and the centroidal polar moment of inertia of the .015-m^2 shaded area shown knowing that $d_2 = .05$ m and that the polar moments of inertia of the area with respect to points A and B are 1.0655×10^{-4} m^4 and 7.908×10^{-5} m^4, respectively.

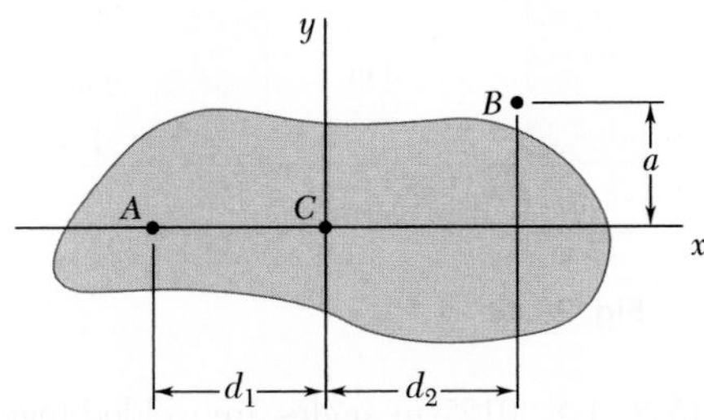

Fig. P9.39 and *P9.40*

9.40 The centroidal polar moment of inertia $\bar{J}_C$ of the .0194-m^2 shaded area shown is 2.1852×10^{-5} m^4. Knowing that $d_1 = d_2 = .06$ m, determine (*a*) the distance a so that $J_B = 3J_A$, (*b*) the polar moment of inertia J_B.

9.41 through 9.44 Determine the moments of inertia $\bar{I}_x$ and $\bar{I}_y$ of the area shown with respect to centroidal axes respectively parallel and perpendicular to side AB.

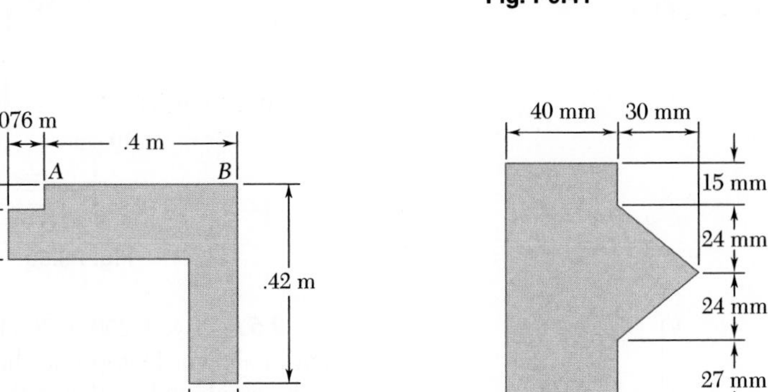

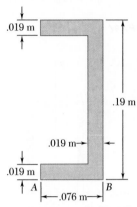

Fig. P9.41

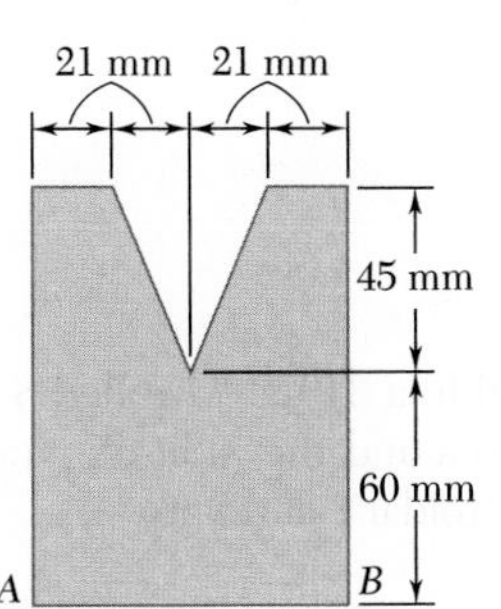

Fig. P9.42

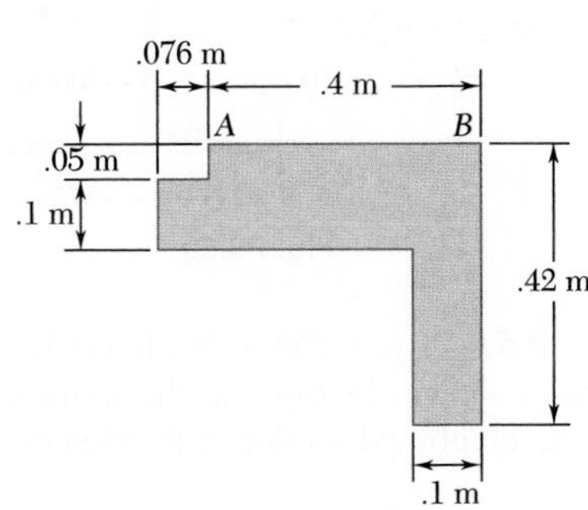

Fig. *P9.43*

Fig. P9.44

9.45 and 9.46 Determine the polar moment of inertia of the area shown with respect to (*a*) point O, (*b*) the centroid of the area.

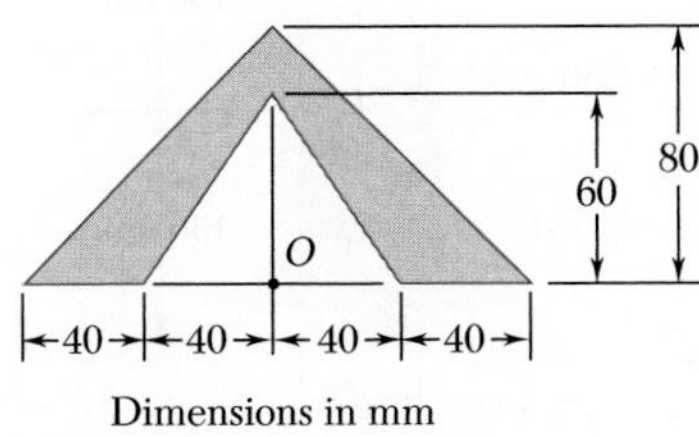

Fig. P9.45

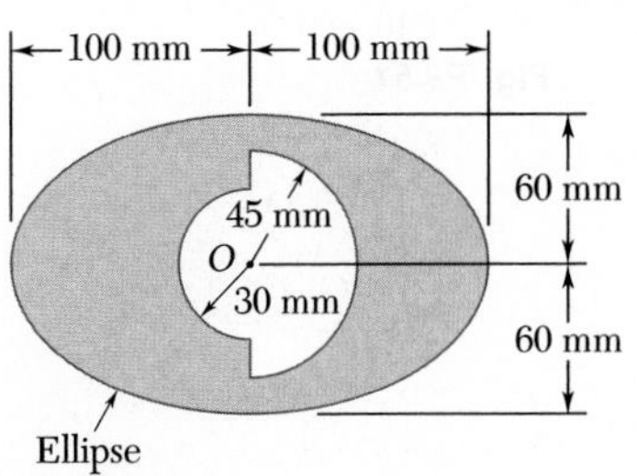

Fig. P9.46

9.47 and 9.48 Determine the polar moment of inertia of the area shown with respect to (*a*) point *O*, (*b*) the centroid of the area.

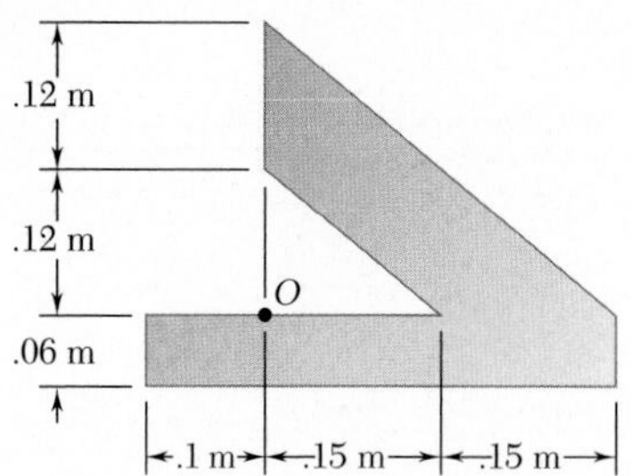

Fig. P9.47

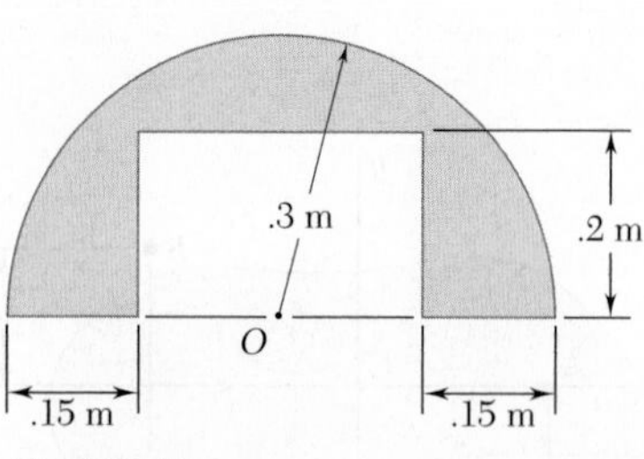

Fig. P9.48

9.49 Two .15 × .1 × .0127-m angles are welded together to form the section shown. Determine the moments of inertia and the radii of gyration of the section with respect to the centroidal axes shown.

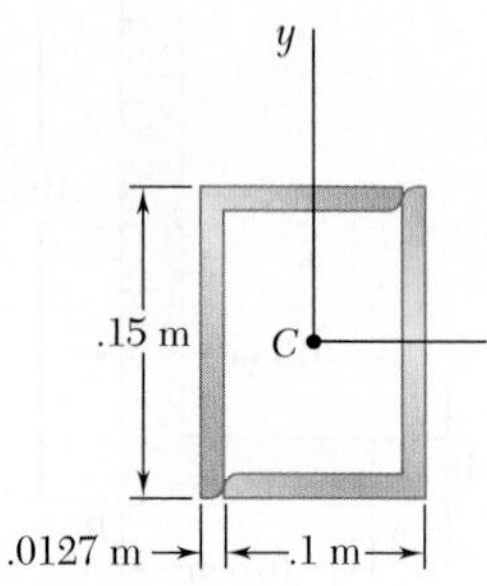

Fig. P9.49

9.50 Two channels and two plates are used to form the column section shown. Determine the moments of inertia and the radii of gyration of the combined section with respect to the centroidal axes shown.

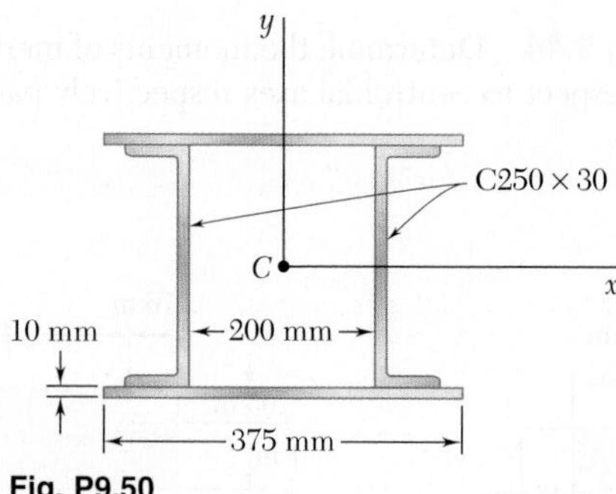

Fig. P9.50

9.51 Two C250 × 30 channels are welded to a 310 × 74 rolled S section as shown. Determine the moments of inertia and the radii of gyration of the combined section with respect to its centroidal x and y axes.

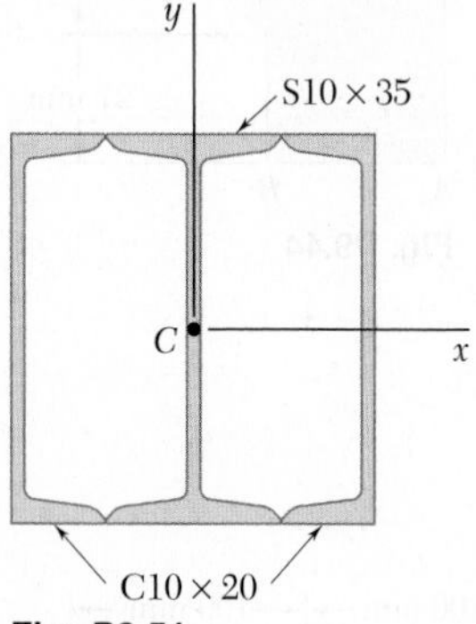

Fig. P9.51

9.52 Two channels are welded to a $d \times 300$-mm steel plate as shown. Determine the width d for which the ratio $\bar{I}_x/\bar{I}_y$ of the centroidal moments of inertia of the section is 16.

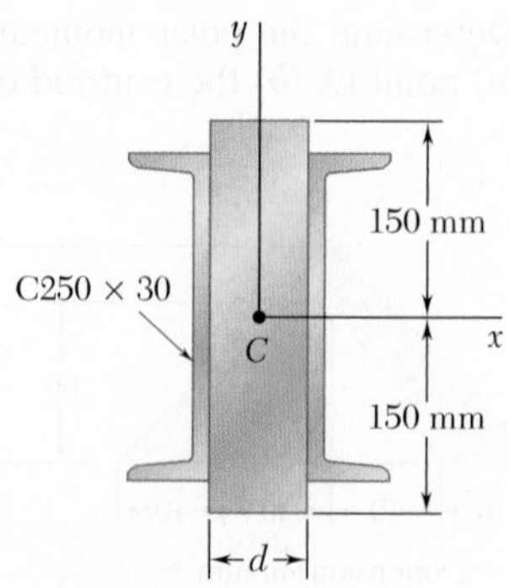

Fig. P9.52

9.53 Two L76 × 76 × 6.4-mm angles are welded to a C250 × 30 channel. Determine the moments of inertia of the combined section with respect to centroidal axes respectively perpendicular and parallel to the web of the channel.

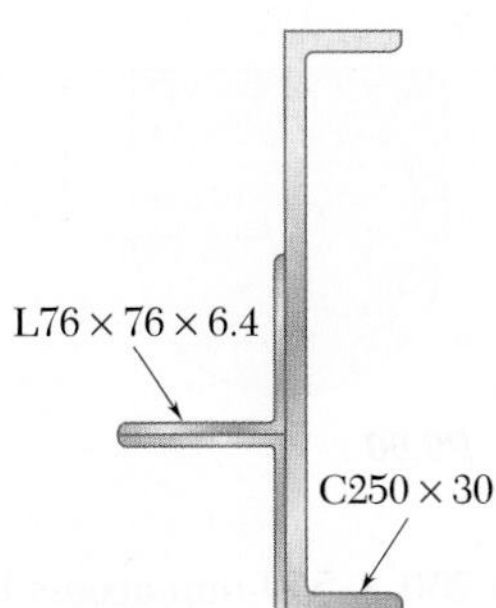

Fig. P9.53

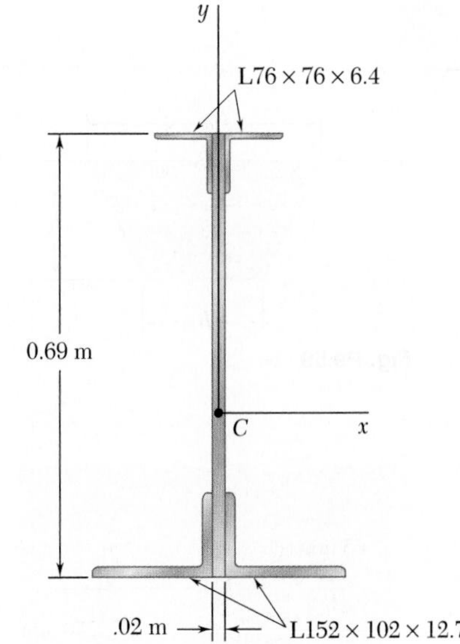

Fig. *P9.54*

9.54 To form a nonsymmetrical girder, two L76 × 76 × 6.4-mm angles and two L152 × 102 × 12.7-mm angles are welded to a .02-m steel plate as shown. Determine the moments of inertia of the combined section with respect to its centroidal x and y axes.

9.55 Two L127 × 76 × 12.7-mm angles are welded to a 10-mm steel plate. Determine the distance b and the centroidal moments of inertia $\bar{I}_x$ and $\bar{I}_y$ of the combined section knowing that $\bar{I}_y = 3\bar{I}_x$.

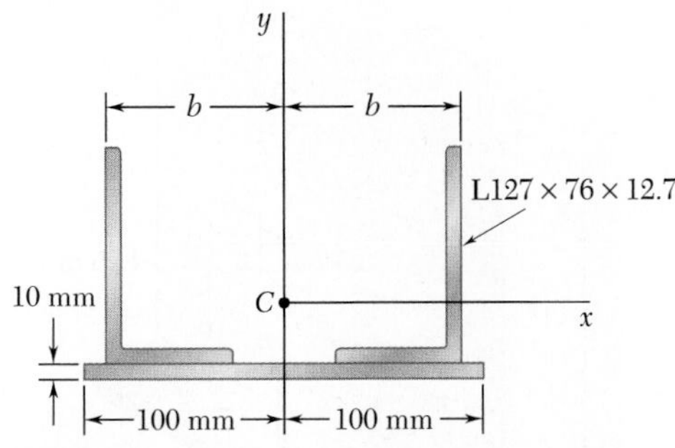

Fig. P9.55

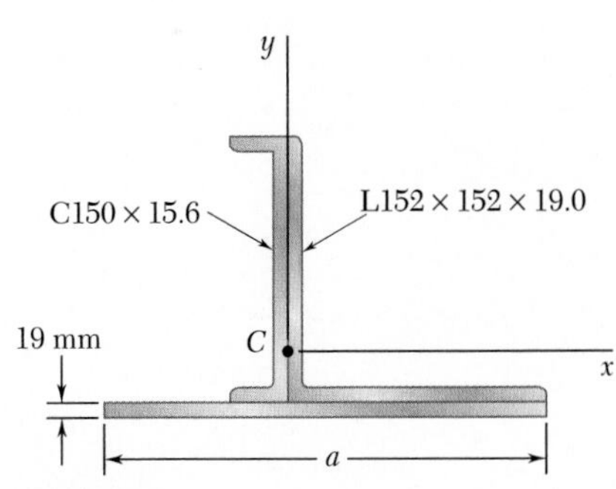

Fig. P9.56

9.56 A channel and an angle are welded to an a × .019-m steel plate. Knowing that the centroidal y axis is located as shown, determine (*a*) the width a, (*b*) the moments of inertia with respect to the centroidal x and y axes.

9.57 and *9.58* The panel shown forms the end of a trough which is filled with water to the line AA'. Referring to Sec. 9.2, determine the depth of the point of application of the resultant of the hydrostatic forces acting on the panel (the center of pressure).

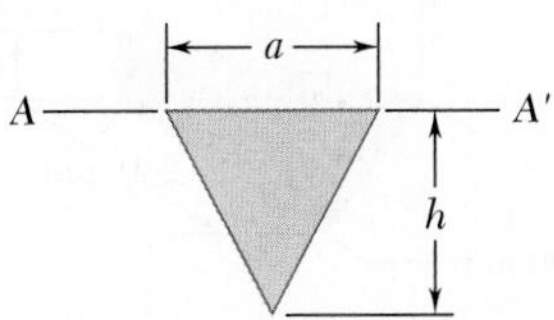

Fig. P9.57

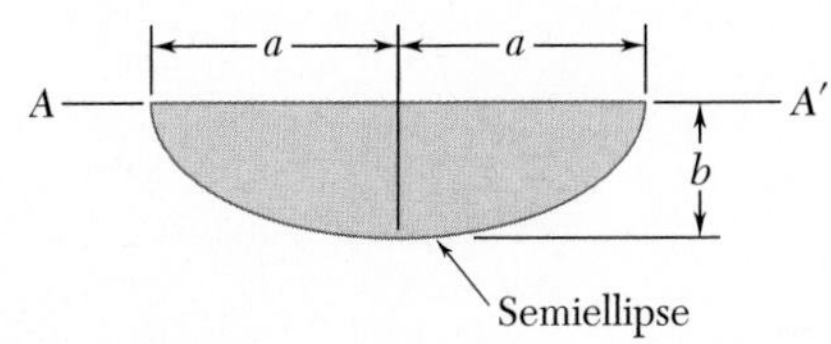

Fig. *P9.58*

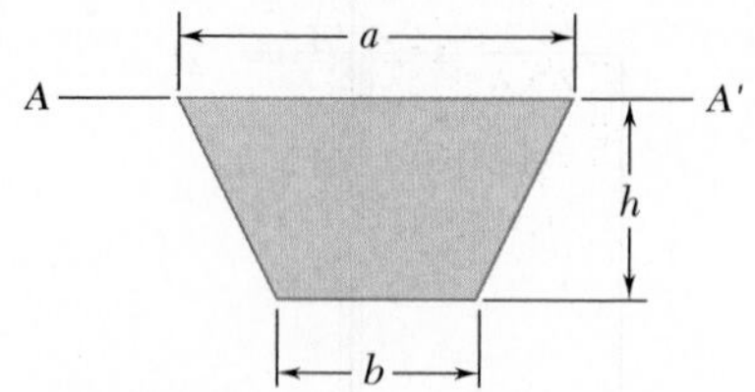

Fig. P9.59

9.59 and *9.60* The panel shown forms the end of a trough which is filled with water to the line AA'. Referring to Sec. 9.2, determine the depth of the point of application of the resultant of the hydrostatic forces acting on the panel (the center of pressure).

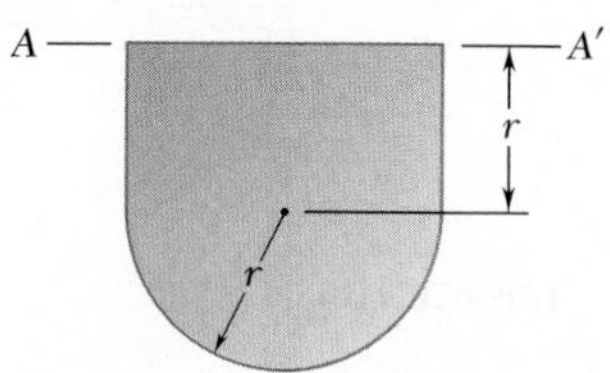

Fig. *P9.60*

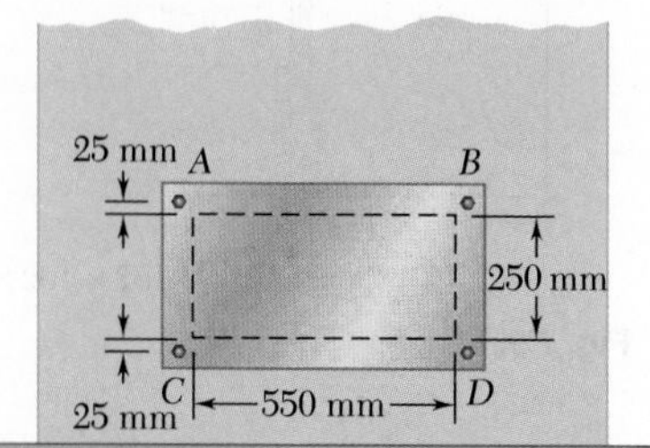

Fig. P9.61

9.61 The cover for a 250 × 550-mm access hole in an oil storage tank is attached to the outside of the tank with four bolts as shown. Knowing that the density of the oil is 920 kg/m³ and that the center of the cover is located 3 m below the surface of the oil, determine the additional force on each bolt because of the pressure of the oil.

9.62 A vertical trapezoidal gate that is used as an automatic valve is held shut by two springs attached to hinges located along edge AB. Knowing that each spring exerts a couple of magnitude 8 kN · m, determine the depth d of water for which the gate will open.

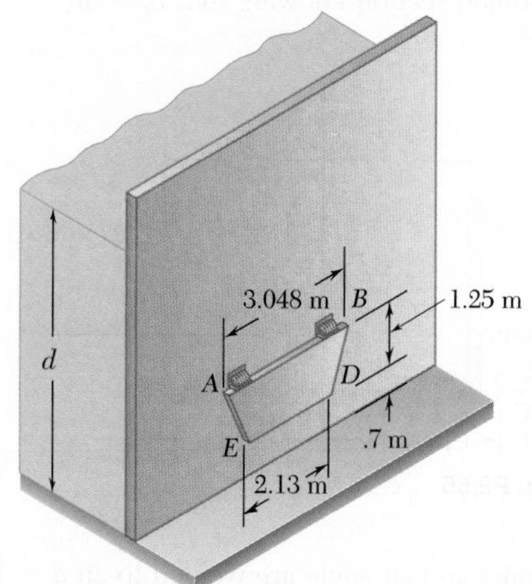

Fig. P9.62

***9.63** Determine the x coordinate of the centroid of the volume shown. (*Hint:* The height y of the volume is proportional to the x coordinate; consider an analogy between this height and the water pressure on a submerged surface.)

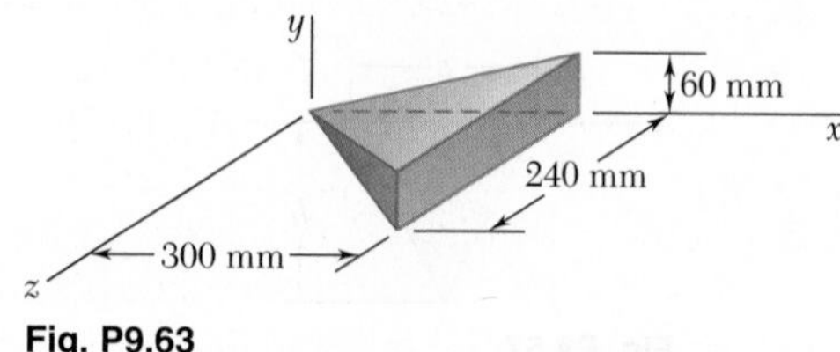

Fig. P9.63

*9.64 Determine the x coordinate of the centroid of the volume shown; this volume was obtained by intersecting a circular cylinder with an oblique plane. (*Hint:* The height y of the volume is proportional to the x coordinate; consider an analogy between this height and the water pressure on a submerged surface.)

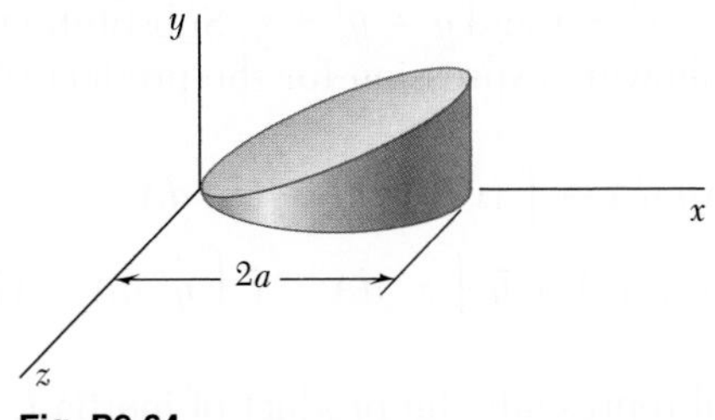

Fig. P9.64

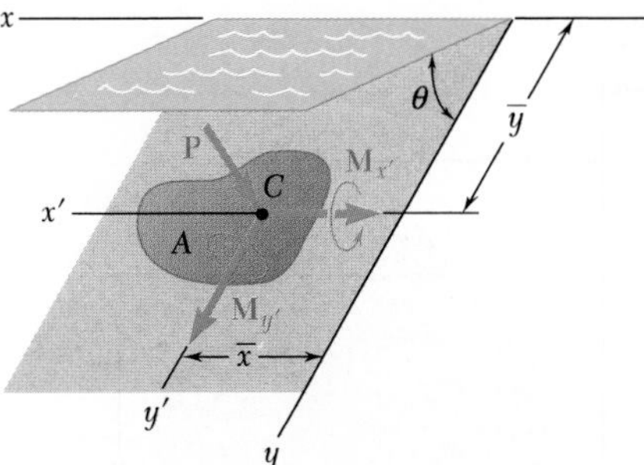

Fig. P9.65

*9.65 Show that the system of hydrostatic forces acting on a submerged plane area A can be reduced to a force $\mathbf{P}$ at the centroid C of the area and two couples. The force $\mathbf{P}$ is perpendicular to the area and is of magnitude $P = \gamma A\bar{y} \sin\theta$, where γ is the specific weight of the liquid, and the couples are $\mathbf{M}_{x'} = (\gamma \bar{I}_{x'} \sin\theta)\mathbf{i}$ and $\mathbf{M}_{y'} = (\gamma \bar{I}_{x'y'} \sin\theta)\mathbf{j}$, where $\bar{I}_{x'y'} = \int x'y'dA$ (see Sec. 9.8). Note that the couples are independent of the depth at which the area is submerged.

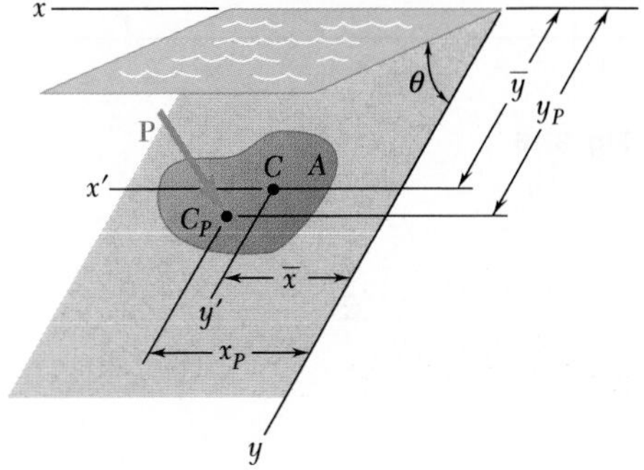

Fig. P9.66

*9.66 Show that the resultant of the hydrostatic forces acting on a submerged plane area A is a force $\mathbf{P}$ perpendicular to the area and of magnitude $P = \gamma A\bar{y} \sin\theta = \bar{p}A$, where γ is the specific weight of the liquid and $\bar{p}$ is the pressure at the centroid C of the area. Show that $\mathbf{P}$ is applied at a point C_P, called the center of pressure, whose coordinates are $x_P = I_{xy}/A\bar{y}$ and $y_P = I_x/A\bar{y}$, where $I_{xy} = \int xy\, dA$ (see Sec. 9.8). Show also that the difference of ordinates $y_P - \bar{y}$ is equal to $\bar{k}_{x'}^2/\bar{y}$ and thus depends upon the depth at which the area is submerged.

*9.8. PRODUCT OF INERTIA

The integral

$$I_{xy} = \int xy\, dA \tag{9.12}$$

which is obtained by multiplying each element dA of an area A by its coordinates x and y and integrating over the area (Fig. 9.14), is known as the *product of inertia* of the area A with respect to the x and y axes. Unlike the moments of inertia I_x and I_y, the product of inertia I_{xy} can be positive, negative, or zero.

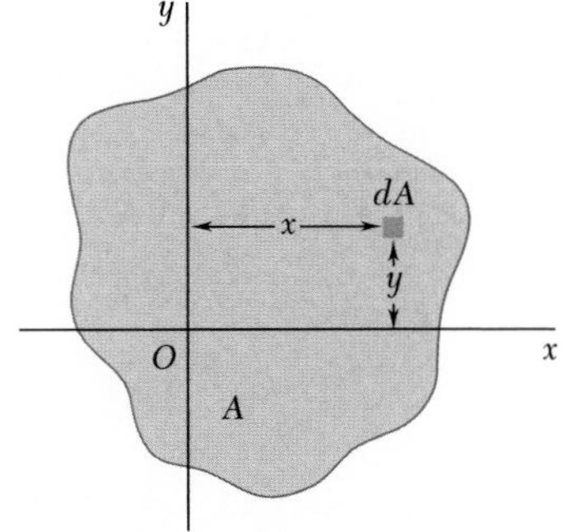

Fig. 9.14

When one or both of the x and y axes are axes of symmetry for the area A, the product of inertia I_{xy} is zero. Consider, for example, the channel section shown in Fig. 9.15. Since this section is symmetrical with respect to the x axis, we can associate with each element dA of coordinates x and y an element dA' of coordinates x and $-y$. Clearly, the contributions to I_{xy} of any pair of elements chosen in this way cancel out, and the integral (9.12) reduces to zero.

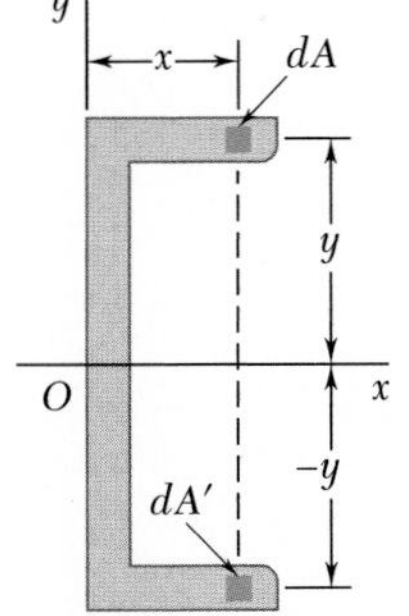

Fig. 9.15

A parallel-axis theorem similar to the one established in Sec. 9.6 for moments of inertia can be derived for products of inertia.

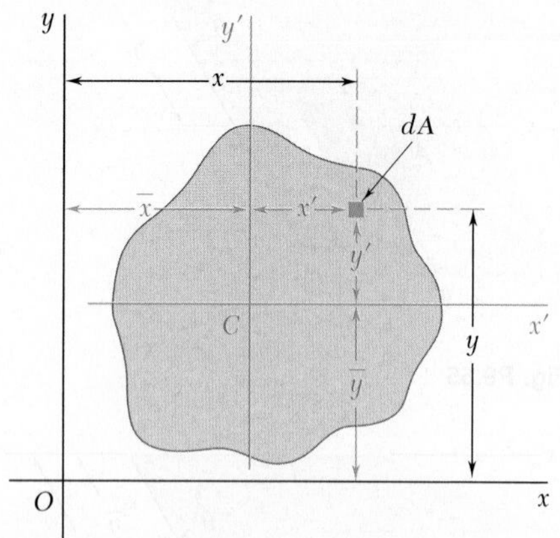

Fig. 9.16

Consider an area A and a system of rectangular coordinates x and y (Fig. 9.16). Through the centroid C of the area, of coordinates $\bar{x}$ and $\bar{y}$, we draw two *centroidal axes* x' and y' which are parallel, respectively, to the x and y axes. Denoting by x and y the coordinates of an element of area dA with respect to the original axes, and by x' and y' the coordinates of the same element with respect to the centroidal axes, we write $x = x' + \bar{x}$ and $y = y' + \bar{y}$. Substituting into Eq. (9.12), we obtain the following expression for the product of inertia I_{xy}:

$$\begin{aligned} I_{xy} &= \int xy\, dA = \int (x' + \bar{x})(y' + \bar{y})\, dA \\ &= \int x'y'\, dA + \bar{y} \int x'\, dA + \bar{x} \int y'\, dA + \bar{x}\bar{y} \int dA \end{aligned}$$

The first integral represents the product of inertia $\bar{I}_{x'y'}$ of the area A with respect to the centroidal axes x' and y'. The next two integrals represent first moments of the area with respect to the centroidal axes; they reduce to zero, since the centroid C is located on these axes. Finally, we observe that the last integral is equal to the total area A. Therefore, we have

$$I_{xy} = \bar{I}_{x'y'} + \bar{x}\bar{y}A \tag{9.13}$$

*9.9. PRINCIPAL AXES AND PRINCIPAL MOMENTS OF INERTIA

Consider the area A and the coordinate axes x and y (Fig. 9.17). Assuming that the moments and product of inertia

$$I_x = \int y^2\, dA \qquad I_y = \int x^2\, dA \qquad I_{xy} = \int xy\, dA \tag{9.14}$$

of the area A are known, we propose to determine the moments and product of inertia $I_{x'}$, $I_{y'}$, and $I_{x'y'}$ of A with respect to new axes x' and y' which are obtained by rotating the original axes about the origin through an angle θ.

We first note the following relations between the coordinates x', y' and x, y of an element of area dA:

$$x' = x \cos \theta + y \sin \theta \qquad y' = y \cos \theta - x \sin \theta$$

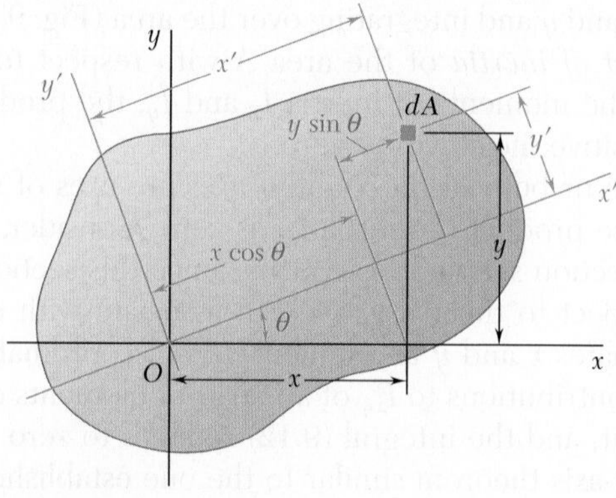

Fig. 9.17

Substituting for y' in the expression for $I_{x'}$, we write

$$I_{x'} = \int (y')^2 \, dA = \int (y \cos \theta - x \sin \theta)^2 \, dA$$
$$= \cos^2 \theta \int y^2 \, dA - 2 \sin \theta \cos \theta \int xy \, dA + \sin^2 \theta \int x^2 \, dA$$

Using the relations (9.14), we write

$$I_{x'} = I_x \cos^2 \theta - 2I_{xy} \sin \theta \cos \theta + I_y \sin^2 \theta \tag{9.15}$$

Similarly, we obtain for $I_{y'}$ and $I_{x'y'}$ the expressions

$$I_{y'} = I_x \sin^2 \theta + 2I_{xy} \sin \theta \cos \theta + I_y \cos^2 \theta \tag{9.16}$$
$$I_{x'y'} = (I_x - I_y) \sin \theta \cos \theta + I_{xy}(\cos^2 \theta - \sin^2 \theta) \tag{9.17}$$

Recalling the trigonometric relations

$$\sin 2\theta = 2 \sin \theta \cos \theta \qquad \cos 2\theta = \cos^2 \theta - \sin^2 \theta$$

and

$$\cos^2 \theta = \frac{1 + \cos 2\theta}{2} \qquad \sin^2 \theta = \frac{1 - \cos 2\theta}{2}$$

we can write Eqs. (9.15), (9.16), and (9.17) as follows:

$$I_{x'} = \frac{I_x + I_y}{2} + \frac{I_x - I_y}{2} \cos 2\theta - I_{xy} \sin 2\theta \tag{9.18}$$

$$I_{y'} = \frac{I_x + I_y}{2} - \frac{I_x - I_y}{2} \cos 2\theta + I_{xy} \sin 2\theta \tag{9.19}$$

$$I_{x'y'} = \frac{I_x - I_y}{2} \sin 2\theta + I_{xy} \cos 2\theta \tag{9.20}$$

Adding Eqs. (9.18) and (9.19) we observe that

$$I_{x'} + I_{y'} = I_x + I_y \tag{9.21}$$

This result could have been anticipated, since both members of (9.21) are equal to the polar moment of inertia J_O.

Equations (9.18) and (9.20) are the parametric equations of a circle. This means that if we choose a set of rectangular axes and plot a point M of abscissa $I_{x'}$ and ordinate $I_{x'y'}$ for any given value of the parameter θ, all of the points thus obtained will lie on a circle. To establish this property, we eliminate θ from Eqs. (9.18) and (9.20); this is done by transposing $(I_x + I_y)/2$ in Eq. (9.18), squaring both members of Eqs. (9.18) and (9.20), and adding. We write

$$\left(I_{x'} - \frac{I_x + I_y}{2}\right)^2 + I_{x'y'}^2 = \left(\frac{I_x - I_y}{2}\right)^2 + I_{xy}^2 \tag{9.22}$$

Setting

$$I_{\text{ave}} = \frac{I_x + I_y}{2} \quad \text{and} \quad R = \sqrt{\left(\frac{I_x - I_y}{2}\right)^2 + I_{xy}^2} \tag{9.23}$$

we write the identity (9.22) in the form

$$(I_{x'} - I_{\text{ave}})^2 + I_{x'y'}^2 = R^2 \tag{9.24}$$

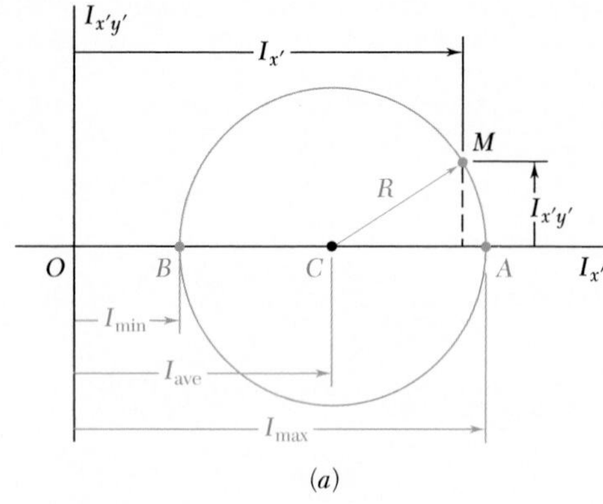

(a)

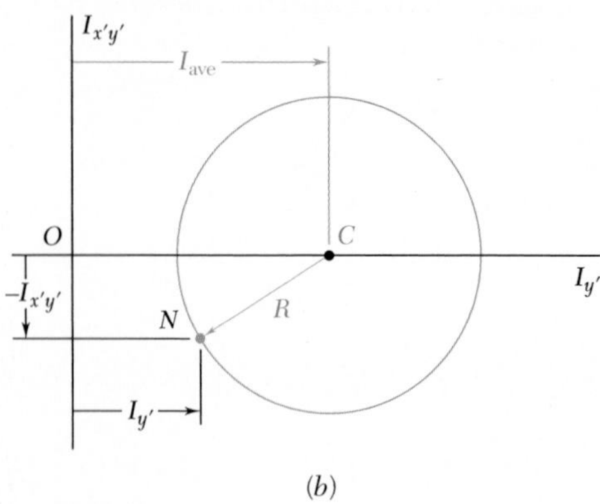

(b)

Fig. 9.18

which is the equation of a circle of radius R centered at the point C whose x and y coordinates are I_{ave} and 0, respectively (Fig. 9.18*a*). We observe that Eqs. (9.19) and (9.20) are the parametric equations of the same circle. Furthermore, because of the symmetry of the circle about the horizontal axis, the same result would have been obtained if instead of plotting M, we had plotted a point N of coordinates $I_{y'}$ and $-I_{x'y'}$ (Fig. 9.18*b*). This property will be used in Sec. 9.10.

The two points A and B where the above circle intersects the horizontal axis (Fig. 9.18*a*) are of special interest: Point A corresponds to the maximum value of the moment of inertia $I_{x'}$, while point B corresponds to its minimum value. In addition, both points correspond to a zero value of the product of inertia $I_{x'y'}$. Thus, the values θ_m of the parameter θ which correspond to the points A and B can be obtained by setting $I_{x'y'} = 0$ in Eq. (9.20). We obtain†

$$\tan 2\theta_m = -\frac{2I_{xy}}{I_x - I_y} \tag{9.25}$$

This equation defines two values $2\theta_m$ which are 180° apart and thus two values θ_m which are 90° apart. One of these values corresponds to point A in Fig. 9.18*a* and to an axis through O in Fig. 9.17 with respect to which the moment of inertia of the given area is maximum; the other value corresponds to point B and to an axis through O with respect to which the moment of inertia of the area is minimum. The two axes thus defined, which are perpendicular to each other, are called the *principal axes of the area about O*, and the corresponding values I_{max} and I_{min} of the moment of inertia are called the *principal moments of inertia of the area about O*. Since the two values θ_m defined by Eq. (9.25) were obtained by setting $I_{x'y'} = 0$ in Eq. (9.20), it is clear that the product of inertia of the given area with respect to its principal axes is zero.

We observe from Fig. 9.18*a* that

$$I_{max} = I_{ave} + R \qquad I_{min} = I_{ave} - R \tag{9.26}$$

Using the values for I_{ave} and R from formulas (9.23), we write

$$I_{max,min} = \frac{I_x + I_y}{2} \pm \sqrt{\left(\frac{I_x - I_y}{2}\right)^2 + I_{xy}^2} \tag{9.27}$$

Unless it is possible to tell by inspection which of the two principal axes corresponds to I_{max} and which corresponds to I_{min}, it is necessary to substitute one of the values of θ_m into Eq. (9.18) in order to determine which of the two corresponds to the maximum value of the moment of inertia of the area about O.

Referring to Sec. 9.8, we note that if an area possesses an axis of symmetry through a point O, this axis must be a principal axis of the area about O. On the other hand, a principal axis does not need to be an axis of symmetry; whether or not an area possesses any axes of symmetry, it will have two principal axes of inertia about any point O.

The properties we have established hold for any point O located inside or outside the given area. If the point O is chosen to coincide with the centroid of the area, any axis through O is a centroidal axis; the two principal axes of the area about its centroid are referred to as the *principal centroidal axes of the area*.

†This relation can also be obtained by differentiating $I_{x'}$ in Eq. (9.18) and setting $dI_{x'}/d\theta = 0$.

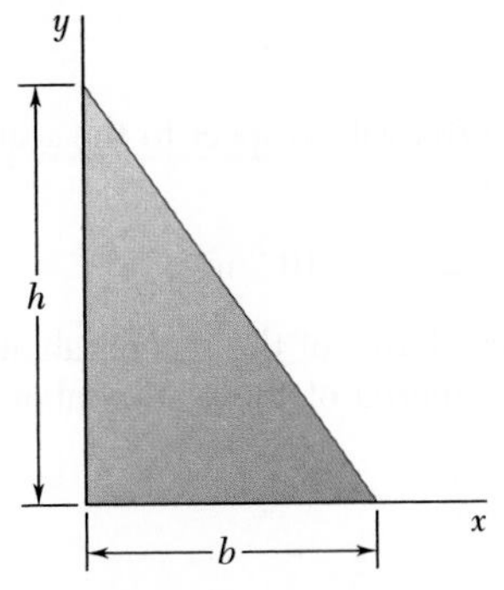

SAMPLE PROBLEM 9.6

Determine the product of inertia of the right triangle shown (*a*) with respect to the x and y axes and (*b*) with respect to centroidal axes parallel to the x and y axes.

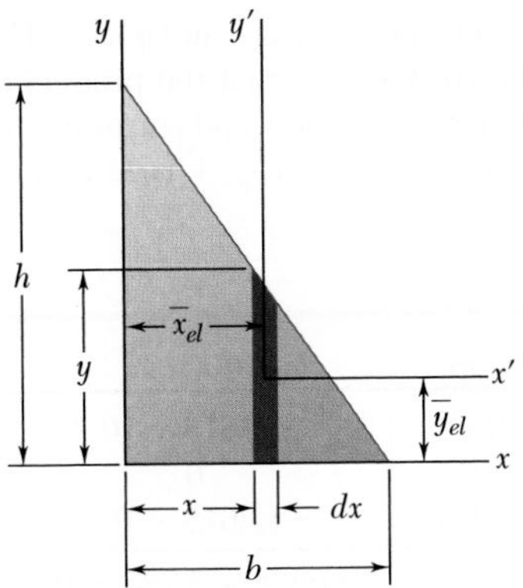

SOLUTION

a. Product of Inertia I_{xy}. A vertical rectangular strip is chosen as the differential element of area. Using the parallel-axis theorem, we write

$$dI_{xy} = dI_{x'y'} + \bar{x}_{el}\bar{y}_{el}\, dA$$

Since the element is symmetrical with respect to the x' and y' axes, we note that $dI_{x'y'} = 0$. From the geometry of the triangle, we obtain

$$y = h\left(1 - \frac{x}{b}\right) \qquad dA = y\, dx = h\left(1 - \frac{x}{b}\right) dx$$

$$\bar{x}_{el} = x \qquad \bar{y}_{el} = \tfrac{1}{2}y = \tfrac{1}{2}h\left(1 - \frac{x}{b}\right)$$

Integrating dI_{xy} from $x = 0$ to $x = b$, we obtain

$$I_{xy} = \int dI_{xy} = \int \bar{x}_{el}\bar{y}_{el}\, dA = \int_0^b x(\tfrac{1}{2})h^2\left(1 - \frac{x}{b}\right)^2 dx$$

$$= h^2 \int_0^b \left(\frac{x}{2} - \frac{x^2}{b} + \frac{x^3}{2b^2}\right) dx = h^2\left[\frac{x^2}{4} - \frac{x^3}{3b} + \frac{x^4}{8b^2}\right]_0^b$$

$$I_{xy} = \tfrac{1}{24}b^2h^2 \quad ◀$$

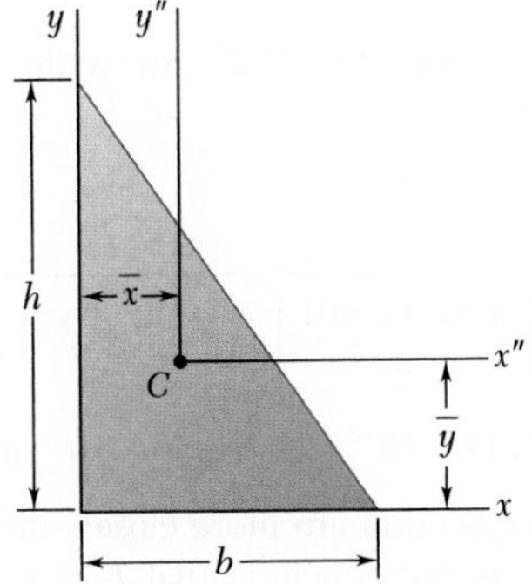

b. Product of Inertia $\bar{I}_{x''y''}$. The coordinates of the centroid of the triangle relative to the x and y axes are

$$\bar{x} = \tfrac{1}{3}b \qquad \bar{y} = \tfrac{1}{3}h$$

Using the expression for I_{xy} obtained in part *a*, we apply the parallel-axis theorem and write

$$I_{xy} = \bar{I}_{x''y''} + \bar{x}\bar{y}A$$

$$\tfrac{1}{24}b^2h^2 = \bar{I}_{x''y''} + (\tfrac{1}{3}b)(\tfrac{1}{3}h)(\tfrac{1}{2}bh)$$

$$\bar{I}_{x''y''} = \tfrac{1}{24}b^2h^2 - \tfrac{1}{18}b^2h^2$$

$$\bar{I}_{x''y''} = -\tfrac{1}{72}b^2h^2 \quad ◀$$

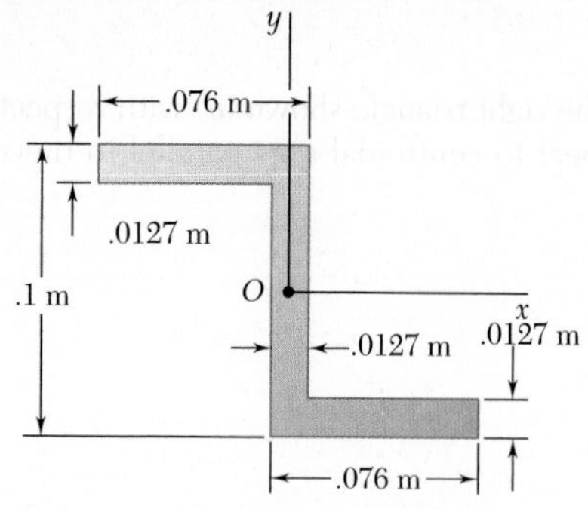

SAMPLE PROBLEM 9.7

For the section shown, the moments of inertia with respect to the x and y axes have been computed and are known to be

$$I_x = 4.32 \times 10^{-6}\ \text{m}^4 \qquad I_y = 2.901 \times 10^{-6}\ \text{m}^4$$

Determine (*a*) the orientation of the principal axes of the section about O, (*b*) the values of the principal moments of inertia of the section about O.

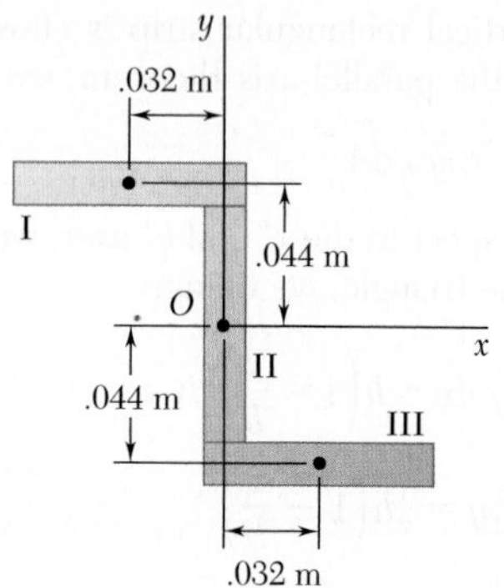

SOLUTION

We first compute the product of inertia with respect to the x and y axes. The area is divided into three rectangles as shown. We note that the product of inertia $\bar{I}_{x'y'}$ with respect to centroidal axes parallel to the x and y axes is zero for each rectangle. Using the parallel-axis theorem $I_{xy} = \bar{I}_{x'y'} + \bar{x}\bar{y}A$, we find that I_{xy} reduces to $\bar{x}\bar{y}A$ for each rectangle.

Rectangle	Area, m²	$\bar{x}$, m	$\bar{y}$, m	$\bar{x}\bar{y}A$, m⁴
I	.000967	−.032	.044	-1.3615×10^{-6}
II	.000967	0	0	0
III	.000967	.032	−.044	-1.3615×10^{-6}
				$\Sigma\bar{x}\bar{y}A = -2.723 \times 10^{-6}$

$$I_{xy} = \Sigma\bar{x}\bar{y}A = -2.723 \times 10^{-6}\ \text{m}^4$$

a. Principal Axes. Since the magnitudes of I_x, I_y, and I_{xy} are known, Eq. (9.25) is used to determine the values of θ_m:

$$\tan 2\theta_m = -\frac{2I_{xy}}{I_x - I_y} = -\frac{2.723 \times 10^{-6}}{(4.32 - 2.901) \times 10^{-6}} = +3.85$$

$$2\theta_m = 75.4° \text{ and } 255.4°$$

$$\theta_m = 37.7° \qquad \text{and} \qquad \theta_m = 127.7° \blacktriangleleft$$

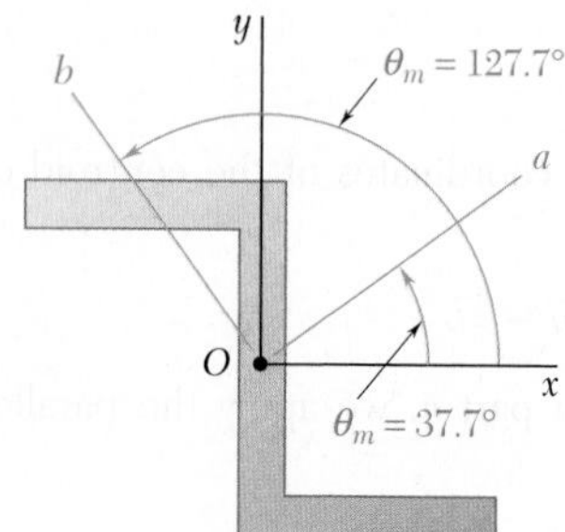

b. Principal Moments of Inertia. Using Eq. (9.27), we write

$$I_{\text{max,min}} = \frac{I_x + I_y}{2} \pm \sqrt{\left(\frac{I_x - I_y}{2}\right)^2 + I_{xy}^2}$$

$$= \frac{(4.32 + 2.901)}{2} \times 10^{-6} \pm \sqrt{\left(\frac{4.32 - 2.901}{2}\right)^2 + (-2.723)^2} \times 10^{-6}$$

$$I_{\max} = 6.4244 \times 10^{-6}\ \text{m}^4 = .7966 \times 10^{-6}\ \text{m}^4 \blacktriangleleft$$

Noting that the elements of the area of the section are more closely distributed about the b axis than about the a axis, we conclude that $I_a = I_{\max} = 6.4244 \times 10^{-6}\ \text{m}^4$ and $I_b = I_{\min} = .7966 \times 10^{-6}\ \text{m}^4$. This conclusion can be verified by substituting $\theta = 37.7°$ into Eqs. (9.18) and (9.19).

SOLVING PROBLEMS ON YOUR OWN

In the problems for this lesson, you will continue your work with *moments of inertia* and will utilize various techniques for computing *products of inertia*. Although the problems are generally straightforward, several items are worth noting.

1. ***Calculating the product of inertia I_{xy} by integration.*** We defined this quantity as

$$I_{xy} = \int xy\, dA \qquad (9.12)$$

and stated that its value can be positive, negative, or zero. The product of inertia can be computed directly from the above equation using double integration, or it can be determined using single integration as shown in Sample Prob. 9.6. When applying the latter technique and using the parallel-axis theorem, it is important to remember that $\bar{x}_{el}$ and $\bar{y}_{el}$ in the equation

$$dI_{xy} = dI_{x'y'} + \bar{x}_{el}\bar{y}_{el}\, dA$$

are the coordinates of the centroid of the element of area dA. Thus, if dA is not in the first quadrant, one or both of these coordinates will be negative.

2. ***Calculating the products of inertia of composite areas.*** They can easily be computed from the products of inertia of their component parts by using the parallel-axis theorem

$$I_{xy} = \bar{I}_{x'y'} + \bar{x}\bar{y}A \qquad (9.13)$$

The proper technique to use for problems of this type is illustrated in Sample Probs. 9.6 and 9.7. In addition to the usual rules for composite-area problems, it is essential that you remember the following points.

a. ***If either of the centroidal axes of a component area is an axis of symmetry for that area, the product of inertia $\bar{I}_{x'y'}$ for that area is zero.*** Thus, $\bar{I}_{x'y'}$ is zero for component areas such as circles, semicircles, rectangles, and isosceles triangles which possess an axis of symmetry parallel to one of the coordinate axes.

b. ***Pay careful attention to the signs of the coordinates $\bar{x}$ and $\bar{y}$ of each component area*** when you use the parallel-axis theorem [Sample Prob. 9.7].

3. ***Determining the moments of inertia and the product of inertia for rotated coordinate axes.*** In Sec. 9.9 we derived Eqs. (9.18), (9.19), and (9.20), from which the moments of inertia and the product of inertia can be computed for coordinate axes which have been rotated about the origin O. To apply these equations, you must know a set of values I_x, I_y, and I_{xy} for a given orientation of the axes, and you must remember that θ is positive for counterclockwise rotations of the axes and negative for clockwise rotations of the axes.

4. ***Computing the principal moments of inertia.*** We showed in Sec. 9.9 that there is a particular orientation of the coordinate axes for which the moments of inertia attain their maximum and minimum values, I_{max} and I_{min}, and for which the product of inertia is zero. Equation (9.27) can be used to compute these values, known as the *principal moments of inertia* of the area about O. The corresponding axes are referred to as the *principal axes* of the area about O, and their orientation is defined by Eq. (9.25). *To determine which of the principal axes corresponds to I_{max} and which corresponds to I_{min}*, you can either follow the procedure outlined in the text after Eq. (9.27) or observe about which of the two principal axes the area is more closely distributed; that axis corresponds to I_{min} [Sample Prob. 9.7].

Problems

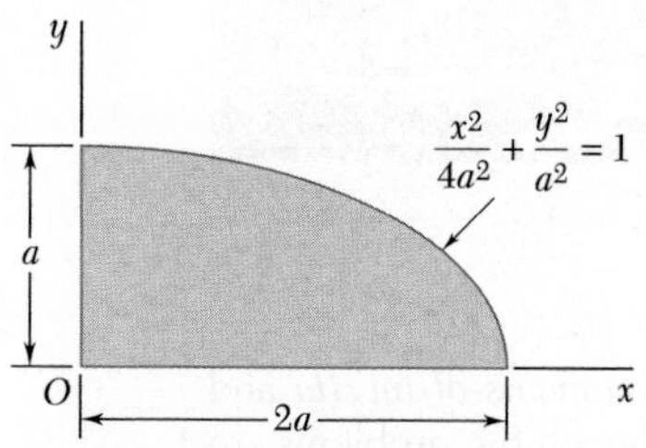

Fig. *P9.67*

9.67 through 9.70 Determine by direct integration the product of inertia of the given area with respect to the x and y axes.

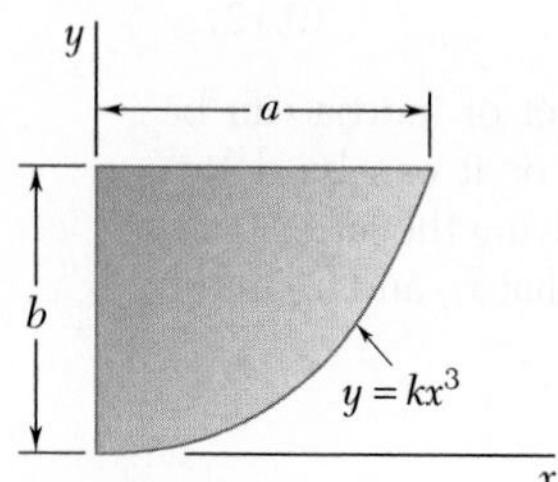

Fig. P9.68

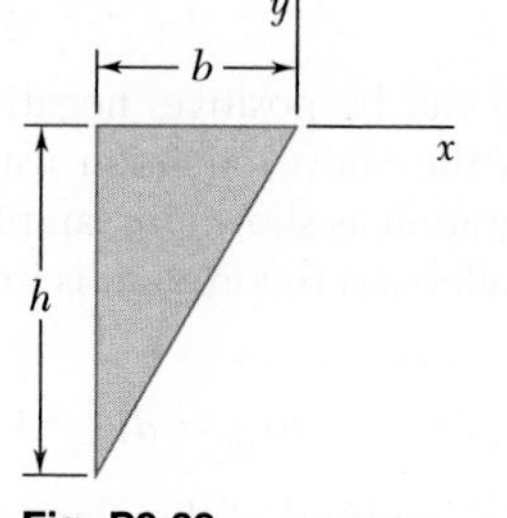

Fig. P9.69

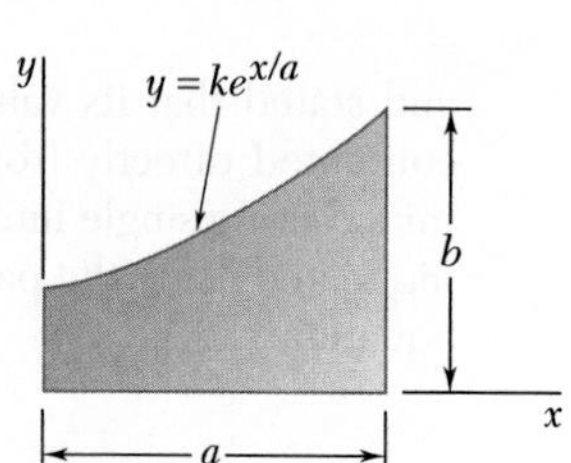

Fig. P9.70

9.71 through 9.74 Using the parallel-axis theorem, determine the product of inertia of the area shown with respect to the centroidal x and y axes.

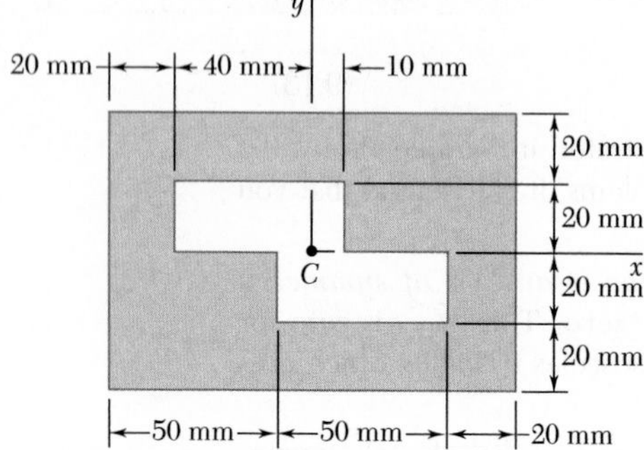

Fig. P9.71

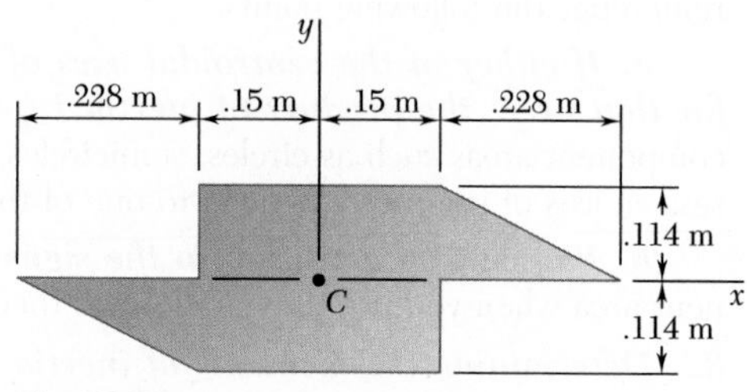

Fig. P9.72

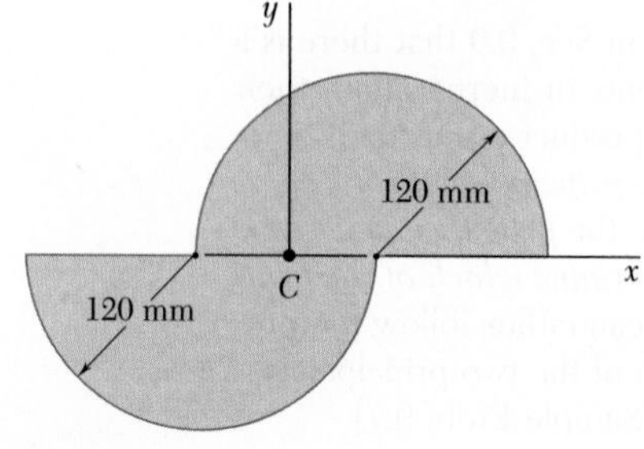

Fig. P9.73

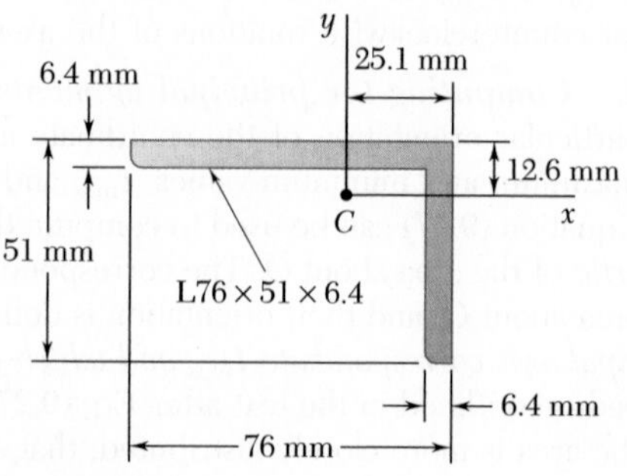

Fig. P9.74

9.75 through 9.78 Using the parallel-axis theorem, determine the product of inertia of the area shown with respect to the centroidal x and y axes.

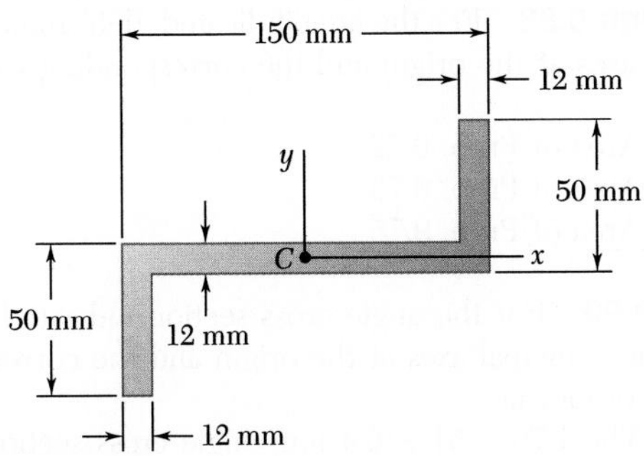

Fig. P9.75

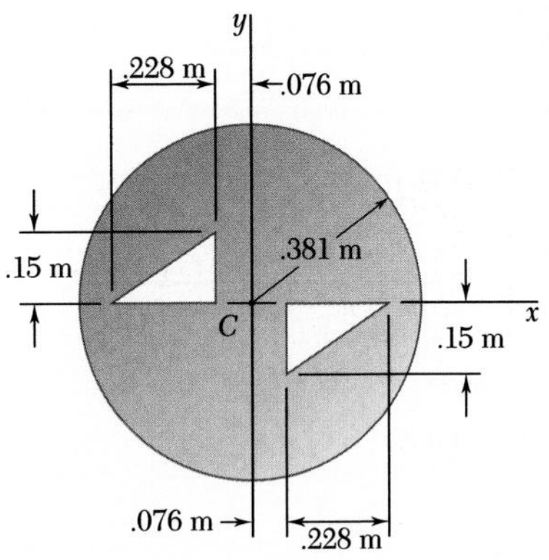

Fig. *P9.76*

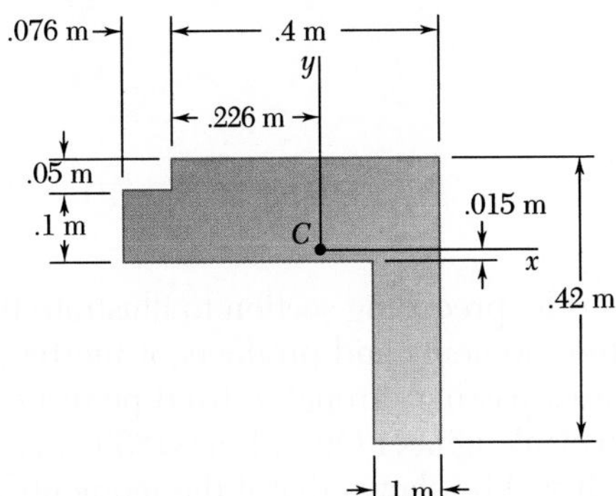

Fig. *P9.77*

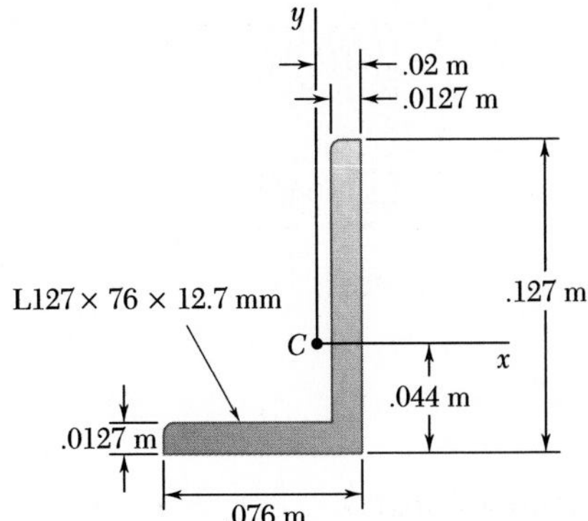

Fig. P9.78

9.79 Determine for the quarter ellipse of Prob. 9.67 the moments of inertia and the product of inertia with respect to new axes obtained by rotating the x and y axes about O (a) through 45° counterclockwise, (b) through 30° clockwise.

9.80 Determine the moments of inertia and the product of inertia of the area of Prob. 9.72 with respect to new centroidal axes obtained by rotating the x and y axes 45° clockwise.

9.81 Determine the moments of inertia and the product of inertia of the area of Prob. 9.73 with respect to new centroidal axes obtained by rotating the x and y axes through 30° clockwise.

9.82 Determine the moments of inertia and the product of inertia of the area of Prob. 9.75 with respect to new centroidal axes obtained by rotating the x and y axes through 60° counterclockwise.

9.83 Determine the moments of inertia and the product of inertia of the L76 × 51 × 6.4-mm angle cross section of Prob. 9.74 with respect to new centroidal axes obtained by rotating the x and y axes through 45° clockwise.

9.84 Determine the moments of inertia and the product of inertia of the L127 × 76 × 12.7-mm angle cross section of Prob. 9.78 with respect to new centroidal axes obtained by rotating the x and y axes through 30° counterclockwise.

9.85 For the quarter ellipse of Prob. 9.67, determine the orientation of the principal axes at the origin and the corresponding values of the moments of inertia.

9.86 through 9.88 For the area indicated, determine the orientation of the principal axes at the origin and the corresponding values of the moments of inertia.

9.86 Area of Prob. 9.72
9.87 Area of Prob. 9.73
9.88 Area of Prob. 9.75

9.89 and 9.90 For the angle cross section indicated, determine the orientation of the principal axes at the origin and the corresponding values of the moments of inertia.

9.89 The L76 × 51 × 6.4-mm angle cross section of Prob. 9.74
9.90 The L127 × 76 × 12.7-mm angle cross section of Prob. 9.78

*9.10. MOHR'S CIRCLE FOR MOMENTS AND PRODUCTS OF INERTIA

The circle used in the preceding section to illustrate the relations existing between the moments and products of inertia of a given area with respect to axes passing through a fixed point O was first introduced by the German engineer Otto Mohr (1835–1918) and is known as *Mohr's circle*. It will be shown that if the moments and product of inertia of an area A are known with respect to two rectangular x and y axes which pass through a point O, Mohr's circle can be used to graphically determine (a) the principal axes and principal moments of inertia of the area about O and (b) the moments and product of inertia of the area with respect to any other pair of rectangular axes x' and y' through O.

Consider a given area A and two rectangular coordinate axes x and y (Fig. 9.19a). Assuming that the moments of inertia I_x and I_y and the product of inertia I_{xy} are known, we will represent them on a diagram by plotting a point X of coordinates I_x and I_{xy} and a point Y of coordinates I_y and $-I_{xy}$ (Fig. 9.19b). If I_{xy} is positive, as assumed in Fig. 9.19a, point X is located above the horizontal axis and point Y is located below, as shown in Fig. 9.19b. If I_{xy} is negative, X is located below the horizontal axis and Y is located above. Joining X and Y with a straight line, we denote by C the point of intersection of line XY with the horizontal axis and draw the circle of center C and diameter XY. Noting that the abscissa of C and the radius of the circle are respectively equal to the quantities I_{ave} and R defined by the formula (9.23), we conclude that the circle obtained is Mohr's circle for the given area about point O. Thus, the abscissas of the points A and B where the circle intersects the horizontal axis represent respectively the principal moments of inertia $I_{\max}$ and $I_{\min}$ of the area.

We also note that, since $\tan(XCA) = 2I_{xy}/(I_x - I_y)$, the angle XCA is equal in magnitude to one of the angles $2\theta_m$ which satisfy Eq. (9.25);

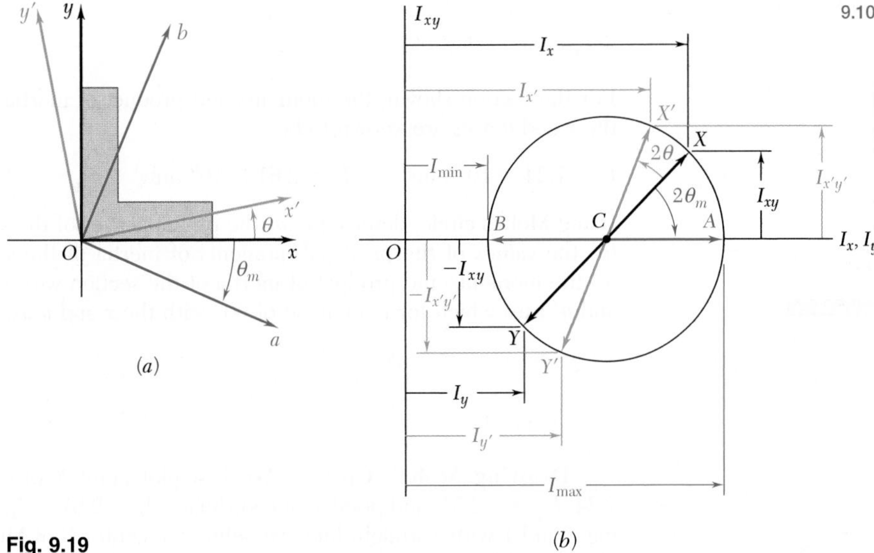

Fig. 9.19

thus, the angle θ_m, which defines in Fig. 9.19*a* the principal axis Oa corresponding to point A in Fig. 9.19*b*, is equal to half of the angle XCA of Mohr's circle. We further observe that if $I_x > I_y$ and $I_{xy} > 0$, as in the case considered here, the rotation which brings CX into CA is clockwise. Also, under these conditions, the angle θ_m obtained from Eq. (9.25), which defines the principal axis Oa in Fig. 9.19*a*, is negative; thus, the rotation which brings Ox into Oa is also clockwise. We conclude that the senses of rotation in both parts of Fig. 9.19 are the same. If a clockwise rotation through $2\theta_m$ is required to bring CX into CA on Mohr's circle, a clockwise rotation through θ_m will bring Ox into the corresponding principal axis Oa in Fig. 9.19*a*.

Since Mohr's circle is uniquely defined, the same circle can be obtained by considering the moments and product of inertia of the area A with respect to the rectangular axes x' and y' (Fig. 9.19*a*). The point X' of coordinates $I_{x'}$ and $I_{x'y'}$ and the point Y' of coordinates $I_{y'}$ and $-I_{x'y'}$ are thus located on Mohr's circle, and the angle $X'CA$ in Fig. 9.19*b* must be equal to twice the angle $x'Oa$ in Fig. 9.19*a*. Since, as noted above, the angle XCA is twice the angle xOa, it follows that the angle XCX' in Fig. 9.19*b* is twice the angle xOx' in Fig. 9.19*a*. The diameter $X'Y'$, which defines the moments and product of inertia $I_{x'}$, $I_{y'}$, and $I_{x'y'}$ of the given area with respect to rectangular axes x' and y' forming an angle θ with the x and y axes, can be obtained by rotating through an angle 2θ the diameter XY, which corresponds to the moments and product of inertia I_x, I_y, and I_{xy}. We note that the rotation which brings the diameter XY into the diameter $X'Y'$ in Fig. 9.19*b* has the same sense as the rotation which brings the x and y axes into the x' and y' axes in Fig. 9.19*a*.

It should be noted that the use of Mohr's circle is not limited to graphical solutions, that is, to solutions based on the careful drawing and measuring of the various parameters involved. By merely sketching Mohr's circle and using trigonometry, one can easily derive the various relations required for a numerical solution of a given problem (see Sample Prob. 9.8).

SAMPLE PROBLEM 9.8

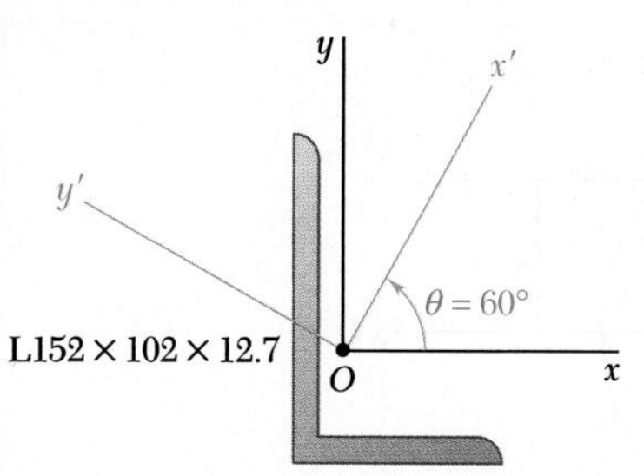

For the section shown, the moments and product of inertia with respect to the x and y axes are known to be

$$I_x = 7.24 \times 10^6 \text{ mm}^4 \qquad I_y = 2.61 \times 10^6 \text{ mm}^4 \qquad I_{xy} = -2.54 \times 10^6 \text{ mm}^4$$

Using Mohr's circle, determine (a) the principal axes of the section about O, (b) the values of the principal moments of inertia of the section about O, (c) the moments and product of inertia of the section with respect to the x' and y' axes which form an angle of 60° with the x and y axes.

SOLUTION

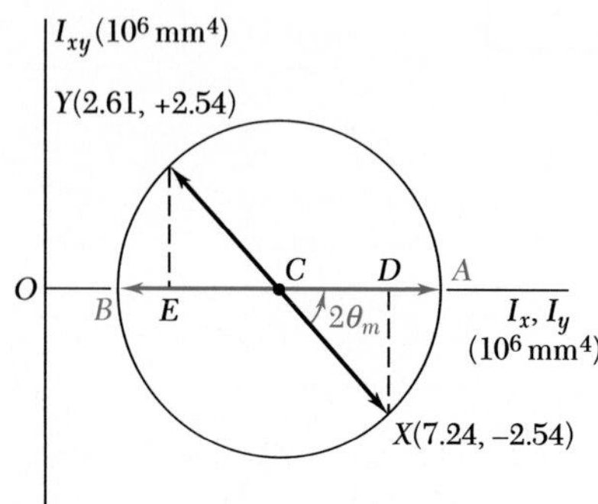

Drawing Mohr's Circle. We first plot point X of coordinates $I_x = 7.24$, $I_{xy} = -2.54$, and point Y of coordinates $I_y = 2.61$, $-I_{xy} = +2.54$. Joining X and Y with a straight line, we define the center C of Mohr's circle. The abscissa of C, which represents I_{ave}, and the radius R of the circle can be measured directly or calculated as follows:

$$I_{\text{ave}} = OC = \tfrac{1}{2}(I_x + I_y) = \tfrac{1}{2}(7.24 \times 10^6 + 2.61 \times 10^6) = 4.925 \times 10^6 \text{ mm}^4$$

$$CD = \tfrac{1}{2}(I_x - I_y) = \tfrac{1}{2}(7.24 \times 10^6 - 2.61 \times 10^6) = 2.315 \times 10^6 \text{ mm}^4$$

$$R = \sqrt{(CD)^2 + (DX)^2} = \sqrt{(2.315 \times 10^6)^2 + (2.54 \times 10^6)^2} = 3.437 \times 10^6 \text{ mm}^4$$

***a.* Principal Axes.** The principal axes of the section correspond to points A and B on Mohr's circle, and the angle through which we should rotate CX to bring it into CA defines $2\theta_m$. We have

$$\tan 2\theta_m = \frac{DX}{CD} = \frac{2.54}{2.315} = 1.097 \qquad 2\theta_m = 47.6° \circlearrowleft \qquad \theta_m = 23.8° \circlearrowleft \quad ◀$$

Thus, the principal axis Oa corresponding to the maximum value of the moment of inertia is obtained by rotating the x axis through 23.8° counterclockwise; the principal axis Ob corresponding to the minimum value of the moment of inertia is obtained by rotating the y axis through the same angle.

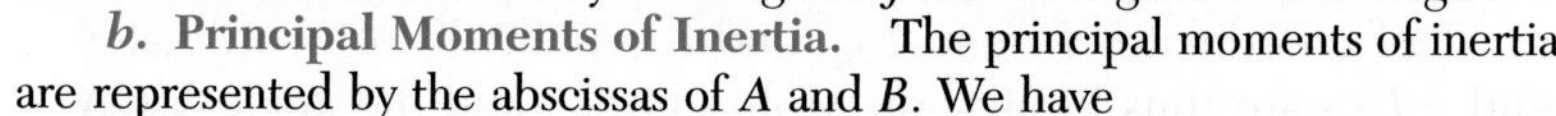

***b.* Principal Moments of Inertia.** The principal moments of inertia are represented by the abscissas of A and B. We have

$$I_{\max} = OA = OC + CA = I_{\text{ave}} + R = (4.925 + 3.437)10^6 \text{ mm}^4$$

$$I_{\max} = 8.36 \times 10^6 \text{ mm}^4 \quad ◀$$

$$I_{\min} = OB = OC - BC = I_{\text{ave}} - R = (4.925 - 3.437)10^6 \text{ mm}^4$$

$$I_{\min} = 1.49 \times 10^6 \text{ mm}^4 \quad ◀$$

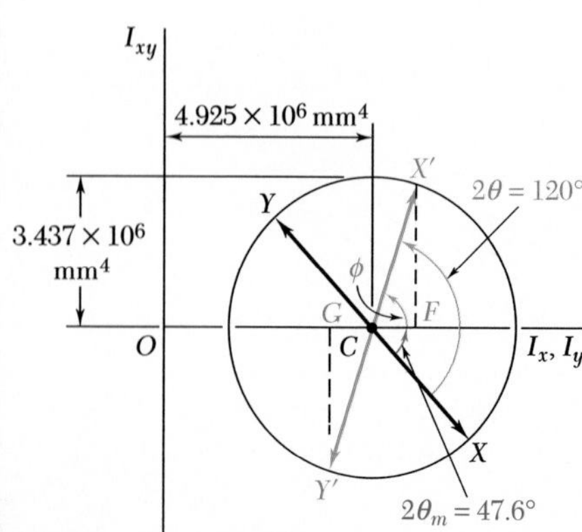

***c.* Moments and Product of Inertia with Respect to the x' and y' Axes.** On Mohr's circle, the points X' and Y', which correspond to the x' and y' axes, are obtained by rotating CX and CY through an angle $2\theta = 2(60°) = 120°$ counterclockwise. The coordinates of X' and Y' yield the desired moments and product of inertia. Noting that the angle that CX' forms with the horizontal axis is $\phi = 120° - 47.6° = 72.4°$, we write

$$I_{x'} = OF = OC + CF = 4.925 \times 10^6 \text{ mm}^4 + (3.437 \times 10^6 \text{ mm}^4) \cos 72.4°$$

$$I_{x'} = 5.96 \times 10^6 \text{ mm}^4 \quad ◀$$

$$I_{y'} = OG = OC - GC = 4.925 \times 10^6 \text{ mm}^4 - (3.437 \times 10^6 \text{ mm}^4) \cos 72.4°$$

$$I_{y'} = 3.89 \times 10^6 \text{ mm}^4 \quad ◀$$

$$I_{x'y'} = FX' = (3.437 \times 10^6 \text{ mm}^4) \sin 72.4°$$

$$I_{x'y'} = 3.28 \times 10^6 \text{ mm}^4 \quad ◀$$

SOLVING PROBLEMS ON YOUR OWN

In the problems for this lesson, you will use *Mohr's circle* to determine the moments and products of inertia of a given area for different orientations of the coordinate axes. Although in some cases using Mohr's circle may not be as direct as substituting into the appropriate equations [Eqs. (9.18) through (9.20)], this method of solution has the advantage of providing a visual representation of the relationships among the various variables. Further, Mohr's circle shows all of the values of the moments and products of inertia which are possible for a given problem.

Using Mohr's circle. The underlying theory was presented in Sec. 9.9, and we discussed the application of this method in Sec. 9.10 and in Sample Prob. 9.8. In the same problem, we presented the steps you should follow to determine the *principal axes,* the *principal moments of inertia,* and the *moments and product of inertia with respect to a specified orientation of the coordinate axes.* When you use Mohr's circle to solve problems, it is important that you remember the following points.

a. Mohr's circle is completely defined by the quantities R and I_{ave}, which represent, respectively, the radius of the circle and the distance from the origin O to the center C of the circle. These quantities can be obtained from Eqs. (9.23) if the moments and product of inertia are known for a given orientation of the axes. However, Mohr's circle can be defined by other combinations of known values [Probs. 9.105, 9.108, and 9.109]. For these cases, it may be necessary to first make one or more assumptions, such as choosing an arbitrary location for the center when I_{ave} is unknown, assigning relative magnitudes to the moments of inertia (for example, $I_x > I_y$), or selecting the sign of the product of inertia.

b. Point X of coordinates (I_x, I_{xy}) and point Y of coordinates (I_y, $-I_{xy}$) are both located on Mohr's circle and are diametrically opposite.

c. Since moments of inertia must be positive, the entire Mohr's circle must lie to the right of the I_{xy} axis; it follows that $I_{ave} > R$ for all cases.

d. As the coordinate axes are rotated through an angle θ, the associated rotation of the diameter of Mohr's circle is equal to 2θ and is in the same sense (clockwise or counterclockwise). We strongly suggest that the known points on the circumference of the circle be labeled with the appropriate capital letter, as was done in Fig. 9.19*b* and for the Mohr's circles of Sample Prob. 9.8. This will enable you to determine, for each value of θ, the sign of the corresponding product of inertia and to determine which moment of inertia is associated with each of the coordinate axes [Sample Prob. 9.8, parts *a* and *c*].

Although we have introduced Mohr's circle within the specific context of the study of moments and products of inertia, the Mohr's circle technique is also applicable to the solution of analogous but physically different problems in mechanics of materials. This multiple use of a specific technique is not unique, and as you pursue your engineering studies, you will encounter several methods of solution which can be applied to a variety of problems.

Problems

9.91 Using Mohr's circle, determine for the quarter ellipse of Prob. 9.67 the moments of inertia and the product of inertia with respect to new axes obtained by rotating the x and y axes about O (*a*) through 45° counterclockwise, (*b*) through 30° clockwise.

9.92 Using Mohr's circle, determine the moments of inertia and the product of inertia of the area of Prob. 9.72 with respect to new centroidal axes obtained by rotating the x and y axes 45° clockwise.

9.93 Using Mohr's circle, determine the moments of inertia and the product of inertia of the area of Prob. 9.73 with respect to new centroidal axes obtained by rotating the x and y axes through 30° clockwise.

9.94 Using Mohr's circle, determine the moments of inertia and the product of inertia of the area of Prob. 9.75 with respect to new centroidal axes obtained by rotating the x and y axes through 60° counterclockwise.

9.95 Using Mohr's circle, determine the moments of inertia and the product of inertia of the L76 × 51 × 6.4-mm angle cross section of Prob. 9.74 with respect to new centroidal axes obtained by rotating the x and y axes through 45° clockwise.

9.96 Using Mohr's circle, determine the moments of inertia and the product of inertia of the L127 × 76 × 12.7-mm angle cross section of Prob. 9.78 with respect to new centroidal axes obtained by rotating the x and y axes through 30° counterclockwise.

9.97 For the quarter ellipse of Prob. 9.67, use Mohr's circle to determine the orientation of the principal axes at the origin and the corresponding values of the moments of inertia.

9.98 through 9.104 Using Mohr's circle, determine for the area indicated the orientation of the principal centroidal axes and the corresponding values of the moments of inertia.

9.98 Area of Prob. 9.72
9.99 Area of Prob. 9.76
9.100 Area of Prob. 9.73
9.101 Area of Prob. 9.74
9.102 Area of Prob. 9.75
9.103 Area of Prob. 9.71
9.104 Area of Prob. 9.77

(The moments of inertia $\bar{I}_x$ and $\bar{I}_y$ of the area of Prob. 9.104 were determined in Prob. 9.43.)

9.105 The moments and product of inertia for an L102 × 76 × 6.4-mm angle cross section with respect to two rectangular axes x and y through C are, respectively, $\bar{I}_x = 0.166 \times 10^6$ mm^4, $\bar{I}_y = 0.453 \times 10^6$ mm^4, and $\bar{I}_{xy} < 0$, with the minimum value of the moment of inertia of the area with respect to any axis through C being $\bar{I}_{\min} = 0.051 \times 10^6$ mm^4. Using Mohr's circle, determine (*a*) the product of inertia $\bar{I}_{xy}$ of the area, (*b*) the orientation of the principal axes, (*c*) the value of $\bar{I}_{\max}$.

9.106 and 9.107 Using Mohr's circle, determine for the cross section of the rolled-steel angle shown the orientation of the principal centroidal axes and the corresponding values of the moments of inertia. (Properties of the cross sections are given in Fig. 9.13.)

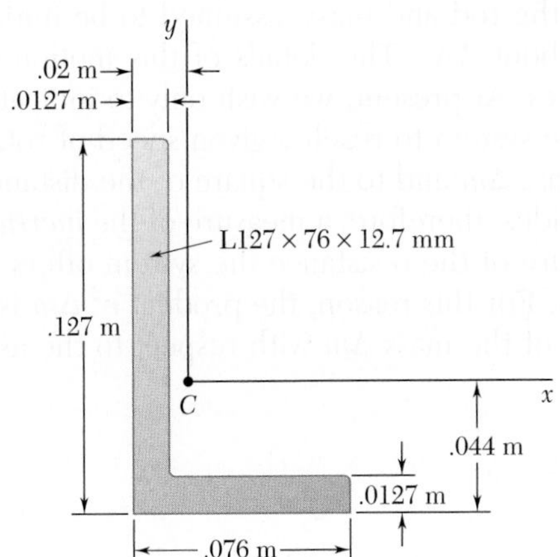

Fig. P9.106

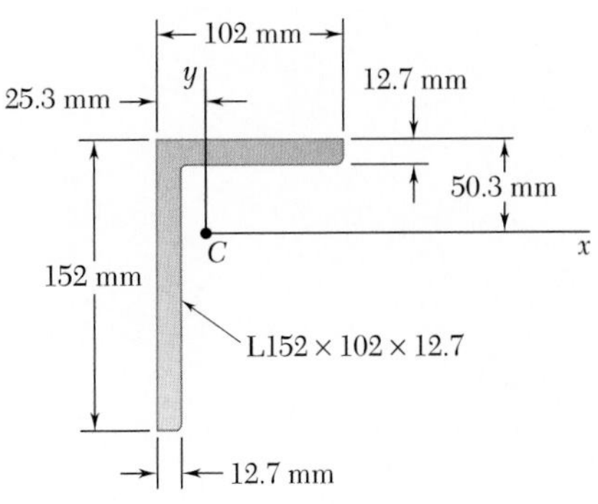

Fig. P9.107

***9.108** For a given area the moments of inertia with respect to two rectangular centroidal x and y axes are $\bar{I}_x = 2.6638 \times 10^{-4}$ m^4 and $\bar{I}_y = 1.1654 \times 10^{-4}$ m^4, respectively. Knowing that after rotating the x and y axes about the centroid 60° clockwise the product of inertia relative to the rotated axes is -7.4922×10^{-5} m^4, use Mohr's circle to determine (*a*) the orientation of the principal axes, (*b*) the principal centroidal moments of inertia.

9.109 It is known that for a given area $\bar{I}_y = 1.24869 \times 10^{-4}$ m^4 and $\bar{I}_{xy} = -5.20289 \times 10^{-5}$ m^4, where the x and y axes are rectangular centroidal axes. If the axis corresponding to the maximum product of inertia is obtained by rotating the x axis 67.5° counterclockwise about C, use Mohr's circle to determine (*a*) the moment of inertia $\bar{I}_x$ of the area, (*b*) the principal centroidal moments of inertia.

9.110 Using Mohr's circle, show that for any regular polygon (such as a pentagon) (*a*) the moment of inertia with respect to every axis through the centroid is the same, (*b*) the product of inertia with respect to every pair of rectangular axes through the centroid is zero.

9.111 Using Mohr's circle, prove that the expression $I_{x'}I_{y'} - I_{x'y'}^2$ is independent of the orientation of the x' and y' axes, where $I_{x'}$, $I_{y'}$, and $I_{x'y'}$ represent the moments and product of inertia, respectively, of a given area with respect to a pair of rectangular axes x' and y' through a given point O. Also show that the given expression is equal to the square of the length of the tangent drawn from the origin of the coordinate system to Mohr's circle.

9.112 Using the invariance property established in the preceding problem, express the product of inertia I_{xy} of an area A with respect to a pair of rectangular axes through O in terms of the moments of inertia I_x and I_y of A and the principal moments of inertia I_{min} and I_{max} of A about O. Use the formula obtained to calculate the product of inertia $\bar{I}_{xy}$ of the 76 × 51 × 6.4-mm angle cross section shown in Fig. 9.13B knowing that its maximum moment of inertia is 524 × 10^3 mm^4.

MOMENTS OF INERTIA OF MASSES

9.11. MOMENT OF INERTIA OF A MASS

Consider a small mass Δm mounted on a rod of negligible mass which can rotate freely about an axis AA' (Fig. 9.20*a*). If a couple is applied to the system, the rod and mass, assumed to be initially at rest, will start rotating about AA'. The details of this motion will be studied later in dynamics. At present, we wish only to indicate that the time required for the system to reach a given speed of rotation is proportional to the mass Δm and to the square of the distance r. The product $r^2 \Delta m$ provides, therefore, a measure of the *inertia* of the system, that is, a measure of the resistance the system offers when we try to set it in motion. For this reason, the product $r^2 \Delta m$ is called the *moment of inertia* of the mass Δm with respect to the axis AA'.

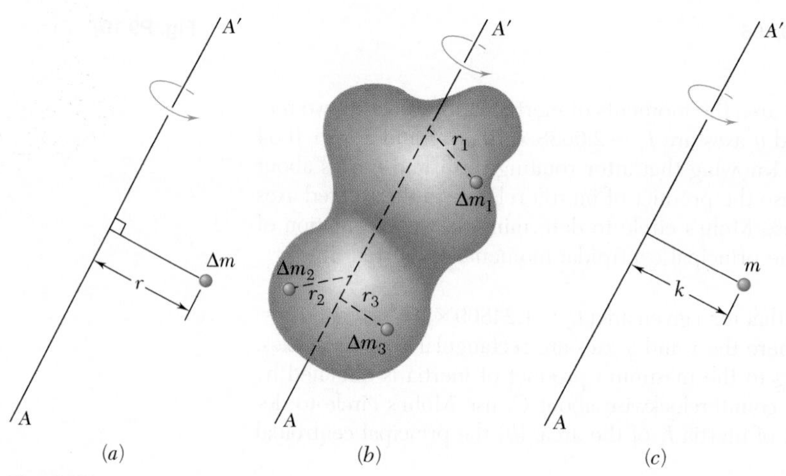

Fig. 9.20

Consider now a body of mass m which is to be rotated about an axis AA' (Fig. 9.20*b*). Dividing the body into elements of mass Δm_1, Δm_2, etc., we find that the body's resistance to being rotated is measured by the sum $r_1^2 \Delta m_1 + r_2^2 \Delta m_2 + \cdots$. This sum defines, therefore, the moment of inertia of the body with respect to the axis AA'. Increasing the number of elements, we find that the moment of inertia is equal, in the limit, to the integral

$$I = \int r^2 \, dm \qquad (9.28)$$

The *radius of gyration* k of the body with respect to the axis AA' is defined by the relation

$$I = k^2 m \qquad \text{or} \qquad k = \sqrt{\frac{I}{m}} \tag{9.29}$$

The radius of gyration k represents, therefore, the distance at which the entire mass of the body should be concentrated if its moment of inertia with respect to AA' is to remain unchanged (Fig. 9.20*c*). Whether it is kept in its original shape (Fig. 9.20*b*) or whether it is concentrated as shown in Fig. 9.20*c*, the mass m will react in the same way to a rotation, or *gyration*, about AA'.

If SI units are used, the radius of gyration k is expressed in meters and the mass m in kilograms, and thus the unit used for the moment of inertia of a mass is $\text{kg} \cdot \text{m}^2$. If U.S. customary units are used, the radius of gyration is expressed in feet and the mass in slugs (that is, in $\text{lb} \cdot \text{s}^2/\text{ft}$), and thus the derived unit used for the moment of inertia of a mass is $\text{lb} \cdot \text{ft} \cdot \text{s}^2$.†

The moment of inertia of a body with respect to a coordinate axis can easily be expressed in terms of the coordinates x, y, and z of the element of mass dm (Fig. 9.21). Noting, for example, that the square of the distance r from the element dm to the y axis is $z^2 + x^2$, we express the moment of inertia of the body with respect to the y axis as

$$I_y = \int r^2\, dm = \int (z^2 + x^2)\, dm$$

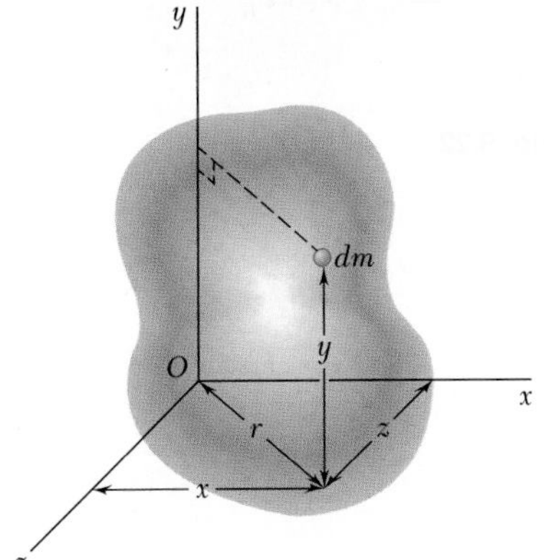

Fig. 9.21

Similar expressions can be obtained for the moments of inertia with respect to the x and z axes. We write

$$\begin{aligned} I_x &= \int (y^2 + z^2)\, dm \\ I_y &= \int (z^2 + x^2)\, dm \\ I_z &= \int (x^2 + y^2)\, dm \end{aligned} \tag{9.30}$$

Photo 9.2 As you will discuss in your dynamics course, the rotational behavior of the camshaft shown is dependent upon the mass moment of inertia of the camshaft with respect to its axis of rotation.

†It should be kept in mind when converting the moment of inertia of a mass from U.S. customary units to SI units that the base unit *pound* used in the derived unit $\text{lb} \cdot \text{ft} \cdot \text{s}^2$ is a unit of force (*not* of mass) and should therefore be converted into newtons. We have

$$1\ \text{lb} \cdot \text{ft} \cdot \text{s}^2 = (4.45\ \text{N})(0.3048\ \text{m})(1\ \text{s})^2 = 1.356\ \text{N} \cdot \text{m} \cdot \text{s}^2$$

or, since $1\ \text{N} = 1\ \text{kg} \cdot \text{m/s}^2$,

$$1\ \text{lb} \cdot \text{ft} \cdot \text{s}^2 = 1.356\ \text{kg} \cdot \text{m}^2$$

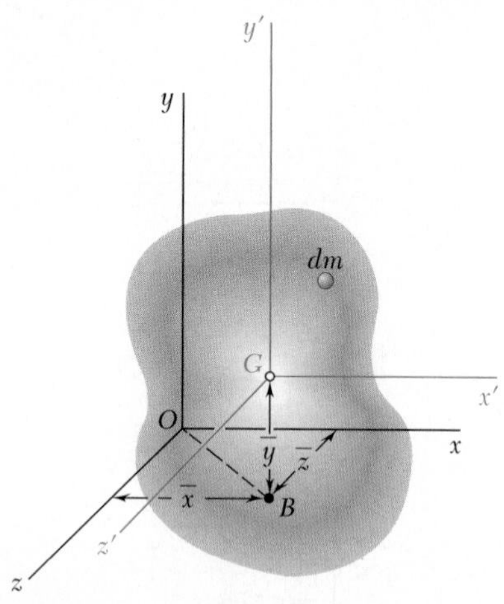

Fig. 9.22

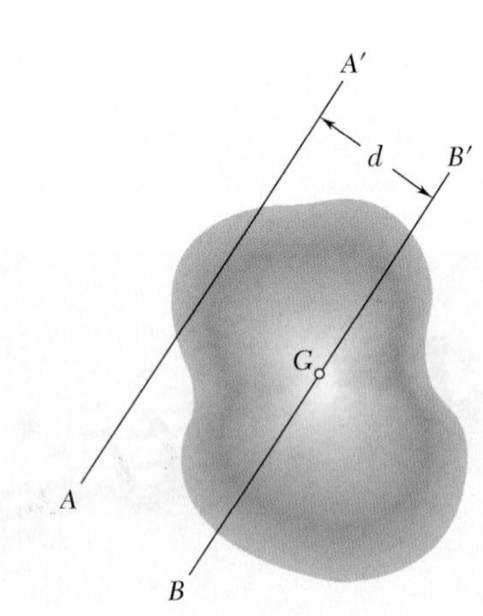

Fig. 9.23

9.12. PARALLEL-AXIS THEOREM

Consider a body of mass m. Let $Oxyz$ be a system of rectangular coordinates whose origin is at the arbitrary point O, and $Gx'y'z'$ a system of parallel *centroidal axes,* that is, a system whose origin is at the center of gravity G of the body† and whose axes x', y', and z' are parallel to the x, y, and z axes, respectively (Fig. 9.22). Denoting by $\bar{x}$, $\bar{y}$, and $\bar{z}$ the coordinates of G with respect to $Oxyz$, we write the following relations between the coordinates x, y, and z of the element dm with respect to $Oxyz$ and its coordinates x', y', and z' with respect to the centroidal axes $Gx'y'z'$:

$$x = x' + \bar{x} \qquad y = y' + \bar{y} \qquad z = z' + \bar{z} \tag{9.31}$$

Referring to Eqs. (9.30), we can express the moment of inertia of the body with respect to the x axis as follows:

$$\begin{aligned} I_x &= \int (y^2 + z^2)\, dm = \int [(y' + \bar{y})^2 + (z' + \bar{z})^2]\, dm \\ &= \int (y'^2 + z'^2)\, dm + 2\bar{y} \int y'\, dm + 2\bar{z} \int z'\, dm + (\bar{y}^2 + \bar{z}^2) \int dm \end{aligned}$$

The first integral in this expression represents the moment of inertia $\bar{I}_{x'}$ of the body with respect to the centroidal axis x'; the second and third integrals represent the first moment of the body with respect to the $z'x'$ and $x'y'$ planes, respectively, and, since both planes contain G, the two integrals are *zero;* the last integral is equal to the total mass m of the body. We write, therefore,

$$I_x = \bar{I}_{x'} + m(\bar{y}^2 + \bar{z}^2) \tag{9.32}$$

and, similarly,

$$I_y = \bar{I}_{y'} + m(\bar{z}^2 + \bar{x}^2) \qquad I_z = \bar{I}_{z'} + m(\bar{x}^2 + \bar{y}^2) \tag{9.32'}$$

We easily verify from Fig. 9.22 that the sum $\bar{z}^2 + \bar{x}^2$ represents the square of the distance OB, between the y and y' axes. Similarly, $\bar{y}^2 + \bar{z}^2$ and $\bar{x}^2 + \bar{y}^2$ represent the squares of the distance between the x and x' axes and the z and z' axes, respectively. Denoting by d the distance between an arbitrary axis AA' and the parallel centroidal axis BB' (Fig. 9.23), we can, therefore, write the following general relation between the moment of inertia I of the body with respect to AA' and its moment of inertia $\bar{I}$ with respect to BB':

$$I = \bar{I} + md^2 \tag{9.33}$$

Expressing the moments of inertia in terms of the corresponding radii of gyration, we can also write

$$k^2 = \bar{k}^2 + d^2 \tag{9.34}$$

where k and $\bar{k}$ represent the radii of gyration of the body about AA' and BB', respectively.

†Note that the term *centroidal* is used here to define an axis passing through the center of gravity G of the body, whether or not G coincides with the centroid of the volume of the body.

9.13. MOMENTS OF INERTIA OF THIN PLATES

Consider a thin plate of uniform thickness t, which is made of a homogeneous material of density ρ (density = mass per unit volume). The mass moment of inertia of the plate with respect to an axis AA' *contained in the plane* of the plate (Fig. 9.24*a*) is

$$I_{AA',\,\text{mass}} = \int r^2\, dm$$

Since $dm = \rho t\, dA$, we write

$$I_{AA',\,\text{mass}} = \rho t \int r^2\, dA$$

But r represents the distance of the element of area dA to the axis

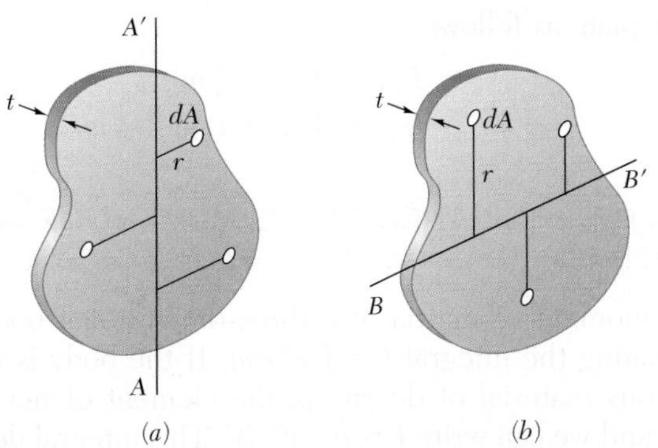

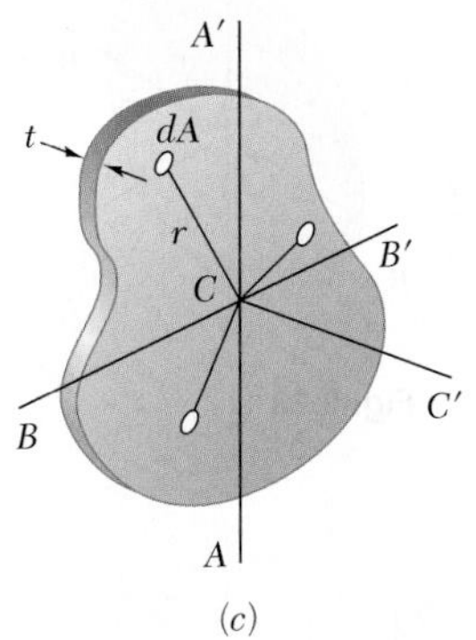

Fig. 9.24

AA'; the integral is therefore equal to the moment of inertia of the area of the plate with respect to AA'. We have

$$I_{AA',\,\text{mass}} = \rho t I_{AA',\,\text{area}} \tag{9.35}$$

Similarly, for an axis BB' which is contained in the plane of the plate and is perpendicular to AA' (Fig. 9.24*b*), we have

$$I_{BB',\,\text{mass}} = \rho t I_{BB',\,\text{area}} \tag{9.36}$$

Considering now the axis CC' which is *perpendicular* to the plate and passes through the point of intersection C of AA' and BB' (Fig. 9.24*c*), we write

$$I_{CC',\,\text{mass}} = \rho t J_{C,\,\text{area}} \tag{9.37}$$

where J_C is the *polar* moment of inertia of the area of the plate with respect to point C.

Recalling the relation $J_C = I_{AA'} + I_{BB'}$ which exists between polar and rectangular moments of inertia of an area, we write the following relation between the mass moments of inertia of a thin plate:

$$I_{CC'} = I_{AA'} + I_{BB'} \tag{9.38}$$

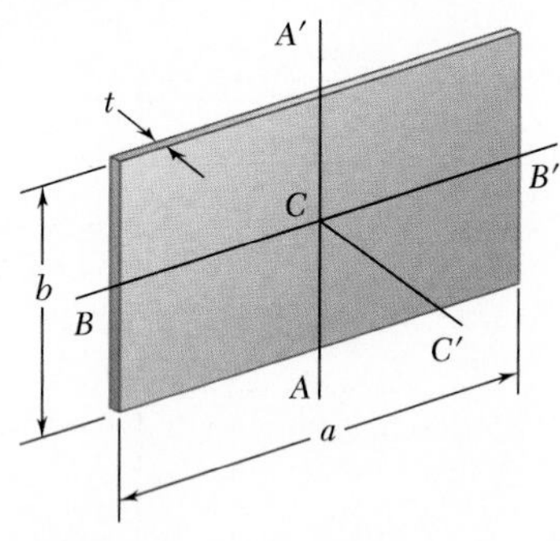

Fig. 9.25

Rectangular Plate. In the case of a rectangular plate of sides a and b (Fig. 9.25), we obtain the following mass moments of inertia with respect to axes through the center of gravity of the plate:

$$I_{AA',\text{ mass}} = \rho t I_{AA',\text{ area}} = \rho t(\tfrac{1}{12}a^3b)$$
$$I_{BB',\text{ mass}} = \rho t I_{BB',\text{ area}} = \rho t(\tfrac{1}{12}ab^3)$$

Observing that the product ρabt is equal to the mass m of the plate, we write the mass moments of inertia of a thin rectangular plate as follows:

$$I_{AA'} = \tfrac{1}{12}ma^2 \qquad I_{BB'} = \tfrac{1}{12}mb^2 \tag{9.39}$$
$$I_{CC'} = I_{AA'} + I_{BB'} = \tfrac{1}{12}m(a^2 + b^2) \tag{9.40}$$

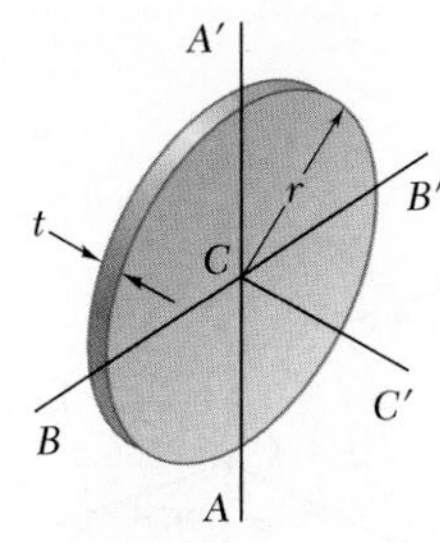

Fig. 9.26

Circular Plate. In the case of a circular plate, or disk, of radius r (Fig. 9.26), we write

$$I_{AA',\text{ mass}} = \rho t I_{AA',\text{ area}} = \rho t(\tfrac{1}{4}\pi r^4)$$

Observing that the product $\rho\pi r^2 t$ is equal to the mass m of the plate and that $I_{AA'} = I_{BB'}$, we write the mass moments of inertia of a circular plate as follows:

$$I_{AA'} = I_{BB'} = \tfrac{1}{4}mr^2 \tag{9.41}$$
$$I_{CC'} = I_{AA'} + I_{BB'} = \tfrac{1}{2}mr^2 \tag{9.42}$$

9.14. DETERMINATION OF THE MOMENT OF INERTIA OF A THREE-DIMENSIONAL BODY BY INTEGRATION

The moment of inertia of a three-dimensional body is obtained by evaluating the integral $I = \int r^2\,dm$. If the body is made of a homogeneous material of density ρ, the element of mass dm is equal to ρdV and we can write $I = \rho\int r^2\,dV$. This integral depends only upon the shape of the body. Thus, in order to compute the moment of inertia of a three-dimensional body, it will generally be necessary to perform a triple, or at least a double, integration.

However, if the body possesses two planes of symmetry, it is usually possible to determine the body's moment of inertia with a single integration by choosing as the element of mass dm a thin slab which is perpendicular to the planes of symmetry. In the case of bodies of revolution, for example, the element of mass would be a thin disk (Fig. 9.27). Using formula (9.42), the moment of inertia of the disk with respect to the axis of revolution can be expressed as indicated in Fig. 9.27. Its moment of inertia with respect to each of the other two coordinate axes is obtained by using formula (9.41) and the parallel-axis theorem. Integration of the expression obtained yields the desired moment of inertia of the body.

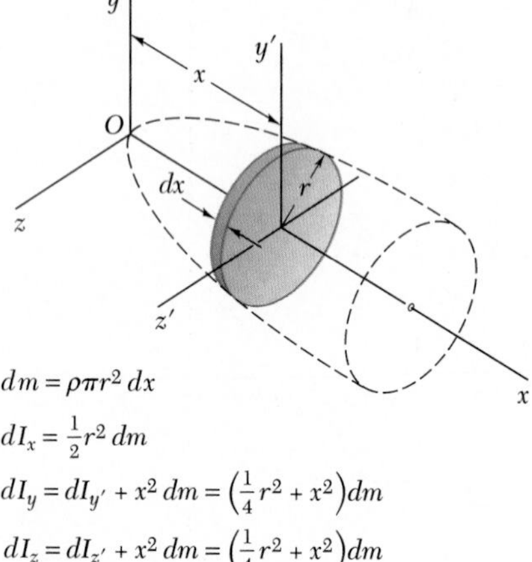

$dm = \rho\pi r^2\,dx$

$dI_x = \frac{1}{2}r^2\,dm$

$dI_y = dI_{y'} + x^2\,dm = \left(\frac{1}{4}r^2 + x^2\right)dm$

$dI_z = dI_{z'} + x^2\,dm = \left(\frac{1}{4}r^2 + x^2\right)dm$

Fig. 9.27 Determination of the moment of inertia of a body of revolution.

9.15. MOMENTS OF INERTIA OF COMPOSITE BODIES

The moments of inertia of a few common shapes are shown in Fig. 9.28. For a body consisting of several of these simple shapes, the moment of inertia of the body with respect to a given axis can be obtained by first computing the moments of inertia of its component parts about the desired axis and then adding them together. As was the case for areas, the radius of gyration of a composite body *cannot* be obtained by adding the radii of gyration of its component parts.

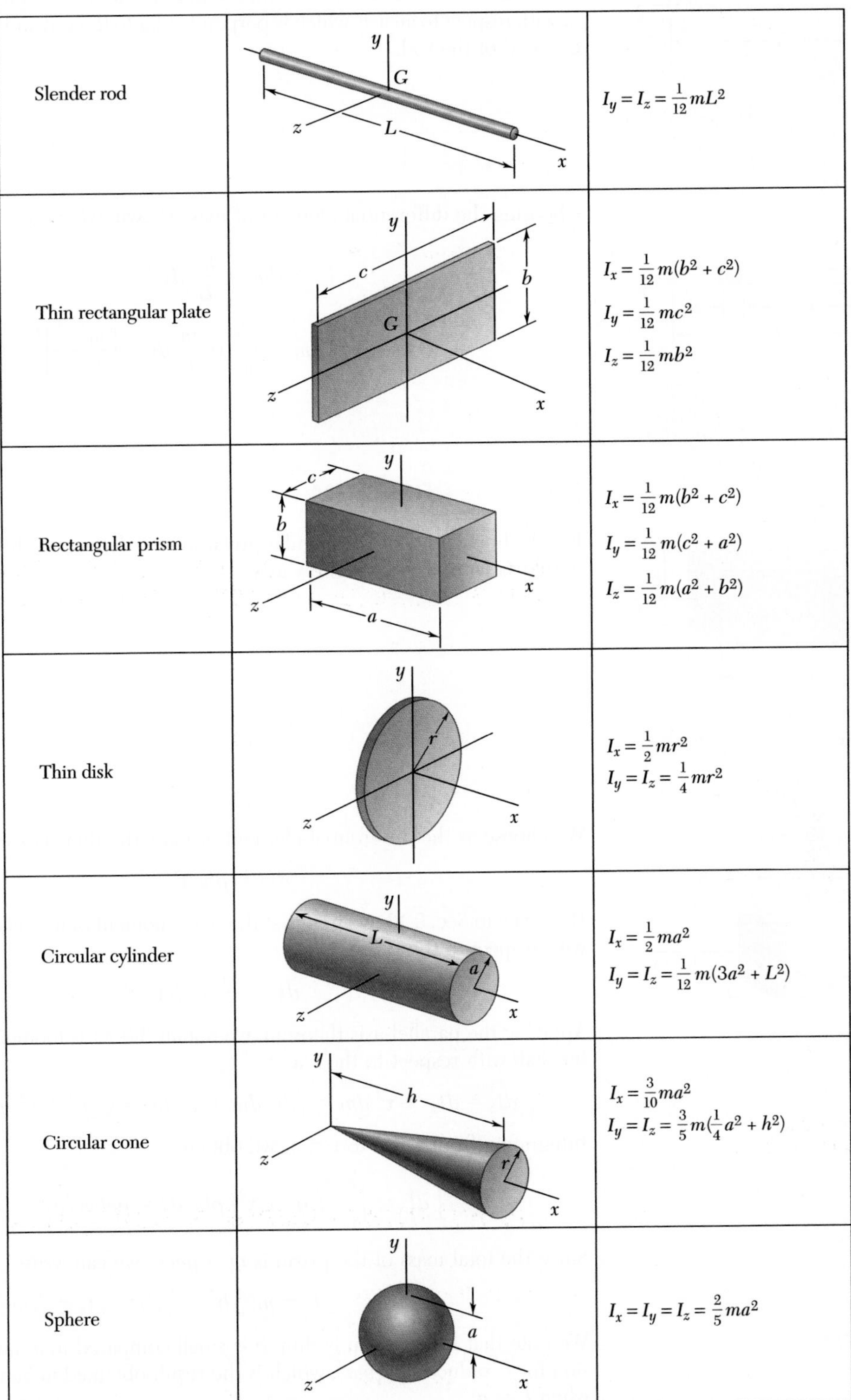

Shape	Mass moments of inertia
Slender rod	$I_y = I_z = \frac{1}{12} mL^2$
Thin rectangular plate	$I_x = \frac{1}{12} m(b^2 + c^2)$ $I_y = \frac{1}{12} mc^2$ $I_z = \frac{1}{12} mb^2$
Rectangular prism	$I_x = \frac{1}{12} m(b^2 + c^2)$ $I_y = \frac{1}{12} m(c^2 + a^2)$ $I_z = \frac{1}{12} m(a^2 + b^2)$
Thin disk	$I_x = \frac{1}{2} mr^2$ $I_y = I_z = \frac{1}{4} mr^2$
Circular cylinder	$I_x = \frac{1}{2} ma^2$ $I_y = I_z = \frac{1}{12} m(3a^2 + L^2)$
Circular cone	$I_x = \frac{3}{10} ma^2$ $I_y = I_z = \frac{3}{5} m(\frac{1}{4} a^2 + h^2)$
Sphere	$I_x = I_y = I_z = \frac{2}{5} ma^2$

Fig. 9.28 Mass moments of inertia of common geometric shapes.

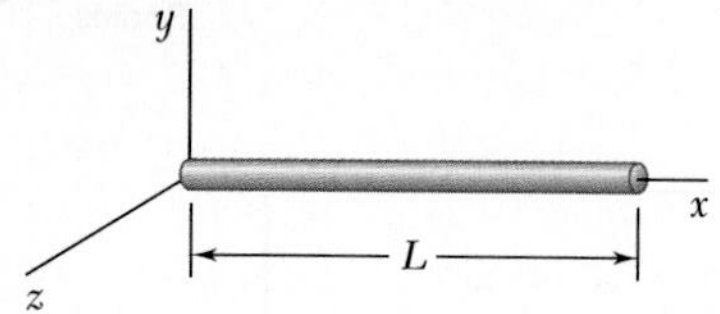

SAMPLE PROBLEM 9.9

Determine the mass moment of inertia of a slender rod of length L and mass m with respect to an axis which is perpendicular to the rod and passes through one end of the rod.

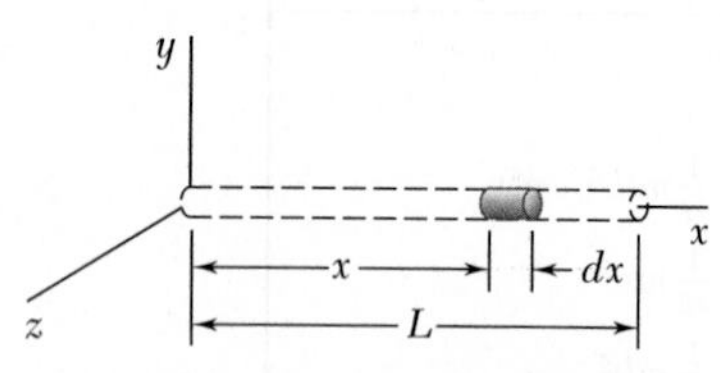

SOLUTION

Choosing the differential element of mass shown, we write

$$dm = \frac{m}{L}\,dx$$

$$I_y = \int x^2\,dm = \int_0^L x^2 \frac{m}{L}\,dx = \left[\frac{m}{L}\frac{x^3}{3}\right]_0^L \qquad I_y = \tfrac{1}{3}mL^2 \blacktriangleleft$$

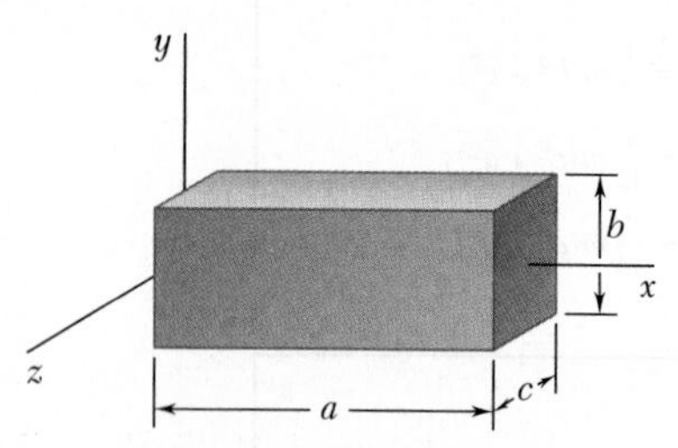

SAMPLE PROBLEM 9.10

For the homogeneous rectangular prism shown, determine the mass moment of inertia with respect to the z axis.

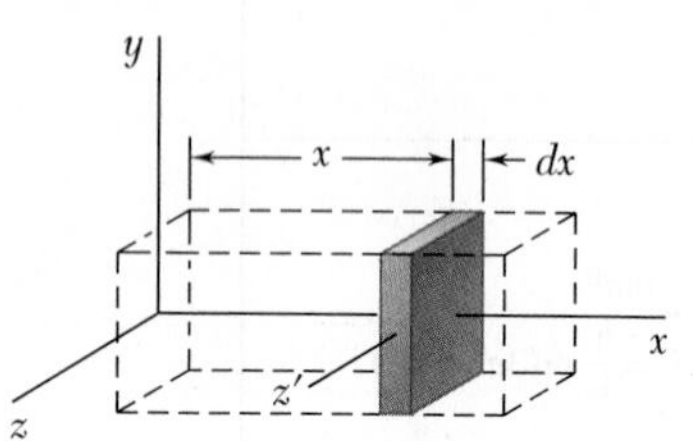

SOLUTION

We choose as the differential element of mass the thin slab shown; thus

$$dm = \rho bc\,dx$$

Referring to Sec. 9.13, we find that the mass moment of inertia of the element with respect to the z' axis is

$$dI_{z'} = \tfrac{1}{12}b^2\,dm$$

Applying the parallel-axis theorem, we obtain the mass moment of inertia of the slab with respect to the z axis.

$$dI_z = dI_{z'} + x^2\,dm = \tfrac{1}{12}b^2\,dm + x^2\,dm = (\tfrac{1}{12}b^2 + x^2)\,\rho bc\,dx$$

Integrating from $x = 0$ to $x = a$, we obtain

$$I_z = \int dI_z = \int_0^a (\tfrac{1}{12}b^2 + x^2)\,\rho bc\,dx = \rho abc(\tfrac{1}{12}b^2 + \tfrac{1}{3}a^2)$$

Since the total mass of the prism is $m = \rho abc$, we can write

$$I_z = m(\tfrac{1}{12}b^2 + \tfrac{1}{3}a^2) \qquad I_z = \tfrac{1}{12}m(4a^2 + b^2) \blacktriangleleft$$

We note that if the prism is thin, b is small compared to a, and the expression for I_z reduces to $\frac{1}{3}ma^2$, which is the result obtained in Sample Prob. 9.9 when $L = a$.

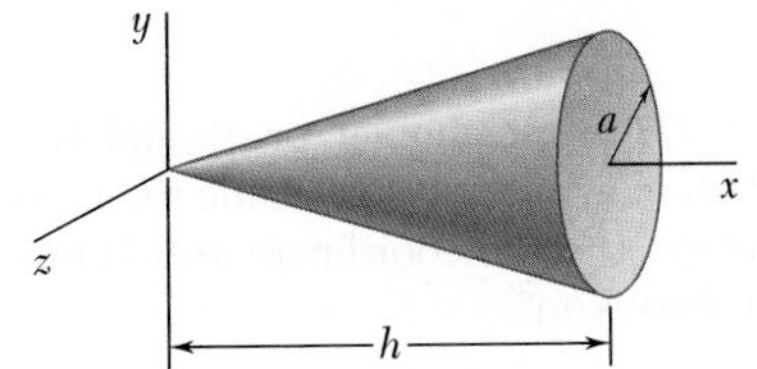

SAMPLE PROBLEM 9.11

Determine the mass moment of inertia of a right circular cone with respect to (*a*) its longitudinal axis, (*b*) an axis through the apex of the cone and perpendicular to its longitudinal axis, (*c*) an axis through the centroid of the cone and perpendicular to its longitudinal axis.

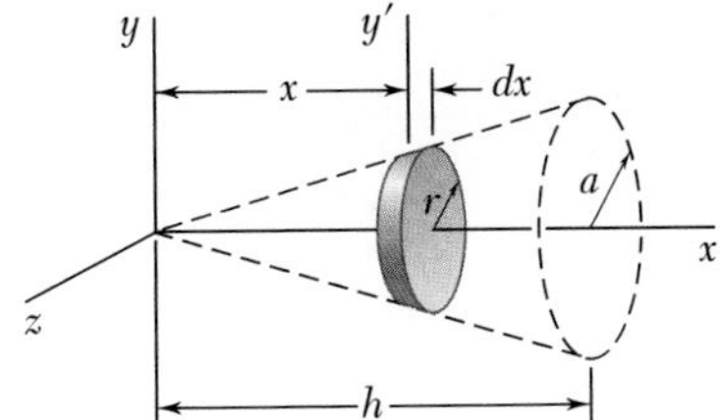

SOLUTION

We choose the differential element of mass shown.

$$r = a\frac{x}{h} \qquad dm = \rho\pi r^2\,dx = \rho\pi\frac{a^2}{h^2}x^2\,dx$$

a. Mass Moment of Inertia I_x. Using the expression derived in Sec. 9.13 for a thin disk, we compute the mass moment of inertia of the differential element with respect to the x axis.

$$dI_x = \tfrac{1}{2}r^2\,dm = \tfrac{1}{2}\left(a\frac{x}{h}\right)^2\left(\rho\pi\frac{a^2}{h^2}x^2\,dx\right) = \tfrac{1}{2}\rho\pi\frac{a^4}{h^4}x^4\,dx$$

Integrating from $x = 0$ to $x = h$, we obtain

$$I_x = \int dI_x = \int_0^h \tfrac{1}{2}\rho\pi\frac{a^4}{h^4}x^4\,dx = \tfrac{1}{2}\rho\pi\frac{a^4}{h^4}\frac{h^5}{5} = \tfrac{1}{10}\rho\pi a^4 h$$

Since the total mass of the cone is $m = \tfrac{1}{3}\rho\pi a^2 h$, we can write

$$I_x = \tfrac{1}{10}\rho\pi a^4 h = \tfrac{3}{10}a^2(\tfrac{1}{3}\rho\pi a^2 h) = \tfrac{3}{10}ma^2 \qquad I_x = \tfrac{3}{10}ma^2 \quad ◀$$

b. Mass Moment of Inertia I_y. The same differential element is used. Applying the parallel-axis theorem and using the expression derived in Sec. 9.13 for a thin disk, we write

$$dI_y = dI_{y'} + x^2\,dm = \tfrac{1}{4}r^2\,dm + x^2\,dm = (\tfrac{1}{4}r^2 + x^2)\,dm$$

Substituting the expressions for r and dm into the equation, we obtain

$$dI_y = \left(\frac{1}{4}\frac{a^2}{h^2}x^2 + x^2\right)\left(\rho\pi\frac{a^2}{h^2}x^2\,dx\right) = \rho\pi\frac{a^2}{h^2}\left(\frac{a^2}{4h^2} + 1\right)x^4\,dx$$

$$I_y = \int dI_y = \int_0^h \rho\pi\frac{a^2}{h^2}\left(\frac{a^2}{4h^2} + 1\right)x^4\,dx = \rho\pi\frac{a^2}{h^2}\left(\frac{a^2}{4h^2} + 1\right)\frac{h^5}{5}$$

Introducing the total mass of the cone m, we rewrite I_y as follows:

$$I_y = \tfrac{3}{5}(\tfrac{1}{4}a^2 + h^2)\tfrac{1}{3}\rho\pi a^2 h \qquad I_y = \tfrac{3}{5}m(\tfrac{1}{4}a^2 + h^2) \quad ◀$$

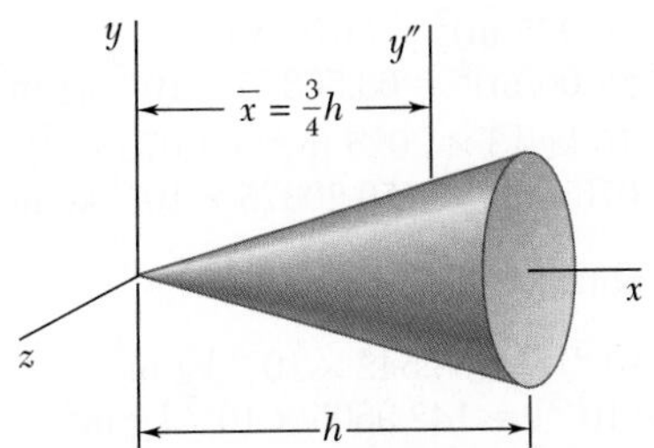

c. Mass Moment of Inertia $\bar{I}_{y''}$. We apply the parallel-axis theorem and write

$$I_y = \bar{I}_{y''} + m\bar{x}^2$$

Solving for $\bar{I}_{y''}$ and recalling from Fig. 5.21 that $\bar{x} = \tfrac{3}{4}h$, we have

$$\bar{I}_{y''} = I_y - m\bar{x}^2 = \tfrac{3}{5}m(\tfrac{1}{4}a^2 + h^2) - m(\tfrac{3}{4}h)^2$$

$$\bar{I}_{y''} = \tfrac{3}{20}m(a^2 + \tfrac{1}{4}h^2) \quad ◀$$

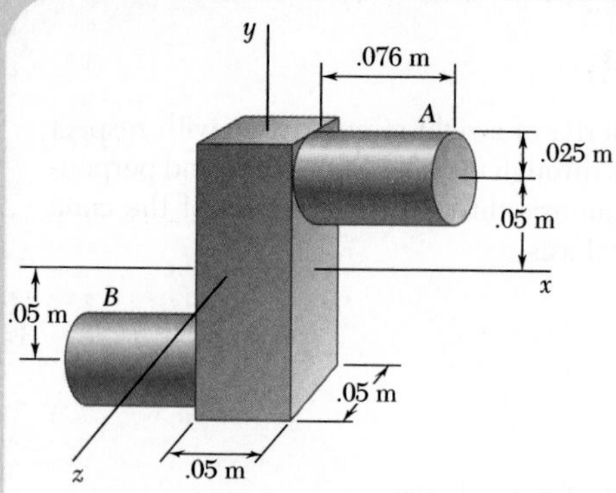

SAMPLE PROBLEM 9.12

A steel forging consists of a .15 × .05 × .05-m rectangular prism and two cylinders of diameter .05 m and length .076 m as shown. Determine the mass moments of inertia of the forging with respect to the coordinate axes knowing that the specific weight of steel is 10,000 N/m³.

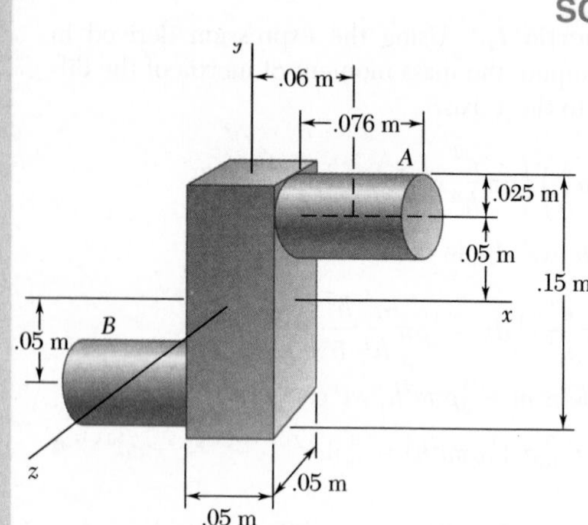

SOLUTION

Computation of Masses

Prism

$$V = (.05 \text{ m})(.05 \text{ m})(.15 \text{ m}) = .000375 \text{ m}^3$$

$$W = (.000375 \text{ m}^3)(10{,}000 \text{ N/m}^3) = 3.75 \text{ N}$$

$$m = \frac{3.75 \text{ N}}{9.8 \text{ m/s}^2} = .38 \text{ kg}$$

Each Cylinder

$$V = \pi(.025 \text{ m})^2(.076 \text{ m}) = 1.49 \times 10^{-4} \text{ m}^3$$

$$W = (1.49 \times 10^{-4} \text{ m}^3)(10{,}000 \text{ N/m}^3) = 1.49 \text{ N}$$

$$m = \frac{1.49 \text{ N}}{9.81} = .15 \text{ kg}$$

Mass Moments of Inertia. The mass moments of inertia of each component are computed from Fig. 9.28, using the parallel-axis theorem when necessary. Note that all lengths are expressed in feet.

Prism

$$I_x = I_z = \tfrac{1}{12}(.38 \text{ kg})[(.15 \text{ m})^2 + (.05 \text{ m})^2] = 7.9167 \times 10^{-4} \text{ kg m}^2$$

$$I_y = \tfrac{1}{12}(.38 \text{ kg})[(.05)^2 + (.05)^2] + \left(\frac{2}{12}\text{m}\right)^2 = 1.5833 \times 10^{-4} \text{ kg m}^2$$

Each Cylinder

$$I_x = \tfrac{1}{2}ma^2 + m\bar{y}^2 = \tfrac{1}{2}(.15 \text{ kg})(.025)^2 + (.15 \text{ kg})(.05 \text{ m})^2$$
$$= 42.1875 \times 10^{-5} \text{ kg m}^2$$

$$I_y = \tfrac{1}{12}m(3a^2 + L^2) + m\bar{x}^2 = \tfrac{1}{12}(.15 \text{ kg})[3(.025 \text{ m})^2 + (.076 \text{ m})^2]$$
$$+ (.15 \text{ kg})(.06 \text{ m})^2 = 63.56375 \times 10^{-5} \text{ kg m}^2$$

$$I_z = \tfrac{1}{12}m(3a^2 + L^2) + m(\bar{x}^2 + \bar{y}^2) = \tfrac{1}{12}(.15 \text{ kg})[3 \times (.025 \text{ m})^2 + (.076 \text{ m})^2]$$
$$+ (.15 \text{ kg})[(.06 \text{ m})^2 + (.076 \text{ m})^2] = 150.20375 \times 10^{-5} \text{ kg m}^2$$

Entire Body. Adding the values obtained,

$$I_x = 7.9167 \times 10^{-4} + 2 \times (42.1875 \times 10^{-5}) = 163.542 \times 10^{-5} \text{ kg m}^2$$
$$I_y = 1.5833 \times 10^{-4} + 2 \times (63.56375 \times 10^{-5}) = 142.9605 \times 10^{-5} \text{ kg m}^2$$
$$I_z = 7.9167 \times 10^{-4} + 2 \times (150.20375 \times 10^{-5}) = 379.5745 \times 10^{-5} \text{ kg m}^2$$

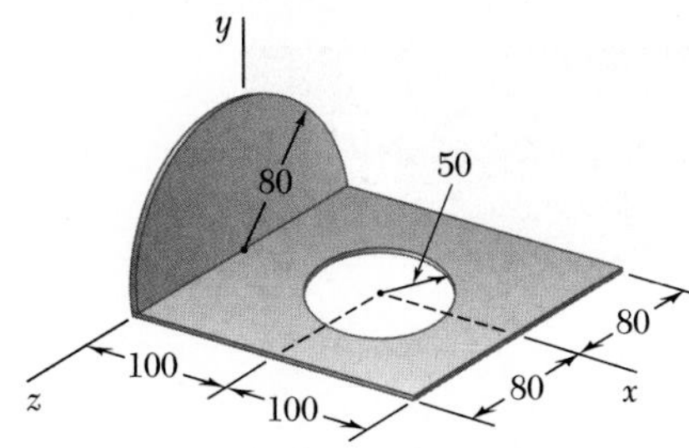

Dimensions in mm

SAMPLE PROBLEM 9.13

A thin steel plate which is 4 mm thick is cut and bent to form the machine part shown. Knowing that the density of steel is 7850 kg/m^3, determine the mass moments of inertia of the machine part with respect to the coordinate axes.

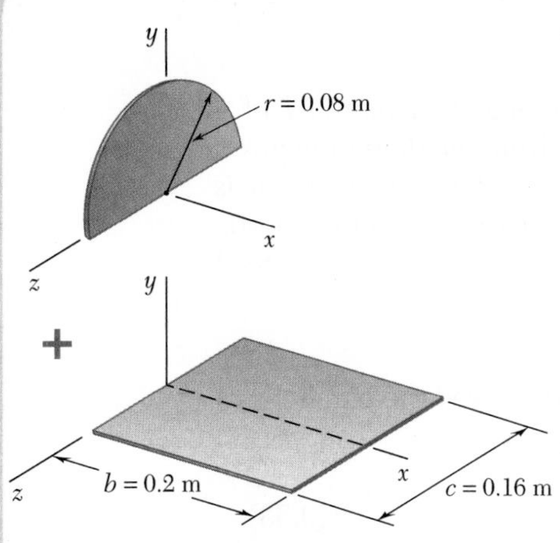

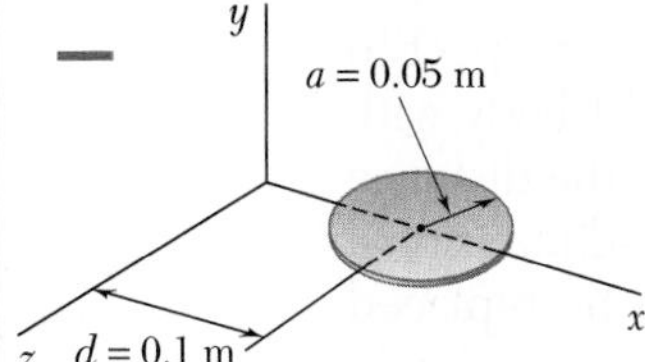

SOLUTION

We observe that the machine part consists of a semicircular plate and a rectangular plate from which a circular plate has been removed.

Computation of Masses. ***Semicircular Plate***

$$V_1 = \tfrac{1}{2}\pi r^2 t = \tfrac{1}{2}\pi(0.08 \text{ m})^2(0.004 \text{ m}) = 40.21 \times 10^{-6} \text{ m}^3$$
$$m_1 = \rho V_1 = (7.85 \times 10^3 \text{ kg/m}^3)(40.21 \times 10^{-6} \text{ m}^3) = 0.3156 \text{ kg}$$

Rectangular Plate

$$V_2 = (0.200 \text{ m})(0.160 \text{ m})(0.004 \text{ m}) = 128 \times 10^{-6} \text{ m}^3$$
$$m_2 = \rho V_2 = (7.85 \times 10^3 \text{ kg/m}^3)(128 \times 10^{-6} \text{ m}^3) = 1.005 \text{ kg}$$

Circular Plate

$$V_3 = \pi a^2 t = \pi(0.050 \text{ m})^2(0.004 \text{ m}) = 31.42 \times 10^{-6} \text{ m}^3$$
$$m_3 = \rho V_3 = (7.85 \times 10^3 \text{ kg/m}^3)(31.42 \times 10^{-6} \text{ m}^3) = 0.2466 \text{ kg}$$

Mass Moments of Inertia. Using the method presented in Sec. 9.13, we compute the mass moments of inertia of each component.

Semicircular Plate. From Fig. 9.28, we observe that for a circular plate of mass m and radius r

$$I_x = \tfrac{1}{2}mr^2 \qquad I_y = I_z = \tfrac{1}{4}mr^2$$

Because of symmetry, we note that for a semicircular plate

$$I_x = \tfrac{1}{2}(\tfrac{1}{2}mr^2) \qquad I_y = I_z = \tfrac{1}{2}(\tfrac{1}{4}mr^2)$$

Since the mass of the semicircular plate is $m_1 = \tfrac{1}{2}m$, we have

$$I_x = \tfrac{1}{2}m_1r^2 = \tfrac{1}{2}(0.3156 \text{ kg})(0.08 \text{ m})^2 = 1.010 \times 10^{-3} \text{ kg} \cdot \text{m}^2$$
$$I_y = I_z = \tfrac{1}{4}(\tfrac{1}{2}mr^2) = \tfrac{1}{4}m_1r^2 = \tfrac{1}{4}(0.3156 \text{ kg})(0.08 \text{ m})^2 = 0.505 \times 10^{-3} \text{ kg} \cdot \text{m}^2$$

Rectangular Plate

$$I_x = \tfrac{1}{12}m_2c^2 = \tfrac{1}{12}(1.005 \text{ kg})(0.16 \text{ m})^2 = 2.144 \times 10^{-3} \text{ kg} \cdot \text{m}^2$$
$$I_z = \tfrac{1}{3}m_2b^2 = \tfrac{1}{3}(1.005 \text{ kg})(0.2 \text{ m})^2 = 13.400 \times 10^{-3} \text{ kg} \cdot \text{m}^2$$
$$I_y = I_x + I_z = (2.144 + 13.400)(10^{-3}) = 15.544 \times 10^{-3} \text{ kg} \cdot \text{m}^2$$

Circular Plate

$$I_x = \tfrac{1}{4}m_3a^2 = \tfrac{1}{4}(0.2466 \text{ kg})(0.05 \text{ m})^2 = 0.154 \times 10^{-3} \text{ kg} \cdot \text{m}^2$$
$$I_y = \tfrac{1}{2}m_3a^2 + m_3d^2$$
$$= \tfrac{1}{2}(0.2466 \text{ kg})(0.05 \text{ m})^2 + (0.2466 \text{ kg})(0.1 \text{ m})^2 = 2.774 \times 10^{-3} \text{ kg} \cdot \text{m}^2$$
$$I_z = \tfrac{1}{4}m_3a^2 + m_3d^2 = \tfrac{1}{4}(0.2466 \text{ kg})(0.05 \text{ m})^2 + (0.2466 \text{ kg})(0.1 \text{ m})^2$$
$$= 2.620 \times 10^{-3} \text{ kg} \cdot \text{m}^2$$

Entire Machine Part

$$I_x = (1.010 + 2.144 - 0.154)(10^{-3}) \text{ kg} \cdot \text{m}^2 \qquad I_x = 3.00 \times 10^{-3} \text{ kg} \cdot \text{m}^2 \blacktriangleleft$$
$$I_y = (0.505 + 15.544 - 2.774)(10^{-3}) \text{ kg} \cdot \text{m}^2 \qquad I_y = 13.28 \times 10^{-3} \text{ kg} \cdot \text{m}^2 \blacktriangleleft$$
$$I_z = (0.505 + 13.400 - 2.620)(10^{-3}) \text{ kg} \cdot \text{m}^2 \qquad I_z = 11.29 \times 10^{-3} \text{ kg} \cdot \text{m}^2 \blacktriangleleft$$

SOLVING PROBLEMS ON YOUR OWN

In this lesson we introduced the *mass moment of inertia* and the *radius of gyration* of a three-dimensional body with respect to a given axis [Eqs. (9.28) and (9.29)]. We also derived a *parallel-axis theorem* for use with mass moments of inertia and discussed the computation of the mass moments of inertia of thin plates and three-dimensional bodies.

1. *Computing mass moments of inertia.* The mass moment of inertia I of a body with respect to a given axis can be calculated directly from the definition given in Eq. (9.28) for simple shapes [Sample Prob. 9.9]. In most cases, however, it is necessary to divide the body into thin slabs, compute the mass moment of inertia of a typical slab with respect to the given axis—using the parallel-axis theorem if necessary—and integrate the expression obtained.

2. *Applying the parallel-axis theorem.* In Sec. 9.12 we derived the parallel-axis theorem for mass moments of inertia

$$I = \bar{I} + md^2 \tag{9.33}$$

which states that the mass moment of inertia I of a body of mass m with respect to a given axis is equal to the sum of the mass moment of inertia $\bar{I}$ of that body with respect to the *parallel centroidal axis* and the product md^2, where d is the distance between the two axes. When the mass moment of inertia of a three-dimensional body is calculated with respect to one of the coordinate axes, d^2 can be replaced by the sum of the squares of distances measured along the other two coordinate axes [Eqs. (9.32) and (9.32′)].

3. *Avoiding unit-related errors.* To avoid errors, it is essential that you be consistent in your use of units. Thus, all lengths should be expressed in meters or feet, as appropriate, and for problems using U.S. customary units, masses should be given in $\text{lb} \cdot \text{s}^2/\text{ft}$. In addition, we strongly recommend that you include units as you perform your calculations [Sample Probs. 9.12 and 9.13].

4. *Calculating the mass moment of inertia of thin plates.* We showed in Sec. 9.13 that the mass moment of inertia of a thin plate with respect to a given axis can be obtained by multiplying the corresponding moment of inertia of the area of the plate by the density ρ and the thickness t of the plate [Eqs. (9.35) through (9.37)]. Note that since the axis CC' in Fig. 9.24*c* is *perpendicular to the plate*, $I_{CC',\text{ mass}}$ is associated with the *polar* moment of inertia $J_{C,\text{ area}}$.

Instead of calculating directly the mass moment of inertia of a thin plate with respect to a specified axis, you may sometimes find it convenient to first compute its mass moment of inertia with respect to an axis parallel to the specified axis and then apply the parallel-axis theorem. Further, to determine the mass moment of inertia of a thin plate with respect to an axis perpendicular to the plate, you may wish to first determine its mass moments of inertia with respect to two perpendicular in-plane axes and then use Eq. (9.38). Finally, remember that the mass of a plate of area A, thickness t, and density ρ is $m = \rho t A$.

5. ***Determining the mass moment of inertia of a body by direct single integration.*** We discussed in Sec. 9.14 and illustrated in Sample Probs. 9.10 and 9.11 how single integration can be used to compute the mass moment of inertia of a body that can be divided into a series of thin, parallel slabs. For such cases, you will often need to express the mass of the body in terms of the body's density and dimensions. Assuming that the body has been divided, as in the sample problems, into thin slabs perpendicular to the x axis, you will need to express the dimensions of each slab as functions of the variable x.

a. ***In the special case of a body of revolution,*** the elemental slab is a thin disk, and the equations given in Fig. 9.27 should be used to determine the mass moments of inertia of the body [Sample Prob. 9.11].

b. ***In the general case, when the body is not of revolution,*** the differential element is not a disk, but a thin slab of a different shape, and the equations of Fig. 9.27 cannot be used. See, for example, Sample Prob. 9.10, where the element was a thin, rectangular slab. For more complex configurations, you may want to use one or more of the following equations, which are based on Eqs. (9.32) and (9.32′) of Sec. 9.12.

$$dI_x = dI_{x'} + (\bar{y}_{el}^2 + \bar{z}_{el}^2)\, dm$$
$$dI_y = dI_{y'} + (\bar{z}_{el}^2 + \bar{x}_{el}^2)\, dm$$
$$dI_z = dI_{z'} + (\bar{x}_{el}^2 + \bar{y}_{el}^2)\, dm$$

where the primes denote the centroidal axes of each elemental slab, and where $\bar{x}_{el}$, $\bar{y}_{el}$, and $\bar{z}_{el}$ represent the coordinates of its centroid. The centroidal mass moments of inertia of the slab are determined in the manner described earlier for a thin plate: Referring to Fig. 9.12 on page 485, calculate the corresponding moments of inertia of the area of the slab and multiply the result by the density ρ and the thickness t of the slab. Also, assuming that the body has been divided into thin slabs perpendicular to the x axis, remember that you can obtain $dI_{x'}$ by adding $dI_{y'}$ and $dI_{z'}$ instead of computing it directly. Finally, using the geometry of the body, express the result obtained in terms of the single variable x and integrate in x.

6. ***Computing the mass moment of inertia of a composite body.*** As stated in Sec. 9.15, the mass moment of inertia of a composite body with respect to a specified axis is equal to the sum of the moments of its components with respect to that axis. Sample Probs. 9.12 and 9.13 illustrate the appropriate method of solution. You must also remember that the mass moment of inertia of a component will be negative only if the component is *removed* (as in the case of a hole).

Although the composite-body problems in this lesson are relatively straightforward, you will have to work carefully to avoid computational errors. In addition, if some of the mass moments of inertia that you need are not given in Fig. 9.28, you will have to derive your own formulas using the techniques of this lesson.

Problems

9.113 A thin semicircular plate has a radius a and a mass m. Determine the mass moment of inertia of the plate with respect to (a) the centroidal axis BB', (b) the centroidal axis CC' that is perpendicular to the plate.

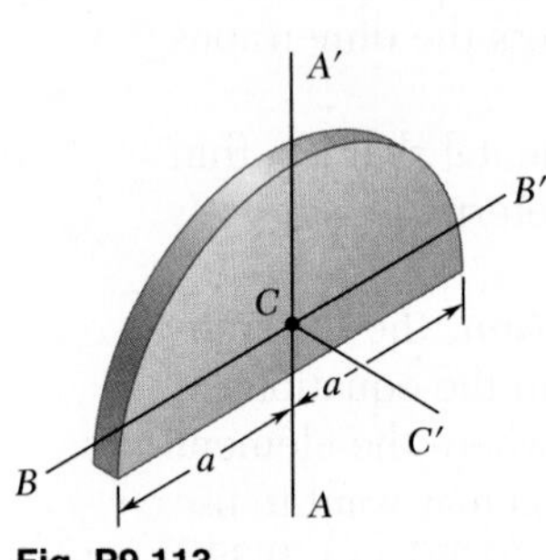

Fig. P9.113

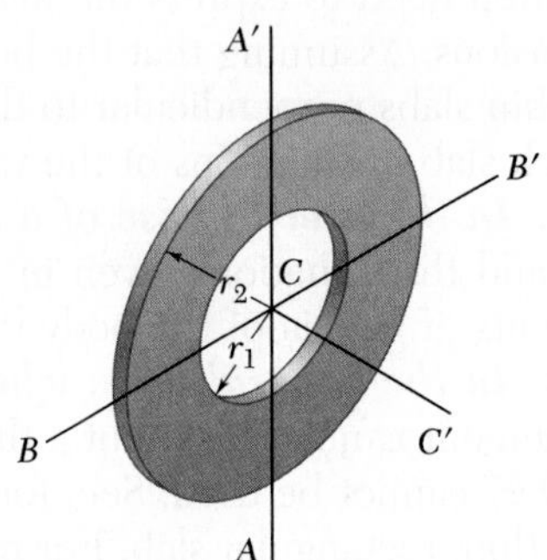

Fig. P9.114

9.114 The thin circular ring shown was cut from a thin, uniform plate. Denoting the mass of the ring by m, determine its mass moment of inertia with respect to (a) the centroidal axis AA' of the ring, (b) the centroidal axis CC' that is perpendicular to the plane of the ring.

9.115 The quarter ring shown has a mass m and was cut from a thin, uniform plate. Knowing that $r_1 = \frac{1}{2}r_2$, determine the mass moment of inertia of the quarter ring with respect to (a) axis AA', (b) the centroidal axis CC' that is perpendicular to the plane of the quarter ring.

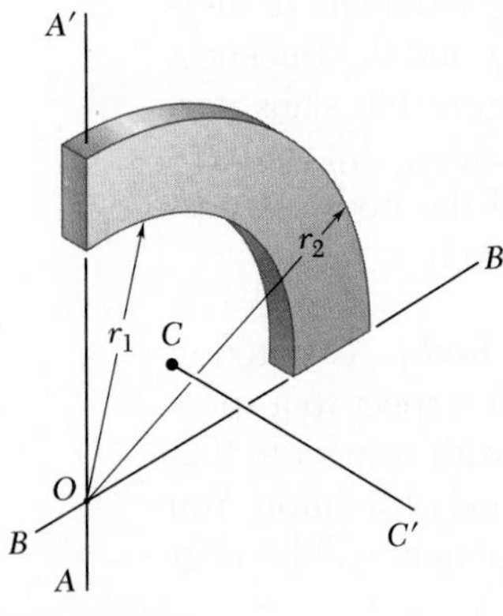

Fig. P9.115

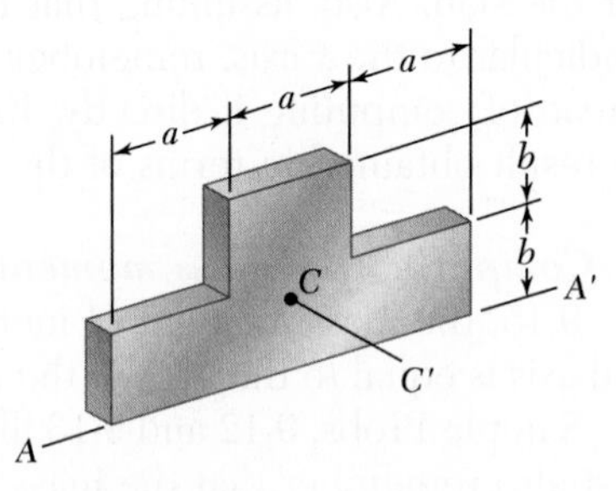

Fig. P9.116

9.116 The spacer shown was cut from a thin, uniform plate. Denoting the mass of the component by m, determine its mass moment of inertia with respect to (a) the axis AA', (b) the centroidal axis CC' that is perpendicular to the plane of the component.

9.117 A thin plate of mass m is cut in the shape of an isosceles triangle of base b and height h. Determine the mass moments of inertia of the plate with respect to (*a*) the centroidal axes AA' and BB' in the plane of the plate, (*b*) the centroidal axis CC' perpendicular to the plate.

9.118 A thin plate of mass m is cut in the shape of an isosceles triangle of base b and height h. Determine the mass moments of inertia of the plate with respect to axes DD' and EE' parallel to the centroidal axes AA' and BB', respectively, and located at a distance d from the plane of the plate.

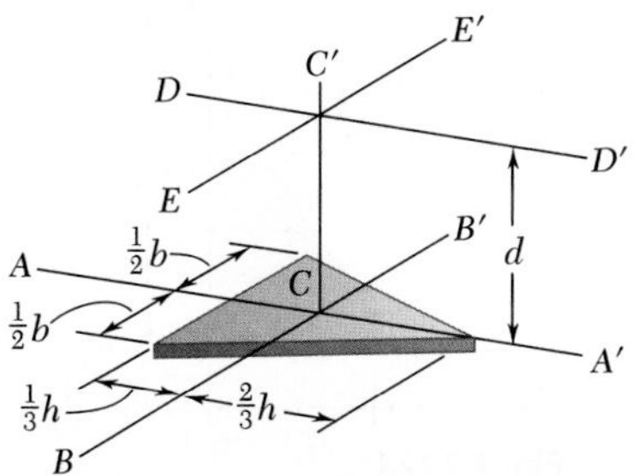

Fig. P9.117 and P9.118

9.119 A thin plate of mass m has the trapezoidal shape shown. Determine the mass moment of inertia of the plate with respect to (*a*) the x axis, (*b*) the y axis.

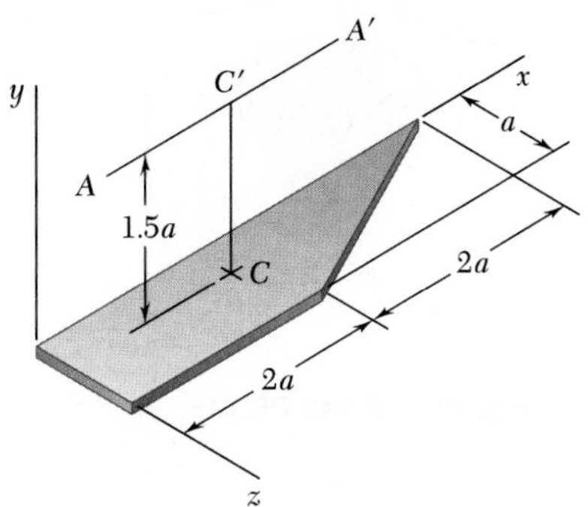

Fig. P9.119 and *P9.120*

9.120 A thin plate of mass m has the trapezoidal shape shown. Determine the mass moment of inertia of the plate with respect to (*a*) the centroidal axis CC' that is perpendicular to the plate, (*b*) the axis AA' which is parallel to the x axis and is located at a distance $1.5a$ from the plate.

9.121 The parabolic spandrel shown is revolved about the x axis to form a homogeneous solid of revolution of mass m. Using direct integration, express the mass moment of inertia of the solid with respect to the x axis in terms of m and b.

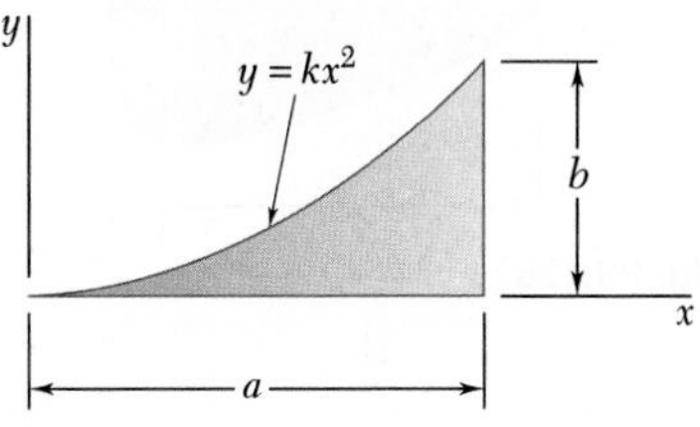

Fig. P9.121

9.122 Determine by direct integration the mass moment of inertia with respect to the z axis of the truncated right circular cone shown knowing that the radius of the base $r_1 = 2r_2$ and assuming that the cone has a uniform density and a mass m.

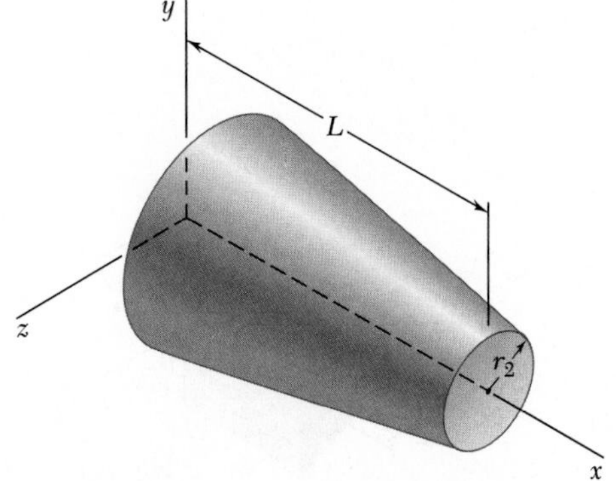

Fig. P9.122

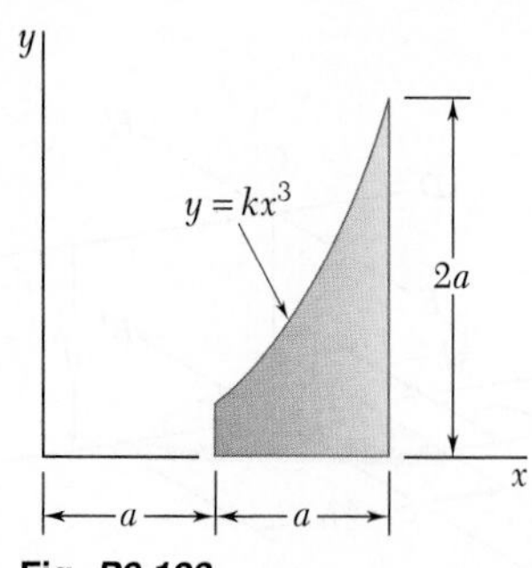

Fig. *P9.123*

9.123 The area shown is revolved about the x axis to form a homogeneous solid of revolution of mass m. Determine by direct integration the mass moment of inertia of the solid with respect to (a) the x axis, (b) the y axis. Express your answers in terms of m and a.

9.124 Determine by direct integration the mass moment of inertia with respect to the x axis of the pyramid shown assuming that it has a uniform density and a mass m.

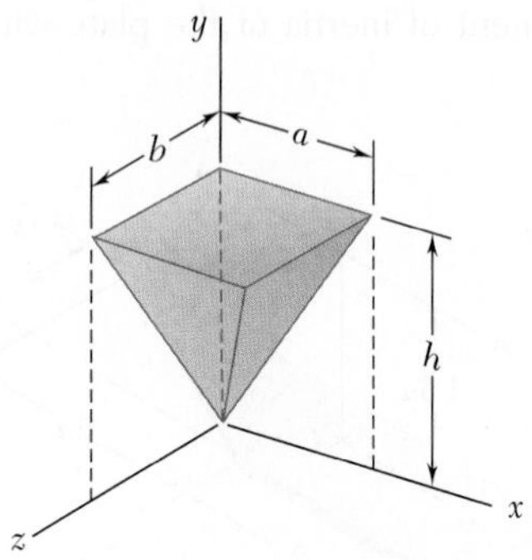

Fig. P9.124 and P9.125

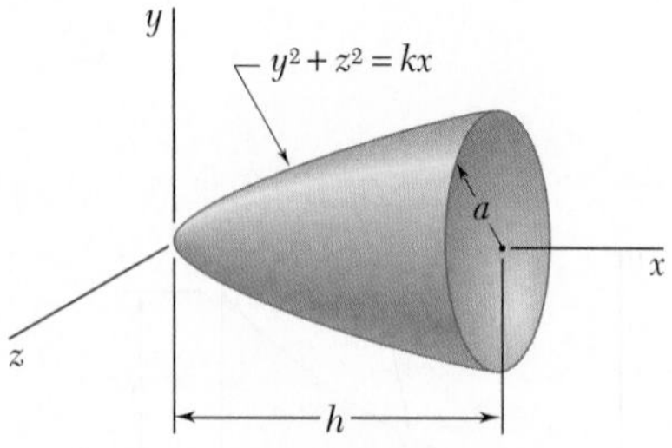

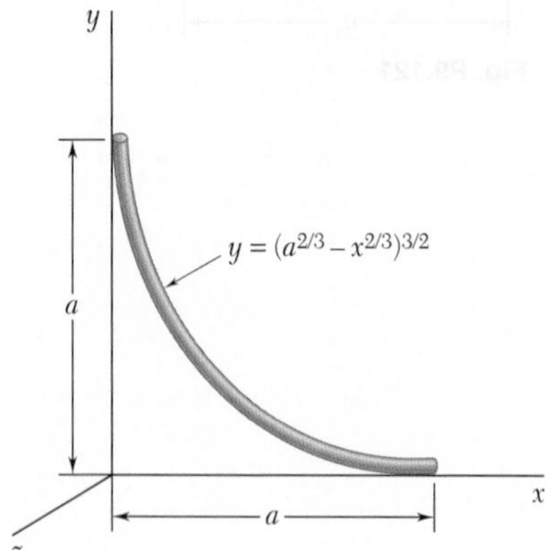

Fig. P9.126

9.125 Determine by direct integration the mass moment of inertia with respect to the y axis of the pyramid shown assuming that it has a uniform density and a mass m.

9.126 Determine by direct integration the mass moment of inertia and the radius of gyration with respect to the y axis of the paraboloid shown assuming that it has a uniform density and a mass m.

***9.127** A thin steel wire is bent into the shape shown. Denoting the mass per unit length of the wire by m', determine by direct integration the mass moment of inertia of the wire with respect to each of the coordinate axes.

Fig. P9.127

9.128 A thin triangular plate of mass m is welded along its base AB to a block as shown. Knowing that the plate forms an angle θ with the y axis, determine by direct integration the mass moment of inertia of the plate with respect to (a) the x axis, (b) the y axis, (c) the z axis.

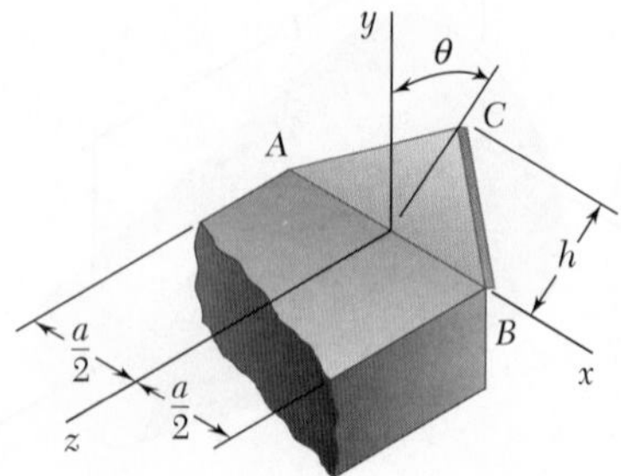

Fig. *P9.128*

9.129 Shown is the cross section of the wheel of a caster. Determine its mass moment of inertia and radius of gyration with respect to axis AA'. (The specific weight of bronze is 9000 kg/m^3; of steel, 8000 kg/m^3; and of hard rubber, 1300 kg/m^3.)

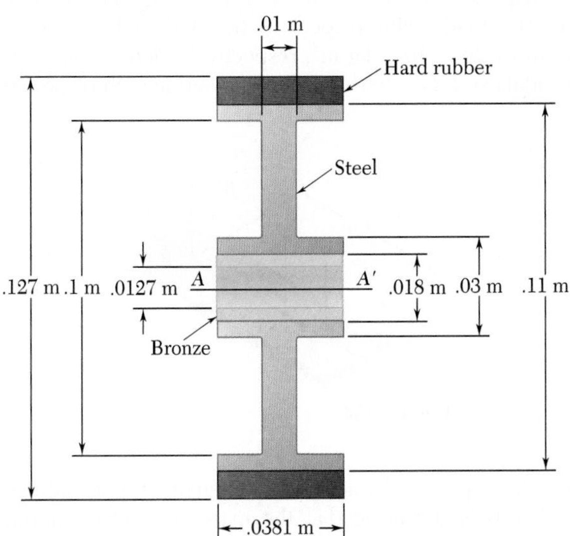

Fig. P9.129

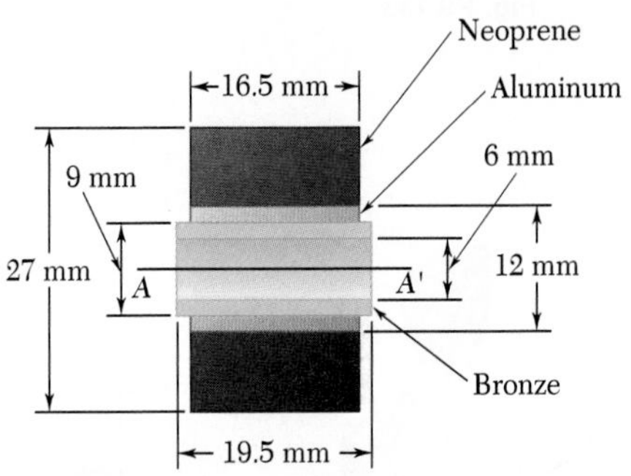

Fig. *P9.130*

9.130 Shown is the cross section of an idler roller. Determine its mass moment of inertia and its radius of gyration with respect to the axis AA'. (The density of bronze is 8580 kg/m^3; of aluminum, 2770 kg/m^3; and of neoprene, 1250 kg/m^3.)

9.131 Knowing that the thin hemispherical shell shown is of mass m and thickness t, determine the mass moment of inertia and the radius of gyration of the shell with respect to the x axis. (*Hint:* Consider the shell as formed by removing a hemisphere of radius r from a hemisphere of radius $r + t$; then neglect the terms containing t^2 and t^3 and keep those terms containing t.)

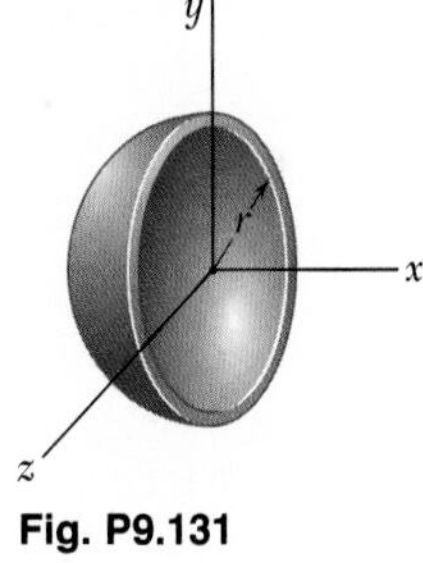

Fig. P9.131

9.132 For the homogenous ring of density ρ shown, determine (*a*) the mass moment of inertia with respect to the axis BB', (*b*) the value of a_1 for which, given a_2 and h, $I_{BB'}$ is maximum, (*c*) the corresponding value of $I_{BB'}$.

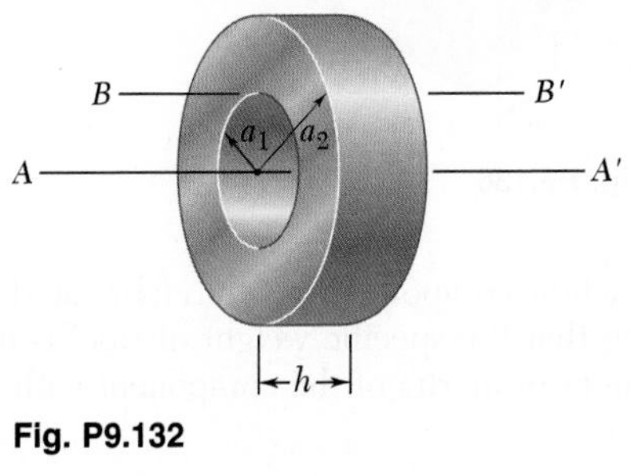

Fig. P9.132

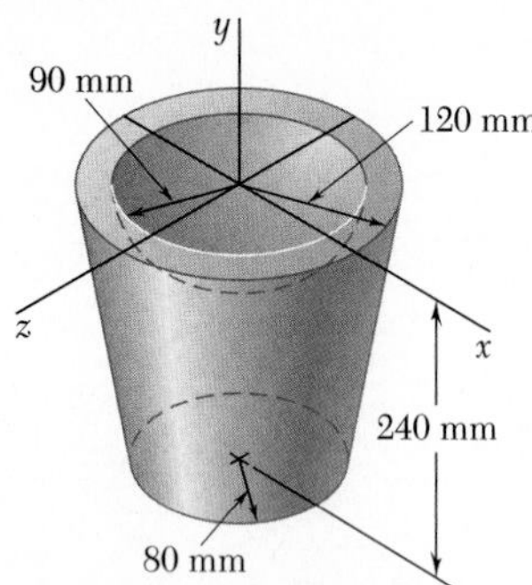

Fig. P9.133

9.133 The steel machine component shown is formed by machining a hemisphere into the base of a truncated cone. Knowing that the density of steel is 7850 kg/m^3, determine the mass moment of inertia of the component with respect to the y axis.

9.134 After a period of use, one of the blades of a shredder has been worn to the shape shown and weighs .4 N. Knowing that the mass moments of inertia of the blade with respect to the AA' and BB' axes are 0.6×10^{-3} kg m^2 and 1.26×10^{-3} kg m^2, respectively, determine (*a*) the location of the centroidal axis GG', (*b*) the radius of gyration with respect to axis GG'.

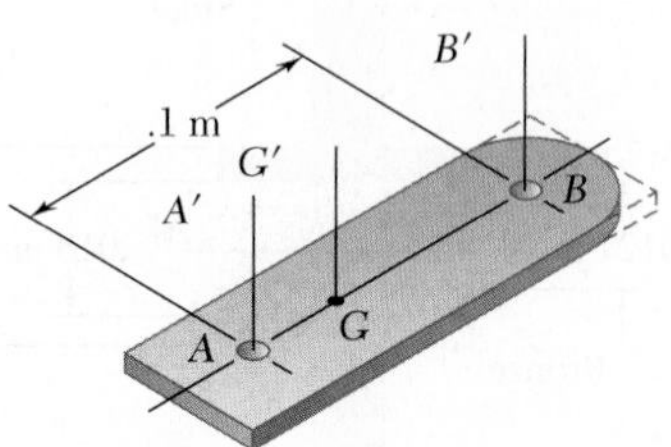

Fig. P9.134

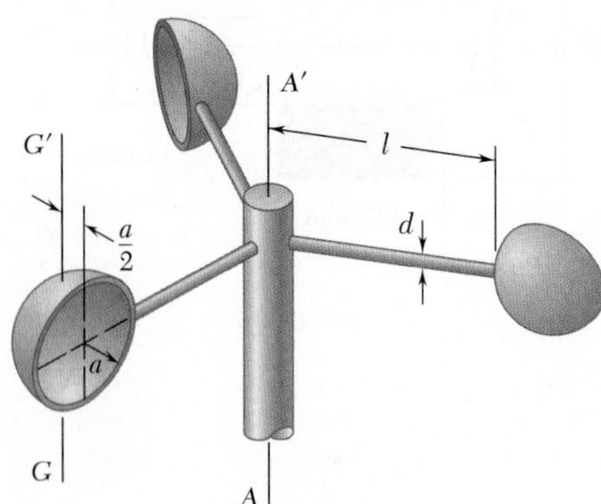

Fig. *P9.135*

9.135 The cups and the arms of an anemometer are fabricated from a material of density ρ. Knowing that the mass moment of inertia of a thin, hemispherical shell of mass m and thickness t with respect to its centroidal axis GG' is $5ma^2/12$, determine (*a*) the mass moment of inertia of the anemometer with respect to the axis AA', (*b*) the ratio of a to l for which the centroidal mass moment of inertia of the cups is equal to 1 percent of the mass moment of inertia of the cups with respect to the axis AA'.

9.136 A square hole is centered in and extends through the aluminum machine component shown. Determine (*a*) the value of a for which the mass moment of inertia of the component with respect to the axis AA', which bisects the top surface of the hole, is maximum, (*b*) the corresponding values of the mass moment of inertia and the radius of gyration with respect to the axis AA'. (The density of aluminum is 2800 kg/m^3.)

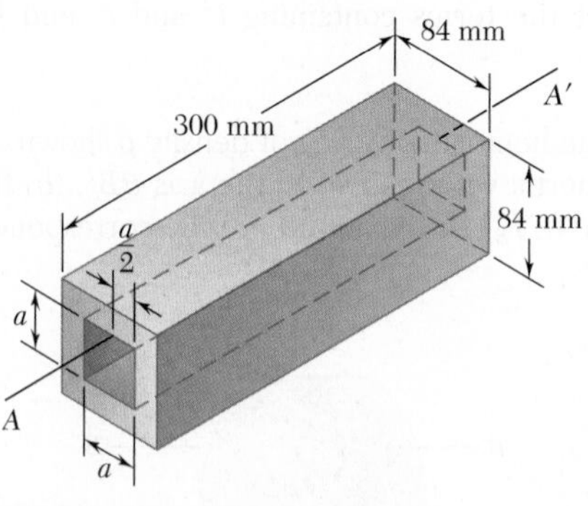

Fig. P9.136

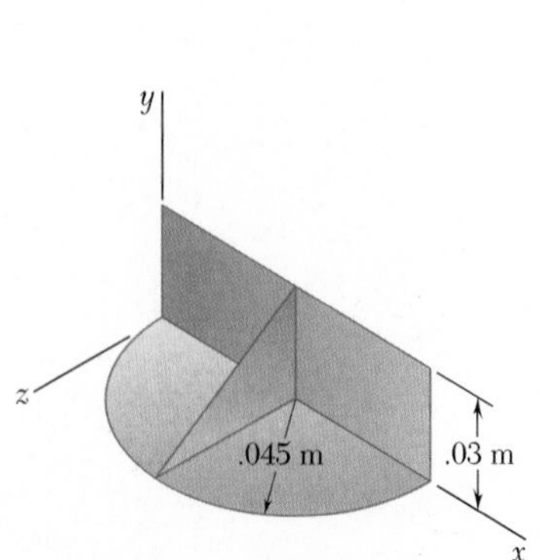

Fig. P9.137

9.137 The machine component shown is fabricated from .002-m-thick sheet steel. Knowing that the specific weight of steel is 9000 kg/m^2, determine the mass moment of inertia of the component with respect to each of the coordinate axes.

9.138 A 3-mm-thick piece of sheet metal is cut and bent into the machine component shown. Knowing that the density of steel is 7850 kg/m^3, determine the mass moment of inertia of the component with respect to each of the coordinate axes.

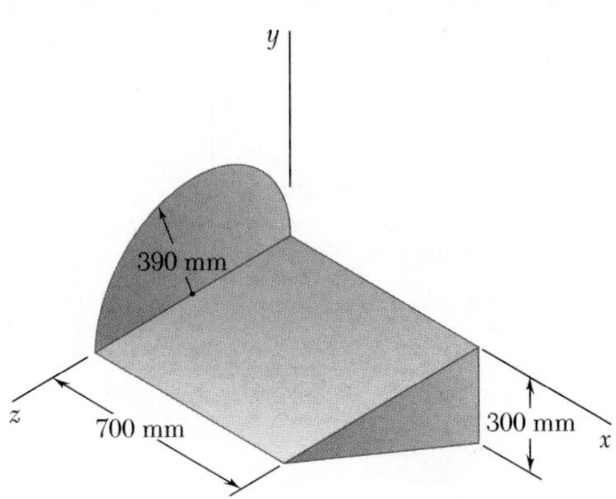

Fig. *P9.138*

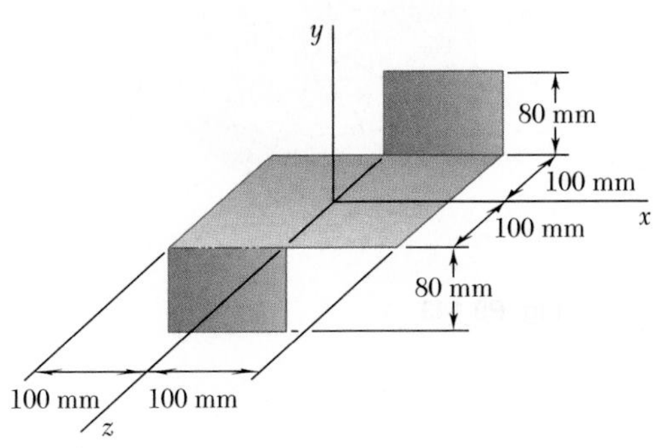

Fig. P9.139

9.139 A 2-mm-thick piece of sheet steel is cut and bent into the machine component shown. Knowing that the density of steel is 7850 kg/m^3, determine the mass moment of inertia of the component with respect to each of the coordinate axes.

9.140 A framing anchor is formed from 2-mm-thick galvanized steel. Determine the mass moment of inertia of the anchor with respect to each of the coordinate axes. (The density of galvanized steel is 7530 kg/m^3.)

9.141 A .0025-m-thick piece of sheet steel is cut and bent into the machine component shown. Knowing that the specific weight of steel is 9000 kg/m^3, determine the mass moment of inertia of the component with respect to each of the coordinate axes.

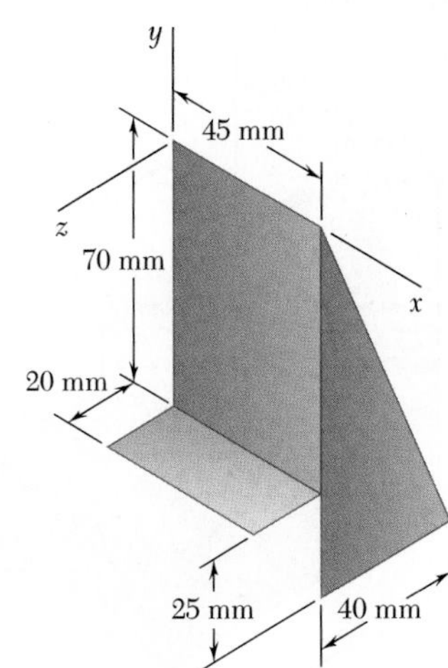

Fig. *P9.140*

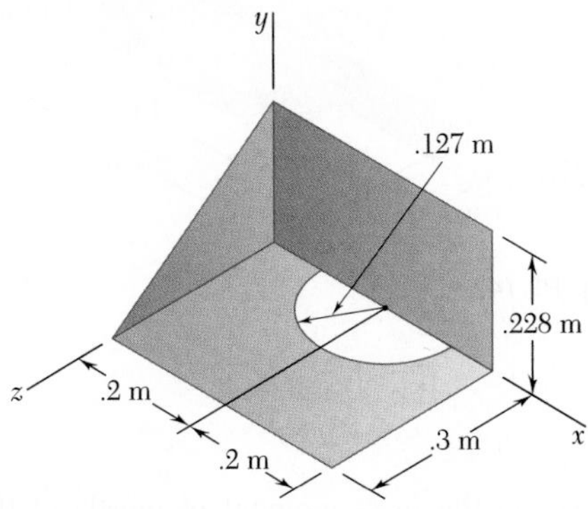

Fig. P9.141

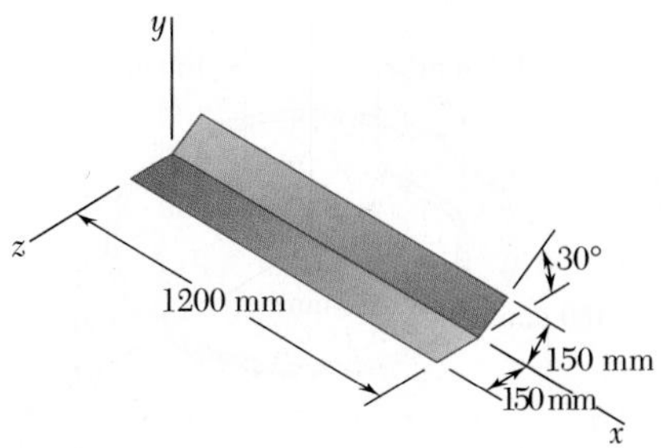

Fig. P9.142

*9.142 The piece of roof flashing shown is formed from sheet copper that is 0.8 mm thick. Knowing that the density of copper is 8940 kg/m^3, determine the mass moment of inertia of the flashing with respect to each of the coordinate axes.

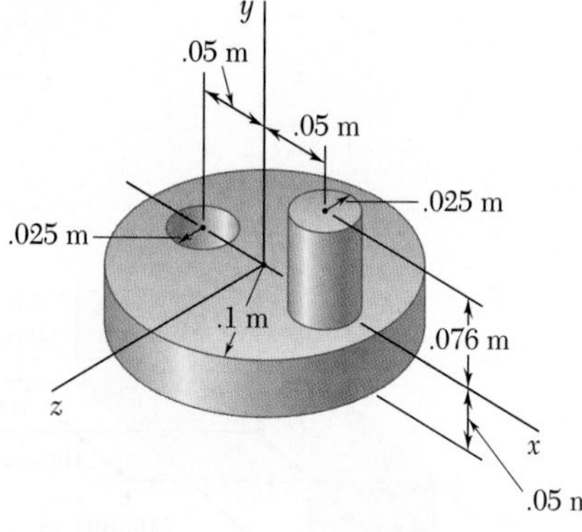

Fig. P9.143

9.143 The machine element shown is fabricated from steel. Determine the mass moment of inertia of the assembly with respect to (*a*) the x axis, (*b*) the y axis, (*c*) the z axis. (The specific weight of steel is 8000 kg/m^3.)

9.144 Determine the mass moment of inertia of the steel machine element shown with respect to the y axis. (The density of steel is 7850 kg/m^3.)

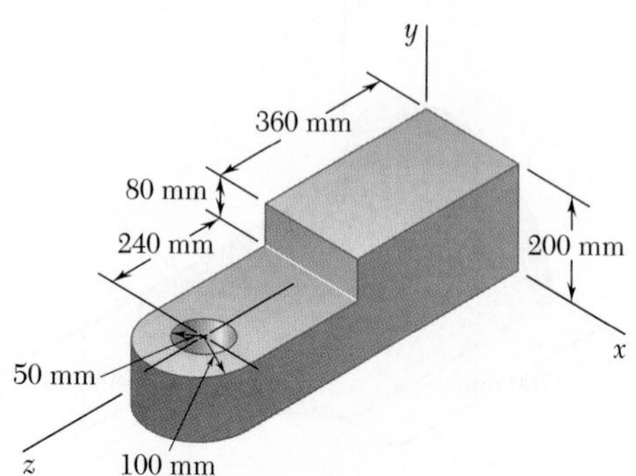

Fig. P9.144 and P9.145

9.145 Determine the mass moment of inertia of the steel machine element shown with respect to the z axis. (The density of steel is 7850 kg/m^3.)

9.146 An aluminum casting has the shape shown. Knowing that the specific weight of aluminum is 3000 kg/m^3, determine the mass moment of inertia of the casting with respect to the z axis.

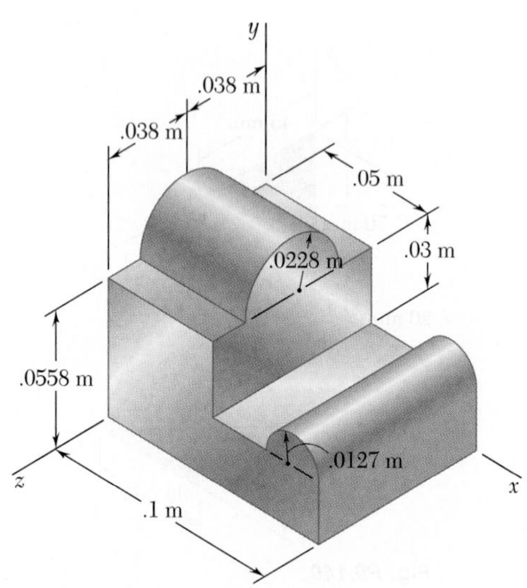

Fig. P9.146

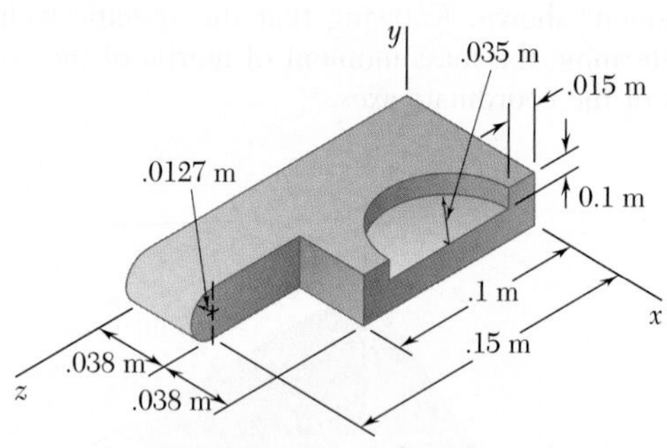

Fig. *P9.147*

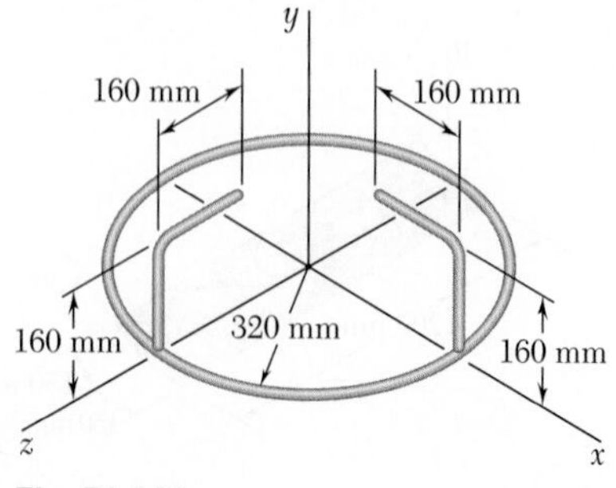

Fig. P9.148

9.147 Determine the mass moment of inertia of the steel machine element shown with respect to (*a*) the x axis, (*b*) the y axis, (*c*) the z axis. (The specific weight of steel is 9000 kg/m^3.)

9.148 Aluminum wire with a mass per unit length of 0.049 kg/m is used to form the circle and the straight members of the figure shown. Determine the mass moment of inertia of the assembly with respect to each of the coordinate axes.

9.149 The figure shown is formed from 3-mm-diameter steel wire. Knowing that the density of the steel is 7850 kg/m^3, determine the mass moment of inertia of the wire with respect to each of the coordinate axes.

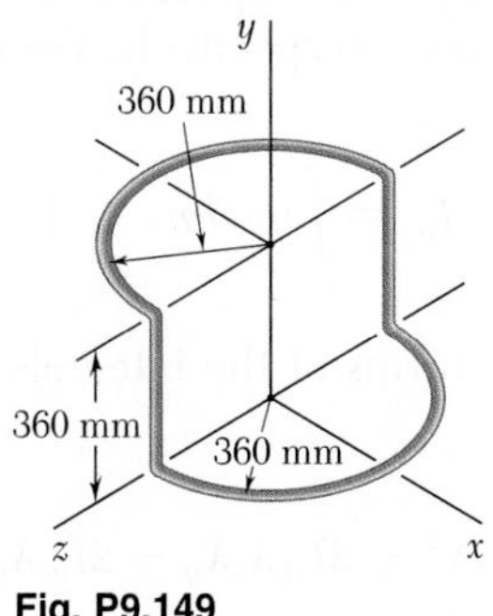

Fig. P9.149

9.150 A homogeneous wire with a weight per unit length of .6 N/m is used to form the figure shown. Determine the mass moment of inertia of the wire with respect to each of the coordinate axes.

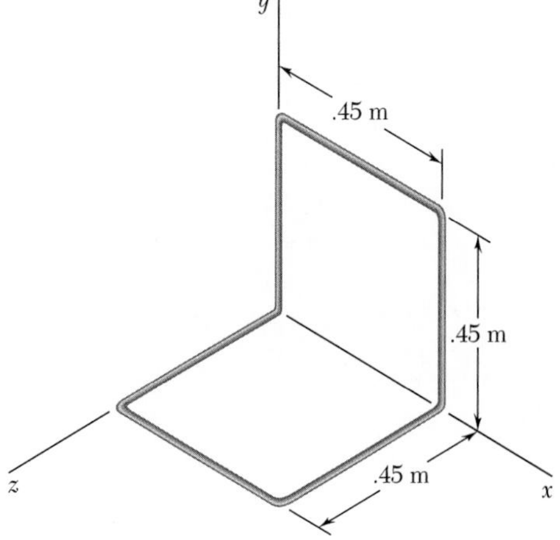

Fig. *P9.150*

*9.16. MOMENT OF INERTIA OF A BODY WITH RESPECT TO AN ARBITRARY AXIS THROUGH *O*. MASS PRODUCTS OF INERTIA

In this section you will see how the moment of inertia of a body can be determined with respect to an arbitrary axis OL through the origin (Fig. 9.29) if its moments of inertia with respect to the three coordinate axes, as well as certain other quantities to be defined below, have already been determined.

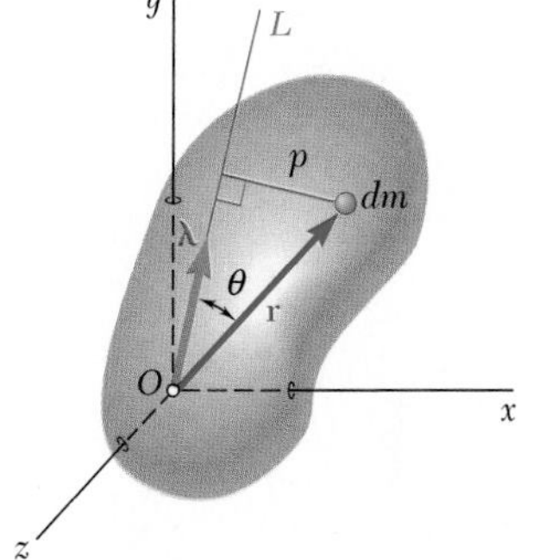

Fig. 9.29

The moment of inertia I_{OL} of the body with respect to OL is equal to $\int p^2\, dm$, where p denotes the perpendicular distance from the element of mass dm to the axis OL. If we denote by $\boldsymbol{\lambda}$ the unit vector along OL and by $\mathbf{r}$ the position vector of the element dm, we observe that the perpendicular distance p is equal to $r \sin\theta$, which is the magnitude of the vector product $\boldsymbol{\lambda} \times \mathbf{r}$. We therefore write

$$I_{OL} = \int p^2\, dm = \int |\boldsymbol{\lambda} \times \mathbf{r}|^2\, dm \tag{9.43}$$

Expressing $|\boldsymbol{\lambda} \times \mathbf{r}|^2$ in terms of the rectangular components of the vector product, we have

$$I_{OL} = \int [(\lambda_x y - \lambda_y x)^2 + (\lambda_y z - \lambda_z y)^2 + (\lambda_z x - \lambda_x z)^2]\, dm$$

where the components λ_x, λ_y, and λ_z of the unit vector $\boldsymbol{\lambda}$ represent the direction cosines of the axis OL and the components x, y, and z of $\mathbf{r}$ represent the coordinates of the element of mass dm. Expanding the squares and rearranging the terms, we write

$$\begin{aligned} I_{OL} = {} & \lambda_x^2 \int (y^2 + z^2)\, dm + \lambda_y^2 \int (z^2 + x^2)\, dm + \lambda_z^2 \int (x^2 + y^2)\, dm \\ & - 2\lambda_x\lambda_y \int xy\, dm - 2\lambda_y\lambda_z \int yz\, dm - 2\lambda_z\lambda_x \int zx\, dm \end{aligned} \tag{9.44}$$

Referring to Eqs. (9.30), we note that the first three integrals in (9.44) represent, respectively, the moments of inertia I_x, I_y, and I_z of the body with respect to the coordinate axes. The last three integrals in (9.44), which involve products of coordinates, are called the *products of inertia* of the body with respect to the x and y axes, the y and z axes, and the z and x axes, respectively. We write

$$I_{xy} = \int xy\,dm \qquad I_{yz} = \int yz\,dm \qquad I_{zx} = \int zx\,dm \tag{9.45}$$

Rewriting Eq. (9.44) in terms of the integrals defined in Eqs. (9.30) and (9.45), we have

$$I_{OL} = I_x\lambda_x^2 + I_y\lambda_y^2 + I_z\lambda_z^2 - 2I_{xy}\lambda_x\lambda_y - 2I_{yz}\lambda_y\lambda_z - 2I_{zx}\lambda_z\lambda_x \tag{9.46}$$

We note that the definition of the products of inertia of a mass given in Eqs. (9.45) is an extension of the definition of the product of inertia of an area (Sec. 9.8). Mass products of inertia reduce to zero under the same conditions of symmetry as do products of inertia of areas, and the parallel-axis theorem for mass products of inertia is expressed by relations similar to the formula derived for the product of inertia of an area. Substituting the expressions for x, y, and z given in Eqs. (9.31) into Eqs. (9.45), we find that

$$\begin{aligned} I_{xy} &= \bar{I}_{x'y'} + m\bar{x}\bar{y} \\ I_{yz} &= \bar{I}_{y'z'} + m\bar{y}\bar{z} \\ I_{zx} &= \bar{I}_{z'x'} + m\bar{z}\bar{x} \end{aligned} \tag{9.47}$$

where $\bar{x}$, $\bar{y}$, and $\bar{z}$ are the coordinates of the center of gravity G of the body and $\bar{I}_{x'y'}$, $\bar{I}_{y'z'}$, and $\bar{I}_{z'x'}$ denote the products of inertia of the body with respect to the centroidal axes x', y', and z' (Fig. 9.22).

*9.17. ELLIPSOID OF INERTIA. PRINCIPAL AXES OF INERTIA

Let us assume that the moment of inertia of the body considered in the preceding section has been determined with respect to a large number of axes OL through the fixed point O and that a point Q has been plotted on each axis OL at a distance $OQ = 1/\sqrt{I_{OL}}$ from O. The locus of the points Q thus obtained forms a surface (Fig. 9.30). The equation of that surface can be obtained by substituting $1/(OQ)^2$ for I_{OL} in Eq. (9.46) and then multiplying both sides of the equation by $(OQ)^2$. Observing that

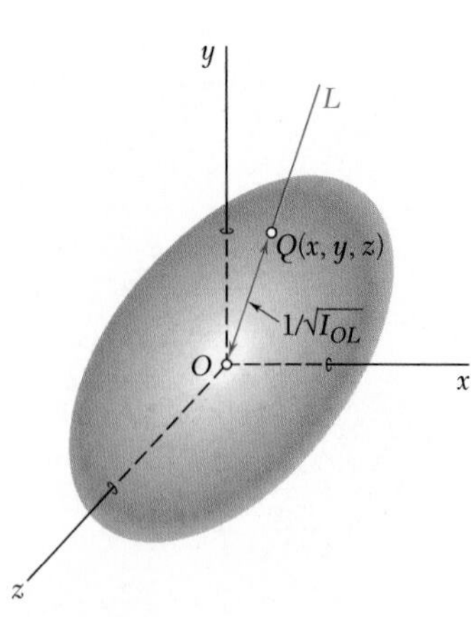

Fig. 9.30

$$(OQ)\lambda_x = x \qquad (OQ)\lambda_y = y \qquad (OQ)\lambda_z = z$$

where x, y, and z denote the rectangular coordinates of Q, we write

$$I_x x^2 + I_y y^2 + I_z z^2 - 2I_{xy}xy - 2I_{yz}yz - 2I_{zx}zx = 1 \tag{9.48}$$

The equation obtained is the equation of a *quadric surface*. Since the moment of inertia I_{OL} is different from zero for every axis OL, no point Q can be at an infinite distance from O. Thus, the quadric surface obtained is an *ellipsoid*. This ellipsoid, which defines the moment of inertia of the body with respect to any axis through O, is known as the *ellipsoid of inertia* of the body at O.

We observe that if the axes in Fig. 9.30 are rotated, the coefficients of the equation defining the ellipsoid change, since they are equal to the moments and products of inertia of the body with respect to the rotated coordinate axes. However, the *ellipsoid itself remains unaffected,* since its shape depends only upon the distribution of mass in the given body. Suppose that we choose as coordinate axes the principal axes x', y', and z' of the ellipsoid of inertia (Fig. 9.31). The equation of the ellipsoid with respect to these coordinate axes is known to be of the form

$$I_{x'}x'^2 + I_{y'}y'^2 + I_{z'}z'^2 = 1 \tag{9.49}$$

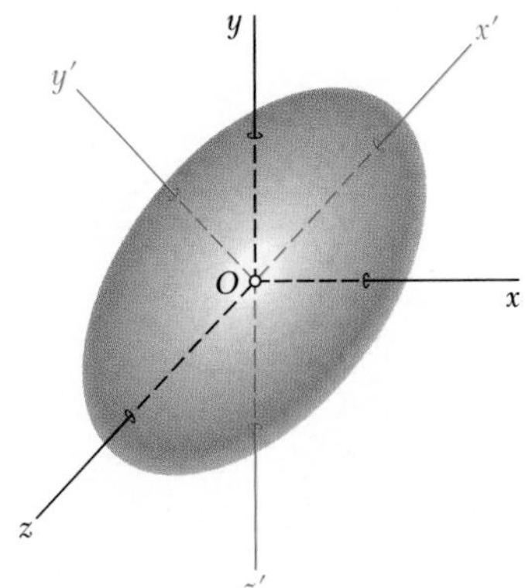

Fig. 9.31

which does not contain any products of the coordinates. Comparing Eqs. (9.48) and (9.49), we observe that the products of inertia of the body with respect to the x', y', and z' axes must be zero. The x', y', and z' axes are known as the *principal axes of inertia* of the body at O, and the coefficients $I_{x'}$, $I_{y'}$, and $I_{z'}$ are referred to as the *principal moments of inertia* of the body at O. Note that, given a body of arbitrary shape and a point O, it is always possible to find axes which are the principal axes of inertia of the body at O, that is, axes with respect to which the products of inertia of the body are zero. Indeed, whatever the shape of the body, the moments and products of inertia of the body with respect to x, y, and z axes through O will define an ellipsoid, and this ellipsoid will have principal axes which, by definition, are the principal axes of inertia of the body at O.

If the principal axes of inertia x', y', and z' are used as coordinate axes, the expression obtained in Eq. (9.46) for the moment of inertia of a body with respect to an arbitrary axis through O reduces to

$$I_{OL} = I_{x'}\lambda_{x'}^2 + I_{y'}\lambda_{y'}^2 + I_{z'}\lambda_{z'}^2 \tag{9.50}$$

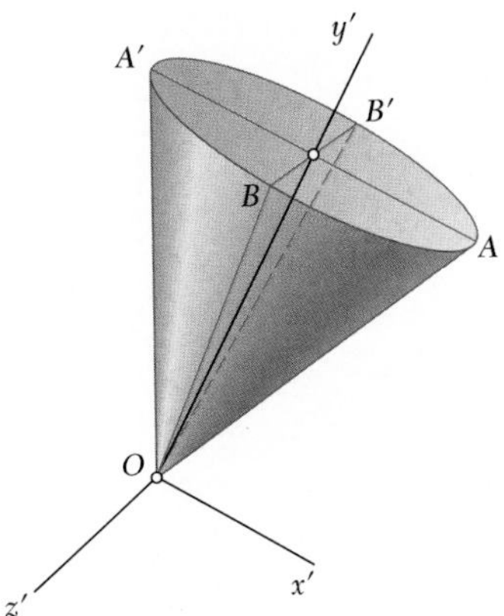

Fig. 9.32

The determination of the principal axes of inertia of a body of arbitrary shape is somewhat involved and will be discussed in the next section. There are many cases, however, where these axes can be spotted immediately. Consider, for instance, the homogeneous cone of elliptical base shown in Fig. 9.32; this cone possesses two mutually perpendicular planes of symmetry OAA' and OBB'. From the definition (9.45), we observe that if the $x'y'$ and $y'z'$ planes are chosen to coincide with the two planes of symmetry, all of the products of inertia are zero. The x', y', and z' axes thus selected are therefore the principal axes of inertia of the cone at O. In the case of the homogeneous regular tetrahedron $OABC$ shown in Fig. 9.33, the line joining the corner O to the center D of the opposite face is a principal axis of inertia at O, and any line through O perpendicular to OD is also a principal axis of inertia at O. This property is apparent if we observe that rotating the tetrahedron through 120° about OD leaves its shape and mass distribution unchanged. It follows that the ellipsoid of inertia at O also remains unchanged under this rotation. The ellipsoid, therefore, is a body of revolution whose axis of revolution is OD, and the line OD, as well as any perpendicular line through O, must be a principal axis of the ellipsoid.

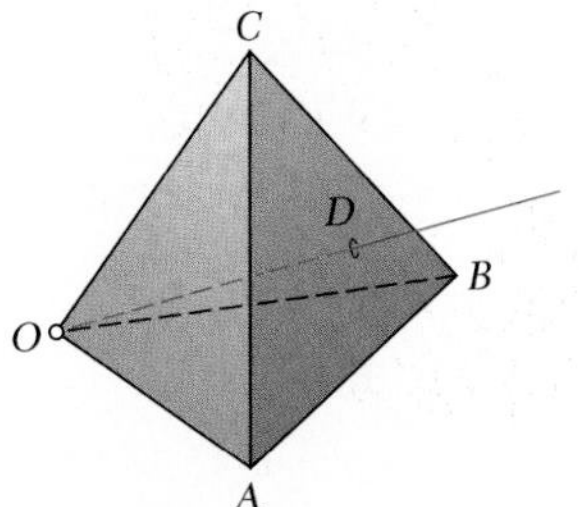

Fig. 9.33

*9.18. DETERMINATION OF THE PRINCIPAL AXES AND PRINCIPAL MOMENTS OF INERTIA OF A BODY OF ARBITRARY SHAPE

The method of analysis described in this section should be used when the body under consideration has no obvious property of symmetry.

Consider the ellipsoid of inertia of the body at a given point O (Fig. 9.34); let $\mathbf{r}$ be the radius vector of a point P on the surface of the ellipsoid and let $\mathbf{n}$ be the unit vector along the normal to that surface at P. We observe that the only points where $\mathbf{r}$ and $\mathbf{n}$ are collinear are the points P_1, P_2, and P_3, where the principal axes intersect the visible portion of the surface of the ellipsoid, and the corresponding points on the other side of the ellipsoid.

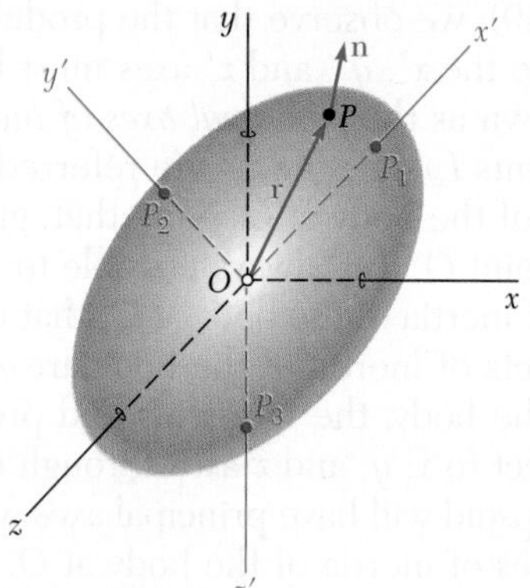

Fig. 9.34

We now recall from calculus that the direction of the normal to a surface of equation $f(x, y, z) = 0$ at a point $P(x, y, z)$ is defined by the gradient ∇f of the function f at that point. To obtain the points where the principal axes intersect the surface of the ellipsoid of inertia, we must therefore write that $\mathbf{r}$ and ∇f are collinear,

$$\nabla f = (2K)\mathbf{r} \tag{9.51}$$

where K is a constant, $\mathbf{r} = x\mathbf{i} + y\mathbf{j} + z\mathbf{k}$, and

$$\nabla f = \frac{\partial f}{\partial x}\mathbf{i} + \frac{\partial f}{\partial y}\mathbf{j} + \frac{\partial f}{\partial x}\mathbf{k}$$

Recalling Eq. (9.48), we note that the function $f(x, y, z)$ corresponding to the ellipsoid of inertia is

$$f(x, y, z) = I_x x^2 + I_y y^2 + I_z z^2 - 2I_{xy}xy - 2I_{yz}yz - 2I_{zx}zx - 1$$

Substituting for $\mathbf{r}$ and ∇f into Eq. (9.51) and equating the coefficients of the unit vectors, we write

$$\begin{aligned} I_x x - I_{xy}y - I_{zx}z &= Kx \\ -I_{xy}x + I_y y - I_{yz}z &= Ky \\ -I_{zx}x - I_{yz}y + I_z z &= Kz \end{aligned} \tag{9.52}$$

Dividing each term by the distance r from O to P, we obtain similar equations involving the direction cosines λ_x, λ_y, and λ_z:

$$\begin{aligned} I_x\lambda_x - I_{xy}\lambda_y - I_{zx}\lambda_z &= K\lambda_x \\ -I_{xy}\lambda_x + I_y\lambda_y - I_{yz}\lambda_z &= K\lambda_y \\ -I_{zx}\lambda_x - I_{yz}\lambda_y + I_z\lambda_z &= K\lambda_z \end{aligned} \tag{9.53}$$

Transposing the right-hand members leads to the following homogeneous linear equations:

$$\begin{aligned} (I_x - K)\lambda_x - I_{xy}\lambda_y - I_{zx}\lambda_z &= 0 \\ -I_{xy}\lambda_x + (I_y - K)\lambda_y - I_{yz}\lambda_z &= 0 \\ -I_{zx}\lambda_x - I_{yz}\lambda_y + (I_z - K)\lambda_z &= 0 \end{aligned} \tag{9.54}$$

For this system of equations to have a solution different from $\lambda_x = \lambda_y = \lambda_z = 0$, its discriminant must be zero:

$$\begin{vmatrix} I_x - K & -I_{xy} & -I_{zx} \\ -I_{xy} & I_y - K & -I_{yz} \\ -I_{zx} & -I_{yz} & I_z - K \end{vmatrix} = 0 \tag{9.55}$$

Expanding this determinant and changing signs, we write

$$\begin{aligned} K^3 - (I_x + I_y + I_z)K^2 + (I_xI_y + I_yI_z + I_zI_x - I_{xy}^2 - I_{yz}^2 - I_{zx}^2)K \\ - (I_xI_yI_z - I_xI_{yz}^2 - I_yI_{zx}^2 - I_zI_{xy}^2 - 2I_{xy}I_{yz}I_{zx}) = 0 \end{aligned} \tag{9.56}$$

This is a cubic equation in K, which yields three real, positive roots K_1, K_2, and K_3.

To obtain the direction cosines of the principal axis corresponding to the root K_1, we substitute K_1 for K in Eqs. (9.54). Since these equations are now linearly dependent, only two of them may be used to determine λ_x, λ_y, and λ_z. An additional equation may be obtained, however, by recalling from Sec. 2.12 that the direction cosines must satisfy the relation

$$\lambda_x^2 + \lambda_y^2 + \lambda_z^2 = 1 \tag{9.57}$$

Repeating this procedure with K_2 and K_3, we obtain the direction cosines of the other two principal axes.

We will now show that *the roots K_1, K_2, and K_3 of Eq. (9.56) are the principal moments of inertia of the given body.* Let us substitute for K in Eqs. (9.53) the root K_1, and for λ_x, λ_y, and λ_z the corresponding values $(\lambda_x)_1$, $(\lambda_y)_1$, and $(\lambda_z)_1$ of the direction cosines; the three equations will be satisfied. We now multiply by $(\lambda_x)_1$, $(\lambda_y)_1$, and $(\lambda_z)_1$, respectively, each term in the first, second, and third equation and add the equations obtained in this way. We write

$$\begin{aligned} I_x^2(\lambda_x)_1^2 + I_y^2(\lambda_y)_1^2 + I_z^2(\lambda_z)_1^2 - 2I_{xy}(\lambda_x)_1(\lambda_y)_1 \\ - 2I_{yz}(\lambda_y)_1(\lambda_z)_1 - 2I_{zx}(\lambda_z)_1(\lambda_x)_1 = K_1[(\lambda_x)_1^2 + (\lambda_y)_1^2 + (\lambda_z)_1^2] \end{aligned}$$

Recalling Eq. (9.46), we observe that the left-hand member of this equation represents the moment of inertia of the body with respect to the principal axis corresponding to K_1; it is thus the principal moment of inertia corresponding to that root. On the other hand, recalling Eq. (9.57), we note that the right-hand member reduces to K_1. Thus K_1 itself is the principal moment of inertia. We can show in the same fashion that K_2 and K_3 are the other two principal moments of inertia of the body.

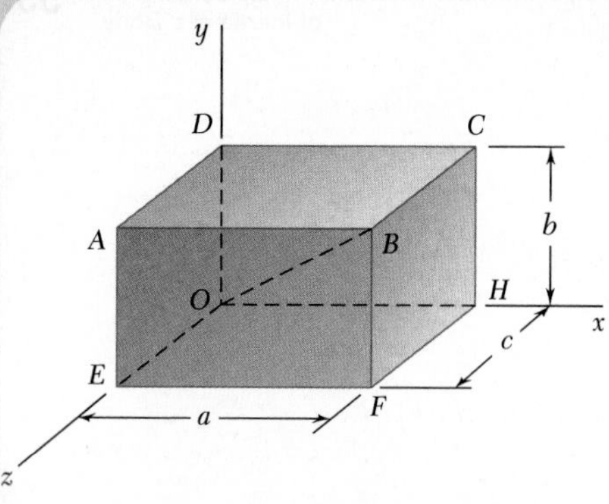

SAMPLE PROBLEM 9.14

Consider a rectangular prism of mass m and sides a, b, and c. Determine (*a*) the mass moments and products of inertia of the prism with respect to the coordinate axes shown, (*b*) its mass moment of inertia with respect to the diagonal OB.

SOLUTION

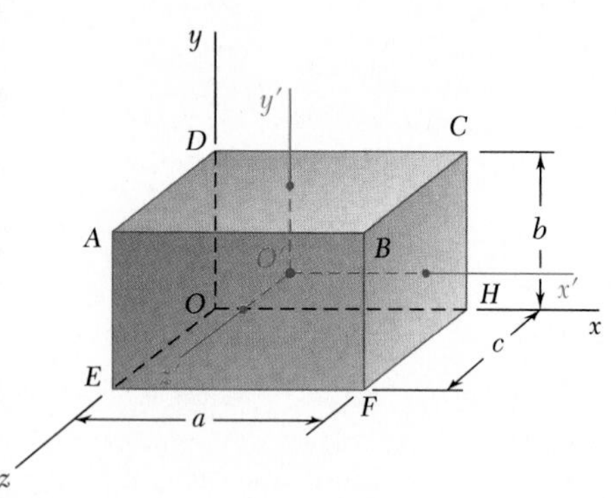

a.* Mass Moments and Products of Inertia with Respect to the Coordinate Axes.** ***Mass Moments of Inertia. Introducing the centroidal axes x', y', and z', with respect to which the mass moments of inertia are given in Fig. 9.28, we apply the parallel-axis theorem:

$$I_x = \bar{I}_{x'} + m(\bar{y}^2 + \bar{z}^2) = \tfrac{1}{12}m(b^2 + c^2) + m(\tfrac{1}{4}b^2 + \tfrac{1}{4}c^2)$$

$$I_x = \tfrac{1}{3}m(b^2 + c^2) \quad ◀$$

Similarly, $\qquad I_y = \tfrac{1}{3}m(c^2 + a^2) \qquad I_z = \tfrac{1}{3}m(a^2 + b^2) \quad ◀$

Mass Products of Inertia. Because of symmetry, the mass products of inertia with respect to the centroidal axes x', y', and z' are zero, and these axes are principal axes of inertia. Using the parallel-axis theorem, we have

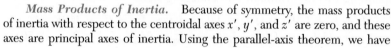

$$I_{xy} = \bar{I}_{x'y'} + m\bar{x}\bar{y} = 0 + m(\tfrac{1}{2}a)(\tfrac{1}{2}b) \qquad I_{xy} = \tfrac{1}{4}mab \quad ◀$$

Similarly, $\qquad I_{yz} = \tfrac{1}{4}mbc \qquad I_{zx} = \tfrac{1}{4}mca \quad ◀$

***b.* Mass Moment of Inertia with Respect to *OB*.** We recall Eq. (9.46):

$$I_{OB} = I_x\lambda_x^2 + I_y\lambda_y^2 + I_z\lambda_z^2 - 2I_{xy}\lambda_x\lambda_y - 2I_{yz}\lambda_y\lambda_z - 2I_{zx}\lambda_z\lambda_x$$

where the direction cosines of OB are

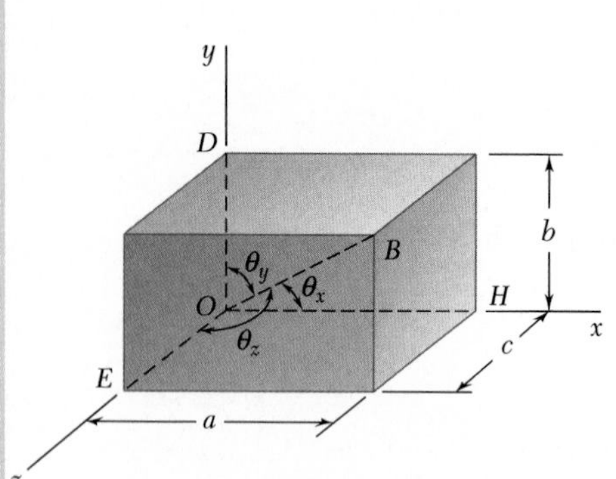

$$\lambda_x = \cos\theta_x = \frac{OH}{OB} = \frac{a}{(a^2 + b^2 + c^2)^{1/2}}$$

$$\lambda_y = \frac{b}{(a^2 + b^2 + c^2)^{1/2}} \qquad \lambda_z = \frac{c}{(a^2 + b^2 + c^2)^{1/2}}$$

Substituting the values obtained for the mass moments and products of inertia and for the direction cosines into the equation for I_{OB}, we have

$$I_{OB} = \frac{1}{a^2 + b^2 + c^2}[\tfrac{1}{3}m(b^2 + c^2)a^2 + \tfrac{1}{3}m(c^2 + a^2)b^2 + \tfrac{1}{3}m(a^2 + b^2)c^2 - \tfrac{1}{2}ma^2b^2 - \tfrac{1}{2}mb^2c^2 - \tfrac{1}{2}mc^2a^2]$$

$$I_{OB} = \frac{m}{6}\,\frac{a^2b^2 + b^2c^2 + c^2a^2}{a^2 + b^2 + c^2} \quad ◀$$

Alternative Solution. The mass moment of inertia I_{OB} can be obtained directly from the principal mass moments of inertia $\bar{I}_{x'}$, $\bar{I}_{y'}$, and $\bar{I}_{z'}$, since the line OB passes through the centroid O'. Since the x', y', and z' axes are principal axes of inertia, we use Eq. (9.50) to write

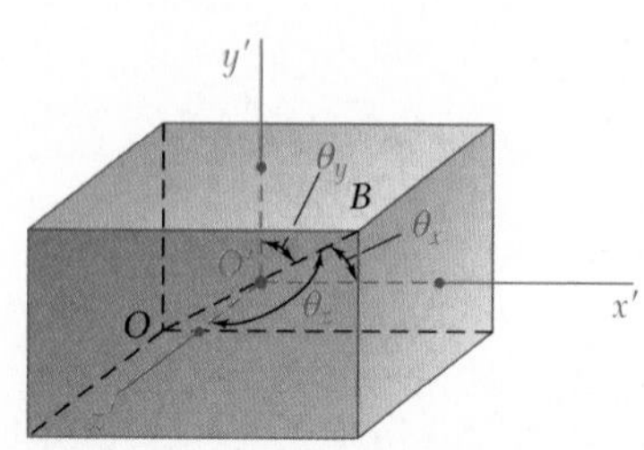

$$I_{OB} = \bar{I}_{x'}\lambda_x^2 + \bar{I}_{y'}\lambda_y^2 + \bar{I}_{z'}\lambda_z^2$$

$$= \frac{1}{a^2 + b^2 + c^2}\left[\frac{m}{12}(b^2 + c^2)a^2 + \frac{m}{12}(c^2 + a^2)b^2 + \frac{m}{12}(a^2 + b^2)c^2\right]$$

$$I_{OB} = \frac{m}{6}\,\frac{a^2b^2 + b^2c^2 + c^2a^2}{a^2 + b^2 + c^2} \quad ◀$$

SAMPLE PROBLEM 9.15

If $a = 3c$ and $b = 2c$ for the rectangular prism of Sample Prob. 9.14, determine (*a*) the principal mass moments of inertia at the origin O, (*b*) the principal axes of inertia at O.

SOLUTION

***a.* Principal Mass Moments of Inertia at the Origin *O*.** Substituting $a = 3c$ and $b = 2c$ into the solution to Sample Prob. 9.14, we have

$$I_x = \tfrac{5}{3}mc^2 \qquad I_y = \tfrac{10}{3}mc^2 \qquad I_z = \tfrac{13}{3}mc^2$$
$$I_{xy} = \tfrac{3}{2}mc^2 \qquad I_{yz} = \tfrac{1}{2}mc^2 \qquad I_{zx} = \tfrac{3}{4}mc^2$$

Substituting the values of the mass moments and products of inertia into Eq. (9.56) and collecting terms yields

$$K^3 - (\tfrac{28}{3}mc^2)K^2 + (\tfrac{3479}{144}m^2c^4)K - \tfrac{589}{54}m^3c^6 = 0$$

We then solve for the roots of this equation; from the discussion in Sec. 9.18, it follows that these roots are the principal mass moments of inertia of the body at the origin.

$$K_1 = 0.568867mc^2 \qquad K_2 = 4.20885mc^2 \qquad K_3 = 4.55562mc^2$$
$$K_1 = 0.569mc^2 \qquad K_2 = 4.21mc^2 \qquad K_3 = 4.56mc^2 \quad ◀$$

***b.* Principal Axes of Inertia at *O*.** To determine the direction of a principal axis of inertia, we first substitute the corresponding value of K into two of the equations (9.54); the resulting equations together with Eq. (9.57) constitute a system of three equations from which the direction cosines of the corresponding principal axis can be determined. Thus, we have for the first principal mass moment of inertia K_1:

$$(\tfrac{5}{3} - 0.568867)\,mc^2(\lambda_x)_1 - \tfrac{3}{2}mc^2(\lambda_y)_1 - \tfrac{3}{4}mc^2(\lambda_z)_1 = 0$$
$$-\tfrac{3}{2}mc^2(\lambda_x)_1 + (\tfrac{10}{3} - 0.568867)\,mc^2(\lambda_y)_1 - \tfrac{1}{2}mc^2(\lambda_z)_1 = 0$$
$$(\lambda_x)_1^2 + (\lambda_y)_1^2 + (\lambda_z)_1^2 = 1$$

Solving yields

$$(\lambda_x)_1 = 0.836600 \qquad (\lambda_y)_1 = 0.496001 \qquad (\lambda_z)_1 = 0.232557$$

The angles that the first principal axis of inertia forms with the coordinate axes are then

$$(\theta_x)_1 = 33.2° \qquad (\theta_y)_1 = 60.3° \qquad (\theta_z)_1 = 76.6° \quad ◀$$

Using the same set of equations successively with K_2 and K_3, we find that the angles associated with the second and third principal mass moments of inertia at the origin are, respectively,

$$(\theta_x)_2 = 57.8° \qquad (\theta_y)_2 = 146.6° \qquad (\theta_z)_2 = 98.0° \quad ◀$$

and

$$(\theta_x)_3 = 82.8° \qquad (\theta_y)_3 = 76.1° \qquad (\theta_z)_3 = 164.3° \quad ◀$$

SOLVING PROBLEMS ON YOUR OWN

In this lesson we defined the *mass products of inertia* I_{xy}, I_{yz}, and I_{zx} of a body and showed you how to determine the mass moments of inertia of that body with respect to an arbitrary axis passing through the origin O. You also learned how to determine at the origin O the *principal axes of inertia* of a body and the corresponding *principal mass moments of inertia.*

1. *Determining the mass products of inertia of a composite body.* The mass products of inertia of a composite body with respect to the coordinate axes can be expressed as the sums of the mass products of inertia of its component parts with respect to those axes. For each component part, we can use the parallel-axis theorem and write Eqs. (9.47)

$$I_{xy} = \bar{I}_{x'y'} + m\bar{x}\bar{y} \qquad I_{yz} = \bar{I}_{y'z'} + m\bar{y}\bar{z} \qquad I_{zx} = \bar{I}_{z'x'} + m\bar{z}\bar{x}$$

where the primes denote the centroidal axes of each component part and where $\bar{x}$, $\bar{y}$, and $\bar{z}$ represent the coordinates of its center of gravity. Keep in mind that the mass products of inertia can be positive, negative, or zero, and be sure to take into account the signs of $\bar{x}$, $\bar{y}$, and $\bar{z}$.

a. *From the properties of symmetry of a component part,* you can deduce that two or all three of its centroidal mass products of inertia are zero. For instance, you can verify that for a thin plate parallel to the xy plane; a wire lying in a plane parallel to the xy plane; a body with a plane of symmetry parallel to the xy plane; and a body with an axis of symmetry parallel to the z axis, *the mass products of inertia* $\bar{I}_{y'z'}$ *and* $\bar{I}_{z'x'}$ *are zero.*

For rectangular, circular, or semicircular plates with axes of symmetry parallel to the coordinate axes; straight wires parallel to a coordinate axis; circular and semicircular wires with axes of symmetry parallel to the coordinate axes; and rectangular prisms with axes of symmetry parallel to the coordinate axes, *the mass products of inertia* $\bar{I}_{x'y'}$, $\bar{I}_{y'z'}$, *and* $\bar{I}_{z'x'}$ *are all zero.*

b. *Mass products of inertia which are different from zero* can be computed from Eqs. (9.45). Although, in general, a triple integration is required to determine a mass product of inertia, a single integration can be used if the given body can be divided into a series of thin, parallel slabs. The computations are then similar to those discussed in the previous lesson for mass moments of inertia.

2. ***Computing the mass moment of inertia of a body with respect to an arbitrary axis OL.*** An expression for the mass moment of inertia I_{OL} was derived in Sec. 9.16 and is given in Eq. (9.46). Before computing I_{OL}, you must first determine the mass moments and products of inertia of the body with respect to the given coordinate axes as well as the direction cosines of the unit vector $\boldsymbol{\lambda}$ along OL.

3. ***Calculating the principal mass moments of inertia of a body and determining its principal axes of inertia.*** You saw in Sec. 9.17 that it is always possible to find an orientation of the coordinate axes for which the mass products of inertia are zero. These axes are referred to as the *principal axes of inertia* and the corresponding mass moments of inertia are known as the *principal mass moments of inertia* of the body. In many cases, the principal axes of inertia of a body can be determined from its properties of symmetry. The procedure required to determine the principal mass moments and principal axes of inertia of a body with no obvious property of symmetry was discussed in Sec. 9.18 and was illustrated in Sample Prob. 9.15. It consists of the following steps.

a. Expand the determinant in Eq. (9.55) and solve the resulting cubic equation. The solution can be obtained by trial and error or, preferably, with an advanced scientific calculator or with the appropriate computer software. The roots K_1, K_2, and K_3 of this equation are the principal mass moments of inertia of the body.

b. To determine the direction of the principal axis corresponding to K_1, substitute this value for K in two of the equations (9.54) and solve these equations together with Eq. (9.57) for the direction cosines of the principal axis corresponding to K_1.

c. Repeat this procedure with K_2 ***and*** K_3 to determine the directions of the other two principal axes. As a check of your computations, you may wish to verify that the scalar product of any two of the unit vectors along the three axes you have obtained is zero and, thus, that these axes are perpendicular to each other.

d. When a principal mass moment of inertia is approximately equal to a mass moment of inertia with respect to a coordinate axis, the calculated values of the corresponding direction cosines will be very sensitive to the number of significant figures used in your computations. Thus, for this case we suggest you express your intermediate answers in terms of six or seven significant figures to avoid possible errors.

Problems

9.151 Determine the mass products of inertia I_{xy}, I_{yz}, and I_{zx} of the steel machine element shown. (The specific weight of steel is 9000 kg/m^3.)

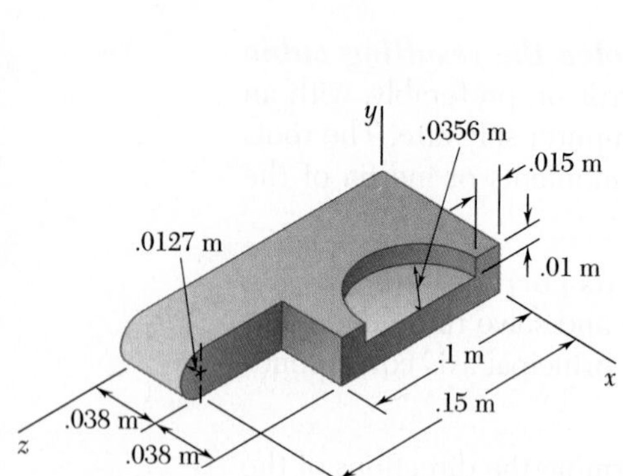

Fig. P9.151

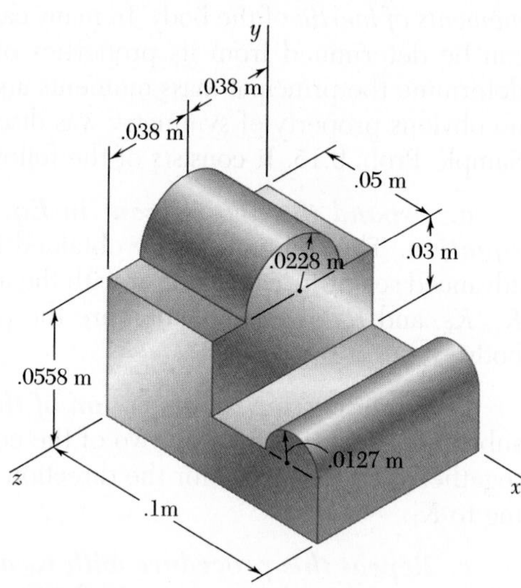

Fig. P9.152

9.152 Determine the mass products of inertia I_{xy}, I_{yz}, and I_{zx} of the aluminum casting shown. (The specific weight of aluminum is 3000 kg/m^3.)

***9.153* and 9.154** Determine the mass products of inertia I_{xy}, I_{yz}, and I_{zx} of the cast aluminum machine component shown. (The density of aluminum is 2700 kg/m^3.)

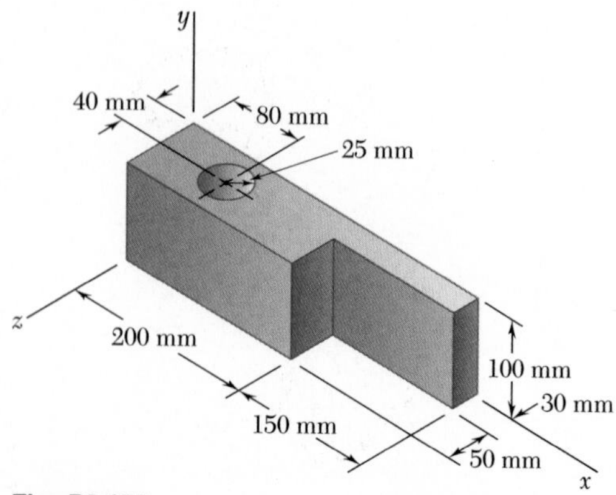

Fig. *P9.153*

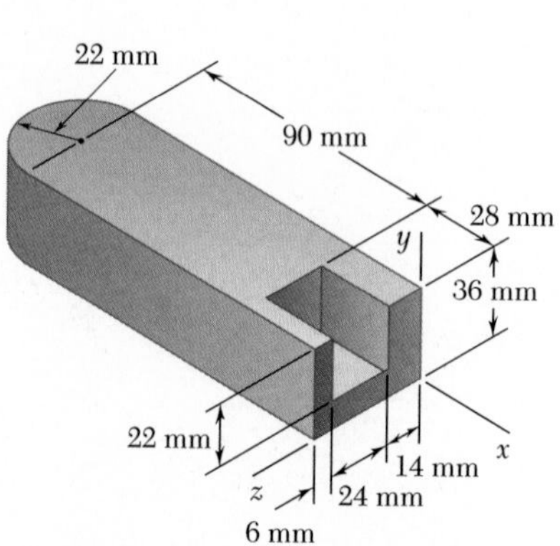

Fig. P9.154

9.155 through 9.157 A section of sheet steel 3 mm thick is cut and bent into the machine component shown. Knowing that the density of the steel is 7860 kg/m^3, determine the mass products of inertia I_{xy}, I_{yz}, and I_{zx} of the component.

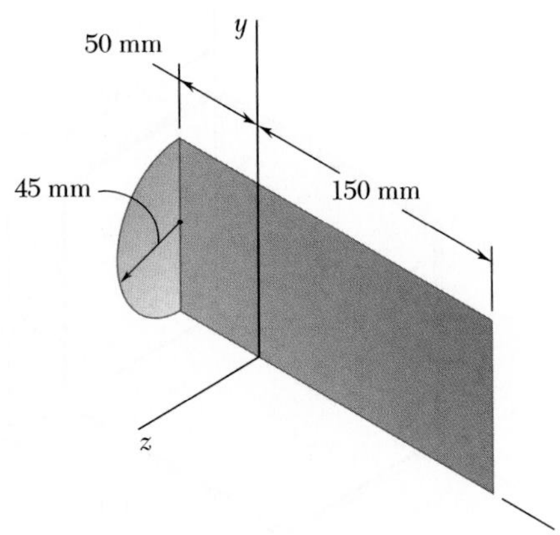

Fig. P9.155

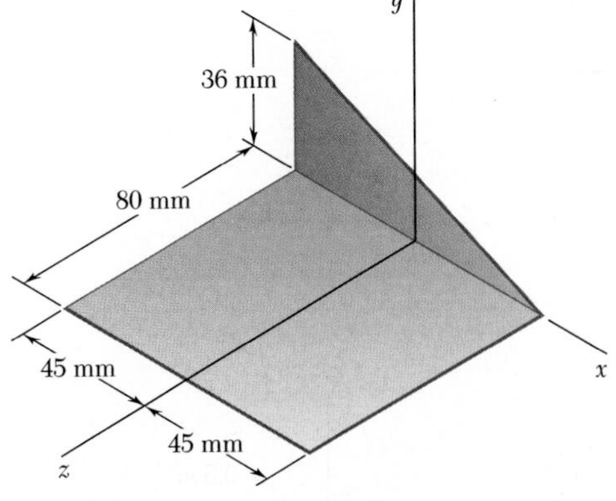

Fig. *P9.156*

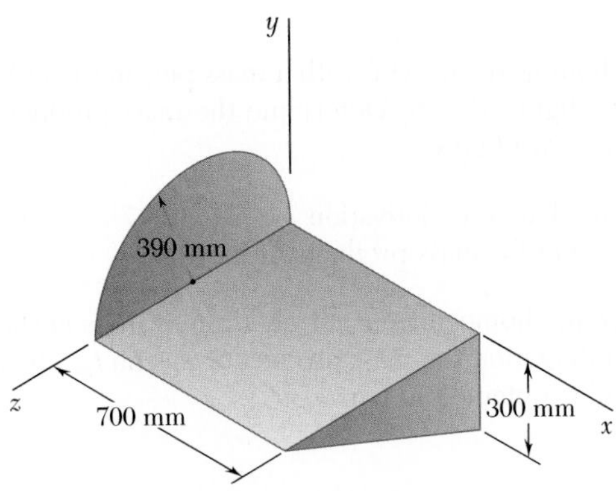

Fig. P9.157

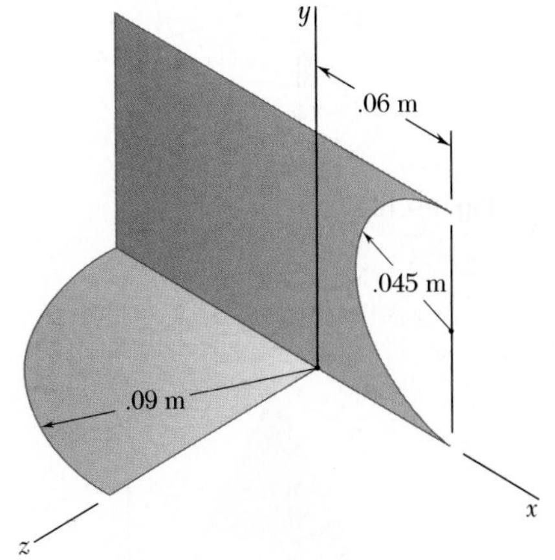

Fig. *P9.158*

9.158 A section of sheet steel .002 m thick is cut and bent into the machine component shown. Knowing that the specific weight of steel is 9000 kg/m^3, determine the mass products of inertia I_{xy}, I_{yz}, and I_{zx} of the component.

9.159 and *9.160* Brass wire with a weight per unit length w is used to form the figure shown. Determine the mass products of inertia I_{xy}, I_{yz}, and I_{zx} of the wire figure.

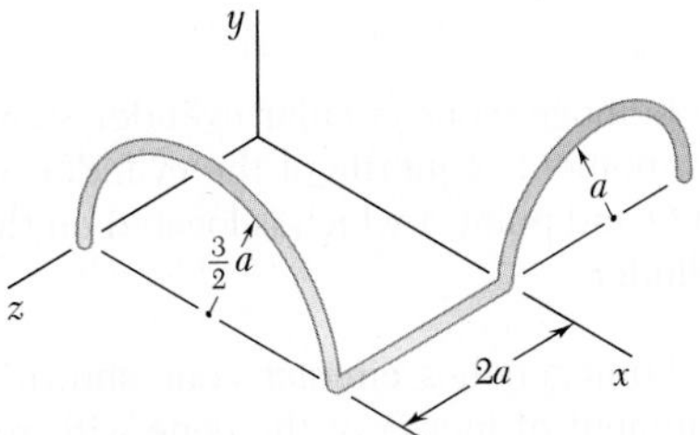

Fig. P9.159

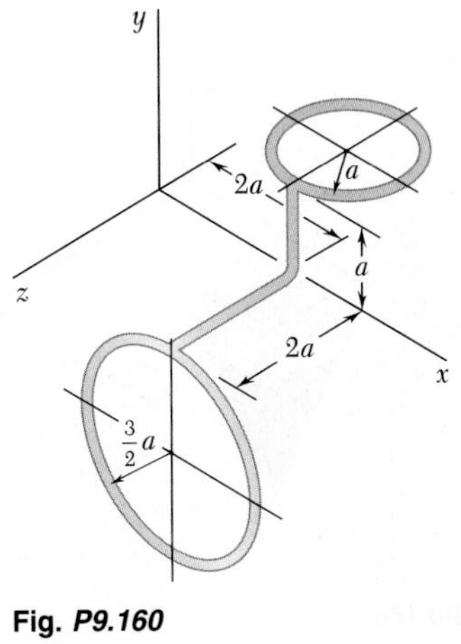

Fig. *P9.160*

9.161 The figure shown is formed from .0019-m-diameter aluminum wire. Knowing that the specific weight of aluminum is 3000 kg/m^3, determine the mass products of inertia I_{xy}, I_{yz}, and I_{zx} of the wire figure.

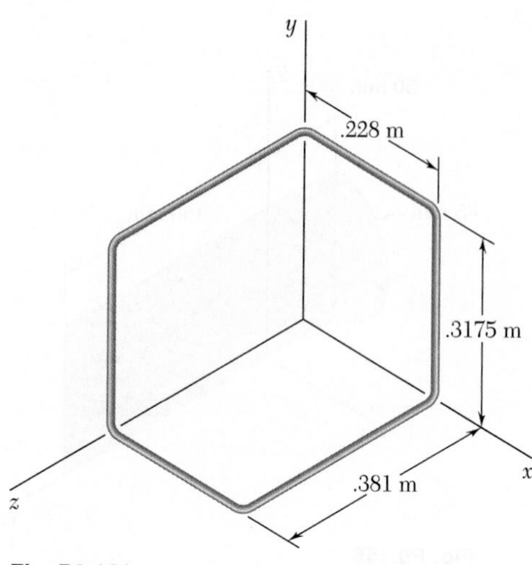

Fig. P9.161

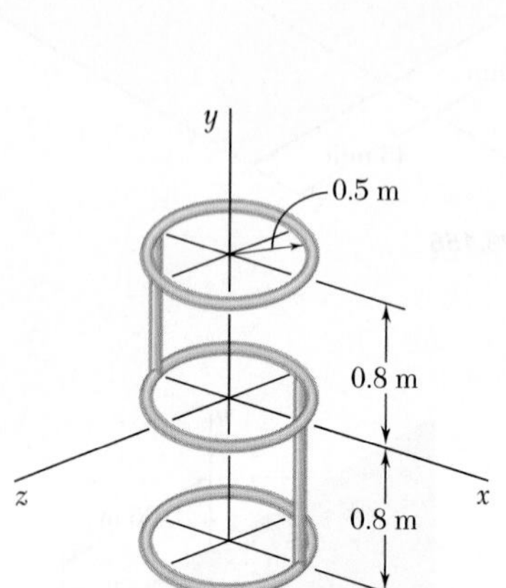

Fig. P9.162

9.162 A homogeneous wire with a mass per unit length of 1.8 kg/m is used to form the figure shown. Determine the mass products of inertia I_{xy}, I_{yz}, and I_{zx} of the wire figure.

9.163 Complete the derivation of Eq. (9.47), which expresses the parallel-axis theorem for mass products of inertia.

9.164 For the homogeneous tetrahedron of mass m shown, (*a*) determine by direct integration the mass product of inertia I_{zx}, (*b*) deduce I_{yz} and I_{xy} from the results obtained in part *a*.

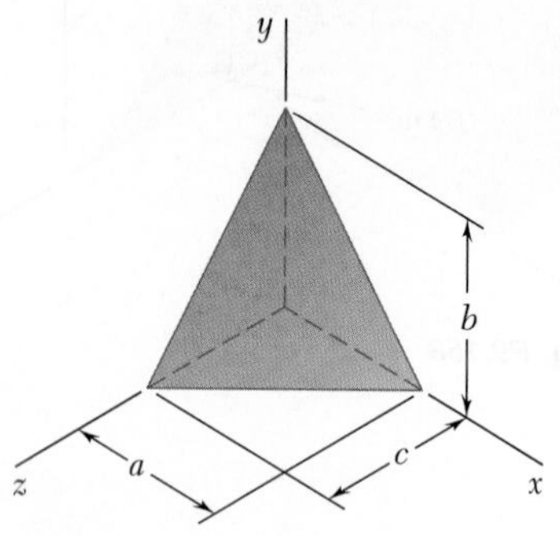

Fig. P9.164

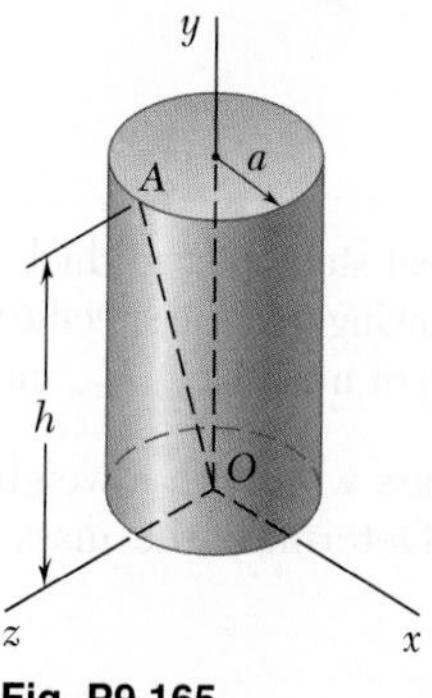

Fig. P9.165

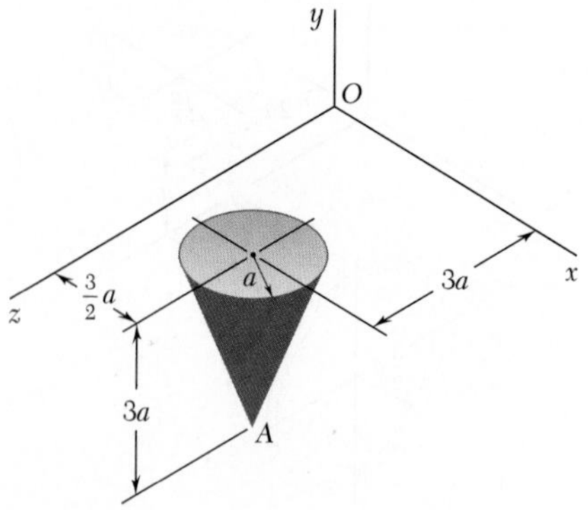

Fig. P9.166

9.165 The homogeneous circular cylinder shown has a mass m. Determine the mass moment of inertia of the cylinder with respect to the line joining the origin O and point A which is located on the perimeter of the top surface of the cylinder.

9.166 The homogeneous circular cone shown has a mass m. Determine the mass moment of inertia of the cone with respect to the line joining the origin O and point A.

9.167 Shown is the machine element of Prob. 9.143. Determine its mass moment of inertia with respect to the line joining the origin O and point A.

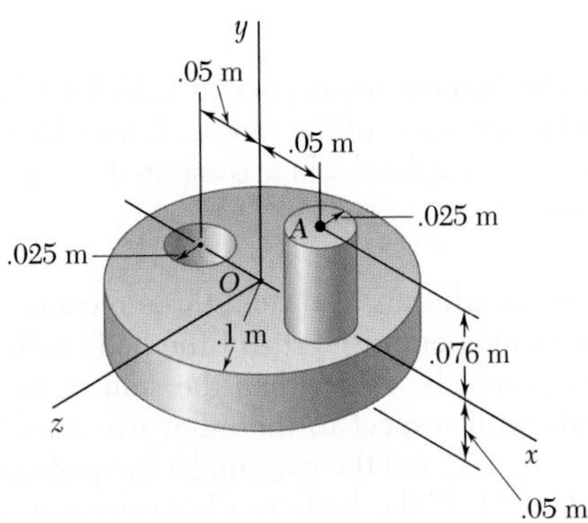

Fig. P9.167

9.168 Determine the mass moment of inertia of the steel machine element of Probs. 9.147 and 9.151 with respect to the axis through the origin which forms equal angles with the x, y, and z axes.

9.169 The thin bent plate shown is of uniform density and weight W. Determine its mass moment of inertia with respect to the line joining the origin O and point A.

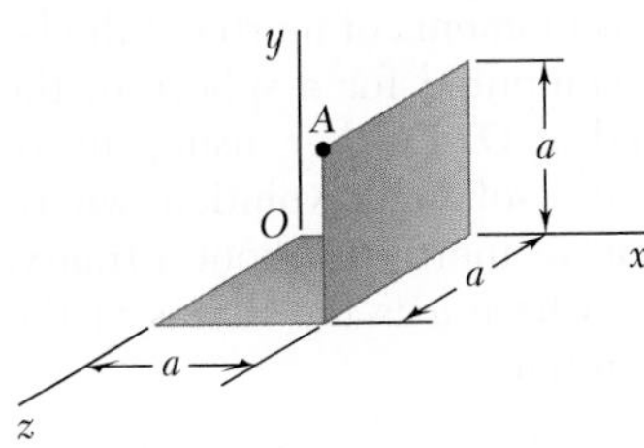

Fig. P9.169

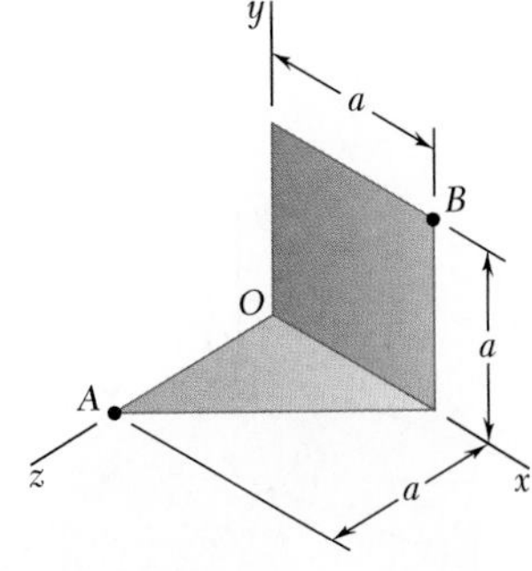

Fig. P9.170

9.170 A piece of sheet metal of thickness t and density ρ is cut and bent into the shape shown. Determine its mass moment of inertia with respect to a line joining points A and B.

9.171 Determine the mass moment of inertia of the machine component of Probs. 9.138 and 9.157 with respect to the axis through the origin defined by the unit vector $\boldsymbol{\lambda} = (-4\mathbf{i} + 8\mathbf{j} + \mathbf{k})/9$.

9.172 through 9.174 For the wire figure of the problem indicated, determine the mass moment of inertia of the figure with respect to the axis through the origin defined by the unit vector $\boldsymbol{\lambda} = (-3\mathbf{i} - 6\mathbf{j} + 2\mathbf{k})/7$.

9.172 Prob. 9.150
9.173 Prob. 9.149
9.174 Prob. 9.148

9.175 For the rectangular prism shown, determine the values of the ratios b/a and c/a so that the ellipsoid of inertia of the prism is a sphere when computed (a) at point A, (b) at point B.

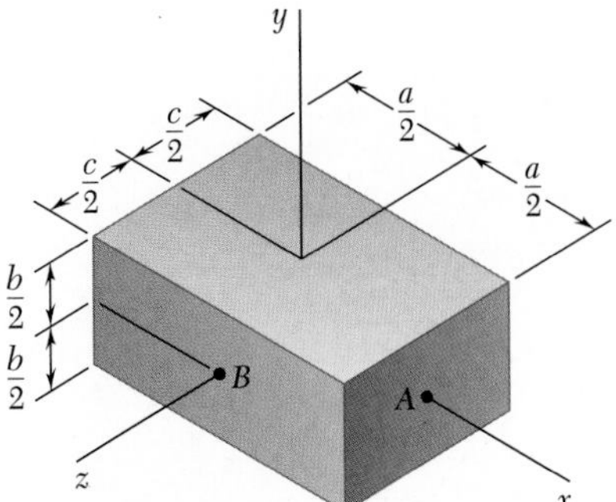

Fig. P9.175

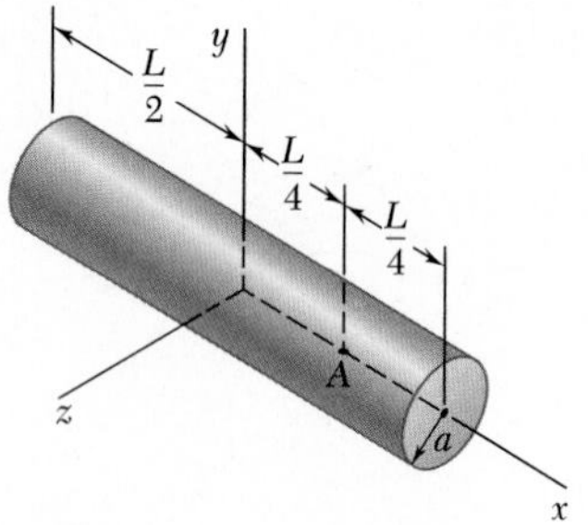

Fig. P9.177

9.176 For the right circular cone of Sample Prob. 9.11, determine the value of the ratio a/h for which the ellipsoid of inertia of the cone is a sphere when computed (*a*) at the apex of the cone, (*b*) at the center of the base of the cone.

9.177 For the homogeneous circular cylinder of radius a and length L shown, determine the value of the ratio a/L for which the ellipsoid of inertia of the cylinder is a sphere when computed (*a*) at the centroid of the cylinder, (*b*) at point A.

9.178 Given an arbitrary body and three rectangular axes x, y, and z, prove that the mass moment of inertia of the body with respect to any one of the three axes cannot be larger than the sum of the mass moments of inertia of the body with respect to the other two axes. That is, prove that the inequality $I_x \leq I_y + I_z$ and the two similar inequalities are satisfied. Further, prove that $I_y \geq \frac{1}{2}I_x$ if the body is a homogeneous solid of revolution, where x is the axis of revolution and y is a transverse axis.

9.179 Consider a cube of mass m and side a. (*a*) Show that the ellipsoid of inertia at the center of the cube is a sphere, and use this property to determine the mass moment of inertia of the cube with respect to one of its diagonals. (*b*) Show that the ellipsoid of inertia at one of the corners of the cube is an ellipsoid of revolution, and determine the principal mass moments of inertia of the cube at that point.

9.180 Given a homogeneous body of mass m and arbitrary shape and three rectangular axes x, y, and z with origin at O, prove that the sum $I_x + I_y + I_z$ of the mass moments of inertia of the body cannot be smaller than the similar sum computed for a sphere of the same mass and the same material centered at O. Further, using the results of Prob. 9.178, prove that if the body is a solid of revolution, where x is the axis of revolution, its mass moment of inertia I_y about a transverse axis y cannot be smaller than $3ma^2/10$, where a is the radius of the sphere of the same mass and the same material.

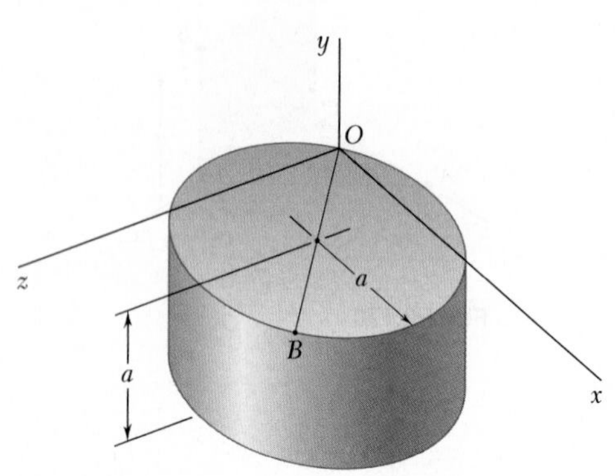

Fig. P9.181

***9.181** The homogeneous circular cylinder shown has a mass m, and the diameter OB of its top surface forms 45° angles with the x and z axes. (*a*) Determine the principal mass moments of inertia of the cylinder at the origin O. (*b*) Compute the angles that the principal axes of inertia at O form with the coordinate axes. (*c*) Sketch the cylinder, and show the orientation of the principal axes of inertia relative to the x, y, and z axes.

9.182 through 9.186 For the component described in the problem indicated, determine (*a*) the principal mass moments of inertia at the origin, (*b*) the principal axes of inertia at the origin. Sketch the body and show the orientation of the principal axes of inertia relative to the x, y, and z axes.

***9.182** Prob. 9.167
***9.183** Probs. 9.147 and 9.151
***9.184** Prob. 9.169
***9.185** Prob. 9.170
***9.186** Probs. 9.150 and 9.172

REVIEW AND SUMMARY FOR CHAPTER 9

In the first half of this chapter, we discussed the determination of the resultant **R** of forces $\Delta\mathbf{F}$ distributed over a plane area A when the magnitudes of these forces are proportional to both the areas ΔA of the elements on which they act and the distances y from these elements to a given x axis; we thus had $\Delta F = ky\,\Delta A$. We found that the magnitude of the resultant **R** is proportional to the first moment $Q_x = \int y\,dA$ of the area A, while the moment of **R** about the x axis is proportional to the *second moment,* or *moment of inertia,* $I_x = \int y^2\,dA$ of A with respect to the same axis [Sec. 9.2].

Rectangular moments of inertia

The *rectangular moments of inertia I_x and I_y of an area* [Sec. 9.3] were obtained by evaluating the integrals

$$I_x = \int y^2\,dA \qquad I_y = \int x^2\,dA \tag{9.1}$$

These computations can be reduced to single integrations by choosing dA to be a thin strip parallel to one of the coordinate axes. We also recall that it is possible to compute I_x and I_y from the same elemental strip (Fig. 9.35) using the formula for the moment of inertia of a rectangular area [Sample Prob. 9.3].

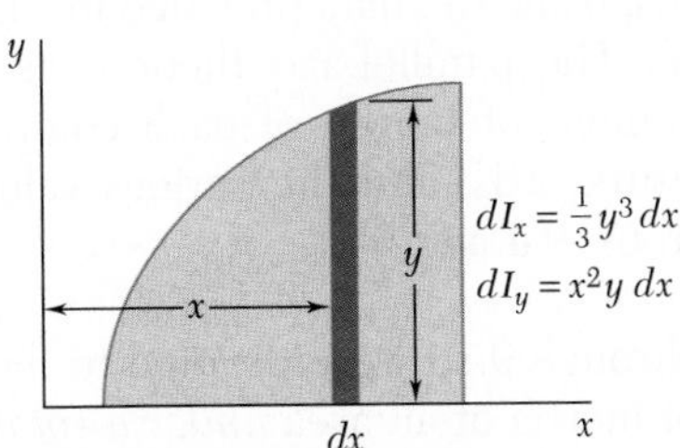

Fig. 9.35

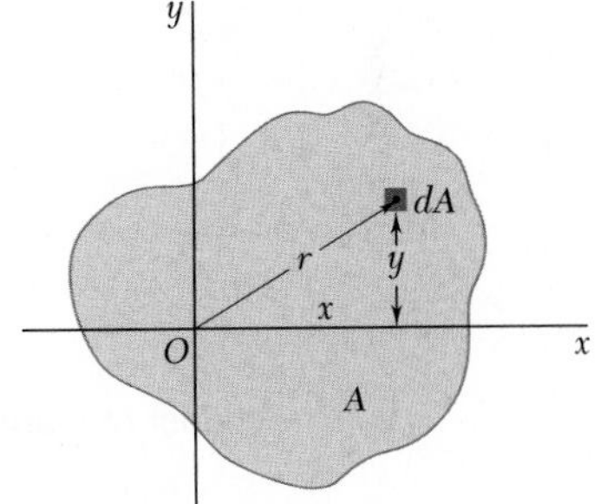

Fig. 9.36

Polar moment of inertia

The *polar moment of inertia of an area A* with respect to the pole O [Sec. 9.4] was defined as

$$J_O = \int r^2\,dA \tag{9.3}$$

where r is the distance from O to the element of area dA (Fig. 9.36). Observing that $r^2 = x^2 + y^2$, we established the relation

$$J_O = I_x + I_y \tag{9.4}$$

Radius of gyration

The *radius of gyration of an area A* with respect to the x axis [Sec. 9.5] was defined as the distance k_x, where $I_x = k_x^2 A$. With similar definitions for the radii of gyration of A with respect to the y axis and with respect to O, we had

$$k_x = \sqrt{\frac{I_x}{A}} \qquad k_y = \sqrt{\frac{I_y}{A}} \qquad k_O = \sqrt{\frac{J_O}{A}} \qquad (9.5\text{–}9.7)$$

Parallel-axis theorem

The parallel-axis theorem was presented in Sec. 9.6. It states that the moment of inertia I of an area with respect to any given axis AA' (Fig. 9.37) is equal to the moment of inertia $\bar{I}$ of the area with respect to the centroidal axis BB' that is parallel to AA' *plus* the product of the area A and the square of the distance d between the two axes:

$$I = \bar{I} + Ad^2 \qquad (9.9)$$

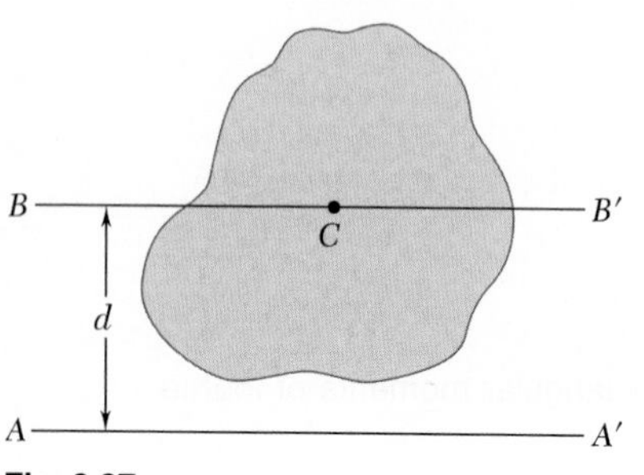

Fig. 9.37

This formula can also be used to determine the moment of inertia $\bar{I}$ of an area with respect to a centroidal axis BB' when its moment of inertia I with respect to a parallel axis AA' is known. In this case, however, the product Ad^2 should be *subtracted* from the known moment of inertia I.

A similar relation holds between the polar moment of inertia J_O of an area about a point O and the polar moment of inertia $\bar{J}_C$ of the same area about its centroid C. Letting d be the distance between O and C, we have

$$J_O = \bar{J}_C + Ad^2 \qquad (9.11)$$

Composite areas

The parallel-axis theorem can be used very effectively to compute the *moment of inertia of a composite area* with respect to a given axis [Sec. 9.7]. Considering each component area separately, we first compute the moment of inertia of each area with respect to its centroidal axis, using the data provided in Figs. 9.12 and 9.13 whenever possible. The parallel-axis theorem is then applied to determine the moment of inertia of each component area with respect to the desired axis, and the various values obtained are added [Sample Probs. 9.4 and 9.5].

Product of inertia

Sections 9.8 through 9.10 were devoted to the transformation of the moments of inertia of an area *under a rotation of the coordinate axes.* First, we defined the *product of inertia of an area A* as

$$I_{xy} = \int xy\, dA \qquad (9.12)$$

and showed that $I_{xy} = 0$ if the area A is symmetrical with respect to either or both of the coordinate axes. We also derived the *parallel-axis theorem for products of inertia.* We had

$$I_{xy} = \bar{I}_{x'y'} + \bar{x}\bar{y}A \qquad (9.13)$$

where $\bar{I}_{x'y'}$ is the product of inertia of the area with respect to the centroidal axes x' and y' which are parallel to the x and y axes, respectively, and $\bar{x}$ and $\bar{y}$ are the coordinates of the centroid of the area [Sec. 9.8].

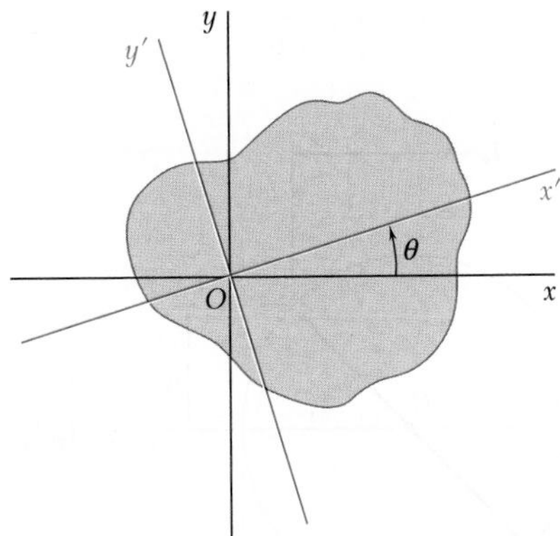

Fig. 9.38

Rotation of axes

In Sec. 9.9 we determined the moments and product of inertia $I_{x'}$, $I_{y'}$, and $I_{x'y'}$ of an area with respect to x' and y' axes obtained by rotating the original x and y coordinate axes through an angle θ counterclockwise (Fig. 9.38). We expressed $I_{x'}$, $I_{y'}$, and $I_{x'y'}$ in terms of the moments and product of inertia I_x, I_y, and I_{xy} computed with respect to the original x and y axes. We had

$$I_{x'} = \frac{I_x + I_y}{2} + \frac{I_x - I_y}{2}\cos 2\theta - I_{xy}\sin 2\theta \qquad (9.18)$$

$$I_{y'} = \frac{I_x + I_y}{2} - \frac{I_x - I_y}{2}\cos 2\theta + I_{xy}\sin 2\theta \qquad (9.19)$$

$$I_{x'y'} = \frac{I_x - I_y}{2}\sin 2\theta + I_{xy}\cos 2\theta \qquad (9.20)$$

Principal axes

The *principal axes of the area about O* were defined as the two axes perpendicular to each other and with respect to which the moments of inertia of the area are maximum and minimum. The corresponding values of θ, denoted by θ_m, were obtained from the formula

$$\tan 2\theta_m = -\frac{2I_{xy}}{I_x - I_y} \qquad (9.25)$$

Principal moments of inertia

The corresponding maximum and minimum values of I are called the *principal moments of inertia* of the area about O; we had

$$I_{\max,\min} = \frac{I_x + I_y}{2} \pm \sqrt{\left(\frac{I_x - I_y}{2}\right)^2 + I_{xy}^2} \qquad (9.27)$$

We also noted that the corresponding value of the product of inertia is zero.

Mohr's circle

The transformation of the moments and product of inertia of an area under a rotation of axes can be represented graphically by drawing *Mohr's circle* [Sec. 9.10]. Given the moments and product of inertia I_x, I_y, and I_{xy} of the area with respect to the x and y

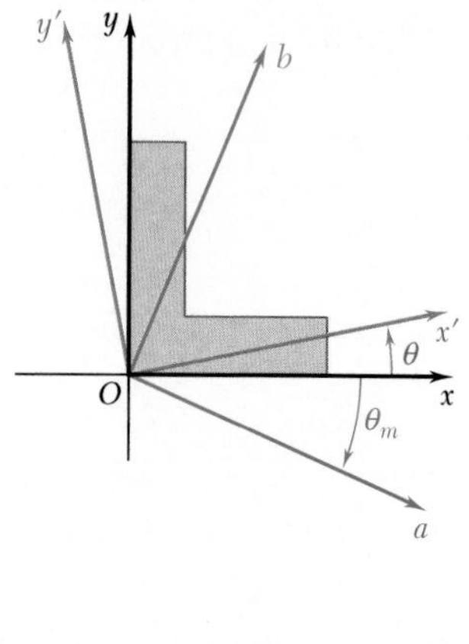

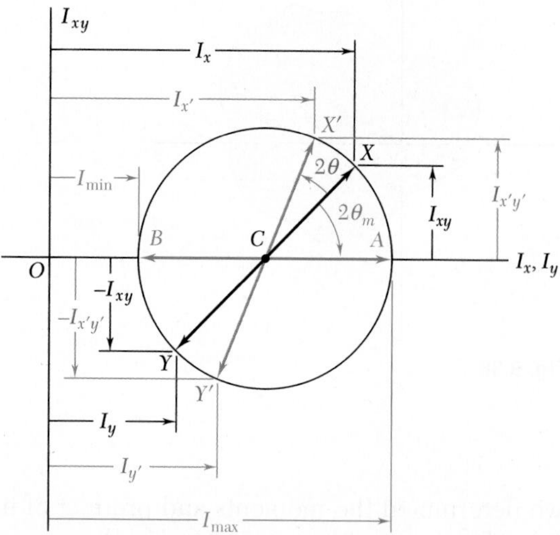

Fig. 9.39

coordinate axes, we plot points X (I_x, I_{xy}) and Y $(I_y, -I_{xy})$ and draw the line joining these two points (Fig. 9.39). This line is a diameter of Mohr's circle and thus defines this circle. As the coordinate axes are rotated through θ, the diameter rotates through *twice that angle,* and the coordinates of X' and Y' yield the new values $I_{x'}$, $I_{y'}$, and $I_{x'y'}$ of the moments and product of inertia of the area. Also, the angle θ_m and the coordinates of points A and B define the principal axes a and b and the principal moments of inertia of the area [Sample Prob. 9.8].

Moments of inertia of masses

The second half of the chapter was devoted to the determination of *moments of inertia of masses,* which are encountered in dynamics in problems involving the rotation of a rigid body about an axis. The mass moment of inertia of a body with respect to an axis AA' (Fig. 9.40) was defined as

$$I = \int r^2\, dm \tag{9.28}$$

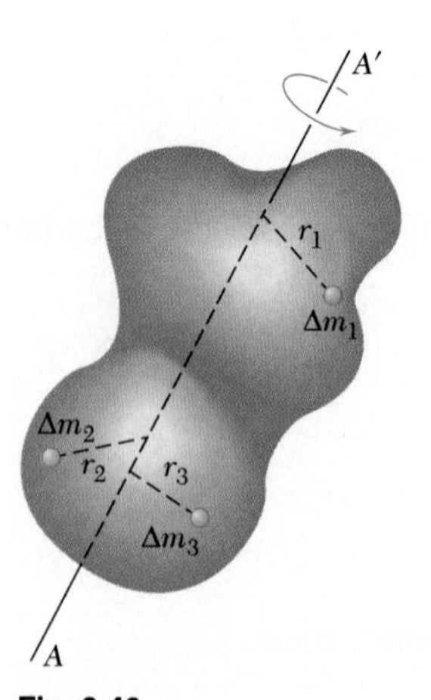

Fig. 9.40

where r is the distance from AA' to the element of mass [Sec. 9.11]. The *radius of gyration* of the body was defined as

$$k = \sqrt{\frac{I}{m}} \tag{9.29}$$

The mass moments of inertia of a body with respect to the coordinate axes were expressed as

$$\begin{aligned} I_x &= \int (y^2 + z^2)\, dm \\ I_y &= \int (z^2 + x^2)\, dm \qquad (9.30) \\ I_z &= \int (x^2 + y^2)\, dm \end{aligned}$$

Parallel-axis theorem

We saw that the *parallel-axis theorem* also applies to mass moments of inertia [Sec. 9.12]. Thus, the mass moment of inertia I of a body with respect to an arbitrary axis AA' (Fig. 9.41) can be expressed as

$$I = \bar{I} + md^2 \tag{9.33}$$

where $\bar{I}$ is the mass moment of inertia of the body with respect to the centroidal axis BB' which is parallel to the axis AA', m is the mass of the body, and d is the distance between the two axes.

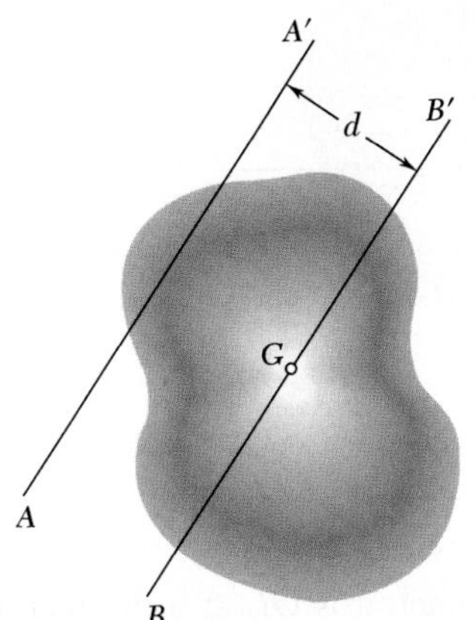

Fig. 9.41

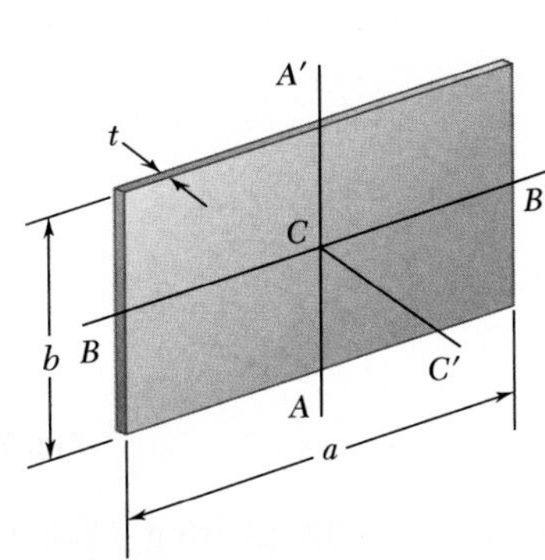

Fig. 9.42

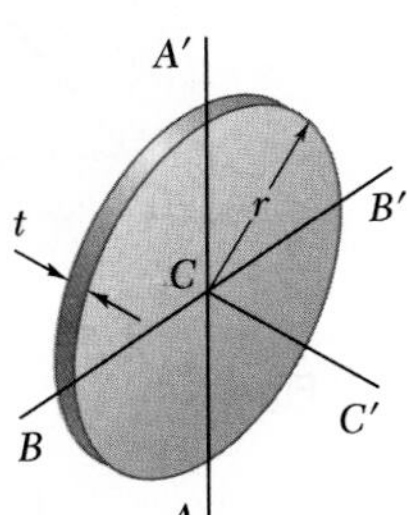

Fig. 9.43

Mass moments of inertia of thin plates

The mass moments of inertia of *thin plates* can be readily obtained from the moments of inertia of their areas [Sec. 9.13]. We found that for a *rectangular plate* the mass moments of inertia with respect to the axes shown (Fig. 9.42) are

$$I_{AA'} = \tfrac{1}{12}ma^2 \qquad I_{BB'} = \tfrac{1}{12}mb^2 \tag{9.39}$$

$$I_{CC'} = I_{AA'} + I_{BB'} = \tfrac{1}{12}m(a^2 + b^2) \tag{9.40}$$

while for a *circular plate* (Fig. 9.43) they are

$$I_{AA'} = I_{BB'} = \tfrac{1}{4}mr^2 \tag{9.41}$$

$$I_{CC'} = I_{AA'} + I_{BB'} = \tfrac{1}{2}mr^2 \tag{9.42}$$

Composite bodies

When a body possesses *two planes of symmetry,* it is usually possible to use a single integration to determine its mass moment of inertia with respect to a given axis by selecting the element of mass dm to be a thin plate [Sample Probs. 9.10 and 9.11]. On the other hand, when a body consists of *several common geometric shapes,* its mass moment of inertia with respect to a given axis can be obtained by using the formulas given in Fig. 9.28 together with the parallel-axis theorem [Sample Probs. 9.12 and 9.13].

Mass moment of inertia with respect to an arbitrary axis

In the last portion of the chapter, we learned to determine the mass moment of inertia of a body *with respect to an arbitrary axis* OL which is drawn through the origin O [Sec. 9.16]. Denoting by

λ_x, λ_y, and λ_z the components of the unit vector $\boldsymbol{\lambda}$ along OL (Fig. 9.44) and introducing the *mass products of inertia*

$$I_{xy} = \int xy\, dm \qquad I_{yz} = \int yz\, dm \qquad I_{zx} = \int zx\, dm \quad (9.45)$$

we found that the mass moment of inertia of the body with respect to OL could be expressed as

$$I_{OL} = I_x\lambda_x^2 + I_y\lambda_y^2 + I_z\lambda_z^2 - 2I_{xy}\lambda_x\lambda_y - 2I_{yz}\lambda_y\lambda_z - 2I_{zx}\lambda_z\lambda_x \quad (9.46)$$

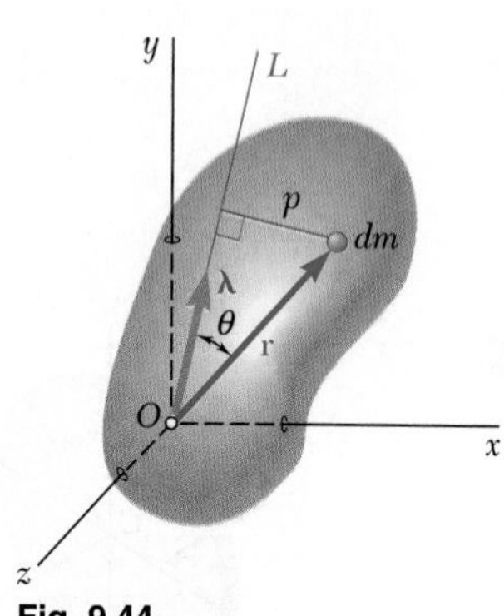

Fig. 9.44

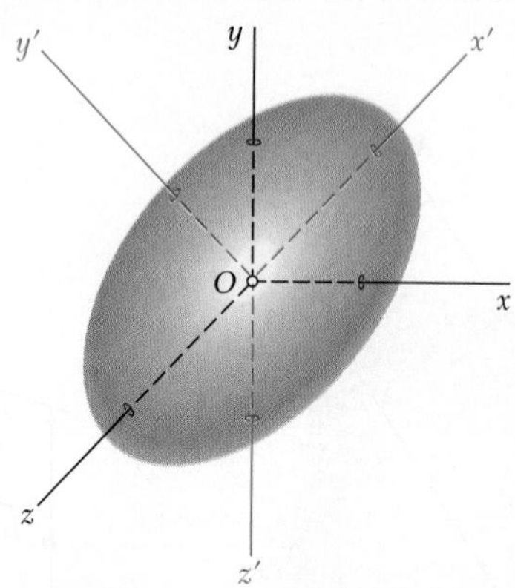

Fig. 9.45

Ellipsoid of inertia

By plotting a point Q along each axis OL at a distance $OQ = 1/\sqrt{I_{OL}}$ from O [Sec. 9.17], we obtained the surface of an ellipsoid, known as the *ellipsoid of inertia* of the body at point O. The principal axes x', y', and z' of this ellipsoid (Fig. 9.45) are the *principal axes of inertia* of the body; that is, the mass products of inertia $I_{x'y'}$, $I_{y'z'}$, and $I_{z'x'}$ of the body with respect to these axes are all zero. There are many situations when the principal axes of inertia of a body can be deduced from properties of symmetry of the body. Choosing these axes to be the coordinate axes, we can then express I_{OL} as

Principal axes of inertia

Principal mass moments of inertia

$$I_{OL} = I_{x'}\lambda_{x'}^2 + I_{y'}\lambda_{y'}^2 + I_{z'}\lambda_{z'}^2 \quad (9.50)$$

where $I_{x'}$, $I_{y'}$, and $I_{z'}$ are the *principal mass moments of inertia* of the body at O.

When the principal axes of inertia cannot be obtained by observation [Sec. 9.17], it is necessary to solve the cubic equation

$$K^3 - (I_x + I_y + I_z)K^2 + (I_xI_y + I_yI_z + I_zI_x - I_{xy}^2 - I_{yz}^2 - I_{zx}^2)K - (I_xI_yI_z - I_xI_{yz}^2 - I_yI_{zx}^2 - I_zI_{xy}^2 - 2I_{xy}I_{yz}I_{zx}) = 0 \quad (9.56)$$

We found [Sec. 9.18] that the roots K_1, K_2, and K_3 of this equation are the principal mass moments of inertia of the given body. The direction cosines $(\lambda_x)_1$, $(\lambda_y)_1$, and $(\lambda_z)_1$ of the principal axis corresponding to the principal mass moment of inertia K_1 are then determined by substituting K_1 into Eqs. (9.54) and solving two of these equations and Eq. (9.57) simultaneously. The same procedure is then repeated using K_2 and K_3 to determine the direction cosines of the other two principal axes [Sample Prob. 9.15].

Review Problems

9.187 Determine by direct integration the moment of inertia of the shaded area with respect to the y axis.

9.188 Determine by direct integration the moment of inertia of the shaded area with respect to the x axis.

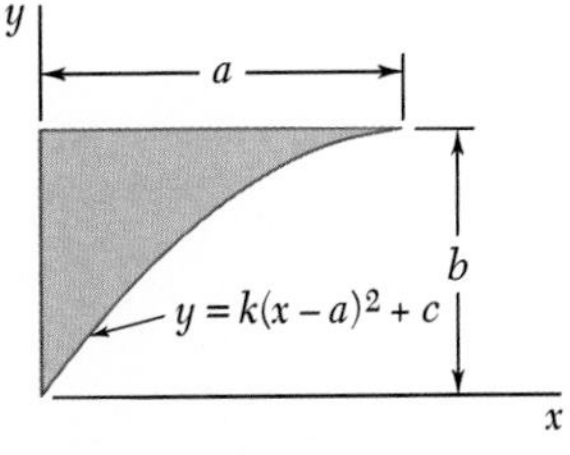

Fig. P9.187 and *P9.188*

9.189 Determine the moment of inertia and the radius of gyration of the shaded area with respect to the x axis.

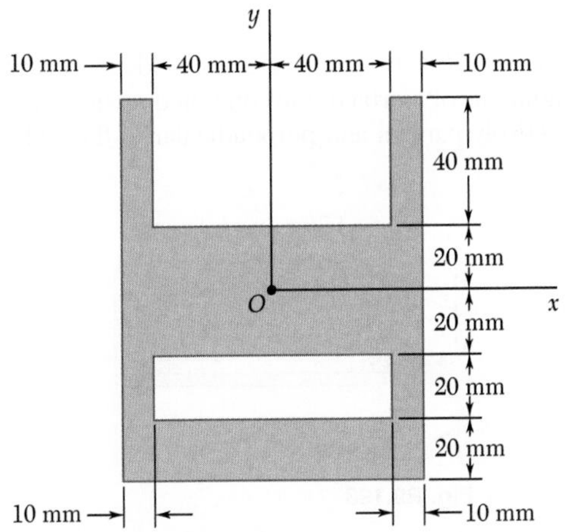

Fig. P9.189 and *P9.190*

9.190 Determine the moment of inertia and the radius of gyration of the shaded area with respect to the y axis.

9.191 Determine the polar moment of inertia of the area shown with respect to (a) point O, (b) the centroid of the area.

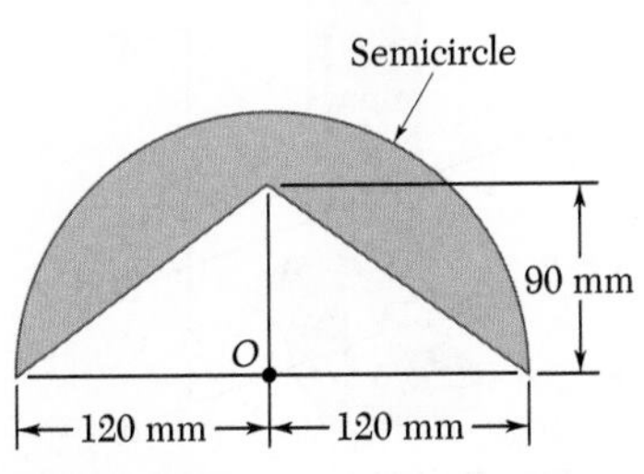

Fig. P9.191

9.192 To form a reinforced box section, two rolled W sections and two plates are welded together. Determine the moments of inertia and the radii of gyration of the combined section with respect to the centroidal axes shown.

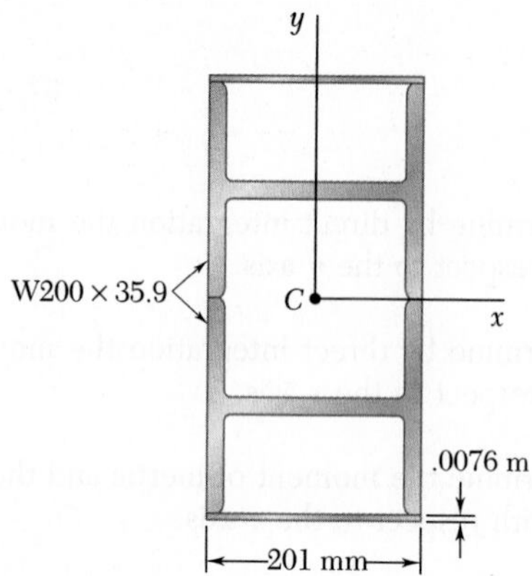

Fig. P9.192

9.193 Two L76 × 76 × 6.4-mm angles are welded to a C250 × 30 channel. Determine the moments of inertia of the combined section with respect to centroidal axes respectively parallel and perpendicular to the web of the channel.

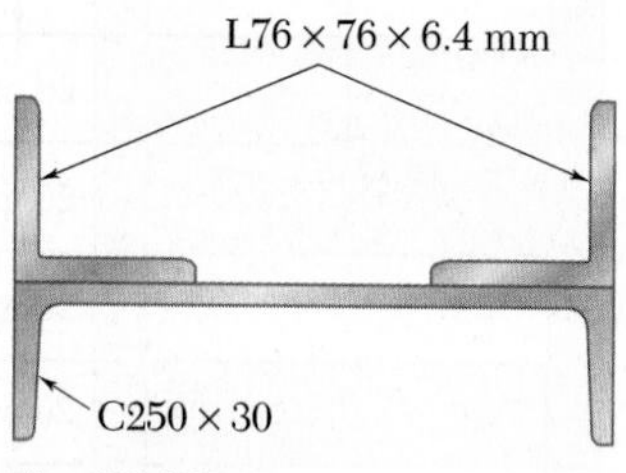

Fig. P9.193

9.194 For the 2-kg connecting rod shown, it has been experimentally determined that the mass moments of inertia of the rod with respect to the centerline axes of the bearings AA' and BB' are $I_{AA'} = 78 \text{ g} \cdot \text{m}^2$ and $I_{BB'} = 41 \text{ g} \cdot \text{m}^2$, respectively. Knowing that $r_a + r_b = 290$ mm, determine (*a*) the location of the centroidal axis GG', (*b*) the radius of gyration with respect to axis GG'.

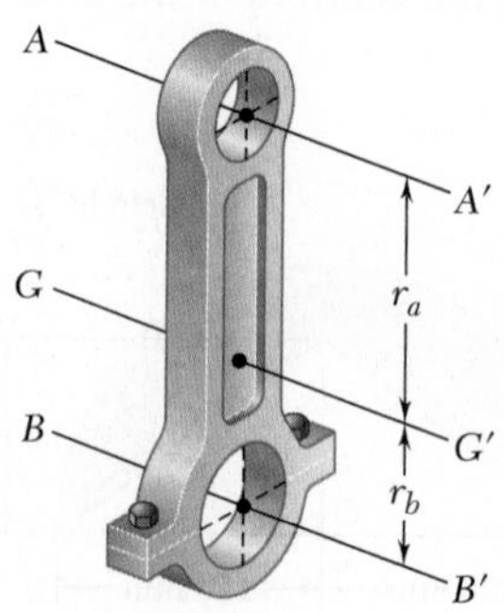

Fig. *P9.194*

9.195 Using the parallel-axis theorem, determine the product of inertia of the area shown with respect to the centroidal x and y axes.

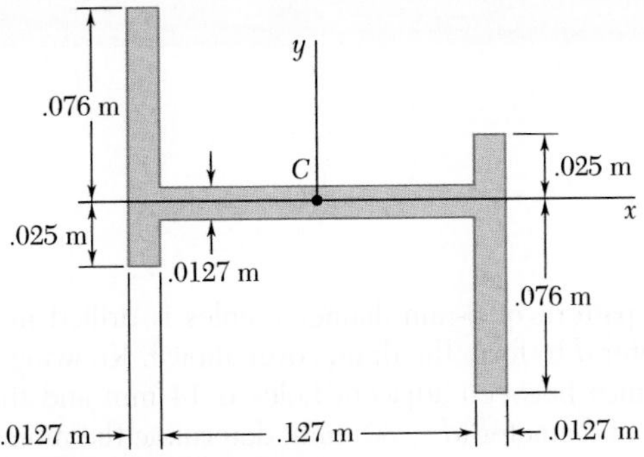

Fig. P9.195 and P9.196

9.196 Using Mohr's circle, determine the orientation of the principal centroidal axes and the corresponding values of the moments of inertia.

9.197 Determine by direct integration the mass moment of inertia with respect to the z axis of the right circular cylinder shown assuming that it has a uniform density and a mass m.

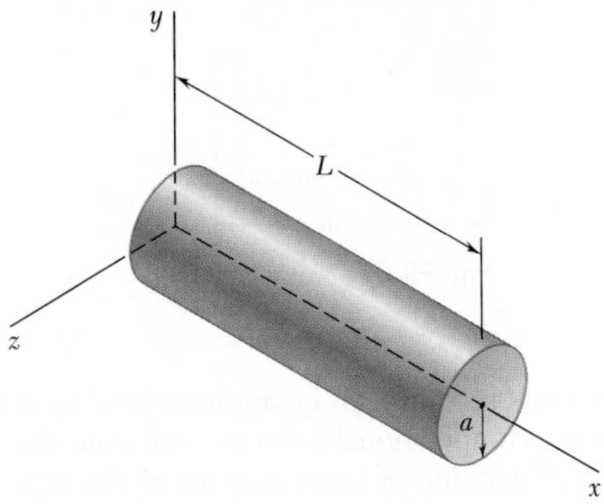

Fig. P9.197

9.198 Determine the mass products of inertia I_{xy}, I_{yz}, and I_{zx} of the steel machine element shown. (The specific weight of steel is 8000 kg/m^3.)

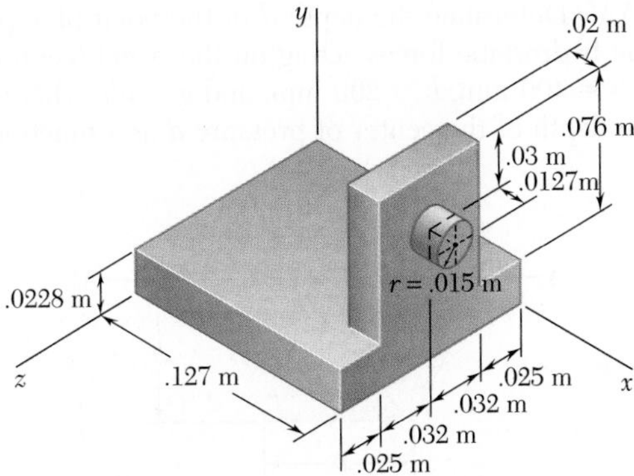

Fig. *P9.198*

Computer Problems

9.C1 A pattern of 6-mm-diameter holes is drilled in a circular steel plate of diameter d to form the drain cover shown. Knowing that the center-to-center distance between adjacent holes is 14 mm and that the holes lie within a circle of diameter $(d - 30)$ mm, determine the moment of inertia of the cover with respect to the x axis when (*a*) $d = 200$ mm, (*b*) $d = 450$ mm, (*c*) $d = 720$ mm.

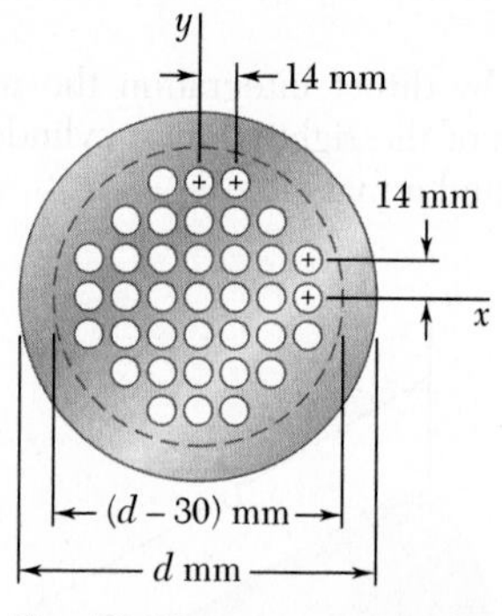

Fig. P9.C1

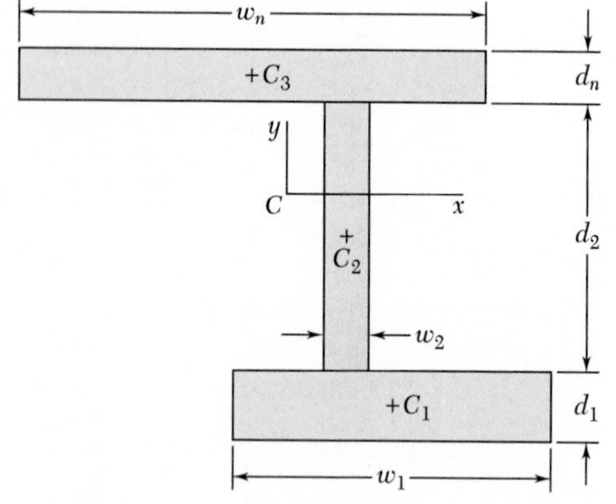

Fig. P9.C2

9.C2 Many cross sections can be approximated by a series of rectangles as shown. Using computational software, calculate the moments of inertia and the radii of gyration of cross sections of this type with respect to horizontal and vertical centroidal axes. Apply the above software to the cross section shown in (*a*) Fig. P9.31 and P9.33, (*b*) Fig. P9.32 and P9.34, (*c*) Fig. P9.41, (*d*) Fig. P9.43.

9.C3 The panel shown forms the end of a trough which is filled with water to line AA'. Determine the depth d of the point of application of the resultant of the hydrostatic forces acting on the panel (center of pressure). Knowing that $h = 400$ mm, $b = 200$ mm, and $a = nb$, where n varies from 1 to 8, plot the depth of the center of pressure d as a function of n.

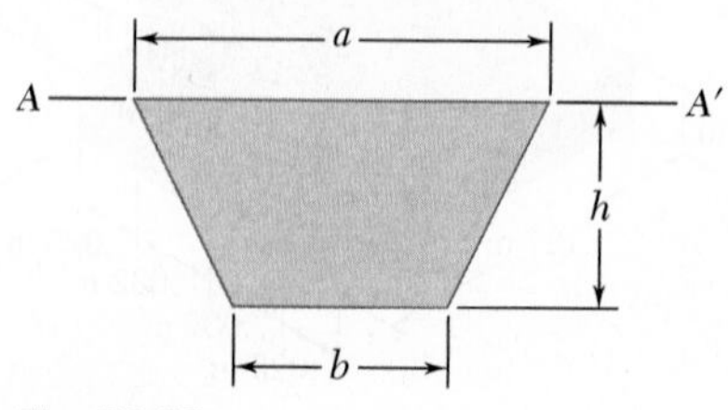

Fig. P9.C3

9.C4 For the area shown, plot I_{xy} as a function of n for values of n from 1 to 10 knowing that $a = 80$ mm and $b = 60$ mm.

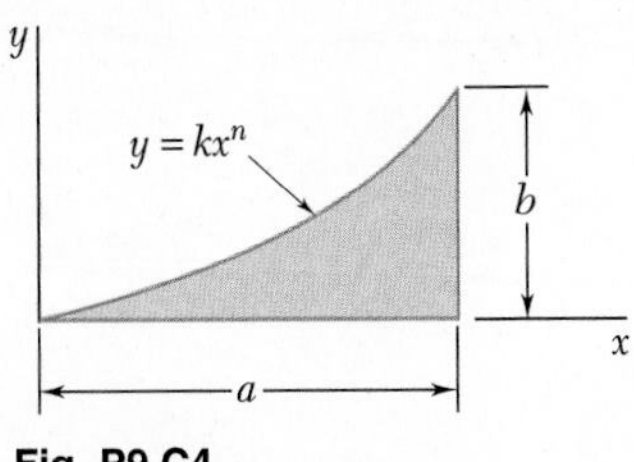

Fig. P9.C4

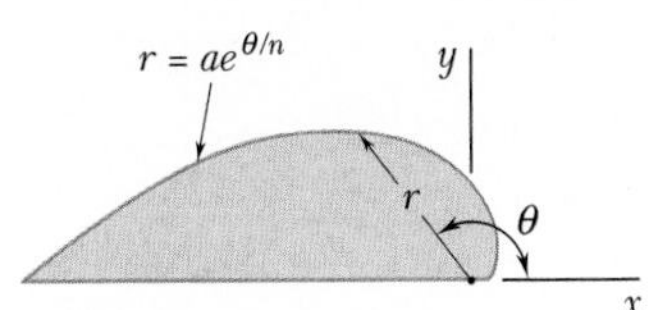

Fig. P9.C5

***9.C5** The area shown is bounded by the logarithmic spiral $r = ae^{\theta/n}$ with $0 \leq \theta \leq \pi$. Using computational software, determine the product of inertia of the area with respect to the x and y axes when $a = 3$ in. and (*a*) $n = 2$, (*b*) $n = 2.5$, (*c*) $n = 4$.

9.C6 An area with known moments and product of inertia I_x, I_y, and I_{xy} can be used to calculate the moments and product of inertia of the area with respect to axes x' and y' obtained by rotating the original axes counterclockwise through an angle θ. Using computational software, compute and plot $I_{x'}$, $I_{y'}$, and $I_{x'y'}$, as functions of θ for $0 \leq \theta \leq 90°$ for the area of Prob. 9.74.

9.C7 A homogeneous wire with a mass per unit length of 0.08 kg/m is used to form the figure shown. Approximating the figure using 10 straight line segments, use computational software to determine the mass moment of inertia I_x of the wire with respect to the x-axis. Using the software, determine I_x when (*a*) $a = 20$ mm, $L = 220$ mm, $h = 80$ mm, (*b*) $a = 40$ mm, $L = 340$ mm, $h = 200$ mm, (*c*) $a = 100$ mm, $L = 500$ mm, $h = 120$ mm.

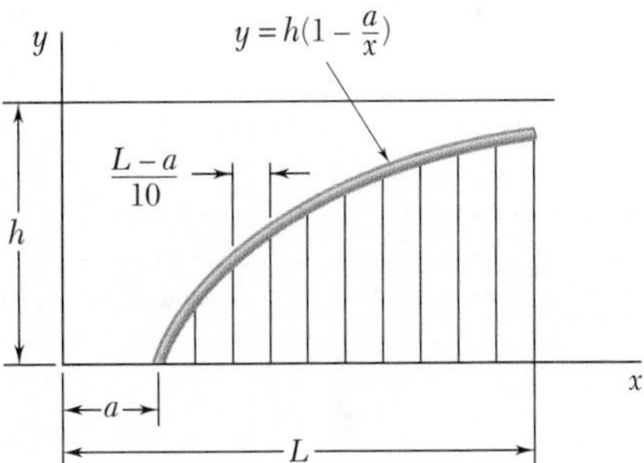

Fig. P9.C7

9.C8 The area shown is revolved about the x-axis to form a homogeneous solid of weight W. Approximating the area using a series of 400 rectangles of the form $bcc'b'$, each of width Δl, use computational software to determine the mass moment of inertia of the solid with respect to the x-axis. Assuming that $W = 16$ N, $a = .127$ m, and $b = .5$ m, use the software to solve (*a*) Prob. 9.121, (*b*) Prob. 9.123.

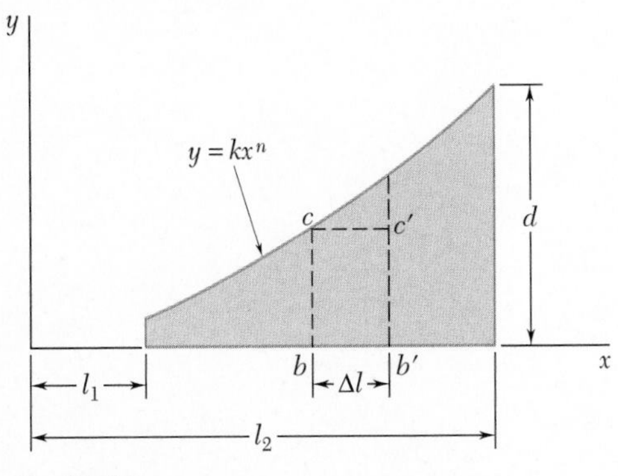

Fig. P9.C8

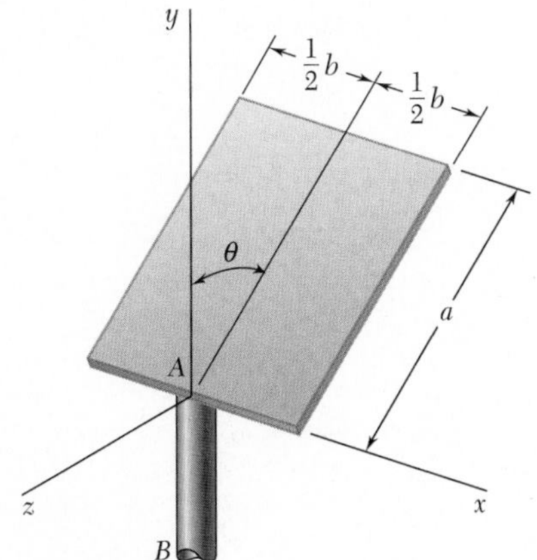

Fig. P9.C9

9.C9 A thin rectangular plate of weight W is welded to a vertical shaft AB with which it forms an angle θ. Knowing that $W = 4$ N, $a = .25$ m, and $b = .2$ m, plot for values of θ from 0 to 90° the mass moment of inertia of the plate with respect to (*a*) the y axis, (*b*) the z axis.

CHAPTER 10

Method of Virtual Work

Using the analytical methods discussed in this chapter, it is easily shown that the force exerted by the hydraulic cylinder to raise and to lower the boom is independent of the workers' location on the platform.

METHOD OF VIRTUAL WORK

*10.1. INTRODUCTION

In the preceding chapters, problems involving the equilibrium of rigid bodies were solved by expressing that the external forces acting on the bodies were balanced. The equations of equilibrium $\Sigma F_x = 0$, $\Sigma F_y = 0$, and $\Sigma M_A = 0$ were written and solved for the desired unknowns. A different method, which will prove more effective for solving certain types of equilibrium problems, will now be considered. This method is based on the *principle of virtual work* and was first formally used by the Swiss mathematician Jean Bernoulli in the eighteenth century.

As you will see in Sec. 10.3, the principle of virtual work states that if a particle or rigid body, or, more generally, a system of connected rigid bodies, which is in equilibrium under various external forces, is given an arbitrary displacement from that position of equilibrium, the total work done by the external forces during the displacement is zero. This principle is particularly effective when applied to the solution of problems involving the equilibrium of machines or mechanisms consisting of several connected members.

In the second part of the chapter, the method of virtual work will be applied in an alternative form based on the concept of *potential energy*. It will be shown in Sec. 10.8 that if a particle, rigid body, or system of rigid bodies is in equilibrium, then the derivative of its potential energy with respect to a variable defining its position must be zero.

In this chapter, you will also learn to evaluate the mechanical efficiency of a machine (Sec. 10.5) and to determine whether a given position of equilibrium is stable, unstable, or neutral (Sec. 10.9).

*10.2. WORK OF A FORCE

Let us first define the terms *displacement* and *work* as they are used in mechanics. Consider a particle which moves from a point A to a neighboring point A' (Fig. 10.1). If $\mathbf{r}$ denotes the position vector corresponding to point A, the small vector joining A and A' may be denoted by the differential $d\mathbf{r}$; the vector $d\mathbf{r}$ is called the *displacement* of the particle. Now let us assume that a force $\mathbf{F}$ is acting on the particle. The *work of the force* $\mathbf{F}$ *corresponding to the displacement* $d\mathbf{r}$ is defined as the quantity

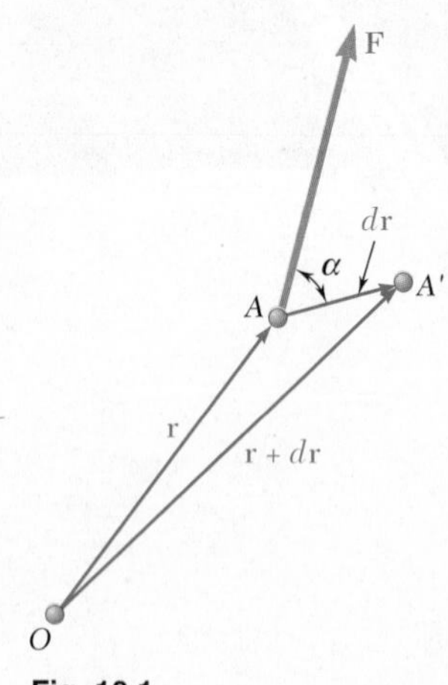

Fig. 10.1

$$dU = \mathbf{F} \cdot d\mathbf{r} \tag{10.1}$$

obtained by forming the scalar product of the force $\mathbf{F}$ and the displacement $d\mathbf{r}$. Denoting respectively by F and ds the magnitudes of the force and of the displacement, and by α the angle formed by $\mathbf{F}$ and $d\mathbf{r}$, and recalling the definition of the scalar product of two vectors (Sec. 3.9), we write

$$dU = F\,ds \cos \alpha \tag{10.1'}$$

Being a *scalar quantity*, work has a magnitude and a sign, but no direction. We also note that work should be expressed in units obtained by multiplying units of length by units of force. Thus, if U.S. customary units are used, work should be expressed in ft · lb or in · lb. If SI units are used, work should be expressed in N · m. The unit of work N · m is called a *joule* (J).†

It follows from Eq. (10.1′) that the work dU is positive if the angle α is acute and negative if α is obtuse. Three particular cases are of special interest. If the force **F** has the same direction as $d\mathbf{r}$, the work dU reduces to $F\,ds$. If **F** has a direction opposite to that of $d\mathbf{r}$, the work is $dU = -F\,ds$. Finally, if **F** is perpendicular to $d\mathbf{r}$, the work dU is zero.

The work dU of a force **F** during a displacement $d\mathbf{r}$ can also be considered as the product of F and the component $ds \cos \alpha$ of the displacement $d\mathbf{r}$ along **F** (Fig. 10.2*a*). This view is particularly useful

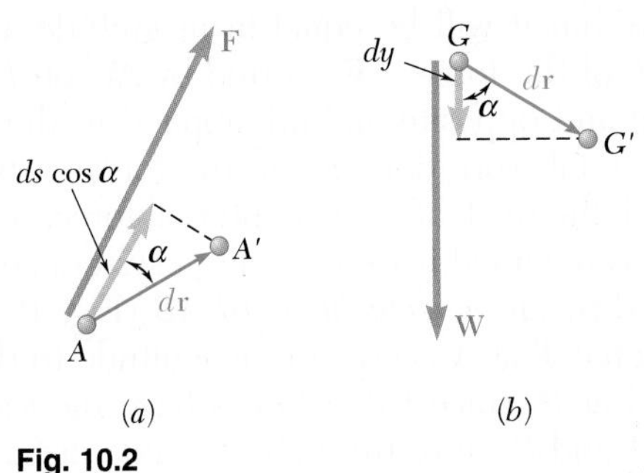

Fig. 10.2

Photo 10.1 The forces exerted by the hydraulic cylinders to position the bucket lift shown can be effectively determined using the method of virtual work since a simple relation exists among the displacements of the points of application of the forces acting on the members of the lift.

in the computation of the work done by the weight **W** of a body (Fig. 10.2*b*). The work of **W** is equal to the product of W and the vertical displacement dy of the center of gravity G of the body. If the displacement is downward, the work is positive; if it is upward, the work is negative.

A number of forces frequently encountered in statics *do no work:* forces applied to fixed points ($ds = 0$) or acting in a direction perpendicular to the displacement ($\cos \alpha = 0$). Among these forces are the reaction at a frictionless pin when the body supported rotates about the pin; the reaction at a frictionless surface when the body in contact moves along the surface; the reaction at a roller moving along its track; the weight of a body when its center of gravity moves horizontally; and the friction force acting on a wheel rolling without slipping (since at any instant the point of contact does not move). Examples of forces which *do work* are the weight of a body (except in the case considered above), the friction force acting on a body sliding on a rough surface, and most forces applied to a moving body.

†The joule is the SI unit of *energy*, whether in mechanical form (work, potential energy, kinetic energy) or in chemical, electrical, or thermal form. We should note that even though N · m = J, the moment of a force must be expressed in N · m, and not in joules, since the moment of a force is not a form of energy.

In certain cases, the sum of the work done by several forces is zero. Consider, for example, two rigid bodies AC and BC connected at C by a *frictionless pin* (Fig. 10.3*a*). Among the forces acting on AC is the force $\mathbf{F}$ exerted at C by BC. In general, the work of this force

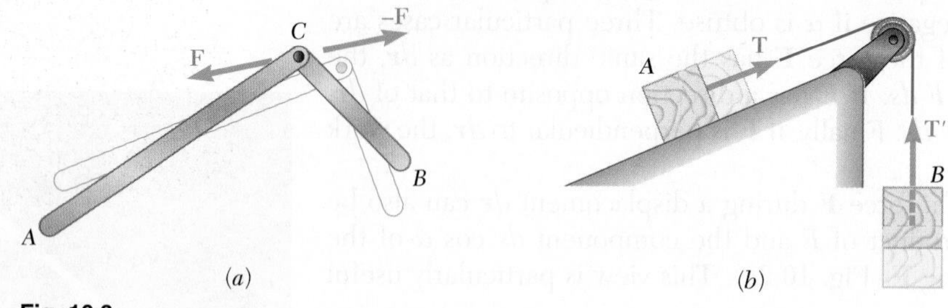

Fig. 10.3

will not be zero, but it will be equal in magnitude and opposite in sign to the work of the force $-\mathbf{F}$ exerted by AC on BC, since these forces are equal and opposite and are applied to the same particle. Thus, when the total work done by all the forces acting on AB and BC is considered, the work of the two internal forces at C cancels out. A similar result is obtained if we consider a system consisting of two blocks connected by an *inextensible cord AB* (Fig. 10.3*b*). The work of the tension force $\mathbf{T}$ at A is equal in magnitude to the work of the tension force $\mathbf{T}'$ at B, since these forces have the same magnitude and the points A and B move through the same distance; but in one case the work is positive, and in the other it is negative. Thus, the work of the internal forces again cancels out.

It can be shown that the total work of the internal forces holding together the particles of a rigid body is zero. Consider two particles A and B of a rigid body and the two equal and opposite forces $\mathbf{F}$ and $-\mathbf{F}$ they exert on each other (Fig. 10.4). While, in general, small dis-

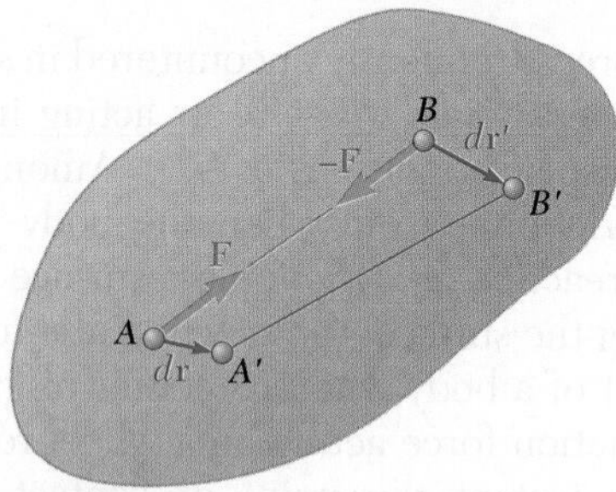

Fig. 10.4

placements $d\mathbf{r}$ and $d\mathbf{r}'$ of the two particles are different, the components of these displacements along AB must be equal; otherwise, the particles would not remain at the same distance from each other, and the body would not be rigid. Therefore, the work of $\mathbf{F}$ is equal in magnitude and opposite in sign to the work of $-\mathbf{F}$, and their sum is zero.

In computing the work of the external forces acting on a rigid body, it is often convenient to determine the work of a couple without considering separately the work of each of the two forces forming the couple. Consider the two forces $\mathbf{F}$ and $-\mathbf{F}$ forming a couple of moment $\mathbf{M}$ and acting on a rigid body (Fig. 10.5). Any small displacement of the rigid body bringing A and B, respectively, into A' and B'' can be divided into two parts, one in which points A and B undergo equal displacements $d\mathbf{r}_1$, the other in which A' remains fixed while B' moves into B'' through a displacement $d\mathbf{r}_2$ of magnitude $ds_2 = r\,d\theta$. In the first part of the motion, the work of $\mathbf{F}$ is equal in magnitude and opposite in sign to the work of $-\mathbf{F}$, and their sum is zero. In the second part of the motion, only force $\mathbf{F}$ does work, and its work is $dU = F\,ds_2 = Fr\,d\theta$. But the product Fr is equal to the magnitude M of the moment of the couple. Thus, the work of a couple of moment $\mathbf{M}$ acting on a rigid body is

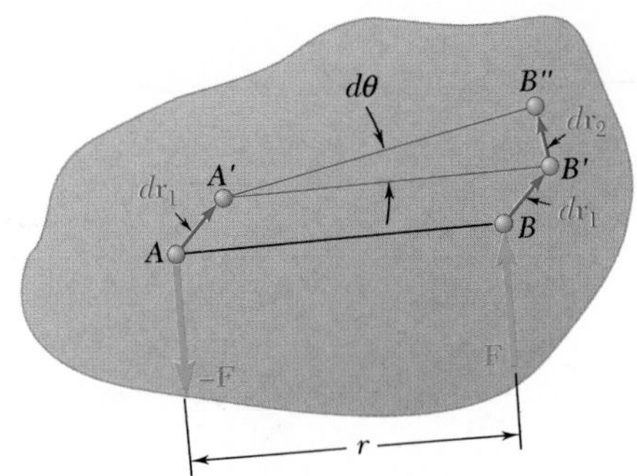

Fig. 10.5

$$dU = M\,d\theta \tag{10.2}$$

where $d\theta$ is the small angle expressed in radians through which the body rotates. We again note that work should be expressed in units obtained by multiplying units of force by units of length.

*10.3. PRINCIPLE OF VIRTUAL WORK

Consider a particle acted upon by several forces $\mathbf{F}_1, \mathbf{F}_2, \ldots, \mathbf{F}_n$ (Fig. 10.6). We can imagine that the particle undergoes a small displacement from A to A'. This displacement is possible, but it will not necessarily take place. The forces may be balanced and the particle at rest, or the particle may move under the action of the given forces in a direction different from that of AA'. Since the displacement considered does not actually occur, it is called a *virtual displacement* and is denoted by $\delta\mathbf{r}$. The symbol $\delta\mathbf{r}$ represents a differential of the first order; it is used to distinguish the virtual displacement from the displacement $d\mathbf{r}$ which would take place under actual motion. As you will see, virtual displacements can be used to determine whether the conditions of equilibrium of a particle are satisfied.

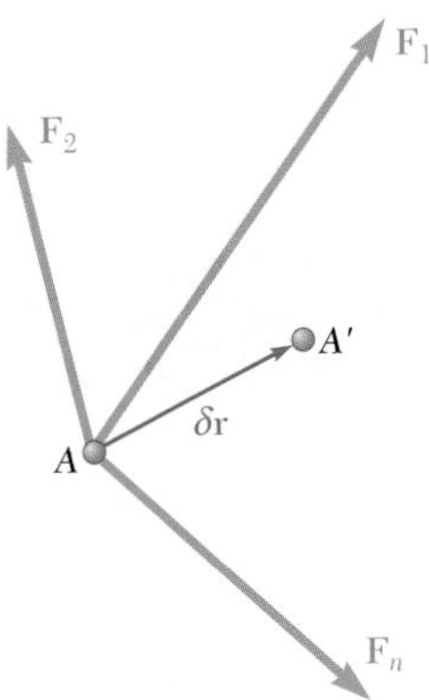

Fig. 10.6

The work of each of the forces $\mathbf{F}_1, \mathbf{F}_2, \ldots, \mathbf{F}_n$ during the virtual displacement $\delta\mathbf{r}$ is called *virtual work*. The virtual work of all the forces acting on the particle of Fig. 10.6 is

$$\begin{aligned}\delta U &= \mathbf{F}_1 \cdot \delta\mathbf{r} + \mathbf{F}_2 \cdot \delta\mathbf{r} + \cdots + \mathbf{F}_n \cdot \delta\mathbf{r} \\ &= (\mathbf{F}_1 + \mathbf{F}_2 + \cdots + \mathbf{F}_n) \cdot \delta\mathbf{r}\end{aligned}$$

or

$$\delta U = \mathbf{R} \cdot \delta\mathbf{r} \tag{10.3}$$

where $\mathbf{R}$ is the resultant of the given forces. Thus, the total virtual work of the forces $\mathbf{F}_1, \mathbf{F}_2, \ldots, \mathbf{F}_n$ is equal to the virtual work of their resultant $\mathbf{R}$.

The principle of virtual work for a particle states that *if a particle is in equilibrium, the total virtual work of the forces acting on the particle is zero for any virtual displacement of the particle*. This condition is necessary: if the particle is in equilibrium, the resultant $\mathbf{R}$ of the forces is zero, and it follows from Eq. (10.3) that the total virtual work δU is zero. The condition is also sufficient: if the total virtual work δU is zero for any virtual displacement, the scalar product $\mathbf{R} \cdot \delta\mathbf{r}$ is zero for any $\delta\mathbf{r}$, and the resultant $\mathbf{R}$ must be zero.

In the case of a rigid body, the principle of virtual work states that *if a rigid body is in equilibrium, the total virtual work of the external forces acting on the rigid body is zero for any virtual displacement of the body*. The condition is necessary: if the body is in equilibrium, all the particles forming the body are in equilibrium and the total virtual work of the forces acting on all the particles must be zero; but we have seen in the preceding section that the total work of the internal forces is zero; the total work of the external forces must therefore also be zero. The condition can also be proved to be sufficient.

The principle of virtual work can be extended to the case of a *system of connected rigid bodies*. If the system remains connected during the virtual displacement, *only the work of the forces external to the system need be considered*, since the total work of the internal forces at the various connections is zero.

*10.4. APPLICATIONS OF THE PRINCIPLE OF VIRTUAL WORK

The principle of virtual work is particularly effective when applied to the solution of problems involving machines or mechanisms consisting of several connected rigid bodies. Consider, for instance, the toggle vise ACB of Fig. 10.7a, used to compress a wooden block. We

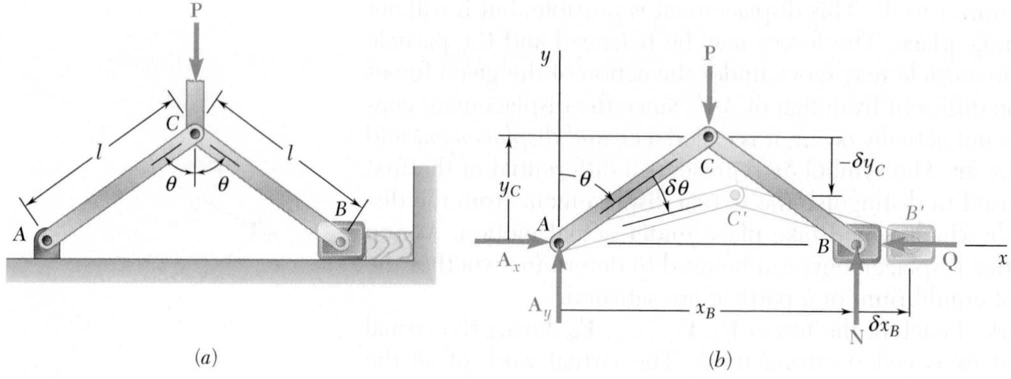

Fig. 10.7

wish to determine the force exerted by the vise on the block when a given force **P** is applied at C assuming that there is no friction. Denoting by **Q** the reaction of the block on the vise, we draw the free-body diagram of the vise and consider the virtual displacement obtained by giving a positive increment $\delta\theta$ to the angle θ (Fig. 10.7b). Choosing a system of coordinate axes with origin at A, we note that x_B increases while y_C decreases. This is indicated in the figure, where a positive increment δx_B and a negative increment $-\delta y_C$ are shown. The reactions $\mathbf{A}_x$, $\mathbf{A}_y$, and **N** will do no work during the virtual displacement considered, and we need only compute the work of **P** and **Q**. Since **Q** and δx_B have opposite senses, the virtual work of **Q** is $\delta U_Q = -Q\ \delta x_B$. Since **P** and the increment shown $(-\delta y_C)$ have the same sense, the virtual work of **P** is $\delta U_P = +P(-\delta y_C) = -P\ \delta y_C$. The minus signs obtained could have been predicted by simply noting that the forces **Q** and **P** are directed opposite to the positive x and y axes, respectively. Expressing the coordinates x_B and y_C in terms of the angle θ and differentiating, we obtain

$$\begin{aligned} x_B &= 2l \sin \theta & \qquad y_C &= l \cos \theta \\ \delta x_B &= 2l \cos \theta \ \delta\theta & \qquad \delta y_C &= -l \sin \theta \ \delta\theta \end{aligned} \tag{10.4}$$

The total virtual work of the forces **Q** and **P** is thus

$$\begin{aligned} \delta U = \delta U_Q + \delta U_P &= -Q \ \delta x_B - P \ \delta y_C \\ &= -2Ql \cos \theta \ \delta\theta + Pl \sin \theta \ \delta\theta \end{aligned}$$

Setting $\delta U = 0$, we obtain

$$2Ql \cos \theta \ \delta\theta = Pl \sin \theta \ \delta\theta \tag{10.5}$$

$$Q = \tfrac{1}{2} P \tan \theta \tag{10.6}$$

The superiority of the method of virtual work over the conventional equilibrium equations in the problem considered here is clear: by using the method of virtual work, we were able to eliminate all unknown reactions, while the equation $\Sigma M_A = 0$ would have eliminated only two of the unknown reactions. This property of the method of virtual work can be used in solving many problems involving machines and mechanisms. *If the virtual displacement considered is consistent with the constraints imposed by the supports and connections, all reactions and internal forces are eliminated and only the work of the loads, applied forces, and friction forces need be considered.*

The method of virtual work can also be used to solve problems involving completely constrained structures, although the virtual displacements considered will never actually take place. Consider, for example, the frame ACB shown in Fig. 10.8*a*. If point A is kept fixed, while B is given a horizontal virtual displacement (Fig. 10.8*b*), we need consider only the work of **P** and $\mathbf{B}_x$. We can thus determine the

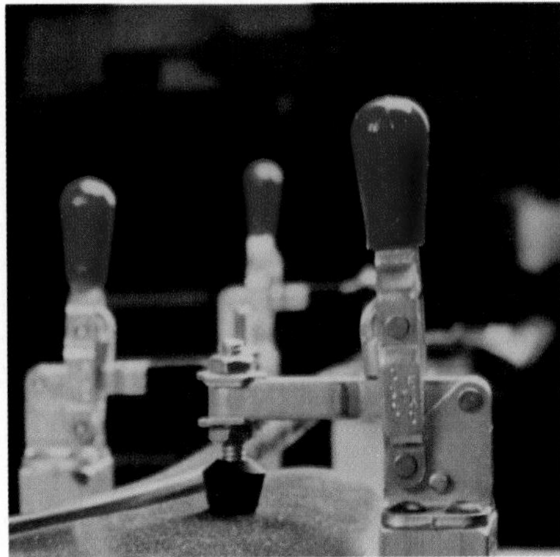

Photo 10.2 The clamping force of the toggle clamp shown can be expressed as a function of the force applied to the handle by first establishing the geometric relations among the members of the clamp and then applying the method of virtual work.

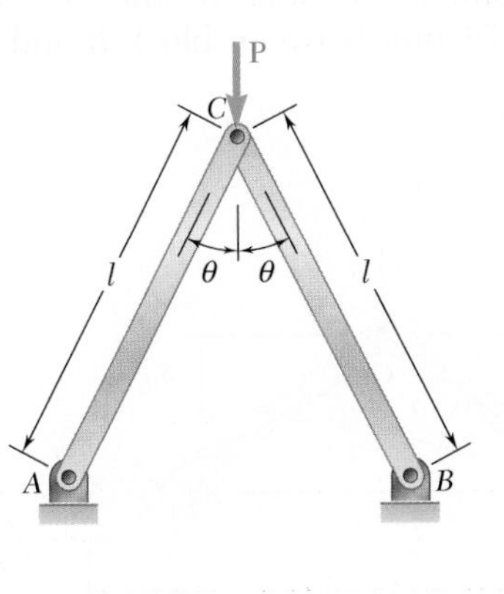

(*a*)

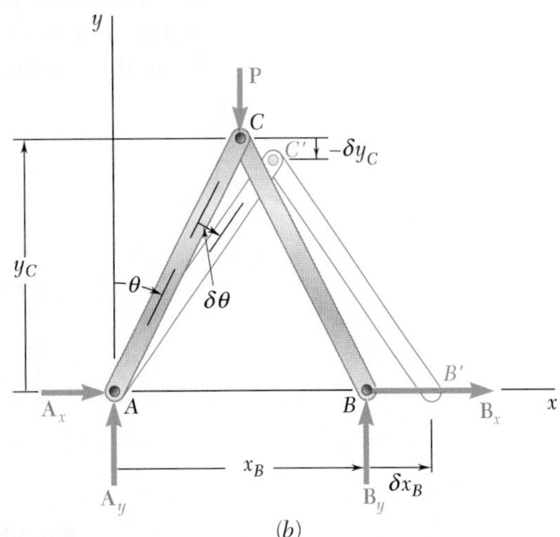

(*b*)

Fig. 10.8

reaction component $\mathbf{B}_x$ in the same way as the force $\mathbf{Q}$ of the preceding example (Fig. 10.7*b*); we have

$$B_x = -\tfrac{1}{2}P \tan \theta$$

Keeping B fixed and giving to A a horizontal virtual displacement, we can similarly determine the reaction component $\mathbf{A}_x$. The components $\mathbf{A}_y$ and $\mathbf{B}_y$ can be determined by rotating the frame ACB as a rigid body about B and A, respectively.

The method of virtual work can also be used to determine the configuration of a system in equilibrium under given forces. For example, the value of the angle θ for which the linkage of Fig. 10.7 is in equilibrium under two given forces $\mathbf{P}$ and $\mathbf{Q}$ can be obtained by solving Eq. (10.6) for $\tan \theta$.

It should be noted, however, that the attractiveness of the method of virtual work depends to a large extent upon the existence of simple geometric relations among the various virtual displacements involved in the solution of a given problem. When no such simple relations exist, it is usually advisable to revert to the conventional method of Chap. 6.

*10.5. REAL MACHINES. MECHANICAL EFFICIENCY

In analyzing the toggle vise in the preceding section, we assumed that no friction forces were involved. Thus, the virtual work consisted only of the work of the applied force $\mathbf{P}$ and of the reaction $\mathbf{Q}$. But the work of the reaction $\mathbf{Q}$ is equal in magnitude and opposite in sign to the work of the force exerted by the vise on the block. Equation (10.5), therefore, expresses that the *output work* $2Ql \cos \theta \, \delta\theta$ is equal to the *input work* $Pl \sin \theta \, \delta\theta$. A machine in which input and output work are equal is said to be an "ideal" machine. In a "real" machine, friction forces will always do some work, and the output work will be smaller than the input work.

Consider, for example, the toggle vise of Fig. 10.7*a*, and assume now that a friction force $\mathbf{F}$ develops between the sliding block B and the horizontal plane (Fig. 10.9). Using the conventional methods of statics and summing moments about A, we find $N = P/2$. Denoting by μ the coefficient of friction between block B and the horizontal

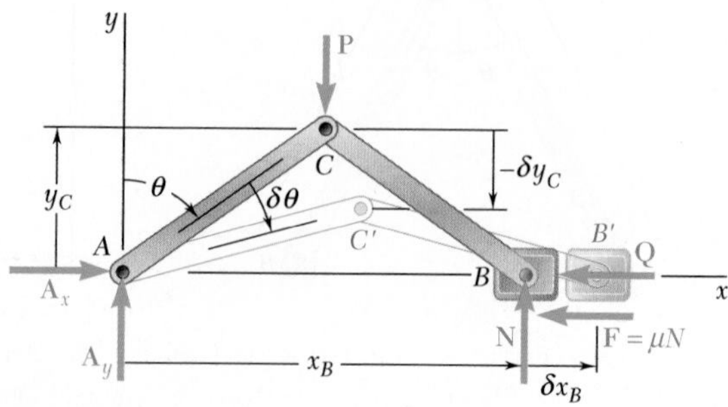

Fig. 10.9

plane, we have $F = \mu N = \mu P/2$. Recalling formulas (10.4), we find that the total virtual work of the forces **Q**, **P**, and **F** during the virtual displacement shown in Fig. 10.9 is

$$\begin{aligned} \delta U &= -Q\,\delta x_B - P\,\delta y_C - F\,\delta x_B \\ &= -2Ql\cos\theta\,\delta\theta + Pl\sin\theta\,\delta\theta - \mu Pl\cos\theta\,\delta\theta \end{aligned}$$

Setting $\delta U = 0$, we obtain

$$2Ql\cos\theta\,\delta\theta = Pl\sin\theta\,\delta\theta - \mu Pl\cos\theta\,\delta\theta \tag{10.7}$$

which expresses that the output work is equal to the input work minus the work of the friction force. Solving for Q, we have

$$Q = \tfrac{1}{2}P(\tan\theta - \mu) \tag{10.8}$$

We note that $Q = 0$ when $\tan\theta = \mu$, that is, when θ is equal to the angle of friction ϕ, and that $Q < 0$ when $\theta < \phi$. The toggle vise may thus be used only for values of θ larger than the angle of friction.

The *mechanical efficiency* of a machine is defined as the ratio

$$\eta = \frac{\text{output work}}{\text{input work}} \tag{10.9}$$

Clearly, the mechanical efficiency of an ideal machine is $\eta = 1$, since input and output work are then equal, while the mechanical efficiency of a real machine will always be less than 1.

In the case of the toggle vise we have just analyzed, we write

$$\eta = \frac{\text{output work}}{\text{input work}} = \frac{2Ql\cos\theta\,\delta\theta}{Pl\sin\theta\,\delta\theta}$$

Substituting from Eq. (10.8) for Q, we obtain

$$\eta = \frac{P(\tan\theta - \mu)l\cos\theta\,\delta\theta}{Pl\sin\theta\,\delta\theta} = 1 - \mu\cot\theta \tag{10.10}$$

We check that in the absence of friction forces, we would have $\mu = 0$ and $\eta = 1$. In the general case, when μ is different from zero, the efficiency η becomes zero for $\mu\cot\theta = 1$, that is, for $\tan\theta = \mu$, or $\theta = \tan^{-1}\mu = \phi$. We note again that the toggle vise can be used only for values of θ larger than the angle of friction ϕ.

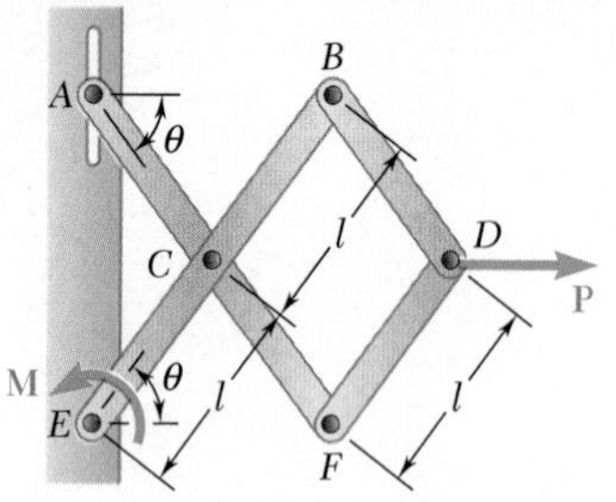

SAMPLE PROBLEM 10.1

Using the method of virtual work, determine the magnitude of the couple **M** required to maintain the equilibrium of the mechanism shown.

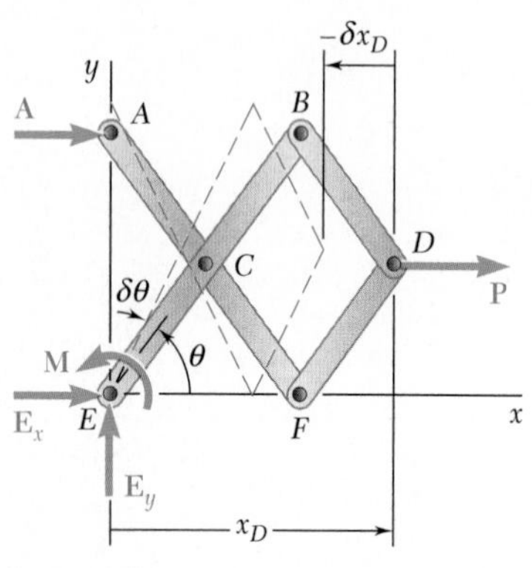

SOLUTION

Choosing a coordinate system with origin at E, we write

$$x_D = 3l \cos \theta \qquad \delta x_D = -3l \sin \theta \, \delta\theta$$

Principle of Virtual Work. Since the reactions **A**, $\mathbf{E}_x$, and $\mathbf{E}_y$ will do no work during the virtual displacement, the total virtual work done by **M** and **P** must be zero. Noting that **P** acts in the positive x direction and **M** acts in the positive θ direction, we write

$$\delta U = 0: \qquad +M\,\delta\theta + P\,\delta x_D = 0$$

$$+M\,\delta\theta + P(-3l \sin \theta \, \delta\theta) = 0$$

$$M = 3Pl \sin \theta \quad ◀$$

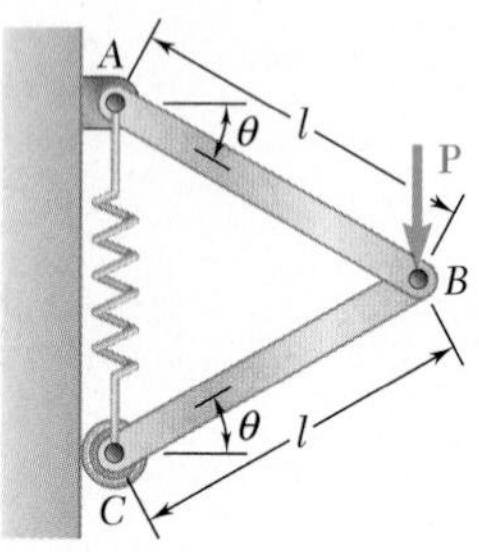

SAMPLE PROBLEM 10.2

Determine the expressions for θ and for the tension in the spring which correspond to the equilibrium position of the mechanism. The unstretched length of the spring is h, and the constant of the spring is k. Neglect the weight of the mechanism.

SOLUTION

With the coordinate system shown

$$y_B = l \sin \theta \qquad y_C = 2l \sin \theta$$

$$\delta y_B = l \cos \theta \, \delta\theta \qquad \delta y_C = 2l \cos \theta \, \delta\theta$$

The elongation of the spring is

$$s = y_C - h = 2l \sin \theta - h$$

The magnitude of the force exerted at C by the spring is

$$F = ks = k(2l \sin \theta - h) \qquad (1)$$

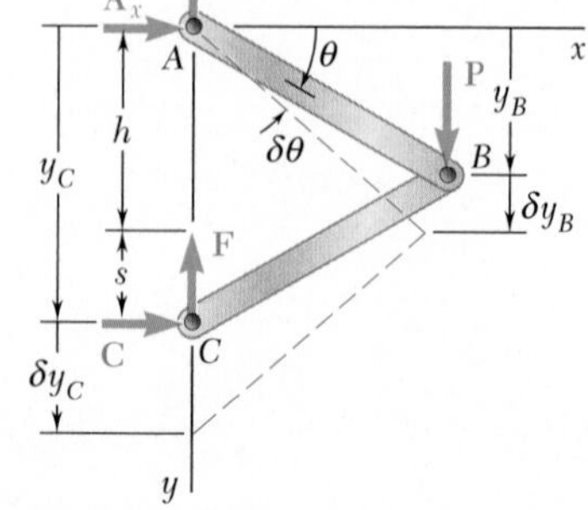

Principle of Virtual Work. Since the reactions $\mathbf{A}_x$, $\mathbf{A}_y$, and **C** do no work, the total virtual work done by **P** and **F** must be zero.

$$\delta U = 0: \qquad P\,\delta y_B - F\,\delta y_C = 0$$

$$P(l \cos \theta \, \delta\theta) - k(2l \sin \theta - h)(2l \cos \theta \, \delta\theta) = 0$$

$$\sin \theta = \frac{P + 2kh}{4kl} \quad ◀$$

Substituting this expression into Eq. (1), we obtain

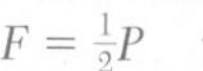
$$F = \tfrac{1}{2}P \quad ◀$$

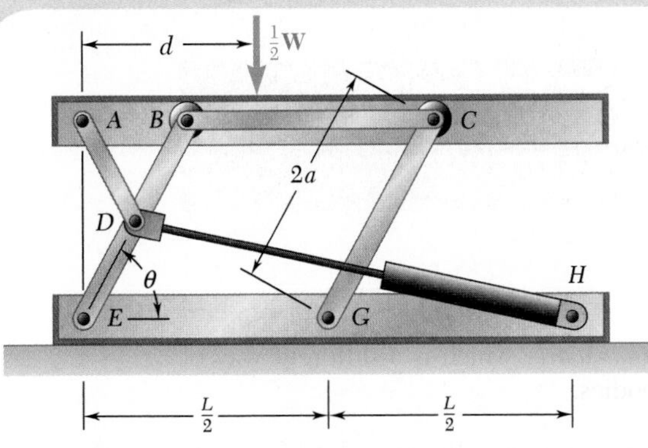

SAMPLE PROBLEM 10.3

A hydraulic-lift table is used to raise a 1000-kg crate. It consists of a platform and of two identical linkages on which hydraulic cylinders exert equal forces. (Only one linkage and one cylinder are shown.) Members EDB and CG are each of length $2a$, and member AD is pinned to the midpoint of EDB. If the crate is placed on the table, so that half of its weight is supported by the system shown, determine the force exerted by each cylinder in raising the crate for $\theta = 60°$, $a = 0.70$ m, and $L = 3.20$ m. This mechanism has been previously considered in Sample Prob. 6.7.

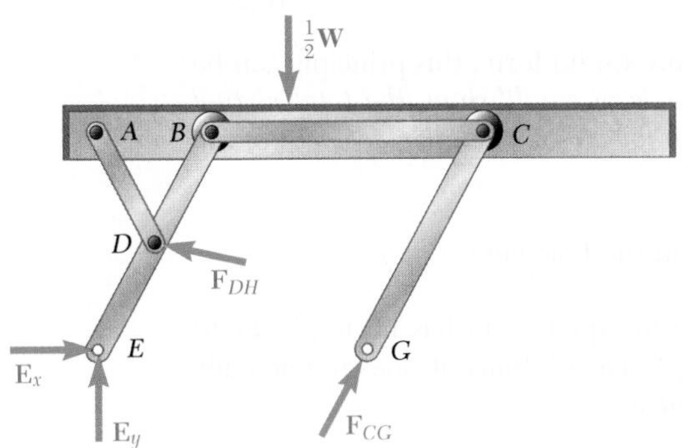

SOLUTION

The machine considered consists of the platform and of the linkage, with an input force $\mathbf{F}_{DH}$ exerted by the cylinder and an output force equal and opposite to $\frac{1}{2}\mathbf{W}$.

Principle of Virtual Work. We first observe that the reactions at E and G do no work. Denoting by y the elevation of the platform above the base, and by s the length DH of the cylinder-and-piston assembly, we write

$$\delta U = 0: \qquad -\tfrac{1}{2}W\,\delta y + F_{DH}\,\delta s = 0 \qquad (1)$$

The vertical displacement δy of the platform is expressed in terms of the angular displacement $\delta\theta$ of EDB as follows:

$$y = (EB)\sin\theta = 2a\sin\theta$$
$$\delta y = 2a\cos\theta\,\delta\theta$$

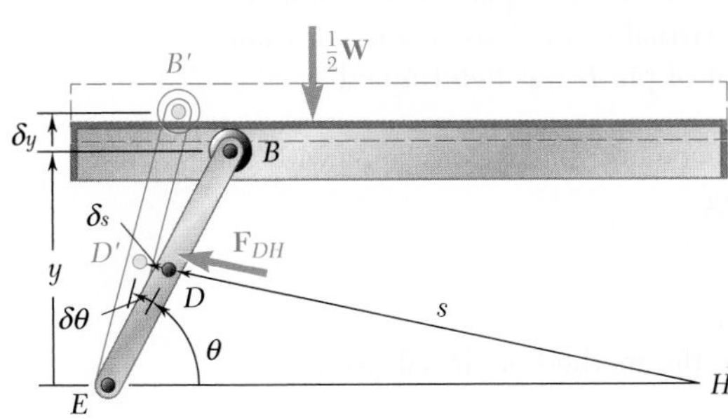

To express δs similarly in terms of $\delta\theta$, we first note that by the law of cosines,

$$s^2 = a^2 + L^2 - 2aL\cos\theta$$

Differentiating,

$$2s\,\delta s = -2aL(-\sin\theta)\,\delta\theta$$
$$\delta s = \frac{aL\sin\theta}{s}\,\delta\theta$$

Substituting for δy and δs into Eq. (1), we write

$$(-\tfrac{1}{2}W)2a\cos\theta\,\delta\theta + F_{DH}\frac{aL\sin\theta}{s}\,\delta\theta = 0$$

$$F_{DH} = W\frac{s}{L}\cot\theta$$

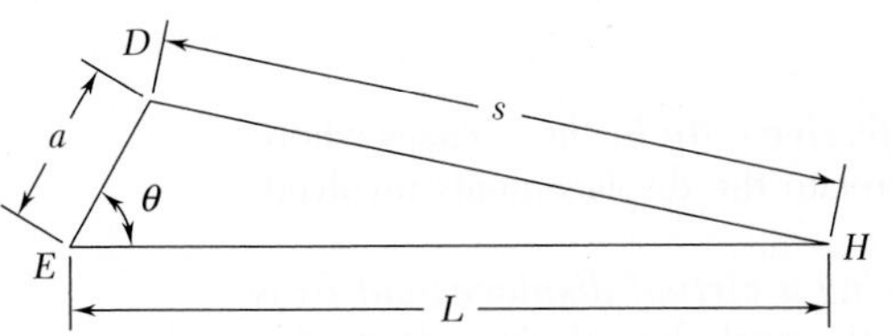

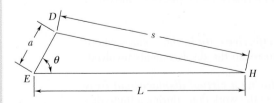

With the given numerical data, we have

$$W = mg = (1000\text{ kg})(9.81\text{ m/s}^2) = 9810\text{ N} = 9.81\text{ kN}$$
$$s^2 = a^2 + L^2 - 2aL\cos\theta$$
$$= (0.70)^2 + (3.20)^2 - 2(0.70)(3.20)\cos 60° = 8.49$$
$$s = 2.91\text{ m}$$

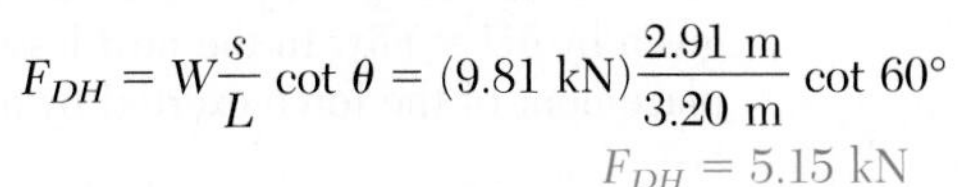

$$F_{DH} = W\frac{s}{L}\cot\theta = (9.81\text{ kN})\frac{2.91\text{ m}}{3.20\text{ m}}\cot 60°$$

$F_{DH} = 5.15$ kN ◀

SOLVING PROBLEMS ON YOUR OWN

In this lesson you learned to use the *method of virtual work,* which is a different way of solving problems involving the equilibrium of rigid bodies.

The work done by a force during a displacement of its point of application or by a couple during a rotation is found by using Eqs. (10.1) and (10.2), respectively:

$$dU = F\,ds\cos\alpha \qquad (10.1)$$

$$dU = M\,d\theta \qquad (10.2)$$

Principle of virtual work. In its more general and more useful form, this principle can be stated as follows: *If a system of connected rigid bodies is in equilibrium, the total virtual work of the external forces applied to the system is zero for any virtual displacement of the system.*

As you apply the principle of virtual work, keep in mind the following:

1. ***Virtual displacement.*** A machine or mechanism in equilibrium has no tendency to move. However, *we can cause, or imagine, a small displacement.* Since it does not actually occur, such a displacement is called a *virtual displacement.*

2. ***Virtual work.*** The work done by a force or couple during a virtual displacement is called *virtual work.*

3. ***You need consider only the forces which do work*** during the virtual displacement. It is important to remember that only the component of a virtual displacement parallel to a given force need be considered when computing the virtual work. This is why, for example, in Sample Prob. 10.2 only the vertical displacement of pin B was determined.

4. ***Forces which do no work*** during a virtual displacement that is consistent with the constraints imposed on the system include the following:

- *a.* Reactions at supports
- *b.* Internal forces at connections
- *c.* Forces exerted by inextensible cords and cables

None of these forces need be considered when you use the method of virtual work.

5. ***Be sure to express the various virtual displacements*** involved in your computations in terms of a *single virtual displacement.* This is done in each of the three preceding sample problems, where the virtual displacements are all expressed in terms of $\delta\theta$. In addition, virtual displacements containing second and higher order terms [for example, $(\delta\theta)^2$ and $(\delta x)^2$] can be ignored when computing the virtual work.

6. ***Remember that the method of virtual work is effective only in those cases*** where the geometry of the system makes it relatively easy to relate the displacements involved.

7. ***The work of the force F exerted by a spring during a virtual displacement*** δx is given by $\delta U = F\delta x$. In the next lesson we will determine the work done during a finite displacement of the force exerted by a spring.

Problems

10.1 and 10.2 Determine the vertical force **P** which must be applied at G so that the linkage is in equilibrium for the position shown.

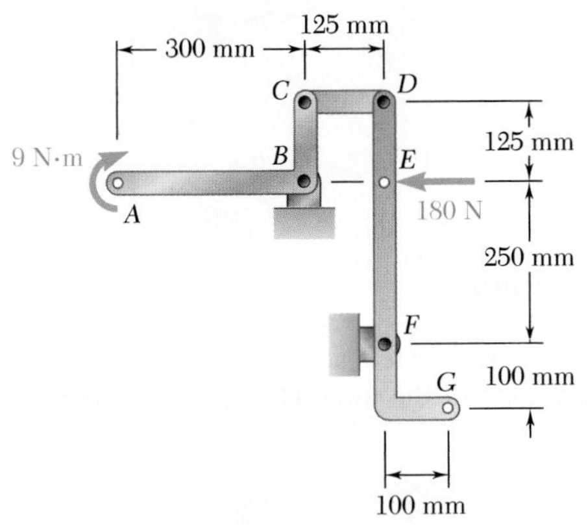

Fig. P10.1 and P10.3

Fig. P10.2 and *P10.4*

10.3 and *10.4* Determine the couple **M** which must be applied to member *DEFG* so that the linkage is in equilibrium for the position shown.

10.5 Determine the horizontal force **P** which must be applied at A so that the linkage is in equilibrium for the position shown.

10.6 An unstretched spring of constant 720 N/m is attached to pins at points C and I as shown. The pin at B is attached to member BDE and can slide freely along the slot in the fixed plate. Determine the force in the spring and the horizontal displacement of point H when a 90-N horizontal force directed to the right is applied (*a*) at point G, (*b*) at points G and H.

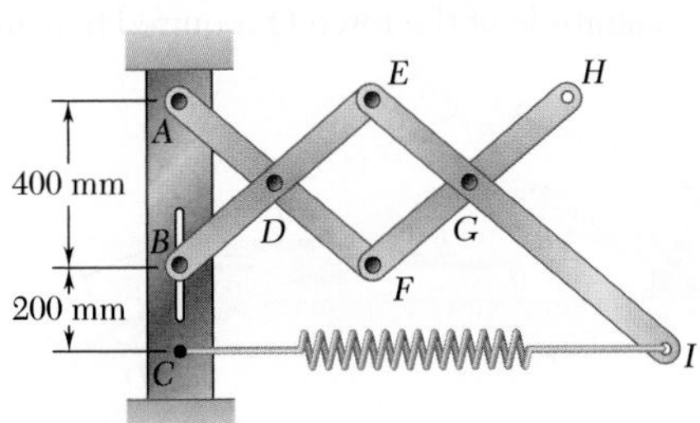

Fig. P10.6 and P10.7

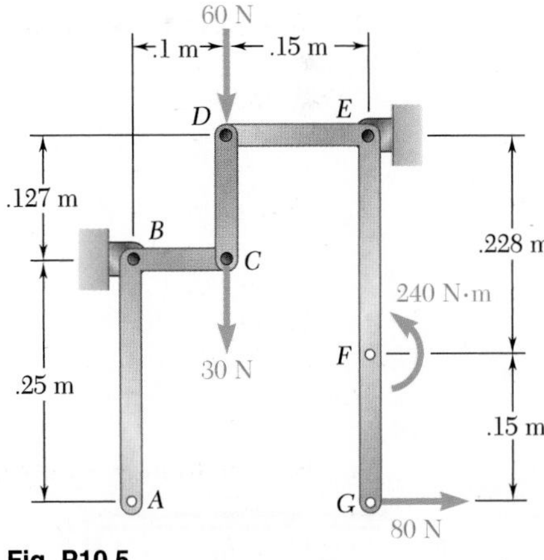

Fig. P10.5

10.7 An unstretched spring of constant 720 N/m is attached to pins at points C and I as shown. The pin at B is attached to member BDE and can slide freely along the slot in the fixed plate. Determine the force in the spring and the horizontal displacement of point H when a 90-N horizontal force directed to the right is applied (*a*) at point E, (*b*) at points D and E.

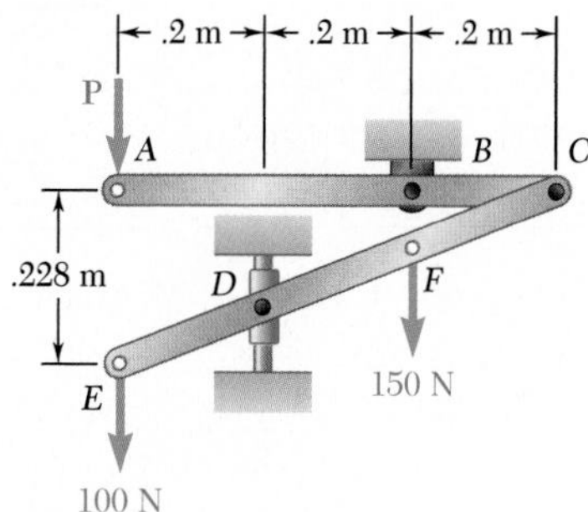

Fig. *P10.8*

10.8 The two-bar linkage shown is supported by a pin and bracket at B and a collar at D that slides freely on a vertical rod. Determine the force **P** required to maintain the equilibrium of the linkage.

10.9 Knowing that the line of action of the force **Q** passes through point C, derive an expression for the magnitude of **Q** required to maintain equilibrium.

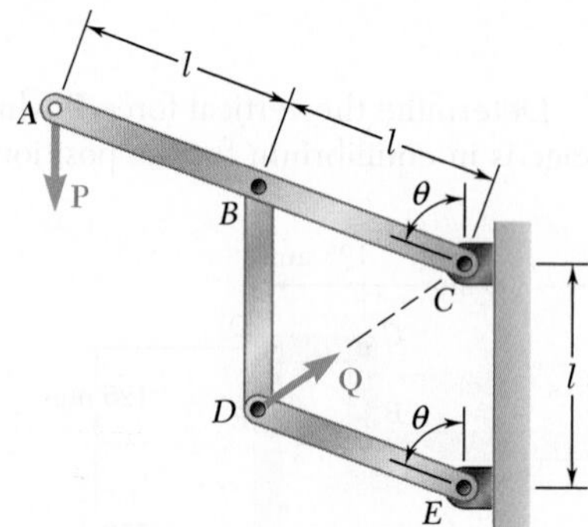

Fig. P10.9

10.10 The mechanism shown is acted upon by the force **P**. Derive an expression for the magnitude of the force **Q** required for equilibrium.

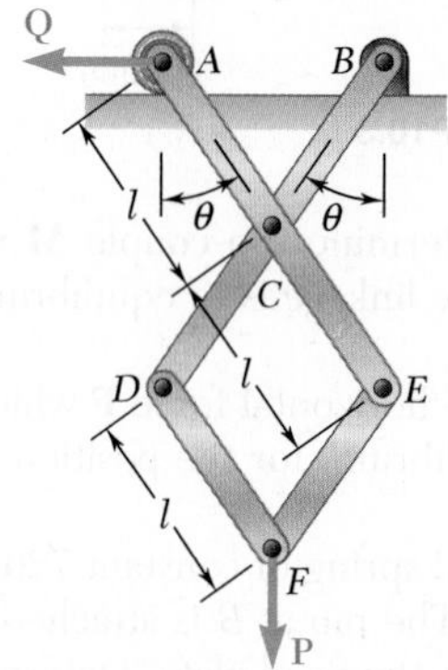

Fig. P10.10

10.11 The mechanism shown is acted upon by the force **P**. Derive an expression for the magnitude of the force **Q** required to maintain equilibrium.

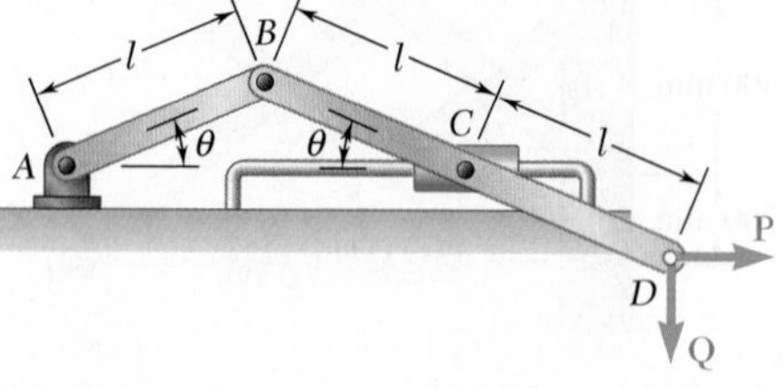

Fig. *P10.11*

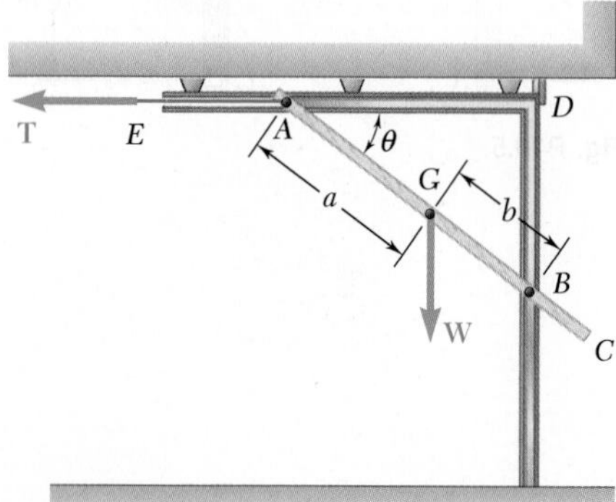

Fig. *P10.12*

10.12 An overhead garage door of weight W consists of a uniform rectangular panel AC that is supported by two sets of frictionless rollers A and B which slide in horizontal and vertical channels, respectively. The door is held in the position shown by a cable attached to the door at the middle of its upper edge. Express the tension T in the cable in terms of W, a, b, and θ.

10.13 A double-scissor lift table is used to raise a 450-kg machine component. The table consists of a platform and two identical linkages on which hydraulic cylinders exert equal forces. (Only one linkage and one cylinder are shown.) Each member of the linkage is of length 600 mm, and pins C and G are at the midpoints of their respective members. The hydraulic cylinder is pinned at A to the base of the table and at F which is 150 mm from E. If the component is placed on the table so that half of its weight is supported by the system shown, determine the force exerted by each cylinder when $\theta = 30°$.

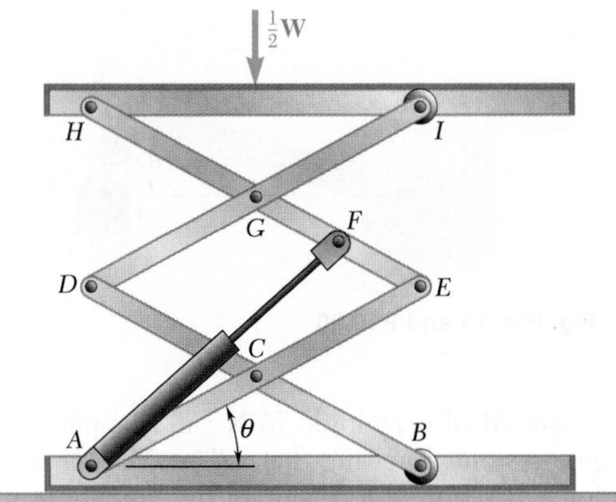

Fig. P10.13 and P10.14

10.14 A double-scissor lift table is used to raise a 450-kg machine component. The table consists of a platform and two identical linkages on which hydraulic cylinders exert equal forces. (Only one linkage and one cylinder are shown.) Each member of the linkage is of length 600 mm, and pins C and G are at the midpoints of their respective members. The hydraulic cylinder is pinned at A to the base of the table and at F which is 150 mm from E. If the component is placed on the table so that half of its weight is supported by the system shown, determine the smallest allowable value of θ knowing that the maximum force each cylinder can exert is 35 kN.

10.15 through 10.17 Derive an expression for the magnitude of the couple **M** required to maintain the equilibrium of the linkage shown.

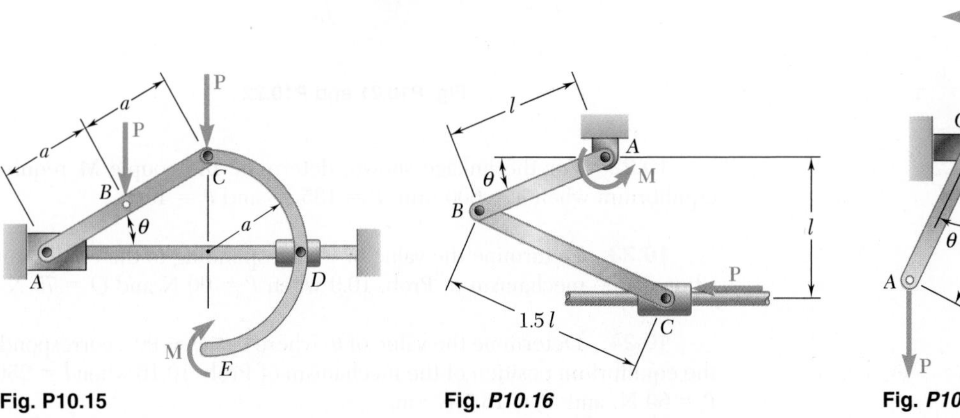

Fig. P10.15

Fig. P10.16

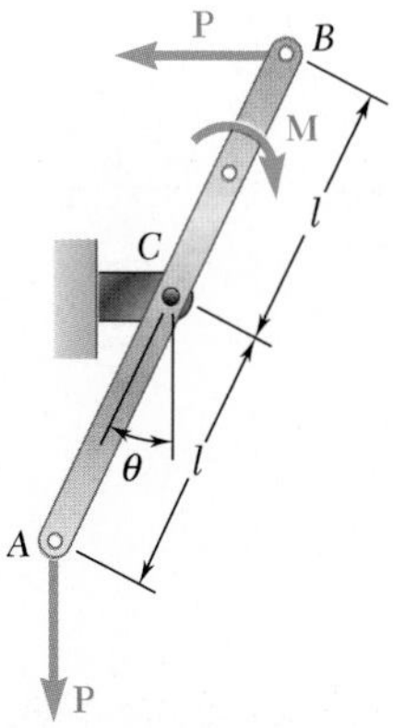

Fig. P10.17

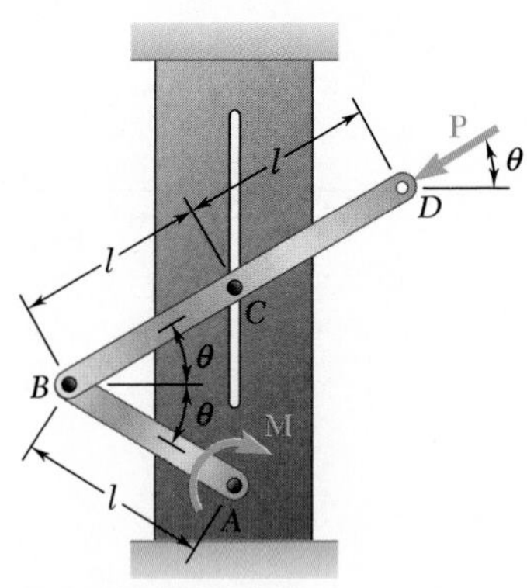

Fig. P10.18

10.18 The pin at C is attached to member BCD and can slide along a slot cut in the fixed plate shown. Neglecting the effect of friction, derive an expression for the magnitude of the couple **M** required to maintain equilibrium when the force **P** which acts at D is directed (*a*) as shown, (*b*) vertically downward, (*c*) horizontally to the right.

10.19 A 1-kN force **P** is applied as shown to the piston of an engine system. Knowing that $AB = .0635$ m and $BC = .25$ m, determine the couple **M** required to maintain the equilibrium of the system when (*a*) $\theta = 30°$, (*b*) $\theta = 150°$.

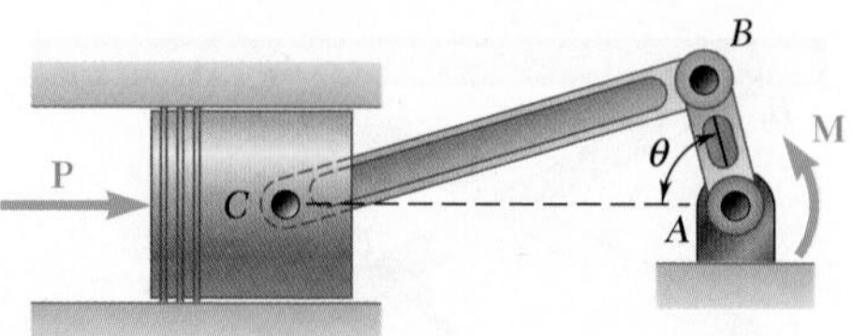

Fig. P10.19 and P10.20

10.20 A couple **M** of magnitude 75 N · m is applied as shown to the crank of an engine system. Knowing that $AB = .0635$ m and $BC = .25$ m, determine the force **P** required to maintain the equilibrium of the system when (*a*) $\theta = 60°$, (*b*) $\theta = 120°$.

10.21 For the linkage shown, determine the force **P** required for equilibrium when $a = 450$ mm, $M = 27$ N · m, and $\theta = 30°$.

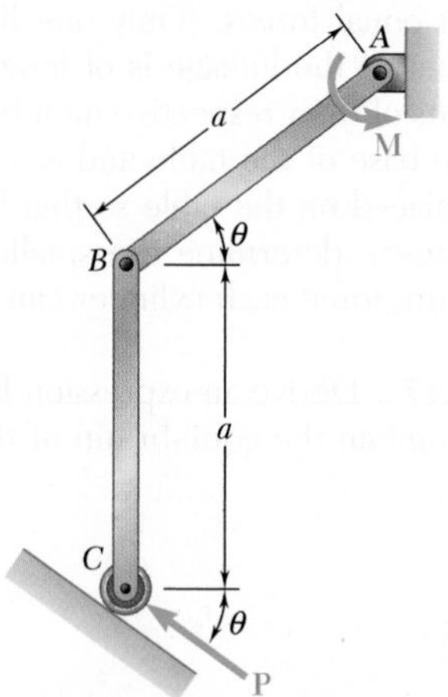

Fig. P10.21 and P10.22

10.22 For the linkage shown, determine the couple **M** required for equilibrium when $a = 600$ mm, $P = 135$ N, and $\theta = 40°$.

10.23 Determine the value of θ corresponding to the equilibrium position of the mechanism of Prob. 10.9 when $P = 60$ N and $Q = 75$ N

10.24 Determine the value of θ, where $0 \leq \theta \leq 90°$, corresponding to the equilibrium position of the mechanism of Prob. 10.16 when $l = 250$ mm, $P = 60$ N, and $M = 13.5$ N · m.

10.25 A slender rod of length l is attached to a collar at B and rests on a portion of a circular cylinder of radius r. Neglecting the effect of friction, determine the value of θ corresponding to the equilibrium position of the mechanism when $l = .381$ m, $r = .11$ m, $P = 15$ N, and $Q = 30$ N.

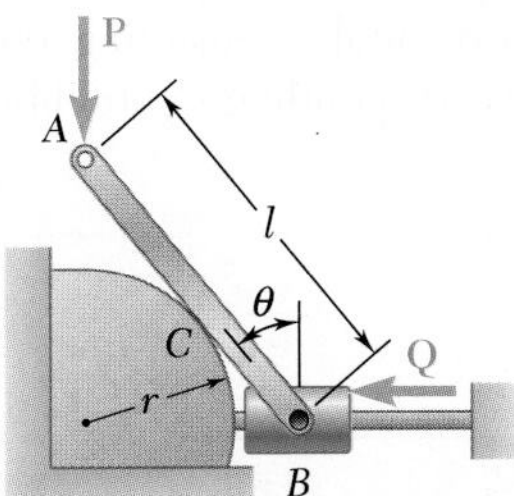

Fig. P10.25 and *P10.26*

10.26 A slender rod of length l is attached to a collar at B and rests on a portion of a circular cylinder of radius r. Neglecting the effect of friction, determine the value of θ corresponding to the equilibrium position of the mechanism when $l = .3556$ m, $r = .127$ m, $P = 75$ N, and $Q = 150$ N.

10.27 In Prob. 10.12, knowing that $a = 1.0668$ m, $b = .71$ m, and $W = 160$ N, determine the tension T in cable AE when the door is held in the position for which $BD = 1.0668$ m.

10.28 The slender rod AB is attached to collar A and rests on a small wheel at C. Neglecting the radius of the wheel and the effect of friction, determine the value of θ corresponding to the equilibrium position of the mechanism when $P = 75$ N and $Q = 135$ N.

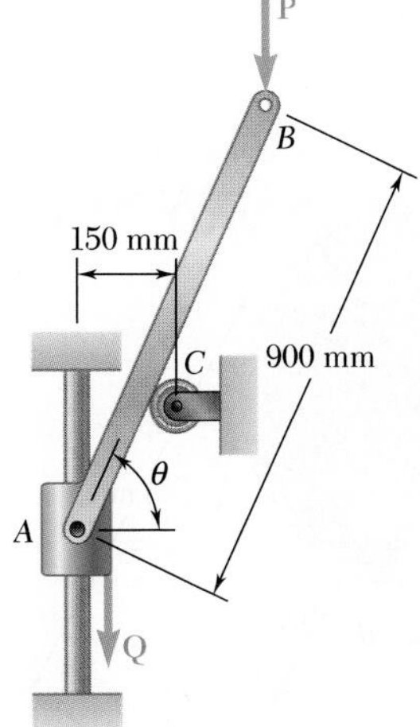

Fig. P10.28

10.29 A force **P** is applied to slider C as shown. The constant of the spring is 1.6 kN/m, and the spring is unstretched when member BD is horizontal. Neglecting friction between the slider and the guide rod and knowing that $BC = BD = 150$ mm, determine the magnitude of **P** so that $\theta = 25°$ when the system is in equilibrium.

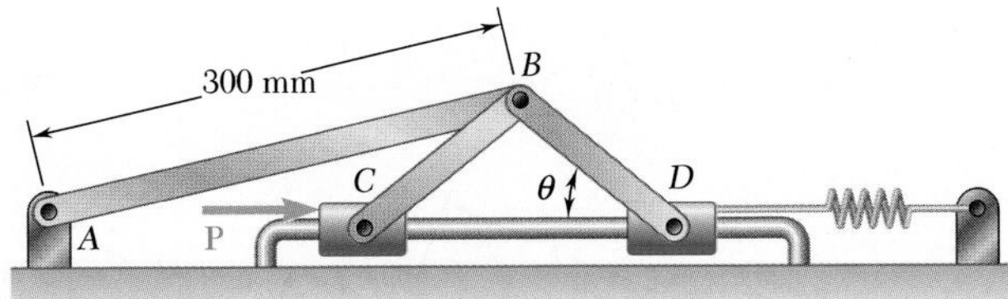

Fig. P10.29

10.30 Two bars AD and DG are connected by a pin at D and by a spring AG. Knowing that the spring is 300 mm long when unstretched and that the constant of the spring is 5 kN/m, determine the value of x corresponding to equilibrium when a 900-N load is applied at E as shown.

10.31 Solve Prob. 10.30 assuming that the 900-N load is applied at C instead of E.

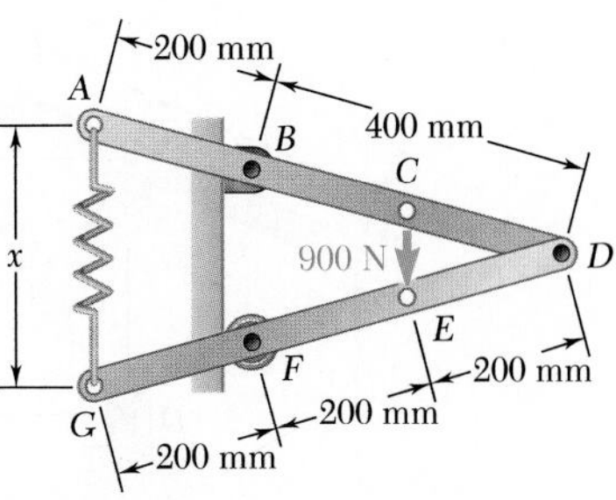

Fig. *P10.30*

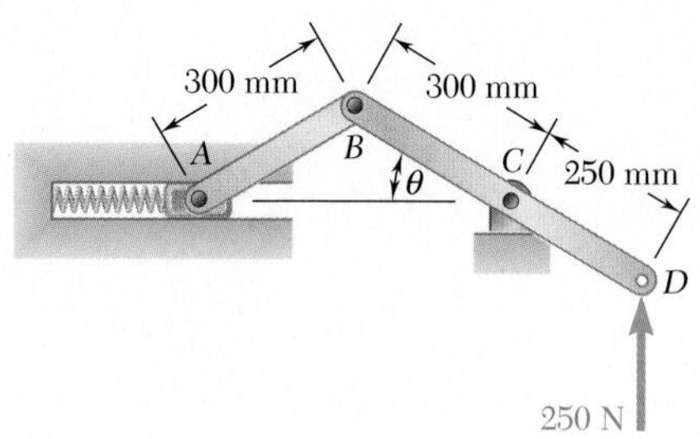

Fig. *P10.32*

10.32 For the mechanism shown, block *A* can move freely in its guide and rests against a spring of constant 2.5 kN/m that is undeformed when $\theta = 45°$. For the loading shown, determine the value of θ corresponding to equilibrium.

10.33 A vertical force **P** of magnitude 150 N is applied to the linkage at *B*. The constant of the spring is 2000 N/m, and the spring is unstretched when *AB* and *BC* are horizontal. Neglecting the weight of the linkage, determine the value of θ corresponding to equilibrium.

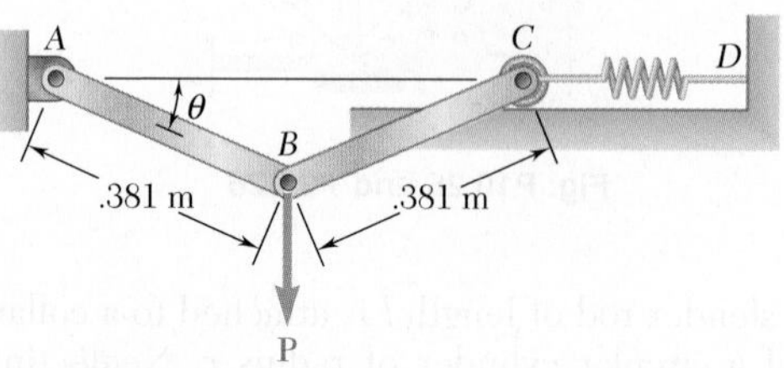

Fig. P10.33 and P10.34

10.34 A vertical force **P** is applied to the linkage at *B*. The constant of the spring is 2000 N/m, and the spring is unstretched when *AB* and *BC* are horizontal. Neglecting the weight of the linkage, determine the magnitude of **P** so that $\theta = 25°$ when the system is in equilibrium.

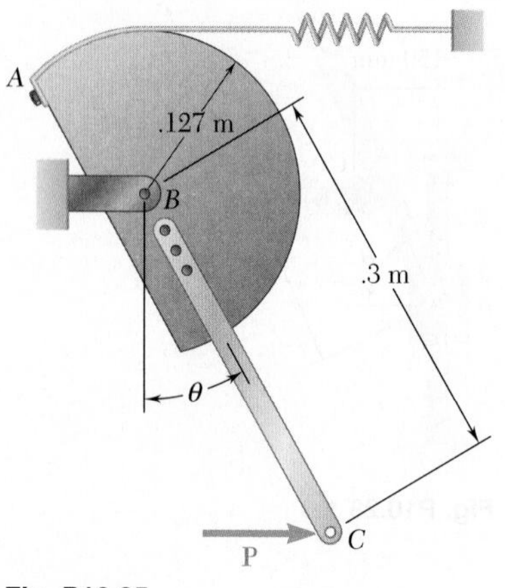

Fig. P10.35

10.35 A horizontal force **P** of magnitude 40 N is applied to the mechanism at *C*. The constant of the spring is $k = 1500$ N/m, and the spring is unstretched when $\theta = 0$. Neglecting the weight of the mechanism, determine the value of θ corresponding to equilibrium.

***10.36* and 10.37** Knowing that the constant of spring *CD* is *k* and that the spring is unstretched when $\theta = 0$, determine the value of θ, where $0 \le \theta \le 90°$, corresponding to equilibrium for the given data.

10.36 $P = 150$ N, $l = .726$ m, $k = 6000$ N/m

10.37 $P = 600$ N, $l = 800$ mm, $k = 4$ kN/m

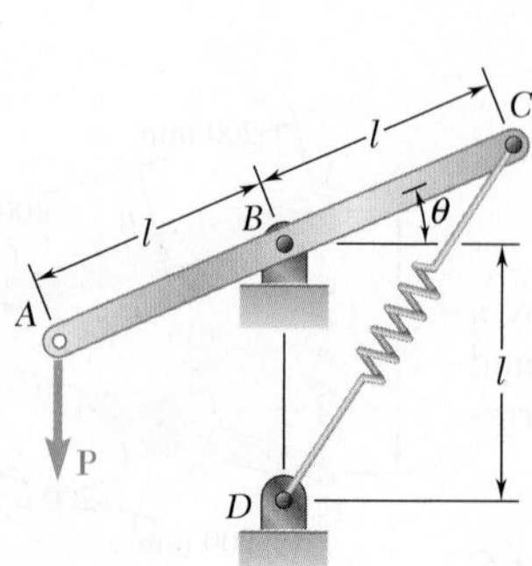

Fig. *P10.36*

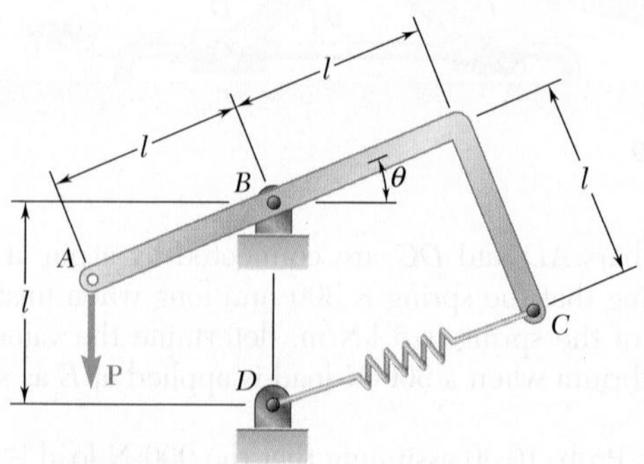

Fig. P10.37

10.38 A cord is wrapped around drum A which is attached to member AB. Block D can move freely in its guide and is fastened to link CD. Neglecting the mass of AB and knowing that the spring is of constant 800 N/m and is undeformed when $\theta = 0$, determine the value of θ corresponding to equilibrium when a downward force **P** of magnitude 480 N is applied to the end of the cord.

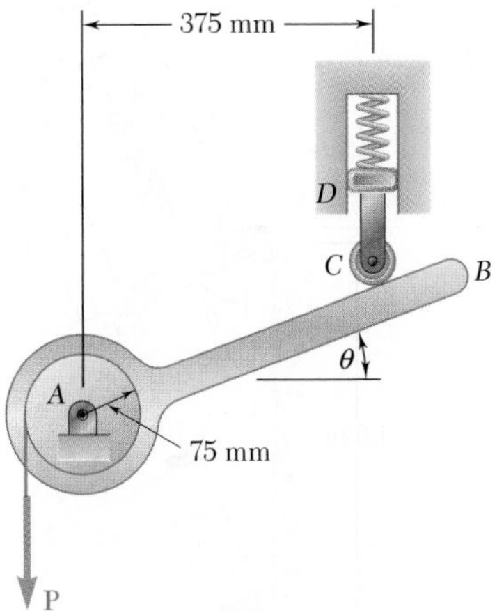

Fig. P10.38

10.39 The lever AB is attached to the horizontal shaft BC which passes through a bearing and is welded to a fixed support at C. The torsional spring constant of the shaft BC is K; that is, a couple of magnitude K is required to rotate end B through 1 rad. Knowing that the shaft is untwisted when AB is horizontal, determine the value of θ corresponding to the position of equilibrium when $P = 2$ kN, $l = 250$ mm, and $K = 225$ N · m/rad.

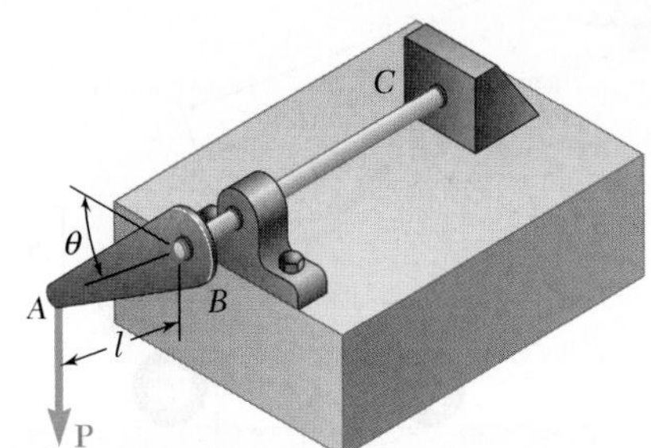

Fig. P10.39

10.40 Solve Prob. 10.39 assuming that $P = 6.3$ kN, $l = 250$ mm, and $K = 225$ N · m/rad. Obtain answers in each of the following quadrants: $0 < \theta < 90°$, $270° < \theta < 360°$, and $360° < \theta < 450°$.

10.41 The position of crank BCD is controlled by the hydraulic cylinder AB. For the loading shown, determine the force exerted by the hydraulic cylinder on pin B knowing that $\theta = 60°$.

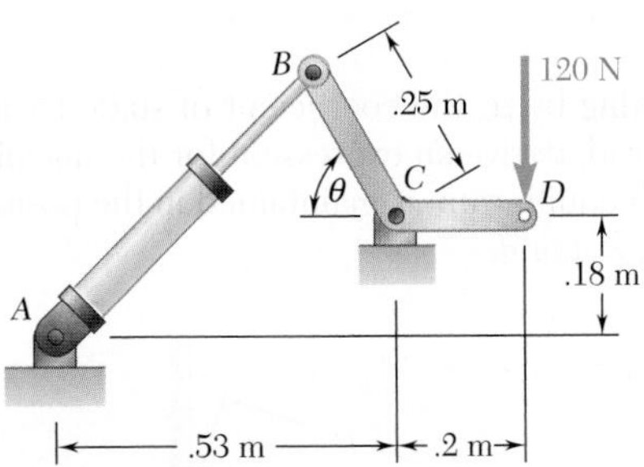

Fig. P10.41 and *P10.42*

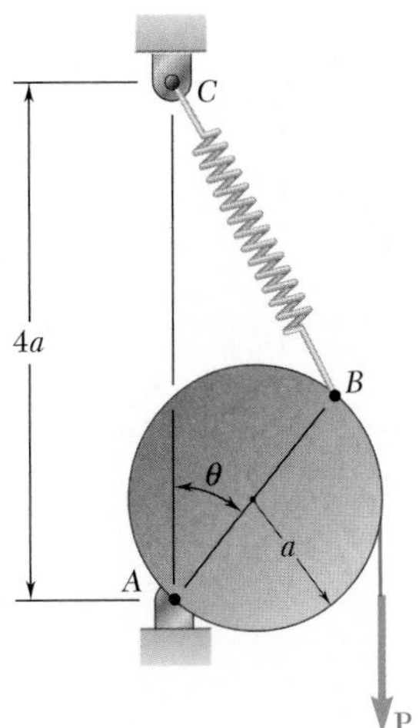

Fig. P10.43

10.42 The position of crank BCD is controlled by the hydraulic cylinder AB. Determine the angle θ knowing that the hydraulic cylinder exerts a 105-N force on pin B when the crank is in the position shown.

10.43 A cord is wrapped around a drum of radius a that is pinned at A. The constant of the spring is 2500 N/m, and the spring is unstretched when $\theta = 0$. Knowing that $a = .19$ m and neglecting the weight of the drum, determine the value of θ corresponding to equilibrium when a downward force **P** of magnitude 12 N is applied to the end of the cord.

10.44 For the linkage shown, determine the force **P** required for equilibrium when $M = 320$ N · m.

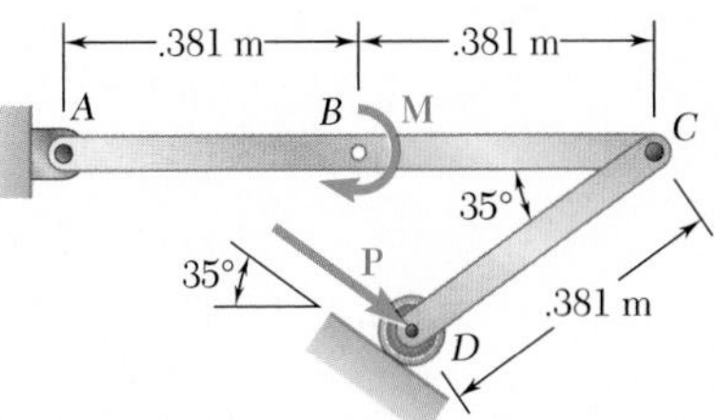

Fig. *P10.44*

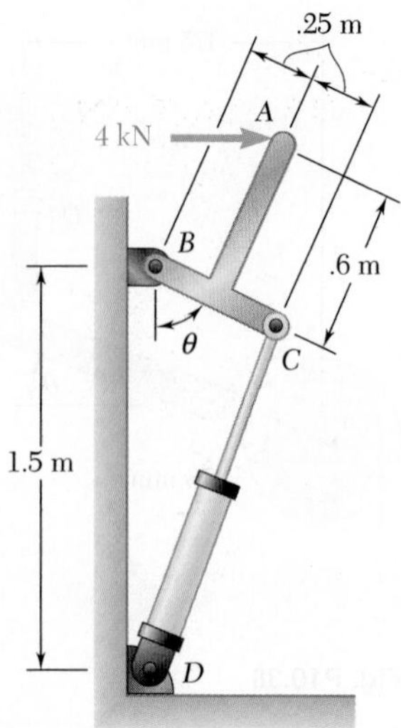

Fig. P10.45

10.45 The position of member ABC is controlled by the hydraulic cylinder CD. For the loading shown, determine the force exerted by the hydraulic cylinder on pin C when $\theta = 60°$.

10.46 The telescoping arm ABC is used to provide an elevated platform for construction workers. The workers and the platform together weigh 500 N, and their combined center of gravity is located directly above C. For the position when $\theta = 20°$, determine the force exerted on pin B by the hydraulic cylinder BD.

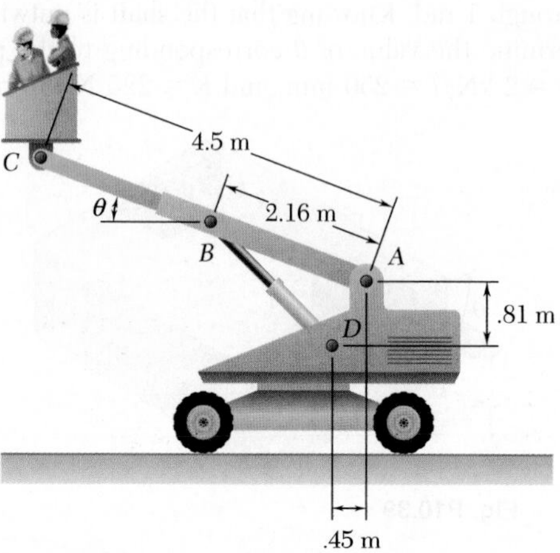

Fig. *P10.46*

10.47 A block of weight W is pulled up a plane forming an angle α with the horizontal by a force $\mathbf{P}$ directed along the plane. If μ is the coefficient of friction between the block and the plane, derive an expression for the mechanical efficiency of the system. Show that the mechanical efficiency cannot exceed $\frac{1}{2}$ if the block is to remain in place when the force $\mathbf{P}$ is removed.

10.48 Denoting by μ_s the coefficient of static friction between collar C and the vertical rod, derive an expression for the magnitude of the largest couple $\mathbf{M}$ for which equilibrium is maintained in the position shown. Explain what happens if $\mu_s \geq \tan\theta$.

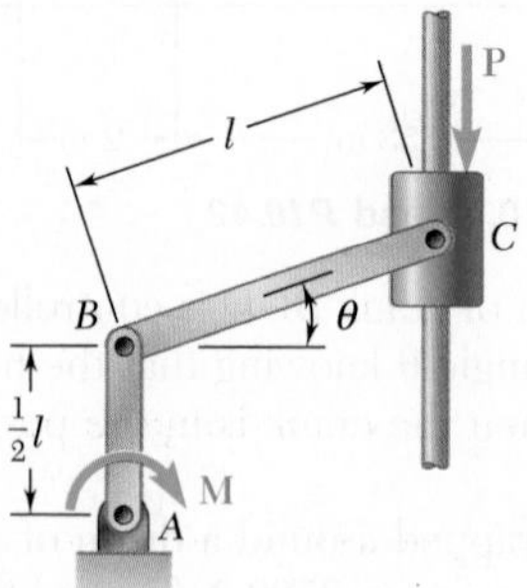

Fig. P10.48 and P10.49

10.49 Knowing that the coefficient of static friction between collar C and the vertical rod is 0.30, determine the magnitude of the largest and smallest couple $\mathbf{M}$ for which equilibrium is maintained in the position shown when $\theta = 35°$, $l = 500$ mm, and $P = 400$ N.

10.50 Denoting by μ_s the coefficient of static friction between the block attached to rod ACE and the horizontal surface, derive expressions in terms of P, μ_s, and θ for the largest and smallest magnitudes of the force **Q** for which equilibrium is maintained.

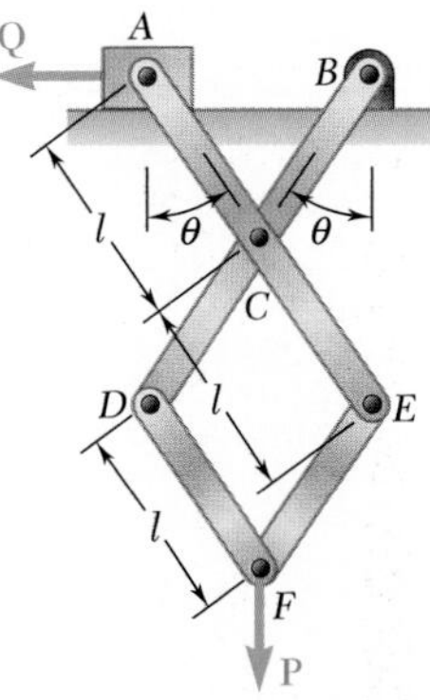

Fig. P10.50 and P10.51

10.51 Knowing that the coefficient of static friction between the block attached to rod ACE and the horizontal surface is 0.15, determine the magnitudes of the largest and smallest force **Q** for which equilibrium is maintained when $\theta = 30°$, $l = 200$ mm, and $P = 40$ N.

10.52 Derive an expression for the mechanical efficiency of the jack discussed in Sec. 8.6. Show that if the jack is to be self-locking, the mechanical efficiency cannot exceed $\frac{1}{2}$.

10.53 Using the method of virtual work, determine separately the force and the couple representing the reaction at A.

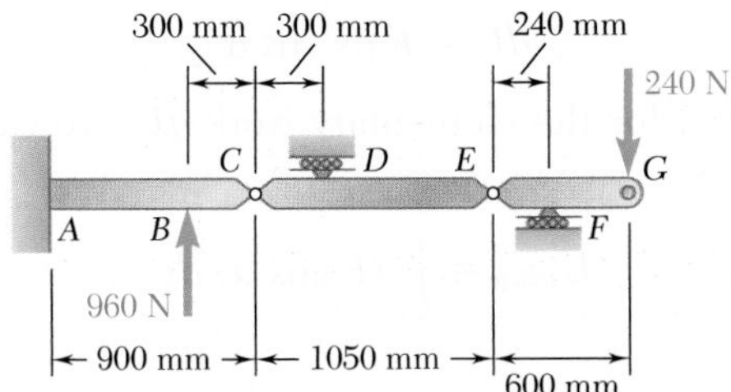

Fig. *P10.53* and *P10.54*

10.54 Using the method of virtual work, determine the reaction at D.

10.55 Referring to Prob. 10.41 and using the value found for the force exerted by the hydraulic cylinder AB, determine the change in the length of AB required to raise the 120-N load .03 m.

10.56 Referring to Prob. 10.46 and using the value found for the force exerted by the hydraulic cylinder BD, determine the change in the length of BD required to raise the platform attached at C .06 m.

10.57 Determine the vertical movement of joint C if the length of member FG is increased 30 mm. (*Hint:* Apply a vertical load at joint C, and, using the methods of Chap. 6, compute the force exerted by member FG on joints F and G. Then apply the method of virtual work for a virtual displacement resulting in the specified increase in length of member FG. This method should be used only for small changes in the lengths of members.)

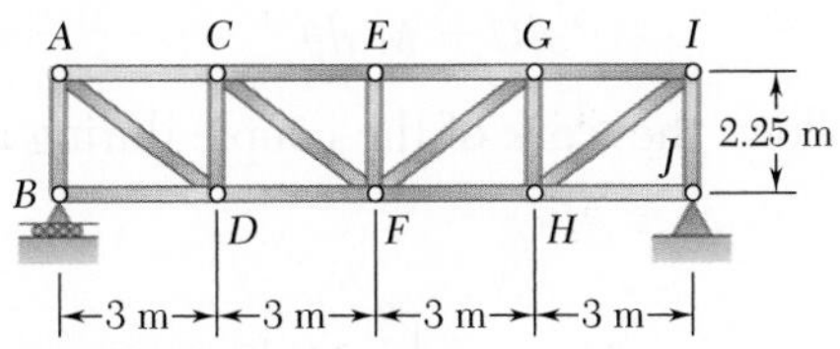

Fig. P10.57 and P10.58

10.58 Determine the horizontal movement of joint C if the length of member FG is increased 30 mm. (See the hint for Prob. 10.57.)

*10.6. WORK OF A FORCE DURING A FINITE DISPLACEMENT

Consider a force **F** acting on a particle. The work of **F** corresponding to an infinitesimal displacement $d\mathbf{r}$ of the particle was defined in Sec. 10.2 as

$$dU = \mathbf{F} \cdot d\mathbf{r} \qquad (10.1)$$

The work of **F** corresponding to a finite displacement of the particle from A_1 to A_2 (Fig. 10.10*a*) is denoted by $U_{1\rightarrow 2}$ and is obtained by integrating Eq. (10.1) along the curve described by the particle:

$$U_{1\rightarrow 2} = \int_{A_1}^{A_2} \mathbf{F} \cdot d\mathbf{r} \qquad (10.11)$$

Using the alternative expression

$$dU = F\, ds \cos \alpha \qquad (10.1')$$

given in Sec. 10.2 for the elementary work dU, we can also express the work $U_{1\rightarrow 2}$ as

$$U_{1\rightarrow 2} = \int_{s_1}^{s_2} (F \cos \alpha)\, ds \qquad (10.11')$$

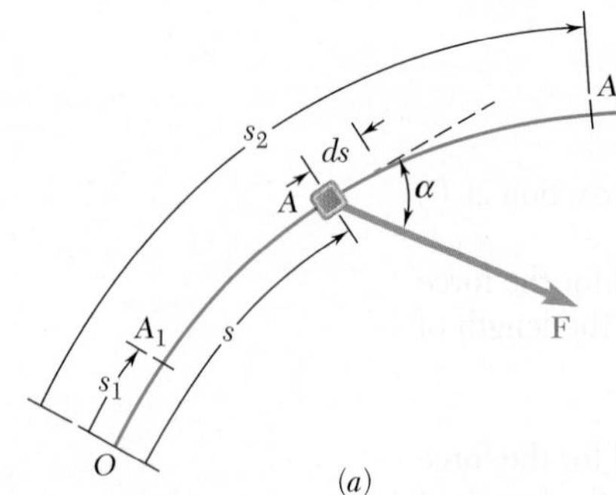

(*a*)

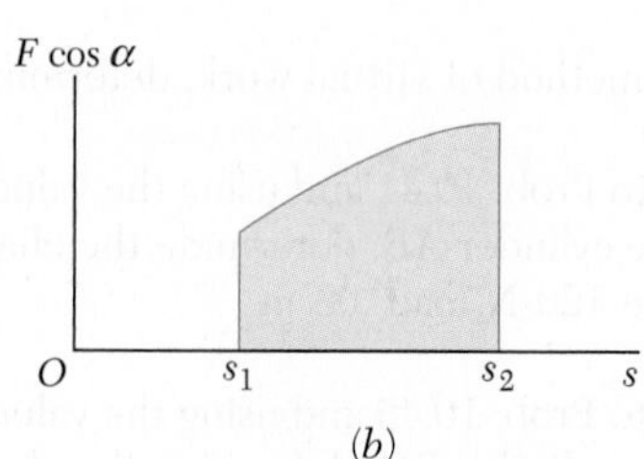

(*b*)

Fig. 10.10

where the variable of integration s measures the distance along the path traveled by the particle. The work $U_{1\rightarrow 2}$ is represented by the area under the curve obtained by plotting $F \cos \alpha$ against s (Fig. 10.10*b*). In the case of a force **F** of constant magnitude acting in the direction of motion, formula (10.11′) yields $U_{1\rightarrow 2} = F(s_2 - s_1)$.

Recalling from Sec. 10.2 that the work of a couple of moment **M** during an infinitesimal rotation $d\theta$ of a rigid body is

$$dU = M\, d\theta \qquad (10.2)$$

we express as follows the work of the couple during a finite rotation of the body:

$$U_{1\rightarrow 2} = \int_{\theta_1}^{\theta_2} M\, d\theta \qquad (10.12)$$

In the case of a constant couple, formula (10.12) yields

$$U_{1\rightarrow 2} = M(\theta_2 - \theta_1)$$

Work of a Weight. It was stated in Sec. 10.2 that the work of the weight **W** of a body during an infinitesimal displacement of the body is equal to the product of W and the vertical displacement of the center of gravity of the body. With the y axis pointing upward, the work of **W** during a finite displacement of the body (Fig. 10.11) is obtained by writing

$$dU = -W\,dy$$

Integrating from A_1 to A_2, we have

$$U_{1\to 2} = -\int_{y_1}^{y_2} W\,dy = Wy_1 - Wy_2 \qquad (10.13)$$

or

$$U_{1\to 2} = -W(y_2 - y_1) = -W\,\Delta y \qquad (10.13')$$

where Δy is the vertical displacement from A_1 to A_2. The work of the weight **W** is thus equal to *the product of W and the vertical displacement of the center of gravity of the body*. The work is *positive* when $\Delta y < 0$, that is, *when the body moves down*.

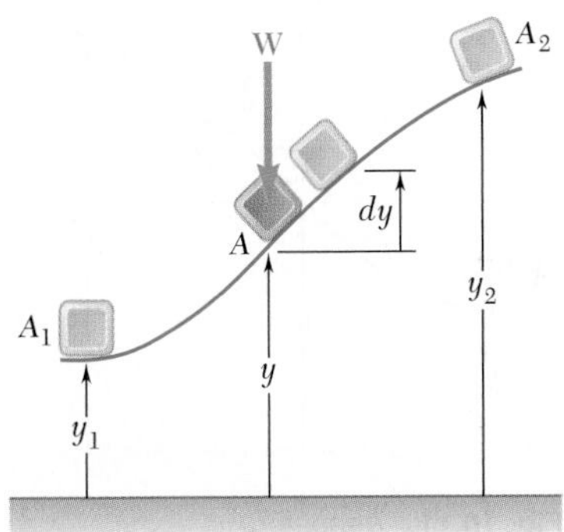

Fig. 10.11

Work of the Force Exerted by a Spring. Consider a body A attached to a fixed point B by a spring; it is assumed that the spring is undeformed when the body is at A_0 (Fig. 10.12*a*). Experimental evidence shows that the magnitude of the force **F** exerted by the spring on a body A is proportional to the deflection x of the spring measured from the position A_0. We have

$$F = kx \qquad (10.14)$$

where k is the *spring constant,* expressed in N/m if SI units are used and expressed in lb/ft or lb/in. if U.S. customary units are used. The work of the force **F** exerted by the spring during a finite displacement of the body from $A_1(x = x_1)$ to $A_2(x = x_2)$ is obtained by writing

$$dU = -F\,dx = -kx\,dx$$

$$U_{1\to 2} = -\int_{x_1}^{x_2} kx\,dx = \tfrac{1}{2}kx_1^2 - \tfrac{1}{2}kx_2^2 \qquad (10.15)$$

Care should be taken to express k and x in consistent units. For example, if U.S. customary units are used, k should be expressed in lb/ft and x expressed in feet, or k in lb/in. and x in inches; in the first case, the work is obtained in ft · lb; in the second case, in in · lb. We note that the work of the force **F** exerted by the spring on the body is *positive* when $x_2 < x_1$, that is, *when the spring is returning to its undeformed position.*

Since Eq. (10.14) is the equation of a straight line of slope k passing through the origin, the work $U_{1\to 2}$ of **F** during the displacement from A_1 to A_2 can be obtained by evaluating the area of the trapezoid shown in Fig. 10.12*b*. This is done by computing the values F_1 and F_2 and multiplying the base Δx of the trapezoid by its mean height $\frac{1}{2}(F_1 + F_2)$. Since the work of the force **F** exerted by the spring is positive for a negative value of Δx, we write

$$U_{1\to 2} = -\tfrac{1}{2}(F_1 + F_2)\,\Delta x \qquad (10.16)$$

Equation (10.16) is usually more convenient to use than Eq. (10.15) and affords fewer chances of confusing the units involved.

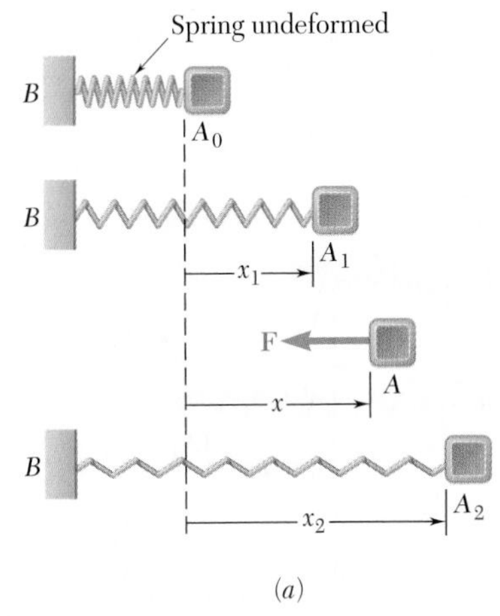

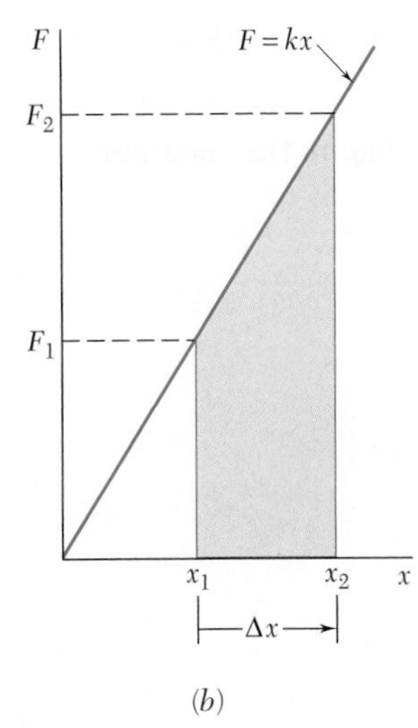

Fig. 10.12

*10.7. POTENTIAL ENERGY

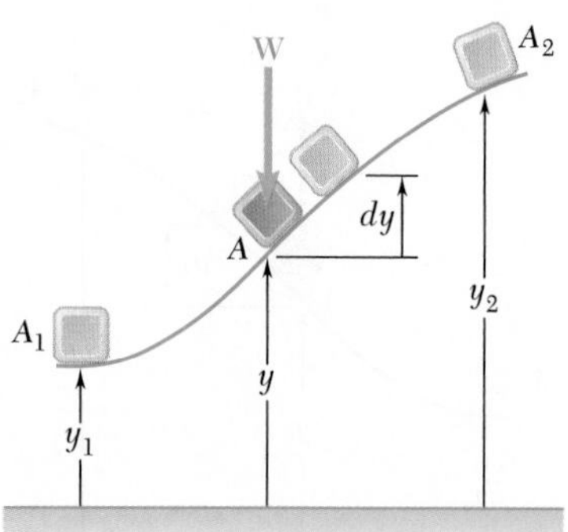

Fig. 10.11 *(repeated)*

Considering again the body of Fig. 10.11, we note from Eq. (10.13) that the work of the weight **W** during a finite displacement is obtained by subtracting the value of the function Wy corresponding to the second position of the body from its value corresponding to the first position. The work of **W** is thus independent of the actual path followed; it depends only upon the initial and final values of the function Wy. This function is called the *potential energy* of the body with respect to the *force of gravity* **W** and is denoted by V_g. We write

$$U_{1\rightarrow2} = (V_g)_1 - (V_g)_2 \qquad \text{with } V_g = Wy \tag{10.17}$$

We note that if $(V_g)_2 > (V_g)_1$, that is, *if the potential energy increases* during the displacement (as in the case considered here), *the work* $U_{1\rightarrow2}$ *is negative*. If, on the other hand, the work of **W** is positive, the potential energy decreases. Therefore, the potential energy V_g of the body provides a measure of *the work which can be done* by its weight **W**. Since only the *change* in potential energy, and not the actual value of V_g, is involved in formula (10.17), an arbitrary constant can be added to the expression obtained for V_g. In other words, the level from which the elevation y is measured can be chosen arbitrarily. Note that potential energy is expressed in the same units as work, that is, in joules (J) if SI units are used† and in ft · lb or in · lb if U.S. customary units are used.

Considering now the body of Fig. 10.12*a*, we note from Eq. (10.15) that the work of the elastic force **F** is obtained by subtracting the value of the function $\frac{1}{2}kx^2$ corresponding to the second position of the body from its value corresponding to the first position. This function is denoted by V_e and is called the *potential energy* of the body with respect to the *elastic force* **F**. We write

$$U_{1\rightarrow2} = (V_e)_1 - (V_e)_2 \qquad \text{with } V_e = \tfrac{1}{2}kx^2 \tag{10.18}$$

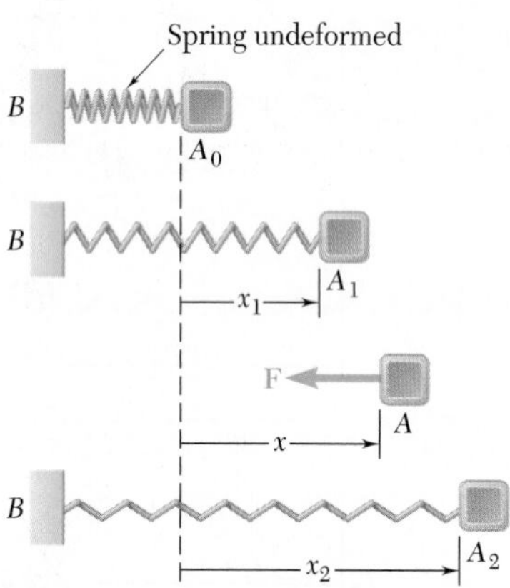

Fig. 10.12a *(repeated)*

and observe that during the displacement considered, the work of the force **F** exerted by the spring on the body is negative and the potential energy V_e increases. We should note that the expression obtained for V_e is valid only if the deflection of the spring is measured from its undeformed position.

The concept of potential energy can be used when forces other than gravity forces and elastic forces are involved. It remains valid as long as the elementary work dU of the force considered is an *exact differential*. It is then possible to find a function V, called potential energy, such that

$$dU = -dV \tag{10.19}$$

Integrating Eq. (10.19) over a finite displacement, we obtain the general formula

$$U_{1\rightarrow2} = V_1 - V_2 \tag{10.20}$$

which expresses that *the work of the force is independent of the path followed and is equal to minus the change in potential energy*. A force which satisfies Eq. (10.20) is said to be a *conservative force*.‡

†See footnote, page 559.

‡A detailed discussion of conservative forces is given in Sec. 13.7 of *Dynamics*.

*10.8. POTENTIAL ENERGY AND EQUILIBRIUM

The application of the principle of virtual work is considerably simplified when the potential energy of a system is known. In the case of a virtual displacement, formula (10.19) becomes $\delta U = -\delta V$. Moreover, if the position of the system is defined by a single independent variable θ, we can write $\delta V = (dV/d\theta)\,\delta\theta$. Since $\delta\theta$ must be different from zero, the condition $\delta U = 0$ for the equilibrium of the system becomes

$$\frac{dV}{d\theta} = 0 \tag{10.21}$$

In terms of potential energy, therefore, the principle of virtual work states that *if a system is in equilibrium, the derivative of its total potential energy is zero*. If the position of the system depends upon several independent variables (the system is then said to possess *several degrees of freedom*), the partial derivatives of V with respect to each of the independent variables must be zero.

Consider, for example, a structure made of two members AC and CB and carrying a load W at C. The structure is supported by a pin at A and a roller at B, and a spring BD connects B to a fixed point D (Fig. 10.13*a*). The constant of the spring is k, and it is assumed that the natural length of the spring is equal to AD and thus that the spring is undeformed when B coincides with A. Neglecting the friction forces and the weight of the members, we find that the only forces which do work during a displacement of the structure are the weight $\mathbf{W}$ and the force $\mathbf{F}$ exerted by the spring at point B (Fig. 10.13*b*). The total potential energy of the system will thus be obtained by adding the potential energy V_g corresponding to the gravity force $\mathbf{W}$ and the potential energy V_e corresponding to the elastic force $\mathbf{F}$.

Choosing a coordinate system with origin at A and noting that the deflection of the spring, measured from its undeformed position, is $AB = x_B$, we write

$$V_e = \tfrac{1}{2}kx_B^2 \qquad V_g = Wy_C$$

Expressing the coordinates x_B and y_C in terms of the angle θ, we have

$$x_B = 2l\sin\theta \qquad y_C = l\cos\theta$$
$$V_e = \tfrac{1}{2}k(2l\sin\theta)^2 \qquad V_g = W(l\cos\theta)$$
$$V = V_e + V_g = 2kl^2\sin^2\theta + Wl\cos\theta \tag{10.22}$$

The positions of equilibrium of the system are obtained by equating to zero the derivative of the potential energy V. We write

$$\frac{dV}{d\theta} = 4kl^2\sin\theta\cos\theta - Wl\sin\theta = 0$$

or, factoring $l\sin\theta$,

$$\frac{dV}{d\theta} = l\sin\theta(4kl\cos\theta - W) = 0$$

There are therefore two positions of equilibrium, corresponding to the values $\theta = 0$ and $\theta = \cos^{-1}(W/4kl)$, respectively.†

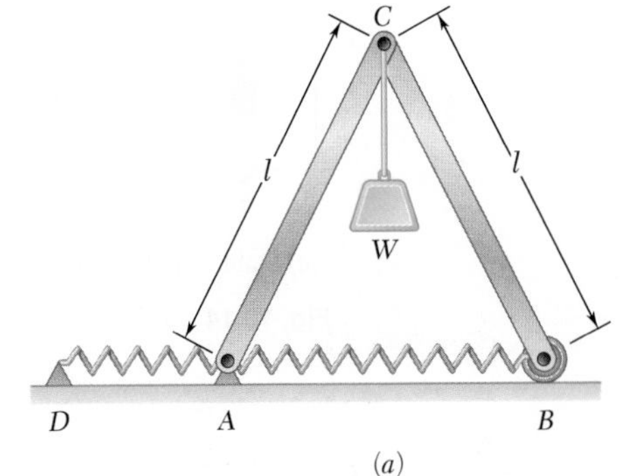

(*a*)

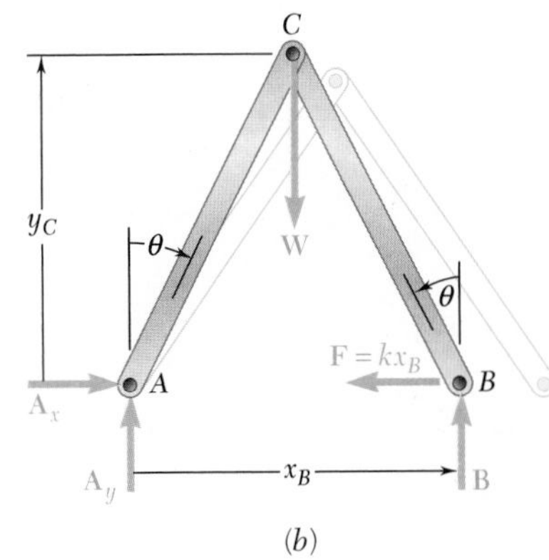

(*b*)

Fig. 10.13

†The second position does not exist if $W > 4kl$.

*10.9. STABILITY OF EQUILIBRIUM

Consider the three uniform rods of length $2a$ and weight **W** shown in Fig. 10.14. While each rod is in equilibrium, there is an important difference between the three cases considered. Suppose that each rod is slightly disturbed from its position of equilibrium and then released: rod a will move back toward its original position, rod b will keep moving away from its original position, and rod c will remain in its new position. In case a, the equilibrium of the rod is said to be *stable;* in case b, it is said to be *unstable;* and, in case c, it is said to be *neutral*.

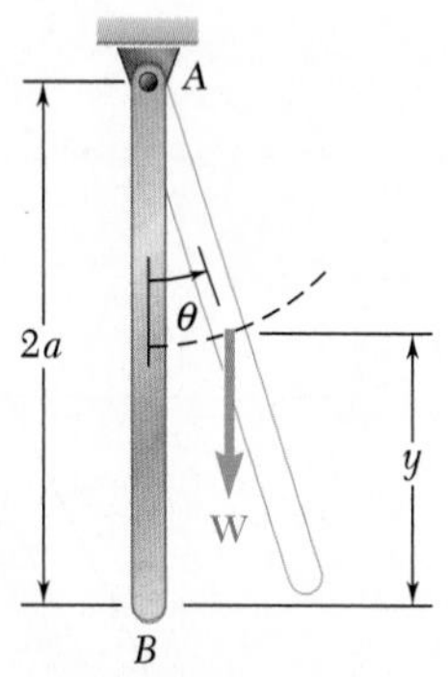

(a) Stable equilibrium

(b) Unstable equilibrium

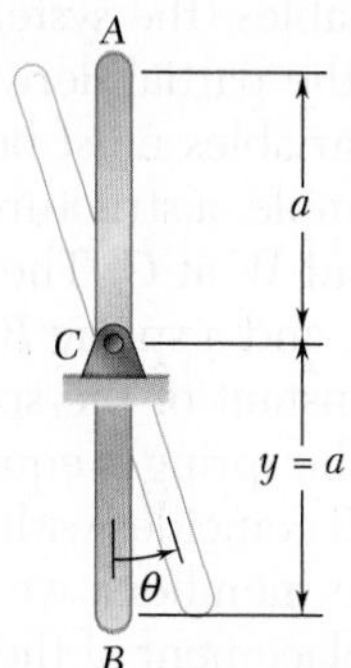

(c) Neutral equilibrium

Fig. 10.14

Recalling from Sec. 10.7 that the potential energy V_g with respect to gravity is equal to Wy, where y is the elevation of the point of application of **W** measured from an arbitrary level, we observe that the potential energy of rod a is minimum in the position of equilibrium considered, that the potential energy of rod b is maximum, and that the potential energy of rod c is constant. Equilibrium is thus *stable, unstable,* or *neutral* according to whether the potential energy is *minimum, maximum,* or *constant* (Fig. 10.15).

That the result obtained is quite general can be seen as follows: We first observe that a force always tends to do positive work and thus to decrease the potential energy of the system on which it is applied. Therefore, when a system is disturbed from its position of equilibrium, the forces acting on the system will tend to bring it back to its original position if V is minimum (Fig. 10.15a) and to move it farther away if V is maximum (Fig. 10.15b). If V is constant (Fig. 10.15c), the forces will not tend to move the system either way.

Recalling from calculus that a function is minimum or maximum according to whether its second derivative is positive or negative, we can summarize the conditions for the equilibrium of a system with one degree of freedom (that is, a system the position of which is defined by a single independent variable θ) as follows:

$$\begin{aligned} \frac{dV}{d\theta} &= 0 \qquad \frac{d^2V}{d\theta^2} > 0\text{: stable equilibrium} \\ \frac{dV}{d\theta} &= 0 \qquad \frac{d^2V}{d\theta^2} < 0\text{: unstable equilibrium} \end{aligned} \tag{10.23}$$

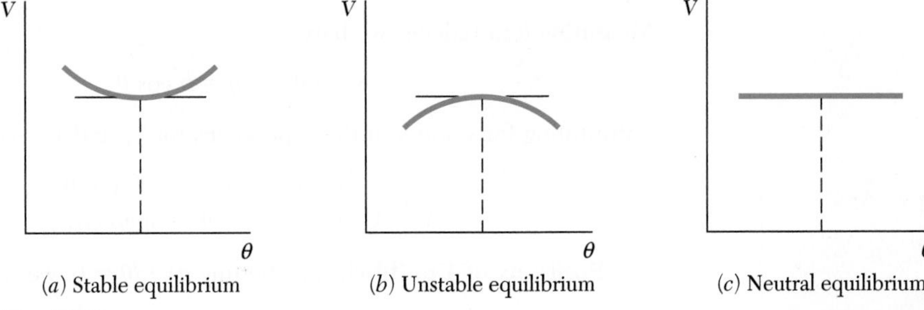

(*a*) Stable equilibrium (*b*) Unstable equilibrium (*c*) Neutral equilibrium

Fig. 10.15

If both the first and the second derivatives of V are zero, it is necessary to examine derivatives of a higher order to determine whether the equilibrium is stable, unstable, or neutral. The equilibrium will be neutral if all derivatives are zero, since the potential energy V is then a constant. The equilibrium will be stable if the first derivative found to be different from zero is of even order and positive. In all other cases the equilibrium will be unstable.

If the system considered possesses *several degrees of freedom,* the potential energy V depends upon several variables, and it is thus necessary to apply the theory of functions of several variables to determine whether V is minimum. It can be verified that a system with 2 degrees of freedom will be stable, and the corresponding potential energy $V(\theta_1, \theta_2)$ will be minimum, if the following relations are satisfied simultaneously:

$$\begin{gathered} \frac{\partial V}{\partial \theta_1} = \frac{\partial V}{\partial \theta_2} = 0 \\ \left(\frac{\partial^2 V}{\partial \theta_1\, \partial \theta_2}\right)^2 - \frac{\partial^2 V}{\partial \theta_1^2}\frac{\partial^2 V}{\partial \theta_2^2} < 0 \\ \frac{\partial^2 V}{\partial \theta_1^2} > 0 \quad \text{or} \quad \frac{\partial^2 V}{\partial \theta_2^2} > 0 \end{gathered} \tag{10.24}$$

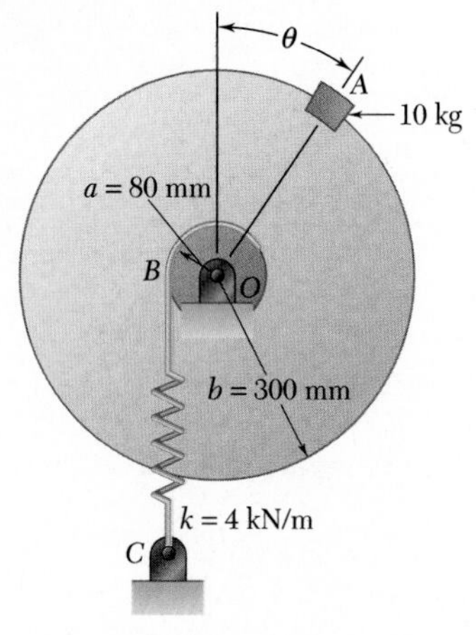

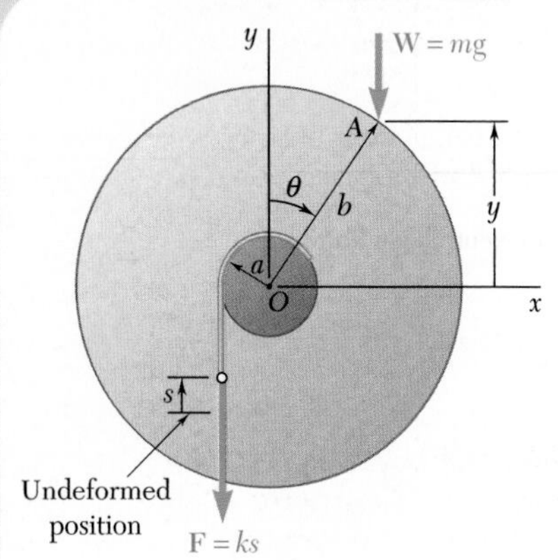

SAMPLE PROBLEM 10.4

A 10-kg block is attached to the rim of a 300-mm-radius disk as shown. Knowing that spring BC is unstretched when $\theta = 0$, determine the position or positions of equilibrium, and state in each case whether the equilibrium is stable, unstable, or neutral.

SOLUTION

Potential Energy. Denoting by s the deflection of the spring from its undeformed position and placing the origin of coordinates at O, we obtain

$$V_e = \tfrac{1}{2}ks^2 \qquad V_g = Wy = mgy$$

Measuring θ in radians, we have

$$s = a\theta \qquad y = b\cos\theta$$

Substituting for s and y in the expressions for V_e and V_g, we write

$$V_e = \tfrac{1}{2}ka^2\theta^2 \qquad V_g = mgb\cos\theta$$
$$V = V_e + V_g = \tfrac{1}{2}ka^2\theta^2 + mgb\cos\theta$$

Positions of Equilibrium. Setting $dV/d\theta = 0$, we write

$$\frac{dV}{d\theta} = ka^2\theta - mgb\sin\theta = 0$$
$$\sin\theta = \frac{ka^2}{mgb}\theta$$

Substituting $a = 0.08$ m, $b = 0.3$ m, $k = 4$ kN/m, and $m = 10$ kg, we obtain

$$\sin\theta = \frac{(4\text{ kN/m})(0.08\text{ m})^2}{(10\text{ kg})(9.81\text{ m/s}^2)(0.3\text{ m})}\theta$$
$$\sin\theta = 0.8699\,\theta$$

where θ is expressed in radians. Solving numerically for θ, we find

$$\theta = 0 \quad \text{and} \quad \theta = 0.902 \text{ rad}$$
$$\theta = 0 \quad \text{and} \quad \theta = 51.7° \quad ◀$$

Stability of Equilibrium. The second derivative of the potential energy V with respect to θ is

$$\frac{d^2V}{d\theta^2} = ka^2 - mgb\cos\theta$$
$$= (4\text{ kN/m})(0.08\text{ m})^2 - (10\text{ kg})(9.81\text{ m/s}^2)(0.3\text{ m})\cos\theta$$
$$= 25.6 - 29.43\cos\theta$$

For $\theta = 0$: $\quad \dfrac{d^2V}{d\theta^2} = 25.6 - 29.43\cos 0 = -3.83 < 0$

The equilibrium is unstable for $\theta = 0$ ◀

For $\theta = 51.7°$: $\quad \dfrac{d^2V}{d\theta^2} = 25.6 - 29.43\cos 51.7° = +7.36 > 0$

The equilibrium is stable for $\theta = 51.7°$ ◀

SOLVING PROBLEMS ON YOUR OWN

In this lesson we defined the *work of a force during a finite displacement* and the *potential energy* of a rigid body or a system of rigid bodies. You learned to use the concept of potential energy to determine the *equilibrium position* of a rigid body or a system of rigid bodies.

1. ***The potential energy V of a system*** is the sum of the potential energies associated with the various forces acting on the system that *do work* as the system moves. In the problems of this lesson you will determine the following:

a. ***Potential energy of a weight.*** This is the potential energy due to *gravity*, $V_g = Wy$, where y is the elevation of the weight W measured from some arbitrary reference level. Note that the potential energy V_g can be used with any vertical force $\mathbf{P}$ of constant magnitude directed downward; we write $V_g = Py$.

b. ***Potential energy of a spring.*** The potential energy, $V_e = \frac{1}{2}kx^2$, is due to the *elastic* force exerted by a spring, where k is the constant of the spring and x is the deformation of the spring *measured from its unstretched position*.

Reactions at fixed supports, internal forces at connections, forces exerted by inextensible cords and cables, and other forces which do no work do not contribute to the potential energy of the system.

2. ***Express all distances and angles in terms of a single variable***, such as an angle θ, when computing the potential energy V of a system. This is necessary, since the determination of the equilibrium position of the system requires the computation of the derivative $dV/d\theta$.

3. ***When a system is in equilibrium, the first derivative of its potential energy is zero.*** Therefore:

a. ***To determine a position of equilibrium of a system***, once its potential energy V has been expressed in terms of the single variable θ, compute its derivative and solve the equation $dV/d\theta = 0$ for θ.

b. ***To determine the force or couple required to maintain a system in a given position of equilibrium***, substitute the known value of θ in the equation $dV/d\theta = 0$ and solve this equation for the desired force or couple.

4. ***Stability of equilibrium.*** The following rules generally apply:

a. ***Stable equilibrium*** occurs when the potential energy of the system is *minimum*, that is, when $dV/d\theta = 0$ and $d^2V/d\theta^2 > 0$ (Figs. 10.14*a* and 10.15*a*).

b. ***Unstable equilibrium*** occurs when the potential energy of the system is *maximum*, that is, when $dV/d\theta = 0$ and $d^2V/d\theta^2 < 0$ (Figs. 10.14*b* and 10.15*b*).

c. ***Neutral equilibrium*** occurs when the potential energy of the system is *constant;* $dV/d\theta$, $dV^2/d\theta^2$, and all the successive derivatives of V are then equal to zero (Figs. 10.14*c* and 10.15*c*).

See page 583 for a discussion of the case when $dV/d\theta$, $dV^2/d\theta^2$ but *not all* of the successive derivatives of V are equal to zero.

Problems

10.59 Using the method of Sec. 10.8, solve Prob. 10.30.

10.60 Using the method of Sec. 10.8, solve Prob. 10.31.

10.61 Using the method of Sec. 10.8, solve Prob. 10.32.

10.62 Using the method of Sec. 10.8, solve Prob. 10.33.

10.63 Using the method of Sec. 10.8, solve Prob. 10.34.

10.64 Using the method of Sec. 10.8, solve Prob. 10.36.

10.65 Using the method of Sec. 10.8, solve Prob. 10.37.

10.66 Using the method of Sec. 10.8, solve Prob. 10.38.

10.67 Show that the equilibrium is neutral in Prob. 10.1.

10.68 Show that the equilibrium is neutral in Prob. 10.2.

10.69 Two uniform rods each of mass m are attached to gears of equal radii as shown. Determine the positions of equilibrium of the system, and state in each case whether the equilibrium is stable, unstable, or neutral.

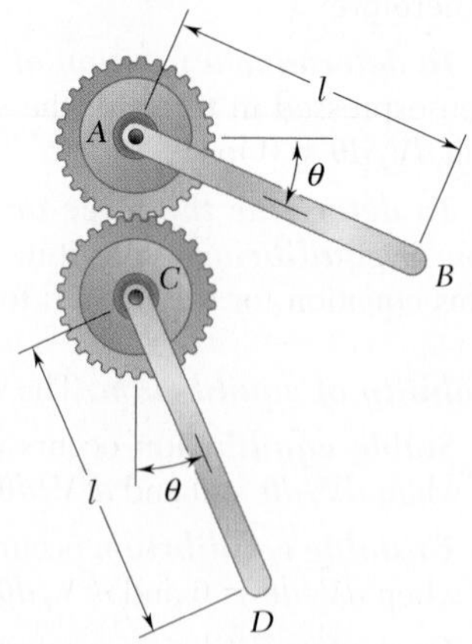

Fig. P10.69 and P10.70

10.70 Two uniform rods, AB and CD, are attached to gears of equal radii as shown. Knowing that $m_{AB} = 300$ g and $m_{CD} = 500$ g, determine the positions of equilibrium of the system, and state in each case whether the equilibrium is stable, unstable, or neutral.

10.71 Two identical uniform rods each of weight W and length L are attached to pulleys that are connected by a belt as shown. Assuming that no slipping occurs between the belt and the pulleys, determine the positions of equilibrium of the system, and state in each case whether the equilibrium is stable, unstable, or neutral.

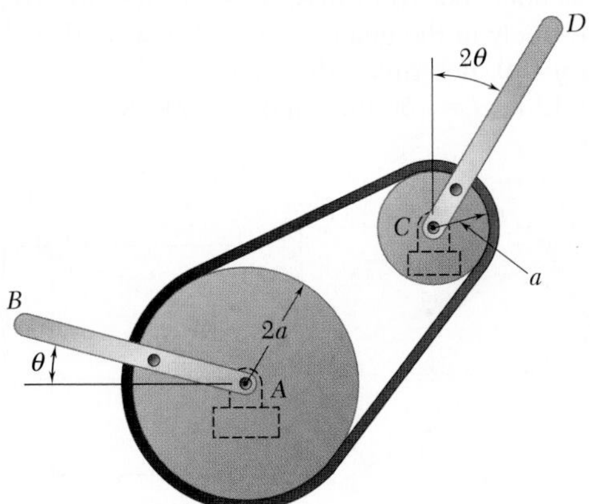

Fig. P10.71

10.72 Two uniform rods each of mass m and length l are attached to gears as shown. For the range $0 \leq \theta \leq 180°$, determine the positions of equilibrium of the system, and state in each case whether the equilibrium is stable, unstable, or neutral.

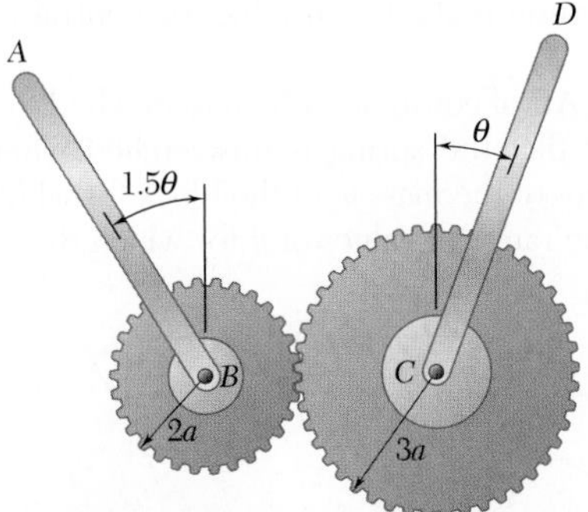

Fig. P10.72

10.73 Using the method of Sec. 10.8, solve Prob. 10.39. Determine whether the equilibrium is stable, unstable, or neutral. (*Hint:* The potential energy corresponding to the couple exerted by a torsional spring is $\frac{1}{2}K\theta^2$, where K is the torsional spring constant and θ is the angle of twist.)

10.74 In Prob. 10.40, determine whether each of the positions of equilibrium is stable, unstable, or neutral. (See the hint for Prob. 10.73.)

10.75 Angle θ is equal to 45° after a block of weight W is hung from member AB as shown. Neglecting the weight of AB and knowing that the spring is unstretched when $\theta = 20°$, determine the value of W, and state whether the equilibrium is stable, unstable, or neutral.

10.76 A block of weight W is hung from member AB as shown. Neglecting the weight of AB and knowing that the spring is unstretched when $\theta = 20°$, determine the value of θ corresponding to equilibrium when $W = 6.6$ N. State whether the equilibrium is stable, unstable, or neutral.

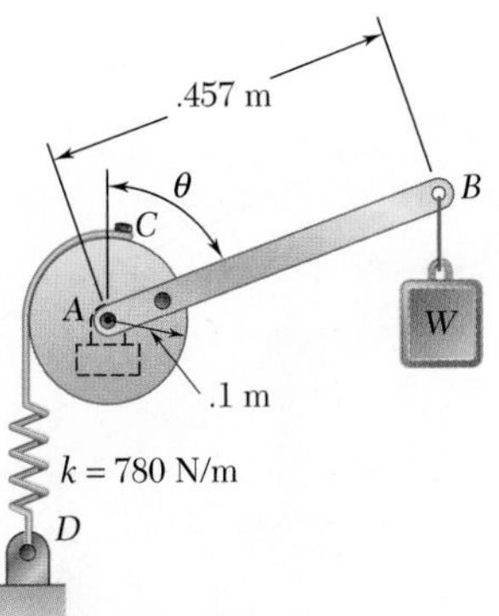

Fig. P10.75 and P10.76

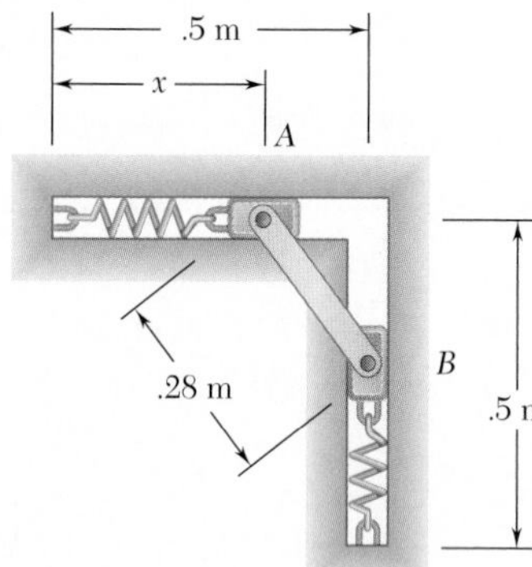

Fig. P10.77

10.77 The slender rod AB of negligible weight is attached to two 10-N blocks A and B that can move freely in the guides shown. Knowing that the constant of the springs is 1 N/m and that the unstretched length of each spring is .19 m, determine the value of x corresponding to equilibrium.

10.78 A slender rod AB of mass m is attached to two blocks A and B which can move freely in the guides shown. Knowing that the spring is unstretched when $y = 0$, determine the value of y corresponding to equilibrium when $m = 12$ kg, $l = 750$ mm, and $k = 900$ N/m.

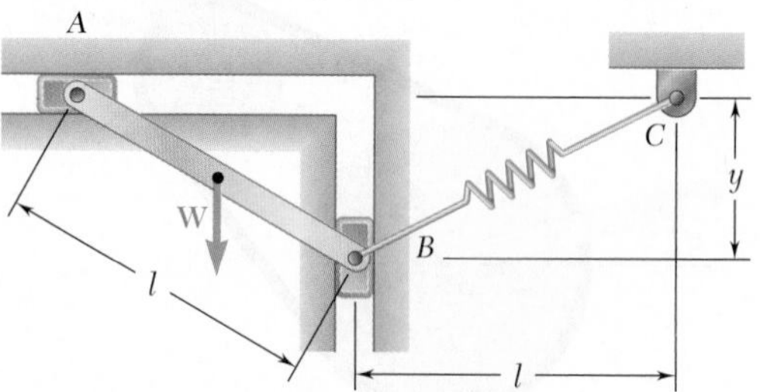

Fig. *P10.78*

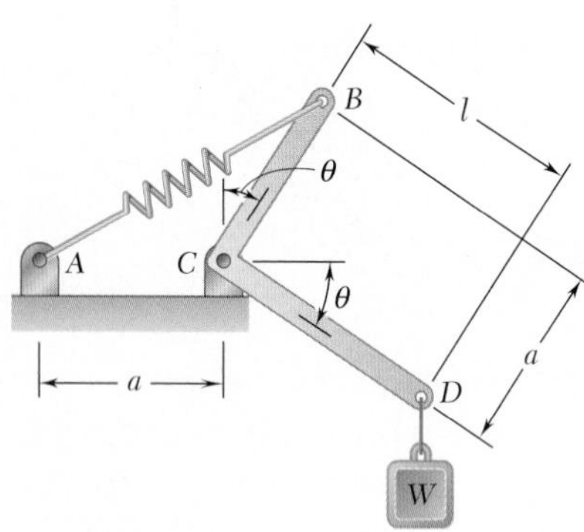

Fig. P10.79

10.79 The constant of spring AB is k, and the spring is unstretched when $\theta = 0$. (a) Neglecting the weight of the rigid arm BCD, derive an equation in terms of θ, k, a, l, and W that is satisfied when the arm is in equilibrium. (b) Determine three values of θ corresponding to equilibrium when $k = 12000$ N/m, $a = .25$ m, $l = .381$ m, and $W = 100$ N. State in each case whether the equilibrium is stable, unstable, or neutral.

10.80 Spring AB of constant 2 kN/m is attached to two identical drums as shown. Knowing that the spring is unstretched when $\theta = 0$, determine (a) the range of values of the mass m of the block for which a position of equilibrium exists, (b) the range of values of θ for which the equilibrium is stable.

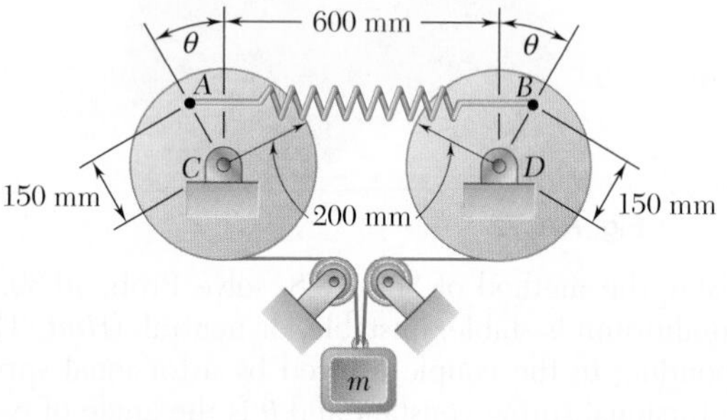

Fig. *P10.80* and P10.81

10.81 Spring AB of constant 2 kN/m is attached to two identical drums as shown. Knowing that the spring is unstretched when $\theta = 0$ and that $m = 20$ kg, determine the values of θ less than 180° corresponding to equilibrium. State in each case whether the equilibrium is stable, unstable, or neutral.

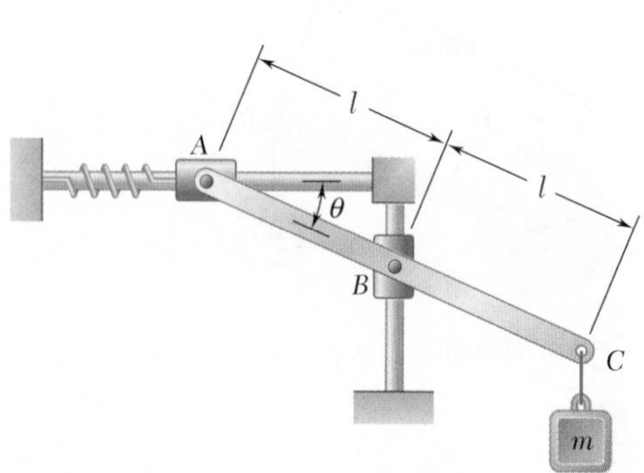

Fig. P10.82

10.82 Bar ABC is attached to collars A and B that can move freely on the rods shown. The constant of the spring is k, and the spring is unstretched when $\theta = 0$. (a) Neglecting the mass of bar ABC, derive an equation in terms of θ, m, g, k, and l that is satisfied when bar ABC is in equilibrium. (b) Determine the value of θ corresponding to equilibrium when $m = 5$ kg, $k = 800$ N/m, and $l = 250$ mm, and check that the equilibrium is stable.

10.83 A slender rod AB of negligible mass is attached to two collars A and B that can move freely along the guide rods shown. Knowing that $\beta = 30°$ and $P = Q = 400$ N, determine the value of the angle θ corresponding to equilibrium.

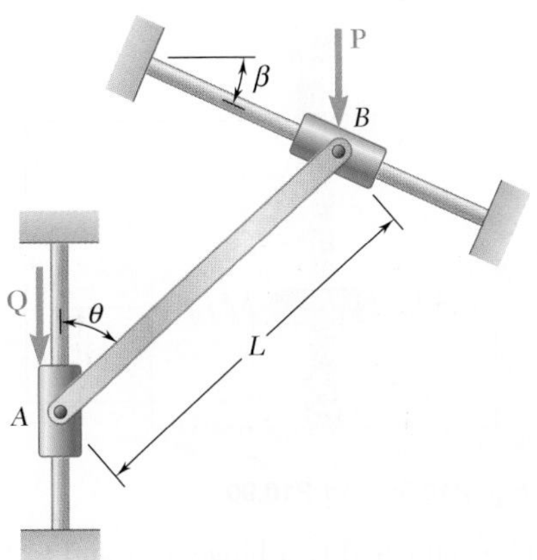

Fig. P10.83 and *P10.84*

10.84 A slender rod AB of negligible mass is attached to two collars A and B that can move freely along the guide rods shown. Knowing that $\beta = 30°$, $P = 100$ N, and $Q = 25$ N, determine the value of the angle θ corresponding to equilibrium.

10.85 The 25-N block D can slide freely on the inclined surface. Knowing that the constant of the spring is 400 N/m and that the spring is unstretched when $\theta = 0$, determine the value of θ corresponding to equilibrium.

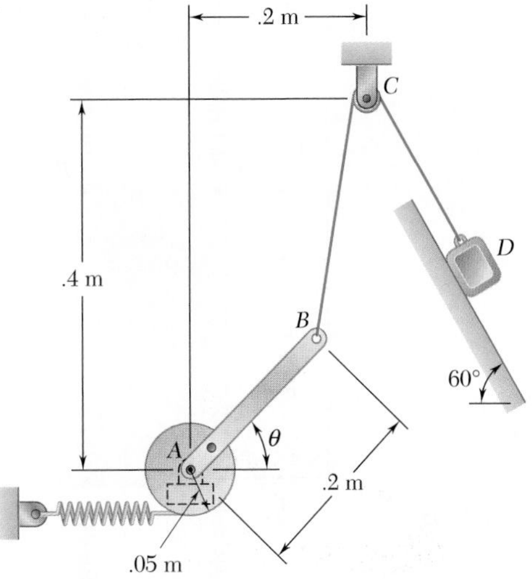

Fig. P10.85

10.86 Cable AB is attached to two springs and passes through a ring at C. Knowing that the springs are unstretched when $y = 0$, determine the distance y corresponding to equilibrium.

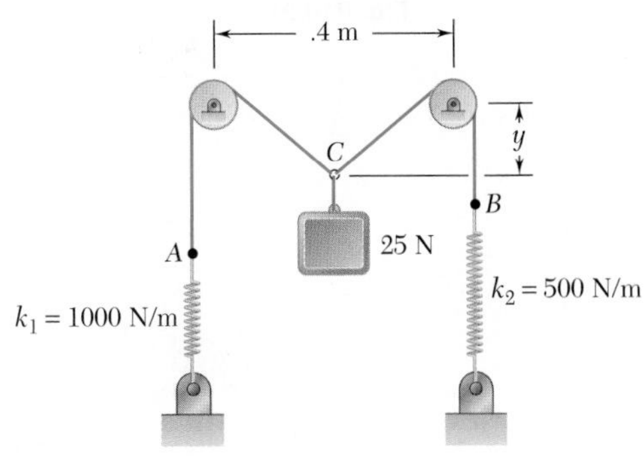

Fig. P10.86

***10.87* and 10.88** Collar A can slide freely on the semicircular rod shown. Knowing that the constant of the spring is k and that the unstretched length of the spring is equal to the radius r, determine the value of θ corresponding to equilibrium when $m = 20$ kg, $r = 180$ mm, and $k = 3$ kN/m.

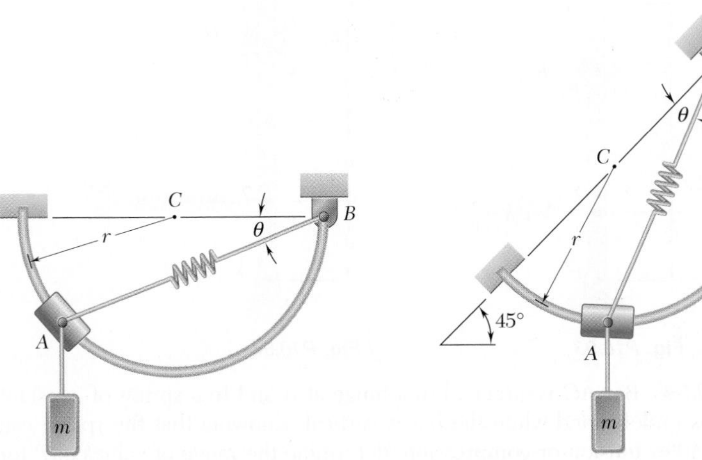

Fig. *P10.87* **Fig. P10.88**

10.89 Rod AB is attached to a hinge at A and to two springs of constant k that are unstretched in the position shown. If h = 1.27 m, d = .6 m, and W = 160 N, determine the range of values of k for which the equilibrium of the rod is stable in the given position. Each spring can act in either tension or compression.

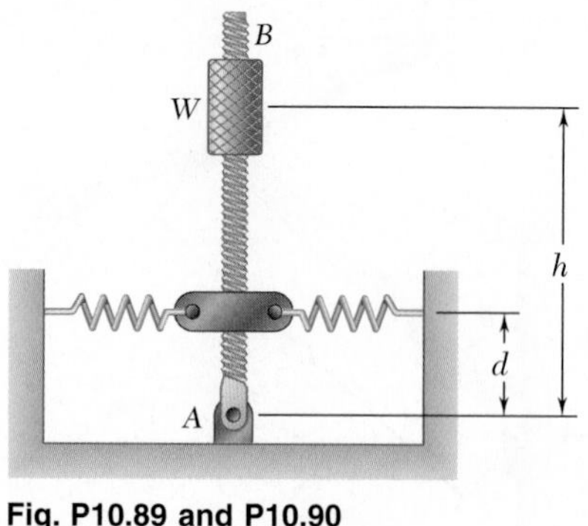

Fig. P10.89 and P10.90

10.90 Rod AB is attached to a hinge at A and to two springs of constant k that are unstretched in the position shown. If h = .762 m, k = 690 N/m, and W = 40 N, determine the smallest distance d for which the equilibrium of the rod is stable in the given position. Each spring can act in either tension or compression.

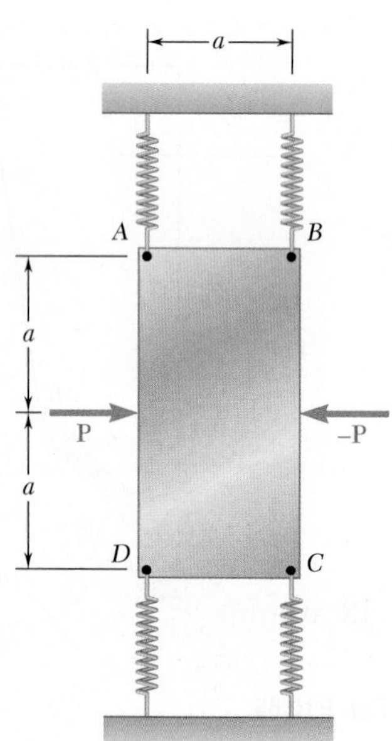

Fig. P10.91

10.91 The uniform plate $ABCD$ of negligible mass is attached to four springs of constant k and is in equilibrium in the position shown. Knowing that the springs can act in either tension or compression and are undeformed in the given position, determine the range of values of the magnitude P of two equal and opposite horizontal forces **P** and –**P** for which the equilibrium position shown is stable.

10.92 and *10.93* Two bars are attached to a single spring of constant k that is unstretched when the bars are vertical. Determine the range of values of P for which the equilibrium of the system is stable in the position shown.

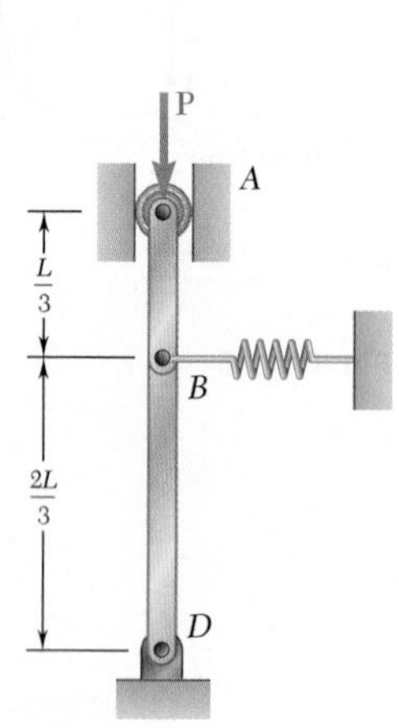

Fig. P10.92

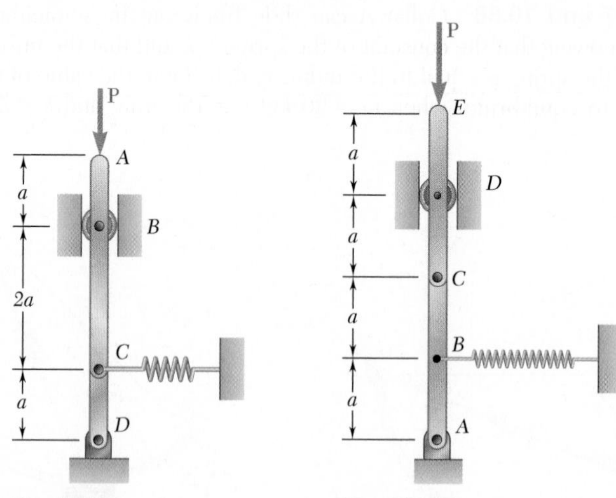

Fig. *P10.93*

Fig. *P10.94*

10.94 Bar AC is attached to a hinge at A and to a spring of constant k that is undeformed when the bar is vertical. Knowing that the spring can act in either tension or compression, determine the range of values of P for which the equilibrium of the system is stable in the position shown.

10.95 Bars BC and EF are connected at G by a pin that is attached to BC and that can slide freely in a slot cut in EF. Determine the smallest mass m_1 for which the equilibrium of the mechanism is stable in the position shown.

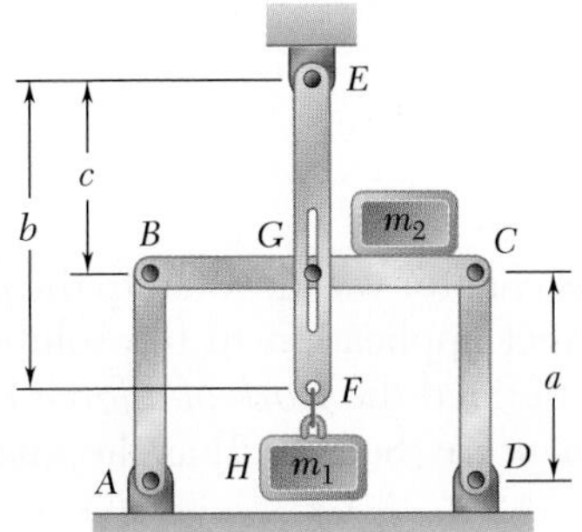

Fig. P10.95

10.96 The horizontal bar BEH is pinned to collar E and to vertical bars AC and GI. The collar can slide freely on bar DF. Determine the range of values of Q for which the equilibrium of the system is stable in the position shown when $a = 480$ mm, $b = 400$ mm, and $P = 600$ N.

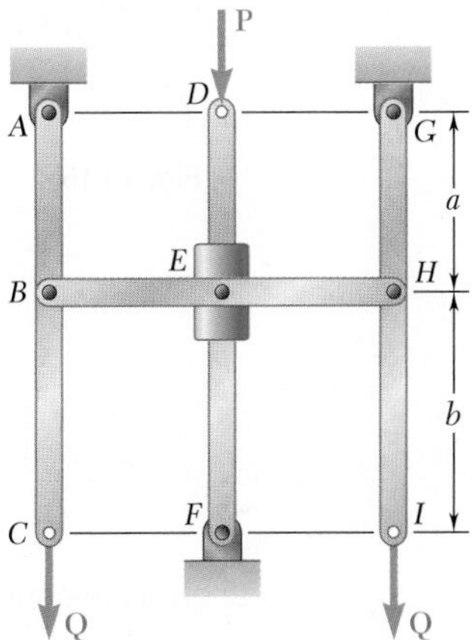

Fig. P10.96

***10.97** Bars AB and BC each of length l and of negligible weight are attached to two springs each of constant k. The springs are undeformed and the system is in equilibrium when $\theta_1 = \theta_2 = 0$. Determine the range of values of P for which this equilibrium position is stable.

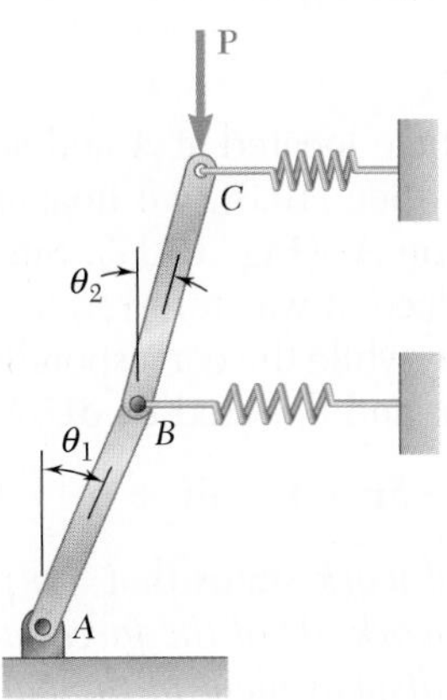

Fig. P10.97

***10.98** Solve Prob. 10.97 knowing that $l = 400$ mm and $k = 1.25$ kN/m.

***10.99** Bar ABC of length $2a$ and negligible mass is hinged at C to a drum of radius a as shown. Knowing that the constant of each spring is k and that the springs are undeformed when $\theta_1 = \theta_2 = 0$, determine the range of values of P for which the equilibrium position $\theta_1 = \theta_2 = 0$ is stable.

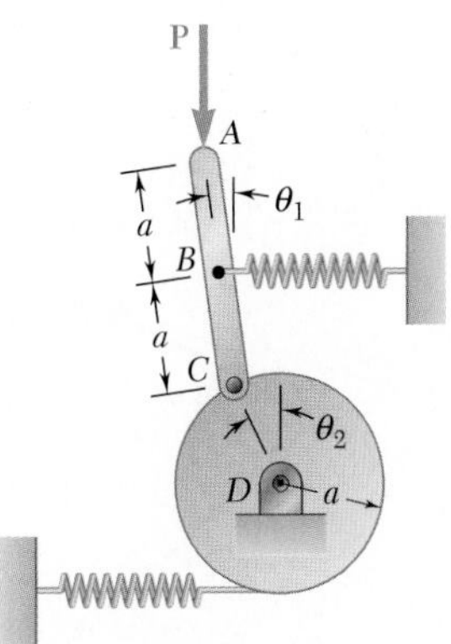

Fig. P10.99

***10.100** Solve Prob. 10.99 knowing that $k = 2$ kN/m and $a = 350$ mm.

REVIEW AND SUMMARY FOR CHAPTER 10

Work of a force

The first part of this chapter was devoted to the *principle of virtual work* and to its direct application to the solution of equilibrium problems. We first defined the *work of a force* **F** *corresponding to the small displacement* $d\mathbf{r}$ [Sec. 10.2] as the quantity

$$dU = \mathbf{F} \cdot d\mathbf{r} \tag{10.1}$$

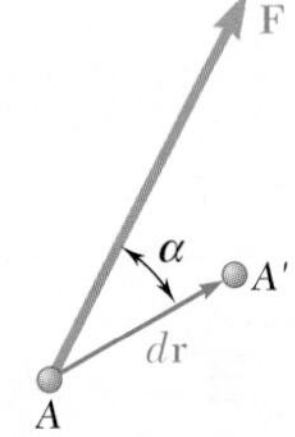

Fig. 10.16

obtained by forming the scalar product of the force **F** and the displacement $d\mathbf{r}$ (Fig. 10.16). Denoting respectively by F and ds the magnitudes of the force and of the displacement, and by α the angle formed by **F** and $d\mathbf{r}$, we wrote

$$dU = F\, ds \cos \alpha \tag{10.1′}$$

The work dU is positive if $\alpha < 90°$, zero if $\alpha = 90°$, and negative if $\alpha > 90°$. We also found that the *work of a couple of moment* **M** acting on a rigid body is

$$dU = M\, d\theta \tag{10.2}$$

where $d\theta$ is the small angle expressed in radians through which the body rotates.

Virtual displacement

Considering a particle located at A and acted upon by several forces $\mathbf{F}_1, \mathbf{F}_2, \ldots, \mathbf{F}_n$ [Sec. 10.3], we imagined that the particle moved to a new position A' (Fig. 10.17). Since this displacement did not actually take place, it was referred to as a *virtual displacement* and denoted by $\delta\mathbf{r}$, while the corresponding work of the forces was called *virtual work* and denoted by δU. We had

$$\delta U = \mathbf{F}_1 \cdot \delta\mathbf{r} + \mathbf{F}_2 \cdot \delta\mathbf{r} + \cdots + \mathbf{F}_n \cdot \delta\mathbf{r}$$

Principle of virtual work

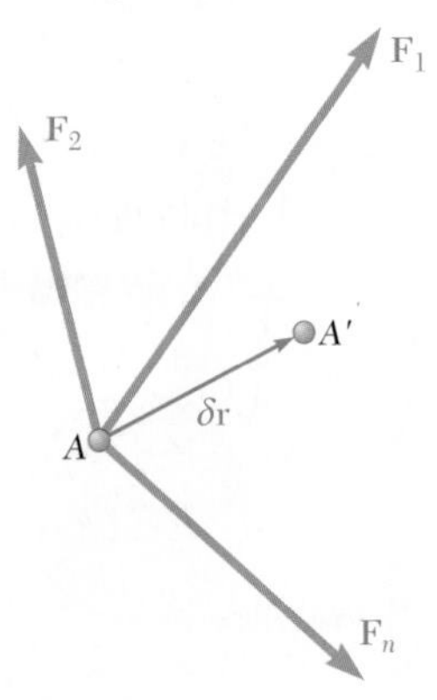

Fig. 10.17

The *principle of virtual work* states that *if a particle is in equilibrium, the total virtual work* δU *of the forces acting on the particle is zero for any virtual displacement of the particle.*

The principle of virtual work can be extended to the case of rigid bodies and systems of rigid bodies. Since it involves *only forces which do work*, its application provides a useful alternative to the use of the equilibrium equations in the solution of many engineering problems. It is particularly effective in the case of machines and mechanisms consisting of connected rigid bodies, since the work of the reactions at the supports is zero and the work of the internal forces at the pin connections cancels out [Sec. 10.4; Sample Probs. 10.1, 10.2, and 10.3].

Mechanical efficiency

In the case of *real machines* [Sec. 10.5], however, the work of the friction forces should be taken into account, with the result that the *output work will be less than the input work*. Defining the *mechanical efficiency* of a machine as the ratio

$$\eta = \frac{\text{output work}}{\text{input work}} \tag{10.9}$$

we also noted that for an ideal machine (no friction) $\eta = 1$, while for a real machine $\eta < 1$.

Work of a force over a finite displacement

In the second part of the chapter we considered the *work of forces corresponding to finite displacements* of their points of application. The work $U_{1\to2}$ of the force $\mathbf{F}$ corresponding to a displacement of the particle A from A_1 to A_2 (Fig. 10.18) was obtained by integrating the right-hand member of Eq. (10.1) or (10.1′) along the curve described by the particle [Sec. 10.6]:

$$U_{1\to2} = \int_{A_1}^{A_2} \mathbf{F} \cdot d\mathbf{r} \tag{10.11}$$

or

$$U_{1\to2} = \int_{s_1}^{s_2} (F \cos \alpha)\, ds \tag{10.11'}$$

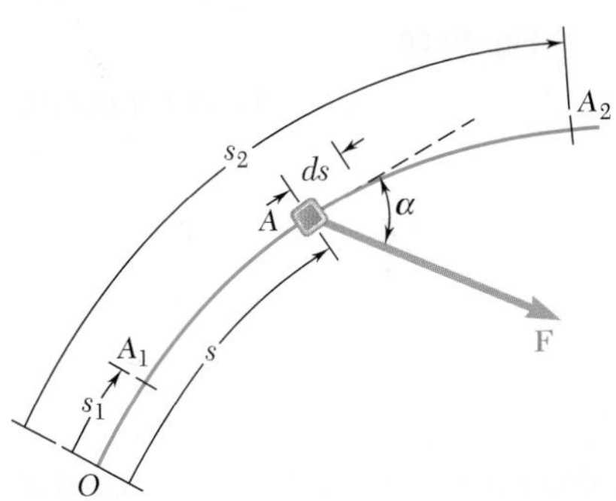

Fig. 10.18

Similarly, the work of a couple of moment $\mathbf{M}$ corresponding to a finite rotation from θ_1 to θ_2 of a rigid body was expressed as

$$U_{1\to2} = \int_{\theta_1}^{\theta_2} M\, d\theta \tag{10.12}$$

Work of a weight

The *work of the weight* $\mathbf{W}$ *of a body* as its center of gravity moves from the elevation y_1 to y_2 (Fig. 10.19) can be obtained by setting $F = W$ and $\alpha = 180°$ in Eq. (10.11′):

$$U_{1\to2} = -\int_{y_1}^{y_2} W\, dy = Wy_1 - Wy_2 \tag{10.13}$$

The work of $\mathbf{W}$ is therefore positive *when the elevation y decreases*.

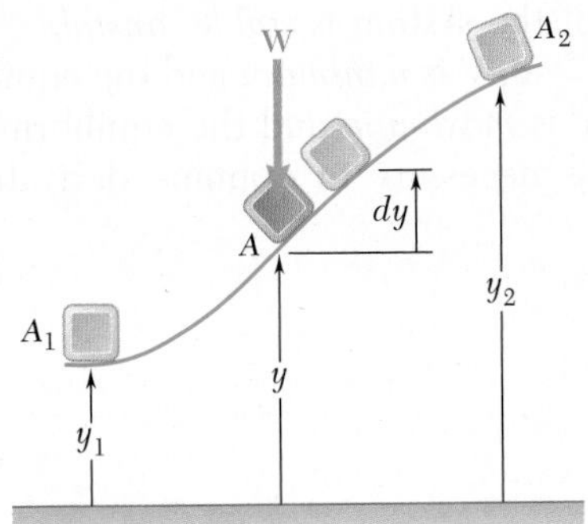

Fig. 10.19

Work of the force exerted by a spring

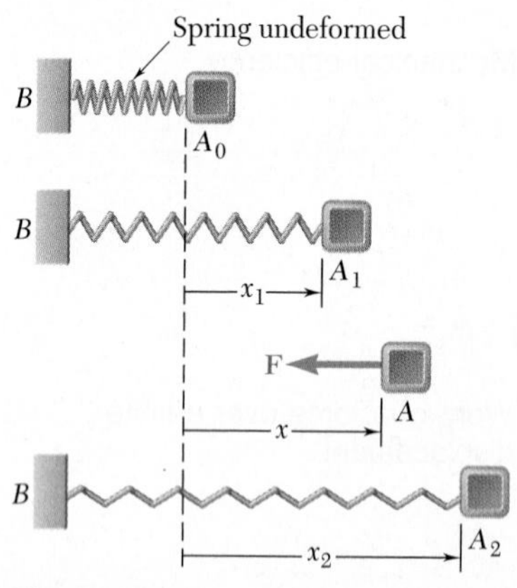

Fig. 10.20

The *work of the force* **F** *exerted by a spring* on a body A as the spring is stretched from x_1 to x_2 (Fig. 10.20) can be obtained by setting $F = kx$, where k is the constant of the spring, and $\alpha = 180°$ in Eq. (10.11′):

$$U_{1\to 2} = -\int_{x_1}^{x_2} kx\, dx = \tfrac{1}{2}kx_1^2 - \tfrac{1}{2}kx_2^2 \qquad (10.15)$$

The work of **F** is therefore positive *when the spring is returning to its undeformed position.*

Potential energy

When the work of a force **F** is independent of the path actually followed between A_1 and A_2, the force is said to be a *conservative force,* and its work can be expressed as

$$U_{1\to 2} = V_1 - V_2 \qquad (10.20)$$

where V is the *potential energy* associated with **F**, and V_1 and V_2 represent the values of V at A_1 and A_2, respectively [Sec. 10.7]. The potential energies associated, respectively, with the *force of gravity* **W** and the *elastic force* **F** exerted by a spring were found to be

$$V_g = Wy \qquad \text{and} \qquad V_e = \tfrac{1}{2}kx^2 \qquad (10.17, 10.18)$$

Alternative expression for the principle of virtual work

When the position of a mechanical system depends upon a single independent variable θ, the potential energy of the system is a function $V(\theta)$ of that variable, and it follows from Eq. (10.20) that $\delta U = -\delta V = -(dV/d\theta)\,\delta\theta$. The condition $\delta U = 0$ required by the principle of virtual work for the equilibrium of the system can thus be replaced by the condition

$$\frac{dV}{d\theta} = 0 \qquad (10.21)$$

When all the forces involved are conservative, it may be preferable to use Eq. (10.21) rather than to apply the principle of virtual work directly [Sec. 10.8; Sample Prob. 10.4].

Stability of equilibrium

This approach presents another advantage, since it is possible to determine from the sign of the second derivative of V whether the equilibrium of the system is *stable, unstable,* or *neutral* [Sec. 10.9]. If $d^2V/d\theta^2 > 0$, V is *minimum* and the equilibrium is *stable;* if $d^2V/d\theta^2 < 0$, V is *maximum* and the equilibrium is *unstable;* if $d^2V/d\theta^2 = 0$, it is necessary to examine derivatives of a higher order.

Review Problems

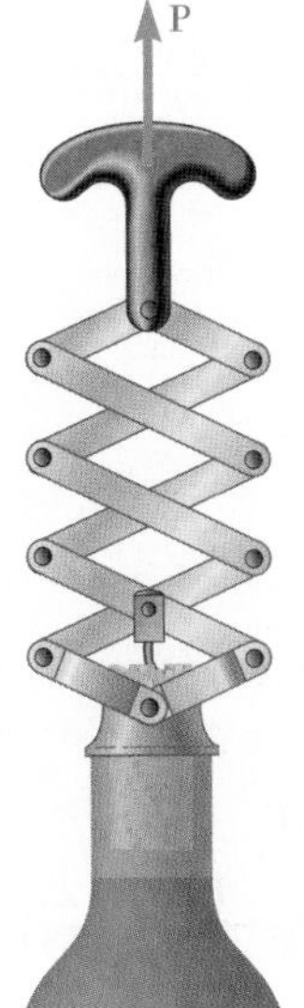

Fig. P10.101

10.101 Knowing that the maximum friction force exerted by the bottle on the cork is 300 N, determine (*a*) the force **P** which must be applied to the corkscrew to open the bottle, (*b*) the maximum force exerted by the base of the corkscrew on the top of the bottle.

10.102 The position of boom *ABC* is controlled by the hydraulic cylinder *BD*. For the loading shown, determine the force exerted by the hydraulic cylinder on pin *B* when $\theta = 70°$.

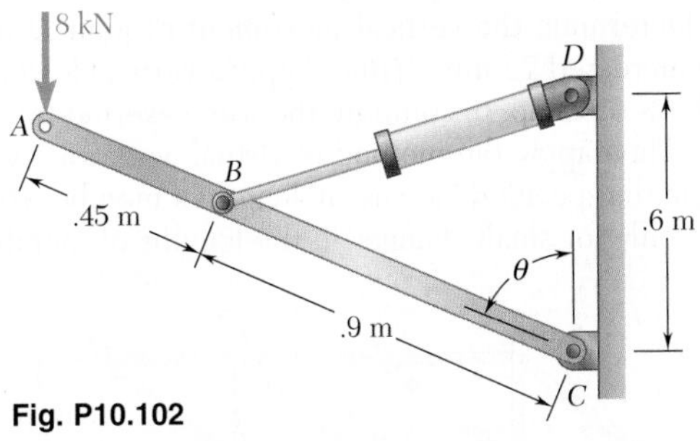

Fig. P10.102

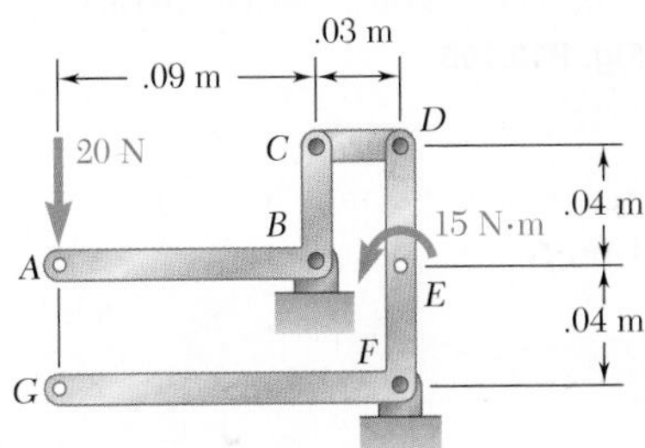

Fig. *P10.103* and P10.104

10.103 Determine the vertical force **P** which must be applied at *G* so that the linkage is in equilibrium for the position shown.

10.104 Determine the couple **M** which must be applied to member *DEFG* so that the linkage is in equilibrium for the position shown.

10.105 Derive an expression for the magnitude of the couple **M** so that the linkage is in equilibrium for the position shown.

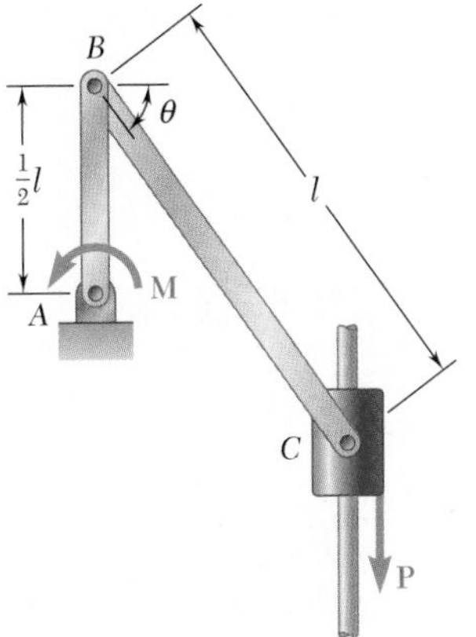

Fig. P10.105

10.106 Two rods *AC* and *CE* are connected by a pin at *C* and by a spring *AE*. The constant of the spring is 27.16 N/m, and the spring is unstretched when $\theta = 30°$. Knowing that $l = .254$ m and neglecting the weight of the rods, determine the value of θ corresponding to equilibrium when $P = 40$ N.

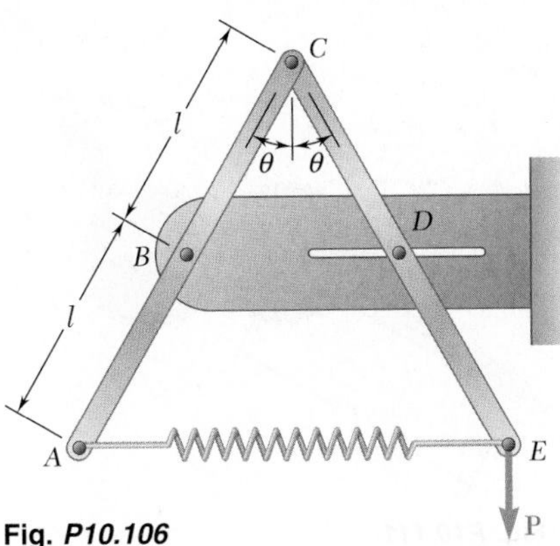

Fig. *P10.106*

10.107 For the linkage shown, determine the couple **M** required for equilibrium when $l = .548$ m, $Q = 40$ N, and $\theta = 65°$.

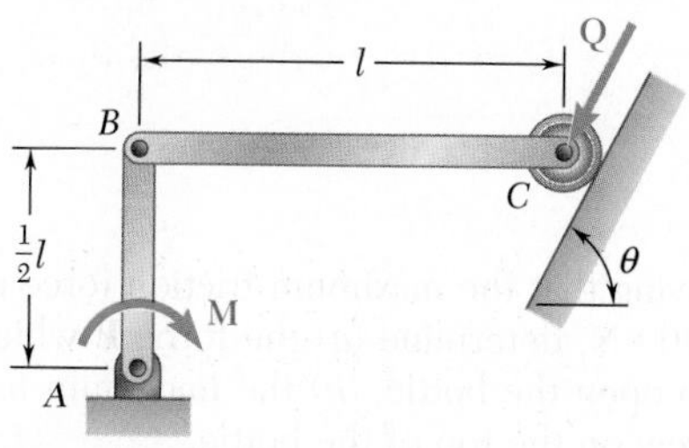

Fig. P10.107

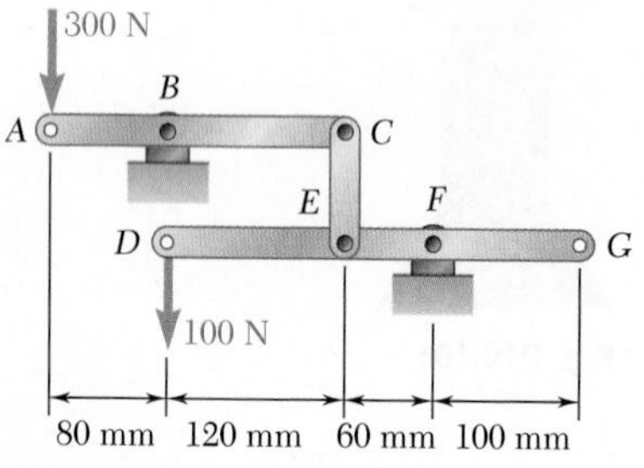

Fig. P10.108

10.108 Determine the vertical force **P** which must be applied at G so that the linkage is in equilibrium for the position shown.

10.109 Determine the vertical movement of joint D if the length of member BF is increased 75 mm. (*Hint:* Apply a vertical load at joint D, and, using the methods of Chap. 6, compute the force exerted by member BF on joints B and F. Then apply the method of virtual work for a virtual displacement resulting in the specified increase in length of member BF. This method should be used only for small changes in the lengths of members.)

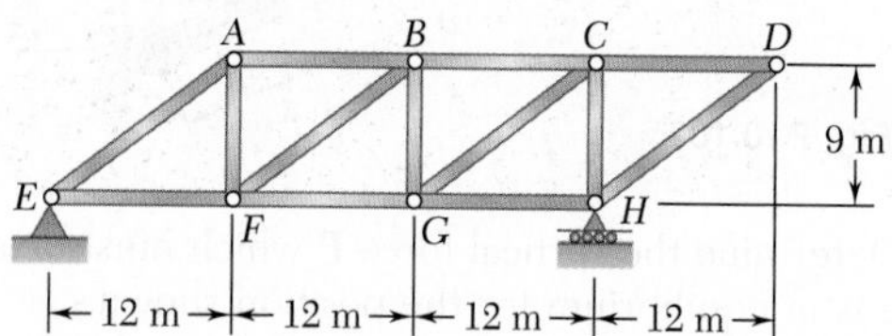

Fig. *P10.109* and P10.110

10.110 Determine the horizontal movement of joint D if the length of member BF is increased 75 mm. (See the hint for Prob. 10.109.)

10.111 Two uniform rods, AB and CD, are attached to gears of equal radii as shown. Knowing that $m_{AB} = 3.5$ kg and $m_{CD} = 1.75$ kg, determine the positions of equilibrium of the system, and state in each case whether the equilibrium is stable, unstable, or neutral.

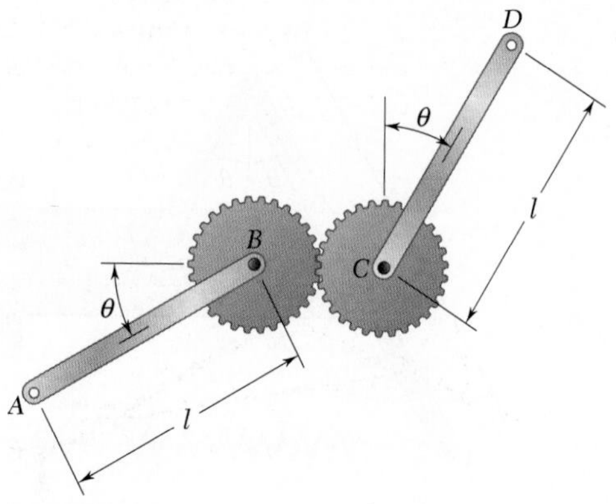

Fig. *P10.111*

10.112 A slender rod AB of mass m is attached to two blocks A and B that can move freely in the guides shown. Knowing that the spring is unstretched when AB is horizontal, determine three values of θ corresponding to equilibrium when $m = 125$ kg, $l = 320$ mm, and $k = 15$ kN/m. State in each case whether the equilibrium is stable, unstable, or neutral.

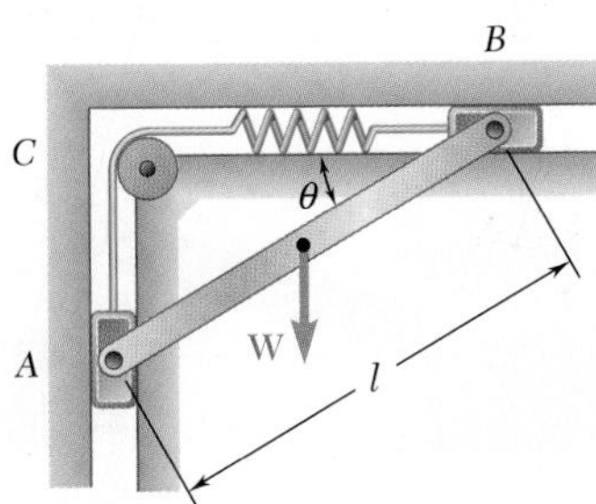

Fig. P10.112

Computer Problems

10.C1 Knowing that $a = .5$ m, $b = .15$ m, $L = .5$ m, and $P = 25$ N, use computational software to plot the force in member BD as a function of θ for values of θ from 30° to 150°. Determine the range of values of θ for which the absolute value of the force in member BD is less than 100 N.

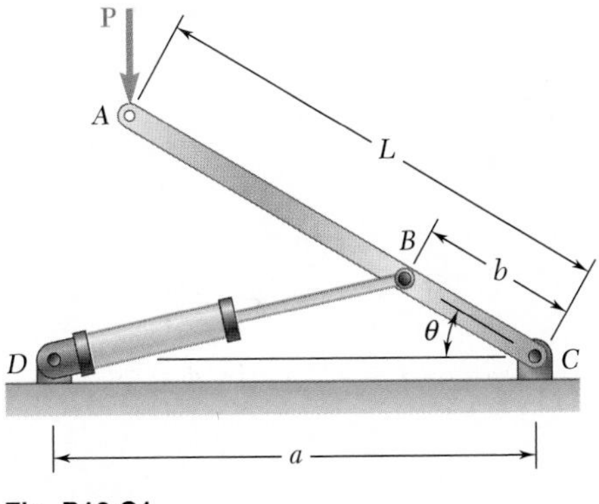

Fig. P10.C1

10.C2 Collars A and B are connected by the wire AB and can slide freely on the rods shown, where rod DE lies in the xy plane. Knowing that the length of the wire is 500 mm and that the mass of each collar is 2.5 kg, (a) use the principle of virtual work to express in terms of the distance x the magnitude of the force $\mathbf{P}$ required to maintain the system in equilibrium, (b) plot P as a function of x for 100 mm $\leq x \leq$ 400 mm.

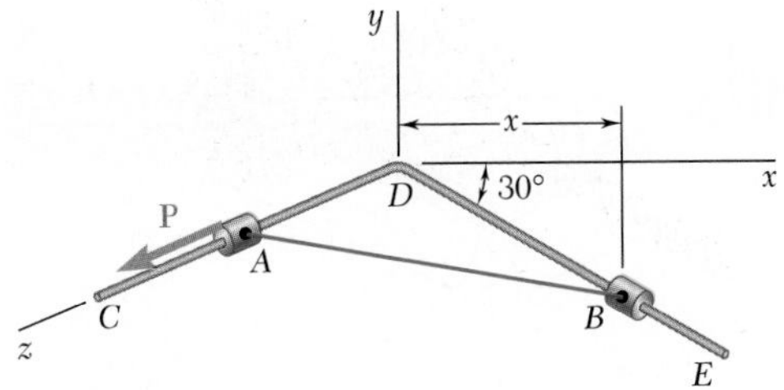

Fig. P10.C2

10.C3 A couple **M** is applied to crank AB to maintain the equilibrium of the engine system shown when a force **P** is applied to the piston. (*a*) Knowing that $b = 48$ mm and $l = 150$ mm, use computational software to plot the ratio M/P as a function of θ for values of θ from 0 to 180°. (*b*) Determine the value of θ for which the ratio M/P is maximum and the corresponding value of M/P.

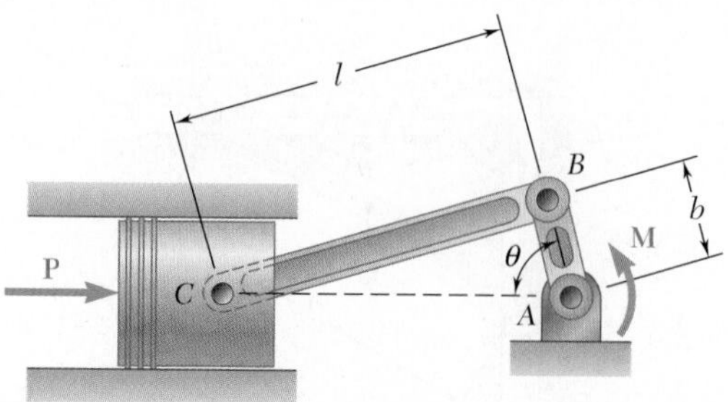

Fig. P10.C3

10.C4 The constant of spring AB is k, and the spring is unstretched when $\theta = 0$. (*a*) Neglecting the weight of member BCD, express the potential energy and its derivative $dV/d\theta$ in terms of a, k, W, and θ. (*b*) Using computational software and knowing that $W = 600$ N, $a = 200$ mm, and $k = 15$ kN/m, plot the potential energy and $dV/d\theta$ as functions of θ for values of θ from 0 to 165°. (*c*) Determine the values of θ for which the system is in equilibrium, and state in each case whether the equilibrium is stable, unstable, or neutral.

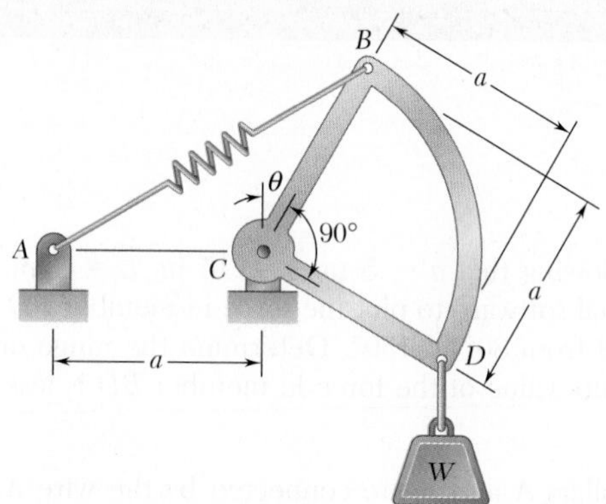

Fig. P10.C4

10.C5 A vertical load **W** is applied to the linkage at B. The constant of the spring is k, and the spring is unstretched when AB and BC are horizontal. For $l = .28$ m and $k = 2000$ N/m, plot W as a function of θ for values of θ from 0 to 80°.

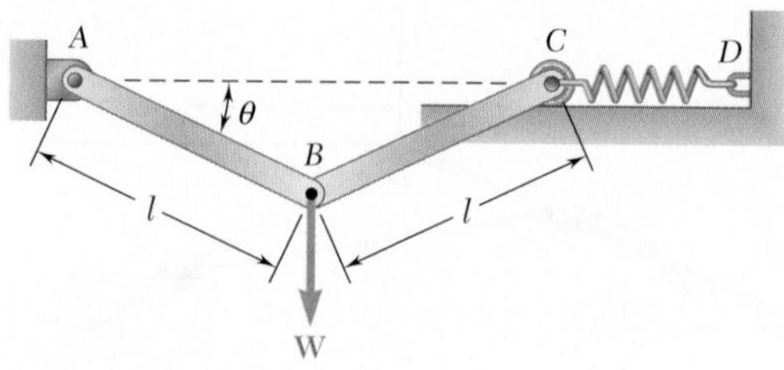

Fig. P10.C5

10.C6 The piston of the boom ABC is controlled by the hydraulic cylinder BD. Using computational software, plot the magnitude of the force exerted by the hydraulic cylinder on pin B as a function of θ for values of θ from 5° to 120°.

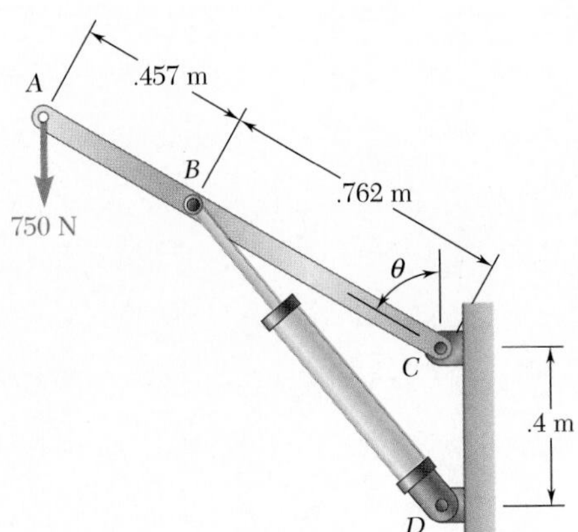

Fig. P10.C6

***10.C7** An 8-kg block is hung from the midpoint C of cable AB that is attached to two springs as shown. Knowing that the springs are unstretched when $y = 0$, plot the distance y corresponding to equilibrium as a function of the spring constant k_2 for 400 N/m $\leq k_2 \leq$ 600 N/m.

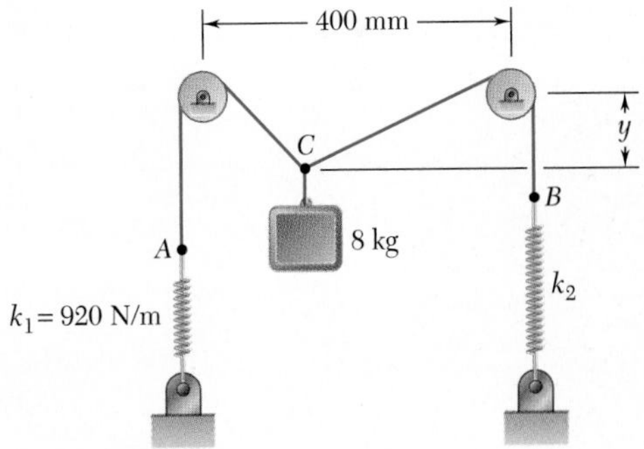

Fig. P10.C7

10.C8 A slender rod AB of weight W is attached to blocks A and B which can move freely in the guides shown. The spring constant is k and the spring is unstretched when AB is horizontal. For l = .5 m and k = 170 N/m, use computational software to determine the three values of the angle θ corresponding to equilibrium for values of W from 1 N to 12 N in 1 N increments.

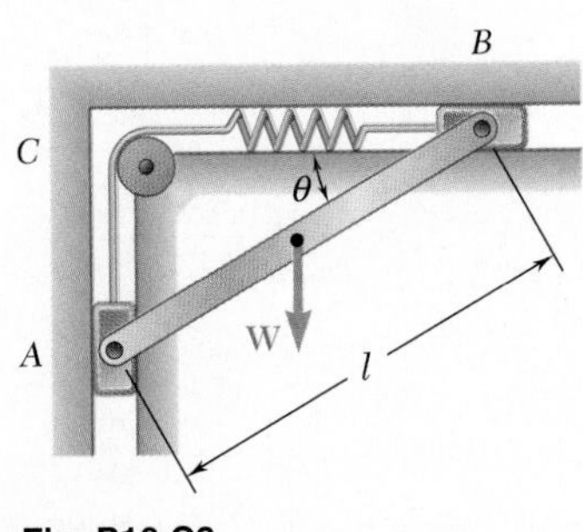

Fig. P10.C8

10.C9 A vertical load **W** is applied to the mechanism at C. Neglecting the weight of the mechanism, use computational software to plot θ as a function of W for values of W from 40 N to 480 N knowing that k = 5 kN/m and that the spring is unstretched when $\theta = 0$.

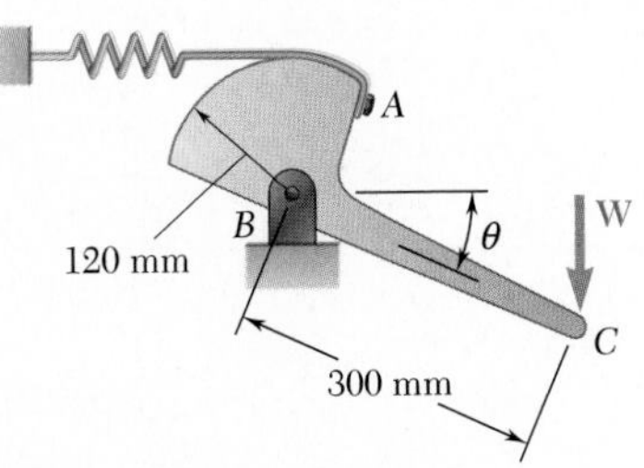

Fig. P10.C9

APPENDIX

Fundamentals of Engineering Examination

Engineers are required to be licensed when their work directly affects the public health, safety, and welfare. The intent is to ensure that engineers have met minimum qualifications involving competence, ability, experience, and character. The licensing process involves an initial exam, called the *Fundamentals of Engineering Examination;* professional experience; and a second exam, called the *Principles and Practice of Engineering*. Those who successfully complete these requirements are licensed as a *Professional Engineer*. The exams are developed under the auspices of the *National Council of Examiners for Engineering and Surveying*.

The first exam, the *Fundamentals of Engineering Examination,* can be taken just before or after graduation from a four-year accredited engineering program. The exam stresses subject material in a typical undergraduate engineering program, including statics and dynamics. The topics included in the exam cover much of the material in this book. The following is a list of the main topic areas, with references to the appropriate sections in this book. Also included are problems that can be solved to review this material.

Concurrent Force Systems (2.2–2.9; 2.12–2.14)
Problems: 2.34, 2.35, 2.40, 2.79, 2.85, 2.90, 2.99

Vector Forces (3.4–3.11)
Problems: 3.16, 3.18, 3.23, 3.28, 3.37, 3.39

Equilibrium in Two Dimensions (2.11; 4.1–4.7)
Problems: 4.3, 4.10, 4.13, 4.21, 4.35, 4.37, 4.67, 4.76

Equilibrium in Three Dimensions (2.15; 4.8–4.9)
Problems: 4.102, 4.104, 4.111, 4.116, 4.120, 4.132, 4.148

Centroid of an Area (5.2–5.7)
Problems: 5.1, 5.3, 5.17, 5.32, 5.53, 5.91, 5.98, 5.99, 5.130, 5.133

Analysis of Trusses (6.2–6.7)
Problems: 6.2, 6.3, 6.7, 6.29, 6.30, 6.42, 6.43, 6.52

Equilibrium of Two-Dimensional Frames (6.9–6.11)
Problems: 6.76, 6.78, 6.84, 6.95, 6.98

Shear and Bending Moment (7.2–7.6)
Problems: 7.22, 7.30, 7.37, 7.41, 7.45, 7.65, 7.74, 7.76

Fiction (8.2–8.5; 8.10)

Problems: 8.1, 8.13, 8.15, 8.21, 8.34, 8.101, 8.102, 8.104, 8.105, 8.111

Moments of Inertia (9.2–9.10)

Problems: 9.1, 9.5, 9.31, 9.33, 9.38, 9.71, 9.75, 9.82, 9.88, 9.94, 9.105

PHOTO CREDITS

CHAPTER 1

Opener (upper, left): © Getty Images; **Opener (upper, middle):** © Abiomed, Inc; **(upper, right):** NASA; **Opener (lower, left):** © Reuters/CORBIS; **Opener (middle):** © Eric Cassano; **Opener (middle, right):** Courtesy of AT&T; **Opener (lower, right):** NASA/JPL-Caltech/Cornell; **p. 2:** © Bettmann/CORBIS; **p. 4:** NASA; **p. 9:** © Robert Rathe, Courtesy of National Bureau of Standards; **p. 10:** © 1998, Lockheed Martin.

CHAPTER 2

Opener: © Image Source/Getty Images; **p. 19:** © Nicolas Russell/ Getty Images; **p. 37:** © H. David Seawell/CORBIS; **p. 57:** © Arthur D'Arazien.

CHAPTER 3

Opener (background): © Profimedia.CZ s.r.o./Alamy; **Opener (inset):** © David De Lossy/Getty Images; **p. 107:** © Elliot Eisenberg; **p. 112:** © Steve Hix/Getty Images; **p. 124:** © Steve Raymer/CORBIS; **p. 125:** © Yogi, Inc./CORBIS; **p. 127, p. 128:** © Elliot Eisenberg.

CHAPTER 4

Opener: © Jochem D Wijnands/Getty Images; **p. 159 (both):** © Elliot Eisenberg; **p. 160 (top):** © Lucinda Dowell; **p. 160 (middle, bottom):** Courtesy Godden Collection, National Information Service for Earthquake Engineering, University of California, Berkeley; **p. 192 (both):** © Elliot Eisenberg.

CHAPTER 5

Opener: © Joseph A. Blum, People & Work; **p. 220:** © Christies Images/SuperStock; **p. 238:** © Annie Griffiths Belt/CORBIS; **p. 248:** © Ghislain & Marie David de Lossy/Getty Images; **p. 249:** © Bruce Hands/Stock, Boston; **p. 259:** NASA.

CHAPTER 6

Opener: © Ron Watts/CORBIS; **p. 286:** Courtesy Godden Collection, National Information Service for Earthquake Engineering, University of California, Berkeley; **p. 288:** © Ferdinand Beer; **p. 289:** © Sabina Dowell; **p. 293:** © EyeWire Collection/Getty Images; **p. 331:** Courtesy of Luxo Lamp Corporation.

CHAPTER 7

Opener: © AP Photo/Christophe Ena; **p. 355:** © Sabina Dowell; **p. 362:** © Elliot Eisenberg; **p. 383:** © Michael S. Yamashita/CORBIS; **p. 386:** © Brian Yarvin/Photo Researchers; **p. 395:** © Steve Kahn/Getty Images.

CHAPTER 8

Opener: © Jeffrey Mazurek; **p. 412:** © Richard Cummins/CORBIS; **p. 416:** © Chuck Savage/CORBIS; **p. 431:** © Ted Spiegel/CORBIS; **p. 451:** © Adam Woolfitt/CORBIS; **p. 452:** © Elliot Eisenberg.

CHAPTER 9

Opener: City of Vancouver National Street Works Yard, LEED Gold, Omicron AEC Designers/Builders. © Terri Meyer Boake/University of Waterloo, School of Architecture; **p. 484:** © Ed Eckstein/CORBIS; **p. 513:** Courtesy of Caterpillar Engine Division.

CHAPTER 10

Opener: Courtesy of Paxton-Mitchell Co.; **p. 559:** Courtesy of Altec Industries; **p. 563:** Courtesy of De-Sta-Co.

Index

Answers to Problems

Answers to problems with a number set in straight type are given on this and the following pages. Answers to problems set in italic are not listed. Answers to computer problems are given at www.mhhe.com/beerjohnston8.

CHAPTER 2

2.1 37 N ⦪ 76.0°.
2.2 57 N ⦫ 86.0°.
2.4 5.4 kN ∡ 12.0°.
2.5 (*a*) 103.0°. (*b*) 276 N.
2.6 (*a*) 25.1°. (*b*) 266 N.
2.7 (*a*) 72.2°. (*b*) 1.391 kN.
2.8 (*a*) 26.9 N. (*b*) 18.75 N.
2.10 (*a*) 7.48°. (*b*) 138.4 N.
2.11 (*a*) 108.6 N. (*b*) 163.9 N.
2.13 (*a*) 45.9 N →. (*b*) 65.5 N.
2.14 (*a*) 4.88 N ⦣ 6.00°. (*b*) 69.8 N.
2.15 37.2 N ⦪ 76.6°.
2.16 56.6 N ⦫ 85.8°.
2.18 1.302 kN ∡ 75.8°.
2.19 41.4 kN ⦪ 72.0°.
2.21 (2.4 kN) 1.543 kN, 1.839 kN; (1.85 kN) 1.738 kN, 0.633 kN; (1.40 kN) 1.147 kN, −0.803 kN.
2.22 (5 kN) 3.83 kN, 3.21 kN; (7 kN) −2.39 kN, 6.58 kN; (9 kN) −8.46 kN, 3.08 kN.
2.24 (204 N) −96.0 N, 180.0 N; (212 N) 112.0 N, 180.0 N; (400 N) −320 N, −240 N.
2.25 (*a*) 1674 N. (*b*) 1371 N.
2.26 (*a*) 39.2 N. (*b*) 25.2 N.
2.28 (*a*) 339 N. (*b*) 218 N ↓.
2.29 (*a*) 47.9 N. (*b*) 16.38 N.
2.31 4.73 kN ∡ 20.6°.
2.32 14.66 kN ⦣ 61.4°.
2.34 905 N ∡ 45.0°.
2.35 45.2 N ⦫ 62.3°.
2.37 1019 N ∡ 26.1°.
2.38 1.295 kN ⦣ 88.3°.
2.39 (*a*) 116.0 N. (*b*) 60.0 N.
2.40 (*a*) 40.3°. (*b*) 1.130 kN.
2.41 (*a*) 56.3°. (*b*) 1021 N.
2.43 (*a*) 169.7 N. (*b*) 348 N.
2.44 (*a*) 2.20 kN. (*b*) 2.43 kN.
2.46 (*a*) 38.6 N. (*b*) 44.3 N.
2.47 (*a*) 405 N. (*b*) 830 N.
2.49 $T_C = 5.87$ kN; $T_D = 9.14$ kN.
2.51 $F_C = 1.433$ kN; $F_D = 1.678$ kN.
2.52 $F_B = 2.99$ kN; $F_D = 1.060$ kN.
2.53 (*a*) 786 N. (*b*) 3.26 kN.
2.54 (*a*) 3.12 kN. (*b*) 20.3 N.
2.55 (*a*) 169.6 N. (*b*) 265 N.
2.57 (*a*) 62.8 N. (*b*) 758 mm.
2.58 (*a*) 19.85 N. (*b*) 62.3 N.
2.59 (*a*) 50.0°. (*b*) 35.0 N.
2.60 (*a*) 1216 N. (*b*) 77.5°.
2.61 (*a*) 1510 N. (*b*) 57.5°.
2.62 4.97 m.
2.65 16.81 cm.
2.66 (*a*) 90.0°. (*b*) 305 N.
2.67 170.5 N ⦫ 7.50°.
2.69 (*b*) 916 N. (*d*) 687 N.
2.70 (*a*) 2.30 kN. (*b*) 3.53 kN.
2.72 $27.4° < \alpha < 223°$.
2.73 (*a*) +557 N, −611 N, +468 N. (*b*) 54.1°, 130.0°, 60.5°.
2.75 (*a*) +706 N, +450 N, −329 N. (*b*) 38.3°, 60.0°, 111.5°.
2.76 (*a*) −611 N, +1785 N, +222 N. (*b*) 108.7°, 20.0°, 83.3°.
2.78 (*a*) +141.3 N, −90.0 N, +65.9 N. (*b*) 38.3°, 120.0°, 68.5°.
2.79 (*a*) −90.1 N, +190.5 N, −63.1 N. (*b*) 114.2°, 30.0°, 106.7°.
2.80 (*a*) 439 N. (*b*) 65.8°, 30.0°, 106.7°.
2.81 $F = 225$ N; $\theta_x = 73.2°$, $\theta_y = 110.8°$, $\theta_z = 152.7°$.
2.83 (*a*) 132.5°. (*b*) $F_x = 53.9$ N, $F_z = 7.99$ N; $F = 74.0$ N.
2.84 (*a*) 153.7°. (*b*) $F_x = -15.37$ N, $F_y = 7.85$ N; $F = 39.0$ N.
2.85 (*a*) $F_y = 75.6$ N, $F_z = 224$ N. (*b*) $\theta_x = 71.3°$, $\theta_z = 26.1°$.
2.87 +30.0 N, −35.0 N, −30.0 N.
2.88 +28.8 N, −36.0 N, +38.4 N.
2.90 +200 N, +1000 N, +740 N.
2.91 −200 N, +370 N, −160.0 N.
2.93 4.28 kN; $\theta_x = 93.7°$, $\theta_y = 31.3°$, $\theta_z = 121.1°$.
2.95 1122 N; $\theta_x = 147.7°$, $\theta_y = 61.6°$, $\theta_z = 104.2°$.
2.96 1122 N; $\theta_x = 150.1°$, $\theta_y = 60.1°$, $\theta_z = 91.6°$.
2.97 (*a*) 1492 N. (*b*) 2040 N; $\theta_x = 90.0°$, $\theta_y = 139.2°$, $\theta_z = 49.2°$.
2.99 (*a*) 360 N. (*b*) 424 N.
2.100 $T_{AB} = 3.25$ kN; $T_{AD} = 1.775$ kN.
2.102 9.71 kN.
2.103 1031 N ↑.
2.105 55.9 N.
2.106 $F_{BA} = 23.5$ N; $F_{CA} = 14.77$ N; $F_{DA} = 26.6$ N.
2.107 6.66 kN ↑.
2.108 8.81 kN ↑.
2.109 $T_{AB} = 86.2$ N; $T_{AC} = 27.7$ N; $T_{AD} = 237$ N.
2.112 $0 \le P \le 0.386$ N.
2.113 $T_{DA} = 62.9$ N; $T_{DB} = T_{DC} = 56.7$ N.
2.114 $T_{DA} = 62.9$ N; $T_{DB} = T_{DC} = 57.8$ N.
2.115 $T_{AB} = 4.33$ kN; $T_{AC} = 2.36$ kN; $T_{AD} = 2.37$ kN.
2.116 $F_{AB} = 1742$ N; $T_{AC} = 1517$ N; $T_{AD} = 403$ N.
2.118 $0 \le P \le 0.1600$ N.
2.120 $T_{AB} = 81.3$ N; $T_{AC} = 22.2$ N.
2.121 $T_{BE} = 1.310$ N; $T_{CF} = 4.38$ N; $T_{DG} = 4.89$ N.
2.122 $T_{BE} = 4.84$ N; $T_{CF} = 1.157$ N; $T_{DG} = 4.58$ N.
2.123 $T_{ADB} = 81.9$ N; $W = 143.4$ N.
2.124 $T_{ADB} = 68.6$ N; $T_{DC} = 14.23$ N.
2.126 (*a*) 221 N. (*b*) 715 N. (*c*) 2060 N.

2.127 (*a*) 2.27 kN. (*b*) 1.963 kN.
2.129 (*a*) 45.6°. (*b*) 27.1 N.
2.131 (*a*) 549 N. (*b*) 315 N.
2.132 (*a*) 5.23 kN. (*b*) 0.503 kN.
2.134 149.1 N ⦥ 32.3° or 274 N ⦤ 32.3°.
2.135 (*a*) 576 N. (*b*) 67.5°, 30.0°, 108.7°.
2.136 (*a*) $F_y = -359$ N, $F_z = -437$ N. (*b*) $\theta_x = 70.5°$, $\theta_y = 126.7°$.
2.137 758 N; $\theta_x = 65.0°$, $\theta_y = 33.0°$, $\theta_z = 69.9°$.
2.139 177.2 N.

CHAPTER 3

3.1 13.02 N · m ↻.
3.2 13.02 N · m ↻.
3.3 16.03 N · m. ↺.
3.5 49.9° or 59.4°.
3.6 (*a*) 386 N · m ↺. (*b*) 160.1 N ∠ 56.0°.
3.7 (*a*) 386 N · m ↺. (*b*) 193.2 N ↑. (*c*) 189.5 N ∠ 78.7°.
3.9 (*a*) 7600 N · cm. ↺. (*b*) 7600 N · cm. ↺.
3.10 250 N.
3.12 140.0 N · m ↺.
3.14 12.54 N · m ↻.
3.16 126.0 mm.
3.17 (*a*) $(-4\mathbf{i} + 7\mathbf{j} + 10\mathbf{k})/\sqrt{165}$.
(*b*) $(-2\mathbf{i} + 2\mathbf{j} - 3\mathbf{k})/\sqrt{17}$.
3.19 (*a*) $-(18.00 \text{ N}\cdot\text{m})\mathbf{i} - (15.75 \text{ N}\cdot\text{m})\mathbf{j} - (40.5 \text{ N}\cdot\text{m})\mathbf{k}$.
(*b*) $(6.38 \text{ N}\cdot\text{m})\mathbf{i} + (1.500 \text{ N}\cdot\text{m})\mathbf{j} + (11.63 \text{ N}\cdot\text{m})\mathbf{k}$.
(*c*) 0.
3.21 $(886 \text{ N}\cdot\text{m})\mathbf{i} + (259 \text{ N}\cdot\text{m})\mathbf{j} - (670 \text{ N}\cdot\text{m})\mathbf{k}$.
3.23 $(236.1 \text{ N}\cdot\text{m})\mathbf{i} - (46.24 \text{ N}\cdot\text{m})\mathbf{j} + (462.4 \text{ N}\cdot\text{m})\mathbf{k}$.
3.24 (*a*) $(1200 \text{ N}\cdot\text{m})\mathbf{i} - (1500 \text{ N}\cdot\text{m})\mathbf{j} - (900 \text{ N}\cdot\text{m})\mathbf{k}$.
(*b*) $-(1200 \text{ N}\cdot\text{m})\mathbf{i} + (1500 \text{ N}\cdot\text{m})\mathbf{j} - (600 \text{ N}\cdot\text{m})\mathbf{k}$.
3.25 $(233.91 \text{ N}\cdot\text{cm})\mathbf{i} - (1187.48 \text{ N}\cdot\text{cm})\mathbf{j} - (25.422 \text{ N}\cdot\text{cm})\mathbf{k}$.
3.27 1.946 m.
3.28 8.9 m.
3.30 1.491 m.
3.31 8.07 cm.
3.32 0.645 m.
3.33 1.141 m.
3.35 $\mathbf{P}\cdot\mathbf{Q} = -23$; $\mathbf{P}\cdot\mathbf{S} = -74$; $\mathbf{Q}\cdot\mathbf{S} = 37$.
3.37 63.6°.
3.39 (*a*) 134.1°. (*b*) −76.6 N.
3.40 (*a*) 65.0°. (*b*) 75.3 N.
3.42 (*a*) 84.0°. (*b*) 26.2 N.
3.43 (*a*) 230 m^3. (*b*) 32.0 m^3.
3.44 13.00.
3.45 $M_x = -1598$ N · m; $M_y = 959$ N · m; $M_z = 0$.
3.46 $M_x = -1283$ N · m; $M_y = 770$ N · m; $M_z = 1824$ N · m.
3.47 15.00 N.
3.49 $P = 186.8$ N; $\phi = 9.87°$; $\theta = 48.1°$.
3.50 28.0 N · m.
3.52 14.75 m.
3.53 −180.0 N · m.
3.54 −222 N · m.
3.55 −24.9 kN · m.
3.56 −35.9 kN · m.
3.57 $aP/\sqrt{2}$.
3.58 (*b*) $a/\sqrt{2}$.
3.60 −225 N · m.
3.62 215 mm.
3.64 8.26 m.
3.65 9.26 m.
3.67 1.741 m.
3.68 (*a*) 24.0 N · m ↺. (*b*) 35.6°. (*c*) 1.000 m.
3.69 (*a*) 26.7 N. (*b*) 50.0 N. (*c*) 23.5 N.
3.70 (*a*) 4.26 N · m. ↻. (*b*) 9.72 cm.
3.71 (*a*) 0.862 N · m. ↺. (*b*) ∠ 53.1°. (*c*) 4.03 N.
3.72 $M = 19.50$ N · m; $\theta_x = 67.4°$, $\theta_y = 90.0°$, $\theta_z = 22.6°$.
3.74 $M = 76.6$ N · m; $\theta_x = 12.20°$, $\theta_y = 90.0°$, $\theta_z = 77.8°$.
3.75 $M = 103.1$ N · m; $\theta_x = 43.4°$, $\theta_y = 52.3°$, $\theta_z = 108.3°$.
3.76 $M = 35$ N · m.; $\theta_x = 33.1°$, $\theta_y = 64.8°$, $\theta_z = 69.9°$.
3.79 (*a*) $\mathbf{F}_B = 135.0$ N ↓; $\mathbf{M}_B = 16.88$ N · m ↺.
(*b*) $\mathbf{F}_B = 225$ N ←; $\mathbf{F}_C = 225$ N →.
3.81 $\mathbf{F}_A = 1.750$ kN ∠ 65.0°; $\mathbf{F}_C = 1.050$ kN ∠ 65.0°.
3.82 $\mathbf{F}_B = 22.5$ N ⦥ 30.0°; $\mathbf{F}_C = 31.5$ N ⦥ 30.0°.
3.83 (*a*) $\mathbf{F}_C = 54.0$ N ⦥ 30.0°; $\mathbf{M}_C = 53.2$ N · m. ↺.
(*b*) $\mathbf{F}_B = 30.3$ N ⦥ 63.0°; $\mathbf{F}_C = 33.0$ N ←.
3.84 (*a*) $\mathbf{F} = 200$ N ↓; $d = 9.00$ m.
(*b*) $\mathbf{F} = 200$ N ↓; $d = 0$.
3.86 $\mathbf{R} = -(60.8 \text{ N})\mathbf{i} - (89.7 \text{ N})\mathbf{k}$; 3.59 m to the right of *A*.
3.87 (*a*) $\mathbf{F}_A = 22.0$ N ∠ 20.0°; $\mathbf{M}_A = 0.65$ N · cm. ↺.
(*b*) $\mathbf{F}_E = 22.0$ N ∠ 20.0°; 0.031 m. below *A*.
3.88 (*a*) 120.0 N; $y = 19.98$ mm. (*b*) −16.26° or −85.0°.
3.90 $\mathbf{F} = -(250 \text{ kN})\mathbf{j}$; $\mathbf{M} = (15.00 \text{ kN}\cdot\text{m})\mathbf{i} + (7.50 \text{ kN}\cdot\text{m})\mathbf{k}$.
3.91 $\mathbf{F} = (6.00 \text{ N})\mathbf{i} - (48.0 \text{ N})\mathbf{j} + (24.0 \text{ N})\mathbf{k}$;
$\mathbf{M} = (540 \text{ N}\cdot\text{m})\mathbf{i} - (135.0 \text{ N}\cdot\text{m})\mathbf{k}$.
3.93 $\mathbf{F} = -(2.00 \text{ kN})\mathbf{i} - (9.50 \text{ kN})\mathbf{j} + (4.00 \text{ kN})\mathbf{k}$;
$\mathbf{M} = (19.00 \text{ kN}\cdot\text{m})\mathbf{i} - (12.00 \text{ kN}\cdot\text{m})\mathbf{j} - (19.00 \text{ kN}\cdot\text{m})\mathbf{k}$.
3.94 $\mathbf{R} = -(190.5 \text{ N})\mathbf{j} - (110.0 \text{ N})\mathbf{k}$;
$\mathbf{M} = (75.7 \text{ N}\cdot\text{m})\mathbf{i} + (22.0 \text{ N}\cdot\text{m})\mathbf{j} - (38.1 \text{ N}\cdot\text{m})\mathbf{k}$.
3.95 $\mathbf{F} = (54.0 \text{ N})\mathbf{i} - (18.00 \text{ N})\mathbf{j} + (27.0 \text{ N})\mathbf{k}$;
$\mathbf{M} = (707 \text{ N}\cdot\text{cm})\mathbf{i} + (778 \text{ N}\cdot\text{cm})\mathbf{j} - (336 \text{ N}\cdot\text{cm})\mathbf{k}$.
3.96 (*a*) $-(2.40 \text{ N})\mathbf{j}$. (*b*) $x = -16.89$ mm, $z = -24.5$ mm.
3.98 (*a*) *Loading a*: $\mathbf{R} = 1000$ N ↓; $\mathbf{M} = 6.00$ kN · m ↺.
Loading b: $\mathbf{R} = 1000$ N ↓; $\mathbf{M} = 6.60$ kN · m ↺.
Loading c: $\mathbf{R} = 1000$ N ↓; $\mathbf{M} = 6.60$ kN · m ↻.
Loading d: $\mathbf{R} = 1000$ N ↓; $\mathbf{M} = 6.60$ kN · m ↺.
Loading e: $\mathbf{R} = 900$ N ↓; $\mathbf{M} = 6.60$ kN · m ↺.
Loading f: $\mathbf{R} = 1000$ N ↓; $\mathbf{M} = 5.80$ kN · m ↺.
Loading g: $\mathbf{R} = 900$ N ↓; $\mathbf{M} = 6.60$ kN · m ↺.
Loading h: $\mathbf{R} = 1000$ N ↓; $\mathbf{M} = 6.60$ kN · m ↺.
(*b*) Loadings *b*, *d*, and *h*.
3.99 Loading *f*.
3.100 (*a*) $\mathbf{R} = 600$ N ↓; 1.500 m. (*b*) $\mathbf{R} = 300$ N ↓; 1.333 m.
(*c*) $\mathbf{R} = 500$ N ↓; 1.600 m.
3.101 Force-couple system at *E*.
3.103 (*a*) 7.82 m. (*b*) 4.48 m.
3.105 (*a*) 158.2 N ⦢ 86.0°. (*b*) 302 mm to the right of *F*.
3.106 (*a*) 72.2°. (*b*) 127.6 N ⦤ 87.4°.
3.107 (*a*) $\mathbf{M} = 115.2$ N · cm. ↺; $\alpha = 39.3°$. (*b*) 56.1 N ⦤ 45.0°.
3.109 (*a*) $\mathbf{R} = 3.72$ kN ⦤ 55.2°; 0.0406 cm. to the left of *EF*.
(*b*) 55.9°.
3.111 350 N ⦢ 21.4°; 92.6 mm from *B* or 27.4 mm from *F*.
3.112 (*a*) 7.35 N ∠ 55.6°. (*b*) 478 mm to the left of *B*.
(*c*) 34.7 mm above and to the left of *A*.
3.113 (*a*) 211 mm. (*b*) 211 mm.
3.114 (*a*) $\mathbf{R} = F$ ⦢ $\tan^{-1}(b^2/2hx)$;
$$\mathbf{M} = \frac{(2h^2 - b^2)x - 2(h/b)^2 x^3}{\sqrt{b^4 + 4h^2x^2}} F \text{ ↺. } (b)\ 0.354 \text{ cm.}$$
3.115 $\mathbf{R} = -(300 \text{ N})\mathbf{i} - (240 \text{ N})\mathbf{j} + (25.0 \text{ N})\mathbf{k}$;
$\mathbf{M} = -(3.00 \text{ N}\cdot\text{m})\mathbf{i} + (13.50 \text{ N}\cdot\text{m})\mathbf{j} + (9.00 \text{ N}\cdot\text{m})\mathbf{k}$.

3.117 **A** = (2.00 N)**i** − (169.1 N)**j** + (12.00 N)**k**; **B** = −(12.00 N)**i** + (169.1 N)**j** − (6.00 N)**k**.
3.118 (*a*) **B** = (2.32 N)**i**; **C** = (1.580 N)**i** − (3.30 N)**j** − (1.110 N)**k**. (*b*) R_y = −3.30 N; M_x = 2.55 N · cm.
3.119 (*a*) 53.1°. (*b*) **R** = (40.0 N)**j** + (5.00 N)**k**; **M** = −(24.0 N · m)**i** + (45.0 N · m)**k**.
3.120 (*a*) **R** = (43.3 N)**j**; **M** = (6.88 N · m)**i** + (5.63 N · m)**j** + (9.74 N · m)**k**. (*b*) Counterclockwise.
3.122 **R** = −(8.00 N)**i** + (56.0 N)**j** − (20.0 N)**k**; **M** = −(81.0 N · m)**i** + (123.0 N · m)**j** + (444 N · m)**k**.
3.123 280 kN; *x* = 0.750 m, *z* = −0.1856 m.
3.124 F_B = 80.0 kN; F_F = 60.0 kN.
3.125 680 kN; *x* = 91.1 m, *z* = 43.2 m.
3.126 *a* = 58.4 m; *b* = 52.4 m.
3.129 (*a*) 2*P*; θ_x = 0°, θ_y = −90.0°, θ_z = 90.0°. (*b*) −0.750*a*. (*c*) *y* = 3.00*a*, *z* = 2.50*a*.
3.131 (*a*) −(21.0 N)**j**. (*b*) 0.571 m. (*c*) Axis of wrench is parallel to the *y* axis at *x* = 0, *z* = 41.7 mm.
3.133 (*a*) **R** = −(35.0 N)**i** − (12.00 N)**k**. (*b*) 5.11 cm. (*c*) *y* = 5.75 cm., *z* = 4.57 cm.
3.135 (*a*) 3*P*(2**i** − 20**j** − **k**)/25. (*b*) −0.0988*a*. (*c*) *x* = 2.00*a*, *z* = −1.990*a*.
3.137 **R** = (4.00 N)**i** + (6.00 N)**j** − (2.00 N)**k**; *p* = 14.7 cm; *y* = −44.21 cm, *z* = −12.375 cm.
3.138 $\mathbf{F}_A = -(M/b)\mathbf{i} + R[1 + (a/b)]\mathbf{j}$; $\mathbf{F}_B = (M/b)\mathbf{i} - (a/b)R\mathbf{j}$.
3.142 (*a*) 80.0 N · m ↻. (*b*) 205 N. (*c*) 177.8 N ∠ 20.0°.
3.144 (*a*) −(22080 N · cm)**i** − (4416 N · cm)**k**. (*b*) −(22080 N · cm)**i** + (25920 N · cm)**j** + (32928 N · cm)**k**.
3.145 38.9°.
3.146 4.00 m.
3.148 (*a*) **F** = 1000 N ⦫ 20.0°; **M** = 1724 N · m ↻. (*b*) **F** = 1000 N ⦫ 20.0°; **M** = 958 N · m ↻.
3.150 **F** = (2.00 N)**i** + (38.0 N)**j** − (24.0 N)**k**; **M** = (792 N · cm)**i** + (708 N · cm)**j** + (1187 N · cm)**k**.
3.151 **R** = 362 N ⦫ 81.9°; *M* = 327 N · m.
3.152 **R** = −(7.00 N)**i** − (8.00 N)**j** − (4.00 N)**k**; **M** = −(12.00 N · cm)**i** + (10.50 N · cm)**j** + (7.50 N · cm)**k**.

CHAPTER 4

4.1 (*a*) 552 N ↓. (*b*) 1152 N ↑.
4.2 (*a*) 5.75 kN ↑. (*b*) 7.25 kN ↑.
4.3 (*a*) 34.0 kN ↑. (*b*) 4.96 kN ↑.
4.4 (*a*) 81.1 kN. (*b*) 134.1 kN ↑.
4.7 (*a*) **A** = 10.05 kN ↑; **B** = 15.35 kN ↑. (*b*) **A** = 8.92 kN ↑; **B** = 16.48 kN ↑.
4.8 (*a*) 0. (*b*) **A** = 10.68 kN ↑; **B** = 14.72 kN ↑.
4.9 56.7 N ≤ T_C ≤ 70 N.
4.10 1.250 kN ≤ *Q* ≤ 27.5 kN.
4.12 4.64 N ≤ W_A ≤ 531 N.
4.13 25.0 mm ≤ *a* ≤ 125.0 mm.
4.15 (*a*) 150.0 N. (*b*) 292 N ∠ 77.5°.
4.16 (*a*) 16 N ∠ 60.0°. (*b*) 16.1 N ⦭ 6.62°.
4.18 (*a*) **A** = 165.0 N ↓; **B** = 165.0 N ↑. (*b*) **A** = 275 N →; **B** = 275 N ←. (*c*) **A** = 141.5 N ⦫ 60.0°; **B** = 141.5 N ⦬ 60.0°.
4.19 (*a*) 300 N. (*b*) 449 N ⦭ 32.3°.
4.21 (*a*) 6.158 N/cm. (*b*) 22.09 N ⦬ 13.60°.
4.23 (*a*) **A** = 258 N ∠ 22.8°; **B** = 187.5 N ←. (*b*) **A** = 253 N ⦫ 20.2°; **B** = 265 N ⦬ 45.0°.
4.24 (*a*) **A** = 238 N →; **B** = 213 N ⦬ 28.1°. (*b*) **A** = 336 N ∠ 45.0°; **B** = 233 N ⦭ 36.3°.
4.26 (*a*) **A** = 54.29 N ∠ 58.5°; **E** = 7.266 N ⦫ 60.0°. (*b*) **A** = 53.4 N ∠ 3.30°; **E** = 42.6 N ⦬ 60.0°.
4.27 (*a*) 594 N. (*b*) 646 N ∠ 24.6°.
4.28 (*a*) 384 N. (*b*) 409 N ∠ 22.4°.
4.29 *T* = 195.0 N; **C** = 216 N ⦭ 33.7°.
4.30 *T* = 65.7 N; **A** = 75 N ⦫ 81.0°.
4.31 *T* = 216.7 N; **A** = 156.1 N ⦫ 87.2°.
4.33 (*a*) 26.6°. (*b*) **B** = $P\sqrt{5}/2$ ⦫ 26.6°; **C** = $P\sqrt{5}/2$ ⦭ 26.6°.
4.34 (*a*) 45.0°. (*b*) **B** = $P\sqrt{2}$ ⦫ 45.0°; **C** = *P* ←.
4.35 *T* = 0.566*P*; **C** = 0.364*P* →.
4.37 (*a*) 600 N. (*b*) **A** = 4.00 kN ←; **B** = 4.00 kN →.
4.38 (*a*) **A** = 953 N ⦬ 80.0°; **B** = 435 N ⦬ 55.0°. (*b*) 415 N →.
4.39 (*a*) 4.24 N. (*b*) $\mathbf{N}_A$ = 5.80 N ⦬ 45.0°; $\mathbf{N}_D$ = 5.80 N ∠ 45.0°.
4.40 (*a*) 0°. (*b*) 3.00 N. (*c*) $\mathbf{N}_A$ = 3.67 N ⦬ 45.0°; $\mathbf{N}_D$ = 3.67 N ∠ 45.0°.
4.41 **A** = **D** = 0; **B** = 868 N →; **C** = 126.1 N ←.
4.42 **A** = **C** = 0; **B** = 422 N ←; **D** = 45.2 N ←.
4.45 (*a*) **A** = 98.1 N ↑; $\mathbf{M}_A$ = 44.1 N · m ↺. (*b*) **A** = 138.7 N ∠ 45.0°; $\mathbf{M}_A$ = 44.1 N · m ↺. (*c*) **A** = 196.2 N ↑; $\mathbf{M}_A$ = 88.3 N · m ↺.
4.46 **C** = 33.9 N ∠ 45.0°; $\mathbf{M}_C$ = 14.4 N · cm. ↺.
4.48 (*a*) **A** = 6 N ↑; $\mathbf{M}_A$ = 140 N · cm. ↺. (*b*) **A** = 3.6 N ↑; $\mathbf{M}_A$ = 44 N · cm. ↺.
4.50 (*a*) **E** = 39.6 kN ↑; $\mathbf{M}_E$ = 64.8 kN · m ↻. (*b*) **E** = 21.6 kN ↑; $\mathbf{M}_E$ = 91.8 kN · m ↻.
4.51 (*a*) 50.4 kN. (*b*) M_E = 51.8 kN · m.
4.52 T_{max} = 1.999 kN; T_{min} = 1.560 kN.
4.53 (*a*) $\sin^{-1}(2M/mgl)$. (*b*) 20.1°.
4.54 (*a*) 30.0°. (*b*) −15.00°.
4.56 32.0°.
4.57 (*a*) $2\sin^{-1}[kl/\sqrt{2}(kl - P)]$. (*b*) 141.1°.
4.59 (*a*) $\tan^{-1}(P/kl)$. (*b*) 63.4°.
4.60 (*a*) $\tan\theta - \sin\theta = W/2kl$. (*b*) 52.94°.
4.61 (1) Completely constrained; determinate; equilibrium; **A** = 116.6 N ∠ 59.0°, **B** = 60.0 N ←. (2) Improperly constrained; indeterminate; no equilibrium. (3) Partially constrained; determinate; equilibrium; **A** = **C** = 50 N ↑. (4) Completely constrained; determinate; equilibrium; **A** = 50 N ↑, **B** = 78.1 N ⦬ 39.8°, **C** = 60 N →. (5) Completely constrained; indeterminate; equilibrium; $\mathbf{A}_y$ = 50 N ↑. (6) Completely constrained; indeterminate; equilibrium; $\mathbf{A}_x$ = 60 N →, $\mathbf{B}_x$ = 60 N ←. (7) Completely constrained; determinate; equilibrium; **A** = **C** = 50 N ↑. (8) Improperly constrained; indeterminate; no equilibrium.
4.63 *P* = 120.0 N; **A** = 150.0 N ⦬ 36.9°.
4.64 *a* ≥ 57.7 mm.
4.65 (*a*) 6.298 N/cm. (*b*) 22.5 N ⦬ 13.35°.
4.67 (*a*) **A** = 150.0 N ↓; **C** = 167.7 N ⦬ 63.4°. (*b*) **A** = 194.5 N ↓; **C** = 253 N ⦬ 77.9°.
4.69 $\mathbf{F}_{nail}$ = 1.018 kN ↑; **B** = 1.027 kN ⦬ 82.7°.
4.70 76.9 mm.

4.71 $\mathbf{F}_{worker} = 314$ N $\measuredangle$ 76.3°; $\mathbf{B} = 227$ N $\searrow$ 70.9°.
4.73 86 N $\searrow$ 80.8°.
4.74 80.8 N $\measuredangle$ 80.9°.
4.76 77.5 N $\measuredangle$ 30.0°.
4.77 (*a*) 88.6 N $\searrow$ 64.6°. (*b*) 98.75 N $\uparrow$. (*c*) 182.7 N.
4.78 (*a*) 5115.9 N $\searrow$ 75.0°. (*b*) 4634.7 N $\nwarrow$ 73.4°.
4.79 (*a*) 440 N. (*b*) 550 N $\swarrow$ 36.9°.
4.80 $T = 177.28$ N; $\mathbf{C} = 273.4$ N $\nwarrow$ 35°.
4.81 (*a*) 20.3 N $\nwarrow$ 45.0°. (*b*) 174.9 N $\searrow$ 85.2°.
4.82 (*a*) 29.8 N $\nwarrow$ 30.0°. (*b*) 176.8 N $\searrow$ 81.6°.
4.84 (*a*) 229 N. (*b*) 172.6 N $\searrow$ 11.5°.
4.86 (*a*) 2.77R.
(*b*) $\mathbf{A} = 1.303mg$ $\measuredangle$ 60.7°; $\mathbf{B} = 0.652mg$ $\swarrow$ 12.15°.
4.87 (*a*) 39.8 N $\searrow$ 39.4°. (*b*) 199.2 N $\measuredangle$ 72.0°.
4.89 34.5°.
4.90 $\tan\theta = 2\tan\beta$.
4.91 (*a*) 43.0°. (*b*) $\mathbf{A} = 45.7$ N $\leftarrow$; $\mathbf{B} = 108.2$ N $\measuredangle$ 65.0°.
9.92 $\sin^{-1}(a/L)^{1/3}$.
4.93 15.04°.
4.95 (*a*) 18.43°. (*b*) $mg/5$.
4.96 $\mathbf{A} = (120.0 \text{ N})\mathbf{j} + (133.3 \text{ N})\mathbf{k}$; $\mathbf{D} = (60.0 \text{ N})\mathbf{j} + (166.7 \text{ N})\mathbf{k}$.
4.97 $\mathbf{C} = (370.5 \text{ N})\mathbf{j} - (342.5 \text{ N})\mathbf{k}$; $\mathbf{D} = -(1170.5 \text{ N})\mathbf{j} + (212.5 \text{ N})\mathbf{k}$.
4.98 $\mathbf{C} = (55.2 \text{ N})\mathbf{j} - (200 \text{ N})\mathbf{k}$; $\mathbf{D} = -(1585.2 \text{ N})\mathbf{j} + (400 \text{ N})\mathbf{k}$.
4.100 (*a*) 150.0 N. (*b*) $\mathbf{C} = -(12.08 \text{ N})\mathbf{j} - (120.0 \text{ N})\mathbf{k}$;
$\mathbf{D} = (52.3 \text{ N})\mathbf{j} - (180.0 \text{ N})\mathbf{k}$.
4.102 $\mathbf{N}_A = 371$ N $\downarrow$; $\mathbf{N}_B = 618$ N $\downarrow$; $\mathbf{N}_C = 679$ N $\downarrow$.
4.103 34.0 kg; $x = 0.600$ m, $z = 1.200$ m.
4.104 $T_A = 9$ N; $T_C = 4.5$ N; $T_D = 40.5$ N.
4.106 (*a*) $\mathbf{A}_y = 1.3$ N $\uparrow$; $\mathbf{B}_y = 1.3$ N $\uparrow$; $\mathbf{C}_y = 0.25$ N $\uparrow$. (*b*) 50.35°.
4.107 $T_A = W/3$; $T_B = 2W(1 - 1/\sqrt{3})/3$; $T_C = 2W/3\sqrt{3}$.
4.108 (*a*) $T_A = T_B = W/3$; $T_C = 4W/3$.
(*b*) $x = L(2 - \sqrt{3})/3$, $z = L[1 - (1/2\sqrt{3})]$.
4.109 (*a*) 450 mm. (*b*) $R_A = 48.2$ N; $R_B = R_C = 43.4$ N.
4.111 (*a*) 27 N $\uparrow$. (*b*) 58.9 N. (*c*) 27 N $\uparrow$.
4.112 $T_{BD} = T_{BE} = 353$ N; $\mathbf{C} = -(100 \text{ N})\mathbf{j} + (433.5 \text{ N})\mathbf{k}$.
4.114 (*a*) $T_{BE} = 857$ N; $T_{BF} = 455$ N.
(*b*) $\mathbf{A} = (73.9 \text{ N})\mathbf{i} + (878 \text{ N})\mathbf{j} - (127.9 \text{ N})\mathbf{k}$.
4.115 (*a*) 29.7°. (*b*) 586 N.
(*c*) $\mathbf{A} = (72.0 \text{ N})\mathbf{i} + (842 \text{ N})\mathbf{j} - (126.0 \text{ N})\mathbf{k}$.
4.116 $T_{AD} = 2160$ N; $T_{BE} = 2990$ N;
$\mathbf{C} = (4480 \text{ N})\mathbf{i} - (213 \text{ N})\mathbf{j} + (320 \text{ N})\mathbf{k}$.
4.117 $T_{AD} = 1890$ N; $T_{BE} = 2610$ N;
$\mathbf{C} = (3920 \text{ N})\mathbf{i} - (76.7 \text{ N})\mathbf{j} + (280 \text{ N})\mathbf{k}$.
4.118 $T_{EG} = 961.6$ N; $T_{CI} = T_{FH} = 1166.7$ N;
$\mathbf{D} = (2573 \text{ N})\mathbf{i} - (280 \text{ N})\mathbf{j} - (30.8 \text{ N})\mathbf{k}$.
4.120 (*a*) 232 N.
(*b*) $\mathbf{A} = -(144.4 \text{ N})\mathbf{j} - (75.5 \text{ N})\mathbf{k}$; $\mathbf{B} = (75 \text{ N})\mathbf{j}$.
4.121 (*a*) 171 N. (*b*) $\mathbf{E} = -(4.37 \text{ N})\mathbf{i} - (68 \text{ N})\mathbf{k}$;
$\mathbf{F} = (104.37 \text{ N})\mathbf{i} + (78 \text{ N})\mathbf{j} + (220 \text{ N})\mathbf{k}$.
4.122 (*a*) 97.1 N. (*b*) $\mathbf{A} = -(23.5 \text{ N})\mathbf{i} + (63.8 \text{ N})\mathbf{j} - (7.85 \text{ N})\mathbf{k}$;
$\mathbf{B} = (9.81 \text{ N})\mathbf{j} + (66.7 \text{ N})\mathbf{k}$.
4.123 (*a*) 233 N. (*b*) $\mathbf{A} = (183.9 \text{ N})\mathbf{i} + (63.8 \text{ N})\mathbf{j} + (139.0 \text{ N})\mathbf{k}$;
$\mathbf{B} = (9.81 \text{ N})\mathbf{j} - (16.35 \text{ N})\mathbf{k}$.
4.125 (*a*) 97.9 N. (*b*) $\mathbf{A} = (50.4 \text{ N})\mathbf{j} - (4.75 \text{ N})\mathbf{k}$;
$\mathbf{B} = -(5.34 \text{ N})\mathbf{i} - (77.8 \text{ N})\mathbf{j} + (22.6 \text{ N})\mathbf{k}$.
4.126 $F_{CE} = 404$ N; $\mathbf{A} = -(112.5 \text{ N})\mathbf{i}$;
$\mathbf{B} = -(112.5 \text{ N})\mathbf{i} + (300 \text{ N})\mathbf{j} - (150 \text{ N})\mathbf{k}$.
4.128 (*a*) 11.2 N. (*b*) $\mathbf{D} = (3 \text{ N})\mathbf{k}$;
$\mathbf{M}_D = (6.6 \text{ N}\cdot\text{cm.})\mathbf{i} + (51.4 \text{ N}\cdot\text{cm.})\mathbf{j} + (4.44 \text{ N}\cdot\text{cm.})\mathbf{k}$.
4.130 (*a*) $F_{CF} = 44.4$ N; $F_{DE} = 18.47$ N.
(*b*) $\mathbf{B} = (81.3 \text{ N})\mathbf{j} - (8.21 \text{ N})\mathbf{k}$;
$\mathbf{M}_B = (1.149 \text{ N}\cdot\text{m})\mathbf{j} + (0.657 \text{ N}\cdot\text{m})\mathbf{k}$.
4.131 (*a*) 39.4 N. (*b*) $\mathbf{B} = -(7.63 \text{ N})\mathbf{i} + (34.3 \text{ N})\mathbf{j} + (17.80 \text{ N})\mathbf{k}$;
$\mathbf{M}_B = -(3.56 \text{ N}\cdot\text{m})\mathbf{j} - (22.3 \text{ N}\cdot\text{m})\mathbf{k}$.
4.132 $T_{BD} = 1.4$ kN; $T_{BE} = T_{CF} = 1.25$ kN;
$\mathbf{A} = (3.51 \text{ kN})\mathbf{i} - (0.56 \text{ kN})\mathbf{k}$.
4.134 $T_{DI} = 164.8$ N; $T_{EH} = 933$ N; $T_{FG} = 187.8$ N;
$\mathbf{A} = (1094 \text{ N})\mathbf{i} + (98.7 \text{ N})\mathbf{j} - (21.3 \text{ N})\mathbf{k}$.
4.135 $T_{DI} = 180.6$ N; $T_{EH} = 960$ N; $T_{FG} = 100.9$ N;
$\mathbf{A} = (1067 \text{ N})\mathbf{i} + (110.4 \text{ N})\mathbf{j} - (11.45 \text{ N})\mathbf{k}$.
4.136 $\mathbf{A} = -(39 \text{ N})\mathbf{j} + (80 \text{ N})\mathbf{k}$; $\mathbf{B} = -(60 \text{ N})\mathbf{i} - (61 \text{ N})\mathbf{j}$;
$\mathbf{C} = (60 \text{ N})\mathbf{i} + (100 \text{ N})\mathbf{j}$.
4.138 $\mathbf{B} = (104.0 \text{ N})\mathbf{k}$; $\mathbf{C} = (36.0 \text{ N})\mathbf{j} - (36.0 \text{ N})\mathbf{k}$;
$\mathbf{D} = -(36.0 \text{ N})\mathbf{j} + (12.00 \text{ N})\mathbf{k}$.
4.140 (*a*) 7.24 N. (*b*) $\mathbf{A} = -(4.48 \text{ N})\mathbf{i} + (20.2 \text{ N})\mathbf{j} - (1.379 \text{ N})\mathbf{k}$;
$\mathbf{N}_B = (3.68 \text{ N})\mathbf{j} + (2.76 \text{ N})\mathbf{k}$.
4.141 (*a*) $(6.4 \text{ N})\mathbf{i} + (8.6 \text{ N})\mathbf{j}$.
(*b*) $\mathbf{A} = -(6.4 \text{ N})\mathbf{i} + (11.4 \text{ N})\mathbf{j} - (6 \text{ N})\mathbf{k}$; $\mathbf{B} = (6 \text{ N})\mathbf{k}$.
4.142 127.6 N.
4.143 125.8 N.
4.144 200 N.
4.145 375 N.
4.146 (*a*) $x = 1.8$ m, $y = 4.05$ m. (*b*) 55 N.
4.147 (*a*) $x = 0$, $y = 8.1$ m. (*b*) 57 N.
4.148 37.8 N.
4.150 65.2 N.
4.152 300 mm $\le d \le$ 800 mm.
4.153 932 N.
4.155 $\mathbf{C} = 915$ N $\searrow$ 88.1°; $\mathbf{M}_C = 3823.6$ N · cm. $\circlearrowright$.
4.157 (*a*) 348.7 N. (*b*) 348.7 N $\searrow$ 35°.
4.158 75.0 mm.
4.159 $\mathbf{A} = (112.3 \text{ N})\mathbf{i} + (41.7 \text{ N})\mathbf{j}$; $\mathbf{B} = (112.3 \text{ N})\mathbf{i} + (125.1 \text{ N})\mathbf{j}$;
$\mathbf{C} = -(225 \text{ N})\mathbf{i}$.
4.161 (*a*) 200.7 N. (*b*) $\mathbf{A} = (66.2 \text{ N})\mathbf{i} + (227.5 \text{ N})\mathbf{j} + (48.8 \text{ N})\mathbf{k}$;
$\mathbf{B} = (57.6 \text{ N})\mathbf{j} + (27.5 \text{ N})\mathbf{k}$.
4.162 $T_{BG} = 796$ N; $T_{DH} = 600$ N; $T_{FJ} = 0$;
$\mathbf{A} = (996.8 \text{ N})\mathbf{i} + (120 \text{ N})\mathbf{j} - (477.6 \text{ N})\mathbf{k}$.

CHAPTER 5

5.1 $\overline{X} = 140.0$ mm, $\overline{Y} = 165.0$ mm.
5.2 $\overline{X} = 8.22$ cm, $\overline{Y} = 4.00$ cm.
5.3 $\overline{X} = 105.0$ mm, $\overline{Y} = 90.0$ mm.
5.5 $\overline{X} = 18.02$ mm, $\overline{Y} = 84.9$ mm.
5.6 $\overline{X} = 8.32$ cm, $\overline{Y} = 3.61$ cm.
5.8 $\overline{X} = 68.2$ mm, $\overline{Y} = 4.55$ mm.
5.9 3.02.
5.10 $\dfrac{r_1 + r_2}{\pi - 2\alpha}\cos\alpha$.
5.11 $\overline{X} = 8.56$ cm, $\overline{Y} = 0$.
5.13 $\overline{X} = -3.17$ cm, $\overline{Y} = 0.668$ cm.
5.14 $\overline{X} = 90.0$ mm, $\overline{Y} = 26.8$ mm.
5.16 $\overline{X} = 80.4$ mm, $\overline{Y} = 82.9$ mm.
5.17 $Q_I = 174.125$ cm^3; $Q_{II} = -174.125$ cm^3.
5.18 $Q_I = 42.3 \times 10^3$ mm^3; $Q_{II} = -42.3 \times 10^3$ mm^3.
5.21 $\overline{X} = 116.7$ mm, $\overline{Y} = 166.7$ mm.
5.22 $\overline{X} = 8.71$ cm, $\overline{Y} = 4.32$ cm.
5.23 $\overline{X} = 54.9$ mm, $\overline{Y} = 71.8$ mm.
5.24 $\overline{X} = 60.1$ mm, $\overline{Y} = -3.16$ mm.
5.25 (*a*) 1.57 N. (*b*) 0.58 N $\searrow$ 83.1°.
5.26 63.6°.
5.27 319 mm.
5.28 (*a*) 1.427r. (*b*) 2.11r.

5.31 $\bar{x} = 2a/3, \bar{y} = 2h/3$.
5.32 $\bar{x} = 2a/5, \bar{y} = 3b/7$.
5.35 $\bar{x} = 2a/3(\pi - 2), \bar{y} = 2b/3(\pi - 2)$.
5.36 $\bar{x} = 0, \bar{y} = \dfrac{2}{3}R\dfrac{3 - \sin^2\alpha}{2\alpha + \sin 2\alpha}\sin\alpha$.
5.37 $\bar{x} = a/4, \bar{y} = 3b/10$.
5.38 $\bar{x} = 39a/50, \bar{y} = -39b/175$.
5.39 $\bar{x} = 2L/5, \bar{y} = 12h/25$.
5.40 $\bar{x} = 18a/19, \bar{y} = 148b/95$.
5.42 $-2r\sqrt{2}/3\pi$.
5.43 $2a/5$.
5.45 $\bar{x} = 0.363L, \bar{y} = 0.1653L$.
5.46 $\bar{x} = 0.549R, \bar{y} = 0$.
5.47 (*a*) $V = 3367.8$ cm^3; $A = 1520.53$ cm^2. (*b*) $V = 9072.9$ cm^3; $A = 3619.1$ cm^2.
5.49 (*a*) $V = 155.5 \times 10^6$ mm^3; $A = 1.885 \times 10^6$ mm^2. (*b*) $V = 2.10 \times 10^6$ mm^3; $A = 3.20 \times 10^6$ mm^2.
5.50 (*a*) $\pi^2 a^2 b$. (*b*) $2\pi^2 a^2 b$. (*c*) $2\pi a^2 b/3$.
5.51 $V = 2.10$ cm^3; $A = 16.83$ cm^2.
5.53 720 mm^3.
5.55 $V = 255 \times 10^3$ mm^3; $A = 37.5 \times 10^3$ mm^2.
5.57 229 kN.
5.58 647 liters
5.59 30.5 g.
5.61 (*a*) $R = 1764$ N; 3.80 m to the right of *A*. (*b*) **A** = 1764 N $\uparrow$; $\mathbf{M}_A$ = 6.70 kN · m $\curvearrowleft$.
5.62 (*a*) $R = 720$ N; 11.25 m to the right of *A*. (*b*) **A** = 270 N $\uparrow$; **B** = 450 N $\uparrow$.
5.63 **A** = 1.280 kN $\uparrow$; **B** = 4.48 kN $\uparrow$.
5.64 **A** = 6.00 kN $\uparrow$; **B** = 4.80 kN $\uparrow$.
5.66 **A** = 90.0 N $\uparrow$; $\mathbf{M}_A$ = 675 N · m $\curvearrowleft$.
5.67 **A** = 7.20 kN $\uparrow$; **B** = 3.60 kN $\uparrow$.
5.69 **B** = 7.04 kN $\uparrow$; **C** = 15.46 kN $\uparrow$.
5.71 (*a*) 1.172 m. (*b*) **A** = 3.53 kN $\uparrow$; **B** = 7.06 kN $\uparrow$.
5.73 $w_A = 556$ N/m; $R_B = 7.25$ kN.
5.74 (*a*) 1.527 kN $\downarrow$. (*b*) 1.630 kN/m.
5.75 (*a*) **H** = 76.28 kN $\rightarrow$; **V** = 511.7 kN $\uparrow$. (*b*) 4.7 m to the right of *A*. (*c*) **R** = 76.7 kN $\nearrow$ 5.71°.
5.76 (*a*) **H** = 176.6 kN $\rightarrow$; **V** = 1350 kN $\uparrow$. (*b*) 5.13 m to the right of *A*. (*c*) **R** = 236 kN $\nearrow$ 41.6°.
5.78 100.0 mm.
5.79 **B** = 103776 N $\rightarrow$; **A** = 117920 N $\rightarrow$.
5.80 4.75%.
5.82 (*a*) 2.35 kN $\leftarrow$. (*b*) 1.782 kN $\downarrow$. (*c*) 5.31 kN $\uparrow$.
5.83 1.337 kN $\leftarrow$.
5.84 **A** = 512 kN $\nearrow$ 65.2°; **B** = 480 kN $\uparrow$.
5.85 17.9 m.
5.87 **A** = 3930 N $\searrow$ 45.4°; **D** = 124.1 N $\rightarrow$.
5.88 0.782 m.
5.90 (*a*) $-1.118R$. (*b*) 0.884.
5.91 $7h/16$.
5.92 $-3a/4\pi$.
5.93 (*a*) $0.548L$. (*b*) $2\sqrt{3}$.
5.94 -1.312 mm.
5.95 51.4 mm.
5.98 0.075 m.
5.99 0.026 m.
5.100 $\overline{X} = 360$ mm, $\overline{Y} = 266$ mm, $\overline{Z} = -60.7$ mm.
5.101 $\overline{X} = 0.06$ m, $\overline{Y} = 0.09$ m, $\overline{Z} = 0.06$ m.
5.102 $\overline{X} = 150.0$ mm, $\overline{Y} = 200$ mm, $\overline{Z} = 40.2$ mm.
5.103 $\overline{X} = 136.2$ mm, $\overline{Y} = 197.8$ mm.
5.104 $\overline{X} = 9.00$ m, $\overline{Y} = -20.4$ m, $\overline{Z} = 12.81$ m.
5.106 $\overline{X} = 340$ mm, $\overline{Y} = 314$ mm, $\overline{Z} = 283$ mm.
5.108 $\overline{X} = 205$ mm, $\overline{Y} = 255$ mm, $\overline{Z} = 75.0$ mm.
5.109 $\overline{X} = 116.7$ mm, $\overline{Y} = 103.0$ mm, $\overline{Z} = 78.7$ mm.
5.111 $\overline{X} = 0.96$ m, $\overline{Y} = 0.87$ m, $\overline{Z} = 0.9$ m.
5.113 5.35 mm.
5.114 50 mm.
5.115 0.086 m. above the bottom of the base.
5.116 $\bar{x}_1 = 21a/88$; $\bar{x}_2 = 27a/40$.
5.117 $\bar{x}_1 = 21h/88$; $\bar{x}_2 = 27h/40$.
5.119 $\bar{x} = 5a/128, \bar{y} = \bar{z} = 0$.
5.121 $\bar{x} = a, \bar{y} = 77b/100, \bar{z} = 0$.
5.122 $\bar{x} = a[1 - (4/\pi^2)]/2, \bar{y} = \bar{z} = 0$.
5.123 $\bar{x} = \bar{z} = 0, \bar{y} = h(2 + \pi)/16$.
5.128 $b(\frac{1}{2}y_0 - \frac{1}{4}y_1 - \frac{1}{3}y_2)/(y_0 - \frac{1}{2}y_1 - \frac{1}{2}y_2)$.
5.129 $\bar{x} = 0, \bar{y} = 5h/16, \bar{z} = -a/4$.
5.130 $\overline{X} = 1.421$ mm, $\overline{Y} = 12.42$ mm.
5.131 $\overline{X} = 0.14$ m, $\overline{Y} = 0.35$ m.
5.133 0.3 m.
5.134 $\overline{X} = 2a/5, \bar{y} = 4h/7$.
5.136 57781.2 cm^3
5.138 **A** = 3.33 kN $\uparrow$; $\mathbf{M}_A$ = 6.33 kN · m $\curvearrowleft$.
5.139 1.54 m.
5.141 $\overline{X} = 20.4$ mm, $\overline{Y} = -4.55$ mm, $\overline{Z} = 29.0$ mm.

CHAPTER 6

6.1 $F_{AB} = 1500$ N *T*; $F_{AC} = 800$ N *T*; $F_{BC} = 1700$ N *C*.
6.2 $F_{AB} = 3.39$ kN *C*; $F_{AC} = 2.60$ kN *T*; $F_{BC} = 3.00$ kN *C*.
6.3 $F_{AB} = 1080$ N *T*; $F_{AC} = 1800$ N *C*; $F_{BC} = 1170$ N *C*.
6.5 $F_{AB} = F_{AE} = 6.71$ kN *T*; $F_{AC} = F_{AD} = 10.00$ kN *C*; $F_{BC} = F_{DE} = 6.00$ kN *C*; $F_{CD} = 2.00$ kN *T*.
6.6 $F_{AB} = 21.9$ kN *C*; $F_{AD} = 40.6$ kN *T*; $F_{BC} = 18.50$ kN *C*; $F_{BD} = 30.4$ kN *C*; $F_{CD} = 18.50$ kN *T*.
6.7 $F_{AB} = 4.00$ kN *T*; $F_{AD} = 15.00$ kN *T*; $F_{BD} = 9.00$ kN *C*; $F_{BE} = 5.00$ kN *T*; $F_{CD} = 16.00$ kN *C*; $F_{DE} = 4.00$ kN *C*.
6.9 $F_{AB} = F_{BC} = F_{CD} = 24.0$ kN *T*; $F_{AE} = 38.4$ kN *T*; $F_{AF} = 30.0$ kN *C*; $F_{BF} = F_{BG} = F_{CG} = F_{CH} = 0$; $F_{DH} = F_{FG} = F_{GH} = 26.0$ kN *C*; $F_{EF} = 24.0$ kN *C*.
6.10 $F_{AB} = F_{FH} = 5.00$ kN *C*; $F_{AC} = F_{CE} = F_{EG} = F_{GH} = 4.00$ kN *T*; $F_{BC} = F_{FG} = 0$; $F_{BD} = F_{DF} = 3.98$ kN *C*; $F_{BE} = F_{EF} = 0.238$ kN *C*; $F_{DE} = 0.286$ kN *T*.
6.12 $F_{AD} = F_{EG} = 17.50$ kN *C*; $F_{AC} = F_{FG} = 15.08$ kN *T*; $F_{BC} = F_{EF} = 2.26$ kN *C*; $F_{BD} = F_{DE} = 15.50$ kN *C*; $F_{CD} = F_{DF} = 9.00$ kN *T*; $F_{CF} = 7.00$ kN *T*.
6.13 $F_{AB} = 15.00$ kN *C*; $F_{AC} = 12.92$ kN *T*; $F_{BC} = 2.26$ kN *C*; $F_{BD} = 13.00$ kN *C*; $F_{CD} = 8.00$ kN *T*; $F_{CF} = 5.60$ kN *T*; $F_{DE} = 10.00$ kN *C*; $F_{DF} = 4.00$ kN *T*; $F_{EF} = 0$; $F_{EG} = 10.00$ kN *C*; $F_{FG} = 8.62$ kN *T*.
6.15 $F_{AB} = 6.01$ kN *C*; $F_{AC} = 3.33$ kN *T*; $F_{BC} = 0.601$ kN *C*; $F_{BD} = 5.41$ kN *C*; $F_{CD} = 0.850$ kN *T*; $F_{CG} = 0.583$ kN *C*; $F_{CI} = 3.47$ kN *T*; $F_{DE} = 9.28$ kN *C*; $F_{DF} = 6.00$ kN *T*; $F_{EF} = 0$.
6.16 $F_{CG} = 0.583$ kN *C*; $F_{CI} = 3.47$ kN *T*; $F_{EF} = 0$; $F_{EG} = 9.28$ kN *C*; $F_{FG} = 6.00$ kN *T*; $F_{GH} = 6.25$ kN *C*; $F_{GI} = 0.500$ kN *T*; $F_{HI} = 0.601$ kN *C*; $F_{HJ} = 6.85$ kN *C*; $F_{IJ} = 3.80$ kN *T*.
6.17 $F_{AB} = 3.61$ kN *C*; $F_{AC} = 4.11$ kN *T*; $F_{BC} = 0.768$ kN *C*; $F_{BD} = 3.84$ kN *C*; $F_{CD} = 1.371$ kN *T*; $F_{CE} = 2.74$ kN *T*; $F_{DE} = 1.536$ kN *C*.

6.18 $F_{DF} = 4.06$ kN C; $F_{DG} = 1.371$ kN T; $F_{EG} = 2.74$ kN T; $F_{FG} = 0.768$ kN C; $F_{FH} = 4.29$ kN C; $F_{GH} = 4.11$ kN T.
6.19 $F_{AB} = 10.06$ kN C; $F_{AC} = 9.00$ kN T; $F_{BC} = 2.81$ kN C; $F_{BD} = 14.64$ kN C; $F_{BE} = 4.16$ kN T; $F_{CE} = 9.43$ kN T; $F_{DE} = 2.05$ kN C; $F_{DF} = 18.45$ kN C; $F_{DG} = 3.43$ kN T; $F_{EG} = 13.72$ kN T.
6.23 $F_{AB} = 8.97$ kN C; $F_{AC} = 8.28$ kN T; $F_{BC} = 3.45$ kN C; $F_{BD} = 14.04$ kN C; $F_{BE} = 4.68$ kN T; $F_{CE} = 8.97$ kN T; $F_{CF} = F_{EF} = 0$; $F_{DE} = 5.61$ kN T; $F_{DG} = 8.60$ kN C; $F_{DH} = 7.10$ kN C; $F_{EH} = 13.14$ kN T.
6.25 $F_{AB} = 430$ N C; $F_{AC} = 255$ N T; $F_{BC} = 1319$ N T; $F_{BD} = 1700$ N C; $F_{CD} = 986$ N T; $F_{CE} = 744$ N T; $F_{DE} = 1050$ N T; $F_{DF} = 1750$ N C; $F_{EF} = 1565$ N T; $F_{EG} = 0$; $F_{FG} = 350$ N C.
6.26 $F_{AB} = F_{BD} = 8.20$ kN T; $F_{AC} = 8.00$ kN C; $F_{BC} = 0.600$ kN C; $F_{CD} = 1.342$ kN T; $F_{CE} = 9.20$ kN C; $F_{DE} = 0.330$ kN C; $F_{DG} = 9.43$ kN T; $F_{EF} = 9.99$ kN C; $F_{EG} = 0.858$ kN T; $F_{FG} = F_{FH} = 7.99$ kN C.
6.27 Trusses of Probs. 6.14, 6.15, and 6.23 are simple trusses.
6.28 Trusses of Probs. 6.21, 6.25, and 6.29 are simple trusses.
6.29 *BE, EI, FG, GH, HI, IJ*.
6.30 *AI, DI, EI, FK, GK*.
6.31 *BC, BE, DE, FH, HI, IJ, OQ, QR*.
6.33 *BC, LM*.
6.35 (*a*) *BF, BG, CG, CH*. (*b*) *BE, EI, FG, GH, HI, IJ*.
6.36 $F_{AB} = 975$ N C; $F_{AC} = 5.00$ N T; $F_{AD} = 5.93$ kN C; $F_{BC} = 611$ N C; $F_{BD} = 4.94$ kN T; $F_{CD} = 1.335$ kN T.
6.37 $F_{AB} = 1.395$ kN C; $F_{AC} = 415$ N C; $F_{AD} = 4.24$ kN C; $F_{BC} = 672$ N T; $F_{BD} = 4.94$ kN T; $F_{CD} = 534$ N C.
6.38 $F_{AB} = 335$ N C; $F_{AC} = 0$; $F_{AD} = 375$ N T; $F_{AE} = 75.0$ N T; $F_{BC} = 100.0$ N T; $F_{BD} = 150.0$ N C; $F_{CD} = 141.4$ N C; $F_{CE} = 50.0$ N C; $F_{DE} = 25.0$ N C.
6.39 $F_{AB} = F_{AD} = F_{BC} = 0$; $F_{AC} = 1.700$ kN C; $F_{AE} = 2.13$ kN T; $F_{BD} = 1.275$ kN T; $F_{BE} = F_{CD} = 1.125$ kN C; $F_{DE} = 600$ N C.
6.40 (*b*) $F_{AE} = 252$ N T; $F_{BE} = 373$ N C; $F_{DE} = F_{EF} = 0$; $F_{EG} = 365$ N T; $F_{EH} = 240$ N C.
6.41 (*b*) $F_{BG} = 348$ N C; $F_{CG} = F_{DG} = F_{FG} = 0$; $F_{EG} = 365$ N T; $F_{GH} = 275$ N C.
6.42 $F_{CF} = 3.25$ kN T; $F_{EF} = 0.1398$ kN T; $F_{EG} = 3.38$ kN C.
6.43 $F_{FI} = 2.75$ kN T; $F_{HI} = 1.258$ kN C; $F_{HJ} = 1.625$ kN C.
6.44 $F_{BD} = 2.14$ kN C; $F_{BE} = 429$ N C; $F_{CE} = 2.47$ kN T.
6.46 $F_{CE} = 14.35$ kN T; $F_{DE} = 11.41$ kN T; $F_{DF} = 25.6$ kN C.
6.48 $F_{DF} = 13.00$ kN C; $F_{DG} = 4.22$ kN C; $F_{EG} = 16.22$ kN T.
6.49 $F_{GI} = 16.22$ kN T; $F_{HI} = 1.000$ kN T; $F_{HJ} = 17.33$ kN C.
6.50 $F_{BD} = 29.8$ kN C; $F_{CD} = 6.25$ kN T; $F_{CE} = 22.5$ kN T.
6.51 $F_{EG} = 16.88$ kN T; $F_{FG} = 8.01$ kN T; $F_{FH} = 22.3$ kN C.
6.52 $F_{CE} = 10.00$ kN C; $F_{DE} = 4.00$ kN C; $F_{EF} = 3.00$ kN T.
6.53 $F_{GI} = 4.00$ kN C; $F_{HI} = 15.00$ kN T; $F_{IJ} = 3.00$ kN T.
6.55 $F_{IK} = 0.707$ kN C; $F_{JL} = 0$; $F_{JM} = 6.35$ kN T.
6.57 $F_{GI} = 7.18$ kN T; $F_{HJ} = 8.03$ kN C; $F_{IJ} = 4.46$ kN C.
6.58 $F_{CE} = 7.34$ kN C; $F_{CF} = 3.58$ kN T; $F_{DF} = 2.35$ kN T.
6.60 $F_{DG} = 1.800$ kN C; $F_{FH} = 1.800$ kN T.
6.62 $F_{HK} = 53.9$ kN C; $F_{IK} = 57.3$ kN C.
6.63 $F_{EG} = 44.1$ kN T; $F_{FI} = 26.2$ kN C.
6.64 $F_{BD} = 15.31$ kN C; $F_{CD} = 2.42$ kN T; $F_{CE} = 13.26$ kN T.
6.65 $F_{BD} = 10.51$ kN C; $F_{BE} = 1.211$ kN T; $F_{CE} = 9.49$ kN T.
6.67 $F_{BE} = 10.00$ kN T; $F_{DE} = 0$; $F_{EF} = 5.00$ kN T.
6.68 $F_{CE} = 15.00$ kN T; $F_{DE} = 25.0$ kN T; $F_{DF} = 30.0$ kN C.
6.70 (*a*) Partially constrained. (*b*) Partially constrained. (*c*) Completely constrained, statically determinate.
6.71 (*a*) Completely constrained, statically determinate. (*b*) Partially constrained. (*c*) Improperly constrained, statically indeterminate.
6.73 (*a*) Improperly constrained. (*b*) Partially constrained. (*c*) Improperly constrained.
6.74 (*a*) Completely constrained, statically determinate. (*b*) Partially constrained. (*c*) Completely constrained, statically indeterminate.
6.76 $\mathbf{A}_x = 120.0$ N $\rightarrow$, $\mathbf{A}_y = 30.0$ N $\uparrow$; $\mathbf{B}_x = 120.0$ N $\leftarrow$, $\mathbf{B}_y = 80.0$ N $\downarrow$; $\mathbf{C} = 30.0$ N $\downarrow$; $\mathbf{D} = 80.0$ N $\uparrow$.
6.78 $\mathbf{C} = 1824$ N $\downarrow$; $\mathbf{D}_x = 1824$ N $\leftarrow$, $\mathbf{D}_y = 480$ N $\downarrow$; $\mathbf{E}_x = 1824$ N $\rightarrow$, $\mathbf{E}_y = 1824$ N $\uparrow$.
6.79 $\mathbf{C} = 1600$ N $\uparrow$; $\mathbf{D}_x = 1600$ N $\rightarrow$, $\mathbf{D}_y = 0$; $\mathbf{E}_x = 1600$ N $\leftarrow$, $\mathbf{E}_y = 1600$ N $\downarrow$.
6.80 (*a*) 7.32 N C. (*b*) $\mathbf{A} = 6.26$ N $\measuredangle$ 16.69°.
6.82 $\mathbf{A}_x = 356$ N $\rightarrow$; $\mathbf{B}_x = 229$ N $\leftarrow$, $\mathbf{B}_y = 127.3$ N $\uparrow$; $\mathbf{C}_x = 127.3$ N $\leftarrow$, $\mathbf{C}_y = 178.2$ N $\uparrow$; $\mathbf{D} = 305$ N $\downarrow$.
6.83 $\mathbf{A}_x = 300$ N $\rightarrow$; $\mathbf{B}_x = 300$ N $\leftarrow$, $\mathbf{B}_y = 0$; $\mathbf{C}_x = 0$, $\mathbf{C}_y = 300$ N $\uparrow$; $\mathbf{D}_y = 300$ N $\downarrow$.
6.84 (*a*) $\mathbf{A}_x = 14.40$ N $\leftarrow$, $\mathbf{A}_y = 9.60$ N $\uparrow$; $\mathbf{E}_x = 14.40$ N $\rightarrow$, $\mathbf{E}_y = 14.40$ N $\uparrow$. (*b*) $\mathbf{A}_x = 6.40$ N $\leftarrow$, $\mathbf{A}_y = 1.600$ N $\uparrow$; $\mathbf{E}_x = 6.40$ N $\rightarrow$, $\mathbf{E}_y = 22.4$ N $\uparrow$.
6.85 (*a*) $\mathbf{A}_x = 120.0$ N $\leftarrow$, $\mathbf{A}_y = 200$ N $\uparrow$; $\mathbf{E}_x = 120.0$ N $\rightarrow$, $\mathbf{E}_y = 120.0$ N $\uparrow$. (*b*) $\mathbf{A}_x = 96.0$ N $\leftarrow$, $\mathbf{A}_y = 96.0$ N $\uparrow$; $\mathbf{E}_x = 96.0$ N $\rightarrow$, $\mathbf{E}_y = 224$ N $\uparrow$.
6.86 (*a*) $\mathbf{A}_x = 19.20$ N $\rightarrow$, $\mathbf{A}_y = 19.20$ N $\uparrow$; $\mathbf{E}_x = 19.20$ N $\leftarrow$, $\mathbf{E}_y = 19.20$ N $\downarrow$. (*b*) $\mathbf{A}_x = 51.2$ N $\rightarrow$, $\mathbf{A}_y = 12.80$ N $\downarrow$; $\mathbf{E}_x = 51.2$ N $\rightarrow$, $\mathbf{E}_y = 12.80$ N $\uparrow$.
6.88 (*a*) $\mathbf{F}_{AB} = 260$ N $\measuredangle$ 22.6°; $\mathbf{F}_{BC} = 480$ N $\rightarrow$; $\mathbf{F}_{GH} = 240$ N $\leftarrow$; $\mathbf{I}_y = 100$ N $\uparrow$. (*b*) $\mathbf{F}_{AB} = 260$ N $\measuredangle$ 22.6°; $\mathbf{F}_{BC} = 240$ N $\rightarrow$; $\mathbf{F}_{FG} = 0$; $\mathbf{I}_y = 100$ N $\uparrow$.
6.89 (*a*) $\mathbf{B}_x = 200$ N $\rightarrow$, $\mathbf{B}_y = 40.0$ N $\downarrow$; $\mathbf{F}_x = 200$ N $\leftarrow$, $\mathbf{F}_y = 160.0$ N $\uparrow$. (*b*) $\mathbf{B}_x = 320$ N $\rightarrow$, $\mathbf{B}_y = 40.0$ N $\downarrow$; $\mathbf{F}_x = 320$ N $\leftarrow$, $\mathbf{F}_y = 160.0$ N $\uparrow$. (*c*) $\mathbf{B}_x = 320$ N $\rightarrow$, $\mathbf{B}_y = 40.0$ N $\downarrow$; $\mathbf{F}_x = 320$ N $\leftarrow$, $\mathbf{F}_y = 160.0$ N $\uparrow$.
6.92 $\mathbf{A}_x = 1315.6$ N $\rightarrow$, $\mathbf{A}_y = 858.3$ N $\uparrow$; $\mathbf{E}_x = 1315.6$ N $\leftarrow$, $\mathbf{E}_y = 1201.7$ N $\uparrow$.
6.93 $\mathbf{A}_x = 1444$ N $\rightarrow$, $\mathbf{A}_y = 1239$ N $\uparrow$; $\mathbf{E}_x = 1444$ N $\leftarrow$, $\mathbf{E}_y = 821$ N $\uparrow$.
6.94 $\mathbf{A}_x = 17.00$ N $\leftarrow$, $\mathbf{A}_y = 94.1$ N $\uparrow$; $\mathbf{E}_x = 17.00$ N $\rightarrow$, $\mathbf{E}_y = 75.9$ N $\uparrow$.
6.95 $\mathbf{A}_x = 45.0$ N $\leftarrow$, $\mathbf{A}_y = 30.0$ N $\downarrow$; $\mathbf{B}_x = 45.0$ N $\rightarrow$, $\mathbf{B}_y = 270$ N $\uparrow$.
6.96 (*a*) $\mathbf{A} = 15.76$ kN $\uparrow$; $\mathbf{B} = 26.2$ kN $\uparrow$. (*b*) $\mathbf{C}_x = 34.6$ kN $\leftarrow$; $\mathbf{D} = 34.7$ kN $\measuredangle$ 4.10°.
6.97 (*a*) $\mathbf{A} = 2.52$ kN $\uparrow$; $\mathbf{B} = 31.5$ kN $\uparrow$. (*b*) $\mathbf{C}_x = 4.93$ kN $\leftarrow$; $\mathbf{D}_x = 4.93$ kN $\rightarrow$, $\mathbf{D}_y = 12.97$ kN $\downarrow$.
6.98 $\mathbf{A}_x = 10.80$ kN $\leftarrow$, $\mathbf{A}_y = 7.00$ kN $\uparrow$; $\mathbf{B}_x = 16.20$ kN $\leftarrow$, $\mathbf{B}_y = 0.500$ kN $\downarrow$; $\mathbf{D}_x = 27.0$ kN $\rightarrow$, $\mathbf{D}_y = 6.50$ kN $\downarrow$.
6.100 $\mathbf{B}_x = 530$ N $\rightarrow$, $\mathbf{B}_y = 385$ N $\downarrow$; $\mathbf{C}_x = 299$ N $\leftarrow$, $\mathbf{C}_y = 385$ N $\uparrow$.
6.101 $\mathbf{B}_x = 60.6$ N $\leftarrow$, $\mathbf{B}_y = 41.7$ N $\downarrow$; $\mathbf{C}_x = 60.6$ N $\rightarrow$, $\mathbf{C}_y = 29.7$ N $\uparrow$.
6.103 (*a*) A' and B'. (*b*) 215 N T.
6.104 (*a*) $\mathbf{A}_x = 27.5$ kN $\rightarrow$, $\mathbf{A}_y = 16.25$ kN $\uparrow$. (*b*) $\mathbf{B}_x = 27.5$ kN $\leftarrow$, $\mathbf{B}_y = 2.25$ kN $\downarrow$.
6.105 (*a*) $\mathbf{A}_x = 28.8$ kN $\rightarrow$, $\mathbf{A}_y = 19.38$ kN $\uparrow$.

(b) $\mathbf{B}_x = 28.8$ kN $\leftarrow$, $\mathbf{B}_y = 1.625$ kN $\uparrow$.
6.106 (a) 1009 N $\nearrow$ 18.18°. (b) 357 N T.
6.108 $a \geq 0.600$ m.
6.109 $F_{CF} = 9.00$ kN C; $F_{DG} = 6.00$ kN T.
6.110 $F_{BF} = 7.20$ kN T; $F_{DG} = 3.00$ kN C.
6.111 $F_{BG} = 6.00$ kN T; $F_{CH} = 3.00$ kN C.
6.113 $\mathbf{A} = 3P/13 \uparrow$; $\mathbf{D} = P/13 \uparrow$; $\mathbf{F} = 9P/13 \uparrow$.
6.114 $\mathbf{A} = P/15 \uparrow$; $\mathbf{D} = 2P/15 \uparrow$; $\mathbf{E} = 8P/15 \uparrow$; $\mathbf{H} = 4P/15 \uparrow$.
6.115 (a) Frame is not rigid. (b) Reactions can be found for an arbitrary value of B_x; frame is rigid. (c) $\mathbf{A} = 2.09P \searrow 16.70°$; $\mathbf{B} = 2.04P \nearrow 11.31°$; frame is rigid.
6.116 (a) $\mathbf{A} = 2.06P \nearrow 14.04°$; $\mathbf{B} = 2.06P \searrow 14.04°$; frame is rigid. (b) Frame is not rigid. (c) $\mathbf{A} = 1.250P \searrow 36.9°$; $\mathbf{B} = 1.031P \nearrow 14.04°$; frame is rigid.
6.117 (a) $\mathbf{A} = 2.24P \nearrow 26.6°$; $\mathbf{B} = 2P \rightarrow$; frame is rigid. (b) Frame is not rigid. (c) $\mathbf{A} = P \uparrow$; $\mathbf{B} = P \downarrow$; $\mathbf{C} = P \uparrow$; frame is rigid.
6.118 (a) 2.86 kN $\downarrow$. (b) 2.70 kN $\swarrow$ 68.5°.
6.119 (a) 420 N. (b) 2.83 kN $\swarrow$ 68.5°.
6.122 (a) 456 N $\leftarrow$. (b) 505 N T.
6.123 113.7 N $\nwarrow$ 16.17°.
6.124 101.8 N $\nwarrow$ 18.89°.
6.125 995 N · m. $\circlearrowright$.
6.127 (a) 3.87 N · m $\circlearrowright$. (b) 5.12 N · m $\circlearrowright$.
6.128 (a) 248 N $\leftarrow$. (b) 187.9 N $\leftarrow$.
6.129 9.38 N · m $\circlearrowright$.
6.130 46.3 N · m $\circlearrowright$.
6.131 9.13 N · m $\circlearrowleft$.
6.132 7.50 N · m $\circlearrowleft$.
6.133 2.77 kN · m. $\circlearrowright$.
6.136 $\mathbf{CD} = 30.0$ kN $\leftarrow$; $\mathbf{F} = 37.5$ kN $\nwarrow$ 36.9°.
6.137 $\mathbf{G} = 7.42$ kN $\downarrow$; $\mathbf{H} = 3.12$ kN $\searrow$ 70.3°.
6.139 720 N.
6.140 2.22 kN.
6.141 156.6 N.
6.142 783 N.
6.143 11.46 N $\swarrow$ 30.0°.
6.144 43.1 N $\nearrow$ 60.0°.
6.146 8.82 kN.
6.147 6.48 kN $\nearrow$ 62.1°.
6.148 (a) 0. (b) $\mathbf{C}_x = 7.20$ kN $\leftarrow$, $\mathbf{C}_y = 1.500$ kN $\downarrow$.
6.150 (a) 7.68 kN C. (b) 21.7 kN C.
6.151 (a) 36.0 mm. (b) 60.0 N · m $\circlearrowright$.
6.152 (a) (9 N · m.)$\mathbf{i}$. (b) $\mathbf{M}_G = (14.4$ N · m.)$\mathbf{i}$; $\mathbf{M}_H = -(10.3$ N · m.)$\mathbf{i}$.
6.154 (a) 43.3 N · m. (b) $\mathbf{B} = -(50.0$ N)$\mathbf{k}$; $\mathbf{D} = (83.3$ N)$\mathbf{k}$; $\mathbf{E} = -(33.3$ N)$\mathbf{k}$.
6.155 $\mathbf{E}_x = 2040$ N $\rightarrow$, $\mathbf{E}_y = 3160$ N $\uparrow$; $\mathbf{F}_x = 540$ N $\rightarrow$, $\mathbf{F}_y = 2410$ N $\downarrow$; $\mathbf{H}_x = 2580$ N $\leftarrow$, $\mathbf{H}_y = 750$ N $\downarrow$.
6.156 $F_{AB} = F_{BD} = 0$; $F_{AC} = 3.00$ kN T; $F_{AD} = 5.00$ kN C; $F_{CD} = 4.00$ kN T; $F_{CE} = 9.00$ kN T; $F_{CF} = 10.00$ kN T; $F_{DF} = 6.00$ kN T; $F_{EF} = 8.00$ kN T.
6.157 $F_{FG} = 1.750$ kN T; $F_{FH} = 2.52$ kN C; $F_{GH} = 0.838$ kN T; $F_{GI} = F_{IK} = F_{KL} = 1.677$ kN T; $F_{HI} = F_{IJ} = F_{JK} = 0$; $F_{HJ} = F_{JL} = 2.12$ kN C.
6.158 $F_{AB} = 61.9$ kN C; $F_{AC} = 56.5$ kN C; $F_{AD} = 30.2$ kN T; $F_{AE} = 19.01$ kN T; $F_{BD} = 43.0$ kN T; $F_{BF} = 56.0$ kN C; $F_{CE} = 82.0$ kN T; $F_{CG} = 84.0$ kN C; $F_{DE} = 44.0$ kN T; $F_{DF} = 67.1$ kN T; $F_{EG} = 0$.
6.160 $F_{AB} = 36.4$ kN T; $F_{AG} = 20.0$ kN T; $F_{FG} = 51.6$ kN C.
6.162 . $\mathbf{A}_x = 4.50$ kN $\leftarrow$, $\mathbf{A}_y = 5.00$ kN $\downarrow$; $\mathbf{F}_{BE} = 2.25$ kN $\rightarrow$; $\mathbf{C}_x = 2.25$ kN $\rightarrow$, $\mathbf{C}_y = 5.00$ kN $\uparrow$.
6.163 $\mathbf{B}_x = 175.0$ N $\leftarrow$, $\mathbf{B}_y = 50.0$ N $\downarrow$; $\mathbf{E}_x = 175.0$ N $\rightarrow$, $\mathbf{E}_y = 125.0$ N $\uparrow$.
6.165 (a) 220 N $\rightarrow$. (b) 254 N T. (c) 280 N $\searrow$ 38.3°.
6.166 1680 N.

CHAPTER 7

7.1 (On EJ) $\mathbf{F} = 0$; $\mathbf{V} = 1200$ N $\leftarrow$; $\mathbf{M} = 180.0$ N · m $\circlearrowright$.
7.3 (On CJ) $\mathbf{F} = 127.3$ N $\leftarrow$; $\mathbf{V} = 178.2$ N $\uparrow$; $\mathbf{M} = 11.46$ N · m $\circlearrowright$.
7.5 (On AJ) $\mathbf{F} = 124.8$ N $\rightarrow$; $\mathbf{V} = 52.0$ N $\downarrow$; $\mathbf{M} = 13$ N · m. $\circlearrowleft$.
7.6 (On CK) $\mathbf{F} = 123.3$ N $\swarrow$ 22.9°; $\mathbf{V} = 24.1 \searrow 67.1°$; $\mathbf{M} = 7.6$ N · m. $\circlearrowright$.
7.7 (On BJ) $\mathbf{F} = 0$; $\mathbf{V} = 0$; $\mathbf{M} = 2.41$ N · m $\circlearrowright$.
7.8 (On BJ) $\mathbf{F} = 0$; $\mathbf{V} = 44.1$ N $\uparrow$; $\mathbf{M} = 4.22$ N · m $\circlearrowleft$.
7.9 (On BJ) $\mathbf{F} = 4.39$ N $\nwarrow$ 60.0°; $\mathbf{V} = 16.39$ N $\swarrow$ 30.0°; $\mathbf{M} = 0.76$ N · m. $\circlearrowright$.
7.11 (On CJ) $\mathbf{F} = 1.482$ N $\nearrow$ 60°; $\mathbf{V} = 103.1$ N$\nwarrow$ 30°; $\mathbf{M} = 10.3$ N · m. $\circlearrowright$.
7.13 (On AJ) $\mathbf{F} = 6260$ N $\searrow$ 19.80°; $\mathbf{V} = 339$ N $\swarrow$ 70.2°; $\mathbf{M} = 346$ N · m $\circlearrowright$.
7.14 $M_{max} = PL/4$; $a = L/2$.
7.15 (On BJ) $\mathbf{F} = 250$ N $\nwarrow$ 36.9°; $\mathbf{V} = 120.0$ N $\nearrow$ 53.1°; $\mathbf{M} = 120.0$ N · m $\circlearrowleft$.
7.16 (On AK) $\mathbf{F} = 560$ N $\leftarrow$; $\mathbf{V} = 90.0$ N $\downarrow$; $\mathbf{M} = 72.0$ N · m $\circlearrowright$.
7.17 (On DJ) $\mathbf{F} = 1036$ N $\nearrow$ 67.4°; $\mathbf{V} = 17.31$ N $\searrow$ 22.6°; $\mathbf{M} = 22.5$ N · m $\circlearrowright$.
7.18 (On AK) $\mathbf{F} = 463$ N $\nearrow$ 53.1°; $\mathbf{V} = 41.1$ N $\searrow$ 36.9°; $\mathbf{M} = 61.7$ N · m $\circlearrowleft$.
7.19 (On CJ) $\mathbf{F} = 733$ N $\nwarrow$ 46.4°; $\mathbf{V} = 87$ N $\swarrow$ 44.6; $\mathbf{M} = 19$ N · m. $\circlearrowleft$.
7.21 (a) (On AJ) $\mathbf{F} = P/2 \downarrow$; $\mathbf{V} = 0$; $\mathbf{M} = 0$.
(b) (On AJ) $\mathbf{F} = 11P/14 \downarrow$; $\mathbf{V} = 2P/7 \leftarrow$; $\mathbf{M} = 2Pa/7$ $\circlearrowright$.
(c) (On AJ) $\mathbf{F} = 5P/2 \downarrow$; $\mathbf{V} = 2P \leftarrow$; $\mathbf{M} = 2Pa$ $\circlearrowright$.
7.23 (On AJ) $\mathbf{M} = 0.0774Wr$ $\circlearrowright$.
7.24 (On AJ) $\mathbf{M} = 0.01085Wr$ $\circlearrowright$.
7.25 $\theta = 27.7°$; (On AJ) $\mathbf{M}_{max} = 0.0777Wr$ $\circlearrowright$.
7.26 $\theta = 66.6°$; (On AJ) $\mathbf{M}_{max} = 0.0362Wr$ $\circlearrowleft$.
7.29 (b) M_0/L; $M_0/2$.
7.30 (b) P; Pa.
7.31 (b) $w_0L/2$; $w_0L^2/6$.
7.32 (b) P; $1.5Pa$.
7.34 (b) 12.63 kN; 8.9 kN · m.
7.36 (b) 3.50 kN; 4.50 kN · m.
7.37 (b) 5.56 kN; 6.59 kN · m.
7.39 (b) 175.0 N; 31.25 N · m.
7.40 (b) 39 kN; 59.4 kN · m.
7.41 (b) 6.00 kN; 6.00 kN · m.
7.43 (b) 4.00 kN; 4.00 kN · m.
7.45 7.00 kN; 7.50 kN · m.
7.47 (b) 495 N; 194.4 N · m.
7.48 (b) 585 N; 290 N · m.
7.49 360 N; 140.0 N · m.
7.51 (a) 0.311 m. (b) 232 N · m.
7.52 (a) 0.43 m. (b) 141 N · m.
7.53 (a) 411 N. (b) 1029 N · m.
7.54 (a) 1.063 m. (b) 8.50 kN · m.
7.56 (a) imaginary.
7.57 (a) 0.414 wL; 0.858 wL^2. (b) $wL/4$; $wL^2/4$.

7.58 (b) M_0/L; $M_0/2$.
7.60 (b) $w_0L/2$; $w_0L^2/6$.
7.61 (b) P; $1.5Pa$.
7.62 (b) 12.63 kN; 8.9 kN · m.
7.64 (b) 780 N; 210 N · m.
7.65 (b) 8.37 kN; 11.02 kN · m.
7.66 (b) 5.56 kN; 6.59 kN · m.
7.68 (b) 175.0 N; 25 N · m.
7.69 (b) 33.0 kN; 9.9 kN · m.
7.70 (b) 124.0 N; 75.4 N · m.
7.72 (b) 1.985 kN · m, 1.260 m from A.
7.74 (a) 23.8 kN · m. (b)
7.75 1011.2 kN · m, 1.59 m from A.
7.76 (b) 52.0 kN · m.
7.78 (b) 6.84 kN · m at E.
7.79 (b) 2.77 kN · m at C.
7.80 (a) $V = (w_0/L)(-2x^2 + Lx)$;
$M = (w_0/6L)(-4x^3 + 3Lx^2)$. (c) $w_0L^2/6$, at $x = L$.
7.81 (a) For $0 \le x \le 2a$: $V = (w_0/2a)(3a^2 - x^2)$,
$M = (w_0/6a)(-9a^3 + 9a^2x - x^3)$. (c) $1.5w_0a^2$, at $x = 0$.
7.82 (b) $1.359w_0a^2$, at $x = 2.10a$.
7.85 (a) **P** = 175.0 N ↓; **Q** = 175.0 N ↓.
7.86 (a) **P** = 600 N ↓; **Q** = 400 N ↓.
(b) M_{max} = 3.40 kN · m, 1.875 m from C.
7.87 (a) **P** = 1.113 N ↓; **Q** = 277 N ↓.
7.88 (a) 1.125 m. (b) $\mathbf{A}_x$ = 4.00 kN ←, $\mathbf{A}_y$ = 2.25 kN ↑.
(c) 5.00 kN.
7.89 (a) 2.26 m. (b) 1.508 m.
7.91 5.00 m.
7.92 (a) 4.65 kN ∠ 23.8°. (b) d_B = 1.112 m;
d_D = 1.641 m.
7.93 (a) 1.385 m.
(b) **A** = 8.45 kN ⦪ 39.7°; **E** = 6.61 kN ∠ 10.46°.
7.94 (a) 1229 N. (b) 11.00 m.
7.96 (a) 29.0 N. (b) 4.06 m.
7.97 a = 1.3 m; b = 3.2 m.
7.98 (a) **A** = 2.08 kN ⦪ 22.6°. (b) 107.0 kg.
(c) T_{AB} = 2.08 kN; T_{BC} = 1.000 kN; T_{CD} = 0.650 kN.
7.101 (a) 33.1 kg. (b) 99.5 N.
7.102 (a) 177.5 kN. (b) 60.1 m.
7.103 (a) 4.50 m. (b) T_1 = 410 N; T_2 = 400 N.
7.104 (a) 16945.17 kN. (b) 1284.8 m.
7.105 (a) 15041.75 kN. (b) 567.2 m.
7.106 (a) 0.08 m. (b) 0.42°.
7.108 1.4 m.
7.110 (a) 58,900 kN. (b) 29.2°.
7.111 (a) 0.36 m from A. (b) 0.04 N.
7.112 (a) 1.713 m. (b) 6.19 m.
7.113 (a) 2.22 m. (b) 5.36 kN.
7.115 2.26 m.
7.116 d_B = 1.112 m; d_D = 1.641 m.
7.120 $y = (w_0L^2/T_0\pi^2)\,[1 - (\cos \pi x)/L]$; $T_{min} = w_0L^2/h\pi^2$;
$T_B = (w_0L/\pi)\sqrt{(L^2/h^2\pi^2) + 1}$.
7.122 (a) 2.92 m. (b) 5.23 N.
7.123 (a) 8.9 m. (b) 61.5 N.
7.124 (a) 123.6 m. (b) 262.5 N.
7.127 (a) 7.94 m. (b) 24.0 m.
7.128 (a) 0.530 m. (b) 114.7 N.
7.129 (a) 30.2 m. (b) 56.6 kg.
7.131 (a) 1.265 m. (b) 80.3°.
7.132 5.23 m.
7.133 2.4 m and 15 m.
7.135 (a) 18.78 m. (b) 3.53 kg/m.
7.136 8.2 N →.
7.137 12.15 N →.
7.138 (a) a = 26.8 m; b = 20.4 m. (b) 35.3 m.
7.139 (a) a = 20.1 m; b = 15.29 m. (b) 26.5 m.
7.140 (a) 3.15 m. (b) 231 N.
7.141 (a) 6.2 m to the left of B. (b) 2.86 N.
7.143 (a) $1.325T_{max}/w$. (b) 12.72 km.
7.146 (a) 0.338. (b) θ_B = 56.5°; $T_{max} = 0.755wL$.
7.147 (On AJ) **F** = 48.7 N ⦩ 60.0°; **V** = 64.3 N ∠ 30.0°;
M = 7.732 N · m. ↓.
7.148 (On EJ) **F** = 50.0 N ↖; **V** = 30.0 N ↙;
M = 27 N · m ↓.
7.150 (b) 8.00 kN; 17.73 kN · m.
7.151 (b) 18.00 kN; 48.5 kN · m.
7.153 (a) 22.5 kN · m, 1.500 m from A.
(b) 30.2 kN · m, 1.350 m from A.
7.154 (a) $V = w_0L\left[\frac{1}{3} - \frac{x}{L} + \frac{1}{2}\left(\frac{x}{L}\right)^2\right]$

$$M = w_0L^2\left[\frac{1}{3}\left(\frac{x}{L}\right) - \frac{1}{2}\left(\frac{x}{L}\right)^2 + \frac{1}{6}\left(\frac{x}{L}\right)^3\right]$$

(c) $0.0642\ w_0L^2$, at $x = 0.423L$.
7.156 (a) 3.35 kN ⦪ 17.35°. (b) 3.88 kN ∠ 34.5°.
7.157 (a) 7.2 m to the left of B. (b) 669 N.

CHAPTER 8

8.1 (a) 31.1 N. (b) 127.0 N.
8.3 Equilibrium; **F** = 4.04 N ⦨ 20°.
8.4 Block moves; **F** = 19.00 N ⦨ 20°.
8.5 7.56 N ≤ P ≤ 59.2 N.
8.6 28.9°.
8.7 (a) 81.7 N. (b) 19.29°.
8.9 (a) $0 \le \theta \le 55.7°$. (b) $167.9° \le \theta \le 180.0°$.
8.12 (a) 361 N ←. (b) 196.2 N ←.
8.13 49.1°.
8.14 23.4°.
8.15 (a) 58.1°. (b) 166.4 N.
8.17 (a) $0.360Wr$. (b) $0.422Wr$.
8.18 (a) 1300 N. (b) 1700 N.
8.20 (a) 17.53°. (b) $0.252W$.
8.21 0.539.
8.23 (a) 4.62° and 48.2°. (b) $0.526W$ and $0.374W$.
8.24 $3.46 \le L/a \le 13.63$.
8.25 2.62 kN ↓.
8.26 0.1865.
8.27 0.1900.
8.28 0.283.
8.30 (a) 0.526. (b) 0.277.
8.32 $21.8° \le \theta \le 62.9°$.
8.34 Equilibrium if 17.82 N ≤ w ≤ 98.2 N.
8.35 66.1 kg ≤ m ≤ 364 kg.
8.36 $2Pl/(\tan\theta - \mu_s)$.
8.37 0.1400.
8.40 (a) 0.614 N · m. ↰. (b) 0.486 N · m. ↰.
8.41 7.72 N.
8.42 (a) 0.322 kg. (b) 3.60 kg.
8.43 0.1757.
8.45 236 N ≤ P ≤ 289 N.
8.46 441 N.
8.47 480 N.

8.50 (*a*) 72.3 kN →. (*b*) 27.0 kN ←.
8.51 (*a*) 99.3 kN ←. (*b*) 45.3 kN →.
8.52 (*a*) 367 N. (*b*) 367 N.
8.54 8.89 kN.
8.55 38.6°.
8.56 117.5 N.
8.57 6.60 N.
8.58 (*a*) Wedge is forced up and out from between plates. (*b*) Wedge binds in the slot.
8.60 714 N ⦨ 20.0°.
8.61 0.203.
8.62 (*a*) 53.2 N →. (*b*) Motion of the plank at *B* is impending.
8.63 (*a*) 61.3 N →. (*b*) Plank does not move.
8.64 0.385.
8.65 0.332.
8.69 224 N · m.
8.72 (*a*) Screw A. (*b*) 1.535 N · m.
8.73 3.07 N · m.
8.74 33.1 N · m.
8.75 15.35 kN.
8.76 126 N.
8.78 81 N.
8.80 (*a*) 0.344. (*b*) 120.2 N.
8.81 T_{AB} = 290 N; T_{CD} = 310 N; T_{EF} = 331 N.
8.82 T_{AB} = 310 N; T_{CD} = 290 N; T_{EF} = 272 N.
8.83 (*a*) 1.177 kN. (*b*) 1.349°.
8.84 253 N.
8.85 250 N.
8.88 (*a*) 5.96 N. (*b*) 3.99 N.
8.89 99.3 mm.
8.90 1.8 N.
8.91 1.596 N · m.
8.95 1.35 N.
8.97 1.200 mm.
8.98 42.7 N.
8.99 (*a*) 56.0 N. (*b*) 54.0 N.
8.100 216 mm.
8.101 (*a*) 0.329. (*b*) 2.67 turns.
8.104 286 N ≤ *P* ≤ 4840 N.
8.105 24.3 N ≤ *P* ≤ 411 N.
8.106 (*a*) 500 N. (*b*) 0.212.
8.107 10.27 N · m.
8.109 (*a*) 47.9 N. (*b*) 1.900.
8.110 (*a*) T_A = 42.0 N; T_B = 98.0 N. (*b*) 0.270.
8.111 (*a*) T_A = 55.7 N; T_B = 104.3 N. (*b*) 10.95 N · m.
8.112 101.1 N · m.
8.114 0.361.
8.115 (*a*) 432 N · m. (*b*) 0.219.
8.116 (*a*) 1.940 kg. (*b*) 63.7 kg. (*c*) 20.2 kg.
8.117 203 kg.
8.118 (*a*) 3.69 N ≤ W_A ≤ 69.3 N. (*b*) 5.61 N ≤ W_A ≤ 45.6 N.
8.120 (*a*) 4.55 N ≤ W_A ≤ 56.2 N. (*b*) 6.92 N ≤ W_A ≤ 37.0 N.
8.122 5.97 N.
8.123 9.56 N.
8.124 (*a*) 538 N · m ↓. (*b*) 1.142 kN ↓.
8.126 0.350.
8.130 21.76 N · m.
8.131 107 N.
8.132 Block moves; **F** = 193.2 N ↗.
8.133 (*a*) 50.5°. (*b*) 66.5°.
8.135 0.1835.
8.136 0.750.
8.137 (*a*) *W* ≤ 4.07 N and *W* ≥ 86.4 N. (*b*) *W* ≥ 246 N.
8.139 2.46 kN ←.
8.141 0.0787.
8.142 10.08 N · m.

CHAPTER 9

9.1 $a^3(b_1 + 3b_2)/12$.
9.2 $5a^3b/33$.
9.3 $a^3b/21$.
9.5 $a(b_1 + b_2)(b_1^2 + b_2^2)/12$.
9.6 $5ab^3/17$.
9.7 $31ab^3/30$.
9.9 $\pi ab^3/8$.
9.11 $0.1107ab^3$.
9.12 $\pi a^3b/8$.
9.14 $0.273a^3b$.
9.16 $59ab^3/30$; $1.086b$.
9.18 $9a^3b/14$; $0.621a$.
9.19 $0.217ab^3$; $0.642b$.
9.20 $1.482a^3b$; $1.676a$.
9.21 (*a*) $4a^4/3$; $a\sqrt{2/3}$. (*b*) $17a^4/6$; $a\sqrt{17/12}$.
9.22 $11ab(a^2 + 3b^2)/6$; $\sqrt{11(a^2 + 3b^2)/30}$.
9.24 $0.415r^4$; $0.822r$.
9.25 (*a*) $3\pi(R_2^4 - R_1^4)/8$. (*b*) $I_x = I_y = 3\pi(R_2^4 - R_1^4)/16$.
9.26 (*b*) −10.56%; −0.772%; −0.0488%.
9.27 $3\pi a^4/64$; $a\sqrt{6}/4$.
9.31 614×10^3 mm^4; 19.01 mm.
9.32 1.869×10^{-4} m^4; 0.067 m.
9.33 1.894×10^6 mm^4; 33.4 mm.
9.34 3.78×10^{-4} m^4; 0.099 m.
9.37 3000 mm^2; 325×10^3 mm^4.
9.38 24.6×10^6 mm^4.
9.39 0.2 m.; 0.7055×10^{-4} m^4
9.41 $\bar{I}_x = 26.76 \times 10^6$ mm^4; $\bar{I}_y = 2650 \times 10^3$ mm^4.
9.42 $\bar{I}_x = 6.51 \times 10^6$ mm^4; $\bar{I}_y = 5.12 \times 10^6$ mm^4.
9.44 $\bar{I}_x = 2.52 \times 10^6$ mm^4; $\bar{I}_y = 1.056 \times 10^6$ mm^4.
9.45 (*a*) 11.57×10^6 mm^4. (*b*) 7.81×10^6 mm^4.
9.46 (*a*) 60.2×10^6 mm^4. (*b*) 60.1×10^6 mm^4.
9.48 (*a*) 511.8×10^6 mm^4. (*b*) 33.4×10^6 mm^4.
9.49 $\bar{I}_x = 18.2 \times 10^6$ mm^4, $\bar{I}_y = 11.2 \times 10^6$ mm^4; $\bar{k}_x$ = 54.5 mm, $\bar{k}_y$ = 42.7 mm.
9.50 $\bar{I}_x = 195.9 \times 10^6$ mm^4, $\bar{I}_y = 190.7 \times 10^6$ mm^4; $\bar{k}_x$ = 114.0 mm, $\bar{k}_y$ = 112.5 mm.
9.52 12.29 mm.
9.53 $\bar{I}_x = 37.7 \times 10^6$ mm^4; $\bar{I}_y = 3.86 \times 10^6$ mm^4.
9.55 *b* = 91.2 mm; $\bar{I}_x = 11.33 \times 10^6$ mm^4.
9.56 (*a*) 363 mm. (*b*) $\bar{I}_x = 46 \times 10^6$ mm^4, $\bar{I}_y = 105.8 \times 10^6$ mm^4.
9.57 $h/2$.
9.59 $h(a + 3b)/(2a + 4b)$.
9.61 $F_A = F_B$ = 918 N; $F_C = F_D$ = 944 N.
9.62 2.55 m.
9.63 225 mm.
9.64 $5a/4$.
9.68 $3a^2b^2/16$.
9.69 $b^2h^2/8$.
9.70 $0.1419a^2b^2$.
9.71 300×10^3 mm^4.
9.72 192.2×10^6 mm^4.
9.73 138.2×10^6 mm^4.
9.74 -0.1596×10^6 mm^4.
9.75 1.573×10^6 mm^4.
9.78 1.17×10^6 mm^4.

9.80 $\bar{I}_{x'} = 1236.7 \times 10^6$ mm^4; $\bar{I}_{y'} = 852.3 \times 10^6$ mm^4; $\bar{I}_{x'y'} = 729.5 \times 10^6$ mm^4.
9.82 $\bar{I}_{x'} = 4.61 \times 10^6$ mm^4; $\bar{I}_{y'} = 3.82 \times 10^6$ mm^4; $\bar{I}_{x'y'} = -3.83 \times 10^6$ mm^4.
9.83 $\bar{I}_{x'} = 149.9 \times 10^3$ mm^4; $\bar{I}_{y'} = 469 \times 10^3$ mm^4; $\bar{I}_{x'y'} = 143.5 \times 10^3$ mm^4.
9.84 $\bar{I}_{x'} = 2.2 \times 10^6$ mm^4; $\bar{I}_{y'} = 2.8 \times 10^6$ mm^4; $\bar{I}_{x'y'} = 1.83 \times 10^6$ mm^4.
9.86 $\theta_m = 7.4°$ and $97.4°$; $\bar{I}_{max} = 1795 \times 10^6$ mm^4, $\bar{I}_{min} = 315 \times 10^6$ mm^4.
9.88 $12.06°$; 8.06×10^6 mm^4, 0.365×10^6 mm^4.
9.89 $-24.0°$ and $66°$, 0.524×10^6 mm^4, 0.0949×10^6 mm^4.
9.90 $\theta_m = -19.6°$ and $70.4°$; $\bar{I}_{max} = 4.35 \times 10^6$ mm^4, $\bar{I}_{min} = 0.64 \times 10^6$ mm^4.
9.92 $\bar{I}_{x'} = 1236.7 \times 10^6$ mm^4; $\bar{I}_{y'} = 852.3 \times 10^6$ mm^4; $\bar{I}_{x'y'} = 729.5 \times 10^6$ mm^4.
9.94 $\bar{I}_{x'} = 4.61 \times 10^6$ mm^4; $\bar{I}_{y'} = 3.82 \times 10^6$ mm^4; $\bar{I}_{x'y'} = -3.83 \times 10^6$ mm^4.
9.95 $\bar{I}_{x'} = 149.9 \times 10^3$ mm^4; $\bar{I}_{y'} = 469 \times 10^3$ mm^4; $\bar{I}_{x'y'} = 143.5 \times 10^3$ mm^4.
9.96 $\bar{I}_{x'} = 22 \times 10^6$ mm^4; $\bar{I}_{y'} = 2.8 \times 10^6$ mm^4; $\bar{I}_{x'y'} = 1.83 \times 10^6$ mm^4.
9.97 $20.2°$; $1.754a^4$, $0.209a^4$.
9.98 $\theta_m = 7.4°$ counterclockwise; $\bar{I}_{max} = 1798.9 \times 10^6$ mm^4, $\bar{I}_{min} = 290.1 \times 10^6$ mm^4.
9.100 $29.7°$; 405×10^6 mm^4, 83.9×10^6 mm^4.
9.101 $-24.0°$; 524×10^3 mm^4, 94.9×10^3 mm^4.
9.103 $2.95°$; 10.67×10^6 mm^4, 4.84×10^6 mm^4.
9.104 $\theta_m = -31.3°$; $\bar{I}_{max} = 2221.3 \times 10^6$ mm^4, $\bar{I}_{min} = 702.5 \times 10^6$ mm^4.
9.105 (a) -215×10^3 mm^4. (b) $-28.1°$. (c) 568×10^3 mm^4.
9.106 $\theta_m = 19.6°$ counterclockwise; $\bar{I}_{max} = 4.84 \times 10^6$ mm^4, $\bar{I}_{min} = 0.152 \times 10^6$ mm^4.
9.107 $-24.0°$; 8.33×10^6 mm^4, 1.509×10^6 mm^4.
9.108 $\theta_m = 7.5°$ clockwise; $\bar{I}_{max} = 269 \times 10^6$ mm^4, $\bar{I}_{min} = 113.9 \times 10^6$ mm^4.
9.112 $\pm 159.4 \times 10^3$ mm^4.
9.113 (a) $0.0699ma^2$. (b) $0.320ma^2$.
9.114 (a) $m(r_1^2 + r_2^2)/4$. (b) $m(r_1^2 + r_2^2)/2$.
9.116 (a) $5mb^2/6$. (b) $m(28a^2 + 13b^2)/48$.
9.117 (a) $I_{AA'} = mb^2/24$; $I_{BB'} = mh^2/18$. (b) $m(3b^2 + 4h^2)/72$.
9.118 $I_{DD'} = m(b^2 + 24d^2)/24$; $I_{EE'} = m(h^2 + 18d^2)/18$.
9.119 (a) $5ma^2/18$. (b) $3.61ma^2$.
9.121 $5mb^2/18$.
9.122 $m(93r_2^2 + 32L^2)/140$.
9.124 $m(b^2 + 3h^2)/5$.
9.125 $m(a^2 + b^2)/5$.
9.126 $m(a^2 + 3h^2)/6$; $\sqrt{(a^2 + 3h^2)/6}$.
9.127 $I_x = I_y = ma^2/4$; $I_z = ma^2/2$.
9.129 2.74×10^{-3} kg · m^2; 0.044 m.
9.131 $2mr^2/3$; $0.816r$.
9.132 (a) $\rho\pi h(a_2^4 + 2a_2^2a_1^2 - 3a_1^4)/2$. (b) $a_2/\sqrt{3}$. (c) $2\rho\pi h a_2^4/3$.
9.133 281×10^{-3} kg · m^2.
9.134 (a) 0.0309 m. (b) 0.117 m.
9.136 (a) 46.0 mm. (b) 8.54×10^{-3} kg · m^2; 45.4 mm.
9.137 $I_x = 4.95 \times 10^{-5}$ kg · m^2; $I_y = 3.34 \times 10^{-4}$ kg · m^2; $I_z = 3.17 \times 10^{-4}$ kg · m^2;
9.139 $I_x = 5.14 \times 10^{-3}$ kg · m^2; $I_y = 7.54 \times 10^{-3}$ kg · m^2; $I_z = 3.47 \times 10^{-3}$ kg · m^2.
9.141 $I_x = 0.1325$ kg · m^2; $I_y = 0.3186$ kg · m^2; $I_z = 0.2706$ kg · m^2
9.142 $I_x = 19.31 \times 10^{-3}$ kg · m^2; $I_y = 1.253$ kg · m^2; $I_z = 1.238$ kg · m^2.
9.143 $I_x = 0.0436$ kg · m^2; $I_y = 0.064$ kg · m^2; $I_z = 0.0446$ kg · m^2
9.144 21.2 kg · m^2.
9.145 3.98 kg · m^2.
9.146 4.807×10^{-3} kg · m^2.
9.148 $I_x = I_z = 6.85 \times 10^{-3}$ kg · m^2; $I_y = 12.63 \times 10^{-3}$ kg · m^2.
9.149 $I_x = 23.2 \times 10^{-3}$ kg · m^2; $I_y = 21.4 \times 10^{-3}$ kg · m^2; $I_z = 17.99 \times 10^{-3}$ kg · m^2.
9.151 $I_{xy} = 7.52 \times 10^{-4}$ kg · m^2; $I_{yz} = 1.786 \times 10^{-3}$ kg · m^2; $I_{zx} = 4.047 \times 10^{-3}$ kg · m^2.
9.152 $I_{xy} = 1.06 \times 10^{-3}$ kg · m^2; $I_{yz} = 1.19 \times 10^{-3}$ kg · m^2; $I_{zx} = 1.75 \times 10^{-3}$ kg · m^2.
9.154 $I_{xy} = -691 \times 10^{-6}$ kg · m^2; $I_{yz} = 203 \times 10^{-6}$ kg · m^2; $I_{zx} = -848 \times 10^{-6}$ kg · m^2.
9.155 $I_{xy} = 786 \times 10^{-6}$ kg · m^2; $I_{yz} = 64.5 \times 10^{-6}$ kg · m^2; $I_{zx} = -71.6 \times 10^{-6}$ kg · m^2.
9.157 $I_{xy} = -0.1931$ kg · m^2; $I_{yz} = 0.310$ kg · m^2; $I_{zx} = 2.26$ kg · m^2.
9.159 $I_{xy} = 12.75wa^3/g$; $I_{yz} = 7wa^3/g$; $I_{zx} = 1.5wa^3(\pi + 4)/g$.
9.161 $I_{xy} = 0.168 \times 10^{-3}$ kg · m^2; $I_{yz} = 0.36 \times 10^{-3}$ kg · m^2; $I_{zx} = 0.225 \times 10^{-3}$ kg · m^2.
9.162 $I_{xy} = -0.576$ kg · m^2; $I_{yz} = I_{zx} = 0$.
9.164 (a) $mac/20$. (b) $I_{xy} = mab/20$; $I_{yz} = mbc/20$.
9.165 $ma^2(10h^2 + 3a^2)/12(h^2 + a^2)$.
9.166 $3.22ma^2$.
9.167 54.7×10^{-3} kg · m^2
9.169 $5Wa^2/18g$.
9.170 $5\rho ta^4/12$.
9.171 6.74 kg · m^2.
9.173 25.3×10^{-3} kg · m^2.
9.174 10.97×10^{-3} kg · m^2.
9.175 (a) $b/a = 2.00$; $c/a = 2.00$. (b) $b/a = 1.000$; $c/a = 0.500$.
9.176 (a) 2.00. (b) $\sqrt{2/3}$.
9.177 (a) $1/\sqrt{3}$. (b) $\sqrt{7/12}$.
9.179 (a) $ma^2/6$. (b) $I_{x'} = ma^2/6$; $I_{y'} = I_{z'} = 11ma^2/12$.
9.181 (a) $K_1 = 0.363ma^2$; $K_2 = 1.583ma^2$; $K_3 = 1.720ma^2$.
(b) $(\theta_x)_1 = (\theta_z)_1 = 49.7°$, $(\theta_y)_1 = 113.7°$;
$(\theta_x)_2 = 45.0°$, $(\theta_y)_2 = 90.0°$, $(\theta_z)_2 = 135.0°$;
$(\theta_x)_3 = (\theta_z)_3 = 73.5°$, $(\theta_y)_3 = 23.7°$.
9.182 (a) $K_1 = 48 \times 10^{-3}$ kg · m^2; $K_2 = 47 \times 10^{-3}$ kg · m^2; $K_3 = 69 \times 10^{-3}$ kg · m^2
(b) $(\theta_x)_1 = (\theta_y)_1 = 90.0°$, $(\theta_z)_1 = 0°$;
$(\theta_x)_2 = 3.43°$, $(\theta_y)_2 = 86.6°$, $(\theta_z)_2 = 90.0°$;
$(\theta_x)_3 = 93.4°$, $(\theta_y)_3 = 3.41°$, $(\theta_z)_3 = 90.0°$.
9.183 (a) $K_1 = 3.42 \times 10^{-3}$ kg · m^2; $K_2 = 31 \times 10^{-3}$ kg · m^2; $K_3 = 33.9 \times 10^{-3}$ kg · m^2.
(b) $(\theta_x)_1 = 72.5°$, $(\theta_y)_1 = 83.0°$, $(\theta_z)_1 = 18.89°$;
$(\theta_x)_2 = 19.38°$, $(\theta_y)_2 = 83.7°$, $(\theta_z)_2 = 108.3°$;
$(\theta_x)_3 = 98.2°$, $(\theta_y)_3 = 9.46°$, $(\theta_z)_3 = 94.7°$.
9.184 (a) $K_1 = 0.1639Wa^2/g$; $K_2 = 1.054Wa^2/g$; $K_3 = 1.115Wa^2/g$.
(b) $(\theta_x)_1 = 36.7°$, $(\theta_y)_1 = 71.6°$, $(\theta_z)_1 = 59.5°$;
$(\theta_x)_2 = 74.9°$, $(\theta_y)_2 = 54.5°$, $(\theta_z)_2 = 140.5°$;
$(\theta_x)_3 = 57.5°$, $(\theta_y)_3 = 138.8°$, $(\theta_z)_3 = 112.4°$.
9.185 (a) $K_1 = 0.203\rho ta^4$; $K_2 = 0.698\rho ta^4$; $K_3 = 0.765\rho ta^4$.
(b) $(\theta_x)_1 = 40.2°$, $(\theta_y)_1 = 50.0°$, $(\theta_z)_1 = 86.7°$;
$(\theta_x)_2 = 56.2°$, $(\theta_y)_2 = 134.5°$, $(\theta_z)_2 = 63.4°$;
$(\theta_x)_3 = 70.8°$, $(\theta_y)_3 = 108.0°$, $(\theta_z)_3 = 153.2°$.

9.186 (a) $K_1 = 29 \times 10^{-3}$ kg · m^2; $K_2 = 53.9 \times 10^{-3}$ kg · m^2; $K_3 = 66.36 \times 10^{-3}$ kg · m^2. (b) $(\theta_x)_1 = 35.2°$, $(\theta_y)_1 = (\theta_z)_1 = 65.9°$; $(\theta_x)_2 = 90.0°$, $(\theta_y)_2 = 45.0°$, $(\theta_z)_2 = 135.0°$; $(\theta_x)_3 = 54.7°$, $(\theta_y)_3 = (\theta_z)_3 = 125.3°$.
9.187 $a^3b/30$.
9.189 7.36×10^6 mm^4; 32.0 mm.
9.191 (a) 122.4×10^6 mm^4. (b) 64.4×10^6 mm^4.
9.192 $\bar{I}_x = 218.2 \times 10^6$ mm^4, $\bar{I}_y = 0.79 \times 10^{-4}$ m^4; $\bar{k}_x = 133.7$ mm, $\bar{k}_y = 0.08$ m.
9.193 $\bar{I}_x = 35.315 \times 10^6$ mm^4; $\bar{I}_y = 23.0 \times 10^3$ mm^4.
9.195 -4.57×10^6 mm^4.
9.196 $\theta_m = -20.1°$; $\bar{I}_{max} = 16.4 \times 10^6$ mm^4, $\bar{I}_{min} = 2.2 \times 10^6$ mm^4.
9.197 $m(3a^2 + 4L^2)/12$.

CHAPTER 10

10.1 180.0 N ↓.
10.2 28.0 N ↓.
10.3 18.00 N · m ↻.
10.5 132.6 N →.
10.6 (a) 54.0 N; 60.0 mm →. (b) 126.0 N; 140.0 mm →.
10.7 (a) 36.0 N; 40.0 mm →. (b) 54.0 N; 60.0 mm →.
10.9 $2P \sin\theta/\cos(\theta/2)$.
10.10 $(3P/2)\tan\theta$.
10.13 7.96 kN.
10.14 5.47°.
10.15 $3Pa/2$.
10.18 (a) $Pl \sin 2\theta$. (b) $3Pl \cos\theta$. (c) $Pl \sin\theta$.
10.19 (a) 38.8 N · m ↺. (b) 24.7 N · m ↺.
10.20 (a) 1206.7 N →. (b) 1568 N →.
10.21 34.6 N ◺ 30.0°.
10.22 96.5 N · m ↺.
10.23 36.4°.
10.24 57.5°.
10.25 40.6°.
10.28 39.1°.
10.29 90.9 N.
10.31 330 mm.
10.33 26°.
10.34 133.17 N.
10.35 25°.
10.37 10.77°.
10.38 16.41°.
10.39 61.2°.
10.40 78.7°; 324°; 379°.
10.41 99.1 N ◸ 44.4°.
10.43 15.27°.
10.45 3.21 kN ↗.
10.47 $\eta = 1/(1 + \mu \cot\alpha)$.
10.48 $Pl/[2(\tan\theta - \mu_s)]$.
10.49 $M_{max} = 250$ N · m; $M_{min} = 100.0$ N · m.
10.50 $Q_{max} = P(3\tan\theta + \mu_s)/2$; $Q_{min} = P(3\tan\theta - \mu_s)/2$.
10.51 37.6 N; 31.6 N.
10.52 $\eta = \tan\theta/\tan(\theta + \phi_s)$.
10.55 0.0363 m (shorter).
10.56 0.0127 m (longer).
10.57 12.50 mm ↓.
10.58 9.38 mm →.
10.60 330 mm.
10.61 15.03° and 36.9°.
10.62 26°.
10.65 10.77°.
10.69 $\theta = 45.0°$, stable; $\theta = -135.0°$, unstable.
10.70 $\theta = 31.0°$, stable; $\theta = -149.0°$, unstable.
10.73 $\theta = 61.2°$, stable.
10.74 $\theta = 78.7°$, stable; $\theta = 324°$, unstable; $\theta = 379°$, stable.
10.75 $W = 10.53$ N, stable.
10.76 $\theta = 31.6°$, stable.
10.77 0.21 m.
10.79 (a) $\cos(\theta/2) - \sin(\theta/2) = [1 - (Wl/ka^2)]\cos\theta$. (b) 6.3°, stable; 90.0°, unstable; 173.8°, stable.
10.81 $\theta = 12.92°$, stable; $\theta = 77.1°$, unstable.
10.82 (a) $(1 - \cos\theta)\tan\theta = 2mg/kl$. (b) 52.0°, stable.
10.83 49.1°.
10.85 62.2°.
10.86 0.165 m.
10.88 46.6°.
10.89 $k > 282.2$ N/m.
10.90 0.15 m.
10.91 $0 \leq P < ka$.
10.92 $0 \leq P < 2kL/9$.
10.95 m_2c^2/ab.
10.96 $Q > 432$ N.
10.97 $0 \leq P < 0.382kl$.
10.99 $0 \leq P < 0.219ka$.
10.101 (a) 75.0 N ↑. (b) 225 N ↓.
10.102 17.90 kN ↗.
10.104 18.65 N · m ↻.
10.105 $Pl/2 \tan\theta$.
10.107 25.9 N · m ↻.
10.108 60.0 N ↓.
10.110 31.3 mm →.
10.112 $\theta = 9.69°$, stable; $\theta = 33.8°$, unstable; $\theta = 90.0°$, stable.

SI Prefixes

Multiplication Factor	Prefix†	Symbol
$1\ 000\ 000\ 000\ 000 = 10^{12}$	tera	T
$1\ 000\ 000\ 000 = 10^{9}$	giga	G
$1\ 000\ 000 = 10^{6}$	mega	M
$1\ 000 = 10^{3}$	kilo	k
$100 = 10^{2}$	hecto‡	h
$10 = 10^{1}$	deka‡	da
$0.1 = 10^{-1}$	deci‡	d
$0.01 = 10^{-2}$	centi‡	c
$0.001 = 10^{-3}$	milli	m
$0.000\ 001 = 10^{-6}$	micro	μ
$0.\ 000\ 000\ 001 = 10^{-9}$	nano	n
$0.000\ 000\ 000\ 001 = 10^{-12}$	pico	p
$0.000\ 000\ 000\ 000\ 001 = 10^{-15}$	femto	f
$0.000\ 000\ 000\ 000\ 000\ 001 = 10^{-18}$	atto	a

† The first syllable of every prefix is accented so that the prefix will retain its identity. Thus, the preferred pronunciation of kilometer places the accent on the first syllable, not the second.

‡ The use of these prefixes should be avoided, except for the measurement of areas and volumes and for the nontechnical use of centimeter, as for body and clothing measurements.

Principal SI Units Used in Mechanics

Quantity	Unit	Symbol	Formula
Acceleration	Meter per second squared	...	m/s^2
Angle	Radian	rad	†
Angular acceleration	Radian per second squared	...	rad/s^2
Angular velocity	Radian per second	...	rad/s
Area	Square meter	...	m^2
Density	Kilogram per cubic meter	...	kg/m^3
Energy	Joule	J	$N \cdot m$
Force	Newton	N	$kg \cdot m/s^2$
Frequency	Hertz	Hz	s^{-1}
Impulse	Newton-second	...	$kg \cdot m/s$
Length	Meter	m	‡
Mass	Kilogram	kg	‡
Moment of a force	Newton-meter	...	$N \cdot m$
Power	Watt	W	J/s
Pressure	Pascal	Pa	N/m^2
Time	Second	s	‡
Velocity	Meter per second	...	m/s
Volume, solids	Cubic meter	...	m^3
Liquids	Liter	L	$10^{-3}\ m^3$
Work	Joule	J	$N \cdot m$

† Supplementary unit (1 revolution $= 2\pi$ rad $= 360°$).

‡ Base unit.

Centroids of Common Shapes of Areas and Lines

Shape		$\bar{x}$	$\bar{y}$	Area
Triangular area	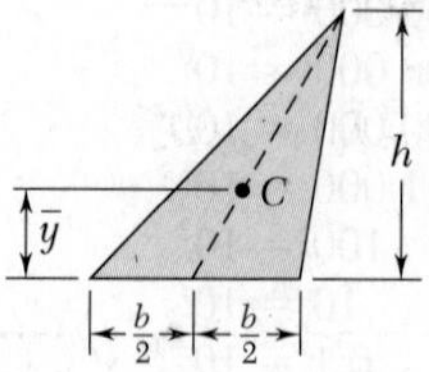		$\frac{h}{3}$	$\frac{bh}{2}$
Quarter-circular area	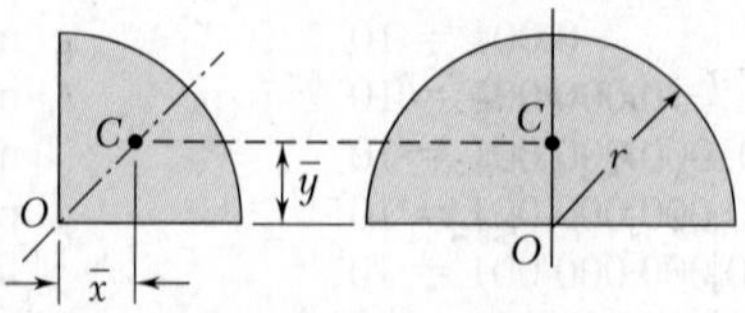	$\frac{4r}{3\pi}$	$\frac{4r}{3\pi}$	$\frac{\pi r^2}{4}$
Semicircular area		0	$\frac{4r}{3\pi}$	$\frac{\pi r^2}{2}$
Semiparabolic area	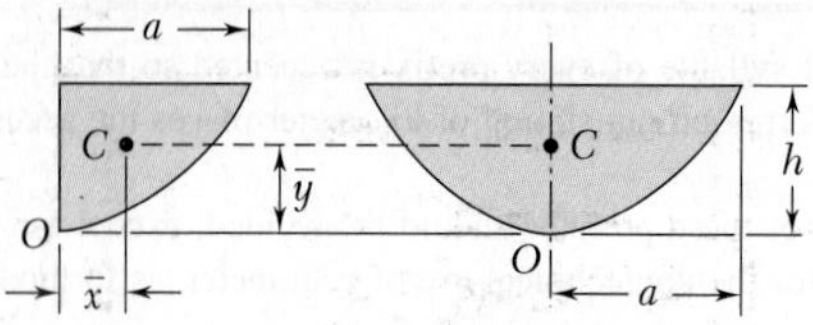	$\frac{3a}{8}$	$\frac{3h}{5}$	$\frac{2ah}{3}$
Parabolic area		0	$\frac{3h}{5}$	$\frac{4ah}{3}$
Parabolic spandrel	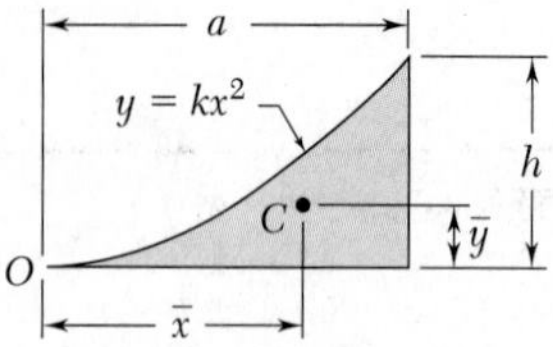	$\frac{3a}{4}$	$\frac{3h}{10}$	$\frac{ah}{3}$
Circular sector	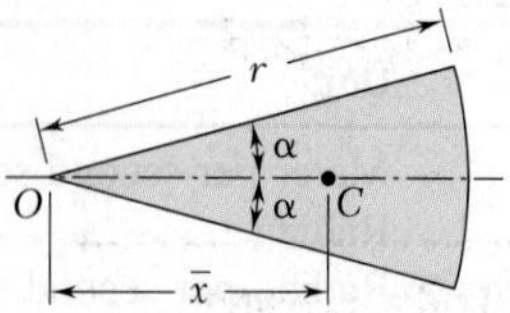	$\frac{2r \sin \alpha}{3\alpha}$	0	αr^2
Quarter-circular arc	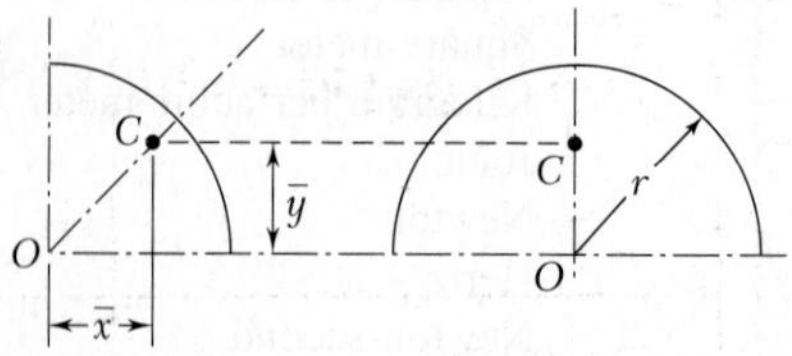	$\frac{2r}{\pi}$	$\frac{2r}{\pi}$	$\frac{\pi r}{2}$
Semicircular arc		0	$\frac{2r}{\pi}$	πr
Arc of circle	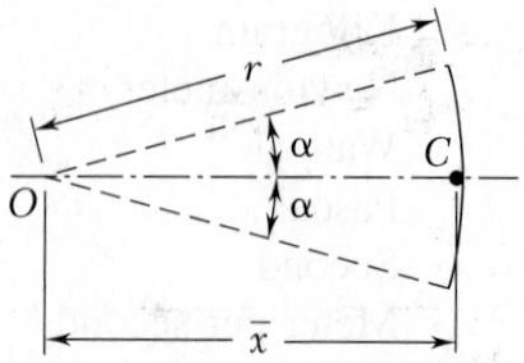	$\frac{r \sin \alpha}{\alpha}$	0	$2\alpha r$